# The Ultimate Montana Atlas and Travel Encyclopedia

## Second Edition

*by*
Michael Dougherty
and Heidi Pfeil Dougherty

UltimatePress
Bozeman, Montana

an *Ultimate*® book



**ISBN: 1-888550-07-4**

***Ultimate* Press**

an imprint of Champions Publishing

1627 W. Main Street #148
Bozeman, Montana 59715
406-585-0237
800-585-0713
www.ultimatemontana.com

**Publisher's Cataloging-in-Publication**
(Provided by Quality Books, Inc.)

Dougherty, Michael, 1951-
The ultimate Montana atlas and travel encyclopedia / by Michael & Heidi Dougherty. -- 2nd ed.
p. cm.
Includes index.
ISBN: 1-888550-11-2

1. Montana--Guidebooks. 2. Montana--Maps, Tourist. I. Dougherty, Heidi. II. Title

F729.3.D68 2002 917.8604'34
QBI02-200554

Printed in Canada

**Attention schools, organizations and non-profit groups:**
Quantity discounts are available on bulk purchases of this book for fund raising.

# Contents

## Acknowledgment

We offer a sincere thank you to all of the sponsors who, without their financial support, this book would not have been possible. Throughout the book, you'll see their names in bold. Stop in and see them when you're in their area. They would like to hear from you.

We especially wish to thank Jessica Jochin for her excellent help in bringing this second edition to press.

## Disclaimer

This guide focuses on recreational activities including traveling to some sites that are off the more frequently traveled roads. As all such activities contain elements of risk, the publisher, author, affiliated individuals and companies included in this guide disclaim any responsibility for any injury, harm, or illness that may occur to anyone through, or by use of, the information in this book. Although the author and publisher have made every effort to ensure that the information was correct at the time of going to press, the author and publisher do not assume and hereby disclaim any liability to any party for any loss or damage to person or property caused by errors, omissions, or any potential travel disruption due to labor or financial difficulty, whether such errors or omissions result from negligence, accident, or any other cause.

Throughout this book, public domain documents of government agencies (National Park Service, USDA Forest Service, Bureau of Land Management, and Montana State Wildlife, Fish and Parks) were reprinted. Also, brochures published by local area chambers of commerce and from the various attractions were reprinted in part or in their entirety. Permissions were obtained where required.

# MONTANA

## THE TREASURE STATE

*Madison River north of West Yellowstone*

## THE TREASURE STATE

Montana—unrivaled splendor and awesome beauty! Over 147,000 square miles of mountains, prairies, farms, forests, rivers and streams await the traveler ready for spectacular scenery and adventure. Montana is a cornucopia of elaborate terrain; every geologic formation known on the planet can be found in Montana. Extraordinary? Yes, and so is Montana.

Although the name of Montana is derived from the Spanish word for mountain, only one third of the state is mountainous. Often described as if it were two states—an eastern prairie and a western mountain range—Montana provides a diverse range of scenery for the traveler. The northern part of Montana borders Canada, Wyoming flanks much of the south, the east borders North and South Dakota, and Idaho lines the west side with the Bitterroot Mountains.

Montana's share of the Rocky Mountains comprise two dozen distinct ranges. The elevations swing from 3,500 feet on valley floors to the peaks of the Beartooth Plateau near Yellowstone National Park that rise above 12,000 feet. The ranges that exist at higher elevations often create their own weather systems, inducing precipitation that supports dense coniferous forests of fir, pine, cedar, spruce, and larch. While snow can pile up hundreds of inches, measurable precipitation only ranges from 14 to 23 inches annually. Powder-white peaks are often still visible on the hottest days of summer.

The valleys that divide Montana's mountain ranges vary from narrow slots to broad floors up to 50 miles wide. The most unforgettable valleys—the Big Hole, Gallatin, Yellowstone, and Madison—are named after the rivers that drain them. Nearly one fourth of Montana, 22.5 million acres, is forested. Most of the forests occur west of the Continental Divide, where moist Pacific Coast air and mountainous areas provide favorable conditions for the growth of approximately twenty-seven types of trees.

Eastern Montana, often deemed as monotonous, has a character of its own and is full of its own topographical surprises such as badlands, sandstone outcropings, glacial lakes, ice caves and even an occasional pine forest or cluster of low mountains. The short grasses that grow in this region support a thriving livestock industry. Out of the wide, endless ranges of grass a legacy grew from the great trail drives that moved cattle and cowboys from Texas to Montana as early as the 1860s. While the prairie is not known for its trees, the savannahs of eastern Montana grow more than sagebrush. Willows take root in the river valleys while pine and cedars spot the hills. Cottonwoods, once prized for firewood and dugout canoes by many Native American tribes and early settlers, grow near river bottoms, while chokecherries and currants grow on lower ground.

Nowhere is the contrast between mountains and plains more striking than along the Rocky Mountain Front which some distinguish as the division of eastern and western Montana. The stretch of highway between Augusta and Browning is remarkable. To the west is a solid wall of peaks; to the east lie the unrelenting expanses of plains. Moods and colors are abundant in the tapestry of the wide open Montana sky as it changes daily, even hourly.

Two of the United States' most extraordinary national parks frame Montana. On the state's northern edge are the chiseled peaks of Glacier National Park, while along the southern Montana-Wyoming border lies the thermal wonder-world of Yellowstone National Park—the oldest national park in the world and largest in the United States. Fire and ice were the artists within Yellowstone, as it was created by a series of volcanic eruptions. These intense geothermal forces are still at work beneath the Earth's shallow crust making Yellowstone Park the largest hotspot on the globe.

## HISTORY

The history of Montana is as remarkable and vast as are its open plains. Ghost towns stand as a reminder of towns once vibrant with life during the mining booms. Stand where General Custer stood; The Little Bighorn Battlefield Monument commemorates the battle of the same name and Custer's "Last Stand" against the Sioux and Cheyenne Indians. Native American culture is still thriving in Montana with seven different Indian reservations, as well as numerous commemorative state parks and historic sites. Two great rivers, the Missouri and the Yellowstone drain the eastern prairies where dinosaurs once roamed and where Crow, Cheyenne and Blackfeet tribes pursued the world's largest herd of American bison across the plains.

Tribes of early people first arrived in Montana from Asia about 10,000–15,000 years ago. Around 5,000 B.C., a desert climate in Asia caused game animals and the peoples who relied on them to migrate in search of more habitable conditions. The Shoshone entered Montana in

## MONTANA AT A GLANCE

**Population (2000):** 902,195
**Entered union:** November 8, 1889
**Capital:** Helena
**Nickname:** Treasure State
**Motto:** "Oro y Plata"(Gold and Silver)
**Bird:** Western Meadowlark
**Flower:** Bitterroot
**Song:** "Montana"
**Stones:** Sapphire and Agate
**Tree:** Ponderosa Pine
**Animal:** Grizzly Bear
**Fish:** Blackspotted Cutthroat Trout
**Fossil:** Maiasaura (Duck-billed Dinosaur)
**Land area:** 147,046 square miles
**Size ranking:** 4th
**Geographic center:** Fergus, 26 miles northeast of Lewistown
**Length:** 630 miles
**Width:** 280 miles
**Highest point:** 12,799 feet (Granite Peak)
**Lowest point:** 1,820 feet (Kootenai River)
**Highest temperature:** 117 deg. on July 5, 1937, at Medicine Lake
**Lowest temperature:** -70 deg. on Jan. 20, 1954, at Rogers Pass

## Cowboy Wave

**Montana is largely rural, and like** largely rural states, it is pretty friendly to most who care to be friendly back. When you're traveling the back roads, particularly the gravel roads, you'll encounter a variety of waves from passing pickups and motorists.

The most common is the one finger wave, accomplished by simply raising the first finger (not the middle finger as is common in urban areas) from the steering wheel. If the driver is otherwise occupied with his hands or if it is a fairly rough road, you may get a light head nod. Occasionally, you may get a two finger wave which often appears as a modified peace sign if the passerby is having a particularly good day. On rare occasions, you may get an all out wave.

The most important things is that whatever wave you get, be sure and wave back.

about 1600, shortly after the Crow Indians settled along tributaries of the Yellowstone River. Over a century later, the Blackfeet came to Montana from the north and east in about 1730. Other tribes later found their way to Montana: Sioux, Cheyenne, Salish, and the Kootenai. Cree and Chippewa tribes entered Montana in the 1870s from Canada.

In the early 1800s, rivers provided the pathway into Montana for the first white explorers. Rivers and riverboats remained the only form of transportation linking Montana and the rest of the nation until the 1880s. Trappers and traders also used the rivers as thoroughfares, and forts were erected to support the lavish trapping and trading of beavers pelts. By 1840, prior to the cessation of this beaver trapping era due to the animal's near extinction, almost three dozen trading forts had been built. As the population of beavers drastically declined, trade continued in buffalo hides.

Mineral wealth, as well as the development of the railroad, fueled Montana's development in the late 1800s. People flocked to Montana searching for gold, creating instant towns in southwestern Montana. Bannack, Virginia City, and Nevada City all began as gold-rush towns. Other gold strikes and later discoveries of silver sparked similar rushes in Last Chance Gulch (now Helena), Confederate Gulch (Diamond City) and many other boom towns. The railroad arrived serendipituously to haul the mineral riches. The Union Pacific built a spur line north from Utah to Butte in 1881. The Northern Pacific spanned the length of Montana linking Portland and Chicago in 1883 and extending its rails across approximately 17 million acres. The Great Northern stretched its service along the Montana-Canada border, joining Minneapolis and Seattle in 1893. With access to the coastal markets, Montana opened wide its doors for development and immigration.

Towns emerged in river valleys and highways were built on their banks. Dams were built to harness water power and reservoirs soon spanned the state altering Montana's geography. Millions of gallons of water are dammed at Fort Peck Reservoir on the Missouri and in Lake Koocanusa on the Kootenai River. The Great Falls of the Missouri, which required Lewis and Clark twenty-two days to painstakingly portage in 1805, are now a series of hydroelectric dams. Further exploits of the Lewis and Clark expedition in Montana are thoroughly chronicled in actual journals they kept.

Montana became a territory in 1864 and gained its statehood in 1889. Although Montana was, in many ways, detached from the rest of the country in its early years of statehood, the state was able to sustain itself by the diverse and rich resources within its borders. Today those same resources travel the world: cattle grown on Montana ranches may end up on the table of a Japanese restaurant, its coal fuels the cities of the Pacific Coast, its timber is used to erect homes across the country, and Montana's gold becomes circuitry in main frame computers and space craft.

Throughout these sections we have provided you enough history of the area to understand its origins. Much of this is provided through the text of historical markers throughout the state. They tell the story of Montana in a colorful way and do an excellent job of spotlighting the important milestones in Montana history. We have provided some background history on over 300 towns and cities in the state, if nothing more than the origin of the town's name. Quite often, the story of the town's name provides insight into its past.

## Lewis & Clark

### The Journey West

The Lewis & Clark Expedition left St. Louis in 1804, heading up the Missouri River to explore the unknown Western Territory, calling themselves the Corps of Discovery. The Corp was traveling upstream, moving up to 25 miles a day when the winds and weather permitted. They had already experienced many trials and tribulations throughout their travels through Nebraska, Iowa, South Dakota, North Dakota and into Montana.

When the Corps of Discovery was nearing the spot where the Missouri and the Yellowstone come together, they were forced to stop for several days due to high wind. The group knew they were close to the Yellowstone River, and on April 25 1805, Meriwether Lewis led a group by foot to the mouth of the Yellowstone to explore the territory that lay ahead. The small group spent the night on the riverbanks, and then headed back to meet the others, and the group completed the journey to the Yellowstone the next day.

This was the first time they reached the Yellowstone River, yet the group continued their journey up the Missouri, leaving the exploration of the Yellowstone for their return route. More miles were traveled through Montana by Lewis & Clark, than any other state. This is due to the fact that the group split up, Clark traveling through Bozeman Pass and following the Yellowstone River, while Lewis returned on the Missouri and explored the Marias River.

## 12,000 Miles of Montana

**There are approximately 12,000** miles of roads in Montana. Many roads are originally routes blazed by the Native Indian tribes and migrating buffalo. The trails were the ones that made passing through mountain passes, around rivers, and other geographical obstacles. The first engineered road was a military supply route to the Northwest which was Mullan from Walla Walla to Fort Benton in 1862. This road linked Montana territory to a natural highway from the Pacific Ocean to the Atlantic Ocean.

Montana's interstate system was completed in 1988 and includes I-90, I-94, and I-15. There are a total of 1,200 Interstate miles in the state. Primary highways cover 5,450 miles in the state. Secondary roads which include county, state, and frontage roads cover a total of 4,760 miles and over a third of those roads are not paved.

### The Return Trip

On July 3, 1806, on their return, Lewis & Clark decided to split up the group, just south of today's city of Missoula. Clark's team, including Sacajawea and her baby Jean Baptiste, proceeded down the Yellowstone, past Pompey's Pillar, and spent the night of July 27 at Castle Rock by today's Forsyth. The next day they passed Rosebud Creek, spotted numerous herds of Elk, and spent the night of July 29, 1806 on an island just across from the Tongue River by Miles City. Clark observed the abundance of coal in the surrounding hills. On July 30, the group passed through a difficult stretch of river and went by Makoshika State Park. The night of July 31 was spent by present day Glendive where they reportedly experienced problems with mosquitoes, grizzly bears and spotted numerous bison. They traveled huge distances of up to 60 miles a day during this time, until they once again returned to the Missouri River on August 4, 1806, where they met up with Lewis and his party.

In each section of the book, you will find an account of the Corps of Discovery's travels through that particular area, mostly in their own words. The markers on the map correspond to the numbered excerpt from their journals in the *On The Trail of Lewis and Clark* sidebar in that section. For more information on the Montana portion of the Lewis & Clark Trail, see local chambers of commerce and look for signs pointing out the trail sites.

## Montana's Native Americans

The Native Americans of Montana were largely nomadic. Their history is characterized by movement with the seasons. They crossed the plains to follow the great herds of bison, then retreated when stronger tribes pushed them off the hunting grounds. As the white man moved in and warfare and disease decimated the tribes, there came the move to the reservations marking the end of an era and a permanent change in lifestyle for the tribes.

Archeological evidence reveals that Native Americans walked these plains and roamed these mountains more than 14,000 years ago. Artifacts link the Kootenai to these prehistoric tribes. The Kootenai made their home in the mountainous terrain west of the divide. They ventured east only to hunt buffalo. The Crow, Salish, and Pend d'Oreilles were probably the first of the "modern" tribes to join the Kootenai on these lands. The

Salish and the Pend d'Oreilles were spread as far east as the Bighorn Mountains. During the 1700s, these tribes co-existed on the same hunting grounds. The Hellgate Treaty took their massive landholdings and confined them to the fertile grounds of the Flathead Reservation.

The Chippewa and Cree were latecomers to Montana. They came to the area after the reservation system was in existence. Today these tribes are intermixed and share the hybrid name, "Chippewa-Cree." They reside on the Rocky Boy's reservation.

Most of Montana's Indians arrived here after 1700. By the time they arrived, the white man's culture was already firmly established. The white man's influence on who would dominate the Montana territory was significant. Guns from the white frontiersman and horses from the Spaniards became deciding factors in a culture completely dependent on the bison.

In the 1880s, the bison-based economy began to crumble. White men were hunting the bison to near extinction, the U.S. and Canadian governments began to drive Indians from their lands, and the diseases brought by the whites all combined to diminish the population of the tribes and shatter their spirits. By the 1870s, large tracts of land were formally reserved for the Indians through various treaties and executive orders.

### Today's Reservations

Today, reservations cover nine percent of the Montana land base. While not all is still owned by native people, all is governed by tribal or federal law. These reservations are not only important for the spiritual ties the Indians have to the land, but because they have become the Indians' last retreat and last chance to preserve the culture of the past. Today, the people of Montana's reservations are working hard to create and sustain strong economic bases to perpetuate the culture for future generations.

Today, these reservations are reservoirs of Native American history. They are havens where the Indian culture can be experienced with a backdrop of sacred landscapes and at annual gatherings—where rituals are performed and traditional dress is worn as it has been for hundreds of years.

There are seven reservations in Montana occupied by eleven tribes. Each maintains a wealth of cultural institutions in their museums. Special events held frequently provide insight into their cultures. Historic sites are plentiful on all seven reservations. While Montana's Native Americans have struggled to adapt to the changing world and conflicting cultures around them, they have managed to maintain the rich culture and traditions of their past. This heritage is a major ingredient in the cultural flavor of Montana.

### Visiting a Reservation

Each of the reservations have special social and cultural events and activities unique to the tribes occupying them. Many, like tribal powwows, rodeos, hand games, and shinny games are social events and usually open to the public. When visiting these events and the public places on the reservation, keep in mind that most of these are not held for the benefit of the public but as important parts of the tribe's culture. Thus it's incumbent on guests to show courtesy and respect when attending these activities.

Most of the cultural and religious ceremonies require a special invitation to attend. In some cases, visitors are not allowed at all. In some tribes, a host family will personally invite visitors and advise them of the protocol in attending. All of the tribes place great importance on their religion and traditions. Sacred sites must be respected and artifacts must not be removed. All reservations have places where mementos may be purchased.

A powwow is a social gathering featuring generations-old dancing and drumming, accompanied by traditional food and dress. Visitors should bring lawn chairs and blankets as seating space is limited at most of these functions. Guests may join in the "Round Dance" where everyone dances in a circle, or by invitation of the emcee. They may also participate by invitation in a "Giveaway," which is a sharing of accomplishment or good fortune. But they should be constantly aware that the dance area is sacred.

All events and points of interest mentioned in this book are open to the public. To be sure about attendance at any other functions, contact the tribal office.

Flash photography is forbidden during contests. If you wish to take a picture of the dancers or singers, ask permission first.

Visitors should be aware that while on the reservation, tribal laws exist that do not exist off the reservation. Most tribes have their own laws regarding the environment and wildlife protection. For information concerning access and recreation, contact the tribal office.

## Economy

Montana, a rural state, claims agriculture, mining, and the timber industry to be its founding trades and are still among its most vital. Tourism continues to increase, drawing revenue to one of the nation's most beautiful states. Agriculture is strictly divided by Montanans between farms, which raise grain, and ranches, which raise livestock. Although many think of Montana as being comprised of huge ranches and roaming cattle, less than 10% of the population make their living from farming and ranching. Beef cattle production is the most common in Montana, with sheep providing a steady alternative. Spring and winter wheat are undoubtedly the most commonly harvested crops, with barley in close contention. Other popular crops, grown predominately in irrigation fields along the Yellowstone River, are corn, soybeans and sugar beets.

Though Montana was born of mining and prospecting camps, most of the gold, silver and copper have been depleted. However, the state remains rich in other mineral wealth such as sapphire, coal and oil. Although the timber industry is a lifestyle for some, early clear-cutting of forests and slow regrowth have limited the state's ability for competition in the world market. Christmas tree farms spot the northwestern part of the state and log-home manufacturers have moved Montana into the forefront of home-kit producers in the world. More log homes are shipped to Japan than remain in Montana.

## Population

People come to Montana to get away from city life, not to find it. A little over 900,000 people live in this state, even though it is the fourth largest state area-wise in the U.S. trailing only Alaska, Texas and California. Montana's largest city, Billings, has less than 100,000 residents, translating to six persons per acre of the state's 145,556 square miles of land. The entire state of Montana has even been likened to a mid-size American city, each town representing a different neighborhood with a unique personality. Each city and town lends itself to a distinct purpose and all contribute to the diversity that is so harmonious with its terrain.



The contrasting values of independence and neighborliness define the character of a typical Montanan. People here still share stories at cozy roadside saloons as glassy-eyed, stuffed animal heads hover as if monitoring the conversations. And when calling anywhere within Montana you just have to remember one area code, 406, and the entire state is on mountain time.

## Arts and Culture

Montana is brimming with art and literary talent, both past and present day. From pioneers who kept journals and sent letters back east to established novelists who make their home in Montana, the literary tradition is a great source of pride to Montanans. A state that can fill a 1,150 page best-selling anthology with its literature is impressive and bespeaks of a tradition worth noting. *The Last Best Place* chronicles the literary history of Montana, from Native American stories to modern cowboy poetry.

Art walks and displays are commonplace and rural cafes will often sell local arts and crafts, from homemade pottery to mountain scenes painted on old barn boards. One of the more famous artists is the Montana painter Charlie Russell who began sketching in bars and around campfires. His studio in Great Falls is now the Charles Russell Memorial Museum.

## Wildlife

Both white-tailed and large-eared mule deer dot the countryside as you drive through the state. Montana is home to more than 150,000 Rocky Mountain elk, which can often be viewed from the roadside. Bighorn sheep, mountain goats and grizzly bears are more likely to be seen high in the slopes of the Rockies. Moose are common but typically avoid humans. Montana's vast wilderness areas serve as valuable homes for many of the country's threatened and endangered species including the gray wolf, whooping crane, white sturgeon, grizzly bear and bald eagle. Mountain lions are also residents of Montana and can show up in unlikely spots, such as the city parks of Missoula or the streets of Columbia Falls, though this is not common.

Magpies, loud, large black & white birds, seem to monopolize Montana's airways, but there are also many other less-aggressive birds. Some to look for in the eastern part of the state are grouse, bobolinks, horned lark, western meadowlark (Montana's state bird), goldfinches and sparrow hawks. In the mountainous western area of the state you may catch the thrill of a bald eagle gliding across the valley or perched on a branch in a tree near the highway. Other birds that frequent the west are owls, woodpeckers, chickadees, ospreys, western tanagers, jays and Rufous hummingbirds. However, these are only a few of the 294 species that have been documented as reliably occurring in Montana.

Over 2,500 species of wildflowers and non-flowering plants can be found in three different areas within Montana: above the timberline (6,000–7,000 feet elevations) in northwestern Montana, mountain forest beginning at 5,000-feet elevations, and those found in open terrain of desert, plains, valleys and foothills.

There are several colorful flowers that can be frequently seen while driving. One is the Shooting Star, which has a rosy purple flower banded with a red and yellow ring pointing downward; elk and deer relish this adornment for meals. Also common is the Wild Rose Scrub, which grows from three to eight feet tall and in the fall produce small red rose-hips (or berries) that make a pleasant tea rich in vitamin C.

The Indian Paintbrush usually has red blossoms that bloom from June to early August in dry to moist soils. The most common flora of Montana is the Wood Violet which comes in a variety of colors ranging from white to purple. It blooms in early spring in wet, wooded areas, usually on slopes and ledges of deciduous forests. The petals of this plant can be eaten in salads or made into jelly, jam or candy. Wildflower meadows of Glacier lilies, Alpine poppies, columbine, asters, arnica spread their colors in midsummer hillsides while Dogtooth violets and Mariposa lilies grow a little farther down the slopes.

A mainstay for the bears of Montana is the huckleberry bush. A grown bear can consume 80 to 90 pounds of food per day, 15% of this poundage may consist of huckleberries. Late July is a good time to hunt huckleberries. They require a good amount of moisture and grow best on a north slope at elevations of 3,500 to 7,000 feet.

Most of western Montana supports lush growth dominated by coniferous forests. This area is usually divided into two categories: lower montane and higher subalpine. Ponderosa pines dominate the lower slopes. A little higher, the Douglas fir takes over and above that are the lodgepole pines so common in Montana-made furniture. Western cedar, grand fir, white pine, aspen and birch are also prevalent.

## Wide Open Spaces

While traveling on the backroads, you will sometimes get a sense that nobody lives here. You can travel for miles without seeing any sign of civilization beyond the occasional small herds of cattle. Occupied houses are rare and outnumbered by abandoned homesteaders shacks and log cabins. Fences often disappear entirely and are replaced by the infrequent "Open Range" signs that warn you cattle may be having their mid-day siesta in the middle of the road.

None-the-less, most of this land is privately owned unless posted otherwise. Before abandoning your car and heading out across these open spaces, it's a good idea and common courtesy to find the property owner and get permission. If you see fenceposts or gates with bright orange blazes, then getting permission isn't an option. They mean "no trespassing" in no uncertain terms.

However, I've never been shot at for stopping the car, getting out and smelling the sage, listening to the sound of silence, or to the voice of the wind, or the gurgle of a stream, the howl of a coyote, or the unidentified song of a prairie bird. I've never been asked to move along when I've stopped to admire a sunset, or simply marvel at the splendor of the endless sky.

Most of those that have bought and paid for a piece of this marvelous state don't mind sharing it with those who come to visit. They simply ask that you respect it and leave no trace you were there.

## The Roads

Gravel roads are the rule rather than the exception in this part of the state. While most of the paved roads are well maintained, they are often narrow and have little or no shoulder. While you may want to slow down on gravel roads, don't expect the locals to do so. The vast distances between towns necessitate speed for those who live here. Remember, until a couple of years ago, Montana didn't even have a posted speed limit. While speed limits are now in effect, it hasn't changed the driving habits of people here much at all.

Be prepared at any time to slow down for riders on horseback. Most horses are accustomed to cars, but can spook if you drive too near. Much of Montana is open range. Cattle may be grazing on the road. A head-on with a steer can be just as deadly as a head-on with another automobile.

And speaking of cattle, don't be surprised if you come upon a cattle drive. If you do, follow the instructions of the drovers. They will make every effort to clear a path to allow you through.

Usually the cattle just part ways and make a path, but don't go on unless you're given instructions to.

Rural unpaved roads have cattle guards at frequent intervals. Good idea to slow down for these. Most often they're not level with the road and can wreak havoc on the suspension, possibly even disabling the car.

Beware of black ice! This is a virtually invisible layer of ice that forms on road surfaces after a fog. Be particularly careful of stretches of road that parallel rivers and creeks. The early morning fog rising from them can settle on the road freezing instantly. If you feel yourself sliding, tap your brakes gently. If you slam on the brakes, it's all but over. Gently steer into the direction of your skid (if your back end is going right—steer right.

### Gumbo

We gave this subject its own headline. It is very important that you read it—and heed it.

While Montana isn't the only state that has gumbo, it certainly seems to have cornered the market. If you become a resident, it is one of the first things you develop a respect (a healthy respect) for. Grizzlys and rattlesnakes might be the hazards you're warned of, but gumbo is the one that will get you.

You'll find it mostly in the eastern half of the state. It lies in wait on what in dry weather appears to be an ordinary rock hard dirt road. Your first clue is the occasional sign that reads *Road Impassable When Wet*. This is a clear understatement. When these roads become even mildly wet, they turn into a monster that swallows all sizes of vehicles—and yes, even 4-wheel drive SUVs. Think you'll get a tow? Forget it. No tow truck operator with a higher IQ than dirt will venture onto it until it dries. If you walk on it, you will grow six inches taller and gain 25 pounds all on the bottom of your shoes. Of course, this is if it doesn't swallow you whole first like an unsuspecting native in a Tarzan movie who steps into quicksand.

Bottomline, heed the signs. If it looks like rain, head for the nearest paved road. When it comes to swallowing things whole, the Bermuda Triangle is an amateur compared to Montana Gumbo.

## Rivers

It is fascinating that Montana has within its borders portions of the three major river drainage systems of North America. From Triple Divide in Glacier National Park, raindrops falling only a few feet apart can take widely differing routes to the seas. Depending on which side of the three-sided point of land on which they fall, the raindrops may flow east into the Missouri and Mississippi rivers, the Gulf of Mexico, and the Atlantic Ocean; west to the Columbia River and the Pacific, or north and east into the rivers that lead to the Hudson Bay.

Rivers and streams that feed upon mountain snow runoff thrive throughout western Montana. They sing to hundreds of fisherman every year and effortlessly carry kayaks, rafts and inner tubes to all who seek beauty and adventure.

## Recreation

In Montana, pristine nature is so prevalent that it is hard to go anywhere and not find beauty and recreation. The abiding treasures of this state are two national parks, a national recreation area, fifteen wilderness areas, ten national forests, eight national wildlife refuges, 370 miles of national wild and scenic river, and several national scenic trails. In addition, there are also forty-two state parks, seven state forests, and approximately 600 miles of prized, blue-ribbon trout streams.

Montana is well-known for its prized fly fishing trout streams. Though it's possible to fish year-round in lakes and rivers, late June through October are the most popular fishing months. The state has more than 300 fishing access areas. A fishing license is reasonably priced and much more affordable than the fine one receives if caught without one. Contact Montana Department of Fish, Wildlife, and Parks (444-2535) for up-to-date information regarding licenses, prices and seasons for both hunting and fishing.

Whitewater rivers send many dancing rafts and kayaks into thrills of summer fun. Relaxing or more invigorating river trips by guides or alone position one to take in some spectacular scenery. Don't forget to take a dip in one of the state's hot springs; indoor or outdoor, they are a real delight both in the winter and warmer seasons. Hot water gurgles up all over the state into a wide variety of resorts, from the most rustic to the chic—there's something for everyone's fancy.

The national forests and mountain ranges provide endless opportunities for hikes on foot or on horseback. Hunters flock to Montana in the fall for elk, antelope, pronghorn, pheasants, deer, and bear. In the winter, both downhill and cross country skiing are all-time favorites.

## Montana's National Forests

The national forests and grasslands of Montana stretch from the prairies and badlands of far eastern Montana, to the rolling hills and isolated ponderosa pine woodlands of the middle part of the state, to the rugged mountain tops and steep timbered canyons in the west.

Recreation opportunities are as diverse as these lands. Everything from sightseeing to motorcycling; horseback riding to picnicking; hunting to snowshoeing; and crosscountry skiing to kayaking await the outdoor enthusiast.

You can get away and experience the solitude and challenges of wildlands. On the other hand, campgrounds and visitor centers provide opportunities to associate with other people and enjoy the convenience of facilities.

Take your pick of the special places available in Montana... enjoy our forests and grasslands.

### Wilderness

"A wilderness, in contrast with those areas where man and his own works dominate the landscape, is hereby recognized as an area where the earth and community of life are untrammeled by man, where man himself is a visitor who does not remain." - From the Wilderness Act September 3, 1964

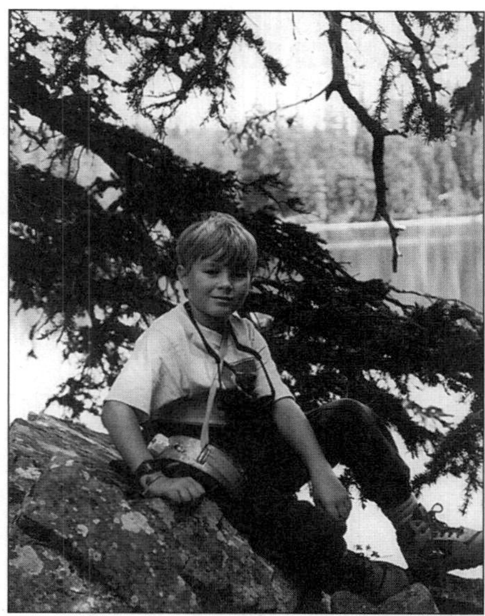

Wildernesses in Montana encompass more than 4 million acres of rugged and beautiful mountain landscapes. Here, in relative solitude, visitors find areas maintained in their natural and undeveloped state providing relief from the pressures of today's society.

### Northern Region Wildernesses:

Absaroka Beartooth
Anaconda Pintler
Bob Marshall
Cabinet Mountains
Gates of the Mountains
Great Bear
Lee Metcalf
Mission Mountains
Rattlesnake
Scapegoat
Selway
Bitterroot
Welcome Creek

### Wildlife & Fisheries

From elk herds roaming the forested mountains of western Montana to antelope racing across the eastern plains, the National Forests are home to a magnificent wildlife and fish resource. Chinook salmon, grizzly bears, northern grey wolves, bald eagles and over 600 other kinds of fish and wildlife thrive here.

There is no place like this vast unspoiled country where wildlife is so diverse and so easily found. It's a great place to watch or photograph animals, large and small. Bighorn sheep, songbirds, moose and prairie dogs are not limited to zoos and refuges. They live everywhere and are part of everyday life.

Some of the best hunting in North America is also found in the region. The state carefully regulates hunting to ensure wildlife populations and quality recreation for future generations.

More stream miles criss-cross this region than any other in the lower 48 states. Names of famous blue ribbon trout streams like the Big Horn, Big Hole and Madison roll off the lips of fishermen like priceless jewels. Hundreds of lakes and reservoirs provide exceptional fishing as well.

Want help finding the best place for photography, hunting or fishing? State licensed guides and outfitters know the country and have the gear to

## Montana Movies

Whether you've ever actually set foot in Montana or not, you've no doubt seen lots of it. If you haven't seen it in any of these movies, you've probably seen it in countless commercials and catalogues. It is a favorite backdrop for film makers. Montana State University has one of the top film schools in the country providing excellent support to film makers shooting in the state. Here is a list of movies filmed here.

2000: *The Flying Dutchman, The Slaughter Rule* (Great Falls) 1999: *Big Eden* (Glacier National Park)

1998: *The Hi-Line* (Livingston/Clyde Park)

1997: *Everything That Rises* (Livingston), *The Horse Whisperer* (Big Timber/ Livingston/Bozeman), *Me and Will, The Patriot* (Ennis), *What Dreams May Come* (Glacier National Park)

1996: *Almost Heros*

1995: *Amanda* (Red Lodge), *Broken Arrow* (Lewistown), *The Real Thing, Under Siege 2: Dark Territory* (MIssoula)

1993: *Beethoven's 2nd* (Glacier National Park/Flathead), *Forrest Gump* (Glacier National Park/Blackfeet Reservation), *Holy Matrimony* (Great Falls), *Iron Will* (West Yellowstone), *The Last Ride* (Livingston/ Deer Lodge), *Montana Crossroads, Return to Lonesome Dove* (Virginia City/ Butte/Billings, *The River Wild* (Libby/ Flathead)

1992: *Ballad of Little Jo* (Red Lodge), *Josh and S.A.M* (Billings)

1991: *A River Runs Through It* (Bozeman/Livingston), *Diggstown* (Deer Lodge), *Far and Away* (Billings), *Keep the Change* (Livingston), *Season of Change* (Bitterroot Valley)

1990: *Common Ground* (Columbia Falls), *Son of the Morning Star* (Billings), *True Colors* (Big Sky)

1989: *Always* (Libby), *Bright Angel* (Billings), *Montana* (Bozeman/Gallatin Gateway), *A Thousand Pieces of Gold* (Nevada City)

1988: *Cold Feet* (Livingston), *Disorganized Crime* (Hamilton/Darby/Missoula)

1987: *Pow Wow Highway* (Hardin/North Cheyenne Reservation/Colstrip), *War Party* (Browning/Cut Bank/Choteau)

1986: *Amazing Grace and Chuck* (Bozeman/Livingston/Helena),*Stacking* (Billings), *Untouchables* (Cascade), *Amy Grant: Home for the Holidays* (Kalispell/ Glacier Park)

1985: *Runaway Train* (Butte/Anaconda)

1983: *The Stone Boy* (Great Falls) , *Triumphs of a Man Called Horse* (Cooke City/Red Lodge)

1982: *Firefox* (Glasgow/Cut Bank)

1980: *Continental Divide* (Glacier National Park), *Fast Walking* (Deer Lodge)

1979: *Heartland* (Harlowton), *Heaven's Gate* (Kalispell/Glacier National Park), *Legend of Walks Far Woman* (Billings/Red Lodge/Hardin), *South by Northwest* (Virginia City/Nevada City)

1978: *Rodeo Red & The Runaway* (Billings), *The Shining* (Glacier National Park)

1977: *Christmas Miracle in Caulfield USA* (Roundup), *Grey Eagle* (Helena), *The Other Side of Hell* (Warm Springs), *Telefon* (Great Falls)

1976: *Beartooth* (Red Lodge), *Damnation Alley* (Lakeside), *Pony Express Rider* (Virginia City/Nevada City)

1975: *Missouri Breaks* (Billings/Virginia City/Red Lodge), *Winds of Autumn* (Kalispell)

1974: *The Killer Inside Me* (Butte), *Potato Fritz* (Helena), *Rancho Deluxe* (Livingston)

1973: *Route 66* (Butte), *Thunderbolt and Lightfoot* (Malpaso/Livingston/Great Falls), *Winterhawk* (Kalispell)

1972: *Evel Knievel* (Butte)

1970: *Little Big Man* (Virginia City/Billings)

1958: *Dangerous Mission* (Glacier National Park)

1954: *Cattle Queen of Montana* (East Glacier)

1953: *Powder River*

1951: *Timberjack, Warpath* (Missoula)

1950: *Red Skies Over Montana* (Missoula)

1920: *Devil's Horse* (Hardin), *Where the Rivers Rise* (Columbia Falls)

ensure an enjoyable trip even in rugged remote country.

### Trails

Trails provide the primary access to most of the undeveloped wildlands and millions of acres of wilderness.

Over 15,000 miles of trails provide a variety of challenges and scenic vistas to hikers, backpackers, horseriders, and cyclists. Most trails are open for recreational use year long; however, in some areas, seasonal restrictions are imposed to protect resources.

### Winter Activities

The national forests of Montana are a winter wonderland.

The 16 alpine ski areas provide slopes for every talent. Winter sports areas have been developed in cooperation with private industry and are operated under national forest special-use permits.

In addition to spectacular downhill runs, there is a vast and diverse landscape for crosscountry skiers and snowmobilers. Crosscountry skiers can follow over 600 miles of designated ski touring trails of varying difficulty across timbered slopes, open meadows, and ridgelines. Or experienced skiers, with appropriate precautions, can do some exploring on their own.

Snowmobilers can tour thousands of miles of designated snowmobile trails. In some areas, wildlife winter ranges are closed to snowmobiling.

There are many rustic cabins and lookouts available for rent, some accessible to only the skier or snowmobiler in winter. A directory is available.

The harsh conditions of winter can turn an outing into a tragedy. Knowledge of the area, weather, route, and the limitations of your body and equipment-plus a little common sense-can ensure safe and enjoyable outings.

### Scenic Drives

There are thousands of miles of roads available within the Region's national forests and grasslands. Some roads are high standard paved routes and others are low-standard "jeep" trails. Seasonal closures to protect resources, such as calving elk or water quality, may affect the use of certain roads. Information about motorized access and road restrictions for each national forest is shown on the forest visitor map.

Scenic drives abound throughout Montana. A few of the more popular routes include the drive around Hungry Horse Reservoir on the Flathead National Forest; the scenic loop around Lake Koocanusa behind Libby Dam on the Kootenai National Forest; and the route around Georgetown Lake on the Beaverhead-Deerlodge National Forest. These roads take you through rugged, scenic country and provide access for fishing and boating as well as to camping and picnicking sites.

For other driving adventures, follow the trail of Lewis and Clark across the Bitterroot Mountains on the Lolo and Clearwater National Forests. Or follow 27 mile Pioneer Mountains National Forest Scenic Byway, along the Pioneer Mountain Range on the Beaverhead-Deerlodge National Forest. Or visit Porphyry Peak Lookout on King's Hill Pass on the Lewis and Clark National Forest. Travel the fabulous Beartooth Highway across 10,942 foot Beartooth Summit on the Custer, Shoshone, and Gallatin National Forests.

Whether you are seeking solitude or scenic splendor, a national forest road will take you there.

### Camping & Picnicking

Visitors can camp and picnic almost anywhere on the national forests and grasslands. For those seeking more convenience, hundreds of developed sites usually contain a parking spur, table, fireplace, and toilets. Water is also provided in some areas. Some sites are accessible to the handicapped or disabled. Showers, laundry facilities, electrical hookups, and hot water are not provided.

Campgrounds requiring a fee for use are signed and limitations on length of stay, if any, are posted. Horses and the shooting of firearms in developed campsites are prohibited.

For the more venturesome, there are numerous isolated roadside and backcountry picnic and campsites. These sites do not contain improvements like toilet, table, or fireplaces.

No matter where you are camping or picnicking, help keep the area clean.

### Lewis & Clark

1101 15th St. No. Box 871 Great Falls, MT 59403. 791-7700

Like two forests in one package, the Lewis & Clark National Forest of west central Montana has two distinct divisions. The rugged mountain peaks of the Rocky Mountain Division often hold snow for 10 months of the year. This long backbone of a mountain range stretches south of Glacier National Park with seemingly endless paralleling ridges and valleys. The six mountain ranges of the Jefferson Division appear to be islands of forest dotting expanses of wheat and ranch lands. Each range has its own unique character, from gently rolling hillsides to rugged, rocky peaks. The Lewis and Clark is truly a forest for everyone to explore.

## Gallatin

P.O. Box 130, Federal Building Bozeman, MT 59771. 587-6701

Yellowstone! Gallatin! Madison! The headwaters of these rivers, world-renowned for "blue ribbon" trout fishing, flow through the heart of some of Montana's most spectacular public lands... the Gallatin National Forest. Located just north of Yellowstone National Park, the 2.1 million acre Gallatin is rich in wildlife, scenic alpine vistas, rugged wildlands, and a spectrum of recreation opportunities. Forest visitors can enjoy wildflowers, trout fishing, big game hunting, photography, alpine and nordic skiing, snowmobiling, camping backpacking, river floating, horseback riding, and more!

## Custer

1310 Main Street P.O. Box 50760 Billings, MT 59105. 657-6361

The lands of the Custer National Forest and National Grasslands lie scattered across 20 counties in Montana, North Dakota and South Dakota. Elevations range from less than 1,000 feet in the Sheyenne Grasslands to 12,799 foot Granite Peak, the highest in Montana. The vast distances across which this Forest is spread result in a very diverse landscape. Ancient sand dunes covered with grasslands, rugged badlands, densely wooded forests, and carpets of alpine wildflowers all await the visitor to the easternmost portion of the Northern Region.

## Kootenai

506 U.S. Highway 2 W. Libby, MT 59923. 293-6211

The Kootenai National Forest lies in the northwest corner of Montana. Its high craggy peaks, deep canyons and mixed conifers stretch from the Canadian border to the Clark Fork valley. Several U.S. and State Highways allow easy access to some of Montana's scenic treasures: the Purcell Mountains, the Yaak River, Ross Creek Scenic Area Giant Cedars, the Kootenai River, Lake Koocanusa, and Libby Dam. Where roads stop, wilderness begins. The heart of the Kootenai is the Cabinet Mountain Wilderness, where majestic peaks tower over the surroundings. The Kootenai is a great place to go to get away from it all!

## Beaverhead-Deerlodge

420 Barrett Street Dillon, MT 59725-3572. 683-3900

The Beaverhead portion of the Beaverhead-Deerlodge National Forest lies tucked away in a great mountainous bowl. The rugged Bitterroot and Centennial Mountain ranges flank the western and southern boundaries. To the east towers the Madison Range. Valley bottoms are about 4,500 feet while many of the peaks exceed 11,000 feet. Cottonwoods and willows line the river bottoms, while grasses and sagebrush carpet foothills. Lodgepole pine and Douglas-fir trees, interspersed with large grassy parks, cover mountain slopes.

The Deerlodge portion straddles the Continental Divide in the heart of richly historic mining country. Many old mines and the ghost town of Elkhorn silently speak of Montana's frontier heritage. The snow capped peaks of the Pintlers and grassy slopes with scattered timber provide excellent habitat for elk and enjoyable hiking and camping. Georgetown Lake offers good fishing, winter or summer.

## Flathead

1935 Third Avenue East Kalispell, MT 59901. 758-5200

The Flathead's spectacular, rugged terrain lies adjacent to Glacier National Park and west of the Continental Divide. The vast expanse of the Bob Marshall Wilderness complex offers forest visitors primitive recreational opportunities. This wild country provides habitat for endangered gray wolves and threatened grizzly bears. The Flathead Wild and Scenic River, a favorite of white-water rafters, and the Swan River, dissect the beauty of the Mission, Swan, and Flathead Mountain ranges. Glaciated peaks and alpine lakes beckon summer users to hike, camp or fish. Fresh powder challenges the alpine enthusiast on The Big Mountain ski area, while nordic skiers and snowmobilers seek the solitude of the backcountry. Try the undiscovered Flathead year-round.

## Helena

2880 Skyway Drive Helena, MT 59626. 449-5201

Montana's "Capital City Forest", the Helena National Forest provides a rather open atmosphere to the visitor, with many grassy parks interspersed amidst lodgepole pine and Douglas-fir forests. Highlighting the forest, the Gates of the Mountains Wilderness, remains as impressive a sight as when Lewis and Clark described them on their journey up the Missouri River. Mountains of the Continental Divide and spectacular alpine scenery characterize the Scapegoat Wilderness and the western portion of the forest. Wildlife and recreational values dominate in the Elkhorn range, southeast of Helena. Montana's rich mining and ranching history are an important part of the Helena National Forest.

## Lolo

Building 24, Fort Missoula Missoula, MT 59804. 329-3750

The Lolo National Forest surrounds the western Montana community of Missoula. The crest of the Bitterroot Mountains divides Montana from Idaho and serve as the forest's western boundary. The Continental Divide through the Scapegoat wilderness defines the forest's eastern boundary. Four major rivers and their streams offer some of the best fishing in the Rocky Mountains. The topography varies from remote, high alpine lakes to whitewater streams and from heavily forested ridges to smooth rolling meadows. The Rattlesnake National Recreation Area offers many recreation opportunities right on the edge of Missoula.

## Bitterroot

1801 North 1st Street Hamilton, MT 59840. 363-3131

Two major mountain ranges separated by the Bitterroot River valley in southeastern Montana and Idaho comprise the Bitterroot National Forest. Breathtaking scenery is provided by 30 deep, rocky, glaciated canyons breaking the sharp face of the Bitterroot range at regular intervals to the west. Most of this rugged range is wilderness. To the east, the Sapphire range presents a gentler horizon. The forest has plentiful big game, high quality water, and backcountry recreation opportunities including wild rivers.

*The above information on the National Forest System in Montana was reprinted from U.S. Forest Service information.*

# Forest Service Cabins

One of the best kept secrets in Montana is the availability of cabins and lookout stations that the U.S. Forest Service makes available to the public at a very nominal fee. At the end of each section we have provided a list of available cabins along with detailed information on each. Following is some general information on reserving and using the cabins.

## Application For Permits

Permits for use of recreational cabins in the National Forests of the Northern Region are issued on a first-come, first-served basis. Permits may be obtained in person or by mail by contacting the Ranger District having administrative responsibility for the cabin of your choice. Advance reservations of a week or more may be required. Lengths of stay are limited to 14 days and in some cases

# The Continental Divide National Scenic Trail

**The Continental Divide National** Scenic Trail (CDNST) was established by Congress under the National Trails System Act of 1968. The trail will extend 3,100 miles, in its entirety, from Canada to Mexico. This northernmost portion follows the backbone of the Rocky Mountains for 795 miles through Montana and Idaho. It passes through some of our nation's most spectacular scenery-Glacier National Park, ten national forests with wildernesses such as the Bob Marshall and Anaconda Pintler, several Bureau of Land Management Resource Areas, State lands and short segments of private lands.

This segment begins at the U.S./Canada border between Glacier and Waterton Lakes National Parks, following a route near the divide and through the Blackfeet Indian Reservation to Marias Pass. Southward the trail passes through the Bob Marshall and Scapegoat Wildernesses, skirting the Chinese Wall. After crossing Rogers and MacDonald Passes, it continues through historic mining districts and ghost towns. West of Anaconda the trail traverses the length of the Anaconda Pintler Wilderness, reaching the Montana-Idaho border near Lost Trail Pass on the 1805 route of Lewis and Clark.

Winding through the Bitterroot Range, the trail passes high above Big Hole National Battlefield, scene of conflict between the Nez Perce Tribe and the U.S. Army in 1877, and on to Lemhi Pass, headwaters of the Missouri River and marked by the Sacajawea Memorial. Continuing on through the Bitterroots, it crosses Monida Pass and winds along the crest of the Centennial Mountains above Red Rock Lakes National Wildlife Refuge. Staying near the divide, the trail crosses Raynolds and Targhee Passes with views of Henry's Lake to the south and Hebgen Lake to the north, before continuing on to the end of this segment of the CDNST, at the western boundary of Yellowstone National Park.

Elevations along the trail through Montana and Idaho vary from 4,200 feet at Waterton Lake to approximately 10,000 feet at Red Conglomerate Peaks in the Bitterroot Range. Over 90 percent of the trail is within 5 miles of the Continental Divide, and much is on the divide itself; the furthest that it deviates from the divide is 8 miles. Annual precipitation varies from 120 inches in Glacier National Park to only 20 inches near Rogers Pass. Because much comes as snow, portions of the trail are passable only in July, August, and September. Temperatures often drop below freezing, and snowstorms can occur even during the summer

Travel on the Continental Divide National Scenic Trail can be a long-remembered adventure. Following are a few tips to help insure a happy and safe trip. Travelers are urged to contact local Forest Service Ranger Stations for specific information.

**Interim Routes:** About 50 of the 795 miles of this northern portion of the trail do not currently exist as constructed trail or primitive road. Temporary "interim routes" serve as detours, pending construction of the preferred route. A special interim route exists in Glacier National Park. Because there are no Canadian Customs officials at Waterton Lake, an interim route for the trail begins at Chief Mountain Customs Station on Montana State Highway 17.

**Modes Of Travel:** While the National Trails System Act intended the trail be established primarily for hiking and horseback use, motorized uses are permitted where previously established. Of the total 795 miles of road and trail, 322 miles permit some type of summertime motorized use. Primitive roads serve as the trail route for 160 miles. Most of the route is lightly used and visitors can expect considerable solitude.

## Special Restrictions

**Glacier National Park:** special regulations apply to travel, camping and stock use. Motorized vehicles are prohibited.

**Wilderness:** travel and camping permits are not required, but some restrictions may apply, including party size limits; motorized transport and bicycles are prohibited.

**U.S. Sheep Experiment Station:** the trail crosses this station two places in the Centennial Mountains. Contact the station for restrictions.

**Stock use:** contact agencies managing the trail for restrictions on grazing, feeding and tying stock.

**Resupply:** There are 34 points on or near roads along this segment of the trail where travelers could prearrange for resupplies of food and equipment. Though land management agencies cannot provide this service, they can help you identify those points.

**Precautions:** Travelers are responsible for recognizing risks inherent in back country travel and taking appropriate precautions. Here are some things to consider:

**Bears:** all of the CDNST in Montana and Idaho is in occupied black bear habitat, and much is also frequented by grizzly bears. To prevent bear-human conflicts, special practices need to be followed in food storage, cooking and disposal of wastes; overnight camping may be prohibited in places.

**Terrain, weather:** the trail passes through remote and rugged terrain. Travelers may encounter a variety of dangerous conditions and face the inherent risks of inclement weather, lightning, isolation, physical hazards, and minimal communications.

**Water:** water in springs, streams and lakes should not be considered safe to drink without proper treatment.

**Mixed uses:** use caution where the trail crosses roads or highways, or where motorized use is allowed

**Be Considerate:** Five miles of the trail lie within the Blackfeet Indian Reservation, and other short sections cross private lands. Please respect these lands and observe special restrictions to ensure they will remain open to travelers in the future. Visitors can expect to observe various management activities, such as logging, mining and grazing on both public and private land along the trail. Agency land management plans and the comprehensive plan for the trail provide for these activities.

**LEAVE NO TRACE!!!!**

Respect those who will follow your footsteps. Leave no trace of your visit.

*Reprinted from National Forest Service pamphlet.*

less. Maps and information may be obtained by Forest Service District maintaining each cabin/lookout.

The daily rate for occupancy is listed. Checks or postal money orders should be made payable to USDA Forest Service.

## Facilities

Cabins and lookouts available through the rental program are rustic and primitive in nature. Most of these cabins are guard stations or work centers located in remote areas that are occasionally used to house Forest Service employees. As the need for these cabins declines, they are being made available to the general public. With the exception of a few cabins, do not expect the modern conveniences that we all are so accustomed to enjoying.

It is suggested that an inquiry be made to the Ranger District that has administrative responsibility for the cabin as to what is and what is not furnished and disabled access information. Based on the information received, you can then plan your needs.

Cabins are generally equipped with the bare basics, including a table, chairs, wood stove and bunks (most with mattresses, some without). Bedding is not furnished. Cooking utensils are available at some cabins but not all of them. Electricity and piped-in water are generally NOT available. It may be necessary to bring safe drinking water or be prepared to chemically treat or boil drinking water. At some cabins, you will need to find and cut your own firewood. Expect to use outdoor toilets. Telephones are not available.

Before leaving, users are requested to: burn all combustible waste materials; make sure fires in stoves are out; pack out all garbage and empty bottles or cans; clean the cabin; leave a supply of firewood and return the key.

## Potential Risks

Travel in the National Forests and use of rustic cabins and lookouts invokes a degree of risk. Recreationists must assume the responsibility to obtain knowledge and skills necessary to protect themselves and members of their party from injury and illness. Weather, snow conditions, personal physical skill and condition along with other factors can influence travel time and difficulty. Parents are strongly discouraged from bringing children under 12 years of age to Lookout Towers. Persons afraid of heights, or lacking physical strength, should also avoid climbing Lookout Towers. Prior to the trip, permit holders are advised to contact the local Ranger District for current conditions. *Reprinted from U.S. Forest Service brochure.*

## Montana's State Park System

Because of the exceptional recreational opportunities on Montana's federal lands, the diversity of opportunities available in the Montana State Park System is sometimes overlooked. This would be a mistake, as the true picture of Montana's natural, cultural, and recreational resources is not complete without the state parks.

Montana's State Park System was created in 1939, when the Montana Legislature created a State Parks Commission. Lewis and Clark Caverns became the state's first state park when the site was transferred to Montana from the federal government. Today, the network of sites has grown to forty-one, in addition to a number of affiliated sites.

State parks are found in every region of the state, offering a wide range of landscapes, natural features, history, and recreational opportunities. Some parks feature a diversity of visitor facilities such as showers, boat launch sites, and concessions, while others are much less developed.

State Park Information: For more detailed state park information, call the Montana Parks Division at 444-3750. Hearing impaired recreationists may call the TDD number at 444-1200.

**Camping:** Camping is offered at many state parks for a modest fee. Campsites are available on a first-come, first-served basis; there is no comprehensive, statewide reservation system. While services vary between individual parks, most sites have a picnic table, a fire ring or grill, and parking for one vehicle and RV.

**Group Camping:** Several state parks have sites set aside for group use. A special brochure is available with more detailed information on group camping opportunities at state parks and fishing access sites.

**Rental Cabins:** Rustic cabins are available for rent at Lewis and Clark Caverns State Park. Call 287-3541 for reservations.

**Day Use Parks:** Some Montana state parks are open for a range of day uses, but do not allow overnight stays.

**Primitive Service Parks:** A primitive parks system was established by the Montana Legislature in 1993. Primitive parks have a minimum of services available, with visitors expected to pack out their own trash.

**Season:** Some parks are open for day use and camping year-round, while others close at least some of their facilities during the winter. For the most current information, call the number listed for each park.

**Fees:** Day use fees are charged at many state parks. Purchase of an annual State Parks Passport allows free entry to all Montana State Parks. Camping fees vary according to the level of service provided.

Camping fees are charged per "camper unit" for a campsite. A "camper unit" is defined as a motorized vehicle, motor home, camping bus, pull-type camper, tent, or any other device designed for sleeping,

A self-registration system is in use at most state parks. Recreation use fees are also charged for designated group use facilities, guided tours, and other services. Fee information is available from the individual parks. Special floater fees are in effect on the Smith River.

Picnicking: Many state parks have developed facilities for picnicking, and some include special facilities for group use. Consult the data given with each state park description. *Reprinted from Montana Fish, Wildlife & Parks brochure.*

## Fishing

### Seasons

You can fish year round in Montana, but seasonal regulations do exist, and water conditions will affect your success. Generally, lakes and larger rivers can be fished all year, while smaller tributaries are closed in the winter and early spring to allow fish to spawn. Ice fishing is popular in the winter. The lakes are usually frozen from December through at least March. During the spring runoff when many freestone rivers are high and muddy, flyfishermen find luck in the smaller streams and spring creeks. The prime fishing season is from late June through October.

### Licenses

A Montana fishing license is required for all anglers 15 years of age and older. You can purchase a license just about anywhere fishing tackle is sold or from any of the Montana Fish, Wildlife and Parks offices. Non-residents can purchase licenses in two-day increments or by the season. There are special requirements for youths under 15, residents 62 years of age or older, and for taking paddlefish. Contact Montana Fish, Wildlife and Parks for a fishing regulations brochure.

### Fishing sites

We have marked over 250 fishing sites on our maps. Each section has a reference chart referring to the numbered sites on the maps. The charts include species available and facilities available. The charts are at the end of each section.

### Maps

While we have marked all of the common fishing sites in the state, there are commercially available maps available. Some of the best for lake fishing are the Kingfisher series. They provide topographic contours showing depths in several of Montana's largest lake fisheries. They also offer some excellent fishing tips. They are available for Fort Peck Lake, Canyon Ferry Lake, Flathead Lake, Holter Lake, and Georgetown Lake. They can be found in many Montana fishing shops or ordered directly by calling 406-585-0237.

## The Fires of 2000

If you paid any attention to the national media during the summer of 2000, you couldn't come to any conclusion other than Montana was a raging inferno and had been blackened beyond recognition. Yes, the skies were smoky for a few weeks, and yes there were thousands of acres burned. The truth is though, you will have to make a serious effort to see any signs of those fires. Most of the fires were in remote regions and back country. If you want to make a game of it with the kids, try to find a single blackened tree while driving the main roads of the state. It will be rare that you will here someone shout "found one!"

## Weather

Montana is known for its unpredictable weather. The weather maintains as much variety as does the state's topography. The lowest temperature recorded in the lower 48 states was -70°F, recorded northwest of Helena. Hot summers are common; 117 degrees has been recorded in both Glendive and Medicine Lake, but the hottest day in Montana is not suffocating due to its low humidity which generally ranges between 20 and 30 percent. The real beauty of Montana's weather, is that it is very dry. Extremes of hot or cold never feel oppressive as a result.

May and June are the wettest months for most of the state. Average rainfall is 15 inches, which can vary from less than 10 inches on the plains and to more than 50 inches in the mountains. July and August are usually Montana's warmest, driest periods and serve as the busiest time for tourism and recreation. Often there is a pleasant Indian summer in September and October. Warm, bright days with cool nights make it an exhilarating time with fishing at its prime. During the fall, Montana's forests may not flaunt the vibrant colors of the eastern woodlands, but its tamaracks are bright yellow contrasting nicely against the ever-

### *Montana Trivia*

T-Shirt Quote:

Feed the Bears.
Ride the Buffalo.
Pet the wolves.
Swim the Hot Pots.
Stick your head in a Geyser.
We thank you for your support.
Montana Paramedics.

greens, and the aspen groves turn a dazzling gold.

The infamous Montana winter rarely settles in for keeps. Even though snow can fall in July, roads can also be clear throughout November. Montana's cold spells and blasts of arctic air bring blizzards which often melt the following week from dry chinook winds blowing from the west. (Native Americans called these winds the "snow eaters.") Even when roads are clear, travelers must be careful as one could hit a patch of ice in a shaded, mountainous area although the road may be dry for miles. While temperatures can be extreme in Montana, the low humidity never causes the weather to be oppressively hot or cold.

## Precautions

**Water Sports:** Beware of high river waters in the spring due to melting snow; it is best to contact knowledgeable people in the area for information before venturing out on your own.

**Animal Caution:** Grizzly bears are found in both Glacier and Yellowstone National Parks and in smaller populations in the northern Rockies. Grizzlies are vicious when provoked, and it doesn't take much to rile them. Check with local rangers for bear updates and guidelines before heading into bear country. When hiking even on trails make noise to warn bears of your presence. If you camp, don't sleep near strong smells or food. Hang all food from branches 100 yards from tents. Also, watch for moose on or near hiking trails. Moose, especially those with offspring, are often known to charge if hikers get too close or the animal feels threatened.

**Rattlesnake Warning:** Rattlesnakes are common primarily in eastern parts of Montana. A bite from the snake can be fatal if not properly treated. These snakes are not aggressive and will usually retreat unless threatened. It is recommended that you wear strong and high top boots when hiking and be mindful of your step. Be especially careful near rocky areas; snakes often sun themselves on exposed rocks. If you hear a rattle, stop and slowly back away. If bitten, immobilize the area and seek medical care immediately.

**Weather:** Extremes are commonplace in Montana without a moment's notice. In high temperatures drink plenty of water; Montana is very dry which aides dehydration in warm weather. Even in warmer weather, nights can be cold so have extra clothes on hand. Sudden storms can blow in; be prepared with rain and wind gear. The windiest areas are Great Falls, Livingston, and Cut Bank. When driving, listen for wind warnings.

Winter weather is the greatest concern. While roads can be treacherous if snow covered, melting snow and ice can also leave small and invisible patches of ice on the road. Also, wildlife commonly descend from the mountains looking for food; be aware of deer or elk on the road particularly at dusk, sunset or at night when visibility is limited. If you travel by automobile during Montana's winter, have plenty of blankets or a sleeping bag, warm clothing, flashlight, and some food and water on hand.

## How to Use this Book

While the state tourism officials divide the state into six tourism "countries," we felt those divisions to be too few and too broad. We divided the state into fifteen sections. Each section has a common personality and at least one major city or town (by Montana standards). We felt doing so makes it much easier to flow through the book. The material in each section is loosely ordered along the highway routes through the section and organized by locator numbers.

### Locator Numbers

These are the numbers on the map in white on a black circle (✂). All information relating to the area on the map marked by that number is presented together in the section. The sections of the book are ordered from southeast to northwest. The numbers in each section are ordered in roughly the same direction. This allows you to follow the routes mile by mile and quickly find information along your path relating to your location on the path. In a nutshell, find the number on the map, then find that number heading in the section and listed under that number is everything there is to see or do at that location on the map.

### Category Classification

Each item listed is classified under one of eight categories. The classification key is the shaded letter immediately preceding the item listed. This makes it very simple to find the type of information you're looking for immediately. If you're hungry, look for any items preceded by an **F**. Looking for something to do? Look for a **T** or **V**. Want to buy something to take home with you? Look for an **S**. Here is a key for the categories:

### H Historic Marker

We have taken the text from over hundreds of historical markers throughout the state and reprinted them here. They're fun reading, and in total provide an excellent background on the history and growth of Montana. We have entered them where they are located. Sometimes this is a different location than the actual item they are referring to. Even though, we've presented the text of these markers here, take the time to stop at everyone you can. They are only a label for the actual site or event they speak of, and the experience is only complete if you are able to view the area surrounding them.

### D Lewis & Clark Corps of Discovery

Under this heading you will find notes from the Lewis & Clark journals as well as other related information relevant to this remarkable journey of exploration.

### T Attraction

This category includes just about anything worth stopping for. It might be a museum, a ghost town, a park, or just some quirky thing on the side of the road that makes traveling through this state so

interesting. Whatever it is, we've tried to provide enough information to let you decide whether you want to plan a stop or not.

### V Adventure

This would be just about anything you would get out of your car and do. A whitewater raft trip, horseback ride, etc.

### A Auto

These are gas stops. A few are repair places as well.

### F Food

We didn't discriminate. If there is prepared food available, we list it. We've listed everything ranging from the finest restaurants in the state (and there are a lot of them), to fast food and hot dog stands. Bottom line, if they'll fix it for you, they're listed here. While we don't rate any of the establishments, we highly encourage you to try the mom and pop eateries and the locally owned fine dining spots. Dayton Duncan, in his excellent book *Out West: American Journey Along the Lewis and Clark Trail* (1987, Penguin Books) gave the best advice we've heard;

> *"Franchises are not for the traveler bent on discovery. Forsaking franchises, like forsaking interstates, means that you're willing to chance the ups and downs, the starts and the stops of gastronomy as well as motoring. It means sometimes finishing a supper so good that you order the piece of pie you hadn't realized you wanted and you're sure you don't need—and spending the night in town just so you can have breakfast in the same place."*

In Montana, you're pretty safe. Just consider the logic. Most of these towns are so small that any place not putting up good grub isn't going to last long anyway. Accountability. While much of America has forgotten that concept, it is still a harsh and unforgiving rule in Montana.

As for fine dining, we'd put scores of our best against the best anywhere outside of Montana. Some of the most talented culinary artists in the world have settled here for the lifestyle and share their talents with us.

## L Lodging

If they'll put a roof over your head and a mattress under your back, they're listed here. Again, we don't discriminate. Truth is, it's hard to find a bad motel in this state. Surviving here is tough, and if you don't put up a good product, you don't last long.

## C Camping

These are private campgrounds that wished to be included in the main portion of each section. Otherwise, all private campgrounds are listed at the back of each section.

## S Shopping

Do we need to explain this one? Obviously, we don't list every place in the state you can buy something. Only those who wanted to be in here. And yes, they paid for the opportunity. It would be impractical to list every place in the state you can buy something. And you probably wouldn't want to wade through all of them to get to the ones that count. So we left it up to the merchants to decide whether or not they might have something of interest to you, and to choose whether or not to include themselves in this book.

## M Misc. Services

This would be just about anything that doesn't fall into one of the other categories above.

## Maps

We've included a map for just about anything you would need a map for. At the beginning of each section is a detailed map of the section. We've also included a map of any town too big to see everything on Main Street standing in one spot—forty-five in all. We've also included a number of maps of special locations. On each of the section maps we've marked where campgrounds, fishing sites, and Lewis & Clark points of interest are.

## Public Campgrounds

Public campgrounds are marked on the map with a number. At the end of each section is a chart listing each campground along with pertinent information about that site. The listings are numbered and the numbers match those on the map. We only listed campgrounds that are maintained in some manner by a state or federal agency. There are countless primitive campgrounds in the state that are not maintained and have no facilities. You'll find almost all of Montana's public campgrounds to be uncrowded. It's not unusual, even at the peak of tourist season, to be the only campers at a site. Most of them charge a small fee to cover the cost of maintaining them.

## Fishing Sites

We've listed over 250 fishing sites in the state and marked and numbered them on the maps. At the end of each section is a chart listing each site in the section along with species and facilities information. There are thousands of places to wet a line in Montana. We have listed the major fisheries and only those that are relatively easy to access.

## Along the Trail of Lewis and Clark

There are numerous sidebars relating to the journey of the Corps of Discovery in addition to those entries under the numbered areas.

## Scenic Drives

We have tried to offer some scenic or interesting side trips wherever possible. Some take you on backroads, others just take you a different way. Some are day trips, some are longer. We feel the book itself offers one long scenic trip, but if you want to get off the path, these offer some choices. Heed the warnings about gumbo and other backroad hazards mentioned earlier in this book.

## Hikes

We have offered you a number of hikes at the end of most sections. There are a few sections of the state that don't offer too many hiking options. We didn't provide a lot of detail about the hikes. We simply pointed them out and tell you how to get there.

## Information Please

Here we give you phone number for just about anything we missed earlier in the section that might be of interest to you.

## What's Happening Here?

We've listed every event we could find that is a recurring event. There are over 650 events listed in total throughout the book.

## Dining and Lodging Quick Reference Guides

These charts allow you to take a quick scan of all of the dining and lodging facilities in a manner that allows you to find information quickly and make quick comparisons. The map locator numbers are listed with each entry to help you find their location and possibly additional information about them in the front of the section.

## Notes

We've allowed you ample room at the back of each section to make notes about your trip or to record additional information about your trip. This is a good place to store reservation confirmation numbers, or schedule information.

We've made every effort to make this book a tool for you to get the most from your visit to the state. If you already live here, we hope it awakens you to the endless things there to do and see in the magnificent chunk of America.

### *Montana Trivia*

Only the state of Texas, with 129 million acres under cultivation, has more farmland than Montana with 58.6 million acres. Approximately 63 percent of Montana land is involved in farming or ranching. Only Kansas and North Dakota harvest more wheat annually than Montana, and only North Dakota harvests more Barley. Montana exports almost 70 percent of its wheat to foreign countries. There are about 24,000 ranchers in Montana at an average age of 60. 5.9 percent of Montana's work force is involved in farming versus 1.9 percent nationwide. While wheat, barley, and hay provide the most total economic benefit, potatoes, sugar beets, and dry beans bring the most money per acre. Farming is the only economic sector in Montana where wages are above the national average

## Montana License Plate Numbers

Montana counties were originally numbered for license plates based on the size of the county. Since the original numbering, populations have shifted—sometimes dramatically. The numbering system, however, has remained the same.

1: Silver Bow (Butte)
2: Cascade (Great Falls)
3: Yellowstone (Billings)
4: Missoula (Missoula)
5: Lewis & Clark (Helena)
6: Gallatin (Bozeman)
7: Flathead (Kalispell)
8: Fergus (Lewistown)
9: Powder River (Broadus)
10: Carbon (Red Lodge)
11: Phillips (Malta)
12: Hill (Havre)
13: Ravalli (Hamilton)
14: Custer (Miles City)
15: Lake (Polson)
16: Dawson (Glendive)
17: Roosevelt (Wolf Point)
18: Beaverhead (Dillon)
19: Choteau (Fort Benton)
20: Valley (Glasgow)
21: Toole (Shelby)
22: Big Horn (Hardin)
23: Musselshell (Roundup)
24: Blaine (Chinook)
25: Madison (Virginia City)
26: Pondera (Conrad)
27: Richland (Sidney)
28: Powell (Deer Lodge)
29: Rosebud (Forsyth)
30: Deer Lodge (Anaconda)
31: Teton (Choteau)
32: Stillwater (Columbus)
33: Treasure (Hysham)
34: Sheridan (Plentywood)
35: Sanders (Thompson Falls)
36: Judith Basin (Stanford)
37: Daniels (Scobey)
38: Glacier (Cut Bank)
39: Fallon (Baker)
40: Sweet Grass (Big Timber)
41: McCone (Circle)
42: Carter (Ekalaka)
43: Broadwater (Townsend)
44: Wheatland (Harlowtown)
45: Prairie (Terry)
46: Granite (Philipsburg)
47: Meagher (White Sulphur Springs)
48: Liberty (Chester)
49: Park (Livingston)
50: Garfield (Jordan)
51: Jefferson (Boulder)
52: Wibaux (Wibaux)
53: Golden Valley (Ryegate)
54: Mineral (Superior)
55: Petroleum (Winnett)
56: Lincoln (Libby)

# Montana Glossary

**Alkali** - white powdery substance appearing on soil surface often around places that have been wet

**Badlands** - bleak, desolate, hostile-looking area

**Basin** - a bowl-shaped valley

**Black ice** - icy stretch of road or highway

**Blizzard** - a very heavy snowstorm with strong winds

**Bull pine** - common name for Ponderosa Pine

**Borrow pit** - a depression beside the road left after the dirt was removed to build the elevated roadway, out-of-staters call them "ditches"

**Chains** - actual chains attached to tires so you get better traction on snow and ice -required on many mountain passes

**Chaps** - ("shaps") leather leg protection for cowboys

**Chinook** - a warm winter wind in winter that melts snow and ice

**Cooley** - miniature valley

**Creek** - medium-sized flow of water, 10-20 feet wide, pronounced "crick"

**Critter** - usually refers to some form of livestock

**Dog hair pine** - very thick pine—trees, need to be thinned

**Dogs** - sometimes refers to coyotes

**Down the road a piece** - Not far - may be a quarter mile or twenty miles (distances seem different in Montana!)

**Draw** - same as a cooley, maybe bigger

**Dryland Farm** - Non-irrigated farm; watered only by rain/snow

**Flood Irrigation** - run ditch water across entire field

**Foothills** - gentle hills at base of mountains

**Gelding** - a male horse that has been castrated

**Good handle** - a good understanding or ability

**Gulley** - like a cooley, maybe smaller. but sharper, more vertical banks

**Gulley washer** - heavy rain storm

**Heave** - where water gets into crack in a road, freezes and expands. When it melts in spring, many depressions and wide cracks are left in the roadways

**Heifer** - a female bovine that hasn't yet had a calf

**Hi-Line** - Hwy. 2 running east to west along the northern part of the state from Bainville to Browning. The route of the Great Northern Railway.

**Jack fence** - x-crossed posts that sit on top the ground, used where it's too rocky to dig post holes

**A little gun shy** - a little jumpy/has had some bad experiences

**Mare** - a female horse

**Missouri Breaks** - canyons, ridges, draws, alongside the Missouri River

**Outfit** - usually refers to a vehicle, sometimes with horse trailer

**Pair** - means a cow and her calf

**Pasty** - a kind of meat pie made with a flour wrapper usually filled with diced beef, onion, turnip, potato and brown gravy. Started as a staple for miners lunch pails. The correct pronunciation is"pass' tee".

**Plow** - usually refers to snowplow - clears roads of snow - usually a pickup or truck

**Plug-in** - outlet at motel where you plug in engine heater of your vehicle so it won't freeze up overnight

**Potbelly** - semi-truck that hauls cattle

**Pulling a big circle** - taking a long trip

**Range land** - native grazing area

**Rattler** - a rattlesnake (beware - poisonous)

**Ridge** - abrupt change in elevation

**Riding with a loose rein** - relaxed, not heavily supervised

**Rise** - like a hill but maybe lower, can't see over it

**River** - a wide creek, maybe 30-40 feet across or more

**Rode hard an' put away wet** - really tired - could be animal or person who has worked hard

**Row crop** - type of farming, usually high-intensity crops planted in rows like potatoes, corn, sugar beets

**Ruminate** - think about something

**Salt grass** - grass that grows in highly alkaline soil

**Sanded road** - icy highways and roads are sanded to cut down skidding and sliding

**Sheep fence** - small mesh wire fence for securing sheep/goats

**Short grass** - doesn't require much moisture and is less than a foot tall

**Snow fences** - built to control drifting snow, usually seen along roadways to help keep roads clear

**Snowblind** - a winter condition where the snow is so bright from the sun it becomes difficult to see

**Spring wheat** - planted in the spring of the year

**Spring** - area where water comes up from deep inside earth

**Stallion** - a male horse that has not been castrated

**Steer** - a male bovine that has been castrated

**Stock** - short for 'livestock'

**Stream** - a small creek, a few feet wide

**Strip farm** - method of farming which rotates crops and controls wind erosion

**Studs** - tires with metal studs imbedded give better traction in snow and ice

**Summer fallow** - farming practice whereby ground is left bare of a crop every other year to conserve moisture and control weeds

**Swather** - machine that cuts hay

**Top a the mornin' to ya** - good morning/have a nice day

**Valley** - lowland surrounded by hills or mountains

**White Out** - snowstorm so heavy that everything looks white, zero visibility, extremely dangerous to drive in

**Wilderness Area** - a Congressionally mandated area within Forest Service land that disallows roads, mining, logging and motorized vehicles

**Winter wheat** - variety of wheat planted in the autumn which germinates then continues growing in the Spring

Some place names you might like a little help with:

**Absarokee**: Ab-SOR-kee
**Charlo**: SHAR-low
**Ekalaka**: EEK-a-lack-a
**Havre**: Hav-er
**Helena**: HELL-en-ah
**Hysham**: HI-shum
**Makoshika**: ma-KOE-sheek-ah
**Marias**: Ma-RYE-us
**Missoula**: Ma-SOO-la
**Rapelje**: Ra-pell-jay
**Ronan**: ROE-nan
Waddie: Cowboy
**Winnett**: WIN-ett

*Montana Trivia*

Only three states have a larger land area than Montana: Alaska, California and Texas.

*Montana Trivia*

The distance from one end of Montana to the other is roughly the distance from Chicago to New York City.

*Montana Trivia*

Montana has a state fossil: the duck-billed dinosaur or Maiasaura peeblesorum (good mother lizard).

All Montana Area Codes are 406

# MONTANA ZIP CODES

|  |  |
|---|---|
| Absarokee | 59001 |
| Acton | 59002 |
| Alberton | 59820 |
| Alder | 59710 |
| Alzada | 59311 |
| Anaconda | 59711 |
| Angela | 59312 |
| Antelope | 59211 |
| Arlee | 59821 |
| Ashland | 59003 |
| Augusta | 59410 |
| Avon | 59713 |
| Babb | 59411 |
| Bainville | 59212 |
| Baker | 59313 |
| Ballantine, | 59006 |
| Basin | 59631 |
| Bearcreek | 59007 |
| Belfry | 59008 |
| Belgrade | 59714 |
| Belt | 59412 |
| Biddle | 59314 |
| Big Arm | 59910 |
| Big Fork | 59911 |
| Bighorn | 59010 |
| Big Sandy | 59520 |
| Big Sky | 59716 |
| Big Timber | 59011 |
| *Billings | 59101 |
| Birney | 59012 |
| Black Eagle | 59414 |
| Bloomfield | 59315 |
| Bonner | 59823 |
| Boulder | 59632 |
| Box Elder | 59521 |
| Boyd | 59013 |
| Boyes | 59316 |
| *Bozeman | 59715 |
| Brady | 59416 |
| Bridger | 59014 |
| Broadus | 59317 |
| Broadview | 59015 |
| Brockton | 59213 |
| Brockway | 59214 |
| Browning | 59417 |
| Brusett | 59318 |
| Buffalo | 59418 |
| Busby | 59016 |
| *Butte | 59701 |
| Bynum | 59419 |
| Cameron | 59720 |
| Canyon Creek | 59633 |
| Capitol | 59319 |
| Cardwell | 59721 |
| Carter | 59420 |
| Cascade | 59421 |
| Cat Creek | 59087 |
| Charlo | 59824 |
| Chester | 59522 |
| Chinook | 59523 |
| Choteau | 59422 |
| Circle | 59215 |
| Clancy | 59634 |
| Clinton | 59825 |
| Clyde Park | 59018 |
| Coffee Creek | 59424 |
| Cohagen | 59322 |
| Colstrip | 59323 |
| Columbia Falls | 59912 |
| Columbus | 59019 |
| Condon | 59826 |
| Conner | 59827 |
| Conrad | 59425 |
| Cooke City | 59020 |
| Coram | 59913 |
| Corvallis | 59828 |
| Corwin Springs | 59030 |
| Crane | 59217 |
| Creston | 59902 |
| Crow Agency | 59022 |
| Culbertson | 59218 |
| Custer | 59024 |
| Cut Bank | 59427 |
| Dagmar | 59219 |
| Danvers | 59429 |
| Darby | 59829 |
| Dayton | 59914 |
| De Borgia | 59830 |
| Decker | 59025 |
| Deer Lodge | 59722 |
| Dell | 59724 |
| Delphia | 59073 |
| Denton | 59430 |
| Dillon | 59725 |
| Divide | 59727 |
| Dixon | 59831 |
| Dodson | 59524 |
| Drummond | 59832 |
| Dupuyer | 59432 |
| Dutton | 59433 |
| Edgar | 59026 |
| E. Glacier Park | 59434 |
| East Helena | 59635 |
| Ekalaka | 59324 |
| Elliston | 59728 |
| Elmo | 59915 |
| Emigrant | 59027 |
| Enid | 59220 |
| Ennis | 59729 |
| Epsie | 59317 |
| Essex | 59916 |
| Ethridge | 59435 |
| Eureka | 59917 |
| *Evergreen | 59901 |
| Fairfield | 59436 |
| Fairview | 59221 |
| Fallon | 59326 |
| Ferdig | 59437 |
| Fishtail | 59028 |
| Flaxville | 59222 |
| Florence | 59833 |
| Floweree | 59440 |
| Forestgrove, | 59441 |
| Forsyth | 59327 |
| Fort Benton | 59442 |
| Fort Harrison | 59636 |
| Fortine | 59918 |
| Fort Peck | 59223 |
| Fort Shaw | 59443 |
| Fort Smith | 59035 |
| Four Buttes | 59263 |
| Frazer | 59225 |
| Frenchtown | 59834 |
| Froid | 59226 |
| Fromberg | 59029 |
| Galata | 59444 |
| Gallatin Gateway | 59730 |
| Gardiner | 59030 |
| Garneill | 59445 |
| Garrison | 59731 |
| Garryowen | 59031 |
| Geraldine | 59446 |
| Geyser | 59447 |
| Gildford | 59525 |
| Glasgow | 59230 |
| Glen | 59732 |
| Glendive | 59330 |
| Glentana | 59240 |
| Goldcreek | 59733 |
| Grantsdale, | 59835 |
| Grass Range | 59032 |
| *Great Falls | 59401 |
| Greenough | 59836 |
| Greycliff | 59033 |
| Hall | 59837 |
| Hamilton | 59840 |
| Hammond | 59332 |
| Hardin | 59034 |
| Harlem | 59526 |
| Harlowton | 59036 |
| Harrison | 59735 |
| Hathaway | 59333 |
| Haugan | 59842 |
| Havre | 59501 |
| Hays | 59527 |
| Heart Butte | 59448 |
| *Helena | 59601 |
| Helmville | 59843 |
| Heron | 59844 |
| Highwood | 59450 |
| Hilger | 59451 |
| Hingham | 59528 |
| Hinsdale | 59241 |
| Hobson | 59452 |
| Hogeland | 59529 |
| Homestead | 59242 |
| Hot Springs | 59845 |
| Hungry Horse | 59919 |
| Huntley | 59037 |
| Huson | 59846 |
| Hysham | 59038 |
| Ingomar | 59039 |
| Inverness | 59530 |
| Ismay | 59336 |
| Jackson | 59736 |
| Jeffers | 59737 |
| Jefferson City | 59638 |
| Joliet | 59041 |
| Joplin | 59531 |
| Jordan | 59337 |
| Judith Gap | 59453 |
| *Kalispell | 59901 |
| Kevin | 59454 |
| Kila | 59920 |
| Kinsey | 59338 |
| Kremlin | 59532 |
| Lake McDonald | 59921 |
| Lakeside | 59922 |
| Lambert | 59243 |
| Lame Deer | 59043 |
| Landusky | 59533 |
| Larslan | 59244 |
| Laurel | 59044 |
| Laurin | 59738 |
| Lavina | 59046 |
| Ledger | 59456 |
| Lewistown | 59457 |
| Libby | 59923 |
| Lima | 59739 |
| Lincoln | 59639 |
| Lindsay | 59339 |
| Livingston | 59047 |
| Lloyd | 59535 |
| Lodge Grass | 59050 |
| Lolo | 59847 |
| Loma | 59460 |
| Lonepine | 59848 |
| Loring | 59537 |
| Lothair | 59461 |
| Lustre | 59225 |
| Luther | 59068 |
| Malmstrom AFB | 59402 |
| Malta | 59538 |
| Manhattan | 59741 |
| Marion | 59925 |
| Martin City | 59926 |
| Martinsdale | 59053 |
| Marysville | 59640 |
| Maudlow | 59714 |
| Maxville, | 59858 |
| McAllister | 59740 |
| McCabe | 59245 |
| McLeod | 59052 |
| Medicine Lake | 59247 |
| Melrose | 59743 |
| Melstone | 59054 |
| Melville | 59055 |
| Mildred | 59341 |
| Miles City | 59301 |
| Mill Iron | 59342 |
| Milltown | 59851 |
| *Missoula | 59801 |
| Moccasin | 59462 |
| Moiese | 59824 |
| Molt | 59057 |
| Monarch | 59463 |
| Moore | 59464 |
| Mosby | 59058 |
| Musselshell | 59059 |
| Nashua | 59248 |
| Nelhart | 59465 |
| Niarada | 59845 |
| Norris | 59745 |
| Noxon | 59853 |
| Nye | 59061 |
| Oilmont | 59466 |
| Olive | 59343 |
| Olney | 59927 |
| Opheim | 59250 |
| Otter | 59062 |
| Outlook | 59252 |
| Ovando | 59854 |
| Pablo | 59855 |
| Paradise | 59856 |
| Park City | 59063 |
| Peerless | 59253 |
| Pendroy | 59467 |
| Perma | 59857 |
| Phillipsburg | 59858 |
| Pinesdale | 59841 |
| Plains | 59859 |
| Plentywood | 59254 |
| Plevna | 59344 |
| Polaris | 59746 |
| Polebridge | 59928 |
| Poison | 59860 |
| Pompeys Pillar | 59064 |
| Pony | 59747 |
| Poplar | 59255 |
| Powderville | 59345 |
| Power | 59468 |
| Pray | 59065 |
| Proctor | 59929 |
| Proctor | 59914 |
| Pryor | 59066 |
| Radersburg | 59641 |
| Ramsay | 59748 |
| Rapelje | 59067 |
| Ravalli | 59863 |
| Raymond | 59256 |
| Raynesford | 59469 |
| Red Lodge | 59068 |
| Redstone | 59257 |
| Reedpoint | 59069 |
| Regina | 59539 |
| Reserve | 59258 |
| Rexford | 59930 |
| Richey | 59259 |
| Richland | 59260 |
| Ringling | 59642 |
| Roberts | 59070 |
| Rock Springs | 59346 |
| Rollins | 59931 |
| Ronan | 59864 |
| Roscoe | 59071 |
| Rosebud | 59347 |
| Roundup | 59072 |
| Roy | 59471 |
| Rudyard | 59540 |
| Ryegate | 59074 |
| Saco | 59261 |
| St. Ignatius | 59865 |
| St. Labre | 59004 |
| Saint Marie | 59231 |
| Saint Marie | 59230 |
| St. Mary | 59417 |
| St. Regis | 59866 |
| St. Xavier | 59075 |
| Saltese | 59867 |
| Sand Coulee | 59472 |
| Sanders | 59076 |
| Sanders | 59038 |
| Sand Springs | 59077 |
| Santa Rita | 59473 |
| Savage | 59262 |
| Scobey | 59263 |
| Seeley Lake | 59868 |
| Shawmut | 59078 |
| Shelby | 59474 |
| Shepherd | 59079 |
| Sheridan | 59749 |
| Shonkin | 59450 |
| Sidney | 59270 |
| Silesia | 59041 |
| Silverbow | 59750 |
| Silver Gate | 59081 |
| Silver Star | 59751 |
| Simms | 59477 |
| Snider | 59869 |
| Somers | 59932 |
| Sonnette | 59348 |
| Springdale | 59082 |
| Stanford | 59479 |
| Stevensville | 59870 |
| Stockett | 59480 |
| Stryker | 59933 |
| Sula | 59871 |
| Sumatra | 59083 |
| Sunburst | 59482 |
| Sun River | 59483 |
| Superior | 59872 |
| Swan Lake | 59911 |
| Sweetgrass | 59484 |
| Teigen | 59084 |
| Terry | 59349 |
| Thompson Falls | 59873 |
| Three Forks | 59752 |
| Toston | 59643 |
| Townsend | 59644 |
| Trego | 59934 |
| Trident | 59752 |
| Trout Creek | 59874 |
| Troy | 59935 |
| Turner | 59542 |
| Twin Bridges | 59754 |
| Twodot | 59085 |
| Ulm | 59485 |
| Utica | 59452 |
| Valier | 59486 |
| Vandalia | 59273 |
| Vaughn | 59487 |
| Victor | 59875 |
| Vida | 59274 |
| Virginia City | 59755 |
| Volborg | 59351 |
| Wagner | 59543 |
| Walkerville | 59701 |
| Warm Springs | 59756 |
| West Glacier | 59936 |
| West Yellowstone | 59758 |
| Westby | 59275 |
| Whitefish | 59937 |
| Whitehall | 59759 |
| White Sulphur Sprngs | 59645 |
| Whitetail | 59276 |
| Whitewater | 59544 |
| Whitlash | 59545 |
| Wibaux | 59353 |
| Willard | 59354 |
| Willow Creek | 59760 |
| Wilsall | 59086 |
| Winifred | 59489 |
| Winnett | 59087 |
| Winston | 59647 |
| Wisdom | 59761 |
| Wise River | 59762 |
| Wolf Creek | 59648 |
| Wolf Point | 59201 |
| Worden | 59088 |
| Wyola | 59089 |
| Yellowtail | 59035 |
| Zortman | 59546 |
| Zurich | 59547 |

*This zip code is for general delivery only. Contact your local post office for other zip codes.

# Montana Counties

# Montana Distances

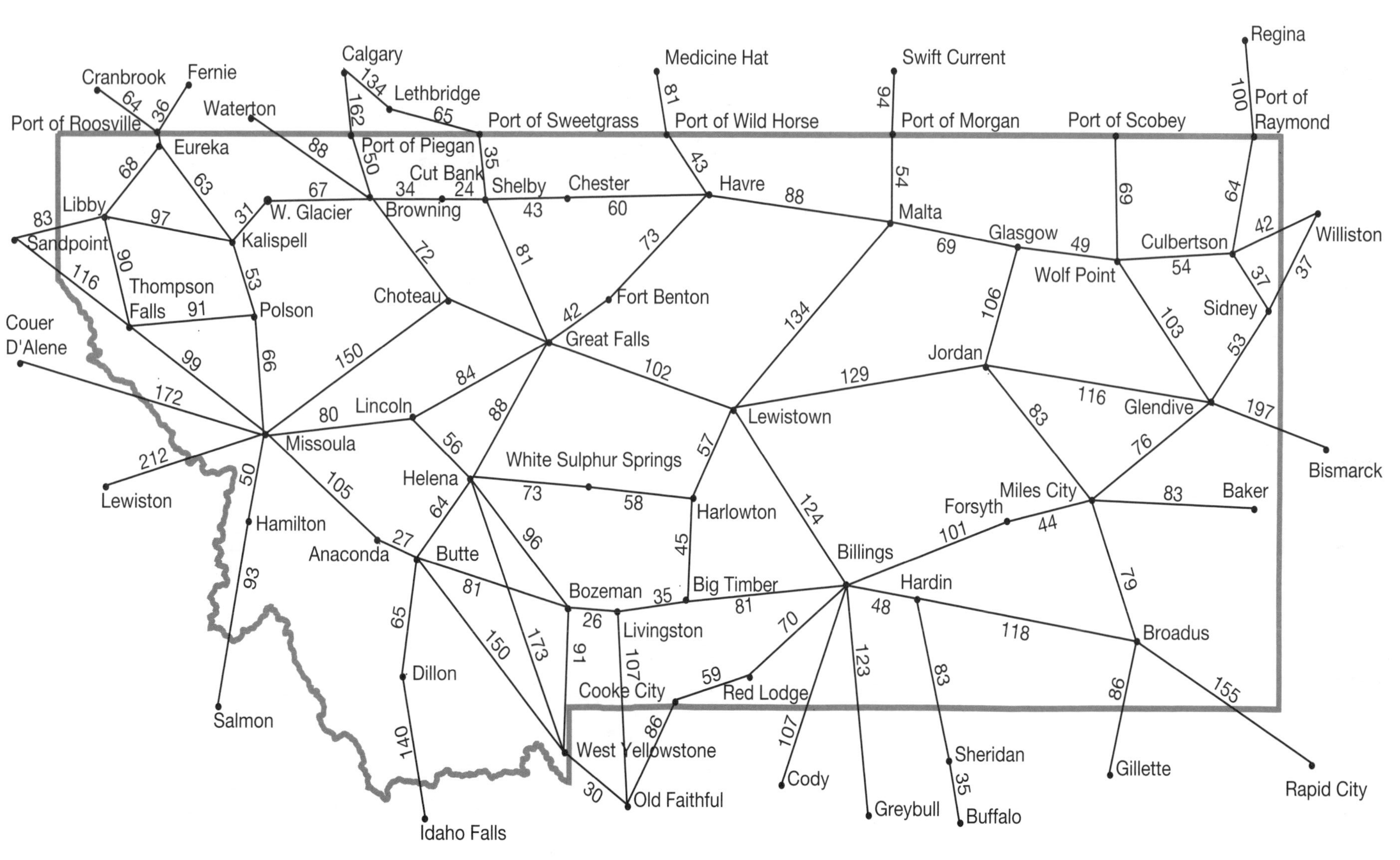

# DRIVING DISTANCE

**Anaconda** to
- Baker 476
- Big Timber 170
- Billings 251
- Boulder 64
- Bozeman 109
- Broadus 419
- Browning 253
- Butte 27
- Chester 290
- Chinook 308
- Choteau 181
- Circle 459
- Columbus 210
- Conrad 223
- Cooke City 244
- Culbertson 548
- Cut Bank 270
- Deer Lodge 27
- Dillon 78
- E. Glacier Park 266
- Ekalaka 511
- Eureka 279
- Forsyth 351
- Fort Benton 216
- Gardiner 188
- Glasgow 445
- Glendive 473
- Grass Range Jct. 293
- Great Falls 172
- Hamilton 126
- Hardin 297
- Harlowtown 205
- Havre 287
- Helena 83
- Hysham 328
- Jordan 392
- Kalispell 213
- Laurel 235
- Lewistown 262
- Libby 295
- Livingston 135
- Malta 375
- Miles City 396
- Missoula 105
- Philipsburg 31
- Plentywood 590
- Polson 171
- Poplar 515
- Red Lodge 258
- Roundup 274
- Ryegate 235
- Scobey 549
- Shelby 248
- Sidney 523
- Stanford 232
- Superior 162
- Sweetgrass 282
- Terry 434
- Thompson Falls 205
- Three Forks 80
- Townsend 106
- Virginia City 99
- West Glacier 234
- W. Yellowstone 177
- Whitefish 227
- W Sulphur Springs 148
- Wibaux 499
- Winnett 316
- Wolf Point 494

**Baker** to
- Anaconda 476
- Big Timber 306
- Billings 225
- Boulder 450
- Bozeman 367
- Broadus 157
- Browning 525
- Butte 449
- Chester 440
- Chinook 359
- Choteau 453
- Circle 120
- Columbus 266
- Conrad 461
- Cooke City 351
- Culbertson 162
- Cut Bank 506
- Deer Lodge 482
- Dillon 479
- E. Glacier Park 538
- Ekalaka 35
- Eureka 670
- Forsyth 125
- Fort Benton 392
- Gardiner 394
- Glasgow 222
- Glendive 71
- Grass Range Jct. 262
- Great Falls 398
- Hamilton 591
- Hardin 200
- Harlowtown 295
- Havre 380
- Helena 426
- Hysham 154
- Jordan 165
- Kalispell 622
- Laurel 241
- Lewistown 293
- Libby 711
- Livingston 341
- Malta 292
- Miles City 81
- Missoula 541
- Philipsburg 507
- Plentywood 209
- Polson 607
- Poplar 185
- Red Lodge 285
- Roundup 226
- Ryegate 265
- Scobey 219
- Shelby 482
- Sidney 125
- Stanford 338
- Superior 598
- Sweetgrass 518
- Terry 110
- Thompson Falls 641
- Three Forks 397
- Townsend 394
- Virginia City 434
- West Glacier 593
- W. Yellowstone 443
- Whitefish 618
- W Sulphur Springs 352
- Wibaux 45
- Winnett 239
- Wolf Point 173

**Big Timber** to
- Anaconda 170
- Baker 306
- Billings 81
- Boulder 144
- Bozeman 61
- Broadus 249
- Browning 299
- Butte 143
- Chester 302
- Chinook 254
- Choteau 227
- Circle 298
- Columbus 40
- Conrad 235
- Cooke City 144
- Culbertson 390
- Cut Bank 382
- Deer Lodge 184
- Dillon 173
- E. Glacier Park 312
- Ekalaka 341
- Eureka 412
- Forsyth 181
- Fort Benton 177
- Gardiner 88
- Glasgow 304
- Glendive 303
- Grass Range Jct. 132
- Great Falls 172
- Hamilton 290
- Hardin 127
- Harlowtown 44
- Havre 252
- Helena 150
- Hysham 158
- Jordan 231
- Kalispell 346
- Laurel 65
- Lewistown 101
- Libby 435
- Livingston 35
- Malta 234
- Miles City 226
- Missoula 263
- Philipsburg 201
- Plentywood 437
- Polson 329
- Poplar 363
- Red Lodge 88
- Roundup 113
- Ryegate 74
- Scobey 397
- Shelby 260
- Sidney 353
- Stanford 112
- Superior 320
- Sweetgrass 294
- Terry 264
- Thompson Falls 363
- Three Forks 91
- Townsend 118
- Virginia City 128
- West Glacier 367
- W. Yellowstone 142
- Whitefish 360
- W Sulphur Springs 94
- Wibaux 329
- Winnett 155
- Wolf Point 351

**Billings** to
- Anaconda 251
- Baker 225
- Big Timber 81
- Boulder 225
- Bozeman 142
- Broadus 168
- Browning 346
- Butte 224
- Chester 310
- Chinook 229
- Choteau 274
- Circle 241
- Columbus 41
- Conrad 282
- Cooke City 126
- Culbertson 309
- Cut Bank 329
- Deer Lodge 265
- Dillon 254
- E. Glacier Park 359
- Ekalaka 260
- Eureka 486
- Forsyth 100
- Fort Benton 224
- Gardiner 169
- Glasgow 279
- Glendive 222
- Grass Range Jct. 97
- Great Falls 219
- Hamilton 371
- Hardin 46
- Harlowtown 93
- Havre 250
- Helena 224
- Hysham 77
- Jordan 174
- Kalispell 420
- Laurel 16
- Lewistown 128
- Libby 509
- Livingston 116
- Malta 209
- Miles City 145
- Missoula 339
- Philipsburg 282
- Plentywood 356
- Polson 405
- Poplar 306
- Red Lodge 60
- Roundup 53
- Ryegate 63
- Scobey 340
- Shelby 307
- Sidney 272
- Stanford 159
- Superior 396
- Sweetgrass 341
- Terry 183
- Thompson Falls 439
- Three Forks 172
- Townsend 192
- Virginia City 209
- West Glacier 414
- W. Yellowstone 218
- Whitefish 434
- W Sulphur Springs 150
- Wibaux 248
- Winnett 98
- Wolf Point 294

**Boulder** to
- Anaconda 64
- Baker 450
- Big Timber 144
- Billings 225
- Bozeman 83
- Broadus 393
- Browning 199
- Butte 37
- Chester 236
- Chinook 252
- Choteau 127
- Circle 412
- Columbus 184
- Conrad 169
- Cooke City 218
- Culbertson 492
- Cut Bank 216
- Deer Lodge 78
- Dillon 93
- E. Glacier Park 212
- Ekalaka 485
- Eureka 289
- Forsyth 325
- Fort Benton 160
- Gardiner 162
- Glasgow 389
- Glendive 447
- Grass Range Jct. 246
- Great Falls 116
- Hamilton 184
- Hardin 271
- Harlowtown 158
- Havre 231
- Helena 27
- Hysham 302
- Jordan 345
- Kalispell 223
- Laurel 209
- Lewistown 215
- Libby 312
- Livingston 109
- Malta 319
- Miles City 370
- Missoula 142
- Philipsburg 95
- Plentywood 534
- Polson 208
- Poplar 459
- Red Lodge 232
- Roundup 227
- Ryegate 188
- Scobey 493
- Shelby 194
- Sidney 487
- Stanford 176
- Superior 199
- Sweetgrass 228
- Terry 408
- Thompson Falls 242
- Three Forks 54
- Townsend 59
- Virginia City 93
- West Glacier 244
- W. Yellowstone 151
- Whitefish 237
- W Sulphur Springs 101
- Wibaux 473
- Winnett 269
- Wolf Point 438

**Bozeman** to
- Anaconda 109
- Baker 367
- Big Timber 61
- Billings 142
- Boulder 83
- Broadus 310
- Browning 267
- Butte 82
- Chester 304
- Chinook 313
- Choteau 195
- Circle 359
- Columbus 101
- Conrad 237
- Cooke City 135
- Culbertson 451
- Cut Bank 284
- Deer Lodge 123
- Dillon 112
- E. Glacier Park 280
- Ekalaka 402
- Eureka 357
- Forsyth 242
- Fort Benton 221
- Gardiner 79
- Glasgow 365
- Glendive 364
- Grass Range Jct. 193
- Great Falls 177
- Hamilton 229
- Hardin 188
- Harlowtown 105
- Havre 292
- Helena 95
- Hysham 219
- Jordan 292
- Kalispell 291
- Laurel 126
- Lewistown 162
- Libby 380
- Livingston 26
- Malta 295
- Miles City 287
- Missoula 202
- Philipsburg 140
- Plentywood 498
- Polson 268
- Poplar 424
- Red Lodge 149
- Roundup 174
- Ryegate 135
- Scobey 458
- Shelby 262
- Sidney 414
- Stanford 173
- Superior 259
- Sweetgrass 296
- Terry 325
- Thompson Falls 302
- Three Forks 30
- Townsend 63
- Virginia City 67
- West Glacier 312
- W. Yellowstone 91
- Whitefish 305
- W Sulphur Springs 80
- Wibaux 390
- Winnett 216
- Wolf Point 412

**Broadus** to
- Anaconda 419
- Baker 157
- Big Timber 249
- Billings 168
- Boulder 393
- Bozeman 310
- Browning 514
- Butte 392
- Chester 472
- Chinook 391
- Choteau 442
- Circle 195
- Columbus 209
- Conrad 450
- Cooke City 294
- Culbertson 241
- Cut Bank 497
- Deer Lodge 433
- Dillon 422
- E. Glacier Park 527
- Ekalaka 192
- Eureka 654
- Forsyth 122
- Fort Benton 389
- Gardiner 337
- Glasgow 276
- Glendive 154
- Grass Range Jct. 259
- Great Falls 387
- Hamilton 539
- Hardin 122
- Harlowtown 261
- Havre 412
- Helena 392
- Hysham 139
- Jordan 163
- Kalispell 588
- Laurel 184
- Lewistown 290
- Libby 677
- Livingston 284
- Malta 346
- Miles City 79
- Missoula 507
- Philipsburg 450
- Plentywood 288
- Polson 573
- Poplar 260
- Red Lodge 228
- Roundup 215
- Ryegate 231
- Scobey 294
- Shelby 475
- Sidney 204
- Stanford 327
- Superior 564
- Sweetgrass 509
- Terry 115
- Thompson Falls 607
- Three Forks 340
- Townsend 360
- Virginia City 377
- West Glacier 582
- W. Yellowstone 386
- Whitefish 602
- W Sulphur Springs 318
- Wibaux 180
- Winnett 237
- Wolf Point 248

**Browning** to
- Anaconda 253
- Baker 525
- Big Timber 299
- Billings 346
- Boulder 199
- Bozeman 267
- Broadus 514
- Butte 236
- Chester 100
- Chinook 181
- Choteau 72
- Circle 420
- Columbus 339
- Conrad 66
- Cooke City 402
- Culbertson 421
- Cut Bank 34
- Deer Lodge 226
- Dillon 292
- E. Glacier Park 13
- Ekalaka 560
- Eureka 145
- Forsyth 408
- Fort Benton 171
- Gardiner 346
- Glasgow 318
- Glendive 469
- Grass Range Jct. 263
- Great Falls 127
- Hamilton 254
- Hardin 392
- Harlowtown 255
- Havre 160
- Helena 172
- Hysham 423
- Jordan 362
- Kalispell 99
- Laurel 362
- Lewistown 232
- Libby 188
- Livingston 293
- Malta 248
- Miles City 444
- Missoula 204
- Philipsburg 263
- Plentywood 463
- Polson 138
- Poplar 388
- Red Lodge 387
- Roundup 307
- Ryegate 283
- Scobey 422
- Shelby 58
- Sidney 458
- Stanford 187
- Superior 224
- Sweetgrass 92
- Terry 483
- Thompson Falls 207
- Three Forks 238
- Townsend 204
- Virginia City 292
- West Glacier 68
- W. Yellowstone 347
- Whitefish 93
- W Sulphur Springs 224
- Wibaux 495
- Winnett 286
- Wolf Point 367

**Butte** to
- Anaconda 27
- Baker 449
- Big Timber 143
- Billings 224
- Boulder 37
- Bozeman 82
- Broadus 392
- Browning 236
- Chester 273
- Chinook 289
- Choteau 164
- Circle 432
- Columbus 183
- Conrad 206
- Cooke City 217
- Culbertson 529
- Cut Bank 253
- Deer Lodge 41
- Dillon 65
- E. Glacier Park 249
- Ekalaka 484
- Eureka 293
- Forsyth 324
- Fort Benton 197
- Gardiner 161
- Glasgow 426
- Glendive 446
- Grass Range Jct. 266
- Great Falls 153
- Hamilton 147
- Hardin 270
- Harlowtown 178
- Havre 268
- Helena 64
- Hysham 301
- Jordan 365
- Kalispell 227
- Laurel 208
- Lewistown 235
- Libby 310
- Livingston 108
- Malta 356
- Miles City 369
- Missoula 120
- Philipsburg 58
- Plentywood 571
- Polson 186
- Poplar 496
- Red Lodge 231
- Roundup 247
- Ryegate 208
- Scobey 530
- Shelby 231
- Sidney 496
- Stanford 213
- Superior 177
- Sweetgrass 265
- Terry 401
- Thompson Falls 220
- Three Forks 53
- Townsend 79
- Virginia City 72
- West Glacier 248
- W. Yellowstone 150
- Whitefish 241
- W Sulphur Springs 121
- Wibaux 472
- Winnett 289
- Wolf Point 475

**Chester** to
- Anaconda 290
- Baker 440
- Big Timber 302
- Billings 310
- Boulder 236
- Bozeman 304
- Broadus 472
- Browning 100
- Butte 273
- Chinook 81
- Choteau 117
- Circle 320
- Columbus 342
- Conrad 67
- Cooke City 409
- Culbertson 321
- Cut Bank 66
- Deer Lodge 263
- Dillon 329
- E. Glacier Park 113
- Ekalaka 475
- Eureka 245
- Forsyth 358
- Fort Benton 129
- Gardiner 353
- Glasgow 218
- Glendive 369
- Grass Range Jct. 213
- Great Falls 130
- Hamilton 319
- Hardin 350
- Harlowtown 258
- Havre 60
- Helena 209
- Hysham 381
- Jordan 312
- Kalispell 199
- Laurel 326
- Lewistown 228
- Libby 288
- Livingston 300
- Malta 148
- Miles City 394
- Missoula 269
- Philipsburg 300
- Plentywood 363
- Polson 238
- Poplar 288
- Red Lodge 370
- Roundup 257
- Ryegate 286
- Scobey 322
- Shelby 42
- Sidney 358
- Stanford 190
- Superior 324
- Sweetgrass 78
- Terry 400
- Thompson Falls 307
- Three Forks 275
- Townsend 241
- Virginia City 329
- West Glacier 168
- W. Yellowstone 384
- Whitefish 193
- W Sulphur Springs 227
- Wibaux 395
- Winnett 236
- Wolf Point 267

**Chinook** to
- Anaconda 308
- Baker 359
- Big Timber 254
- Billings 229
- Boulder 252
- Bozeman 313
- Broadus 391
- Browning 181
- Butte 289
- Chester 81
- Choteau 191
- Circle 239
- Columbus 270
- Conrad 148
- Cooke City 355
- Culbertson 240
- Cut Bank 147
- Deer Lodge 281
- Dillon 345
- E. Glacier Park 194
- Ekalaka 394
- Eureka 326
- Forsyth 277
- Fort Benton 96
- Gardiner 342
- Glasgow 137
- Glendive 288
- Grass Range Jct. 132
- Great Falls 136
- Hamilton 355
- Hardin 269
- Harlowtown 210
- Havre 21
- Helena 225
- Hysham 300
- Jordan 231
- Kalispell 280
- Laurel 245
- Lewistown 153
- Libby 369
- Livingston 289
- Malta 67
- Miles City 313
- Missoula 305
- Philipsburg 318
- Plentywood 282
- Polson 319
- Poplar 207
- Red Lodge 289
- Roundup 176
- Ryegate 215
- Scobey 241
- Shelby 123
- Sidney 277
- Stanford 161
- Superior 362
- Sweetgrass 159
- Terry 319
- Thompson Falls 388
- Three Forks 291
- Townsend 257
- Virginia City 345
- West Glacier 249
- W. Yellowstone 396
- Whitefish 274
- W Sulphur Springs 233
- Wibaux 314
- Winnett 155
- Wolf Point 186

**Choteau** to
- Anaconda 181
- Baker 453
- Big Timber 227
- Billings 274
- Boulder 127
- Bozeman 195
- Broadus 442
- Browning 72
- Butte 164
- Chester 117
- Chinook 191
- Circle 357
- Columbus 267
- Conrad 50
- Cooke City 330
- Culbertson 431
- Cut Bank 97
- Deer Lodge 154
- Dillon 220
- E. Glacier Park 85
- Ekalaka 488
- Eureka 217
- Forsyth 336
- Fort Benton 99
- Gardiner 274
- Glasgow 328
- Glendive 406
- Grass Range Jct. 191
- Great Falls 55
- Hamilton 210
- Hardin 320
- Harlowtown 183
- Havre 170
- Helena 100
- Hysham 351
- Jordan 290
- Kalispell 171
- Laurel 290
- Lewistown 160
- Libby 260
- Livingston 221
- Malta 258
- Miles City 372
- Missoula 160
- Philipsburg 191
- Plentywood 473
- Polson 210
- Poplar 398
- Red Lodge 315
- Roundup 235
- Ryegate 211
- Scobey 432
- Shelby 75
- Sidney 432
- Stanford 115
- Superior 217
- Sweetgrass 109
- Terry 411
- Thompson Falls 260
- Three Forks 166
- Townsend 132
- Virginia City 220
- West Glacier 140
- W. Yellowstone 275
- Whitefish 165
- W Sulphur Springs 152
- Wibaux 432
- Winnett 214
- Wolf Point 377

**Circle** to
- Anaconda 459
- Baker 120
- Big Timber 298
- Billings 241
- Boulder 412
- Bozeman 359
- Broadus 195
- Browning 420
- Butte 432
- Chester 320
- Chinook 239
- Choteau 357
- Columbus 282
- Conrad 365
- Cooke City 367
- Culbertson 98
- Cut Bank 386
- Deer Lodge 441
- Dillon 462
- E. Glacier Park 433
- Ekalaka 155
- Eureka 565
- Forsyth 163
- Fort Benton 296
- Gardiner 386
- Glasgow 102
- Glendive 49
- Grass Range Jct. 166
- Great Falls 302
- Hamilton 521
- Hardin 238
- Harlowtown 254
- Havre 260
- Helena 385
- Hysham 192
- Jordan 67
- Kalispell 519
- Laurel 257
- Lewistown 197
- Libby 608
- Livingston 333
- Malta 172
- Miles City 119
- Missoula 471
- Philipsburg 478
- Plentywood 140
- Polson 537
- Poplar 65
- Red Lodge 301
- Roundup 188
- Ryegate 227
- Scobey 99
- Shelby 362
- Sidney 75
- Stanford 242
- Superior 528
- Sweetgrass 398
- Terry 80
- Thompson Falls 571
- Three Forks 387
- Townsend 353
- Virginia City 426
- West Glacier 488
- W. Yellowstone 440
- Whitefish 513
- W Sulphur Springs 311
- Wibaux 75
- Winnett 143
- Wolf Point 53

**Columbus** to
- Anaconda 210
- Baker 266
- Big Timber 40
- Billings 41
- Boulder 184
- Bozeman 101
- Broadus 209
- Browning 339
- Butte 183
- Chester 342
- Chinook 270
- Choteau 267
- Circle 282
- Conrad 275
- Cooke City 114
- Culbertson 350
- Cut Bank 322
- Deer Lodge 224
- Dillon 213
- E. Glacier Park 352
- Ekalaka 301

All Montana Area Codes are 406

Introduction

Eureka 452
Forsyth 141
Fort Benton 217
Gardiner 128
Glasgow 320
Glendive 263
Grass Range Jct. 138
Great Falls 212
Hamilton 330
Hardin 87
Harlowtown 84
Havre 291
Helena 190
Hysham 118
Jordan 215
Kalispell 386
Laurel 25
Lewistown 141
Libby 475
Livingston 75
Malta 250
Miles City 186
Missoula 303
Philipsburg 241
Plentywood 397
Polson 369
Poplar 347
Red Lodge 48
Roundup 94
Ryegate 104
Scobey 381
Shelby 300
Sidney 313
Stanford 152
Superior 360
Sweetgrass 334
Terry 224
Thompson Falls 403
Three Forks 131
Townsend 158
Virginia City 168
West Glacier 407
W. Yellowstone 182
Whitefish 400
W Sulphur Springs 134
Wibaux 289
Winnett 139
Wolf Point 335

**Conrad** to
Anaconda 223
Baker 461
Big Timber 235
Billings 282
Boulder 169
Bozeman 237
Broadus 450
Browning 66
Butte 206
Chester 67
Chinook 148
Choteau 50
Circle 365
Columbus 275
Cooke City 342
Culbertson 388
Cut Bank 47
Deer Lodge 196
Dillon 262
E. Glacier Park 79
Ekalaka 496
Eureka 211
Forsyth 344
Fort Benton 107
Gardiner 286
Glasgow 285
Glendive 414
Grass Range Jct. 199
Great Falls 63
Hamilton 252
Hardin 328
Harlowtown 191
Havre 127
Helena 152
Hysham 359
Jordan 298
Kalispell 165
Laurel 298
Lewistown 168
Libby 254
Livingston 233
Malta 215
Miles City 380
Missoula 202
Philipsburg 233
Plentywood 430
Polson 204
Poplar 355
Red Lodge 323
Roundup 243
Ryegate 219
Scobey 389
Shelby 25
Sidney 425
Stanford 123
Superior 259
Sweetgrass 59
Terry 419
Thompson Falls 273
Three Forks 208
Townsend 174
Virginia City 262
West Glacier 134
W. Yellowstone 317
Whitefish 159
W Sulphur Springs 160
Wibaux 440
Winnett 222
Wolf Point 334

**Cooke City** to
Anaconda 244
Baker 351
Big Timber 144
Billings 126
Boulder 218
Bozeman 135
Broadus 294
Browning 402
Butte 217
Chester 409
Chinook 355
Choteau 330
Circle 367
Columbus 114
Conrad 342
Culbertson 435
Cut Bank 389
Deer Lodge 258
Dillon 233
E. Glacier Park 415
Ekalaka 386
Eureka 492
Forsyth 226
Fort Benton 321
Gardiner 56
Glasgow 405
Glendive 348
Grass Range Jct. 223
Great Falls 279
Hamilton 364
Hardin 172
Harlowtown 188
Havre 376
Helena 230
Hysham 203
Jordan 300
Kalispell 426
Laurel 110
Lewistown 245
Libby 515
Livingston 109
Malta 335
Miles City 271
Missoula 337
Philipsburg 275
Plentywood 482
Polson 403
Poplar 432
Red Lodge 66
Roundup 179
Ryegate 189
Scobey 466
Shelby 367
Sidney 398
Stanford 256
Superior 394
Sweetgrass 401
Terry 309
Thompson Falls 437
Three Forks 165
Townsend 198
Virginia City 176
West Glacier 447
W. Yellowstone 92
Whitefish 440
W Sulphur Springs 182
Wibaux 374
Winnett 224
Wolf Point 420

**Culbertson** to
Anaconda 548
Baker 162
Big Timber 390
Billings 309
Boulder 492
Bozeman 451
Broadus 241
Browning 421
Butte 529
Chester 321
Chinook 240
Choteau 431
Circle 98
Columbus 350
Conrad 388
Cooke City 435
Cut Bank 387
Deer Lodge 521
Dillon 561
E. Glacier Park 434
Ekalaka 197
Eureka 566
Forsyth 209
Fort Benton 336
Gardiner 478
Glasgow 103
Glendive 91
Grass Range Jct. 264
Great Falls 376
Hamilton 595
Hardin 284
Harlowtown 352
Havre 261
Helena 465
Hysham 238
Jordan 165
Kalispell 520
Laurel 325
Lewistown 295
Libby 609
Livingston 425
Malta 173
Miles City 165
Missoula 545
Philipsburg 558
Plentywood 47
Polson 559
Poplar 33
Red Lodge 369
Roundup 286
Ryegate 325
Scobey 88
Shelby 363
Sidney 37
Stanford 340
Superior 602
Sweetgrass 399
Terry 126
Thompson Falls 628
Three Forks 481
Townsend 451
Virginia City 518
West Glacier 489
W. Yellowstone 527
Whitefish 514
W Sulphur Springs 409
Wibaux 117
Winnett 241
Wolf Point 54

**Cut Bank** to
Anaconda 270
Baker 506
Big Timber 282
Billings 329
Boulder 216
Bozeman 284
Broadus 497
Browning 34
Butte 253
Chester 66
Chinook 147
Choteau 97
Circle 386
Columbus 322
Conrad 47
Cooke City 389
Culbertson 387
Deer Lodge 243
Dillon 309
E. Glacier Park 47
Ekalaka 541
Eureka 179
Forsyth 391
Fort Benton 154
Gardiner 333
Glasgow 284
Glendive 435
Grass Range Jct. 246
Great Falls 110
Hamilton 288
Hardin 375
Harlowtown 238
Havre 126
Helena 189
Hysham 406
Jordan 345
Kalispell 133
Laurel 345
Lewistown 215
Libby 222
Livingston 280
Malta 214
Miles City 427
Missoula 238
Philipsburg 280
Plentywood 429
Polson 172
Poplar 354
Red Lodge 370
Roundup 290
Ryegate 266
Scobey 388
Shelby 24
Sidney 424
Stanford 170
Superior 258
Sweetgrass 58
Terry 466
Thompson Falls 241
Three Forks 255
Townsend 221
Virginia City 309
West Glacier 102
W. Yellowstone 364
Whitefish 127
W Sulphur Springs 207
Wibaux 461
Winnett 269
Wolf Point 333

**Deer Lodge** to
Anaconda 27
Baker 482
Big Timber 184
Billings 265
Boulder 78
Bozeman 123
Broadus 433
Browning 226
Butte 41
Chester 263
Chinook 281
Choteau 154
Circle 441
Columbus 224
Conrad 196
Cooke City 258
Culbertson 521
Cut Bank 243
Dillon 92
E. Glacier Park 239
Ekalaka 517
Eureka 252
Forsyth 357
Fort Benton 189
Gardiner 202
Glasgow 418
Glendive 479
Grass Range Jct. 275
Great Falls 145
Hamilton 129
Hardin 311
Harlowtown 187
Havre 260
Helena 56
Hysham 342
Jordan 374
Kalispell 186
Laurel 249
Lewistown 244
Libby 269
Livingston 149
Malta 348
Miles City 402
Missoula 79
Philipsburg 57
Plentywood 563
Polson 145
Poplar 488
Red Lodge 272
Roundup 256
Ryegate 217
Scobey 522
Shelby 221
Sidney 516
Stanford 205
Superior 136
Sweetgrass 255
Terry 440
Thompson Falls 179
Three Forks 94
Townsend 88
Virginia City 113
West Glacier 207
W. Yellowstone 191
Whitefish 200
W Sulphur Springs 130
Wibaux 505
Winnett 298
Wolf Point 467

**Dillon** to
Anaconda 78
Baker 479
Big Timber 173
Billings 254
Boulder 93
Bozeman 112
Broadus 422
Browning 292
Butte 65
Chester 329
Chinook 345
Choteau 220
Circle 462
Columbus 213
Conrad 262
Cooke City 233
Culbertson 560
Cut Bank 309
Deer Lodge 92
E. Glacier Park 305
Ekalaka 514
Eureka 344
Forsyth 354
Fort Benton 253
Gardiner 191
Glasgow 468
Glendive 476
Grass Range Jct. 296
Great Falls 209
Hamilton 163
Hardin 300
Harlowtown 208
Havre 324
Helena 120
Hysham 331
Jordan 395
Kalispell 278
Laurel 238
Lewistown 265
Libby 361
Livingston 138
Malta 398
Miles City 399
Missoula 171
Philipsburg 109
Plentywood 602
Polson 237
Poplar 527
Red Lodge 261
Roundup 277
Ryegate 238
Scobey 561
Shelby 287
Sidney 526
Stanford 262
Superior 228
Sweetgrass 321
Terry 437
Thompson Falls 271
Three Forks 83
Townsend 209
Virginia City 57
West Glacier 299
W. Yellowstone 141
Whitefish 292
W Sulphur Springs 161
Wibaux 502
Winnett 319
Wolf Point 515

**E. Glacier Park** to
Anaconda 266
Baker 538
Big Timber 312
Billings 359
Boulder 212
Bozeman 280
Broadus 527
Browning 13
Butte 249
Chester 113
Chinook 194
Choteau 85
Circle 433
Columbus 352
Conrad 79
Cooke City 415
Culbertson 434
Cut Bank 47
Deer Lodge 239
Dillon 305
Ekalaka 573
Eureka 132
Forsyth 421
Fort Benton 184
Gardiner 359
Glasgow 331
Glendive 482
Grass Range Jct. 276
Great Falls 140
Hamilton 241
Hardin 405
Harlowtown 268
Havre 173
Helena 185
Hysham 436
Jordan 375
Kalispell 86
Laurel 375
Lewistown 245
Libby 175
Livingston 306
Malta 261
Miles City 475
Missoula 191
Philipsburg 265
Plentywood 476
Polson 125
Poplar 401
Red Lodge 400
Roundup 320
Ryegate 296
Scobey 435
Shelby 71
Sidney 471
Stanford 200
Superior 211
Sweetgrass 105
Terry 496
Thompson Falls 194
Three Forks 251
Townsend 217
Virginia City 305
West Glacier 55
W. Yellowstone 360
Whitefish 80
W Sulphur Springs 237
Wibaux 508
Winnett 299
Wolf Point 380

**Ekalaka** to
Anaconda 511
Baker 35
Big Timber 341
Billings 260
Boulder 485
Bozeman 402
Broadus 192
Browning 560
Butte 484
Chester 475
Chinook 394
Choteau 488
Circle 155
Columbus 301
Conrad 496
Cooke City 386
Culbertson 197
Cut Bank 541
Deer Lodge 517
Dillon 514
E. Glacier Park 573
Eureka 705
Forsyth 160
Fort Benton 427
Gardiner 429
Glasgow 257
Glendive 106
Grass Range Jct. 297
Great Falls 433
Hamilton 626
Hardin 235
Harlowtown 330
Havre 415
Helena 461
Hysham 189
Jordan 200
Kalispell 657
Laurel 276
Lewistown 328
Libby 746
Livingston 376
Malta 327
Miles City 116
Missoula 576
Philipsburg 542
Plentywood 244
Polson 642
Poplar 220
Red Lodge 320
Roundup 261
Ryegate 300
Scobey 254
Shelby 517
Sidney 160
Stanford 373
Superior 633
Sweetgrass 553
Terry 145
Thompson Falls 676
Three Forks 432
Townsend 429
Virginia City 469
West Glacier 628
W. Yellowstone 478
Whitefish 653
W Sulphur Springs 387
Wibaux 80
Winnett 274
Wolf Point 208

**Eureka** to
Anaconda 279
Baker 670
Big Timber 412
Billings 486
Boulder 289
Bozeman 357
Broadus 654
Browning 145
Butte 293
Chester 245
Chinook 326
Choteau 217
Circle 565
Columbus 452
Conrad 211
Cooke City 492
Culbertson 566
Cut Bank 179
Deer Lodge 252
Dillon 344
E. Glacier Park 132
Ekalaka 705
Forsyth 553
Fort Benton 316
Gardiner 436
Glasgow 463
Glendive 614
Grass Range Jct. 408
Great Falls 272
Hamilton 231
Hardin 532
Harlowtown 393
Havre 305
Helena 262
Hysham 563
Jordan 507
Kalispell 66
Laurel 477
Lewistown 377
Libby 68
Livingston 383
Malta 393
Miles City 589
Missoula 181
Philipsburg 255
Plentywood 608
Polson 115
Poplar 533
Red Lodge 500
Roundup 452
Ryegate 423
Scobey 567
Shelby 203
Sidney 603
Stanford 332
Superior 191
Sweetgrass 237
Terry 628
Thompson Falls 158
Three Forks 328
Townsend 294
Virginia City 365
West Glacier 77
W. Yellowstone 437
Whitefish 52
W Sulphur Springs 336
Wibaux 640
Winnett 431
Wolf Point 512

**Forsyth** to
Anaconda 216
Baker 392
Big Timber 177
Billings 224
Boulder 160
Bozeman 221
Broadus 389
Browning 171
Butte 197
Chester 129
Chinook 96
Choteau 99
Circle 296
Columbus 217
Conrad 107
Cooke City 321
Culbertson 336
Cut Bank 154
Deer Lodge 189
Dillon 253
E. Glacier Park 184
Ekalaka 427
Eureka 316
Fort Benton 275
Gardiner 269
Glasgow 242
Glendive 122
Grass Range Jct. 145
Great Falls 281
Hamilton 466
Hardin 75
Harlowtown 170
Havre 298
Helena 301
Hysham 29
Jordan 129
Kalispell 497
Laurel 116
Lewistown 176
Libby 586
Livingston 216
Malta 257
Miles City 45
Missoula 416
Philipsburg 382
Plentywood 256
Polson 482
Poplar 228
Red Lodge 160
Roundup 101
Ryegate 140
Scobey 262
Shelby 369
Sidney 172
Stanford 221
Superior 473
Sweetgrass 403
Terry 83
Thompson Falls 516
Three Forks 272
Townsend 269
Virginia City 309
West Glacier 476
W. Yellowstone 318
Whitefish 501
W Sulphur Springs 227
Wibaux 148
Winnett 146
Wolf Point 216

**Fort Benton** to
Anaconda 216
Baker 392
Big Timber 177
Billings 224
Boulder 160
Bozeman 221
Broadus 389
Browning 171
Butte 197
Chester 129
Chinook 96
Choteau 99
Circle 296
Columbus 217
Conrad 107
Cooke City 321
Culbertson 336
Cut Bank 154
Deer Lodge 189
Dillon 253
E. Glacier Park 184
Ekalaka 427
Eureka 316
Forsyth 275
Gardiner 265
Glasgow 233
Glendive 345
Grass Range Jct. 130
Great Falls 44
Hamilton 263
Hardin 267
Harlowtown 133
Havre 75
Helena 133
Hysham 298
Jordan 229
Kalispell 270
Laurel 240
Lewistown 99
Libby 359
Livingston 212
Malta 163
Miles City 311
Missoula 213
Philipsburg 226
Plentywood 378
Polson 279
Poplar 303
Red Lodge 265
Roundup 174
Ryegate 161
Scobey 337
Shelby 132
Sidney 371
Stanford 65
Superior 270
Sweetgrass 166
Terry 350
Thompson Falls 313
Three Forks 199
Townsend 165
Virginia City 253
West Glacier 239
W. Yellowstone 308
Whitefish 264
W Sulphur Springs 141
Wibaux 371
Winnett 153
Wolf Point 282

**Gardiner** to
Anaconda 188
Baker 394
Big Timber 88
Billings 169
Boulder 162
Bozeman 79
Broadus 337
Browning 346
Butte 161
Chester 353
Chinook 342
Choteau 274
Circle 386
Columbus 128
Conrad 286
Cooke City 56
Culbertson 478
Cut Bank 333
Deer Lodge 202
Dillon 191
E. Glacier Park 359
Ekalaka 429
Eureka 436
Forsyth 269
Fort Benton 265
Glasgow 392
Glendive 391
Grass Range Jct. 220
Great Falls 223
Hamilton 308
Hardin 215
Harlowtown 132
Havre 338
Helena 174
Hysham 246
Jordan 319
Kalispell 370
Laurel 153
Lewistown 189
Libby 459
Livingston 53
Malta 322
Miles City 314
Missoula 281
Philipsburg 219
Plentywood 525
Polson 347
Poplar 451
Red Lodge 122
Roundup 201
Ryegate 162
Scobey 485
Shelby 311
Sidney 441
Stanford 200
Superior 338
Sweetgrass 345
Terry 352
Thompson Falls 381
Three Forks 109
Townsend 142
Virginia City 138
West Glacier 391
W. Yellowstone 54
Whitefish 384
W Sulphur Springs 126
Wibaux 417
Winnett 243
Wolf Point 439

**Glasgow** to
Anaconda 445
Baker 222
Big Timber 304
Billings 279
Boulder 389
Bozeman 365
Broadus 276
Browning 318
Butte 426
Chester 218
Chinook 137
Choteau 328
Circle 102
Columbus 320
Conrad 285
Cooke City 405
Culbertson 103
Cut Bank 284
Deer Lodge 418
Dillon 468
E. Glacier Park 331
Ekalaka 257
Eureka 463
Forsyth 242
Fort Benton 233
Gardiner 392
Glendive 151
Grass Range Jct. 182
Great Falls 273
Hamilton 492
Hardin 317
Harlowtown 260
Havre 158
Helena 362
Hysham 271
Jordan 113
Kalispell 417
Laurel 295
Lewistown 203
Libby 506
Livingston 339
Malta 70
Miles City 197
Missoula 442
Philipsburg 455
Plentywood 145
Polson 456
Poplar 70
Red Lodge 339
Roundup 226
Ryegate 265
Scobey 104
Shelby 260
Sidney 140
Stanford 248
Superior 499
Sweetgrass 296
Terry 182
Thompson Falls 525
Three Forks 393
Townsend 359
Virginia City 432
West Glacier 386
W. Yellowstone 446
Whitefish 411
W Sulphur Springs 317
Wibaux 177
Winnett 189
Wolf Point 49

**Glendive** to
Anaconda 473
Baker 71
Big Timber 303
Billings 222
Boulder 447
Bozeman 364
Broadus 154
Browning 469
Butte 446
Chester 369
Chinook 288
Choteau 406
Circle 49
Columbus 263
Conrad 414
Cooke City 348
Culbertson 91
Cut Bank 435
Deer Lodge 479
Dillon 476
E. Glacier Park 482
Ekalaka 106
Eureka 614
Forsyth 122
Fort Benton 345
Gardiner 391
Glasgow 151
Grass Range Jct. 215
Great Falls 351
Hamilton 570
Hardin 197
Harlowtown 292
Havre 309
Helena 423
Hysham 151
Jordan 116
Kalispell 568
Laurel 238
Lewistown 246
Libby 657
Livingston 338
Malta 221
Miles City 78
Missoula 520
Philipsburg 504
Plentywood 138
Polson 586
Poplar 114
Red Lodge 282
Roundup 223
Ryegate 262
Scobey 148
Shelby 411
Sidney 54
Stanford 291
Superior 577
Sweetgrass 447
Terry 39
Thompson Falls 620
Three Forks 394
Townsend 391
Virginia City 431

West Glacier .537
W. Yellowstone .440
Whitefish .562
W Sulphur Springs 349
Wibaux .26
Winnett .192
Wolf Point .102

**Grass Range Jct.** to
Anaconda .293
Baker .262
Big Timber .132
Billings .97
Boulder .246
Bozeman .193
Broadus .259
Browning .263
Butte .266
Chester .213
Chinook .132
Choteau .191
Circle .166
Columbus .138
Conrad .199
Cooke City .223
Culbertson .264
Cut Bank .246
Deer Lodge .275
Dillon .296
E. Glacier Park .276
Ekalaka .297
Eureka .408
Forsyth .145
Fort Benton .130
Gardiner .220
Glasgow .182
Glendive .215
Great Falls .136
Hamilton .355
Hardin .137
Harlowtown .88
Havre .153
Helena .219
Hysham .168
Jordan .99
Kalispell .362
Laurel .113
Lewistown .31
Libby .451
Livingston .167
Malta .112
Miles City .181
Missoula .305
Philipsburg .312
Plentywood .306
Polson .371
Poplar .231
Red Lodge .157
Roundup .44
Ryegate .83
Scobey .265
Shelby .224
Sidney .241
Stanford .76
Superior .362
Sweetgrass .258
Terry .220
Thompson Falls .405
Three Forks .221
Townsend .187
Virginia City .260
West Glacier .331
W. Yellowstone .274
Whitefish .356
W Sulphur Springs 145
Wibaux .241
Winnett .23
Wolf Point .219

**Great Falls** to
Anaconda .172
Baker .398
Big Timber .172
Billings .219
Boulder .116
Bozeman .177
Broadus .387
Browning .127
Butte .153
Chester .130
Chinook .136
Choteau .55
Circle .302
Columbus .212
Conrad .63
Cooke City .279
Culbertson .376
Cut Bank .110
Deer Lodge .145
Dillon .209
E. Glacier Park .140
Ekalaka .433
Eureka .272
Forsyth .281
Fort Benton .44
Gardiner .223
Glasgow .273
Glendive .351
Grass Range Jct. .136
Hamilton .219
Hardin .265
Harlowtown .128
Havre .115
Helena .89
Hysham .296
Jordan .235
Kalispell .226
Laurel .235
Lewistown .105
Libby .315
Livingston .170
Malta .203
Miles City .317
Missoula .169
Philipsburg .182
Plentywood .418
Polson .235
Poplar .343
Red Lodge .260
Roundup .180
Ryegate .156
Scobey .377
Shelby .88
Sidney .377
Stanford .60
Superior .226
Sweetgrass .122
Terry .356
Thompson Falls .269
Three Forks .155
Townsend .121
Virginia City .209
West Glacier .195
W. Yellowstone .264
Whitefish .220
W Sulphur Springs .97
Wibaux .377
Winnett .159
Wolf Point .322

**Hamilton** to
Anaconda .126
Baker .591
Big Timber .290
Billings .371
Boulder .184
Bozeman .229
Broadus .539
Browning .254
Butte .147
Chester .319
Chinook .355
Choteau .210
Circle .521
Columbus .330
Conrad .252
Cooke City .364
Culbertson .595
Cut Bank .288
Deer Lodge .129
Dillon .163
E. Glacier Park .241
Ekalaka .626
Eureka .231
Forsyth .466
Fort Benton .263
Gardiner .308
Glasgow .492
Glendive .570
Grass Range Jct. .335
Great Falls .219
Hardin .417
Harlowtown .296
Havre .334
Helena .165
Hysham .448
Jordan .254
Kalispell .165
Laurel .355
Lewistown .324
Libby .240
Livingston .255
Malta .422
Miles City .511
Missoula .50
Philipsburg .124
Plentywood .637
Polson .116
Poplar .562
Red Lodge .378
Roundup .365
Ryegate .326
Scobey .596
Shelby .277
Sidney .596
Stanford .279
Superior .107
Sweetgrass .311
Terry .549
Thompson Falls .150
Three Forks .200
Townsend .197
Virginia City .219
West Glacier .186
W. Yellowstone .297
Whitefish .179
W Sulphur Springs 239
Wibaux .596
Winnett .378
Wolf Point .541

**Hardin** to
Anaconda .297
Baker .200
Big Timber .127
Billings .46
Boulder .271
Bozeman .188
Broadus .122
Browning .392
Butte .270
Chester .350
Chinook .269
Choteau .320
Circle .238
Columbus .87
Conrad .328
Cooke City .172
Culbertson .284
Cut Bank .375
Deer Lodge .311
Dillon .300
E. Glacier Park .405
Ekalaka .235
Eureka .532
Forsyth .75
Fort Benton .267
Gardiner .215
Glasgow .317
Glendive .197
Grass Range Jct. .137
Great Falls .265
Hamilton .417
Harlowtown .139
Havre .290
Helena .270
Hysham .52
Jordan .204
Kalispell .456
Laurel .62
Lewistown .168
Libby .555
Livingston .162
Malta .249
Miles City .120
Missoula .385
Philipsburg .328
Plentywood .331
Polson .451
Poplar .303
Red Lodge .106
Roundup .93
Ryegate .109
Scobey .337
Shelby .353
Sidney .247
Stanford .205
Superior .442
Sweetgrass .387
Terry .158
Thompson Falls .485
Three Forks .218
Townsend .238
Virginia City .255
West Glacier .460
W. Yellowstone .264
Whitefish .480
W Sulphur Springs 196
Wibaux .223
Winnett .138
Wolf Point .291

**Harlowtown** to
Anaconda .205
Baker .295
Big Timber .44
Billings .93
Boulder .158
Bozeman .105
Broadus .261
Browning .255
Butte .178
Chester .258
Chinook .210
Choteau .183
Circle .254
Columbus .84
Conrad .191
Cooke City .188
Culbertson .352
Cut Bank .238
Deer Lodge .187
Dillon .208
E. Glacier Park .268
Ekalaka .330
Eureka .393
Forsyth .170
Fort Benton .133
Gardiner .132
Glasgow .260
Glendive .292
Grass Range Jct. .88
Great Falls .128
Hamilton .296
Hardin .139
Havre .208
Helena .131
Hysham .170
Jordan .187
Kalispell .327
Laurel .109
Lewistown .57
Libby .416
Livingston .79
Malta .190
Miles City .215
Missoula .246
Philipsburg .224
Plentywood .394
Polson .312
Poplar .319
Red Lodge .132
Roundup .69
Ryegate .30
Scobey .353
Shelby .216
Sidney .329
Stanford .68
Superior .303
Sweetgrass .250
Terry .253
Thompson Falls .346
Three Forks .133
Townsend .99
Virginia City .172
West Glacier .323
W. Yellowstone .186
Whitefish .341
W Sulphur Springs .57
Wibaux .318
Winnett .111
Wolf Point .307

**Havre** to
Anaconda .287
Baker .380
Big Timber .252
Billings .250
Boulder .231
Bozeman .292
Broadus .412
Browning .160
Butte .268
Chester .60
Chinook .21
Choteau .170
Circle .260
Columbus .291
Conrad .127
Cooke City .376
Culbertson .261
Cut Bank .126
Deer Lodge .260
Dillon .324
E. Glacier Park .173
Ekalaka .415
Eureka .305
Forsyth .298
Fort Benton .75
Gardiner .338
Glasgow .158
Glendive .309
Grass Range Jct. .153
Great Falls .115
Hamilton .334
Hardin .290
Harlowtown .208
Helena .204
Hysham .321
Jordan .252
Kalispell .259
Laurel .266
Lewistown .174
Libby .348
Livingston .285
Malta .88
Miles City .334
Missoula .284
Philipsburg .297
Plentywood .303
Polson .298
Poplar .228
Red Lodge .310
Roundup .197
Ryegate .236
Scobey .262
Shelby .102
Sidney .298
Stanford .140
Superior .341
Sweetgrass .138
Terry .340
Thompson Falls .367
Three Forks .270
Townsend .236
Virginia City .324
West Glacier .228
W. Yellowstone .379
Whitefish .253
W Sulphur Springs 212
Wibaux .335
Winnett .176
Wolf Point .207

**Helena** to
Anaconda .83
Baker .426
Big Timber .150
Billings .224
Boulder .27
Bozeman .95
Broadus .392
Browning .172
Butte .64
Chester .209
Chinook .225
Choteau .100
Circle .385
Columbus .190
Conrad .152
Cooke City .230
Culbertson .465
Cut Bank .189
Deer Lodge .56
Dillon .120
E. Glacier Park .185
Ekalaka .461
Eureka .262
Forsyth .301
Fort Benton .133
Gardiner .174
Glasgow .362
Glendive .423
Grass Range Jct. .219
Great Falls .89
Hamilton .165
Hardin .270
Harlowtown .131
Havre .204
Hysham .301
Jordan .318
Kalispell .196
Laurel .215
Lewistown .188
Libby .285
Livingston .121
Malta .292
Miles City .346
Missoula .115
Philipsburg .93
Plentywood .507
Polson .181
Poplar .432
Red Lodge .238
Roundup .200
Ryegate .161
Scobey .466
Shelby .167
Sidney .460
Stanford .149
Superior .172
Sweetgrass .201
Terry .384
Thompson Falls .215
Three Forks .66
Townsend .32
Virginia City .120
West Glacier .217
W. Yellowstone .175
Whitefish .210
W Sulphur Springs .74
Wibaux .449
Winnett .242
Wolf Point .411

**Hysham** to
Anaconda .328
Baker .154
Big Timber .158
Billings .77
Boulder .302
Bozeman .219
Broadus .139
Browning .423
Butte .301
Chester .381
Chinook .300
Choteau .351
Circle .192
Columbus .118
Conrad .359
Cooke City .203
Culbertson .238
Cut Bank .406
Deer Lodge .342
Dillon .331
E. Glacier Park .436
Ekalaka .189
Eureka .563
Forsyth .29
Fort Benton .298
Gardiner .246
Glasgow .271
Glendive .151
Grass Range Jct. .168
Great Falls .296
Hamilton .448
Hardin .52
Harlowtown .170
Havre .321
Helena .301
Jordan .158
Kalispell .497
Laurel .93
Lewistown .199
Libby .586
Livingston .193
Malta .280
Miles City .74
Missoula .416
Philipsburg .359
Plentywood .285
Polson .482
Poplar .257
Red Lodge .137
Roundup .124
Ryegate .140
Scobey .291
Shelby .384
Sidney .201
Stanford .236
Superior .473
Sweetgrass .418
Terry .112
Thompson Falls .516
Three Forks .249
Townsend .269
Virginia City .286
West Glacier .491
W. Yellowstone .295
Whitefish .511
W Sulphur Springs 277
Wibaux .177
Winnett .169
Wolf Point .245

**Jordan** to
Anaconda .392
Baker .165
Big Timber .231
Billings .174
Boulder .345
Bozeman .292
Broadus .163
Browning .362
Butte .365
Chester .312
Chinook .231
Choteau .290
Circle .67
Columbus .215
Conrad .298
Cooke City .300
Culbertson .165
Cut Bank .345
Deer Lodge .374
Dillon .395
E. Glacier Park .375
Ekalaka .200
Eureka .507
Forsyth .129
Fort Benton .229
Gardiner .319
Glasgow .113
Glendive .116
Grass Range Jct. .99
Great Falls .235
Hamilton .454
Hardin .204
Harlowtown .187
Havre .252
Helena .318
Hysham .158
Kalispell .461
Laurel .190
Lewistown .130
Libby .550
Livingston .266
Malta .183
Miles City .84
Missoula .404
Philipsburg .411
Plentywood .207
Polson .470
Poplar .132
Red Lodge .234
Roundup .121
Ryegate .160
Scobey .166
Shelby .323
Sidney .142
Stanford .175
Superior .461
Sweetgrass .357
Terry .123
Thompson Falls .504
Three Forks .320
Townsend .286
Virginia City .359
West Glacier .430
W. Yellowstone .373
Whitefish .455
W Sulphur Springs 244
Wibaux .142
Winnett .76
Wolf Point .120

**Kalispell** to
Anaconda .213
Baker .622
Big Timber .346
Billings .420
Boulder .223
Bozeman .291
Broadus .588
Browning .99
Butte .227
Chester .199
Chinook .280
Choteau .171
Circle .519
Columbus .386
Conrad .165
Cooke City .426
Culbertson .520
Cut Bank .133
Deer Lodge .186
Dillon .278
E. Glacier Park .86
Ekalaka .657
Eureka .66
Forsyth .497
Fort Benton .270
Gardiner .370
Glasgow .417
Glendive .568
Grass Range Jct. .362
Great Falls .226
Hamilton .165
Hardin .466
Harlowtown .327
Havre .259
Helena .196
Hysham .497
Jordan .461
Laurel .411
Lewistown .331
Libby .89
Livingston .317
Malta .347
Miles City .542
Missoula .115
Philipsburg .189
Plentywood .562
Polson .49
Poplar .487
Red Lodge .434
Roundup .396
Ryegate .357
Scobey .521
Shelby .157
Sidney .557
Stanford .286
Superior .125
Sweetgrass .191
Terry .580
Thompson Falls .108
Three Forks .262
Townsend .228
Virginia City .299
West Glacier .31
W. Yellowstone .371
Whitefish .14
W Sulphur Springs 270
Wibaux .594
Winnett .385
Wolf Point .466

**Laurel** to
Anaconda .235
Baker .241
Big Timber .65
Billings .16
Boulder .209
Bozeman .126
Broadus .184
Browning .362
Butte .208
Chester .326
Chinook .245
Choteau .290
Circle .257
Columbus .25
Conrad .298
Cooke City .110
Culbertson .325
Cut Bank .345
Deer Lodge .249
Dillon .238
E. Glacier Park .375
Ekalaka .276
Eureka .477
Forsyth .116
Fort Benton .240
Gardiner .153
Glasgow .295
Glendive .238
Grass Range Jct. .113
Great Falls .235
Hamilton .355
Hardin .62
Harlowtown .109
Havre .266
Helena .215
Hysham .93
Jordan .190
Kalispell .411
Lewistown .144
Libby .500
Livingston .100
Malta .225
Miles City .161
Missoula .328
Philipsburg .266
Plentywood .372
Polson .394
Poplar .322
Red Lodge .44
Roundup .69
Ryegate .79
Scobey .356
Shelby .323
Sidney .288
Stanford .175
Superior .385
Sweetgrass .357
Terry .199
Thompson Falls .428
Three Forks .156
Townsend .183
Virginia City .193
West Glacier .430
W. Yellowstone .202
Whitefish .425
W Sulphur Springs 159
Wibaux .264
Winnett .114
Wolf Point .310

**Lewistown** to
Anaconda .262
Baker .293
Big Timber .101
Billings .128
Boulder .215
Bozeman .162
Broadus .290
Browning .232
Butte .235
Chester .228
Chinook .153
Choteau .160
Circle .197
Columbus .141
Conrad .168
Cooke City .245
Culbertson .295
Cut Bank .215
Deer Lodge .244
Dillon .265
E. Glacier Park .245
Ekalaka .328
Eureka .377
Forsyth .176
Fort Benton .99
Gardiner .189
Glasgow .203
Glendive .246
Grass Range Jct. .31
Great Falls .105
Hamilton .324
Hardin .168
Harlowtown .57
Havre .174
Helena .189
Hysham .199
Jordan .130
Kalispell .331
Laurel .144
Libby .420
Livingston .136
Malta .133
Miles City .212
Missoula .274
Philipsburg .281
Plentywood .337
Polson .340
Poplar .262
Red Lodge .188
Roundup .75
Ryegate .85
Scobey .296
Shelby .193
Sidney .272
Stanford .45
Superior .331
Sweetgrass .227
Terry .251
Thompson Falls .374
Three Forks .190
Townsend .156
Virginia City .229
West Glacier .300
W. Yellowstone .243
Whitefish .325
W Sulphur Springs 114
Wibaux .272
Winnett .54
Wolf Point .250

**Libby** to
Anaconda .295
Baker .711
Big Timber .435
Billings .509
Boulder .312
Bozeman .380
Broadus .677
Browning .188
Butte .310
Chester .288
Chinook .369
Choteau .260
Circle .608
Columbus .475
Conrad .254
Cooke City .515
Culbertson .609
Cut Bank .222
Deer Lodge .269
Dillon .361
E. Glacier Park .175
Ekalaka .746
Eureka .68
Forsyth .586
Fort Benton .359
Gardiner .459
Glasgow .506
Glendive .657
Grass Range Jct. .451
Great Falls .315
Hamilton .240
Hardin .555
Harlowtown .416
Havre .348
Helena .285
Hysham .586
Jordan .550
Kalispell .89
Laurel .500
Lewistown .420
Livingston .406
Malta .436
Miles City .631
Missoula .190
Philipsburg .264
Plentywood .651
Polson .138
Poplar .576
Red Lodge .523
Roundup .485
Ryegate .446
Scobey .610
Shelby .246
Sidney .646
Stanford .375
Superior .159
Sweetgrass .280
Terry .669
Thompson Falls .90
Three Forks .351
Townsend .317
Virginia City .382
West Glacier .120
W. Yellowstone .460
Whitefish .103
W Sulphur Springs 359
Wibaux .683
Winnett .474
Wolf Point .555

**Livingston** to
Anaconda .135
Baker .341
Big Timber .35
Billings .116
Boulder .109
Bozeman .26
Broadus .284
Browning .293
Butte .108
Chester .300
Chinook .289
Choteau .221
Circle .333
Columbus .75
Conrad .233
Cooke City .109
Culbertson .425
Cut Bank .280
Deer Lodge .149
Dillon .138
E. Glacier Park .306
Ekalaka .376
Eureka .383
Forsyth .216
Fort Benton .212
Gardiner .53
Glasgow .339
Glendive .338
Grass Range Jct. .167
Great Falls .170
Hamilton .255
Hardin .162
Harlowtown .79
Havre .285
Helena .121
Hysham .193
Jordan .266
Kalispell .317
Laurel .100
Lewistown .136
Libby .406
Malta .269
Miles City .261
Missoula .228
Philipsburg .166
Plentywood .472
Polson .294
Poplar .398
Red Lodge .123
Roundup .148
Ryegate .109
Scobey .432
Shelby .258
Sidney .388
Stanford .147
Superior .285
Sweetgrass .292
Terry .299
Thompson Falls .328
Three Forks .56
Townsend .89
Virginia City .93
West Glacier .338
W. Yellowstone .107
Whitefish .331
W Sulphur Springs .73
Wibaux .364
Winnett .190
Wolf Point .386

**Malta** to
Anaconda .375
Baker .292
Big Timber .234
Billings .209
Boulder .319
Bozeman .295
Broadus .346
Browning .248
Butte .356
Chester .148
Chinook .67
Choteau .258
Circle .172
Columbus .250
Conrad .215
Cooke City .335
Culbertson .173
Cut Bank .214
Deer Lodge .348
Dillon .398
E. Glacier Park .261
Ekalaka .327
Eureka .393
Forsyth .257
Fort Benton .163
Gardiner .322
Glasgow .70
Glendive .221
Grass Range Jct. .112
Great Falls .203
Hamilton .422
Hardin .249
Harlowtown .190

Havre 88
Helena 292
Hysham 280
Jordan 183
Kalispell 347
Laurel 225
Lewistown 133
Libby 436
Livingston 269
Miles City 267
Missoula 372
Philipsburg 385
Plentywood 215
Polson 386
Poplar 140
Red Lodge 269
Roundup 156
Ryegate 195
Scobey 174
Shelby 190
Sidney 210
Stanford 178
Superior 429
Sweetgrass 226
Terry 252
Thompson Falls 455
Three Forks 323
Townsend 289
Virginia City 362
West Glacier 316
W. Yellowstone 376
Whitefish 340
W Sulphur Springs 247
Wibaux 247
Winnett 135
Wolf Point 119

**Miles City** to
Anaconda 396
Baker 81
Big Timber 226
Billings 145
Boulder 370
Bozeman 287
Broadus 79
Browning 444
Butte 369
Chester 394
Chinook 313
Choteau 372
Circle 119
Columbus 186
Conrad 380
Cooke City 271
Culbertson 165
Cut Bank 427
Deer Lodge 402
Dillon 399
E. Glacier Park 457
Ekalaka 116
Eureka 589
Forsyth 45
Fort Benton 311
Gardiner 314
Glasgow 197
Glendive 78
Grass Range Jct. 181
Great Falls 317
Hamilton 511
Hardin 180
Harlowtown 215
Havre 334
Helena 346
Hysham 74
Jordan 84
Kalispell 542
Laurel 161
Lewistown 212
Libby 631
Livingston 261
Malta 267
Missoula 461
Philipsburg 427
Plentywood 212
Polson 527
Poplar 184
Red Lodge 205
Roundup 146
Ryegate 185
Scobey 218
Shelby 405
Sidney 128
Stanford 257
Superior 518
Sweetgrass 439
Terry 39
Thompson Falls 561
Three Forks 317
Townsend 314
Virginia City 354
West Glacier 512
W. Yellowstone 363
Whitefish 537
W Sulphur Springs 272
Wibaux 104
Winnett 158
Wolf Point 172

**Missoula** to
Anaconda 105
Baker 541
Big Timber 263
Billings 339
Boulder 142
Bozeman 202
Broadus 507
Browning 204
Butte 120
Chester 269
Chinook 305
Choteau 160
Circle 471
Columbus 303
Conrad 202
Cooke City 337
Culbertson 545
Cut Bank 238
Deer Lodge 79
Dillon 171
E. Glacier Park 191
Ekalaka 576
Eureka 181
Forsyth 416
Fort Benton 213
Gardiner 281
Glasgow 442
Glendive 520
Grass Range Jct. 305
Great Falls 169
Hamilton 50
Hardin 385
Harlowtown 246
Havre 284
Helena 115
Hysham 416
Jordan 404
Kalispell 115
Laurel 326
Lewistown 274
Libby 190
Livingston 228
Malta 372
Miles City 461
Philipsburg 74
Plentywood 587
Polson 66
Poplar 512
Red Lodge 351
Roundup 315
Ryegate 276
Scobey 546
Shelby 227
Sidney 546
Stanford 229
Superior 57
Sweetgrass 261
Terry 499
Thompson Falls 100
Three Forks 173
Townsend 147
Virginia City 192
West Glacier 136
W. Yellowstone 270
Whitefish 129
W Sulphur Springs 189
Wibaux 546
Winnett 328
Wolf Point 491

**Philipsburg** to
Anaconda 31
Baker 507
Big Timber 201
Billings 282
Boulder 95
Bozeman 140
Broadus 450
Browning 263
Butte 58
Chester 300
Chinook 318
Choteau 191
Circle 478
Columbus 241
Conrad 233
Cooke City 275
Culbertson 558
Cut Bank 280
Deer Lodge 57
Dillon 109
E. Glacier Park 265
Ekalaka 542
Eureka 255
Forsyth 382
Fort Benton 226
Gardiner 219
Glasgow 455
Glendive 504
Grass Range Jct. 312
Great Falls 182
Hamilton 124
Hardin 328
Harlowtown 224
Havre 297
Helena 93
Hysham 369
Jordan 411
Kalispell 189
Laurel 266
Lewistown 281
Libby 264
Livingston 166
Malta 385
Miles City 427
Missoula 74
Plentywood 600
Polson 140
Poplar 525
Red Lodge 289
Roundup 293
Ryegate 254
Scobey 559
Shelby 258
Sidney 553
Stanford 242
Superior 131
Sweetgrass 292
Terry 465
Thompson Falls 174
Three Forks 111
Townsend 125
Virginia City 130
West Glacier 210
W. Yellowstone 208
Whitefish 203
W Sulphur Springs 167
Wibaux 530
Winnett 335
Wolf Point 504

**Plentywood** to
Anaconda 590
Baker 209
Big Timber 437
Billings 356
Boulder 534
Bozeman 498
Broadus 288
Browning 463
Butte 571
Chester 363
Chinook 282
Choteau 473
Circle 140
Columbus 397
Conrad 430
Cooke City 482
Culbertson 47
Cut Bank 429
Deer Lodge 563
Dillon 602
E. Glacier Park 476
Ekalaka 244
Eureka 608
Forsyth 256
Fort Benton 378
Gardiner 525
Glasgow 145
Glendive 138
Grass Range Jct. 306
Great Falls 418
Hamilton 637
Hardin 331
Harlowtown 394
Havre 303
Helena 507
Hysham 285
Jordan 207
Kalispell 562
Laurel 372
Lewistown 337
Libby 651
Livingston 472
Malta 215
Miles City 212
Missoula 587
Philipsburg 600
Polson 601
Poplar 80
Red Lodge 416
Roundup 328
Ryegate 367
Scobey 41
Shelby 405
Sidney 84
Stanford 282
Superior 644
Sweetgrass 441
Terry 173
Thompson Falls 670
Three Forks 527
Townsend 493
Virginia City 565
West Glacier 531
W. Yellowstone 574
Whitefish 556
W Sulphur Springs 451
Wibaux 164
Winnett 283
Wolf Point 96

**Polson** to
Anaconda 171
Baker 607
Big Timber 329
Billings 405
Boulder 208
Bozeman 268
Broadus 573
Browning 138
Butte 186
Chester 238
Chinook 319
Choteau 210
Circle 537
Columbus 369
Conrad 204
Cooke City 403
Culbertson 559
Cut Bank 172
Deer Lodge 145
Dillon 237
E. Glacier Park 125
Ekalaka 642
Eureka 115
Forsyth 482
Fort Benton 279
Gardiner 347
Glasgow 456
Glendive 586
Grass Range Jct. 371
Great Falls 235
Hamilton 116
Hardin 451
Harlowtown 312
Havre 298
Helena 181
Hysham 482
Jordan 470
Kalispell 49
Laurel 394
Lewistown 340
Libby 138
Livingston 294
Malta 386
Miles City 527
Missoula 66
Philipsburg 140
Plentywood 601
Poplar 526
Red Lodge 417
Roundup 381
Ryegate 342
Scobey 560
Shelby 196
Sidney 596
Stanford 295
Superior 97
Sweetgrass 230
Terry 565
Thompson Falls 91
Three Forks 239
Townsend 213
Virginia City 258
West Glacier 70
W. Yellowstone 336
Whitefish 63
W Sulphur Springs 255
Wibaux 612
Winnett 394
Wolf Point 505

**Poplar** to
Anaconda 515
Baker 185
Big Timber 363
Billings 306
Boulder 459
Bozeman 424
Broadus 260
Browning 388
Butte 496
Chester 288
Chinook 207
Choteau 398
Circle 65
Columbus 347
Conrad 355
Cooke City 432
Culbertson 33
Cut Bank 354
Deer Lodge 488
Dillon 527
E. Glacier Park 401
Ekalaka 220
Eureka 533
Forsyth 228
Fort Benton 303
Gardiner 451
Glasgow 70
Glendive 114
Grass Range Jct. 231
Great Falls 343
Hamilton 562
Hardin 303
Harlowtown 319
Havre 228
Helena 432
Hysham 257
Jordan 132
Kalispell 487
Laurel 322
Lewistown 262
Libby 576
Livingston 398
Malta 140
Miles City 184
Missoula 512
Philipsburg 525
Plentywood 80
Polson 526
Red Lodge 366
Roundup 253
Ryegate 292
Scobey 62
Shelby 330
Sidney 70
Stanford 307
Superior 569
Sweetgrass 366
Terry 145
Thompson Falls 595
Three Forks 452
Townsend 418
Virginia City 491
West Glacier 546
W. Yellowstone 505
Whitefish 481
W Sulphur Springs 376
Wibaux 140
Winnett 208
Wolf Point 21

**Red Lodge** to
Anaconda 258
Baker 285
Big Timber 88
Billings 60
Boulder 232
Bozeman 149
Broadus 228
Browning 387
Butte 231
Chester 370
Chinook 289
Choteau 315
Circle 301
Columbus 48
Conrad 323
Cooke City 66
Culbertson 369
Cut Bank 370
Deer Lodge 272
Dillon 261
E. Glacier Park 400
Ekalaka 320
Eureka 500
Forsyth 160
Fort Benton 265
Gardiner 122
Glasgow 339
Glendive 282
Grass Range Jct. 157
Great Falls 260
Hamilton 378
Hardin 106
Harlowtown 132
Havre 321
Helena 238
Hysham 137
Jordan 234
Kalispell 434
Laurel 44
Lewistown 188
Libby 525
Livingston 123
Malta 269
Miles City 205
Missoula 351
Philipsburg 289
Plentywood 416
Polson 417
Poplar 366
Roundup 113
Ryegate 123
Scobey 400
Shelby 348
Sidney 332
Stanford 200
Superior 408
Sweetgrass 382
Terry 243
Thompson Falls 451
Three Forks 179
Townsend 206
Virginia City 216
West Glacier 455
W. Yellowstone 158
Whitefish 448
W Sulphur Springs 182
Wibaux 308
Winnett 158
Wolf Point 354

**Roundup** to
Anaconda 274
Baker 226
Big Timber 113
Billings 53
Boulder 227
Bozeman 174
Broadus 215
Browning 307
Butte 247
Chester 257
Chinook 176
Choteau 235
Circle 188
Columbus 94
Conrad 243
Cooke City 179
Culbertson 286
Cut Bank 290
Deer Lodge 256
Dillon 277
E. Glacier Park 320
Ekalaka 261
Eureka 452
Forsyth 101
Fort Benton 174
Gardiner 201
Glasgow 226
Glendive 223
Grass Range Jct. 44
Great Falls 180
Hamilton 365
Hardin 93
Harlowtown 69
Havre 197
Helena 200
Hysham 124
Jordan 121
Kalispell 396
Laurel 69
Lewistown 75
Libby 485
Livingston 148
Malta 156
Miles City 146
Missoula 315
Philipsburg 293
Plentywood 328
Polson 381
Poplar 253
Red Lodge 113
Ryegate 39
Scobey 387
Shelby 268
Sidney 263
Stanford 120
Superior 372
Sweetgrass 302
Terry 184
Thompson Falls 415
Three Forks 202
Townsend 168
Virginia City 241
West Glacier 375
W. Yellowstone 255
Whitefish 400
W Sulphur Springs 126
Wibaux 249
Winnett 45
Wolf Point 241

**Ryegate** to
Anaconda 235
Baker 265
Big Timber 74
Billings 63
Boulder 188
Bozeman 135
Broadus 231
Browning 283
Butte 208
Chester 286
Chinook 215
Choteau 211
Circle 227
Columbus 104
Conrad 219
Cooke City 189
Culbertson 325
Cut Bank 266
Deer Lodge 217
Dillon 238
E. Glacier Park 296
Ekalaka 300
Eureka 423
Forsyth 140
Fort Benton 161
Gardiner 162
Glasgow 265
Glendive 262
Grass Range Jct. 83
Great Falls 156
Hamilton 326
Hardin 109
Harlowtown 30
Havre 236
Helena 161
Hysham 140
Jordan 160
Kalispell 357
Laurel 79
Lewistown 85
Libby 446
Livingston 109
Malta 195
Miles City 185
Missoula 276
Philipsburg 254
Plentywood 367
Polson 342
Poplar 292
Red Lodge 123
Roundup 39
Scobey 326
Shelby 244
Sidney 302
Stanford 96
Superior 333
Sweetgrass 278
Terry 223
Thompson Falls 376
Three Forks 163
Townsend 129
Virginia City 202
West Glacier 351
W. Yellowstone 216
Whitefish 371
W Sulphur Springs 87
Wibaux 288
Winnett 84
Wolf Point 280

**Scobey** to
Anaconda 549
Baker 219
Big Timber 397
Billings 340
Boulder 493
Bozeman 458
Broadus 294
Browning 422
Butte 530
Chester 322
Chinook 241
Choteau 432
Circle 99
Columbus 381
Conrad 389
Cooke City 466
Culbertson 88
Cut Bank 388
Deer Lodge 522
Dillon 561
E. Glacier Park 435
Ekalaka 254
Eureka 567
Forsyth 262
Fort Benton 337
Gardiner 485
Glasgow 104
Glendive 148
Grass Range Jct. 255
Great Falls 377
Hamilton 596
Hardin 337
Harlowtown 353
Havre 262
Helena 466
Hysham 291
Jordan 166
Kalispell 521
Laurel 356
Lewistown 296
Libby 610
Livingston 432
Malta 174
Miles City 218
Missoula 546
Philipsburg 559
Plentywood 41
Polson 560
Poplar 62
Red Lodge 400
Roundup 287
Ryegate 326
Shelby 364
Sidney 125
Stanford 341
Superior 603
Sweetgrass 400
Terry 179
Thompson Falls 629
Three Forks 486
Townsend 452
Virginia City 525
West Glacier 490
W. Yellowstone 539
Whitefish 515
W Sulphur Springs 410
Wibaux 174
Winnett 242
Wolf Point 55

**Shelby** to
Anaconda 248
Baker 482
Big Timber 260
Billings 307
Boulder 194
Bozeman 262
Broadus 475
Browning 58
Butte 231
Chester 42
Chinook 123
Choteau 75
Circle 362
Columbus 300
Conrad 25
Cooke City 367
Culbertson 363
Cut Bank 24
Deer Lodge 221
Dillon 287
E. Glacier Park 71
Ekalaka 517
Eureka 203
Forsyth 369
Fort Benton 132
Gardiner 311
Glasgow 260
Glendive 411
Grass Range Jct. 224
Great Falls 88
Hamilton 277
Hardin 353
Harlowtown 216
Havre 102
Helena 167
Hysham 384
Jordan 323
Kalispell 157
Laurel 323
Lewistown 193
Libby 246
Livingston 258
Malta 190
Miles City 405
Missoula 227
Philipsburg 258
Plentywood 405
Polson 196
Poplar 330
Red Lodge 348
Roundup 268
Ryegate 244
Scobey 364
Sidney 400
Stanford 148
Superior 282
Sweetgrass 36
Terry 442
Thompson Falls 265
Three Forks 233
Townsend 199
Virginia City 287
West Glacier 126
W. Yellowstone 342
Whitefish 151
W Sulphur Springs 185
Wibaux 437
Winnett 247
Wolf Point 309

**Sidney** to
Anaconda 523
Baker 125
Big Timber 353
Billings 272
Boulder 487
Bozeman 414
Broadus 204
Browning 458
Butte 296
Chester 358
Chinook 277
Choteau 432
Circle 75
Columbus 315
Conrad 425
Cooke City 398
Culbertson 37
Cut Bank 424
Deer Lodge 516
Dillon 526
E. Glacier Park 471
Ekalaka 160
Eureka 603
Forsyth 172
Fort Benton 371
Gardiner 441
Glasgow 140
Glendive 54
Grass Range Jct. 241
Great Falls 377
Hamilton 596
Hardin 247
Harlowtown 329
Havre 298
Helena 460
Hysham 201
Jordan 142
Kalispell 557
Laurel 288
Lewistown 272
Libby 646
Livingston 388
Malta 210
Miles City 128
Missoula 546
Philipsburg 553
Plentywood 84
Polson 596
Poplar 70
Red Lodge 332
Roundup 263
Ryegate 302
Scobey 125
Shelby 400
Stanford 317
Superior 603
Sweetgrass 436
Terry 89
Thompson Falls 646
Three Forks 444
Townsend 428
Virginia City 481
West Glacier 526
W. Yellowstone 490
Whitefish 551
W Sulphur Springs 386
Wibaux 80
Winnett 218
Wolf Point 91

**Stanford** to
Anaconda 232
Baker 338
Big Timber 112
Billings 159
Boulder 176
Bozeman 173
Broadus 327
Browning 187
Butte 213
Chester 190
Chinook 161
Choteau 115
Circle 242
Columbus 152
Conrad 123
Cooke City 256
Culbertson 340
Cut Bank 170
Deer Lodge 205
Dillon 260
E. Glacier Park 200
Ekalaka 373
Eureka 332
Forsyth 221
Fort Benton 65
Gardiner 200
Glasgow 248
Glendive 291
Grass Range Jct. 76
Great Falls 60
Hamilton 279
Hardin 205
Harlowtown 68
Havre 140
Helena 149
Hysham 236
Jordan 175
Kalispell 286
Laurel 175
Lewistown 45
Libby 375
Livingston 147
Malta 18
Miles City 257
Missoula 229
Philipsburg 242
Plentywood 282
Polson 295
Poplar 307
Red Lodge 200
Roundup 120
Ryegate 96
Scobey 341
Shelby 148
Sidney 317
Superior 286
Sweetgrass 182
Terry 296
Thompson Falls 329
Three Forks 187
Townsend 153
Virginia City 240
West Glacier 255
W. Yellowstone 254
Whitefish 280
W Sulphur Springs 111
Wibaux 317
Winnett 99
Wolf Point 295

**Superior** to
Anaconda 162
Baker 598
Big Timber 320
Billings 396
Boulder 199
Bozeman 259
Broadus 564
Browning 224
Butte 177
Chester 324
Chinook 362
Choteau 217
Circle 528
Columbus 360
Conrad 259
Cooke City 394
Culbertson 602
Cut Bank 258
Deer Lodge 136
Dillon 228
E. Glacier Park 211
Ekalaka 633
Eureka 191
Forsyth 473
Fort Benton 270
Gardiner 338
Glasgow 499
Glendive 577
Grass Range Jct. 362
Great Falls 226
Hamilton 107
Hardin 442
Harlowtown 303
Havre 341
Helena 172
Hysham 473
Jordan 461
Kalispell 125
Laurel 385
Lewistown 331
Libby 159
Livingston 285
Malta 429
Miles City 518
Missoula 57
Philipsburg 131
Plentywood 644
Polson 97
Poplar 569
Red Lodge 408
Roundup 372
Ryegate 333
Scobey 603
Shelby 282
Sidney 603
Stanford 286
Sweetgrass 316
Terry 556
Thompson Falls 69
Three Forks 230
Townsend 204
Virginia City 249
West Glacier 156
W. Yellowstone 327
Whitefish 139
W Sulphur Springs 246
Wibaux 603
Winnett 385
Wolf Point 548

**Sweetgrass** to
Anaconda 282
Baker 518
Big Timber 294

Billings 341
Boulder 228
Bozeman 296
Broadus 509
Browning 92
Butte 265
Chester 78
Chinook 159
Choteau 109
Circle 398
Columbus 334
Conrad 59
Cooke City 401
Culbertson 399
Cut Bank 58
Deer Lodge 255
Dillon 321
E. Glacier Park 105
Ekalaka 553
Eureka 237
Forsyth 403
Fort Benton 166
Gardiner 345
Glasgow 296
Glendive 447
Grass Range Jct. 358
Great Falls 122
Hamilton 311
Hardin 287
Harlowtown 250
Havre 138
Helena 201
Hysham 418
Jordan 357
Kalispell 191
Laurel 357
Lewistown 227
Libby 280
Livingston 292
Malta 226
Miles City 439
Missoula 261
Philipsburg 292
Plentywood 441
Polson 230
Poplar 366
Red Lodge 382
Roundup 302
Ryegate 278
Scobey 400
Shelby 36
Sidney 436
Stanford 182
Superior 316
Terry 478
Thompson Falls 299
Three Forks 267
Townsend 233
Virginia City 321
West Glacier 160
W. Yellowstone 376
Whitefish 185
W Sulphur Springs 219
Wibaux 473
Winnett 281
Wolf Point 345

**Terry** to
Anaconda 434
Baker 110
Big Timber 264
Billings 183
Boulder 408
Bozeman 325
Broadus 115
Browning 483
Butte 407
Chester 400
Chinook 319
Choteau 411
Circle 80
Columbus 224
Conrad 419
Cooke City 309
Culbertson 126
Cut Bank 466
Deer Lodge 440
Dillon 437
E. Glacier Park 496
Ekalaka 145
Eureka 168
Forsyth 83
Fort Benton 350
Gardiner 352
Glasgow 182
Glendive 39
Grass Range Jct. 220
Great Falls 356
Hamilton 549
Hardin 148
Harlowtown 253
Havre 340
Helena 384
Hysham 112
Jordan 123
Kalispell 580
Laurel 199
Lewistown 251
Libby 669
Livingston 299
Malta 252
Miles City 39
Missoula 499
Philipsburg 465
Plentywood 173
Polson 565
Poplar 145
Red Lodge 243
Roundup 184
Ryegate 223
Scobey 179
Shelby 442
Sidney 89
Stanford 296
Superior 556
Sweetgrass 478
Thompson Falls 599
Three Forks 355
Townsend 352
Virginia City 392
West Glacier 551
W. Yellowstone 401
Whitefish 576
W Sulphur Springs 310
Wibaux 65
Winnett 197
Wolf Point 133

**Thompson Falls** to
Anaconda 205
Baker 461
Big Timber 363
Billings 439
Boulder 242
Bozeman 302
Broadus 607
Browning 207
Butte 220
Chester 307
Chinook 388
Choteau 260
Circle 571
Columbus 403
Conrad 273
Cooke City 437
Culbertson 628
Cut Bank 241
Deer Lodge 179
Dillon 271
E. Glacier Park 194
Ekalaka 676
Eureka 158
Forsyth 516
Fort Benton 313
Gardiner 381
Glasgow 525
Glendive 620
Grass Range Jct. 405
Great Falls 269
Hamilton 150
Hardin 485
Harlowtown 346
Havre 367
Helena 215
Hysham 516
Jordan 504
Kalispell 108
Laurel 428
Lewistown 374
Libby 90
Livingston 328
Malta 455
Miles City 561
Missoula 100
Philipsburg 174
Plentywood 670
Polson 91
Poplar 595
Red Lodge 451
Roundup 415
Ryegate 376
Scobey 629
Shelby 265
Sidney 646
Stanford 329
Superior 69
Sweetgrass 299
Terry 599
Three Forks 273
Townsend 247
Virginia City 292
West Glacier 139
W. Yellowstone 370
Whitefish 122
W Sulphur Springs 289
Wibaux 646
Winnett 428
Wolf Point 574

**Three Forks** to
Anaconda 80
Baker 397
Big Timber 91
Billings 172
Boulder 54
Bozeman 30
Broadus 340
Browning 238
Butte 53
Chester 275
Chinook 291
Choteau 166
Circle 387
Columbus 131
Conrad 208
Cooke City 165
Culbertson 481
Cut Bank 255
Deer Lodge 94
Dillon 83
E. Glacier Park 251
Ekalaka 432
Eureka 328
Forsyth 272
Fort Benton 199
Gardiner 109
Glasgow 393
Glendive 394
Grass Range Jct. 221
Great Falls 155
Hamilton 200
Hardin 218
Harlowtown 133
Havre 270
Helena 66
Hysham 249
Jordan 320
Kalispell 262
Laurel 156
Lewistown 190
Libby 351
Livingston 56
Malta 323
Miles City 317
Missoula 173
Philipsburg 111
Plentywood 527
Polson 239
Poplar 452
Red Lodge 179
Roundup 202
Ryegate 163
Scobey 486
Shelby 233
Sidney 444
Stanford 187
Superior 230
Sweetgrass 267
Terry 355
Thompson Falls 273
Townsend 34
Virginia City 61
West Glacier 283
W. Yellowstone 110
Whitefish 276
W Sulphur Springs 76
Wibaux 420
Winnett 244
Wolf Point 440

**Townsend** to
Anaconda 106
Baker 394
Big Timber 118
Billings 192
Boulder 59
Bozeman 63
Broadus 360
Browning 204
Butte 79
Chester 241
Chinook 257
Choteau 132
Circle 353
Columbus 158
Conrad 174
Cooke City 198
Culbertson 451
Cut Bank 221
Deer Lodge 88
Dillon 109
E. Glacier Park 217
Ekalaka 429
Eureka 294
Forsyth 269
Fort Benton 165
Gardiner 142
Glasgow 359
Glendive 391
Grass Range Jct. 187
Great Falls 121
Hamilton 197
Hardin 238
Harlowtown 99
Havre 236
Helena 32
Hysham 269
Jordan 286
Kalispell 228
Laurel 183
Lewistown 156
Libby 317
Livingston 89
Malta 289
Miles City 314
Missoula 147
Philipsburg 125
Plentywood 493
Polson 213
Poplar 418
Red Lodge 206
Roundup 168
Ryegate 129
Scobey 452
Shelby 199
Sidney 428
Stanford 153
Superior 204
Sweetgrass 233
Terry 352
Thompson Falls 247
Three Forks 34
Virginia City 89
West Glacier 249
W. Yellowstone 143
Whitefish 242
W Sulphur Springs 42
Wibaux 417
Winnett 210
Wolf Point 406

**Virginia City** to
Anaconda 99
Baker 434
Big Timber 128
Billings 209
Boulder 92
Bozeman 67
Broadus 377
Browning 292
Butte 72
Chester 329
Chinook 345
Choteau 220
Circle 426
Columbus 168
Conrad 262
Cooke City 176
Culbertson 518
Cut Bank 309
Deer Lodge 133
Dillon 57
E. Glacier Park 305
Ekalaka 469
Eureka 365
Forsyth 309
Fort Benton 253
Gardiner 138
Glasgow 432
Glendive 431
Grass Range Jct. 260
Great Falls 209
Hamilton 219
Hardin 255
Harlowtown 172
Havre 324
Helena 120
Hysham 286
Jordan 359
Kalispell 299
Laurel 193
Lewistown 229
Libby 382
Livingston 93
Malta 362
Miles City 354
Missoula 192
Philipsburg 130
Plentywood 565
Polson 258
Poplar 491
Red Lodge 216
Roundup 241
Ryegate 202
Scobey 525
Shelby 287
Sidney 481
Stanford 240
Superior 249
Sweetgrass 321
Terry 392
Thompson Falls 292
Three Forks 61
Townsend 89
West Glacier 320
W. Yellowstone 84
Whitefish 313
W Sulphur Springs 131
Wibaux 457
Winnett 283
Wolf Point 479

**West Glacier** to
Anaconda 234
Baker 593
Big Timber 367
Billings 414
Boulder 244
Bozeman 321
Broadus 582
Browning 68
Butte 248
Chester 168
Chinook 249
Choteau 140
Circle 488
Columbus 407
Conrad 134
Cooke City 447
Culbertson 489
Cut Bank 102
Deer Lodge 207
Dillon 299
E. Glacier Park 55
Ekalaka 628
Eureka 77
Forsyth 476
Fort Benton 239
Gardiner 391
Glasgow 386
Glendive 537
Grass Range Jct. 331
Great Falls 195
Hamilton 186
Hardin 460
Harlowtown 323
Havre 228
Helena 217
Hysham 491
Jordan 430
Kalispell 31
Laurel 430
Lewistown 300
Libby 120
Livingston 338
Malta 316
Miles City 512
Missoula 136
Philipsburg 210
Plentywood 531
Polson 70
Poplar 546
Red Lodge 455
Roundup 375
Ryegate 351
Scobey 490
Shelby 126
Sidney 526
Stanford 255
Superior 156
Sweetgrass 160
Terry 551
Thompson Falls 139
Three Forks 283
Townsend 249
Virginia City 320
W. Yellowstone 392
Whitefish 25
W Sulphur Springs 291
Wibaux 563
Winnett 354
Wolf Point 435

**W. Yellowstone** to
Anaconda 177
Baker 443
Big Timber 142
Billings 218
Boulder 151
Bozeman 91
Broadus 386
Browning 347
Butte 150
Chester 384
Chinook 396
Choteau 275
Circle 440
Columbus 182
Conrad 317
Cooke City 92
Culbertson 527
Cut Bank 364
Deer Lodge 191
Dillon 141
E. Glacier Park 360
Ekalaka 478
Eureka 437
Forsyth 318
Fort Benton 308
Gardiner 54
Glasgow 445
Glendive 440
Grass Range Jct. 274
Great Falls 264
Hamilton 297
Hardin 264
Harlowtown 186
Havre 379
Helena 175
Hysham 295
Jordan 373
Kalispell 371
Laurel 202
Lewistown 243
Libby 460
Livingston 107
Malta 376
Miles City 363
Missoula 270
Philipsburg 208
Plentywood 574
Polson 336
Poplar 505
Red Lodge 158
Roundup 255
Ryegate 216
Scobey 539
Shelby 342
Sidney 490
Stanford 254
Superior 327
Sweetgrass 376
Terry 401
Thompson Falls 370
Three Forks 110
Townsend 143
Virginia City 84
West Glacier 392
Whitefish 385
W Sulphur Springs 171
Wibaux 466
Winnett 297
Wolf Point 493

**Whitefish** to
Anaconda 227
Baker 628
Big Timber 360
Billings 434
Boulder 237
Bozeman 305
Broadus 602
Browning 93
Butte 241
Chester 193
Chinook 274
Choteau 165
Circle 513
Columbus 400
Conrad 159
Cooke City 440
Culbertson 514
Cut Bank 127
Deer Lodge 200
Dillon 292
E. Glacier Park 80
Ekalaka 653
Eureka 52
Forsyth 501
Fort Benton 264
Gardiner 384
Glasgow 411
Glendive 562
Grass Range Jct. 365
Great Falls 220
Hamilton 179
Hardin 480
Harlowtown 341
Havre 253
Helena 210
Hysham 511
Jordan 455
Kalispell 14
Laurel 454
Lewistown 325
Libby 103
Livingston 331
Malta 341
Miles City 537
Missoula 129
Philipsburg 203
Plentywood 556
Polson 63
Poplar 481
Red Lodge 448
Roundup 400
Ryegate 371
Scobey 515
Shelby 151
Sidney 551
Stanford 280
Superior 139
Sweetgrass 185
Terry 576
Thompson Falls 122
Three Forks 276
Townsend 242
Virginia City 313
West Glacier 25
W. Yellowstone 385
W Sulphur Springs 284
Wibaux 588
Winnett 379
Wolf Point 460

**W Sulphur Springs** to
Anaconda 148
Baker 352
Big Timber 94
Billings 150
Boulder 101
Bozeman 80
Broadus 318
Browning 224
Butte 121
Chester 227
Chinook 233
Choteau 152
Circle 311
Columbus 134
Conrad 160
Cooke City 182
Culbertson 409
Cut Bank 207
Deer Lodge 130
Dillon 151
E. Glacier Park 237
Ekalaka 387
Eureka 336
Forsyth 227
Fort Benton 141
Gardiner 126
Glasgow 317
Glendive 349
Grass Range Jct. 145
Great Falls 97
Hamilton 239
Hardin 196
Harlowtown 57
Havre 212
Helena 74
Hysham 227
Jordan 244
Kalispell 270
Laurel 159
Lewistown 114
Libby 359
Livingston 73
Malta 247
Miles City 272
Missoula 189
Philipsburg 167
Plentywood 451
Polson 255
Poplar 376
Red Lodge 182
Roundup 126
Ryegate 87
Scobey 410
Shelby 185
Sidney 386
Stanford 111
Superior 246
Sweetgrass 219
Terry 310
Thompson Falls 289
Three Forks 76
Townsend 42
Virginia City 131
West Glacier 291
W. Yellowstone 171
Whitefish 284
Wibaux 375
Winnett 168
Wolf Point 364

**Wibaux** to
Anaconda 499
Baker 45
Big Timber 329
Billings 248
Boulder 473
Bozeman 390
Broadus 180
Browning 495
Butte 472
Chester 395
Chinook 314
Choteau 432
Circle 75
Columbus 289
Conrad 440
Cooke City 374
Culbertson 117
Cut Bank 461
Deer Lodge 505
Dillon 502
E. Glacier Park 508
Ekalaka 80
Eureka 640
Forsyth 148
Fort Benton 371
Gardiner 417
Glasgow 177
Glendive 26
Grass Range Jct. 241
Great Falls 377
Hamilton 596
Hardin 233
Harlowtown 318
Havre 335
Helena 449
Hysham 177
Jordan 142
Kalispell 594
Laurel 264
Lewistown 272
Libby 683
Livingston 364
Malta 247
Miles City 104
Missoula 546
Philipsburg 530
Plentywood 164
Polson 612
Poplar 140
Red Lodge 308
Roundup 249
Ryegate 288
Scobey 174
Shelby 437
Sidney 80
Stanford 317
Superior 603
Sweetgrass 473
Terry 65
Thompson Falls 646
Three Forks 420
Townsend 417
Virginia City 457
West Glacier 563
W. Yellowstone 466
Whitefish 588
W Sulphur Springs 375
Winnett 218
Wolf Point 128

**Winnett** to
Anaconda 316
Baker 239
Big Timber 155
Billings 98
Boulder 269
Bozeman 216
Broadus 237
Browning 286
Butte 289
Chester 236
Chinook 155
Choteau 214
Circle 143
Columbus 139
Conrad 222
Cooke City 224
Culbertson 241
Cut Bank 269
Deer Lodge 298
Dillon 319
E. Glacier Park 299
Ekalaka 274
Eureka 431
Forsyth 146
Fort Benton 153
Gardiner 243
Glasgow 189
Glendive 192
Grass Range Jct. 23
Great Falls 159
Hamilton 378
Hardin 138
Harlowtown 111
Havre 176
Helena 242
Hysham 169
Jordan 76
Kalispell 385
Laurel 114
Lewistown 54
Libby 474
Livingston 190
Malta 135
Miles City 158
Missoula 328
Philipsburg 335
Plentywood 283
Polson 394
Poplar 208
Red Lodge 158
Roundup 45
Ryegate 84
Scobey 242
Shelby 247
Sidney 218
Stanford 99
Superior 385
Sweetgrass 281
Terry 197
Thompson Falls 428
Three Forks 244
Townsend 210
Virginia City 283
West Glacier 354
W. Yellowstone 297
Whitefish 379
W Sulphur Springs 168
Wibaux 218
Wolf Point 128

**Wolf Point** to
Anaconda 494
Baker 173
Big Timber 351
Billings 294
Boulder 438
Bozeman 412
Broadus 248
Browning 367
Butte 475
Chester 267
Chinook 186
Choteau 377
Circle 53
Columbus 335
Conrad 334
Cooke City 420
Culbertson 54
Cut Bank 333
Deer Lodge 467
Dillon 515
E. Glacier Park 380
Ekalaka 208
Eureka 512
Forsyth 216
Fort Benton 282
Gardiner 439
Glasgow 49
Glendive 102
Grass Range Jct. 219
Great Falls 322
Hamilton 541
Hardin 291
Harlowtown 307
Havre 207
Helena 411
Hysham 245
Jordan 120
Kalispell 466
Laurel 310
Lewistown 250
Libby 555
Livingston 386
Malta 119
Miles City 172
Missoula 491
Philipsburg 504
Plentywood 96
Polson 505
Poplar 21
Red Lodge 354
Roundup 241
Ryegate 280
Scobey 55
Shelby 309
Sidney 91
Stanford 295
Superior 548
Sweetgrass 345
Terry 133
Thompson Falls 574
Three Forks 440
Townsend 406
Virginia City 479
West Glacier 435
W. Yellowstone 493
Whitefish 460
W Sulphur Springs 364
Wibaux 128
Winnett 196

## NOTES:

# CITY/TOWN LOCATOR

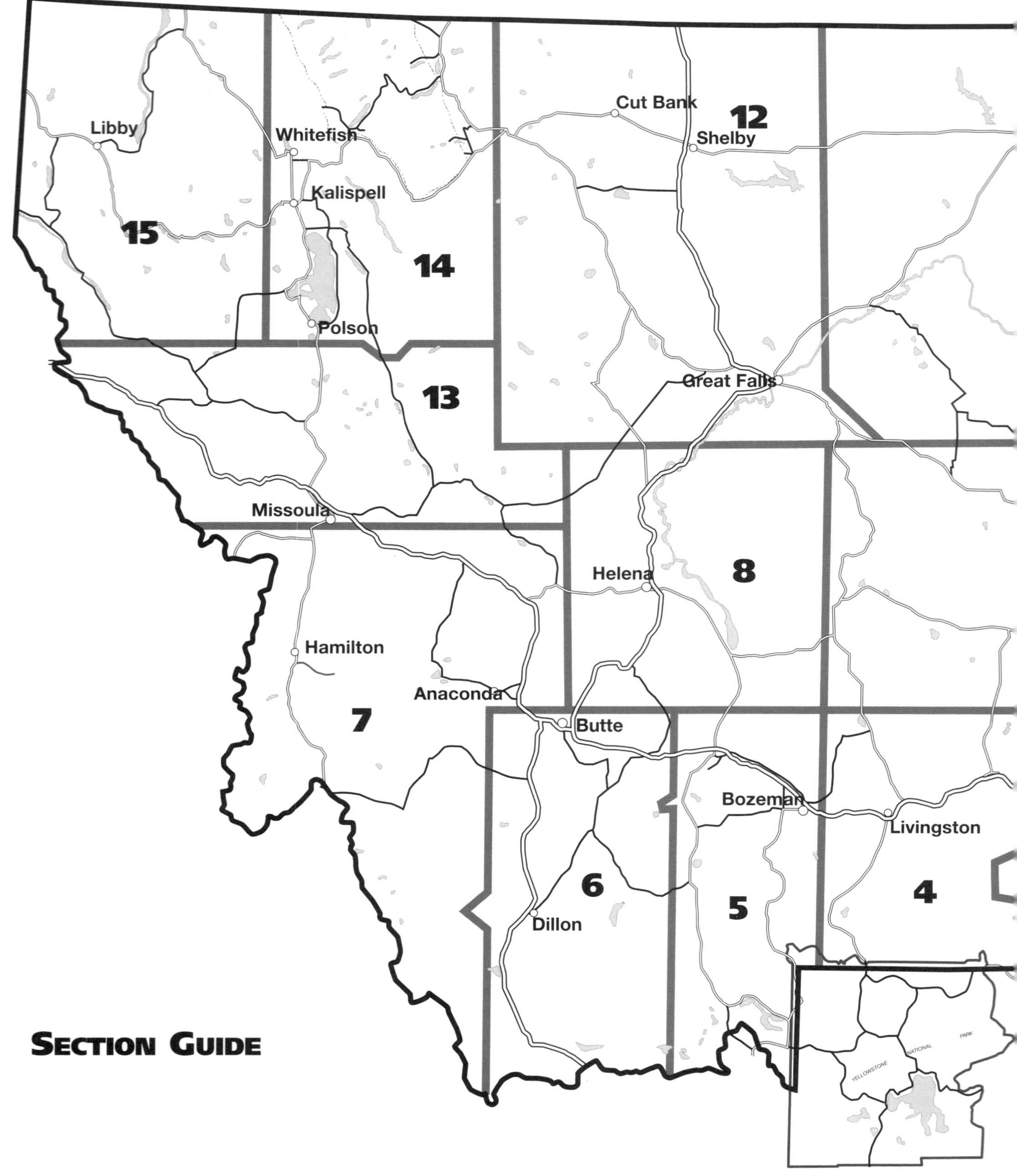


## Section Guide

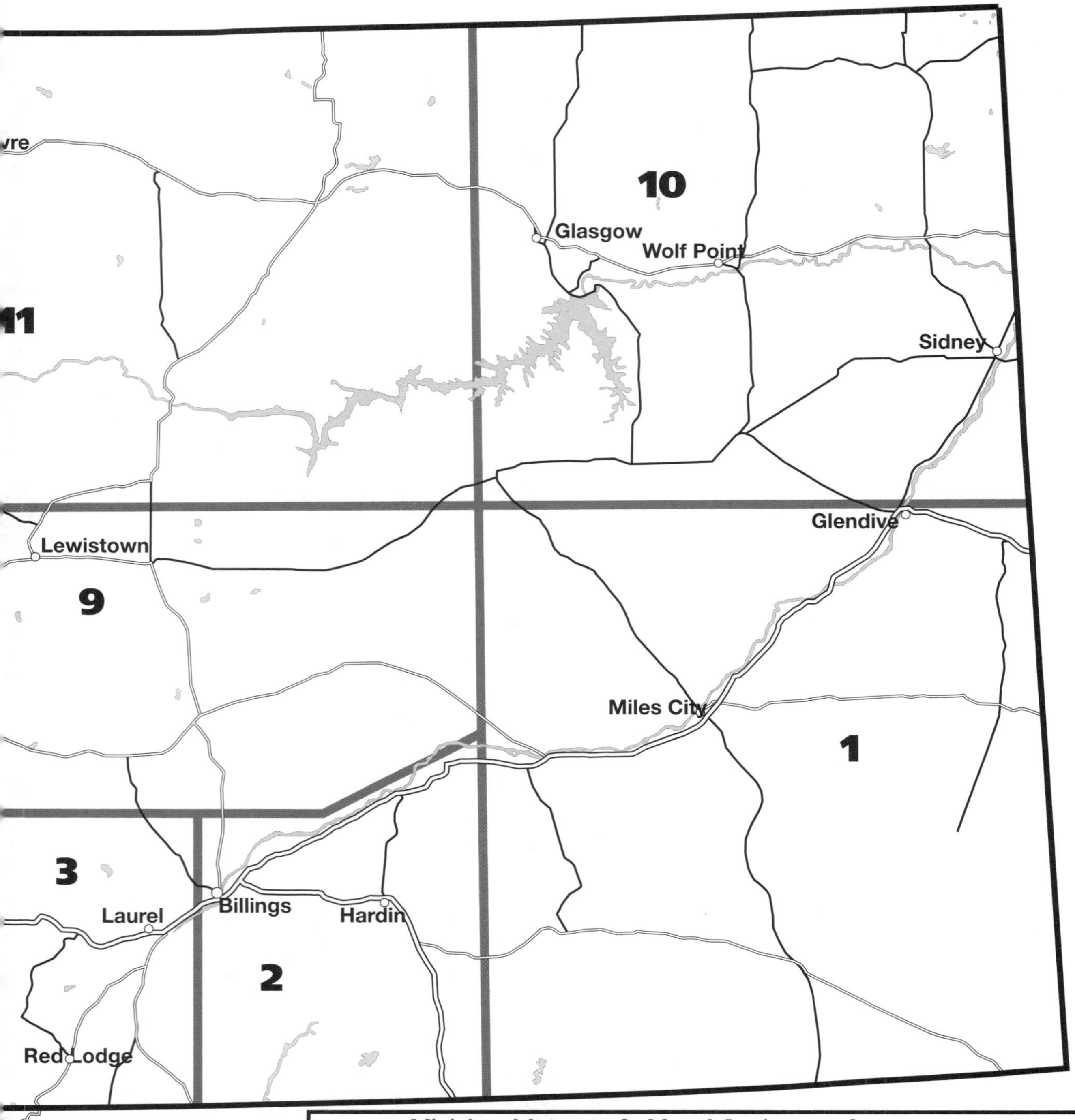

vre
10
Glasgow
Wolf Point
11
Sidney
Glendive
Lewistown
9
Miles City
1
3
Laurel
Billings
Hardin
2
Red Lodge

Port of Roosville
Port of Chief Mtn.
Port of Piegan
Port of Del Bonita
Port of Sweetgrass
Port of Whitlash
Yaak
Rexford
Eureka
Fortine
Trego
Polebridge
Stryker
Olney
Troy
Libby
Whitefish
Columbia Falls
Coram
Martin City
Hungry Horse
West Glacier
Apgar
Essex
Kalispell
Marion
Kila
Somers
Lakeside
Creston
Bigfork
Woods Bay
Swan Lake
Happy's Inn
Heron
Noxon
Manicke
Trout Creek
Belknap
Thompson Falls
Proctor
Dayton
Elmo
Big Arm
Niarada
Lonepine
Camas
Hot Springs
Polson
FLATHEAD
INDIAN
RESERVATION
Pablo
Ronan
Charlo
Moiese
St. Ignatius
Plains
Paradise
Perma
Dixon
Ravalli
Arlee
Saltese
Haugan
De Borgia
St. Regis
Superior
Tarkio
Alberton
Frenchtown
Huson
Evaro
Missoula
Milltown
Bonner
Potomac
Clinton
Lolo
Lolo Hot Springs
Florence
Stevensville
Victor
Pinesdale
Corvallis
Woodside
Hamilton
Grantsdale
Darby
Conner
Sula
Condon
Seeley Lake
Ovando
Lincoln
Helmsville
Drummond
Hall
Gold Creek
Maxville
Philipsburg
Anaconda
Opportunity
Warm Springs
Galen
Garrison
Avon
Elliston
Helena
E. Helena
Marysville
Austin
Rimini
Clancy
Montana City
Winston
Alhambra
Jefferson City
Basin
Boulder
Butte
Rocker
Whitehall
Cardwell
LeHood
Silver Star
Waterloo
Harrison
Pony
Norris
Three Forks
Willow Creek
Amsterdam
Churchill
Manhattan
Belgrade
Bozeman
Trident
Logan
Toston
Lombard
Townsend
Radersburg
Canyon Ferry
York
Wise River
Dewey
Divide
Melrose
Wisdom
Jackson
Polaris
Glen
Twin Bridges
Sheridan
McAllister
Laurin
Alder
Ruby
Nevada City
Virginia City
Ennis
Jeffers
Cameron
Gallatin Gateway
Big Sky
Bannack
Dillon
Grant
Dell
Lima
Monida
Lakeview
Gardiner
Jardine
Corwin Springs
Miner
Emigrant
Pray
Chico
Pine Creek
Livingston
McLeod
Springdale
Clyde Park
Wilsall
Ringling
Martinsdale
White Sulphur Springs
Checkerboard
Sixteen
Maudlow
Cascade
Craig
Wolf Creek
Canyon Creek
Ulm
Sand Coulee
Centerville
Eden
Stockett
Tracy
Belt
Raynesford
Geyser
Monarch
Neihart
Great Falls
Black Eagle
Sun River
Vaughn
Simms
Ft. Shaw
Augusta
Fairfield
Power
Dutton
Collins
Brady
Conrad
Ledger
Valier
Dupuyer
Heart Butte
Choteau
Bynum
Pendroy
Cut Bank
Shelby
Ethridge
Santa Rita
Kevin
Oilmont
Ferdig
Sunburst
Sweetgrass
Whitlash
Galata
Devon
Dunkirk
Lothair
Chester
Joplin
Inverness
Rudyard
Hingham
Box Elder
Virgelle
Loma
Fort Benton
Carter
Floweree
Portage
Montague
Highwood
Shonkin
Geraldine
Babb
St. Mary
Kiowa
Browning
Blackfoot
East Glacier Park
BLACKFEET
INDIAN
RESERVATION
Mammoth
Tower Jct.
Norris
Canyon Jct.
Madison Jct.
West Yellowstone
Old Faithful
West Thumb
Grant Village
YELLOWSTONE
NATIONAL
PARK
Silver Gate
Flathead Lake
Hebgen Lake
Clark Canyon Reservoir

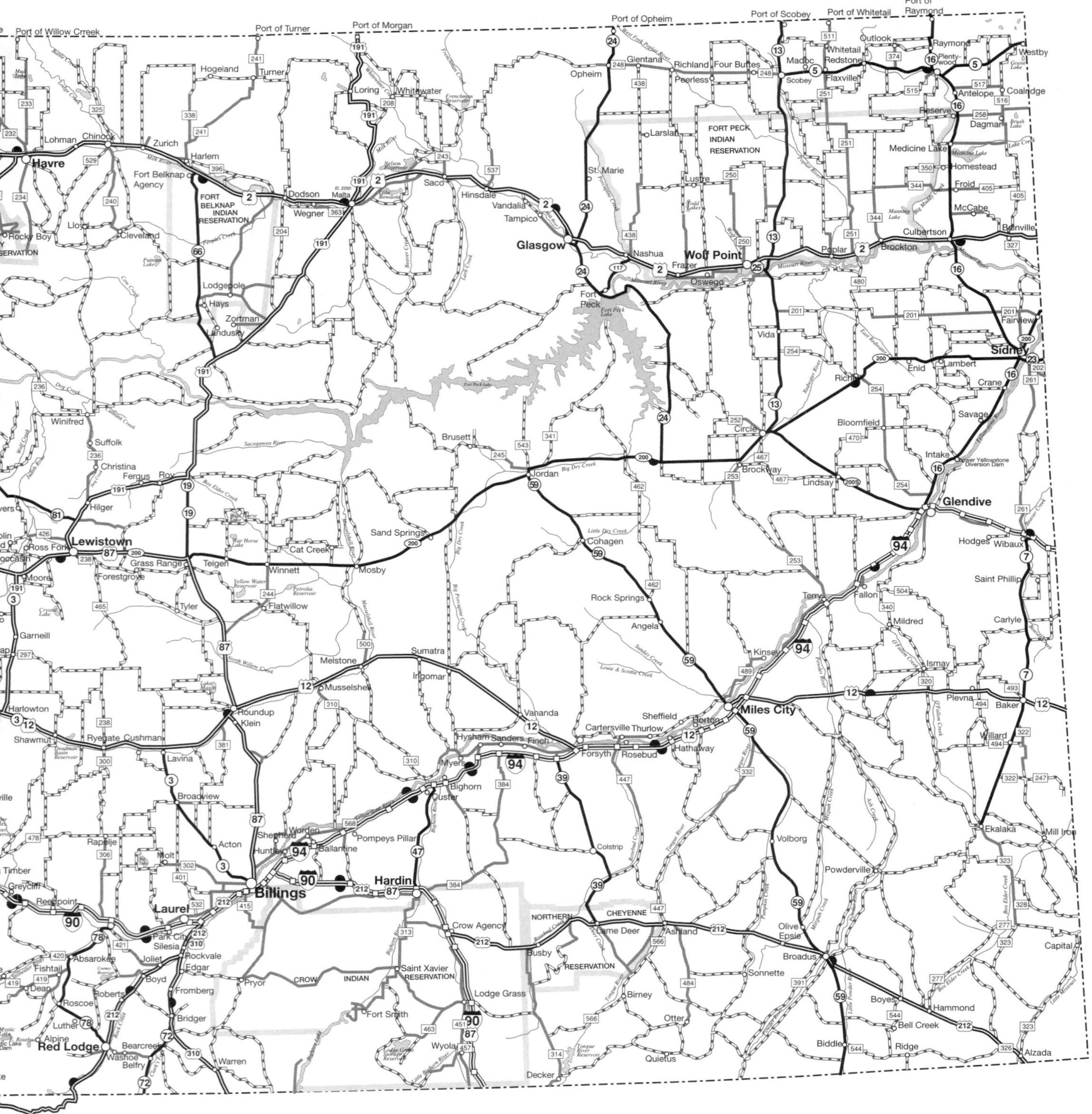
Port of Willow Creek
Port of Turner
Port of Morgan
Port of Opheim
Port of Scobey
Port of Whitetail
Port of Raymond
Hogeland
Turner
Loring
Whitewater
Opheim
Glentana
Richland
Four Buttes
Peerless
Scobey
Madoc
Whitetail
Redstone
Flaxville
Outlook
Raymond
Plentywood
Westby
Antelope
Coalridge
Reserve
Dagmar
Lohman
Chinook
Zurich
Havre
Harlem
Fort Belknap Agency
FORT BELKNAP INDIAN RESERVATION
Dodson
Malta
Wegner
Saco
Hinsdale
Vandalia
Tampico
St. Marie
Larslan
FORT PECK INDIAN RESERVATION
Lustre
Medicine Lake
Homestead
Froid
McCabe
Bainville
Culbertson
Brockton
Poplar
Lloyd
Rocky Boy
Cleveland
Glasgow
Nashua
Wolf Point
Frazer
Oswego
Fort Peck
Lodgepole
Hays
Zortman
Landusky
Vida
Fairview
Sidney
Lambert
Enid
Richey
Crane
Savage
Bloomfield
Circle
Brockway
Lindsay
Intake
Glendive
Winifred
Suffolk
Christina
Fergus
Roy
Brusett
Jordan
Hilger
Lewistown
Ross Fork
Moore
Forestgrove
Grass Range
Teigen
Cat Creek
Winnett
Mosby
Sand Springs
Cohagen
Hodges
Wibaux
Saint Phillip
Tyler
Flatwillow
Rock Springs
Angela
Terry
Fallon
Mildred
Carlyle
Garneill
Melstone
Sumatra
Ingomar
Kinsey
Ismay
Harlowton
Musselshell
Roundup
Klein
Miles City
Plevna
Baker
Shawmut
Ryegate
Cushman
Vananda
Sheffield
Cartersville
Thurlow
Horton
Willard
Lavina
Hysham
Sanders
Finch
Forsyth
Rosebud
Hathaway
Myers
Bighorn
Custer
Broadview
Pompeys Pillar
Shepherd
Worden
Huntley
Ballantine
Acton
Rapelje
Molt
Colstrip
Volborg
Ekalaka
Mill Iron
Timber
Greycliff
Reedpoint
Billings
Hardin
Laurel
Park City
Silesia
Crow Agency
NORTHERN CHEYENNE
Lame Deer
Ashland
Powderville
Olive
Epsie
Broadus
Capitol
Absarokee
Fishtail
Joliet
Rockvale
Edgar
Busby
RESERVATION
Sonnette
Dean
Boyd
Fromberg
Pryor
CROW INDIAN RESERVATION
Saint Xavier
Lodge Grass
Birney
Roscoe
Roberts
Bridger
Luther
Alpine
Red Lodge
Fort Smith
Otter
Boyes
Hammond
Bell Creek
Bearcreek
Washoe
Belfry
Warren
Wyola
Quietus
Biddle
Ridge
Alzada
Decker

# Montana Phone Exchanges

## Alphabetical

| Exchange | Prefix |
|---|---|
| Absarokee | 328 |
| Alberton | 722 |
| Alberton S. | 864 |
| Alta | 849 |
| Alzada | 828 |
| Alzada S. | 878 |
| Amsterdam | 282 |
| Anaconda | 563 |
| Arlee | 726 |
| Ashland | 784 |
| Augusta | 562 |
| Avon | 492 |
| Babb | 732 |
| Bainville | 769 |
| Baker | 778 |
| Baker | 978 |
| Belfrey | 664 |
| Belgrade | 388 |
| Belt | 277 |
| Big Fork | 837 |
| Big Sandy | 378 |
| Big Sky | 995 |
| Big Timber | 932 |
| Billings | 245 |
| Billings | 248 |
| Billings | 252 |
| Billings | 254 |
| Billings | 255 |
| Billings | 256 |
| Billings | 259 |
| Billings | 657 |
| Billings | 698 |
| Billings | 855 |
| Billings W. | 652 |
| Billings W. | 655 |
| Billings W. | 656 |
| Billings W. | 976 |
| Billings Shepherd | 373 |
| Birney | 984 |
| Bloomfield | 583 |
| Boulder | 225 |
| Box Elder | 352 |
| Bozeman | 581 |
| Bozeman | 585 |
| Bozeman | 586 |
| Bozeman | 587 |
| Bozeman | 994 |
| Bozeman Cellular | 580 |
| Brady | 753 |
| Bridger | 662 |
| Broadus | 436 |
| Broadus N. | 554 |
| Broadus S. | 427 |
| Broadview | 667 |
| Brockton | 786 |
| Browning | 338 |
| Busby | 592 |
| Butte | 490 |
| Butte | 496 |
| Butte | 723 |
| Butte | 782 |
| Butte-south | 494 |
| Canyon Creek | 368 |
| Canyon Ferry | 475 |
| Carlyle | 588 |
| Carter | 734 |
| Cascade | 468 |
| Charlo | 644 |
| Chester | 759 |
| Chester S. | 456 |
| Chinook | 357 |
| Choteau | 466 |
| Circle | 485 |
| Circle | 974 |
| Clancy | 933 |
| Clark | 645 |
| Clinton | 825 |
| Clyde Park | 686 |
| Colstrip | 748 |
| Columbia Falls | 892 |
| Columbus | 322 |
| Condon | 754 |
| Conrad | 278 |
| Conrad E. | 627 |
| Cooke City | 838 |
| Corvallis | 961 |
| Crow Agency | 638 |
| Culbertson | 787 |
| Custer | 856 |
| Cutbank | 873 |
| Cut Bank N. | 336 |
| Dagmar | 483 |
| Darby | 821 |
| Decker | 750 |
| Decker | 757 |
| Deer Lodge | 846 |
| Denton | 567 |
| Devon | |
| Dillon | 683 |
| Divide | 267 |
| Dixon | 246 |
| Dodson | 383 |
| Drummond | 288 |
| Dupuyer | 472 |
| Dutton | 476 |
| E. Carlyle | 688 |
| E. Glacier Park | 226 |
| Ekalaka | 775 |
| Ekalaka | 975 |
| Elmo | 849 |
| Ennis | 682 |
| Ethridge | 339 |
| Eureka | 296 |
| Eureka Rural | 889 |
| Fairfield | 467 |
| Fairview | 742 |
| Fairview | 747 |
| Fallon | 486 |
| Finley Point | 887 |
| Flaxville | 474 |
| Flaxville Rural | 779 |
| Forsyth | 356 |
| Fort Benton | 622 |
| Fort Peck | 526 |
| Fortshaw | 264 |
| Fort Smith | 666 |
| Fortine | 882 |
| Frazer | 695 |
| Frenchtown | 626 |
| Froid | 766 |
| Froid Rural E. | 963 |
| Fromberg | 668 |
| Gallatin Gateway | 763 |
| Gardiner | 848 |
| Geraldine | 737 |
| Geyser | 735 |
| Gildford | 376 |
| Glasgow | 228 |
| Glasgow | 263 |
| Glasgow N. | 367 |
| Glendive | 345 |
| Glendive | 359 |
| Glendive | 365 |
| Glendive | 377 |
| Glendive Cellular | 939 |
| Glentana | 724 |
| Grant | 681 |
| Grass Range | 428 |
| Great Falls | 452 |
| Great Falls | 453 |
| Great Falls | 454 |
| Great Falls | 455 |
| Great Falls | 727 |
| Great Falls | 731 |
| Great Falls | 761 |
| Great Falls | 771 |
| Great Falls | 788 |
| Great Falls | 791 |
| Great Falls | 799 |
| Great Falls | 833 |
| Great Falls | 966 |
| Hamilton | 363 |
| Hardin | 665 |
| Hardin | 679 |
| Harlem | 353 |
| Harlowton | 632 |
| Harrison | 685 |
| Haugan | 678 |
| Havre | 265 |
| Havre N. | 398 |
| Havre S. | 390 |
| Havre S. | 395 |
| Hays | 673 |
| Heart Butte | 338 |
| Helena | 439 |
| Helena | 439 |
| Helena | 441 |
| Helena | 442 |
| Helena | 443 |
| Helena | 444 |
| Helena | 447 |
| Helena | 449 |
| Helena E. | 227 |
| Helena E. | 458 |
| Highwood | 733 |
| Hingham | 397 |
| Hinsdale | 364 |
| Hinsdale N. | 648 |
| Hobson | 423 |
| Hopp Illiad | 386 |
| Hot Springs | 741 |
| Hungry Horse | 387 |
| Huntley | 348 |
| Hysham | 342 |
| Jackson | 834 |
| Joliet | 962 |
| Joplin | 292 |
| Jordan | 557 |
| Jordan | 977 |
| Judith Gap | 473 |
| Kalispell | 253 |
| Kalispell | 257 |
| Kalispell | 752 |
| Kalispell | 755 |
| Kalispell | 756 |
| Kalispell | 758 |
| Kevin-oilmont | 337 |
| Kremlin | 372 |
| Lakeside | 844 |
| Lambert | 774 |
| Lame Deer | 477 |
| Larslan | 725 |
| Laurel | 628 |
| Lavina | 636 |
| Lewistown | 538 |
| Lewistown Cellular | 366 |
| Libby | 293 |
| Lima | 276 |
| Lincoln | 362 |
| Lindsay | 584. |
| Livingston | 222 |
| Lodge Grass | 639 |
| Lolo | 273 |
| Loma | 739 |
| Malta | 654 |
| Malta S. | 658 |
| Mammoth, Wy | 344 |
| Manhattan | 284 |
| Marion | 854 |
| Martinsdale | 572 |
| Mcgregor Lake | 858 |
| Medicine Lake | 789 |
| Melrose | 835 |
| Melstone | 358 |
| Melville | 537 |
| Miles City | 232 |
| Miles City | 233 |
| Miles City | 234 |
| Miles City | 853 |
| Miles City | 874 |
| Miles City S. | 421 |
| Milltown | 258 |
| Missoula | 240 |
| Missoula | 243 |
| Missoula | 251 |
| Missoula | 329 |
| Missoula | 523 |
| Missoula | 542 |
| Missoula | 543 |
| Missoula | 544 |
| Missoula | 549 |
| Missoula | 721 |
| Missoula | 728 |
| Molt | 669 |
| Moore | 374 |
| Musselshell | 947 |
| Nashua | 746 |
| Nashua N. | 785 |
| Neihart | 236 |
| N. Ryegate | 575 |
| Noxon | 847 |
| Old Faithful, Wy | 545 |
| Olney | 881 |
| Opheim | 762 |
| Opportunity | 797 |
| Outlook | 895 |
| Ovando | 793 |
| Pablo | 675 |
| Park City | 633 |
| Peerless | 893 |
| Pendroy | 469 |
| Philipsburg | 859 |
| Plains | 826 |
| Plentywood | 765 |
| Plevna | 772 |
| Plevna | 971 |
| Polson | 883 |
| Pompeys Pillar | 875 |
| Poplar | 768 |
| Poplar N. | 448 |
| Potomac | 244 |
| Power | 463 |
| Pray | 333 |
| Rapelje | 663 |
| Raynesford | 738 |
| Redlodge | 425 |
| Redlodge | 446 |
| Reedpoint | 326 |
| Reserve | 286 |
| Richey | 773 |
| Richey | 979 |
| Roberts | 445 |
| Rock Springs | 354 |
| Ronan | 676 |
| Rosebud | 347 |
| Roundup | 323 |
| Roy | 464 |
| Rudyard | 355 |
| Ryegate | 568 |
| Saco | 527 |
| Saint Ignatius | 745 |
| Saint Mary | 732 |
| Saint Regis | 649 |
| Savage | 776 |
| Scobey | 487 |
| Scobey Rural | 783 |
| Seeley Lake | 677 |
| Shelby | 434 |
| Shepherd | 373 |
| Sheridan | 842 |
| Sidney | 422 |
| Sidney | 433 |
| Sidney | 482 |
| Sidney | 488 |
| Sidney E. | 481 |
| Simpson | 394 |
| Somers | 857 |
| S. Wolf Point | 525 |
| Stanford | 566 |
| Stevensville | 777 |
| Stockett | 736 |
| Sunburst | 937 |
| Superior | 822 |
| Swan Lake | 886 |
| Sweetgrass | 335 |
| Terry | 635 |
| Terry | 637 |
| Thompson- Falls | 827 |
| Three Forks | 285 |
| Townsend | 266 |
| Troy | 295 |
| Turner | 379 |
| Twin Bridges | 684 |
| Ulm | 866 |
| Valier | 279 |
| Valley Industrial Park | 524 |
| Vaughn | 965 |
| Victor | 642 |
| Virginia City | 843 |
| Warm Spring | 693 |
| W. Glacier | 888 |
| W. Glendive | 687 |
| W. Sidney | 798 |
| W. Yellowstone | 646 |
| W.by | 385 |
| W.by E. | 985 |
| White Sulphur Springs | 547 |
| Whitefish | 862 |
| Whitehall | 287 |
| Whitewater | 674 |
| Wibaux | 795 |
| Wibaux | 796 |
| Wilsall | 578 |
| Winifred | 462 |
| Winnett | 429 |
| Wisdom | 689 |
| Wise River | 832 |
| Wolf Creek | 235 |
| Wolf Point | 653 |
| Wolf Point N. | 392 |
| Worden | 967 |
| Wyola | 343 |
| Yellow Bay | 982 |

## Numerical

| Prefix | Exchange |
|---|---|
| 222 | Livingston |
| 225 | Boulder |
| 226 | East Glacier |
| 227 | Helena East |
| 228 | Glasgow |
| 232 | Miles City |
| 233 | Miles City |
| 234 | Miles City |
| 235 | Wolf Creek |
| 236 | Neihart |
| 240 | Missoula |
| 243 | Missoula |
| 244 | Potomac |
| 245 | Billings |
| 246 | Dixon |
| 248 | Billings |
| 251 | Missoula |
| 252 | Billings |
| 253 | Kalispell |
| 254 | Billings |
| 255 | Billings |
| 256 | Billings |
| 257 | Kalispell |
| 258 | Milltown |
| 259 | Billings |
| 263 | Glasgow |
| 264 | Fortshaw |
| 265 | Havre |
| 266 | Townsend |
| 267 | Divide |
| 273 | Lolo |
| 276 | Lima |
| 277 | Belt |
| 278 | Conrad |
| 279 | Valier |
| 282 | Amsterdam |
| 284 | Manhattan |
| 285 | Three Forks |
| 286 | Reserve |
| 287 | Whitehall |
| 288 | Drummond |
| 292 | Joplin |
| 293 | Libby |
| 295 | Troy |
| 296 | Eureka |
| 322 | Columbus |
| 323 | Roundup |
| 326 | Reedpoint |
| 328 | Absarokee |
| 329 | Missoula |
| 333 | Pray |
| 335 | Sweetgrass |
| 336 | Cut Bank North |
| 337 | Kevin-oilmont |
| 338 | Browning |
| 338 | Heart Butte |
| 339 | Ethridge |
| 342 | Hysham |
| 343 | Wyola |
| 344 | Mammoth,Wy |
| 345 | Glendive |
| 347 | Rosebud |
| 348 | Huntley |
| 349 | Alta |
| 352 | Box Elder |
| 353 | Harlem |
| 354 | Rock Springs |
| 355 | Rudyard |
| 356 | Forsyth |
| 357 | Chinook |
| 358 | Melstone |
| 359 | Glendive |
| 362 | Lincoln |
| 363 | Hamilton |
| 364 | Hinsdale |
| 365 | Glendive |
| 366 | Lewistown Cellular |
| 367 | Glasgow North |
| 368 | Canyon Creek |
| 372 | Kremlin |
| 373 | Billings-shepherd |
| 373 | Shepherd |
| 374 | Moore |
| 376 | Gildford |
| 377 | Glendive |
| 378 | Big Sandy |
| 379 | Turner |
| 383 | Dodson |
| 385 | Westby |
| 386 | Hopp Illiad |
| 387 | Hungry Horse |
| 388 | Belgrade |
| 390 | Havre South |
| 392 | Wolf Point North |
| 394 | Simpson |
| 395 | Havre South |
| 397 | Hingham |
| 398 | Havre South |
| 421 | Miles City South |
| 422 | Sidney |
| 423 | Hobson |
| 425 | Red Lodge |
| 427 | Broadus South |
| 428 | Grass Range |
| 429 | Winnett |
| 431 | Helena |
| 432 | Devon |
| 433 | Sidney |
| 434 | Shelby |
| 436 | Broadus |
| 439 | Helena |
| 441 | Helena |
| 442 | Helena |
| 443 | Helena |
| 444 | Helena |
| 445 | Roberts |
| 446 | Redlodge |
| 447 | Helena |
| 448 | Poplar North |
| 449 | Helena |
| 452 | Great Falls |
| 453 | Great Falls |
| 454 | Great Falls |
| 455 | Great Falls |
| 456 | Chester South |
| 458 | Helena East |
| 462 | Winifred |
| 463 | Power |
| 464 | Roy |
| 466 | Choteau |
| 467 | Fairfield |
| 468 | Cascade |
| 469 | Pendroy |
| 472 | Dupuyer |
| 473 | Judith Gap |
| 474 | Flaxville |
| 475 | Canyon Ferry |
| 476 | Dutton |
| 477 | Lame Deer |
| 481 | E Sidney, Nd |
| 481 | Sidney East |
| 482 | Sidney |
| 483 | Dagmar |
| 485 | Circle |
| 486 | Fallon |
| 487 | Scobey |
| 488 | Sidney |
| 490 | Butte |
| 492 | Avon |
| 494 | Butte-south |
| 496 | Butte |
| 523 | Missoula |
| 524 | Valley Industrial Park |
| 525 | South Wolf Park |
| 526 | Fortpeck |
| 527 | Saco |
| 537 | Melville |
| 538 | Lewistown |
| 542 | Missoula |
| 543 | Missoula |
| 544 | Missoula |
| 545 | Old Fthfl, Wy |
| 547 | White Sulfur Springs |
| 549 | Missoula |
| 554 | Broadus North |
| 557 | Jordan |
| 562 | Augusta |
| 563 | Anaconda |
| 566 | Stanford |
| 567 | Denton |
| 568 | Ryegate |
| 572 | Martinsdale |
| 574 | Silvertip, Wy |
| 575 | North Ryegate |
| 578 | Wilsall |
| 580 | Bozeman Cellular |
| 581 | Bozeman |
| 583 | Bloomfield |
| 584 | Lindsay |
| 585 | Bozeman |
| 586 | Bozeman |
| 587 | Bozeman |
| 588 | Carlyle |
| 592 | Busby |
| 622 | Fortbenton |
| 626 | Frenchtown |
| 627 | Conrad East |
| 628 | Laurel |
| 632 | Harlowton |
| 633 | Park City |
| 635 | Terry |
| 636 | Lavina |
| 637 | Terry |
| 638 | Crow Agency |
| 639 | Lodge Grass |
| 642 | Victor |
| 644 | Charlo |
| 645 | Clark |
| 646 | West Yellowstone |
| 648 | Hinsdale North |
| 649 | Saint Regis |
| 652 | Billings West |
| 653 | Wolf Point |
| 654 | Malta |
| 655 | Billings West |
| 656 | Billings West |
| 657 | Billings |
| 658 | Malta South |
| 659 | N Parkma, Wy |
| 662 | Bridger |
| 663 | Rapelje |
| 664 | Belfry |
| 665 | Hardin |
| 666 | Fort Smith |
| 667 | Broadview |
| 668 | Fromberg |
| 669 | Molt |
| 673 | Hays |
| 674 | Whitewater |
| 675 | Pablo |
| 676 | Ronan |
| 677 | Seeley Lake |
| 678 | Haugan |
| 679 | Hardin |
| 681 | Grant |
| 682 | Ennis |
| 683 | Dillon |
| 684 | Twin Bridges |
| 685 | Harrison |
| 686 | Clyde Park |
| 687 | West Glendive |
| 688 | East Carlyle |
| 689 | Wisdom |
| 693 | Warm Springs |
| 695 | Frazer |
| 698 | Billings |
| 721 | Missoula |
| 722 | Alberton |
| 723 | Butte |
| 724 | Glentana |
| 725 | Larslan |
| 726 | Arlee |
| 727 | Great Falls |
| 728 | Missoula |
| 731 | Great Falls |
| 732 | Babb |
| 732 | Saint Mary |
| 733 | Highwood |
| 734 | Carter |
| 735 | Geyser |
| 736 | Stockett |
| 737 | Geraldine |
| 738 | Raynesford |
| 739 | Loma |
| 741 | Hot Springs |
| 742 | Fairview |
| 745 | Saint Ignatius |
| 746 | Nashua |
| 747 | Fairview |
| 748 | Colstrip |
| 750 | Decker |
| 752 | Kalispell |
| 753 | Brady |
| 754 | Condon |
| 755 | Kalispell |
| 756 | Kalispell |
| 757 | Decker |
| 758 | Kalispell |
| 759 | Chester |
| 761 | Great Falls |
| 762 | Opheim |
| 763 | Gallatin Gateway |
| 765 | Plentywood |
| 766 | Froid |
| 768 | Poplar |
| 769 | Bainville |
| 771 | Great Falls |
| 772 | Plevna |
| 773 | Richey |
| 774 | Lambert |
| 775 | Ekalaka |
| 776 | Savage |
| 777 | Stevensville |
| 778 | Baker |
| 779 | Flaxville Rural |
| 782 | Butte |
| 783 | Scobey Rural |
| 784 | Ashland |
| 785 | Nashua North |
| 786 | Brockton |
| 787 | Culbertson |
| 788 | Great Falls |
| 789 | Medicine Lake |
| 791 | Great Falls |
| 793 | Ovando |
| 795 | Wibaux |
| 796 | Wibaux |
| 797 | Opportunity |
| 798 | West Sidney |
| 799 | Great Falls |
| 821 | Darby |
| 822 | Superior |
| 825 | Clinton |
| 826 | Plains |
| 827 | Thompson Falls |
| 828 | Alzada |
| 832 | Wise River |
| 833 | Great Falls |
| 834 | Jackson |
| 835 | Melrose |
| 837 | Big Fork |
| 838 | Cooke City |
| 842 | Sheridan |
| 843 | Virginia City |
| 844 | Lakeside |
| 844 | E. Fairview |
| 846 | Deer Lodge |
| 847 | Noxon |
| 848 | Gardiner |
| 849 | Elmo |
| 853 | Miles City |
| 854 | Marion |
| 855 | Billings |
| 856 | Custer |
| 857 | Somers |
| 858 | Mcgregor Lake |
| 859 | Philipsburg |
| 862 | Whitefish |
| 864 | Alberton South |
| 866 | Ulm |
| 873 | Cut Bank |
| 874 | Miles City |
| 875 | Pompeys Pillar |
| 878 | Alzada South |
| 881 | Olney |
| 882 | Fortine |
| 883 | Polson |
| 886 | Swan Lake |
| 887 | Finley Point |
| 888 | West Glacier |
| 889 | Eureka Rural |
| 892 | Columbia Falls |
| 893 | Peerless |
| 895 | Outlook |
| 932 | Big Timber |
| 933 | Clancy |
| 937 | Sunburst |
| 939 | Glendive Cellular |
| 947 | Musselshell |
| 961 | Corvallis |
| 962 | Joliet |
| 963 | Froid Rural East |
| 965 | Vaughn |
| 966 | Great Falls |
| 967 | Worden |
| 971 | Plevna |
| 974 | Circle |
| 975 | Ekalaka |
| 976 | Billings West |
| 977 | Jordan |
| 978 | Baker |
| 979 | Richey |
| 982 | Yellow Bay |
| 984 | Birney |

# Section 1

## Southeastern Area
## Including Miles City and Glendive

Rodeo reigns in here. Photo provided by Miles City Chamber of Commerce

Photo: John Riggs

## Weather

The climate here is one of extremes. The summer can bring blistering dry days reaching 100° or more. The winter can create an arctic environment with subzero and windy, blustery days. The area has the record high temperature for Montana (117° in Glendive) and one of the lowest temperatures on record (-65° at Fort Keogh). The summer days are usually sunny with frequent but short thundershowers. Evenings are usually cool enough for a sweater or light jacket.

Traveling in the winter can be down right scary with blowing snow and icy roads. If you're traveling across this area in the winter, be sure and bring blankets, food and water. If you should break down, it may be hours before a passing motorist finds you. A tow truck may be more than 50 miles away if your car should break down. Before traveling across this area in the winter, a call to the Montana Road Conditions number at 800-332-6171.

The best time to travel here is in the late spring and early fall. You'll find warm comfortable days, and cool evenings.

## Averages

**Miles City**

| | |
|---|---|
| January | |
| Average High: | 26.7° F |
| Average Low: | 6.2° F |
| Average Precip.: | 0.51 in |
| April | |
| Average High: | 58.0° F |
| Average Low: | 33.8° F |
| Average Precip.: | 1.26 in |
| July | |
| Average High: | 88.6° F |
| Average Low: | 60.7° F |
| Average Precip.: | 1.56 in |
| October | |
| Average High: | 61.1° F |
| Average Low: | 35.6° F |
| Average Precip.: | 0.96 in |

**Baker**

| | |
|---|---|
| January | |
| Average High: | 27.6° F |
| Average Low: | 2.2° F |
| Average Precip.: | 0.53 in |
| April | |
| Average High: | 57.1° F |
| Average Low: | 29.7° F |
| Average Precip.: | 1.41 in |
| July | |
| Average High: | 87.4° F |
| Average Low: | 55.5° F |
| Average Precip.: | 1.87 in |
| October | |
| Average High: | 61.4° F |
| Average Low: | 31.1° F |
| Average Precip.: | 1.00 in |

**Glendive**

| | |
|---|---|
| January | |
| Average High: | 26.2° F |
| Average Low: | 3.5° F |
| Average Precip.: | 0.40 in |
| April | |
| Average High: | 60.0° F |
| Average Low: | 32.8° F |
| Average Precip.: | 1.21 in |
| July | |
| Average High: | 89.1° F |
| Average Low: | 59.1° F |
| Average Precip.: | 1.79 in |
| October | |
| Average High: | 62.8° F |
| Average Low: | 34.3° F |
| Average Precip.: | 0.80 in |

**1.** *Historic Marker, Gas, Attraction, Food, Lodging, Shopping*

### Wibaux

At the eastern edge of the state, Wibaux is known as the "Gateway to Montana." The tiny farming and ranching community has a rich history dating back to the 1880s when a Frenchman named Pierre Wibaux moved to the area and began cattle ranching.

Wibaux's family was in the textile business, but the young Pierre didn't want to join the family business, so at age 27 he moved to America and made his way to eastern Montana. Wibaux knew nothing about cattle ranching when he established the W-Bar Ranch along Beaver Creek 12 miles north of town. He eventually became one of the largest cattleman in the state, with a herd that reportedly numbered over 70,000 that grazed in both Montana and North Dakota. Just over the border, Wibaux's friend Teddy Roosevelt was ranching in the badlands of North Dakota.

During the hard winter of 1890, Wibaux bought up cattle at bargain prices when many of his fellow stockmen had to sell out. A shrewd businessman, Wibaux is still remembered for his humor, good nature and fairness.

The town was originally called Mingusville and was one of the largest cattle shipping points on the Northern Pacific Railroad. Both the town and the county were named after Wibaux and some reports say that Wibaux himself carried petitions to get the name changed. The post office was established there in 1895.

A brochure outlining the walking tour through Wibaux is available at the museum. On the tour you'll pass by the historic St. Peter's Catholic Church, built in 1985 with funds donated by Wibaux. The original frame structure has been covered with beautiful, native lava rock.

Wibaux also has a new state visitor's center located along Interstate 94 at Exit 242. The information center and rest area was built in 1998 to greet travelers entering Montana from the east.

Outside of town, the land is a mix of badlands and gentle rolling hills. The area is great for hunting, hiking and photography, and Beaver Creek is known to produce some lunker walleye, northern pike and catfish.

### H Pierre Wibaux

*In 1876, this was strictly buffalo and Indian country. There wasn't a ranch between Bismarck, North Dakota, and Bozeman, Montana. But the U.S. Cavalry rounded up the hostile Indians from 1876 to 1881 and forced them onto reservations while the buffalo hunters were busy clearing the range for the cattle boom of the Eighties.*

*Pierre Wibaux ran one of the biggest cattle spreads around here in the early days. His will provided a fund to erect a statue of himself "overlooking the land I love so well." It stands a mile west of the town of Wibaux.*

*From this end of Montana to the west end is just about the same distance as from New York to Chicago. You have to push a lot of ground behind you to get places in this state.*

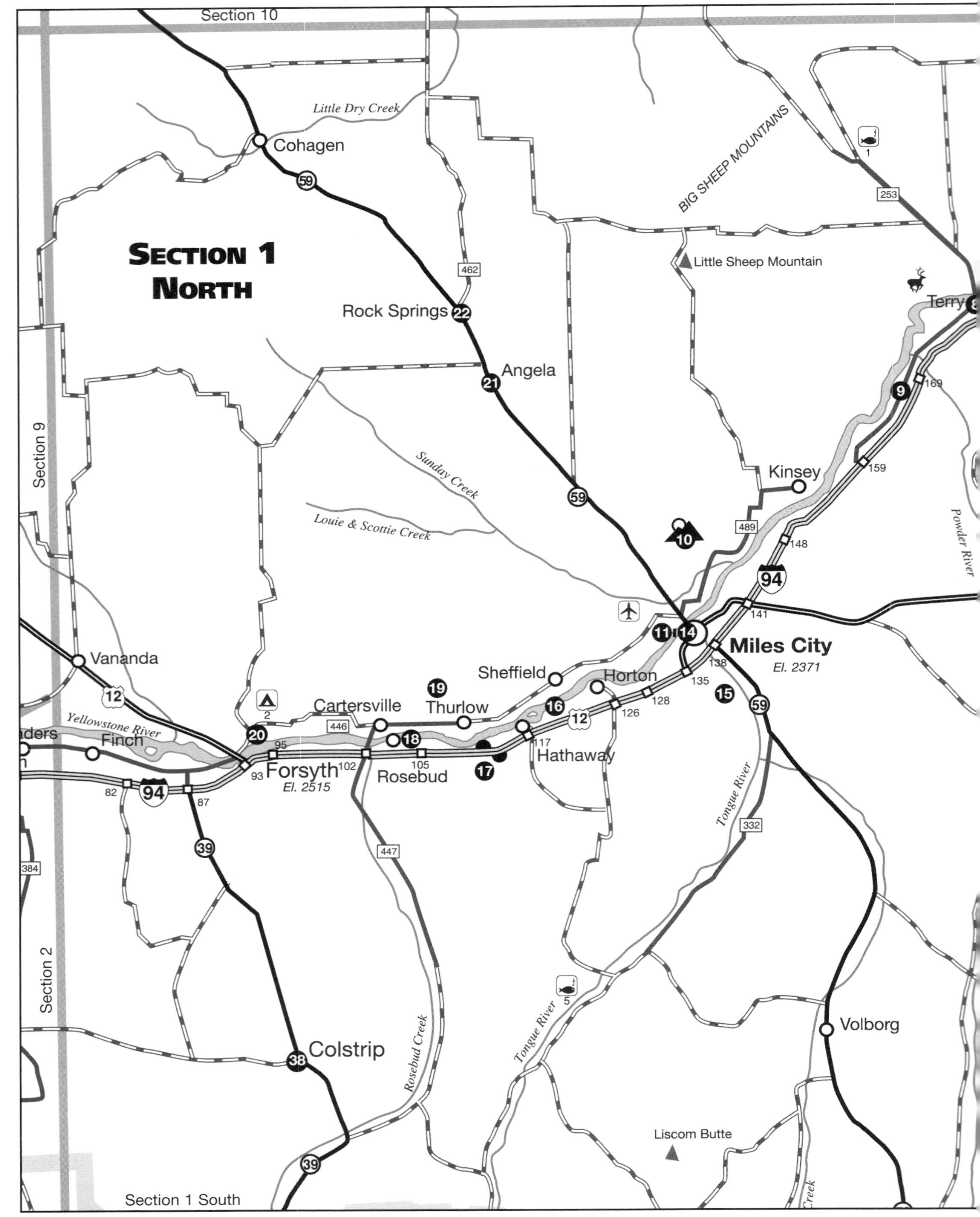
Section 10
Section 1 North
Little Dry Creek
Cohagen
BIG SHEEP MOUNTAINS
Little Sheep Mountain
Rock Springs
Angela
Terry
Section 9
Sunday Creek
Louie & Scottie Creek
Kinsey
Powder River
Miles City
El. 2371
Vananda
Sheffield
Horton
Cartersville
Thurlow
Yellowstone River
Finch
Forsyth
El. 2515
Rosebud
Hathaway
Tongue River
Section 2
Rosebud Creek
Colstrip
Volborg
Liscom Butte
Section 1 South

# Section 1 Northeast

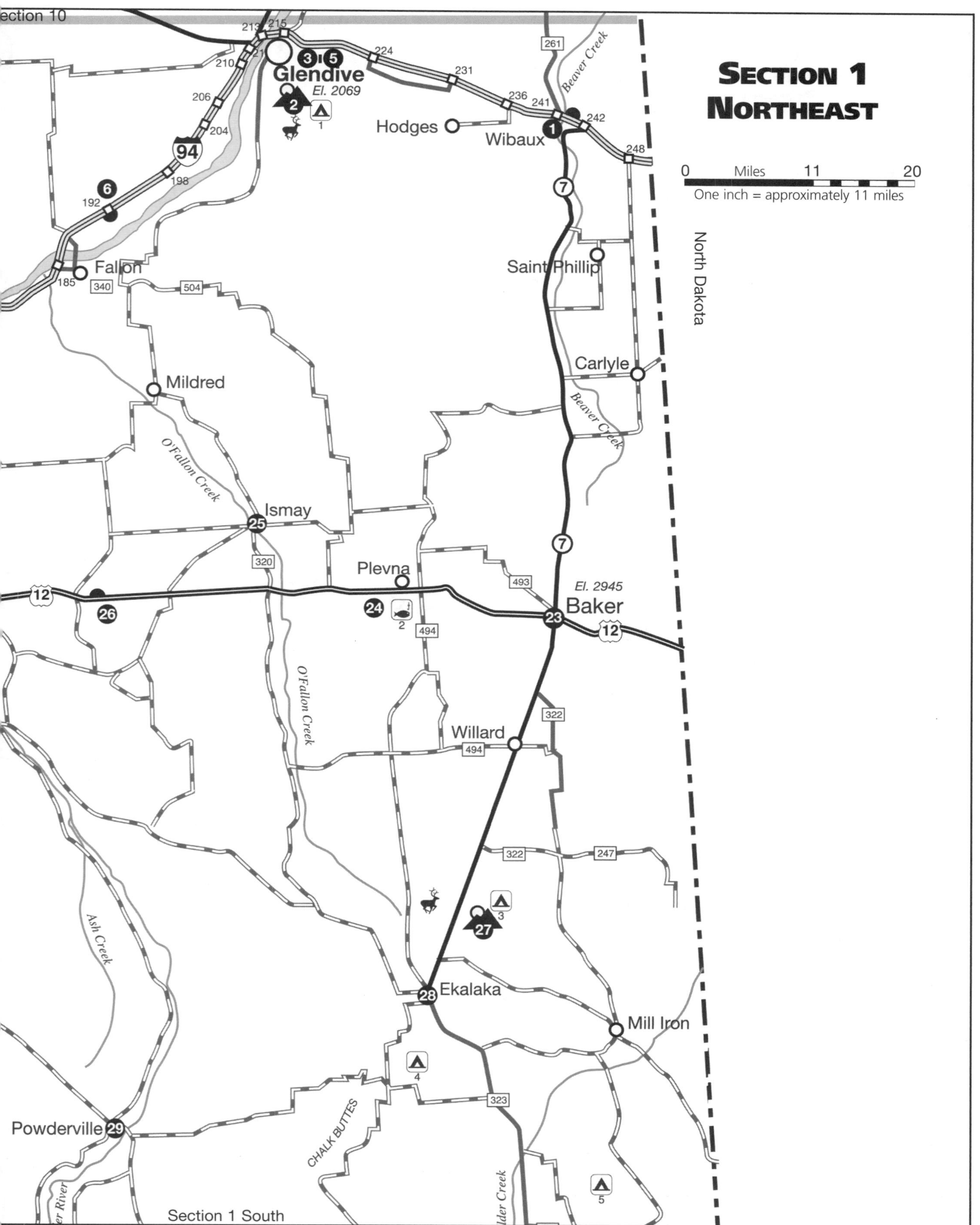

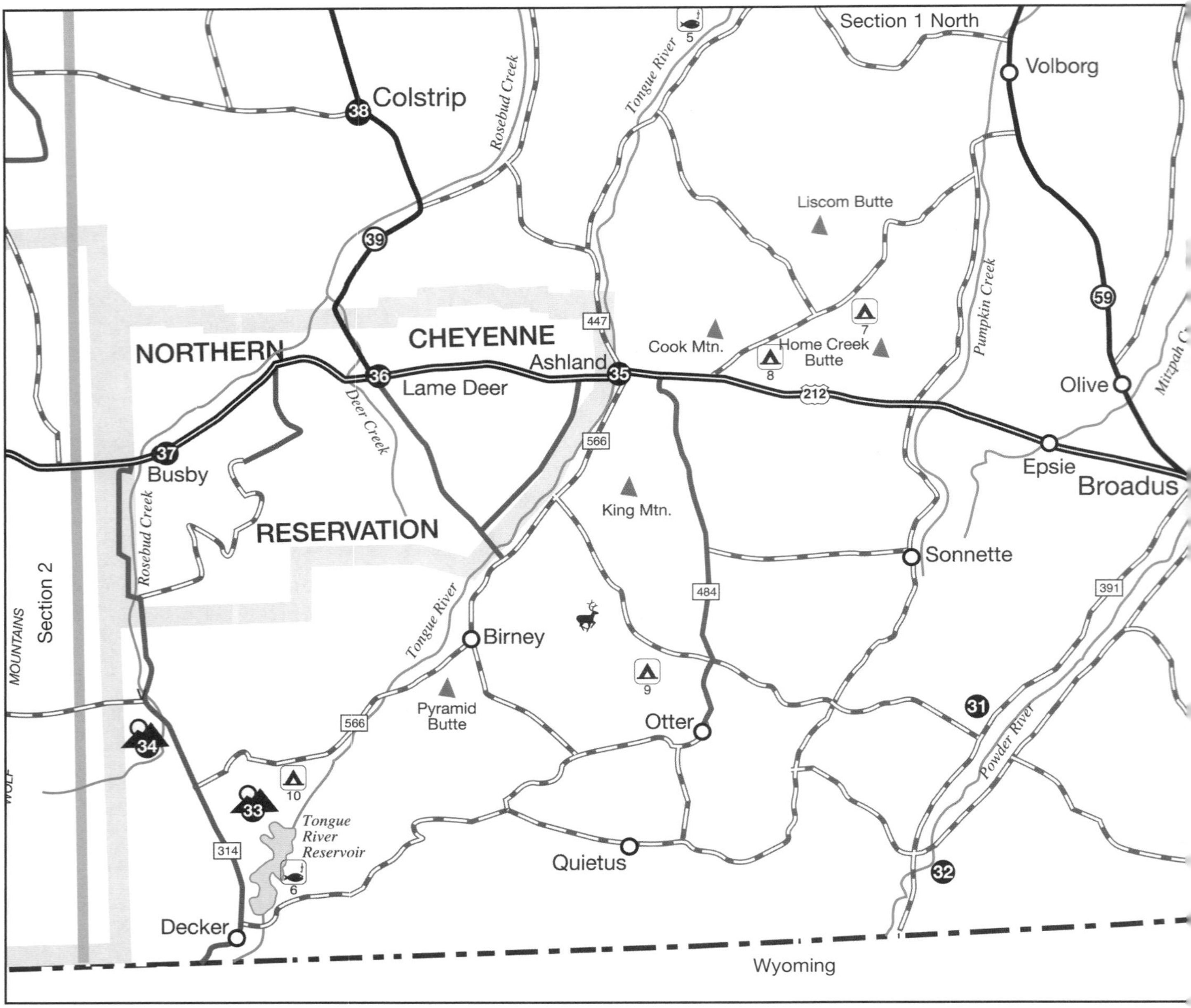

Section 1 North
Volborg
Colstrip
38
Rosebud Creek
Tongue River
5
Liscom Butte
39
59
447
7
NORTHERN
CHEYENNE
Cook Mtn.
Home Creek Butte
Pumpkin Creek
Ashland
8
36
35
Lame Deer
212
Olive
Mizpah C
Deer Creek
37
566
Epsie
Busby
Broadus
King Mtn.
Rosebud Creek
RESERVATION
Sonnette
Section 2
MOUNTAINS
484
391
Tongue River
Birney
9
Pyramid Butte
566
31
Otter
34
10
33
Powder River
Tongue River Reservoir
314
6
Quietus
32
Decker
Wyoming

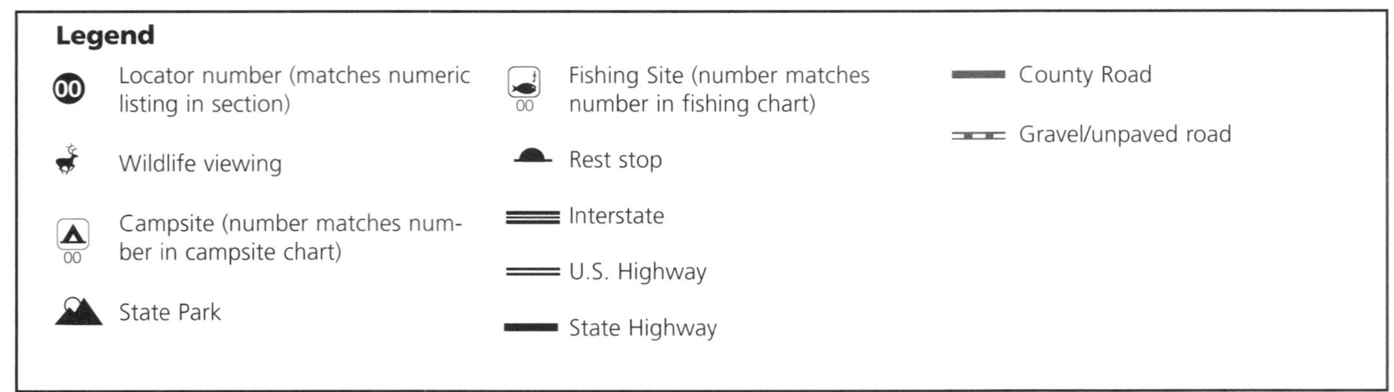

# Section 1 South

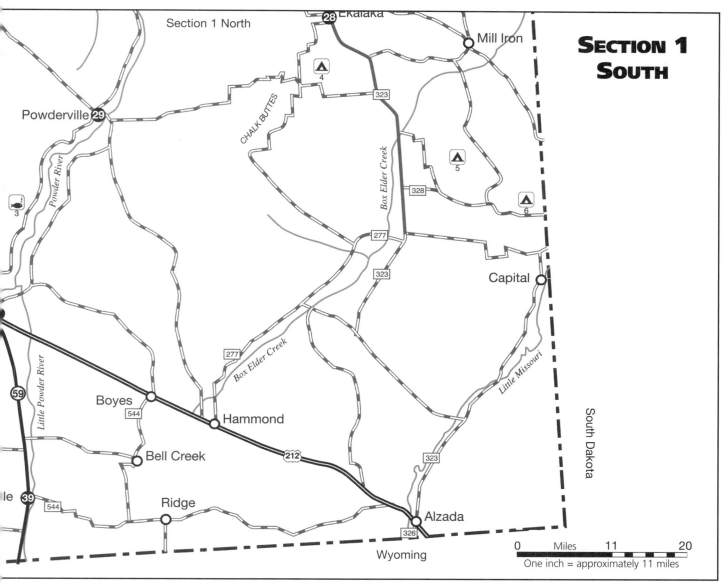

Section 1 North
Ekalaka
Mill Iron
Powderville
Chalk Buttes
Powder River
Box Elder Creek
Capital
Boyes
Hammond
Bell Creek
Ridge
Alzada
Little Powder River
Little Missouri
South Dakota
Wyoming
0 Miles 11 20
One inch = approximately 11 miles

## H St. Peter's Catholic Church

Glendive

*Dismayed that his son's adoptive home had no Catholic church, Frenchman Achille Wibaux instructed Pierre to build one here. The rancher contributed $2,000 for the construction of this wood-frame, vernacular Gothic Revival structure. It was built in 1895 by R. R. Cummings and Eugene Blias of Glendive. The Wibaux congregation being at that time a mission of Miles City, Father Van der Broeck of Miles City superintended the church's construction. In 1938, the church was enlarged and its exterior walls covered with scoria, a lava rock common to the badlands of the area. Father Leahy, pastor of the church beginning in 1931, conceived the idea of a scoria facing, and volunteers from the congregation went rock-picking in wagons and pick-up trucks. Father Leahy recorded that "patient men did a beautiful job of laying the rock up to and on the steeple." The building served as Wibaux's Catholic church until 1965, when a new church was built and this building was converted to a catechism school.*

## T Wibaux County Museum Complex

E. Oregon Ave., Wibaux. 795-2381 or 796-9969

The Town of Wibaux and the County of Wibaux are both named for Pierre Wibaux, a Frenchman who gave up opportunities in his family's textile business to seek his fortune in the cattle industry of the American northwest.

Arriving in the area in 1883, a young man of 27, Pierre established his ranch headquarters, the W-Bar, 12 miles north of town on Beaver Creek. He ran cattle on the open range in an area covering nearly 70,000 acres. Among his western friends were Teddy Roosevelt, who was then ranching about 30 miles east of Wibaux in the Dakota badlands, and the Marquis de Mores, a fellow Frenchman who had undertaken a grandiose meat packing and meat marketing enterprise in Dakota.

Many ranchers were devastated by the hard, cattle-killing winter of 1886-87, but Wibaux remained optimistic about the future of cattle raising on the plains. He sought additional financing and bought up the surviving livestock, knowing they would be a hardy base for his expanded herds. By 1889, he had accumulated more than 40,000 head of livestock and employed 25 to 30 cowboys.

The town which had been known as Mingusville, one of the largest cattle shipping points on Northern Pacific Railroad, was renamed Wibaux in 1895. Some reports say Pierre himself carried petitions for the name change.

As the 19th century and the days of open grazing came to a close, Pierre Wibaux was diversifying into banking and mining. He died in 1913 at the age of 55.

### On the National Register of Historic Places

While his ranch home burned in the 1920s, one building which belonged to Pierre Wibaux still exists. The Pierre Wibaux Museum, listed on

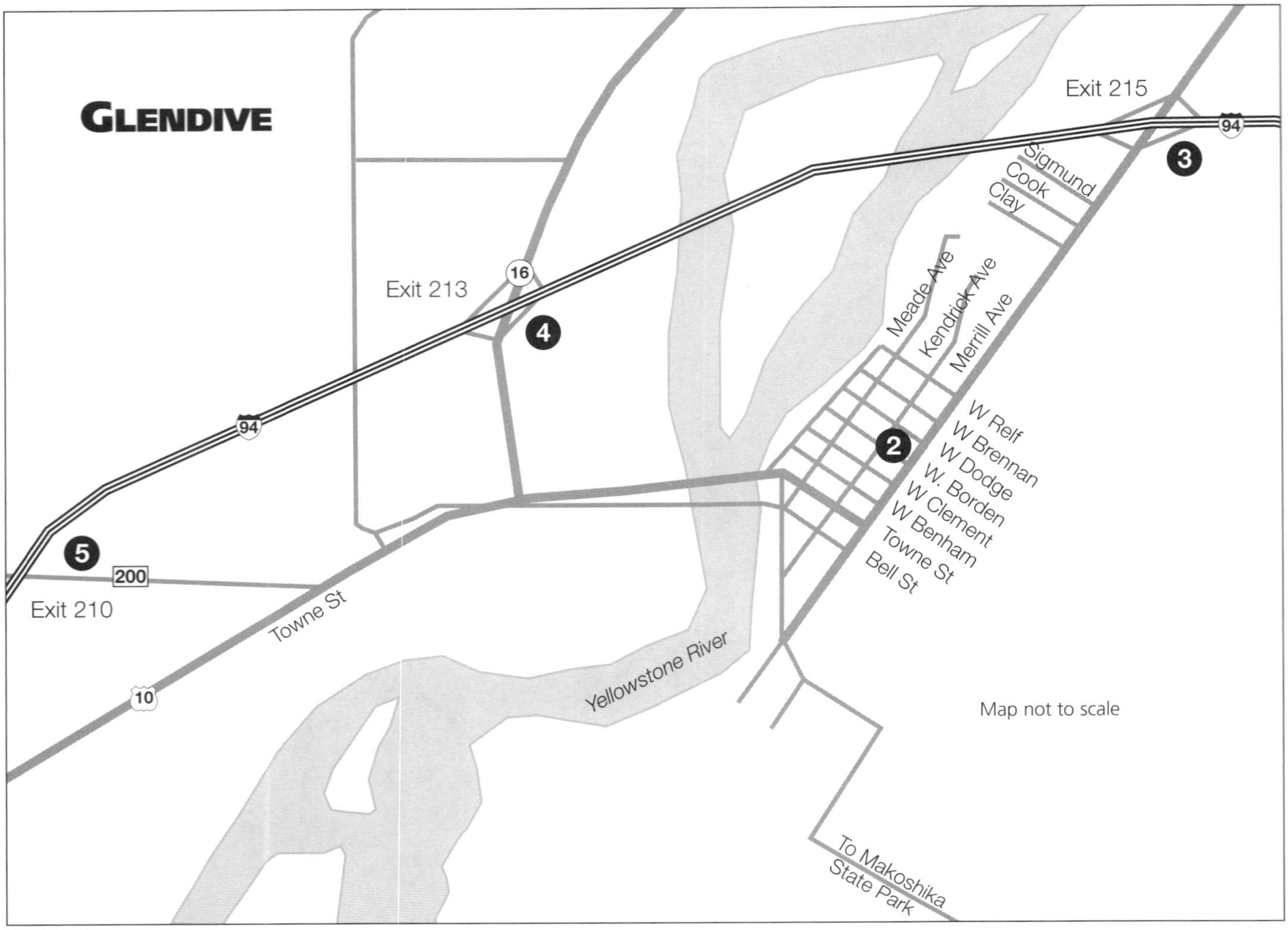

## Glendive

Exit 215
Sigmund
Cook
Clay
Exit 213
Meade Ave
Kendrick Ave
Merrill Ave
W Relf
W Brennan
W Dodge
W. Borden
W Clement
W Benham
Towne St
Bell St
Exit 210
Towne St
Yellowstone River
To Makoshika State Park
Map not to scale



the National Register of Historic Places, was built in 1892 by Pierre Wibaux and Henry Boice of the Berry-Boice Cattle Company as a town office building. Within a year of its construction, Wibaux had bought out Boice's interest in the building and hired a French gardener to landscape the grounds. The complex became known as "The Park," a well known landmark to railroad travelers. It originally faced north, toward the railroad tracks.

The office building was restored in 1972 and is now the heart of the Wibaux community's museum complex. It displays items which once belonged to Pierre Wibaux, such as his desk and dishes, as well as other items relating to area ranching history.

Other exhibits include:

### Barber Shop

The 1900s barbershop and bath house building on the museum grounds was originally built in 1889 as an assay office. Almost a hundred years later, it was moved to the museum grounds and restored with the aid of a Cultural and Aesthetic Projects Grant from the State of Montana. In addition to early-day barbershop furnishings and a beautiful barbershop back bar, the building houses local history items, including the first indoor bathroom in Wibaux County, completely reassembled.

### Livery Stable

A third component of the museum complex is a livery stable decorated on the outside with area brands. Inside are forges, horse shoes, branding irons and other furnishings of a livery stable,

early-day machinery such as a 1925 Rumley Oil Pull tractor and the first fire wagon used by county firefighters, and O.M. Helvik's shoe repair shop equipment.

### Centennial Car

Additional museum items, such as a heavy chain used to fight prairie fires from horseback, school memorabilia, arrowheads, wildlife mounts and even a petrified oyster found along Beaver Creek, can be seen in a railroad car which was once part of the Montana Territorial Centennial Train which was on display at the World's Fair in New York City in 1964. The car also serves as an information center for visitors seeking Montana maps and travel brochures.

### Pierre Wibaux Statue

Mr. Wibaux requested in his will to be buried beneath a twice life-size statue depicting himself as a cowboy, overlooking the "land he loved so well." This statue is located on west Oregon Avenue.

*Pierre Wibaux home.*

### Old St. Peter's Catholic Church

Also on west Oregon Avenue is the old St. Peter's Catholic Church. A stained glass window at the back of the church notes that the church was constructed in 1895 through the generosity of

Pierre Wibaux in honor of St. Peter. Originally a frame structure, the church was later covered with beautiful, native lava rock.

Tours daily from Memorial Day–Labor Day. Admission is free. *Reprinted from Pierre Wibaux Museum brochure.*

**2.** *Lewis & Clark, Food, Lodging, Shopping,*

## Glendive

Glendive, the county seat for Dawson County, has a population of just over 4,800 and is the state's 15th largest city. The town was thought to have been named by Sir George Gore, a wealthy Irish sportsman who hunted extensively in the area in the 1850s and reportedly named the area Glendale. The name "Glendive" is thought to have evolved from that.

Like many towns in Montana, Glendive took hold when the Northern Pacific pushed through in the late 1880s. It was home to a locomotive repair shop and serves as an important commercial hub for ranchers and farmers in the area who produce cattle, sugar beets, grain and forage crops.

Glendive is known as "Paddlefish and Caviar Capital of the World." Located on the Yellowstone River near the North Dakota Border, it is here that the ancient Paddlefish comes to spawn each year, swimming against the mighty current to deposit eggs on flooded gravel bars in the Yellowstone. (see sidebar)

Glendive has also set up a self-guided walking tour through the historic downtown area. Guide brochures are located at the Glendive Chamber office at 200 N. Merrill in the downtown area. The walking tour also includes the historic Bell Street Bridge, which spans the Yellowstone River.

### D William Clark

August 1, 1806

*"we had Showers of rain repetedly all day at the intermition of only a fiew minits between them. My Situation a very disagreeable one. in an open Canoe wet and without a possibility of keeping my Self dry."*

### T Makoshika State Park

2 miles southeast of Glendive, 377-6256.

## The Badlands Of Eastern Montana

Rising from the Yellowstone valley and surrounding prairies is a broad region of seeming disarray—bad lands. Hogback ridges, fluted hillsides, pinnacles, and caprocks ornament a network of buttes. The mineral-banded, soft, sedimentary rocks with their decor of contrasting pines and junipers create a panorama of unique shapes and colors that has a chameleon character, changing with the ever-varying pattern of light and shadow from the passing sun, clouds, moon, and seasons.

When this intriguing, rugged, yet delicate land was set aside as a state park in 1953 it was called Makoshika (Mako'-she-ka). The name is a variant spelling of a Lakota phrase meaning land of bad spirits, "badlands."

## A Look At the Past...

These badlands expose older rock layers than those in the badlands of the Dakotas. Here, the Yellowstone River and its tributaries cut into a fascinating transition in time: the passing from the Age of Reptiles, so dramatically represented by the dinosaurs, to the Age of Mammals.

Most of these strata are the brownish-gray sediments of the Hell Creek Formation dating back 65 million years ago when the Rocky Mountains were rising in the west. At that time, this area was rivers and flood plains similar to the present southeastern United States with sub-tropical climate and vegetation. It was the Cretaceous Period, the "Age of Reptiles." Rivers draining the western mountains deposited layer upon layer of sediments which over millions of years compacted to form the sandstones, mudstones, clays, and shales that form the badlands landscape.

*Makoshika State Park.*

Above the Hell Creek Formation and visible in the upper 100 feet or so of the highest areas of the park are the yellowish sediments of the Fort Union Formation. These Paleocene age strata mark the beginning of the "Age of Mammals" that began about 64 million years before the present.

One of the criteria geologists use to determine the age of rock formations is fossil evidence (remains of prehistoric life). Here, in the Hell Creek Formation, over 10 species of dinosaurs are found. The most well known are Triceratops, Edmontosaurus and Tyrannosaurus rex. Parts of fish (sturgeon and gar) turtles, lizards, crocodiles, birds, and early mammals are found in these Cretaceous-Age strata. In the Paleocene-Fort Union Formation no dinosaur remains are found. These Paleocene sediments were deposited after the dinosaurs and many other reptilians became extinct. Mammal remains are present but in scant numbers. Plant fossils like ginko and sequoia are more common.

It is only within the past several million years that erosion dissected these ancient sediments offering us the opportunity to look into the past to that time of evolutionary transition. But imagination is required to envision those primeval, tropical environments and creatures, for the setting is quite different now.

## The Present. . .

Erosion has carved an island of contemporary upland prairie, studded by pines and divided into finger-like mesas by the mostly barren, steep-walled, gullied slopes. Instead of Triceratops and Tyrannosaurus Rex we might see mule deer, cottontails and turkey vultures.

As much as water is a factor in eroding the shapes of this land so it is a critical factor in determining what kind and how much life this land can support. Average annual precipitation is from 12" to 13". But the badlands topography has inherent extremes. South-facing slopes are sun-baked, with little vegetation. Nevertheless, some birds have found advantages in this setting: prairie falcons, golden eagles, and turkey vultures select nesting sites on sandstone ledges or in cavities. In contrast, the north facing slopes, retaining more moisture, maintain dense groves of Rocky Mountain juniper and ponderosa pine.

During warm months, over 150 species of wildflowers mix with grasses and shrubs. Sagebrush lizards and bull snakes are less visible residents. Down in the draws, snowberry, wild plum, and chokecherry find more moisture and in turn provide needed cover for animals and nesting birds. Early morning or evening hours provide the best photographic opportunities of badlands scenes and inhabitants.

## And with the Visitor Center...

You can take a self-guided tour that chronicles 74 million years of Eastern Montana history through the educational, interpretive and interactive displays. The tour is highlighted with fossils and artifacts like invertebrates of early sea life, a triceratops skull, and stone tools used by early man.

Makoshika State Park is open for day use, recreation and camping 365 days each year. The Visitor Center is open from 10:00 a.m. to 6:00 p.m. every day from Memorial Day through Labor Day and 9:00 a.m. to 5:00 p.m., Monday through Saturday and 1:00 p.m. to 5:00 p.m., Sundays, Labor Day to Memorial Day.

## New Perspectives

Makoshika is an island in time-a vantage point from which to look back millions of years, to imagine a vastly different environment right here, to ponder the extinction of the dinosaurs, to contemplate the development of mammals, the change of climates, the creation of these badlands, and man's place in all of this.

Part of man's history here was the establishment of this area as a state park. Makoshika is a preserve of 8,832 acres—a place for recreation, education, escape from the everyday, and reflec-

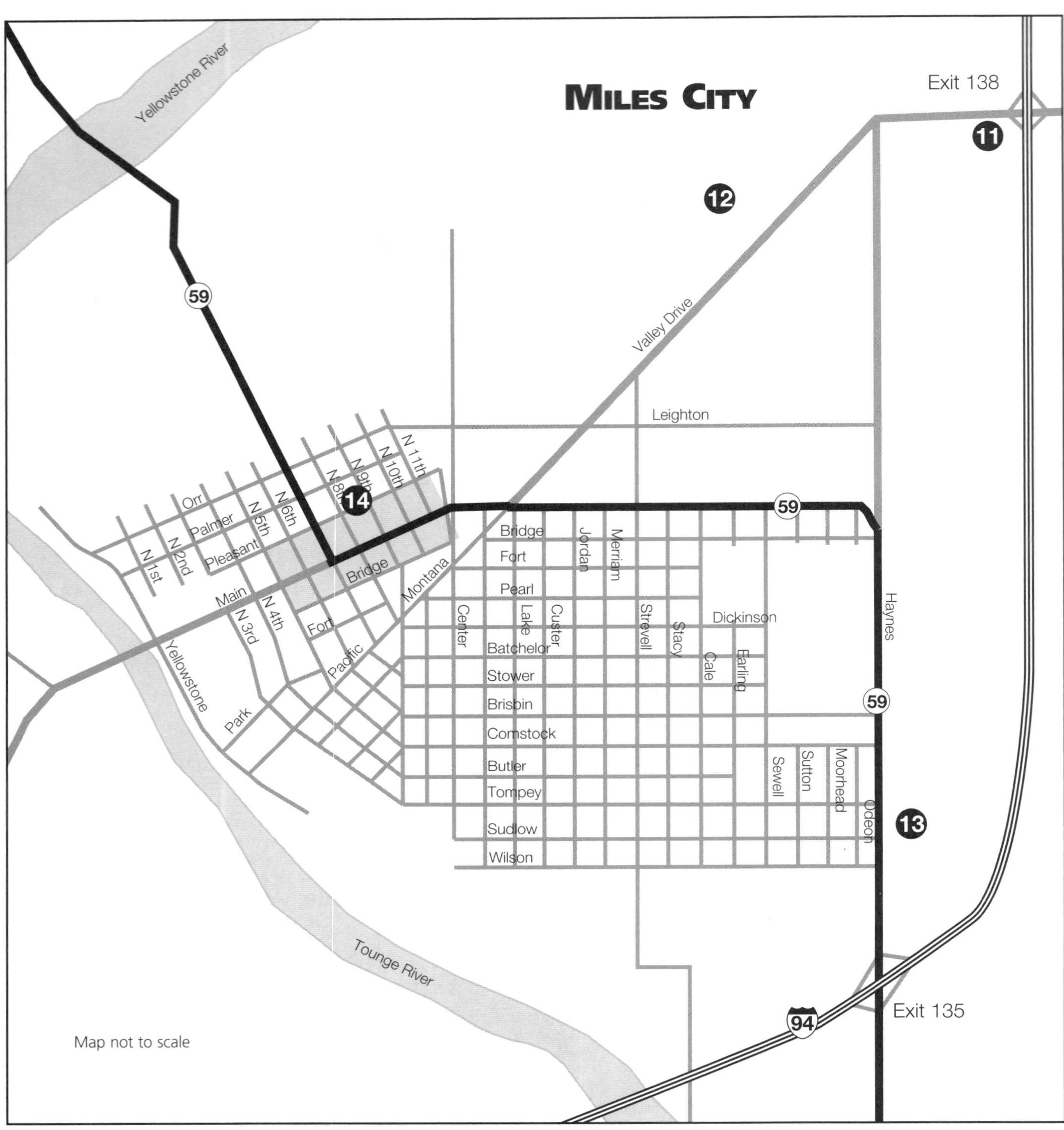


## WIBAUX SKI FESTIVAL

**One doesn't expect to find ski festivals** in July. You especially doesn't expect to find a ski festival in Wibaux. The town has had a three day ski festival every year since the early 1990's. There isn't any cross-country or downhill skiing, but there are a lot of Jablonski and Bjoorniski families and other Polish and Norwegian families who's names end with "ski". This is a celebration of those Wibaux residents who make up a large part of the 500 or so folks who live there.

This is one big family event and includes things like wild cow milking, cattle penning, hide ride (like skijoring on a hide), horse saddling, greased pole climb, and ranch rodeo, just to name a few. There is lots of food, of course including "Polish Hot Dogs". On Sunday, mass at St. Peter's Church is livened up with hymns and a polka beat. Sunday the festivities come to a close with a massive horseshoe tournament. The festival is not exclusive even if you are a Smith, Jones, or Olson you can join in the fun.

Wibaux Chamber of Commerce. 796-2412

tion. Your participation in preserving this special place is needed. All natural things are protected here. Please leave fossil remains in place, and report significant discoveries to a Department employee so that a professional team can be sent to study and preserve them. Please visit with care so that future generations of all living things will be enriched by the experience of Makoshika.

Included within the park are archery and shooting ranges as well as scenic drives and nature trails, a campground with 8 sites, a group picnic area, and many picnic sites. The largest of Montana's State Parks encompasses 8,834 acres at an elevation of 2,374 feet. The park offers a visi-

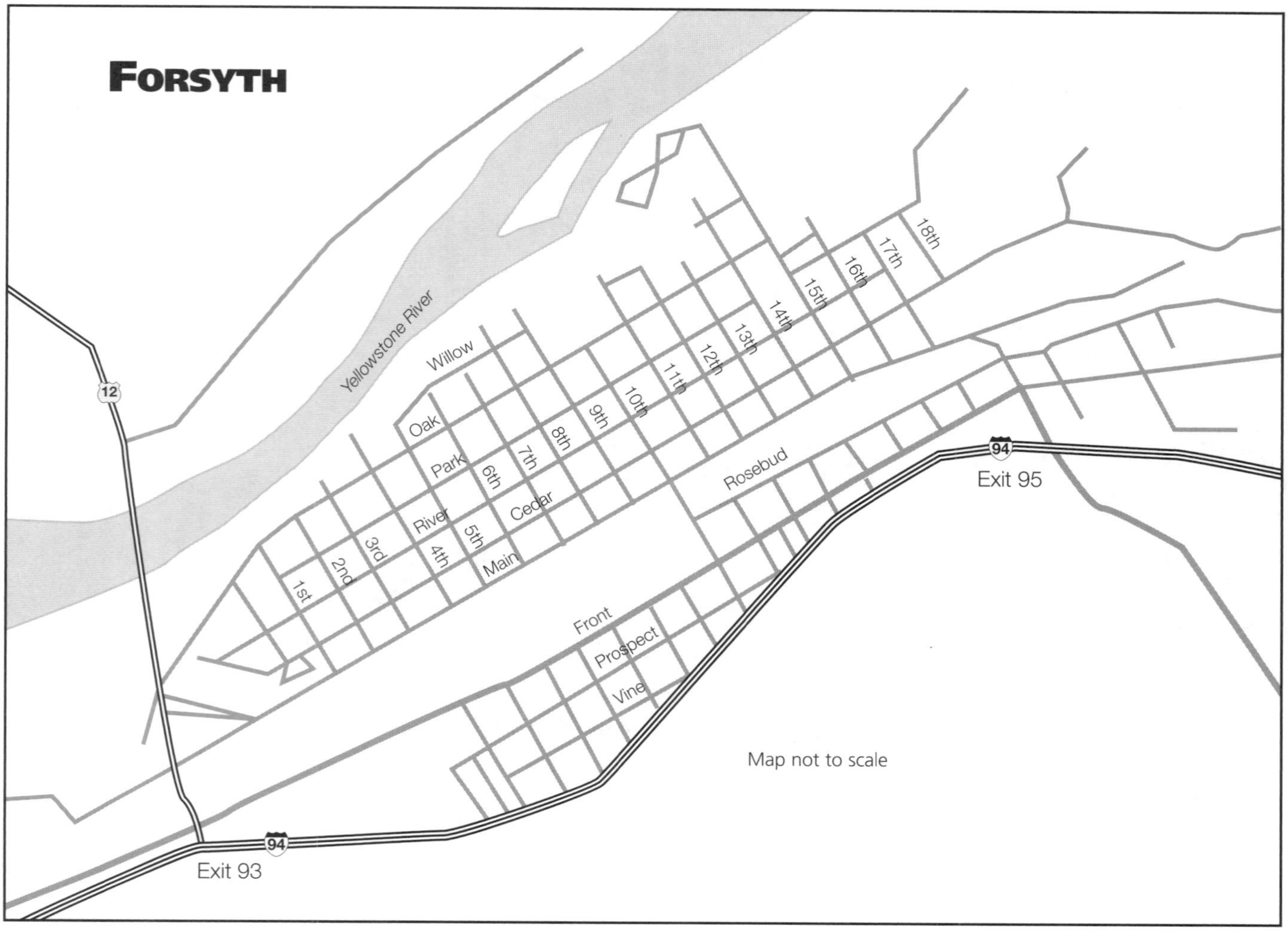

## FORSYTH

Yellowstone River
Willow
Oak
Park
River
Main
Cedar
Rosebud
Front
Prospect
Vine
1st
2nd
3rd
4th
5th
6th
7th
8th
9th
10th
11th
12th
13th
14th
15th
16th
17th
18th
12
94
Exit 93
94
Exit 95
Map not to scale

tors center, both flush and vault toilets, a public phone, grills/fire rings, picnic tables, trash cans, drinking water, interpretive displays, and special events throughout the summer. Visitors may camp 14 days during a 30 day period. Camping: $8.00. Entrance Fee Day Use:Vehicle $3.00 Person $0.50 walk-in/bicycle. Season of Operation: Open All Year. *—Reprinted from park brochure*

### FS Book 'n' Bear Nook & The Coffee Den

104 S. Merrill Ave. Glendive. 377-4938

The Book 'n' Bear Nook and The Coffee Den, located in the historic Dion Building in downtown Glendive, is a great place to browse while enjoying your favorite coffee or non-coffee drink. The Book 'n' Bear Nook provides gifts for residents and visitors of all ages in Glendive since 1986. They carry Big Sky Carvers, Boyd's bears, gifts for the new baby, Made In Montana items, inspirational gifts, gifts for the hunter or fisherman, books and much more. The Coffee Den was added to the Book 'n' Bear Nook in 2001 to provide a place to sit back and relax while enjoying a great cup of coffee, and a wonderful place to meet friends. They offer espresso drinks and specialize in made from scratch goodies, including pies, cheesecakes, soup and breads.

### FL Best Western Jordan Inn

223 N. Merrill Ave., Glendive. 377-5555 or (888) 453-3483

Conveniently located in Glendive's city center is the Jordan Inn dating back to 1901, offering 86 clean guest rooms in a family atmosphere. There are non-smoking rooms available, some with kitchenettes, microwaves and refrigerators, and an indoor heated pool and sauna. Breakfast, lunch and dinner is served in the coffee shop, offering homestyle cooking at affordable prices. They also have fine dining in The Blue Room restaurant—both are open 7 days a week. They offer a lunch buffet Monday through Friday and a Sunday Super Brunch every Sunday from 8 a.m.–1:30 p.m. There is a full service lounge and casino, and room service is available as well.

### L Charley Montana Bed & Breakfast

103 N. Douglas, Glendive. 365-3207 or toll free 888-395-3207. charley-montana.com

### L El Centro Motel

11 S. Kendrick, Downtown, Glendive. 377-5211

### L The Hostetler House Bed & Breakfast

113 N. Douglas, Glendive. 377-4505 or toll free 800-965-8456. bnbinns.com/hostetlerhouse.inn

### C Green Valley Campground

124 Green Valley Lane, Glendive. 377-1944

### S The Gift Shop - Jordan Inn

223 N. Merrill, downtown Glendive. 365-9833. montana-giftshop.com

The Gift Shop at the Jordan Inn is conveniently located in the heart of downtown Glendive. They offer a variety of "Montana Made" items, including Glendive-made rag rugs to famous, locally crafted Montana Moss Agate jewelry. The whole family will find something from their large selection of Montana T-shirts, sweatshirts, and caps. If you are

*The Gift Shop-Jordan Inn*

hunting for a special Ty Beanie Baby™, The Gift Shop is the only authorized dealer in Glendive. Stop in to visit this unique shop and select a memorable gift from their complete line of Montana souvenirs and receive a warm welcome to Glendive - "Where the Best Begins. . ."

### S Bridger Bronze
112 W. Benham, Downtown Glendive. 377-8505

If you are a beginning bronze collector or adding to an existing collection be sure and visit Bridger Bronze. You will also meet internationally recognized sculptor/owners, Pamela Harr and Harvey Rattey. A warm welcome brings you into their world of over 800 different creations that cover a range from Western, wildlife, historical, and contemporary bronze sculptures especially well known throughout the Western art world. Pamela's love of people and animals, combined with a ranching background, significantly influences her work. The West has been a way of life for Harvey, a rancher and rodeo competitor of Native American ancestry. Together, their work reveals individual deep insight and emotional involvement in each piece. Beginning in Bozeman over twenty years ago, they relocated to Glendive and have five school aged children where the creativity never stops.

### S The Enchanted Room
222 W. Towne St., Glendive. 377-4745.
www.Enchanted-Room.com

The Enchanted Room is known throughout the area for outstanding customer service. Enter this classic shop and you will find lovely accessories for your home and garden. You'll be welcomed by the many fragrances of Village and Lang candles. Select from exquisite tabletop items from Signature, Momma Ro, and Foreside, along with beautiful florals and floral accessories. Refreshing bath and body products are available from Crabtree and Evelyn and Thymes. Their quilting department is a gorgeous splash of over 4,000 bolts of the finest quality quilting fabric. They also carry every quilting gadget or tool available from creative grid rulers to glass beads. You'll also find over 300 quilting book titles and numerous patterns to please every interest.

### S Trinkets n' Treasures Giftware & Antiques
212 S. Merrill, Glendive. 377-7662

You're always welcome to browse at Trinkets n' Treasures. They are a small friendly shop filled with antiques, collectibles, and giftware. They not only offer large items such as wardrobes, china cabinets, and primitive cupboards, but also have inexpensive, hard to find items from vintage clothing and linens to kitchen gadgets. It's like taking a peek into Grandma's attic. You do not need a fortune to find a fortune of fun at Trinkets n' Treasures.

### S Clothing Exchange & Picture That Custom Framing
109 N. Merrill, Glendive. 377-7559

The Clothing Exchange and Picture That are two delightful stores in one. The Clothing Exchange is located in the front of the building. They offer new and like new family apparel, lovely Montana-made jewelry, sterling silver and genuine gemstone jewelry. Where you can look good for less. The also carry Montana-made aroma therapy, and a wide selection of Emu oil products, Martinson's Ranch Chocolates (seasonal), Davidson teas and wickless candles. Picture That at the back of the store is a full-service custom framing and matting center. You'll find beautiful handcrafted greeting cards, a large selection of decorative frames, a wide variety of local artists pottery, and many unique prints and posters. You'll enjoy a warm welcome along with a fun shopping experience.

### S Strokes & Stitches, Your Country Store
217 W. Towne St., Glendive. 377-7614

A beautiful historical house is home to Strokes and Stitches - Your Country Store. This enchanting store offers nine delightful rooms creating a shopping adventure with a different country themes in each room. The lovely array of items includes everything from collectibles to primitive

# Custer National Forest

**The lands of the Custer National** Forest and National Grasslands lie scattered across 20 counties in Montana, North Dakota, and South Dakota. Elevations range from less than 1,000 feet in the Cheyenne Grasslands to 12,799 foot Granite Peak, the highest in Montana. The vast distances across which this Forest is spread results in a very diverse landscape. Ancient sand dunes covered with grasslands, rugged badlands, densely wooded forests, and carpets of alpine wildflowers all await you.

**Directions**

From Billings, follow Interstate 90 east approximately 60 miles to State Hwy 212 east. Follow State 212 for about 60 miles to reach the forest.

Custer National Forest
USDA Forest Service
1310 Main Street
P.O. Box 50760
Billings, MT 59105
Phone: 248-9885
Email:Mailroom_R1_Custer@fs.fed.us

Reprinted from www.recreation.gov

to Victorian. Customers' favorites begin with Montana Made, Boyd's Bears, Department 56, Burt's Bees, to handmade country crafts and exquisite gifts. You'll find items to delight everyone on your list, including yourself. Relax and enjoy a beverage from the full espresso bar and take a break on their country porch while enjoying one of their fresh-baked pretzels.

### S J & S Feeds, Gifts, and Jewelry

1000 N. Merrill Ave., Glendive. 377-2180

J & S Feed is the most intriguing feed store you will ever have an opportunity to visit! Not only will you find a large selection of pet food and supplies, livestock feed, and horse tack, but you will also find top names in jewelry, accessories, and gifts for yourself or someone special. They carry a complete line of Montana's own Silversmith jewelry and a tempting selection of Brighton bags, wallets, and accessories, and hats for every personality. Stop in for a free sample of Exclusive pet food for cats and dogs. They also carry a full line of Purina products, feed for all animals large and small, including a variety of bird feed.

# The Oldest Surviving Big Game Animal in North America

**On North Dakota's far Northwest, at** the border with Montana, lies the Confluence of the Yellowstone and Missouri Rivers. Each Spring, swollen with mountain runoff, the wild and murky Yellowstone swells and rushes head-long to spill its waters into the wide Missouri, unchanged from its discovery by Lewis & Clark.

The Confluence site has played a major role in the history of the American West. It is just one-half mile from Fort Buford, where Sitting Bull surrendered to the U.S. Army in 1881; the Little Bighorn wounded were brought here by steamboat; and two miles from the reconstructed Fort Union, where John Jacob Astor's American Fur Company conducted a thriving business. Between 1829 and 1866, whites traded peacefully their guns, knives, pots, cloth, and beads to Indian Tribes (Assiniboine, Cree, Crow, Blackfoot, and Sioux) in exchange for beaver, buffalo, and other valuable furs. Today, Fort Union holds perhaps the most complete collection of original trade beads in North America.

It is in this area that the ancient Paddlefish comes to spawn each year, swimming against the mighty current to deposit their eggs on flooded gravel bars in the Yellowstone. The largest females snagged each year are between 15 and 50 years old. Plankton feeders, paddlefish are thought to use their "paddle" (rostrum) to help keep them level as they move through the water with their mouths open, filtering food through filament-like gill rakers. The rostrum also helps detect food organisms through tiny sensory pores.

Modern paddlefish (Polyodon Spathula) are classic examples of millions of years of ecological fine-tuning. Paddlefish have adapted remarkably to their environment since they were introduced into the Yellowstone River in 1963. They may be the oldest big-game animal surviving in North America!

Paddlefish skin is tough, smooth and scaleless except for the upper portion of its tail. The most striking feature of the paddler is its elongated paddle-shaped snout which is used as an antenna for detecting concentrations of food and helping the fish react to the changing water current. Adult paddlefish can weigh from 60 to 120 pounds! The state record paddlefish was 142 pounds, caught in 1973.

The Intake Diversion Dam 17 miles north of Glendive, Montana is famous for paddlefishing and the production of caviar. Glendive is considered the "Paddlefish Capitol of the World" and draws over 3,000 anglers annually to this short stretch of the Yellowstone River.

It takes a special fishing skill and a heavy duty tackle to challenge this senior denizen of the river. Because paddlefish feed on microscopic organisms, they cannot be caught by conventional fishing methods. Live bait and lures are useless against these formidable foes...they must be snagged!

Despite the unconventional fishing methods, their prehistoric origins and rather home-

ly appearance, paddlefish are an excellent tasting fish. They can be prepared as you would any other fish. A paddlefish can yield a large quantity of top-quality meat. The meat can be frozen, canned, poached, steamed, smoked, baked, or sliced into steaks and grilled.

In recent years, paddlefish roe has been harvested, processed into caviar, and shipped from Glendive. Fisherman are encouraged to donate the roe to the Glendive Chamber of Commerce who, in turn, process the roe into world-class caviar. The proceeds from the venture are used to improve fisheries and recreation in Eastern Montana, as well as provide grants given to area organizations for historical and cultural projects. And here's the best part, if you donate your roe they will clean your paddlefish for you!

Paddlefish season runs from May 15th through June 30th every year. You will need a Montana fishing license and a special paddlefish tag. Tags are two for $5 for Montana residents and $7.50 for non-residents.

# Agate Hunting

**Agate hunting is a popular sport along** the banks of the Yellowstone River, and it's a fun way to spend an afternoon. The agates found in this area are popular worldwide, due to their high quality.

Agate is translucent and often has unique patterns imbedded into the interior of the rock The outside of the rock is rough and the rock is usually tan or gray in color. Most of the rocks are found in gravel deposits in the hills surrounding the Yellowstone River, and on the gravel beds in the river. The Agate hunting season is from early spring through the fall.

Agate is formed when the igneous rock layer cools and leaves behind gas bubbles. The bubbles are later filled with mineral rich water and silica solution that hardens and creates a colored layer. The layers build up creating the agate.The agates found in Montana are often referred to as Montana Moss Agate or Plume agates.

For more information on where to begin your hunt, contact the local area Chambers of Commerce. Guided hunts are also available.

## M Dawson Community College

300 College Drive, Glendive. (800) 821-8320, www.dawson.cc.mt.us

Dawson Community College was established in 1940 as a public junior college to meet the educational needs of eastern Montana. Students can earn associate degrees and vocational certificates both at the Glendive campus and at the extension site in Sidney, Montana. Approximately 700 students are enrolled at DCC annually.

## 3. *Lewis and Clark, Attraction, Gas, Food, Lodging, Camping*

### D William Clark

August 1, 1806

*"at 2 P.M. I was obliged to land to let the Buffalow Cross over. not withstanding an island of half a mile in width over which this gangue of Buffalo had to pass and the Chanel of the river on each Side nearly 1/4 of a mile in width, this gangue…was entirely across and as thick as they could Swim."*

### D William Clark

August 1, 1806

*"We had Showers of rain repeetedly all day at the intermition of only a fiew minits between them. My Situation a very disagreeable one. in an open Canoe wet and without a possibility of keeping my Self dry."*

### T Frontier Gateway Museum

I-90 Exit 215 on Belle Prairie Rd., Glendive. 377-8168.

The museum is historical and chronological in content. Displays range from prehistoric times to the 20th century.

Major displays include fossils, buffalo, Indian, homesteaders, cattlemen, settlers, railroad, Civil War, and numerous miscellaneous displays that fit into those eras.

The museum complex of seven buildings is located on an acre of land. Besides the main building, there are on the grounds a blacksmith shop, two country stores, buggy shed, a fire hall, log cabin, a restored country school and a large display of farm machinery. All are from this area.

A street named "Merrill West" is located in the basement of the museum's main building, and the store names are those which were in existence in Glendive from 1881 to mid-1900's.

Murals on the exterior walls depict actual historic events of Glendive and the immediate surrounding area; Indian encampment, the buffalo which roamed the prairies, the wagon train of early settlers, Camp Canby - which was a military post - and the first site of the city itself.

Three recent notable acquisitions are a restored and working 1915 windmill, and a 1918 155mm cannon in the park area west of the main building and an NP caboose.

Open June through August from 9-12 a.m. and 1-5 p.m., Monday through Saturday. 1-5 p.m. on Sundays and holidays. May and September, 1-5 p.m. daily. Free admission.

### *Montana Trivia*

The town of Mingusville, later to be called Wibaux was a popular cattle shipping point. Cowboys filled the saloons on weekends and literally shot up the town. It has been reported that one storekeeper built a sidewalk in front of his store from the empty cartridge shells he picked up off the street.

### L Comfort Inn

1918 N. Merrill Ave., Glendive. 365-6000

### L Super 8 Motel

1904 N. Merrill Ave., Glendive. 365-5671

### C Glendive Campground

201 California St., Glendive. 377-6721, www.glendivervpark.com

## 4. *Gas, Food, Lodging, Camping*

### L Parkwood Motel

1002 W. Bell, Glendive. 377-8222

### C Green Valley Campground

124 Green Valley Lane, Glendive. 377-1944

## 5. *Historic Marker, Gas*

### H Glendive

A yachting party consisting of Capt. Wm. Clark, of the Lewis and Clark Expedition, six of his men, Sacajawea and her child floated by here August 1, 1806, navigating a craft made by lashing together two hollowed-out cottonwood logs. It was Clark's birthday and the outfit had to land that afternoon to let a herd of buffalo swim the river ahead of them.

Sir George Gore, a 'sporting' Irish nobleman, arrived on the scene to hunt in 1855 with Jim Bridger as a guide. Gores harvest during an eleven-month stay in the Yellowstone Valley included 105 bears, over 2,000 buffalo, and 1,600 elk and deer. He hunted for the thrill of the chase and trophies, only infrequently using the meat. The Crows, who occupied this country, hotly protested the devastation of their food supply.

It was Sir George who named the local tributary to the Yellowstone River "Glendive," and the town assumed the same name 25 years later. During the cattle boom of the 1880s Glendive became the 'Queen City of the Cow Land." In 1884, 12,800 "pilgrims" or eastern cattle were unloaded here in one week to help stock the range. They may have been "barnyard stock" but their progeny grew up rough, tough and hard to curry.

## 6. *Historic Marker, Food*

### H The Yellowstone River

Near Fallon at Mile Marker 192

## On the Trail of Lewis & Clark

**On July 3, 1806, on their return,** Captains Lewis & Clark decided to split up the group, just south of today's city of Missoula. Clark's team, including Sacajawea and her baby Jean Baptiste, proceeded down the Yellowstone, past Pompeys Pillar, and spent the night of July 27 at Castle Rock by today's Forsyth.

The next day they passed Rosebud Creek, spotted numerous herds of Elk, and spent the night of July 29, 1806 on an island just across from the Tongue River by Miles City. Clark observed the abundance of coal in the surrounding hills.

On July 30, the group passed through a difficult stretch of river and went by Makoshika State Park.

The night of July 31 was spent by present day Glendive where they reportedly experienced problems with mosquitoes, grizzly bears and spotted numerous bison.

They traveled huge distances of up to 60 miles a day during this time, until they once again returned to the Missouri River on August 4, 1806, where they met up with Lewis and his party.

*Interstate 90 generally follows the Yellowstone River from Glendive to Livingston, Montana. This river originates south of Yellowstone National Park and terminates when it joins the Missouri River north of here. It is the longest undammed river in the lower 48 states.*

*When the West was won, most rivers were lost to damming and dewatering. This river is the exception; it remains wet, wild and damfree over its entire length. The Yellowstone flows free for over 650 miles, draining a watershed greater in area than all of the New England states combined.*

*In the 1970s Montanans held a great debate over this mighty river's future. When the dust settled, the state reserved a substantial amount of water to remain instream so that the Yellowstone might never be depleted and might forever remain free-flowing.*

*Other uses of the river—municipal, agricultural and industrial—are also provided for. Today, this waterway is in balance with all its users, including nature's creatures. Few American rivers can still make that claim.*

## 7. *Lewis & Clark, Attraction*

### D William Clark

July 31, 1806

*"I was much disturbed last night by the noise of the buffalow which were about me. one gang Swam the river near out Camp which alarmed me a little for fear of their Crossing our Canoes and Splitting them into pieces."*

### D William Clark

July 30, 1806

Referring to country surrounding Terry: *"entirely bar of timber…great quantities of coal…in every bluff and in the high hills at a distance."*

### T Terry Badlands

232-4333

These badlands near the town of Terry provide a dramatic backdrop and recreational opportunities.

## 8. *Attraction, Gas, Food, Lodging, Camping*

### Terry

Terry is nestled by the Yellowstone River in the heart of agate country and is the county seat of Prairie County, located about half way between Miles City and Glendive. It was named for General Alfred Terry, who commanded an 1876 expedition against the Indians.

Sheep herding and wool production were an important part of Terry's early economy. In 1897, the Northern Pacific Railroad built a wool storage house there. Early accounts say that before that, the wool was stored in the school house and it was impossible to hold classes there when the building was full. In 1906, nearly a million pounds of wool was shipped from Terry, bringing in an estimated $275,000 in revenue.

Today, Prairie County is still an agricultural area with Terry serving as its hub. The Yellowstone River is broad and gentle as it flows through Terry. After highwater in July and August, it's ideal for boating, floating and fishing. It also offers a treasure-trove of Montana agate. Prairie County has plenty of good hunting and the famed Terry Badlands are an excellent place to hike.

### T Cameron Gallery

Logan St., Terry

In the late 1800s, those living along the Yellowstone River in eastern Montana were likely to encounter a woman lugging a large format camera. She carried her 5x7 Graflex camera everywhere and, after nearly 30 years of taking photographs, she had amassed an incredible archive of life on the frontier.

An English couple, Ewen and Evelyn Cameron were among the earliest to settle near Terry. Evelyn was a child of the London aristocracy. Ewen's dream was to raise polo ponies and ship them to Europe. When most of his first shipment of horses died, the Camerons, broke, had to struggle to survive. Evelyn was forced to take in boarders, sell vegetables from her garden, and cook for roundup crews to make ends meet. She purchased a mail order camera and taught herself photography. She photographed everything and everyone around her.

Cowboys, sheepherders, frontier families, people working, riverboats, weddings, wildlife and landscapes. Farmers and their wives all going about their daily activities were her subjects.

In addition to her photographs, Lady Cameron also kept copious notes to detail her photos and life in Terry. Her legacy offers a rare glimpse into that era. While many photographs exist of that time and place, Cameron's work is unique because she took so many photos and because they are such good photos — sharp, clear and well composed. Cameron's work is on display at the Cameron Gallery in Terry. Her photos and memoirs have also been compiled in a book, *Photographing Montana 1984-1920: The Life and Work of Evelyn Cameron.*

The gallery is part of the Prairie County Museum. The main museum is housed in the old State Bank of Terry, an architectural gem built in 1916 with marble floors, intricate woodwork and leaded glass.

### T Prairie County Museum

105 Logan Ave., Terry. 637-5595

The gallery is part of the Prairie County Museum. The main museum is housed in the old State Bank of Terry, an architectural gem built in 1916 with marble floors, intricate woodwork and leaded glass.

The museum was founded in 1975 and now includes the 1906 Bank of Terry building, the only steam heated outhouse west of the Mississippi, a pioneer homestead, a Burlington Northern train depot, and the Cameron Gallery.

### L Kempton Hotel & Wagon Wheel Antiques

204 Spring Street, Terry. 635-5543

1904 Historic Hotel.

## 9. *Lewis & Clark, Historic Marker*

### H Powder River

SE of Terry

*This is the river that exuberant parties claim is a mile wide, an inch deep, and runs uphill. The statement is exaggerated. Captain Clark of the Lewis and Clark Expedition, named it the Redstone in 1806 and afterwards found out that the Indians called it the same thing but they pronounced it 'Wahasah' He camped just across the Yellowstone from the mouth of the Powder on the night of July 30th, 1806.*

*Generals Terry and Custer, moving from the east to take part in a campaign against the Sioux and Cheyenne Indians, camped on the Yellowstone about 25 miles west of here June 10, 1876. From that point Major Reno was sent with six troops of the 7th Cavalry to scout the Powder and Tongue valleys for Indian sign. He swung further west and picked up a fresh trail on the Rosebud. It was this trail that led Custer into contact with the hostiles resulting in the Battle of the Little Big Horn.*

### D William Clark

July 30, 1806

*"This is by far the worst place which I have Seen on this river from the Rocky mountains to this place. . .which I call Buffalow Sholes from the Circumstance of one of those animals being in them."*

## 10. *Lewis & Clark, Attraction*

### D William Clark

July 30, 1806

*"The elk on the banks of the river were So abundant that we have not been out of sight of them to day....Beaver plenty"*

### D William Clark

July 30, 1806

Probably refering to the Powder River: *"its Chanel is 88 yards and in this there is not more water than could pass through an inch auger hole. I call it Yorks dry R."*

### T Pirogue Island State Park (Day Use Only)

1 mile north of Miles City on Montana 59, then 2 miles east on Kinsey Road, then 2 miles south on county road. 232-0900

Pirogue Island is on the Yellowstone River just a few miles north of Miles City. The densely wooded area is an oasis for abundant wildlife including beavers, deer and many different species of birds. Moss agate hunting and floating are popular recreational activities at this park. Sheltered by mature cottonwoods, floaters find this isolated and undeveloped Yellowstone River island an excellent spot to view wildlife and hunt for Montana moss agates. During low water, a small channel can be forded by vehicle to obtain access to the island from the mainland.

## 11. *Gas, Food, Camping*

### Miles City

The Old West is still alive and well in Miles City—the Cow Capital of Montana. With the world famous Miles City Bucking Horse Sale, the annual Beef Breeders Show, the Fort Keogh Days, the Range Rider's Museum, three historic districts and impressive collections of historic photographs, Miles City keeps the Old West alive through events and exhibits.

The confluence of the Tongue and Yellowstone rivers has been an important spot for centuries. Native Americans, early explorers and trappers all camped in the area and the spot was an excellent place for fording the Yellowstone and for trading. The military set up a temporary base in 1877, and after the battle of the Little Bighorn, Col. Nelson Miles established Fort Keogh and soon a civilian settlement sprang up nearby.

In 1887, the new community was named Miles City in honor of the commanding officer. As the city became established and began to grow, it developed into an important stopping place for the long cattle drives from Texas. Soon, cattle men began establishing large ranches in the area.

In 1881, the Northern Pacific arrived in town, and from then on Miles City had rail access — the thread that stitched the early West together. The railroad also helped Miles City become a center for the cattle industry in the region.

Now, 100 years later, Miles City is still a regional center, a cattle ranching and agricultural hub and a thriving community. Events and activities are planned throughout the year. It's home to Miles Community College, a two-year school with a solid reputation. The Livestock and Range Research Station at Fort Keogh conducts important research on swine, poultry, sheep, horses and dairy cows.

## 12. *Attraction, Food, Lodging, Shopping*

### T Ursuline Convent

1411 Leighton Blvd, Miles City. 232-4146

The first Ursuline Convent in the Rocky Mountains opened in Miles City on January 18, 1884. Six teaching sisters of the order of St. Ursula from Toledo, Ohio, came to Montana invit-

Downtown Miles City

ed by Father Lindesmith, Fort Keogh chaplain. Bishop Brondel requested that three of the sisters settle in Miles City. The three remaining "Lady Blackrobes" traveled south led by Superior Mother Amadeus Dunne to establish St. Labre's Mission among the Northern Cheyenne.

The Convent of the Sacred Heart enrolled both sons and daughters of settlers from all over eastern Montana. Twenty dollars a month paid for their "board, tuition and washing." In 1897, fire destroyed the convent. Local ranchers and merchants donated land and prominent Helena architect Charles S. Haire was commissioned to design a new academy. The three-story brick and stone structure, constructed in formal Colonial Revival style with distinctive Romanesque and Queen Anne elements was completed in 1902.

A central entrance pavilion with four wooden columns supports a triangular pediment. Palladian windows and a rounded tower capped by a conical roof add pleasing visual interest. The well preserved landmark is an apt tribute to the Ursuline Sisters, marking their contribution to the building of Montana and dedicated service to her children.

Dominican Sisters of Everett, Washington, and Presentation Sisters of Aberdeen, South Dakota, taught from the Convent until 1978. From 1978–1991, the Mental Health Center leased the Convent for clinical offices and day treatment. In the fall of 1991, when the parish decided to demolish the Convent, a small group of volunteers banded together as "Convent Keepers." With $9,000 pledged from area people in ten days, the Convent was saved for a Community Center. Monthly rental of rooms and hospitality offered for special events keep up the maintenance expenses. Generous donations and fund raisers keep exterior restoration in progress. Reprinted from Ursuline Convent brochure.

## Montana Trivia

What would you do with a few hundred extra cowboy boots? Well, Harry Landers tops his fence posts with them. In fact he's past 300 posts and that's over a mile. You can't miss them. After rounding up a few dozen to get started, the donations keep coming and he'll just keep going. You can see them on Hwy. 59 just south of Miles City.

### F Alta Saloon & Dance Hall
2410 Valley Drive E., Miles City. 232-6851

1940's Dance Hall & Honky Tonk.

### S Red Rock Sporting Goods
2900 Valley Drive E., Miles City. 232-2716

## 13. *Gas, Food, Lodging*

### F Jewels' Steakhouse & Lounge
1111 S. Haynes Ave., Miles City. 232-7288

Jewels', Steak House & Lounge is a full service restaurant with one smoking and two nonsmoking dining rooms, a lounge with an 80 inch TV, plus a brand new casino off the lounge. A wholesome atmosphere welcomes the entire family. The menu includes, aged steaks, 16 oz. lobster, 8, 12 and 18 oz. prime rib, king crab, shrimp, halibut, gourmet burgers, chicken, a large variety of pastas and desserts, and that's not all. A kid's menu is available. You'll enjoy fast and friendly service that will provide a memorable dining experience. Jewels' is located just 3 blocks north of Exit 138 at Miles City across from McDonalds on Haynes Avenue. "Where everyone is treated like a gem!"

## Dinosaur Remains in Montana

**This area is abundant with fossilized** dinosaur remains dating back as far as 65 million years. Paleontologists have had numerous finds, and even locals and tourists have turned up interesting fossils by chance. It is said that back when the dinosaurs roamed this area, the land was covered by large riverbeds and marshlands with a sandy floor. Throughout the years this turned into the sandstone formations seen in Makoshika State Park.

In 1990, a museum volunteer stumbled across the skull of a Triceratops that is now on display at the Makoshika State Park Visitor Center. In 1994, a student came across the fossilized remains of a duck-billed dinosaur just west of Hysham. In 1997, a volunteer at Makoshika State Park discovered a very rare species called the Thescelosaurus. This medium sized dinosaur somewhat resembles a lizard and is displayed at the Museum of the Rockies in Bozeman.

These are a few examples of the exciting surrounding area that can be explored today. Much of this landscape has been valuable in helping give researchers a glimpse of what existed up to 65 million years ago. Now this area can be explored by you. Maybe you will stumble across something…

### L Holiday Inn Express
1720 S. Haynes, Miles City. 232-1000 or 888-700-0402

The Holiday Inn Express is one of the newest hotels in Miles City, and winner of the "Torchbearer Award"—the most prestigious award given by Holiday Inn. You can choose from the King suites with jacuzzi tubs, microwaves and refrigerators or the Queen suites also with microwaves and refrigerators. All rooms have an attractive decor, cable TV with HBO, ESPN and Disney, free local calls and data ports on all phones. There is an indoor pool and hot tub, complimentary extended breakfast bar, gym workout privileges at a nearby location, laundry facilities, meeting space, freshly baked cookies daily, and tea and coffee available 24 hours at the 24-hour front desk.

## L GuestHouse Inn & Suites

3111 Steel Street, Miles City. 232-3661 or fax 232-8943

The GuestHouse Inn & Suites Miles City anticipates guests' needs by filling the wide variety of room types it offers with an array of amenities. All rooms are equipped with a TV, VCR, digital cable, pay-per-view movies, microwave, refrigerator, coffee maker with coffee, iron and ironing board, hairdryer, voicemail, alarm clock/radio and dataports. Additionally, guests enjoy access to an indoor pool, hot tub, fitness center, and guest laundry. You can relax and get off to a great start in the morning while they serve their famous hot breakfast buffet, which includes favorites like scrambled eggs, sausage, biscuits and gravy, plus piping hot waffles. An extended continental breakfast bar is also provided for the light eater.

## L Budget Inn

1006 S. Haynes Ave., Miles City. 232-3550 or 800-525-6303

## L Comfort Inn

1615 S. Haynes Ave., Miles City. 232-3141

# 14. *Attraction, Gas, Food, Lodging, Camping, Shopping*

## T Riverside Park and Oasis Swimming Lake

Southwest edge of Miles City. 232-3462

The kids will love this man-made swimming lake. There are plenty of picnic tables amidst giant cottonwoods. The Tongue River runs alongside the park and is the source of the water for the swimming area. The water is filtered and chlorinated before feeding into the pool. There is a sandy beach, tennis courts and a ballpark.

## T Custer County Art Center

Water Plant Rd., West of Miles City. 232-0635

Housed in the historic Miles City Water Works and built in 1910 and 1924, the Custer County Art Center is a unique venue for art displays. The old water tanks now hold art, sculpture, photographs and other displays. The art center fills nearly 7,000 square feet of exhibit and work space and earned the Governor's Historic Preservation Award for best adaptation of a historic structure in 1979. The facility is located on the banks of the Yellowstone River, so the grounds are just as beautiful as the building itself. Open Feb.–Dec., Tues.–Sat. 1–5.

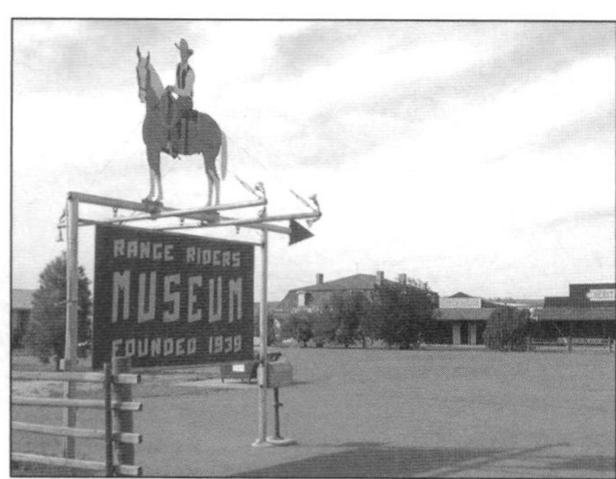


## T Range Riders Museum

West end of Main St., Miles City. 232-6146

From its humble beginnings in 1940s, the Range Riders Museum has become one of the finest museums in the northwest. Located on the original Fort Keogh cantonment, the museum features a fascinating variety of extensive displays.

Over the years, volunteers have scaled down a number of historic sites from Miles City's past, including the old Milwaukee Road locomotive repair shops, an Indian village, Fort Keogh and the old LO Ranch, the largest working ranch in the area in the early part of the century.

The life-sized exhibits include the Heritage Center, which, as the name implies, has a little bit of everything from the early days. The Milestown street has a hotel, a post office, a blacksmith's shop, a bank, a store and a saloon.

Two new additions to the museum are the Bert Clark Family Gun Collection, which includes over 400 pieces dating back to the Revolutionary War. The museum also added a Charles M. Russell Gallery to display prints donated to the museum.

The Range Riders Museum takes pride in having a little bit of everything and something to represent all walks of life in the early days — from cowboys and sheepherders, to homesteaders, businessmen, teachers and just plain ordinary folk.

Range Riders Museum is a true cowboy museum housing over 1000 cowboy hats! Open April 1–Oct. 31, 8 a.m.–8 p.m., cost is $3.50.

### Montana Trivia

During the 1960s and 1970s, Miles City was home to a nationally known television station. It's claim to fame was that it was the smallest television station in the country. KYUS (Kay-use) was owned and operated by Dave and Ella Rivenes. This dynamic duo wrote, produced, and broadcast two and a half hours of news and local programming each day.

## T Woolhouse Gallery

419 N. 7th St. in Miles City. 232-0769

This 1909 wool warehouse was once owned by the Milwaukee Railroad. Today it features railroad artifacts and memorabilia, an art gallery, Hoffman prints and steel sculptures.

## FL Historic Olive Hotel, Lounge, Dining Room, & Casino

501 Main St., MIles City, 232-2450

Downtown Miles City, with updated historical rooms and fine dining.

## S Miles City Saddlery

808 Main St. in Miles City. 232-2512. www.milescitysaddlery.com

The Miles City Saddlery has been in business since 1909 and has everything that you and your horse might want! They have clothing, boots, and hats for men, women, and children; a wide variety of Montana Silversmith jewelry and accessories, specialty gifts; and an impressive selection of tack and equine accessories. They are famous for their beautiful hand carved custom saddles, and also carry factory saddles. They also make leather products such as saddlebags, scabbards, chinks, and chaps. You'll be sure to enjoy yourself exploring two floors of quality westernwear and tack

### It Happened in Montana

March 17, 1876. The Seventh Cavalry, commanded by Colonel Reynolds, attacks Chief Two Moon's camp at dawn near the present-day town of Broadus. The Northern Cheyenne, caught by surprise, are forced to retreat leaving behind their tipis, buffalo robes, supplies and a herd of almost 700 horses. Colonel Reynolds orders the camp burned and captures the horses. Later that night, a band of Cheyenne braves returns to recapture all but 200 of the herd. Reynolds had left the herd unguarded and was court-martialed for the incident.

and a third floor features a great collection of old custom saddles and spurs. Visit their web site and preview what this great store has to offer.

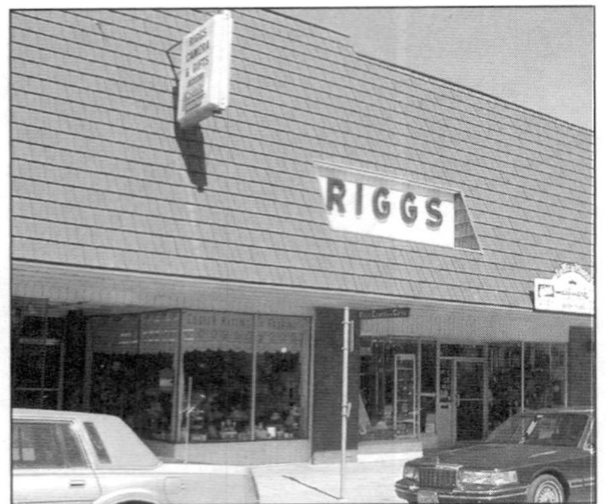


### S Riggs Camera and Gifts, Inc
807 Main, Miles City. 232-1838 or fax 232-1843

Do you like collectibles, limited edition prints, superb scenic photographs or old photos such as circa 1890s? Visit Riggs Camera and Gifts for these and much more. Many photos by owner John Riggs, photographs, like the first one in section 1 of this book, are available for framing or as a refrigerator magnet made to order if you don't see the one you want. Their selection of collectibles includes Precious Moments, Boyd,s Bears, Dreamcycles, Snow Babies, and more. The art gallery offers limited edition prints, and reproductions of old photographs (circa 1890s) by Christian Barthelmess, Evelyn Cameron, R.C. Morrison, and others. Services include a 1-hour photo lab and custom framing and matting. They are a Hallmark Gold Crown store, too.

### S Copper Thimble Fabrics & Quilts
709 Main St., Miles City. 232-7226

The Copper Thimble is a quilter's dream! The largest quilt store in Eastern Montana promises thousands of bolts of fabric to choose from. Specializing in quilt fabrics, patterns, and books, they offer a fantastic variety for the discriminating or beginning quilter. You will want to feast your eyes on all the store samples in this bright and open store located in the heart of Miles City's Main Street. You will find that "frontier friendly" service at it's best. Husqvarna Viking sewing machines and creative notions for embroidery are also featured in the store. The owners are always ready to make a great deal! They are open 9 a.m. to 5:30 p.m., Monday through Saturday.

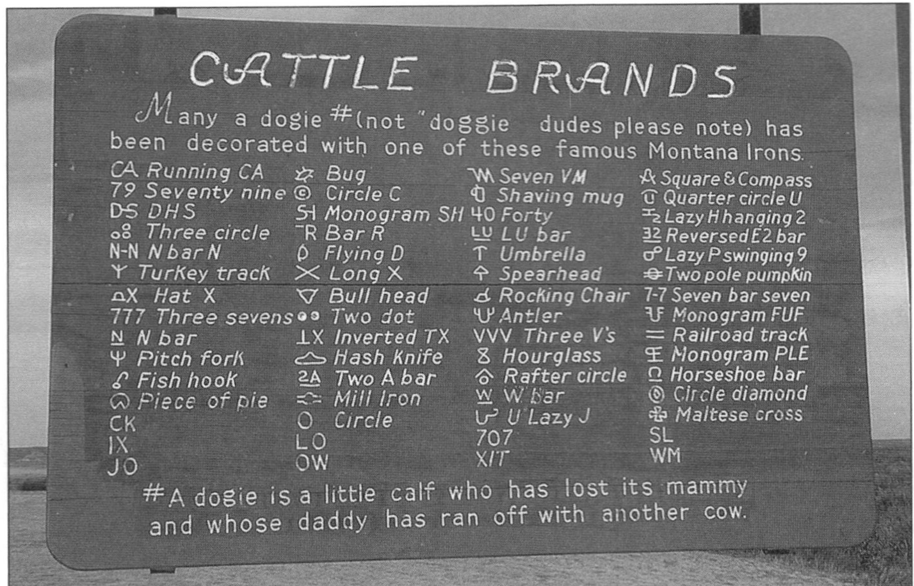


### S Valley Furniture, Gifts, & Antiques
3 N. 5th, Miles City. 232-0641 or toll free 866-227-0641

### M Miles Community College
2715 Dickinson Street, Miles City. 234-3031 or 800-541-9281, www.mcc.cc.mt.us

Miles City Community College was founded in 1939 as Custer County Junior College in Miles City, a town with a colorful history. It is a fully accredited two year associate degree institution that strives to maintain the values of it's Western heritage with everything from ranching to rodeo. The current enrollment is approximately 525 students.

## Montana Trivia

In 1882, Miles City's most infamous election was held. The polling place was Charlie Brown's, a saloon that was a local's favorite. It took the judges five days to count over 1,700 ballots. At the time, the town had a population of 1,200, including women and children. Ballots came from one precinct called Wooley's Ranch. To this day, Wooley's Ranch has never been located.

## 15. *Attraction*

### T Fort Keogh
2 miles southwest of Miles City.

This was, at one time the, largest army post in Montana. It served from 1877-1908 as a major post at the close of the Indian wars. Several of the original buildings remain and the old parade grounds are still intact. The notorious John "Liver Eatin" Johnson was attached to General Mile's command at the fort in 1877, after the Battle at Little Big Horn. An interesting fact is that 15 inch snowflakes, still the largest ever recorded anywhere, fell at Fort Keogh in January of 1887. Today, the Range Riders Museum is built on the Fort Keogh cantonment. The Fort Keogh Officers' Quarters, Coach House, Homestead House, and a One-Room School are full of donated artifacts and reflect much of the history of the area and Fort Keogh.

## 16. *Lewis & Clark*

### Hathaway and Horton

Hathaway and Horton are both communities that sprang up along the Northern Pacific Railroad in the early part of the century. Both are located between Miles City and Forsyth along Interstate 94.

Hathaway was named for Major Hathaway, a U.S. Army officer. And like many former station stops along the railroad, now that passenger service has been discontinued and freight traffic consists mainly of long haul shipping, Hathaway and Horton are a cluster of buildings along the tracks.

### D William Clark
July 29, 1806

*"The river widens I think it may be generally Calculated at from 500 yards to half a mile in width."*

## 17. *Historic Marker*

### H Rosebud

*From July 28, 1806, when Wm. Clark passed Rosebud Creek on his way down the Yellowstone, this river valley has served as one of the major avenues for development and trade in eastern Montana. Innumerable trappers and traders followed Clark's route, including the American Fur Co. which constructed Ft. Van Buren at the juncture of the Rosebud and Yellowstone in 1835. The fort proved unprofitable and was abandoned in 1843.*

*Buffalo hunters took over 40,000 robes from this area alone during the 1860s and 1870s, shipping them out by river boat. The slaughter disrupted eastern Montana's Indian culture and precipitated several years of bloody confrontation culminating in the Battle of the Rosebud on June 17, 1876, and the Battle of the Little Big Horn eight days later.*

*In late 1882, the Northern Pacific R.R. established a siding in the Rosebud vicinity as it pushed westward. Soon a town sprang up as a livestock shipping center with Butte Creek and the Rosebud forming a natural corral. Rail and auto transportation quickly replaced wagon and river traffic. As Rosebud grew it even acquired its own car dealership, the Otis Davis Agency featuring the E.M.E. line. Many an old-timer assumed the initials meant "Every Morning Fix 'em."*

### H Cattle Brands

See photo above.

## 18. *Lewis & Clark, Historic Marker*

### H The Rosebud River

*This stream was noted by Captain Wm. Clark July 28th, 1806, when he was descending the Yellowstone River.*

*In June, 1876, the columns of General Gibbon and General Custer, both under command of General Terry, met here, the former coming from the west and the latter from the east. They were under orders to campaign against the Sioux and Cheyenne Indians.*

*The Generals held a conference aboard the supply steamer "Far West" and it was decided that Custer take his column up the Rosebud on a fresh Indian trail which had been found by a scouting party under Major Reno. He started June 22nd. Terry and Gibbon were to proceed to the mouth of the Big Horn and follow that stream up to the valley of the Little Big Horn where they believed the hostiles would be found. Custer was expected to contact Gibbon June 26th and the two columns would cooperate in an attack.*

*Custer reached and attacked the Indian camp June 25th and his entire command was all but wiped out.*

### Montana Trivia

During the 1880's cattle rustling was a lucrative trade in the hills and badlands of southeastern Montana. One of the more notorious gangs was led by George Excelbee. During a February snowstorm in 1884, the streets of Stoneville (present day Alzada) witnessed a shootout between a sheriff's posse and Excelbee's gang. The gang escaped leaving behind one dead sheriff and two cowhands killed by stray bullets. One gang member was cornered shortly after by the posse, and was riddled with bullets.

### D William Clark

July 28, 1806

*"passed a river…which I call Table Creek from the tops of Several mounds in the Plains to the N.W. resembling a table"*

## 19.

### Cartersville/Sheffield

Cartersville and Sheffield are both located along the former Milwaukee Railroad main line that ran along the north side of the Yellowstone River. Cartersville was named in honor of former U.S. Senator Thomas Carter, who was also Montana's first congressman. Sheffield was known as Calabar, but the name was changed when the post office was established in 1929.

## 20. *Lewis & Clark, Attraction, Gas, Food, Lodging*

### Forsyth

Forsyth is an area that is rich with history, and is located on the banks of the Yellowstone River. In their exploration of the great Northwest Territory, Lewis and Clark passed through this area on their journey up the Yellowstone River. Forsyth is located on what is now called the Lewis and Clark Trail. On July 28, 1806, Capt. William Clark traveled along the Yellowstone River, by what was to become Rosebud County, on his way downriver to meet Meriwether Lewis who was traveling down the Missouri River.

General Custer also traveled through Rosebud County on his way to the Little Bighorn in his ill-fated campaign against the Cheyenne in 1876. That same year, Forsyth became the first settlement along the Yellowstone River. In 1882, residents chose a name for their town after General Forsyth, who was in charge of U.S. Troops in what was to become eastern Montana, and there they opened the first post office.

During that time, side wheel steamers, the only reliable method of transporting freight and supplies, traveled up and down the Yellowstone. Forsyth blossomed when the Northern Pacific Railroad pushed through the area. In 1909, the Chicago, Milwaukee and St. Paul Railroad completed its line through Montana to Seattle, giving Forsyth two transcontinental railroads! During the early part of the century, the railroads promoted the West to try and get people to move to Montana. But the harsh weather, the hard farming life and financial crises of the 1930s combined to drive many off the land. Yet some stayed and moved to Forsyth.

When the Northern Pacific built a spur line and the opening of the large strip mining operation in the Colstrip area in 1923, it helped business in Forsyth, and the line continues to be an important part of Forsyth's financial stability.

The Rosebud County Pioneer Museum is an interesting collection of old relics that were tucked away in the attics, bunk houses and sheds throughout the county.

Today, Forsyth is a prosperous city with plenty to do in and around town. With its spot on the Yellowstone River, fishing and water sports are popular and many rock hounds and collectors visit this area every year. The Yellowstone banks have a plentiful supply of Montana moss agate, which is found in gravel deposits in the middle and lower Yellowstone valleys. Montana moss agate are nodules of gray, translucent chalcedony, which, when cut and polished, contain small manganese dendrites of pleasing appearance.

Like most of eastern Montana, the Forsyth area offers plenty of hunting opportunities with large antelope herds, mule deer and whitetail deer. The bird hunting is some of the best anywhere.

### D William Clark

July 28, 1806

*"Set out this morining at day light and proceeded on glideing down this Smooth Stream passing many Isld. and Several Creeks and brooks."*

### T Rosebud County Museum

1300 Main St., Forsyth. 356-7547

This museum is home to many items used by early settlers, and a collection of photographs from the founding families of Forsyth and Rosebud County. You will find Indian artifacts and beadwork, vintage clothing, barbed wire display and farm implements. Open May through September and admission is free.

### T Rosebud County Courthouse

Forsyth. 356-7318

This three-story, neoclassical building is listed on the National Register of Historic Places. It is capped with an ornate copper dome. Inside are murals and stained glass.

### FL Rails Inn & Motel

3rd Ave. & Front St., Forsyth. 356-2242

The 50 clean and comfortable rooms at The Rails Inn are complete with non-smoking units, queen size beds, refrigerators and cable TV. Enjoy breakfast, lunch, or dinner in the restaurant with daily specials and a salad bar. They serve a full dinner

menu and offer a relaxed family atmosphere, with a banquet room downstairs. The Sidetrack Lounge is open Monday through Saturday at 5 p.m., with darts, a pool table, casino machines, and free popcorn. AAA rated.

### L Best Western Sundowner Inn

1018 Front St., Forsyth. 356-2216 or 877-356-2215

From many of the rooms at the Sundowner Inn, you can view the thousands of coal carrying train cars that pass through Forsyth on a daily basis. The newly remodeled rooms feature in-room coffee, refrigerators, cable TV with Showtime, and a high standard of cleanliness you expect from a Best Western. They also offer non-smoking rooms, guest laundry and winter plug-ins. Enjoy an indoor Olympic size pool, tennis courts, a golf course, and two city parks within walking distance of the motel. Forsyth and the surrounding area offer a variety of opportunities for outdoor enthusiasts including float trips on the Yellowstone River, wildlife viewing, agate hunting and much more.

### L Westwind Motor Inn

225 Westwind Lane, Forsyth. 356-2038

The Westwind Motor Inn is "Forsyth's Newest & Finest." This 33 room motel is AAA rated, clean and quiet, and just off I94 at exit 93 and Hwy.12. Easy on and off the freeway. The Westwind offers large rooms with queen size beds, cable TV, HBO, air conditioning, free local calls, and both smoking and nonsmoking rooms. You'll enjoy the friendly atmosphere served up with a continental breakfast. The motel is close to restaurants, shopping, golf, and the Yellowstone River.

L **Restwell Motel**
810 Front Street, Forsyth. 356-2771 or reservations at 800-548-3442.

L **Nansel Ranch Hunting, Guest House & Western Adventures**
23 Nansel Ranch Lane, Forsyth. 356-7253 or fax 356-2902. www.HuntingNanselRanch.com or email: tmansel@rangeweb.net

C **Wagon Wheel Campsite**
1/4 mile south, Hwy 94, Exit 95, Forsyth. 356-7982 or 356-2454

## 21. *Attraction*

T **Angela Well**
Hwy 59, 30 miles north of Miles City

The hottest and most isolated geothermal resources in Montana is on private property.The owners don't mind soakers, but the road is rough, the water has strong sulphur odors and there are horseflies in the warm months. The water comes from a well head at 185 degrees F at 1,200 gallons per minute. Just remember there is no ranger to guide you and the terraced crust created by the flowing waters may not be as solid as they look.

## 22.

### Rock Springs

Rock Springs is located in Rosebud County along state Highway 59 north of Miles City. The town was named after Rock Springs Creek, which is fed by a spring that bubbles out of a rock outcrop. The post office was established there in 1911 and is still run in conjunction with a general store and gas station.

Wild roses grow all over Montana, a fact that led many early-day residents to choose the name "Rosebud" for rivers, towns, and counties. That led to some confusion along the way, particularly with the small town of Rosebud, located just east of Forsyth along Interstate 94. At various times in its history, the tiny town had different names, including Rosebud, Albright and Beeman.

### *Montana Trivia*

Because Miles City's first jail was a stockade that did little to prevent escapes, the jail was guarded round the clock by an armed guard and the sheriff's pet bear.

## 23. *Historic Marker, Attraction, Gas, Food, Lodging, Camping, Shopping, Miscellaneous*

### Baker

Baker is the county seat for Fallon County at the eastern edge of the state. The boom in Baker hit in 1915 when a driller looking for water hit a pocket of natural gas. The well ignited and burned for years, and since that time the oil and gas industry has been an important part of Baker's economic picture.

Baker began as a camping spot on the Trail, no doubt because there were surface springs in the area, as well as abundant grasses for the livestock. If you look closely, you can still see the wagon ruts of the old trail near town.

Originally called Lorraine, Baker was renamed in 1908 for A.G. Baker, a construction engineer who worked on the Milwaukee Railroad main line.

Recreational opportunities are plentiful in and around Baker — fishing, hunting, water skiing, golf, tennis, hiking, motocross and, in the winter, snowmobiling and cross country skiing. Baker Lake and nearby Sandstone Reservoir offer plenty of summer water sports, and fishing for walleye, perch, pike and crappie is excellent. The O'Fallon Historical Museum is a must see.

H **Wagon Road**
Just north of Baker

*Around these gumbo buttes and across these ridges and valleys, the old trail wended its way between Ft. Lincoln on the Missouri River in Dakota Territory and Ft. Keogh on the Yellowstone River in Montana. Government mail stages, covered wagons, soldiers, people searching for homes, wealth, or adventure—with horses, ox teams, and mules plunged or plodded along this undulating trail. In 1887, one freight train Of 95 wagons, each drawn by 4 to 6 horses or mules, and each loaded with civilian goods of all kinds made up the largest train to make the trip. All were constantly watched and harassed by the Indians, whose lands and way of life were, by trick and treaty being forever forced from them. With the building of the Northern Pacific Railroad, and also the fences by homesteaders, the trail was abandoned. A few grassy ruts may be seen on the ridge to the southwest.*

T **O'Fallon Historical Museum**
2nd St. & Fallon, Baker. 778-3265

This five building museum features the old jailhouse, two homestead houses, antique cars, homestead antiques, dinosaur bones and much more. You can also check out the old teepee rings and wagon ruts left over from the old days.

The O'Fallon Museum is actually several museums in one. The original O'Fallon Museum was first located in the old library, and then moved to the former jail and sheriff's living quarters in 1975. This building houses Steer Montana, "The World's Largest Steer." It was born east of Baker in 1923. Steer Montana grew to 5' 11" in height and weighed 3,980 pounds. Other exhibits in the museum include a 1920 parlor, kitchen, homestead items, a beauty parlor, World War I and II displays, a Christmas store, a drug store, Indian artifacts and much more.

The Forrest Duffield Museum is a private museum which faithfully portrays a way of life in the area in the early part of the 20th century. The museum is a replica of a claim shack. Some of the contents are: a Majestic cook stove which was truly the heart of the home with a warming oven and hot water heater, a butter churn, oil paintings by Forrest's mother and some rugs she made including an unusual Button Rug. Also on display is Jessie's J. Tredle sewing machine which was purchased before coming to Montana.

The Lambert House was built by Amos and Corida Lambert in the summer of 1907. Up until that time the Lamberts had lived in a dugout. The Lamberts raised nine children in this house located in the Lame Jones community. They had what

*The world's largest steer weighed as much as the combined weight of eleven professional football linesmen.*

was known as squatter's rights, as the land had not yet been surveyed.

Another building houses machinery and antique cars.

T **Sandstone Lake Recreation Area**
Hwy 12, 13 miles west of Baker, 7 miles south.

Free camping and fishing.

## 24.

### Plevna

Just up the road from Baker is the little town of Plevna. This homestead-era boomtown was founded by immigrants from Russia. It received its name from a town in Bulgaria captured by Russian troops in 1877. Every October, the residents of the town and surrounding areas congregate at the fire hall for the annual sausage supper. Nearby is Dead Man's Butte. It was at this spot that a stage line driver named Fritz lost his life. The stage line ran from Fort Lincoln, near Bismarck, ND, to Fort Keogh near Miles City.

### *Montana Trivia*

As you travel down I-94 look north between mileposts 166 and 167. This is where the worst commercial train wreck in Montana history, and one of the five worst in U.S. history, occurred on June 19th, 1938. Six inches of rain in three hours created a flash flood in Custer Creek that hit the bridge at almost precisely the same time as the Milwaukee Olympian Express was crossing it. Bodies were fished out of the Yellowstone as far away as Glendive and Sidney. There were 165 passengers on board. 47 died that night and 75 were injured.

## 25.

### Ismay

The Milwaukee Railroad named the town of Ismay after the two daughter's (Isabelle and May) of a company executive. The residents there, hearing that a passenger on the titanic named Ismay pushed his way onto a lifeboat ahead of women and children, wanted to change the name of the town. For whatever reason, this didn't happen.

In 1990, Ismay was Montana's smallest incorporated town with only 31 people. In 1993, a Kansas City radio station looking for a gimmick, asked the town fathers to change the name to Joe, Montana in honor of the Chief's famous quarterback. The residents, drunk with fame and thirsty for more, held a July 4th parade, rodeo, and fireworks extravaganza. Over 2,000 people showed up and the town netted over $70,000. Pretty good for a town whose mayor is only paid $4 a month. And hey, if it worked once, why not try it again? Assured of a spot on the David Letterman show, they geared up for an even greater extravaganza the next year. The spot didn't materialize. No one showed. The maps still call it Ismay.

## 26. *Historic Marker*

### H Powder River

Just east of Miles City

*When a top rider from this part of the country is forking the hurricane deck of a sun-fishing, fuzztail, some of his pals are prone to sit on the rope rail of the corral, emitting advice and hollering "Powder River! Let 'er buck!!" by way of encouragement. The 91st Division adopted that war cry during the first World War and spread it far and wide. Well, this is the famous Powder River, that enthusiasts allege is a "mile wide, an inch deep, and runs up hill"*

*The entire Powder River country was favorite buffalo hunting range for the Sioux and Cheyenne Indians before the day of cattle men. Many intertribal battles were fought in this region as well as frequent skirmishes between Indians and the U.S. troops. The country is rich in Indian lore and tales of the subsequent reign of the cattle kings.*

### H After The Roundup

Just east of Miles City

*D. J. O'Malley grew up living at frontier forts because his stepfather served in the 19th Infantry. He lived at Fort Keogh, near Miles City, for five years before going to work in 1882 at age 16 for the Home Land and Cattle Co. (N-Bar-N) for $45 a month. His 14-year tenure with the outfit included three trail drives from Texas.*

*In O'Malley's day, writing verse about life on the range was a common cowboy pastime, and O'Malley was one of the best. His poem, "After the Roundup," appeared in the Miles City Stockmens journal in 1893. Thirty years later, it had become the classic, "When the Work's All Done This Fall." Here is the refrain from the original poem:*

*After the round up's over,*
*After the shipping's done,*
*I'm going straight back home, boys,*
*Ere all my money's gone.*
*My mothers dear heart is breaking,*
*Breaking for me, that's all;*
*But, with God's help I'll see her,*
*When work is done this fall.*

> ### *Montana Trivia*
>
> From its beginnings as two tent saloons and a gambling hall, Miles City was a tough, rowdy town. In March of 1880 the local newspaper declared in an article "We have 23 saloons in our town and they all do a good business. We are to have one church soon."

## 27. *Attraction*

### T Medicine Rocks State Park

25 miles south of Baker on Montana 7.
230-0900

*Cattle drives are a common sight in southeastern Montana.*

In the late 1800s, Teddy Roosevelt said the area was "as fantastically beautiful a place as I have ever seen." Covering one square mile, Medicine Rocks was referred to by the Sioux Indians as "Rock with Hole In It" due to the tunnels and holes burrowed in the stone. They also called it "Medicine Butte" and believed that this was a sacred area where spirits resided. The medicine man often prayed here, but it is said that the tribe itself camped on the outskirts. The sandstone formations have been created by years of weathering. Carved by the wind into odd shapes, some of the pillars tower 80 feet above the pine-clad prairie. Millions of years ago a flood plain flowed through these high plains, and as the climates changed sandstone was created. Many fossils are embedded in the rock formations, telling a story of the past. Indian artifacts can be seen ranging from tepee rings to a few rock drawings. The area is known for its abundant wildlife, including deer, pronghorn antelope, grouse, pheasants, bass and bluegill.

### The Rocks

Medicine Rocks State Park manifests but a small portion of a complex sequence of geological events that took place some 50 million years ago. At that time, a huge inland lake covered much of the Northern Great Plains. The climate was warm and tropical.

This was the age of the mammal, for the giant lizard-like dinosaur had already succumbed to changes in its environment. The swampy, forested margins of this huge, ancient sea teemed with mollusks (clams and other forms of ocean life), turtles and small mammals, as well as palm trees, water lillies and other vegetation. Fossils, or the preserved remains attesting to the existence of

*Unusual rock formations at Medicine Rocks State Park.*

prehistoric plants and animals, have been found in the rocky formations of the park.

Cutting through the lush swamps were slow-moving, shallow, silt-laden rivers. These rivers, resembling present day waterways in the south-eastern United States, transported sediments from the newly forming Rocky Mountains to the west. Some of these sediments were deposited as sand bars and channel deposits. Medicine Rocks represents the fossilized river channel of one of these ancient streams.

Through the ensuing ages, the climate changed. Dryer conditions caused the inland sea to retreat, leaving the continent high and dry. Some streams dried, others changed their courses. Compaction, great pressure and eons of time turned the sediments to sandstone.

Some parts of the sandstone were cemented together more solidly than other areas, making them harder and more weather resistant. Over the ages wind, water and temperature extremes constantly wore away the rock. The more resistant materials survived this weathering process, called erosion, and are the knobs and pillars we view today.

The park's formations owe their grossly pock-marked features to natural and dynamic events, for it is the selective weathering process that gives the rock a Swiss cheese-like effect.

Geologic processes are at work today just as they were millions of years ago. Pounding wind, runoff from snowmelt and rain, and freezing and thawing action continuously eats away at the land, giving shape, form and life-like qualities to the Medicine Rocks.

There are approximately 15 camping sites with vault toilets, a group-use area, grills/fire rings, picnic tables, and drinking water. The RV/trailer size limit is 20' and campers may stay 14 days during a 30-day period. Due to its "Primitive" park designation, it is a pack-in/pack-out site and there are no fees to enter or stay there. The park is open all year. For more information, call 232-4365

## Montana Trivia

Most of the towns in this section are tiny remnants of days past. While much of the history of settlement in Montana started here, much of the history of the past thirty years has led to its decline. A diminished importance of the rail lines, a decline in cattle and agricultural prices, and confiscatory estate taxes which caused the breakup of family farms and ranches, has put many of these small towns on the verge of disappearing.

## 28. *Historic Marker, Attraction, Food, Lodging*

### Ekalaka

Ekalaka is the "town at the end of the road," located on State Highway 7 south of Baker in eastern Montana, this town of about 650 residents is the county seat of Carter County.

Ekalaka began as a saloon for cowboys working the area in the late 1800s. According to local legend, buffalo hunter Claude Carter was hauling a load of logs along intending to build himself a saloon in another location. When his wagon became bogged down in a mud hole, Carter decided to build the Old Stand Saloon in a spot that became Ekalaka.

David Harrison Russell was the first homesteader in the area. In 1875, Russell married an Indian woman named "Ekalaka," which means "Swift One." Ekalaka was Sitting Bull's niece. She lived in the area until her death in 1901. In the early days, Ekalaka also became known as "Pup Town" because of the large number of prairie dog towns around.

### H Ekalaka
at Ekalaka

*Some people claim an old buffalo hunter figured that starting a thirst emporium for parched cowpunchers on this end of the range would furnish him a more lucrative and interesting vocation than downing buffalo. He picked a location and was hauling a load of logs to erect this proposed edifice for the eradication of ennui when he bogged down in a snowdrift. "Hell," he exclaimed, "Any place in Montana is a good place for a saloon," so he unloaded and built her right there. That was the traditional start of Ekalaka in the 1860s and the old undaunted pioneer spirit of the West still lingers here.*

*When it became a town it was named after an Indian girl, born on the Powder River, who was the daughter of Eagle Man, an Ogalala Sioux. She was a niece of the War Chief, Red Cloud, and was also related to Sitting Bull. She became the wife of David H. Russell, the first white man to settle permanently in this locality.*

### T Carter County Museum
Main St., Ekalaka. 775-6886.

Features dinosaur fossil remains dating back 65 million years ago when many dinosaurs roamed this area. Among the paleontological finds housed within the museum are a mounted skeleton of an Anatotitan Copei, one of three known skeletons found in the world. This giant Duck-billed Dinosaur lived in the Marshlands of Eastern Montana 75 Million years ago; complete skulls of Triceratops horridus (three horns); Pachycephalosaurus wyomingenisi (dome head); and a Nannotyrannus lancensis (tiny Tyrannosaur) all collected in local exposures of the Hell Creek cretaceous formation. The museum is known throughout the country as having one of the best collections of dinosaur bones.

The museum is also a great place to see an extensive collection of Western rifles and firearms, they have a military room, honoring the U.S armed forces, and Indian artifacts, all capturing bits of local history. Open Tues.–Sat. 1–4 p.m.

## 29.

### Powderville

About 35 miles northeast of Broadus is the little town of Powderville. This site was originally known as the Elkhorn Crossing of the old Deadwood Stage. If you look real hard, you can still see the route the wagons took where they forded the river here. Just west of the Powderville Post Office is the Boot Hill Cemetery which is maintained by the Powder River Historical Society. The post office here was established in 1872.

## 30. *Historic Marker, Attraction, Gas, Food, Lodging, Shopping*

### Broadus

Just up the road from Alzada at the junction of U.S. 212 and state highway 59 is Broadus, the county seat of Powder River County. In the center of the County and right in the middle of some of the finest wildlife in the country, Broadus is it an excellent destination for photographers and hunters.

The Powder River Valley was considered the last great hunting ground of the natives. It's common to find arrowheads and artifacts as you hike through these ancient lands. Many of the world's finest skeletal remains were discovered in this former coastal region and the mighty T-rex was the ruler of this land millions of years ago. Check your Jurassic maps dinosaur enthusiasts; you have just found a very special place. This was an ancient coastal region and therefore one of the best deposits of fossilized bone and plant life ever found.

## Montana Trivia

Carter's Old Stand Saloon, which was the beginning of the town of Ekalaka, finally met its demise when the drought drove out the homesteaders, and Congress passed prohibition. The local newspaper recorded it as an obituary edged in black: "Death came peacefully in the presence of a few fond mourners whose hearts were too full for utterance."

### H The Powder River Country
On U.S. Hwy 212 at milepost 79 at the Broadus rest area

*From its source in central Wyoming to its union with the Yellowstone River, the Powder River is 250 miles Long "A mile wide and an inch deep; too thick to drink and too thin to plow." During World War I, Montana's 91st Division gained national notoriety for the river with its war cry of 'Powder River let 'er buck!' The origin of the river's name, however, is obscure.*

*In July, 1806, Captain William Clark christened it the "Red Stone" river. Later renamed the Powder River, historians supposed it took its name from the dark gunpowder-colored soil and sand along its banks. But army scout William Drannan maintained that the river was inadvertently named by Vierres Roubidoux, a French guide, who shouted "Cache la Powder!" (Hide the Powder!) when a group of soldiers he was escorting was attacked by Indians.*

*Located in the center of Powder River County, Broadus was once situated 20 miles upstream on the Powder River in 1900. Named for a pioneer family, Broadus was relocated to this site at the beginning of the Homestead Boom in 1907. The community's strategic location at the junction of two important highways made Broadus an important trade center despite its great distance from any railroads. Designated the county seat of the newly created Powder River County in 1919, Broadus was once described as one of the "Biggest Little Towns in the West."*

### H Southeastern Montana
On U.S. Hwy 212 at milepost 79 at the Broadus rest area

*The first white man to enter Montana was Pierre de La Verendrye, a French explorer, who arrived in this corner of the state on New Year's Day, 1743. His party had traveled southwest from a Canadian fur trading post to investigate Indian tales of the Land of the Shining Mountains.*

*Next came the trappers, following the Lewis and Clark Expedition of 1804-06. Like the rest of Montana east of the mountains this portion remained unsettled Indian and buffalo country until the Texas trail herds overran the range in the 1880s. Up to that time it was a favorite hunting ground for roving bands of Cheyenne Indians and the various Sioux tribes.*

*With the coming of the cowman the buffalo gave way to the beef critter and high-heeled boots replaced buckskin moccasins.*

## *Montana Trivia*

Nelson A. Miles was one of the West's most successful military leaders. His success was almost exceeded by his ego. His abrasive personality was tolerated by his superiors only because he consistently won victories over the Cheyenne, Sioux, and Nez Perce Indians. In 1876 Miles grew weary of the civilian loafers and gamblers hanging out at his Tongue River Cantonment and threw them out. He placed a marker two miles away and ordered them not to cross it. The outcasts set up two tent saloons and a gambling hall at this spot. Just to show what great guys they really were, they not only invited Miles to a dinner of wild game and liquor, but they decided to name the new town after Miles, toasting him as "our future President".

*Yellowstone River near Rosebud.*

### T Powder River Historical Museum

102 Wilson, Broadus. 436-2862

The rich history of the area is captured in the Powder River Historical Museum. Antique cars, pioneer photographs, memorabilia and other artifacts that represent the ranching heritage of the area. Other exhibits include displays of fossilized remains of the mighty T-Rex, triceratops, ancient sharks, seashells, petrified bison bones, dinosaur eggs and signs from the beginnings of time. A favorite item is the buggy used by Colonel Biddle at least 100 years ago. The buggy was designed to ford the deeper streams in the area. Behind the museum itself is the original county jail. This was home to many an outlaw and cattle rustler.

Several room setting exhibits, contain artifacts from local pioneers and recreate local history. There is a reading library where visitors can comfortably sit for hours reading through pages and pages of Montana history. One exceptional building, among several on the museum's property, contains "Mac's Museum", a collection of literally thousands of items in collections of everything from arrowheads to seashells. All items were carefully collected and cataloged in Mac McCurdy's living room before the collection of collections found a permanent home in the museum. The museum is open Monday through Saturday during the summer months or you can call for an appointment. Plan to spend the day! Admission is free but donations are helpful.

### T Arches of Broadus

Arches of Broadus was constructed years ago by several local builders and are a unique feature in town. The first arch, located along the highway, is large and quite stout. The second, near the town-square, is much smaller—in fact it's too short to walk through. It's made from petrified wood, gathered from the hills around the county.

### T Historic Helm House

Broadus

Visit the Historic Helm House where you will find the best example in the region of lava rock walls, terraces, fireplaces, an underground rock garage and the two largest of the arches, all built by Mr. Helm. This is a great spot for bird watching, and the recently restored gardens were long the finest flowerbeds of the area. Some say the house is haunted.

## 31. *Attraction*

### T Powder River Taxidermy Wildlife Museum

At Reynolds Battlefield 23 miles south of Broadus. 436-2538

This museum features wildlife mounts, antique and commemorative guns and local art. It is open year-round.

## 32. *Attraction*

### T Reynolds Battlefield National Monument

35 miles south of Broadus.

This is the site of Col. Joseph Reynold's unprovoked attack on a peaceable Indian camp of Cheyennes, Oglalas, and Miniconjous on the Powder River. The Indians counter-attacked causing Reynolds to retreat and sending Gen. George Crook back to Fort Fetterman. It was this battle that told the Indians the Government was serious about moving them to the reservation.

## 33. *Attraction*

### T Tongue River Reservoir State Park

6 miles north of Decker on Secondary 314, then 1 mile east on county road. 232-0900.

The Tongue River Reservoir State Park was formed when the Tongue River was dammed, resulting in a 12-mile long reservoir that winds through scenic red shale, juniper canyons and open prairies of southeastern Montana. Boating and other water sports are popular here, and the park boasts excellent bass, crappie, walleye, and northern pike fishing. Four state record fish have been pulled from its waters. This is a great spot for fun and relaxation.

The use of metal detectors, digging, collecting or removal of artifacts is restricted. Bikes are allowed on existing roadway. The leash law for pets is in effect from April 1st until the opening day of upland bird season. Visitors should watch for rattlesnakes. The park is undeveloped and is adjacent to the Crow Indian Reservation.Daily entrance fee of $4/vehicle, $1/walk-in and $7/night camping. Camping at 106 sites is limited to 14 days during a 30-day period.

## 34. *Attraction*

### T Rosebud Battlefield State Park (Day Use Only)

25 miles east of Crow Agency on U.S. 212, then 20 miles south of Secondary 314, then 3 miles west on county road. 232-0900.

See sidebar at right.

## 35. *Attraction, Gas, Food, Lodging, Camping*

### Ashland

Ashland, Montana is located along U.S. Highway 212—the shortest route between the Black Hills and Yellowstone National Park. Nestled between the Cheyenne Indian Reservation to the west and the Custer National Forest to the east, it is located along the Tongue River and is an ideal spot to take a break if you're driving along 212. The Ashland post office was established in 1886 and the town may have been named for the abundance of ash trees in the area. Ashland is cattle country and is also the headquarters for one ranger district of the Custer National Forest.

The Cheyenne Indian Reservation was created in 1884 and encompassed Ashland.

The St. Labre Mission is in Ashland. In 1883, Private George Yoakam, who was stationed at Fort Keogh in Miles City, convinced a Catholic bishop to intervene and help the Cheyenne people. The bishop purchased some land and on March 24, 1884 set up the St. Labre Indian school. Four Ursuline Sisters responded to the bishop's request for nuns and priests and began teaching in a log cabin. Today, St. Labre provides accredited education to over 700 children at three locations on the Northern Cheyenne and Crow Indian reservations. Native American Day is celebrated on the fourth Friday in September. Visitors should stop and see the unique teepee-style church and the Cheyenne Indian Museum. The Ashland Ranger District was originally known as the Otter Forest Reserve, and later became the original site of the Custer National Forest Supervisor's Office.

The Supervisor's Office was later moved to Miles City, and then to Billings, where it is currently located. The Ashland Ranger District has the largest contiguous block of Federal ownership in eastern Montana. The district has the largest grazing program of any national forest ranger district in the nation. The district is popular with trophy deer hunters, and turkey hunters. The land on the district offers everything from rolling grasslands to steep rock outcrops. The vegetation varies from prairie to dense stands of ponderosa pine. Picnic and camping facilities are available at Red Shale, Holiday Springs, Cow Creek and Poker Jim Overlook.

In addition, the Forest Service offers Whitetail Cabin for rent throughout the year. The cost is $15 per night with a maximum limit of four nights. The cabin will sleep four persons, has electricity, and wood is provided; water must be brought in by the user. The cabin provides a good location for hunting and cross-country skiing. There are three riding and hiking areas on the district totalling about 40,000 acres — Cook Mountain, King Mountain, Tongue River Breaks. Motorized travel is not permitted and there are no developed trails within the areas at this time.

As you can see, you can stop in Ashland for a quick break or for an extended stay. The town has all the creature comforts — a motel, cafe, groceries and shops — and the surrounding area offers a variety of terrain for hikers and hunters.

While in Ashland visit the St. Labre Mission and the Cheyenne Indian Museum with its large collection of artifacts and art that help illustrate the rich Northern Cheyenne, Crow, Sioux, and other tribal history from this part of the state. Tours are available by calling 784-2741.

*The Tongue River.*

### T St. Labre Mission

Ashland. 784-4500, www.stlabre.org

In 1883, Private George Yoakam, who was stationed at Fort Keogh in Miles City, convinced a Catholic bishop to intervene and help the Cheyenne people. The bishop purchased some land and on March 24, 1884 set up the St. Labre Indian school. Four Ursuline Sisters responded to the bishop's request for nuns and priests and began teaching in a log cabin.

Today St. Labre provides accredited education to over 700 children at three locations on the Northern Cheyenne and Crow Indian reservations. Native American Day is celebrated on the fourth Friday in September. Visitors should stop and see the beautiful campus with a unique teepee-style church and the excellent Cheyenne Indian Museum.

### T Cheyenne Indian Museum

Ashland. 784-2741

## 36. *Gas, Food, Miscellaneous*

### Lame Deer

Lame Deer is located at the center of the Northern Cheyenne Indian Reservation and serves as the tribal headquarters and the site for the offices of the Bureau of Indian Affairs.

Lame Deer was named for Chief Lame Deer, of the lakota Sioux, who was killed in a battle with the US Calvary in May of 1877. Today, Lame Deer is the site of the annual Northern Cheyenne Pow Wow that takes place every July 4th, complete with competitive dancing, parades and tribal gatherings in native dress. Northern Cheyenne arts and crafts can be purchased at many businesses in town, along with the Northern Cheyenne Chamber of Commerce. The Dull Knife Memorial College is also located in Lame Deer.

### M Dull Knife Memorial College

Lame Deer. 477-6215, www.dkmc.cc.mt.us/

Dull Knife Memorial College, originally chartered in 1975, by Tribal Ordinance as the Northern Cheyenne Indian Action Program. It is named after Chief Dull Knife, also known as Chief Morning Star and is located on the Northern Cheyenne Indian Reservation. It serves the reservation and surrounding communities by offering associate degrees and certificate programs.

> *Montana Trivia*
>
> US Highway 212, which runs through Broadus was gravel until the late 1950's. The road was in such poor condition, that one area resident planted sunflowers in one pothole to provide a warning to motorists.

### M Northern Cheyenne Reservation

Southeastern Montana.

Approximately 5,000 Northern Cheyenne, along with members of other tribes, live in the rugged country of the Northern Cheyenne Reservation. The 445,000 acre reservation is bounded on the east by the Tongue River and on the west by the Crow Reservation. The reservation was established in 1884.

# Rosebud Battlefield State Monument

**On June 17, 1876, 1300 soldiers,** scouts, and miners were met in battle by an equal number of Sioux and Cheyenne. The hills and rocky outcroppings overlooking Rosebud Creek were the setting for one of the most intense battles ever waged between Indians, attempting to retain their cultural way of life, and the United States Army who were enforcing an edict from Washington.

In 1876, the various bands of Sioux and Cheyenne had combined for common defense creating a fighting force uncommonly large and aggressive for Plains Indians. Over 2,500 participants from both sides were involved in a titanic struggle, which lasted more than six hours and encompassed an area over ten square miles. The battle of the Rosebud symbolizes the Indians' first stiff resistance in the Sioux War of 1876. Its outcome contributed to Lt Col. George A. Custer's devastating defeat on the Little Bighorn a week later.

## Causes of the Indian Wars

The 1868 treaty guaranteed the rights of Indians to ownership of lands, roughly the western half of South Dakota, eastern Montana and Wyoming. The U.S. Government promised protection "against the commission of all depredations by people of the United States." Rights were forgotten or ignored with the discovery of gold in 1874. Soldiers were sent in to evict the miners but to no avail. Indians, disenchanted with reservation life, and angered over treaty violations joined the ranks of Sitting Bull and Crazy Horse who vowed never to relinquish their lands. The Commissioner of Indian Affairs in December 1875, ordered the Indians to return to the reservation by January 31, 1876, or face military action. When the ultimatum was ignored, soldiers were ordered to force them back to reservations.

## The Campaign of 1876

Army strategy called for a three-prong movement to trap the Indians between Col. John Gibbon's command moving down the Yellowstone River from Ft. Ellis, Montana; Brig. General Alfred H. Terry's Dakota Column advancing west from Ft. Lincoln, near Bismarck, and George Crook's force marching north from Wyoming.

## Crook Marches

Crook, with the largest force of the three columns departed Ft. Fetterman, Wyoming, May 29. He numbered over 1,000 men including 15 companies of the 2nd and 3rd Cavalry, and five companies of the 5th and 9th Infantry. On June 14, Crook reached present-day Sheridan. Here the column received reinforcements with the arrival of 276 Shoshone and Crow scouts. Acting on information, later to prove false, that an Indian village was on the Rosebud, Crook stripped his column to light marching order in an attempt to overtake the village. By the evening of the 16th, the army camped on the upper reaches of Rosebud Creek.

## The Battle of the Rosebud

The next morning Crook moved down the Rosebud but halted around 8 a.m. after covering 5 miles. Men unsaddled their horses, officers congregated to chat or play a quick game of cards. Meanwhile, the Sioux, alerted the night before of Crook's advance, raced from their village located on a tributary of the Little Bighorn some 30 miles distant to intercept Crook's troops. An exact count of the number of warriors engaged is not known; estimates range from 700-1,500. Prominent in leading the Sioux contingent was the Oglala warrior Crazy Horse. Two Moon, Young Two Moon, and Spotted Wolf led the Cheyenne.

At 8:30 a.m. soldiers heard firing to the north. Most gave it little thought believing it to be the scouts hunting buffalo. But the shots grew in intensity and within minutes Crow and Shoshones could be seen charging down the hills towards the soldiers pursued by Sioux. The scouts halted and fought within 500 yards of the camp, buying Crook precious minutes to mount his defense.

Crook sent the 2nd Cavalry under Captain Henry B. Noyes with support from the foot soldiers to dismount and occupy the low hills immediately north of the camp while Captain Anson Mills' battalion of the 3rd Cavalry mounted and charged the warriors on Noyes' right .According to Mills:

*We met the Indians at the foot of this ridge, and charged right in and through them, driving them back to the top of the ridge. These Indians were most hideous, every one being painted in most hideous colors and designs, stark naked, except their moccasins, breech clouts and head gear … the Indians proved then and there that they were the best cavalry soldier on earth. In charging up towards us they exposed little of their persons, hanging on with one arm around the neck and one leg over the horse, firing and lancing from underneath the horses' necks, so that there was no part on the Indian at which we would aim.*

To the left Colonel William B. Royall with the remaining four companies of the 3rd Cavalry pursued warriors who retreated before his advance. About one mile north of the creek, a high knoll commanded the valley of the Rosebud. Mills' second charge cleared the hilltop, which Crook immediately seized as his command post.

For several hours, the battle ebbed and flowed. Indians retreated as soldiers advanced, then when the troops became scattered, the warriors would concentrate a superior force and drive them back. Another trooper commented: *"They were in front, rear, flanks, and on every hilltop, far and near, I had been in several Indian battles, but never saw so many Indians at one time before … or so brave."*

By 11 a.m. Crook decided to force the issue. Still believing the Indian camp was nearby on the Rosebud, he ordered Mills to take eight companies of cavalry and strike the village. But Mills' withdrawal prompted a general advance by the Indians who believed the soldiers were preparing to retreat. Concentrating on Crook's left, they nearly overwhelmed Col. Royall's detachment struggling to unite with Crook. The beleaguered battalion was extricated from disaster by the fortunate arrival of the infantry. Confronted by aggressive warriors and mounting casualties, Crook reluctantly recalled Mills. With Mills' return, the Indians abandoned the battlefield.

## Aftermath

Crook's casualties were high for Indian fighting—10 dead, 21 wounded. With his supplies and ammunition running low, Crook buried his dead on the field and returned to his supply base at Sheridan.

For the Sioux and Cheyenne, their losses are unknown but considered similar. Bolstered by their stoppage of Crook, the Indians returned to their camp. The battle of the Rosebud was to be a prelude to their still greater victory eight days later at Little Bighorn.

The park is 3,052 acres and is at 4,445 feet in elevation. It is open all year long for day use only. Self guided tours are set up with interpretive signs.

*Reprinted from Montana State Parks brochure. Article written by Neil Mangum. For more information, read "Battle of the Rosebud" by Neil Mangum available from the Custer Battlefield Historical and Museum Association. 665-2060.*

## 37. *Gas, Attraction*

### Busby

Busby, located on the Cheyenne Reservation in southeastern Montana, was established in 1904. On June 24, 1876, Custer camped there before leaving to head north for the Indian encampment on the Little Big horn.

### T Two Moons Monument

Busby

In 1936, W.P. Moncure, an Indian trader, with the help of a store employee named Jules, reburied the body of Chief Two Moons along with personal items of his and other Cheyennes from the Battle for the Little Bighorn, and a sealed envelope of documents. On the monument he wrote:

*"Why I erected the Two Moons Monument 1)History and location of Starved to Death Rock; 2) Bozeman Expedition 1874 up Rosebud Creek, 3) Two soldiers got away from Custer Battle alive; 4) History, Indian fort up Busby Creek; 5) Hiding place and location of money and trinkets taken from dead soldiers on Custer Battlefield; 6) To be opened June 25, 1986. Key removes screws with offset screwdriver. W.P. Moncure, Busby, Montana, June 25, 1936.*

Unfortunately, the vault was broken open and the items and the sealed envelope were taken around October, 1960.

## 38. *Attraction, Gas, Food, Lodging, Shopping*

### Colstrip

When steam locomotives were in their heyday, crisscrossing Montana, hauling passengers, freight, mail and other goods, the coal to fire those locomotives came from an area in southeastern Montana that has become synonymous to coal mining. Even the name, Colstrip, is a combination of the word "coal" and the process used to extract it from the ground "strip mining."

Just under the surface of the ground is a rich

vein of lignite, a type of low sulphur coal that burns more cleanly than coal from other parts of the country. The coal deposit here is nearly flat, making it relatively easy to mine.

In 1959 — about the time the railroad was switching to diesel engines — the Northern Pacific Railroad sold the coal leases to the Montana Power Company — a deal that included all the machinery to mine the coal and the Colstrip town site. A Montana Power subsidiary started mining the coal in the late 1960s, and at that time Colstrip consisted of about 60 houses, two churches, a school, a grain elevator. Today, Colstrip is a thriving community in the shadow of the huge electric generation plants.

### T Colstrip Visitor Center
6200 Main St., Colstrip. 748-3756

Take a tour of the Rosebud Mine in Colstrip. You can't miss the operation when you head for the town. The visitor center has video presentations of the surface coal mine, the Colstrip power generating plants and the town site. It is open year round and admission is free. The tour takes about 90 minutes to complete.

*At Colstrip, a giant shovel with a base as large as a house strips coal from the surface of the earth.*

## Rock Hounding

**This is one of the best areas o**f the state for rock and fossil hunting. Particularly abundant are Montana agates or moss agates—one of the state's official gemstones. The best place to hunt these prized stones is along the banks and beds of the Yellowstone throughout this section as well as the tributaries that feed into the Yellowstone. To find these treasures, you have to know what to look for. It's a good idea to visit a rock shop first and view an unpolished specimen. The rough skinned translucent stones have been described as looking like a potato before being polished.

The best place to look for fossils in this area is at Makoshika State Park adjacent to Glendive. You must get a permit to collect any fossils in the park, and any rare or unusual finds should be reported.

Another excellent area for fossil hunting is at the Strawberry Hills Recreation Area. This is part of the large Fort Union Formation predominant in the eastern part of Montana. Here the red "clinker" beds bear lots of surprises. Directions to this area can be found under the hiking section above.

Near Colstrip look for abandoned "scoria" pits and mine tailings. These are very good places to search for fossils. Layers have been turned here that you would never get to otherwise. Be very careful when examining these areas as they are often populated by rattle snakes. It is best to turn over stones with a rock hammer or heavily gloved hand as black widow spiders reside beneath. Avoid active mining areas, and check locally to avoid trespassing on private property.

### T Schoolhouse History & Art Center
Colstrip. 748-4822

The gallery is housed in the first school house in Colstrip, and provides visitors a look at Colstrip's history with photographs and other exhibits.

## 39.
### Biddle

Biddle, Montana is located along state Highway 59 just north of the Wyoming border along the Little Powder River. The area was named for the Biddles, owners of the Cross Ranch, who imported Scottish Highlander cattle in the early part of the century.

## 40.
### Alzada

On the banks of the Little Missouri River, in the extreme southeast corner of Montana, is the tiny town of Alzada. Settled in the late 1870s by cattle ranchers, the town was established in 1880 under the name of Stoneville, in honor of Louis Stone, who owned a saloon there at the time. There was some confusion, however, because another Montana town had a similar name, so in 1885 the town was renamed Alzada, in honor of Mrs. Alzada Sheldon, the wife a pioneer rancher who came to the area in 1883.

Alzada was a stage stop on the route between Deadwood, South Dakota and Miles City. In its early days, it was renowned for the "Shoot out at Stoneville," when the famous Exelby Gang met their match in 1884. The gang had been running roughshod over the area since it was formed in 1877, rustling cattle and horses, and generally making life miserable for the residents. The shoot out culminated a series of arrests and led to the ultimate breakup of the gang.

## Scenic Drives

While touring off the main highways in this area, be sure and carry plenty of water, some food, and a full tank of gas when possible. Check your spare and make sure it's ready to go. Both of these tours take you on a considerable amount of gravel roads.

**Tongue River Reservoir Tour**

This 121-mile loop will take you through some spectacular badland country crowned with rock spires and arid plateaus while dipping into river bottoms and open rangeland. On the northern part of the loop, you will wind around knobby hills on the Crow and Cheyenne Indian Reservations. Special attractions along the way include the Northern Cheyenne Tribal Museum, Rosebud Battlefield, the Tongue River and Tongue River Reservoir, and the Saint Labre Mission. While you can do this drive year round, you may find some of the gravel roads closed in the winter time when there is severe weather.

The loop starts at the town of Lame Deer. Take the Hwy. 39 exit six miles west of Forsyth towards Colstrip. Go 51 miles to the town of Lame Deer. This popular meeting place for the Northern Cheyenne people was named after an Indian Chief who was killed by U.S. soldiers under the command of General Nelson A. Miles. At this site, the General's soldiers looted and burned Lame Deer's camp. Stop and visit the tribal museum here. At the nearby cemetery are the graves of two chiefs who fought at the Battle of Little Big Horn—Dull Knife and Little Wolf. If you can time it right, the Fourth of July Powwow here has Native American dance contests, a parade, and drumming exhibitions.

At Lame Deer, proceed west on Hwy. 212

### *Montana Trivia*

The area surrounding the Yellowstone in this section was once home to one of the largest herds of bison in North America. The size was estimated at over 1.5 million animals. This area was also the site of the biggest slaughter of animals in the nation's history. Montana's bison hunters had perfected the art of mass killing working in the southern Great Plains. They hunted in winter when the bison were slow and their coats were thick. They simply stood beside the herd and shot the bison with Sharps rifles. Killing as many as 100 per hunter per day, they skinned the hides quickly before the hide froze to the carcass. They kept their hands warm by sticking them in the entrails. The meat was left to rot. Within a few short years, the great herd had vanished.

# Paddling Adventures

**This section has two canoeable** rivers. The Yellowstone and the Tongue River.

## The Yellowstone

When you float this section of the Yellowstone, you are following the same route that Captain Clark followed on his return trip shortly before meeting up with Meriwether Lewis at the junction of the Yellowstone and the Missouri. It is on this section where Captain Clark and the Corps of Discovery were dumbstruck by the incredible numbers of wildlife. It is also here that you will view, even today, abundant wildlife.

This section is part of the "prairie" section of the river and braids slowly through the area. It is the islands, sandbars, and backwaters that create an exceptional wildlife habitat.

This is the area where fur trappers came to trap countless beavers, as well as mink, muskrat, and otter. Here you will see whistling swans and sandhill cranes. Other avian species here include eared grebes, white pelicans, doubled breasted cormorant, occasional whooping cranes and numerous wild turkeys.

The river is easy to navigate for beginners except during runoff. Watch for diversion dams at Forsyth and Intake. Both of these have difficult and unmarked portages at river right.

## The Tongue River

One argument that may never be settled is how the Tongue got its name. Most agree the Indians named it. Some attribute the name to the prominent buttes at the upper sections of the river, which look somewhat like a tongue. Some say it's a euphamism for "talking river". Others think the Indians called it the Tongue because it meanders in every direction.

The put in is right below the Tongue River Dam. For the first 10 miles the river winds through the Tongue River Canyon. This is arguably the most scenic stretch of the river. After leaving the canyon, the river winds through thick stands of cottonwoods. Frequently the paddler will see thick seams of coal on the river banks.

In the cottonwood bottoms you will see whitetail deer, beaver, and ducks. Watch also for the unusually large turtles. If you pull ashore, watch for rattlesnakes on the rocky banks. Avian species include vultures, sandhill cranes, white pelicans, and double-crested cormorants. This is an easy float for beginners, but watch for cables, barbed wire, and occasional diversion dams.

toward Busby. This little hamlet sits where Custer allegedly made his last camp. Stop and visit the Chief Two Moon Monument where the remains of seventeen Indians killed in nineteenth century battles are buried. These remains were buried in 1993 after being held at the Smithsonian Institution, the Harvard University's Peabody Museum, and the National Museum of Health and Medicine for studies.

Just west of Busby, look for the Tongue River Road turnoff. This road is paved single lane with no shoulder until the turnoff to Tongue River Reservoir. As you look around you, imagine buffalo herds, grazing antelope, and Indian encampments. This land looks pretty much the way it did 100 years ago. Crossing scattered forest and rangeland, it follows the bottomlands of Rosebud Creek. If you go through here in the fall, you'll be greeted by the brilliant reds and golds of turning cottonwoods and dogwoods. Over to the west are the low lying Wolf Mountains. Stay alert for cattle, antelope and deer crossing the road.

After about 20 or so miles, begin to watch for signs directing you to Rosebud Battlefield State Park. Stop awhile here and breathe in the history. A description of the battle here can be found earlier in this section. Had this battle not occurred, General Crooks men would have joined with Custer's troops and the outcome of the Battle of the Little Bighorn may have had a different outcome.

Leaving the park, head south on CR314 and follow the signs to Decker for approximately 12 miles where you'll find the turnoff to Tongue River Reservoir State Park. This area is rich with the yellow, red, and brown bluffs which create the badlands carved out by the Tongue River and its tributaries. Stop here and play as long as you like. There is boating, fishing, and campsites. There is also a marina with limited supplies.

When you're ready to go, take the road around the reservoir heading east. You'll find it very curvy with several steep pitches. If the road has been graded, it is a decent road to drive on. However, the summer travel can turn it into a washboard surface late in the summer. As you head north, you will pass the earthen dam which creates the reservoir. From this point on you are traveling through the Tongue River Canyon. As much of the land along the river bottom is private, watch for cattle on the road.

It's a good idea to move slow along this stretch. The road is gravel, often narrow, and there are no guardrails. Whenever you come to an intersection, follow the signs to Birney. Turn right on Four-Mile Road (CR 566). In about two miles the road splits. Bear left. A couple of miles past Deadman's Gulch, the road crosses the river and takes you up to the plateau. Here you can see Pyramid Butte and the red bluffs to the north.

Continue on the the little town of Birney. It is here that General Nelson Miles attacked a band of Oglala Sioux, led Chief Crazy Horse, and a band of Cheyenne led by Two Moon. As you head north out of town you will go up the hill to another fork. Bear left. The Tongue River Road now becomes the Ashland-Birney Road. About 6 miles north of Birney you will come to a major fork in the road. If you wish to bail out, now's the time to do it. Go left on the fork and cross the river. Here you can choose to follow the paved road back to Lame Deer, or follow the western bank of the Tongue River to Ashland. This road is also paved.

For the adventurous, the rest of this scenic drive takes the gravel road following the east bank of the Tongue River. You will also skirt the edge of the Custer National Forest. You are no longer on reservation here, so you can feel free to explore. Look for golden eagles, wild turkeys, and antelope. In the evening look for bats. After you pass O'Dell Creek, look for the white frostlike patches along the road. These are saline seeps. Water, lying just beneath the surface absorbs the salts and minerals in the ground. Once rising to the surface, it evaporates, leaving behind the crusty residue.

As you're driving this stretch, don't forget to stop and look behind you at the badland vistas. Continue on through the Otter Creek lowlands to US 212 in downtown Ashland.

While you're here, be sure and visit the Saint Labre Mission. This Indian school has a small museum. Here you can also get a tour of the mission.

From here head west to Lame Deer where you can retrace your steps through Colstrip and back to I-94, or continue west to Crow Agency and the Little Bighorn Battlefield.

**The Black's Pond Drive**

It is a good idea to tackle this drive only if you have good clearance and a 4WD vehicle. It's 23 miles through the Custer National Forest and it is not for the faint of heart. It is impassable from November through April. A complete brochure describing this drive is available from the Ashland Ranger District office. This is an excellent drive for viewing wildlife. You'll see pronghorn antelope, deer, wild turkeys, songbirds, and more. To get there from Ashland go three miles east on US 212.

*A giant conveyer belt carries the coal from the mine area for miles to loading stations and ultimately to the power plant in Colstrip.*

Go south on CR 484 (Otter Creek Road) for 19 miles to CR 95 (Cow Creek Road). This is where the drive begins.

**Long Pines**
This is another drive where 4WD and a high clearance is recommended. The pine forests and aspen groves south of Ekalaka shelter the nation's highest reported nesting density of merlins. You will also spot great horned owls and eagles here. Wild Turkeys abound. From Ekalaka, take CR 323 south for 23 miles. Go left (east) on Tie Creek Road for a little over 11 miles to Forest Road 118. Go left (north) one mile to the forest boundary and the start of the tour. You can get a brochure describing this drive in detail from any Custer National Forest office.

**Powder River Trail**
This drive is short and doesn't require a lot of description. Many of the sights along this trail have been described earlier in this section. Consider this an alternative route to I-94.

Exit I-94 at Wibaux, just west of the North Dakota border and head south on Hwy. 7 to Baker. Just before you reach Baker stop at mile marker 44 where you can still see the ruts of wagon trains that passed through here. Because of it's ample grasses to feed the horses and livestock, and its many springs, Baker was a favorite stopping point for wagon trains heading west.

While in Baker, be sure and stop at the O'Fallon Historical Museum. If you ask, the museum personnel will guide you to teepee rings and wagon ruts nearby.

From here you can move on to Miles City, or take a side trip to Ekalaka. The side trip is worthwhile.

Go south on Hwy. 7 for 25 miles to Medicine Rocks State Park. Indian hunting parties once gathered at these unique sandstone formations to pray to spirits. The pockmarked buttes make an excellent habitat for raptors. Here you can spot golden eagles, ferruginous hawks, kestrils, prairie falcons, and merlins. On the ground look for pronghorn antelope, mule deer, fox, and coyote. The Sioux Indians called this area *inyan oka lo ka*, or "rock with hole in it."

After visiting the park, move on down to the little town of Ekalaka. This cowboy watering hole has a fine little museum worth a visit. The Carter County Museum has an excellent collection fossils and dinosaur remains. The only Pachycephalosaurus remains in the world were unearthed by museum curator Marshall Lambert. They now reside in New York, but a plaster cast of the original is in the museum.

Head back to Baker and catch US 12 to Miles City. For the next few miles, you will be traveling through farm country dotted with random oil wells. At the town of Plevna you can turn south on Plevna Road and drive 7 miles to the South Sandstone Recreation area.

Continue on US 12 past Plevna for 12 miles. Here you can take CR 320 north to what was once the town of Ismay. It is now Joe. In 1993, the twenty two people in the town changed the name to honor the football player of the same name. The only real reason to go here (aside from their annual rodeo) is to say you've seen Joe Montana. From here to Miles City you will drive through badlands of coulees, buttes, and bluffs and crumbly black deposits left by an ancient inland sea. You will cross over the Powder River traveling through what was once prime buffalo hunting grounds for the Sioux and Cheyenne Indians before connecting with I-94.

## Area Hikes

While this part of the state doesn't offer the majesty of the mountains with its lush flora, cascading waterfalls, and fast moving creeks and streams, it does offer a beauty unlike anywhere else. When hiking these areas, carry plenty of water (and drink it), be prepared for relentless heat in the summer, and watch for rattlesnakes. It's prudent to carry a snake bite kit. Be aware that while it may be blistering heat in the daytime, the evenings can cool rapidly. It's a good idea to carry a light jacket if you're going to be on the trail in the evening.

**Camps Pass Trails**
This is the only developed trail in the Ashland Ranger District of the Custer National Forest. There are three trails here perfect for easy day hikes. The area here is abundant with wildlife. From Ashland, go east for eighteen miles to Forest Road 785. The trailhead is marked and just off the highway there.

**The William L. Matthews Recreation & Habitat Management Area**
This is a short loop trail in a riparian area along the Yellowstone River. You'll see a large variety of birds here. Watch for ring necked pheasants, foxes, deer, and raccoon. To reach it, take old US 10 out of Miles City for about 10 miles to the Kinsey Road turnoff.

**Tongue River Breaks**
This 7-mile end to end (14-mile round trip) hike takes you through thick ponderosa pine forest teeming with wildlife. Look especially for the wild turkey. You will also see many unique rock hoodoos along the trail.

To get there, drive south out of Ashland on the Tongue River Road for about 25 miles till the road intersects the road to Lame Deer. Turn left on Poker Jim Creek Road. Drive for as far as you are comfortable (usually about two miles) and park. From here follow the cow paths along the South Fork of Poker Jim Creek. As you reach the lower end of the trail, you will reach open grasslands followed by thick stands of ponderosa pine. When you reach Poker Jim Butte, climb up the butte to a fire lookout. The views from here of the Tongue River Breaks and the Bighorn Mountains make the trek worthwhile.

If you want to start from the Poker Jim Butte side, stay on Tongue River Road to Birney. Go left at Birney on for about two miles. Turn left again at the East Fork Road and look for the Poker Jim Butte turnoff. Turn left again and you will see the lookout on the north side of the road.

**The Terry Badlands**
Here you'll find an abundance and a variety of wildlife and fowl. The area swarms with white-tailed jackrabbits and desert cottontails which provide ample prey for the resident raptors. To get there from Terry, take Rt. 253 north for two or so miles. Turn left onto a dirt road and head west for about six miles to a scenic overlook. This road becomes impassable when wet. You can either hike in from the south on the old railroad grade, or hike in from the overlook.

**Buffalo Creek Wildlands**
Chances are if you find this place, you'll have it to yourself. This little known wild area is just south of Broadus. But it is beautiful and worth the visit. Take US 59 about 1.5 miles south out of Broadus. Turn right on the first road you can (Powder River East Road) and drive till you see the brown carsonite posts marking the wilderness study area. Park at any of the turnouts on the south side of the road. There are no constructed trail heads here. This is a wandering kind of place. Explore freely.

**Strawberry Hills**
This easy dayhike just 8 miles east of Miles City takes you through a mix of buttes, badlands, and prairie scenery.
Travel east on US 12 for 8 miles until you see the sign for the Strawberry Hills Recreation Area. The Strawberry Hills get their name from the red layer of rock which theoretically was formed when coal seams underneath caught fire and baked the upper layers of sedimentary rock.

**Makoshika State Park**
There are hiking and nature trails throughout this dreamscape terrain. Brochures describing the various walks through the 8,123 acres are available at the Park Visitor Center. If you camp in the park, rise early and head for one of the overlooks to watch the sunrise. It's an experience that will stay with you forever.

## Cross-Country Ski Trails

### Custer National Forest

*For more information contact District Ranger, Red Lodge, MT 59068 (406) 446-2103*

**Camps Pass-18 mi. E Ashland via US 212**
*2 km Easiest, 2 km More Difficult, 6 km Most Difficult; no grooming*
Two loops; parking at trailhead on US 212.

## Information Please

All Montana area codes are 406

### Road Information

| | |
|---|---|
| Montana Road Condition Report | |
| 800-226-7623, 800-335-7592 or local | 444-7696 |
| Montana Highway Patrol | 444-7696 |
| **Local Road Reports** | |
| Glendive | 365-2314 |
| Miles City | 232-2099 |

### Tourism Information

| | |
|---|---|
| Travel Montana | 800-847-4868 outside Montana |
| | 444-2654 in Montana |
| | http://travel.mt.gov/. |
| Custer Country | 800-346-1876 or 665-1671 |
| **Chambers of Commerce** | |
| Montana | 442-2405 |
| Baker | 778-2266 |
| Broadus | 436-2818 |
| | 436-9976 |
| Colstrip | 748-5046 |
| Ekalaka | 775-6658 |
| Forsyth | 356-2123 |
| Glendive | 365-5601 |
| Miles City | 232-2890 |
| N. Cheyenne | 477-8844 |
| Terry | 637-2126 |
| Wibaux | 796-2253 |

### Airports

| | |
|---|---|
| Broadus | 436-2361 |
| Colstrip | 748-2217 |
| Ekalaka | 775-6539 |
| Forsyth | 356-7129 |
| Glendive | 989-2054 |
| Miles City | 232-1354 |
| Terry | 637-5459 |

### Government Offices

| | |
|---|---|
| State BLM Office | 255-2885, 238-1540 |

| | |
|---|---|
| Custer National Forest Supervisor | 784-2344 |
| Miles City District BLM Office | 233-2800 |
| Dept. Fish, Wildlife & Parks-Regional Information Officer | 232-4365 |
| Montana Board of Outfitters | 444-3738 |

## Indian Reservations

| | |
|---|---|
| Northern Cheyenne Reservation | 477-8844 |

## Hospitals

| | |
|---|---|
| Fallon Medical Complex • Baker | 778-3331 |
| Rosebud Health Center • Forsyth | 356-2161 |
| Glendive Medical Center • Glendive | 345-3306 |
| Holy Rosary Hospital • Miles City | 232-2540 |
| Prairie Community Hospital • Terry | 637-5511 |

## Public Golf Courses

| | |
|---|---|
| Lakeview Country Club • Baker | 778-3166 |
| Forsyth Country Club • Forsyth | 356-7710 |
| Cottonwood Coun. Club • Glendive | 365-8797 |
| Town & Country Club • Miles City | 232-1600 |
| Ponderosa Butte Public • Colstrip | 748-2700 |

## Bed & Breakfasts

| | |
|---|---|
| **Charley Montana** • Glendive | 365-3207 |
| **The Hostetler House** • Glendive | 377-4505 |
| Lakeview • Colstrip | 748-3653 |
| The Teddy Bee Ranch • Ashland | 784-6139 |
| Oakland Lodge • Broadus | 427-5474 |
| SunSet House • Forsyth | 356-2647 |
| Nunberg's N Heart Ranch • Wibaux | 795-2345 |
| Helm River Bend • Miles City | 421-5420 |

## Vacation Homes/Condos/Cabins

| | |
|---|---|
| Ringneck Rendezvous • Baker | 853-5688 |
| R Lazy 4 Ranch & Retreat • Miles City | 853-5688 |

## Guest Ranches and Resorts

| | |
|---|---|
| Bay Horse Vacations • Biddle | 427-5746 |

## Forest Service Cabins

*Custer National Forest*

**Whitetail Cabin**

18 mi. E of Ashland, MT (Beaver Cr.) 784-2344
Capacity: 4 Nightly fee: $20 Available: All year (max. stay 4 days)
Corral available; no water, power available. New refrigerator & cooking stove, wood stove for heat (wood provided). Depending on road condition, type of vehicle, you may have to hike last 100 yards.

## Private Campgrounds

| | |
|---|---|
| **Wagon Wheel Campsite** • Forsyth | 356-2454 |
| **Green Valley Campground** • Glendive | 377-4156 |
| Black Kettle RV Park • Lame Deer | 477-8844 |
| Beaver Valley Haven • Wibaux | 796-2280 |
| La Rue's Wayside RV Park • Broadus | 436-2510 |
| White Buffalo Campground • Broadus | 436-2626 |
| Green Valley Campground • Glendive | 359-9944 |
| Wayside RV Park • Broadus | 436-2510 |
| Glendive Campground • Glendive | 377-6721 |
| Spring Grove Trailer Court • Glendive | 365-2018 |
| Big Sky Camp & RV Park • Miles City | 232-1511 |
| KOA Kampgrounds • Miles City | 232-3991 |
| Diamond Motel • Terry | 637-5407 |
| Terry's RV Oasis • Terry | 637-5520 |

## Car Rental

| | |
|---|---|
| Avis Rent-A-Car | 365-8032 |
| Hertz Rent-A-Car | 365-2331 |
| Mac's Frontierland | 232-2456 |

## Outfitters & Guides

*F=Fishing H=Hunting R=River Guides*
*E=Horseback Rides G=General Guide Services*

| | | |
|---|---|---|
| Cheyenne Trailriders | G | 784-6150 |
| Doonan Gulch Outfitters | H | 427-5474 |
| Otter Creek Outfitters | HGE | 784-2808 |
| Powder River Outfitters | G | 427-5497 |
| Trophies Plus Outfitters | H | 853-5688 |
| Spur of the Moment | GE | 784-2732 |
| Rumph Ranch Outfitters | H | 427-5452 |
| Golden Sedge Drifters | F | 554-3464 |
| Indian Creek Adventures | HGE | 784-2889 |
| Mitchell Outfitting | H | 436-2522 |
| J&J Guide Service | H | 775-8991 |
| Montana Trails Trophy Outfitters | H | 686-4761 |
| Sage & Sun Outfitting | H | 354-7461 |
| Yellowstone River Hunting | H | 342-5830 |
| Badland Bucks & Bull | H | 232-0535 |
| Cottonwood Outfitters | H | 232-4910 |
| Sage & Sun Outfitting | H | 354-7461 |
| Ray Perkins | H | 232-4283 |
| Bales Hunts | H | 784-2487 |
| Cat Track Outfitters H | F | 347-5499 |
| Robert Dolatta Outfitters | H | 486-5736 |
| Hidden Valley Outfitters | H | 795-8286 |

### *Montana Trivia*

Sir George Gore. Never was a gentleman so aptly named. He came to Montana to hunt along with an entourage of 112 horses, 14 hounds, 6 wagons, 12 yoke of oxen, 21 carts loaded with luxuries and more than 40 employees. He stocked an arsenal that many armies would covet. With Jim Bridger as his guide, he proceeded to shoot any creature that moved in his sights. By his own estimate, he slaughtered over 2,500 bison, 40 grizzly bears, and countless antelope, elk, and deer. Today we know him as the man who crossed a small tributary to the Yellowstone and called it Glendive. It is from this site that the town of Glendive grew.



## Public Campgrounds

## Campsite Directions

| | Season | Camping | Trailers | Toilets | Water | Boat Launch | Fishing | Swimming | Trails | Stay Limit | Fee |
|---|---|---|---|---|---|---|---|---|---|---|---|
| **1•Makoshika FWP**<br>2 mi. SE of Glendive on Snyder Ave. | All Year | 15 | • | D | • | | | | N | 14 | • |
| **2•Rosebud (East Unit) FWP**<br>I-94 at Forsyth•E Exit•N to Yellowstone River | 3/15-11/30 | 10 | • | • | • | C | • | | | 7 | • |
| **3•Medicine Rocks FWP**<br>25 mi. S of Baker on MT 7•Primitive | All Year | • | 20' | • | • | | | | | 14 | |
| **4•Ekalaka Park FS**<br>3 mi. SE of Ekalaka on Rt. 323•1 mi. W on Cty. Rd.•5 mi. S on Forest Rd. 813 | 5/1-11/15 | 10 | 30' | • | • | | | | | 14 | |
| **5•Lantis Spring FS**<br>3 mi. W of Camp Crook, SD•on SD 20 SE of Ekalaka•11 mi. NW on Forest Rd. 117 | 5/1-11/15 | 10 | 30' | • | • | | | | | 14 | |
| **6•Wickham Gulch**<br>4.5 mi. NW of Camp Cook, SD | 5/1-11/15 | 1 | 14' | • | • | | | | | 14 | |
| **7•Holiday Springs FS**<br>5 mi. E of Ashland on US 212•9.5 mi. NE on Forest Rd. 423•E on Forest Rd. 777 | All Year | 5 | • | | | | | | | | |
| **8•Red Shale FS**<br>6 mi. SE of Ashland on US 212 | 5/11-11/15 | 14 | 30' | • | • | | | | | 14 | • |
| **9•Cow Creek FS**<br>4 mi. E of Ashland on US 212•20 mi. S on Cty. Rd. 484•5 mi. W on Forest Rd. 95 | 5/15-11/1 | 8 | 32' | • | | | • | | | 14 | • |
| **10•Tongue River Reservoir FWP**<br>6 mi. N of Decker on Rt. 314•1 mi. E on Cty. Rd. | All Year | 100 | • | • | • | C | • | | | 14 | • |

| Fishery | Cold Water Species | | | | | | | | | | | | Warm Water Species | | | | | | | | | | Services | | | | | |
|---|---|---|---|---|---|---|---|---|---|---|---|---|---|---|---|---|---|---|---|---|---|---|---|---|---|---|---|---|
| | Brook Trout | Mt. Whitefish | Lake Whitefish | Golden Trout | Cutthroat Trout | Brown Trout | Rainbow Trout | Kokanee Salmon | Bull Trout | Lake Trout | Arctic Grayling | Burbot | Largemouth Bass | Smallmouth Bass | Walleye | Sauger | Northern Pike | Shovelnose Sturgeon | Channel Catfish | Yellow Perch | Crappie | Paddlefish | Vehicle Access | Campgrounds | Toilets | Docks | Boat Ramps | Motor Restrictions |
| 1.Homestead Reservoir | | | | | | | | | | | | | • | • | | | | | | | | | • | | | | | |
| 2.South Sandstone Reservoir | | | | | | | | | | | | | • | • | • | | • | | | • | • | | • | • | • | | • | • |
| 3.Powder River | | | | | | | | | | | | | | | | • | | • | • | | | | • | | | | | |
| 4.Castle Rock Lake | | | | | | | | | | | | | • | | • | | • | | | | • | | • | | • | | | • |
| 5.Tongue River | | | | | | | | | | | | | | • | • | • | • | • | • | | | | • | | | | | |
| 6.Tongue River Reservoir | | | | | | | | | | | | | | • | • | | • | | | • | • | | • | • | • | | • | |

**Notes:**

Section 1

All Montana Area Codes are 406

## Dining Quick Reference

Price Range refers to the average cost of a meal per person: ($) $1-$6, ($$) $7-$11, ($$$) $12-up. Cocktails: "Yes" indicates full bar; Beer (B)/Wine (W), Service: Breakfast (B), Brunch (BR), Lunch (L), Dinner (D). Businesses in bold print will have additional information under the appropriate map locator number in the body of this section.

| RESTAURANT | TYPE CUISINE | PRICE RANGE | CHILD MENU | COCKTAILS BEER WINE | SERVICE | CREDIT CARDS | MAP LOCATOR NUMBER |
|---|---|---|---|---|---|---|---|
| Gennie's Kitchen | Family | $/$$ | Yes | | B/L | | 1 |
| Shamrock Club | Steakhouse | $$ | | Yes | L/D | | 1 |
| Tastee Hut | Family | $/$$ | Yes | | L/D | | 1 |
| **Best Western Jordan Inn** | Family | $—$$$ | Yes | Yes | B/L/D | Major | 2 |
| Gust-Hauf | Family | $ | | B/W | L/D | | 2 |
| Taco John's | Fast Food | $ | Yes | | L/D | | 2 |
| C C's Family Cafe | Family | $$ | No | | B/L/D | | 3 |
| King's Inn | Family | $/$$ | | Yes | B/L/D | Major | 3 |
| Dairy Queen | Fast Food | $ | Yes | | L/D | | 3 |
| Hardee's | Fast Food | $ | Yes | | B/L/D | | 3 |
| Doc & Eddie's | Family | $$ | Yes | B/W | L/D | V/M | 4 |
| McDonald's | Fast Food | $ | Yes | | B/L/D | | 4 |
| Pizza Hut | Pizza | $/$$ | Yes | B | L/D | V/M/D | 4 |
| Subway | Fast Food | $ | Yes | | L/D | | 4 |
| Lazy JD Bar & Cafe | | | | | | | 6 |
| Bud & Bette's Bar & Cafe | | | | | | | 8 |
| Overland Restaurant | Family | $/$$ | Yes | | B/L/D | | 8 |
| Roy Rodger's Restaurant & Lounge | American | $/$$ | | Yes1 | L/D | V/M | 8 |
| **Alta Saloon & Dance Hall** | Bar | | | Yes | | | 11 |
| Dairy Queen | Fast Food | $ | Yes | | L/D | | 11 |
| Thad's Restaurant | Family | $ | Yes | | B/L/D | Major | 11 |
| **Jewels' Steakhouse & Lounge** | Fine Dining | $/$$$ | Yes | Yes | L/D | Major | 13 |
| 4B's Restaurant | Family | $ | Yes | | B/L/D | V/M/D | 13 |
| Gallagher's Family Restaurant | Family | $ | Yes | | B/L/D | Major | 13 |
| Hardee's | Fast Food | $ | Yes | | B/L/D | | 13 |
| Kentucky Fried Chicken | Fast Food | $ | Yes | | L/D | | 13 |
| Little Caesar's | Pizza | $ | | | L/D | | 13 |
| McDonald's | Fast Food | $ | Yes | | B/L/D | | 13 |
| New Hunan Chinese & American | Chinese/American | $$ | Yes | | L/D | V/M/D | 13 |
| Pizza Hut/Taco Bell | Pizza/Mexican | $/$$ | Yes | B | L/D | V/M/D | 13 |
| Subway | Fast Food | $ | Yes | | L/D | | 13 |
| Taco John's | Fast Food | $ | Yes | | L/D | | 13 |
| The Boardwalk Restaurant | Steakhouse | $/$$ | Yes | | D | V/M | 13 |
| The Stage Coach | American | $–$$$ | Yes | Yes | B/L/D | | 13 |
| Wendy's | Fast Food | $ | Yes | | L/D | | 13 |
| **Historic Olive Hotel** | Steaks & Seafood | $$/$$$ | | Yes | L/D | Major | 14 |
| 600 Cafe | Family | $ | Yes | Yes | B/L/D | V/M | 14 |
| Airport Inn | Family | $ | Yes | Yes | L/D | | 14 |
| Blimpie's Subs | Fast Food | $ | Yes | | L/D | | 14 |
| Hole In The Wall Supper Club/Casino | Steaks & Seafood | $$/$$$ | Yes | Yes | L/D | V/M | 14 |
| Shirley's Cafe | American | $ | | | B/L | | 14 |
| The Cellar Restaurant | Family | $/$$ | Yes | B/W | B/L/D | Major | 14 |
| **Rails Inn & Motel** | Family | $/$$ | | B/W/C/L | B/L/D | Major | 20 |
| B & L Big Sky Cafe | American | $ | | | B/L/D | | 20 |
| Bloomin Onion | American | $–$$$ | Yes | W/B | B/L/D | V/M | 20 |
| Dairy Queen | Fast Food | $ | Yes | | L/D | | 20 |
| Far West Cafe & Lounge | Family | $ | | Yes | B/L/D | | 20 |
| Hong Kong Restaurant | Chinese | $ | | B/W | L/D | Major | 20 |
| M & M Pizza | Pizza | $ | | B | L/D | V/M | 20 |
| Speedway Diner | American | $ | | | B/L/D | | 20 |
| Top That! | Deli | $ | | | B/L/D | | 20 |
| Gramma Sharon's Family Restaurant | Family | $ | Yes | | B/L/D | Major | 23 |
| Green Dragon Pizza | Pizza | $ | Yes | Yes | L/D | Major | 23 |
| Jane's Home Cookin | Family | $ | Yes | | B/L/D | Major | 23 |
| Sakalaris' Kitchen | Family | $ | Yes | | B/L/D | V/M | 23 |
| The Loft Steaks & Seafood | Steaks & Seafood | $$/$$$ | Yes | Yes | L/D | Major | 23 |
| The Tavern | Steaks & Seafood | $ | Yes | Yes | L/D | Major | 23 |
| Wagon Wheel Cafe | American | $ | | | B/L/D | | 28 |
| Cashway Cafe | Homestyle | $ | Yes | | B/L/D | | 30 |
| Chuck's Tastee Freez | Fast Food | $ | | | L/D | | 30 |

## Dining Quick Reference

Price Range refers to the average cost of a meal per person: ($) $1-$6, ($$) $7-$11, ($$$) $12-up. Cocktails: "Yes" indicates full bar; Beer (B)/Wine (W), Service: Breakfast (B), Brunch (BR), Lunch (L), Dinner (D). Businesses in bold print will have additional information under the appropriate map locator number in the body of this section.

| RESTAURANT | TYPE CUISINE | PRICE RANGE | CHILD MENU | COCKTAILS BEER WINE | SERVICE | CREDIT CARDS | MAP LOCATOR NUMBER |
|---|---|---|---|---|---|---|---|
| Homestead Inn | Family | $ | Yes | | B/L/D | V/M | 30 |
| Judges Chambers | Fine Dining | $/$$ | | B/W | L/D | Major | 30 |
| Powder River Lanes | Family | $/$$ | | B/W | B/L/D | | 30 |
| Hitching Post Cafe | American | $ | | | B/L/D | V/M | 35 |
| Justus Inn | American | $/$$ | | B | B/L/D | | 35 |
| Chicken Coop | Fast Food | $ | | | L/D | | 36 |
| Dull Knife Cafe | American | $ | | | D | | 36 |
| Bob's Place | American | $/$$ | Yes | Yes | B/L/D | Major | 38 |
| Pizza Hut/Taco Bell | Pizza/Mexican | $/$$ | Yes | B | L/D | V/M/D | 38 |
| Subway | Fast Food | $ | Yes | | L/D | | 38 |

## Motel Quick Reference

Price Range: ($) Under $40 ; ($$) $40-$60; ($$$) $60-$80, ($$$$) Over $80. Pets [check with the motel for specific policies] (P), Dining (D), Lounge (L), Disabled Access (DA), Full Breakfast (FB), Cont. Breakfast (CB), Indoor Pool (IP), Outdoor Pool (OP), Hot Tub (HT), Sauna (S), Refrigerator (R), Microwave (M) (Microwave and Refrigerator indicated only if in majority of rooms), Kitchenette (K). All Montana area codes are 406.

| HOTEL | PHONE | NUMBER ROOMS | PRICE RANGE | BREAKFAST | POOL/ HOT TUB SAUNA | NON SMOKE ROOMS | OTHER AMENITIES | CREDIT CARDS | MAP LOCATOR NUMBER |
|---|---|---|---|---|---|---|---|---|---|
| Wibaux Super 8 Motel | 796-2666 | 35 | $$ | CB | | Yes | P/DA | Major | 1 |
| **Best Western Jordan Inn** | 377-5555 | 86 | $$ | | IP/S | Yes | K/P/D/M/R/L | Major | 2 |
| **El Centro Motel** | 377-5211 | 27 | $ | | | Yes | K/P/M/R | Major | 2 |
| **Charley Montana Bed & Breakfast** | 365-3207 | 7 | $$$ | FB | | Yes | | Major | 2 |
| **Hostetler House Bed & Breakfast** | 377-4505 | 3 | $$ | FB | HT | Yes | | Major | 2 |
| **Comfort Inn** | 365-6000 | 48 | $$ | CB | IP/HT | Yes | P/M/R/DA | Major | 3 |
| **Super 8 Motel** | 365-5671 | 52 | $$$ | CB | | Yes | P/DA | Major | 3 |
| King's Inn | 365-5636 | 35 | $ | | IP/HT | Yes | P/M/R/DA | Major | 3 |
| Budget Motel | 377-8334 | 24 | $/$$ | | | Yes | K/P/M/R | Major | 3 |
| Days Inn | 365-6011 | 59 | $$ | CB | | Yes | P/DA | Major | 3 |
| **Parkwood Motel** | 377-2349 | 17 | $ | | | Yes | K/P | Major | 4 |
| Riverside Inn-Budget Host | 365-2349 | 36 | $$ | CB | | Yes | K/P | Major | 4 |
| Kempton Hotel & Wagon Wheel Antiques | 635-5543 | 14 | $/$$ | | | | K/P/L | V/M | 8 |
| Diamond Motel & Campground | 637-5407 | 1 | $ | | | | K/P/D/R/DA | V/M/D | 8 |
| Gingham Lady Motel | 232-9919 | 20 | $ | | | | | V/M | 11 |
| **Holiday Inn Express** | 232-1000 | 52 | $$$ | CB | DA | | | Major | 13 |
| **Guesthouse Inn** | 232-3661 | 61 | $$$ | CB | | Yes | | | 13 |
| **Budget Inn** | 232-3550 | 49 | $$ | CB | OP | Yes | DA | Major | 13 |
| **Comfort Inn** | 232-3141 | 49 | $$$ | CB | IP/HT | Yes | M/R/DA | Major | 13 |
| Best Western War Bonnet Inn | 232-4560 | 54 | $$$ | CB | IP/HT/S | Yes | M/R | Major | 13 |
| Motel 6 | 232-7040 | 88 | $ | | | Yes | DA | Major | 13 |
| Super 8 Motel | 232-5261 | 58 | $$ | CB | | Yes | DA | Major | 13 |
| **Historic Olive Hotel** | 232-2450 | 59 | $–$$$ | | | Yes | P/D/L/DA | Major | 14 |
| **Rails Inn & Motel** | 356-2242 | 50 | $$ | FB | | Yes | FB/P/D/L/DA | Major | 20 |
| **Best Western Sundowner Inn** | 356-2216 | 40 | $$ | | | Yes | P/M/R | Major | 20 |
| **Westwind Motor Inn** | 356-2038 | 33 | $$ | CB | | Yes | P/DA | | 20 |
| **Nansel Ranch Guest House** | 356-7253 | | $$$$ | | HT | | | Major | 20 |
| **Restwel Motel** | 356-2771 | 16 | $ | | | Yes | K/P/M/R | Major | 20 |
| Montana Inn | 356-7947 | 27 | $ | | | Yes | K/P/R | V/M | 20 |
| Montana Motel | 778-3315 | 11 | $$ | | | Yes | | Major | 23 |
| Roy's Motel | 778-3321 | 22 | $ | | HT | Yes | P | Major | 23 |
| Sagebrush Inn | 778-3341 | 40 | $$ | | | Yes | P/DA | Major | 23 |
| Guest House Motel | 775-6337 | 5 | $ | | | | P | Major | 28 |
| Midway Motel | 775-6619 | 6 | $$ | | | | | Major | 28 |
| Buckskin Inn | 436-2929 | | | | | | | | 30 |
| C-Bar-J Motel | 436-2671 | | | | | | | | 30 |
| Quarter Horse Motor Inn | 436-2626 | | | | | | | | 30 |
| Western 8 Motel | 784-2400 | 19 | $ | | | Yes | DA | Major | 35 |
| Fort Union Inn | 748-2553 | 20 | $ | | | Yes | P/DA | Major | 38 |
| Super 8 Motel | 748-3400 | 40 | $$ | CB | | Yes | DA | Major | 38 |

# SECTION 2

## BILLINGS AND SURROUNDING AREA

*Billings viewed from the rimrocks.*

### WEATHER AVERAGES

**Billings**

| January | |
|---|---|
| Average High: | 31.8° F |
| Average Low: | 13.7° F |
| Record High : | 68.0° F |
| Record Low : | -30.0° F |
| Average Precip.: | 0.90 in |
| Rain/Snow Days: | 8 days |

| April | |
|---|---|
| Average High: | 57.1° F |
| Average Low: | 34.0° F |
| Record High : | 92.0° F |
| Record Low : | -5.0° F |
| Average Precip.: | 1.74 in |
| Rain/Snow Days: | 10 days |

| July | |
|---|---|
| Average High: | 86.7° F |
| Average Low: | 58.3° F |
| Record High : | 106.0° F |
| Record Low : | 41.0° F |
| Average Precip.: | 0.94 in |
| Rain/Snow Days: | 7 days |

| October | |
|---|---|
| Average High: | 60.6° F |
| Average Low: | 37.5° F |
| Record High : | 90.0° F |
| Record Low : | -7.0° F |
| Average Precip.: | 1.14 in |
| Rain/Snow Days: | 6 days |

**Bighorn Lake**

| January | |
|---|---|
| Average High: | 33.2° F |
| Average Low: | 4.9° F |
| Average Precip.: | 0.20 in |

| April | |
|---|---|
| Average High: | 61.5° F |
| Average Low: | 30.9° F |
| Average Precip.: | 0.49 in |

| July | |
|---|---|
| Average High: | 90.9° F |
| Average Low: | 53.5° F |
| Average Precip.: | 0.54 in |

| October | |
|---|---|
| Average High: | 65.9° F |
| Average Low: | 31.1° F |
| Average Precip.: | 0.34 in |

**Bighorn River**

| January | |
|---|---|
| Average High: | 33.2° F |
| Average Low: | 4.9° F |
| Average Precip.: | 0.780 in |

| April | |
|---|---|
| Average High: | 61.5° F |
| Average Low: | 30.9° F |
| Average Precip.: | 1.77 in |

| July | |
|---|---|
| Average High: | 90.9° F |
| Average Low: | 53.5° F |
| Average Precip.: | 0.99 in |

| October | |
|---|---|
| Average High: | 65.9° F |
| Average Low: | 31.1° F |
| Average Precip.: | 0.76 in |

**1.** *Lewis & Clark, Attraction, Gas, Food*

### Hysham

At the turn of the century, shortly after Montana territory received statehood, Hysham was part of vast open area known as Custer County. The Flying E Ranch had thousands of cattle grazing the Yellowstone River Valley, and many of them grazed along the railroad tracks that ran through this area. The trainmen of the Northern Pacific railroad often left supplies ordered by Charlie J. Hysham, an associate of the Flying E, labeled "for Mr. Hysham." The association between the site, the Flying E, and Mr. Hysham stuck and the spot became known as simply Hysham. Today, Hysham is the county seat of Treasure County and is bordered on the north by the Yellowstone River, and to the south by beautiful rolling hills.

This area is rich in history of the early days in the settlement of Montana. Near here, Manuel Lisa built a fur trading post near the mouth of the Bighorn River in 1807. This was the first building in the state of Montana. Fort Cass, the first fort built by the American Fur Company on the Yellowstone, was constructed just three miles below the mouth of the Bighorn. Near the mouth of the Bighorn, the stockade of Fort Pease was built in 1875 as a defense against a part of Sioux Indians and also to serve as a trading post. There are still some remnants of Fort Pease on the original site, but the locations of the other forts remain a mystery.

*David Manning's theater.*

Today, Hysham is a clean, friendly little town. As you enter the town, the historic Yucca Theater stands guard at the end of main street. This distinctive stucco building and its Santa Fe art deco style of architecture seem oddly out of place in this small farming community. Constructed in 1931 by David Manning, a local contractor, the theater was the focal point of entertainment in the area for more than 50 years. The first film shown there was the 1914 classic *A Room With A View*. The last film to grace its screen in 1986 was *Tillie's Punctured Romance*.

David Manning later went on to become one of Montana's most prominent legislators serving in the Montana House of Representatives continuously for 52 years until his retirement in 1985. In 1990, the Manning family donated the theater to the museum across the street. It seemed fitting as most of the museum contains the memorabilia and inventions of Senator Manning.

Section 2

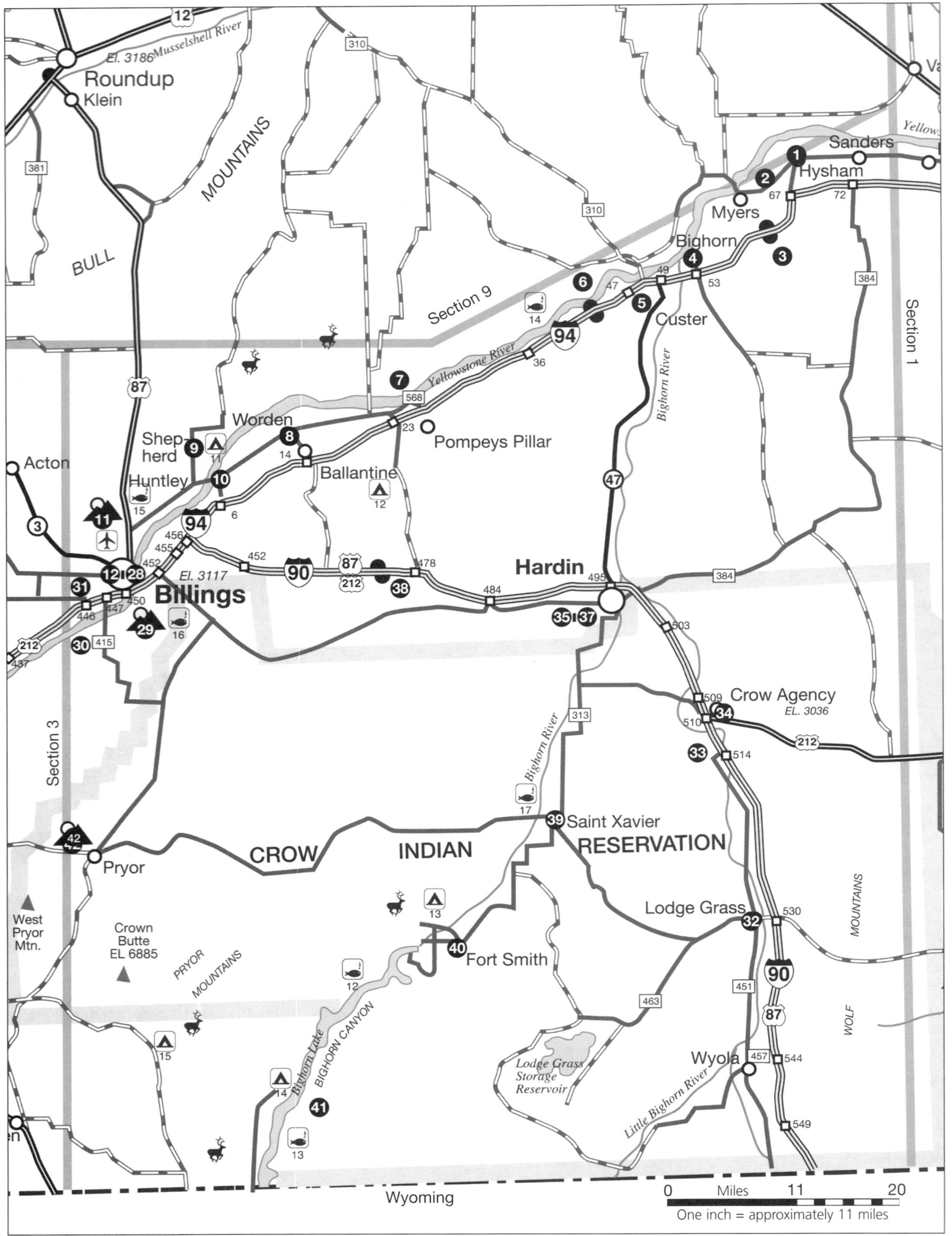

Roundup
Klein
El. 3186
Musselshell River
BULL
MOUNTAINS
Section 9
Sanders
Hysham
Myers
Bighorn
Custer
Yellowstone River
Bighorn River
Section 1
Worden
Shepherd
Pompeys Pillar
Acton
Huntley
Ballantine
Hardin
El. 3117
Billings
Crow Agency
EL. 3036
Section 3
Saint Xavier
CROW
INDIAN
RESERVATION
Pryor
West Pryor Mtn.
Crown Butte EL 6885
PRYOR MOUNTAINS
Lodge Grass
Fort Smith
BIGHORN CANYON
Bighorn Lake
Lodge Grass Storage Reservoir
Wyola
Little Bighorn River
WOLF MOUNTAINS
Wyoming
0 Miles 11 20
One inch = approximately 11 miles

**Legend**

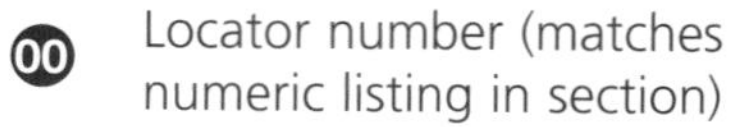
Locator number (matches numeric listing in section)

Wildlife viewing

Campsite (number matches number in campsite chart)

State Park

Fishing Site (number matches number in fishing chart)

Rest stop

Interstate

U.S. Highway

State Highway

County Road

Gravel/unpaved road

### D William Clark
July 27, 1806

*"when we pass the Big Horn I take my leave of the view of the tremendious chain of Rocky Mountains white with Snow in view of which I have been Since the 1st of May last."*

### T Treasure County 89ers Museum
Elliott Ave., Hysham. 342-5252

Local history is preserved with displays called "Tales of Treasure County. There is also a restored early day soda fountain that is open for special occasions. It is directly across the street from the Yucca Theatre. Open Memorial Day through Labor Day.

## 2. *Attraction*

### T Howrey Island
7 miles west of Hysham. 232-7000

This 560-acre Montana Watchable Wildlife area on the Yellowstone River island has numerous trails and lots of waterfowl throughout the year. Bald eagles can be seen throughout the summer. A self guided 1.3 mile nature trail winds through a typical riparian cottonwood forest.

## 3. *Historic Marker*

### H Yellowstone River Trading Posts
south of Hysham

*Even before the Lewis and Clark Expedition returned to St. Louis in 1806, enterprising fur traders looked to the upper Missouri and Yellowstone rivers as a source of profit. At various times between 1807 and 1876, eight trading posts were located between the mouths of the Big Horn and Tongue rivers. Most were owned and operated by the American Fur Company—a firm organized in 1808 by John Jacob Astor. Rather than rely on the rendezvous system and the mountain men, the "Company" built a series of fixed posts designed to encourage the local tribes to trade at the forts. American Fur Company forts were virtual duplicates—each was about 100 square feet with cottonwood palisades and block houses at opposite corners. The forts included Fort Remon or Manuel Lisa (1807-1809), the first Fort Benton (1821), the second Big Horn Post (1824), Fort Cass (1832-1835), Fort Van Buren (1835-1843), Fort Alexander (1842-1850) and two Fort Sarpys.*

*Nearly all the existing accounts of the forts tell stories of a lively trade that was often filled with danger for both trader and Native American. By 1876, the fur trade was no longer profitable and the trading post was abandoned. While their presence was fleeting; they significantly impacted the lives of Native Americans and those who chose to garrison these isolated places. The trading posts represented a colorful era in Montana's history.*

## 4. *Lewis & Clark*

### Big Horn

Seldom does such a small town have such big history. The site of this town has been occupied almost continuously since Capt. William Clark camped here in 1806. In 1807, Manuel Lisa built a trading post here. Fort Van Buren was built near here in 1822 at the mouth of the Big Horn River. In 1876, General Gibbon and a band of 450 men crossed the Yellowstone here on their way to help an already doomed General Custer.

### D William Clark
July 27, 1806

*"about Sunset I Shot a very large fat buck elk from the Canoe near which I encamped, and was near being bit by a rattle Snake."*

## 5. *Historic Marker, Gas, Food*

### Custer

No mystery where this town got its name. It was built after floods washed away the town of Junction City across the river. It served at one time as a freight station for traders hauling supplies to the Crow Indian Reservation. Prior to that it was a favorite camping spot for those traveling to and from Fort Custer at the junction of the Bighorn and Little Bighorn Rivers.

### H Junction
Custer

*The frontier town of Junction was just across the Yellowstone River. It was a stage station for outfits heading for old Fort Custer which used to be twenty-five or thirty miles south of here on the Crow Reservation. The original Reservation took in everything in Montana west of the Tongue River and south of the Yellowstone.*

*There isn't anything left of Junction except a few unkept graves along the hillside but she was lurid in her days. Calamity Jane sojourned there awhile and helped whoop things up. Calamity was born in Missouri, raised in Virginia City, Montana, and wound up at Deadwood, South Dakota. She had quite a dazzling social career.*

*Several years ago they found a skeleton of a three-horned dinosaur in the formation which makes the bluffs on the north side of the river. It must have bogged down some time before Junction did, probably a couple of million years.*

## 6. *Historic Marker*

### H Buffalo Country
west of Custer

*Buffalo meant life to the Plains Indians, and the mountain Indians used to slip down from the hills for their share, too. Some tribes would toll buffalo into a concealed corral and then down them; another system was to stampede a herd over a cliff, but the sporting way was to use bows and arrows and ride them down on a trained buffalo horse.*

*Fat cow was the choice meat. The Indians preserved their meat long before the whites ever had any embalmed beef scandals. They made pemmican by drying and pulverizing the meat, pouring marrow bone grease and oil over it, and packing it away in skin bags. It kept indefinitely, and in food value one pound was worth ten of fresh meat.*

*Tanned robes and rawhide were used for bedding, tepees, clothes, war shields, stretchers, travois, canoes, and bags. Horns and bones made tools and utensils. The buffalo played a prominent part in many of their religious rites and jealousy of hereditary hunting grounds brought on most of the intertribal wars.*

### H Junction of Big Horn and Yellowstone Rivers
west of Custer

*The area which surrounds the mouth of the Big Horn River as it enters the Yellowstone 13 miles east of here is one of the most significant areas in the early history of Montana.*

*The Yellowstone was known universally to the Indians as Elk River, early French explorers called it Riviere Roche Jaune. The Big Horn was called Le Corne.*

*Captain William Clark of the Lewis and Clark Expedition, on his return trip from their journey to the Pacific Ocean, camped on the east bank of the Big Horn River, Saturday, July 26th, 1806.*

*The following year, on November 21st, 1807, an expedition led by Manuel Lisa, a St. Louis fur trader, arrived at the mouth of the Big Horn River. He built a fur trading post which he named Fort Remon in honor of his two-year-old son. This was the first building erected in what is now the State of Montana. From here Lisa sent John Colter to make contact with the Indians who were in winter camp to induce them to come to his post and trade their furs for goods. On this journey Colter discovered the wonders of present-day Yellowstone National Park.*

*In 1876 during the Sioux and Cheyenne Indian campaign of that year, General Terry and Colonel Gibbon marched up the Big Horn River to the site of Custers defeat at the Battle of the Little Big Horn. They arrived two days after the battle. The steamer Far West, carrying supplies, plied the waters of both rivers and brought the wounded from that encounter back to Fort Abraham Lincoln, Dakota Territory.*

## 7. *Historic Marker, Lewis & Clark, Attraction*

### H Camp #44 of the 1873 Yellowstone Expedition
near Pompeys Pillar

*In June, 1873, a Northern Pacific Railroad surveying party escorted by 1,500 soldiers, including the 7th Cavalry under the command of George Armstrong Custer, and 526 civilians, left Dakota Territory for the Yellowstone Valley to survey a route for the second transcontinental railroad.*

*The Lakota Sioux and Cheyenne were opposed to the railroad and dashed with the soldiers on several occasions throughout July. On August 11th, the expedition camped for a well-earned rest at this site. Five*

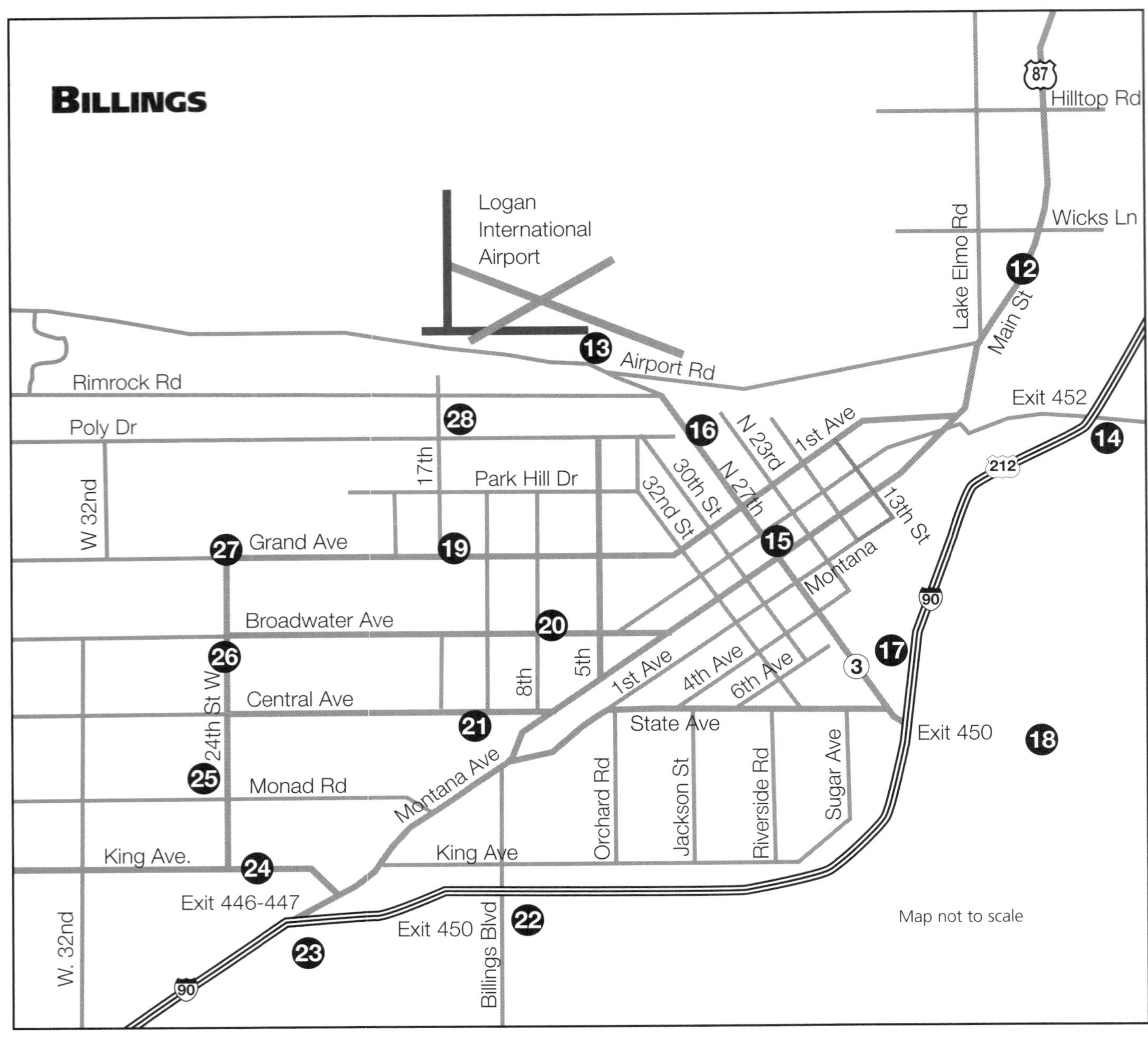


*days later, shots were fired at them by six Lakota warriors hiding near Pompeys Pillar. One man later humorously reported that in the "ensuing scramble for cover, nude bodies [scattered] in all directions on the north bank. Shirts, pants and boots decorated the area along the north bank for a hundred yards" The soldiers returned fire and eventually drove the Indians away; no one was killed in the skirmish. Perhaps figuring that discretion was the better part of valor, the soldiers thereafter chose to "bear the heat rather than risk another swim in the Yellowstone" It was not reported if Custer was among those caught with his pants down by the Lakota on that hot August day in 1873.*

### H Pompey's Pillar
near Pompey's Pillar

*Called lishbiia Anaache or "Place Where the Mountain Lion Dwells' by the Apsaalooka (Crow) people, Pompey's Pillar was a well-known landmark to the Plains Indians. It was here, at a strategic natural crossing of the Yellowstone, or Elk River as it was known to the Apsaalooka, that the Indian people met to trade and exchange information. They painted pictographs and etched petroglyphs onto the sheer cliffs of the feature. Apsaalooka legend reports that Pompey's Pillar was once attached to the sandstone bluffs on the north side of the river. At one point, however, the rock detached itself from the cliffs and rolled across the river to it present site.*

*Pompey's Pillar was also a significant landmark for Euro-American explorers, fur trappers, soldiers and emigrants. It was discovered by Canadian North West Company employee Francois Larocque in 1805. A little less than a year later, on July 25, 1806, it was visited by a 12-man detachment under the command of William Clark that included Sacajawea. and her infant son. Clark carved his name and the date on the rock and named it in honor of Sacajawea's son. He was just one of hundreds of individuals who have left their marks on the rock for generations.*

*Pompey's Pillar is now a National Historic Landmark administered by the Bureau of Land Management and is once again a meeting place for people on the northern Great Plains.*

### D William Clark
July 25, 1806

*The Indians hav made 2 piles of Stone on the top of this Tower. . .have engraved on the face of this rock the figures of animals &c. near which I marked my name and the day of the month & year.*

### D William Clark
July 25, 1806

*"I employed my Self in getting pieces of the rib of a fish which was Semented within the face of the rock it is 3 feet in length tho a part of the end appears to hav been broken off."*

### T Pompey's Pillar
I-94 Exit 23, 30 miles east of Billings. 875-2233

How many times have you traveled somewhere and thought about who had been there before? Pompeys Pillar is like a sandstone history book that reads like a who's who of western frontier history. Look on the rockface for the remains of animal drawings created by people who used the area

# Billings Tour

**Since the American West's early days,** Billings has hosted a cast of famous figures: Custer, Calamity Jane, Buffalo Bill, Crazy Horse, Lewis & Clark and others.

To follow Billings' official beginnings as a city, you only need to follow rivers and railroads. After Lewis & Clark finished their historic expedition across the West, numerous explorers began pushing westward along the many wild rivers, laying railroad tracks as they went.

The Northern Pacific Railroad followed the Yellowstone River, and trainloads of people followed soon after. Just a mile upriver from an established trans-shipment point on the Yellowstone and Missouri Rivers was a valley surrounded by Rimrocks and mountains—an ideal place for a settlement. And so Billings, the "Magic City" was born.

Today, you'll still find glimpses of yesterday throughout the valley. With mansions, museums, galleries and many other historic sites, this city never forgets its past.

Your tour starts at the Billings Chamber Visitor Center where you can get loads of good information on the area. The tour covers nine miles and about 25 minutes of drive time, but you will want to allow at least four hours to stop at every site along the way. Turn right out of the Visitor Center parking lot and head northwest on 27th Street toward downtown. Turn right on Montana Ave. approximately three blocks to...

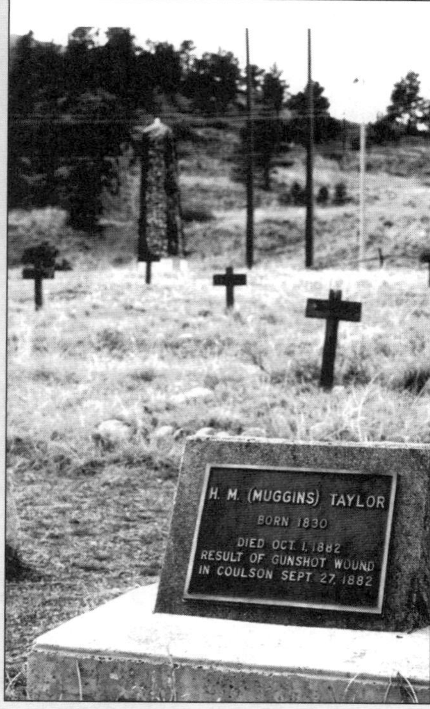


*Boothill Cemetery.*

1. Union Depot. The arrival of the Northern Pacific Railroad in 1882 signaled the real beginning of the private town of Billings, named for the President of the railroad, Frederick Billings. This depot, built in 1909, replaced the first temporary station. From here continue on northeast and bear left on Main Street and follow Main to...

*Yellowstone Art Center*

2. Metra Park. This is the host to events such as rodeos, ice shows, sporting events, concerts and large trade shows. The grounds are the site of Montana's largest event: MontanaFair. Immediately past Metra Park you will turn left to begin winding your way up the rim. You are on...

3. Black Otter Trail. This is a scenic drive which climbs Kelly Mountain, and follows the edge of the Rimrocks where it descends to the valley. Black Otter Trail is named after a Crow chief who was killed here by a Sioux war party. One of the first things you will come upon is...

4. Boot Hill Cemetery. This cemetery marks the only remains of the original river town of Coulson (1877-1885). Many of its occupants met with violent deaths, including Sheriff "Muggins Taylor," the army scout who first carried the news of the Custer Battle to the outside world. Continue on the trail to...

5. Yellowstone Kelly's Grave. Yellowstone Kelly, who lived from 1849 to 1928, was the epitome of a frontiersman, army scout, dispatch rider and hunter. At his own request, he is buried on Kelly Mountain overlooking the Yellowstone River, where he lived his most interesting days. Five mountain ranges can be viewed from here—clockwise from the southeast: the Big Horns, the Pryors, the Beartooths, the Crazys, and the Snowys. Continue up the trail to the airport. Directly across from the airport is...

6. The Peter Yegen Jr. Museum. This museum houses many artifacts of early history. In the basement is an authentic Roundup Wagon and a diorama featuring pioneer life. Outside you'll find No. 1031, the last Northern Pacific Steam Engine operated in Billings. There's also a lifesize statue, the "Range Rider of the Yellowstone," depicting the days of the open range. Open Tuesday through Friday, 10:30 a.m. to 5 p.m., Sundays 2–5 p.m. Turn left out of the parking lot and catch the turn back down the Rimrocks. Follow this back to 27th Street. Bear right toward downtown. As you enter downtown you will find on your left...

7. The Yellowstone Art Center. This premier museum in a four-state region exhibits western and contemporary art from nationally and internationally acclaimed artists. Leave the museum and continue southeast on 27th Street for a block to 3rd Ave. North. Turn right here and go one block to...

8. The Alberta Bair Theater. This performing arts theater opened in January of 1987. It is now the largest performing arts theater between Minneapolis and spokane. It is also home to the Billings Symphony, Community Concerts and the Fox Committee for the performing arts. Leave the theater again on 3rd Ave. North heading southwest to Division Street. Turn left here. On your right will be ...

9. The Moss Mansion. Built in 1901 for the Preston B. Moss family, the elegant home was designed by H. J. Hardenbergh, architect of the Waldorf-Astoria and Plaza Hotels in New York City. It was purchased in 1987 with original furnishings from the estate of Melville Moss. Tours are available March through October and at Christmas time. When you leave the Mansion, continue south on Division to Montana Ave. Turn left here and go to N. 28th Street. Just across the intersection to your right is...

10. The Western Heritage Center. This regional museum was originally built in 1909 as the Parmly Billings Library, and is named for the son of the founder of Billings. Exhibits change every six weeks (themes include saddle makers, steam power, quilts and western art). This museum is open Tuesday to Saturday, 10 a.m. to 5 p.m. and Sunday 1 p.m. to 5 p.m.

*Partially reprinted from Billings Chamber of Commerce brochure.*

for rendezvous, campsites, and hunting.

Pompey's Pillar National Historic Landmark contains exceptional cultural, recreational and wildlife values. It represents the legacy of the early West and its development. At the Pillar, there is evidence of Native Americans, early explorers, fur trappers, the U.S. Cavalry, railroad development and early homesteaders, many of whom left their history embedded in this sandstone pillar. Captain William Clark, his guide, Sacagawea, her 18-month old son (nicknamed "Pompey") and a crew of 11 men stopped near the 200-foot-high rock outcropping on the return leg of the Lewis and Clark Expedition.

On July 25, 1806, Clark carved his signature and the date in the rock and recorded doing so in his journal. "I marked my name and the day of the month and year," wrote Captain William Clark in his journal on Friday, July 25, 1806. This inscription is the only surviving on-site physical remains of the Lewis and Clark Expedition. Clark named this rock Pompy's Tower. Pompy was Clark's nickname for young Baptiste Charbonneau whose mother, Sacagawea, was the party's interpreter. Pompy means "little chief" in the Shoshoni language. In 1814 the landmark was renamed when the journals of the Lewis and Clark Expedition were published. The historic signature remains today, and visitors can walk on a boardwalk to see it.

A river landmark and rendezvous point for early travelers, Pompey's Pillar stands 150 feet above the Yellowstone River. A stairway ascends up 220 steps to the top of the pillar for an outstanding view of the surrounding area. You can get a closer look at Clark's signature half way up the

*Pompey's Pillar.*

climb. Admission is $3 per vehicle, open Memorial Day–September. Walk-in visits are allowed in the off-season. *Reprinted from www.recreation.gov and the BLM site brochure.*

## 8. *Attraction, Gas, Food*

## Worden

Named after a prominent Montana family, Worden has also prospered in farming due to the irrigation project. Stop into the Huntley Project Museum of Irrigated Agriculture, located in Worden, for an interesting look at farming artifacts, machinery and displays.

### T Huntley Project Museum of Irrigated Agriculture

2561 S. 22nd Rd., Worden

This is a great stop for visitors interested in agriculture and irrigation. The museum features a unique display of farming and irrigation machinery and artifacts and has a neat gift shop attached.

## 9.

## Shepherd

Shepherd was named after R.E. Shepherd, owner of the Billings Land and Irrigation Company and the Merchants National Bank. This area was used for cattle ranching in the early part of the 1900s, until the creation of an irrigation canal throughout the area was built for farmlands. Many immigrants poured into the area to try and start a new life in farming, but eastern Montana is known for drought, thistle, coyotes, prairie dogs and grasshoppers, and a combination of all of these forced the land back to ranching. It has become a suburb of Billings.

## 10. *Gas, Food*

## Huntley

The town of Huntley was established in 1877 just a mile from today's Huntley. The post office was a stopping point for travelers and traders on the Yellowstone River, and served as the base for steamboat travel on the river. Huntley still remains an area with rich farmlands.

## 11. *Attraction*

### T Lake Elmo State Park

Billings. 254-1310 (summer), 247-2940 (winter)

Located in the Billings Heights area, the 64-acre Lake Elmo is a popular recreation area for locals and visitors. There is a great beach that is well maintained and features lifeguards on duty during summer high-use times. Wind surfing has become a favorite activity of this area, fishing is excellent with lots of large mouth bass, yellow perch and crappie, and the hiking/biking trail is wheel-chair accessible.

## 12. *Historic Marker, Attraction, Gas, Food, Lodging, Shopping*

## Billings

Billings, established in 1882, was named for Frederick Billings, president of the Northern Pacific Railroad, and is Montana's largest and perhaps most economically diverse city. Here you'll find the warm hospitality and rugged beauty of the West blended with the modern conveniences and opportunities of a dynamic, vigorous and progressive community.

Native Americans ventured throughout this area over 10,000 years ago, leaving their traces behind through different pictographs and petroglyphs. Due to the abundance of wildlife and the flowing Yellowstone River, the area was later inhabited by the Sioux, Shoshone, Crow, and Blackfeet tribes, all at different times throughout history.

The first white inhabitants came to this area in 1877, setting up the first trade center and McAndow's store, and they called the town Coulson. Coulson was the largest early settlement on the Upper Yellowstone at that time. They set up a ferry crossing across the Yellowstone River which made the passing from the army base of Fort Custer to Bozeman possible. They made a prosperous living selling food, grain and goods to soldiers passing through.

The city is nicknamed "The Magic City," as it developed "like magic" during the railroad's westward expansion. From its humble beginnings as a railhead for the Northern Pacific, Billings has blossomed into a sophisticated city whose population doubles nearly every 30 years.

Billings' primary trading area, in excess of 125,000 square miles, is one of the largest in the United States. In addition to its roles as a regional trade, energy, and service center, Billings is the educational and medical center for the region. With two state-of-the-art hospitals, sixteen clinics, and hundreds of physicians, the area offers every major medical specialty, along with a complete range of surgical services and emergency care. The area is also home to MSU-Eastern Montana College, Rocky Mountain College, and Billings Vocational Center.

Recreational opportunities in the area are abundant. A short drive takes you to the Little Bighorn Battlefield where General Custer took his "Last Stand." Yellowstone Park is also only a brief distance away. The drive there takes you onto the scenic Beartooth Highway referred to by Charles Kuralt as "the most beautiful road in America." Though an engineering triumph as it teeters up switchbacks and hairpin curves with names like "Mae West" and "Frozen Man," it can be very tedious driving and should not be undertaken if you want to get to Yellowstone Park quickly. The highway can close without notice due to snow in this high country. The alternate route on I–90, though not as exciting or scenically beautiful, is much safer and better suited for one who is short on time.

The Billings area is surrounded by seven mountain ranges: the Pryors, Big Horns, Bulls, Snowys, Crazys, Absarokas and Beartooths. Standing on the north rim of the city, the splendor of Montana is visible all around. The city itself is home to Lake Elmo, one of Montana's state parks. Other nearby natural attractions include Pompey's Pillar, and the Pictograph Caves.

In addition to the outdoor recreational opportunities, Billings is host to hoards of entertainment. Year-round theaters host nationally known entertainers, concerts, dramatic and musical productions, as well as symphony performances. Located in the heart of Downtown Billings, the 5.12 million dollar Alberta Bair Theater serves as the hub of cultural entertainment in the city, as it is home to the Billings Community Concert Association and the Billings Symphony.

Metra, Yellowstone County's 12,000 seat arena and civic center, is located at MetraPark, the area's county fairgrounds. The arena hosts major entertainment events, as well as indoor sports events such as rodeos, ice hockey, and tractor pulls. MetraPark itself contains a 7,000 seat grandstand and horse racing track. Races run during August and September.

Billings is also equipped with a plethora of museums for those wanting to relax. The Yellowstone Art Center, The Western Heritage Center, and the Peter Yegen Jr. Museum are three of the top choices. There are also more historic sites in town than can be seen in a day. The Moss Mansion is one highlight that shouldn't be missed. Built at the turn of the century for Preston Moss, one of Montana's wealthiest men, the mansion is maintained as it was originally furnished and decorated. It cost $105,000 in 1903, a time when the average house cost was about $3,000.

Whatever your pleasure, Billings has it! From fun entertainment to exciting recreation, fine dining to excellent shopping, you will find it here.

### H The Place Where the White Horse Went Down

Billings Heights area

*In 1837-38 a smallpox epidemic spread from the American Fur Trading Company steamboat St. Peter which had docked at Fort Union. The terrible disease for which the Indians had no immunity eventually affected all Montana tribes. A story is told among the Crow of two young warriors returning from a war expedition who found their village stricken. One discovered his sweetheart among the dying, and both warriors, grieving over loss of friends and family, were despondent and frustrated because nothing could alter the course of events. The young warriors dressed in their finest clothing and mounted a snowwhite horse. Riding double and singing their death-songs, they drove the blindfolded horse over a cliff and landed at what is now the eastern end of the Yellowstone County Exhibition grounds. Six teenage boys and six teenage girls who were not afflicted with the disease witnessed the drama; they buried the dead warriors and left the camp. Great loss of life among the tribe followed in the wake of the epidemic. Although time has reduced the height of the cliff, the location is remembered even today as The Place Where the White Horse Went Down.*

### T Metra Park

308 6th Ave. N, Billings. 256-2422
or 800-366-8538

Recreational opportunities in and around the Billings area are abundant. Metra Park is the 12,000 seat arena and civic center at the county fairgrounds. The arena hosts major entertainment events, indoor sports and rodeos. It also features a horse racing track that runs during August and September.

### A FAS-Break Auto Repair

605 Main St., Billings. 248-2673

### A Zane's 24 Hour Road Service

Airport Rd. & Main, Billings. 246-5405

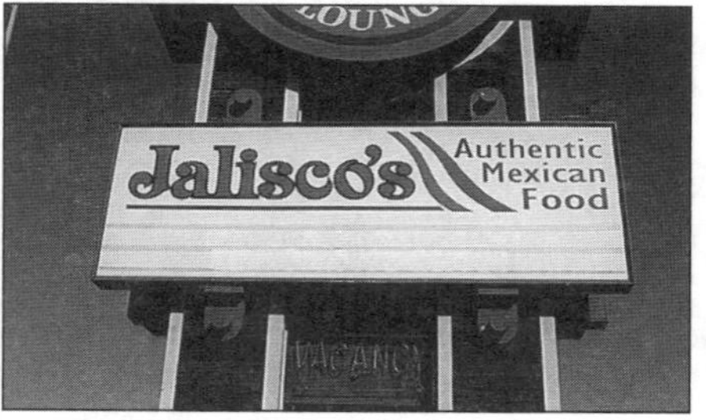


### F Jalisco's

403 Main St., Billings. 245-7077.

Run by the Salazar family, Jalisco's offers a variety of dining choices with Mexican, Italian, and American items on the menu. The restaurant has a good reputation and a warm atmosphere. The recipes have been created by the family after years of research, using only the finest ingredients. Their Mexican food is authentic, with everything made from scratch—absolutely no canned food! They offer daily specials that are always different, with prime rib on Fridays and Saturdays. You will find a nice, quiet atmosphere, perfect for families. Located next to a lounge and casino on Main Street in Billings Heights.

### F Godfather's Pizza

905 Main St., Billings Heights, 252-0865.

The fun atmosphere at Godfather's Pizza is great for group gatherings, family dinners, or just a relaxing meal out. Offering two locations in Billings, they feature a wide variety of pizzas to choose from, with golden and thin crusts and many topping choices. If you're not in the mood for pizza, try the salad bar or a variety of sandwiches. Offering dine in, carry out, and delivery seven days a week. Godfather's also serves specialty buffets and welcomes large groups.

> *Montana Trivia*
>
> In 1873, 1,508,000 bison hides were shipped to St. Louis from Montana. In 1874, only 158,000 were shipped.

### F Golden Phoenix Chinese Restaurant

Airport Rd. & Main, Billings. 256-0319

### F Peking House Express

1414 Main St., Billings. 245-9711

### L Lewis and Clark Inn

1709 1st Ave. N., Billings. 252-4691 or toll free 800-821-6741

The Lewis and Clark Inn, named for the great explorers, is conveniently located within minutes of the Billings Metra Park, Logan International Airport, and beautiful downtown Billings. The Inn offers 57 clean, quiet rooms, modestly priced, with microwaves, refrigerators, and cable TV. They also feature 24 hour desk service, wake up calls, and guest laundry facilities. An added attraction is the Lewis and Clark Café serving breakfast and lunch, including their specialty, The Expeditioner's Delight. The Lewis and Clark Inn is a great headquarters while visiting Yellowstone Park, The Little Big Horn Battlefield, Zoo Montana, and other area attractions.

**L Boothill Inn & Suites**
242 E. Airport Rd., Billings. 245-2000
or 266-boothill(266-8445) or fax 245-8591.
www.boothillinn.com

Located at the foot of Billings' historic rimrocks, just below the original Boot Hill Cemetery, the Boothill Inn and Suites offers you all of the comforts of home, with the conveniences sought after by business and leisure travelers alike. Amenities include an indoor swimming pool with two jacuzzis, a complete fitness center, complimentary continental breakfast each morning and a bedtime snack of fresh baked cookies and milk each evening. Free high speed internet access is available in every guest room. A courtesy van is available to transport you to and from the Airport and Billings' Metrapark and fairgrounds. Call for more information or check out the web site at www.boothill.com.

**L Heights Inn**
1206 Main St., Billings. 252-8451

**S Bottles & Shots Heights**
247 Main St., Billings. 245-8118.

Cigars, Liquor Store & Casino.

## 13. *Attraction*

**T Rimrocks**
Northern edge of Billings

The landmark that seems to stand out most in Billings are the Rimrocks. These sandstone cliffs run along the northern edge of the city and offer spectacular views of the city and the surrounding mountain ranges-the Pryors, Bighorns, Snowys, Crazys and Beartooths. The Black Otter Trail, named after a Crow Indian chief who was buried here, offers a great opportunity for exploring the Rimrocks. Along the trail, you will come across Boothill Cemetery, the site where many residents of Coulson are buried. Coulson was a rough Old West town in the 1800s and outlaws and violence was commonplace. Muggins Taylor, the army scout who spread news of Custer's defeat, is buried here along with 52 Coulson residents. Yellowstone Kelly's grave is just west of Boothill Cemetery. Kelly was known for being adventuresome and quite a frontiersman. He spoke both Crow and Sioux languages and guided the army after Custer's defeat.

### On the Trail of Lewis and Clark

It is on this stretch that the only physical evidence of the Lewis and Clark Expedition can be found. Clark reached a large sandstone landmark he named Pompy's Tower after Sacajawea's son. Here he carved his name and the date and climbed to the top of the tower. His carving can still be seen today.

**T Peter Yegen Jr. Yellowstone County Museum**
At Logan International Airport, Billings. 252-0163

The Museum incorporates an 1893 log cabin built by Paul McCormick, Sr., a pioneer Montana cattleman. McCormick used the cabin as a social center and hosted many lively get togethers there, including entertaining his close friend, President Teddy Roosevelt. The cabin still has its original sod roof and several artifacts belonging to the McCormick family. An observation platform covers the lower addition, giving a breathtaking view of the Yellowstone Valley, including the city of Billings and the snow-capped Beartooth, Pryor, Crazy and Bighorn mountain ranges.

The permanent collection of the Museum contains over 20,000 artifacts dating from prehistory through the Fur Trade Era, the Post-Reservation Period and both World Wars. The Museum's extensive collection of Plains Indian artifacts includes feather bonnets, coups sticks, pipes and pipe bags, a rare dog travois, moccasins, parfleche bags, articles of clothing, saddles, and many other items of everyday use. Cowboy memorabilia includes saddles, chaps, bridles, spurs, firearms, branding irons and other western gear from early area cowboys. Everyday house hold goods display what life was like for the area's pioneers. The facility has several thousand historic photographs depicting local and regional history. Located on the Museum grounds is one of the last steam switch engines to operate in the Billings yards, American Locomotive Company #1031, It was donated to the Museum by the Northern Pacific Railroad Company in 1956. A short distance away is a statue of 1920s silent film star William Hart, in his role as Range Rider of the Yellowstone. It was sculpted by C.C. Cristadoro and presented by Hart to the people of Billings in 1923.

The Museum's Landmarks Gallery features changing exhibits which have recently included internationally known artists LeRoy Greene and J. K. Ralston. They are open Monday-Friday from 10:30 a.m.–5:00 p.m. and Saturday from 10:30 a.m. –3:00 p.m. www.pyjrycm.org. Admission is free. *Reprinted from Museum brochure.*

**14.** *Gas, Food*

**15.** *Attraction, Gas, Food, Lodging, Shopping, Miscellaneous*

### T Western Heritage Center
2822 Montana Ave., Billings. 256-6809

The Western Heritage Center is located in the Billings Historic District on Montana Avenue. It resides in the old Parmly Library that was donated to the city in 1901 by Fredrick Billings Jr. The museum features wonderful historic displays of the Yellowstone River Region. There is a large collection of historic photographs, artifacts and other memorabilia that invite you to revisit the past of the frontier life. Relief maps give a good overview of the region's natural landforms. The Center also offers tours, educational programs and organizes a number of cultural events Admission is free and it is open daily year round, except closed the month of January. See their web site at www.ywhc.org for more information.

### T Yellowstone Art Museum
401 N. 27th St. in downtown Billings. 256-6804. http://yellowstone.artmuseum.org

There is no lack of cultural experiences in Billings. The Yellowstone Art Museum resides in the restored old jailhouse, and over the years it has acquired a reputation as one of the finest contemporary art museums in the Northern Rockies. The large permanent collection offers an array of some of the most important artists working in the west. The temporary galleries show interesting exhibitions of international acclaim, and change throughout the year. The museum also features different educational programs and classes for all ages.

More than a snapshot, more than a picture, the Yellowstone Art Museum is a rich tapestry of the visions and voices that make up the West. It has quickly acquired a reputation as the finest contemporary art museum in the Northern Rockies. With a Permanent Collection of more than 1,900 pieces and temporary galleries which house exhibitions of international acclaim, the museum represents the most comprehensive resource in this region for the appreciation of 20th Century art.

The museum's Permanent Collection encompasses a wide range of aesthetic experiences. The Montana Gallery is home to some of the most important artists currently working in the West. With sculpture by Deborah Butterfield, paintings by Ted Waddell, and drawings by Bill Stockton, the Montana Collection represents a thorough cross-section of today's most interesting visual expression.

The Virginia Snook Collection, in the gallery of the same name, is the largest publicly held collection of author and illustrator Will James' work in the United States. It extends the museum's scope and broadens its appeal to visitors who identify with the traditions of the west. Also included in the Snook Collection are works by C.M. Russell, Joseph Henry Sharp, and other notable historic artists. *Source: Museum brochure*

### T Moss Mansion
914 Division St., Billings. 256-5100

The Moss Mansion is a unique historical look into the wealthy lifestyle that was present in the early 1900s. This turn-of-the-century mansion built in 1902 for Preston B. Moss, a Billings banker, has become a monument to the wealth of Montana in those early years. The house cost $105,000 to build when the average house cost only $3000. The three-story home contains original furnishings of Preston B. Moss and the grounds are well-kept with magnificent gardens of perennials, annuals and roses. The architect was Henry Janeway Hardenbergh, designer of the original Waldorf Astoria, Astoria, Plaza, and other fine hotels. Regular tours are also available. The mansion is open to the public with admission charged.

### T Alberta Bair Theater
Broadway & 3rd Ave. N, Billings. 256-6052

Billings is a great spot to catch some local entertainment. Year-round theatres host nationally known entertainers, concerts, dramatic and musical productions as well as symphony performances. Located in the heart of Downtown Billings is the Alberta Bair Theater that is home to the Billings Community Concert Association and the Billings Symphony.

### T Museum of Women's History
2423 Pine, Billings. 245-4871 or 657-2191

## Montana Trivia

Billings has been called the "Wall Street of the West." Over $150 million in livestock is sold annually at Billings' public Auction Yards.

### A Cono Mart Super Store #5
2701 6th Ave. N., Billings. 252-6504

Locally owned & operated, convenience store, friendly service, clean restrooms, and 24-hour fuel pumps.

### A L.P. Anderson Tire Company
3741 Montana Ave., Billings. 252-5151

### F Club Carlin
2501 Montana Ave., Downtown Billings. 245-2500, www.clubcarlin.com

The Club Carlin is Billings' new hot night spot, featuring quality live entertainment in a classy and comfortable atmosphere. Located in the Billings Historical District, the club is part of the beautifully restored 1912 Hotel Carlin. They maintain the turn-of-the-century decor and hospitality. The Carlin offers fantastic food, drinks, and service with a variety of entertainment weekly including Big Band, Jazz, and many others. You never know who may be dropping in for an evening jam. Give them a call for the latest performance line-up.

### F McCormick Cafe
2419 Montana Ave., Downtown Billings. 255-9555, www.mccormickcafe.com

The McCormick Cafe has quickly become a jewel in the crown of the beautifully restored Billings Historical District. The cafe opened to fantastic reviews and is a perfect mix between New York class and Montana warmth and hospitality. Guests are treated to a fabulous selection of breakfasts, lunches, desserts, and coffees prepared with the care and experience that turns a simple meal into a memorable event. Experience the cafe's sensational soups and unique sandwiches weekdays 7 a.m.–4 p.m. & Sat. 8 a.m.–3 p.m.

### F The Rex
2401 Montana Ave., Billings. 245-7477.

In the turn-of-the-century building in the heart of Billings Historic District, The Rex has built its reputation on great food. They pride themselves on serving fresh seafood flown in twice weekly and top quality certified angus beef. The Rex's menu has something for everyone—prime rib, steaks, seafood, pasta, chops, and specialties. The Rex has a full bar and has received awards from Wine Spectator Magazine for its high quality wine list. In 1998 a Patio Bar & Grill was added, serving lunch Monday through Friday from 11:30 a.m. They feature unique sandwiches, pizzas, salads, appetizers, rotisserie chicken, and daily specials. Outside dining is available in season. The Rex has become known by locals as one of "Billings best."

### F Rocket Burritos Gourmet Burritos & Sodas
111 N. 29th St., Billings. 248-5231

### F Juliano's
2912 7th Ave. N., Billings. 248-6400

### F Bruno's Italian Specialties
1002 1st Ave. N., Billings. 248-1589

## Montana Trivia

One scout and a horse named Commanche were the sole survivors from General George Custer's unit of 215 men at the Battle of the Little Big Horn. Custer was not the only member of his family to perish at the battle. Along with him went a nephew, a brother-in-law, and his brother Tom.

### L The Josephine Bed & Breakfast
514 N. 29th St., Billings. 248-5898.
www.thejosephine.com

This charming historic home offers comfortable, elegant rooms and delicious gourmet breakfasts. All rooms are complete with a private bath, and a whirlpool suite is available. The rooms are also modem friendly and have cable television. Enjoy the comfort and elegance of The Josephine, with the uncompromising convenience of the pleasant downtown location. The Josephine has received a Double Diamond AAA rating. For more information and photos go to www.thejosephine.com. Reservations are suggested.

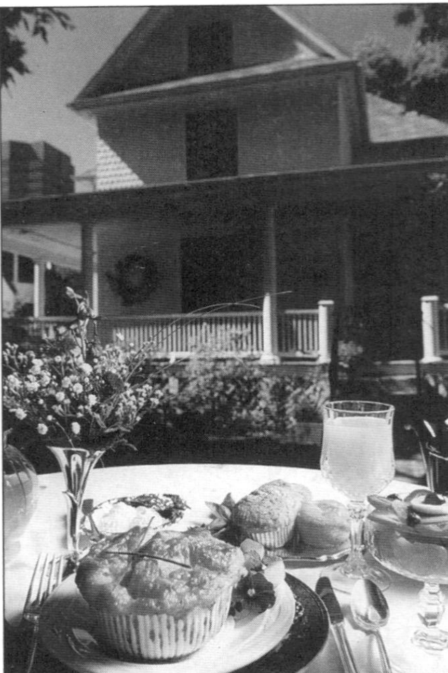

*The Josephine Bed & Breakfast*

## Montana Trivia

General George Armstrong Custer was 34th out of 34 in his graduation class at West Point.

### L Sheraton Billings
27 27th Ave., Billings. 252-7400 or 800-588-7666

### L Town House Motel
3420 1st Ave. N, Billings. 245-4191

### M The Wellness Center
19 N. 25th St., Downtown Billings. 896-9000.

The Wellness Center, located just off Montana Avenue in the Historic District, specializes in urgent care, family practice, internal medicine, and women's health. They are a complete primary care facility with an on-site laboratory and radiology. Complimentary modalities include acupuncture, naturopathic medicine, massage therapy, Reiki, reflexology, hydrotherapy, and fitness assessment. They accept all insurance for medical care. Six massage therapists are available seven days a week. Stop in for a relaxing massage, or for any of your medical needs.

### M The Yoga Center
2417 Montana Ave., Downtown Billings. 896-9000.

Located in Billings Historic District, The Yoga Center offers yoga classes seven days a week, and drop-ins are more than welcome. They cater to all levels of experience from advanced to those interested in learning more about yoga. They have yoga for all ages. They also sell videos, books, eyebags, and mats. Located right next to the fitness center which features rock climbing, exercise machines, and supervised programs. If you are traveling through the area, drop in and try a yoga class or get a good workout.

### S Lou Taubert Ranch Outfitters
123 N. Broadway, Billings. 245-2248.

Lou Taubert is "One of the Nation's Leading Western Stores." Carrying Wrangler, Justin, Lucchese, Olathe, Pendleton, Cowtown, Laredo, Tony Lama, Resistol, Bailey, Charlie One Horse—some of the most famous brands in the west. They carry men's, women's and children's western wear and will fit you in boots of any size and width. See the exotic boot selection. Specialty items include turquoise jewelry, Vogt Jewelry, leather belts and wallets, Montana Silversmith buckles, bolos, and a wide selection of jewelry. Visit the Fine Ladies Department where they are "Romancing the West." Lou Taubert is easy to find right downtown. Stop in Mon.–Sat. 9:30 a.m.–5:50 p.m.

### S Yesteryears Antiques & Crafts
114 N. 29th St., Billings. 256-3567

Take a step back in time and find that perfect home accent, Montana souvenir or gift. At Yesteryears Antiques and Crafts you'll find treasures steeped in history or handmade by local artisans. This beautifully arranged store has some of the most knowledgeable dealers in the area, supplying an extensive variety of collectibles, furniture, jewelry, glassware, dolls, books, Indian artifacts, and much more. Upstairs you'll enjoy the Crafters Mall where you will find Montana-made items such as ceramics, textiles table accents, quillos, toys, baby gifts, and quilts. The Fireside Room features framed artwork, wall decor, and Christmas collectibles. The pantry is filled with items that will give your kitchen personality! Enjoy their comfy, homey, and relaxed shopping experience.

### S Custer Battlefield Trading Post
2519 Montana Ave., Billings. 256-1876.
www.lastsdtand.com

The Custer Battlefield Trading Post, located on Montana Avenue, is a new addition to the exciting Historic District. Contemporary Native American and Western Art & Antiquities represent some of the finest examples available today. In addition to the exquisite crafts and artwork, Custer Battlefield Trading Post sells fine gift items for those traveling through the region. The store's namesake is the world famous Custer Battlefield Trading Post located directly across from the entrance to the Little Bighorn Battlefield. Many of the artifacts for sale are the result of many years of collecting by the proprietors, Putt & Jill Thompson. Come on down to the Historic District and see the finest Montana has to offer.

S **Oxford Hotel Antiques**
2411 Montana Ave., Billings. 248-2094

**16.** *Attraction, Food, Lodging, Miscellaneous*

T **Mindworks Museum**
1500 N. 30th St., MSU Billings. 657-2242

F **Matthew's Taste of Italy**
1233 N. 27th St., Billings. 254-8530

L **Rimview Inn**
1025 N. 27th, Billings. 248-2622 or reservations only at 800-551-1418

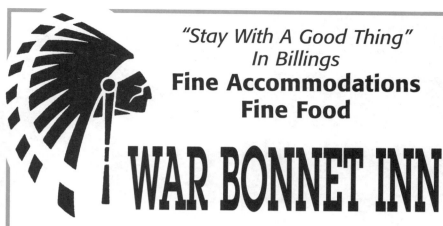

The Rimview Inn is the home of Montana's largest saltwater aquarium It is also conveniently located to Logan Airport, MetraPark, Downtown, MSU Billings, and in walking distance to both hospitals and medical facilities. They provide spacious rooms with all the comforts of home and a free continental breakfast and free 24 hour airport shuttle. A full range of extras include king or queen size beds, and furnished apartments for extended stays. Also available is a guest laundry, headbolt heater plug-ins, and freezer space. They offer conference facilities for up to 40 people. The Rimview Inn is locally owned and operated and you'll find that the management takes great pride in providing quality service and accommodations at affordable daily and weekly rates.

## Montana Trivia

Billings, the seat of Yellowstone County, is the most urban county seat in the state with almost ninety thousand people. It also has the highest population density with 48,3 people per square mile. It is known as "The Magic City" because its population doubles every thirty years. Only seven towns in Montana have populations greater than twenty-five thousand.

L **Juniper Inn**
1315 N. 27th St., Billings. 245-4128.

Welcome to the Juniper Inn—located close to the airport, medical community, hospitals, and both colleges. This family operated motel offers a variety of rooms from comfortable queen size beds to large elegant jacuzzi suites with king size beds. They have a shuttle service and continental breakfast for all guests.

L **Cherry Tree Inn**
823 N. 28th St., Billings. 252-5603 or Reservations at 800-237-5882

The Cherry Tree Inn of Billings was built by George Washington. That is George Washington's namesake thus the clever name for his business. The current owners have expanded the Washington connection by decorating the Inn's lobby with art depicting Colonial America and the

Revolutionary War. They even provide an excellent lending library on Colonial America for guests. The Inn is located near the Billings Medical Center, Downtown, MSU, and the airport. You'll also find everything you need for a comfortable stay including a free continental breakfast, 24 hour coffee, elevator, electronic security, non-smoking rooms, 24 hour desk, kitchenettes, and guest laundry. Small pets are welcome, and they have very affordable rates. It's a great place to stay!

S **Al's Bootery & Repair Shop**
1820 1st Ave. North, Billings. 245-4827 or toll free at 800-745-4827. www.alsbootery.com

M **Montana State University/Billings**
1500 N. 30th St., Billings. 657-2011 or 800-565-6782, www.msubillings.edu

The Billings campus of Montana State University features programs in liberal arts, education, special education and business and professional degrees. Students are offered bachelor's and master's degrees.

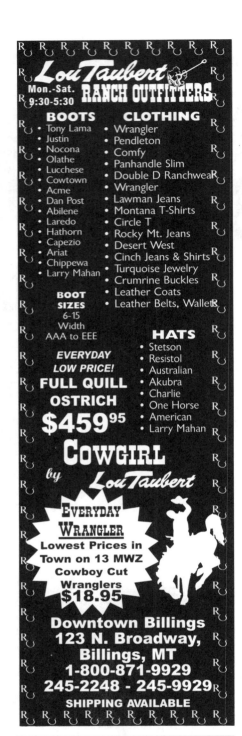

## Montana Trivia

In 1862, Congress passed the Free Homestead Act granting each family 160 acres. In 1878, USGS director John Wesley Powell suggested to Congress that a single homesteading family needed 2,560 acres to survive in Montana. More than thirty years later, Congress increased the allotment to 320 acres. Over 80,000 came to Montana to claim their land. Over 60,000 left after the drought of 1919. Today, the average size farm in Montana is 2,714 acres.

*Big Ice Cave is one of the favorite destinations in the Pryors. A picnic area is only a short distance from the cave.*

# Wild Horses and More!

### Pryor Mountains

In the extreme southeast corner of Carbon County you'll find one of the last remaining herds of wild horses in the country. The 44,000 acre Pryor Mountains National Wild Horse Range was set aside by the Secretary of the Interior in 1968.

Theories of where these horses originated are varied. Some believe they are descendants of those brought to the region by Spanish conquistadors in the 16th century. Others believe they are escaped from domestic herds of local ranchers. Probably, they are a mix of both. Common mustang social units form around a dominant stud, his harem of mares, and their foals.

Getting to them isn't easy, but the trip is worth it. The best route through Montana is via Hwy 310 south out of Laurel. Follow that for 50 miles to Warren. Another 20 miles of gravel road will put you in the canyons of the Pryors.

If you want to go the whole way on paved road, continue on past Warren to Lovell, WY. Just on the east side of town you'll see the turnoff to Hwy. 37. Follow this to the Bighorn Recreation area. If you are more adventurous you can take the turnoff to Barry's Landing.

While exploring this area, watch for Bighorn sheep. They have been restocked in the Pryors and are plentiful.

Keep your eyes open for teepee rings left by ancient tribes. If you look hard enough, you may find pictographs or other archeological evidence of civilizations past.

There is also an abundance of caves here. Big Ice Cave is the most notable. These caves are usually gated and closed off to prevent vandalism. However the Forest Service does conduct weekend tours of Big Ice Cave during the summer. Access these caves from Warren on a long gravel road. When (if) you reach the caves continue on for a short distance to Dry Head Vista. Here you will find a spectacular panorama of the Bighorn Canyon area dropping away for over 4,000 feet.

For access to these caves and additional information about them, contact the Custer National Forest Supervisor's Office in Billings. Write to them at 2602 1st Ave. N., Billings, MT 59103 or call them at (406) 657-6361.

### The Pryor Mountains Are Unique

The Pryor Mountains were named after Sergeant Nathaniel Pryor of the Lewis and Clark Expedition which traversed the nearby Yellowstone River Valley in 1806. The Pryor mountain range is actually an extension of the Bighorn Mountains but is separated from the Bighorns by the Bighorn Canyon.

The Pryor Mountains are unique in many ways. Some of the more notable aspects are the rainfall/snowfall zones and related vegetation from the southern foothill regions to the highest points in the mountain range. Annual rainfall varies from less than five inches in the foothills to twenty inches in the high country. Most of the southern portion of the Wild Horse Range is northern cold desert country.

Differences in rainfall/snowfall contribute to the most diverse plant community in Montana. As you move from the southern desert portion to the upper, lush, sub-alpine portions of the Pryor Mountains, you can see the progression of desert, low bushes to fir trees and grasses. In between these zones is a graduation of plant species. In addition, the bladderpod and Shoshonea are two examples of rare and sensitive plants that are found in the Pryors.

For centuries, the Pryors were home to small bands of Native American people. The warm, dry southern slopes provided a favorable environment during the harsh winter months, while the high elevation lands were occupied at other times of the year. This environment provided a variety of both plant and animal foods. Bighorn sheep, mule deer, bison and elk provided meat and skins while berries, roots and possibly ants supplemented diets.

Hard stone deposits called chert, exist in the Pryors and were used by Native Americans to make projectile points and scraping tools. In fact, the Crow Indian tribe used to refer to the Pryors as the "Arrow-head" mountains.

The Crow Tribe considers many sites within the Pryors sacred. Cultural resources are protected by federal law on public lands and should be left as found for scientific investigation and enjoyment by future visitors.

*Excerpted from BLM pamphlet.*

## 17. *Gas, Food, Lodging, Miscellaneous*

### A Cono Mart Super Store #4

1240 S. 27th St., Billings. 252-6105

Locally owned & operated, convenience store, friendly service, clean restrooms, and 24-hour fuel pumps.

### L War Bonnet Inn

2612 Belknap Ave., Exit 450, I-90 & 27th South, Billings. 248-7761 or Reservations only at 888-242-6023

The War Bonnet Inn is easy to find, but some consider it hard to leave! The 101 cheerful rooms have cable, air conditioning and queen and king sized beds, with a pool for hot summer days. The War Bonnet Inn offers complete facilities for weddings, receptions, meetings, and banquets and many extra services to make your stay comfortable and carefree, including airport shuttle. You'll enjoy relaxing in their Apache Lounge or dining in the Arapaho Dining Room. The War Bonnet has been serving the Billings area for over 30 years and is a proud sponsor of Team Roping and the Northern International Livestock Expo. You'll always enjoy their friendly, warm service and helpful staff.

### M Billings Chamber of Commerce

815 S. 27th St., Billings. 245-4111. 800-735-2635

## 18. *Attraction*

### T Sacrifice Cliff

Across the Yellowstone River south of Billings.

Sacrifice Cliff is unmarked but is located south of the Yellowstone River, opposite Boothill Cemetery. This legendary cliff of the Rimrocks, was believed to be a place of meditation for Crow Indian boys coming of age. A story is also told of two teen Crow brothers who returned to their tribe to find that their sweethearts and much of their tribe had fallen victim to smallpox. They were so filled with anguish that they blindfolded their horses and rode over the 60-foot cliff. Another version of the story says that a Crow party found their village destroyed by the deadly small pox and rode off the cliff in despair.

## 19. *Gas, Food*

### A Champion Auto Store

1447 Grand Ave., Billings. 259-5100 or 800-959-5104

### F Pork Chop John's

1223 Grand Ave., Billings. 252-4650.

John's original pork chop sandwich has been a tradition of quality for over 60 years. Originating in Butte, Montana in 1924, founder John Burkland sold his pork chop sandwich from the back of a wagon. The quality and delicious flavors still remain today with locations in Butte, Bozeman, and Billings. Stop in and see why this famous, mouth-watering sandwich has become a unique part of the Montana experience.

### S Angels on Broadway, Montana Made Angels & Gifts

1212 Grand Ave., Billings. 896-0174
or toll free 866-MTANGEL(682-6435).
www.anglesonbroadway.com

## 20. *Gas, Food*

## 21. *Gas, Food, Lodging, Camping*

### A Hanser's Auto & Wrecker Co.

430 S. Billings Ave., Billings. 248-7795
or 800- 345-1754.

Hanser's is a 33-year old family corporation that is dedicated to the service of the motoring public. Specializing in accident recovery & cleanup, air cushion recovery, damage-free motor home transport, cargo transfer & cleanup, and fuel spill cleanup—they can tow just about anything! With 24 wreckers and full-service emergency roadcare service, Hanser's is on duty 24-hours a day.

### A North Star Auto Body & Trailor Repair

121 Moore Lane, Billings. 245-4895

## Pryor Mountain National Wild Horse Range

**The Pryor Mountain Wild Horse Range** was established after a two-year grassroots effort by citizens concerned about the long-term welfare of the Pryor Mountain horses. In 1968, interested individuals and groups convinced Interior Secretary Stewart Udall to set aside 31,000 acres in the Pryor Mountains as a public range for the wild horses. This was the first of its kind in the nation.

### Unique Horses

For more than a century, the Pryor Mountains have been home to free-roaming bands of wild horses. This herd of horses is a genetically unique population. Blood typing by the Genetics Department of the University of Kentucky has indicated that these horses are closely related to the old type European Spanish horse.

As you explore the range, look for horses with unusual coloring which may correspond to their Spanish lineage, such as dun, grulla, blue roan and the rare sabino.

Also watch for primitive markings such as a dorsal stripe down their back, wither stripes, and zebra stripes on their legs. These unusual features are considered typical of Spanish characteristics.

So, where did the horses come from? The origins are unclear, but a common belief is that the horses escaped from local Native American Indian herds and eventually found a safe haven in the Pryors.

Like many wild horse populations, the Pryor horses live within family groups. As you travel throughout the Range, you may find over 25 family groups and assorted "bachelor" stallions. Most families (or harems) average 5-6 animals, with a dominant stallion, a lead mare, and a variety of other mares and young animals. Horses love to follow a good leader and the Pryor horses are no different. The Pryor stallions seem to make the daily decisions for the rest of the family group, but in other populations the decision makers are often the lead mares.

Scientific studies have shown that the genetic diversity of the horses is high and the current level of inbreeding within the population is low. In some populations, inbreeding can be a problem if the numbers of horses in the herd are too low. The Pryor population has been historically managed at a successful size of between 120 and 160 horses. The population appears to be confined to this range by both natural and manmade barriers, and thus the only source of new horses are the 20-30 foals born each year. Since the horses have few natural enemies, it is necessary to limit the number of animals. The Bureau of Land Management gathers and removes animals every 2-3 years in order to maintain a desired number of horses.

### Where Can I View Wild Horses?

Most visitors will have opportunities to view wild horses along Bad Pass Highway within the Bighorn Canyon National Recreation Area. Small bands of horses are often visible from this paved road year round. Look for horses in the low elevation lands north of the Mustang Flat interpretive sign.

Adventurous visitors will find that most of the wild horses can be found in the higher mountain meadows surrounding Penn's cabin during the summer and early fall months. However, four wheel drive vehicles will be required to make the journey to the Penn's cabin vicinity.

Photography and filming opportunities in the Pryor Mountains are excellent. All photographers and filmers are cautioned to respect the comfort zone around wild horses at all times and not to, in any way disrupt the horse's natural behavior.

Casual use activities such as noncommercial still photography or recreational video taping do not require a permit or fees. Commercial filming and certain categories of commercial photography do require a permit and fees. For further information, please contact the BLM Billings Field Office.

*Reprinted from BLM brochure.*

### *Montana Trivia*

Almost 7,500 Native Americans live on the Crow Reservation. 85% of them speak Crow as their first language. Chief Plenty Coups of the Crow Tribe acted as the head of state of the Indian Nation at the dedication of the Tomb of the Unknown Soldier in Washington, D.C. Susie Walking Bear Yellowtail, a Crow Indian, became the first Native American Registered Nurse in 1923.

**L Days Inn**
843 Parkway Ln., I-90 Exit 446 or 447, Billings. 252-4007 or Reservations only at 800-329-7466

Whether you are in Billings for business or pleasure, you will enjoy the friendly atmosphere, courteous staff and clean quiet rooms at Day's Inn. They offer expanded cable, HBO and in-house movies, and there is a large, secluded hot tub to soothe the body. After a good night's sleep, enjoy their expanded continental breakfast in a lovely breakfast room. All guest rooms come with a coffee pot, hair dryer and data port phones for laptops. Business rooms are also available with king-size beds, a large desk and end table, refrigerator, microwave, along with an iron and ironing board. A Guest laundry is also available. Don't forget your free *USA Today!* Your pet is welcome, see their listing on www.petswelcome.com.

**L Super 8 Motel Of Billings**
5400 Southgate Dr., Billings. 248-8842.

Life's great at the Billings Super 8! Guests relax in the cozy atmosphere of the lobby, where they can sit by the fireplace and enjoy free coffee and a toast bar every morning. They specialize in clean rooms and friendly service, with a 24-hour front desk, wake-up service, non-smoking rooms, suites units, some rooms with microwaves & refrigerators, guest laundry and cable T.V. with HBO. There are also outside plug-ins for those cold nights and children under 12 are free when accompanied by an adult. Located near the Rimrock Mall, Zoo Montana, Little Bighorn Battlefield, Pompey's Pillar, Yellowstone National Park and much more.

**C Billings Big Sky Campground & Magic Carpet RV**
5516 Laurel Rd, Billings. 259-4110

## 22. *Gas, Food, Lodging*

**A Cono Mart Super Store #7**
4903 Southgate Dr., Billings. 254-0600

Locally owned & operated, convenience store, friendly service, clean restrooms, and 24-hour fuel pumps.

## 23. *Gas, Food, Lodging*

**L Holiday Inn Grand Montana**
5500 Midland Rd., Billings. 248-7701 or 877-55GRAND. www.holiday-inn.com/billings-west

Experience the Holiday Inn Grand Montana—Billings' most recently renovated hotel and convention center. Featuring the spectacular atrium's towering expanse and cascading waterfall, and boundless meeting space that captures the "Big Sky" spirit of Montana. For business and leisure travellers alike, you will enjoy the convenient and centralized Billings location, beautiful newly appointed guest rooms, an indoor pool & sauna, an exercise room, a full service restaurant & lounge, convenient business services, data port access, voice mail, acres of free parking and a friendly tradition of Montana-style service and hospitality.

**L Ramada Inn Limited**
1345 Mullowney Lane, Billings. 252-2584 or

800- 2-RAMADA (726232).

Located just one block south of I-90 at Exit 446, the Ramada Limited is conveniently located to all Billings area attractions, Yellowstone National Park, great restaurants and shopping. Featuring 116 "Green Air" Rooms with queen beds, a complimentary light breakfast buffet, an exercise room, guest laundry, free local calls, 24-hour coffee, fax & copy services non-smoking and physically challenged rooms and more! For that special occasion, try the 2-room suite with a conference area and large jacuzzi bath. Stay at the Ramada Limited and enjoy friendly service and excellent quality accommodations.

### Montana Trivia

Before Charles Lindbergh made his famous non-stop flight from New York to Paris, he lived in Billings where he made a living performing as a barn-storming aviator.

**L Red Roof Inn**
5353 Midland Road, Billings. 248-7551 or reservations at 800-RED-ROOF, www.redroof.com

## 24. *Gas, Food, Lodging*

**A Hank's Body Repair**
1845 Lampman Dr., Billings. 652-8686

**F MacKenzie River Pizza Co.**
403 Main, Billings. 254-0066

Famous for gourmet pizzas, super sandwiches and extraordinary salads, everything is made fresh daily right down to the salad dressings and the pizza dough! They are located in the Target Center near the Metra. This is the perfect place to enjoy pizza and a brew before or after your next Metra event.

### L C'mon Inn
Exit 446, Kings Avenue & I-90, Billings. 655-1100 or 800- 655-1170.

At the C'mon Inn they believe it is their responsibility to ensure that every guest is well taken care of and enjoys their visit. All the beds are queen size to enhance a restful sleep, whether you stay in a single, double, or suite unit. The suites are complete with a personal jacuzzi, microwave, refrigerator, and family area for added comfort. All guests are invited to use the exercise room, the large swimming pool, children's pool, or one of the five hot tubs located in the spacious tropical courtyard. Enjoy the arcade, ping pong table, and shuffleboard for family fun, as well as 24-hour dining next door. There is a complimentary continental breakfast and children under 12 are free.

### L Quality Inn
2036 Overland Ave., Billings. 652-1320 or 800- 228-5151.

Famous for their complimentary cooked to order breakfast, you must see it to believe it! Including eggs, pancakes, bacon & sausage, hash browns, a large continental selection, and more! Have a bite to eat at The Lobby Soup Bar in the evening. You always have a choice when it comes to guest rooms—the Deluxe room includes two queen beds, the Junior Suite offers a queen bed with a recliner, and the King Suite features two separate rooms, a wet bar with refrigerator, hair dryer, two televisions and telephones, a king size bed, sofa sleeper and a spacious vanity area. All rooms offer in-room coffee, HBO and data ports. The Indoor Swim Center offers a spacious sauna, 15 person hot tub and indoor pool. They also have meeting facilities, golf and fitness privileges and a complimentary airport shuttle. If you're looking for Value and Comfort, look no further than the Quality Inn Homestead Park!

### L Comfort Inn
2030 Overland Ave., Billings. 652-5200

Comfort Inn Billings truly has your personal comfort in mind. They are are conveniently located at I-90 Exit 446, King Ave., and near many great restaurants and shopping. They offer 60 rooms with amenities including in-room movies, cable TV, air conditioning, safety deposit box, free local calls, irons, and ironing boards. Those who prefer will find nonsmoking rooms, connecting rooms, suites, and handicap accessible rooms. Relax after a busy day in the whirlpool, hot tub, or indoor swimming pool. There is also an on-site game room. Guests are hosted to a complimentary continental breakfast and newspaper every morning. There is even an outdoor picnic area and parking for all sizes of vehicles.

### L Fairfield Inn
2030 Overland Ave., Billings. 652-5200

Comfort Inn Billings truly has your personal comfort in mind. They are are conveniently located at I-90 Exit 446, King Ave., and near many great restaurants and shopping. They offer 60 rooms with amenities including in-room movies, cable TV, air conditioning, safety deposit box, free local calls, irons, and ironing boards. Those who prefer will find nonsmoking rooms, connecting rooms, suites, and handicap accessible rooms. Relax after a busy day in the whirlpool, hot tub, or indoor swimming pool. There is also an on-site game room. Guests are hosted to a complimentary continental breakfast and newspaper every morning. There is even an outdoor picnic area and parking for all sizes of vehicles.

## 25. *Food*

## 26. *Adventure, Gas, Food, Lodging, Shopping*

### A Cono Mart Superstore
1st Ave. N., Billings

Locally owned & operated, convenience store, friendly service, clean restrooms, and 24-hour fuel pumps.

### F Godfather's Pizza
503 24th St. W., Billings. 652-3150

The fun atmosphere at Godfather's Pizza is great for group gatherings, family dinners, or just a relaxing meal out. Offering two locations in Billings, they feature a wide variety of pizzas to choose from, with golden and thin crusts and many topping choices. If you're not in the mood for pizza, try the salad bar or a variety of sandwiches. Offering dine in, carry out, and delivery seven days a week. Godfather's also serves specialty buffets and welcomes large groups.

### SVL Big Horn Fly & Tackle
485 S. 24th St. W., Billings. 656-8257

Bighorn Fly and Tackle Shop has earned a reputation as one of Montana's premium fly shops, lodging and guide services. Guide services are offered on the Bighorn, Yellowstone, and Stillwater Rivers. They are an all-inclusive outfitter with friendly guides and employees. Their services will insure a pleasurable experience whether you're a novice or experienced fisherman. Painstaking measures are taken to hire and retain some of the most knowledgeable and friendly guides in the region. All of their gear is top of the line—boats, float tubes, and fly fishing gear and available for rent or purchase. They offer a variety of clean and comfort-

*Pryor Mountains south of Billings*

able accommodations for every angler's needs, including a hearty continental breakfast each morning. They offer the convenience of shuttle services, including intakes and outtakes. Plan a day or a week and they'll do everything possible to assure that you'll have the best fly fishing adventure possible. Look for their locations in Hardin and Ft. Smith. Visit them at www.bighorn-fly.com for more information.

## 27. *Gas, Food, Shopping*

### A Cono Mart Super Store #6

2402 Grand Ave., Billings. 656-7775

Locally owned & operated, convenience store, friendly service, clean restrooms, and 24-hour fuel pumps.

### F MacKenzie River Pizza Co.

3025 Grand Ave., Billings. 651-0068

Famous for gourmet pizzas, super sandwiches and extraordinary salads, everything is made fresh daily right down to the salad dressings and the pizza dough! Located in the Grand Avenue Mall off of Rehberg. You can enjoy a pizza and brew in the Pub or on their patio.

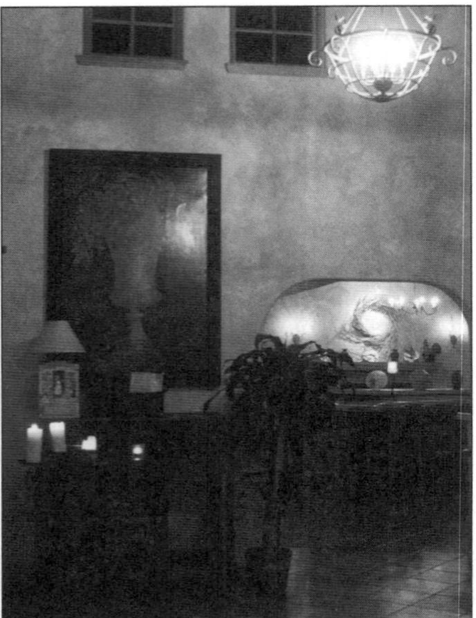

### F Enzo Mediterranean Bistro

Rehberg Lane @ Grand, Billings. 651-0999.

Enzo is a neighborhood bistro for all seasons. The inviting interior glows in Mediterranean shades of ochre and olive, with two levels and half moon pine bars. The menu features mesquite grilled Pacific fish & aged meats, authentic Naples pizza made in an Italian wood burning oven, superb handmade pastas, sandwiches & salads, and legendary contemporary desserts. They also feature a fine selection of microbrews and regional wines. In a recent review, New York food critic and travel writer Steven Shaw wrote, "Who would have believed that Billings, Montana could be the home of a restaurant as good as Enzo?"

### F Billings Burrito Company

2922 Grand Ave., Billings. 651-4961

### F Bruno's Italian Specialties

2658 Grand Ave., Billings. 248-4146

### S Bottles & Shots West

3925 Grand Ave., Billings. 655-3394.

Cigars, Liquor Store & Casino.

### S Jan's Gifts

2646 Grand Ave. #7, Billings. 652-0009.

Full line of Montana products, including sausage, cheese, jelly, jam, syrup, candy, jerky, cups, cards, puzzles, postcards, gift boxes & baskets, diet products and shipping services. Visa and Mastercard accepted. Take 24th St. W. north to Grand, turn left and go two blocks.

> *Montana Trivia*
>
> The red sandstone rimrock cliffs surrounding Billings rise 400 feet above the Yellowstone River valley. They were created by a giant inland sea millions of years ago.

## 28. *Gas, Food, Miscellaneous*

### M Rocky Mountain College

1511 Poly Drive, Billings. 761-7885 or 800-877-6259, www.rocky.edu.

Rocky Mountain College a small highly respected liberal arts college, was founded in 1878 and is Montana's first institution of higher learning based in Christianity. RMC offers students a uniquely integrated curriculum that joins professional programs and traditional liberal arts education for approximately 800 students.

## 29. *Attraction*

### T Pictograph Cave State Park

I-90, exit 452, south of Lockwood, Billings. 247-2940

Pictograph Cave State Park is a truly unique glimpse into the past and a dreamland for archaeologists. Pictograph and Ghost Caves served as shelters for Native American inhabitants over 5,000 years ago. They would stop here to rest during hunting trips to make tools and left behind over 100 paintings that line the back walls in red, black and white. In 1937, excavations began in the caves, resulting in a huge finding of Native American artifacts, tools, jewelry and much more. This excavation also discovered the pictographs that date back to between 500 and 1900 A.D., depicting animals, men on horses, rituals and costumes just to name a few.

William T. Mulloy was brought in around 1940, to study the findings of the major excavation. Through his observations, Mulloy discovered that Native Americans inhabited this area from as far back as 2600 B.C. Through this study, he also came up with a system for dating artifacts that is used by archeologists to this day.

The park is open April through October. There is a day use fee.

## 30. *Attraction*

### T Oscar's Dreamland Yesteryear Museum

3100 Harrow Dr., Billings. 656-0966

Oscar Cooke had a dream of building the largest steam tractor museum in the world. He did. For years the museum had no other in the world like it. When Oscar and his wife passed away, his daughter was forced to sell off many of the pieces to pay off the confiscatory estate taxes imposed by the government. There is still enough here to fill a day looking.

### T Riverfront Park

I-90 Exit 446 to S. Billings Ave., Billings.

Located on the Yellowstone River, this park is a great place to relax, walk, jog, fish and enjoy a picnic.

## 31. *Attraction, Lodging*

### T Zoo Montana

2100 Shiloh Road, Billings. 652-8100

If you haven't gotten your fill of wildlife viewing just driving around the state, visit this 70-acre zoo situated along the Canyon Creek. Zoo Montana is the only zoo in Montana that features animals that reside in a natural habitat wildlife park. They specialize in animals that can survive the climate in Montana, and also have a botanical gardens. The zoo is still in the early stages of development, but definitely worth the trip. Kids and adults will enjoy the Siberian tigers, otters, children's zoo and sensory garden. The zoo also has a farm animal petting area and a discovery center with hands-on exhibits that kids love, a one mile nature loop and a wetlands area. Open all year at 10 a.m. daily. Closed on major holidays. Take I-90 exit 446 to King Avenue West. Follow King Avenue West to Shiloh Road. Follow Shiloh Road south approximately 1 1/2 miles to zoo.

### L Sanderson Inn

2038 S. 56th St. W., Billings. 656-3388

## 32. *Gas*

### Lodge Grass

Lodge Grass is the first full service gas stop on I-90, if you are heading from Wyoming, and is part of the Crow Indian Reservation. Located on the Little Bighorn River, Lodge Grass was named for Lodge Grass Creek that flows into the Little Bighorn. The Crows used this area as hunting grounds in the early days and they called the Creek "Greasy Grass" because of the rich grass that was said to make the animals fat. The words "grease" and "lodge" are very similar in the Crow language, and the name of the creek was interpreted as Lodge Grass instead of Greasy Grass by accident. The grazing lands here are still lush and widely used by ranchers.

A nice stop on your way through town is White Arm Park in town, and Willow Creek Reservoir, just southwest of town. Every 4th of July, Lodge Grass hosts the Valley of the Chiefs Celebration, a four day event.

### L Westwood Ranch Bed & Breakfast

Lodge Grass Exit, 80 miles east of Billings. Turn left at Cenex Farmers Union Station to Westwood Ranch sign. Turn left and drive to 3rd house on road. 639-2450 or reservations at 800-551-1418

The Westwood Ranch Bed and Breakfast is surrounded by breathtaking scenery on a working ranch. It is in the middle of the Crow Indian

Reservation and only 12 miles from the Little Bighorn Battlefield. A six-acre lake provides an ever changing visual feast with wild birds, water fowl, and domestic trumpeter swans. The lake and the Little Bighorn River, which runs through the property, provide endless recreational opportunities. The swimming pool has cooking facilities, a guest cabana, and hot tub nearby. A special feature on the property is a Tug Boat Playhouse, docked on the edge of the lake at a dock that wraps around three sides. The ranch will provide an unforgettable experience for children and adults alike.

## 33. *Historic Marker, Attraction, Gas, Food, Lodging, Camping, Shopping*

### H Garryowen
I-90 Exit 514

*Garryowen, the old Irish tune, was the regimental marching song of the 7th Cavalry, General Custer's command.*

*The Battle of the Little Big Horn commenced in the valley just east of here June 25, 1876, after Custer had ordered Major Marcus A. Reno to move his battalion into action against the hostile Sioux and Cheyennes, led by Gall, Crazy Horse, Two Moons and Sitting Bull.*

*Reno, with 112 men, came out of the hills about 2 1/2 miles southeast of here and rode within 1/4 mile of the Indian camp where he was met by the hostiles who outnumbered the soldiers ten to one. Dismounting his men, Reno formed a thin skirmish line west across the valley from the timber along the river. After severe losses he was forced to retreat to high ground east of the Little Big Horn where he was joined by Major Benteen's Command. The combined force stood off the Indians until the approach of Gibbon's column from the north on the following day caused the hostiles to pull out. Reno and Benteen were not aware of Custer's fate until the morning of the 27th.*

### T Little Bighorn Battlefield National Monument
Highway 212 (I-90 Exit 510), Crow Agency. 638-2621

Located 15 miles east of Hardin, this national monument, commemorates the Battle of the Little Bighorn. In the visitor center, a thorough account is presented, explaining historical aspects of the battle while displays and artifacts reinforce the realism of the scene. The battle claimed the lives of 260 soldiers and military personnel of the Seventh Cavalry under Custer's command as well as 99 men under the command of Major Benteen. Between 60 to 100 Sioux and Cheyenne were killed out of several thousand. Guided tours of the battlefield are available. Open year round: Spring & Fall 8 a.m.–6 p.m.. Summer 8 a.m.–7:30 p.m., Winter 8 a.m.–4:30 p.m. $6 per vehicle.

### T Custer's Last Stand Reenactment
Hardin Chamber of Commerce, 665-3577 or toll free at 888-450-3577

Watch history come alive! Feel the whirlwinds of epic forces clashing on the high plains of Montana. Relive history as warriors of the Sioux, Cheyenne and Arapaho fight the Seventh Cavalry at Custer's Last Stand Reenactment.

Surrounded by the vast sky and rolling hills of Montana, you have a front row seat to watch galloping warriors battle charging cavalry troops to the last man! Each performance reenacts the most famous and mysterious battle in American history. See legendary leaders portrayed in the context of history—Sitting Bull, medicine man of the Hunkpapa Sioux; Crazy Horse, fearless Lakota war

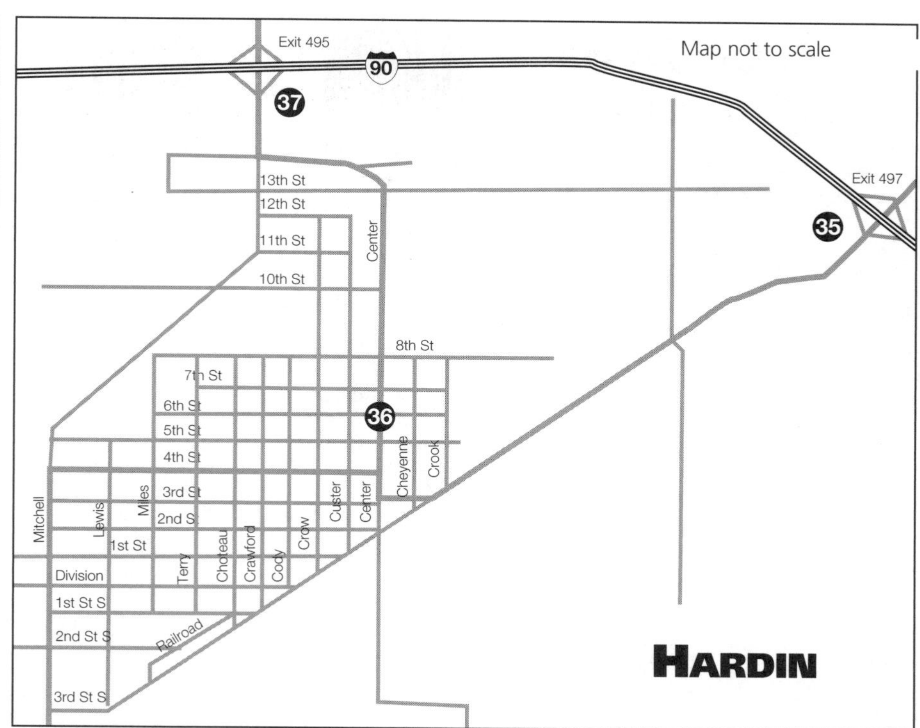


chief and conqueror of General Crook on the Rosebud; George Armstrong Custer, flamboyant Civil War hero and controversial Plains Indian fighter.

You are there and participate in the sweep of epic American adventure as sight, sound and smell bring the past alive. Experience history that is real. History you can taste, more powerful and exciting than television, movies or video games!

Custer's Last Stand Reenactment is history alive. Crow Tribal elder and historian, Joe Medicine Crow, has crafted a script based on translations of Native American oral histories retold for generations. The narrative portrays nations on the move and cultures colliding. See firsthand the struggles of the Sioux, the Cheyenne, the Crow, and the Americans. Share the epic of the West beginning more than two hundred years ago. See the buffalo culture of the Plains Indian. See direct descendants of fighting warriors in full regalia attack and destroy the Seventh Cavalry in the great Sioux War of 1876!

World fascination with the Battle of the Little Big Horn has never been more intense. Custer's Last Stand Reenactment has been the focus of two A&E productions, CNN and BBC coverage, and filming for the Hollywood movie *Legend of Crazy Horse*. Don't miss this performance, listed for five years as one of the "Top 100 Events in America" by Destinations Magazine. Witness, in person, the excitement which has attracted hundreds of journalists and film makers, enthralled Americans and brought visitors from Canada, Mexico, China, Great Britain, France, Australia, and Germany.

Meet Indian warriors, face to face. Shake hands with U.S. Cavalry troopers. Talk to General Custer.

Experience living history. Walk traders row on the reenactment grounds. Sample Native American food and shop for unique Native American and cavalry merchandise. Come and watch, or come in costume and dance at the 1876 Grand Ball. Enjoy Little Bighorn Days and the other special events that surround Custer's Last Stand Reenactment.

As one recent Reenactment visitor exclaimed, "it's like really being there—smack dab in the middle of history!"

For more information, visit the Reenactment on the world wide web at: http: //www. mcn. net/~custerfight, or send email to custerfight@mcn.net. For tickets call 1-888-450-3577 or 406-665-3577.—*Reprinted from Hardin Chamber of Commerce brochure.*

### FS Custer Battlefield Trading Post & Cafe
Highway 212 (I-90 Exit 510), Crow Agency. 638-2001

### F Crow's Nest
Highway 212 (I-90 Exit 510), Crow Agency. 638-0900

## 34. *Gas, Food, Miscellaneous*

### Crow Agency
The Crow Nation spans across 3,565 square miles and is spread out to seven different communities-Crow Agency, Wyola, Lodge Grass, Garryowen, St. Xavier, Fort Smith and Pryor. Crow Agency serves as the Crow Reservation's agency headquarters-taking care of tribal management and government. Every August Crow Agency hosts one of Montana's largest powwows during the Crow Fair celebration. The Little Bighorn College is a tribal community college that has a great tourism department and offers cultural tours of the area.

# A Clash of Cultures

**Little Bighorn Battlefield National** Monument memorializes one of the last armed efforts of the Northern Plains Indians to preserve their ancestral way of life. Here in the valley of the Little Bighorn River on two hot June days in 1876, more than 260 soldiers and attached personnel of the U.S. Army met defeat and death at the hands of several thousand Lakota and Cheyenne warriors. Among the dead were Lt. Col. George Armstrong Custer and every member of his immediate command. Although the Indians won the battle, they subsequently lost the war against the white man's efforts to end their independent, nomadic way of life.

The Battle of the Little Bighorn was but the latest encounter in a centuries-long conflict that began with the arrival of the first Europeans in North America. That contact between Indian and white cultures had continued relentlessly, sometimes around the campfire, sometimes at treaty grounds, but more often on the battlefield. It reached its peak in the decade following the Civil War, when settlers resumed their vigorous westward movement. These western emigrants, possessing little or no understanding of the Indian way of life, showed slight regard for the sanctity of hunting grounds or the terms of former treaties. The Indians' resistance to those encroachments on their domain only served to intensify hostilities.

In 1868, believing it "cheaper to feed than to fight the Indians," representatives of the U.S. Government signed a treaty at Fort Laramie, WY., with the Lakota, Cheyenne, and other tribes of the Great Plains, by which a large area in eastern Wyoming was designated a permanent Indian reservation. The government promised to protect the Indians "against the commission of all depredations by people of the United States."

Peace, however, was not to last. In 1874 gold was discovered in the Black Hills, the heart of the new Indian reservation. News of the strike spread quickly, and soon thousands of eager gold seekers swarmed into the region in violation of the Fort Laramie treaty. The army tried to keep them out, but to no avail. Efforts to buy the Black Hills from the Indians, and thus avoid another confrontation, also proved unsuccessful. In growing defiance, the Lakota and Cheyenne left the reservation and resumed raids on settlements and travelers along the fringes of Indian domain. In December 1875, the Commissioner of Indian Affairs ordered the tribes to return before January 31, 1876, or be treated as hostiles "by the military force." When the Indians did not comply, the army was called in to enforce the order.

Maj. Marcus A. Reno was Custer's second in command. His handling of the retreat from the valley during the Little Bighorn fight was severely criticized. An 1879 court of inquiry exonerated him from any direct responsibility for the defeat, but the stigma of the controversy haunted him for the rest of his life.

## The Campaign of 1876

The army's campaign against the Lakota and Cheyenne called for three separate expeditions- one under Gen. George Crook from Fort Fetterman in Wyoming Territory, another under Col. John Gibbon from Fort Ellis in Montana Territory, and the third under Gen. Alfred H. Terry from Fort Abraham Lincoln in Dakota Territory. These columns were to converge on the Indians concentrated in southeastern Montana under the leadership of Sitting Bull, Crazy Horse, and other war chiefs.

Crook's troopers were knocked out of the campaign in mid-June when they clashed with a large Lakota-Cheyenne force along the Rosebud River and were forced to withdraw. The Indians, full of confidence at having thrown back one of the army's columns, moved west toward the Little Bighorn River. Meanwhile, Terry and Gibbon met on the Yellowstone River near the mouth of the Rosebud. Hoping to find the Indians in the Little Bighorn Valley, Terry ordered Custer and the 7th Cavalry up the Rosebud to approach the Little Bighorn from the south. Terry himself would accompany Gibbon's force back up the Yellowstone and Bighorn Rivers to approach from the north.

The 7th Cavalry, numbering about 600 men, located the Indian camp at dawn on June 25. Custer, probably underestimating the size and fighting power of the Lakota and Cheyenne forces, divided his regiment into three battalions. He retained five companies under his immediate command and assigned three companies each to Maj. Marcus A. Reno and Capt. Frederick W. Benteen. A twelfth was assigned to guard the slow-moving pack train.

Benteen was ordered to scout the bluffs to the south, while Custer and Reno headed toward the Indian village in the valley of the Little Bighorn. When near the river, Custer turned north toward the lower end of the encampment.

Reno, ordered to cross the river and attack, advanced down the valley to strike the upper end of the camp. As he neared the present site of Garryowen Post Office, a large force of Lakota warriors rode out from the southern edge of the Indian village to intercept him. Forming his men into a line of battle, Reno attempted to make a stand, but there were just too many Indians. Outflanked, he was soon forced to retreat in disorder to the river and take up defensive positions on the bluffs beyond. Here he was joined by Benteen, who had hurried forward under orders from Custer to "Come on; Big village, be quick, bring packs."

No one knew precisely where Custer and his command had gone, but heavy gunfire to the north indicated that he too had come under attack. As soon as ammunition could be distributed, Reno and Benteen put their troops in motion northward. An advance company under Capt. Thomas B. Weir marched about a mile downstream to a high hill (afterwards named Weir Point), from which the area now known as the Custer battlefield was visible. By now the firing had stopped and nothing could be seen of Custer and his men.

When the rest of the soldiers arrived on the hill, they were attacked by a large force of Indians, and Reno ordered a withdrawal to the original position on the bluffs overlooking the Little Bighorn. Here these seven companies entrenched and held their defenses throughout that day and most of the next, returning the Indians' fire and successfully discouraging attempts to storm their position. The siege ended finally when the Indians withdrew upon learning of the approach of the columns under Terry and Gibbon.

Meantime, Custer had ridden into history and legend. His precise movements after separating from Reno have never been determined, but vivid accounts of the battle by Indians who participated in it tell how his command was surrounded and destroyed in fierce fighting. Northern Cheyenne Chief Two Moon recalled that "the shooting was quick, quick. Poppop-pop very fast. Some of the soldiers were down on their knees, some standlng.... The smoke was like a great cloud, and everywhere the Sioux went the dust rose like smoke. We circled all around him, swirling like water around a stone. We shoot, we ride fast, we shoot again. Soldiers drop, and horses fall on them."

In the battle, the 7th Cavalry lost the five companies (C, E, F, 1, and Q under Custer, about 210 men Of the other companies of the regiment, under Reno and Benteen, 53 men were killed and 52 wounded. The Indians lost no more than 100 killed. They removed most of their dead from the battlefield when the large village broke up. The tribes and families scattered, some going north, some going south. Most of them returned to the reservations and surrendered in the next few years.

## Battlefield Tour

The Battle of the Little Bighorn continues to fascinate people around the world. For most, it has come to illustrate a part of what Americans know as their western heritage. Heroism and suffering, brashness and humiliation, victory and defeat, triumph and tragedy these are the things people come here to ponder.

The battlefield tour begins at the Reno-Benteen site, 4.5 miles from the visitor center. The exhibit panels are best viewed in sequence on the return trip. Stop at the visitor center before starting your tour; park rangers can answer your questions and help you plan your day. Museum exhibits and literature also help to explain these historical events. The tour stop descriptions are keyed to the map.

**1. Reno-Benteen:** Battlefield Major Reno, leading three companies of Custer's divided command, attacked the Indian village lying in the valley on the afternoon of June 25, 1876.

Forced to retreat, his battalion took position on these bluffs, where it was soon joined by Captain Benteen's men. Until the Indians left the next day, Reno and Benteen were surrounded in this position.

**2. Custer's Lookout:** From the ridge on your right (east), Custer watched Reno's attack underway in the valley. He also saw, for the first time, a portion of the enormous Indian village in the valley, perhaps the largest gathering of Plains Indians ever seen. The estimated 1,000 lodges held approximately 7,000 people; at least 1,500 were warriors. In this vicinity Custer sent back the first of two messengers with orders for Captain McDougall and the pack train to reinforce him. From here Custer's five-company battalion continued marching northward, trying to locate the upper end of the village. The marble marker honors Vincent Charley, farrier of Company D, who was killed in this area during Reno's retreat.

**3. Weir Point:** Late on the afternoon of June 25, Capt. Thomas Weir led his company to this hill, where he was soon joined by other companies of Reno's command. Although heavy firing had been heard earlier, only dust and great numbers of Indians moving on the hills to the north could be seen. The Indians soon spotted the cavalry on Weir Point and attacked, pushing Reno and Benteen back to their first position on the bluffs.

**4. Medicine Tall Ford:** At this point the Little Bighorn River's low banks and shallow depth offered Custer his first opportunity to cross into the Indian village. Indian accounts indicate that at least part of Custer's battalion came to the ford, whether to attack or simply to reconnoiter is not known. Perhaps as many as three of the companies remained on Nye-Cartwright Ridge, probably to attract Benteen. At first only a small number of warriors defended the ford from the west side. They were soon reinforced, compelling the troopers to fall back. Soon hundreds of warriors, released from the fight with Reno, pushed across the ford and pursued Custer's command onto the hills.

**5. Calhoun Ridge:** Indian accounts, supported by archeological evidence, suggest that one of the companies charged into the coulee on your left to break up the massed warriors. The soldiers came under heavy fire and were forced back to the ridge, where most were killed. Lame White Man, a Cheyenne, led the attack; he fell a short time later.

**6. Calhoun Hill:** Markers here show where members of Company L were overwhelmed by Lakota warriors. As you proceed along Battle Ridge, you will see many markers along the right (east) side. For the most part these represent the men of Capt. Miles Keogh's Company 1. A Lakota force, led by the famed warrior Crazy Horse, struck Keogh's company, now combined with the survivors of C and L Companies, as they fled toward Custer Hill. Keogh and most of his soldiers perished here.

**7. Custer Hill:** Here Companies E and F, along with a few survivors from the other three companies, reunited to make a stand. The markers scattered on the low ridge below, toward the river, may represent a short-lived attempt to stem Indians advancing from the west. The cluster of markers within the fence shows where the last remnant of Custer's battalion fell. Custer, his brothers Tom and Boston, and his nephew Autie Reed were all found in this group.

On June 28, the bodies of Custer and his men were buried in great haste at or near the places they had fallen. These shallow graves were improved in the next few years. In 1881, those graves that could be found were reopened and the bones reinterred in a common grave around the base of the memorial shaft bearing the names of the soldiers and civilians killed in the battle. The remains of 11 officers and two civilians already had been exhumed for reburial elsewhere at the request of relatives. Custer's remains were reburied at the U.S. Military Academy in West Point, N.Y., on October 10, 1877.

The Lakota and Cheyenne warriors killed in the battle, estimated at between 60 and 100, were removed from the field by friends and relatives.

Little Bighorn Battlefield National Monument lies within the Crow Indian Reservation in southeastern Montana, one mile west of I-90/U.S. 87. Crow Agency is two miles north. Billings, Mont., is 65 miles northwest, and Sheridan, WY., is 70 miles to the south.

*Tombstones mark the spots where cavalrymen fell.*

No camping or picnicking facilities are in the park. Federal law prohibits the removal or disturbance of any artifact, marker, relic, or historic feature. Metal detecting on park land or adjacent Indian lands is prohibited. Remember, you are in rattlesnake country; stay on the pathways while walking the battlefield. Rangers will offer prompt assistance in case of accidents, but you can prevent them from happening by being cautious.

For more information write: Superintendent, Little Bighorn Battlefield National Monument, RO. Box 39, Crow Agency, MT 59022; Call: 406-638-2621; or Internet: www.nps.gov/libi.

*Reprinted from National Park Service Brochure*

## M Crow Reservation

Of the Crow tribe's approximately 9,300 enrolled members, about 75 percent live on or near the reservation. Eighty-five percent speak Crow as their first language.

The Crow Indians derived their name from the Hidatsa tribes, their ancestors who were originally from the area along the headwaters of the Mississippi. The Hidatsa word "Absarokee" is translated as the "Children of the Large Beaked Bird", referred to by the white man as the Crow. The Crow split from the larger tribe in the early 1600s, and resided in the Black Hills of South Dakota. Because their lifestyle was dependent on hunting, the Crow region continued to expand, and by the late 1700s, they had moved to the banks of the Yellowstone and Bighorn Rivers. The Crow have been known as hunters and horse people, and from the beginning they managed to maintain friendly relations with the white man, and formed a strong alliance. Their prominent leader Chief Plenty Coups promoted education and peace among the reservation, and spoke out for peace among all races. The reservation was established in 1851.

## M Little Big Horn College

1 Forestry Lane, Crow Agency. 638-3104.
www.lbhc.cc.mt.us

Little Big Horn College is a public two year college chartered by the Crow Tribe of Indians. It offers a number of associate degrees and other areas, with a strong emphasis on college preparatory programs. The campus is located in the capital of the Crow Indian Reservation and has an enrollment of approximately 300 students.

**35.** *Attraction*

## Hardin

Hardin was established in 1907 and named after Samuel Hardin, a rancher and early settler who lived south of Hardin, in Ranchester, Wyoming. As one of the last areas in the Montana plains to be settled, Hardin was originally set up by the Lincoln Land Company as a trading spot alongside the railroad. Samuel Hardin was a good friend of the Lincoln Land Company's president. Hardin was named Bighorn County seat in 1913, and by 1922 the town was well established with a developed business district.

Ranching and farming are still popular in this area today. Hardin is a great base camp for The Little Bighorn Battlefield, visits to Bighorn Canyon National Recreation Area and the many other area activities and sites. Little Bighorn Days is a four day festival that takes place every year towards the end of July, featuring Custers Last Stand Re-enactment which is based on Crow Tribal Elder Joseph Medicine Crow's translation of Native American writings and talks dating back 200 years ago. With a staged battle occurring in nearby plains, visitors can see a first hand account of what the battle was like. The festival also features ethnic food and wonderful performances.

### *Montana Trivia*

Charlie Russell said of the artist Edgar S. Paxson: "His brush told stories that people like to read." Paxson painted nearly 2,000 paintings of the Battle of Little Big Horn.

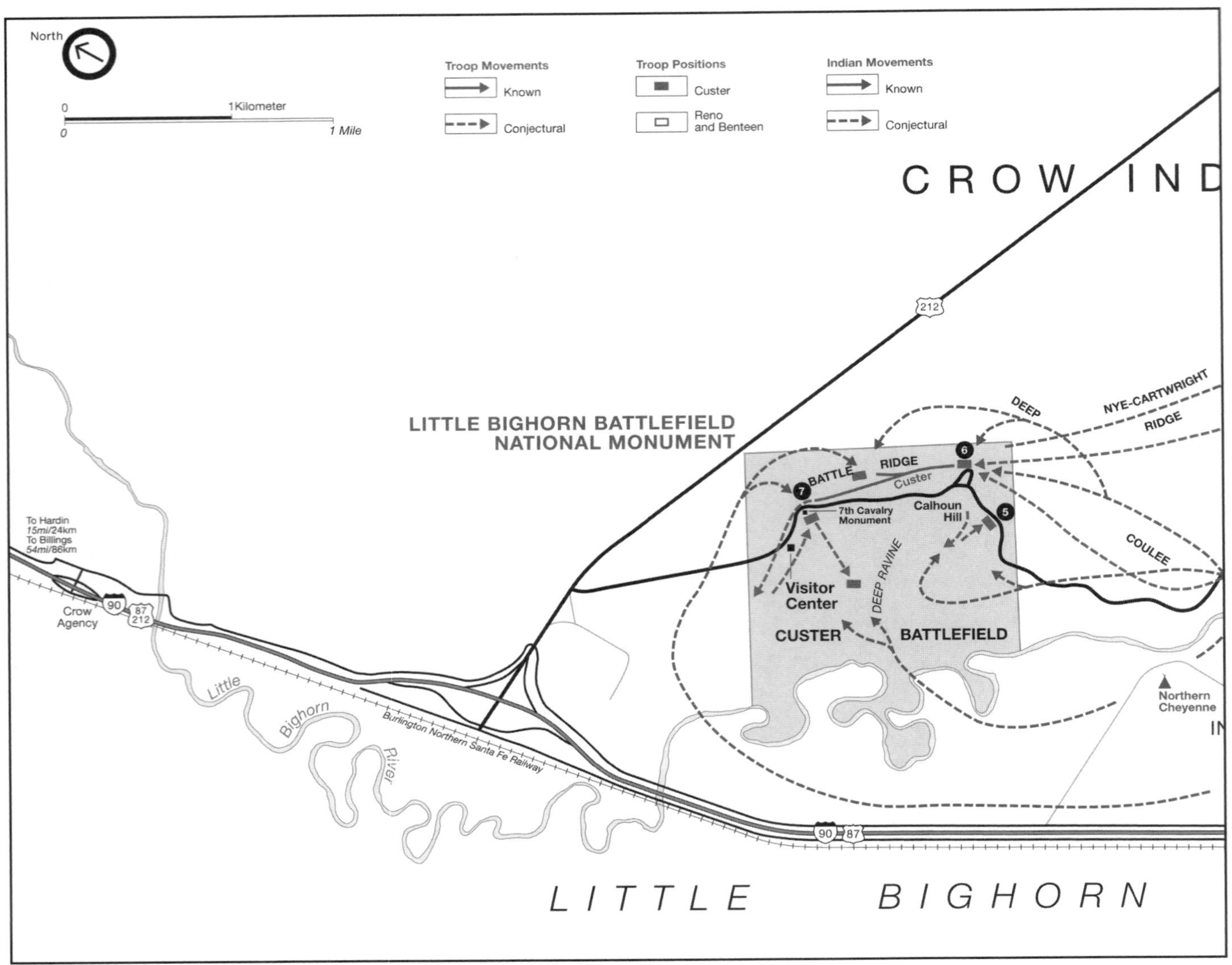


**T Big Horn County Historical Museum & Visitors Center**
I-90, exit 497, Hardin. 665-1671

See sidebar

## 36. *Attraction, Gas, Food, Lodging, Camping*

**T The Jail House Gallery**
218 N. Center, Hardin. 655-3239.

This gallery promotes artists within Bighorn County and the Crow & Cheyenne Reservations. The exhibits change regularly.

**L Western Motel**
830 3rd St. W., Hardin. 665-2296

## 37. *Gas, Food, Lodging, Camping*

**SV Big Horn Fly & Tackle Shop**
1426 N. Crawford, Hardin. 665-1321

## 38. *Historic Marker*

**H Buffalo Country**
Hardin

*Buffalo meant life to the Plains Indians, and the mountain Indians used to slip down from the hills for their share, too. Some tribes would toll buffalo into a concealed corral and then down them; another system was to stampede a herd over a cliff, but the sporting way was to use bows and arrows and ride them down on a trained buffalo horse.*

*Fat cow was the choice meat. The Indians preserved their meat long before the whites ever had any embalmed beef scandals. They made pemmican by drying and pulverizing the meat, pouring marrow bone grease and oil over it, and packing it away in skin bags. It kept indefinitely, and in food value one pound was worth ten of fresh meat.*

*Tanned robes and rawhide were used for bedding, tepees, clothes, war shields, stretchers, travois, canoes, and bags. Horns and bones made tools and utensils. The buffalo played a prominent part in many of their religious rites and jealousy of hereditary hunting grounds brought on most of the intertribal wars.*

## 39. *Historic Marker, Food, Camping*

**St. Xavier**

In 1887, Fr. Peter Paul Prondo, a Jesuit Priest, established the first mission at St. Xavier. The church still stands today and is in use as a school affiliated with the St. Labre Mission in Ashland. It is now called the Pretty Eagle School after a famous Crow Chief.

**H Fort C. F. Smith**
north of Saint Xavier on Hwy. 313, milepost 23

*The ruins of this military post are about 25 miles west of here. In August 1866, two companies of soldiers guided by Jim Bridger established the fort on a plain overlooking the Big Horn River between Spring Gulch and Warrior Creek. It was built of logs and adobe, the third, last and most northerly of three posts built to protect emigrants and freighters on the Bozeman or Bonanza Trail from the Sioux and Cheyennes defending their hunting grounds.*

*The "Hayfield Fight" occurred August 1st, 1867, three miles east of the fort when a handful of soldiers in a log corral stood off an attacking band of Cheyennes estimated at several hundred strong. The Cheyenne had not anticipated the soldiers new repeating rifles which were quickly reloadable.*

*The Sioux under Red Cloud forced the closing of the trail and abandonment of the fort under the Fort Laramie Treaty in 1868. The Indians lost the battle but won the war, though their victory would be short-lived given the ever-increasing encroachment by the settlers.*

**FC Big Horn RV Park & Cafe**
Hwy 313 Mile Marker 30, St. Xavier. 666-2460

## 40. *Attraction, Adventure, Shopping, Lodging*

**Fort Smith**

Fort C.F. Smith was established in August of 1866, built by the U.S. army to protect those traveling on the Bozeman Trail from the Sioux & Cheyenne

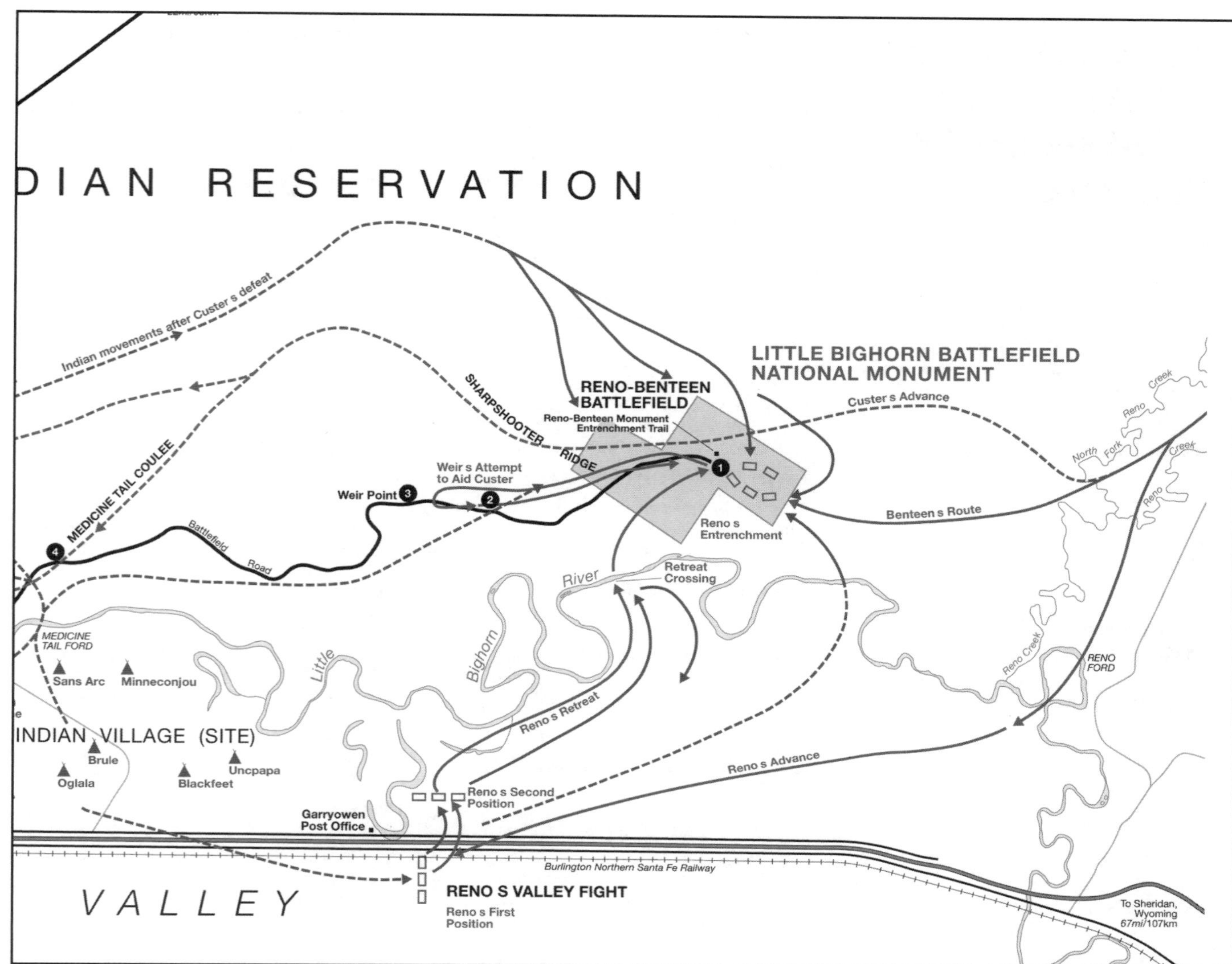




Indian attacks. Remnants of the old Fort C.F. Smith site, located along the Bighorn River, is 4 miles north of the present day Fort Smith. In 1868, the Sioux destroyed Fort C.F. Smith, after two years of fighting with the army along the Bozeman Trail.

Today, Fort Smith is a great place to try your hand at trout fishing on the blue ribbon trout waters of the Bighorn River, known as one of the finest trout streams in the U.S. You can stop through town for supplies, fishing advice, guide services and boat rentals.

### T Yellowtail Dam Visitor Center and Power Plant

Fort Smith. 666-2412

The dam and visitor center was named for Robert Yellowtail who was a prominent tribal leader of the Crow throughout the 1900s. The dam spans 1,480 feet across the Bighorn Canyon and stands 525 feet tall. The visitor center provides information about the dam and how it was built. An interesting fly-fishing exhibit compares man-made flies with their natural counterparts.

### SV Big Horn Fly & Tackle Shop

1 Main St., Ft. Smith. 666-2253

## 41. *Attraction*

### T Bighorn Canyon

See sidebar

### T Devil Canyon Overlook

SE on U.S. Hwy. 310 to Lovell, WY then north on Hwy. 37. (307) 548-2251

This vista offers a scenic view of the Bighorn River 1,000 feet below where it cuts through the Bighorn Canyon. Immediately west of the canyon, you can see where the Pryor Mountains have been uplifted along fault lines. Nearby is the Pryor Mountains Wildhorse Refuge where about 130 wild, free-roaming mustangs make their home. Along the drive from the Visitor's Center in Lovell to the overlook, you will probably see mountain goats along the side of the road.

## 42. *Attraction*

### Pryor

Pryor is located 35 miles south of Billings on the Crow Indian Reservation and is the site of Chief Plenty Coups State Park and is adjacent to the Bighorn Canyon Recreation Area. Named after the Pryor Mountain Range that lines the Montana-Wyoming border, Sgt. Nathaniel Pryor was a member of the Lewis & Clark Expedition that came through this area. These mountains are famous for the herd of wild horses that roams the area, and can be seen at the Wild Horse Range that is set aside for their protection.

### T Chief Plenty Coups State Park (Day use only)

1 mile west of Pryor on county road. 252-1289.

The fascinating and honorable life of Chief Plenty Coups is remembered at this location. He was the respected tribal chief of the Crow people from 1904-1932 and was the tribe's most revered leader; loved by his people, as well as respected by white leaders. With many achievements during his leadership, he was the most respected chief the Crows would ever have, and was not replaced after his death.

Chief Plenty Coups was a brave warrior and leader, enforcing his beliefs that education was the way to deal with the white man. He adapted to the changing times, replacing his tepee for a two story cabin by the Pryor Mountain Range, where he cultivated the land. This was a show of peace to the white man, and he was a great mediator, explaining the importance of peace between all people.

After frequent trips to Washington D.C., in 1924 he was asked to represent American Indians in the dedication of the tomb of the unknown soldier at Arlington National Cemetery. Here, Plenty

# Big Horn County Historical Museum & Visitors Center

Situated on 24 acres, the Big Horn County Historical Museum was established in 1979. The Museum complex consisting of twenty permanent buildings represents the interest and involvement that local residents, the business community, the Big Horn County Historical Society, the Historical Museum Foundation, and local and state government have taken to preserve, exhibit and interpret the areas past.

As you walk through the buildings that make up the museum, you are walking through the pages of history and touching the footsteps of such people as the first Americans who roamed the high plains in search of buffalo; traders and settlers that came in search of adventure; and the early day homesteaders who toiled out a living by farming and raising livestock. They all wrote their chapters.

## Main Exhibit Building/State Visitor Center

The main building features a rotating exhibit, which changes each year, a museum gift shop which offers a large selection of books, locally crafted Indian bead work, Montana made gift and other items. Also inside the main building you will discover a staffed State Visitor Center, where you will find a wide variety of state and regional travel information.

## 1911 Farmhouse

Your tour of the Big Horn County Historical Museum begins with the 1911 farmhouse.

It's located to the East of the main exhibit building.

The farmhouse was built in 1911, about five years after this part of Montana was opened for homesteading and about ten years after the military abandoned Fort Custer, which was located on the bluffs, south of here across the Big Horn River.

The home and the barn located at the rear of the structure stand on their original site. The farmhouse contains a fine collection of items from the turn of the century and will give you an idea of the quality of life during that time.

## LaForge Cabin

The LaForge log cabin was built in Lodge Grass, Montana, by Thomas and Tom LaForge. Thomas LaForge, served as a scout for military campaigns led by some of the West's most notable military commanders, including Custer, Terry and Gibbons.

Thomas was born in Ohio in 1850. He came to Montana with his parents in 1865 and at the age of about nineteen he chose to live among the Crow Indians and was later adopted into the tribe.

This 18' x 24' cabin was built out of logs from the Wolf Mountains and stood through three generations of occupancy until 1981 when it was moved to the museum site.

The interior of the cabin features only the necessities needed to make it a home.

## Barn and Blacksmith Shop

The barn was built in 1916 as a part of the original farm site and was a practical addition to the working farm of the era. Today, the barn is used to display a variety of horse tack, branding irons, traps, garden tools, a large collection of woodworking tools and items needed in tending farm animals.

The items displayed in the blacksmith shop were used for years to keep a vast variety of farm machinery in operating condition to farm the thousands of acres under tillage by Campbell Farming Corporation, which once operated the world's largest privately owned wheat farm.

Towering over the barn is a windmill used to pump water from a well before rural electricity was available. Some area ranches still use windmills to provide water for animals in remote areas where electricity is cost prohibitive.

## Farm Exhibit Area

A 1919 Altman Taylor tractor, powered with a gasoline engine; a Mac truck and threshing machines of various models can be seen in and around the Farm Exhibit area.

Part of the equipment is fully restored and operational and some of the equipment needs restoration as funds and time allow.

The tractors, rakes, mowers, planters, and other farm equipment depict the rapid change in technology in farming during this century. The major crops raised in this county include hay, barley, wheat, sugar beets and corn.

## Corinth Store and Post Office

The small community of Corinth, 23 miles northwest of Hardin, was established in 1908 and grew up around the Chicago, Burlington and Quincy Railroad line.

L.R. Good, of Sheridan, Wyoming, moved to Corinth in 1918 and built this store with living quarters in the back. This building also became the Corinth Post Office.

The interior of the store has been restocked to give our visitors a taste of what was available in a small country store. The post office boxes are original and were in the building when it was moved to the museum in 1986.

## Fly Inn

Fly Inn was a cafe and filling station that was built between Hardin and Billings, Montana to meet the needs of the new transportation system that was developing in the region.

In 1928, U.S. Highway 87 was under construction between Billings and Hardin. The highway was completed in 1933. To meet the needs of the travelers on this 50 mile stretch of road, the original Fly Inn was opened by Lee Fly. This 12" by 12" structure was an addition built in 1937. Interstate 90 followed a different route and the Fly Inn was closed in 1958.

The exhibit in the building represents the tools and other equipment that was necessary to keep those wonderful automobiles in running condition. Maps, soda and other items that were needed to assist those weary travelers were also found available in the local "filling stations".

The station was moved to the museum in 1986 and continues to bring nostalgic memories to those who found help along what is now known as the "old road".

## Fort Custer Stage Station

The Fort Custer Stage Station was built in 1994, with funds raised by the Historical Society, to house their growing collection of horse drawn wagons and buggies. This large wooden building was designed to resemble one of the barns at Fort Custer.

Fort Custer, the finest cavalry post in the world, was built on the bluffs south east of this site in 1877. The Fort was abandoned in 1898 and in 1903 the buildings were demolished and nothing was left at the site.

While in the stage barn you will see the mud coach which ran from Fort Custer to Rock Springs, Wyoming, grain wagons used on the Campbell Farming Corporation, a surrey, a variety of buggies and wagons, as well as vintage motorized vehicles.

## Christ Evangelical Lutheran Church

The Christ Evangelical Lutheran Church of Hardin was built by German settlers in 1917. Intense anti-German sentiment in the community forced a brief closure during World War I.

The church was saved from destruction, when the historical society moved it to the museum complex in 1981. This was the first building to be moved to the museum.

Restoration included building a new steeple, complete with bell, plastering the walls and furnishing with all the original furniture and fixtures.

Regular nondenominational services are held each Sunday from June through August and visitors are invited to attend the church services.

## Doctor's Building

Hardin's first hospital was built in 1915, by Dr. O.S. Haverfield on 3rd Street. The hospital, known as the Haverfield General Hospital, brought modern medicine to our area.

Recruiting RN's became difficult due to the lack of housing, so this small building, which originally served as the rectory for the Catholic Priest, was moved from its original site and placed behind the Haverfield Hospital to serve as a home for nurses. The young nurses didn't care for renting the small house, but felt it would be a great place for breaks and resting.

A new community hospital was constructed in 1945 and the Haverfield Hospital was used as a nursing home and the small house once again became a rental.

In 1991, the house was moved to its final resting place at the museum and is used to interpret those early days of medicine.

## Halfway School

The 1922 Halfway School recalls the one-room school days of the past.

The school, which once served area children between Hardin and St. Xavier, Montana, approximately 12 miles south of Hardin on State Highway 313, was moved to the museum in 1983.

The school offered a fully equipped classroom of the period, as evidenced by the various sizes of desks, books and other items used by teachers as they taught several grade levels in one room.

To the west of the school is the historic 1922, merry-go-round that was once located in Custer Park. The City of Hardin donated the merry-go-round in 1996.

*The Lodge Grass Depot Railroad Exhibit.*

The scene is complete with the old school bell well pump and out house.

### Campbell Farming Corporation Camp 4

The humming sound of fifteen gasoline powered 3060 Aultman Taylor tractors plowing unbroken sod was heard for the first time 80 years ago when the Campbell Farming Corporation leased land on the Cheyenne and Crow Indian Reservations to raise wheat to help alleviate food shortages following World War I.

The Campbell Farming Corporation was founded in 1919 by Thomas D. Campbell, who was born in 1882 near Grand Forks, N.D. At the young age of 17, Tom managed his father's 4,000 acre wheat farm.

Campbell approached President Wilson with the idea of raising wheat on a large scale using mechanized farming. He entered into a contract with the government to lease Indian lands on the Fort Peck and Crow Reservations of Montana. By the fall of 1918, Campbell had 7,000 acres in production, but due to the drought of 1919, most of the crop was destroyed. Campbell then moved his equipment out of the Fort Peck area and concentrated on the Crow reservation land. By 1923, Campbell Farming Corporation employed 100 men and cultivated 10,000 acres.

Thomas soon became known as the "King of Wheat Growers" because of the mechanized farming technique he developed to raise wheat in Montana's semi-arid climate.

Campbell Farming Corporation discontinued their farming operations in 1987 and in 1996, the cookhouse, a bunkhouse, shower house and commissary from the Camp 4 site were donated to the Big Horn County Historical Society by the Campbell Farming Corporation. They were moved to the museum site in 1997 and restoration was completed in 1998 with funding from the Corporation and the Campbell Family Foundation.

Camp 4 symbolizes the triumph of mechanized farming in Big Horn County. Only images are left of the lines of wooden grain wagons and granaries, the rows of identical combines setting records for bushels of wheat harvested in a day, and the workers gathering for dinner in the cookhouse.

### Lodge Grass Depot Railroad Exhibit

The Chicago, Burlington & Quincy Railroad opened a station in 1906 at Lodge Grass, Montana.

The depot, which originally didn't have running water or electricity, became the center of the flourishing small community in southeastern Big Horn County. Almost everything came by train to Lodge Grass-even the news.

The depot came to rest on the museum grounds in 1987.

The main floor includes a waiting room, agents office-complete with some of the early day equipment, and the warm and cold freight rooms. Displays include early day railroad equipment, carts, lanterns and photographs.

The second story living quarters is furnished with items from the Arthur Westwood family, who once resided there. Westwood was the Lodge Grass depot agent from 1906-1944.

Resting on the railroad track is one of the last wooden stock cars, a turn of the century Way car and an 1880s drover's car. The drover's car is where the ranchers rode when they shipped their livestock. The drover's car is very similar to early day coach cars.

### Teepees

Teepees, which served as the early day homes of the American Indian, are erected each summer. Eighteen lodge pole pines, which grow in the area mountains are used as the structure for the teepees. Two poles are used to keep the flaps open and allow the smoke to escape. The opening or door of the teepee faces the east to prevent the northwest winds from entering.

### Centennial Park/Picnic Area

Montana celebrated its Statehood Centennial in 1989 and the museum honored that birthday by developing the park and picnic area.

The park serves as a home to 41 trees that signify Montana's admission as the 41st state to enter the union, and allows our guests a great spot to enjoy a picnic.

Open year round, daily May to September and week days only during remaining months.

Coups gave an unforgettable short speech and prayer for peace.

Chief Plenty Coups donated his land and home to be used by all people of all races in friendship. At his death in 1932, the land became Chief Plenty Coups State Park and consists of a 40 acre homestead with a Crow Indian Museum, the Chief's home and store, his grave and a gift shop.

The Park is open from May 1 through September 30, 8 a.m. to 8 p.m. The visitor center hours are 10 a.m. to 5 p.m. A fee is charged.

*Montana Trivia*

80,730 wolves were killed in Montana between 1883 and 1915.

Section 2

*The view from Dryhead Overlook*

## Scenic Drives

**Dryhead Overlook**

This is a long bumpy drive over gravel road. Toward the end, it is not much more than a cattle trail. Four-wheel drive is almost mandatory here. If it's anything but dry out, forget it. Those "Impassable When Wet" signs aren't kidding. That being said, the drive here is worth it. At the end of the drive, you'll be standing atop an 8,500 foot rim looking thousands of feet down into the Bighorn Canyon. It's a view you normally only get from an airplane. Just before the Overlook, you'll pass the Big Ice Cave picnic area. Stop here for a break and take the short walk to the ice cave. Continue up the road for another four miles till you get to the end. You'll know when you get there. This is also the northern edge of the Pryor Mountain Wild Horse Range. Keep your eyes open for these magnificent descendants of the horses left by the Spanish Conquistadors when they explored this area.

To get here, take Hwy. 310 to the little town of Warren just short of the Wyoming border. There is nothing more here than a limestone processing plant and railroad siding. Turn east at the plant, and then take an immediate left on the road heading north. Go about 10 miles to the first major junction you reach (Rd. 211) and turn east toward Sage Creek campground. This road will take you to the overlook.

## Hikes

### Bighorn Canyon Hikes

As parts of the Bighorn Canyon NRA are in Wyoming, we have included some hikes that are partially in Wyoming.

**Trail Safety**

Bighorn Canyon is a dry, desert area. For your safety, please abide by the following precautions whenever hiking:

1. Carry water on all hikes longer than one mile, especially on hot summer days.

2. Wear good, sturdy shoes with closed toes. The canyon trails are rocky and have a lot of spiny vegetation. Sandals and sneakers do not give adequate protection.

3. There may be rattlesnakes anywhere in Bighorn Canyon. Watch where you put your hands and feet. Generally, they are shy and will move away from people, if given the chance.

4. Do not get too close to the canyon rim. In some places there may be overhangs.

5. If you are fair skinned or are not acclimated to the sun, wear sunscreen, a broad brimmed hat, and long sleeves.

6. After any springtime hike, check your skin for ticks.

7. If hiking alone, let someone know where you are going.

**Sykes Mountain Trail**

*Description: Hard, 2-3 miles round trip.*

This is a rugged cross-country hike up a desert mountain. It is for experienced hikers only! Just after you turn onto the Horseshoe Bend access road, take the first drainage that you see on your right (south). Follow this drainage until you see a small game trail on your right (west). Follow this game trail to a rockslide. The game trail then crosses to the left (east) side of the drainage and then disappears. From here, pick your way upward for about a mile through small canyons and rock formations until you come to a deep canyon that forces you to go left (east). Follow the ridge east (left) to an outcropping that overlooks Bighorn Canyon and Horseshoe Bend.

**Crooked Creek Trail**

*Description: Easy, about .5 miles*

This desert nature trail can be reached from the amphitheater in Loop B of the Horseshoe Bend Campground. Head out the back of the amphitheater and go up the ridge directly In front of you. Follow the cairns around loop C of the campground to the marked nature trail. You may request a copy of the trail Interpretive guide at the Lovell Visitors Center.

**Mouth of the Canyon Trail**

*Description: Moderate, 3-Miles Round Trip*

On the north end of Loop B (to your left if you are facing the water). In the Horseshoe Bend Campground you will find a service road that leads toward a water storage tank. Follow this road until it meets up wIth an abandoned road that veers off to the right just before you reach the water storage tank. Follow this abandoned road to where Crooked Creek runs into the canyon. Double back through a juniper lined draw to the top of the ridge. Follow the cairns back to the old road just east (left) of the water tank. This trail offers spectacular views of the Pryor and Bighorn Mountains and the red badlands surrounding Horseshoe Bend.

**State Line Trail**

*Description: Easy to Moderate, I Mile Round Trip*

Just north of the Montana State line, you will find a cairn marking the beginning of this trail. Follow the cairns along an old road that leads to the rim of the canyon. You may then follow the canyon rim for several hundred feet. This trail leads through juniper forest and limestone plateaus to unique views of the canyon.

**Lower Layout Creek Trail**

*Description: Easy to Moderate, Approximately 3.5 Miles Round Trip*

The end of the Wild Horse Range is marked with a cattle guard. Follow an old two-track road, which begins to the right of the cattle guard and runs parallel to Layout Creek, to the juncture where Layout Creek Canyon joins with Bighorn Canyon. You may then follow the canyon rim for several hundred feet. This hike offers several opportunities to stray from the main trail and view Layout Creek Canyon and offers spectacular views of Bighorn Canyon as well. This trail is also located in the Pryor Mountain Wild Horse Range, so there is a possibility of viewing some wild horses from afar. Ultimately, this road loops in a horseshoe shape and meets the main road approximately .5 miles from where the two-track road began. However, you may alternately follow a well trodden horse trail which begins near the canyon rims and eventually re-joins the two-track road near it's beginning. This route will shorten your round trip hike to approximately 3 miles.

**Hillsboro**

*Description: Easy to Moderate, I to 3 Miles Round Trip*

Follow the turn off for Barry's Landing down past the campground. On your right hand side, you will see a red dirt road extending up a hill. Drive or walk the half mile to a gate and kiosk. From here it is another half mile into Hillsboro by foot trail. The trail continues beyond the ranch itself and becomes the original wagon road into the ranch. Spend some time exploring the ranch as well as the views of trail creek canyon.

**Sullivan's Knob Trail**

*Description: Easy to Moderate, I Mile Round Trip*

Roughly 1 mile north of Devil's Canyon Overlook, you will find a turnout around a geological formation known as Sullivan's knob. Turn into the parking lot at Sullivan's knob. Follow the cairns and the trail to the right of the hill directly in front of you (East). Follow the cairns to the canyon rim. From there it's possible to see the north side of Devil's Canyon Overlook.

**Upper Layout Creek Trail**

*Description: Moderate, 4 Miles Round Trip*

Approximately 5 miles from the turnoff for Devil's Canyon Overlook you will find a turnoff on the left side of the road marked "historic site." Turn off here and follow the road into the parking area east (left) of the corrals. Go through the corrals and follow an old road along Layout Creek to where the creek enters Layout Creek Canyon. This trail goes between a limestone plateau and a lush river area up to the base of East Pryor Mountain.

**Barry's Island Trail**

*Description: Moderate, 5 MIles Round Trip*

Follow the turnoff for Barry's Landing until the road dead ends In a parking area. To the north (your left if you are facing into the parking area), you will see a red road leading away from the parking area. Follow this road 1/4 of a mile until you meet a gate. On foot, follow this road until it submerges underwater. You will then see a game wall, which will lead you to where the road emerges. Continue on the old road about half a mile beyond the Medicine Creek Campground to Wassin Canyon.

**Lockhart Ranch**

*Description: Easy, 1.5 Miles Round Trip*

Beyond Barry's Landing, Highway 37 becomes a dirt road. Follow this dirt road 2.5 miles to Lockhart Ranch. You may park in the pull-out across from the gate to the ranch. To the left of the gate you will find a cutout in the fence. Use this to gain access to the ranch. Beyond the gate you will find a kiosk and a trail into the ranch. East (left) of the corrals, you will find a garage, which lies just north of an old road that runs along Davis Creek and offers views of the Pryor Mountains. At the end of this trail, take a left to continue on the main dirt road, which meets up with the main road, or follow the Davis Creek Trail back to the ranch. Then take a right to finish the loop through the ranch and head back to the parking area.

**Om-Ne-A Trail**

This is a rim-top trail that provides some awesome views of the magnificent Bighorn Canyon. The 3-mile trail goes from Yellowtail Dam to Ok-A-Beh marina. The trail starts at Yellowtail Dam and is steep for the first quarter mile.

# Fly Fishing at its Finest

by Mike DuFresne

The fly fishing in the Billings area of south central Montana is some of the best in the state. It's so good that the Bighorn River is rated as one of the best trout fisheries in the world. Here is some information on our favorite local waters.

## Bighorn River

This is the world renowned fishery that anglers are most familiar with. The portion of the river most commonly fished is a 13 mile section below the Yellowtail Dam on the Crow Indian Reservation near the small government community of Fort Smith (Yellowtail). This is approximately 90 miles southeast of Billings and 45 miles south of Hardin.

Because of the year round stable flows of cold clear water, this river sustains an incredibly

large population of aquatic insects, which in turn can support a population of catchable trout that numbers over 6,000 per mile. There is a mixture of rainbow and brown trout in the river with brown trout being the most abundant. An average fish is over 14 inches with four-year-old trout averaging 20 inches. The primary food sources are freshwater shrimp, aquatic sowbugs, midges, and incredible mayfly and caddis fly hatches.

Whether you like to fish dry flies, nymphs or streamers, this is a great river for all. With so many fish, this is also a great river to learn how to fly fish as your opportunities of catching fish are more than double any other river in Montana. A guide is always recommended for your first outing on this river to ensure the best fishing experience.

## The Stillwater River

This classic freestone river is located approximately 45 miles west of Billings and flows into the Yellowstone River just outside of Columbus. This river is much more typical when picturing a Montana trout stream. A free-flowing river that is the farthest thing from still, the Stillwater has fast water riffles, deep pools, large meanders, slippery boulders and incredible scenery. The best fishing is from April through September for brown and rainbow trout that readily take flies from the surface. An average fish on this river will be around ten inches with a large fish being fifteen inches or more. For a quick getaway from Billings, this is your best bet. There are at least ten public access points along over 30 miles of river. Primarily fished with a large dry fly with a bead head dropper, the fishing can be fast and furious. Streamers work well for those die-hards looking for the big one. A guided float trip in a raft is the recommended method of fishing, however, with the large amount of access, this is one that's fun to fish on your own.

## The Lower Yellowstone River

The portion of the Yellowstone below Livingston holds a large population trout that are most easily caught from a drift boat. This wild and scenic river is home to rainbow, brown and cutthroat trout along with whitetail and mule deer, bald eagles, and many other furred and feathered creatures. Because of the size of the river and limited access points, the Yellowstone is best fished with a guide and a drift boat. April and May and then July to October is prime time to fish. June is usually high water month from the melting mountain snow and for much of the month is virtually unfishable. Large dry flies with droppers, streamers and late summer grasshoppers provide some incredible fishing. This is the river for you if you want to be away from the crowds and want the experience of Montana and the longest free-flowing river in the country.

## Monster Lake

If you want to catch a real Monster, this one is for you. With the average fish weighing over 4 pounds, this private lake is your best shot at fish weighing in the double digits. Just a two-hour drive from Billings, Monster Lake is approximately 10 miles southeast of Cody, Wyoming. The lake is one of the richest in food in our region supporting large numbers of very big rainbow, brown, brook and even a few cutthroat trout. This 150-acre lake is limited to twelve fly fishers a day and all fish must be released. Either fished with a guide or on your own, you can count on some trophy photos to take back home.

For more information on fly fishing the local area, contact:

Bighorn Fly & Tackle Shop
485 S. 24th St West, Billings, MT 59102
Phone 656-8257
E-mail: info@bighornfly.com
Or see them on the web at
www.bighornfly.com
http://www.bighornfly.com

# Information Please

All Montana area codes are 406

## Road Information

| | |
|---|---|
| Montana Road Condition Report | |
| 800-226-7623, 800-335-7592 or local | 444-7696 |
| Montana Highway Patrol | 444-7696 |
| **Local Road Reports** | |
| Billings | 252-2806 |
| Billings Weather Reports | 652-1916 |

## Tourism Information

| | |
|---|---|
| Travel Montana | 800-847-4868 outside Montana<br>444-2654 in Montana<br>http://travel.mt.gov/. |
| Custer Country | 800-346-1876 or 665-1671 |
| Northern Rodeo Association | 252-1122 |
| **Chambers of Commerce** | |
| Montana | 442-2405 |
| Billings | 245-4111 |
| Hardin | 665-1672 |
| Laurel | 628-4504 |
| Hysham | 342-5457 |

## Airports

| | |
|---|---|
| Billings | 657-8495 |
| Fort Smith | 666-2412 |
| Hardin | 665-2301 |
| Hysham | 342-5563 |

## Government Offices

| | |
|---|---|
| State BLM Office | 255-2885, 238-1540 |
| Bureau of Land Management | |
| Billings Field Office | 896-5013 |
| Custer National Forest | 657-6200 |
| Montana Fish, Wildlife & Parks | 247-2940 |
| U.S. Bureau of Reclamation | 247-7295 |

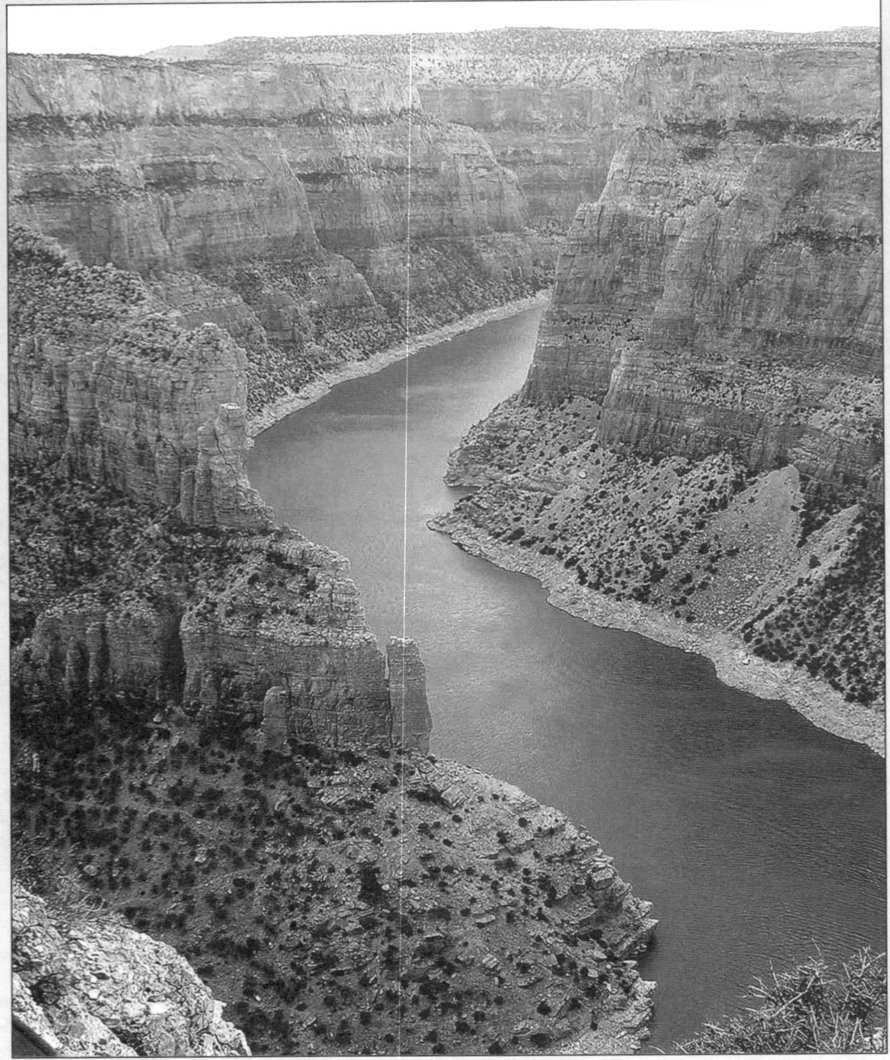

# Bighorn Canyon

At first glance, time seems to have stopped at Bighorn Canyon. The lake and the steep-sided canyons provide a peaceful setting for those seeking a break from the daily routine. The focus of the area is 71 -mile-long Bighorn Lake, created by Yellowtail Dam near Fort Smith. Dedicated in 1968, the dam provides electric power, water for irrigation, flood control, and recreation. Boating, water skiing, fishing, swimming, and sightseeing are main attractions.

While you enjoy the play of light and shadow on rock and water, take time to contemplate the changes that the land and the life upon it have undergone. Time and water are keys to the canyon, where the land has been shaped by moving water since upheavals of the Earth's crust built the Pryor and Bighorn mountains millions of years ago. For 15 miles upstream from the dam, the lake bisects a massive, arching anticline, exposing fossils that tell of successive times when this land was submerged under a shallow sea, when it was a tropical marsh, and when its conifer forests were inhabited by dinosaurs. Humans arrived here more than 10,000 years ago, living as hunters and gatherers. In modern times people have further altered the land.

Most of Bighorn's visitors come to enjoy the recreational opportunities the lake offers. Boaters, water skiers, anglers and scuba divers are all attracted here. But the park offers more than just the lake: from the wild flowers in spring and summer to more than 200 species of birds; from the stories of life forms adapting to a harsh environment to the modern search for energy. You can get more information on what the park offers at visitor centers near Lovell, WY, and Fort Smith, MT. Find your own place of solitude to relax and to enjoy the diversity and timelessness of this uncommon canyon water land.

## A Challenging Land

In North America people have traveled and made their living along rivers and streams for more than 40,000 years. But the Bighorn River was too treacherous and too steep-walled. People here lived near the Bighorn but avoided navigating it—until the dam tamed the river.

The broken land here also challenged the ingenuity of early residents, forcing them to devise unusual strategies of survival. More than 10,000 years ago, Indian hunters drove herds of game into land traps. These Indians lived simply, gathering wild roots and seeds to balance and supplement their meat diet. They made clothes of skins, baskets and sandals of plant fibers, and tools of stone, bone, and wood. The many caves of the Bighorn area provided seasonal shelters and storage areas for the Indians, as well as for early traders and trappers.

Absaroke means "People of the largebeaked bird," in the Siouan language of the Crow. Their reservation surrounds most of Bighorn Canyon. Originally a farming people, the Crow split off from the Hidatsa tribe more than 200 years ago. They became a renowned hunting people, described by one of the Lewis and Clark Expedition as "the finest horsemen in the world."

After 1800, explorers, traders, and trappers found their way up the Bighorn River. Charles Larocque met the Crow at the mouth of the Bighorn in 1805; Captain William Clark traveled through a year later. Jim Bridger claimed he had floated through the canyon on a raft. Later fur traders packed their goods overland on the Bad Pass Trail, avoiding the river's dangers.

During the Civil War the Bozeman Trail led to mines in western Montana by crossing the Bighorn River. Open from 1864 to 1868, the trail was bitterly opposed by Sioux and Cheyenne; the Crow were neutral. The Federal Government closed the trail in 1868 after the Fort Laramie Treaty. Fort C.F. Smith, now on private land, guarded the trail as an outpost. A stone monument commemorates the Hayfield Fight, a desperate but successful defense against Sioux and Cheyenne warriors. In this skirmish a party of soldiers and civilian haycutters, working three miles north of Fort C.F. Smith, fought for eight hours until rescued by the fort's troops on August 1, 1867.

After the Civil War, cattle ranching became a way of life. Among the huge open-range cattle ranches was the Mason-Lovell (the ML); some of those buildings remain. Dude ranching, reflected in the remains of Hillsboro, was popular in the early 1900s.

The Crow made the transition from hunter-gatherers to ranchers in one generation. In 1904, after 12 years of labor, they completed an irrigation system and opened 35,000 acres of land to irrigated farming. Water was diverted into the Bighorn Canal by a 416-foot diversion dam, moving 720 cubic feet of water per second. Near Afterbay Campground is Bighorn Canal Headgate, remains of this human response to the challenge of the land.

Congress established Bighorn Canyon National Recreation Area in 1966 as part of the National Park System to provide enjoyment for visitors today and to protect the park for future generations.

## Bighorn Canyon Visitor Center

The solar-heated visitor center near Lovell, WY., symbolizes the energy-conscious concerns of the National Park Service and of modern Americans. The heating is accomplished by storing heat from the sun in a rock bin, then blowing hot air through the building. The Yellowtail Dam Visitor Center, in the park, is two miles past the community of Fort Smith. It is approachable from the north by car.

## Bighorn Wildlife

The wildlife of the Bighorn Canyon country is as varied as the land, which can be divided into four climate or vegetative zones. In the south is desert shrub land inhabited by wild horses, snakes, and small rodents. Midway is juniper woodland with coyotes, deer, bighorn sheep, beaver, wood rats, and porcupine. Along the flanks of the canyon is pine and fir woodland with mountain lions, bear, elk, and mule deer. In the north is shortgrass prairie, once home to herds of buffalo. Many of the smaller animals, such as cottontails, skunks, coyotes, and rattlesnakes, are seen frequently throughout the park. More than 200 species of birds, including many kinds of water fowl, have been seen here. Each plant and animal species is adapted to the particular conditions of temperature, moisture, and landform within one or more of the park's four primary zones.

*Bighorn sheep are a common sight in the canyon.*

## Yellowtail Dam

The dam is named in honor of Robert Yellowtail, former Crow tribal chairman and reservation superintendent. The dam creates one of the largest reservoirs on the Missouri River tributary system. This arch type dam is 525 feet high.

## Yellowtail Wildlife Habitat Management Area

Riparian, cottonwood forest, shrub land, and wetlands provide habitat for whitetail deer, bald eagles, pelicans, heron, water fowl, wild turkeys, and other species. The area is managed by the Wyoming Game and Fish Department through agreements with the National Park Service, Bureau of Land Management, and Bureau of Reclamation.

## Ranch Sites

**Mason-Lovell Ranch:** A.L. Mason and H.C Lovell built cattle ranch headquarters here in 1883. Cattle roamed the Bighorn Basin in a classic open-range operation.

**Hillsboro:** A one mile round trip trail takes you to the site of Grosvenor William Barry's Cedarvale Guest Ranch and the 1915 to 1945 Hillsboro post office.

**Lockhart:** Caroline Lockhart, a reporter, editor, and author, began ranching at age 56. The well preserved buildings give a feel for ranch life; one mile roundup.

**Ewing-Snell:** This site was in use for nearly 100 years.

## Bad Pass Trail

American Indians camped along this trail 10,000 years ago, and in prehistoric and historic times Shoshone used it to get to the buffalo plains. Early trappers and traders used it to avoid the dangers of the Bighorn River. You can see rock calms left along the route between Devil Canyon Overlook and Barry's Landing. Before the arrival of the horse, life changed little here for thousands of years. Small family groups wintered in caves near the canyon bottoms. In early spring they moved out of the canyon bottoms in search of plants and small animals, and in summer they moved to the highlands in search of game and summer maturing plants. Large groups gathered in fall for a communal bison hunt.

### Devil Canyon Overlook

Here the canyon crosscuts the gray limestone of the Devil Canyon Anticline, a 1,000-foot high segment of the fault blocks that make up the Pryor Mountains.

## What to See and Do

A film at Bighorn Canyon Visitor Center highlights park activities. Exhibits explain the canyon's history and natural features.

Boating enthusiasts will find a marina, snack bar, camp store (gas and oil), and boat ramp at Horseshoe Bend and OkABeh. Ramps are also at Afterbay Dam and Barry's Landing. All boaters should sign registration sheets at the ramps when entering and leaving the lake. If mechanical problems develop while you are on the lake, stay with your boat; hail other boaters and ask them to notify a ranger. Carry both day and night signaling devices. Do not try to climb the lake's steep canyon walls.

Swimmers are encouraged to use the lifeguarded areas at Horseshoe Bend and Ok-A-Beh.

Camping is restricted to designated sites in developed areas. It is also allowed in the back country and below the highwater mark along Bighorn Lake. Fire restrictions during periods of high fire danger may close certain areas to camping. Check with a ranger for the restrictions on fires or back country camping.

Hiking is available in the national recreation area and in nearby forests. Ask at the visitor centers for more information.

Hunting is allowed in designated areas in accordance with state laws. Trapping is prohibited.

Fishing in Montana or Wyoming requires the appropriate state fishing license. Fine game fish, such as brown and rainbow trout, sauger, ling, and perch, abound.

The most popular game fish, a gourmet's delight, is the walleye. Winter ice fishing around Horseshoe Bend is good. The Bighorn River provides excellent brown and rainbow trout fishing.

Regulations and Safety: Firearms are prohibited in developed areas and areas of concentrated public use, unless they are unloaded and cased. Pets must be on a leash in developed areas and in areas of concentrated public use. Trash and waste disposals into area waters are prohibited; all vessels must have a waste receptacle on board. Carry a first-aid kit as a precaution against poisonous snake bites.

All plants, animals, natural and cultural features, and archeological sites are protected by federal law. Collecting is prohibited.

*Reprinted from National Park Service brochure.*

## Indian Reservations

| | |
|---|---|
| Northern Cheyenne Reservation | 477-8844 |
| Crow Reservation | 638-2601 |

## Hospitals

| | |
|---|---|
| Ask-A-Nurse • Billings | 657-8778 |
| Billings Inter-Hospital Onclay •Billings | 259-2245 |
| Deaconess Medical Center • Billings | 657-4000 |
| St. Vincents Hospital • Billings | 657-7000 |
| US PHS Hospital • Crow Agency | 638-2626 |
| Big Horn County Memorial Hospital Hardin | 665-2310 |

## Golf Courses

| | |
|---|---|
| Lake Hills Golf Club Pro Shop Billings | 252-9244 |
| Par-3 Exchange City Golf Course Club House Billings | 652-2553 |
| Peter Yegen Jr. Golf Club • Billings | 656-8099 |

## Bed & Breakfasts

| | |
|---|---|
| **The Josephine B&B** Billings | 248-5898 |
| **Sanderson Inn** • Billings | 656-3388 |
| **Westwood Ranch B&B** Lodge Grass | 248-2622 |
| Cowdin's Carriage House B&B Billings | 652-5108 |
| Cross A Guest Ranch • Lodge Grass | 639-2697 |
| Hotel Becker B&B • Hardin | 665-2707 |
| Pine Hills Place B&B • Billings | 252-2288 |
| Tight Lines Lodge • Saint Xavier | 666-2240 |
| Sisters Inn • Billings | 252-9350 |
| V Lazy B B&B and Horse Motel Molt | 669-3885 |
| Wald Ranch • Lodge Grass | 639-2457 |
| Westwood Ranch B&B • Lodge Grass | 639-2450 |

## Private Campgrounds

| | |
|---|---|
| **Big Sky Campground & RV** Billings | 259-4110 |
| **Big Horn RV Park** • St. Xavier | 666-2460 |
| Battlefield Express Center • Crow | 638-4452 |
| Casa Village • Billings | 656-3915 |
| Cottonwood Camp • Fort Smith | 666-2391 |
| Fort Custer Campground • Custer | 856-4191 |
| Eastwood Estates • Billings | 245-7733 |
| Glentana Mobile Home Ct • Billings | 259-2177 |
| Grandview Campground • Hardin | 665-2489 |
| KOA Kampgrounds • Hardin | 665-1635 |
| KOA Inc • Billings | 248-7444 |
| KOA Kampgrounds • Billings | 252-3104 |
| Little Big Horn Camp • Crow Agency | 638-2232 |
| Trailer Village • Billings | 248-8685 |
| Yellowstone River RV Park & Campground Billings | 259-0878 |

## Guest Ranches & Resorts

| | |
|---|---|
| Bighorn River Country Lodge Fort Smith | 666-2332 |
| Big Sky Roping Ranch • Huntley | 348-2460 |
| Cross A Guest Ranch • Lodge Grass | 639-2697 |
| Double Spear Ranch • Pryor | 259-8291 |
| Eagle Nest Lodge • Hardin | 665-3712 |
| Seventh Ranch • Garryowen | 638-2438 |

## Car Rental

| | |
|---|---|
| AA-A Auto Rental | 245-9759 |
| Ace-Rent-A-Car | 252-2399 |
| Avis Rent-A-Car | 252-8007 |
| Budget Rent-A-Car | 259-4168 |
| Dollar Rent-A-Car | 259-1147 |
| Enterprise Billings West | 652-2000 |
| Enterprise Rent-A-Car | 259-9999 |
| Hertz Rent-A-Car | 248-9151 |

National Car Rental 252-7626
Rent A Wreck 245-5982
Thrifty Car Rental 259-1025
U Save Auto Rental 655-4440

## Outfitters & Guides

*F=Fishing H=Hunting R=River Guides*
*E=Horseback Rides G=General Guide Services*

**Bighorn Fly & Tackle Shop** G F 656-8257
**Bighorn Fly & Tackle Shop** G F 666-2253
Angler's Edge Outfitters F 666-2417
Big Horn Angler HF 666-2233
Big Horn Trout Outfitters RF 666-2224
Big Horn River Country Lodge F 666-2351
Big Horn Trout Shop F 666-2375
Bighorn River Lodge F 666-2368
Brad Downey's Anglers' Edge HRF 666-2417
Cat Track Outfitters HF 347-5499
Eagle Nest Lodge & Outfitters G 665-3711
East Slope Outfitters HF 666-2320
Elk River Outfitters G F H 656-4271
Fort Smith Flyshop F 666-2550
George Kelly Bighorn Country HF 666-2326
Forrester's Bighorn River Resorts GHF 666-9199
Kingfisher Lodge/Big Horn Country Outfitters G F 666-2326
Last Stand Lodge R F 665-3489
Last Stand Outfitters G H 665-3489
Montella From Montana RF 666-2360
MT Adventures in Angling GFREG 248-2995
MT River Discoveries R 651-0537
Phil Gonzalez's Bighorn River Lodge G 666-2368
Schneider's Guide Service G 666-2460
Stillwaters Outfitting FR 652-8111
Sunshine Sports R 252-3724
Two Leggins Outfitters HFR 665-2825
Western Waters G F R 252-5212

## NOTES:

## Public Campgrounds

## Campsite Directions

| Campsite Directions | Season | Camping | Trailers | Toilets | Water | Boat Launch | Fishing | Swimming | Trails | Stay Limit | Fee |
|---|---|---|---|---|---|---|---|---|---|---|---|
| **11•Huntley Diversion Dam USBR**<br>1 mi. W of I-94.Huntley Exit on gravel road | All Year | • | | | | B | • | | | 14 | |
| **12•Anita Reservoir USBR**<br>4 mi. S of I-94•Pompeys Pillar Exit | All Year | • | | | | A | • | | | 14 | |
| **13•BIGHORN CANYON NATIONAL RECREATION AREA•Afterbay NPS•**<br>1 mi. NE of Yellowtail Dam | All Year | 48 | | D | • | C | • | | N | 14 | |
| **14•BIGHORN CANYON NATIONAL RECREATION AREA•Barry's Landing NPS•**<br>27 mi. N of Lovell, WY•on WY 37 | All Year | 9 | • | D | | C | • | | • | 14 | |
| **15•Sage Creek FS**<br>3 mi. S of Bridger on US 310•22 mi. SE on Cty. Rd.•1 mi. E on Forest Rd. 50 | 6/15-9/15 | 12 | 20' | • | | | • | | | 10 | |

**Agency**
FS—U.S.D.A Forest Service
FWP—Montana Fish, Wildlife & Parks
NPS—National Park Service
BLM—U.S. Bureau of Land Management
USBR—U.S. Bureau of Reclamation
CE—Corps of Engineers

**Camping**
Camping is allowed at this site. Number indicates camping spaces available

H—Hard sided units only; no tents

**Trailers**
Trailer units allowed. Number indicates maximum length.

**Toilets**
Toilets on site. D—Disabled access

**Water**
Drinkable water on site

**Fishing**
Visitors may fish on site

**Boat**
Type of boat ramp on site:
A—Hand launch
B—4-wheel drive with trailer
C—2-wheel drive with trailer

**Swimming**
Designated swimming areas on site

**Trails**
Trails on site
B—Backpacking N—Nature/Interpretive

**Stay Limit**
Maximum length of stay in days

**Fee**
Camping and/or day-use fee

## Fishery

| Fishery | Cold Water Species | | | | | | | | | | | | Warm Water Species | | | | | | | | | | Services | | | | | |
|---|---|---|---|---|---|---|---|---|---|---|---|---|---|---|---|---|---|---|---|---|---|---|---|---|---|---|---|---|
| | Brook Trout | Mt. Whitefish | Lake Whitefish | Golden Trout | Cutthroat Trout | Brown Trout | Rainbow Trout | Kokanee Salmon | Bull Trout | Lake Trout | Arctic Grayling | Burbot | Largemouth Bass | Smallmouth Bass | Walleye | Sauger | Northern Pike | Shovelnose Sturgeon | Channel Catfish | Yellow Perch | Crappie | Paddlefish | Vehicle Access | Campgrounds | Toilets | Docks | Boat Ramps | MotorRestrictions |
| 12. Yellowtail Afterbay | | | | | | • | • | | | | | | | | | | | | | | | | • | • | • | • | • | |
| 13. Bighorn Lake | | | | | | • | • | | | | | | • | | • | • | | | • | • | • | | • | | • | • | • | |
| 14. Yellowstone River | | | | | | • | • | | | | | | | • | • | • | • | • | • | | | • | • | • | • | | • | |
| 15. Lake Elmo | | | | | | | | | | | | | • | | | | | | • | • | • | | • | | • | | • | • |
| 16. Lake Josephine | | | | | | | | | | | | | • | | | | | | • | • | • | | • | | • | | | • |
| 17. Bighorn River | | • | | | | • | • | | | | | • | | • | | | | | • | | | | • | • | • | | • | • |

## Notes:

## Dining Quick Reference

Price Range refers to the average cost of a meal per person: ($) $1-$6, ($$) $7-$11, ($$$) $12-up. Cocktails: "Yes" indicates full bar; Beer (B)/Wine (W), Service: Breakfast (B), Brunch (BR), Lunch (L), Dinner (D). Businesses in bold print will have additional information under the appropriate map locator number in the body of this section.

| RESTAURANT | TYPE CUISINE | PRICE RANGE | CHILD MENU | COCKTAILS BEER WINE | SERVICE | CREDIT CARDS | MAP LOCATOR NUMBER |
|---|---|---|---|---|---|---|---|
| Patrick's Cafe | American | $$ | | Yes | L/D | | 1 |
| Junction City Saloon | American | $ | | Yes | L/D | | 5 |
| Fort Custer | American | $ | | Yes | B/L/D | Major | 5 |
| Jud's Longbranch Bar & Cafe | American | $$ | | Yes | L/D | | 8 |
| Country Kitchen | Family | $-$$ | Yes | | B/L/D | Major | 8 |
| Miller's Darkhorse Saloon | | | | | | | 8 |
| Bluecat Inn | | | | | | | 10 |
| Sam's Cafe | Family | $/$$ | | Yes | B/L/D | Major | 10 |
| **Godfather's Pizza** | Pizza | $ | Yes | B | L/D | V/M/D | 12 |
| **Golden Phoenix Chinese Restaurant** | Chinese | $/$$ | | | L/D | Major | 12 |
| **Jalisco's** | Mexican | $/$$ | Yes | Yes | L/D | Major | 12 |
| **Peking House Express** | Chinese | $ | | | L/D | Major | 12 |
| Applebee's Neighborhood Grill | Eclectic | $$/$$$ | Yes | Yes | L/D | Major | 12 |
| Burger Barb's | Burgers | $$ | Yes | B/W | L/D | Major | 12 |
| Burger King | Fast Food | $ | Yes | | B/L/D | | 12 |
| Dairy Queen | Fast Food | $ | Yes | | L/D | | 12 |
| Elmer's Pancake & Steak House | Family | $-$$ | Yes | | B/L/D | Major | 12 |
| Grand Bagel Company | Deli | $ | | | B/L | | 12 |
| Kit Kat Cafe | American | $ | Yes | | B/L/D | | 12 |
| McDonald's | Fast Food | $ | Yes | | B/L/D | | 12 |
| Papa John's Pizza | Pizza | $ | Yes | | L/D | | 12 |
| Subway | Fast Food | $ | Yes | | L/D | | 12 |
| Taco John's | Fast Food | $ | Yes | | L/D | | 12 |
| Arby's | Fast Food | $ | Yes | | B/L/D | | 12 |
| Blimpie's Subs | Fast Food | $ | Yes | | L/D | | 12 |
| Bugz's Restaurant | American | $ | | Yes | B/L/D | | 12 |
| Circle Inn | American | $ | | Yes | | | 12 |
| Doc & Eddy's Restaurant | Family | $$ | Yes | B/W | L/D | V/M | 12 |
| Domino's Pizza | Pizza | $ | | | L/D | | 12 |
| Pizza Hut | Pizza | $/$$ | Yes | B | L/D | V/M/D | 12 |
| Taco Bell | Fast Food | $ | Yes | | L/D | | 12 |
| Wendy's | Fast Food | $ | Yes | | L/D | | 12 |
| Blimpie's Subs | Fast Food | $ | Yes | | L/D | | 14 |
| Burger King | Fast Food | $ | Yes | | B/L/D | | 14 |
| Jackpot Diner | Family | $/$$ | Yes | | | | 14 |
| Subway | Fast Food | $ | Yes | | L/D | | 14 |
| Arby's | Fast Food | $ | Yes | | B/L/D | | 14 |
| Wolfy's Diner | Family | $/$$ | Yes | | B/L/D | Major | 14 |
| **Club Carlin** | Fine Dining | $$/$$$ | | Yes | D | Major | 15 |
| **McCormick Cafe** | Eclectic | $/$$ | Yes | | B/L | Major | 15 |
| **The Rex** | Regional American | $–$$$ | Yes | Yes | L/D | Major | 15 |
| **Juliano's** | Fine Dining | $$$ | | Yes | L/D | Major | 15 |
| **Bruno's Italian Specialties** | Italian | $/$$ | Yes | Yes | L/D | Major | 15 |
| **Rocket Burritos Gourmet Burritos & Sodas** | Gourmet Burritos | $ | | | L/D | | 15 |
| The Beanery Bar & Grill | American | $$/$$$ | Yes | B/W | L/D | Major | 15 |
| La Soledad | Mexican/American | $$ | Yes | Yes | L/D | MC/V | 15 |
| Montana Brewing Company | Brew Pub | $$ | | B/W | L/D | | 15 |
| Puerta Vallarta Mexican Restaurant | Mexican | $$ | Yes | B/W | L/D | | 15 |
| Scooter's Java Pub | Coffee House | | | | | | 15 |
| Burger King | Fast Food | $ | Yes | | B/L/D | | 15 |
| Denny's | Family | $ | Yes | | B/L/D | V/M | 15 |
| Hardee's | Fast Food | $ | Yes | | B/L/D | | 15 |
| Jake's | Steakhouse | $$ | | Yes | L/D | Major | 15 |
| Kentucky Fried Chicken | Fast Food | $ | Yes | | L/D | | 15 |
| Perkins Family Restaurant | Family | $/$$ | Yes | | B/L/D | Major | 15 |
| Walkers Grill | American Bistro | $$/$$$ | Yes | Yes | D | Major | 15 |
| Athenian | Greek | $$/$$$ | Yes | B/W | L/D | Major | 15 |
| El Burrito Cafeteria | Mexican | $$ | | | B/L/D | | 15 |
| George Henry's Restaurant | Gourmet | $$/$$$ | | Yes | L/D | Major | 15 |
| Maxines Eatery | American | $$ | | | B/L | | 15 |
| Stella's Kitchen & Bakery | American | $/$$ | | | B/L | | 15 |

## Dining Quick Reference—Continued

Price Range refers to the average cost of a meal per person: ($) $1-$6, ($$) $7-$11, ($$$) $12-up. Cocktails: "Yes" indicates full bar; Beer (B)/Wine (W), Service: Breakfast (B), Brunch (BR), Lunch (L), Dinner (D). Businesses in bold print will have additional information under the appropriate map locator number in the body of this section.

| RESTAURANT | TYPE CUISINE | PRICE RANGE | CHILD MENU | COCKTAILS BEER WINE | SERVICE | CREDIT CARDS | MAP LOCATOR NUMBER |
|---|---|---|---|---|---|---|---|
| Wendy's | Fast Food | $ | Yes | | L/D | | 15 |
| Cafe Jones | Coffee House | | | | | | 15 |
| Grand Bagel Company | Deli | $ | | | B/L | | 15 |
| Little Bangkok Restaurant | Asian | $$ | | | L/D | Major | 15 |
| NaRa Oriental Restaurant | Japanese/Korean | $$ | | | L/D | Major | 15 |
| O'Hara's Restaurant | Family | $ | Yes | | B/L/D | | 15 |
| Pug Mahon's | Irish Pub | $$/$$$ | Yes | Yes | L/D | Major | 15 |
| Quizno's Classic Subs | Subs | $ | Yes | | L/D | | 15 |
| Thai Orchid Restaurant | Thai/Chinese | $/$$ | | | L/D | V/M | 15 |
| Cattin's Family Dining | Family | $ | Yes | | B/L/D | | 15 |
| **Matthew's Taste of Italy** | Italian | $$/$$$ | Yes | Yes | L/D | V/M/A | 16 |
| Pizza Chef | Pizza | $$ | | | L/D | | 16 |
| Pizza Hut | Pizza | $/$$ | Yes | B | L/D | V/M/D | 16 |
| Twisters | Coffee House | | | | | | 16 |
| **The Bungalow** | American | $-$$$ | Yes | Yes | L/D | V/M | 17 |
| Blondies | Deli | $ | | | B/L/D | | 17 |
| Dairy Queen | Fast Food | $ | Yes | | L/D | | 17 |
| Lucky Cuss Casino | American | $$ | | Yes | L/D | Major | 17 |
| Pizza Hut | Pizza | $/$$ | Yes | B | L/D | V/M/D | 17 |
| Subway | Fast Food | $ | Yes | | L/D | | 17 |
| 4B's Restaurant | Family | $ | Yes | | B/L/D | V/M/D | 17 |
| Burger King | Fast Food | $ | Yes | | B/L/D | | 17 |
| McDonald's | Fast Food | $ | Yes | | B/L/D | | 17 |
| McDonalds | Fast Food | $ | Yes | | B/L/D | | 17 |
| Subway | Fast Food | $ | Yes | | L/D | | 17 |
| **Pork Chop John's** | Fast Food | $ | Yes | | L/D | | 19 |
| Arby's | Fast Food | $ | Yes | | B/L/D | | 19 |
| Burger King | Fast Food | $ | Yes | | B/L/D | | 19 |
| China Buffet | Chinese | $$ | | | L/D | Major | 19 |
| Dairy Queen | Fast Food | $ | Yes | | L/D | | 19 |
| Four Seas Restaurant | Family | $ | | Yes | | | 19 |
| Great Wall Chinese Restaurant | Chinese | | Yes | B/W | L/D | Major | 19 |
| Happy Diner | American | $ | Yes | | B/L/D | | 19 |
| J B'S Restaurant | Family | $ | Yes | | B/L/D | V/M | 19 |
| Khanthaly's Eggrolls II | Oriental | | | | | | 19 |
| Little Caesar's | Pizza | $ | | | L/D | | 19 |
| Marco Polo Gardens | Chinese | $$ | | | L/D | Major | 19 |
| McDonald's | Fast Food | $ | Yes | | B/L/D | | 19 |
| Pizza Hut | Pizza | $/$$ | Yes | B | L/D | V/M/D | 19 |
| Subway | Fast Food | $ | Yes | | L/D | | 19 |
| Taco Bell | Fast Food | $ | Yes | | L/D | | 19 |
| Taco John's | Fast Food | $ | Yes | | L/D | | 19 |
| Taco Treat | Fast Food | $ | Yes | | L/D | | 19 |
| Wendy's | Fast Food | $ | Yes | | L/D | | 19 |
| Chelsea's Yogurts | Fast food/Frozen Yogurt | $ | | | L/D | | 19 |
| Gulliver's Restaurant | American | $/$$ | | | B/L/D | | 19 |
| Musgrave's | Coffee House | $/$$ | | | | | 19 |
| PK's Pizza | Pizza | $ | | | L/D | | 19 |
| Red Robin Restaurant | American | $$ | Yes | Yes | L/D | Major | 19 |
| Shooter's Grill | American | $$ | | Yes | L/D | Major | 19 |
| Domino's Pizza | Pizza | $ | | | L/D | | 20 |
| Sports Page Restaurant | American | $$/$$$ | Yes | Yes | L/D | Major | 20 |
| Muzzle Loader Cafe | American | $$ | Yes | | L/D | Major | 21 |
| West Parkway Truck Stop Rstrnt | American | $$ | Yes | | B/L/D | Major | 21 |
| The Hop Drive In | Fast Food | $ | | | L/D | | 21 |
| Cracker Barrel | Family | $ | Yes | | B/L/D | V/M | 23 |
| Yellowstone Valley Steakhouse | Steakhouse | $$/$$$ | Yes | Yes | B/L/D | Major | 23 |
| Silver Dollar Restaurant | American | $ | | B/W | B/L/D | V/M | 23 |
| Southern Empire Emporium | American | $ | Yes | | B/L/D | V/M | 23 |
| Torres Cafe | American | $$ | | | L/D | V/M | 23 |
| **MacKenzie River Pizza Co.** | Pizza | $/$$ | | B/W | L/D | Major | 24 |

## Dining Quick Reference—Continued

Price Range refers to the average cost of a meal per person: ($) $1-$6, ($$) $7-$11, ($$$) $12-up. Cocktails: "Yes" indicates full bar; Beer (B)/Wine (W), Service: Breakfast (B), Brunch (BR), Lunch (L), Dinner (D). Businesses in bold print will have additional information under the appropriate map locator number in the body of this section.

| RESTAURANT | TYPE CUISINE | PRICE RANGE | CHILD MENU | COCKTAILS BEER WINE | SERVICE | CREDIT CARDS | MAP LOCATOR NUMBER |
|---|---|---|---|---|---|---|---|
| 5 & Diner | American | $/$$ | Yes | | B/L/D | Major | 24 |
| Applebee's Neighborhood Grill | Eclectic | $$/$$$ | Yes | Yes | L/D | Major | 24 |
| Cactus Creek Steak Outfitters | Steaks & Seafood | $/$$ | Yes | Yes | L/D | Major | 24 |
| Dairy Queen | Fast Food | $ | Yes | | L/D | | 24 |
| Dos Machos Mexican Food | Mexican | $/$$ | Yes | Yes | L/D | Major | 24 |
| Old Country Buffet | Buffet | $/$$ | Yes | | L/D | Major | 24 |
| Pizza Hut | Pizza | $/$$ | Yes | B | L/D | V/M/D | 24 |
| Quizno's Classic Subs | Subs | $ | Yes | | L/D | | 24 |
| Teriyaki Bowl Express | Oriental | $ | | | L/D | | 24 |
| Western Empire Emporium | American | $ | Yes | Yes | | Major | 24 |
| Burger King | Fast Food | $ | Yes | | B/L/D | | 24 |
| Denny's | Family | $ | Yes | | B/L/D | V/M | 24 |
| Fuddruckers | American | $-$$ | Yes | Yes | L/D | Major | 24 |
| Gusick's Restaurant | American | $/$$ | | Yes | L/D | V/M | 24 |
| Jade Palace Chinese | Chinese | $/$$ | Yes | Yes | L/D | Major | 24 |
| Olive Garden | Italian | $$ | | B/W | | Major | 24 |
| Outback Steakhouse | American | $$/$$$ | Yes | Yes | D | Major | 24 |
| Perkins Family Restaurant | Family | $/$$ | Yes | | B/L/D | Major | 24 |
| Red Lobster Restaurant | Seafood | $$ | Yes | B/W | L/D | Major | 24 |
| Subway | Fast Food | $ | Yes | | L/D | | 24 |
| Taco John's | Fast Food | $ | Yes | | L/D | | 24 |
| Arby's | Fast Food | $ | Yes | | B/L/D | | 25 |
| Baja Burrito | Mexican | | | | | | 25 |
| Bob's Pizza | Fast Food | $ | Yes | | L/D | | 25 |
| Cinnabon World Famous Cinnamon | Bakery/Coffee | $ | | | L/D | | 25 |
| Fuddrucker's Express | Fast Food | $-$$ | Yes | Yes | L/D | | 25 |
| Neon Pretzel | Fast Food | $ | | | L/D | | 25 |
| Noodle Express | Oriental | $ | | | L/D | | 25 |
| Papa John's Restaurant | Pizza | $$ | | | L/D | Major | 25 |
| Sidney's Pizza Cafe | Family | $/$$ | | Yes | L/D | Major | 25 |
| Sleeping Giant Brew Pub | Casual Brew Pub | $$/$$$ | Yes | W/B | L/D | Major | 25 |
| **Godfather's Pizza** | Pizza | $ | Yes | B | L/D | V/M/D | 26 |
| Chuck E Cheese's | Pizza | $$ | Yes | | L/D | Major | 26 |
| Golden Corral Family Steak House | Steakhouse | $ | Yes | | L/D | | 26 |
| Great American Bagel | Deli | $ | | | B/L | | 26 |
| Guadalajara Family Mexican Restaurant | Mexican | $/$$ | Yes | Yes | L/D | Major | 26 |
| Hardee's | Fast Food | $ | Yes | | B/L/D | | 26 |
| J B'S Restaurant | Family | $ | Yes | | B/L/D | V/M | 26 |
| Pratts Lunch & Dinner Club | American | $ | | Yes | L/D | Major | 26 |
| Riverboat Dining | Mexican | $$/$$$ | Yes | Yes | L/D | Major | 26 |
| Subway | Fast Food | $ | Yes | | L/D | | 26 |
| C J'S Restaurant | Steakhouse | $$ | Yes | Yes | L/D | Major | 26 |
| Elmer's Pancake & Steak House | Family | $-$$ | Yes | | B/L/D | Major | 26 |
| Little Caesar's | Pizza | $ | | | L/D | | 26 |
| McDonalds | Fast Food | $ | Yes | | B/L/D | | 26 |
| Mongolian Grill | Asian | $$ | | | L/D | Major | 26 |
| Pepper's Pizza & Pasta | Pizza/Italian | $$ | | B/W | L/D | | 26 |
| Taco Bell | Fast Food | $ | Yes | | L/D | | 26 |
| Taco John's | Fast Food | $ | Yes | | L/D | | 26 |
| Wendy's | Fast Food | $ | Yes | | L/D | | 26 |
| **MacKenzie River Pizza Co.** | Pizza | $/$$ | | B/W | L/D | Major | 27 |
| **Billings Burrito Company** | Mexican | $ | | | B/L/D | | 27 |
| **Bruno's Italian Specialties** | Italian | $/$$ | Yes | Yes | L/D | Major | 27 |
| **Enzo Mediterranean Bistro** | Bistro | $$ | Yes | W/B | L/D/BR | Major | 27 |
| 4B's Restaurant | Family | $ | Yes | | B/L/D | V/M/D | 27 |
| Grand Bagel Company | Deli | $ | | | B/L | | 27 |
| Kentucky Fried Chicken | Fast Food | $ | Yes | | L/D | | 27 |
| Korum's Pizzeria | Pizza | $ | | | L/D | | 27 |
| Mayflower of China | Chinese | $$ | Yes | | L/D | V/M/D/DC | 27 |
| T C'S Diner & Casino | American | $ | Yes | Yes | B/L/D | | 27 |
| Village Inn Pizza | Pizza | $/$$ | Yes | B | L/D | V/M | 27 |

## Dining Quick Reference—Continued

Price Range refers to the average cost of a meal per person: ($) $1-$6, ($$) $7-$11, ($$$) $12-up. Cocktails: "Yes" indicates full bar; Beer (B)/Wine (W), Service: Breakfast (B), Brunch (BR), Lunch (L), Dinner (D). Businesses in bold print will have additional information under the appropriate map locator number in the body of this section.

| RESTAURANT | TYPE CUISINE | PRICE RANGE | CHILD MENU | COCKTAILS BEER WINE | SERVICE | CREDIT CARDS | MAP LOCATOR NUMBER |
|---|---|---|---|---|---|---|---|
| Domino's Pizza | Pizza | $ | | | L/D | | 27 |
| Hero's Subs | Deli | $ | | | L/D | | 27 |
| McDonald's | Fast Food | $ | Yes | | B/L/D | | 27 |
| Subway | Fast Food | $ | Yes | | L/D | | 27 |
| Sweet Surrender Cafe | Cafe/Bakery | $ | | | B/L | Major | 27 |
| Teanna's Tea Room | tearoom | $ | | L | Major | | 27 |
| 17th St. Station | Coffee House | | | | | | 27 |
| The Granary Restaurant | Steaks & Seafood | $$$ | | Yes | D | Major | 28 |
| **Crow's Nest** | Native American | $ | | | B/L/D | | 33 |
| **Custer Battlefield Trading Post & Cafe** | Family | $ | Yes | | B/L/D | Major | 33 |
| Shake & Burger Hut | Fast Food | $ | | | L/D | | 34 |
| Little Big Man Pizza | Pizza | $ | | B/W | L/D | | 36 |
| Merry Mixer | Regional American | $-$$$ | Yes | Yes | B/L/D | Major | 36 |
| Blimpie's Subs | Fast Food | $ | Yes | | L/D | | 37 |
| Dairy Queen | Fast Food | $ | Yes | | L/D | | 37 |
| Far West Restaurant | Family | $/$$ | Yes | Yes | B/L/D | Major | 37 |
| Kentucky Fried Chicken | Fast Food | $ | Yes | | L/D | | 37 |
| McDonald's | Fast Food | $ | Yes | | B/L/D | | 37 |
| Pizza Hut/Taco Bell | Pizza/Mexican | $/$$ | Yes | B | L/D | V/M/D | 37 |
| Purple Cow Restaurant | Family | $$ | Yes | B/W | B/L/D | Major | 37 |
| Subway | Fast Food | $ | Yes | | L/D | | 37 |
| Taco John's | Fast Food | $ | Yes | | L/D | | 37 |
| **Big Horn RV Park & Cafe** | American | $/$$ | | | B/L/D | | 39 |

**NOTES:**

Section 2

## Motel Quick Reference

Price Range: ($) Under $40 ; ($$) $40-$60; ($$$) $60-$80, ($$$$) Over $80. Pets [check with the motel for specific policies] (P), Dining (D), Lounge (L), Disabled Access (DA), Full Breakfast (FB), Cont. Breakfast (CB), Indoor Pool (IP), Outdoor Pool (OP), Hot Tub (HT), Sauna (S), Refrigerator (R), Microwave (M) (Microwave and Refrigerator indicated only if in majority of rooms), Kitchenette (K). All Montana area codes are 406.

| HOTEL | PHONE | NUMBER ROOMS | PRICE RANGE | BREAKFAST | POOL/ HOT TUB SAUNA | NON SMOKE ROOMS | OTHER AMENITIES | CREDIT CARDS | MAP LOCATOR NUMBER |
|---|---|---|---|---|---|---|---|---|---|
| **Heights Inn** | 252-8451 | 33 | $ | | | Yes | DA/K/P/M/R | Major | 12 |
| **Boot Hill Inn & Suites** | 245-2000 | 69 | $$$$ | CB | IP/HT | Yes | M/R/DA | Major | 12 |
| Airport Metra Inn | 245-6611 | 104 | $ | | | Yes | DA | Major | 12 |
| Metra Inn | 245-6611 | 104 | $$$ | | OP | Yes | P/M/R | | 12 |
| Twin Cubs Motel | 252-9851 | 11 | $$ | | | | P | Major | 12 |
| **Lewis & Clark Inn** | 252-4691 | 57 | $$ | | IP/HT | Yes | R/M/R/DA | Major | 15 |
| **The Josephine Bed & Breakfast** | 248-5898 | | | | | | | | 15 |
| Radisson Northern Hotel | 245-5121 | 160 | $$$ | CB | | Yes | DA/P/D | Major | 15 |
| **Sheraton** | 252-7400 | 282 | $$$ | | IP | Yes | P/D/L/DA | Major | 15 |
| Billings Inn | 252-6800 | 60 | $$ | | | Yes | DA/P | Major | 15 |
| Dude Rancher Lodge | 259-5561 | 57 | $$$ | | | Yes | P/D/M/R | Major | 15 |
| Esquire Motor Inn | 259-4551 | 5 | $ | | | Yes | K/R/L/R | Major | 15 |
| Town House Motel | 245-4191 | 24 | $ | | | Yes | P/DA | Major | 15 |
| Travelodge | 245-6345 | 38 | $$ | | | | P/DA | Major | 15 |
| Best Western Ponderosa Inn | 259-5511 | 130 | $$/$$$ | | OP/S | Yes | P/R/M/R/DA | Major | 15 |
| Lazy K-T Motel | 252-6606 | 26 | $ | | | Yes | P | Major | 15 |
| Big Five Motel | 245-6645 | 34 | $ | | | Yes | DA/P | Major | 15 |
| Billings Travel West Inn | 245-6345 | 38 | $$ | CB | | Yes | P | Major | 15 |
| Historic Northern Hotel | 245-5121 | 160 | $$$$ | CB | | yes | R/L/DA/P | Major | 15 |
| **Cherry Tree Inn** | 252-5603 | 65 | $$ | CB | | Yes | DA/P | Major | 16 |
| **Juniper Inn** | 245-4128 | 47 | $ | CB | | Yes | P/M/R/DA | Major | 16 |
| Hilltop Inn | 245-5000 | 57, | $$ | CB | | Yes | DA/P | Major | 16 |
| Rimrock Inn | 252-7107 | 83 | $ | CB | HT | Yes | P/DA | Major | 16 |
| **Rimview Inn** | 248-2622 | 54 | $/$$ | CB | HT | Yes | K/P/M/R/DA | Major | 16 |
| Hojo Inn | 248-4656 | 173 | $$$ | | | Yes | D/L/DA/P | Major | 17 |
| Howard Johnsons | 248-4656 | 172 | $$/$$$ | CB | | Yes | P/M/R/DA | Major | 17 |
| War Bonnet Inn | 248-7761 | 102 | $$ | | IP | Yes | P/D/L/DA | Major | 17 |
| Sleep Inn | 254-0013 | 75 | $$ | CB | | Yes | DA | Major | 17 |
| **Super 8 Motel Of Billings** | 248-8842 | 114 | $$/$$$ | CB | | Yes | P/M/R/DA | Major | 21 |
| Days Inn | 252-4007 | 63 | $$/$$$ | CB | HT | Yes | P/DA | Major | 21 |
| Hampton Inn | 248-4949 | 80 | $$$ | CB | IP/HT | Yes | DA/M/R | Major | 21 |
| Parkway Motel | 245-3044 | 26 | $$ | | | | | Major | 21 |
| Picture Court Motel | 252-8478 | 20 | $ | | | Yes | | Major | 21 |
| **Holiday Inn Billings Plaza** | 248-7701 | 315 | $$$ | | IP/HT | Yes | R/L/DA | Major | 23 |
| Best Western Billings | 248-9800 | 80 | $$/$$$ | CB | IP/HT/S | Yes | P/M/R/DA | Major | 23 |
| Billings Hotel & Convention Center | 248-7151 | 242 | $$ | | IP | Yes | P/R/L/DA | Major | 23 |
| Kelly Inn | 252-2700 | 88 | $/$$ | CB | OP/HT/S | Yes | K/P/M/R/DA | Major | 23 |
| Motel 6 N. | 248-7551 | 117 | $$ | | IP | Yes | DA/P | Major | 23 |
| **Ramada Inn Limited** | 252-2584 | 116 | $$/$$$ | CB | OP | Yes | P/M/R/DA | Major | 23 |
| **Red Roof Inn** | 252-0093 | 99 | $$ | | | Yes | P/DA | Major | 23 |
| **Sanderson Inn Bed & Breakfast** | 656-3388 | | | | | | | | 23 |
| **C'mon Inn** | 655-1100 | 80 | $$$ | CB | HT/IP | Yes | M/R/DA | Major | 24 |
| **Comfort Inn** | 652-5200 | 60 | $$$/$$$$ | CB | IP/HT | Yes | P/DA | Major | 24 |
| **Fairfield Inn** | 652-5330 | 63 | $$$ | | IP | Yes | DA | Major | 24 |
| **Quality Inn** | 652-1320 | 62 | $$-$$$ | FB | IP/HT/S | Yes | FB/P/R/DA | Major | 24 |
| Picture Court Motel | 252-8478 | 20 | $$ | | | Yes | P | Major | 31 |
| Little Big Horn Camp | 638-2232 | 8 | $ | | | | | V/M/D | 33 |
| **Western Motel** | 665-2296 | 28 | $ | | | Yes | P/M/R/DA | Major | 36 |
| Camp Custer Motel | 665-2504 | 8 | $ | | | | P | V/M | 36 |
| Lariat Motel | 665-2683 | 18 | $ | | | Yes | P/M/R | Major | 36 |
| American Inn | 665-1870 | 42 | $$ | | OP/HT | Yes | P/D | Major | 37 |
| Super 8 Motel | 665-1700 | 53 | $$ | | | Yes | P/M/L | Major | 37 |
| Big Horn Angler Motel | 666-2233 | 9 | $$ | CB | | Yes | D | Major | 40 |



**NOTES:**

# Section 3

## Red Lodge, Laurel, Columbus and Surrounding Area

*Atop the Beartooth Plateau.*

### Weather Averages

**Red Lodge**

| | |
|---|---|
| January | |
| Average High: | 32.7° F |
| Average Low: | 10.8° F |
| Average Precip.: | 1.11 in |
| April | |
| Average High: | 51.0° F |
| Average Low: | 27.7° F |
| Average Precip.: | 3.02 in |
| July | |
| Average High: | 78.6° F |
| Average Low: | 50.1° F |
| Average Precip.: | 1.51 in |
| October | |
| Average High: | 56.0° F |
| Average Low: | 32.0° F |
| Average Precip.: | 1.67 in |

**1.** *Gas, Miscellaneous*

### Laurel

Laurel has railroad tracks going through the center of town, that reflect the town's history as the railroad hub in the early 1900s. As the coal mining production grew in the Red Lodge area, the demand for transportation became greater and Laurel became a division point for different railroad companies. Because Laurel is only 16 miles from Billings, it has also become a suburb of the big city. Toward the end of her life, Calamity Jane was said to have resided about 9 miles from Laurel near the Canyon Creek Battleground. Laurel is said to have the largest fireworks show in the state on the 4th of July. The Mountain Man Rendezvous, is a yearly celebration, held towards the end of July. It recaptures the Lewis & Clark Expedition that charted the Yellowstone River.

Laurel is considered by many to be the "recreational hub of Montana." From this small town, Yellowstone National Park can be entered four different ways. It is straddled on both sides by a complex labyrinth of railroad tracks, the largest and busiest rail yard in Montana. The first post office opened its doors in 1886, and the city was incorporated in 1908. The "Laurel Leaf" refinery began operation in 1930 with the present-day name of CENEX.

Laurel is replete with history: On Lewis & Clark's return trip from the West Coast, they split up into two teams exploring the rivers. Clark's party camped near the junction of the Clarks Fork of the Yellowstone and the Yellowstone River which is near present day Laurel. Downtown you will find a statue in Fireman's Park commemorating the great Nez Perce leader, Chief Joseph.

Laurel is near many recreational areas. To the south there is the majestic Big Horn Canyon with the Yellowtail Reservoir, known for its sheer beauty and as an adventureland for boaters. Below the reservoir lies the Bighorn River, which carries with it some of the finest trout fishing. Northeast of Laurel is the nation's largest earth-filled dam at Fort Peck; to the west is the renowned Yellowstone River.

Also, observe Montana's largest free Fourth of July fireworks display in Laurel each year if in the area during this holiday.

### D William Clark

July 24, 1806

*"for me to mention or give an estimate of the differant Species of wild animals on this river. . .would be incredible. I shall therefore be silent on the Subject further."*

### A Riverside Repair

1813 Thiel Road, Laurel. 628-4046

Riverside Repair is a NAPA Auto Care Center that has been family owned and operated for over 10 years. Their Master Certified technicians have over 40 years experience. They do a full range of services on foreign and domestic models of cars, vans, pick-ups, RVs, and semi trucks. With up to date computer diagnostic testing, fast turn around on repairs, and friendly service at very fair prices, Riverside is the place to go so you can get back on the road. All the work is guaranteed. Tech net Professional Auto Service.

## Beartooth Mountains

The Beartooth Mountains, part of the Rocky Mountains, are the result of about seventy million years of geological formations, leaving a spectacular mountain range that is full of geological wonders and leaves the sightseer awe struck. In 1931, local Red Lodge physician J.C.F Siegfriedt had a vision of a "high road" to connect Red Lodge to Cooke City, and draw tourists to this beautiful spot. After the local mines had closed, the area needed prosperity, and the Beartooth Highway was the key. With the help of O.H.P. Shelley, the owner of the Carbon County News, Siegfriedt convinced congress of the need for "approach highways" that lead tourists to National Parks. The building started in 1931, and after spending $2.5 million, the road opened in June of 1936.

Visitors can drive the Scenic 65-mile Beartooth Highway that connects Red Lodge to Cooke City and Yellowstone National Park. The highway consists of major switchbacks, as you climb to the elevation of 10,942 ft. At the top, on a clear day, you will experience amazing views of up to 75 miles in distance, with mountain lakes, glaciers, mountain ranges and field of wildflowers in the summer. Because of the elevation, snow often covers some fields through most of July, and you may even spot skiers throughout the summer months. The Beartooths are home to Granite Peak, the highest peak in Montana at 12,799 ft. In 1989, the Beartooth Highway received recognition as one of the most beautiful drives in America, and was made one of 52 other National Scenic Byways. The driving is slow going, due to the many switchbacks, and many necessary stops to soak in the awesome views.

### Montana Trivia

The Absaroka-Beartooth Wilderness is the home of the largest single expanse of land above ten thousand feet in elevation in the lower forty-eight states. It is also the home of the fifty highest points in Montana.

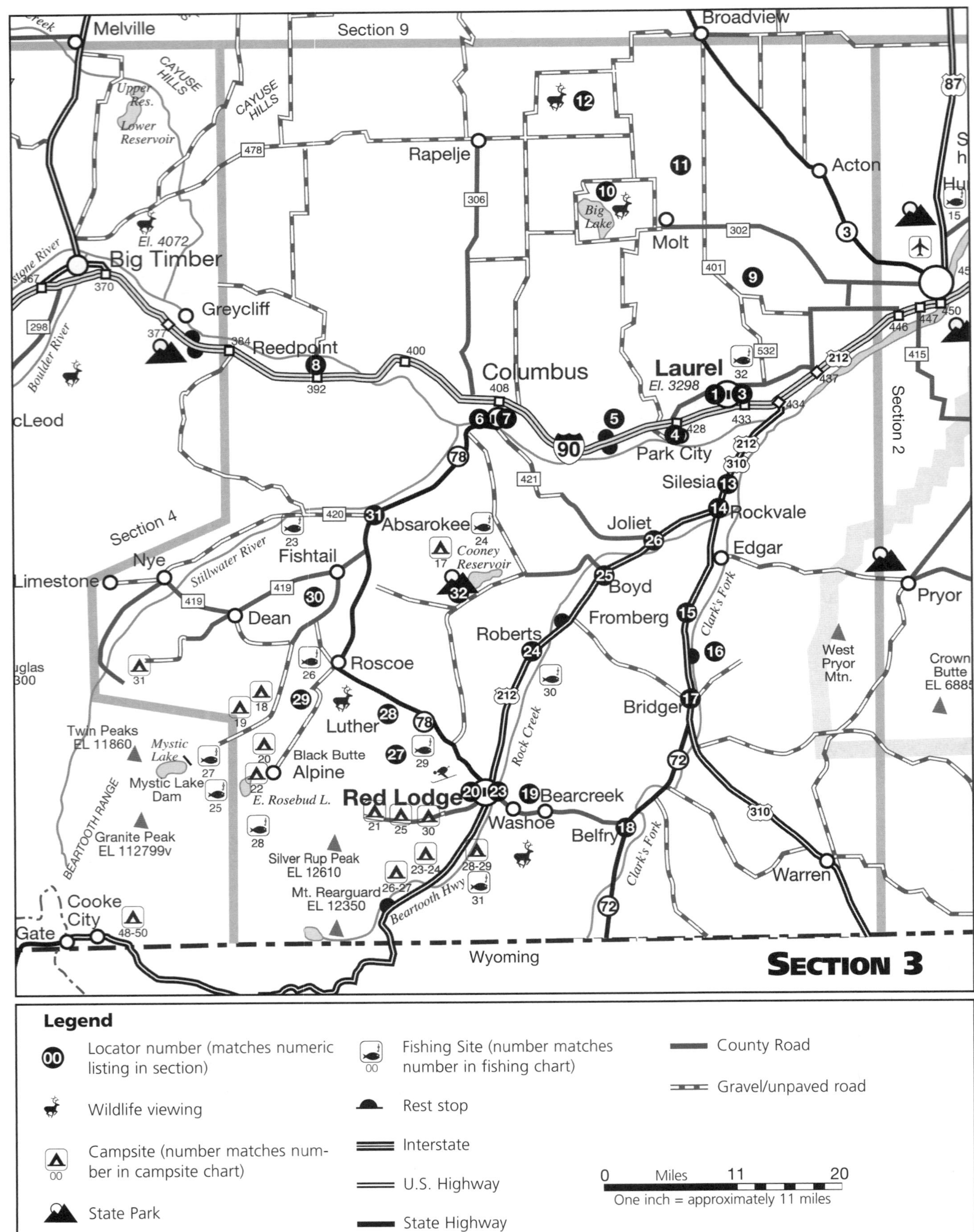
Melville
Section 9
Broadview
CAYUSE HILLS
CAYUSE HILLS
Upper Res.
Lower Reservoir
478
Rapelje
306
Acton
87
Big Lake
Molt
302
El. 4072
Big Timber
367
370
401
298
Greycliff
377
384
Reedpoint
400
392
Columbus
408
Laurel
El. 3298
532
212
446
447
450
415
434
437
433
428
Park City
90
212
310
Silesia
Rockvale
421
Section 2
cLeod
Section 4
420
Absarokee
Cooney Reservoir
Joliet
Edgar
Nye
Fishtail
Stillwater River
Limestone
419
419
Dean
Boyd
Fromberg
Pryor
Roberts
West Pryor Mtn.
Crown Butte EL 6885
Roscoe
Bridger
212
Rock Creek
Clark's Fork
Luther
Twin Peaks EL 11860
Mystic Lake
Black Butte
Alpine
72
Mystic Lake Dam
E. Rosebud L.
Red Lodge
Bearcreek
BEARTOOTH RANGE
Washoe
Belfry
310
Granite Peak EL 112799v
Silver Rup Peak EL 12610
Clark's Fork
Warren
Mt. Rearguard EL 12350
Beartooth Hwy
Cooke City
Gate
72
Wyoming
SECTION 3
Legend
Locator number (matches numeric listing in section)
Wildlife viewing
Campsite (number matches number in campsite chart)
State Park
Fishing Site (number matches number in fishing chart)
Rest stop
Interstate
U.S. Highway
State Highway
County Road
Gravel/unpaved road
0 Miles 11 20
One inch = approximately 11 miles

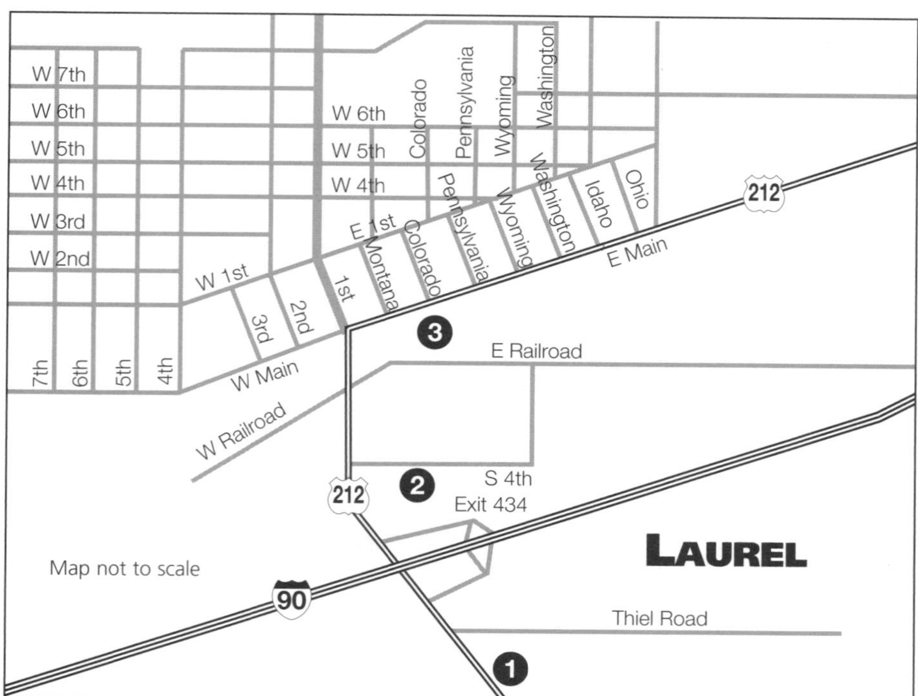

## M Laurel Sports Center

1547 U.S. Hwy 212 S., Laurel. 628-2932

## 2. *Gas, Food, Lodging*

### A Conomart Super Store #2

1st Ave. N., Laurel. 628-2018

Locally owned & operated, convenience store, friendly service, clean restrooms, and 24-hour fuel pumps.

### A Expert Lube & Wash

203 4th St. S.E., Laurel. 628-2293

This family owned and operated service center will get you on the road quickly with new oil and a clean vehicle. Featuring Pennzoil products, they carry all major brands of oil. A comfortable waiting area with fresh coffee is available while your car is being serviced. They can also service your transmission and radiator. Mechanics are on duty from 7:30 a.m. to 7 p.m. Monday through Saturday. Once your car's vital fluids have been serviced, give it a new look at their convenient car wash. An RV bay is available for motor homes and trailers.

### A Rapid Tire Inc.

101 W. Railroad St. in Laurel. 628-4604

### L Laurel Super 8

205 S.E. 4th Street, Laurel. 628-6888 or 800-800-8000

Just a few minutes from Billings, the new Super 8 Motel is Laurel is designed for the comfort of each guest. It has earned the "Pride of Super 8 " distinction, awarded to upscale motels in the franchise providing outstanding facilities and service. Guests may select from standard rooms to king sized suites equipped with whirlpool tubs, microwave ovens, and refrigerators or even a conference table. All guest rooms have cable TV, HBO, and computer data ports. You'll also appreciate the convenience of a guest laundry, game room, exercise room, fully handicapped accessible rooms, and complimentary "Super Start" breakfast. They also offer a heated pool and hot tub for their guests enjoyment.

### L Best Western Locomotive Inn

310 S. 1st Ave., Laurel. 628-8281

## 3. *Attraction, Gas, Food, Lodging, Shopping*

### T Fireman's Park

Laurel

### A Conomart Super Store #3

519 W. Main St., Laurel. 628-2034

Locally owned & operated, convenience store, friendly service, clean restrooms, and 24-hour fuel pumps.

### A Mel's Auto Clinic

619 E. Main St. Laurel. 628-1299

### A Modern Auto

601 E. Main St., Laurel. 628-7145

### F Caboose Saloon & Casino

704 W. Main, Laurel. 628-7414

There are stops along every journey that become highlights of a trip remaining etched in one's memory for years to come. In Laurel, the Caboose has a long and honorable history. It began as the old Laurel Bar and grew during the boom years of the refinery and railroad. While it has changed locations over the years, at its present site since 1977, it's name was changed to the Caboose and decorated with an antique back bar that was said to have come across the country on a covered wagon. Old wagon wheels for overhead lighting and old coins , some dating back to the 1800s, are deeply imbedded in the top of bar. What really makes this establishment unique, is a large collection of bronze sculptures from many of the finest artists in the country. They range in size from miniatures to life-size moose, elk, and a mountain lion, by such well-known names as R. F. Rains, Bill Rains, Jim Knight, Lyle Johnson, and Don Hershberger, just to name a few. Over 30 life-size bronzes are on permanent display. The newest, Jeremiah Johnson and his horse, greet you at the entrance. Whether it's western art, country music, friendly wagering, cold drinks, or friendly faces you're after, you'll find them at the Caboose.

> ### *It Happened in Montana*
>
> On February 27, 1943, an explosion ripped through the Smith Mine just south of Red Lodge. Seventy-four miners perished making it the worst mine disaster in Montana history. This disaster was the beginning of the end of the coal industry in Carbon County.

### F Dragon Palace Chinese Cuisine

409 W. Main St., Laurel. 628-8268

### L Welcome Traveler's Motel

620 W. Main St. Laurel. 628-6821

### L Russell Motel

711 E. Main St. Laurel. 628-6513

## S Sassy 2nds Antique Mall

103 E. Main St. Laurel. 628-6065

## S Montana Country Pines

113 E. Main St., Laurel. 628-8535 or Toll free at 877-628-8535. WWW.MTcountrypines.com

Montana Country Pines is located in the heart of downtown Laurel. The ultimate shopping experience for the country spirit. The owners of this truly Montana business specialize in building and decorating log homes. If you're looking for anything with the lodge or western look, they probably have it. Best of all, most of it is made right here in Montana! You'll find everything from log furniture to antler lighting, bear skin rugs, animal mounts, Native American art, great Montana gift items and much, much more. Check out the log cabin in their showroom. Le them design, build and furnish the log home of your dreams.

### Montana Trivia

The town of Columbus holds the state record for the most name changes. At various times it has been named Stillwater, Eagle's Nest, and Sheep Dip.

## 4. *Gas, Food, Lodging*

### Park City

Park City used to be a docking point for boats traveling on the Yellowstone River, and was called Young's Point. A group of settlers from Wisconsin settled here and planted many elm and maple trees on their land. When the railroad came through, the area was named Rimrock because of the dry sandstone landscape, but the settlers were aiming for more trees and green grass and chose the name Park City instead.

## 5. *Historic Marker, Attraction*

### H Columbus

*The town of Columbus is located about 9 miles west of here. There is probably no town (or city) in Montana that had a more spectacular career, or more hectic embarrassment in finally "lighting" on an incorporated name than did the county seat of Stillwater. From 1875, when the Countryman stage station was known as Stillwater, until its incorporation in 1907, its name was changed every time the whims of a merchant moved his stock of merchandise, or a new business appeared. First it was "Eagle's Nest," about two miles west of town; then an Indian trading post was listed as "Sheep Dip," and it was not until the Northern Pacific built a station here in 1882 and named it Stillwater that the town's location attained permanence. Even this name didn't last long, however, as the N.P. had already listed a Stillwater, Minnesota, on their main line and the similarity of Minnesota and Montana led to misdirected shipments, so the name of Columbus replaced Stillwater on January 1, 1894*

*There was just reason, perhaps, that this part of the Yellowstone was slow in getting settled. It was borderland on the north side of the Crow Reservation, and there were constant raids on the area by Sioux and Cheyenne war parties who would just as soon attack the white invaders. This ever-present danger didn't appeal to many prospective home-seekers, who high-tailed it over to the Gallatin or other points farther west.*

### H Park City

*The town of Park City is located about seven miles east of here. In 1882, a colony from Ripon, Wisconsin, making the trip in the prairie schooners, settled in this region. It was to be their future home, so they planted trees and made what improvements they could to ultimately beautify the little city. A section of land was donated to them, and things started off in a prosperous pleasant manner. The railroad soon came through and established a station. The bare, sandstone bluffs north of town inspired the officials to christen the place Rimrock, but not so with the persons who had planted sprigs and started a city of trees. Bravely they clung to the name Park City, and Rimrock finally disappeared with the list of unused titles. This was unfortunate inasmuch as the general manager of the N.P. resented this stubbornness on the part of the homesteaders, and in retaliation he changed the location of the proposed railroad yards and shops from this townsite to Laurel.*

### D William Clark

July 18, 1806

*" I observed a Smoke rise to the S.S.E in the plains . . .this Smoke must be raisd, by the Crow Indians. . .as a Signal for us, or other bands."*

### T Buffalo Mirage Access

Buffalo Mirage Access: This is the spot where Lewis and Clark dug out two canoes to continue their exploration of the Yellowstone River.

## 6. *Lewis & Clark, Gas, Food, Lodging*

### Columbus

Columbus dates back to 1875 when a man by the name of Horace Countryman opened a trading post and stage station stop along the Yellowstone Trail a few miles west of present day Columbus. This area used to be part of the Crow Indian Reservation lands, and Countryman followed the Crow Agency from Mission Creek to Rosebud Creek. He opened his business just off the reservation. Countryman built the Log Hotel to accommodate visitors that were traveling between Miles City and Bozeman, and by 1882 this area became a major stop on the Northern Pacific Railroad. The railroad named this stop Stillwater Village. In 1894, the railroad renamed the town Columbus, due to shipping mixups with Stillwater, Minnesota.

Hagar & Co. opened a sandstone quarry in the mid 1890s, which supplied building materials for a large portion of the Montana State Capitol Building in Helena. At this time there was a population of about 550, with many small businesses sprouting up. The main business was, and still is agriculture and ranching. Columbus is the Stillwater County seat. Located at the confluence of the Stillwater River and Yellowstone River, Columbus offers plenty of outdoor recreation with great trout fishing, whitewater rafting, hunting, hiking, horseback riding and much more.

### D William Clark

July 17, 1806

*I can See no timber Sufficient large for a Canoe which will Carry more than 3 men and Such a one would be too Small to answer my purpose"*

### D William Clark

July 16, 1806

*"the emence Sworms of grass Hoppers have distroyed every Sprig of Grass for maney miles."*

### It Happened in Montana

On March 24, 1978, Congress establishes the Absarokee-Beartooth Wilderness area. This remote and rugged alpine wilderness comprises the largest single expanse of land above 10,000 feet in the lower 48 states. The entire area covers over a million acres and includes two national forests. 28 peaks over 12,000 feet tower over more than 950 lakes and nine major drainages.

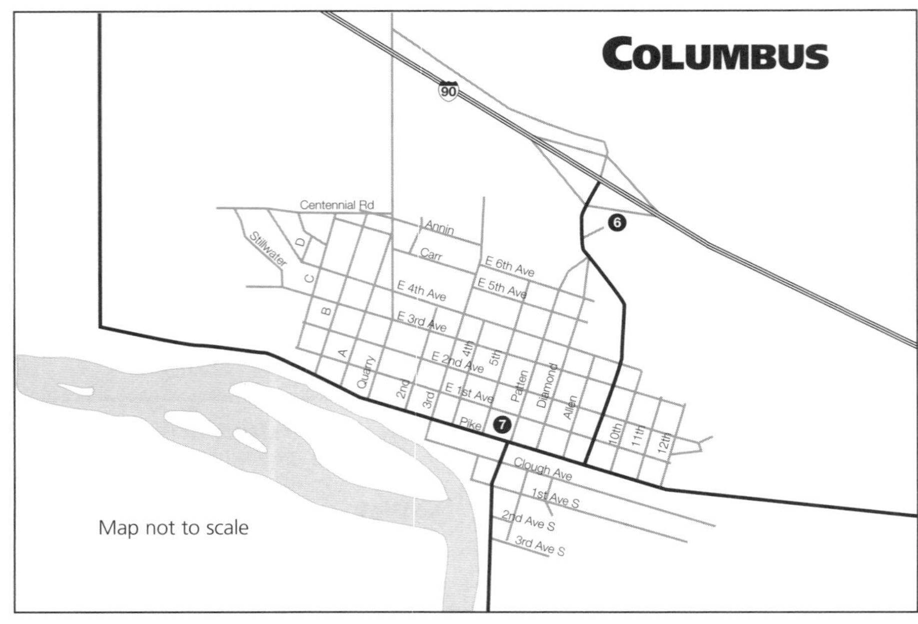

**F** **Apple Village Cafe & Gift Shop**
725 N. 9th St., Columbus. 322-5939

Offering the very finest to their guests. Great home style food for the weary traveler, homemade pies and cinnamon rolls, and Montana-made gifts are among their many specialties.

**F** **Peggy Sue's Coffee**
Drive Thru next to McDonalds, Exit 408, Columbus. 321-JAVA(5282

**S** **Art is Everywhere**
725 N. 9th St., Columbus. 322-4001

## 7. *Gas, Food, Lodging, Shopping, Miscellaneous*

**T** **Museum of the Beartooths**
I-90 Exit 408 in Columbus. 322-4588

The Museum of the Beartooths is a great place to visit the history of the homestead era. The museum offers displays of farm equipment and machinery showing the rich agricultural history in the area and carries artifacts of the Rosebud River Crow Indians, Northern Pacific railroad memorabilia and World War II history. Open seasonally. Look for the red NP caboose at the corner of 5th and 5th North.

**A** **J.C. Tire**
310 N. 9th St., Columbus. 322-5389

**F** **The New Atlas Bar**
528 Pike, Columbus. 322-4033

Opened in 1906, The New Atlas is the oldest licensed bar in Montana. The unique western atmosphere is complete with over 50 mounted animals on display throughout the bar, and a large variety of antiques. It is a full service bar with air conditioning and keno & poker machines. Stop in on your way through for a cold drink in an air conditioned, one-of-a-kind Montana bar.

**F** **Steel Horse Saloon**
927 E. 4th Ave. N., Columbus. 322-4718

**LA** **Git's Conoco & Big Sky Motel**
740 E. Pike Ave., Columbus. 322-4111

**S** **Arolyn's of the Rockies Factory Outlet**
325 E. 1st Ave. N., Columbus. 322-4143

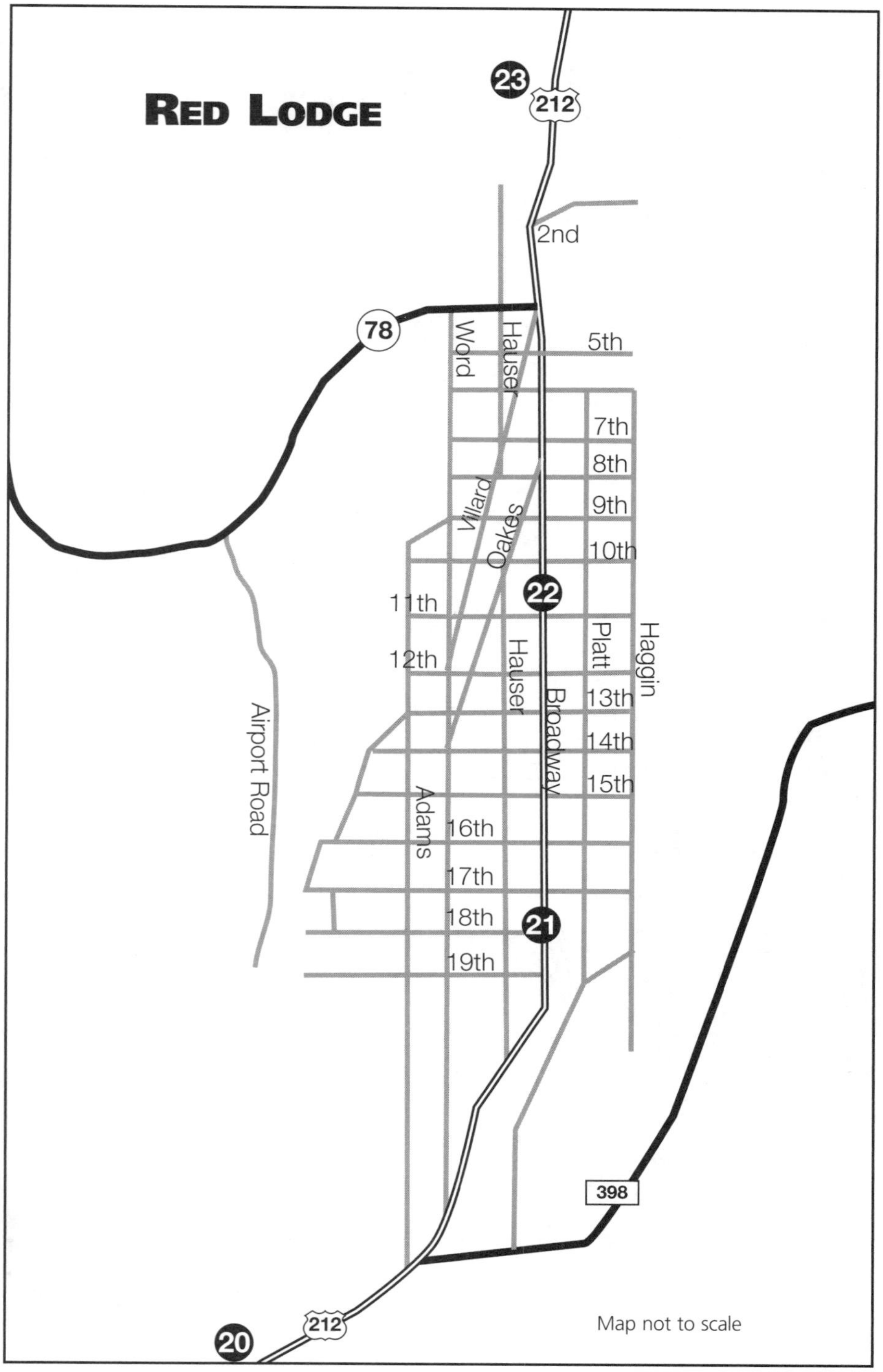

## Red Lodge

23 212 2nd 78 5th Word Hauser 7th 8th 9th Villard Oakes 10th 11th 22 12th Hauser Platt Haggin 13th Broadway 14th Airport Road 15th Adams 16th 17th 18th 21 19th 398 212 20

Map not to scale

Tee's, sweats, jackets, union suits, sizes 6 mo. thru 6XL adults; gifts.

**S** **Bruursema Jewelers**
522 E. Pike Ave., Columbus. 322-4778

**S** **The Shed Antiques & Liquor**
927 E. 4th Ave. N., Columbus. 322-4718

**M** **Johansen & Associates Real Estate**
904 E. 2nd Ave. N., Columbus. 322-5522.

Whether you are interested in buying or selling property, Johansen & Associates offers expertise and integrity that can do it for you! Specializing in residential, commercial, acreage, recreational, and farm & ranch land, they can show you any property listed by any realtor in any county in Montana. Discover the wonders of south central Montana where wildlife abounds, you are surrounded by 17 "Blue Ribbon" trout waters, and the majestic Beartooth Mountain Range. Stop in or call ahead and let Johansen & Associates show you what is available in this beautiful area.

## 8. *Gas, Food, Lodging*

### Reed Point

Reed Point is a town that has a genuine feeling of the wild west, and is one of the smallest communities along the Yellowstone River. It was a boom-

*Bellies to the bar for Italian Sodas at the Montana Hotel in Reed Point.*

ing little town in the early part of the century with 54 operating businesses. Most of the surrounding area was homesteaded and after a three year drought and realization by the homesteaders that they needed more than the 320 acre allotment in order to make a living in this area, they picked up and moved on further west. The little town began its slow demise at that time.

The focal point of this town is the Hotel Montana. Built in approximately 1909, this two story brick building was originally Walkers Store, a mercantile that sold anything from farm equipment (as evidenced by the original McCormick Deering-Walkers Store sign on the south wall of the restaurant) to fancy bloomers from New York. Upstairs was a doctor's office, a lawyer's office and living quarters of the Walkers. The downstairs was always a mercantile or general store and in later years a grocery store. The upstairs was turned into a boarding house for students and teachers and in later years into three separate apartments.

It was purchased in 1994 by long time Reed Point residents Russ and Connie Schlievert. At the time, the downstairs had been a grocery store that was closed up three years prior to their purchase and the upstairs was full of tenants in the three apartments. After about a year of using the downstairs as a warehouse for antiques and running the apartments, Russ and Connie decided to use their great store of antiques and Russ's extensive collection of old west saloon items to create the building you see today. The project, of course, cost three times their original estimate, and took approximately 18 months to complete.

*Guests at the Montana Hotel can "dress" for dinner in the period costumes found in each room.*

But complete it they did, and opened it as the Hotel Montana in 1997. Everything used to create Hotel Montana is antique and original and was collected from many other old buildings, in Montana primarily, and put together here. Each item you see in the building has its own story to tell and little pieces of history attached.

The public is welcome to tour the upstairs rooms and stay the night in them if you are so moved (it is, after all, a hotel). The costumes hanging in the rooms are for the guests. Connie says a large number of the guests dress up in the costumes and come downstairs for dinner and maybe some pictures.

### D William Clark

July 16, 1806

*"two of the horses was So lame owing to their feet being worn quit Smooth and to the quick... I had Mockersons made of... Buffalow Skin... which Seams to releve them very much in passing over the Stoney plains."*

### 9. *Attraction*

### T Battle At Canyon Creek

Hwy. 532, 9 miles north of Laurel.

In 1877, just after The Battle at the Big Hole, the Nez Perce, led by Chief Joseph, started heading towards Yellowstone National Park in hopes of fleeing to Canada. On September 13, 1877, as they crossed the Yellowstone River just nine miles from Laurel, they Nez Perce were confronted by Colonel Sturgis and the new Seventh Cavalry, which led to the Battle at Canyon Creek. This battle took three of the cavalry men and wounded three Nez Perce. There is a small marker at the site.

## 10. *Attraction*

### T Halfbreed National Wildlife Refuge

Halfbreed National Wildlife Refuge is another great spot to view birds and Pronghorn Sheep.

## 11.

### Acton

Acton is a very small town that is supported by a sprawling ranching community, even though the population is said to be 10. The town originally served as a stop along the Great Northern Railroad.

### Molt and Rapelje

Molt and Rapelje are both very small agricultural communities that are tucked away on the in the northern part of Stillwater County. The area is popular among hunters.

## 12. *Attraction*

### T Hailstone National Wildlife Refuge

This is a great stop for Birdwatchers-with the large lake and prairie lands that attracts a large amount of waterfowl including white pelicans, mallards, teals, grebes and many more-especially during migration. There is a viewpoint on the hill, where you may also spot, pronghorn, eagles, owls and hawks.

## 13. *Food*

### Silesia

Just south of Laurel, Silesia is a small town named after a local family that was from the German Province Silesia.

### F El Rancho Inn

Hwy 212, Siliesia. 962-3251

Open 7 days, 11 a.m..–11 p.m.., Fri. & Sat. open until 2 a.m.

## 14. *Gas, Camping*

### Rockvale

Once a main stop along the Northern Pacific Railroad. A few businesses get business from tourists and skiers going to and from Red Lodge. A few buildings remain along with a few residents.

### *Montana Trivia*

The Yellowstone River is the longest free-flowing river in the U.S. It begins in the south of Yellowstone National Park and terminates at the confluence of the Missouri River at the Montana/North Dakota border.

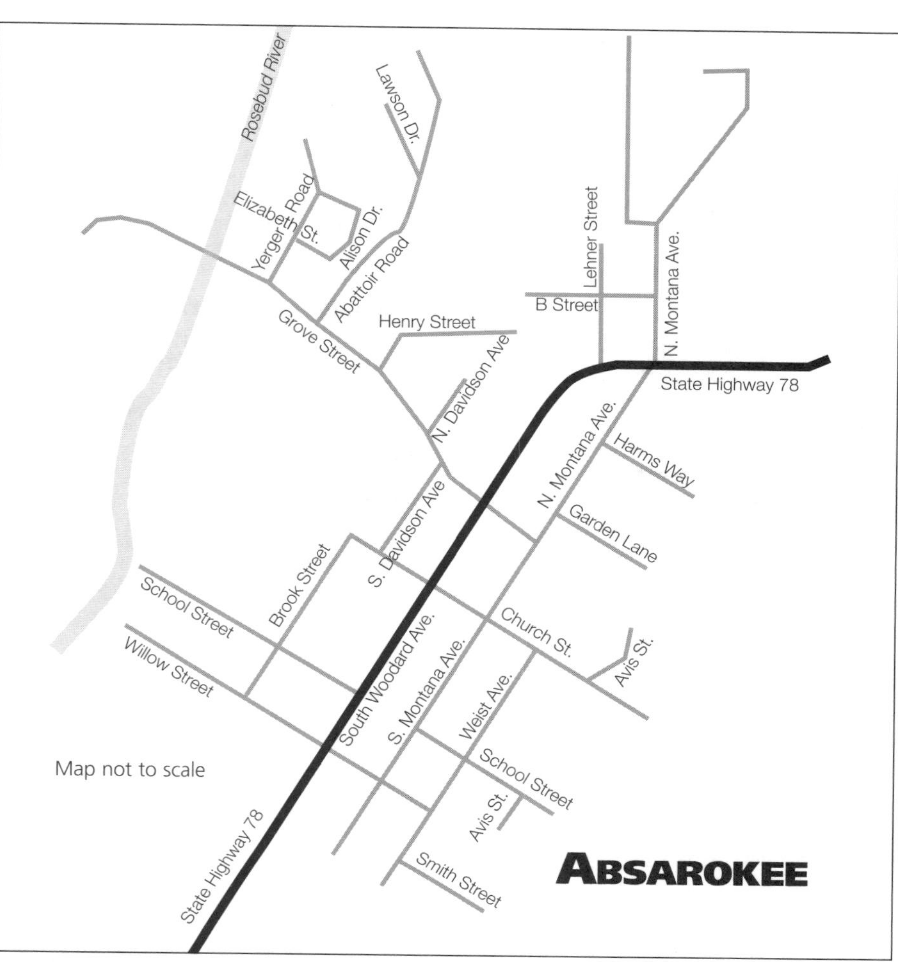

### F Quick Stop Drive In

Junction of Hwy 310 & 212, Rockvale. 962-3311

Open from March 15 through October 15, this family owned and operated restaurant cooks everything to order for better taste. They offer fast service and great food, with a large variety of menu options ranging from specialty burgers, steak strips, salads, steak, chicken and halibut dinners to shareable snack items. They feature daily specials as well. They serve ice cream for shakes, malts, and sundaes, cyclones, and their own specialty drinks like the Elvis Shake and Dr. Malt. This is a family atmosphere with a kids' playground and outdoor dining on clean picnic tables.

## 15. *Attraction, Food*

### Fromberg

Fromberg is a Slavic name, that was given to the town by the large population of Slavics who moved here in the early 1900s and started farmlands. It was originally called Gebo after a man who started a coal mine in this town. The area was called "Poverty Flats" because of droughts that occurred, almost causing locals to starve. After the irrigation system was installed, the land prospered and still remains rich farming land.

### T Clark Fork Valley Museum

101 E. River St. in Fromberg. 668-7650

### TF Little Cowboy Bar & Museum

Fromberg. 668-9502

A trip through Fromberg wouldn't be right without a stop at the Little Cowboy Bar. In fact, it wouldn't be right not to plan a trip to Fromberg for the Little Cowboy Bar. The bar is a great place for a cold beer, but the museum in the back is what will keep you there for a while. Shirley Smith, the owner, has amassed a fascinating collection of memorabilia about the Greenough Ranch and the Greenough family dynasty. If you didn't know already, you'll soon learn that the Greenoughs were some of the world's most celebrated rodeo stars. Shirley's husband worked for the Greenoughs and became very good friends. The museum is a living tribute to the Greenoughs and their colorful history as stars and brushes with stars. True Montana legends!

## 16. *Historic Marker*

### H The Pryor Mountains

At Bridger Rest Area on U.S. 310

*The Pryor Mountains to the east cover roughly 300,000 acres. Once entirely Crow Indian territory, now only the north end of the range is on the Crow Reservation. The south end is in the Custer National Forest. The range is bound on the east by Bighorn Reservoir and on the south by the Pryor Mountain National Wild Horse Range. The mountains came by their name indirectly from Pryor Creek, which Captain William Clark named for Lewis and Clark Expedition member Sergeant Nathaniel Pryor.*

*The Pryors hold many intriguing features, including ice caves, sinks, and caverns, and archeological finds, such as Clovis Points indicating human occupation as long as 10,000 years ago. In the south end of the range, remains of log and frame houses and barns attest to the homesteads staked after passage of the Forest Homestead Act in 1906. Most of the settlers came from this area. Though they cultivated some crops, for many homesteading was a pretense for mountain grazing on adjacent forest and reservation ranges. One forest ranger observed that some claimants had applied for places where it would be impossible to winter over, though to hear them talk "one would think that Pryor Mountain contained the biggest part of the Banana Belt and that pineapples grew wild."*

## 17. *Historic Marker, Gas, Food, Lodging*

### Bridger

The town of Bridger is named after explorer Jim Bridger, who was one of the first white men to travel through this area and into Yellowstone National Park. The town was originally called Georgetown, after the coal mine that was started up by a man named George Town. Mining became extremely popular in this area, and another small community developed, and was called Stringtown. In 1864, Jim Bridger came through the area, leading a wagon train to the mining areas in Virginia City. On his way through, he led the train across the Clark's Fork River-which they referred to as "Bridger's Crossing." Eventually the name of the whole town was changed to Bridger.

### H Jim Bridger, Mountain Man

Bridger

*Jim Bridger arrived in Montana in 1822 as a member of a Rocky Mountain Fur Co. brigade. For years he had no more permanent home than a poker chip. He roamed the entire Rocky Mountain region and often came through this part of the country. A keen observer, a natural geographer and with years of experience amongst the Indians, he became invaluable as a guide and scout for wagon trains and Federal troops following the opening of the Oregon Trail.*

*He shares honors with John Colter for first discoveries in the Yellowstone Park country. He was prone to elaborate a trifle for the benefit of pilgrims, and it was Jim who embroidered his story of the petrified forest by asserting that he had seen "a peetrified bird sitting in a peetrified tree, singing a peetrified song"*

*The Clarks Fork of the Yellowstone was named for Capt. Wm. Clark of the Lewis and Clark Expedition. Chief Joseph led his band of Nez Perce Indians down this river when he made his famous retreat in the summer of 1877.*

### F Buckeye Bar Grill & Casino

121 N. Main St., Bridger. 662-3230

### F Jungle Jayne's Stringtown Saloon & Eatery

215 S. Main St., Bridger. 662-3494

## 18. *Gas, Food*

### Belfry

Named after Dr. William Belfry, the town started out as the headquarters for the railroad. The Yellowstone Park Railroad Company started building a road that would connect Belfry to the park, but the project was never completed.

## 19. *Historic Marker, Attraction*

### Washoe

Washoe is on Hwy 308 between Belfry and Red Lodge. Washoe is most notable for the Smith Mine Disaster, which took the lives of 74 coal miners in 1943. In 1907, the town was the base of the Anaconda Copper Mining Company and Washoe Coal Mine. The Northern Pacific Railroad came through town, delivering hundreds of tons of coal to Anaconda on a daily basis. The formation of Montana Power Co. in 1912, cut back the need for coal operations. The unique coal mines of the area were beginning to decline by the late 1920s, following a period of strikes and labor disturbances.

Newer mines were established about the same time and remained busy until World War II. One being the Smith Mine that stayed busy until the disaster effectively ended coal mining in the area. Remnants of the mine still stand, but to truly understand the impact of such a disaster, visit the Bearcreek Cemetery. A handful of people, along with a few remnants of the mine, still live in Washoe which was once home to 3,000. Details of the Smith Mine and the ending disaster are available at the Peaks to Plains Museum in Red Lodge. Call them at 446-3667.

*Many of the tombstones in the nearby cemetery mark the same tragic date in history.*

### H Smith Mine Disaster

Washoe

*Smoke pouring from the mine entrance about 10 o'clock the morning of February 27, 1943, was the first indication of trouble. "There's something wrong down here. I'm getting out" the hoist operator called up. He and two nearby miners were the last men to leave the mine alive.*

*Rescue crews from as far away as Butte and Cascade County worked around the clock in six-hour shifts to clear debris and search for possible survivors. There were none. The night of March 4, workers reached the first bodies. More followed until the toll mounted to 74. Some died as a result of a violent explosion in No. 3 vein, the remainder fell victim to the deadly methane gasses released by the blast.*

*The tragedy at Smith Mine became Montana's worst coal mine disaster, sparking investigations at the state and national level. Montana Governor Sam C. Ford visited the scene, offered state assistance and pushed a thorough inquiry into the incident.*

*Today's marker of the Smith Mine Disaster follows a simpler one left by two of the miners trapped underground after the explosion, waiting for the poisonous gas they, knew would come.*

*"Walter & Johnny. Goodbye. Wives and daughters. We died an easy death. Love from us both. Be good."*

### H Bearcreek

Washoe

*Platted in 1905 by George Lamport and Robert Leavens, Bearcreek was the center of an extensive underground coal mining district. At its height during World War I, Bearcreek boasted a population of nearly 2,000 people. The community was ethnically diverse and included Serbians, Scotsmen, Montenegrans, Germans, Italians and Americans. They were served by seven mercantiles, a bank, two hotels, two billiard halls, a brickyard, and numerous saloons. The town also boasted concrete sidewalks and an extensive water system. No church was ever built in Bearcreek. Foundations of many of the town's buildings, in addition to some structures themselves, consisted of sandstone quarried in the nearby hill. The local railway, the Montana Wyoming and Southern, carried coal from the mines through Bearcreek where it was distributed to communities across Montana.*

*The Lamport Hotel was once located on the foundation to the right of this marker. Built in 1907, it was described as "well furnished … the beds being especially soft and sleep producing. [The] meals are served with a desire to please the guests and no one leaves without a good impression and kindly feelings for the management." The hotel was razed about 1945.*

*In 1943, Montana's worst coal mining disaster at the nearby Smith mine took the lives of 74 men, many of whom lived in Bearcreek.The tragedy hastened the decline of the town. Many buildings in Bearcreek were moved to other communities or demolished, leaving haunting reminders of their presence along Main Street. The railroad tracks were removed in 1953 and the last mining operation closed in the 1970s. Today, Bearcreek is the smallest incorporated city in the state.*

### T Bear Creek & Pig Races

3 miles west of Red Lodge

A few people and abandoned mine buildings still remain after the Smith Mine disaster of 1943. During the past two decades it is better known for the state's only pig races. Every weekend from Memorial Day to Labor Day the town's population of 50 residents grows to 500 or more for the pig event. The races have been held since 1989 at Bearcreek Downs next to the Bear Creek Saloon where you can also get one heck of a steak dinner. This nonprofit fundraiser is perfectly legal and the four-legged racers, like all sports celebrities are pampered, live high on the hog. The winning pigs pays $25 on a $2 ticket that buys a spot on the sports pool-style board. The race has become a

*Downtown Red Lodge.*

widely known event and has attracted media and people from all over the world. Bring the whole family and know that the little squealers are racing for a good cause—scholarships for Carbon County high school students.

## 20. *Historic Marker, Food, Lodging*

### Red Lodge

The story varies on how Red Lodge got its name. One version has the Crow Indians applying red clay to their tipis, or the clay adhering to the tipis as they were pulled on travois behind the horses. Another version tells of a Crow leader named Red Bear whose tipi was painted red.

The first Europeans in the area were probably Spaniards. A Spanish expedition led by Cabezo de Vaca may have visited the area in 1535. It would be 200 years before Lewis & Clark came through the area along the Yellowstone River north of here. Shortly after that, a trickle of explorers turned into a flood. John Colter, one of the Lewis & Clark members, returned to explore this area along the Clarks Fork just east of Red Lodge. Jim Bridger trapped here, and a town nearby bears his name.

The Red Lodge area was, for a period, a part of the Crow reservation. But as often happened in the history of the West, discovery of minerals led the government to change the deal. In this case it was the rich coal deposits discovered in 1886. At that time there were three Indians to every settler and four men for every woman. The Rocky Fork Coal Company opened the area's first mine in 1887 and shortly thereafter the Rocky Fork and Cooke City Railways came to the area. The area prospered as Red Lodge became the shipping point for the vast area to the south.

Red Lodge has had its share of colorful characters. In addition to John Colter and Jim Bridger, Buffalo Bill Cody used the railway to supply his Cody enterprises. Calamity Jane frequented the area. "Liver Eating" Johnson, who the Robert Redford character in the movie "Jeremiah Johnson" was modeled after, moved here in 1894. Johnson's cabin is preserved at the south end of town.

With the growth of the coal mines came a diversity of ethnic backgrounds. Finnish, Irish, Scottish, Slavic, Italian, and Scandinavian miners and their families settled here. When Red Lodge was made the seat of newly-formed Carbon County in 1896, the town boasted twenty saloons. In 1906, there were six churches, 14 fraternal orders, two newspapers, public schools, two telephone systems, three banks, an electric plant, three hotels and a population of 4,000. Before its decline, the population reached 6,000, almost triple today's population.

In the mid 20s, the depression forced mines to close. The town turned to manufacturing bootleg liquor, which was marketed as cough syrup and sold as far away as Chicago and San Francisco. In 1943, the Smith Mine disaster at Bear Creek killed 74 miners. This pretty much led to the end of coal mining in Carbon County. Today, the community is largely supported by agriculture and tourism.

### H The Beartooth Highway

*Although these mountains were criss-crossed by trails used by Native Americans since prehistory, it was not until the early 20th century that many sought a permanent route over the mountains to Cooke City and Yellowstone National Park.*

*Beginning in 1924, a group of Red Lodge businessmen, led by Dr. J. C. E. Siegfriedt and newspaper publisher O. H. P. Shelley, lobbied Montana's congressional delegation to construct a road between their community and Cooke City. Because of their efforts, President Herbert Hoover signed the Park Approach Act into law in 1931. The Act funded the construction of scenic routes to the country's national parks through federally-owned land. The Beartooth Highway was the only road constructed under the Act. Construction on the $2.5 million project began in 1932.*

*The Beartooth Highway is an excellent example of "Seat-of-Your-Pants" construction with many of the engineering decisions made in the field. Some 100 workers employed by five companies blasted their way up the side of the 11,000-foot plateau. The workmen gave names to many features of the road that are still used today, including Lunch Meadow, Mae West Curve and High Lonesome Ridge. The road officially opened on June 14, 1936. The spectacular Beartooth Highway is a testimonial to the vision of those who fought for its construction and a tribute to those who carved it over the mountains.*

## 21. *Historic Marker, Adventure, Gas, Food, Lodgiing,*

### H Red Lodge

Hwy. 212 in Red Lodge

*Coal was discovered in the Rock Creek Valley nearly two decades before Red Lodge was established as a mail stop on the Meteetsee Trail in 1884. In 1887, the Rocky Fork Coal Company opened the first large-scale mine at Red Lodge sparking the community's first building boom, consisting mostly of "hastily constructed shacks and log huts." The completion of the Northern Pacific Railway branch line to Red Lodge in 1890 resulted in the construction of many brick and sandstone buildings that now line the city's main street.*

*Like all mining camps, Red Lodge had a large population of single men and an abundance of saloons. For many years, the notorious "Liver-eating"Johnson kept the peace as the town's first constable. Red Lodge also boasted several churches and social clubs for those not inclined toward the city's more earthier entertainment.*

*Hundreds of people came to Red Lodge in the 1890s and early 1900s. Immigrants from all over Europe worked shoulder-to-shoulder in the coal mines, but settled in neighborhoods called Finn Town, Little Italy and Hi Bug. Their cultural traditions endured and are celebrated at the city's annual Festival of Nations.*

*Production in the coal mines declined after World War I, eventually leading to their closure by 1932. The completion of the scenic Beartooth Highway in 1936 revitalized Red Lodge by linking it directly to Yellowstone National Park. Today, Red Lodge's past is represented by its historic buildings and by the pride its citizens take in its history and traditions.*

### H The Red Lodge Country

Hwy. 212 at Red Lodge

*According to tradition, a band of Crow Indians left the main tribe and moved west into the foothills of the Beartooth Range many years ago. They painted their council tepee with red clay and this old-time artistry resulted in the name Red Lodge.*

*This region is a bonanza for scientists. It is highly fossilized and Nature has opened a book on Beartooth Butte covering about a quarter of a billion years of geological history. It makes pretty snappy reading for parties interested in some of the ologies, paleontology for example.*

*Some students opine that prehistoric men existed here several million years earlier than heretofore believed. Personally we don't know, but if there were people prowling around that long ago, of course they would pick Montana as the best place to live.*

### V Adventure Whitewater

P.O. Box 636, 446–3061 or 800-897-3061.
www.redlodge.com; www.adventure.com

Known as Red Lodge's first rafting company, Adventure Whitewater is AAA rated, offering family rafting on the beautiful Stillwater River in South Central Montana. Enjoy their private launch and private parking for your half day, full day or paddle & saddle trips. Private float with Elvis, $2 million. Private float with owner slightly less.

## L Bear Bordeaux B&B

302 S. Broadway, Red Lodge. 446-4408

The Bear Bordeaux offers four stunningly decorated guest rooms, all designed with guests' needs & comforts in mind. All rooms are equipped with cozy down comforters, VCRs & color TVs, and some rooms offer fireplaces and private jacuzzi-baths. A great place to return after a full day of hiking or skiing, this amenity laden lodge offers stunning views of the Beartooth & Absaroka Mountains as well as Downtown Red Lodge. For those in need of quiet time, the Bear Bordeaux offers a 3,000-volume library, and for the movie buff they offer a 450+ video movie library with something to suit any taste. They offer a full breakfast with freshly brewed Gevalia coffee every morning, and with advance notice they can prepare special dinners or picnic lunches. Maid service is offered twice daily. They also offer massage therapy for extra comfort after that rough hike. Special occasions are welcome. Let them know and they'll help you create something special!

## L Chateau Rouge

1505 S. Broadway, Red Lodge. 446-1601

The Chateau Rouge Lodge is comprised of 24 adjoining chalet-style units in Red Lodge, only 6 miles from the ski area. All units feature fully equipped kitchen facilities with coffee. The condo style two bedroom apartments have fireplaces with stocked wood. The larger units sleep up to six with comfortable living rooms, separate kitchens, two separate bedrooms, and a tub/shower combination. The single floor studio units are convenient and spacious—sleeping up to four people in a large living area with a breakfast nook. The lodge has queen beds in the studios and king size beds in the master bedroom of the two bedroom units. All units have cable TV. Enjoy the indoor swimming pool and spa after a long drive, a great ski day, or a day of cross-country skiing on one of the many surrounding trails. A large common area with a huge natural fireplace and living room atmosphere is available to all guests and is a great place to hold meetings or receptions.

## L Willows Inn

224 S. Platt, Red Lodge. 446-3913.
www.bbhost.com/willowsinn

Come home to the Willows Inn, nestled below the majestic Beartooth Mountains in majestic Red Lodge. A home away from home, this quaint bed & breakfast has captured turn-of-the-century Victorian splendor. Travelers are luxuriously accommodated in five distinctly appointed guest rooms or two storybook cottages, each with breathtaking views of the surrounding countryside. Awake mornings to a scrumptious full breakfast offering homemade pastries baked on the premises. A variety of recreational pleasures also await guests of the Willows Inn. Nature lovers will thrill at the abundance of wildlife, while anglers will revel in the renowned Rock Creek, which runs behind the Inn.

*An excellent firearms exhibit is one of the many features of the Peaks to Plains Museum in Red Lodge.*

## L Best Western Lupine Inn

702 S. Hauser, Red Lodge. 446-1321

Close to all nearby attractions, the Best Western Lupine Inn is a great place to stay while enjoying all that Red Lodge has to offer. Within walking distance to downtown and just miles from Red Lodge Ski Area, Beartooth Pass, Yellowstone National Park, and a variety of outdoor activities. Guests can enjoy the indoor heated pool, sauna and spa after a long day of activities. There is also a complimentary continental breakfast, indoor playground, fitness room, kitchenette units, laundry facilities, a ski waxing room, a meeting room and separate guest houses. Pets are welcome.

## L Eagles Nest Motel

702 S. Broadway, Red Lodge. 446-2312

Set back off the highway, right by Rock Creek, sits The Eagles Nest Motel. The 17 units all have cable TV, queen and extra long beds, phones, and coffee. There are four family units, some with galley kitchens, and one cottage that sleeps eight. Guests can relax in the jacuzzi after a long day of hiking or skiing, enjoy the outside picnic area and the gift shop. The motel is within walking distance to downtown Red Lodge, and a great base camp for excursions to Red Lodge Mountain Ski Area, Beartooth Pass and Wilderness Area, Custer National Forest, and the many other surrounding activities.

## L Super 8 Motel

1223 S. Broadway, Red Lodge. 446-2288 or 800-800-8000 or fax 446-3162

# 22. *Historic Marker, Attraction, Adventure, Gas, Food, Lodging, Shopping*

## H Chief Plenty Coups Statue marker

Red Lodge

Plenty Coups—Chief of the Crows

(Circa 1848-March 4, 1932)

*"The buffalo gone and freedom denied him, the Indians was visited by two equally hideous strangers, famine and tuberculosis. He could cope with neither. His pride broken he felt himself an outcast, a beggar in his own country. It was now that Plenty Coups became the real leader of his people."*

*"All my life I have tried to learn as the chickadee learns, by listening, profiting by the mistakes of others, that I may help my people. I hear the white man say there will be no more war. But this cannot be true. There will be other wars. Men have not changed, and whenever they quarrel they will fight, as they have always done. We love our country because it is beautiful, because we were born here. Strangers will covet it and someday try to possess it, as surely as the sun will come tomorrow. Then there must be war, unless we have grown to be cowards without love in our hearts for our native land. And whenever war comes between this country and another, your people will find my people pointing their guns with yours. If ever the hands of my people hold the rope that keeps this country's flag high in the air, it will never come down while an Absarokee (Crow) warrior lives."*

-Linderman's Biography of Plenty Coups

*Crow country once ranged from Three Forks to the Black Hills, from the Musselshell to the Big Horn Mountains. Red Lodge was a place of worship, food and protection for the Crow people when it was theirs. Please respect it and love it. It is a very good place.*

### T Peaks to Plains Museum

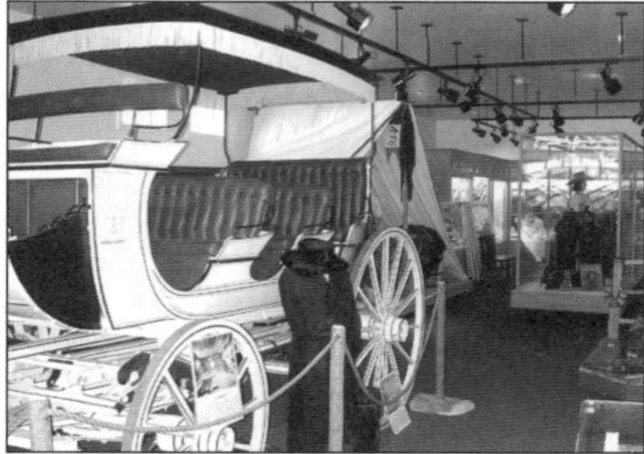

224 N. Broadway Ave. in downtown Red Lodge. 446-3667

This new location for the Carbon County Historical Society's museum is in the renovated 1909 Labor Temple at the north end of downtown Red Lodge. Inside is a variety of exhibits portraying the rich cultural and natural history of the region.

Featured here is a walk-through simulated coal mine in the downstairs portion of the museum along with associated mining tools and photographs. Upstairs exhibits include: a fully restored 1890s Yellowstone National Park touring coach; the Greenough Collection of cowboy and rodeo memorabilia, including many of the items used by the renowned "Riding Greenough's" as they performed throughout the world; an early 19th century trade tent and a display of authentic costumes and items from the fur-trade era; and a display of the Waples Family collection of more than 80 historic guns and accessories.

There are exhibits portraying the local history of the Crow Indians, trappers and mountain men, early immigrants, paleontology and geology. There is also an eclectic collection of artifacts from the more recent past, including an old electroshock therapy machine.

The museum is open daily during the summer from 10 a.m. to 5 p.m. There is a small admission charge.

### V Headwaters and High Country Outfitters

13 N. Broadway, Red Lodge. 446-2679

Hunting and fishing in Montana is truly a great and memorable experience. Headwaters and High Country is proud to offer you some of the best hunting and fishing in the state of Montana. Their hunting lease is located in a game-rich area known as the Bull Mountains. Elk, whitetail, mule deer and antelope are their specialty. They offer fly fishing instruction and classes through their full service fly shop. Follow up your class with a wade or float trip on the Yellowstone, Big Horn or Stillwater Rivers or on Rock Creek located in Red Lodge. They are not only outfitters, but a full service bike shop with trail info and repairs.

### F Bridge Creek Backcountry Kitchen & Wine Bar

116 S. Broadway, Historic Downtown Red Lodge. 446-9900. www.eatfooddrinkwine.com

Dinner at Bridge Creek features locally raised, all-natural beef, fresh seafood and an award-winning wine list. They are rapidly becoming a real Montana legend. Their "quick-service" lunch menu is packed with salads, sandwiches, wraps and burgers. Soups and breads are made fresh daily including their signature clam chowder—locals claim it's the "best in the West!" Enjoy a locally brewed beer by the fireplace. Dine in a warm and comfortable surrounding. Watch their talented chef at work in his open kitchen. The Coffee Bar is open daily at 7 a.m. serving some of the finest espresso and freshly baked pastries in Red Lodge. A full selection of hot and iced coffee drinks are also available. Enjoy their comfortable seating area, including a patio which overlooks downtown Red Lodge. Private dining rooms and custom menus are available for groups of 12 to 120.

### F Bull Moose Bistro

17 S. Broadway, Red Lodge. 446-2840

Located in the heart of downtown Red Lodge, the Bull Moose Bistro features a unique regional cuisine that stands apart from other local restaurants.

The menu changes with the seasons, offering a broad range of meats and seafood from steaks, pork dishes, and lamb to shrimp scampi and daily seafood specials. The interesting selection of appetizers and the great salads are perfect for lunch or dinner. Featuring a great list of micro-brews and fine wines to go along with the menu, as well as a full service bar. The warm, relaxed atmosphere, experienced staff, and great food will make for a truly unique dining experience.

### FL The Pollard
2 N. Broadway, Red Lodge. 446-0001 or 800-POLLARD(7655273), www.pollardhotel.com.

Built in 1893 as Red Lodge's first brick structure, The Pollard has been the cornerstone of the community for over one hundred years. This historic hotel has been meticulously restored and offers a variety of charming guest rooms. Modern additions include an elevator and a health club with racquetball courts, saunas, and a hot tub. Enjoy outstanding food and selections from their award-winning wine list in the dining room. Arthur's Grill at The Pollard offers impeccable service in a distinguished, yet comfortable atmosphere. A full breakfast is included in their room rates. Reservations are recommended. The Pollard is entirely non-smoking.

### F Red Lodge Café & Lounge/Casino
16-18 S. Broadway, Red Lodge. 446-1619

The Red Lodge Café has been open since the early 1900s and still has a big reputation for family dining and "home cooking at it's finest." They cater to locals but are sought out by visitors. In addition to great meals, you'll be dazzled by their salad bar, home baked goods, and daily specials. Plan to have plenty of fun with karaoke on weekends, casino machines, poker, and keno. You'll even find one of the only two right-angle pool tables in the state of Montana. Enjoy your favorite cocktail, cold beer, or wine, too. Stop by for breakfast, lunch, or dinner. They are open daily from 6 a.m. to 9 p.m.

### F Bogart's
11 S. Broadway, Red Lodge. 446-1784

Enjoy this unique establishment adorned with old Hollywood shots of rustic Montana and old Humphrey Bogart himself. A must stop while in town, Bogart's has been featured in Bon Appetit magazine for their fabulous Mexican food and hamburgers. Their diverse menu also features pizza & pasta, sandwiches, excellent margaritas, a kid's menu with mini-pizzas, and lots of great vegetarian items. Try their homemade salsa and seasonal micro-brews brewed especially for Bogart's. For your enjoyment, Bogart's is always entirely non-smoking. Don't miss this fun & funky place with great food in true Montana fashion!

### F Coffee Factory Roasters
6 S. Broadway, Red Lodge. 446-3200

### S Common Ground Western Art & Gifts
3 N. Broadway, Red Lodge. 446-2800 or fax 446-2513. www.comngrndartgallery.com or email comngrnd@wtp.net

## Beartooth Highway

Author Charles Kurault described the Beartooth Scenic Highway as "the most beautiful drive in America." In 1989, the highway received national recognition when it was designated a National Scenic Byway. Only 52 other drives in the country share this distinction. This spectacular 65-mile drive reaches the highest drivable points in both Wyoming and Montana. Leaving Red Lodge, U.S. Hwy. 212 climbs 11,000 feet to Beartooth Pass and drops down to the northeast entrance to Yellowstone Park.

After mine closings wrecked the economy of Red Lodge, J.C.F. Siegriedt, a Red Lodge physician, lobbied the U.S. Government to rebuild the old "Black and White Trail" which ran along Rock Creek south of Red Lodge. He and O.H.P. Shelby, the local newspaper publisher persuaded the congress to authorize the Secretary of the Interior to build "approach highways" to the national parks. Herbert Hoover signed the bill, and construction began in 1931. The highway, at a cost of $2.5 million, opened on June 14, 1936.

The 64-mile corridor provides a panoramic view at the 10,942 ft. summit of peaks, varied topography, glaciers, plateaus, alpine lakes, cascading streams, wildflowers, and wildlife. The Beartooth Plateau is unique. After endless climbing you come to what appears to be an expansive plains rather than the top of a mountain range. Had you just been dropped here, you would think you were on a vast prairie filled with deep gorges. Glaciation missed this area leaving it relatively flat and smooth, unlike the jagged sculpted peaks in the distance. There are 25 features here labeled "Beartooth" all taken from the name of the conspicuous spire the Crow Indians called *Na Pet Say*—the "bears tooth." At its highest points, you can play in snow fields along the highway.

Allow yourself at least three hours to cross the highway. The limitless views demand that you stop every few minutes. The winding switchbacks do not allow speed. Check your film supply before heading up. You'll take many photos. And anticipate cool, if not cold weather at the top along with almost constant wind. Take your time and savor this trip, it's only open a few short months of the year.

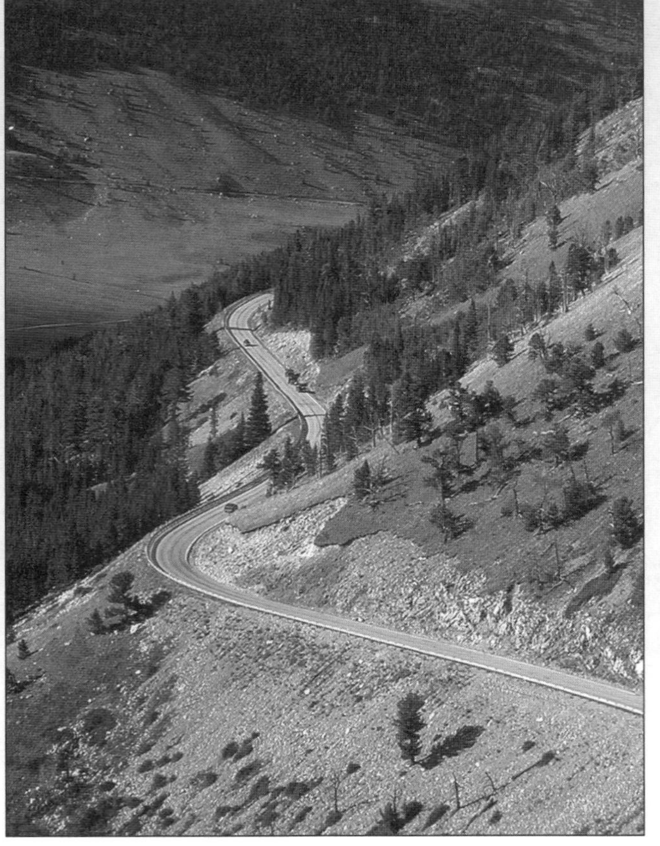

Common Ground Western Art and Gifts representing Bradford J. Williams, artist and sculptor, also pays tribute to other outstanding artists they show in their exquisite gallery. On display are decoys by carver David Ritter, beautiful photographic landscapes by Carter E. Gowl, original oils by Brent Flory and Chuck Dayton, original water colors by Luke Buck, and original Pastels by Dale Martin. There are belt buckles and watches, sterling silver and 18-caret gold jewelry, along with iron décor. Owner Mary L. Allen will acquaint you with the history of each piece and provide information about the artist. Common Ground also carries numerous other items including Aspen Bay Candles, Big Sky Carvers picture frames and gifts, and Leanin' Tree cards.

### S Shades & Specs

20 S. Broadway, Red Lodge. 446-2135

Sunglasses, ski goggles and sports specific eyewear are Shades & Specs specialty, with both prescription and brand name, non-prescription styles available. Licensed optician Jeff Warner has one of the largest eyewear inventories in the area. He also has over twenty years experience filling and dispensing eye doctors prescriptions for eyeglasses, and is the only full-time optical dispensary in Carbon County. Shades & Specs can provide you with quality optics to enhance your sport, recreational and eyewear needs. Stop in for a chat and see what Jeff can do for you. Check out some of the fun new products now on the market for prescription and non-prescription eyeglass buffs and outdoor enthusiasts.

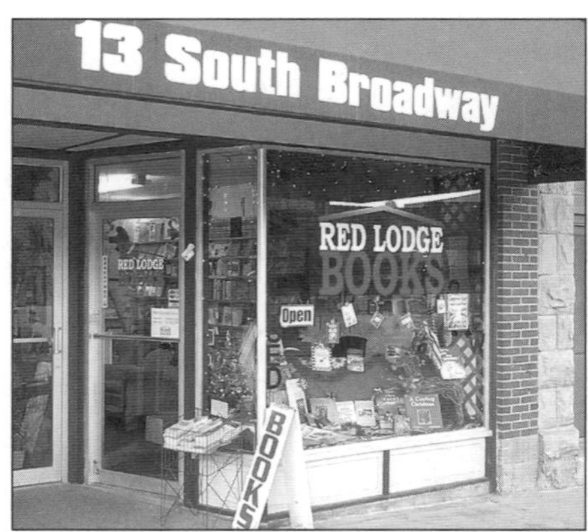


### S Red Lodge Books

13 S. Broadway, Red Lodge. 446-2742.
www.redlodgebooks.com or
email gary@redlodgebooks.com

Red Lodge Books, formerly the Broadway Bookstore, has been a fixture in Red Lodge for 15 years. If you're looking for information on the area, this is the place to find it. Red Lodge Books carries both new and used books, with an extensive selection on local and Western history. In the new section, you'll also find guidebooks for hiking, driving, camping, fishing, and hunting as well as books about Native Americans, ranching, farming, horses, cowboys, rodeo, and even a collection of popular novels. The used section is an eclectic collection, ranging from inexpensive paperbacks to collectibles and first editions.

### S The Glass Rabbit

112 S. Broadway, Red Lodge. 446-2805 or
fax 446-2929

A visit to The Glass Rabbit will bring years of fond memories long after you return home from your visit to Red Lodge. Share the memories of Montana with gifts for that special someone. The Glass Rabbit offers a selection of decorative accent pieces to warm every room of your home or office. Find jewelry to match your individual style from Western to Victorian, including Montana's finest selection of Native American jewelry. Explore all natural aromatherapy products from candles to bath and beauty accessories. Collectibles are available from Boyds Bears, Beanie Babies, and Dreamsicles. Treat yourself to gourmet chocolate sauce made in Red Lodge. They are open daily, year round, and will ship for your convenience.

### S Magpie Toymakers

115 N. Broadway, Red Lodge. 446-3044

Step back in time as you browse this charming shop in historic Red Lodge. Here you will find classic toys and games including tops, yo-yos, marbles, and jacks, as well as old-fashioned paper dolls and a tremendous selection of Dover Books. The heart of this store is the toymaker's workshop where fascinating toys, puzzles, and art pieces are expertly hand-crafted from fine hardwoods. These original designs are both whimsical and elegant. If you're looking for kids' travel activities, unique gifts, or a piece of the past, amuse yourself at the store where toys are powered by the imagination, not batteries.

### S Montana Candy Emporium

7 S. Broadway, Red Lodge. 446-1119

### S Sylvan Peak

9 S. Broadway, Red Lodge. 446-1770
or 800-425-0076. sylvanpk@wtp.net;
www.redlodge.com/sylvanpeak

Sylvan Peak specializes in custom-made outdoor clothing for all ages. You can choose your own colors and they will fit your build and ship to any location. The downstairs shop concentrates on cross country, telemarking, and snowshoe rental, sales and service in the winter months. In the summer you can find all your hiking and backpacking supplies, as well as trail suggestions and up to the minute conditions from the knowledgeable staff. Visit their quaint town and discover the vastness of their back door playground, with some of the most beautiful scenery in world. Call or stop in for a free catalogue. Open everyday year-round.



### S The Body Lodge

22 S. Broadway Suite B, Red Lodge. 446-3668.

Owner Kim Greenough invites you to pamper yourself in their comfortable atmosphere where her friendly staff will literally wait on you hand and foot. This full service salon offers massage, body wraps, tanning, steam treatments, artificial nails, spa manicures and pedicures, facials and waxing. While you're there, browse through their line of unique gifts, skin care products, nail care products, bath products, candles and jewelry. They are located in the heart of Red Lodge behind Waters Department Store on the corner of Broadway and 12th, or check out their second location at 302 Woodard Ave. in Absorkee.

### S Cottage Quilts

316 S. Broadway, Red Lodge. 446-2581.
www.cottage-quilts.com or
email: CottQuilts@peoplepc.com

## 23. *Attraction, Gas, Lodging, Camping, Miscellaneous*

### TS Depot Gallery

Red Lodge. 446-1370

This outstanding gallery, located in Red Lodge's original railroad depot at the north end of town has rotating exhibits and sales. Most work is by local artists, including members of the Carbon County Arts Guild who operate the Gallery. Open Tuesday-Saturday 11–5 and summer Sundays 11-3.

### T Beartooth Nature Center

900 N. Bonner, Red Lodge. 446-1133

Located in Coal Miner's Park, the Nature Center takes in animals that can not be left alone in nature, and nurtures them back to good health. On site are mountain lions, bears and many others, with a petting zoo for the kids. It is a great spot to view the surrounding wildlife up close. Open in the summer from 10 a.m.–6 p.m., children $2, adults $4.

### *Montana Trivia*

Montana is a pretty crowded place. Per square mile there are 1.4 elk, 1.4 pronghorn antelope, 3.3 deer, 896 catchable fish and fewer than six people.

### A Napa Auto Parts
121 E. 5th St., Red Lodge. 446-1830

### L Comfort Inn of Red Lodge
612 N. Broadway, Red Lodge. 446-4469 or toll free at 888-733-4661

A "Gold Award Winner" featuring rooms with a warm lodge look, the Comfort Inn of Red Lodge offers a cozy yet luxurious atmosphere. With king size, queen size and even double extra long beds, each guest enjoys a good night's sleep and feels right at home.

### M Silver Strike Casino
609 N. Broadway, Red Lodge, 446-3131. www.redlodge.com

Located at the north end of Red Lodge, next to the visitor's center, the Silver Strike is a great place to stop in for great family fun. This air conditioned casino, sports bar & bowling alley has full beverage service, the latest in adult gaming machines, and a slew of televisions, including a big screen, for watching that game you don't want to miss. You will also find two regulation size pool tables, eight newly resurfaced bowling lanes, and some of the most popular video games available. Happy hour is from 4–7 p.m. daily, and they offer an all-day drink special. The drink prices at the Silver Strike are the best in town. Adjoining the establishment is Becker's Kitchen & Steakhouse serving breakfast, lunch & dinner daily.

## 24. *Gas, Food, Shopping*

### Roberts
Roberts is a small town that lays on Rock Creek. It was one of the stops on the Northern Pacific Railroad, and dates back to the late 1800s.

### S Hayseed's Antiques
101 1st Ave. N., Roberts. 445-2378

## 25. *Gas*

### Boyd
The town of Boyd was named for the homesteader John Boyd, who settled in this area in the early 1900s. The farmland around Boyd is irrigated with water that melts from the Beartooth Mountains.

### A M & M Sales & Service
First & Montana, Boyd. 962-3486

## 26. *Attraction, Gas, Food, Lodging*

### Joliet
Located along Rock Creek, Joliet is an agricultural community named by a Railroad worker from Joliet, Illinois.

*The Sermon on the Mount.*

### T Pathway Through the Bible
2 miles north of Joliet

A German immigrant, Adolph Land, moved to Montana from Iowa in 1952 with his wife, Helen, and a small pile of rocks. While supporting themselves by selling honey and trees, he decided to build a rock garden similar to "The Grotto" in West Bend, Iowa. The project turned into a 23 year endeavor that resulted in the "Pathway Through the Bible", an elaborate display of biblical stories represented in rocks.

Over the years the Land's collected rocks from all corners of the state and created gardens of flowers, shrubs, and rock formations of biblical characters and stories. After Adolph passed on, Helen sold the property to Verdine and Rick White who were willing to maintain the property with the reverence it earned over the years.

The garden gate is always open for public enjoyment. Guests are free to wander and only asked to respect the property owner's privacy.

### F Frontier Bar & Bone Pile
108 Main St., Joliet. 962-9972

## 27. *Lodging*

### L Blessing House Bed & Breakfast
4 miles west of Red Lodge. 446-4269

## 28. *Attraction*

### Luther
This town was named for the Luther family who ran the post office and general store here. A blacksmith, lumberyard and saloon graced the site in years past.

## Calamity Jane

Calamity Jane, was born, Martha Jane Canary, in Princeton, Missouri in 1852, the oldest of six children.As a child she was a tomboy and had a passion for riding horses. In 1865, at the age of 13 the Cannary family made the five month journey, stopping in Virginia City, to take part in the quest for gold on their way to Salt Lake City. During their migration Martha practiced hunting with the men, and by the time they reached Virginia City, she was an accomplished rider and gun handler.

From 1866 on, she and her family moved around quite a bit-to Salt Lake City where her father died the next year, and then onto Wyoming where she helped scout for the army. During her travels she worked when she could find it, and even took up prostitution, although she always seemed to prefer men's work.

In the early 1870s Martha Jane Cannary was christened "Calamity Jane," known for her reckless daring riding and good aim. In 1876 Calamity Jane crossed paths with Wild Bill Hickok, and they remained good friends, (she told some they were married) until his death. She was known for causing a bit of trouble by stirring up the occasional saloon fight, and was said to have had a problem with alcoholism. Calamity Jane moved around most of her life and found it difficult to settle in one place. She did however spend some time in Montana, residing in Livingston for a period, and outside of Laurel where her cabins still stand today. She also called Big Timber, Castle, and Harlowton home for brief periods. When she died in 1903 at the age of 51, Calamity Jane was buried, at her request, next to Wild Bill in Deadwood, South Dakota.

### T Wild Bill Lake
This is a popular fishing, hiking and swimming spot, with trails that go up the West Fork of Rock Creek. It is handicapped accessible.

## 29. *food*

### Roscoe
Roscoe is a small town half way between Red Lodge and Columbus. Originally names Morris after a local family, the mail was often confused with the town of Norris. Therefore, the name was changed to Roscoe in 1905, after the postmaster's favorite horse. It is the gateway to East Rosebud Canyon and Lake.

## 30. *Gas, Food, Lodging*

### Nye
A small town started during the mining boom years and a handful of residents still live here. Children still attend classes in a one room school house. Located in the upper Stillwater Valley, the town is named for Jack Nye, an agent for the Minneapolis Mining Co. in the 1880s.

### Dean
A small hamlet that borders the Beartooths. Don't be surprised to see a wolf or a grizzly stop through town.

## Excerpts From The Beartooth Report

1882 by General Philip H. Sheridan

August 26, resumed the march, passing through Cooke City, a mining town on the divide between the waters of the east fork of the Yellowstone River and Clark's Fork. Many of the mines here are considered valuable. There are about 100 houses in the city, with fair prospects of as many more in a few months, indicated by the quantities of freshly hewn logs lying about and the number of town lots for sale. After stopping for only a short time to make some inquiries of the courteous inhabitants we continued on our way.

Just as we reached the summit of the divide, where the waters of Soda Butte Creek and Clark's Fork take their respective watersheds, we met a hunter, Mr. Geer, who considered himself so familiar with the Beartooth range of mountains that I was induced to abandon the old Clark's Fork trail and make an effort to cross that range, thus saving about three days in our journey to Billings station on the Northern Pacific railroad.

After meeting him and employing him as a guide, somewhat against the judgment of older guides, we passed down the mountain with much difficulty, on account of the burning forests, the fire extending across our line of march. The journey this day was through high mountain peaks, covered on top with perpetual snow. We encamped at the base of Index peak and Pilot knob, on the banks of Clark's Fork of the Yellowstone. This camp was named Camp Clark, after Captain W.P. Clark, second cavalry, our Indian interpreter. Distance marched, 31 miles; altitude of camp, 7,100 feet.

On the morning of August 27, under the direction of our new guide, we crossed to the north side of Clark's Fork and began the ascent of the Beartooth Range. This was long, but gradual, and quite feasible for a wagon road so far as grade is concerned. The only difficulties which presented themselves during the day were bodies of densely growing timber at one or two places. However, we got through these without much delay, and about 12 o'clock encamped immediately under a very prominent land mark, called on the map Red butte. The camp was beautiful and was named Camp Gregory, after Colonel Gregory of my staff.

Section 3

### Fishtail

You would think that this tiny town's name somehow relates to its proximity to some of the finest fishing in Montana. Some of the residents there say that a local mountain formation that looks like a fishtail had something to do with the name. There is even a Fishtail River nearby. In truth, this little community located about 25 miles southwest of Columbus, was named for a Mr. Fishtail who resided in the area at the end of the 19th century. In about 1901 the town became official when a post office was established to service the surrounding Fiddler, Fishtail and, and Rock Creek area. Stressley Tunnell established a store at the time which was later purchased by the Columbus Mercantile in 1908. The store is still in operation today. The town sits in the foothills and the shadow of the Absaroka Mountain range. Today the town is only one block long, but manages to muster up a two mile long parade during the festival it sponsors every summer. Its also known to host one of the biggest yard sales in the state during that same festival.

### V Benbow ATV Rentals LLP

60 Trinity Trail, Fishtail. 328-4352. www.benbowatvrentals.com

### F Montana Hanna's

Dean. 328-6780

### S Fishtail General Store

In Fishtail on Hwy. 419. 328-4260

The Fishtail General Store has been operating in the same location since it opened in 1900. You'll love the old meat market section of the store which features its world famous "Fishtail General Store Special Sausage," a delicacy treasured by its regular customers. This is truly a "general" store with a little of everything including food, hardware, provisions for camping and hunting and fishing licenses. If need something or just plain curious, it's a gosh darn fun place to browse. The original pot belly stove still keeps the place warm. Handmade crafts, toys, wall hangings, candles and soaps made by local folks are displayed on floor to ceiling maple shelves complete with a rolling ladder for the high reaches. If you get lucky, you'll get fresh baked cookies, warm from the oven. This place is worth a side trip!

### S Nye Trading Post

1997 Nye Rd., Nye. 328-6262

## 31. *Gas, Food, Lodging*

### Absarokee

Absarokee is a small town with a lot of character. The name originates from the Crow Indians who, in the Hidatsa language, were referred to as Absarokee or "Big Beaked Bird." The white man referred to them as The Crow. The town of Absarokee used to be part of the Crow Reservation and the Old Crow Agency is just outside of town, marked with a plaque. Located on the Stillwater and Rosebud Rivers, the town sits about a mile away from the Bozeman Trail. Oliver Hovda built the first house, a pre-fab from Sears and Roebuck, in 1904.

### V Absaroka River Adventures, LCC

113 Grove St., Absarokee. 328-7440 or 800-334-RAFT(7238). www.absarokariver.com or email info@absarokariver.com

Absaroka River Adventures is a family owned and operated business dedicated to providing personalized high quality river rafting trips on the Stillwater River. The Stillwater River is a snowmelt, spring-fed river entirely free-flowing (no dams). Peak flows generally occur in May or June. Half-day and full-day trips are available along with horseback/rafting combo trips, with paddle or oar. The managing partner and head guide has over 20 years' experience floating and fishing the Stillwater River and their professional guides are trained in river rescue and first aid. Experience the thrills, friendships, and natural beauty that you'll enjoy on the Stillwater River.

### A J.C. Tire

135 Woodward, Absarokee. 328-4766

F **Stake-Out**
Main Street, Absarokee, 328-6566

Offering some of the best steaks around, a great selection of burgers, a rib menu with different sauce selections, and all-you-can-eat crab and prime rib on weekends. The Stake-Out has a charming rustic, yet modern, atmosphere, that is great for families or a nice romantic dinner. There is a fresh salad bar, homemade soups, and hand-cut meats. Breakfast is served on weekends, but they try to accommodate anyone's tastes any time. You will also enjoy their friendly staff and great selection of music. The 5 Spot Bar is connected with occasional entertainment. Stop in for a great hearty meal in a warm, inviting atmosphere.

F **Dew Drop Inn**
3328 Hwy 78, Absarokee. 328-4121

Stop in for old-fashioned hamburgers and milk-shakes made to order. You will experience a clean, family oriented atmosphere and friendly service. This locally owned and operated restaurant was established in 1958. Visit for lunch or dinner, they offer daily specials, easy access, an outdoor deck, and a spectacular view of the Beartooth Mountain Range. Spend a few days at the "New" Dew Drop Inn RV Park, and enjoy nearby gift shops, fishing, hiking, river rafting and horseback riding. The 10 full service hookups are adjacent to the restaurant. Turn south at Columbus, I-90 Exit 408, at Absarokee on Highway 78 (14 miles up the Stillwater River Valley) on the scenic route to the Absaroka-Beartooth Backcountry Wilderness or Yellowstone National Park, via Red Lodge.

L **Bed & No Breakfast Bunkhouse**
18 Woodard St., Absarokee. 328-7418.
Email: bnnob@mcn.net

This brand new establishment offers a smoke-free environment with unique Western-style rooms, each decorated in a different theme using customized Western iron art and local Artesian Pine log furnishings. Each room has cable TV and a telephone. The bunkhouse is conveniently located near downtown and within walking distance of local shops and restaurants. All rooms are non-smoking and no pets are allowed. For prolonged stays there are five one-bedroom efficiency apartments available at reduced rates. A laundromat is conveniently located next door, and pay showers are also available for the public. Come enjoy a Western stay in beautiful Absarokee, close to the Beartooth Mountains.

L **Stoney Lonesome Ranch & JR Outfitters**
1390 Bridger Creek Rd. 20 miles north of Absarokee. 932-4452

JR Outfitters and the Stoney Lonesome Ranch are owned and operated by the same family. The ranch is located in the foothills and mountains of one of the most prime and beautiful places in Montana. Cabins, horse back riding, great food, and hospitality combined with the abundant wild life and surrounding views make this ranch a place next to heaven. Hunting in the fall and riding, camping, and rafting the Stillwater River in the summer make this a unique and pleasurable combination for all. They are only 20 miles north of Absarokee, 35 miles south of Big Timber, and 21 south of Reedpoint.

S **Charmed, Inc. Antiques & Home Furnishiings**
15 S. Woodard Ave. in Absarokee. 328-7444

Montana Made gift items and beautiful antiques beckon you to stop in Absarokee at Charmed, Inc. Located right downtown along Highway 78, this is the prefect place to stop and stretch your legs, and appeal to all your senses. Let aromatic decorative fragrances welcome you as you enter this haven for yesteryear's favorite furniture, linens, vintage jewelry, and all of Grandma's things that you fondly remember. Artfully mixing the old and not so old, with today's decorating trends. Locally hand crafted wind chimes, birdhouses, candles, and soap; there is something to interest everyone in your family. Ask them for a free sample of Stillwater Chocolate River Rocks!

**32.** *Attraction*

T **Cooney Lake State Park**
22 miles southwest of Laurel on U.S. 212, then 5 miles west of Boyd on county road. Summer, 445-2326 Winter, 252-4654.

One of the most popular recreation areas in south-central Montana, the lake is actually a reservoir, with a great view of the Beartooths in the background. This is a popular spot for fishing, swimming and boating, and has some nice camping as well. Attractions include good walleye and rainbow trout fishing. Boating and camping opportunities are abundant, and the Beartooth Mountains loom in the distance.

## Scenic Drives

**Beartooth Scenic Byway (U.S. Route 212)**
This drive certainly ranks as one of the most spectacular drives in the United States. Driving south out of Red Lodge, the highway follows Rock Creek through several layers of forest and climbs to high alpine tundra revealing a rugged panorama. Once you cross the high plateau, the drive continues on to the little town of Cooke City and the northeast entrance to Yellowstone National Park. While the mileage for this drive is relatively short, allow yourself the better part of the day for the round trip. You will be stopping often and using a lot of film.

**East Rosebud Lake**
To start this drive from Red Lodge, take MT Hwy. 78 (the turnoff is just north of downtown) west and drive to the town of Roscoe. This route offers some spectacular uninterrupted views of the Beartooth Range to the south. On clear days you can view the Crazy Mountains to the northwest. Turn into the town of Roscoe and stay left through the town. When you cross the bridge over East

*Gas pumps party outside the Charles Ringer studio just north of Red Lodge.*

## It Happened in Montana

On November 11, 1965,Bill Linderman, the legendary rodeo champion from the Belfry-Bridger area dies in a commercial airplane crash at Salt Lake City. Just hours before the crash, Linderman wrote a counter check for $20 at a friend's tavern. Under his signature, he gave his address as "Heaven." At the time of the crash, his friends speculated as to whether Linderman had a premonition, was referring to his home in Montana, or was just playing one of his pranks.

Rosebud River look for an immediate right turn. This road will take you to East Rosebud Canyon and the lake. Make sure your dentures are glued on tight. This is usually a pretty bumpy road. The steep granite walls of the canyon tower over the lake creating one of the more photographic settings in the area. In 1997, the Shepard Mountain Fire burned clear much of the old lodgepole pine forest. Now thousands of aspen seedlings and wildflowers blanket the slopes. This is a great place to fish, hike and enjoy an afternoon picnic.

## Wildlife Viewing

This area, with the Absaroka-Beartooth Wilderness, Beartooth Mountains and many river valleys, offers unlimited wildlife viewing opportunities. The area is abundant with prairie dogs which tend to stand up for lookout by their holes. The prairie dog towns increase the habitat for many other animals that feed off of the dogs, such as hawks, fox, and ferrets. It is very common to see deer standing in the fields or crossing the roads-be careful of this! Pronghorn are often spotted in the flat prairie lands, and keep an eye out for eagles.

Although much wildlife can be seen just driving through this area if you are paying attention, there are spots that can almost guarantee a viewing and of course hiking in the backcountry is your best bet. The Hailstone and Half Breed Wildlife Refuge areas are both located north of Laurel. Both offer spectacular birdwatching opportunities.

## Hikes

The Beartooth Mountains are the source of all hikes in this section. One of the most popular areas is the East Rosebud drainage which takes you past countless waterfalls and mountain lakes. Numerous trails depart from the Beartooth Scenic Highway area also, and many of these make nice day hikes while traveling the highway. This is Grizzly country so be watchful, make a lot of noise and pack bear spray.

**Elk Lake**
This four mile hike starts at East Rosebud Lake and climbs about 500 feet. To get to East Rosebud Lake, take Forest Road 2177 south from Roscoe. This is a slow, rough road.

**Granite Peak Trail**
You'll find the trailhead for this trail at East Rosebud Lake also. This trail takes you approximately six miles through a creek bottom canyon to Mystic Lake.

**Wild Bill Lake Area**
Head south on U.S. 212 and watch for Forest Road #71. This is the road to the Red Lodge Ski area. Follow this to the lake. An easy trail goes partway around the lake. There is some excellent fishing here as well. At the end of the road are several more trailheads. One is a short hike (approximately three miles) up to Lake Gertrude and Timberline Lake.

**Basin Lakes National Recreation Trail**
Approximately one mile past Wild Bill Lake is the trailhead for this hike. This is about a 2.5 mile hike to Lower Basin Creek Lake. If you're feeling energetic, you can go an additional 1.5 miles to Upper Basin Creek Lake. It's worth the hike to see this shimmering lake nestled in a glacial cirque. Much of this trail follows an old logging road.

**Lake Fork Lake**
To reach this trail head, follow the Beartooth Scenic Highway south of Red Lodge to Lake Fork Road on your right. If you reach the campgrounds, you've gone too far. The trailhead for this hike is just 1.25 miles up Lake Fork Road. These are fairly short hikes leading either upstream or downstream on Lake Fork Creek.

**Parkside National Recreation Trail**
A bit further up the road is the Parkside Picnic Area. The trailhead for this hike starts here and heads north for a little over two miles up to Greenough Lake.

**Glacier Lake**
Continue to follow the Beartooth Scenic Highway south of Red Lodge to the first turnoff to campgrounds on your right. These will be about a mile past the Lake Fork Road turnoff. If you've reached the switchbacks of the highway, you've gone too far. Take Forest Road #421 across Rock Creek and head south for about seven miles following the creek. This is a rough road and a high clearance is recommended. At the end of the road is a parking area and the trailhead for the two-mile hike to the lake. This lake is the source of Rock Creek and sits in the shadow of the 12,350-foot high Mt. Rearguard. The trail takes you through some spectacular alpine country.

## Cross-Country Ski Trails

### Custer National Forest

*For more information contact District Ranger, Red Lodge, MT 59068. Phone, 446-2103*

**Silver Run-5 mi. W Red Lodge via West Fork Rock Creek Road**
*Range of difficulty depends on snow conditions. No grooming*
One-way mountain touring trail; 4 loops (4 km;7 km; 11 km; and 13 km); closed to snowmachines.

**Lake Fork-10 mi. S Red Lodge via Hwy 212**
*Range of difficulty depends on snow conditions. No grooming*
Two loops (2 km and 5 km); closed to snowmachines. Park at junction of Hwy 212 and Lake Fork Road.

**West Fork Rock Creek Road–6 mi. W Red Lodge via West Fork Rock Creek Road**
*1 km Easiest, 11 km More Difficult; no grooming*
No loops; dead end route. Shared with snowmachines.

## Information Please

All Montana area codes are 406

### Road Information

Montana Road Condition Report
800-226-7623, 800-335-7592 or local 444-7696
Montana Highway Patrol 444-7696
Local Road Reports
Billings 252-2806
Billings Weather Reports 652-1916

### Tourism Information

Travel Montana
800-847-4868 outside Montana
444-2654 in Montana http://travel.mt.gov/.
Yellowstone Country 800-736-5276 or 646-4383
Northern Rodeo Association 252-1122
**Chambers of Commerce**
Laurel 628-8105
Red Lodge 446-1718
Stillwater 322-4505

### Airports

Bridger 662-3319
Columbus 322-4843
Laurel 628-6373

### Government Offices

State BLM Office 255-2885, 238-1540
Bureau of Land Management
Billings Field Office 896-5013
Custer National Forest, Beartooth Ranger District 446-2103
Montana Fish, Wildlife & Parks 247-2940
U.S. Bureau of Reclamation 247-7295

### Hospitals

Ask-A-Nurse • Billings 657-8778
Billings Inter-Hospital Onclay 259-2245
Deaconess Medical Center • Billings 657-4000
St. Vincents Hospital • Billings 657-7000
Stillwater Community Hospital
Columbus 322-5316
Carbon County Memorial Hospital
Red Lodge 446-2345

### Golf Courses

Red Lodge Mt. Resort • Red Lodge 446-3344
Stillwater Golf & Rec. • Columbus 322-4298

### Bed & Breakfasts

**Bear Bordeaux B&B** • Red Lodge 446-4408
**Blessing House B&B** • Red Lodge 446-4269
**Bed & No Breakfast Bunkhouse**
Absarokee 328-7419
**Willows Inn** • Red Lodge 446-3913
Hotel Montana • Reed Point 326-2288
Inn On The Beartooth • Red Lodge 446-1768
Magnolia Mae Inn • Red Lodge 446-2900
Wolves Den B & B • Red Lodge 446-1273
Abigail Inn• Absarokee 328-6592
Magpie's Nest • Absarokee 328-4925
River Haven • Absarokee 328-4138

### Forest Service Cabins

Custer National Forest
**Meyers Creek**
60 mi. SE of Red Lodge 446-2103
Capacity: 6 Nightly fee: $40 Available: 5/1-10/15
Summer use only. Refrigerator, lights, water, shower, flush toilet and forced air heat. 2 bedroom house. Corral for horses.

## Private Campgrounds

Beck's Alpine Motel • Red Lodge 446-2213
Cedar Hills Campground • Reed Point 326-2266
City Park Campground • Bridger 662-3677
Clark's Camp • Laurel 652-7561
KOA Kampgrounds • Red Lodge 446-2364
Mountain Range RV Park • Columbus 322-1140
Perry's Camper Park • Red Lodge 446-2722
Rock Creek Campground • Rockvale 962-3459

## Guest Ranches & Resorts

**Stoney Lonesome Ranch** • Absarokee 932-4452
Sugarloaf Mountain Outfitters
Absarokee 328-4939
Lonesome Spur Ranch • Bridger 662-3460
Calamity Jane's Horse Cache • Molt 628-6000
Small Ranch • Reed Point 326-2327
Lazy E-L Working Guest Ranch
Roscoe 328-6855

## Vacation Homes & Cabins

Bighorn River Country Lodge
Fort Smith 666-2332
Big Sky Roping Ranch • Huntley 348-2460
Canyon Cabin • Red Lodge 446-2421
Cross A Guest Ranch • Lodge Grass 639-2697
Double Spear Ranch • Pryor 259-8291
Eagle Nest Lodge • Hardin 665-3712
Fiddler Creek Cabins • Absarokee 328-4949
Green Ranch • Fishtail 537-4472
Hammond Guest House • Melville 328-4229
Johnson Place • Absarokee 328-4195
Lena's Cabins • Fishtail 328-4878
Little Cabin in Red Lodge • Red Lodge 245-7360
Mountain View Condo • Red Lodge 245-1704
Picket Pin Ranch • Nye 328-7004
Pitcher Guest Houses • Red Lodge 446-2859
Red Lodging • Red Lodge 446-1272
Reels End • Columbus 322-5539
Riverside Guest Cabins • Columbus 322-5066
Rosebud Retreat • Fishtail 328-4220
Seventh Ranch • Garryowen 638-2438
Torgirimson Place • Fishtail 328-4412
Whipple Cabin • Fishtail 328-6907

## Car Rental

AA-A Auto Rental 245-9759
Ace-Rent-A-Car 252-2399
Avis Rent-A-Car 252-8007
Budget Rent-A-Car 259-4168
Dollar Rent-A-Car 259-1147
Enterprise Billings West 652-2000
Enterprise Rent-A-Car 259-9999
Hertz Rent-A-Car 248-9151
National Car Rental 252-7626
Rent A Wreck 245-5982
Thrifty Car Rental 259-1025
U Save Auto Rental 655-4440
Ray-Judd Ford 446-1400

## Outfitters & Guides

*F=Fishing H=Hunting R=River Guides*
*E=Horseback Rides G=General Guide Services*

**Absaroka River Adventures** R 328-7440
**Adventure Whitewater Inc** R 446-3061
**Headwaters & High Country** FH 446-2679
7 C Quarter Circle Outfitters G 445-2280
Beartooth Mountain Guides G 446-1952
Beartooth Plateau Outfitters GF 445-2293
Beartooth Whitewater R 446-3142
Calamity Jane Horse Cache E 628-6000
Chatlain Dennis & Jane G 445-2280
Fish Montana Fly Shop GF 328-6548
Paint Brush Adventures Inc GFE 328-4158
Slow Elk Trail Inc E 446-4179
Sugarloaf Mountain Outfitters H 328-4939
Beartooth River Trips R 446-3142

| | Cold Water Species | | | | | | | | | | | | Warm Water Species | | | | | | | | | | Services | | | | | |
|---|---|---|---|---|---|---|---|---|---|---|---|---|---|---|---|---|---|---|---|---|---|---|---|---|---|---|---|---|
| **Fishery** | Brook Trout | Mt. Whitefish | Lake Whitefish | Golden Trout | Cutthroat Trout | Brown Trout | Rainbow Trout | Kokanee Salmon | Bull Trout | Lake Trout | Arctic Grayling | Burbot | Largemouth Bass | Smallmouth Bass | Walleye | Sauger | Northern Pike | Shovelnose Sturgeon | Channel Catfish | Yellow Perch | Crappie | Paddlefish | Vehicle Access | Campgrounds | Toilets | Docks | Boat Ramps | MotorRestrictions |
| 23. Stillwater River | • | • | | | | • | • | | | | | | | | | | | | | | | | • | • | • | | | |
| 24. Cooney Reservoir | | | | | | • | • | | | | | | | | • | | | | | | • | | • | • | • | • | • | |
| 25. West Rosebud Lake | • | • | | | • | • | • | | | | | | | | | | | | | | | | | • | • | | | |
| 26. Emerald Lake | • | • | | | • | • | • | | | | | | | | | | | | | | | | | • | • | | | |
| 27. Mystic Lake | • | | | | • | | | | | | | | | | | | | | | | | | | | | | | |
| 28. Beartooth Plateau Alpine Lakes | • | | | • | • | • | • | | | • | | | | | | | | | | | | | | | | | | |
| 29. Wild Bill Lake | | | | | | | • | | | | | | | | | | | | | | | | • | | • | | | |
| 30. Rock Creek | • | | | | | • | • | | | | | | | | | | | | | | | | • | | | | | |
| 31. Greenough Lake | | | | | | | • | | | | | | | | | | | | | | | | • | • | • | | | |
| 32. Laurel Pond | | | | | | | • | | | | | | | | | | | | | | | | • | | | | | |

## NOTES:

Section 3

All Montana Area Codes are 406

## Campsite Directions

| Campsite Directions | Season | Camping | Trailers | Toilets | Water | Boat Launch | Fishing | Swimming | Trails | Stay Limit | Fee |
|---|---|---|---|---|---|---|---|---|---|---|---|
| **16•Itch-Kep-Pe Park**<br>S of Columbus on MT 78 | 4/1-10/31 | 30 | • | • | • | • | • | • | | 14 | |
| **Cooney FWP**<br>22 mi. SW of Laurel•Milepost 90•8 mi. W on Cty. Rd. | All Year | 70 | • | D | • | C | • | • | | 14 | • |
| **Pine Grove FS**<br>1 mi. W of Fishtail on Rt. 419•6 mi. SW on Cty. Rd. 425•8 mi. S on Forest Rd. 72 | 5/27-9/15 | 46 | 30′ | D | • | | • | | | 10 | • |
| **Emerald Lake FS**<br>1 mi. W of Fishtail on Rt. 419•6 mi. SW on Cty. Rd. 425•12 S on Forest Rd. 72 | 5/27-9/5 | 32 | 30′ | D | • | | • | | | 10 | • |
| **Jimmy Joe FS**<br>9 mi. S of Roscoe on Cty. & Forest Rd. 177 | 5/27-9/5 | 10 | 16′ | • | | | • | | | 10 | |
| **Cascade FS**<br>2 mil S of Red Lodge on US 212•10 mi. W on Forest Rd. 71<br>Reservations 800-280-CAMP or 202-205-1760 | 5/27-9/5 | 31 | 30′ | • | • | | • | | | 10 | • |
| **East Rosebud Lake FS**<br>12 mi.S of Roscoe on Cty. & Forest Rd. 177 | 5/27-9/5 | 14 | 16′ | • | • | • | • | | • | 10 | • |
| **M-K FS**<br>12 mi. SW of Red Lodge on US 212•4 mi. SW on Forest Rd. 421 | 5/30-9/5 | 10 | 16′ | • | | | • | | • | 10 | |
| **Limber Pine FS**<br>12 mi. SW of Red Lodge on US 212•1 mi. SW on Forest Rd. 421<br>(Reservations:800-280-CAMP or 202-205-1760 | 5/27-9/5 | 13 | 35′ | • | • | | • | | • | 10 | • |
| **Basin FS**<br>1 mi. S of Red Lodge, US 212•7 mi. W on Forest Rd. 71 (800-280-CAMP or 202-205-2760) | 5/27-9/5 | 30 | 30′ | D | • | | • | | • | 10 | • |
| **Parkside FS**<br>12 mi. SW of Red Lodge on US 212•1 mi. SW on Forest Rd. 421<br>(Reservations 800-280-CAMPor 202-205-1760) | 5/27-9/5 | 28 | 30′ | D | • | | • | | • | 10 | • |
| **Greenough Lake FS**<br>12 mi. SW of Red Lodge on US 212•1 mi. SW on Forest Rd. 421<br>(Reservations: 800-280-CAMPor 202-205-1760) | 5/27-9/5 | 18 | 30′ | D | • | | • | | • | 10 | • |
| **Ratine FS**<br>5 mi. SW of Red Lodge on US 212•3mi. SW on Forest Rd. 379<br>(Reservations: 800-280-CAMPor 202-205-1760) | 5/27-9/5 | 7 | | • | • | | • | | • | 10 | • |
| **Sheridan FS**<br>5 mi. SW of Red Lodge on US 212•2 mi. SW on Forest Rd. 379<br>(Reservations 800-280-CAMP or 202-205-1760) | 5/27-9/5 | 8 | 22′ | • | • | | • | | • | 10 | • |
| **Palisades FS**<br>1 mi. W of Red Lodge on Forest Rd. 71•2 mi. W on Cty. & Forest Rd.3010 | 6/15-9/15 | 6 | 16′ | • | | | | | | 10 | |
| **Woodbine FS**<br>8 mi. SW of Nye on Rt. 419 | 6/15-9/15 | 44 | 30′ | D | • | | • | | • | 10 | • |

**Agency**
FS—U.S.D.A Forest Service
FWP—Montana Fish, Wildlife & Parks
NPS—National Park Service
BLM—U.S. Bureau of Land Management
USBR—U.S. Bureau of Reclamation
CE—Corps of Engineers

**Camping**
Camping is allowed at this site. Number indicates camping spaces available
H—Hard sided units only; no tents

**Trailers**
Trailer units allowed. Number indicates maximum length.

**Toilets**
Toilets on site. D—Disabled access

**Water**
Drinkable water on site

**Fishing**
Visitors may fish on site

**Boat**
Type of boat ramp on site:
A—Hand launch
B—4-wheel drive with trailer
C—2-wheel drive with trailer

**Swimming**
Designated swimming areas on site

**Trails**
Trails on site
B—Backpacking N—Nature/Interpretive

**Stay Limit**
Maximum length of stay in days

**Fee**
Camping and/or day-use fee

## Notes:

## Dining Quick Reference

Price Range refers to the average cost of a meal per person: ($) $1-$6, ($$) $7-$11, ($$$) $12-up. Cocktails: "Yes" indicates full bar; Beer (B)/Wine (W), Service: Breakfast (B), Brunch (BR), Lunch (L), Dinner (D). Businesses in bold print will have additional information under the appropriate map locator number in the body of this section.

| RESTAURANT | TYPE CUISINE | PRICE RANGE | CHILD MENU | COCKTAILS BEER WINE | SERVICE | CREDIT CARDS | MAP LOCATOR NUMBER |
|---|---|---|---|---|---|---|---|
| Burger King | Fast Food | $ | Yes | | B/L/D | | 2 |
| Curt's Saloon | Pizza | $/$$/$$$ | Yes | Yes | L/D | Major | 2 |
| Hardee's | Fast Food | $ | Yes | | B/L/D | | 2 |
| Locomotive Inn Restaurant | Family | $$ | Yes | Yes | D | Major | 2 |
| Pizza Hut | Pizza | $/$$ | Yes | B | L/D | V/M/D | 2 |
| Stageline Pizza | Pizza | $/$$ | | | L/D | | 2 |
| Subway | Fast Food | $ | Yes | | L/D | | 2 |
| Taco John's | Fast Food | $ | Yes | | L/D | | 2 |
| **Caboose Saloon & Casino** | Bar | | | Yes | | | 3 |
| **Dragon Palace Chinese Cuisine** | Chinese | $$ | Yes | B/W | L/D | V/M/D | 3 |
| Sid's Place | American | $ | | Yes | L/D | | 3 |
| Cafe Mabel's | Mexican | $$ | | | L/D | Major | 3 |
| Dairy Queen | Fast Food | $ | Yes | | L/D | | 3 |
| Pelican Truck Plaza | Family | $$ | Yes | | B/L/D | Major | 3 |
| Owl Junction Owl Junction Diner | Eclectic | $–$$$ | Yes | | B/L/D | Major | 3 |
| Railside Diner | American | $ | Yes | | B/L/D | | 3 |
| Pop's Inn | American | $ | | Yes | L/D | | 4 |
| Park City Cenex Car & Truck Stop | American | $$ | Yes | | B/L/D | Major | 4 |
| **Apple Village Cafe & Gift Shop** | American | $-$$$ | Yes | | B/L/D | Major | 6 |
| **Peggy Sue's Coffee** | Coffee House | $/$$ | | | B/L/D | | 6 |
| McDonalds | Fast Food | $ | Yes | | B/L/D | | 6 |
| **New Atlas Bar** | Bar | | | Yes | | | 7 |
| **Steel Horse Saloon** | American | $-$$$ | | Yes | L/D | | 7 |
| 307 Restaurant | American | $-$$$ | | Yes | L/D | V/M | 7 |
| Sports Hut | American | $/$$ | | Yes | L/D | Major | 7 |
| Uncle Sam's Eatery | Deli | $ | | | L | | 7 |
| Hotel Montana | American | $$/$$$ | Yes | Yes | B/L/D | Major | 8 |
| El Rancho Inn | Mexican American | $–$$$ | Yes | Yes | L/D | Major | 13 |
| Quick Stop Drive In | Fast Food | $ | Yes | | L/D | | 14 |
| Fort Rockvale Restaurant | American | $–$$$ | Yes | Yes | B/L/D/BR | V/M | 14 |
| **Little Cowboy Bar & Museum** | Bar | | | Yes | | | 15 |
| **Buckeye Bar Grill & Casino** | Steakhouse | $–$$$ | Yes | Yes | L/D | V/M/D | 17 |
| **Jungle Jayne's Stringtown Saloon & Eatery** | American | $–$$$ | Yes | Yes | L/D | | 17 |
| Bridger Cafe & Casino | Family | $$ | Yes | B/W | B/L/D/BR | | 17 |
| Maverik Country Store | Fast Food | $ | | | B/L/D | Major | 17 |
| The Trapper Drive-In Restaurant | Family | $/$$ | Yes | | B/L/D | | 17 |
| Country House Cafe | American | $ | Yes | | B/L | | 18 |
| Silvertip Restaurant & Casino | American | $–$$$ | Yes | Yes | B/L/D/BR | | 18 |
| Bear Creek Saloon & Steakhouse | Steakhouse | $$/$$$ | | Yes | D | V/M | 19 |
| Kiva Restaurant | American | $/$$ | Yes | Yes | B/L/BR | Major | 20 |
| Old Piney Dell | Steaks & Seafood | $$$ | Yes | Yes | D | Major | 20 |
| P D Mc Kinney's Family Dining | Family | $/$$ | Yes | | B/L | V/M/D | 21 |
| Red Box Car Drive-In | Fast Food | $ | Yes | | L/D | | 21 |
| Subway | Fast Food | $ | Yes | | L/D | | 21 |
| **Bull Moose Bistro** | Regional | $/$$$ | Yes | Yes | L/D | V/M | 22 |
| **The Pollard** | Regional | $$$ | Yes | Yes | B/L/D/BR | Major | 22 |
| **Red Lodge Ale House Pub & Grill** | Pub Grub | $-$$$ | Yes | B/W | L/D | V/M | 22 |
| **Bogart's** | Family/ Eclectic | $/$$ | Yes | Yes | L/D | V/M | 22 |
| **Coffee Factory Roasters** | Coffee House | $ | | | B/L | V/M | 22 |
| **Bridge Creek Backcountry Kitchen & Wine Bar** | Seafood/American | $-$$$ | Yes | B/W | L/D | Major | 22 |
| **Red Lodge Cafe, Lounge & Casino** | Family | $-$$$ | | Yes | B/L/D | V/M | 22 |
| Bull & Bear Saloon | Pizza/burgers | $$ | | Yes | L/D | Major | 22 |
| China Town Restaurant | Chinese | $$ | | | L/D | V/M | 22 |
| Carbon County Steakhouse | Steakhouse | $$/$$$ | | Yes | D | Major | 22 |
| Genesis Natural Foods | Deli | $ | | | L | Major | 22 |
| Red Lodge Pizza Co. | Pizza | $/$$ | Yes | Yes | L/D | Major | 22 |
| Gunsmoke BBQ | Barbeque | $–$$$ | | | L/D | | 23 |
| Rock Creek Texaco Novasio Hamburgers | Fast Food | $ | | | L/D | | 23 |
| Round Barn Restaurant | Buffet | $/$$ | Yes | | B/L/D | Major | 23 |
| Becker's Kitchen | Homestyle | $$ | Yes | Yes | B/L | Major | 23 |
| Brown Bear Inn | Steakhouse | $–$$$ | | Yes | L/D | Major | 24 |

## Dining Quick Reference-Continued

Price Range refers to the average cost of a meal per person: ($) $1-$6, ($$) $7-$11, ($$$) $12-up. Cocktails: "Yes" indicates full bar; Beer (B)/Wine (W), Service: Breakfast (B), Brunch (BR), Lunch (L), Dinner (D). Businesses in bold print will have additional information under the appropriate map locator number in the body of this section.

| RESTAURANT | TYPE CUISINE | PRICE RANGE | CHILD MENU | COCKTAILS BEER WINE | SERVICE | CREDIT CARDS | MAP LOCATOR NUMBER |
|---|---|---|---|---|---|---|---|
| Lost Village Saloon and Eatery | American | $$ | | Yes | L/D | | 24 |
| **Frontier Bar & Bone Pile** | American | $ | | Yes | L/D | | 26 |
| Homestead Cafe | American | $ | Yes | Yes | B/L/D | | 26 |
| Grizzly Bar Steaks & Burgers | Steakhouse | $-$$$ | Yes | Yes | L/D | Major | 29 |
| **Montana Hanna's** | American | $-$$$ | Yes | B/W | L/D | V/M/D | 30 |
| Cowboy Bar & Supper Club | Steak/Seafood | $-$$$ | | Yes | B/L/D | V/M | 30 |
| **Stake-Out** | Family/American | $-$$$ | Yes | Yes | L/D/BR | V/M/D | 31 |
| **Dew Drop Inn** | Fast Food | $ | Yes | | L/D | | 31 |

## Motel Quick Reference

Price Range: ($) Under $40 ; ($$) $40-$60; ($$$) $60-$80, ($$$$) Over $80. Pets [check with the motel for specific policies] (P), Dining (D), Lounge (L), Disabled Access (DA), Full Breakfast (FB), Cont. Breakfast (CB), Indoor Pool (IP), Outdoor Pool (OP), Hot Tub (HT), Sauna (S), Refrigerator (R), Microwave (M) (Microwave and Refrigerator indicated only if in majority of rooms), Kitchenette (K). All Montana area codes are 406.

| HOTEL | PHONE | NUMBER ROOMS | PRICE RANGE | BREAKFAST | POOL/ HOT TUB SAUNA | NON SMOKE ROOMS | OTHER AMENITIES | CREDIT CARDS | MAP LOCATOR NUMBER |
|---|---|---|---|---|---|---|---|---|---|
| **Best Western Locomotive Inn** | 628-8281 | 52 | $$$ | CB | IP | Yes | DA | Major | 2 |
| **Laurel Super 8** | 628-6888 | 60 | | CB | IP/HT | Yes | P/DA | Major | 2 |
| **Welcome Traveler's Motel** | 628-6821 | 10 | $ | | | Yes | K/P/M/R | V/M/D | 3 |
| **Russell Motel** | 628-6513 | 13 | $/$$ | | | Yes | K/P/M/R | Major | 3 |
| Pelican Truck Plaza | 628-4324 | 12 | $$ | | | Yes | DA/P | Major | 3 |
| Laurel Ridge Motel | 628-2000 | 10 | $ | | | | K/P/R | V/M | 3 |
| Lohof Motel | 628-6216 | 14 | $$ | | | Yes | K/R | V/M | 3 |
| Wagon Wheel Motel | 628-8084 | 11 | $/$$ | CB | | Yes | K/P/M/R/DA | V/M/D | 3 |
| Lazy RL Motel | 633-2352 | 9 | $ | | | | K/R/DA | A/V/M | 4 |
| CJ's Motel | 633-2352 | 9 | $ | | | | | Major | 4 |
| **Git's Conoco & Big Sky Motel** | 322-4111 | 20 | $ | | | Yes | L | Major | 7 |
| Super 8 | 322-4101 | 72 | $$ | | HT | Yes | DA/P | Major | 7 |
| Riverside Guest Cabins | 322-5066 | 7 | $ | CB | | Yes | K/R | V/M | 7 |
| Hotel Montana | 326-2288 | 5 | $/$$ | FB | | Yes | PB/P/L | Major | 8 |
| Bridger Motel | 662-3212 | 8 | $ | | | Yes | K/R/DA | | 17 |
| Rock Creek Resort | 446-1111 | 88 | $$$$ | | IP/HT/S | Yes | K/D/L/DA | Major | 20 |
| **Super 8 Motel** | 446-2288 | 50 | $$/$$$$ | | IP/HT/S | Yes | K/P/DA | Major | 21 |
| **Yodeler Motel** | 446-1435 | 23 | $$/$$$ | | HT/S | Yes | K/P/M/R/DA | Major | 21 |
| **Bear Bordeaux B&B** | 446-4408 | | | | | | | | 21 |
| **Willows Inn B&B** | 446-3913 | | | | | | | | 21 |
| **Chateau Rouge** | 446-1601 | 24 | $$-$$$$ | | IP/HT | Yes | K/P/M/R | Major | 21 |
| **Best Western Lupine Inn** | 446-1321 | 46 | $$/$$$ | CB | IP/HT/S | Yes | K/P/M/R/DA | Major | 21 |
| **Eagles Nest Motel** | 446-2312 | 17 | $/$$$$ | | | | HTK/P | Major | 21 |
| Red Lodge Inn | 446-2030 | 14 | $$ | | HT | Yes | K/P/M/R/DA | Major | 21 |
| **The Pollard** | 446-0001 | 39 | $$$/$$$$ | FB | HT/S | Yes | D/PB/DA | Major | 22 |
| **Comfort Inn of Red Lodge** | 446-4469 | 55 | $$/$$$$ | CB | IP/HT | Yes | P/M/R/DA | Major | 23 |
| Beck's Alpine Motel | 446-2213 | 15 | $$ | | HT | Yes | P | Major | 23 |
| Joliet Motel & Trailer Park | 962-3693 | | | | | | | | 26 |
| **Blessing House B&B** | 446-4269 | | | | | | | | 27 |
| Juro's Aspen Lodge | 328-4284 | | | | | | | | 30 |
| Stillwater Lodge | 328-4899 | 6 | $/$$ | | | Yes | P/DA | Major | 31 |
| **Bed & No Breakfast Bunkhouse** | 328-7418 | 8 | $/$$ | | | Yes | K | | 31 |

**NOTES:**

Section 3

**NOTES:**

Section 3

# Section 4

## Livingston, Big Timber, Gardiner and Surrounding Area

*The Yellowstone River in Paradise Valley.*

### Weather Averages

**Livingston**

| | |
|---|---|
| January | |
| Average High: | 32.5° F |
| Average Low: | 14.7° F |
| Average Precip.: | 0.55 in |
| April | |
| Average High: | 52.7° F |
| Average Low: | 30.0° F |
| Average Precip.: | 1.33 in |
| July | |
| Average High: | 83.4° F |
| Average Low: | 51.3° F |
| Average Precip.: | 1.36 in |
| October | |
| Average High: | 58.7° F |
| Average Low: | 34.6° F |
| Average Precip.: | 1.31 in |

### Introduction

This section covers a unique landscape with an interesting past, including parts of Sweetgrass and Park County, and the area called Paradise Valley. The area consists of plains with rich soil and grasslands that are perfect for ranching and farming, surrounded by the Crazy and Absaroka Mountain Ranges in the background. Pioneers and settlers were drawn here in the 1800s for the wide open spaces, mining opportunities and railroad jobs. Park County was formed in 1887 and Sweetgrass County came about in 1896, from parts of Meagher, Yellowstone and Park Counties, and was named for the "creek of fragrant grasses." The Northern Pacific Railroad had a large impact on the population in this area and set up numerous job opportunities in Livingston. The railroad also carried an influx of people coming through to see the wonders of Yellowstone, the first National Park.

The Homestead Act, passed in 1862, gave 162 acres of land to every citizen over 21, or to the heads of the family who intended to become a citizen. This act, and the development of the railroad, brought many people out west to start a new life. Many Norwegians were drawn to Montana, attracted to the landscape that reminded them of their native homeland. Norwegians started their own communities in Sweetgrass County, Melville being the first, and introduced sheep to the area in 1881. Cattle ranching and sheep herding were popular among the settlers, and brought them prosperity in Sweetgrass County.

**1.** *Historic Marker, Attraction*

### Grey Cliff

Grey Cliff, named for the sandstone bluffs near the town, was established in 1882. The little town was located under the bluffs on the south side of Interstate 90 just east of the present site. There was a coal dock, water tank and a "Y" to turn the engines around on the railroad. A general store, saloon and boarding house with a few year-round residents made up the town. In 1890, the Northern Pacific Railroad moved Grey Cliff nearer to the tracks and the Yellowstone River. The first school was built in 1910. In 1949, the town was moved again to its present site. Between 1910 and 1924, Grey Cliff thrived. It boasted two general stores, a blacksmith shop, garage, livery barn, lumber yard, grain elevator, railroad depot, hotel, saloon, saddle shop, restaurant, post office, pool hall, dance hall and cigar factory. With the increase of motorized transportation, making it easier for the local people to get to the larger towns, the little town slowly became the close knit community it is today. Near Grey Cliff is the Pelican Fishing Access on the Yellowstone River. Across the Interstate is the Prairie Dog Town State Park. You can enjoy lunch while watching these little creatures in their natural habitat.

*Reprinted from Sweetgrass Chamber information sheet.*

### H The Thomas Party

East of Greycliff

*In 1866, William Thomas, his son Charles, and a driver named Schultz left southern Illinois bound for the Gallatin Valley, Montana. Traveling by covered wagon, they joined a prairie schooner outfit at Fort Laramie, Wyoming, and started over the Bridger Trail. The train was escorted by troops detailed to build a fort (C. E Smith) on the Big Horn River.*

*From the site of this fort the Thomas party pushed on alone. A few days later they were killed at this spot by hostile Indians. Emigrants found the bodies and buried them in one grave.*

*The meager details which sifted back greatly impressed William Thomas's seven-year old nephew. Seventy-one years later (1937), this nephew closely followed the Bridger Trail by car and succeeded in locating the almost forgotten grave.*

### H Captain Wm. Clark

*You are now following the historic trail of the Lewis and Clark Expedition. On his return from the Pacific in July 1806, Captain Clark camped for six days about forty miles downstream, near Park City. The Expedition had been looking for timber suitable for building canoes ever since striking the river near Livingston. They found a couple of large cottonwoods here that would serve. They fitted their axes with handles made from chokecherry and went to work making two canoes. When finished they laced them together with a deck of buffalo hides between. Seven men, Sacajawea and her child went curving down the river on this makeshift yacht, arriving at the mouth of the Yellowstone August 3rd. Captain Lewis split off north on the return trip and explored the Marias River and returned via the Missouri, joining them on August 12th.*

### H The Crazy Mountains

Called Awaxaawippiia by the Apsaalooka (Crow) Indians, the Crazy Mountains, which you can see to the northwest, are an igneous formation forged about 50 million years ago. For the Apsaalooka, they are the most sacred and revered mountains on the northern Great Plains. Awaxaawippiia was a place of refuge and protection. The Apsaalooka's enemies would not follow them into the mountains. Because of their great spiritual power, Awaxaawippiia continues to be an important vision quest site for the tribe. Famed Chief Plenty Coups had a vision there in 1857 in which, he said, the end of the plains Indian way-of-life was shown to him.

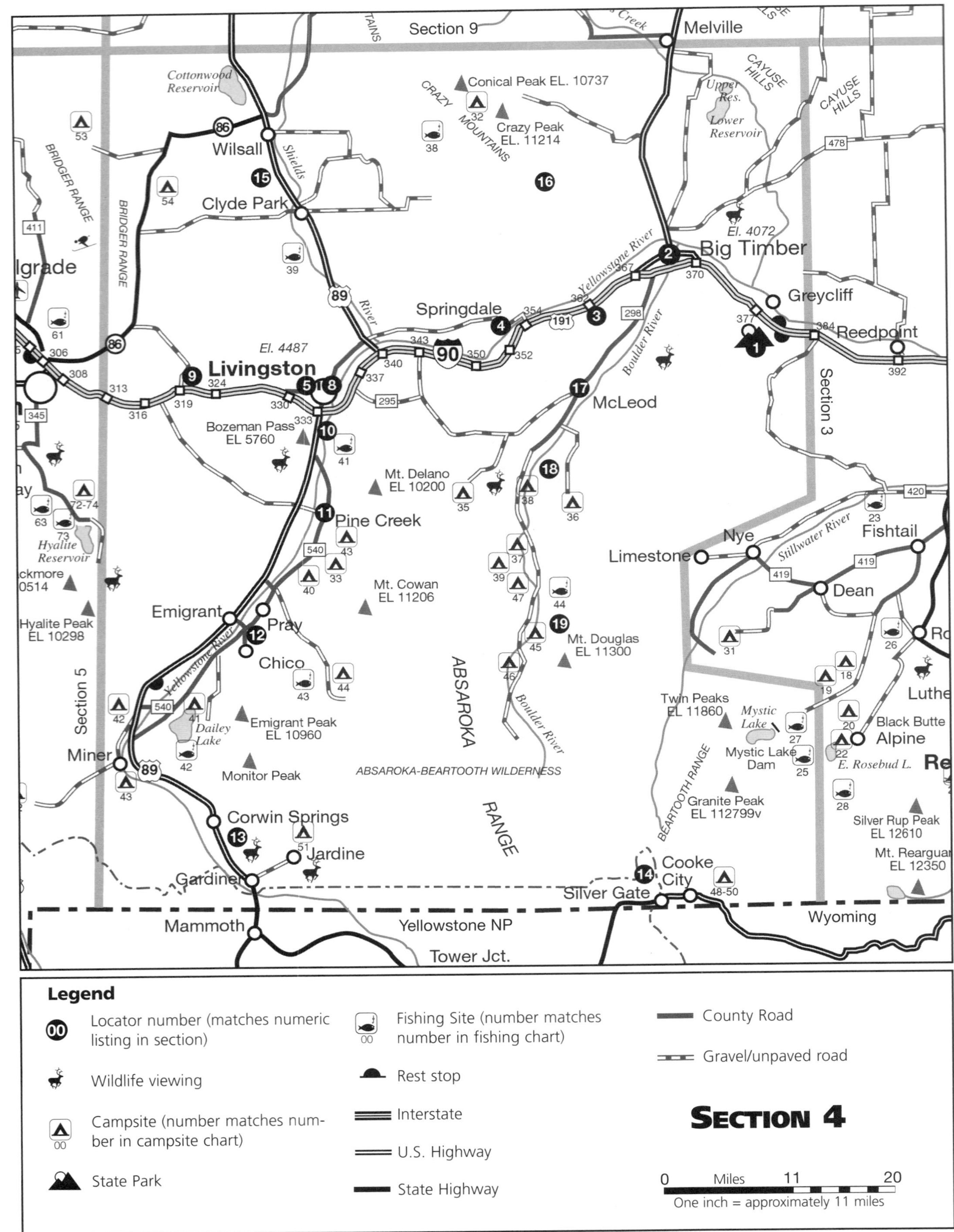
Section 9
Melville
Cottonwood Reservoir
Conical Peak EL. 10737
CRAZY MOUNTAINS
Crazy Peak EL. 11214
CAYUSE HILLS
Upper Res.
Lower Reservoir
478
BRIDGER RANGE
Wilsall
Shields
Clyde Park
411
El. 4072
Big Timber
Yellowstone River
Belgrade
89
River
Springdale
191
298
Greycliff
Reedpoint
El. 4487
Livingston
90
Boulder River
Section 3
345
Bozeman Pass EL 5760
295
McLeod
Mt. Delano EL 10200
Hyalite Reservoir
Pine Creek
540
Nye
Stillwater River
Fishtail
420
Limestone
419
Dean
Mt. Cowan EL 11206
Emigrant
Pray
Hyalite Peak EL 10298
Chico
Mt. Douglas EL 11300
ABSAROKA
Section 5
Twin Peaks EL 11860
Mystic Lake
Black Butte
Alpine
Dailey Lake
Emigrant Peak EL 10960
Mystic Lake Dam
E. Rosebud L.
Miner
Monitor Peak
ABSAROKA-BEARTOOTH WILDERNESS
BEARTOOTH RANGE
Granite Peak EL 112799v
Silver Rup Peak EL 12610
Corwin Springs
RANGE
Jardine
Cooke City
Mt. Rearguard EL 12350
Gardiner
Silver Gate
Mammoth
Yellowstone NP
Wyoming
Tower Jct.
Legend
Locator number (matches numeric listing in section)
Wildlife viewing
Campsite (number matches number in campsite chart)
State Park
Fishing Site (number matches number in fishing chart)
Rest stop
Interstate
U.S. Highway
State Highway
County Road
Gravel/unpaved road
SECTION 4
0 Miles 11 20
One inch = approximately 11 miles

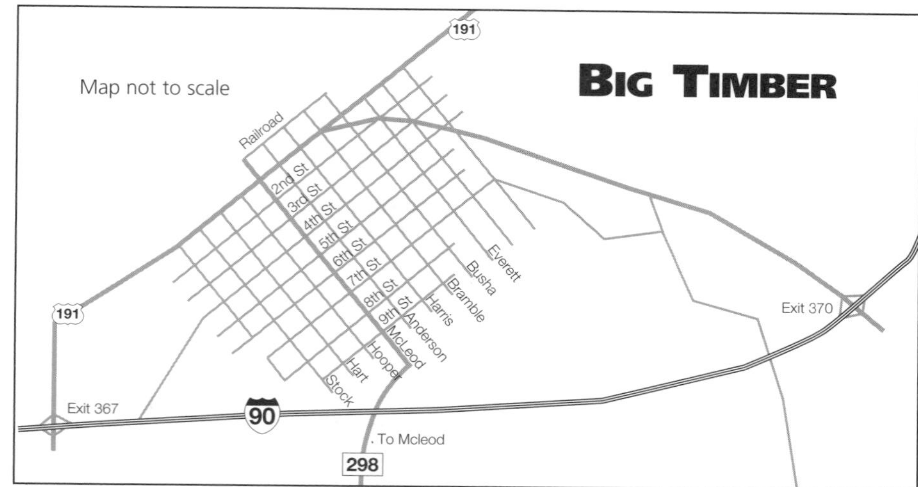


There are several stories about how the mountains got their current name. The most popular story goes that a woman traveling across the plains with a wagon train went insane. She escaped from the party and was found near these mountains. So they were called the Crazy Woman Mountains, a name which was eventually shortened. Perhaps the mountains were named, as others have claimed, because of their crazy appearance. The Crazy Mountains were an important landmark for Bozeman Trail emigrants in the Yellowstone Valley. This district was great cow and sheep country in the days of the open range, and there are still a number of large ranches in this vicinity, though now under fence.

### D William Clark

July 15, 1806

*"in the evening after usial delay of 3 hours to give the horses time to feed and rest and allowing our Selves time also to Cook and eate Dinner, I proceeded on down the river on an old bufalow road."*

### T Greycliff Prairie Dog Town State Park

9 miles east of Big Timber on 1-90, at Greycliff exit. 247-2940

See sidebar.

### V Big Timber Waterslide

I-90 exit 377, 8 miles east of Big Timber, 705 Hwy 10 East. 932-6570

Big Timber Waterslide, the first waterpark in Montana, is conveniently located just off I-90, and offers economical fun for all ages. They offer over ten different adventures. In addition, full service concessions, picnic areas, and group rates are also available. This is a great place to spend a day or even two. You'll want to bring the entire family and enjoy a picnic under beautiful shade trees, or give mom a break and eat at their extensive snack bar. For rates, hours or reservations give them a call. They are conveniently located next door to the beautiful Big Timber KOA campground.

### L Buckin' Horse Bunkhouse, Log Cabin Bed & Breakfast

361 Bridger Creek Rd., east of Big Timber, Reedpoint, 932-6537. www.buckinhorse.com

### C Big Timber KOA Campground

I-90 exit 377, 8 miles east of Big Timber, 693 Hwy 10 East. 932-6571 or fax 932-6569

This KOA is nestled among many shade trees in the heart of the state. There are six camping cabins and many lovely grassy campsites for tents under large trees. Full hookups and 50 amp big rig sites. Besides having a game room, mini golf, deluxe showers and restrooms, and a heated pool, this KOA is located next door to the Big Timber Waterslides, fun for young and old. You can enjoy wading pools, swimming pools, slow slides, or the wild suicide slide. Something for everyone! This is the perfect stay and play location for vacations, weekends, family reunions and all around family fun. For information or reservations on sites or cabins, give them a call.

## 2. *Historic Marker, Attraction, Gas, Food, Lodging, Shopping*

## Big Timber

Big Timber, 33 miles east of Livingston, is located near a geographical transition point. West of town, the Absaroka Range rises to lofty heights, while east stretch the vast Great Plains. The Crazy Mountains' jagged summits rise to the north of Big Timber towering more than 11,000 feet. Predominantly a livestock producing and recreational community, Big Timber is surrounded by the Gallatin National Forest.

Sweet Grass-land of livestock knee-deep in

good grass, sparkling clear water and air scented by sage and pine-became a county in 1895. The history of this 1,849 square mile area goes back many years before that to the Indian tribes who hunted the area. Crow, Cheyenne, Blackfoot, and raiding Sioux all claimed the area as hunting grounds.

William Clark came through the region in 1806 on his way back from the Pacific. "Rivers Across" in his journal refers to the spot on the Yellowstone just below Big Timber where, directly across from one another, the Boulder River and Big Timber Creek empty into the Yellowstone. Clark named Big Timber Creek for the unusually large cottonwood trees growing by its mouth.

The early 1880s brought the railroad to the country. At its projected westward advancement for the winter of 1882, at the spot Clark named Rivers Across, a few enterprising individuals constructed the settlement of Dornix, meaning "large, smooth stones". Unfortunately, due to an open winter, the railroad didn't stop but went on to the foot of the Bozeman Hill. Having hurt Dornix, the railroad now gave it a purpose for existence. To build the roadbed, vast numbers of ties were cut in the mountains during the winter, then floated down the creeks during spring high water to points on the railroad. With its position, Dornix was the logical spot for docking ties coming down the Boulder.

Again the railroad interfered. Dornix was just below a hill; it was difficult for the trains to stop and then make a standing start at the hill. They preferred to run on up to the long flat above Dornix and then stop. In 1883, Dornix was moved lock, stock and barrel to its present site. Within several months of the move, nothing remained of Dornix. Several years after the move, the railroad again high-handedly affected the town when the officials in St. Paul renamed it Big Timber.

*Parts are reprinted from Sweetgrass Chamber information sheet.*

### H The Bonanza or Bozeman Trail

BIg Timber

*In the early 1860s there wasn't a ranch in this country from Bismarck to Bozeman and from the Platte River to Canada. To whites it was land considered "fit only to raise Indians" and while some of them were hoping for a crop failure, the majority were indifferent. They didn't care how much the tribes fought amongst themselves. They were like the old-timer whose wife was battling a grizzly bear. He said he never had seen a fight where he took so little interest in the outcome.*

*Then the white man's greed asserted itself and he looked for a shortcut from the Oregon Trail at Laramie, Wyoming, to the gold diggin's of western Montana. The Bonanza or Bozeman Trail across Indian hunting grounds was the result. It forded the Yellowstone near here, coming from the southeast. It was a trail soaked with the blood of warriors, soldiers, and immigrants.*

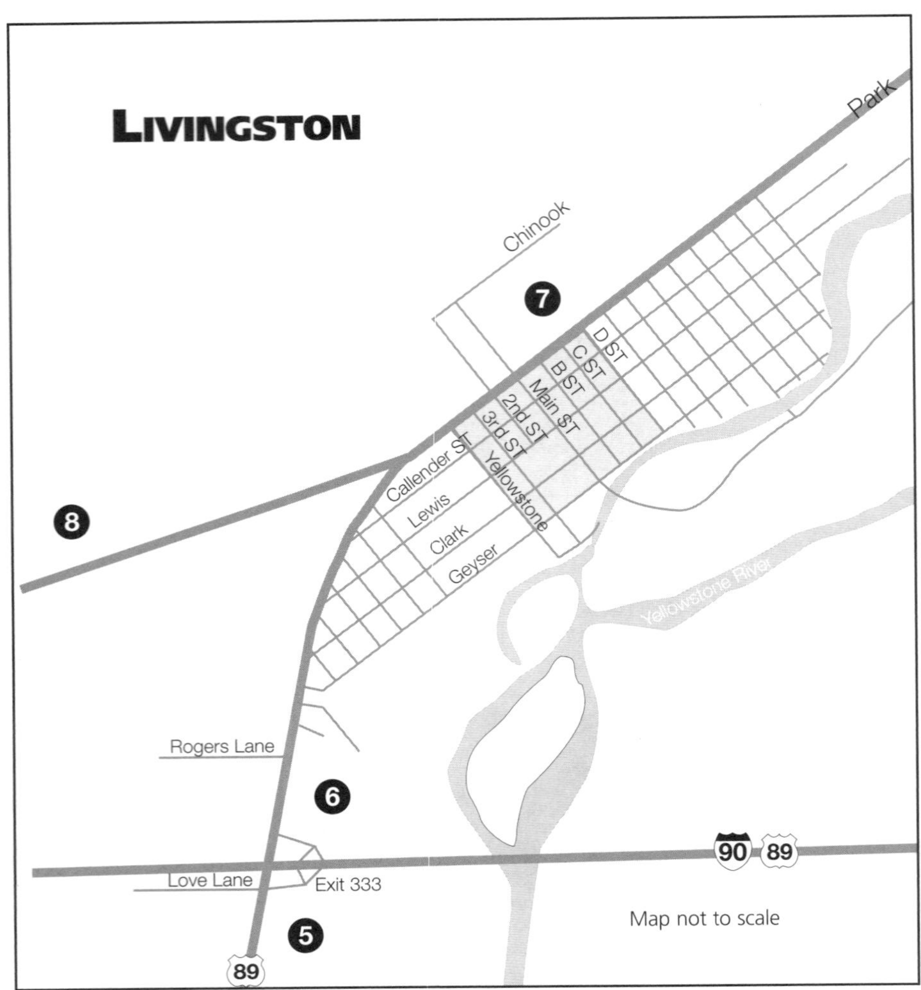


*Thousands of Sioux warriors, primarily under Red Cloud, bolstered by hundreds of Cheyennes and some Arapahos, fought the trail for six years and forced its closure by the Government in 1868.*

## T Crazy Mountain Museum

Cemetery Road, Big Timber. 932-5126

Crazy Mountain Museum encompasses the historical background of Sweet Grass County and the surrounding areas. One of the more exceptional displays is a model replica of Big Timber in 1907. It includes 184 buildings which took 6 years to research and build. The model, a representation of miniature artistry and meticulous craftsmanship, is a historically accurate replica built on a scale of 1/16"=1' and depicts 12 1/2 square blocks of the town. 184 buildings—1,018 windows—406 doors—143 chimneys—152 power and telephone poles—135 people—22 vehicles—6 bicycles—35 horses—18 sheep—4 cows—20 chickens—8 dogs—4 cats—and 4 pigeons. The details are incredible. Look for clothes on a line, merchandise in windows, a hobo under a tree, axes in woodpiles, gardens, a blacksmith, wool sacks, coal bins, wheelbarrows, manure piles, milk cans, bars on jail and salon windows, a drunk, an apple tree, a red light on the porch of a female boarding house, a dog in a trash can, ladders, hitching posts, horse troughs, spokes on poles for linemen, a picture in front of the Auditorium, and a towel on a wall in back of the bathhouse, and more!

On the grounds of the museum is a unique structure known as a stabbur. The Stabbur was built as a memorial to the Norwegian pioneers who helped build Sweet Grass County. Buildings like these were a common site in Norway and often had flowers and small trees growing out of their sod roof. They were built as storehouses, and were often decorated with wood carvings. A farmer's wealth in Norway was measured by the contents of his stabbur. It was his security and signature and was assurance of food for the long winters. The stabbur was usually two stories with the stairs leading to the lower locked door built a distance from the building— "greater than a rat could jump." The first level was where the grain and other foods were stored including the salted or dried fish, hams and mutton which hung from hooks in the ceiling. The second floor was for clothing, trunks, and other valuables.

## T Shiloh Rifle Mfg. Co

201 Centennial Dr. or PO Box 279, Big Timber. 932-4454

## V Sweetcast Angler Guide Service & Raft Rental

119 N. 1st, Big Timber. 932-4469

## SA The Fort

PO Box 1343, Hwy 10 East, Big Timber. 932-5992 or fax 932-5772

The Fort is a Big Timber landmark where you can take care of just about any of your traveling needs whether fishing and hunting supplies or groceries. Gas up the car, get your licenses, stock up on ammo, lures, flies, maps, adult beverages, and snacks for the whole family. They are much more than a gas stop and convenience store. You'll also enjoy taking a stroll through the delightful gift shop on the upper level. You'll find special gifts, including Montana specialties for yourself or someone back at home. Make the Fort a priority stop in Big Timber. They are conveniently located on Hwy. 10 E., just off I-90 and open 7 days a week 6 a.m. to 10 p.m.

## F City Club Lanes & Steakhouse

202 Anderson St., Big Timber. 932-5485

City Club Lanes and Steak House, new in 2000, is only one block off Main Street in Big Timber. The Steak House was added on to the existing bowling alley and casino that includes full bar service. Prime rib is the house specialty and you can enjoy it seven nights a week. They will also charbroil your favorite cut of steak in sizes that will suit any appetite. One favorite from their menu is the jumbo prawns served battered or sautéed. If pasta is your choice, you'll find a great selection of dishes. They also offer 8 ounce juicy burgers and a kiddy menu. This is a fun place to spend an evening of dining, bowling, pool or gaming!

## F American Legion Post No. 19

110 E. 3rd Ave., Big Timber. 932-5486

### It Happened in Montana

October 31, 1987. Near the Bozeman Pass, three Burlington Northern locomotives derail after they were cut loose from a train in Livingston. The engines careened driverless through the mountains reaching speeds in excess of 80 miles per hour before leaving the track. A transient riding in one of the cars is injured. Mysteriously, the incident happens immediately after a judge orders the end of a strike by railroad workers. On that same day, Missoula billionaire Dennis Washington purchases a portion of the Burlington Northern and names it Montana Rail Link.

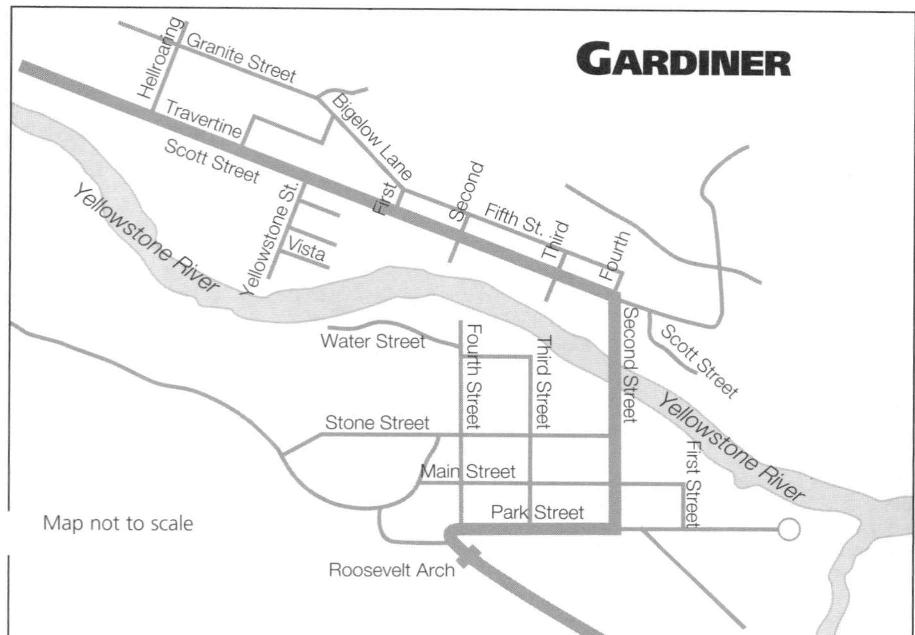


**F** **Timber Bar**
116 McLeod St., Big Timber. 932-4040

**F** **Frosty Freez**
403 E. Boulder, Big Timber. 932-5799

**FL** **Carriage House Ranch Bed & Breakfast**
8 miles north of Big Timber, Hwy. 191, 7/10 miles past mile marker 7. 932-5339 or toll free at 877-932-5339. www.carriagehouseranch.com

Carriage House Ranch, 8 miles north of Big Timber, is a working horse ranch and historical property with Bed & Breakfast accommodations, guest house lodging, equestrian activities, a cafe, and space for special meetings, weddings, retreats, and reunions. The scenery is spectacular, with the Crazy Mountains as a breathtaking backdrop and 1 1/2 miles of Big Timber Creek running through this 700 acre ranch. Many use it as their base camp before venturing into the Crazies on foot or horseback. (Plentiful overnight stabling.) Bird watching, wild animal viewing, hiking, fishing, horseback riding and carriage driving available. The ranch's history is rich and entertaining: Native Americans,followed by the Lewis & Clark Expedition, trappers, Dutch settlers, and finally the former owner who entertained writers and artists from around the world at the ranch.

**L** **Budget Host Big Timber**
I-90 Exit 367, 600 W. Second, Big Timber. 932-4943

**S** **Sweetgrass & Sage Fine Art & Gifts**
1 mile west at I-90, Exit 367, Big Timber. 932-5228

Only two artists, Jessica Zemsky and Jack Hines, supply the vast variety of beautiful artworks in this gallery. Both accomplished professionals, the couple address their work to those who appreciate fine realism in paint. The human element is foremost in their work, speaking directly to mankind's tender side. Originals and less costly museum quality reproductions are available. Teri, in the gift shop, has elegant, sensibly priced jewelry and clothing items reflecting the west, books, decorative arts and novelty items, all worthy of inclusion in the art gallery setting. Stop and see us. You'll be glad you did! Off I-90 at exit 367.

**S** **Country Crossroads Antiques**
406 East 1st Ave., Big Timber. 932-4649

If you enjoy a wonderful adventure finding local antiques, unusual gifts and crafts, then don't miss Country Crossroads Antiques. This is a special shop where you will find a great selection of reasonably priced furniture, small items and collectibles, including many "Made in Montana" items. They are known for offering the lowest antique prices in the area. The beautiful handcrafted wood shelves and doll furniture sold in the shop are made on the premises and feature many unique and original designs. For all of you movie fans, the shop is located in the building that was formerly the headquarters for making of the movie The Horse Whisperer by Robert Redford. The movie features scenery from the Big Timber area.

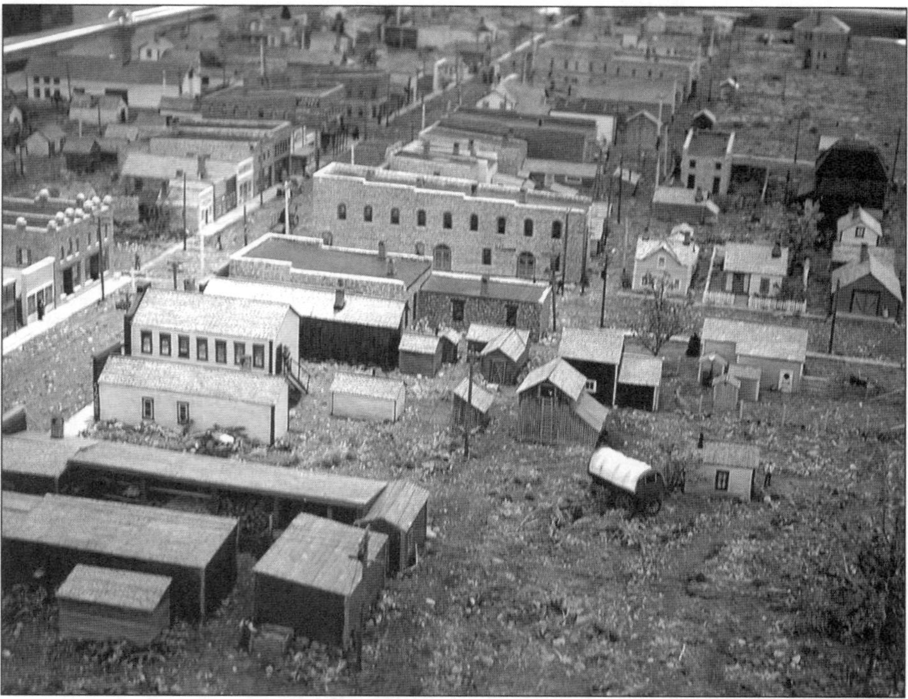

*This remarkable model of the town of Big Timber is on display at the Crazy Mountains Museum in Big Timber. It is precise in every detail.*

Section 4

# Sweetgrass and Sage

**The main exhibit is ongoing at** *Sweetgrass and Sage*. It is comprised of the heartfelt warmth and the caring about each person who walks through the doors. That quality is upfront each day, regardless of the changing shows of paintings that grace the walls year round,. The people at *Sweetgrass and Sage* are devoted to learning about their visitors and helping those folks to learn about the variey of art being shown. Besides the paintings on display, the content of the gift shop is selected in a highly creative manner.

*Jack Hines and Jessica Zemsky at their home in Big Timber.*

The gallery and its art are unusual in that only two artists are represented. Jessica Zemsky and Jack Hines are painters who share over 120 years as professional artists. They also share a constant thirst to expand their knowledge and their subject matter. Their marriage and their intense curiosity about the world around them has resulted in extensive travel and artistic recording of places far and near. These products of wanderlust come to rest on the gallery walls at *Sweetgrass and Sage*. To be seen are paintings of many European countries, some of Africa, the Caribbean, marine subjects, wildlife, landscapes, still life, cowboys, indians, sports activities and the sheer beauty of humankind.

An example of the spirit that Jessica and Jack share is in the story of their honeymoon. It was spent living in a tipi in company with a small group of still-nomadic indians in Alberta, Canada. That is typical of their determination to gain thorough intimacy with subject.

That particular quest for knowledge has resulted in a very close set of relationships with indian tribes in the west. In fact, two sacred plants of the plains and mountain indians are, sweetgrass and sage. The purity and spiritual qualities of these two gave rise to the gallery's name *Sweetgrass and Sage*. The artist couple try, in every way, to live up to the purity and the spiritual in their art. Their work has gained them devoted followers and collectors nationwide and overseas.

Jessica and Jack both delight in the times when they can be in the gallery to talk with visitors. Every painting has a story to be told about it. Those stories lend a living quality to each piece. Every one becomes an adventure which the artists love to share. The picture and the story always involves the viewer in the total experience and enriches the life of the listener.

No less fascinatiing is the story of Teri Schlabach who is the guiding spirit of the GIFT segment of *Sweetgrass and Sage*. Central to the selection is her thoughtfully assembled collection of jewelry of Native American Creation. Teri is also gifted with a wanderlust, making her an ideal reflection of Jessica and Jack's philosopy of living. She is a Montana girl, born and brought up on a ranch, is conversant with horses and mules, fluent in their behavorial languages. She is a thoroughly frontier creature with the taste and sensibility of an aesthete.

Teri travels many times a year to find what has become an almost revlolutionary output of jewelry, artistically put together by Indians, but with eyes to modernity. The end product is almost an anthropological study in the graceful evolution of a native art form. It is entirely appropriate for such work to be on exhibition in an art gallery setting.

Travelers are invited to stop and enjoy the *Sweetgrass and Sage* experience... to meet the unique people who have made this place a special oasis of culture that lives in the true west, reflects its honesty and values, but respects and celebrates worldwide cultures.

Here is art that speaks all languages, in concert with a gift selection that effectively echoes the pictorial aesthetic. The gallery is off I-90 at exit 367.

## S Little Timber Quilts

108 McLeod, Big Timber. 932-5404 or Fax 932-5511

**3.** *Historic Marker*

## H The Original Voges Bridge

Milepost 362, I-90

*In late 1913, Sweet Grass County residents petitioned the County Commissioners to build a bridge across the Yellowstone River west of Big Timber. The petition was submitted to the commissioners by New York millionaire oil man and part-time Montana rancher, W. Dixon Ellis of the Briggs-Ellis Cattle Company. Dixon offered to donate $5,000 toward the construction of the bridge if the commissioners agreed to build it the following year. In April, 1914, the county contracted with the Security Bridge Company to construct a 2-span pin-connected Pratt through truss bridge at this site for $14,995. Designed by Sweet Grass County Surveyor J. B. Kleinhesselink and County Assessor D. J. Walvoord, the 378-foot long bridge included an experimental floor system that allowed use of the bridge by the new 20-ton tractors of the time. The Security Bridge Company completed the structure in June, 1914 and it eventually became known as the Voges Bridge by area residents. Charles Voges owned a nearby sheep ranch and donated the land for the existing one-room school on the north bank of the river in 1920. When completed, the Voges Bridge provided access to the transportation systems on the south side of the river to the farmers and ranchers living north of the Yellowstone. The bridge was also the last pin-connected bridge built across the Yellowstone River.*

**4.** *Lewis & Clark*

## Springdale

This was a railroad station and a stopping place for travelers on their way to Hunter's Hot Springs. It took its name from the many springs that surround the area. The only thing left of Hunter's today is a fire hydrant sitting mysteriously in a field. This is near the spot where Capt. Lewis and his group lost their horses to Indian raiders. They were forced to travel down the Yellowstone in bull boats.

## D William Clark

July 14, 1806

*"I proceeded up this plain... and Crossed the main Chanel of the river. ...and nooned it ...the river is divided and on all the small Streams inoumerable quanitities of beaver dams, tho' the river is yet navigable for Canoes."*

## D William Clark

July 15, 1806

*"in the evening after usial delay of 3 hours to give the horses time to feed and rest and allowing our Selves time also to Cook and eate Dinner, I proceeded on down the river on an old bufalow road."*

**5.** *Lewis & Clark, Lodging, Miscellaneous*

## Livingston

Located between the Gallatin and Crazy Mountain ranges and surrounded by the Absaroka-Beartooth Wilderness Area, the town of Livingston was established around the railroad in the 1880s. The Crow Indians occupied the land along the Yellowstone River for thousands of years before the white settlers moves in, and the Absaroka Mountains are named after the Crow. Lewis & Clark were among the first white men to travel through this area, and were followed by traders and trappers. As the Northern Pacific Railroad was making it's way through, they chose Livingston as their base camp, and set up a town that revolved around the railroad with repair shops and a thriving downtown.

It all started in 1882 with a man named Joseph McBride who was sent to find a location to open a store that would supply workers on the new railroad. He chose the site of present day Livingston, bypassing the settlement of Benson's Landing, a settlement that existed just a few miles down the Yellowstone. The store started out of tents, but it was not long until the downtown began to develop. Originally named Clark City after William Clark, the name Livingston became widely accepted after the director of the Northern Pacific, Crawford Livingston.

The historic Main Street is a reminder of the past, with grand old buildings that have been restored and preserved. Many of the buildings date back to the turn of the century, and much local effort was put into their restoration, that gives the downtown area a real charm. Many of these old building were hotels for the tourists who came through Livingston on their way to Yellowstone National Park. Back in the day, tourists had to change trains in Livingston to get to Gardiner and many spent the night.

The Historic Depot Center was built by the Northern Pacific Railroad in 1902, was used until the 1970s, and still stands today as the Chamber of Commerce and a railroading museum. By 1882, Livingston was a thriving community, complete with 30 saloons, six general stores, two hotels, two restaurants and more. At one time, up to 2,200 men worked for the railroad and were based in Livingston. Calamity Jane spent a fair amount of time in Livingston, it is said that she lived in a local hotel and even spent some time in the town's jailhouse.

Today, Livingston has much to offer the locals and tourists visiting Montana. Located on the Blue

Ribbon Trout waters of the Yellowstone River, Livingston is a fly fishing community, with many outfitters and guides to accommodate the visitors. The city has over 13 art galleries to browse through, two playhouses, four museums, many unique downtown shops, and some great restaurants to choose from. Whitewater rafting is also popular on the Yellowstone River. The Livingston Roundup Rodeo is held every year from July 2–July 4 and draws competitors and visitors from all over the country.

### D Sgt. Ordway

July 13, 1806

*"Capt. Clark & party leaves us hear to cross over the River Roshjone. So we parted I and 9 more proceeded on down the river with the canoes verry well."*

### L Livingston Comfort Inn

114 Loves Ln., at I-90 exit 330 and Hwy 89, Livingston. 222-4400

Featuring 49 rooms complete with king, queen or double beds, cable TV with HBO, air conditioning, and some rooms with microwaves and refrigerators. The Livingston Comfort Inn offers complimentary continental breakfast, non-smoking rooms, guest laundry, and special suites are available. Relax in the hot tub and enjoy the pool area. Located just 30 miles from the airport and one hour from Yellowstone National Park, the Comfort Inn is close to restaurants, shopping, galleries and museums. This is a great place to enjoy the wonderful outdoor recreational opportunities and small town charm of Livingston.

### M Livingston Visitor Center

1 mile south of I-90 Exit 330 on Hwy. 89

**6.** *Gas, Food, Lodging*

**7.** *Attraction, Gas, Food, Lodging, Shopping*

### T Livingston Depot Center

200 W. Park St. in Livingston. 222-2300

Built by the Northern Pacific Railroad in 1902, the grand Italian style Passenger depot complex holds an art and cultural museum with records of railroading in the Pacific Northwest and Montana. There are exhibits of photographs describing one of America's most important industries. Hands-on displays for children, including a small train, make this a really fun stopover. Tours are also available through The Mountain Rockies Rail Tours. The museum is open May through September and there is a modest admission fee.

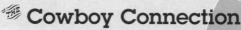

### T Yellowstone Gateway Museum

118 W. Chinook in Livingston. 222-4184

Experience the pioneer days in this museum filled with interesting artifacts, railroad memorabilia, and archaeological finds. Located in a turn-of-the-century schoolhouse, the museum also offers displays of the early explorers, including a real-life stagecoach, a caboose from the 1890s, and a covered wagon. Open Memorial Day–Labor Day, 10 a.m.–5 p.m.

### T Federation of Fly Fishers Fly Fishing Museum

215 E. Lewis in Livingston. 222-9369

This Fly Fishing Center is the only one of its kind in the nation. The center has live fish, explanations about fish habits and habitats, informative displays, a coldwater fish room with a tank of Yellowstone cutthroat trout and a warmwater fish room with an aquarium display of bass, sturgeon and others. Free fly-fishing classes are also available during the summer months.

#### *Montana Trivia*

The Absarokee (Crow) Indians are thought to be the the only Plains tribe that never made war against the white man.

# Prairie Dog Town

This 98-acre facility is operated by the Parks Division of Montana Fish, Wildlife & Parks to preserve the black-tailed prairie dog ecosystem for the public's educational and viewing enjoyment. Protection of this prairie dog town is due to the efforts of Edward Boehm of Livingston, Montana, who spearheaded the efforts to save it as the Interstate Highway was being built. Cooperative efforts by the Nature Conservancy and the Montana Department of Highways also helped preserve the park. Interpretive displays and picnic tables are provided. A day-use fee is charged at the park entrance to support ongoing maintenance. Restrooms are available about 1 mile east. Camping facilities are located at the KOA about 1/4 mile west.

## Range

Five species of prairie dogs are native to North America. The black-tailed prairie dog (*Cynomys ludovicianus*), inhabits Greycliff Prairie Dog Town State Park and is the most common species. These ground dwelling squirrels live on the plains from southern Canada to northern Mexico. Large prairie dog towns, or colonies, are further divided into coteries. One coterie (the family territory) is usually comprised of one adult male, three to five adult females and their offspring.

It is typical for black-tailed prairie dogs to dig 15-40 burrow entrances per acre, many more than other species. Each burrow usually has two entrances which lead to a tunnel 4-7 feet deep and perhaps 15-25 feet long. Look for tunnel entrances marked by mounds of excavated soil compacted into a crater of dome shape. Often two feet high, these mounds serve as good lookouts and prevent running water from entering the tunnels. Burrowing aerates and mixes soil types, as well as incorporating organic matter to enhance soil formation.

## Life Cycle

Black-tailed prairie dogs are usually sexually mature after their second winter and will breed in March each year. One to ten pups (average of 5) are born about 34 days after conception. The pups are born hairless and blind. They remain in the safety of their burrow for 48-49 days before emerging above ground. Prairie dogs are fully grown by October or November, averaging 1-3 pounds and 14-17 inches long. When late spring arrives, black-tailed prairie dogs may remain in the coterie in which they were born. If they cannot replace another member of the coterie who has left or died, the young prairie dog must leave. Young prairie dogs are most vulnerable during this time of dispersal. Watch for conflicts between males as the young attempt to join existing family territories or establish new coteries. If they survive their first two years of turmoil, prairie dogs may live five years or more.

## Communication

Watch for a variety of postures or displays, such as lifting their heads or standing on their hind legs to scrutinize the terrain for signs of danger. Listen for at least 11 different calls used to communicate with each other. If a predator approaches, the prairie dog scampers to his burrow mound and sounds a series of short nasal yips to alert others. A jump-yip, or "whee-oo," call is given as an "all clear" message when danger has passed. Different calls and displays are used depending upon the relationship between caller and target (ie. resident vs. nonresident of the caller's coterie). Coterie members engage in a greeting ceremony by touching teeth, followed by elaborate grooming. This display seems to encourage harmony among the family and helps to identify intruding prairie dogs.

## Activities

Black-tailed prairie dogs and Mexican prairie dogs do not hibernate as do the three white-tailed species. You should easily spot a few prairie dogs during daylight hours. They may retreat to their burrow seeking relief from the summer's midday heat or shelter from a winter storm. Prairie dogs can be seen eating green grasses, broad leafed, non-woody plants (forbs), and digging for roots and bulbs. Seeds and insects add variety to their diet. They are adept at removing the spines from prickly-pear cactus before eating the leaves.

## Predators

Coyotes, foxes, and bobcats may be seen stalking along the outer perimeters of prairie dogtowns, or they may sit and wait at burrow entrances to make captures. Ferruginous hawks and golden eagles perch or soar near towns hunting prey. Look for enlarged burrow entrances, evidence of badgers who can dig deep into the burrows. Weasels have streamlined bodies allowing them to prowl through the tunnels. Keep an eye out for prairie rattlesnakes and bull snakes which occasionally use the tunnels for shelter and may dine on the young prairie dogs.

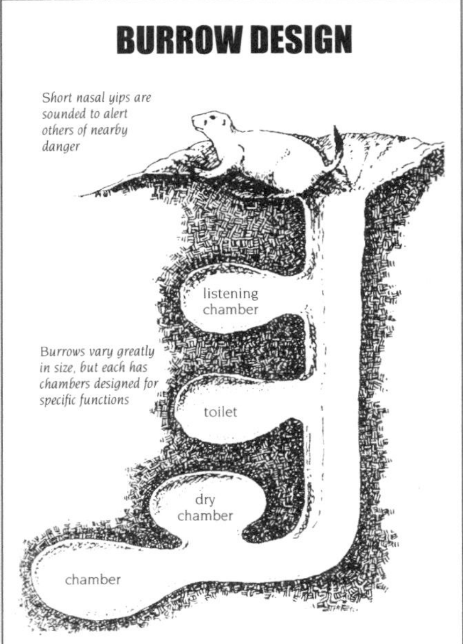


## Can Prairie Dogs and Man Coexist

Black-tailed prairie dogs have long been viewed as a detriment to successful livestock production because they create dangerous holes and compete with livestock for grasses and forbs. In reality, prairie dogs have a variable effect on livestock production depending on habitat conditions and climate. In some areas, new plant growth is more nutritious and compensates for loss of forage volume.

Black-tailed prairie dogs have been reduced by 80-90% in various. portions of their range. This reduction has had an impact on some species that use prairie dog towns. The most famous of these is the black-footed ferret which lives only in prairie dog towns and feeds almost exclusively (85-90%) on prairie dogs. The black-footed ferret is an endangered species, extinct in the wild except for one site in Wyoming. A recovery program is underway to restore this ferret to certain portions of its range. Over 101 vertebrate species inhabit the special ecosystem found near prairie dog towns, including the burrowing owl, golden eagle, ferruginous hawk, mountain plover, and swift fox.

## Please Do Not Feed the Prairie Dogs

The digestive tracts of wild animals are specifically adapted to utilize their natural foods. Human foods, often with preservatives and chemicals, can compromise their ability to survive, especially during times of stress. Wild animals may ingest foil, plastic or paper wrappers which smell or taste like food. The results could be fatal.

*Reprinted from Greycliff Prairie Dog Town State Park brochure. Montana Fish, Parks & Wildlife.*

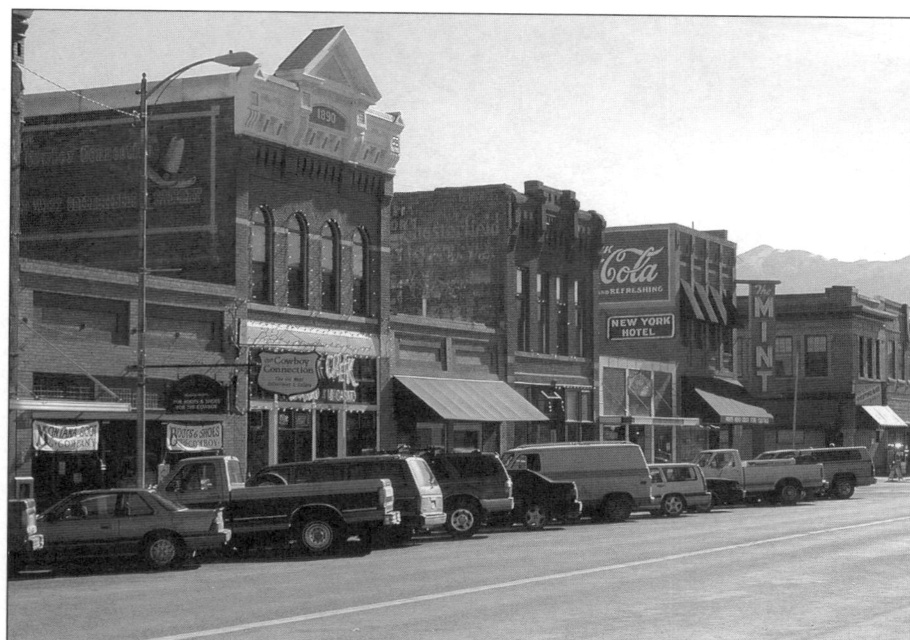

*Downtown Livingston.*

## L Murray Hotel

201 W. Park, Downtown Livingston. 222-1350, www.murrayhotel.com

The Murray Hotel's guests have ranged from Will Rogers to the Queen of Denmark, Calamity Jane to Sam Peckinpah. In the 1930s Walter Hill, son of a railroad magnate, tried to bring his prized pinto horse up the elevator. One might find the cast of one of the many movies filmed in the area, most recently, "The Horse Whisperer", residing there on a temporary basis. The Murray is still using its original hand-crank, glass door, 1905 Otis elevator. Restored to its original splendor the Murray offers one of the Livingston area's premier dining, drinking, and meeting places. When you think back to a stay at the "Murray", what you remember won't be what you watched on TV. Enjoy all the comforts of modern lodging, while experiencing the Old West.

## L Guest House Motel

105 W. Park St., Livingston. 222-1460 or reservations at 888-222-1460

This Guest House Motel is conveniently located in historic downtown Livingston. They offer spacious rooms, including bridal and executive suites, with plenty of friendly service. An elevator, off-street parking, and complimentary coffee in the lobby, cable TV, and air conditioning are provided for additional convenience. There is also a cocktail lounge, dance floor, and game room. The motel is located within walking distance of Livingston's

famous restaurants, downtown shopping, art galleries, and museums. The historical Depot Center Museum is directly across the street. Livingston's only movie theater is also within walking distance, or enjoy live entertainment in local restaurants and bars. Senior and family rates are available.

## L Rainbow Motel

5574 E. Park St., Livingston. 222-3780 or toll free 800-788-2301. www.rainbowmotelmt.com

The Rainbow Motel is located on the quiet side of Livingston with direct fishing access to the Yellowstone River. All rooms are ground floor with plenty of parking for all sizes of vehicles. The clean newly remodeled rooms are available with kitchenettes, microwaves and refrigerators, and all are equipped with individually controlled air conditioning and heat, phones and cable TV. Guest laundry facilities are available on the property. Pet are welcome and there is a lovely lawn with picnic tables for relaxing. Livingston attractions and restaurants are 3 minutes down the road. Off season weekly rates are offered. Visit the Rainbow Motel on the web.

## S Cowboy Connection

110 N. Main, Upstairs, Downtown Livingston. 222-0272, www.thecowboyconnection.com

You are in for a true wild west fantasy when you experience the passel of Old West collectables Jerry and Vangie Lee have for you to claim. You'll find the real thing here! You might find a gun that was once used by your favorite western character or something made and used long before there were cinema cowboys. This place is filled with items from the low end to the high minded! Spurs, saddles, Colts, Winchesters, Western art, old photos, and genuine Indian turquoise jewelry. Also open by appointment. Take a look at their collection at www.thecowboyconnection.com.

## S Bob & Lu's

219 S. Main St., Livingston. 222-9225

Bob & Lu's is an old fashioned second hand store with just about anything you can imagine, right on Main St. in downtown Livingston. They are known by the local folks as a great source for almost any needed or useful thing. The store also has a delightful mix of collectibles, art work, antiques, and all kinds of unique things. Browsing

through their vast selection of merchandise is a regular treasure hunt, and you'll always find a real surprise. There is everything from fishing and camping gear, western memorabilia and art work, books, old advertising, vintage kitchen items, furniture, appliances, and much more. They pay cash for almost anything, including households and estates.

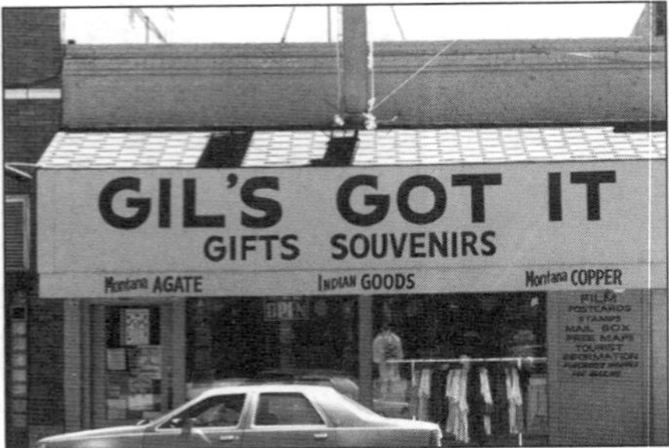


### S Gil's Got It!

207 W. Park, Livingston. Across from Depot Center. 222-0112

Gil's is the perfect souvenir shop! You will find everything from copper items, silver and turquoise, a large selection of moccasins, Montana clay, Black Hills Gold, and more costume jewelry than you can imagine. From the traditional to the curious, you'll find it in the store with the big yellow sign. Gifts to bring lasting memories and gifts to make you smile. Run by the nicest folks you'll find anywhere, with a great selection of goods. This is the place to stock up on film. The store is open year round. Hours are 8 a.m. to 9 p.m. daily, during the summer.

### S White Buffalo Lodges & Anvil Wagon Works

522 E. Park, Livingston. 222-7390 or fax 222-5926. Whitebuffalolodges.com or email at tipisandwagons@aol,com

White Buffalo Lodges specializes in the production of authentic native American tipis of the Sioux, Cheyenne, Crow, and Blackfeet. They make the most authentic and durable tipis, using the finest materials, and paying attention to every detail. They also offer wall tents, range tipis, diamond shelters, backrests, wagon covers, kids and pets tipis, cowboy bedrolls and more. Anvil Wagon Works specializes in restoration and construction of historic wagons, sheep camp wagons, chuck wagons, grain wagons, farm wagons, covered wagons, spring wagons and goat carts. They offer wheelwrighting and many accessories. Rentals are available for parties and weddings. A general store and trading post offers various Native American and Western gift items. See how they keep the old west alive. Watch a tipi being sewn or painted, wagons in restoration, wheel being rebanded, or even a blacksmith at the forge. Custom work is available. If you can dream it they can make it!

### S Tom's Jewelry

114 W. Lewis St., Livingston. 222-1413

### S Little Buckaroos

202 S. Main St., Livingston. 222-5532. www.littlebuckaroos.com

**8.** *Gas, Food*

**9.** *Historic Marker*

### H Bozeman Pass

Milepost 321 on I-90

*Sacajawea, the Shoshone woman who guided portions of the Lewis and Clark Expedition, led Captain Wm. Clark and his party of ten men over an old buffalo road through this pass on July 15, 1806. They were eastward bound and planned to explore the Yellowstone River to its mouth where they were to rejoin Captain Lewis and party who were returning via the Missouri River.*

*In the 1860s John M. Bozeman, an adventurous young Georgian, opened a trail from Fort Laramie, Wyoming, to Virginia City, Montana, across the hostile Indian country east of here. He brought his first party through in 1863 and the next year guided a large wagon train of emigrants and gold-seekers over this pass, racing with an outfit in charge of Jim Bridger. Bridger used a pass north of here. These pioneer speed demons made as much as fifteen to twenty miles a day—some days. The outfits reached Virginia City within a few hours of each other.*

**10.** *Food, Lodging*

**11.** *Lodging, Camping*

### Pine Creek

This tiny community located at the base of the Absaroka Mountainsis a great place for flyfishing on the Yellowstone or hiking to Pine Creek Lake.

### LC Luccock Park Camp & Cabins

263 Luccock Park Rd,.6 mi. south of Pine Creek, Livingston. 222-3025. www.imt.net/~luccock

**12.** *Historic Marker, Attraction, Gas, Food, Lodging*

### Emigrant

Tucked away in Paradise Valley, Emigrant is located halfway between Livingston and Gardiner on the Yellowstone River. Named after Emigrant Peak, the back drop of the town, the town prospered with the discovery of gold back in 1862. The locals used to soak in the natural hot springs at the base of Emigrant Peak.

Emigrant was named for Emigrant Peak, towering nearby at 10,960 feet. Gold was discovered in Emigrant Gulch in 1862 and the area also served as a spa for early trappers and prospectors who enjoyed the natural hot springs.

### H Emigrant Gulch

Milepost 28 on Hwy. 89 south of Emigrant

*A party of emigrants who had traveled with a wagon train across the Plains via the Bozeman or Bonanza Trail arrived in this gulch August 28, 1864. Two days later three of these men explored the upper and more inaccessible portion of the gulch and struck good pay. A mining boom followed.*

*When cold weather froze the sluices the miners moved down to the valley, built cabins and "Yellowstone City" began its brief career. Provisions were scarce that winter. Flour sold for $28 per 96 lb. sack, while smoking tobacco was literally worth its weight in gold.*

*The strike was not a fabulous one, but snug stakes rewarded many of the pioneers for their energy and hardships.*

### H The Absaroka-Beartooth Wilderness

Milepost 24 on Hwy. 89, south of Emigrant

*The Absaroka-Beartooth Wilderness, which lies to the east, contains the largest single expanse of land above 10,000 feet in elevation in the United States. The U.S. Forest Service set aside portions of the region as primitive areas in 1932, and Congress voted it a wilderness area in 1978. Visitors spent 392,000 collective days here in 1983, making it the fourth most visited wilderness in America.*

*Artifacts and pictographs indicate that people have hunted in these mountains for thousands of years, but it has always been country for people to visit, not live in. Reserved by treaty for the Crow in the early 1800s, the tribe shared with the less-rugged mountains on the west side of the wilderness (that you can see from here) their name for themselves, Absaroka (Absoarkey). The rugged mountains on the east side they named Beartooth, after one tooth-shaped peak. Gold discoveries in the 1860s attracted prospectors to Emigrant Gulch, and an 1880 treaty moved the reservation boundary eastward to allow previously clandestine mining claims to be developed.*

*The entire wilderness is a watershed for the Yellowstone, the longest undammed river left in the United States. It flows over 670 miles from its sources out of Yellowstone National Park and is the lifeblood of about one-third of Montana and much of northern Wyoming.*

### T Old Chico

Old Chico Road, 5 miles south of Chico Hot Springs

Chico began as a mining camp when a group of miners moved up the gulch from Yellowstone City. Some of them took up farming. It wasn't a fun place to live for the early families there. The Crow Indians constantly attacked the settlement and stole their horses. During the winters, many of the families would take boats up the Yellowstone River for warmer parts of Montana. At one time, the town supported a hotel, meat market, blacksmith shop, store, schoolhouse, a post office, and sixty cabins. Mining operations ceased in 1933 and the town pretty much went away. A few people still live in this ghost town. Few buildings remain as reminders from busier days, but the scenery is spectacular.

## 13. *Attraction, Gas, Food, Lodging*

### Jardine

Jardine is an old western mining town that once supported a gold mine up until World War II. This town can only be reached by a gravel road that heads west from Gardiner. You can see the old bunkers and other remnants of the mine, and the town is a great place to take advantage of some hiking or biking opportunities.

### T Corwin Hot Springs

Hwy 89, 6 miles north of Gardiner

Corwin Hot Springs runs off into the Yellowstone River and is located on Forest Service land. Nearby is La Duke Springs which is extremely dangerous for soaking. The springs are surrounded by the Royal Teton Ranch that until recently was owned by the Church Universal and Triumphant. The ruins of a bathhouse and elegant resort built in the early 1900s are nearby. A much safer place to soak on the Yellowstone River is 10 miles south, at Boiling River, inside the North entrance to Yellowstone Park at Gardiner.

### Gardiner

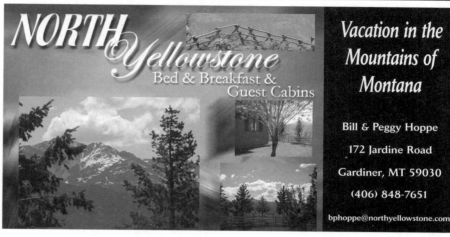

The town of Gardiner began to prosper when Yellowstone National Park opened in 1872, and is the north entrance to this first National Park. Gardiner began serving tourists when the Northern Pacific Railroad brought them from Livingston to the small town called Cinnabar, where they would get on stagecoach to finish the journey to Gardiner. After many disputes, the railroad expanded the last few miles to Gardiner, making it the new gateway to the park. Roosevelt Arch was built in 1903, marking the entrance to the world's first National Park. Gardiner is a quaint town with lots of lodging, shopping and dining to accommodate the large volume of tourists. Sitting in between the Absaroka-Beartooth Wilderness and Yellowstone National Park, seasonal outdoor activities abound in Gardiner. Fishing, hunting, horseback riding, whitewater rafting and kayaking are all popular. Elk, deer, bighorn sheep, and an occasional bear will often be seen roaming on the various lawns throughout town.

Gardiner, the first gateway to Yellowstone, is located in southwest Montana, along the Yellowstone River. Gardiner was founded in 1880 at the North Entrance to the Yellowstone Park and became a center of activity for visitors to the region, as it served as the original and only year-round entrance to the park. Gardiner offers a fine selection of motels, restaurants, shops, art galleries, churches, a small airport and related visitor services. Campgrounds and trailer parks with hookups offer overnight services.

Sandwiched between the Absaroka-Beartooth Wilderness to the north and the world's most famous park to the south, seasonal outdoor activities abound in Gardiner. Spring, summer and fall offer fishing, hunting, pack trips, river-rafting and kayaking. During the winter, Yellowstone Country is magically transformed under a blanket of snow and cross-country skiing and snowmobiling are the activities of popular demand.

Viewing wild antelope on the hills and in the meadow across Park Street in Gardiner is a thrill that few towns can boast. Listen carefully and coyotes can be heard in the foothills. Bears will occasionally wander into town, while Elk roam freely throughout town.

Gardiner has survived a rough and tumble existence of gold rushes, the railroad and destructive fires. A tough little frontier town, it fed and sheltered miners, entertained the early soldiers who ran Yellowstone Park, and learned to host the pioneer visitor. Gardiner has matured, tempered and grown to meet the needs of today's visitor. It's a good place, rich in history, in the heart of some of the West's finest country.

### T Roosevelt Arch

Gardiner. North Entrance to Yellowstone Park. 848-7971

# An Angler's Guide to Paradise Valley

*by Mathew Long—Long Outfitting*

As fishing has grown in popularity, so has the desire to fish in the northern gateway to Yellowstone Park, Paradise Valley. The majestic mountains seem to have an overpowering effect to draw anglers from around the globe to its abundance of blue ribbon trout fisheries. The valley, 50 miles in length, offers dozens of opportunities to fish for trout of various species and sizes, in a variety of waters from the mighty Yellowstone River to remote alpine lakes. A bit of exploration by an angler, or a day of fishing with one of the area's professional guides can make for a successful and pleasant outing. The following brief descriptions of some of the area's most popular fisheries are designed to lead you in the proper direction in relation to the type of water you desire to fish, the species and size of trout you would like to catch, and the amount of money you would like to spend.

## The Yellowstone River

By far, the most popular of all the angling activities is a float trip down the Yellowstone river. This wild and scenic river provides anglers with over 60 miles of floatable, fishable water in Paradise Valley. Some of the sections throughout the valley support up to 1,000 fish per mile. Do not overlook the sections upstream in Yellowstone Park and downstream towards Big Timber, though. These areas hold excellent populations of larger trout. The types of water, as well as the speciation of the trout change rapidly throughout the rivers length.

Depending on the time of the year, trout will feed on various orders of insects. Spring and fall provide excellent mayfly and midge hatches, while the hot, dry summer days make for excellent terrestrial and caddis action.

Take a comfortable drift boat down the river, or use one of the public access areas to gain access for wade fishing. Remember that once you have legally gained access to the river, everything below the high-water mark is public property. The most effective way to fish this large river is to hire a guide and cover a lot of water in a drift boat. Look for the pods of trout in back eddies containing foam lines and on deeper shelves off of cut banks and current seams. Yellowstone River trout usually average between 10 and 18 inches.

## The Spring Creeks

For the discriminating fly fisherman, the spring creeks are among the most famous in the world. Located in the northern end of Paradise Valley and minutes from Livingston, Montana, Armstrongs, Depuys, and Nelsons spring creeks are a convenient and popular destination. Gin clear water, prolific, complex hatches, and tricky currents all combine to make for a challenging, yet hopefully rewarding day. Breathtaking views of the lush weed beds, dimpling trout, and white-tailed deer combined with the backdrop of the Absaroka-Beartooth Wilderness to the east and the Gallatin Mountains to the west offer picturesque moments.

Catching trout here is anything but easy. Reading the feeding trout, matching the hatch, floating perfect drifts, and presenting accurate casts all can increase your odds of taking these selective trout. Brown, rainbow, and cutthroat trout can all be found in the privately-owned spring creeks.

All the streams are managed as fee fishing areas and have limited access to insure a quality experience for all of the anglers. Rod dates book early and it is wise to call in advance. Approximate cost per fisherman is $75.00 per day. Some local fly shops reserve extra rods for client's use, so don't be afraid to stop in and ask questions. Despite all the rumors about the damage done by the floods of 1996 and 1997, the creeks fish just as well now as before.

## Private Lakes

Another option that fly fishermen often take advantage of, especially during the snow-melt run-off, are the numerous private lakes located in Paradise Valley. Fishing these still waters often produces large trout in the 14-25 inch range. Some of these lakes can be fished effectively from shore, while others are large enough to require the use of a drift boat or float tube. Some lakes require fishermen to be accompanied by a guide, while others just require a daily access rate.

Often times, fish can be caught on a variety of fly patterns from tiny midge to large leeches. The famous damsel hatch in mid-July is a wonderful time to fish dry flies. Just to give you an example of the quality of some of these fisheries, Merrell Lake, located in Tom Miner Basin, has been rated by Fly Fisherman Magazine as one of the top six privately owned lakes in North America. This is a pretty impressive status for a 90-acre trout lake in the heart of Paradise Valley.

Other local lakes can produce some great fishing for very large rainbow, cutthroat, and brown trout. Check with a Livingston fly shop on access and price information. Prices range from $50 per angler, while others are free when fishing with a guide.

## Alpine Lakes and Small Tributaries

For the fisherman who likes to get away to a "less traveled to" location, many small tributaries to the Yellowstone River and the high-altitude lakes of the Absaroka and Gallatin ranges can provide solitude, serenity and excellent fishing. Many of the fish are small, but are eager to feed on flies and are certainly some of the feistier fish you will ever encounter.

A topographic map can help you locate some destinations including Mill Creek, Big Creek, Rock Creek, Tom Miner Creek, Bear Creek, Emerald Lake, Thompson Lake, Shelf Lake, and Ramshorn Lake. There are too many of these small streams and lakes to even begin to list them all. Take your hiking shoes and some bear spray, and check your fishing regulation book before going on your trek. Some of these lakes are in Yellowstone Park and some are located in forest service and wilderness areas.

It is easy to see how Paradise Valley has received its name. For anglers, it is truly an angling paradise. For non-anglers, it is a geological and wildlife paradise. Come see for yourself the impressive scenery and the awesome fishing south of Livingston. Fond memories and feeding trout await your arrival.

For more information on fishing Paradise Valley call:

Matthew Long
222-6775 or Email: longoutfit@ycsi.net
www.longoutfitting.com

This imposing stone archway on the edge of Gardiner is the North Entrance to Yellowstone Park and has marked the only year-round, drive-in entrance since 1903. In that year, it was dedicated by President Theodore Roosevelt before an estimated 5,000 spectators.

### AS Sinclair Tank 'n' Tackle

Park Ave. & 2nd Street, Gardiner. 848-7501

Sinclair Tank n' Tackle not only takes care of your gasoline and diesel needs, but you can also purchase your Yellowstone and Montana fishing licenses here. Stock up on everything you'll need from lures, flies and fishing poles, to a wide selection of beer, soda pop, picnic supplies, and snacks. Sinclair Tank n' Tackle is the only lottery retailer in town for those Power Ball and Scratch tickets. In addition to your automotive needs there are video rentals, ice, and an ATM machine to make it all happen. Just around the corner is the Town Club for a fantastic meal before heading out for your next adventure.

### F The Yellowstone Mine & Rusty Rail Lounge & Casino

Hwy. 89 S. on west edge of Gardiner. 848-7336

Enjoy some of Montana's best dining at the famous Yellowstone Mine Restaurant. Relax by the fire in the gold mine atmosphere. They feature fine dining with steaks, prime rib, seafood, pasta, salads, exceptional appetizers and specialty desserts, along with a full service bar. Be sure and check out the Chef's nightly special! They also serve up all your favorites for breakfast at very reasonable prices. A breakfast buffet is featured during the summer months. They are open seven days a week. Breakfast is served from 6 a.m. to 11 a.m. and dinner from 5 p.m. to 9:30 p.m. The casino is open until 2 a.m. They are adjacent to the Best Western Mammoth Hot Springs and Gold Strike Gifts.

### FS The Four Winds at Cinnabar Gifts and Deli

Hwy 89 S., north of Gardiner. 848-7891 or toll free 800-775-1445. www.the4winds.com

The Four Winds has many faces. The ambiance is filled with lovely music and the aroma of sweet fragrances interspersed with aromas from the deli kitchen. The store offers items from around the globes, lovely pictures, jewelry, statuary, sparkling crystal gifts and a wide selection of books from Montana interests to your own personal transcendence. Additionally there are complete lines of skincare items, food supplements and healthy snacks and food items. The deli, offers a whole-foods lunch buffet including a seasonal salad bar, sandwiches, croissants, muffins, desserts and much more. Exceptional soups are made fresh daily and renowned throughout Paradise Valley. Order a box lunch for your trip into the park, or stay and enjoy the music and friendly atmosphere.

### FLS Town Club Motel, Lounge, & Gift Shop

122 Park Street, Gardiner. 848-7322 or fax 848-2336

A warm welcome from the management and crew at The Town Café will greet you with their fine dining and family style menus. The Café opens at 6 a.m. for one of the heartiest breakfasts you will ever eat. Check out their "Belly Buster!" If you can eat it all, it's free! They switch to lunch at 11:30 a.m. and offer a family lunch and dinner menu until 9 p.m. Try The Town Loft upstairs for seafood and steaks, while enjoying incredible views of Yellowstone Park. The Loft is open from 5:30 p.m. to 10 p.m. and features a 30+ item salad bar. You'll find a complete line of Montana and Yellowstone souvenirs in the Town Gift Shop. They also have a Casino Lounge for a late night drink or try your luck at the Poker and Keno machines. There are 11 rooms available at the adjoining motel.

### F Outlaws Pizza and Casino

Hwy. 89 S., in the Outpost Mall, Gardiner. 848-7733

#### *Montana Trivia*

Alzada in the southeast corner of Montana is closer to the Texas panhandle, than it is to Yaak, Montana in the far northeast corner of the state. It is 800 miles, or 12 hours driving from Alzada to Yaak.

### L North Yellowstone Bed & Breakfast

179 Jardine Road, Gardiner. 848-7651. www.northyellowstone.com or email bphoppe@northyellowstone.com

The North Yellowstone Bed and Breakfast is located high above Gardiner, on the Hoppe Ranch, near the North entrance to Yellowstone Park and situated high above any traffic. Two guest cabins are available, the Sheep Mountain Cabin and the Electric Peak Cabin. Spend a night, week, or month in Yellowstone Country. Enjoy gold medal fly-fishing at it's best. Ride horses through the Absaroka Wilderness or deep into Yellowstone Park. Start your day each morning with a hearty Montana Breakfast prepared by hosts Bill & Peggy Hoppe. Historic Livingston, Cooke City, Red Lodge, Cody. Billings and Bozeman are day trips for shopping or sight seeing. North Yellowstone Guest Cabins can establish contacts for everything you would like to do while vacationing in the area.

### L Yellowstone Basin Inn

4 Maiden Basin Dr., MP 5, Hwy 89 S., Gardiner. 848-7080 or fax 848-7083 or 800-624-3364 www.yellowstonebasin.com

The Yellowstone Basin Inn offers fine western lodging just outside of Gardiner amid pristine mountains. Relax under the covered deck in the heated outdoor spa and enjoy views of the Gallatin and Absaroka ranges. Select from comfortable luxurious accommodations. The Montana Suite, is a two bedroom family unit, complete with a fully equipped kitchen and a washer and dryer. The rustic log Paradise room treats guests to a taste of the West and includes a private kitchenette. The Yellowstone Suite features cathedral ceilings, views of Electric Peak, plus a private spa tub. The La Duke room offers king size comfort and is handicap accessible. There are several other custom rooms to choose from. A continental breakfast and cable TV is included with all accommodations. Enjoy the many year around activities the area offers and know that the Yellowstone Basin Inn is your home away from home in Yellowstone.

**L Yellowstone Comfort Inn**
107 Hellroaring Dr., North Entrance to Yellowstone Park, Gardiner. 848-7536 or 800-228-5150, www.yellowstonecomfortinn.com

Open throughout the year, the West Yellowstone Comfort Inn offers true western hospitality. Enjoy the largest heated pool in West Yellowstone, along with a spa, exercise room, complimentary continental breakfast, local airport shuttle, guest laundry, conference room, non-smoking rooms, fax services, handicap access, winter plug-ins, and much more. The 78 spacious guest rooms are complete with cable TV, direct dial phones, and full climate control. Experience the thrill of a true western adventure with Yellowstone National Park right at your doorstep offering blue ribbon trout streams, hunting, hiking, snowmobiling from your door, cross country skiing, and horseback riding. Most rooms have fantastic views!

**L Best Western Mammoth Hot Springs**
Hwy. 89 S., Gardiner. 848-7311 or reservations at 800-828-9080, www.bestwestern.com/mammoth-hotsprings

The Best Western is conveniently located one mile from the North Entrance to Yellowstone National Park on the banks of the Yellowstone River. Enjoy spectacular views of the park, river, wildlife, and surrounding mountains from your room. The hotel offers 85 deluxe rooms, some with jacuzzis, family suites, and kitchenettes are also available. Other hotel amenities include a large indoor heated pool and jacuzzi, two saunas, restaurant, lounge, casino and gift shop. They also offer snowmobile day rentals. Be sure and ask about their discounted snowmobile and cross-country ski packages. This is a three star AAA rated property. Senior discounts. Check them out on the web!

### Montana Trivia

In his 1994 book, *Nothing But Blue Skies*, author Tom McGuane chronicles the happenings in the fictional town at Deadrock. He is taking a humorous jab at the town of Livingston ("living stone") where he resides.

**L Jim Bridger Court Cabins**
Hwy. 89 S., Gardiner. 848-7371 or reservations at 888-858-7508

The Jim Bridger Court Cabins are conveniently located near the North Entrance to Yellowstone National Park. Enjoy your stay in affordable, clean, and comfortable cabins. All cabins feature private showers, cable television, and are an easy walking distance from dining and shopping. Whitewater rafting, fishing, horseback riding, and hiking are only minutes away.

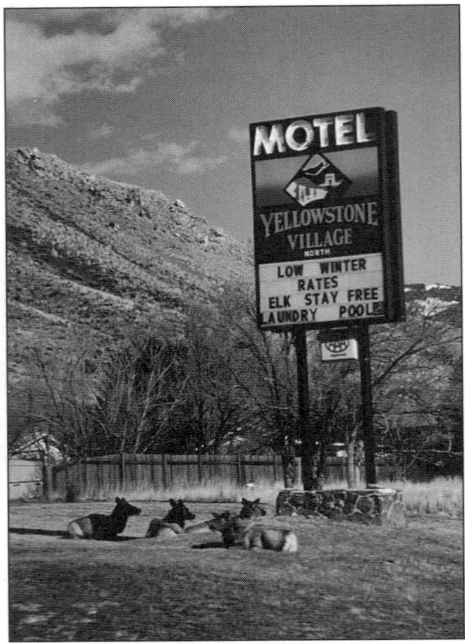


**L Yellowstone Village Inn**
North Gate, Yellowstone National Park, Hwy 89, Gardiner. 848-7417 or reservations at 800-228-8158. www.YellowstoneVinn.com

The Yellowstone Village Inn is located at Teddy Roosevelt's Arch, the first entrance to Yellowstone Park in historical Gardiner. They are open year-round and AAA approved, offering 43 rooms, 3 kitchen suites, one suite, along with an indoor pool and sauna, basketball court, laundromat, horseback riding, rafting, flyfishing, and park bus tours right from the Inn. Winter activities available from the Inn include snowshoeing, X-country skiing, snowmobiling, snowcoach tours, and ice skating. Don't be surprised to see Elk grazing right out your front door! They also provide guests with continental breakfast. Ask them about customized activity packages and discount programs. You can also visit them on the web!

### Montana Trivia

John Steinbeck said of Montana: "For other states I have admiration, respect, recognition, even some affection, but with Montana it is love, and it's difficult to analyze love when you're in it.

**L Yellowstone Super 8 Motel**
Hwy 89 S., Gardiner. 848-7401 or national reservations at 800-800-8000. www.yellowstonesuper8.com

Located at the North Entrance to Yellowstone National Park, Gardiner offers year-round adventure for everyone. East access to the park allows for some of the best wildlife viewing in Yellowstone. Photographers, hikers, bikers, fishermen/women and skiers will find the Yellowstone Super 8 to be a convenient place to explore Yellowstone and the surrounding area. They offer economy lodging with excellent customer service, and clean and comfortable rooms that include family rooms with micro/fridge and a full kitchen suite. Amenities include indoor heated pool, continental breakfast and 24 hour coffee. The Yellowstone Super 8 Motel is where memories are made and spirits renewed!

**L Absaroka Lodge**
Hwy 89 in Gardiner. 848-7414 or reservations at 800-755-7414. www.yellowstonemotel.com or email: ablodge@aol.com

This beautifully appointed lodge is located directly on the banks of the Yellowstone River. There are 41 rooms including eight suites. Each room has it's own private balcony or deck overlooking the Yellowstone River. You can even see Yellowstone Park in the near distance. The suites also offer fully equipped kitchens. You'll find delightful gift shops along with the fishing and hunting shops, and great eating establishments, all within walking distance. Complimentary coffee and tea are available in the lobby through the evening. Check out their special Montana-made jewelry and gifts. Enjoy sitting on the park benches in their front lawn or your own private balcony and enjoy the views. Visit their web site for more information.

**L Above The Rest Lodge**
Gardiner. 848-7747

**L Westernaire Motel**
Hwy 89 in Gardiner. 848-7397 or reservations only at 888-273-0358

**S E.L.K., Inc**
224 Park St., Gardiner. 848-7997 or toll free at 800-272-4355

See article ar right.

**S Silvertip Bookstore**
Hwy 89 in Gardiner. 848-2225.
Email: DERA@prodigy.net

The Silvertip Bookstore offers over 25,000 new, used and out-of-print, paperback and hardback books. Most used books are half cover price including best sellers, sci-fi, westerns, Yellowstone Park, history, nonfiction, reference, romance, children's, mystery, self-help, cookbooks, women's, travel, sports, health, audio-books, first editions, CD's. You can even get Internet access! They have great espresso, bagels, pastries, and a friendly trained staff to help you find what you are looking for. Open everyday year-round. They buy collections and will do valuation on estate collections. Questions are always welcome! Stop in to enjoy and relax, give them a call, or email at DERA@prodigy.net.

**14.** *Historic Marker, Gas, Food, Lodging, Shopping*

## Cooke City

Cooke City is located on the northeastern edge of the Yellowstone National Park boundary, and is accessed either by the Beartooth National Scenic Byway or by driving through the park.

Shoo-Fly, the original name of the mining town now known as Cooke City was changed by the miners in 1880 to honor Jay Cooke, Jr. Cooke, a Northern Pacific Railroad contractor and the son of an investor in the Northern Pacific Railroad, promised not only to promote the area's development, but also to help bring a railroad to the town. However, he got into financial difficulties, forfeited his bond, and his bonded mining claims reverted back to the original owners. by the 1870s, the town was booming. A few years later, Chief Joseph and the Nez Perce stormed through town and burnt down much of the gold mining facilities. Although they were reconstructed, due to it's hard to reach location, the boom did not last very long. Old cabins are left over from the mining days and the town reflects the past very well.

The town of Cooke City and the land around it were within the Crow Reservation until 1882, when the boundaries of the reservation were shifted eastward. Shortly after moving these boundaries, 1,450 mining claims were staked and recorded in the New World District. Most of these

## Building a Better Elk Call

**E.L.K., Inc. is not located in a fancy**, many-thousand square foot facility decorated with trophy animals and racks of designer clothes. Rather it occupies a modest 600 square-foot storefront on Park Street in Gardiner, MT. Its only trophy decorations are a few antlers hanging here and there throughout the store and some hunter's snapshots. Its designer clothing consists of a few embroidered and camouflage hunting caps.

There are no smooth-talking sales people selling high-dollar equipment and promising successful hunting with each purchase. In fact E.L.K.'s best salesman is its owner, Don Laubach, an easy going, western-shirted Montanan with a great sense of humor. Don just happens to be an expert, 53-year veteran hunter and the inventor of "Cow Talk", the call that revolutionized elk hunting.

Don says, "Before 1984 I was a self-employed accountant who had started hunting with my dad for our freezer and not for sport when I was nine years old. As seasons passed and I gained experience it became obvious to me that to call a bull elk effectively any time of the year, not just rutting season, I needed to sound like a cow elk. So I made a simple device for my own use that proved my theory.

"In 1984 Gordon Eastman a renowned outdoor movie-maker from Wyoming asked me to help produce an elk calling video and when he found out how I called elk he informed me I had something that would revolutionize the elk hunting world. Little did I know how true his statement was!

"Like any fisherman with a favorite fishing hole, I was reluctant to share my invention. But Gordon convinced me to market the call and in 1985 we formed E.L.K., Inc. (Eastman Laubach Kreations, Inc.). We did not have the funding to have calls molded nor the foresight to realize the demand. We operated our business entirely from my home and in the first year I built over 10,000 calls in my basement. I could not keep up with the demand.

"Major hunting magazines began featuring articles about 'Cow Talk' and our volume of mail grew to 10 to 20 pounds a day! I still thought my call was just a fad but the next year we sold over 50,000 and again I could not keep up with the demand.

"I hired people to help and this allowed me time to exhibit at trade shows, attend markets, develop new products, write books and work with Gordon on new videos. When Gordon died 6 years ago, I bought 'Eastman's Outdoor World' video business and started producing videos on my own. Soon I will offer DVDs. Today we have over 40 distributors that sell our products worldwide, including Japan, France, England, Germany, Canada and Australia. We have increased our line of products from one call to over 70 related items."

The shelves at E.L.K., Inc. are stocked with calls and related accessories for attracting elk, deer, turkeys and coyotes along with instruction books and videos - most sell for $10 to $25. Besides the products Don developed there are other related items including binoculars, scents and lures. Part of Don's success has been a darn good product and his niche market. A much greater factor has been Don's "down to earth" approachability and the power of "word of mouth" advertising. He comments' "I'm not in this business to promote myself; I'm here to help people". And people do call and they do come – some for help learning to use his calls, some to say "thanks", some to meet the inventor, and some just to find out where the best sightings are. All are welcome.

Section 4

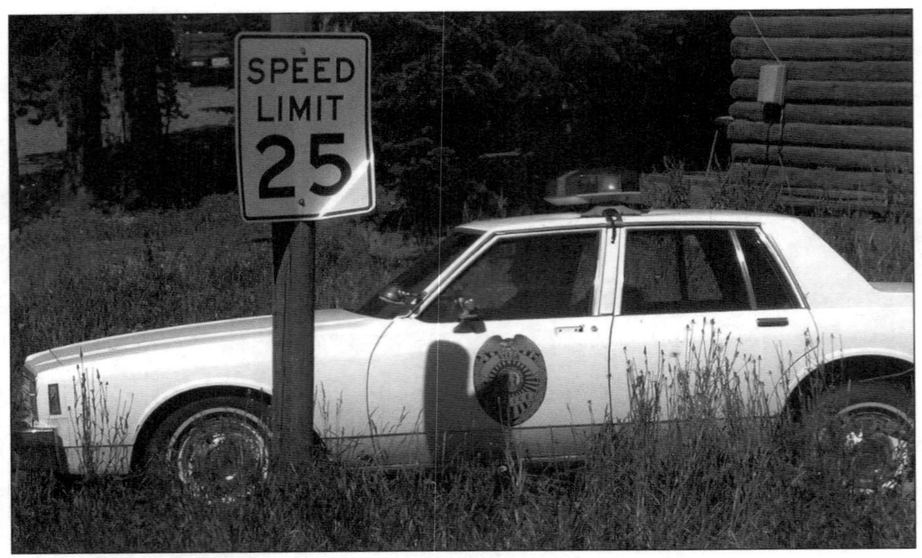


*The local law in vintage police car sits at both ends of Main Street in Cooke City asking you to slow down when you enter town.*

claims lapsed after a year. By 1883, Cooke City had grown to a community of about 135 log huts and tents.

John P. Allen was the first person to drive a four-horse team and loaded wagon to town. In 1883 he built the Allen Hotel, later renamed the Cosmopolitan. Eventually he opened three mines: the O-Hara, War Eagle and McKinley.

The town site was platted in 1883, had two hundred twenty seven voters, two smelters, two sawmills three general stores, two hotels, two livery stables and a meat market. However, because of the large number of irregularly shaped mining claims and the problems of organizing them, it took eight years to complete the surveying and platting.

Today, Cooke City has a year around population of approximately 90 people. The population expands to over three hundred when summer residents arrive The town has a rustic "old west" atmosphere, which can be traced to its mining roots. However, tourism is currently the main stay of the economy.

This is a tourist destination, with people pouring in from both sides, but with Cooke City's past, it is easy to see why.

*Source: Cooke City Chamber of Commerce*

## Silver Gate

The town of Silver Gate is located on land home steaded by Horace S. Double, for which he was granted a patent on May 2, 1897. In 1932, John L Taylor and J. J. White later founded the town of Silver Gate on part of the homestead. They intended to create a rustic, western town to serve the tourist trade and to provide building sites for summer recreationists. The year-round population includes only a few, but the summer population is well over a hundred. Covenants written for the original town site covered setbacks, signs, and building standards requiring log construction and rustic architecture.

*Source: Cooke City Chamber of Commerce*

## H Cooke City
Cooke City

*In 1868 a party of prospectors came into this country by way of Soda Butte Creek. They found rich float but were set afoot by Indians. Caching their surplus supplies on the stream now called Cache Creek they made it back to the Yellowstone and reported their find. In the next few years many prospectors combed these mountains; the first real development began about 1880 with Jay Cooke's infusion of eastern capital.*

*Chief Joseph's band of fugitive Nez Perce Indians came through here in 1877. In 1883 there were 135 log cabins in the settlement, two general stores and thirteen saloons.*

*Cooke City had been waiting years for reasonable transportation connections to the outside world so that her promising ore deposits could be profitably mined. She's no blushing maiden, but this highway was the answer to her prayers.*

## 15. *Historic Marker, Gas, Food*

## Clyde Park

Originally named Sunnyside, Clyde Park was chosen because the post office was on a ranch that raised Clydesdale horses and the town resembled a park. This small town revolved around farming and ranching and with the help of the Northern Pacific Railroad, the trains still haul the harvest goods to larger towns.

## H Shields River Valley
Wilsall

*This river was named by Capt. Wm. Clark of the Lewis and Clark Expedition in honor of John Shields, a member of the party. Capt. Clark and his men, guided by Sacajawea, the Shoshone woman, camped at the mouth of the river July 15, 1806, while exploring the Yellowstone on their return trip from the coast.*

*Jim Bridger, famous trapper, trader and scout, guided emigrant wagon trains from Fort Laramie, Wyoming, to Virginia City, Montana, in the 1860s, crossing hostile Indian country via the Bonanza Trail. Bridger's route came up this valley from the Yellowstone, followed up Brackett Creek, crossed the divide west of here to strike Bridger Creek and thence down the latter to the Gallatin Valley.*

## 16. *Food,*

## T Crazy Mountains
I-90 Exit 367, Big Timber

This island mountain range stands in stark contrast to the surrounding plains. Its rugged granite peaks are snow capped a good part of the year.

The majestic peaks, alpine lakes, cascading streams and infinite views make this one of Montana's most magnificent alpine areas. The Robert Redford movie *Jeremiah Johnson* was based on the life of Liver Eatin' Johnson, who frequented these mountains.

The Crazy Mountains were formed by igneous rock and carved by glaciers. They have been inhabited by man for 11,500 years and now provide beauty and recreation to the people of Big Timber and her visitors. Indians, most recently the Shoshone and Crow, have camped in the canyons, drunk the clear water from the streams, and eaten of the vast herds of deer, antelope, and elk. Between 1860 and 1880 the Indians gave way to trappers, traders, and settlers.

The Crazies weren't named until the 1860s with fact blending with fiction about how they came by their title. In the first theory, Indians called them the "Mad Mountains" for their steepness, rugged beauty, and haunting winds that blow down the canyon. Geology plays a part in the second theory. The lava upthrusts are young in perspective of time and do not fit in with the neighboring rock formations, hence the name "Crazy". In the third, and most widely accepted, a woman-some say Indian and some say white-went mad on the prairie, possibly due to the death of her family, and took refuge in the mountains. Indian belief required the crazy people be left alone and so she was.

However the name came about, the fact remains, the Crazy Mountains are a beautiful backdrop for the surrounding area, and offer much in the way of recreation.

## 17. *Food, Lodging*

## McLeod

In 1882, W.F. McLeod drove a herd of 125 cattle and 200 horses into the Boulder Valley from Oregon. He was recognized as the first permanent homesteader in the valley, with the little town named after him. The Boulder Valley residents conducted their first election in 1884. On June 11, 1886, the McLeod Post Office was established with the mail coming in on horseback from Big Timber. In the spring of 1887, the first school started with five children.

Settlers moved into the valley, including Thomas Hawley, who assisted in the discovery of the valuable mineral deposits farther up the river valley. Prospecting had started in 1869, so by the spring of 1887, the mining operations had attracted considerable attention. A pack trail was cut through the timber and the Independence Mining Company took the first stamp mill up the mountain in 1888. Independence Mine was running full blast in '92 and '93, boasting a population of 500 or more persons. One long street with a few cabins, four saloons and two general stores made up the town. All that remains of Independence and the other mining camps today are a few tumbled down log structures and the glory of this magnificent mountain valley. Hiking trails lead to hidden valleys and lakes where wildlife such as moose, bear, elk and the many small animals make their home.

The little town of McLeod has a school, post office, cabins, camping and the infamous Road Kill Cafe. Take a drive south to one of the most beautiful mountain valleys in Montana. Enjoy the peaceful surroundings of the valley, fish in the pristine waters of the Boulder River, and picnic at the Natural Bridge and Falls.

*Reprinted from Sweetgrass Chamber information sheet.*

### F Road Kill Cafe

Hwy 298, McLeod. 932-6174

A trip to McLeod wouldn't be complete without a stop at the Roadkill Cafe and Bar. Their motto is "From Your Grille to Ours"! Get a darn good meal and rub elbows with the locals. It's a great place to get local information and some unusual Montana souvenirs.

### C Spring Creek Campground & Trout Ranch

On the Boulder River, 2 1/2 miles on Hwy 298 S. of Big Timber. 932-4387. www.springcreekcampground.com

Spring Creek is located in the heart of "The Horse Whisperer" Country. Truly one of the most beautiful and quiet campgrounds you'll every find, located on a shaded setting along the scenic Boulder River and a trout stream. Bring your RV or tent to one of Montana's best kept secret spots. Wander through acres of unspoiled back country, or enjoy a sunset. Fishing, photography, golf, horseback rides, family float trips, are just minutes away. Spring Creek has camping facilities with full hook-ups, cabins, tent sites, laundry, free showers, store, ice cream parlor, email service, exchange library, pancake breakfasts, and private fish ponds (no license required). They even have a pet bear! Visit their web site for more information.

## 18. *Attraction*

### T Natural Bridge

27 miles south of Big Timber on Hwy. 298. 932-5131

This is one of the more unusual waterfalls you will ever see. The Boulder River literally drops into a hole and exits out of the face of a 100 foot cliff. If you catch it at the right time during spring runoff (usually early to mid-June) the river rises above the hole and cascades over the bridge to the gorge below. The appearance is that of a mini-Niagara. The river and canyon below the falls is equally spectacular. The viewpoints for the falls are wheelchair accessible and much of the walk to and around the falls is paved. A parking area and points along the trail have interpretive signs explaining the geology of the falls.

## 19. *Attraction*

### T Independence Ghost Town

Hwy 298, south of McLeod

It's a little challenging to get to the mine shafts, cabins, and brothel that still stand here. You might even see an occasional moose, elk, deer, or grizzly bear. Located at an altitude of about 10,000 feet, the view of the Absaroka-Beartooth Wilderness area is stunning from Independence. Plan on using 4WD or a good pair of hiking boots. Both wouldn't be a bad idea.

## Scenic Drives

### Boulder River Valley

Big Timber marks the confluence of the Boulder and Yellowstone Rivers. The Boulder River Valley is a beautiful drive just south of Big Timber on Route 298. Occupied by the Crow Indians until 1882, the area was opened to settlers shortly after. The discovery of gold and silver drew many settlers to the area, and farming and ranching became the mainstay that is still popular today. Many settlers built guest ranches along the Boulder Valley to accommodate travellers, and a few still remain today.

On this beautiful drive, you will pass Natural Bridge State Park and travel through the Gallatin National Forest which lines much of the Boulder River. The historic ranger station built in 1905 sits along Route 298. Native American Caves can be seen from the road just west of the ranger station, and used to shelter the Crow. There are pictographs on the walls of one of the caves. As you head further down the Main Boulder, you can visit the ghost town Independence.

### Paradise Valley

Paradise Valley has been carved by the Yellowstone River running through the land, separating the Gallatin Range to the west and the Absaroka Range to the east. Leading from Livingston to the Gardiner entrance to Yellowstone National Park, the valley offers spectacular landscape and great fly fishing and recreational activities. The Crow Indians inhabited this area along the river for many years before the white man settled here. Today celebrities such as Dennis Quaid, Peter Fonda and others call it home much of the year.

After striking gold in Emigrant Gulch in 1862, a few small mining towns sprouted up along the valley, including Old Chico and Yellowstone City. By the late 1800s, coal mines exceeded gold mines, and much was extracted from this area. Nowadays ranching is how the locals make a living in the area, among other things.

## Hikes

**Pine Creek Lake**

This isn't a hike for couch potatoes. It will take you into some gorgeous mountain scenery with a pristine alpine lake at the end. To get there, travel south of Livingston on Hwy. 89 to East River Road. Cross the Yellowstone and travel another nine miles. Turn left and follow the signs to the Pine Creek campground. The trailhead starts here and takes you immediately to a spectacular waterfall. From here it begins a steep ascent climbing 3,000 feet in 4 miles.

**Blue Lake**

This 5 mile hike can be a bit rugged, particularly the second half that takes a pretty steep ascent. The trails switch back frequently though and are not that strenuous. The trail starts into Big Timber Canyon as a jeep trail and gradually narrows to a hiking trail. Along the way you will pass Big Timber Falls, a beautiful cascading falls on Big Timber Creek. The source of this stream is your destination. About 2 miles along the trail, you will come to a clearly marked trailhead for Blue Lake. The trail immediately crosses the creek and begins switching back and forth up the mountain. The lake itself is a beautiful post card scene of an alpine lake. There are several excellent camp sites around the lake and a trail completely circles it. There is excellent fishing here. If you walk to the far side of the lake to the roaring sound you will see where the lake spills down the mountain side and the beginnings of Big Timber Creek.

**East Fork Boulder River Trail 27**

From Big Timber head south on McLeod Street (the main street) through the residential area of town until it takes a sharp right and turns into Hwy. 298. Follow this for 19 miles past McLeod to the East Boulder Road turnoff on your left (east). Follow this road for 6 miles on a bumpy gravel road past the Ricks Park Campground and Upsidedown Creek Trailhead to the Box Canyon Trailhead. The trailhead is well signed. This trail used to be an old wagon road. It is a 3.5 mile hike to a log bridge that is an excellent picnic area.

**West Boulder Trail 41**

This easy trail goes 16 miles to Mill Creek Pass if you go the whole way. The trail pretty much follows the river into the wilderness area. The lower part of the trail passes through some private property and you may share some of it with cattle grazing the area. From Big Timber head south on McLeod Street (the main street) through the residential area of town until it takes a sharp right and turns into Hwy. 298. Follow the highway for 16 miles to Hwy. 35 on your right (west). Drive 6.5 miles to a major fork in the road. Go left and follow this road for 8 miles till you see the sign marking the turn to the campground. To reach the trailhead, go straight past the campground for a few hundred feet. You will see the sign marking the trailhead.

## Cross-Country Ski Trails

### Gallatin National Forest

*For more information contact District Ranger, Gardiner, MT 59030 (406) 848-7375*

**Bannock Trail—Cooke City to Silver Gate**
*4.8 km*
Easiest trail is on groomed snowmobile trail.

**Republic Creek—Cooke City**
*3 km More Difficult; no grooming*
Trail enters Wyoming and the North Absaroka Wilderness.

**Woody Creek-Cooke City**
*2 km More Difficult, 1 km Most Difficult; no grooming*
Steep climb through timber near Cooke City; trail breaks into open timber and meadows.

**Bear Creek Trail System— Jardine**
*7 km Easiest, 7.5 km more difficult; intermittantly groomed*
Easy climb through timber along Bear Creek Road. Climbs through timber along old logging road to a meadow on the ridge.

**Tom Miner—Tom Miner Basin, 26 mi. W Gardiner**
*6.4 km Easiest; no grooming*
Road plowed by County; stay on road—do not trespass on private land.

**Sheep Creek-Cooke City**
*4 km Easiest; no grooming*
Follow Miller Loop snowmobile trail for first mile.

## Gallatin National Forest

*For more information contact District Ranger, Livingston, MT 59047 (406) 222-1892*

**Suce Creek—8 mi. SE Livingston**
*2.0 miles Moderate; no grooming. Trail crosses private property, please stay on trail.*
Suce Creek Forest Service road #201 is plowed to a private driveway in Section 20, T3S, R10E. Do Not block driveway. Parking capacity 3 cars. Please respect private property.

**Trail Creek-15 mi. SW Livingston**
*1.9 miles Moderate; no grooming. Trailhead and trail crosses private lands, please stay on trail.*
Trail begins at the Trail Creek Trailhead on Park County's Newman Creek Rd; parking capacity 10 cars; shared with snowmobiles. Depending upon snow and road conditions Park County's Newman Creek Rd may be impassable to wheeled vehicles. Parking then would be at the junction of Park County's Trail Creek and Newman Creek Roads; parking capacity 8 cars. This will add 1.2 mi. to the trail length. Please respect private property.

# Information Please

All Montana area codes are 406

## Road Information

Montana Road Condition Report
800-226-7623, 800-335-7592 or local 444-7696
Montana Highway Patrol 444-7696
**Local Road Reports**
Bozeman 586-1313
Statewide Weather Reports 453-2081

## Tourism Information

Travel Montana 800-847-4868 outside Montana
444-2654 in Montana
http://travel.mt.gov/.
Yellowstone Country 800-736-5276 or 646-4383
Northern Rodeo Association 252-1122
**Chambers of Commerce**
Big Timber 932-5131
Cooke City 838-2495
Gardiner 848-7971
Livingston 222-0850

## Airports

Big Timber 932-4389
Gardiner 848-7794
Livingston 222-0520
Red Lodge 446-2537
Wilsall 222-0520

## Government Offices

State BLM Office 255-2885, 238-1540
Bureau of Land Management
Billings Field Office 896-5013
Custer National Forest, Beartooth Ranger District 446-2103
Gallatin National Forest, 522-2520
Montana Fish, Wildlife & Parks 994-4042
U.S. Bureau of Reclamation 247-7295

## Hospitals

Sweet Grass Community Hospital
Big Timber 932-5449
Stillwater Community Hospital
Columbus 322-5316
Livingston Memorial Hospital
Livingston 222-3541

## Golf Courses

Overland Golf Course 932-4297
Livingston Golf Club 222-1031

## Bed & Breakfasts

**Yellowstone Basin Inn** • Gardiner 848-7080
**Carriage House Inn** • Big Timber 932-5339
**Buckin' Horse Bunkhouse**•Big Timber 932-6537
**North Yellowstone B & B** • Gardiner 848-7651
The River Inn • Livingston 222-2429
Burnt Out Lodge • Big Timber 932-6601
Big Timber Inn B&B • Big Timber 932-4080
Davis Creek B&B • Livingston 333-4768
Java Inn B&B • Big Timber 932-6594
Gibson Cassidy House • Clyde Park 686-4490
Teneagles Lodge • Clyde Park 686-4285
Medicine Bow Ranch • Big Timber 932-4463
Cabin By The River • Corwin Springs 848-2223
Dome Mountain Ranch • Emigrant 333-4361
Paradise Gateway B & B • Emigrant 333-4063
Querencia B & B • Emigrant 333-4500
Yellowstone Riverview Lodge B & B
Emigrant 848-2156
Johnstad's B & B & Log Guest House
Emigrant 333-9003
Yellowstone Country B & B•Emigrant 333-4917
Headwaters B & B • Gardiner 848-7073
Yellowstone Suites B & B • Gardiner 848-7937
The Elliott Guest House • Livingston 222-2055
Blue Winged Olive • Livingston 222-8646
Greystone Inn B & B • Livingston 222-8319
O'Carroll's B&B on the Yellowsone
Livingston 333-9099
Pleasant Pheasant B & B• Livingston 333-4659
Remember When B & B • Livingston 222-8367
Log Cabin Cafe And B & B•Silver Gate 838-2367
Wickiup B&B • Emigrant 333-4428
The Grand • Big Timber 932-4459

## Guest Ranches & Resorts

**Luccuck Park Camp & Cabins**
**Livingston** **222-3025**
Chico Hot Springs • Pray 333-4933
Dome Mountain Ranch • Emigrant 333-4361
B Bar Guest Ranch • Emigrant 848-7523
Hawley Mountain Guest Ranch
Mc Leod 932-5791
High Country Motel • Cooke City 838-2272
High Country Outfitters Fly Fishing Lodge
Pray 333-4763
Lazy K Bar Ranch • Big Timber 537-4404
Logans Guest Ranch • Clyde Park 686-4684
Ten Eagles Lodge• Clyde Park 686-4285
Mcleod Resort • Mcleod 932-6167
Mountain Sky Guest Ranch • Emigrant 333-4911
Point Of Rocks Guest Ranch•Emigrant 848-7278
Range Riders Ranch • Big Timber 932-6538
Soda Butte Lodge • Cooke City 838-2251
Sweet Grass Ranch • Big Timber 537-4477
Yellowstone Yurt Hostil • Cooke City 586-4659
Triple R Corporation • Livingston 222-8363

## Vacation Homes & Cabins

**Above the Rest** • Gardiner 848-7747
**Jim Bridger Court** • Gardiner 848-7371
Absaroka Cabins • Livingston 222-6519
Bearclaw Service & Cabins
Cooke City 838-2336
Big Timber Creek Vacation Cabin
Big Timber 932-4790
Cabin on the Yellostone • Livingston 222-1404
Cedar Bluffs • Livingston 222-0190
Crystal Spring Ranch • Big Timber 932-6238
CWC Ranch Houses • Big Timber 932-4359
Deep Creek Guest Cabin • Livingston 222-2380
Dome Mountain Ranch • Emigrant 333-4361
Dupuy Spring Creek Villa
Livingston 222-5432
Elliot Guest House • Livingston 222-2055
Emigrant Creek Cabin • Pray 333-4396
4M Ranch Log Guest House • Pray 333-4784
Island Guest House • Livingston 222-3788
Montana Getaway • Mcleod 932-6141
Mountain Retreat • Gardiner 848-7272
Paradise Valley Vacation Home
Emigrant 848-7477
Patricia Blume Properties
Livingston 222-3793
Pine Creek Lodge • Livingston 222-3628
Shields River Home • Livingston 222-5264
Silver Gate Cabins • Silver Gate 838-2371
The Arch House • Gardiner 848-2205
The Centennial • Livingston 222-5456
The Holler • Reed Point 932-6532
The Pond Cabin • Pray 222-4499
The River House • Livingston 222-2658
The School House • Livingston 222-2527
The Trout House & Tipi • Pray 333-4763
White Pines Cabin • LIvingston 222-6765

## Forest Service Cabins

*Gallatin National Forest*
**Battle Ridge Cabin**
20 mi. NE of Bozeman, MT 587-6920
Capacity: 4 Nightly fee: $25 Available: All year
Road access to cabin. Plowed within .25 miles of cabin.

**Big Creek Cabin**
35 mi. S of Livingston, MT on U.S. Highway 89, then 5 mi. W on Big Creek Road. 222-1892
Capacity: 10 Nightly fee: $25
Available: All year
Wood cook/heating stoves, lantern, no drinking water. Big Creek Rd access within 1/2 mi of cabin; walk or ski last 1/2 mi from Mountain Sky Guest Ranch.

**Deer Creek Cabin**
33 mi. S. of Big Timber, MT on I-90, ll mi. on W. Bridger Cr. Rd., 4 mi S & SE by trail on foot or horseback. 932-5155
Capacity: 4 Nightly fee: $20 Available: All year
Primitive road last 1/2 mile to trailhead. Not recommended for low clearance vehicles. Hikers need to ford Lower Deer Cr. numerous times. Corrals for horses, supplemental feed required. Wood heat cookstove. No power or drinking water.

**Fourmile Cabin**
42 mi. S of Big Timber, MT in Main Boulder Canyon 932-5155
Capacity: 5 Nightly fee: $30 Available: All year
Between 6/1 - 9/30 reservations taken no more than 2 weeks in advance. Access by snowmobiles, cross-country skis, or snowshoes in winter. Grazing of livestock is not allowed in either of administrative pastures. Power, electric stove and refrigerator.

**Ibex Cabin**
15 mi. E of Clyde Park, MT 222-1892
Capacity: 4 Nightly fee: $25 Available: All year
Wood heating stove, lantern, no drinking water. Plowed within 5 miles of cabin. Accessible by snowmobile or cross-country skis, in winter. High clearance vehicles in summer.

**Kersey Lake Cabin**
4 mi. E of Cooke City, MT on Kersey Lake 848-7375
Capacity: 10 Nightly fee: $30
Available: 6/15 - 9/15 & 12/15 - 03/15
Winter skis or snowmobiles from Cooke City. Summer hike 1.5 mi. along Russell Creek Trail. Can also bike or use ATV along Kersey Lake Jeep Road. - foot access last 400 yds.

**Mill Creek Guard Station**
15 mi. Hwy. 89 S Livingston, MT 12 mi. E Mill Creek Road 486 222-1892
Capacity: 4 Nightly fee: $25 Available: All year
Wood stove for heat, electric stove, lights, lantern, no drinking water. Road is plowed to Snowbank Snowmobile Parking Area which is adjacent to Mill Creek area.

**Porcupine Cabin**
16 mi. NE of Wilsall, MT. 222-1892
Capacity: 8 Nightly fee: $25 Available: All year
Wood heating stove, lantern, no drinking water. Road access to cabin plowed within 1.5 miles; accessible by snowmobile or cross-country skis in winter, high clearance vehicles in summer.

**Round Lake Cabin**
4.5 mi. N of Cooke City, MT 848-7375
Capacity: 4 Nightly fee: $20 Available: 6/15 - 9/15 Winter
Snowmobile or ski from Cooke City. Summer hike or 4x4 up Round Lake Road (primitive) from Fish Creek Rd.

**Trail Creek Cabin**
20 mi. SW of Livingston, MT (N end Gallatin Mtn. Range) 222-1892
Capacity: 4 Nightly fee: $25 Available: All year
Wood heat stove, lantern, no drinking water. Access via Goose Creek Rd. Summer the last 5 mi. restricted to vehicles 50 wide or less. Winter access varies with snow conditions.

**West Boulder Cabin**
30 mi. SW of Big Timber, MT on W Boulder River. Adjacent to FS campground. 932-5155
Capacity: 6 Nightly fee: $30 Available: All year
Between 6/1 - 9/30 reservations taken no more than 2 weeks in advance. 14 mi. on gravel road. Winter; ski, snowshoe or snowmobile short distance on county road. Power, electric stove, wood stove & refrigerator available. No drinking water.

**West Bridger Station**
27 mi. SE of Big Timber, MT on W. Bridger Road 932-5155
Capacity: 4 Nightly fee: $20 Available: All year
1/4 mile driveway to cabin; slick in wet weather. Winter access varies with snow conditions. Wood heat and cook stove. Pasture available for horses. No power or drinking water.

## Private Campgrounds

**KOA Kampgrounds** • Big Timber 932-6569
**Rainbow Motel & Campground**
Livingston 222-3780
Livingston Campground • Livingston 222-1122
McLeod Resort • McLeod 932-6167
Osen's Campground • Livingston 222-0591
Spring Creek Camp • Big Timber 932-4387
Rocky Mountain Campground
Gardiner 848-7251
Yellowstone RV Park & Campground
Gardiner 848-7496
Paradise Valley/KOA Kampgrounds
Livingston 222-0992
Rock Canyon RV Park • Livingston 222-1096
Windmill Park • Livingston 222-2784
Yellowstone Edge RV Park • Livingston 333-4036

## Car Rental

Bob Faw Chevrolet-Oldsmobile, Inc. 932-5465
Livingston Ford 222-7200
Rent A Wreck 222-0071
Yellowstone Country Motor 222-8600

## Outfitters & Guides

*F=Fishing H=Hunting R=River Guides*
*E=Horseback Rides G=General Guide Services*

| | | |
|---|---|---|
| Silver Run Outfitting | GF | 328-4694 |
| Absaroka Beartooth Outfitters | HF | 287-2280 |
| Anchor Outfitting | H | 537-4485 |
| Anderson's Yellowstone Angler | GF | 222-7130 |
| Bear's Den Outfitters | G | 222-0746 |
| Bear Paw Outfitters | HFE | 222-6642 |
| Beartooth Plateau Outfitters | HFER | 838-2328 |
| Big Bear Lodge | F | 838-2267 |
| Big Sky Flies & Guides | GF | 333-4401 |
| Big Sky Guides & Outfitters | GHRFE | 578-2270 |
| Big Sky Whitewater | R | 848-2112 |
| Big Timber Fly Fishing | RF | 932-4368 |
| Big Timber Guides | FREHG | 932-4080 |
| Black Mountain Outfitters | HFR | 222-7455 |
| Black Otter Guide Service | G | 333-4362 |
| Blue Rbbon Fishing Tours | F | 222-7714 |
| Brant Oswald Fly Fishing Services | F | 222-8312 |
| Castle Creek Outfitters & Guide | HEF | 333-4763 |
| Chan Welin's Big Timber Fly Fishing | GF | 932-4368 |
| Chimney Rock Outfitters | G | 222-5753 |
| Country Angler | F | 222-7701 |
| Covered Wagon Outfitters | HFRG | 222-7274 |
| Cudney Guide Service | RF | 223-1190 |
| Crazy Mountain Outfitter | GFHEF | 686-4648 |
| Dan Bailey's Fly Shop | F | 222-2673 |
| Dave Handl Fly Fishing Outfitter | FR | 222-1404 |
| Depuy's Spring Creek Reservations | F | 222-0221 |
| Dome Mountain Ranch Outfitters | G | 333-4361 |
| Double Creek - Running M | HFER | 632-6121 |
| Elk Creek Outfitters | HRE | 578-2216 |
| Elk Ridge Outfitters | GFHRE | 578-2379 |
| Fish Hawk Outfitting | F | 222-0551 |
| Flying Diamond Guide Service | GE | 222-1748 |
| Greater Yellowstone Flyfishers | F | 838-2468 |
| Hatch Finders Fly Shop | F | 222-0989 |
| Hawley Mountain Guides | HE | 932-5791 |
| Hell's A' Roarin Outfitters | HEF | 848-7578 |
| High Country Outfitters | ERG | 333-4763 |
| Horse Creek Outfitters | EFR | 333-4977 |
| Hubbard's Yellowstone Lodge | F | 848-7755 |
| James Marc Spring Creek Specialist | F | 222-8646 |
| John Greene's Fly Fishing | F | 222-4562 |
| J R Outfitters | H | 932-4452 |
| Johnson Edwin Outfitting | H | 848-7265 |
| Jumping Rainbow Ranch | F | 222-5425 |
| Lazy Heart Horse & Mule | GHFR | 222-7536 |
| Lone Creek Outfitters | HFRG | 222-7155 |
| Long Outfitting | GF | 222-6775 |
| Lost Creek Outfitters | H | 222-1167 |
| Lucky Day Outfitter | HFGRE | 686-4402 |
| Montana Guide Service | FREHG | 848-7265 |
| Montana's Master Angler | HF | 222-2273 |
| Montana Whitewater | R | 848-7398 |
| North Fork Creek Outfitters | HFE | 848-7859 |
| Paradise Valley Planes & Reins | E | 333-4788 |
| Park's Fly Shop | F | 848-7314 |
| Paul Tunkis Flyfishing Guide | F | 222-8480 |
| Pine Mountain Outfitters | GH | 848-7570 |
| Rendevous Outfitters | G | 848-7110 |
| Rising Sun Outfitters | H | 333-4624 |
| Roy Senter | F | 222-3775 |

*Continued next page*

Section 4

| Fishery | Cold Water Species | | | | | | | | | | | | Warm Water Species | | | | | | | | | | Services | | | | | |
|---|---|---|---|---|---|---|---|---|---|---|---|---|---|---|---|---|---|---|---|---|---|---|---|---|---|---|---|---|
| | Brook Trout | Mt. Whitefish | Lake Whitefish | Golden Trout | Cutthroat Trout | Brown Trout | Rainbow Trout | Kokanee Salmon | Bull Trout | Lake Trout | Arctic Grayling | Burbot | Largemouth Bass | Smallmouth Bass | Walleye | Sauger | Northern Pike | Shovelnose Sturgeon | Channel Catfish | Yellow Perch | Crappie | Paddlefish | Vehicle Access | Campgrounds | Toilets | Docks | Boat Ramps | MotorRestrictions |
| 38.Crazy Mountains alpine lakes | • | | | • | • | | • | | | | | | | | | | | | | | | | | | | | | |
| 39. Shields River | | • | | | • | • | • | | | | | | | | | | | | | | | | | | | | | |
| 40. Hyalite Reservoir | | | | | • | | | | | | | | | | | | | | | | | | • | • | • | • | • | • |
| 41. Yellowstone River | | • | | | • | • | • | | | | | • | | | | | | | | | | | • | • | • | | • | • |
| 42. Dailey Lake | | | | | | | • | | | | | | | | • | | | | | • | | | • | • | • | | • | |
| 43. Sixmile Creek | | | | | • | • | | | | | | | | | | | | | | | | | • | | | | | |
| 44. Boulder River | • | • | | | • | • | • | | | | | | | | | | | | | | | | • | • | • | | | |

Rubber Ducky River Services & Shuttles R 222-3746
Shiplet Ranch Outfitters H 686-4696
63 Ranch GHRFE 222-0570
Slip & Slide Ranch GHREF 848-7648
Stevenson's Montana Wild F 222-0341
Story Cattle Co. & Outfitting GFHEF 333-4739
Sun Raven Guide Service F 333-4454
Sweet Cast Angler F 932-4469
Track Outfitter & Guide HG 222-0406
Troutwest HFR 222-8233
Wild West Rafting R 848-2252
Wilderness Connection Inc GHE 848-7287
Wilderness Pack Trips RF 333-9046
Williams Guide Service RF 222-1386
Wine Glass Mountain Trail Rides E 222-5599
Yellowstone Flyfisher F 222-7385
Yellowstone International Fly Fisherman's Lodge F 222-7437
Yellowstone Raft Co R 848-7777
Bear Paw Outfitters GE 222-5800
Big Bear Lodge G 838-2267
Parks' Fly Shop GF 848-7314
Wildlife Outfitters H 848-7675

## Cross-Country Ski Centers

B Bar Guest Ranch • Basin 848-7523

## Snowmobile Rentals

Cooke City Exxon & Polaris/Ski-doo Cooke City 838-2244
Soda Butte Lodge • Cooke City 838-2251
Yellowstone Village Inn • Gardiner 848-7417



## Motel Quick Reference

Price Range: ($) Under $40 ; ($$) $40-$60; ($$$) $60-$80, ($$$$) Over $80. Pets [check with the motel for specific policies] (P), Dining (D), Lounge (L), Disabled Access (DA), Full Breakfast (FB), Cont. Breakfast (CB), Indoor Pool (IP), Outdoor Pool (OP), Hot Tub (HT), Sauna (S), Refrigerator (R), Microwave (M) (Microwave and Refrigerator indicated only if in majority of rooms), Kitchenette (K). All Montana area codes are 406.

| HOTEL | PHONE | NUMBER ROOMS | PRICE RANGE | BREAKFAST | POOL/ HOT TUB SAUNA | NON SMOKE ROOMS | OTHER AMENITIES | CREDIT CARDS | MAP LOCATOR NUMBER |
|---|---|---|---|---|---|---|---|---|---|
| **Carriage House B & B** | 932-5339 | | | | | | | | 2 |
| **Budget Host** | 932-4943 | 22 | $$ | | | Yes | DA/R | Major | 2 |
| **Buckin' Horse Bunkhouse B & B** | 932-6537 | | | | | | | | 2 |
| The Grand Hotel B&B | 932-4459 | 11 | $$$$ | FB | | Yes | P/D/L | V/M/D | 2 |
| Big Timber-Super 8 Motel | 932-8888 | 39 | $$ | | | Yes | P/D/R | Major | 2 |
| Lazy J Motel | 932-5533 | 15 | $ | | | | P | Major | 2 |
| **Livingston Comfort Inn** | 222-4400 | 49 | $$$$ | CB | IP/HT | Yes | M/R/DA | Major | 5 |
| Super 8 Motel | 222-7711 | 36 | $$ | | HT | Yes | DA | Major | 5 |
| The River Inn | 222-2429 | | | | | | | | 5 |
| Paradise Inn Motel | 222-6320 | 43 | $$$ | | IP | Yes | P/D/L/DA | Major | 6 |
| Yellowstone Inn & Conference Center | 222-6110 | 99 | $$/$$$ | | IP | Yes | K/P/D/DA | Major | 6 |
| Budget Host Parkway Motel | 222-3840 | 28 | $$ | | OP | Yes | K/P | Major | 6 |
| Del Mar Motel | 222-3120 | | | | | | | | 6 |
| Econo Lodge | 222-0555 | 50 | $$$$ | CB | IP/HT | Yes | P/M/R/DA | Major | 6 |
| Livingston Inn Motel & Recreational Vehicl | 222-3600 | | | | | | | | 6 |
| Remember When Bed & Breakfast | 222-8367 | | | | | | | | 6 |
| **Murray Hotel** | 222-1350 | 30 | $$-$$$$ | | HT | Yes | K/P/D/R/L | Major | 7 |
| **Rainbow Motel** | 222-3780 | 24 | $$ | | | Yes | P | Major | 7 |
| **Guest House Motel** | 222-1460 | 40 | $ | | | Yes | P/L | Major | 7 |
| Country Motor Inn | 222-1923 | 24 | $$/$$$ | | | Yes | P/DA | Major | 7 |
| Greystone Inn Bed & Breakfast | 222-8319 | | | | | | | | 7 |
| Pine Creek Lodge | 222-3628 | 5 | $$/$$$ | | | | P/D/L/R | Major | 10 |
| Luccock Park Camp & Cabins | 222-3025 | | | | | | | | 11 |
| **Yellowstone Village Inn** | 848-7417 | 43 | $ | CB | IP/S | Yes | K/M/R/DA | Major | 13 |
| **Above The Rest Lodge** | 848-7747 | | | | | | | | 13 |
| **North Yellowstone B & B** | 848-7651 | | | | | | | | 13 |
| **Yellowstone Comfort Inn** | 848-7536 | 80 | $$$/$$$$ | CB | HT | Yes | DA | Major | 13 |
| **Best Western Mammoth Hot Springs** | 848-7311 | 85 | $$/$$$$ | | IP/HT | Yes | K/P/D/M/R/DA | Major | 13 |
| **Jim Bridger Court Cabins** | 848-7371 | 21 | $/$$ | | | | P/D/L | Major | 13 |
| **Yellowstone Basin Inn** | 848-7080 | 13 | $$/$$$$ | CB | HT | Yes | K/M/R/DA | Major | 13 |
| Absaroka Lodge | 848-7414 | 44 | $$/$$$$ | | | Yes | K/P/DA | Major | 13 |
| Super 8 Motel | 848-7401 | 66 | $$$ | CB | IP | | P/DA | Major | 13 |
| **Town Cafe Motel** | 848-7322 | 11 | $/$$$ | FB | | | P/D | V/M/D | 13 |
| **Westernaire Motel** | 848-7397 | 10 | $/$$$ | | | Yes | P | Major | 13 |
| Hillcrest Cottages | 848-7353 | 14 | $$ | | | Yes | | Major | 13 |
| Motel 6 | 848-7520 | 40 | $$$ | | | Yes | | Major | 13 |
| Yellowstone Suites Bed & Breakfast | 848-7937 | | | | | | | | 13 |
| Soda Butte Lodge | 838-2251 | 32 | $$$ | IP/HT | | Yes | D/L/DA | MAjor | 14 |
| Alpine Motel | 838-2262 | 27 | $$$ | | | Yes | K | Major | 14 |
| Elkhorn Lodge | 838-2332 | 8 | $ | | | Yes | P/K | Major | 14 |
| High Country Motel | 838-2272 | 15 | $$ | | | | P/K | Major | 14 |
| Edelweiss Cabins | 838-2332 | | | | | | | | 14 |
| Grizzly Lodge | 838-2219 | 17 | $$ | HT | | Yes | DA/K/P | Major | 14 |
| Silver Gate Cabins | 838-2371 | | | | | | | | 14 |
| Range Riders Lodge | 838-2371 | 18 | $ | | | | L/P | | 14 |

## Dining Quick Reference

Price Range refers to the average cost of a meal per person: ($) $1-$6, ($$) $7-$11, ($$$) $12-up. Cocktails: "Yes" indicates full bar; Beer (B)/Wine (W), Service: Breakfast (B), Brunch (BR), Lunch (L), Dinner (D). Businesses in bold print will have additional information under the appropriate map locator number in the body of this section.

| RESTAURANT | TYPE CUISINE | PRICE RANGE | CHILD MENU | COCKTAILS BEER WINE | SERVICE | CREDIT CARDS | MAP LOCATOR NUMBER |
|---|---|---|---|---|---|---|---|
| **American Legion Post No. 19** | American | $/$$ | | Yes | L/D | | 2 |
| **Timber Bar** | American | $ | | Yes | L/D | | 2 |
| **City Club Lanes & Steakhouse** | Steakhouse | $$/$$$ | | Y | D | All Major | 2 |
| **Frosty Freez** | Family | $ | | | B/L/D | No | 2 |
| Prospector Pizza Plus | Pizza | $ | | B/W | L/D | V/M/D | 2 |
| The Grand Hotel B&B | Fine Dining | $$$ | | Yes | D | V/M/D | 2 |
| Crazy Jane's Conoco | Family | $/$$ | Yes | B/W | B/L/D | Major | 2 |
| Hardee's | fast Food | $ | Yes | | B/L/D | | 5 |
| McDonald's | Fast Food | $ | Yes | | B/L/D | | 5 |
| Subway | Fast Food | $ | Yes | | L/D | | 5 |
| Buffalo Jump Steaks | Steakhouse | $$/$$$ | Yes | Yes | L/D | Major | 5 |
| Crazy Coyote Mexican Food | Mexican | $$ | Yes | | L/D | | 6 |
| Dairy Queen | Fast Food | $ | Yes | | L/D | | 6 |
| Domino's Pizza | Pizza | $ | | | L/D | | 6 |
| Mark's In & Out | Fast Food | $ | Yes | | L/D | | 6 |
| Pizza Hut | Pizza | $/$$ | Yes | B | L/D | V/M/D | 6 |
| The Homemade Cafe | Family | $ | Yes | | B/L | | 6 |
| Paradise Inn Motel | American | $$ | Yes | Yes | B/L/D | Major | 6 |
| **Murray Lounge & Grill** | American | $$ | | Yes | L/D/BR | Major | 7 |
| Beartooth Diner & Bakery | Family | $ | Yes | | B/L | | 7 |
| Coffee Crossing | Coffee/Soup | $ | | | B/L | | 7 |
| Pinky's | Deli | $ | | | B/L | Major | 7 |
| 49er | American | $$ | | Yes | L/D | Major | 7 |
| Java Bean | Coffee house | | | | | | 7 |
| Chatham's Livingston Bar & Grille | Continental | $$$ | Yes | Yes | D | Major | 7 |
| Martin's Cafe | Family | $$ | Yes | | | | 7 |
| Pastime Bar & Grille | Steakhouse | $$ | | Yes | L/D | | 7 |
| Pickle Barrel | Deli | $ | | | L/D | | 7 |
| Pizza Garden | pizza | $$ | | | | | 7 |
| Stockman | Steak | | | | | | 7 |
| T Rumours | Eclectic | $-$$$ | | B/W | B/L/D | Major | 7 |
| Taco John's | Fast Food | $ | Yes | | L/D | | 7 |
| The Sport | American | $$ | Yes | Yes | L/D | V/M/D | 7 |
| Peterson's Spirits & Eatery | Bistro | $$$ | Yes | Yes | D | Major | 7 |
| Sister's Cafe | Cafe | $$ | Yes | | B/L | | 8 |
| Road Kill Cafe | American | $$ | Yes | Yes | L/D | | 8 |
| Rosa's Pizza | Pizza | $ | | | L/D | V/M | 10 |
| Pine Creek Cafe | Family | $$ | Yes | B/W | B/L/D | | 11 |
| Chico Hot Springs | Casual Gourmet | $$/$$$ | Yes | Yes | B/L/D | Major | 12 |
| Livery Stable & Old Saloon | Steakhouse | $–$$$ | Yes | Yes | B/L/D | V/M | 12 |
| Deli Cafe | deli | $ | | | L/D | | 12 |
| **The Yellowstone Mine & Rusty Rail Lounge** | Steaks & Seafood | $–$$$ | Yes | Yes | B/D | Major | 13 |
| **Outlaws Pizza and Casino** | Pizza | $/$$ | | B/W | L/D | Major | 13 |
| **Town Club** | American | $$/$$$ | Yes | Yes | B/L/D | Major | 13 |
| **Four Winds Deli** | Deli | $/$$ | | | B/L | Major | 13 |
| Bear Country Restaurant | American | $$ | Yes | | B/L/D | V/M | 13 |
| Cecil's Restaurant | Family | $/$$ | Yes | B/W | B/L/D | V/M | 13 |
| Corral Drive Inn | Fast Food | $ | | | | | 13 |
| Red's Blue Goose Saloon | Steaks & Barbeque | $–$$$ | Yes | Yes | L/D | Major | 13 |
| Sawtooth Deli | Deli | $/$$ | | B/W | L | | 13 |
| Two Bit Saloon | Regional American | $ | Yes | Yes | B/L/D | Major | 13 |
| Beartooth Cafe | American | $$ | Yes | B/W | L/D | | 14 |
| Big Bear Lodge | American | $$/$$$ | Yes | B/W | B/L/D | Major | 14 |
| Village Market Coffee House | Deli/ Coffee House | $ | | | B/L | | 14 |
| Soda Butte Lodge, Tavern, & Prospector Restaurant | Regional | $$/$$$ | Yes | Yes | B/L/D | Major | 14 |
| Clyde Park Tavern | American | $ | | Yes | L/D | | 15 |
| Stageline Pizza | Pizza | $/$$ | | | L/D | | 15 |
| Wilsall Bar & Cafe | American | $$ | Yes | Yes | B/L/D | V/M | 15 |

## Campsite Directions

| Campsite Directions | Season | Camping | Trailers | Toilets | Water | Boat Launch | Fishing | Swimming | Trails | Stay Limit | Fee |
|---|---|---|---|---|---|---|---|---|---|---|---|
| **32•Half Moon FS**<br>11 mi. N of Big Timber on US 191<15 mi. W on Cty. Rd 25 (Big Timber Canyon Rd.) | All Year | 8 | 22′ | • | • | | • | | • | 16 | |
| **33•Mallard's Rest FWP**<br>13 mi. S of Livingston on US 89 to Milepost 42 | All Year | 20 | • | • | • | B | • | | | 7 | • |
| **34•Pine Creek FS**<br>9 mi. S of Livingston on US 89•6 mi.E on Pine Creek Rd. | 5/26-9/1526 | 26 | 22′ | D | • | | • | | • | 16 | • |
| **35•West Boulder FS**<br>16 mi. S of Big Timber on Rt.298•6.5 mi. SW on Cty. Rd. 30•8 mi. SW on W Boulder Rd. | All Year | 10 | 20′ | • | • | | • | | • | 16 | |
| **36•East Boulder FS**<br>19 mi. S of Big Timber on Rt. 298•6 mi. E on E Boulder Rd. | All Year | 2 | 16′ | • | | | • | | | 16 | |
| **37•Big Beaver FS**<br>25 mi. SW of Big Timber on Rt. 298•8 mi. S on Cty. Rd. 212 | All Year | 5 | 32′ | • | | | • | | | 16 | |
| **38•Falls Creek FS**<br>25 mi. SW of Big Timber on Rt. 298•5 mi. S on Cty. Rd. 212 | All Year | 8 | | • | • | | • | | | 16 | |
| **39•Aspen FS**<br>25 mi. SW of Big Timber on Rt. 298•8.5 mi. S on Cty. Rd. 212 | All Year | 8 | 32′ | D | • | | • | | | 16 | |
| **40•Loch Leven FWP**<br>9 mi. S of Livingston on US 89 to Milepost 44•2 mi. E•4 mi. S on Rt. 540 | All Year | 30 | • | • | • | C | • | | | 7 | • |
| **41•Dailey Lake FWP**<br>1 mi. E of Emigrant•4 mi. S on Rt. 540•6 mi. SE on Cty. Rd. | All Year | 35 | • | • | • | C | • | | | 7 | |
| **42•Carbella BLM**<br>20 mi. N of Gardiner on US 89•1 mil. W at Miner•Primitive | All Year | 5 | 35′ | • | | B | • | | | 14 | |
| **43•Yankee Jim Canyon FS**<br>18 mi. N of Gardiner on US 89 | All Year | 12 | 48′ | • | | | | | | 16 | |
| **44•Snow Bank FS**<br>15 mi. S of Livingston on US 89•13 mi. SE on Mill Creek Rd. (Forest Rd. 486) | 5/26-9/15 | 11 | 22′ | • | • | | • | | • | 16 | • |
| **45•Hells Canyon FS**<br>25 mi. SW of Big Timber on Rt. 298•15.5 Mi. S on Cty Rd. 212 | All Year | 11 | 16′ | • | | | • | | • | 16 | |
| **46•Hicks Park FS**<br>25 mi. SW of Big Timber on Rt. 298•21 mi. S on Cty. Rd. 212 | All Year | 16 | 32′ | D | • | | • | | 0 | 16 | |
| **47•Chippy Park FS**<br>25 mi. SW of Big Timber on Rt. 298•9.5 mi. S on Cty Rd. 212 | All Year | 7 | 32′ | D | • | | • | | | 16 | |
| **48•Soda Butte FS**<br>1 mi. E of Cooke City on US 212 | 7/1-9/15 | 21 | 22′ | • | • | | • | | | 16 | • |
| **49•Colter FS**<br>2 mi. E of Cooke City on US 212 | 7/15-9/15 | 23 | 48′ | • | • | | • | | • | 16 | • |
| **50•Chief Joseph FS**<br>4 mi. E of Cooke City on US 212 | 7/1-9/30 | 6 | 20′ | • | • | | | • | • | 16 | • |
| **51•Eagle Creek FS**<br>2 mi. NE of Gardiner on Jardine Rd. | All Year | 12 | 30′ | D | • | | | | | 16 | |
| **52•Tom Miner FS**<br>20 mi. N of Gardiner on US 89•12 mi. SW on Tom Miner Rd. (Forest Rd. 63)<br>•4 mi. SW on Forest Rd. 63 | 6/1-9/30 | 16 | 22′ | • | • | | | | • | 16 | • |
| **53•Fairy Lake FS**<br>22 mi. N of Bozeman on MT 86•5 mi. W on Fairy Lake Rd. | 7/15-9/15 | 9 | | D | • | | • | • | | 16 | |
| **54•Battle Ridge FS**<br>22 mi. NE of Bozeman on MT 86 | 6/10-9/30 | 13 | 16′ | D | • | | | | | 16 | |

**Agency**
FS—U.S.D.A Forest Service
FWP—Montana Fish, Wildlife & Parks
NPS—National Park Service
BLM—U.S. Bureau of Land Management
USBR—U.S. Bureau of Reclamation
CE—Corps of Engineers

**Camping**
Camping is allowed at this site. Number indicates camping spaces available
H—Hard sided units only; no tents

**Trailers**
Trailer units allowed. Number indicates maximum length.

**Toilets**
Toilets on site. D—Disabled access

**Water**
Drinkable water on site

**Fishing**
Visitors may fish on site

**Boat**
Type of boat ramp on site:
A—Hand launch
B—4-wheel drive with trailer
C—2-wheel drive with trailer

**Swimming**
Designated swimming areas on site

**Trails**
Trails on site
B—Backpacking N—Nature/Interpretive

**Stay Limit**
Maximum length of stay in days

**Fee**
Camping and/or day-use fee

# SECTION 5

## GALLATIN RIVER CANYON AND MADISON RIVER VALLEY
## INCLUDING BOZEMAN, BIG SKY, ENNIS, THREE FORKS AND WEST YELLOWSTONE

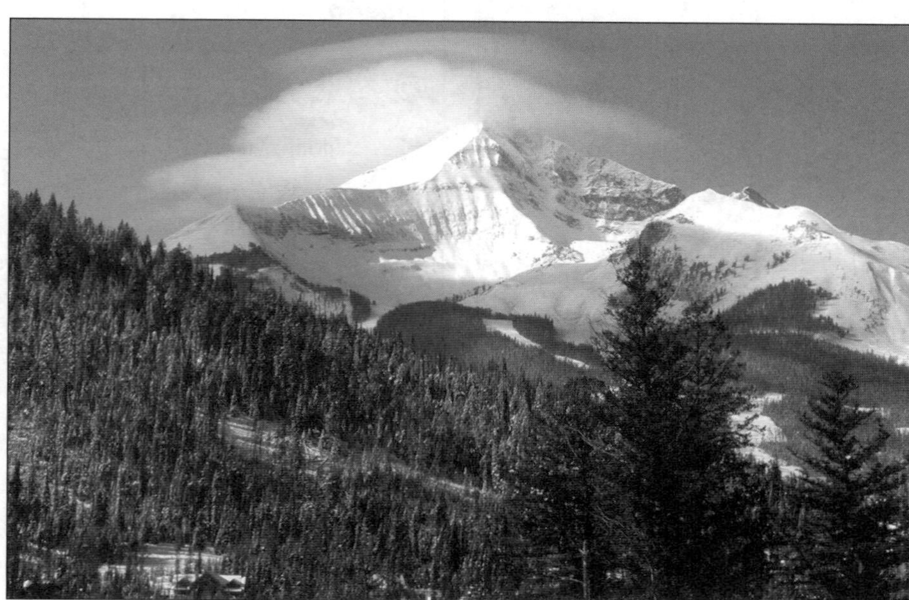

*Majestic Lone Mountain towers over the Big Sky area.*

### WEATHER AVERAGES

**Bozeman**

**January**

| | |
|---|---|
| Average High: | 29.0° F |
| Average Low: | 5.3° F |
| Average Precip.: | 0.63 in |

**April**

| | |
|---|---|
| Average High: | 54.3° F |
| Average Low: | 28.7° F |
| Average Precip.: | 1.26 in |

**July**

| | |
|---|---|
| Average High: | 83.9° F |
| Average Low: | 48.9° F |
| Average Precip.: | 1.15 in |

**October**

| | |
|---|---|
| Average High: | 58.5° F |
| Average Low: | 29.5° F |
| Average Precip.: | 1.10 in |

**Bridger Bowl**

**January**

| | |
|---|---|
| Average High: | 31.4° F |
| Average Low: | 11.6° F |
| Average Precip.: | 0.88 in |

**April**

| | |
|---|---|
| Average High: | 53.9° F |
| Average Low: | 30.6° F |
| Average Precip.: | 1.84 in |

**July**

| | |
|---|---|
| Average High: | 81.5° F |
| Average Low: | 51.6° F |
| Average Precip.: | 1.39 in |

**October**

| | |
|---|---|
| Average High: | 58.2° F |
| Average Low: | 33.1° F |
| Average Precip.: | 1.54 in |

**Big Sky**

**January**

| | |
|---|---|
| Average High: | 34.3° F |
| Average Low: | 17.6° F |
| Average Precip.: | 0.38 in |

**April**

| | |
|---|---|
| Average High: | 55.7° F |
| Average Low: | 33.2° F |
| Average Precip.: | 1.08 in |

**July**

| | |
|---|---|
| Average High: | 84.9° F |
| Average Low: | 54.4° F |
| Average Precip.: | 1.29 in |

**October**

| | |
|---|---|
| Average High: | 60.3° F |
| Average Low: | 37.3° F |
| Average Precip.: | 0.88 in |

**West Yellowstone**

**January**

| | |
|---|---|
| Average High: | 24.1° F |
| Average Low: | -0.6° F |
| Average Precip.: | 2.13 in |

**April**

| | |
|---|---|
| Average High: | 47.7° F |
| Average Low: | 19.8° F |
| Average Precip.: | 1.52 in |

**July**

| | |
|---|---|
| Average High: | 79.2° F |
| Average Low: | 39.6° F |
| Average Precip.: | 1.49 in |

**October**

| | |
|---|---|
| Average High: | 52.5° F |
| Average Low: | 22.1° F |
| Average Precip.: | 1.52 in |

**1.** *Historic Marker, Gas, Food, Lodging, Camping*

### Bozeman

Bozeman is nestled in the midst of the pristine jewel of the Rockies, the Gallatin Valley. Located in the "Heart of Yellowstone Country" just 90 miles north of Yellowstone National Park, Bozeman is sophisticated, yet down to earth. It is happily isolated in the open and beautiful "Valley of the Flowers," as early Native Americans named it, yet remains almost entirely surrounded by the Rockies. The Bridger Mountains rise ruggedly on the east, the Tobacco Roots to the west, the Big Belts to the north and the Spanish Peaks and Gallatin Range to the south.

Bozeman was named after John Bozeman, who blazed a trail across Wyoming and in 1864 guided the first train of immigrants into the Gallatin Valley. When the first wagon train made its way through the canyon, frontiersman Jim Bridger was leading the way, thus the canyon, mountain range, and area trails now bear his name.

The area of Bozeman is brimming with adventure and an abundance of outdoor recreational possibilities, one of the most popular being fly fishing. The rivers, streams, and lakes in the region provide some of the finest fly fishing in the world with a backdrop of spectacular scenery. Over 2,000 miles of blue-ribbon trout streams weave through this sportsman's paradise, while golf courses, first-class tennis courts, indoor and outdoor pools and hot springs make Bozeman a city of diverse recreational opportunities. Just minutes away is the Bridger Bowl ski area featuring 1,200 acres inside the Gallatin National Forest. Ski the well groomed slopes of 50 different runs.

The Yellowstone, Gallatin, and Madison rivers provide excellent rafting and kayaking for whitewater enthusiasts travelling to the Bozeman area, while the Gallatin National Forest is a wonderful place for nature or pleasure hikes.

Bozeman is an exceptional town offering many opportunities for recreational experiences, while retaining its flavor as a thriving arts and culture community. Here culture and entertainment are as abundant as the blue sky. Bozeman uniquely combines the classic Old West with the comforts and amenities of the new. Bozeman boasts art galleries, historic museums, symphony,and the state's only opera company. It is also home to the main campus of Montana State University, the Museum of the Rockies, and Compuseum.

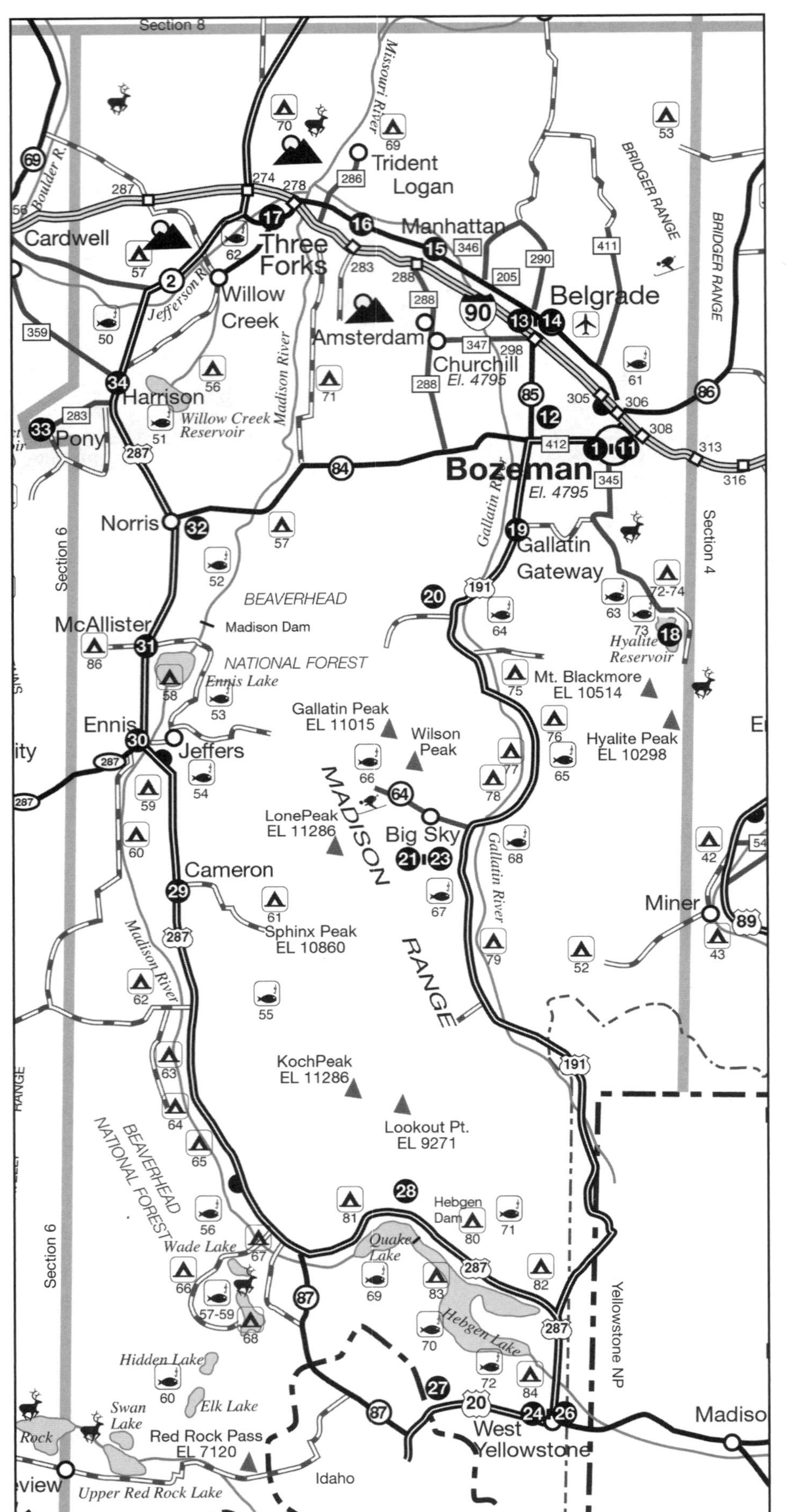


# SECTION 5

0 Miles 11 20
One inch = approximately 11 miles

**Legend**

- Locator number (matches numeric listing in section)
- Wildlife viewing
- Campsite (number matches number in campsite chart)
- State Park
- Fishing Site (number matches number in fishing chart)
- Rest stop
- Interstate
- U.S. Highway
- State Highway
- County Road
- Gravel/unpaved road

## On The Trail of Lewis & Clark

**Clark's advance party had reached** the Three Forks of the Missouri on July 25. They saw the prairie had recently been burned, and there were horse tracks which appeared to be only a few days old. Clark left a note for Lewis telling him he was going to continue on in search of the Shoshones; if he didn't find them he would return to the Three Forks.

The main party arrived at the Three Forks on July 27, making camp where Clark had left the note. Lewis ascended a prominent rock bluff to view the area which he believed "to be an essential point in the ge-ography of this western part of the Continent."

The officers named the east fork of the Three Forks in honor of Treasury Secretary, Albert Gallatin, the south fork in honor of Secretary of State James Madison, and the west fork in honor of President Jefferson.

On their westward journey the band camped near here for two days for rest and repairs and heard Sacajawea tell of her abduction by Hidatsa raiders five years earlier as her band of Shoshone camped at the same spot.

On the return trip Clark's party separated at the Three Forks. Sergeant John Ordway and nine men continued down the Missouri with the dugouts. Clark and the rest of the party headed east along Gallatin River on to explore the Yellowstone River. Clark crossed Clark's Pass (the current Bozeman Pass), and hit the Yellowstone near present-day Livingston.

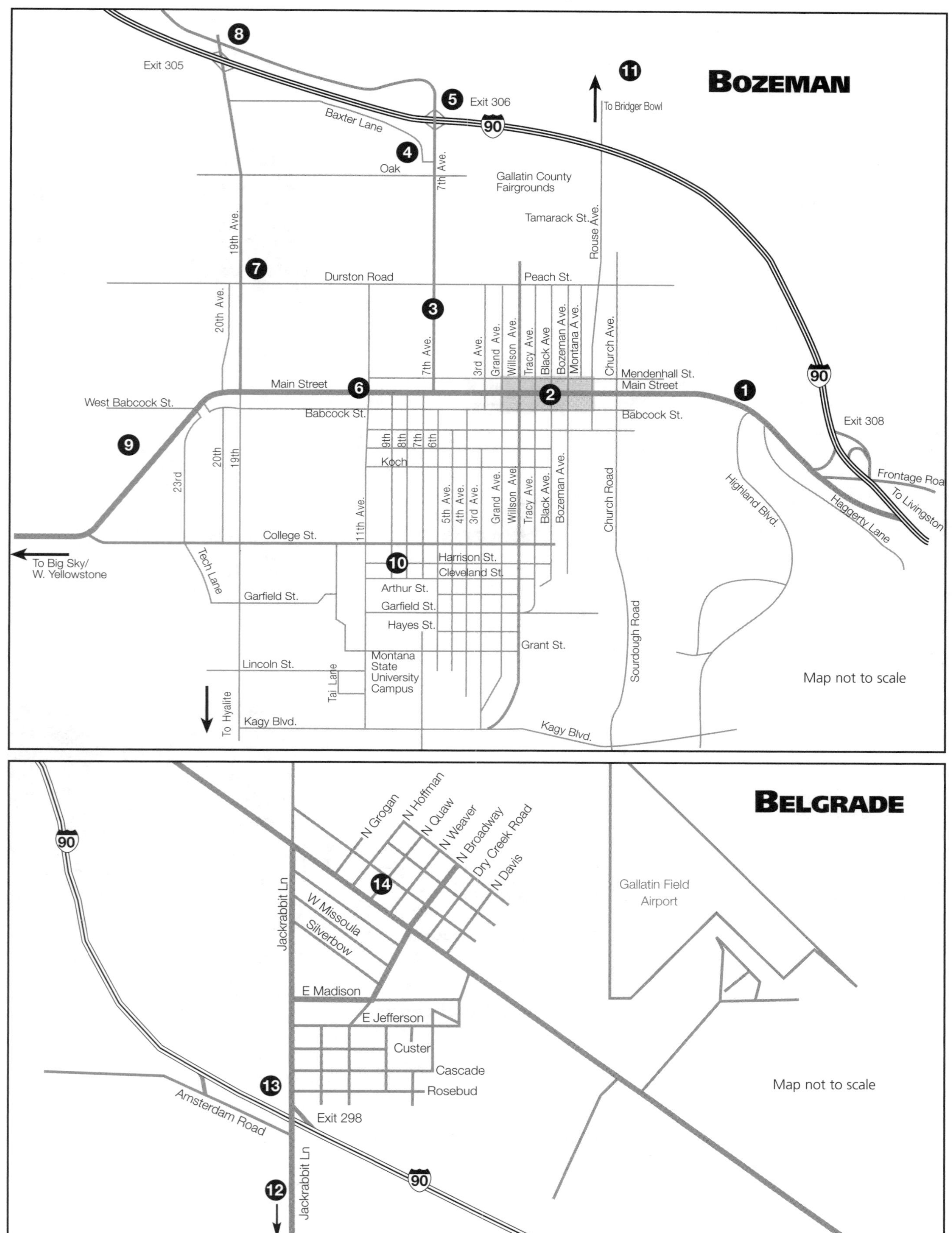

Bozeman
Exit 305
Exit 306
90
To Bridger Bowl
Baxter Lane
Oak
7th Ave.
Gallatin County Fairgrounds
Tamarack St.
Rouse Ave.
19th Ave.
Durston Road
Peach St.
20th Ave.
7th Ave.
3rd Ave.
Grand Ave.
Willson Ave.
Tracy Ave.
Black Ave
Bozeman Ave.
Montana Ave.
Church Ave.
Mendenhall St.
Main Street
Main Street
West Babcock St.
Babcock St.
Babcock St.
Exit 308
9th
8th
7th
6th
Koch
23rd
20th
19th
Frontage Road
To Livingston
Haggerty Lane
Highland Blvd.
11th Ave.
5th Ave.
4th Ave.
3rd Ave.
Grand Ave.
Willson Ave
Tracy Ave.
Black Ave.
Bozeman Ave.
Church Road
College St.
To Big Sky/ W. Yellowstone
Tech Lane
Harrison St.
Cleveland St.
Garfield St.
Arthur St.
Garfield St.
Hayes St.
Grant St.
Sourdough Road
Lincoln St.
Tai Lane
Montana State University Campus
To Hyalite
Kagy Blvd.
Kagy Blvd.
Map not to scale
Belgrade
90
N Grogan
N Hoffman
N Quaw
N Weaver
N Broadway
Dry Creek Road
N Davis
Jackrabbit Ln
W Missoula
Silverbow
Gallatin Field Airport
E Madison
E Jefferson
Custer
Cascade
Rosebud
Amsterdam Road
Exit 298
Jackrabbit Ln
90
Map not to scale


Section 5

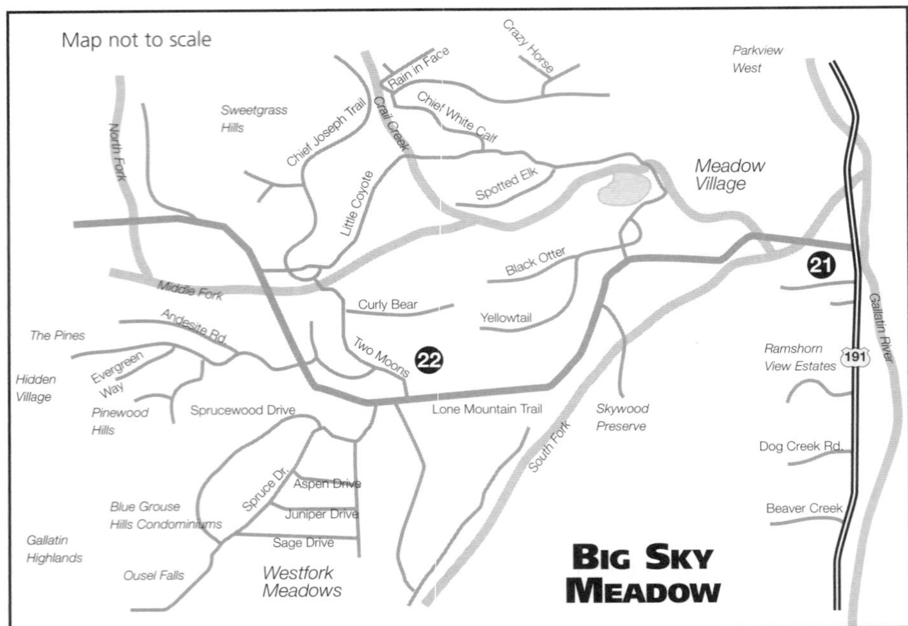


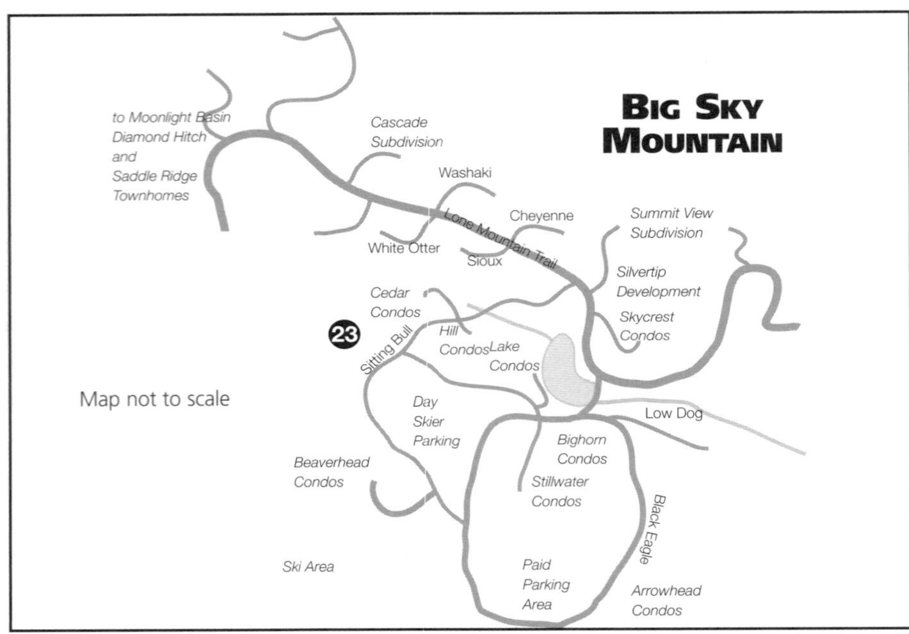






## H Gallatin Valley

Hwy 10, east of Bozeman

*Captain Wm. Clark, of the Lewis and Clark Expedition, with a party of ten men, passed through this valley July 14, 1806, eastward bound, and guided by the Shoshone woman, Sacajawea. They camped that night at the toe of the mountains on the eastern edge of the valley. Captain Clark wrote in his journal: "I saw Elk, deer and Antelopes, and great deel of old signs of buffalow. their roads is in every direction…emence quantities of beaver on this Fork … and their dams very much impeed the navigation of it."*

*In the early 1860s John Bozeman, young adventurer, and Jim Bridger, grand old man of the mountains, guided rival wagon trains of emigrants and gold-seekers through here over the variously called Bonanza Trail, Bridger Cutoff, or Bozeman Road, from Fort Laramie, Wyo., to Virginia City, Mont. The trail crossed Indian country in direct violation of treaty and was a "cut off" used by impatient pioneers who considered the time saving worth the danger. Traffic was not congested.*

## F East Side Diner

1104 East Main, Bozeman. 585-0124

## C Sunrise Campground

31842 Frontage Rd., Bozeman. 587-4797

## 2. *Attraction, Gas, Food, Lodging, Shopping*

## T Emerson Cultural Center

111 S. Grand Ave., Bozeman. 587-9797

The Emerson Cultural Center is home to many visual and performing arts as well as galleries that rotate exhibits of contemporary, Native American and local artists' work. Art related activities are sponsored through this community center.

## T Bogert Park and City Pool

300 block of S. Church St. in Bozeman. 587-4724

If you want to cool off in an outdoor pool and enjoy a picnic in a nice shady park, this is a great place. On Saturday mornings beginning in July, the Farmer's Market fills the grounds. This is one of the largest and most popular farmer's markets in the state. Only items grown or made by the seller can be sold here, with lots of fresh flowers, fruits and vegetables, as well as baked goods and handmade crafts and clothing.

## T Gallatin County Pioneer Museum

317 W. Main St. next to the courthouse in Bozeman. 582-3195

Located amidst the town of Bozeman is the Gallatin County Pioneer Museum which includes a former county jail, jailhouse isolation chambers, an actual gallows, a 12' x 14' hand-hewn log cabin, and various artifacts and exhibits that bring to life the county's colorful history. The museum is open year round and admission is free.

## T South Willson Historic District

Willson St., Bozeman. 586-5421

The drive on Willson St. from the downtown area of Bozeman south takes you through a residential district featuring houses that range from large mansions to small cottages, all preserved and maintained in the style they were originally constructed.

## T Compuseum - American Computer Museum

234 E. Babcock, Downtown Bozeman. 587-7545.
www.compuseum.org

Over 4,000 years of the history of computing and computers on display. See the story of mechanical calculators, slide rules, typewriters & office appliances, room-sized mainframe computers, an original Apollo Spacecraft Guidance Computer & astronaut items, the story of the Personal Computer, a working industrial robot and the computer pioneer timeline. Only one of two museums of its type in the world. As seen in The New Yorker Magazine and The New York Times! The ideal family destination, no computer background needed to enjoy! See sidebar.

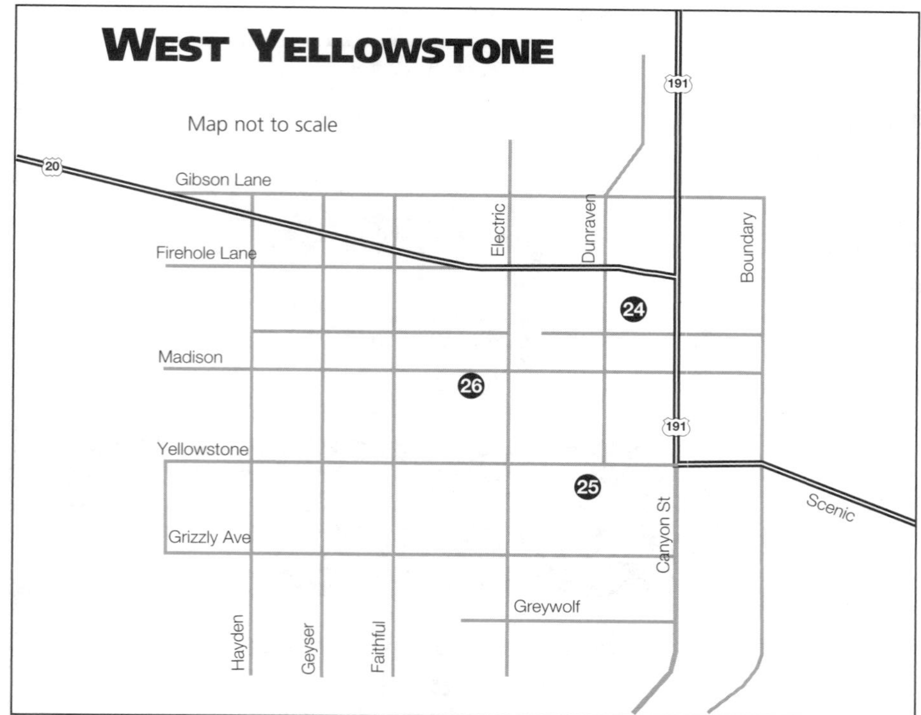

## F Montana Ale Works

611 E. Main, Bozeman. 587-7700

Here you will find creative fine dining, traditional Pub fare, 42 brews on tap, billiards, snooker, and gaming room all located in the beautifully restored Little Montana Transport building on Bozeman's Happenin' east end. You will find Bozeman's only fully non-smoking gaming and dining establishment created by the same great people who brought MacKenzie River Pizza to Montana. Casual fine dining, casual good fun!

## F Boodles

215 E. Main, Historic Downtown Bozeman. 587-2901

Boodles is a favorite dining destination in Historic Downtown Bozeman. Be sure and plan to enjoy their Regional American Cuisine. Their menu consists of hand cut steaks, fresh seafood, wild game and pasta. Compliment your meal with their offerings from a full service bar and extensive wine list. Their wine list has received the Wine Spectator's Award of Excellence. Boodles' atmosphere is casual and the service is attentive. They provide a non-smoking atmosphere until 10 p.m. Enjoy lunch Mon. through Sat. Dinner is offered seven nights a week and the bar is open nightly until 2 a.m. Reservations are suggested at Boodles.

## F MacKenzie River Pizza Co.

232 E. Main, in Historic Downtown Bozeman. 587-0055 See photo in previous column.

Famous for gourmet pizzas, super sandwiches and extraordinary salads, everything is made fresh daily right down to the salad dressings and the pizza dough! Established in 1993 and located in historic downtown Bozeman, this is the original store that launched the spread across the state.

## F John Bozeman's Bistro

125 W. Main, Downtown Bozeman. 587-4100

"The Bistro" is renowned for legendary cooking in Downtown Bozeman for over seventeen years. It's no secret that this is a local favorite for it's warm inviting atmosphere and eclectic menu. Chef/Owner Tyler Hill loves to cook and everyone who has dined there knows it! If you are hungry for a traditional meal or something refreshing and different this is where you'll find it. Enjoy a menu that offers selections of fresh fish, steaks, pasta, sushi, wild game or Southeast Asian. To accompany your meal they offer an assortment of beers from Montana microbrews or wines from an extensive list. Open for lunch and dinner Tuesday through Saturday. Reservations accepted.

## F O'Brien's

312 E. Main, Historic Downtown Bozeman. 587-3973

A long time mainstay in Downtown Bozeman this popular restaurant is open for breakfast, lunch, and dinner. Owned and operated by award winning chefs, Carolyne and David Mumford, featured in Gourmet Magazine. Menu items such as exquisite fresh baked pastries, made-from-scratch pancakes, waffles and french toast are a breakfast gourmet's delight, and offered through 2 p.m. For lunch, select from unique daily specials offered along with their time tested standards. For dinner, choose from items such as succulent filet mignon, savory crabcakes, and flavorful vegetarian dishes to name a few. Complement your meal with selections from their offerings of beer and wine and heavenly desserts. Open seven days a week and reservations are recommended.

### *Montana Trivia*

The nation's longest river begins in this part of Montana. The Gallatin, Madison, and Jefferson Rivers meet near Three Forks as the headwaters of the Missouri River.

### F Leaf & Bean

35 W. Main, Historic Downtown Bozeman.
587-1580.

Bozeman's original coffee house was established in 1977 and continues to be a favorite meeting place for locals and out-of-towners alike. Freshly air-roasted coffee and gourmet espresso drinks, exotic teas, pastries that are baked in-house all day long, and superior service make this wonderful place addictive. In the Bean's authentic coffee house atmosphere you can surround yourself with original art from local studios, and enjoy live entertainment several nights a week. It's a Bozeman tradition. Open early seven days a week for people on the go.

**Montana Trivia**

Famous newscaster, Chet Huntley, was the driving force behind the construction of the Big Sky Ski Resort. He was born in Cardwell, Montana and died only three days before the grand opening of the resort.

### F Spanish Peaks Brewing Co.

Corner of Main & Church, Downtown Bozeman.
585-2296 or 800-810-2484
www.spanishpeaks.com

Home of the award-winning Black Dog Ale, now open at their new downtown location, serving a distinct Italian menu in a casual atmosphere. Their traditional selections include brick oven pizza, fresh pasta, seafood, and family-style Italian dinners. Compliment your meal with selections from their own Spanish Peaks signature brand of ales, lagers, ciders, and cigars, or choose from their full bar offering fine wines, spirits, and specialty coffees. Enjoy dinner for two or bring a large group to the balcony banquet area. Always a smoke-free atmosphere and open daily for lunch, dinner, and late night cocktails. Don't forget to pick up a copy of their mail order catalog, and as always: No Whiners!

**Montana Trivia**

World famous paleontologist Jack Horner, who served as character model and technical advisor for the *Jurassic Park* series, struggled in school with dyslexia. He found his first dinosaur bone at the age of seven.

### F Burger Bob's

39 W. Main, Downtown Bozeman. 585-0080

You'll find the locals eating here day and night for good reason. They serve gourmet hamburgers with fresh-daily Montana beef and cooked to order. This restaurant, opens at 11:00 a.m. every day of the week and also provides such scrumptious delights as grilled chicken, tuna steaks, chicken strips, sirloin steak, hot dogs and Polish sausages, and much more. Burger Bob's is located in the heart of downtown Bozeman. Burger Bob's

American Computer Museum

# Compuseum

American Computer Museum

## The national museum of communications, computers & the Internet

Experience this award winning museum as seen in the *New Yorker Magazine, the New York Times, USA Today, C-Span, AAA Tour Book*… Join thousands of visitors from 50 states and over 30 countries that have already visited us! Make sense of the modern Information Age by viewing its history. The ideal family destination! Be you a technology novice or techie fanatic

**See the information highway…**

**when it was a dirt road!**

234 East Babcock Street • Downtown Bozeman, MT 59715
www.compuseum.org Tel: (406) 587-7545

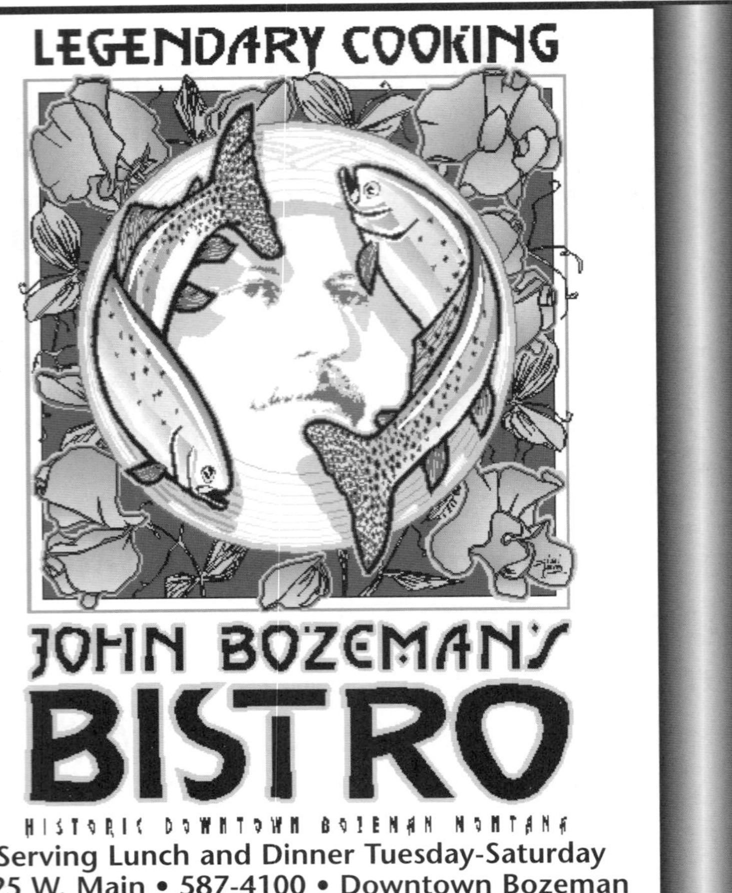




takes pride in the fact that they sell more fresh Wheat Montana Hamburger Buns than anyone in the world. Come in for the best burger around and say and say "Hi" to Bob!

**F The Point After**
15 N. Rouse, Bozeman Hotel, Bozeman. 587-7982

The Point After is the Bobcat Bar and Grill! They offer Phil Schneider's famous fantastic food, great drinks, several big screen TV's for your favorite sports event and banquet facilities for up to forty-five people. Enjoy checking our their extensive collection of Bobcat memorabilia. Satisfy your appetite from a menu loaded with appetizers, salads, sandwiches, pasta dishes, or steak, shrimp and chicken entrees. The Point After is a local favorite and a memorable Bozeman stop if you are passing through. They are open at 11:30 a.m. daily and serve lunch and dinner seven days a week. In the historical Bozeman Hotel at the corner of E. Main and Rouse. Go Cats!

**F Pickle Barrel**
209 E. Main, Downtown Bozeman. 582-0020

**F Soby's Mexican/American Restaurant**
321 E. Main, in the Historic Bozeman Hotel, Bozeman. 587-8857

**F Western Cafe**
443 E. Main St., Bozeman. 587-0436

**L Best Western City Center**
507 W. Main at west end of downtown Bozeman. 587-3158 or 800-870-3661

The Best Western City Center is a short walk from Downtown Bozeman and easy access to all area attractions. You will enjoy their 64 beautifully decorated extra large rooms that feature only queen and king size beds for quiet restful sleep. Additionally, they offer a guest fitness center, convention facilities, and adjacent restaurant and casino. Family dining is available at 4B's, a "Montana Tradition", just next door. After a busy day you can relax and enjoy their newly remodeled indoor pool and Jacuzzi. Lodging at the Best Western City Center offers everything you need to feel totally refreshed and ready for another day of adventure, fun, or business.

### L Mountain Home-Montana Vacation Rentals

104 E. Main, Suite 209, Bozeman. 586-4589 or toll free at 800-550-4589. www.mountain-home.com or email: info@mountain-home.com

Did you know that vacationing at a home or cabin can be as affordable, if not less expensive, than staying at a motel? Plus you get all of the comfort & privacy, not to mention great views, of a Montana home. Cozy mountain cabins, beautiful ranch lodges and downtown Bozeman homes. Mountain Home has them all. With over 40 carefully screened, high quality properties throughout southwest Montana, you'll experience first class service, recommendations for activities, and much more. Homes are complete with linens, fully equipped kitchens and include complimentary housekeeping. Call or check out their website for full details. You'll be surprised!

### L Bozeman Cottage Vacation Rentals

Homes in and around Bozeman. 580-3223 or toll free at 888-415-9837. info@bozemancottage.com. www.bozemancottage.com

### S Montana Gift Corral

237 E. Main, in Historic Downtown Bozeman. 585-8625 or 800-242-5055 www.giftcorral.com

The Montana Gift Corral offers sensational products by talented and creative artists. They bring you the best of Montana. Many of the outstanding craftsmen represented live right here in the Gallatin Valley, sharing the friendly western lifestyle the area is known for. Enjoy a complimentary cup of coffee and convenient parking behind the store. The helpful staff at this special store invites you to visit the home of breathtaking scenery, rodeos, magnificent wildlife, world famous trout streams, ski resorts, and museums. They are also located at Gallatin Field Airport offering the same prices or visit them on the web.

### S Barrel Mountaineering

240 E. Main, Downtown Bozeman. 585-1335. www.barrelmountaineering.com

Barrel Mountaineering is widely known for featuring the best in climbing equipment, backpacking supplies, telemark gear and functional outdoor apparel. The store was founded on technical, yet personalized, customer service. They feature the best selection of outdoor equipment for any mountain endeavor from Patagonia, Kavu, Marmot, Mountain Hardwear, and Arc'Teryx. Barrel celebrates mountaineering's rich heritage, while promoting the future of climbing, backpacking, telemark skiing, and the outdoor lifestyle.

Local customers recognize Barrel Mountaineering for the best gear, genuine expertise, no attitude, and experienced, helpful staff. They are open seven days a week. Give them a call or surf to www.barrelmountaineering.com.

#### Montana Trivia

The Bozeman based Vigilante Theater Company once toured with an original musical revue called *FTV: The Fishing Channel*. It was based on a twenty-four-hour channel devoted to fishing.



Section 5

## S Chaparral Fine Art

24 West Main St., Downtown, Bozeman. 585-0029. www.chaparralfineart.com

Chaparral Fine Art, located on Bozeman's historic Main Street since 1994, is widely regarded as one of Montana's preeminent collections of fine art. The gallery represents works by renowned Western artists and emerging young talents, including; Lorenzo Chavez, Beth Loftin, Taylor Lynde, Robert Moore, Richard Murray, Sherry Sander, and Jeff Walker. Chaparral Fine Art is famous for innovative exhibition programs. The annual Masters in Montana invitational gathers artists from around the country to create work on location in the beautiful Gallatin Valley and the Plein Air Exchange sends artists around the globe to paint in the world's most magnificent cultural centers. Worth a visit!

## S Gem Gallery

402 E. Main, Downtown Bozeman. 587-9330 or fax 587-9320, toll free 800-856-3709

The Gem Gallery is a unique jewelry store, offering everything from repair services to in-house custom gem-cutting. Their gem selection features Montana's best sapphires, with colors ranging from the rainbow hues found in western Montana, to the cornflower blue of the famous Montana Yogo Sapphires. They offer an impressive collection of the very rare, larger Yogos, along with exceptional-quality Antwerp diamonds and Burmese rubies. The Gem Gallery is proud of their award-winning goldsmiths, who encourage their customers to bring in their own designs, and work with them to create a truly custom piece in gold or platinum. Stop in and browse, and take advantage of their personal, professional service, as well as the jelly beans.

## S T. Charbonneau's

402 E. Main, Downtown Bozeman. 587-9198

Established in 1990, T. Charbonneau's was conceived as retail store reflecting Montana's Rustic Heritage. Charbonneau was the trapper, trader, translator, and significant other of Sacajawea, on the Lewis and Clark Expedition. With this rich history in mind the store emulates those earlier days with wood floors, chinked walls and river rock fireplaces. T. Charbonneau's staff will warmly welcome you with a wonderful collection of updated clothing, leathers, accessories, jewelry, furniture, home accents, and gifts with Montana tradition in mind. Find them at the corner of East Main and Rouse with convenient parking adjacent to the building.

### Montana Trivia

Producers of the 1993 film *Josh and S.A.M.* chose Montana as a main location because they wanted a single state that could look like seven different states.

## Montana Ballet

**In the late 70s and early 80s ballet** wasnt taken very seriously in Montana. Ann Bates, Artistic Director of Montana Ballet, appealed to state legislators for a portion of the state coal-tax arts money to no avail. She finally persuaded Rep. Francis Bardanouve that it was unfair to ignore dance while supporting other arts. Lawmakers subsequently awarded her a $10,000 grant. She sent the venerable Bardanouve a tutu which he gamely wore on his head.

Today Montana Ballet is the only small dance company in the rural west with big company goals: 1) To educate the youth of the Gallatin Valley in dance at the professional level; 2) To present a season of international dance companies, world-known ballet stars, and local talent of amazingly high caliber; and 3) To offer a variety of outreach opportunities to schools as far as 100 miles away from Bozeman.

Comments about productions reflect astonishment that the Bozeman area could be the home to a ballet company equal to comparable companies in much larger communities.

The motivation for this excellence stems from the pride Montana Ballet staff and Board of Directors take in making art that surprises and delights. Visiting companies for each Fall's international performance have included *Woofa* from New Guinea, *Tangokinesis* from Buenos Aires, *Jose Greco* from Madrid, and the *Dance Masters of Bali*.

The full season of Montana Ballet Company's performances also includes the much-anticipated and usually sold-out holiday *Nutcracker* extravaganza presented the first weekend of every December, coinciding with Bozeman's Christmas Stroll. Another favorite of the community is the *New York Connection* production presented as part of the two-week New York Connection workshop offered each August in association with Montana State University's College of Arts and Architecture. Professional dance teachers offer classes in a variety of subjects and join the dancers in the two culminating productions performing works by Balanchine as well as classical repertoire.

More information about Montana Ballet Company and its affiliate, the privately-owned Montana Ballet School, is available at www.montanaballet.com.

# COMPUSEUM

**See the information highway when it** was a dirt road! Here at the American Computer Museum in Bozeman, the Compuseum will show you the most comprehensive display of the history of the information age. From the ancient cave paintings of southern France to the ideologies of the Enlightenment, the knowledge based American Revolution to the explorations of Lewis & Clark, the Pony Express, the telegraph, the telephone, radio, television, computers and the Internet are interwoven and presented in a 30,000 year timeline with thousands of historic artifacts and supporting materials.

Visitors from all 50 states and over 30 countries have marveled at the vast scope of the Compuseum's collection ranging from 4,400 year old Babylonian Clay tablets through an original copy of Sir Isaac Newton's revolutionary book, Principia (the foundation of physics) to rare documents from American and world-wide contributors to the rise of the Information Age including signed documents by Thomas Jefferson, James Madison, Alexander Graham Bell, Samuel Morse, Ada Lovelace, Claude Shannon with original first editions of books by Charles Babbage, John Von Neuman, etc. to spectacular exhibits of antique office equipment and furniture including typewriters, cash registers, time pieces, slide rules, adding machines on through the enormous room-sized computers of the 1940s through the 1970s.

The stories of radio, television, the transistor, the microprocessor and other important inventions are showcased with world-class artifacts including an original Apollo Moon Mission Guidance Computer, a piece of the ENIAC computer and the first generations of the personal computer including the Altair, Apple I, the IBM PC, the first portable computers and hundreds of hand-held electronic calculators including the prototype of the very first one!

The best part of the Compuseum is that those visitors with little if any computer background have left extremely positive comments regarding their ability to, for the first time, understand the computer revolution. Individuals with backgrounds and interests spanning antiques, human history, the story of writing and mathematics, philosophy and the arts have found the Compuseum equally as engaging as those particularly interested in the history and evolution of science and technology. Those who are fascinated with technology: computer and communications specialists and professional historians of science and technology have been impressed with the depth of the Compuseum's historic coverage. Children as well as adults enjoy the hands-on opportunities to try for themselves some early devices including typewriters, adding machines, slide rules and early games in the Compuseum is interactive area.

The Compuseum has been written about in quality media outlets such as, The New Yorker Magazine, The New York Times, USA Today, The Los Angeles Times, QST Magazine, PC Week Magazine, National Public Radio, C-Span and national network television.

The Compuseum is located at the American Computer Museum building at 234 East Babcock Street in Downtown Bozeman, one block from Main Street. There is plenty of free parking available. The admission fee is $3 per adult (13 yrs. and older), $2 per child (6 to 12 yrs.) and free for children under 6.

Hours: September through May: Tuesdays, Wednesdays, Fridays and Saturdays, Noon-4 p.m. June, July & August: 9 a.m. to 5 p.m., 7 days a week. Closed July 4th, Christmas and New Year's Days.

## S Miller's Jewelry

2 E. Main, Downtown Bozeman. 586-9547 or toll free 800-946-9547

Miller's Jewelry is a landmark in the heart of Bozeman's downtown. This is a unique jewelry store that was established in 1892. They have continued to offer many well known brands and styles for jewelry gifts, china and crystal, as well as Waterford crystal. You will be mesmerized by their collection of Montana Yogo Sapphires. They are the only store in Bozeman with Keepsake wedding rings and the Absolute Ideal cut Diamonds. You'll appreciate their warm hometown service while you enjoy shopping for that special gift for yourself or someone special. They are conveniently located at the corner of East Main and South Tracy.

## S Poor Richard's News & Tobacco

33 W. Main, Historic Downtown Bozeman. 586-9041.

A mainstay in Bozeman for decades, Poor Richard's offers an unrivaled selection of fine cigars, pipes, specialty tobaccos and smokers accessories. This downtown landmark also carries an enormous variety of magazines, including hard-to-find titles, and local interest books. Stop by for regional and national newspapers, including the Sunday New York Times. Open 7 days a week.

## M bozemanrealestate.com

Bozeman. 388-0208 or toll free 888-388-0208. www.bozemanrealestate.com or info@bozemanrealestate.com

It's no wonder so many people turn to bozemanrealestate.com for homebuying assistance. Their members save time. They save money. Best of all, they enjoy the freedom of buying a home in their own time, at their own pace, with background and insight into every property for sale in and around the Bozeman area. Tired of surfing for tidbits of property information? Flipping through magazines? Scouring the newspaper? Want detailed, up-to-the-minute listing information from someone you can trust? Put the power of their network to work for you. Call or visit their website to experience an easier, more enjoyable way to find and transact your ideal Montana property.

## 3. *Adventure, Gas, Food, Lodging*

## F Burrito Shop

203 N. 7th Ave., Bozeman. 586-1422

If you like Mexican cuisine, you'll love the Burrito Shop. Known locally as the place to go for the best-handmade burritos you'll find anywhere, like their Super Burrito - a twelve inch flour tortilla stuffed with pinto or blacks beans, rice, sour cream and salsa. A full pound! Have it with 911 sauce! Try their Grilled Meat Super Burrito with charbroiled chicken breast or hand-cut marinated and charbroiled beef steak. We dare you to finish a whole order of their 4-Door Cadillac Nachos. Enjoy their salsa bar, fresh guacamole and a wide selection of beers. Open seven days a week. They also offer delivery and take-out service.

## F Ferraro's Restaurant and Lounge

726 N. 7th Ave, Bozeman. 587-2555

Ferraro's is known throughout Montana for their excellent authentic Italian cuisine, fresh pasta that is made daily, the most extensive list of Italian wines in the state, and their knowledgeable and attentive staff. You can enjoy your favorite cocktail or cigar in their lively lounge. Then enjoy an exquisite dinner of pollo, veal, seafood, and other wonderful combinations, with fabulous sauces, appetizers, and desserts, in their smoke-free dining room. You will leave planning to return! They are open for dinner seven days a week at 5 p.m.

Section 5

# THE BOZEMAN CEMETERY

There are few plots of land n Montana that have as much history buried in them as the Bozeman Cemetery. The stories of the individuals buried here—their dreams, achievements, and failures—give us a rich picture of not only Bozeman's history, but also the history of the West. Here are the stories of a select few.

**John Bozeman**
*b. 1835 in Georgia d. 1867*

When gold was discovered in Colorado, John Bozeman left Georgia in 1860 and headed West, leaving a wife and three children behind. By 1862 Bozeman had traveled to the gold strike in Bannack in what was to become Montana Territory.

The 1860s were turbulent years in Montana's history. The successive gold strikes brought thousands of fortune seekers within weeks of each discovery. The rich mining camps were terrorized by thieves and murderers; vigilante committees were organized. Meanwhile, the steady stream of wagon trains through Indian hunting grounds convinced the Sioux and Cheyenne that they must fight to keep their land. Back in the States the Civil War raged, creating tensions between Montana's Northern and Southern emigrants as well as between Southerners who were Confederate Army veterans and those who had avoided military service. It was indeed, the Wild West.

The mining camps of Bannack and Alder Gulch (Virginia City) were dependent on potatoes and flour freighted in from Salt Lake City 400 miles away. The immensely fertile Gallatin Valley was only 60 miles from Virginia City, and it was here in 1863 that John Bozeman conceived the idea of starting a farming community that could supply the miners. Bozeman guided several wagon trains into the area on a trail that shortened the trip by almost two weeks. Over time, it became known as the Bozeman Trail, but after 1864 his energy went into fostering the growth of his town site.

John Bozeman did not fit the typical image of the frontiersman in fringed buckskins. Various contemporaries described him as over six-feet tall, strong, brave, handsome, kind, stalwart, and tireless, with "the looks and ways of a manly man." He was a Southern gentleman, a well dressed Beau Brummel, and no doubt a heart throb.

He was murdered in 1867, only three years after the establishment of the town of Bozeman. While on a trip with Tom Cover to solicit business for the town's flour mill, he was shot on the banks of the Yellowstone River. The accepted story has been that he was murdered by Blackfeet Indians, but inconsistencies in the information have over time resulted in a mystery that variously points the finger of blame at Tom Cover (an interesting individual who was himself murdered under mysterious circumstances years later) or at a jealous husband of one of the few women in town.

John Bozeman's death insured the survival of his town. Fear of Indian attacks led to the establishment in 1867 of Fort Ellis three miles east of the town which provided both protection and a ready market for Bozeman's farms and merchants. Bozeman's remains were returned to the town three years later. His friend, fellow Georgian William McKenzie, died in 1913 and is buried next to him.

**Nelson Story**
*b. 1838 in Ohio d. 1926*

**Ellen Trent Story**
*b. 1844 in Kansas d. 1924*

Nelson and Ellen met and married in Kansas before coming to Bannack and Alder Gulch in 1863. Nineteen-year-old Ellen baked pies and bread to sell to the miners while Nelson operated a store and mined a claim from which he took $40,000 in gold.

It was in Alder Gulch that Story's famous participation in frontier justice took place. Road agent (robber) George Ives had been charged with murder by an informal judge and jury. A crowd of several thousand spectators gathered as darkness fell. Ives stood on a packing box with a noose around his neck. A rescue party of his friends stood up with their guns, but "quick as thought" Story pulled the box (or kicked it, depending on whose version you hear) out from under Ives and he was hanged.

The Storys decided to settle in Bozeman and Ellen stayed there in 1866 while Nelson went down to Texas to drive his famous herd of 3,000 longhorns and a wagon train up to Montana. Not only did he fight his way through thousands of hostile Indians, but he also had to outwit the U.S. Army who wanted to turn back the expedition for its own safety. Story had to sneak 3,000 longhorns past the troops in the dark. These cattle that were driven into the Gallatin Valley formed the nucleus for Montana's cattle industry.

Ellen gave birth to seven children. Three sons and one daughter survived. Nelson's successes in cattle, a flour mill and other business ventures enabled them to build a 17 room mansion in the 1880s. This exquisite building was torn down in 1938. Marble columns from the mansion were salvaged to decorate the family plot.

The Ellen Theatre on Main Street was named for Mrs. Story. Nelson Story was instrumental in bringing Montana State College to Bozeman. Both lived long and productive lives and were major figures in building the Bozeman community.

**James D.Chesnut**
*b. 1834 in Ohio d. 1886*

The life of James Chesnut was full of adventure. At the age of 19 he left for the California gold fields by steamer, but the boat exploded, killing 100 people. James escaped with only a slight scald. In San Francisco, after doing well in several merchandising enterprises, the 19-year-old Chesnut joined up with the audacious military adventurer, William Walker.

The prevailing mood of the times was that American civilization had a right and duty to expand itself; the lines between idealism and piracy were blurred. To the Hispanic South there were people to be liberated and great fortunes to be made in silver, gold and cattle ranching. As part of Walker's illegal Independence Brigade, Chesnut was one of 300 mercenaries to invade and conquer without a shot, the small, sleepy, coastal towns of Western Mexico. Walker proclaimed himself President of the Republic of Lower California and led his ill-equipped army on a rugged march to "liberate" mineral-rich Sonora. The brutal landscape and lack of food took its toll in desertions and death. The group never reached Sonora. All that remained of Walker's army were 34 men who surrendered at the U.S. border and returned to San Francisco.

A year later, Chesnut chose not to accompany Walker on his next venture, the bloody and successful invasion of Nicaragua, where he made himself President. Instead, Chesnut exchanged all his valuables for $7,000 in gold, and booked passage on a steamer bound for New York. The launch that was taking him to the steamer sank, and while 38 people drowned, Chesnut swam back to shore, hired a diver, retrieved his gold and boarded the steamer in time for departure.

Later, during the Kansas border wars, Chesnut was arrested and jailed for high treason. When the Civil War began, he worked at the unique job of enlisting Indians and blacks for the Union Army. He enlisted a regiment of Delaware Indians and himself commanded a regiment of black troops, achieving the rank of Colonel.

In 1867, he came to Montana and discovered coal in the Rocky Canyon Trail Creek area. For 15 years he developed his coal mining enterprise, benefiting the growth of the community. Chesnut liked to say that the coal in his claim ran all the way down to China, thereby making the famous coal mines of England an infringement on his rights. Coal was welcomed since wood was becoming scarce and high priced. But stove grates were not suited to coal, and the Colonel had difficulty promoting his product. The small town of Chestnut was named for him, however the name was misspelled.

Chesnut owned extensive real estate, including the Chesnut Corner, an elegantly appointed saloon, complete with a reading room and a club room in back. This club room was Bozeman's nerve center, where its leading male citizens discussed public problems and their genial host encouraged new enterprises for the rapidly growing town. The large upstairs floor was a social center, and in summer the Fort Ellis band played from its balcony on Main street. Although Chesnut was the focus of several romantic stories, he never married.

**"Lady" Mary Blackmore**
*b. in England d. 1872*

The sad story of 'Lady' Mary Blackmore and her husband William is part of Bozeman's lore. In 1872 they came from England to visit Yellowstone, stopping in Bozeman on their way because Lady Mary had become suddenly ill. She died of peritonitis at General Lester Willson's home and was buried on five acres purchased by 'Lord' Blackmore and given to the town for use as a cemetery.

Further investigation reveals that 'Lord' Blackmore was in fact not a lord, although he did expect to be knighted. It was Emma Willson who started referring to them as 'Lord' and 'Lady.' William Blackmore was, however, an extraordinary man. He had become quite wealthy working as a middle man between English investors and promoters in the American West. He and Mary lived on an extensive estate where they entertained a dazzling array of guests including Oliver Wendell Holmes, Charlotte Bronte, Alfred Lord Tennyson, and "Mark Twain". The beautiful Mary was a

London social leader and an intimate of Queen Victoria. William had made several trips to the U.S., and from all evidence he loved the West. He had provided generous financial assistance to photographer William Jackson, artist Thomas Moran, and explorer Dr. Ferdinand Hayden. He had a deep interest in anthropology and in Native American life and customs. His fourth trip to the U.S. in 1872 was to check on investments in the Southwest, as well as to join Hayden on his expedition to The Yellowstone. Mary and a nephew accompanied him on this trip, and the couple agreed that if either should die on their travels they would be buried where they died. Dr. Hayden named Mt. Blackmore in Mary's honor. Looking south from the grave site the mountain's pyramid-shaped peak can be seen. Hayden also named a newly discovered mineral Blackmorite in William's honor. In 1878 Blackmore's American investments brought him to financial ruin. In the library of his estate he committed suicide by shooting himself in the head.

**Henry T.P. Comstock**
*b. 1820 in Canada d. 1870*

Henry Comstock, nicknamed "Old Pancake" was said to have enough badness in him for three men. Lazy and conniving, he was making a meager living in 1859 mining for gold in western Nevada. When two naive Irish immigrants made a strike, Old Pancake showed up, said that the land was his (it wasn't), and demanded partnerships for himself and a friend if he were to allow the Irishmen to continue digging.

The odd-looking gold that came from the claim was soon discovered to be mostly silver. Comstock was a loudmouth and talked about "his" discovery and "his" claim so much that it became known as the Comstock Lode. The four prospectors sold out to a developer, and Comstock received $11,000 for his share. As was typical of the times, none of the discoverers held onto an interest in the mine that was to become the single greatest mineral strike in history, producing 400 million dollars in precious metals. The developers who took over the claim became phenomenally wealthy; many of the great American fortunes were founded with revenues from the mines in the Comstock Lode. Comstock quickly spent his money. Drifting and demented, he ended up in Bozeman where he lived in a shack just off the east end of Main Street. Dead broke and lonely, he committed suicide by shooting himself.

**Monroe "Beaver" Nelson**
*b. 1861 in Iowa d. 1932*

**Frank "Doc" Nelson**
*b. 1867 in Montana d. 1964*

Beaver and Doc were two of the seven children of John and Lavine Nelson. The couple came to the Gallatin Valley in 1864, just in time for the arrival of their son Pike, one of the first white children born in the area. Monroe "Beaver" Nelson was a boy at the time, but grew up to become foreman of the Two Dot Willson Cattle Co. Kid Curry of Butch Cassidy's "Hole in the Wall Gang" and the Logan boys rode under Beaver, as did Charlie Russell, who proclaimed Nelson the most ideal cowboy he had ever known and used him as the subject for many of his paintings.

In 1879, while drinking with two other cowboys at the Headquarters Saloon on Main Street, Beaver was involved in one of Bozeman's biggest shoot-outs. One of the cowboys drinking with Beaver got into a fight with a local trouble maker, beat him up, and ran him out of the saloon. The trouble maker sneaked back in and shot him in the back. The dying cowboy, Beaver, and the other cowboy all spun around and fired at the trouble maker. The cowboy and the trouble maker both hit the floor dead.

In another incident Beaver and his younger brother Doc witnessed the famous Lewistown shootout in which Rattlesnake Jake and three others were killed. Elsewhere in Montana, Doc was also around when a cowboy got into a gunfight and accidentally shot the local schoolmarm. This made the boys in town so mad that they hanged the cowboy and shot his body full of lead. The schoolmarm survived.

Doc had been a little boy of three when his father took him to see some friends who had just returned from the Rosebud Expedition. One of the men had a bloody mass of fresh Sioux scalps hung on a wire which he whirled through the air at the petrified child. At age 11, Doc helped on a drive of 1,000 head of cattle. At 14 he met 16-year-old Charlie Russell on another cattle drive and for several years the two wrangled for big brother Beaver's cattle outfit. One morning, Doc and an ornery pony bucked right through the cook's fire and became the subject of C.M. Russell's popular painting "Bronc to Breakfast." This image is engraved on Doc's tombstone, and Doc is in the National Cowboy Hall of Fame.

**Chester R. "Chet" Huntley**
*b. 1911 in Montana d. 1974*

Chet Huntley was born in the Cardwell Railroad Depot where his father worked as a telegrapher. In 1929, he came to Montana State College to study entomology, later transferring to the University of Washington. After getting a start in radio broadcasting, he went to Los Angeles where he eventually worked for all three television networks—CBS, ABC and NBC. During the nationally televised political conventions of 1956, he was teamed with David Brinkley. The two became a popular news team which lasted until Huntley quit in 1970. The Huntley/Brinkley Report won every major TV news award, including 7 Emmy awards. When Chet Huntley resigned from NBC, he returned to Montana to develop Big Sky, Inc., of Montana, a resort and ski complex in Gallatin Canyon. He died a few years later from lung cancer.

*Reprinted with permission from "Who's Who in the Bozeman Cemetery—A Guide to Historic Gravesites" The Bozarts Press. Copyright 1987 by Anne Garner.*

Section 5

### F The Wok

319 N. 7th. Ave. Bozeman. 585-1245

The Wok is a local favorite for diners, specializing in authentic Cantonese and Mandarin style lunches and dinners serving many items, including house specialties such as Chinese Hot Pot, Moo Shui (pork or chicken), and their Sizzling Seafood Platter. The atmosphere is fresh, elegant, casual, and relaxing. The first location opened in Livingston, and soon met the demands in Bozeman and Belgrade. Now they have three conveniently located restaurants, only minutes from most area lodging. Enjoy domestic and oriental beers and wines with your meal. They are open seven days a week and the Bozeman location offers a lunch buffet daily. Delivery available.

### L Royal 7 Motel

310 N. 7th, Bozeman. 587-3103 or 800-587-3103. www.avicom.net/royal7/

The Royal 7 motel invites you to join their many loyal guests and make the Royal 7 your home away from home whenever you are in Bozeman. Whether you are coming to Bozeman and the beautiful Gallatin Valley on business or pleasure, the Royal 7 welcomes you and the courteous staff will make your stay a pleasant one. All of the sparkling clean and spacious guest rooms are on the ground floor, offering great beds, cable TV with HBO, front door parking and smoking & non-smoking rooms. Guests can enjoy morning coffee & donuts, an indoor hot tub, and just a short stroll to many fine restaurants. See their web site for more information.

## 4. *Gas, Food, Lodging*

### L Bozeman Inn

1235 N. 7th Ave., Bozeman. 587-3176, fax 585-3591 or toll free at 800-648-7515. www.avicom.net/bozemaninn/

The owners of the Bozeman Inn believe in great customer service along with room rates to fit anyone's budget. This makes it an ideal place to stop. They are easy to find off I-90, exit 306, with easy access to shopping, service stations, car washes, and dining. Guests will take comfort in a soothing hot tub, in-house restaurant, laundry facilities, continental breakfast, and fresh clean rooms. During the summer months guests can enjoy sunshine and mountain views in an outdoor heated pool. The staff at this locally owned and operated motel go the extra mile to assure a great stay for all their guests. Visit them on the web and see for yourself!

### L Best Western GranTree Inn

1325 N. 7th Ave., Bozeman. 587-5261 or toll free 800-624-5865. www.bestwestern.com/grantreeinn

The Best Western GranTree Inn is conveniently located just off I-90 in Bozeman and provides exceptional service to both business and vacation travelers. The warm rustic lobby sets the tone for their Montana hospitality. There are 119 guest rooms with outstanding amenities, including hair dryers, voicemail, and irons. For the discriminating traveler, they offer 23 suites. The restaurant features a wide selection for breakfast, lunch, and dinner. After a long day, join the fun in their lively lounge and casino. You might find yourself relaxing in their large indoor pool or adjacent hot tub. As an added bonus their fitness room has a great view of the mountains. Learn more about the GranTree by checking their web site.

### L Bozeman Comfort Inn

1370 N. 7th Ave., Bozeman. 587-2322 Reservations 800-587-3833.

The Bozeman Comfort Inn combines quality, service, and that "special touch" to make your stay in Bozeman both comfortable and memorable. You'll sleep under the stars in your room, and enjoy spectacular mountain views from your window. They offer 121 spacious sleeping rooms, specialty, and business suites. Business amenities include such features as a fully equipped business center, T-1 hi-speed access, and a professional workout facility. Additionally, they provide an indoor pool and hot tub, guest laundry, and free deluxe continental breakfast where you will enjoy "homemade" muffins. Their meeting facilities can host groups from 20 to 150 and the Comfort Inn staff will personally see to all meeting needs. They are located close to I-90, most area attractions, dining, and shopping. Learn more this great place to stay by checking their web site.

### L Holiday Inn

5 Baxter Lane, Bozeman. 587-4561 or reservations: 800-366-5101. www.holidayinnbozeman.com

The Holiday Inn specializes in the comforts you are looking for after a long day whether you are in town for business or pleasure. After checking in, wander over to the lounge and try the daily special and free hors d'oeuvres during happy hour. When in the room enjoying a movie, or checking the latest news, order room service and relax for the evening. Take in a massage from the certified massage therapists on site. After a restful night in a comfortable, newly renovated room, start the day by working out in the fitness room while the kids swim in the largest pool of any Bozeman hotel. The professional, personable staff of the Holiday Inn will make your stay as enjoyable as possible.

### L Hampton Inn

75 Baxter Lane, Bozeman. 522-8000

The Bozeman Hampton Inn offers luxury rooms at great prices —100% guaranteed! Located just off I-90, they offer free airport shuttle service, a deluxe breakfast bar, an indoor pool and spa, an on-site fitness facility, in-room coffee & ironing boards, guest laundry, free local calls and much more. The business traveler will enjoy the convenience of in-house business center, phones with data ports, and the hospitality/meeting suite. Many rooms are complete with mountain views, and the friendly staff can help you plan skiing, whitewater rafting, hiking, golfing, visits to Yellowstone National Park, and many of the opportunities that this area holds.

## 5. *Attraction, Gas, Food, Lodging*

### T East Gallatin Recreation Area

Griffith Drive, Bozeman

Known simply as "the Beach" by locals, the lake here has a 300 acre beach front which is a great spot for swimming, sun bathing, and picnicking. There are several shelters here maintained by the Sunrise Rotary Club and plenty of picnic tables. You can fish here for trout, perch, and sunfish. On any given day, you will see a number of windsurfers, kayakers, and canoeists practicing their skills.

### F Apple Tree Restaurant

At exit 306 in Bozeman. 712 Wheat Dr. 586-1748

Join Tom Huber and his friendly staff for a home-style meal "made from scratch." Located right at the Bozeman 7th St. exit (360) and convenient to most of the motels in the area, they offer a family atmosphere in a country decor and a full menu at affordable prices. For almost 20 years this family owned business has served up some of the finest breakfasts, lunches, and dinners to area visitors and continues to be a local's favorite. Enjoy your favorite beer or wine with your meal. They are open daily from 6 a.m. to midnight Memorial Day to Labor Day and 6 a.m. to 11 p.m. the rest of the year.

### L TLC Inn

805 Wheat Dr. at I-90 Exit 306, Bozeman. 587-2100, reservations at 877-466-7852. www.tlc-inn.com/www.tlc-inn.com

The TLC Inn specializes in luxury accommodations at economy rates. Featuring 42 clean and comfortable rooms, a complimentary continental breakfast, a 24-hour hot tub, free local calls and cable TV, you get all that you need in a motel at

# Shakespeare in Montana

**Montana Shakespeare in the Parks is** a theatrical outreach program of Montana State University Bozeman. The Company's mission is to bring quality, live theatrical productions of Shakespeare and other classics communities in Montana and vicinity at a reasonable cost with an emphasis on small, underserved communities. Shakespeare in the Parks opened in the summer of 1973. Since that time the company of professional actors has traveled over 250,000 miles, over 44 plays, presenting over 1,800 performances mostly in Montana to a cumulative audience of over half a million.

Since it's inception Montana Shakespeare in the Parks has employed a company of professionals who combine their theatrical talents with a love and appreciation for Montana and the audience they serve. Because of the Company's desire to bring a quality performance to people who would not otherwise have access to theatre of any kind, many company members have found the tour to be a rejuvenating professional experience, reminding them of "why they went into theatre to begin with." This unique combination of invested performer and receptive audience coupled with outdoor performances which make the actor even more accessible to the audience, has evolved into a unique performance style for the Company.

Recognition of SIP's unique contribution to the cultural fabric of Montana has been both regional and national in scope. The performances continue to entertain audiences of all ages, usually free of charge, due to the financial support of generous sponsors throughout the state. For a complete performance schedule and additional information call the office on the campus of Montana State University at 994-3901 or visit them at www.montana.edu/shakespeare

very affordable prices. Located just off the highway and one of the closest motels to the airport. To make your stay more enjoyable, the friendly staff can help you plan your stay in the Bozeman area. Stop in or call for reservations and quality accommodations. Learn even more on their web site!

## L Microtel Inn & Suites

At exit 306 in Bozeman. 712 Nikles Drive.
586-3797 or 888-771-7171.
microtel@montana.com

One of Bozeman's newest motels boasts 61 rooms with nine suites, all containing chiropractic-approved mattresses. The many amenities include complimentary remote cable TV (ESPN, CNN and HBO) and free Continental breakfast. Computer hookups are available in each guestroom along with built-in desktop workspaces and data port telephones.When you're not on the computer, you can relax in the room's window seat or visit their indoor pool and spa. For the businessperson, a DSL Internet Business Center is available with spacious conference and meeting rooms. Children under 16 stay free in the parent's room, and complimentary cribs are available. ADA-compliant accessible rooms are available for those with disabilities. AAA, senior and corporate rates are offered.

## L Ramada Limited

2020 Wheat Dr., at I-90 Exit 306, Bozeman.
585-2626 or toll free 800-2RAMADA(272-6232),
Email: ramada@bigsky.net

## 6. *Gas, Food, Lodging, Shopping*

## T Bozeman Recreation Center

1211 W. Main St. next to High School. 587-4724

This is the only indoor 50 meter 8-lane swimming pool in the state. The pool is open year round with generous open swim hours. The kids will love the two waterslides in the pool. There is a hot tub and some exercise equipment available.

### *It Happened in Montana*

December 3, 1866. Nelson Story arrives in the Gallatin Valley (Bozeman area) with 3,000 longhorns. Not only did he fight his way through thousands of hostile Indians, but he also had to outwit the U.S. Army who wanted to turn back the expedition for its own safety. Story and his two dozen cowboys had to sneak the cattle past the Indians in the dark. Colonel Carrington offered to buy the cattle to provide beef for the soldiers at Fort Phil Kearney. Story declined. The cattle that he brought into the Gallatin Valley formed the nucleus for Montana's cattle industry.

### FS Community Food Co-op

908 W.Main Street., Bozeman. 587-7955

The Community Food Co-op is easy to find in Bozeman and is Southwest Montana's largest natural foods market. The Co-op's full service deli is locally famous for the incredibly cheap "One World Lunch", which is served most days from 11:30 AM until is sells out. The deli also serves sandwiches, hot dinners, desserts, and a whole lot more. The Co-op features organic produce, groceries, beer and wine, over 800 items in bulk, and everything else you'd expect from a natural food store. Visitors are welcome with no added surcharge. They are open daily.

### F Café Zydeco

1520 West Main, Bozeman. 994-0188

Named after true Southwestern Louisiana Zydeco music, Café Zydeco specializes in good ol' Cajun grub. The authentic Cajun cuisine includes legendary one-pot dishes such as jambalaya, gumbo, catfish tchoupitoulas, and crawfish etouffee. Sandwiches adapted from the French Market originals include a selection of Po-Boys, hot and cold subs, blackened tuna, Rueben, veggie sandwiches and more. Great breakfast sandwiches, wraps, salads, sweets, coffee and espresso drinks, and beignets (Saturdays and Sundays) round out the popular menu at Bozeman's home to Cajun grub. Open for lunch and dinner Monday through Saturday and breakfast Friday through Sunday. Visit their other location, at 4 Corners, on your way to the Gallatin Canyon. What good? Everything!

### F Perkins Family Restaurant

2505 W. Main, Bozeman. 587-9323

Perkins Family Restaurant is open 24 hours and serves a wide variety of delicious breakfast, lunch and dinner items. Relax in the casual, family atmosphere, and enjoy fluffy pancakes, hearty omelets, salads served in fresh-baked bread bowls, and melt sandwiches. Breakfast any time of the day! Dinner selections include steak, chicken, lasagna, and shrimp. Top off your meal with a scrumptious piece of their famous pie or huge cookie fresh from their in-house bakery. You'll want to grab some of their mammoth muffins for the road! Great dining for the entire family. You can count on Perkins to fill your plate without emptying you wallet. Find them under the big American flag on West Main on the way to Yellowstone.

### F Pork Chop John's

1631 W. Main., Bozeman. 587-8040

John's original pork chop sandwich has been a tradition of quality for over 60 years. Originating in Butte, Montana in 1924, founder John Burkland sold his pork chop sandwich from the back of a wagon. The quality and delicious flavors still remain today with locations in Butte, Bozeman, and Billings. Stop in and see why this famous, mouth-watering sandwich has become a unique part of the Montana experience.

### S Antique Mall

1530 West Main St, Bozeman. 587-5281

The Antique Mall, owned by Paul and Pam Landsgaard, is conveniently located in Bozeman, near 19th Street and West Main Street next to American Bank. The historic red barn is home to an eclectic mix of antiques, collectibles, and second hand furniture. The extensive collection of items includes Victorian Walnut and Mission Oak furniture, fine china, glassware, and pottery such as North Dakota Rosemeade. They also offer in interesting selection of western, Yellowstone National Park, and other regional memorabilia, such as postcards, pictures, and Gary Carter prints. If you are looking for an unusual treasure from the past you're sure to find it among toys, dolls, clocks, cookware, books, bottles, juke boxes, slot machines, old cash registers, antique cars and trucks, and even a stage coach.

### S Montana Bowhunters Supply

1716 W. Main, Bozeman. 586-7722

### M Christine Delaney/Absaroka Realty

1516 W. Main, Bozeman. 581-7542 or fax 522-5446. www.bozemanmove.com

Christine Delaney, a Colorado native now living in her dream community, is a Realtor with Bozeman's Absaroka Realty. In Denver she owned a retail magic store and came to Yellowstone every autumn to recharge her batteries. The opportunity to relocate presented itself and she couldn't be happier. Customer Service has always been her passion, whether it's magic or real estate. She knows what it's like to rush into town, find a dream home, and struggle to coordinate everything long distance. Moving is a stressful time and

Christine has been there and done that. She is there to dot the i's and cross the t's for her clients. Christine is an expert at putting the FUN back in the fundamentals of real estate. Visit Absaroka Realty's web site for more information or give her a call.

**7.** *Gas, Food, Lodging, Shopping*

**VS Fins and Feathers of Bozeman**
1500 N. 19th, Suite B, Bozeman. 586-2188, fax 586-2462. www.finsandfeathersonline.com

Fins and Feathers in the Bridger Peaks Town Center is the area's only authorized full ORVIS dealer for rental equipment, flies, rods, reels, accessories and current river conditions. This Bozeman owned and operated family business is committed to offering quality products service for everyone in your family. Their guides are topnotch and will take you for the best experience you can imagine on the area's famous trout waters. You will find an enormous selection of flies, fly-tying gear, and all needs for the flyfishing enthusiast. Additionally, they carry a wide variety of gifts, luggage, clothing and accessories for the non-fisherman. Be sure and ask about their wing-shooting accouterments and adventures. For more information or area fishing news visit them at www.finsandfeathersonline.com.

**F Denny's Classic Diner**
1510 N. 19th Ave, Bozeman. 522-0402

Journey back to the 50s at Denny's Classic Diner. With great deals on meals 24 hours a day where you can get whatever you're hungry for any time of the day. Seven days a week! Try their famous breakfast combinations, delicious soups, salads, sandwiches, famous burgers, appetizers and homestyle dinners. Select from a huge selection of breakfast entrees served all day and night. Their pies are mouth-watering! You will find great food, great prices, great service, a friendly staff, all in a unique family atmosphere. Take out available. Call them ahead or find them in the Bridger Peaks Shopping Center on the north side of Bozeman.

**F MacKenzie River Pizza Co.**
145 Rawhide Ridge & N. 19th Street, Bozeman. 582-0099

The Outpost is also famous for gourmet pizzas, super sandwiches and extraordinary salads, everything is made fresh daily right down to the salad dressings and the pizza dough! They are located just off the North 19th Street stretch of Bozeman. Pick up dinner or grab a quick lunch. This location specializes in eating on the fly. Delivery to local motels and carry out for your tired traveling family needs is available here.



**F Leaf and Bean**
1500 N. 19th Ave., Bridger Peaks Shopping Center. Bozeman. 587-2132

**8.** *Gas, Food, Lodging*

**9.** *Gas, Food*

**T Bozeman Ponds**
Next to the Gallatin Valley Mall on Huffine Lane in Bozeman.

This pond recently received a complete makeover by the Bozeman Breakfast Optimist Club turning three separate ponds into one large one. The area has picnic tables, a pavilion, rest rooms, and walking trails. Swimming is allowed but there are no lifeguards present. The pond is stocked with rainbow, brook, and brown trout and perch.

### A Big Sky RV Inc.

8466 Huffine Lane, west of Bozeman. 587-0039 or 800-877-9606, www.bigskyrv.com

If you love RV's, you'll love Big Sky RV. You'll be dazzled by over 150 new and used units in stock. They are recognized as a leading dealer for Jayco's Designer trailers and fifth wheels. In addition to sales they offer professional service, parts, sewer dump station, propane and hitch repair. You'll find an easy drive-through access and prompt travelers' emergency service. Located 2 1/2 miles west of the Gallatin Valley on Hwy 191. See them on the web at www.bigskyrv.com.

### F Fuddrucker's

2905 W. Main, Bozeman. 585-2890

Is there anyone who doesn't love Fuddruckers? The World's Greatest Hamburger is waiting for you in Bozeman! Enjoy your favorite burger, chicken breast and other sandwiches made with the freshest ingredients possible and top it yourself with plentiful garden fresh toppings. Finish your meal with a fresh cookie, slice of pie, or other desserts made daily in their in-house bakery. Choose your favorite beverage from a selection of serve yourself soft drinks, or enjoy ice cold beer, wines, or a frosty margarita or daiquiri, juices, and smoothies. They are open at 11 a.m. seven days a week for lunch and dinner. The spacious dining room is perfect for a large family gathering or a small business lunch. Located in front of the Gallatin Valley Mall.

### F Godfather's Pizza

200 S. 23rd Ave., University Square, Bozeman. 586-8551

The fun atmosphere at Godfather's Pizza is great for group gatherings, family dinners, or just a relaxing meal out. Featuring a wide variety of pizzas to choose from, with golden and thin crusts and many topping choices. If you're not in the mood for pizza, try the salad bar or a variety of sandwiches. Offering dine in, carry out, and delivery seven days a week. Godfather's also serves specialty buffets and welcomes large groups.

### L Bobcat Lodge

2307 W. Main, Bozeman. 587-5241 or 888-587-5241

The Bobcat Lodge conveniently located close to Montana State University and the Museum of the Rockies, the Gallatin Valley Mall and many area restaurants, has been a transit home to Montanans and students for over twenty years. You will enjoy their heated indoor pool with sauna and a spacious, quiet, courtyard that is perfect for family picnics. They also offer winter plug-ins, kitchenettes, pet stays, and laundry. Whether you are a single or a family, let their friendly and professional staff find one of their oversized rooms or apartments to accommodate your particular needs and length of stay.

### L Intermountain Property Management

2006 W. Babcock, Ste. A, Bozeman. 586-1503 or toll free at 888-871-7856. www.montanavacation.com or Email: ipm@montanavacation.com

Intermountain Property Management, Inc. proudly represents more than 30 vacation rental homes and cabins in Southwest Montana for your perfect Montana Vacation experience. They offer homes in the heart of historical downtown Bozeman, near Yellowstone Park, Paradise Valley, Ennis, Big Sky, and Bridger Bowl, and surrounding areas. All homes are fully furnished, which means all you will need to bring are your clothes, food and your favorite fly rod! For a sampling of what they offer visit web site, www.montanavacation.com. Let them help you plan your next Montana Vacation and know that you have found the key to a great vacation.

### S High Country Gifts

2825 W. Main #4-J, Gallatin Valley Mall, Bozeman. 586-3991 or fax 586-3691. 888-465-6614. www.highcountrygifts.com

High Country Gifts welcomes you to browse the

#### *It Happened in Montana*

July 17, 2001, Bozeman hosted the world premiere of *Jurassic Park III*. The model for actor Sam Neills character is Bozeman's own Jack Horner, world famous paleontologist and curator of paleontology at the Museum of the Rockies in Bozeman. In one of the early scenes actress Laura Dern mentions she's using Horner as a source for her latest book. The next scene supposedly takes place at Fort Peck Lake in eastern Montana. In it, actor Neill is driving a Museum of the Rockies vehicle. Horner was the technical advisor for this movie as he was for the two previous Jurrasic Park thrillers.

Sprit of the West, captured in a selection of the finest Montana gifts and home accents. Visit their store conveniently located in Bozeman's Gallatin Valley Mall or on-line at www.highcountrygifts.com. High Country is well-known for helping customers find that perfect item for any special occasion. They offer regional and huckleberry foods, comfy clothing for the entire family, western reading and music, Lewis & Clark celebration items, art gallery, hand crafted items from local artists, and even a western wedding section. In store engraving is available to personalize that special gift.

## S Madison House

2504 W. Main, Bozeman. 587-0587

The Madison House is a well known source for wonderful gifts, accessories, and home furnishings. If you are looking for a unique accent for your home or a special gift to take home as a memory from Montana, their talented staff can help you make a personal selection. This exquisite store offers a large selection of unusual picture frames, richly scented candles, hand crafted furniture, stunning bedding, pillows, throws, and one-of-a-kind lamps. Madison House specializes in rustic accessories and furniture with a warm "Rocky Mountain flavor". They are open Monday through Saturday 10 a.m. - 5:30 p.m.

**10.** *Attraction, Gas, Food*

## T Museum of the Rockies

On the MSU campus at 600 W. Kagy Blvd., Bozeman. 994-225. www.museumoftherockies.org

When you walk through the Museum of the Rockies, you travel through more than four billion years in time. Learn about history and prehistory of the northern Rockies region through exhibits ranging from paleontology and Native American artifacts to historic photography and antique vehicles. Start your walk through time with a look at the universe and Montana's Big Sky in the Taylor Planetarium. The Taylor Planetarium is one of 25 facilities in the world with a computer graphics system that can simulate flight through space. It is the only major public planetarium in the surrounding three-state region.

The museum is well known for its paleontology research. On display are several important finds including the skulls of Torosaurus, Tyrannosaurus Rex and Triceratops and an 80 million-year-old nest of dinosaur eggs. Working at Montana sites, the museum's curator of paleontology, Jack Horner, has discovered important information about dinosaur biology and in recent years has made discoveries of international significance. One of the most spectacular finds, a Tryannosaurus Rex, has been cast in bronze and the 38 foot long and 15 foot tall skeleton stands in front of the museum.

Montana's rich agricultural history is portrayed at the museum's living history farm where the daily life of early homesteaders is recreated for visitors.

The Museum of the Rockies is open daily from 8am–8pm (summer) and 9am–5 pm Monday through Saturday and 12:30–5pm Sundays (winter). An admission fee is charged to nonmembers. For more information call or visit the web site.

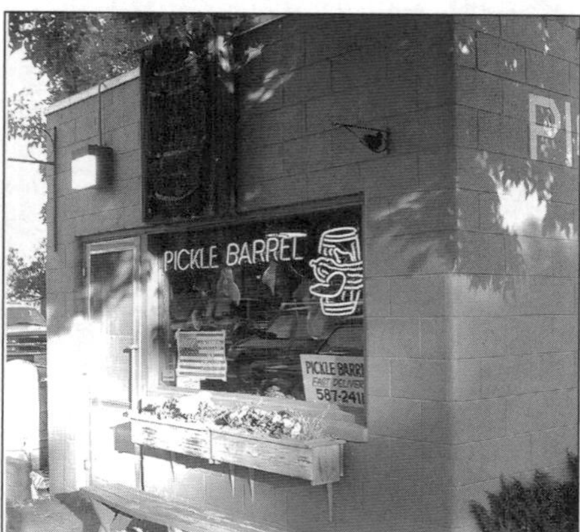


## F Pickle Barrel

809 W. College, Bozeman. 587-2411

Be sure and visit Montana's most renowned sandwich shop. The Pickle Barrel has been making some of the best subs in Montana and maybe even the world for over twenty-eight years! Well known throughout the United States their selection of great stuffed cold and hot sandwiches are made to order for eating in, take out or delivery. Vegetarian varieties are also available. Save room for great desserts that include ice cream in fresh made absolutely delicious waffle cones and outrageously good brownies and cookies. You can also enjoy their legendary sandwiches at 209 E. Main in Downtown Bozeman located inside the Rocking R Bar.

## S Quilting In the Country

5100 19th Street, Bozeman. 587-8216, www.QuitingInTheCountry.com

Quilting in the Country is a nationally recognized shop located in the Big Sky Country. The setting is a restored 110-year-old farmstead. Surrounding mountains and streams provide year-round recreational activities. We are noted for our original patterns, "Soups On" quilt kit and cookbook, 100% wool fabric and classes taught by enthusiastic local and nationally known teachers. Classes are in the old bunkhouse and outside under huge willows, weather permitting! Unique to QIC is the Annual Outdoor Quilt Show. The show held in August features nearly 500 quilts, demos, and venders, classes and lectures by internationally known teachers. American Patchwork & Quilt Sampler has featured this spectacular event.

## M Bridger Realty

2001 Stadium Drive, Ste. A, Bozeman. 586-7676 or toll free 888-586-7676. www.bridgerrealty.com

Bridger Realty is one of Bozeman's most successful independent real estate brokerages. In business since 1980, there are currently 21 brokers and sales associates with expertise in residential, commercial and land sales. The Realtors at Bridger Realty are full-time professionals with a history of sales and marketing productivity, and a commitment to the Bozeman community. The brokerage is a member of the Southwest Montana Multiple Listing Service and RELO, a leading national relocation company. The web site offers continually updated information on real estate listings, and also helpful links for those contemplating a move to Bozeman. A Relocation Guide is available upon request.

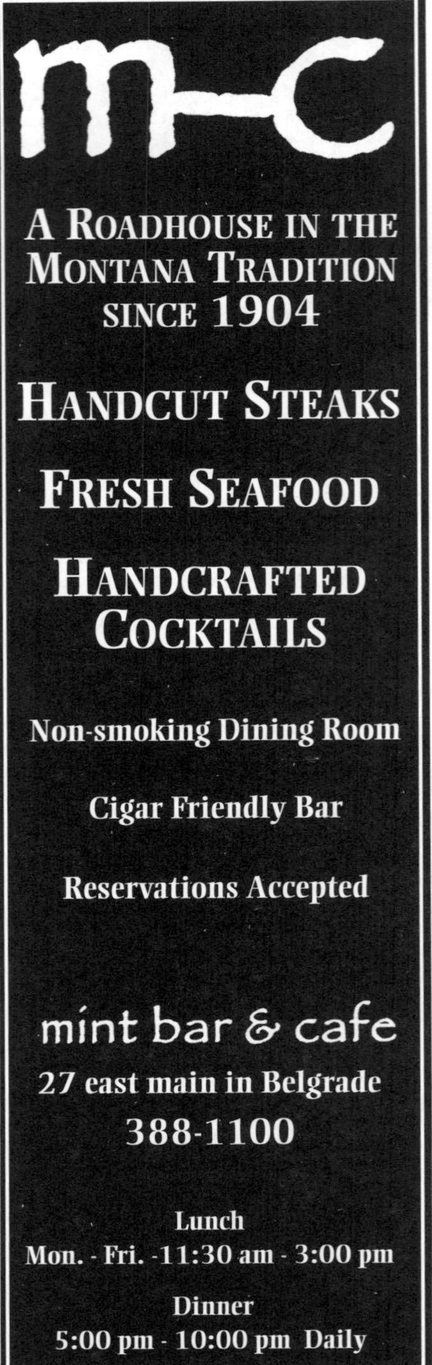


### M Montana State University/Bozeman

994-0211 or 888-678-2287, www.montana.edu

Montana State University received its charter as Montana's oldest public education institution in 1893, as the state's Land Grant University. It is home to the fighting "Bobcats". The university has grown and changed to meet the needs of the people of Montana, and is now a multi-campus university offering over 46 majors, master's degrees in over 37 fields, and doctorates in twelve fields. It is also home to KUSM-Montana Public Television and the Museum of the Rockies. Approximately 11,000 students are enrolled at the Bozeman campus.

## 11. *Adventure, Gas, Shopping*

### ASV Panda Sports Rentals

621 Bridger Dr., Bozeman. 587-6280

Panda offers rentals for all of your outdoor recreation sports needs from canoes, mountain bikes, rafts, skis, snow boards, avalanche beepers, and more for year round fun at great, very affordable rates. They also sell a special line of fleece vests and jackets. Overnight repairs and ski tuning is also available. This is also a one-stop shop for food, snacks, beer, cold drinks, Sinclair gas and propane when you are in a hurry to get to that next adventure. They are located on the northeast corner of Bozeman, on the way to Bridger Bowl, as well as close to major hotels and motels. They are open seven days a week.

### V Campbell's Guided Fishing Trips, L.L.C.

Bozeman. 587-0822. Email: flyrod@imt.net or www.rodneycampbell.com

Fish with a third-generation Montana fishing outfitter, licensed to guide all of Montana with over 18 years guiding experience in SW Montana. Fish for native Cutthroats, Grayling, Mountain Whitefish, or Rainbows, Browns, Brookies, and Goldens. Select from a variety of magnificent trips that range from river float trips in a McKenzie-style drift boat, walk/wade trips, fishing private ranch water to float tubing a private trophy lake. Fish any of Montana's famous rivers including the Yellowstone, Madison, Missouri, Gallatin, Big Hole, Jefferson, and Big Horn. They offer half or full day trips. Whichever trip you choose, you'll be assured a first-class fishing trip with Rodney Campbell. Visit them on the web at www.rodneycampbell.com for more information.

### L Lehrkind Mansion Bed and Breakfast

719 N. Wallace Ave., Bozeman. 585-6932. www.bozemanbedandbreakfast.com

The Lehrkind Mansion Bed and Breakfast provides a glimpse into 1897 Bozeman. Originally built as the residence of brewmaster Julius Lehrkind, it anchors Bozeman's Historic Brewery District. The mansion is filled with period antiques, including a

rare seven foot tall music box. Comfortable overstuffed chairs and cozy beds provide a place to curl up with a great book. Streams of morning sunlight join with calming music, adding elegance to your candlelit gourmet breakfast after savoring your first cup of coffee and views of the Bridger Mountains from the porch swing. They are only 15 minutes from Bridger Bowl and within walking distance of Bozeman's many fine restaurants. Whether inside surrounded by century old furnishings , or soaking in the outdoor hot tub, you will enjoy an oasis at the historic Lehrkind Mansion.

**12.** *Gas, Food, Shopping, Miscellaneous*

### F Kountry Korner Cafe

81820 Gallatin Rd, at Four Corners, Bozeman.
586-2281

The Kountry Korner is a family-style café located at Four Corners just west of Bozeman. They are open for breakfast, lunch or dinner and offer daily home-cooked specials, offering a wide selection of family favorites. Homemade pies and soups are made fresh daily. Locals love to eat here and are partial to the homemade chicken-fried steaks. You can enjoy a great meal anytime between 6 a.m. and 9 p.m. or have them pack a sack lunch to take on your outing. They are also known for a fantastic Sunday brunch buffet. A children's play area is available for the little ones and a large dining room is available for private parties and large groups. Look for the bear sitting on the roof!

### *Montana Trivia*

While driving in Montana, the most likely item to collide with is another automobile. The second most common item is wildlife. Over 1,800 cars collide with wild animals every year.

## Museum of the Rockies

**When you walk through the Museum** of the Rockies at Montana State University, you travel through more than four billion years in time. Visitors to one of Montana's top ten tourist destinations experience the Northern Rocky Mountain region and life that emerged upon it from the beginning of time to the present.

*"Big Mike," the first free-standing full-size bronze Tyrannosaurus rex in the world, welcomes you to the Museum of the Rockies. Cast from the actual bones of T. rex excavated in eastern Montana by Jack Horner and the museum's paleontology crew, the skeleton measures 38 feet in length, stands 12 feet tall and weighs 6,000 pounds.*

Start your travels outside the Taylor Planetarium where a huge wall mural orients you to our place in the universe. Then test your knowledge of space at the interactive "space station." Your next stop is Landforms/Lifeforms where you learn about the geologic formation of this region including the mountain building in Yellowstone, Glacier and Teton National Parks. Spectacular dioramas introduce you to the earliest life forms that lived here and show their fossilized counterparts. There's also a video about the supercontinent, Pangea, a pinball game about extinction, and a number of artifacts and activities to touch or try.

Then it's on to the Berger Dinosaur Hall. One Day 80 Million Years Ago takes you back in time to the Egg Mountain dinosaur nesting colonies near present-day Choteau, Montana. You meet Maiasaura peeblesorum and her babies and the other animals who lived there, and see skulls of T. rex and Gigantosaurus. You'll also see Torosaurus, whose nine-foot skull was the largest of any dinosaur. Fossils from current research projects are on display on the balcony overlooking the hall and volunteers in the Bowman Fossil Bank will be happy to answer your questions about fossil preparation techniques. Moving on you encounter Mammoths and the Great Ice Age, featuring fossils of animals that lived at least 10,000 years ago.

At your next stop you discover the presence of humans in the Northern Rockies. Enduring Peoples: Native Cultures of the Northern Rockies and Plains traces the origins and development of Indians who have occupied Montana and other parts of the region for more than 11,000 years. The reasons fur trappers and white settlers came west and the life styles they carved out for themselves are reflected in Montana On The Move in the Paugh History Hall. Historic artifacts, photographic wall murals and pieces from the Museum's extensive textile collection add to your understanding of Montana's past. Here you'll see evidence collected from the only Lewis and Clark campsite to ever be scientifically verified.

The Museum of the Rockies is also home to the world-class Taylor Planetarium. It is the only public planetarium in a three-state region and one of the few with a computer graphics system that can simulate 3-D effects and flight through space. In addition to its main features which change quarterly, the planetarium offers live narrated tours of the night sky, laser shows, and a children's show on Saturday mornings. There's a constantly changing schedule of exhibits, too, so there's always something new to see at the Museum of the Rockies. You can see what's currently showing and what's coming next by logging onto the web site at museumoftherockies.org.

Your children will love the Martin Discovery Room, an interactive play area with dinosaurs, pioneers, a play station, earthquake table and a cozy reading nook with a huge plush teddy bear. Everyone will enjoy at stop at the Museum Store, one of the best places in the area for children's activity kits, educational toys, books and unique gifts. During the summer months, you can lunch at the T.rextaurant on the Bair Plaza, where the menu includes Big Mike burgers and Dino nuggets for the kids.

The Museum is open from 9 a.m. to 5 p.m. Monday through Saturday and Sunday afternoons from 12:30 to 5 p.m. From mid-June through Labor Day, hours are 8 a.m. to 8 p.m. daily. A $9 adult ticket and $6.50 student ticket for children 5-18 (children under 5 are free) gets access to the museum and planetarium. Admission to the museum only is $7 for adults and $4 for children; planetarium shows are $3 and laser shows tickets are $5. For information on current exhibits and programs, call (406) 994-2251 or (406) 994-DINO or check our web site at museumoftherockies.org.

The Museum is located on the Montana State University campus at 600 West Kagy Boulevard. The most direct route is via the 19th Street exit from Interstate 90. Travel through Bozeman on 19th Street until you reach the stoplight at Kagy Boulevard; turn left and follow the street signs.

*The Living History Farm with its lovely heirloom and Native American gardens are open during the summer months. Through daily activities, programs and livestock it illustrates life on a Montana homestead a century ago.*

# Colter's Run

*Excerpted from "John Bradbury's Travels in the Interior of America, 1809-1811" in Thwaites, Reuben G., (ed.) Early Western Travels, 1784-1846, Vol. V, Arthur H. Clark Co., Cleveland, 1904.*

The year was 1806. The Lewis and Clark Expedition was heading down the Missouri on its way back to civilization. The group met two trappers—Dickson and Hancock—who were on their way west to the rich beaver country. The two persuaded one member of the Expedition, 35-year-old John Colter, to accompany them.

The three spent the winter of 1806-1807 trapping by the Yellowstone River. Following a quarrel with his partners, Colter left in the spring and once again made his way down the Missouri. At its junction with the Platte River, he met a large party of trappers, the newly-formed Missouri Fur Company headed by Manuel Lisa. The company included several veterans of the Lewis and Clark Expedition: George Drouillard, John Potts and Peter Wiser. The group intended to establish a trading post on the Yellowstone at the mouth of the Bighorn and felt that Colter's previous experience in the area would be invaluable. Colter was easily persuaded to fall in with his old companions and headed up the Missouri again.

Arriving at the Bighorn in October 1807, the trappers built their post. They sent Colter into the surrounding country to contact local bands of Indians, tell them about the post and invite them in to trade. This seemingly simple mission turned out to be the first of John Colter's amazing travels through the Rocky Mountains.

## Yellowstone Geysers Discovered

Struggling through heavy snows and frigid temperatures of a Montana winter, Colter's journey took him to the smoking geyser basins in the vicinity of present-day Cody, Wyoming (which later became known as Colter's Hell) through the Wind River Mountains to the Tetons, then up past Yellowstone Lake and possibly through the Lamar Valley near what is now Cooke City. John Colter was thus the first white person to see the wonders of Yellowstone Park, but his accounts of the geological oddities sounded so farfetched that he was the butt of many a mountain man's jokes for years afterward.

Passing the summer at the Bighorn, Colter traveled west in the fall of 1808 toward the Missouri Headwaters with a band of Crow and Flathead Indians. One day's journey from the Three Forks, Blackfeet attacked the party. Wounded in the leg, Colter managed to survive, but the Blackfeet noted his presence with the Crow. This set the pattern of Blackfeet hostility toward whites in the Headwaters area, an antagonism which lasted for sixty years.

## Colter at the Headwaters

This encounter with the Blackfeet didn't discourage the trapper from returning to the Headwaters. In later years, John Colter told of his adventure to John Bradbury, whose account is reprinted below:

"This man came to St. Louis in May, 1810, in a small canoe, from the head waters of the Missouri, a distance of three thousand miles, which he traversed in thirty days. I saw him on his arrival, and received from him an account of his adventures after he had separated from Lewis and Clark's party: one of these, from its singularity, I shall relate."

"Soon after he separated from Dixon, and trapped in company with a hunter named Potts...They were examing their traps early one morning, in a creek about six miles from that branch of the Missouri called Jefferson's Fork, and were ascending in a canoe, when they suddenly heard a great noise, resembling the trampling of animals... Colter immediately pronounced it to be occasioned by Indians... In a few minutes afterwards their doubts were removed, by a party of Indians making their appearance on both sides of the creek, to the amount of five or six hundred, who beckoned them to come ashore. As retreat was now impossible, Colter turned the head of the canoe to the shore; and at the moment of its touching, an Indian seized the rifle belonging to Potts; but Colter... immediately retook it, and handed it to Potts, who remained in the canoe, and on receiving it pushed off into the river. He had scarcely quitted the shore when an arrow was shot at him, and he cried out, "Colter, I am wounded." Colter remonstrated with him on the folly of attempting to escape, and urged him to come ashore. Instead of complying, he instantly levelled his rifle at an Indian, and shot him dead on the spot... He was instantly pierced with arrows so numerous, that, to use the language of Colter, "he was made of riddle of." They now seized Colter, stripped him entirely naked, and began to consult on the manner in which he should be put to death. They were first inclined to set him up as a mark to shoot at, but the chief interfered, and seizing him by the shoulder, asked him if he could run fast?"

## Colter's Run

[Colter] knew that he had now to run for his life, with the dreadful odds of five or six hundred against him, and those armed Indians; therefore cunningly replied that he was a very bad runner, although he was considered by the hunters as remarkably swift. The chief... led Colter out on the prairie three or four hundred yards, and released him, bidding him to save himself if he could. At that instant the horrid war whoop sounded in the ears of poor Colter, who, urged with the hope of preserving life, ran with a speed at which he was himself surprised. He proceeded toward the Jefferson, having to traverse a plain six miles in breadth, abounding with the prickly pear, on which he was every instant treading with his naked feet. He ran nearly half way across the plain before he ventured to look over his shoulder, when he perceived that the Indians were very much scattered, and that he had gained ground to a considerable distance from the main body; but one Indian, who carried a spear, was much before all the rest, and not more than a hundred yards from him. He had now arrived within a mile of the river, when he distinctly heard the appalling sound of footsteps behind him, and every instant expected to feel the spear of his pursuer. Again he turned his head, and saw the savage not twenty yards from him. Determined if possible to avoid the expected blow, he suddenly stopped, turned round, and spread out his arms. The Indian, surprised by the suddenness of the action, also attempted to stop, but exhausted with running, he fell whilst endeavoring to throw his spear, which stuck in the ground, and broke in his hand. Colter instantly snatched up the pointed part, with which he pinned him to the earth, and then continued his flight. The foremost of the Indians, on arriving at the place, stopped till others came up to join them, when they set up a hideous yell. Every moment of this time was improved by Colter, who, although fainting and exhausted, succeeded in gaining the skirting of the cottonwood trees, on the borders of the fork, through which he ran, and plunged into the river."

## Escape

Fortunately for him, a little below this place there was an island, against the upper point of which a raft of drift timber had lodged. He dived under the raft, and after several efforts, got his head above water amongst the trunks of trees, covered over with smaller wood to the depth of several feet. Scarcely had he secured himself, when the Indians arrived on the river, screeching and yelling, as Colter expressed it, "like so many devils." ... In horrible suspense he remained until night, when hearing no more of the Indians, he dived from under the raft, and swam silently down the river to a considerable distance, when he landed, and traveled by night. Although happy in having escaped from the Indians, his situation was still dreadful: he was completely naked, under a burning sun; the soles of his feet were entirely filled with the thorns of the prickly pear; he was hungry, and had no means of killing game, although he saw abundance around him, and was at least seven days journey from Lisa's Fort, on the Bighorn branch of the Yellowstone River. These were circumstances under which almost any man would have despaired. He arrived at the fort in seven days, having subsisted on a root much esteemed by the Indians of the Missouri, now known by naturalists as *psoralca esculenta*."

**F The Sandwich Co.**
8192 Huffine Lane, at Thriftway Concoco, Bozeman. 582-1393

**S Antique Post**
81550 Gallatin Road, at 4 Korners, Bozeman. 585-3554 or fax 585-3593

The Antique Post is located in the Four Corners area on your way to or from Big Sky. Discover 7,600 square feet of light and open floor space that is filled with everything from Western treasures to European antiques from 40 different dealers. Enjoy the friendly service they are known for while you explore jewelry, antiques, collectibles, primitives, Western Art, and furniture. You'll delight in finding everything from treasured pieces of Montana's historic past to antique skis and other unique furnishings to complement the decor of your new Montana home. They are open seven days a week with plenty of convenient parking.

**S Antler Art by Frank Long**
8189 Huffine Ln., Bozeman. 587-5255 or 800-242-5255

Located at Four Corners, just 8 miles west of Bozeman. Frank Long has over 30 years experience in designing and building antler lighting fixtures and furniture. Come on in, visit the showroom, and see the one-of-a-kind buffalo chair. Open Monday–Friday 8:30 a.m.–5 p.m. Mention this ad and receive one free deer antler.

**M Bozeman Hot Springs**
81123 Gallatin Road, US Hwy 191, 4 Corners, Bozeman. 586-6492. Spa: 522-9563

The Bozeman Hot Springs has been a popular destination in the Bozeman area for over 100 years. Today you'll find a beautifully remodeled modern state of the art health and fitness center that provides every amenity to pamper and rejuvenate yourself after enjoying Montana's beautiful outdoors. A trip to the Bozeman Hot Springs offers ten pools that range in temperatures from cold to very hot and everything in between. Sun bathe on the deck of the outdoor pool! All pools are drained and refreshed nightly. No chemicals are used in this naturally pure water. Not only can you soak in these therapeutic waters, but you can also enjoy the steam room, sauna, tanning beds,

and state of the art extensive fitness center. Fully equipped dressing rooms provide private showers and lockers.

Pamper yourself at the luxurious spa with a massage, manicure, pedicure, waxing, facial with lymph drainage and infrared, body wraps, salt glows, and chi machine. There's even more! Enjoy healthy refreshments at their juice bar, babysitting service on site, and buy or rent swimsuits if you forget yours! You'll find everything you need to enjoy a day of fun and rejuvenation at the Bozeman Hot Springs Spa and Fitness Center! They are open seven days a week. Single admission as well as various membership packages are available.

## 13. *Gas, Food, Lodging*

### Belgrade

In 1882, Thomas B. Quaw, an entrepreneur, located land along the newly surveyed Northern Pacific Railway about ten miles from Bozeman. He found this property greatly to his liking, and thus, the community had its beginning. At that time, many European financiers invested money to complete the Northern Pacific Line. As a complimentary notice of appreciation to the Serbian investors, this blind siding was named Belgrade after the capital of Serbia.

From the turn of the century through the 1930s, Belgrade continued to expand, gaining businesses, professionals and the trappings of an established community. However, speculation in the community slowed, the depression took its toll, and Belgrade settled into the quiet farming community it was to remain for some time.

During the 1990s, Belgrade has experienced significant growth due largely to the boom environment of Gallatin County. While it is now somewhat of a bedroom community of Bozeman, it maintains its own character as a community. *Partially reprinted from Belgrade Chamber of Commerce brochure.*

**A Power Train Plus**
5174 Jackrabbit Ln., Belgrade. 388-1887

Power Train Plus has an excellent reputation for quality auto repair. They will repair any kind of vehicle including complete auto, truck, motor home, and muffler service. With six full-time auto technicians, they can also perform diagnostic repairs on newer vehicles. Located right off I-90 there is plenty of room for parking in front of the shop. Open Monday–Friday.

**F Country Kitchen**
6269 Jackrabbit Ln and I 90., Belgrade. 388-0808

Enjoy family oriented dining in this attractive, smoke-free, relaxing restaurant. Located next to the Holiday Inn Express, the Country Kitchen has easy access to I-90. They are "kid friendly" offering snacks, coloring, and Game Boys for the kids. This is a convenient stop on your way to Yellowstone National Park and Big Sky. The menu offers home-style cooking and a break for the traveler who is tired of fast food. Menu selection to satisfy every appetite. Breakfast, lunch and dinner are served daily from 6 a.m. to 10 p.m.

### L Holiday Inn Express
6261 Jackrabbit Lane, Belgrade. Manhattan.388-0800 or Reservations 800-542-6791

Conveniently located close to the Gallatin Field Airport, this new Holiday Inn Express offers exceptional accommodations for business travelers and families alike. Their 67 spacious guest rooms feature cable TV with HBO, air conditioning, non-smoking rooms, beautiful decor and luxurious comfort. Enjoy their hot tub and complimentary continental breakfast. The lobby has a spacious sitting area that is a perfect place to relax with a book. Family dining is available next door at the Country Kitchen. The friendly staff, excellent service, and modern accommodations at the Holiday Inn Express will make your stay unforgettable.

### L Super 8 Motel Of Belgrade
6450 Jackrabbit Lane, I-90 Exit 298 S., Belgrade. 388-1493 or Reservations at 800-800-8000

The Super 8 of Belgrade is conveniently located at I-90 and minutes from Gallatin Field Airport. They offer 72 newly renovated rooms that provide excellent, yet economical accommodations. Enjoy cable television, air conditioning, indoor heated pool, and free deluxe continental breakfast, served in their spacious and comfortable lobby. You can select from nonsmoking rooms and suites. Their suites are available for every need, with extras such as sleeper sofas, refrigerators, microwaves, kitchenettes, and some with jetted tubs. Whether you stay for a day or a week you will enjoy the excellent customer service the folks at the Super 8 in Belgrade are known for.

## 14. *Gas, Food*

### V Wapiti Basin Outfitters
13607 Springhill Road, Belgrade. 388-4941. www.wapitibasinoutfitters.com

What makes Wapiti Basin Outfitters different is their dedication to hunting Montana Bull Elk. If you are looking for a true western mountain hunt-

## Gallatin City

**In the 1860s, gold was discovered** in Colorado, Idaho and Montana, and a flood of emigrants poured into the Northern Rockies. Mining camps with names like Bannack, Virginia City and Last Chance Gulch sprang up in western Montana.

Fortunes were not only made with pick and shovel; often larger ones were made by those who could supply and feed the hungry miners. One group of enterprising Missourians realized that existing freight routes into Bannack and Virginia City from Utah were long, arduous and uncertain. An easier route lay to the northwest-the Missouri River. By 1860, steamboats were beginning regular service to Fort Benton; if their service could be extended up to the Three Forks of the Missouri, it would then take only two or three days of easy overland travel to reach the gold camps.

### City at the Headwaters

In 1862, the Missourians organized the Gallatin Town Company and received permission to navigate to the Three Forks. By January 1863, a town named Gallatin City had been laid out on the north bank of the combined Madison-Jefferson rivers, opposite the mouth of the Gallatin. The town was a speculative venture; the founders hoped it would become the commercial capital of the region. Their expectations never materialized, however, and the town was gradually deserted. Some of the cabins were moved to established farms on the south bank of the river, where a small community-also called Gallatin City-was incorporated February 2, 1865.

This second Gallatin City experienced brief prosperity. Its ferry became a busy link from the booming gold towns of Virginia City and Bannack to Last Chance Gulch (Helena). Food and wheat from Gallatin City farmers was much less expensive and more readily available for the gold camps than the supplies which had to be shipped in from "the States." At its height in the early 1870s, Gallatin City would boast of a grist mill, several stores, a hotel, a fairground and even a racetrack.

But the good days were fleeting ones. The ferry provided unreliable passage across the river; by 1871 several bridges had been constructed at more convenient points up the river. The neighboring town of Bozeman attracted more and more settlers and by the late 1879's perceptive Gallatin City merchants were disposing of their properties. The final blow was dealt by the railroad which came in 1883, bypassing Gallatin City by two miles.

*Excerpted from the Headwaters Herald, Montana Fish, Wildlife & Parks.*

ing experience and understand the effort involved and challenges that "result oriented" bull elk hunting presents, you will leave their camp satisfied. You will experience the finest in food, equipment, horses and facilities, not to mention good times. Serious hunters will have an unforgettable experience that will bring a lifetime of memories. Hunting bull elk in Montana represents one of the most exciting and challenging experiences any hunter will ever have and Wapiti Basin Outfitters has a lifetime of experience to deliver just that.

### F The Mint Bar & Cafe

27 East Main, Belgrade. 388-1100

The Mint brings back the spirit of the great Montana roadhouses of the 40s and 50s, when each saloon had it's own personality and was measured by the quality of their beef and the dryness of their martinis. Eat in the cigar friendly bar or the non-smoking dining room. Enjoy hand-cut steaks, fresh seafood and pasta or just come in, pull a seat up to the bar, try fabulous hand-made cocktails, maybe sing along with Sinatra, and let some time go by. You will find that a very special dining experience will always be enjoyed at The Mint! Open daily for dinner from 5 p.m. to 10 p.m. Open Monday through Friday from 11:30 a.m. to 3 p.m. for lunch. Reservations recommended.

### F MacKenzie River Pizza Co.

409 West Main St., Belgrade. 388-0016

Famous for gourmet pizzas, super sandwiches and extraordinary salads, everything is made fresh daily right down to the salad dressings and the pizza dough! Conveniently located on the West end of the business loop, perfect for when you are on your way to Yellowstone or Big Sky, or even the airport.

### F The Wok

307 E. Main Street, near the airport, Belgrade. 388-4850

### S Montana Gift Corral at Gallatin Field

Gallatin Field Airport, Belgrade. 585-2655. www.giftcorral.com

A trip in or out of the Gallatin Field Airport would not be complete without a stop at the Montana Gift Corral located on the main floor. This is not an ordinary airport gift shop. The store offers western, fishing, and outdoor themed gift items, sculpture, jewelry, home accents, books, Montana foods, and toys. Sensational items to remind you of your visit to Montana. They can also help you with the sundry and snack items you might need for the trip ahead. All items are the same price as at the downtown store. Visit them at their web site their downtown store.

## 15. *Gas, Food, Lodging, Camping, Shopping*

### Amsterdam/Churchill

As you would guess, this area was settled and named by Hollanders. The area is still largely occupied by families of Dutch descent who carry on many of the community oriented traditions of the old country, including dairy farming.

### Manhattan

Manhattan, 20 miles northwest of Bozeman, is a small town which once had a profitable malting business until the time of prohibition. The stone malt house still stands and the town remains branded with a name given to it by investors who operated the Manhattan Malting Company. Originally called Moreland, a group from a land-holding company in New York City renamed the town in 1891. Today it remains primarily an agricultural community.

### T Manhattan Area Museum

A quaint museum located in downtown Manhattan gives visitors a taste of the railroad and rural roots of the area. Open during the summer months, Tuesday through Saturday, 10 a.m. to 4 p.m.

### F Sir Scott's Oasis

204 W. Railroad Ave. S., Downtown Manhattan. 284-6929

This nationally known restaurant is the Sir Scott's of the "Real Beef in Manhattan" commercials. Locally famous for their outstanding steaks and seafood served up daily. Your entree selection comes with appetizers, soup, salad, choice of potato, dessert and coffee. The generous portions are something you won't forget! All of Sir Scott's beef is USDA Choice beef aged and cut daily on the premises. Try their Jo Jo fries and don't say no to their soups. The atmosphere is pure Montana and open seven days a week for lunch and dinner. They also offer a carry out menu. Reservations are highly recommended.

### F Garden Café

107 S. Broadway, Manhattan. 284-3366

The Garden Café, originally built as the Kid Johnson Theater in 1917, is owned by Ann Tappan and Nick Schmutz, who trained in Switzerland, cooked in Europe, the Caribbean and San Francisco. The café is known for it's warm, friendly atmosphere and home style food. The burgers are made from fresh ground beef. Real ice cream shakes, and lunch specials ranging from spaghetti, chicken-fried steak, smothered pork chops, enchiladas, and fresh homemade pies and cookies fill out the fare. Saturdays, enjoy amazing omelets and the perennial favorite, Biscuits and Sausage Gravy. They use local, fresh ingredients, such as potatoes for homemade French Fries and pork for the Smoked Pork Chop Breakfast. The Billings Gazette wrote, "travelers from all over Montana stop by for their on the road meal." Open 6 a.m. to 4 p.m. Monday-Saturday. They occasionally feature live music and can accomodate private parties. Call for reservations or information at 284-3366.

### M Gallatin River Ranch Residential Ranch Community

3200 Nixon Gulch Rd., Manhattan. 284-3200 or 800-232-3295. www.gallatinriverranch.com

Residents at Gallatin river Ranch truly "live their vacation"! Private flyfishing access to the Gallatin River, horseback riding, hiking, and biking. You can enjoy it all at GRR where you can have your own "little piece of the West". They are offering 20 acre parcels at affordable prices, including underground power and phone, in this scenic 6,000 acre Residential Ranch Community. Their world-class equestrian center features a stable, indoor and outdoor arenas, training, and instructors. Visit them, take a trail ride, or schedule a tour of this scenic community to select a site that is perfect for you and your family. Visit their web site for additional information.

## 16. *Lewis & Clark, Food*

### Logan

At one time this was a major railroad town and had a roundhouse. The train still goes through town, but doesn't have much need to stop. The railroad bought the right-of-way from Odelia Logan in 1885 and named the town for her. Today its main business is the legendary The Land of Magic Steakhouse. They hold Annual Branding Parties the first weekend in May and area ranchers leave their marks on the walls of the restaurant.

### Trident

Named for the three forks of the Missouri River that meet near here. Today it is mostly a cement company town.

### D William Clark

July 14, 1806 (along the East Gallatin River)

*"I proceeded up this plain...and Crossed the main Chanel of the river,...and nooned it... the river is divided and on all the small Streams inoumerable quantities of beaver dams, tho' the river is yet navigable for Canoes."*

### T Madison Buffalo Jump State Park (Day use only)

23 miles west of Bozeman on I90 at Logan exit, than 7 miles south on Buffalo Jump Road. 994-4042.

As early as 2000 years ago and as recently as 200 years ago, the trampling of hoofs could be heard as Indians stampeded herds of buffalo off the cliffs to claim their meat and fur. Buffalo bone piles up to 60 inches deep and tepee rings on the plateau have left an unmistakable record of this form of buffalo hunting.

The story of the site is described in an outdoor display. Diagrams and descriptions point out the location of rock piles that formed drive lanes, the area below the cliff where Indian women butchered the bison, and a more settled site where Indians processed their trappings. Here you can experience the history and the breathtaking view of the Madison Valley and the Tobacco Root Mountains from the overlook.

### F Land of Magic Dinner Club

I-90 Exit 283, 11060 Front Street, Logan. 284-3794

This historic restaurant in the tiny historical railroad hamlet of Logan is widely known as "The Place for Steak". Also famous for their exceptional twice baked potatoes, the Land of Magic offers a wide variety of charbroiled steaks, seafood entrees and other house entrees such as Duck a l'orange and baby back ribs. Enjoy your favorite cocktail, beer, or wine with dinners that include everything from appetizers to dessert. The rustic atmosphere is just the way you would expect it to be in Montana. They hold an Annual Branding Party and Steak Barbeque the first Sunday in May. Reservations are recommended.

## 17. *Historic Marker, Lewis & Clark, Attraction, Gas, Food, Lodging, Camping, Shopping*

### Three Forks

Three Forks is situated near the convergence point of the three rivers of the Missouri River about 30 miles from Bozeman. The three forks making the confluence of the Missouri River are: the Jefferson River, the Gallatin River and the internationally-famous Madison River. The town lies at 4,081 feet and is protected by the Rocky Mountains leaving the eastern side mild in the winter with cool mountain breezes in the summer.

Historically, the three tributaries of the Missouri have brought people of various cultures together. The Indians came together at this point because it was a convergence for wildlife and a crossroads of hunting trails. Fur traders found these river junctions a useful trading location. Today the Headwaters Heritage Museum and Missouri Headwaters State Park preserve the history of this confluence of peoples and rivers.

The areas at the headwaters and of Three Forks has some of the most colorful early history in Montana. Three Forks was the crossroads of Indian trails. Just west of town, Sacajawea as a child was captured from her tribe, the Shoshones. She married a French-Canadian trapper, Toussaint Charbaneau, and together they guided the Lewis and Clark Expedition through the area in 1805.

The Corps of Discovery arrived at the headwaters of the Missouri River in July 1805. They camped for a week along the Jefferson River just above the headwaters, while Clark recovered from a fever. In 1806, Clark was guided by Sacajawea across the valley from the three forks to the pass leading directly into the Yellowstone River.

Three Forks is also the site of one of the bloodiest battles ever fought between the Blackfeet, the Flatheads and the Crow. John Colter took part in this fight on the side of the Flatheads and the Crows in 1808. Colter's allies, though fewer in number, won the battle. In April 1810, the Missouri Fur Company established Fort Three

## Fort Three Forks

In the spring of 1810, Manuel Lisa sent Andrew and Pierre Menard with a party of about 30 men and John Colter as a guide to the Three Forks area to build a trading post. The resulting fort, Fort Three Forks, was one of the first trading posts between the Missouri and the Pacific Coast. The fort was built as a base for trapping beaver over the entire area of the Missouri river and its branches above the Great Falls.

Life was always interesting at the Fort. Eight of the party were killed by raiding Blackfeet Indians. When they weren't harassed by Indians, critters like rattlesnakes and grizzlies kept them on their toes. The business of beaver trapping was so hazardous that the fort was abandoned in 1811.

Nothing is left of the fort today. Time and the meandering river has destroyed most of the ground the fort stood on. A modern motel with the fort's name stands nearby the original site. However, an anonymous surveyor has given us a description of the fort: "A double stockade of logs set three feet deep, enclosing an area of 300 sq. feet situated upon the tongue of land about a half a mile wide, between the Jefferson and Madison Rivers, about two miles above the confluence, upon the south bank of the channel of the former stream, now called the Jefferson Slough. The store and warehouse were built on each side of the gates, and on the other side next to the interior of the fort, two buildings were connected by a gate, the space between buildings and stockade filled in with pickets, making a large strong room without any covering overhead. In each store, about five feet from the ground, was a hole 18 inches square, with a strong shutter fastening inside, opening into the enclosed space between the gates.

When the Indians wanted to trade, the inner gate was closed; a man would stand at the outer gate until a number of Indians had passed in and then lock the outer gate. He would then climb through the trading hole into the store. The Indians would pass whatever each one had to trade through the hole into the store and the trader would throw out of the hole whatever the Indians wanted to the value of the article received."

Forks, but because of constant Indian attacks, the fort was abandoned before it was completed. Kit Carson narrowly escaped from a Blackfeet brave whom he killed on the bluffs north of Three Forks. This fascinating history is displayed on plaques at the Headwaters State Park or from the Headwaters Heritage Museum in downtown Three Forks.

Only eighteen miles west of Three Forks is the Lewis and Clark Caverns State Park, a treasure you won't want to miss! This is Montana's first state park and has perhaps the most impressive limestone caves in northwestern United States. It is truly an underground fairyland of ancient stalactites and stalagmites created millions of years ago. There is a gradual sloping trail leading to the caverns entrance and once inside be prepared for over 600 steps leading through hands-and-knees crawl space, narrow rock slides and cathedral-size chambers. The cave's interior is a constant 50 degrees.

## Willow Creek

The town was named for the creek that flows nearby, which in turn was named for the willows that line the banks of the creek.

## H The Three Forks of the Missouri

Hwy 10, east of Three Forks

*This region was alive with beaver, otter and game before the white man came. It was disputed hunting territory with the Indian tribes. Sacajawea, the Shoshone who guided portions of the Lewis and Clark Expedition, was captured near here when a child, during a battle between her people and the Minnetarees. Her memories of this country were invaluable to the explorers. The Expedition, westward bound, encamped near here for a few days in the latter part of July, 1805. The following year Captain Clark and party came back, July 13, 1806, on their way to explore the Yellowstone River.*

*In 1808, John Colter, discoverer of Yellowstone Park, and former member of the Lewis and Clark Expedition, was trapping on a stream in this vicinity when captured by a band of Blackfeet. His only companion was killed. Colter was stripped, given a head start, and ordered to run across the flat which was covered with prickly pear. The Indians were hot on his heels but Colter undoubtedly made an all-time record that day for sprints as well as distance events. He outran the Indians over a six-mile course and gained the cover of the timber along the Jefferson River. Once in the stream he dove and came up under a jam of driftwood. This hideout saved him from a lot of disappointed and mystified Indians. When night came he headed east, weaponless and outnuding the nudists. He traveled in this condition for seven days to Fort Lisa, his headquarters, at the mouth of the Big Horn River.*

*In 1810, the Missouri Fur Co. built a fur trading post close by but due to the hostility of the Blackfeet Indians were forced to abandon it that fall.*

## D Sgt. Ordway

July 13, 1806 (at the Three Forks)

*"Capt. Clark & party leaves us hear to cross over to the River Roshjone. So we parted I and 9 more proceeded on down the river with the canoes verry well."*

## D William Clark

July 13, 1806

*"The indian woman who has been of great Service to me as a pilot through this Country recommends a gap in the mountain more South which I shall cross."*

## T Parker Homestead State Park (Day use only)

8 miles west of Three Forks on Montana 2. 994-4042.

This is probably the smallest park in the system and officially lists visitation as zero. In fact, if you weren't looking for it, you would just pass right on by. There is no sign marking the site, and no interpretative displays explaining its history. It is simply a sod-roofed log cabin tucked under a few large cottonwoods on 1.67 acres. The state brochure lists it as "This sod-roofed log cabin is representative of the frontier homes of pioneers who settled Montana." It was built by Nelson and Rosie Parker and is a good example of log homesteads built in the late 1800s and early 1900s.

The state originally had plans to repair the cabin, erect signs, and create a parking area. Those plans were abandoned long ago. The state tried unsuccessfully to give it to the county. It is still a state park costing the state literally nothing. There is no caretaker and the state collects no fees from the property. It is a fascinating place and offers a glimpse of life for settlers at the turn of the century.

## T Missouri Headwaters State Park

Just off I-90 east of Three Forks. 994-4042

If you love to see moving waters, this is the place. The park embraces the wild rivers of the Gallatin, Jefferson, and Madison that converge near Three Forks and flow into the Missouri River. Missouri Headwaters was a geographical focal point important to early Native Americans, trappers, traders, and settlers. The now obliterated site of the Three Forks Post, built in 1810 by a group of trappers, is believed to be near here. Sacajawea lived near here as a teenager before she was kidnapped by a band of Hidatsa Indians and taken to North Dakota where she later met the Lewis and Clark Expedition. John Colter visited this area several times, and it was from here that he made his historic run over cactus, rocks and sagebrush after being stripped naked by a band of Blackfeet. It is now a wonderful place for outdoor activities such as hiking, fishing, camping and wildlife viewing.

## T Luzenac America Talc Mine

2150 Bench Road, Three Forks. 285-5300

The second largest talc mine in the world is located between Three Forks and Willow Creek. Call for tour information.

## T Headwaters Heritage Museum

Cedar & Main St., Three Forks. 285-4778

Housed in what was originally one of the first banks in Three Forks, the museum portrays the history of Three Forks through various displays and artifacts, including a turn-of-the-century village on the second floor. In 1925, the building suffered considerable damage from an earthquake but was restored to its original design.

The museum contains thousands of artifacts and memorabilia depicting the local history, such as a small anvil, all that remains of a trading post established here in 1810. The largest fish ever caught in the state of Montana—a 29 1/2 pound brown trout caught at Wade Lake in 1966 by a resident of Three Forks—is on display.

Nostalgic scenes from the past include a dental office, kitchen, laundry nook, schoolroom, blacksmith shop, beauty salon and millinery shop. The military room holds remembrances of our local veterans. Three Forks began as a railroad community, and the Milwaukee Railroad station agent's office holds an interesting assortment of memorabilia of those bygone days. Another excellent exhibit is 701 different types of barbed wire.

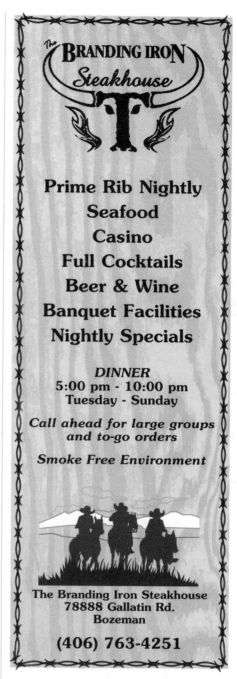

A log cabin from Gallatin City, built in the 1860s of cottonwood logs, can be seen in the picnic area directly behind the museum. The interior is furnished with the necessities of pioneer life, and prickly pear cactus grow and bloom on its rooftop.

The museum is open from May through September Monday through Saturday from 9 a.m. to 5 p.m. and Sunday from 1-5 p.m. Admission is free, but donations are appreciated.

*Reprinted from museum brochure.*

## T Lewis & Clark Caverns State Park

19 miles west of Three Forks on Montana 2. 287-3541

Located in the rugged Jefferson River Canyon, Lewis and Clark Caverns features one of the most highly decorated limestone caverns in the Northwest. Naturally air conditioned, these spec-



Section 5

tacular caves are lined with stalactites, stalagmites, columns, and helictites. The Caverns—which are part of Montana's first and best known state park—are electrically lighted and safe to visit. Guided cave tours are offered at Lewis and Clark Caverns State Park, including special candle light tours in December. To avoid peak use periods, call the park for suggested visitation and tour times.

Lewis and Clark Caverns are the largest limestone caves in Montana and have fascinated children as well as adults for many years. The labyrinth of these underground caves leads you through narrow passages among stalactites and stalagmites which glitter and drip. Truly a limestone fairyland decorated by nature, these colorful and intriguing formations make for a worthwhile two-hour tour. Also within the park are breathtaking views of the Tobacco Root Mountains and the Jefferson River valley.

### F Willow Creek Cafe & Saloon

21 Main Street, Willow Creek. 285-3698

Take a scenic drive to Willow Creek and find the wonderful history of Montana embodied in this landmark built in 1907. While enjoying the down home atmosphere and great homestyle cooking check out the bullet holes in the molded tin ceiling that date back to its early days as the Babcock Saloon. The best part of the wonderful country drive to Willow Creek will be the food once you've arrived. The hand cut steaks, pasta dishes, their signature chicken fried steak with pan gravy and more can be enjoyed with your favorite beverage. Legendary baby back ribs are served Tuesday through Sunday nights. Also check for daily specials. Breakfast is served Sundays at 8:00 a.m. Open for lunch and dinner Tuesday through Saturday.

### F Historic Headwaters Restaurant

105 S. Main, Downtown Three Forks. 285-4511, www.headwatersrestaurant.com

Built in 1908 as a restaurant, the Headwaters has been restored to its original charm and beauty. Stuart, a graduate of the Culinary Institute of America in Hyde Park, NY and his partner Michelle specialize in handmade American food with flavor. The seafood is flown in daily, the buffalo is raised locally, the beef is organic longhorn and they use as many regionally produced ingredients as are available. Their menu offers not only American Regional but also, Oriental, Italian and Mexican selections. Enjoy the smoke-free dining room or the gardens and fresh air deck and a variety of micro-brews and American wines to compliment your meal. Their hours are Wed. through Sun., 11 a.m. to 5 p.m. for lunch, and dinner from 5 p.m. to 10 p.m. And. . .they always play the blues! Learn more at their web site at www.headwatersrestaurant.com.

### F Wheat Montana Farms & Bakery

10770 U.S. Hwy 287, I-90 Exit 274, Three Forks. 285-3614, www.wheatmontana.com

Wheat Montana Farms & Bakery is an experience in itself. It is a 13,000 acre working wheat farm producing two very special varieties of chemical-free wheat. It is also a bakery producing about 10,000 loaves of bread a day from the wheat they grow. Additionally, it is a gift shop featuring Montana made products. For the traveler, Wheat Montana is a deli/restaurant featuring farm fresh baked rolls, muffins and breads, plus coffees, refreshments and incredible soups and sandwiches. This is a perfect stop for a unique Montana experience and a taste of homemade, natural goodness. A large parking area and easy access from I-90 is convenient for all vehicles. Be sure and visit them at their web site.

### L The Broken Spur Motel

124 W. Elm, Hwy 2 W., Three Forks. 285-3237
Reservations only 888-354-3048

The Broken Spur Motel is a western motel with old fashioned hospitality, located in historic Three Forks, featuring deluxe rooms at reasonable rates. The rooms are complete with queen size beds, non-smoking rooms, cable TV, phones, kitchenettes, special suites for families or meetings and handicapped accessible rooms. Enjoy complimentary continental breakfast with fresh coffee, tea, hot chocolate, juice, and homemade cinnamon rolls, muffins and toast served in the spacious lobby. Browse the gift shop with Montana-made gifts and souvenirs. The Broken Spur is close to many activities and sites in the area. See them at www.brokenspurmotel.com.

### L Fort Three Forks Motel & RV Park

10776 US Hwy. 287, Three Forks. 285-3233
Reservations 800-477-5690, www.forthreeforks.com

Fort Three Forks features deluxe rooms and western hospitality at reasonable rates. Named for the fort known as Fort Three Forks, and also known as Old Fort Henry, one of the first trading posts between the Mississippi and the Pacific Coast. The motel offers complimentary continental breakfast, balconies overlooking the Bridger Mountains, special suite units, satellite TV, laundry facilities, handicapped and nonsmoking rooms, and extensive parking. The RV park has full hook ups. Enjoy touring their frontier village complete with a homestead cabin, tepees and wagon! Their friendly staff will help you with any of your accommodation needs. They are located just off I-90 near Wheat Montana. Visit them at www.fortthreeforks.com or at www.fort3forks@aol.com.

## 18. *Attraction*

### T Hyalite Canyon Recreation Area

17 miles south of Bozeman on S. 19th St. 587-6920

This is the most used recreation area in the state,

> ## THREE RIVERS
>
> **Captain Lewis, July 28th, 1805:**
> Both Capt. C. and myself corrisponded in opinon with rispect to the impropriety of calling either of these streams the Missouri and accordingly agreed to name them after the President of the United States and the Secretaries of the Treasury and state having previously named one river in honour of the Secretaries of War and Navy. In pursuance of this resolution we called the S.W. fork, that which we meant to ascend, Jefferson's River in honor of that illustrious personage Thomas Jefferson. *[the author of our enterprise.}* the Middle fork we called Madi-son's River in honor of James Madison, and the S.E. Fork we called Gallitin's River in honor of Albert Gallitin [Gallatin]. the two first are 90 yards wide and the last is 70 yards, all of them run with great velocity and th[r]ow out large bodies of water. Gallitin's River is reather more rapid than either of the others, is not quite as deep but from all appearances may be navigated to a consider-able distance. Capt. C. who came down Madison's river yesterday and has also seen Jefferson's some distance thinks Madison's reather the most rapid, but it is not as much so by any means as Gallitin's. the beds of all these streams are formed of smooth pebble and gravel, and their waters perfectly transparent; in short they are three noble streams...

# Earthquake Lake

**A severe earthquake caused a massive** landslide on August 17, 1959 at 11:37 p.m. Several faults in the Madison River area moved at the same time causing an earthquake that triggered a massive landslide.

The slide moved at 100 mph and happened in less than one minute. Over 80 million tons of rock crashed into the narrow canyon, burying an open meadow where some campers had stopped for the night.

The landslide completely blocked the Madison River and caused it to form Earthquake Lake. The force of the slide displaced both the air in the canyon and water of the Madison River. It created high velocity winds and a wall of water that swept through the area, just downstream from the slide, killing five people in its path.

## Earthquake at Hebgen Lake

The Hebgen Lake Earthquake measured 7.5 on the Richter scale. At least three blocks of the earth's crust suddenly dropped as two faults moved simultaneously... the Red Canyon fault and the Hebgen Lake fault.

The north shore of Hebgen Lake dropped 19 feet and cabins fell into the water. Hebgen Lake sloshed back and forth. Huge waves called seiches crested over Hebgen Dam. This earth filled dam cracked in at least four places, but held. Three sections of Highway 287 fell into the lake. Hundreds of campers were trapped.

28 people lost their lives as a result of the earthquake. Their names appear on a bronze plaque on one of the massive dolomite boulders carried across the canyon by the slide. The dolomite boulder serves as a memorial.

## Madison River Canyon Earthquake Area

This immense earthquake's impact shocked and chilled the world. Families gradually rebuilt their lives, structures and roads were reconstructed.

In 1960, a 38,000 acre area in the canyon was designated as the "Madison River Canyon Earthquake Area." This portion of the Gallatin National Forest is of great scientific and general interest.

As you travel through this area, the effects of the ever-changing earth can be seen all around you.

The Visitor Center is located on Highway 287, 17 miles west of Highway 191, and 25 miles to the town of West Yellowstone, Montana.

*Two people died at Cliff Lake Campground, 15 miles southwest of the Madison Canyon landslide, when a large boulder bounced over the picnic table and landed on their tent. Their three sons, sleeping a few feet away, were not injured. 1959 U.S. Forest Service photo.*

This facility is accessible to people with disabilities.

Open: Memorial Day - late September, 7 days a week, 8:30 - 6:00 p.m. Telephone: 646-7369 (V/TDD)

## Map Guide

1. A Spillway was cut across the slide by the U.S. Army Corps of Engineers. On September 10, 1959 water passed through the 250 ft. wide and 14 ft. deep channel. On October 17, 1959 the channel was deepened another 50 ft.

2. Visitor Center and Slide - Come and view the slide from the observation room. Listen to the interpreter's story. Walk the trail to the Memorial Boulder and overlook.

3. Rock Creek Turnout - A Forest Service campground lies under 100 feet of water just off this point. Some campers escaped and others perished from the rising waters.

4. Earthquake Lake - The slide dammed the Madison River to form Earthquake Lake, which filled in three weeks and created a new body of water 190 ft. deep and 6 miles long.

5. Boat Launch - This portion of the old highway continues to serve the public. The old highway lies beneath the waters of Earthquake Lake.

6. Refuge Point - This ridge provided a place of protection during the night of August 17 for many survivors of the earthquake. The next morning Forest Service smoke jumpers parachuted to this point and set up rescue operations. Later that day helicopters evacuated the survivors.

7. Ghost Village - These deserted cabins were displaced here from the waters of Earthquake Lake.

8. Cabin Creek Scarp - At this site a 21 foot fault scarp severed the old campground.

9. Hebgen Dam - The earth fill dam held, although it suffered damage from tremors and huge earthquake caused waves called seiches.

10. Building Destruction - A short walk will take you through this area. You can see the old resort cabins that are submerged in Hebgen Lake.

11. Road Destruction - One of the three places where the road collapsed into Hebgen Lake. Look along the old roadbed to see where the land shifted during the earthquake.

12. Red Canyon - You can view the fault scarp that extends 14 miles in this area. A fault scarp is a cliff created by movement along a fault.

13. Duck Creek Y - This is where the epicenter of the earthquake occurred.

*Reprinted from U.S. Forest Service brochure.*

*The north shore of Hebgen Lake was submerged when the rock on which it rests dropped down adjacent to the new Hebgen fault scarp. The main residence at Hilgard Lodge dropped off its foundation into the lake and floated to this location. 1959 U.S. Forest Service photo.*

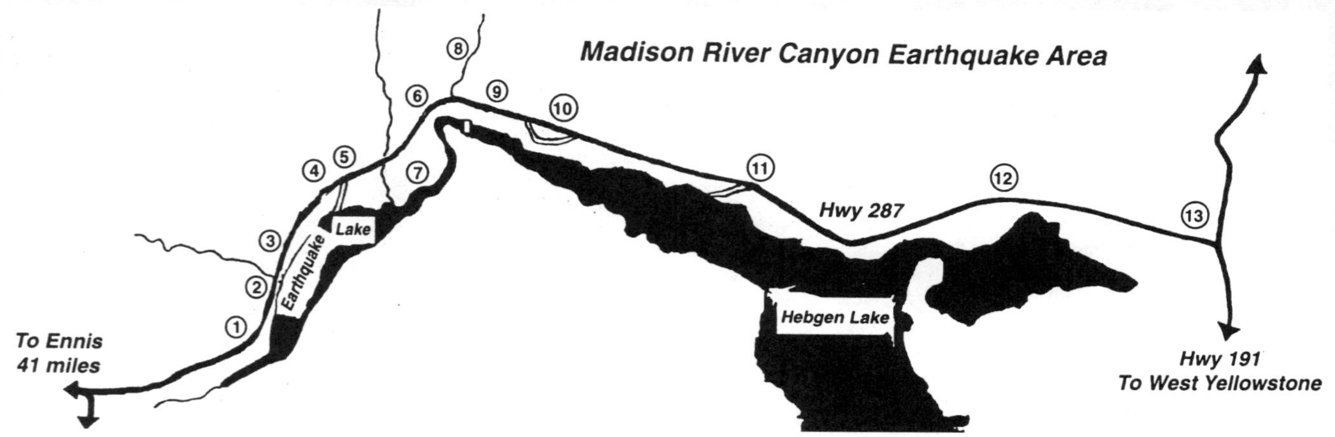


Section 5

and for good reason. A beautiful mountain lake sits at the end of a beautiful drive up the canyon of Hyalite Creek. The dam was constructed in the late 1940s, and the reservoir provides water for the community of Bozeman. Surrounding the lake are several campsites, picnic areas, and hiking trails. Fishing is good here and there is a boat launch with parking.

## 19. *Gas, Food, Lodging*

### Gallatin Gateway

Named for its proximity to the entrance of the Gallatin Canyon. The town was originally named Salesville for the Sales brothers who were storekeepers and ran a sawmill in the area in the late 1860s.

### AF Buffalo Station

75770 Gallatin Rd., Hwy 191, 6 miles south of 4 Corners, Gallatin Gateway. 763-4762. www.buffalostation.com

The Buffalo Station is the complete stop for all your needs when traveling from Bozeman to the Big Sky area and Yellowstone Park. Gas up the car or RV, stock up on snacks from the general store which offers the largest selection of chilled beverages around, or sit down to a great meal from the grill and enjoy indoor or patio dining. There's tantalizing selection of great food to choose from, including Buffalo burgers, delicious barbeques, or fresh-made deli sandwiches, complemented by a variety of soups and salads, and their famous "shaped" ice cream made with Montana's own Wilcoxen's Ice Cream. The Saloon features live music, with live poker and video machines in the Casino. You will find plenty of convenient parking for any sized vehicle at the Buffalo Station.

### F Branding Iron Steakhouse

78888 Gallatin Rd., Bozeman. 763-4251

The Branding Iron Steakhouse offers Old West atmosphere at its flavor-best and with a tantalizing selection of steaks, seafood or prime rib nightly. The restaurant has a lovely open airy atmosphere. You'll enjoy a Western decor, your favorite cocktail, beer or wine, and quiet rural setting with smoke free dining. There is a separate bar area, and casino away from the dining area. Show your Big Sky or Bridger Bowl ski pass and receive a free drink. When weather permits, diners can enjoy the beautiful outdoor patio with great views of the Bridger Mountain Range. Calling ahead for large groups is recommended, and to order food to go.

## 20.

### T Flying D Ranch: Bison Viewing Area

Just south of Gallatin Gateway.

This is the private property of media mogul Ted Turner. One of the first things he did when he bought the ranch was to remove all of the fences on the 130,000 acres to allow his bison herd (as many as 5,000) to roam as freely as they did in times past. Fortunately for visitors, there is a Forest Service road that traverses his property. The hundreds of "Turner Enterprises" signs along the road are a clear reminder that you are on private property if you leave the road. The road terminates at a trailhead and National Forest Access area.

While following the road, it is highly likely that you will see at least a few of the bison. On a good day, you may see hundreds if not thousands of them on the hillsides. This is probably the closest you will ever come to seeing a herd close to the size of herds that once roamed these areas. If you want to take pictures, do so from your car window. DO NOT get out of your car if bison are anywhere nearby. The can accelerate from standing still to 50 mph in seconds. They will charge suddenly and be on top of you before you can take your finger off the shutter. Almost every year, a tourist gets gored by a bison somewhere in the state because they got to close.

To find the ranch take Hwy. 191 into the Gallatin Canyon just south of Gallatin Gateway. Immediately after you enter the Canyon, watch for Spanish Creek Road veering off to the right of the paved road. As soon as you pass through the gate just a few yards ahead, you are on Turner property.

### V Arnaud Outfitting, Inc.

Gallatin Gateway. 763-4235. www.arnaudoutfitting.com

Arnaud Outfitting Inc. is a professional hunting company that specializes in trophy hunting of big game animals. One of the premier hunting destinations offered by this company is the famous Flying D Ranch with a professionally managed wild and free ranging elk herd that numbers 2,500 head. Complementing this world-class herd of elk is a magnificent herd of bison. Arnaud Outfitting, Inc. offers bison hunts that vary from trophy bison that inhabit the expanse of the Ranch to meat harvests that are designed to fit any pocketbook. They also offer hunts on fourteen other premier ranches in Montana, Colorado, California and Utah. Species offered for trophy hunting are, North American bison, Rocky Mountain elk, Tule elk, mule deer, white-tailed deer and Shiras moose. Hunting is limited on each property insuring that only mature animals are harvested.

## 21. *Attraction, Gas, Food, Lodging, Shopping*

### Big Sky

In 1902, Frank Crail first set foot in the Big Sky area. While hunting elk in the shadow of Lone Peak he fell in love with the beauty of the surroundings. He purchased the land from the original homesteaders and established the first cattle ranch in the area. Today, the original Crail Ranch house still stands in the meadow area by the golf course.

Following his lead, others moved into the area. Cattle ranching was soon superceded by dude ranches. Most of these, The 320 Ranch, Elk Horn Ranch, Lone Mountain Ranch, Covered Wagon Ranch and the Nine Quarter Circle Ranch are still in full operation today. This was the beginning of the Big Sky tourist trade.

Native Montanan Chet Huntley had a dream for the area as well. In 1969, Huntley and a group of investors including Conoco, Burlington Northern, Montana Power, Chrysler Corporation and Northwest Orient Airlines purchased the Crail Ranch land. In 1973, his dream of creating a year round resort community began to materialize with the official opening of Big Sky Ski & Summer Resort. In 1976, the Boyne Corporation acquired the property and began steps to develop and improve the area. Today it is a bustling year round resort community.

The drive to Big Sky through the Gallatin Canyon is arguably the most beautiful drive in the state, and the area surrounding the resort is arguably some of the most beautiful and dramatic mountain scenery found anywhere in the country. From atop the singular and majestic Lone Peak the view is one of endless mountain peaks. To the immediate north are the dramatic Spanish Peaks and the Spanish Peaks Wilderness area. Just 18 miles to the south is the boundary of Yellowstone National Park. Over 3 million acres of pristine land surrounding Big Sky is set aside as wilderness area. Big Sky sits in the middle of the greater Yellowstone ecosystem, which has some of the cleanest air and water quality in the world. It's not unusual to see moose, mountain goats, elk, big horn sheep, eagles, bear, deer or coyotes wandering around. The nearby Gallatin river is one of the best blue-ribbon trout streams in the world and was the site where "A River Runs Through It" was filmed.

### T Soldier's Chapel

Just south of entrance to Big Sky

This structure was built in 1955 as a World War II memorial. The inscription on the plaque in front of this beautiful little chapel reads: "In tribute to those immortal soldiers of the 163rd infantry who with courage and devotion died in pain, defending their country and the cause of freedom for all men. The 163rd Infantry, 41st Division, of Montana.

### V Gallatin Riverguides

PO Box 160212, Big Sky. 995-2290 or toll free at 888-707-1505 or Fax 995-4588. www.montanaflyfishing.com or email info@montanaflyfishing.com

Gallatin Riverguides is a Montana fly fishing tradition! They are a full-service outfitter and offer unparalleled accessibility to Montana's legendary trout streams: the Madison, Yellowstone, Missouri and Gallatin Rivers, with year round fly fishing trips available. They are located on the banks of the Gallatin River and their shop offers the widest selection of flies, clothing, tackle, and equipment in the area. A 3-acre spring fed casting pond adjacent to the shop provides a setting for clinics, demos, and instruction. They have cozy, riverside accommodations for groups of up to six. Additionally, they are a fully licensed Yellowstone Park outfitter. Call them or visit their web site at www.montanaflyfishing.com for a complete information packet.

### V Wild Trout Outfitters

Hwy. 191, 1/4 mile south of Big Sky entrance at Canyon Square. 995-2975 or 800-423-4742. www.wildtroutoutfitters.com

### F Big Horn Cafe

Hwy 191, Big Sky. 1/4 mile north of the entrance to Big Sky Resort. 995-3350

People frequent the Big Horn Cafe because of its wonderful home-cooked food, warm atmosphere and western hospitality. They are known by locals for the delicious homemade soups, mouth watering hot pastrami, and the Cuban sandwich. The homemade potato chips are to die for. A regular's favorite is the Huevos Rancheros for breakfast. The cafe has some of the best coffee in the area, along with espressos and lattes. When it's cold outside you can relax by the fire and sip a "Grandma's Mocha" (Grandma liked hers with a little Frangelico), or enjoy a local draft beer. They are open Tues. through Sun. at 7:30 a.m. until 3:30 p.m.

### FL 320 Guest Ranch

12 miles south of Big Sky, Hwy 191, Marker 36. 995-4283 or 800-243-0320. www.320ranch.com

A truly western experienceand vacation of a lifetime awaits you at the 320 Guest Ranch. Relax along the banks of the Gallatin River in the heart of the Gallatin National Forest as you cast your line into the stream or ride to an area mountain lake complete with float tube and fins. In the summer experience trail rides to 10,000 foot mountain peaks, white water rafting, hiking, mountain biking, barbecues by the river, and abundant wildlife. For winter, ski, snowmobile or snowshoe in deep powder, the "cold smoke" for which the area is renowned. Located only a few minutes from Yellowstone National Park, experience an incredible variety of activities and year-round accommodations. Choose from deluxe duplex cabins, 2 bedroom riverside cabins, with fireplace and kitchenettes or 3 bedroom/2 bath log homes with fireplace, jetted tubs and full-size kitchens. Stay for a day, a month, or anything in between. The 320 family will help you arrange your vacation, host your wedding, family reunion or company retreat.

### FL Cinnamon Lodge

37090 Gallatin Road, Gallatin Gateway, south of Big Sky. 995-4253

Visit a slice of heaven at the Cinnamon Lodge. The cabins are the original buildings that were built in the late 1940's and you'll enjoy a bit of the Wild West, but with modern-day amenities. The lodge, cabins and restaurant sit just off the shores of the beautiful Gallatin River. They cater to individuals who wish to experience the adventure of unspoiled back country, the high mountain trails and lakes, and the beauty of the Gallatin Canyon.

### *Montana Trivia*

In 1984, the Big Sky area was the scene of a Wild West drama that captured and held national attention. Kari Swenson, a world-class biathlete, was kidnapped by two self-professed mountain men. Soon after, Don Nichols and his son Dan shot and killed a would-be rescuer and wounded Swenson. They escaped and for five months were hunted by Sheriff Johnny France of Madison County, a former rodeo champion. A tip led him to their camp where he captured them without firing a shot.

The restaurant is widely acclaimed for their authentic Mexican cuisine, as well as Montana steaks, and desserts.

### FL Best Western Buck's T-4 Lodge

Hwy 191, 1 mile south of Big Sky entrance. 995-4111 or 800-822-4484

You will discover a friendly, inviting atmosphere the moment you step into Buck's T-4. A warm welcoming blaze in the stone hearth, big game trophies, and antique sporting gear hint at the establishment's beginnings as a hunting & fishing lodge. The richly appointed guest rooms provide western style accommodations at affordable prices. The restaurant offers exquisite Montana fine dining. Chef Chuck Schommer's creations feature wild game, steaks and daily specialties to tempt your palate. Buck's award winning wine list features 150 selections. They have been recognized by national publications such as Gourmet, Wine Spectator, Eating Well, and Bon Appetit.

### FL Rainbow Ranch Lodge

Hwy 191, 5 miles south of Big Sky entrance, 995-4132 or 800-937-4132, www.rainbowranch.com

Dine and stay with the Rainbow Ranch. It's the civilized way to enjoy the wild west on the banks of the world famous Gallatin River. The luxurious guest units have a unique western decor complete with lodgepole beds, down comforters, satellite TV, fireplace and private decks on the river. Join them for dinner in their renowned restaurant to experience elegant dining, Montana style. Chef, Michael McAuliffe brings together local, regional and international cuisines to provide you with a wide variety of superb dining choices. Also enjoy appertifs, fine cognacs, and Montana's largest selection of wines. The Rainbow Ranch continues the tradition of honoring guests with a rare combination of warm, attentive hospitality, rustic elegance and unparalleled wilderness beauty. Visit their web site and be dazzled.

### FL Corral Bar, Café, Steakhouse & Motel

5 miles south of Big Sky on Hwy. 191 at mile marker 43, 42895 Gallatin Rd. 995-4249. www.corralbar.com

The Corral has been a Gallatin Canyon landmark for over 50 years. A true Montana roadhouse with excellent dining offering steaks, seafood, fresh fish, chicken and pasta. You'll be satisfied after eating their outstanding breakfast, lunch, and dinner fare seven days a week. They offer a full beverage selection with your favorite beer, wine, or cocktail. They have some of the most affordable motel rooms in Big Sky and are just minutes from skiing, snowmobiling, fishing, golf and Yellowstone National Park. Live entertainment is often on the menu and there's always plenty of local color, western hospitality and great atmosphere. Ride the Snow Express Shuttle from the slopes for free during the ski season.

### L Comfort Inn Big Sky

Hwy 191, 1/2 mile south of entrance to Big Sky Resort, Big Sky. 995-2333 or reservations at 877-466-7222, www.comfortinnbigsky.com

The Comfort Inn of Big Sky is the newest motel in the scenic Gallatin Canyon! They feature free deluxe continental breakfast, spacious air conditioned rooms, and an indoor pool with a 90-foot

waterslide. Their convenient location allows easy access to fishing, skiing, hiking, horseback riding, shopping and dining in the canyon. Discounted ski passes are available at the front desk. They also offer great parking access for vehicles of all sizes. The Comfort Inn is the perfect place to stay year round for accommodations whether you are driving through the canyon or staying for several days. You can learn more about them at www.comfortinnbigsky.com.

### L Big EZ Lodge

7000 Beaver Creek Rd. at Big Sky. 995-7000 or toll free 877-244-3299 or fax 995-7007. www.bigezlodge.com

The award winning Big EZ Lodge is where luxury meets the wilderness. Situated on 4,300 private acres on the outskirts of Big Sky and Yellowstone Park, each of the individually appointed rooms offer the finest appointments, amenities, and outstanding views of the surrounding mountain ranges. Executive Chef, John Rolfe and his culinary team create fantastic delights with new menu's daily. Nightly rates are either inclusive, with three gourmet meals and spirits per day or just a room and breakfast. Both packages allow use of all on site amenities including stocked trout ponds, massive hot-tub, billiards and championship putting course. Preview this exquisite lodge at the web site.

## 22. *Food, Lodging*

### F Edelweiss Restaurant

Meadow Village, Big Sky. 995-4665

The Edelweiss Restaurant is a special Alpine café conveniently located in Big Sky's Meadow Village. A "must stop" for any visitor to the Gallatin Canyon. Savor the hand carved wood decor and Old World charm that will surround you. The eclectic menu, prepared by their Award winning

Chef, offers European and Continental cuisine along with the chefs' own creations. Succulent dinners feature veal, poultry, steaks, game and fresh seafood. Enjoy your favorite cocktail or make a selection from their impressive list of imported beer and wine. With seating for 50 people this is a perfect location for a special group or private gathering. Reservations are highly recommended.

### FL Lone Mountain Ranch

Lone Mountain Ranch Access Road, between Meadow and Mountain Village, Big Sky. 995-4644 or 800-514-4644. www.lmranch.com

Lone Mountain Ranch is a historic ranch dating back to 1925. It is now a top quality, highly acclaimed resort specializing in family ranch and winter ski vacations. Summer activities include horseback riding, hiking, guided trips into Yellowstone, canoeing, llama treks and an active kids' program. Winter brings 75 km of groomed cross-country ski trails, snow shoeing, downhill skiing at Big Ski Ski Resort, and Yellowstone ski adventures. An ORVIS® endorsed fly fishing lodge, they offer guided trips year-round to the many nearby blue-ribbon trout streams. Their acclaimed cuisine, cozy, comfortable log cabins, and on site massage therapists provide exceptional creature comforts after a day of fun and adventure.

## 23. *Adventure, Food, Lodging*

### V Gondola Ride

Big Sky Ski Resort. 995-5000

Want to see Lone Peak up close and personal. Then take the newly renovated gondola to the top. Take your camera along—the views from the top of the lift are spectacular. You'll go to the 11,150 foot summit of Lone Peak on a 8,500 foot ride up. There are three ways to get down: take the gondola back, hike back, or ride your mountain bike down. The gondola is open daily in the summer.

Section 5

### L East West Resorts

1 Mountain Loop Road, Big Sky. 995-7600 or 800-845-4428. www.eastwestresorts.com. Email: bigskyres@eastwestresorts.com

East West Resorts located in the heart of Big Sky at the beautiful Moonlight Lodge, offers condominiums, homes, log cabins, and luxury penthouse vacation rentals. Select from accommodations in several Big Sky locations: Moonlight Basin Ranch for ski-in and ski-out, Mountain Village for slope side, or Meadow Village on the golf course. All properties have fully equipped kitchens and linens, most have fireplaces, hot tubs, and washer dryers. Rates range from budget to luxury with sizes from studios to five bedrooms. Let them help you find that perfect vacation home to fit your budget and desired amenities. Learn more at their website: www.eastwestresorts.com.

### L Mountain Meadows Guest Ranch

7055 Beaver Creek Road, Big Sky. 995-4997 or toll free 888-644-6647. www.mountainmeadowsranch.com.

Visit a place where time stands still and stay at the exclusive Mountain Meadows Guest Ranch nestled in the midst of rolling hills, lush forests, ponds and streams. The Guest Ranch can accommodate 28 guests in two log cabins and luxurious rooms in a stunning 10,000 square foot lodge in the heart of Big Sky country. No amenities are overlooked in the fabulous surroundings and activities provided by the Severn Family, that owns and operates the ranch. They offer special events, many extra services, restaurant, hay rides & BBQ's, Thirsty Moose Bar, outdoor activities, along with a breathtaking setting will assure guests that they will enjoy a vacation of a lifetime. Visit them on the web.

## 24. *Historic Marker, Attraction, Gas, Food, Lodging, Camping, Shopping*

### West Yellowstone

West Yellowstone is located at the West Gate to

# Polo Under the Big Sky

**Polo "The Cowboy Way," played** across Montana each summer from Missoula to Billings and Great Falls to Bozeman. Now it might not look like white pants and English saddles, but these western horsemen sure have a lot of fun when they get together to battle over the ball. The game is played in rodeo style arenas with two five player teams. Each player is armed with a mallet, and the object is to knock an inflatable rubber ball through the other teams goal. All that is needed is a horse, a mallet, the ability to ride, and the love of adventure.

Players use western tack, helmets with face guards, and padded chaps. Competition consists of two teams on the field, a player from each team in each of the five zones. The 15 minute periods are called chukkers— four of which constitutes the game. Teams change goal directions at the beginning of each chukker, and the ball changes possession after a score. A score is made when the ball is whacked through the opposing teams goal. If a score is made from within the first zone, it counts as one point, if made from the second zone, two points, and if made from the center zone, three points. Each game is run by two referees, who ensure the rules are followed and determine if a score counts for one or more points. In addition, there is one goal spotter at each end of the field who informs the referees when the ball goes through the goalposts. Other game officials consist of a scorekeeper, timekeepers, and an announcer to call the play-by-play. If you like beautiful horses and things western, and want to see them at their best, bring your lawn chair, pull up some shade, and enjoy the next Montana Cowboy Polo match.

For more information call 587-5088.

Yellowstone Park and offers four seasons of recreational opportunity. Although the town only has 900 year-round residents, well over one million people enter the park each year via this small town. Visitors across the globe come to take advantage of the endless possibilities for outdoor enjoyment, be it fishing the many blue-ribbon streams, or snowmobiling the nearly 1,000 miles of groomed trails accessible from hotel rooms, and cross country skiing. West Yellowstone is ideally located at the center of fun and recreation.

West Yellowstone may well be one of the finest meccas for fly fishing enthusiasts. Many scenes from the movie "A River Runs Through It" were filmed on the Gallatin River north of West Yellowstone. Professional guides and outfitters throughout the area offer advice and service to visiting fisher-folk, and are eager to help you make the most of your fishing excursion in Yellowstone Country.

With Yellowstone National Park at the front door, the hiking, biking, sightseeing, wildlife watching opportunities are endless, and the national forest lands which border West Yellowstone on the remaining three sides offer one breathtaking vista after another! Learn more at www.wyellowstone.com.

## H The 1959 Earthquake

West Yellowstone

*On August 17, 1959, at 11:37 P.M., this spectacularly scenic section of Montana became the focus of world-wide attention and made modern history. A heavy shock smashed the soft summer night, earth and rock buckled, lifted and dropped. In several mighty heaves Mother Earth reshaped her mountains in violent response to an agony of deep-seated tensions no longer bearable. A mountain moved, a new lake was formed, another lake was fantastically tilted, sections of highway were dropped into a lake, the earth's surface was ripped by miles of faults, and 28 persons were missing or dead. The area is now safe and much of it has been preserved and marked by the Forest Service for all to see. The Madison River Canyon Earthquake area, located a few miles northwest of here, is an awesome testimonial to Nature's might.*

## F The Gusher Pizza Sandwich Shop

40 Dunraven, West Yellowstone. 646-9050, gusher-pizza@westyellowstone.com

"A Yellowstone tradition," The Gusher has served literally millions of guests since it opened in 1957. They feature pizza, steaks, shrimp, sandwiches, soups, salads and daily specials, all served in a clean and pleasant atmosphere. They offer wine and an extensive array of domestic, import, micro-

brew and "craft" beers both bottled and on tap. All orders are available "to go" with free delivery within West Yellowstone. Kids can enjoy the game room, separate from the dining area. After dining you are invited to enjoy video poker and keno in the friendly pub right next door.

## F Texas Rose

335 Hwy 20, West Yellowstone. 646-0095

Texas Rose offers authentic Tex-Mex cuisine, tantalizing aroma of spices, relaxed dining, and welcoming smiles. You'll feel like you crossed the border as a personal guest in Doris's kitchen. Her homemade specialties such as chimichangas, enchiladas, and chili Relenos have been enjoyed by diners for over 10 years. The colossal size chilies are special delivered from Texas and guacamole and a variety of salsas are prepared daily, including Mother Sophie's Famous Salsa Roja, a family secret for generations. On "Taco Tuesday" enjoy Doris's favorite taco for 79 cents each. The menu also features vegetarian entrees and American selections. Open for breakfast, lunch and dinner from 7 a.m. to 3 a.m. 7 days a week. Dine or take out. Catering is available for any size group. Reservations are recommended.

### L One Horse Motel

216 Dunraven St., West Yellowstone. 646-7677 or reservations only at 800-488-2750 1horse@wyellowstone.com.

Locally owned and operated, the One Horse Motel offers clean, quiet, down-home accommodations. Located across the street from the City Park, 1/2-mile from the West Entrance of Yellowstone National Park and within walking distance to all restaurants and shops. The One Horse Motel is one story with exterior corridors and off-street parking near all rooms. All rooms have telephones, tub/shower combinations, remote control color TV, movie channels, microwaves and refrigerators. A guest laundry is on-site, as is a hot-tub for winter use. Hosts Nick & Becky welcome phone calls or email; they are happy to answer questions and help with reservations and trip planning. Visit them at their web site.

### LC Brandin' Iron Inn & RV Park

201 Canyon St., West Yellowstone. 646-9411 or 800-217-4613. info@brandiniron.com; www.brandiniron.com

Located just two blocks from the west entrance of Yellowstone National Park, the 79 clean and comfortable rooms at the Brandin' Iron Inn are complete with refrigerators, cable TV and laundry facilities. Guests can relax in the hot tubs and visit the city park right across the street. The 16 RV sites have full hook-ups with access to laundry facilities, showers, picnic tables and the hot tubs. Gift shops and fine dining are within walking distance. Ask about the snowmobile packages. Don't miss out on these great accommodations for your summer or winter vacation. Check their web site and learn more!

### L Big Western Pine Motel and Rustler's Roost Restaurant & Lounge

234 Firehole Lane, West Yellowstone. 646-7622 or 800-646-7622, fax 646-9443. www.wyellowstone.com/bigwesternpine/

Your home away from home! A stay at the Big Western Pine includes everything you need for a great visit to West Yellowstone. You will enjoy your stay from the time you meet their knowledgeable and friendly staff. They are located only 4 blocks from the West entrance to Yellowstone, and walking distance to great shopping. The Big Western Pine is also home to the popular Rustler's Roost Restaurant and Lounge. Enjoy their heated pool during the summer or their year-round indoor whirlpool and sauna. Let them arrange a snowmobile or snow coach tour during your winter stay. All of their impeccably clean rooms include cable, phones, and tub shower combinations. Family rooms with kitchenettes are also available.

### L Best Western Executive Inn

236 Dunraven, West Yellowstone. 646-7681 or fax 646-9549 www.taylorhotelgroup.com/yellowstone.htm

This is the perfect headquarters for your Yellowstone adventure. It is a a full service hotel, centrally located in West Yellowstone behind the city park and shopping is within walking distance. Guest rooms are large and comfortable with in-room coffee, irons with ironing boards, and hair dryers. Many rooms also include refrigerators and large screen TV's. Whether you visit in winter to enjoy snowmobiling, cross country skiing, and snowshoeing or in summer to visit Yellowstone Park, fly fish, or hike, you'll want to start your day with breakfast in their Parkside Restaurant. End your day with a relaxing soak in the large outdoor hot tub, a glass of wine or micro-brew beer in the Tavern, and a special dinner in the restaurant.

## 25. *Historic Marker, Adventure, Gas, Food, Lodging*

### H Madison Hotel

On Yellowstone Ave. in West Yellowstone

*The Forest Service granted Jess Pierman a special-use permit to build a hotel and restaurant here in 1910. A large tent accommodated guests until the present hotel was under constrtiction in the fall of 1912. Doll Bartlett began cooking for Pierman in 1910, saving much of her weekly ten-dollar paycheck. Her husband Roxy drove the stage between Monida and West Yellowstone. By the time the hotel was under construction, the Bartletts had saved enough money to buy the business which they ran until Roxy died in the 1920s. Doll continued to run the hotel with her second husband, George Pickup. The two-story rectangular plan is of simple log construction with saddle-notched corner timbering and a prominent front dormer. The original six upstairs rooms, warmed by a cut stone fireplace in the downstairs lobby, catered to rail and stage travelers. Each room had a pitcher, a wash basin and a chamber pot. Water came from a well across the street. The hotel expanded adding fourteen rooms in 1921 and a bar and dance floor soon after, but there was no running water until the 1900s. In 1923, President Harding was a guest and antiquated registers show that such Hollywood greats as Wallace Beery and Gloria Swanson enjoyed the hospitality of the Madison Hotel. Log support columns and beams, wood floors, light fixtures, the stone fireplace and many of the room furnishings are original. Although not the first hotel in West Yellowstone, the Madison is the only hotel that remains from this early period when tourism was in its infancy.*

### H Union Pacific Dining Hall

Yellowstone Ave. next to Museum of the Yellowstone

*As tourism blossomed during the first decades of the twentieth century, the Union Pacific Railroad considered how to better accommodate travelers. Officials conceived the idea of building restaurants and pavilions architecturally similar to the monumental lodges being constructed in national parks. Acclaimed architect Gilbert Stanley Underwood, whose mastery of the Rustic style set the standard for national park architecture, designed this splendid dining lodge for the Union Pacific. Completed in 1926, it was an intermediate project built while Underwood was designing the world-renowned Ahwahnee Hotel at Yosemite National Park. The Rustic style of this lodge, its wood and welded tuff in grand harmony with the landscape, echoes that of the the famed hotel. Featuring mammoth walk-in fireplaces, the multi-level interior is characteristic of Underwood's designs. As part of a national collection of Underwood's work, the lodge gains added significance as a rare surviving example of a railroad dining hall constructed to mimic park architecture.*

### T Yellowstone IMAX Theater

West entrance to Yellowstone Park, West Yellowstone. 646-4100 or 888-854-5862

Grizzlies, geysers, and grandeur is what the centerpiece film, "Yellowstone", provides on a six story high screen with over 12,000 watts of digital surround sound. The IMAX experience will transport you to places you've only dreamed of. You are drawn into the film and become a player in the movie. Ten times the size of 35mm, the Imax experience is one of such detailed and crisp realism that it will become a memory of a lifetime. The theatre seats 354 and is open year round! IMAX movies all day and Hollywood blockbusters at night with new movies added often. Call for more information on shows and rates.

### T Grizzly Discovery Center

201 S. Canyon Street, West Yellowstone. Manhattan.646-7001 or 800-257-2570 www.grizzlydiscoveryctr.com.

Section 5

All Montana Area Codes are 406

Experience views rarely seen and discover first-hand the habits and surprisingly playful behaviors of grizzly bears and a gray wolf pack. The center presents a broad range of interactive exhibits, films, presentations and wildlife themed gift shop suitable for all ages. Experience this unparalleled educational facility devoted to the preservation of these threatened wildlife species. A portion of the proceeds from entrance fees and gift sales is donated to the International Grizzly Fund. The center is open daily all year long. Visit their web page at www.grizzlydiscovery.ctr.com.

### T Museum of the Yellowstone

124 Yellowstone Ave. in West Yellowstone.
646-1100. www.yellowstonehistoriccenter.org

Located in the 1909 Union Pacific Depot, this museum has historic exhibits featuring cowboys, mountain men, Native Americans, and Yellowstone Park. Come face to face with the wildlife of Yellowstone, including bison, elk and the legendary grizzly "Old Snaggletooth." Catch their fly-fishing exhibit that chronicles the history of the fly-fishing shops in West Yellowstone. Get derailed in the exhibit on the history of the Union Pacific railroad; complete with models of the train and the Northern and Union Pacific Depots. Transport yourself back to the fires of 1988. Experience the reality of man's struggle to save the famous Old Faithful Inn and the Town of West Yellowstone. Discover how the infernos rejuvenated the ecosystem of Yellowstone National Park and how the beauty still prevails. Shake, rattle, and roll with the quake that rocked the entire Yellowstone area. Can you build a structure to withstand an earthquake? Their earthquake table will give you the answer. Experience the Yellowstone of 1908-1960. With a train whistle, your trip to "Wonderland" begins. Put on your "duster" and take a magical tour through the finest souvenirs of yesteryear, including stagecoaches, memorabilia, and historic film footage. An admission is charged. The museum is open from July–August from 9 a.m. to 9 p.m. and September–October from 9 a.m. to 7 p.m.

### VS Free Heel & Wheel

40 Yellowstone Ave., West Yellowstone.
646-7744

Free Heel and Wheel is just a few steps from the west entrance to Yellowstone National Park. They are Nordic and cycling specialists and your headquarters for the greater Yellowstone area. They sell or rent everything for your summer play and bike needs or winter ski adventure, including both a full service ski and full service bike shop for tune ups and repairs on all makes and models. Complete your gear with clothing, accessories, and jewelry that has been selected for the outdoor enthusiast. You can enjoy their famous Zebra Mocha and a light lunch at the in-house espresso bar while planning your next great adventure. Let their knowledgeable staff help you or learn more by visiting www.freeheelandwheel.com.

### A Yellowstone Automotive

555 Yellowstone Ave., West Yellowstone. 646-4047

Yellowstone Automotive is located close to the West Entrance to Yellowstone National Park and believes in the highest quality of repair work for your vehicle. They have a great deal of experience in electronic, diagnostic, computer problems, engine work, drive-ability problems, and also take care of general maintenance and offer computerized 4-wheel alignment. The ASE Master Certified Technician would be happy to answer any of your questions and help you with any of your automotive problems when in the Yellowstone area.

### F Timberline Café

135 Yellowstone Ave., 646-9349.
http://my.montana.net/timberlinecafe/

The Timberline Cafe, in operation since it was built in the early 1900's, offers a charming family atmosphere in a smoke-free environment. Homemade soups, entrees, pies, and pastries are prepared daily from fresh ingredients. They feature a full soup and salad bar. Check out the Idaho Spud with all the fixings. The menu offers the finest steak, chicken, buffalo steaks, classic burgers, gourmet entrees like fresh made lasagna, fabulous fresh breakfasts, cinnamon rolls and great snacks anytime. Their menu will please even the most discriminating appetites any time of the day. Stop in, say hello to Tom, Dee, and the crew while enjoying a memorable meal while you are in West Yellowstone. Visit them on the web.

### L Fairfield Inn

105 S. Electric, West Yellowstone. 646-4892 or 800-565-6803 www.wyellowstone.com/FairfieldInn

The West Yellowstone Fairfield Inn offers a wide range of thoughtful amenities at an economical price. Guests can enjoy the complimentary continental breakfast, indoor pool and jacuzzi, fitness center, cable TV with HBO, spacious guest rooms, 24-hour fax service, non-smoking and handicapped units, some rooms with refrigerators, microwaves, and wet bars and one jacuzzi suite. This is a great place to stay while visiting the many nearby attractions. Check their web site for more information.

### L Kelly Inn

104 S. Canyon St., West Yellowstone, 646-4454 or 800-259-4672, fax 646-9838,
www.wyellowstone.com/KellyInn

While visiting the breathtaking expanse of Yellowstone National Park, stay at this new beautiful rustic log style property. The 78 large, comfortable guest rooms have a charming decor, king or queen size beds, cable TV, pay-per-view movies and Nintendo. Try one of the specialty suites with a whirlpool, wet bar, refrigerator, microwave and hairdryer. Also enjoy a complimentary continental breakfast, heated indoor pool, sauna, and extra large whirl pool. Open year 'round. Visit their web site!

### FL Holiday Inn Sunspree Resort & Conference Center Hotel Oregon Shortline Iron Horse Lounge

315 Yellowstone Ave., West Yellowstone. 646-7365

Located just three blocks from Yellowstone National Park's west entrance, this resort is the finest, most complete lodging facility in West Yellowstone. They are equipped to provide superb facilities for groups as small as 10 or as large as 500, while their professional staff takes the guess work out of your event. Their 123 spacious rooms offer a range of luxury appointments & floor plans. All rooms include mini-fridges, microwaves, hair dryers, irons & ironing boards, coffee makers & sofas. The Yellowstone Country Activities Desk can arrange snowcoach or snowmobile rental in the winter, or mountain bike rental, whitewater rafting and numerous other excursions in the summer! Additionally, enjoy the wild-game cuisine in a turn of the century setting at the Oregon Short Line Restaurant. More information is available at their web site.

### L Madison Motel

139 Yellowstone, West Yellowstone. 646-7745 or 800-838-7745

The Madison Motel is an excellent economical choice for a restful stay in West Yellowstone. They offer all nonsmoking, clean rooms with showers and cable TV. Additionally, deluxe rooms have queen beds, tubs, and air conditioning. Public phones are available. They don't have kitchens or pools. Just plain good value. They are close to restaurants and all of the great activities available nearby.

### L West Yellowstone Hostel at Madison Hotel

139 Yellowstone, West Yellowstone.
646-7745 or toll free 800-838-7745
www.madisonhotel@wyellowstone.com/lodging

## *Montana Trivia*

Many of the scenes for the Robert Redford production *A River Runs Through It* were filmed in the Gallatin Canyon on the Gallatin River. The actual story was supposed to take place on the Blackfoot river

Section 5

### S Madison Hotel and Gift Shop

139 Yellowstone Ave. 646-7745
or toll free at 800-838-7745
www.madisonhotel@wyellowstone.com

The Madison Hotel is a historical landmark. Originally built by Roxy and Dolly Bartlett, who settled in "West" during the spring of 1912. Dolly worked in the Timberline Cafe next door and Roxy was a driver who took tourists on the five day trip through Yellowstone Park by stagecoach. They built the Madison Hotel as a hunting lodge, replacing the tent hotel on the property directly across the street from the railroad station. The hotel was a hub of excitement for the next forty years as it grew to 28 rooms, with a dance hall and bar. Important visitors like Presidents Harding and Hoover, Clark Gable, and Gloria Swanson graced it's rooms. In 1959 the Hadley's purchased the hotel with new attitudes and styles while maintaining the historical atmosphere. Downstairs rooms were replaced with a gift shop, where visitors today can still entertain themselves with the unique collection of souvenirs, gifts, and other collectibles. Open seven days a week. The hotel still offers rooms with clean linens, comfortable beds, and pleasant friendships. The lobby has been carefully preserved with original furnishings. Visit them on the web. Visitors are welcome to tour unrented rooms before 6 p.m.

### S SilverHeels Jewelry

115 Yellowstone Ave., in the Montana Outpost. West Yellowstone. 646-7796

SilverHeels is known around the world for exquisite custom jewelry made by the owners Greg and Beverly Huth. They have been in business since 1970 and create and repair fine jewelry right in West Yellowstone. Bring them your elk ivories and special stones or select from their collection of Montana Yogo Sapphires, Montana Garnets, or many precious and semi precious stones, and let them create a custom piece that you will always treasure. You'll enjoy exploring their extensive cases of jewelry for sale as well as the collection of gems ready to be combined with gold or silver and made into a special bracelet, necklace, earrings or other special creation. Be sure and see the fossil art carvings while you are there.

### S Bargain Depot Outlet Stores

22 Canyon Street & 25 Yellowstone Ave,
West Yellowstone. 646-9047

The Bargain Depot Outlet Stores are proud of over 20 years of outstanding values and service, offering savings of 40% to 70% off retail prices on clothing for the entire family, including, outerwear, travel gear, and Yellowstone Park T-shirts and sweat shirts. They are considered by many to be one of the truly outstanding bargain stores in the entire Northwest. Stop by and see them, you will be pleasantly surprised to find out that there are indeed bargains in a tourist town! Find them on Main Street (22 Canyon) next to the Canyon Street Grill and across from the Visitors Center at 25 Yellowstone Ave.

## 26. *Gas, Food, Lodging*

### FL Three Bears Lodge & Restaurant

205 Yellowstone Ave. in West Yellowstone.
646-7811 or toll free 800-646-7353.
Email reev@three-bear-lodge.com.
www.three-bear-lodge.com

Three Bear Lodge has been a Yellowstone tradition for 30 years. Located just two blocks east of the West Gate entrance to Yellowstone you will find yourself within walking distance to every major attraction in West Yellowstone. Their restaurant is known as one of the best in town and is a locals favorite. As your vacation headquarters Three Bear Lodge can book activities for both summer and winter activities which include snowmobile, snowcoach, and van tours, as well as horse back riding. Whether you're visiting Yellowstone for the first time or returning as a guest, Three Bear Lodge is an excellent choice for all of your vacation needs. Reservations are strongly encouraged in the summer and required in the winter.

### L West Yellowstone Comfort Inn

638 Madison Ave., West Yellowstone. 646-4212 or 888- 264-2466, www.wyellowstone.com/comfortinn/

Open throughout the year, the West Yellowstone Comfort Inn offers true western hospitality. Enjoy the largest heated pool in West Yellowstone, along with a spa, exercise room, complimentary continental breakfast, local airport shuttle, guest laundry, conference room, non-smoking rooms, fax services, handicap access, winter plug-ins, and much more. The 78 spacious guest rooms are complete with cable TV, direct dial phones, and full climate control. Experience the thrill of a true western adventure with Yellowstone National Park right at your doorstep offering blue ribbon trout streams, hunting, hiking, snowmobiling from your door, cross country skiing, and horseback riding. Most rooms have fantastic views!

### L Buckboard Motel

119 Electric, West Yellowstone. 646-9020
or toll free 800-548-4117

The Buckboard Motel is located just 4 blocks from the entrance to Yellowstone Park in the heart of West Yellowstone. You can walk to West Yellowstone's great shopping and dining. If you bring your own snow machine or ski equipment you'll find the area's great miles of trails begin at the Buckboard's doorstep. They provide plenty of off street parking for trailers and large vehicles. For your comfort they offer smoking and non-smoking rooms, all equipped with cable TV and showers with plenty of hot water. You will also enjoy their hot tub/spa after a day of summer or winter activity and fresh complimentary morning coffee.

### L Sleepy Hollow Lodge

124 Electric St., West Yellowstone. 646-7707
www.sleepyhollowlodge.com or
email: sleepyhollowlodge.com

## 27. *Adventure, Food, Lodging*

### V Yellowstone Rental & Sports

1630 Targhee Pass Hwy, West Yellowstone. 646-9377, www.wyellowstone.com/yellowstonerentals/

Yellowstone Rental & Sports carries all types of rental items from heavy equipment to hand & power tools, from garden tools, boats and camping equipment to floor polishers & carpet cleaners. They even have baby accessories, party & wedding supplies, and more! They also rent ATVs, mountain bikes & canoes. Call ahead to secure time for some of the most scenic unguided horseback riding found in the West Yellowstone area. Travel along streams and down wooded trails surrounded by aspens to the high mountain meadows with scenic overviews of the Hebgen Valley. They have what you need, be it for an hour, day, week or month!

### H Targhee Pass

Hwy 20, west of West Yellowstone

*This pass across the Continental Divide takes its name from an early-day Bannack Chief. Free trappers and fur brigades of the Missouri River and Rocky Mountain Fur companies were familiar with the surrounding country in the early part of the last century.*

*Chief Joseph led his band of Nez Perce Indians through this pass in 1877 while making his famous 2,000-mile march from the central Idaho country in an effort to evade U.S. troops and find sanctuary in Canada. He was closely followed through the pass by the pursuing forces of General Howard. Joseph repulsed or outdistanced all the commands sent against him until finally forced to surrender to Col. Nelson A. Miles at the Battle of the Bear's Paw, when within a comparatively few miles of the Canadian line.*

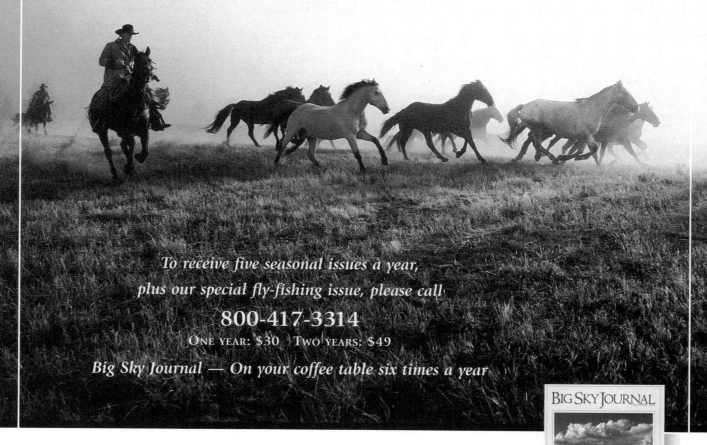

## 28. *Attraction, Food, Lodging*

### T Earthquake Lake

See sidebar.

## 29. *Lodging*

### Cameron

Cameron is the namesake of the Cameron family who were early pioneers in the area. In the settlement originally known as Bear Creek, Addison Cameron owned a building that contained the post office, a general store and a dance hall upstairs.

## 30. *Historic Marker, Attraction, Gas, Food, Lodging, Camping, Shopping, Miscellaneous*

### Ennis

Ennis is a bustling and picturesque western town in the heart of the Madison Valley, east of the Tobacco Root Mountains and 13 miles from historic Virginia City. Primarily a hunting and fishing center, Ennis' three blocks of downtown businesses boast Old West-style facades.

Ennis, like most of the towns in this area, was spawned from the discovery of gold in the area. Within months after gold was discovered at Alder Gulch, William Ennis homesteaded the site along the Madison that is now the town of Ennis. A Mr. Jeffers homesteaded the site across the river. Ranchers, farmers, and businesses soon flocked to the area. By the late 1880s there were three major stage lines servicing the community. The tall grass and favorable climate created an excellent environment to raise horses, cattle, and sheep. Chief White Cloud's tribe of Bannack Indians was friendly to the settlers and whites and Indians existed in harmony. Today this small town of 1,000 is known for its Black Angus and prize Herefords. Timber is harvested from the surrounding forests, and gold mining is making a comeback in the area. But nationally, Ennis is known as a staging area for some of the finest fly-fishing in the world on the blue ribbon Madison River. Another of Ennis' assets, The Ennis National Fish Hatchery, is located only twelve miles south of Ennis.

Nowhere is the love affair with livestock more apparent than in Ennis during Rodeo Weekend. This small town swells with excitement as people from all over come to celebrate one of Montana's most popular Fourth of July rodeos.

### H Raynold's Pass

Hwy 287, south of Ennis

*The low gap in the mountains on the sky line south of here is Raynold's Pass over the Continental Divide.*

*Jim Bridger, famous trapper and scout, guided an expedition of scientists through the pass in June of 1860. The party was led by Capt. W. F. Raynolds of the Corps of Engineers, U.S. Army. They came through from the south and camped that night on the Madison River near this point. Capt. Raynolds wrote "The pass is ... so level that it is difficult to locate the exact point at which the waters divide. I named it Low Pass and deem it to be one of the most remarkable and important features of the topography of the Rocky Mountains."*

*Jim Bridger didn't savvy road maps or air route beacons but he sure knew his way around.*

### T Ennis National Fish Hatchery

12 miles SW of Ennis. 682-4845

This hatchery is different from most others. Most hatcheries produce fish of various sizes and then stock these fish in public lakes and streams, providing anglers with hours of fun, whereas the Ennis Hatchery is a broodstock hatchery. There are only three rainbow trout broodstock hathcheries in the Nationwide Federal Hatchery System. A broodstock hatchery raises fish to adult size, then takes eggs from those fish, incubating them and shipping them to production hatcheries. A visitor center is open seven days a week, year round.

### T Wildlife Museum of the West

121 W. Main St., Ennis. 682-7141

### FL Sportsman's Lodge

310 US Highway 287 N., 682-4242 or 800-220-1690.

Sportsman's Lodge has become a landmark to many vacationers traveling southwest Montana. The lodge is situated on six acres, in a rustic setting with modern facilities and all the comforts of home. Whether you stay in one of the 18 lodgepole pine log cabins or in the 11-unit motel, you will enjoy the casual country atmosphere with the abundant recreational opportunities all around. Relax in the cocktail lounge and enjoy a hearty meal in the cozy dining room. Spend your days viewing nearby historic ghost towns, hiking in pristine wilderness areas, or shopping in Ennis. A public golf course and tennis courts are just around the corner. Make this vacation a genuine old west experience the whole family will remember for a lifetime.

### L El Western Resort

Ennis, 1 mile south on US Hwy 287 N. 682-4217 or reservations at 800-831-2773. www.elwestern.com

The El Western offers guests western hospitality, comfort and incredible surroundings for more that 50 years. Accommodations are available to meet the needs of vacationers and sportsmen for overnight or extended stays. Seventeen acres of wide green lawns, towering spruce trees and a rushing creek with views of the majestic Madison range are included whether you choose a cozy overnight cabin, a kitchen cabin suite, or a spacious deluxe cabin or lodge. Many of their cabins have fireplaces and kitchens completely equipped for your convenience. Their conference center provides facilities for retreats, family gatherings or seminars. All cabins have large picture windows, porches, cable TV, phones with data ports, daily housekeeping and they are spotlessly clean. El Western Resort is conveniently located to Yellowstone Park and Virginia City.

### L Rainbow Valley Lodge

1 mile S. of Ennis. 682-4264 or 800-452-8254. www.rainbowvalley.com

The Rainbow Valley Lodge, one mile south of Ennis, is open year-round and hosted by Ed and Jeanne Williams, both well known in the world of fly fishing. They offer 24 immaculate deluxe log cabin style units for full service lodging that includes fully equipped kitchens, private patios, phones, Fax service, cable television, movies, heated pool, barbecue picnic area, horse corrals, winter plug ins, coin laundry, handicapped accessible, and guide and shuttle services. Enjoy their breathtaking park-like setting, spectacular views of the Rocky Mountains, all in walking distance of the Madison River. Guests have been returning year after year for over four decades to enjoy fishing, hunting and family vacations. You'll also want to see the pine needle baskets and fishing flies made by Jeanne, a nationally recognized artist.

### L Fan Mountain Inn

204 N. Main, Ennis. 682-5200 or 877- 682-5200, fanmountaininn.com

The Fan Mountain Inn offers small town country hospitality with clean, spacious rooms and beautiful views of the Madison mountains. The 28 units are complete with king or queen size beds, cable TV, air conditioning and telephones. Adjoining units, handicap units, and non-smoking units are available, as well as a deluxe suite and a conference or meeting room. There is easy access to downtown Ennis for a variety of shopping and restaurants. The Fan Mountain Inn is also within walking distance to the renowned Madison River, where you can walk along the scenic banks or fish for blue-ribbon trout. Visit them at their web site.

### C Ennis RV Village

5034 Highway 287 N., Ennis. 682-5272, www.Ennisrvvillage.com

Located in the heart of the Madison Valley with stunning mountain views, clear running streams flowing into the famed Madison River, and a one-of-a-kind community noted for its friendliness. The Ennis RV Village features 41 large pull-thru, full-service sites with 50 amp electric, sewer, water, and phone hook-up available at some sites. The clean, convenient restrooms have never ending hot showers that are heated from a geothermic source. There are over eight acres of private park with walking trails for you and your pet, a large

picnic area with BBQ pits and tables, and a convenience store geared to the RV owner. Tent camping is also available. This is a great base camp for guests to enjoy the many surrounding activities. Learn even more about them at their web site.

### S Ennis Trading Post

113 Main Street, Ennis. 682-4329

Looking for fine men or women's clothing, superb jewelry, unique fragrance, or maybe a sharp hat, classy belt or great socks? Stop in to visit Shad, Cammie and Susan at Ennis Trading Post, a rustic, upscale clothing store, and choose from such brands as Double D Ranch, Barn Fly, Wrangler, Woolrich, Bushwacker and more. They offer beautifully hand crafted jewelry made from silver, gold, turquoise, coral or lapis. You'll also find an outstanding selection of Brighton watches and purses. Maybe you'll find a new pair of moccasins, fabulous cologne or perfume, or pick up a great Tee or sweatshirt while in the Trading Post. You'll love shopping at the Ennis Trading Post!

### S The Plant & Flower Shop

202 1st St., Ennis. 682-4218 or 888- 682-7343

Gift baskets, 3 wire services, fruit baskets—when you are away from home, remember your family and friends with flowers.

### M Reed Real Estate

105 E. Main, Ennis. 682-4288 or fax 682-4280. www.reedrealestate.com

Ever dream of an over two million acre backyard? The area around the town of Ennis could be your dream come true with 2.2 million acres of publicly accessible mountainous land. Ennis is located in Madison Valley, southwest Montana and is surrounded by three major mountain ranges, the Gravely Range, Madison Range and Tobacco Roots. Reed Real Estate has specialized in Madison Valley properties for 25 years and is an active member of the Multiple Listing Service. They can help you with information regarding all properties for sale in the Madison Valley and surrounding areas. Call Reed Real Estate for all your real estate needs or visit them on the web.

### M Madison Valley Real Estate

201 E. Main, Ennis. 682-5002 or 888-592-5002

## 31. *Attraction, Gas, Food, Lodging*

## McAllister

The namesake of the McAllister family, local ranchers who settled the area in the late 1800s. In 1887, one of the first churches in Madison County was built here. The Methodist church still stands today.

### H Madison Valley

On scenic view turnout just south of McAllister on Hwy. 287

*Settlement of the Madison Valley followed on the heels of the Gold Rush to Alder Gulch in the mid 1860s. Homesteaders grazed their livestock in the lush meadows of the valley and surrounding mountains, raising beef and mutton to feed the miners.*

*Today, in addition to meat production, these ranches serve another important ecological role—maintaining open space and a place for wildlife to prosper.*

*Thousands of elk, mule deer, whitetail deer, antelope, and other smaller animals live, eat, and migrate through the valley. While public lands of the Beaverhead-Deerlodge National Forest provide protected habitat in the mountains surrounding the valley, ranch lands of the valley bottom provide essential food, security, and freedom of movement for many animals, particularly in winter.*

*One of the greatest threats to wildlife is the loss of this critical habitat to human encroachment. As ranches are subdivided, the open space and abundant food supply these area ranches provide are lost.*

### T Kobayashi Beach on Ennis Lake

McAllister. 683-2337

Ennis Lake is relatively shallow and acts like a giant solar collector. The waters in the lake can heat up to 85° (the temperature of a very warm swimming pool) in the summertime making it a great place to swim. Kobayashi Beach is a favorite locals hangout. Its sandy beach is managed by the BLM for Montana Power Company. It's easy to find and makes a great place to take a break from the traveling. At the tiny town of McAllister just north of Ennis, take the road heading east out of town for a little over 3 miles. After you pass through a housing area, you will see the signed beach.

## 32. *Historic Marker, Gas, Food, Lodging*

## Norris

As were many towns in this area, Norris was named for a rancher. The cattle from the rich pasturelands south of here were driven to Norris for shipment on the railroad. Cowboys, miners and travelers liked to partake of the nearby hot springs.

### H Bozeman Trail

US Hwy 287, 5 miles south of Norris





*In 1840, the Oregon Trail was the primary emigration route across the northern part of the United States. Two decades later, when gold was discovered west of here, a trail called the "Corrine Road" was used to bring supplies north from Salt Lake City to Bannack and Virginia City. John Bozeman, determined to shorten the time and distance to the gold strikes, scouted another route, departing from the Oregon Trail at the North Platte River. The Bozeman Trail, or Montana Cutoff, crossed here and can be seen on the opposite hillside.*

*This trail was used from 1863 to 1868. Sioux Indians frequently attacked the wagons and freight trains as they crossed the eastern leg of the trail. Consequently, Fort Reno, Fort Phil Kearney and Fort C. E. Smith were established to protect travelers but were also the target of Indian attacks.*

## T Beartrap Canyon

Hwy 84, between Ennis and Norris

This part of the Lee Metcalf Wilderness is popular for hiking, fishing and whitewater sports on the Madison River. The canyon is carved by the river cutting through 1,500 feet of granite rock.

## T Norris Hot Springs

East of Norris on Hwy. 84. 685-3303

Near the Madison River this swimming hole has changed very little since the 1880s era open-air wooden pool and bath house were built. The water in the privately owned pool is about 105 degrees F. The hot springs has had a wild reputation over the years, primarily for the swimsuit-optional "buff nights" which were discontinued in the late 1990s in order to appeal to a wider base of clientele. The springs are open year round with an admission fee.

## 33. *Attraction, Food, Lodging, Camping*

## Pony

Pony is located 30 miles southwest of Three Forks on Hwy 287. This old mining town is perched on a steep incline deep in the Tobacco Root Mountains. Pony took its name from Tecumseh "Pony" Smith who mined here in 1868. The approach to Pony is so steep and so tight in the nook it occupies that one resident penned, "Pony, Pony, the beautiful little town where train backed in 'cause it couldn't turn around." Though it may seem like a ghost town, there are about 115 residents. Many of the historic buildings are standing and some are still in use. Pony is a pleasant blend of the past and the present. Nearby is the ghost Strawberry Camp that was named because a miner swinging his pick axe in a strawberry field discovered a vein that was rightly named the Strawberry. Several other ghost mines are above Pony. Pony is the nearest town to Potosi Hot Springs.

## T Upper Potosi Hot Springs

West of Pony

Two primitive high-country hot springs pools on public land high in the Tobacco Root Mountains. The road to the nearby campground is unplowed during the winter. A little hiking and dodging cattle is about the only restriction to getting into the soaking pools. Water temperatures in the pools vary from 104 to 110 degrees F.

## LC Potosi Hot Springs Resort

S. Willow Creek Road, PO Box 269, Pony. 888-685-1695, www.potosiresort.com

Potosi Hot Springs Resort is a truly unique Montana experience. A 75 acre private inholding in the Tobacco Root Mountains of the famous Madison Valley, they have the finest accommodations, cuisine and soaking in the West. With four luxurious cabins perched on two miles of private water on South Willow Creek, guests can catch rainbow, brown, brook, and cutthroat trout right out the front door of their private cabin. The resort also prides itself on their gourmet organic restaurant and amazing natural hot springs. Potosi Hot Springs Resort is the ultimate base camp for all your fishing and hunting needs while you enjoy Montana's finest country. For more information visit them on the web.

## 34. *Gas, Food*

## Harrison

This ranch town in the Madison River valley was named for Henry C. Harrison who settled at Willow Creek in 1865. He was known for his Morgan horses and shorthorn cattle. He also operated a large steam dairy.

## Scenic Drives

### Gallatin Canyon

This 85 mile drive is arguably one of the most beautiful and breathtaking drives in Montana, if not in the country. The drive parallels the Gallatin River and skirts the majestic Spanish Peaks where it ends at the northwest corner of Yellowstone National Park. The yellow cliffs rising from the river on much of the route are constant backdrops for the paintings of the world famous Gary Carter.

## Hikes

### Bozeman Area

Bozeman has a number of "urban" hikes within the city limits. Some of these trails turn into cross country ski trails in the winter.

**Gallagator Trail**
From Main St. on the east side of downtown take Church St. south.The trail starts on the right on Story Street just past Bogert Park. The trail follows what was once the Gallatin Valley Electric Railroad right-of-way. The trail goes 1.5 miles to the Museum of the Rockies. A half mile extension goes around the museum and continues south.

**Peet's Hill and the Highland Ridge Trail**
Peet's Hill provides great views of the city and the surrounding mountain ranges. The hill itself is the ultimate sledding hill for residents in the winter time. A short, but steep walk takes you to the ridge from the parking lot. The trail at the top of the ridge heads south to Kagy Blvd. for 2.3 miles and connects with some of the other trails. The parking lot is on the corner of S. Church Ave. and Story Street near Bogert Park.

**Sourdough Trail**
This hike on the south side of Bozeman follows a tree-lined creek from Goldenstein Lane to Kagy Blvd. There are plenty of access spots to the creek. The best place to access this trail is from the south end. Take 19th Ave. south from Main St. Drive on 19th for 3 miles to Goldenstein. Turn left (east) and drive until the road crosses Sourdough Creek. The trail starts here.

**Painted Hills Trail**
This trail on the outskirts of Bozeman is more rural than urban. It travels 1.25 miles up and down through a gully area. To find the trailhead take Church St. south of Main St. to Kagy Blvd. Turn left (east) on Kagy and go .7 mile to a small parking area on the right.

**Triple Tree Trail**
This is a longer wooded trail on the outskirts of Bozeman which takes you 6 miles towards the mountains. Take 19th Ave. south of Main St. to Kagy Blvd. Turn left (east) and drive to Sourdough Road. Turn right (south) and drive about 2 miles. The trailhead is on the left side of the road. There is a small parking lot here.

### North of Bozeman

Traveling up Springhill Road along the base of the Bridger Mountains you will find several trails leading into the mountains. Cruise the gravel roads to the east of Springhill Road and you will stumble on to several trailheads.

**Sypes Canyon Trail**
This trail winds up the west side of the Bridger Mountains through mostly wooded areas. There are several spots along the trail that offer scenic vistas of the Gallatin Valley. Take 19th Ave. north of Main St. until it crosses over the interstate. Immediately after that it terminates at Springhill Road. Turn right here and go about 1 mile to Sypes Canyon Road. Turn right (east) and follow the road to the end. There is a parking area and clearly marked trailhead.

**South Cottonwood Trail 422**
This trail follows the South Cottonwood Creek drainage and is a relatively easy hike. You can follow this for as far as you can handle hiking back. It is not a loop trail. Take 19th Ave. south of Main St. until it takes a sharp right. The next main road

after the Hyalite Recreation area turnoff is Cottonwood Road. Turn left (south) here and go 2.1 miles to Cottonwood Canyon Road. Go left again for 2.2 miles to the signed trailhead.

## Hyalite Recreation Area

### Palisades Falls

This is one of the more popular destinations for locals. It really isn't as much of a hike as a short walk. But it is worth the trip to see the spectacular falls which plummet over a basalt cliff. Take S. 19th to Hyalite Canyon Road and go to Hyalite Reservoir.Cross the dam continuing around the far side of the lake. You will come to a fork in the road. Bear left and look for the parking lot just a short distance down the road. Because of snow, you probably won't want to attempt this trip until very late May or early June.

### Mount Blackmore

Take S. 19th to Hyalite Canyon Road and go to Hyalite Reservoir. The trailhead for this pleasant hike starts at the parking lot of the Reservoir. It is a very well maintained trail and a moderate hike to a small mountain lake. From Blackmore Lake you can continue on up to the top of 10,514 ft. Mt. Blackmore, but the trail becomes more difficult. The lake alone is worth the hike, but the view from the top of Blackmore is incredible.

### Hyalite Peak (Grotto Falls) Trail

Follow the directions to Palisades Falls, but stay right at the fork. The road will terminate a couple of miles down at a large parking lot. The trailhead is here. This hike is 5.5 miles to a small lake sitting at the base of massive cliffs. Along the trail are 11 waterfalls, some visible from the trail, some only a few yards off the trail.

### History Rock Trail 424

This is a short hike to a large rock where early pioneers carved their names and the dates they were there. It is a challenge finding the historical carvings in between the more recent carvings of local graffiti artists. It is still a nice short hike through a mostly wooded area. The trailhead and parking area are very clearly marked and are approximately 10 miles from the start of Hyalite Canyon Road.

## Bridger Canyon Area

### The "M"

No doubt one of the most traveled trails in the area. Sitting on the south flank of Mt. Baldy at the Bozeman end of the Bridger Range, the "M" is one of Bozeman's most visible landmarks. It's a short hike and their are two routes—the easy way, and the hard way. If you take the trail straight up, it is literally that. There are no real switchbacks and the climb is totally vertical. The other route switches back and forth up the mountain and is a more moderate hike. Once you reach the "M" you can continue on up Mt. Baldy for some incredible views of the valley and surrounding mountain ranges.

To get there take N. Rouse until it turns into Bridger Canyon Drives. You'll find the parking lot and trailhead just before entering the canyon.

### Sacajawea Peak

This is a great hike at the end of a scenic drive. There are few residents here who haven't taken this trip at one time or another. The hike starts at the scenic little Fairy Lake and switches up the mountain to a saddle between Sacajawea Peak to the south, and Hardscrabble Peak to the north. Once you reach the saddle, the view of the Gallatin Valley is incredible. It's best to take this hike later in the summer as snow stays in the bowl beneath the saddle well into August. In fact, it seldom ever melts completely and you will have to traverse part of it just about anytime. To get there take Bridger Canyon Drive about 20 miles continuing past the Bridger Bowl Ski Area. You'll soon see the sign for the turnoff to Fairy Lake. Follow the road about 8 miles to the lake and campground. The trailhead starts just above the campground.

### Bridger Bowl Trail

Take Bridger Canyon Drive northeast of Bozeman for approximately 15 miles to the Bridger Bowl Ski Area. Turn here and follow the road to the lodge. When you reach the lodge follow the road to the right and wind up the hill. You will reach a (usually) closed gate and a small parking area. The trail starts here and winds up to the ridge for approximately two miles. This is a moderate to difficult hike and follows some steep and sometimes difficult terrain. You will climb about 2,100 feet in elevation. At the top you will see the helicopter landing platform used by HawkWatch volunteers for viewing and observing raptors during the fall migration. You will also have an incredible view of at least six mountain ranges.

## Gallatin Canyon

### Golden Trout Lakes Trail 83

This is an easy to moderate 2.5 mile trail with a little climbing. The hike takes you to three picturesque alpine lakes. The first is the only one with fish. Take Hwy. 191 south into the Gallatin Canyon. Portal Creek Road is about 3 miles south of Moose Flats Campground. Turn left on Portal Creek Road and drive about 6 miles to the parking area and trailhead.

### South Fork of Spanish Creek Trail

To find this trail take Hwy. 191 into the Gallatin Canyon just south of Gallatin Gateway. Immediately after you enter the Canyon, watch for Spanish Creek Road veering off to the right of the paved road. As soon as you pass through the gate just a few yards ahead, you are on media mogul Ted Turner's property. There's a good chance you will see anywhere from a few to possibly thousands of bison roaming the area. If any are nearby stay in your car. You are trespassing if you leave the road. The trailhead starts at the end of this road.

This is a very popular hike and you will more than likely pass others along the way. The full loop of this trail goes 26 miles. That is too long for a family hike, but hard core hikers may want to give it a go. The trail travels through sections of the Lee Metcalf Wilderness Area and provides some awesome scenery.

### Swan Creek Trail 186

This is an easy 2-mile hike along the creek bottom. It's a good area to see wild roses, and at the right time of the year wild berries. The trail ultimately ends at Hyalite Peak. Take Hwy. 191 south of Bozeman into the Gallatin Canyon about 32 miles to the very visible Swan Creek Campground sign. Turn left (east) and go 1 mile to the campground road. Follow this to the end of the road.

### Beehive Basin Trail 40

This hike takes you into the beautiful Beehive Basin where you can explore little Beehive Lake and an alpine meadow. You may very well spot moose or bighorn sheep up here on a good day. This hike is 8 miles round trip, but seems to be a family favorite. Take Hwy. 191 south of Bozeman into the Gallatin Canyon. When you come to the entrance to Big Sky, turn right (west) and drive up the mountain to the Mountain Village area. Instead of turning into the resort at the sign, continue straight on the road for 2.7 miles to the second trailhead parking lot. If you want a longer hike, start at the parking lot a mile back. The trailhead leaves from the left side of the road.

### Porcupine Creek Trail 34

This is an easy 4.5 mile trail through a creek bottom and along low ridges. If you look closely, you may find some petrified wood in the creek and along the banks of Porcupine Creek. Take Hwy. 191 south of Bozeman into the Gallatin Canyon. Drive just past the entrance to Big Sky Resort and look for the Ophir school building on the right. Turn left just past this and cross the Gallatin River. The trailhead is a quarter mile past the river. This trail can be confusing because of the excessive horse usage and the numerous horse trails leading off the main path. Stay on the main trail.

### Lava Lake

This 3-1/2 mile hike takes you to a beautiful mountain lake in the Spanish Peaks area of the Madison Range. The trail follows Cascade Creek through thick woods past a waterfall or two. You emerge from the woods at a small lake. This hike is best taken from mid to late summer. The lake can be covered in ice until at least mid-summer. To get there go south on Hwy. 191 from Bozeman into the Gallatin Canyon and watch for the Lava Lake parking area to your right.

## Other areas

### Bear Trap Canyon

This is an excellent early season hike through a magnificent canyon. The stretch of the Madison River that runs through here is a favorite of whitewater enthusiasts. The hike is along a fairly level trail along the Madison River. It is 7 miles long from end to end. To get there drive west of Bozeman to Four Corners. Continue straight on Hwy. 84 for about a half hour and watch for the signs to the Bear Trap Recreation Area. When you see the river you are close. Follow the 3 mile dirt road to the parking area and trail head. Keep your eyes open for rattlesnakes that frequent this area.

### Cliff and Wade Lakes Interpretive Trail

These lakes are surrounded by tall cliffs created a billion years ago by a geologic shift. The cliffs are a natural nesting area for a variety of raptors including bald eagles, prairie falcons and ospreys. A signed interpretive trail connects the two lakes between Wade Lake Campground and the Hilltop Campground. It's a 1.4 mile round trip with a 400 foot elevation gain from Wade Lake to Hilltop. To get there take Hwy. 287 40 miles south of Ennis. Look for the turnoff on the right signed for the lakes. Go west here for about 6 miles. The trailhead is just before the Wade Lake Campground with parking at the trailhead. Start here as there is no parking at the Hilltop end.

# Hiking the Bridger Ridge

## Take a Walk Through Time

*"The old Lakota was wise. He knew that man's heart away from nature becomes hard: he knew that lack of respect for growing, living things soon led to lack of respect for humans, too. So he kept his youth close to its softening influence."*

-Chief Luther Standing Bear, Oglala Sioux

Few places in Montana offer the adventurous and observant hiker a better opportunity to walk through time than do the Bridger Mountains. Pay close attention and you can experience the natural world much like the Native Americans and early explorers who traveled through these mountains in the past. Like them, you will discover that wildflowers still grow in profusion along the trails. Hawks and eagles still circle and soar overhead as they migrate home. Mountain goats, ground squirrels, pikas and marmots still skitter along the rocks and if you look closely, you'll discover that even the rocks themselves have a story to tell.

Stop, look, and listen as you walk along this spectacular ridge, and enjoy your walk through time.

## Follow the Footsteps Of Early Explorers

Many of the early mountain tribes, including the Salish, the Pend d'Oreille, and the Kootenai, crossed Bridger Ridge to hunt buffalo in the Shields and Yellowstone valleys. Sacajawea, the Shoshone interpreter who traveled with Lewis and Clark, knew this area well. on their journey home, the two explorers separated. Lewis traveled a northern route while Clark headed south. When Clark entered the Gallatin Valley, two major routes across the mountains were visible to him. One was the Flathead Pass, north of here. The other was the Rocky Canyon, now known as the Bozeman Pass. On the advice of Sacajawea, Clark chose the Rocky Canyon route which brought him directly to the Yellowstone River near what is now Livingston, Montana. This route was also preferred by John Bozeman, and became part of the Bozeman Trail.

Jim Bridger preferred Sacajawea's other route. The Bridger Range was named in honor of Jim Bridger, the famous trail blazer who scouted a trail that passed through this mountain range.

## Discover the Geological Past

The Bridger mountain range is the result of over 1.5 billion years of mountain building, a process which has included faulting, thrusting and folding. These so-called "tectonic" events are responsible for most of the mountain ranges in Western Montana. As recently as 10,000 years ago, large glaciers pushed their way through the area, carving the wide open valleys and cirque basins we see today.

But there's more to look for as you explore these ancient geological wonders. Sedimentary rocks such as the sandstone and limestone you see at the top of the Sacajawea Trail were once deposited at the bottom of ancient seas. These rocks have since been uplifted and folded to form many of the ridges along which the trail follows. Look closely, and you will see signs of the sea, including bits of coral, shells, and other small aquatic animals and plants embedded in the rock.

## Be Prepared for Weather

Because the Bridger Mountains trend north and south, weather often moves in from the west. So while the west side of the Bridgers receives more sun and wind (creating the thermals on which the raptors ride), it is cooler with more snow on the east side of the range. As you hike up the ridge, notice where the wind funnels the snow between Sacajawea and Hardscrabble Peaks above Fairy Lake. As the snow melts in the late spring and into the summer, you can still see bedrock scratched and smoothed by an ancient glacier which carved those open bowls and left behind stacks of tumbled rocks.

Watch for signs of how the wind and weather have created different growing environments as you proceed up the mountain. Above Fairy Lake, there is less soil and smaller, more dwarfed and twisted trees known as krummholz. Notice, too, how little, sheltered growing environments are created on the downward side of many of these wind-twisted trees. Here, only the hardiest alpine plants are able to survive in this harsh environment.

But pay close attention: these same windswept conditions can contribute to fast-moving changes of weather year-round. As you hike on the east side of the mountain, rain, hail, wind and lightning can move in suddenly from the west and put hikers at real risk. Always be prepared for a variety of conditions, and if the weather is questionable, plan your outing for earlier in the day.

## Enjoy the Flowers

In the late spring and summer, the Bridger Mountains are awash with the bright colors of wildflowers. Depending on the time of year and where you are in the Bridgers, look for glacier lilies pushing through the lingering snow, followed by buttercups, alpine bluebells, columbine, and sandwort.

Even those knowledgeable in alpine wildflowers can have difficulty distinguishing one species from another, so bring along a field guide to identify each flower by name. Your world will be richer for knowing them. Please remember, though, that wildflowers are delicate and often struggle to survive, particularly in these higher elevations. Stay on the trails so you do not disturb them and their habitat.

## Scan the Sky for Raptors

Bridger Ridge is one of the best places in the country to view migrating golden eagles. During the peak migration period, early to mid-October, hikers might see more than 100 eagles in a day as well as up to sixteen other species of raptors, including hawks, ospreys, and falcons as they migrate home.

You know how skiers get to the top of the mountain, but did you know that raptors also catch a "lift" up to the ridge? The sun heats the ground and the warm air rises, drawing cooler air underneath. Raptors simply spread their wings and catch these rising "thermals," sometimes traveling thousands of feet into the air. They then glide for miles without even flapping their wings.

Although fall is the best time to view the largest number and variety of raptors along Bridger Ridge, look for these magnificent birds soaring overhead no matter what time of the year.

## Look & Listen for Wildlife

If you're walking along the trail above Fairy Lake and hear a high-pitched call, it could be the sound of a pika warning of your arrival. These small mammals keep busy in the summer storing up "haystacks" of grasses upon which they feed all winter long.

You might encounter a number of other animals as they, too, forage for food. Watch for yellow bellied marmots, snowshoe hares, and weasels. You may even see a mountain goat or two, scrambling along the ridge. Moose and an occasional black bear have also been viewed along both the Bridger and Fairy Lake trails.

Remember, all of these animals are wild and should never be approached.

Listen too for the songs of birds in the forest and sub alpine meadows. You might hear the calls of pine siskins, whitecrowned sparrows, mountain bluebirds, American robins and rosy finches, to name a few. You may also hear the drumming of various woodpeckers as they communicate or search out insects in the trunks of trees. if you hear a strange call that you can't identify, it could very well be that of one of the jay species, which are noted for their ability to mimic a variety of sounds.

### Have a Great Hike

The Bridger Bowl and Sacajawea trails will transport you through some of the most beautiful country in Montana. Stop, look, listen and enjoy the rich diversity of biology, geology, botany and history you encounter along the way. Like the earliest travelers who passed along this ridge before, explore it—and enjoy it.

*Reprinted from National Forest Service brochure*

## Cross-Country Ski Trails

### Beaverhead-Deerlodge National Forest

*For more information contact District Ranger. 5 Forest Service Road. Ennis, MT 59279 (406) 682-4253 or Wade Lake Resort (406) 682- 7560*

**Wade Lake Ski Trails-40 mi. S Ennis on Hwy. 287 to Wade Lake Access Road and 6 mi. to Resort**
*35 km; groomed*
Several routes of set track provide skiers with touring of Cliff and Wade Lakes and scenic vistas of the area; food and lodging are available from the Resort. Trail map available.

### Gallatin National Forest

*For more information contact District Ranger, 3710 Fallen, Bozeman. MT 59715 (406) 522-2520*

**Brackett Creek/Fairy Lake Roads-20 mi. N Bozeman**
*24 km More Difficult; no grooming*
Shared with snowmobiles.

**New World Gulch-6 mi. S Bozeman**
*16 km Most Difficult; no grooming*

**Bozeman Creek—5 mi. S Bozeman**
*10 km More Difficult; intermittent grooming*
Snowmobiles prohibited.

**Moser Creek/Bozeman Creek–10 mi. S Bozeman**
*4.5 km Most Difficult; no grooming*

**Moser Creek/Face Draw Loop—11 mi. S Bozeman**
*5 km More Difficult; no grooming*
Snowmobiles prohibited.

**Hyalite Loop 15 miles S. Bozeman (Hyalite Reservoir)**
*24 km Most Difficult; no grooming;*
Sections of loop trail are shared with snowmobiles

**Wildhorse - Lick Creek 15 miles S. Bozeman**
*12.9 km More Difficult; no grooming.*
Shared with snowmobiles

**Bear Canyon 8 miles E. Bozeman**
*9.6 km More Difficult, no grooming.*
Shared with snowmobiles

**Spanish Creek 27 miles S. Bozeman**
*Starting point varies, depending on the condition of the Spanish Cr. rd. 5.6 km from the end of gravelled county road to Spanish Cr. parking area. From here there are many options for ski routes into the Lee Metcalf Wilderness. More/Most difficult, no grooming.*
Spanish Creek recreation/rental cabin available for extended trips. Trips further up the canyon to the high country are recommended for strong and experienced ski parties only. Avalanche hazard areas are common.

**Beehive Basin**
*5 km Most Difficult, no grooming.*
Avalanche hazard areas are common. Ski route gose into Lee Metcalf Wilderness.

*For more information on the following trails contact District Ranger, West Yellowstone, MT 59758 (406) 823-6961*

**Rendezvous Complex—West Yellowstone**
*16 km Easiest; daily grooming for classic/skate*
U. S. Olympic Team official fall training camp in November; dogs • snowmobiles prohibited. Fees 12/1-3/31-$3.00 daily per person; $20 season pass; $40 family season pass.

**Dead Dog Loop-West Yellowstone**
*5.5 km More Difficult; daily grooming for classic/skate*
Access via Rendezvous system. Fees apply.

**Windy Ridge-West Yellowstone**
*7 km More Difficult; intermittent grooming in November and December only for classic/skate* See above
Access via Rendezvous system. Fees apply.

## Information Please

All Montana area codes are 406

### Road Information

Montana Road Condition Report
800-226-7623, 800-335-7592 or local 444-7696
Montana Highway Patrol 444-7696
**Local Road Reports**
Bozeman 586-1313
Statewide Weather Reports 453-2081

### Tourism Information

Travel Montana 800-847-4868 outside Montana
444-2654 in Montana
http://travel.mt.gov/.
Yellowstone Country 800-736-5276 or 646-4383
Gold West Country 800-879-1159 or 846-1943
Northern Rodeo Association 252-1122
**Chambers of Commerce**
Belgrade 388-1616
Big Sky 995-3000
Bozeman 586-5421
Ennis 682-4388
Manhattan 284-6094
Three Forks 285-4556
West Yellowstone 646-7701

### Airports

Bozeman 388-6632
Ennis 682-7431
West Yellowstone 444-2506

### Government Offices

**State BLM Office** 255-2885, 238-1540
**Bureau of Land Management**
Billings Field Office 896-5013
Butte Field Office 494-5059
**Gallatin National Forest,** 522-2520
**Beaverhead/Deerlodge National Forest**
Butte 522-2520
**Lee Metcalf National Wildlife Refuge** 777-5552
**Red Rock Lake Wildlife Refuge** 276-3536
**Montana Fish, Wildlife & Parks** 994-4042
**U.S. Bureau of Reclamation**
Dillon Field Office 683-6472
Helena Field Office 475-3310

### Hospitals

Bozeman Deaconess Hospital
Bozeman 585-5000
Same Day Surgical Center •Bozeman 586-1956
Madison Valley Hospital • Ennis 682-4274

### Golf Courses

Big Sky Resort • Big Sky 995-5780
Bridger Creek • Bozeman 586-2333
Cottonwood Hills • Bozeman 587-1118
Headwaters Public • Three Forks 285-3700
Madison Meadows • Ennis 682-7468

### Bed & Breakfasts

**Lehrkind Mansion Bed & Breakfast**
**Bozeman** 585-6932
**West Yellowstone Hostel** 646-7745
Artful Lodger B&B • Belgrade 5887-2015
Aspen Grove B & B • Gallatin Gateway 763-5044
Bear Creek Angler Inn • Manhattan 282-9491
Bridger Inn • Bozeman 586-6666
Bridger Mountains Highland House 587-0904
Chokecherry Guest House • Bozeman 587-2657
Cottonwood Inn Bed & Breakfast 763-5452
Covered Wagon Ranch • Big Sky 995-4237
Fox Hollow B&B At Baxter Creek
Bozeman 582-8440
Gooch Hill B&B • Bozeman 586-5113
Gallatin River Lodge • Bozeman 388-0148
Howlers Inn • Bozeman 586-0304
Lindley House Bed & Breakfast
Bozeman 587-8403
Rachie's Crows Nest • Ennis 682-7371
Silver Forest Inn • Bozeman 586-1882
Voss Inn Bed & Breakfast • Bozeman 587-0982
Wild Rose B&B • Gallatin Gateway 763-4692

### Guest Ranches & Resorts

**320 Guest Ranch** 995-4283
**Big EZ Lodge** 995-7000
**East West Resorts At Big Sky** 995-2665
**Lone Mountain Ranch** 995-4644
**Mountain Meadows Guest Ranch** 995-4997
**Rainbow Ranch Lodge** 995-4132
**Potosi Hot Springs Resort** 685-3330
Bar N Ranch 646-7121
Elk Lake Resort 276-3282
Firehole Ranch 646-7294
Kirkwood Resort & Marina 646-7000
Big River Lodge 763-3033
Elkhorn Ranch 995-4291
Big Sky Resort 995-5000
Cliff Lake Resort 682-4982
Gallatin River Lodge 388-0148
International Backpackers Hostel 586-4659
Nine Quarter Circle Ranch 995-4276
Wade Lake Resort 682-7560
Castle Rock Inn 763-4243
Lionshead Resort 646-9584
B Bar Ranch 848-7729
Centennial Guest Ranch 682-7292
Diamond J Ranch Main Ranch 682-4867
Covered Wagon Ranch 995-4237
Nine Quarter Circle Ranch 995-4276
Twin Rivers Ranch 284-6485

Section 5

Parade Rest Guest Ranch 646-7217
Yellowstone Holiday RV & Marina 646-4242

## Vacation Homes & Cabins

**Intermountain Property Management**
Bozeman 586-1503
**Mountain Home-Montana Vacation Rentals**
Bozeman 586-4589
**Bozeman Cottage Vacation Rentals**
Bozeman 580-3223
**East West Resorts** • Big Sky 995-2665
**Cinnamon Lodge** • Big Sky 995-4253
Battle Ridge Ranch • Bozeman 686-4723
Bear Canyon Cabin • Bozeman 587-4749
Black Dog Ranch • Bozeman 686-4948
Bozeman Cottage • Bozeman 585-4402
Bozeman Vacation.com • Bozeman 580-1080
Brook Trout Inn • West Yellowstone 646-0154
Canyon Cabins • Gallatin Gateway 763-4248
Canyon Pines Cottage • Bozeman 586-1741
Darham Vacation Rentals • Bozeman 586-0091
DJ Bar Guest House • Belgrade 388-7463
Faithful Street Inn • West Yellowstone 646-4329
Gallatin River Guest Cabin • Big Sky 995-2832
Gallatin River Hideaway • Bozeman 586-8446
Gallatin Riverhouse • Big Sky 995-2290
Hyalite Creek Guest House • Bozeman 585-3458
Laura's Lilac Cottage • Bozeman 586-4140
Madison River Lodge • Ennis 682-4915
Magpie Guest House • Bozeman 585-8223
McClain Guest House • Bozeman 587-3261
Middle Creek Lodging • Bozeman 522-5372
Moose Haven • West Yellowstone 646-9295
Quarter Circle JK • West Yellowstone 646-4741
ResortQuest • Big Sky 995-4800
Sportsman's High Vacation Rental
West Yellowstone 646-7865
Tamarack Guest House • Bozeman 585-2496
Twin Rivers Ranch • Manhattan 284-6485
Wagon Wheel RV Campground & Cabins
West Yellowstone 646-7872
Wildflower Guest & Mountain Cabin
Bozeman 586-6610
Yellowstone Townhouses
West Yellowstone 646-9331
Yellowstone Village Condominiums
West Yellowstone 646-7335

## Forest Service Cabins

***Beaverhead-Deerlodge National Forest***

**Bear Creek Bunkhouse**
21 mi. S of Ennis, MT 682-4253
Capacity: Nightly fee: $20 Available: 12/1 - 4/30
On border of Lee Metcalf Wilderness; several trails available for cross-country skiing. $40/night for both bunkhouse & cabin.

**Bear Creek Cabin**
21 mi. S of Ennis, MT 682-4253
Capacity: 4 Nightly fee: $30 Available: 12/1 - 4/30
On border of Lee Metcalf Wilderness; several trails available for cross-country skiing.

**Wall Creek Cabin**
24 mi S of Ennis, MT 682-4253
Capacity: 4 Nightly fee: $20 Available: 5/16 - 12/1
Not available in winter.
West Fork Cabin
40 mi S of Ennis, MT 682-4253
Capacity: 3 Nightly fee: $30 Available: 7/2 - 3/31
Access by road in summer. Up to 30 mi. of snowmobile or ski travel required in winter.

**Landon**
50 mi. S of Ennis 682-4253
Capacity: 4 Nightly fee: $25 Available: 10/21-3/30
One room cabin w/propane stove & lights. High clearance or 4-wheel drive vehicle required. Winter access by snowmobile or skis

Gallatin National Forest

**Basin Station Cabin**
6.25 mi. W of West Yellowstone, MT. 646-7369
Capacity: 4 Nightly fee: $25 All year
Accessible by cross-country skiing or snowmobile. Plowed within 3 miles of cabin. Road access in summer.

**Beaver Creek Cabin**
21 mi. NW of West Yellowstone, MT. 646-7369
Capacity: 4 Nightly fee: $25 Available: All year
Plowed within 3 miles of cabin. Accessible by cross-country skis or snowmobile in winter. Road access in summer.

**Cabin Creek Cabin**
22 mi. NW of West Yellowstone, MT. 646-7369
Capacity: 4 Nightly fee: $25 Available: All year
Access by horseback or hiking in summer and by snowmobile and cross-country skis in winter.

**Fox Creek Cabin**
14 mi. S of Bozeman, MT 587-6920
Capacity: 2 Nightly fee: $25 Available: 12 /1 - 10/15
Trail access from nearest road is 2.5 miles. Winter access distance varies with snow conditions.

**Garnet Mountain (Lookout Cabin)**
19 mi. SW of Bozeman, MT 587-6920
Capacity: 4 Nightly fee: $25 Available: 12/1 - 10/15
Trail access from nearest road is 3.5 miles in summer. 10 mile ski or snowmobile in winter.

**Little Bear Cabin**
14 mi. S of Gallatin Gateway, MT 587-6920
Capacity: 4 Nightly fee: $25 Available: All year
Approximately 10 miles to cabin via snowmobile or skis in winter. Can drive to cabin in summer.

**Mystic Lake Cabin**
8 mi. SE of Bozeman, MT (S of Mystic Lake) 587-6920
Capacity: 4 Nightly fee: $25 Available: 12/1 - 10/15
Two access routes - more difficult, 5.3 miles; or easier, 10 mile route. Area closed to motorized vehicles.

**Spanish Creek Cabin**
23 miles SW of Bozeman, MT 587-6920
Capacity: 4 Nightly fee: $25 Available: 12/1 - 4/30
Normally plowed within 3.5 miles of cabin.

**Wapiti Cabin**
19 mi. SW of Big Sky, MT. 646-7369
Capacity: 4 Nightly fee: $25 Available: 11/1 - 4/30
Plowed within 3 miles of cabin. Accessible by cross-country skis or snowmobile in winter. Road access in fall and spring.

**Window Rock Cabin**
15 mi. S of Bozeman, MT (S of Hyalite Reservoir) 587-6920
Capacity: 4 Nightly fee: $25 Available: Year around
Road access to cabin in summer. Winter access distance varies with snow conditions.

**Windy Pass Cabin**
28 mi. S of Bozeman, MT 587-6920
Capacity: 4 Nightly fee: $25 Available: 6/1 - 10/15
Trail access from road is 2.5 miles, 1300 foot elevation gain.

**Yellow Mule Cabin**
35 mi SW of Bozeman, MT. 14 mi W of US 191 587-6920
Capacity: 2 Nightly fee: $25 Available: 12/1 - 10/15
Not recommended for ski parties (14 mile trip); 8 mile hike during summer..

## Private Campgrounds

**Sunrise Campground** • Bozeman 587-4797
**Ennis RV Village** • Ennis 682-5272
**Fort Three Forks Motel & RV Park**
Three Forks 285-3233
**Madison Arm Resort & Marina**
West Yellowstone 646-9328
Bear Canyon RV Park • Bozeman 587-1575
Gallatin County Campgrounds
Bozeman 587-9054
KOA Kampgrounds • Bozeman 586-6492
Sunset Motel & Trailer Park •Bozeman 587-5536
Slide Inn • Cameron 682-4804
Camper Corner • Ennis 682-4514
Elkhorn Store & Recreational Vehicle
Ennis 682-4273
Castle Rock Inn • Gallatin Gateway 763-4243
Madison River Cabins & RV • Ennis 682-4890
Manhattan Camper Court-Trailer
Manhattan 284-6930
Lainey's Lakeview Cabin • Mc Allister 682-4687
Lake Shore Cabins & Campground
Mc Allister 682-4424
La Siesta RV Park • West Yellowstone 646-7536
Norris-Bear Trap Hot Springs • Norris 685-3303
KOA Kampgrounds • Three Forks 285-3611
Brandin' Iron Motel & RV
West Yellowstone 646-9411
Fort JAX RV Park • West Yellowstone 646-7729
Hideaway RV Campground
West Yellowstone 646-9049
KOA • West Yellowstone 646-7606
Lionshead • West Yellowstone
Moonlight Enterprises RV
West Yellowstone 646-7276
Pony Express Motel & RV Park
West Yellowstone 646-7644
Rustic Wagon RV Campground
West Yellowstone 646-7387
Three Forks KOA • Three Forks 285-3611
Wagon Wheel Trailer Park
West Yellowstone 646-7872
Yellowstone Grizzly RV Park
West Yellowstone 646-4466
Yellowstone Holiday RV Campground & Marina
West Yellowstone 646-4242
Yellowsotne Park KOA
West Yellowstone 646-7606

## Car Rental

Avis-Rent-A-Car 388-6414
Budget Rent -A-Car 388-4091
Dollar Rent-A-Car 388-1323

| | |
|---|---|
| Free Spirit Car Rental | 388-2002 |
| Rent A Wreck | 388-4189 |
| Thrifty Car rental | 388-3484 |
| Enterprise Rent-A-Car | 586-8010 |
| Hertz Rent-A-Car | 388-6939 |
| National Car Rental | 388-6694 |
| Practical Rent-A-Car | 586-8373 |
| Big Sky Car Rentals | 646-9564 |
| Budget Car & Truck Rental | 646-7882 |

## Outfitters & Guides

*F=Fishing H=Hunting R=River Guides*
*E=Horseback Rides G=General Guide Services*

| | | |
|---|---|---|
| **Campbell's Guided Fishing Trips** | GF | 587-0822 |
| **Arnaud Oufitting** | H | 763-4235 |
| **Wapati Basin Outfitters** | H | 388-4941 |
| **Wild Trout Outfitters** | F | 995-4895 |
| **320 Guest Ranch** | FRE | 995-4283 |
| **Gallatin Riverguides** | GHF | 995-2290 |
| **Lone Mountain Ranch** | GFER | 995-4644 |
| **Panda Sport Rentals** | R | 587-6280 |
| Arrick's Fishing Flies | G | 646-7290 |
| Beartooth Outfitting | F | 682-7525 |
| Big Sky Outfitters | HFRE | 587-2508 |
| The Bozeman Angler | F | 587-9111 |
| Bridger Outfitters | GFHER | 388-4463 |
| Buffalo Horn Outfitters | G | 587-0448 |
| C Francis & Co Sporting Agents | F | 763-4042 |
| Clark's Guide Service | FR | 682-4679 |
| Bar 88 Horses | HEF | 682-4827 |
| Bear Trap Express | R | 682-4263 |
| Bear Trap Outfitters | HEF | 646-7312 |
| Beardsley Outfitting & Guide | G | 682-7292 |
| Bleu Sky Pack Station Inc | G | 685-3647 |
| Blue Ribbon Flies | HR | 646-7642 |
| Bob Cleverly | FR | 682-4371 |
| Boojum Expeditions | G | 587-0125 |
| Broken Hart Ranch | EHF | 763-4279 |
| The Bozeman Angler | GF | 587-9111 |
| Bud Lilly's Trout Shop | F | 646-7801 |
| Buffalo Jump Outfitting | G | 682-7900 |
| B.W. Outfitters | HEF | 284-6562 |
| Canoe Rentals-shuttles & Fly Fishing Outfitter | GFR | 285-3488 |
| Cutthroat Services & Sales Inc | G | 522-7723 |
| Daniel E. Glines | FR | 682-7247 |
| Diamond "P" Ranch | E | 646-7246 |
| Diamond K Outfitters | E | 995-4132 |
| Diamond P Ranch | E | 646-7246 |
| Diamond R Stables | E | 388-1760 |
| Diamond Wing | HFREG | 682-4867 |
| Doud Gregory J | G | 682-7336 |
| Eaton Outfitters | ER | 682-4514 |
| East Slope Anglers | GF | 995-4369 |
| Firehole Ranch LLC | FE | 646-7294 |
| Flying D Ranch | H | 763-4930 |
| Flyfishing Montana Co. | F | 585-9066 |
| Flyfishing-Wild Trout Outfitters | GF | 995-4895 |
| Gallatin River Ranch Equestrian Center | E | 284-3782 |
| Gerald R. Clark | EFR | 682-7474 |
| Geyser Whitewater Expeditions | R | 995-4989 |
| Gone Clear Outfitters | F | 388-0029 |
| Greater Yellowstone Flyfishers | F | 585-5321 |
| Grossenbacher Guides | F | 582-1760 |
| Hawkridge Outfitters & Rods | F | 585-9608 |
| Headwaters Guide Service | FR | 763-4761 |
| Highlands to Islands Guide Service | HF | 682-7677 |
| Howard Outfitters | F | 682-4834 |
| Jake's Horses | GFEH | 995-4630 |
| Jack River Outfitters | F | 682-4948 |
| Jacklin's Outfitters For The World Of Fly Fishing | G | 646-7336 |
| Jim Danskin | F | 646-9200 |
| Kicking Ass Outfitters | G | 682-4488 |
| Kokopelli's Travels | EF | 686-4475 |
| Madison River Fishing Company | F | 682-4293 |
| Madison River Outfitters | GF | 646-9644 |
| Macgregor Fogelsong Flies | F | 652-4252 |
| Mcguire Dick | G | 682-4370 |
| McNeely Outfitting | HF | 585-9896 |
| Medicine Lake Outfitters | GF | 388-4938 |
| Montana Flycast Guide Service | GF | 587-5923 |
| Montana Horses | E | 285-3541 |
| Montana Troutfitters | GF | 587-4707 |
| Montana Whitewater Inc | ER | 763-4465 |
| Montana Rivers to Ridges | F | 580-2328 |
| Nine Quart Circle Ranch | EF | 995-4276 |
| Randy Brown's Madison Flyfisher | F | 682-7481 |
| The River's Edge | GF | 586-5373 |
| Riverside Motel & Outfitters | F | 682-4241 |
| RJ Cain & Co. Outfitters | F | 586-8524 |
| Rod-n-Dog Outfitting & Guide Service | GF | 682-7419 |
| Running River Fly Guide | F | 586-1758 |
| Sphinx Mountain Outfitting | HREF | 682-7336 |
| Saunders Floating | F | 682-7128 |
| S & W Outfitters | H | 995-2658 |
| T Lazy B Ranch | HER | 682-7288 |
| The Tackle Shop Outfitters | HRF | 682-4263 |
| Thompson's ANgling Adventures | HF | 682-7509 |
| Wild Trout Outfitters Fly Fishing Guide Service | F | 995-4895 |
| Yellowstone Adventures | F | 585-7494 |
| Yellowstone LLamas | F | 586-6872 |
| Yellowstone Mountain Guides | HF | 646-7230 |
| Yellowstone Net | R | 388-2100 |
| Yellowstone Raft Company | R | 995-4613 |

## Cross-Country Ski Centers

| | |
|---|---|
| Bohart Ranch • Bozeman | 586-9070 |
| Lone Mountain Ranch • Big Sky | 995-4644 |
| Wade Lake Resort • 30 mi. W of West Y ellowstone | 682-7560 |
| Yellowstone Expediitons West Yellowstone | 646-9333 |

## Downhill Ski Areas

| | |
|---|---|
| Big Sky Resort | 995-5000 |
| Bridger Bowl | 586-2787 |

## Snowmobile Rentals

| | |
|---|---|
| Bar T Z • Belgrade | 388-7228 |
| Team Bozeman Rentals • Bozeman | 587-4671 |
| Big Boys Toys • Bozeman | 587-4747 |
| Summit Motor Sports Inc • Bozeman | 586-7147 |
| Canyon Adventures •Gallatin Gateway | 995-4450 |
| Yellowstone Motor Sport Rentals & Snovan Tours West Yellowstone | 646-7656 |
| Alpine West Snowmobiles Of West Yellowstone West Yellowstone | 646-7633 |
| Back Country Adventures Snowmobile Rentals West Yellowstone | 646-9317 |
| Big Western Pine Motel West Yellowstone | 646-7622 |
| Days Inn • West Yellowstone | 646-7656 |
| Dude Motor Inn / Roundup Motel West Yellowstone | 646-7301 |
| Gray Wolf Inn & Suites West Yellowstone | 646-0000 |
| Hi Country Snowmobile Rental West Yellowstone | 646-7541 |
| High-mark Snowmobile Rentals West Yellowstone | 646-7586 |
| Old Faithful Snowmobile Rentals West Yellowstone | 646-9695 |
| Rendezvouz Snowmobile Rental West Yellowstone | 646-9564 |
| Roundup Motel • West Yellowstone | 646-7301 |
| Ski-doo Snowmobiles West Yellowstone | 646-7735 |
| Stage Coach Inn • West Yellowstone | 646-7381 |
| Targhee Snowmobiles West Yellowstone | 646-7900 |
| Targhee Snowmobiles Karl Cook West Yellowstone | 646-7700 |
| Three Bear Lodge Motor Lodge West Yellowstone | 646-7353 |
| Two-top Snowmobile Rental Inc West Yellowstone | 646-7802 |
| Westgate Station-snowmobile Rentals West Yellowstone | 646-7651 |
| Yellowstone Adventures West Yellowstone | 646-7735 |
| Yellowstone Arctic/Yamaha West Yellowstone | 646-9636 |
| Yellowstone Lodge • West Yellowstone | 646-0020 |
| Yellowstone Snowmobile West Yellowstone | 646-7301 |



**Notes:**

## PUBLIC CAMPGROUNDS

# Campsite Directions

| Campsite Directions | Season | Camping | Trailers | Toilets | Water | Boat Launch | Fishing | Swimming | Trails | Stay Limit | Fee |
|---|---|---|---|---|---|---|---|---|---|---|---|
| **55•Lewis & Clark Caverns FWP•** 19 mi. W of Three Forks on MT 2•Milepost 271 | All Year | 50 | • | • | • | | • | | N | 7 | • |
| **56•Harrison Lake FWP•** 5 mi. E of Harrison on Cty. Rd. | All Year | 25 | • | • | | B | • | | | 7 | • |
| **57•Red Mountain BLM•** 9 mi. NE of Norris on SR 289 | All Year | 8 | 35′ | • | • | A | • | | B | 14 | • |
| **58•Valley Garden FWP** US 287 1/4 mi. S of Ennis•Milepost 48•2 mi. N. on Cty. Rd | 4/1-11/30 | • | • | • | | C | • | | | 7 | • |
| **59•Ennis FWP•** US 287 E of Ennis•Milepost 48 | 4/1-11/30 | 25 | • | • | • | C | • | | | 7 | • |
| **60•Varney Bridge FWP•** 2 mi. W of Ennis on US 287•10 mi. S on Cty. Rd. | All Year | • | • | • | | C | 0 | | | 7 | • |
| **61•Bear Creek FS•** 11 mi. S of Ennis on US 287•9 mi. E of Cameron Community Center | 6/1-11/30 | 12 | • | • | • | | | | • | 16 | |
| **62•West Madison BLM•** 18 mi. S of Ennis on US 287•3 mi. S on Cty. Rd. | All Year | 22 | 35′ | • | • | | • | | | 14 | • |
| **63•South Madison BLM•** 26 mi. S of Ennis on US 287•1 mi. W | All Year | 11 | 35′ | • | • | C | • | | | 14 | • |
| **64•West Fork FS•** 24 mi. S of Cameron on US 287.1 mi. W on Forest Rd. 8381 | 6/1-9/15 | 7 | | • | • | | • | | | 16 | • |
| **65•Madison River FS•** 24 mi. S of Cameron on US 287•1 mi. SW on Cty. Rd. 8381 | 6/1-9/30 | 10 | 22′ | • | • | | • | | | 16 | • |
| **66•Wade Lake FS•** 8 mi. N of West Yellowstone on US 191•27 mi. W on US 287•6 mi. SW on Forest Rd. 5721 | 6/1-9/30 | 30 | 24′ | D | • | C | • | • | • | 16 | • |
| **67•Hilltop FS•** 8 mi. N of West Yellowstone on US 191•27 mi. W on US 287•6 mi. SW on Forest Rd. 5721 | 6/1-9/30 | 20 | 22′ | • | • | | • | | • | 16 | • |
| **68•Cliff Point FS•** 8 mi. N of West Yellowstone on US 191•27 mi. W on US 287•6 mi. SW on Forest Rd. 5721 | 6/1-9/15 | 6 | 16′ | • | • | C | • | • | • | 16 | • |
| **69•Fairweather FWP•** 1 mi. W of Logan on Rt. 205•3 mi. N on Logan-Trident Rd.•7 Mi. NE on Clarkston Rd. | All Year | 10 | 16′ | | | | • | | | 7 | |
| **70•Missouri Headwaters FWP•** 3 mi. E of Three Forks on Rt. 205•3 mi. N on Hwy 286 | All Year | 20 | • | • | • | • | • | | • | 7 | • |
| **71•Greycliff FWP•** 23 mi. W of Bozeman on MT 84•6 mi. S on Madison River Rd. | All Year | 30 | • | • | • | C | • | | | 7 | • |
| **72•Langhor FS•** 11 mi. S of Bozeman on S 19th Ave. & Hyalite Canyon Rd. (Forest Rd. 62) | 5/15-9/15 | 12 | 16′ | D | • | | • | | • | 16 | • |
| **73•Hood Creek FS** 17 mi. S of Bozeman on S 19th Ave. & Hyalite Canyon Rd. (Forest Rd.62) | 6/1-9/15 | 18 | 30′ | D | • | C | • | | | 16 | • |
| **74•Chisholm FS•** 18 mi. S of Bozeman on S 19th Ave. & Hyalite Canyon Rd. (Forest Rd. 62) | 5/15-9/15 | 10 | 40′ | D | • | | • | | • | 16 | • |
| **75•Spire Rock FS•** 26 mi. S of Bozeman on US 191•2 mi. E on Forest Rd. 1321 | 5/15-9/15 | 17 | 30′ | • | | | • | | | 16 | • |
| **76•Greek Creek FS•** 31 mi. S of Bozeman on US 191 | 5/15-9/15 | 14 | 40′ | D | • | A | • | | • | 16 | • |
| **77•Swan Creek FS•** 32 mi. S of Bozeman on US 191•1 mi. E on Forest Rd. 481 | 5/15-9/15 | 13 | 30′ | • | • | | • | | | 16 | • |
| **78•Moose Flat FS•** 32 mi. S of Bozeman on US 191 | 6/1-9/15 | 13 | 40′ | D | • | A | • | | | 16 | • |
| **79•Red Cliff FS•** 48 mi. S of Bozeman on US 191 | 5/15-9/15 | 68 | 30′ | • | • | A | • | | • | 16 | • |
| **80•Cabin Creek FS•** 8 mi. N of West Yellowstone on US 191•14 mi. W on US 287 | 5/22-9/15 | 15 | 32′ | D | • | | • | | • | 16 | • |

**Agency**
FS—U.S.D.A Forest Service
FWP—Montana Fish, Wildlife & Parks
NPS—National Park Service
BLM—U.S. Bureau of Land Management
USBR—U.S. Bureau of Reclamation
CE—Corps of Engineers

**Camping**
Camping is allowed at this site. Number indicates camping spaces available
H—Hard sided units only; no tents

**Trailers**
Trailer units allowed. Number indicates maximum length.

**Toilets**
Toilets on site. D—Disabled access

**Water**
Drinkable water on site

**Fishing**
Visitors may fish on site

**Boat**
Type of boat ramp on site:
A—Hand launch
B—4-wheel drive with trailer
C—2-wheel drive with trailer

**Swimming**
Designated swimming areas on site

**Trails**
Trails on site
B—Backpacking N—Nature/Interpretive

**Stay Limit**
Maximum length of stay in days

**Fee**
Camping and/or day-use fee

## Public Campgrounds

### Campsite Directions

| Campsite Directions | Season | Camping | Trailers | Toilets | Water | Boat Launch | Fishing | Swimming | Trails | Stay Limit | Fee |
|---|---|---|---|---|---|---|---|---|---|---|---|
| **81•Beaver Creek FS•**<br>8 mi. N of West Yellowstone on US 191•16 mi. W on US 287 | 6/15-9/15 | 64 | 32′ | D | • | C | • | | | 16 | • |
| **82•Rainbow Point FS•**<br>5 mi. N of West Yellowstone on US 191•3 mi. W on Forest Rd. 610 •2 mi. N on Forest Rd. 6954 | 5/22-9/15 | 85-H | 32′ | | • | C | • | • | | 16 | • |
| 83•Lonesomehurst FS•<br>8 mi. West of West Yellowstone on Hebgen Lake Rd. | 5/22-9/15 | 26 | 32′ | D | • | C | • | • | | 16 | • |
| **84•Bakers Hole FS•**<br>3 mi. N of West Yellowstone on US 191 | 5/22-9/15 | 72-H | 32′ | D | • | | • | | | 16 | • |
| **85•Potosi FS•**<br>3 mi. SE of Pony on Cty. Rd. 1601•5 mi. SW on Forest Rd. 1501 | 6/1-9/30 | 15 | 32′ | • | • | | • | | • | 16 | |
| **86•Branham Lakes FS•**<br>6 mi. E of Sheridan on Cty. Rd. 1111•5 mi. E on Forest Rd. 1112•3 mi. N on Forest Rd. 1110 | 7/1-9/15 | 6 | 22′ | • | | C | • | • | • | 16 | |

## Fishery

| Fishery | Cold Water Species | | | | | | | | | | | | Warm Water Species | | | | | | | | | | Services | | | | | |
|---|---|---|---|---|---|---|---|---|---|---|---|---|---|---|---|---|---|---|---|---|---|---|---|---|---|---|---|---|
| | Brook Trout | Mt. Whitefish | Lake Whitefish | Golden Trout | Cutthroat Trout | Brown Trout | Rainbow Trout | Kokanee Salmon | Bull Trout | Lake Trout | Arctic Grayling | Burbot | Largemouth Bass | Smallmouth Bass | Walleye | Sauger | Northern Pike | Shovelnose Sturgeon | Channel Catfish | Yellow Perch | Crappie | Paddlefish | Vehicle Access | Campgrounds | Toilets | Docks | Boat Ramps | MotorRestrictions |
| 50. Jefferson River | | • | | | | • | • | | | | | | | | | | | | | | | | • | • | • | | • | |
| 51. Harrison Lake | | | | | | • | • | | | | | | | | | | | | | | | | • | • | • | | • | |
| 52. Madison River | | • | | | | • | • | | | | | | | | | | | | | | | | • | • | • | | • | • |
| 53. Ennis Lake | | | | | | • | • | | | | • | | | | | | | | | | | | • | • | • | | • | |
| 54. Odell Creek | | | | | | • | • | | | | | | | | | | | | | | | | • | | | | | |
| 55. Madison alpine lakes | | | | | • | | • | | | | | | | | | | | | | | | | | | | | | |
| 56. West Fork Madison River | | | | | | • | • | | | | | | | | | | | | | | | | • | • | • | | | |
| 57. Cliff Lake | | | | | • | | • | | | | | | | | | | | | | | | | • | • | | | • | |
| 58. Wade Lake | | | | | | • | • | | | | | | | | | | | | | | | | • | • | • | • | • | |
| 59. Hidden Lake | | | | | | | • | | | | | | | | | | | | | | | | | | | | | |
| 60. Elk Lake | | | | | • | | | | | • | • | | | | | | | | | | | | • | • | • | • | | |
| 61. East Gallatin River | • | • | | | | • | • | | | | | | | | | | | | | | | | • | | | | | |
| 62. Three Forks ponds | | | | | | | • | | | | | | • | | | | | | | | | | • | | | | | |
| 63. Hyalite Creek | • | | | | • | | • | | | | | | | | | | | | | | | | • | • | • | | | |
| 64. Squaw Creek | • | | | | | • | • | | | | | | | | | | | | | | | | • | • | • | | | |
| 65. Gallatin Mountains alpine lakes | | | | • | • | | • | | | | • | | | | | | | | | | | | | | | | | |
| 66. West Fork Gallatin River | | | | | | • | • | | | | | | | | | | | | | | | | • | | | | | |
| 67. Taylor Fork | | | | | • | • | • | | | | | | | | | | | | | | | | • | • | | | | |
| 68. Gallatin River | • | • | | | | • | • | | | | | | | | | | | | | | | | • | • | | | | • |
| 69. Quake Lake | | | | | | • | • | | | | | | | | | | | | | | | | • | • | • | • | • | |
| 70. Hebgen Lake | | | | | | • | • | | | | | | | | | | | | | | | | • | • | • | • | • | |
| 71. Grayling Creek | | | | | • | | • | | | | | | | | | | | | | | | | • | | | | | |
| 72. South Fork Madison River | | | | | | • | • | | | | | | | | | | | | | | | | • | • | | | | |

**Notes:**

## Dining Quick Reference

Price Range refers to the average cost of a meal per person: ($) $1-$6, ($$) $7-$11, ($$$) $12-up. Cocktails: "Yes" indicates full bar; Beer (B)/Wine (W), Service: Breakfast (B), Brunch (BR), Lunch (L), Dinner (D). Businesses in bold print will have additional information under the appropriate map locator number in the body of this section.

| RESTAURANT | TYPE CUISINE | PRICE RANGE | CHILD MENU | COCKTAILS BEER WINE | SERVICE | CREDIT CARDS | MAP LOCATOR NUMBER |
|---|---|---|---|---|---|---|---|
| **East Side Diner** | Family | $$/$$$ | Yes | | B/L/D | Major | 1 |
| **Montana Ale Works** | Fine Dining/Pub Fare | $$/$$$ | | B/W | L/D | Major | 2 |
| **Boodles** | Creative | $$$ | | Yes | L/D | Major | 2 |
| **John Bozeman's Bistro** | Eclectic | $$/$$$ | Yes | B/W | L/D/ | Major | 2 |
| **MacKenzie River Pizza Co.** | Pizza | $/$$ | | B/W | L/D | Major | 2 |
| **Spanish Peaks Brewing Co.** | Italian | $$/$$$ | | Yes | L/D | V/M/D | 2 |
| **O'Brien's** | Continental | $$/$$$ | yes | B/W | B/L/D | V/MC | 2 |
| **Pickle Barrel** | Deli | $ | | | L/D | | 2 |
| **Soby's** | Mexican | $ | Yes | B/W | L | V/M | 2 |
| **The Point After** | American | $/$$ | | Yes | L/D | Major | 2 |
| **Western Cafe** | American | $ | | | B/L/D | | 2 |
| **Burger Bob's** | American | $$ | Yes | Yes | L/D | | 2 |
| **Leaf & Bean** | Coffee House/Bakery | $ | | | B/L/D | V/MC | 2 |
| 4B's Restaurant | Family | $ | Yes | | B/L/D | V/M/D | 2 |
| Azteca | Mexican | $$ | | | L/D | Major | 2 |
| Black Angus Steak House | Fine Dining | $$ | | Yes | L/D | V/M/A | 2 |
| Sunrise Cafe | Fresh Deli | $/$$ | | | B/L | | 2 |
| Cat Eye Cafe | Eclectic | $/$$ | Yes | B/W | B/L/D | MC/V | 2 |
| Charlie's Deli & Coffee House | Deli/Coffee House | $ | | | L | | 2 |
| **Ferraro's Restaurant and Lounge** | Italian | $$/$$$ | | Yes | D | V/M/D | 3 |
| **Burrito Shop** | Mexican | $ | Yes | B/W | L/D | Major | 3 |
| **The Wok** | Chinese | $$ | | B/W | L/D | Major | 3 |
| Brandi's Restaurant | American | $/$$ | Yes | Yes | B/L/D | Major | 3 |
| Dairy Queen | Fast Food | $ | Yes | | L/D | | 3 |
| Frontier Pies Restaurant | Family | $/$$ | Yes | | B/L/D | Major | 3 |
| Hipshots | American | $$ | | | B/L/D | Major | 3 |
| Taco Bell | Fast Food | $ | Yes | | L/D | | 3 |
| Taco John's | Fast Food | $ | Yes | | L/D | | 3 |
| Village Inn Pizza | Pizza | $/$$ | Yes | B | L/D | V/M | 3 |
| Applebee's Neighborhood Grill | Eclectic | $$/$$$ | Yes | Yes | L/D | Major | 4 |
| Arby's | Fast Food | $ | Yes | | B/L/D | | 4 |
| **Cantrell's** | American | $$ | Yes | Yes | B/L/D | Major | 4 |
| **Best Western Grantree Inn** | American | $—$$$ | Yes | Yes | B/L/D | Major | 4 |
| **AppleTree Restaurant** | American | $/$$ | Yes | | B/L/D | Major | 5 |
| Santa Fe Reds | Mexican | $$/$$$ | Yes | Yes | L/D | Major | 5 |
| Grum's Deli & Gourmet Restaurant | Deli | $$ | Yes | | L/D | Major | 5 |
| McDonald's | Fast Food | $ | Yes | | B/L/D | | 5 |
| **Pork Chop John's** | Fast Food | $ | Yes | | L/D | | 6 |
| **Community Food Co-op** | Natural Foods | $ | | | B/L/D | V/D | 6 |
| **Café Zydeco** | Cajun | $/$$ | | | | | 6 |
| **Perkins Family Restaurant** | Family | $/$$ | Yes | | B/L/D | Major | 6 |
| Cosmic Gourmet Pizza | Pizza | $$ | | | L/D | V/M | 6 |
| Arby's | Fast Food | $ | Yes | | B/L/D | | 6 |
| Bagel Works | Coffee House/ Deli | $ | | | B/L | | 6 |
| Chinatown | Chinese | $ | | | L/D | V/M | 6 |
| Hardee's | Fast Food | $ | Yes | | B/L/D | | 6 |
| It's Greek To Me | Greek | $ | | | L/D | | 6 |
| La Parrilla | Wraps | $ | Yes | B/W | L/D | | 6 |
| McDonald's | Fast Food | $ | Yes | | B/L/D | | 6 |
| Subway | Fast Food | $ | Yes | | L/D | | 6 |
| Wendy's | Fast Food | $ | Yes | | L/D | | 6 |
| Lewis & Clark Motel & Family Restaurant | Family | $/$$ | | B/W | B/L/D | Major | 6 |
| **Denny's Classic Diner** | Family | $ | Yes | | B/L/D | V/M | 7 |
| **Leaf & Bean** | Coffee House | $ | | | B/L/D | V/MC | 7 |
| Taco Del Sol | Fast Food | $ | | | L/D | V/MC | 7 |
| Johnny Carino's | Italian | $$/$$$ | Yes | B/W | L/D | Major | 7 |
| Bennigans | Family | $$/$$$ | Yes | Yes | L/D | Major | 7 |
| Mongolian Grill | Asian | $/$$ | | | LD | V/M | 7 |
| A&W Root Beer/Kentucky Fried Chicken | Fast Food | $ | Yes | | L/D | | 7 |
| 19th Hole Grill | American | $ | | Yes | L/D | Major | 8 |
| **Fuddrucker's** | American | $-$$ | Yes | Yes | L/D | Major | 9 |

## Dining Quick Reference-Continued

Price Range refers to the average cost of a meal per person: ($) $1-$6, ($$) $7-$11, ($$$) $12-up. Cocktails: "Yes" indicates full bar; Beer (B)/Wine (W), Service: Breakfast (B), Brunch (BR), Lunch (L), Dinner (D). Businesses in bold print will have additional information under the appropriate map locator number in the body of this section.

| RESTAURANT | TYPE CUISINE | PRICE RANGE | CHILD MENU | COCKTAILS BEER WINE | SERVICE | CREDIT CARDS | MAP LOCATOR NUMBER |
|---|---|---|---|---|---|---|---|
| **Godfather's Pizza** | Pizza | $ | Yes | B | L/D | V/M/D | 9 |
| Casey's Corner | Fast food | $ | | | B/L/D | Major | 9 |
| Burger King | Fast Food | $ | Yes | | B/L/D | | 9 |
| Domino's Pizza | Pizza | $ | | | L/D | | 9 |
| Duck-In Cafe | | | | | | | 9 |
| J B'S Restaurant | Family | $ | Yes | | B/L/D | V/M | 9 |
| Pizza Hut | Pizza | $/$$ | Yes | B | L/D | V/M/D | 9 |
| Quizno's Classic Subs | Subs | $ | Yes | | L/D | | 9 |
| Taco Time | Fast Food | $ | Yes | | L/D | | 9 |
| The Bay Bar & Grill | Steakhouse | $$/$$$ | Yes | Yes | L/D | Major | 9 |
| **Pickle Barrel** | Deli | $ | | | L/D | | 10 |
| Casa Sanchez | Mexican | $$ | Yes | B/W | L/D | Major | 10 |
| Colombo's Pizza & Pasta | Pizza | $ | | B/W | L/D | | 10 |
| Hero's Subs | Deli | $ | | | L/D | | 10 |
| Spectators Sports Bar & Grill | American | $$ | | Yes | L/D | V/M | 10 |
| Stageline Pizza | Pizza | $/$$ | | | L/D | | 10 |
| **Kountry Korner Cafe** | Family | $/$$ | Yes | B/W | B/L/D/BR | Major | 13 |
| **Sandwich Company** | Cajun | $/$$ | | | B/L | | 12 |
| B&H Restaurant | American | $$ | Yes | Yes | B/L/D | Major | 12 |
| Puerto Vallarta Mexican Food | Mexican | $$ | | Yes | L/D | | 12 |
| Corner Store Exxon/Grand Slam Grill | Fast Food | $ | | | B/L/D | Major | 13 |
| **Country Kitchen** | Family | $-$$ | Yes | | B/L/D | Major | 13 |
| Burger King | Fast Food | $ | Yes | | B/L/D | | 13 |
| Dairy Queen | Fast Food | $ | Yes | | L/D | | 13 |
| Hero's Subs | Deli | $ | | | L/D | | 13 |
| McDonald's | Fast Food | $ | Yes | | B/L/D | | 13 |
| Pizza Hut | Pizza | $/$$ | Yes | B | L/D | V/M/D | 13 |
| Rosa's Pizza | Pizza | $ | | | L/D | V/M | 13 |
| Subway | Fast Food | $ | Yes | | L/D | | 13 |
| Taco Time | Fast Food | $ | Yes | | L/D | | 13 |
| Mama Mac's Bakery & Sandwich Shop | Family | $/$$ | Yes | | B/L/D | | 13 |
| **The Mint Bar & Cafe** | Eclectic | $$$ | | Yes | L/D | Major | 14 |
| **MacKenzie River Pizza Co.** | Pizza | $/$$ | | B/W | L/D | Major | 14 |
| **The Wok** | Chinese | $$ | | B/W | L/D | Major | 14 |
| It's Greek to Me | Greek | $ | | | L/D | | 14 |
| Stageline Pizza | Pizza | $/$$ | | | L/D | | 14 |
| **Sir Scott's Oasis** | Steakhouse | $$$ | Yes | Yes | D | Major | 15 |
| **Garden Cafe** | Family | $/$$ | Yes | | B/L | | 15 |
| Broken Arrow Cafe | American | $$ | | Yes | L/D | | 15 |
| Cafe on Broadway | Family | $/$$ | Yes | | B/L/D | | 15 |
| Margarita's Steakhouse | Mexican | $$ | Yes | Yes | D | Major | 15 |
| Stageline Pizza | Pizza | $/$$ | | | L/D | | 15 |
| **Land of Magic Dinner Club** | Steaks & Seafood | $$ | | Yes | L/D | Major | 16 |
| **Historic Headwaters Restaurant** | Creative | $$/$$$ | Yes | B/W | L/D | Major | 17 |
| **Wheat Montana Farms & Bakery** | Deli | $ | | | B/L | | 17 |
| **Willow Creek Cafe & Saloon** | American | $$ | Yes | Yes | L/D/BR | V/M | 17 |
| Custer's Last Root Beer Stand | Family | $ | Yes | | L/D | | 17 |
| Longhorn Cafe | Family | $/$$ | | | B/L | | 17 |
| Stageline Pizza | Pizza | $/$$ | | | L/D | | 17 |
| Three Forks Cafe | Family | $/$$ | | | B/L | | 17 |
| Three Forks Candy Co. | Deli/Candy shop | $ | | | B/L/D | Major | 17 |
| Steer In | Steaks, Chops | $$$ | Yes | Yes | L/D | V/M | 17 |
| Subway | Fast Food | $ | Yes | | L/D | | 17 |
| **MacKenzie River Pizza Co.** | Pizza | $/$$ | | B/W | L/D | Major | 18 |
| Gourmet Gas Station | Casual Gourmet | $/$$$ | Yes | B/W | B/L/D | Major | 19 |
| Post Office Pizza | Pizza | $$ | | | L/D | | 19 |
| Castle Rock Inn | American | $$ | | Yes | B/L/D | | 19 |
| Gallatin Gateway Inn | Regional American | $$$ | Yes | Yes | D | Major | 19 |
| **Big Horn Cafe** | Deli | $$ | | B/W | B/L | Major | 21 |
| **Best Western Buck's T-4 Lodge** | Steaks/Wild Game | $$$ | Yes | Yes | D | Major | 21 |
| **Rainbow Ranch Lodge** | Continental | $$$ | Yes | Yes | D | Major | 21 |

Section 5

## Dining Quick Reference-Continued

Price Range refers to the average cost of a meal per person: ($) $1-$6, ($$) $7-$11, ($$$) $12-up. Cocktails: "Yes" indicates full bar; Beer (B)/Wine (W), Service: Breakfast (B), Brunch (BR), Lunch (L), Dinner (D). Businesses in bold print will have additional information under the appropriate map locator number in the body of this section.

| RESTAURANT | TYPE CUISINE | PRICE RANGE | CHILD MENU | COCKTAILS BEER WINE | SERVICE | CREDIT CARDS | MAP LOCATOR NUMBER |
|---|---|---|---|---|---|---|---|
| **320 Guest Ranch** | Steakhouse | $$/$$$ | Yes | Yes | B/L/D | Major | 21 |
| **Corral Steakhouse Cafe & Motel** | Steakhouse | $$ | Yes | Yes | B/L/D | Major | 21 |
| Canyon Conoco and Cafe | American | $/$$ | | | B/L | | 21 |
| **Lone Mountain Ranch** | Gourmet | $$$ | Yes | Yes | D | Major | 22 |
| **Edelweiss Restaurant** | European/Continental | $$$ | | Yes | D | Major | 22 |
| Country Market & Deli | Deli | $ | | B/W | B/L/D | Major | 22 |
| First Place Restaurant | Fine Dining | $$$ | | Yes | D | Major | 22 |
| Gallatin Gourmet Deli | Bistro | $/$$ | Yes | Yes | B/L/D | Major | 22 |
| Huckleberry Cafe | American | $$ | Yes | | | | 22 |
| Rocco's Restaurant | Mexican/Italian | $$ | Yes | Yes | D | V/M | 22 |
| Allgood's Bar & Grill | Barbeque | $/$$ | Yes | Yes | B/L/D | Major | 22 |
| Blue Moon Bakery | Bakery/ Deli | $ | | | B/L | | 22 |
| Hungry Moose Market & Deli | Deli | $ | Yes | | L/D | Major | 22 |
| Dante's Inferno | Regional | $$ | | Yes | L/D | Major | 22 |
| M R Hummers | Steaks/Seafood | $$/$$ | yes | Yes | D | major | 23 |
| Mountain Top Pizza | pizza | $$ | | | | | 23 |
| Scissorbills Bar & Grill | American | $$ | | Yes | L/D | Major | 23 |
| Sun Dog Cafe | coffee house/deli | $/$$ | | | B/L | | 23 |
| Twin Panda | Chinese | $$ | | Yes | D | AX/Vi/MC | 23 |
| **The Gusher Pizza Sandwich Shop** | Pizza/Sandwiches | $/$$ | | B/W | L/D | | 24 |
| **Texas Rose** | Tex Mex | $/$$/$$$ | Yes | | B/L/D | Major | 24 |
| Canyon Street Grill | American | $/$$ | | | B/L/D | | 24 |
| Cappy's Espresso Cafe | coffeehouse | | | | | | 24 |
| D&M Cafe | Mexican/American | $/$$ | | | L/D | | 24 |
| Dairy Queen | Fast Food | $ | Yes | | L/D | | 24 |
| McDonald's | Fast Food | $ | Yes | | B/L/D | | 24 |
| Mountain Mike's Cafe | American | $/$$ | | | B/L/D | | 24 |
| Pete's Rocky Mountain Pizza | Pizza & Pasta | $$ | | | L/D | | 24 |
| Silver Spur Cafe | Family | $/$$ | | B/W | B/L/D | | 24 |
| Subway | Fast Food | $ | Yes | | L/D | | 24 |
| Totem Cafe & Lounge | Steaks & Seafood | $$-$$$ | Yes | Yes | D | V/M | 24 |
| Wolf Pack Microbrewery & Pub | Sandwiches | $$ | | B | L/D | Major | 24 |
| **Timberline Café** | American | $$ | | | B/L | | 25 |
| Oregon Shortline Restaurant | Wild Game | $–$$$ | Yes | Yes | B/L/D/BR | Major | 25 |
| Outpost Restaurant | American | $$ | | | B/L/D | | 25 |
| **Three Bears Motel & Restaurant** | Family | $/$$ | Yes | | B/L/D | Major | 26 |
| **Rustler's Roost Restaurant** | American | $$ | Yes | Yes | B/L/D | Major | 26 |
| Ernie's Big Horn Deli | Deli | $ | | | | | 26 |
| Firehole Grill | American | $-$$$ | | Yes | B/L/D | Major | 26 |
| Kentucky Fried Chicken | Fast Food | $ | Yes | | L/D | | 26 |
| Montana Cafe | Family | $ | Yes | | B/L | | 26 |
| Uncle Laurie's Riverside Cafe | Family | $ | Yes | | B/L | | 26 |
| Bullwinkles Saloon & Eatery | American | $$ | Yes | Yes | L/D | Major | 26 |
| Chinatown Restaurant | Chinese | $ | | | L/D | V/M | 26 |
| Old Town Cafe | Family | $/$$ | Yes | | B/L/D | V/M | 26 |
| Running Bear Pancake House | American | $ | | | B/L | | 26 |
| Days Inn & Trappers Family Restaurant | Family | $/$$ | Yes | | B/L/D | Major | 26 |
| Alice's Restaurant | Regional | $$ | | Yes | B/D | Major | 27 |
| The Campobelo Lodge @ the Bar N Ranch | Steakhouse | $$ | | Yes | D | V/MC | 27 |
| Eino's Tavern | American | $ | | Yes | L/D | | 28 |
| **Sportsman's Lodge** | Family | $/$$ | Yes | Yes | B/L/D/BR | Major | 30 |
| Continental Divide | Gourmet | $$/$$$ | | Yes | L/D | Major | 30 |
| Dairy Queen | Fast Food | $ | Yes | | L/D | | 30 |
| Ennis Cafe | Family | $/$$ | Yes | | B/L/D | | 30 |
| Junction 287 Fine Food | Family | $—$$$ | | | B/L | V/M | 30 |
| Madison River Pizza | Pizza | $ | | | L/D | V/M | 30 |
| Main St. Diner | Family | $/$$ | Yes | | B/L/D | Major | 30 |
| Scotty's Long Branch Supper | Steakhouse | $$/$$$ | | Yes | L/D | M/V | 30 |
| Silver Dollar Bar & Grill | American | $ | | Yes | B/L/D | | 30 |
| Yesterday's Restaurant & Soda Fountain | Soda Fountain | $ | Yes | | B/L/SB | Major | 30 |
| Bear Claw Bar & Grill | Steakhouse | $$/$$$ | | Yes | L/D | V/M | 31 |

## Dining Quick Reference-Continued

Price Range refers to the average cost of a meal per person: ($) $1-$6, ($$) $7-$11, ($$$) $12-up. Cocktails: "Yes" indicates full bar; Beer (B)/Wine (W), Service: Breakfast (B), Brunch (BR), Lunch (L), Dinner (D). Businesses in bold print will have additional information under the appropriate map locator number in the body of this section.

| RESTAURANT | TYPE CUISINE | PRICE RANGE | CHILD MENU | COCKTAILS BEER WINE | SERVICE | CREDIT CARDS | MAP LOCATOR NUMBER |
|---|---|---|---|---|---|---|---|
| Norris Bar | American | $ | | Yes | L/D | V/M | 32 |
| Old Norris Schoolhouse Cafe | Mexican | $/$$ | Yes | B/W | L/D | Major | 32 |
| **Potosi Hot Springs Resort** | Organic | $$$ | | | B/L/D | MC/V | 33 |
| B & S Diner | American | $ | Yes | | B/L/ | Major | 34 |

**NOTES:**

Section 5

## Motel Quick Reference

Price Range: ($) Under $40 ; ($$) $40-$60; ($$$) $60-$80, ($$$$) Over $80. Pets [check with the motel for specific policies] (P), Dining (D), Lounge (L), Disabled Access (DA), Full Breakfast (FB), Cont. Breakfast (CB), Indoor Pool (IP), Outdoor Pool (OP), Hot Tub (HT), Sauna (S), Refrigerator (R), Microwave (M) (Microwave and Refrigerator indicated only if in majority of rooms), Kitchenette (K). All Montana area codes are 406.

| HOTEL | PHONE | NUMBER ROOMS | PRICE RANGE | BREAKFAST | POOL/ HOT TUB SAUNA | NON SMOKE ROOMS | OTHER AMENITIES | CREDIT CARDS | MAP LOCATOR NUMBER |
|---|---|---|---|---|---|---|---|---|---|
| Alpine Lodge | 586-0356 | 15 | $$ | CB | | Yes | K/P/M/R | Major | 1 |
| Blue Sky Motel | 587-2311 | 27 | $/$$ | CB | HT | | K/P/M/R | Major | 1 |
| Continental Motor Inn | 587-9231 | 60 | $/$$ | CB | HT | Yes | K/P/M/DA | Major | 1 |
| Ranch House Motel | 587-4278 | 16 | $ | | | | | Major | 1 |
| Western Heritage Inn | 586-8534 | 38 | $$/$$$ | CB | HT/S | Yes | K/P/M/R/DA | Major | 1 |
| **Montana Home-Montana Vacation Rentals** | 586-4589 | 30 | $$$$ | | HT | Yes | K/P/M/R/DA | Major | 2 |
| **Bozeman Cottage Vacation Rentals** | 580-3223 | | $$$/$$$$ | | HT | Yes | K/M/R | V/M | 2 |
| Best Western City Center | 587-3158 | 63 | $$$$ | | IP/HT | Yes | D/DA | Major | 2 |
| Imperial Inn | 587-4481 | 37 | $$ | | | Yes | P | Major | 2 |
| **Royal 7 Motel** | 587-3103 | 47 | $$ | CB | HT | Yes | P/R | Major | 3 |
| Rainbow Motel | 587-4201 | 43 | $$ | | OP | Yes | P | Major | 3 |
| **Bozeman Comfort Inn** | 587-2322 | 87 | $$$ | CB | IP/HT/S | Yes | M/R/P/DA | Major | 4 |
| **Hampton Inn** | 522-8000 | 70 | $$$$ | CB | IP/HT | Yes | M/R/DA | Major | 4 |
| **Bozeman Inn** | 587-3176 | 49 | $$$ | CB | HT/S | Yes | P/D/M/R/L | Major | 4 |
| Days Inn | 587-5251 | 79 | $$$$ | CB/FB | HT | Yes | P/M/R/DA | Major | 4 |
| Holiday Inn | 587-4561 | 179 | $$$$ | | IP/HT | Yes | K/P/D | Major | 4 |
| Best Western Grantree Inn | 587-5261 | 103 | $$$$ | | IP/HT | Yes | D/DA | Major | 4 |
| **TLC Inn** | 587-2100 | 42 | $$/$$$ | CB | HT/S | Yes | P/DA | Major | 5 |
| **Microtel Inn & Suites** | 586-3797 | 61 | $$ | CB | HT/IP | Yes | P/DA | Major | 5 |
| Ramada Limited | 585-2626 | 50 | $$/$$$$ | CB | IP/HT | Yes | K/P/M/R/DA | Major | 5 |
| Sleep Inn of Bozeman | 585-7888 | 56 | $$$ | CB | IP/HT | Yes | P/DA | Major | 5 |
| Fairfield Inn | 587-2222 | 57 | $$$ | CB | IP/HT | Yes | P/DA | Major | 5 |
| Super 8 Motel Of Bozeman | 586-1521 | 108 | $$/$$$ | | | Yes | P/M/R/DA | Major | 5 |
| Lewis & Clark Motel & Family Restaurant | 586-3341 | 50 | $$ | | IP/HT/S | Yes | D/L/DA | Major | 6 |
| Wingate Inn of Bozeman | 582-4995 | 86 | $$$$ | CB | IP/HT | Yes | K/M/R/DA | Major | 8 |
| **Bobcat Lodge** | 587-5241 | 78 | $$ | | IP/S | Yes | K/P/R | Major | 9 |
| **Holiday Inn Express** | 388-0800 | 67 | $$/$$$ | CB | HT | Yes | P/M/R/DA | Major | 12 |
| **Super 8 Motel Of Belgrade** | 388-1493 | 72 | $$ | CB | IP/HT | Yes | P/DA | Major | 12 |
| Belgrade Inn & Suites | 388-2222 | 65 | $$$$ | CB | IP/HT | Yes | P/DA | Major | 12 |
| **The Broken Spur Motel** | 285-3237 | 24 | $$ | CB | | Yes | K/P/M/R/DA | Major | 17 |
| **Fort Three Forks Motel & RV Park** | 285-3233 | 24 | $$ | CB | HT | Yes | P/M/R/DA | Major | 17 |
| Bud Lillie's Fly Fishing Retreat | 586-5140 | 6 | $$$ | | | Yes | K/PB/M/R/DA | V/M | 17 |
| Lewis & Clark Sportsman's Lodge | 285-3454 | 4 | $$$ | | | | R/L | Major | 17 |
| Castle Rock Inn | 763-4243 | 8 | $$ | | | Yes | R/L/P | Major | 19 |
| Gallatin Gateway Inn | 783-4672 | 35 | $$$$ | | OP/HT | | D/L/DA | Major | 19 |
| **Best Western Buck's T-4 Lodge** | 995-4111 | 74 | $$/$$$$ | | HT | Yes | | Major | 21 |
| **Rainbow Ranch Lodge** | 995-4132 | 21 | $$$ | | HT | Yes | D/L/DA | Major | 21 |
| **Comfort Inn Big Sky** | 995-2333 | 62 | $$$$ | CB/FB | IP | Yes | K/P/M/R/DA | Major | 21 |
| **Corral Steakhouse Cafe & Motel** | 995-4249 | 8 | $$ | | HT | Yes | R/L/P | Major | 21 |
| **Cinnamon Lodge** | 995-4253 | 6 | $$$ | | | Yes | D/L/P/DA | Major | 21 |
| **East West Resorts Big Sky** | 995-4800 | 225+ | $$ | | OP/HT | Yes | K/R/L/M/F/D | V/M/D | 23 |
| **Mountain Meadows Guest Ranch** | 995-4997 | | | | | | | | 23 |
| Holiday Inn Express/Mountain Inn Hotel | 995-7858 | 90 | $$$$ | CB | IP/HT | Yes | L | Major | 23 |
| Big Sky Ski & Summer Resort Huntley | 995-5000 | 200+ | | | | | | | 23 |
| **Kelly Inn** | 646-4544 | 78 | $$$$ | CB | IP/HT/S | Yes | P/DA | Major | 24 |
| **One Horse Motel** | 646-7677 | 19 | $$/$$$ | | HT | Yes | M/R | Major | 24 |
| **Brandin' Iron Inn & RV Park** | 646-9411 | 79 | $$–$$$$ | CB | HT | Yes | K/R/DA | Major | 24 |
| Best Western Desert Inn | 646-7376 | 76 | $$-$$$$ | CB | IP/HT | Yes | M/R/DA | Major | 24 |
| Best Western Weston Inn | 646-7373 | 65 | $/$$ | | OP/HT | Yes | P/D/DA | Major | 24 |
| Ho Hum Motel | 646-7746 | 23 | $$ | | | Yes | K/P/DA | V/M | 24 |
| **Best Western Executive Inn** | 646-7681 | 82 | $$$ | | OP/HT | Yes | P/D/M/R | Major | 24 |
| **Fairfield Inn** | 646-4892 | 77 | $$$$ | CB | IP/HT | Yes | DA | Major | 25 |
| **Holiday Inn Sunspree Resort** | 646-7365 | 123 | $$$$ | | IP/HT/S | Yes | M /D/L/DA | Major | 25 |
| Gray Wolf & Suites | 646-0000 | 102 | $$$$ | CB | IP/HT | Yes | P/DA | Major | 25 |
| Hibernation Station | 646-4200 | 26 | $$$$ | | HT | Yes | DA/P | Major | 25 |
| Yellowstone Lodge | 646-0020 | 77 | $$$$ | CB | IP/HT | Yes | P/DA | Major | 25 |
| Al's Westward Ho Motel | 646-7331 | 34 | $$ | | | Yes | DA | Major | 25 |
| Traveler's Lodge | 646-9561 | 46 | $$ | CB | IP/HT | Yes | P/D/DA | Major | 25 |
| **Three Bears Motel & Restaurant** | 646-7811 | 75 | $$$ | | IP/HT | Yes | R/L | Major | 26 |
| **West Yellowstone Comfort Inn** | 646-4241 | 78 | $$$$ | CB | IP/HT | Yes | M/R/DA | Major | 26 |
| **Big Western Pine** | 646-7622 | 46 | $$$ | | IP/HT | Yes | P/D/L | Major | 26 |

## Motel Quick Reference

Price Range: ($) Under $40 ; ($$) $40-$60; ($$$) $60-$80, ($$$$) Over $80. Pets [check with the motel for specific policies] (P), Dining (D), Lounge (L), Disabled Access (DA), Full Breakfast (FB), Cont. Breakfast (CB), Indoor Pool (IP), Outdoor Pool (OP), Hot Tub (HT), Sauna (S), Refrigerator (R), Microwave (M) (Microwave and Refrigerator indicated only if in majority of rooms), Kitchenette (K). All Montana area codes are 406.

| HOTEL | PHONE | NUMBER ROOMS | PRICE RANGE | BREAKFAST | POOL/ HOT TUB SAUNA | NON SMOKE ROOMS | OTHER AMENITIES | CREDIT CARDS | MAP LOCATOR NUMBER |
|---|---|---|---|---|---|---|---|---|---|
| **Buckboard Motel** | 646-9020 | 24 | $$$ | | HT | Yes | DA/P | Major | 26 |
| **Sleepy Hollow Lodge** | 646-7707 | 13 | $$$ | CB | | | DA/P | Major | 26 |
| Days Inn & Trappers Family Restaurant | 646-7656 | 118 | $$$$ | CB | IP/HT | Yes | D/DA | Major | 26 |
| Rustic Wagon RV Campground & Cabins | 646-7387 | | | | | | | | 26 |
| Crosswinds Best Western | 646-9557 | 72 | $$/$$$$ | CB | IP/HT | Yes | P/M/R/DA | Major | 26 |
| Evergreen Motel | 646-7655 | 16 | $$$ | | | Yes | P | Major | 26 |
| Pine Shadows Motel | 646-7541 | 14 | $$ | | | Yes | DA/P | Major | 26 |
| Pony Express Motel | 646-7644 | 17 | $$ | | | Yes | P | Major | 26 |
| Yellowstone Cabins | 646-9350 | 8 | $$$ | CB | | | DA/P | Major | 26 |
| Yellowstone Inn | 644-7633 | 10 | $$/$$$$ | | S | Yes | K/P/M/R | Major | 26 |
| Alpine Motel | 646-7544 | 12 | $$ | | | Yes | K/P | Major | 26 |
| City Center Motel | 646-7337 | 25 | $$$ | CB | IP/HT | Yes | DA | Major | 26 |
| Dude Motor Inn | 646-7301 | 30 | $$ | | | Yes | D/L | Major | 26 |
| Golden West Motel | 646-7778 | 12 | $$ | | | Yes | | Major | 26 |
| Pioneer Motel | 646-9705 | 20 | $$$ | | | Yes | DA/P | Major | 26 |
| Stage Coach Inn | 646-7381 | 80 | $$$$ | | HT | Yes | D/DA | Major | 26 |
| Westwood Lodge | 646-7713 | 24 | $$-$$$$ | | | Yes | K/R | V/M | 26 |
| Crow's Nest Motel | 646-7873 | 10 | $$$$ | CB | IP/HT | Yes | R/DA/P | Major | 27 |
| Super 8/Lionshead Resort | 646-9584 | 44 | $$/$$$ | | HT/S | Yes | | Major | 27 |
| Kirkwood Ranch Motel | 646-7200 | 9 | $$$ | | | Yes | DA | Major | 28 |
| Lakeview Cabins On Hebgen Lake | 646-7257 | | | | | | | | 28 |
| Slide Inn | 682-4804 | 9 | $$ | | | | DA/K | V/M | 29 |
| **El Western Resort** | 682-4217 | 29 | $$$/$$$$ | | | Yes | P/K | Major | 30 |
| **Rainbow Valley Lodge** | 682-4264 | 24 | $$/$$$ | | OP | Yes | DA/R/M/K | Major | 30 |
| **Sportsman's Lodge** | 682-4242 | 29 | $$/$$$ | CB | | Yes | P/D/L/DA | Major | 30 |
| **Fan Mountain Inn** | 682-5200 | 28 | $$ | | | Yes | P/M/R/DA | Major | 30 |
| Riverside Motel | 682-4240 | 12 | $$ | | | Yes | K/P | Major | 30 |
| Silvertip Lodge-Downtown Ennis | 682-4384 | 9 | $$ | | | Yes | P/K | Major | 30 |
| **Potosi Hot Springs Resort** | 685-3330 | 4 | $$$$ | | HT/OP | Yes | K | | 33 |

Section 5

**NOTES:**

**NOTES:**

# SECTION 6

## BUTTE, DILLON AND VIRGINIA CITY AREA

*Historic Virginia City*

### WEATHER AVERAGES

| | |
|---|---|
| **Butte** | |
| January | |
| Average High: | 28.8° F |
| Average Low: | 4.0° F |
| Average Precip.: | 0.55 in |
| April | |
| Average High: | 50.3° F |
| Average Low: | 25.7° F |
| Average Precip.: | 1.00 in |
| July | |
| Average High: | 79.7° F |
| Average Low: | 45.1° F |
| Average Precip.: | 1.23 in |
| October | |
| Average High: | 55.6° F |
| Average Low: | 26.1° F |
| Average Precip.: | 0.74 in |
| **Dillon** | |
| January | |
| Average High: | 30.4° F |
| Average Low: | 9.5° F |
| Average Precip.: | 0.33 in |
| April | |
| Average High: | 53.4° F |
| Average Low: | 27.6° F |
| Average Precip.: | 0.86 in |
| July | |
| Average High: | 83.8° F |
| Average Low: | 49.2° F |
| Average Precip.: | 0.82 in |
| October | |
| Average High: | 58.1° F |
| Average Low: | 30.8° F |
| Average Precip.: | 0.55 in |

**1.** *Gas, Camping*

### Cardwell

This town is the birthplace of Chet Huntley—famous TV newscaster and founder of Big Sky Resort. The town took its name from Edward Cardwell, a man with extensive property holdings in the area when the town was established. At one time, Cardwell was a station on the Northern Pacific Railroad. It saw a short boom time when the Mayflower Mine was in operation.

### LaHood

This town started as a stopping point for travelers and freighters that traveled between Butte and the Madison River. The town is the namesake of Shadan LaHood, a Lebanese immigrant who came to Montana in 1902. From 1902 to 1919, he traveled between Butte, Dillon, Missoula and Madison County in a covered wagon canvassing for a dry goods firm. In 1909, he and his wife opened a general merchandise store at Jefferson Island. He built a park there that bears his name.

### A Cardwell Store & RV Park

I-90 Exit 256

This full service gas station, convenience store, casino, and RV park has just about anything you could possibly need. Located just off I-90 you will find grocery items, snacks, gifts, souvenirs, and friendly service. They offer level pull-throughs and full hook-ups for the RV sites. Tent sites are available as well as showers and a laundromat. The camp sites are nicely situated with access to three rivers—the Jefferson, North Boulder and South Boulder. Hiking and biking trails are nearby.

**2.** *Historic Marker, Lewis & Clark, Attraction, Gas, Food, Lodging*

### Whitehall

Old Whitehall was the name E. G. Brooke gave his large white ranch house in the mid-1800s. The house served as a stage stop for the stages running from Helena to Virginia City. The modern community of Whitehall was developed when the railroad ran a branch line from Garrison to Logan through the area. Today, the Golden Sunlight Mine on a nearby mountainside offers much of the economic fuel to the town.

### H Father De Smet

I-90 Frontage Rd, Whitehall

*The Lewis and Clark Expedition passed here, westward bound, August 2, 1805. Captain Lewis named the Boulder River "Fields Creek" for one of the party.*

*In August, 1840, Pierre Jean De Smet, S.J., a Catholic missionary of Belgian birth, camped near the mouth of the Boulder River with the Flathead Indians and celebrated the holy sacrifice of the Mass. Father De Smet left the Indians soon after to go to St. Louis. He returned the following year and established the original St. Mary's Mission in the Bitter Root Valley, hereditary home of the Flatheads. Fearless and zealous, his many experiences during the pioneer days have been chronicled and form a most interesting chapter in the frontier annals of Montana.*

### H Lewis and Clark Expedition

*On August 1, 1805, the Lewis and Clark Expedition camped at a point 200 yards west from this spot, on the south bank of the river facing the mouth of the creek which flows into the river from the north. Meriwether Lewis and three others, on a scouting expedition in the hope of finding Sacajawea's people, had crossed the mountains to the northeast of here and coming down the North Boulder Valley had reached here at 2:00 p.m. They found a herd of elk grazing in the park here and killed two of them. After taking time out for an elk steak lunch, they headed on upstream leaving the two elk on the bank of the river for the expeditions dinner.*

*Captain Clark with the expedition reached here late in the evening after a strenuous day spent in snaking the boats up the canyon rapids by means of a long rawhide tow line which had broken in the rapids immediately below here with near calamitous results. At sight of the two elk, the hungry men called it a day and pitched camp. Reuben and Jo Fields went on a short hunt up the creek and killed five deer in the willow brakes which caused the stream to be named Field's Creek, now known as North Boulder. A large brown bear was seen on the south side of the river; Clark shot a big horn sheep in the canyon and Lewis shot two antelope a short distance up stream. Near camp was seen the first Maximilan Jay known to science. The temperature at sunrise on August 2 was fifty degrees above zero.*

# Section 6

0 Miles 12 20
One inch = approximately 12 miles

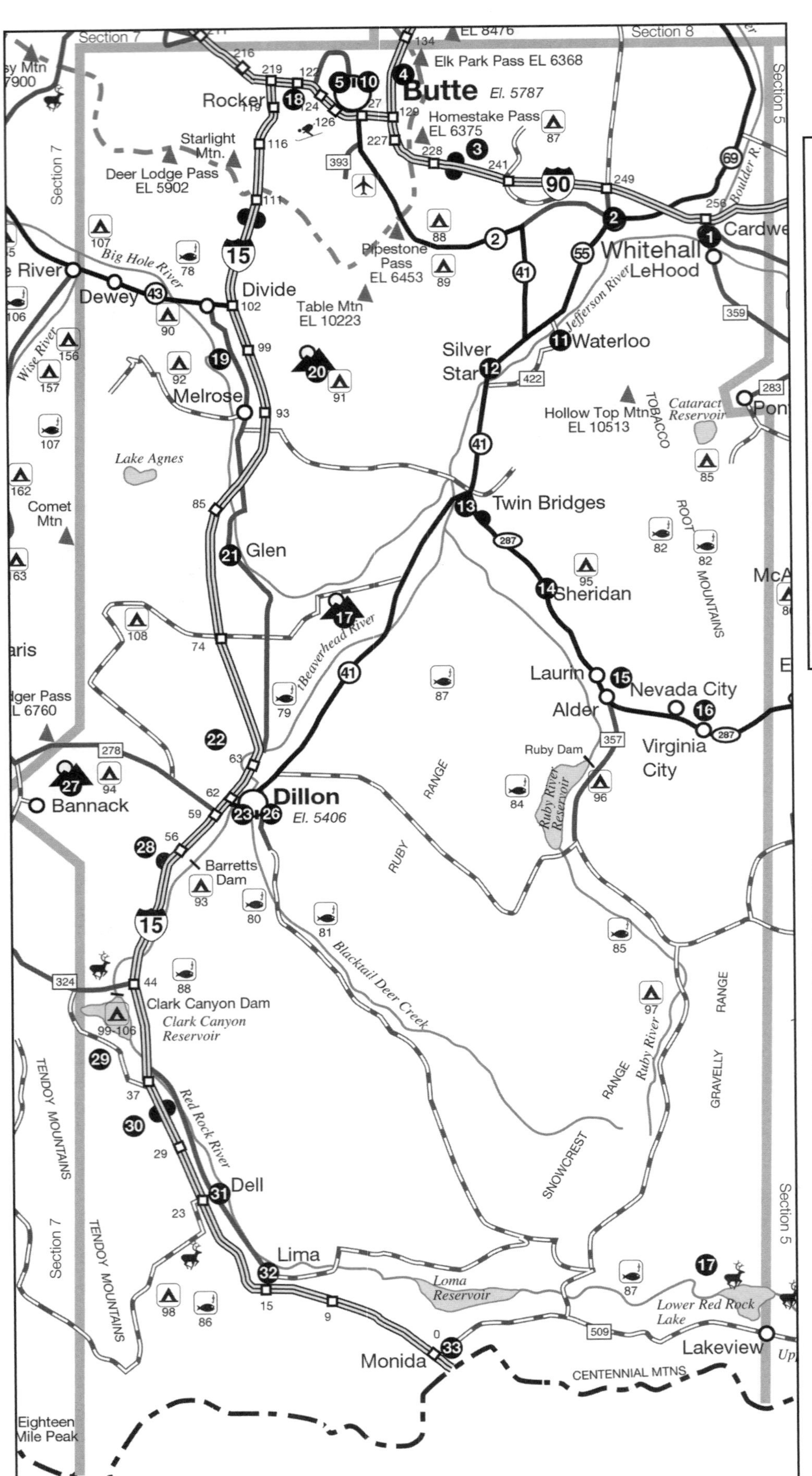


## Legend

- Locator number (matches numeric listing in section)
- Wildlife viewing
- Campsite (number matches number in campsite chart)
- State Park
- Fishing Site (number matches number in fishing chart)
- Rest stop
- Interstate
- U.S. Highway
- State Highway
- County Road
- Gravel/unpaved road

## *It Happened in Montana*

The first Montana legislative assembly convened at Bannack. The meeting was not held in a bastion of concrete, stone and marble; but rather in a cold log cabin with a dirt floor. They practiced the democratic principles of a country they were yet to be a part of as they huddled around a wood stove. The meeting was not without dissension. When Governor B. F. White called the meeting to order, he told the elected officials that they needed to recite the oath of allegiance to the United States. Most didn't hesitate to do so, but three vociferously disagreed. One, a man named Rogers, resigned rather than take the oath. Interestingly, Montanans have always been some of the most fiercely independent citizens of any state in the union. They are also the first to answer the call to defend our freedoms. They consistently send a higher percentage of their population to war than any other U. S. state.

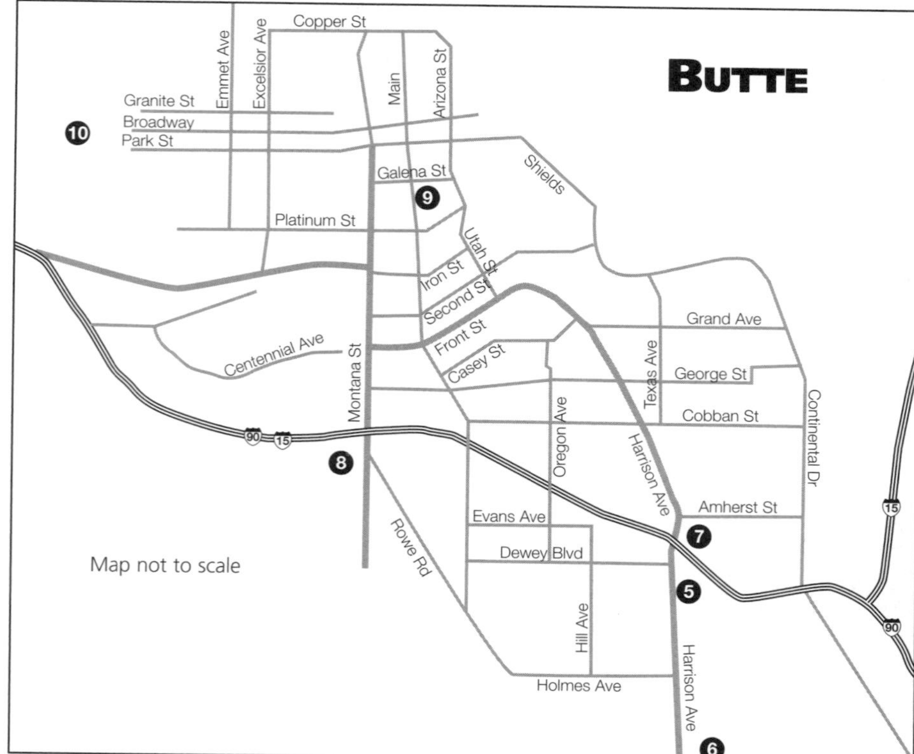


D **Mer. Lewis**
August 2, 1805

*"we say some very large beaver dams today. . .the brush. . .acquires a strength by the irregularity with which they are placed by the beaver that it would puzzle the engenuity of man to give them."*

D **Mer. Lewis**
August 2, 1805

*"After passing the river this morning Sergt. Gass lost my tommahawk in the thick brush and we were unable to find it, I regret the loss of this usefull implement, however accedents will happen in the best families"*

T **Golden Sunlight Mine**
Whitehall, 287-2018

If you're driving on I-90 near Whitehall, you'll notice the mountain to the north doesn't look quite right. In fact, it looks like it's been shaved off. This is the Golden Sunlight gold mine, and much of the smooth side of the mountain you see are mine tailings. From mid-June to mid-September, tours are offered daily at 10 a.m. If you would like to view an operational gold mine, this is the place. To get to the mine take the Cardwell Exit 256 and head north. The road curves around and parallels the interstate. Follow this road for almost 3 miles to Mine Road. Head north to the mine.

T **Jefferson Valley Museum**
303 S. Division in Whitehall.

The bright red barn that houses this museum was built in 1914. In 1992, the owners donated the barn to use as a museum. As you would expect, the historical exhibits center on life in the Jefferson River Valley. The museum is open from Memorial Day through Labor Day. Admission is free.

T **Cape Horn Taxidermy Museum**
Whitehall

T **Parrot Ghost Camp**
Near Whitehall on the Jefferson River

A few building foundations are the only reminders that the town of Parrot, stood on the banks of the river back in the 1890s.

T **The City of Murals**
Throughout town of Whitehall

When you enter the small community of Whitehall, your attention is immediately drawn to a giant mural on the side of a building at the junction of the two main streets in the town. The 9' x 28' mural depicts Lewis and Clark's Corps of Discovery pulling boats upstream on the Jefferson River. An excerpt from Capt. Lewis' journal is in the lower corner. As you drive through the town, more of these murals pop into view. Currently there are ten gracing the sides of buildings in the town--all depicting scenes from the journey of the Corps of Discovery. Two more are planned by

summer of 2002. The Whitehall Chamber of Commerce organized the mural project in 1999 funded by over $17,000 in grants and local contributions. The first mural was painted by local residents Kit Mather and Michelle Tebay. The rest were done by many of the local residents who painted the base colors while Mather completed the detail. The wall space and even the paint and materials were donated by the building owners. All of the murals depict actual activities or events that took place in the Jefferson Valley when the Corps passed through the area in 1805 and 1806. Mather did extensive research of the Corps of Discovery journals prior to painting the murals. When you visit Whitehall you can pick up a publication printed by the local newspaper which provides detailed information on each mural and shows you where to find it. The publication is available at most of the area businesses and is free.

F **Crazy Bear Pizza**
13 W. Legion, Whitehall. 287-9934

Located in the heart of downtown Whitehall, Crazy Bear Pizza is a great family restaurant. They are known for their ribs and Mexican fare as well as their outstanding pizzas. The restaurant has a family atmosphere, with a game room in the back. They have meeting rooms and can cater out to private parties. Take out and delivery is available.

F **Land of Magic, Too**
27 W. Legion, Whitehall. 287-5252

This steakhouse named for the original Land of Magic in Logan is widely known as "The Place for Steak" just like the Logan location. Also famous for their exceptional twice baked potatoes, the Land of Magic offers a wide variety of charbroiled steaks, seafood entreés and other house entrees such as Duck a l'orange and baby back ribs. Open Sunday through Friday for lunch and dinner. Saturday open for dinner only. Reservations are recommended.

L **Rice Motel**
7 North A, Whitehall. 287-3895 or 287-5497

S **Meriwether's Gallery & Gift**
1-AE Legion Ave., Whitewhall. 287-9252

**3.** *Historic Marker, Attraction*

H **The Humbug Spires Primitive Area**
I-15, south of Butte

*Named for its unique granite peaks, this primitive area is part of a geologic system of large-scale volcanic intrusions known as the Boulder Batholith, which extends north beyond Helena and south into Idaho.*

*Humbug Spires, which can be seen to the southeast, is part of the Highland Mountains. In 1866, rich gold placers were discovered near the Spires. Most of the mining occurred on the east and south sides of the area and produced large amounts of silver, lead, copper, and gold. Total value of production between 1876 and 1947*

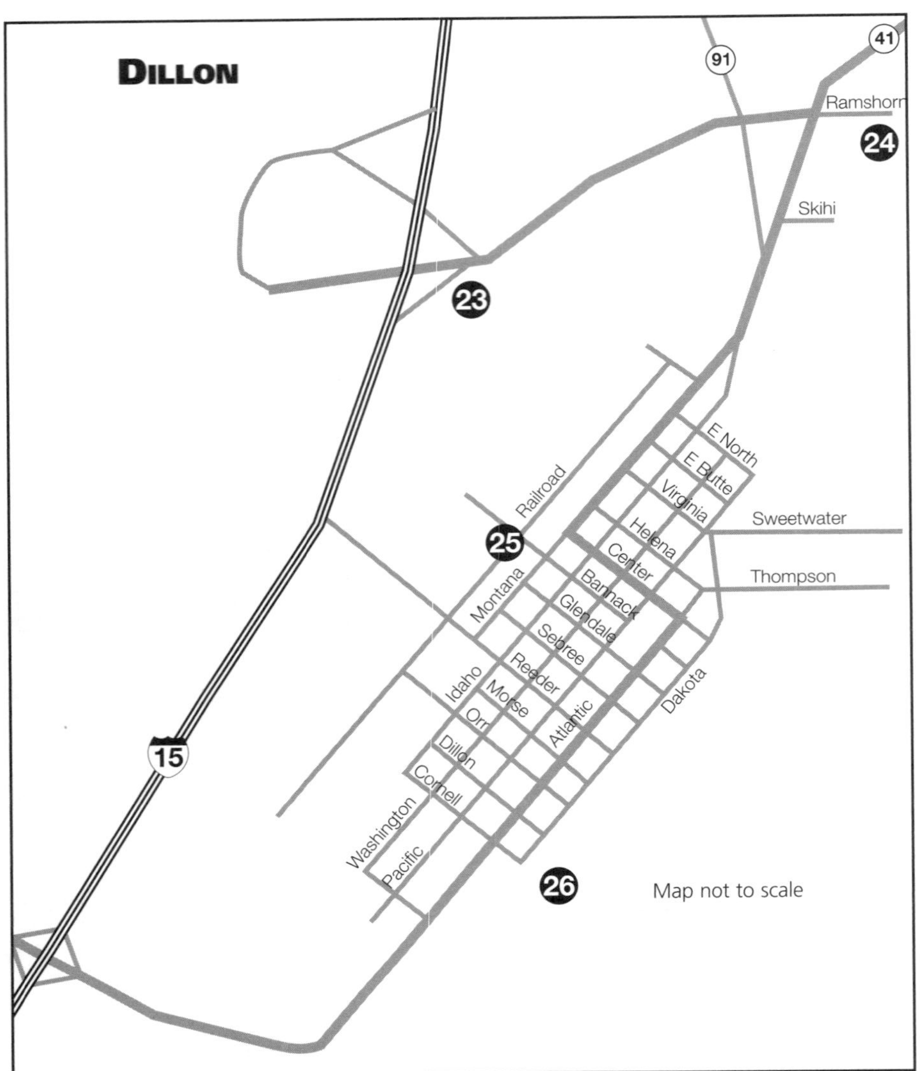


*is estimated to have been as much as $3 million. Although there currently (1999) is no mining in the Humbug Spires Primitive Area, prospecting is done on surrounding lands.*

*The Spires offer the finest high quality hard-rock climbing in Montana and are an excellent place to hike, ride horses, sightsee, fish, and hunt.*

### T Homestake Lake
I-90 Exit 233

This is a pleasant spot to picnic, swim and do a little fishing. From the exit go north for 1.5 miles to the right hand turn marked "Homestake Lake."

## 4. *Historic Marker*

### H Meaderville
I-15, Butte

*William Allison and G. 0. Humphreys had the Butte hill, richest hill on earth, entirely to themselves when they located their first quartz claims there in 1864.*

*They discovered an abandoned prospect hole which had evidently been dug by unknown miners a number of years before. These mysterious prospectors had used elk horn tines for gads, and broken bits of these primitive tools were found around the shafts. Allison and Humphreys died, their property passed into other hands, and they never knew that they were the potential owners of untold wealth.*

### H Butte
I-15, Butte

*The "greatest mining camp on earth" built on "the richest hill in the world." That hill, which has produced over two billion dollars worth of gold, silver, copper and zinc, is literally honeycombed with drifts, winzes and stopes that extend beneath the city. There are over 3,000 miles of workings, and shafts reach a depth of 4,000 feet.*

*This immediate country was opened as a placer district in 1864. Later Butte became a quartz mining camp and successively opened silver, copper and zinc deposits.*

*Butte has a most cosmopolitan population derived from the four corners of the world. She was a bold, unashamed, rootin, tootin', hellroarin' camp in days gone by and still drinks her liquor straight.*

## 5. *Attraction, Gas, Food, Lodging, Shopping*

### Butte

Butte's history is revealed in its skyline, the omnipresent black steel headframes, and the gaping hole in the earth known as Berkeley Pit. These are two of the more vivid reminders of a town that started as a mining camp and grew to a city of over 100,000 by 1917.

Before the gold rush of the 1860s brought prospectors and settlers to the area, Native Americans and fur traders frequented this semi-arid valley. When the placer ran out in 1867, the population of about 500 dwindled to around 240. It wasn't long though before the potential for mineral riches in the quartz deposits was recognized.

While the cost of smelting the complex copper-bearing ore was high, investors like William Andrews Clark and Andrew Jackson Davis began to develop Butte's mines and erect mills to extract the silver and gold. The riches in the hills made Davis Montana's first millionaire.

By 1876, Butte had become a prosperous silver camp with over 1,000 inhabitants. Marcus Daly arrived that year representing the Walker brothers, entrepreneurs from Salt Lake City. His mission was to inspect the Alice Mine for possible purchase by the brothers. Daly purchased the mine and successfully managed it for the Walkers. The town of Walkerville, which still overlooks the city of Butte, sprang up around the mine and other mines in the area.

In 1880, Daly sold his interest in the Walkers' properties and bought the Anaconda Mine. He did so with investment money from several San Francisco capitalists, including George Hearst, the father of media mogul William Randolph Hearst. Clark and Davis also attracted investors from Denver and points east. It wasn't long before capitalists from New York and Boston bought into the huge potential of the area. During the 1880s, copper mining came into the forefront and Butte became the world's greatest copper producer. The Union Pacific Railroad came to the area in 1881 allowing developers to build and equip smelters. The Butte smelters quickly became the best in the world at extracting the metal from the ore.

It wasn't long before Butte began to pay a price for the riches. The air filled with toxic sulfurous smoke. Daly responded by building a giant smelter in Anaconda, just 30 miles west of Butte. To this day, the giant smokestack remains a landmark. Shortly after Daly built the smelter, the Boston and Montana Co., with holdings only second to Daly's, built one in Great Falls. Trains carried the ore from Butte's mines to both smelters.

In 1899, Daly teamed up with Rockefeller's Standard Oil to create the giant Amalgamated Copper Mining Co., one of the largest trusts of the early Twentieth Century. By 1910, it had changed its name to the Anaconda Copper Mining Company swallowing several smaller mining companies along the way. The Company dominated Butte for the next 70 years. The battle between the Copper Kings Clark and Daly is a large chapter in Montana history. To stir the mix, another Copper King, F. Augustus Heinze, fought the dominance of Amalgamated, providing excitement to an already interesting chapter in Montana's legal history.

The mines brought whole families from every corner of the nation and around the world. They crowded into tiny houses and occupied apartment buildings called flats. The earlier skilled miners were Cornish, but the Irish soon followed, tempted by the prospects of steady pay. They came in droves and soon became the largest ethnic group. Suburbs of Butte, with names like Finntown, Meaderville, Dublin Gulch, Chinatown, Corktown, and Parrot Flat were soon filled with Italians, Croatians, Serbians, Finns, French Canadians, Lebanese, Scandinavians, Chinese, Mexicans, Germans, Austrians, and African-Americans.

Economic exploitation and the dangers of working in the mines led to the labor movement—an important part of Butte's heritage. The city soon had the tag of the "Gibraltar of

Unionism." Butte's Miners Union, founded in 1878, became Local No. 1 of the Western Federation of Miners. At the 1906 International Workers of the World founding convention in Chicago, Butte's delegation was the largest.

In the late 1800s, the mining companies competed for scarce labor. This gave the unions leverage and many successes. But, as the Anaconda Company consolidated operations, the unions lost their leverage and their power. In the early 1900s, worker frustration and company opposition combined to form a violent atmosphere. The Miner's Union Hall was bombed in 1914, and in 1917 IWW organizer Frank Little was lynched. A fictional account of this incident is told in Dashiell Hammett's *Red Harvest*.

In 1917, the Speculator Mine fire killed 168 men—to this day the most lives lost in a hardrock mining disaster in American History. Despite the dangers, mining flourished. At an altitude of 5,775 feet above sea level, Butte claimed it was "a mile high and a mile deep." But like most mining camps, the riches extracted here—more than $22 billion by the 1980s—went to the speculators and investors far away from the mountains of Montana.

1955 saw the abandonment of labor intensive underground work when the Anaconda Company switched to more cost effective open-pit mining. The excavation of the Berkeley Pit and surrounding area, changed the face and the skyline of Butte. The population declined and the new method of mining wiped away hundreds of homes, flats, boarding houses, bars and corner groceries which once proliferated on Butte's East Side. Whole communities like Meaderville and McQueen vanished. Columbia Gardens was an elegant, old-fashioned amusement park with an elaborate dance pavilion nestled alongside the East Ridge. For generations it provided fun and amusement to Butte families. It too fell victim to the open pit mining. Anaconda Mining Company merged with Atlantic Richfield Co. (ARCO) in 1977. In 1985, ARCO's holdings were purchased by Montana billionaire Dennis Washington.

When you visit uptown Butte and it's older sections, much of its history can be seen by looking up. By viewing the ornate architecture, fading signs on the sides of buildings, and the headframes surrounding the area, one can get a small sense of the grandeur this city once knew.

## On The Trail of Lewis & Clark

On July 31, the Expedition reached the third range of mountains which forms another close canyon. They were out of fresh meat. No game was killed on this day; indeed, no buffalo had been seen since entering the mountains. Lewis wrote: "When we have plenty of fresh meat I find it impossible to make the men take any care of it or use it with the least frugallity. Tho' I expect that necessity will probably teach them this art,"

On Aug. 1, Lewis, and three men, went ahead in search of Indians. Near his camp on the morning of Aug. 3, Clark discovered Indian tracks which he followed to an elevation where the Indians had apparently spied on his camp. But Clark found no Indians.

By now, the arduous task of pulling the eight heavily laden dugouts was taking its toll. At one place a tow line broke, at another they were dragging the vessels over rocks, Clark wrote: "The men were so much fatiegued today that they wished much that navigation was at an end that they might go by: land."

Lewis reached Big Hole River on Aug. 4, and after some investigation decided this was not the route the Expedition should follow. He left a note on a green willow for Clark, telling him not to go that way, but to wait there. By the time Clark's party arrived at the Big Hole River, a beaver had gnawed down the green willow upon which Lewis had left the note, and had taken off with it. Consequently, Clark's party began the difficult task of ascending the swift waters of that treacherous river. One boat turned over and two others filled with water before Lewis' party arrived and told them they would have to return to the Jefferson.

It had been 21 days since they left the Great Falls of the Missouri. The 33 travelers had used up enough provisions to warrant leaving one canoe on shore to be retrieved on me return journey.



A statue weighing 51 tons, rising 90 feet high and requiring 6 years to construct is set atop the rugged Rocky Mountain ridge. This monument of Our Lady of the Rockies was built in the likeness of Mary, Mother of Jesus, but is intended to be a tribute to all women regardless of religion. Perched on the east ridge overlooking Butte, the statue is lit at night and can be seen glowing on Butte's skyline. A bus tour is available, and a possible gondola ride is under consideration.

**T Our Lady of the Rockies (Visitor Center)**
3100 Harrison Ave., Butte. 494-2656

*The richest hill on earth.*

# "GALLOWS" FRAMES

**There is no skyline in the world like** Buttes. Standing like sentries on the surrounding hillsides are stark black headframes of several mines no longer in use. The Orphan Girl headframe at the World Museum of Mining is visible from the interstate. Dominating the landscape are the Kelley, Steward, the Original, Belmont, Granite Mountain, Bell Diamond, Badger State, Travona, Lexington, Centerville's mighty Mountain Con and the Anselmo gallows frames.

To put it simply, headframes are like the tops of elevators, but not hidden in the inside of a tall building. The frames held the cables that lowered men, equipment, timbers, dynamite, ore cars and, in earlier days, the mules to pull the cars. Once the men and equipment were inside the mines, the frames hauled to the surface the copper ore which was then loaded on trains and shipped to the smelter in Anaconda.

At its peak, the Butte Hill was alive with the bright lights of the mine yards at night. The sound of bells used as signals for the hoist operators, the shrill mine whistles signaling the shift changes, and the throaty "toots" of the trains as they hauled their ore loaded cars through town could be heard around the clock.

**T U.S. High Altitude Sports Center**
Butte. 494-7570

When you first exit the Homestake Pass driving west into Butte, one of the first things you see is a large oval track. This track has been the training ground for several Olympic speedskating champions, including Bonnie Blair and Dan Jansen. The outdoor speed skating facility was completed in 1987, and has been the venue for several national and world speedskating competitions. In 1994, the Women's World Championship was held here. The World Cup Competition has been held here on six different occasions. What makes the Center unique is its altitude. At a 5,500 foot elevation, it is a premier training facility providing athletes from around the world a chance to build stamina through exercise programs tailored for varying competitions.

**T Stodden Park and Community Pool**
Corner of Holmes and Hills Avenue, Butte.
494-3686

Stodden Park is Butte's main city park. There are tennis courts, a ball diamond, horseshoe pits, and large areas of shaded grassy areas for taking an afternoon nap while the kids play in the public swimming pool here.

**L Butte Super 8 Motel**
2929 Harrison Ave.

The Butte Super 8 offers 104 rooms complete with queen size beds, cable TV with remotes, alarm clocks, free local calls, air conditioning, and a complimentary continental breakfast. There is easy access from I-90 and I-15 and large vehicle parking with plug-ins. They are located adjacent to shopping and many dining choices. The front desk is open 24-hours for your safety and convenience and they offer discounted rates for seniors, AAA members, corporates, truckers, government and state workers.

**L Hampton Inn**
1/2 mile south of I-90 exit 127 on Harrison Ave.
494-2250 or 800-426-7866

Experience Butte's newest hotel. They offer a complimentary deluxe breakfast bar and serve fresh baked cookies, coffee and tea in the lobby every evening. The Inn features all of the amenities and comforts you expect from a first rate motel: in-room coffeemakers, data ports, in-room voice mail, 25" TV screens, free HBO, pay-per-view movies and Nintendo, irons, ironing boards, hairdryers, and complimentary copy of USA Today each morning. Other amenities include an indoor pool, hot tub, and state-of-the-art fitness center open each day from 6 a.m. to midnight. Their rooms on the front of the property offer stunning views of "Our Lady of the Rockies," a Butte icon located atop the Continental Divide.

**L Best Western Butte Plaza Inn**
2000 Harrison, Butte. 484-7611

## 6. *Attraction, Gas*

**T Silver Bow**
15 miles south of Butte on Rte.2

Also known as Highland City, many of the several hundred miners cabins that were built still exist near the graveyard. The city once had a fierce reputation for wild gun play and rich with gold during its boom years between 1865 and 1875. The site is accessible on a good Forest Service logging road.

**F Grama's Homestyle Buffet**
3502 Harrison Ave., Butte. 494-2510

**FL Ramada Inn Copper King Hotel and Convention Center**
4655 Harrison Ave., Butte. 494-6666,
fax 494-3274 or toll free at 800-332-8600.
www.ramada.com

The Copper King is a full service hotel and provides comfortable accommodations at reasonable prices and will care for all your travel needs. Each of the 146 spacious guest rooms come with a coffee maker, voice mail, data parts, personal safe, remote-control color television, and free local calls. You'll be able to relax and enjoy Butte's largest indoor pool, sauna, spa, and fitness center during your stay. There is plenty of free parking available too. The café serves an American Breakfast Buffet for only $4.99 and also offers complete breakfast, lunch, and dinner menus. The Dining Room offers casual family style dining with nightly specials. The lounge features live entertainment. Fax, Internet access, and copy services are also available.

## 7. *Gas, Food, Lodging*

**F Pork Chop John's**
2400 Harrison Ave., Butte. 782-1783

John's original pork chop sandwich has been a tradition of quality for over 60 years. Originating in Butte, Montana in 1924, founder John Burkland sold his pork chop sandwich from the back of a wagon, and later opened this Butte landmark location in 1932. The quality and delicious flavors still remain today with locations in Butte (2), Bozeman, and Billings. Stop in and see why this famous, mouth-watering sandwich has become a unique part of the Montana experience.

**F Great Harvest Bread Co.**
1803 Harrison, Butte. 723-4988

**L Holiday Inn Express**
1 Holiday Park Dr., Butte. 494-6999

**S Keenan Jewelers**
3100 Harrison, Butte. 494-2897, www.keenanjewelers.com

## 8. *Attraction, Gas*

**T Butte Chamber, Visitor & Transportation Center**
1000 George St., I-90 Exit 126, Butte. 723-3177 or 800-735-6814

This new visitor's center is more than just a good place to pick up literature on the area. Inside is a small museum that highlights the forming of the geology and early settlement of the area, the gold and silver era of Butte, the development of the richest hill on earth, the mining and smelting industry and the all-important transportation corridors.

Also inside the center is the George F. Grant Fly Collection. Even if you don't know a thing about fly fishing, you'll marvel at these works of art. A legend in fly fishing circles, George's unique woven hackle monofilament bodied flies are artistic masterpieces and are prized by collectors. Learn more at www.butteinfo.org.

## 9. *AttractionGas, Food, Lodging, Shopping*

**T Berkeley Pit**
Mercury St., Butte. 723-3177

Think you've seen some big holes? Wait till you see this one. The pit was started in 1955 as a large truck-operated open-pit copper mine until mining ceased in 1982. By that time, nearly 1.5 billion tons of material had been removed including more than 290 million tons of copper ore.

Two communities and a large part of the one time populous East Side were consumed to create the pit. The homes, businesses and schools of the working-class towns of Meaderville and McQueen east of the pit site were purchased by the Anaconda Mining Company. Several deep shaft mines were also obliterated. The headframe of the Leonard was part of Meaderville's main street.

The pit is 7,000 feet long, 5,600 feet wide, and 1,600 feet deep. Groundwater seeping from the several thousand miles of interconnected tunnels that honeycomb the hills surrounding the pit has created a small lake in the pit. In April of 1996, pumping operations began to pump and treat 2.5 million gallons daily to prevent surface flows from entering the Pit. Today, copper is being recovered from the water in the pit for use in industry.

The Pit water is acidic from water contact with mineralized zones. Since it is a hazard to waterfowl, a number of devices are being used to keep the birds from landing on the water. Flares, shell crackers and electronic noise makers are some examples.

The Pit is just off of Continental Drive. An observation stand is open at the site from dawn to dusk late spring through early fall. There is no admission fee.

**T Piccadilly Museum of Transportation**
20 W. Broadway in uptown Butte. 723-3034

Butte's newest museum features oil company collectables, underground train (subway) memorabilia from the United States and Europe, a vintage replica 1920s service station complete with original gas pumps, license plates from around the world, and a small but interesting collection of motorized and non-motorized vehicles. Included in the collection is an exhibit of commercial advertising art and Coca Cola® and Pepsi® memorabilia. The museum is open June through September Tuesday through Sunday. Admission is free.

**T Granite Mountain Memorial**
In Butte head north on Main Street and turn right at the directional sign just beyond the St. Lawrence Church in Walkerville. 723-3177

168 men lost their lives in the tragic "Spec fire" disaster on June 8, 1917. This was the greatest loss of life in hardrock mining history. Interpretive plaques tell the story of this disaster and the turbulent times that surrounded this episode. From this point you can view an unforgettable panorama of the 10,000 ft. Highland Mountains and the scattered remnants of a once booming mining industry.

**T The Mother Lode Theater**
316 W. Park St. in Uptown Butte. 723-3602

This beautiful building is located in Butte's historic district and is a showplace for the performing arts. Its proscenium theater seats 1,230 people.

**T The Mai Wah Museum**
17 W. Mercury, Butte. 723-3177

When the history of Butte's mining era is told, most of the focus is on the Irish. The Chinese played an important role as well. As the placer mining era declined, Chinese miners came to Butte to work the mines. As that work declined, they were relegated to work in laundries, domestic service and noodle parlors. The Mai Wah and Wah Chong Tai buildings are adjacent to China Alley, a narrow thoroughfare which runs between Galena and Mercury Streets. In the building you'll see exhibits which interpret the history of Asians in Butte and the Rocky Mountain West.

The Mai Wah Society, was established for educational, charitable, and scientific purposes, including research and public education about the history, culture, and conditions of Asian people in the Rocky Mountain West. The Mai Wah Society is the caretaker for Montana's only authentic ceremonial parade dragon, a generous gift of the government of Taiwan to the people of Montana. Each summer an exhibit in the museum interprets aspects of the lives of Asian immigrants to the region. The museum is open June through August, Tuesday through Saturday from 11 a.m. to 3 p.m.

**T The Dumas Brothel**
45 E. Mercury, Butte. 723-6128

For more than 90 years, the Dumas operated continuously as a house of prostitution. The run from 1890 to 1982 gives it the dubious honor of being the longest-running house of ill repute in the United States. It is now the only remaining remnant of what was once a thriving red light district in Butte. When the building was threatened with demolition, Butte native Rudy Giecek purchased the building and began to restore it in 1990. Today, it is open as a museum depicting the history of this industry that was so vital to the miners of yesterday. The museum is open May through September from 9 a.m. to 5 p.m.

**T St. Lawrence O'Toole Church**
1308 N. Main in Butte.

In 1897, miners and local families raised $25,000 in donations to build this church. A European artist painted 40 frescoes on the ceilings and a number of paintings in other parts of the church



Section 6

*The Berkeley Pit—one mile wide, one mile high, and a mile deep.*

in 1907. The church is no longer used for services and is only open to visitors on Fridays and Saturdays from noon to 5 p.m.

## T Arts Chateau

321 W. Broadway, Butte. 723-7600.
www.artschateau.org

Charles Clark, the son of Copper King William A. Clark, built this mansion in 1898. It now serves the community as an arts center and museum.

When you first step into the entry way of this magnificent building, notice the beveled glass windows, ornate wrought iron, sandstone and vaulted brick ceiling. A free-standing spiral staircase inside is surrounded by 26 rooms adorned with exotic woods from around the world, several stained glass windows, hand-painted wallpaper by Marshall Field, and a redwood paneled 4th floor ballroom. Thousands of historic artifacts are on display in the museum including textiles, books, vintage clothing and accessories. The furniture collection here is on permanent loan from the University of Montana.

Inside the mansion are four fine art galleries featuring works by local, regional and national artists.

The Chateau is open all year. In the summer, hours are 10 a.m. to 5 p.m. Tuesday through Saturday and noon to 5 p.m. on Sunday. Winter hours are Tuesday through Saturday 11 a.m. to 4 p.m. An admission fee is charged.

## T Copper King Mansion

219 W. Granite St., Butte. 782-7580

The Copper King Mansion was built by William Clark, one of the world's richest men. The 34 room home was constructed from 1884-1888 at a cost of $260,000, a significant amount of money at the time. In 1971 it was designated as a National Historical Place, and in 1972 it became the first home in Montana to be designated a Montana Historic Site. It is now the only privately owned mansion in the state that is accessible to the public.

As you step inside, you will see the intricately carved wood of the entryway. The hall and staircase present the work of the finest craftsman of the times. Panels of birds and flowers carved in the golden oak staircase represented all the nations of the world when the home was built. Other lavish touches include embellishments of bronze, silver, and copper on the walls, nine original fireplaces, French beveled glass and Tiffany-style stained glass windows. The staircase landing surrounds a seven by thirteen foot window. Parquet floors, hand painted "fresco" ceilings, combed plaster designed walls and nine different kinds of wood contribute to the opulence of the manor. Anticipating the arrival of electricity, Clark had all of the chandeliers equipped for gas and electricity. The octagon shaped reception room, the massive dining room, the billiard room and library all reflect the lavish lifestyle of Mr. Clark.

In addition to the mansion itself, the current owners have numerous collections on display including dolls, toys, clocks, hats, demitasse cups and steins. The Mansion also operates as a bed and breakfast, so if you plan ahead you can spend the night. The mansion is open daily May 1 through September 30th from 9 a.m. to 4 p.m. From October through April it is open by appointment only.

## Chinese Pioneers

Chinese pioneers were one of the first distinctive ethnic groups to come to Montana during the late 19th century. During the 1870s ten percent of the state's residents were Chinese. These hardworking and often courageous immigrants worked in mining, railroad construction and numerous service industries.

Most of the Chinese immigrants who followed the lure of quick riches of "Gold Mountain" were young men who left villages and families. China was plagued with economic difficulties. Many Westerners were frightened by Chinese food, dress, customs, clannishness and religious beliefs. This resulted in name-calling, obstruction of their legal rights, anti-Chinese laws, and violence.

The Chinese immigrants sacrificed blood and dreams to help build the American West. The Mai Wah Society, an organization to preserve the Chinese cultural history of Butte, Montana, is researching the contributions that Chinese pioneers made to the settlement of the Montana area. The Chinese, who left behind their families and lives to travel east, also helped to build the foundation of our nation with their dreams and hopes for a better future.

Notable Chinese in the state are immortalized at the Mai Wah museum such as: Tommie Haw, who came on the first cattle drive into Beaverhead, came to Montana in 1850, adopted by a local rancher William Orr, and later raised cattle and sheep in the Dillon area; Dr. Rose Hum Lee, graduated from Butte High School in 1921. Her father came to the Butte area in the 1870s. He worked in ranching and mining, and had a laundry business. Dr. Lee later became the head of the sociology department at Roosevelt University, Chicago in 1956, according to the Mai Wah Society. Our nation was built on the dreams of all immigrants who came in search of a new beginning.

## F Uptown Cafe

47 E. Broadway, Uptown Butte. 723-4735

Unique dishes are the rule, not the exception at this surprising spot located in Historic Uptown Butte. The owners have created a modern gourmet cafe that blends very nicely into the old neighborhood. They offer convenient cafe lunches weekdays and fine dining and early dining specials every night with French, Cajun, Italian, and other regional specialties. The unique atmosphere in the Uptown Cafe is similar to an art gallery, with different displays by local and nationally known artists. You will find it a perfect place to dress up for a night out, or enjoy a casual dining experience. The friendly staff can help you choose the right bottle of wine, and will tell you about the wonderful desserts that include New York cheesecake and white chocolate mousse pie.

## F Pork Chop John's

8 West Mercury, Butte. 782-3159

John's original pork chop sandwich has been a tradition of quality for over 60 years. Originating in Butte, Montana in 1924, founder John Burkland sold his pork chop sandwich from the back of a wagon. The quality and delicious flavors still remain today with locations in (2) Butte, Bozeman, and Billings. Stop in and see why this famous, mouth-watering sandwich has become a unique part of the Montana experience.

## F Columbian Garden Espresso

27 N. Main, Butte. 782-8808

This quaint café is nestled in the heart of Historic Uptown Butte. They specialize in a variety of fresh, homemade sausages without preservatives, made on the premises. Start the day with an espresso and a sausage breakfast sandwich. Return later in the day for yummy luncheon specials, and

topped with a fresh baked treat or a scoop of Montana-made Wilcoxson's ice cream. This friendly café offers a variety of daily lunch specials with hot home-style soups and fresh baked rolls. Deli sandwiches are served on fresh Wheat Montana Breads. Also available are lattes, cappuccinos, milkshakes and more. They also provide space for groups, parties and family get-togethers. Ask about the Montana-made gift items, including pottery, candles and framed pictures on display from a nearby gallery.

## F Northwest Noodles 'n Wraps

33 W. Park Street, Butte. 723-5651

Northwest Noodles 'n Wraps features a mouthwatering range of noodle styles, a variety of top-quality meats, tofu, vegetables and other taste sensations. Northwest Noodles 'n Wraps offers delicious, wholesome, quick Asian-style foods that are both affordable and nutritious. Good food at its best. The wraps and noodle dishes are prepared from scratch. Each wrap is made fresh with a combination of flavor-infused flatbread wrapped around char-broiled meats and vegetables. Add to this delicious seasonings and sauces, and you will definitely leave feeling satisfied. Wraps are high in complex carbohydrates and low in fat. If you are looking for flavorful and healthy food you'll love Northwest Noodles 'n Wraps. Eat in or take it with you.

## F Spaghettini's Italian Restaurante

27 N. Main, Butte. 782-8855

## L Finlen Hotel & Motor Inn

100 E. Broadway, Uptown Butte. 723-5461 or 800-729-5461, www.finlen.com

Opened on New Years Day 1924, the design of the Finlen Hotel is French Empire with a copper Mansard roof. Built by financier James Finlen, the hotel was modeled after the Hotel Astor in New York City. Over the years many notable people

have stayed here including Charles Lindbergh, Mrs. Herbert Hoover, Senator & Mrs. John F. Kennedy and Richard Nixon. A beautiful renovated lobby awaits you upon check-in. There are many restaurants within walking distance and the Cavalier Lounge in the Finlen is open nightly for cocktails. For the visitor on the go, the same level of comfort is offered at the adjacent Finlen Motor Inn.

## L Capri Motel

220 N. Wyoming, Butte. 723-4391 or toll free 800-342-2774

The Capri is a clean, comfortable motel located in historic uptown Butte, a superb place to visit and shop for all your heart desires. The motel is at the site of the Old Butte Brewery and close to all major attractions. Take a leisurely stroll Uptown and return for a soak in the hot tub or play in the game room. There's a great selection of restaurants nearby. Take the Montana Street exit north 1.4 miles, then right on Granite and 3 blocks to Wyoming. Let the Capri Motel be your home while visiting Butte and its historic uptown area and enjoy their quiet and convenient location.

## FL Acoma Restaurant & Lounge

60 E. Broadway, Butte. 782-7001

The doors of the Hotel Acoma first opened in 1914 when the Copper Kings still battled over the richest hill on earth. When it was converted into a supper club and lounge, the Acoma became Butte's hot spot for dining, dancing, and cavorting. Now The Acoma is a silent reminder of Butte's notorious history, where you can experience the splendor of one of Butte's historic landmarks and enjoy fine dining and fun. The menu offers choice cuts of certified Angus beef, seafood, veal, lamb, gourmet sauces, and delicious desserts in an atmosphere that is casual, yet elegant. Located in Historic Uptown Butte. Reservations are recommended.

### L The Scott Bed & Breakfast Inn
15 West Copper, Butte. 723-7030 or 800-844-2952. www.scottinn.com

### S Pipestone Mountaineering
829 S. Montana, Butte. 782-4994. www.pipestonemtng.com

Step over the threshold of Pipestone Mountaineering's door and find an exciting world of outdoors waiting for you. A especially unique feature of Pipestone is that within the retail space of the store, is a 2,900 Sq. ft. climbing gym, which can be rented for parties or just to practice your climbing skills. Lessons are also available. They also have a large rental department with everything from sleeping bags, tents, canoes, and kayaks. The store offers a variety of the best quality gear with brands such as Patagonia, Black Diamond, Osprey, Marmot, Sierra Designs, and Dagger. This is also the perfect place to stock up from a large selection of guidebooks and Forest Service maps.

### S Munchkins
55 W. Park, Uptown Butte. 782-2856

Munchkins, a specialty store with quality children's clothes and educational toys. They carry clothes from birth to size 8 for boys and girls. Some of the great quality clothes they offer are from Mulberribush, Chicken Noodle, Baby Lulu, Zutano and many more lines that are perfect for that special little one. You'll love their wonderful selection of baby gifts from newborn toys to picture frames to specialty silk blankets from Barefoot Dreams. Munchkins carries truly special christening gowns and gifts. Educational toys include books, creative kits for your kids to enjoy and unique items to keep children busy while traveling. Stop by Munchkins in uptown Butte for children's clothes as cute as your kids.

### S Rediscoveries
83 E. Park, Butte. 723-2176

Rediscoveries is a wonderful collection of extraordinary items from the past. Located in historic Uptown Butte for over ten years, this shop features antiques, vintage jewelry, dolls, linens and vintage clothing. Discover a remarkable selection of antique fabrics for the decorator, collector, and quilting enthusiast. Rediscoveries also enjoys a wide reputation for its costume rentals, with a great selection of period and whimsical costumes. The shop, housed in one of Butte's exquisite historic buildings, has retained the original turn-of-the-century cast iron support columns and pressed tin ceiling architecture. Be sure and stop at Rediscoveries for a step back in time and discover a treasure or bring back a memory for yourself or someone special!

### S Garden of Beadin'
43 W. Park, Butte. 782-0661. www.beadin.com

Experience the largest bead store in Montana, the Garden of Beadin'. In addition to thousands of beads, including glass, semi-precious, bone, ceramic, wood, and vintage, they carry a full line of stringing and finding supplies. Truly a bead-lovers paradise! Furthermore, in this dazzling and spacious store, you'll find a wide selection of unique jewelry, batiked and embroidered clothing, and an eclectic array of items including incense, cards, handbags, tapestries, and sarongs. You'll also find beading books, beading classes, jewelry repair, custom jewelry design, and expert advice from their helpful staff is always available.

### S Beveled Mirror Gallery & Livings Stones Granite
743 S. Wyoming St., Butte. 782-4688, fax 782-4397. www.bigskyglass.com

### S Sophie's Shoe & Accessories
31 W. Park, Butte. 782-1712

### S D & G Antiques
16 N. Montana, Butte. 723-4552

## 10. *Attraction, Miscellaneous*

### T Mineral Museum
Montana Tech Campus, Butte. 496-4414

This is a rock hounds paradise. Butte's rich mining history is on display here through an impressive array of fine-quality mineral specimens from the underground mines.

Although it is impossible to permanently display the entire collection of 15,000 specimens, a large number are incorporated in the exhibits. At present, about 1,500 specimens are displayed in the Museum.

The Highland Centennial Gold Nugget, weighing 27,475 troy ounces, was recently donated to the Mineral Museum for permanent display. This very large nugget was found in September 1989 during placer mining in the Highland Mountains south of Butte. Also on display is a huge 400 pound quartz crystal.

A display of fluorescent minerals is exhibited in a separate room. Minerals in these cases are illuminated in both long and short wavelength ultraviolet light.

Two other cases deserve special mention. One is the exhibit of minerals from Butte, and the other is a display of some of the wide variety of minerals found in Montana.

The museum is open daily year round. Seasonal hours apply. There is no admission fee.

## T World Museum of Mining

W. Park St., Butte. 723-7211

One of Butte's most popular attractions is nestled beneath the massive headframe of the once active Orphan Girl underground mine. Spread over 12 acres, this 1889 mining camp has displays both inside and outdoors and is appealing to the whole family.

This extensive Mining Museum and reconstructed 1899 Mining Camp are built on the original Orphan Girl Mine site and provide insights into the mining era that can only be captured here. The museum was built entirely with volunteer help and donations. A replica of an actual mining camp, complete with cobblestone streets and boardwalks, shows the interiors of more than thirty businesses filled with antiques from the same era. The antiques can be viewed through the windows as the visitor strolls along the boardwalks of a time long ago past. Unique displays include a Chinese laundry, a sauerkraut factory, a funeral parlor, an ice house, a school, a general store, and of course, a saloon. On specific days, one can pan for gold; call ahead for days and times.

The Orphan Girl Express is a three car train pulled by an underground trammer engine. You can take the 20 minute train ride around the grounds while the engineer points out historic features along the way.

At the Hardrock Mining Building early day mining life is depicted in the photo archives of over 6,000 photographs.

The museum is open April 1 through October 31 from 9 a.m. to 6 p.m. daily. To get there go up the hill to the Montana Tech campus and past the Marcus Daly statue. Just beyond th statue, you will see the sign pointing to the museum. An admission fee is charged.

## T Anselmo Mine Yard

North Excelsior Street, Butte. 497-6275 or 800-735-6814

This is the best surviving example of the surface support facilities that served Butte's underground copper mines. A guided tour reveals the colorful labor history of miners, pipefitters, carpenters, hoist operators and trainmen. Also on display is the B.A. & P. "Cow & Calf", a restored G.E. 1909 heavy haul electric locomotive & cars. The mine yard and surrounding Historic District was designated a National Historic Landmark in 1961. The Anselmo is open mid-June to mid-August Monday through Friday from 10 a.m. to 6 p.m.

*A statue of Marcus Daly guards the entrance to Montana Tech.*

## M Montana Tech of The University of Montana

1300 West Park Street, Butte. 496-4178 or 800-445-8324. www.mtech.edu

Originally the Montana School of Mines, founded in 1895, Montana Tech now offers programs with a focus on the technical sciences. Montana's Bureau of Mines and Geology, and the Division of Technology have expanded the school's offerings. The current enrollment is approximately 1,800 students.

### Montana Trivia

The "richest hill on earth" has given up over twenty-one billion pounds of copper, ninety million ounces of silver, ninety million pounds of molybdenum, and three million ounces of gold. The veins of copper at Butte extended nearly a mile down. Over 70 percent of Montana's mineral wealth is concentrated in Silver Bow County.

## 11. *Attraction*

## Waterloo

Settlers began coming to this area as early as 1864. A woolen mill was started here at one time, but failed. A pottery mill did survive for a while. The story goes the town got its name when a battle ensued over the location of the post office. The settlers thought Waterloo was an appropriate name.

## T Renova Hot Springs

Hwy 55, near Waterloo on the Jefferson River

Pools along the shoreline are accessible year-round and located on public land. Volunteers have built the rock pools to allow the water to mix with the seeps that are about 112 degrees F. Due to the changing levels of the river the soaking temperatures vary widely throughout the year. Midsummer and early fall are the most ideal times for soaking. The scenery on the river and view of the Tobacco Root Mountains are spectacular.

## 12. *Lewis & Clark, Attraction*

## D William Clark

August 3, 1805

*"in my walk I saw a fresh track which I took to be an Indian,...I think it probable that this Indian Spied our fires and Came to a Situation to view us from the top of a Small knob on the Lard. [left] Side."*

## T Silver Star

Silver Star is the third oldest town in Montana and took its name from a nearby mining claim. It was at one time the only town between Helena and Virginia City and served as a supply point for silver miners in the area. Legend has it that Edward, Prince of Wales, and the son of Queen Victoria, spent three days at the Silver Star Hotel in 1878.

Now, with a population of about 40, you might think you could blink and miss the town as you drive through. You won't miss Lloyd Harkin's place though. Seven acres on Rte 41 are surrounded by a chain link fence that holds his enormous collection of mining equipment. He once had visions of creating a museum, later deciding that he didn't want to be tied down.

Today, as folks drive past they won't miss the seventy-eight-foot head frame that was used to lower cages of workers into a mine shaft or several twenty-one-foot wheels standing upright along the fence line. That's just part of it. The collection contains tons and tons of mining equipment from the 138 mines that Butte was once home to, and some from a few others. He managed to haul away just about everything imaginable from the mines, except the 4,000 miles of tunnel that still lie under the city of Butte.

The metallic assemblage contains everything from ore cars, pumps, railroad cars, pulleys, gas pumps, and some curious items not necessarily mining related. None of the items are a mystery to

Lloyd. He was a miner in Butte for twenty-five years and knows the entire story behind each piece. He'll buy, sell, or trade for the right deal. You can get a pretty good idea of what just went into all those mines as you drive by. A few of the items were purchased by Walt Disney's set designers and used in movies. Lloyd's museum never materialized but a great deal of his collection has been donated to Butte's World Museum of Mining.

**13.** *Historic Marker, Lewis & Clark, Attraction, Adventure, Gas, Food, Lodging*

## Twin Bridges

This town was founded by two brothers, M.H. and John T. Lott. A year after it was established, the brothers built two bridges, one across the Big Hole River and one across the Beaverhead River. Assured that this would be the hub of the valley, they proceeded to build roads to and from the town. 130 years later their descendents still occupy the valley. The area today is a farming and ranching community. Alfalfa, grains and potatoes grow in the fields surrounded by the Tobacco Root, Highland, McCartney and Ruby Mountains. Near the Twin Bridges school, four Indian trails converged at a natural ford on the Beaverhead.Twin Bridges is now known as a quintessential Montana fly fishing town and home to R.L. Winston Rod, internationally known maker of custom fly rods.

The town sits at the conjuncture of four rivers: the Big Hole, Beaverhead, Ruby and Jefferson. When Lewis and Clark camped near hear in 1805, they decided to name the three rivers that formed the Jefferson River for the three "cardinal virtues" of their president and benefactor for whom they had just named the Jefferson River. Unfortunately, the names of Philosophy, Philanthropy, and Wisdom were a little hard for settlers that later came through and the rivers were renamed the Big Hole, Ruby, and Beaverhead.

### H Jefferson Valley

north of Twin Bridges

*The Lewis and Clark Expedition, westward bound, came up the Jefferson River in August, 1805. They were hoping to find the Shoshone Indians, Sacajawea's tribe, and trade for horses to use in crossing the mountains west of here. Just south of here the river forks, the east fork being the Ruby and the west fork the Beaverhead. They followed the latter and met the Shoshones near Armstead, which is now under the Clark Canyon Reservoir 20 miles south of Dillon.*

*On the return trip from the coast in 1806, Capt. Wm. Clark retraced their former route down this valley to Three Forks, and then crossed the Yellowstone. Capt. Lewis left Clark in the Bitter Root Valley, crossed the Divide via the Big Blackfoot River and thence to Great Falls. They met near the mouth of the Yellowstone, arriving within nine days of each other.*

### D Mer. Lewis

August 6, 1805

*...we therefore determined that the middle fork was that which ought of right to bear the name we had given to the lower portion or River* Jefferson, *and called the bold rapid an[d] clear streem* Wisdom, *and the more mild and placid one which flows in from the S.E.* Philanthrophy, *in commemoration of two of those cardinal virtues, which have tso eminently marked that deservedly selibrated character through life.*

### T Rochester

10 miles northwest of Twin Bridges.

Rochester was once the major gold mining area in the region and at one time had a population of almost 5,000. Today all that remains is a few stone foundations and a fenced in cemetery, most of the town's buildings lost to vandalism. To get there drive west on Hwy. 41 out of Twin Bridges to just past where the road curves. Turn right on Melrose Twin Bridges County Road. Follow this road a little more than two miles until it crosses over Rochester Creek. A few yards on the other side of the creek is a road that follows the creek. Turn north here. The town is approximately seven miles down this road.

### T Montana Children's Center

Twin Bridges, Twin Bridges Historical Association. 684-5701

The economy of Twin Bridges was waning after the decline of the mining boom at the end of the 1800s. That's when the Montana Children's Center was established to give the local economy a boost. Better known as the orphanage, the 223 acre complex on the Beaverhead River was home to over 6,000 children through it's 80 year history. Children were delivered to the orphanage for many reasons over the eighty-two years of it's duration.

The Children's Center was a self-sustaining community where residents were taught to be proficient in life skills. It had it's own hospital, swimming pool, dairy, livestock, and elementary school. The Center provided well for the children who lived there, teaching true work ethics and lifelong skills. The orphanage has been vacant since closing in 1975 and the buildings have fallen into disrepair, but remain an imposing part of the Twin Bridges landscape. The Twin Bridges Museum has preserved remnants and the history of the Children's Center.

### V Four Rivers Fishing Company

205 S. Main St., Twin Bridges. 684-5651 or 888-4RIVERS. www.4rivers.com

This full service fly shop is located in the center of the blue ribbon trout fishing waters of four great rivers—the Ruby, Beaverhead, Bighole and Jefferson. The experienced guides and knowledgeable staff can lead you to great fishing holes and help you pick out the right flys and gear. They offer personalized walk/wade trips, float trips, and fishing/lodging multi-day packages. Gear is supplied on guided trips if necessary, and the shop is a retail outlet for Winston Fly Rods. These outstanding guides are in high demand and get booked up early. Call for your reservations as soon as possible and stop in on your way through to stock up on supplies and get some good local fishing advice.

### FS The Weaver's Studio

108 Main Street, Twin Bridges. 684-5744

Rugs, saddle blankets, beadwork & espresso.

### L King's Motel

307 S. Main St., Twin Bridges. 684-5639

### S Timeless Treasures Quilt Gallery

1/2 mile west of Hwy.41, Twin Bridges. 684-5719

**14.** *Gas, Food, Lodging*

## Sheridan

Many of the miners who came to this area in the 1860s were Civil War veterans. The town was named for Gen. Phillip H. Sheridan, a Union cavalry leader.

### F Sheridan Bakery & Cafe

201 S. Main St., Sheridan. 842-5716

The Sheridan Bakery & Café is open year around and offers award winning breads, donuts, and pastries made on the premises. Stop by for breakfast and lunch in a hometown atmosphere. This is a great place to meet the locals and enjoy fresh pastries at their best. Breakfast and lunch specials are posted on the chalkboard and are very popular, so don't be late. They are located in the heart of the area's Blue Ribbon trout streams, big game hunting, and just minutes from Historic Virginia and Nevada Cities. Sheridan's Main Street offers a variety of shopping pleasures as well as services to enjoy.

### L Moriah Motel

Corner of Poppleton & Main, Sheridan. 842-5491. moriah@sellit-montana.com

You can't miss the Moriah Motel, located right in the heart of downtown Sheridan. The 12 clean and comfortable rooms are complete with cable TV, queen size beds, direct dial phones and handicapped facilities. Non-smoking rooms and laundry facilities are also available. The Moriah is conveniently located near wonderful recreation areas, many outdoor activities, and it is within walking distance to local restaurants. The friendly staff will help make your stay a very pleasant one.

**15.** *Historic Marker, Gas, Food, Lodging, Camping*

## Alder

Once served as a shipping center during the early gold rush days, gold dredging operations at the turn of the century left large gravel mounds west of town. Near Alder Ponds lie piles of processed rock, called windrows, as well as the dredge

## *Montana Trivia*

The only Kentucky Derby winner to come from Montana came from the Bayer Ranch near Twin Bridges. Spokane won the 1886 Derby with six-to-one odds. The unusual wedding cake type barn of the Bayer Ranch can be seen from the highway to the east while driving south of Twin Bridges.

ponds from the operation of one of the largest dredges to be used in 1911. Two of Harry Plummer's road agents were hanged near here in 1864. It's estimated over $100 million dollars in gold was extracted from this area. Even today, visitors can pan for gold at Alder Gulch River of Gold. A few buildings remain, along with a few residents.

### Laurin

The town was a station on the Northern Pacific railroad between Sheridan and Alder. Originally know as Cicero, the name was changed to honor John Baptiste Laurin who ran a trading store nearby. John and his wife prospered by trading with the Indians and selling goods to the miners. He and his wife were in the mercantile and livestock business for almost forty years. While they had no children of their own, they raised fourteen who had been left to their care for one reason or another. They built a magnificent Catholic church of native stone and donated it to the community. The church still stands. Perhaps Laurin is best know for its "Hangman's Tree" where members of the Plummer Gang were dispatched at the end of a rope on January 4, 1864.

### H Robbers' Roost
south of Sheridan

*In 1863, Pete Daly built a road house on the stage route between Virginia City and Bannack to provide entertainment for, man. and beast. The main floor was a shrine to Bacchus and Lady Luck. The second floor was dedicated to Terpsichore and bullet holes in the logs attest the fervor of ardent swains for fickle sirens. Occasionally a gent succumbed.*

*Pete's tavern became a hangout for unwholesome characters who held up stage coaches and robbed lone travellers. One of the road agents is alleged to have left a small fortune in gold cached in the vicinity.*

*In later years, time and neglect gave the building its present hapless look and it became known as Robbers' Roost. It is in the cottonwood grove just across the railroad tracks. Drive over and pay your respects but please don't dig up the premises trying to locate the cache.*

### H The Ruby Valley
near Alder

*The Ruby River was called the Passamari by the Indians and became known as the Stinking Water to the whites in the pioneer days. It joins the Beaverhead to form the Jefferson Fork of the Missouri.*

*Fur trappers, Indians, prospectors and road agents have ridden the trails through here in days gone by.*

*The large gravel piles to the west are the tailings resulting from gold dredging operations over about a twenty-year period beginning in 1899. The dredges are reported to have recovered between eight and nine million dollars in gold from the floor of the valley and the lower end of Alder Gulch.*

### L Lynch's Lair Bed & Breakfast
2477 Hwy 287, Alder, 10 miles N. of Virginia City. 842-5699. www.lynchslair.com

Lynch's Lair offers tastefully decorated, comfortable lodging with great food and that famous western hospitality in the beautiful Ruby Valley. Innkeeper Jeannette Lynch will welcome you with a touch of the blarney and a heart felt smile! She's well known as a great cook and is delighted to share her home with those who would like a touch of the Montana lifestyle. Lynchstyle! Hot and cold beverages, fruit, and Jeanette's homemade cookies are always available. Jeannette's mother and daughter also help out, and her granddaughter has been known to entertain! That's four generations! Truly a family operation. Relax in this quiet environment while visiting Virginia City and the surrounding area. Pets by prior arrangement.

### LC Chick's Motel & RV Park
Hwy 287, Alder. 842-5366

## 16. *Historic Marker, Attraction, Food, Lodging, Camping, Shopping*

### Virginia City

Stories of colorful mining-era boomtowns in the American West are abundant. But, few are quite as colorful as the story of Virginia City. On May 26, 1863, six frustrated prospectors set up a camp on the banks of a small creek in the Tobacco Root Mountains. All they wanted was to find enough gold to buy tobacco when they returned to Bannack. Within hours, they had collected $12.30 in gold, and that there might be more here than a few days worth of tobacco. The area was named Alder Gulch for the bushes that grew along the creek.

The town of Virginia City was born, and within a year grew to 10,000 people. Within two years almost 30,000 people lived within 20 miles of the town. Within three years, Alder Gulch coughed up more than $30 million in gold, and to this day is the richest placer gold discovery in history yielding over $130 million in flakes, nuggets, and gold dust.

The stories that go with this town are just as rich. Henry Plummer, the criminal sheriff who plundered the area for years. The Montana Vigilante movement that finally hung the crooked sheriff and contributed numerous graves on the local Boot Hill. And, of course, the political intrigue and wrangling when the town served as Montana's Territorial Capital.

Probably the most unique thing about Virginia City is that most of it is still standing today—intact and preserved. Most of the buildings here have stood in the same spot for more than 130 years. The "downtown" of Virginia City is arguably one of the best collection of "boomtown" buildings still standing on their original sites. Ranks Mercantile, established in 1864, is Montana's oldest continuously operating general store.

Charles and Sue Bovey visited Virginia City in 1944 and immediately recognized its historic value. Their efforts to restore and preserve the town lasted for years until the Bovey estate sold the town to the State of Montana. Today, you can shop, dine, and sleep in a town so authentic you'll feel you've stepped back in time. Learn more about this rare historical treasure at www.virginiacity.com and www.virginiacitychamber.com.

### Nevada City

A celebrated ghost town, Nevada City recreates the mining era so authentically that it has been filmed in western movies such as *Little Big Man* and *Return to Lonesome Dove*. Buildings include five streets of shops, homes, a schoolhouse and Chinatown. The most popular exhibition is the Music Hall which contains one of the world's largest collections of mechanical music machines.

### H Nevada City
Nevada City

*A ghost town now, but once one of the hell roarin' mining camps that lined Alder Gulch in the 1860s. It was*

Virginia City

*a trading point where gold dust and nuggets were the medium of exchange: where men were men and women were scarce. A stack of whites cost twenty, the sky was the limit and everyone was heeled.*

*The first Vigilante execution took place here when George Ives, notorious road agent, was convicted of murder and hanged.*

*The gulch was once filled with romance, glamour, melodrama, comedy and tragedy. It's plumb peaceful now.*

### H Virginia City
Virginia City

*All of Montana has the deepest pride and affection for Virginia City. No more colorful pioneer mining camp ever existed. Dramatic tales of the early days in this vicinity are legion.*

*Rich placer diggin's were discovered in Alder Gulch in the spring of 1863 and the stampede of gold-seekers and their parasites was on. Sluices soon lined the gulch and various "cities" blossomed forth as trading and amusement centers for freehanded miners. Virginia City, best known of these and the sole survivor, became the Capital of the Territory. Pioneers, who with their descendants were to mold the destinies of the state, were among its first citizens. If you like true stories more picturesque than fiction, Virginia City and Alder Gulch can furnish them in countless numbers.*

### H Adobetown
Northwest of Virginia City

*Placer riches in Alder Gulch spawned many colorful communities. Among them, Adobetown flourished briefly as the center of mining activity in 1864. In that year alone, miners extracted over $350,000 in gold from nearby streams.*

*Taking its name from the numerous adobe shacks the miners constructed in the vicinity Adobetown assumed permanence in the fall of 1865 when Nicholas Carey and David O'Brien erected a large log store. The building's central location contributed to the growth of the settlement and the development of other businesses. Stages from Salt Lake City and later the Union Pacific Railroad at Corinne, Utah, made regular stops at the Adobetown store for passengers and mail.*

*The town received an official post office in 1875 with Carey as postmaster. He, and later his wife Mary, served as the community's only postmasters until her retirement and the subsequent close of the office in the fall of 1907.*

*Once in lively rivalry with Virginia City for social and political leadership of Alder Gulch, Adobetown's population and importance waned after 1865 as the placer gold gave out in the immediate area.*

### H Elling Bank
Virginia City

*Bankers Nowland and Weary set up business in this brick-veneered building, one of the town's oldest stone structures, in 1864. Three well-proportioned gothic arches with elaborate tracery, removed during 1910 remodeling, originally graced its stone facade. In 1873, Henry Elling took over the banking business. His first fortune, made in merchandising, had disappeared along with his partner, but Elling quickly recouped his losses. The buying of gold dust proved a most profitable venture and Elling became an expert, able to determine the exact location of extraction from the texture and color of the dust. Under his shrewd direction, Elling's tiny bank became the first financial capital of Montana. The ornate vault, still intact, always carried large amounts of the dust. The Elling State Bank was organized in 1899 and Elling died a millionaire the following year. His family continued to operate the bank for another thirty years.*

### H Metropolitan Meat Market
Virginia City

*George Gohn was one of the first to arrive at Alder Gulch in 1863 where he and Conrad Kohrs set up a meat market in a log cabin. Alkali dust sifted through the chinks and covered the meat prompting Gohn to experiment with various other locations until he settled on this site in 1880. When fire destroyed much of the block in 1888, only Gohn rebuilt. The present building, completed that year, long stood solitary on this section of Wallace Street. Decorative pilasters, brackets and imitation quarried stone highlight the cast iron storefront manufactured by George Mesker of Evansville, Indiana. Recent interior renovation included restoration of the tin ceiling. In the process, owners discovered a hidden treasure behind a plastered drywall: Gohn's elaborate oak meat cooler with beveled mirrors intact. This unusual example of 1880s state-of-the-art equipment stands sixteen feet high. Gohn advertised that his cooler was always well stocked with beef, veal, pork, game fowl and mutton and that his peddling wagons were "run regularly up and down the gulch."*

### H Pfouts and Russel (Rank's Drug-Old Masonic Temple)
Virginia City

*Paris Pfouts, Vigilante president and Virginia City's first mayor, was instrumental in laying out the town. He and his partner, Samuel Russell, built a log store on this site in summer, 1863. Local hell-raiser Jack Slade was arrested here on March 10, 1864 and, in an execution controvesial even amoung the Vigilantes, hanged on a corral gatepost behind the building. Pfouts and Russell constructed the present building in 1865. Lime was not yet available for mortar, so the stone walls were secured with adobe mud. A loyal Mason, Pfouts gave the second floor to the Masonic Lodge. There the Grand Lodge of Montana A.F. & A.M. was founded on January 24, 1866. W.W. Morris moved his drug store, established in the Hangman's Building in 1864, to this location circa 1877. C.W. Rank bought the business in 1889. He and his wife ran it until 1946. Now housing the oldest continuously-operated business in Montana, the building has been little altered since the 1860s.*

### T Virginia City Historical Museum
Virginia City

### T Alder Gulch Short Line
Virginia City. 843-5377

The Short Line is a narrow gauge railroad that runs between Virginia City and Nevada city. The 1.25 mile trip is a favorite with kids. The train's engineer entertains you during the entire trip with narratives of the area's history. Early June to late-August. There is an admission charge.

### T Alder Gulch River of Gold
Virginia City. 843-5402

Whether you just want to see how placer gold was mined during Virginia City's gold boom, or do a

## It Happened in Montana

January 2, 1865. For 185 rounds, Con Orem and Hugh O'Neill battled bare-knuckled to a draw in Virginia City. The fight was best described by Granville Stuart:

*"...each man toed the mark and the battle begun and lasted three hours and five munutes, in which one hundred eighty-five rounds were fought. At this junction a sudden feeling seemed to animate the backers of both men. The referee was called on by both parties to stop the fight. (the men themselves were still game and ready to go.) This was accordingly done to the satisfaction of most people present. Bets were declared off and the ring money was divided evenly."*

The prize purse was $1,000. As it was a draw, each man ended up receiving $425 and half of all the gold dust "pokes" thrown into the ring.

## *Montana Trivia*

The six prospectors who dipped their pans in Alder Creek in 1863 were only looking for enough gold to pay for their tobacco. Over $10 million in gold was eventually taken out of history's richest placer gold discovery. In todays dollars that would equal $2.5 billion.

little gold panning yourself, you'll find this an enjoyable stop for every member of the family. An outdoor mining museum displays dredging equipment and other mining artifacts. You can pan for gold and garnets with a little professional help.

### F Banditos at the Wells Fargo

320 W. Wallace, Virginia City. 843-5556

### L The Bennett House Country Inn

115 E. Idaho St., Virginia City. 843-5220
or toll free 877-843-5220.
http://bennetthouseinn.com/inside.html

Located just northwest of Yellowstone National Park in historic Virginia City is the Bennett House. Built in 1879 for Alden J. Bennett, this Queen Anne style Victorian home offers six uniquely furnished guest rooms along with a hot tub ( call ahead to determine availability); a log cabin is also available. The Inn is open all year long and hosts, Karla, Nancy & Garry include a delightful full breakfast with all room rates. The Inn is within walking distance to all area attractions. Guests will enjoy the haunting beauty of Virginia City's century old buildings. Find the spirit of the Old West as you walk along wooden sidewalks just one block from this historic Country Inn.

### L Just an Experience B&B

1570 Hwy. 287 N., Virginia City. 843-5402

### S Rank's Mercantile

211 W. Wallace, Virginia City. 843-5454 or
800-494-5442. www.gold-rush-adventures.com

Rank's Mercantile is the oldest continually operated store in Montana, established in 1863 when gold was discovered up Alder Gulch near Virginia City. Murder and robbery led honest men to taking the law into their own hands when Paris Pfouts, one of the Vigilantes, established Rank's. The infamous Jack Slade was arrested there and hanged from a corral out back. Rank's mercantile is an old-time general store offering wild west period clothing, groceries, patent medicines, jewelry, gifts and notions. They specialize in books on women of the west, fur trappers, Native Americans, ghost towns and Montana's rich history.

**17.** *Historic Marker, Lewis & Clark, Attraction*

### H Beaverhead Rock

Hwy 41, north of Dillon

*On August 10, 1805, members of the Lewis and Clark expedition pushed their way up the Jefferson River's tributaries toward the Continental Divide and the Pacific Ocean beyond. Toward afternoon they sighted what Clark called a "remarkable Clift" to the west. Sacajawea (or, as Lewis spelled it: Sahcahgarweah), their Indian guide for this portion of the trip, said her tribe called the large promontory "Beaver's head."*

*Both Lewis and Clark agreed on the rock's likeness to the fur-bearing animal and recorded the name in their journals. They continued south only to encounter a heavy rain and hail storm. "the men defended themselves from the hail by means of the willow bushes but all the party got perfectly wet," Lewis said. They camped upstream from the Beaver's head, enjoyed freshly killed deer meat, then pushed on the next day.*

*Beaverhead Rock served as an important landmark not only for Lewis and Clark, but also for the trappers, miners, and traders who followed them into the vicinity. It is the namesake for the county in which it is now located, retaining the same appearance that inspired Sacajawea and her people to name it centuries ago.*

## On The Trail of Lewis & Clark

### The Beaver's Head

A few miles below the mouth of Ruby River, Sacagawea recognized a prominent point of land known to her people as the Beaver's Head. She informed the captains that they were not far from the summer retreat of her people, which, she said, was on a river beyond the moun-tains (Lcmhi River.)

On Aug. 9, Lewis, along with three men, again set out ahead of the main party in an attempt to find the Shoshones.

About 9 1/2 miles by water from the Beaver's Head, the main party reached an island which they named 3000-Mile Island—a refer-ence to their distance up the Missouri River.

### Fourth Range Of Mountains

Lewis's party, which was following an Indian road, passed through the fourth range of mountains on Aug. 10, and from the number of rattlesnakes about the cliffs called it "Rattlesnake Cliffs." The main party entered this canyon four days later and both Clark and Sacagawea were in danger of being struck by these serpents.

Lewis continued on the Indian road, and soon came to a fork at the head of the Jefferson River. He left a note here on a dry willow to inform Clark of his decision to follow the west fork. At about 15 miles from the forks, on Horse Prairie, Lewis finally saw a Shoshone on horseback—the first Indian the Expedition had seen in 1400 miles. The native, wary of the strangers, would not allow them to approach, and soon disappeared into the mountains.

### Fifth Range Of Mountains

Lewis fixed a small U.S. flag onto a pole as a symbol of peace, which was carried along as they followed the horse's tracks. They camped that night at the head of Horse Prairie. They were now about to enter the fifth range of mountains.

The following morning they came upon recently inhabited willow lodges, and a place where the Indians had been digging roots. They continued on until they reached what Lewis described as "the most distant fountain of the waters of the Mighty Missouri in surch of which we have spent so many toilsome days and wristless nights. Thus far I had accomplished one of those great objects on which my mind has been unalterably fixed for many years..." He then wrote that Private McNeal "exultingly stood with a foot on each side of the little rivulet and thanked his god that he had lived to bestride the mighty & heretofore deemed endless Missouri."

*Reprinted from U.S. Forest Service pamphlet "Lewis and Clark in the Rocky Mountains"*

Section 6

## Montana Trivia

R.E. Mather and F.E. Boswell describe the fatal Virginia City shooting of Deputy Dillingham in "Gold Camp Desperadoes":

*...a Virginia City miners' court met to settle a claim dispute. The courtroom was a conical tent of willows interlaced with brush, which stood on the creek bank at the foot of Wallace Street. Though the tent was barely large enough to hold judge, clerk, plaintiff, defendant, and attorneys, curious spectators followed the proceedings by peeping through gaps in the brush. As Charley Forbes (the former Ed Richardson) sat at Judge William Steele's elbow taking notes [he was clerk of the court], deputies Buck Stinson and Hayes Lyons burst through the doorway and whispered something in Charley's ear. They then hurried outside to confront Deputy D.H. Dillingham. Charley followed a few steps behind. An argument had arisen a few days earlier when Dillingham had stated that Stinson, Lyons, and Forbes intended to rob a miner. Now as the deputies faced off a few steps from the willow tent, Lyons cursed at Diilingham and then demanded, "Take back those lies." As hands moved toward revolver butts, Charley cried, "Don't shoot, don't shoot!" From that point on, events moved too rapidly for observers to determine exactly what happened, but in the end Dillingham lay dead with a shot in the thigh and a second in the chest. Deputy Jack Gallagher disarmed Stinson, Lyons, and Forbes and ordered them bound with logging chains and placed under guard in a cabin on Daylight Creek. But the memory of the Carson City shackles was still strong in Charley's mind, and when his turn to be chained came, he refused, declaring he would rather die first. Six guards drew on him, however, and he was forced to submit to the chains and padlock.*

### D William Clark

August 5, 1805

*"Men much fatiqued from their excessive labours in hauling the Canoes over the rapids & very weak being in the water all day."*

### D William Clark

August 8, 1805

*"the Indian woman recognized the point of a high plain to our right which she informed us was not very distant from the summer retreat of her nation on a river beyond the mountains which runs to the west. this hill she says her nation calls the beaver's head from a conceived remblance of it's figure to the head of the animal. . .I determined to proceed tomorrow. . .untill I find the Indians. . . "*

### T Beaverhead Rock State Park

14 miles south of Twin Bridges on MT 41. 834-3413

Sacajawea recognized this huge landmark, resembling the head of a swimming beaver, while traveling with Lewis and Clark in 1805, helping the party with their orientation. Day use only.

## 18. *Gas, Food, Lodging*

### Rocker

This town has had its ups and downs. It first grew up around the Bluebird Mine, but faded when the mine closed in 1893. It was reborn when the Pacific Railroad chose Rocker as the division point where ore cars were made up between Butte and Anaconda. The name came from a cradle-like machine called a rocker which was used to wash gold from gravel by early miners.

### A Rocker Repair & Tire

1100 Grizzly Trail, at Rocker Exit. 723-1117

At Rocker Repair & Tire, they try their hardest to take good care of the motoring public. They specialize in tire repair, and will work on just about everything else. If there is something they can not fix, they will make referrals and make sure you get the help you need. Located right next to the truck stop and weigh scale in Rocker, they will fix large truck tires 24 hours-a-day. Stop in for friendly and extremely helpful service, with exceptionally affordable rates.

### L Rocker Inn

12201 W. Brown's Gulch Road, I-15 Rocker Interchange, west of Butte. 723-5464 or 800-828-5311

Just off Hwy. 15 and I-90, and away from the hustle and bustle of the city, the Rocker Inn has clean rooms in a friendly, quiet atmosphere, with great views of the highlands. There is a lounge on the premises serving beer and wine. 50 rooms, with non-smoking options, in room microwave & refrigerator, air conditioning, irons and ironing boards and a guest laundry facility, and 24 hours desk. Great access to all area activities. Pets are allowed with fee and certain restrictions. Ask about senior, AAA, and commercial discounts.

## 19. *Attraction*

### Melrose

Just off of I15 south of Butte on the Big Hole River, is the town of Melrose. Some of the log cabins have survived the years and are still used as residences. Other original buildings that have been vacated are still standing from the days when this town was a supply depot for mining camps. There is also a motel, guest ranch, and Bed and Breakfast in the area and plenty of fishing.

### Divide

Divide is named for the town's proximity to the Continental Divide. At one time the town was a station on the Union Pacific and was a distribution and stock shipping point for farms and ranches of the Big Hole Valley.

## Montana Trivia

The six men who discovered Alder Gulch were not real adept at keeping a secret. Their plan was to "sneak" out of Bannack with the horses and supplies they had purchased with their new gold. The discoverers--Bill Fairweather, Tom Cover, Henry Edgar, Barney Hughes, Harry Rogers, and Mike Sweeney--just had that "look" about them and spent a little too freely. When they left town they were followed by 200 men who had been observing their behavior for the past week. Just before reaching Alder Gulch, they realized there was no fooling the followers and confessed to the new find. Not before sending Barney Hughes ahead to secure their claims though. On the trail they called a miner's meeting with the followers to establish some rules. No miner could possess more than two claims. A claim was 200 feet wide in the bed of the gulch or to the center of the stream in wider parts. A miner had to work his claim at least three days a week to retain title to it. Stuart Granville no doubt used a little hyperbole when he claimed "The Alder Gulch diggings were the richest gold placer diggings ever discovered in the world." They were rich. According to Granville "the district extended from the foot of Old Baldy to twelve miles down the creek, and the bed of the creek and the bars on both sides were uniformly rich; the bed rock being literally paved with gold." Virginia City was established here and grew to nearly 10,000 inhabitants before the gold played out.

### T Glendale

West of Melrose.

To reach this town, take Trapper Creek Road west out of Melrose for about 15 miles. This was the largest of several towns in the Bryant Mining District. The others, Lion City, Greenwood, Trapper City and Hecla have virtually vanished. At one time Glendale had a population of over 1,500 people, a school for 200 students, a Methodist church, commercial stores, and a water works system. The Hecla Mining Company was the main employer from 1881 to 1900. During it's short life, it mined ore that was valued at over $22 million. The most interesting remains are those of the old Coke ovens which provided over 100,000 bushels of charcoal a month for the smelter. The ovens and the smelter stack are still in evidence on the road north of town. When the Hecla Mine shut down in 1904, the residents quickly deserted the town.

## 20. *Attraction*

### T Humbug Spires Primitive Area

I-15 Exit 99

*Old train station adjacent to the Beaverhead County Museum in Dillon.*

The gently rolling countryside here is starkly disrupted by nine 300 to 600-foot granite monoliths. No one knows how old these spires are. Estimates range from 70 million to 2 billion years old. They are part of the Boulder batholith that you see driving over Homestake Pass near Butte and are a remarkable piece of Montana geology.

**21.** *Historic Marker*

### H Browne's Bridge

mile north of Glen

*Browne's Bridge was constructed as a toll bridge by Fred Burr and James Minesinger in late 1862 and early 1863. The bridge was located on the Bannack to Deer Lodge Road. Joseph Browne, a miner, bought the bridge in 1865. The territorial legislature granted him a charter to maintain the bridge and charge travelers for its use. Within a few years, Browne had acquired about 3,000 acres near the bridge and had developed nearby Browne's Lake for recreational purposes. A post office was located just west of the bridge from 1872 until the early 1880s. Even though most of Montana's counties assumed control of the state's toll facilities by 1892, Browne operated the bridge until his death in 1909. Beaverhead and Madison counties assumed joint ownership of the bridge in 1911.*

*In 1915 the counties petitioned the Montana State Highway Commission for a new bridge. The Commission designed the bridge in 1915; a Missoula company built it during the autumn and winter of that year. A riveted Warren through truss bridge, it was one of the first structures designed by the Commission's bridge department. In 1920 high water destroyed the old structure, which was located slightly upstream from this bridge.*

*Beaverhead County rehabilitated this bridge with funds provided by the Montana Department of Transportation.*

**22.** *Attraction*

### T Argenta

Hwy. 278, to Argenta Flats Road, west of Dillon

Argenta (formerly Montana) was the site of Montana's first silver-lead mine in Montana, The Legal Tender. It once had a population of over 1,500. Granville Stuart, in speaking of Argenta wrote, "The wealth of the Rothchilds is as nothing compared to the riches which lie concealed in the bowels of the Rattlesnake hills awaiting the coming of the enchanters with their wands (in the shape of greenbacks), to bring forth these treasures." In 1866, the St. Louis and Montana Mining Company funded and built the first smelter in the Montana Territory here. The only remnants of this town are mine shafts, slag heaps, some abandoned mine structures, and several private residences.

**23.** *Lodging*

### Dillon

Dillon was born with the screech of a steam whistle. The Utah and Northern Railroad (present day Union Pacific) was forging north, toward Butte in 1880, as winter converged the railroad halted construction at Richard Deason's ranch. The location of the town was determined coincidentally when the rancher owning the land refused the railroad passage. Some enterprising businessmen travelling with the train bought the ranch to form a town site company. During the winter the railroad remained at the end of the track and when it moved north again in the spring, the town remained. Dillon was named after the president of the Union Pacific Railroad, Sidney Dillon.

With a population of about 4,000, Dillon is an agricultural community and the regional trade center for southwestern Montana. At one point it was the largest wool shipping point in Montana. It is also the county seat of Beaverhead County and boasts an "Entrance to Montana" Visitors Information Center located in the old Union Pacific Depot Building alongside the Chamber of Commerce. Western Montana College, built here in the early 1900s, has assisted Dillon's economic stability and development.

Nestled within the surrounding mountain ranges of the Beaverhead, the Tendoys, the Centennial Range and the Pioneer Mountains, Dillon enjoys a pocket of mild weather and a variety of geographical splendor.

## Montana's Vigilantes

The Vigilante movement began the winter of 1863 in Alder Gulch. While thousands came to the fields to mine gold others came with them who had other ideas for making money. Gamblers, dance-hall girls, and crooks flooded into the area with the miners. While every part of the west had its share of criminals, Alder Gulch had someone to organize them in the personage of Henry Plummer. A smooth, shrewd con man with a rap sheet going back 10 year, Plummer arrived in Bannack in the winter of '62-'63. By spring, he had conned everyone and was wearing the sheriff's badge. Now in control of the law, he began to organize the criminal elements into a cohesive unit that terrorized the thousands in the area.

After suffering through a year of Mr. Plummer's reign, the honest miners took matters into their own hands. A three day trial in Nevada City claimed its first "Road Agent," and George Ives was hanged, and the Montana Vigilantes were formed. During the next two months, the Vigilantes cleaned up the area. The nucleus of the Plummer gang were either hanged or banished and the consummate conman finished his reign at the end of a noose.

### L GuestHouse Inns & Suites

580 Sinclair Street, Dillon. 683-3636 or 800-21-guest (48378). www.guesthouse.net

GuestHouse Inn & Suites is committed to quality, customer service and quality. Spacious rooms are equipped with extra amenities that include a coffee maker, microwave, refrigerator, VCR, hairdryer, iron and ironing board. Enjoy plenty of adventure with world-class trout fishing, big-game hunting, or a stroll in the footsteps of Lewis and Clark. Visit a ghost town, a mining operation or an Indian battleground, and return in the evenings for some relaxation in the indoor pool and spa. They also offer an exercise room, guest laundry, and business center for your convenience. A complimentary hot breakfast buffet including scrambled eggs, potatoes, bacon, sausage and gravy, waffle sticks, hot and cold cereals, fruit and donuts is included with your stay.

**24.** *Attraction, Gas, Food, Lodging*

### T Clark's Lookout State Park

In Dillon on 490 at Montana 41 exit, .5 miles east, then .5 miles north on county road. 834-3413

This is the location of an observation site used by William Clark of the Lewis and Clark Expedition on August 13, 1805. This area has some great views. Undeveloped land makes it a great place for adventure and primitive camping.

### L Super 8 Dillon
550 N. Montana St., Dillon. 683-3636

## 25. *Attraction, Gas, Food, Lodging, Shopping*

### T Beaverhead County Museum
15 S. Montana St. in downtown Dillon. 683-5027

The Beaverhead County Museum is a time machine reopening the past.

A tour of the museum will unfold the county's history… its inhabitants, wildlife, agriculture, mining and lifestyle. Included with Indian artifacts, early ranching relics and mining memorabilia, is a huge, mounted Alaskan brown bear towering over the exhibits.

Exhibits depict the manner in which Indians, early pioneers and the medical profession served as caretakers of land and man. A second room features the local mining industry, while another invites you into the domestic side of early life in Beaverhead County.

Outside, you can read 1,700 branded boards along the boardwalk, leading to an authentic homesteader's cabin and Dillon's first flush toilet. Mining equipment, a sheepherder's wagon, and an old Ford tractor are other interesting outdoor displays.

Continue south on the boardwalk to the 1909 Union Pacific Depot, now housing the Travel Montana Visitors' Center, the Beaverhead Chamber of Commerce, the Old Depot Theatre and a large diorama of Lewis and Clark.

Take a walk through time and enjoy your visit. Our friendly hosts and hostesses will be happy to answer your questions.

The museum is open year round. While no admission is charged there is a suggested donation. *Reprinted from Dillon Chamber of Commerce brochure.*

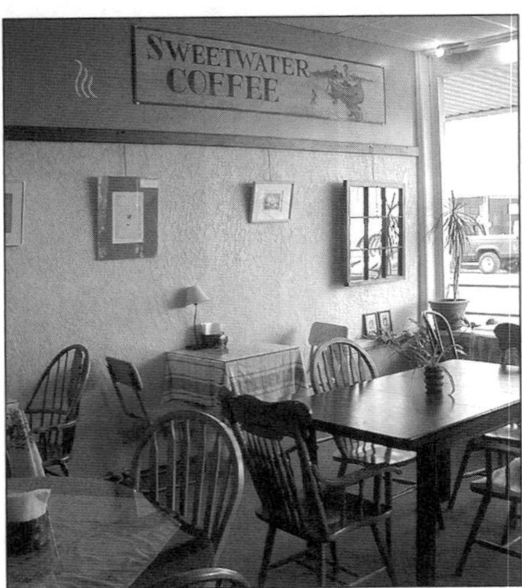


### F Sweetwater Coffee
26 E. Bannack, Dillon. 683-4141

If you're looking for great food at reasonable prices and great service then be sure and visit this unique and friendly restaurant. They serve great homemade food, and the best coffee around, all with a warm welcome. Located in the heart of downtown Dillon, the Sweetwater offers wonderful sandwiches, generous salads, delicious pastas, hearty soups, homemade cookies baked daily, and of course, a wide selection of wonderful freshly brewed coffee. You'll find a cozy and relaxing atmosphere, a friendly staff that is friendly and helpful, and food that is second-to-none. Enjoy their fabulous food always served with a side of that special Montana charm.

### F Blacktail Station
26 S. Montana St., Dillon. 683-6611

### L Sundowner Motel
500 N. Montana, Dillon. 683-2375
or reservations at 800-524-9746

### S Crafty Quilter
104 N. Montana St., Dillon. 683-5884

Visit The Crafty Quilter in an 1880s historic building and select from a dazzling selection of over 4,000 bolts of fabric, including a large selection of Western prints, Hoffman, Marcus Brothers and more. The Crafty Quilter boasts one of the best flannel selections in Southwest Montana and is their specialty, with many kits and fabric packs available. People travel from far and wide for these fabrics. Take time to enjoy a one-day quilting class with Susy McCall and her staff between hunting and fishing trips. Chances are you'll get hooked on quilt offered with mention of this book.

### S Mitchell Drug
125 E. Glendale in Dillon. 683-2316.
www.mitchelldrug.com

A walk into Mitchell Drug is like coming home.

The friendly, homey atmosphere will welcome you, and the aisles are filled with a variety of gifts. Take a few minutes to peruse the aisles and visit with the folks at Mitchell Drug. The store's selection includes a variety of candles, Beanie Babies, a wide selection of camera equipment and some of the best quality gifts available in Dillon. Of course, there is a full service pharmacy and a convenient one hour photo lab for those special photos you've taken in Montana. If the folks at Mitchell Drug can't help you find that perfect gift, they will point you in the right direction to other friends in Dillon who can.

### L Centennial Inn B&B
122 S. Washington, Dillon. 683-4454.
www.bmt.net/~centenn

### S P & L Antiques & More
236 N. Idaho, Dillon. 683-9863

Lynn Westad has a shop filled with a large selection of furniture, wonderful collectibles, and miscellaneous timeless treasures. You might just find that piece you've been searching for. You can find items that suit every budget from beautiful hard-to-find antiques to sentimental objects that will bring a smile to your face. You'll enjoy exploring an extensive collection of glassware, estate jewelry, china, and much more. P & L Antiques is located at the corner of Idaho and Virginia Streets and open from 10 a.m. to 6 p.m. daily. You are welcome to call Lynn at home (683-4102) if your schedule doesn't fit regular hours.

### S Silverado Jewelers
30 E. Bannack, Dillon. 683-4350

Dillon draws those adventurers who like to get off the beaten path. When in town enjoy a unique, uncrowded, pleasant shopping experience at Silverado. This is a store that specializes in friendly down home service. They offer a huge selection of half-priced silver jewelry, including rings, necklaces, earrings, and bracelets! They also offer affordable one of a kind gifts from all over the world. They have developed a steady reputation throughout southwest Montana as a "must see" shopping experience for the discriminating adventurer. Find them in the heart of the downtown area, conveniently located on the corner of Bannack and Idaho Streets. You'll be glad you did!

### S Delightfully Yours Gifts, Granola, & More
32 S. Idaho, Dillon. 683-8243.
www.mountainmunchies.com

### S Fins & Feathers Tropical Fish, Birds, & Supplies
31 N. Idaho, Dillon. 683-2600

### S Rocky Mountain Gifts
16 S. Montana, Dillon. 683-4238 or fax 683-3693

### S The Good Life
2 S. Montana, Dillon. 683-9000

**M Bramlette & Co. Realtors**
8 South Idaho, Dilllon. 683-4316 or Ruby Valley Office, 842-5028, www.bramlettecompany.com

Montana! A state rich in history and in traditions. A place where the land is a part of life and the people are unique as each sunset. The folks at Bramlette and Company understand Montana and the people who live and work here. They are proud to provide Southwest Montana with a service oriented and knowledgeable staff. People trust them with their property to sell and are confident of their professional representation of the property. Buyers seek them out through the exposure they create for their Sellers through efficient, productive marketing and advertising. Their professionalism and reputation for excellence are recognized throughout the industry. Featuring fine homes, recreational property, working ranches, and commercial opportunities. Bramlette and Co. offers their great services in their Ruby Valley office in Sheridan at 114 S. Main, 842-5028.

## 26. *Gas, Food, Lodging, Miscellaneous*

**F Crosswinds Restaurant**
1004 S. Atlantic St., Dillon. 683-6370

**L Creston Motel**
335 S. Atlantic St., Dillon. 683-2341. www.crestonmotel.uswestdx.com

The Creston Motel is a small, family-owned motel located in the heart of recreational southwestern Montana. The motel is located in a quiet residential neighborhood and offers 22 immaculately clean rooms. Amenities include air conditioning, queen size beds, cable TV, free local calls, and winter plug ins. Conveniently located with easy access to I-15, Western Montana College, the hospital, local restaurants and shopping. Hunting, fishing, camping, skiing, Sate parks, and snowmobiling are all nearby. In addition to their reasonable rates, they offer senior discounts and government/contractor rates. Pets are accepted.

**M Western Montana College of The University of Montana**
710 S. Atlantic, Dillon. 683-7011 or 800-962-6668. www.wmc.edu

Beginning in 1893 at Montana State Normal College, today Western Montana College has approximately 1,100 students. The school is known for it's liberal arts studies, especially in elementary and secondary education.

## 27.

**T Bannack State Park**
5 miles south of Dillon on 1-15, then 21 miles west on Secondary 278, then 4 miles south on county road. 834-3413

Bannack was the site of the state's first big gold strike in 1862 and the birthplace of Montana's government. Gold was discovered in Grasshopper Creek on July 28, 1862. This strike set off a massive gold rush that swelled Bannack's population to over 3,000 by 1863. The remnants of over 60 buildings show the extent of development reached during the town's zenith. When the gold ran out, the town died.

Montana's first territorial capital, was the site of many "firsts" in the state's history. Bannack had the first jail, hotel, chartered Masonic Lodge, hard rock mine, electric gold dredge, quartz stamp mill, and commercial sawmill. Bannack's two jails, built from hand-hewn logs, tell the story of the lawlessness that terrorized Grasshopper Gulch and the road to Virginia City. Road Agent's Rock, just a few miles from Bannack, was the lookout point for an organized gang of road agents, toughs, robbers, and murders. The infamous sheriff of Bannack, Henry Plummer, was secretly the leader of this gang called "The Innocents." The gang is said to have murdered over 102 men and robbed countless others during the eight months that Plummer served as sheriff. Many of their escapades were planned in Skinner's Saloon, which still stands in Bannack today. It could not last. Bannack's law-abiding citizens rose up and organized a vigilance group. In conjunction with a similar group in Virginia City, they quickly hunted down 28 of the "Innocents," including Henry Plummer, and hanged them on the gallows Plummer had just built.

"The Toughest Town in The West" soon grew quiet due to the reign of the vigilantes and a population of transient gold seekers that left to follow better gold strikes. However, gold mining activity continued for many years. The reputation of Bannack lives on today in Western history and fiction, forming the basis of many Western novels and movies. Many actors in the drama of early-day Bannack went on to play key roles in

Montana history. The mines and placer diggings are quiet now, but the streets of Bannack still echo with the footsteps of those who seek the rich lode of Western history that Bannack hoards like the gold once hidden in its hills and creeks. Over 50 buildings remain at Bannack today, each one with a story to tell…from tumble-down, one-room bachelor cabins to the once-stately Hotel Meade. The diggin's are quiet now, but the streets still ring with the footsteps of those seeking the rich lode of Western history that Bannack hoards like the gold once hidden in its hills…a moment in time for modern-day visitors to discover and enjoy.

Walk the deserted streets of Bannack, and discover for yourself the way the West really was. Bannack is one of the best preserved of all of Montana's ghost towns. Bannack is unique…preserved rather than restored…protected rather than exploited. Reprinted from Bannack State Park brochure.

### It Happened in Montana

January 11, 1864. A band of Vigilantes hangs Dutch John Wagner in Bannack from the beam of a building. Not finished with their work for the day, they proceed to the cabin of a man they call Mexican Frank. Two of the vigilantes storm through the cabin door but are shot and manage to scramble to safety. The Chief Justice of the Idaho Territory, Sidney Edgarton, lends them a small howitzer and shells. The men fire three of the shells into the cabin collapsing the structure. The Vigilantes find the suspect trapped under a beam. They tie a clothesline around his neck and hoist him to a pole before firing more than a hundred shots into the strangling man. They then create a bonfire from the remains of the cabin and throw the corpse on the pyre. Unfortunately, Mexican Frank was not home that day. The unfortunate victim was a man named Joe Pizanthia. He was not on their list of suspected road agents. Rather than admit the screwup, the Vigilantes spread the rumor that Pizanthia was "one of the most dangerous men that ever infested our frontier."

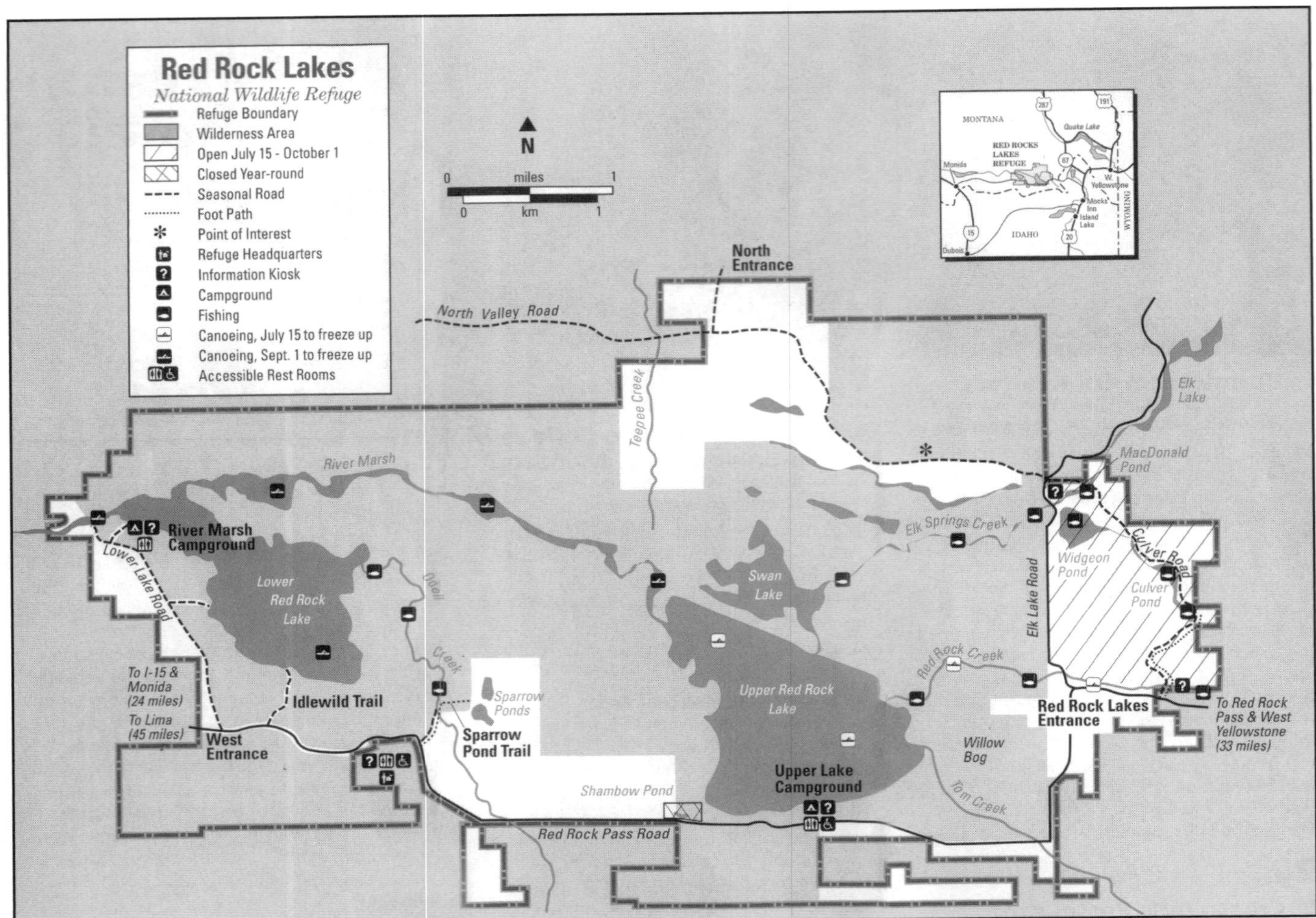


## 28. *Historic Marker, Lewis & Clark, Gas, Food*

### H Bannack

I-15. MP 55

*The Lewis and Clark Expedition, westward bound, passed here in August, 1805.*

*The old mining camp of Bannack is on Grasshopper Creek about twenty miles west of here. The first paying placer discovery in Montana was made in that vicinity by John White, July 28, 1862, and Bannack became the first capital of Montana Territory. They should have built it on wheels. The following spring six prospectors discovered Alder Gulch and practically the entire population of Bannack stampeded to the new diggings where the new camp of Virginia City eventually became the capital until it was changed to Helena.*

*Henry Plummer, sheriff and secret chief of the road agents, was hanged at Bannack in 1864 by the Vigilantes. It tamed him down considerably.*

### D Mer. Lewis

August 11, 1805

*"he suddonly turned his horse about, gave him the whip leaped the creek and disapeared in the willow brush in an instant. . .I now felt quite as much mortification and disappointment as I had preasure and expectation at the first sight of this indian."*

### D Mer. Lewis

August 17, 1805

*"Capt. Clark arrived with the Interpreter Charbono and the Indian woman who proved to be the sister of the Chief Cameahwait, tge meeting of those people wsa really affecting. . .we had the satisfaction. . .to find ourselves. . .with a flattering propect of being able to abtain as many horses shortly as would enable us to prosicute our voyage by land should that by water be deemed unadvisable."*

### D William Clark

July 12, 1806

*"this morning I was detained untill 7 A M makeing Paddles and drawing the nails of the Canoe to be left a this place and the one we had before left here."*

## 29. *Attraction*

### T Camp Fortunate Overlook and the Clark Canyon Recreation Area

I-15 S. of Dillon. 638-6472

Here Lewis and Clark expedition received horses from Sacajawea's brother, Chief Cameahwait, which were needed to cross the mountain ranges into the Columbia River drainage. The area is perfect for fishing, boating and camping. An interpretive memorial to Sacajawea is here. Clark Canyon Recreation Area has a man-made lake with great fishing for rainbow trout, or try the local favorite spot for water skiing.

### T Big Sheep Creek

I-15 exit at Dell, 24 miles north of the Montana-Idaho border. Northern terminus is Montana Route 324 west of Clark Canyon Dam.

This isolated, spectacular mountain valley is a narrow canyon with a good dirt road that often provides exceptional opportunities to view bighorn sheep and other wildlife.

### T Clark Canyon Reservoir

South of Dillon.

Clark Canyon Reservoir ranks as one of the finest places to catch large trout. Located 20 miles from Dillon it covers some six thousand acres and contains two major islands.

This great fishing haven didn't exist until 1964. Before this date, it was the location of the town named Armstead. The town was named after Harry Armstead, a local miner. It became the starting point of the Gilmore-Pacific Railroad, which

## Rockhounding

**Radar Creek area near Toll Mountain** southeast of Butte on Hwy. 2. Look here for smokey quartz crystals. At the Toll Mountain Campground look for limonite cubes. At the Boulder Batholith just east of Butte, look for quartz crystals.

Crystal Butte is about 8 miles west of Twin Bridges. This is a good place to find white quartz crystals.

Virginia City area. The gold rush may be over but you can still find placer deposits of gold in the tailings between Virginia City and Alder.

Sheridan area. Near Indian Creek west of town you can find white and honey-colored, banded masses of calcite.

Ruby Dam south of Alder is a good place to find calcite, garnets and opalite.

# Red Rock Lakes National Wildlife Refuge

## A Quiet Retreat for Wildlife and People

Red Rock Lakes National Wildlife Refuge (NWR) was established in 1935 to protect the rare trumpeter swan. Today, this 45,000-acre Refuge continues to be one of the most important habitats in North America for these magnificent migratory birds. The Refuge lies in the eastern end of the Centennial Valley near the headwaters of the Missouri River. The Centennial Mountains border the Refuge on the south and east and catch the heavy snows of winter, providing a constant supply of water that replenishes the Refuge's 14,000 acres of lakes and marshes. The flat, marshy lands of the valley floor merge into the rolling foothills of the Gravelly Range to the north. This ideal habitat provides the solitude and isolation that are so essential to the trumpeter swan.

The Refuge includes a designated Wilderness Area and is also a registered National Natural Landmark. These special habitats are managed to retain as much of the wilderness character and landscape as possible. Likewise, public use is managed to provide visitors the rare opportunity to experience isolation and solitude.

Red Rock Lakes National Wildlife Refuge is one of more than 500 refuges in the National Wildlife Refuge System - a network of public lands set aside specifically for wildlife. The U.S. Fish and Wildlife Service manages these lands to conserve wildlife and habitat for people today and for generations to come.

## Early Valley Visitors

The Centennial Valley was well known to the Bannock Indians as a favored travel route between the headwaters of the Big Hole River and Yellowstone country. Trapper Osborne Russell, in the mid-1800s, found many bison and signs of Blackfeet Indians in the valley. Settlement by the white man did not occur until 1876. With settlement, herds of livestock were driven into the valley, and homesteads sprang up at scattered locations.

In the early days, market hunting for waterfowl and big game brought some revenue to local residents, but most settlers concentrated on livestock and sporadic lumbering. The long winters, great distances to market, and small land parcels combined to make subsistence difficult. Few survived the depression of the 1930s. Visitors can still see some of the original homesteads on the Refuge today.

## Return of the Trumpeters

The trumpeter swan once ranged over much of the interior of the United States, but their numbers decreased as they were shot for their plume feathers and as their habitat diminished. By the early 1900s, only a remnant population was left in the tri-state area of southwestern Montana, southeastern Idaho, and northwestern Wyoming, as well as in parts of Canada and Alaska. Less that 100 swans were in the tri-state area in 1935 when the Refuge was established. The Refuge provided protection and seclusion, and swan populations increased. Their slow, steady growth continued until the nesting population peaked in the early 1960s.

Current trumpeter swan summer populations for the tri-state area average about 400 birds. This population grows to more than 2,000 trumpeter swans during fall as migrating birds arrive from Canada. Most winter in the nearby Madison River Valley, at Ennis Lake, along the Henry's Fork River, and further south into Idaho. About 25 trumpeter swans winter in secluded sites on the Refuge.

During the winter, the birds are limited to the confines of the open water on the Refuge and elsewhere within the tri-state area. In earlier years, wildlife managers believed that naturally available foods were insufficient to maintain the growing population. As a result, grain was provided for the swans at MacDonald and Culver Ponds during the severe winters. Wintering swan numbers increased and became crowded enough on the small Refuge ponds to raise concern for the potential spread of diseases. In 1992, biologists throughout the traditional migration route of the swan agreed that the birds should be encouraged to migrate to areas with larger natural bodies of open water. Consequently, the feeding program was discontinued.

The U.S. Fish and Wildlife Service has introduced swans from the Refuge to repopulate their former habitats in other areas. As a result, wild flocks of trumpeters are now reestablished in Oregon, Nevada, South Dakota, Nebraska, and Minnesota. Zoos and parks throughout the United States, Canada, and Europe exhibit trumpeter swans originating from Red Rock Lakes birds.

## Wildlife Refuge Throughout the Seasons

The diverse habitats of the Refuge attract a variety of wildlife species throughout the year. Each spring, greater sandhill cranes nest in the Refuge meadows and marshes. These long-legged birds are most easily observed in the open areas near Upper Red Rock Lake from April through September. Their courtship display and dance take place in April and May. Great blue herons, willets, avocets, and long-billed curlews are other conspicuous waders and shorebirds that frequently nest on the Refuge.

The Refuge's lakes, marshes, and creeks provide attractive habitats for a multitude of ducks. Eighteen different kinds of waterfowl, including the Barrows goldeneye, raise their young here each year. In October and November, thousands of ducks and geese congregate on the Refuge before their southward migration. Tundra swans often make their appearance on the Refuge in November.

The timber-covered slopes and aspen stands on the south side of the Refuge prove attractive to blue and ruffed grouse and many different songbirds and raptors. Brewer's sparrows are among the more common sagebrush residents.

Moose are year-round residents, but most of the elk, deer, and pronghorn are forced to migrate out of Centennial Valley due to the severe winters. Refuge visitors will encounter other familiar mammals such as red fox, badger, striped skunk, and Richardson's ground squirrel.

## Enjoy Your Visit

Feel free to enjoy recreational activities such as fishing, hunting, wildlife observation, photography, hiking, and camping at Red Rock Lakes NWR. The best time to visit the Refuge for most activities is from May through September.

Much of the Refuge can be seen from your car when the weather is good. To preserve the wilderness explorer spirit, there are no artificially-maintained back country hiking trails. Instead, nature provides many routes created by big game animals. You are welcome to cross-country hike throughout open areas of the Refuge, or follow big game routes and see the Refuge from the wildlife point of view.

Animals are best seen in the summer and fall during morning and evening hours. Visitors are encouraged to learn the habitats and behavior of specific animals, such as moose foraging in willow-covered streams, badgers digging holes in grasslands, and falcons swooping on concentrations of shorebirds. This is the key to successful wildlife viewing on the primitive, undeveloped landscape of the Refuge where artificial facilities have been minimized and wildlife is on the move.

Beginning in May, look for a myriad of wildflowers starting to appear on the Refuge. By July, the Refuge becomes a wildflower paradise. Shooting stars, buttercups, sticky geranium, and Indian paintbrush color the grasslands in hues of reds, pinks, blues, and yellows.

Staff is available at the Refuge headquarters during weekdays from 7:30 am to 4:00 pm to help you get oriented, answer questions, or provide more information.

*Reprinted from U.S. Department of the Interior Fish and Wildlife Service pamphlet.*

began operation in 1910 only to meet financial failure in 1941. The post office was active until 1962. After that most of the buildings were moved, the dam was built, and the area was flooded in 1964.

The dam is under the control of the East Bench Irrigation District and supplies most of the irrigation water to Dillon. It has easy access from I-15, has a perimeter road around the reservoir, picnic areas and a marina.

Fishing brings many people to try their luck at Clark Canyon. A boat or floating device is the preferred way to fish. Rainbow and brown trout, along with ling are the main species in the lake. Some trout can get as big as 10 pounds, thus making this a great destination spot for anyone who likes to catch big fish. Water skiing and jet skiing can also be enjoyed here.

### L Hildreth Livestock Guest Ranch

I-15 Exit 44, Hwy 324, to Medicine Lodge Road, south of Dillon. 681-3111.
www.greatdivideadventure.com

Hildreth Livestock Ranch is a nature adventurers' paradise in pristine Rocky Mountain country. Escape and be mesmerized by panoramas and sounds that delight the soul while being serenaded by abundant wildlife. Explore the mountainous territories including the Great Divide summit for nine continuous miles by hiking, cycling, or driving. Fish mountain lakes, streams, and the ranch's ponds. Two contemporary and ranch-style guesthouses are available with homemade sumptuous feasts. Notably, this ranch is the highest elevation home based ranch in Montana and one of the oldest continuously owned and operated in Beaverhead County. They are well known for the Chiangus cattle bred on the ranch. The area is geologically renowned for the Smithsonian Institute's Shatter Cone site. Complete information and directions are on web site.

## 30. *Historic Marker*

### H The Montana-Utah Road

I-15, Red Rocks

*Interstate 15 is the latest in a series of roads that have traversed this area since prehistory. Although used for generations by Native Americans, the first recorded use of this route was by the Lewis and Clark Expedition on August 10, 1805. They named cliffs to the north of here after the scores of rattlesnakes they encountered on their trip upriver. With the discovery of gold at nearby Grasshopper Creek and Alder Gulch in the early 1860s, thousands of people came to southwest Montana to mine gold and to "mine the miners." The road originated in Corinne, Utah and traversed a series of high plateaus and narrow canyons on its way north to southwestern Montana, The road was the best route into the territory for the freighters who supplied the mining camps. Drawn by teams of mules or oxen, each wagon carried up to 12,000 pounds of freight. The trip from Utah typically took three weeks and a freighting outfit could usually make three or four round trips each year, Just south of here near Dell, the Montana-Utah Road branched into three separate trails that led to Bannack, Deer Lodge, Virginia City and Helena. This section of the road terminated at Helena. With the arrival of the Utah & Northern Railroad in 1880, the Montana-Utah Road became obsolete. In the 1920s, however, it again became an important travel corridor first as the Vigilante Trail/Great White Way, then as U.S. Highway 91 and, finally, as Interstate 15.*

### H Old Trail to the Gold Diggins'

I-15, Red Rocks

*Along in the early 1840s the Americans were like they are now, seething to go somewhere. It got around that Oregon was quite a place. The Iowa people hadn't located California yet. A wagon train pulled out across the plains and made it to Oregon. Then everyone broke out into a rash to be going west.*

*They packed their prairie schooners with their household goods, gods, and garden tools. Outside of Indians, prairie fires, cholera, famine, cyclones, cloud bursts, quick sand, snow slides, and blizzards they had a tolerably blithe and gay trip.*

*When gold was found in Montana some of them forked off from the main highway and surged along this trail aiming to reach the rainbow's end. It was mostly one-way traffic but if they did meet a backtracking outfit there was plenty of room to turn out.*

## 31. *Attraction, Food*

### Dell

This town took its name from the topography of the surrounding area. It was once a station on the Union Pacific and was a trading center for valley ranchers. Not much there today except for one of the quirkiest little cafes you'll find anywhere. The Calf-A and Yesterday's Museum appear at first glance to be an old brick building with a junk shed next door. Don't turn away, the diner serves over 30,000 meals a year to people from all over the world. The diner is housed in the old schoolhouse with high ceilings and bare pine floors. Memorabilia lines the walls, the menu is written on the old blackboard, and the salad is on the teachers desk. The museum next door isn't your run-of-the-mill gallery either. It is a warehouse of everything left behind when the mining and lumbering petered out. The original owner, Ken Berthelson, is now deceased. Before going he left a number of wildlife sculptures in an outdoor sculpture corral. No, these aren't the magnificent bronze sculptures that seem to dominate Montana. They are created from just about anything Ken could put his hands on. There are lots of fine cafes in Montana, but not too many that you'll take pictures of for the folks back home.

### TF Yesterday's Cafe

I-90 Exit 23, Dell.

What do you do with an old school building in a virtual ghost town on an interstate exit? You could turn it into a cafe. That's what Ken Berthelson did. Actually, he only wanted the bell from the school, but got the whole building. The brick school building in the heart of "downtown" Dell was built in 1903 and stopped operating in 1963. Ken didn't just stop with starting a cafe. He gathered up a lot of the scraps from the fading community and started a museum next door. Today the diner serves more than 30,000 customers a year. The

guestbook logs visits from all over the world. It's certainly worth a stop.

## 32. *Gas, Food, Lodging*

### Lima

This hamlet sits close to the Idaho border on the Red Rock River. Like many towns in Montana, it has gone through several name changes. First Allerdice, then Spring Hill. The name that stuck was Lima, named after the Lima, Wisconsin hometown of settler Henry Thompson.

### Monida

Monida gets its name from its proximity to the Montana-Idaho border. Monida was once an important stop on the old Utah & Northern narrow-gauge railway which ran from Salt Lake City to Butte and Garrison. It was also a stage stop for the Monida-Yellowstone Park stagecoaches that met the trains.

## 34. *Attraction*

### H Sawtell's Ranch

Red Rock Lakes National Wildlife Refuge

*In 1868, Gilman Sawtell started a dude ranch and Henry's Lake fishery that did much to develop this natural resort area.*

*Sawtell did everthing from supplying swans for New York's Central Park zoo to building a network of roads for tourist access to Yellowstone National Park. His commercial fishery served Montana mining markets. His pioneer Henry's Lake ranch was a major attraction here for a decade before rail service brought more settlers to this area.*

### H The Shambo Stagecoach Station

Red Rock Lakes National Wildlife Refuge

*The historic Shambo waystation was once located on the opposite side of Shambo Pond. The station served as a livery and overnight stop for the M & Y stage line (Monida and Yellowstone) which acted as a link between the railhead at Monida, Montana and Yellowstone National Park The original outfit consisted of twelve 11-passenger and four 3-passenger Concord coaches with eighty horses and forty employees in 1898.*

*By 1915 the line brought In over forty percent of the more than twenty thousand people who entered Yellowstone National Park. In that year the "Red Line" was operating forty-five 11-passenger four-horse coaches; eight 11-passenger four-horse stages; thirteen 3-passenger two-horse surries; and sixty-one 5-passenger two-horse surries.*

*It was a big-time operation. The M & Y Line sold three different excursion trips from Monida through the park with either a return to Monida or to and exit from another gateway. It took one day to get from Monida to Dwell's, a ranch-hotel near the western boundary of the park—a distance of approximately 70 miles.*

*The Shambo family managed this station and were among the earliest settlers in the Centennial Valley. This pond and immediate area still carry their name.*

### T Red Rock Lakes National Wildlife Refuge

85 miles southeast of Dillon. 276-3536

The Red Rock Lakes National Wildlife Refuge is one of more than 500 National Wildlife Refuges across the United States. The Refuge was established in 1935 for the protection of trumpeter swans and other wildlife. Visitors to the Refuge will find a wildlife watcher's paradise. Trumpeter swans, bald, eagles, peregrine falcons, moose, elk, sandhill cranes, and a number of other species are often seen. Much of the Refuge lies within a 32,350-acre wilderness area that provides additional protection and habitat. The Refuge has been designated as a National Natural Landmark, recognizing its significance as one of the best remaining examples of the geologic and biologic character of our Nation's landscape.

For centuries, the Centennial Valley has been rich in fish and wildlife resources. Indians favored the Valley as a summer hunting area. Mountain men, trappers, cowboys, and settlers all left their mark on this remote corner of Montana. It was in this Valley and in Yellowstone National Park, that the last remaining trumpeter swans in the continental United States found refuge from the plume hunters of the early 1900s.

Today, The Centennial Valley is known for its abundant wildlife, scenic beauty, primitive landscape, and secluded tranquility. The 45,000-acre Red Rock Lakes National Wildlife Refuge is an integral part of the Valley and helps to maintain a balance between human needs and the needs of wildlife.

## Scenic Drives

**Highlands**

The Highlands offer several opportunities for scenic drives accessing the Highland Lookout and Humbug Spires. One drive provides a scenic loop which winds through the Highlands and Burton Park and ends at the Feeley interchange on Interstate 15. From Butte take Montana Highway 2 south eight miles to Roosevelt Drive (Forest Service Road #84). Follow the road for 19 miles to Interstate 15. The drive provides scenic vistas of the Highland Mountains and meadows with opportunities to view moose, elk and deer throughout the drive. To return to Butte from the Feeley interchange, take I-15 north to Interstate 90 and continue east to Butte four miles. This drive will take approximately one and a half to two hours to complete and will accommodate two-wheel drive vehicles during the summer.

**Delmoe Lake**

From Whitehall, head west on Interstate 90 to the Pipestone exit just below Homestake Pass and continue north on Forest Service Road #222. The road will take you through sagebrush grasslands, into the timber, provide spectacular mountain vistas, and then return to Interstate 90 at Homestake pass 20 miles later. Approximately ten miles from Pipestone is Delmoe Lake campground and picnic area. Delmoe Lake has the same oblong rounded boulder landforms that you see along Homestake Pass. It also has fishing opportunities and a boat ramp (no docking facility). The drive will take you approximately one and half to two hours to complete and is maintained for two-wheel drive vehicles during the summer.

**South Boulder, Tobacco Roots**

This drive will take you up into a scenic canyon with high peaks, alpine meadows and lakes. From Whitehall, head east on Interstate 90 to the Cardwell exit where you will take Montana Highway 359 south approximately six miles to the South Boulder turnoff, heading southwest. The road turns into Forest Service Road #107 and continues for approximately 14 miles passing through the old mining town of Mammoth. The road will lead into the canyon through several dispersed recreation areas which are popular for picnicking. At the upper end of the canyon there are opportunities to park and take short hikes to several alpine lakes. The road can be rough. The first 13 miles can be traveled in a passenger car, but high clearance or 4-wheel drive is recommended beyond. The road is generally open from mid May to mid September depending on snow conditions.

*Reprinted from U.S. Forest Service information handout.*

**Red Rocks Lake Wildlife Refuge Tour**

At one time, only a handful of the beautiful and graceful trumpeter swans remained in the Montana-Wyoming-Idaho area. To prevent their extinction in the area, Red Rock Lakes Wildlife Refuge in the Centennial Valley, was formed to offer the Trumpeters a refuge. Today, 400-500 swans call this area their home. Winter populations have been observed to reach as high as 1,500. Once you reach the refuge, the best place to observe the swans is in the open areas near Upper Red Rock Lake. April through September are the best viewing months.There are 18 other types of waterfowl at the refuge as well as moose, antelope, deer, and elk.

Depart from Dillon south on 1-15. Clark Canyon Reservoir is 21 miles from Dillon. Great fishing and boating here (many public campgrounds and one marina.) Camp Fortunate Historical Point from Lewis and Clark journey.

Continue south on 1-15 and drive 14 miles to Dell, Montana. From here you could elect to take the Sheep Creek/Medicine Lodge Backcountry Byway that ends back on Hwy 324—roads permitting. Also at Dell is the historic hotel that has been renovated and the old school house that is now a cafe.

From Dell, travel 9 miles south to Lima. Lima is a great little town with places to eat, sleep, camp, and a city park to picnic in.

From Lima continue on 1-15 for 14 miles to Monida, Montana. Go through this tiny town, heading east on a gravel road.

*Reprinted from Dillon Chamber of Commerce brochure.*

**Glendale-Vipond Park Loop Tour**

Take Interstate 15 north from Dillon 30 miles to Melrose exit.

Get off of 1-15, turn left into Melrose. Do not take any turns but continue through Melrose, across the bridge over the Big Hole River. Head west on the gravel road approximately 7 miles where you will come to a fork in the road. Take the Canyon Creek Road on the right. Continue approximately 7 miles to the site of the town of Glendale. Just above the townsite, you will find the famous Charcoal Kilns, where coal was made for the silver extraction process. The kilns have been under restoration the past few years by the Forest Service.

In the summer/fall (when roads are dry) you can continue on past the town on the back country by-way through the scenic Vipond Park area that eventually comes out on Hwy 43 near the small town of Dewey. From here you can either return to Dillon by turning right and traveling back to 1-15 or you can turn left and head west on Hwy 43 to Wise River and Wisdom.

Travel approximately 26 miles east to Lakeview and the Red Rock Lakes National Wildlife Refuge. Visit the Refuge Visitor Center. (This is an opportunity for great wildlife viewing and photography opportunities). Ask for road conditions and directions at the visitor center to return to Dillon via the scenic Blacktail Road. Elk Lake is also near this area.

*Reprinted from Dillon Chamber of Commerce brochure.*

**Yellowstone National Park via Virginia City**

Leave Dillon on Hwy 41 and travel 28 miles to Twin Bridges. In Twin Bridges turn right on Hwy 287 heading southeast 30 miles to Nevada City and Virginia City. Stop and enjoy both of these towns reminiscent of frontier days in Montana... many displays, exhibits, museums, etc.

From Virginia City, continue on Hwy 287 to Ennis, another fun town to visit with several large sculptures on display along the main street.

From Ennis, go south on Hwy 287, 41 miles to junction on Hwy 87 and Hwy 287. Continue on Hwy 287 around Hebgen Lake. Take time to stop at the Earthquake Area Visitor Center. Continue the 22 miles to the junction of Hwy 287 and Hwy 191. Turn right and go 8 miles to West Yellowstone. Stop at the Visitor Center for information concerning the Park.

*Reprinted from Dillon Chamber of Commerce brochure.*

## Hikes

### Whitehall Boulder Area

**Lost Cabin Lake Trail #150** (National Recreation Trail) Tobacco Root Mountains

The Lost Cabin Lake Trail begins at the west end of Bismark Reservoir. The trail is five miles in length, is well maintained and is on an easy grade. A few sections are steep, but they can be traveled by young persons or older individuals who are in good physical condition. The peaks surrounding the lake reach elevations above 10,000 feet. Mountain goats can often be seen on the cliffs to the south and east of the lake. Depending on snow, the trail is usually open from July 1 to the middle of October. Snow drifts on the trail may be abundant during years of late thaws.

From Interstate 90 take the Cardwell exit seven miles east of Whitehall. Take Montana Highway 359 south for approximately five miles to the South Boulder Road #107. Travel south on Road #107 for approximately 15 miles to the trailhead at Bismark Reservoir. Passenger cars can drive this road, but the last two miles are best traveled by high clearance vehicles.

**Louise Lake Trail #168** (National Recreation Trail)

Louise Lake Trail offers very scenic views. This is a new trail 3.5 miles in length and replaces a shorter steeper trail that was hard to maintain and partly located on private land. Louise Lake is a high alpine lake cradled among the 10,000-foot peaks that surround the lake. Mountain goats can often be spotted on the sheer rock faces. The trail is open from July 1 to the middle of October. Snowdrifts on the trail may be abundant during years of late thaws.

From Interstate 90, take Cardwell exit seven

# Beaverhead National Forest

**Located in Southwest Montana, the** Beaverhead-Deerlodge National Forest is the largest of the national forests in Montana. The forest offers breath-taking scenery for a wide variety of recreation pursuits. Whether it's wilderness trekking in the Anaconda-Pintler or Lee Metcalf wildernesses, driving the Gravelly Range Road or Pioneer Mountains Scenic Byway, or camping in one of the 50 small to medium-sized campgrounds in the forest, the Beaverhead-Deerlodge has it all. Winter enthusiasts find snowmobiling, cross-country skiing trails, as well as downhill skiing at Discovery, near Anaconda, and Maverick Mountain, near Dillon. Summertime affords chances to hike and drive primitive routes to high-mountain lakes or to drive more improved roads to places like Delmoe and Wade lakes. The Continental Divide National Scenic Trail and Nez Perce Historic Trail pass through the forest. Georgetown Lake offers winter and summer recreation near Philipsburg. At the ghost towns of Elkhorn and Coolidge, you can relive Montana's boom and bust past. Sheepshead Recreation Area, north of Butte, offers pleasant picnicking and lake fishing, accessible for the disabled. The Forest covers 3.32 million acres.

Directions:
The headquarters in Dillon is located on Interstate 15 just 63 miles north of the Utah border.

Beaverhead-Deerlodge National Forest
USDA Forest Service
420 Barrett Street
Dillon, MT 59725-3572
Phone: 406-683-3900
Email:Mailroom_R1_Beaverhead_Deerlodge@fs.fed.us

*Reprinted from www.recreation.gov*

miles east of Whitehall. Take Montana Highway 359 south for approximately five miles to South Boulder Road #107. Travel south on Road #107 approximately 15 miles to the trailhead at Bismark Reservoir. This road can be driven by passenger cars, but the last two miles are best traveled by a high clearance vehicles.

**Brownback Trail #156**
Brownback Trail follows Brownback Gulch, a scenic narrow rocky canyon. The lower portion of the trail is mostly open country covered with grass, shrubs, and a few trees. It offers viewing of wildflowers, occasionally elk, deer, and a variety of other plants, animals, and birds. The trail is four miles long one way, and has an easy grade. The trail is open from mid May to mid November. This is a good trail to hike when the rest of the high country is still snowed in.

From Interstate 90, take the Cardwell exit seven miles east of Whitehall. Take Montana Highway 359 south for approximately five miles to South Boulder Road #107.

Travel south on Road #107 for four miles. Just past the Indiana University Geological Field station turn right on Forest road #5104 and travel one mile to the trailhead. There is parking for several cars and a horse unloading ramp.

*Reprinted from U.S. Forest Service pamphlet*

**"M" Trail**
The "M" that looks down on Montana Tech was constructed in 1910 by students. Since its construction it has been fitted with lights so it can be seen at night. Unlike the "M"s in Missoula and Bozeman, you can actually drive up to the base of this landmark or hike to it from the college. It does provided some excellent views of the city. To get there take the Montana St. Exit on I-90 and head north to Park Ave. Go left to Excelsior St. and turn right. Follow Excelsior to Hornet and go left to the J.F. Kennedy Elementary School on Emmet and Hornet streets. Drive up the hill past the school for about .3 miles to a dirt road which turns to the left. Follow this to the turnaround just below the "M" and park.

**Humbug Spires**
is 26 miles south of Butte, Montana, along the western foot-hills of the Highland Mountains. It was designated a Primitive Area in 1972. About 8,800 acres of the 11,175-acre Humbug Spires Wilderness Study Area has been recommended for inclusion in the National Wilderness Preservation System.

Humbug Spires is characterized by rolling hills of Douglas fir and lodgepole pines accentuated by majestic granite spires. Lush meadows, dense forests and grassy flats are found throughout the area. Humbug offers many opportunities for primitive and unconfined recreation. The primary uses are hiking, stream fishing, rock climbing, backpacking, wildlife watching, nature photography, hunting, snowshoeing, cross country skiing and horseback riding.

To reach the area, take 1-15 to the Moose Creek interchange and go east about 3 miles along the creek on an improved gravel road. Park at the trail head parking lot. To reach the hiking trail, cross the foot bridge just downhill from rest room and the visitor information board. Humbug's main trail goes northeast from here along Moose Creek, passing through stands of Douglas fir trees more than 250 years old.

After about 1.5 miles, the trail forks. Take the right fork marked by white arrows. The trail continues for .3 miles up a small side drainage over a ridge, and then along the northeast fork of Moose Creek. From this drainage, numerous game trails leading in all directions are available to the adventurous hiker. These trails provide access to the rock spires located throughout the northern part of the area. To reach the "Wedge," one of the more prominent spires, continue 1.3 miles up the main trail along the intermittent creek. The Wedge is about a hundred yards uphill from an abandoned miner's cabin at the head of the drainage.

Given the diverse topography of the heavily timbered terrain, visitors hiking off the designated trail should have topographic maps, a compass, and drinking water. United States Geologic Survey 7-1/2 minute quadrangle maps cover the area and are available locally. You will need the Tucker Creek, Mount Humbug, Melrose and Wickiup quads for full coverage.

Offsite camping facilities are provided at BLM's Divide Bridge Campground, about 2 miles west of the Divide Interchange along Highway 43 on the west side of the Big Hole River.

*Reprinted from BLM brochure.*

## Cross-Country Ski Trails

### Beaverhead-Deerlodge National Forest

*For more information contact District Ranger Dillon, MT 59725 (406) 683-3900*

**Elkhom Hot Springs Ski Trails-37 mi. NW Dillon**
*233 km Most Difficult; no grooming*
Trail begins at plowed parking lot near Elkhom Hot Springs Resort Trail system consists of several loops with approximately 1000 ft of climb- Trail map available.

**Birch Creek-21 mi. NW Dillon**
*5.0 km More Difficult; no grooming*
Trail begins across Birch Creek bridge on the Birch Creek road about 1 mile west of the junction with the Willow Creek road. Trail map available.

## Information Please

All Montana area codes are 406

### Road Information

Montana Road Condition Report
800-226-7623, 800-335-7592 or local 444-7696
Montana Highway Patrol 444-7696
**Local Road Reports**
Butte 494-3666
Statewide Weather Reports 453-2081

### Tourism Information

Travel Montana 800-847-4868 outside Montana
444-2654 in Montana
http://travel.mt.gov/.
Gold West Country 846-1943 or 800-879-1159
www.goldwest.visitmt.com
Northern Rodeo Association 252-1122
**Chambers of Commerce**
Butte-Silver Bow 723-3177
Twin Bridges 684-5259
Virginia City 843-5555
Whitehall 287-2260

### Airports

Butte 494-3771
Dell 444-2506
Twin Bridges 684-5574

### Government Offices

State BLM Office 255-2885, 238-1540
Bureau of Land Management
Billings Field Office 896-5013
Butte Field Office 494-5059
Beaverhead/Deerlodge National Forest, Butte 522-2520
Helena National Forest 449-5201
Red Rock Lake Wildlife Refuge 276-3536
Montana Fish, Wildlife & Parks 994-4042
U.S. Bureau of Reclamation
Dillon Field Office 683-6472
Helena Field Office 475-3310

### Hospitals

Highland View • Butte 782-2391
St. James Community Hospital • Butte 782-8361
Barrett Memorial Hospital • Dillon 683-2323
Ruby Valley Hospital • Sheridan 434-5536

### Golf Courses

Beaverhead Golf Club • Dillon 683-9933
Red Rock Golf Course • Lima 276-3555

Highland View Golf Course • Butte 494-7900

## Bed & Breakfasts

**Copper King Mansion B&B** • Butte 782-7580
**Bennett House Country Inn**
Virginia City 843-5220
**Just An Experience** • Virginia City 843-5402
**Scott Inn Bed & Breakfast** • Butte 723-7030
**The Centennial Inn** • Dillon 683-4454
**Lynch's Lair B&B** • Alder 842-5699
Bannock Pass Ranch • Dillon 681-3229
Horse Prairie Inn • Dillon 681-3144
Healing Waters Lodge • Twin Bridges 684-5960
Iron Wheel Guest Ranch • Whitehall 494-2960
Montana Mountain Inn • Sheridan 842-7111
Stonehouse Inn • Virginia City 843-5504

## Guest Ranches & Resorts

**Hildreth Livestock Guest Ranch**
Dillon 681-3111
**Fairmont Hot Springs Resort**
Fairmont 797-3241
Broken Arrow Lodge & Outfitters
Alder 842-5437
Canyon Creek Guest Ranch • Melrose 276-3288
Centennial Guest Ranch • Ennis 682-7292
Crane Meadow Lodge • Twin Bridges 684-5773
Diamond J Ranch • Ennis 682-4867
Divide Wilderness Ranch • Lakeview 276-3300
Elk Lake Resort • Lima 276-3282
Great Waters Inn • Melrose 835-2024
Healing Waters Fly Fishing Lodge
Twin Bridges 684-5960
Hidden Valley Guest Ranch • Dillon 683-2929
Madison Valley Ranch • Ennis 682-4514
Ruby Springs Lodge • Alder 842-5250
T Lazy B Ranch • Ennis 682-7288
Upper Canyon Ranch & Outfitting
Alder 842-5884

## Vacation Homes & Cabins

**Mountain Home-Montana Vacation Rentals**
Bozeman 586-4589
Arrow Cross Cabins • Dillon 835-2103
Back Country Angler • Dillon 683-3462
Beaverhead Rock Ranch Guest House
Dillon 683-2126
Big Hole River Bunkhouse • Dillon 835-2501
Big Trout Ranch • Twin Bridges 684-5995
Centennial Outfitters • Lima 276-3463
CT Cabin Rentals • Dillon 683-2791
Goose Down Ranch • Dillon 683-6704
Hawke's Nest • Alder 842-5698
Jim McBee Outfitters • Dillon 276-3478
Rod & Rifle Inn • Sheridan 842-5960
Torrey Mountain Log Cabin Rental
Dillon 683-4706

## Forest Service Cabins

***Beaverhead-Deerlodge National Forest***

**Hells Canyon Cabin**
30 mi. SW of Whitehall, MT 287-3223
Capacity: 4 Nightly fee: $20 Available: All year
Road to cabin not plowed. Access distance varies with snow conditions.

**Black Butte Cabin**
30 mi S of Ennis MT 20 mi NW on Standard Cr Rd 682-4253
Capacity: 4 Nightly fee: $20 Available: 7/1 - 4/30
Depending on snow conditions, snowmobile travel may be necessary. Refer to Travel Plan Map regulations.

**Canyon Creek Cabin**
13 mi. W of Melrose, MT 832-3178
Capacity: 4 Nightly fee: $15 Available: All year
Winter access varies with snow conditions, normally can drive to cabin with 4-wheel unit; otherwise, road may be blocked 6 miles from cabin.

**Notch Cabin**
41 mi S of Sheridan, MT 682-4253
Capacity: 3 Nightly fee: $20 Available: 7/2 - 12/1
Remote cabin. Access by road with 4-wheel drive vehicle. Access to Snowcrest Trail.

**Antone Cabin**
34 mi. SE of Dillon 682-4253
Capacity: 3 Nightly fee: $20 Available: 12/1-3/1
Depending on snow conditions, snowmobile travel of up to 6 miles may be required. Access is from Blacktail Road.

**Vigilante**
25 mi. S of Alder 682-4253
Capacity: 6 Nightly fee: $50 Available: All year
Frame house w/2 bedrooms, living room, kitchen, electric lights. Water not available in fall & winter.

**Fleecer**
20 mi. SW of Butte 494-2147
Capacity: 6 Nightly fee: $40 Available: 11/1-5/1
Has electricity, heat, water. Winter access by snowmobile or skis.

**High Rye**
16 mi. SW of Butte 494-2147
Capacity: 4 Nightly fee: $20 Available: 5/15-12/1
High clearance vehicle access. Has three beds.

## Private Campgrounds

Armstead Campground • Dillon 683-4199
Countryside RV Park • Dillon 683-9860
Hunter's Beaverhead Marina & RV Park
Dillon 683-5556
KOA Kampgrounds • Alder 842-5677
KOA Kampgrounds • Butte 782-0663
LA Rue Mountain View • Butte 494-3211
Beaverhead Marina & RV Park • Dillon 683-5556
KOA Kampgrounds • Dillon 683-2749
Pipestone Campground • Butte 287-5224
Skyline RV Park • Dillon 683-4692
Southside RV Park • Dillon 683-2244
Lee's RV Park • Lima 276-3535
Red Rock RV Park • Lima 276-3555
Stardust RV Park • Twin Bridges 684-5648
2 Bar Lazy H RV Park & Campground
Butte 782-5464
Virginia City Campground • Virg. City 843-5493

## Car Rental

Avis Rent-A-Car 494-3131
Budget Rent-A-Car of Butte 494-7573
Enterprise Rent-A-Car 494-1900
Hertz Rent-A-Car 782-1054
U-Save Auto Rental 494-6001

## Outfitters & Guides

*F=Fishing H=Hunting R=River Guides*
*E=Horseback Rides G=General Guide Services*

Allaman's Montana Adventure Trips G 843-5550
Al Wind's Trout Futures F 684-5512
Atcheson Outfitting H 782-2382
Back Country Angler F 683-3462
Beaverhead Anglers F 683-5565
Beavertail Outfitters F 683-6232
Bloody Dick Outfitters HFE 681-3163
Broken Arrow Lodge & Outfitters GE 842-5437
Cargill Outfitters GHFE 494-2960
Centennial Outfitters GHF 276-3463
Cougar Ridge Outfitters HFE 2767-3288
Coyote Outfitters Inc G 684-5769
Crane Meadow Lodge GFH 684-5773
Curry Comb Outfitters FH 276-3306
Dave Wellborn Outfitter FH 681-3117
Diamond Hitch Outfitters FHE 683-5494
Divide Wilderness Ranch GHFW 276-3300
Eric Troth Fly Fishing Guide F 683-9314
Experience Montana FG 842-5134
Fish Montana/Bar Six Outfitters F 683-4005
Five Rivers Lodge F 683-5000
Flatline Outfitter & Guide Service GF 684-5639
Four Rivers Fishing Company GF 684-5651
Frontier Anglers HF 683-5276
Garrett's Guide Service F 683-5544
Great Divide Outfitters GHFE 267-3346
Greg Lilly Fly Fishing Services GF 684-5960
Harmon's Fly Shop F 842-5868
Horse Prairie Outfitters HF 681-3173
Jim McBee Outfitters & Guides HF 276-3478
Last Best Place Tours G 681-3131
Lone Tree Fly Goods F 683-2090
M&M Outfitters HF 683-4579
Montana High Country Tours FG 683-4920
Montana Peaks Fly Fishing F 683-3555
Mossy Horn Outfitters HFE 491-2236
Southwest Montana Fishing Co. F 842-5364
Sundown Outfitters GHEF 835-2751
Tim Tollett's Frontier Anglers GF 683-5276
Tom's Fishing & Bird Hunting Guide Service
GF 723-4753
Watershed Fly Fishing Adventures F 683-6660
Uncle Bob's Fishing Supplies GF 683-5565
Upper Canyon Ranch & Outfitting GE 842-5884
Watershed Fly Fishing Adventures GF 683-6660

## Cross-Country Ski Centers

Elkhorn Hot Springs
50 mi. NW of Dillon 586-9070

## Snowmobile Rentals

All Seasons Adventures • Butte 723-4637

## Notes:

| Fishery | Brook Trout | Mt. Whitefish | Lake Whitefish | Golden Trout | Cutthroat Trout | Brown Trout | Rainbow Trout | Kokanee Salmon | Bull Trout | Lake Trout | Arctic Grayling | Burbot | Largemouth Bass | Smallmouth Bass | Walleye | Sauger | Northern Pike | Shovelnose Sturgeon | Channel Catfish | Yellow Perch | Crappie | Paddlefish | Vehicle Access | Campgrounds | Toilets | Docks | Boat Ramps | MotorRestrictions |
|---|---|---|---|---|---|---|---|---|---|---|---|---|---|---|---|---|---|---|---|---|---|---|---|---|---|---|---|---|
| | **Cold Water Species** | | | | | | | | | | | | **Warm Water Species** | | | | | | | | | | **Services** | | | | | |
| 78. Big Hole River | • | • | | | | • | • | | | | | | | | | | | | | | | | • | • | • | | • | |
| 79. Beaverhead River | | • | | | | • | • | | | | | | | | | | | | | | | | • | • | • | | • | |
| 80. Poindexter Slough | | • | | | | • | • | | | | | | | | | | | | | | | | | | | | | |
| 81. Blacktail Deer Creek | • | • | | | • | | • | | | | | | | | | | | | | | | | | | | | | |
| 82. Branham Lakes | • | | | | | | | | | | | | | | | | | | | | | | • | | | | | |
| 83. Twin Lakes | • | | | | | | | | | • | | • | | | | | | | | | | | • | • | • | | • | • |
| 84. Ruby River Reservoir | | • | | | | • | • | | | | | | | | | | | | | | | | • | • | • | | • | |
| 85. Ruby River | | • | | | • | • | • | | | | | | | | | | | | | | | | • | • | • | | | |
| 86. Big Sheep Creek | | • | | | | • | • | | | | | | | | | | | | | | | | • | • | • | | | |
| 87. Red Rock River | | • | | | | • | • | | | | | | | | | | | | | | | | | | | | | |
| 88. Clark Canyon Reservoir | | • | | | | • | • | | | | | • | | | | | | | | | | | • | • | • | • | • | |

**NOTES:**

## Motel Quick Reference

Price Range: ($) Under $40 ; ($$) $40-$60; ($$$) $60-$80, ($$$$) Over $80. Pets [check with the motel for specific policies] (P), Dining (D), Lounge (L), Disabled Access (DA), Full Breakfast (FB), Cont. Breakfast (CB), Indoor Pool (IP), Outdoor Pool (OP), Hot Tub (HT), Sauna (S), Refrigerator (R), Microwave (M) (Microwave and Refrigerator indicated only if in majority of rooms), Kitchenette (K). All Montana area codes are 406.

| HOTEL | PHONE | NUMBER ROOMS | PRICE RANGE | BREAKFAST | POOL/ HOT TUB SAUNA | NON SMOKE ROOMS | OTHER AMENITIES | CREDIT CARDS | MAP LOCATOR NUMBER |
|---|---|---|---|---|---|---|---|---|---|
| **Rice Motel** | 2887-3895 | 10 | $ | | | | P | Major | 2 |
| Chief Motel | 287-3921 | 16 | $ | | | | K/P/D/M/R/L | Major | 2 |
| Whitehall Super 8 | 287-5588 | 33 | $$ | | HT | Yes | P/DA | Major | 2 |
| **Best Western Butte Plaza Inn** | 494-3500 | 134 | $$$/$$$$ | FB | IP/HT/S | Yes | P/D/M/R/L/DA | Major | 5 |
| **Butte Super 8 Motel** | 494-6000 | 104 | $/$$ | CB | | Yes | P/DA | Major | 5 |
| **Hampton Inn** | 494-2250 | 91 | $$$ | CB | IP/HT | Yes | DA | Major | 5 |
| Comfort Inn Of Butte | 494-8850 | 150 | $$ | CB | HT | Yes | P/DA | Major | 5 |
| Motel 6 | 782-5678 | 66 | $$ | | | Yes | P | Major | 5 |
| Red Lion Hotel | 494-7800 | 131 | $$$ | | HT/IP | Yes | R/L/P | Major | 5 |
| **Ramada Copper King Inn** | 494-6666 | 148 | $$$ | | IP/HT/S | Yes | P/D/L/M/R/DA | Major | 6 |
| Skookum Motel & Restaurant | 494-2153 | 25 | $$ | | | Yes | D/L/P | Major | 6 |
| **Holiday Inn Express** | 494-6999 | 83 | $$-$$$ | CB | | Yes | M/R/DA | Major | 7 |
| War Bonnet Inn | 494-7800 | 131 | $$$ | | IP/HT/S | Yes | P/M/R/DA | Major | 7 |
| Days Inn | 494-7000 | 74 | $$-$$$ | CB | HT | Yes | P/M/R/DA | Major | 7 |
| **Scott Bed & Breakfast** | 723-7030 | | | | | | | | 9 |
| **Copper King Mansion B&B** | 723-7580 | | | | | | | | 9 |
| **Capri Motel** | 723-4391 | 30 | $$ | CB | HT | Yes | DA | Major | 9 |
| **Finlen Hotel & Motor Inn** | 723-5461 | 50 | $/$$ | | | Yes | M/F | Major | 9 |
| Eddy's Motel | 7234364 | 28 | $$ | | | Yes | D/L | Major | 9 |
| **King's Motel** | 684-5639 | 12 | $$ | | | Yes | K/R | Major | 13 |
| Hemingways Lodging & Fly Shop | 684-5648 | 6 | $ | | | Yes | P | Major | 13 |
| **Moriah Motel** | 842-5491 | 12 | $$ | | | Yes | DA | Major | 14 |
| Mill Creek Inn | 842-5442 | 6 | $$ | | | Yes | D/L/DA/P | Major | 14 |
| **Chick's Motel & RV Park** | 842-5366 | 4 | $$ | | | Yes | DA/P | Major | 15 |
| **Lynch's Lair B&B** | 842-5699 | | | | | | | | 15 |
| **The Bennett House Country Inn** | 843-5220 | 5 | $$$ | FB | HT | Yes | | Major | 16 |
| **Just an Experience B&B** | 843-5402 | 5 | $$$ | FB | | Yes | | Major | 16 |
| Nevada City Hotel & Cabins | 843-5377 | 30 | $$–$$$$ | | | Yes | P/DA | V/M/D | 16 |
| Fairweather Inn | 843-5377 | 15 | $$ | | | Yes | | Major | 16 |
| Stonehouse Inn | 843-5504 | 5 | $$$ | FB | | | FB | | 16 |
| **Rocker Inn** | 723-5464 | 50 | $$ | | | Yes | P/L/M/F | Major | 18 |
| Big Hole River Inn | 823-3296 | 6 | $ | | | Yes | D/L | | 19 |
| Sportsman Motel | 835-2141 | 8 | $$ | | | Yes | P | Major | 19 |
| **GuestHouse Inns & Suites** | 683-3636 | 58 | $$/$$$ | | IP/HT | Yes | K/P/M/R/DA | Major | 23 |
| Comfort Inn | 683-6831 | 48 | $$ | CB | IP | Yes | | Major | 23 |
| **Super 8 Dillon** | 683-4288 | 48 | $$ | | | Yes | P/M/R/DA | Major | 24 |
| Best Western Paradise Inn | 683-4214 | 65 | $$ | | IP/HT | Yes | P/D/L | Major | 24 |
| Sacajawea Motel | 683-2381 | 15 | $ | | | Yes | K/P | V/M/D | 24 |
| **Sundowner Motel** | 683-2375 | 32 | $$ | CB | | Yes | P | Major | 25 |
| **Centennial Inn Bed & Breakfast** | 683-4454 | | | | | | | | 25 |
| Metlen Hotel Bar & Cafe | 683-2335 | 32 | $ | | | | | | 25 |
| **Creston Motel** | 683-2341 | 22 | $$ | | | Yes | P/DA | Major | 26 |
| **Hldreth Livestock Guest Ranch** | 681-3111 | | | | | | | | 29 |
| Red Rock Inn | 276-3501 | 7 | $$$ | | | Yes | R/L | Major | 31 |
| Sportsman Inn | 276-3535 | 18 | $ | | | Yes | K/P/M/R | Major | 32 |

**NOTES:**

## Dining Quick Reference

Price Range refers to the average cost of a meal per person: ($) $1-$6, ($$) $7-$11, ($$$) $12-up. Cocktails: "Yes" indicates full bar; Beer (B)/Wine (W), Service: Breakfast (B), Brunch (BR), Lunch (L), Dinner (D). Businesses in bold print will have additional information under the appropriate map locator number in the body of this section.

| RESTAURANT | TYPE CUISINE | PRICE RANGE | CHILD MENU | COCKTAILS BEER WINE | SERVICE | CREDIT CARDS | MAP LOCATOR NUMBER |
|---|---|---|---|---|---|---|---|
| **Crazy Bear Pizza** | Pizza | $ | Yes | | L/D | Major | 2 |
| **Land of Magic, Too** | steaks | $$ | yes | | D | major | 2 |
| A & W Family Restaurant | Fast Food | $ | Yes | | L/D | | 2 |
| Borden's Cafe | American | $ | Yes | Yes | B/L/D | | 2 |
| Subway | Fast Food | $ | Yes | | L/D | | 2 |
| Two-Bit Saloon & Grill | Regional American | $ | Yes | Yes | B/L/D | Major | 2 |
| 4B's Restaurant | Family | $ | Yes | | B/L/D | V/M/D | 5 |
| Arby's | Fast Food | $ | Yes | | B/L/D | | 5 |
| Asia Gardens | Asian | $$ | | | L/D | Major | 5 |
| Burger King | Fast Food | $ | Yes | | B/L/D | | 5 |
| Four B'S Restaurant | Family | $-$$ | Yes | | B/L/D | Major | 5 |
| Kentucky Fried Chicken/A&W | Fast Food | $ | Yes | | L/D | | 5 |
| McDonald's | Fast Food | $ | Yes | | B/L/D | | 5 |
| Perkins Family Restaurant | Family | $/$$ | Yes | | B/L/D | Major | 5 |
| Pizza Hut | Pizza | $/$$ | Yes | B | L/D | V/M/D | 5 |
| Plaza Royale Casino & Restaurant | American | $$ | | Yes | B/L/D | Major | 5 |
| Subway | Fast Food | $ | Yes | | L/D | | 5 |
| Taco Bell | Fast Food | $ | Yes | | L/D | | 5 |
| Taco John's | Fast Food | $ | Yes | | L/D | | 5 |
| Wendy's | Fast Food | $ | Yes | | L/D | | 5 |
| **Grama's Homestyle Buffet** | Buffet | $ | | Yes | L/D/BR | V/M | 6 |
| Dairy Queen | Fast Food | $ | Yes | | L/D | | 6 |
| Lamplighter Inn | American | $$$ | Yes | Yes | D | Major | 6 |
| Lydia's | Steakhouse | $$/$$$ | Yes | Yes | D | Major | 6 |
| Ponderosa Club | American | $$/$$$ | | Yes | L/D | Major | 6 |
| Prospector Cafe | Steaks/Seafood | $/$$ | | Yes | B/L/D | V/M/D | 6 |
| Silver Bow Pizza Parlor | Pizza | $ | Yes | Yes | L/D | V/M | 6 |
| Skookum Motel & Restaurant | American | $$ | | Yes | L/D | | 6 |
| **Pork Chop John's** | Fast Food | $ | Yes | | L/D | | 7 |
| Arctic Circle | Fast Food | $ | Yes | | L/D | | 7 |
| Copper City Restaurant | American | $ | | Yes | B/L/D | | 7 |
| Denny's | Family | $ | Yes | | B/L/D | V/M | 7 |
| Domino's Pizza | Pizza | $ | | | L/D | | 7 |
| El Taco | Fast Food | $ | Yes | | L/D | | 7 |
| Hardee's | Fast Food | $ | Yes | | B/L/D | | 7 |
| It's Greek To Me | Greek | $ | | | L/D | | 7 |
| Joe's Pasty Shop | Pastys | $ | | B/W | L/D | | 7 |
| Little Caesar's | Pizza | $ | | | L/D | | 7 |
| Papa John's Pizza | Pizza | $ | Yes | | L/D | | 7 |
| Taco John's | Fast Food | $ | Yes | | L/D | | 7 |
| The Derby | American | $/$$ | Yes | Yes | L/D | V/M | 7 |
| War Bonnet Inn | Fine Dining | $/$$ | Yes | Yes | B/L/D | Major | 7 |
| **Uptown Cafe** | Eclectic | $-$$$ | | Yes | L/D | Major | 9 |
| **Pork Chop John's** | Fast Food | $ | Yes | | L/D | | 9 |
| **Columbian Garden Espresso** | Coffee House | $ | Yes | | B/L | Major | 9 |
| **Northwest Noodle 'n Wrap** | Asian | $ | Yes | | L/D | V/M | 9 |
| **Acoma Restaurant & Lounge** | Continental | $$/$$$ | no | Yes | L/D | Majors | 9 |
| Bonanza Freeze | Fast Food | $ | Yes | | L/D | | 9 |
| Dairy Queen | Fast Food | $ | Yes | | L/D | | 9 |
| El Taco Dos | Fast Food | $ | Yes | | L/D | | 9 |
| Gold Rush Casino | Family | $/$$ | Yes | Yes | B/L/D/SB | V/M/D | 9 |
| Joker's Wild Restaurant | Family | $ | Yes | Yes | B/L/D | Major | 9 |
| La Cosina Mexican Restaurant | Mexican | $$ | Yes | Yes | L/D | V/M | 9 |
| M&M Bar & Cafe | American | $ | | Yes | B/L/D | | 9 |
| Metals Banque | Bistro | $$ | | Yes | L/D | Major | 9 |
| Ming's Chinese Restaurant | Chinese | $/$$ | | | L/D | V/M | 9 |
| Rancho Los Arcos Mexican | Mexican | $ | Yes | | L/D | V/M | 9 |
| Spaghettini's | Italian | $/$$ | Yes | W/B | L/D | V/M | 9 |
| Subway | Fast Food | $ | Yes | | L/D | | 9 |
| Blue Anchor Cafe | Family | $—$$$ | Yes | Yes | B/L/D | | 13 |
| The Old Hotel | Fine Dining | $$ | | B/W | D | V/M | 13 |

## Dining Quick Reference-Continued

Price Range refers to the average cost of a meal per person: ($) $1-$6, ($$) $7-$11, ($$$) $12-up. Cocktails: "Yes" indicates full bar; Beer (B)/Wine (W), Service: Breakfast (B), Brunch (BR), Lunch (L), Dinner (D). Businesses in bold print will have additional information under the appropriate map locator number in the body of this section.

| RESTAURANT | TYPE CUISINE | PRICE RANGE | CHILD MENU | COCKTAILS BEER WINE | SERVICE | CREDIT CARDS | MAP LOCATOR NUMBER |
|---|---|---|---|---|---|---|---|
| The Shack Homemade Pizza & Subs | Pizza/Sub | $$ | | | L/D | | 13 |
| **The Weaver's Studio** | Coffee House | $ | | | | | 13 |
| Three Rivers Cenex | Fast Food | $ | | B | L/D | Major | 13 |
| Prospector Drive-in | Fast Food | $ | Yes | | L/D | | 14 |
| Ruby Hotel Steakhouse | American | $/$$ | | Yes | L/D | | 14 |
| Sheridan Bakery & Cafe | Homestyle | $ | | | B/L | | 14 |
| Alder Steakhouse | Steakhouse | $$ | Yes | Yes | D | V/M | 15 |
| Star Bakery | Gourmet | $$/$$$ | | | B/L/D | | 16 |
| Banditos at the Wells Fargo | Southwestern | $$/$$$ | Yes | Yes | L/D/BR | V/M | 16 |
| Bob's Place | Deli | $/$$ | Yes | | L/D | Major | 16 |
| Lynch's Virginia City Cafe | Family | $/$$ | | Yes | B/L/D | | 16 |
| Madison Dinner House | American | $/$$$ | Yes | | B/L/D | Major | 16 |
| Mexican Frank's Restaurant | Fast Food | $ | Yes | | L/D | | 16 |
| Roadmaster Grill | American | $-$$$ | | B/W | B/L/D | Major | 16 |
| Arby's | Fast Food | $ | Yes | | B/L/D | | 18 |
| Four B'S Restaurant | Family | $-$$ | Yes | | B/L/D | Major | 18 |
| Thad's Flying J Restaurant | Family | $ | Yes | | B/L/D | Major | 18 |
| Big Hole River Inn | Family | $$ | | Yes | B/L/D | | 19 |
| Dessert Daves Pizza & Pastry | Pizza | $ | | | L/D | | 19 |
| Melrose Cafe | Family | $ | | | B/L/D | V/M | 19 |
| Kentucky Fried Chicken | Fast Food | $ | Yes | | L/D | | 24 |
| McDonald's | Fast Food | $ | Yes | | B/L/D | | 24 |
| Pizza Hut | Pizza | $/$$ | Yes | B | L/D | V/M/D | 24 |
| Subway | Fast Food | $ | Yes | | L/D | | 24 |
| The Lion's Den | American | $$$ | Yes | Yes | L/D | V/M/D | 24 |
| Best Western Paradise Inn | Family | $$ | | Yes | B/L/D | Major | 24 |
| **Blacktail Station** | Steaks & Seafood | $$/$$$ | Yes | Yes | L/D | Major | 25 |
| **Sweetwater Coffee** | coffee house | $ | | | B/L | | 25 |
| Klondike Cafe & Supper Club | Family | $$ | | Yes | B/L/D | V/M | 25 |
| Las Carmelitas | Mexican | $ | Yes | | L/D | V/M/D | 25 |
| Papa T'S | Family | $/$$ | Yes | Yes | L/D | V/M | 25 |
| Stageline Pizza | Pizza | $/$$ | | | L/D | | 25 |
| The Peppermint Stick | Family/Ice Cream | $/$$ | Yes | B/W | L/D | V/M/D | 25 |
| Rookies | Family | $/$$ | | Yes | B/L/D | | 25 |
| Western Wok | Chinese | $$ | Yes | Yes | L/D | Major | 25 |
| **Crosswinds Restaurant** | Family | $/$$ | | | B/L/D | V/M | 26 |
| Dairy Queen | Fast Food | $ | Yes | | L/D | | 26 |
| Rookies Sports Pub & Grill | American | $ | Yes | B/W | L/D | V/M/D | 26 |
| Blondies Burgers | Fast Food | $ | | | L/D | | 26 |
| Taco John's | Fast Food | $ | Yes | | L/D | | 26 |
| Big Sky Truck Stop | Family | $ | Yes | B | B/L/D | Major | 28 |
| **Yesterday's Café** | Family | $/$$ | Yes | | B/L/D | | 31 |
| Jan's Cafe 'n' Cabins | Family | $/$$ | Yes | | B/L/D | V/M | 32 |

**NOTES:**

## Public Campgrounds

# Campsite Directions

| Campsite Directions | Season | Camping | Trailers | Toilets | Water | Boat Launch | Fishing | Swimming | Trails | Stay Limit | Fee |
|---|---|---|---|---|---|---|---|---|---|---|---|
| **87•Delmoe Lake FS**<br>Homestake Exit off I-90 E of Butte•10 mi. on Forest Rd. 222 | 5/26-9/17 | 25 | 32′ | • | • | • | • | • | | 16 | • |
| **88•Toll Mountain FS**<br>15 mi. W of Whitehall on MT 2•3 mi. N on Forest Rd. 240 | 5/25-9/15 | 5 | 22′ | D | | | | | • | 16 | |
| **89•Pigeon Creek FS**<br>15 mi. W of Whitehall on MT 2•5 mi. S on Forest Rd. 668. | 5/25-9/15 | 6 | | • | • | | • | | • | 16 | |
| **90•Divide Bridge BLM**<br>2.5 mi. W of Divide on MT 43 | All Year | 25 | 24′ | D | • | A | • | | B | 14 | • |
| **91•Humbug Spires BLM**<br>I-15 S of Divide•Moose Creek Exit•3 mi. NE on Moose Creek Rd. | All Year | • | 24′ | • | | | | | B | 14 | |
| **92•Maidenrock FWP**<br>I-15 at Melrose•Milepost 93•6 mi. W & N on Cty. Rd. | All Year | 30 | • | • | • | B | • | | | 7 | |
| **93•Barretts Park USBR**<br>5 mi. S of Dillon on I-15 | All Year | • | • | D | • | B | • | | | 14 | |
| **94•Bannack FWP**<br>5 mi. S of Dillon on I-15•21 mi. W on Rt. 278•4 mi. S on Cty. Rd. | All Year | 20 | • | D | • | | • | | | 7 | • |
| **95•Mill Creek FS**<br>7 mi. E of Sheridan on Mill Creek Rd. | 6/1-10/31 | 13 | 22′ | • | •f | | | | | 16 | |
| **96•Ruby Reservoir BLM**<br>S of Twin Bridges on MT 287 to Alder•S to E shore of Ruby River Reservoir | All Year | 10 | 35′ | • | | C | • | • | | 14 | |
| **97•Cottonwood FS**<br>36 mi. S of Alder•Follow Ruby Reservoir Rd. off MT 287 | 5/26-11/30 | 10f | • | • | | | | | | | |
| **98•East Creek FS**<br>8 mi. SW of Lima on Cty. Rd. 1791•1 mi. S on Forest Rd. 3929•1 mi. SE on Forest Rd. 3930 | 5/15-10/1 | 4 | 16′ | • | • | | | | | 16 | |
| **99•CLARK CANYON RESERVOIR USBR•Lonetree USBR**<br>Clark Canyon Reservoir•20 mi. S of Dillon on I-15 | All Year | • | • | D | • | B | • | | | 14 | |
| **100•CLARK CANYON RESERVOIR USBR•Hap Hawkins USBR**<br>Clark Canyon Reservoir•20 mi. S of Dillon on I-15 | All Year | • | • | D | • | | • | | | 14 | |
| **101•CLARK CANYON RESERVOIR USBR•West Cameahwait USBR**<br>Clark Canyon Reservoir•20 mi. S of Dillon on I-15 | All Year | • | • | d | • | | • | | | 14 | |
| **102•CLARK CANYON RESERVOIR USBR•Cameahwait USBR**<br>Clark Canyon Reservoir•20 mi. S of Dillon on I-15 | All Year | • | • | D | 0 | | • | | | 14 | |
| **103•CLARK CANYON RESERVOIR USBR•Horse Prairie USBR**<br>Clark Canyon Reservoir•20 mi. S of Dillon on I-15 | All Year | • | • | D | • | C | • | | | 14 | |
| **104•CLARK CANYON RESERVOIR USBR•Lewis & Clark**<br>Clark Canyon Reservoir•20 mi. S of Dillon on I-15 | All Year | • | • | D | • | | • | | | 14 | |
| **105•CLARK CANYON RESERVOIR USBR•Fishing Access USBR**<br>Clark Canyon Reservoir•20 mi. S of Dillon on I-15 | All Year | • | • | D | • | C | • | | | 14 | |
| **106•CLARK CANYON RESERVOIR USBR•Beaverhead USBR**<br>Clark Canyon Reservoir•20 mi. S of Dillon on I-15 | All Year | • | • | D | • | C | • | | | 14 | |
| **107•Beaver Dam FS**<br>5 mi. W of Butte on I-90•12 mi. S on I-15•6 mi. W on Forest Rd. 96 | 5/25-9/15 | 15 | 50′ | • | • | | • | | • | 16 | • |
| **108•Dinner Station FS**<br>12 mi. N of Dillon on I-15•12 mi. NW on Birch Creek Rd. | 5/15-9/15 | 7 | 16′ | D | • | | • | | • | 16 | |

**Agency**
FS—U.S.D.A Forest Service
FWP—Montana Fish, Wildlife & Parks
NPS—National Park Service
BLM—U.S. Bureau of Land Management
USBR—U.S. Bureau of Reclamation
CE—Corps of Engineers

**Camping**
Camping is allowed at this site. Number indicates camping spaces available
H—Hard sided units only; no tents

**Trailers**
Trailer units allowed. Number indicates maximum length.

**Toilets**
Toilets on site. D—Disabled access

**Water**
Drinkable water on site

**Fishing**
Visitors may fish on site

**Boat**
Type of boat ramp on site:
A—Hand launch
B—4-wheel drive with trailer
C—2-wheel drive with trailer

**Swimming**
Designated swimming areas on site

**Trails**
Trails on site
B—Backpacking N—Nature/Interpretive

**Stay Limit**
Maximum length of stay in days

**Fee**
Camping and/or day-use fee

Section 6

# Section 7

## The Bitterroot Valley, Bighole Valley, and Georgetown Lake Including Anaconda, Hamilton and Deer Lodge

*Along the Bitterroot River*

## Weather Averages

**Hamilton**

| January | |
|---|---|
| Average High: | 34.5° F |
| Average Low: | 16.2° F |
| Average Precip.: | 1.04 in |
| **April** | |
| Average High: | 59.0° F |
| Average Low: | 32.7° F |
| Average Precip.: | 0.91 in |
| **July** | |
| Average High: | 84.9° F |
| Average Low: | 49.9° F |
| Average Precip.: | 0.88 in |
| **October** | |
| Average High: | 60.2° F |
| Average Low: | 32.7° F |
| Average Precip.: | 0.91 in |

**Discovery Basin Ski Area**

| January | |
|---|---|
| Average High: | 30.8° F |
| Average Low: | 14.6° F |
| Average Precip.: | 0.80 in |
| **April** | |
| Average High: | 50.8° F |
| Average Low: | 29.5° F |
| Average Precip.: | 1.06 in |
| Average High: | 79.5° F |
| Average Low: | 51.3° F |
| Average Precip.: | 1.32 in |
| **October** | |
| Average High: | 55.0° F |
| Average Low: | 33.8° F |
| Average Precip.: | 0.89 in |

**Lost Trail/Powder Mountain Ski Area**

| January | |
|---|---|
| Average High: | 30.8° F |
| Average Low: | 14.6° F |
| Average Precip.: | 0.55 in |
| **April** | |
| Average High: | 50.8° F |
| Average Low: | 29.5° F |
| Average Precip.: | 1.00 in |
| **July** | |
| Average High: | 79.5° F |
| Average Low: | 51.3° F |
| Average Precip.: | 1.23 in |
| **October** | |
| Average High: | 55.0° F |
| Average Low: | 33.8° F |
| Average Precip.: | 0.74 in |

**1.** *Historic Marker, Attraction, Gas, Food, Lodging*

### Anaconda

Anaconda was founded in 1883 by Marcus Daly, one of the Copper Kings of the area who personally picked this spot for the smeltering process because of its ample water and limestone. It is home to the largest smokestack in the world, a remnant of the glory days of mining. The town in the mouth of a narrow valley near the Continental Divide grew up around the giant smelter built by Marcus Daly. Daly picked the site for his smelter when the air quality in the booming town of Butte was being fouled by Butte's smelters. Only 35 miles from Butte, Daly liked this site because it was near ample water and limestone.As the story goes, Daly saw a cow grazing in the valley, pointed to it and said he wanted the Main Street of his new town to run north and south right through the cow. The town was platted in 1883 and named Copperopolis. Shortly after that, the postmaster found out there was already in Copperopolis in Meagher County, and renamed the city for the giant mine in Butte.

It is said that when copper is in demand, both smelter and town prosper; but when the mines are quiet, so is Anaconda. Interestingly, the name Anaconda is not related to copper, but comes from a newspaper reference to the large, South American snake bearing this name. Michael Hickey was a Union Army veteran and an adventurous Irish miner. He had once read an article by Horace Greeley describing Grant's army "encircling Lee's forces like a giant anaconda." As Hickey recalled, "That word struck me as a mighty good one. I always remembered it, and when I wanted a name for my mine, I remembered Greeley's editorial and called it the 'Anaconda.'" Hickey's mine led to one of Butte's richest copper veins. Later, the world's largest copper mining, smeltering and fabricating organization took the name—the Anaconda Copper Mining Company.

Anaconda opens the door to the Pintler Primitive area, Deerlodge National Forest, Lost Creek State Park, Discovery Ski Basin, the Big Hole Battlefield, Georgetown Lake and ghost towns west of town. In nearby mountains, sapphires, garnets, fossils and gold can be found to the delight of rock-hunters of every age.

### Fairmont

Fairmont, known for the Fairmont Hot Springs and Resort, is located between Anaconda and Butte just off of I-90. The hot springs fill four pools, two of them olympic size. Into the pools are water slides which makes this a great place for kids. Pools are open year round and average temperatures in the various pools range from 86 to 105 degrees F. The pools are open to the public with admission charged. Early records show that hot springs were first settled in the 1860s and has been operated as a resort since 1869. The springs were named Fairmont Hot Springs in 1972, and named after the owner's similar property in British Columbia. Today, soakers have a choice of indoor and outdoor pools in a modern, upscale environment.

### H Atlantic Cable Quartz Lode

west of Anaconda

*This mining property was located June 15, 1867, the name commemorating the laying of the second transatlantic cable.*

*The locators were Alexander Aiken, John B. Pearson and Jonas Stough. They were camped on Flint Creek and their horses drifted off. In tracking them to this vicinity the men found float that led to the discovery.*

*Machinery for the first mill was imported from Swansea, Wales, and freighted by team from Corinne, Utah, the nearest railroad point.*

*The mine was operated with indifferent success until about 1880 when extremely rich ore was opened up, a 500 ft. piece of ground producing $6,500,000 in gold. W. A. Clark paid $10,000 for one chunk of ore taken from this mine in 1889 and claimed it was the largest gold nugget ever found.*

### H Anaconda

east edge of Anaconda

*Selected by Marcus Daly as a smelter site in 1883 because of an abundant supply of good water, Anaconda was the home of the Washoe Smelter of the*

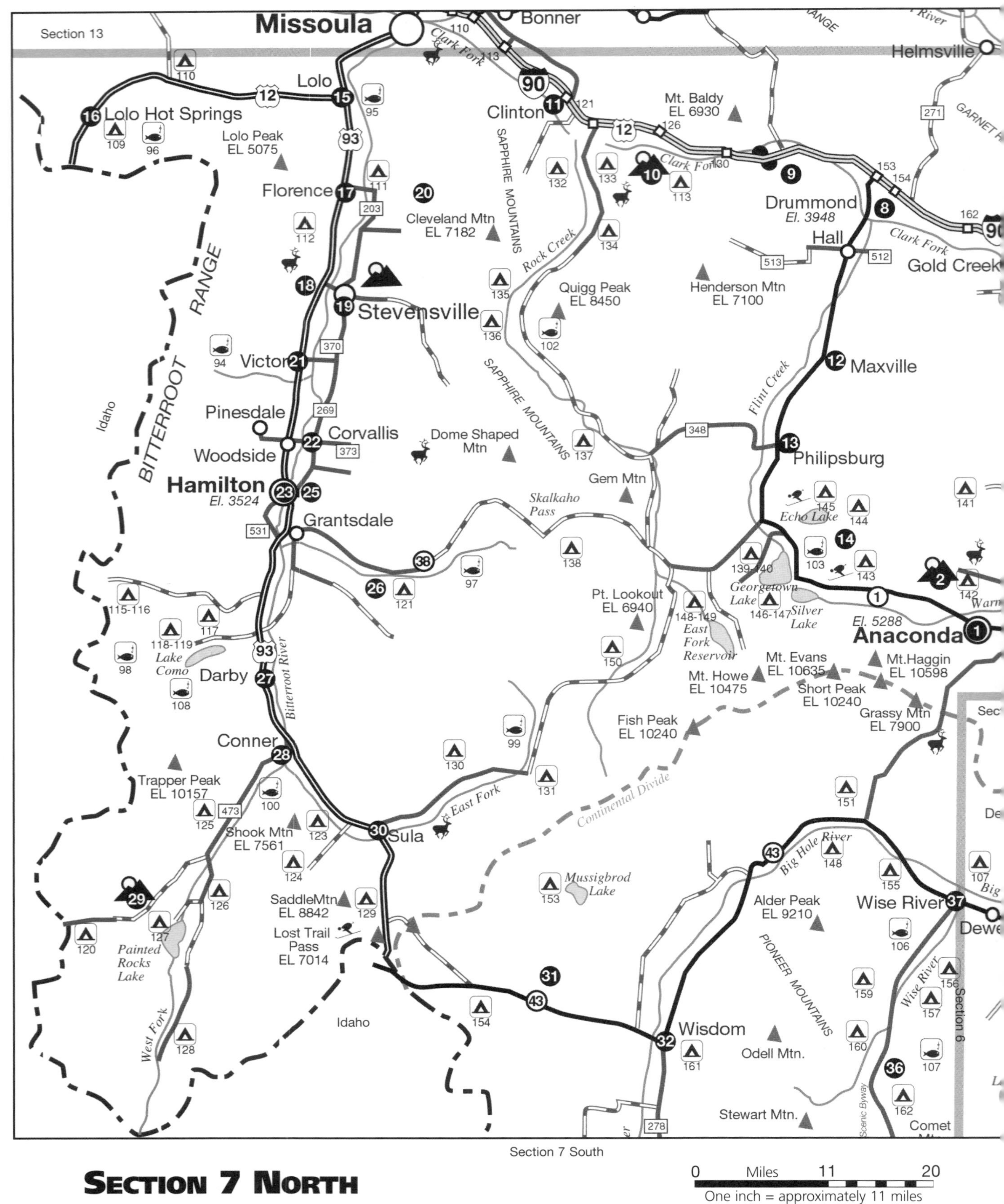


Section 7 South

# Section 7 North

0 Miles 11 20
One inch = approximately 11 miles

Section 13
Stemple Pass EL 6376
279
Section 8
Nevada Creek
141
Dearborn Mtn. EL 7460
Mullan Pass EL 5902
Avon
Elliston
Garrison
Blackfoot R.
Little
McDonald Pass EL 6320
104
105
179
180
184
Deer Lodge
El. 4531
4
5
187
90
182
183
Basin
197
3
181
184-185
151
156
122
15
201
Warm Springs
Opportunity
186
138
Whitetail Peak EL 8476
211
134
216
219
Elk Park Pass EL
Butte
El. 5787

Legend
Locator number (matches numeric listing in section)
Wildlife viewing
Campsite (number matches number in campsite chart)
State Park
Fishing Site (number matches number in fishing chart)
Rest stop
Interstate
U.S. Highway
State Highway
County Road
Gravel/unpaved road

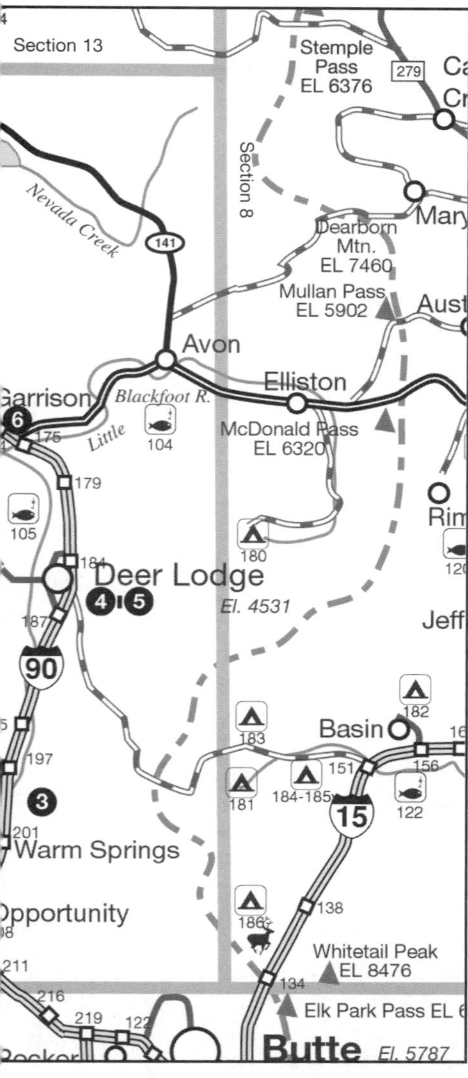

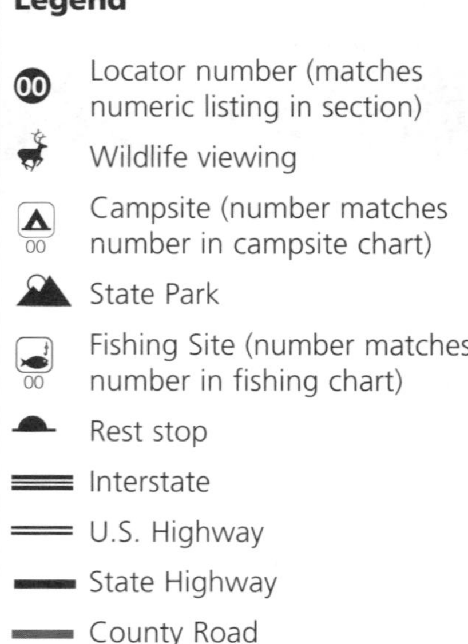

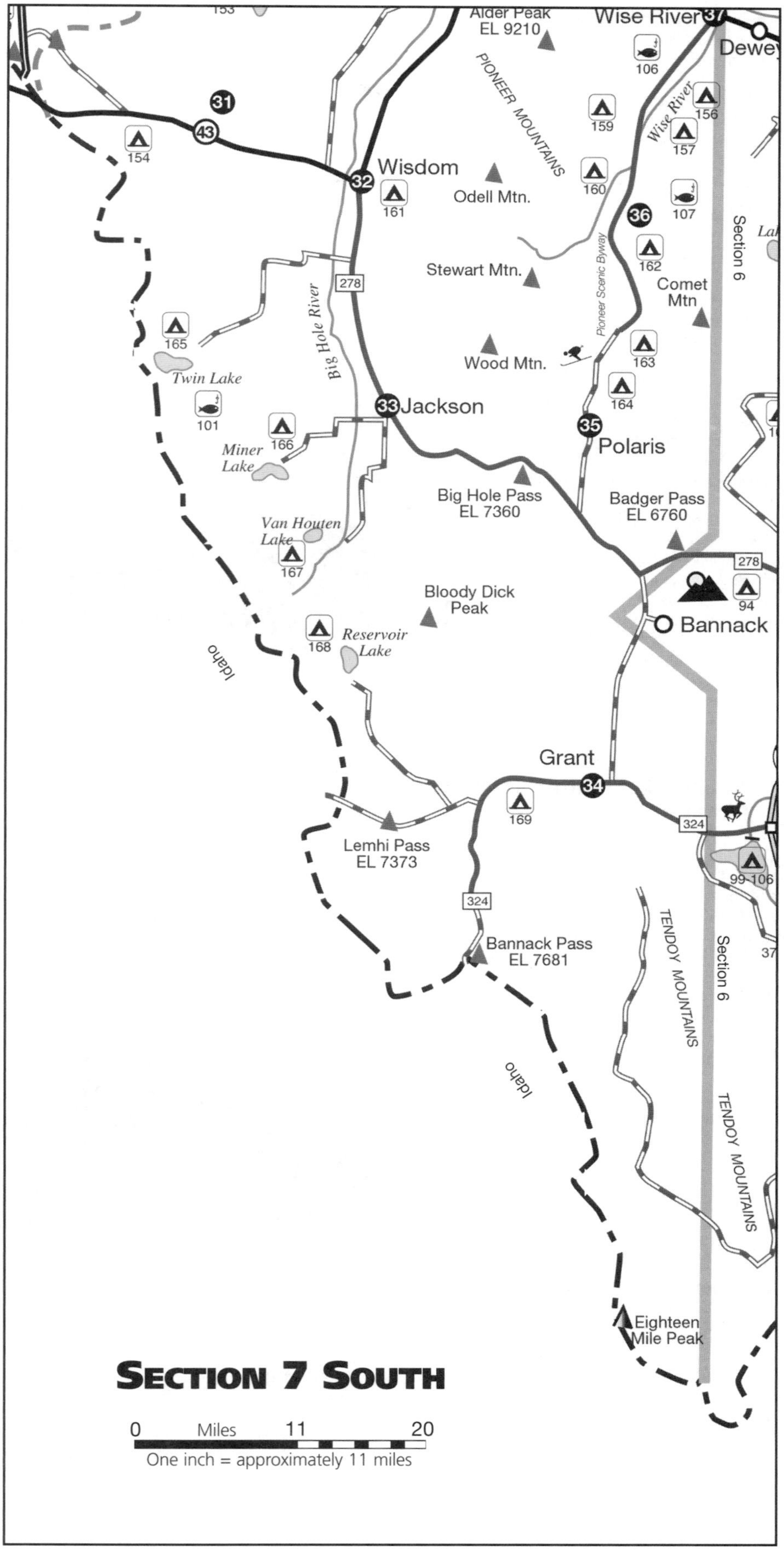

Alder Peak EL 9210
Wise River
37
Dewey
106
31
43
154
PIONEER MOUNTAINS
159
156
157
Wise River
Wisdom
32
161
Odell Mtn.
160
107
36
162
Section 6
278
Stewart Mtn.
Comet Mtn
Pioneer Scenic Byway
165
Big Hole River
Wood Mtn.
163
Twin Lake
164
101
33 Jackson
35
166
Polaris
Miner Lake
Big Hole Pass EL 7360
Badger Pass EL 6760
Van Houten Lake
167
278
Bloody Dick Peak
94
168
Reservoir Lake
Bannack
Idaho
Grant
34
169
324
Lemhi Pass EL 7373
99-106
324
Bannack Pass EL 7681
TENDOY MOUNTAINS
Section 6
Idaho
TENDOY MOUNTAINS
Eighteen Mile Peak
Section 7 South
0 Miles 11 20
One inch = approximately 11 miles

*Anaconda Copper Mining Company until 1980. History has been made here in the science of copper smelting, and the plant is famous throughout the mining and metallurgical world.*

From a straggling tent town Anaconda grew to be a modern city, but retained all of the aggressive spirit of the pioneer days. This spirit refused to die with the Anaconda Co. pullout and the town remains a vital community.

### H Washoe Theater
Downtown Anaconda

*Seattle-based theater architect B. Marcus Pinteca (890-1971) drew the plans for this remarkable structure in 1930. However, the Depression delayed interior finishing and the $200,000 movie theater did not open until 1936. The Washoe Theater and Radio City Music Hall in New York were the last two American theaters built in the Nuevo Deco style, a lavish form popular for vaudeville theaters. From the street, the Washoe's restrained brick exterior gives little indication of the breath-taking splendor that lies beyond the etched glass doors. Designer Nat Smythe of Hollywood created the sumptuous interior, adorning the walls and ceilings with murals. Colors of cerulean blue, salmon, rose, beige and yellow are enhanced by abundant copper plating, silver and gold leaf, and ornamental ironwork. Two magnificent stags are hand-painted on the blue silk plush curtain that graces the stage. Early advertisements extolled the fine "Mirrophonic Sound" system and the large capacity auditorium that seated 1,000 movie-goers. Admission for first-run films was thirty-five cents. Today, the Washoe is one of the best preserved theaters in the United States, with original fixtures and equipment still in place and in use. It is all the more remarkable for its Depression-era birth when movie theaters were built on a grand scale but no longer so opulently furnished.*

### T Anaconda Smelter Stack (No direct access)
In Anaconda on Montana 1. 542-5500.

This giant chimney holds two titles: it is the largest free-standing masonry structure on earth, and the highest chimney on earth. Constructed in 1918, it is all that remains of the once largest non-ferrous copper smelter in the world. It's outside diameter is 86 feet at the base and 75 feet inside. It tapers to 60 feet wide at the top. It is 585 feet tall and was constructed with 2,464,672 acid-resistant blocks (equal to 6,672,214 ordinary bricks), and weighs 23,810 tons. To place the blocks required 41,350 sacks of cement, 77 cars of sand (50 tons a car) and 37 cars of fire clay. The base was created with 20,891 sacks of cement, 50 cars of sand, 118 cars of crushed rock, and 5,100 cubic yards of concrete. Construction took 142 actual eight-hour shifts with 12 bricklayers a shift. The workers used 305,000 board feet of lumber. It is large enough to hide the Washington Monument inside its massive structure. There is no direct access to the stack, but you won't miss seeing it from the road.

### T Washoe Theater
Main between 3rd and 4th in Anaconda

The Washoe Theater in Anaconda is ranked as the fifth most beautiful theater in the nation by the Smithsonian Institute. While the exterior appears as many smalltown theaters of times gone by, the interior is stunning in its decor. Original Art Deco light fixtures and furnishings are set off by ornate silver, copper, and gold leaf accents. Ceiling and wall murals decorate the interior hallways. Elegant light fixtures look down on the deep carpet of the stairs and second floor. Sitting inside the 1,000 seat theater, the visitor is overwhelmed by the opulent decor. Hand painted curtains depict rearing deer in gold and red against a turquoise background. Mosaic murals line the walls and hand carved ram's heads line the ceiling. The dome of the theater is decorated with a mural done in soft pastel shades of powder blue, red, and yellow. The scene illustrates modern civilization's dependence on copper. The pilasters and proscenium surrounding the stage are decorated in eight shades of gold and accented with copper leaf.

The Washoe was designed by Seattle architect B. Marcus Priteca and built during the glory days of the movie industry. During that time, huge, elaborate movie palaces were constructed in homage to the filmmakers. Few but the Washoe still stand today.

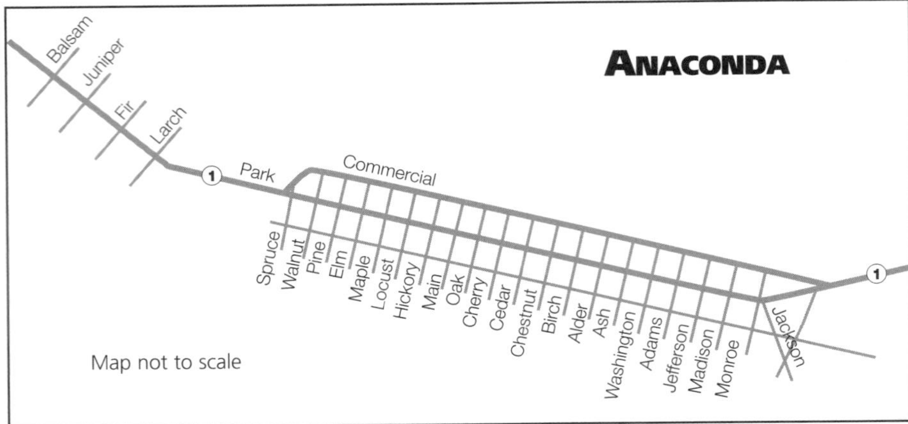

### T Copper Village Museum & Art Center
401 E. Commercial Ave., Anaconda. 563-2422

A dream of copper magnate Marcus Daly was to make Anaconda the state capital. For that reason, he spared no expense in making Anaconda's buildings spectacular. One example of his largess is the Anaconda City Hall which was built in 1895. Constructed of local materials, its pressed brick and Anaconda granite is trimmed with Anaconda copper. In its day, it was the finest city hall in the northwest. In 1976 the building was boarded up and abandoned when the city moved its offices to the County Courthouse. In 1982, Copper Village Museum and Arts Center along with the local Historical Society renovated the building and transformed it into a regional cultural center. Today, the building houses an art gallery, retail shops, a crafts center and the historical museum.

### T City Hall Historical Museum
401 E. Commercial Ave., Anaconda. 563-2422

The artifacts and information collected here tell not only the story of Anaconda, the smelter, and the county, but of the settlement of the west reflecting the perspective of individuals, and the political, social and industrial milieu of the time. The museum is open Tuesday through Saturday from 1–4 p.m.

### F Barclay II Supper Club & Lounge
1300 E. Commerical Ave., Anaconda. 563-5541

Sandy Mattson and the Barclay II Supper Club will welcome you to elegant dining in Anaconda. This superb restaurant has been family owned and operated by three generations for over 20 years. Prepare yourself to enjoy a full seven course meal. There are menu choices from a large selection of steak, seafood, chicken, veal, and pasta entrees. The lounge offers a full bar, and with one of the friendliest bartenders around. Barclay II is well known for the excellent selection of wines, beers and of course, Barclay's own "ice cream drinks." People who visit Anaconda return to this elegant, yet relaxed restaurant time after time. The food is memorable and delicious, just like the dining experience you will enjoy here.

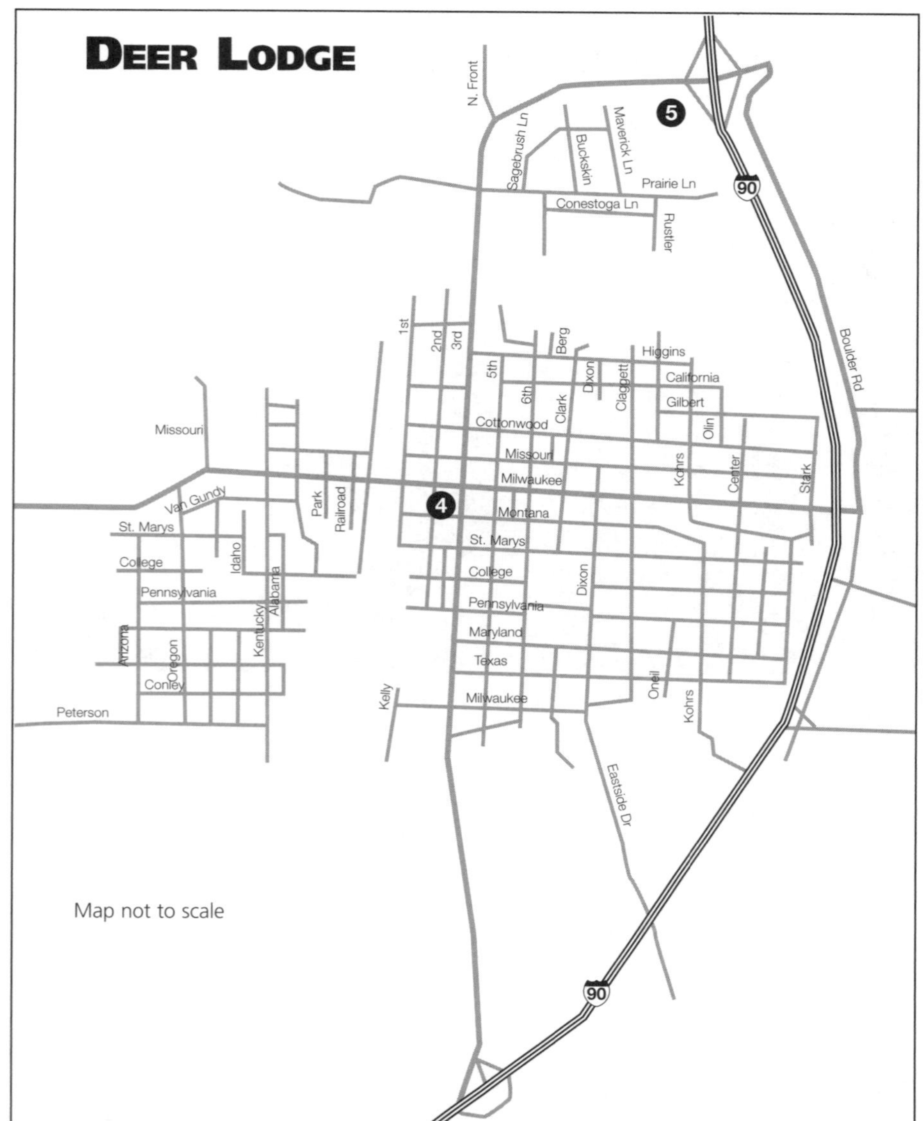

## F Subway Sandwiches

200 Main Street, Anaconda. 563-6570.
www.subway.com

Savor Subway's famous sandwiches while enjoying the surroundings of the historical Montana Hotel built in the late 1800's. Subway offers a variety of wraps, freshly baked breads, soups and salads made fresh daily. The Subway menu is known for fresh, low fat, great tasting, custom made delicious sandwiches for every taste. The dining area at this store is light and airy with a great view of the downtown shopping area. Enjoy the atmosphere as well as the internationally acclaimed sandwiches, always made and served with a smile. A great place to simply stop in for a refreshing beverage or coffee and desert between visits to the surrounding shops in Anaconda.

## F Chat & Chew

123 E. Park, Anaconda. 563-2352

Stop by the Chat & Chew if you're looking for homemade food like grandma used to make. They make everything from soups and bread to famous homemade cinnamon rolls and pies. Drop in for a yummy homemade pastry, or find your favorite from a wide variety of sandwiches that range from hoagies to hamburgers. This homey café is located in uptown Anaconda and offers friendly service that attracts legions of the locals daily. Bring the kids along, play some pool, chat and chew! Take-out orders are also available for your outdoor adventures and the delivery is free in the Anaconda area if you prefer to eat in.



## F Donivan's Family Restaurant & Catering

211 East Park St., Anaconda. 563-6241

## F Stageline Pizza

211 Cherry St., Anaconda. 563-2338

## F The Fudge Factor Inc

116 1/2 East Park St., Anaconda. 563-4365
or 888-772-7444 or fax 563-4375.
www.thefudgefactor.com

# Washoe Theater

**The following article appeared in the** Anaconda Standard on Thursday, September 24, 1936 announcing the opening of the Washoe Theater:

## Doors Of Finest Theater Of Size To Be Opened To Patrons Tonight

### Masterfully Decorated Interior of Building. Will Thrill Proud Residents; Three Shows Arranged.

A new chapter in the theatrical history of Anaconda, now in its fifty-third year, will be written tonight when the doors of the new Washoe Theater are opened to its first patrons—Smelter City residents—who are boasting proudly of the new addition to the community's entertainment sphere.

The theater, its massive walls erected on the site of the old Margaret showhouse, which for 30 years was the center of entertainment in this city, was built at the cost of approximately $200,000. This large expenditure is not only an expression of confidence in the economic future of the community but gives Anaconda the finest showhouse of any city of its size in the country.

From the smallest article of furniture to the magnificent stage, from the smallest light fixture to the handsome chandelier, the best obtainable and the most modern has been placed in the new building. Added to its exquisite lighting, its beautiful furnishings and elaborate decorations are the latest in sound equipment and picture projection, machines.

In finishing the interior of the structure, which was built in 1931, Joseph A. English, manager of the theater for the Washoe Amusement Company, sought and demanded the best. As a result the Washoe becomes the peer of theaters in Montana and a model for others to follow throughout the country.

Manager English selected for the opening picture "The Texas Rangers" King Vidor's historical epic of the men who molded a state from the territory of Texas. This picture has a general appeal. It featured an all-star cast headed by Fred MacMurray and Jack Oakie. Included in its headliners is Jean Parker, a Montana contribution in filmdom.

Doors of the theater will open at 6:30 o'clock for the first show. The box office will open at 6 o'clock. Two other shows will follow at 8:30 and 10:30 o'clock. The three shows were arranged to permit thousands to attend the first night. The theater will seat 1,000 persons in roomy and comfortable seats.

Last details for the opening of the new theater were finished yesterday. There will be no formal opening. The welcome and greetings of the Washoe Amusement Company will be carried in a feature "trailer" on the screen. The board of directors of the company is composed of Albert Nadeau, president; Mrs. M. Rimboud, vice president, and J.A. English, secretary and treasurer. A history of the theatrical enterprises of this city, an interpretation of the decorations of the new theater and a description of the sensational Mirrophonic sound , apparatus and projection machines appear in other pages of this theater edition.

The depression postponed the opening of the new theater until this fall. The new showhouse is a step from the Sundial theater which was destroyed by fire in 1929. The old Margaret theater was revamped in 1927 at the cost of $60,000 to become the ill-fated Sundial. The Washoe becomes the third theater to occupy that particular site.

The new building was designed by that master architect, B. Marcus Priteca. He has designed many of the famous theaters of the west coast.

The building was erected by Gus Forseen, Missoula contractor, who also built the Junior high school. Decoration work was done under the direction of Nat Smythe. Mural paintings in the theater are by that young, talented painter, Colville Smythe.

The Electrical Research Products corporation, distributors of Western Electric sound equipment, was called in at the time plans were made for construction. This action has given Anaconda, one of the few theaters built as a perfect instrument for sound pictures.

Heaton Randall, Salt Lake City, representative of the National Theater Supply company, carried out his firm's contract for the finishing of the theater. Mr. Randall has constantly been on the job, directing this important phase of the new theater. He left nothing undone to give Anacondans one of the finest theaters for its size in the country today.

Many thrills are in store for the patrons of the theater. Not only will they be strongly impressed with the elaborate decorations of the theater, but they will be thrilled by the clarity and closeness of the pictures on the screen and the true-tone sound development.

Anacondans have eagerly awaited the opening of the showhouse. They will be joined tonight and this week by hundreds of visitors from nearby communities in attending the first picture in the finest theater in the Treasure state.

**F The Celtic House Inn & Harp Pub**
23 Main St., Anaconda. 563-2372, www.harppub.com

**FL Fairmont Hot Springs**
1500 Fairmont Rd., Fairmont. 797-3241 or 800-332-3272. www.fairmontmt.com

Fairmont Hot Springs Resort is a year-round family recreation and convention destination located between Butte and Anaconda. Only three miles off I-90 and eight miles from the I-90 and I-15 Interchange, Fairmont's 500 acres is cradled by the Continental Divide. They feature four hot spring pools (open 24 hours for guests), a 350-foot water slide, 18-hole golf course, massage services, wildlife zoo, skiing nearby, and lots more. You can have your choice of two restaurants—the coffee shop for informal dining, and the dining room, serving steaks and seafood. The lounge has live entertainment five nights a week and a video gaming casino. Join Fairmont for a "funtastic" vacation.

**L 1880's Ranch**
1600 North Cable Road, Anaconda. 491-2336 or fax 563-6665. www.1880sranch.com

The 1880's Ranch has everything you'd expect to find in a genuine Old West town including saloon, boarding house, jail, log cabin, teepee, dugout, sheep wagon, Indian bark Lodge, cord-wood building, and 1880's Mercantile for your shopping pleasure. All lodgings convey the heart of the Old West in the late 19th century, but with all the conveniences of the late 20th century. They offer all sorts of recreation on 1,328 acres of scenic Big Sky splendor. Ringed by mountains reaching as high as 10,400 feet providing the best horseback riding opportunities, along with horses and staff anywhere. Their chef will satisfy your appetite with fresh produce and beef and pork raised right on the ranch. For an unforgettable Old West experience plan a trip to the 1880's Ranch. Be sure and visit their website!

**L Hickory House Inn B & B**
608 Hickory, Anaconda. 563-5481. www.hickoryhouseinn.com or email hickoryhouseinn@mcn.com

The Hickory House Inn sits at the foot of the Pintler Mountains, providing a breathtaking backdrop for every outdoor activity imaginable. You'll enjoy backpacking in the wilderness, downhill skiing at Discovery Ski Area, cross-country skiing at Mt. Haggin recreational area, fishing and boating at Georgetown Lake, miles of snowmobiling trails, golfing at the Old Works Golf Course, or exploring the past at Granite Ghost Town. The elegant house was built in 1893 and beautifully restored in 1999. Now open as a Bed and Breakfast with four rooms each with a private bath. The Garden Room accommodates 4 to 5 people and the three other rooms comfortably sleep 2 to 3 people. After a busy day enjoy their hot tub and wake up to a full gourmet breakfast.

**S Beyond Necessity Gifts**
301 E. Park St., Anaconda. 563-3218

**S MacIntyre's Family Clothing**
205 E. Park, Anaconda. 563-3731

**S Memories on Park Avenue**
1200 E. Park Ave., Anaconda. 563-4308

**S Anaconda Antiques**
601 E. Park, Anaconda. 563-3209

## 2. *Attraction*

**T Lost Creek State Park**
1.5 miles east of Anaconda on Montana 1, then 2 miles north on Secondary 273, then 6 miles west. 542-5500

The drive through this park takes you through a narrow 3,000 ft. deep canyon. The road is narrow and winding and not friendly to large trailers. In fact, several stretches of the road are single lane only. Lost Creek Falls cascade over a 50 foot drop to provide one of the most scenic and popular spots in the park. Mountain goats, bighorn sheep and other wildlife are frequently seen on the cliffs above the creek. Interpretive displays, camping, picnic area, fishing, trails, and disabled access (toilet).

## 3. *Gas*

### Warm Springs

Named for the hot water springs nearby, the town is the home of the state mental facility. Native Americans and early settlers referred to Warm Springs as "the deer lodge", because of the large rust colored 40-foot-tall travertine mound that the springs flow from. Large number of deer were often seen grazing near the mound. The mound is now covered and protected and no bathing is allowed.

A small resort was built at Warm Springs in the 1860s. The property was later sold to two doctors who were partners in a contract to care for those residents of the Territory of Montana who were, back then, called insane. The asylum opened in 1873. In 1912 the state purchased the mental institution and has continued to expand and renovate the property. All of the original buildings have been demolished as age took its toll on them.

## 4. *Attraction, Gas, Food, Lodging, Shopping*

### Deer Lodge

Deer Lodge is nestled in the beautiful Deer Lodge Valley and has three mountain ranges towering nearby: the Flint Creek Mountain Range to the west, the Garnet Mountain Range to the north, and the Pintler Mountain Range to the south. The Clark Fork River traverses the valley, as do many lakes and streams in the area. The valley was once called "Lodge of the White-Tailed Deer" by Native Americans, but Deer Lodge actually got its name from a salt lick popular with deer during the frontier days. Deer Lodge is an early mining town from the 1860s, that didn't die, but turned to other pursuits.

Today, at the heart of this town is a huge array of history as well as recreation. Some attractions of this town are: the Old Montana Prison, Yesterday's Playthings, Montana Auto Museum, Little Joe Engine, and the Powell County History Museum and Gallery. The prison, which predates the statehood of Montana, was opened in 1871.

**T Montana Auto Museum**
1106 Main St., Deer Lodge. 846-3111

Trace the development of the automobile and the use Montanans put it to in this newly refurbished museum. Over 110 cars on display from the 1903 Ford Runabout to the Muscle Cars of the early 70s. Historical photographs show the cars in use. "Vintage Camping Vehicles" highlighted by a 1928 Pierce Arrow Motor Home and "Mustangs and Muscle Cars" are some of the recent exhibits. Open daily 8 a.m.–8 p.m. June–Aug.; 8:30 a.m. –5:30 p.m. Apr.–May and Sept.–Oct.; otherwise varies.

**T Old Montana Prison**
Located off I-90 Exit 184 or 187. 1106 Main St., Downtown Deer Lodge. 846-3111

This building functioned as a prison from 1871–1979. It is comprised of 12 historic structures surrounded by a high sandstone wall. Enjoy self-guided tours around the cell house, maximum security areas and walled prison grounds. Signs of the 1959 riot are still visible. The experience provides a view of early prison life and area history. Guided tours available in summer. Open daily 8 a.m.–8 p.m., June–Aug.; 8:30 a.m.–5:30 a.m. April–May and Sept.–Oct.; otherwise varies.

**T Law Enforcement Museum**
At the Old Montana Territorial Prison in Deer Lodge. 846-1480

This is one of the few museums of its kind in the United States which is actually open to the public. The museum is not only a history of Montana's peace officers, but a memorial as well. The museum is open from May 16 through October 1, Tuesday through Saturday, 9 a.m. to 5 p.m.

*Aerial view of the Grant-Kohr's ranch.*

### T Yesterday's Playthings Doll & Toy Museum

1106 Main St., Downtown Deer Lodge. 846-1480

See over 1,000 dolls from the Hostetter collection, over 2,000 clown dolls from the Patricia Campbell collection, and china dolls, and paper mache dolls from the 1800s. There are working model railroad sets and many other toys spanning more than a century. These include cars and trucks, toy soldiers, farm animals, boats, and a large collection of marbles. Open daily 9:30 a.m.–5 p.m. mid-May to Sept.

### T Frontier Montana Museum

1106 Main St., Downtown Deer Lodge. 846-0026

The museum features the largest collection of handguns, spurs, chaps and all the cowboy collectables between Cody and Calgary. See Civil War Items and American Indian artifacts. Old Desert John's Saloon treats visitors to the most complete whiskey memorabilia collection in the U.S. The Mule Barn, built in 1918, has a classic embossed metal ceiling and a unique end-grain wood block floor. Open mid-May to Sept., 9 a.m.–5 p.m.

### T Powell County Historical Museum

1106 Main St. in Deer Lodge. 846-3294 or 846-3111

Trace the steps through the history of the Deer Lodge Valley at this museum. On display here is the extensive Paul Elberson gun collection. This eclectic collection contains a blend of frontier era firearms, muskets, and World War I and II weapons. There is also an excellent collection of slot machines, and a fascinating collection of old Wurlitzer juke boxes dating from 1938-1948. In the back room is a typical home from the 1920-1940 era with a kitchen, parlor and nursery. In addition to the permanent exhibits, there is a steady stream of changing exhibits. The museum is open from noon to 5 p.m. daily. Admission is free.

### L Downtowner Motel

500 Fourth St., Deer Lodge. 800-253-4093 and ask for 846-9823

Located in the heart of Downtown Deer Lodge, the Downtowner Motel features newly remodeled rooms in a friendly and quiet atmosphere. The 11 rooms offer a complimentary continental breakfast, queen size beds, direct dial phone with internet availability, cable TV, and plug-ins for cars—all at very reasonable rates. Jacuzzi suites and non-smoking rooms are available. The motel is within walking distance to all local attractions and is an excellent location for hunting and fishing trips.

### S Trading Post/The Wren's Nest

232 Main St., Deer Lodge. 846-1962. pamela@imine.net

This unique shop in the heart of downtown Deer Lodge features antiques, collectables, Montana-made handcrafted items, and locally crafted jewelry. They buy, sell, and trade new and used goods and carry a large selection of used books and music. The Trading Post is a full service fax & copy shop and notary public. Internet service is available so tourists can check their e-mail on the way through. Stop in to this unique shop, and you will find just about anything you can imagine.

## 5. *Attraction, Gas, Food, Lodging, Camping, Shopping*

### T Grant-Kohrs National Historic Site

West edge of Deer Lodge. 849-2070

This ranch was originally settled by Johnny Grant, the proprietor of a local trading post, in 1862. Four years later he sold his holdings to a hard-working German named Conrad Kohrs. The ranch grew to become Montana's largest ranch boasting more than 10 million acres. At one time cattle with the GK brand could be found grazing on open range from the Canadian border to Colorado. Each year between 8,000 and 10,000 head were shipped to market.

A stroll through the ranch gives you a small feel for what life was like on a frontier ranch in the open range days. Everything here is authentic to the site. Today it is a dynamic living museum with cattle, horses, and chickens. Take the self guided tour through bunkhouse row, the blacksmith shop, the tack room, the carriage barn and other buildings. There are 90 historic structures in all, and 37,000 artifacts covering 130 years of ranch history. Nowhere is the life of a cowboy preserved so well. There is a visitor center, The Cottonwood Creek Nature Trail combines a short walk with information about ranching, cattle grazing and ecosystems. The park is open daily from April through September from 9 a.m. to 5:30 p.m. It's open the rest of the year with reduced hours. There is a modest admission charge.

### C Indian Creek Campground

745 Maverick Lane, Deer Lodge. 846-3848

### FA Country Village

141 I-90 N. Interchange, Deer Lodge. 846-1443

Country Village is your complete stop on your way through the Deer Lodge area. Located right off the highway, they are complete with gas, a convenience store with lots of snacks, groceries, gifts, books, a casino, and a food court. They have food selections to satisfy anyone's needs. Take your pick from Perky's Pizza, Sully's Subs, TJ's Tacos, an espresso stand, a variety of ice cream and lots of comfortable seating. Stop into the "West of the Story Bookstore" and choose from a variety of regional books, stories from the Northwest and bestsellers. Country Village is a great stopping point for fast, casual dining and lots more.

### L Super 8 Motel of Deer Lodge

1150 N. Main, Deer Lodge. 846-2370 or 800-800-8000

The Deer Lodge Super 8 Motel has 57 clean and quiet rooms equipped with cable TV with remotes, direct dial phones, free local calls, plug-ins for autos, non-smoking rooms, and plenty of truck parking. A complimentary continental breakfast is also offered with your room. They have discounts for seniors, AAA, off-season, commercial, state, VIP card members, and AARP. Located just off Exit 184 on I-90.

## 6. *Historic Marker, Gas*

### Garrison

The town was named in honor of William Lloyd Garrison, an anti-slavery Yankee veteran who came for the Gold Rush and settled in the valley. The first post office was established in 1883.

# THE FRONTIER CATTLE INDUSTRY

They were a rugged set of men, these pioneers, well qualified for their self-assumed task. In the pursuit of wealth a few succeeded and the majority failed, as in all other spheres of activity… the range cattle industry has seen its inception, zenith, and partial extinction all within a half-century. The changes of the past have been many; those of the future may be of even more revolutionary character. —Conrad Kohrs, 1913

Dreams of wealth lured the first cattlemen to Montana. The range was open and unfenced, and ranchers could fatten their cattle on the lush bunchgrass and push on to new pasture when the old areas were overgrazed. The main obstacles were buffalo and the Indians, and by the 1860s both were fast being overcome.

Many of the herds were built through trade with westward-bound emigrants, who gladly swapped two or more trail-worn cows for a single well-fed one. In the late 1870s cowboys drove herds of rangy longhorns up from Texas to the better grazing lands of Montana, adding a Spanish strain to the English shorthorn breeds already established there and greatly multiplying the herds.

Frontier military posts and mining camps bought most of the first beef produced. When the railroads opened up this region in the 1870s, the big market was back east. Beef was becoming the favorite meat of the teeming populations of eastern cities, and it could now be shipped long distances economically in refrigerator cars. By 1885, cattle raising was the biggest industry on the High Plains, and foreign investors and eastern speculators rushed to get in on the bonanza. As ranches multiplied and the northern herds grew, there came a predictable consequence: overgrazing. This and the fierce winter of 1886-87 caused enormous losses, estimated at one third to one-half of all the cattle on the northern plains. Many cattlemen never recovered.

If the snows of '86-87 foreshadowed the end of open range ranching, the homesteaders, with their barbed wire and fenced-in 160-acre claims, finished it off. By 1890, many cattlemen were practicing a new kind of range management: they brought the feed and water to the cattle. As feed crops replaced native grasses, river bottoms became useful for growing hay, and water-or the right to it-became a valuable asset, making the land far more productive than it otherwise might be. The quality of livestock became more important than the quantity. Improved range management and selective breeding produced cattle that yielded more beef and better withstood the rigorous winters. With these changes, the old life of the cowboy passed. He now spent less time herding cattle and more time growing feed and repairing fences.

*The ranch house at the Grant-Kohr's Ranch.*

The open-range cattle industry lasted only three decades. Few of its pioneering men and women made their fortunes are remembered today. But from their beginnings has evolved the more scientific ranching of today, with its own risks and uncertainties. That is the legacy of the Grants and the Kohrs, whose pioneer ranch, complete with original furnishings, is a reminder of an important chapter in the history of the West.

## Ranch Life

The ranch house and the bunkhouse, though only 50 feet apart, were two different worlds. The cowboy's day was spent tending cattle, mending fences, and taking care of horses and equipment. It was a strenuous, often monotonous life, relieved by spring or fall roundups or a few days in a railroad town after a cattle drive. On the occasional trip to town he had a chance to replace worn-out boots or buy a pair of pants. Since a cowboy made only $20 to $30 a month, and a new hat might cost $20, he had to shop carefully and buy clothes and gear that were functional and durable.

The bunkhouse—home for the cowboys and ranch hands—lacked the amenities of the ranch house. Its pleasures were few and simple but appreciated. The food was plain. Yet, the meals at the long table were banquets compared with the rough fare on the trail or during roundups. A Chinese cook served beef, beans, and sourdough bread, a menu sometimes varied by bacon and eggs, vegetables, pies, cakes, and sweet biscuits called "bannocks." In the evening the cowboys gathered around the stove to chew tobacco or smoke, swap stories, or listen to news brought in by cowboys from other parts of Kohrs' far-flung empire.

While the rancher and his family might have been better fed and clothed, they hardly had an easy existence, at least in the early years. A rancher worked as hard as the hands, and his wife had to endure isolation and loneliness, not to speak of her labor on countless everyday chores. When they did achieve some success, their prosperity showed in the furnishings of the ranch house. The rancher's wife tried to make her home as comfortable and gracious as possible and a good place for raising children and entertaining friends. The Kohrs, better off than most, lavished improvements on their house—the latest furniture, a brick addition, indoor plumbing, lighting, and central heat—and traveled widely.

For all the tangencies of their lives, the rancher and the cowboy were partners in an intricate, often risky business: a rancher depended on good cowboys; a cowboy appreciated a rancher who could make the ranch pay and was sensible and fair. They shared the common bonds of open grasslands, cattle, horses, and hard work.



## H The Valley of a Thousand Haystacks

Garrison

*The Little Blackfoot Valley is filled with lush hay fields. You already may have noticed the rounded haystacks and commented on the strange lodgepole structures standing in many of the fields. This contraption that looks like a cross between a catapult and a cage is a hay-stacker that actually acts like a little of both. It was invented before 1910 by Dade Stephens and H. Armitage in the Big Hole Valley about sixty miles south of here. The device, called a beaverslide, revolutionized haying in Montana. It helped keep the wind from blowing the hay away and cut stacking time considerably.*

*To work the beaverslide, a large rake piled high with hay is run up the arms of the slide (the sloping portion of the "catapult"). At the top the hay dumps onto the stack. The side gates (the cage part) keep the stack in a neat pile and make it possible to stack higher. The sides were added to the system in the late 1940s. Although the lifting of the rake is usually powered by a takeoff from a tractor, truck or car axle, on some operations horse teams still provide the rpm's to muscle the hay up the slide.*

*Aside from minor improvements, the beaverslide has remained unchanged since its inception. Once used throughout a good portion of the northern west, modern technology that can shape hay into bales, loaves or huge jelly rolls have replaced it in many areas. The Little Blackfoot is one of several valleys in Montana where you can still see the beaverslide and its distinctive haystacks.*

## Montana Trivia

The smelter smokestack in Anaconda is the biggest free-standing masonry structure in the world. The Washington Monument could fit inside it with room to spare, and a car could drive around its rim.

**7.** *Historic Marker, Attraction*

### H First Discovery of Gold in Montana

east of Gold Creek

*Opposite this point a creek flows into the Clark Fork River from the west. In 1852, a French halfbreed, Francois Finlay, commonly known as "Benetsee," prospected the creek for placer gold. Finlay had some experience in the California goldfields but was inadequately equipped with tools. However, he found colors and in 1858 James and Granville Stuart, Reece Anderson and Thomas Adams, having heard of Benetsee's discovery, prospected the creek. The showing obtained convinced them that there were rich placer mines in Montana. The creek was first called "Benetsee Creek" and afterwards became known as Gold Creek.*

*The rumors of the strike reached disappointed "Pikes Peakers" as well as the backwash of prospectors from California and resulted in an era of prospecting that uncovered the famous placer deposits of Montana.*

### T Pioneer Ghost Town

South of Gold Creek on I-90

Pioneer was built in 1862 before the Gold Creek placers were abandoned for the big strike in Bannack. At one time there were several hotels, general stores, black smith shops and so on. The piles of tailings surrounding the remains are highly visible remnants of the ugly side of mining operations. The road is easy to drive.

### T Gold Creek Ghost Town

I-90 between Drummond and Garrison

Some consider this the site of the first discovery of gold in Montana. Very little remains of the town, and most information has been found in the diaries of two brothers, Granville and James Stewart. There are a lot of opinions with dates from 1852 to 1858, but Gold Creek was without a doubt among the first. It never became a booming town because other gold discoveries did seem more promising. The infamous Bannack sheriff Henry Plummer made his Montana debut in Gold Creek after arriving from Idaho.

*Drummond has the nickname "World Famous Bullshippers". Could that be referring to the used cow salesmen?*

**8.** *Attraction, Gas, Food, Lodging*

### Drummond

Drummond, originally the Packers Ranch, was officially named Drummond when the Northern Pacific Railroad completed its east-west line with nearby Drummond Camp. There is some confusion as to where it got its name. Some say was named after Drummond in South Wales. Others say it was taken from the name of the winningest horse in the regular horse races on Main Street. It quickly became a shipping point for goods, mine ores and cattle from Granite County. Though many towns became ghost towns after the mineral boom dwindled, Drummond has sustained growth for over one hundred years. A ranching town from the start, Drummond continues to ship cattle to markets all over the country. The town is known worldwide for the quality of its various registered herds which include Angus, Herfords and Salers. Hence the nickname "World Famous Bullshippers." Just north of Drummond is Garnet, considered by many to be one of the best-preserved ghost towns in Montana.

### T Sunrise

Rt 1, near Hall

The first patented mine in Montana was Sunrise and it was given two chances at the mining life. The first faded away with the silver panic in the early 1900s. The second came about fifty years later when it was reopened with hopes of producing silver through large-scale dredging. The hopeful miners soon discovered that the silver couldn't be mined economically and Sunrise was once again abandoned. Only a few decaying structures remain.

### T New Chicago School Museum

44 Old Hwy 10A in Drummond. 288-3223

A rest stop on the Mullan Trail for freighters, New Chicago was called the "Gateway to the Gold Fields." Located three miles south of the present town of Drummond, it was established in 1874 as the first town at this end of the Flint Creek Valley. At one time the town boasted a telegraph station, a flour mill, hotel, Methodist church, livery stable, school and other businesses. Its demise came when the Northern Pacific railroad came through in 1883 and established the town of Drummond.

The Old Schoolhouse was moved to the west end of Drummond in 1988 and has been restored by volunteers. Among the exhibits here is the story of Emma Davis Wilson (1844-1917), a pioneer teacher who homesteaded with her husband and two sons near New Chicago in 1874. Another fascinating exhibit is the quilt depicting the history of the Drummond area. The museum offers a number of other exhibits giving the visitor a glimpse of the history of this area. It is open Tuesday through Friday from mid-June to mid-August, 10 a.m. to 4 p.m.

### FL Wagon Wheel Motel & Cafe

310 Front St., Drummond. 288-3201

**9.** *Historic Marker, Attraction*

## Montana Trivia

Powell County, with Deer Lodge as it's county seat, has the greatest ratio of men to women in Montana. 139 males to every 100 females.

### H Bearmouth

west of Drummond

*Bearmouth, across the river to the south, was a trading point for the placer camps at Beartown, Garnet and Coloma located in the hills north of here. A pioneer family named Lannen operated the gold exchange and a ferry boat.*

*The river, officially known as Clark Fork of the Columbia and so named for Capt. Wm. Clark of the Lewis and Clark Expedition, has many local names. Its source is Silver Bow Creek, then it becomes the Deer Lodge River, changes to the Hellgate River, is then called the Missoula and winds up as the Clark Fork.*

*It had one other name given to it by a white man. In September, 1841, the intrepid Jesuit priest, Pierre Jean De Smet, traveled westward through here on his way from St. Louis to establish a mission for the Flathead Indians in the Bitter Root Valley. He crossed the river at the present site of Garrison and named it the St. Ignatius.*

### T Bearmouth Ghost Town

I-90 between Clinton and Drummond

Bearmouth was a stopover point for stage coaches and depended on the survival of other towns that were mining camps. Coaches traveled old Mullan Road between Fort Benton, Montana and Walla Walla, Washington. When the nearby mining camps of Garnet and Beartown died, so did Bearmouth. The beautiful Inn that provided accommodations for travelers still stands. Also nearby is the ghost camp of Coloma, that lasted until the 1930s and a few buildings are still standing.

**10.** *Attraction*

### T Beavertail Hill State Park

26 miles southeast of Missoula on 1-90 to Beavertail Hill exit, then .25 miles south on county road.

Beavertail Hill includes a half-mile of frontage on the Clark Fork River. Visitors enjoy fishing and camping in the shade provided by a stand of river cottonwoods.

**11.** *Gas, Food, Lodging*

### Clinton

Clinton is an old lumber and mining town. At one time, the Charcoal Mine yielded thousands of dollars worth of silver and lead. The town was originally known as Better's Station and was a stage stop on the Mullan Road. The name was later changed to honor a fellow by the name of Henry Clinton.

### Rock Creek Area

This popular recreation area is nestled in the Sapphire Mountain Range and in the Lolo National Forest, a fly fishing mecca. The stream has rainbow, cut throat, brown, brook and bull trout. Bighorn sheep are plentiful on the rocky bluffs. As you pass through this beautiful valley, watch for moose, bear and mountain lions. Bald eagles and hawks are plentiful as well as a number of waterfowl. The road leaves the interstate and immediately enters a canyon where it winds along Rock Creek for 49 miles. There are six trailheads along the road into the National Forest and the Welcome Creek Wilderness area. Along this road you'll also find the ghost town of Quigley. Not much left here but a sign.

### L The Blue Damsel

I-90 Exit 126, 10.8 mi. south. 825-3077.
niki@thebluedamsel.com. www.thebluedamsel.com.

This magnificent log lodge is located on 17 private acres of tumbling Rock Creek frontage. The lodge has accommodations for up to 14 people. Guests enjoy huge breakfasts of crepes, waffles, souffles, and omelets on silver and china in front of a huge stone fireplace. Several of the rooms have fireplaces and jacuzzis. All are furnished with antiques and art. Guests can also share the library, tell stories around the huge fire pit, and stargaze through their telescope. Luxuriate in the thick terry cloth robes provided each guest during their visit. Stroll the creekside and watch eagles swoop past on their way to lunch or moose foraging the riverbanks.

The inn is a masterpiece in itself. Owner Aldo Sardot has incorporated twisted log handrails with carved trout, basketwoven wood ballasters, and amazing workmanship throughout the lodge. His wife Niki is an artist who has filled the Blue Damsel with murals, tile paintings, unusual tile rugs and hand-carved fireplace surrounds of wild animals. They are located in the Lewis & Clark discovery triangle between Missoula and Helena in the Gold Region, just 40 minutes from the Missoula airport, and only a short trip from four blue-ribbon trout fishing streams.

### FLC Bearmouth Chalet

1610 W. Drummond Frontage Rd., Clinton.
825-9950

### LS Rock Creek Fisherman's Mercantile & Motel

73 Rock Creek Road, Clinton. 825-6440

## 12. *Food, Lodging*

### Maxville

This town sat on the Northern Pacific spur to Philipsburg. It was named for the storekeeper and postmaster R. R. MacLeod. The town was supposed to be Macville, but a postal employee copied it to the postal records as Maxville. The name stuck.

## 13. *Attraction, Gas, Food, Lodging, Camping, Shopping, Miscellaneous*

### Philipsburg

Philipsburg emerged almost overnight. It was born of the mineral boom and named after a prominent mining engineer, Philip Deidesheimer. In August of 1867, the town was "scarcely thirty days old" but by December of that same year the town boasted a population of about 1500 and over 250 houses had been built. By 1869, the town dissolved as quickly as it grew and was referred to as "the Deserted Village." In 1869 only 36 people remained at the end of summer, but the town slowly recovered. In 1873, growth was sparked partially by the reorganization of Northwest Mining Company and Hope Mining Company. In 1874, the Northern Pacific Railroad made it possible to ship ore and merchandise which had previously been transported by ox teams and wagons from the Utah territory. Manganese deposits, vital for war production and the richest in the United States, kept the town sprouting during World War I. Later manganese dioxide needed for drycell batteries continued the demand well into 1925.

Philipsburg survived while others remained only as ghost towns. Today, the town is a National Historic District full of unique architecture. In 1997, it was named one of the five "Prettiest Painted Places in America." Old fashioned street lights with American and Montana flags flying from their standards line the main street. Among the many historical buildings is the original county jail, constructed in 1895 and still in use today. The Philipsburg School is the oldest in the state

## A Kingdom of Cattle

Cattle ranching began in the Deer Lodge Valley in the late 1850s. Johnny Grant-a Canadian trader—settled there and became one of the first ranchers in Montana. In less than a decade he built a herd of 2,000 cattle, mostly by trading along the Oregon Trail. In 1862 he moved his ranching operation close to the present town of Deer Lodge. Here, he built a two-story log house for his wife Quarra—a Bannock Indian—and his large family. It was the finest house in Montana, said a newspaper. It looked as if "it had been lifted by the chimneys from the banks of the St. Lawrence and dropped down in Deer Lodge Valley. It has twenty-eight windows, with green painted shutters, and looks very pretty."

Grant worked this ranch for only a few years. He sold out in 1866 for $19,200- "farmhouses with household furniture, stables, corrals, ricks of hay, all my farming implements, wagons ... cattle, sheep, goats and grain"—and returned to Canada. The new owner was Conrad Kohrs, a German immigrant and by trade a butcher. He had already shown his skill in the frontier cattle business by shrewd trading and by selling beef to mining camps. He owned a sizable herd, and the Grant ranch gave him a base for his operations.

The ranch at this time was a fairly primitive place. On a trip back east in 1868, Kohrs found a wife. She was Augusta Kruse, a 19-year-old of German background. After a whirlwind courtship and marriage, they set out for Montana. The trip took 7 weeks by riverboat and 6 days in a wagon in the rain. After this daunting start Augusta settled in and brought a much needed order to the ranch. She cooked, cleaned, milked cows, made soap and candles, roasted coffee, ran the house, and began to raise a family.

Shortly after Kohrs took over the ranch, he brought in his half-brother John Bielenberg as partner. Kohrs handled the business end and Bielenberg supervised day-to-day work. Under them, the ranch became one of the best known in the region. They grazed their cattle far beyond the Deer Lodge Valley. At one point they ran their herds on ten million acres of land in four states and Canada. They also greatly improved the quality of their cattle. In the 1870s and '80s, they brought in as breeding stock registered Shorthorns and Herefords.

Part of Kohrs' success lay in diversifying. He went into partnership with other ranchers, and he invested in mining, real estate, and water rights. This enabled him to ride out market fluctuations, epidemics, and bad weather. Kohrs not only survived the killing winter of 1886-87, but he fairly prospered. His registered herds came through virtually intact, partly because of their sheltered location in the valley. There were less cattle all around competing for range, and he was in a good position to rebuild.

The hard winter marked a divide for the cattle business. The old freewheeling days of nomadic grazing gave way to more settled ranching based on good range management, supplemental feeding, and upgraded bloodlines. Kohrs and Bielenberg were equally successful in the transformed industry. Their home ranch holdings increased to 30,000 acres and became a center for stock breeding. For a quarter of a century after '86-87, they shipped to market each year between 8,000 and 10,000 cattle. During the 1890s, Kohrs left the management of the ranch to his son-in-law John Boardman and Bielenberg and turned his attention to his other business interests.

On the eve of World War 1, Kohrs and Bielenberg saw still another fundamental shift coming. Homesteaders had pretty well fenced in the range, and it was no longer possible to swing big herds across the plains in search of grass and water. Had they been younger men they might have acted differently. But, Kohrs was 75 and Bielenberg 65. Moreover, their heir apparent William, Kohrs' only son, had died in 1901, and there was no one to operate the ranch on the scale required. Reducing their holdings seemed the best move. By the time of their deaths in the early 1920s, they had sold all but 1,000 acres around the home ranch. It was this remnant that Conrad Kohrs Warren, a grandson, began to manage in the 1930s. In 1940 he bought the ranch from the Kohrs Trust and began breeding the registered Hereford cattle and Belgian horses for which he became widely known.

Augusta Kohrs still loved the old ranch. Until she died in 1945 at age 96, she spent part of every summer there, cherishing the pictures, furnishings, and household items of her younger years. Conrad Warren and his wife Nell carded this work further. They carefully preserved the old buildings and their furnishings and gathered together the ranch's working documents, so essential to reconstructing its history. Others became interested in saving the ranch, and in response Congress in 1972 set the ranch aside as a National Historic Site for the purpose of providing "an understanding of the frontier cattle era of the nation's history."

*Reprinted from National Park Service brochure.*

## THEY WORKED UNDERGROUND

**Trammer**—pushed ore cart or cage to surface or away from face

**Topman**—pulled cars on and off the cage

**Bar down**—barred loose slabs and rock

**Mucker**—Shoveled rock into car or chute

**Smitty**—blacksmith (fashioned and sharpened tools)

**Miner**—drilled, blasted, mucked and timbered

**Hoistman**—ran engine for hoisting and watched compressor

**Station Tender**—loaded cars on cage from different levels

**Shifter**—The boss directly over the mine crew

and celebrated its centennial in 1996. The McDonald Opera House is another must-see piece of architecture. It is the oldest theater still in operation in Montana and has been on the National Historic Building Registry for years.

### T Granite County Museum & Cultural Center

S. Sansome St. in Philipsburg. 859-3388

This museum focuses on the mining legacy of the surrounding area. Upstairs in the museum, view the revolving historical exhibits, including archival photos, clothing and artifacts from Granite County.

Downstairs, experience a miner's daily life. You'll begin your tour here by viewing a mural depicting the above-ground activities of actual miners of the area. View an authentic assay office with all of its equipment, then enter a bank, complete with a coin collection found beneath old floorboards of a miner's cabin.

Next, step into the world of the miner's cabin—a completely furnished cabin has been reconstructed to depict the bare necessities the miner would have required at the end of his exhausting work day.

Explore a mining adit and tunnel. You'll feel yourself in the miner's well-worn boots as you experience the lighting and special effects of this mining experience. You'll see what a real vein would have looked like lit by the soft glow of the miner's candle. When you exit, you'll be greeted by a 1,200-cubic-foot compressor and learn how it worked, as well as a display of mining tools, an ore car with its own design blueprint, and much more.

Also on display is an extensive mineral collection including the Bielenberg Sapphire Collection. Other exhibits include Indian artifacts, a pewter saddlebag altar used by the circuit riding priest, period clothing, and artifacts from early ranchers and blacksmiths.

The museum is open from mid-May through October daily.

### T Granite Ghost Town

Located approximately 5 miles southeast of Philipsburg. Go south on Sansome Road, then east on rough dirt road opposite Center Street. Inquire locally about road conditions. 542-5500

This remote, difficult-to-reach ghost town is "rich" in mining history. For adventurous history buffs, this small park preserves an evocative fragment of the past—the "superintendent's house" and the ruins of an old miner's union hall. A high clearance four-wheel drive vehicle is recommended to reach Granite.

### FA Sunshine Station

3830 Hwy 1, Philipsburg. 859-3450

Sunshine Station is a family owned and run operation that is centered around fun. It's the home to what the locals call the BOB, or the Big 'ol Burger. They serve hand pressed burgers, homemade Montana gourmet pizzas, and delicious steak dinners. They have a full bar, lounge, and casino area with billiards. For family fun, you can enjoy a game of volleyball or horseshoes. The convenience store is complete with groceries, gifts, fishing supplies, maps, and an RV dump site. Sunshine Station is a great stopping off point between Anaconda and Rock Creek on the Pintler Scenic Highway.

### L Blue Heron - A Bed & Breakfast

138 W. Broadway, Philipsburg. 859-3856.
www.blueheronmt.com

Your hosts Myrlin & John look forward to welcoming you as their guest at the Blue Heron. This fine bed & breakfast is located in the rich, historic district of Philipsburg in a quaint, restored 19th century building. Accommodations feature eye-pleasing combinations of color, unique artwork and antiques. Tracing its origin back to the 1800s the building served as a boarding house for locals and adventurous travellers. Enjoy one of the uniquely decorated guest rooms with shared bath or the private bath suite. Awaken to a hearty breakfast featuring homemade breads, preserves and fresh ground coffee. At the Blue Heron you are sure to have a one of a kind experience enjoying historic Philipsburg and the beautiful surrounding area. Visit them at www.blueheronmt.com.

### LC Inn at Philipsburg

915 W. Broadway, Philipsburg. 859-3959.
www.theinn-philipsburg.com, theinn@montana.com

This family inn and RV park is located at the edge of town, in the heart of the Philipsburg valley. It provides a base to explore the historic ranch land,

mining ghost towns, national forests, sapphire mines, and year-round recreation possibilities of this Montana paradise. Non-smoking rooms are available, and some rooms are equipped with kitchenettes. There are RV sites with full hook-ups, as well as camp sites and trailer parking. Pets are welcome.

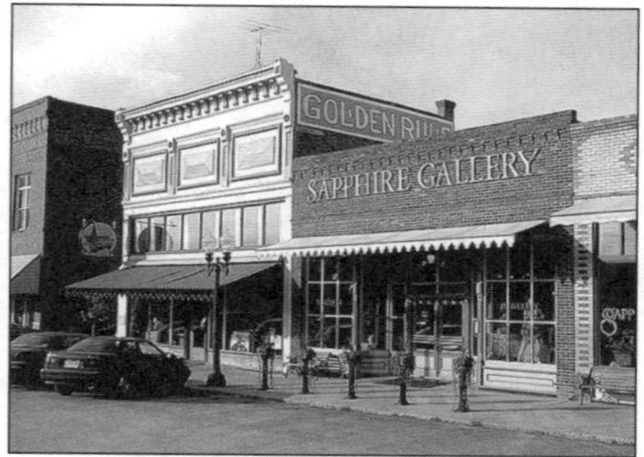


## S The Sapphire Gallery/Sweet Palace.

115 E. Broadway, Philipsburg. 859-3631. www.sapphire-gallery.com and www.sweetpalace.com

The Sapphire Gallery features the widest range of sapphire colors in the United States—from Montana and worldwide sapphire and ruby deposits. Mine sapphires in the mining room year round and create fine heirloom jewelry of your very own. When you are finished, step next door where chocolates, taffy and fudge are made daily. Over 750 royal treats to choose from in the Sweet Palace. The friendly folks at the Sweet Palace and Sapphire Gallery are awaiting you in the elegantly restored Victorian buildings. Open year round Monday–Friday and every Sunday. This is an attraction that should not be missed! Visit them at their web sites and be dazzled.

## S Pickle Dish Quilt and Gift Shop

208 E. Broadway, Anaconda. 859-3750

## M Waldbillig Realty

5 Andre Lane, Philipsburg. 859-(LAND)5263 or fax 859-5263. www.pburgproperties.com

The folks at Waldbillig Realty are specialists in Western Montana and have been helping people find dream properties in the Philipsburg, Drummond, Georgetown Lake, Discovery Ski Basin, and Rock Creek areas since 1958. The Granite County area offers beautiful vistas, undiscovered mountain lakes, and endless scenic drives. The Georgetown Lake area is loaded with recreational opportunities including fishing, boating, water sports, hiking, biking, and camping. Discover Discovery Basin with its downhill and X-country skiing, snowmobiling, and breathtaking views. If you're a hunter, the area offers unlimited cow elk tags, non-typical B&C bulls, and an abundance of mule and whitetail deer. These folks are some of the most experienced people you will find in the area and will help you find the property you've dreamed of in Montana.

*The Sayrs Building is just one of many unique and colorful historic buildings in Philipsburg.*

## M Pintlar Territories Real Estate

14 W. Broadway, Philipsburg. 859-3522, f ax 859-4522 or toll free at 877-859-3522. www,pintlarterritories.com.

Pintlar Territories has the largest "For Sale" inventory in Granite County. They specialize in the sale of homes, land, lots, ranches, and commercial properties. Several members of their team are lifetime Philipsburg residents who thoroughly know the area, it's facilities, and many recreational opportunities available. They make Pintlar Territories a true hometown real estate company.

These folks take great pride in getting things done with a professional and personal touch. If you plan to be in the area give them a call. Not only will they help with your real estate needs, but they can also help you make arrangements for your stay.

## 14. *Attraction, Food, Lodging*

## T Southern Cross

Hwy 10, above Georgetown Lake

This once busy gold and silver mining town settled by Swedish and Finnish immigrants in the 1860s continued operations for eighty years. The

Section 7

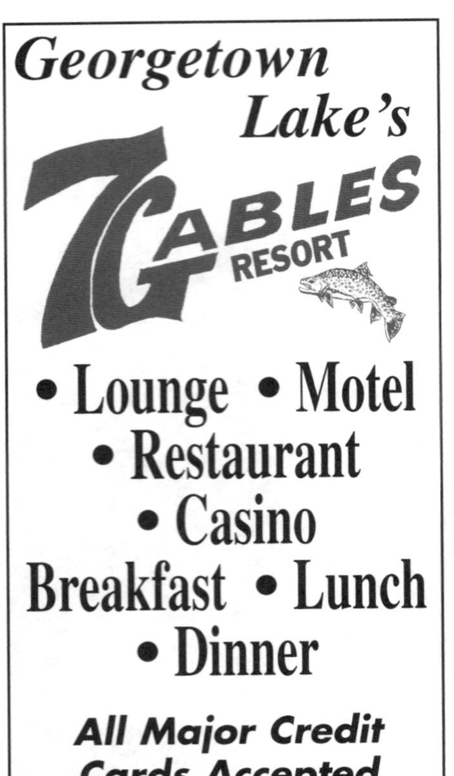


Section 7

town is still home to a handfull of residents and frequent wildlife. Residents have preserved the many buildings that reflect an important part of Montana's history.

### T Red Lion Ghost Town
Near Discovery Basin Ski Area off Hwy 1

There are still a few log cabins and tramway towers, mixed with some beautiful scenery that was once home to about 500 in the early 1900s. The town dates back to 1875 when gold was discovered in the area.

### T Georgetown Lake
18 miles west of Anaconda on MT Highway 1.

Georgetown Lake, well-known for its superb fishing and stunning grandeur, is surrounded by the Deerlodge National Forest and the Anaconda-Pintler Wilderness to the southwest. This area is a haven for wildlife as well as a wide range of outdoor activities.

### T Cable Ghost Camp
Hwy 10, near Georgetown Lake

Some say that the world's largest gold nugget was found here and bought by W.A. Clark for $19,000. The mine was originally discovered when three prospectors made camp for the night and lost their horses. While looking for the horses they discovered a quartz vein and of course, the rest is history. The operation had it's ups and downs from 1867 until 1940 when the entire operation closed for good. The property is closed to visitors due to vandalism.

### V Discovery Ski Area
P.O. Box 221, northwest of Anaconda. 563-2184

Discovery Ski Area is located in the Beaverhead-Deer Lodge National Forest and known for light powder, inexpensive prices, uncrowded slopes, delicious food, and friendly atmosphere. The terrain ranges from gentle beginner slopes to extreme skiing on the back side. There are 380 acres of skiable terrain equally divided between beginner, intermediate, advanced and expert slopes. Group and private lessons are available, including beginner packages. A complete rental and repair shop is located in the main lodge, and The Sport Shop offers ski clothing and accessories for all seasons. Enjoy the full-service cafeteria with delicious homemade foods, or relax in the bar with your favorite drink. Discovery is located 95 miles southeast of Missoula and 45 miles northwest of Butte.

### FL Seven Gables Resort
Hwy 1 on Georgetown Lake. 563-5052. www.sevengablesmontana.com

With beautiful views of Georgetown Lake, Seven Gables has great homestyle dining, 10 recently remodeled rooms, and 6 RV sites with electrical hookups. The restaurant serves breakfast, lunch, and dinner with daily specials, has a full service bar, and a fun, relaxed atmosphere with gaming machines. The rooms are complete with queen size beds, kitchenettes, and coffee pots. They also have a store with souvenirs and gift items. Seven Gables is a great place to relax after a long day skiing Discovery, snowmobiling, or fishing.

*The Gold Coin min just south of Anaconda on Pintler Scenic Highway.*

## 15. *Historic Marker, Lewis & Clark, Attraction, Gas, Food, Lodging, Camping, Shopping*

### Lolo
Lolo abounds with history. Referred to as "Travelers Rest" by Lewis & Clark, Lolo is located south of Missoula just east of the Bitterroot Range. Here the Corps of Discovery rested and planned to hunt wild game before crossing the Bitterroots. As game was scarce, the Corps headed over the mountains and hunted along the way. Several times the expedition was forced to kill their colts for food; when no colts remained they went hungry. This portion of the expedition proved to be the harshest the Corps encountered.

The Lolo Pass (elev. 5233-ft.) has well-marked trails for cross-country skiing and snowmobiling. When the snow disappears, hiking is available along parts of the original Lewis & Clark Trail. Take a camera and venture down this "Wild and Scenic River Corridor."

### H Traveler's Rest
south of Lolo

*The Lewis and Clark Expedition, westward bound,*

*Georgetown Lake*

# On the Trail of Lewis & Clark

## The Continental Divide And The Shoshone Indians

The four men soon crossed the Continental Divide and began their descent on the western side of the Bitterroot Mountains along an Indian road. The next day, Aug. 13, they saw on an eminence, about a mile ahead, two women, a man and some dogs. When they came within a half mile of the Indians, Lewis set his accouterments on the ground, unfurled the flag, and advanced alone towards them. But the wary Indians disappeared behind a hill.

Continuing on about a mile, Lewis came upon three Shoshone females. One young woman began to run, but an elderly woman and a girl of about 12 years remained. Lewis laid down his gun and approached the two. He gave them beads, moccasin awls, mirrors and some paint. At Lewis' request, the elderly woman called back the young woman. The three agreed to lead the men to their village. After about two miles, they met 60 warriors mounted on excellent horses coming rapidly toward them. Convinced of Lewis's peaceful mission, the Indians smoked the pipe with the white men.

They then went down Lemhi River four miles to the village. The lodges were all made of sticks because the *Pahkees* (the Indians who inhabited the area around the Great Falls of the Missouri) had raided them that spring. They took or killed 20 Shoshones, took all their skin lodges, and a great number of horses.

At the village Lewis was told that he would not be able to reach the ocean by way of Salmon River. Lewis hoped that the description of the river was exaggerated and that the Expedition could, in fact, navigate these waters.

Lewis told the Indians that another chief of the white men (Clark) was waiting at the forks of the Jefferson with baggage. He asked the Indians to come with him and bring 30 horses that would be used to transport the baggage over the Divide to their village. The Expedition would then trade with them for horses.

Many of the Indians still felt that the whites were in league with the Pahkees and were trying to lead them into an ambush. Nevertheless, 28 men and three women agreed to accompany Lewis back to the forks of the Jefferson. Sixteen of the Indians bravely camped with Lewis at the forks even though the promised "chief" and baggage were not to be seen. Clark's party arrived at the forks the next day (Aug. 17). The band of Shoshones with Lewis just happened to be the band to which Sacagawea belonged. It also turned out, to the advantage of the Expedition, that Sacagawea's brother, Cameahwait, was now chief of that band.

## Searching For Navigable Waters And Bargaining For Horses

The camp of Aug. 17–23 was named Camp Fortunate in commemoration of the meeting with the Shoshones. Lewis and dark informed the Indians of their mission, and told them that once they had portaged over the Divide to the Indians' village, they would buy horses from them, if horses were needed to Find a navigable river to the ocean.

On Aug. 18, Lewis bartered for two horses, which Clark and 11 men would need on their reconnaissance over the Divide to satisfy in their own minds whether the Salmon was a navigable route to the Columbia. Sacagawea and Charbonneau accompanied Clark's party to the Shoshone village to encourage the Indians to bring horses to Camp Fortunate. In the meantime, Lewis purchased another horse for the hunters. His men also purchased a horse.

On Aug. 20, Lewis selected a site three-fourths of a mile below Camp Fortunate to cache more excess baggage. And while they waited the return of the Indians who were to bring horses, they made harnesses and pack saddles for the portage.

On the same day, Clark reached the Shoshone village. He hired a Shoshone named Toby for a guide on his reconnaissance. Clark was informed of a route over the Bitterroots which the Nez Perce used to go to the Missouri. On this route game was scarce, and the Nez Perce suffered excessively from hunger. He learned that the mountains there were broken, rocky and so thickly covered with timber that the Indians could scarcely pass. Clark reasoned that should the Salmon prove unnavigable, the party would take the Nez Perce trail, for if thosc Indians could cross the mountains with their women and children, certainly the Expedition could do likewise.

On Aug. 22, Sacagawea, Charbonneau, Cameahwait, and about 50 men with a number of women and children arrived back at Camp Fortunate with the horses needed to cross the Divide. At this time Lewis purchased five more horses at a cost of about six dollars worth of merchandise for each.

Clark's party reached the North Fork of the Salmon on the same day. They continued down the Salmon along a very steep and rocky mountain. As they went along they looked for trees suitable for making dugouts in case the river was navigable. They found only one such tree.

On Aug. 23, back at Camp Fortunate, Lewis had the canoes taken out of the river and sunk in a nearby pond so they wouldn't be lost by high water or burned in one of the fires the natives made on the prairies. The Indians had sold Lewis all the horses they could spare until they returned to their village.

Clark's party continued down the north side of Salmon River with great difficulty, traveling over large, sharp rocks. Still not totally convinced that the river was unnavigable, Clark had some of his party halt to hunt and fish while three men and Toby continued on with him to further examine the river. Clark finally conceded that the Indian information was accurate: the Salmon was not navigable. He marked his name on a tree at the mouth of Indian Creek.

Before Lewis' party left Camp Fortunate, 50 men, women and children came to the camp on their way to hunt buffalo. Lewis managed to purchase three more horses and a mule from these people. Then as much baggage as possible was packed on the horses for the portage. The Indian women carried the balance.

## Three Options

Clark sent a private on horseback with a note to Lewis stating three possible plans for their route to the ocean. The first was to procure one horse for each man, hire Toby as a guide, and proceed by land to some navigable part of the Columbia. The second plan was to divide the men into two parties, make dugouts, and have one party attempt the treacherous Salmon with whatever provisions were on hand, and have the remaining party go by horseback procuring what food they could by use of their guns, and occasionally meeting up with the party on the river. A third possibility would be to divide into two parties, have one go over the mountains to the north while the other returned to the falls of the Missouri to collect provisions, go up Sun River, and over the route used by the Hidatsas to get to the country of the Flatheads (near present Missoula). Both parties would meet there and continue on to the ocean.

On Aug. 26, Clark's messenger arrived at the Shoshone village with the note about the same time Lewis arrived, Clark recommended that the first plan be used, and that a horse be purchased for every member of the Expedition. The chief, however, informed Lewis that the Pahkees had stolen many of their horses that spring and that they could not spare that many.

Lewis sent word for Clark to come to the village and get the 22 horses he had been able to purchase. Clark managed to purchase another horse for his pistol, 100 balls, powder, and a knife. Another horse was bought for a musket.

The explorers set out with Toby as their guide, and soon began their ascent of the North Fork. Two days later they found the mountains close to the creek on both sides. They were forced to travel along the steep mountain walls. Several of the horses slipped and injured themselves quite badly. It was also at this place that they had the misfortune of breaking their last thermometer. It snowed about two inches, then began to rain, and then sleet. Shortly before reaching Lost Trail Pass, Toby, for some unknown reason, led the party in the wrong direction. They encamped that evening about three miles west of the pass, having taken a much more difficult routethan necessary.

*Text and drawings excerpted from U.S. Forest Service pamphlet "Lewis and Clark in the Rocky Mountains"*

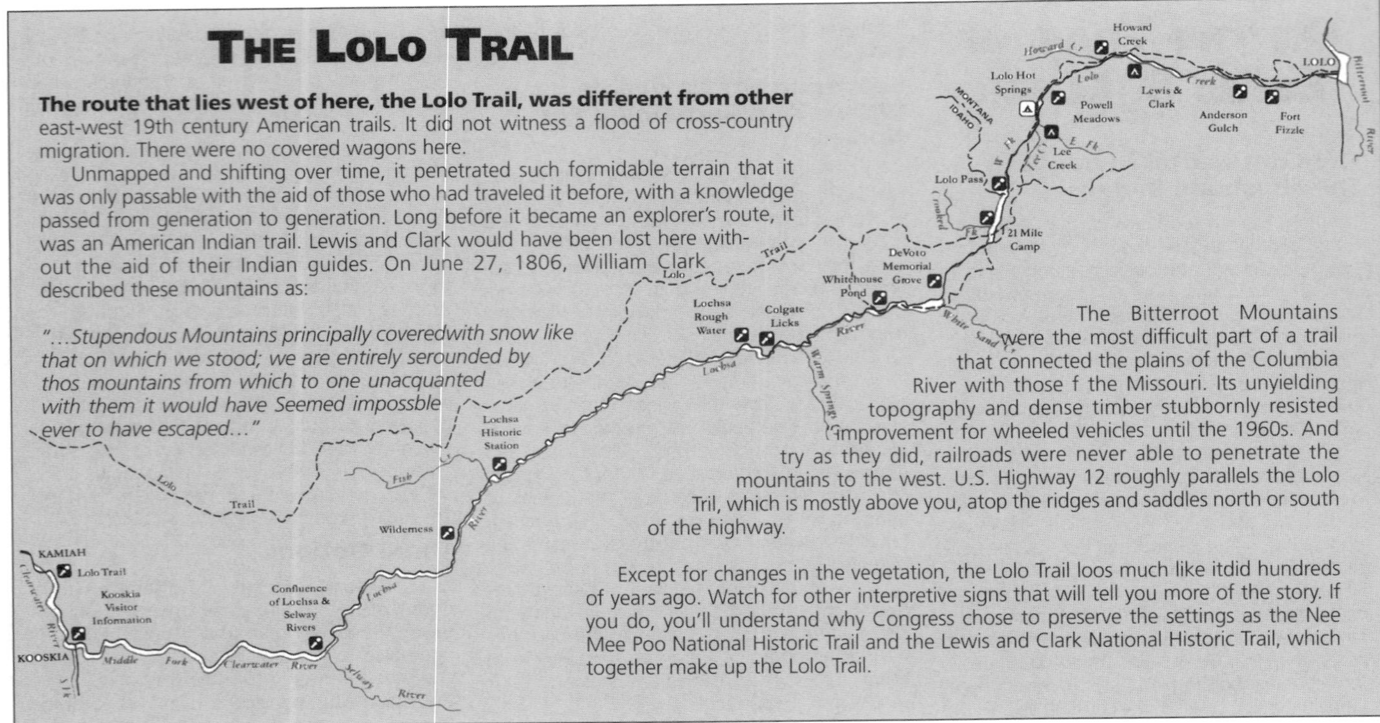


## THE LOLO TRAIL

**The route that lies west of here, the Lolo Trail, was different from other** east-west 19th century American trails. It did not witness a flood of cross-country migration. There were no covered wagons here.

Unmapped and shifting over time, it penetrated such formidable terrain that it was only passable with the aid of those who had traveled it before, with a knowledge passed from generation to generation. Long before it became an explorer's route, it was an American Indian trail. Lewis and Clark would have been lost here without the aid of their Indian guides. On June 27, 1806, William Clark described these mountains as:

*"...Stupendous Mountains principally coveredwith snow like that on which we stood; we are entirely serounded by thos mountains from which to one unacquanted with them it would have Seemed impossble ever to have escaped..."*

The Bitterroot Mountains were the most difficult part of a trail that connected the plains of the Columbia River with those f the Missouri. Its unyielding topography and dense timber stubbornly resisted improvement for wheeled vehicles until the 1960s. And try as they did, railroads were never able to penetrate the mountains to the west. U.S. Highway 12 roughly parallels the Lolo Tril, which is mostly above you, atop the ridges and saddles north or south of the highway.

Except for changes in the vegetation, the Lolo Trail loos much like itdid hundreds of years ago. Watch for other interpretive signs that will tell you more of the story. If you do, you'll understand why Congress chose to preserve the settings as the Nee Mee Poo National Historic Trail and the Lewis and Clark National Historic Trail, which together make up the Lolo Trail.

*camped at the mouth of Lolo Creek September 9th, 10th, 1805. They had been traveling down the Bitter Root Valley and halted here to secure a supply of venison before crossing the mountains to the west via Lolo Pass. They named the spot Traveler's Rest, and it was at this camp that they first learned of the Indian road up Hell Gate leading to the buffalo country east of the main range of the Rockies.*

*Returning from the coast they again camped here from June 30th, 1806, to July 3rd. When the party divided, Lewis took the Indian "Road to the Buffalo" and after exploring the Marias River descended the Missouri while Clark went via the Big Hole, Beaver Head, Jefferson and Gallatin Valleys and the Yellowstone River.*

*They reached their rendezvous near the mouth of the Yellowstone within 9 days of each other.*

*Considering distance and unexplored terrain, they were tolerably punctual.*

### H The Changing Landscape

Highway 12 west of Lolo

*The Lewis and Clark and the Nez Perce National Historic trails, collectively referred to as the Lolo Trail, follow the ridges north of U.S. Highway 12. The landscape you see along Lolo Creek has changed in many ways since this land was the aboriginal territory of the Nez Perce and Salish people. They viewed the Lewis and Clark Expedition as a business venture into a very old cultural landscape—the territory of sovereign nations with richly developed cultures. The people who followed Lewis and Clark practiced a more visually evident style of land management than did the American Indians. American Indians utilized resources made available by natural events. Today, on the other hand, we often create disturbances to make resources available. The look of the landscape along Lolo Creek reflects that style.*

*Land ownership had a different meaning to the American Indians who had been here for centuries. Since that time, these lands have been claimed and managed in a variety of ways. Most of the bottom land east of here along lower Lolo Creek is owned by small private landowners. The upper reaches of Lolo Creek near Lolo Hot Springs and visible from Highway 12 are a "checkerboard" of Nationa Forest and private timber company lands.*

*This "checkerboard" ownership pattern began in 1908 when the U.S. Government granted the Northern Pacific Railroad alternate sections of land along their proposed railroad route. This was our nation's second attempt to build a railroad across these mountains. But the 1854 assessment of Lt. John Mullan during the first attempt to build a railroad here proved correct when he wrote:*

"It is thoroughly and utterly impractical for a railroad rout...an immense bed of rugged pinnacles and difficult mountains that can never be converted to any purpose for the use of man...I have never met with a more ininviting and rugged set of mountains."

Though the railroad was never completed, the checkerboard ownership pattern still remains.

Railroads, fire management, windstorms, timber management practices, subdivisions and road construction all affect the way this land looks today.

*On December 4, 1995, a huge windstorm blew down millions of board feet of timber across thousandsof acres along Lolo Creek. That wind event played a big role in how the forest looks today. Some of the blown-down timber left on the hillsides and some of the timber from this natural disturbance was utilized for lumber. Look closely as you travel along Highway 2 and you can see where the trees were blown over and are pointing in the same direction.*

### H Nez Perce Sikum

*Sikum is the Nez Perce word for horse. The Nez Perce people were introduced to the horse in the 1730s. The word "appaloosa" was created by white settlers. The Nez erce learned through selective breeding that they could produce a horse uniquely suited to their homeland and the country around you where they frequently traveled.*

*The Nez Perce National Historic Trail travels down Lolo Canyon and was a critical and frequently used route for the Nez Perce between their homeland and the bison rich plains to the east. According to Samuel Penny, Chairman of the Nez Perce Tribal Executive Committee:*

"This was our commerce trail. We followed this trail east to hunt buffalo. We came here for camas. We came here in our flight from the oldiers."

*On February 15, 1806, Meriwether Lewis rote of the Nez Perce horses in hi journal:*

"Their horses appear to be of an excllent race; they are lofty, elegantly formed, active and durable, in short, many of them look like fine

English corsers and would make a figure in any country."

*The rich history of the sikum lives on today with the Nez Perce through their Young Horseman Program. The Nez Perce maintain an active horse breeding program in Lapwai, Idaho. The Nez Perce horse of oday is a unique cross between the Akhal-Teke of Turkmenistan and the Appaloosa. Through this program they maintain their reputation as accomplished equestrians.*

### D Mer. Lewis
September 9, 1805

*"It is hear a handsome stream about 100 yards wide and affords a considerable quantity of very clear water, the banks are low and it's bed entirely gravel. the stream appears navigable, but from the circumstance of thier being no sammon in it I believe that there must be a considerable fall in it below."*

### D Mer. Lewis
Return Trip, June 29, 1806

*"both the men and indians amused themselves with the use of a bath this evening."*

### D Wm. Clark
Return Trip, June, 30, 1806

*"Descended the mountain to Travellers rest leaveing those tremendious mountaines behind us in passing of which we have experienced Cold and hunger of which I shall ever remember. . .a little before sunset we arrived at our old encampment on the south side of the creek."*

### D Wm. Clark
Return Trip, July 3, 1806

*"I took My leave of Capt Lewis and the indians at 8 A M Set out with 19 men interpreter Shabono & his wife & child. ..with 50 horses."*

### D Mer. Lewis
Return Trip, July 3, 1806

*"All arrangements being now compleated for carrying into effect the several schemes we had planed for execution on our return, we saddled our horses and set out."*

### T Fort Fizzle
Four miles west of Lolo

To block the Nez Perce from entering Montana, Captain Rawn, 7th Infantry, with thirty enlisted men and four officers from nearby Fort Missoula, entrenched themselves behind log breastworks in a small opening along the Lolo Creek drainage adjacent to the Lolo Trail. About 150 settlers joined the soldiers. The 750 Nez Perce, with their 1000+ horses, were camped about five miles to the west.

At a meeting of the Nez Perce chiefs and Army officers, the Nez Perce made four things very clear: they had no intention of molesting settlers or property; they wanted to travel in peace; they would not surrender their horses, arms and ammunition; and they were not ready to return to the hostile environment in Idaho.

*"I had a talk with Chiefs Joseph, White Bird and Looking Glass, who proposed if allowed to pass unmolested, to march peaceably through the Bitter Root Valley."*

Captain Rawn.

Soon after the meeting, many settler volunteers returned home. Some reports say they were convinced that the Nez Perce wanted a peaceful trip through the valley.

*"Others, at the sight of so many Indians…deserted,"* said Corporal Loynes, 7th Infantry.

*"Now could we see the Indians passing within sight of us. Of course they did not want us to see them, and we did not."* reported Corporal Loynes, 7th Infantry.

Captain Rawn had clear orders. He said the Nez Perce could not pass; however, the barricade failed when the Nez Perce, with their horses and possessions, climbed a steep ravine behind the ridge to the north and bypassed the soldiers. This maneuver earned White Bird the nickname of the "Indian Hannibal" and the previously unnamed barricade became a ridiculed "Fort Fizzle."

*"How easy any Indian force, whether seeking pillage or only escape, could pass around, through and by our untrained troops. So far as infantry goes, except to defend the larger towns or some fortified position, thereby are as useless as boys with popguns."* The Helena Daily Herald, July 30, 1877.

*"The Indians were fagged out, their cayuses scarcely able to walk, and their cartridge belts almost empty. To let them go by was equivalent to giving them new horses, plenty of ammunition and ample provisions. It was in a word, breathing new life into a corpse."* Sergeant T. A. Sutherland, Volunteer aide-de-camp to General Howard.

## 16. *Lewis & Clark, Attraction, Food, Lodging*

### D Wm. Clark
September 12, 1805

*"passed Some most intolerable road on the Sides of the Steep Stoney mountains"*

### D Wm. Clark
September 16, 1805

*"I have been wet and as cold in every part as I ever was in my life, indeed I was at one time fearull my feet would freeze in the thin mockersons which I wore"*

### T Lolo Hot Springs
Hwy 12, 15 miles west of Lolo

Lolo Hot Springs Indoor and outdoor pools are located on a private resort and open to the public year round with an admission fee. Lolo hot springs has a history longer than Montana. The first written record of visitors to Lolo Hot Springs were Lewis and Clark in 1805. In journals, Captain Clark described the wildlife, hot water, and bathing hole made by local Indians, but did not have time to linger. They were desperate to cross the Continental Divide before winter set in. On their return from the Pacific Coast the following June, Clark wrote about the soaks and bathing when the members of the Corp of Discovery enjoyed more leisure time. The hot springs and trail were later named after a French fur trapper, Lolo, who trapped beaver in the nearby streams. The springs were popular through the 1800s and 1900s closing in 1964, and reopening in 1988 when the current owner purchased the resort.

## 17. *Gas, Food*

### Florence
The earliest Irish immigrants who settled here called the town "One Horse" for the little creek that runs through it. It was later named for the wife of A.B. Hammond, a prominent resident of Missoula. Hammond was instrumental in developing the area for timber production. He brought the railroad to the area to transport the lumber and built a sawmill to process it. Florence grew up at the center of a prime wheat producing area also. At one time, history records as many as 100 carloads of wheat per day were shipped out of the area.

## 18. *Historic Marker, Gas, Food, Lodging, Camping, Shopping*

### Stevensville
Stevensville is the oldest town in the state and claims a number of other important "firsts." The first church—St. Mary's Mission—was established in 1841, along with the first school in the Northwest. With the Mission came agriculture; Stevensville grew the first grain, ground the first flour, milled the first lumber, had the first planted fruit trees and practiced the first irrigation in Montana. John Owen established his trading post in 1850, and filed Montana's oldest water right in 1852.

The peaceful community of Stevensville, nestled in the beautiful Bitterroot Valley between the Sapphire and Bitterroot Mountain Ranges, has weathered both boom and bust in agriculture, mining and timber industries. Through the years Stevensville has managed to retain the simplicity and charm of its rural roots.

### H Fort Owen
Stevensville Junction

*Between 1831 and 1840 the Flathead Indians sent out three delegations, with St. Louis as their objective, to petition that "Black Robes" be sent to teach them. As a result Father De Smet, a Catholic missionary; established the original St. Mary's Mission here in 1841. He and his assistants hewed logs and built a dwelling, carpenter and blacksmith shops, and a chapel. They drove in the first oxen with wagons, carts, and plows that year and in 1842 brought cows from Colville, Washington, and raised a crop of wheat and garden produce, probably the first in Montana.*

*In 1843, assisted by Father Ravalli and others, he built the first grist mill. The stones were brought from Antwerp, Belgium, via the Columbia River.*

*The Mission was sold to Major John Owen in 1850. On its site he built a trading post and fort, the north wall of which stands. The Major was a genial and convivial host when travelers came that way, and for many years Fort Owen was an important trading center for whites as well as Indians.*

### S Bitterroot Emporium
3946 Hwy. 93, Mile Marker 67, Stevensville.
777-7138 or fax 777-4451

The Bitterroot Emporium is often referred to as one of Montana's most interesting stores. They feature the finest quality antiques, vintage spurs and bits, guns, and artifacts of the American West. You'll find a premium variety of art and prints by well known artists. The collection of unique cabin and ranch furniture and decor also includes, lighting, candles, pillows and more will help you achieve that special touch in your home or cabin. This is also a great place to find that special gift or fabulous piece of jewelry. Absolutely the best of the old and new. Find the Emporium just 20 minutes south of Missoula, on Hwy. 93 at Mile Marker 67.

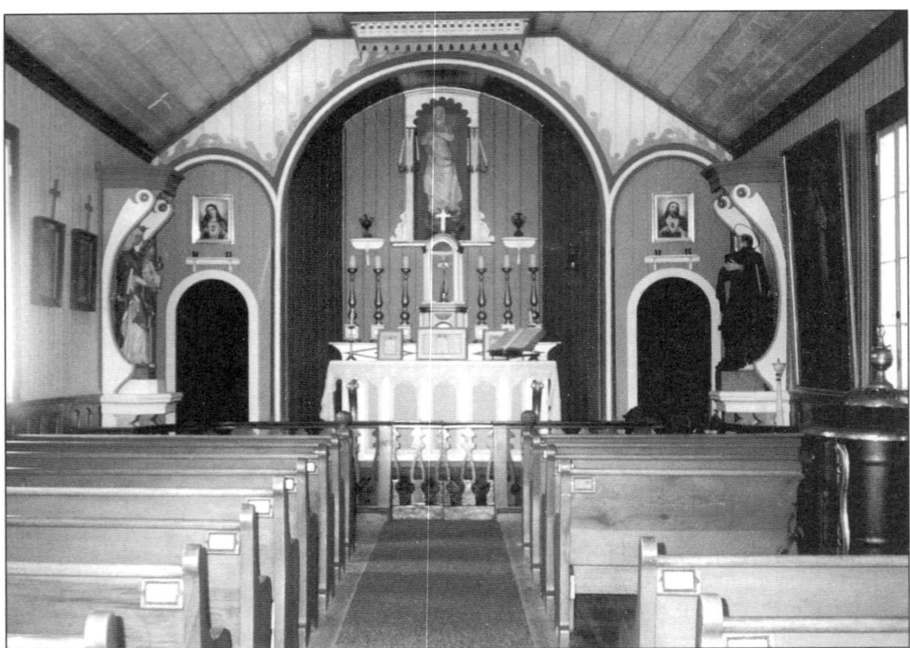
The chapel at St. Mary's Mission.

## 19. *Attraction, Gas, Food, Lodging, Camping, Shopping*

### T Fort Owen Monument State Park (Day Use Only)

25 miles south of Missoula on U.S. 93 to Stevensville Junction, then .5 miles east of Secondary 269. 444-2535

Fort Owen State Park in the Bitterroot Valley of western Montana is the site of many "firsts" in the state. Its history intertwines with that of Montana's first Catholic church and is the site of the first permanent white settlement in Montana. The first saw mill, the first grist mill, the first agricultural development, the first water right and the first school are all credited to the Fort Owen site.

Lewis and Clark passed the future site of Fort Owen on their way to the Pacific in 1805. Soon the entire Northwest was the new fur bonanza for Great Britain and the United States.

Christian Indians from the East brought Catholicism to the Bitterroot Valley. In 1841, Father Pierre Jean DeSmet came here to establish the first Christian Mission in what is now Montana.

The early years at St. Mary's Mission were encouraging and productive. However, by the late 1840s the missionaries were beleaguered by lack of funds, apostasy among the converts, and continual harassment from the Blackfeet Indians. In 1850, the Jesuits decided to close St. Mary's temporarily. At this point, John Owen stepped into Montana history.

### John Owen

John Owen was born in Philadelphia, Pennsylvania on June 27, 1818. He came west as a licensed trader or sutler with a regiment of United Slates Mounted Riflemen, recruited to man military posts along the Oregon Trail. The regiment wintered near Fort Hall, Idaho, in 1849-1850. Near Fort Hall, Owen also met Nancy, a Shoshoni woman whom he formally married in 1858. Owen resigned his sutlership and by autumn of 1850 he arrived in the Bitterroot Valley to begin trading the Indians and the growing numbers of immigrants.

### The Agency Years

In 1856, John Owen was appointed acting agent to the Flathead Nation and in 1857 the position was confirmed. Fort Owen was the Flathead Agency Headquarters until 1860 when the reservation headquarters was moved north to the Jocko Valley.

As agent Owen had problems with governmental indifference and negligence. He frequently drew on his personal funds and supplies to relieve the bitter hardships for his charges. He was also plagued with pressures from illegal white squatters.

A weary and disgusted John Owen resigned as Flathead Agent in July of 1862.

### Fort Owen Transitional Years

The decade of the 1860s brought many changes to the Bitterroot Valley. A trading establishment built by Frank H. Worden and C. P. Higgins at Hell Gate Ronde on the recently completed Mullan Road (west of the present-day Missoula) competed with Fort Owen. The gold camps provided an outlet for the agricultural produce from the bitterroot, but Fort Owen was no longer the only "bastion of civilization."

After Nancy's death in 1868, Owen's mental health began to deteriorate. Always a social drinker, he now drank heavily and in 1871, diagnosed as suffering from "dementia," Owen was committed to St. John's Hospital in Helena. In 1874 Governor Benjamin Potts declared John Owen legally insane and deported him from Montana Territory. Owen's old friend William Bass accompanied him to Philadelphia, where Owen remained with his family until his death on July 12, 1889.

### After John Owen

The Fort Owen property was purchased by Washington J. McCormick at a sheriff's sale in 1872. Ironically, McCormick outlived Owen by only few months.

In 1937, an acre of land enclosing the historic ruins of Fort Owen was donated by the McCormick heirs to the State of Montana to be administered by the State Department of Fish, Wildlife and Parks as a State Monument. In 1971, the Monument was entered on the National Register of Historic Places.

1. East Barracks. Completed during the adobe reconstruction of 1860, the east barracks contains four separate rooms for distinct uses—Owen's bedroom, his office, the guest room, and the dormitory room.

2. Root Cellar. The root cellar was completed in 1860 and used for food storage. The foundations are all that remain.

3. Well House. The original 1860 wellhouse cov-

*Fort Owens. The East Barracks as viewed from the southeast corner of the fort.*

ered a stone-lined shaft from which water was drawn. The present wellhouse is reconstruction based on old photographs and archaeological evidence.

*Reprinted from Montana Fish, Wildlife & Parks article.*

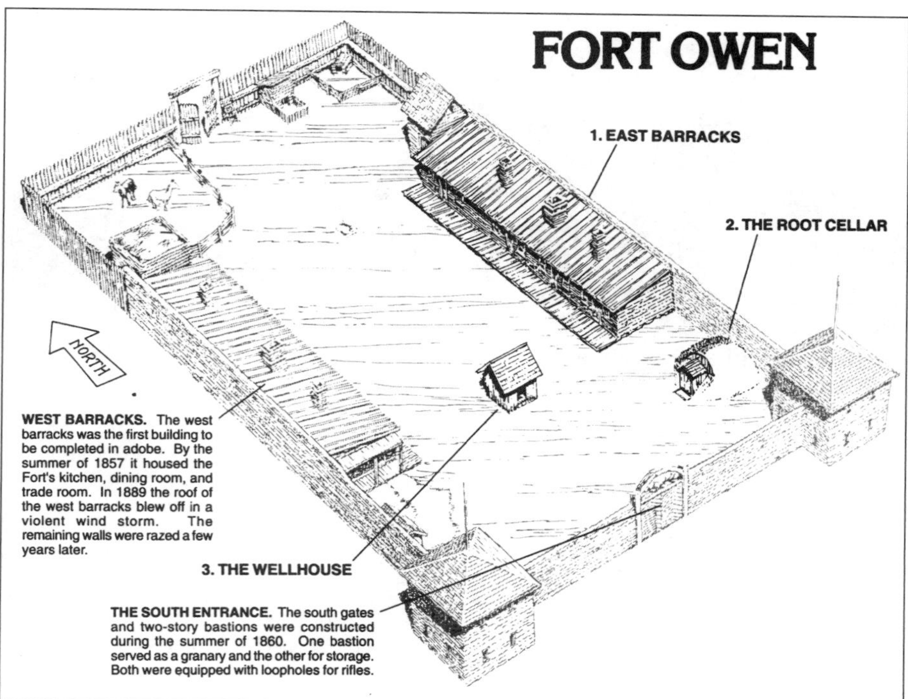

FORT OWEN
1. EAST BARRACKS
2. THE ROOT CELLAR
NORTH
WEST BARRACKS. The west barracks was the first building to be completed in adobe. By the summer of 1857 it housed the Fort's kitchen, dining room, and trade room. In 1889 the roof of the west barracks blew off in a violent wind storm. The remaining walls were razed a few years later.
3. THE WELLHOUSE
THE SOUTH ENTRANCE. The south gates and two-story bastions were constructed during the summer of 1860. One bastion served as a granary and the other for storage. Both were equipped with loopholes for rifles.

## T St. Mary's Mission

4th St. W., Stevensville

Established in 1841 by Father Pierre DeSmet, the St. Mary's Mission was the first permanent white settlement in Montana. The site has a restored log chapel and priest's quarters, a pharmacy, and cemetery. Many notably significant people are buried here with headstones that reflect both white settlers as well as Indians.

A tour of Historic St. Mary's Mission is a visit to the cradle of civilization in Montana-a truly historical experience.

The history of St. Mary's Mission begins with arrival in the Northwest of twenty-four Iroquois Indians employed as trappers by the Hudson's Bay Company. During the 1823-24 season, twelve of these Iroquois remained among the Flatheads in the Red Willow (now Bitterroot) valley. They were adopted into the tribe and married the Flathead women.

Coming from a nation which had been introduced to Christianity some two hundred years earlier, when they gathered around the campfire in the evenings the Iroquois talked about white men who wore long black gowns, carried crucifixes, did not marry and whose practice it was to instruct people, bringing them to know God and all things to enable them to live after death. The Flatheads, together with their neighbors the Nez Perce, became so interested in these stories that between 1831 and 1839 they sent four delegations to St. Louis to obtain a Black Robe to live among them to teach them all these things to which the Iroquois referred.

It was September 24, 1841, when Father Pierre Jean DeSmet, together with his fellow Jesuit missionaries, Fathers Gregory Mengarini and Nicolas Point, and three Lay Brothers arrived in the Bitterroot valley with their belongings and supplies in three carts and a wagon, the first vehicles to enter the area. They established the first white settlement in what became Montana on the east bank of the Bitterroot river, immediately west of the present town of Stevensville. The new mission, as well as the river and the tallest mountain peak to the west, was named "St. Mary's." Fifty years later the name of the river was changed to "Bitterroot" by the Forest Service.

The first chapel measured 25'x 33', with two galleries in order to accommodate the entire tribe. Father DeSmet made a trip to Fort Colville of the Hudson Bay Company and returned with supplies to tide them over the winter, plus wheat, oats, potatoes and garden seeds for the first crops.

The news of the Black Robes' arrival spread, and within a short time Indians from many tribes came to visit. The following year, a larger church, 30'x60', was built a few hundred yards east of the river. Following a trip to Fort Vancouver on the west coast, from where he brought into Montana the first cattle, swine and poultry, Father DeSmet returned to St. Louis. After seeing off a group of helpers to travel overland to St. Mary's, he left for Europe to seek recruits and funds for the new mission area in the Northwest.

One of his recruits was a true renaissance man, Father Anthony Ravalli, S. J., an Italian, who arrived at St. Mary's in November 1845. In addition to being a Jesuit priest, he was Montana's first physician, surgeon and pharmacist. He was an architect, an artist and sculptor. He built the first grist mill and saw mill. Religion classes were held twice a day. Also, there were classes in reading, writing and arithmetic, taught in the Salish language. There was a band which played numbers by German and Italian composers. They were taught to plow, plant, cultivate, irrigate and harvest crops, and to tend cattle, sheep, pigs and poultry.

A larger church was under construction in 1846. Before it's completion, problems with the Flatheads' traditional enemies, the Blackfeet, forced what was intended to be a temporary closure of the Mission. By terms of a Conditional Bill of Sale in November 1850, John Owen, a former army sutler, bought the improvements for $250. Should the Jesuits return within two years the mills and fields would revert to them. When they were unable to return by the designated time, the Jesuits sent word to burn the church to save it from desecration. The former mission site became Fort Owen, a trading post.

It was sixteen years later (1866) when Father Joseph Giorda, Superior for the Rocky Mountain area, called back Father Ravalli and Brother William Claessens and reestablished St. Mary's Mission about a mile south of Fort Owen. Brother Claessens built a little chapel, the fourth he had built for St. Mary's, to which he attached a study, dining room, kitchen and a story and a half barn. Father Giorda made the "new" St. Mary's the Jesuit mission headquarters for the Rocky Mountain province. In 1879 an addition to the front of the building doubled the size of the chapel. The entire mission complex has been restored to that date-the peak of its beauty.

Today Old St. Mary's stands as a monument to those heroic sons of the mountains, through whose efforts the first trail into Montana was blazed with the Cross, and to those dedicated Jesuits who were the pioneers of Montana's pioneers. The mission complex includes the chapel/residence, Father Ravalli's log house/pharmacy, Chief Victor's house (now a small Indian museum), and DeSmet Park, with picnic facilities. Most chapel and residence furnishings are the handiwork of Father Ravalli.

Tours of the Mission are available from April through October from 10:15 a.m. to 4:00 p.m. daily.

*Reprinted from Historic St. Mary's Mission, Inc. brochure.*

### Montana Trivia

The bitterroot is Montana's state flower. It can live for over a year without water and can be revived even after it has been dried and pressed. It was considered a luxury food item by Native Americans.

Section 7

**T Stevensville Historical Museum**
517 Main St. in Stevensville. 777-2269

This museum features displays and artifacts emphasizing the early history of the Bitterroot Valley and Stevensville, which is the earliest white settlement in Montana, established around St. Mary's Mission. Open Memorial Day to Labor Day on Thursday, Friday & Saturday 11 a.m. to 4 p.m. and on Sunday from 1 p.m. to 4 p.m.

**A Rocky Mountain Express Lube & Service Center**
Hwy 93, 1/2 mile North of the Y, Stevensville. 777-0747

Don't let car troubles affect your vacation travel plans. Stop into Rocky Mountain Express Lube for any of your car troubles, oil change, tune-ups or general questions about your vehicle. With ASE certified mechanics, you are guaranteed to get quick, honest and reliable service. One of the only places around that can service semi trucks, motor homes and RVs. Offering senior citizen discounts and crazy days specials on Wednesdays.

**F Stevi Café**
202 Main St., Stevensville. 777-2171

Stevi Café is where home-cooked specialties are featured and everyone is treated like a friend. Stop in to join locals at a favorite place to enjoy home-made breads, rolls and pies baked fresh daily. You'll also be tempted with a variety of lunch specials. Prime rib is served Friday and Saturday nights, and evening buffets are offered Friday through Sunday. They serve an exceptional breakfast buffet on Saturdays and Sundays from 9 a.m. to noon. Stevi Café is open Monday through Saturday, 6 a.m. to 8 p.m., and Sunday until 4 p.m. The café can also accommodate weddings and parties for large groups of up to 100. A non-smoking dining room is available.

**F Mary's Place Café and Drive Thru**
110 N. Main St., Stevensville. 777-5097

The locals love Mary's Place Café and Drive Thru and so will you. Enjoy the quaint atmosphere in this friendly café. Daily specials that will tantalize your taste buds, and on Friday nights they serve succulent steaks and prime rib on Saturday night, among many favorite dinners. Throughout the week you can choose anything from burgers to full dinners. A variety of delicious soups made from scratch are always available. Other home-made specialties include rolls, Hoagie buns, and ice cream sandwiches on chocolate chip cookies. The café includes an ice cream shop with all your favorite treats. In a hurry or ready to relax over a great meal? Either way you'll enjoy Mary's Place.

**F Olde Coffee Mill**
225 Main St., Stevensville. 777-2939

**S Majestic Mountains Gift Shop & Gallery**
205 Main St., Stevensville. 777-0302.
www.majesticmountains.com

Majestic Mountains Gift Shop and Gallery is a wonderful new shop, located in downtown Stevensville in the heart of the Bitterroot Valley. The shop is beautifully appointed and offers everything from everyday gifts to elegant treasures from around the world. The owner, Kathy Marcus, offers art from international artists as well as locally known artists and craftsmen. There is a delightful "Always Christmas" corner tucked in the store. Browse an exciting variety of limited edition gifts, collectibles, and one-of-a-kind items, clocks, bronze, jewelry, tableware, porcelain, carvings, crystal, art glass, and furthermore, a home decorating catalog center. They are open Tuesday through Saturday.

**M Chantilly Theatre - Bitterroot Valley Community Theatre**
319 Main Street, Stevensville. 777-2722

The Chantilly Theatre, nestled in the heart of the Bitterroot Valley, has provided art patrons with original and classic theatrical productions for over 13 years. The community theatre entertains with a diverse set of productions, from side splitting comedies to large scale musicals and interactive murder mystery dinner theatres and special holiday productions. Their repertoire includes everything from Western flavor to Broadway hits. The Chantilly has attracted audiences from as far away as Seattle and Los Angeles with shows throughout the year. Call a find out what is playing while you are in the area.

**M Eickert Realty**
307 Main Street, Stevensville. 777-3696 or fax 777-5921.

## 20. *Attraction*

**T Lee Metcalf National Wildlife Refuge**
located 25 miles south of Missoula, and two miles north of Stevensville. 777-5552

Located in the Bitterroot Valley of southwestern Montana; 25 miles south of Missoula. Majestic scenery dominates with the 9,000 foot Bitterroot Mountains located across the Bitterroot River to the west. Between 100,000 and 150,000 people visit the refuge annually. Habitat is primarily riparian and consists of cottonwood and ponderosa pine overstory with 13 man-made impoundments ranging in size from 5 to 80 acres. Wildfowl Lane, a county road, bisects the lower half of the refuge and provides excellent, diverse "watchable wildlife" viewing and provides year-round access to a fully accessible 140-acre nature trail recreation area along the river. Waterfowl hunting and archery hunting for white-tailed deer are allowed. A resident pair of bald eagles and several pair of osprey nest annually on the refuge, which provides habitat for 235 bird species including 105 confirmed nesters. Common mammals include white-tailed deer, coyote, otter, porcupine, Columbian ground squirrel, and yellow-bellied marmots. The refuge maintains a tremendous environmental education program for the local schools and University systems, and serves as the State Coordinator for the annual Junior Duck Stamp Art Contest, as part of the national "Conservation Through the Arts" program.

From Missoula, follow Highway 93 south to Florence. Take Eastside Highway 203 south eight miles to Wildfowl Lane. The Refuge can also be accessed from Highway 93 at the Stevensville cut-off road (269). Follow this road one mile into Stevensville. Turn left at Hwy. 203, then one block to Wildfowl Lane or continue on into Stevensville along Main Street to Third Street. The Refuge office is located at 115 W. Third.

*Reprinted from www.recreation.gov*

## 21. *Lewis & Clark, Attraction, Gas, Food*

### Victor

Originally named Garfield, the name was changed to honor Chief Victor of the Salish tribe.

**D Sgt. Ordway**
September 8, 1805

*"passed over Smooth plains in this valley. the Mountains are rough on each side and are covred with pine and on the tops of which are covd. with Snow."*

**T Willoughby Environmental Education Area**
2 miles north of Victor.

Encompassing 40 acres at the base of the Sapphire Range, this area provides a 1-mile nature trail loop through three different habitats. An interpretive

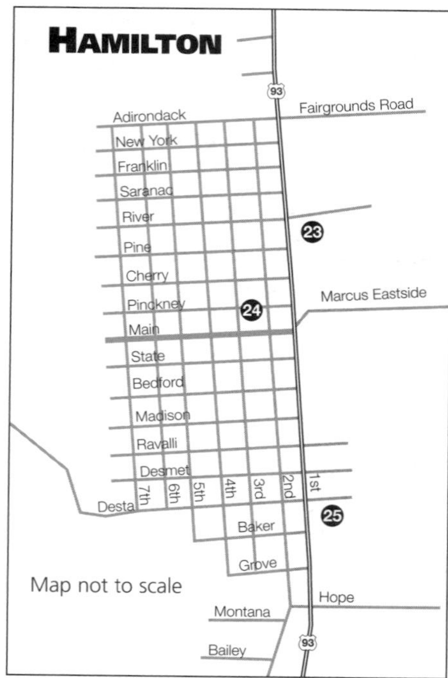


brochure that describes their ecology is furnished for visitors' benefit—a wonderful hike that is also educational!

## T Victor Heritage Museum

Blake and Main in Victor. 642-3997

Housed in the old railroad depot the museum is run by volunteers and preserves the rich heritage of railroading, American Indians, schools, churches and natural resources. Open Memorial Day through Labor Day. No admission charged but donations are always welcome.

## F Victor Steakhouse

2424 Meridian Road, Victor. 642-3300

The Victor Steakhouse is the perfect setting for a large family dinner, or a quiet, romantic meal for two. Certified angus steaks are their specialty, but they also offer a wide range of seafood and chicken dishes. They have many micro-brews on tap, an extensive wine list to choose from, and poker machines in the lounge area for entertainment. The decor at the Victor Steakhouse is rustic, with a casual, yet elegant atmosphere.

# On the Trail of Lewis & Clark

### The Bitterroot Valley And The Flathead Indians

On the morning of Sept. 4, everything was wet and frozen, and the ground covered with snow. They went over the crest and down the other side of the mountain range, a distance of about twelve miles, where they met a village of the Flathead nation consisting of 33 lodges, some 440 people, and 500 horses.

Lewis and Clark were able to purchase 13 more horses from the Flatheads. On Sept. 6, they set out down the Bitterroot River and reached the wide valley of that river on Sept. 7. They passed down the valley with no peculiar incident until they reached Lolo Creek. They named their camp Travellers Rest.

Toby informed the captains that they were only four days from the Missouri, if they should continue down the Bitterroot about nine miles to the Clark's Fork; go up that river to the Blackfoot River; and then on to the Great Falls. He also told them that they were now to leave the Bitterroot River and turn west up Lolo Creek on the Nez Perce trail.

One of the hunters met three Flatheads up Lolo Creek and brought them back to Travellers Rest. One of them agreed to accompany the Expedition as a guide over the Bitterroots, and introduce them to his people who lived on the other side at a place where they could build dugouts and sail to the ocean.

### To The Ocean

On Sept. 11, the explorers set out again, and two days later reached Lolo Pass. On the 14th they began what was to be the most difficult part of their entire journey. Horses fell on the steep trail, one nearly 100 yards down the mountain side. There was no game and they were forced to eat candles, horses, and their insipid "portable soup." There were times when they had no water. At other times there was nothing at all to eat. Poor diet caused the men to weaken and sores developed on their bodies. In spite of these hardships, they eventually reached the Nez Perce on the Clearwater River. They left their horses with these people, made another cache, built five dugouts, and navigated the Clearwater, Snake and Columbia rivers until finally, in November, they reached the Ocean.

They built a winter fort near the coast and christened it "Fort Clatsop" in honor of their neighbors, the Clatsop Indians.

On March 26, 1806, the Expedition began its return up the Columbia on tile homeward journey. They collected their horses from the Nez Perce, and on June 30 arrived back at Travellers Rest.

### The Return Journey

At Travellers Rest, on July 3, the party separated. Clark with 50 horses, 20 men, Sacagawea and her baby, headed up the Bitterroot River to the place they had met the Flatheads the year before. They then crossed the Continental Divide at Gibbon's Pass; crossed the head of the Big Hole valley, in a southeasterly direction, passing a place where the Indians had recently been digging roots; stopped at a hot springs; and then crossed Big Hole Pass; and arrived at Camp Fortunate on July 8. Here they recovered their dugouts and the supplies which had been cached the year before.

*Text and drawings excerpted from U.S. Forest Service pamphlet "Lewis and Clark in the Rocky Mountains"*

## L Sweet Sage Guest House

838 Seathouse Creek Rd., Victor. phone or fax 642-6400

## L Time After Time Bed & Breakfast

197 Pistol Lane, Victor. 642-3258.
www.montana.com/timeaftertime

## L Blackbird's Flyfishing Lodge

1754 Hwy 93, Victor. 642-6375 or fax 642-6375. Toll free 800-210-8648. www.blackbirds.com

## S Painted Mountain Gallery

1771 US Hwy 93 N., Mile Post 56, Victor. 642-6966. wwwpatbakerart.com

Pat Baker welcomes you to a gallery filled with her beautiful country, western and wildlife paintings, including limited editions of Lewis & Clark. The gallery is also a consignment gallery for many local artists, offering hand built furniture, stonework, metalwork, woodwork, wood boxes made from wood collected around the world, carved bears, and sculpture. A collection of Native American handmade jewelry and bronzes are also offered. Enjoy incredible views from the gallery on it's hilltop setting just 3 miles south of Victor Items in the gallery change frequently, so visit more than once and find that special treasure for yourself or a special gift. Visit their web site for a preview!

**22.** *Historic Marker, Gas, Food, Shopping*

## Corvallis

Just seven miles north of Hamilton lies the village of Corvallis surrounded by some of the most productive agricultural land in Montana. Several orchards also survive here. The town was named for Corvallis, Oregon, by some of the early settlers who came from there to settle in this fertile Montana valley.

## H The Welcome Creek Wilderness

Rock Creek

Rock Creek, one of the nation's most celebrated blue-ribbon trout streams, is bordered on the west, just a few miles southwest of here, by the Welcome Creek Wilderness Area, established in 1977.

Not a typical wilderness area, Welcome Creek is a small enclave of undisturbed forest designated to protect an important watershed and contains no grand-scale scenic wonders. But to one retired forest ranger it is "a major island in an ocean of roads and logged areas." Welcome Creek is providing a unique opportunity to study long-term changes that logging and management produce on tree growth, soil fertility, wildlife diversity, and watershed protection. It is also a favorite summer home and migration route for about 300 elk that winter in the state's Threemile Game Range in the western foothills of the Sapphire Mountains.

### S The Brooks

Corvallis, 961-6895

The grandeur of The Brooks is back. Located in a beautiful Victorian House dating from 1894, The Brooks is a landmark for the Bitterroot Valley and a perfect stop for the traveler heading to Missoula. Offering a wide-array of gifts, this is a perfect stop for all of your Christmas shopping. Stop in and check out their 17 theme decorated trees.

## 23. *Historic Marker, Attraction, Gas, Food, Lodging, Shopping*

### Hamilton

Hamilton is the county seat for Ravalli County, the third largest county in the state. In 1887, Marcus Daly was shopping for a business endeavor other than mining and started a lumber industry on the banks of the Bitterroot River. Daly began acquiring land to develop a 22,000 acre stock farm in the late 1880s. Robert O'Hara and James Hamilton were brought in by Daly to design and develop the town. The town was named after Hamilton, and O'Hara became the town's first mayor.

### H Rocky Mountain Laboratory

Hamilton

*In earlier days, Rocky Mountain spotted fever was a dreaded malady in the West. The first case of spotted fever was recorded in the Bitterroot Valley in 1873. Neither cause nor cure was known and mortality was high.*

*Through efforts of the Montana State Board of Health and Entomology, scientists were brought in to solve the mystery. By 1906 they had proved that the bite of a wood tick was the cause of the disease, which was found later to exist throughout the United States. A preventive vaccine was finally developed in this remote laboratory. Yearly vaccination of those who may become exposed to tick bite and effectual treatment methods have solved the problem.*

*A modern laboratory, now operated by the U.S. Public Health Service, has replaced the tents, log cabins, woodsheds and abandoned schoolhouses that served the first handful of workers. Research has been expanded to include many infectious diseases that are problems in the West.*

### Montana Trivia

Chief Joseph conducted one of the most masterful retreats in military history. Up to that time he had never fought a battle. He led his band of men, women, children, cows and horses from the Ronde Grande in Idaho through Lolo Pass, into Yellowstone Park and through Montana to what he thought was the Canadian border, only to find he was forty miles short. During this time he fought eleven battles against four U.S. armies. All but the last successful.

### H Marcus Daly Mansion

north of Hamilton

*Hamilton's Daly Mansion was a summer retreat for Butte's "Copper King" Marcus Daly and his wife, Margaret. Daly came to the United States as a poor Irish immigrant at age 15. Attracted to western mining camps, he quickly learned mining skills. Through ingenuity and hard work, he made a fortune from copper and was influential in Montana's politics and economy for many years.*

*Daly began acquiring land to develop a 22,000 acre stock farm in the late 1880s and platted the town of Hamilton in 1890. His prized thoroughbreds, raised and trained in the Bitterroot Valley, set new records at Eastern tracks. Now open for tours, this 42 room Georgian revival style mansion contains many exquisite Italian marble fireplaces and an elegant central staircase. Newspapers of that period termed this mansion one of Montana's largest homes, and also one of the West's most pretentious and costly dwellings. Surrounding landscaped grounds include many exotic trees and graceful flowerbeds. Other structures include a greenhouse, playhouse, laundry, servant's quarters and a heated swimming pool.*

*Daly's mansion is located to your left, just off the Eastside Highway.*

### Montana Trivia

Clarence Birdseye of frozen food fame once worked in the Bitterroot Valley as a field naturalist for the U.S. Biological Survey. In 1909 he studied which animals are carriers of ticks and Rocky Mountainspotted fever

### T Daly Mansion

251 Eastside Hwy in Hamilton. 363-6004. www.bitterroot.net/dmpt/daly.html

Marcus Daly, an Irish immigrant, made his fortune in the mines of Butte and founded the Anaconda Mining Company. One of Montana's colorful "Copper Kings" he established the towns of Anaconda, with his smelter, and Hamilton, with his lumber industry. In the late 1880s, Marcus Daly built his family a summer home in Hamilton, the heart of the beautiful Bitterroot Valley.

The Daly Mansion and the estate known as "Riverside", were once part of Daly's 22,000 acre Bitterroot Stock Farm. The Mansion occupies 24,000 square feet on three floors, with 24 bedrooms, 14 bathrooms, and 7 fireplaces, 5 of which are faced with Italian marble.

The Mansion today, a Georgian Revival Style residence, was designed by A. J. Gibson and completed in 1910 for Margaret Daly, Marcus Daly's widow. After Mrs. Daly's death in 1941, the Mansion was closed and boarded up until 1987, when it was opened to the public. The Mansion grounds feature a wide variety of trees, a tennis court, swimming pool, children's playhouse, greenhouse, laundry building and boat house.

Today, the Mansion and fifty acres of grounds surrounding it are owned by the State of Montana, managed by the Daly Mansion Preservation Trust, and recognized as a National Historic Site. The Mansion is open from April 15 to October 15. Tours are available by appointment in the off season.

*Reprinted from Daly Mansion brochure.*

### F B J'S Family Restaurant & Lounge

900 N. First St., Hamilton. 363-4650

Enjoy this fantastic family oriented establishment decorated with artwork from a local gallery. BJ's is famous among locals for their homemade pizzas & pies. They offer daily lunch & dinner specials, a range of homestyle cooking, as well as prime rib and seafood every night. Breakfast is served all day, and Sunday offers a breakfast buffet. They are handicap accessible and have a private banquet facility which can accommodate 60 people. The adjacent lounge offers a happy hour. Don't miss this fabulous restaurant with friendly staff in a great location. Locals love it!

### Montana Trivia

Montana has more species of mammals than any other state. An average square mile in Montana carries 1.4 elk, 1.4 pronghorn antelope, 3.3 deer, and 6.2 humans. The state also has more than two thousand species of flowering plants. On the domestic side, cows outnumber humans by three to one.

**L Holiday Inn Express-Bitterroot River Inn**
139 Bitterroot Plaza Drive (North edge of town). 375-2525

Enjoy the latest in lodging convenience during your stay in Hamilton. Nestled on the Bitterroot River, the Inn offers breathtaking views of the stunning Bitterroot Mountain Range right from your room. Fishing access to one of Montana's finest rivers is available right outside your room.The area's newest facility offers lodge-style sleeping rooms with extended continental breakfast, 25" TV's with HBO; data ports, in-room microwaves and refrigerators; in-room coffee makers and blow driers; and indoor heated pool, hot tub and sauna. Deluxe king suites with garden-size whirlpool tubs, king suites with whirlpool tubs, and junior suites are available. For business meetings, the Inn offers a deluxe conference suite with board room for six people, and a 4,000 sq. ft. conference center for up to 400 people.

**L Hamilton Super 8 Motel**
1325 N. 1st, Hwy 93 N., Hamilton. 363-2940 or 800-800-8000

The Hamilton Super 8 has had the "Pride of Super 8" award every year it's been open. With a clean, friendly atmosphere, the motel offers quiet rooms overlooking the mountains, a complimentary morning toast bar and coffee, cable TV, non-smoking rooms, free local calls, air conditioning, and guest laundry. When checking in at the 24-hour front desk, you may want to ask about the AARP/Senior, AAA, VIP, and group rates. The motel also has jacuzzi suites available, for an utterly relaxing vacation.

## 24.

**T Ravalli County Museum**
3rd & Bedford, Hamilton. 363-3338

Built in 1900 as the Ravalli County Courthouse, the museum displays extensive Flathead Indian artifacts, a veteran's exhibit, and "Apple Boom Days" relics. The museum houses the catalogued archives of all of the old newspapers published in the valley. Items are also exhibited from the Rocky Mountain Lab Tick Museum which contributed to important research on spotted fever and wood ticks responsible for disease since World War I. On Sundays you can enjoy a special program on such things as history, cowboy poetry or folk music.

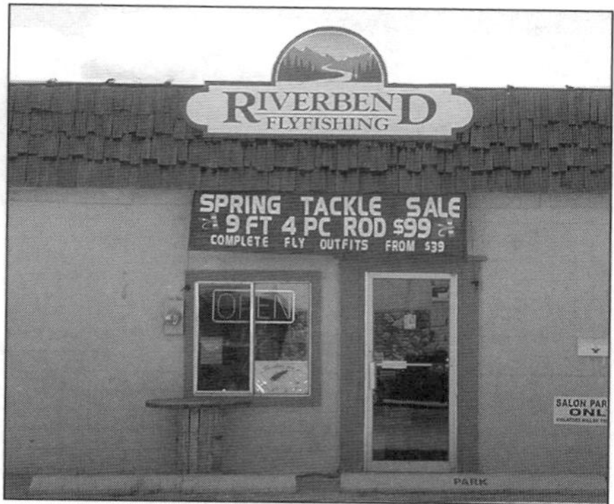


**VS Riverbend Flyfishing**
105 State St. in Hamilton. 363-4197, www.riverbendfly.com

Step into this shop and you'll probably see an "old guy" tying flies. Take a moment to chat with him and you'll quickly find Chuck Stranahan to be one of the most knowledgeable people you've ever heard speak on the subject. Chuck is a regular seminar speaker at sports shows, teaching fly tying and casting. He's also a writer, whose work appears nationally in flyfishing books and magazines. Most of the time, though, you'll find him tying flies and dispensing practical fishing advice in his shop. His whole shop harkens back to an era when quality was more important than fashion. Everything he stocks is there because of its quality and value, not its trendiness. Many of his flies started as local favorites and are now standards throughout the West. His guides are not only seasoned veterans, but some of the most respected in the industry. Casual anglers, those just getting started, and "old pro's" feel equally at home with Chuck and his crew. A stop at the shop is a treat in itself, and can be the makings of a memorable vacation.

**F The Spice of Life Eclectic Cafe**
163 S. 2nd St., Hamilton. 363-4432

Spice of Life is where a culinary adventure awaits! Using the valley's freshest ingredients, they create fabulously flavored food from all over the world. The setting has a historical, rustic decor with a relaxed atmosphere. You can sit in the dining room, on the comfortable couches, or at the espresso bar. The Spice of Life invites you to come as you are, kick back and enjoy good food, good company, live music on Wednesday nights, and delicious coffee and desserts. Check out their great, yet moderately priced, wine list and choice of locally brewed beers.

## The Big Ditch

The history of Montana is rich with the tales of entrepreneurs and ambitious communities seeking ways to attract settlers. The early residents of the Bitterroot saw an opportunity when they noticed how well trees grew in the Valley. The logic was, if the native trees grew so well, then planted orchard trees would do just as well. They dreamed of a fruit growing region that would rival those in Washington State. The idea was to develop the orchards, then sell them to buyers out east.

They planned a huge irrigation system. The $3.5 million required to build the system was provided by investors from Chicago after the federal government turned down the project and attempts to raise the money locally failed.

Work on the ditch began. The dam at Lake Como was raised by 50 feet and by 1906, the first 17 miles of the 6 foot deep, 24 foot wide ditch was finished. The next 75 miles required siphoning and making flumes of the water across many canyons and creeks and under the Bitterroot River. By 1910, although there was still insufficient water, additional orchards were being planted up and down the Valley. Barrels of water were hauled in to water the seedlings.

In 1910, fruit from orchards planted in the 1890s was sent to the East in hopes of attracting buyers. The prospective buyers were treated like royalty—for a while. They were given train tickets to Missoula and met in chauffer driven cars. They were wined and dined in hopes of closing the sale. Once they signed, they were left alone to do as they please. The investors who bought before arriving weren't treated as regally. They were met in Missoula, then taken to their orchard and dumped. By 1918 the Big Ditch Company was bankrupt and the Chicago investors foreclosed. Today few of the orchards remain. The land is used for other crops. The federal government took over the ditch and now sells the water to farmers and ranchers.

### *Montana Trivia*

The Bitterroot Mountains are the longest mountain range in the state and form the western border of Montana. They are the eastern edge of the largest wilderness area in the country—the Bitterroot Selway National Wilderness Area.

## F Nap's Grill

220 N. 2nd St., Hamilton. 363-0136. www.cybernet1.com/naps

Nap's Grill has been known as one of the local's favorites ever since they were awarded "Best Steaks and Best Burgers" by local businesses in the Hamilton area. David Letterman even stopped in during his visit to Hamilton. Try one of their famous steaks with mouth watering sauteed mushrooms! The pleasant, family atmosphere and quick service adds to the overall good time you will enjoy at Nap's, for lunch or dinner any day of the week. Visit Nap's on-line!

## F A Place to Ponder Bakery & Café

166 Second Street, Hamilton. 363-0080

## L City Center Motel

415 West Main St., Hamilton. 363-1651

Conveniently located in downtown Hamilton, the City Center Motel offers 14 clean and comfortable rooms. Seven of the rooms are complete with kitchens, one of which is wheel chair accessible, and all have expanded cable TV with remotes and HBO, AT&T long distance service and free local calls. Their guests especially enjoy the quiet off-highway location which is within walking distance to main street shops and restaurants. Stay in the heart of Hamilton while you enjoy the many local sites including Painted Rocks Lake, Lake Como, Daly Mansion, the Hamilton Golf Course and much more.

### Montana Trivia

When officials in Idaho Territory agreed to cede some land to form the new state of Montana, they expected the line to be drawn at the Continental Divide. Political shenanigans caused the boundary to be the Bitterroot Mountains instead. The left Idaho with its strange panhandle.

## L Red Willow Bed & Breakfast

147 West Bridge Road, Hamilton. 375-1101. www.Redwillowinn.com

The Red Willow Inn Bed and Breakfast will take you into the past, just one mile from downtown Hamilton. The guest rooms have private baths, and the king size room has a jetted tub for pure relaxation. A healthy, hearty breakfast that can be enjoyed inside or outdoors on a large wraparound deck with beautiful views. Located in the heart of the Bitterroot Valley, many activities are convenient from The Red Willow Inn, including fishing, hunting, hiking, biking, walks, rafting, golfing, great shopping and restaurants and wonderful weather. An easy walk to town and the Bitterroot River. Also on the premises is an antique and gift shop. They are located only 40 miles south of Missoula international airport.

## S Out West

202 W. Main, Hamilton. 375-0017, spike1733@aol.com

Out West offers Montana's best & more! From t-shirts & sweatshirts to vests & western decor, from western souvenirs & gifts to furniture, linens & rocks, Out West has it all in an elegant & friendly atmosphere. Browse their selection of Montana-made huckleberry products. Adjacent is a soda-fountain featuring Wilcoxin's ice-cream made in Livingston, Montana. Enjoy their wonderful desserts, sodas, sundaes and espressos!

## S Robbins

209 W. Main, Hamilton. 363-1733

Unwrap the magic at Robbins. As an award winning Hallmark Gold Crown Gallery, they offer absolutely unique items for gifts, decorating, celebrating & fun! Browse their selection of gourmet cookware for your kitchen and check out their Heritage Lace collection displaying over 20 lace patterns. Let their breathtaking exhibit of Swarovski Crystal catch your eye. Remember there is always something new at Robbins.

## S Art Focus Fine Arts & Framing

215 W. Main, Hamilton. 363-4112

Robert Neaves, professional artist and owner of Art Focus Fine Arts and Framing, invites you to invest in a beautiful piece of art that will remain with you for a lifetime. The gallery offers original art from a variety of artists in oil, watercolor, pastels, and original graphics, with an emphasis on local Montana scenery. Limited edition prints are available, and this gallery has access to most images offered on today's market. Discover locally made ceramics that are art pieces as well as functional. You will also find jewelry in glass, silver, ceramic, and semiprecious stones in necklaces, earrings, and pins created by various local artisans. Sculpture and decorative posters are also offered. Custom framing is available to complete that special piece.

## S Curious Goods a/k/a The Clothes Tree

301 W. Main St., Hamilton. 363-7003

Enjoy Curious Goods also known as The Clothes Tree, a fun store that offers a wonderful selection of the old and the new. Curious Goods specializes in vintage costume jewelry. You've never seen so many earrings, all sorted by color! You will also find a delightful assortment of small antiques and a variety of collectibles. You'll marvel at the great selection of vintage clothing. Take your pick from a fantastic collection of classy and consignment clothes. They offer a unique collection of vintage hats to top off that one-of-a-kind outfit only Judie Deaver, the proprietress, can provide at super prices. This is a really fun place to visit.

### S The Mill Antiques

140 Cherry Street, at 2nd & Cherry, Hamilton. 363-1968

The Mill Antiques is a distinctive old feed mill which now houses several distinctive shops. The rooms were once used for wheat, barley, and corn cribs. This wonderful building is filled with antiques, collectibles, and quality used items. Many different vendors supply items such as turn-of-the-century glass crystal, jewelry, furniture, books, violins, pictures, paintings, old kitchen relics, primitives, Western memorabilia, and numerous collectible and unique items. There is an up and operational train room where a collection of trains consisting of Lionel, HO, and a selection of old railroad memorabilia is available. You can always expect the unexpected at The Mill.

### S MIkesell's Fine Jewery

128 Main Street, Hamilton. 363-6236

### M Bitterroot Clock Repair & Custom Jewelry

241 N. 2nd St. Hamilton. 363-4006

## 25. *Gas, Food, Lodging*

### F Twin Kitchens

1094 S. First St., Hamilton. 363-3801

Twin Kitchens prides itself in offering "Choices in Family Dining." You can choose from a wide variety of Mexican, Oriental, and American style foods. The decor is fun for dining in a smoke-free, family atmosphere, with a kid's menu available. They also feature an espresso bar with a wide variety of specialty coffee drinks. The pick-up window makes it convenient for take-out food. Stop in for one of their famous breakfast burritos. Open for breakfast, lunch and dinner Monday–Saturday.

### F Coffee Cup Cafe

500 First St., Hamilton. 363-3822

Everything at the Coffee Cup Cafe is made from scratch, ranging from great homemade pies, to soups, chili, and tasty gravy. They have a great collection of antiques hanging on the walls, and lots of old time charm. With a 14-page menu, daily specials, great salads, and delicious home cooking, the Coffee Cup is popular among locals and travellers alike. Enjoy breakfast, lunch, and dinner any time of the day. Located right in downtown Hamilton.

### L Best Western Hamilton Inn

409 S. First St., Hamilton. 363-2142 or reservations at 1800426-4586

The Best Western Hamilton Inn is located 45-miles south of Missoula, in the heart of the Bitterroot Valley where western hospitality remains a way of life. The perfect choice for comfort, convenience & value, their ideal location allows guests to enjoy all Hamilton has to offer while the management and staff make every stay enjoyable. The city's best restaurants are within walking distance. Enjoy area recreation and attractions. Fly fishing, golfing, hiking, skiing & snowmobiling opportunities abound in the majestic Bitterroot Valley. Relax in their large outdoor hot tub after that long day of recreation and sight-seeing.

### L Bitterroot River Lodge

1182 Hwy 93, S, Hamilton. 363-0708.

The Bitterroot River Lodge is located on a peaceful and secluded four-hundred-acre property, with beautiful views in all directions. The Bitterroot River runs through the property and there are four lakes which may be used for fishing, along with the one mile of river. Wild life is seen daily. Guests may take a walk, play horseshoes, go for a bike ride, use the patio/barbeque area, or just relax in one of many comfortable areas. Rustic, cozy, and quiet describe the Bitterroot River Lodge where the sound of the river will soothe you to sleep. It is only ten minutes from downtown Hamilton.

### L Deffy's Motel

321 S. 1st St., Hwy 93, Hamilton. 363-1244 or reservations toll free at 800-363-1305

Deffy's Motel is a clean, comfortable motel, for the short or long term guest, offering suites with full kitchens. They are conveniently located in walking distance of downtown attractions. There are 1, 2, and 3 bed units with kitchens. Other amenities include cable TV, free local calls, hot tub, and convenient parking at your door. The motel is situated off the main street, providing a pleasant and

quiet atmosphere. A short walk takes you to Hamilton's wonderful restaurants, gift shops, antique stores and art galleries. And just around the corner you'll find a city park, movie theater, museum and the local post office. Smoking and nonsmoking rooms are available and some pets are permitted.

### S Candy Bouquet

822 S. 1st., Hamilton. 363-YUMM (9866). www.yumshop.com or email: candybouquet@montana.com

The Candy Bouquet can help you make a lasting impression with a special gift that won't fade, wilt, or die. Each bouquet comes in a creative theme container filled with delicious hand-wrapped candies and chocolates from around the world. Unique accessories and cellophane accents help make each hand made bouquet one-of-a-kind to your specifications. Choose from their own selection of popular designs or they will custom design a bouquet for your special occasion. They also create sugar free bouquets. A nice selection of Montana gifts are also available and can be included in your special bouquet. They will deliver locally or ship anywhere in the world.

## 26. *Attraction*

### T Skalkaho Pass and Wildlife Area

3 miles south of Hamilton and east on Hwy. 38.

Highway 38 just a few miles south of Hamilton is also known as the Skalkaho Highway. This drive into the mineral rich Sapphire Mountains takes you on some of Montana's least traveled mountain roads. The highway was once a heavily used trail for Indians. A road was built over the route in 1924 to link the mining areas in the mountains with the agricultural communities of the Bitterroot Valley. This is a gentle winding drive that offers some excellent views and takes you past Skalkaho Falls. You can turn around at the falls, or continue on the Pintlar Scenic Highway near Philipsburg.

If you're adventurous, take a sidetrip to the Skalkaho Basin. This was once a wildlife preserve and still offers excellent opportunities to view a wide range of wildlife. In the fall, you can find large herds of elk here and hear them bugling, especially east of Kneaves and Fool Hen lakes. There is also the possibility you may see moose, mule deer, wolverines, badgers, coyotes, and black bear. When you reach the pass, about 27 miles from Hwy. 93, turn north on FR 1352 and drive approximately five miles to the basin.

### *Montana Trivia*

From 1990 to 2000, Ravalli County in the Bitterroot Valley, was the fastest growing county in Montana. It recorded a 40% growth in population.

# The Big Hole Valley

## The Land of 10,000 Haystacks

This spectacular high mountain valley stretches 59 miles along the western border of Beaverhead County and is framed by the Bitterroot Mountain Range, whose peaks soar to elevations nearing 11,000 feet. The average elevation of the valley is 6,245 feet—nearly 1.2 miles above sea level. This elevation is nearly twice as high as the average Montana elevation of 3,400 feet.

The valley today is an unusual blend of history and contemporary living. If you travel through at the right time of year, you might find yourself caught up in a cattle drive. If you drive through in the haying season, you might witness a unique method of haying that has changed little since the turn of the century. On the valley floor, 39 miles wide at its broadest point are expansive ranches reminiscent of the early West. Famed not only for its cattle, the area also was acclaimed as the "Land of 10,000 Haystacks", derived from its nutritious wild hay which boasts a worldwide reputation as having no parallel.

From its source in the south end of the valley, to just above Wise River, the Big Hole River falls more than 1,650 feet in elevation. 149 lakes feed into this river with around 58 found in the mountains surrounding the valley.

Population centers include Wisdom (120), Jackson and Wise River (50 each). Annual events, attract national audiences, feature black powder shoots, Old Timer's Day, Big Hole Battlefield celebration, Big Hole Valley Days, and cow pasture golf tournament.

In addition to the customary recreational activities, the Big Hole also lists such specialties as snowmobiling, dog sledding, trap shooting, hang gliding, brandings, gun shows and fiddler's contests.

### VFL Skalkaho Lodge & Outfitters/Steakhouse

1380 Skalkaho Rd., Hamilton. 363-3522.
www.montanahunt.com

John and Sandy Rose have been outfitters and offering lodging for over 30 years, at the beautiful Skalkaho Lodge, located in the heart of the Bitterroot Valley, 60 miles south of Missoula. Hunters leave the ranch each morning by vehicle, and return each evening to a family style dinner and hot shower. A wide range of hunts is available, including a 10 day cougar hunt, 7 day bow hunt, a 6-day big game rifle hunts, or a 7-day spring bear hunt. Something for every hunter. For those nonhunters who just want a great meal, call for reservations at the steakhouse located at Skalkaho Lodge. John is also licensed to guide in Alaska. Sandy is a Realtor, for those wishing to buy property in Montana.

# Rockhounding

Crystal Park is located on the Pioneer Mountains Scenic Byway about 26 miles south of Wise River. It is one of the most unique collecting sites in western Montana. This is a good place to find crystals of amethyst and smokey quartz.

Philipsburg area. There are a number of mining sites around Philipsburg. In the dumps and tailings surrounding the mines, look for tiny crystals of manganese minerals.

Anaconda area. Cable Mountain, northeast of Georgetown Lake has several piles of old mine tailings. Look in these for scheelite and epidote. On the western side of Georgetown Lake argillites and quartzites can be found.

## 27. *Lewis & Clark, Attraction, Gas, Food, Lodging, Camping*

### Darby

South of Lake Como on Highway 93 lies the town of Darby. Darby originated when James Darby built a cabin and started a post office. Later, he added a grocery and general store, as people came to get their mail and needed other supplies. Originally the settlers voted to name the town Harrison after the then President Benjamin Harrison, but this name was not accepted by the U.S. Postal Service because another Harrison, Montana already existed. In 1888, James Darby named the town for himself after consulting its inhabitants.

While in Darby stop in the first building in Montana to have electricity and an elevator, The Historic Ranger Station & Visitor Center. Built in the 1930s and designed in the French Prison tradition to look imposing, this former Forest Service Administration building is located on Main Street and houses a wealth of artifacts from the 1940s.

### D William Clark

Return trip, July 4, 1806

*"This being the day of the decleration of Independence of the United States and a Day commonly Scelebrated by my Country I . . .halted early and partook of Sumptious Dinner of a fat Saddle of Venison and Musch of buscuitroot."*

### T Pioneer Museum

Main St., Darby. 821-4503

Located on Main Street in Darby is the Pioneer Museum featuring exhibits and memorabilia of bygone days. Explore the history of Darby's settlement during the 1800s through exhibitions including Darby's original telephone switchboard with the kid's favorites being the old photo albums and stereoscope.

### T Lake Como Recreation Area

Hwy 93, Darby

Originally called "Lake of the White Moose" by the Indians because of an albino moose that once visited its shores, the scenic 906-acre lake is now the setting of many water sports. The name was changed when a settler named Wilson Harlan came to the area. He thought the beautiful lake sitting against the backdrop of the snowcapped Bitterroot Mountains reminded him of Lake Como in Italy. His ranch later became the Como Ranch, and the peaks beyond became the Como Peaks. This recreational site is excellent for swimming, skiing, boating or fishing and offers a seven-mile trail around the lake. Facilities include: 9 camping units, an equestrian campground with a livestock ramp, picnic areas and toilets.

### T Darby Historical Visitor Center

Darby Ranger Station. 821-4503

### F Sawmill Saloon & Silverspoon Cafe

123 Main St., Darby. 821-3020

The Sawmill Saloon is located in the historic, 100-year-old bank building in downtown Darby. It has a very rustic atmosphere, with existing vaults and a collection of antique logging memorabilia. Serving a wide array of American style food, including charbroiled burgers, steaks and pizza.

### FL Bud & Shirley's Motel, Restaurant and Pizza

212 Main St. in Darby. 821-3401

Bud and Shirley's aims to please, whether it's the motel, restaurant, or the pizza palace. The motel has twenty one units, four are suites with Jacuzzi tubs.There's also a laundromat, teen center with pool table, arcade, and video rentals. The family restaurant serves breakfast, lunch and dinner with the largest salad bar in the valley. Fill up at the buffet seven days a week and at the breakfast buffet on Saturdays and Sundays. For food on the go you can use the drive-in window or get a take-and-bake for pizza hot to go when you are ready. Bud says they can seat 1,000 people, 100 at a time and serve T-bones weekly for 50 cents or $14.95 with meat.

### L Trapper Creek Lodge

158 Trapper Road, West Fork, Darby. 821-4970 or toll free at 888-821-4970.
www.trappercreeklodge.com or
email: trapper@blackfoot.net

Trapper Creek Lodge offers modern, rustic log cabins. Cabins overlook Trapper Creek, a cutthroat and brook trout stream, less than 100 yards away. The West Fork of the Bitterroot River is about 300 yards away where rainbow trout can be caught and enjoyed at your cabin. Two catch and release trout ponds are offered for the less adventuresome fisherman. Horseback riding from the ranch, skiing, and snowmobiling, or fall big game hunting are available in season. Relax in a secluded creek side hot tub for an afternoon or midnight soak. Mountain bikes, sauna, and a fitness room are provided to guests free of charge. See wild game from your cabin on this 175-acre ranch bordered by National Forest. There are four deluxe vacation cabins and one guesthouse, including a family cabin with full kitchen, a sleeping cabin without kitchen, and a three bedroom guesthouse. Open year round.

### L Triple Creek Ranch

5551 West Fork Rd. 821-4600 or fax 821-4666.
www.triplecreekranch.com

An unforgettable retreat awaits you at Triple Creek Ranch, a mountain hideaway in the heart of the Montana Rockies. Known for its hospitality, gourmet meals and fine wines, this all-inclusive Relais & Chateaux resort offers 19 custom log cabins nestled in 400 wooded acres surrounded by the Bitterroot National Forest. After a day of exhilarating activities, guests gather at the lodge to relax in the library, dine in the casually elegant restaurant or share stories of the day in the rooftop lounge. Winter activities include downhill/cross-country skiing, sleigh rides, horseback rides and snowshoeing. Summer activities include hiking, fishing, horseback rides, swimming and tennis.

## Pioneer Mountain Scenic Byway

The Pioneer Mountain Scenic Byway extends north from Hwy 278 between Dillon and Jackson, Montana, to Hwy 43 at Wise River. You will see mountain meadows, lodgepole pine forests and broad "willow bottoms", not to mention numerous varieties of wildlife.

The first sight on your tour is the tiny rural town of Polaris. Then the Grasshopper Creek Valley widens to spectacular views. Ranching is the economic mainstay for the valley and the valley is dotted with haystacks built by "Beaverslides".

As you travel you will pass Maverick Mountain Ski Area, where visitors can enjoy the 18 trails, with a 2,100' vertical drop and an average annual snowfall of about 200 inches. After a long day of skiing you can then visit Elkhorn Hot Spring and soak in their outdoor natural hot pools year-round. Traveling on you will come upon the meadows of Moose Park and Crystal Park.

Rock hounds come to Crystal Park in the summer to dig for quartz crystals and amethyst. The park is open to the public free of charge.

As you descend the 7,800 foot divide between Grasshopper Creek and Wise River, you will see the old railroad bed of the Montana Southern Railway, the last narrow-gauge railroad built in the U.S. The railroad served the Elkhorn Mine, one of the largest ore-mill structures in the U.S., It also served the town of Coolidge, which grew up around the mill. Elkhorn and Coolidge offer an interesting side trip from the byway.

The byway ends at the ranching community of Wise River, situated along the Big Hole River. Fishing enthusiasts arrive seasonally to try their skill on the blue ribbon river. This byway features great sight-seeing along with wonderful recreational opportunities.

*Reprinted from Dillon Chamber of Commerce brochure.*

### LC Wilderness Motel RV & Tent Park

308 S. Main St., Darby. 821-3405 or 800-820-2554

Built in the 1930s but recently renovated, it still maintains its old charm and character. The units are modern, but each has its own personality. Reasonable rates. Many units have full kitchens, all have cable TV. An economical bunkhouse is available. The RV park with full hook-up sites has mature trees and green grass. Tent/camping sites are available.

### L River Bend Fishing Lodge

2498 Old Darby Rd, Darby. 821-1999.
www.montanafishinglodge.net

### M Alpine Realty

808 N. Main, Darby. 821-3771 or fax 821-3771.
email: info@montanaoutback.com

Looking for that perfect Montana get away, Montana vacation home, or place to live out your retirement in the Bitterroot Valley? Alpine Realty offers full real estate brokerage services in the Bitterroot Valley. If you are either a buyer or a seller, they can assist you from finding the perfect property, to listing and advertising your property, to completing the deal to closing. As a member of the Bitterroot Valley Board of Realtors, the Montana Board of Realtors, and the National Association of Realtors, they work with other brokers to find and sell properties while maintaining professionalism. Dorene Sain, the Owner/Broker of Alpine Realty, Inc., has been a resident of the Bitterroot Valley for 26 years with a reputation for quality services for her clients.

### M Realty 2000

120 Main Street, Darby. 821-0051 or Fax 821-0917.
Email: R2000mt@aol.com

## 28. *Historic Marker, Gas, Food, Lodging*

### Conner

The Aaron Conner family settled the area known as Whitesell Flats in 1882. A notable and well-respected speaker, Aaron Conner was elected as a representative from Ravalli County to the Montana House of Representatives in 1900. When he died of injuries resulting from an accident in his sawmill, the post office and town were named for him. Both were later moved to Conner's current location south of Darby.

### H Medicine Tree

south of Darby

*This Ponderosa Pine has been standing guard here on the bend of the river for nearly 400 years. Somewhere, imbedded in its trunk, a few feet above the ground, is the horn of a Big Horn ram, the basis of a legend which across the centuries has established the historical significance of the pine as a Medicine Tree.*

*Once upon a time, when the tree was small, according to Salish Indian lore, a mountain sheep of giant stature and with massive, curling horns, accepting a challenge from his hereditary enemy, Old Man Coyote, attempted to butt it down. The little pine stood firm, but one of the ram's horns caught in the bole, impaling the luckless sheep, causing his death. A Salish war party chased the coyote away from his anticipated feast and then hung offerings of beads, cloth, ribbon and other items on the ram's horns as good medicine tokens to his bravery, and to free the scene of evil.*

*Countless succeeding Indian tribes followed the practice until, less than 100 years ago, the horn disap-*

## Battle of the Big Hole

In the summer of 1877 five bands of Nez Perce Indians-about 800 people, including 125 warriors-began a 1,300 mile journey from northeastern Oregon and central Idaho over the Bitterroot Mountains and through the Montana Territory. Though they were herding more than 2,000 horses and carrying whatever possessions they could manage, the Nez Perce made this long and difficult trek in less than four months—not because they were eager to reach their destination, but because they were being chased by United States Army troops under Gen. Oliver O. Howard with orders to place them on a reservation. The Nez Perce had hoped to elude the Army but they were forced to stop and face their pursuers several times. One of the major encounters of this epic odyssey, the battle with the most loss of life, took place in the Big Hole Valley of southwestern Montana. The Battle of the Big Hole was a tragic turning point of what came to be called the Nez Perce War of 1877.

Battle Mountain
Big Hole National Battlefield
Twin Trees
North Fork Big Hole River
Overlook
Monument
Site of Nez Perce Camp
Howitzer Capture Site
Siege Area Trail
Nez Perce National Historic Trail
Picnic Area
Nez Perce Camp Trail
Visitor Center
Trail Creek
Ruby Creek
To 93
43
To Wisdom 10mi 16km
0 0.1 0.5 Kilometer
0 0.1 0.5 Mile

The Nez Perce arrived in the lush Big Hole Valley on the morning of August 7, and their principal leader, Chief Looking Glass, chose an old camp site at which to stop and set up their tipis. Believing that they were far enough ahead of Howard's soldiers to be out of danger, Looking Glass did not post guards. Unknown to the Nez Perce, a second military force—Col. John Gibbon and 162 men of the 7th U.S. Infantry out of Fort Shaw and four other western Montana forts—had joined the chase and was advancing up the Bitterroot Valley toward them.

Gibbon's scouts spotted the Nez Perce tipis on the afternoon of August 8. Before dawn on the 9th, most of the soldiers and 34 civilian volunteers were forming a skirmish line on the west bank of the North Fork of the Big Hole River, within 200 yards of the Nez Perce camp. Here they would wait tensely for first light, when they would attack. The attack started prematurely, however, when a lone Nez Perce, out to check his horses, stumbled onto the concealed soldiers and volunteers and was shot and killed. When the troops crossed the river and fired into the village, some of the Nez Perce scattered quickly while others were slow to awaken. In the confusion of the faint predawn light, men, women, and children were shot indiscriminately. The soldiers soon occupied the south end of the camp, while the Nez Perce warriors, urged on by Chiefs Looking Glass and White Bird, quickly took up sniper positions. Their deadly shooting eventually forced Gibbon's men to retreat back across the river to a point of pines projecting from Battle Mountain. The troops dug in and were pinned down for the next 24 hours. The soldiers suffered many casualties.

During the attack, some of Gibbon's men had been struggling to haul a 12-pounder mountain howitzer through the dense lodgepole pine forest. They managed to place it on the hillside above the siege area just as the soldiers were digging in. The crew fired two rounds before a group of Nez Perce horsemen galloped forward, captured the gun and dismantled it, and rolled the wheels down the hill.

As the siege continued, some of the Nez Perce warriors began withdrawing to help Chief Joseph and others care for the injured, bury the dead, gather their horses, and break camp. Others remained to keep the soldiers under fire while the bands headed south, leaving much of their belongings behind. Finally, in the early morning of the second day of fighting August 10th the remaining warriors fired parting shots and left to join their people. The battle was over.

General Howard's troops arrived the next day and found Gibbon wounded and his command out of action. In a military sense, the Nez Perce had won the battle, but the "victory" was a hollow one. Sixty to ninety members of the tribe had been killed, only about thirty of whom were warriors: the rest were women, children, and old people. The Nez Perce now realized the war was not over, that they must flee for their lives. Eventually they decided to go to Canada and join Sitting Bull.

The military's losses were also high, with 29 dead and 40 wounded, but they knew that they had greatly damaged the fighting ability of the Nez Perce. Furthermore, the 7th Infantry had not retreated, as other units of the army that fought the Nez Perce had been forced to do. Subsequently, seven enlisted men were awarded the Congressional Medal of Honor, and those officers who survived received brevet promotions. But the horrors of what they had seen at the Battle of the Big Hole would haunt them for the rest of their lives.

*Reprinted from National Park Service Brochure.*

*peared within the tree. But the Indians continue to regard it as a shrine and even the white men honor its sacred legend.*

### H Ross' Hole
south of Darby

*Alexander Ross, of the Hudson Bay Company, with 55 Indian and white trappers, 89 women and children and 392 horses, camped near here on March 12, 1824, enroute from Spokane House to the Snake River country. Nearly a month was spent here in a desperate attempt to break through the deep snow across the pass to the Big Hole, and from their hardships and tribulations, Ross called this basin "The Valley of Troubles."*

### S West Fork Mountain Crafts
4955 Sawmill Lane, Connor. 821-2007.
www.westforkmountaincrafts.com

West Fork Mountain Crafts is visible from the Conner cutoff, close to the point where Lewis and Clark crossed the Bitterroot River. The hand peeled cabin once stood on the west fork of Rock Creek. The warm history of the structure provides the perfect atmosphere for their classroom, workshop, showroom and bead outlet. This delightful shop located on the banks of the Bitterrroot offers a wonderful line of Made in Montana products along with flies, rods, reels, and licenses. The resident artist, Gay Findley is a Montana native. Many other artists are enjoying this outlet for their paintings, bead work, leather work, and other unique creations.

## 29. *Attraction*

### T Painted Rocks State Park
17 miles south of Hamilton on U.S. 93, then 23 miles southwest on Route 473. 542-5500

Administered by Montana Fish, Wildlife and Parks, Painted Rocks State Park is located 17 miles south of Hamilton on U.S. 93, then 23 miles southwest on Secondary 473. Contained within the Bitterroot Valley, this park is surrounded by history. Open year-round as a "primitive" park, Painted Rocks offers a multitude of recreational opportunities. Winter opportunities include snowshoeing, cross-country skiing and wildlife viewing. Summer opportunities include camping, fishing, boating, hiking, and water skiing. All this within a scenic, western pine forest setting!

### Are The Rocks Really Painted?

Painted Rocks received its name from the green, yellow and orange lichens which cover the grey and black rock walls of the granitic and rhyolite cliffs. The lichen forms out of the symbiotic relationship between the algae growing on the cliffs and fungi. Different combinations of each plant forms various colored lichen.

### Geology of Painted Rocks

Painted Rocks State park is located in the val-

# The Nez Perce War

## A Long Journey to Surrender

The traditional homeland of the Nez Perce was that place where Oregon, Washington, and Idaho meet. Mistakenly called Nez Perce (pierced nose) by French-Canadian trappers, these powerful, wealthy, semi-nomadic people grazed horses and cattle on the valley grasslands, gathered edible roots on the prairies, fished for salmon, and hunted buffalo east of the mountains.

In the mid-1800s, calling it their "Manifest Destiny," settlers, stockmen, and gold miners began moving onto Nez Perce lands. Desiring peace, the tribe agreed to a treaty in 1855 that confined them to a spacious reservation that included much of their ancestral land. The treaty promised that non-Indians could live on the reservation only with the Nez Perce's consent.

But gold was discovered on the reservation in 1860. Settlers and miners, wanting more of the Nez Perce's land, forced a new treaty in 1863 that reduced the reservation to one-tenth its original size. Those chiefs whose lands lay within the diminished reservation reluctantly signed the treaty, but those whose lands fell outside the new reservation boundary (about a third of the tribe) refused. The five bands who refused to participate became known as the "nontreaty" Nez Perce.

The non-treaty bands remained in their homeland for several years. In 1877, however, increasing demands for settlement and mining caused the Indian Bureau to order all Nez Perce bands to move onto the smaller reservation. Gen. Oliver 0. Howard was instructed to make sure the order was obeyed. In mid-May Howard issued an ultimatum that the Nez Perce must be on the reservation within 30 days.

Chief Joseph, one of the non-treaty spokesmen, probably reflected the general reaction of most of the non-treaty Nez Perce when he asked for more time. " I cannot get ready to move in 30 days," he said. "Our stock is scattered and Snake River is very high. Let us wait until fall, then the river will be low." General Howard refused the appeal and threatened to use force if the deadline was not met.

Reluctantly, the non-treaty chiefs persuaded their people to obey the ultimatum. They rounded up as much of their far-ranging livestock as they could, took all the possessions they could pack, struggled across the swollen Snake and Salmon Rivers, and made their way to a camp within a few miles of the reservation. The Nez Perce had almost met the 30-day deadline when, on June 15, three young warriors, seeking revenge, attacked several white settlers who earlier had cheated or killed members of their families. Other warriors soon joined them, killing 17 settlers in two days of raids. Fearing retaliation, most of the non-treaty Nez Perce fled to White Bird Canyon, where they could defend against a surprise attack.

When General Howard learned of the killings, he sent a force of 99 cavalrymen and 11 civilian volunteers to quell the uprising. At White Bird Canyon, on June 17, the troopers were routed by a poorly armed and smaller group of warriors and suffered heavy losses.

During the following month, the Nez Perce attempted to avoid the army, their journey marked by small encounters and skirmishes. General Howard summoned troops from up and down the West Coast to begin an encircling movement to trap the elusive Nez Perce. Then on July 11, Howard's forces met the Nez Perce near the Clearwater River where they fought for two days with neither side winning. Finally the Nez Perce withdrew, leaving behind many of their supplies and tipis.

It was now clear to the non-treaty Nez Perce that they could not escape from the army in Idaho Territory. In council, the five bands agreed to follow the leadership of Chief Looking Glass, who persuaded them to leave their homelands and head east to Montana and join their allies, the Crow, in buffalo country. They would follow the Lolo Trail, which Nez Perce hunters had used for centuries. The Nez Perce wished only to find a place where the army would leave them alone and where they would be far enough from settlements to avoid further clashes.

By early August, the non-treaties had crossed the Lolo Trail and reached the Bitterroot Valley in Montana. They decided they were now among friendly settlers, and General Howard was far behind. But a second force, under Col. John Gibbon, who commanded the 7th U.S. Infantry in the western part of Montana Territory, had been ordered to join the pursuit of the Nez Perce. Chief Looking Glass, unaware of Gibbon's forces, slowed the pace of travel even though some of the chiefs and warriors urged haste. The result: disastrous losses at the Battle of the Big Hole.

After the Big Hole, the Nez Perce, now under Lean Elk's leadership, headed south to Shoshone country where they hoped to pick up warriors to replace those lost in the battle. Some young warriors began raiding ranches along the way. The Nez Perce again defeated Howard's men at Camas Meadow, Idaho, then headed through Yellowstone National Park. Col. Samuel D. Sturgis' 7th Cavalry tried unsuccessfully to block their path at Clark's Fork Canyon. On September 13 the Nez Perce defeated Sturgis' troopers at Canyon Creek. When the Nez Perce reached Crow country they found that their old allies could not help them, and knew that they must now try to join Sitting Bull in Canada.

Finally, on September 30, near the Bear Paw Mountains of Montana, just 40 miles south of the Canadian border, the Nez Perce were surprised by army troops under the command of Col. Nelson A. Miles. The chiefs rallied their followers, but after five days of fighting and intermittent negotiations, and the deaths of four chiefs (including Looking Glass, who had replaced Lean Elk as leader), Chief Joseph surrendered to Miles. They had traveled almost 1,300 miles.

Of the nearly 800 non-treaty Nez Perce who had started the trek, only 431 remained to surrender. Of the rest, some had been killed in battles enroute, over 200 had succeeded in reaching Canada, and some were hiding in the hills. In the end, it was the loss of fighting men, as well as the emotional blow at the Big Hole, that broke the Nez Perce's power to resist.

The Nez Perce War was a result of cultural conflicts. As the United States expanded westward, the settlers felt it was their "Manifest Destiny" to take the land. The Nez Perce hoped only to preserve theirs. The war seemed unavoidable. It is a dramatic example of the price paid in human lives for the westward expansion of our nation.

*Reprinted from National Park Service Brochure.*

ley of the West Fork of the Bitterroot River. The Bitterroot Mountains that surround the park rise to an elevation of 10,700 feet. The Bitterroot Range is formed of granitic rock from approximately 70 to 90 million years ago.

### Vegetation of Painted Rocks Area

A typical western pine forest setting, the Painted Rocks State Park is composed of Ponderosa and Lodge Pole pines, Douglas Fir, as well as Engleman Spruce. On site are also several species of grasses, shrubs, and forbs including bluebunch wheatgrass, huckleberry, mountain mahogany, snowberry and beargrass.

### Historical Use of the Painted Rocks Area

The Lewis and Clark Expedition passed through the forks of the Bitterroot River on September 7, 1805. Fifteen years later, the valley had become an important corridor for American and English fur companies as well as the "mountain men" of the era. The Bitterroot provided the only safe passage for trappers from raiding Blackfeet Indians, between the Snake, Columbia and Flathead Rivers. The main trapping era lasted approximately 25 years from 1820 to 1845. At that time Christian missionaries began to arrive in the area and permanent European American settlement followed.

Homesteaders, believing that the railroad would follow up the Bitterroot Valley into Idaho, began settling the West Fork Valley. They hoped that when the railroad came they could sell their land and make a profit. Unfortunately, the railroad never made it past Darby, (22 miles to the north).

On February 22, 1897, President Theodore Roosevelt established the Bitterroot Forest Reserve, now the Bitterroot National Forest. Just south of Painted Rocks State Park lies one of the first ranger stations in the United States. Erected in 1899 at Alta, Montana, by two local rangers, this was also one of the first Forest Service buildings to fly the American flag.

The West Fork of the Bitterroot, like the rest of the Bitterroot Valley and much of western Montana, has been part of the homeland of the Salish people for countless millennia—since the very beginning of human history. To this day, tribal elders know the traditional Salish place—names and cultural sites scattered throughout the area. Many of them refer to the deeds of Coyote when he created the world we know today. These stories reach back to the time of the last ice age and beyond.

The West Fork, in particular, was one of the connecting routes between the Salish and the Nez Perce in Idaho, and it was always a place of great importance to the Salish as a particularly good hunting area, as well as a place rich in other important traditional foods, including huckleberries, serviceberries, bitterroot, trout and other fish, and mountain tea. Tribal oral histories contain references to many Salish place-names in the West Fork area, beginning with the Conner area, known as Ep MsaWiy (Place of the Wild Violets).

In 1939, the Montana Water Conservation Board began construction on Painted Rocks Dam. Originally constructed for agricultural use, the Painted Rocks Reservoir now provides water for irrigation, stockwater, domestic use, instream flows and for fish.

The 143 foot high and 800 foot long dam receives its water from the West Fork of the Bitterroot watershed (316 square miles). At full capacity, the reservoir stores over 45,000 acre-feet of water.

## Recreational Opportunities at Painted Rocks State Park

All Montana state boating regulations apply to Painted Rocks Reservoir. There is a boat ramp and dock available for access to the reservoir. After August 1, water levels can be poor due to irrigation usage.

There are 25 sites available for camping, with vault toilets available on site. This area limits RV/trailer size to 25' in length. There is a 14-day limit for camping within a 30 day period.

Swimming is available at Painted Rocks State Park; however, there is no lifeguard on duty. Swim at your own risk!

Wildlife abounds in the area around Painted Rocks. Elk, mule deer, whitetailed deer, black bear, and moose can be found in the area. In the 1980s, bighorn mountain sheep as well as peregrine falcons were reintroduced to the area. The reservoir is used as a stopping ground for waterfowl during spring and autumn migrations. Don't be surprised if you see osprey, great blue heron, water ouzels, spotted sandpiper or kill-deer.

Six species of game fish call Painted Rocks Reservoir home; mountain whitefish, westslope cutthroat trout, rainbow trout, brown trout, brook trout and dolly varden.

There are two shelters available for picnics. For groups of 30 and over, please call the regional parks office at (406) 542-5531 for a special recreation permit. Since this is a primitive park, please follow the pack-it-in/pack-it-out policy.

*Reprinted from Montana Fish, Wildlife & Parks article.*

## 30. *Lewis & Clark, Attraction, Gas, Food, Lodging, Camping*

### Sula

Sula is named for the first white child born in the Ross Hole Country, Ursula. The Ross Hole area is named for the Alexander Ross expedition which traveled through the area in 1824 and consisted of 55 Native Americans and white trappers, 89 women and children, and 329 horses. The basin came to be called "The Valley of the Troubles" as the expedition suffered many hardships when forced to spend the winter here.

### D Wm. Clark

September 4, 1805

*. . .we met a party of the Tushepau (Flathead) nation, of 33 lodges about 80 men 400 Total and at least 500 horses, those people recved us friendly, threw white robes over our Sholders & Smoked in the pipes of peace. . .I was the first white man who ever wer on the waters of this river."*

### D Wm. Clark

September 6, 1805

*"Proceeded on Down the River which is 30 yds. wide Shallow & Stoney. . .rained this evening nothing to eat but berries, our flour out, and but little Corn, the hunters killed 2 pheasents only."*

### T Lost Trail Hot Springs

Mile marker 6 on U.S. Hwy 93 just south of Sula. 821-3574

Here, natural mineral hot springs provide a soak in a rustic facility including a large medium-hot pool, a smaller hot pool, and a sauna. The pool temperature averages 95 degrees F year round. The Lost Trail Pass was named after an error by the Lewis and Clark Expedition. Although, they were lost in the area of the current Lost Trails Hot Springs, they didn't see it at that time. The recorded first inhabitant was in 1892 when a woman built a cabin nearby to provide therapeutic soaks for her ailing son. Now open daily from June until Labor Day with a pool fee and some winter hours.Camping, lodging, and dining are all available year round.

### T East Fork Bighorn Sheep Herd Viewing Area

Approximately 5 miles east of Sula on East Fork Road.

This is one of the spots in Montana where you are almost sure to get a glimpse of these magnificent creatures. They tend to congregate on the hills and slopes above the East Fork of the Bitterroot River. You can see them year round, but the best viewing is in the winter time.

### *Montana Trivia*

The men of the Lewis and Clark Expedition were all paid for their efforts. Captain Lewis was paid $40 per month, Captain Clark $25 per month, and the privates were paid $5 per month. Sacajawea, their female Indian guide, received nothing. Neither did York, Clark's personal slave.

### FLAC Sula Country Store & KOA Campground

7060 Hwy 93 S., Sula. 821-3364 or 800-562-9867. www.koakampgrounds.com, sulakoa@montananet.com

The Sula Country Store & Sula KOA Campground has just about everything you could possibly need. Nestled in the heart of the Bitterroot National Forest, their cabins, cottages, RV park, and tent sites are bordered by the East Fork of the Bitterroot River. You can enjoy homestyle cooking for breakfast (served all day), lunch, and dinner. The handicapped accessible general store features unique selections of clothing, gifts, and jewelry, as well as grocery items. They offer brand name gas/diesel with 24-hour credit card access. Come visit the beautifully situated 16-acre campground that is open all year. Check out their web site for more information.

### L A Li'l Bit of Heaven - Classy Rental Cabins

7987 Hwy 93 S. Sula. 821-3433. www.alilbitofheaven.com

A Li'l Bit of Heaven "Classy Rental Cabins" has 2 new beautiful log cabins and is located on the Lewis and Clark Trail. "The Lupine" is 800 square feet of delightfully relaxing atmosphere with lots of deck space. Very comfortable for 4 people. It houses everything one might need for a home away from home. "The Bitterroot" is a 3 bedroom/2 bath with private hot tub on a wraparound deck, with a dishwasher and lots of relaxing space. Both "Classy Rentals" contain full stoves, refrigerators, complete kitchens including microwaves, toasters, coffee makers, pots and pans, washers & dryers, queen size beds, all linens, satellite with HBO, propane barbeques, deck chairs as well as picnic tables. All you'll need is your toothbrush and food!

## 31.

### T Big Hole Battlefield National Monument

10 miles west of Wisdom on Hwy 43. 689-3155. Open Daily Summer: 8:30 a.m. to 6:00 p.m.; Winter: 9:00 a.m. to 5:00 p.m. Closed: Thanksgiving, Christmas, and New Years Day.

*Along the Big Hole River.*

Big Hole National Battlefield is a memorial to the people who fought and died here on August 9 and 10, 1877; combatants in a five month conflict that came to be called the Nez Perce War of 1877. Like other Indian Wars in the late 1800s, the Nez Perce War involved two very different groups with very different outlooks on land rights, civilian authority, government powers, social organization, and the responsibilities of the individuals to society.

In 1992, legislation incorporated Big Hole National Battlefield with Nez Perce National Historical Park, making it part of a unique park consisting of 38 different sites located in five states; Oregon, Washington, Idaho, Montana, and Wyoming. Two Visitor Centers service the park, one at Spalding, Idaho, 11 miles east of Lewiston, and the other at Big Hole National Battlefield, 10 miles west of Wisdom, Montana. Both facilities are staffed year round by uniformed personnel who can answer your questions about the local area, the Nez Perce People and the War of 1877. Movies, museum exhibits, and guided tours are available at both facilities covering a variety of topics on the Nez Perce Culture and History. Although there is no Visitor Center at Bear Paw Battlefield located in Chinook, Montana, there is a nice display and video on the battle at the Blaine County Museum in Chinook.

The Visitor Center houses a small museum with exhibits of Nez Perce, military clothing and equipment, a 12 minute introductory video presentation, books sales, area information, and a Junior Ranger activity program for first through eighth grade.

A minimum of four hours is recommended to view the museum exhibits, watch the introductory film and walk the battlefield trails. Fishing (state license required), photography and wildlife watching (moose, elk, raptors) are additional recreational opportunities that are available within the park.

## Trails, Roads

All are welcome to take a self-guided walk through the battlefield from sunrise to sunset, daily. Guided walks are offered during the summer months.

The road to the battlefield is closed in late autumn due to snow. The Visitor Center remains open daily, and the battlefield is accessible to skiers or snowshoers. The road normally reopens in late April, but the exact date of reopening is weather dependent.

**The Nez Perce Camp Trail** leads 1.2 miles round trip, to the site where the Nez Perce were camped and attacked by United State Army soldiers and civilian volunteers on the night of August 9, 1887.

**The Siege Trail** leads 1 mile round trip, to the area where the soldiers and volunteers were held under siege by Nez Perce warriors.

## Programs, Activities

Regularly scheduled ranger guided tours are available daily in the summer. Educational programs for schools are given throughout the school year. Other groups are welcome and will be accommodated as staffing permits. Reservations for school programs and other group tours required.

Nez Perce, Military, and Volunteer descendants come to the battlefield to commemorate all those who fought here each year in early August. Call for dates and event listings at 689-3155.

*Reprinted from National Park Service brochure.*

**32.** *Lewis & Clark, Attraction, Gas, Food, Lodging*

## Wisdom

This town took its name from the original name of the Big Hole River which flows through town. The river was originally named by Lewis and Clark for one of the "cardinal virtues" of their president, Thomas Jefferson. For some reason, the name didn't sit well with later settlers and was changed to the Big Hole. The name of the town here stayed the same though. The town had already gone through two name changes. Originally it was Crossings, but was briefly changed when the post office moved to the Noyes Ranch and Mrs. Noyes was appointed postmaster. The name sounded too much like Norris which was a little ways to the east, so the name Wisdom was assigned.

### D William Clark

Sepember 2, 1805

*. . .we. ..proceded on thro' thickets in which we were obliged to Cut a road over rockey hill Sides where our horses were in perpeteal danger of Slipping to their certain distruction & up & Down Steep hills, where Several horses fell, Some turned over, and others Sliped down Steep hill Sides, one horse Crippeled & 2 gave out.*

### T Nez Perce National Historic Trail

Hwy 43, Wisdom.

Congress passed the National Trails System Act in 1968 establishing a frame work for a nationwide system of scenic, recreational, and historic trails. The Nez Perce (Ne-Me-Poo) Trail, extending approximately, 170 miles from the vicinity of Wallowa Lake, Oregon, to the Bear Paw Battlefield near Chinook, Montana, was added to this System by Congress as a National Historic Trail in 1986.

The Nez Perce Indians, composed originally of a number of independent villages and bands, were long known as friends of the whites. They had welcomed Lewis and Clark, fur trappers, and missionaries to their homeland in the mountains, valleys, and along the rivers of southeastern Washington, northeastern Oregon, and northcentral Idaho. In 1855, Washington Territorial governor, Isaac I. Stevens, responding to increasing white expansion, negotiated a treaty with the Nez Perce chiefs, recognizing their peoples' right their traditional homeland and establishing it as reservation of some 5,000 square miles.

In 1860, prospectors, encroaching on Nez Perce lands, struck gold. In the ensuing rush, thousands of miners, merchants, and settlers, disregarding Stevens's treaty, overran large parts the reservation, appropriating the Indians' lands and livestock and heaping miscreant and misjustices on the Nez Perce. To cope with the situation, the United States Government engaged the angered Nez Perce in new treaty talks that culminated in a large treaty council in 1863. Nearly all tribal bands were represented. When the Government tried to get some of the bands to cede all or most of their lands, they refused to do so and left the council. In their absence, other chiefs, without tribal authority to speak for the departed bands, did just that, ceding the lands of those who had left the council. Their act resulted in a division of the tribe. Those who had signed were praised by the whites as "treaty" Indians; those who did not sign became known as the "non-treaty" Nez Perce.

For some years, the "non-treaty" bands continued to live on their lands, insisting that no one had the right to sell them. But conflicts with the growing white population increased, particularly in the Wallowa country of northeastern Oregon, the homeland of Chief Joseph's band. In May, 1877, the Army finally ordered the non-treaties to turn over their countries to the whites and move onto a small reservation. Rather than risk war with the Army, the "non-treaty" chiefs decided to move onto the reservation at Lapwai, Idaho. Pent-up emotions, stemming from years of highhandness and miscreant by whites and from the order to leave their homelands, moved several embittered young warriors to ride out to the Salmon River and kill some whites, avenging the past murders of tribal members. The hope for a peaceful move to the small reservation at Lapwai, thus ended, and the flight of the Nez Perce began on June 15, 1877.

Pursued by the Army, the nontreaties left

Idaho, intending initially to seek safety with their Crow allies on the plains to the east. When this failed, flight to Canada became their only hope. Their long desperate and circuitous route, as they traveled and fought to escape pursuing white forces, is what we now call the Nez Perce National Historic Trail.

This route was used in its entirety only once; however, component trails and roads that made up the route bore generations of use prior to and after the 1877 flight of the "non-treaty" Nez Perce. Trails and roads perpetuated through continued use often became portions of transportation systems, though some later were abandoned for more direct routes or routes better suited for modem conveyances. Most abandoned segments can be located today but are often overgrown by vegetation, altered by floods, power lines, and other manmade structures, or cross a variety of ownerships.

General William Tecumseh Sherman called the saga of the Nez Perce "the most extraordinary of Indian wars." Precipitated into a fight they did not seek by the impulsive actions of the few revengeful young men, some 750 "non-treaty" Nez Perce only 250 of them warriors, the rest women, children, and old or sick people, together with their 2,000 horses, fought defensively for their lives in some 20 battles and skirmishes against a total of more than 2,000 soldiers aided by numerous civilian volunteers and Indians of other tribes. Their route through four states, dictated by topography and their own skillful strategy, covered over 1,100 miles before they were trapped, and surrendered at Montana's Bear Paw Mountains just short of the Canadian border and safety on October 5, 1877.

There is irony in the tragic fate of the Nez Perce. In addition to having been loyal friends and allies of the whites for almost three quarters of a century their conduct during the war was free of traits which whites usually associated with Indian warfare. Following what the whites regarded as a civilized code of conduct, the Nez Perce refrained from scalping, mutilating bodies, or torturing prisoners, and generally avoided attacks on noncombatant citizens. Nevertheless, as defeated Indians, the surviving Nez Perce were sent to several years of exile in present day Oklahoma before they were allowed to return to reservations in the Northwest.

*Reprinted from Forest Service Brochure.*

### L Nez Perce Motel
Hwy 43, Wisdom. 689-3254.
nezpercemotel@montana.com

The locally owned and operated Nez Perce Motel offers warm hospitality and small town charm in a clean, quiet, comfortable atmosphere. It is a great location for hunting, fishing, downhill & cross-country skiing, hiking, and only 10 miles from the Big Hole National Battlefield. Owners Wayne & Barb Challoner can tell you about all of the local attractions, like the wonders of haying and calving seasons, to help you plan your stay. They can even sell you a fishing license. The motel is open year-round with very affordable rates.

### S Conover's Trading Post
Highway 43, Wisdom. 689-3272 or fax 689-3354

## 33. *Lewis & Clark, Attraction, Food, Lodging*

### Jackson
It is said that Jackson is 45 miles from Idaho by car, and 25 miles by snowshoe. Today it is more of a winter sports resort than a town. It was named for Anton Jackson, who served as the first postmaster when the post office opened there in 1896.

### D Mer. Lewis
Near Reservoir Lake, August 19, 1805

*"Notwithstanding their extreem poverty they are not only cheerfull but even gay, fond of gaudy dress and amusements. . .they are frank, communicative, fair in dealing, generous with the little they possess, extreemly honest, and by no means beggarly."*

### D Mer. Lewis
Near Miner Lake,August 20, 1805

*" I . . .asked Cameahwait by what rout the Pierced nosed indians (Nez Perce), who. . .inhabited this river below the mountains came over to the Missouri; this informed me was ot the north, but added that the road was a very bad one. . .however knowing that the Indians had passed, and did pass, at this season on that side of this river to the same below the mountains, my rout was instantly settled. . ."*

### D Wm. Clark
Return trip, July 7, 1806

*"this Spring. . .actually blubbers with heat for 20 paces below where it rises. . .I directt Sergt. Pryor and John Shields to put each a peice of meat in the water of different Sises. the one about the Size of my 2 fingers cooked dun in 25 minuts the other much thicker was 32 minits before it became Sufficiently dun."*

### T Jackson Hot Springs
Rte 278, 15 miles south of Wisdom

The springs provide water for the entire town of Jackson in the Big Hole Valley. The privately owned Jackson Hot Springs Lodge is open year round for soaks in the Big Hole Valley. Admission is charged. The 9,000 square foot very Western lodge is also worth the trip. Members of the Lewis and Clark Expedition on their way back from the Pacific were the first to write about the springs here, when Clark cooked meat in the bubbling waters. Fur trappers were known to have enjoyed the springs but not commercially used until 1884. From then on it has had a number of owners and improvements.

## 34. *Lewis & Clark*

### D Mer. Lewis
At Lemhi Pass, August 13, 1805

*". . .we met a party of about 60 warriers mounted on excellent horses who came in nearly full speed. . .the chief and two others who were a little in advance of the main body spoke to the women and they informed them who we were and exultingly shewed the presents which had been given them. . .bothe parties now advanced and we wer all carresed and besmeared with their grease and paint till I was heartily tired of the national hug. I now had the pipe lit and gave them smoke. . ."*

### D Wm. Clark
Return trip, July 10, 1806

*"proceeded. . .into that butifull and extensive Valley open and fertile which we Call the beaver head Valley which is the Indian name in their language from the north of those animals in it & a pt. of land resembling the head of one."*

### D Wm. Clark
Return Trip, July 11, 1806

*"at 7 P M I arrived at the Enterance to Wisdom River and Encamped. in the Spot we had encamped the 6th of August last. here we found a Bayonet which had been left & the Canoe quite safe."*

### Grant
This little town on Prairie Creek was originally known as Amesville, but was renamed Grant when the post office opened in 1899. That post office closed in 1967 and most of what remains is a store and a historic old hotel.

## 35.

### Polaris
In January of 1885, six men discovered the Polaris Mine in the Lost Cloud mining district. It is believed to be the most important silver lode discovered in the region at the time. At one time, a 100 ton smelter with four blast furnaces operated near the mine. The smelter was destroyed by fire in 1922. The original town site was two miles south of the present site of Polaris.

## 36. *Attraction*

### T Coolidge
On the Pioneer Mountains National Scenic Byway.

Coolidge was founded in 1911 with the construction of the Elkhorn Mine. The mine was the hub of a large mining operation which was started by former Lieutenant Governor, William Allen. Coolidge was the terminus of a 40-mile narrow-gauge railroad, the Montana Southern, which came from Divide. This was the last narrow-gauge line built in America. Following a disastrous flood, the railroad was abandoned and torn up. While much of Coolidge has been stripped for its lumber, part of the huge mill and several of the buildings still stand. The turnoff for the town is about a half mile south of Mono Creek Campground on the Pioneer Mountains Scenic Byway. Head east on the road. Bear left at the fork and continue on to a junction. Go left here and drive to the end of the road. It is approximately four miles from the highway.

### T Crystal Park
25 miles south of Wise River on the Pioneer Mountains Scenic Byway. 683-3900

Crystal Park is a unique recreation area at an elevation of 7,800 feet in the Pioneer Mountains in southwest Montana. The Butte Mineral and Gem Club maintain mining claims at Crystal Park open to the public for digging quartz crystals. You are welcome to dig for quartz crystals here, but are asked to follow the rules of the Park. The park is open from May 15 through October 15, but those dates are subject to change depending on snow and road conditions. There is no charge, although donations for support of operations and maintenance of the site are welcome.

### Park Geology
Like most of the eastern Pioneer Mountains, the "country rock" or bedrock at Crystal Park is granite. About 68 million years ago, the Pioneer Batholith intruded the area, pushing up molten granite to form the Pioneer Mountain range. The granite was about 300° C or approximately 600° F. As the granite cooled, super-heated water circulated through it, carrying quartz, pyrite, and other minerals in solution. As the granite and the water continued to cool, the minerals precipitated out and were deposited in veins and cavities (called

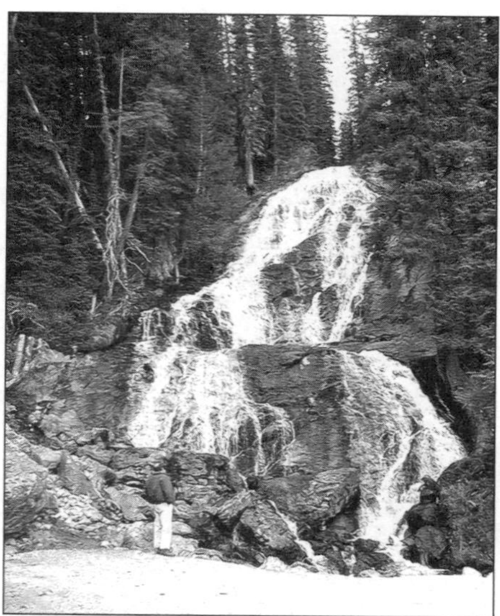

*Skalkaho Falls*

"vugs"). The molten granite continued to cool and solidified for several thousand years.

Later, glaciers, surface and ground water, weathering and other erosional processes exposed the minerals and crystals to air and ground water. The original crystals remained unchanged, but when the rock temperature was 30° to 50° C, and iron (from pyrite) was available, amethyst quartz crystals were formed. Amethyst crystals sometimes formed directly on another colorless crystal.

Quartz crystals at Crystal Park seem randomly distributed because weathering of the granite has freed them from veins where they formed. Careful digging can sometimes expose traces of veins seen as reddish-brown zones in the light-colored granite. By tracing remnant veins, "pockets" of crystals are sometimes found.

## Park Facilities

About 30 of the nearly 200 acres set aside for crystal digging are currently open. Digging areas are a short walk from paved parking. Facilities include: a hand pump water well, three picnic sites with tables and grills, information signs, toilets, and a paved trail with benches and an overlook. The facilities are designed to be universally accessible. Crystal Park is open for day use. There are Forest Service campgrounds along the Scenic Byway to the north and south of Crystal Park. A host is usually present to assist visitors, maintain the facilities, and to ensure the rules are followed.

Information on digging for quartz crystals is available at the Park. You will need to bring your own tools. For digging, a shovel, hand trowel, gardener's hand cultivator, and gloves are useful. A daypack to carry your tools in is handy.

*Reprinted from Forest Service brochure.*

### T Elkhorn Hot Springs

Off Rt 278, north of Polaris

The pools are open year round with admission charged to soak in the pools at the rustic privately owned resort. There is also a dark and steamy "Grecian wet Sauna", where temperatures average 105 degrees F. The pool temperature averages 95 degrees F. Elkhorn Hot Springs was originally owned by the federal government as part of the Beaverhead National Forest until 1905, when Samuel Engelsjard filed water rights on the springs. Through a number of owners and hard times the springs has survived and with many improvements still retains rustic charm.

## 37. *Gas, Food, Lodging, Shopping*

### Wise River

This tiny town sits at the junction of the Big Hole and the Wise River. The Big Hole was at one time named the Wisdom River by Lewis and Clark after one of Thomas Jefferson's "cardinal virtues." For some reason, this name didn't sit well with later settlers and they renamed the river the Big Hole. Perhaps as a consolation, this tributary to the Big Hole was given the name Wise River.

### FL Wise River Club

Hwy 43, Wise River. 832-3258

Known as the "World Famous Wise River Club," they offer home-style cooking, six newly renovated cabins, full RV hookups, and a wide range of fishing and hunting supplies as well as cards and gifts right on the premises. There is great fishing, hunting, snowmobiling, and downhill skiing in the Wise River area. The lounge is equipped with gambling machines and pool tables for entertainment, and the restaurant serves breakfast, lunch and dinner every day of the week.

### S Big Hole Gift & Gear

Hwy 43, Wise River

## Scenic Drives

**Spring Emery Road**

From Deer Lodge, take Forest Service Road #705 to Forest Service Road #1504 for approximately 11 miles to Forest Service Road #82. Turn right and head back to Deer Lodge. The drive will take you through scenic vistas and mountain meadows for a total of 25 miles. The road is maintained and suitable for two wheel drive vehicles during the summer months. An interpretive auto tour brochure is available.

**Deer Lodge/Champion Pass/Bernice**

From Deer Lodge, take Forest Service Road #82 over Champion Pass (Continental Divide) and down into the Headwaters of Boulder Creek for approximately 20 miles where it will end at the Bernice interchange on Interstate 15. From Bernice to Butte is 20 miles, and then 37 miles on Interstate 90 back to Deer Lodge. The drive will take approximately three to four hours in which there are four campgrounds along the route to stop for a picnic or fishing along Boulder Creek.

**Skalkaho Highway**

From Philipsburg, drive south six miles on Montana Highway 1 . (Pintler Scenic Highway) to Montana Highway 38 (Skalkaho Highway) where the drive will take you to Hamilton, approximately a 65 mile drive one way. The drive is very scenic and will take you over Skalkaho Pass, passing a waterfall and picnic area. The drive provides wildlife viewing and fishing opportunities in many of the Creeks on the way to Hamilton. The highway is open from June to September depending on snow conditions. Contact the Forest Service office in Philipsburg for road conditions prior to leaving. The road is generally open to two-wheel vehicles, without trailers, but has narrow road widths in some places.

**Rock Creek**

From Philipsburg, head north one half mile to Montana Highway 348 and continue on 348 for approximately 14 miles. Take Forest Service Road #102 along Rock Creek for approximately 35 miles where it will end at the Rock Creek interchange on Interstate 90. From there you are 25 miles from Missoula or 24 miles from Drummond where you can exit and take Montana Highway 1 back to Philipsburg, 27 miles from Drummond. The drive is very scenic and provides excellent fishing opportunities along Rock Creek, a blue ribbon trout stream. There are wildlife viewing opportunities for moose, bighorn sheep and elk. The road is maintained and will accommodate two wheel vehicles during the summer. The road is generally open from mid-May through mid-September depending on snow conditions.

**Beaverhead Scenic Loop/Pioneer Mountains National Scenic Byway**

Begin this loop at exit 59 on Hwy. 278. Stop at Bannack then return to the highway. Continue west across the Big Hole Divide to Jackson. The stretch from Jackson to Wisdom parallels the Big Hole River, one of the top blue-ribbon trout streams in America. This stretch is one of the last areas where rare arctic grayling trout survive. Lewis and Clark first named this fish as a "silvery trout" in 1806. Continue to Wisdom through the "Valley of 10,000 Haystacks." Follow Hwy. 43 east to Wise River.

At Wise River pick up the Pioneer Mountains National Scenic Byway and head south. Follow this highway, stopping often to enjoy the scenery, through Polaris and the Grasshopper Valley. Along this highway, you travel the length of the Pioneer Mountain Range. To the west you will see gentle forested terrain while the east reveals dramatic granite peaks reaching 10,000 feet in elevation. Along the way are lodgepole pine forests, mountain meadows, and broad willow bottoms. The road winds its way up a gentle assent to a 7,800 foot divide. If you wish to stretch your legs and lace up your hiking boots, there are numerous trailheads along the Byway leading into the Pioneer Mountains. If you have the time, you may want to stop and soak in the hot pools at Elkhorn Hot Springs. Connect with Highway 278 to complete the loop.

**Pintlar Scenic Drive**

This highway forms a loop that takes you over high mountain passes to the towns of Anaconda, Philipsburg, and Drummond. It skirts the shores of the scenic Georgetown Lake with the magnificent backdrop of the Anaconda Pintler Wilderness. Start at either end of MT Hwy. 1 at the I-90 Drummond exit or the Anaconda exit.

## Hikes

**Bear Creek Trail**

On Hwy 93, drive approximately seven miles north of Hamilton, turn west onto Bear Creek Rd. Continue about two miles and turn right on Red Crow Rd. Travel less than a mile and turn left on

# THE BITTERROOT

## The Bitterroot At a Glance

The Bitterroot Range and Wilderness Area border the valley to the west, and the Sapphires roll toward the Continental Divide to the east. The landscape is dotted with stands of trees, log home companies, a winding river and its tributaries, family farms and small towns. The largest, Hamilton, is still "small town" in character, but in a way that offers pleasing amenities.

**The fishing:** There are 80 fishable miles in the Bitterroot River, another 40 in the East and West Forks.

Currents are gentle and easily fished by wading or floating. The forks are primarily wade fisheries. The character of the river is varied and intimate, with plenty of suitable habitat for larger trout.

There are five species of wild trout, primarily rainbows and westslope cutthroats; browns are also available. Bull trout and brookies are also taken occasionally.

**Dry fly fishing:** There are abundant and varied hatches throughout the season, some of them unique to the area.

Through the course of summer, dry flies in larger sizes flies predominate, along with outstanding nymph and streamer opportunities.

This is a river, as one observer noted, to delight the beginner and challenge the veteran. We'd like to share it with you.

## About the Bitterroot

The late Joe Brooks, pioneer international flyfisher and angling legend in his own time, once listed the Bitterroot among his top ten favorite rivers. His reasons could have had to do with the tranquil yet spectacular beauty of the river and the valley, but more than likely had to do with the variety and quality of the angling itself.

Today, the Bitterroot beckons a dedicated group of anglers to return annually. They might enjoy the warmth of non-touristy accommodations, ranging from quaint and rustic B&B's to deluxe full service lodges, or camping in the wilderness -- which is surprisingly accessible. The idyllic valley is bordered by the jagged peaks of the Bitterroot Range, part of the largest wilderness area in the lower forty-eight. Over a dozen streams and trailheads are just minutes from the valley floor.

The Bitterroot winds for more than eighty

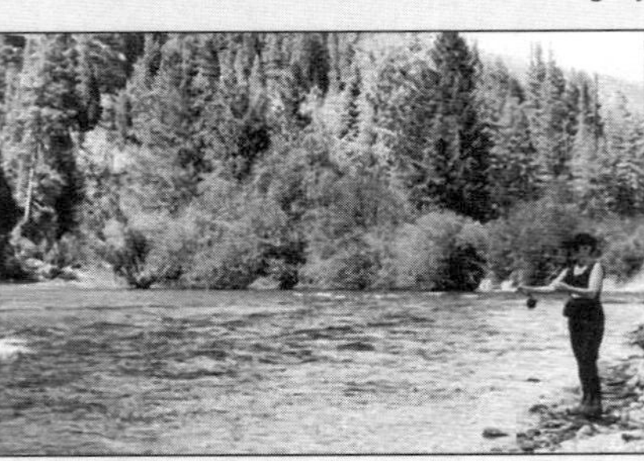

varied miles through its valley on the western border of Montana. It offers superb fly fishing, much of it with dries, in a variety of conditions for three major species of trout -- Rainbow, Brown, and the beautiful and feisty West-slope Cutthroat. Brook and Bull trout are also available, and a few lucky anglers hit a five specie grand slam every summer.

The East and West Forks of the Bitterroot are delightful small rivers, gliding through meadows or, more frequently, tumbling and bubbling through rocky runs and boulder- studded glides that are easy to wade and offer good numbers of fish, some of them sizable. The streams are for the most part gentle and intimate, yet cast in rugged and lush mountain settings.

*Article by Chuck Stranahan of Riverbend Flyfishing. www.riverbendfly.com*

Middle Bear Creek Road. Continue for three miles to the trailhead. This trail takes you to Bear Creek Falls and is approximately 4 miles round trip. The grade is moderate.

**Blodgett Overlook Trail**
Turn west on Main St. in Hamilton off Hwy. 93 (at second stop light). Continue as Main St. becomes West Bridge Rd. (keep to the right). At the end of West Bridge Road turn left on Blodgett Camp Road and follow the signs to the Canyon Creek Trailhead. This trail provides spectacular views of Canyon Creek, Blodgett Canyon, and the valley below. It is approximately 1.5 miles to Blodgett Overlook, and is a moderate grade.

**Boulder Creek Trail**
On Hwy. 93, four miles south of Darby, turn west onto the West Fork Road. Travel 15 miles and turn right into the Sam Billings campground. The trailhead is at the end of the campground. Boulder Creek Falls, which is your destination, is located within the Selway Bitterroot Wilderness. The hike there is about 4.5 miles on a moderate grade.

**Camas Creek Trail**
On Hwy. 93, four miles south of Darby, turn west onto the West Fork Road, to south of Hamilton approximately nine miles and turn west (right) on Lost Horse Road. Travel a little more than two miles and turn right at the FS Camas Creek sign. The trailhead is six miles past this sign. Camas Lake is approximately 3.5 miles and is your destination. The hike is on a moderate grade.

**Kootenai Creek Trail**
From the Stevensville junction on Hwy. 93, travel north one mile. Turn west on Kootenai Creek Road and continue two miles to the trailhead. This is a 14.5 mile hike on varied grades.

**Lake Como North Trail and Rock Creek Trail**
On Hwy. 93, 12 miles south of Hamilton, turn right on Lake Como Road. Drive approximately 3 miles and turn right on FS Road 5623. Continue to the Upper Como campground where the trailhead begins. Stock use is restricted on the North trail. There is access across the dam making this hike a complete loop around the lake. This loop is also a suggested mountain bike trail. North trail ends at the bridge/falls. This is the point of access to the Rock Creek trail. The entire hike around the lake is approximately 7 miles. There are very few inclines making it a very easy trail.

**St. Mary's Peak Trail**
3.5 miles south of the Stevensville junction on Hwy. 93, turn west on Indian Prairie Loop. Continue west 1.8 miles to St. Mary's Road, turn right and continue for one mile to the junction of McCalla Ridge Road and St. Mary's Peak Road (#739) approximately 14 miles to the road's end at the trailhead. The total climb from the trailhead to the lookout is 2,500'. St. Mary's Peak Summit is within the Selway Bitterroot Wilderness. The grade on this hike is moderate.

**Warm Springs Trail**
On Hwy. 93, approximately 4 miles north of Sula, turn west on Medicine Springs Road (FS #5728). Continue for approximately four miles to the Crazy Creek campground. Follow the signs to the trailhead. This nine mile trail is easy for the first 7 miles, but difficult on the final 2 miles.

**Storm Lake**
Between mile markers 21 and 22 on the Pintlar Scenic Highway is an unpaved road taking you to Storm Lake. Park at Storm Lake and pick up the trail on the lake's western shore. A trail register marks the trailhead. Take the trail up to Storm Lake Pass and Goat Flats for some astounding views. If you're lucky, you may run into a mountain goat or two. This hike is best taken in July or later as snow may make it impassable before that.

**Canyon Falls**
These are some of the more accessible falls in the Bitterroot Range. The stream tumbles in a series of cataracts in a drop of nearly 200 feet. To reach the trail head, go west on Main Street through Hamilton and continue to Ricketts Road. Ricketts is about .1 miles past the left bend on Main. Go right (north) to Blodgett Camp Road. Go left (west) for just under 2 miles where Blodgett Camp Road takes a sharp right. Go right for about .5 miles to Canyon Creek Road. Follow this road to the trailhead on Canyon Creek.

**Charles Waters Memorial Natural Area**
This area contains a nature trail and a fitness trail with several fitness stations which kids seem to love. Bass Creek trail begins at the first switchback on the main road west of the campground. This 2.5 mile interpretive fire ecology trail wanders through a dry, pine forest area. To get there, take Hwy. 93 approximately four miles north of the Stevensville turnoff. Turn west at the signed entrance and go about 1.75 miles to the parking area. Here is where the nature trail and fitness trail begin.

## CROSS-COUNTRY SKI TRAILS

### Beaverhead-Deerlodge National Forest

*For more information contact District Ranger, Wisdom, MT 59761(406)689-3243*

**Cabinet Creek-26 mi. W Wisdom**
*9.6 km More Difficult; no grooming*
Trail begins at plowed parking area on Highway 43; follows Cabinet Creek to junction with Anderson Mountain Road; has some steep pitches. Can use either Anderson Mountain Road or Richardson Ridge Trail to make semi-loops. Trail map available.

**Chief Joseph Cross Country Trails-28 mi. W Wisdom**
*8 km Easiest, 14.5 km More Difficult; 2.1 Most Difficult; weekly grooming*
Trail system starts on north side of Highway 43 at Chief Joseph Pass. Parking for 55-60 cars; toilet and maps at trailhead. Trail system consists of several loops which provide a variety of lengths and skill levels. Groomed by Bitterroot Ski Club. No pets, please. Warming hut open 12/1 to 04/15.

**Shoofly-22 mi. W Wisdom**
*7.2 km More Difficult; no grooming*
Parking at plowed lot on Highway 43. Trail starts on north side of highway; accesses Hogan Rental Cabin. Trail map available.

**Richardson Creek-26 mi. W Wisdom**
*6.1 km More Difficult; no grooming*
Parking at plowed lot on Highway 43; trail starts from lot. Can use Cabinet Creek Trail or Anderson Mountain Road to make semi-loops. Trail map available.

**Scotter Creek Trail-26 mi. W Wisdom**
*4.8 km More Difficult; no grooming*
Trail connects Chief Joseph Pass groomed trail system with Shoofly Trail and Hogan Rental Cabin-Trail map available.

**Anderrick Trail-28 mi. W Wisdom**
*3.2 km Easiest; no grooming*
Trail connects Anderson Mtn. Road and Richardson Creek Trail to form a loop. Trail map available.

**Anderson Mountain Road-28 mi. W Wisdom**
*12.8 km More Difficult; no grooming*
Trail begins on south side of Chief Joseph Pass. Can use Richardson Creek or Cabinet Creek Trails to make semi- loops. Trail map available.

**Gibbons Pass Road—off Hwy. 43 at Chief Joseph Pass, 28 mi. W Wisdom**
*3.2 km Easiest, 4.3 km more difficult; no grooming*
About 7.5 km of excellent skiing with moderate slope and open areas for telemarking. Open to snowmobiles. Accesses Hogan Rental Cabin, Trail map available.

**May Creek Trail-16 mi. W Wisdom**
*9.6 km More Difficult; no grooming*
Trail begins from May Creek Campground; joins Cabinet Creek Trail at end. Can use Cabinet Creek and May Creek Ridge Trails to form loop. Accesses May Creek Rental Cabin. Trail map available.

**May Creek Ridge Trail-16 mi. W Wisdom**
*13.7 km Most Difficult; no grooming*
Trail begins from May Creek Campground; not marked as ski trail; does have standard trail blazes. Can use with Cabinet Creek Trail and May Creek Trail to form loop. Trail map available.

**LaMarche Creek-20 mi. W Wise River**
*8 km Easiest, 3.4 km More Difficult; intermittent grooming*
For more information contact Sundance Lodge, Wise River, MT 59762 (406)689-3611
Loop trails out of Sundance Lodge; grooming by Lodge as needed.

*For more information on following trails contact District Ranger, Philipsburg, MT 59858 (406) 859-3211*

**Lodgepole Ridge Ski Trails-Georgetown Lake**
*7.7 km More Difficult, 1.1 km Most Difficult; no grooming*
Parking available at Red Bridge Boat Launch. Trail map available at Forest Offices.

**Cable Campground Ski Trails—Discovery Basin Ski Area**
*5.2 km More Difficult; no grooming*
Parking available at Discovery Basin Ski Area. Trail map available at the Ski Area and Forest Offices.

**Discovery Basin Ski Trails- Discovery Basin Ski Area**
*5.2 km Easiest intermittent grooming; 3. 1 km More Difficult, 9.6 km Most Difficult; no grooming*
Parking available at Discovery Basin Ski Area. Trail map available at the Ski Area and Forest Offices.

### Bitterroot National Forest

*For more information contact District Ranger, Sula, MT 59871(406)821-3201*

**Saddle Mountain-Lost Trail Pass**
*4.8 km Most Difficult (mountain touring); no grooming*
Mountain touring trail; begins at Lost Trail Ski Area. follows the road up to Saddle Mountain.

**Wildfire Trail-Lost Trail Pass**
*5 km More Difficult, 1 km Most Difficult (mountain touring); no grooming*
Mountain touring trail takes off from Saddle Mountain Trail and follows ridge out into the Saddle Mountain Bum. Provides 3 separate routes through the bum; 1 most difficult and 2 more difficult. Trails are marked, signed, and maintained.

**Saddle Mountain Bum Trail-Lost Trail Pass**
*1.3 km Easiest, 1.3 km More Difficult, 1.4 km Most Difficult (mountain touring); no grooming*
Mountain touring trail begins in Lost Trail Pass Ski Area parking lot and ends on Hwy. 93 at the East Camp Creek Road.

## INFORMATION PLEASE

All Montana area codes are 406

### Road Information

Montana Road Condition Report
800-226-7623, 800-335-7592 or local 444-7696
Montana Highway Patrol 444-7696
**Local Road Reports**
Missoula 728-8553
Statewide Weather Reports 453-2081

### Tourism Information

Travel Montana 800-847-4868 outside Montana
444-2654 in Montana
http://travel.mt.gov/.
Gold West Country 846-1943 or 800-879-1159
Glacier Country 837-6211 or 800-338-5072
Northern Rodeo Association 252-1122
**Chambers of Commerce**
Anaconda 563-2400
Powell County 846-2094
Bitterroot Valley 363-2400
Philipsburg 859-3388

### Airports

Anaconda 563-8275
Conner 821-3069
Deer Lodge 846-1771
Dillon 683-4447
Drummond 288-3405
Hamilton 363-4740
Philipsburg 826-3605
Stevensville 777-2006
Wisdom 683-5242
Wise River 832-3219

### Government Offices

State BLM Office 255-2885, 238-1540
Bureau of Land Management
Missoula Field Office 329-3914
Butte Field Office 494-5059
Bitterroot National Forest 363-7161
Lolo National Forest 329-3750
Beaverhead/Deerlodge National Forest
Butte 522-2520
Lee Metcalf National Wildlife Refuge 777-5552
Montana Fish, Wildlife & Parks 542-5500
U.S. Bureau of Reclamation
Dillon Field Office 683-6472

### Hospitals

Community Hospital of Anaconda 563-5261
Powell Cnty Memorial •Deer Lodge 846-2212
Marcus Daly Hospital • Hamilton 363-2211
Granite Cnty Memorial•Philipsburg 859-3271

### Golf Courses

Anaconda Country Club • Anaconda 797-3220
Old Works Golf Course • Anaconda 563-5989
Fairmont Hot Springs Resort Public Golf Course • Fairmont 797-3241
Deer Lodge Golf Club • Garrison 846-1625
Hamilton Golf Club • Hamilton 363-4251
Pete's Pitch & Putt • Lolo 273-3333
Whitetail Golf Course • Stevensville 777-3636

### Bed & Breakfasts

**Time After Time B&B** • Victor 642-3258
**Blue Heron B&B** • Philipsburg 859-3856
**Hickory House Inn** • Anaconda 563-5481
**Bearmouth Chalet** • Clinton 825-9950
**The Blue Damsel** • Clinton 825-3077
**Red Willow Inn** • Hamilton 375-1101
A Cosie Place • Helmville 793-5523
Alpine Meadow Ranch • Hamilton 363-1582
Bitterroot River Lodge • Hamilton 363-0708
Big Horn B&B • Philipsburg 859-3109
Big Creek Pines B&B • Stevensville 642-6475
Camp Creek Inn • Sula 821-3508
Coleman-Fee Mansion • Deer Lodge 846-2922
Country Caboose • Stevensville 777-3145
Deer Crossing B&B • Hamilton 363-2232
Haus Rustika B&B • Florence 777-2291
Heavenly View Hideaway • Corvallis 961-5220
Inn at the Call of the Wild • Hamilton 961-5235
Flying R Guest Cabins • Darby 821-4631
Green Thumb B&B • Florence 273-6522
Mystical Mountain Inn • Stevensville 642-3464
Moose Walk Inn B&B • Victor 961-3037
Trout Springs B&B • Hamilton 375-0911
Red Sun Labyrinth B&B • Victor 327-0590
Roaring Lion Inn • Hamilton 363-6555
Sleeping Child Creek B&B • Hamilton 363-4462
Starfire Farm Lodge • Hamilton 363-6240
Roaring Lion Inn • Hamilton 363-6555

### Guest Ranches & Resorts

**1880's Ranch** • Anaconda 491-2336
**Rive Bend Fly Fishing Lodge** • Darby 821-1999
**Skalkaho Lodge & Outfitters**
Hamilton 363-3522
**Trapper Creek Lodge** • Darby 821-4970
**Triple Creek Lodge** • Darby 821-4600
**Fairmont Hot Springs** • Anaconda 797-3241
**Seven Gables Resort** • Anaconda 563-5052
**Lolo Hot Springs** • Lolo 273-2290
Alpine Meadows Guest Ranch • Retreat
Darby 821-4486
Alta Meadow Ranch • Hamilton 349-2464
Alta Ranch • Darby 349-2142
Bear Creek Lodge • Victor 642-3750
Flying R Guest Cabins • Darby 821-4631
Under Wild Skies Lodge • Philipsburg 859-3000
Wildlife Adventures Inc • Victor 642-3262
Pepperbox Ranch • Darby 349-2920
Georgetown Lake Lodge • Anaconda 563-3402
Teller Wildlife Refuge • Corvallis 961-3204
West Fork Billabong • Darby 821-1853
Star Haven • Hamilton 363-6675
Starfire Farm Lodge • Hamilton 800-363-9918
Elkhorn Hot Springs • Polaris 834-3434
Lost Trail Hot Springs Resort • Sula 821-3574
Lost Horse Creek Lodge • Hamilton 363-6107
Rock Creek Lodge • Clinton 825-4868
Rye Creek Lodge • Darby 821-3366

Sundance Lodge • Wise River 689-3611
Wildlife Adventures • Victor 642-3262
White Birch Ranch • Darby 349-2141

## Vacation Homes & Cabins

**A L'il Bit of Heaven - Classy Cabins**
Sula 821-3433
**Sweet Sage Guest House** • Victor 646-6400
**Wise River Club** • Wise River 832-3258
Angler's Lodge • Hamilton 363-0980
Broad Axe Lodge • Sula 821-3878
Cut Off Cabin Rental • Troy 295-4339
Elk Ridge Cabin • Sula 642-3187
Flying R Guest Cabins • Darby 821-4631
Harlan Cabin • Hamilton 363-6265
Kootinai Crest Lodge • Troy 295-9056
Kootinai River Vaction Homes • Troy 295-4630
Nez Perce Ranch • Darby 349-2100
Overdale Lodge LLC • Troy 295-4057
Reimel Creek Ranch • Sula 363-0747
Starfire Farm Lodge • Hamilton 363-6240
West Fork Bitterroot Vacation Retreat
Darby 821-3817
West Fork Meadows Ranch • Darby 349-2468

## Forest Service Cabins

*Beaverhead-Deerlodge National Forest*

**Birch Creek Cabin**
20 mi. NW of Dillon, MT 683-3900
Capacity: 3 Nightly fee: $20 Available: All Year
Winter: Most years the Birch Creek Road provides access to within 1/4 mile.

**Bloody Dick Cabin**
23 mi. S of Jackson, MT 683-3900
Capacity: 3 Nightly fee: $20 Available: All Year
Winter: Depending on snow conditions, may need to travel up to 23 miles by snowmobile or skis to reach cabin.

**Doney Cabin**
11 mi NW of Deer Lodge , MT 846-1770
Capacity: 6 Nightly fee: $15 Available: All year
Access distance varies with snow conditions; under normal winter conditions, can drive within 5 miles. No water.

**Douglas Creek Cabin**
10 mi. SE of Hall, MT 846-1770
Capacity: 6 Nightly fee: $15 Available: All year
Take Hwy. l S. from Hall, approx. 2 1/2 miles to Douglas Creek. Take Forest Road 707 approx. 7 1/2 miles to cabin site. No water.

**Foolhen Cabin**
l2 miles W of Wise River, MT (north end of Pioneer Mtns.) 832-3178
Capacity: 4 Nightly fee: $20 Available: 12/1 8/31
Winter: Recommended for snowmobile access only, nearest road is 12 miles. Summer: Access by trail, 2.5 miles from nearest road.

**Hogan Cabin**
25 mi. W of Wisdom, MT 689-3243
Capacity: 4 Nightly fee: $20 Available: 12/1—3/31
Access from nearest road by snowmobile is 5 miles and for skiers, 3.2 miles by trail.

**Horse Prairie Guard Station**
44 mi. SW of Dillon, MT 683-3900
Capacity: 3 Nightly fee: $20 Available: All Year
Winter: Road normally plowed to junction, about 1.5 miles from cabin.

**May Creek Cabin**
18 mi. W of Wisdom, MT 689-3243
Capacity: 4 Nightly fee: $20 Available: 07/5-8/25 and 12/-3/31
Take Hwy. 43, 16 miles West from Wisdom to May Creek Campground. Trail into cabin is approx. 2 1/2 miles.

**Moose Lake Guard Station**
24.3 mi. SW of Philipsburg, MT 859-3211
Capacity: 4 Nightly fee: $20 Available: All year
May require about a 1/4 mile walk in for 12/1 - 4/1, depending on snow conditions.

**Stony Cabin**
19.4 mi. NW of Philipsburg 859-3211
Capacity: 4 Nightly fee: $20 Available: All year
May require about a 1/4 mile walk-in from 12/2 - 4/1 depending on snow conditions

**Twin Lakes Cabin**
26 mi SW of Wisdom, MT 689-3243
Capacity: 4 Nightly fee: $20 Available: 12/01 - 3/31
Access on snowmobile trail. 12 miles from end of plowed county road to cabin.

*Bitterroot National Forest*

**McCart Lookout Tower**
20 mi. E of Sula, MT 821-3201
Capacity: 4 Nightly fee: $30 Available: 05/01 - 10/30 (max. stay 7 days)
Winter access depends on snow conditions. 1.5 mile easy trail access from end of road, Lookout restored to 1930s era. No water available. Ideal family getaway.

**East Fork Guard Station**
16 mi. E of Sula, MT on E Fork Bitterroot Road 821-3201
Capacity: 8 Nightly fee: $30 Available: All year (max. stay 7 days)
Winter access may require 3/4 mile travel by snowmobile or skis/snowshoes. Electricity & fire-wood provided.

**Horse Heaven Cabin**
75 miles SW of Darby, MT on Magruder Road to Elk City, ID 821-3269
Capacity: 4 Nightly fee: $25 Available: All year (max. stay 7 days)
Located in road corridor between two of largest Wildernesses in Lower 48 States. Primitive road; winter access about 57 miles by snowmobile.

**Magruder Ranger's House**
52 miles SW of Darby, MT in Magruder Corridor, Adjacent to Selway River. 821-3269
Capacity: 5 Nightly fee: $40 Available: 6/1 - 10/31 & 12/1 - 2/28
Propane stove, refrigerator and lights. Wood fur-nace. Hot/cold water, shower, flush toilet (summer only).

**Twogood Cabin**
10 mi. SW of Sula, MT 821-3201
Capacity: 6 Nightly fee: $25 Available: Year round except 10/15 - 12/01
Water, woodstove, firewood, propane cooking stove, kitchen utensils. Range line cabin built in 1952. Located on Porcupine Creek in Allen Mtn. Roadless Area. Access via 6 mi. hike or ride up Trail 103.Winter access may require 9 mi. travel with ski's or snowshoes.

**Woods Cabin**
8 mi.NW of Darby, MT on Lake Como 821-3913
Capacity: 15 Nightly fee: $50
Available: 05/01 - 9/30
Water, wood heating stove, propane cooking stove. 3 bedrooms, large meeting room, deck.

**Medicine Point Lookout Tower**
8 mi. W of Sula 821-3201
Capacity: 4 Nightly fee: $30 Available: 7/1-10/1
3 mi. difficult hike trail, 7 mi. medium horse trail. Newly restored (1999) lookout, propane eating/cooking stove, kitchen utensils provided. No water. Several loop trails in area.

*Lolo National Forest*

**West Fork Butte (Lookout Cabin)**
25 mi. W of Lolo, MT S of Hwy. 12 329-3814
Capacity: 4 Nightly fee: $20 Available: All year
14 ft. by 14 ft. building on ground; access and availability varies by season; winter access by skis or snowmobile for last 7.5 miles with elevational rise of 2,300 ft. Summer availability depends on weather.

## Private Campgrounds

**Indian Creek Campground**
Deer Lodge 846-3848
**Sula Country Store, Campground. RV, & KOA**
Sula 821-3364
**Wise River Club** • Wise River 832-3258
**Chalet Bearmouth Campground**
Clinton 825-9950
**Seven Gables Resort & RV**
Georgetown Lake 563-5052
**Wilderness Motel RV & Tent Park**
Darby 821-3405
Angler's Roost • Hamilton 363-1268
Big Sky RV Park & Campground
Anaconda 563-2967
Bitterroot Family Campground
Hamilton 363-2430
Black Rabbit RV Park • Hamilton 363-3744
Denton's Point • Anaconda 563-6030
Fairmont RV Park • Anaconda 797-3505
Georgetown Lake Lodge • Anaconda 563-7020
Ekstrom's Stage Station • Clinton 825-3183
Elkhorn Guest Ranch • Clinton 825-3220
Hunter's Trailer Court • Anaconda 563-7860
Lakeview RV Park • Georgetown Lake 563-3116
Lick Creek Campground • Hamilton 821-3840
Lolo Hot Springs RV Park • Lolo 273-2294
Turah Store & Campground • Clinton 258-6628
Moosehead Campground • Conner 821-3327
Indian Creek RV Campground
Deer Lodge 846-3848
KOA Kampgrounds • Deer Lodge 846-1629
Ravalli Store Campgroud • Ravalli 745-4554
Riverfront RV Park • Garrison 846-2158
Riverside RV Park • Hamilton 363-3744
Square Dance Center • Campground
Lolo 273-0141
The Inn at Philipsburg • Philipsburg 859-3959
Wilderness Motel & RV Park • Darby 821-3405
St Mary's Motel • Stevensville 777-2838
Tucker RV Park • Victor 642-3752

## Car Rental

Avis Rent-A-Car 549-4711
Budget of Missoula 543-7001
Dollar Rent-A-Car 542-2311
Enterprise Rent-A-Car 721-1888
Grizzly Auto Center 721-5000
Hertz Rent-A-Car 541-9511
National Car Rental 543-3131
Paradise RV Rentals 721-6729
Practical Rent-A-Car 721-4391
Rent A Wreck 721-3838
Thrifty Car Rental 549-2277

| | |
|---|---|
| Xpress Rent-A-Car | 542-8459 |
| Payless Car Rental | 563-5256 |
| Mildenberger Motors | 363-4100 |
| Rent A Wreck | 363-1430 |

## Outfitters & Guides

*F=Fishing H=Hunting R=River Guides*
*E=Horseback Rides G=General Guide Services*

| | | |
|---|---|---|
| **Skalkaho Lodge** | HGEF | 363-3522 |
| **Riverbend Flyfishing** | GF | 363-4197 |
| **Blackbird's Fly Shop & Lodge** | F | 642-6375 |
| Anglers Afloat | F | 777-3421 |
| Backdoor Outfitters | F | 777-3861 |
| Bartlett Creek Outfitters • Deer Lodge | | 693-2433 |
| Big Velvet Ranch | H | 821-3131 |
| Bloody Dick Outfitters | G | 681-3163 |
| Big Wild Adventures | G | 821-3747 |
| Birch Creek Outfitters | G | 961-3511 |
| Bitterroot Fly Company | GFR | 821-1624 |
| Bitterroot Anglers | F | 777-5667 |
| Bunky Ranch Outfitters | HFR | 821-3574 |
| Carl Mann's Montana Experience | GF | 273-6966 |
| Catch Montana | F | 363-4494 |
| Complete Fly Fisher | GF | 832-3176 |
| Craig Fellin's Big Hole Outfitters | FG | 832-3252 |
| Fairmont Trail Rides | E | 797-3377 |
| The Fishhook | F | 832-3317 |
| Fishhaus Fly Fishing | F | 363-6158 |
| Fly Fishing Adventures | F | 363-2398 |
| Fly Fishing Always | F | 363-0943 |
| Flying W Outfitters | G | 821-4900 |
| High Country Connection | FFE | 821-3389 |
| Iron Horse Outfitters | HFEG | 821-4474 |
| JM Bar Outfitters & Trailrides | GHFE | 825-3230 |
| Lapham Outfitters | HF | 834-3134 |
| Lightening Creek Outfitters | HE | 363-0320 |
| Lolo Hot Springs | E | 273-2290 |
| Lone Tree Outfitting | H | 777-3906 |
| Lost Horse Creek Lodge | E | 363-1460 |
| McCormick's Sunset Ranch | HF | 793-5574 |
| M&M Flyfishing | F | 375-2459 |
| Montana Fly Fishing Adventures | F | 846-0002 |
| North West Force | R | 642-3251 |
| Painted Rock | HFE | 349-2909 |
| Parsons Pony Farm | E | 273-3363 |
| Party Roundup | E | 375-0758 |
| Peterson's Horse Corral | EG | 797-3377 |
| Pioneer Outfitter | G | 832-3128 |
| Rainbow Outfitters | GF | 834-3444 |
| Rivers Edge Sporting Goods | GF | 846-2926 |
| R.L. Sourbrine & Sons Outfitting | HF | 642-3251 |
| Scully's Gude Service | F | 846-2582 |
| Smith & Baker Outfitting | FHE | 859-3948 |
| Stockton Outfitters | H | 689-3609 |
| Troutfitters | GF | 832-3212 |
| Trout Fishing Only | F | 363-2408 |
| Under Wild Skies Outfitters | FH | 859-3000 |
| Wapati Waters | 642-6548 | 642-6548 |
| WW Outfitters | R | 821-3622 |
| Whistling Elk Work Shops | G | 832-3195 |
| Wildlife Adventures Inc | G | 642-3262 |

## Cross-Country Ski Centers

| | |
|---|---|
| Mt. Haggin Nordic Ski Center<br>15 mi. S of Anaconda | 494-4235 |
| Sundance Lodge<br>20 mi. W of Wise River | 689-3611 |

## Downhill Ski Areas

| | |
|---|---|
| Discovery Ski Area | 563-2184 |
| Lost Trail Ski Area | 821-3211 |
| Maverick Mountain | 834-3454 |

## Snowmobile Rentals

| | |
|---|---|
| Bitterroot Adventures Rentals<br>Hamilton | 961-3392 |
| Lolo Hot Springs • Lolo | 273-2290 |
| Powder Hound Rental • Lolo | 273-6420 |

## NOTES:

Section 7

## Public Campgrounds

# Campsite Directions

| Campsite Directions | Season | Camping | Trailers | Toilets | Water | Boat Launch | Fishing | Swimming | Trails | Stay Limit | Fee |
|---|---|---|---|---|---|---|---|---|---|---|---|
| **109•Lee Creek FS**<br>26 mi. W of Lolo on US 12 | 5/20-9/30 | 22 | 30′ | • | • | | • | | • | 14 | • |
| **110•Lewis & Clark FS**<br>15 mi. W of Lolo on US 12 | 5/20-9/30 | 18 | 30′ | • | • | | • | | | 14 | • |
| **111•Chief Looking Glass FWP**<br>14 mi. S of Missoula on US 93 to Milepost 77•1 mi. E on Cty. Rd. | 5/1-11/30 | 19 | • | • | • | A | • | | | 7 | • |
| **112•Charles Waters FS**<br>2 mi. NW of Stevensville on Cty. Rd. 269•4 mi. N on US 93<br>•2 mi. W on Cty. Rd. 22•1 mi. W on Forest Rd. 1316 | 5/25-9/10 | 22 | 35′ | D | • | | • | | • | 14 | • |
| **113•Beavertail Hill FWP**<br>26 mi. SE of Missoula on I-90 •Milepost 130•Beavertail Hill Exit•1/4 mi. on S on Cty Rd. | 5/1-9/30 | 26 | 28′ | • | • | A | • | | N | 14 | • |
| **114•Blodgett Canyon Campground**<br>5 mi. NW of Hamilton | 5/15-9/15 | 6 | 30′ | • | | | • | | • | 5 | |
| **115•Schumaker FS**<br>7 mi. N of Darby on US 93•2 mi. W on Cty. Rd.•<br>16 mi. W on Forest Rd. 429•2 mi. N on Forest Rd. 5505 | 7/15-9/15 | 5 | 18′ | • | | A | • | | • | 14 | |
| **116•Bear Creek Pass FS**<br>7 mi. N of Darby on US 93•18 mi. W on Forest Rd. 429 (Lost Horse Rd.) | 7/15-0/15 | 7 | 32′ | • | | | | | • | 14 | |
| **117•Rock Creek Horse Camp FS**<br>4 mi. N of Darby on US 93•4.2 mi. W on Cty. Rd. 82 | 5/15-9/15 | 10 | 50′ | D | | | • | | • | 14 | • |
| **118•Lake Como Upper Campground FS**<br>4 mi. N of Darby on US 93•5.3 mi. W on Cty. Rd. 82 | 6/1-9/15 | 10 | 16′ | D | • | • | • | • | • | 14 | • |
| **119•Lake Como Lower Campground FS**<br>4 mi. N of Darby on US 93•4.8 mi. W on Cty. Rd. 82 | 5/31-9/5 | 12 | 50′ | D | • | C | • | • | • | 14 | • |
| **120•Slate Creek FS**<br>4 mi.S of Darby on US 93•24 mi. W on Cty. Rd. 473•2 mi. S on Cty. Rd. 96 | 5/1-12/1 | 4 | 30′ | • | | • | • | • | | 14 | |
| **121•Black Bear FS**<br>3 mi. S of Hamilton on US 93•l3 mi. E on MT 38 | 6/1-9/15 | 6 | 18′ | D | | | | • | | 14 | |
| **122•Warm Springs FS**<br>5 mi. NW of Sula on US 93•1 mi. SW on Cty. Rd. 100 | 5/15-9/10 | 14 | 26′ | • | • | | • | | | 14 | • |
| **123•Spring Gulch FS**<br>5 mi. NW of Sula on US 93 | 5/15-9/15 | 10 | 50′ | • | • | | • | | • | 14 | • |
| **124•Crazy Creek & Crazy Creek Horse Camp FS**<br>5 mi. NW of Sula on US 93 •1 mi. SW on Cty. Rd. 100•3 mi. SW on Forest Rd. 370 | 5/15-12/1 | 6 | 26′ | | | | | | | 14 | |
| **125•Sam Billings Memorial FS**<br>4 mi. S of Darby on US 93•13 mi. SW on Rt. 473•1 mi. NW on Forest Rd. 5631 | 5/1-12/1 | 12 | 30′ | • | | | • | | • | 14 | |
| **126•Rombo FS**<br>4 mi. S of Darby on US 93•18 mi. SW on Rt. 473 | 5/1-12/1 | 16 | 40′ | • | • | | • | | | 14 | • |
| **127•Painted Rocks FWP**<br>17 mi S of Hamilton on US 93• | All Year | 32 | • | • | | C | • | | | 14 | |
| **128•Alta FS**<br>4 mi. S of Darby on US 93•30 mi. on Rt. 473 | 5/1-12/1 | 15 | 50′ | • | • | | • | | • | 14 | • |
| **129•Indian Trees FS**<br>6 mi. S of Sula on US 93•1 mi. SW on Forest Rd. 729 | 5/15-9/10 | 17 | 50′ | • | • | | | | | | |
| **130•Jennings Camp FS**<br>1 mi. W of Sula on US 93•10 mi. NE on Cty. Rd. 472 | 5/15-12/1 | 4 | 25′ | • | | | • | | | 14 | |
| **131•Martin Creek FS**<br>1 mi. W of Sula on US 93•4 mi. NE on Cty. Rd. 472•12 mi. NE on forest Rd. 80 | 5/15-12/1 | 7 | 35′ | 0 | • | | | | | 14 | • |
| **132•Norton FS**<br>5 mi. SE of Clinton on I-90 to Rock Creek Exit•11 mi. S on Forest Rd. 102 | All Year | 10 | 16′ | • | • | | | | | 16 | |
| **133•Grizzly FS**<br>5 mi. SE of Clinton on I-90 to Rock Creek Exit•11 mi. S on Forest Rd. 102 | 5/20-9/30 | 10 | 32′ | • | •f | | • | | • | 14 | • |

**Agency**
FS—U.S.D.A Forest Service
FWP—Montana Fish, Wildlife & Parks
NPS—National Park Service
BLM—U.S. Bureau of Land Management
USBR—U.S. Bureau of Reclamation
CE—Corps of Engineers

**Camping**
Camping is allowed at this site. Number indicates camping spaces available
H—Hard sided units only; no tents

**Trailers**
Trailer units allowed. Number indicates maximum length.

**Toilets**
Toilets on site. D—Disabled access

**Water**
Drinkable water on site

**Fishing**
Visitors may fish on site

**Boat**
Type of boat ramp on site:
A—Hand launch
B—4-wheel drive with trailer
C—2-wheel drive with trailer

**Swimming**
Designated swimming areas on site

**Trails**
Trails on site
B—Backpacking N—Nature/Interpretive

**Stay Limit**
Maximum length of stay in days

**Fee**
Camping and/or day-use fee

## Public Campgrounds

# Campsite Directions

| Campsite Directions | Season | Camping | Trailers | Toilets | Water | Boat Launch | Fishing | Swimming | Trails | Stay Limit | Fee |
|---|---|---|---|---|---|---|---|---|---|---|---|
| **134•Dalles FS**<br>5 mi. SE of Clinton on I-90 to Rock Creek Exit•13 mi. S on Forest Rd. 102 | 5/20-9/30 | 10 | 32′ | • | • | | • | | • | 14 | |
| **135•Harry's Flat FS**<br>5 mi. SE of Clinton on I-90 to Rock Creek Exit•18 mi. S on Forest Rd. 102 | 5/20-9/30 | 18- | 32′ | • | • | | • | | | 14 | • |
| **136•Bitterroot Flat FS**<br>5 mi. SE of Clinton on I-90 to Rock Creek Exit•24 mi. S on Forest Rd. 102 | 5/20-9/30 | 15 | 32′ | • | • | | • | | | 14 | • |
| **137•Squaw Rock FS**<br>19 mi. W of Philipsburg off Rock Cr. Rd. (Forest Rd. 102) | 4/1-10/30 | 7 | 32′ | D | • | | • | | | 16 | |
| **138•Crystal Creek**<br>6 mi. S of Philipsburg on MT 1•21 mi. SW of Philipsburg on MT 38 | 7/1-9/30 | 3 | 16′ | • | | | | | • | 16 | |
| **139•Cable Mountain FS**<br>16 mi. S of Philipsburg off Discovery Basin Rd.•Adjacent to N Fork of Flint Cr. | 5/29-9/15 | 11 | 22′ | • | • | | • | | | 14 | • |
| **140•Lodgepole FS**<br>11 mi. S of Philipsburg on MT 1 | 5/22-9/30 | 31 | 32′ | • | • | C | • | | | 14 | • |
| **141•Racetrack FS**<br>3 mi. E of Anaconda on MT 1•7 mi. NW on Cty. Rd.•2 mi. NW on Forest Rd. 169 | 5/25-9/15 | 13 | 22′ | D | • | | • | | | 16 | • |
| **142•Lost Creek FWP**<br>1.5 mi. E of Anaconda on MT 1•Milepost 5•2mi. N on Rt. 273•6 mi. W | 5/1-11/30 | 25 | • | D | • | | • | | N | 14 | |
| **143•Springhill FS**<br>11 mi. NW of Anaconda on MT 1 | 4/1-10/30 | 7 | 32′ | D | • | | | | | 16 | • |
| **144•Warm Springs FS**<br>11 mi. NW of Anaconda on MT 1•2.5 mi. N on Forest Rd. 170 | 5/25-9/25 | 6 | 16′ | • | • | | • | | | 16 | |
| **145•Flint Creek FS**<br>8 mi. S of Philipsburg on MT 1 | 5/1-10/30 | 16 | 16′ | D | | | • | | | 16 | |
| **146•Philipsburg Bay FS**<br>11 mi. S of Philipsburg at Georgetown Lake | 9/15-9/30 | 69 | 32′ | D | • | C | • | | | 14 | • |
| **147•Piney FS**<br>13 mi. S of Philipsburg on MT 1 on Georgetown Lake Rd. | 5/15-9/15 | 49 | 48′ | D | • | C | • | | | 14 | • |
| **148•East Fork FS**<br>6 mi. S of Philipsburg on MT 1•6 mi. SW on MT 38•<br>5 mi. SE on Forest Rd.672•1 mi. SE on Forest Rd. 9349 | 5/1-9/30 | 10 | 22′ | • | • | | • | | | 16 | |
| **149•Spillway FS**<br>18 mi. SW of Philipsburg off East Fork Rd. (Forest Rd. 672) | 5/25-9/5 | 15 | 22′ | • | • | | | | | 16 | • |
| **150•Copper Creek FS**<br>8 mi. S of Philipsburg on MT 1•9 mi. SW on MT 38•10 mi. S on FR 5106 | 5/15-9/30 | 7 | 22′ | D | • | | • | | • | 16 | • |
| **151•Seymour FS**<br>11 mi. W of Wise River on MT 43•4 mi. N on Rt. 274•8 mi. NW on Forest Rd. 934 | 5/25-9/15 | 17 | 16′ | • | • | | • | | • | 16 | |
| **152•East Bank BLM**<br>8 mi. W of Wise River on MT 43 | All Year | 5 | 24′ | D | | C | • | | | 14 | |
| **153•Mussigbrod FS**<br>1.5 mi. W of Wisdom on MT 43•9 mi. N on Lower North Fork Rd.<br>•10 mi. W on Musigbrod Lake Rd.•Follow signs. | 6/26-9/6 | 10 | • | • | • | • | • | | • | 16 | • |
| **154•May Creek FS**<br>17 Mi. W of Wisdom on MT 43 | 6/25-9/6 | 21 | 32′ | • | • | | • | | • | 16 | • |
| **155•Dickie Bridge BLM**<br>18 mi. W of Divide on MT 43 | All Year | 8 | 24′ | • | | | • | | | 14 | |
| **156•Fourth of July FS**<br>11 mi. SW of Wise River on Pioneer Mtns. Scenic Byway | 6/15-9/15 | 5 | 24′ | • | • | | • | f | • | 16 | • |
| **157•Boulder FS**<br>12 mi. SW of Wise River on Pioneer Mtns. Scenic Byway | 6/15-9/15 | 12 | 24′ | • | f• | | • | | • | 16 | • |
| **158•Lodgepole FS**<br>13 mi. SW of Wise River on Pioneer Mtns. Scenic Byway | 5/25-9/15 | 11 | 16′ | • | • | • | | | • | 16 | • |
| **159•Willow FS**<br>14 mi. SW of Wise River on Pioneer Mtns. Scenic Byway | 6/1509/30 | 9 | 16′ | • | • | | • | | • | 16 | • |
| **160•Little Joe FS**<br>20 mi. SW of Wise River on Pioneer Mts. Scenic Byway (Forest Rd. 484) | 5/25-9/15 | 4 | 16′ | • | • | | • | | • | 16 | • |
| **161•Steel Creek FS**<br>1 mi. N of Wisdom•6 mi. E on Steel Creek Rd. | 6/26-9/6 | 7 | • | • | • | • | • | | • | 16 | • |
| **162•Mono Creek FS**<br>23 mi. SW of Wise River on Lower Elkhorn Rd. 2465 | 6/15-9/30 | 5 | 16′ | • | • | | • | | • | 16 | • |
| **163•Price Creek FS**<br>4 mi. S of Dillon on I-15•27 mi. W on Rt. 278•17 mi. N on Pioneer Mtns. Scenic Byway | 5/22-9/15 | 28 | • | • | • | | | | • | 16 | • |

Section 7

## PUBLIC CAMPGROUNDS

# Campsite Directions

| Campsite Directions | Season | Camping | Trailers | Toilets | Water | Boat Launch | Fishing | Swimming | Trails | Stay Limit | Fee |
|---|---|---|---|---|---|---|---|---|---|---|---|
| **164•Grasshopper FS**<br>4 mi. S of Dillon on I-15•27 mi. W on Rt. 378•11.5 mi. N on Pioneer Mtns. Scenic Byway | 6/f16-9/15 | 24 | 16′ | • | • | | | | • | | |
| **165•Twin Lakes FS**<br>7 mi. S of Wisdom on Rt. 278•8 mi. W on Cty. Rd. 12<br>•5 mi. S on Forest Rd. 945•6 mi. SW on Forest Rd. 183 | 6/25-9/6 | 21 | 32′ | • | • | C | • | | • | 16 | • |
| **166•Miner Lake FS**<br>19 mi. S of Wisdom at Jackson on Rt. 278•7 mi. W on Cty. Rd. 95•3 mi. W on Forest Rd. 182 | 6/1-9/15 | 18 | 32′ | • | • | C | • | | • | 16 | |
| **167•South Van Houten FS**<br>1 mi. S of Jackson•10 mi. on Skinner Meadows Rd. | 6/25-9/6 | 3 | | • | • | | • | | | 16 | |
| **167•North Van Houten FS**<br>1 mi. S of Jackson•10 mi. on Skinner Meadows Rd. | 6/25-9/6 | 4 | | • | • | • | • | | | 16 | |
| **168•Reservoir Lake FS**<br>19 mi. S of Dillon on I-15 •17 mi. W on Rt. 324•NW on Cty. Rd. 1814•5 mi. on Forest Rd. 1813 | 6/16-9/15 | 16 | 16′ | • | • | C | • | • | • | 16 | |
| **169•Sacajawea Memorial FS**<br>Lemhi Pass•10 mi. off Rt. 324.•W of Grant | 6/16-9/15 | 2 | | | | | | | | | |

**Agency**
FS—U.S.D.A Forest Service
FWP—Montana Fish, Wildlife & Parks
NPS—National Park Service
BLM—U.S. Bureau of Land Management
USBR—U.S. Bureau of Reclamation
CE—Corps of Engineers

**Camping**
Camping is allowed at this site. Number indicates camping spaces available
H—Hard sided units only; no tents

**Trailers**
Trailer units allowed. Number indicates maximum length.

**Toilets**
Toilets on site. D—Disabled access

**Water**
Drinkable water on site

**Fishing**
Visitors may fish on site

**Boat**
Type of boat ramp on site:
A—Hand launch
B—4-wheel drive with trailer
C—2-wheel drive with trailer

**Swimming**
Designated swimming areas on site

**Trails**
Trails on site
B—Backpacking N—Nature/Interpretive

**Stay Limit**
Maximum length of stay in days

**Fee**
Camping and/or day-use fee

Section 7

All Montana Area Codes are 406

# Fishery

| Fishery | Cold Water Species | | | | | | | | | | | | Warm Water Species | | | | | | | | | | Services | | | | | |
|---|---|---|---|---|---|---|---|---|---|---|---|---|---|---|---|---|---|---|---|---|---|---|---|---|---|---|---|---|
| | Brook Trout | Mt. Whitefish | Lake Whitefish | Golden Trout | Cutthroat Trout | Brown Trout | Rainbow Trout | Kokanee Salmon | Bull Trout | Lake Trout | Arctic Grayling | Burbot | Largemouth Bass | Smallmouth Bass | Walleye | Sauger | Northern Pike | Shovelnose Sturgeon | Channel Catfish | Yellow Perch | Crappie | Paddlefish | Vehicle Access | Campgrounds | Toilets | Docks | Boat Ramps | MotorRestrictions |
| 94. Bear Creek | | | | | • | | | | | | | | | | | | | | | | | | • | | | | | |
| 95. Bitterroot River | • | • | | | • | • | • | | | | | | | | | | | | | | | | • | • | • | | • | |
| 96. Lolo Creek | • | • | | | • | • | • | | • | | | | | | | | | | | | | | • | • | • | | | |
| 97. Skalkaho Creek | | • | | | • | | | | | | | | | | | | | | | | | | • | | | | | |
| 98. Bitterroot alpine lakes | | | | | • | | | | | | | | | | | | | | | | | | | | | | | |
| 99. East Fork Bitterroot River | | • | | | • | | • | | • | | | | | | | | | | | | | | • | | | | | |
| 100. West Fork Bitterroot River | | • | | | • | • | • | | | | | | | | | | | | | | | | • | • | • | | | |
| 101. West Big Hole alpine lakes | • | | | • | • | | • | | | | • | • | | | | | | | | | | | • | • | | | • | |
| 102. Rock Creek | • | • | | | • | • | • | | • | | | | | | | | | | | | | | • | • | • | | | |
| 103. Georgetown Lake | • | | | | | | • | • | | | | | | | | | | | | | | | • | • | • | | • | |
| 104. Little Blackfoot River | | • | | | • | • | • | | | | | | | | | | | | | | | | | | | | | |
| 105. Clark Fork River | • | • | | | | • | • | | • | | | | | | | | | | | | | | • | • | • | | • | |
| 106. Wise River | • | • | | | • | • | • | | | | | • | | | | | | | | | | | • | • | • | | | |
| 107. East Pioneer alpine lakes | • | | | • | • | | • | | | | • | | | | | | | | | | | | | • | | | | |
| 108. Lake Como | | | | | | | • | | | | | | | | | | | | | | | | • | • | • | | | • |

## Dining Quick Reference

Price Range refers to the average cost of a meal per person: ($) $1-$6, ($$) $7-$11, ($$$) $12-up. Cocktails: "Yes" indicates full bar; Beer (B)/Wine (W), Service: Breakfast (B), Brunch (BR), Lunch (L), Dinner (D). Businesses in bold print will have additional information under the appropriate map locator number in the body of this section.

| RESTAURANT | TYPE CUISINE | PRICE RANGE | CHILD MENU | COCKTAILS BEER WINE | SERVICE | CREDIT CARDS | MAP LOCATOR NUMBER |
|---|---|---|---|---|---|---|---|
| **Fairmont Hot Springs** | Continental | $$ | Yes | Yes | B/L/D | Major | 1 |
| **Barclay II Supper Club** | Steaks & Seafood | $$$ | | Yes | D | Major | 1 |
| **Chat & Chew** | Family | | | | | | 1 |
| **Donivan's Family Restaurant** | Family | $ | Yes | B/W | B/L/D | Major | 1 |
| **Stageline Pizza** | Pizza | $/$$ | | | L/D | | 1 |
| **Subway** | Fast Food | $ | Yes | | L/D | | 1 |
| ACM Sports Bar Grill | American | $$ | | B/W | L/D | Major | 1 |
| Copper Bowl Cafe | American | $ | | Yes | B/L/D | Major | 1 |
| Daily Grind & Deli | Deli/Coffee | $ | | | B/L | | 1 |
| First Quarter Restaurant | American | $/$$ | | B/W | B/L/D | V/M | 1 |
| Granny's Kitchen | Family | $/$$ | Yes | Yes | B/L/D | V/M | 1 |
| Hardee's | Fast Food | $ | Yes | | B/L/D | | 1 |
| Haufbrau Restaurant | Family | $$ | Yes | Yes | B/L/D | Yes | 1 |
| Jim & Clara's Dinner Club | American | $/$$ | | Yes | D | Major | 1 |
| Joe's Place | American | | | | | | 1 |
| McDonald's | Fast Food | $ | Yes | | B/L/D | | 1 |
| New China Cafe | Chinese | $/$$ | | | L/D | | 1 |
| Peppermint Patty's | Sandwich | $ | | | B/L/D | | 1 |
| Pizza Hut | Pizza | $$ | Yes | Yes | L/D | V/M/D | 1 |
| Taco Time | Fast Food | $ | Yes | | L/D | | 1 |
| A & W Family Restaurant | Fast Food | $ | Yes | | L/D | | 4 |
| Broken Arrow Steak House | Steakhouse | $$/$$$ | Yes | Yes | L/D | Major | 4 |
| Chalet Coffee House | Deli | $ | Yes | | B/L | | 4 |
| Deer Lodge Bakery | Bakery | | | | | | 4 |
| Paul's Supper Club | American | $$ | | Yes | B/L/D | | 4 |
| Pizza Hut | Pizza | $/$$ | Yes | B | L/D | V/M/D | 4 |
| R B Drive IN | Fast Food | | | | | | 4 |
| Spanky's People Feeders | Family | $ | Yes | W/B | B/L/D | | 4 |
| Hot Stuff Pizza/Smash Hit Subs | Fast Food | $ | Yes | | B/L/D | | 4 |
| **Country Village** | Food Court | $ | Yes | | B/L/D | Major | 5 |
| Four B'S Restaurant | Family | $-$$ | Yes | | B/L/D | Major | 5 |
| McDonald's | Fast Food | $ | Yes | | B/L/D | | 5 |
| **Wagon Wheel Motel & Cafe** | Family | $/$$ | Yes | B/W | B/L/D | V/M | 8 |
| Frosty Freeze | Fast Food | $ | | | L/D | | 8 |
| Korner Cafe | Family | | | | | | 8 |
| Montana Maggies | Home Cooking | $ | Yes | | B/L/D | | 8 |
| Papa Noelly's Pizza Palace | Pizza | | | | | | 8 |
| Poor Henry's Cafe | American | | | | | | 11 |
| Rock Creek Lodge | American | $ | | Yes | B/L/D | V/M | 11 |
| **Sunshine Station** | Family | $/$$ | | Yes | B/L/D | Major | 13 |
| Chuckwagon | Family | $ | | | L/D | | 13 |
| The Gallery Cafe | American | $ | Yes | B/W | B/L | V/M | 13 |
| The Rendezvous | Southwestern | $$ | | B/W | B/L/D | V/M | 13 |
| **Seven Gables Resort** | Family | $$ | | Yes | B/L/D | Major | 14 |
| Georgetown Lake Lodge | American | $$ | Yes | Yes | B/L/D | V/M/D | 14 |
| The Pintler Inn | Family | $$ | Yes | Yes | B/L/D | Major | 14 |
| Eagle Cafe & Store | Family | $ | | | B/L/D | | 15 |
| Bad Bubba's BBQ | Barbeque | | | | | | 15 |
| Cinnamon Street Bakery | Bakery | | | | | | 15 |
| Dairy Queen | Fast Food | $ | Yes | | L/D | | 15 |
| Double Front South Restaurant | American | $$ | Yes | Yes | D | Major | 15 |
| Fort Fizzle Inn | American | $$ | Yes | Yes | B/L/D | Major | 15 |
| Grizzly Café | Family | $/$$ | Yes | Yes | B/L/D | V/MC | 15 |
| Guy's Lolo Creek Steakhouse | Steakhouse | $$/$$$ | | | L/D | Major | 15 |
| Hot Stuff Pizza | Fast Food | $ | Yes | | B/L/D | | 15 |
| KT'S Hayloft Restaurant | American | $ | | Yes | L/D | | 15 |
| Lolo Trail Cafe | Family | $ | Yes | | B/L/D | | 15 |
| Subs | | | | | | | 15 |
| Subway | Fast Food | $ | Yes | | L/D | | 15 |
| Wagon Wheel Pizza | Pizza | $/$$ | | | L/D | Major | 15 |
| Dee Dee's Drive In | Fast Food | | | | | | 17 |

## Dining Quick Reference-Continued

Price Range refers to the average cost of a meal per person: ($) $1-$6, ($$) $7-$11, ($$$) $12-up. Cocktails: "Yes" indicates full bar; Beer (B)/Wine (W), Service: Breakfast (B), Brunch (BR), Lunch (L), Dinner (D). Businesses in bold print will have additional information under the appropriate map locator number in the body of this section.

| RESTAURANT | TYPE CUISINE | PRICE RANGE | CHILD MENU | COCKTAILS BEER WINE | SERVICE | CREDIT CARDS | MAP LOCATOR NUMBER |
|---|---|---|---|---|---|---|---|
| Glen's Cafe | American | | | | | | 17 |
| Wagon Wheel Pizza | Pizza | $/$$ | Yes | B/W | L/D | Major | 17 |
| Dyna Mart Sinclair | Fast Food | $ | | | B/L/D | Major | 17 |
| Town Pump Conoco/Arby's | Fast Food | $ | | | B/L/D | Major | 17 |
| **Olde Coffee Mill** | Deli | $ | | | B/L/D | | 18 |
| Dairy Queen | Fast Food | $ | Yes | | L/D | | 18 |
| Figaro's | Pizza | $ | | | L/D | V/M | 18 |
| Fireside Pizza | Family | $ | Yes | B/W | L/D | Major | 18 |
| Frontier Cafe | Family | $/$$ | Yes | | B/L/D | Major | 18 |
| Kodiak Jax | Pizza | $ | Yes | B/W | L/D | V/M | 18 |
| Mary's Place Cafe | American | | | | | | 18 |
| Mini Market Hamburgers & Deli | Fast Food | $ | | Yes | L/D | Major | 18 |
| Plum Loco | Stea/Seafood | $$/$$$ | | Yes | L/D | Major | 18 |
| Rooter's Grill & Lounge | Family | $$ | Yes | Yes | D/BR | Major | 18 |
| Royal Flush Bar & Grill | American | $$ | | Yes | L/D | | 18 |
| Salvador's Mexican Restaurant | Mexican | | | | | | 18 |
| Stageline PIzza | Pizza | $/$$ | | | L/D | | 18 |
| Subway | Fast Food | $ | Yes | | L/D | | 18 |
| Country Store Cenex | Fast Food | $ | | | L/D | Major | 18 |
| Ole's Conoco | Fast Food | $ | | | B/L/D | Major | 18 |
| **Mary's Place Café & Drive Thru** | Family | $/$$ | Yes | | B/L/D | | 19 |
| **Stevi Cafe** | Family | $/$$/$$$ | Yes | | B/L | | 19 |
| **Ole Coffee Mill** | Deli | $ | | | B/L | | 19 |
| **Victor Steakhouse** | Steakhouse | $$/$$$ | Yes | Yes | D | Major | 21 |
| Cantina La Cocina Mexican Restaurant | Mexican/American | $$ | Yes | Yes | D | Major | 21 |
| The Hamilton — A Public House | British | $$ | Yes | Yes | L/D | | 21 |
| Amigos Taco Shop | Mexican | $ | Yes | | L/D | | 22 |
| Corvallis Grill | American | $ | | Yes | L/D | | 22 |
| Memories Cafe | American | $$ | Yes | | B/L/D | MC/V | 22 |
| **B J'S Family Restaurant & Lounge** | Family | $ | Yes | Yes | B/L/D | Major | 23 |
| 4B's Restaurant | Family | $ | Yes | | B/L/D | V/M/D | 23 |
| Cheng Family International Cuisine | Chinese | | | | | | 23 |
| Dairy Queen | Fast Food | $ | Yes | | L/D | | 23 |
| El Sol De Mexico Restaurant | Mexican | $$ | Yes | | L/D | | 23 |
| Far East Restaurant | Chinese | $/$$ | | | L/D | | 23 |
| Hardee's | Fast Food | $ | Yes | | B/L/D | | 23 |
| Kentucky Fried Chicken/A&W | Fast Food | $ | Yes | | L/D | | 23 |
| McDonald's | Fast Food | $ | Yes | | B/L/D | | 23 |
| Pizza Hut | Pizza | $/$$ | Yes | B | L/D | V/M/D | 23 |
| Subway | Fast Food | $ | Yes | | L/D | | 23 |
| Taco Bell | Fast Food | $ | Yes | | L/D | | 23 |
| **The Spice of Life Eclectic Cafe** | Eclectic | $$ | Yes | B/W | L/D | V/M/A | 24 |
| **Nap's Grill** | American | $$ | | | L/D | | 24 |
| **A Place to Ponder Bakery & Café** | Bakery Cafe | $ | | | L/D | | 24 |
| Signal Bar & Grill | American | $ | | Yes | B/L/D | | 24 |
| Back Door Deli | Deli | $ | Yes | | B/L | | 24 |
| The Banque Supper Club | Fine Dining | $$/$$$ | | Yes | L/D | Major | 24 |
| The Hamilton Kitchen | Family | $ | Yes | | B/L/BR | | 24 |
| Wild Oats Cafe & Coffee House | Regional/Seasonal | $–$$$ | Yes | | B/L/D | | 24 |
| **Twin Kitchens** | International | $$ | Yes | | B/L/D | Major | 25 |
| **Coffee Cup Cafe** | American | $ | Yes | | B/L/D | Major | 25 |
| Homestead Bar & Cafe | American | $ | | Yes | L/D | | 25 |
| Sundance Cafe | Mexican | $ | | B/W | L/D | V/M | 25 |
| **Sawmill Saloon & Silverspoon Café** | American | $/$$ | Yes | Yes | B/L/D | | 27 |
| Bud & Shirley's Pizza Palace | Pizza | $$ | | | L/D | Major | 27 |
| Dorothy's Good Food | Home Cooking | $ | | | B/L | | 27 |
| Montana Cafe | Family | $ | Yes | | B/L | | 27 |
| Robin's Cafe | Creative | $ | Yes | | B/L | | 27 |
| Trapper's Family Restaurant | Family | $/$$ | | | L/D | | 27 |
| Bud & Shirley's Motel & Restaurant | American | $/$$ | Yes | No | B/L/D | Major | 27 |
| Conner Grocery & Deli | Deli | $ | | | B/L/D | | 28 |

## Dining Quick Reference-Continued

Price Range refers to the average cost of a meal per person: ($) $1-$6, ($$) $7-$11, ($$$) $12-up. Cocktails: "Yes" indicates full bar; Beer (B)/Wine (W), Service: Breakfast (B), Brunch (BR), Lunch (L), Dinner (D). Businesses in bold print will have additional information under the appropriate map locator number in the body of this section.

| RESTAURANT | TYPE CUISINE | PRICE RANGE | CHILD MENU | COCKTAILS BEER WINE | SERVICE | CREDIT CARDS | MAP LOCATOR NUMBER |
|---|---|---|---|---|---|---|---|
| Outpost | Steaks & Seafood | $$-$$$ | | Yes | D | Major | 28 |
| Rocky Knob Lodge | Steakhouse | $$ | | Yes | L/D | V/ M | 28 |
| **Sula Country Store & KOA Campground** | Family | $ | | | B/L/D | Major | 30 |
| Antler Saloon | Pizza | $$ | | Yes | L/D | | 32 |
| Big Hole Crossing | Family | $ -$$$ | Yes | B/W | B/L/D | V/M | 32 |
| Fetty's Bar & Cafe | Family | $/$$ | Yes | Yes | B/L/D | | 32 |
| Rose's Cantina | | | | | | | 33 |
| **Wise River Club** | American | $/$$ | Yes | | B/L/D | V/M | 37 |
| H-J Saloon & Cafe | Family | $/$$ | | Yes | B/L/D | | 37 |

## Motel Quick Reference

Price Range: ($) Under $40 ; ($$) $40-$60; ($$$) $60-$80, ($$$$) Over $80. Pets [check with the motel for specific policies] (P), Dining (D), Lounge (L), Disabled Access (DA), Full Breakfast (FB), Cont. Breakfast (CB), Indoor Pool (IP), Outdoor Pool (OP), Hot Tub (HT), Sauna (S), Refrigerator (R), Microwave (M) (Microwave and Refrigerator indicated only if in majority of rooms), Kitchenette (K). All Montana area codes are 406.

| HOTEL | PHONE | NUMBER ROOMS | PRICE RANGE | BREAKFAST | POOL/ HOT TUB SAUNA | NON SMOKE ROOMS | OTHER AMENITIES | CREDIT CARDS | MAP LOCATOR NUMBER |
|---|---|---|---|---|---|---|---|---|---|
| **Fairmont Hot Springs** | 797-3241 | 152 | $$-$$$$ | | OP | Yes | D/L/DA | Major | 1 |
| **1880's Guest Ranch** | 491-2336 | | | | | | | | 1 |
| **HIckory House B&B** | 563-5481 | | | | | | | | 1 |
| Marcus Daly Motel | 563-3411 | 19 | $$ | | | Yes | | Major | 1 |
| Trade Wind Motel | 563-3428 | 32 | $$ | | IP/HT | Yes | | Major | 1 |
| Vagabond Lodge | 563-5251 | 18 | $$ | | | Yes | | Major | 1 |
| **Downtowner Motel** | 846-1897 | 11 | | CB | | Yes | | Major | 4 |
| Western Big Sky Inn | 846-2590 | 21 | $$ | | | Yes | | Major | 4 |
| **Super 8 Motel of Deer Lodge** | 846-2370 | 54 | $$ | | | Yes | P | Major | 5 |
| Scharf Motor Inn | 846-2819 | 44 | $$ | | | Yes | K/P/R/DA | V/M/D | 5 |
| Western Big Sky Inn | 846-2590 | 21 | $$ | | | Yes | | Major | 5 |
| **Wagon Wheel Motel & Cafe** | 288-3201 | 11 | $ | | | Yes | P | V/M | 8 |
| Drummond Motel | 288-3272 | 9 | $ | | | Yes | K/P/R/DA | Major | 8 |
| Sky Motel | 288-3206 | 15 | $ | | HT | Yes | K/P/M/R | Major | 8 |
| **Blue Damsel B&B** | 825-3077 | | | | | | | | 11 |
| **Bearmouth Chalet** | 925-9950 | | | | | | | | 11 |
| **Rock Creek Fisherman's Motel** | 825-6440 | 6 | $$ | | OP | Yes | P | Major | 11 |
| Big M Outfitters | 859-3746 | 2 | $$ | | | Yes | R | V/M | 12 |
| **Blue Heron - A Bed & Breakfast** | 859-3856 | | | | | | | | 13 |
| **Inn at Philipsburg** | 859-3959 | 12 | $ | | | Yes | K/P/R/M | Major | 13 |
| **Seven Gables Resort** | 563-5052 | 10 | $$ | | | Yes | K/P/R/L/F/D | Major | 14 |
| Georgetown Lake Lodge | 563-7020 | 10 | $$/$$$ | | | | P/D/L/DA | V/M/D | 14 |
| The Pintler Inn | 563-5072 | 7 | $ | FB | | | K/P/D/R/L/DA | Major | 14 |
| Fort Fizzle Inn | 273-6993 | 8 | $$ | | | | L/P/D | Major | 15 |
| Days Inn Of Lolo | 273-2121 | 40 | $$$ | CB | | Yes | K/P/M/R/DA | Major | 15 |
| **Lolo Hot Springs Mountain Lodge** | 273-2201 | | $$$ | | IP/OP | Yes | K/L/D | Major | 16 |
| St. Mary's Motel & RV Park | 777-2838 | 14 | $$ | | | Yes | K/M/R/DA | V/M/D | 18 |
| **Sweet Sage Guest House** | 646-6400 | | | | | | | | 21 |
| **Time After Time B&B** | 646-3258 | | | | | | | | 21 |
| **Blackbeard's Fly fishing Lodge** | 646-6375 | | | | | | | | 21 |
| **Holiday Inn Express-Bitterroot River Inn** | 375-2525 | 65 | $$$/$$$$ | | IP/HT/S | Yes | DA | Major | 23 |
| **Hamilton Super 8 Motel** | 363-2940 | 40 | $$ | CB | | Yes | DA | Major | 23 |
| Comfort Inn | 363-6600 | 65 | $$$ | CB | HT/S | Yes | | Major | 23 |
| **City Center Motel** | 363-1651 | 14 | $ | | | Yes | K/P/M/R/DA | Major | 24 |
| **Best Western Hamilton Inn** | 363-2142 | 36 | $$-$$$ | CB | HT | Yes | M/R/DA | Major | 25 |
| Angler's Lodge | 363-0980 | 6 | $$$/$$$$ | | HT | | K/P/R | V/M | 25 |
| Bitterroot Motel | 363-1142 | 11 | $ | | | Yes | K/P/M/R | Major | 25 |

## Motel Quick Reference

Price Range: ($) Under $40 ; ($$) $40-$60; ($$$) $60-$80, ($$$$) Over $80. Pets [check with the motel for specific policies] (P), Dining (D), Lounge (L), Disabled Access (DA), Full Breakfast (FB), Cont. Breakfast (CB), Indoor Pool (IP), Outdoor Pool (OP), Hot Tub (HT), Sauna (S), Refrigerator (R), Microwave (M) (Microwave and Refrigerator indicated only if in majority of rooms), Kitchenette (K). All Montana area codes are 406.

| HOTEL | PHONE | NUMBER ROOMS | PRICE RANGE | BREAKFAST | POOL/ HOT TUB SAUNA | NON SMOKE ROOMS | OTHER AMENITIES | CREDIT CARDS | MAP LOCATOR NUMBER |
|---|---|---|---|---|---|---|---|---|---|
| **Bitterroot River Lodge** | 363-0708 | 2 | $$$ | | | | K | Major | 25 |
| **Deffy's Motel** | 363-1244 | 16 | $ | | | Yes | K/P/M/R | Major | 25 |
| **Skalkaho Lodge** | 363-3522 | | | | | | | | 25 |
| **Bud & Shirley's Motel & Restaurant** | 821-3401 | 22 | $$ | | HT | Yes | K/P/D/M/R | Major | 27 |
| **Wilderness Motel RV & Tent Park** | 821-3405 | 12 | $/$$ | | | Yes | K/P/M/R/DA | Major | 27 |
| **Trapper Creek Lodge** | 821-4970 | | | | | | | | 27 |
| **River Bend Fishing Lodge** | 821-1999 | | | | | S | | | 27 |
| **Triple Creek Ranch** | 821-4600 | | | | | Yes | | | 27 |
| Tin Cup Lodge | 821-1620 | 4 | $$$$ | FB | HT | Yes | Lodge | Major | 27 |
| West Fork Lodge | 821-3069 | | | | | | | | 27 |
| Log Cabin Motel | 821-3282 | 6 | $$ | | | Yes | K/R | V/M | 27 |
| Rocky Knob Lodge | 821-3520 | 5 | $ | | | | | V/M | 28 |
| **A L'il Bit of Heaven Rental Cabins** | 821-3433 | | | | | | | | 30 |
| **Sula Country Store & KOA Campground** | 821-3364 | 6 | $ | | HT | Yes | K/D/R/HT/DA | Major | 30 |
| Camp Creek Inn | 821-3508 | | | | | | | | 30 |
| **Nez Perce Motel** | 689-3254 | 8 | $$ | | | Yes | K | A/V/M | 32 |
| Sandman Motel | 689-3218 | 9 | $ | | | | K/P | V/M | 32 |
| Maverick Mountain Ski Area | 834-3454 | | | | | | | | 33 |
| Grasshopper Inn | 834-3456 | | | | | | | | 35 |
| **Wise River Club** | 832-3258 | 6 | $ | | S | | P/D/L | V/M | 37 |

### NOTES:

Section 7

All Montana Area Codes are 406

# SECTION 8

## HELENA AND SURROUNDING AREA

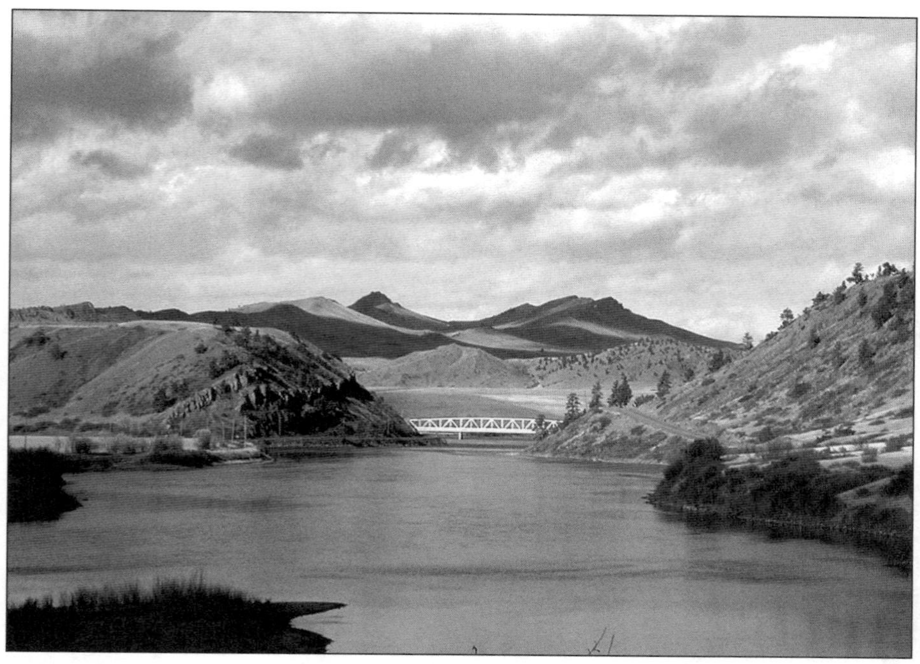

*Missouri River Bridge near Holter Lake.*

## WEATHER AVERAGES

**Helena**

| January | |
|---|---|
| Average High: | 29.6° F |
| Average Low: | 9.6° F |
| Record High : | 62.0° F |
| Record Low : | -42.0° F |
| Average Precip.: | 0.63 in |
| Rain/Snow Days: | 8 days |
| **April** | |
| Average High: | 56.1° F |
| Average Low: | 30.6° F |
| Record High : | 86.0° F |
| Record Low : | 1.0° F |
| Average Precip.: | 0.97 in |
| Rain/Snow Days: | 8 days |
| **July** | |
| Average High: | 85.0° F |
| Average Low: | 53.4° F |
| Record High : | 102.0° F |
| Record Low : | 36.0° F |
| Average Precip.: | 1.10 in |
| Rain/Snow Days: | 8 days |
| **October** | |
| Average High: | 58.5° F |
| Average Low: | 31.6° F |
| Record High : | 85.0° F |
| Record Low : | -8.0° F |
| Average Precip.: | 0.60 in |
| Rain/Snow Days: | 6 days |

**Canyon Ferry Lake**

| January | |
|---|---|
| Average High: | 29.4° F |
| Average Low: | 10.1° F |
| Average Precip.: | 0.56 in |
| **April** | |
| Average High: | 55.3° F |
| Average Low: | 31.2° F |
| Average Precip.: | 0.93 in |
| **July** | |
| Average High: | 83.3° F |
| Average Low: | 53.2° F |
| Average Precip.: | 1.12 in |
| **October** | |
| Average High: | 57.9° F |
| Average Low: | 32.7° F |
| Average Precip.: | 0.67 in |

**Great Divide Ski Area**

| January | |
|---|---|
| Average High: | 29.4° F |
| Average Low: | 10.1° F |
| Average Precip.: | 0.56 in |
| **April** | |
| Average High: | 55.3° F |
| Average Low: | 31.2° F |
| Average Precip.: | 0.93 in |
| **June** | |
| Average High: | 73.0° F |
| Average Low: | 47.5° F |
| Average Precip.: | 2.07 in |
| **July** | |
| Average High: | 83.3° F |
| Average Low: | 53.2° F |
| Average Precip.: | 1.12 in |
| **October** | |
| Average High: | 57.9° F |
| Average Low: | 32.7° F |
| Average Precip.: | 0.67 in |

**1.** *Lewis & Clark*

### Lombard

This railroad town sat at the crossroads of the Northern Pacific and the Milwaukee railroads. For years, the only access to the town was by rail as there were no automobile roads to the community. It is the namesake of A.G. Lombard who was the chief engineer of the Montana Railroad during its construction. The town was originally known as Castle Junction and was dominated by the "Jaw Bone" Railroad. In the 1890s, the town had a Chinese mayor named Billy Kee. A man-about-town, he built the famous two-story High Point Inn. The hotel served good meals and featured a bathroom with hot and cold running water. Kee was known as a "flexible" proprietor. When he retired at night, he would leave the light on for any latecomers and the cash register open. The guests would scrawl their name in the register, put their money in the till, and take a key to a room.

### Radersburg

Several mining camps nearby have been abandoned but it has never become a complete ghost town. The first gold was discovered in the early 1860s and in 1866 Jahn A. Keating's mine brought people to town. The hills behind Radersburg still harbor the remains of various mine shafts. About 400 people live in the Toston and Radersburg area. Montana's own Myrna Loy was born nearby in Parker which no longer exists.

### Toston

Toston was named for Thomas Toston, an early homesteader and the first postmaster. From 1883–1899, the town enjoyed prosperity while the giant Toston Smelting Company was in operation. Loads of ore from Radersburg and coal from the Big Springs area were hauled to the smelter by six horse teams. Mining, smelting, trading and land development made Toston a regional marketing center for a brief period, while earthquakes, fires and mine closings nearly killed it. Today it consists of a small collection of residences, whose only service is a post office.

### D Mer. Lewis

July 27, 1805

*"we are now several hundred miles within the boseom of this wild and mountainous country, whre game may rationally be expected shortly to become scarce and subsisitence precaious without any information with reispect to the country*

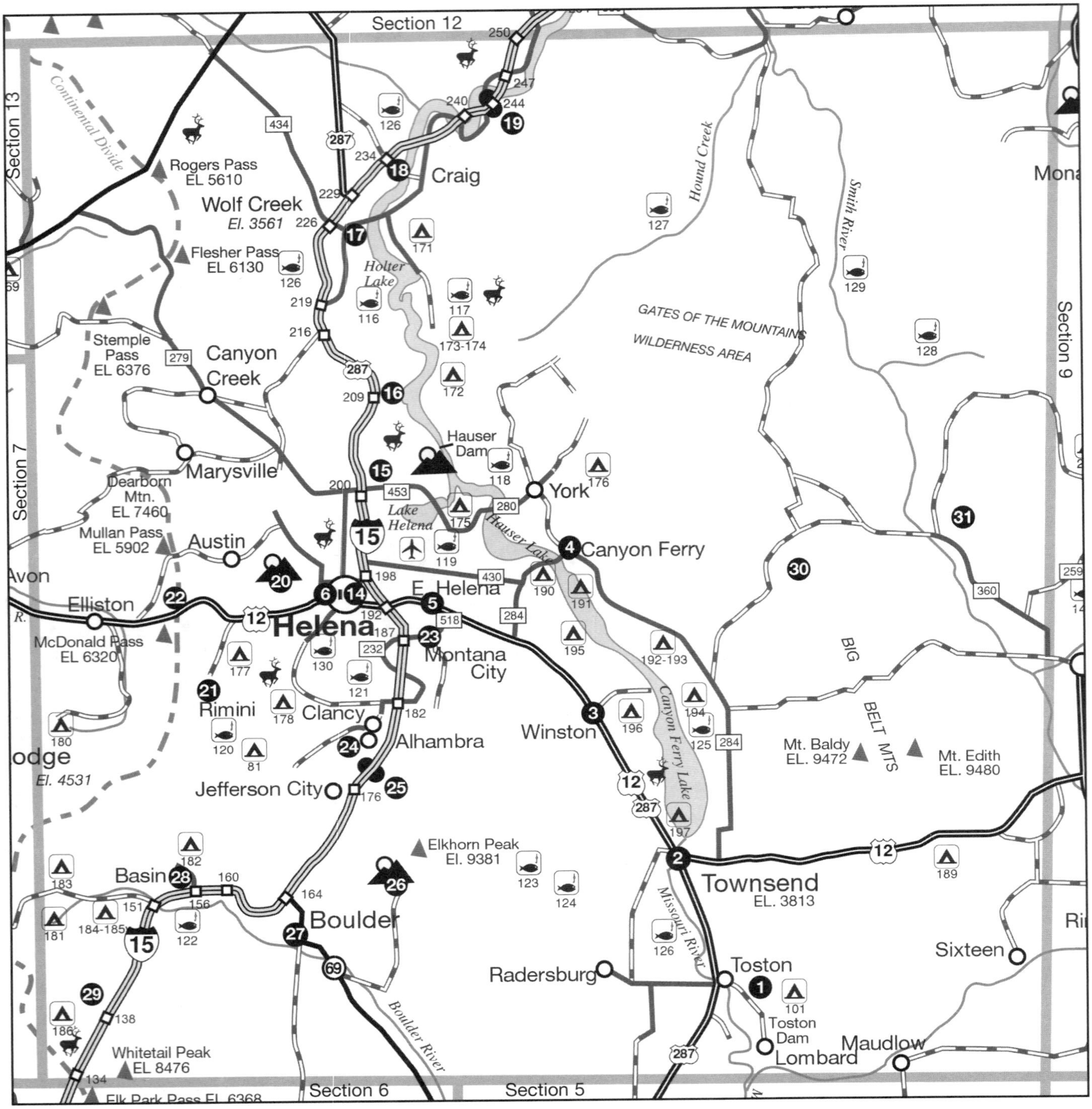

Section 12
Section 13
Section 9
Section 7
Section 6
Section 5
Continental Divide
Rogers Pass
EL 5610
Wolf Creek
El. 3561
Flesher Pass
EL 6130
Stemple Pass
EL 6376
Canyon Creek
Marysville
Dearborn Mtn.
EL 7460
Mullan Pass
EL 5902
Austin
Avon
Elliston
McDonald Pass
EL 6320
Lodge
El. 4531
Helena
E. Helena
Montana City
Rimini
Clancy
Alhambra
Jefferson City
Basin
Boulder
Whitetail Peak
EL 8476
Elk Park Pass EL 6368
Elkhorn Peak
El. 9381
Boulder River
Craig
Holter Lake
Hauser Dam
York
Lake Helena
Hauser Lake
Canyon Ferry
Canyon Ferry Lake
Winston
Townsend
EL. 3813
Missouri River
Radersburg
Toston
Toston Dam
Lombard
Maudlow
Sixteen
Hound Creek
Smith River
GATES OF THE MOUNTAINS
WILDERNESS AREA
BIG BELT MTS
Mt. Baldy
EL. 9472
Mt. Edith
EL. 9480
Mona


## Legend

- Locator number (matches numeric listing in section)
- Wildlife viewing
- Campsite (number matches number in campsite chart)
- State Park
- Fishing Site (number matches number in fishing chart)
- Rest stop
- Interstate
- U.S. Highway
- State Highway
- County Road
- Gravel/unpaved road

## SECTION 8

0 Miles 11 20

One inch = approximately 11 miles

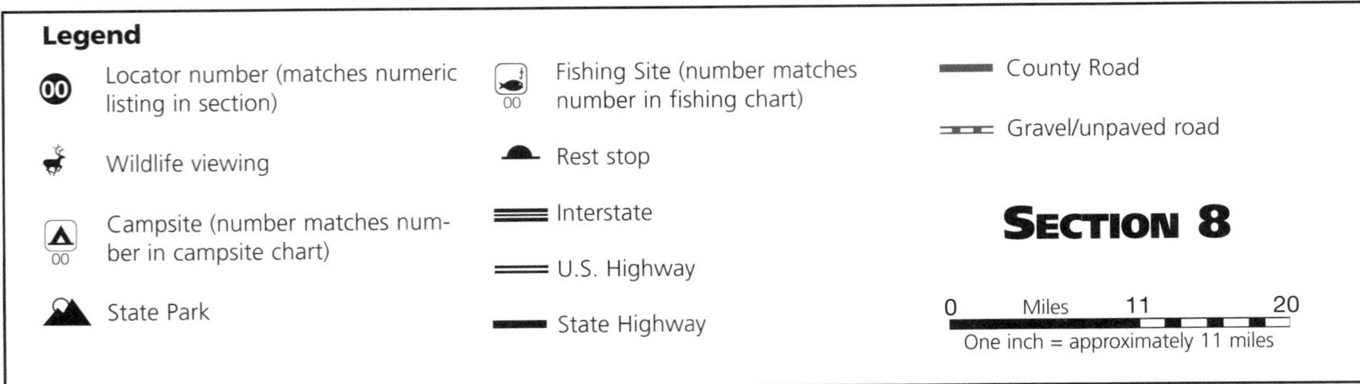

*not knowing how far these mountains continue, or wher to direct our course ot pass them to advantage or intersept a navigable branch of the Columbia."*

### It Happened in Montana

January 9, 1962. The record for the highest barometric pressure in the contiguous United States was set in Helena at 31.40 inches.

**2.** *Lewis & Clark, Attraction, Adventure, Gas, Food, Lodging, Shopping, Miscellaneous*

### Townsend

Townsend is the county seat of Broadwater County and was reportedly named in honor of the wife of Charles B. Wright, president of the Northern Pacific Railroad from 1874–1879. Her maiden name was Townsend. The first passenger train to travel from St. Paul to Portland in 1883 stopped at Townsend. The town had been laid out and developed in anticipation of the railroad. The first town lots sold for $5 a piece. Today it is a thriving agricultural community nestled along the Missouri River and sitting in the shadows of the Big Belt Mountains.

### D Mer. Lewis

July 24, 1805

*"our trio of pests still invade and obstruct us on all occasions, these are the Musquetoes eye knats and prickley pears, equal to any three curses that ever poor Egypt laiboured under, except the Mahometant yoke."*

### D Mer. Lewis

July 26, 1805

*"these barbed seed penetrate our mockersons and leather legings and give use great pain untill they are removed. my poor dog suffers with them excessively, he is cnstantly biting and scratching himself as if in a rack of pain."*

### D William Clark

July 26, 1805

*"We continud. thro a Deep Vallie without a Tree to Shade us Scorching with heat,. . .I was fatigued mhy feet with Several blisters & Stuck with prickley pears."*

### T Broadwater County Museum & Library

133 N. Walnut in Townsend. 266-5252

Local history is featured here with exhibits that reflect mining, a dental office, general store, homestead cabin, and rural school, along with fossil and military collections. There are many artifacts from the area dating back to 10,000 years ago. The museum is open from May to September. No admission charge, but donations are helpful.

### T The Maize - Corn Maize

250 Dry Creek Rd, Townsend.

### A Townsend Body Shop

110 Broadway, Downtown Townsend. 266-3453

With over 30 years experience in roadside service and technical training, Townsend Body Shop is a great place to go for any kind of repair. They do all types of mechanical work ranging from minor repairs to major overhauls. They also concentrate on body work and frame straightening. No job is too big or too small to receive their full attention and personalized service. Townsend Body Shop puts a guarantee on all of their work.



### A Townsend Sinclair

401 Broadway, Townsend. 266-5251

### F Silo's Inn

6999 US Hwy 287, 7 miles north of Townsend. 266-5622

Silo's Inn overlooks the beautiful Canyon Ferry Lake and Big Belt Mountains. You will enjoy great views and out-of-this-world Barbecue, in a warm inviting atmosphere. Owners, Ernie and Carolyn Nunn offer old fashioned Montana hospitality and will even cater and provide facilities for special occasions like weddings or family reunions. Winter ice fishing and ice boating in the Silo's area is great. Stop in and refuel in their cozy surroundings. Enjoy views of the Lewis and Clark Trail along the mighty Missouri River Headwaters. Among all the special sauces served, sampling the Sacajawea Sauce is a must! This is the place to satisfy that hunger for great views, a taste of history, great food, and Sunday Brunch.

### F The Mint

305 Broadway, Townsend. 266-9991

The Mint is a proud contributor to several Montana traditions. They are recognized throughout the state for serving some of the "heartiest and tastiest" family style cuisine. You'll find a staff of the "downright friendliest" people around with the personality and skills to guarantee a pleasurable experience. The Mint Bar has a real family atmosphere. Additionally, patrons can play live Keno, video keno and poker, and arcade games. Travelers find the Mint to be a one stop travel center with a wide range of services including, hotel rooms, public showers, Laundromat, barber shop, beauty shop, and bus depot.

*A rail line follows the Missouri River near Townsend.*

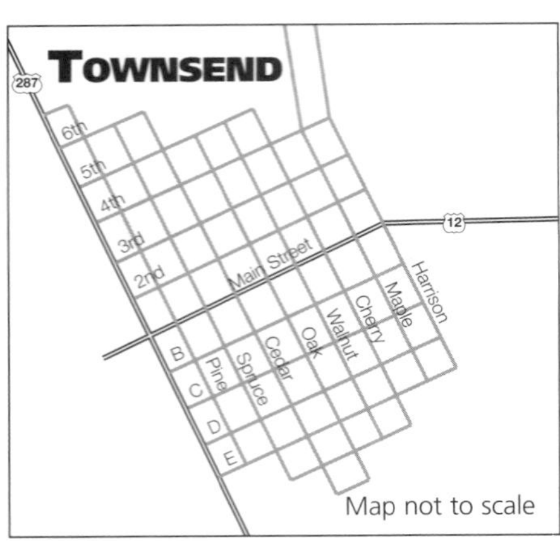


### F Lucky Lanes & Lounge

217 Broadway, Townsend. 266-3315

The Lucky Lanes Family Fun Center has been providing family entertainment in Townsend since 1956 and has been newly remodeled providing a six lane bowling center with automatic scoring. They also feature cosmic bowling along with music to enhance your enjoyment of the bowling experience you'll find there. A full bar, poker keno machines and snack bar round out the facilities to make your visit comfortable and enjoyable. The friendly service and clean facilities make Lucky lanes a must see attraction on your visit to the area.

### F A & W Drive Inn

512 N. Front St., Townsend. 266-3814

### LV Litening Barn Bed and Breakfast/Float Trips/Horseback Riding

290 Litening Barn Rd., Townsend. 266-4554 or 800-654-2845, www.ewwatson.com

This family owned outfitting business offers a wide variety of summer activities, hunting expeditions, and a unique lodging experience. Join their river expeditions on the headwaters of the Missouri, the Gallatin, Madison, Jefferson and Yellowstone Rivers for float trips, wade walks, horseback camping and cast & blast trips. Their five day Hi Mountain Lake Horseback Trip is a unique and memorable experience for families, groups or individuals, with great food and a comfortable relaxing camp. The MT High Country Cattle Drive should not be missed. This true working cattle drive offers a true western experience. Reservations are required. If just passing through town, you will enjoy the B&B experience on this family owned ranch. Call, write, or check out their web site for more information.

#### Montana Trivia

Over 1,200 earthquakes shook Helena in the fall and winter of 1935. One was a magnitude 6.3,another 6.0. These two caused widespread damage and killed two people.

### L Canyon Ferry Mansion Bed & Breakfast

7408 Hwy 287 N., at Canyon Ferry Lake, Townsend. 266-3599 or toll free at 888-732-5583. www.canyonferrymansion.com

This exquisitely restored, 1915 mansion was once home to A.B. Cook, King of Cattle Kings, and stood in the middle of what is now Canyon Ferry Lake. It is an ideal place to be pampered, relax, and unwind. The Mansion is a perfect location for meetings, corporate retreats, weddings, and reunions. Schedule a five-course Murder Mystery Dinner evening, with a ghostly mansion tour. This is the ultimate location for your lake resort wedding, with exceptional cuisine and affordable elegance with a personal touch, overlooking Canyon Ferry Lake with sweeping views of the Big Belt and Elkhorn Mountains. During your stay enjoy the available jacuzzi or day spa complete with a professional massage. Visit their antique store. They also offer 3 new cabins for sportsmen and families.

### S Jack Farm Crafts Etc.

510 N. Front St., Townsend. 266-5886

Owners, Ernie Forrey and Linda Huth, would be pleased to have you stop by and browse through their store. With hand crafted items from over 70 Montana craftsmen and artists, they carry unique, one-of-a-kind gifts that cannot be found in any other shops. Many of these local artists have chosen Jack Farm Crafts as their only outlet in the state. A sampling of items carried include: black metal frames, western office supplies, clocks, horse-drawn wagons to scale, Lewis & Clark items, belt buckles, western pottery, leather work, wooden toys, and lots more.

### S Sweet Thing Curios & Candy

319 Broadway, Townsend. 266-4408

Under the green awning on the main street of Townsend, you will find an air-conditioned delight. Sweet Thing offers hand dipped homemade chocolates, hard candy by the pound, and harking back to the 1950's, two for a penny and penny candy. This is a great place to find unique

*A calm afternoon on Canyon Ferry Reservoir.*

*The Silos near Winston on Canyon Ferry Lake are a familiar landmark.*

toys, including play in the car toys for kids. Select Montana gift baskets brimming with local products that can be shipped or ordered from home. There is also an interesting selection of antique china and glass, fragrances, and wonderful fine jewelry. All this can be found just one mile from Canyon Ferry. Be sure and check out their store, Tori's Antiques, at Last Chance Gulch in Helena, too.

### S JL Wright Trading Post

123 Broadway in Townsend. 266-3032

### M Broadwater Realty

306 Broadway, Townsend. 266-3160 or 800-850-9928. bdwtreal@ixi.net

Broadwater Realty represents both buyers and sellers in all areas of their real estate needs. Broadwater County, of which Townsend is the County Seat, is an agricultural area that supports a mining and timber industry. Recreation has become a fast new business opportunity in the area due to the excellent fishing, big game and bird hunting, water and snow sports and access to thousands of acres of national forest. Marcia Bieber, Broker Owner, is a longtime county resident, loves Broadwater County, and would like to share her knowledge of the area with you.

## 3. *Historical Marker, Lewis & Clark, Adventure*

### Winston

Winston was platted by the Northern Pacific Railroad and soon settled by ranchers and farmers. It began with Fred Goudy's Saloon, and was followed by the Duncan Hotel, a combined rooming house and restaurant. The Dodge brothers operated a rooming house in a rock building which, deserted and crumbling, stands today. Gold, silver, copper and lead mines were active in the area from 1908–1918 and 1926–1928. Winston was named for P. B. Winston, a contractor for the Northern Pacific Railroad.

One of Winston's most notable characters was George Beatty, a young New York man who was "doomed to die" presumably from tuberculosis. He set out for Montana in the 1860s hoping the mountain air would add a couple of years to his life. He was so resolved to his fate that he brought his tombstone with him. Carved on it was:

*My mother's prayers kept me out of Hell.*
*Thank God for a blessed hope beyond the grave.*

Beatty stored the tombstone in a back shed. When he died at the ripe old age of ninety-two, it was placed on his grave in Helena where it can be seen today.

### H Thar's Gold in Them Thar Hills

Montana City

*The mountains to the west are the Elkhorns. Those to the east across the Canyon Ferry Lake are the Big Belts. Both of these ranges are highly mineralized. Confederate Gulch of the Big Belts was famous in the 1860s for its rich placer diggings. Its Montana Bar, at the old boom camp of Diamond City, now a ghost town, has always been known as "the richest acre of ground in the world." The pay streak ran as high as $2,000 to the pan.*

*Most of the gulches in the Elkhorns were active as placer camps in the early days and this range is dotted with quartz mines still producing lead, zinc, silver and gold. Like most of the mountains in Montana they have been here a long time.*

*The Lewis and Clark Expedition came up the Missouri River through this valley in July, 1805.*

### D Mer. Lewis

July 22, 1805

*"The Indian woman recognizes the country and assures us that this the river on which her relations live, and that the threee forks are at no great distance. this peice of information has cheered the speirts of the party who now begin to console themselves with the anticipation of shortly seeing the head of the missouri yet unkown to the civilized world."*

### D Mer. Lewis

July 22, 1805

*"I killed an otter which sunk to the bottom on being shot. . .the water was about 8 feet deep yet so clear that I could see it at the bottom; I swam in and obtained it by diving."*

### V Staubach Creek Ranch

112 Pole Creek Road in Winston. 227-6918.
Email staubachcreek@aol.com

## 4. *Lewis & Clark, Attraction*

### D William Clark

July 20, 1805

*"I left Signs to Shew the Indians if they should come on our trail that we were not their enemeys."*

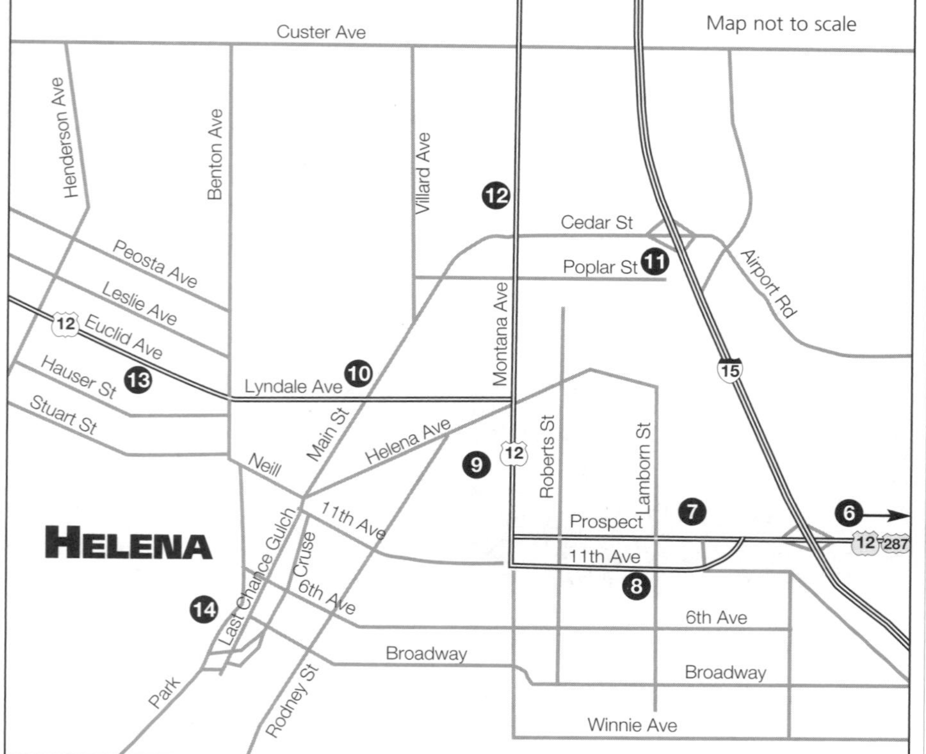


Section 8

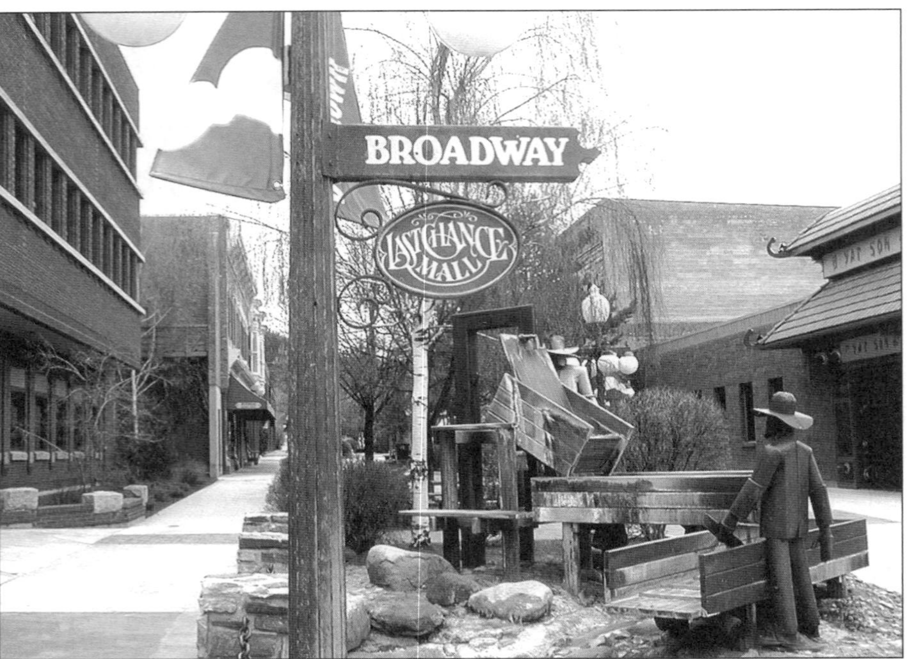

*Last Chance Gulch.*

### T Canyon Ferry Wildlife Management Area
Hwy 12 E., Townsend.

This 5,000-acre area is a bird watcher's paradise, as the wetland is a landing field for numerous species of migrating birds. You can expect to see osprey, American white pelicans, Caspian terns, bald eagles, sand cranes, Canada geese and double-crested cormorants, as well as large congregations of common loons in the spring and fall. Tundra swans are present for a short time during March. In the delta area there are often beavers, raccoons, deer and otters.

### T Canyon Ferry Visitor Center
20 miles east of Helena. 475-3128

The easiest way to get here is to take Hwy. 12 southeast out of Helena for about 10 miles. At the flashing yellow light turn left on Hwy. 284. Go another 10 miles to the Visitor Center. The Center is small but packed with informative and interesting exhibits. There are picnic tables here and an outdoor interpretive display.

### T Canyon Ferry Lake
Hwy.12/287 between Helena and Townsend.

This is Montana's most popular state park offering over 76 miles of shoreline notched with quiet coves perfect for swimming, fishing, and picnics. The lake has 25 recreation and camping areas with boat ramps in many of them. It is one of the most popular lakes in the state for water skiing and sailing. It is also a popular area for watching the migration of eagles in November and December. The lake covers a total of 35,000 acres and is 160 feet deep at the north end.

The lake covers an area Lewis and Clark described as a beautiful 10 or 12 miles wide and extending as far upriver as the eye could see. Today, the lake is surrounded by a rich agricultural area. The cottonwood studded valley is one of the more diverse agricultural areas in the state growing hay, grain, sugar beets, seed potatoes and cattle.

The name "Canyon Ferry" originated when John Oakes started ferrying miners and prospectors across the Missouri River Canyon in 1865.

## 5. *Attraction, Gas, Food*

### East Helena

East Helena, a smelter town for the Anaconda Copper Mining Company, was named for its location in relation to Helena. Many of its original settlers came from the Balkan countries shortly after the turn of the century. It is the home of one of the world's few remaining smelters which can be seen on the south side of the road. Ore for gold, silver, lead, zinc, and other metals are shipped here from Montana and Idaho.

### T Kleffner Ranch
Helena. 227-6645

At the Kleffner Ranch, return to the Gold West Country as it was 110 years ago and learn interesting details about the history of this area. This octagonal stone house and three-story barn is the largest stone and timber barn in the United States. This is still a working ranch. Regular tours are available.

## 6. *Gas, Food*

### Helena

Helena found its beginning in the discovery of rich mineral resources, as did many cities in Montana. Helena not only survived its initial boom, it prospered. Helena was once the camp of one of history's richest gold strikes, Last Chance Gulch, which still serves as the city's main street. In 1888, an estimated 50 millionaires lived in this town, making it the richest city per capita in the United States. Not only was the area replete with gold, but silver and lead as well. When the gold boom subsided, Helena was equipped to forge a new identity. Strategically located along early travel routes and in the center of Montana's mining district, it easily became a major trade center. Later, Helena won the right to be Montana's permanent capital.

No other Montana city's history approaches the magnitude of Helena's which remains evident in its monuments and architecture. Helena is graced with the elegance of the State Capitol Building, the towering Cathedral of St. Helena, as well as excellent museums and galleries that preserve the best of Montana's past and present. An extravagant conglomeration of Baroque, Romanesque, Gothic, Neoclassic and Italianate designs speak loudly of late 19th Century architecture. The century-old mansions on the west side of town boast an opulent mix of styles including the original Governor's Mansion, open to the public for tours. Today Helena is a bustling city of culture and tourism yet it owes its sustenance to government. Much of the state's business is conducted in the State Capitol and state offices are located in buildings throughout the town.

Helena lacks nothing for those interested in nature. Close by is Mount Helena, and the city is surrounded by national forests offering the best of recreational pleasure. Helena combines a rich brew of history with numerous outdoor activities. Visit ghost towns within a short distance, choose boating and fishing at nearby lakes on the Missouri River, or hike and ski in the Helena National Forest.

## 7. *Gas, Food, Lodging, Shopping, Miscellaneous*

### L Days Inn Helena

2001 Prospect Ave., Helena. 442-3280 or 800-325-2525

Located off I-15, the Helena Days Inn is nestled in the valley of the Rocky Mountains, and in the heart of Montana's history. The 94 comfortable guest rooms consist of king or queen size beds, large executive suites, non-smoking rooms, free local calls, and cable TV with HBO. The hotel also offers a hot tub, sauna, exercise room, guest laundry, complimentary hot cooked-to-order and continental breakfasts, copy and fax services, and a board room is available. Tour the State Capital, the Original Governor's Mansion, and ride the tour train. Experience Helena's colorful past and explore nearby sites and recreational activities. Friendly service awaits you at your home away from home at the Days Inn Helena.

**L Shilo Inn**
2020 Prospect Ave., Helena. 442-3020
or 800-222-2244

The newly remodeled Shilo Inn is conveniently located off I-15 and offering 48 newly remodeled rooms that include a microwave, refrigerator, coffee maker, iron, hair dryer, free local calls, and cable TV. Kitchen units and a spacious 3 bed mini-suite are also available. They also feature an indoor heated pool, Jacuzzi, steam room, sauna, and laundry facility. Unique to Shilo are exterior electrical outlets for battery chargers or block heaters. If you aren't traveling by car they also provide a complimentary 24-hour shuttle. Each morning brings Complimentary Continental Breakfast and USA Today. The lobby displays brochures on local attractions and restaurants, including the Country Harvest next door.

**M Helena College of Technology of The University of Montana**
1115 N. Roberts, Helena. 444-6800
or 800-241-4882 www.hct.umontana.edu

Established in 1939 the Helena College of Technology is recognized for two-year programs in the technologies, trades, business, protective services and allied health services.

## 8. *Gas, Food, Lodging, Shopping*

**T Montana State Capital**
1301 6th Ave., Helena. 444-4789

Situated against a backdrop of the hills of Helena, the Montana State Capital commands a panoramic view of the Helena Valley. Explorers Meriwether Lewis and William Clark called this area "Prickly Pear Valley" when they traversed it in 1805. A century of exploration, trapping, prospecting, mining, settlement and development occurred in what became Montana, before the construction of a State Capital was achieved.

The mining camp of Last Chance Gulch was born with the discovery of placer gold by the "Four Georgians" in 1864. The fledgling camp soon changed to Helena. Surprisingly, the community did not die when the gold ran out because the merchants turned it into a banking and supply center. By 1875 Helena had wrested the Montana Territorial capital from Virginia City.

When Montana joined the Union in 1889, a battle for the permanent state capital ensued. In 1894 Helena (backed by Copper King William A. Clark) opposed Anaconda (supported by Copper King Marcus Daly) for this honor. Helena's victory assured it a state capitol building, yet the National Crash of 1893 initially delayed construction.

Finally, optimism about the state's future led the 1895 legislature to enact laws authorizing a $1 million Capital, its design to be chosen in a nationwide architectural competition. Cash prizes were awarded and a design selected before funding problems were understood to be insurmountable. To make matters worse, scandal erupted when it was discovered that the Capital commissioners themselves planned to defraud the state of substantial portions of the building's cost. Investigations were conducted in time to prevent the graft, replace the commissioners, and begin anew.

The 1897 legislature then authorized a more modest statehouse. The completed, furnished building, located on its donated parcel of land, cost approximately $485,000—less than one-half the price of the abandoned design.

In 1898 Charles Emlen Bell and John Hackett Kent of Council Bluffs, Iowa, were selected as the Capital architects, on the condition that they would relocate to Helena to fulfill a legislative provision requiring selection of a Montana architect. Although denounced by the state's resident architects, the selection proved to be a fortunate one, resulting in a handsome design that was promptly realized. After a festive corner stone-laying ceremony on Independence Day, 1899, Bell and Kent's "Greek Ionic" neo classical Capital was constructed, faced in sandstone from a Columbus, Montana Quarry. The building was dedicated with much appreciative fanfare on July 4, 1902.

After its first decade, the Capital was enlarged (1909-1912) to accommodate the growing executive, legislative and judicial branches of government. East-and West-wing additions were designed by New York architect Frank M. Andrews in association with Montanans John G. Link and Charles S. Haire. The much-debated

## Take a Pass Around Helena

**The Continental Divide skirts Helena** to the west, and there is more than one way to cross it—each offering spectacular scenery.

### McDonald Pass

This 6,323-foot pass 15 miles southwest of Helena on Hwy.. 12 has a vista point at the top that has stunning views of the valley below. If you can visit it in the evening you will be rewarded with a spectacular view of the lights of Helena.

### Flesher Pass

To reach this and Stemple Pass, take Montana Ave. north to Lincoln Road. Head west toward the mountains. The road begins a quick winding ascent once it reaches the mountain. Plenty of switchbacks offer incredible views of the Helena National Forest. From the top of the pass at 6,350 feet, you can see a beautiful panorama of the Blackfoot River Valley. By the way, when you cross the pass, you are not too far from Ted Kazinski's hideaway. Make no mistake, the folks around here are not proud of that fact.

### Stemple Pass

Follow the directions to Flesher Pass, but watch for Stemple Pass Road about eight miles after you pass through Canyon Creek and before you reach Flesher. It will be on your left. This is a more isolated pass and the road here is gravel.

### Mullan Pass

While the road to this pass is gravel, and fourwheel drive is recommended, it is certainly the most interesting pass if you're a history buff. The pass was discovered by U.S. Army Capt. John Mullan in 1853. He drove the first wagon over it a year later. In 1860—four years before prospectors discovered gold in Last Chance Gulch—he supervised construction of the road over the pass. Helena simply didn't exist at that time which is why the road didn't bother to swing through town.

Mullan Road stretched 624 miles from Walla Walla, Washington to Fort Benton, Montana. An interesting side note for those of you who are Masons, the campground at the top of the Divide was the site of the Montana Territory's first Masonic meeting in July 1862.

To get to Mullan Pass, take Birdseye Road northwest out of Helena and turn southwest on Austin Road. It's gravel from here. You'll see a long railroad tunnel that was built in 1882. After transiting the pass, the road reconnects with Hwy.. 12 just below McDonald Pass.

*McDonald Pass just a few miles from Helena offers spectacular views of the surrounding area.*

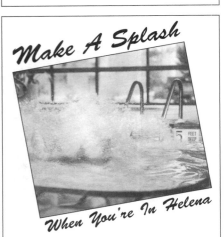

*Montana State Capitol building.*

selection of stone for facing the wings required a special session of the legislature, which chose Jefferson County granite. A good match for the Columbus sandstone used in the original building, the granite held the added advantage of durability. The State Capital is a structure with several historical dimensions. Interwoven with Montana's development as a state, the building's origins recall people and practices from another age. These turn-of-the-century Montanans, conscious of their place in the progression of time, chose architecture and art that described a remote classical past as well as the passing era of the frontier. Yet they focused optimistically on the future as well. Today the Capital is listed on the National Register of Historic Places and continues to be associated with events significant to the citizens and government of Montana.

*Excerpted from "Montana's Capital Building", a publication of the Montana Historical Society*

Note: A two-year renovation project of Capital was completed in early 2001. The building was restored to it's original elegant charm. Years ago many of the buildings treasures were removed as attempts were made to earthquake proof the structure. Many of those items had been purchased by Charles Bovey of Nevada and Virginia City fame. The items were in storage and once again became property of the state and were reinstalled during the project. Items that couldn't be salvaged were replicated. The entire restoration was done at a cost of $26 million. Tours of the Capitalaa are hourly weekdays from 9 a.m. to 4 p.m. and weekends noon to 4 p.m. There is no charge for tours which are led by members of the Montana Historical Society.

### T Montana Historical Society Museum

225 N. Roberts, Helena. 444-4710

This is Montana's largest museum displaying artifacts covering 12,000 years of history. Paintings of Montana landscapes and people give a rich perspective into life in Montana through the eyes of artists. It has the largest collection of books and periodicals about Montana in the world. Permanent galleries also exhibit the photography of F. Jay Haynes and another to the works of Charlie Russell. The Montana Historical Society is the oldest organization in the West. Founded in 1865 it was initially a private exclusive organization for prominent Montana pioneers. The museum and Museum Store are open year round and no admission is charged.

### T State Capital Grounds (Day use only)

Located in Helena at the junction of 6th and Montana Ave. 449-8864

While this area does not resemble a state park, the formal grounds and flower gardens are visited by thousands of people each year. The capital grounds include 50 acres around the capital building, Montana Historical Society Museum, and state office complex.

### F Planet Gyros

1431 11th Ave. Butte. 449-2550

### L Fairfield Inn

2150 11th Ave., Helena. 449-9944 or 800-228-2800

Positioned halfway between Glacier and Yellowstone National Parks, this Fairfield Inn by

Marriott is located in the heart of the rockies. Offering the 70 year Marriott Tradition of service in the Capital City of Montana you will experience clean, fresh accommodations in a warm and friendly atmosphere. Guests can enjoy a complimentary continental breakfast, indoor pool and whirlpool, fitness center, guest laundry, cable TV with HBO & ESPN and many non-smoking units. Business travelers will enjoy the spacious guest rooms with well-lit desks and 24-hour fax service. Some rooms also have microwaves and refrigerators and whirlpools. Enjoy the sites of the Capital City with the Fairfield by Marriott as your base camp.

**L West Coast Colonial Hotel**
2301 Colonial Drive, Helena. 443-2100 or toll free at 800-325-4000. www.westcoasthotels.com

West Coast Colonial Hotel is conveniently located in the heart of Montana's State Capital. All of Helena's historical districts, the Gulch, shopping, and cultural opportunities are easily accessible from the hotel. 149 rooms and suites all feature king or queen beds with in-room coffee, irons, and hair dryers. The full service Colonial Restaurant and Lounge are on site. You can relax and unwind in the outdoor and indoor swimming pools, hot tubs, or fitness center. This is also a great place to plan your next meeting or special occasion with over 15,000 feet of meeting and banquet space available.

**L Helena's Country Inn & Suites**
2101 11th Ave., Helena. 443-2300 or 800-541-2743

## 9. *Gas, Food, Shopping*

**S Capital Sports & Western Wear**
1092 Helena Ave., Helena. 443-2978 or fax 442-8136

Located in the heart of Helena since 1970, this is an old-time, full-line favorite and popular with locals and outdoor enthusiasts. You'll find a full line of sporting goods, clothing and footwear along with a wide variety of top branded merchandise and services such as gunsmithing, ski tuning and bicycle repair. This is a great place to get the current scoop on fishing, pick up a map and find out about local hiking trails, get the latest ski-snow report, or share tall tales of hunting season. Everyone should stop in for a look at their fabulous big game display, including Montana's largest non-typical elk.

# On the Trail of Lewis and Clark

## Gates Of The Mountains

Upon leaving "canoe camp" just above the Great Falls, on July 15, Lewis and dark, along with two privates, walked on shore to lighten the burden of the excessively loaded canoes. The next day they found willow shelters and horse tracks which appeared to be about 10 days old. They supposed these to be signs of the Shoshones, whom they were anxious to meet and bargain with for horses. Lewis, two privates, and York went ahead of the party in an unsuccessful attempt to find these Indians.

On July 18, Clark, with a small party, ventured out along an Indian road in search of the natives. The next day they saw where the Indians had peeled bark off pine trees. Sacagawea later informed them that her people obtained sap and the soft part of the wood and bark for food.

Meanwhile Lewis and the main party were using tow lines and poles to ascend the ever-more challenging Missouri. On July 19 they reached the ."most remarkable cliffs" they had yet seen. It looked as though the river had worn a passage just the width of its channel through these 1,200-foot-high cliffs for a distance of three miles. Lewis called this the Gates of the Rocky Mountains.

## The Rocky Mountains

On July 20, Lewis saw smoke up a creek near Gates of the Mountains, and on the same day Clark saw smoke up Prickly Pear Creek. The officers determined that these fires were set by Indians to alert distant tribesmen. However, the Indians kept themselves hidden.

Clark's party followed the Indian road up Prickly Pear Creek. As they walked they left items of clothes, paper and linen tape along the trail to inform the Indians that they were white men and not their enemies.

On July 22, Sacagawea, for the first time since leaving Fort Mandan, began to recog-nize the country. Lewis wrote: "The In-dian woman recognizes the country and as-sures us that this is the river on which her relations live, and that the three forks are at no great distance, this piece of information has cheered the sperits of the party..."

On this same day Lewis's party reunited with Clark's. In the four days they were out, Clark's detachment was unable to make contact with any Indians

The following morning, Clark, with Charbonneau and three privates, again went in pursuit of the Shoshones. Certain they were getting close to the Indians, Lewis ordered small U.S. flags hoisted on the canoes so the natives would understand they were not enemy Indians.

The river became ever more difficult as the days passed. With growing fatigue, the men struggled to pull the boats over rapids. Not only was the river forbidding, Lewis also noted that, "our trio of pests still invade and obstruct us on all occasions, these are the musquetoes eye knats and prickly pear, equal to any three curses that ever poor Egypt laiboured under, except the Mahometant Yoke."

On July 24, they passed a remarkable bluff of red colored earth. Sacagawea told them this was the clay the Indians used for paint. For her people red was emblematic of peace.

On July 25 Lewis's party reached the "Little Gates of the Mountains," also referred to as the "second range of mountains." The Indians at Mandan had informed them of this place.

Excerpted from U.S. Forest Service pamphlet "Lewis and Clark in the Rocky Mountains."

## 10. *Gas, Food, Lodging, Shopping, Miscellaneous*

**M Carroll College**
1601 North Benton Ave, Helena. 447-4300 or 800-992-3648, www.carroll.edu

Founded in 1909 as an independent, four-year, private liberal arts college, of Catholic affiliation. It is located on 64 acres in the heart of Helena with a student body size of approximately 1,300. Carroll College is considered on of the top colleges in the Northwest.

## 11. *Gas, Food*

**F Mother Lode Restaurant & Sports Bar**
1428 Cedar, Helena. 443-3510

Stop into the Mother Lode for a casual home cooked meal. Enjoy breakfast, lunch and dinner with daily specials, homemade soups, weekend

Section 8

## Finding the "Big One"

**Helena and its surrounds are well** known for world famous gemstones. Tourists and rockhounders alike love to search for the "Big One."

Montana sapphires are a variety of the mineral corundum that is transparent or translucent. The best known sapphires are commonly known as the ruby.

Except for the diamond, the sapphire is the hardest stone in the world. Because sapphires are four times more rare than diamonds, a large one can almost equal the value of a fine diamond in value. While a Montana sapphire appears dull and glassy in its rough state, when cut and polished, it can approach the luster of a diamond.

The sapphire is the birthstone for September. They have always been prominent throughout history. In the Bible, the Ten Commandments were engraved in tablets of sapphire. The ancient Persians believed the earth sat on a great sapphire and that the sky took its blue color from the reflection of the stone.

Searching for sapphires can be an exciting treasure hunt. The techniques are as simple as sifting gravel through a screen then washing it to find the heavier sapphire. The concentrators used to wash the sand are usually available at digging sites. Some of the better digging sites charge a fee, but have the equipment available for rental.

Now that you found your "big one" the fun really begins. Stones that appear cloudy can be heat treated to enhance the brilliance. Those that are clear need only be faceted. Faceting is the process jewelers use to turn the rough stone into a finished gem. Helena has the only heat treatment facility in the state and several expert lapidaries that can facet your stone. There are also several expert jewelers nearby who can mount your stone and turn it into a beautiful piece of jewelry.

There are seven pay digging sites in the Helena area. These are your best bet for finding that treasure stone:

The Eldorado Bar Sapphire Mine is on the east shore of Hauser Lake. 449-1907.

French Bar Sapphire Mine. Just downstream from the Canyon Ferry Dam. 475-3380.

Castles Sapphire Mine is located about eight miles downstream from the Canyon Ferry Dam. 227-5485.

Lovestone Sapphire Mine is located just a few miles downstream from the Canyon Ferry Dam on the east side of the Missouri River.

steak & lobster specials, prime rib, and a Sunday all-you-can-eat breakfast buffet with an omelet bar, pastries, coffee and juice. Also enjoy entertainment with live poker nightly and a great selection of poker & keno machines. The sports bar is complete with 17 T.V.s showing the NFL package—football is spoken here! Enjoy 16 oz. pints for $1.25 and complimentary drinks while gambling. The Mother Lode is a great place to enjoy a great meal, gamble and watch your favorite sports.

**12.** *Gas, Food, Shopping*

### F Godfather's Pizza

2216 N. Montana Ave., Helena. 443-7050

The fun atmosphere at Godfather's Pizza is great for group gatherings, family dinners, or just a relaxing meal out. They feature a wide variety of pizzas to choose from, with golden and thin crusts and many topping choices. If you're not in the mood for pizza, try the salad bar or a variety of sandwiches. Offering dine in, carry out, and delivery seven days a week. Godfather's also serves specialty buffets and welcomes large groups.

### F Jade Garden Restaurant

3128 N. Montana Ave., Helena. 443-8899

The Jade Garden has been serving authentic Chinese cuisine in Helena for years and has continually been voted the city's Best Restaurant. Chef-Owner Lum Lee chooses only the finest meats and vegetables for his dishes. Sauces are made with the best spices available worldwide, and each of his many entrees is cooked fresh to your order and portioned generously. Whether it's a promptly served lunch, convenient call-ahead take-out, or their fabulous Peking Duck, Jade Garden offers a culinary experience second to none. They are open daily at 11 a.m., serving until 9:30 p.m., and until 10 p.m. Friday and Saturday. They are located at the corner of Montana and Custer.

**13.** *Attraction, Gas, Food, Lodging*

### T Broadwater Hot Springs

Hwy. 12, westside of Helena.

Once an elegant hot springs resort stood near the location of the Broadwater Athletic Club and Hot Springs. The springs were originally developed with the arrival of gold prospectors to Last Chance Gulch in 1864. The first owner advertised it's medicinal properties and built a hotel. Water rights were given to Charles A. Broadwater in 1874, who built an elegant and lavish Hotel and Natatorium in 1888 with an investment of $500,000. Broadwater died three years later and so did most of the direction for the grand resort. It closed in the 1890s and reopening in the 1930s but didn't survive Prohibition and the threat of the coming World War. In 1935, a severe earthquake severely damaged the building, which was later demolished. The health club is open to the public year round with pools, jacuzzis, weight rooms, raquetball, handball, indoor running track, outdoor running trails and modern dressing rooms.

### L Knights Rest Motel

1831 Euclid Ave., Helena. 442-6384
or 888-442-6384

Conveniently located on the quiet west side of Helena, the Knights Rest Motel is close to seven fine restaurants, two golf courses, and Spring Meadow Lake. The 12 guest rooms are complete with queen size beds, kitchenettes, air conditioning, TV and VCR, microwaves and refrigerators. Non-smoking units are available and pets are allowed. This family run motel is a big enough motel to meet all of your needs, yet small enough to care about each one of their guests. Enjoy a complimentary continental breakfast and the Knight's Rest Drive-thru, offering espresso drinks, mini donuts, juice, pastries, and sandwiches—guests can enjoy complimentary regular coffee and 50% off espresso & mini-donuts. Discounts are offered for seniors, AAA, off-season, corporates, and veterans.

### L Lamplighter Motel

1006 Madison Ave., Helena. 442-9200

## 14. *Historic Marker, Attraction, Gas, Food, Lodging, Shopping*

### H Last Chance Gulch
Helena

*The city of Helena started as a group of placer miners' cabins and Main Street follows the bottom of Last Chance Gulch. The gulch is formed by the convergence of Oro Fino and Grizzly Gulches and its colorful history began when gold was discovered July 14, 1864, by a party returning to Alder Gulch from an unsuccessful prospecting trip. They agreed to camp and give this locality a try as their "last chance' It proved to be a bonanza.*

*It is estimated that the Gulch produced thirty million in pay dirt and there is plenty left beneath the present business district. After a cloudburst, colors and nuggets have been found in the gutters.*

*Main Street is very irregular in width and alignment. Some opine that it was laid out in this matter to restrict the shooting range of impetuous, hot-blooded gents in the roaring days gone by.*

### H Reeder's Alley
At entrance to Reeder's Alley

*Pennsylvania brick mason Louis Reeder came to Helena in 1867 to practice his trade. Reeder invested in real estate and among his properties were these lots along the steep hillside of West Cutler Street. Between 1875 and 1884 Reeder constructed a series of apartments and bunkhouses offering single miners a comfortable alternative to log cabin accommodations. The simple masonry provided permanence and resistance to fire, a menace that plagued the early community. The complex included some thirty-five housing units in a collection of stone and brick buildings, including an existing log cabin Reeder ingeniously incorporated into the largest structure. The area was already known as Reeder's Alley when Reeder died after a fall in 1884. The miners moved on, but over the years tenants remained mostly single and male. Twenty-three pensioners lived at Reeder's Alley in 1961 when these buildings were rescued from demolition and rehabilitation begun. The narrow alleyway and closely-spaced buildings nestled against the slope of Mt. Helena today comprise the town's most complete remaining block of the territorial period.*

### H The Morrelli Bridge
At Reeders Alley

"*Where Benton Avenue swings by the Stonehouse and joins Reeder's Alley, forming a "Y", is the Helena end of the old Benton Road. During the 1860s and 1870s, when Montana was still a Territory, settlers from the "States" were brought up the Missouri by riverboat to Fort Benton, thence by oxen or mule team to Helena. The Benton Road avoided the mud and dust of Last Chance Gulch by continuing along the side hill. Cargo was unloaded at various points down the "Gulch". Above the Stonehouse is Morrelli Bridge, said to be fashioned after the Morrelli Bridge in Milan, Italy.*" (Helena, Her Historic Homes, *Jean Baucus, Vol. 1, 1976*).

### T Mount Helena City Park
Northwest of Downtown Helena

Mount Helena rises 1,300 feet above the Last Chance Gulch giving panoramic views of Helena and the surrounding area. The 800-acre city park is a perfect place for a walk or a hike on twenty miles of hiking trails with lots of mule deer in the area. A wonderful place for exploration is the "Devil's Kitchen," a fire-blackened cave in the limestone cliffs of the mountains. To get to the parking area follow W. Main just southwest of Last Chance Gulch (downtown) and follow the signs up the hill. There is a historic sign at the parking lot which reads:

*Mount Helena stands out "grandly and cleancut," a dramatic backdrop for the city that has grown in its shadow. Since picnickers first enjoyed its quiet refuge during mining camp days, Mount Helena has served the community. First miners searched in vain for its minerals. Settlers next stripped its slopes of timber and quarried its limestone. In 1883, residents by the hundreds trekked up the mountain side to watch the railroad, smoking slowly westward across the valley to Helena. Then on November 12,1894, a huge bonfire at the summit lit the night sky, confirming Helena's victory as state capital. Near the century's turn, forest fires further decimated the near-barren mountain. A city park was proposed in 1898 and on Arbor Day in 1899 Helena school children armed with baskets of evergreen seedlings hiked the lightning-scorched slopes. Accompanied by Fred Kuphal's violin, they began reforestation. From the ashes also came the "1906 Mount Helena Trail," actually constructed by the city in 1903. Far-sighted city fathers envisioned a wind-blown seed, and inch of shade, a little snow, and peace … to make a beautiful tree upon the mountain.' And so it was in 1906 that through the cooperative efforts of the Helena Improvement Society and the newly-created U.S. Forest Service, 30,000 seedlings were hand-planted upon the eastern slope. Many still flourish. Today the city's century-old invitation still stands: "Do not deny yourself the health and pleasure of the…delightful walk. Go all and go often."*

For hikes on Mount Helena see the "Hikes" section at the end of this chapter.

### T Holter Museum of Art
12 E. Lawrence, Helena. 442-6400

This museum exhibits quality visual arts in all media from local, national, and international artists, as well as traveling shows.The museum is located in the historic downtown area. It was founded in 1987 and showcases contemporary art in two exhibition galleries and a museum shop feature ceramics, paintings, prints, fibers, woodwork, jewelry, and cards. Open year round and closed on Mondays.

### T Montana Arts Council
316 N. Park Ave. in Helena. 444-6430

### T Reeder's Alley
308 S. Park Ave.in downtown Helena, 449-2552

The need for lodging in the new camp of Last Chance Gulch prompted Lewis Reeder to build the winding series of one-room brick shanties for the many bachelors in the camp. The buildings at the far west end of what was known as "Bridge Street" were constructed of native materials and brick brought by steamboat from St. Louis to Fort Benton and hauled overland to the Gulch. For nearly 20 years Reeder continued to expand his hostelry. A devastating series of fires destroyed "Bridge Street," but each time the Alley was spared.

Along this cobblestone lane of Reeder's Alley lie some of the few remaining original buildings from the Last Chance Gulch mining era of the 1860s. An important piece of history comes alive through the Pioneer Cabin, the oldest cabin in Helena, that sits at the entrance of the alley. Authentically reconstructed, this small building is a museum of Montana's pioneering days and a monument to the gold rush era that gave birth to this area.

### T Cathedral of Saint Helena
509 N. Warren, Helena. 442-5825

A must-see Helena landmark, this magnificent cathedral was modeled after the Vienna Votive Church and the German Cologne Cathedral. The superb architecture includes 46 beautiful stained glass windows, 21 carved marble statues of scientists and statesman and twin majestic spires towering over the city skyline.

### T Montana's Original Governor's Mansion
304 N. Ewing in Helena. 444-4789

### The Mansion

For over a century, the Original Governor's Mansion has stood as a symbol of Helena's wealth and political prominence. In 1888 entrepreneur William A. Chessman, built the home for his wife Penelope and their two children. After 1900, railroad contractor Peter Larson and his wife, Margaret resided in the house, followed in 1911 by Harfield and Kathryn Conrad of the influential

Section 8

Conrad family of Great Falls.

The State of Montana acquired the handsome brick mansion in 1913 to serve as the first official governor's residence. For nearly half a century, Montana's governors and their families lived here, beginning with Samuel V. Stewart and ending with J. Hugo Aronson.

Restoration of the building began in 1969 with the support of the City of Helena. Since 1981, the Montana Historical Society has administered the Mansion as an historic-house museum. Restoration has continued with the assistance of the Original Governor's Mansion Restoration Board, a dedicated group of local citizen advocates. Guided tours of the Original Governor's Mansion offer the opportunity to explore a part of Montana's and Helena's past.

## Private Lives...and Public Roles

The Original Governor's Mansion has enjoyed both private and public roles in the history of Montana and its capital city. From 1888 until 1959, the Ewing Street residence served as home to three consecutive private owners, and a succession of nine "first" families. The history of the Mansion is as much a history of these people as it is of a building.

For the Chessman family, their new Queen Anne style house reflected William Chessman's wealth and influence in the Helena community. Thanks to his success and the work of their servants, the Chessmans led the comfortable domestic life expected of the well-to-do Victorian family. Though financial difficulties forced the Chessmans to give up this lifestyle, the Larsons and the Conrads continued the pattern of affluence into the 1900s.

When the private home became the official governor's residence in 1913, the occupant families represented Montana's elite, again supported by a staff of servants. Politics were endured as an important element of domestic life. Governors relied primarily on state funding to run their household, and they used the residence as a family home, as well as to host important guests.

Since 1888 the residents of the Mansion have changed frequently. The Mansion itself has changed less than its occupants. The structure has remained intact, and the furnishings were updated only partially over the years. The appearance of the building today closely resembles the Mansion during its years of prominence.

Tours to the mansion are provided Tuesday through Saturday from noon to 5 p.m. between April and Memorial Day and Labor Day through December. From Memorial Day through Labor Day tours are held from Tuesday through Sunday from noon to 5 p.m. Tours begin on the hour with the last tour starting at 4 p.m. The mansion is closed from January through March. Admission is free, but donations are encouraged to fund restoration projects.

## T Last Chance Gulch

The downtown area of Helena is a virtual outdoor museum. It was here that Helena was born when gold was discovered on July 14, 1864. Prickly Pear Creek meandered down the mountain through a maze of mining claims here. The gulch is now the state's only downtown outdoor walking mall. Up and down the mall you'll see a restored streetcar, a bullwhacker statue, bronze statues of miners (by Billings sculptor L. Pomeroy), a newsboy statue, a mural that pays tribute to Montana women, a "frontier log" play area for children, and more.

If you really want to see the history, look up.

Many of the oddly shaped buildings match the oddly shaped claims they were built on. Much of the unique and elaborate architecture attests to the wealth and power that originated here.They also attest to the fact that the main occupation of Helena has been commerce rather than mining. The Colwell Building, near the library, is long and narrow—just like a claim. The Power Block at 58 N. Last Chance Gulch was constructed in 1889. Look at the windows on the southeast corner. Notice anything unusual? The Windbag Saloon at 19 S. Last Chance Gulch, was underneath a bordello until 1973. The Atlas Building at 7 N. Last Chance Gulch, is one of Helena's more interesting buildings. On the cornice upheld by Atlas, lizards and a salamander do battle. The Securities Building at 101 N. Last Chance Gulch was constructed in 1886. The Romanesque building has mysterious thumbprints carved between the first-floor arches. Stop at the Chamber of Commerce for a walking tour map of the area.

## T Montana Club

24 W. 6th, Helena. 442-5980

You can almost feel the power oozing out of the mortar in this wedge shaped building. In the inner sanctum of these walls, much of Montana's history was shaped in smoke filled rooms behind closed doors. This was Montana's most prestigious club with membership open only to millionaires and is the oldest private club in the Northwest. Originally constructed in 1885, it was burned by an arsonist in 1903 and rebuilt in 1905.

Over the years many notables have graced the inside of this building. Copper kings, millionaires and politicians played host to such notable personalities as presidents Theodore Roosevelt and Howard Taft, humorist Will Rogers, author Mark Twain, movie stars Robert Montgomery, Donna Reed, Gary Cooper, Myrna Loy, and a wide assortment of royalty and other dignitaries. The building is listed in the National Register of Historic Places. Today it is a dinner club for men and women. Tours of the building are available.

## T Wells Fargo Museum of Gold

350 N. Last Chance Gulch in Helena. 447-2000

This museum is in the lobby of the Wells Fargo bank and has a gold collection worth over $600,000. There are gold flakes, nuggets, wires, coins, and "character" nuggets. "Character" nuggets are chunks of gold that come in interesting shapes like the "Cowboy Boot" nugget on display. The museum is open when the bank is open.

### *Montana Trivia*

The government is the largest employer in the state, employing 21 percent of the work force. In Helena, 25 percent of the full time jobs are related to running the state government.

## T Old Fire Tower

Sitting on a hill overlooking Last Chance Gulch is a structure the locals affectionately call "Guardian of the Gulch." The Old Fire Tower is the city's symbol. The tower was built in 1876 to keep a watchful eye for fire. It was manned 24 hours a day with the watchman ready to sound the alarm should smoke or fire be spotted. At one time there were several of these in town. Today it is only one of five left standing in the United States.

## F Salvatore's Trattoria

42 S. Park Ave., Helena. 443-0358

Specializing in traditional Italian Cuisine, Salvatore's Trattoria has an authentic and elegant atmosphere to go along with the fine cuisine. Everything is made from scratch including all the pasta, sauce, and dessert. The menu offers Sicilian chicken, roast pork and a wonderful selection of Italian desserts. The marinara sauce is "world famous" and a favorite among locals. The dinner is unique in that there is no menu. You will notice the sign on the wall that reads "You will eat what the kitchen cooks." What the kitchen cooks is an elegant seven course traditional Italian fare that is not to be missed. Stop in for lunch Mon.–Fri. and dinner Thurs.–Sat.

## F Stonehouse Restaurant

120 Reeder's Alley in Helena. 449-2552

Enjoy an elegant 1890's atmosphere while dining at the Stonehouse Restaurant located at the top of

# Mann Gulch Tragedy

## What Happened in Mann Gulch?

On August 5, 1949, about 6:00 p.m., fifteen USDA Forest Service Smokejumpers and a Helena National Forest fire guard were entrapped by a wildfire in Mann Gulch that was caused by lightning struck trees. Ten jumpers and the forest guard perished that evening, two jumpers died later from burn injuries and three jumpers survived. The jumpers, dispatched from Missoula, had parachuted into Mann Gulch to help fight a lightning caused fire burning on the ridge between Meriwether and Mann Gulch.

The jump plane arrived over the fire with the jumpers at 3:10 p.m. Spotter Earl Cooley and Jumper Foreman Wag Dodge chose a jump site up canyon in Mann Gulch. The fire size was estimated at 60 acres, but was still considered a routine fire. The air was quite turbulent, requiring a higher than normal approach causing the jumpers and cargo to scatter widely. Also, the cargo chute for the radio failed to open, leaving the jumpers without outside communication.

By 5:00 p.m., the men had gathered their gear and were eating before attacking the fire. Foreman Dodge left squad leader Bill Hellman in charge and crossed to the south side of Mann Gulch to meet Meriwether Guard Harrison. He told Hellman to take the crew toward the river on the north side of the canyon and said he would tie in with them later.

Dodge and Harrison caught up with the crew around 5:40 p.m. They had continued down Mann Gulch for about 5 minutes when Dodge noticed the fire had crossed to the north side of the gulch. Realizing the danger, he told the men to head back up Mann Gulch. The wind had increased and the fire was beginning to blow up, burning rapidly toward them in light grass and brush.

The men had only traveled 300 yards when Dodge gave instructions to drop their gear. Flames were estimated at 50 feet high and were moving 50 yards every 10 seconds. The men quickly became exhausted due to the steep slopes, high temperature and smoke filled air.

The crew traversed another 200 yards when Foreman Dodge realized the fire was going to catch them. Dodge lit an escape fire hoping it would quickly burn out, allowing his men to get into the burned area and survive. For unknown reasons, the crew did not follow Dodge's instructions and continued toward the ridgetop.

Jumpers Rumsey and Sallee followed the edge of the escape fire to the ridgetop where they escaped the flames. After the blowup had subsided, they found Hellman, badly burned, but alive. Wag Dodge, who had survived inside the escape fire area, joined Rumsey and Sallee and reported he had found Jumper Sylvia alive, but badly burned. Dodge and Sallee proceeded down Rescue Gulch to the Missouri river to find help while Rumsey stayed with Hellman.

A rescue crew arrived on the scene at 12:30 a.m. on August 6th. At 1:50 a.m., the rescue crew found Jumpers Sylvia and Hallman. The two injured men were evacuated at 5:00 a.m., but both died in a Helena hospital later in the morning. Before the day was over, 11 bodies would be found. All had died within 300 yards of each other.

During the blow up stage, the Mann Gulch fire covered an estimated 3,000 acres in 10 minutes and eventually burned 5,000 acres.

The fatal smoke and flames that roared on that hot, August afternoon have long since cooled and vanished. However, the events of the Mann Gulch Fire will forever be etched in our hearts and continue to influence wildfire safety and suppression tactics. Today, firefighters nationwide analyze fire behavior from investigative conclusions and follow the Ten Standard Fire Orders that were influenced in part, by the events that occurred in Mann Gulch.

## How to Experience Mann Gulch

Reaching Mann Gulch today is nearly as difficult as it was in 1949. There are still no roads in the area and one must still boat, hike or ride horseback to reach the site.

For those who choose to hike or ride horseback to visit the area, there are three main Forest Service trails leading from north, east and south of Mann Gulch. These trails range in length from seven to 18 miles and offer overnight or day hike opportunities.

By far the easiest way to reach Mann Gulch is by boat. Many visitors take a commercial tour boat originating at the Gates of the Mountains Boat Club. This tour offers seasonal transportation to and from Meriwether picnic area with boats arriving and departing every two hours. By taking the morning tour boat and returning on the last tour boat of the day, many people visit Mann Gulch by hiking from Meriwether picnic area. Visitors choosing this two-mile route will need to maintain a brisk walking pace to visit the site and return to the picnic area in order to catch the tour boat.

Private or rental boats can also reach the mouth of Mann Gulch from launching facilities located on both Upper and Lower Holter Lakes. Visitors choosing to boat to the mouth of Mann Gulch should be advised that there are no docking facilities provided and that landing and launching are done at the operator's risk. Once beached at the mouth of the canyon, a two-mile hike up the bottom of the gulch will take a visitor to the area of the firefighters' memorials.

## For Your Safety

Visitors to Mann Gulch should be prepared for a backcountry experience with all its inherent risks and dangers. In keeping with the rugged and wild character of the area, there are no trails or directional signs in Mann Gulch. The footing is sometimes treacherous, the slopes are steep, and boulder fields are numerous. Watch for rolling rocks from above as you approach the ridge between Mann Gulch and Rescue Gulch. Wear good hiking shoes and carry a map. There is no water and temperatures in the canyon frequently exceed 100 degrees during the summer months, so take along plenty of drinking water.

Among the wild creatures that call Mann Gulch home are rattlesnakes and ticks. Be prepared to encounter both critters during your hike. Wearing tight-fitting clothing will keep the ticks on the outside of your clothes—where they belong—and closely watching where you place your hands and feet during the hike will help prevent you from waking a dozing snake.

## Visiting the Memorials

Since that tragic August day, families, friends and colleagues have remembered those who lost their lives in Mann Gulch. In 1950, white crosses were designed and cast in Missoula, Montana by smokejumper comrades of those who perished. They were placed in the location where each body was recovered.

Harsh weather and time have caused the crosses to become fragile and crumble. Respectfully the Forest Service and the Smokejumpers have placed marble plaques next to the original crosses. The memory of those 13 men has been renewed and the memorials serve as a lasting reminder of all women and men who have served as wildland firefighters, especially those who have paid the ultimate price for that service.

*Reprinted from U.S. Forest Service brochure*

Section 8

Helena's Reeder's Alley. The historical building has retained the rock walls, waterfalls and fireplaces in the main dining room that provides a truly special experience. Chef, Jason Lehmans, presents his award winning menu that features, New American French Cuisine, for your total enjoyment. Select from award winning menu items such as Moroccan Fire Grilled Salmon, Tournedos Rossini, Proscuitto wrapped Chilean Sea Bass Stack, Sautéed Wild Mushroom Medley with Black Truffles and Sage, just to name a few. Accompany meal with your favorite cocktail or fine wine. They also provide catering facilities and a banquet room for large parties.

### F Last Chance Casino

1001 N. Last Chance Gulch, Helena. 442-4474

Helena's Last Chance Casino is ready to serve you with the most friendly and courteous service you'll find anywhere. The staff takes pride in serving the best meals at the best prices in the area. Their full service restaurant is where you can have breakfast, including their famous old fashioned ham and eggs, all day long starting at 7 a.m. until closing. The bar and casino have an array of video Poker and Keno machines to choose from. Live Keno is available 7 days a week, and is the only electronic and the hottest game in town. You'll be back time after time once you've been to the Last Chance Casino conveniently located n Last Chance Gulch.

*Last Chance Casino.*

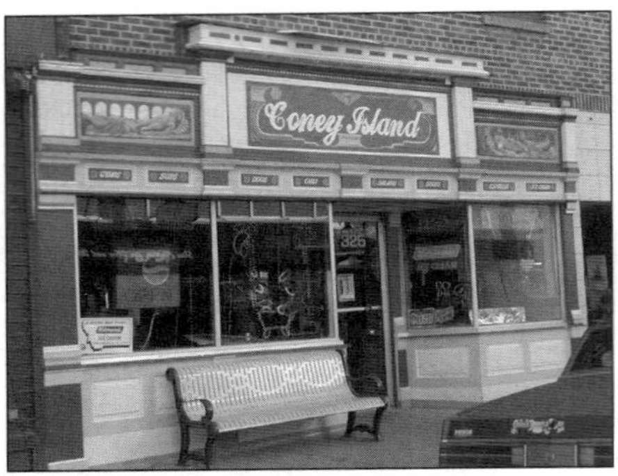


**F Coney Island**
325 N. Last Chance Gulch, Helena. 443-9664

Coney Island has been a Last Chance Gulch fixture for 27 years. Outside paintings on this diner/restaurant are as charming as the colorful murals inside. Families enjoy the pony carousel where the owner is known to pass out quarters to the children. The Werner family and employees make everyone feel welcome and know many of the customers by their first name. The relaxed and fun atmosphere draws a regular following of locals and tourists alike. You'll find a tempting menu of hot dogs, coney dogs, polish dogs, homemade soups and chilies. Gyros and sub sandwiches are their specialties! Try the old fashioned shakes and malts! Rumor has it that their Mexican menu is the best in town. A great place for variety, good food, and reasonable prices when you are near or in Helena.

**L Budget Inn Express**
524 N. Last Chance Gulch, Helena. 442-0600 or toll free 800-862-1334 or fax 443-1770

**S The Leather Store & More**
438 N. Last Chance Gulch in Helena. 443-2007

The Leather Store and More is located in the heart of historic downtown Helena and offers a fantastic variety of high quality leather goods at reasonable prices. Personal service is at the cornerstone of your shopping experience. You will find leather apparel ranging from soft lambskin trench coats and plush furs all the way to rough and tough motorcycle coats and chaps. They also specialize in licensed NFL leather sports apparel and accessories. In addition to leather goods they custom make horsehair belts, bridals, hatbands, or just about anything that can be made with horsehair. A very special store!

### Montana Trivia

In the 1920s, it was proposed (and voted down) to change the spelling of Helena to Hellena. It seems the locals were bothered by the common mispronunciation as Hel-EEN-a.

**S Tori's Antiques, Curios & Candy**
424 N. Last Chance Gulch, Helena. 442-5595

The squeaky wind-blown wooden sign invites you to enter the old store front on Historic Last Chance Gulch. Tories has been there for over 25 years and is well-known for exquisite jewelry, fine antique furniture, stunning glassware and china, along with ranch and Yellowstone Park primitives. Don't forget Dad and the kids. They'll want to check out their candy store, Sweet Thing, offering a large selection of homemade candy and treats. You'll be pleasantly surprised with the selection of interesting local antiques and the array of unusual fun items such as designer socks, silk screened cottons. You always be welcomed with air conditioning and a smile. Be sure and visit their store, Sweet Thing, in Townsend too.

**S Pan Handler Plus**
40 S. Last Chance Gulch, Downtown Helena. 443-1916 or fax 442-2239

A trip to Helena is not complete without a trip to The Pan Handler. You'll find them on the walking mall near the old Trolley. The store is a cook's dream! You'll find unique and specialty gift items along with a very impressive extensive selection of gourmet kitchen products and kitchen gadgets. They take pride in offering a selection of brands known for outstanding quality. You'll love their gourmet foods and selection of quality wines from around the world. The perfect picnic starts here! Not only is the Pan Handler a fun place to shop, but they offer complementary gift wrap for those special gifts. Gift baskets and shipping are also available.

## 15. *Attraction, Food, Lodging*

**T Hauser Lake**
Take Hwy. 280 11 miles east out of Helena.

The historic Hauser dam was Samuel T. Hauser's idea for creating electricity to sell to the mining companies in Butte and Anaconda. The dam is the second of three on the upper Missouri River. The lake created by the dam is a great place to watch bald eagles feed on the spawning salmon in the fall. Black Sandy, one of Helena's most popular beaches, sits on the shore of Hauser. Crossing the York bridge on Hwy. 280 will take you to some great sapphire hunting mines. The Lake has the most prolific kokanee salmon fishery. Four pound salmon are not uncommon here. There is a Visitor Center in the dam area.

**T Black Sandy State Park**
7 miles north of Helena on I-15, then 4 miles east on Secondary 453, then 3 miles north on county road. 449-8864

One of the few public parks on the shores of Hauser Reservoir, Black Sandy is an extremely popular weekend boating, fishing, and water skiing take-off point. Proximity to Helena makes Black Sandy State Park a convenient and great recreational area. It's a good place to watch bald eagles during their fall migration or to fish for salmon and trout. There are campground facilities and the nearby Lakeside Resort offers a marina and other recreational facilities.

## 16.

**T Gates of the Mountains Boat Tour**
Hwy 15, north of Great Falls. 458-5241

This spectacular boat cruise along a stretch of the Missouri has been in operation for over 100 years. It retraces the areas traveled by Lewis and Clark in 1805 beginning at the Upper Holter Lake and passing through the incredible limestone cliffs where many forms of wildlife are commonly spotted. You'll see many birds, bighorn sheep, mountain goats, and possibly even a black bear or mountain lion.

Meriwether Lewis named this stretch of the Missouri River. The sheer limestone cliffs appear to open or close as you approach or depart the canyon. Lewis wrote *"The rocks approached the river on both sides, forming a most sublime and extraordinary spectacle. Nothing can be imagined more tremendous than the frowning darkness of these rocks, which project over the river and menace us with destruction. This extraordinary range of rocks we called the Gates of the Rocky Mountains."*

In 1886, Nicholas Hilger began giving boat tours of the area. Today there are three open-air river boats that provide tours of the canyon. The 105 minute cruise begins at the marina three miles off of Exit 209 on I-15 just north of Helena. The cruise through here appears just as it did when first seen by Lewis and Clark.

The cliffs are so shear here that there are very few places to beach a boat. One of the few places is the Meriwether Picnic Area, named after the explorers it is believed camped here. The tour boat does stop here for a break. If you wish, you can take a hike up to Mann Gulch where 13 smokejumpers died in a raging forest fire in 1949.

### Montana Trivia

Nate Vestal made a fortune from the Penobscot gold mine near Helena, one of the richest in the world. Unfortunately he lost it in the stock market and had to take a job as a laborer—in the mine he once owned.

The tour boat operator will pull in close to the walls to observe Indian pictographs. There is a good chance that you will also see mountain goats along the rugged walls.

## 17. *Historic Marker, Attraction, Gas, Food, Lodging*

### Wolf Creek

There are several versions of how the creek which this town took its name from got its name. All agree that it was from a name the Indians gave it. Some say it was "Creek where the wolf jumped too." Others say it was "Creek where the wolf jumped to." The files of the Great Northern Railroad claim the origin is "Creek that the wolf jumped in." In each case, the wording changes the story behind the name. One thing is for sure—it had something to do with a wolf.

### H The Mann Gulch Fire

Northeast of Wolf Creek, frontage road.

*At an isolated gulch about three miles northeast of here on August 5, 1949, twelve smokejumpers and a Forest Service employee died when a routine fire unexpectedly turned deadly. The lightning-caused fire at Mann Gulch was spotted by a Forest Ranger about noon on August 5th. Within hours, fourteen of the Forest Service's crack smokejumpers were on the ground in the gulch and moving toward the 55 acre fire. Wind, combined with tinder dry grass and the steep terrain in the gulch, caused a rare and little understood phenomenon called a "blow up" The result was an inferno that quickly enveloped Mann Gulch. The fire jumped the mouth of the gulch and cut off escape to the Missouri River. The men then sought the protection afforded by the ridge line to the north. The raging wall of flame moved faster than the men could climb the steep slope to safety. Realizing they could not outrun the holocaust, the crew's foreman set a back-fire to provide a makeshift shelter for the smokejumpers. Tragically, fear drove the men on and no one sought shelter with the foreman; the last words he recalled hearing before being engulfed by the flames were "To hell with this; I'm getting out of here!" Within minutes, eleven men lay dead on the hillside, killed by the super-heated air generated by the fire. Two other smokejumpers died the following day from severe burns. Three men, including the foreman, survived the fire. Only the 1994 South Canyon Fire in Colorado was deadlier for the National Forest Service's elite smokejumpers.*

*This marker is dedicated to the thirteen men who died in the Mann Gulch Fire.*

### D Mer. Lewis

July 19, 1805

*"We entered much the most remarkable clifts that we have yet seen. . .the river appears to have forced it's way through this immence body of solid rock for the distance of 5 and three quarters miles. . .mor is ther in the 1st 3 miles of this distance a spot except one of a few yards in extent on which a man could rest the soal of his foot."*

### T Holter Lake

Interstate 15 exits 209 and 226 take you directly to the lake.

Holter Dam was completed in 1918 and created this 4,800-acre lake just east of Wolf Creek.

### T Holter Lake Recreation Area

Hwy 15, north of Helena.

Nestled in the Big Belt Mountains, Holter Lake is a great fishing area for trout, walleye and salmon. The lake is a great place to play or lounge on the beach and also offers a chance to see many birds, such as, peregrine falcons, American white pelicans, great blue herons and loons. Don't forget to look up on the rock outcroppings above the lake for bighorn sheep and mountain goats. Holter Lake is nearby the Gates of the Mountains Wilderness, Beartooth Wildlife Management Area, and Sleeping Giant Wilderness Study Area which offer wonderful hiking adventures, horseback riding, boat-in camping and beautiful picnic spots.

### VL Rocking Z Ranch

2020 Sieben Canyon Rd., I-90 Exit 216. Wolf Creek. 458-3890 or fax 458-6287. www.rockingz.com

Rocking Z is a full service guest ranch owned by Zack and Patty Wirth, fourth generation Montana ranchers. They offer a superb horseback riding program for Day Riders, as well as ranch guests. Lessons are available for all levels of riders, and take you from valleys to mountain tops. Guest rooms are new, large, luxurious, furnished with log furniture, have private baths, and heated with a cast iron stoves. Fantastic ranch meals are prepared with only fresh ingredients, and include breads, pies, and cookies made in their own kitchen. Evening activities include campfires, dancing, storytelling, and singing, topping days filled with hiking, birding, fishing, history, and Lewis & Clark lore. Reservations are recommended, but not always necessary. Stay for one night or several. They are conveniently located between Helena and Great Falls.

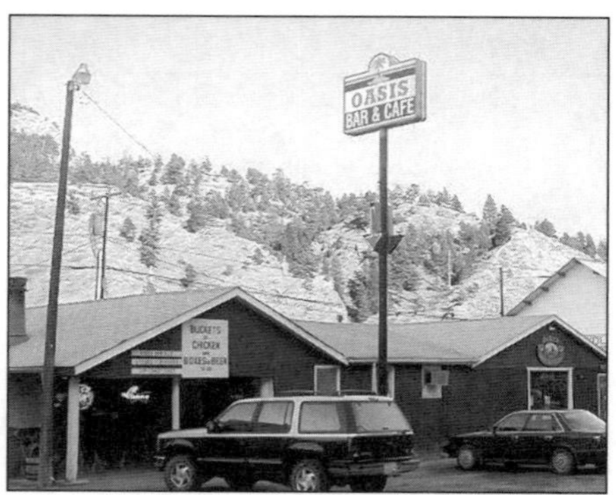


### F Oasis Family Café

250 Recreation Road, Old Hwy 91, Wolf Creek. 235-9992. www.corpsofdiscovery.com/oasis.htm

Discover Wolf Creek and the Oasis Family Restaurant and dine on delicious home cooked meals, soup and pies in a friendly family atmosphere. The Oasis is nestled along the scenic Little Prickly Pear Creek close to prime blue-ribbon trout fishing on the fabled upper Missouri River mentioned in Norman McLean's A River Runs Through It. Just minutes from Lewis & Clark's famous Gates of the Mountains in prime wildlife habitat, where ancient Indian petroglyphs are found along the cliffs, and elk, deer, mountain goats and sheep are easily seen. They are located less than an hour's drive from either Helena or Great Falls and open for breakfast, lunch or dinner.

*Holter Lake*

## 18. *Food, Lodging*

### Craig

The town was named for its original settler, Warren Craig. The town is the site of a ferry that once ran across the Missouri to the little settlement of Stickney across the river in the late 1800s.

## 19. *Historic Marker*

### H The Montana Central Railroad

North of Craig.

*The Montana Central Railroad used to run on the tracks that follow Little Prickly Pear Creek and the highway. It was part of the railroad tycoon James J. Hill's plan to build a vast transcontinental transportation system. As the Helena Weekly Herald reported: "The Montana Central was a scheme inaugurated by Col. Broadwater [of Helena] and countenanced by James J. Hill of St. Paul, president of Manitoba Railroad. Its birth was coetaneous with the decision of Mr. Hill to begin the extension of the Manitoba to Montana and the West."*

*Hill and other railroad magnates took the first through train from St. Paul to Helena on Nov. 18, 1887. At the very hour that locals were dressing the city in flags and bunting to welcome Hill and party the Northern Pacific Railroad attempted to keep the Montana Central track laying crew from building across its line. The blockage attracted much attention and a hot exchange of words, but was settled quickly and without further incident, the track was completed. The Nov. 21 celebration was held as scheduled.*

*Helenans had rejoiced five years earlier when the Northern Pacific came to town because it meant competition for the stage companies and bull-team freighters. In turn, arrival of the Montana Central broke the NP's monopoly.*

*The Manitoba Railway became the Great Northern in 1890 and Montana Central sold out to them in 1907. Burlington Northern now owns these lines as well as most of the others in Montana.*

### H Fort Shaw

I-15 at Milepost 245

*Barring fur trading posts, the first important white settlements in Montana were the mining camps in the western mountains. Everything to the east belonged to the plains Indians and was buffalo range. To protect the miners and settlers from possible incursions of hostile tribes, a series of military posts was established around the eastern border of the mining camps and settlements. Fort Shaw, established in 1867, was one of these. It also protected the stage and freight trail from Fort Benton, head of navigation on the Missouri, to the Last Chance Gulch placer diggings at Helena. Everything north of the Sun River was Blackfeet Indian Territory at that time. The fort was built by the 13th U.S. Infantry, under Major Wm. Clinton.*

*General Gibbon led his troops from here in 1876 to join General Terry and General Custer on the Yellowstone just prior to the latter's disastrous fight with the Sioux and Cheyenne Indians at the Battle of the Little Big Horn.*

## 20. *Historical Marker, Lewis & Clark, Attraction*

### H The Mullan Road

West of Helena at McDonald Pass

*From this point west to the Idaho line I-90 follows the route of a military road located and constructed during 1858-62 by Captain John Mullan, 2nd Artillery, U.S. Army. The road was 624 miles long and connected Fort Benton, Montana, with Fort Walla Walla, Washington. An average wagon outfit required a minimum of forty-seven days to travel it.*

*The Captain, aside from his engineering ability, was a man of considerable acumen as evidenced by the following excerpts from his final report. He prophesied "… the locomotive engine will make passage of the … wild interior at rates of speed which will startle human credulity."*

*Mullan himself might have been incredulous had he seen the freight train that crossed this divide in 1865. Seven camels, each laden with 600 pounds of flour, made the trek from Helena to the Deer Lodge mines. One of the less successful experiments in American transportation history the dromedary carried tremendous loads, was sure footed, and had great stamina, but the horses, mules and oxen of the teamsters and mule train packers stampeded at the sight and smell of them. The camels were gone from Montana by 1867.*

### H Continental Divide—Elevation 6,325

West of Helena at McDonald Pass

*MacDonald Pass joins two other Continental Divide crossings as vital links between east and west in Montana. Both Mullan and Priest Passes, just north of this route, had roads as early as the 1850s. In 1870, E. M. "Lige" Dunphy built a toll road over this portion of the Divide making extensive use of log "corduroying" in muddy spots. He hired Alexander "Red" MacDonald to manage the toll gate with charges for all types of transportation except pedestrians and those traveling after dark. During the early 1880s a half dozen six-horse stages a day passed this way to and from Helena and western Montana.*

*In September of 1911, Cromwell Dixon earned a $10,000 prize when he became the first aviator in America to fly over the Continental Divide not too far from this spot. Today a four-lane highway and an air beacon replace buckboards and biplanes of earlier eras.*

### D Sgt. Gass

July 16, 1805

*"This day we went about 20 miles."*

### D Mer. Lewis

July 16, 1805

*"early this morning we passed about 40 little booths formed of willow bushes to shelter them from the sun; they appeared to have been deserted about 10 days; we supposed that they were snake Indians. they apperaed to have a number of horses with them- this appearance gives me much hope of meeting with these people shortly."*

### D Mer. Lewis

July, 17, 1805

*"The sunflower is in bloom and abundant in the river bottoms. The Indians of the Missouri particularly those who do not cultive maze make great uce of the seed of this plant for bread, or use it in thickening their soope."*

### D William Clark

July 18, 1805

*"in the evening I passed over a mountain on an Indian rode by which rout I cut off Several miles of the Meandering of the River, the roade. . .is wide and appears to have been dug in maney places."*

### D Mer. Lewis

July 19, 1805

*"every object here wears a dark and gloomy aspect. the tow(er)ing and projecting rocks in many places seem ready to tumble on us. . .from the singular appearance of this place I called the gates of the rocky mountains."*

### T Spring Meadow Lake (Day use only)

State 12 West, North on Joslyn to Country Club. 449-8864.

Located on the western edge of Helena, this 30 acre spring fed lake is noted for its clarity and depth. Open to non-motorized boats only, the lake is popular for swimming, sunbathing, scuba diving, wildlife viewing, and fishing for trout, bass, and sunfish. A nature trail circles the lake.

## 21. *Attraction*

### T Rimini Ghost Camp

West of Helena. on Hwy 12.

Rimini is still home to a few residents. Many of the original buildings are still standing and some in good condition thanks to care given by the residents who live in them. Porphyry Dike Mine is also nearby.

## 22. *Attraction, Gas, Food, Lodging*

### Elliston

This town was established to service the gold, quartz and placer mines in the area.

### T Frontier Town

McDonald's Pass 15 miles west of Helena on Hwy. 12. 449-3031

John R. Quigley was a descendent of Montana pioneers. One day he got the bug to carve a monument to his forefathers. While doing that, he decided to carve himself a log and rock village out of the mountain at the top of the Continental Divide. Over a period of ten years, four block houses, massive log gates and buildings grew from the mountainside. His crowning structure was an eighty seat log and stone non-denomination chapel dedicated to his creator. This he finished in 1957. In 1979, old John passed on. His wife continued to operate the compound as "Frontier Town" until 1992 when she sold it to D. Richard Pegg, a Seattle contractor. As a builder, Pegg felt a kinship with Quigley and promised the widow to preserve and protect the Quigley compound.

Pegg had planned to use the compound as a private residence, but decided to share his dream home with the public. He did away with the entrance fee and opened the gates to the public. Since the place had received no maintenance, he invested $100,000 in minor renovations "to keep it standing." Some hard times hit Pegg and he was forced to sell it in 1996. The place deteriorated rapidly out of his custody. It 1998, he re-acquired it and was given a second chance to make good on his promise to the widow Quigley. Today Pegg and partners are operating it as a resort and first class seafood restaurant.

## Helena National Forest

Mullan Pass Located in central Montana, the Helena National Forest surrounds the capital city of Helena. The Forest contains 976,000 acres and is one of 10 National Forests in the state.

Directions
From Helena, south on State highway 287 to State highway 284 will lead you to the forest. See our map for help in getting there.
Helena National Forest
USDA Forest Service
2880 Skyway Drive
Helena, MT 59601
Phone: 406-449-5201
Email:Mailroom_R1_Helena@fs.fed.us

*Reprinted from www.recreation.gov*

## 23. *Gas, Food, Lodging, Shopping*

### Montana City

Montana City began as a Great Northern Railroad station and lies only a few miles from Helena.

### LA Elkhorn Mountain Inn

1 Jackson Creek Rd, Montana City. 442-6625

The Elkhorn Mountain Inn is locally owned and operated, and the Calnan Family is prepared to give their guests the personalized attention that they deserve. The Inn has been designed around locally handcrafted furnishings that portray a true taste of Montana hospitality. All rooms are complete with cable TV and VCR, with movies available right downstairs. The convenience store is connected by an interior passage, offering a full line of groceries, fast food, gas, and a full service post office. Located just 4 miles from Helena, the Elkhorn Mountain Inn is a great place to enjoy the beautiful Montana landscape, with the convenience of city life nearby. Ask about the luxurious honeymoon/jacuzzi suite and possibility of special arrangements for groups and tours.

### F Montana City Grill & Saloon

Exit on I-15, Montana City. 449-8890

Located just five short minutes from Helena, The Montana City Grill & Saloon is well worth the drive! Featuring a great selection of steaks, barbeque, seafood, pasta, Italian specialties, and world famous Huckleberry BBQ Pork Ribs that should not be missed. Lunch & dinner specials are also served daily. Montana City Grill has been recently remodeled and is perfect for both formal and casual occasions, with a banquet room available for private parties. Enjoy the full service bar and casino for after dinner fun. Open for lunch & dinner daily, and breakfast Saturday & Sunday. Just look for the bright lights!

### S The Artful Framer's Gallery

1 Jackson Creek Rd., Montana City, 442-5996 or 888-442-5996.

Nestled at the base of the beautiful Elkhorn Mountains, The Artful Framer's Gallery specializes in unique gifts and products that reflect Montana and beyond. They feature several Montana artists with originals and prints, bronze sculptures, pottery and custom framing. The unique gift selection also includes custom made jewelry and silver. They offer professional, friendly service, will ship your purchases for you, and will special order any prints by your favorite artists. Some featured artists include Monte Dolack, Nancy Glazier, Terry Redlin, Robert Morgan, Charles Petersen, Thomas Kinkade, and Becky Eiker. Stop in to experience it for yourself.

## 24. *Gas, Food*

### Clancy

Clancy sits in the heart of a famous silver camp. In the late 1800s the Clancy district mined ore so rich that it could be hauled by bull team to Ft. Benton, put on steamers headed east, shipped over the ocean to Swansea, Wales for smelting, and still show a profit. The town took its name from a colorful old-timer known as "Judge" Clancy.

## 25. *Historical Marker, Attraction*

### Jefferson City

This town had its beginnings as a stage station of the freight and passenger line that linked Virginia City and Fort Benton. The town took its name from the Jefferson River nearby.

### H Freighters

North of Jefferson City on I-15.

*Time was when ox and mule teams used to freight along this route. A five-ton truck doesn't look as picturesque but there hasn't been much change in the language of the drivers.*

*Jerk-line skinners were plumb fluent when addressing their teams. They got right earnest and personal. It was spontaneous, no effort about it. When they got strung out they were worth going a long ways to hear. As a matter of fact you didn't have to go a long ways, providing your hearing was normal. Adjectives came natural to them but they did bog down some on names. They had the same one for each of their string.*

*Those times have gone forever.*

### H The Prickly Pear Diggings

North of Jefferson City on I-15.

*The Fisk or Northern Overland Expedition camped on the future site of Montana City just east of the highway in September, 1862. The outfit consisting Of 125 emigrants had left St. Paul June 16, 1862, under the leadership of Capt. James L. Fisk for the purpose of opening a wagon route to connect at Ft. Benton with the eastern terminal of the Mullan Road from Walla Walla.*

*They found "Gold Tom," one of Montana's first prospectors, holed up in a tepee near here scratching gravel along Prickly Pear Creek in a search for the rainbow's end. The few colors he was panning out wouldn't have made much of a dent in the national debt, but about half of the Fisk outfit got the gold fever and decided to winter here.*

*Montana City swaggered into existence in September 1864 as a roaring mining town that is only a memory now. Today it is a suburb of metropolitan Helena.*

### T Wickes Ghost Camp

I-15, 20 miles south of Helena.

Remains of huge smelters and refineries are all that are left in the ghost town of Wickes. Once a thriving mining town that produced $50,000,000 in gold and silver before operations ceased in the early 1890s. Folks continued to live there for a number of years, until most of the town was destroyed by fire. The road to Wickes is easily traveled by car. Also nearby is the Alta Mine and the Corbin camp.

## 26. *Attraction*

### T Elkhorn Ghost Town State Park

I-15 at Boulder exit, 7 miles south on Montana 69, then 11 miles north on country road. 449-8864

Wander through a once-thriving silver mining town. Booming in 1870, Elkhorn, with only a few residents, is now considered a ghost town by many. Many of the original buildings are still intact though they are privately owned. Two buildings that have not been renovated are the

*Fraternity Hall.*

Fraternity Hall and Gillian Hall, both of which you can explore. An old cemetery holds the tragic memory of the 1888 diphtheria epidemic during which many children died.

The Elkhorn Mine was discovered in 1870 by Peter Wye, a native of Switzerland. Peter Weiss, William Hahn and Herman Koch had discovered the first mine in this area only two years earlier.

A. M. Holter, an Alder Gulch pioneer, developed the Elkhorn Mine in 1875. A mill was built in 1884 and a smelter the following year. By February of 1888, the mine's monthly production was valued at more than $30,000. Daily rail service started in 1887.

Much of the surrounding timbered areas near Elkhorn were clear-cut prior to 1887 to provide fuel for power in the mines and heat for homes. More than 500 woodsman and 1,500 mules worked in the woods. Elkhorn's population reached 2,500 in the 1880s, additional hundreds lived in the surrounding gulches.

An English syndicate purchased the mine for $500,000 in 1889. By 1900 the Elkhorn Mine had produced a total of 8,902,000 ounces of silver, 8,500 ounces of gold and more than 4 million pounds of lead. The 1897 silver market crash pretty much ended the operations of the mine, although there were a few short-lived revivals in 1901 and 1905.

The cemetery tells a sad tale of hardship. Notice the large number of children's graves dated September 1888 through August 1889. It is believed their deaths resulted from a particularly severe winter.

When visiting Elkhorn, realize that the land, buildings and other property is in private ownership. There are still people who live here year round. Please do not molest the property or disturb the residents.

When visiting the town, there are a number of hay meadows north of the town that are excellent spots for spotting large groups of bull elk.

### *Montana Trivia*

In the 1880s, Helena boasted more millionaires per capita than any other community in the nation. There were more than fifty.

**27.** *Historical Marker, Attraction, Gas, Food, Lodging, Shopping*

*Boulder courthouse.*

## Boulder

Boulder, originally Boulder Valley, was named for the mammoth stones strewn around the valley. It was initially established as an early stage coach stop in the 1860s along the Fort Benton–Virginia City route. The area later became a frontier trading center for the surrounding mining and agricultural area. The town retains much of its original essence with its red-brick storefronts in the town's center. The Montana Home for the Feeble Minded and the Jefferson County Courthouse, both built in the late 19th Century, are listed upon the National Registry of Historic Places. The courthouse is a particularly impressive building. Built by a local architect influenced by his German training, the courthouse has a three-story entry and gargoyles perched on 24-inch-thick stone walls.

### H The Boulder River Bridge
South of Boulder on Hwy. 59

*The trusses on this structure were salvaged from the "Hubbard" or "Red" Bridge. The original structure was built by the Gillette-Herzog Manufacturing Company in 1899. The company was one of several Minnesota-based bridge construction firms active in Montana from the late 19th century to the early 1920s. The bridge was one of eight pinconnected Pratt through truss spans built by the company over a ten year period beginning in 1891. It provided access to Boulder from the rich mining and ranching operations located on the west side of the river. The design of this structure represents an accord between local citizens wanting to preserve some aspect of the original bridge, while providing a structure that could accommodate modern traffic needs. The new bridge represents the best of late 19th century and late 20th century technologies.*

### H Boulder Hot Springs
South of Boulder

*For centuries Native Americans have been coming to these pure, flowing hot water springs for rest and healing. Legend tells that they called this area Peace Valley. They agreed to lay down their weapons when they sojourned here, believing that the land and the waters were for everyone to share and could not be owned. In the 1860s prospector James Riley chanced upon the springs and filed a land and water rights claim. In 1864 he built a crude bathhouse and tavern. When Riley succumbed to smallpox in 1882, new owners built a small, more fashionable hotel. In 1891 it was remodeled and enlarged in the Queen Anne style and boasted fiftytwo rooms, electricity, facilities for invalids, a resident physician, gymnasium and various entertainments. Between 1910 and 1913, the present bathhouse, east wing and an addition at the west were built. The older building was also remodeled with raised parapets and a covering of stucco, creating a grand hotel in the present California Mission style. Opulent interior appointments included Tiffany glass lighting, beamed ceilings and hand-stenciled walls in the Arts and Crafts tradition. Under various names and owners, Boulder Hot Springs has catered to a widely varying clientele. Architecturally significant as vintage Queen Anne remodeled to a newer style, Boulder Hot Springs is the last vestige of the many large-scale hot spring retreats that provided respite and recreation to early Montanans.*

### T The Radon Health Mines of Boulder
Found in hills surrounding Boulder and Basin.

Montana is the radon capital of the United States, and the Boulder/Basin area is the radon capital of Montana. Each year thousands of people come to visit the radon health mines surrounding the towns of Boulder and Basin. Radon is an odorless, colorless, tasteless gas that results from the breakdown of uranium. What many spend large sums of money to get rid of, others are spending money to inhale. They flock here for relief from arthritis, emphysema, bursitis, cataracts, and any number of other ailments. Many of them have been coming for decades. They come from all over the world to find relief from what ails them by sitting in the mines. There are several mines in the hillsides surrounding these towns including the Merry Widow, the Free Enterprise, Radon Tunnel, Sunshine and Earth Angel. While there are several radium hot springs in the country, Montana is the only state that has underground radon mines.

*Radiation therapy in the Merry Widow Health Mine.*

### LF Boulder Hot Springs
31 S. Hot Springs Road, Hwy 69, Boulder.
225-4339, www.boulderhotsprings.com

Nestled in the foothills of Montana's snowpeaked Elkhorn Mountains is Peace Valley, home of Boulder Hot Springs. One of the last remaining grand hotels from the golden age of Montana's hot springs resorts is now a bed and breakfast and incredible views of the Boulder Valley. This historic landmark once catered to presidents and wealthy ranchers. The pools, indoor and outdoor, range from 95 to 104 degrees F. Thirty two springs throughout the hillside provide water for the facility which was established with the arrival of gold prospectors in the area in the 1860s. The resort has survived a series of ups and downs through the 20th century. In 1990, it was purchased by Anne Wilson-Schaef a highly respected and well-known psychologist in the field of addiction and recovery, who grew up a few miles from Boulder. She and her business partners have restored the hotel to its former glory and continue to make improvements to this wonderful alcohol and tobacco free Montana landmark.The hotel was built in 1888 and renovated in the summer of 1991. The spa buildings, dining room, and the east wing of the hotel have been completely refurbished. Boulder Hot Springs now offers a conference or retreat facility for large and small groups, bed and breakfast rooms, a weekly Sunday Buffet, along with swimming and soaking in the healing mineral laden geo-thermal waters. They offer a

### Montana Trivia

Excavation for the Placer Hotel in Helena yielded enough placer gold to pay for the cost of construction of the building.

healing, relaxing, and healthy non-smoking, non-alcohol environment for people seeking a place of peace, calm, and fun. The pools are open year round. Check for more information at www.boulderhotsprings.com.

## 28. *Historical Marker, Attraction, Food*

*Basin schoolhouse.*

### Basin

This town came into existence when two miners started a trading center to service the prospectors in the gold fields nearby. Many of the original buildings are still standing with the two story false fronts typical of western towns in the nineteenth century. The area is still well known for its radon mines which are reputed to offer health benefits to those exposed to the radiation inside them.

### H Mining Country

*This is about the center of a rich mining district extending from Butte to Helena. The mountains are spurs of the Continental Divide.*

*Ghost and active mining camps are to be found in almost every gulch. The ores yield gold, silver, copper, lead and zinc. The district has been producing since quartz mining came into favor following the first wave of placer mining in the 1860s. In those days placer deposits were the poor man's eldorado. They needed little more than a grub stake, a pick and a shovel to work them. Quartz properties, seldom rich at the surface, required machinery and capital, transportation and smelting facilities.*

*Before smelters were built in Montana, ore from some of the richest mines in this region was shipped by freight team, boat and rail to Swansea, Wales, and Freiburg, Germany, for treatment.*

### T Comet

I-15 Exit 160, near Basin

Many of the buildings are still standing. Like many of Montana's ghost towns Comet was once vandalized by treasure seekers who have spoiled much of the historic longevity of these wonderful buildings.

### T Merry Widow Mine

I-15 at Basin Exit

## 29.

### T Sheepshead Mountain Recreation Area

Hwy 15, 13 miles north of Butte

This is a wonderful recreational area primarily because it was designed to allow everyone enjoyment of nature regardless of physical challenges or age. Twelve years of effort created a fun place providing a variety of outdoor facilities, such as a volleyball court, softball field, horseshoe pits and a wheelchair-accessible fishing pier. A 4.5-mile trail is paved and ready for wheelchairs or rollerblades. The trail traverses grassy meadows cutting through a beautiful lodgepole pine forest and around Maney Lake.

## 30.

### T Diamond City

Diamond City, which emerged in Confederate Gulch on the east side of present day Canyon Ferry Lake, was the hub of the area's gold activity and became one of Montana Territory's most populated early communities. Its population once reached more than 10,000 but dwindled to 255 by 1870. Eventually it slid into obscurity leaving barely a trace.

Placer gold, remarkable for its incredible wealth, was discovered in the area by two former Confederate soldiers. The gravels here were among the richest washed anywhere in the world. Single pans were said to contain more than $1,000 of gold at a time when gold's worth was $20 an ounce. Most remarkable was that these gravels existed within only a two-acre area which by its end yielded over $16 million (over two and a half tons) of gold in 1860s standards of money. Weekend prospectors and some commercial placer miners still work the same areas in hopes of hitting paydirt.

Just like the ghost towns created by the gold rush era, evidence of much earlier activities can be found at various locations throughout the area. Ancient tepee rings, campsites, underground ovens, arrow heads and spear heads have been found throughout the region, some of which have been calculated to be 10,000 years old. A collection of such artifacts is displayed at the Broadwater County Museum in Townsend.

## 31. *Attraction*

### T Smith River State Park

16 miles northwest of White Sulphur Springs on Rte 360, then 7 miles north on county road. 454-5840

A 61-mile float trip down the remote Smith River Canyon provides outstanding scenery and excellent trout fishing. There are 27 boat camps along the river from the put-in point at Camp Baker to the take-out at Eden Bridge. In order to help preserve the unique wild quality of the Smith, a reservation and permit are required to float the river; call the number above for more details.

## 32.

### Marysville

Just north of Helena off Hwy. 279 you can find Marysville, which isn't quite deserted and some mining still goes on, but not like the days when the Drumlummon Mine was going strong during the 1880s and 1890s. The mine was named by an Irishman, Thomas Cruse, who named it after his birthplace in Ireland, once Montana's leading gold producer. It is estimated that over $50,000,000 in gold production came out of the town. Unique to the mining camp is the baseball field and bleachers that still stand. Many buildings still stand from the years when 3,000 people lived there.

### Canyon Creek

This town is the namesake of a nearby creek that flows to the Missouri River through a canyon.

## Section 8 Drives

**Elk Park**

Drive 1. From Butte, take Interstate 15 north to Helena to the Elk Park exit, turn left off the exit ramp and drive west on Forest Service Road #442 past Sheepshead Recreation Area for approximately ten miles where the road connects to Forest Service Road #82 and continue out to Interstate 15 at the Bernice interchange. The drive will take you down through an old mining area where you can view tailings from past mining operations. This drive will take approximately one and a half to two hours to complete. Passenger cars can travel this road during the summer.

Drive 2. Take Interstate 15 north to Helena, exit at Elk Park and continue on Forest Service Road #442 for six miles until it intersects with Forest Service Road #9485. Take #9485 approximately 15 miles where it will join Road #85 and return to Interstate 90 at the Rocker interchange. The drive will take approximately one and a half to two hours to complete. Passenger cars can travel this road during the summer.

**Canyon Ferry**

This tour starts in Helena and heads south on Hwy.. 12/287. The wide open meadows just before you reach Townsend are home to a herd of antelope that are visible practically anytime. Turn into Townsend on Hwy.. 12 and follow it through town and east until you reach Hwy.. 284. Turn here and follow the road along the eastern shore of the lake. Keep your eye open for St. Joseph's Canton Church and cemetery which is listed on the National Historic Register. Continue past the dam to York. There are several sapphire mines here. The Spokane Sapphire Mine is open seven days a week. If you wish to dig for gems, check first with the Helena Chamber of Commerce to make arrangements. As you leave York and cross the bridge on 280, watch the dramatic landscape change. Continue on back to Helena.

**Hogback Lookout**

While it's a bit of a drive to this spot, the breathtaking views are ample payback. From Nelson to the lookout, you will drive among 1,500-foot limestone cliffs and stark rock spires. The top gives you a 360° panorama. Take I-15 Exit 200 and go east for 5.2 miles. Turn right onto Lake Helena Drive at the stop sign where the roads join. Drive .4 miles to the Helena Causeway Fishing Access Site. Cross the causeway and drive for 1.8 miles to a left-hand turn. In a little less than 3 miles you will come to York Road. Turn left and drive about 3 miles to York Bridge across the Missouri. Go another 3 miles to the town of York. At York turn north to Nelson and drive about 15 miles to an open saddle, Indian Flats. This is the divide between the Trout Creek and Beaver Creek drainages. Go right at the saddle and continue about 3 miles to the Hogback mountain Lookout.

## Hikes

### Mount Helena

From the parking area of Mount Helena there are several hikes.

**1906 Trail**

The trail begins west of the parking lot. This is the most popular route to the summit, it passes close underneath Mt. Helena's limestone cliffs and "Devil's Kitchen." This trail has a gradual climb of 1.6 miles from the trailhead to the summit.

**The Prairie Trail**

This trail leaves the 1906 Trail to the right .3 miles from the parking lot. It is fairly level through meadows for .9 miles, then climbs with easy switchbacks for another .5 miles to Bitterroot

Meadows. From there you may hike left .1 mile to the Backside Trail and gain the summit by the Backside and Hogback Trails. From trailhead to summit via this route is 2.6 miles. Or you may continue left from the Bitterroot Meadows .2 miles to join the 1906 Trail to the summit. From trailhead to summit via this route is 2.2 miles.

**The Prospect Shafts Trail**
The trail begins south out of the parking lot with a fairly level grade for .5 miles to the picnic table near the charcoal kilns. From that point the trail begins to climb gradually through timber, followed by a steeper ridge climb for 1 mile to the junction of Backside and Hogback Trails. You may continue up the steep hogback to the summit another .3 miles or follow the Backside Trail to the junction of Prairie Trail at Bitterroot Meadows, .5 miles.

**The Backside Trail**
This interesting trail passes through a typically open and grassy woodland of ponderosa pine. Notice the pines at the trail's western end have a little fire-blackening at the base of their trunks. Quick burning grass fires happen often here, but these pines are well adapted to thrive in spite of them.

**The Hogback Trail**
This trail is more rough and rocky than the others. It leads from the peak of the mountain southward along the exposed Hogback Ridge. It is certainly more enjoyable descending it than going up, but any effort is rewarded with spectacular views in all directions, and the closest thing to a windswept alpine experience on this mountain.

**Mount Helena Ridge National Recreation Trail**
This trail leaves the Mount Helena Park trail system at Bitterroot Meadows and follows Mount Helena Ridge southwest on National Forest Lands providing many striking vistas to the east or west. The trail is approximately 6 miles long from the park border to the trailhead and parking lot at Park City near the head of Grizzly Gulch.

## Elkhorn Mountains

**Cottonwood Lake Trail #65**
Cottonwood Lake is located in the headwaters of Boulder Creek. The trail is an easy hike for two and a half miles to the lake. Fishing opportunities are fairly good with additional trails leading from the lake to Thunderbolt Mountain and toward Electric Peak.

From Butte, take Interstate 15 north to Helena and exit at Bernice. Drive west on Forest Service Road #82 toward Whitehouse campground. Turn right at Whitehouse campground onto Forest Service Road #65. Drive approximately three miles to the trailhead. The trailhead is not well marked, but the road ends in an open area. The trail is restricted to non-motorized use only.

**Trout Creek Canyon**
This is one of the more popular hikes in the Helena area. Take Hwy.. 280 northeast out of Helena past the small town of York to the Vigilante campground. This easy hike ascends only 800 feet over a distance of three miles. The hike takes you to some spectacular views of steep-walled limestone formations in the canyon. The trail mostly follows a segment of an old road that was washed out in 1981 by a spring flood.

**Missouri-Beaver Creek**
This 2.5 mile trail is a great family hike. Park at Hauser Dam just northeast of Helena and walk across the dam to the east side of the Missouri River. Follow the trail north to the Beaver Creek fishing access site. On the hike you will view some beautiful geologic formations. Bird and wildlife viewing is also excellent along this trail. Keep a watch out for rattlesnakes along the trail.

**Casey Meadows Trail**
This hike in the Elkhorn Mountains is a popular one for locals. Take I-15 south of Helena to Montana City. Turn right at the school and follow the road past Saddle Mountain Estates to Forest Road 294. The trailhead is here. This is an easy hike with a gradual elevation gain of about 1,300 feet on a three-mile walk to the meadows. This trail takes you through part of the 1988 Warm Springs Fire burn area.

## Elkhorn Mountains/Radersburg Area

Several hikes originate near here and connect with each other. The whole area in the Elkhorns surrounding Radersburg was heavily mined in the past and the mountains are laced with roads and trails. To get to Radersburg take Hwy.. 287 south of Townsend to the Toston/Radersburg turnoff. Head west to the little burg of Radersburg. Follow the road through town and follow it as it winds up the Crow Creek drainage. Along this road you will find the Eagle Creek Ranger Station and pick up the following trailheads. It's best to have a USGS map of the area to find the exact location of the trails.

**Eagle Creek Interpretive Trail**
This is a gentle four-mile loop that takes you past several old cabin sites along Eureka Creek.

**Trail 127**
This trail takes you to the South Fork Lakes. This two-mile hike will get you to some good fishing for rainbow and brook trout at the lakes.

**Trail 109**
This trail begins at the lower part of the Crow Creek Valley and follows the valley for nearly eight miles. You'll pass the old Crow Creek Power Dam here and excellent fishing along the way.

**Trail 112**
This trail begins above the Eagle guard Station and takes you 11 miles along the Longfellow Clear Creek and other drainages to the Tizer Basin. If you want to see wildlife, this is an excellent trail. Elk, mountain goats, bighorn sheep, black bears, and eagles are often seen here.

**Tizer-Poe Park Trail 110**
This is the shortest hike to the Tizer Basin covering only four miles. Wildflowers and wildlife are routine observances along this trail.

**Big Belts**
This is another heavily mined area laced with roads and trails. There are still several private claims along the banks of Confederate and Avalanche creeks.

**Edith Lake Trail 152**
This is the most popular hike in the Big Belts. Aside from the outstanding scenery along the way, it ends up and four small lakes which offer excellent fishing. Take highway 12 east out of Townsend approximately 12 miles to the North Fork Road turnoff. Follow this road northeast for about eight miles until the road turns south. Just after the bend is the trailhead. This four mile hike is well signed and leads to the central peak in the range.

**Skidway Trail 124**
This trail begins at the Skidway campground about 15 miles east of Townsend just off Hwy. 12. The trail is actually a road that takes you to the top of Grassy Mountain. Great wildlife viewing.

**Bear Gulch Trail 123**
This easy 4-mile hike follows Bear Gulch to Bear Meadows. The first mile is on an old Jeep trail. Take I-15 south of Helena to Exit 151. Go east about 100 yards and turn right on FR 8481. Follow this to the trail head.

## Other Hikes

**Meriwether Picnic Area: Vista Point Trail**
This is a short half mile trail that takes you to a great vista of the Missouri River. Take the Gates of the Mountains tour boat to Meriwether Picnic Area. The trail starts at the shelter and goes up Meriwether Canyon. Turn left immediately after the old Forest Service building. There is a sign indicating the start of Vista Point Trail. In a short distance the trail forks. The right side goes to the Mann Gulch Fires site and the left takes you to the Vista Point.

**Missouri River Canyon Trail 257 to Coulter Campground**
This is another trail taking off from the Meriwether Picnic Area. The trailhead starts behind the vault toilet just beyond the picnic shelter. The short hike takes you to views of the river and the spectacular limestone cliffs of the canyon.

**Refrigerator Canyon Trail 259**
Refrigerator Canyon gets its name from the abrupt drop in temperature as you enter the canyon. At certain points the narrow limestone canyon is only 10 feet wide in places while the walls tower almost 200 feet overhead. A "refrigerator" effect drops the temperature by 10 to 20 degrees when evaporative cooling from breezes that blow over the stream channel into the canyon. Take I-15 Exit 200 and go east for 5.2 miles. Turn right onto Lake Helena Drive at the stop sign where the roads join. Drive .4 miles to the Helena Causeway Fishing Access Site. Cross the causeway and drive for 1.8 miles to a left-hand turn. In a little less than 3 miles you will come to York Road. Turn left and drive about 3 miles to York Bridge across the Missouri. Go another 3 miles to the town of York. At York turn north to Nelson. At Nelson, go right (east) toward the Hogback Mountain Lookout. Drive about 5 miles to the trailhead which is clearly marked.

**Trout Creek Canyon Trail**
This is a magnificent hike into the Big Belt Mountains. The trail winds through a narrow canyon of yellow and gray limestone cliffs. The canyon walls are full of interesting rock configurations. Follow the directions to the Refrigerator Canyon trail. At York continue straight to the Vigilante Campground about 6 miles further. The trailhead starts at the upstream end of the parking lot or in the campground. The trail is not signed, but you'll know you're OK if you are following the creek.

**Missouri-Beaver Creek Trail**
This is a great family hike along the river. Don't be fooled by the rugged beginning of the trail. That's as bad as it gets. There are a lot of spur trails that take you down to the river. Take the I-15 Exit 200 and go east for 5.2 miles to a T intersection. Go left here toward Black Sandy State Park for 3 miles. Steer left just before the park entrance and go 1.5 miles to Hauser Dam. The trailhead is across the dam and immediately to the left.

## Cross-Country Ski Trails

### Helena National Forest

*For more information contact District Ranger, Helena, MT 59601. 449-5490*

**MacDonald Pass—15 mi. W Helena**
*4.5 km Easiest, 17 km More Difficult, 5.6 km Most Difficult; groomed*
Snowmobiles prohibited; parking capacity, 25 cars near MacDonald Pass.

*For more information on trails below contact District Ranger, Lincoln, MT 59639. 362-4265*

**Stemple Pass—37 mi. N Helena**
2 km Easiest, 20 km More Difficult, 10 km Most Difficult; no grooming. Parking for 40 cars.

**Maupin/Willard Cr—15 mi. SE Helena**
*4.5 km Easiest, some grooming.* Parking for 6 cars.

## Information Please

All Montana area codes are 406

### Road Information

Montana Road Condition Report
800-226-7623, 800-335-7592 or local 444-7696
Montana Highway Patrol 444-7696
**Local Road Reports**
Great Falls 453-1605
Statewide Weather Reports 453-2081

### Tourism Information

Travel Montana 800-847-4868 outside Montana
444-2654 in Montana.
http://travel.mt.gov/.
Gold West Country 846-1943 or 800-879-1159
Russell Country 761-5036 or 800-527-5348
Northern Rodeo Association 252-1122
**Chambers of Commerce**
Helena 442-4120
Townsend 266-3333

### Airports

Boulder 225-3552
Canyon Ferry 444-2506
Helena 442-2821
Townsend 266-4208

### Government Offices

State BLM Office 255-2885, 238-1540
Bureau of Land Management
Great Falls Field Office 791-7700
Butte Field Office 494-5059
Lewis & Clark National Forest 791-7700
Helena National Forest 449-5201
Beaverhead/Deerlodge National Forest
Butte 522-2520
Lee Metcalf National Wildlife Refuge 777-5552
Montana Fish, Wildlife & Parks 444-4720
U.S. Bureau of Reclamation
Helena Field Office 475-3310

### Hospitals

Shodair Hospital • Helena 444-7500
St Peter's Community Hosp. • Helena 442-2480
Broadwater Health Center • Townsend 266-3186

### Golf Courses

Fox Ridge Golf Course • Helena 227-8304
Bill Roberts Golf Course • Helena 442-2191

### Bed & Breakfasts

**Boulder Hot Springs** • Boulder 225-4339
**Canyon Ferry Mansion** • Townsend 266-3599
**Litening Barn B&B** • Townsend 266-3741
Appleton Inn B&B • Helena 449-7492
Barrister B&B • Helena 443-7330
Birdseye B&B • Helena 449-4380
Bungalow B&B • Wolf Creek 235-4276
Carolina B&B • Helena 495-8095
Castoria Motel B&B • Boulder 225-3549
Flyaway Ranch • Wolf Creek 235-4116
Grizzly Gulch B&B • Helena 495-9535
Missouri River Trout Lodge • Craig 235-4474
Missouri River Lodge • Wolf Creek 468-2224
Mountain Meadow Inn • Helena 443-7301
Sanders-Helena's B&B • Helena 442-3309

### Guest Ranches & Resorts

**Staubach Creek Ranch** • Winston 227-6918
**Rocking Z Guest Ranch** • Wolf Creek 458-3890
Battle Creek Ranch • Townsend 266-4426
Blacktail Ranch • Wolf Creek 235-4330
Flynn Ranch Vacations • Townsend 266-3534
Hidden Hollow Hideaway • Townsend 266-3322
Merry Widow & Health Mine • Basin 225-3220
Sunshine Health Mine Resort•Boulder 225-3670
Lakeside Resort & Marina • Helena 227-6076
Yacht Basin Marina • Helena 475-3440
Holter Lake Lodge • Wolf Creek 235-4331

### Vacation Homes & Cabins

**Canyon Ferry Mansion** • Townsend 266-3599
Alta Vista Lodge • Helena 443-5359
Boarding House Overniter • Marysville 449-0854
End of the Line Retreat • Craig 468-9111
Helena Accommodations • Helena 449-4812
Ingersoll Ranch • Wolf Creek 235-4395
Little Blackfoot River Retreat • Helena 442-3045
Mona's Place • Wolf Point 235-4370
Mountain Stream Loft • Helena 449-4322
River View Guest House • Craig 468-3074
Springhill Studio • Helena 443-4817

### Forest Service Cabins

*Helena National Forest*

**Bar Gulch Cabin**
24 mi. NE of Helena. 266-3425
Capacity: 6 Nightly fee: $20
All year (max stay 5 nights)
Barrier-free parking area, cabin entry, and toilet. Road access to cabin most of year. Winter distance varies with snow conditions and may require ski or snowmobile access last 3.5 miles.

**Eagle Guard Station**
14 mi. W of Townsend. 266-3425
Capacity: 6 Nightly fee: $20
Available: 12/2 - 5/15
Last 4 mi. not open to motorized vehicles. 2 night min. on holiday weekends.

**Indian Flats Cabin**
40 mi. NE of Helena. 449-5490
Capacity: 4 Nightly fee: $25
Available: All year (max. stay 5 nights)
Access in winter by cross-country skis or snowmobile last 7 miles. Access mlay be restricted during spring breakup.

**Strawberry Cabin**
18 mi. SW of Helena 449-5490
Capacity: 2 Nightly fee: $25
Available: 12/1 - 3/31 (max stay 5 nights)
Road access plowed to within 2-3/4 mi. of cabin. Last 3/4 mi. not open to motorized vehicles.

**Thompson Guard Station**
27 mi. NE of Townsend; 17 mi. W of White Sulphur Springs 266-3425
Capacity: 6 Nightly fee: $25
Available: All year (max stay 5 nights)
Drive to cabin in summer (approx. 6/1 - 9/15); trails and high mtn. lakes nearby; corral available. Winter access varies, but best from White Sulphur Springs with 4WD, to within 3 mi., then ski or snowmobile to cabin.

**Kading Cabin**
40 mi. SW of Helena 449-5490
Capacity: 4 Nightly fee: $25 Available: All year, except 4/15 to 6/1 (Max stay 5 nights)
Access via Little Blackfoot Road at Elliston. Road plowed within 7 miles of cabin. Access may by restricted during spring breakup.

### Private Campgrounds

Alhambra RV Park • Clancy 993-8020
Branding Iron • Helena 443-9703
Buzz In RV & Campground • E. Helena 227-9002
Canyon Ferry RV Park • Helena 458-4714
High Ore Health Mine• Boulder 225-3754
RC RV Park • Boulder 225-9122
Sunset Trailer Court • Boulder 225-3387
Free Enterprise Health Mine • Boulder 225-3383
H & C RV Campground • Helena 458-6390
Helena Campground • Helena 458-4714
Kim's Marina RV Park • Helena 475-3723
Lakeside Resort & Marina • Helena 227-6076
Lincoln Road RV Park • Helena 458-3725
Merry Widow Health Mine • Basin 225-3220
Verns Canyon Ferry RV Park • Helena 475-3811
Goose Bay Marina • Townsend 266-3645
Roadrunner RV Park • Townsend 266-9900
Silo's RV Park • Townsend 266-3100

### Car Rental

Avis Rent-A-Car 442-4440
Cents-ible Rent-a-Car 443-7436
Enterprise Rent-A-Car 449-3400
Hertz Rent-A-Car 449-4167
National Car Rental 442-8620
Rent A Wreck 443-3635

### Outfitters & Guides

*F=Fishing H=Hunting R=River Guides*
*E=Horseback Rides G=General Guide Services*

| | | |
|---|---|---|
| Big Sky Expeditions | F | 442-2630 |
| Big Sky Horse Leasing | E | 266-3285 |
| Blacktail Ranch | HFE | 235-4428 |
| Elk Ridge Outfitters | GHFER | 227-6625 |
| E.W. Watson & Sons Outfitting | FEH | 266-3741 |
| Four Seasons Outfitting | G | 458-5257 |
| Holter Lake Lodge | G | 235-4331 |
| John Maki Outfitters | HF | 442-6129 |
| Lewis & Clark Expeditions | F | 449-4632 |
| Missouri River Lodge | F | 468-2224 |
| Missouri River Trout Shop | F | 235-4474 |
| Montana Fly Goods | F | 442-2630 |
| Montana River Anglers | F | 261-2033 |
| Montana River Outfitters | R | 235-4350 |
| Wild West Outfitters | HFE | 439-3030 |
| Paul Roos Outfitters | GF | 442-5489 |
| Shining Times Outfittings | H | 266-3882 |
| Top Rod River Expeditions | EFR | 266-3741 |
| McDonough Outfitters | HFE | 235-4428 |
| Wolf Creek Guide Service | F | 442-5148 |

### Cross Country Ski Centers

Maupin Willard Trail Center
20 mi. SE of Helena 443-5360

## Public Campgrounds

### Campsite Directions

| Campsite / Directions | Season | Camping | Trailers | Toilets | Water | Boat Launch | Fishing | Swimming | Trails | Stay Limit | Fee |
|---|---|---|---|---|---|---|---|---|---|---|---|
| **171•Holter Lake BLM**<br>3 mi. N of Wolf Creek on Rec. Rd.•across bridge•3 mi. E on Cty. Rd. | All Year | 50 | 35′ | • | • | C | • | • | | 14 | • |
| **172•Coulter FS**<br>20 mi. N of Helena on Missouri River•4 mi. by boat | 6/1-9/15 | • | | • | 0 | | • | | • | 14 | • |
| **173•Log Gulch BLM**<br>Holter Lake•3 mi. N of Wolf Creek on Rec. Rd.•across bridge•7 mi. SE on Cty. Rd. | All Year | 80 | • | • | • | C | 0 | | | 14 | • |
| **174•Departure Point BLM**<br>Holter Lake•3 mi. N of Wolf Creek on Rec. Rd.•8 mi. SE on Cty. Rd. | All Year | 10 | 50′ | • | | A | • | | | 14 | • |
| **175•Hauser Lake/Black Sandy Beach FWP**<br>7 mi. N of Helena on I-15 to Lincoln Rd. Exit•4 mi. E on Rt. 453•3 mi. N | All Year | 30 | • | D | • | C | • | • | | 7 | • |
| **176•Vigilante FS**<br>20 mi. NE of Helena on Rt. 280•12 mi. NE on Cty. Rd. | 5/15-9/10 | 22 | • | D | • | | | | • | 14 | • |
| **177•Cromwell Dixon FS**<br>15 mi. W of Helena on US 12 | 6/1-9/15 | 15 | • | • | • | | | | | 19 | • |
| **178•Moose Creek FS**<br>10 mi. W of Helena on US 12•4 mi. SW on Rimini Rd. | 6/15-9/15 | 10 | • | • | • | | | | • | 14 | • |
| **179•Park Lake FS**<br>1 mi. N of Clancy on Cty. Rd.•8 mi. W on Cty. Rd.•6 mi. W on Forest Rd. 4009 | 6/15-9/15 | 22 | • | • | • | A | • | | | 14 | • |
| **180•Kading FS**<br>1 mi. E of Elliston on US 12•4 mi. S on Cty. Rd.•9 mi. SW on Forest Rd. 227 | 6/1-9/15 | 14 | • | • | • | | • | | • | 14 | |
| **181•Orofino FS**<br>13 mi. SE of Deer Lodge on Forest Rd.82 | 5/25-9/15 | 10 | 22′ | • | • | | | | | 16 | |
| **182•Basin Canyon FS**<br>5 mi. NW of Basin on Forest Rd. 172 | 5//25-9/15 | 2 | 16′ | • | | | | | | 16 | |
| **183•Whitehouse FS**<br>4 mi. W of Basin on I-15•8 mi. W on Forest Rd. 82 | 5/25-12/1 | 5 | 22′ | • | • | | • | | • | 16 | |
| **184•Ladysmith FS**<br>4 mi. W of Basin on I-15•4 mi. W on Forest Rd. 82 | 5/25-12/1 | 6 | 16′ | • | | | | | | 16 | |
| **185•Mormon Creek FS**<br>4 mi. W of Basin on I-15•2 mi. W on Forest Rd. 82 | 5/25-12/1 | 16 | 16′ | • | | | | | | 16 | |
| **186•Lowland FS**<br>8 mi. NE of Butte on I-15•8 mi. W on Forest Rd. 442•2 mi. S on Forest Rd. 9485 | 5/15-9/15 | 11 | 22′ | D | • | | | | | 16 | • |
| **187•Indian Road USBR**<br>1 mi. N of Townsend on US 287•Milepost 75 | All Year | 25 | • | • | • | C | • | | | 14 | • |
| **188•Toston Dam BLM**<br>13 mi. S of Townsend on US 287•E to Toston Dam | All Year | 10 | 24′ | • | | C | • | | | 14 | |
| **189•Skidway FS**<br>23 mi. E of Townsend on US 12•2 mi. S on Forest Rd. 4042 | 6/1-10/1 | 11 | • | • | • | | • | | • | 14 | |
| **190•CANYON FERRY RESERVOIR•Riverside BLM**<br>Canyon Ferry•9 mi. E of Helena on US 287•9 mi. NE on Rt. 284<br>•1 mi. NW on Forest Rd. toward power plant | All Year | 34 | • | D | • | C | • | | | 14 | • |
| **191•CANYON FERRY RESERVOIR BLM•Court Sherriff BLM**<br>Canyon Ferry•9 mi.E of Helena on US 287•9 mi. NE on Rt. 284 | All Year | 65 | • | Df | • | B | • | • | | 14 | • |
| **192•CANYON FERRY RESERVOIR•Chinaman's Gulch BLM**<br>Canyon Ferry•9 mi. E of Helena on US 287•10 mi. NE on Rt. 284 | All Year | 40 | • | D | • | B | • | • | | 14 | • |
| **193•CANYON FERRY RESERVOIR•Jo Bonner BLM**<br>Canyon Ferry•9 mi. E of Helena on US 287•12 mi. NE on Rt. 284 | All Year | 12 | • | D | • | B | • | | | 14 | • |
| **194•CANYON FERRY RESERVOIR BLM•Hellgate BLM**<br>Canyon Ferry•9 mi. E of Helena on US 287•18 mi. NE on Rt. 284 | All Year | 130 | • | D | • | C | • | • | | 14 | • |
| **195•CANYON FERRY RESERVOIR BLM•White Earth BLM•**<br>13 mi.N of Townsend on US 287 to Winston•5 mi. E on Cty. RD. | All Year | 40 | • | D | • | C | • | | | 14 | • |

**Agency**
FS—U.S.D.A Forest Service
FWP—Montana Fish, Wildlife & Parks
NPS—National Park Service
BLM—U.S. Bureau of Land Management
USBR—U.S. Bureau of Reclamation
CE—Corps of Engineers

**Camping**
Camping is allowed at this site. Number indicates camping spaces available
H—Hard sided units only; no tents

**Trailers**
Trailer units allowed. Number indicates maximum length.

**Toilets**
Toilets on site. D—Disabled access

**Water**
Drinkable water on site

**Fishing**
Visitors may fish on site

**Boat**
Type of boat ramp on site:
A—Hand launch
B—4-wheel drive with trailer
C—2-wheel drive with trailer

**Swimming**
Designated swimming areas on site

**Trails**
Trails on site
B—Backpacking N—Nature/Interpretive

**Stay Limit**
Maximum length of stay in days

**Fee**
Camping and/or day-use fee

## Public Campgrounds

### Campsite Directions

| Campsite Directions | Season | Camping | Trailers | Toilets | Water | Boat Launch | Fishing | Swimming | Trails | Stay Limit | Fee |
|---|---|---|---|---|---|---|---|---|---|---|---|
| **196•CANYON FERRY RESERVOIR BLM•Silos BLM**<br>Canyon Ferry•7 mi. N of Townsend on US• 287•Milepost 70•1 mi. E on Cty. Rd. | All Year | 80 | • | D | • | C | • | | | 14 | • |
| **197•CANYON FERRY RESERVOIR BLM•Indian Road BLM**<br>Canyon Ferry•1 mi. N of Townsend on US 287 at Milepost 75 | All Year | 15 | • | D | | B | • | | | 14 | |

## Fishery

| Fishery | Cold Water Species | | | | | | | | | | | | Warm Water Species | | | | | | | | | | Services | | | | | |
|---|---|---|---|---|---|---|---|---|---|---|---|---|---|---|---|---|---|---|---|---|---|---|---|---|---|---|---|---|
| | Brook Trout | Mt. Whitefish | Lake Whitefish | Golden Trout | Cutthroat Trout | Brown Trout | Rainbow Trout | Kokanee Salmon | Bull Trout | Lake Trout | Arctic Grayling | Burbot | Largemouth Bass | Smallmouth Bass | Walleye | Sauger | Northern Pike | Shovelnose Sturgeon | Channel Catfish | Yellow Perch | Crappie | Paddlefish | Vehicle Access | Campgrounds | Toilets | Docks | Boat Ramps | MotorRestrictions |
| 114. Missouri River | • | • | | | • | • | • | | | | | | | | | | | | | | | | • | • | • | | • | • |
| 115. Little Prickly Pear Creek | • | • | | | | • | • | | | | | | | | | | | | | | | | • | • | • | | | |
| 116. Holter Lake | | | | | | • | • | • | | | | | | | • | | | | | • | | | • | • | • | • | • | |
| 117. Beaver Creek | | | | | | • | • | | | | | | | | | | | | | | | | • | • | • | | | |
| 118. Hauser Lake | | | | | | | • | • | | | | | | | | | | | | • | | | • | • | • | • | • | |
| 119. Helena Valley Regulating Res. | | | | | | | | • | | | | | | | | | | | | | | | • | | • | | • | • |
| 120. Park Lake | | | | | • | | | | | | • | | | | | | | | | | | | • | • | • | | | • |
| 121. Prickly Pear Creek | • | | | | | • | • | | | | | | | | | | | | | | | | | | | | | |
| 122. Boulder River | • | | | | | • | • | | | | | | | | | | | | | | | | | | | | | |
| 123. Elkhorn Mtns alpine lakes | • | | | | • | • | | | | | | | | | | | | | | | | | | | | | | |
| 124. Crow Creek | • | | | | | | • | | | | | | | | | | | | | | | | | | | | | |
| 125. Canyon Ferry Lake | | | | | | • | • | | | | | • | | | | | | | | • | | | • | • | • | • | • | |
| 126. Missouri River | • | • | | | • | • | • | | | | | | | | | | | | | | | | • | • | • | | • | • |
| 127. Hound Creek | | • | | | | • | • | | | | | | | | | | | | | | | | • | • | • | | | |
| 128. Sheep Creek | • | • | | | | • | • | | | | | | | | | | | | | | | | • | • | • | | | |
| 129. Smith River | • | • | | | | • | • | | | | | • | | | | | | | | | | | • | • | • | | • | • |
| 130. Spring Meadow Lake | | | | | | | | | | | | | • | | | | | | | • | | | • | | | | | |

**Notes:**

Section 8

## Dining Quick Reference

Price Range refers to the average cost of a meal per person: ($) $1-$6, ($$) $7-$11, ($$$) $12-up. Cocktails: "Yes" indicates full bar; Beer (B)/Wine (W), Service: Breakfast (B), Brunch (BR), Lunch (L), Dinner (D). Businesses in bold print will have additional information under the appropriate map locator number in the body of this section.

| RESTAURANT | TYPE CUISINE | PRICE RANGE | CHILD MENU | COCKTAILS BEER WINE | SERVICE | CREDIT CARDS | MAP LOCATOR NUMBER |
|---|---|---|---|---|---|---|---|
| Bunkhouse Bar & Cafe | American | $ | | Yes | L/D | V/M | 2 |
| Broadwater Creamery | Family/Ice Cream | $ | | | B/L/D | Major | 2 |
| Full Belli Deli | Deli | $ | | | L/D | | 2 |
| Horseshoe Cafe | Family | $ | Yes | B/W | B/L/D | Major | 2 |
| Jasper's Pizza & Pub | Family | $ | Yes | B/W | L/D | | 2 |
| **The Mint** | Steakhouse | $/$$ | Yes | Yes | B/L/D | V/M | 2 |
| **Townsend A&W** | Fast Food | $ | Yes | | L/D | | 2 |
| **Silos Inn** | Family | $$/$$$ | Yes | Yes | L/D | V/M | 3 |
| Winston Bar | Fast Food | $ | | Yes | L/D | | 3 |
| 14 West Restaurant | American | | | | | | 5 |
| A & W Family Restaurant | Fast Food | $ | Yes | | L/D | | 5 |
| Ali's Pizza & Pasta | Pizza | $ | | B/W | L/D | | 5 |
| Brino's Diner | Family | | | | | | 5 |
| Burger King | Fast Food | $ | Yes | | B/L/D | | 6 |
| Hot Stuff Pizza/Smash Hit Subs | Fast Food | $ | Yes | | B/L/D | | 6 |
| Howard's Pizza | Pizza | $/$$ | | | D | | 6 |
| Stageline Pizza | Pizza | $/$$ | | | L/D | | 6 |
| Subway | Fast Food | $ | Yes | | L/D | | 6 |
| Town Pump Conoco | Fast Food | $ | | | B/L/D | Major | 6 |
| J B'S Restaurant | Family | $ | Yes | | B/L/D | V/M | 7 |
| Taco Bell | Fast Food | $ | Yes | | L/D | | 7 |
| Dairy Queen | Fast Food | $ | Yes | | L/D | | 7 |
| Big Cheese Pizza | Pizza | $/$$ | | | L/D | | 7 |
| Frontier Pies Restaurant | Family | $/$$ | Yes | | B/L/D | Major | 7 |
| Pizza Hut | Pizza | $/$$ | Yes | B | L/D | V/M/D | 7 |
| Subway | Fast Food | $ | Yes | | L/D | | 7 |
| Dragon Wall Chinese Buffet | Chinese | $/$$ | | | L/D | | 7 |
| Bulls Eye Restaurant | American | $$ | | Yes | L/D | Major | 7 |
| Kentucky Fried Chicken/A&W | Fast Food | $ | Yes | | L/D | | 7 |
| Taco Treat | Fast Food | $ | Yes | | L/D | | 7 |
| Patrick's Paddock Irish Pub & Eatery | American | $ | | Yes | L/D | V/M | 7 |
| Village Inn Pizza | Pizza | $/$$ | Yes | B | L/D | V/M | 7 |
| Wendy's | Fast Food | $ | Yes | | L/D | | 7 |
| McDonald's | Fast Food | $ | Yes | | B/L/D | | 7 |
| Country Harvest Buffet | Buffet | $ | Yes | | B/L/D | V/M | 7 |
| Burger King | Fast Food | $ | Yes | | B/L/D | | 7 |
| **Colonial Restaurant** | American | $$/$$$ | Yes | Yes | B/L/D | Major | 8 |
| **Planet Gyros** | Greek | $ | | | L/D | | 8 |
| Papa John's Pizza | Pizza | $ | Yes | | L/D | | 8 |
| L&D Chinese Buffet | Chinese | $$ | | | L/D | | 8 |
| Café Montana | American | $$ | | | L/D | | 8 |
| Overland Express | American | $$ | Yes | Yes | B/L/D | Major | 8 |
| Dragon Seed Restaurant | Chinese | $$ | Yes | B/W | L/D | V/M/D | 8 |
| Lucky Lil's Restaurant | American | $$ | Yes | Yes | B/L/D | Major | 8 |
| Bob's Pizza | Fast Food | $ | Yes | | L/D | | 8 |
| Mrs. Powells Cinnamon Rolls | Bakery | $ | | | B/L/D | | 8 |
| Orange Julius | Fast Food | $ | Yes | | B/L/D | | 8 |
| Taco John's | Fast Food | $ | Yes | | L/D | | 8 |
| Last Chance Restaurant | American | $$ | Yes | Yes | B/L/D | Major | 9 |
| The Bagel Company | Deli | $ | | | B/L | | 9 |
| Donut Hole | Bakery | $ | | | B | | 10 |
| Sleeping Giant Brew Pub | Casual Brew Pub | $$/$$$ | Yes | W/B | L/D | Major | 10 |
| Arctic Circle | Fast Food | $ | Yes | | L/D | | 10 |
| **Mother Lode Restaurant & Sports Bar** | American | $ | | Yes | L/D | V/ M | 11 |
| Pizza Hut | Pizza | $/$$ | Yes | B | L/D | V/M/D | 11 |
| Perkins Family Restaurant | Family | $/$$ | Yes | | B/L/D | Major | 11 |
| Subway Sandwiches | fast food | $ | Yes | | L/D | | 11 |
| **Jade Garden Restaurant** | Chinese | $$ | | | L/D | Major | 12 |
| **Godfather's Pizza** | Pizza | $ | Yes | B | L/D | V/M/D | 12 |
| **MacKenzie River Pizza** | Pizza | $$ | Yes | B/W | L/D | Major | 12 |
| Grub Stake | Family | $$ | | Yes | B/L/D | | 12 |

## Dining Quick Reference-Continued

Price Range refers to the average cost of a meal per person: ($) $1-$6, ($$) $7-$11, ($$$) $12-up. Cocktails: "Yes" indicates full bar; Beer (B)/Wine (W), Service: Breakfast (B), Brunch (BR), Lunch (L), Dinner (D). Businesses in bold print will have additional information under the appropriate map locator number in the body of this section.

| RESTAURANT | TYPE CUISINE | PRICE RANGE | CHILD MENU | COCKTAILS BEER WINE | SERVICE | CREDIT CARDS | MAP LOCATOR NUMBER |
|---|---|---|---|---|---|---|---|
| Taco John's | Fast Food/ Mexican | $ | Yes | | L/D | | 12 |
| Applebee's Neighborhood Grill | Eclectic | $$/$$$ | Yes | Yes | L/D | Major | 12 |
| River Grille The | Steak/Seafood | $$/$$$ | | Yes | D | Major | 12 |
| Steffano's Pizza & Subs | Pizza | $/$$ | Yes | | L/D | V/M | 12 |
| Whistle Stop Family Restaurant | Family | $ | Yes | Yes | B/L/D | V/M | 12 |
| Chili O'Brien's Cafe | Sandwiches | $$ | | Yes | B/L/D | V/M | 12 |
| Suds Hut | Family | $ | Yes | B/W | B/L/D | Major | 12 |
| House of Wong | Chinese | $$ | | B/W | L/D | V/M | 12 |
| Arby's | Fast Food | $ | Yes | | B/L/D | | 12 |
| Taco Bell | Fast Food | $ | Yes | | L/D | | 12 |
| Dairy Queen | Fast Food | $ | Yes | | L/D | | 12 |
| McDonald's | Fast Food | $ | Yes | | B/L/D | | 12 |
| Pizza Hut | Pizza | $/$$ | Yes | B | L/D | V/M/D | 13 |
| Ming's Chinese Kitchen | Chinese | $$ | | | L/D | V/M | 13 |
| Hardee's | Fast Food | $ | Yes | | B/L/D | | 13 |
| Emiliano's Mexican Food | Mexican | $$ | | | L/D | | 13 |
| Montana Nugget | American | $$ | | Yes | L/D | Major | 13 |
| Boomer's Sports Pub | American | $/$$ | | Yes | L/D | V/M | 13 |
| Wong's Chinese Kitchen | Chinese | $$ | | | L/D | | 13 |
| Bullwinkle's Saloon | American | $ | | B/W | B/L/D | V/M | 13 |
| Moose Magoo's Steaks & Seafood | Steakhouse | $$/$$$ | | B/W | L/D | Major | 13 |
| **Stonehouse Restaurant** | Fine Dining | $$$ | Yes | Yes | D | Major | 14 |
| **Salvatore's Trattoria** | Italian | $$/$$$ | | | L/D | | 14 |
| **Last Chance Casino** | American | $/$$ | | Yes | B/L/D | V/M | 14 |
| Wall Street Lunch Cafe | Sandwich | $/$$ | | | L | | 14 |
| Brewhouse Pub & Grill | American | $$/$$$ | | BW | L/D | Major | 14 |
| Benny's | Deli | $ | | | B/L | | 14 |
| Morning Light | Coffee House | $ | | | | | 14 |
| Big Al's Deli | Deli | $ | | | L | | 14 |
| Flicker's Coffee House | Coffee House | $ | | | B/L | | 14 |
| Bullwhackers Western Grill | American | $ | Yes | | B/L | | 14 |
| Coney Island | Coney Island | $ | Yes | | L/D | | 14 |
| Bert & Ernie's Saloon | Family Fine Dining | $/$$ | Yes | B/W | L/D | Major | 14 |
| Toi's Thai Cuisine | Thai | $$ | | | D | V/M | 14 |
| Rialto Grill | American | | | | | | 14 |
| Windbag Saloon | Steaks & Seafood | $$ | | B/W | L/D | Major | 14 |
| Miller's Crossing | Pub | $$ | | Yes | L/D | V/M | 14 |
| Riley's Bar & Restaurant | American | $$ | | Yes | L/D | Major | 15 |
| Lakeside Resort & Marina | American | $$/$$$ | | | | | 15 |
| **Oasis Family Restaurant** | Family | $$ | | Yes | B/L/D | V/M | 17 |
| Hookers Grill | American | | | Yes | L/D | Major | 17 |
| The Frenchman & Me | Family | $/$$$ | | Yes | B/L/D | | 17 |
| Holter Lake Lodge | Fine Dining | $/$$$ | Yes | Yes | B/L/D | V/M | 17 |
| Stoner's Last Chance Saloon | Fast Food | $ | | Yes | L/D | | 22 |
| **Montana City Grill & Saloon** | Family | $$/$$$ | Yes | Yes | B/L/D | Major | 23 |
| Jackson Creek Saloon | American | $ | | Yes | L/D | | 23 |
| Papa Ray's Casino & Pizzeria | Pizza | $ | | Yes | L/D | V/M | 23 |
| Legal Tender Restaurant | Family | $$ | Yes | Yes | D | Major | 24 |
| Singletree Saloon & Steakhouse | Steakhouse | $$/$$$ | | Yes | L/D | Major | 24 |
| Dairy Queen | Fast Food | $ | Yes | | L/D | | 27 |
| Mountain Good Restaurant | American | $/$$ | Yes | | B/L/D | | 27 |
| Phil & Tim's Cafe | American | $ | | Yes | L/D | | 27 |
| Pizza Parlor | Pizza | $/$$ | Yes | | L/D | | 27 |
| Leaning Tower of Pizza | Pizza | $$ | | | L/D | | 28 |

## Motel Quick Reference

Price Range: ($) Under $40 ; ($$) $40-$60; ($$$) $60-$80, ($$$$) Over $80. Pets [check with the motel for specific policies] (P), Dining (D), Lounge (L), Disabled Access (DA), Full Breakfast (FB), Cont. Breakfast (CB), Indoor Pool (IP), Outdoor Pool (OP), Hot Tub (HT), Sauna (S), Refrigerator (R), Microwave (M) (Microwave and Refrigerator indicated only if in majority of rooms), Kitchenette (K). All Montana area codes are 406.

| HOTEL | PHONE | NUMBER ROOMS | PRICE RANGE | BREAKFAST | POOL/ HOT TUB SAUNA | NON SMOKE ROOMS | OTHER AMENITIES | CREDIT CARDS | MAP LOCATOR NUMBER |
|---|---|---|---|---|---|---|---|---|---|
| **Canyon Ferry Mansion B&B** | 266-3599 | | | | | | | | 2 |
| **Litening Barn B&B** | 266-4554 | | | | | | | | 2 |
| Lake Townsend Motel | 266-3461 | 13 | $$ | | HT | Yes | K/P | Major | 2 |
| Mustang Motel | 266-3491 | 22 | $$ | | | Yes | P/M/R/DA | Major | 2 |
| **Days Inn Helena** | 442-3280 | 93 | $$ | FB | HT/S | Yes | FB/P/DA | Major | 7 |
| **Shilo Inn** | 442-0320 | 47 | $$$ | CB | IP/HT/S | Yes | K/P/M/R/DA | Major | 7 |
| Holiday Inn Express | 449-4000 | 75 | $$ | CB | IP | Yes | DA | Major | 7 |
| Comfort Inn | 443-1000 | 56 | $$ | CB | IP/HT/S | Yes | P/M/R/DA | Major | 7 |
| Motel 6 | 442-9990 | 80 | $$ | | OP | Yes | P/DA | Major | 7 |
| **Fairfield Inn** | 449-9944 | 60 | $$$/$$$$ | CB | IP/HT | Yes | M/R/DA | Major | 8 |
| **Helena's Country Inn & Suites** | 443-2300 | 70 | $$/$$$ | CB | IP/HT/S | Yes | P/D/L/M/R | Major | 8 |
| Super 8 Motel | 443-2450 | 102 | $$ | CB | | Yes | P/M/R/DA | Major | 8 |
| **WestCoast Colonial Inn** | 443-2100 | 149 | $$$$ | | IP/OP/HT/S | Yes | P/D/L/DA | Major | 8 |
| Helena Inn | 442-6080 | 69 | $$ | CB | OP/S | Yes | K/P/M/R/DA | Major | 9 |
| **Knights Rest Motel** | 442-6384 | 12 | $ | CB | | Yes | M/R | Major | 13 |
| **Lamplighter Motel** | 442-9200 | 16 | $/$$ | | | Yes | K/M/R/DA | Major | 14 |
| Holiday Inn Hotel Downtown | 443-2200 | 71 | $$$$ | | IP | Yes | D/M/R/L/DA | Major | 14 |
| Budget Inn Express | 442-0600 | 47 | $/$$ | | HT | Yes | K/P/M/R | Major | 14 |
| Lakeside Resort & Marina | 227-6413 | | | | | | | | 15 |
| Kim's Marina & RV Resort | 475-3723 | 5 | $$ | | | | K | Major | 15 |
| Holter Lake Lodge | 235-4331 | 12 | $$ | | | | D | V/M | 17 |
| Frenchy's Motel | 235-4251 | 12 | $ | | | | | V/M | 17 |
| The Fly Shop Motel & Cabins | 235-0244 | 8 | $$ | | | | | Major | 17 |
| Last Chance Motel | 492-7250 | 4 | $ | | | | | V/M | 22 |
| **Elkhorn Mountain Inn** | 442-6625 | 22 | $$ | CB | | Yes | P/R/DA | Major | 23 |
| **Boulder Hot Springs** | 225-4339 | 7 | $$$$ | FB | OP/HT | Yes | BB/PB | V/M | 27 |
| Merry Widow Health Mine | 225-3220 | 26 | $ | | | | DA/P | Major | 27 |
| O-Z Motel | 225-3364 | 9 | $ | | | Yes | K/P | V/M | 27 |

**NOTES:**

# SECTION 9

## WHITE SULPHUR SPRINGS, LEWISTOWN, ROUNDUP AND MUSSELSHELL RIVER VALLEY

The Big Open.

### WEATHER AVERAGES

**Lewistown**

| | |
|---|---|
| January | |
| Average High: | 29.4° F |
| Average Low: | 7.5° F |
| Average Precip.: | 0.77 in |
| April | |
| Average High: | 52.1° F |
| Average Low: | 28.1° F |
| Average Precip.: | 1.16 in |
| July | |
| Average High: | 80.8° F |
| Average Low: | 49.8° F |
| Average Precip.: | 1.79 in |
| October | |
| Average High: | 57.9° F |
| Average Low: | 31.8° F |
| Average Precip.: | 1.12 in |

**Harlowton**

| | |
|---|---|
| January | |
| Average High: | 30.8° F |
| Average Low: | 10.6° F |
| Average Precip.: | 0.77 in |
| April | |
| Average High: | 52.6° F |
| Average Low: | 27.7° F |
| Average Precip.: | 1.19 in |
| July | |
| Average High: | 81.1° F |
| Average Low: | 48.3° F |
| Average Precip.: | 1.47 in |
| October | |
| Average High: | 56.9° F |
| Average Low: | 30.6° F |
| Average Precip.: | 1.05 in |

**Showdown Ski Area**

| | |
|---|---|
| January | |
| Average High: | 30.8° F |
| Average Low: | 10.6° F |
| Average Precip.: | 0.53 in |
| April | |
| Average High: | 52.6° F |
| Average Low: | 27.7° F |
| Average Precip.: | 1.16 in |
| July | |
| Average High: | 81.1° F |
| Average Low: | 48.3° F |
| Average Precip.: | 1.74 in |
| October | |
| Average High: | 56.9° F |
| Average Low: | 30.6° F |
| Average Precip.: | 0.83 in |

**1.** *Gas, Food*

### Ingomar

Upon completion of the Milwaukee Railroad in 1910, Ingomar became the hub of commerce in an area bounded by the Missouri River to the north, the Musselshell River to the west and the Yellowstone River to the south and east. Ingomar was an ideal location for a railhead and shipping center for the thousands of acres between the Yellowstone and the Missouri Rivers. The town site was platted in 1910 by the railroad and named by railroad officials. The depot was completed in 1911.

Contributing to the growth of the area north to the Missouri and south to the Yellowstone was the Homestead Act of 1862, later amended to give settlers 320 acres of land which, if proved up in 5 years, became their own. The railroad advertised the area as "Freeland" and was responsible for bringing settlers into the area.

Ingomar was also the sheep shearing center to the migratory sheep men using the free spring, summer and fall grass. Ingomar became the site of the world's largest sheep shearing and wool shipping point. Two million pounds of wool a year were shipped from Ingomar during the peak years. Shearing pens in Perth, Australia, were designed using the Ingomar pens as a model. Wool was stored in the wool warehouse located adjacent to the shearing pens, and shipped out by rail through 1975, when the wool warehouse was sold to William Magelssen. Rail service was discontinued in 1980.

Since potable water could not be found at the town site, water was supplied by the Milwaukee Railroad using a water tender. The water tender was left in Ingomar as a gift by the Milwaukee Railroad when services were discontinued. In late 1984, a water system was installed for the few remaining Ingomar residents.

Between 1911 and 1917, there were an average of 2,500 homestead filings per year in this area. The post office was established in 1910, with Si Sigman as the postmaster. Ingomar soon became a bustling town of 46 businesses, including a bank, 2 elevators, 2 general stores, 2 hotels (of which, one remains), 2 lumber yards, rooming houses, saloons, cafes, drug store, blacksmith shop, claims office, doctor, dentist, maternity home and various other essential services. To the northeast of the town site is what remains of Trout Lake, a body of water impounded by the embankment of the railroad, which provided boating and swimming in summer, skating in winter, and a source of ice that was cut, harvested and stored in 3 ice houses to provide summer refrigeration. Fires, drought and depression have wreaked havoc on this community over the years. The dreams of homesteaders vanished as rain failed to come in quantities to assure a crop with sufficient frequency to enable them to make a living. A reluctance to abandon the town has kept it alive through the devastating fire of 1921, which destroyed a large portion of it. Some businesses rebuilt, but others moved on.

The Jersey Lilly

The Ingomar Hotel located at the corner of Main Street and Railway Avenue was built in 1922 and connected to an older dining room which was managed by Mrs. H. J. Broom, and by Stena Austin after Mrs. Broom's death. The mortgagor, Emil Lura, took over ownership and management of the property, after twice foiling Stena's efforts to torch the hotel. At that time rates were 50 cents per night and no women allowed; after World War II rates were raised to $1 per night. The building was purchased by Bill Seward in 1966 and is no longer operated as a hotel.

The present day Jersey Lilly had its beginning as a bank in 1914, known as Wiley, Clark and

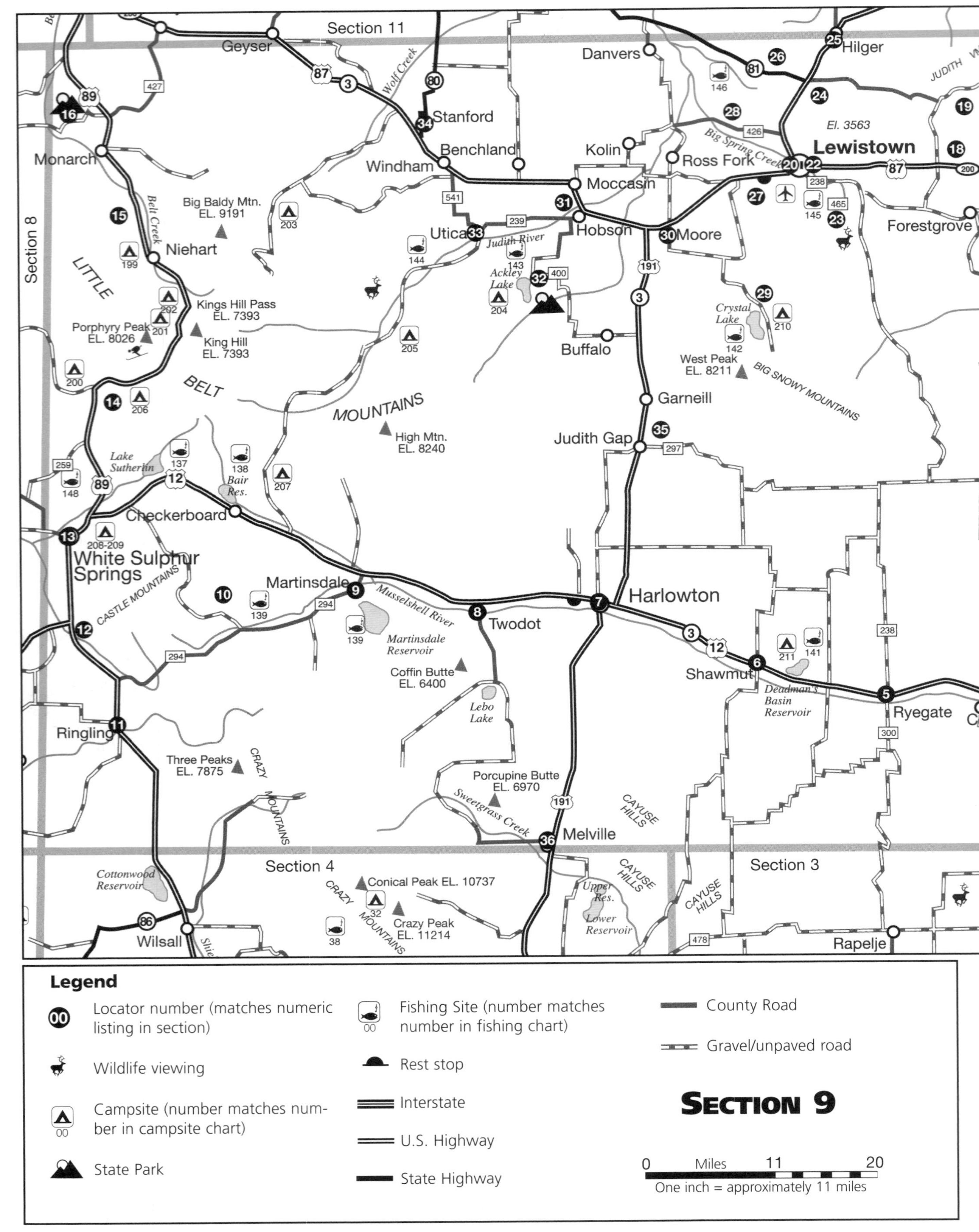
Section 11
Section 8
Section 4
Section 3
Geyser
Monarch
Stanford
Windham
Benchland
Danvers
Hilger
Kolin
Ross Fork
Lewistown
El. 3563
Moccasin
Hobson
Moore
Forestgrove
Utica
Niehart
Big Baldy Mtn. EL. 9191
Kings Hill Pass EL. 7393
King Hill EL. 7393
Porphyry Peak EL. 8026
LITTLE
BELT
MOUNTAINS
High Mtn. EL. 8240
Ackley Lake
Buffalo
Crystal Lake
West Peak EL. 8211
BIG SNOWY MOUNTAINS
JUDITH MOUNTAINS
Garneill
Judith Gap
Lake Sutherlin
Bair Res.
Checkerboard
White Sulphur Springs
CASTLE MOUNTAINS
Martinsdale
Musselshell River
Martinsdale Reservoir
Twodot
Harlowton
Shawmut
Deadman's Basin Reservoir
Ryegate
Coffin Butte EL. 6400
Lebo Lake
Ringling
Three Peaks EL. 7875
CRAZY MOUNTAINS
Porcupine Butte EL. 6970
Sweetgrass Creek
Melville
CAYUSE HILLS
Cottonwood Reservoir
Wilsall
Conical Peak EL. 10737
Crazy Peak EL. 11214
Upper Res.
Lower Reservoir
Rapelje
Wolf Creek
Belt Creek
Judith River
Big Spring Creek
Legend
Locator number (matches numeric listing in section)
Wildlife viewing
Campsite (number matches number in campsite chart)
State Park
Fishing Site (number matches number in fishing chart)
Rest stop
Interstate
U.S. Highway
State Highway
County Road
Gravel/unpaved road
SECTION 9
0 Miles 11 20
One inch = approximately 11 miles

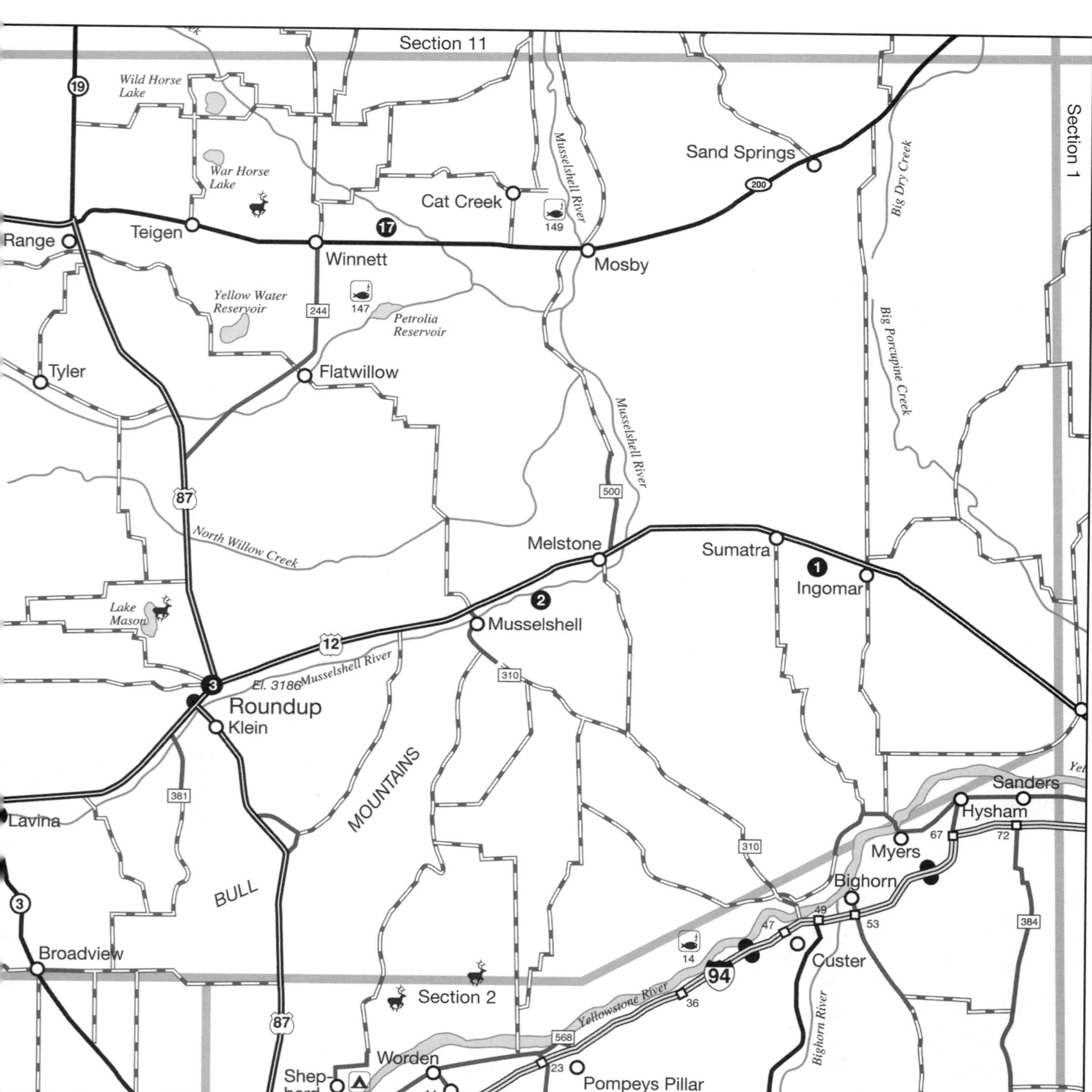




Greening, Bankers. On Jan. 1, 1918, the bank was reorganized from a probate bank to Ingomar State Bank; it received a federal charter, and operated as the First National Bank of Ingomar from January until July 21, 1921, when it closed. On October 13, 1921, the bank went into receivership. In June, 1924, William T. Craig was charged in Federal Court in Billings with misapplying certain funds of the bank. Craig was found guilty and sentenced to 16 months and fined $1,000. In April, 1925, the Circuit Court of Appeals in San Francisco reversed the Montana decision and the indictment was ordered quashed. Craig was dismissed. The money lost by the bank customers was never repaid.

In 1933, Clyde Easterday established the Oasis bar in the bank building; Bob Seward took over the bar in 1948 and named it the Jersey Lilly after Judge Roy Bean's bar of the same name in Langtry, Texas. Bob's son, Bill, purchased the building in 1958, and the Jersey Lilly continued under his ownership, serving as the local watering hole, cafe and general gathering place for area residents until August, 1995, when it was purchased by Jerry J. Brown. The Jersey Lilly is internationally known for its beans and steaks. The cherry wood, back bar of the Jersey Lilly is one of two which were transported from St. Louis by boat up the Missouri and Yellowstone rivers and installed at Forsyth in the early 1900s. This bar was stored at Forsyth during Prohibition, sold to Bob Seward, and installed here in 1933; the other back bar was destroyed in 1912, when the American Hotel burned in Forsyth.

The original frame school building, the Jersey Lilly and Bookman Store were all placed on the National Registry of Historic places in September, 1994. Both the original frame school building and the Milwaukee Depot are now privately owned.

Ingomar retains its post office and one rural route with mail delivered every Friday in spite of snow, rain, heat or gloom of night.

Area residents banded together to construct a rodeo arena, which has become the home of one of the best NRA rodeos. Rodeos are held throughout the summer and early fall.

Across the street from. the Jersey Lilly, the local 4-H club has constructed a park with horse-

Ingomar sits like an island on the open plains.

shoe pits and picnic tables for public use.

A campground with hookups is open throughout the year. If you are planning a stay in Ingomar, call the Jersey Lilly at 358-2278 for information.

From the grazing of buffalo to Texas cattle to early sheep men and through the homestead era, this land has completed a cycle, bringing it back to its primary use, production of natural grasses. Ingomar survives today because of the social needs of the people of this vast and sparsely populated area.

*Source: Town brochure*

## H Ingomar

Ingomar

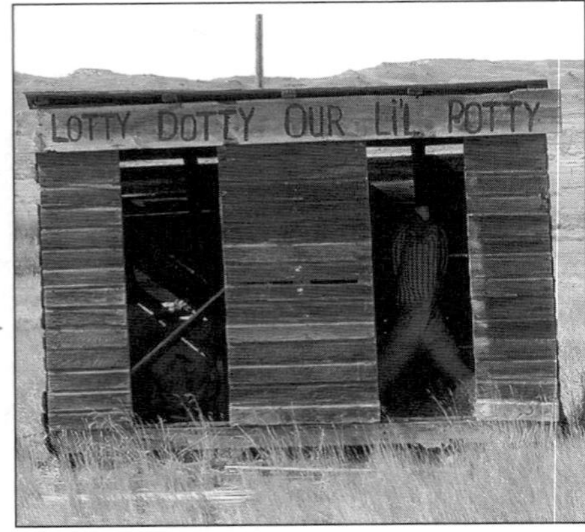


This outhouse greets you at the entrance to Ingomar.

*Upon completion of the Milwaukee Railroad in 1910, Ingomar became a hub of commerce in the area bounded by the Missouri, Musselshell and Yellowstone Rivers. From Ingomar, horses and wagons carried supplies to the settlers and brought produce back to the community. The railroad promoted the growth of the area by encouraging settlers to use the 1909 Homestead Act to stake 320 acre claims. There were an average of 2500 homestead filings per year in this area between 1911 and 1917.*

*Ingomar claimed the title of "Sheep Shearing Capital of North America." Shearing at Ingomar was advantageous because of its vital location on the route between the winter pastures and the free summer grass. From Ingomar, the wool was loaded directly onto the railroad cars without risk of weather damage or delayed delivery to the buyers. Two million pounds of wool a year were shipped from Ingomar during the peak years of the 1910s.*

*A devastating fire in 1921, drought and depression have taken their toll on the area but the original frame school building, Bookman's store and the Jersey Lilly Saloon are recognized by the National Register of Historic Places.*

## H Greening Bank

Ingomar

*Completion of the "Milwaukee Road" brought hundreds of homesteaders to Ingomar during the 1910s. By 1914, wood-frame homes and a small commercial district proclaimed the town a permanent settlement. On July 2, 1914, the Ingomar Index announced that a bank would soon open, marking an important milestone in the community's development. Investors H.B. Wiley, C.M. Greening and E.B. Clark hired bookkeeper W.T. Craig. All, declared the Index, were businessmen of sterling reputations. When the new building was completed that October, the newspaper declared it a "pippin, " noting that "cashier Craig feels like a kid with a new toy." It was Ingomar's first brick building. The bank indeed prospered, reorganizing and expanding in 1917 as a state bank, and reorganizing again in 1921 under federal charter. Economic reversal led to the bank's sudden closure later that year. Craig was convicted of misuse of bank funds, a ruling that was later overturned on appeal. The bank stood empty, a painful reminder of delinquent loans and failed homesteads. In 1933, the Oasis Bar opened in the building and the Jersey Lilly Bar and Cafe moved here in 1948. The former bank has since served as a community gathering place with a devoted clientele. Original pressed tin ceilings, bank vaults and the outline of teller cages on unfinished hardwood flooring suggest the building's previous function. Its dignified outward appearance reflects the time when Ingomar was the commercial and social center of a vital agricultural community.*

## H J. A. Bookman General Store

Ingomar

*J. Abraham "Abe" Bookman came from Ireland with his wife, Anna, and brother-in-law, Simon Sigman. By 1912, they had settled in Ingomar where Bookman operated the town mercantile and Sigman served as postmaster. The business was so prosperous that once, when Bookman was at the depot to receive a shipment of groceries and clothing, settlers waiting for the next train bought every single item before it could be carried to the store. In 1914, Bookman's success allowed him to finance Sigman's opening of a general store in nearby Vananda. Although Rosebud County's economy was obviously in trouble by 1921 and many homesteaders had moved on, Ingomar's commercial area remained relatively stable. When fire devastated the small district that year, this prominent brick building with its lively diamond pattern of polychromatic brick was built to replace Bookman's original store. Now connected to its neighbor through an interior doorway, the well-preserved vintage building is a classic example of the commercial structures once common in small prairie settlements. The intact survival of its two-bay storefront is particularly noteworthy. Although most Ingomar businesses closed during the 1920s and 1930s, the Bookmans struggled through hard times and loss of their property at sheriff's sale in 1933. They repurchased the store in 1935, and Abe hung on to the business until his death in 1941. Anna retired two years later, closing the store for good. Its closure marked the true end of Ingomar's pioneer era.*

The old Ingomar schoolhouse is now "The Bunk and Biscuit." The dormitory style bunkhouse offers beds by the night for $15 per person—no matter how many people in a bed. The biscuits are over at the Jersey Lilly across the road. The sign on the bell tower claims "The only place to sleep in 100 miles." No doubt it is.

## H Ingomar Public School

Ingomar

*As hundreds of farmers and ranchers homesteaded the arid , treeless plains of northwestern Rosebud County, the townsite of Ingomar was platted along the tracks of the Chicago, Milwaukee & St. Paul Railway in 1912. That year, one teacher and a borrowed building served Ingomar's first public school students. By the following year the western one-room portion of the present building was completed and fourteen students attended classes. In 1915, the school district contracted with Melstone builder Neils Hanson to construct an addition. At a cost of $9,000, the enlarged schoolhouse would serve not only local children, but would also provide a place for community functions. The teachers and their thirty-seven scholars presented a dedication program on November 24, 1915, for the visiting State Inspector of Schools. The school continued to be well attended during the 1920s and 1930s partly because of the closure of other area rural schools. A second build-*

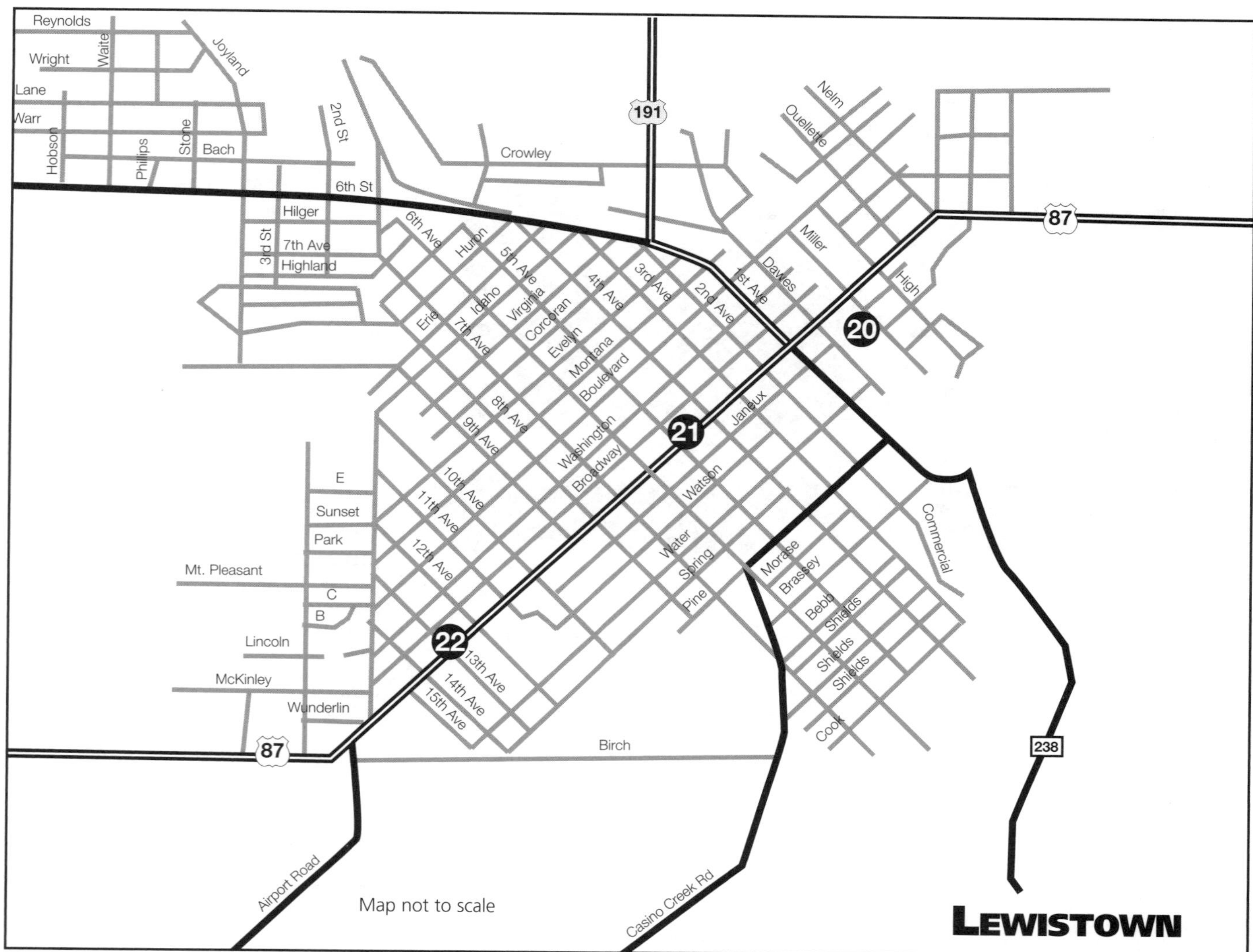


*ing, no longer standing, was built in 1922 to accommodate elementary students, and this building was then converted for use as a high school. It served as such until 1951 and again briefly during the 1960s. Activity at the site ended permanently when Ingomar's school district closed in 1992. Today the spacious, well-lighted classrooms with hardwood floors, wood wainscot walls and pressed tin ceilings remain intact. One of the area's few surviving examples of public architecture, it is also eastern Montana's most outstanding example of post frontier prairie schoolhouse design. This splendid landmark is all the more remarkable because time and service have left its appearance virtually unchanged.*

## Sumatra

This town was a station and the highest point between Miles City and Harlowton on the Milwaukee rail line. The trains required a "pusher" engine to get them to the top of the hill in Sumatra. The town was originally called Summit, and no one knows exactly where the new name came from. Before the railroad came, the town was on the trail between Fort Musselshell and Fort Custer. Years ago, a fire destroyed much of the town and it was never rebuilt. Now only a white church and a few old buildings remain.

## 2.

## Musselshell

The town takes its name from the river that was named by Lewis and Clark: "...the stream which we suppose to be called by the Minetarus, the Musselshell River...." The name came from the mussel shells found along the river bed. Opposite the present townsite is the Musselshell Crossing, an old stockman's landmark. Here in the 1880s, herds of Texas Longhorn cattle were bedded down just prior to being distributed to their ultimate Montana owners. The trail that connected Fort Custer and Fort McGinnis passed through here as well.

## 3. *Historical Marker, Attraction, Gas, Food, Lodging*

## Roundup

Roundup was once the gathering point for huge herds of cattle which grazed throughout the valley. It remained a cowtown until 1903, when settlers arrived and homesteads were fenced closing off the land and inhibiting grazing. Roundup is located at the crossroads of Highways 12 and 87. Since Montana's statehood centennial in 1989, the Roundup Cattle Drive has become an annual tradition.

### T Musselshell Valley Historical Museum

524 1st St. W., Roundup. 323-1662

When you enter this museum, you can sign in on the old registry of the Adams Hotel of Lavina. The museum tells the story of the birth of Roundup and includes a pioneer-era cabin and a five-room house. Its main exhibit is a coal mine and tunnel with a wooden car, carbide lamps, lunchpails, photos and maps. Other exhibits include local Indian artifacts, fossils, and paintings by local artists. Special exhibit rooms include the old Rothiemy Store and post office, a one room rural school, the original operating rooms of the old Vicars Hospital, and a dressmaker shop. On the grounds are a print shop, a blacksmith shop, and the old NF Ranch home which was originally built in 1884. Admission is free.

### H Cow Country

Roundup

*In the 1880s, days of the open range, many a roundup outfit worked this country. The spring roundup gathered the cattle in order to brand and tally the calf crop. The fall roundup gathered beef critters for shipping.*

*An outfit consisted of the captain, the riders, the "reps" from neighboring ranges, the cavvy or horse herd in charge of the day herder and night hawk, the four horse chuck wagon piloted by the cook and the bed wagon driven by his flunkey. Camp moved each day.*

*The cowboys rode circle in the morning, combing the breaks and coulees for cattle and heading them toward the central point to form a herd. In the afternoons of spring roundup the guards kept the herd together, the cutters split out the cows with calves, the ropers dabbed their loops on the calves, took a couple of dally welts around the saddle horn and dragged 'em*

*Lavina today.*

*to the fire. There the calf wrestlers flanked and flopped them and the brander decorated them with ear notches, or dew laps, and a hot iron. It wasn't all sunshine and roses.*

### L Big Sky Motel
740 Main, Roundup. 323-2303

## 4.

### Lavina

Walter Burke operated a stage line in the late 1800s. He built a trading post and stage stop at this site for his Billings to Lewistown route. It was Burke's job to establish stage stops, build corrals and barns for the horses, and lodging and dining (and drinking) facilities for the passengers and drivers. Of all he built, his favorite was the one on the south bank of the Musselshell River. He named it Lavina, after an old sweetheart. By 1883, a fleet of fine Concord stage coaches were leaving Lavina headed toward Roundup, Billings, and Lewistown.

When the railroad came through town in the early 1900s, prosperity followed and many of the town's buildings were built. The historic Adams Hotel was one of the first and still stands on Main Street. The town was nicknamed "White City," referring to all the buildings in the town painted white.

## 5. *Gas, Food*

### Ryegate

Like many towns in Montana, this one was named by railroad officials. It was a rye field on the Sims-Garfield ranch that was the inspiration for the name. The town is built at the base of a three mile long stretch of rimrocks on what was once part of that ranch. These rimrocks were once the shore of a large lake. As a result, the area is a good place to hunt for marine fossils. The rimrocks themselves still have a number of prehistoric inscriptions visible, including a crudely drawn picture of six men and three antelope. Ruth Lane Garfield was the first woman sheriff in Montana and had her office in Ryegate. She was appointed to fill out her husband's position after he was shot by a demented farmer in 1920.

### T Ryegate Testicle Festival
Ryegate. 568-2330

Ryegate has hosted the Montana Testicle Festival the second Saturday of June, every year for nearly two decades. Festivities gear up with a traditional rodeo on Friday night and a rancher's rodeo on Saturday. The festival started as a local event has grown to well over 2,000 guests each year. The event continues to be a family affair that you can bring the kids to, complete with a street dance and lot's of great food for those who want more than the delicacy that is also known as Rocky Mountain oysters.

## 6. *Food*

### Shawmut

Once a station on the Milwaukee railroad, the town was named for a local rancher. A Avaceratops dinosaur was found in the area and is now on display in the Upper Musselshell Museum in Harlowton.

## 7. *Historical Marker, Attraction, Gas, Food, Lodging*

### Harlowton

Nestled between the snow-capped peaks and forests of three mountain ranges, Harlowton offers the fresh air and close knit harmony characteristic of Rural America. The Musselshell Valley in which it resides boasts a climate few Montana communities can claim, including moderate winters. Summer temperatures rarely top 90 degrees with pleasantly cool evenings. Winter temperatures seldom drop below zero and humidity generally remains under 35 percent.

Harlowton is historic ground. Professional and amateur paleontological teams have been uncovering a tremendous array of finds dating from prehistoric animals, birds and fish clear through the days when the Crow and Blackfeet pursued buffalo herds in the area.

Chief Joseph and his Nez Perce crossed the Musselshell River near here during their historic retreat to Canada, and Army troopers were an important part of the country's history in the 1870s and 80s. Chief Joseph Park in Harlowton is dedicated to the memory of a great Indian chief and his band of loyal followers. The park is located right along the highway within the city limits, and provides camping facilities, as well as a fishing pond, rodeo grounds and high school athletic track facility. A covered picnic shelter and children's playground add to the attractiveness of the area as a resting place for travelers.

The Musselshell Valley first became home to ranchers who took full advantage of the lush grazing for cattle and sheep herds. Homesteaders moved onto the land that was more suitable for tilling. They were followed by the railroad, first by the "Jawbone" or Montana Railroad which later became part of the Milwaukee Railroad. Harlowton served as a division point and was the eastern end of the electrified lines until the Milwaukee went out of existence in 1980. The E-57B electric engine is still maintained in Harlowton as a monument to that era.

The agricultural heritage continues to dominate the area's economy. Herds of cattle and sheep are spread over the valley, and fields of wheat, oats, barley and hay add color to the country throughout the growing season.

### H The Crazy Mountains
West of Harlowtown.

*The Crazy Mountains, which you can see to the southwest, are an outlying range. They are far more rugged and beautiful than they appear at a distance. The story goes that a woman traveling across the plains with a wagon train of emigrants went insane. She escaped from the party and was found near these mountains. So they were called the Crazy Woman Mountains, which in time was shortened.*

*This district was great cow country in the days of the open range, and there are still a number of large cattle ranches in this vicinity, though under fence. The town of Two Dot gets its name from an early day brand.*

### H E57B The Last Electric Locomotive
Harlowtown

*The Milwaukee Road's 656-mile electrified railroad ended at 11:40 P.M. June 15, 1974, when Engineer Art Morang stopped the E57B & E34C on the Harlowton Roundhouse Track. They were the last operating locomotives of the original 84 locomotives built by General Electric in 1915.*

*The electric locomotive roster had totaled 116 locomotives of 5 different types operating from Harlowton, Montana, 440 miles to Avery, Idaho, and 216 miles from Othello, Washington, to Tacoma, Washington, over 5 mountain ranges.*

*The E57B is 57' 8-3/4" long, 16' 8" high, 10' 0" wide and weighs 144 tons. Rated at 1500 H.P. it could develop 2395 H.P. starting effort, a 62% overload. Operated in 1 to 4 unit consists, they were very trouble-free locomotives. The 3000 volt D.C. trolley restricted them to a small portion of the 11,248 mile railroad and they were replaced by the more versatile diesel electric locomotives.*

### T Upper Musselshell HIstorical Society Museum
11 S. Central Ave. in Harlowtown. 632-5519

Inside this museum you will find a general store, a pioneer home, Native American artifacts, and varied items that tell the history of the area. The Avaceratops dinosaur found in the Shawmut area is also on display. Its statement of purpose says it all, "Historical preservation of the Upper Mussellshell River history of the past five million years". Open May through October.

## L Graves Hotel

106 S. Central Ave., at Highways 12 & 191, Harlowtown. 632-5798 or toll free at 866-632-5798

The Graves Hotel, built in 1908, is on the national historic register. This three story Victorian sandstone overlooks the Crazy mountains, Mussellshell river and vast ranch lands. Dine and relax in their lounge and casino, or sip a cool one on the wrap-around verandah, enjoy the spectacular views, and imagine the history that took place here. The restaurant is open for breakfast, lunch, and dinner. The Old Milwaukee Railroad, St. Joseph Park, rodeo grounds, and Pioneer Museum are all with in walking distance. This is a wonderful headquarters to enjoy the area's golf, fishing, hunting, exploring, or just plain relaxing.

*This was the first building in Martinsdale. It was built in the late 1890s by William Coates and served as a livery stable and the home of Coates' Coulson Martinsdale Stage Company. Martinsdale's wide Main Street can be attributed to the need for space to turn the stagecoaches around. Frank Rognlie ran a bar in the south part of the livery stable, which later became a barber shop. Through the years, this building has served as a garage, a restaurant and once housed the Martinsdale power plant. —Historical marker on building.*

## 8.

### Two Dot

This town is the namesake of cattleman H. J. "Two Dot" Wilson. Wilson was sensitive to the risk of theft by rustlers so he made his brand by putting a dot on the shoulder and another on the thigh. This ingenious marking was pretty difficult to alter. Thus the nickname "Two Dot."

## 9. *Attraction, Gas, Food, Lodging*

### Martinsdale

In 1876, Frank Gaugler built a hotel and general store near the forks of the Musselshell. He named the place Gauglersville. In August the following year, a gentleman named Richard Clendennin moved his family to the North Fork of the Mussellshell directly across from Gauglersville. In time, the two men joined forces and established the town of Martinsdale. They named the town for the Montana Territory's Congressional Delegate, Martin McGinnis. Soon, wool growers, discovering the mild climate of the Musselshell valley, began to move in and the area flourished.

In 1875, a wool growers stock company was established and within three years the association had more than 20,000 sheep. Fortunes were made here, including those of John Smith, whose ranch grew to 86,000 acres and C.M. Bair with 80,000 acres. These were two of the biggest sheep outfits in the state. In 1910, records show that Bair shipped out forty-four carloads of wool with an estimated worth of $500,000. This was the largest shipment of wool to ever leave Montana. False fronts on the buildings still standing in Martinsdale reflect the era of the 1880s.

The Milwaukee depot in Martinsdale sat quiet for most of the year, but became a bustling place when the cattle and sheep from the local ranches were brought in for shipping. Today, Martinsdale still serves as a small ranching community and stands as a testament to the pioneers of Montana.

*The Crazy Mountain Inn in Martinsdale.*

### Checkerboard

This town has never been much more than a friendly stop on the road for travelers. It sits on land which was once owned by the Bair Livestock Company. In the early 1900s, Bair was one of the state's largest sheep ranchers.

## The Woodpeckers of Ryegate

**As you drive the stretch between** Ryegate and Harlowton on U.S. Highway 12, a bird parked on a pole might catch your eye. Soon another one just like it on a fencepost, then one on a building, then they seem to be everywhere. What you'll notice about these birds immediately is that they are large, they are colorful, and they are made of plywood. A sign along the way that reads "Woodpecker Crossing Next 30 Miles" gives you a clue to the species.

These semi-lawn ornaments are the work of Earl Osse and Jerry Gantz, two guys who just wanted to brighten up an otherwise dull stretch of highway. Between the two of them, they've hung over 1,500 of them. If you'd like one of your very own, pick one up at the store in Ryegate or Shawmut.

## T Charles M. Bair Family Museum

One mile south of the Martinsdale turnoff on Hwy 12 between White Sulphur Springs and Harlowton. 727-8787

Charles M. Bair came to Montana in 1883 as a conductor on the Northern Pacific Railroad and went into the ranching business in 1893. He established his fortune in the Alaskan Gold Rush and went on to invest in mining, oil and real estate along with his ranching interests. Bair became one of the largest sheep owners in the world, at one time running as many as 300,000 head. He counted among his friends Charlie Russell, Joseph Henry Sharp, Tom Mix, Will Rogers, William Hart, Chief Plenty Coups, and many U.S. Presidents.

It was the wish of Charlie Bair's daughters that

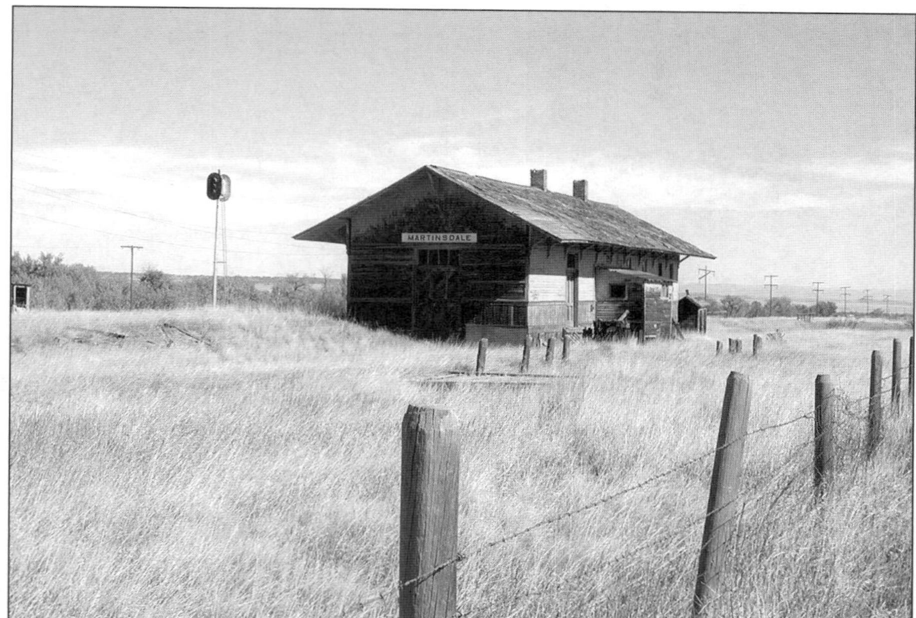


*The Martinsdale train station, once a bustling cattle and sheep depot, now sits idle.*

Charles M. Bair Museum.

their home be left as a museum for others to enjoy. The house is a rich repository of Indian artifacts, paintings by renowned artists such as Russell and Sharp, and some of the finest period antiques.

Charles Bair purchased the ranch in 1913, and it became the family's permanent residence in 1934 after remodeling the old John Grant ranch house. They continued to add to the residence until it consisted of 26 rooms, filled with the antiques and paintings collected by Charlie's daughters, Alberta and Marguerite, on their many trips to Europe.

Charles Bair collected Native American artifacts and western paintings while his daughters amassed Louis XV furniture, Scottish china, Sevres pottery, English silver, and a collection of the late French Impressionist paintings by Edouard Cortes. The contrasts and immense abundance of antiques and fine art from all over the world located through this Montana ranch house will absolutely astonish you. This is easily one of Montana's most captivating sites.

*Source: Museum brochure*

**10.** *Historical Marker, Attraction*

## H Lennep Mercantile
Lennep

*Built in 1914 by M. T. Grande, this building housed a grocery store with a small supply of dry goods. It also served as the post office, which had been established in 1903 in the log home across the road. A succession of store keepers leased the building through the years.*

*The large hall upstairs witnessed community dances, the annual What-Not -Club Sale and fund raising events for the Red Cross and other entities during World War II.*

*Most of the ranches had telephone service with privately built and maintained lines. Each house boasted a crank telephone with different combinations of long and short rings to signal each other. Every ring rang in every home so it was not difficult to keep up with neighborhood news. Long distance calls were made by ringing the storekeeper who switched the private line to a line to Martinsdale Hardware where it was switched to the long distance carrier. After store hours, a caller drove to the store and did the switching himself.*

*In the sixties, the Milwaukee trains no longer stopped to leave groceries and mail. Sam and Mildred Berg moved their inventory to Martinsdale. They hoped to broaden their market as ranches were consolidated, cattle replaced sheep on the range, and the many sheep camps were shut down. AT&T ran their lines through the neighborhood and provided direct services at all hours. A rural route delivers mail from the Martinsdale post office.*

*The Grande family still owns the building.*

## T Lennep and the Lennep Church
Hwy. 294, south of Martinsdale.

The Trinity Lutheran Church in Lennep is the second oldest Lutheran church in the state. The beautiful clapboard structure was built in 1914 and is nestled in the heart of Lennep. The school built in 1910 is still being used as well. A few empty buildings and a few families still occupy this little hamlet.

## T Castle Ghost Town
Rt 294, off Hwy. 89 near White Sulphur Springs.

The town tucked away under the Castle Mountains started in 1882, and mushroomed as a silver camp during the next few years. It had a schoolhouse, eighty dwellings, a jail, fourteen saloons, and seven brothels at its peak. Calamity Jane and her buddies tried the restaurant business in Castle for a spell. Three stage lines served the town on a daily basis. A railroad built by Richard A. Harlowe didn't materialize in time to serve the mining needs of the town, it was completed in 1903 after the boom had faded and most everyone had left Castle. The last two residents remained until the 1930s. Many of the buildings are still standing. Find Castle and enjoy a nice drive on good roads.

**11.** *Food*

## Ringling
Yes, it was named for one of the Ringling Bros. of circus fame. John Ringling was also the president and builder of the Yellowstone Park and White Sulphur Springs Railroad which eventually became a branch of the Milwaukee railroad. The Ringlings at one time owned over 100,000 acres in the area and at one time contemplated establishing a circus headquarters here. At one time it was a bustling little town with several businesses as a junction for White Sulphur Springs transfer customers.

After several devastating fires, the last in 1931, and the demise of the railroads Ringling dwindled to a few people and the surrounding ranches. Today it has a post office, school, and restaurant and bar.

Partial remains of Castle.

The town was immortalized by Jimmy Buffet when he wrote of the town in his song *Ringling, Ringling* on the *Living and Dying in Three Quarter Time* album. And yes, *Livingston Saturday Night* was about Livingston, Montana down the road a piece.

## 12.

Junction Highway 12 to Townsend.

## 13. *Historical Marker, Attraction, Gas, Food, Lodging*

### White Sulphur Springs

White Sulphur Springs is so named because of white deposits around the hot sulphur springs that were found in this area. The springs are still active and provide commercial opportunities for the community. Indians came from long distances to use the medicinal waters from these springs. Situated in the Smith River Valley, White Sulphur Springs, frequented by buffalo and originally a trading center, has since become famous for its fine cattle. Learn more about the area at www.meagherchamber.com.

### H The Smith River Valley

South of White Sulphur Springs.

*The mountains to the west are the Big Belts, and those to the east are the Castle Mountains. The gulches draining the west slope of the Big Belts were famous in the 1860s and 1870s for their gold placer diggings. Montana Bar in Confederate Gulch was called the "richest acre of ground in the world." The Castle Mountains are also well known for their quartz mines.*

*Fort Logan, first established as Camp Baker in November, 1869, as a military outpost to protect the mining camps and ranches to the west from possible attack by Indians, was located towards the north end of the valley. The White Sulphur Springs, typical of the many thermal springs in Montana, were discovered in 1866 by Jas. Scott Brewer. Analysis of the water is said to be almost identical with that, at the famous spa, Baden Baden, Germany.*

### T Copperopolis

Hwy. 89, near White Sulphur Springs.

A few deserted shacks and mine shafts are all that remain of a mining camp that back in in the 1890s, hoped to compete for size and fame with Butte.

### T The Castle and Carriage House

Hwy. 89 and 12 in White Sulphur Springs. 547-2324

Familiarly known as the "Castle", this house was built by B.R. Sherman, stockman and mine owner in 1892. The gray stone structure has long been a landmark on its hilltop overlooking the town of White Sulphur Springs. The Castle was sold in 1905 to Michael Donahoe, and in 1960 his heirs gave the house to the Meagher County Historical Association.

The antique furnishings come from families throughout the county in memory of their pioneer ancestors. This is a locally supported effort to preserve the history of Meagher County.

Open daily May 15 to September 15 from 10 a.m. to 6 p.m. There is an admission charge.

### T Meagher County Historical Association

White Sulphur Springs. 547-3520

### L Spa Hot Springs Motel

202 West Main, White Sulphur Springs. 547-3366

Native Americans traveling through this valley were the first to discover and make use of the hot springs that are now part of the Spa Hot Springs Motel. The native people believed that the hot mineral water had a strong medicinal effect, healing the body and strengthening the spirit. These natural waters have continued to provide a variety of health benefits for hundreds of years. Visitors today can choose to stay in the newly remodeled and refurnished motel where every room has firm beds, is geothermally heated, and has cable TV. Relax in two wonderful natural hot mineral pools, naturally drained and cleaned daily without chemicals. The Spa Hot Springs Motel offers the best example of solar and wind generating systems, along with geothermal heating, in Montana. White Sulphur Springs is a year round outdoor paradise and the Spa Hot Springs Motel is the perfect place to relax.

### L All Seasons Super 8

808 Third Ave. SW & Hwy.. 89 S., White Sulphur Springs. 547-8888 or reservations 800-800-8888 www.Super8Montana.com

Whether you are staying for business or leisure, you will love your stay at the "All Seasons Super 8". Your Montana connection from "geysers to glaciers". Scenic Hwy. 89 takes you from the North entrance of Yellowstone Park to East Entrance to Glacier Park. White Sulphur Springs is surrounded by the Big Belt, Little Belt, and Castle Mountains. This brand new motel offers non-smoking, handicapped accessible rooms, suites, cable TV, guest laundry, hot tub, pets with deposit, ample parking, and complimentary continental breakfast. They are only a short drive away from many area attractions from museums to river sports, to snow sports and golfing. We their web site at www.Super8montana.com.

## 14. *Adventure, Gas, Food, Lodging*

### T Kings Hill National Scenic Byway

547-3361

This 71 mile scenic drive on U.S. Hwy.. 89 bisects the Little Belt Mountains. It runs between U.S. Hwy.. 12 at the south end and U.S. Hwy.. 87 at the north end. This is a beautiful, winding mountain drive. Along this route is Sluice Boxes State Park which offers great fishing and hiking opportunities. Former mining camps Neihart and Monarch are still active communities, along beautiful Hwy. 89 winding through the Little Belt Mountains. The drive through these areas offers a blend of the present with remnants of their lively past.

## 15.

### Niehart

The discovery of silver-lead ore in this area in 1881 proved to be one of the richest strikes in the Little Belt Mountains. James L. Neihart was one of a group of prospectors who first discovered the ore and the town was named for him. The town was built with exceptionally wide streets. The main street was eighty feet wide and all cross streets were 60 feet. One of the buildings still standing in the town has a sign over it reading:

*Wu Tang Laundry*
*Drugs*
*1882*

Sapphire mining also proved to be a profitable enterprise here. An estimated $3 million worth of sapphires ranging in color from pale to royal blue have been extracted from these mines.

### Monarch

In 1890, the Great Northern constructed a branch line from Great Falls to Monarch to haul ore from the nearby mines. The name of Monarch is thought to come from the relationship to the nearby mines of "King," "Czar," and "Emperor." Amateur prospectors still pan the streams surrounding the town.

## 16. *Attraction*

### T Sluice Boxes State Park

North of Monarch on U.S. 89, then 2 miles west on county road. 454-5840.

A primitive trail follows an abandoned railroad grade through the scenic, Belt Creek Gorge. The trail provides access to numerous stream fishing opportunities, and a nearby ghost town. The trail requires numerous fords, which are possible only during low water. There are no developed facilities at Sluice Boxes.

## 17. *Gas, Food*

### Mosby

William Henry Mosby drove a team and wagon over the Rocky Mountains from Oregon to this town's present site on the east bank of the Musselshell River in 1891.

### Winnett

This town took its name from a rather colorful character named Walter John Winnett. Winnett was born in the Crystal Palace—now the Queen's Hotel—in Toronto. As a boy, he ran away from home seeking adventure in "Indian Country." He was a sharpshooter with a rifle, a skill which easily landed jobs providing fresh meat to outfits. He was captured by the Sioux Indians and later was adopted into the tribe. They gave him the name Eagle Eyes because of his remarkable shooting skills.

In 1879, Winnett established a ranch near an active trading post and the Hangman's Tree utilized by the vigilantes in the area. In 1900, he built a massive ranch house which not only housed his family, but served as a gathering place for the community.

Winnett built a freight line to Billings to haul supplies. His outfits each consisted of ten to twenty horses pulling huge wagons. In 1910, he built a store and petitioned for a post office. The town of Winnett was born.

Winnett built the Log Cabin Saloon to protect his horses. Seems his ranch hands and wagon drivers were stealing horses out of his barn to ride to Grass Range for a drink. He thought a nearby saloon would be a lot easier on his horses.

In 1914, when land was opened to homesteading, the dry land farmers poured in. Drought and grasshoppers soon sent them packing.

The town saw a small revival when a sizable pool of oil was discovered at Cat Creek. At one time the town had thirty hotels and rooming houses packed to capacity. One hotel was just a big tent with bunks. They didn't rent by the month, week, or day—they rented by the shift.

### Grass Range

Before the Milwaukee Railroad made this town a station on the branch line to Winnett, it existed as a trading center to local settlers. Surrounding the new town was some of the finest open grassland which was home to the early cattle herds that grazed the area. These magnificent grasslands were later plowed under by homesteaders.

## 18. *Attraction*

### T Maiden

Northeast of Lewistown

See information in Historical Marker at number 24.

### T Fort Maginnis

Northeast of Lewistown

See information in Historical Marker at number 19.

## 19. *Historical Marrker*

### H Fort Maginnis

East of Lewistown.

*Fort Maginnis, the last army post created in Montana, was built about 8 miles north of here in 1880. This country was great buffalo range before that time but cattlemen were bringing in stock from the western valleys and the Texas longhorns were being trailed in from the southeast. There wasn't room for both cattle and buffalo, so the latter had to go. The soldiers were to protect the cattle from being mistaken for buffalo by hungry Indians, to encourage settlement of the Judith Basin west of here and to patrol the Carroll Road to keep supplies rolling between Carroll (near the mouth of the Musselshell River) and Helena. By 1890 the post was no longer needed, the threatening Indians having been relegated to reservations, and the fort was abandoned with civilian blessings.*

*There were also quite a number of palefaced parties who were handy with a running iron and prone to make errors as to brands and ownership. Such careless souls were known as "rustlers". Sometimes the cattlemen called on these pariahs with a posse and intimated that they were unpopular. Usually such a visitation cured a rustler or two permanently.*

**Editor's note:** Fort Maginnis was actually not the last fort built in Montana. Fort William Henry Harrison was established by the army near Helena in 1892.

### H Lewistown

Lewistown

*This area, the final hunting ground for Montana Indians, was the site of battles fought over the buffalo. In 1874 on the Carroll Trail, Reed and Bowles ran a trading post known as "Reed's Fort." Chief Joseph and his band stopped at the post on their retreat across Montana. Camp Lewis was built near the post to guard freight wagons from Indian raiding parties. During the winter, soldiers of the Seventh Infantry relieved boredom by playing cards and that's how two nearby creeks were called Big and Little Casino. Lewistown, named after the camp, was first inhabited by Metis, French Canadian Indians, who migrated into Montana and possibly gave some Montana communities their French names.*

## 20. *Attraction, Gas, Food, Lodging, Shopping*

### Lewistown

Lewistown, a lively trading center for both farmers and ranchers, is considered to be the hub of Central Montana. The address of 1105 W. Main in Downtown Lewistown is the exact center of Montana. Agriculture remains a key to Lewistown's economy. Winter wheat, feed barley, and some spring wheat comprise most of the local production. Fergus County has the state's largest acreage dedicated solely to growing hay.

Located along the Big Spring Creek at the foot of the Judith, Big Snowy and Moccasin Mountains, Lewistown has one of the prettiest settings in the state. The town is endowed with graceful turn-of-the-century architecture that is a tribute to the fantastic backdrop of scenery surrounding it and bears testimony to a long-standing stability. From the spectacular mountain ranges abundant with elk and deer, to its fertile valleys full of pronghorn, waterfowl and wild turkeys, this is a hunter's paradise.

### T Central Montana Historical Association Museum

408 N.E. Main St. in Lewistown. 482-2401

The museum contains history from Lewistown's early history as a trading post during the homestead era. You will see pioneer relics, blacksmith and cowboy tools, guns, Native American artifacts and artwork. Open year round.

### FL Yogo Inn & Garden Restaurant

211 E. Main, Downtown Lewistown. 538-8721 or 800-860-9646 www.yogoinn.com, email, yogo@lewsitwon.net.

The Yogo Inn of Lewistown, named after the rare yogo sapphires minded locally, is located just blocks from the geographical center of Montana. It is Lewistown's largest motel with 121 guest rooms and convention facilities with various sized meeting rooms for up to 350 people. The Inn offers an indoor pool, hot tub, guest laundry, game room, gift shop, beauty shop, lounge, casino, and restaurant. The Garden Restaurant specializes in the finest prime rib dinners and its famous Sunday Champagne Brunch. They serve breakfast, lunch, and dinner daily. The Yogo Inn is located within easy walking distance to shopping, the Historic District, and blue-ribbon trout fishing. For more information find them at www.yogoinn.com.

### L The Sunset Motel

115 N.E. Main St., Lewistown. 538-8741

The Sunset Motel provides convenience and safety to all its guests. Rooms are located on ground level, with room front parking. The units are exceptionally clean and comfortable with direct dial phones, cable TV, air conditioning, winter plug-ins, and a quiet atmosphere. They are an easy walk to restaurants and shopping. The modern accommodations and friendly service at the Sunset Motel will put a smile on your face.

## 21. *Attraction, Gas, Food*

### T Lewistown Art Center

801 W. Broadway in Lewistown. 538-8278

This eclectic structure is a combination of bits and pieces of old buildings and other items collected from throughout Central Montana. From the stained glass windows of the old hospital to the old stone walls of the Center itself, volunteers have combined these things into a truly fascinating place. The gallery features rotating exhibits of local, state, and regional artists in a variety of mediums and styles. Open Tuesday through Saturday, all year.

*Lewistown Art Center*

**FS Crabtree Coffee & Gifts**
618 W. Main in Lewistown. 538-5262

**L Historic Calvert Hotel**
216 7th Ave.. S. in Lewistown. 538-5411

**L Trails End Motel**
216 NE Main in Lewistown. 538-5468.

## S Owl Card & Gift Gallery

410 W. Main in Lewistown. 538-9357
or fax 538-6530

Treat yourself to the wonderful smells of fragrant candles and potpourrithat welcome you to the Owl Card & Gift Gallery. The store offers two levels of fine shopping, with theme rooms beautifully decorated and chockfull of lovely gifts and collectibles. This gallery boasts the largest selection of Boyd's Bears in the state. Collectibles available also include a wide selection of Fenton glass, Dreamsicles, Precious Moments, Ty collectibles, Russell Stover candies, and a large selection of cuddly plush items. They also provide a bridal registry and friendly service always abounds. Your visit to Lewistown should include a stop at this delightful store.

## S Center of the Universe

323 W. Main, Lewistown. 538-2815
or toll free at 888-863-8103

This store is the most unexpected place you will find in central Montana. Step inside and you could be in Seattle, New York, Los Angeles or any metropolitan area. This trendy one-of-a-kind department store carries cutting-edge street wear and skateboard clothing and accessories, body-piercing jewelry and over a hundred types of incense and candles. Collectibles from fantasy to fine art reproductions are part of the treasures you'll find. A complete skateboard shop is located on the upper level, and a smoke shop for the over-18 crowd is located within the store. Downstairs contains a giant black-light room with a mural that spans a 60-foot wall. The "Center" is well known throughout Montana. They are open

seven days a week.

## S Country Junction

211 W. Main in Lewistown. 538-8402
or toll free 800-756-8402

Walk in to a lovely, friendly setting of pure country and enjoy a free cup of fresh-brewed gourmet coffee as you browse through a wonderful selection of kitchen supplies, gourmet foods, candies and linens. Pamper yourself with a variety of bath and body items from Crabtree and Evelyn, The Thymes, and Camille Beckman. Also available are country and lodge selections of pottery and accent pieces featuring moose, bear, fish, elk and deer. check out their variety of silk flowers and small decorative trees to bring a touch of the outdoors to your home or office. They also offer Yankee candles and Montana Candle Scentasions, made here in Lewistown. The owner, Ruth Hertel, adds her personal touch and Montana friendliness to

make Country Junction a place you will want to shop at again and again.

## S Don's

120 2nd Ave., S, Lewistown. 538-9408 or tollfree at 800-879-8194 or fax 538-9461.
wwwdons-store.com or
email: donstore@lewistown.net

Don's Store, located in beautiful downtown Lewistown, is one of the town's oldest family businesses. The store is 56 years old and is now run by three generations of the family. Don's Store is a general sporting goods and clothing store selling everything from fishing and hunting equipment to boots and western wear. "The store for everyone." They also feature a fantastic display of Montana's own Yogo Sapphires, mined locally. The staff is a pleasure to work with and is available to offer any information they can that will help you enjoy

Central Montana. For more information email them or visit their web site.

## S Moccasin Mountain Art Gallery

408 W. Main in Lewistown. 538-5125

Moccasin Mountain Gallery and Frame Shop, located on Main Street, represents a wide range of Western and Wildlife art featuring Montana artists. They offer originals and limited edition prints and the highest quality custom framing for all your needs. They offer a great selection of Montana Made pottery from artists such as Julie Wagner and Betty Filius. A few of the many Montana artists they represent are: Mike Capser, Diana Brady, Monte Dolack, Don Greytak, and Joe Ziolkowski. They are also an authorized dealer for many limited edition prints from other fine Western and Wildlife artists. They are open Monday through Saturday for your convenience.

## S Footprints Shoe Store

205 W. Main in Lewistown. 538-2928
or email: footprints@midrivers.com

### *Montana Trivia*

In 1900

Cowboys earned an average of $32 per month.

Cooks earned $39 per month. If you were a woman, you earned only $26 per month.

The first Texas to Montana cattle drive was in 1869. The last was in 1888.

In 1879, the total cattle shipment was between 60 to 70 thousand head

The average cost of a horse was $50, a saddle was $32, and a months worth of grub was $15-$20.

### *Montana Trivia*

In 1905, Charles Bair, who owned the largest flock of sheep in the nation at the time (300,000 head) filled forty-four railroad cars with 1.5 million pounds of wool.

## Upper Missouri National Wild and Scenic River and Missouri Breaks

White Cliff of Lewis & Clark This 149-mile section of the Missouri River is the only major portion that has been preserved in a natural and free-flowing state. It is a remarkable float trip for canoers and rafters, and is suitable for beginners. Along the way, habitats change from rolling grasslands to beautiful white cliffs to rugged badlands. Turkeys are common, and the chances of seeing bighorn sheep are very good, particularly after August of each year.

Directions

The main access points on the Marias are at Tiber dam, the Circle Bridge on state Highway 223 between Fort Benton and Chester, and U.S. Highway 87 at Loma. No visitor services are provided on the Marias river.

Bureau of Land Management
P.O. Box 1160
Lewistown, MT 59457
Phone: 406-538-7461
Email:lfoinfo@mt.blm.gov

*Reprinted from www.recreation.gov*

### S Roger's Jewelry, Home of the Yogo Sapphire
311 W. Main in Lewistown. 538-3188
or fax 538-2262

## 22. *Gas, Food, Lodging*

### L Mountain View Motel
1422 W. Main in Lewistown. 538-3457
or reservations at 800-862-5786

Relax in comfort at this friendly motel located at the west end of Lewistown, while enjoying the many activities the area has to offer. The Mountain View Motel is conveniently located within walking distance to downtown restaurants and shopping. The motel offers clean, spacious rooms at affordable prices. The 33 guest rooms have cable TV with HBO, air conditioning, in-room coffee, and winter plug-ins. Two houses with kitchenettes are available for nightly rentals, perfect for families, reunions, and hunting or fishing trips winter and summer. Pets are allowed.

## 23. *Attraction*

### T Big Spring Trout Hatchery
South of Lewistown. Hwy.. 238. 538-5588

This is the state's largest coldwater production station for several species of trout and kokanee salmon. It is also the site of one of the largest natural springs in the world.

## 24. *Historical Marker*

### H Maiden's Gold
North of Lewistown.

*The old mining camp of Maiden, now a ghost town, is located about 10 miles east of here. She roared into existence in May, 1880, when gold was discovered by "Skookum Joe" Anderson, David Jones, Frank "Pony" McPartland, J. R. Kemper, C. Snow and others.*

*"Skookum Joe" and Jones located placer claims in Virgin Gulch and later moved to Alpine Gulch. Several good placer diggings were opened the following month.*

*The first quartz mine was also located by Anderson and Jones. The Maginnis, the Spotted Horse and the Collar were the best quartz producers. The ore in the Spotted Horse was "high grade" and was found in pockets.*

*Over three millions in gold were taken from Maiden. Her population was 1,200 at the top of the boom. Ten years later it had dwindled to less than 200. The camp was prosperous for about 15 years.*

## 25.

### Hilger
Named for David Hilger who founded the community when the Winifred branch of the Milwaukee Railroad came through in the early 1900s.

## 26. *Attraction*

### T Gigantic Warm Springs
Begin this tour by taking U.S. 191 north of Lewistown about 9.5 miles; turn left on Montana Highway 81 and drive about 3.5 miles where you will see a sign. Turn right to the Spring which is on private property and there is a small admission charge. The spring is huge. Almost 50,000 gallons of 68 degree F water emerges every minute! It is open June to September with a lifeguard on duty during the summer months. A great family spot with swimming pool, wading pool, picnic area, sunbathing, and a roomy open air shelter.

## 27. *Historical Marker*

### H The Judith Basin Country
West of Lewistown.

*The first white man to explore this district was Hugh Monroe, called "Rising Wolf" by the Blackfeet Indians. The Judith Basin was favorite hunting ground for this Nation, and Monroe, as an adopted member of the Piegan Tribe, often came here with them during the first half of the last century.*

*Reed's Fort, a typical Indian trading post, was located near here. Operated by Major Reed and Jim Bowles, the latter a friend of Jim Bridger, the post was going strong during the 1870s.*

*In the early 1880s cattlemen and prospectors moved in. Rich mines were opened in the Judith Mountains and range stock replaced the vanishing buffalo. This country is rich in frontier history and tales of the pioneers.*

## 28. *Attraction*

### T Hanover (Spring Creek) Trestle
Hwy. 426, northwest of Lewistown

Drive north from Lewistown on Hwy.. 191 about three miles. Go west on MT Hwy.. 426 about eight miles and look for the trestle on your left. The trestle is a railroad bridge 78 feet high and 1,391 feet long constructed entirely of milled timber. The only exception are the two rectangular steel firebreak bents which divide the bridge into approximate thirds.

## 29. *Attraction*

### T Crystal Lake and Big Snowy Mountains
566-2292

From Lewistown, take Hwy.. 87 west for approximately 12 miles. At the Crystal Lake sign, turn left on a gravel road for about 10 miles to FS road 275. Follow this road for another nine miles to the lake. This shallow alpine lake is nestled on the northwestern slope of the Big Snowy Mountains at about 6,000 feet. It is stocked with rainbow trout each year and is an excellent place to fish. There are a number of trails in the area including several accessible to handicapped persons.

## 30. *Gas, Food*

### Moore
This town was named for a Mr. Moore of Philadelphia. Moore was a significant financial backer of Richard Harlow's "Jaw Bone" railroad which stretched from Harlowton to Lewistown.

## Hay! What Was That?

**The longest celebration in the** state is organized by some of the smallest towns in the state. The exhibits stretch for twenty-five miles and the population along that route is about one person per mile. Utica days has been celebrated for quite a few years and now Hobson is helping out. The main attraction is the competition involving sculptures made of bails of hay and not a whole lot more, but a whole lot of hay! The creativity will astound and amuse you! Competition has grown quite fierce and "grows" every year, even involving other neighboring communities. There is even a bazaar and various venders, including the local church and others. To find out when the festival is held or more information, call 423-5248.

## 31. *Historical Marker*

### Hobson
S. S. Hobson was an early day cowboy and rancher who owned the Campbell and Clendenan ranches on the Judith River between present day Hobson and Utica.

As homesteaders crowded into the area, Hobson prospered and businesses grew. One of these was a house of ill repute that was run out of a tar paper shack near the stockyards. Since the Milwaukee owned the land the shack was on, the leaders of the local women's club asked the railroad to shut the house down and evict the two sisters running it. When the railroad refused, a

### *Montana Trivia*

Walter Winnett (after whom the town of Winnett was named) built the Log Cabin Saloon to keep his ranchhands on the ranch. Apparently some had been sneaking his horses out to ride to nearby Grass Range for a drink.

mysterious fire destroyed the shack. Unfazed, the sisters rebuilt on the same land a larger house with a solid foundation. The club women, now faced with the prospect of a permanent business, pressed the railroad again to evict the sisters. This time the company agreed. The sisters, undaunted, put their house on wheels and moved it to the main street of town directly across from the post office. Proudly denying they had been evicted, they claimed they were simply moving closer to their clientele.

### H The Judith River

West of Hobson.

*When the Lewis and Clark Expedition came up the Missouri River in 1805 Capt. Clark named the Judith River for one of the girls he left behind him.*

*Southwest of here is the Pig-eye Basin and beyond that, in the Little Belt Mountains, is Yogo Gulch. Yogo sapphires are mined there. They are the deepest colored sapphires found in the world and the only ones mined from a lode. When combined with Montana nuggets they make a mighty pretty and unique combination for rings, cuff links, pins and similar fancy doodads. Oriental, as well as all other Montana sapphires are found in placer ground.*

*The Judith Basin country was the early-day stomping ground of Charley M. Russell, famous and beloved Montana cowboy artist. Charley is now camped somewhere across the Great Divide where the grass is good and there aren't any fences.*

## 32. *Attraction*

### T Ackley Lake State Park

17 miles west of Lewistown on U.S. 87 to Hobson. then 5 miles south on Secondary 400, then 2 miles southwest on county road. 454-5840

Ackley Lake, named after an early settler and frontiersman, offers diverse water sports opportunities. The lake provides good angling for 10 to 15 inch rainbow trout.

## 33. *Attraction*

### Utica

This was the headquarters of the Judith Basin Cattle Pool and the site of the big Judith Basin roundup of the 1880s. Each fall as many as 500 cowboys gathered here. When they showed up Utica became a very lively town. To entertain themselves they raced their horses on the only street and hung out in the local saloons. One of the more prominent cowboys who spent time here was Charlie "Kid" Russell.

A fellow named Jake Hoover found sapphires in Yogo Gulch just north of town. Four New York prospectors heard of the strike and came rushing to the area. Unfortunately there wasn't enough sapphires to make a living for all four. The story goes that the four, during a particularly severe blizzard, decided they must have been crazy to have come here in the first place. They decided to name the place in memory of their hometown of Utica, New York because that was also where the state insane asylum was located. The miners, J. D. Waite, Frank Wright, John Murphy, and Joseph Cutting decided to settle in the area. Cutting became the first postmaster.

In 1881 John Murphy's cabin served as a post office for the convenience of the nearby settlers. It was a severe winter and the roads were often blocked by deep snow. The mail carrier's buckboard broke forcing him to leave on horseback. Because of his limited capacity, he took only the letters and left a heavier sack to pick up on his next trip through in a couple of months. Murphy kicked the sack under his bunk on the dirt floor of the cabin where the dog slept on it. It gathered dust and he pretty much forgot about it. About the middle of May, a detachment of soldiers from Fort McGinnis rode in and said they were searching for a sack of money that had disappeared. Murphy remembered the sack the dog had been sleeping on all winter. As he pulled it from under his bunk, a soldier gasped and said, "That's it, that's the $40,000 we've been moving heaven and earth to find."

This was a frequent campsite for Blackfeet and Crow Indians as they traveled cross-country between the Hardin and Browning areas. The route they followed was generally the same one used by stage and freight drivers.

### T Utica Historical Museum

Rte 541, Main Street, Utica. 423-5208

The museum is a large collection of artifacts from the Homestead Era. Everything from household items to farm tools. There is also a large photo collection. Open Memorial Day through Labor Day, Wednesday through Sunday.

## 34. *Attraction, Gas, Food, Lodging*

### Stanford

Stanford is the county seat of Judith Basin County and had its beginnings as a station on the Fort Benton-Billings stage route. It was also a favorite hangout for the cowboys who worked for the numerous cattle companies surrounding the area before the homesteaders and sheep ranchers moved in. In 1880, the Bower brothers, Calvin and Edward brought a thousand head of sheep and purchased 100,000 acres to graze them on. When the settlement got a post office, the Bowers named the town for their old hometown, Stanfordville, in New York.

For years legends of white wolves roaming the area proliferated. One huge one, "Old Snowdrift," was a legendary outlaw. A mounted white wolf can be seen at the Basin Trading Post.

## Charlie Russell Chew Choo

This is one of the country's premier dinner trains. People from all over the world come here to experience this truly unique adventure. The ride includes great scenery, wildlife viewing opportunities, live entertainment, and a great Western style dinner you'll be talking about years after your trip. The train has grown from two cars to five since its inception in 1994. There is one car used for food preparation and a bar area, three used for dining, and one containing a gift shop and modern restrooms.

The train crosses three 150 foot high trestles ranging in length from 1,300 to 1,900 feet. The train also passes through a half-mile long tunnel enroute. It's almost a guarantee that you'll see abundant wildlife along the route. The train passes through four railroad towns, three of which were built specifically by the railroad companies—Ware, Danvers, and Husac. And while you're watching the scenery, keep your eyes out for outlaws who may be staking out a potential train job. The train turns around at Denton and dessert is served on the return trip.

An average of 184 people make each trip. The train runs a regular schedule and does charters for groups and organizations. It's a good idea to make reservations well in advance (at least two weeks). Reservations can be made by calling 538-2527. The current cost (subject to change) is $75 which includes a prime rib dinner. There is a cash bar available on the train. 408 NE Main, Lewistown, 538-5436.

### Montana Trivia

Thomas Meagher, for whom Meagher was named, was an Irish rabble-rouser who, during his lifetime, was convicted of treason, was sentenced to life-imprisonment in the penal colonies of Tasmania, escaped and fled to America, became an editor, lawyer, and major general, and served as the acting governor of the Montana Territory. His name is pronounced "Mar" if you're from Montana, and "Meager" if you're a tourist.

### Montana Trivia

Petroleum County is the least populated county in Montana with a population of only 518. It was the last Montana county established, in 1925. The county seat is Winnett.

Section 9

## The Winter of 1886

Few, if any, winters in the written history of the West were as devastating as the winter of 1886.

The summer preceding it was unusually hot and dry. Some areas received no more than two inches of rain all summer. Others received less and the range was parched and overgrazed. At the time, there were over a million head of cattle grazing in the state. The ranchers prayed for a wet autumn and an easy winter.

On December 24th it began to snow and the temperatures plummeted. By the 27th, the temperatures had dropped below zero and the Missouri River was frozen at Fort Benton.

The cattle couldn't break through the snow to feed. The cowboys, in what was mostly a futile attempt, worked round the clock in temperatures reaching -55° F with wind chills approaching -95° to get feed to the cattle.

The storm continued into March when it finally broke. The ranches were so devastated, many didn't recover.

The toll was significant. Almost 60% of the million head of cattle perished. A cowboy could walk from carcass to carcass and never touch ground. Food was in such short supply that a bag of flour sold for $7 in 1886 prices.

A young cowboy here got his 15 minutes of fame when he rode a horse the local cowboys said couldn't be rode. "Kid" Amby Cheney took the bet and rode the horse. He earned $65 for his effort when a hat was passed around for his benefit.

### T Judith Basin Historical Museum

21 Third St. S., Stanford. 566-2281

### Montana Trivia

The now defunct town of Ubet, near Judith Gap, was named when the town father, A. R. Barrows, was asked if he could think of a name for the town. He replied, "You bet!"

### T Basin Trading Post

Stanford

The famous White Wolf is on display at this historic stop in downtown Stanford.

### T Judith Basin Historical Society

Stanford. 566-2277 Ext. 122

## 35. *Gas, Food*

### Judith Gap

Judith Gap was named for its location in a gap between the Snowies and the Little Belt Mountains. The area served as the easy way to the Judith Basin. At one time it was a division point on the Great Northern railroad as attested to by the remains of the coal chute and water tanks. Because of the railroad, it was a busy grain shipping center as well. The path through the gap was originally established by Indian warriors and hunters defending or seeking the rich hunting grounds of the Judith Basin. It was later used as a vital route by freighters, cattle drivers, prospectors, hunters and settlers passing northward into the Judith Basin or southward to the Yellowstone or Musselshell valleys. It was named for the nearby Judith River which was named by Lewis and Clark.

## 36.

### Melville

In 1877, only nine people lived in the "Norwegian Settlement" north of Big Timber. Three log cabins were the beginning of Melville, named for Col. Melville, the famed arctic explorer. Mail was collected in a cigar box for the Stage to pick up on its way to Bozeman. Odd miners from Virginia city purchased land and sent word to their relatives in Minnesota of the abundant water, grass and timber so much like their native Norway. The first child of Norwegian descent was born in November 1881. The Midwife used an oilcloth from the table to shelter the mother and baby until the men finished the sod roof on their new home. The first post mistress, Mrs. Puett, kept her prize stallion in a specially made stall in her kitchen to protect him from Indian raids, which continued as late as 1880. As more settlers arrived, the first English speaking school in Sweet Grass County was established in Melville in 1882. The school was used for all church and social functions, including the first election in the Melville Precinct. Of the 14 votes cast in the election, nine were Republican, five Democratic and no Populist or Prohibition votes were cast. By 1883, Melville was receiving weekly mail from Big Timber.

In its heydey, Melville had a flourmill, a cheese factory, a hotel, at least four saloons, two stores and a drug store. The railroad in Big Timber made such luxuries as dried fruits and green coffee available. From its humble beginnings, Melville was destined to earn the reputation as one of the toughest little towns in the state. The individuals who helped it earn that name were such men as Mel Jewell, Charlie Brown, Sim Roberts and "Tench" Hannon. It became a saying that if you wanted to get out-fought, out-rode, or out-run, come to Melville. Melville was the gathering point for miles around for Saturday night dances. Horse racing was especially popular in Melville, where stakes were high, not only for money, but cattle and horses, too.

The settlers organized the first Lutheran Congregation in the State of Montana in 1885 and built their Church in 1914. There were 18 services held at the Melville Church in 1915—two in English and 16 in Norwegian. Then, in 1924, church minutes were recorded in English for the first time. At the annual meeting in 1932, it was voted to allow women members of the church to vote and hold church office. A resolution was also passed that "fewer sermons be preached in Norwegian".

Bad winters and droughts or good weather and high prices—you never know what will happen in the ranching industry. People have come and gone in "the Settlement". Most of the supplies are purchased in Big Timber now. The Melville school is in session and the church still stands in its place at the foot of the Crazies. There have been changes in the town, but the country remains largely the same as it was when the first settlers found this wild and beautiful country. Soak in the peaceful vastness of the prairie, and imagine the early days of the cattle and sheep ranches built by the Norwegian settlers of Sweet Grass County. *Reprinted from Sweetgrass Chamber information sheet.*

## Scenic Drives

### Lewistown Ghost Town Tour

Begin by driving east on Hwy.. 87 approximately 12 miles to the Cheadle turnoff and go north approximately 7 miles to the town of Gilt Edge.

There are several ruins still standing in this town. Probably the most interesting building here is the house of prostitution which still has some of the tattered silk wallpaper hanging. This house is best viewed from the outside looking in as it is in serious decay and a danger to enter. Across the street from the house is an old jail, not much larger than a small horse stall. Legend has it that the notorious Calamity Jane spent a winter here in the late 1890s. There are many accounts of her presence there and a photo of her in the town with Teddy Blue Abbott, author of *"We Pointed Them North."*

From there continue on the road through Maiden Canyon. While driving this short but beautiful drive, you can take a sidetrip up to Judith Peak for a spectacular view of the surrounding mountains and prairie landscapes. From the top you can see the Snowy Mountains (30 miles south), Little Belts (70 miles southwest), North and South Moccasin Mountains (20 miles west), Highwood Mountains (70 miles west), Bear Paw Mountains (70 miles northwest), Little Rockies (70 miles northeast), and the Missouri River nestled in the Missouri River Breaks about 50 miles to the north. When you come back down the mountain continue west to the town of Maiden.

Maiden got its name when a fellow named Maden showed up late for the rush. He was rudely told to move on. He went up the valley to another gulch which he named "Camp Maden" for himself. The word "camp" was eventually dropped and an "i" was added. This was once a town of over 1,200 people with 154 houses and six saloons. It also had a department store, the ruins of which are still visible. The ruins are just east of the current town.

Leave Maiden heading west. In a couple of miles you'll come to an old stage coach road. Turn right here and go approximately six miles to Hilger. (If it has been raining recently or is currently raining—don't take this road! You will be buried alive in gumbo.) Otherwise continue on to Hwy.. 191 and head north to Hilger. From Hilger, take the country road west to the Kendall ghost town. This is the best preserved of the three local ghost towns.

On the return trip, take a right at the fork in the road and head south toward Brooks. This scenic stretch takes you along a beautiful valley and through the foothills of the North Moccasin Mountains. Turn left and go to Highway 191 where you will turn right for the return leg to Lewistown.

### Fort Maginnis

Begin by driving east from Lewistown on Hwy.. 87 approximately 12 miles to the Cheadle turnoff and go north. Head toward the ghost town of Gilt Edge and follow the signs to the Fort. This site features the historic ruins of the 1880 frontier military post which was crucial in the development of the area. Near the Fort is a small cemetery with several graves, including the grave of Teddy Blue Abbott, a famous western author. If you have the time, include a visit to the Fort on the ghost town tour.

**Spring Creek Tour**
From Lewistown drive 4.5 miles south on MT 238 to MT 466. Go right and drive two miles. Located in the Snowy Mountains, Big Spring is the third largest fresh water spring in the world, and is the source of Spring Creek. Over 90 million gallons of water a day flow out of the Spring. Also here is the Montana State Fish Hatchery. It is one of the three largest fish hatcheries in the west. More than 3 million trout are raised here each year. From the hatchery, go back to Hwy.. 238 and head south for about 12 miles to the East Fork Recreation Area. There is fishing and a boat launch site here, plus picnic tables and grills, restrooms, and a camp ground.

## Hikes

### Kings Hill Area

**Pioneer Ridge Trail #734**
**Access:** *5 miles north of Neihart and 03. miles north of the Belt Creek Information Station on the east side of U.S.Hwy. 89. Limited parking.*
**Elevation:** Beginning 5080 ft. Ending 7280 ft.
Attractions: Excellent 1 to 3 day hike. Trail is 7 miles long. Use is medium. Difficulty of the trail is rated as Difficult. Recommended season is early summer to mid-autumn. Provides access to other trails in the area. Ask permission to go on private land. USGS Map(s):Neihart. Baker, Belt Park Butte. Monarch Quads. (MT)

**Memorial Palls Trail #321**
**Access:** *1.6 miles southeast of Neihart on U.S.Hwy. 89. The trailhead is on the east side of the road.*
**Attractions:** The trail winds adjacent to the creek. Length of the trail is 0.5 mile and use is heavy. Difficulty is rated at easy. Recommended season of use is early summer to mid-autumn. There are two falls on the trail. Very enjoyable for sight-seeing and photography. Pleasant short day trip. USGS Map: Neihart (MT)

**North Fork Crawford Creek Trail #329**
**Access:** *4.8 miles north of Neihart at the Belt Creek Information Station.Trail starts behind the station.*
**Elevations:** Beginning, 5200 ft. (west across Belt Creek from the Belt Creek'Wormation Station) Ending, 6212 ft. (at the Belt Park Road in Belt Park).
**Attractions:** A good one day trip. Length of the trail is 3.2 miles and use is light. Difficulty is rated at easy. Recommended season of use is early summer to mid-autumn.Trail crosses back and forth across the creek. Please leave all gates as you find them.The last 0.7 mile of this route is across private land - PLEASE obtain permission from the owner. USGS Map: Belt Park Butte (MT)

**Paine Gulch Trail #737**
**Access:***1.2 miles south of Monarch on U.S. Hwy. 89.*
**Elevations:** Beginning, 4642 ft. (0.2 mile north of the Lazy Doe Bar on east side of U.S. 89. Ending, 5800 ft. (at base of Servoss Mountain).
Attractions: A one day in-out trip. Length of trail is 3.8 miles with use moderate. Difficulty is rated at easy. Recommended season of use is early summer to mid-antumn. The trail leads up Paine Gulch which has been nominated as a Research Natural area. No wheeled motorized vehicles are permitted. USGS Map: Monarch Quad (MT)

**North Fork Deep Creek Trail #303**
**Access:** *2.7 miles south of Logging Creek Campground on Forest Road #839 to Mill Creek.*
**Elevations:** Beginning, 5120 ft. (2.7 miles south on Forest Road at Mill Creek).Ending, 4180 ft (at junction with Trail #308 in the bottom of Deep Creek).
**Attractions:** The start of the trail in Mill Creek is the start of the Deep Creek Figure 8 Loop National Recreation Trail. Length of the trail is 8.8 miles and use is heavy. Difficulty is rated at more difficult. Recommended season of use is late spring to mid-autumn.This trail can be used to access the Smith River and for fishing in the North Port of Deep Creek. Use of the upper 6.1 miles of the trail by horses and motorized vehicles is heavy. USGS Map(s): Blankenbaker Flats, Deep Creek Park Quads (MT)

**South Fork Deep Trail #316**
**Access:** *6 miles west of junction of Forest Road #839 and Forest Road #268 past Monument Peak. Trail junction is along Forest Road #268.*
**Elevations:** Beginning, 6440 ft. (2 miles west of Monument Peak on Forest Road #268). Ending, 44480 ft. (junction of North Fork Deep Creek and South Fork Deep Creek).
**Attractions:** Trail crosses back and forth across the South Fork of Deep Creek. Length is 4.9 miles and use is heavy. Difficulty is rated at more difficult. Recommended season of use is late spring to late autumn. USGS Map(s): Deep Creek Park. Blankenbaker Hats. Monument Peak Quads (MT)

**Deep Creek Ridge Trail #338**
**Access:** *1.6 miles west on Forest Road #268 from the junction of Forest Roads #839 and #268 to Trail #339. North 1.1 miles on Trail #339 to trail #338. Ample parking at trailhead.*
**Elevations:** Beginning, 7223 ft. (2.2 miles north of Monument Peak). Ending, 4560 ft. (South Pork of Deep Creek on Trail #316).
**Attractions:** Part of the Deep Creek Figure 8 Loop National Recreation Trail. Length is 3.2 miles with usage heavy. Difficulty is rated at moderate. Recommended season of use is late spring to late autumn. Good portion for a 3-4 day trip into Deep Creek area. Road to trailhead 4x4 or other high clearance vehicle. USGS Map(s): Blankenbaker Hats, Deep Creek Park Quads (MT)

**Sawmill Trail #306**
**Access:** *1.2 miles north of Logging Creek Campground on Forest Road #839 to junction with Forest Road #6416 to the Private Land. 0.6 mile southwest through private lands from the gate trail. No parking at the trailhead with very little room to turn a vehicle around.*
**Elevations:** Beginning, 4640 ft. (at boundary of private land in Sawmill Gulch 1.2 miles northwest of Logging Creek Campground). Ending, 5148 ft. (bottom of Sand Coulee at the Forest Boundary).
Attractions: Access to the trail is limited on both ends because of private land. Only public access is via Ming Coulee Trail #307. The trail length is 7.0 miles with usage light. Difficulty of the trail is rated at moderate. Recommended season of use is late spring to late autumn. By backpacking, it can be used as part of a 2-5 day trip.USGS Map(s): Blankenbaker Rats, Evans Quads (MT)

**Blankenbaker Trail #320**
**Access:** *2.7 miles south of Logging Creek Campground on Forest Road #839 to Mill Creek and Trail #303. 1 mile east on Trail #303 to Trail #307. 2.8 miles north easterly on Trail #307 to junction of Trail #320.*
**Elevations:** Beginning, 6840 ft. (4.5 miles southwest of logging Creek Campground). Ending, 4860 ft. (ends at Trail #303 in the bottom of the North Fork of Deep Creek)
**Attractions:** The trail receives heavy motorized vehicle and horse use. Length of the trail is 2.8 miles and is heavy. Difficulty is rated at moderate. Recommended seasor of use is late spring to late autumn. The trail is located almost entirely in parks, meadows or open country. Much of the surrounding country can be observed from the trail. This trail comprises part of a very nice 2-5 day trip. USGS Map(s):Blankenbaker Hats, Deep Creek Park Quads (MT)

**Ming Coulee Trail #307**
**Access:** *2.7 miles south of Logging Creek Campground on Forest Road #839 to Mill Creek and Trail #303; 1 Mile east on Trail #303 to Junction of Trail #303 and Trail #307.*
**Elevations:** Beginning, 6200 ft. (3.5 miles north of Monument Peak at Trail #303). Ending, 5320 ft. (private land and NW Forest boundary at Ming Coulee).
**Attractions:** The upper portion of the trail is part of the Deep Creek Figure 8 Loop National Recreation Trail. The length of the trail is 6.9 miles and use is moderate. Difficulty of the trail is moderate. Recommended season of use is late spring to late autumn. Heavy use on the upper loop from horses and motorized vehicles. Good view points offer the user chances to observe surrounding country.

**Ming-Sand Coulee Crossover Trail #312**
*Access: 0.2 mile sooth from the end of Trail #307 in the bottom of Ming Coulee to the junction with Trail #312.*
**Elevations:** Beginning, 5240 ft. (2 miles from end of Ming Coulee Trail #307 in Ming Coulee). Ending, 5400 ft (at the Sand Coulee Trail #306).
Attractions: This is a short cut to get to Ming or

## Yogo Sapphires

Yogo Gulch is south of Hwy.. 87 between Windham and Utica in the Judith Basin. This is where the Montana sapphire bonanza was started. Jake Hoover, a friend of cowboy artist Charles Russell, made one of the earliest discoveries of Yogo sapphires. Looking for gold, he found the blue pebbles in the gravels of Yogo Creek in 1896. After sending a few samples off to Tiffany's in New York he was surprised to receive a check for $17,000. The Yogo mines attracted wide attention and capital. The U.S. Geological Survey termed the location "America's most important gem location."

The mining operation has had its up and downs through various owners through the years. The mining operations have been streamlined with new technology and about $40 million worth of the sapphires are mined annually. Yogo sapphires are admired for their ability to retain their amazing brilliance under all forms of light. They are formed very slowly, over 50 million years, allowing impurities to be purged through intense heat and pressure. Sapphires come in nearly all colors except red. Blue is of course the most common and desirable color. Yogo Gulch's signature "Cornflower Blue" sapphire is known throughout the world and was adopted as Montana's state gemstone in 1969.

Another well known sapphire mining area in Montana is located near Philipsburg, at Gem Mountain, where Montana Sapphires are found. Montana Sapphire is also legendary for the spectacular array of colors, clarity and brilliance. Some areas around Gem Mountain are open to the public. The Sapphire Gallery in Philipsburg is an excellent source for information about Gem Mountain.

Sand Coulee (one to the other). Length of the trail is 1.5 miles and use is light Difficulty is rated at moderate. Recommended season of use is late spring to late autumn. An excellent loop type trail for a 1-5 day trip in the Deep Creek Area.

**Temple Gulch Trail #308**
**Access:** *2.7 miles south of Logging Creek Campground on Forest Road #839 to Mill Creek and Trail #303; 5.2 miles west on Trail #303 to Trail #316; 0.6 mile south on Trail #316 to Trail #317; 1.8 miles west on Trail #317 & Trail #309; 1 mile northwest on Trail #309 to junction with Trail #308.*
**Elevations:** Beginning, 5340 ft (1.2 miles west of Robertson Spring in Deep Creek Park). Ending, 5520 ft. (Forest boundary north of Deep Creek Park).
**Attractions:** Trail ends at the forest boundary north of Deep Creek Park. No right-of-way across the private land on the north. Check with land owner before crossing. Length of the trail is 3.8 miles with use light. Difficulty is rated at moderate. Recommended season of use is late spring to late autumn or early winter. USGS Map: Deep Creek Quad (MT)

**Parker Ridge Trail #309**
**Access:** *2.7 miles south of Loggmg Creek Campground on forest Road #839 to Mill Creek and Trail #303; 6.2 miles west on Trail #303 to junction with Trail #316; 0,4 mile south on Trail #316 to junction with Trail #317; 1.8 miles west on Trail #317 to junction with Trail #309.*
**Elevations:** Beginning, 5320 ft. (4 miles east of the Smith River in Deep Creek Park). Ending, 3800 ft. (Smith River).
**Attractions:** One of the few access routes to the Smith River from the nationall forest Length of the trail is 4.0 miles and use is light. Difficulty of the trail is rated at moderate. Recommended season of use is mid-spring to late autumn. The first two (2) miles of the trail are used by 4x4 vehicles. The last mile of the trail is very steep and rough. Most of the trail is in open country and provides a good view of the surrounding area. USGS Map(s): Deep Creek Park and Millegan Quads (MT)

**Robertson Spring Trail #317**
**Access:** *2.7 miles south of Logging Creek Campground on Forest Road #839 to Mill Creek and Trail #303; 5.2 miles west on Trail #303 to Trail #316; 0.4 mile south on Trail #316 to junction with Trail #317.*
**Elevations:** Beginning, 4560 ft. (1,2 miles east of Robertson Spring in Deep Creek Park). Ending, 5300 ft. (in Deep Creek Park at junction with Trail #311).
**Attractions:** The length of the trail is 2.0 miles and use is heavy. Difficulty is rated at most difficult Recommended season of use is late spring to mid-autumn. The upper portion of the trail is located on private land. Please stay on the trail. USGS Map: Deep Creek Park Quad (MT)

**Smart Fork Trail #322**
**Access:** 2 miles west of Monument Peak on Forest Road 268; then 2 miles west onTrail #301. Parking at the trailhead is limited.
**Elevations:** Beginning, 7202 ft. (0.7 mile northwest of Desolation Peak on Trail #301). Ending, 4600 ft. (bottom of South Fork of Deep Creek at junction with Trail #316).
**Attractions:** The trail is steep and heads into South Pork Deep Creek. The length of thetrail is 2.5 miles with use moderate. Difficulty of the trail is rated at more difficult. Recommended season of use is late spring to late autumn. View from the trail is limited the last mile. USGS Map: Deep Creek Park Quad (MT)

**Strawberry Ridge Trail #311**
**Access:** *2 miles west of Monument Peak on Forest Road 268; 3 miles west on Trail #301 to the junction with Trail #311.*
**Elevations:** Beginning, 6850 ft. (Strawberry Ridge 1.7 miles west of Desolation Peak). Ending, 3880 ft. (private land in the Smith River)
**Attractions:** The entire trail offers a very good view of the surrounding country. Length of the trail is 6.5 miles with use moderate. Difficulty is rated at more difficult. Recommended season of use is late spring to late autumnGood access route to the Smith River. Excellent route to use with other trails for a 2-5 day trip. USGS Map(s):Deep Creek Park and Millegan Quads (MT)

**Old Baldy Trail #301**
**Access:** *2 miles west of Monument Peak on Forest Road 268 to Daisy Spring.*
**Elevations:** Beginning, 6440 ft. (2 miles west of Monument Peak on Forest Road 268). Ending, 5925 ft. (8.1 miles west of Monument Peak at junction of trails #310 and #331).
**Attractions:** Excellent trail to use if planning a 2-4 day trip into the Deep Creek area. Length of the trail is 6.1 miles with use heavy. Difficulty of the trail is rated at more difficult. Recommended season of use is mid-spring to late autumn. This trail is only a fair access route to reach either Smith River or Tenderfoot Creek. Most of the trail is along ridge tops and offers an excellent view of the surrounding country. USGS Map(s): Monument Peak and Bald Hills Quads (MT)

**Cow Coulee #331**
**Access:** *2 miles west of Monument Peak on Forest Road 368; 4.2 miles west on trail #301.*
**Elevations:** Beginning: 5860 ft. (1.2 miles west of Old Baldy on Trail #301) Ending, 4000 ft. (on private land on the Smith River).
**Attractions:** One of the access routes to the Smith River. Length is 4.4 miles with moderate use. Difficulty of the trail is rated at moderate. Recommended season of use is late spring to late autumn. There is moderate use by horses and motorized vehicles on this trail. The trail crosses private land and ends on private land on the Smith River. Good 2+day trip. USGS Map(s): Bald Hills and Lingshire Quads (MT)

**Bear Gulch Trail #310**
**Access:** *2 miles west of Monument Peak on Forest Road 268; 6.2 miles west on Trail #301.*
**Elevations:** Beginning, 5925 ft. (1.2 miles west of Old Baldy at the end of Trail #301) Ending, 3960 ft. (ends at the Smith River)
**Attractions:** One of the access routes to the Smith River. Length of the trail is 3.3 miles with light use. Difficulty of the trail is rated at more difficult. Recommended season of use is late spring to mid-autumn. The trail crosses private land; landowner allows use of the trail without permission. Very little use by horses of motorized vehicles. The trail is not well maintained in places. At the Smith River (end of trail) there is a nice camp spot. USGS Map(s): Bald Hills, Deep Creek Park and Millegan Quads (MT)

**Double Gulch Trail #354**
**Access:** 2 miles west of Monument Peak on Forest Road 268; 5.8 miles west on Trail #301. Parking at the trailhead is limited.
**Elevations:** Beginning, 6560 ft. (.7 mile west of Old Baldy on Trail #301). Ending, 4360 ft. (Tenderfoot Creek at the Mouth of Double Gulch). Attractions: This is an excellent trail for a 1-5 day trip providing access to Tenderfoot Creek and can be used as part of a loop with other trails. Trail length is 3.2 miles with light use. Difficulty is rated at more difficult. Recommended season of use is late spring to late autumn. Use of the trail is mostly by horses. USGS Map: Bald Hills Quad (MT)

## Montana Trivia

On July 31, 1884, The Husbandman reported:

"Nec-Tie parties are becoming very fashionable in eastern Meagher county. Horse thieves are usually the most conspicuous participants. The farmers, stock growers, and cowboys are having some rare enjoyment at these parties nowdays. There is certainly something very fascinating about horse stealing and having people turn out en mass and show so much respect to the thieves. It is an 'elevating' pursuit to say the least."

**Bald Hills Trail #345**
**Access:** *20.6 miles southwest on Forest Road 839 to Forest Road 268; 6 miles on Forest Road 268 (end of road). Limited parking at the trailhead.*
**Elevations:** Beginning, 6280 ft. (at the end of Forest Road 268 at Daisy Spring east of Monument Peak). Ending, 4688 ft. (trail ends at Tenderfoot creek).
**Attractions:** This is a good trail for access to Tenderfoot Creek. The length of the trail is 4.0 miles with medium use. Difficulty of the trail is rated at moderate. Recommended season of use is late spring to mid-autumn. The trail does pass through private land. Land owner allows foot and horse traffic on the trail within private land. Good 1-2 day trip. USGS Map(s): Monument Peak and Bald Hills Quads (MT)

**Taylor Hills Trail #344**
**Access:** *6.9 miles west on Forest Road 839 from the junction of Forest Road 839 and Forest Toad 3484. There is ample parking at the trailhead.*
**Elevations:** Beginning. 7440 ft. (2.8 miles west of Green Mountain of Forest Road 839). Ending, 5240 ft. (Tenderfoot Creek on Trail #342).
**Attractions:** The first 3.5 miles of the trail is used by 4x4 vehicles. The last 0.5 mile is steep and not usable by vehicles. Total length of the trail is 4.0 miles with heavy use. Difficulty is rated at more difficult. Recommended season of use is late spring to late autumn. USGS Map(s): Monument Peak and Blankenbaker Flats Quads (MT)

**Taylor Connector Trail #351**
**Access:** *2.8 miles west on Forest Road 839 from the junction of Forest Road 839 and Forest Road 3484, to the trailhead of Trail #343; 3.2 miles southwest on Trail #343, to the junction of Placer Creek and Balsinger Creek. Limited parking at the trailhead.*
**Elevations:** Beginning, 5840 ft (junction of Placer Creek and Balsinger Creek on Trail #343). Ending, 5930 ft. (private land 0.2 mile east of Taylor Hills).
**Attractions:** This is a short cut from Balsinger to Taylor Hills. The length of the trail is 1.8 miles with light use. Difficulty is rated at moderate. Recommended season of use is early summer to late autumn. USGS Map(s): Monument Peak and Bubbling Springs Quads (MT)

**Balsinger Trail #343**
**Access:** *19.1 miles northwest of Kings Hill on Forest Road 839. Very limited parking at the trailhead.*
**Elevations:** Beginning, 7200 ft. (2 miles west of Central Park on Forest Road 839). Ending, 5400 ft. (at Tenderfoot Creek in mouth of Balsinger Creek)

**Attractions:** Very good 1-2 day hike. Length of the trail is 4.0 miles with light use. Difficulty is rated at more difficult Recommended season of use is early summer to mid-autumn. Very little motorized or horse use on the trail. Not a good access route to Tenderfoot Creek. Crosses Balsinger Creek numerous times. USGS Map(s): Bubbling Springs and Monument Peak Quads (MT)

**Lost Stove Trail #346**

**Access:***16.1 miles northwest on Forest Road 839 from U.S. Hwy. 89 at Kings Hill junction of Forest Road 839 and Forest Road 3483; 4 miles south-westerly on Forest Road 3484 to Trail #346.*

**Elevations:** Beginning, 6600 ft. (2.8 miles south-west of Central Park). Ending, 5760 ft. (Tenderfoot Creek on Trail #342). This is the quickest and shortest route into the upper part of Tenderfoot Creek. Total length of the trail is 1.0 mile with moderate use. Difficulty rating of the trail is more difficult. Recommended season of use is early summer to late autumn.

**Attractions:** Sedans and short motorhomes can travel the roads in dry weather. USGSMap: Bubbling Springs Quad (MT)

**Tenderfoot Trail #342**

**Access:** *10.6 miles west of Kings Hill on Forest Road 839 to Forest Road 586; 1.2 miles west on Forest Road 586 to east side of Onion Park; 0.5 mile north on the old Divide Road to Trail #342.*

**Elevations:** Beginning, 7280 ft. (north end of Onion Park). Ending, 3960 ft. (Smith River at the mouth of Tenderfoot Creek).

**Attractions:** The trail provides access to some excellent trout fishing in Tenderfoot Creek. Length of the trail is 21.0 miles with heavy use. Difficulty of the trail is rated at more difficult. Recommended season of use is early summer to late autumn or early winter.There are 23 creek crossings from the start of the trail to the Zehntner Ranch. Do not use until after low water or runoff. View of steep walls is good in the lower portion of the canyon. Excellent 3-10 day trip possibilities. USGS Map(s): Belt Park Butte, Bubbling Springs. Monument Peak, Bald Hills and Lingshire Quads (MT)

**Williams Mountain Trail #347**

**Access:** *10.6 miles west of Kings Hill on Forest Road 839 to junction with Forest Road 585; 6.6 miles west on Forest Road 586 to junction with Forest Road 3465; 2.6 miles north on Forest Road 3465 to junction with Trail #347.*

**Elevations:** Beginning, 6700 ft. (1.5 miles north of Williams Mountain). Ending. 5800 ft. (Tenderfoot Creek on Trail #342)

**Attractions:** Access to the trail via Forest Road 3465 is restricted to foot and horse use 10/15 to 12/1 by locked gate at the junction of Forest Road 586 and Forest Road 3465. Total length of the trail is 1.0 mile and use is light. Difficulty rating is moderate. Recommended season of use is early summer to mid-autumn. The road is open for wheeled vehicle traffic; starting 6/15. Good trail to access Tenderfoot Creek in the summer. USGS Map: Bubbling Springs Quad (MT)

**Reynolds Park Trail #349**

**Access:** *10.6 miles west on Forest Road 839 from Hwy. 89 on Kings Hill to junction with Forest Road 586; 11 miles west on Forest Road 586 to junction of Forest Road 3472 in Eagle Park; north 2.1 miles on Forest Road 3472 to the start of Trail 3349. Road leading to Reynolds Park is not designed for sedans or other low vehicles.*

**Elevations:** Beginning, 600 ft. (2.5 miles north of Eagle Park). Ending, 5360 ft. (Tenderfoot Creek Trail #342)

**Attractions:** Good access route to Tenderfoot Creek from the south. Trail is 1.0 mile is length and use is light. Difficulty is rated at moderate. Recommended season of use is early summer to mid-autumn. Some of the road used to access the trail and part of the trail is located on private land. Obtain permission to cross Reynolds Park. Do Not use road in wet weather. USGS Map: Monument Peak Quad (MT)

**Monument Ridge Trail #339**

**Access:** *7.6 miles north of Logging Creek Campground on Forest Toad 839 to junction with Forest Road 268; 1.6 miles west of Forest Road 268 to junction with Trail 3339.*

**Elevations:** Beginning. 6977 ft. (1.7 miles west of Monument Peak on Forest Toad 268). Ending, 6220 ft. (Mill Creek Saddle at junction with Trail #303).

**Attractions:** The first 1.1 mile can be driven in a 4x4 or other high clearance vehicle. The last 1.6 mile is very steep and rough, even for hiking. Total length of the trail is 2.7 miles and use is high. Difficulty rating is more difficult. Recommended season of use is early summer to mid-autumn. Trail is part of the Deep Creek Figure 8 Loop National Recreation Trail. USGS Map: Blankenship Flats Quad (MT)

## Little Belt Mountains

**Dry Wolf Trail #401**

**Access:** *No. 1 - From Hwy. 87 at Stanford; follow Dry Wolf Road #251 to Wolf Campground. Drive through the campground to the picnic site where the trailhead is located.*

*No. 2 - From Hwy. 87 at Stanford, follow Diy Wolf Road #251 to Dry Wolf Campground. Follow the road approximately 600 feet and then turn right on a primitive road. Travel about 1 mile through a grassy park to Freddies Meadow dispersed campsite. The old Dry Wolf Trail starts at Freddies Meadow campsite and can still be followed, though you have to cross the deep creek. You also can follow trail #402 for about 1000 ft. then take a trail to the right which leads over a bridge to trail #401.This way the trail is only 4.2. miles in length.*

**Elevations:** Beginning, 5950 ft. (Dry Wolf Campground; trailhead is at picnic site). Ending, 7500 ft. (Yogo-Big Baldy Jeep Trail, Forest Road #3300 on the Jefferson Divide).

**Attractions:** The trail climbs continually, first at an easy slope following Dry Wolf Creek through meadows and timber, then at a steeper slope following a ridge through the forest. Length of the trail is 5.2 miles and use is medium. Difficulty is rated from easy to moderate. The trail ends at the meadows on Jefferson Divide, providing a beautiful panorama view. The upper part of the trail can be snowbound until the middle of July. USGS Map: Yogo Peak Quad (MT)

**Butcherknife Trail #417**

**Access:** *No. 1, From Hwy. 87 at Stanford, follow Dry Wolf Road #251 to Butoherknife Gulch; here take Butoherknife Road #2093, there is a trail sight after about a mile (to the right).*

*No. 2 - Via Trail #416 from Big Baldy Mountain.*

**Elevations:** Beginning, 5800 ft. (Butoherknife Road #2093). Ending. 7800 ft. (Big Baldy Trail #416 on ridgetop).

**Attractions:** Length of the trail is 3 miles; low use. Difficulty is rated at moderate. After a hard, steep climb to the ridgetop, you walk through meadows, with a beautiful view. The trail will follow the ridgetop until it terminates at the Big Baldy Trail, which leads to the highest mountain in the Little Belts: Big Baldy Mountain, 9176 ft. USGSMap: Mixes Baldy Quad (MT)

**Placer Creek Trail #419**

**Access:** *No. 1 - From Hwy. 87 at Stanford; follow Dry Wolf Road #251. After 20 miles, mere is a sign "Placer Creek" and a primitive road branching to the right. The first half mile of this road leads through private land. You need to ask permission to cross it. The trail-head is 1.5 miles from Dry Wolf Road at the forks of Placer Creek and Snow Creek.*

*No. 2 - By trail #416 from Big Baldy Mountain.*

**Elevations:** Beginning. 6000 ft. (Placer Creek Jeep Trail, 1.5 miles from Dry Wolf Road). Ending, 7400 ft. (Big Baldy Trail #416 on ridgetop).

**Attractions:** The trail is 2 miles (3.5 miles when starting at Dry Wolf Road) and use is medium. Difficulty is rated at easy. The trail follows the Snow Creek drainage through heavy, mixed conifer timber stands up to the meadows on the ridgetop where there is a panorama view in all directions. Here it terminates at trail #416, a trail that follows the ridgetop. USGS Map(s): Mixes Baldy and Yogo Peak Quads (MT)

**North Fork Highwood Trail #423**

**Access:** *No. 1, Half a mile west of Thain Creek Campground, North Fork Road #8840 goes south, following the creek. The trailhead is 1 mile up.*

*No. 2 - Kirby Creek Trail #426.*

**Elevations:** Beginning, 4600 ft. (North Fork Road #8840). Ending, 4750 ft. (Cottonwood Creek Jeep Trail, east forest boundary).

**Attractions:** The trail is 3.5 miles in length and use is medium. Difficulty is rated from easy to difficult.The trail leads through meadows and follows the North Fork to its headwaters. Here is the junction with Kirby Creek Trail #426. The trail then climbs over a saddle (highest point 6000 ft.) and descends in the drainage ofCottonwood Creek. It follows the creek to the forest boundary. USGSMap: Arrow Peak Quad (MT)

**Kirby Creek Trail #426**

**Access:** *No 1, From Geraldine, MT via Shonkin Creek to Kirby Creek, then following the trail through private land (ask permission before you cross).*

*No. 2, Via Briggs Creek Trail #431.*

*No. 3, Via North Fork Highwood Trail #423.*

**Elevations:** Beginning, 4700 ft. (fence boundary between private land and National Forest in Kirby Creek). Ending, 5400 ft. (North Fork Highwood Trail #423).

**Attractions:** Length of the trail is 2.0 miles with low use. Difficulty is rated at moderate (hard to find trail).The trail is mainly a small cow-path through scenic meadows, following Kirby Creek up towards the headwaters. Just before that point, the trail climbs over a saddle and comes down to the North Fork Highwood Trail #423. USGS Map: Arrow Peak Quad (MT)

**Windy Mountain Trail #454**

**Access:** *No. 1, From Thain Creek Campground, follow Road #1074 to the north of Thain Creek Campground.*

*No. 2, Briggs Creek Trail #431.*

**Elevations:** Beginning, 4500 ft. (Trailhead at the end of road #1074). Ending, 5400 ft. (trail terminates at Briggs Creek #431).

**Attractions:** This trail forms together with Briggs Creek Trail #431, a 6.5 miles loop from Thain Creek Campground. The trail leads up to a saddle just south of Windy mountain and then down through meadows to Briggs Creek Trail #431. Use of the trail is medium with difficulty rated at easy. USGS Map: Arrow Peak Quad (MT)

**Briggs Creek Trail #431**

**Access:** *No.1, Follow the road to the east from Thain Creek Campground. The road ends after 3000 ft. The trail starts here.*

*No.2, Via windy Mountain Trail #454.*
**Elevations:** Beginning, 4580 ft. (end of road going from Thain Creek Campground to the east) Ending, 4900 ft. (Kirby Creek Trail #426)
**Attractions:** Length of the trail is 3.5 miles with moderate use. Difficulty is rated at easy to difficult; (trail is hard to find).
This trail can be used for a day hike loop from Thain Creek Campground by going either north via the Windy Mountain Trail #454 or south via Kirby Creek Trail #426. This trail climbs up to a saddle following Briggs Creek to its origin. The trail then climbs up to a saddle where it junctions with the Windy Mountain Trail. Here the Briggs Creek Trail starts descending to Kirby Creek following the Grant Creek drainage. USGSMap: Arrow Peak Quad (MT)

### Snowy Mountains

The following trails are located on the Judith Ranger District portion of the Snowy Mountains.

**Crystal Lake Shoreline Loop Trail #404**
**Access:** From Stanford, Hwy. 87 east to Moore. Turn south (right) onto the road to Crystal Lake. Pick up the trail either at the picnic area or campground.
**Elevations:** Beginning, 6000 ft. (Crystal Lake Campground and Grandview Picnic area). Ending, 6000 ft. (Crystal Lake Campground and Grandview Picnic area).
**Attractions:** Length of trail is 1.7 miles. Use is high with difficulty rated at easy. The trail follows the shoreline of Crystal Lake and is almost level with access to the entire shore and opportunities for sunbathing, swimming, fishing, picnicking, etc. The whole trail forms a loop, bringing you back to the place you started. USGS Map: Crystal Lake Quad (MT)

## Cross-Country Ski Trails

*For more information on the following trails contact Belt Creek Ranger Station, Neihart, MT 59465 (406) 236-5511*

**North Waldron Trails North Fork Teton—Teton Pass Ski Area**
*5 km More Difficult; no grooming*
Access from Teton Pass Ski Area; parking available.

**Mizpah Ridge—7 mi. SE Neihart**
*2.1 km Easiest; 2.2 km More Difficult, 1.2 km Most Difficult; no grooming*
Park in lot near Kings Hill Campground. Trailhead on west side of Hwy..

**O'Brien Creek-7 mi. SE Neihart**
*2 km Easiest, 2.5 km More Difficult, 2.2 km Most Difficult; no grooming*
Park in lot near Kings Hill Campground. Trailhead on west side of Hwy..

**Silver Crest—same as above**
*4.7 km Easiest, 10.3 km More Difficult, 4.2 km Most Difficult: intermittent grooming*
Park in Kings Hill winger recreation lot (2 miles N of Pass).

**Deadman—same as above**
*2 km Easiest, 1.2 km More Difficult, 3.2 km Most Difficult; no grooming*
Park in lot near Kings Hill Campground Trailhead on E side of Hwy..

*For more information on the following trails contact: District Ranger, Stanford, MT 59479 (406) 566-2292*

**Green Pole-35 mi. SW Lewistown**
*2.4 km Easiest; no grooming*
Parking for 10 cars; check on road conditions.

**Rock Creek—same as above**
*2.9 km Easiest; no grooming*
Parking for 10 cars; check on road conditions.

## Information Please

All Montana area codes are 406

### Road Information

Montana Road Condition Report
800-226-7623, 800-335-7592 or local 444-7696
Montana Highway Patrol 444-7696

**Local Road Reports**
Great Falls 453-1605
Lewistown 538-7445
Billings 252-2806
Statewide Weather Reports 453-2081

### Tourism Information

Travel Montana 800-847-4868 outside Montana
444-2654 in Montana
http://travel.mt.gov/.
Custer Country 665-1671 or 800-346-1876
Russell Country 761-5036 or 800-527-5348
Missouri River Country
653-1319 or 800-653-1319
Northern Rodeo Association 252-1122

**Chambers of Commerce**
Harlowton 632-4694
Lewistown 538-5436
Roundup 323-1966
Stanford 735-6948
White Sulphur Springs 547-3366

### Airports

Harlowtown 632-4545
Lavina 444-2506
Lewistown 538-3264
Roundup 323-1011
Ryegate 444-2506
Sand Springs 557-6144
Stanford 566-2236
White Sulphur Spgs. 547-3412

### Government Offices

State BLM Office 255-2885, 238-1540
Bureau of Land Management
Great Falls Field Office 791-7700
Lewistown Field Office 538-7461
Lewis & Clark National Forest 791-7700
Montana Fish, Wildlife & Parks 444-4720
U.S. Bureau of Reclamation
Helena Field Office 475-3310
Charles M. Russell National Wildlife Refuge
538-8706

### Hospitals

Wheatland Memorial Hospital
Harlowton 632-4351
Central Montana Medical Center
Lewistown 538-7711
Roundup Memorial Hospital
Roundup 323-2301
Basin Medical Center • Stanford 566-2773
Mountain View Memorial Hospital
White Sulphur Springs 547-3321

### Golf Courses

Judith Shadows Golf Course
Lewistown 538-6062
Pine Meadows Golf Course
Lewistown 538-5885
Pine Ridge Golf Club • Roundup 323-2880
Arrowhead Meadows Golf Association
White Sulphur Springs 547-3993
Jawbone Creek Country Club
Harlowton 632-4206

### Bed & Breakfasts

Duvall Inn • Lewistown 538-7063
Meadow Brook Farm B&B Inn
Hobson 423-5537
Pheasant Tales Bed & Bistro
Lewistown 538-7880
Montana Mountain Lodge
White Sulphur Springs 547-3773
Foxwood Inn•White Sulphur Springs 547-2224
Symmes Wicks House • Lewistown 538-9068
Sky Lodge B&B•White Sulfur Springs 547-3999
The Columns • White Sulphur Springs547-3666

### Guest Ranches & Resorts

Bonanza Creek Country • Martinsdale 572-3366
Careless Creek Ranch Getaway
Shawmut 632-4140
Circle Bar Guest Ranch • Utica 423-5454
Checkerboard Inn • Checkerboard 572-3373
Camp Maiden • Lewistown 538-9869
Forest Green Resort
White Sulphur Springs 547-3496
Prairie Skys Retreat • Shawmut 537-4492
Hougen Ranch • Melstone 358-2204
Homestead Ranch • Utica 423-5301
Solberg's Pine Valley Cabins
Martinsdale 572-3322
Trophy Trout Springs Ranch & Fly Fishing
Hobson 423-5542

### Vacation Homes & Cabins

Camp Baker Outfitters
White Sulphur Springs 547-2173
The Creek House • Lewistown 538-4961
Golden Bear Outfitters • Judith Gap 473-2312
Grassy Mountain Lodge
White Sulphur Springs 547-3357
Leninger Ranch Log Cabin Rentals
Lewistown 538-5797
The Montana Bunkhouse • Moore 538-5543
Pigeye Basin Outfitters • Utica 423-5494
Rocking J Cabins & Campground
Monarch 236-5535
Sadie Creek House • Harlowton 632-4246
Solberg's Pine Valley Cabins
Martindsdale 572-3322

### Forest Service Cabins

***Gallatin National Forest***
**Bennett Creek Guard Station**
20 mi. N of Wilsall on Hwy. 89 on Shields River Rd. 222-1892
Capacity: 5 Nightly fee: $25 Available: All year
Wood heat/propane cook stove, lanterns, no drinking water. Cross-country ski or snowmobile for 5 miles, in winter. High clearance vehicles in summer.

***Lewis and Clark National Forest***
**Calf Creek Cabin**
20 mi. N of White Sulphur Springs 547-3361
Capacity: 4 Nightly fee: $30 Available: All year
Access Forest Road No. 119. Not plowed. Cabin 8 mi. from Hwy. 89. Wood stove & firewood provided.

**Crystal Lake Cabin**
35 mi. SW of Lewistown. 566-2292

Capacity: 6 Nightly fee: $25 Available: 10/15 - 4/30 (max. stay 7 days)
Plowed within 6 mi. Early late season snow conditions may be marginal. No water. Lights, wood stove & firewood provided.

**Dry Wolf Cabin**
15 mi. SW of Stanford.
Capacity: 5 Nightly fee: $25 Available: All year
Late season road vehicle access may be marginal. Four-wheel drive advised. No water. Propane cookstove, lights, woodstove & firewood provided.

**Hunters Spring Cabin**
40 mi. NW of Harlowton 632-4391
Capacity: 8 Nightly fee: $20 Available: 12/1 - 3/31
Plowed within 7 mi. of cabin. Propane stove, refrigerator, wood stove, firewood & water provided.

**Kings Hill Cabin**
Kings Hill Pass. 31 mi. N of White Sulphur Springs 547-3361
Capacity: 6 Nightly fee: $40 Available: All year
l00 yards from Hwy. 89. Parking, plowed in winter. Near cross-country & snowmobile trails. Firewood, electrical lighting, refrigerator & cooking facilities provided. No water.

## Private Campgrounds

| | |
|---|---|
| Little Montana Truck Stop Grass Range | 428-2270 |
| Chief Joseph Park • Harlowtown | 632-5532 |
| Conestoga Campground White Sulphur Springs | 547-3890 |
| Fergus Country Fairgrounds Lewistown | 538-4060 |
| Hilltop Campgrounds • Winnett | 429-5321 |
| Historic Jersey Lilly Campground Ingomar | 358-2278 |
| J&M RV Park • Stanford | 566-2289 |
| Judith Landing • Winifred | 386-2202 |
| Mountain Acre RV Park & Campground Lewistown | 538-7591 |

## Car Rental

| | |
|---|---|
| Budget Rent-A-Car of Lewistown | 538-7701 |

## Outfitters & Guides

*F=Fishing H=Hunting R=River Guides*
*E=Horseback Rides G=General Guide Services*

| | | |
|---|---|---|
| Al Bassett, Montana Outfitter | H | 947-5335 |
| Avalanche Basin Outfitters | G | 547-3962 |
| Bales Hunts | H | 784-2487 |
| Beaver Creek Outfitters | H | 538-5706 |
| Birch Creek Outfitters | H | 547-2107 |
| Bull Mountain Outfitters | G | 947-3337 |
| Camp Baker Outfitters | H | 547-2173 |
| Castle Mountain Fly Fishers | HF | 547-3918 |
| Circle Bar Guest Ranch | HF | 423-5454 |
| Crow Creek Outfitters | HF | 266-3742 |
| DC Outfitting | HF | 538-7821 |
| Golden Bear Outfitters | HF | 473-2312 |
| Headwaters Angling | F | 547-2390 |
| Homestead Ranch | HF | 423-301 |
| Howard Zentner Hunting | HF | 547-3483 |
| Kibler Outfitting & Charter | F | 557-2503 |
| MBK Outfitters | HF | 323-3062 |
| McFarland & White Ranch | H | 632-5637 |
| Missouri Breaks Adventures | H | 428-2222 |
| Musselshell Outfitters | HF | 323-3043 |
| Pigseye Basin Outfitters | HF | 423-5494 |
| Starwest Adventures | F | 538-8670 |
| Sundance Outfitting Service | GFH | 575-4215 |
| Tri Mountain Outfitters | HF | 547-2177 |
| Twin Buttes Outfitters | H | 554-3495 |
| Virgelle Mercantile & Missouri River Canoe Co. Virgelle | R | 378-3110 |
| West Fork Outfitters | H | 251-5542 |
| Yellowater Outfitters | G | 428-2119 |

## Downhill Ski Areas

| | |
|---|---|
| Showdown Ski Area | 236-5522 |

## Snowmobile Rentals

| | |
|---|---|
| Montana Snowmobile Adventures Niehart | 236-5358 |
| Lewistown | 538-5436 |

## Notes:

Section 9

## Dining Quick Reference

Price Range refers to the average cost of a meal per person: ($) $1-$6, ($$) $7-$11, ($$$) $12-up. Cocktails: "Yes" indicates full bar; Beer (B)/Wine (W), Service: Breakfast (B), Brunch (BR), Lunch (L), Dinner (D). Businesses in bold print will have additional information under the appropriate map locator number in the body of this section.

| RESTAURANT | TYPE CUISINE | PRICE RANGE | CHILD MENU | COCKTAILS BEER WINE | SERVICE | CREDIT CARDS | MAP LOCATOR NUMBER |
|---|---|---|---|---|---|---|---|
| Jersey Lilly Bar & Cafe | American | $-$$$ | | Yes | B/L/D | V/M | 1 |
| A & W Family Restaurant | Fast Food | $ | Yes | | L/D | | 3 |
| Blue Star Espresso | Coffee House | $ | | | | | 3 |
| Busy Bee Family Dining & Gift | Family | $ | Yes | B/W | B/L/D | Major | 3 |
| Pioneer Cafe | Family | $ | Yes | B/W | B/L/D | Major | 3 |
| Stella's Supper Club | Steaks & Seafood | $-$$$ | Yes | Yes | L/D | Major | 3 |
| Buffalo Trail Cafe | Family | $/$$ | | B/W | B/L/D | Major | 5 |
| Ryegate Cafe | | | | | | | 5 |
| Stage Stop Store & Cafe | Family | $ | | | B/L | | 6 |
| Hitching Post Cafe | American | $ | | | B/L/D | V/M | 7 |
| **Graves Hotel** | American | $/$$ | Yes | Yes | B/L/D | Major | 7 |
| Eat Shop Drive In | Fast Food | $ | No | | L/D | | 7 |
| Merino Inn | Family | $ | Yes | | B/L/D | | 7 |
| Sportsman's Bar & Steakhouse | Steakhouse | $$ | Yes | Yes | D | Major | 7 |
| The Cornerstone Restaurant | Family | $ | Yes | B/W | L/D | V/M | 7 |
| Wade's Drive Inn & Cafe | Family | $ | Yes | | B/L/D | Major | 7 |
| The Mint | Burgers/Hot Dogs | $ | | All | L/D | No | 9 |
| J T'S Bar & Supper Club | | | | | | | 11 |
| Dori's Cafe | American | $ | | | B/L/D | | 13 |
| The Connexion | American | $ | Yes | Yes | L/D | | 13 |
| Truck Stop Cafe | Family | $ | | | B/L/D | | 13 |
| Lazy Doe Bar & Restaurant | American | $ | | | L/D | | 15 |
| Bob's Restaurant, Motel & Gas | American | $ | | Yes | L/D | Major | 15 |
| Kozy Korner Bar & Cafe | American | $ | Yes | Yes | B/L/D | | 17 |
| **Yogo Inn & Garden Restaurant** | Family | $$ | Yes | Yes | B/BR/L/D | Major | 20 |
| Dairy Queen | Fast Food | $ | Yes | | L/D | | 20 |
| Dash Inn | Fast Food | $ | Yes | | L/D | | 20 |
| Little Big Men Pizza | Pizza | $ | | B/W | L/D | | 20 |
| Taco Time | Fast Food | $ | Yes | | L/D | | 20 |
| 4 Aces Casino & Restaurant | American | $$ | | Yes | L/D | Major | 20 |
| Bon Ton Cafe | Soda Fountain | $ | | | | | 21 |
| Bullseye Bagels | Bagel Shop | $ | | | | | 21 |
| Dominga's Specialty Cafe | Oriental | $ | | | B/L/D | | 21 |
| Empire Cafe | Family | $ | Yes | | B/L/D | | 21 |
| Main St. Bistro | Continental | $/$$ | | Yes | L/D | V/M | 21 |
| Poor Man's Books & Coffee | Coffee House | $ | | | B/L | | 21 |
| Saphire Cafe | Family | $ | Yes | | B/L | | 21 |
| The China Garden | Chinese | $ | | | L/D | V/M | 21 |
| The Mint Bar & Grill | Steakhouse | $$/$$$ | | Yes | D | Major | 21 |
| The Whole Famdamily Cafe | Deli & More | $ | Yes | B/W | L/D | Major | 21 |
| Newlan Creek Club | Steaks & Seafood | $-$$$ | | Yes | L/D | | 21 |
| Crabtree Coffee & Cafe | Coffee House | $ | | | B/L | Major | 22 |
| Hackamore Supper Club | Steaks & BBQ | $$ | | Yes | D | Major | 22 |
| McDonald's | Fast Food | $ | Yes | | B/L/D | | 22 |
| Pizza Hut | Pizza | $/$$ | Yes | B | L/D | V/M/D | 22 |
| Sportsman Restaurant | American | $$ | | Yes | B/L/D | V/M | 22 |
| Subway | Fast Food | $ | Yes | | L/D | | 22 |
| Eddie's Corner Inc | American | $$ | | B/W | B/L/D | Major | 30 |
| By-Way Cafe | Family | $$ | | | | | 34 |

**NOTES:**

## Motel Quick Reference

Price Range: ($) Under $40 ; ($$) $40-$60; ($$$) $60-$80, ($$$$) Over $80. Pets [check with the motel for specific policies] (P), Dining (D), Lounge (L), Disabled Access (DA), Full Breakfast (FB), Cont. Breakfast (CB), Indoor Pool (IP), Outdoor Pool (OP), Hot Tub (HT), Sauna (S), Refrigerator (R), Microwave (M) (Microwave and Refrigerator indicated only if in majority of rooms), Kitchenette (K). All Montana area codes are 406.

| HOTEL | PHONE | NUMBER ROOMS | PRICE RANGE | BREAKFAST | POOL/ HOT TUB SAUNA | NON SMOKE ROOMS | OTHER AMENITIES | CREDIT CARDS | MAP LOCATOR NUMBER |
|---|---|---|---|---|---|---|---|---|---|
| Bunk & Biscuit Bunkhouse Dormitory | 932-5799 | | | | | | | | 1 |
| **Big Sky Motel** | 323-2303 | 22 | $ | | | Yes | P/R/DA | Major | 3 |
| Best Inn | 323-1000 | 20 | $ | CB | | Yes | K/M/R | Major | 3 |
| Ideal Motel & Trailer Court | 323-3371 | 10 | $ | | | Yes | K/M/R | Major | 3 |
| **Graves Hotel** | 632-5798 | 45 | $$/$$$ | | | Yes | D/L | Major | 7 |
| Corral Motel | 632-4331 | 18 | $ | | | Yes | K/P | Major | 7 |
| Country Side Inn | 632-4119 | 15 | $$ | | HT/S | Yes | P/R | Major | 7 |
| Troy Motel | 632-4428 | 7 | $ | | | Yes | P | | 7 |
| Crazy Mountain Inn | 572-3307 | 10 | $/$$ | | | Yes | P/D/L | V/M | 9 |
| **Spa Hot Springs Motel** | 547-3366 | 21 | $$ | | IP/OP | Yes | P | Major | 13 |
| **All Seasons Super 8** | 547-8888 | 32 | $$ | CB | HT | Yes | DA | Major | 13 |
| Gordon's Highland Motel | 547-3880 | 10 | $ | | | Yes | P | Major | 13 |
| Tenderfoot Motel | 547-3303 | 14 | $ | | | Yes | K/P/R/DA | Major | 13 |
| Bob's Restaurant, Motel & Gas | 236-5955 | 12 | $$ | | HT | Yes | D/L/DA | Major | 15 |
| Cub's Den Motel | 236-5922 | 14 | $$ | CB | OP/HT | Yes | P/D/L/DA | Major | 16 |
| **Yogo Inn** | 538-8721 | 122 | $$$ | | IP/OP/HT | Yes | P/D/R/L/DA | Major | 20 |
| **The Sunset Motel** | 538-8741 | 16 | $ | | | Yes | K/P/M/R | Major | 20 |
| B & B Motel | 538-5496 | 38 | $$ | CB | | Yes | K/P/R | Major | 20 |
| **Trails End Motel** | 538-5468 | 18 | $ | | OP | Yes | K/P/M/R/DA | V/M/D | 21 |
| **Historic Calvert Hotel** | 538-5411 | 45 | $ | | | | | Major | 21 |
| **Mountain View Motel** | 538-3456 | 33 | $/$$/$$$ | | | Yes | P/K | Major | 22 |
| Lewistown Super 8 | 538-2581 | 44 | $$ | | | Yes | DA | Major | 22 |
| Triangle Motel | 538-9914 | 5 | $$ | | | Yes | K/P/R | V/M/D | 22 |
| Eddie's Corner | 374-2471 | 4 | $ | | | | D/L/DA | Major | 7 |
| Sundown Motel | 566-2316 | | | | | | | Major | 34 |
| Runway Motel | 566-2943 | 4 | $$ | | | | DA | Major | 34 |

Section 9

## Fishery

| Fishery | Cold Water Species | | | | | | | | | | | | Warm Water Species | | | | | | | | | | Services | | | | | |
|---|---|---|---|---|---|---|---|---|---|---|---|---|---|---|---|---|---|---|---|---|---|---|---|---|---|---|---|---|
| | Brook Trout | Mt. Whitefish | Lake Whitefish | Golden Trout | Cutthroat Trout | Brown Trout | Rainbow Trout | Kokanee Salmon | Bull Trout | Lake Trout | Arctic Grayling | Burbot | Largemouth Bass | Smallmouth Bass | Walleye | Sauger | Northern Pike | Shovelnose Sturgeon | Channel Catfish | Yellow Perch | Crappie | Paddlefish | Vehicle Access | Campgrounds | Toilets | Docks | Boat Ramps | MotorRestrictions |
| 136. Belt Creek | • | • | | | | • | • | | | | | | | | | | | | | | | | • | • | • | | | |
| 137. Lake Sutherlin | | | | | | | | | | | | • | | | | | | | | | | | • | • | • | | • | |
| 138. Bair Reservoir | | | | | | | • | | | | | | | | | | | | | | | | • | • | • | | • | |
| 139. Martinsdale Reservoir | | | | | | • | • | | | | | | | | | | | | | | | | • | • | • | | • | |
| 140. Musselshell River | • | • | | | | • | • | | | | | | | | | | | | | | | | • | • | • | | | |
| 141. Deadman's Basin Reservoir | | | | | | • | • | | | | | | | | | | | | | | | | • | • | • | | • | |
| 142. Crystal Lake | | | | | | | • | | | | | | | | | | | | | | | | • | • | • | | • | • |
| 143. Ackley Lake | | | | | | | • | | | | | | | | | | | | | | | | • | • | • | | • | |
| 144. Judith River | • | • | | | | • | • | | | | | | | | | | | | | | | | • | • | • | | | |
| 145. Big Spring Creek | | • | | | | • | • | | | | | | | | | | | | | | | | • | | • | | | |
| 146. Warm Springs Creek | | | | | | | • | | | | | | | • | | | | | | | | | • | | | | | |
| 147. Petrolia Reservoir | | | | | | | | | | | | | | | • | | • | | | • | | | • | • | • | | • | |
| 148. Newlan Creek Reservoir | | | | | • | | • | | | | | | | | | | | | | | | | • | • | • | | • | |
| 149. Musselshell River | | • | | | | • | | | | | | | | • | | | | | • | | | | • | • | • | | | |
| 150. Broadview Pond | | | | | | | • | | | | | | • | | | | | | | | • | | • | | | | | |

## Campsite Directions

| Campsite Directions | Season | Camping | Trailers | Toilets | Water | Boat Launch | Fishing | Swimming | Trails | Stay Limit | Fee |
|---|---|---|---|---|---|---|---|---|---|---|---|
| **198•Logging Creek FS**<br>11 mi. S of Belt on US 89 to Sluice Boxes State Pk.<br>•6 mi. W on Cty. Rd. to Forest Rd. 67•4 mi. S to Forest Rd. 839, then 2 mi. SW | Summer/Fall | 26 | 22′ | D | • | | • | | • | 14 | • |
| **199•Aspen FS**<br>6 mi. N of Neihart on US 89 | Summer/Fall | 6 | 22′ | D | • | | • | | • | 14 | • |
| **200•Moose Creek FS**<br>18 mi. N of White Sulphur Springs on US 89•6 mi. W on Forest Rd. 119<br>•3 mi. W on Forest Rd. 204 | Summer/Fall | 6 | 22′ | • | • | | • | | | 14 | • |
| **201•Kings Hill FS**<br>9 mi. S of Neihart on US 89 | Summer/Fall | 18 | 16′ | D | • | | • | | • | 14 | • |
| **202•Many Pines FS**<br>4 mi. S of Neihart on US 89 | Summer/Fall | 23 | 22′ | D | • | | • | • | | 14 | • |
| **203•Dry Wolf FS**<br>20 mi. SW of Stanford on Cty. Rd.• 6 mi. SW on Forest Rd. 251 | Summer | 26 | 32′ | • | • | | • | | • | 14 | • |
| **204•Ackley Lake FWP**<br>23 mi. W of Lewistown at Hobson•Milepost 58•5 mi. S on Rt. 400•2 mi. SW on Cty. Rd. | All Year | 18 | • | • | • | C | • | | | 14 | • |
| **205•Indian Hill FS**<br>12 mi. W of Hobson on Rt. 239•12 mi. SW on Cty. Rd.•3 mi. SW on Forest Rd. 487 | Summer | 7 | 22′ | • | | | • | | • | 14 | |
| **206•Jumping Creek FS**<br>22 mi. NE of White Sulphur Springs on US 89 | Summer/Fall | 15 | 22′ | D | • | | • | | • | 14 | • |
| **207•Spring Creek FS**<br>30 mi. W of Harlowton on US 12•4 mi. N on Forest Rd. 274 | Summer/Fall | 10 | 22′ | • | • | | | | • | 14 | • |
| **208•Grasshopper Creek FS**<br>7 mi. E of White Sulphur Springs on US Forest Rd. 211 | Summer/Fall | 12 | 16′ | • | • | | • | | • | 14 | |
| **209•Richardson Creek FS**<br>7 mi. E of White Sulphur Springs on US 12•5 mi. S on Forest Rd. 211 | Summer/Fall | 3 | 16′ | • | | | • | | • | 14 | |
| **210•Crystal Lake FS**<br>9 mi. W of Lewistown on US 87•16 mi. S on Cty. Rd.• 8.5 mi. S on Forest Rd 275 | Summer | 28 | 22′ | • | • | • | < | • | • | 14 | • |
| **211•Deadman's Basin FWP**<br>20 mi. E of Harlowton on US 12 | All Year | • | • | • | • | A | • | | | 14 | |

**Agency**
FS—U.S.D.A Forest Service
FWP—Montana Fish, Wildlife & Parks
NPS—National Park Service
BLM—U.S. Bureau of Land Management
USBR—U.S. Bureau of Reclamation
CE—Corps of Engineers

**Camping**
Camping is allowed at this site. Number indicates camping spaces available
H—Hard sided units only; no tents

**Trailers**
Trailer units allowed. Number indicates maximum length.

**Toilets**
Toilets on site. D—Disabled access

**Water**
Drinkable water on site

**Fishing**
Visitors may fish on site

**Boat**
Type of boat ramp on site:
A—Hand launch
B—4-wheel drive with trailer
C—2-wheel drive with trailer

**Swimming**
Designated swimming areas on site

**Trails**
Trails on site
B—Backpacking N—Nature/Interpretive

**Stay Limit**
Maximum length of stay in days

**Fee**
Camping and/or day-use fee

**Notes:**

# Section 10

## Northeast Corner

## Including Glasgow, Sidney, Wolf Point and Surrounding Area

*The gulches surrounding Plentywood offered plenty of hiding places for outlaws in the late 1800s.*

## Weather Averages

**Glasgow**

| | |
|---|---|
| January | |
| Average High: | 19.9° F |
| Average Low: | 1.2° F |
| Record High : | 57.0° F |
| Record Low : | -47.0° F |
| Average Precip.: | 0.37 in |
| Rain/Snow Days: | 8 days |
| April | |
| Average High: | 56.5° F |
| Average Low: | 32.0° F |
| Record High : | 91.0° F |
| Record Low : | -3.0° F |
| Average Precip.: | 0.69 in |
| Rain/Snow Days: | 7 days |
| July | |
| Average High: | 84.7° F |
| Average Low: | 56.7° F |
| Record High : | 104.0° F |
| Record Low : | 41.0° F |
| Average Precip.: | 1.72 in |
| Rain/Snow Days: | 8 days |
| October | |
| Average High: | 58.7° F |
| Average Low: | 33.3° F |
| Record High : | 90.0° F |
| Record Low : | -6.0° F |
| Average Precip.: | 0.61 in |
| Rain/Snow Days: | 5 days |

**Wolf Point**

| | |
|---|---|
| January | |
| Average High: | 21.2° F |
| Average Low: | -1.3° F |
| Average Precip.: | 0.32 in |
| April | |
| Average High: | 58.7° F |
| Average Low: | 30.4° F |
| Average Precip.: | 0.92 in |
| July | |
| Average High: | 87.6° F |
| Average Low: | 56.0° F |
| Average Precip.: | 2.09 in |
| October | |
| Average High: | 61.1° F |
| Average Low: | 31.7° F |
| Average Precip.: | 0.68 in |

**Fort Peck Lake**

| | |
|---|---|
| January | |
| Average High: | 20.9° F |
| Average Low: | -0.7° F |
| Average Precip.: | 0.42 in |
| April | |
| Average High: | 57.0° F |
| Average Low: | 31.1° F |
| Average Precip.: | 0.90 in |
| July | |
| Average High: | 86.2° F |
| Average Low: | 56.6° F |
| Average Precip.: | 1.57 in |
| October | |
| Average High: | 59.4° F |
| Average Low: | 32.5° F |
| Average Precip.: | 0.71 in |

**Sidney**

| | |
|---|---|
| January | |
| Average High: | 24.1° F |
| Average Low: | 2.0° F |
| Average Precip.: | 0.38 in |
| April | |
| Average High: | 58.5° F |
| Average Low: | 31.0° F |
| Average Precip.: | 1.14 in |
| July | |
| Average High: | 87.1° F |
| Average Low: | 56.8° F |
| Average Precip.: | 1.81 in |
| October | |
| Average High: | 60.8° F |
| Average Low: | 33.3° F |
| Average Precip.: | 0.84 in |

**Jordan**

| | |
|---|---|
| January | |
| Average High: | 28.7° F |
| Average Low: | 2.8° F |
| Average Precip.: | 0.45 in |
| April | |
| Average High: | 60.0° F |
| Average Low: | 30.0° F |
| Average Precip.: | 1.06 in |
| July | |
| Average High: | 89.8° F |
| Average Low: | 54.9° F |
| Average Precip.: | 1.56 in |
| October | |
| Average High: | 63.3° F |
| Average Low: | 30.8° F |
| Average Precip.: | 0.75 in |

**1.** *Historical Marker, Attraction, Gas, Food, Lodging, Shopping*

### Sidney

When the railroad arrived at Glendive, so did hundreds of settlers and homesteaders spreading out along the Yellowstone Valley. Near Lone Tree Creek, the current site of Sidney, homesteads began to dot the countryside. When the telegraph line connecting Fort Keogh to Fort Buford crossed the town site in 1878, this remote part of the nation was connected with the rest of the world. Soon after, the townspeople, tired of making the trip to Newlon 10.5 miles away to post their mail, petitioned for a post office under the name Eureka. Imagine their disappointment when Washington D.C. officials informed them that the name had already been taken by another community in northwestern Montana.

The man responsible for submitting the petition, Judge H. L. Otis, employed a family named Walters. The judge, a long time bachelor, was fond of their six-year-old son Sidney. Sidney was his constant companion and steadfast fishing buddy.. When Judge Otis suggested the name of his young friend for the new post office, not an objection was heard. The community on the banks of the Lone Tree had a name. Today it is nicknamed the "Sunrise City" and is the largest town in northeast Montana.

At one time, one of the largest herds of buffalo on the North American continent roamed the area between the Yellowstone and Missouri Rivers over the land that is now present day Richland County. These massive herds stretched for as far as the eye could see.

### H Old Fort Gilbert

north of Sidney on Mt 200.

"Old Fort Gilbert" was situated directly east of this point on the west bank of the Yellowstone River. The Fort was named after Colonel Gilbert, one-time commanding officer at Fort Buford, and existed between the years 1864 and 1867. It was used as a trading center in the lower Yellowstone Valley. This point also marks the south boundary

All Montana Area Codes are 406

Section 10

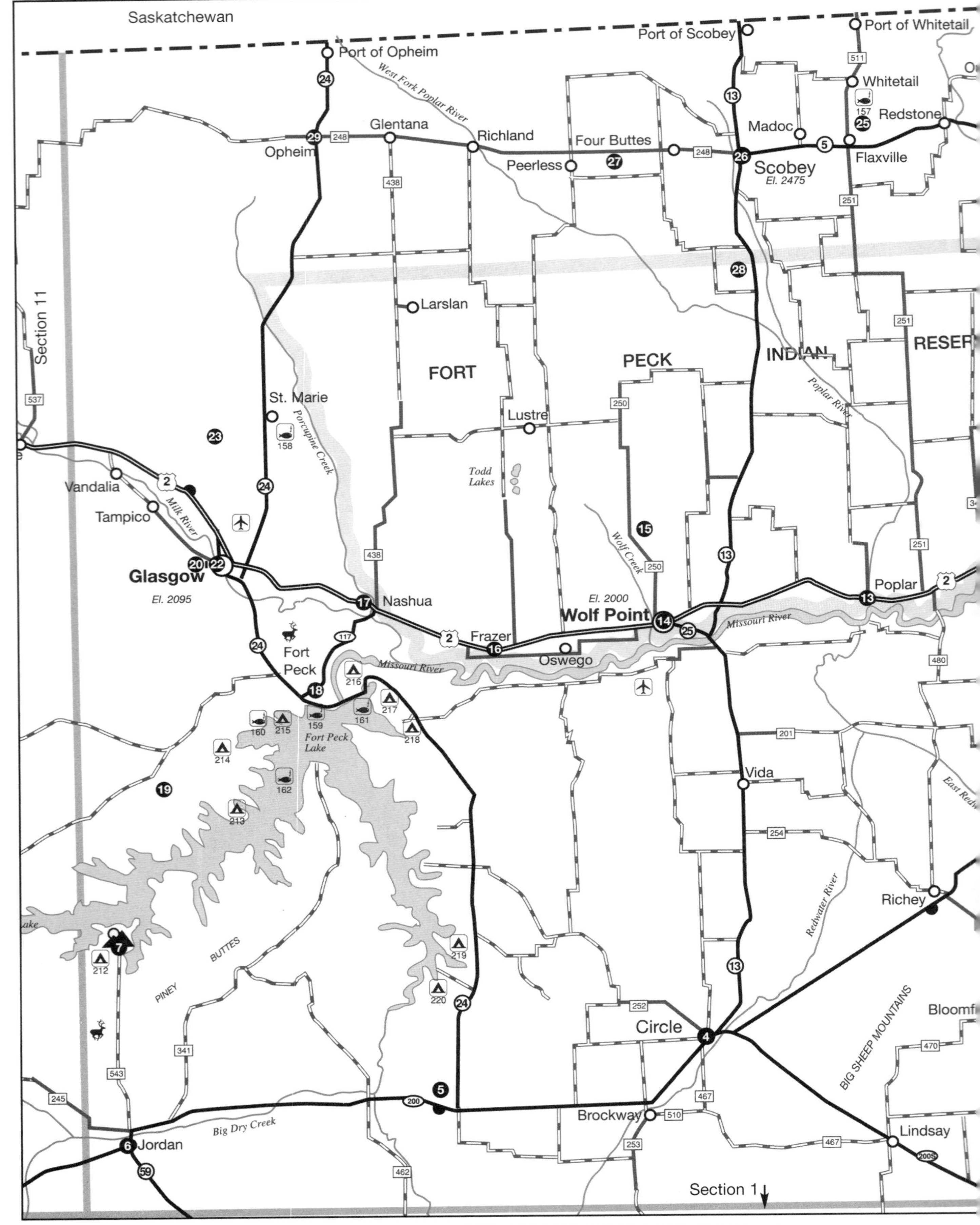

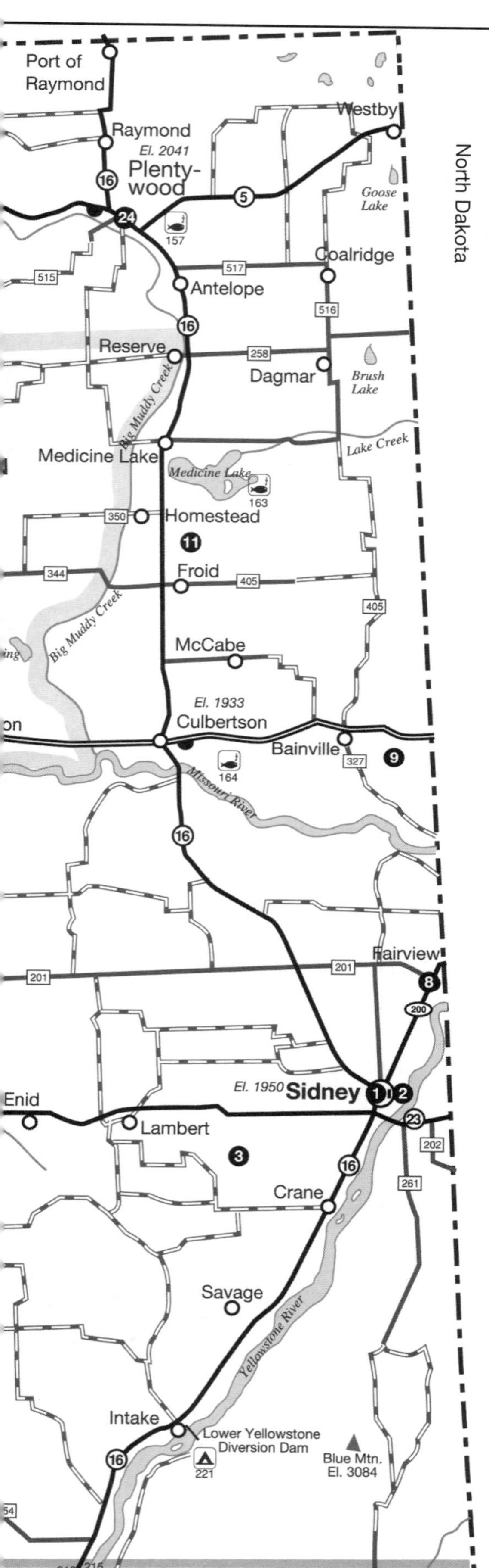


# Section 10

0 Miles 13 20

One inch = approximately 13 miles

**Legend**

- Locator number (matches numeric listing in section)
- Wildlife viewing
- Campsite (number matches number in campsite chart)
- State Park
- Fishing Site (number matches number in fishing chart)
- Rest stop
- Interstate
- U.S. Highway
- State Highway
- County Road
- Gravel/unpaved road

## On the Road

The paved highways and gravel backroads of this part of the state are passable in all but the worst weather. However, many of the less traveled backroads are impassable when wet (see gumbo in general info section). In some places, the back roads roll with the terrain like a roller coaster. Fun for the kids. The roads here are narrower and the local population is not used to seeing many cars on them. You may very well come over a rise and find yourself head-on with a local's pick-up truck. Stay far to the right and drive at a prudent speed that allows you time to react. Follow the same rule on blind curves.

It's a good idea to carry plenty of water with you. Stops are far between, and on the backroads, services are non existent. The dry Montana air can quickly dehydrate you.

For the sheer beauty of it, May through July is the best time to travel through here. The grasses and wheat fields are green and stretch forever, a paintbox of wildflowers blanket the countryside, cloud patterns accent the endless sky, and the sunsets last forever. As the summer matures, the landscape turns to gold. In the fall the colors return as the low lying shrubbery turns red and the cottonwoods turn to orange.

The following item appeared in the August 15, 1913 edition of *The Plentywood Herald:*

## Speed Limit 90 Miles an Hour

The above sign is the first thing that greets the eye of every visitor coming to Fairview from any direction.

The sign has caused no end of comment, the remarks of an auto touring party last Friday were typical of many.

"That's sure going some! Then we stopped to read the sign again and decided that the town with no speed limit must have some 'live wires' in it. So, here we are to look her over. Ain't she a dandy? Never saw so much building going on before at one time, and [the] town is growing! It's no wonder you took off the speed limit on autos and everything else." —*Fairview Times*

She sure is a dandy as a representative of the *Herald* and J.W. McKee autoed down there last Sunday. A $30,000 hotel and a $15,000 theater is in the course of construction, to say nothing of the other business places and private homes that are being built.

Chas. Johnson, the genial lumber man told us, while his good wife fed us on fried spring chicken and other good things, of their enthusiastic commercial club and how hard it was to keep a stock of lumber on hand as the demand was so great.

*Reprinted with permission from the "Outlaw News", a publication of Missouri River Country.*

of the Fort Buford Military Reservation, which post operated for many years on the north bank of the Missouri River at the mouth of the Yellowstone.

By taking the side road just north of here and going west a short distance to Fort Gilbert Lookout Point, on the bluffs, you have an excellent view of the Yellowstone Valley. Well worth the drive.

## T Mondak Heritage Center
Downtown Sidney. 853-1912

This is a history museum and a regional art center. It includes an extensive historical library. A wide, curving staircase delivers you to a complete "town" that has been re-created and furnished down to the last detail with artifacts from the homesteader days. It's easy to imagine you've stepped back in time as you leisurely wander through their street scene.

The displays include a church, school, bank, post office, sheriff's office, leather and tack shop, dental office, soda fountain and depot. Also on display are brands from ranchers in the area, a model of Fort Union Trading Post with accompanying information, and display cases full of fascinating artifacts. Other highlights include an old jail door and leather handcuffs found in the sheriff's office; an increasingly rare wooden altar painted to look like marble in the church; a fully equipped dentistry office that even smells like the real thing; and a 1919 Model T and a vintage Fisk-brand tire sign found in the service station. The museum is open year round except January from 1-4 p.m. There is a nominal admission charge.

## D William Clark
August 2, 1806

*"about 8 A.M this morning a Bear of the large vicious Species being on a Sand bar raised himself up on his hing feet and looked at us as we passed down near the middle of the river. he plunged into the water and Swam towards us."*

### Montana Trivia

The easternmost town in Montana is the little burb of Westby in the extreme northeast corner of the state. How did it get the name *West*by? Until the railroads came through and moved it across the border, it was the westernmost town in North Dakota The suffix by means "town" in Danish.

## FS Homestead Books and Clothes & South 40 Restaurant and Casino
207 2nd Ave. NW, Sidney. 482-5571
or toll free 800-788-4419

The Homestead and South 40 have celebrated over 25 years in Sidney. The main level comprises the Homestead, home of an ever-evolving selection of apparel and accessories for sizes ladies sizes, 4 - 24. The upper level accommodates the largest selection of books for miles, with a vast selection of Western, Americana, and regional titles. There is also a complete health and vitamin department. The award-winning South 40 Restaurant serves lunch and dinner 7 days a week. Their enormous Soup and Salad Bar accompanies most entrées or can be a meal in itself. They also bring people back with juicy prime rib and sizzling steaks. The South 40 Lounge features a full casino, darts, trivia games, karaoke, appetizers, and cocktails for your enjoyment.

## F Sadie's Stockyard Homecooking Cafe
Sidney Livestock Center, Rt. 2, Sidney. 482-9949

## S Quilts & More - Full Line Quilt Shop
2 miles north, Hwy. 200, to Co Rd. 127, south on Co. Rd. 352, Sidney. 482-3366 or fax 482-6772

## 2. *Gas, Food, Lodging*

## 3. *Gas, Food*

### Enid
This town was named for a child—Enid Montana Dawe. Her father, L.A. Dawe was one of the early settlers in the area and the first postmaster. This town boomed during the homesteader area with a railroad depot, a two-story schoolhouse and a number of shops and stores.

### Richey
Richey sits in the middle of productive ranching and farming country. Cattle and sheep co-exist amidst fields of wheat, oats, and barley. The author pulled into this town right at the start of the high school's homecoming parade. Had to wait almost 90 seconds for it to pass. It's a fun little town.

### Savage
The namesake of H. M. Savage, a supervising engineer for the U.S. Reclamation Service.

## T Historical Society Museum
Lambert. 774-3439

While this museum traces the area's beginnings from 1914, emphasis is placed on its native son, former Governor Nutter. Open May through September, Tuesdays and Thursdays, 9 a.m. to 3 p.m. Admission is free.

## T Richey Historical Museum
Main St. & Antelope Ave. in Richey. 773-5656

Like most of the small museums throughout Montana, this one has its collection of items from Montana's past. The museum actually consists of several small buildings including the Lisk Creek School No. 92 which was used from 1914-1918; a homestead shack; and another small building displaying items from the Richey Mercantile, the area's first store. Over 5,000 items are on display. Some of the items include a Model A mail car, pioneer kitchen, blacksmith shop, church and school memorabilia, and newspaper files from 1916 to 1948. There are also several articles of clothing on display: World War I and II uniforms, wedding dresses, and coats made of buffalo hides, raccoon, horsehide, and muskrat. The museum is open from Memorial Day through Labor Day in the afternoons.

## 4. *Historical Marker, Attraction, Gas, Food, Lodging, Shopping*

### Circle
Circle is located halfway between Glendive and the Fort Peck Reservoir and the Big Sheep Mountains lie to the north. Circle got its start as a cattle town; the name is derived from a circle brand used by one of Montana's first cattle outfits.

## H Circle
Circle

*Major Seth Mabry, a Confederate Army officer, came to the Redwater Valley about 1883, driving a herd of longhorns from Texas. President of the Mabry Cattle Co., he branded with a plain circle iron. From the brand, the operation became known as the Circle Ranch. They sold three to four thousand beeves each fall for about 13 years.*

*Other cattlemen ran the ranch until about 1900 when Peter Dreyer and Hans Grue bought it and used it as a summer camp for sheep and as a stopover for themselves and other ranchers going to and from Glendive. Two bachelors ostensibly cared for the ranch, but actually they started a saloon there. Since strong drink spoiled the sheepherders' work habits, Dreyer and Grue offered the place to Dreyer's brother-in-law, Peter Rorvik, in 1903. During an absence of the saloonkeepers, the Rorviks and their six children moved in. The next summer saw 100,000 sheep on the Redwater River. The herders and ranchers needed a supply source, so Rorvik opened a store on the ranch.*

*So began the town of Circle about one-half mile southeast of here. In 1907, the surrounding lands were opened to homesteading and the area has been producing grain as well as livestock ever since.*

## T McCone County Museum
Hwy.. 200 on west edge of Circle. 485-2414

Features the 35 year old accumulated wildlife collection of Orville Quick and his sons. While driving through town, don't be surprised to see a brontosaurus towering over Orville Quick's house. Once you find the museum though, you'll find an extensive collection of mounted birds and animals of Eastern Montana are set in their natural habitat. In addition there are over 5,000 items on display including a large firearm collection, a replica homesteader's shack, a military display, Indian artifacts, agricultural tools and equipment, and more. Open year round from 9 a.m. to 5 p.m. on weekdays. Admission is free.

**5.** *Historical Marker*

### H Dinosaurs

MT 200, east of Jordan.

*Difficult to believe now, but 80 million years ago the middle of our continent was a shallow sea. This area, when not underwater, was part of a hot, humid tropical coastline of marshes, river deltas, and swamps, bearing dense vegetation probably similar to that found on the southern coast of Louisiana today.*

*Fossils tell us that turtles, crocodiles, lizards, toads, fishes, small primitive mammals, and dinosaurs lived on this coastal plain. Many of the most complete dinosaurs on display in the world were gathered here in Garfield County. The first Tyrannosaurus rex skeleton came out of its hills in 1902. In fact, four of the six tyrannosaurs found in the world are from Garfield County and five of the six are from Montana. The Garfield County Museum in Jordan holds replicas of a tyrannosaur skull, a duckbill dinosaur skull, and a triceratops skeleton.*

*Paleontologists were puzzled by the scarcity of young dinosaurs and eggs in this rich fossil area. One explanation was discovered in 1978 on the eastern front of the Rocky Mountains about 300 miles west of here. Hundreds of eggs from at least three different dinosaur species and thousands of whole and partial dinosaur skeletons were found. This new evidence indicates that the dinosaurs migrated from the coast to the mountains to lay their eggs and raise their young. One may see fossils from this site at the Museum of the Rockies in Bozeman, Montana.*

**6.** *Historical Marker, Attraction, Gas, Food, Lodging*

### Jordan

Jordan is the site of three of the world's six Tyrannosaurus Rex skeleton finds. Located within Garfield County in the heart of eastern Montana, dinosaur tours are the town's main attraction. Jordan began as a small cow town in the 1890s. The post office opened in 1899 with Arthur Jordan as postmaster. The most isolated county seat in the lower 48 states, Jordan is 175 miles from the nearest airport, 85 miles from the closest bus line and 115 miles from the nearest train.

### H Indian Country

MT 59, south of Jordan

*Until the early 1880s this portion of Montana was wild unsettled country where roving parties of Sioux, Crow and Assiniboine Indians hunted buffalo and clashed in tribal warfare. Sitting Bull's band of Hunkpapa Sioux frequently ranged through here and except for a few nomadic trappers there were no white men.*

*With the coming of the Texas trail herds the buffalo were slaughtered to clear the range for beef critters and the cattle kings held sway for many years.*

*In 1910 the first wave of homesteaders surged in and the open range dwindled before their fences and plowed fields. The glamour of the frontier days is gone.*

### T Garfield County Museum

Hwy. 200 in Jordan. 557-2517

A one-room school house sits beside the museum and is completely furnished with everything from old text books to the water pail and double desks from old schools in the area.

## On the Trail of Lewis & Clark

**April 27, 1805:** The Corps of Discovery left their campsite where Fort Union is now located and followed the Missouri River into what is now Montana. Besides the two captains, there were three sergeants, 23 enlisted men, Clark's black slave, York, two inter-preters, Drouillard and Charbonneau, Charbonneau's wife, Sacajawea and her 2-month-old son, Baptiste (nicknamed Pomp) and Seaman, Lewis's Newfoundland dog. They came in six canoes and two round boats called pirogues. They camped that night across the river from what is now the community of Nohly in Richland County.

**April 28, Sunday:** They covered 24 miles. Lewis: *"the beaver have cut great quantities of timber; saw a tree nearly 3 feet in di-ameter that had been felled by them."* Camped on the south side of the river near Otis Creek.

**April 29, Monday:** Lewis saw and shot his first Grizzly bear which pursued him 70 or 80 yards before the second shot killed him. He wrote: *"...this anamal ap-peared to me to differ from the black bear; it is a much more furi-ous and formidable anamal, and will frequently pursue the hunter when wounded."* Camped just above Big Muddy Creek in Roosevelt County.

**April 30, Tuesday:** Clark, Charbonneau and Sacajawea walked along the shore most of the day. Lewis shot a bull elk which men-sured 5 feet 3 inches from hoof to top of the shoulder. Camped on the north side near the present Brockton.

**May 1, Wednesday:** Lewis wrote: *"...the wind being favorable—we used our sales which carried us on a a good pace untill about 12 OCk. when the wind became so high that the small canoes were unable to proceed."* Spent the rest of the day and night on the south side in the vicinity of the later Elkhorn Point.

**May 2, Thursday:** *"...at daylight it began tosnow...ground was covered with an inch deep, forming a striking contrast with the veg-etation, which is considerably advanced, put-ting flowers forth..."* Camped 15 miles below Porcupine River (now Poplar River) on the north side.

**May 3, Friday:** Went several miles up Porcupine River and named a *"bold running stream"* 2000 Mile Creek, (Redwater now) because that is how far they figured they had come. They camped three or four miles above the present town of Poplar. This site is not certain.

**May 4, Saturday:** *"We were detained this morning untill about 9 OCk. in order to repare the rudder irons...which were broken last evening in landing;... passed several old Indian hunting camps..."* Traveled 18 miles and camped on the north shore (Roosevelt County).

**May 5, Sunday:** *"saw the carcases of many Buffaloe lying dead along the shore partially devoured by the wolves and bear."* Clark found a den of young wolves, possibly coy-otes. *"my dog caught a goat (antelope) which he over-took by superior fleetness, the goat it must be understood was with young and extreemly poor."* They camped southeast of the present town of Wolf Point. Due to shifts in the river, the campsite is now on the opposite side and a mile or two from the river.

**May 6, Monday:** Lewis: *"a fine morning ... passed two Creeks and a River today on the Lard ... the countrey on both sides butifull."* Camped on a point on the south side of the river (now McCone County), a few miles south-west of the present town of Oswego.

**May 7, Tuesday:** *"the country we passed today on the North side of the river is one of the most beautifull plains we have yet seen, it rises gradual-ly ... then becoming level as a bowling green.... as far as the eye can reach;"* Camped on the south bank, a few miles south-west of the present town of Frazer.

**May 8, Wednesday:** Lewis wrote: *"We saw a great number of buffaloe, elk, common and blacktailed deer, goats, beaver and wolves."* Camped on south side (of old river bed) about 7.5 river miles below Fort Peck Dam. Site is now in Valley County.

**May 9, Thursday:** Passed Big Dry on the south side. Lewis wrote: *"today we passed the bed of the most extraordinary river that I ever beheld, it is as wide as the Missouri is at this place or 1/2 a mile wide and not containing a single drop of runing water;"* They traveled 24 1/2 miles (9 1/2 past the Big Dry) and camped on the north side near what is now Duck Creek.

**May 10, Friday:** Set out at sunrise but only traveled 4 1/2 miles when a violent storm came up and they had to seek shelter on the south side. A dog wandered into their shelter, and they watched for Indians but saw none. Group is bothered with boils and sore eyes.

**May 11, Saturday:** Woke to frost. River very crooked, banks caving in and strong winds. Bratton was chased by bear he had, shot. Hunters went back and killed the bear. It took two men to carry the hide. They ren-dered the bear's oil—about eight gallons. Traveled 17 miles and camped on the south shore, close to where "The Pines" is today.

**May 12, Sunday:** Lewis describes choke cherries in *"blume."* Strong winds. Traveled 18 3/4 miles and camped early on the south side.

**May 13, Monday:** Did not start until after-noon because of strong winds. *"... courant weather stronger than usual and the water contin-ues to become reather clearer, from both which I anticipate a change of country shortly."* wrote Lewis. They started saving skins to make a leather boat to use above the falls. Traveled seven miles and camped on the south side about one or two miles above the former entrance of today's Crooked Creek.

*Excerpted from Missouri River Country brochure, "Montana's Lewis and Clark Trail Through Missouri River Country."*

Section 10

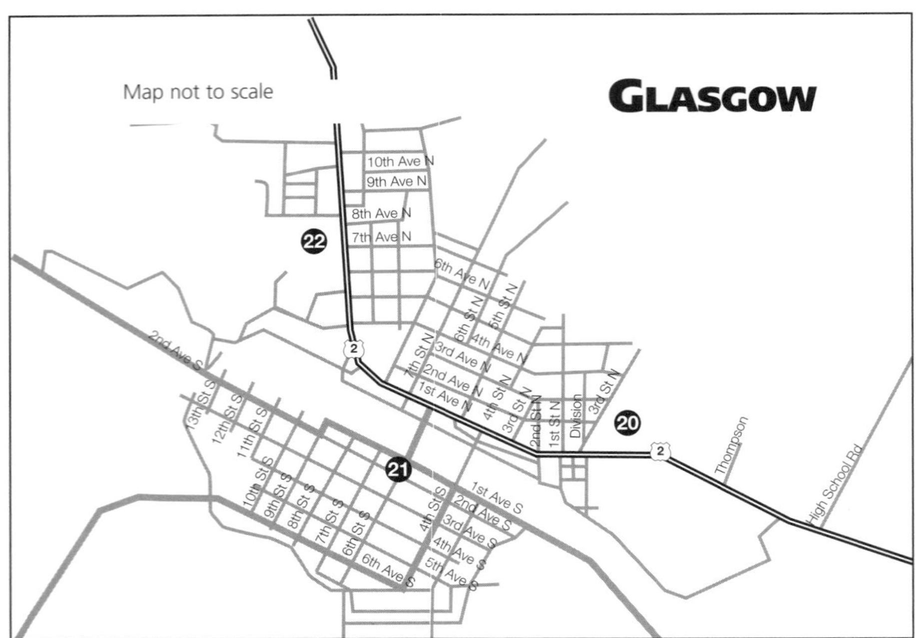

Sugarbeet monument in Fairview

Dr. Farrand practiced in the county for over 50 years and delivered around 3,000 babies. There is a special display of pictures of many of "his" babies and his medical tools.

This summer the museum is starting a Hall of Fame featuring early settlers. The first section will be of people who came before 1910. If you know someone who should be in this section, please drop the museum a note and picture, if possible.

Garfield County, then part of Dawson County, was one of the last areas to be homesteaded. Arthur Jordan arrived at the Big Dry in the summer of 1896 and by 1900 had a small trading post and a post office.

### Montana Trivia

Jordan has been called the "lonesomest town in the world." It is 175 miles from the nearest airport and 115 miles from the nearest rail depot. It sits in the middle of an area known as "The Big Open".

Most of the homesteaders came to the area around 1912. At one time before the dry 1930s, there were around 8,000 people in the county. Now there are around 1,500 and a third of them live in Jordan.

There has never been a train so they came in wagons and later cars and trucks. Many of the things they brought with them are housed in this museum that opened in 1984.

Displays include a bedroom, a parlor, a dining room and kitchen decorated by local ladies' clubs, drug and hardware store collections, a blacksmith shop, early photography, World War I uniforms, animals of the area, and an almost complete file of old Jordan Tribunes.

An addition to the west side of the museum houses antique farm machinery.

A fiberglass replica of a triceratops, which may have weighed 12 tons and stood ten feet tall in real life, stands in its diorama along the north wall.

Harley Garbani from the Los Angeles Museum of Natural History dug up the original on the Frank McKeever ranch about 25 miles northwest of Jordan in 1965.

In the Cretaceous sediments of the badlands along the Missouri River, paleontologists have made some of the first and most important fossils finds.

Just after the turn of the century Dr. Barnum Brown of the American Museum of Natural History found the first Tyrannosaurus Rex in the Hell Creek area north of Jordan.

In 1989 a Garfield County couple found an almost complete Tyrannosaurus skeleton along the shore of Fort Peck Lake, the seventh in the area. It is now in the Museum of the Rockies.

Smaller fossils such as mollusks, fish, leaf prints, figs and even dinosaur eggs are found in the gumbo hills. Many of these are displayed in the museum. *Reprinted from museum brochure*

## 7. *Attraction*

### T Hell Creek State Park

North of Jordan on Rte. 543.

The road into this park passes through rugged badlands. A beautiful park weaving through fossil and dinosaur land offers a prime wildlife viewing area. Elk, foxes, deer and coyotes are a few of the animals you might see. Eighteen miles from Jordan, a pullout provides a magnificent view.

## 8. *Attraction, Gas, Food, Lodging, Shopping*

### Fairview

Nestled in the heart of the valley at the confluence of the Yellowstone and Missouri Rivers, lies the friendly, quiet, and a little bit strange town of Fairview. As Montana's easternmost town it has the unique feature of two states meeting on Interstate Avenue more commonly known to residents as State Street. Part of the town lies in North Dakota, while the majority is in Montana. You can literally drive down State Street with the driver in Montana and the passenger in North Dakota. To compound the weirdness, the line dividing the Mountain time zone from the Central time zone also passes through town. You need to be pretty careful when making appointments in this town.

Fairview is the Sugar Beet Capital of both Montana and North Dakota with a large part of its irrigated farm land devoted to the growing of sugar beets. While there are other parts of both states that produce more sugar beets, they got the title because they asked for it. Since no one else had ever asked, the governors from both states said—"Okay." During the fall harvest, you will see millions of beets being hauled on endless streams of trucks carrying what looks like large potatoes. In fact, the industry is so big here that there is a monument in the center of town dedicated the humble beet.

The people here are pretty mellow—honest, friendly, and proud of their community, but laid-back. Call the police department just about any time after 5:00, at lunchtime, or on weekends and you may get an answering machine. The residents here have pretty much always been known for their laid-back attitude. The story goes that in the beginning, a bar sat on the bench overlooking the valley below. A patron of the bar, sitting on the back porch commented, "Now that's a fair view." The name stuck.

### T The Twin Bridges of Fairview and Snowden

North Dakota border.

One of the oddities of Fairview is the pair of bridges just outside of town. The Fairview Bridge in North Dakota and its twin bridge, the Snowden Bridge in Montana were both obsolete before they were built. While both were designed as "lift" bridges, neither has ever had to be raised as commercial traffic on the Missouri and Yellowstone Rivers had ceased years before 1913 when construction began. In spite of that, the federal government through the infinite wisdom of bureaucrats, insisted that the lift functions of the bridges were a requirement. And so they were built. The only recorded time the bridge was raised was when it was tested at the completion of construction in 1914.

Over time, the bridges have served as a little-used branch line for passenger and freight trains. Passenger service saw its end in the 1950s and freight service ended around 1986. At one time planking was placed between the bridge rails so

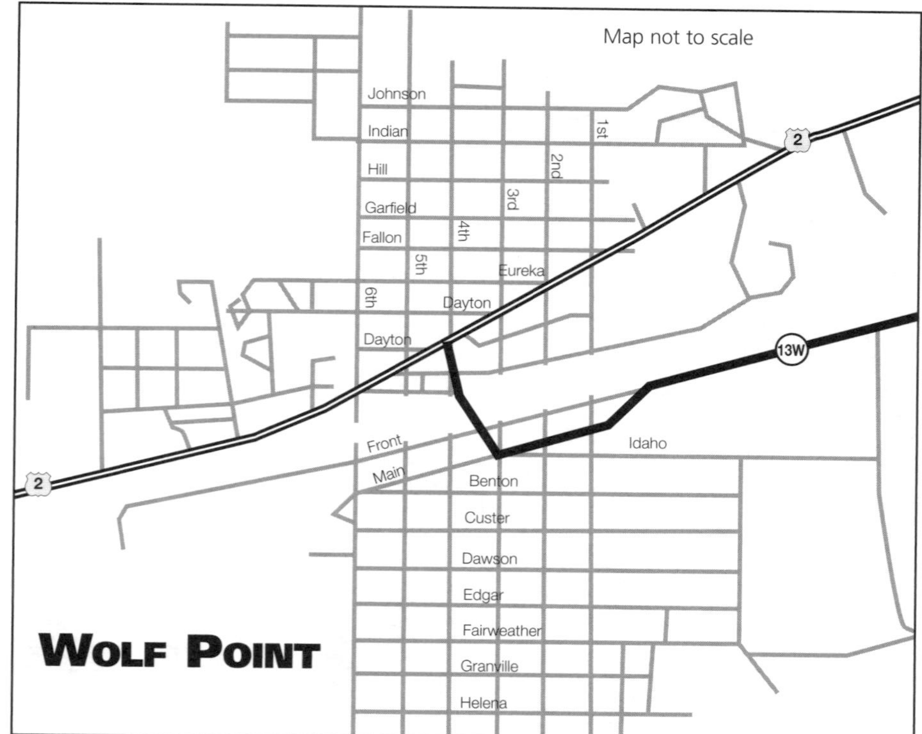


that automobiles could use the bridges. This was a problem as trains were still using the bridge. This necessitated a watchman at the bridge to control the traffic. Until 1937, the Great Northern charged a toll for cars using the bridge. The state took over the bridge at that time and assumed responsibility. The bridge continued to be used for auto traffic until a new highway bridge was built in 1955. These are the last two bridges of their kind in the country.

The Snowden Bridge stayed open to traffic until the mid 1980s and is used today as a branch line by the railroad.

## Montana Trivia

The town of Fairview is split between Montana and North Dakota. It also has two different time zones.

**9.** *Historical Marker, Lewis & Clark, Attraction, Gas, Food*

### H Snowden Bridge

East of Bainville.

*The only vertical lift bridge in Montana is located 10 miles south of here on the Missouri River. Built for Great Northern Railway by the Union Bridge and Construction Co. of Kansas City in 1913, it consists of three 275-foot fixed spans and one 296-foot lift span that raised to allow passage of river traffic. All of the spans are Parker riveted through trusses. When completed, it was the longest vertical lift bridge in existence and had the second largest clear opening of all movable bridges in the world.*

*In 1926, the one-track bridge was modified by the addition of timber approach ramps and a plank deck to accommodate local vehicular traffic. A signal system regulated direction of flow and tolls were collected from motorized and horse-drawn vehicles.*

*No record exists of the number of times the lift span was operated, but it was rare due to declining navigation on the Missouri. The last time there was need for it, when Fort Peck Dam was being built in the 1930s and barges loaded with construction materials needed the bridge raised to pass upstream, the mechanism no longer worked. The original hoist mechanism is still in place, but the operating machinery was retired in 1943.*

*Snowden Bridge was closed to auto traffic in 1985 when a new bridge was built three miles downstream.*

### H Fort Union

East of Bainville.

*Fort Union, one of the largest and best known trading posts of the fur days, was located on the Missouri near the mouth of the Yellowstone, about 14 miles southeast of here. Built by the American Fur Company in 1828 for trade with the Assiniboine Indians, its importance increased with the arrival of the first steamboat from St. Louis, the "Yellowstone" about June 17, 1832.*

*The Blackfeet, influenced by British fur companies, had refused to trade with Americans until Kenneth McKenzie, in charge of Fort Union, succeeded in having a band of this nation brought to the fort in 1831.*

### T Fort Union Trading Post

Bainville. 701-572-9083

### Outpost on the Missouri

John Jacob Astor's American Fur Company built Fort Union in 1829 near the junction of the Missouri and Yellowstone rivers in what is now North Dakota. The post soon became headquarters for trading beaver furs and buffalo hides with the Assiniboine Indians to the north, the Crow Indians on the upper Yellowstone, and the Blackfeet who lived farther up the Missouri.

Much of the fort's early success was due to Kenneth McKenzie. He not only supervised its construction but served as the first bourgeois, or superintendent, of the Astor-affiliated Upper Missouri Outfit, as the operation at the trading post was called. The Scottish-born McKenzie came to the United States by way of Canada, where he

## ON THE TRAIL OF LEWIS & CLARK

### The Return

In the 1930's the largest hydraulically tilled earth dam in the world was built on the Missouri River, backing water up for about 134 miles and forming Fort Peck Lake. Fifteen Lewis and Clark campsites along this section of the river are now under lake water. The lake has many bays and inlets, giving it 1,520 miles of shoreline (Elev. 2234). It is surrounded by the Charles M. Russell National Wildlife Refuge.

On the return trip in 1806 Lewis and Clark separated July 3, 1806. Clark would explore the Yellowstone River, Lewis would explore the Marias and retrace their route along the Missouri and pick up their cached materials.

**August 3:** Lewis, in a hurry to meet Clark, did not stop for lunch and set out the next morning, August 4, at 4 a.m. That day they passed the mouths of the Big Dry (which had water this time) and the Milk River.

**August 5:** The group waited, in vain, until noon for Colter and Collins, who had gone hunting, to catch up with them. That night, a violent storm arose and lasted through the next day, August 6, hampering their progress.

**August 7:** Lewis: "*..at 8 A.M. we passed the entrance of Marthy's river (Big Muddy Creek) which has changed it's entrance since we passed it last year,...*" They arrived at the mouth of the Yellowstone at 4 P.M., and found a note that Clark had left August 4, saying: "*Musquetors excessively troublesom So much So that the men complained that they could not work at their Skins for those troublesom insects, and I find it entirely impossible to hunt in the bottoms,....The torments of those Missquetors ....induce me to deturmine to proceed on to a more eliagiable Spot...*" Both men (Clark on the **4th** and Lewis on the **7th**) left Mon-tana worried about each other and bothered by mosquitoes.

On **August 12**, Colter and Collins caught up with Lewis along the Missouri River at a point which is now under Garrison Reservoir. The same day he wrote: "*...at 1 P.M. I overtook Capt. Clark and party and had the pleasure of finding them all well.*"

*Excerpted from Missouri River Country brochure, "Montana's Lewis and Clark Trail Through Missouri River Country."*

## Montana Trivia

A sign hangs over the dining area of the Hell Creek Bar in Jordan:

This is not a Burger King
You don't get it your way
You get it my way
Or you don't get the son of a bitch
Have a Nice Day

Section 10

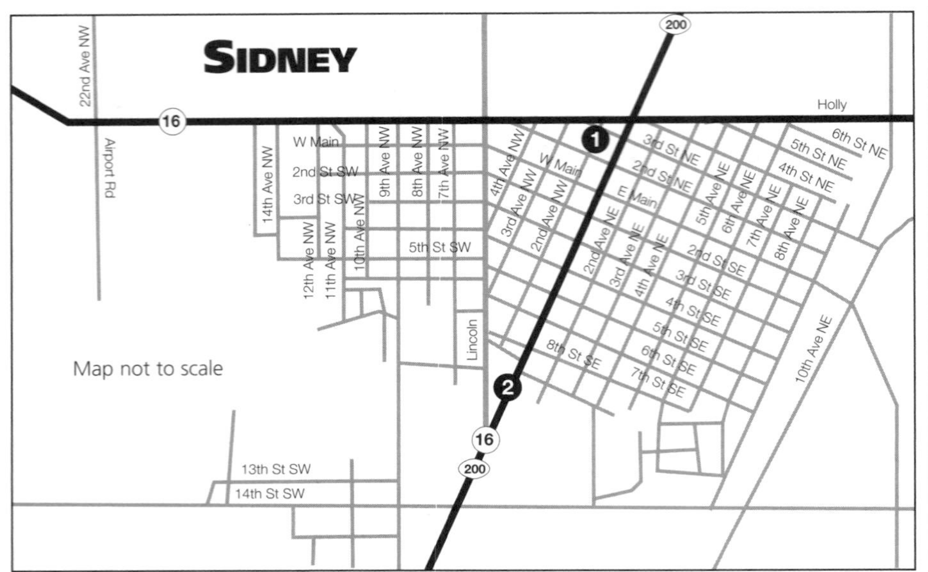


gained experience in the fur trade by working for that country's North West Company. He was a proud, ruthless man and he set out to dominate the upper Missouri trade. Others would compete with him, but none succeeded for long.

Fort Union stood on a grassy plain that stretched away to the north for a mile, thus providing ample space for Indian camps at trading time. A stout palisade of vertical logs enclosed a quadrangle 220 by 240 feet. Employees occupied rooms in a long building on the west side of the interior. A similar building on the east side contained a retail store and storerooms for furs and various food items. At the north end stood the imposing bourgeois house and, behind it, a bell tower and kitchen. The main gate, used by freight wagons and the trading public opened on the south or river side; another gate on the opposite side led to the prairie. Near the main gate were a reception room for Indians and shops for the blacksmith and the tinner. Other structures included an icehouse, a powder magazine, and enclosures for animals. Impressive two-story stone bastions at the northeast and southwest corners of the fort served as observation posts and defensive positions. A great flagstaff stood in the center of the court.

The American Fur Company's policy of helping travelers to visit its posts on the Missouri brought many famed men—adventurers, scientists, artists, priests—to Fort Union. One of the first, artist George Catlin, arrived in 1832 on board the Yellowstone, the first upper Missouri steamboat to reach the fort. Prince Maximilian of Wied, Father Pierre De Smet, John James Audubon, Karl Bodmer, and Rudolph Frederich Kurz were among other early visitors who made paintings of the fort or wrote vivid accounts of life there. The company also encouraged its bourgeois and clerks to collect and prepare specimens for scientific study. Edwin Thompson Denig, for example, who started out as a clerk at Fort Union and retired 25 years later as bourgeois, spent considerable time during those years compiling information about the Indian tribes of the upper Missouri which proved of inestimable value to ethnologists. He also contributed many skins and skulls of upper Missouri mammals and birds to the Smithsonian Institution in Washington, D.C.

When McKenzie established Fort Union, beaver had been in great demand for nearly three decades. Starting in the early 1830s, however, silk hats began to replace beaver hats as status symbols and the demand for beaver skins declined. But the demand for tanned buffalo robes increased, and this, coupled with improved river transportation, caused Fort Union to thrive. Trade remained brisk until 1837, when smallpox wrought havoc among the Indian tribes. Despite the tragedy the robe trade continued, slowly for a time but gradually increasing in volume again.

As Fort Union approached its quarter century, signs of coming change were apparent on the upper Missouri. Buffalo herds were still immense, but white civilization was beginning to encroach on the homelands of the Plains Indians. The Sioux became more and more hostile. In 1857 smallpox struck again, and many of the Plains tribes broke

*An excellent museum inside the Bourgeois House has numerous displays depicting and interpreting the life and times of the Fort.*

up into bands and scattered to escape the scourge. As a result, not many Indians traded at Fort Union that summer. By the time the Civil War began four years later, trade in general had declined and the post was in need of repair. In the summer of 1864, Gen. Alfred Sully, who had been sent west as part of the Army's efforts to curb the ongoing Sioux depredations, described Fort Union as "an old dilapidated affair, almost falling to pieces." An infantry company was stationed there during the winter to guard supplies until a regular Army post could be built.

In June 1866, a new infantry company arrived on the upper Missouri and commenced the construction of an Army post, Fort Buford, at the site of old Fort William, the earliest Fort Union competitor. By then Fort Union had been sold to the Northwest Fur Company, which tried to continue the trading activity but finally gave up and sold the post to the Army in 1867. Troops dismantled the fort and used the materials to complete Fort Buford. Only remnants of the foundations remained.

## Bourgeois, Craftsmen, and Traders

*"A craftsman or workman receives $250 a year; a workman's assistant is never paid more than $120; a hunter receives $400, together with the hides and horns of the animals he kills; an interpreter without other employment, which is seldom, gets $500. Clerks and traders who have mastered [Indian languages] … may demand from $800 to $1,000 without interest. All employees are furnished board and lodging free of charge."*

*Fog from the Missouri River enshrouds the Fort as it has done countless times during its lifetime.*

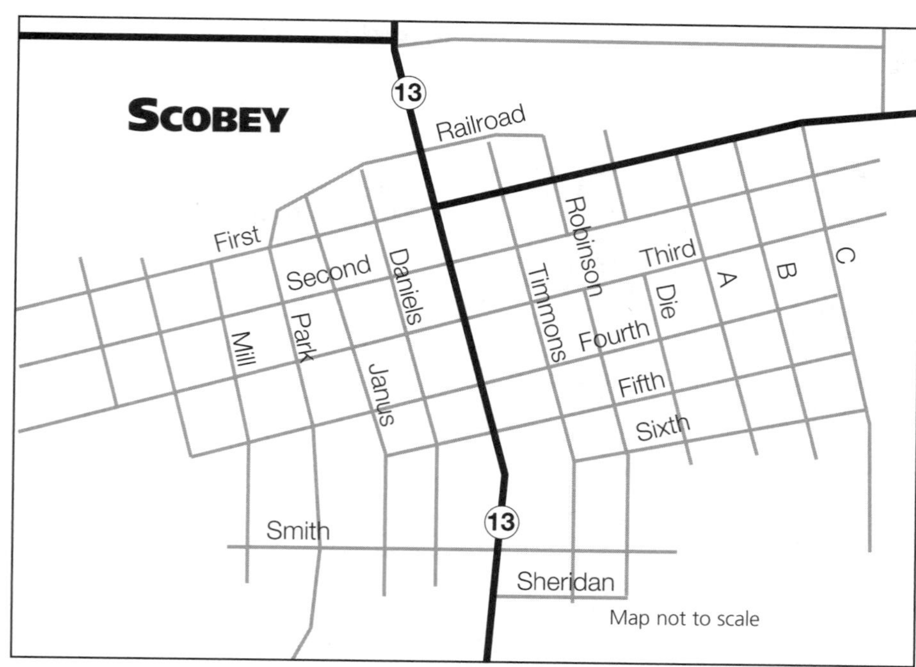


-Rudolph F. Kurz, clerk at Fort Union 1851-52

In its heyday, Fort Union Trading Post was a busy place and employed up to 100 persons, many of whom were married to Indian women and had families. A visitor in the 1830s noted the cosmopolitan mix of the fort's inhabitants, and it was not unusual to see Americans (including blacks), Englishmen, Germans, Frenchmen, Russians, Spaniards, Italians, Indians, wives, and children stream down to the landing to greet the arrival of the annual steamboats.

The man in charge of the post was called the bourgeois. Starting with Kenneth McKenzie, Fort Union witnessed a succession of outstanding bourgeois, including Alexander Culbertson and Edwin Denig. Other important members of the fort's staff were the clerks, responsible for maintaining inventories of trade goods and furs and hides. They also kept track of the fort's tools, equipment, animals, and a dozen other things. Interpreters, another key group, had to know several Indian languages as well as English and French.

Hunters, often men of mixed blood, supplied the tables with fresh meat, whether buffalo, elk, or deer. Craftsmen, such as carpenters, masons, and blacksmiths, were essential in constructing and maintaining the fort and its equipment and tools. The tinner had the task of preparing such trade goods as rings, bracelets, and kettles. Herders cared for the horses and cattle. Traders sent to Indian camps during the winter returned in the spring, hopefully with a load of furs and no left-over trade goods.

All in all, fort employees were rough and ready, often hard-drinking men, and violence was a common event in the daily routine. Yet, with a strong bourgeois, the fort's mission was met and the American Fur Company reaped the profits of its labor.

## The Fort Today

Grass covered the entire site when the National Park Service acquired the property in 1966. Four low ridges forming a near square indicated the line of the palisades and two mounds at the northeast and southwest corners the location of the stone bastions.Two other mounds within the enclosure marked the powder magazine and the bourgeois house.

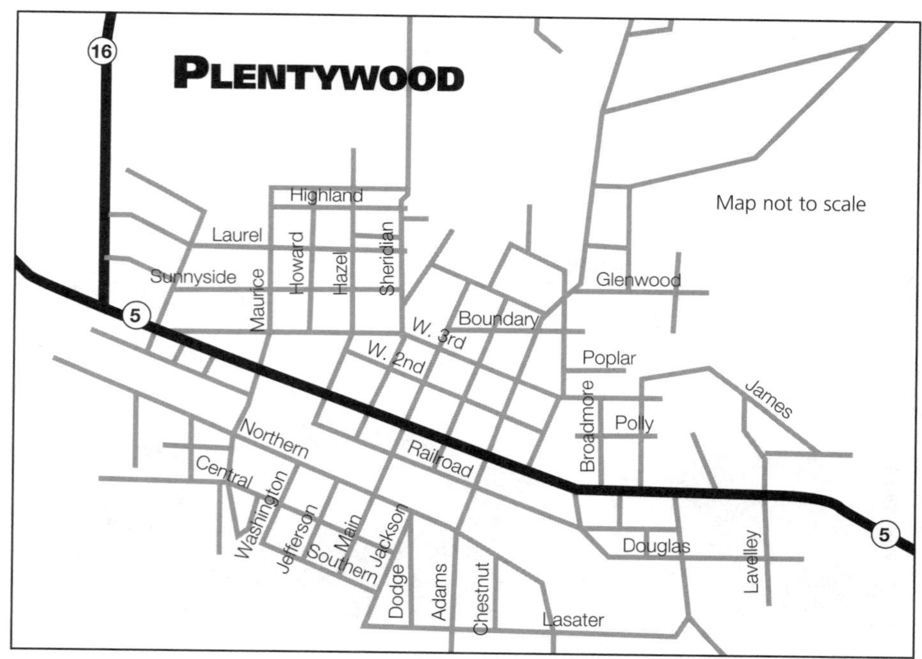


The National Park Service has excavated the stone foundations of the palisades, the main house and its kitchen, the Indian reception building, and the main gate. It has uncovered artifacts relating to life at the fort, including eating utensils, beer bottles, buttons, metal parts of trapping gear and harnesses, china, pottery, and glass.

Between 1985 and 1991 the National Park Service reconstructed portions of Fort Union Trading Post, including the walls, stone bastions, Indian trade house, and Bourgeois House. The surrounding lands are also being controlled to provide an authentic mid-19th century setting for the post.

Fort Union Trading Post National Historic Site is 25 miles southwest of Williston, N.D., and 24 miles north of Sidney, Mont. The fort is open daily from 9 a.m. to 5:30 p.m., with extended hours in summer. The fort is closed on Thanksgiving, December 25, and January 1. Groups must make arrangements in advance.

More information Write: Superintendent, Fort Union Trading Post National Historic Site, 15550 HWY. 1804, Williston, ND 58801-8680. Call: 701-572-9083. www.nps.gov/fous.

### D Mer. Lewis

August 7, 1806

*"at 8 A.M. we passed the entrance of Marthy's river which has changed it's entrance since we passed in last year, falling in at preasent about a quarter of a mile lower down."*

### D William Clark

April 28,1805

*"coal is in great abundance and the salts still increase an quantity; the banks of the river and sandbars are incrusted with it in many places and appear perfectly white as if covered with snow of frost."*

### T Pioneer Pride Museum

Bainville. 769-2596

This museum features the old jail from Mondak. Other exhibits include rooms furnished as they were in the days of the pioneers, and a 1929 fire truck. Open Memorial Day to Labor Day, Tuesdays through Sundays 1:30 to 4:30. Admission is free.

## 10. *Attraction, Gas, Food, Lodging*

## Culbertson

The old cowtown of Culbertson was born on the prairie in 1887 with the arrival of the railroad. While buffalo and Indians roamed freely over the plains, a townsite was established and horse ranching was the order of the day, with constant demand for cavalry mounts by military posts along the Missouri River. Big scale cattle ranching replaced the horse trade and with the arrival of homesteaders, the little cowtown gradually became an agriculture and livestock center.

The town is thought to be named after Alexander Culbertson, a manager and partner in the American Fur Co. Culbertson married an Indian princess named Natawis. While ranchers

# The Indians and Fort Union

The Assiniboines claimed the land on which Fort Union was built. This tribe occupied both sides of the border with Canada and thus had a choice of trading with either the Hudson's Bay Company or the American Fur Company. The Crow Indians lived on the upper Yellowstone River and its tributaries. This was a pleasant, bountiful land, and the Crow were considered the richest tribe east of the Rocky Mountains.

Farther up the Missouri, the Blackfeet also claimed land on both sides of the international boundary. Since the days of Lewis and Clark, when a Blackfoot warrior had been killed by the exploration party, these Indians considered American whites their enemies. The Blackfeet, however, welcomed British traders in their midst. Bourgeois Kenneth McKenzie took advantage of this situation when a trapper named Jacob Berger wandered into Fort Union. Berger had worked for the British and had learned the Blackfeet language. McKenzie sent the man to the Blackfeet with an invitation to visit the fort. The scheme worked and the Blackfeet eventually allowed the American Fur Company to establish a trading post in their territory.

The Indians were shrewd bargainers and the trading companies were in fierce and constant competition. Rarely did any of these tribes threaten Fort Union with violence. Occasionally, a disgruntled leader gathered his followers and attempted a takeover. None achieved success. Violence often did occur among the Indians themselves, especially at trading time. Every year the traders smuggled alcohol into the upper Missouri country, despite laws to the contrary. Many trading sessions concluded with the Indians becoming thoroughly intoxicated and settling old scores with one another

Liquor was not the only scourge the traders introduced to the upper Missouri. In 1837 the steamboat St. Peters arrived at Fort Union bringing with it the smallpox. The disease struck the fort's employees just when a band of Assiniboine arrived to trade. Fort traders went out to meet them, taking along trade goods and urging the Indians not to approach any closer. The Assiniboine paid no heed. Their bodies had little resistance against the foreign virus, and of the approximately 1,000 people in the band who caught the disease, only about 150 survived. Other bands kept coming in that summer and the smallpox spread throughout the tribe. The Blackfeet were also ravaged by the disease. The Crow Indians, somehow, escaped the pestilence. Twenty years later, in 1857, the smallpox struck again. The Assiniboine suffered once more and, this time, the disease swept through the Crow tribe, striking down young and old alike.

The first Sioux appeared in the vicinity of Fort Union in 1847. Before this, they had lived farther downstream, but white expansion from the east forced them to roam westward in increasing numbers. By the 1860s their hostility towards whites, and even other Indian tribes, made them a menace to life at Fort Union. After the Minnesota uprising of 1862, the U.S. Army undertook inconclusive campaigns against the Sioux. This led to the establishment of Fort Buford a short distance downriver from Fort Union. The Sioux continued to harass both forts and anyone traveling between them. Fort Union was finally abandoned and dismantled in 1867. The romance of the fur trade on the high plains and in the Rocky Mountains was now but a memory.

*Reprinted from National Park Service brochure.*

Fort Union Trading Post in 1833 by Karl Bodmer

had run cattle and horse herds in the area as early as the 1860s, the Culbertson's son Jack founded one of the first ranches in the area in 1879.

When the railroad arrived, Culbertson became a stock shipping center and a rowdy cowtown which at one time boasted fourteen saloons. A boom in new businesses came with the homesteaders. Banks, shops, and services appeared overnight. Today Culbertson is an agricultural and livestock area with a significant oil industry.

## T Culbertson Museum

1 mile east of Culbertson on U.S. Hwy. 2. 787-6320

The Culbertson museum is filled with unique items which take you back to the turn of the century. The nine rooms include: a chapel which contains a traveling alter; a school room from the 20s and 30s; a barber shop with a portable barber chair; and an examining chair-table from one of the first physicians in the area. A general store is stocked with original items, including a collection of old calendars. In the farm and ranch section you will find a side saddle that dates back to 1886 along with a pair of angora chaps. You'll find mannequins dressed in period clothing and original photos from the early years of the area. Open 9 a.m. to 6 p.m. daily in May and September. Open 8 a.m. to 8 p.m. daily from June through August. Admission is free.

## 11. *Attraction, Gas*

### Froid

The best theory for the naming of this town of 200, comes from the French word "froid" for cold.

### Homestead

This town, originally a siding for the Northern Pacific Railroad, was named to honor the homesteaders that the town owed its beginning to.

### Medicine Lake

Named for the nearby lake which was named because Indians found many of their medicinal roots and herbs on the shore of the lake. The Indians also believed that lake's waters had medicinal properties.

## T Medicine Lake National Wildlife Refuge

Approximately 30 miles north of Culbertson. 789-2305

The Medicine Lake National Wildlife Refuge is located between Culbertson and Plentywood and covers over 31,000 acres of lake, wetlands and prairie. It is home to many species of waterfowl as well as deer and antelope. More than 100,000 migrating waterfowl call the refuge home in the summer. Watch for great blue herons, white pelicans, sandhill cranes, grebes and ten different species of ducks. In 1976, over 11,000 acres of the refuge were declared wilderness. Only non-motorized vessels are allowed on the lake. Wildlife watching and photo opportunities are abundant on the self-guided auto tour. There is a 100-foot observation tower you can climb for a panoramic view of the area. At the Teepee Hills Natural Area, you can find a number of teepee rings which mark the sites of early Indian lodges.

## 12. *Lewis & Clark*

### Brockton

This little village on the prairie sits near the famous landmark of the Twin Buttes a few miles to the north of town. This was the site of a famous battle between the Crow and the Sioux Indians. The Crow, having stolen about 150 horses from the Sioux, were ambushed as they camped between the two buttes and massacred.

## D William Clark

April 29, 1805

*"we call this river Martheys river in honor to the Selebrated M.F."*

## D Mer. Lewis

May 2, 1805

*"The flesh of the beaver is esteemed a delecacy among us; I think the tale a most delicious morsal, when boiled it resembles in flavor the fresh tongues and sounds (air bladders) of the codfish, and is usually sufficiently large a plentifull meal for two men."*

## D Mer. Lewis

May 3, 1805

*"met with 2 porcupines,. . .this anamal is exceedingly clumsy and not very watchfull I approached so near one of them before it perceived me that I touched it with my espontoon."*

## 13. *Historical Marker, Attraction, Gas, Food, Lodging, Shopping, Miscellaneous*

### Poplar

This town was no doubt named for the trees that line the banks of the Poplar and Missouri Rivers that join here. The town sprang up around Fort Peck. The fort was built to protect cattle ranchers from hostile Indians. Today it is the home of the Fort Peck Indian Reservation.

## H Fort Peck Indian Reservation

Poplar

*Fort Peck Indian Reservation is the home of two tribes, the Assiniboines, whose forefathers were living in this vicinity when Lewis and Clark came up the Missouri in 1805, and the Dakota (Sioux), descendants of the "hostiles" who fiercely resisted the white invasion of their homelands. Some of the Dakotas took part in the Minnesota uprising of 1862 and moved west when the Army tried to round them up. Others took part in Custer's demise at the Battle of the Little Big Horn in 1876. The Assiniboines, also of Dakota descent, split from the Yanktonai band in the early 1600s and migrated west. They shared the vast Blackfeet hunting territory set aside by the Treaty of 1855 from which Fort Peck Reservation was created in 1888 when 17,500,000 acres were ceded to the government. Part of the tribe resides on the Fort Belknap Reservation, 160 miles west of here.*

*Named for Campbell Kennedy Peck, Fort Peck was originally a fur trading post established near the mouth of the Milk River by Abel Farwell for the Durfee and Peck Co. in 1866-67. In 1873, the Bureau of Indian Affairs began using part of the post as Fort Peck Indian Agency. Flooded out by an ice jam on the Missouri in 1877, the agency was moved to the present site at the mouth of the Poplar River. The earlier site now rests under the waters behind Fort Peck Dam.*

## T Fort Peck Indian Reservation

395-4282

In 1886, the Assiniboine and Sioux Tribes exercised their sovereign powers and signed an agreement with the United States Government to create the Fort Peck Indian Reservation. After three years of negotiations, the Congress of the United States ratified the agreement in 1888.

Today, descendants of six of the 33 bands of Assiniboines call the reservation home: the Canoe Paddlers, the Rock Band, the Red Bottom, the Cree Speakers, the Fat Horse Band, and the Canoe Paddlers of the Prairie Band. The Sioux represent all three divisions of the Dakota Indians. The largest of these groups is the Cuthead Yanktonai Band. Other bands include the Sisseton, Wahpeton and Hunkpapa Bands. The Yanktonais moved from northern Minnesota to the Dakotas and divided into the upper and lower divisions.

Today, over 10,000 members are enrolled as members of the Fort Peck Tribes. A little more than half of these reside on the reservation which covers 2,093,318 acres of land within the reservation boundaries. The reservation inhabitants pay high regard to the traditional ways of life. Each year they hold numerous tribal celebrations and encampments. The reservation was established in 1888. Much of the economy today is derived from manufacturing, ranching, farming and oil extraction.

## D William Clark

May 4, 1805

*"We were detained this morning untill about 9 Ock. in order to repare the rudder irons of the red perogue which were broken last evening in landing"*

## M Fort Peck Community College

Poplar. 768-5551 www.montana.edu/wwwfpcc

This tribally-controlled community college on the Port Peck Indian Reservation is chartered by the government of the Fort Peck Assiniboine and Sioux Tribes in 1978. An additional campus is located in Wolf Point. The college offers associate's degrees and a number of certification programs. Approximately 400 students attend the school.

## T Fort Peck Assiniboine & Sioux Cultural Center and Museum

Poplar. 768-5155 Ext 2328

This is a traditional teepee village located on the Missouri River near Wolf Point. The museum also features exhibits of Assiniboine and Sioux heritage and culture, along with arts and crafts. Open year round from 8 a.m. to 4:30 p.m. daily. Admission is free.

## The Assiniboine & Sioux Nations

The Assiniboine and Sioux nations living on the Fort Peck Reservation, like so many of the native American tribes living in Montana, migrated to this area from what is now Canada. In the early 1600s Europeans were forcing Indians on the east coast westward. At the end of the 1600s, the Sioux had migrated as far west and south as central Minnesota. A large and powerful nation, the Sioux are comprised of seven bands. Each of these bands speak a language of Siouan descent. Over time these seven bands evolved to the present day three. The Dakotas (Santee Sioux), the Nakotas (Yankton and Yanktonai Sioux) and the Lakotas (Teton Sioux) each have a distinct language.The Sioux residing on the Fort Peck Reservation are of the Nakota band.

During the migration to Minnesota, one band of the Sioux split into two: the Yankton and the Yanktonai. While the Yanktonai Band stayed to the north, the Yankton Band moved south across the northern plains. Today it is the Yanktonai band which resides on the Fort Peck reservation and at reservations in North Dakota, South Dakota and in Canada.

Sometime in the 1600s, the Assiniboine broke from the Yanktonai Sioux and returned as a distinct tribe on the Reservation in the 1860s. Their Siouan ancestry is reflected in their name. The word *ass-ni-pwan* means "stone Sioux," and refers to the Assiniboine method of cooking food with hot stones and boiling water. Sometime during the 17th century, the Assiniboine split into two groups. While one stayed in Canada, the other migrated south to hunt buffalo on the Great Plains. In 1744, the southern group once again divided. This time one group went to the Missouri Valley region while the other went west and north into the valleys of the Assiniboine and Saskatchewan Rivers. When the U.S. -Canada border was established in 1818, the north and south tribes were further separated. The southern group were plains hunters and adapted well to the fur traders who were entering the area.

The Assiniboine, small in numbers, were vulnerable to other Plains Indian tribes. Not only had their size been diminished by their several divisions, but smallpox wiped out nearly two-thirds of the tribe. Unable to adequately defend their hunting grounds, they readily accepted the terms of the Fort Laramie Treaty in 1851. They were included in the Friendship Treaty made by the Blackfeet tribe and Isaac Stevens.

In 1869, smallpox further reduced the numbers in the Upper Assiniboine band. To avoid the same fate, the Lower Assiniboine avoided the Upper Assiniboine and followed their chief, Red Stone, to live with the Yanktonai Sioux who had moved into the northeastern part of Montana to hunt buffalo. In 1871, the Fort Peck agency was established for the Sioux who were unable to get along with anyone other than their newly found friends, the Lower Assiniboine. The alliance between these two tribes has remained in effect to this day.

Today, almost 6,000 members of the Sioux and Assiniboine occupy the two million acre reservation. The expansive reservation is approximately 110 miles long by 40 miles wide.

The Assiniboine and Sioux Cultural Center and Museum in Poplar has permanent exhibits depicting the tribal heritage. Throughout the Fort Peck Reservation are interesting artifacts and historical areas including teepee rings, buffalo jumps and sacred sites.

## T Poplar Museum

212 F West, Poplar. 768-5212

Poplar Museum contains the best display of Native American culture to be found on the Fort Peck Reservation with superb beadwork and exquisite star quilts. It is housed in the 1920 jailhouse, and the Poplar Pride ferryboat straddles the yard—this boat made countless crossings on the Missouri from 1949 to 1969. There is also an emphasis is on the fur trade from the 1840s through the 1860s. Open June 15th to September 15th, 11 a.m. to 5 p.m., Monday through Friday. Admission is free.

**14.** *Historical Marker, Attraction, Gas, Food, Lodging, Shopping*

## Wolf Point

Nobody knows for sure where Wolf Point got its name. The most accepted account is that during a late cold 1860s winter, wolf hunters (wolfers) killed hundreds of gray wolves. Before the hunters could skin the pelts, the carcasses froze. They stacked them in piles in their campsites along the Missouri River waiting for the spring thaw. Before spring came around, Indians ran off the wolfers and took over the campsite. The putrid piles remained as a visible landmark to the steamboats coming up river in the spring. Thus the name Wolf Point.

### Montana Trivia

In 1861, an American Fur Trading Company steamboat exploded near Wolf Point when a deckhand tried to tap a keg of alcohol by candlelight. There were twenty-five kegs of powder on board.

Its difficult to find documentation of Wolf Point's birth. It was probably first settled as a trading post for the fur trade. When the huge cattle herds came from Texas to graze on the rich tall grasses of northern Montana, it evolved into a cow town. The early town was a genuine frontier outpost featuring a dugout hotel along the river.

In 1914, homesteaders flooded the area creating a growth spurt. When Congress opened the Fort Peck Reservation to non-Indians, the town took another spurt. Today the town is part of the Fort Peck Indian Reservation. This mix of residents hasn't changed much since the early 1900s. It is still about 50% Indian and 50% non-tribal residents. The Fort Peck Reservation is the home to the Nakota (Assiniboine) and the Dakota-Lakota-Nakota (Sioux) nations.

## H Wolf Point

Wolf Point

*The Lewis and Clark Expedition passed here, westward*

*bound in 1805. Fur trappers and traders followed a few years later. Steamboats began making it from St. Louis up the Missouri as far as Fort Benton in the early 1860s and this was considered the halfway point between Bismarck and Fort Benton. Wood choppers supplied cord wood for boats stopping to refuel. An American Fur Company packet burned and blew up in 1861 not far from here. A deck hand tapped a barrel of alcohol by candle light with a gimlet. The fumes, the candle, and 25 kegs of powder did the rest.*

*This district was favorite buffalo country for the Assiniboines and Sioux.*

*A party of trappers poisoned several hundred wolves one winter, hauled the frozen carcasses in and stacked them until spring for skinning. It taught the varmints a lesson. No one in Wolf Point has been bothered by a wolf at the door since then.*

### H The Wolf Point Bridge

Southeast of Wolf Point on Missouri.

*The Wolf Point Bridge was the result of many years of lobbying by Roosevelt and McCone county citizens led by Wolf Point businessman William Young. In 1927, the Montana Highway Commission and Bureau of Public Roads approved the project. The Missouri Valley Bridge and Iron Company of Leavenworth, Kansas began construction of the bridge in 1929.*

*The company's construction camp on the north bank of the river included a powerhouse, workshops, office, a dance hall, bunkhouse and several small cottages to house the workers' families. For most of 1929 and 1930, the site was the most popular tourist attraction in northeastern Montana.*

*The Wolf Point Bridge was dedicated on July 9, 1930. The celebration included speeches, bands, a float, cowboys, and a daylight fireworks show. The bridge was blessed by tribal elders from the Fort Peck Reservation. A crowd of perhaps 15,000 people attended the festivities.*

*The Wolf Point Bridge is the longest and most massive through truss in Montana. The structure is 1,074-feet long and contains 1,150 tons of steel. The 400-foot span is the longest in the state. When dedicated in 1930, the bridge was called "A memorial to those whose lives have been lost in the Missouri and a monument to those whose cooperation made possible its erection."*

### D Sgt. Gass

August 4, 1806

*"Having proceeded 88 miles we encamped for the night."*

### D William Lewis

May 5, 1805

*"The country is as yesterday beautifull in the extreme."*

### T Wolf Point Area Historical Museum

200 2nd Ave. S., Wolf Point. 853-1912

Wolf Point Museum is a small and very interesting museum containing a life-sized statue of the cowboy and artist Charles M. Russell, as well as artifacts from early-day white settlers and Native Americans. Some of the items on display include Sherman T. Cogswell's 1910 National cash register, antique printing presses, pendulum clocks, two 1890 Edison phonographs and cylinder records, a 1915 Bible, the 1913 oak dresser from the first rooming house in Wolf Point, an excellent arrowhead collection, and paintings by local artists Magnhild Holum, Tenny DeWitt and Marlene Toavs. Seven miles down the road the Lewis and Clark Memorial Park provides a glimpse of where locals sold wood for use on steamboats. Open Memorial Day through Labor Day Monday through Friday from 10 a.m. to 5 p.m.

## What's Growing

In northeast Montana, agriculture is the economy. Much of the landscape you'll see as you drive down the road grains, grasses for cattle, or undisturbed prairie and badlands.

Most of the crops you see are spring wheat. This is planted in May and is harvest from early to mid-September. Some farmers will take their chances with winter wheat. While there's always a chance of winter kill, the yield in bushels-per-acre is higher than spring wheat.

Wonder what the long rows of green or golden grain alternating with the dark earth stretching endlessly are? It's called strip farming. This practice reduces wind erosion of the soil and conserves moisture. The strip that remains fallow will have more moisture in it when it is planted the next year. The strips are alternated each year.

## 15. *Attraction*

### T Louis Toavs' John Deere Collection

North of Wolf Point. 392-5224

If you're a fan of John Deere tractors, you have to make a stop at Louis Toavs' farm north of Wolf Point. Louis has managed to acquire every model of John Deere made from 1923 to 1953—over 500 in all. This is a private collection, but Louis insists he enjoys showing off his tractors to visitors. Allow yourself an entire afternoon just to skim the surface. A proper visit would take the best of two days. To schedule an appointment to view the collection, call Louis at 392-5224.

## 16. *Historical Marker, Lewis & Clark*

### Frazer

The town of Frazer sits on the Fort Peck Indian Reservation, the home of the Sioux and Assiniboine. Named after a railroad official, the town had the humble beginnings of a siding on the railroad. The first trading post in the county was established here in 1908.

### H In Memoriam

East of Frazer.

*In the summer of 1837 an American Fur Trading Company steamboat laden with trade goods made its way from St. Louis to Fort Union. Smallpox broke out among the crew, but the boat continued to its destination. Contact with the steamboat's crew during the distribution of trade goods exposed the Wichiyabina or Little Girls' Band of Assiniboine, starting a terrible epidemic which eventually affected all the tribes of what is now northeastern Montana. Many of the tribes had never been exposed to this virulent European disease and were extremely susceptible. The disease seemed to strike the young, vigorous and most able-bodied family members with such swiftness that burial in many cases was impossible. Ninety-four percent of the Wichiyabina or Little Girls' Band of Assiniboine died. By the winter of 1838, when the disease had run its course, the Wichiyabina or Little Girls' Band of Assiniboine were no more. The 8o remaining Band members banded with other smallpox survivors and formed the Redbottom Band (Hudesabina) of Assiniboines. Today the Assiniboine people still mourn the untimely passing of so many of their ancestors, innocent victims of this dreadful pestilence.*

### D Sgt. Gass

May 7, 1805

*"Having this day made sixteen miles we encamped on the South side."*

### D Mer. Lewis

May 9, 1805

*"Capt. Clark killed 2 buffaloe. . .our wrighhand cook Charbono, calls boudin blanc, and immediately set him about preparing them for supper. . .About 6 feet of the lower extremity of the large gut of the Buffaloe is the first morsel. . .the mustle lying underneath the shoulder blade next to the back, and fillets are next saught, these are needed up very fine with a portion of kidney to suit: to this composition is then added a just proportion of pepper and salt and a small quanitity of flour. . .all is compleatly filled with something good to eat, it is tyed at the other end.. . .it is then baptized in the missouri with two dips and a flirt, and bobbed into the kettle; from whence, after it be well boiled is taken and fried in bears oil untilit browns, when it is ready to esswage the pangs of a keen appetite, or as such travelers in the wilderness are seldom at a loss for. . ."*

### D Mer. Lewis

May 10, 1805

*"The Hunters returned this evening having seen no tents or Indians nor any fresh sign of them"*

## 17.

### Nashua

The name Nashua comes from the Indian word meaning "meeting of the waters." The town was founded by a second cousin of Robert E. Lee named Charles Sargent. Sargent served under Lee during the Civil War. He was part of the contingent that the army sent to build Fort Buford at the confluence of the Yellowstone and the Missouri. In 1886, Sargent "squatted" on the public land at the site of Nashua and waited for the arrival of the railroad to set up a town site.

## 18. *Historical Marker, Lewis & Clark, Attraction, Gas, Food, Lodging*

### Fort Peck

The community of Fort Peck overlooks the Fort Peck Dam and is home to about 350 residents. Many of the buildings are of the 1930s vintage that were built along with the dam.

### H Old Fort Peck

Fort Peck

*On the west bank of the Missouri River about 1 mile from the Dam was located Old Fort Peck.*

*The stockade was about 300 feet square with walls 12 feet high of cottonwood logs set vertically, 3 bastions and 3 gateways on the front, and 2 bastions on the rear, enclosed quarters for men, store houses, blacksmith shops, stables and corral. Built in 1867 by the firm of Durfee & Peck as a trading post, the fort was named for Colonel Campbell K. Peck. Although not an Army post, it often served as temporary headquarters for military men and commissioners sent out by the Government to negotiate with the Indians.*

*To peaceful Indians it was an important trading post, to trappers and rivermen a safe shelter from war-*

### *Montana Trivia*

Fort Peck Lake has almost 1,600 miles of shoreline—equal to the total coastal front of the state of California.

*like Indians. Sternwheel steamers loaded and unloaded here and took on wood for steam for their journeys.*

*Old Fort Peck is history. Its site lies peacefully, with its memories, covered by a man-made lake which is formed by the largest earthfilled dam ever built by man.*

## D Mer. Lewis

May 11, 1805

*"Bratton. . .had shot a brown bear which immediately turned on him and pursued him a considerable distance. . .we at length found him concealed in some very thick brush and shot him through the skull with two balls. . .Bratton had shot him through the center of the lungs. . .these bear being so hard to die reather intimedates us all; I must confess that I do not like the gentlemen and had reather fight two Indians than one bear. . ."*

## T Fort Peck Theatre

In Fort Peck. 228-9219

The small town of Fort Peck nestled alongside the Fort Peck Dam is the last place you'd expect to find a summer stock theater. But the Historic Fort Peck Theater has been the home to summer stock theater and other special event for almost 70 years. The theater attracts audiences from all over the country. It is the only summer stock theater in northeastern Montana and is on the National Register of Historic Places. In 1996, no less than the National Symphony Orchestra from the John F. Kennedy Center in Washington, D.C. performed here.

The theater is one of the most unusual and exquisite buildings in Montana. Constructed in 1934, its carved and painted wood chalet motif displays touches of the fine craftsmanship that was abundant in that time. At the time it was built, the 1,209 seats gave it the largest seating capacity for any theater in the state.

During the dam construction days, the theater operated around the clock to provide the 30,000 workers and their families affordable entertainment. The theater lobby still displays movie posters from those days with the likes of Shirley Temple, Clark Gable, Great Garbo, Claudette Colbert, Jimmy Stewart, and many others. An adult ticket then was 30¢ and children got in for a dime.

Today, the theater has had the stage expanded to allow for live theater. Air conditioning has been added to keep theater goers comfortable. Performances run from mid-June through August. Curtain time is at 8 p.m. every Friday, Saturday, and Sunday night. Dress is casual and admission is only a little bit more than 30¢.

## T Fort Peck Dam & Lake

A product of FDR's New Deal, construction on Fort Peck Dam began in October of 1933. It was constructed by hydraulic methods and to this day is the largest hydraulically earth filled dam in the world. Electrically operated dredge boats dredged Missouri River bottom sands, silts and clays which were then pumped through 28" pipelines to the dam site. The dredged area is covered by the Fort Peck Lake today.

At its construction peak, nearly 11,000 people were employed. At one time during the construction years, the population of the area exceeded 50,000 in 18 construction boom towns surrounding the lake. Life magazine featured one of these towns in the November, 1936 issue. Today the population of Fort Peck Lake is but a mere 235.

To allow construction of the dam, the waters of the Missouri River were diverted through four flood control tunnels. The lake created by the dam is 130 miles long, 16 miles wide at its widest and 220 feet deep at its deepest.

The U.S. Army Corps of Engineers build Fort Peck Dam initially for flood control, irrigation, navigation and domestic water supply. Hydroelectric power generation and recreation were later authorized for use. Two hydroelectric powerhouses are located below the dam.

Most of the area surrounding Fort Peck Lake is remote and desolate. When boating or fishing on the lake, be prepared to stay overnight in case of bad weather or mechanical breakdown. Check the weather forecast before going onto the lake. The weather can be unpredictable with winds change direction and speed rapidly, especially when a thunderstorm is approaching. It's a good idea to leave a float plan at the Marina or with someone you know.

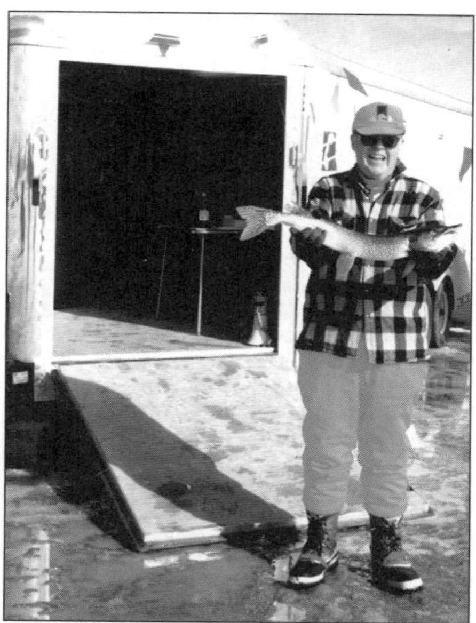

*Ice fishing on Fort Peck Lake is some of the finest anywhere. Photo courtesy of Glasgow Chamber of Commerce.*

### Fishing

Fort Peck Lake enjoys nationwide recognition as a hot spot for walleye fishing. The lake also offers excellent fishing for sauger, smallmouth bass, lake trout, chinook salmon and northern pike. The introduction of cisco as a forage fish in 1983 proved successful and has increased both the size and number of game fish.

Walleye and sauger are found throughout the lake and are usually caught in water less than 25 feet deep. Walleyes in the 2- to 4-pound class are common, and 8 to 10-pounders are caught with increasing regularity.

Smallmouth bass are most abundant in the middle portion of the lake between Hell Creek and Devil Is Creek. Smallmouth bass are most commonly caught by those fishing from rocky points and submerged islands. Fish in the 2- to 3-pound class are common and some weighing more than five pounds are occasionally taken.

Lake trout and chinook salmon are found in the deep water at the lower end of the lake. The trout and salmon can be caught in shallow water in the early spring or late fall, and in deep water during the summer. Salmon and lake trout weighing 15 to 20 pounds are common and fish in excess of 30 pounds have been taken.

Additional information on fishing and hunting can be obtained by contacting the Montana Fish, Wildlife and Parks Dept., Route 1, Box 4210, Glasgow, MT 59230.

### Recreation

The vast size of Fort Peck Lake and its remoteness from major population centers provide a variety of high quality outdoor experiences. Popular recreation activities include camping, boating, fishing, hunting, sightseeing, watching wildlife and just relaxing.

Fifteen hundred miles of pristine shoreline serve as a haven for those wishing to get away from the stresses of modem life.

The recreation areas near and around the dam offer paved roads, electricity, showers and playgrounds while facilities around the rest of the lake are more primitive with gravel roads, picnic tables and vault toilets. Roads to many of the remote areas may be impassable in inclement weather.

### Wildlife

Wildlife is abundant throughout the project due to an active wildlife management program and the presence of the Charles M. Russell Wildlife Refuge. This 1.1 million-acre refuge completely surrounds the lake.

Game species found along the lake include mule deer, pronghorns, elk, bighorn sheep, white-tailed deer, sage grouse, sharp-tailed grouse and waterfowl. A wildlife exhibition pasture near the town of Fort Peck displays buffalo, pronghorns, elk and deer.

Bald eagles wintering along the open water below the dam provide a rare opportunity for bird watchers. Nesting osprey can be observed at Hell Creek, The Pines and Flat Lake.

### Prehistoric Graveyard

Another intriguing aspect of Fort Peck Dam and Lake, is that it's widely recognized by scientists as one of the most fossiliferous localities in the world.

Between 1907 and 1914, the rich Fort Peck fossil field was revealed to the world through the discoveries of Dr. Barnum Brown, a leading authority on dinosaurs.

His finds include some of the most outstanding fossil discoveries of all time, most of which were assembled at the American Museum of Natural History in New York.

The most spectacular findings include the only skeleton of the akylosaurus ever found, and the skeleton of the tyrannosaurus rex, the flesh-eating king of the dinosaurs.

More than 400 specimens - including the massive skull of a triceratops - are on display at the museum inside the Fort Peck power plant. Models and exhibits which focus on the building, operation, and benefits of Fort Peck Dam are located in the adjacent power plant lobby.

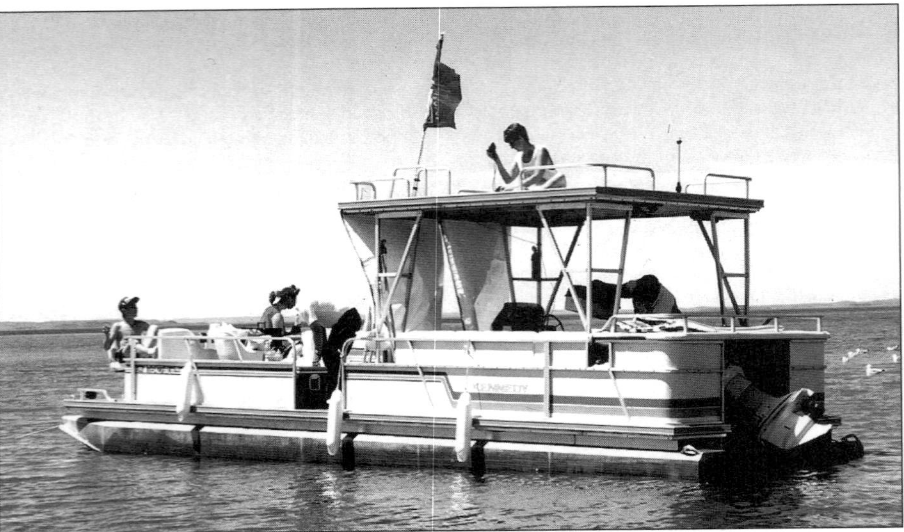

*One of the better ways to enjoy the lake. Photo courtesy of Glasgow Chamber of Commerce.*

## Historical

The area surrounding Fort Peck was first charted by Lewis and Clark in 1804, and the pristine natural condition of the river and surrounding area awed the renowned explorers.

The Old Fort Peck trading post was built in 1867 on a narrow ledge of shale about 35 feet above the river, its rear wall abutting the hillside. The front of the stockade was so close to the ledge that it was an effective steamboat landing for stern wheelers that made frequent trips upstream. But the site of the old stockade was lost to the river in the 1870s.

Fort Peck Dam was the first dam built in the upper Missouri River basin. When President Franklin D. Roosevelt authorized the Fort Peck project in 1933, thousands of Depression-bled people from all over the country migrated to Montana in hopes of earning a living.

More than 7,000 men and women signed on to work on the dam in 1934 and '35, during the midst of the Great Depression. Employment peaked at nearly 11,000 dam workers in 1936, and thousands more swarmed to Montana to set up businesses including food markets, hardware stores, butcher shops, general stores, saloons and brothels.

Eighteen boom towns sprang up in the vicinity, and the "wild west" was reborn as a tiny and obscure township swelled from a population of a few hundred to nearly 40,000 people.

Maj. Clark C. Kittrell, who served as Corps of Engineers district engineer at Fort Peck in the '30s, defined the complexity of the mission: "No engineering job of this magnitude had ever been attempted with so short a time for planning."

New techniques had to be learned and developed as rapidly as ingenuity would allow. Countless technical problems arose and were solved, and a shipyard in dry and dusty Montana quickly turned out the "Fort Peck Navy," which would dredge the river bottom and pump the slurry that ultimately formed the dam.

Dam workers overcame a massive slide in 1938, a year after closure was made, and with completion of the dam in sight. The last load of material was dumped in October 1940, almost seven years to the day after FDR authorized the dam.

The legacy that is Fort Peck provides visitors a fascinating look into yesteryear. The town of Fort Peck, now an independent municipality, is a rare treasure. Neither progress nor modernization can erase the etchings of time that allow visitors a glimpse back at another era.

Many of the early buildings - some of which are listed on the National Register of Historic Buildings - still stand, symbols of a distant past, with an integrity that allows them to function yet today. *Reprinted from Corps of Engineers brochure.*

## Model of Design

The World Almanac lists Fort Peck Dam as the largest embankment dam in the United States with the fifth largest man-made reservoir. It is also the second largest volume embankment dam and the largest "hydraulic fill" dam in the world.

Hydraulic fill dams are comprised of sediment pumped from the river bottom. The slurry was pumped through miles of huge pipelines to the centerline of the dam. The "core pool," as it was called, ran the length of the dam, with water slowly draining back to the river while impervious material settled and formed the center of the dam.

Railroad cars then hauled rock and fill material via bridges, dumping their cargo on top of the layered embankment of the dam.

The Fort Peck Dam served as a model of design for the vast majority of major earth fill dams built after it.

The embankment stretches four miles across the Missouri River Valley and contains 126 million cubic yards of earth fill.

Fort Peck Lake is 134 miles long at normal operating level, with 1,600 miles of shoreline. Ninety-nine percent of the water released from Fort Peck Dam - or about 6.5 billion gallons per day - passes through the power plant. That translates into 2.8 million kilowatt hours of pollution-free energy produced each day, on average.

*Reprinted from Corps of Engineers brochure.*

### T The Pines Recreation Area

MT Hwy. 24 N., Fort Peck

The outstanding features of this recreation area are the tall ponderosa pine trees. This unique campground on the Fork Peck Lake offers a wilderness experience with the conveniences of a shelter building, fire grill, potable water, toilets, boat ramp and access to untamed beaches.

### T Powerhouse Museum

Fort Peck. 526-3421

A pictorial history of the dam construction is supplemented by models and exhibits. In addition to the displays on the workings of the powerhouse itself, there is a collection of over 400 fossil specimens including the skull of a Triceratops. Open year round from 9 a.m. to 5 p.m. daily. Admission is free.

### FL Historic Fort Peck Hotel/Mikel's Restaurant

175 S. Missouri Ave., Fort Peck. 526-3266 or 800-560-4931

This registered historic site just off scenic U.S. Route 2 is in the center of some of the best hunting, fishing, and outdoor recreation in Northeastern Montana. Their simple rustic decor will take you back to the 1930s and 40s. Mikel's Restaurant, located in the hotel, offers exceptional dining with an emphasis on Cajun fare. In season, you can dine on their front porch. Relax on their front porch while watching deer wander through the beautiful park directly across the street. They are only a short walk from the Fort Peck Theater, and only minutes away from the dam, the Powerhouse Museum, and one of the largest man-made lakes in the country. Their comfortable lobby lounge is the perfect place to relax with your favorite cocktail and talk about the one that got away.

## 19. *Lewis & Clark, Attraction*

### D William Clark
May 14, 1805

*"Six good hunters of the party fired a Brown or Yellow Bear several times before they killed hem, & indeed he had like to have defeated the whole party, he pursued them Separately as they fired on him, and was near Catching Several of them one he pursued into the river . . . "we proceeded on verry well untill about 6 oClock a Squawl of wind Struck our Sale broad Side and turned the perogue nearly over, and in this Situation the Peroque remained untill the Sale wa Cut down in which time She nearly filed with water."*

### D William Clark
May 17, 1805

*"we were roused late in the night and warned wo the danger of fire from a tree which had Cought and leaned over our Lodge"*

### D William Clark
May 18, 1805

*" at about 12 oClock it began to rain and continued moderately for about 1 and a half hours, not Sufficient to wet a man thro' his clothes; this is the first rain Since we Set out this Spring"*

### D Mer. Lewis
May 19, 1805

*"one of the party wounded a beaver, and my dog as usual swam in to catch it; the beaver bit him through the hind leg and cut the artery; it was with great difficulty that I could stop the blood; I fear it will yet prove fatal to him."*

### D Mer. Lewis
August 4, 1806

*"during our halt we killed a very large rattlesnake. . . it had 176 scuta on the abdomen and 25 on the tail, it's length 5 feet"*

### T Charles M. Russell National Wildlife Refuge

Named after the prized Montana cowboy-artist, this refuge is the third largest in the United States and the second largest in the lower 48 states with over one million acres of prairies, badlands and rolling hills. The refuge surrounds Fort Peck Lake and portions of the Missouri River, making it a paradise for any lover of the great outdoors.

The refuge is remote, rough and spectacular. The 1,000 feet deep canyons harbor abundant wildlife and make it an ideal spot for wildlife viewing. Here you can see bighorn sheep, antelope, deer and prairie dog towns. The nation's largest remaining prairie elk herd makes its home here and can be seen along the river most prominently in September during mating season. Over 230 species of birds have been identified here including the great blue heron, golden eagle and great horned owl.

Lewis and Clark were the first through here and were soon followed by fur trappers and steamboats. Some of the wild west towns of legend, now gone, were situated on the banks of the river.

The loop Slippery Ann wildlife tour, 6 miles east of U.S. Highway 191 offers excellent wildlife viewing and photo opportunities. Many of the roads into the refuge are gravel and dirt. Access is limited. There are established campgrounds at James Kipp State Park, Fred Robinson Bridge and at the Crooked Creek Recreation Area.

> **Montana Trivia**
>
> The area surrounding Fort Peck Lake is one of the richest sources of fossils and dinosaur remains in the world. At the Hell Creak area north of Jordan, paleontologists discovered a virtually complete skeleton of Tyrannosaurus. The Fort Peck Power House Plant & Museum has over 400 specimens on display. If you would like to hunt on your own, you can obtain a permit by calling the Corps of Engineers in Fort Peck at 526-3411.

> **Montana Trivia**
>
> As of 1999, twenty tyrannosaurs have been discovered on the North American Continent. Almost half of those were found in Montana.

## 20. *Gas, Food, Lodging, Shopping*

### Glasgow

Like many names for towns picked by the railroads, a spin of the globe determined this town's name. Glasgow was named after Glasgow, Scotland. It began as a railroad town on the tracks of the Great Northern Railway in 1887. Its original name was Siding 45. It was the 45th siding west of Minot, North Dakota. It remained a sleepy little livestock and grain town until 1933 when construction of the Fort Peck dam began 18 miles southeast. While many of the construction workers lived in the boom towns surrounding the lake, many stayed in Glasgow.

### L Cottonwood Inn
US Hwy. 2, eastern edge of Glasgow. 321-8213 or 800-321-8213

This is one of Montana's premier hotels and convention centers. Ninety-two quiet comfortable rooms featuring valet and room service. The Cottonwood Inn caters to the needs of the weary traveller and busy executive alike. They have an excellent dining room and lounge, indoor pool, sauna, and jacuzzi. For the business traveler they have executive rooms with a full-size desk, computer and fax outlets, recliner, and even a telephone in the bathroom. If you really want to indulge, try their hot tub rooms complete with a wet bar, refrigerator and king-size bed. With over 3,200 sq. Ft. of banquet & convention space, and a first-class catering staff, they can accommodate almost any event or meeting.

### F Cottonwood Inn Prairie Rose Restaurant
US Hwy. 2, eastern edge of Glasgow. 228-8213

This fine restaurant specializes in good ol' home-style cooking. They feature two homemade soups which are prepared fresh daily. Their deliciously prepared lunch buffet has a selected entreé and full salad bar served from 11 a.m.–2 p.m. daily. Evening meals are expertly prepared and served with a fresh baked mini loaf and soup or salad bar. The perfect ending to any meal selection is a piece of their fresh baked pie.

## 21. *Food*

## 22. *Attraction, Food, Lodging*

### T Leo Coleman Wildlife Exhibition Pasture
US Hwy. 2 & MT Hwy. 24, Glasgow.

This 250-acre wildlife pasture offers a wonderful wildlife viewing opportunity for spotting plains buffalo, elk, antelope and deer.

### T Valley County Pioneer Museum
Hwy.. 2, Glasgow. 228-8692

In Valley County, Montana, a person is still able to find the fossilized remains of prehistoric creatures, tipi rings, buffalo jumps and artifacts of past Indian cultures in the hills and prairie lands where only a century ago huge buffalo herds roamed. Cattle, sheep and homestead shacks can still be seen.

Steamboats and forts once graced the banks of the Missouri River. Fur traders, buffalo hunters, woodhawks, and Indian agents have called this "home." Sheepherders and cowboys still ply their trades today. Golden fields of grain and vast stretches of grazing land inhabit the hills, prairie lands and river bottoms.

Small rural towns conveniently situated to accommodate their benefactors-the farmers and ranchers-have prospered to the present.

You can see evidence of the past and present at the Valley County Pioneer Museum.

**Specimens of Fossils.** Many fossils of the numerous species of prehistoric animals that roamed present Valley County 100 million years ago are found every year. A 30 foot vertebrae of the Plesiosaur is on display.

**Naming Milk River.** Lewis and Clark, the first white men in present Valley County, named the largest northern tributary of the Missouri "Milk River," noting that its water had "the colour of a cup of tea with the admixture of a tablespoonful of milk." A diorama of this event is displayed here.

**Indian Artifacts.** When the first white men arrived in present Valley County, the land was the hunting grounds of the nomadic Assiniboine Indians. The Wetsit Collection includes fabulous Indian artifacts and the Wetsit tipi made from 23 elk hides.

**The Last Hunt.** Shortly after white man's horse was introduced to the plains Indians, the men of the hunting tribes became skilled horsemen as depicted in Georgia Montfort's action packed "Last Hunt" diorama.

**Old Fort Peck.** A number of "forts" were erected along the southern border of Valley County during the fur trade days. Old Fort Peck was established in the mid-1860s and served as a trading post and Indian agency until 1877. A diorama of Old Fort Peck is featured here.

**The Buffalo Bone Trade.** Present Valley County abounded in buffalo before the final slaughter in the 1880s. The abandoned carcasses left on the prairies to rot produced thousands of tons of bones that were later gathered for commercial use.

**The Cattlemen.** Thousands of cattle were trailed into present Valley County in the 1880s to graze on the rich grasses of the late buffalo herds. The chuck wagon and stone cart on exhibit made the trip up the Texas Trail.

**The Sheepmen.** Close on the heels of the cattlemen came the sheep ranchers. In the spring of 1906, there were more than 250,000 sheep sheared in the Valley County area. The sheep wagon displayed in the museum served its purpose for 70 years on the prairies.

**Early Day Businesses.** At first Glasgow was no more than clusters of tents along the railroad track which began to grow into the present day town. Businesses and professions developed. Opheim General Store, Hinsdale Doctor's Office, Lustre Post Office, and the Frazer Barber Shop are displayed.

**The Homesteaders.** Squatters came into the area immediately following the arrival of the railroad. Homestead acts were approved, and between 1900 and 1917, 80,000 persons came into eastern Montana to file homestead claims. A diorama by Georgia Montfort depicts the Homesteaders way of life.

*St. Marie—Montana's largest ghost town.*

**Jim Hill's Railroad.** In the 1850s, a survey was made to determine a practicable rail route from St. Paul to Puget Sound. The approved route cut across present Valley County. It was not until the 1880s that the railroad was finally laid. Exhibits depict this era.

**The Unprecedented Fort Peck Dam.** During the Depression of the 1930s, the Public Works Administration approved an unprecedented engineering project which provided employment for an estimated 50,000 workers and created the world's largest earth filled dam. The entire Fort Peck Dam Project is featured in miniature form.

**The History of Local Aviation.** Valley County's history of aviation began with "barnstorming" in 1913. With the advent of war and the need for military operations came the construction of the World War II bomber base, the Opheim Radar Base and the Glasgow Air Force Base. Valley County's T.G. Kirkland hurled Valley County and the rest of the world into the space age with his design of the fuel cell for the Gemini V Space Craft.

**Nationally Recognized Sculptor.** Some years ago "Ripley's Believe It or Not" column featured the world's tiniest workable violin. The violin, created by the late Frank Lafournaise, as well as his tools and other samples of his masterful woodcarvings are on display.

In addition to all of this, you'll see the fantastic exhibit of wildlife mountings, artifacts, saddles, horns, antlers and furs from the Stan Kalinski Collection. The collection is handsomely displayed in a specially designed 30 x 70 foot room for maximum viewing.

You'll see the beautifully ornate and historical Buffalo Bill Cody bar which still sports a bullet hole and lead slug reminiscent of the wild west; the mounted head of the buffalo butchered for a celebration honoring President Franklin D. Roosevelt during his visit here in the 1930s; the albino mule deer, the white fox, the extinct Audubon sheep, 20-foot snake skins, record size elk, and many more varieties of birds, mammals, and reptiles.

The museum is located on Hwy.. 2 in Glasgow and is open from Memorial Day to Labor. Admission is free. *Reprinted from museum brochure.*

## Old Scobey

One of the last homesteading opportunities existed along the Montana-Saskatchewan border. While much of the country had been populated by the 1880s, the region that encompasses present-day Daniels County and the town of Scobey was not brought into the fold of civilization until the 1910s. The arm of the law was little felt or heeded by many inhabitants of this wide open country. The close proximity of the Canadian and North Dakota borders provided markets for stolen cattle or horseflesh and sanctuaries from local authorities.

Founder Mansfield Daniels and brother-in-law Jake Timmons established Old Scobey on the west bank of the Poplar River where they started a general store. The Hole in the Wall dugout saloon located in Old Scobey was the hangout of many shady characters like "Dutch" Henry, Pidgeon-Toed Kid and Frank Jones. The dreams of Daniels and Timmons for their town were dashed when the railroad decided to build their tracks on the other side of the river about a mile and a half from their townsite.

In those days it was customary to open your home to strangers. The Code of the West required any decent sort to offer a traveler a hot meal and bed. One morning an outlaw known as Old Scarface ate breakfast at the Hughes ranchhouse north of Scobey. Another guest, Jake Davis had just ridden in on a fine sorrel horse. Old Scarface coveted the animal and said, "Mister Davis, how would you like to trade horses?"

Jake responded, "No, I don't care to."

To which Old Scarface declared, "Well, I generally trade whether the other guy wants to or not."

Jake and his host resolved not to allow Scarface to take the sorrel without a scrap. Perhaps sensing this resistance, after breakfast the outlaw rode off ... on his own horse.

Jake Davis had come to Old Scobey in 1904 and was the area's first undertaker, simply because there was no one else to do the job. Some of Jake's colorful experiences in the early undertaking business included the time a man died suddenly at the Hole in the Wall Saloon. The unfortunate was placed in a box and left overnight on the hill near where he died. The next morning the body and coffin had disappeared. Nothing supernatural had occurred. A strong wind had blown through the country in the night and deposited the body and coffin in a deep coulee. On another occasion, a bereaved father gave the wrong measurements of his son who was an accidental gunshot victim. The coffin was too small so the boy was buried with his feet sticking out of the box.

*(Source: Homesteaders Golden Jubilee 1963) Reprinted with permission from the "Outlaw News," a publication of Missouri River Country.*

## The Big Muddy

The extreme northeast corner of Montana is now a quiet area of ranches and farms and few people. It wasn't always that way. In fact, this whole area, particularly the badlands of Big Muddy Creek, was at one time one of the wildest and most colorful areas of the American West. The three counties of Daniels, Sheridan, and Valley were once one big county (Valley). A stock inspector noted in his files that "Valley County is the most lawless and crookedest country in the union and the Big Muddy is the worst of it." Over time there were Indians, horse and cattle thieves, outlaws, bootleggers, homesteaders, baseball rivalries, newspaper wares, political battles, communists and car thieves.

Near present day Plentywood, Sitting Bull and his Sioux followers surrendered to the US Army. The Outlaw trail crossed into Canada just north of Plentywood carrying along it a large number of stolen cattle and horses across the border. The trail was named by none other than the infamous Butch Cassidy who actually established a rest station west of Plentywood in the Big Muddy Valley. At the turn of the century, the gulches surrounding Plentywood harbored every species of outlaw. This was, in fact, "The Old West" of legend.

After 1910, homesteaders brought civilization with them and the area began to settle down.

## 23. *Historical Marker, Attraction*

### H Buffalo Country

West of Glasgow.

*Buffalo meant life to the Plains Indians, and the mountain Indians used to slip down from the hills for their share, too. Some tribes would toll buffalo into a concealed corral and then down them; another system was to stampede a herd over a cliff, but the sporting way was to use bows and arrows and ride them down on a trained buffalo horse.*

*Fat cow was the choice meat. The Indians preserved their meat long before the whites ever had any embalmed beef scandals. They made pemmican by drying and pulverizing the meat, pouring marrow bone grease and oil over it, and packing it away in skin bags. It kept indefinitely, and in food value one pound was worth ten of fresh meat.*

*Tanned robes and rawhide were used for bedding, tepees, clothes, war shields, stretchers, travois, canoes, and bags. Horns and bones made tools and utensils. The buffalo played a prominent part in many of their religious rites and jealousy of hereditary hunting grounds brought on most of the intertribal wars.*

### H Liquid Gold

Vandalia

*Water is the life blood of Montana. During the state's early settlement, the rivers provided transportation and trading routes; later they sustained the livestock and crops of ranchers and homesteaders; and they still provide Montana's base for agriculture, industry, and tourism. The Milk River that parallels Highway 2 from Glasgow to Hinsdale is one of the most important rivers in the north-central part of the state.*

*One of the earliest Milk River users was Augustin Armel (AKA Hamel) who arrived about 1820. He worked at all the major American Fur Co. posts on the Missouri River until the 1850s. In 1855, he opened Hammel's House, the first trading post on the Milk River, located about 7 miles southwest of here (near Vandalia). Tom Campbell's House followed, built near the same site in 1870. Neither lasted very Long and no physical remains of them have been found.*

*Later comers to this region raised mostly cattle, sheep, and wheat. They needed water on more of the land than was blessed with it and today you can see the irrigation system along Highway 2. The Lower Milk River Valley Water Users Association promoted the construction of the Vandalia Dam and Canal in the early 1900s. Area rancher, H. H. Nelson, interested in attracting settlers, became involved in irrigation after establishing Vandalia in 1904. Nelson was director and superintendent for construction of the dam at Vandalia and the canal that runs from there east to Nashua. The dam was completed in 1917. Nelson's hopes for a sizable settlement at Vandalia never materialized.*

### T St. Marie

Driving on Hwy.. 24 to Opheim one expects to see little more than endless rolling wheat fields. The sign pointing to St. Marie suggests a small one-elevator town on an old railroad siding. But a quick glance in that direction tells you there's something different about this community. Gigantic buildings loom on the horizon. Several water towers fill the skyline. What appears to be a community larger than any other in this part of Montana sits eerily quiet only a few hundred yards from the highway. Driving into this town, one gets the feeling that they are entering a community where a strange virus has wiped out the population, or aliens have abducted the entire populace.

*Gigantic abandoned hangers sit eerily silent.*

Row after row of weathered, abandoned buildings in disrepair suggest a hasty retreat by the residents. The spooky thing is that the buildings aren't from a past century, but appear to have been built in the 1950s, 60s or 70s. A good sized hospital sits abandoned, along with a sizable school building and a large number of other buildings. A baseball field has knee-high grass on its infield. Clearly not too long ago, people got up every morning and went to work here, children went to school, and at night families sat down to dinner.

Looking toward the huge buildings to the north of town an air traffic control tower is visible hovering over runways suitable for a large international airport in a large metropolitan area. A city with an airport! Abandoned! Roads leading to the airfield are blocked by ominous signs warning that trespassers will be prosecuted (mysteriously disappear?). The authority behind the signs is Marco Aviation Research. A CIA front. And where are they? There appears to be no sign of life on the airfield.

## "Dutch" Henry Dead or Alive

"Dutch" Henry, Henry Jauch or Jeuch was born in Holland and trailed north to Montana from Texas with the great cattle herds. He found rustling more profitable and easier than honest cowboy work and formed a gang comprised of like-minded characters including his brother known as Coyote Pete, a little Irishman known as Duffy, Tom Reed, Seffick, Ernie Stines, a former Mountie named Frank Carlyle and "Kid" Trailor.

To coin a phrase from the wag Mark Twain, rumors of his death were greatly exaggerated. Referring to the horsethief and outlaw "Dutch" Henry the reports were so frequent that you would think Henry was the proverbial cat with nine lives. The voice of reason in the wild border town of MonDak, *The Yellowstone News* reports on Saturday January 15, 1910... "DUTCH" HENRY KILLED Moose Jaw, Sask., Jan. 11 -*"Dutch" Henry, the scourge of the cattle country for many years, was killed yesterday in a desperate gunfight with a mounted policeman in the badlands south of here and near the border.*

*He had been sought by the police on both sides of the line for years and had maintained a constant war with civilization in company with his desperate gang all that time. He recognized no authority but that of the six-shooter and Winchester.*

*While a lone mounted policeman was scouting along the Big Muddy Creek, in the haunts of the daring outlaw, he sighted his man and he immediately attempted his capture. "Dutch" Henry opened fire at once with his Winchester, killing the policeman's horse at the first shot. The officer rolled over when his horse fell but returned the bandit's fire at once, killing his antagonist with a bullet through the breast, his second shot.*

Apparently that was not the end of "Dutch" Henry however, because in the January 22. 1910 edition of *The Yellowstone News* appeared this announcement ... *It is now said that there is no truth in the report that "Dutch" Henry, the notorious border cattle rustler was killed in a fight with a member of the Royal Northwest Mounted Police near Moose Jaw, Canada.*

It is curious that five years earlier a Mounted Police Superintendent included this paragraph in his annual report ... *This is a very sparcely settled part of the country, and its importance is due to the fact of being near the boundary, and on account of several gangs of horse thieves which, within the last two or three months have been operating on both sides of the line. The principals however, of these gangs are now dead and the notorious "Dutch" Henry was murdered by a friend last December 6.*

The rumors flew fast and furious. Henry's dead body found in a brush heap was positively identified in Minnesota. He apparently plied his trade down south because there's a report that "Dutch" was hanged in Mexico. Another story has "Dutch" Henry married and living peacefully in Stillwater, Minnesota until he died of a gunshot wound in 1928 or 29. The truth is in there somewhere, or is it?

*Reprinted with permission from the "Outlaw News", a publication of Missouri River Country.*

Section 10

## Steamboats Navigate the Missouri River

In the years immediately following the Great War between the states, the Montana goldrush was booming along with the riverboat traffic on the Upper Missouri River. The head of navigation in 1866 was Fort Benton located about 200 miles north of the gold strikes of Alder Gulch, Bannack, Virginia City and Last Chance Gulch. Thirty-one steamers tied up to shore at Fort Benton that season, a startling increase over the half a dozen boats that arrived the prior year. Steamboat operators stood to earn huge profits, averaging $22,000 on voyages to the west to deliver staples and returning to St. Louis with passengers and freight that included the remnants of the fur trade and gold dust. But the risk was great and not a venture for the faint-hearted.

Captain Grant Marsh, though only 34, struck all who met him as a commanding presence and the steamboat under his authority, the *Luella*, made history before the summer was over. Twice that season Marsh plied the tricky shoals, sandbars and rapids of the Big Muddy. Steamboat captains generally hastily unloaded their cargo at Fort Benton and wasted no time pushing off and heading downstream. It was considered wise to "travel light" to avoid entrapment in the rapidly shallowing river of mid-summer.

Marsh, who instilled confidence in his crew and passengers, decided to delay his final departure until September. As the *Luella* offered the last opportunity of the year for leaving the country, there was a great rush of applications for passage. Many rough characters would employ any trick to avoid paying the established rates set as high as $350 for passage to St. Louis. Payment was demanded in advance, in gold dust. Some cagey miners tried to mix black sand with their dust which, if left undetected, would save some of their hard-earned wealth. Marsh foiled their scheme by requiring the passengers to pan their dust in the presence of the shipping clerk before boarding, thereby washing out all the sand.

When the voyage began September 2nd. the *Luella* had aboard 230 passengers and $1,250,000 in gold dust. It was the richest treasure ever carried down the Missouri River.

Marsh's great skill through the torturous river bends, shallows and narrows made the trip uneventful until the *Luella* reached the mouth of the Milk River 347 miles below Fort Benton. It was at this point the *Luella* ran aground on a sandbar. One of the passengers. a man named McClellan, was on deck observing the crew as they labored to dislodge the boat. When the deck heaved and rocked, McClellan accidently fell overboard. Though the water was barely two feet deep the current was swiFort McClellan, apparently weighed down by a leather belt filled with gold dust hidden under his clothes. was swept off his feet and was unable to regain his balance on the slippery riverbottom. So great was the weight of his treasure belt that he was dragged down and drowned before help could reach him. The powerful current swept away his body which was never recovered.

Indians, who happened upon the scene of the floundering paddlewheeler, began firing upon the *Luella* from a high bluff overlooking the river. Marsh simply called his 230 passengers to the deck who along with the 40 crew members, unholstered their shooting irons and drove the tribesmen off the skyline with the first, noisy fusillade.

Marsh got his boat, passengers, cargo and crew to St. Louis without further incident, earning for himself, respect rarely accorded to a new captain on the Missouri and an everlasting place in steamboating lore.

*(Source material: "The Conquest of the Missouri" by Joseph Hanson 1909. "The Rivermen" Time-Life Books Inc. 1975. "Steamboats of the Fort Union Fur Trade" Michael M. Caster 1999)*

### The Steamboat Josephine on the Yellowstone

Josephine At A Glance

- Wood hull
- Originally owned by the Coulson Family
- 183 feet long. 31 feet wide, and 4 feet deep
- Named for the daughter of General Stanley
- Had two boilers to supply steam to the engines
- Made 50 trips to Montana
- Was used during the Sioux-Cheyenne War in 1876
- Crashed due to ice on March 3, 1907, at Running Water, South Dakota
- Engines salvaged for use in a Yukon River steamboat in Alaska

The steamboat *Josephine*, a sternwheel packet, was one of three boats to get any distance above the narrow, fast portion of the river around Pompeys Pillar. The others were the F.Y. *Batchelor* and the *Key West*. The Yellowstone was thought to be impassible beyond the mouth of the Bighorn River to steamboat travel. However in 1875, Captain Grant Marsh piloted the *Josephine* beyond the Bighorn confluence to the vicinity of present day Billings. The *Josephine* made a total of ten trips up the Yellowstone until her destruction in 1907. Steamboats were a big part of life along the river in the late 1860s and 1870s until the transcontinental railroad line was completed.

*Reprinted with permission from the "Outlaw News", a publication of Missouri River Country.*

Occasionally an automobile or two can be seen parked amid the maze of streets lined with abandoned houses. Suddenly a lone jogger appears. When asked about the nature of this town she replies "I think it used to be an Air Force base."

What was the name of it?

"I really don't know. I guess I should, but I don't. We're bringing it back though."

### The Story Behind the Town

In the 1950s the Air Force built Glasgow Air Force Base, and along with it a thriving community of over 10,000. There were schools, churches, a hospital, a movie theater and a bowling alley. All of the elements of a normal, healthy, community are still there today, with the exception of one-the people. The air base grew and prospered during the Vietnam War until 1976 when the war ended. Major cutbacks in military spending forced the base to close, and virtually overnight, the people were gone.

Efforts to revive the town over the years have more or less failed. AVCO, an ammunitions-support business, moved in for a while. They moved out in a few short years. The Mountain-Plains/Family Training Center, Inc. tried to open a center for training low income citizens and welfare recipients. That lasted about ten years. More than a dozen businesses have tried to survive here and failed. As each effort ended, the town slipped more and more into disrepair.

The federal government, eager to get it off their hands, gave complete ownership to Valley County. In 1985, a developer purchased the whole town, airstrip and all, from Valley County. The developer named the town after an infant daughter he and his wife had lost. His plan? To build a retirement community, complete with a golf course, fitness center, and medical facility. He did sell about 200 of the 1,200 units. But a number of these units were hauled off to other parts of the state, and following the death of the developers wife, the town was sold to another developer in 1966. The new developer generated substantial debt and enough legal tangles to fill the town with lawyers.

So what did the jogger mean when she said "we're bringing it back?" Perhaps she was referring to the talk that NASA is looking at the site as a base for its next generation of Space Shuttles (Venture Star). And why not? The 13,500 foot airstrip is one of the longest anywhere, and it was built extra thick to handle the northern Montana winters. The large amount of water needed to cool the new space craft is nearby in Fort Peck Reservoir. It's isolated (the government loves secrecy), and it has an infrastructure in place. The power, water, and sewer systems are in place, and a little paint and spackle will bring the churches, schools, hospital, and houses back to shape in no time.

The community is 17 miles north of Glasgow on Hwy.. 24. Drive in and look around, but heed the warning signs. You are being watched.

**24.** *Attraction, Gas, Food, Lodging*

### Plentywood

Plentywood is a high plains community tucked away in the northeast corner of Montana and serves as a 24-hour port entry into Canada. Approximately 2,200 people dwell in this town which has very little water and few mountains. Called the "gateway to Saskatchewan," this small town claims grain and livestock as the kings of the local economy.

You might wonder how a little town sitting on the high prairie would get a name like this. The story goes that a bunch of cowboys and a cook were attempting to build a fire out of buffalo chips. Old Dutch Henry came along and told them "If you'll go a couple of miles up this creek, you'll find plenty wood." When it came time to name the town, these words of wisdom were remembered.

(The following is an item from the front page of *The Plentywood Herald* Friday, July 11, 1913)

## Kid Trailor Arrested

Kid Trailor was arrested at or near Froid and brought up to Plentywood where he was taken before Judge Bolster and placed under heavy bonds to appear on the 15th.

Some of his friends came up and signed his bond. They claim that the Kid has been leading a quiet life trying to overcome a bad reputation for horse stealing and that in this case he has been wrongly accused. It will be up to him and his friends to prove this.

(A similar item appeared in *The Sheridan County News* on the same date.)

## Kid Trailor Made Us A Visit

Kid Trailor, thief, horse rustler, general tramp and gun man, of whom it is claimed wouldn't harm a chicken, spent a few hours in the city Tuesday the guest of Sheriff "Jack" Bennett. It seems that Trailor was rounded up in the vicinity of Froid by one Cy Matthews, a rancher, and was taken into Froid at the point of a gun Monday evening, where he remained over night and on Tuesday was brought to the county seat. After arriving here and being lodged in jail it was found that there was no one to appear or make complaint against the so called bad man, hence the officers having nothing to hold Trailor for he was released and that evening wended his way for other parts.

*Reprinted with permission from the "Outlaw News", a publication of Missouri River Country.*

### T Big Sky's Lil' Norway Reindeer Farm

3 miles west of Plentywood on Hwy. 5. 895-2489

OK, so you've seen the elk, deer, antelope, moose, bears, bison and scores of other critters that reside in Montana—but have you seen the reindeer? It's easy to pass right by if you're not looking. You may not see the reindeer from the road because they'd rather hide from the flies in their shed.

### T Sheridan County Museum

Hwy. 16, Plentywood. 765-2219

### 25. *Gas, Food*

### Flaxville

When the Great Northern built its branch line across the northeastern part of Montana, several new towns sprung up at the sidings and depots that the rail line created. The second of these was Flaxville. It was originally to be named Boyer after the Henry Boyer family at whose home the early railroad construction workers were fed. However, there was some confusion with the name that was to be given the next siding west, and this new town was named after the only crop that was grown in the area—Flaxville. The next one down became Madoc.

Flaxville was at one time a bustling community with more than thirty businesses operating during its peak. However, its reliance on the railroad would turn that around as other forms of transportation took people and business away.

### Whitetail

While it is the town at the end of the Soo Line railroad, it did not begin as a railroad town. The Soo Line planned to build farther west, but ended up stopping at Whitetail. When the railroad arrived, the town began to boom. It sits in a beautiful valley along Whitetail Creek next to a reservoir at its outskirts.

In the 1920s a rumor spread that several gallons of oil were pumped out of a well in town. This created a frenzy. Oilmen came in from Wisconsin and the Whitetail Oil Syndicate was formed. In 1928 drilling began and continued for several years. Unfortunately no oil was ever recovered, although enough natural gas was found to power the steam power unit for a while.

Whitetail at one point was an industrial center. In the late 30s, the Schlecter Bros. invented the power-take-off grain blower. This revolutionized grain handling. A factory was built and by the 40s every farm truck had a "Whitetail Grain Blower". As often happens, new technology was the downfall of the business.

### 26. *Attraction, Gas, Food, Lodging*

### Scobey

This idyllic prairie town, like so many towns in this part of the state, began as a railroad town. Actually, it was the child of two railroads, the Great Northern, and the Soo Line (see sidebar). The town took its name from Major Scobey, an agent at the Fort Peck Reservation.

### T Pioneer Town and Museum

On western edge of Scobey. 487-5965 or 487-5502

The first settlers to arrive in Daniels County never would have dreamed that the rustic homesteads and storefronts they constructed would still be standing in 100 years. But rather than tear down the old to make way for the new, the residents of Daniels County painstakingly relocated their ancestors' buildings to the outskirts of Scobey. Through the years they collected a total of 42 original structures throughout the area. Soon an entire Old Western Main Street had been rescued, renovated and christened—Pioneer Town. This is not a recreation, it is the real thing. Here you can wander through original Old West shops and homes.

Pioneer Town is situated at the crossroads of two famous old west trails and the Great Northern Railroad. The Indian followers of Sitting Bull traveled the "Wood Mountain Trail" as they made their desperate retreat to Canada. Butch Cassidy led his band of misfits up the "Outlaw Trail" to evade the law. The town is open from Memorial Day to Labor Day.

## A Tale of Two Railroads

Before branchlines of the railroads were built in the northeast part of Montana, supplies were freighted in from the "main line" by team and wagon. A stage route followed the same route as the ancient Wood Mountain Trail for years carrying mail and passengers.

At that time the two railroads—the Soo and the Great Northern—were fierce competitors. When word got out that the Soo planned to build a branch line just south of the Canadian border, the Great Northern hurried up to build one of its own. That competition created two railroad lines only seven miles apart, both within 15 miles of the border. The next closest railroad line was 50 miles to the south.

The railroad had a custom of setting up a siding and depot about every six miles. Towns sprung up at these depots. Look at the distances between the towns of Flaxville, Madoc, Scobey, Four Buttes, Gluten and Peerless.

### 27. *Gas, Food*

### Four Buttes

A town that got its name from, where else, the four unique buttes that stand on the prairie west of the town. Known as "Whiskey Buttes" in days past because they were a frequent rendezvous point for whiskey traders and Indians. Like so many towns in Montana, Four Buttes began in 1926 when the Great Northern Railroad was extended from Scobey. That same year a grain elevator was constructed with a capacity of 35,000 bushels. The original elevator burned in 1944, but was replaced by the one that stands there today. Until 1967, Four Buttes children attended a one room schoolhouse. The children now are bussed to Scobey. The bar and dance hall building constructed in 1942 still stands as the Whiskey Buttes Supper Club.

*House of ill repute? In the early days of this area, "One-eyed Molly's" was a hotel/house of pleasure in what is now Scobey. When Daniels County was formed, the hotel was for the most part abandoned. The County purchased it and turned it into a courthouse. A few years later an addition was added. The building still serves as one of Montana's more colorful county capitols and is listed on the National Register of Historic Places.*

## Peerless
## The Town Named After a Beer

One of the more colorful towns in Montana is the little town of Peerless, named after Peerless Beer around 1912. The story goes that during a meeting in a local saloon to pick a name for the new post office, a traveling salesman was drinking a bottle of Peerless Beer and suggested that as a name for the new town. The name stuck.

In its early days, the town was known for its moonshiners and boozerunners. It even had a house of ill repute. The town was full of colorful characters. In the early days "Whitey the Gambler" shot and killed a man and was given 30 days to leave town. Then there's the mysterious local farmer, John Brown. No one knew where he came from or anything about his past. In the late 50s, they found him dead with quite a sum of money, a .38 strapped to his chest, and another alongside his bed.

## 28. *Historical Marker, Gas, Food, Lodging*

## Opheim

Between 1900-1918, during the homestead era, this community and some of the smaller ones to the south were much bigger. The town was named for Alfred Opheim, the second postmaster for the area. His wife was the first.

### H Wood Mountain Trail

Rte. 13, south of Scobey.

*This Indian trail extended from the Yellowstone River past this point to the Wood Mountains in Canada. It was used for decades by the Sioux and the Assiniboine tribes in pursuit of the migrating buffalo. Also stalking this meat staple on the hoof were the Metis, a French Canadian band of Indians who used the trail. In the 1800s fur hunters and trappers made continual use of the passage and at the turn of the century, settlers and homesteaders followed. It was over this trail in July of 1891 that Sitting Bull and his Sioux warriors were escorted from Canada by Canadian Mounties and Jean Louis Le Gare, the man responsible for Sitting Bull's surrender at Fort Buford.*

*Scobey, Montana, was named for Major Scobey who served at Fort Buford and. later worked with the Indian Bureau on the Fort Peck Reservation.*

## Scenic Drives

As you travel through this vast open area of Montana, your first impulse is to hurry through it. The seemingly endless roads surrounded by vast plains or stretches of badlands seem like an obstacle on your way to the mountains of the west.

Slow down. Savor the experience. Stop your car every now and then and step out into the Big Open to experience the solitude and the power of the surrounding landscape. The scale and power of this country has a way of seeping inside your soul. Try to envision the grandeur that Lewis and Clark saw when they passed this way along the Missouri River. Picture in your mind the vast herds of bison, elk, antelope, and deer that they encountered. Imagine the awesome loneliness that might have struck their group as they journeyed through here.

### Four Buttes, Poplar River and Rock Creek Badlands Route

Glasgow is your starting point for this trip. This trip is a 202 mile circle so plan your time accordingly. We'd recommend at least 2 days. This route will take you through endless miles of strip wheatfields and rolling grasslands. Head two miles east of town and take Route 24 north to Opheim. To the west of you, beyond a few farm roads, is some of the wildest prairie lands in the northern part of Montana—Bitter Creek.

After visiting Opheim go east on Highway 248. Along the way you'll pass through the towns of Glentana, Richland, Peerless, and Four Buttes. Stop at each one if you can.

A stop in Peerless isn't complete without a visit to Dutch Henry's Bar. The place is named for an outlaw who roamed these parts in times past. You actually learn a lot about the history of the area from the photos on the bar's walls.

When you get to Four Buttes notice the stately buttes to the northwest from which the town got its name. Continue on to Scobey where you'll want to be sure and visit Pioneer Town, arguably one of the finest exhibits of its kind in the west.

Head south out of Scobey on Highway 13 through the Poplar River Valley to Highway 2 and the Missouri River Valley. Turn right on Highway 2 to Wolf Point and on back to Glasgow.

For another tour of this area, drive west on Highway 2 to Hinsdale. Another railroad town, this one was named after a town in New Hampshire. Its first building was a boxcar which served as a railroad depot. North of here you will find some of the most spectacular and remote badlands in Montana. About three miles east of Hinsdale, pick up Rock Creek Road and head north. Within about 18 miles you'll be skirting the western edge of a true prairie wilderness—the Bitter Creek region. There is a loop trip through these badlands which will take about eight hours. Check at the BLM office in Glasgow for a map and information about the loop. A 4-wheel drive vehicle is recommended for this sidetrip. The stretch along Rock Creek is true cowboy country. The ranches are big here and there is a lot of space between people.

When you return to Glasgow on Highway 2, take a side trip at the sign to Vandalia and take Highway 246 back to Glasgow via Vandalia and Tampico.

### Jordan Country, Circle Range and CMR Wildlife Refuge Route

This area was dubbed "The Big Open" by the late 1800s photographer L. A. Huffman. Others have called it "The Big Dry." Until the 1990s it was a fairly unknown area to the rest of the country when the standoff between the Federal agents and the Freeman brought it national attention. Jordan was founded in 1896 by Arthur Jordan. However, it wasn't named after him. He asked that the town take the name of a friend in Miles City who was also named Jordan. The first building or structure in Jordan was Arthur Jordan's tent. A post office

# Lewis and Clark Meet Mr. Griz

Editor's Note: The creative spelling and punctuation found in the journals has been faithfully reproduced to give you the true flavor of the time.

**The Corps of Discovery led by** Meriwether Lewis and William Clark entered Montana in April of 1805. The explorers had wintered with the Mandan Indians in what is now central North Dakota. They spent the winter gathering information from the local tribesmen to determine what lay ahead. The Indians and French traders they encountered no doubt warned the white men about the ferocious *"great white bear."* The explorers did not faithfully record these warnings in their journals. The Indians told how they prepared for a grizzly hunt as if they were going on the war path against neighboring tribes and would not think of challenging the bear with fewer than six to eight warriors and the likelihood that one or two of their number would not survive the encounter. On Monday, April 29th, 1805, Lewis recorded the following after the group's first close encounter near the confluence of the Missouri and Yellowstone Rivers,

*"... the Indians may well fear this animal equipped as they generally are with their bows and arrows of indifferent fuzees, but in the hand of skillful rifle men they are by no means as formidable or dangerous as they have been represented."*

By this comment Lewis exhibits a quality of confidence, if not arrogance, shared by intrepid explorers everywhere that feel virtually invincible. This feeling of superiority depended on their own physical qualities, character and experience, not to mention their Kentucky flintlocks. Lewis recognized the differences between the eastern black bear, of his and his fellow's experience and this animal. Lewis described the beast killed on that date,

*"... it was a male not fully grown, we estimated his weight at 300 lbs. not having the means of ascertaining it precisely. The legs of this bear are somewhat longer than those of the black, as are it's tallons and tusks incomparably larger and longer."*

Though far from the first description of a grizzly, this is the first detailed one. Henry Kelsey, in 1691, was probably the first white man to see a grizzly.

It was not only the physical characteristics that separated this bear from his eastern cousins, but its temperament and attitude toward men. A child with a stick could easily frighten off the timid black bear, while this giant carnivore of the western plains was used to having his own way and feared no living creature including man and was more likely to attack especially when provoked. Sgt. Patrick Gass wrote,

*"The natives call them white, but they are more of a brown grey. They are longer than the common black bear, and have much larger feet and talons."*

Lewis and Clark and their men became believers when they met a much larger specimen on May 5th. Clark wrote,

*"The river rising & current Strong & in the evening we saw a Brown or Grizzly beare on a sand beech, I went out with one man Geo Drewyer & killed the bear, which was verry large and a turrible looking animal, which we found very hard to kill we Shot ten Balls into him before we killed him, & 5 of those Balls through his lights. This animal is the largest of the carnivorous kind I ever saw"*

Lewis' description was more detailed,

*"It was the most tremendious looking anamal, and extremely hard to kill notwithstanding he had five balls through his lungs and five others in various parts he swam more than half the distance across the river to a sandbar, & it was at least twenty minutes before he died: he did not attempt to attack, but fled and made the most tremendous roaring from the moment he was shot. We had no means of weighing this monster; Capt. Clark thought he would weigh 500 lbs. for my part I think the estimate too small by 100 lbs. he measured 8 Feet 7 1/2 Inches from the nose to the extremety of the hind feet, 5 F. 10 1/2 Ins. arround the breast."* The following day Lewis wrote, *"I find the curiossity of our party is pretty well satisfyed with rispect to this anamal, the formidable appearance of the male bear killed on the 5th added to the difficulty with which they die when even shot through the vital parts, has staggered the resolution (of) several of them, others however seem keen for action with the bear; I expect these gentlemen will give us some amusement shortly as they (the bears) soon begin now to coppolate."*

Amusement was probably not the word that came to mind as several of the party were forced to flee after discharging their single~shot rifles and seeing little effect, besides enraging the bears, as described in the journal of Sgt. John Ordway.

*"Saturday 11th May 1805 ...one of the party which had a lame hand was walking on Shore. towards evening he came running and hollowing to the perogues chased by a brown bair which he had wounded, bad. Some of the hunters went out with him and killed it. It was nearly of the Same description as the one killed Some days past, but much fatter."* Then on the 14th Ordway reported, *"... abt. 4oClock the men in the canoes Saw a large brown bear on the hills on the S.S. 6 men went out to kill it. they fired at it and wounded it. it chased 2 of them into a canoe, and anoth(er) (into) the River and they Steady fireing at after shooting eight balls, in his body Some of them through the lites, he took the River and was near catching the Man he chased in, but he went up against the Stream and the bear being wounded could not git to him one of the hunters Shot him in the head which killed him dead. we got him to Shore with a canoe and butchred him we found him to be nearly the Same discription of the first we killed only much larger."*

As the expedition continued westward they had several more hair-raising adventures with Mr. Grizzly. (Source material: *"The Journals of Lewis & Clark"*, Bernard DeVoto, *"The Journals of Patrick Gass," "The Journals of John Ordway"*, *Undaunted Courage*, Stephan E. Ambrose, 1996)

*Reprinted with permission from* "Outlaw News", *a publication of Missouri River Country.*

and store were soon added and a cow town was born. The place maintains an old west flavor with its false front buildings on main street, many of which are over 80 years old.

This town is the gateway to some of the most remote and beautiful river canyons, badlands and prairie wilderness in the west. Much of this rugged terrain is in the Charles M. Russell Wildlife Refuge which stretches for almost 200 miles and surrounds Fort Peck Lake. The loop route you'll take out of here is about 227 miles long, so you should give yourself a couple of days.

Leave Jordan headed east on Highway 200 to Circle. Almost immediately you'll see red and yellow colored buttes and badlands. This is dinosaur country and is a favorite hunting ground for paleontologists. One of the first dinosaurs of record, a Tyrannosaurus Rex was discovered near Jordan in the Hell Creek Formation in 1904. Since then its been the source of many excellent finds.

Circle is another "cow town" which got its name from the Circle Brand, one of Montana's earliest ranches. This is still primarily a farm and ranch town. To the south of Circle you'll see a unique range of high sandstone hills. The Big Sheep Mountains were named after the Audubon Sheep that lived there until eliminated by the homesteaders in the early 1900s.

Take Highway 13 north out of Circle toward Wolf Point. When you reach Highway 2, turn east and continue through Wolf Point and the Missouri River Valley to Nashua. Turn left at Nashua onto Highway 117 to Fort Peck Dam and the town of Fort Peck. Just beyond that you'll reach Montana 24. Go right on this and drive over the dam. This area east of Fort Peck Lake is called Dry Arm. Continue on Highway 24 to Highway 200 and turn right to Jordan.

## The Missouri and Yellowstone Route

Twenty miles to the northeast of present day Sidney on April 27, 1805, Lewis and Clark and the Corps of Discovery first entered Montana. A couple of days earlier, they camped at the confluence of the Yellowstone and Missouri Rivers just across what is now the border. Their journals tell the story of abundant wildlife in the area:

*"we saw great quantities of game today; consisting of the common and mule deer, Elk, Buffaloe, and Antelopes; also 4 brown bear, one of which was fired on and wounded by one of the party, but we did not get it; the beaver have out great quantities of timber; saw a tree nearly 3 feet in diameter that had been felled by them."* The next day, they encountered their first grizzly bear... *"I walked on shore with one man about 8 A.M. we fell in with two brown or yellow bear."*

Almost a year and a half later on August 16, 1806, they met each other on their return trip. Previously, the two captains had agreed to split up on the western side of Montana. Lewis took the northern route retracing their steps west, and Clark took a southern route primarily following the Yellowstone river.

Sidney is your hub for several short tours. Before leaving Sidney, be sure and visit the MonDak Heritage Center.

For a great view of the Yellowstone Breaks and Badlands, follow Highway 16 three miles south to Route 23. Go left and drive another three miles until you reach Highway 261. Turn right heading

# WHAT MAKES THE BADLANDS "BAD"?

Much of this region was covered by a continental glacier which flowed out of Canada approximately 15,000 years ago. It moved as far south as the current Highway 2. By the time it reached this area it was thinning and didn't do the carving that alpine glaciers do in the mountains. It did, however, move the channel of the Missouri and Milk Rivers. The Milk now occupies the old Missouri River Valley and the Missouri is now further south than it was then. The glacier also covered the area with rich glacial deposits creating the most extensive grain growing region in this half of the state.

Badlands are found in pockets throughout this part of the state. This terrain is a desert environment created when fire or other disruption destroys the plant cover that would normally protect the surface from erosion. Rain water hits the stripped surface and compacts it preventing new seeds from taking hold.

The runoff then forms gullies and begins to carve the strange looking formations. Unusual and strange formations that look like mushrooms are scattered through these areas. They are sandstone that has been carved by the winds.

As you travel through the area, you'll see hills that have a distinct red banding to them. Often referred to as scoria, their proper name is clinker. Clinker is red sandstone and shale that has had the misfortune of lying above a burning coal seam. The seam may have been ignited by prairie fire or lightning, and "cooked" the overlying formation. As the coal heated it to extreme temperatures, oxygen combined with iron in the rock forming iron oxide which produced the bands of red rust color visible in these hillsides. Clinker is tough stuff and is often used for resurfacing some of the eastern Montana roads.

south. This road is known locally as "The Lost Highway." Drive about 17 miles and go right on Road 106 to the river. This is a very scenic route, but you are crossing private land, so stay on the road.

Another day trip out of Sidney takes you west on Highway 200 to Lambert and Fox Lake Wildlife Management Area. When you leave Lambert work your way back on the back roads toward Crane on Highway 16 just south of Sidney.

If you head north out of Sidney on Highway 200 you will reach Fairview in about 12 miles. This town has the distinction of being in two states. Ask the locals how to get to the Snowden Bridge. Just about anybody there will tell you its story. From Fairview, head north on Highway 58 to Fort Union Trading Post National Historic Site.

You can take a 95 mile loop out of Sidney to explore the varied river breaks, the Missouri River, and badlands scenery. Leave Sidney on Highway 16 northwest to Culbertson. At Culbertson, go right on Highway 2 to Bainville. Explore Bainville for a bit before heading south on the Bainville-Snowden road.

### Outlaws, Old trails and the Sioux and Assiniboine Nations Route.

You will cover 188 miles on this circle trip so allow yourself some time. You will probably need to take at least a couple of days even if you hurry through.

Lewis and Clark camped near Wolf Point where you begin this tour on May 5, 1805. They recorded killing a large grizzly bear on the banks of the Missouri which measured 8 feet 7 1/2 inches long and weighed in at 500-600 pounds.

Leave Wolf Point and head east on Highway 2 to Poplar. The headquarters of the Sioux and Assiniboine tribes is located here. Take some time to visit the cultural center and museum located on the east end of town.

Lewis and Clark camped on the Poplar River near here, about 3 1/2 miles upstream from where it enters into the Missouri River. Because of the abundance of porcupine in the area, the team named the river the Porcupine River. The name was later changed to the Poplar River reflecting the abundance of poplar trees along the river's banks.

Six mile past Poplar, turn left on Highway 151and head to Flaxville a little more than 50 miles away. While driving this road it can't be explained, but you'll know you are driving north and uphill. You'll see why. Most of this stretch consists of vast open wheatfields stretching to the horizon.

Somewhere south of Flaxville, you'll cross the old Wood Mountain Trail. This trail was practically a highway leading to Wood Mountain in Saskatchewan, Canada. It was a popular wintering place for plains tribes because of its abundant water, trees, and good habitat for game. This is the route Sitting Bull took when escaping to Canada after the Battle of Little Bighorn. This trail began somewhere near the Yellowstone River to the southeast and went through Fort Union near Sidney. Not only was it only a popular trail for Indians, but for hunters, trappers, and eventually homesteaders.

When you reach Flaxville at the junction of Highway 5 continue north through town on Highway 511 to Whitetail. When you reach the rise just before town, you can get a great photo of the town nestled in the valley of Whitetail Creek.

When you're finished visiting Whitetail, head back to Flaxville and go west on Highway 5. When you get to Scobey, be sure and visit Pioneer Town, a recreation of a turn-of-the-century homestead town (see sidebar).

When you've finished in Scobey, head back east to Plentywood. On the way stop in Redstone. This town took its name around 1900 from the red shale in the area. You are now entering the "Wild West" of legend.

Leave Plentywood southward toward Culbertson. On the way, spend some time at

## Montana Trivia

In 1924, Scobey became the largest single primary wheat loading center in North America. With only limited facilities, the town managed to load out close to three million bushels on the Great Northern Railroad. It was also suspected to be one of the largest centers for smuggling wheat from Canada when Canadian grain prices were low.

## Montana Trivia

The infamous Outlaw Trail which extended from Mexico to Canada crossed much of this area. As a result, there is a colorful history of early-day outlaws (mostly horse thieves) passing through the region. A stock inspector named Halle wrote in his files that *"Valley County, Montana is the most lawless and crookedest county in the Union..."*

The outlaws were seldom a problem to the local residents. Just southwest of Scobey are the remains of a known outlaw hangout called the "Dugout Saloon". It is situated near where the Outlaw Trail and the Wood Mountain Trail cross. Attempts are underway to make this a national historic site.

Medicine Lake National Wildlife Refuge (see sidebar). When you reach Culbertson drive south a few miles on Highway 16 to the Missouri River for a great view of the "Big Muddy" and surrounding badlands. Back in town, stop at the Culbertson Museum and Visitors Center on the east side of town.

From Culbertson, head back to Wolf Point on Highway 2. This was the Minnesota Wagon Road in the late 1800s. You can still see a roadhouse from those days where Big Muddy Creek meets the Missouri River. In 1883 a toll bridge was built there, and in 1867, Pony Express riders from Minneapolis rode the area that parallels today's US Highway 2. If you have the time take a side road down to the Missouri. Try to picture the trappers in their dugout boats and the steamboats parading upriver to Fort Benton.

## INFORMATION PLEASE

All Montana area codes are 406

### Road Information

Montana Road Condition Report
800-226-7623, 800-335-7592 or local 444-7696

| | |
|---|---|
| Montana Highway Patrol | 444-7696 |
| Local Road Reports | |
| Wolf Point | 653-1692 |
| Billings | 252-2806 |
| Glasgow Weather Reports | 228-4042 |
| Statewide Weather Reports | 453-2081 |

### Tourism Information

| | |
|---|---|
| Travel Montana | 800-847-4868 outside Montana<br>444-2654 in Montana<br>http://travel.mt.gov/. |
| Custer Country | 665-1671 or 800-346-1876 |
| Missouri River Country | 653-1319 or 800-653-1319 |
| Northern Rodeo Association | 252-1122 |
| **Chambers of Commerce** | |
| Circle | 485-2414 |
| Culbertson | 787-5821 |
| Fairview | 747-5259 |
| Glasgow | 228-2222 |
| Jordan | 557-2248 |
| Poplar | 768-3800 |
| Richey | 773-5634 |
| Scobey | 487-5502 |
| Sidney | 482-1916 |
| Wolf Point | 653-2012 |

### Airports

| | |
|---|---|
| Circle | 485-2481 |
| Culbertson | 787-6620 |

| | |
|---|---|
| East Poplar | 783-5372 |
| Fairview | 482-2415 |
| Glasgow | 228-4023 |
| Jordan | 557-2565 |
| Opheim | 762-3277 |
| Plentywood | 765-1400 |
| Poplar | 768-3800 |
| Richey | 773-5835 |
| Scobey | 487-2725 |
| Sidney | 482-2415 |
| West Poplar | 476-2320 |
| Wolf Point | 653-1852 |

## Government Offices

| | |
|---|---|
| State BLM Office | 255-2885, 238-1540 |
| Bureau of Land Management | |
| Glasgow Field Office | 228-4316 |
| Lewistown Field Office | 538-7461 |
| Malta Field Office | 654-1240 |
| Miles City Field Office | 232-4333 |
| Montana Fish, Wildlife & Parks | 228-3700 |
| Army Corps of Engineers | 526-3411 |
| U.S. Bureau of Reclamation | |
| Tiber Field Office | 456-3226 |
| Charles M. Russell National Wildlife Refuge | 538-8706 |
| Medicine Lake National Wildlife Refuge | 789-2305 |

## Hospitals

| | |
|---|---|
| McCone County Medical Assist Circle | 485-2444 |
| Roosevelt Memorial Hospital Culbertson | 787-6281 |
| Garfield County Health Center Inc. Jordan | 557-6262 |
| Sheridan Memorial Hospital Plentywood | 765-1420 |
| Poplar Community Hospital • Poplar | 768-3452 |
| Community Memorial Hospita•Sidney | 482-2120 |
| Trinity Hospital • Wolf Point | 653-2100 |

## Golf Courses

| | |
|---|---|
| Sunnyside Golf & Country Club N W Of Glasgow | 228-9519 |
| Plentywood Golf Club • Plentywood | 765-2532 |
| Scobey Golf Course • Scobey | 487-5322 |
| Airport Golf Course • Wolf Point | 653-2161 |
| Truels Golf Course • Opheim | 762-3221 |
| Sidney Country Club • Sidney | 482-1894 |

## Bed & Breakfasts

| | |
|---|---|
| Box Canyon Guest Ranch • Sidney | 569-2478 |
| Buckfield B&B • Vandalia | 367-5353 |
| Double J B&B • Vandalia | 367-5353 |
| Gray's Coulee Guest Ranch • Lambert | 774-3778 |
| Hilltop House B&B • Westby | 385-2533 |
| IOU Ranch • Jordan | 557-2544 |
| The Meadowlark • Wolf Point | 525-3289 |
| Sandcreek Clydesdale Ranch Vacations Jordan | 557-2865 |

## Guest Ranches & Resorts

| | |
|---|---|
| Hell Creek Guest Ranch • Jordan | 557-2224 |
| Montana River Ranch • Bainville | 769-2500 |
| Wolff Farms • Circle | 485-2633 |

## Private Campgrounds

| | |
|---|---|
| Bolster Dam Campground Plentywood | 765-1700 |
| Five Wheels Inc. • Sidney | 482-7676 |
| Hi-Line Terrace RV Park • Glasgow | 228-8587 |
| Jordan RV Park • Jordan | 557-6116 |
| Kamp Katie • Jordan | 557-2851 |
| Lions Campground • Scobey | 783-5666 |
| Montana Smiles • Poplar | 774-3730 |
| RBW-Campground • Wolf Point | 525-3740 |
| Rock Creek Marina • Fort Peck | 485-2560 |
| Shady Rest RV Park • Glasgow | 228-2769 |
| Scheer's Trailor Court • Circle | 485-2285 |
| Smith's Mobile Park • Poplar | 768-3841 |
| Trail's West Campground • Glasgow | 228-2778 |
| Rancho Motel & Campground Wolf Point | 653-1382 |

## Car Rental

| | |
|---|---|
| Budget of Glasgow | 228-9325 |
| Avis Rent-A-Car | 482-4402 |
| Gem City Motors | 482-1445 |
| Larson Motor Co., Inc. | 482-1810 |
| Way-Out-West Car Rentals | 653-1310 |

## Outfitters & Guides

*F=Fishing H=Hunting R=River Guides*
*E=Horseback Rides G=General Guide Services*

| | | |
|---|---|---|
| Antelope Creek Outfitters | H | 367-5582 |
| Billingsley Ranch Outfitters | G | 367-5577 |
| Burke Ranch | HF | 367-5247 |
| Fort Peck Dinosaur Discoveries | G | 228-9530 |
| Fort Peck Fishing Guide Service | GF | 526-3565 |
| Hell Creek Guest Ranch | HF | 557-2224 |
| KG Guides & Outfitters | HF | 388-7616 |
| Montana River Ranch | G | 769-2200 |
| Timber Creek Ranch | H | 798-7770 |
| Twitchell Bros. Snap Creek Ranch | HF | 557-2554 |
| Uncle Fester's Montana Hunts | H | 367-5122 |

## NOTES:

Section 10

## Dining Quick Reference

Price Range refers to the average cost of a meal per person: ($) $1-$6, ($$) $7-$11, ($$$) $12-up. Cocktails: "Yes" indicates full bar; Beer (B)/Wine (W), Service: Breakfast (B), Brunch (BR), Lunch (L), Dinner (D). Businesses in bold print will have additional information under the appropriate map locator number in the body of this section.

| RESTAURANT | TYPE CUISINE | PRICE RANGE | CHILD MENU | COCKTAILS BEER WINE | SERVICE | CREDIT CARDS | MAP LOCATOR NUMBER |
|---|---|---|---|---|---|---|---|
| **Sadie's Stockyard Homecooking Café** | family | $ | | | B/L | | 1 |
| Baker Boy Bakery | Bakery | $ | Yes | | L/D | Major | 1 |
| Bean Bag | Coffee House | $ | | | B/L | Major | 1 |
| Cattle-ac Steakhouse | Steakhouse | Yes | Yes | | L/D | Major | 1 |
| Gullivers Restaurant | Deli | $ | | | B/L | | 1 |
| Kentucky Fried Chicken | Fast Food | $ | Yes | | L/D | | 1 |
| La Fiesta Cafe | Mexican | $ | | | L/D | | 1 |
| **South 40 Restaurant** | American | $$ | | Yes | L/D | Major | 1 |
| Dairy Queen | Fast Food | $ | Yes | | L/D | | 2 |
| Footers Pizza Subs & Pasta | Italian | $ | | | L/D | | 2 |
| Hardee's | Fast Food | $ | Yes | | B/L/D | | 2 |
| M & M Cafe | Family | $ | | | B/L/D | V/M/D | 2 |
| McDonald's | Fast Food | $ | Yes | | B/L/D | | 2 |
| New China Restaurant | Chinese | $/$$ | | | L/D | V/M | 2 |
| Pizza House | Pizza | $ | | B | L/D | V/M | 2 |
| Pizza Hut | Pizza | $/$$ | Yes | B | L/D | V/M/D | 2 |
| Taco John's | Fast Food | $ | Yes | | L/D | | 2 |
| The Depot Restaurant | Pizza | $ | Yes | | L/D | Major | 2 |
| Farmer's Kitchen | American | $ | | | B/L/D | | 3 |
| Tastee Freez | Fast Food | $ | Yes | | L/D | | 4 |
| Wooden Nickel Family Restaurant | Family | $ | Yes | B/W | L/D | | 4 |
| Rancher's Bar & Cafe | American | $ | | Yes | L/D | | 6 |
| Albert Hotel Dining Room | | | | | | | 8 |
| Stockman Cafe | American | $$ | | Yes | L/D | | 8 |
| Valley Cafe | | | | | | | 8 |
| Welcome Stop | | | | | | | 9 |
| M & M's Place | American | $$ | Yes | | L/D | | 10 |
| Stagecoach Station | American | $$ | | Yes | B/L | | 10 |
| Wild West Diner | Family | $/$$ | Yes | | B/L/D | | 10 |
| Missouri Breaks Truckstop | Family | $ | | | B/L/D | | 10 |
| 4J Mexican Cafe | Mexican | | | | | | 13 |
| Buck Horn Bar & Restaurant | Bar/Cafe | $ | | Yes | B/L/D | | 13 |
| Frostees | Fast Food | $ | Yes | | L/D | | 13 |
| Hempels' Bakery & Coffee Shop | Bakery | $ | | | | | 13 |
| Jasper's | Family | $ | | B/W | L/D | | 13 |
| Espresso Madness | Coffee House | $ | | | L | | 14 |
| Golden Dragon Restaurant | Chinese | $$ | | Yes | L/D | MC/V | 14 |
| McDonald's | Fast Food | $ | Yes | | B/L/D | | 14 |
| Old Town Grill | American | $ | | | L | Major | 14 |
| Stockmans Cafe | Family | $ | | | B/L/D | | 14 |
| Subs & Such | Deli | $ | Yes | | L/D | Major | 14 |
| Subway | Fast Food | $ | Yes | | L/D | | 14 |
| Tastee Freez | Fast Food | $ | Yes | | L/D | | 14 |
| The Pizza Place Restaurant | Pizza | $ | Yes | B/W | L/D | V/M/D | 14 |
| Wolf Point Cafe | American | $ | | | B/L | | 14 |
| Bergies | Cafe | $ | | | B/L/D | | 17 |
| **Mikel's Restaurant** | Cajun/American | $$/$$$ | Yes | Yes | B/L/D | Major | 18 |
| Gateway Inn | Family | $/$$ | Yes | Yes | B/L/D | | 18 |
| Park Grove Bar & Cafe | American | $$ | Yes | Yes | L/D | | 18 |
| **Cottonwood Inn Prairie Rose Restaurant** | Family | $$ | Yes | Yes | B/L/D | Major | 20 |
| Aces & 8's | American | $ | Yes | B/W | L/D | V/M/D | 20 |
| Clansman Chinese American Restaurant | Chinese | $/$$ | | | L/D | Major | 20 |
| Dairy Queen | Fast Food | $ | Yes | | L/D | | 20 |
| Eugene's Pizza | Pizza | $ | | | L/D | | 20 |
| McDonald's | Fast Food | $ | Yes | | B/L/D | | 20 |
| Sam's Supper Club | American | $$ | | Yes | D | | 20 |
| Subway | Fast Food | $ | Yes | | L/D | | 20 |
| The Hanger | Pizza/American | $/$$ | | Yes | L/D | | 20 |
| Fourth St. Espresso | Coffee House | $ | | | B/L | | 21 |
| Hong Kong Restaurant | Chinese | $ | | | L/D | | 21 |
| Johnnie's Cafe | Family | $ | Yes | | B/L/D | | 21 |

## Dining Quick Reference-Continued

Price Range refers to the average cost of a meal per person: ($) $1-$6, ($$) $7-$11, ($$$) $12-up. Cocktails: "Yes" indicates full bar; Beer (B)/Wine (W), Service: Breakfast (B), Brunch (BR), Lunch (L), Dinner (D). Businesses in bold print will have additional information under the appropriate map locator number in the body of this section.

| RESTAURANT | TYPE CUISINE | PRICE RANGE | CHILD MENU | COCKTAILS BEER WINE | SERVICE | CREDIT CARDS | MAP LOCATOR NUMBER |
|---|---|---|---|---|---|---|---|
| Oasis Lounge & Eatery | American | $ | | Yes | B/L | | 21 |
| Soma-dis Deli | Deli | $ | Yes | | L/D | V/M | 21 |
| Pizza Hut | Pizza | $/$$ | Yes | B | L/D | V/M/D | 22 |
| Quick-N-Tasty | Fast Food | $ | Yes | | L/D | | 22 |
| Subway | Fast Food | $ | Yes | | L/D | | 22 |
| Taco John's | Fast Food | $ | Yes | | L/D | | 22 |
| Cousins Family Restaurant | Family | $ | Yes | | B/L/D | V/M | 24 |
| Dairy Queen | Fast Food | $ | Yes | | L/D | | 24 |
| E-Z Way Bakery & Coffee Shop | Bakery | $ | Yes | | L/D | Major | 24 |
| Fergie's Pizza | Pizza | $ | | | L/D | | 24 |
| Four Winds Cafe | Family | $/$$ | Yes | | | | 24 |
| Fryer Tucks Supper Club & Steakhouse | Steakhouse | $$/$$$ | Yes | Yes | D | Major | 24 |
| Randy's Restaurant | American | $ | | | B/L/D | | 24 |
| The Loft | American | $/$$ | Yes | Yes | L/D | | 24 |
| Burger Hut | Fast Food | $ | Yes | | B/L/D | | 26 |
| Ponderosa Pizza | Pizza | $ | | Yes | L/D | | 26 |
| Rosewood Cafe | Family | $ | Yes | | L/D | Major | 26 |
| Shu's Kitchen | Chinese | $ | | | L/D | | 26 |
| Slipper Lounge Restaurant | American | $ | | Yes | D | | 26 |
| Uncle Al's | Pizza & Subs | $ | | | L/D | | 26 |
| Dutch Henrys Supper Club | Steakhouse | $$ | | Yes | L/D | | 27 |
| Silver Dollar Bar & Cafe | American | $ | | Yes | B/L/D | | 27 |

## Motel Quick Reference

Price Range: ($) Under $40 ; ($$) $40-$60; ($$$) $60-$80, ($$$$) Over $80. Pets [check with the motel for specific policies] (P), Dining (D), Lounge (L), Disabled Access (DA), Full Breakfast (FB), Cont. Breakfast (CB), Indoor Pool (IP), Outdoor Pool (OP), Hot Tub (HT), Sauna (S), Refrigerator (R), Microwave (M) (Microwave and Refrigerator indicated only if in majority of rooms), Kitchenette (K). All Montana area codes are 406.

| HOTEL | PHONE | NUMBER ROOMS | PRICE RANGE | BREAKFAST | POOL/ HOT TUB SAUNA | NON SMOKE ROOMS | OTHER AMENITIES | CREDIT CARDS | MAP LOCATOR NUMBER |
|---|---|---|---|---|---|---|---|---|---|
| Lone Tree Motor Inn | 482-4520 | 40 | $$ | | | Yes | P/DA | Major | 2 |
| Park Plaza Motel | 482-1520 | 55 | $ | CB | | Yes | P | Major | 2 |
| Richland Motor Inn | 482-6400 | 62 | $$ | CB | | Yes | P/DA | Major | 2 |
| Sunrise Inn Motel | 482-3826 | 36 | $ | | | Yes | K/P/M/R | | 2 |
| Traveller's Inn | 485-3323 | 14 | $ | | | Yes | P | Major | 4 |
| Fellman's Motel | 557-2209 | 45 | $ | | | Yes | P | Major | 6 |
| Garfield Motel | 557-6215 | 13 | $ | | | Yes | DA | Major | 6 |
| Korner Motel | 747-5259 | 6 | $ | | HT | | DA/P | | 8 |
| Diamond Willow Inn | 787-6218 | 12 | $ | | | Yes | | Major | 10 |
| Kings Inn Motel | 787-6277 | 20 | $ | | | Yes | | Major | 10 |
| Lee Ann's Motel | 768-5442 | 15 | $ | | | Yes | | Major | 13 |
| Big Sky Motel | 653-2300 | 22 | $ | | | Yes | | Major | 14 |
| Homestead Inn | 653-1300 | 47 | $ | | | Yes | P/DA | Major | 14 |
| Sherman Motor Inn | 653-1100 | 46 | $ | | | Yes | P/D/L/DA | Major | 14 |
| **Historic Fort Peck Hotel** | 526-3266 | 38 | $$ | | | Yes | P/D/L/DA | Major | 18 |
| **Cottonwood Inn** | 228-8213 | 92 | $$ | | IP/HT/S | Yes | P/D/M/R/L/DA | Major | 20 |
| Koski's Motel | 228-8282 | 24 | $ | | | Yes | P/DA | Major | 20 |
| La Casa Motel | 228-9311 | 13 | $ | | | Yes | | Major | 20 |
| Campbell Lodge | 228-9328 | 31 | $ | CB | | Yes | P/DA | Major | 21 |
| Star Lodge Motel | 228-2494 | 30 | $ | | | Yes | | Major | 22 |
| Plains Motel | 765-1240 | 30 | $ | | | Yes | P | Major | 24 |
| Sherwood Inn | 765-2810 | 65 | $$ | | | Yes | K/P/L/DA | Major | 24 |
| Cattle King Motor Inn | 487-5332 | 29 | $$/$$$ | CB | | Yes | P/DA | Major | 26 |
| Homestead Hotel & Cafe | 762-3343 | 10 | $ | | | | | | 28 |

Section 10

## Campsite Directions

| Campsite | Season | Camping | Trailers | Toilets | Water | Boat Launch | Fishing | Swimming | Trails | Stay Limit | Fee |
|---|---|---|---|---|---|---|---|---|---|---|---|
| **212•Hell Creek FWP**<br>26 mi. N of Jordan on Cty. Rd.•Seasonal water system | All Year | 40 | • | • | • | C | • | | | 14 | • |
| **213•The Pines CE**<br>33 mi. SW of Fort Peck on Cty. Rd.•12 mi. on Willow Cr. Rd. off MT 24•12 mi. E•Primitive | All Year | • | • | • | • | C | • | | | 14 | |
| **214•Duck Creek CE**<br>4 mi. SW of Fort Peck on Duck Cr. Rd.•Primitive | All Year | • | • | • | | C | • | | | 14 | |
| **215•West End CE**<br>2 mi. SW of Fort Peck on MT 24 | 5/31-9/6 | 12 | 35′ | D | • | C | • | | | 14 | • |
| **216•Downstream CE**<br>.5 mi. E of Fort Peck on MT 117•Reservations: 526-3224 | 5/1-10/30 | 69 | • | D | • | C | • | | • | 14 | • |
| **217•Flat Lake CE**<br>6 mi. E of Fort Peck on MT 24 | All Year | • | • | • | | C | • | | | 14 | |
| **218•Bear Creek CE**<br>14 mi. SE of Fort Peck on MT 24•7 mi. W on Cty. Rd.•Primitive | All Year | • | • | • | | | • | | | 14 | |
| **219•McGuire Creek CE**<br>41 mi. SE of Fort Peck on MT 24•7 mi. W on Cty. Rd.•Primitive | All Year | • | • | • | | | • | | | 14 | |
| **220•Nelson Creek CE**<br>45 mi. SE of Fort Peck on MT 24•7 mi. W on Cty. Rd.•Primitive | All Year | • | • | • | | C | • | | | 14 | |
| **221•Intake FWP**<br>16 mi. N of Glendive on MT 16•S on Cty. Rd. | | 40 | • | • | • | C | • | | | 7 | • |

**Agency**
FS—U.S.D.A Forest Service
FWP—Montana Fish, Wildlife & Parks
NPS—National Park Service
BLM—U.S. Bureau of Land Management
USBR—U.S. Bureau of Reclamation
CE—Corps of Engineers

**Camping**
Camping is allowed at this site. Number indicates camping spaces available
H—Hard sided units only; no tents

**Trailers**
Trailer units allowed. Number indicates maximum length.

**Toilets**
Toilets on site. D—Disabled access

**Water**
Drinkable water on site

**Fishing**
Visitors may fish on site

**Boat**
Type of boat ramp on site:
A—Hand launch
B—4-wheel drive with trailer
C—2-wheel drive with trailer

**Swimming**
Designated swimming areas on site

**Trails**
Trails on site
B—Backpacking N—Nature/Interpretive

**Stay Limit**
Maximum length of stay in days

**Fee**
Camping and/or day-use fee

## Fishery

| Fishery | Brook Trout | Mt. Whitefish | Lake Whitefish | Golden Trout | Cutthroat Trout | Brown Trout | Rainbow Trout | Kokanee Salmon | Bull Trout | Lake Trout | Arctic Grayling | Burbot | Largemouth Bass | Smallmouth Bass | Walleye | Sauger | Northern Pike | Shovelnose Sturgeon | Channel Catfish | Yellow Perch | Crappie | Paddlefish | Vehicle Access | Campgrounds | Toilets | Docks | Boat Ramps | MotorRestrictions |
|---|---|---|---|---|---|---|---|---|---|---|---|---|---|---|---|---|---|---|---|---|---|---|---|---|---|---|---|---|
| | **Cold Water Species** | | | | | | | | | | | | **Warm Water Species** | | | | | | | | | | **Services** | | | | | |
| 156. Whitetail Reservoir | | | | | | | | | | | | | | | | | • | | | • | | | • | • | • | | | • |
| 157. Box Elder Reservoir | | | | | | | | | | | | | | | | | • | | | • | • | | • | | • | | • | |
| 158. Glasgow AFB Pond | | | | | | | • | | | | | | | | | | | | | • | | | • | • | • | | | |
| 159. Fort Peck Dredge Cuts | | | | | | | | | | • | | • | | | • | • | • | • | • | | | • | • | • | • | • | • | |
| 160. Dredge Cut trout pond | | | | | | | | | | | | | • | | • | | • | | | • | | | • | • | • | • | • | • |
| 161. Flat Lake | | | | | | | • | | | | | | | | | | | | | | | | • | | • | | | |
| 162. Fort Peck Lake | | | | | | | | | | • | | • | | • | • | • | • | • | • | • | | | • | • | • | | • | |
| 163. Medicine Lake | | | | | | | | | | | | | | | | | • | | | | | | • | • | • | | | • |
| 164. Missouri River | | | | | | | • | | | • | | | | | • | • | • | • | • | | | • | • | • | • | • | • | |
| 165. Kuester Reservoir | | | | | | | | | | | | | | | | | • | | | • | | | • | • | • | | | |

**Notes:**

# Section 11

## The Hi-Line

## Including Havre, Chinook, Malta and Fort Benton

*Spacious grasslands mixed with striped wheat fields characterize much of this area.*

### Weather Averages

| Havre | |
|---|---|
| January | |
| Average High: | 25.7° F |
| Average Low: | 4.3° F |
| Average Precip.: | 0.43 in |
| April | |
| Average High: | 57.3° F |
| Average Low: | 30.7° F |
| Average Precip.: | 1.01 in |
| July | |
| Average High: | 85.4° F |
| Average Low: | 53.9° F |
| Average Precip.: | 1.54 in |
| October | |
| Average High: | 59.9° F |
| Average Low: | 32.2° F |
| Average Precip.: | 0.67 in |
| **Fresno Reservoir** | |
| January | |
| Average High: | 24.0° F |
| Average Low: | 2.8° F |
| Average Precip.: | 0.43 in |
| April | |
| Average High: | 56.7° F |
| Average Low: | 30.8° F |
| Average Precip.: | 1.01 in |
| July | |
| Average High: | 84.2° F |
| Average Low: | 53.4° F |
| Average Precip.: | 1.54 in |
| October | |
| Average High: | 59.6° F |
| Average Low: | 31.4° F |
| Average Precip.: | 0.67 in |

**1.** *Attraction, Gas, Food, Lodging*

### Hinsdale

Like many towns in this part of the state, Hinsdale began as a railroad siding, its first building, a railroad boxcar, that served as a depot. The town is nestled along the Milk River surrounded by cottonwoods, ash and willows. Ranches here stretch endlessly (from front gate to front porch can easily be 30 miles).

### Saco

No one quite knows where Saco got its name. Some say that it comes from a contraction of Sacajawea, the name of the Shoshone woman who guided Lewis and Clark. Another is that it came from the railroad's practice of spinning the globe and stopping randomly on a name.

### T Chet Huntley Schoolhouse

U.S. Hwy 2 East of Saco.

This schoolhouse is preserved as the typical country school it was when the nationally known newscaster, Chet Huntley, attended.

### T Sleeping Buffalo Springs

Hwy 2, 18 miles east of Malta.

The only hot springs along Montana's highline, is actually a 3,500 foot deep well that produces more than 700 gallons of 108 degree F. water per minute. There is an admission charge to soak in the three pools that are on private property. Chose from pools that range in temperatures from 90 to 110 degrees F. The resort is open year round with a restaurant, lodging, gift shop, golf, baseball, and volley ball. The well was discovered in 1924 when a wildcat oil driller struck a highly pressurized mix of hot water and natural gas. The area is named for Sleeping Buffalo Rock, named by Native Americans, because of it's resemblance to a buffalo sleeping on the prairie.

**2.** *Attraction*

### T Bowdoin National Wildlife Refuge

Northeast of Malta. 654-2863

The 15,000 acre Bowdoin National Wildlife Refuge is a haven for migrating and nesting waterfowl. You will find resident and migratory waterfowl, ducks of all species, Canadian geese, colonial nesting birds and upland game birds. Over 800 pair of nesting pelicans and rarer birds like white faced ibises and night herons reside here, along with deer and antelope. This refuge protects 208 bird species.

**3.** *Gas, Food, Lodging, Camping, Shopping*

### Malta

Malta is a town that was raised on cattle. During the late 1800s, the town was the hub of a vast cattle empire. It originated as a town to service the cattle industry, but when the Northern Pacific Railroad came through it turned into an important siding to load livestock. Today, it still serves the cattle industry as well as the agriculture industry. The name was picked by a railroad official who spun a world globe and put his finger on the place where it stopped—Malta. The town was named after the Mediterranean island of Malta.

### LC Edgewater Inn & RV Park

Junction US Hwy 2 and Hwy 191 N., Malta. 654-1302 or 800-821-7475 (in state)

### L Royals Inn

117 N. 1st St., Hwy. 2, Malta. 654-1150

**4.** *Attraction, Gas, Food, Lodging*

### T Phillips County Museum

At the junction of Hwy. 2 and Hwy. 191 in Malta. 654-1037

Included in displays here are early plains Indian artifacts from the McClellan and Sullivan collections. You will also find exhibits on the homesteading days, ranching and farming in Phillips County, mining, early day schools, mercantile, an early day doctor's office, and many wildlife mounts. On display is a very fine dinosaur collection including many marine fossils found in the area, and a life size Albertosaurus. An informative display of early day outlaw, Kid Curry, is featured telling the story of his infamous train robbery in 1901, just to the west of Malta. The robbery netted the gang $40,000 and was never recovered. There is also a Brand Board showing family

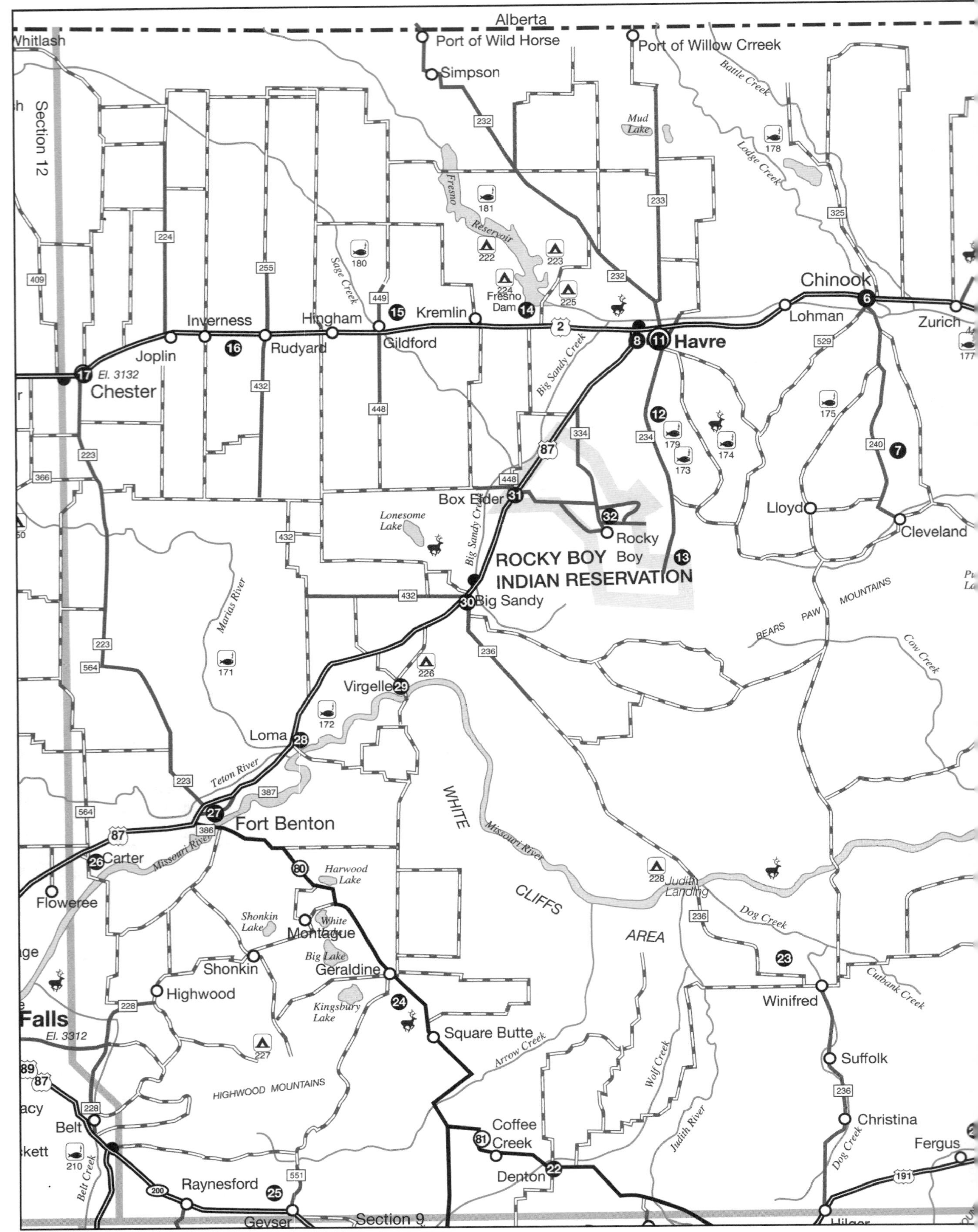
Alberta
Port of Wild Horse
Port of Willow Crreek
Simpson
Section 12
Battle Creek
Mud Lake
Lodge Creek
Fresno Reservoir
Sage Creek
Fresno Dam
Chinook
Lohman
Zurich
Inverness
Hingham
Kremlin
Joplin
Rudyard
Gildford
Havre
Chester
El. 3132
Big Sandy Creek
Box Elder
Lonesome Lake
Rocky Boy
ROCKY BOY INDIAN RESERVATION
Lloyd
Cleveland
Big Sandy
Marias River
BEARS PAW MOUNTAINS
Cow Creek
Virgelle
Loma
Teton River
Fort Benton
WHITE CLIFFS AREA
Missouri River
Carter
Floweree
Harwood Lake
Shonkin Lake
White Lake
Montague
Big Lake
Shonkin
Geraldine
Highwood
Kingsbury Lake
Square Butte
Falls
El. 3312
HIGHWOOD MOUNTAINS
Arrow Creek
Judith Landing
Dog Creek
Winifred
Cutbank Creek
Wolf Creek
Judith River
Suffolk
Christina
Fergus
Coffee Creek
Denton
Belt
Belt Creek
Raynesford
Geyser
Section 9
Hilger

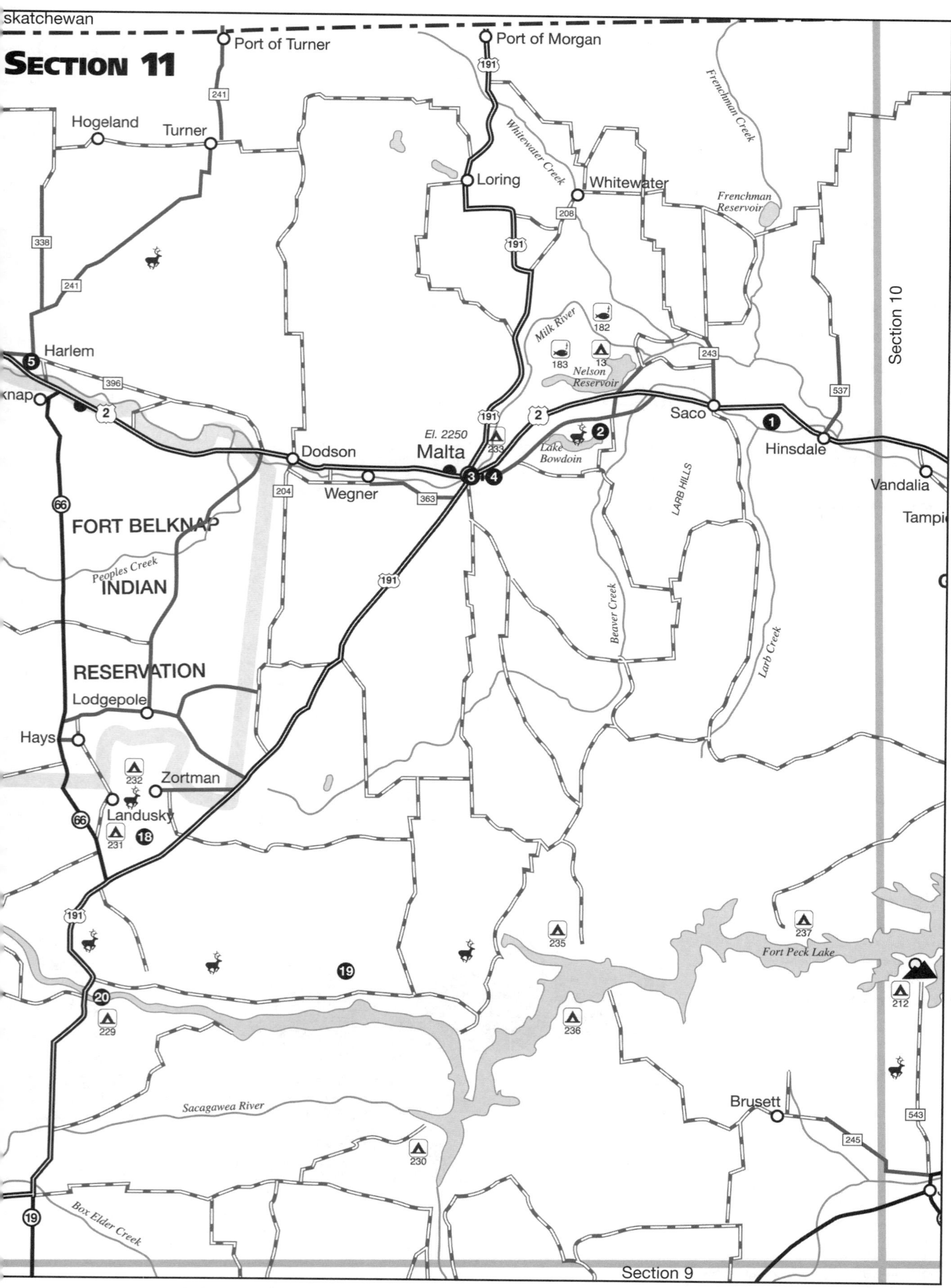
Section 11
skatchewan
Port of Turner
Port of Morgan
Hogeland
Turner
Loring
Whitewater
Frenchman Creek
Whitewater Creek
Frenchman Reservoir
Harlem
Milk River
Nelson Reservoir
Saco
Hinsdale
Vandalia
Dodson
Malta
El. 2250
Lake Bowdoin
Wegner
LARB HILLS
Beaver Creek
Larb Creek
FORT BELKNAP
INDIAN
RESERVATION
Peoples Creek
Lodgepole
Hays
Zortman
Landusky
Fort Peck Lake
Sacagawea River
Brusett
Box Elder Creek
Section 10
Section 9

**Map Legend**

- Locator number (matches numeric listing in section)
- Wildlife viewing
- Campsite (number matches number in campsite chart)
- State Park
- Fishing Site (number matches number in fishing chart)
- Rest stop
- Interstate
- U.S. Highway
- State Highway
- County Road
- Gravel/unpaved road

0 Miles 13 20
One inch = approximately 13 miles

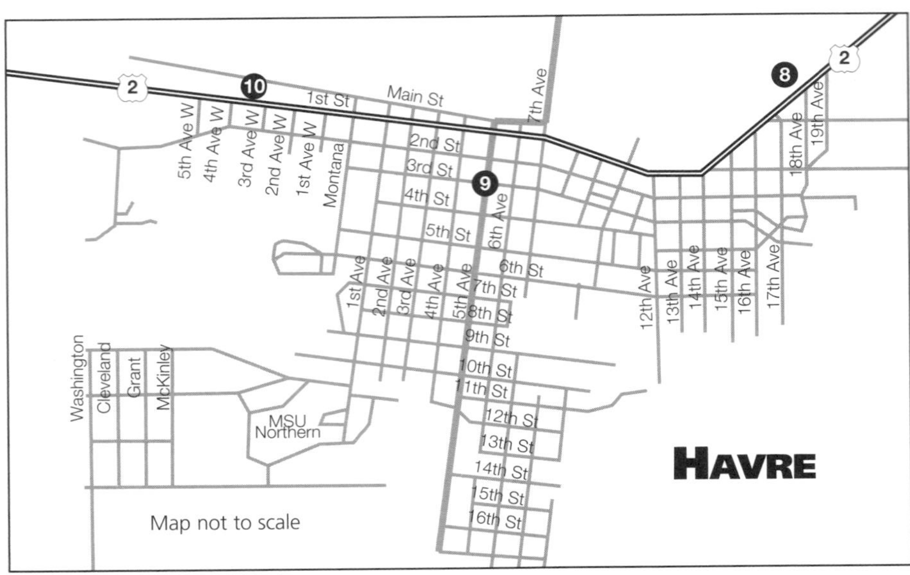


brands burned into wood. Some of the original brands seen on the Texas trail herds, are still being used on the local cattle herds. A stage coach is exhibited which was used to travel from Malta to Zortman, a 50 mile trip, through mud, snow and mosquitoes. Open mid-May through mid-September. Admission is free.

### F Stockman's Bar & Steakhouse

64 S. 1st Street, Malta. 654-1919

## 5. *Historical Marker, Attraction, Gas, Food, Lodging*

### Fort Belknap

Named for Robert E. Belknap, the town was a station on the Great Northern Railroad and the agency headquarters for the Fort Belknap Indian Reservation.

### Harlem

This town grew up as a trading center for the nearby Fort Belknap Indian Reservation. This is another town that won its name by a spin of the globe by railroad officials. In this case, the finger landed on Harlem in the Netherlands.

### H Fort Belknap Reservation

Hwy 2 & Rte 66, east of Harlem.

*Fort Belknap Reservation was established in 1888 when the Gros Ventres, Blackfeet, and River Crows ceded to the government 17,500,000 acres of their joint reservation that had covered all of northern Montana east of the Rocky Mountains. Home for the Gros Ventres and Assiniboines, who had shared hunting rights on the reservation, it was named for Wm. W. Belknap, secretary of war under President U. S. Grant.*

*The Gros Ventres (French for "big belly" and pronounced "Grow Von") got the name courtesy of the early French fur trappers. Also known as Atsina, the tribe's own name for themselves is Aa'ninin or "White Clay People." Always a small tribe, they lived in the Red River Valley, North Dakota, from about 1100 to 1400 A.D., then moved west, splitting into two tribes around 1730. One group moved southwest and became the Arapaho, the other northwest, ending up in Montana by the early 1800s. They were close allies to the Blackfeet.*

*Tradition credits the Assiniboine tribe as separating from the Yanktonai Sioux in the early 1600s. Two of the first ladies of the tribe, wives of leaders, quarreled over an epicurean delicacy, viz. a buffalo heart. The gentlemen chipped in and the tribe split. One faction headed west and became known as the Assiniboine. They call themselves Nakota, meaning "The Peaceful Ones." When the reservation was created, part of the tribe enrolled here and the remainder at Fort Peck, about 180 miles to the east.*

### H The Vision Quest

Hwy 2 & Rte 66, east of Harlem.

*High points such as mountain tops and tabletop buttes are considered powerful and sacred areas by many Indian peoples. Snake Butte is one such location, often used as a place for the spiritual rite of vision questing.*

*The individual vision quest is an intensely private ritual in which a man or woman seeks supernatural power, or medicine. The Supreme Being grants this power through an intermediary spirit which can be a living or nonliving entity such as an animal, a spider, a snake, or a rock. The devout quester may acquire powers of war, wealth, love, doctoring, or prophesy which must be used only to good ends; misuse brings very serious consequences, even death. First cleansing the body through a sweatlodge purification ceremony, the quester then withdraws to a secluded location for three to four days. Fasting and praying, the quester seeks contact with a spiritual being. The successful vision quest takes great concentration and courage. Not all quests are successful, but for those so chosen, acceptance of the power offered is a great responsibility, sometimes not without a price. It is said that those who acquire certain powers never live a long life.*

*For a brief period, the town of Saco was in the Guiness Book of World Records for the cooking the world's largest hamburger. The hamburger weighed 6,000 pounds and took the title away from Seymour, Wisconsin. The next year, Seymour regained the title with an 8,266 pound burger. Seventeen cows went into Saco's burger. The next day the leftovers were used for biscuits and gravy at breakfast and sloppy joes for dinner.*

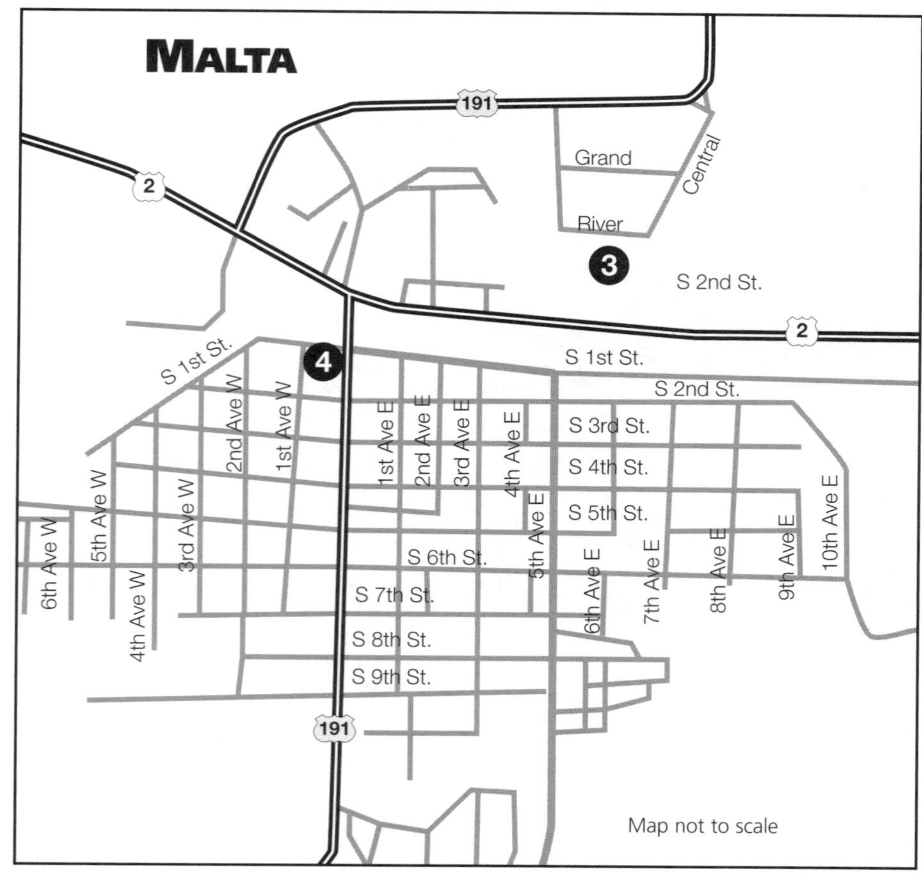


## T Fort Belknap Indian Reservation

Northcentral Montana. 353-2205

Located between the Milk River and the Little Rocky Mountains, the 650,000 acre reservation is home to the Assiniboine and Gros Ventre tribes, Snake Butte, Mission Canyon, Bear Gulch and St. Paul's Mission. The combined tribal enrollment is about 4,000. Some of the wildlife viewable on the reservation includes a bison herd, deer, antelope, rare black-footed ferrets, migratory waterfowl and upland game birds. The reservation was established in 1888. The Bureau of Indian Affairs and the tribe are the major employers here today, developing tourism and marketing Native American arts and crafts.

## M Fort Belknap Community College

353-2607 www.fortbelknap.cc.mt.us

The college was established by the Community Council in 1984, to maintain the cultural integrity of the Gros Ventre and Assiniboine Tribes and encourage success in an American Technological society. Fort Belknap College is a fully accredited, two-year Tribal College.

## 6. *Historical Marker, Attraction, Gas, Food, Lodging, Shopping*

## Chinook

Chinook was named after the Indian word for the winds that often whisk through this area during January and February causing temperatures to rise as much as 70 degrees in only a few hours. Charles Russell captured the impact of these winds to cattlemen on the range in his painting of a starving cow entitled *"Waiting for a Chinook."*

Many cattle have been spared by the merciful chinook winds that melt snow and expose grass for grazing.

The county seat of Blaine County, is a small, rural, community located on the Milk River in north central Montana. Originally, it was founded on the south side of the river, but relocated on the north side of the Milk bringing it closer to the Great Northern Railroad.

The Chinook area offers one of the most historic regions of the state. Seventeen miles south is the site of the last Indian battle in the United States. The Bear's Paw Battlefield, the very spot where a major encounter between the U.S. Cavalry and the American Indian began in September of 1877 and ended on October 5, 1877. Chief Joseph of the Nez Perce surrendered to Colonel Miles with the infamous words: *"From where the sun now stands, I will fight no more forever"*.

The topography of Chinook and the surrounding Blaine County is as diverse as its agriculture, gas and oil industries. From the Milk River Valley, which divides Blaine County from east to west, rolling plains of grain fields and cattle pasture stretch north to the Canadian border. To the south dryland grain farming reaches to meet the Bear Paw Mountains where cattle and sheep are raised, and on to the rugged breaks of the Missouri River, Blaine County's southern border. Irrigated farms fill the narrow Milk River Valley. The oil and gas industry is evidenced by the presence of Northern Natural Gas Co. as well as Ronco and other oil companies.

Recreational opportunities in Chinook are limited to the extent of one's imagination. Antelope, deer, waterfowl and upland game bird hunting is unmatched anywhere. Bighorn sheep and elk roam the Missouri Breaks area. Also, for the fishing enthusiast, nearby reservoirs are filled with everything from trout to the crafty walleye.

*Source: Chinook Chamber of Commerce brochure*

## History Of The Sleeping Buffalo

In 1922, a wildcatter, exploring for oil, encountered a tremendous flow of hot mineral water at 3200 feet, and went broke trying to cap the flow. Legend has it that cowboys made use of the hot water for their Saturday night baths. A Saco rancher built a wooden tub around the water and soaked his polio-stricken son in the mineral water which is very similar to that of the Warm Spring, Georgia sanatorium made famous by President Franklin Delano Roosevelt.

In the early '30s, a joint partnership between the Soil Conservation Service and the Phillips County American Legion developed the complex with the help of Roosevelt's Work Project Administration (WPA). Several permanent buildings of rock were erected, and the "Saco Health Plunge" became a prominent recreational facility.

Following a stoppage the previous year, a new well was drilled in 1958, and over 2500 visitors attended the grand opening of the "Malta Legion Health Plunge." By now, everyone just called this favorite swimming place "The Plunge." The following year, the disastrous West Yellowstone earthquake broke the well casing and another well had to be drilled.

The Sleeping Buffalo Recreation Association (SBRA) was formed in 1965, with Dennis Mahoney as President. The resort's new name was in honor or a particular rock resembling a buffalo which signifies the staff of life for several Native American tribes, including the Chippewa, Cree, Assiniboine and Sioux. This rock, which originally was part of a group of rocks that looked like a herd of buffalo from a distance, laid upon a ridge above Cree Crossing just a couple miles north of the resort. It was moved to the town of Malta, and later still to old U.S. Highway #2 south of the resort, where it was joined with the "Medicine Rock." Today these ancient glacial boulders, which are listed on the National Record of Historic Places, are enshrined at the junction of Highway 2 and State Highway 243, and mark the entrance to the resort which is a short distance up the hill on the right. Nelson Reservoir and the Bureau of Reclamation Park on the left.

*Reprinted from Sleeping Buffalo Resort brochure.*

## H The Battle of Bears Paw

Chinook

*This battle was fought September 30 to October 5, 1877, on Snake Creek, about 20 miles south of here near the Bears Paw Mountains, where after a five days' siege Chief Joseph, one of five remaining Nez Perce leaders, surrendered to Col. Nelson A. Miles of the U.S. Army.*

*The usual forked-tongue methods of the whites, which had deprived these Indians of their hereditary*

Section 11

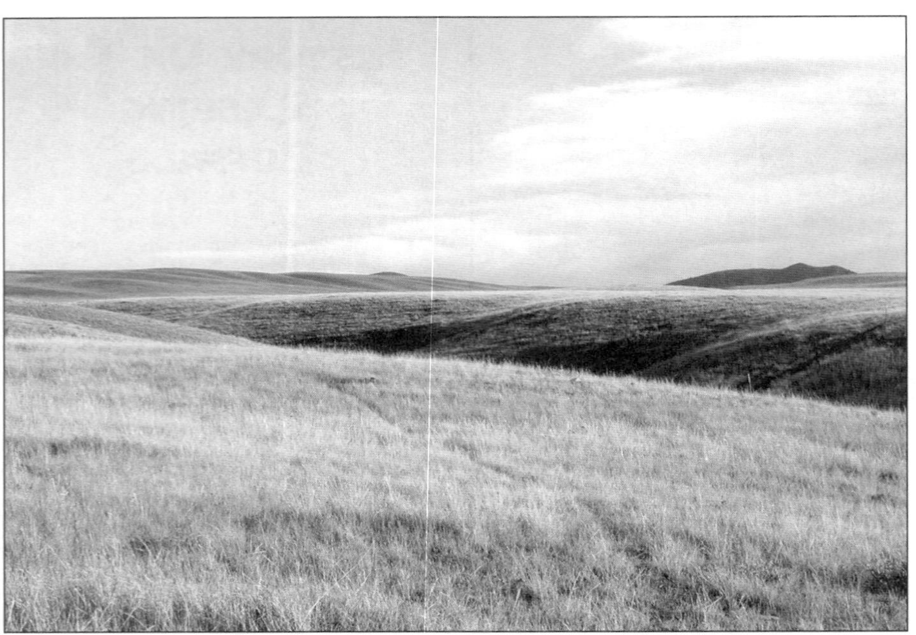

*Standing on these lonely hill you can almost hear the gunfire and the cries of the combatants during the Battle of Bear Paw.*

*lands, caused Joseph and six other primary chiefs to lead their people on a tortuous 2,000 mile march from their home in Idaho to evade U.S. troops and gain sanctuary in Canada.*

*These great Indian generals fought against fearful odds. They and their warriors could have escaped by abandoning their women, children and wounded. They refused to do this.*

*Joseph's courage and care for his people were admired by Col. Miles who promised him safe return to Idaho. One of the blackest records in our dealings with the Indians was the Government's repudiation of this promise and the subsequent treatment accorded Joseph and his followers.*

*The Blaine County Museum should be your first stop before visiting the Bear's Paw Battlefield.*

## T Blaine County Museum

South side of downtown Chinook. 357-2590

Experience the West, from prehistoric to pioneer, through thought provoking exhibits, that tell the story of this land, its people, and its times. Native American artifacts and culture make up an important part of the museum's collection, together with early photographic records of Nez Perce life.

Military and Indian artifacts from the Bear Paw Battlefield are on exhibit, but a visit to the battlefield itself, just sixteen miles south of Chinook, should be on your itinerary. Interpretive signage and markers line the footpath through the battlefield.

Exploration of northern Montana began with the fur traders of the mid 1700s and Lewis and Clark's Corps of Discovery expedition in 1804. Settlement did not begin in earnest until the Great Northern Railroad was completed in 1887. Prior to that time access was by means of the Missouri and riverboats. 1888 saw the boom of the cattle and sheep ranching era, and their associated range wars. Large scale homesteading began only as recently as 1910.

Extensive exhibits tell the story of the Nez Perce Indians, the pioneer days of the cowboy, the hardships of the homestead era, and follow Blaine County through two World Wars. Reconstructions feature strongly in the museum, with an early church, schoolrooms, country dentist and doctors offices, complete with "torture tools", and even a reconstructed "Tar paper" homestead, with period furnishings, on display inside the museum.

The most incredible journeys we make are not measured in miles, they are instead, voyages of the imagination, transporting us back through the ages to very different times than these. In fact, back as far as worlds inhabited by the giant dinosaurs, which lived, hunted and died in what is now Blaine County. The paleontology department exhibits many unique fossil remains of paleo-life from the seas, which periodically covered this region, and the dinosaurs that ruled the land 75 million years ago.

The audiovisual presentation "40 Miles to Freedom" is one of the highlights of the museum. Combining video, sound, lighting effects, and photography, centered around artist Lorenzo Ghiglieri's spectacular paintings, the presentation details the events leading up to the Battle and siege of the Bear Paw. Which event ended one of the most remarkable and tragic retreats in this nations history, Inspiring Chief Joseph to utter the now immortal line "*From where the sun now stands, I will fight no more forever.*"

The museum is located just south of downtown Chinook and is open daily Memorial day to Labor day. Hours are reduced off season to 1 p.m.-5 p.m. weekdays only. There is no admission charge and guided tours are available.

*The monument to those who fell at the Bear's Paw Battlefield is decorated with offerings in tribute to the dead. Small piles of offerings like those shown below are found along the paths of the battlefield. The cigarette seen in the collection above is not litter. Tobacco is considered sacred by the Native Americans.*

# Battle of Bear Paw

## Chronology of Events - 1877

**September 23:** Nez Perce cross Missouri River at Cow Island

**September 24/25:** General Miles' forces cross Missouri River near mouth of Squaw Ck about 70 miles east of Cow Island

**September 29:** Nez Perce arrive at Bear Paw, while Miles camps 12 miles southeast

**September 30:** Miles: Breaks camp in pre-dawn; Discovers NP trail about 8 a.m.; Attacks about 10 a.m.

Nez Perce discover approaching military about 9 a.m.

Nez Perce repel four direct assaults

2nd Cavalry and Cheyenne/Sioux scouts take Nez Perce horse herd

Miles decides to lay siege to camp

Approx. 200 Nez Perce escape to Canada early in battle, and 430 remain in camp

**October 1:** Joseph taken prisoner under flag of truce

Lt. Jerome taken prisoner by Nez Perce

**October 2:** Prisoner exchange. Looking Glass killed by sniper

**October 4:** Woman and child killed by cannon fired into shelter area (Yellow Wolf's date)

Howard arrives with an escort, reporte.rs and two "treaty Nez Perce" (about 30 total)

**October 5:** Nez Perce meet in council with "treaty Nez Perce"; Joseph's speech delivered there

White Bird refuses to surrender; Joseph "quits the fight" at 2 p.m. with short speech

Under cover of darkness White Bird and about 30 others escape to Canada

**October 6/7:** Prepare and then leave for Fort Keogh on the Yellowstone River

## Why Did The Nez Perce Stop?

They were exhausted and short on supplies. The area provided time to gather food and rest. They were unaware of Miles. They expected to rest a couple of days before continuing on to Fort Walsh, Canada.

## Who were the principle participants & leaders?

Nez Perce "leadership" was through a counsel of equals. The weight of character and strength of argument determined leadership which was fluid. Primary leaders included Husis Kut (Wawawai Band), Heinmot Tooyalakeket (or Joseph of Wallowa Band), Alalymya Takaniin (or Looking Glass of Alpolwai Band), Peopeo Kiskiok Hihih (or White Bird of Lamtama Band), Tuhuulhuuthulsuit (Pikunan Band), and Lean Elk. Col. Nelson A Miles was in command of the military including elements of the 2nd (Co G, H, F) & 7th (Co A, D, K) Cavalry and 5th Infantry (Co B, C, D, F, G, 1, K) and Cheyenne and Sioux Scouts. Upon General Oliver 0. Howard's arrival command remained with Miles.

## How do we know what happened here?

Nez Perce oral and written traditions, much of it recorded by L.V. McWhorte.r. Also, numerous military and civilian records provide information.

## What are the "survey markers" on the battlefield?

In the 1920s & 30s, L.V. McWhorte.r recorded much of the Nez Perce story. He walked the battlefield with Nez Perce survivors including Chief Many Wounds & White Hawk. As the story was told, markers identified the location of events. In 1936, McWhorte.r requested county surveyor C.R. Noyes to record the story on a survey map. This was done with some stakes replaced and added. In 1963, Noyes, his sons and the Chinook Lions Club replaced all wooden markers with the metal markers now seen using the survey map as a reference.

## What is the caged area on the hill above the camp?

The Nez Perce Monument was placed in the 1920s by L.V. McWhorte.r and others to honor those who suffered at this site. Locally it is referred to as the Looking Glass Monument because of its proximity to the rifle pit in which Looking Glass was killed. The concrete bust of an "Indian in head dress" capped the concrete post. Because of potential damage, the headpiece is in the NPS office in Chinook. This and one at Big Hole are two of the five original placed along the Nez Perce Trail.

## What happened at Death's Point of Rocks?

During the battle on Sept 30, Chief Tuhhuulhuulhutsuit and seven other warriors were attempting to re-enter the main camp area and the main battle. They were caught in the rocky outcrop. To the west were the 2nd Cavalry, and Cheyenne and Sioux scouts. Unable to find a defensible position, the seven warriors were caught in the open. Six died in battle while the wounded Eagle Necklace Jr and Tamyahnin entered the main camp.

## What was the location and role of Cannons?

Miles had a large twelve pound Napoleon Cannon and a smaller Hotchkiss Rifle. The Napoleon was located on the prairie west of the highway (now private property). The Hotchkiss was placed on the high point above Snake Creek, south from the picnic shelter. It is reporte.d that both weapons were used to fire on the Nez Perce camp to keep morale down and force an early surrender.

*Reprinted from National Park Service brochure.*

### FL Chinook Motor Inn & Restaurant

100 Indiana St. & Hwy 2, Chinook, 357-2248, www.chinookmotorinn.com

Chinook Motor Inn, locally owned and operated, is a complete modern facility with 38 clean, comfortable rooms, a full service restaurant, and a lounge & casino. Offering economy rates, this AAA motor inn also provides free local calls, cable TV with HBO, winter plug-ins, ample parking, non-smoking rooms, queen-size beds, air-conditioning, cribs and rollaways at no extra charge, a handicap room, and kids stay free! They invite you to have your parties and meetings either upstairs or downstairs in the carpeted meeting rooms. The friendly staff along with the fine food served in the restaurant will make your stay a pleasant one! Stay and enjoy Chinook's historical museum, fall hunting, and year-round hospitality.

**7.** *Attraction*

### T Bear Paw Battlefield

Chinook. 357-3130

## The Nez Perce Campaign of 1877

In the summer of 1877, five bands of Nez Perce, including some Palouse allies, began a 1,300 mile journey from northeastern Oregon and central Idaho through Montana Territory. In less than four months, about 800 people, including 125 warriors, herded more than 2,000 horses and carried whatever possessions they could manage on this long and difficult trek. They pushed forward, not because of an eagerness to reach their destination, but because they were being pursued by U.S. Army troops under the command of General Oliver 0. Howard.

Howard had orders to place them on a reservation in Idaho, in compliance with US policy at that time to place all tribes on reservations. Although the Nez Perce tried to evade the pursuing soldiers, they were attacked or forced into battle at White Bird Canyon (Idaho), Clearwater River (Idaho), Big Hole (Montana), Camas Meadow (Idaho), and Canyon Creek (Montana). The Nez Perce traveled first to the buffalo country of the Yellowstone River to seek assistance from their Crow allies.

When the Crow were unable to assist, the Nez Perce bands turned north to join Sitting Bull, who had taken refuge in Canada after the Little Bighorn Battle, just one year earlier. Knowing they

### Montana Trivia

About 6 percent of Montana's population is comprised of Native Americans. There are seven Indian reservations in the state covering approximately 13,055 square miles—9 percent of the state.

were several days' march ahead of their pursuers, the exhausted Nez Perce stopped to rest on September 29 along Snake Creek, just north of the Bear Paw Mountains and about forty miles short of the Canadian border.

The Nez Perce were unaware that Colonel Nelson A. Miles had been dispatched from the Tongue River Cantonment (near today's Miles City, Montana) to intercept them. With elements of the 7th and 2nd Cavalries, the 5th Mounted Infantry and 30 to 40 Cheyenne and non-Indian scouts, Miles' command totaled 400 men. The troops crossed the Missouri River by steamer and approached the Nez Perce camp. On September 29, Miles ordered his men to camp 12 miles southeast of the Nez Perce.

### The Battle

About 4 a.m. on September 30, army scouts alerted Colonel Miles of the Nez Perce camp. Miles ordered his troops to march, expecting to surprise and overwhelm the Nez Perce with a sudden attack. In the Nez Perce camp, people awoke to cold weather. Early morning calm was soon shattered as the alarm went out, "Enemies right on us … soon the attack!" The 7th Cavalry's frontal attack resulted in heavy hand-to-hand combat. The 2nd Cavalry made a flanking movement and separated the Nez Perce from their horses. The 5th Infantry secured a high bench to the south, but the Nez Perce held their position and prevented any further advance.

Both sides suffered heavy casualties the first day. Unable to defeat the Nez Perce, the troops besieged the camp. On October 4, General Howard's troops arrived as reinforcements. During the battle, the Army lost 23 men, and 45 more were wounded. The Nez Perce lost 30 people with another 46 wounded. Chief White Bird and about 150 Nez Perce managed a night escape from camp and fled to Canada.

On the afternoon of October 5, the final day of the battle, Chief Joseph, speaking for the remaining Nez Perce, agreed to quit fighting and offered his rifle to Colonel Miles. Thus ended the Battle of the Bear Paw, and the Nez Perce Campaign.

*"Hear me, my chiefs, I am tired; my heart is sick and sad, From where the sun now stands, I will fight no more forever."*

### Exile

During the surrender negotiations, Colonel Miles agreed that the Nez Perce could return to the Nez Perce Reservation in Idaho. He was soon overruled by his superiors. The 431 Nez Perce were first escorted to the Tongue River Cantonment in eastern Montana, then to Fort Abraham Lincoln in North Dakota, next to Fort Leavenworth in Kansas, and eventually to Indian Territory in Oklahoma. Chief Joseph and Yellow Bull lobbied for the return of their people to Idaho for the next eight years. Many of the Nez Perce died in Oklahoma, a place so foreign to them.

In 1885, with the support of Miles and others, 118 Nez Perce were returned to Idaho. The remaining 150, including Chief Joseph, were sent to the Colville Reservation in the state of Washington.

### Visiting Bear Paw Battlefield

Bear Paw Battlefield is located 16 miles south of Chinook, Montana, via US Route 2 and County Road 240. A self guided trail, picnic tables, and restrooms are available. Overnight camping is not permitted. Bear Paw Battlefield is a unit of Nez Perce National Historical Park, and is managed by the National Park Service.

Bear Paw Battlefield is the final stop on the Nez Perce National Historic Trail. The 1,300 mile trail starts in Joseph, Oregon, and follows the path of the non-treaty Nez Perce bands during the 1877 Campaign. The trail passes through federal, tribal, state, local and privately owned lands.

*Reprinted from National Park Service brochure.*

*The only life size statue of James T. Hill stands in front of the train station in Havre.*

## 8. *Historical Marker, Gas, Food, Lodging*

### Havre

Havre got its start in 1879 when Fort Assiniboine, the largest military fort west of the Mississippi, was constructed. As the first trains forged across the Great Plains, Havre quickly became the transportation hub of the area. Havre was vital to trappers, miners and military stationed at Fort Assiniboine. The town was originally known as Bull Hook Bottoms, later changed to Bull Hook Siding when the rail station at Assiniboine was abandoned. James Hill, president of the Great Northern Railroad and the founder of Havre thought the name too undignified to attract business and settlers to the area. Several of the first settler in the town were Frenchmen. After much debate, they chose the name LeHavre after a french sea port of the same name and telegraphed Hill. He wasn't too fond of the suggestion, but agreed to accept the French spelling if it was pronounced Have-Er.

Havre was a true Old West "cow town." Cowboys from the surrounding cattle ranches used it as a trading center and a place to "hole up" in the winter. The town gained national notoriety when a dispute arose as to the legality of tying horses up to the parking meters. The cowboys maintained that as long as they paid the meters, that the horses had as much right to park there as the automobiles.

Prior to 1901, the area was primarily devoted to raising sheep, cattle and horses, but ranches soon became lesser in number as farms began to produce some of the world's greatest spring and winter wheat. Agriculture and ranching are still the undisputed mainstay of Havre with 100 miles of grain field to its west and 300 miles of ranches to the east. However, the area's economy is also diversified with health services, education, professional and retail businesses; manufacturing and railroad industries also thrive in Havre—the largest town on the Hi-Line.

Havre is a focal point of commercial activity, while wide open spaces envelop the area offering many recreational opportunities. Beaver Creek Park, a 10,000-acre strip within the Bear Paw Mountains, is one of the largest county parks in the nation. Rolling grasslands, pine woods, aspen and cottonwood groves, rocky cliffs and chilly, rushing streams provide nature's most beautiful patchwork. Beaver Creek, Bear Paw Lake and the Lower Beaver Creek Lake are full of rainbow and brook trout.

The badlands exposed along the Milk River just north of Havre combine geology, paleontology and scenery all in just a 5 mile drive. Fossils found in these badlands have proven the existence of marine animals, dinosaurs and even tropical plants that lived in the area millions of years ago.

### H Hurry, Honyocker, Hurry!

*"Honyocker, scissorbill, nester … He was the Joad of a quarter century ago, swarming into hostile land; duped when he started, robbed when he arrived; hopeful, courageous, ambitious: he sought independence or adventure, comfort and security. Or perhaps he sought wealth; for there were some who did not share the Joad's love of the soil, whose interest was speculative….*

*"The honyocker was farmer, spinster, deep-sea diver; fiddler, physician, bartender, cook. He lived in Minnesota or Wisconsin, Massachusetts or Maine. There the news sought him out—Jim Hill's news of free land in the Treasure State:*

*"'More Free Homesteads; Another Big Land Opening; 1,400,000 Acres Comprising Rocky Boy Indian Lands Open to Settlers; MONTANA….*

*"'By order of the secretary of the interior, the lands shown on the map herein will be opened to homestead settlement March 10, 1910, and to entry at the Glasgow, Montana, land office'"*

*Thus Joseph Kinsey Howard described Montana's last frontier of settlement in* Montana High, Wide and Handsome. *Promoted by railway, by government, and by the American dream, train loads of newcomers rolled in and filed homestead entries. They fenced the range and plowed under the native grasses. With the optimism born of inexperience and promoters' propaganda they looked forward to bumper crops on semi-arid bench land, but the benches were never meant for a Garden of Eden. There were a few years of hope, then drought with its endless cycle of borrowing and crop failure. Between 1921 and 1925, one out of every two Montana farmers lost his place to mortgage foreclosure. Those who survived learned the lessons of dry-land farming and irrigation.*

### H Havre

*Cowpunchers, miners, and soldiers are tolerably virile persons as a rule. When they went to town in the frontier days seeking surcease from vocational cares and solace in the cup that cheers it was just as well for the urbanites to either brace themselves or take to cover. The citizens of any town willing and able to be host city for a combination of the above diamonds in the rough had to be quick on the draw and used to inhaling powder smoke.*

*Havre came into existence as a division point when the Great Northern Railroad was built and purveyed pastime to cowboys, doughboys and miners on the side. It is hard to believe now, but as a frontier camp, she was wild and hard to curry.*

### F Box Cars Restaurant & Casino
619 1st W., Havre. 265-2233

### F Uncle Joe's Steakhouse
1400 1st St., Havre. 265-5111

### L El Toro Inn
521 First St., Havre, 265-5414

The El Toro Inn, with its Spanish design, offers you Western hospitality at reasonable rates. There are 41 comfortable guest rooms to accommodate you, whether you are here for business or pleasure.

### L Havre Budget Inn Motel
115 9th Ave., Havre, 265-8625 or 888-868-8625

At the Havre Budget Inn, they go out of their way to satisfy their guest's every need. The 40 clean, quiet and affordable rooms are complete with queen sized beds, cable TV, and air conditioning. The kitchenette rooms feature a fully equipped kitchen with a stove, microwave, refrigerator and kitchen sink. They offer non-smoking rooms and an exercise room. The motel is in a quiet downtown neighborhood, within walking distance to shopping and restaurants. Ask about rates for AAA, seniors, off-season, and corporates.

### L Siesta Motel
538 1 St., Havre. 265-5863

## 9. *Attraction, Gas, Food, Lodging, Shoppinp, Miscellaneous*

### T Havre Beneath the Streets
Tours start at the Havre Railroad Museum at 120 3rd Ave., Havre. 265-8888

Probably one of the most popular attractions in northcentral Montana is the historical tour through Havre's underground. In January of 1904 a devastating fire wiped out a large part of the Havre business. A shortage of building materials made it difficult to rebuild immediately, so the businesses moved their stores to the steam tunnels running under the city until their buildings could be replaced above ground. This created what was probably one of the first shopping malls in the country.

*History is alive at Havre Beneath the Streets.*

When prohibition ended, so did the use of the tunnels. Over time the underground was largely forgotten. But talk of the passages below the streets was common among Havre's older residents, and more than one schoolboy yearned to explore the mysteries of the passages. Frank DeRosa, Lyle Watson, and a group of Havre residents and history buffs decided to explore for themselves the stories of businesses and bootleggers using the underground. What they discovered was not just a bootlegging past, but a whole world of businesses and history that had largely been forgotten. They formed the Havre Beneath the Streets Committee and began the restoration.

It took over four years to bring the project to fruition. Easements needed to be obtained, garbage and rubble needed to be removed, hallways needed to be created, old plumbing and electrical wiring had to be moved or removed. The highway through town had already destroyed a part of the area. In all, the community effort took countless hours to complete. But complete it they did. Since it opened in 1994, over 80,000 people have taken the tour.

Today it is one of the finest museums of Montana history anywhere. The one hour tour will take you through a post office, the Holland and Son Mercantile, Wright's Dental Office, the Sporting Eagle Saloon, a bordello, the Bruce Clyde Dray & Tack Shop, the Casady Blacksmith Shop, a sausage shop, the Pioneer Meat Market, C.W. "Shorty" Young's Office and Game Room, the Gourly Brothers Bakery, Tamale Jim's, Boones Drug Store, Wah Sing Laundry, an opium den, and the Fountain Barber Shop. Two new exhibits just opened include a motor service garage and Studebaker dealership and the old Havre Herald.

The museum is open daily in the summer from 9 a.m. to 5 p.m. Winter hours are Monday through Saturday from noon to 5 p.m. An admission fee is charged.

### T The Heritage Center/ H. Earl Clack Museum
306 3rd Ave. in Havre. 265-7258. www.theheritage-center.com

The old post office built in 1932 and now listed on the National Register of Historic Places, is the home of The Heritage Center and the H. Earl Clack Museum. The building is a well preserved example of Neo-Classical architecture. The original architectural motif and character of the building such as marble steps and wainscot, the terrazzo floor and the beautiful wood and glass arches in the main lobby, have been maintained through the years and still exists today.

The museum has a number of featured exhibits including a bison exhibit with a fully articulated bison skeleton allowing a rare opportunity to see within the animal so vital to the Native American way of life.

The Bob Scriver diorama depicts Chief Joseph during his famous "Hear Me My Chiefs" speech. Chief Joseph led his tribe on a 1,500 mile journey trying to get to Canada.

The Dinosaur exhibit features a Lambeosaur embryo unique to the Havre area. Dinosaur eggs are also featured in this one-of-a-kind exhibit.

Fort Assiniboine, built in 1879 in response to

the Indian Wars, was the last built in the U.S. and was home to the famous Buffalo Soldiers of the 10th Cavalry. Exhibits here depict life on the fort.

The Jim Pasma diorama shows the "Great Northern Rodeo" which "Long George" Francis played a major role in establishing. Every figure is based on a person who lived during this time period. The museum has seasonal hours and admission is charged.

*Founder Frank DeRosa with some of the railroad paraphernalia in the Havre Railroad Museum.*

### T Havre Railroad Museum
120 Third Ave., Havre. 265-8888

This is the newest museum in Havre, but a must for railroad buffs. The small museum is packed with all sorts of railroad artifacts, information and memories. According to museum spokesman Frank DeRosa, there were 10 different railroads rolling through Havre and the Hi-Line in the past. The Old St. Paul and Pacific rolled through Havre until it went bankrupt in 1862. The Great Northern served Havre from 1893 until 1970 when it became the Burlington Northern. The BN's green engines rolled through town until it merged with the Santa Fe Railroad to become the Burlington Northern Santa Fe Company. One of the main attractions in the museum for kids and adults alike, is the giant model train exhibit. Other items on display are a wire center used by rail offices along the lines, an old railroad pull cart with a collection of tools for laying track, and lanterns used by car men. DeRosa also plans a reference library with books and journals for the public to use and review. The museum is open daily in the summer from 9 a.m. to 5 p.m. Winter hours are Monday through Saturday from 9 a.m. to 4 p.m. An admission fee is charged.

### Montana Trivia

The Northern Pacific Railroad was granted 39 million acres in Montana and Idaho—the largest land grant ever given a railroad.

### S Northern Casuals
220 3rd. Ave., Atrium Mall, Downtown, Havre. 265-7413

### S Carousel Decor & Crafts
220 3rd Ave., Atrium Mall, Downtown, Havre. 265-8655Located in the Lower Level Atrium Mall.

### S High Plains Gallery
215 3rd Ave., Havre. 265-3125

### S Crazy Quilters
126 3rd Ave., Havre. 265-7212

### M Flynn Realty, Inc.
201 3rd. Ave., Havre. 265-7845 or fax 265-8782. www.flynnrealty.com or Email:flynn@flynnrealty.com

## 10. *Historical Marker, Attraction, Gas, Food, Lodging, Shopping*

### H Wahkpa Chu'gn Meat Market
Havre

*Just behind this modern shopping center is a market of an earlier vintage. Located on the Milk River (called Wahkpa Chu'gn or "Middle River" by the Assiniboine) is a communal bison kill and meat-processing camp used extensively from about 2000 to 600 years ago. This site contains both a bison jump (where the buffalo would be run over a cliff to their deaths below) and an impoundment (where the animals would be corralled, then killed). The hunter could choose the more efficient method for the situation at hand. The grazing area for the buffalo was southeast of Havre below Saddle Butte Mountain. It is farm land today, but you can visualize the browsing herds and the Indians' drive lanes leading toward the kill site.*

*The site, listed on the National Historic Register as "Too Close for Comfort" because of its proximity to Havre, is owned by Hill County and administered by the H. Earl Clack Museum. They may be contacted for tours during the summer season.*

### T Wahkpa Chu'gn National Historic site
Behind Holiday Village Mall, Havre, 265-6417

### Site Discovery

The Wahkpa Chu'gn site (pronounced "wock-pajew-kon") is a prehistoric Indian bison kill and campsite which was frequently used from approximately 2,000 to 600 years ago. It is one of the largest known bison kill sites in northern Montana. "Wahkpa Chu'gn" is the Assiniboine name for the Milk River.

The site was discovered in the fall of 1961 and is largely situated on lands owned by Hill County. This site is now managed on Hill County's behalf by the H. Earl Clack Museum.

### Prehistoric Use Of The Site

Three archaeological cultures used the site at different times. The earliest of these is known as Besant. Besant peoples used the site extensively a number of times between 2,000 and 1,500 years ago. After its use by Besant peoples, the site was abandoned for a 200-300 year period. Then it was used briefly by a culture known as Avonlea somewhere between 1,200 and 1,300 years ago. Almost immediately thereafter it started being used by a third culture known as Saddle Butte who continued using the site extensively until about 600 years ago when the site was again abandoned for the last and final time.

### Site Displays And Tours

The museum conducts guided walking tours of the site approximately 1 hour long, which provide a unique and unequaled view of the area's cultural prehistory as well as illustrating the techniques employed by archaeologists to discover and interpret it.

On your tour of the site you will view extensive archaeological bison kill and campsite deposits at various depths up to 20 feet below surface. These materials are displayed at five locations throughout the site within wooden display houses constructed to protect the deposits and make them accessible for public display.

Tours available from mid-May through Labor Day, Tuesday through Saturday from 10 a.m. to 5 p.m. Admission is charged. *Reprinted from site brochure*

### F P J'S Restaurant & Casino
15 3rd Ave., Havre. 265-3211

### L Super 8 Motel Of Havre
1901 US Hwy. 2 W., Havre, 265-1411
or reservations at 800-800-8000

Enjoy your trip to Historic Havre and enjoy your rest at The Super 8. They are conveniently located near shopping, the fairgrounds, the airport, and golf course, and provide 63 quiet rooms for the single traveler or the vacationing family. Fax and copy service are available. You'll find ample parking for all vehicles large and small. The rooms and suites are equipped with queen size beds, cable TV with HBO, free local calls, free cribs, continental breakfast, and outside outlets. They will allow pets with permission, handicapped access, Senior Discounts are available., and children 12 & under are free with parents.

## 11. *Attraction, Miscellaneous*

### T MSU Northern Collections
300 W. 11th, Math Science Bldg, Havre. 265-3757

On campus is an excellent exhibit of the area's natural history and Native American artifacts.

### M Montana State University/Northern
Havre, 265-3700 or 800-662-6132.
www.msun.edu

The Havre campus, "Northern" emphasis is in degree programs of applied and engineering technologies, along with professional teacher education programs, nursing programs and business technology. MSUN also has an educational center in Lewistown, located at the Central Montana Medical Center.

## 12. *Historical Marker, Attraction*

### H Fort Assinniboine
Rte 234, south of Havre

*Established in 1879, Fort Assinniboine was one of the most strategically placed U.S. Army posts in the northwest. Headquarters for the District of Montana, the fort and military reserve encompassed the entire Bears Paw mountain range. The post was constructed by the 18th U.S. infantry under the command of Colonel Thomas Ruger. When completed, the 51 substantial brick buildings included officers' quarters, barracks, a large hospital, chapel, gymnasium, officers' club, stables, and warehouses. The fort was built to protect settlers to the south from possible raids by Sitting Bull's Hunkpapa Sioux who fled to Canada after Custer's defeat on the Little Big Horn in 1876. The military's fears proved groundless, however, as no serious Indian disturbances occurred in the area.*

*General John J. Pershing served here in the 1890s, earning his nickname "Black Jack" because of his association with the Afro-American 10th Cavalry—the famed "Buffalo Soldiers." For many years, Fort Assinniboine soldiers worked with the Canadian Mounties to quell smuggling across the border.*

*In 1911, the War Department abandoned the post. A few years later, the landless Chippewa and Cree Indians found a home on the southern part of the military reserve when it was set aside as Rocky Boy's Reservation. The State of Montana purchased the fort's remaining buildings and 2,000 acres for use as the Northern Agricultural Research Center of Montana State University—Bozeman.*

### T Fort Assiniboine
Fort Assiniboine, the largest military post constructed in Montana, was established in 1879. Within four years, a stately, impressive complex of some one hundred brick, stone and wood buildings, was clustered around the parade ground overlooking the quiet meandering of Beaver Creek, and in the shadow of the beautiful Bear Paw Mountains. The Fort buildings were surrounded by a vast military reservation of a half million acres.

The Fort was designed to house ten companies of soldiers, both infantry and cavalry. The troopers were in charge of monitoring the activities of the many Indian groups living in the region, and protecting them and the citizens of Montana from hostile incursions of Canadian tribal bands. In its heyday, nearly 1,000 officers, enlisted men, and civilians called Assiniboine home.

The Fort, one of northern Montana's earliest white outposts, was a busy self contained city. Bakery, laundry, and blacksmith facilities were in operation, as were a general store, post office, hotel and restaurant. For recreation, the post band gave regular concerts, and the men engaged in such sport activities as baseball, track and boxing. Other diversions offered included a library for reading, cardplaying and checkers; plus an enlisted man's amusement center housed in the regimental band barracks. The lifestyle was routine, with the men largely spared from battle activity.

By the early twentieth century, Montana's frontier was drawing to a close, and the Fort was surrounded by homesteads and the trappings of "Civilization." The post was finally closed in 1911, and the state of Montana turned the site into an agricultural experiment station. Today much of it is gone, but the surviving buildings are a proud and majestic reminder of Montana's Frontier Heritage.

The site of old Fort Assiniboine is now the home of the Northern Agricultural Research Center, operated by Montana State University. It is not open to individual visitors; however, the Fort Assiniboine Preservation Association conducts regular guided tours of the site during the summer months. Tour schedules and other information may be obtained from the Havre Area Chamber of Commerce (406) 265-4383. Reprinted from Fort Assiniboine Preservation Association brochure.

## 13. *Attraction*

### T Beaver Creek Park
South of Havre on Hwy. 234.

This mile wide and 17 mile long strip stretches along the north slopes of the Bear Paw Mountains. At 10,000 acres, it is one of the largest county parks in the country. Within its boundaries are rolling grasslands, pine woods, aspen and cottonwood groves, cold rushing streams, and rocky cliffs. The flora ranges from cool leafy cottonwood, aspen, lodge pole pine, ponderosa, and Douglas fir on the south end to box elder, willow, alder, and buffalo berry on the north end. Bear Paw Lake, Beaver Creek and Lower Beaver Creek are well stocked with Rainbow and Brook trout. The park is teeming with wildlife including mule and whitetail deer, bobcat, coyote, beaver, fox, mink, grouse, pheasants, Golden Eagles, and hawks. The geology of the area varies from glacial deposits at the north end through volcanic strata and dikes, to metamorphic and sedimentary rocks full of fossils.

### Montana Trivia

In 1888, the now defunct town of Cypress once boasted a restaurant, a store, two bordellos, and thirty-two saloons. In 1889, it withered down to one saloon when the commanding officer of nearby Fort Assiniboine declared it off-limits to troops.

## 14. *Attraction, Miscellaneous*

### T Fresno Reservoir
13 miles west of Havre. 265-6177

This is one of the more popular recreation areas in this part of the state. There are four relatively primitive campgrounds, a swimming area, boat ramps and picnic facilities. Go 13 miles west of Havre and look for the signs to the lake. The turnoff is just across from Blackie's Tavern. Head north for the lake. The first left takes you to the beach area, the second to the boat ramp.

### M Northern Lights Ranch
13300 River Rd., East of Havre, 394-2262

Northern Lights Ranch is the home of 20+ Arabian Horses, including NL Montana Tsunrise, their breeding stallion. They breed for halter conformation, performance ability, Arabian beauty, and good dispositions. Their horses' quality speaks for itself.

## 15. *Gas, Food*

### Gildford
Like many of the railroad towns along the Hi Line, Gildford was named for a city in another part of the world, in this case, the town of Gildford in England. A mile from today's town site, trappers wintered at Sage Creek Crossing where there was good feed and water for their horses. When the waters of Sage Creek rose with the spring thaw, they would load their furs on crude rafts and float them to Fort Benton. During the hard days of poor crops and low grain prices, G. Fred Mundy built a flour mill here. He found grain for the impoverished homesteaders and gave them cereal to eat and feed for their animals. The mill is a landmark today and Gildford's primary industry is as a marketing town for Northern Plains farmers who produce excellent quality hard spring wheat.

### Hingham
At one time, Hingham was euphemistically known as "the progressive city, a city built on the square." In 1911 Hingham's *Review* reported, "This time last year there was no semblance of a town here. Now, we have a thriving town in which over twenty firms are each doing business." Today it is a shipping and storing station for grain and stock.

### Kremlin
There is some debate over how this town got its name. It is a fact that many of the early settlers were Russian. Some way they "saw the citadels of Moscow in the mirages that appear of the surrounding prairie." Others say the settlers named it for the Russian word meaning fortress. In 1913 the Great Northern Railroad built a depot here to handle the implement and equipment shipments that were pouring in for the homesteaders. The Kremlin *Chancellor* reported, *"it is a bustling, booming, growing trade center for the hundreds of homesteaders who have filed on 600,000 acres of highly productive chocolate loamsoil."*

## 16. *Attraction, Gas, Food*

### Inverness
"Scotty" Watson, a local pioneer, named this town for his hometown in his native Scotland.

### Joplin
Joplin began as a Hi-Line train station where hundred's of homesteaders arrived to settle on "free land." Once a battleground of Piegan, Blood, and Gros Ventre Indians, the area became a land where homesteaders battled grasshoppers and the elements.

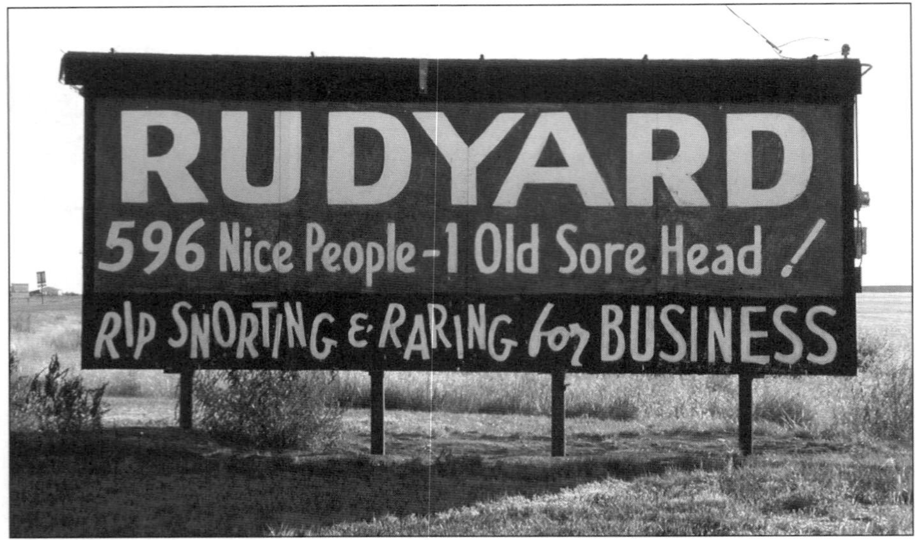


## Rudyard

The best theory is that this town was named for Rudyard Kipling who traveled west to the Pacific Coast passing through Montana in 1889.

### T The Depot Museum

Rudyard, 355-4322

Except for the sign on Hwy. 2 that points to Rudyard and advertises "596 people and 1 old sorehead," you wouldn't think there's much to see and cruise right on through. There's no big sign advertising the Depot Museum. The folks of Rudyard think that word-of-mouth is the best advertising. But if you love history, you'll want to turn off the cruise control and swing into this small town.

The museum is called the Depot Museum because it's in the old Great Northern depot that once sat next to the tracks just south of town. The Rudyard Historical Society purchased the building for $1 and moved it to its new home several years ago. This is more than just a Rudyard Museum. This is a museum of the Hi-Line. The grounds are home to a blacksmith shop, a one-room schoolhouse, and a homesteaders shack. The museum itself houses photographs, glassware, uniforms, and artifacts from across the Hi-Line.

Probably the most important part of the museum sits at the corner of the complex. The "Paper Museum" is a climate controlled concrete building that houses old Hingham newspapers from 1911 to 1952. The Inverness and Rudyard papers are stored there also. Written documents, school and graduation documents, photographs, and anything that ties people to the community are stored there.

When you park there take special notice of the 100-foot long and 42-inch high wall. It is filled with colored stones each with the name of a homesteader, veteran, or other deceased Hi-Line resident whose name has been carefully penciled on the stone.

The museum is open from June 1 through the middle of September, Tuesday through Sunday, 2 p.m. to 5 p.m.

**17.** *Historical Marker, Attraction, Gas, Food, Lodging, Shopping*

## Chester

Before the Great Northern railroad came through, ranchers had to drive their cattle all the way to Minot, North Dakota to market. This was a favorite resting spot of theirs on the way east. The town was named by the first telegraph operator there after his home town in Pennsylvania. Of all the homestead communities between Havre and Shelby, Chester was the shining star. It beat Joplin in an election for the designation of county seat for Liberty County in 1919. Much of its early growth was attributed to the efforts of two men—Brown B. Weldy and Charles Baker.

Weldy owned a ramshackle hostelry called the Prairie Inn. At a time when homesteaders were living in tents for temporary shelter, the Prairie Inn was filled to overflowing. Weldy was a man of many talents. He was a land locator, postmaster, merchant, justice of the peace, and newspaper editor. His biggest talent was as a booster for the town. As one historian noted "Weldy seemed to be the sort of person that made you think you heard an enthusiastic brass band in the background when he spoke and the urge to fall into step was overwhelming."

Another landmark building in the early days of Chester was the Chester Trading Company. It was well established in 1908 when Charles F. Baker and his partner Alex Wright purchased it. Baker started out as a traveling merchant carrying his clothing and wares in covered wagons to the ranches along the Canadian border. Baker's store sported a sign that claimed "We Sell Everything." If there was a buyer for it, they sold it. Baker and Wright often granted customers credit that ran for years. His pride and joy was his tiled meat case. When asked why he entered his store unarmed to chase away a burgler he answered "We mighta got shootin' back and forth and hit my meat case."

### H The Sweet Grass Hills

East of Chester

*You can see the Sweet Grass Hills or the Three Buttes to the north of here on a reasonably clear day. The Indians used them as watch towers from which they could locate buffalo herds. Things sure grow in this country. Some old-timers claim that when they arrived those buttes weren't much bigger than prairie dog mounds.*

*In 1884 a Blackfoot Indian found gold in them thar hills and the usual stampede followed. The middle peak is called Gold Butte. It was claimed that the placer ground in Two Bits Gulch produced twenty-five cents in colors for every shovel full of gravel.*

*The pay dirt has been pretty well worked out and the glamour of boom days is gone, but a few old-timers still prospect the gulches, hoping some day to find that elusive pot of gold at the rainbow's end, called the Mother Lode.*

### H First Methodist Episcopal Church of Chester

At Liberty County Museum

*The first two decades of the twentieth century saw railroad promotion and homestead settling along Montana's Hi-Line. Chester was one of the first communities to spring up along the new Great Northern Railway Line in the 1890s. The town incorporated in 1910 and the local newspaper noted, '...a progressive city like Chester is not taking the right course by neglecting the building of churches." At that time church services were held in several locations including the Grand Bar and Hotel. The community unanimously decided a proper church was an immediate necessity. The congregation of the First Episcopal Methodist Church bought the land and construction began in June of 1911. Furnished with items donated in memory of lost family and friends, the first service was held the following November 5. Because the church was built with community labor, it was fitting that the fruits be shared with Catholics, Lutherans and Presbyterians who helped in the construction. Sundays were divided so that each congregation could use the church for services until each had its own place of worship. In the summer of 1946, the church was turned to face the east and a cry room and office added. Services were held until 1968 and in 1970, the Liberty County Museum Association purchased the building for one dollar. Students of Chester's graduating high school class of 1997 researched and prepared the nomination for listing on the National Register of Historic Places in conjunction with the Montana Heritage Project.*

### T Liberty County Museum

3 blocks south of Hwy 2 on 2nd St. E., Chester. 759-5256

The museum resides in the former Methodist Church building, built in 1911. As with most small Montana museums, the exhibits focus on the history of the area. Exhibits include a one room homesteader household. The clothes washing equipment display has more items than can be listed. If you've heard of the different ways clothes have been washed throughout the decades, you can bet they are all included in this display. U.S., English, German and Japanese made rifles and shotguns are represented in a wide array of guns on display, some date back to 1826. Inside a display case is a beautiful collection of antique dishes, including cut glass, carnival glass and assorted china, some 75 to 100 years old. A unique military display encompasses uniforms from World

### Montana Trivia

The town of Havre was originally named Bullhook Bottoms after a nearby stream of the same name.

War I through the Korean Conflict. A World War I uniform is complete with a gas mask. The museum is open from the end of May through middle September.

## FS Wired Inn Coffee Shop & Computer Center

30 Main Street, Chester. Computer Center 759-5090 or Coffee Shop & Deli 759-5079.
www.wired-inn-mt.com

Wired Inn takes the definition of "cyber cafe" to a new level. Established by two sisters, Barbara Wolfe and Jackie Watson, it incorporates a full service computer center with a coffee shop and deli. The computer center has four stations, including scanner, laser printer, and copier available for any publishing you may also want to do. Wired Inn is a Gateway dealer, the local Internet provider, with repair, troubleshooting, and large selection of computer supplies. The coffee shop has espresso, teas, and specializes in made-from-scratch soups, large deli sandwiches, and specialty salads made in-house or packaged to go for your adventure. A take-home-and-bake deli pizza is available in it's own bake-and-serve pan. On-line ordering is available from the web site, and pick up at the drive-up window. Wired Inn has a relaxing atmosphere and a welcome stop when traveling the Hi-Line.

**18.** *Historical Marker, Attraction, Gas, Food, Lodging, Camping*

## T The Little Rockies

South of Malta.

See sidebar

## Zortman

This quirky, but historic little mining town is nestled in the Little Rockies just above Landusky. One of the favorite activities for visitors here is panning for gold. Candy and John Kalal, the proprietors of the Zortman Garage and Motel will give you guidance on this fun and sometimes rewarding activity. This little town sits in the heart of some of the more colorful history of Montana. Lewis and Clark named this range in 1805. Gold mining arrived in 1884. Kid Curry and his Wild Bunch homesteaded nearby and left a number of graves with stories to tell behind them. As you drive into Zortman, you will see the old jail still standing.

### Montana Trivia

Pike Landusky, founder of the town that bears his name, was so mean that the townsfolk buried him twelve feet under and piled rocks on his grave just to make sure he didn't get out. His grave can be seen in Landusky today.

## H Our Lady of the Little Rockies

Hays

*This shrine was erected in 1931 by Father B. Feusi S.J. and Tom Flack, (a German Immigrant), in honor of the Virgin Mary. Inside is a hand-carved statue of Mary, an exact copy of the miraculous one in the little Swiss town of Einsiedeln. Mass is celebrated in this shrine on the Saturdays of May.*

## H The Story of the Miraculous Statue

Hays

*In the little Swiss town of Einsiedeln lived an aged and holy wood-carver who had great devotion to the Blessed Mother of God. Towards the close of his life, he desired to carve a statue in honor of our Lady. He spent many laborious but happy hours praying as he carved and making each stroke an act of love for Mary, the mother of God. A few days after the statue had been completed, this holy man died. When his friends came to dispose of his belongings, they saw this beautiful statue and, not wishing it to remain the natural brown of the wood, they decided to paint it and then put it in the village church. That evening many neighbors came to the house of the old wood-carver to watch his two friends paint the statue. The face and arms of the child Jesus and his blessed mother were tinted a delicate pink, the robe of the divine child was colored white and Our Lady's mantle was made blue. When the work was completed all left for their homes. Late the next day the neighbors came to move the statue to the church. Great was their surprise to find that all the paint had fallen in tiny flakes around the foot of the statue and the image of our lady and her divine son was again just as it had left the hands of the old wood-carver. The people realized this miracle was our Blessed Lady's way of showing her appreciation of the holy man's loving work and her desire that the statue should-remain as he had carved it.*

## H St. Paul's Mission

Hays

*Est. in 1886 by the Jesuit Fathers under the authority of Fr. Frederick Ebbschweiler S.J. on Sept. 14, 1887 the Ursuline Sisters opened a boarding school for the Native Americans of Ft. Belknap. The year 1936 saw the Franciscan Sisters assume the duties of Ursulines. The Jesuit volunteer corps have been sending their members to St. Paul's since 1969. The Dominican Sisters arrived in the fall of 1973, on Dec. 5, 1973. A fire razed the school building. The last high school class graduated in 1974. Since then an elementary school has been staffed and maintained through the combined efforts of these men and women. Sister Clare Hartman S.E. is the resident historian of this area, having arrived in Aug. 1939. Sister M. Giswalda Kramer O.S.F. (1903-1988)—after serving 46 years at the mission is in death. A guardian angel of St. Paul's School.*

*Little church on the hill in Zortman.*

## T Zortman Mine

Hwy 19, Little Rockies area . 673-3162

At one time, the mine was one of the largest producing gold mines in the nation. It is in the scenic Little Rocky Mountains and is a national historic site. Once embroiled in controversy in the late 1980s, the mine is now closed, and land reclamation efforts are being made.

Section 11

# The Little Rockies

*This is a view of the Little Rockies similar to what Lewis and Clark would have seen as they passed through the area.*

**When exploring the Little Rockies, you** have to divide the exploration into four areas: the Zortman area, the Landusky area, the Hays area, and the north area around Lodgepole.

## Landusky

Much of the history of this area revolves around mining and Landusky is where it began. On July 3, 1884, Frank Aldridge found gold in his sluice box on Alder Creek. Dutch Lewis and Pike Landusky were right there with him. Landusky, not exactly the quiet type, headed for Lewistown immediately with news of the strike and plans to create a mining district. The rush was on. Within a week the first hopeful prospectors were staking out claims up and down the creek. A month later a mining district was formed, and within two months the little camp had turned into a bustling, rowdy, lawless community of tent saloons, dugouts and hastily ramshackle log cabins. A dance hall and grocery store also sprang up. The town was robust and the gulches were lined with prospectors working their claims. Arguments erupted which were often resolved with gunfire. Indians and prospectors jostled each other on the main street. Deals were made daily for claims, lumber for sluice boxes, liquor, and news of more profitable sites. The calvary from Fort Assiniboine camped in a clearing nearby, sent to keep the peace.

*Old Zortman Jail*

But the gold didn't pan out. Optimism was maintained by the salting of mines, of false reports of strikes up or down the creek. It was said the same nuggets turned up in one sluice box after another. In fact, the miners worked hard just to buy their beans and bacon. By fall it was all over.

It was 10 years before the ever optimist Landusky and his partner Bob Ormond struck it rich at the August mine.

Landusky is mostly a ghost town today. This was the town where Kid Curry shot Landusky in the saloon Landusky owned. This was where the "Kid" starte.d his life of crime and ended it in these parts. You can still see the grave where Pike is buried here under a pile of rocks with a carved wood grave marker.

## Zortman

Pete Zortman arrived soon after gold was disovered here. He and his partner built a mill near the town named for him. They proved that you could extract gold from low grade ore and make a profit. The mill ran for five years.

Soon after the Ruby Gulch Mine was discovered, followed by the Independent, and the Carte.r, Mint and Divide. Four partners including Charley Whitcomb acquired and developed the mine and constructed a mill which at one time was producing as much as $14,000 a day in gold bullion. The Ruby Gulch Mill was built in 1904, enlarged in 1914 and later destroyed by fire. A new 600 ton mill was built to replace it. All work was suspended when World War I broke out, and the town quickly became a ghost town. The new mill burned to the ground in 1923. Whitcomb was the only one of the original partners to keep his interest in the mine and in the 30s he returned to purchase the August Mine, found a new strike and built another mill. The first car of ore they shipped from the August returned close to $15,000. Whitcomb later opened the Ruby Gulch Mine again. The mill still stands now hidden in growths of brush and trees. The mill was the second largest cyanide mill in the world at the time it was operating. WW II forced the closing of the mines and in 1936 a terrible fire swept the Little Rockies. Since that time there have been no big mining developments.

*Mission Canyon*

History records that the Whitcombs made and lost several fortunes through the years. At times, they occupied a mansion in Helena. When their fortunes faded, they would move back to their homes in Zortman or over the divide near Beaver Creek. The old cemetery in Zortman has a special place for the Whitcombs. It is an impressive part to see and a testimony to the influence they had on this community. Townsfolk today can point out the Whitcomb house in Zortman and give directions to the ghostly Dutch-style house that still sits, deserte.d and intriguing. Mine officials will sometimes allow visitors to another Whitcomb house by the old Ruby Mill. That house, built by the only Whitcomb boy, George, has a fireplace constructed of high grade ore. It is a unique house with an incredible view from the long glassed in porch looking out through the Little Rockies across the vast eastern prairies.

When you're in Zortman, visit the tiny Catholic church that sits high on a hill watching over the small town. The church was built around 1910. One of the favorite activities for visitors here is gold panning. Stop in and see Candy Kalal at the Zortman Garage and Motel. She'll set you up and tell you where to hunt the precious metal. If you like old mines, you can explore Alder Gulch. On the bluffs to the east of town there are caves and indentations filled with tiny fossils.

## Hays and the Mission Canyon

On the southwest side of the Little Rockies is the tiny town of Hays. You are on the Fort Belknap Reservation here which is home to the members of the Assiniboine and Gros Ventre Tribes. In Hays is a mission founded by Father Eberschweiler before the turn of the century. The mission still stands and is still in use today. Driving up to the mission you will pass Our Lady of the Lil Rockies shrine to a religious statue. The story is told of the miracle of the statue on a sign outside the shrine.

Leaving the mission and heading east you drive into a canyon of towering limestone cliffs and a very narrow gorge. The road follows Mission Creek. One of the first things you come upon is the Natural Bridge. While this is the one most people come to see, there are others further from the road but visible as you drive. The upper canyon is home to powwows each summer as well as religious ceremonies. Along the road you will see interpretive signs describing various Indian personalities important to the tribe's history. There are several picnic spots along the way.

## Lodgepole

At the north end of the Little Rockies is a road which connects the Malta highway and the Harlem highway. The road skirts Lodgepole pine forests. In the distance you can see massive limestone cliffs separating the mountains from the prairies. There are some natural warm springs near here.

### T Landusky/Mission Canyon

Landusky is the home of Mission Canyon, and features a natural limestone bridge that arches more than 50 feet above the canyon floor. In mid-June each year the Hays Mission Canyon Dance is held and is open to the public. For more information call 673-3281.

### T Ruby Gulch Mine

North of Zortman.

The most easterly of all Montana gold producing areas. This area was rich with gold for a few years, but its ghosts are some of liveliest stories about the likes of Pike Landusky, Kid Curry, and his brothers. The mine stayed busy until 1935, and finally closed in 1942 when the U.S. Government order L.28 forced all gold mines to close.

*Natural bridges are abundant among the limestone formations of the Little Rockies.*

### T Mission Canyon

Hays

This beautiful canyon features a natural limestone bridge that arches more than 50 feet above the canyon floor. In mid-June each year the Hays Mission Canyon Dance is held and is open to the public. For more information call 673-3281.

### T Little Rockies Recreation Management Area

From Malta, drive about 40 miles south on US 191. Watch for a sign pointing west toward Zortman, and follow that road about 7 miles, turning at the Camp Creek Campground turnoff. 228-4316

This heavily-timbered, isolated mountain range rises abruptly from the surrounding plains, providing habitat for a unique mix of mountain and prairie wildlife. Many species found infrequently in eastern Montana are found here. Bighorn sheep can often be seen on the south side of Saddle Butte and Silver Peak, especially in winter.

### LC Zortman Garage & Motel

302 Main St., Zortman. 673-3160

## 19. *Attraction*

### T UL Bend National Wildlife Refuge

Hwy 191, then 40 miles east of Robinson Bridge. 538-8706

This isolated and beautiful refuge, a designated wilderness area, is located inside the C.M. Russell Refuge deep in the Missouri Breaks. The roads are rough getting there, and impassable when wet. Bighorn sheep, elk, deer, bobcats and pronghorn antelope thrive here. It also provides nesting and feeding habitat for ducks, geese, swans, raptors, and other migratory birds. Fort Peck Reservoir surrounds the southern half of the area. There are no maintained trails in the area, but camping and hiking are allowed.

*The Missouri River at Fred Robinson Bridge.*

## 20. *Lewis & Clark, Attraction*

### D William Clark

May 14, 1805

*"We proceeded on verrry well untill about 6 oClock a Squawl of wind Struck our Sale broad Side and turned the perogue nearly over, and in this Situation the Perogue remained untill the Sale was Cut down in which time She nearly filled with water."*

### D William Clark

May 14, 1805

*"Six good hunters of the party fired at a Brown or Yellow Bear several times before they killed him, & indeed he had like to have defeated the whole party, he pursued them Seperately as they fired on him, and was near Catching Several of them one he pursued into the river."*

### T James Kipp Recreation Area

US Hwy. 191 near Robinson Bridge. 538-7461

This is a key access point for the Upper Missouri National Wild & Scenic River. For centuries, Native Americans were attracted to this area to gather plants and hunt game. The Ancient camps and bison kill sites here are evidence of human dependence along the river corridor.

Lewis and Clark and their Corps of Discovery passed here on May 24, 1805, during the second year of their adventure. They camped just 2-1/2 miles down river. The members of the expedition averaged about 13 miles a day by sailing, poling, and mostly pulling their boats upriver against the formidable currents. In July, 1806, Captain Lewis and his party returned down the Missouri through this area.

Few names stand out in Missouri River history than James Kipp. Born in Montreal in 1788, he was a fort builder, fur trader, and steamboat captain. In 1831, he established Fort Piegan near Loma, 128 river miles upstream from this spot. It was the first American Fur Company trading post

*The Missouri Breaks just west of Fred Robinson Bridge.*

## Kid Curry and the Wild Bunch

For some 10 to 15 years the four Curry brothers, Henry, John, Loney and Harvey (The Kid) made the Little Rockies their home and headquarte.rs. Their real name was Logan and the fact that they came to Montana under an assumed name suggests that their past was not pristine before they arrived here in the 1890s. The brothers, along with Harry Longabaugh (The Sundance Kid) and Butch Cassidy made up the infamous "Wild Bunch."

Bill Kellerman was an orphan befriended and adopted by the colorful Pike Landusky. Kellerman recalls, *"A Christmas dance was being held in Landusky. That night the Curry Gang shot up the town, including the dance hall. They shot the piano to splinters, broke guitars over the musicians' heads and generally wrecked the place. The Curry boys were pretty active around the old mining camp the first few months after I arrived. One time three or four of them rode into a pool hall and played a game on horseback. One of the horses broke through the floor and horse and rider dropped into a dirt cellar. They were always coming into town, getting liquored up and shooting up the camp."*

The Currys had a special beef with Pike Landusky. At one time, the Currys and Landusky were neighbors and got along fine for several years. But somewhere along the line a feud starte.d between them over Loney Curry's courtship of Landusky's daughter. Pike had a chance to vent his anger one day when two of the brothers John and Harvey "The Kid" were arrested for altering a cattle brand. Pike was the deputy sheriff and reporte.dly roughed them up pretty good while they were incarcerated. The brothers were released for lack of evidence and swore revenge on Pike.

Christmas of 1894 Pike threw a pretty good party for the town. He had four dozen quarts of Baltimore select oysters shipped in for the celebration. Word got out that Landusky was throwing a grand party. As reporte.d in the *Great Falls Tribune*, "From that time until the big day the camp was all feverish activity. The big time was all the topic of conversation and fully a barrel of bourbon was licked up in considering details and devising new features. Word had gone over all that sparsely settled country that Landusky was entertaining; they all heard it and they all came.... They drifted in from the badlands 60 miles away, from grassy valleys in the foothills, from the alkali flats farther out, from remote places in the river breaks and from the gulches of far reaches of the mountains. They came in all the vehicles that were known to the time and they brought food enough to feed the multitude in the wilderness, those who didn't get a break on the loaves and fishes."

About 100 people showed up for the party. They danced, drank, and ate nonstop for two days and nights. But throughout the celebration there was a tenseness—a feeling that something might explode between the Curry's and Landusky. On the morning of December 27th Pike made his usual mid-morning visit to Jew Jake's saloon. Within minutes of his arrival, Kid Curry entered the saloon. He slapped Landusky on the shoulder, and when Landusky turned around his jaw received a load of knuckles. Onlookers ordered the patrons of the saloon at gunpoint not to interfere. The Kid's blow knocked Landusky to the floor and the Kid beat him relentlessly to a bloody pulp. When he was certain Landusky was finished, he got up only to see Pike rise and draw his gun. According to the *Great Falls Tribune*, *"It was one of the new fangled automatics that had just come out at that time, and either Pike didn't know how to use it or it went wrong. ... Anyway, it didn't work. The Kid found himself in a moment, drew his .44 and it was all over. He shot Pike twice in the head—and missed the third time—and Pike battled no more."*

The Curry Gang rode out of town after the killing and hid on the ranch they had established south of the mountains. The ranch was strategically located for a quick get-away and was a good headquarte.rs for the meetings of the Wild Bunch. Sheriff's officers were sent from Fort Benton and scoured the country following up every lead in search of the Currys.

Sometime towards the spring of 1895 Kellerman recalls walking to the Curry ranch. The Kid, Longabaugh and the cook greeted him cordially and invited him in. The Kid was watching a team and buckboard headed towards the ranch through a powerful field glass. He figured it was the "law" and he and Longabaugh slipped out the back door, mounted their horses and headed for the Missouri River. Kellerman says "I was fooling with the Currys' pet gopher when the buckboard stopped at the ranch. A man wearing a star stepped down and asked me if anyone was at home. I said 'no'—figured the less I said the better off I'd be. I'd learned a lot in the short time I had been in Montana."

John Curry was involved in a shooting episode at the Jim Winters ranch south of the mountains that not only resulted in his death, but, ultimately, the death of Jim Winters. Dan Tressler and his wife had separated and John Curry, whom she planned to marry, took her to a friend's ranch on the Missouri River. Tressler sold the ranch to Jim Winters and his half-brother Abram Gill. Mrs. Tressler didn't like the fact that she'd been cut out of the deal and persuaded John Curry to retrieve the ranch for her. Curry sent Winters a note to vacate within a certain period or face the consequences. Winters knew what the consequences would be and kept a loaded rifle behind the door. When the deadline arrived Winters saw Curry approaching the place on horseback. A few shots later, John Curry lay dead. Six months later, Jim Winters took two shots to the stomach while walking to his outhouse. Several agonizing hours later he was dead.

Later, Abram Gill sold the ranch for $10,000 to the Coburn Cattle Company. He left with a down payment check of $2,000 in hand. He and his white horse vanished somewhere between the ranch and Lundusky. No trace of him was ever found.

The robbery of the Great Northern "Flyer" at Exeter Creek was probably the most famous escapade of Kid Curry. By now his brothers were dead. John killed by Jim Winters, Loney killed by lawmen, and Henry dead from tuberculosis. This was the last robbery credited to the Wild Bunch. The holdup was believed to have been planned by Curry and Butch Cassidy.

On July 3, 1901, the "Flyer" stopped for water at Malta. Kid Curry and another accomplice boarded the train. After the train was underway, they made their way to the engine and stuck a gun in the engineer's back ordering him to stop the train. They ordered the fireman to open the express car where they proceeded to blow the safe and a load $40,000 in currency and cash into a sack. The money was never recovered and historians differ on what ultimately happened to the Kid.

established on the Missouri west of Fort Union. He made the return trip the following spring with more than 4,000 beaver pelts and other furs in tow. After 41 years in the fur trade business, he retired in 1859.

Today, this stretch of the Upper Missouri is a national treasure under the careful stewardship of government agencies and private landowners. 149 miles upriver to Fort Benton is designated as a National Wild and Scenic River. Downriver to Fort Peck, the land surrounding the river forms the heart of the C.M. Russell National Wildlife Refuge.

### T Fred Robinson Bridge

Approximately 70 miles south of Malta on Highway 191.

Looking from the bridge you are viewing much of the same scenery that Lewis and Clark viewed when passing through this area. On May 23, 1805, the Corps of Discovery camped about seven miles downstream from this spot. While their journals are vague on this, they viewed from the hills above the campsite the Little Rocky Mountains about 25 miles to the northwest. They camped the next day about 2 miles upstream from the bridge.

## 21. *Gas, Food*

### Fergus

This town was named for Andrew Fergus, one of the original settlers here and a prominent cattleman. The town began as a station on the Milwaukee Railroad branch line.

### Roy

The name of this town was supposed to be "Ray" but as sometimes happened, the Post Office Department made an error and the town was named Roy. W. H. Peck, an early settler, named it for a member of his family. The population of Roy reached its peak during the homesteader era. People came from all around by horseback or buggy to attend the Saturday night dances here. When World War I came, most of the homesteaders left and their land was bought up by larger concerns, mostly cattle ranchers.

## 22. *Food*

### Denton

This town was named for the Dent brothers who originally owned the land the town sits on. The name was considered too short for a town name so it was lengthened to Denton. This town is the turnaround point for the Charlie Russell Chew Choo Dinner Train out of Lewistown.

## 23. *Historical Marker, Lewis & Clark, Attraction*

### H Claggett Hill Trail

northwest of Winifred

*In 1866, the U.S. army established Camp Cooke on the west bank of the Judith River near here to protect local settlers from Indian raids. Shortly thereafter, steamboat entrepreneur and trader T C. Power built a small trad-*

*ing post near the camp to supply goods and services to the soldiers. The post was named Fort Claggett in honor of William Claggett, one of Montana Territory's most respected politicians and capitalists. After Camp Cooke closed in 1870, Power built a second Fort Claggett east of the Judith River about two miles from this marker. Strategically located near a river ford, the fort obtained supplies from steamboats plying the Missouri and shipped out beaver pelts, buffalo hides and cattle. By 1884, this segment of the Claggett Trail was heavily used by freighters, cowboys, businessmen, Indians and miners seeking their fortunes in the nearby Judith Mountains. In the mid-1880s, Power and Gilman Norris formed the Judith Mercantile and Cattle Company with its headquarters at Fort Claggett. At its peak in the late 1880s, Fort Claggett consisted of a store, hotel, saloon, warehouse, mail station, stables and sheep sheds. Although Fergus County has actively maintained portions of the Claggett Trail, this section exists unaltered and is representative of late 19th century freighting roads.*

### H The Judith Landing
Hwy. 236 just south of the Missouri River

*This area, which surrounds the confluence of the Missouri and Judith Rivers, was designated a National Historic District in 1974 because of its historic importance to Montana's transportation system. Missouri River steamboats en route to Fort Benton tied up at Judith Landing to buy fuel from "woodhawks." The rotted stumps of trees cut for fuel can still be seen in the area. At the Judith's mouth, Camp Cooke was built (1866) to protect river travellers from Indian attacks. In 1872, T. C. Power erected the Fort Claggett Trading Post just below the mouth of the Judith. Renamed Judith Landing, the site became a bustling community including (1885) a large stone warehouse, saloon, hotel, stable, blacksmith shop, and store. The PN (Power-Norris) Ferry provided transportation across the Missouri. The Lohse Family started (1923) a new ferry downstream, and it operated until the Winifred Bridge was built in 1982.*

### H Fort Chardon
Rte 236

*Captains Meriwether Lewis and William Clark passed through this area (1805) on their expedition to the Pacific Ocean, and the landscape here remains much as they described it. Fur trappers and traders then followed them into the Upper Missouri region. Fort Chardon was erected (1844) on this bank, but local Indian hostilities forced its closure two years later. The north bank also was the site of two important treaty councils. In 1846, Father Pierre Jean De Smet convened the Blackfeet and the Salish here to end their open warfare. In 1855, Governor Isaac I. Stevens organized a meeting of more than 3,000 Blackfeet, Gros Ventres, Nez Perces, and Salish to produce a major treaty between the tribes and the government. This area first was homesteaded in the 1880s. Traces of early homestead irrigation systems can still be seen within the National Historic District.*

### D Mer. Lewis
August 1, 1806

*"a white bear came within 50 paces of our camp before we perceived it; it stood on it's hinder feet and looked at us with much apparent unconsern"*

### D Sgt. Gass
May 27, 1805

*"There are Indian paths along the Missouri and some in other parts of the country. . .There are also roads and paths made by the buffaloe andother animals; some of the buffaloe roads are at least ten feet wide."*

### D William Clark
May 28, 1805

*"The Creek. . .I call Thompsons Creek after a valuable member of our party."*

### D Sgt. Ordway
May 30, 1805

*"we discover in many places old encampments of large bands of Indians, a fiew weeks past & appear to be makeing up the River."*

### T Judith Landing Historic District
40 miles from Big Sandy on Hwy. 236

This is the site of a trading post built by James Wells in 1882 in partnership with T.C Power and I.G. Baker of Fort Benton, developers of Fort Benton's leading commercial businesses in the 1860s through 1880s. The sandstone and granite building is one Montana's most historic buildings and stands at the landing. The post office, three ranch houses and the town's original log schoolhouse still stand. The buildings are on private property and must be viewed from a distance.

James Wells was a Pony Express rider, stagecoach driver, fur trapper and cattle rancher. He was married to a Gros Ventre Indian woman and became immersed in the customs of her tribe. Wells had great insight into the future of Montana, but could not have predicted the unjust treatment his Indian wife and children would receive after his death. The story of the development of Judith Landing and the Wells family is found in *"James Wells of Montana"* written by James A. Franks.

### T Missouri Breaks Backcountry Byway
Rte. 236, Winifred. 538-7461

This 81 mile loop starts in Winifred. Highlights along the route include the Lewis and Clark and Nez Perce national historic trails, C.M. Russell National Wildlife Refuge and a side trip to the free McClelland Ferry which crosses the Missouri River from April through October.

## 24. *Atraction*

### Geraldine

This town was named for the wife of Milwaukee Railroad executive William Rockerfeller. Nearby Winchell Springs was a long time stopping off point for travelers and was the water source for Geraldine until artesian wells were drilled in 1959. The stage coach stop at Winchell was called the Dew Drop Inn.

### T Square Butte Natural Area
Hwy.. 80, south of Geraldine. 538-7461

A scenic recreational area. This imposing rock butte is home to plentiful deer, elk, mountain goats and hawks. The flat topped butte stands 2,400 feet above the surrounding plains.

## 25. *Historical Marker*

### Geyser

This town began as an overnight stop on the stage route from Lewistown to Great Falls. It later became a railroad stop when the Great Northern was built from Billings to Great Falls. This area at the turn of the century was primarily a sheep ranching area dominated by the J. B. Long Sheep Company. Homesteaders, mainly Finnish, flooded the area lured here by offers of free land. The town got its name from a nearby bubbling mud springs. The geysers were most active during the dry years of the 1930s, but dried up when the rains returned and never came back.

## Powell "Pike" Landusky

Pike Landusky had a reputation as being one of the toughest fighters in the West. At one point, while trapping and trading with the Indians on the Musselshell River, he was captured by a war party of Brules. He began beating one of the warrior braves with a frying pan. The remaining party, awed by the violent spectacle, retreated and left two ponies to calm the wild man down. He later ran a trading post he called Lucky Fort on Flatwillow Creek in what is now Petroleum County. There, after a Piegan brave shot him and shattered his jaw, Landusky tore out the loose fragments of four broken teeth and threw them away.

In 1893 he and his partner, Bob Orman, found gold in the gulches of the Little Rockies and named their mine after the month. Believing they were on the Fort Belknap Indian Reservation they initially snuck the gold ore out at night. When they discovered they were a few miles south of the reservation, they relaxed their guard and word leaked out of the discovery. In a matter of months a gold rush was on and hundreds of miners flooded the area. A town was born.

Landusky's luck finally ran out when he had a showdown with "Kid" Curry. The Curry brothers lived five miles to the south and used Landusky as a trading center. "Kid Amby" Cheney, a local cowboy who witnessed the event tells the story:

"Pike was known as a mean devil. He always carried a gold headed, weighted cane and he used it often, sometimes hitting a bystander at the bar whether he was making trouble or not. Pike owned the Landusky Saloon and he had a business rival just across the street named 'Jew Jake,' a one-legged guy who had lost the other one in a shooting scrape in Great Falls. Jew Jake used his rifle as a crutch when he walked and kept it slung around his neck when he sat down. He used to sit out on the porch of his saloon waiting for some trouble with Pike. One day Kid Curry and Pike got into an argument: some say it was over a woman, others that it was over a plow that the Currys had borrowed from Pike and returned badly broken. The Kid was standing at the bar in Pike's saloon when the argument, began. Pike reached for his gun, but Curry was quicker on the draw and killed Landusky with the first shot. Curry escaped and by the time the sheriff had come from Fort Benton (200 miles away) the smoke had cleared away and the officer told the boys in Landusky that if they ever happened to see the Kid to tell him to come on in and give himself up. They wouldn't do much to him because of Pike's quarrelsome reputation. After Landusky's death, John Curry, one of the Kid's brothers, sort of throwed-in with Mrs. Landusky."

When Pike died, it is said that the townspeople buried him six feet deeper than usual and piled rocks on top of his grave so he couldn't get out. The rock is still there along with a carved wood grave marker.

# On the Trail of Lewis & Clark

**May 14, Tuesday:** Two events happened toward evening. Six men went after a bear. Two had to jump off a 20-foot cliff into the water to get away from him. He jumped in after them, but someone on shore fired and hit the bear in his brain. While butchering him, the men found that eight shots had passed through his body. Also the pirogue almost tipped over, losing some papers and medications. Sacajawea saved most of it. The hunters came in after dark. Lewis wrote: "*We thought it a proper occasion to console ourselves and cheer the sperits of our men and ac-cordingly took a drink of grog and gave each man a gill of sper-its.*" Traveled 16 1/2 miles and camped on the north side where they had the accident, a few miles above present Snow Creek.

**May 15, Wednesday:** Camped all day and tried to dry papers.

**May 16, Thursday:** Didn't get starte.d until about 4 P.M. Fired on a panther. Traveled seven miles and camped, probably on south side.

**May 17, Friday:** Passed Seven Blackfoot Creek just below camp. Clark saw some coal, a recently deserte.d Indian camp, and almost stepped on a rattlesnake. Traveled 20 1/2 miles. Camped on the south bank. Were awakened during the night by a fire, probably starte.d from their campfire. Just got moved when a burning tree fell where they had been.

**May 18, Saturday:** Traveled 21 miles and camped two miles up stream from the present Devil's Creek.

**May 19, Sunday:** Heavy fog, late start, Lewis's dog was bitten by a beaver. From a hill Clark saw the Musselshell River and the Little Rockies. Traveled 20 1/4 miles. Camped near or at site which was later Long Point.

**May 20, Monday:** Arrived at the Musselshell River about 11 a.m. and stopped for the day to make the necessary observations. It was 110 yards wide and entered the Missouri 2,270 miles from its mouth. At this point the Missouri was 222 yards wide.

**May 21, Tuesday:** They traveled 20 miles and camped on north side.

**May 22, Wednesday:** Stormed all night and morning. Did not get starte.d until 10 a.m. Traveled 16 1/2 miles, killed a bear and ren-dered lard. Camped on the north side just below the present Kannuck Creek.

**May 23, Thursday:** "*Set out early this morn-ing, the frost was severe last night, the ice appeared along the edge of the wa-ter, water also freized on the oars.... Just above the entrance of Teapot Creek on the stard. there is a large assemblage of the burrows of the Burrowing Squirrel.*"(prai-rie dog)"*The wild rose which is now in blume are very abundant.*" Traveled 27 miles. Camped on the north side, a little below the mouth of Rock (North Mountain) Creek in Phillips County.

**May 24, Friday:** They passed Rock Creek and camped about three miles above the present location of the Robinson Bridge on Highway 191.

## The Return

In the 1930's the largest hydraulically tilled earth dam in the world was built on the Missouri River, backing water up for about 134 miles and forming Fort Peck Lake (see Section 10). Fifteen Lewis and Clark campsites along this section of the river are now under lake water. The lake has many bays and inlets, giv-ing it 1,520 miles of shoreline (Elev. 2,234). It is surrounded by the Charles M. Russell National Wildlife Refuge.

On the return trip in 1806 Lewis and Clark separated on July 3. Clark would explore the Yellowstone River, Lewis would explore the Marias and retrace their route along the Missouri and pick up their cached materials. It was raining as Lewis and the 15 men who were with him entered the area that is now the Charles M. Russell National Wildlife Refuge. That night, July 31, [they] "*took shelter in some Indian lodges built of sticks, about 8 ms. below the entrance of North mountain creek... (Rock Creek, in Phillips County) ...these lodges appeared to have been built in the course of the last winter, these lodges with the addition of some Elk skins afforded us a good shelter from the rain which continued to fall powerful-ly all night.*"

**August 1:** Again they found shelter in aban-doned Indian lodges and stayed 2 days to dry out.

## Raynesford

This was the maiden name of a woman who pro-vided room and board for the Great Northern sur-vey crew while the railroad was under construction.

### H "Mining Plays Second Fiddle"

East of Geyser

*"MINING PLAYS SECOND FIDDLE—FOR THE FIRST TIME IN MONTANA'S HISTORY AGRICUL-TURAL PRODUCTS TAKE THE LEAD" Newspaper headlines in 1910 proclaimed the change brought about by settlement of more than one million acres of Montana land. By 1922 over 40% of the entire state would have claims filed on it.*

*This immediate area got a big influx of homestead-ers between 1900 and 1910. Many Finns settled the benchland northeast of here, thereafter called Finn Bench. Many of them got their stake in Montana as coal miners in Sand Coulee, Belt, or Stockett or as sil-ver miners in Neihart.*

*Once on the freight and stage route between Great Falls and Lewistown, Judith Basin was occupied mainly by a few stockgrowers before that homestead boom. Arrival of the Great Northern Railway in 1908 sig-naled the end of the isolated range. It advertised "Wheat—Forty Bushels to the Acre" and "Stockmen's Paradise Has Become the Home Builders Garden Spot" to attract farmers to stake their claims here. Great Northern was motivated by its need to fill its box cars for the return trips east. What better way than to pro-mote the government's free land to farmers who would have to ship their crops to eastern markets?*

## 26. *Lewis & Clark*

## Carter

This small community features one of the three remaining ferry crossings on the Missouri River.

### D William Clark

June 4, 1805

*"those who accompanied me were Serjt. Gass Jos: & Ruben Fields G. Shannon & my black man York, and we St out to examine the South fork. . .Struck the river at . . .13 miles at which place we encamped in an old Indian lodge made of sticks and bark"*

### D Mer. Lewis

July 28, 1806

*"we heared the report of several rifles very distinctly on the river to our right, we quickly repared to this joyfull sound and on arriving at the bank of the river had the unspeakable satisfaction to see our canoes coming down."*

## 27. *Historical Marker, Attraction, Gas, Food, Lodging, Shopping, Miscellaneous*

## Fort Benton

Fort Benton, one of the oldest communities in Montana, is built at the head of navigation on the Missouri River. The town operated as a major trading post for the American Fur Co. between 1850 to the late 1880s, and was the world's inner-most port. Here supplies were unloaded and taken on freight wagons to gold camps in Helena, Virginia City and other western locations within Montana. River rapids near Fort Benton prevented steamboats from going any further.

From 1860 to 1887, the town was known as "the toughest town in the West." Today it is the gateway for exploration of the Wild & Scenic Upper Missouri River.

The Grand Union Hotel, once the "finest hostelry between Seattle and the Twin Cities," was erected in 1882. This landmark hosted an array of guests who were stopping at the head of the Missouri, including Army officers, trappers, river captains, stockmen, missionaries and Indian agents. The hotel has been restored to its original grandeur for guests to enjoy today.

The lucrative trading diminished seemingly overnight when the Great Northern Railroad reached Helena in 1887. Ruins of the 250-foot square trading post and blockhouse still remain in the present-day tourist park; it is said that one wall on the back of the buildings was originally 32 feet thick. Many original buildings are still in use in Fort Benton.

### H Fort Benton

Fort Benton

*Capt. Clark with members of the Lewis and Clark Expedition camped on the site of Fort Benton June 4, 1805.*

*Originally a trading post of the American Fur Co., it became head of navigation on the Missouri with the arrival of the first steamboat from St. Louis in 1859. She boomed in the early 1860s as a point of entry to the newly discovered placer mines of western Montana. Supplies were freighted out by means of ox teams and profanity.*

*An early observer states, "Perhaps nowhere else were ever seen motlier crowds of daubed and feathered Indians, buckskin-arrayed halfbreed nobility, moc-casined trappers, voyageurs, gold seekers and bull driv-ers ... on the opening of the boating season...'*

### T Old Shep

City Park on the Missouri, Fort Benton.

The body of Shep's master was placed on a train

*Tepees line the shore across the river from Fort Benton.*

headed east for a burial. Old Shep was left behind. For over five years, Shep stayed at the depot on the northern edge of town waiting for his owner to return. He wore a mile-long trail to the

Missouri River where he would go for water. Sympathetic railyard workers fed him. He slept beneath one of the wooden platforms at the station. A story was published about the faithful canine and he became famous. Travelers would route their trips through Fort Benton just to get a look at the famous dog. Shep got so much fan mail that the station master hired a secretary just to handle it. Each day he would faithfully meet every train that arrived hoping to greet his absent master.

He may have waited longer if he hadn't slipped on an icy track one day and fallen under the wheels of a train in 1942. He was given a fitting funeral by hundreds of local citizens and buried on the hill above the depot. His casket was carried by the local boy scouts, a eulogy was read and "Taps" were played. A lot of tears fell that day. His grave and memorial can be seen from the old depot. A bronze statue of Shep was erected by the Great Northern Railroad on the levee on Front Street.

### T Museum of the Northern Great Plains

1205 20th St., Fort Benton. 622-5316

### T Museum of the Upper Missouri

City Park on the Missouri, Fort Benton. 622-3766

This museum focuses on the colorful history of Fort Benton which is depicted through dioramas, photos and many interesting artifacts. One such artifact is the rifle of Nez Perce leader Chief Joseph who surrendered to Colonel Nelson A. Miles at the Bear's Paw Battlefield. The museum highlights the important role Fort Benton played in the settlement of the American West as a trading post, military fort and head of steamboat navigation on the Missouri River. There is an admission fee to visit the museum which is open May to September. It is also available by appointment during other months.

### T Upper Missouri River Visitor Center

1718 Front St., Fort Benton. 622-5185

This riverfront center outlines the Lewis and Clark travels with archaeological displays and a multimedia presentation; maps of their campsites are also provided. It's a wonderful place to learn about the Missouri River, its history or obtain information concerning today's most popular activity—floating the river. Also, interpretive exhibits explain the historical impact the Missouri River has had on both this area and the entire nation.

### T Montana Agricultural Center & Museum

20th & Washington in Fort Benton. 622-5316

This is the largest agricultural museum in the state. The museum explores the culture, traditions and struggles of early settlers in the area. Exhibits include a variety of antique machinery and the Hornaday Buffalo on loan from the Smithsonian Institution. Open during the summer months or by appointment.

#### *Montana Trivia*

For 115 years the clock on the Fort Benton courthouse read 12:20. Seems that during the construction, the money ran out. The townsfolk put up a fake clock made of plywood. Schoolchildren of the town finally raised the $750 to put up a real clock.

### V Canoe Montana - Montana River Expeditions

1312 Front Street, Fort Benton. 622-5882 or toll free 800-500-4538. www.montanariver.com

Canoe Montana offers unique guided explorations of the Upper Missouri River Breaks National Monument. Your adventure begins in Fort Benton, a town which has prevailed in western history for over 200 years. Experience the river as Lewis and Clark did, while retreating into the splendor of Montana's great natural wonders. Guided expeditions are designed for people with no canoeing, kayaking, or camping experience. Safety will be a priority as you learn to paddle, read the river, and spot wildlife, while sharing Canoe Montana's commitment to the preservation of the pristine beauty of Montana's rivers and the earth. Their goal is to provide each guest with a relaxed and memorable experience, while luxurious camping methods have been perfected to minimize the impact of human contact. Visit their web site to learn more.

### V Double Circle Ranch Hayride

453 Double Circle Lane, east of Fort Benton. 622-3875

The Double Circle Ranch hayrides will make you feel like you are stepping into the Old West. The Tweets enjoy sharing their ranch with guests while providing a safe, pleasant visit rich in Western ranching heritage. In addition to ranch livestock, you'll see deer, water fowl and an occasional pheasant. Draft horses pulling the wagon will take you moseying along the Shonkin Creek to the Missouri River while you obsrve a working ranch from the inside. The mouth of Shonkin Creek was once the location of a construction yard for mackinaws. The Tweets also cater to private parties with sizzling steak fries. Everyone is welcome. Find them at on Hwy. 80 over the Missouri River Bridge just past mile marker 4.

### F Bob's Riverfront Restaurant

1414 Front Street, Fort Benton. 622-3443

Bobs Riverfront Restaurant takes home-style cooking to a new level. Daily home-cooked specials are

Section 11

## Montana Trivia

The first dinosaur fossil ever found in the western hemisphere was a single tooth of a Troodon found near the Judith River east of Fort Benton in 1854

offered for breakfast, lunch and dinner. They even make their own wonderful orange marmalade and sun tea. The meats served are hand-cut to order. Hamburgers are served on homemade hoagie buns, that are baked fresh daily along with pies, pastries and muffins. Bob's Riverfront is located in the center of downtown with scenic views of the Missouri River. An interesting collection of historic photos, including a portrait of Old Shep, are displayed for your enjoyment. Catering is offered and there is a Back Alley Banquet Room available for large groups up to 40 people.

### F Trailhead Pizza Pro
809 14th Street, Fort Benton. 622-3324
or fax 622-5538

### FL The Grand Union Hotel & Restaurant
1 Grand Union Square, Ft. Benton. 622-1882 or 888- 838-1882

Listed on the National Register of Historic Places and elegantly restored to its 1882 splendor, the Grand Union commands impressive views of the Missouri River where long ago Lewis & Clark traveled and broad bottom steamboats docked. The 27 guest rooms have been exquisitely renovated with luxurious private baths, phones, voicemail, cable television and individually controlled heat and air conditioning. A European breakfast is provided. Meet new friends in the Saloon or relax in the lobby. The Grand Union is also the perfect setting for group meetings, conferences or private receptions. You'll also enjoy the Grand Union's riverside restaurant.

### L Pioneer Lodge
1700 Front Street, Fort Benton. 622-5441
or 800-622-6088.
www.fortbenton.com/accomodation/PioneerLodge

## Montana Trivia

In 1859 the first steamboat arrived in Fort Benton. In 1862, four made the trip. At the peak of steamboat travel in 1867 thirty-nine came. The last one came in 1888. The railroads killed the steamboat business. Approximately twenty percent of the steamboats that left St. Louis bound for Fort Benton via the Missouri River never made it back.

### S RJ's Toggery & Liquor Store
1506 Front Street, Benton. 622-5130

### M Fort Benton Realty, LLP
1512 Front Street, Fort Benton. 622-3803
or fax 622-3464. www.fbrealty.com

Historic Fort Benton sits on the banks of the Missouri River and is located just 40 miles northeast of Great Falls. Fort Benton is a rural agricultural community with strong ties to Montana's grand beginnings and fascinating history. Fort Benton Realty specializes in Farm & Ranch, Commercial, Residential and 1031 Exchanges and serves the Golden Triangle area. They have agents throughout the state to assist in all of your real estate needs. Their office is located just across the street from the walking bridge over the Missouri River. Stop in and visit with their friendly staff or give them a call. Fort Benton Realty has an up-to-date, comprehensive web site that offers information and photos on their available properties.

## 28. *Historical Marker, Lewis & Clark, Attraction, Gas, Food, Lodging, Shopping*

### Loma

This is near one of the recorded campsites of the Lewis and Clark Expedition. They camped here on June 3, 1805, and named the smaller river here after a cousin of Capt. Lewis, Maria Wood. In 1831, James Kipp of the American Fur Co. established Fort Piegan here. The fort was abandoned a year later when it was burned by Indians. It was replaced shortly after by Fort McKenzie. For many years there was a ferry here.

### H A Montana Crossroads
northeast of Loma

*The Missouri River once flowed northeasterly through this valley to Hudson Bay. During the Bull Lake Ice Age, an ice dam near Loma diverted the river into its current channel. This channel began filling with glacial sediment, preventing the river from returning to its original course when the dam finally broke about 70,000 to 130,000 years ago. Several sections of the highway between Loma and Havre follow Big Sandy Creek, which is located in the old river channel.*

*From this point you also have a panoramic view of the drainages of three major Montana river systems: the Teton, Marias and Missouri. To the southwest, the Teton and Marias Rivers merge near Loma before joining the Missouri about a mile downstream. In the background are the Bear's Paw Mountains to the east, Square Butte and Round Butte to the southeast, the Highwood Mountains toward the south, and the Little Belt Mountains in the southwest.*

*Because of the geography, this area was the crossroads for many events important to Montana history. The Lewis and Clark Expedition passed through here in 1805. They were followed by fur traders, the steamboats, the Great Northern Railway and the homesteaders.*

### H Marias River
Loma

*The Lewis and Clark Expedition camped at the mouth of this river just east of here June 3, 1805. Lewis named it Maria's River in honor of his cousin, Miss Maria Wood (over time the apostrophe was dropped) Until exploration proved otherwise, most members of the party believed this river to be the main channel of the Missouri.*

*On his return trip from the coast in 1806 Capt. Lewis explored the Marias almost to its source.*

*In the fall of 1831 James Kipp of the American Fur Co. built Fort Piegan at the mouth of the river, as a trading post for the Blackfoot Indians, and acquired 2,400 beaver "plews" or skins by trade during the first 10 days. In 1832 the post was abandoned and the Indians burned it.*

### H Great Northern Railway
Milepost 51 on U.S. 87 south of Loma

*The railroad grade you see before you was the St. Paul, Minneapolis and Manitoba Railway, a precursor of the Great Northern Railway. James J. Hill, owner and builder, constructed this line in record time in 1887 to serve wealthy mining communities. There he offered more competitive freight rates to take business away from the Northern Pacific and Union Pacific transcontinental railroads.*

*As railroads competed for ascendancy, Montana's cities vied for transportation facilities. Fort Benton had prospered as the head of steamboat navigation and the hub of freight and stage lines to settlements in Montana, Idaho and Canada. As railroads replaced steamboats as carriers, this line bypassed Fort Benton, ending its economic importance in transportation. This line went directly to Great Falls, enabling that city to grow as an industrial and rail center.*

### D William Clark
June 3, 1805

*"the wild rose which grows here in great abundance in the bottoms of all these rivers is now in full bloom, and adds not a little to the beaty of the cenery.."*

### D William Clark
June 3, 1805

"An interesting question was now to be deter-

## Ferries Across the Missouri

Just when it look's like you'll never get to the other side of the Missouri, help is on its way. Catch a ferry at three different locations along Hwy.. 87. The state owned ferries are free, but tips sure help keep the operators happy. The ferries make about 6 trips a day during the summer. It's not for those travelers that are in a rush, but you'll get there safely and enjoy a unique experience in the process.

The ferries are best suited for an average size car or maybe two. They each run on two cables, one for power, and one to keep them from floating downstream. Your RV will make the trip and crossing at Virgelle and Carte.r, but the road to the landing at McClelland is probably too steep and rough to bother trying.

Carter is 20 miles northeast of Great Falls off Hwy. 87, 734-5335. Virgelle is 30 miles northeast of Fort Benton on Hwy. 87, 378-3194. The McClelland ferry is 45 miles north of Lewistown on Rd. 300, 462-5513.

*mined; which of these rivers was the Missouri. . .the utmost circumspection and caution was necessary in deciding on the stream to be taken."*

### D Mer. Lewis
June 6, 1805

*"I now became will convinced that this branch of the Missouri had it's direction too much to the North for our rout to the Pacific"*

### D Mer. Lewis
June 5, 1805

*"it is astonishing what a quantity of water it takes to saturate the soil of this country."*

### D Mer. Lewis
June 7, 1805

*"I now laid myself down on some willow boughs to a comfortable nights rest, and felt indeed as if I was fully repaid for the toil and pain of the day, so much will a good shelter, a dry bed, and comfortable supper revive the speirts of the waryed, wet and hungry traveler."*

### T Lewis & Clark Decision Point
US Hwy. 87, Loma

This is certainly one of the most historic spots in America and is a must see for Lewis and Clark history buffs. When Lewis and Clark arrived at this point, the Marias River was flooding. They were uncertain which of these two branches was the main channel of the Missouri. They made the decision to split up and each explore a branch until they were sure which was the Missouri. After nine days of exploring they chose what turned out to be the correct channel. Enjoy a short walk on a trail that leads to an overlook on the Missouri and Marias rivers. Loma now sits at that confluence 11 miles north of Fort Benton. Interpretive exhibits are provided.

History also records a fort built at or near this spot called Fort Pigeon. It was probably built prior to Fort Benton.

Another event that occurred here is the founding of the town of Ophir. In the early days, steamboats would stop here to unload freight and transport it overland to Fort Benton. The river was too shallow to go any further during certain times of the year. Some entrepreneurs decided to build a city here to compete with Fort Benton for the trade coming up the river. One day while the work crew of eleven men were constructing the site, they were all killed. No one knows for sure who killed them. Some think Blackfeet Indians. Others think it may have been a group from Fort Benton who wished to stop the project for good. Whatever happened, the town was never completed.

To get to this site, turn south on the gravel road just past the Marias Bridge at Loma. Drive a short distance to the pole fence which opens to a parking lot. The overlook is just a short distance on a well maintained path.

### T House of One Thousand Dolls
106 1st St., Loma. 739-4338

A small and unusual privately owned museum has a wonderful collection of dolls and toys dating back to the 1830s to the present. Open seasonally or by appointment.

### T Richard Wood Watchable Wildlife Area
Hwy. 87, 5 miles south of Loma

A wildlife enhancement area adjacent to the Missouri and Marias Rivers.. Plenty of waterfowl here including geese and pelicans. Have the kids watch for turtles, beavers and muskrats along the river shore. Winter offers an opportunity to see



bald and golden eagles. Wildlife viewing opportunities area available all year round. The area provides opportunities for hiking, biking, and boating. Several dirt roads traverse the area.

### T Earth Science Museum
106 Main St., Loma. 739-4224

This museum is home to a large collection of rocks, fossils and minerals with parts of the museum displaying hands-on exhibits for children. There is also an excellent collection of train memorabilia and Indian artifacts. Of special interest are items found along the Fort Benton to Fort Assinniboine Trail.

## 29. *Lewis & Clark, Attraction*

### Virgelle
Virgelle is the site of one of three ferries that still cross the Missouri River. It is a popular launch point for float trips on the "Wild and Scenic Missouri River" stretch.

### D Mer. Lewis
May 31, 1805

*"The hills and river Clifts which we passed today exhibit a most romantic appearance. The bluffs of the river rise to the hight of from 2 to 300 feet and in most places nearly perpendicular; they are formed of remarkable white sandstone."*

### D Pvt. Whitehouse
June 1, 1805

*"And there lies some handsome barren plains, which lay a small distance back from the River. We saw likewise here Mountains, which lay a short distance from the River, on the North side, and some Mountains, lying on the South side of the River, at a considerable distance up it."*

### D Mer. Lewis
July, 29, 1806

*"the river is now nearly as high as ithas been this season and is so thick with mud and san that it is with difficulty I can drink it."*

### T Upper Missouri National Wild and Scenic River
538-7461

If you enjoy float trips, this is one of the best. The Upper Missouri stretches 149 miles down river from Fort Benton. Lewis and Clark explored this river and camped on its banks. Some of the highlights along the route include the scenic White Cliffs area, Citadel Rock, Hole in the Wall, Lewis and Clark Camp at Slaughter River, abandoned homesteads and abundant wildlife. There are commercial boat tours, shuttle services and rentals at Fort Benton and Virgelle.

## 30. *Attraction, Gas, Food*

### Big Sandy
The Blackfeet Indians called the creek running near this town Un-es-putcha-eka which translated to "Big Sandy Creek" and the town was named for the creek. This is one of the more colorful towns of the Old West. Novelist B.M. Bower lived here and used this town as the model for "Dry Lake" in her Flying U novels. Charles Russell worked on some of the nearby ranches.

John Willard, in his book Adventure Trails in Montana writes, "Big Sandy was a cow town of long tradition and a freighting center when goods were unloaded at the Coal Banks Landing just south of here on the Missouri River. Materials for Fort Assiniboine were delivered at Coal Banks by river steamer, then freighted overland to the fort."

The railroad found the water source to its liking and erected a water tower nearby along with the McNamara freight depot. History records that a saloon was opened in a tent near McNamara and Marlow's freight depot in 1886 followed soon after by another saloon, the Log Cabin. These two depots, the saloons (nine in all—mostly tents with wood floors), a warehouse, and a boxcar that the section foreman lived in made up the beginnings of the town. As the town grew, and the number of cowboys, settlers, and railroad men increased, the Spokane Hotel was built to accommodate the increased traffic.

By 1912 the town was booming with homesteaders and the Great Northern Railroad moved its depot into town. Before that a horse-drawn shuttle bus carted passengers to and from the train a short distance away. The 1-1/2 mile ride cost a mere 50¢. By 1919, the homesteader boom was a bust. Many sold out and moved on. Those that stayed bought what the others sold and became sustainable sized farms.

### T A Gathering of Memories Museum
Just west of Hwy.. 87 near the center of Big Sandy.

This museum's displays chronicle the history of the Big Sandy area. It is housed in the old Burlington Northern Dept. When you first enter the old B.N. waiting room, your first impression is that there is little more to see. Even entering the old freight room area, you still wonder what there is to see here. It is the newer portion of the building that houses the bulk of the display area.

Walking into this section you feel you just

## The Trail of Clubfoot George

(This article is reprinted from a 1930s news clipping)

When during the winter of 1864-65 a band of Gros Ventres Indians discovered the trail of Clubfoot George Boyd in the snow in the Milk River country and ascertained that it was headed towards Fort Benton, they thought it was that of an evil spirit. They made an emergency ride to the Fort to warn the white men there that a demon was coming to their place. But they arrived too late.

The Indians' finding of Boyd's trail and their belief that it was that of an evil spirit attended a long, lonely, dangerous trek Boyd made on foot from Fort Pierre in the Dakotas to Fort Benton, at the behest of the American Fur Co., which had trading posts at both places. The post at Fort Pierre ran out of sugar, a very serious shortage because it was one of the things which the Indian customers were very fond of, using it to sweeten the tea which the traders had taught them to brew and drink.

There was no hope of obtaining a new supply before navigation opened in the spring, and it would be impossible to go to get it then unless a messenger was dispatched to Fort Benton with a request that a supply be on the first river boat after the ice had gone out. The bulk of supplies came from St. Louis, but the upstream boats would not arrive until much later, whereas a boat would be dispatched down river from Fort Benton with furs at the earliest possible date.

The journey from Fort Pierre to Fort Benton would have to be made on foot and was attended by many perils, not the least of which were from being lost, frozen, killed by Indians, or attacked by wild animals in some lonely night camp. There was at the post, however, a man equal to the occasion. It was George Boyd. Although handicapped by nature with two club feet, he was as fearless, as resourceful and as intrepid as any pioneer of the period. He left a remarkable trail, but his enemies, both red and white, found it a good trail not to follow. He volunteered to make the trip.

With his bed blankets in a back pack, and his rifle, he set out one day on his lonely tramp. He relied upon his gun to supply him with food.

When an Indian brave of a hunting party of Gros Ventres discovered George's trail in the snow along the Milk River, he gazed at it long and wonderingly. He had roamed that country for many years, but had never before seen tracks like these. He called his hunting companions together, and after inspecting the trail they held council.

The more they gazed upon George's trail, the more bewildered and fearful they became. Those tracks, they felt sure, had been made by an evil spirit embodied in some animal hitherto unknown to them. They abandoned their hunting, returned to the main camp and consulted the medicine man.

That worthy communed with himself for 24 hours before announcing that he would provide the bravest warriors with charms to ward off the influence of the evil spirit, or failing that, to guarantee them good hunting in the Happy Hunting Grounds.

Thus equipped, a party of braves starte....d to follow the strange trail to death or glory. In the meantime, George had a good start and had reached Fort Benton. Not many hours later the party of Gros Ventres hove in sight and their head man asked for a conference with the chief of the fort. To him the Indians confided they had come to warn the white men of an evil spirit they had trailed there from their own country. By signs and with gesticulations they endeavored to explain the nature of the trail they had followed. Presently one of their audience exclaimed, "I'll bet they have been following George Boyd's trail."

Boyd was called. When he stumped into the room, the Indians gazed at him in astonishment for several minutes. They then turned and filed slowly from the room.

*Source; Roosevelt County's Treasured Years 1976) Reprinted with permission from the "Outlaw News," a publication of Missouri River Country.*

entered a secret tomb filled with buried treasure. A 40 foot mural by Vernon The Boy depicts a scene from a Native American encampment. There is a turn-of-the-century schoolhouse, a homestead shack, a general store. The store is well stocked with day-to-day items such as foot warmers and charcoal burning irons. Antique boxes of Corn Flakes sit with early toasters.

A "stone boat" is displayed along with numerous mannequins in period dress. A trappers cabin and a "McClellan Saddle" are also on display. A crank style telephone hangs just a few feet from a cylinder record player. Standing in the corner is a horse and buggy complete with fringe and life-size horse.

## 31.

### Box Elder

The town's name came from the name of the creek it sits on. The banks are lined with Box Elder trees, thus the name. At the end of the 1880s the railroad moved 40 families from Ohio to settle the area. They didn't last long and after the hot dry summers of 1889 and 1890 only two families remained. Today the town is the headquarters for the Rocky Boy Reservation.

### M Stone Child College

Box Elder, 395-4313,
www.montana.edu/~www.ai/scc

Stone Child College is a tribally-controlled community college of the Chippewa-Cree Tribe, offering programs fro Associates of Arts and Associate of Science degrees and certificates. Chartered in 1984 and dedicated to meeting the needs of and promoting the pride in each tribal member's Chippewa-Cree heritage. The College is located at the Rocky Boy Agency, 14 miles from Box Elder, Montana. Approximate enrollment is 280 students.

## 32.

### Rocky Boy's Reservation

Hwy. 87, west of Box Elder, 395-4282

The Rocky Boy's R eservation is home to about 2,500 members of the Chippewa-Cree tribe. The name came from the name of a leader of a band of Chippewa Indians. The Indian name meant "stone boy" but the meaning was lost in the translation from Chippewa to English and it evolved to "Rocky Boy." The Bear Paw Mountains on the reservation provide a sharp contrast to the flat bottomlands of the rest of the reservation. The reservation was established in 1916.

### *Montana Trivia*

Thomas Jefferson paid the French three cents per acre in 1803 for the Louisanna Purchase. Today, the average price per acre of Montana crop land is $502.

## Scenic Drives

### Fred Robinson Bridge Tour

The Fred Robinson Bridge over the Missouri River is approximately 70 miles south of Malta on Highway 191. Looking from the bridge you are viewing much of the same scenery that Lewis and Clark viewed when passing through this area. On May 23, 1805, the Corps of Discovery camped about seven miles downstream from this spot. While their journals are vague on this, they viewed from the hills above the campsite the Little Rocky Mountains about 25 miles to the northwest. They camped the next day about 2 miles upstream from the bridge.

While most of northeastern Montana witnessed the "Old West," this area experienced the "Wild West." Outlaws, vigilantes, sprawling ranches, frontier towns, gold mines, trappers, cowboys, and steamboats were all a part of this colorful era.

From the bridge you can start exploring the backroads of the C.M. Russell Wildlife Refuge. James Kipp Park is near the bridge and has camping facilities. Head up the hill to the south to the Slippery Ann Wildlife Station and refuge office. The name Slippery Ann is a corrupted spelling of the fur trader, Cyprian Mat. In the late 1880s he was the proprietor of a trading post just south of the Little Rockies.

An excellent 20-mile long self guided tour starts here. The duty personnel here can give you a map and information about the tour. This tour will take you near Lewis and Clark's May 22, 1805, campsite as well as two frontier towns—Rocky Point and Carroll. Make sure you carry plenty of water with you on the refuge. There is very little, if any, drinking water available on the refuge.

When you're finished at the refuge go back to Highway 191 and head north. You will rise out of the Missouri Breaks and soon catch a view of the Little Rocky Mountains, arguably one of the most colorful and storied mountain ranges in the west. When you reach the Highway 66 junction, take a left and go a short distance to the old mining town of Landusky.

The town was named for Pike Landusky, a brutish character who roamed the territory in search of gold in the late 1800s (see sidebar).

When you're finished in Landusky, backtrack to Highway 191 and continue north about 20 miles to the turnoff to Zortman. If you're in the mood, there are backroads and trails from here that will take you high into the hills where you can get some great views of the surrounding prairies.

Leaving Zortman and heading north on 191

CATTLE BRANDS
Many a dogie# (not "doggie" -dudes please note) has been decorated with one of these famous Montana irons.
CA Running CA
79 Seventy nine
DS DHS
Three circle
N-N N bar N
Turkey track
Hat X
777 Three sevens
N bar
Pitch fork
Fish hook
Piece of pie
CK
IX
JO
Bug
Circle C
Monogram SH
R Bar R
Flying D
Long X
Bull head
Two dot
IX Inverted TX
Hash knife
2A Two A bar
Mill iron
O Circle
LO
OW
VM Seven VM
Shaving mug
40 Forty
LU L U bar
Umbrella
Spearhead
Rocking Chair
Antler
VVV Three V's
Hour glass
Rafter circle
W W bar
U Lazy J
707
XIT
Square & Compass
Quarter circle U
Lazy H hanging 2
Reversed E 2 bar
Lazy P swinging 9
Two pole pumpkin
7-7 Seven bar seven
Monogram FUF
Railroad track
Monogram PLE
Horseshoe bar
Circle diamond
Maltese cross
SL
WM
#A dogie is a little calf who has lost its mammy and whose daddy has run off with another cow.

*Historical marker south of Malta.*

you will cross the trail of the legendary "Long Drives" of Longhorn cattle that Texans drove 1,800 miles to winter in Montana. You'll soon enter the Milk River Valley and reach the ranching town of Malta.

### Ranching Country and Milk River Route

This tour through this section's northeast country begins in Malta on U.S. Highway 2, the Hi-Line highway. This tour will take you through unique prairie country, and a mix of beautiful canyons, benchlands, and river bottoms. Head north on Highway 242 for about 16 miles. Here you will find a side road that climbs to a high point. The view from here is spectacular. To the east you will see the Milk River and its banks lined with cottonwoods. To the west are the canyons of Cottonwood Creek. If you follow this road for about four to six miles, you will be treated to a view of the deep gorge to the north of Little Cottonwood Creek Canyon.

Return to the main highway and head north to Loring. After stopping in the little community of Loring head back south on 242 for about 20 miles. Turn left on a road that stretches east through the Milk River valley for about 23 miles to Highway 243. On the way, you'll pass the Hewitt Lake National Wildlife Refuge and an access road to Nelson Reservoir. This is one of the region's most popular recreation areas for both water sports and fishing. On this road, you will see more deer and antelope than people.

When you reach Highway 243, turn right to Saco. From Saco, you can go several directions. Continue through Saco to the Larb Hills. Stories have been told of cowboys roping grizzly bears here for amusement. Of course, there are no longer grizzly bears in this part of the state. Head west to the Nelson Reservoir and the nearby Sleeping Buffalo Resort. Or continue back toward Malta and visit the Bowdoin National Wildlife Refuge about 8 miles east of Malta.

## Hikes

### Beaver Creek Park

**Rotary Falls and Canyon Hike**
Just to the north of Bear Paw Lake is a great area for hiking. Crude trails in the canyon on both sides of Beaver Creek can be accessed from the dam, the Beaver Creek Hwy.. just north of the lake at the bottom of Rotary Hill, or by side roads above the canyon. The canyon is spectacular and Rotary Falls is beautiful year round.

**Mount Otis**
This gentle winding set of switchbacks begin at Mooney's Coulee and meanders to the top of Mount Otis. The trail was originally built by the CCC in the 1930s and is still in excellent condition. While it is a climb, the numerous switchbacks make it a relatively gentle climb. The trail moves around all four sides of the mountain offering beautiful views and at times meanders beside a lush fir forest on the north side of the mountain. To get there drive up the Beaver Creek Hwy.. past the Taylor Road turn to a marked coulee called Mooney's Coulee. Drive up the coulee to the marked trail head sign on the north side of the road.

**Beaver Creek Trail**
The Beaver Creek Trail is the name of the first road through the upper reaches of Beaver Creek Park. The road hangs above the valley floor and goes several miles to the Rocky Boy's Reservation. From there it continues almost to Baldy. After an initial gain in elevation, the trail levels out all the way through the park. This trail will take you to some of the best berry picking in the park. The best place to access this trail is from the Lion's Group Picnic area shelter. The trail is just above the valley floor to the west.

**Blackie Coulee Overlook Trail**
This hike is arguably the most beautiful in the park. The only catch is you have to work to find the trail. Blackie Coulee is the last coulee to the east of the park before it joins the Rocky Boy's Reservation. Cross the Beaver Creek ford in the middle of a camping area, and start up the narrow and winding road. Watch closely after going up a steep hill for a culvert fording Blackie Creek. Stop here. A clearly marked trail heads through a meadow and hillside to the north and winds up at an overlook with incredible views of the Beaver Creek valley. There is a mysterious rock monument at the vista point. Similar to one sheepherders might use to mark hills, this one is larger and there have never been sheep in Beaver Creek Park. While it is difficult to find, it is worth the effort.

### Glasgow Area

**Bitter Creek Badlands**
There really are no trails here, but it's really tough to get lost in this open country. Walking across this open country gives you a feel of what early Indians or explorers may have seen when they first walked this land. Watch for sage and sharp-tailed grouse. Drive west of Glasgow on Hwy.. 2 for about 20 miles or East from Hinsdale for about 5 miles to Britsch Road. This is opposite the turnoff to Vandalia. Head north for 17 miles. Signs will direct you to the Wildlife viewing area. Park on the side of the road and explore.

## Information Please

All Montana area codes are 406

### Road Information

Montana Road Condition Report
800-226-7623, 800-335-7592 or local 444-7696
Montana Highway Patrol 444-7696

**Local Road Reports**

| | |
|---|---|
| Havre | 265-1416 |
| Great Falls | 453-1605 |
| Glasgow Weather Reports | 228-4042 |
| Great Falls Weather Reports | 453-5469 |
| Statewide Weather Reports | 453-2081 |

### Tourism Information

Travel Montana 800-847-4868 outside Montana
444-2654 in Montana
http://travel.mt.gov/.
Russell Country 761-5036 or 800-527-5348
Missouri River Country
653-1319 or 800-653-1319
Northern Rodeo Association 252-1122

**Chambers of Commerce**

| | |
|---|---|
| Big Sandy | 378-3220 |
| Chester | 759-5215 |
| Chinook | 357-2100 |
| Fort Benton | 622-3864 |
| Fort Belknap Reservation | 353-2205 |
| Havre | 265-4383 |
| Malta | 654-1776 |
| Saco | 527-3218 |

### Airports

| | |
|---|---|
| Big Sandy | 378-2534 |
| Chester | 759-5116 |
| Chinook | 357-2429 |
| Denton | 567-2571 |
| Fort Belknap | 353-2205 |
| Fort Benton | 622-5249 |
| Geraldine | 737-4286 |
| Harlem | 353-2305 |
| Havre | 265-1129 |
| Hinsdale | 364-2272 |
| Hogeland | 379-2582 |
| Malta | 654-1021 |
| Turner | 379-2303 |
| Winifred | 462-5425 |

### Government Offices

State BLM Office 255-2885, 238-1540
Bureau of Land Management

Section 11

*Somewhere south of Malta.*

| | |
|---|---|
| Havre Field Office | 265-5891 |
| Lewistown Field Office | 538-7461 |
| Malta Field Office | 654-1240 |
| Great Falls Field Office | 791-7700 |
| Montana Fish, Wildlife & Parks | 454-5840 |
| Army Corps of Engineers | 526-3411 |
| U.S. Bureau of Reclamation Tiber Field Office | 456-3226 |
| Charles M. Russell National Wildlife Refuge | 538-8706 |
| Benton Lake National Wildlife Refuge | 727-7400 |
| Bowdoin National Wildlife Refuge | 654-2863 |

## Hospitals

| | |
|---|---|
| Big Sandy Medical Center • Big Sandy | 932-5917 |
| Liberty County Hospital • Chester | 759-5181 |
| Missouri River Medical Center Fort Benton | 622-3331 |
| Northern Montana Hospital • Havre | 265-2211 |
| Phillips County Hospital • Malta | 654-1100 |

## Golf Courses

| | |
|---|---|
| Chinook Golf & Country Club Chinook | 357-2112 |
| Signal Point Golf Club • Fort Benton | 622-3666 |
| Beaver Creek Golf Course Pro Shop Havre | 265-4201 |

## Bed and Breakfasts

| | |
|---|---|
| Long's Landing B&B Fort Benton | 622-3461 |
| Our Home B&B • Havre | 265-1055 |
| West Prairie Inn B&B • Havre | 265-7281 |

## Guest Ranches and Resorts

| | |
|---|---|
| Beaver Creek • Malta | 658-2111 |
| Rock Creek lodge • Hinsdale | 648-5524 |
| Tillman's • Malta | 658-2154 |
| Whiskey Ridge Lodge • Winifred | 462-5514 |

## Private Campgrounds

| | |
|---|---|
| **Edgewater Inn & Campground** • Malta | 654-1302 |
| Evergreen Campground • Havre | 265-8228 |
| Bear Paw Court • Chinook | 357-2221 |
| Emporium Food & Fuel Store • Havre | 265-8861 |
| Havre RV Park & Travel Park • Havre | 265-8861 |

## Car Rental

| | |
|---|---|
| Power Motors Ford-Mercury | 622-3321 |
| Budget Rent-A-Car of Havre | 265-1156 |
| Havre Ford | 265-2246 |
| Rent A Wreck | 265-1481 |
| Tilleman Motor Company | 265-7865 |
| Delta Ford | 654-1850 |

## Outfitters & Guides

*F=Fishing H=Hunting R=River Guides*
*E=Horseback Rides G=General Guide Services*

| | | |
|---|---|---|
| **Canoe Montana** | GR | 622-5882 |
| Big Sky Trails | HFE | 654-1989 |
| Heartland | HF | 674-5271 |
| Little Rockies Outfitting | HF | 673-3559 |
| L S Adventures | H | 357-2300 |
| Missouri River Outfitters | R | 622-3295 |
| Montana Breaks Outfitting | H | 6524-2259 |
| Montana Prairie Adventures | HFR | 654-1649 |
| Montana Wilderness Outfitters | HF | 538-6516 |
| Rock Creek Outfitters | H | 648-5524 |

| Fishery | Cold Water Species | | | | | | | | | | | | Warm Water Species | | | | | | | | | | Services | | | | | |
|---|---|---|---|---|---|---|---|---|---|---|---|---|---|---|---|---|---|---|---|---|---|---|---|---|---|---|---|
| | Brook Trout | Mt. Whitefish | Lake Whitefish | Golden Trout | Cutthroat Trout | Brown Trout | Rainbow Trout | Kokanee Salmon | Bull Trout | Lake Trout | Arctic Grayling | Burbot | Largemouth Bass | Smallmouth Bass | Walleye | Sauger | Northern Pike | Shovelnose Sturgeon | Channel Catfish | Yellow Perch | Crappie | Paddlefish | Vehicle Access | Campgrounds | Toilets | Docks | Boat Ramps | MotorRestrictions |
| 171. Marias River | | • | | | | • | • | | | | | • | | • | • | • | • | • | • | | | | • | • | • | | • | |
| 172. Missouri River | | • | | | | • | • | | | | | • | | • | • | • | • | • | • | | | • | • | • | • | • | • | • |
| 173. Beaver Creek | • | | | | • | • | • | | | | | | | | | | | | | | | | • | • | • | | | |
| 174. Bearpaw Lake | | | | | • | | • | | | | | | | | | | | | | | | | • | • | • | | | • |
| 175. Grasshopper Reservoir | | | | | | | • | | | | | | | | | | | | | | | | • | | | | | • |
| 176. Faber Reservoir | | | | | | | • | | | | | | | | | | | | | | | | • | | • | | | • |
| 177. Milk River | | | • | | | | • | | | | | • | | • | • | • | • | | | • | | | • | • | • | | | |
| 178. Reser Reservoir | | | | | | | • | | | | | | • | | | | | | | • | • | | • | | | | | |
| 179. Beaver Creek Reservoir | | | | | | | • | | | | | | | | • | | • | | | • | | | • | • | • | | • | • |
| 180. Bailey Reservoir | | | | | | | | | | | | | • | | | | • | | | • | | | • | | • | | • | • |
| 181. Fresno Reservoir | | | • | | | | | | | | | | | | • | | • | | | • | | | • | • | • | | • | |
| 182. Milk River | | | | | | | | | | | | | | • | • | • | • | • | • | • | | • | • | • | • | | | |
| 183. Nelson Reservoir | | | | | | | | | | | | | | | • | | • | | | • | | | • | • | • | | • | |

## Public Campgrounds

# Campsite Directions

| Campsite Directions | Season | Camping | Trailers | Toilets | Water | Boat Launch | Fishing | Swimming | Trails | Stay Limit | Fee |
|---|---|---|---|---|---|---|---|---|---|---|---|
| **222•Kremlin USBR**<br>W of Havre on US 2•2 mi. N on Cty. Rd. | All Year | • | | C | | • | • | | | 14 | |
| **223•Kiehns USBR**<br>W of Havre on US 2•2 mi. N on Cty. Rd. | All Year | • | • | D | | • | • | | | 14 | |
| **224•Fresno Beach USBR**<br>W of Havre on US 2•2 mi. N on Cty. Rd. | All Year | | | D | | C | • | • | | 14 | |
| **225•River Run USBR**<br>W of Havre on US 2•2 mi. N on Cty. Rd. | All Year | • | | B | | | • | | | 14 | |
| **226•Coalbanks BLM**<br>11 mi. S of Big Sandy on US 87•S at sign for Upper Missouri Wild & Scenic River | All Year | 10 | 24' | • | | C | • | | | 14 | |
| **227•Thain Creek FS**<br>6 mi. E of Great Falls on US 89•13 mi. E on Rt. 228•16 mi. E on Cty. Rd. 121 •2 mi. E on Forest Rd. 8840 | Summer | 20 | 22' | d | • | | • | | • | 14 | • |
| **228•Judith landing BLM**<br>26 mi. NW of Winifred on Rt. 236 | 515-10/15 | 10 | 48' | • | • | C | • | | | 14 | |
| **229•James Kipp BLM**<br>64 mi. NE of Lewistown on US 191 | 4/1-12/1 | 34 | 48' | • | • | C | • | | • | 14 | • |
| **230•Crooked Creek CE**<br>48 mi. NE of Winnett on Cty. Rd.•429-2999 | All Year | | | • | | | | | | 14 | |
| **231•Montana Gulch BLM**<br>1 mi. S of Landusky on Cty. Rd. | All Year | 15 | 24' | • | | | | | | 14 | • |
| **232•Camp Creek BLM**<br>1 mi. NE of Zortman on Cty. Rd. | All Year | 21 | 24' | • | • | | | | | 14 | • |
| **233•Trafton Park**<br>N of junction of US 2 in Malta | All Year | 20 | • | | • | | • | | | | |
| **234•Nelson Reservoir USBR•**<br>18 mi. E of Malta on US 2•2 mi. N on Cty. Rd. | All Year | • | • | • | | C | • | • | | | |
| **235•Fourchette Creek CE**<br>60 mi. S of Malta on Cty. Rd.•Primitive | All Year | • | • | • | | C | • | | | 14 | |
| **236•Devils Creek CE**<br>48 mi. NW of Jordan on Cty. Rd.•Primitive | All Year | • | 16' | • | | C | • | | | 14 | |
| **237•Bone Trail CE**<br>60 mi. SW of Fort Peck on Willow Creek Rd.•Primitive | All Year | • | 16' | • | | C | • | | | 14 | |

**Agency**
FS—U.S.D.A Forest Service
FWP—Montana Fish, Wildlife & Parks
NPS—National Park Service
BLM—U.S. Bureau of Land Management
USBR—U.S. Bureau of Reclamation
CE—Corps of Engineers

**Camping**
Camping is allowed at this site. Number indicates camping spaces available
H—Hard sided units only; no tents

**Trailers**
Trailer units allowed. Number indicates maximum length.

**Toilets**
Toilets on site. D—Disabled access

**Water**
Drinkable water on site

**Fishing**
Visitors may fish on site

**Boat**
Type of boat ramp on site:
A—Hand launch
B—4-wheel drive with trailer
C—2-wheel drive with trailer

**Swimming**
Designated swimming areas on site

**Trails**
Trails on site
B—Backpacking N—Nature/Interpretive

**Stay Limit**
Maximum length of stay in days

**Fee**
Camping and/or day-use fee

## Notes:

Section 11

## Dining Quick Reference

Price Range refers to the average cost of a meal per person: ($) $1-$6, ($$) $7-$11, ($$$) $12-up. Cocktails: "Yes" indicates full bar; Beer (B)/Wine (W), Service: Breakfast (B), Brunch (BR), Lunch (L), Dinner (D). Businesses in bold print will have additional information under the appropriate map locator number in the body of this section.

| RESTAURANT | TYPE CUISINE | PRICE RANGE | CHILD MENU | COCKTAILS BEER WINE | SERVICE | CREDIT CARDS | MAP LOCATOR NUMBER |
|---|---|---|---|---|---|---|---|
| Circle V Cafe | American | | | | | | 1 |
| Buffalo Barn Supper Club | Steaks & Seafood | $$$ | Yes | Yes | D | | 1 |
| Raider's Quick Stop | American | $ | | | B/L/D | Major | 1 |
| Dairy Queen | Fast Food | $ | Yes | | L/D | | 3 |
| Hitchin Post Cafe | Family | $ | | | B/L/D | | 3 |
| L&L Meats Deli | Deli | $ | | | L | | 3 |
| **Stockman's Bar & Steakhouse** | Steakhouse | $$/$$$ | | Yes | D | V/M | 4 |
| Great Northern Coffee House | Family | $ | Yes | | B/L/D | Major | 4 |
| Great Northern Steak House | Steaks & Seafood | $$$ | Yes | Yes | L/D | Major | 4 |
| Homesteaders Pizza | Pizza | $ | | B/W | L/D | Major | 4 |
| Joe's In & Out | Fast Food | $ | Yes | | L/D | | 4 |
| Mustang Lanes Cafe | Family | $ | Yes | Yes | L/D | Major | 4 |
| Deb's Diner | American | $ | | | B/L/D | | 5 |
| Hitching Post Pizza | Pizza | $ | | | B/L/D | | 5 |
| Pizza Pro | Pizza | $ | | | L/D | | 6 |
| Tastee Bite Cafe | American | $ | Yes | | B/L/D | | 6 |
| **Chinook Motor Inn & Restaurant** | Family | $/$$ | Yes | Yes | B/L/D | Major | 6 |
| **Box Cars Restaurant & Casino** | American | $$ | | Yes | B/L/D | Major | 8 |
| Navlika's Pizza | Pizza | $ | | | L/D | | 8 |
| Plainsman Steak House & Lounge | Steakhouse | $$ | | Yes | L/D | Major | 8 |
| **Uncle Joe's Steakhouse** | Full Menu | $$ | | Yes | L/D | V/M/D | 8 |
| Lunch Box | American | | | | L/D | | 9 |
| Rod's Drive Inn | Fast Food | $ | Yes | | L/D | | 9 |
| Taco John's | Fast Food | $ | Yes | | L/D | | 9 |
| Taco Treat | Fast Food | $ | Yes | | L/D | | 9 |
| Wolfer's Diner | 50s Diner | $ | Yes | | B/L/D | | 9 |
| Yummy Yogurt | Fast Food | $ | | | L/D | | 9 |
| **P J'S Restaurant & Casino** | American | $$ | | Yes | B/L/D | Major | 10 |
| 15 West | American | $ | | Yes | L/D | V/M | 10 |
| 4B's Restaurant | Family | $ | Yes | | B/L/D | V/M/D | 10 |
| Andy's Supper Club | Steaks & Seafood | $$ | | Yes | D | V/M | 10 |
| Arctic Circle | Fast Food | $ | Yes | | L/D | | 10 |
| Canton Chinese Restaurant | Chinese | $$ | | | L/D | | 10 |
| Kentucky Fried Chicken/A&W | Fast Food | $ | Yes | | L/D | | 10 |
| McDonald's | Fast Food | $ | Yes | | B/L/D | | 10 |
| Pizza Hut | Pizza | $/$ | | B | L/D | V/M/D | 10 |
| Pizza Pro | Pizza | $ | | | L/D | | 10 |
| Roadrunner Pizza | Pizza | | | | | | 10 |
| Subway | Fast Food | $ | Yes | | L/D | | 10 |
| Taco Time | Fast Food | $ | Yes | | L/D | | 10 |
| The Park Restaurant | Family | $ | Yes | | B/L/D | V/M | 10 |
| Wendy's | Fast Food | $ | Yes | | L/D | | 10 |
| Kelly's Pub & Grub | Burgers | $$ | | Yes | L/D | | 15 |
| HI Way Bar & Service | American | $ | Yes | | L/D | Major | 15 |
| Inverness Bar and Steakhouse | Steakhouse | $$ | | Yes | L/D | Major | 16 |
| **Wired Inn & Coffee Shop & Computer Center** | Deli | $ | | | | | 17 |
| Homestead Cafe | American | $–$$$ | Yes | B/W | B/L/D | V/M/D | 17 |
| Naez Place Restaurant | Family | $/$$$ | Yes | B/W | B/L/D | Major | 17 |
| Red Onion Restaurant | Steakhouse | $$/$$$ | | Yes | L/D | Major | 17 |
| Spud's Cafe | Family | $ | Yes | | L/D | Major | 17 |
| Sugar Shack Diner | Original Diner | $ | | | L/D | | 17 |
| **Jose's Place Family Restaurant** | Family | $ | Yes | Yes | L/D | | 18 |
| The Kalamity Kafe | Family | | | | | | 18 |
| Bohemian Corner Cafe | Family | $ | | B | B/L/D | V/M/D | 21 |
| Denton Cafe | Family | $ | | | | | 22 |
| **The Grand Union Hotel & Restaurant** | Continental | $–$$$ | | Yes | B/L/D | | 27 |
| **Bob's Riverfront Restaurant** | Family | $ | Yes | B/W | B/L/D | Major | 27 |
| **Trailhead Pizza Pro** | Pizza | $ | | L/D | | V/M | 27 |
| A&K Pizza | Pizza | $ | | B/W | L/D | | 27 |
| L & R Meats & Sandwich Shop | Deli | $ | | | L | | 27 |
| Missouri River Eatery | American | $/$$ | Yes | Yes | L/D | | 27 |

## Dining Quick Reference-Continued

Price Range refers to the average cost of a meal per person: ($) \$1-\$6, ($$) \$7-\$11, ($$$) \$12-up. Cocktails: "Yes" indicates full bar; Beer (B)/Wine (W), Service: Breakfast (B), Brunch (BR), Lunch (L), Dinner (D). Businesses in bold print will have additional information under the appropriate map locator number in the body of this section.

| RESTAURANT | TYPE CUISINE | PRICE RANGE | CHILD MENU | COCKTAILS BEER WINE | SERVICE | CREDIT CARDS | MAP LOCATOR NUMBER |
|---|---|---|---|---|---|---|---|
| Banque Club Steakhouse | Steakhouse | $$ | | Yes | L/D | Major | 27 |
| Ma's Loma Cafe | Family | | | | | | 28 |
| Mint Bar & Cafe | American | $$ | | Yes | L/D | | 30 |
| Pep's Cafe | American | $$ | | Yes | L/D | | 30 |
| Pizza Pro | Pizza | $ | | | L/D | | 30 |

## Motel Quick Reference

Price Range: ($) Under $40 ; ($$) $40-$60; ($$$) $60-$80, ($$$$) Over $80. Pets [check with the motel for specific policies] (P), Dining (D), Lounge (L), Disabled Access (DA), Full Breakfast (FB), Cont. Breakfast (CB), Indoor Pool (IP), Outdoor Pool (OP), Hot Tub (HT), Sauna (S), Refrigerator (R), Microwave (M) (Microwave and Refrigerator indicated only if in majority of rooms), Kitchenette (K). All Montana area codes are 406.

| HOTEL | PHONE | NUMBER ROOMS | PRICE RANGE | BREAKFAST | POOL/ HOT TUB SAUNA | NON SMOKE ROOMS | OTHER AMENITIES | CREDIT CARDS | MAP LOCATOR NUMBER |
|---|---|---|---|---|---|---|---|---|---|
| Sleeping Buffalo Resort | 527-3370 | 31 | $ | | IP/OP/HT | | K/P/D/M/R/L/DA | | 1 |
| Saco Motel | 527-3261 | 8 | $ | | | Yes | DA | Major | 1 |
| **Royals Inn** | 654-1150 | 16 | $ | | | Yes | K/P/M/R | Major | 3 |
| Riverside Inn | 654-2310 | 21 | $ | | | Yes | P | Major | 3 |
| Sportsman Motel | 654-2300 | 15 | $ | | | Yes | P | Major | 3 |
| **Edgewater Inn & RV Park** | 654-1302 | 32 | $$ | | IP/HT | Yes | | Major | 3 |
| Great Northern Motor Hotel | 654-2100 | 28 | $$ | | | Yes | P/D/L | Major | 4 |
| Maltana Motel | 654-2610 | 19 | $$ | | | Yes | | Major | 4 |
| Mc Guire's Motel | 353-2433 | 14 | $ | | | | DA | Major | 5 |
| **Chinook Motor Inn & Restaurant** | 357-2248 | 38 | $$ | | | Yes | P/D/DA | Major | 6 |
| Bear Paw Court | 357-2221 | 16 | $$ | | | Yes | | Major | 6 |
| **Havre Budget Inn Motel** | 265-8625 | 40 | $ | | | Yes | K/P/M/R | Major | 8 |
| Circle Inn Motel | 265-9655 | 12 | $ | | | Yes | P | Major | 8 |
| **El Toro Inn** | 265-5414 | 41 | $$ | CB | | Yes | P/M/R/DA | Major | 8 |
| **Siesta Motel** | 265-5863 | 23 | $$ | | | Yes | R | V/M | 8 |
| Rails Inn Motel | 265-1438 | 32 | $ | | | Yes | P | Major | 9 |
| Hi-Line Motel | 265-5512 | 12 | $ | | | | K/P/R | V/M | 10 |
| Park Hotel | 265-7891 | 29 | $$ | | | Yes | D/DA | Major | 10 |
| **Super 8 Motel Of Havre** | 265-1411 | 64 | $$ | CB | | Yes | P/DA | Major | 10 |
| Townhouse Inns Of Havre | 265-6711 | 104 | $$ | CB | IP/HT/S | | P/L | Major | 10 |
| M X Motel | 759-7165 | 17 | $ | | | Yes | DA | Major | 17 |
| **Zortman Garage & Motel** | 673-3160 | 25 | $ | | | Yes | K/P/M/R/D | Major | 18 |
| Buckhorn Store, Cabins & RV | 673-3162 | 7 | $ | | | Yes | D/P | Major | 18 |
| **The Grand Union Hotel & Restaurant** | 622-1882 | 27 | $$$/$$$$ | | HT | Yes | D/L/DA | V/M | 27 |
| **Pioneer Lodge** | 622-5441 | 9` | $$ | CB | | Yes | DA | Major | 27 |
| Fort Motel | 622-3312 | 11 | $$ | | | | P | Major | 27 |
| Rose River Inn | 739-4242 | | | | | | | | 28 |
| Q's Cafe & Motel | 378-2461 | 8 | $ | | | Yes | P/D/DA | V/M | 30 |

**NOTES:**

**Notes:**

Section 11

# SECTION 12

## GREAT FALLS AND SURROUNDING AREA
## INCLUDING SHELBY, CUT BANK AND CHOTEAU

*Highway 287 near Augusta.*

## WEATHER AVERAGES

**Great Falls**

| January | |
|---|---|
| Average High: | 30.6° F |
| Average Low: | 11.6° F |
| Record High : | 67.0° F |
| Record Low : | -37.0° F |
| Average Precip.: | 0.91 in |
| Rain/Snow Days: | 9 days |

| April | |
|---|---|
| Average High: | 55.3° F |
| Average Low: | 31.9° F |
| Record High : | 89.0° F |
| Record Low : | -6.0° F |
| Average Precip.: | 1.41 in |
| Rain/Snow Days: | 9 days |

| July | |
|---|---|
| Average High: | 83.3° F |
| Average Low: | 53.2° F |
| Record High : | 105.0° F |
| Record Low : | 40.0° F |
| Average Precip.: | 1.24 in |
| Rain/Snow Days: | 8 days |

| October | |
|---|---|
| Average High: | 59.3° F |
| Average Low: | 35.8° F |
| Record High : | 91.0° F |
| Record Low : | -11.0° F |
| Average Precip.: | 0.78 in |
| Rain/Snow Days: | 6 days |

**Cut Bank**

| January | |
|---|---|
| Average High: | 27.7° F |
| Average Low: | 7.3° F |
| Average Precip.: | 0.38 in |

| April | |
|---|---|
| Average High: | 52.1° F |
| Average Low: | 28.2° F |
| Average Precip.: | 0.89 in |

| July | |
|---|---|
| Average High: | 79.3° F |
| Average Low: | 49.9° F |
| Average Precip.: | 1.49 in |

| October | |
|---|---|
| Average High: | 56.1° F |
| Average Low: | 31.1° F |
| Average Precip.: | 0.51 in |

**Lake Elwell**

| January | |
|---|---|
| Average High: | 30.9° F |
| Average Low: | 8.9° F |
| Average Precip.: | 0.32 in |

| April | |
|---|---|
| Average High: | 54.5° F |
| Average Low: | 28.9° F |
| Average Precip.: | 1.00 in |

| July | |
|---|---|
| Average High: | 80.8° F |
| Average Low: | 50.8° F |
| Average Precip.: | 1.52 in |

| October | |
|---|---|
| Average High: | 58.8° F |
| Average Low: | 33.1° F |
| Average Precip.: | 0.61 in |

**1.** *Gas, Food, Lodging*

### Galata

Galata is virtually a ghost town, but at one time it was a booming railroad center. David R. McGinnis, a Great Northern executive, thought the area was so beautiful that he filed a claim for the land near where the small Galata Creek ran down from the Sweet Grass Hills. He built a ten room hotel and a number of commercial buildings, but nobody showed up. His dream of building a town had failed. He later recalled, "Cowboys, jam-full of life, coming there to ship stock, in their excess of joy of living would playfully shoot the doorknobs off the vacant buildings." He closed up and moved to Kalispell. He later received a check in the mail marked "back rent". A cowhand had moved into the deserted store and had done a fair amount of business with dryland farmers who were settling the area.

**2.** *Lewis & Clark, Attraction*

### T Lake Elwell and Tiber Dam

Tiber Dam and its reservoir, Lake Elwell, are on the Marias River in north-central Montana. The dam and reservoir are features of the Lower Marias Unit of the Pick-Sloan Missouri Basin Project. The reservoir has 17,678 surface acres and 181 miles of shoreline. Major game fish include northern pike, walleye, and rainbow trout. Concrete boat ramps, campgrounds, marina, picnic shelters. Reprinted from www.recreation.gov

### D Mer. Lewis

July 27, 1806

*"my design was to hasten to the entrance of Maria's river as quick as possible in the hope of meeting with the canoes and party at that place. . .after refreshing ourselves we again set out by moon light and traveled leasurely, heavy thunderclouds lowered arround us on every quarter but that from which the moon gave us light."*

**3.** *Lewis & Clark, Attractino, Gas, Food, Lodgng, Shopping*

### Shelby

Shelby was born when the Great Northern Railroad, forging through this area, threw off a boxcar and called it a station. Allan Manvel, the General Manager of the Montana line at that time, was tasked with naming the new stations along Montana's Hi-Line. An easy and common practice for naming sidings was to name them after company personnel. This one he named after Peter P. Shelby, the General Superintendent of the Great Northern Montana line. His response? "I don't know what Manvel was thinking of when he named that mudhole, God-forsaken place after me. It will never amount to a damn".

Truth is, had a geologist named Gordon Campbell not discovered oil here during the worst drought of the century, Peter Shelby may have been right. In the midst of a grand exodus, oil was discovered (a vein leading all the way to the Canadian border) and the town exploded in growth.

This place, "twenty miles from water and 40 miles from wood," quickly grew to be a distribution center for a 50-mile radius.

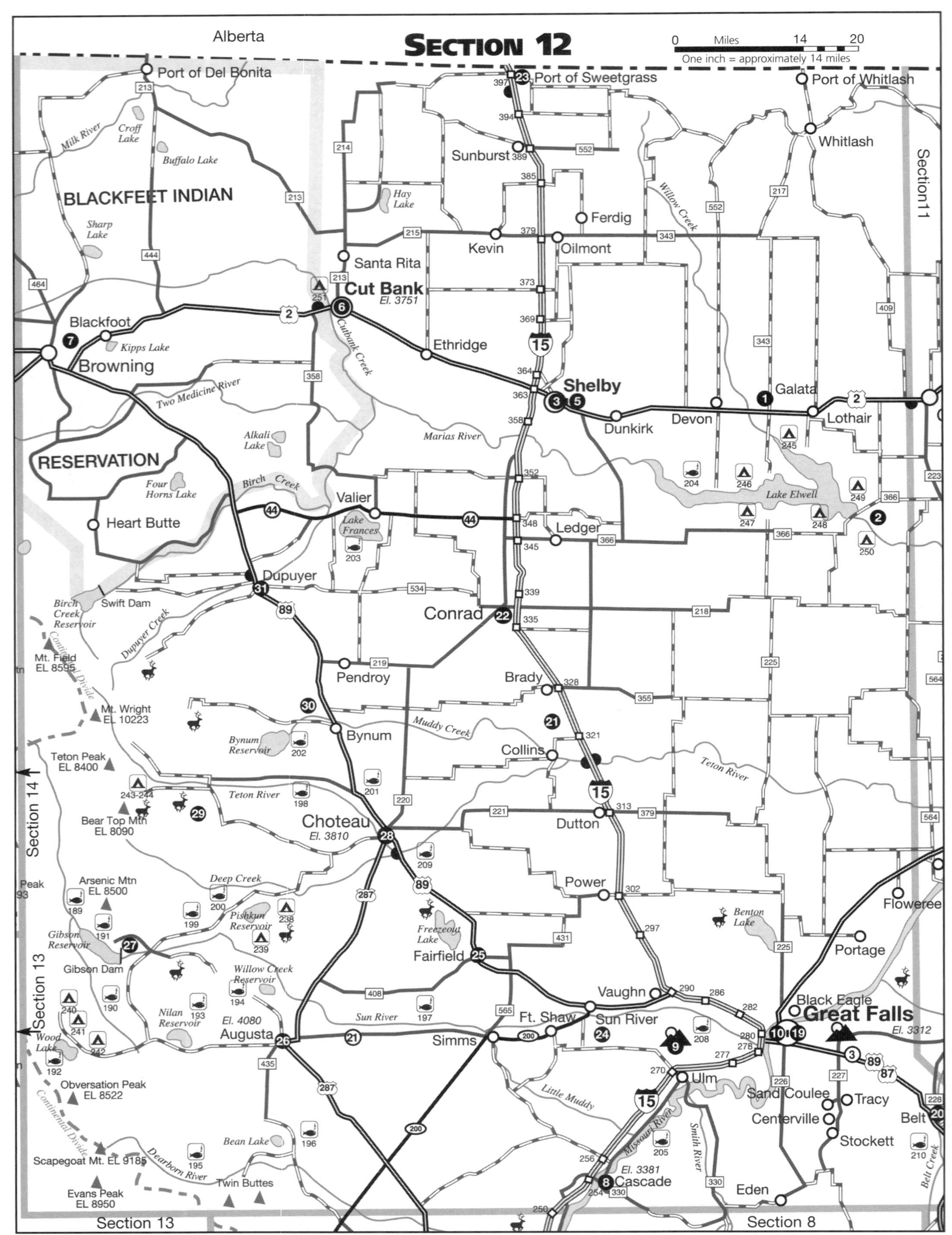
Section 12
Section 12
Alberta
0 Miles 14 20
One inch = approximately 14 miles
Port of Del Bonita
Port of Sweetgrass
Port of Whitlash
Whitlash
Sunburst
Ferdig
Kevin
Oilmont
Santa Rita
Cut Bank
El. 3751
Blackfoot
Browning
Ethridge
Shelby
Galata
Lothair
Dunkirk
Devon
BLACKFEET INDIAN
RESERVATION
Heart Butte
Valier
Ledger
Dupuyer
Conrad
Pendroy
Brady
Bynum
Collins
Choteau
El. 3810
Dutton
Power
Floweree
Portage
Fairfield
Vaughn
Black Eagle
Great Falls
El. 3312
Augusta
El. 4080
Simms
Ft. Shaw
Sun River
Ulm
Sand Coulee
Tracy
Centerville
Belt
Stockett
Cascade
El. 3381
Eden
Twin Buttes
Milk River
Croff Lake
Buffalo Lake
Hay Lake
Sharp Lake
Kipps Lake
Cutbank Creek
Willow Creek
Two Medicine River
Alkali Lake
Marias River
Birch Creek
Four Horns Lake
Lake Frances
Lake Elwell
Swift Dam
Birch Creek Reservoir
Dupuyer Creek
Continental Divide
Mt. Field EL 8595
Mt. Wright EL 10223
Teton Peak EL 8400
Bear Top Mtn EL 8090
Arsenic Mtn EL 8500
Bynum Reservoir
Muddy Creek
Teton River
Deep Creek
Pishkun Reservoir
Freezeout Lake
Benton Lake
Gibson Reservoir
Gibson Dam
Willow Creek Reservoir
Nilan Reservoir
Wood Lake
Sun River
Little Muddy
Missouri River
Smith River
Belt Creek
Obversation Peak EL 8522
Scapegoat Mt. EL 9185
Dearborn River
Bean Lake
Evans Peak EL 8950
Section 14
Section 13
Section 13
Section 8
Section11

*Entering Shelby.*

## D Mer. Lewis

July 20, 1806

*"the day has proved excessively warm and we lay by four hours during the heat of it."*

## D Mer. Lewis

July 21, 1806

*"being convinced that this stream came from the mountains I determined to pursue it as it will lead me to the most northern point of which the waters of Maria's river extend which I now fear will not e as far north as I wished and expected."*

## T Williamson Park

Shelby. 434-5222

This pleasant park sits in a wooded area along the Marias River. This is a great place for a picnic and a little waterplay in the river. Locals like to float the river from the golf course to the park. Take I-15 5 miles south of Shelby to exit 358. Go east to the frontage road and follow that south for 4 miles to the park.

## T Marias Museum of History & Art

206 12th Ave., Shelby. 434-2551

This museum is known for its collection of memorabilia from the celebrated Heavyweight Championship in 1923 when Jack Dempsey held off Tommy Gibbons for 15 rounds. Among the interesting items are a model of the arena and a pair of Tommy Gibbons' gloves, as well as dozens of photos and other artifacts. With a population thought to be around 500, the citizens of Shelby hosted the fight and built a wooden arena to accommodate 40,000 people was built in what is now the west end of town. The fascinating story unfolds through actual documents and photos.

Other room exhibits include the country store, featuring items from the old Gardener store in Devon; a doctor-dentist area; a blacksmith tack area with equipment from the Gold Butte smithy; a school; a bedroom; a parlor; a homestead kitchen; and a room for oil and railroad related items.

The numerous exhibits also feature several early 20th Century room replicas. Open from June through August daily, and on Tuesday afternoons the rest of the year.

# On The Trail of Lewis & Clark

## The Great Falls

Entering present Montana on April 27, 1805, the corps passed Milk River, the largest northern tributary of the Missouri, on May 8, and came to another large northern tributary on June 2, which was equal in size to theMissouri. For some reason the Indians at Mandan had not told them about this river, and because of its size the explorers were not sure which course to follow. After a week of investigating the two rivers, they finally determined that the south course was that of the Missouri. The river flowing from the north was given the name Maria's River in honor of Lewis'cousin, Maria Wood.

At Marias River (as it is known today) they left one of the pirogues, and cached a good deal of the baggage they could do without until they returned from the ocean.

On June 13, Lewis and a small party, which had gone ahead of the boats, reached the Great Falls of the Missouri. Rather than onewaterfall, as they had anticipated, there was a series of five cascades around which they would have to portage boats and baggage, dark arrived with the boats on June 16 and found the shortest and best portage route was on the south side of the river and nearly 18 miles long.

In order to haul six dugouts and baggage around the falls, they had to build two wagons. Slabs from a 22" cotton-wood tree were cut for wheels. Harnesses were made and strapped to the men who were to pull the wagons. When the wind was favorable, the sails were raised on the dugouts to help the men move the wagons across the rugged prairie. The pirogue was too large to portage. It was dragged ashore and left below the falls. More baggage was cached near the lower portage campsite.

The portage required four round trips and two weeks to complete. However, the party remained at the falls for an additional week completing construction on a collapsible iron-frame boat which Lewis designed and had built at Harper's Ferry during the summer of 1803. His initial plan was to navigate the keelboat (which he had also designed) up the Missouri to the Rocky Mountains. The Expedition would then portage over the mountains to navigable waters on the western side, assemble the iron-frame boat, and sail to the ocean.

Unfortunately, it was not that simple. And now they suffered another setback. They were unable to find the necessary pine pitch, and they did not have the proper needles to sew the hides together. The iron-frame boat had to be abandoned. In its place they built two more cottonwood dugouts. The failure of the iron-frame boat made it necessary to cache more baggage, this time at the upper portage camp.

The delay at the Great Falls gave the hunters and fishermen an opportunity to prepare a large quantity of dried fish, meat, and pemmican. They had learned at Fort Mandan that game would be scarce once they reached the mountains—a warning that proved only too accurate. *Excerpted from U.S. Forest Service pamphlet "Lewis and Clark in the Rocky Mountains".*

# Dempsey vs. Gibbons

In a day when a steak dinner cost 50 cents, Shelby, Montana, asked $50 for ringside seats to the famous July 4, 1923, World's Heavyweight Championship Fight between Jack Dempsey and Tommy Gibbons. An octagon-shaped wooden arena, with a seating capacity of 40,208 was constructed for the event at a cost of $82,000. The arena covered six acres, measured 558-1/2 feet in diameter, had 85 rows of seats and 16 entrances.

## F Sports Club Cattle Baron

210 Main Street, Shelby. 434-9214.
www.babbbarcattlebaron.com

The Sports Club Cattle Baron is the second location for the famous Babb Bar Cattle Baron Supper Club that is run by the Burns family. Both restaurants are famous for the size and flavor of the steaks they serve. Their unique secret sauce is the key ingredient and many people proclaim it as the best steak they have ever had. The menu also includes seafood, chicken, and lamb. This upscale steak house caters to their customers in every way possible. Not only is the food outstanding, but the atmosphere is unforgettable, and the Native American art collection on display is another fascinating element of the Cattle Baron restaurants.

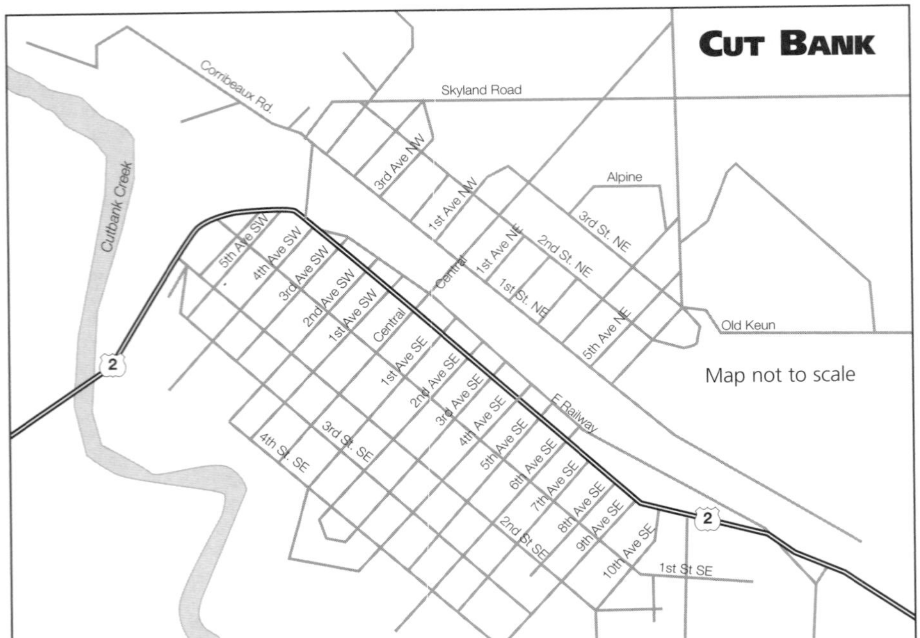


**F** **Hong Kong Chan's**
200 Front St., Shelby. 424-2646

**L** **The Sherlock Motel, Inc.**
133 5th Ave. S., and Main St. 434-5216 or 800-477-5216

Located in the heart of downtown Shelby, the Sherlock Motel spreads across 5th Avenue, just off Highway 2 (Main Street) in a quiet residential neighborhood. Owners Mark and Sonja Wilson take pride in attentively pampering their guests. The accommodations are true to their motto, "service is our signature, cleanliness…our commitment, graciousness…our guarantee." They make everyone feel like a VIP. The Sherlock features a check-in refreshment, door-side parking, soft water, plush towels, expanded cable TV, and complimentary local shuttle service. Standard amenities include in-room coffee, and free local and 800 phone calls.

**4.** *Gas, Food, Lodging*

**5.** *Historical Marker,*

**H** **The Oily Boid Gets the Woim**
Hwy 2, East of Shelby

*A narrow gauge railroad nicknamed the "turkey track" used to connect Great Falls, Montana, and Lethbridge, Alberta. When the main line of the Great Northern crossed it in 1891, Shelby Junction came into existence. The hills and plains around here were cow country. The Junction became an oasis where parched cowpunchers cauterized their tonsils with forty-rod and grew plumb irresponsible and ebullient.*

*In 1910 the dry-landers began homesteading. They built fences and plowed under the native grass. The days of open range were gone. Shelby quit her swaggering frontier ways and became concrete sidewalk and sewer system conscious.*

*Dry land farming didn't turn out to be such a profitable endeavor but in 1921 geologists discovered that this country had an ace in the hole. Oil was struck between here and the Canadian line, and the town boomed again.*

**F** **Dixie Inn Dining Room**
I-15 Exit 363, Shelby. 434-5817

**F** **Papa's Taco**
1100 Roosevelt Hwy., Shelby. 434-5781

**L** **Crossroads Inn**
1200 W. US Hwy. 2, Shelby. 434-5134
or 800-779-7666

**L** **Glacier Motel & RV Park**
744 Roosevelt Hwy., Shelby. 434-5181
or 800-764-5181

**6.** *Lewis & Clark, Attraction, Gas, Food, Lodging*

### Cut Bank

Cut Bank, located halfway between Browning and Shelby, was named after the deep gorge nearby made by the Cut Bank Creek. The Blackfeet Indians called it "the river that cuts into the white clay banks." The population, which numbered 845 people in 1939, ballooned into the thousands as natural gas and oil fields were discovered and sustained for many years. Gas piped from this region is used in Helena, Great Falls, Butte and Anaconda.

**D** **Mer. Lewis**
Great Falls

*"The Blackfoot indians rove through this quarter of the country and as they are a vicious lawless and reather anabandoned set of wretches I wish to avoid an interview with them if possible"*

**D** **Mer. Lewis**
July 25, 1806

*"I now begin to be apprehensive that I shall not reach the United States within this season inless I make every exertion in my power."*

## On The Trail of Lewis & Clark

### The Return: Lewis Explores the Marias

From Travellers Rest, Lewis and nine men headed down the Bitterroot River to the Clark Fork. They crossed that river and headed upstream to Blackfoot River, which they ascended, following the route to the plains used by the Nez Perce on their buffalo hunts.

On July 6, they crossed "the prairie of the knobs" (at present day Ovando), Lewis identified the path they were following as a warpath of the Hidatsas. They passed the remains of many Indian lodges, and crossed the Continental Divide at Lewis and Clark Pass, and the next day saw the first buffalo since entering the mountains a year earlier. Two days later they reported see-ing 10,000 buffalo in a 2-mile circle. They reached Sun River, and followed it to their upper portage camp at the Great Falls. As with Clark's horses on the Yellowstone, seven of Lewis' horses were stolen by Indians who were never seen.

On July 16, Lewis and three men set out overland from the Great Falls to explore Marias River. They wanted to see if it reached 50 degrees north, thus determining the northern boundary of the Louisiana Territory, and satisfying the conditions of the 1783 U.S. Treaty with England.

On July 18, Ordway's party arrived at the Great Falls with the boats which would be portaged to below the falls.

Also on the 18th, Lewis's party reached the Marias. Three days later they reached the headwaters of the Marias, and headed up the northern branch (Cut Bank River). They finally came to a place where they could see the river exiting from the mountains. Because the river did not reach 50 degrees north, Lewis named his camp "Camp Disap-pointment". It was the northernmost camp of the entire Expedition. Lewis was hopeful that the Milk River would reach the 50th Parallel, but he wouldn't have time to check it out.

On their return to the Missouri River, Lewis' party met eight Blackfeet Indians. From them, Lewis learned that a large band of their tribe was on its way to the mouth of the Marias River. The Indians camped with Lewis's party on Two Medicine River and were awakened when the Indians attempted to steal their horses. In the ensuing fight, two of the Indians were killed.

Lewis' party made a hasty retreat to the Missouri River where they had the good fortune of meeting the boats coming down the river from the Great Falls. They abandoned the horses, boarded the boats, and sailed down to the mouth of the Marias, picked up the items they had cached the year before, and took off before any Blackfeet arrived.

*Excerpted from U.S. Forest Service pamphlet "Lewis and Clark in the Rocky Mountains".*

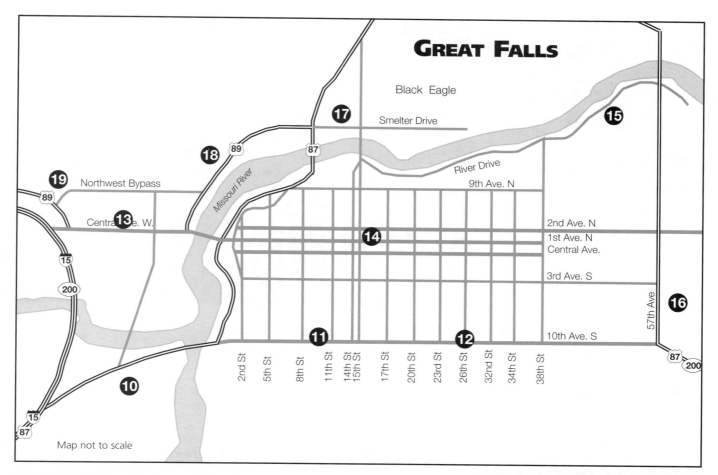

## GREAT FALLS

Black Eagle
Smelter Drive
River Drive
Missouri River
Northwest Bypass
Central Ave. W.
9th Ave. N
2nd Ave. N
1st Ave. N
Central Ave.
3rd Ave. S
10th Ave. S
57th Ave
2nd St
5th St
8th St
11th St
14th St
15th St
17th St
20th St
23rd St
26th St
32nd St
34th St
38th St
Map not to scale

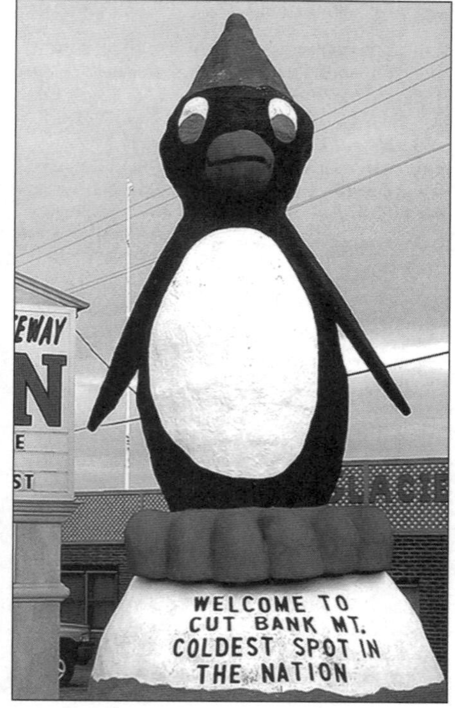


**D Mer. Lewis**
July 26, 1806

*"I believie they (8 Piegan Indians) were more allarmed at this accedental interview than we were. . .as soon as they found us all in possession of our arms they ran and endeavored to drive off all the horses."*

**T Glacier County Historical Museum**
113 E. Main St., Cut Bank. 873-4904

Many fascinating exhibitions about the life of the Blackfeet Indians, the oil business, and the history of the white settlers include farming, town life, oil production, and homestead-era railroads. The exhibits occupy over 13 acres of land. The Museum is open year round Tuesday through Saturday 1-5 p.m. Suggested donation of $1.00 per person.

### *Montana Trivia*

Between the time the Lewis and Clark Corps of Discover entered the eastern part of Montana until they prepared to leave the western part of the state, they did not encounter a single human being. About 25 percent of the expedition took place in the current boundaries of Montana.

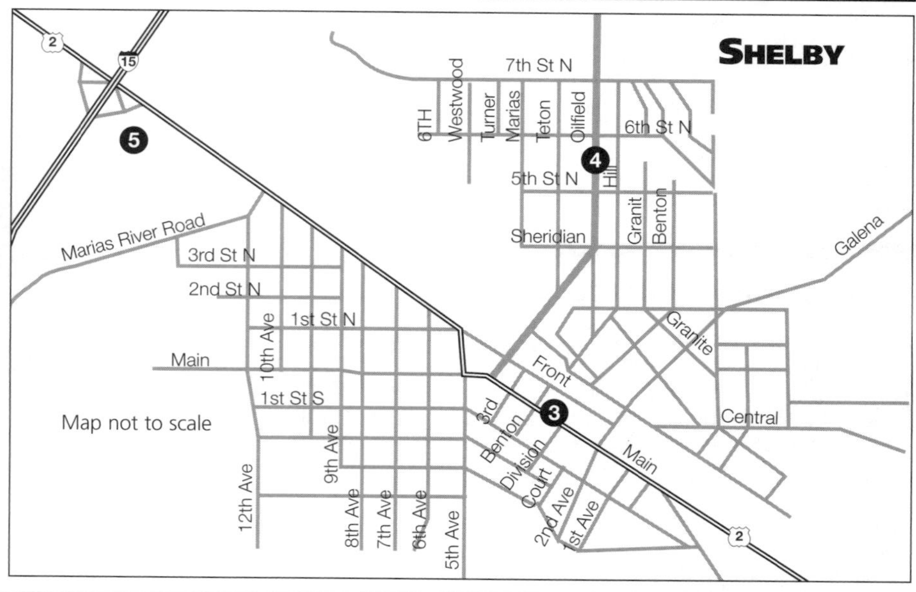


Section 12

## F C & L Country Café

112 N. Central, Cut Bank. 873-5335

C & L Country Café is known for their family atmosphere and delicious selection of homemade pies, soups, specials, breakfasts, enormous pancakes and fantastic omelets. Stop in with an appetite and leave with a smile. They use hormone-free beef in all hamburgers, served on homemade buns. Locally grown W Diamond Pure Beef is served and a selection of cuts available in the freezer, available for purchase. The beef is raised on the café owners ranch with no hormones or antibiotics. You will taste the difference. The café also offers specialty dishes, a variety of homemade soups that change daily, and a great salad bar. Buy one of their famous homemade pies for the road!

## F Java Time & Specialty Gifts

502 W. Main, Cut Bank. 873-5688

## S Coop Consignment & Secondhand Store

317 E. Railroad, Cut Bank. 873-2302

The Coop is a great little store with wide appeal. You will enjoy finding a wonderful selection of everything to make your house a home or something unique and special for yourself. Perhaps you are looking for a specific item, but chances are you'll find yourself in a fun treasure hunt. The store contains everything you can imagine, from a library, sewing room, tool room, to furniture, jewelry, bedding, kitchenware, dolls, toys, vintage clothing and lots of antiques without antique prices. The Coop will buy or consign entire estates, many are from local families going back generations. You will be sure to find real treasures and gems at the Coop.

### It Happened in Montana

The winter of 1886-87 was described by one cowboy as "hell without heat." Eighty of the two hundred cattle operations went bankrupt after 60 percent of the cattle in the state starved. 350,000 cattle and countless sheep died. In 1886 before the devastating winter, there were over 700,000 head of cattle and over a million sheep in Montana.

*Endless wheat fields characterize this area.*

## S W Diamond Pure Beef

112 1/2 N. Central, Cut Bank. Phone or Fax 873-2224. www.purebeef.net

From the wide open plains of Montana, this lean, juicy beef is wonderfully tender, protein dense and quick cooking. W Diamond beef is raised under the most ideal conditions, using only pure sandstone filtered spring water, no hormones, implants or antibiotics. Cattle eat all natural corn, barley, oats, peas and high plains roughage, and they are grown on a family operated farm to insure quality. This commitment to quality has paid off in producing a super lean beef breed called Piedmontese. Combined with the already lean Charolais cattle, W Diamond Pure Beef has produced a blend of very lean and surprisingly juicy and tender beef. Try some on your table today! Products are packaged and shipped with dry ice.

## S DrugMart

601 West Main, Hwy. 2, Northern Village Shopping Center, Cut Bank. 873-5631

DrugMart is the first drugstore east of Glacier National Park. The store offers a wide variety of products and services to suit your traveling needs. It is loaded with special souvenirs, greeting cards, postcards, books, magazines, CD's, health and beauty aids, toys, games, and much more. There is a full line giftware section featuring: Lang Candles, Enesco Precious Moments, Ambassador Cards, Russ, Ganz, Pacific Rim, and many unique gift items. This is a great place to experience the fast and friendly independent pharmacy tradition. They are a Good Neighbor Pharmacy.

**7.** *Lewis & Clark, Historical Marker, Attraction, Gas, Food, Lodging*

## Blackfeet Reservation

Northwestern Montana along the eastern slopes of the Rocky Mountains north and south of Hwy 2. 338-7276

The 1.5 million acre Blackfeet reservation is the home of the Blackfeet tribe. Approximately 7,000 of the 14,750 enrolled tribal members live on or near the reservation. Close to 27 percent of the enrolled members are of three quarter or greater Indian blood. It is thought that the Blackfeet were named for their black or near-black moccasins which they painted or darkened with ashes. The reservation was established in 1851.

## Blackfoot

While it is clear this town took its name from the Blackfeet Indians, it is not so clear where the tribe

### Lewis & Clark National Forest

**In mountain country located in west** central Montana, lies the Lewis and Clark National Forest encompassing 1.8 million acres scattered into seven separate mountain ranges. The forest boundaries spread east from the rugged, mountainous Continental Divide onto the plains. When looking at a map, the Forest appears as islands within oceans of prairie. Because of its wide-ranging land pattern, the Forest is separated into two Divisions: the Rocky Mountain and the Jefferson.

US highways 89 and 287 skirt the east side of the forest and provide access points into the forest. 791-7700.

got its name. One story has the name coming from the legend of the Sun telling an old man in a vision to paint the feet of the eldest with black medicine which Sun provided. Doing so gave the old man's sons power to catch the buffalo. The old man then decreed that his descendents should be called Blackfeet.

In another legend the Blackfeet were named so because their mocassins became blackened when they crossed the burnt prairies. The name in their language is *Siksiksa* which literally translates to "Blackfoot." However, the constitution under which their tribal council was formed translates to "Blackfeet."

## Browning

Browning is the convergence point for Native Americans and tourists, as it is the headquarters of the Blackfeet Tribe. Located near the East Entrance of Glacier National Park, the town was founded in 1895.

### H The Blackfeet Nation

Hwy 2 east of Browning

*The Blackfeet Nation consists of three tribes, the Pikunis or Piegans, the Bloods and the Blackfoot. Each tribe is divided into clans marking blood relationship. The majority of the Indians on this reservation are Piegans.*

*Many years ago the Blackfeet ranged from north of Edmonton, Alberta to the Yellowstone River. They were quick to resent and avenge insult or wrong, but powerful and loyal allies when their friendship was won.*

*They were greatly feared by early trappers and settlers because of the vigor with which they defended their hereditary hunting grounds from encroachment.*

*No tribe ever exceeded them in bravery. Proud of their lineage and history they have jealously preserved their tribal customs and traditions. They have produced great orators, artists, and statesmen.*

*The Government record of the sign language of all American Indians, started by the late General Hugh L. Scott, was completed by the late Richard Sanderville, who was official interpreter of this reservation.*

### H Old Agency, 1880-1894

Hwy 89 south of Browning

*The second Indian Agency on the Blackfeet Reservation was built at Old Agency in 1879. Agent John Young moved the buildings from Upper Badger Creek with help from the Blackfeet Indians. Both men and women dug cellars, hauled stone and mixed mortar. The women covered the exterior with lime from Heart Butte. Built in stockade shape, the Agency had two bastions at diagonal corners to protect against enemy attack. The Indians called it "Old Ration Place" after the government began issuing rations. The "Starvation Winter" of 1883-1884 took the lives of about 500 Blackfeet Indians who had been camping in the vicinity of Old Agency. This tragic event was the result of an inadequate supply of government rations during an exceptionally hard winter. In 1894, after the Great Northern Railway had extended its tracks across the Reservation, the Agency moved to Willow Creek at the present site in Browning. Today, the Museum of the Plains Indian in Browning houses a fine collection of artifacts that illustrate Blackfeet culture before and after the establishment of the Reservation.*

### H Camp Disappointment

Browning

*The monument on the hill above was erected by the Great Northern Railway in 1925 to commemorate the farthest point north reached by the Lewis and Clark Expedition, 1804-06. Captain Meriwether Lewis, with three of his best men, left the main party at the Missouri River and embarked on a side trip to explore the headwaters of the Marias River. He hoped to be able to report to President Jefferson that the headwaters arose north of the 49th parallel, thus extending the boundaries of the newly acquired Louisiana Purchase.*

*The party camped on the Cut Bank River July 22-25, 1806, in a "beautifull and extensive bottom." Deep in the territory of the dreaded Blackfeet, the men were uneasy. Lewis wrote, "gam[e] of every discription is extremly wild which induces me to believe that the indians are now, or have been lately in this neighbourhood" Lewis could see from here that the river arose to the west rather than to the north, as he had hoped. Disheartened by this discovery, by the cold, rainy weather, and by the shortage of game, Lewis named this farthest point north Camp Disappointment, the actual site of which is four miles directly north of this monument.*

### D Mer. Lewis

July 26, 1806

*"We set out biding a lasting adieu to this place which I now call camp disappointment."*

### T Museum of the Plains Indians

Junction of U.S. Hwy. 2 and U.S. Hwy. 89 in Browning.

The history of the Northern Great Plain tribes is made visible in this small but outstanding museum in Browning. The exhibits document the history and migration of the Plains Indian from the Blackfeet Tribe to the Assiniboine and Sioux. Also documented are the cultures, lifestyles, clothing and history of the Plains Indian. The museum contains a wonderful collection of Indian art and beadwork along with contemporary items for sale. The multi-media show, Winds of Change, is a must see. The museum is open year round. From June through September and an admission is charged.

### T Bob Scriver Hall of Bronze & Museum of Montana Wildlife

U.S. Highway 2 & 89 in Browning. 338-5425

This privately owned museum was established in 1956 and provides a very special view and understanding of the wildlife native to Montana. The museum is now a tribute to Bob Scriver, known as "The Cowboy's National Sculptor." He passed on in 1999, leaving a legacy of work that earned national recognition and honor. The Hall of Bronze houses Scriver's bronze creations, depicting the wildlife of Montana, early Americans, cowboys, Blackfeet Indians and major sculptures of famous people. Scriver lived in Browning, and here is the most complete collection of his work.

Bob Scriver started as a taxidermist, and his superb knowledge of the mountain animals shows not only in his taxidermy but also in the sculptures that followed. There are over 1,000 works in the museum, grouped by theme. Taxidermied animals include a grizzly and black bear, moose, wolf, buffalo, and antelope—creatures of the mountains and the plains that surround Browning. In addition to Scriver's bronzes and taxidermied pieces, the museum also showcases Scriver's books, including the *Rodeo* series and *No More Buffalo*, which focuses on Indian themes.

He has been called the "foremost sculptor in America today—bar none" (Dr. Harold McCracken, Director Emeritus, Whitney Gallery of Western Art, Cody, Wyoming). His bronzes of cowboys at work, Indians on the high plains, or animals such as bighorn sheep seem to freeze in time the essence of the frontier, and they are

## The Falls

If you're like most folks visiting Great Falls for the first time, one of the first questions that comes to mind is—where are the falls? Actually they were more a series of falls, five in all within a stretch of ten miles. Notice the word "were." When Lewis and Clark first portaged the area they portaged a total of five falls. Starting from Great Falls going downriver is Black Eagle Falls followed by Rainbow Falls and Crooked Falls. These three can be seen from the south bank of the Missouri River by taking River Drive or the River's Edge Trail. Colter Falls was located between Black Eagle and Rainbow when the Corps of Discovery made their legendary portage. Today it is gone, a victim of the construction of Rainbow Dam. The largest of the falls, and the most majestic, is the Great Falls at Ryan Dam. The are accessible from the north side of the river by driving north on Highway 87 for approximately five miles and following the signs.

Section 12

found in museums throughout the West.

Don't miss a chance to visit this treasure. It is open from Mother's Day to the late fall. There is anominal admission charge.

### M Blackfeet Community College

Browning. 338-5441, www.montana.edu/wwwbcc

The Blackfeet Community College is located in Browning, Montana, on the Blackfeet Indian Reservation adjacent Glacier National Park. This fully accredited college was chartered in 1974. The Blackfeet Tribal Business Council chartered the Blackfeet Community College by Executive Action for the Blackfeet Indian Reservation community.

## 8. *Lewis & Clark, Gas, Food, Lodging*

### Cascade

This is the town that should have been Great Falls. It was named for the falls on the Missouri though not very near them, and is much older than Great Falls. At one time it was the rival of Great Falls for the county seat. Charlie Russell lived here for awhile.

### D Lewis and Clark

June 13 through July 15, 1805

*The portage around the Great Falls took a solid month of prime travel days. They were exposed to flash floods, pelted with hailstroms, stalked by grizzly bears, tormented by prickly pear cactus, in addition to the menacing task of portaging their gear and dugout canoes past the five waterfalls.*

### D Sgt. Ordway

July 4, 1805

*"It being the 4th of Independence we drank the last of our ardent Spirits except a little reserved for Sickness."*

### D Mer. Lewis

July 15, 1805

*"We arrose very early this morning, assigned the canoes their loads and had it put on board. we now found our vessels eight in number all heavily laden, notwithstanding our several deposits."*

### D Sgt. Ordway

July 15, 1805

*"we loaded the 8 Canoes and could hardly find room in them for all our baggage about 10 oClock A.M. we Set out. . .and proceeded on verry well."*

## 9. *Attraction, Gas, Food*

### Ulm

Named for William Ulm, an early rancher whose ranch included the land the town sits on. When the Great Northern came through the town became a shipping center for the wheat grown in the surrounding benchlands.

### T Ulm Pishkun State Park (Day use only)

10 miles south of Great Falls on I-15 at Ulm Exit, then 6 miles northwest on county road. 454-5840.

For more than 1,000 years, prehistoric men and women of the Great Plains hunted bison by driving them over cliffs. One of the most spectacular yet least commercially developed "buffalo jumps" can be seen today at Ulm Pishkun State Park, a dozen miles west of Great Falls.

"Pishkun" comes from a Blackfeet word meaning "deep blood kettle." With good reason. Certainly dozens, probably hundreds, possibly thousands of buffalo at a time were driven over the cliff at Ulm Pishkun and slaughtered.

Recently, archaeologists from Montana State University researched and excavated the site. They found:

- Ulm Pishkun is perhaps the largest buffalo jump in the world.
- Human activity at the site dates back to at least A.D. 500.
- Buffalo apparently were killed and processed throughout the year, not just fall or winter, as was previously believed.

To the nomadic people who inhabited the Great Plains for thousands of years, the buffalo meant survival: hides for clothing and shelter, bones for utensils, sinew for bow strings and meat to eat.

But the most efficient method for killing buffalo-the horse-didn't appear on the plains until the

*Ulm Pishkun State Park.*

early to mid-1700s. Faced with the enormous size, quickness and toughness of the buffalo, these people used a readily available means: drive them over cliffs. *Reprinted from Montana Department of Fish, Wildlife & Parks pamphlet.*

## 10. *Gas, Food, Lodging, Shopping*

### Great Falls

Great Falls, headquarters for the state's agricultural industry, straddles the Missouri River where a series of water falls once roared. Not only did it receive its name from these cascading falls but today's hydroelectric power harnessed by dams gave the city another nickname: the "Electric City." One of the most extraordinary chapters of the Lewis and Clark Expedition was the legendary portage of the Great Falls, which is the present site of Ryan Dam. At first sight Meriwether Lewis proclaimed the falls a "sublimely grand specticle" but later bemoaned them when Lewis and Clark stalled at this site for almost a month. They were required to portage 18 miles around the falls before continuing upriver which took two weeks to cover a distance normally travelled by water in a single day.

Great Falls, with a population of about 60,000, is the second largest city in Montana. Located near the center of the state, Great Falls is a windy city averaging 13 mph winds all day. It has roots as a regional trade center and is the resting place for 200 long-range missiles, as well as a modern center of national air defense. It is considered to have a very diversified economy with the river supporting a thriving wheat and barley crop on the northern hills.

The mountains surrounding the city also provide exceptional recreational opportunities; some of the finest and most readily accessible hunting and fishing in the country lie near Great Falls. There are endless possibilities for camping, hiking, boating, water skiing and fishing.

Montana's north-central region was named the Russell Country after the cowboy artist who captured the vast and vivid landscapes on canvas. Great Falls is the adopted home for Charles M. Russell, the nation's most acclaimed frontier painter. Russell loved the west and created over 4,000 works of art. Great Falls has preserved the most complete collection of his art in the C. M. Russell Museum; the museum complex also includes Russell's log-cabin studio and house. Great Falls' natural beauty is enhanced by the artistic flavor of the world-renowned C. M. Russell Museum, a well-established symphony, and four professional theater groups.

Great Falls offers extraordinary sights and experiences that thrilled and inspired Lewis & Clark as well as Charles Russell. Discover the natural wonders and visit the special monuments which bear tribute to a rich heritage. Don't miss the Ulm Pishkun Buffalo Jump or the Lewis and Clark Interpretive Center.

## 11. *Gas, Food, Lodging, Shopping*

### F MacKenzie River Pizza Co.

1220 9th Street S. Great Falls. 761-0085

Famous for gourmet pizzas, super sandwiches and extraordinary salads, everything is made fresh daily right down to the salad dressings and the pizza dough! They are located one block South of the 10th Street light, in the Joe's Place Pub building smack dab in the middle of Lewis and Clark Country.

### F Godfather's Pizza

1300 10th Ave. S., Great Falls. 761-7722

The fun atmosphere at Godfather's Pizza is great for group gatherings, family dinners, or just a relaxing meal out. Featuring a wide variety of pizzas to choose from, with golden and thin crusts and many topping choices. If you're not in the mood for pizza, try the salad bar or a variety of sandwiches. Offering dine in, carry out, and delivery seven days a week. Godfather's also serves specialty buffets and welcomes large groups.

### F Big Sky Bagel Bakery

1227 10th Ave. S., Great Falls. 453-5747

### FL Townhouse Inn

1411 10th Ave. S., Great Falls.761-4600 or 800-442-4667, www.townpump.com

Townhouse Inn of Montana has a welcoming atmosphere with a 24-hour front desk, queen & king size beds, and specialty rooms featuring recliners, whirlpool baths, suites and kitchenettes. Located close to convenience stores, gas stations, restaurants and a shopping mall. Guests enjoy free local calls, free parking, a full service restaurant with room service, and indoor swimming pool, spa, sauna, casino with a live poker room, and discounts for AAA, senior citizens and corporates.

### L Super 8 Motel Great Falls

1214 13th St. S., Great Falls. 727-7600 or 800-800-8000

Conveniently located off of I-15, no more than 15 minutes away from all of the many attractions in the Great Falls area. Adjacent to Holiday Village Mall, the largest shopping center in Great Falls. Many fine restaurants and movie theatres are within walking distance. Enjoy complimentary coffee, tea, juice and an expanded toast bar in the hospitality room each morning. AAA approved, free local calls, all queen sized beds, remote control cable TV with HBO, and an elevator for the guest's convenience.

### S Bos Best of Show Gallery & Frame House

609 10th Ave. S., Great Falls. 453-5560 or fax 453-3707. www.bestofshowgallery.com

### S House of Bargains Fine Unfinished Furniture, Home Decor, & Collectibles

816 13th Street S., Great Falls. 454-3402

## 12. *Historical Marker, Attraction, Gas, Food, Lodging, Shopping, Miscellaneous*

### H Lewis and Clark Portage Route

Great Falls

*To avoid the series of waterfalls along the Missouri River north of this point, the Expedition portaged their canoes and several tons of baggage, crossing the highway right here. At the lower camp, some 12 miles NE the crew made crude wagons, the wheels sliced off a cottonwood tree. The upper camp, named after the bears which inhabited the islands, was located some 5 miles SW.*

*The portage was near man-killing: "the men has to haul with all their strength wate & art," Clark wrote.*

### Montana Trivia

North America's first fossilized dinosaur eggs were found at Egg Mountain, in Pine Butte Swamp Nature Preserve near Choteau. They provided evidence that some dinosaur species were good mothers, tending their nests and babies.

# HISTORIC TAVERNS IN GREAT FALLS

by Ralph Pomnichowski, Great Falls

**Taverns were gathering places and** information exchanges in frontier Montana and they keep that niche in the Treasure State to this day. Their proprietors and barkeeps frequently are historians a couple of notches above amateur.

Unlike many western towns that "jest growed," Great Falls was planned from the start with residential and business areas, streets crossed at right angles, railroad rights of way established and very large areas reserved for parks.

The makeup of settlers coming here also was unusual for a western town. Most of the men were young, well-educated and interested in making a home-not making a stake and moving on.

Even the cowpokes and sheepherders toting a year's pay after roundup didn't shoot up bars and brawl nonstop as you see in the movies. But they did live here. Many still do. There wasn't much of a desperado quotient up here compared to, say, the legends of the lower Midwest or the Southwest. Some of the U.S. Army's black buffalo soldiers stationed west of here at Fort Shaw caused a little excitement once in a while, just like the coal and silver miners did a little east of here, but not the stuff of which legends are made.

In Montana, people take cover in taverns during storms. Kids get off the school bus there. You can get directions from there to anywhere. They offer a cold drink on a hot day, or a hot one when it's snowing. Nowadays you can place a bet there and some taverns outside the cities were convenience stores before they were called that, carrying snacks, toilet paper, .22 shells and the other necessities of life.

Visitors are always welcome and unlike taverns in bigger states, you'll find fairly often that the owner is pouring your drink or fixing your food. Many of the taverns and their suppliers in this area have been in the same family for several generations and many of those families are intermarried.

You'll find velvet and chrome in a few of the places and worn stools in others, but you'll find some history in all of them, whether it's the building, the clientele or the locale. Dress is casual in all of these taverns. The guy on the next stool could be a college graduate wheat farmer with thousands of acres whose bank accounts could buy and sell you many times over.

We have the 1868 Whoop-Up Trail that led into Canada, the Bootlegger Trail that led here from Canada, and a lot of happy trails between. You can still take the Prohibition-era Bootlegger north from here through the wheat fields to Canada, or you can take a drive up the Missouri River toward Helena to the make-believe Canadian border crossing near Hardy seen in the motion picture "The Untouchables," starring Sean Connery.

### City Bar & Casino
*709 Central Avenue*

Founder Charlie Watson was a man we would call entrepreneur in today's business jargon. He already was his own boss, working as a barber, and he kept moving in that direction.

Shortly after the start of Prohibition in 1917, he was a partner in a cigars, confectionery and billiards enterprise downtown. Right at the end of Prohibition in 1933, even though it was the depth of the Great Depression, he risked buying the first of his own bars, the Montana Bar, just down the avenue from this one,

He built his next venture, the City Bar, in 1939, the same year World War II broke out and "*Gone With The Wind*" was breaking box office records. Some people told Charlie his new bar would go broke because it was too far out of the core business district. Today's Tenth Avenue South business strip was nothing more than sand hills back then.

The City Bar's huge Brunswick back bar, a pre-Prohibition piece, was resurrected by Charlie from under an ash heap in the basement of the former Great Falls Hotel downtown.

Charlie, who hailed from California, and his Finn wife, Anna, who had moved here from Alberta, then ran both the Montana Bar and City Bar for five years. When Charlie passed away in 1943, the Montana was sold for $2,500 and the City was managed by one of Anna's nephews until the Watson sons were ready to run it.

Bill and Bob Watson took over in 1955, when the City's barkeeps still wore starched whites and the place was only half as large as it is now. It had a tile floor, Venetian blinds and chrome and plastic tables and chairs. Additions in 1956 and 1976 brought it to the current 50-by-70-foot size.

The Radiant Estate nickel-plated wood-burning stove, installed during the latest addition, originally was a coal burner in a northeastern North Dakota hotel parlor in the late 1800s.

Bob succumbed to an unexpected heart attack in 1986 and the City Bar & Casino now is owned by Bill and his son, Brad. One of them is almost always there to answer questions.

### Club Cigar Saloon & Eatery
*208 Central Ave.*

This tavern is in a very changed business block that was practically all bars only a few decades ago. People could easily read newspapers at night by the glare of all the neon signs.

The famous western artist Charlie Russell used to spend a lot of time in long-gone taverns on this block-mainly in Sid Willis' Mint Saloon and Billy Rance's Silver Dollar. And now Jon Tovson's Club Cigar is the only old-time tavern left in the whole block.

Working girls in rooms near the rear of the Club Cigar made it a popular locale years ago. The pay-for-fun girls are gone, but the remodeled Club remains a popular night spot for singles. Cosmopolitan magazine said so.

The Club has been a tavern in continuous operation at various addresses since 1914, under the management of some pretty colorful characters from time to time, including a madam.

It's been at this location since 1931. But it didn't look anything like it does now until Tovson bought it in 1978 and remodeled into gentility what had been more or less a rough-and-tumble barroom.

The largest item in the Club Cigar is the 14-by-30-foot Brunswick mirrored mahogany back bar. It is the largest of the Brunswick back bars in Great Falls and is highlighted in this setting by the wood wall wainscoting and other woods throughout the place in furniture, ceiling, divider and other uses.

The stained glass windows, the ancient orangeade machine and some of the other older touches in decor were rescued from a heap in the basement where they had accumulated over the years.

Adaptive of a pretty casual atmosphere, today's Club Cigar has lighters proclaiming: "We cheat the other guy and pass the savings on to you."

The Club serves a great lunch featuring homemade soups, sandwiches, Mexican food and daily specials. The newest addition is the 5¢ gambling parlor in the back room-ideal for those who might be "feelin' lucky"!

### 3D International
*1825 Smelter Ave., Black Eagle*

Tommy Grasseschi followed his father and grandfather as a worker at the nearby copper and zinc smelter, toiling in the works until he was 33, when he opened the door here the day before Independence Day in 1946.

This little bistro only had 10 tables in the bar and 10 in the dining room then. But Smelter Hill today doesn't look anything like it did before demolition of the plant in the early 1980s either. The 506-foot smelter stack dominated the skyline and was a landmark for travelers approaching Great Falls from all directions.

The hill looks barren now but the block after block of small, neat houses in this former smelter town haven't changed a great deal. Life goes on here for the older families as if the steam whistles still blew at the smelter to start and end the shifts.

The main floor of the 3D originally was a butcher shop and the second story was a boarding house, both in a single-lot brick structure stretching back from Smelter Avenue. Today's main dining room was the first addition, in 1948, Ten years after that, another addition enclosed the stage and dance floor. The landmark 3D neon sign (signifying drink, dine and dance) came in 1951 and serves as a handy beacon for travelers trying to find the place.

Today's menu is truly international in theme and variety. The outstanding cuisine features specialties from Oriental (Cantonese, Szechwan and Thai), as well as Italian and American menu favorites. A children's menu is available, as is seating in either smoking or non-smoking areas. The 3D is handicapped accessible and accepts

Master Card, Visa and Discover cards. Enjoy the history of Black Eagle in the city's only art-deco style surrounding.

Tommy and his wife, Dorothy, were big on live entertainment through the years and booked many of the top acts traveling between Chicago and Seattle. They even had a small ice rink built to accommodate a few of the ice revues.

Tommy is gone now but the caliber of service carries on under his son, Mark, who will be your maitre'd many nights of the week. The 3D opens nightly at 4:30 p.m.

**Little Chicago Club**
*113 15th Street, Black Eagle*

The small town of Black Eagle north of the Missouri River from Great Falls was called Little Chicago long ago because it existed in the actual shadow of the mighty copper and zinc smelters and refineries of the Anaconda Copper Mining Co.

It took its moniker from Chicago, Illinois, the American industrial colossus of the period.

The copper and zinc ores and concentrates were brought by rail from Butte and Anaconda, Montana, for processing, taking advantage of the cheap hydroelectric power produced by Black Eagle Dam at the foot of what was-and still is-Smelter Hill.

And, like its namesake, Little Chicago was heavily populated with immigrants who still give it a unique flavor with ethnic foods, games and traditions exhibited on special occasions in the nearby Black Eagle Park.

They treasure their enclave's independence too. They told the Great Falls city manager to take a hike recently when he suggested annexation.

The huge industrial complex was closed in 1980 by ARCO, its latest owner, and dismantled for salvage. The last step was blowing up the legendary 506-foot smokestack in the fall of 1982. It is difficult for visitors nowadays to imagine the extent of the works judging only by the few foundations left in place that they can see from scenic overlooks on the bluffs on the Great Falls side of the river.

"I kept the name 'Little Chicago' when I bought the place 18 years ago because it's part of the past here," says moustachioed owner Bill Lindsey. His tavern's block used to have the Croatian Brotherhood Hall at one corner. "There's a continuing mystique in the name too. It causes people to come here just to look, for gangsterism or something, I guess."

It is amazing that shelf after shelf of pool-playing trophies don't pull down the walls in this establishment. "Those are just the major ones I've kept from the teams I sponsor," Lindsey says casually "We've given away 600 or 700 smaller ones." Little Chicago is a mecca for serious pool players in this area. Lindsey wields a respectable cue himself and can show you how if you stop by.

**Cowboy's Bar & Museum**
*311 3rd St. NW*

You can step into a slice of the Old West in this log-built place and sip your favorite dust-cutter as you walk around a working cowhand's museum.

Rodeo is spoken here (but not every minute) and if you appreciate fine old saddles and tack and neat old photographs of the nags that used to be under'em, this is the place for you to spend an hour or two.

There's also a splendid collection of Indian artifacts donated over the years by the ranchers and cowboys who first obtained them.

Guns, branding irons, bedrolls, buffalo-hide coats and just about every kind of horseshoe in creation are among thousands of other items in nicely done displays that trace some of the history of north central Montana.

Children are welcome.

The Cowboy's Bar is managed right well by Bill & Dee Davis but it's always been owned by the Montana Cowboys Association founded in 1938. This spacious, twin-fireplace structure was built as a gathering place for cowboys and sympathizers by the federal Works Progress Administration in the late 1930s right across the street from the Montana State Fairgrounds.

The relics inside this cottonwood-shaded building are a tribute to the pioneer and later stockmen who battled disease, drought, blizzards, and two- and four-legged predators to create a stable industry that now is the biggest single agricultural moneymaker in Montana.

Cowboy film star Gene Autry has wet his whistle in here and most of today's working rodeo cowboys who appear across the street in professional events also stop in regularly.

Electronic poker machines have replaced the one-armed bandits and you can either get your fill of live horse racing across the street at certain times of year, or relive the races in the Cowboy's by watching the videotapes later in the day.

## T Galerie Trinitas

University of Great Falls campus next to Trinitas Chapel.

This gallery contains many of the works of Sister Mary Trinitas. During her lifetime she created a legacy of religious-themed art work. She also taught art and French at the university. The gallery exhibits her works as well as those of faculty and students of the university.

## F The Prospector Casino & Restaurant II

616 10th Ave. S., Great Falls. 454-1766

The family owned and operated Prospector Casino and Restaurant features an attractive casino with video poker and keno, as well as a full service bar. They offer an extensive menu complete with daily specials and good home-style cooking, featuring steaks, sandwiches, soups and salads. Live keno is available here as well. Right next to the 8-Ball Casino.

## F Cattin's Family Dining

2001 10th Ave., Great Falls. 727-6874

A visit to Cattin's Restaurant is like going to a friends house for a very special meal. They have been well known for serving high quality food, fresh and quickly prepared, in their squeaky clean kitchen to residents and visitors since 1984. They start with the freshest high quality food around and then use that great food to create your meal. Breakfast, Lunch, and Dinner are served 24 hours a day to satisfy any craving and any age. Kids' and Seniors menus are available. They are a wonderful choice for family dining and value when you are in the Great Falls area.

## L Wagon Wheel Motel

1818 10th Ave. S in Great Falls. 761-1300

Wright Nite Inns in Great Falls offers three properties: Wagon Wheel Motel, Sahara Motel, and Rendezvous Motel, with over 130 rooms, executive suites, and themed for their guests. Larry and Anne Wright will have just the room to help you

unwind, relax, and rejuvenate, while you enjoy a truly unique lodging experience. They even offer limo service throughout the "Electric City" in their Ultra Stretch Limo for the best of night life while you are in Great Falls. Select from themed rooms that feature romance, such as the 50s, Jungle, and Arabian rooms. Or maybe just plain fun and adventure. Other themes include the Barn Room, the Sports Room, or the Disney Room, with wonderful characters from your favorite Disney movies. Other amenities available are, indoor pool, sauna, jacuzzi, no smoking rooms, Showtime, complimentary coffee, fruit and popcorn.

## S Best of Montana Company

2912 10th Ave. S., Great Falls. 761-1233 or 877-761-1233. www.mtgifts.com

Best of Montana carries a complete line of Montana souvenirs, from shirts and caps to jams and jellies. They feature Montana Huckleberry products, including jams, chocolates and lotions.

They offer pottery from several local artisans and crafts from around the region. Their food selection includes coffee, tea, honey, syrups, soups, candy, jams/preserves, and much more! Samples are available daily. Stop on in for friendly helpful service, and visit them on-line for shopping at home. They can ship your purchases across town or across the world, just ask!

### M Montana State University College of Technology/Great Falls

2100 16th Ave.S., Great Falls. 771-4300 or 800-662-6132. www.msugf.edu

The Montana State University College of Technology in Great Falls has the charge for programs in allied health, business and office technology, trades and industry and related general education. It is also the site for the Montana University System Higher Education Center for Great Falls.

### M Montana State University Fire Services Training School

2100 16th Ave. South, Great Falls. 771-4100 or 800-446-2698, www.montana.edu/www.fire

The Fire Services Training School FSTS is the state level agency charged with providing professional development for community fire and rescue services and is attached to the Extension Service of Montana State University serving all of Montana's fire departments,companies and districts with an estimated 9,600 members in 355 organizations, 95% of which are volunteers. The FSTS develops and operates programs which make local government effective in their mission of providing quality fire and rescue service to the public.

### M University of Great Falls

1301 20th South, Great Falls. 761-8210 or 800-848-3431, www.ugf.edu

The University of Great Falls (UGF) is a private four-year Catholic University founded in 1932 as the College of Great Falls. It achieved university status in 1995 and offers an extensive telecom site program covering over 300,000 square miles, enabling students to earn degrees in 30 communities in Alberta, Canada, Montana, and Wyoming. The approximate enrollment is over 1,200 students.

### L Rendezvous Wright Nite Motel

10th Ave. S at Fox Farm Road in, Great Falls. 452-9525 or toll free 800-800-6483. www.wrightnite.com

## 13. *Gas, Food, Lodging*

## 14. *Attraction, Gas, Food, Lodging, Shopping*

### T Ursuline Centre

2300 Central Ave., Great Falls. 452-8585

The Ursuline Centre is a fully preserved Catholic academy-boarding school. When you visit the museum take note of the gargoyles over the front door. Inside the museum view the Native American relics and antique furnishings. Visit the third floor Chapel and view the exquisitely beautiful murals painted by Mother Raphael Schweda which have been preserved there since 1927. The collection covers over 100 years of history of the Ursuline Sisters lives and how they contributed to the history of Montana.

### T Gibson Park

Central Ave. & Park Ave. N, Great Falls.

The largest park in Great Falls was appropriately named for the city's founder. Colorful flower gardens, green lawns, majestic trees, a children's playground and an improved walking path fill the park. There is plenty of room for picnics and family gatherings. And kids love the Gibson Pond, home to a wide variety of waterfowl, including beautiful swans.

### T Cascade County Historical Society

422 2nd St. S. in Great Falls. 452-3462

From the first rough and tumble cowboys who camped here to the homesteaders who created a new life on this western edge of the great American prairie, to the visionaries who built the city of Great Falls, this museum traces their deeds and actions in history that informs and entertains. It's collection contains over 60,000 permanent items. The museum and gift shop are open year round.

### T C.M. Russell Museum

400 13th St. N., Great Falls. 727-8787

Charlie Russell captured the spirit of the Old West more clearly and lovingly than any other artist. His watercolors, oil paintings, bronzes and sketches offer a personal view of Montana life at the turn of the century. The C. M. Russell Museum has the most complete collection of his works, letters, and personal objects you'll find anywhere. On display is the original log Cabin Studio, built in 1903, where Russell not only entertained friends with his lively stories and campfire cooking, but also completed most of his works. The Russell Home, a designated National Historic Landmark, is located right next door. The museum and gift shop are open year round. There is a modest admission fee.

### T Children's Museum of Montana

22 Railroad St., Great Falls. 452-6661

This museum is full of hands-on activities and interactive exhibits. Exhibits include a Human Kaleidoscope, bubbles-bubble and more bubbles, a dinosaur dig, and the body shop—an actual hospital with X-rays and a life-size doll with removable organs, Indian village and sod house . It offers fun and interactive educational experience for the young and the young at heart. There's also a full schedule of special programs and events for children, parents, grandparents and more. You can perform in a puppet show, generate your own electricity, or build a model city in the Construction Zone. It's guaranteed family fun.

### T Paris Gibson Square Museum of Art

1400 1st Ave. N., Great Falls. 727-8255

Great Fall' s first high school, built in 1896, named for the City's founder, now houses the Paris Gibson Square. This is Great Falls premier cultural center and a nationally registered landmark. It is one of Great Falls more recognizable buildings with its gray sandstone walls and bright orange roof.The Square features a unique and ever-changing mix of contemporary art, focusing on the cultural diversity of the Northwest. In addition the building houses the Cascade County Historical Museum. There is also a gift shop and cafe. Open Tuesday through Sunday year round.

### H Chicago, Milwaukee and St. Paul Depot

9 1st Ave. N in Great Falls

The Chicago, Milwaukee and St. Paul Railway was constructed between 1907 and 1909, the last transcontinental railroad to cross Montana. Its service to Great Falls during the homestead boom supported the city's establishment as a major urban center for central Montana. When the Milwaukee Road completed this passenger depot in January of 1915, railway officials hailed it as the finest of its kind between Spokane and Chicago. The terminal is the only building in Great Falls made of "flash" brick, which is burned and unevenly fired. The 135-foot tower became a Great Falls landmark, acting as a giant marker of the depot's location. The corporate logos 100 feet up on each side of the tower were the first of this type, designed to be used on any railway station in the United States. They are composed of small, high-grade tiles pointed with tinted mortar to create a seamless effect—even if viewed close up. Each sign measures 17 feet by 10 feet. This grand railroad depot compares favorably with the Milwaukee Road's Passenger depots in Miles City (1909), Butte (1916-17) and Missoula (1910).

### F Primrose Tea Cottage

118 Central Ave., Great Falls. 452-3283

Primrose Tea Cottage is one of the most unique and charming restaurants in Great Falls. They serve delicious lunches and dreamy deserts every Monday through Saturday from 8:00 am to 4:30 p.m., with a different homemade soup each day of the week, hearty sandwiches served on fresh bread, and a variety of luscious cakes, pies and English scones made from scratch daily. They also serve numerous teas, coffees & lattes in a Victorian style tea room, old English pub, or delightful garden room. The owners are 3 sisters from the Great Falls area who serve their customers with wonderful cooking and a pleasant and warm atmosphere, along with their truly caring employees. Each one wears a smile on her face and loves serving guests.

### F Bert & Ernie's

300 1st Ave. S., Great Falls. 453-0601

Bert & Ernie's made a name for itself in Great Falls, known among locals and visitors for their great food, fun atmosphere and occasional live entertainment. Locally owned and operated for the past 23 years, the menu features a variety of choices ranging from burgers, chicken sandwiches and salads, to steaks and pasta dishes. Lunch and dinner specials are featured daily. The bar serves a unique selection of micro-brews and wines, and the friendly staff will charm you with western hospitality. Stop in for lunch or dinner Monday through Saturday.

### F Serendipity Café

200 Central Ave., Great Falls. 452-5895

*Montana Trivia*

Country and Western music star Charlie Pride once played semi-professional baseball in Great Falls.

### FL Perkins Family Restaurant & Mid Town Motel

526 2nd Ave. N., Great Falls. 453-2411 or 800-457-2411

### L Charlie Russell Manor

825 4th Ave. N., Great Falls. 455-1400 or fax 727-3771. Toll free 877-2076131. www.charlie-russell.com

The Charlie Russell Manor offers gracious western hospitality, from the house built in 1916, located on the original townsite of Great Falls. The Manor is located in the heart of the Northside Historic District and registered as a National Historic site. Five spacious rooms are equipped with private baths, telephones, data ports, televisions, Egyptian cotton linens, and air conditioning. The elegantly appointed rooms such as Jefferson Suite, Sacagawea/Charbonneau Room, York Room, and Shoshone/Blackfeet/Nez Perce Room, are exquisitely furnished by theme. Enjoy shaded patios surrounded by a lovely large lawn. Inside, relax in the drawing room, bright sun room, or den with a big screen television. A fine art collection, including bronze pieces and unique items of historical interest, is housed at the Manor. Of course, a hearty breakfast is served to guests! An experience waiting to happen. Visit their web site!

### L Collins Mansion Bed & Breakfast and Catering

1003 Second Ave. NW, Great Falls. 452-6798 or fax 452-6787. www.collinsmansion.com

The Collins Mansion, built in 1891, is listed on the National Historic Register. Beautifully landscaped grounds, a covered carriage entrance and gazebo, make the mansion a perfect setting for any special occasion. The home was restored to it's original grandeur and opened as a B & B and catering service in 1998. There are five beautifully appointed quest rooms, all with private baths. Enjoy the fresh Montana air and big sky from the wraparound veranda and recall times gone by. Gourmet breakfasts are served to their overnight guests. The Collins Mansion is delightful lodging centrally located for travel between Yellowstone and Glacier National Parks. Check their web site for more information.

### L O'Haire Motor Inn

7th & 1st Ave. S., Great Falls. 454-2141 Or 800-332-9819

Located in Downtown Great Falls, the O'Haire Motor Inn has 72 comfortably decorated guest rooms with cable TV and free local calls. The downtown location is close to shopping, many businesses, and government offices. The O'Haire Motor Inn Restaurant offers family style dining at reasonable rates with room service available. In the unique "Sip-N-Dip" Lounge you can watch the swimmers from under the surface of the indoor heated pool. Best of all, the indoor parking garage keeps the snow off all winter and provides protection from the sun in the summer. The friendly staff of this family owned and operated motel look forward to greeting you in Great Falls.

### L The Old Oak Inn

709 4th Ave. N., Great Falls. 727-5782 or 888-727-5782, www.mtbba.com

### S Candy Masterpiece Confectionery

120 Central Ave., Great Falls. 727-5955

Stepping into Candy Masterpiece Confectionery is a tantalizing, fun experience. A visual treat for your eyes and something to appeal to every sweet tooth. The shop is filled with wonderful gifts that

Section 12

can be shipped anywhere. Choose from a mouth watering selection of fine chocolates, homemade cream and butter fudge in 30 flavors, fresh-pulled salt water taffy, and candy to suit any craving. The shop also offers a great selection of sugar-free products. The friendly people working behind the counter are ready to help you "experience the flavor" with choice samplings to help you choose. Candy Masterpiece is located on the "Fun Hundred Block", downtown Great Falls.

### S In Cahoots for Tea

118 Central Ave., Great Falls. 452-2225. www.in-cahoots-for-tea.com

In Cahoots is located along the "Fun Hundred Block". You will be amazed to step inside and find a wonderful assortment of beautiful china, Lomonosov from Russia, fine Belleek from Ireland, and lovely bone china. Delight yourself with nearly 200 loose teas from all over the world, in addition to an enormous selection of bagged teas. The staff is always available for tea talk, sharing their knowledge of the world of tea and to help with all your tea enjoyment needs. A little "British Pantry" is chock full of many tasty treats that will bring back fond memories. Find an extensive variety of Heritage Lace that is washable, reasonably priced and made in the USA. In Cahoots offers shipping and special orders are always welcome.

### S Wood Express Home Furnishings

420 Central Ave., Downtown Great Falls. 453-9591, toll free 888-453-9591. www.woodexpress.net

Wood Express offers emotion and charm among many other things important to furnishing your home. The elegance of old style log furniture that allows your mind to drift back in time to the metal counter stools with rodeo events themes. From the smell of leather to the fabric upholstery designs of today, you'll find it at Wood Express. If you are looking for a special custom piece for your home they can build it in aspen, lodge pole pine, or cabinet oak. You can even order pieces unfinished so that you can finish them to match your woods. You won't find a friendlier place to shop and learn about the special needs for your home or retreat, right down to the artwork on the walls.

*Giant Springs*

## 15. *Lewis & Clark, Historical Marker, Attraction*

### H Black Eagle Falls

*The uppermost of the Great Falls of the Missouri bears west of this point. The name is a modern one derived from an entry for June 14th, 1805 in the journal of Capt. Meriwether Lewis of the Lewis and Clark Expedition. He discovered the falls on that date and wrote, "… below this fall at a little distance a beautifull little Island well timbered is situated about the middle of the river. in this Island on a Cottonwood tree an Eagle has placed her nest; a more inaccessable spot I believe she could not have found; for neither man nor beast dare pass those gulphs which separate her little domain from the shores."*

*After viewing the falls, Capt. Lewis ascended the hill to the former location of the smelter stack and saw "… in these plains and more particularly in the valley just below me immence herds of buffaloe…."*

*Roe River*

### T Giant Springs State Park

4600 Giant Springs Road, Great Falls. 454-5840

The Giant Springs Heritage State Park is a 218-acre facility which includes the spring, hatchery, and the regional headquarters and visitor center for the Montana Department of Fish, Wildlife and Parks. The spring is an unforgettable experience. About 7.9 million gallons of water run through the spring each hour making it the largest freshwater spring in the United States. Lewis and Clark were astonished at its size and Lewis wrote that it was the "largest fountain I ever saw…"

Not only does it claim the "largest spring" status, but the Roe River which flows from the Springs to the Missouri is the shortest river in the world at a mere 53 feet long. There is also a fish hatchery here where more than one million Rainbow Trout are raised each year and you're more than welcome to feed the fish. Keep your eyes open here for raccoons, beaver, pelicans, bald eagles, deer and more.

Madison Limestone lied under most of eastern Montana and is about 250 million years old. Rainfall and melted snow soaks into the limestone where it is exposed on the slopes of the Little Belt Mountains. The water drains downward and then flows through openings in the limestone to the Great Falls area where it flows upward about 700 feet through fractures. It is then forced out at Giant Springs by a force of about 300 pounds per square inch. Giant Springs discharges about 134 thousand gallons per minute. It contains calcium, magnesium, bicarbonate, and sulfate. It is excellent for growing Trout. The entire trip of 38 miles from the Little Belts to Giant Springs takes many hundres of years. *Text of interpretive sign at site.*

### T Lewis & Clark National Historical Trail

Inside Giant Springs Heritage State Park, Great Falls. 791-7717

### T River's Edge Trail

Great Falls. 761-4434

This trail stretches along the beautiful Missouri River for 13.3 miles and offers spectacular views, plenty of space and the chance to see bald eagles, pelicans and many other birds feeding at the river. Bike, skate, walk, or jog this splendid trail.

## T Lewis & Clark Interpretive Center

4201 Giant Springs Road, Great Falls. 727-8733

Centrally located along the 4,000-mile Lewis and Clark National Historic Trail, Great Falls is the heart of Montana country where Lewis and Clark and the rest of the Corps of Discovery camped more often and trekked more miles than any other trail state. Surrounded by the historic landscape, Interpretive Center visitors come to hike, fish, birdwatch, re-energize and re-live the Lewis and Clark adventure.

To see everything, plan a two-hour visit at the Interpretive Center. Spend your time in the theater with a feature film produced by Ken Burns, learn more at a costumed interpreter's presentation, tour the exhibit hall, stroll the paved trails or experience the Missouri River shoreline with a visit to River Camp.

Imagine the untamed prairie, prickly pear poking underfoot, a smoke scent drifting on the wind, an eagle soaring silently overhead, and the rumbling roar of a waterfall pounding the stillness.

Photo courtesy: USDA Forest Service, Lewis and Clark National Historic Trail Interpretive Center

Photo courtesy: USDA Forest Service, Lewis and Clark National Historic Trail Interpretive Center

Awaken your senses by stepping back in time to the open prairie where antelope grazed amongst roaming herds of bison, and Meriwether Lewis and William Clark with a small party of devoted companions known as the Corps of Discovery explored the landscape in the early 19th century. Indians called this land home; explorers called it paradise. Lewis wrote of the countryside in 1805, "*… I overlooked a most beatifull and extensive plain reaching from the river to the base of the snowclad mountains … I also observed the missoury stretching … through this plain to a great distance filled to it's even and grassey brim …*" The beauty of the prairie awaits those who visit the Lewis and Clark National Historic Trail Interpretive Center where the past meets the future. (Note: the spelling is just as it was in the journals)

Center exhibits feature the epic travels of Lewis and Clark through Indian Country, the West in 1805. Celebrate the successes, feel the frustrations.

From the lobby, enjoy panoramic views of the Missouri River and explore the centerpiece exhibit highlighting the expedition's struggle portaging the Great Falls of the Missouri River.

"*… I deturmined to examine & Survey the Portage find a leavel rout if possible- The 2 men despatched to examine the Portage gave an unfavourable account of the Countrey, reporting that the Creek & 2 deep reveens cut the Prarie in such a manner between the river and mountain as to render a portage in their oppinion for the Canoes impossible- we Selected 6 men to make wheels & to draw the Canoes on as the distance was probably too far for to be carried on the mens Shoulders…*" [Clark, June 16th of Sunday 1805] (Spelling is just as it was in the journals)

The story unfolds in the 6,000 square-foot exhibit hall. Journey back to 1804 and follow the Corps of Discovery from their departure in St. Charles, Missouri, up the Missouri River, across the expansive plains, through the white cliffs, and over the treacherous snow-capped mountains to the Columbia River and their ultimate goal, the Pacific Ocean shores. Feel their labors and pain by gripping a rope and pulling your own canoe against the incessant current; gauge your daily towing capacity using the mile-o-meter. Try your hand at building the iron boat; enjoy the cottonwood fragrance as you ring the doorbells and enter the Mandan lodge; translate four foreign languages as you negotiate for horses; and scribe your name at Pompey's Pillar.

With every step, meet the people who unselfishly embraced the explorers. Experience the Indian lifestyles so intriguing to the explorers, and witness the elaborate, often imperfect, diplomacy of the exploring party. Experience the struggles and successes of these early explorers traveling across the continent through the American West.

Seasonally, interpretive programs move outdoors. Enjoy guided walks on summer mornings; keep an eye open for a pelican swooping for the catch of the day; watch the native plants surrounding the facility burst to flower; and listen for the songbirds calling for a mate.

In River Camp along the shores of the Missouri, try your hand at hide scraping, cooking over an open fire, or pitching a tipi - daily survival skills essential to the enterprise.

Less than two miles upstream of the Interpretive Center today lies Black Eagle Falls. "*below this fall at a little distance a beatifull little Island well timbered is situated about the middle of the river. in this Island on a Cottonwood tree an Eagle has placed her nest …. the water is also broken in such manner as it descends over this pitch that the mist or sprey rises to a considerable hight.*" [Lewis, Friday June 14th 1805]

During the school year, thousands of schoolchildren engage in special programs integrating science, English, history, anthropology, ecology, geology, and leadership into their classroom instruction. Reservations are required for school groups. Call ahead for openings.

Like the tribes and the exploring party, nothing stays static at the Interpretive Center. Changing temporary exhibits, on loan from other national facilities, complement the Center's permanent collection.

The Center's bookstore, the Portage Cache, offers innovative selections for the discerning buyer. For scholars, the Archives Library of the Lewis and Clark Trail Heritage Foundation boasts a superior assemblage of collectable books. Schedule a research visit with the librarian.

Return time and again to see a new interpretive program, new exhibit, or new selection in the gift store.

Fees: Adults - $5.00; Seniors (62+) and Students with valid college ID - $4.00; Youths (6-17) - $2.00; Children (under 6) - free. Group rates available by pre-arrangement. Annual family and individual passes available. Golden Age, Golden Access, and Golden Eagle passes accepted.

Hours: Memorial Weekend–September 30, 9:00 a.m. to 6:00 p.m. Daily; October 1–Memorial Weekend, 9:00 a.m. to 5:00 p.m. Tuesday - Saturday and noon to 5:00 p.m. Sunday; closed

New Years, Thanksgiving, Christmas.

Press releases, events calendars and links to other Lewis and Clark groups are posted on the Interpretive Center's website: www.fs.fed.us/r1/lewisclark/lcic.htm

*Article provided by Lewis & Clark Interpretive Center*

### T Ryan Dam & Falls Overlook & Picnic Area

Hwy 87 approximately 4 mi. north of Great Falls to Ryan and Morony Dam turnoff. Follow signs. 761-4434

This great picnic spot is on Ryan Island and is accessed by crossing a large suspension bridge. Once on the island there is a short walk to the Ryan Falls Overlook.

### T Montana Department of Fish, Wildlife & Parks Visitors' Center

East side of the Missouri River; 3.7 miles on River Dr., Great Falls. 454-5840

There is a lot to learn about the area's wildlife at this center. There are a number of mounted animals and interpretive displays.

### D Mer. Lewis

June 13, 1805

*". . .a roaring too tremendious to be mistaken for any cause short of the great falls of the Missouri. . .this truly magnifficent and sublimely grand object"*

### D Mer. Lewis

June 14, 1805

*". . .presented by one of teh most beautifull objects in nature, a cascade of about fifty fee perpendicular streching at rightangles across the river from side to side to the distance of at least a quarter of a mile. . .the water descends un one even and uninterupted sheet to the bottom wher dashing against the rocky bottom rises into foaming billows of great hight and rappiedly glides away, hising flashing and sparkling as it departs."*

### D William Clark

June 23, 1805

*"The men has to haul with all their Strength wate & art, maney times every man all catching grass & knobes & Stones with their hands to give them more force in drawing in the Canoes & Loads, and notwithstanding the Coolness of the air in high presperation and every halt (the men) are asleep in a moment, maney limping from the Soreness of their feet"*

### D Pvt. Whitehouse

June 25, 1805

*"all of us amused ourselves with dancing until 10 oC. all in cheerfulness and good humor."*

### D Mer. Lewis

June 27, 1805

*"my dog seems to be in a constant state of alarm with these bear and keeps barking all night."*

### D Mer. Lewis

June 29, 1805

*"I have scarely experienced a day since my first arrival in this quarter without experiencing some novel occurrence among the party or witnessing the appearance of some uncommon object."*

### D Mer. Lewis

June 23, 1805

*"their fatiegues are incredible; some are limping from the soreness of their feet, others faint and unale to stand for a few minutes, with heat and fatiegue, yet no one complains all go with cheerfullness.*

## 16. *Attraction*

### T Malmstrom Heritage Center & Air Park

Malmstrom Air Force Base in Great Falls. 731-2705

This museum portrays the history of the base and the local area relating to aviation. Displays include the Lewis and Clark expedition of 1805, the WWII era with a barracks room and flight line diorama, the Strategic Missile Mission, including a simulated Launch Control Center and Re-entry Vehicle, the Air Defense Mission, and various other base missions or functions. There is a very extensive military model collection.

This is a great museum for aviation buffs. You'll find a large collection of past and present military aircraft including the F-86A Sabre Jet, F-102A Delta Dagger, a KC-97G Stratotanker, a Minuteman missile, a F-101B/F Voo Doo and more. The museum is open year round with shortened hours in the winter.

## 17. *Attraction, Gas, Food*

### Black Eagle

Named for the nearby falls on the Missouri which was named by Lewis and Clark for the many eagles in the area. In the early 1900s, it was nicknamed "Little Chicago" because of the refineries and smelters that fed its existence. The town was populated early on by people of Slavic descent who, for many years, retained the habits, customs and dialects of the old country.

### T Tenth Street Bridge

10th St. spanning the Missouri River, Great Falls.

This bridge is the oldest open-span, multi-arched bridge in Montana. It is the longest bridge of its type in all the Great Plains states stretching for 1,330 feet across the Missouri River. It is listed on the National Register of Historic Places. The bridge almost met its demise when a new modern span was constructed to replace it. A group of citizens filed suit to halt the demolition. The city of Great Falls now owns the bridge and plans to restore it are underway.

### T Benton Lake National Wildlife Refuge

9 miles north of Great Falls on 15th St.

See sidebar.

### F The Prospector Casino & Restaurant

907 Smelter Ave., Great Falls. 452-5266

The family owned and operated Prospector Casino features an attractive casino with video poker and keno, as well as a full service bar. They offer an extensive menu complete with daily specials and good home-style cooking, featuring steaks, sandwiches, soups and salads. Live keno is available here as well. Enjoy the Silver City Casino while you are there!

> **Montana Trivia**
>
> The Roe River in Great Falls is the world's shortest river. It flows 201 feet from Giant Springs to the Missouri River.

### F Borrie's Family Restaurant

1800 Smelter Ave., Great Falls. 761-0300

## 18. *Attraction, Gas, Food, Lodging*

### T Montana Cowboys Association Museum

311 3rd St. NW, Great Falls. 761-9299

The Cowboys Museum is one of the many projects the Montana Cowboys Association has undertaken to perpetuate the historical importance of Western heritage. Built in the late 1930s by the National Youth Administration and opened in 1941, the Cowboys Museum is an authentic log cabin with double fireplaces and replicas of hitching posts from Montana's frontier days.

Exhibits include a lady's intricately fashioned side-saddle, a trickrope saddle, numerous Indian artifacts, and a Kimball-Reed organ that was brought down-river from St. Louis to Fort Benton, Montana in 1876. There is also a gun collection that even avid gun collectors would be in awe of, a rivet set made by Kid Curry, and local cowboy artist Charlie Russell's black boots, and a list that goes on with over 500 momentos of a romantic era in our nation's history and is an integral part of Montana's past. The museum opens at 11 a.m. daily, year round. You can even enjoy a cold beer while you are there! Admission to the museum is free.

### F The Feedlot West

1701 3rd St. NW, Great Falls. 727-3563

### L Days Inn Great Falls

101 14th Ave., Great Falls. 727-6565 Or 800-329-7466. wwwdaysinn.com.

Conveniently located off I-15 in Northwest Great Falls, the Days Inn is close to shopping, entertainment, restaurants, casinos, museums, golfing, the City Convention Center, Lewis & Clark Interpretive Center, and State Fairgrounds. The 62 clean and quiet guest rooms feature queen size beds, cable TV with remote, in-house movies, free local calls, non-smoking rooms, guest laundry and a complimentary continental breakfast. Whether you are in Great Falls for business or pleasure you are sure to be pleased with their friendly staff and affordable rates.

**19.** *Gas, Food, Lodging*

**20.** *Historical Marker, Attraction, Gas, Food*

## Belt

Belt is named for a nearby mountain with a surrounding belt, or girdle, of rocks. Coal mining first began here and supplied fuel for nearby smelters in Great Falls. In 1930, the smelters were converted to natural gas and the coal market plummeted.

### H Belt Jail

Belt

*Lewis and Clark or early trappers named nearby Belt Butte for its girdle or rocks. In 1877, John Castner founded the town that would finally be called Belt. Coal brought Castner here, and Fort Benton was the first market for his Castner Coal Company. In 1894, Castner merged his company with the Anaconda Mining Company, whose Great Falls reduction works had already been using Castner's coal. Their mine soon employed a thousand men. The town experienced a boom time and in 1900 was Cascade County's second-largest community, with a population above 2,800, including French, Finnish, Slav, German and Swedish immigrants. The sandstone jail was constructed for $1,500 during the boom, when 32 saloons flourished in town. Fire destroyed the Anaconda mine in 1915, and in 1930 the smelters stopped using coal. While small wagon mines operated and the town served as an agricultural center, Belt's population fell off. The jail itself survived major floods in 1909 and 1953, and a 1976 fire caused by a train derailment.*

### T Mehmke's Steam Museum

10 miles east of Great Falls on Hwy 89. 452-6571

This museum gives visitors a first-hand look at prairie farm life. From its collection of fully operational steam traction and gas engines to the charming display of household items, this museum offers a glimpse into Montana's homestead roots. One of the more interesting exhibits here is an antique bar that once was in a Great Falls saloon at the turn of the century.

### T Belt Museum

Belt. 277-3616

The museum is located in the town's original jail building, dating back to 1895. Open Memorial Day through Labor Day or by appointment. No admission charged.

### F Black Diamond Supper Club

64 Castner St., Belt. 277-4118

**21.** *Historical Marker, Gas, Food*

## Brady

There is some disagreement as to where this town got its name. Some say it was named for a Dr. Brady who came to this area to treat an outbreak of smallpox while the narrow gauge railroad from Shelby to Great Falls was under construction here. Another theory is that it was named for the attorney for the rail line. Today it is a grain marketing and distribution center.

## Collins

The Great Falls and Canada Railroad was a narrow gauge line built around 1890 and ran from Great Falls to Lethbridge. The town's namesake, Timothy Collins was stockholder and director of the line.

## Dutton

Dutton began as a railroad siding and was named for a little known employee of the Great Northern Railroad. "Sinker Bill" Frixel first settled this land in 1909. He got his name from the roundup crews he cooked for. They described his biscuits as "sinkers." Frixel later sold his land to George Sollid. After five years, George sold his ranch but stayed in the area as a "land locater." As one of the first real estate agents in the state he is credited with most of the original growth of this town. George advertised the area with brochures and booklets to people in the midwest offering cheap land, a good life, and bounteous crops. He eventually located land for 85 per cent of the homesteaders who came to the area. Many of his clientele were sent to him by his brother in Conrad. According to one source, newcomers were told: *"Just go down to the depot and sit around looking like a sucker. It won't be long before George will show up."*

## Power

The town of Power started as a wheat shipping point on the Great Northern Railroad. The town was named for T.C. Power, a homesteader in the early 1900s. At one time two bars were built so close to the tracks that the train engineer could reach out the window and grab a beer as he went by. When he blew his whistle, some thought it was to warn the horse and buggy traffic crossing the tracks to beware. It was really a signal to the bar owners—"Here I come, have my beer ready."

### H The Whoop-Up Trail

I-15, north of Dutton.

*During the 1860s and 1870s supplies and trade goods that came up the Missouri River from St. Louis were transferred at Fort Benton from steamboat to wagon freight for inland distribution. In 1868, a freight trail was open from Fort Benton to Fort McLeod, a military post in Canada located west of Lethbridge. Traders, who eagerly swapped firewater for furs, soon found*

### Montana Trivia

Giant Springs, in Great Falls, is the largest freshwater spring in the world. It pumps an amazing 7.9 million gallons of water every hour at a constant temperature of 54 degrees. The water is carbon dated at three thousand years old.

## Benton Lake National Wildlife Refuge

**Benton Lake National Wildlife** Refuge is located on the western edge of the northern Great Plains near Great Falls, Montana. The "lake" is actually a 5,800 acre shallow marsh in a closed basin created by the last continental glacier to occupy the area. The gently rolling refuge uplands are dominated by 6,000 acres of native short grass prairie. Approximately 700 acres of former cropland has been planted to dense nesting cover, a mix of tall growing grasses and legumes. Water for refuge marshes is supplied by natural runoff from the small Lake Creek watershed and by water pumped from Muddy Creek, a stream 15 miles west of the refuge. The refuge wetlands support a great variety of water birds with both nesting and migration habitat. Up to 100,000 ducks, 40,000 geese, 5,000 tundra swans, and occasionally bald eagles and peregrines may be observed in migration. Up to 20,000 ducks, 500 canada geese, 10,000 franklin's gulls are produced each year along with many shorebirds, eared grebes, white-faced ibis and other species. A nine mile auto tour route is open to the public for wildlife observation. About 4,000 acres is open to public hunting of game birds.

Directions:

From Great Falls, MT, drive north on 15th Street/US 87 to its junction with Bootlegger Trail on the northern outskirts of the city. Look for the "Benton Lake Wildlife Refuge" sign. Turn left onto Bootlegger Trail (paved) and drive north 9.25 miles. Turn left on the Refuge Entrance Road (gravel) and drive 1.75 miles west to the refuge office.

Benton Lake NWR
Fish and Wildlife Service
National Wildlife Refuge System
922 Bootlegger Trail
Great Falls, MT 59404-6133
Phone: 406-727-7400
Email:r6rw_bnl@fws.gov

*Reprinted from www.recreation.gov*

*themselves in need of protection from their patrons who sometimes felt they hadn't been given a square deal. This encouraged the building of "whiskey forts" or trading posts along the trail. The exact origin of the name "Whoop-up" is lost, but one old-timer told this story: "When Johnny LaMotte, one of the traders, returned to [Fort] Benton from across the border, he was asked, 'How's business 'Aw, they're just whoopin' 'er up!' was the reply."*

*The Whoop-up Trail was the precursor in reverse of Alberta-Montana rum-running channels of the noble experiment era. Though its prime traffic furthered the trading of headaches for hides it did gain a modicum of respectability by becoming a supply route for a few legitimate wares consigned to old Fort McLeod. The trail ran near here.*

### Montana Trivia

The buttes prevelant in this area are known as laccoliths. They are formed when magma rises, but is unable to break through the surface, then hardens. It is later revealed by erosion.

**22.** *Lewis & Clark, Gas, Food, Lodging*

## Conrad

Conrad is named for W. G. Conrad, a significant figure in the Conrad Investment Company which owned much of the land in this area. The town is located near the old trading post where Fort Conrad was located. Close by, Lake Francis, Lake Elwell, and the Marias River extend adventure for both fishing and boating. Occasionally, the only company in these parts is a wide variety of wildlife.

### D Sgt. Gass
July 11, 1806

*"came to the Missouri at the Bear islands, nearly opposite our old encampment."*

### D Mer. Lewis
July 19, 1806

*"the river bottoms. . .possess a considerable quantity of timber entirely cottonwood; the underbrush is honeysuckle rose bushes the narrow leafed willow and bufaloberry. . .the plants are beautiful and level but the soil is but thin."*

**23.** *Attraction, Gas, Food, Lodging*

### T Gold Butte
I-15, on the Canadian border.

The Blackfeet Indians were no doubt the first to discover gold in the Sweet Grass Hills. In the 1870s a survey party found gold but didn't develop the area. In 1884 prospectors found gold, wintered in the area, and eventually built the town, that lasted for about five years, yet several of the few buildings still stand.

## Sweetgrass

Today Sweetgrass is the last town on I-15 before crossing the border to Canada. In 1890 a narrow-gauge railroad called the Turkey Track ran from Great Falls to the Canadian town of Lethbridge. The dry land farmers came with the railroad and Sweetgrass became a booming trade center. The town gets its name from the "sweet" grass which grows in abundance around the town.

**24.** *Historical Marker, Gas, Food, Lodging*

## Fort Shaw

Fort Shaw, located on the Sun River twenty-four miles west of Great Falls, has been coined the "Queen of Montana's Posts." Boasting one building 125 feet long, the first professional stage performance in Montana was presented here. The theater had log seats, and the entire orchestra rose in unison and turned down the kerosene lamps that lined the stage to dim the lights during a play. First a military post and later a school for Native Americans, Fort Shaw remains today to tell of a lively past.

## Sun River

This is one of the oldest settlements still active in the state—though barely. Travelers going from Fort Benton the the gold fields in western Montana crossed through here. Before the railroad came it was a boisterous town where trappers, miners and bull whackers got together for a good time. The town got its name from the nearby river. French trappers interpreted the Indian name for the river, *Natae-oeti* to mean "medicine" or "sun."

## Simms

Now dominated by farmers, the town was one time a cattleman's town. It was named for an early settler.

### H Fort Shaw
Rte. 21, Fort Shaw.

*Barring fur trading posts, the first important white settlements in Montana were the mining camps in the western mountains. Everything to the east belonged to the plains Indians and was buffalo range. To protect the miners and settlers from possible incursions of hostile tribes, a series of military posts was established around the eastern border of the mining camps and settlements. Fort Shaw, established in 1867, was one of these. It also protected the stage and freight trail from Fort Benton, head of navigation on the Missouri, to the Last Chance Gulch placer diggings at Helena. Everything north of the Sun River was Blackfeet Indian Territory at that time. The fort was built by the 13th U.S. Infantry, under Major Wm. Clinton.*

*General Gibbon led his troops from here in 1876 to join General Terry and General Custer on the Yellowstone just prior to the latter's disastrous fight with the Sioux and Cheyenne Indians at the Battle of the Little Big Horn.*

**25.** *Attraction, Food*

## Fairfield

Beer lovers bow down. This is the malting barley capital of the world. It began as a station on the Milwaukee Railroad and now serves as a trading center for the farmers on the Greenfield Bench. The name is descriptive of the abundant hay and grain fields surrounding the town.

### T Freezout Lake Wildlife Area
Hwy 89, south of Choteau.

With easy access from Highway 89, this 12,000-acre management area is a magnificent place to enjoy the splendor of millions of birds that migrate here. At peak migration times (March–May, September–November) up to 300,000 snow geese and 10,000 tundra swans have been seen here. Ibis, herons, sandhill cranes, gulls, eagles, hawks and owls are just a few other birds spotted here. This area is a great place to camp or bike.

**26.** *Lewis & Clark, Historical Marker, Gas, Food, Lodging, Shopping*

## The Métis

**At one time over 30,000 Métis** lived in Manitoba and Saskatchewan, Canada. The Métis are a mixed breed of Cree, Chippewa, French, English and Scottish heritage. They were driven out of Canada in the late 1880s with the death of their leader, Louis Riel, following the Red River Rebellion. Many of them fled into Montana fearing reprisals following the rebellion to continue their traditional lifestyle. They found homes in the sharp canyons and mountains to the west of Choteau.

Public Order 103 went out on May 1, 1883 calling for the expulsion of the Cree Indians that resulted in a death march through Augusta and Choteau. Many of the Montana Métis were swept up in this process, in spite of having been well established in the area communities.

While the story of the Canadian Métis is well documented, the story of the Montana Métis is just beginning to be understood. The Métis Cultural Recovery Trust has organized the historic cabin at the Old Trail Museum in Choteau and has re-created a "Red River" car at the museum grounds.

## Augusta

Lewis and Clark passed through this area in 1806. Their presence here was well documented in their journals. Historians conclude that the prominent landmark they mentioned was the now-famous Haystack Butte.

Around 1862, cattlemen brought large herds to the area. The South Fork of the Sun River gained a reputation for being one of the stock paradises of Montana. Before the winter of '86-'87, it was estimated that there were more than a half million head of cattle grazing in the area. That disastrous winter claimed almost 70% of the herds.

In 1901, a booming Augusta caught fire and within two hours the entire business section burned to the ground. The gutsy residents rebuilt and the town reached its peak in 1914.

This is a town with a real Western flavor. The western facades on the buildings, the general store, and the Buckhorn saloon all take you to days past. Latigo & Lace is one of the more contemporary establishments with an old west flavor. Augusta was named after the daughter of rancher J.D. Hogan. When the railroad bypassed it and built its 1912 station a few miles to the north, Augusta's existence was threatened by the new town of Gilman which was built on that site. By 1942, however, Augusta was still alive while the upstart town had faded. Today it remains the economic center for the surrounding ranch area.

### H Sun River
Augusta

*The Sun River was called the Medicine River by the Indians in the days of the Lewis and Clark Expedition (1804-06). The Indian name was probably given because of an unusual mineral deposit possessing marked medicinal properties which exist in a side gulch of the Sun River Canyon west of here.*

*This country was claimed and occupied by the Blackfeet Nation in the frontier days. After the Indians were relegated to reservations it became cattle range.*

*In 1913 the U.S. Reclamation Service built a storage and diversion dam near the mouth of the canyon and the water is used for irrigation on the valleys and bench lands east of here.*

### D Mer. Lewis

July 7, 1806

*"saw some sighn of boffaloe early this morning. . .from which it appears that the buffaloe do sometimes penetrate these mountains a few miles."*

### D Mer. Lewis

July 6, 1806

*"much rejoiced at finding ourselves in the plains of the Missouri which abound with game."*

### VL Benchmark Wilderness Outfitter & Guest Ranch

Benchmark Road, 28 miles west of Augusta. Phone or fax 562-3336, outfitter, 467-3110

### L Viewforth Bed & Breakfast

4600 Hwy 287, 7 miles north of Augusta. 467-3884. www.viewforth.com or email at info@viewforth.com

Viewforth Bed & Breakfast is located on the fabled Rocky Mountain Front. The dining area looks out onto the high plains to the east, the mountains to the west. Cattle, sheep, haystacks and abundant bird life are part of the surrounding landscape. Dramatic skyscapes of day give way to spectacular sunsets and moonlight walks under a billion stars confirm that you are in Big Sky Country. Guest rooms are quietly elegant with private baths. Heirloom linens and silver grace the breakfast table where aromas, tastes, and visual pleasures all combine perfectly. The lovely garden and front porch are much favored spots. Nearby attractions include hiking trails, Nature Conservancy sites, buffalo jumps, and dinosaur digs. Viewforth is on the most scenic route between Yellowstone and Glacier.

### S Latigo & Lace

124 Main St., Augusta. 562-3665

This unique store has been referred to as "a cultural watering hole on the Eastern Front" and is a necessary stop. You can find award-winning art by regional artists, fine bronzes and antler carvings, antiques, great books, music, unusual pottery, blown glass, hand-woven rugs and baskets by local artists, beautiful quilting and beadwork, one-of-a-kind clothing, jewelry, wood and antler buttons, and a great kids section, just to name a few. Since opening in 1992, Latigo and Lace has made a name for itself across Montana. Stop in for something refreshing from the cappuccino bar and some local color while you browse through the unique collection of gifts and art in this authentic western town. Open seven days a week summer through Christmas.

## 27. *Attraction*

### T Gibson Reservoir

Northwest of Augusta. 791-7700

Gibson Dam, the principal structure of the Sun River Project, is on the Sun River, 70 miles west of Great Falls, Montana. It is a concrete arch dam and contains 167,500 cubic yards of concrete. The reservoir, with 1,296 surface acres and 15 miles of shoreline, offers fair fishing for rainbow trout, cutthroat trout, and brown trout. Recreation is managed for Reclamation by the U.S. Forest Service as part of the Lewis and Clark National Forest which can be reached at 791-7700. *Reprinted from www.recreation.gov*

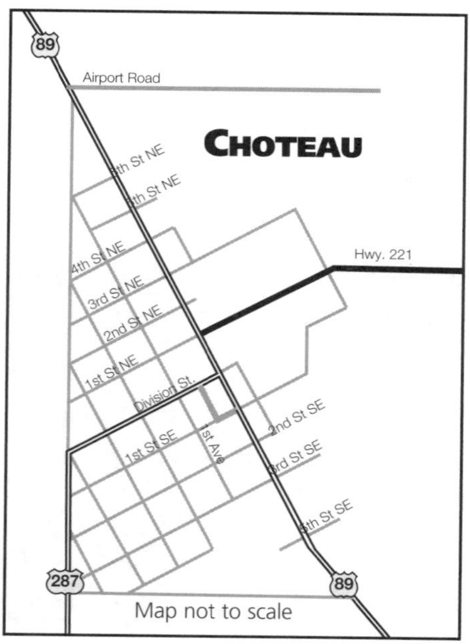


### T Sun River Canyon

From Augusta take Willow Creek Rd. northwest approximately 4 miles to Sun River Rd. Follow Sun River Rd., 15 miles to the Canyon. 466-5341

This 4,000 acre area is one of the best places in the state to view bighorn sheep. In November and December you can hear the clashing of horns as they fight for mating rights. During the rest of the year, you can see them grazing on the canyon floor, or leaping from cliff to cliff overhead.

## 28. *Historical Marker, Attraction, Gas, Food, Lodging, Shopping*

## Choteau

Choteau was named to honor Pierre Choteau, Jr., the president of the American Fur Company and the first to bring a steamboat up the Missouri. It is one of the oldest towns still alive in Montana which began as a trading post. Once a center for large cattle ranchers, cattle and sheep raising continues as an important key to the economy of the area.

Early Native Americans migrated along the Old North Trail in the foothills west of Choteau. For centuries, buffalo and Blackfeet Indians claimed the endless prairies. Later, fur trappers and traders worked their way through the area followed by stockmen and farmers of the present. The cultures of the German Hutterites and French-Indian Metis add to the unique texture and history of Choteau.

The historic quarrystone courthouse stands imposingly on the "village green," the center of town. Cottonwood-lined streets extend out to the grasslands with mountains beyond. Congenial and open, Choteau area residents reach out to visitors sharing their special Western hospitality.

### H Old Agency on the Teton

Northwest of Choteau.

*About 1/4 mile SE of this point, a huge native stone marks the site of "Old Agency" of the former Blackfeet Indian Reservation. The agency was established in 1868-69 and with unusual generosity, the whites in authority permitted Blackfeet chiefs to select the location. They chose the spot known to them as "Four Persons" because of the pleasant memories associated with it. Some of their warriors had overtaken and dispatched four furtive Crees there a few years before.*

*At Old Agency, in 1869, the first government agricultural experiment was conducted. In 1872 the first public school was opened for the benefit of the Blackfeet. Neither project attained notable popularity with the beneficiaries. However, that same year they were impressed by young "Brother Van," a circuit-riding Methodist lay preacher, not so much by the sincere fervor of his oratory as by his courage, skill and stamina during a buffalo hunt staged in his honor.*

*The Northwest Fur Company and I. G. Baker and Brother operated licensed Indian trading posts near the agency where they pursued the tolerably lucrative business of bartering tobacco, beads, and other essential goods for furs.*

*At his request, Big Lake, a great chief of the Blackfeet, was buried on a high point overlooking Old Agency so that his spirit could look down on his people as they came to trade.*

*Reservation boundaries were moved north to Birch Creek by a Congressional Act of April 15, 1874 and in 1876 Old Agency on the Teton was abandoned.*

### H Blackfeet and Buffalo

Northwest of Choteau.

*In the days of the fur traders and trappers immediately following the time of the Lewis and Clark Expedition (1804-06) all of this country bordering the Rocky Mountains from here north into Canada and south to the three forks of the Missouri and to the Yellowstone River was buffalo range and the hunting grounds of the Blackfeet Nation. These Indians were fierce and willing fighters who jealously guarded their territory from invasion.*

*Like all of the Plains Indians they were dependent upon the buffalo for their existence. The herds meant meat, moccasins, robes, leggings and tepees. Board and room on the hoof. Some Indian legends say that the first buffalo came out of a hole in the ground. When the seemingly impossible happened and the buffalo were wiped out there were Indians who claimed the whites found the spot, hazed the herds back into it, and plugged the hole.*

### T Old Trail Museum

823 N. Main, Choteau. 466-5332

This museum is chock full of perfectly preserved fossils, life-sized dinosaur models, and educational dioramas. It possesses a unique dinosaur room where you can view fossils and watch a video about the nearby finds. It also showcases the history of Native American culture along the Rocky

*The Marias River Valley.*

Mountain Front. Other attractions are an A. C. Robinson railroad collection, an antique medical instruments collection, homesteader artifacts, a grizzly bear exhibit, and the Old North Trail Exhibit. Open May through September.

### T Teton Spring Creek Bird Reserve
823 N. Main in Choteau. 466-5332

### F Circle N Restaurant
925 N. Main, Choteau.466-5531

The Circle N Restaurant boasts all home-style cooking, serving locals and visitors for over 30 years. They use only fresh vegetables and cut their own meat to order. The homemade soups and daily specials are very popular with a different offering for lunch and dinner every day. Ask your waitress for the wine list for a selection to complement your steak, seafood or chicken dinner choice. They also offer waist watcher meals in addition to a variety of salad selections. All food orders can be prepared to go, and catering is available for special occasions of any size. The restaurant is open daily from 11 a.m. to 10 p.m.

### F Log Cabin Café
102 S. Main, Choteau. 466-2888

The Log Cabin Café has a reputation for offering the some of the best food and service along the Rocky Mountain Front! Try their hearty homemade soups, delectable desserts, pies and huge sweet rolls. If variety is what you're looking for, the Log Cabin Café offers hearty breakfasts, fresh salads, fresh pasta dishes and their mouthwatering prime rib, served on Friday and Saturday nights.

Enjoy a game menu with Montana-grown buffalo or elk. The café has a Sunday breakfast buffet from 8:00 A.M. to noon. They make great lunches to go from a carry out menu with an outdoor adventure in mind. Open 7 days a week during the summer from 7:00 A.M. to 9:00 P.M. and closed Mondays in the winter. Blue Jeans Cuisine at it's finest!

### F Outpost Deli & Ice Cream Parlor
819 N. Main, Choteau. 466-5330

The Outpost Deli and Ice Cream Parlor, with a log cabin atmosphere is the place to satisfy that urge for yummy homemade cinnamon rolls, deli sandwiches, hamburgers and fries, or Meadow Gold Ice Cream. They serve a full breakfast where people help themselves to coffee. The Outpost Deli is like a home away from home for many locals, friends and repeat customers throughout the states who stop in on their visits to Choteau. Word of mouth has brought many customers in for the cinnamon rolls or just to relax and visit. They also offer artwork and gifts, including a crochet from some of the ladies in town, and framed photographs by the owner's husband. Easy to find across the street from the Old Trail Museum.

### L Stage Stop Inn
1005 N. Main, Choteau. 466-5900
or fax 466-5907 and toll free 888-466-5900.
www.stagestopinn.com

The Stage Stop Inn is found at the "Wild Edge of the Rockies and offers spectacular views of the Rocky Mountain Front, beautiful western decor, and stunning trophy mounts. They offer 43 rooms, including nonsmoking and handicapped accessible, and all specially designed to minimize noise. You'll enjoy other services such as free local phone service, indoor pool, hot tub, cable television, children under 12 free, free continental breakfast, and outdoor kennels available for your pets. They also have meeting and banquet facilities for business or pleasure. You'll find pure western hospitality at the Stage Stop Inn and a super location to some of the state's great attractions. Be sure and visit their web site.

### L Bella Vista Motel
614 N. Main St., Choteau. 466-5711

The Bella Vista Motel offers a quaint cottage-type motel that has been serving guests for about 40 years. They boast a bed and breakfast atmosphere, without the breakfast. Enjoy this jewel on your stop in Choteau. Each room is uniquely decorated with lovely wallpaper, hardwood floors and cozy and comfortable furnishings. Non smoking rooms are available. The Bella Vista Motel is located at the quiet north end of town, and is an easy walk to Choteau's great shopping and dining. Pam Price will be there to greet you and make your visit memorable.

### *It Happened in Montana*

On January 23, 1870, 200 cavalrymen opened fire on a Blackfeet Indian village. 173 were killed. The 140 survivors had to walk ninety miles for help. The temperature was 35 below zero. Only one cavalryman died.

**L Gunther Motel & Apartments**
20 7th Ave. SW, Choteau. 466-5444
or toll free 877-491-5444

**S Grandma's Attic**
304 N. Main Street, Choteau. 466-3669

## 29. *Attraction*

**T Egg Mountain**
Go south on Hwy. 287 to sign for Pishkun Reservoir (at Triangle Meat Packing Plant). Head south on Bellview Rd. for approximately six miles to fork. Go right at the fork. Choteau. 994-2251 or 466-5332

Egg Mountain isn't really a mountain, but a rounded hill among many other similar hills. It is known for the discovery of the first dinosaur egg in the Western Hemisphere. In 1978 more than 300 specimens of the duck-billed Maiasaura dinosaur were unearthed from a nesting area known as the Two Medicine formation. That is where the name "Egg Mountain" was derived. The eggs were discovered by Jack Horner, paleontologist, the Museum of the Rockies in Bozeman.

The land, now owned by the Nature Conservancy, covers about 3,600 square miles in a 2,000-foot-deep layer of sandstone dating back 80 million years. This mountain is a perfect place to acquaint oneself with these massive creatures of long ago.

**T Pishkun Reservoir**
Go south on Hwy. 287 to sign for Pishkun Reservoir (at Triangle Meat Packing Plant). Head south on Bellview Rd. for approximately six miles to fork. Go left at the fork. Choteau. 466-5332

Pishkun Dikes and Reservoir are part of the Sun River Project. The Reservoir is an offstream storage reservoir, about 15 miles northeast of Gibson Dam and is formed by 8 earthfill dikes with heights ranging from 12 to 50 feet and an overall length of 9,050 feet. This reservoir, with 1,550 surface acres and 13 miles of shoreline, offers major game fishing for kokanee salmon, northern pike, and rainbow trout. Picnic shelter available. (Reprinted from www.recreation.gov.)

**T Pine Butte Swamp Preserve**
Approximately 20 miles west of Choteau.

This 18,000 acre preserve offers excellent wildlife viewing including grizzly bears and golden eagles. On this site is Egg Mountain, the first location in North America to yield dinosaur nests. The site has yielded two new species of dinosaurs. There are a number of well marked short hikes. Hiking in some areas of the preserve is limited to protect the bears.

## 30. *Food*

### Bynum

The town of Bynum took its name from Stephen Bynum, one of the early settlers in the area. The town today still has a one room schoolhouse with an enrollment of around 40 students.

> **Montana Trivia**
>
> Smallpox devasted the Blackfeet tribe in 1837 when a steamboat with an infected crew docked at Fort Benton. The disease swept through the tribe killing more than 6,000—two-thirds of the tribe.

**TS T-rex Agate Shop - Bynum Rock & Gift Shop**
161 S. Front, Bynum. 469-2314.
www.trexagateshop.com or email: trex@3rivers.net

The Bynum Rock and Gift Shop, also known as T-rex Agate Shop, has been serving the public for 65 years from a a turn-of-the-century church building. Dinosaur murals painted on the building provide the first evidence of the shop's unique history and product offerings. It was in the museum portion of this shop that Jack Horner, Montana's own noted paleontologist, identified the first remains of baby dinosaurs known in North America. Marion Brandvold, the lady who found them, can still be found overseeing the store. The Rock Shop offers a wide variety of gift items as well as rocks, minerals, crystals, books, and jewelry. It is widely known for its quality merchandise at excellent prices, and for the friendly staff. They are open seven days a week.

**V Timescale Adventures**
121 2nd Ave. S., Bynum. 469-2211
or fax 469-2241 or Toll free at 800-238-6873.
www.timescale.org or email: info@timescale.org

Are you ready for a real adventure? A "Timescale Adventure"? This is a hands-on, educational science center specializing in dinosaur research. As a nonprofit organization, Timescale Adventures decided early on that it's mission would be to provide the public with access to and involvement in it's research projects. The team is led by David Trexler, who is best known for his work on duck-billed dinosaurs. The current research quarry contains the remains of 2 dinosaur species thought to be new to science. You, too, can be a part of this exciting project. Participation in Timescale Adventures' programs is by advance registration only. Give Timescale Adventures a call or check their website and get ready for an adventure you won't forget.

> **Montana Trivia**
>
> Glacier County, which encompasses the Blackfeet Indian Reservation, produces the world's highest per-acre yield of flax.

### Pendroy

Established in 1916 when the Great Northern railway extended its branch line from Bynum, 11 miles to the south. Named for Levi Boots Pendroy, a personal friend of railroad magnate James J. Hill, this town was the terminus of the branch line.

**T Blackleaf Wildlife Management Area**
15 miles west of Bynum. 278-7754 or 454-5840

The sharp canyon walls and wetlands of this 10,000 acre refuge are home to a wide variety of wildlife including black and grizzly bears, mountain goats, elk, mule and whitetail deer, golden eagles and prairie falcons.

## 31.

### Dupuyer

This is one of the oldest towns along the Rocky Mountain Front. It takes its name from Dupuyer Creek. The name came from the French word *depouilles*, which fur trappers and explorers used to describe the back fat of a buffalo. This was a delicacy revered by both the whites and the Indians. The town came was a stage stop on the bull team freight route between Fort Benton and Fort Browning.

### Valier

Named in honor of Peter Valier of LaCombre, Wisconsin, who supervised the construction of the Montana Western Railroad. The Montana Western connected Valier with the main line of the Great Northern. The area was settled by a group of Belgian immigrants that arrived in 1913 by train.

**H Captain Meriwether Lewis**
North of Dupuyer.

*Captain Meriwether Lewis of the Lewis and Clark Expedition, accompanied by three of his men, explored this portion of the country upon their return trip from the coast. On July 26, 1806, they met eight Piegans (Blackfeet), who Lewis mistakenly identified as Gros Ventres, and camped with them that night on Two Medicine Creek at a point northeast of here. Next morning the Indians, by attempting to steal the explorers' guns and horses, precipitated a fight in which two of the Indians were killed.*

*This was the only hostile encounter with Indians that the Expedition encountered in their entire trip from St. Louis to the Pacific and back. Lewis unwittingly dropped a bombshell on the Piegans with the news that their traditional enemies, the Nez Perce, Shoshoni and Kootenai, were uniting in an American-inspired peace and would be getting guns and supplies from Yankee traders. This threatened the Blackfeet's 20-year domination of the Northern Plains made possible by Canadian guns.*

**H Dupuyer**
Hwy 89, north of Dupuyer.

*Dupuyer, a colorful frontier cattle town and 1880s stop on the Fort Shaw-Fort Macleod Trail, is the oldest town between Fort Benton and the Rocky Mountains. Joe Kipp and Charlie Thomas, whiskey traders, settled here to raise cattle in 1874 and sold their holdings to Jimmy Grant in 1877. Jimmy was killed by an Indian and is buried east of the highway.*

To the west, following the base of the mountains, lies one of the oldest trails in the United States. It began when early North American natives used it as a primary north-south route. Jim Bridger and his kind knew it as "The Old Travois Trail," when white men bootlegged whiskey into Canada, it became known as the "Pondera Trail."

*The refugees of the Riel Rebellion came to Dupuyer*

*Creek in 1885 and many remained to make this area their home. The Home Ranch on Dupuyer Creek was headquarters for the famous Seven Block Cattle spread of the Conrads and a frequent stopping place for Montana's noted western artist, Charlie Russell.*

## H Chief Mountain and Old North Trail

Hwy 89, north of Dupuyer.

*Chief Mountain, NINASTAQUAY, has always been known to the Blackfeet people. Identified on maps as King Mountain as early as 1796, this outstanding landmark has long been revered for its supernatural powers. Generations of Blackfeet have used Chief Mountain for fasting and prayer. In 1992, the Blackfeet Tribe, by Tribal Resolution, limited public access into the area.*

*The ancient Old North Trail, well worn by centuries of Indian travois, entered the United States from the north, a few miles west of present day Port of Piegan Customs. It ran along the east slope of the Rocky Mountains from Edmonton, Alberta, to at least as far as Helena, Montana. Perhaps one of the great migration routes of early man, the Trail more recently served the Northwest Plains Indians as the route for war parties and exchanging goods between Canada and the United States. The Museum of the Plains Indian in Browning relates the story of Plains Indian culture including native travel patterns from earliest times to the present.*

## T Theodore Roosevelt Memorial Ranch

11 miles west of Dupuyer. 472-3380

This ranch is operated by the Boone and Crockett Club, a national conservation organization. Theodore Roosevelt established the Boone and Crockett Club in 1887. It is one of the oldest conservation organizations in the world. In 1986, the club purchased a working ranch here and opens portions to the public for wildlife viewing. It has an excellent 1.375 mile watchable wildlife trail that is open nine months of the year. It is only closed during hunting season. You can expect to see a wide range of wildlife here including grizzlies, black bears, mule deer, elk, bobcats, beaver, mountain lions, golden eagles, and a variety of bird life.

### Montana Trivia

Great Falls is called the "Electric City" because of the five dams on the Missouri River that drowned the Great Falls. It took Lewis and Clark thirty days to portage around these once magnificent falls.

## HIKES

### Sun River Area (west of Augusta)

**Home Gulch-Lime gulch Trail #267**

This is a moderate 15 mile long trail. The trailhead for this hike starts near the first campground in the Sun River Canyon and heads south. The trail will take you to an excellent view of the Sawtooth Ridge, the sheer rock walls on the west side of the two gulches. There are also some great vistas from the passes. You may spot bighorn sheep, elk, deer or bear on this trek. If you take the hike in the fall, the colors add to the beauty as the aspens, mountain maples, and other shrubs change color.

**Hannon Gulch Trail #240**

This trail also begins near the first campground in the Sun River Canyon, but heads north. This moderate to difficult trail travels a distance of 6.5 miles through an open gulch which allows good views of the Sun River Canyon. Bighorn sheep, deer, and bear frequent this area. The aspen groves in the lower part of the gulch are spectacular in the fall.

**Blacktail Creek Trail #223**

This trail begins near the second campground in the Sun River Canyon. The 11 mile hike is easy to moderate running through primarily forested areas. It climbs over the pass into open meadows with great views of the Sawtooth Ridge, Sun River Canyon and Deep Creek.

**Mortimer Gulch Trail #252**

To reach this trail follow the directions to trail #223. Take #223 for approximately five miles. The junction with this trail will be on your left. Mortimer Gulch is mostly open with scattered stands of aspen, lodgepole pine, and Douglas fir. This hike will take you to great views of Sawtooth Ridge, Norwegian and French Gulch and Gibson Reservoir.

**Big George Gulch Trail #251**

This trail begins just beyond the second campground in Sun River Canyon just before reaching the reservoir. The trail skirts the reservoir for a bit before heading into the gulch. The trail crosses a pass and is steep in places. Bighorn sheep, deer, mountain goats and bear are frequent visitors here.

### Teton River Area (West of Choteau)

From Choteau take Hwy. 89 north about five miles to the Teton Canyon Road turnoff. Follow Teton Canyon Road west for approximately 15 miles. All of these trails start from this area.

**Rierdon Gulch Trail #126**

Take the turnoff to the left at Twin Lakes. Bear right at the junction and follow the road past the ranger station. The trailhead is about four miles down the road. The Rierdon Gulch Trail will be on your left. This trail takes you through open, grassy areas with stands of lodgepole pine, aspen, and Douglas fir with a few scattered limber pine. There is a very steep but scenic pass into Slim Gulch and the north fork of Deep Creek.

**Green Gulch Trail #127**

The trailhead to this trail is about one mile past the trailhead to the Rierdon Gulch Trail. This is a moderate to more difficult trail. It is heavily forested and green with lush vegetation in early summer. Steep avalanche chutes can be observed here. Bighorn sheep, deer, and bear are common here.

**South Fork Teton Trail #168**

This trailhead is about one mile past the Green Gulch trailhead. This moderate to difficult hike is about 12 miles. It offers some spectacular views west to the high ridges of Rocky Mountain and northwest to Old Baldy Peak.

**Our Lake Trail**

The trailhead for this hike is about one mile past Trail #168. This alpine lake is accessible by a 3.5 mile long hiking trail that does include some steep terrain. A large interpretive sign about 50 yards up the trailhead interprets the natural history of the lake. Good opportunities in this area to see mountain goats and sheep, pikas, marmots and pocket gophers.

**Clary Coulee Trail #177**

Find the trailhead for this trail on Canyon Road about three miles past the Twin Lakes just before the first campground (Cave Mountain). This moderate to difficult trail takes you about six miles on a line between two contrasting geographic features: the high rocky walls and peaks of the front range to the west, and the vast plains to the east.

**North Fork Teton Trail #107**

Follow Canyon Road to the second campground. The trailhead is near here. This is an easy to moderate hike for about four miles. You will hike through the narrow and winding walls of Box Canyon. The trail crosses the Teton River which might be too high to cross in the early spring.

**Mount Wright Trail**

Follow Trail #107 for about five miles to the junction with Trail #114. Go west on this trail for about a mile to the junction of the Mount Wright Trail. This trail is steep to the top of Mount Wright, but your efforts are rewarded with a spectacular view from the top.

**Jones Creek Trail #155 and West Fork Trail #156**

The trailhead for both of these is just before the second campground at the end of Canyon Road. Start at the trailhead and hike for about two miles. The trail splits. Take your pick. From either trail you'll have a spectacular view of Choteau Mountain.

**Middle Fork of Teton River Trail #108**

This trail starts at the first campground (Cave Mountain). This is a river bottom trail that follows the river and is mostly wooded. This is an easy walk, and while there are no magnificent views on this trail, you may see a beaver dam or two.

**Ear Mountain Outstanding Natural Area and Trail**

Take the turnoff just past Twin Lakes onto South Fork Teton Road. After you cross the river, you will see Ear Mountain on your right. The trailhead is another 2 miles. Ear Mountain was a sacred site for the Blackfeet Indians and was used for centuries as a vision quest site. The 2.1 mile trail wanders gently up and down along Yaeger Flats, an area of open prairie lands. This is prime grizzly habitat and chances are high of seeing a griz. In fact, the area is closed from mid-December to mid-July because of high grizzly bear use.

**Mill Falls Trail**

Take the turnoff to the left at Twin Lakes. Bear right at the junction and follow the road past the ranger station. The trailhead is about 9.5 miles down the road at the end of the campground road. This is a very short walk in a wooded area ending at a small waterfall.

**A. B. Guthrie, Jr. Memorial Trail**

Take the turnoff just past Twin Lakes onto South Fork Teton Road. After you cross the river, continue straight for about 3.5 miles. You will see a kiosk on the left hand side of the road and the trailhead across from that on the right. This trail was named for the Pulitzer Prize-winning novelist, A. B. Guthrie, Jr. who wrote a series of books on Montana. It is a short, but steep trail with interpretive information at the kiosk and interpretive signs along the way.

## Great Falls Area

**Lewis and Clark Overlook and the Cochrane Dam Trail**
The trailhead and overlook are a little over a mile downstream from Giant Springs heritage State Park. There is a parking area here. The overlook provides a view of Crooked Falls, the only falls on the Missouri yet undammed. The trail to the dam begins at the parking lot.

## INFORMATION PLEASE

All Montana area codes are 406

### Road Information

Montana Road Condition Report
800-226-7623, 800-335-7592 or local 444-7696
Montana Highway Patrol 444-7696
**Local Road Reports**
Great Falls 453-1605
Statewide Weather Reports 453-2081

### Tourism Information

Travel Montana 800-847-4868 outside Montana
444-2654 in Montana
http://travel.mt.gov/.
Gold West Country 846-1943 or 800-879-1159
Russell Country 761-5036 or 800-527-5348
Northern Rodeo Association 252-1122
**Chambers of Commerce**
Browning 338-7911
Conrad 278-7791
Choteau 466-5316
Cut Bank 873-4041
Fairfield 467-2531
Great Falls 761-4434

### Airports

Browning 444-2506
Choteau 466-2968
Conrad 278-5672
Cutbank 873-4722
Dutton 476-3337
Fairfield 467-2336
Great Falls 727-3404
Shelby 434-2462
Sunburst 377-2980
Sweetgrass 355-2911
Valier 279-3467

### Government Offices

State BLM Office 255-2885, 238-1540
Bureau of Land Management
Great Falls Field Office 791-7700
Butte Field Office 494-5059
Lewis & Clark National Forest 791-7700
Benton Lake National Wildlife Refuge 727-7400
Montana Fish, Wildlife & Parks 454-5840
U.S. Bureau of Reclamation
Tiber Field Office 456-3226

### Hospitals

Blackfeet Community Hospital
Browning 388-6100
Teton Medical Center Hospital
Choteau 466-5763
Pondera Medical & Dental Clinic
Conrad 278-3211
Glacier County Medical Cente
Cut Bank 873-2251
Benefis West Health Care • Great Falls 727-3333
Benefis East Health Care • Great Falls 761-1200
U S Air Force Hospital • Great Falls 731-3863
Toole County Hospital • Shelby

### Bed & Breakfasts

**Viewforth Bed & Breakfast** • Fairfield 467-3884
**Charlie Russell Manor** • Great Falls 455-1400
**Collins Mansion B&B** • Great Falls 452-6798
**Old Oak Inn** • Great Falls 727-5782
Aspenwood Country Inn • Browning 338-7911
Inn Dupuyer • Dupuyer 472-3241
Murphy's House B&B • Great Falls 452-3598
Stone School Inn B&B • Valier 279-3796

### Guest Ranches & Resorts

**Benchmark Wilderness Ranch Outfitters**
Augusta 562-3336
Diamond Bar X Christian Guest Ranch
Augusta 562-3505
Bull Run Guest Ranch • Cascade 468-9269
Blixrud Chuck • Choteau 466-2044
Fishing Lodge • Cascade 468-9391
Fly Fishers' Inn • Cascade 468-2529
H Lazy 6 Ranch & Flyfishing Lodge
Choteau 466-2550
Heaven on Earch Ranch • Ulm 866-3316
JJJ Wilderness Ranch • Augusta 562-3653
Missouri Riverside Outfitters & Lodge
Cascade 468-9385
Seven Lazy P Ranch • Choteau 466-2044
Sun Canyon Lodge • Augusta 562-3654
Why Lazy T Ranch • Stockett 736-5416

### Vacation Homes & Cabins

Styren Ranch Guest House • Choteau 266-2008
Russell Country Inn • Great Falls 761-7125

### Private Campgrounds

Bridge Creek RV Park • Belt 277-3656
Choteau City Park & Campground
Choteau 466-2510
Choteau KOA • Choteau 466-2615
Dick's RV Park • Great Falls 452-0333
Fort Ponderosa Campground • Belt 277-3232
Farmers Campground • Browning 338-2500
Glacier RV Park • Shelby 434-5181
Great Falls KOA • Great Falls 727-3191
Horizon Park • Shelby 434-2211
KOA Kampgrounds • Great Falls 727-3191
Lake Shel-oole Campground • Shelby 434-5222
Lewis & Clark RV Park • Shelby 434-2710
Meriwether Meadows • Cut Bank 338-7737
Missouri Meadows Campground
Great Falls 452-0408
Pondera RV Park •Conrad 949-3090
Riverview Campground • Cut Bank 873-4151
Shady Grove Campground • Cut Bank 336-2475
Sunrise Trailer Court • Conrad 271-5901
Williamson Park Camground • Shelby 434-5222

### Car Rental

Bell Motor Company 873-5515
Northern Ford 873-5541
Avis Rent-A-Car 761-7610
Budget Rent-A-Car 454-1001
Daketo Kacate Auto-Limo 727-5440
Enterprise Rent-A-Car 761-1600
Hertz Rent-A-Car 761-6641
National Car Rental 453-4386
Rent A Wreck 761-0722
U-Save Auto Rental 771-1111
Shelby Motors 434-5593

### Outfitters & Guides

*F=Fishing H=Hunting R=River Guides*
*E=Horseback Rides G=General Guide Services*

**Benchmark Wilderness Outfitter & Guest Ranch**
HEFG 562-3336
A Lazy H Outfitters 466-5564
Bull Run Outfitting GHRFE 468-9268
Central Montana Outfitters GFH 799-7984
Cut Bank Creek Outfitters HF 338-5567
DL Elk Outfitters H 468-2642
Fallon Creek Outfitters H 278-3948
The Fishing Lodge FR 468-9391
Fly Fishers' Inn GF 468-2529
Ford Creek Outfitters E 562-3672
H Lazy 6 Fly Fishing Lodge F 466-2552
Mills Outfitting-ron & Tucker G 562-3335
Missouri Riverside Outfitters G 468-9385
Montana River Outfitters GFR 761-1677
Montana Safarsi G 466-2004
Morningstar Troutfitters F 338-2785
Mountain Leisure & Trading Co G 452-9000
Parsons Ranch HFR 468-2828
Triple R Recreation River Rentals R 799-7238
Wolf Creek Outfitters GFR 235-9000
Montana Ranch Adventures E 338-3333
Shadow Cast Outfitters GF 727-2119
Wolverton's Fly Shop GF 454-0254

## NOTES:

## Public Campgrounds

# Campsite Directions

| Campsite Directions | Season | Camping | Trailers | Toilets | Water | Boat Launch | Fishing | Swimming | Trails | Stay Limit | Fee |
|---|---|---|---|---|---|---|---|---|---|---|---|
| **238•Home Gulch FS**<br>20 mi. NW of Augusta on Sun River Canyon Rd.•2mi. W on Forest Rd. 108 | Summer/Fall | 12 | 16′ | D | • | B | • | • | • | 14 | • |
| **239•Mortimer Gulch FS**<br>20 mi. NW of Augusta on Sun River Canyon Rd.•4 mi. W on Forest Rd. 1082 •3 mi. N on Forest Rd. 8984 | Summer/Fall | 28 | 22′ | • | • | B | • | • | • | 14 | • |
| **240•South Fork FS**<br>31 mi. W of Augusta on Benchmark Rd. 235 (wilderness access) | Summer/Fall | 7 | 22′ | D | • | | • | | • | 14 | • |
| **241•Benchmark FS**<br>14 mi. W of Augusta on Cty. Rd. 235•16 mi. SW on Forest Rd. 235 (wilderness access) | Summer/Fall | 25 | 22′ | • | f• | | • | | • | 14 | • |
| **242•Wood Lake FS**<br>24 mi. W of Augusta on Benchmark Rd. 235 | Summer | 9 | 22 | •f | • | | • | • | • | 14 | • |
| **243•West Fork FS**<br>6 mi. N of Choteau on US 89•33 mi. NW on Cty. Rd. 144 (wilderness access) | Summer | 6 | | • | • | | • | | • | 14 | |
| **244•Cave Mountain FS•**<br>5 mi. N of Choteau on US 89•23 mi. W on Forest Rd. 144 (wilderness access) | Summer | 14 | 22′ | • | • | • | | • | • | 14 | • |
| **245•Lake Elwell Willow Creek USBR**<br>17 mi. S of Chester on Rt. 223•7 mi. W on Cty. Rd.•(public marina and RV park•• | All Year | • | • | D | | C | • | | | 14 | |
| **246•Lake Elwell North Bootlegger USBR**<br>13 mi. S of Chester on Rt. 223•7 mi. W on Cty. Rd.•(public marina and RV park• | All Year | • | • | D | | C | • | | | 14 | |
| **247•Lake Elwell South Bootlegger USBR**<br>15 mi. S of Chester on Rt. 223•7 mi. W on Cty. Rd.•(public marina and RV park• | All Year | < | • | D | | C | • | | | 14 | |
| **248•Lake Elwell VFW Campground USBR**<br>16 mi. S of Chester on Rt. 223•7 mi. W on Cty. Rd.•(public marina and RV park• | All Year | • | • | D | | C | • | | | 14 | |
| **249•Lake Elwell Island Area USBR**<br>12 mi. S of Chester on Rt. 223•7 mi. W on Cty. Rd.•(public marina and RV park• | All Year | • | • | D | | C | • | | | 14 | |
| **250•Lake Elwell Sanford Park USBR**<br>14 mi. S of Chester on Rt. 223•7 mi. W on Cty. Rd.•(public marina and RV park• | All Year | • | • | D | • | B | • | | | 14 | |
| **251•Gary Smith Memorial**<br>5th Ave. NW in Cut Bank | 5/1-10/1 | 5 | 30′ | • | • | | | | | | |

**Agency**
FS—U.S.D.A Forest Service
FWP—Montana Fish, Wildlife & Parks
NPS—National Park Service
BLM—U.S. Bureau of Land Management
USBR—U.S. Bureau of Reclamation
CE—Corps of Engineers

**Camping**
Camping is allowed at this site. Number indicates camping spaces available
H—Hard sided units only; no tents

**Trailers**
Trailer units allowed. Number indicates maximum length.

**Toilets**
Toilets on site. D—Disabled access

**Water**
Drinkable water on site

**Fishing**
Visitors may fish on site

**Boat**
Type of boat ramp on site:
A—Hand launch
B—4-wheel drive with trailer
C—2-wheel drive with trailer

**Swimming**
Designated swimming areas on site

**Trails**
Trails on site
B—Backpacking N—Nature/Interpretive

**Stay Limit**
Maximum length of stay in days

**Fee**
Camping and/or day-use fee

## Notes:

| Fishery | Brook Trout | Mt. Whitefish | Lake Whitefish | Golden Trout | Cutthroat Trout | Brown Trout | Rainbow Trout | Kokanee Salmon | Bull Trout | Lake Trout | Arctic Grayling | Burbot | Largemouth Bass | Smallmouth Bass | Walleye | Sauger | Northern Pike | Shovelnose Sturgeon | Channel Catfish | Yellow Perch | Crappie | Paddlefish | Vehicle Access | Campgrounds | Toilets | Docks | Boat Ramps | MotorRestrictions |
|---|---|---|---|---|---|---|---|---|---|---|---|---|---|---|---|---|---|---|---|---|---|---|---|---|---|---|---|---|
| | Cold Water Species | | | | | | | | | | | | Warm Water Species | | | | | | | | | | Services | | | | | |
| 189. North Fork Sun River | | | | | | | • | | | | | | | | | | | | | | | | | | | | | • |
| 190. South Fork Sun River | | | | | • | | • | | | | | | | | | | | | | | | | | | | | | • |
| 191. Gibson Reservoir | | | | | | | • | | | | | | | | | | | | | | | | • | • | • | | • | |
| 192. Wood Lake | | | | | | | • | | | | | | | | | | | | | | | | • | • | • | | • | |
| 193. Nilan Reservoir | | | | | | | • | | | | | | | | | | | | | | | | • | • | • | | • | |
| 194. Willow Creek Reservoir | | | | | | | • | | | | | | | | | | | | | | | | • | • | • | | • | |
| 195. Dearborn River | | • | | | • | • | • | | | | | | | | | | | | | | | | • | | | | | |
| 196. Bean Lake | | | | | | | • | | | | | | | | | | | | | | | | • | • | • | | • | |
| 197. Sun River | | • | | | | • | • | | | | | | | | | | | | | | | | • | • | • | | • | |
| 198. Teton River | • | • | | | • | • | • | | | | | | | | | | | | | | | | • | • | • | | | |
| 199. Split Rock Lake | | | | | | | | | | | | | | | | | • | | | • | | | • | | | | | |
| 200. Pishkun Reservoir | | | | | | | • | | | | | | | | | | • | | | • | | | • | • | • | | • | |
| 201. Eureka Reservoir | | | | | | | • | | | | | | | | | | | | | | | | • | • | • | | • | |
| 202. Bynum Reservoir | | | | | | | | | | | | | | | • | | | | | • | | | • | • | • | | • | |
| 203. Lake Frances | | | | | | | | | | | | • | | | • | | • | | | • | | | • | • | • | | • | |
| 204.Tiber Reservoir | | | | | | | • | | | • | | • | | | • | | • | | | • | | | • | • | • | | • | |
| 205. Missouri River | | • | | | | • | • | | | | | • | | | | | | | | | | • | • | • | • | • | • | • |
| 206. Kipps Lake | • | | | | | | • | | | | | | | | | | | | | | | | | | | | | |
| 207. Mission Lake | | | | | | | • | | | | | | | | | | | | | | | | | | | | | |
| 208. Wadsworth Pond | | | | | | | | | | | | | • | | • | | | | | • | | | • | | | | | |
| 209. Priest Butte Lake | | | | | | | | | | | | | | | | | | | | • | • | | • | | | | | |

**Notes:**

## Dining Quick Reference

Price Range refers to the average cost of a meal per person: ($) $1-$6, ($$) $7-$11, ($$$) $12-up. Cocktails: "Yes" indicates full bar; Beer (B)/Wine (W), Service: Breakfast (B), Brunch (BR), Lunch (L), Dinner (D). Businesses in bold print will have additional information under the appropriate map locator number in the body of this section.

| RESTAURANT | TYPE CUISINE | PRICE RANGE | CHILD MENU | COCKTAILS BEER WINE | SERVICE | CREDIT CARDS | MAP LOCATOR NUMBER |
|---|---|---|---|---|---|---|---|
| U S 89 Espresso To Go | Coffee | | | | | | 1 |
| Sully's Bar & Cafe | American | $$ | | Yes | L/D | | 1 |
| **Hong Kong Chan's** | Chinese | $-$$$ | | | L/D | V/M | 3 |
| Kow Loon Chinese Restaurant | Chinese | $$ | | Yes | L/D | Major | 3 |
| Treehouse Cafe | American | $/$$ | Yes | | B/L/D | Major | 3 |
| Sports Club Dining Room | Steaks & Seafood | $$ | | Yes | D | Major | 3 |
| Main St. Exxon/Hot Stuff Pizza | Fast Food | $ | Yes | | B/L/D | | 3 |
| The Pizza Depot | Family | $ | | B/W | B/L/D | V/M | 4 |
| **Dixie Inn Dining Room** | Steaks & Seafood | $-$$$ | Yes | Yes | L/D | Major | 5 |
| **Papa's Taco** | Fast Food | $ | Yes | B/W | L/D | | 5 |
| McDonald's | Fast Food | $ | Yes | | B/L/D | | 5 |
| Pizza Hut | Pizza | $/$$ | Yes | B | L/D | V/M/D | 5 |
| Frontier Bar and Supper Club | Steakhouse | $ | Yes | | L/D | Major | 5 |
| Golden Harvest Cafe | American | $ | | | B/L/D | | 6 |
| J R'S Dining & Lounge | American | $$$ | | B/W | L/D | Major | 6 |
| Java Time | Coffeehouse | $ | | | | | 6 |
| Maxie's Ribs | Family | $$ | Yes | B/W | D | | 6 |
| McDonald's | Fast Food | $ | Yes | | B/L/D | | 6 |
| Pizza Hut | Pizza | $/$$ | Yes | B | L/D | V/M/D | 6 |
| Point Drive Inn | Fast Food | $ | | | L/D | | 6 |
| Smokehouse Deli | Deli | $ | | | L/D | | 6 |
| Taco John's | Fast Food | $ | Yes | | L/D | | 6 |
| The Village Dining & Lounge | Family | $ | | Yes | B/L/D | Major | 6 |
| Browning Cafe | American | $ | | | B/L | | 7 |
| Glacier Restaurant | American | $/$$ | | | L/D | | 7 |
| Subway | Fast Food | $ | Yes | | L/D | | 7 |
| Angus Cafe | American | $/$$ | | Yes | B/L/D | | 8 |
| Badger Cafe | American | $ | | | B/L/D | | 8 |
| Driftwood Grill | American | $ | | B/W | L/D | | 8 |
| Pizza Pro | Pizza | $ | | | L/D | | 8 |
| Griffins Restaurant | Steak/Seafood | $$/$$$ | | Yes | D | Major | 9 |
| Quigleys Last Jump Exxon/Hot Stuff Pizza | Fast Food | $ | Yes | | L/D | | 9 |
| Mama Mia's West Side | Pizza/Italian | $ | | | L/D | Major | 10 |
| McDonalds | Fast Food | $ | Yes | | B/L/D | | 10 |
| Elmer's Pancake & Steak House | Family | $-$$ | Yes | | B/L/D | Major | 10 |
| Chinatown Restaurant | Chinese | $ | | | L/D | V/M | 10 |
| Dairy Queen | Fast Food | $ | Yes | | L/D | | 10 |
| Mardi Gras Cafe | American | $/$$ | | | L/D | | 10 |
| **Godfather's Pizza** | Pizza | $ | Yes | B | L/D | V/M/D | 11 |
| J B'S Restaurant | Family | $ | Yes | | B/L/D | V/M | 11 |
| Taco Bell | Fast Food | $ | Yes | | L/D | | 11 |
| Jaker's Steak Ribs & Fish House | Steak/Seafood | $$ | | Yes | L/D | Major | 11 |
| Country Kitchen | Family | $-$$ | Yes | | B/L/D | Major | 11 |
| Pizza Hut | Pizza | $/$$ | Yes | B | L/D | V/M/D | 11 |
| Subway | Fast Food | $ | Yes | | L/D | | 11 |
| Papa John's Pizza | Pizza | $ | Yes | | L/D | | 11 |
| Burger King | Fast Food | $ | Yes | | B/L/D | | 11 |
| McDonald's | Fast Food | $ | Yes | | B/L/D | | 11 |
| Dairy Queen | Fast Food | $ | Yes | | L/D | | 11 |
| A & W Family Restaurant | Fast Food | $ | Yes | | L/D | | 11 |
| Bob's Pizza Plus | Fast Food | $ | Yes | | L/D | | 11 |
| Coffee Etc | Coffee | | | | | | 11 |
| Little Athens | Greek | $ | | | L/D | | 11 |
| Orange Julius | Fast Food | $ | Yes | | B/L/D | | 11 |
| Pepper's Grill & Bar | Family | $/$$ | Yes | Yes | L/D | Major | 11 |
| Posh Taco | Mexican | $ | | | L/D | | 11 |
| Great Wall Orient Buffet | Chinese | $$ | | | L/D | V/M | 11 |
| **MacKenzie River Pizza Co.** | Pizza | $/$$ | | B/W | L/D | Major | 12 |
| **The Prospector Casino & Restaurant II** | American | $ | | Yes | B/L/D | Major | 12 |
| **Cattin's Family Dining** | Family | $ | Yes | | B/L/D | | 12 |
| Ming's Chinese Restaurant | Chinese | $/$$ | | | L/D | V/M | 12 |

## Dining Quick Reference-Continued

Price Range refers to the average cost of a meal per person: ($) $1-$6, ($$) $7-$11, ($$$) $12-up. Cocktails: "Yes" indicates full bar; Beer (B)/Wine (W), Service: Breakfast (B), Brunch (BR), Lunch (L), Dinner (D). Businesses in bold print will have additional information under the appropriate map locator number in the body of this section.

| RESTAURANT | TYPE CUISINE | PRICE RANGE | CHILD MENU | COCKTAILS BEER WINE | SERVICE | CREDIT CARDS | MAP LOCATOR NUMBER |
|---|---|---|---|---|---|---|---|
| Prime Cut Restaurant | Family | $ | Yes | | L/D | Major | 12 |
| Fuddruckers | American | $-$$ | Yes | Yes | L/D | Major | 12 |
| Prime Time Grill | American | $ | | Yes | B/L/D | Major | 12 |
| R&R Restaurant | American | $ | | Yes | B/L/D | Major | 12 |
| 4B's Restaurant | Family | $ | Yes | | B/L/D | V/M/D | 12 |
| Loft Restaurant | Family | $ | | | B/L | V/M | 12 |
| Taco John's | Fast Food | $ | Yes | | L/D | | 12 |
| Taco Treat Mexican Restaurant | Fast Food | $ | Yes | | L/D | | 12 |
| Mama Mia's Eastside | Pizza/Italian | $$ | Yes | | L/D | Major | 12 |
| Burger Master | Fast Food | $ | Yes | | B/L/D | | 12 |
| Peking Garden East | Chinese | $$ | | Yes | L/D | Major | 12 |
| Maria's Mexican Food | Mexican | $$ | Yes | | L/D | Major | 12 |
| Chi Chi's Mexican Restaurant | Mexican | $$ | | B/W | L/D | | 12 |
| Eggroll & Bar-B-Q Place | Oriental | $$ | | | | | 12 |
| Hardee's | Fast Food | $ | Yes | | B/L/D | | 12 |
| Arby's | Fast Food | $ | Yes | | B/L/D | | 12 |
| Wendy's | Fast Food | $ | Yes | | L/D | | 12 |
| Kentucky Fried Chicken | Fast Food | $ | Yes | | L/D | | 12 |
| Joe's Place | American | $ | | Yes | L/D | V/M | 12 |
| Ford's Drive In | Fast Food | $ | Yes | | L/D | | 13 |
| Kentucky Fried Chicken/A&W | Fast Food | $ | Yes | | L/D | | 13 |
| Candie's Soup Dujours & Specialties | Deli | $ | | | B/L | V/M/D | 13 |
| Dairy Queen | Fast Food | $ | Yes | | L/D | | 13 |
| **Bert & Ernie's** | American | $/$$ | Yes | B/W | L/D | Major | 14 |
| **Perkins Family Restaurant & Mid Town Motel** | Family | $/$$ | Yes | | B/L/D | Major | 14 |
| **Big Sky Bagel Bakery** | Deli | $ | | | B/L | | 14 |
| **Primrose Tea Cottage** | tea house/café | $/$$ | | | B/L | Major | 14 |
| **Serenditpity Café** | Deli | $ | | | B/L/D | | 14 |
| Daily Grind | Coffee House | $ | | | B/L | | 14 |
| Stein Haus | Tavern | $$ | | B/W | L/D | Major | 14 |
| Dairy Queen | Fast Food | $ | Yes | | L/D | | 14 |
| Park & Ponder Coffee House Etc | Coffee | $ | | | | | 14 |
| Baker Bobs & Back Alley Pub | Bakery/Deli | $ | | B/W | B/L/D | | 14 |
| Tracy's Family Restaurant | American | $ | Yes | | B/L/D | | 14 |
| Club Cigar | American | $$ | | Yes | L/D | Major | 14 |
| Ristorante Portofino | italian | $/$$$ | Yes | B/W | B/L/D | Major | 14 |
| Hardee's | Fast Food | $ | Yes | | B/L/D | | 14 |
| Charlies Restaurant | Homestyle | $/$$ | Yes | Yes | B/L/D | Major | 14 |
| Subway | Fast Food | $ | Yes | | L/D | | 14 |
| 5th Street Diner | Family | $/$$ | Yes | | B/L | Major | 14 |
| Coffee Stop | Coffee | $ | | | | | 14 |
| Brian's Top Notch Cafe | Family | $ | | | B/L | | 14 |
| Zandy's Drive In | Fast Food | $ | Yes | | L/D | | 14 |
| The Kitchen | American | $ | Yes | | L/D | | 14 |
| Taco Treat Mexican Restaurant | Fast Food | $ | Yes | | L/D | | 14 |
| **The Prospector Casino & Restaurant** | American | $ | | Yes | B/L/D | Major | 17 |
| **Borrie's Family Restaurant** | Family | $/$$ | Yes | Yes | L/D | V/M/D | 17 |
| Christina's Italian Restaurant | Italian | $$ | | | L/D | | 17 |
| 3-D International | International | $$ | | Yes | L/D | V/M | 17 |
| Peking Garden West | Chinese | $$ | | Yes | L/D | Major | 17 |
| **The Feedlot West** | American | $ | | | L/D | | 18 |
| Arby's | Fast Food | $ | Yes | | B/L/D | | 18 |
| The Lost Woodsman Restaurant | Regional | $$ | Yes | Yes | L/D | | 18 |
| Subway | Fast Food | $ | Yes | | L/D | | 18 |
| New Peking | Chinese | $$ | | Yes | L/D | Major | 18 |
| Taco Bell | Fast Food | $ | Yes | | L/D | | 18 |
| Taco Treat Mexican Restaurant | Fast Food | $ | Yes | | L/D | | 18 |
| McDonald's | Fast Food | $ | Yes | | B/L/D | | 18 |
| Pizza Hut | Pizza | $/$$ | Yes | B | L/D | V/M/D | 18 |
| Burl's Broiled Burgers | Fast Food | $ | Yes | | B/L/D | | 19 |
| Taco John's | Fast Food | $ | Yes | | L/D | | 19 |

## Dining Quick Reference-Continued

Price Range refers to the average cost of a meal per person: ($) $1-$6, ($$) $7-$11, ($$$) $12-up. Cocktails: "Yes" indicates full bar; Beer (B)/Wine (W), Service: Breakfast (B), Brunch (BR), Lunch (L), Dinner (D). Businesses in bold print will have additional information under the appropriate map locator number in the body of this section.

| RESTAURANT | TYPE CUISINE | PRICE RANGE | CHILD MENU | COCKTAILS BEER WINE | SERVICE | CREDIT CARDS | MAP LOCATOR NUMBER |
|---|---|---|---|---|---|---|---|
| Halftime Sportsbar Restaurant | American | $$ | | Yes | L/D | Major | 19 |
| Burger King | Fast Food | $ | Yes | | B/L/D | | 19 |
| Yellowstone Truck Stop | American | $$ | Yes | | B/L/D | Major | 19 |
| Holiday Exxon/Blimpies Subs | Fast Food | $ | Yes | | L/D | | 19 |
| **Black Diamond Supper Club** | American | $–$$$ | | Yes | D | V/M | 20 |
| Belt Creek Brew Pub | Deli/Sausage | $ | | Yes | L/D | | 20 |
| Belt Creek Cafe | American | $ | | | B/L/D | | 20 |
| Dutton Cafe | American | $ | | | B/L/D | | 21 |
| Arby's | Fast Food | $ | Yes | | B/L/D | | 22 |
| Branding Iron Steak & Dinner | Steakhouse | $$ | Yes | Yes | B/L/D | Major | 22 |
| Durango Dining Room | Steakhouse | $$ | Yes | | B/W | V/M/D | 22 |
| Home Cafe | American | $ | | | B/L | | 22 |
| Keg Family Restaurant | Family | $ | Yes | B/W | L/D | | 22 |
| Pizza Hut | Pizza | $/$$ | Yes | B | L/D | V/M/D | 22 |
| Pizza Pro | Pizza | $ | | | L/D | | 22 |
| The Lobby Cafe | American | $ | | Yes | L/D | V/M | 22 |
| Four Corners Cafe | Family | $ | | Yes | | | 23 |
| Charlie's Pizza | Pizza | $ | | Yes | D | Major | 23 |
| Glocca Morra Inn & Cafe | Family | $ | | Yes | B/L/D | | 23 |
| Fireside Inn Supper Club | Family | $$ | | Yes | B/L/D | | 24 |
| Silver Spur Bar And Supper Club | Steaks | $$ | | Yes | L/D | Major | 24 |
| Harvest Cafe & Casino | Family | $/$$ | Yes | B/W | B/L/D | V/M | 25 |
| Bowman's Corner | Steakhouse | $/$$ | | Yes | L/D | | 26 |
| Buckhorn Bar | American | $ | | Yes | L/D | | 26 |
| Lazy B Bar & Cafe | American | $$ | Yes | Yes | B/L/D | | 26 |
| Mel's Diner | Family | $ | | | B/L/D | | 26 |
| Mountain Pie Pizza Co. | Pizza | $$ | | | L/D | | 26 |
| Western Bar | American | $$ | | Yes | L/D | | 26 |
| Wagons West Motel & Restaurant | Family | $/$$ | | Yes | B/L/D | V/M/D | 26 |
| Choteau Seafood & Steakhouse | Steaks & Seafood | $–$$$ | Yes | Yes | B/L/D | V/M | 28 |
| **Circle N Restaurant** | Family | $$ | Yes | B/W | L/D | V/M | 28 |
| **Log Cabin Family Restaurant** | Family | $/$$ | Yes | | B/L/D | V/M | 28 |
| **Outpost Deli** | Deli | $ | Yes | | B/L | | 28 |
| Hot Stuff Pizza/Smash Hit Subs | Fast Food | $ | Yes | | B/L/D | | 28 |
| John Henry's | Family | $$ | Yes | B/W | L/D | V/M | 28 |
| The Buckaroo Coffee House | Coffee House | $ | | | B/L | | 28 |
| Trading Post Cafe | Family | $ | | | L | V/M | 28 |
| Rose Room | Steaks & Seafood | $$/$$$ | Yes | Yes | D | | 30 |
| Double Barrel Family Dining | Family | $$ | Yes | | B/L/D | | 31 |

### NOTES:

## Motel Quick Reference

Price Range: ($) Under $40 ; ($$) $40-$60; ($$$) $60-$80, ($$$$) Over $80. Pets [check with the motel for specific policies] (P), Dining (D), Lounge (L), Disabled Access (DA), Full Breakfast (FB), Cont. Breakfast (CB), Indoor Pool (IP), Outdoor Pool (OP), Hot Tub (HT), Sauna (S), Refrigerator (R), Microwave (M) (Microwave and Refrigerator indicated only if in majority of rooms), Kitchenette (K). All Montana area codes are 406.

| HOTEL | PHONE | NUMBER ROOMS | PRICE RANGE | BREAKFAST | POOL/ HOT TUB SAUNA | NON SMOKE ROOMS | OTHER AMENITIES | CREDIT CARDS | MAP LOCATOR NUMBER |
|---|---|---|---|---|---|---|---|---|---|
| Galata Motel | 432-2352 | 8 | $ | | | | P | | 1 |
| **The Sherlock Motel, Inc.** | 434-5216 | 23 | $$ | | | Yes | K/R/DA | Major | 3 |
| O'Haire Manor Motel of Shelby | 434-5555 | 37 | $$ | | HT | Yes | K/P/M/R | Major | 3 |
| Williams Court | 434-2254 | 11 | $ | | | | K/R | V/M | 3 |
| Shelby Motel | 434-5164 | 14 | $ | | | | | Major | 4 |
| Totem Motel | 434-2930 | 8 | $$ | | | | P/M/R | Major | 4 |
| **Crossroads Inn** | 434-5134 | 52 | $$ | CB | IP/HT | Yes | P/M/R/DA | Major | 5 |
| **Glacier Motel & RV Park** | 434-5181 | 17 | $ | | | Yes | K/P/M/R | Major | 5 |
| Comfort Inn | 434-2212 | 72 | $$ | CB | IP/HT | Yes | P/D/L/DA | Major | 5 |
| Glacier Gateway Plaza | 873-2566 | 19 | $$$ | CB | P/HT | Yes | DA | Major | 6 |
| Terrace Motel | 873-5031 | 17 | $ | | | Yes | P | Major | 6 |
| Billman's Terrace Motel | 873-5031 | 17 | $ | | | Yes | P | | 6 |
| Corner Motel | 873-5588 | 11 | $ | | | Yes | K/P/M/R/DA | Major | 6 |
| Glacier Gateway Inn | 873-5544 | 18 | $$ | CB | HT | Yes | K/P/M/R/DA | Major | 6 |
| Glacier Motor Inn | 873-4022 | 53 | $$$ | | | Yes | D/L/DA | Major | 6 |
| Northern Motor Inn | 873-5662 | 61 | $$ | | IP/HT | Yes | D | Major | 6 |
| Parkway Motel | 873-4582 | 5 | $$ | | | Yes | P | Major | 6 |
| The Point Motel | 873-5544 | 11 | $ | | | Yes | K/P/M/R | Major | 6 |
| Glacier Motel | 338-7004 | 9 | $ | | | | K | | 7 |
| War Bonnet Lodge | 338-7610 | 40 | $$ | | | Yes | P/D | Major | 7 |
| Western Motel | 338-7572 | 15 | $$ | | | Yes | P/DA | Major | 7 |
| A & C Motel | 468-2513 | 8 | $$ | | | | | Major | 8 |
| Badger Motel | 468-9330 | 5 | $$ | | | Yes | P | Major | 8 |
| Holiday Inn Express | 445-1000 | 95 | $$$ | CB | | Yes | DA | Major | 10 |
| Budget Inn | 453-1602 | 60 | $$ | CB | IP/HT/S | Yes | P/DA | Major | 10 |
| Best Western Heritage Inn | 761-1900 | 65 | $ | | | Yes | K/P/M/R | Major | 10 |
| **Wright Nite Inns** | 761-6150 | | | | | | | | 11 |
| **Townhouse Inn** | 761-4600 | 109 | $$ | | IP/HT | Yes | P/D/L/DA | Major | 11 |
| **Super 8 Motel Great Falls** | 727-7600 | 117 | $$ | | | Yes | P/DA | Major | 11 |
| Plaza Inn | 452-9594 | 20 | $$ | | | Yes | P | Major | 11 |
| **Rendezvous Wrigth Nite Motel** | 452-9525 | 43 | $$ | | HT | Yes | | Major | 12 |
| **Sahara Wright Nite Motel** | 761-6150 | 20 | $$ | | | Yes | DA | Major | 12 |
| Highwood Village Motel | 452-8505 | 65 | $ | | | Yes | K/P/M/R | Major | 12 |
| Town & Country Motel | 452-5643 | 10 | $ | | | Yes | P/M/R/DA | Major | 12 |
| Western Motel | 453-3281 | 25 | $$ | | | Yes | P | Major | 12 |
| Wagon Wheel Motel | 761-1300 | 64 | $$ | | | Yes | K/P/M/R/DA | Major | 12 |
| Holiday Inn | 727-7200 | 169 | $$/$$$ | | IP/HT/S | Yes | P/D/L/DA | Major | 12 |
| Village Motor Inn | 727-7666 | 34 | $$ | | | Yes | P | Major | 12 |
| Fairfield Inn | 454-3000 | 63 | $$/$$$ | CB | IP/HT | Yes | M/R/DA | Major | 12 |
| Comfort Inn | 454-2727 | 64 | $$$ | CB | IP/HT | Yes | P/DA | Major | 12 |
| Alberta Motel | 452-3467 | 10 | $ | | | Yes | | Major | 13 |
| Central Motel | 453-0161 | 32 | $$ | | | Yes | P | Major | 13 |
| Edelweiss Motor Inn | 452-9504 | 20 | $ | | | Yes | P | Major | 13 |
| **Perkins Family Restaurant & Mid Town Motel** | 453-2411 | 40 | $ | | | Yes | P/D/M/R | Major | 14 |
| **The Old Oak Inn** | 727-5782 | | | | | | | | 14 |
| **O'Haire Motor Inn** | 454-2141 | 69 | $$ | | IP | Yes | D/L | Major | 14 |
| Imperial Inn | 452-9581 | 30 | $$ | | | Yes | P | Major | 14 |
| Midtown Motel | 453-2411 | 40 | $$ | | | Yes | D/P | Major | 14 |
| Royal Motel | 452-9548 | 22 | $ | | | Yes | P | Major | 14 |
| Howard Johnson Ponderosa Inn | 761-3410 | 105 | $$/$$$ | | OP/S | Yes | P/D/M/R/DA | Major | 14 |

**NOTES:**

## Motel Quick Reference

Price Range: ($) Under $40 ; ($$) $40-$60; ($$$) $60-$80, ($$$$) Over $80. Pets [check with the motel for specific policies] (P), Dining (D), Lounge (L), Disabled Access (DA), Full Breakfast (FB), Cont. Breakfast (CB), Indoor Pool (IP), Outdoor Pool (OP), Hot Tub (HT), Sauna (S), Refrigerator (R), Microwave (M) (Microwave and Refrigerator indicated only if in majority of rooms), Kitchenette (K). All Montana area codes are 406.

| HOTEL | PHONE | NUMBER ROOMS | PRICE RANGE | BREAKFAST | POOL/ HOT TUB SAUNA | NON SMOKE ROOMS | OTHER AMENITIES | CREDIT CARDS | MAP LOCATOR NUMBER |
|---|---|---|---|---|---|---|---|---|---|
| Triple Crown Motor Inn | 727-8300 | 49 | $ | | | Yes | P/R/DA | Major | 14 |
| **Days Inn Great Falls** | 727-6565 | 62 | $$ | CB | | Yes | CB/DA | Major | 18 |
| Conrad Motel | 278-7544 | 23 | $ | | | Yes | P | Major | 22 |
| Northgate Motel | 278-3516 | 5 | $ | | | Yes | P | Major | 22 |
| Super 8 Motel | 278-7676 | 49 | $$ | | | Yes | P/D/L/DA | Major | 22 |
| Glocca Morra Inn & Cafe | 335-2850 | | | | | | | | 23 |
| Bob & Ethel's Ramble Inn | 264-9435 | | | | | | | | 24 |
| Office Bar & Motel | 965-9982 | 4 | $ | | | | P | | 24 |
| Wagons West Motel & Restaurant | 562-3295 | 14 | $$ | | | Yes | P/D/L | V/M/D | 26 |
| Bunkhouse Inn | 562-3387 | | | | | | | | 26 |
| Sun Canyon Lodge | 562-3654 | | | | | | | | 26 |
| **Stage Stop Best Western** | 466-5900 | 43 | $$$ | CB | IP | Yes | M/DA | Major | 28 |
| **Viewforth B&B** | 467-3110 | | | | | | | | 28 |
| **Bella Vista Motel** | 466-5711 | 14 | $$ | | | Yes | K/P/M/F/D | Major | 28 |
| Big Sky Motel | 466-5318 | 13 | $$ | | | Yes | K/P | Major | 28 |
| Western Star Motel | 466-5737 | 7 | $ | | | Yes | DA | V/M | 28 |
| **Gunther Motel & Apartments** | 466-5444 | 22 | $/$$ | | | Yes | P | Major | 29 |
| Lake Francis Inn | 279-3476 | 12 | $ | | | | DA | Major | 31 |

## NOTES:

Section 12

# SECTION 13

## MISSOULA AREA

## INCLUDING I-90 TO IDAHO BORDER, SEELEY LAKE, LINCOLN, AND RONAN

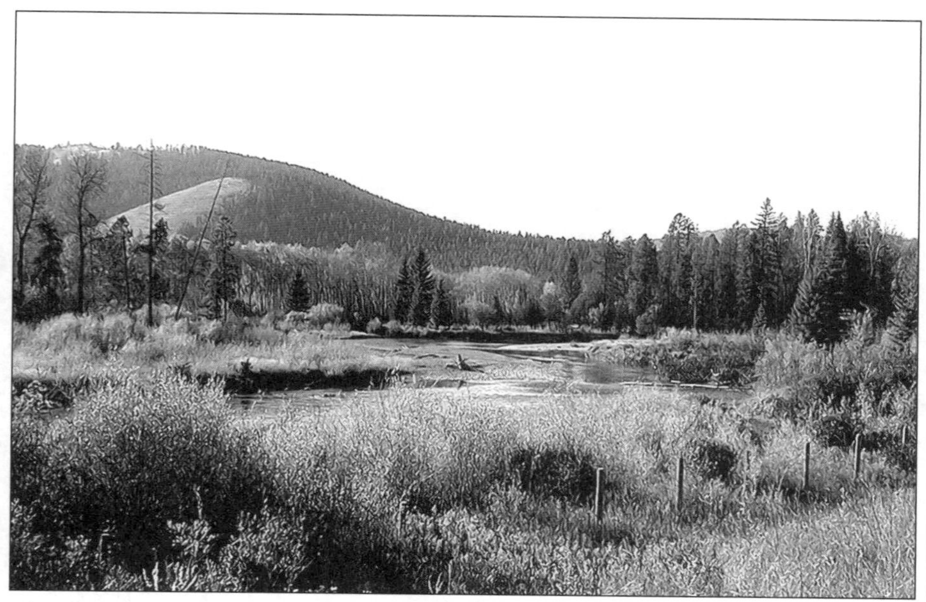

The Blackfoot River.

### WEATHER AVERAGES

**Missoula**

| January | |
|---|---|
| Average High: | 30.0° F |
| Average Low: | 15.4° F |
| Record High : | 59.0° F |
| Record Low : | -33.0° F |
| Average Precip.: | 1.24 in |
| Rain/Snow Days: | 14 days |

| April | |
|---|---|
| Average High: | 57.5° F |
| Average Low: | 30.9° F |
| Record High : | 87.0° F |
| Record Low : | 14.0° F |
| Average Precip.: | 0.96 in |
| Rain/Snow Days: | 10 days |

| July | |
|---|---|
| Average High: | 83.4° F |
| Average Low: | 50.1° F |
| Record High : | 105.0° F |
| Record Low : | 31.0° F |
| Average Precip.: | 0.91 in |
| Rain/Snow Days: | 7 days |

| October | |
|---|---|
| Average High: | 57.0° F |
| Average Low: | 31.3° F |
| Record High : | 85.0° F |
| Record Low : | 0.0° F |
| Average Precip.: | 0.74 in |
| Rain/Snow Days: | 8 days |

**Montana Snowbowl Ski Area**

| January | |
|---|---|
| Average High: | 29.8° F |
| Average Low: | 14.3° F |
| Average Precip.: | 1.04 in |

| April | |
|---|---|
| Average High: | 57.1° F |
| Average Low: | 31.9° F |
| Average Precip.: | 1.02 in |

| July | |
|---|---|
| Average High: | 83.9° F |
| Average Low: | 49.7° F |
| Average Precip.: | 0.93 in |

| October | |
|---|---|
| Average High: | 57.0° F |
| Average Low: | 31.4° F |
| Average Precip.: | 0.91 in |

**1.** *Historical Marker, Gas, Food*

### Bonner

This was the site of one of the state's first large sawmills. It was named for E.L. Bonner who settled here in 1888. He was the first president of the Missoula and Bitter Root Valley Railroad.

### Milltown

Originally called Riverside because of its proximity to the Clark Fork and Blackfoot Rivers. The name was later changed to avoid confusion with another town of the same name near Butte. The town's name was then changed to Finntown to honor the large number of Finnish residents. Later members of the community objected and changed to name to Milltown. The lumber mill that was erected here was sold in 1898 to Marcus Daly whose mines had an insatiable appetite for lumber.

### H Junction of the Hell Gate and Big Blackfoot Rivers

West of Milltown

*An important Indian road came east through the Hell Gate and turned up the Big Blackfoot. It followed that river almost to its source, then crossed the Continental Divide to the plains country. The Indians called the river the Cokalahishkit, meaning "the river of the road to the buffalo."*

*Capt. Clark and Capt. Lewis, of the Lewis and Clark Expedition, divided forces near the present site of Missoula on their return trip from the coast. Capt. Lewis and his party followed this Indian road and passed near here July 4th, 1806.*

*Capt. John Mullan, U.S.A., locator and builder of the Mullan Military Road from Fort Benton to Fort Walla Walla, maintained a construction camp here during the winter of 1861-62 which he named Cantonment Wright. He was the first engineer to bridge the Blackfoot.*

### H Hell Gate and Missoula

East of Missoula

*In the Indian days the mountain tribes had a road through here which led across the Continental Divide to the buffalo. The Blackfeet, from the plains, used to consider it very sporting to slip into this country on horse-stealing expeditions and to ambush the Nez Perce and Flathead Indians in this narrow part of the canyon. Funeral arrangements were more or less sketchy in those days even amongst friends, so naturally, enemies got very little consideration. In time the place became so cluttered with skulls and bones that it was gruesome enough to make an Indian exclaim "Isul" expressing surprise and horror. The French trappers elaborated and called it "La Porte d'Enfer" or Gate of Hell.*

*From these expressions were derived the present-day names Missoula and Hell Gate. If the latter name depresses you it may be encouraging to know that Paradise is just 79 miles northwest of here.*

### H The Big Blackfoot Railway

East of Missoula

*The Blackfoot River has been a transportation corridor for hundreds of years, first serving Indian travelers, then later fur trappers, miners, and loggers. The first large-scale timber cutting started in 1885 when the Big Blackfoot Milling Co. located at Bonner. The mill's principal customer was Butte copper magnate, Marcus Daly. The expanding mines created an insatiable appetite for lumber, and in 1898 Daly's Anaconda Copper Mining Co. bought the mill.*

*The mill started the Big Blackfoot Railway to move timber from outlying cuts to the river. The main line ran from Greenough to McNamara Landing which was on the river about five miles north of here. Logs were skidded by horses to temporary branch lines, then transferred to the main line for the trip to the river. At high water the logs were floated down to Bonner. Once an area was cleared of timber, the temporary rail lines would be moved to the next cut.*

*The Milwaukee Railroad acquired the Big Blackfoot Railway as a branch line about 1910 and the trains ran until 1916, when logging ceased for ten years. Both resumed in 1926, but the railway's years were numbered. Logging trucks came on the scene in the 1920s and by 1948 had dominated the industry. Hauling by rail had ended by 1957. Trucks also eliminated the need for logging camps, so most of the small communities disappeared too.*

*One of the locomotives, specially geared for rough track and steep grades, can be seen in the Bonner park.*

**2.** *Attraction, Gas, Food, Lodging, Shopping*

### Missoula

Missoula, with a population of about 45,000, sits on the Clark Fork River at the intersection of five river valleys. Surrounded by mountains on all sides, the university town (University of Montana spreads across 150 acres) is unquestionably one of Montana's most attractive communities. Missoula,

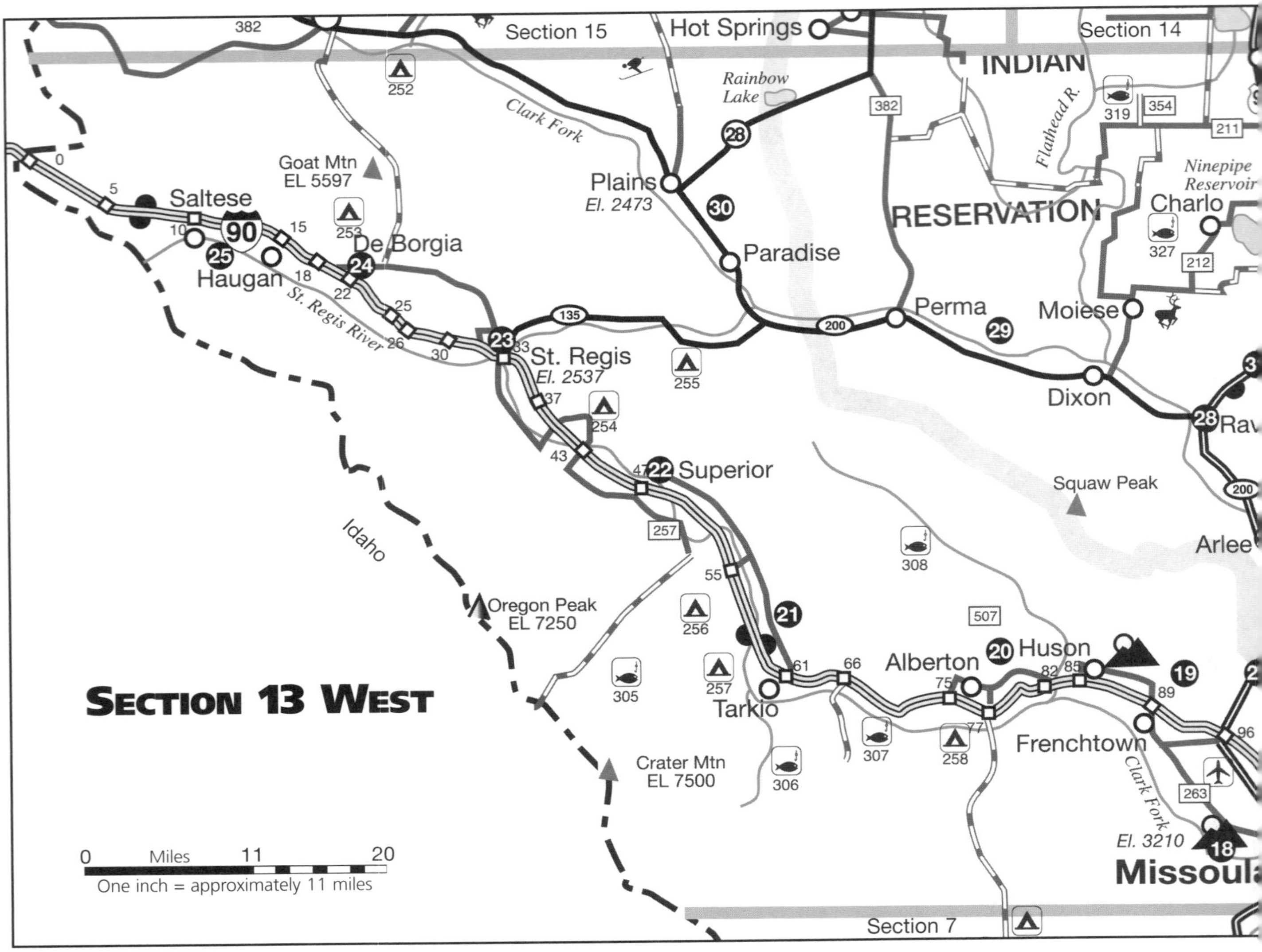

# Section 13 West

0 Miles 11 20
One inch = approximately 11 miles

**Legend**

 Locator number (matches numeric listing in section)

 Wildlife viewing

 Campsite (number matches number in campsite chart)

 State Park

 Fishing Site (number matches number in fishing chart)

 Rest stop

 Interstate

 U.S. Highway

 State Highway

 County Road

Gravel/unpaved road

intellectually and artistically oriented, is perhaps Montana's most cultured town. Jeanette Rankin, the first women representative in the U.S. Congress, was born in Missoula.

This colorful city is also in the heart of some of the most beautiful outdoor splendor. The Rattlesnake Wilderness area, which bans motorized travel, begins just a mile from the city. The broad Clark Fork flows through Missoula, making Missoula truly a mecca for backpacking, river rafting and fishing. Within minutes one can leave the conveniences of the city and be amidst secluded forests, pristine rivers or rugged mountains.

Missoula is known as the "Garden City" for its imported Vermont maple trees, profuse flower gardens and lush, green landscape. The city is the hub of shopping, recreation, education and entertainment for western Montana. A shopper's paradise, Missoula has a variety of specialty shops, art galleries, as well as a modern mall with over one hundred stores.

The town acquired its name from the British explorer David Thompson who mapped the area in 1812 and dubbed it Ne-missoola-takoo, meaning "at the cold chilling waters" in the Salish language. Another theory is that it came from the Salish "In mis sou let ka," meaning "river of awe." In 1860 the first settlement made its home here and the town developed quickly as a regional center for mining, logging and the railroad industry.

If you're a history buff, you'll love Missoula. Twenty-seven city buildings are on the National Register of Historic Places, including the old Northern Pacific Depot. Other highlights are The Missoula Museum of Arts, Historical Museum of Fort Missoula, Missoula Memorial Rose Garden, and the Smokejumper Training Center and Aerial Fire Depot—the largest smoke-jumper base in the United States.

### T Rattlesnake Recreation Area

I-90 Exit 105 and north on Van Buren. Missoula

This 61,000 acre recreation area has 33,000 acres designated as wilderness. The Sawmill-Curry trail system provides an entire network of hiking trails here. See the map on the next page

### *Montana Trivia*

Glacial Lake Missoula covered much of western Montana ten thousand years ago. The lake was formed by ice sheet dams. It filled and emptied between thirty-six and forty times as the ice dams broke and reformed. The resulting floods ran with a volume ten times greater than all of the world's rivers combined and moved at a rate of 387,000 cubic feet per second.

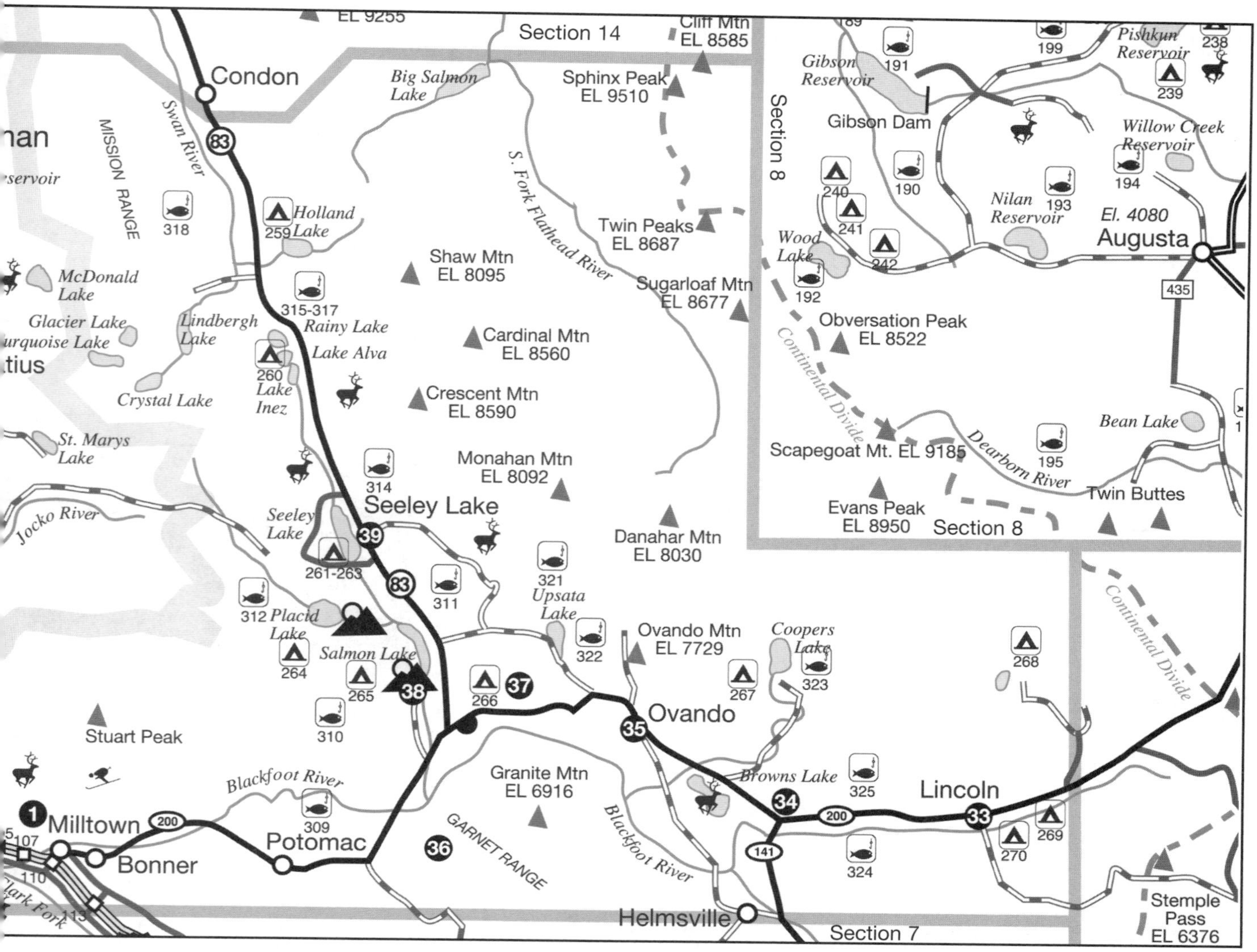

## V 10,000 Waves - Rafts & Kayak Adventures

1311 E. Broadway, Missoula. 546-6670 or toll free 800-537-8315. www.10000-waves.com.0

10,000 Waves offers quality whitewater and scenic rafting, inflatable and sit-on-top kayak adventures, kayak instruction, and whitewater guide schools on Montana's premier rivers. Their trips are in the pristine places Montanans treasure, such as the Alberton Gorge (Class III-IV), some of the finest whitewater in the Northwest, and various trips down the Blackfoot and Bitterroot Rivers. Each of their guides are versed in the geologic and natural histories of the area and waterways and share this information along the way, making the trips not only thrilling and fun, but enriching and memorable leaving you with reason to return to Montana and memories that will last a lifetime!

## L Holiday Inn Express Hotel Riverside

1021 E. Broadway, Missoula. 549-7600 or 800-HOLIDAY(465-4329)

The Holiday Inn Express Riverside offers complete comfort and convenience for the traveler. All of the 95 guest rooms overlook the beautiful Clark Fork River, which flows through the center of Missoula. The hotel is within walking distance to the University of Montana and just a half mile from downtown, with easy access to I-90. Offering a complimentary breakfast bar, king suites with whirlpool tub, a fitness center, business center, free HBO, free local calls, guest laundry, complimentary airport shuttle, and a meeting room for up to 100 people. The friendly staff can help you with any of your business or recreation needs. Enjoy the wonders of Missoula and the surrounding area from the Holiday Inn Express Riverside.

### Montana Trivia

It took John Mullan and his 250-man crew only three years (1859-1862) to build a road that stretched 624 miles from Fort Benton to Walla Walla, Washington. The road was the last link in the transportation route between the Atlantic and the Pacific. It took the average traveler forty-seven days to travel the full length of the road. The road was built at a cost of $100,000. A century later, it cost $1.2 billion to build the interstate highway system in Montana.

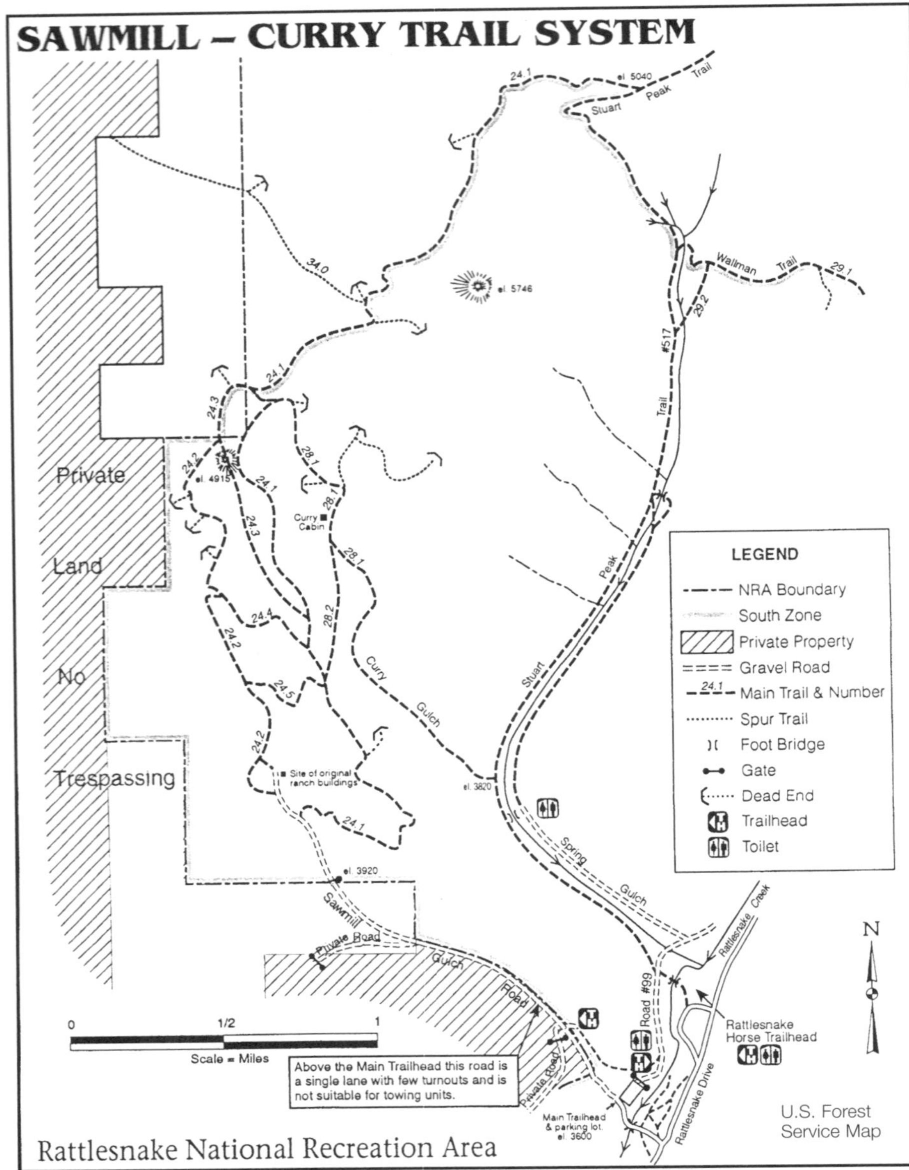

## L Thunderbird Motel

1009 E. Broadway, Missoula. 543-7251 or 800- 952-2400

At the Thunderbird Motel you can have your choice of rooms with king or queen size beds, the family unit with three beds, or the jacuzzi suite. Some rooms are complete with recliners and all rooms have refrigerators, free local calls, dataports, and cable TV with HBO, CNN, and ESPN. Enjoy a complimentary continental breakfast with coffee, juice, bagels, and muffins. You can enjoy a swim in the indoor pool, or relax in the jacuzzi. Guests can use the fax and copy machine at the front desk and a meeting room is available for special events. A microwave, guest laundry and winter plug-ins are available as well.

## L Foxglove Cottage B&B

2331 Gilbert in Missoula. I-90 Exit 105, north on Van Buren, left on Gilbert. 543-2927. foxglovecottage@msn.com. www.foxglovecottage.net.

## L Creekside Inn

630 E. Broadway, Missoula. 549-2387

## 3. *Attraction, Gas, Food, Lodging, Shopping*

## T Missoula Museum of the Arts

335 N. Patee, Downtown Missoula. 728-0447

This museum is housed in the old Carnegie Library and has a small permanent collection. It also features periodic traveling exhibits of regional, national, and international art with an emphasis on art of the West.

## L City Center Motel

338 E. Broadway, Missoula. 543-3193

Located close to all downtown Missoula activities, Montana State University, and right across the street from the Missoula Children's Theatre, the City Center Motel is a great central spot to stay. All rooms are complete with cable TV with HBO and microwaves & refrigerators. Enjoy this quiet location, off the highway, and within walking distance to many fine downtown restaurants.

## L Holiday Inn Missoula Parkside

200 S. Patee in downtown Missoula. 721-8550. 800-399-0408. http://www.montana.com/parkside. info@park-side.com.

## 4. *Attraction, Food, Lodging, Shopping*

## T A Carousel for Missoula

1 Caras Park, Downtown Missoula. 549-8382

A Carousel for Missoula is the place where you can "Ride the Dream." Not only is it one of the first fully hand-carved carousels built in America since the Great Depression, but it is also one of the fastest carousels in the country. It has the largest band organ in continuous use in the United States, making for great music for your ride. Thirty-eight ponies, two chariots, and many other carvings are housed in a specially designed building .The Carousel is available for tours and private rentals. Also stop in to The Gift Shop at the Carousel where you will find work by local artists & craftsmen, carousel collectables, souvenirs, and gift items for all occasions. The Carousel is a labor of love by citizens of Missoula and beyond. It is open year round from 11 a.m. to 7 p.m. June through August, and 11 a.m. to 5:30 p.m. September through May.

## F MacKenzie River Pizza Co.

137 W. Front Street, Missoula. 721-0077

Famous for gourmet pizzas, super sandwiches and extraordinary salads, everything is made fresh daily right down to the salad dressings and the pizza dough! Their Front Street store is in the middle of Downtown Missoula. You can enjoy warm weather seating over looking Caras Park and Clark's Fork River, or stay inside and enjoy a glass of wine and a great dinner.

## FS Butterfly Herbs

232 N. Higgins Ave., Missoula. 728-8780

Many people feel that Butterfly Herbs is the essence of Missoula—an exotic blend of aromas wafting from coffees, teas, spices and essential oils from around the world. This is the home of "Evening in Missoula" tea as well as a large selection of other specially blended herbal teas, unique Montana-made gifts and eclectic imported treasures. Nestled in the back of the historic store is Butterfly Espresso Bar, Missoula's oldest operating coffee house established in 1980. Enjoy a refresh-

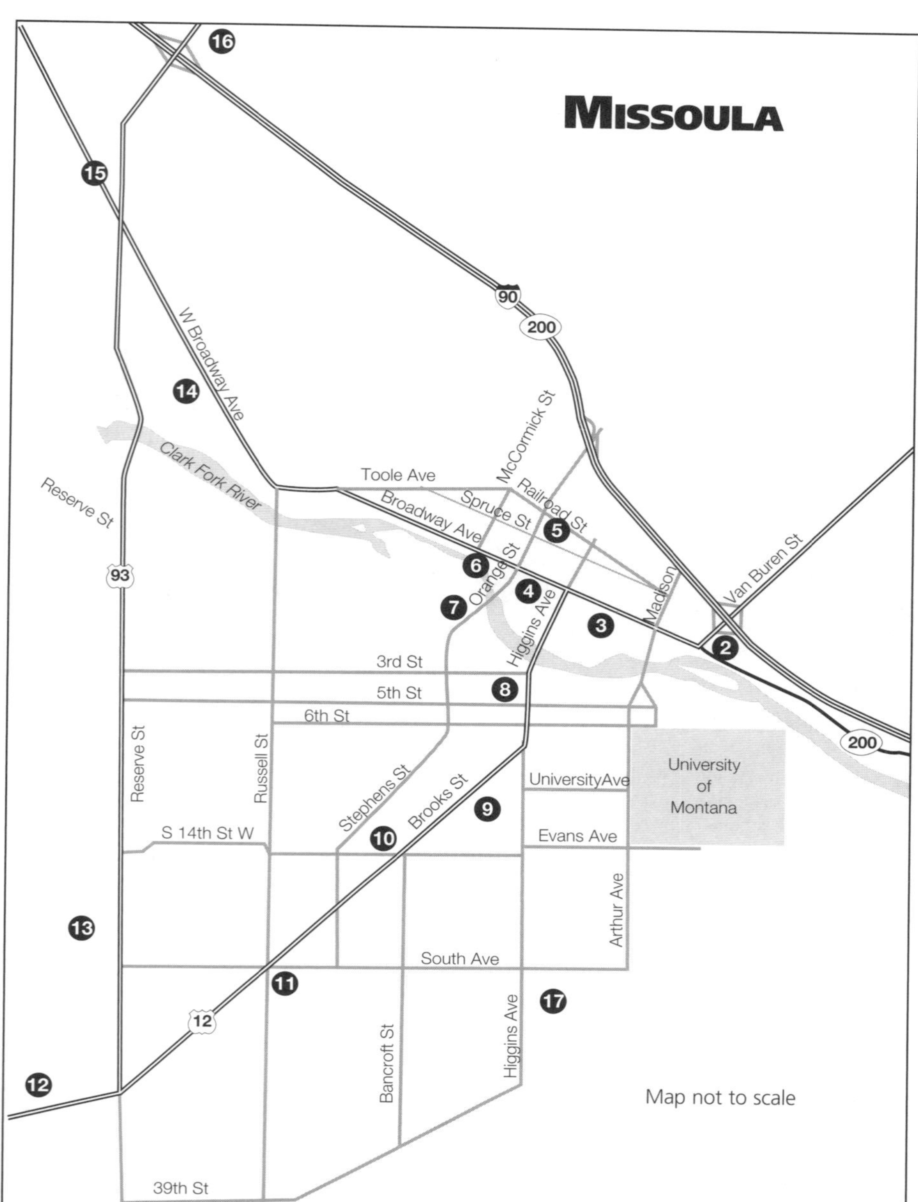


ing coffee soda or a rich and creamy Butterfly Mocha. Lattes, cappuccinos, and straight shots are also available. Also serving lunch with homemade soups, bagels and cream cheese, or simple sandwiches served on herb seed rolls.

## L Uptown Motel

329 Woody St., Missoula. 549-5141 or 800-315-5141

The Uptown Motel is across from the Missoula courthouse and near St. Patrick's Hospital, and close to all downtown activities. They are within walking distance to many of Missoula's wonderful restaurants. The 13 affordable guest rooms are complete with cable TV with HBO, microwaves and refrigerators. Pets are welcome.

### *Montana Trivia*

Hellgate is the narrow gap in the mountains east of Missoula. It was so named because Indian battles throughout the ages left it littered with bones. It is seventy-nine miles from Hellgate to Paradise.

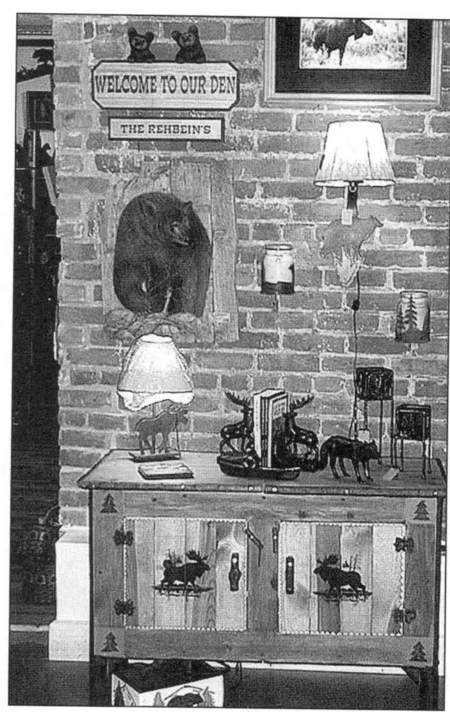


## S Moose Creek Mercantile

314 N. Higgins Ave., Missoula. 543-6503.

This unique store features a western, wildlife, nature theme which is very creatively displayed. It is the perfect place to find decorations for the home or cabin and unique gifts. They have a large collection of furniture, bedding, lighting, kitchenware, artwork, and gifts. All the products are carefully selected both locally and nationally. This retail establishment has acquired a reputation as one of Montana's most unique and appealing stores, and it draws people from all over the country. Come on in and see for yourself!

## S Monte Dolack Gallery

139 W. Front St., Downtown Missoula. 549-3248, www.dolack.com

Located on Front Street in the heart of historic Downtown Missoula, the Monte Dolack Gallery is a must see. The gallery contains the most complete collection of fine art, prints, posters and notecards by Montana artists Monte Dolack and Mary Beth Percival. Their limited edition prints, posters and notecards are also distributed worldwide. Monte has gained national recognition for his posters and his love of the natural world and extensive travel has helped shape the content of his imagery. They invite you to stop by the gallery and view this work, as well as jewelry, prints and sculpture by other talented Montana artists. Visit their web site!

**S Ovilla Antique & Gift Emporium**
115 W. Front St., Missoula. 728-3527

Built in 1888, in the oldest part of town, featuring antiques, collectables, gifts, espresso, locally made fine chocolates.

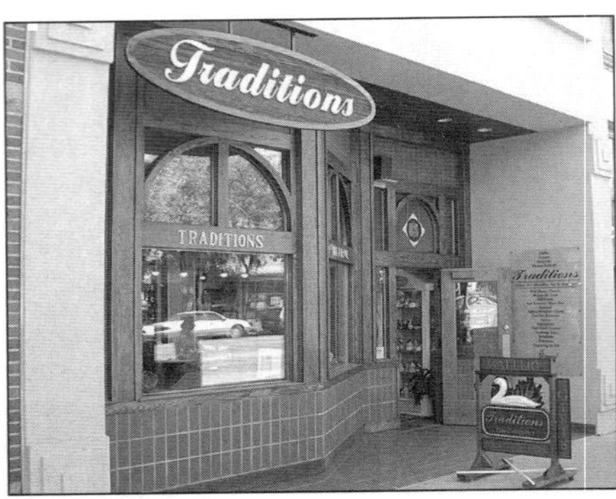


**S Traditions**
228 N. Higgins, Missoula. 543-3177
or fax 543-3178

**5.** *Gas, Food, Lodging*

**FS Worden's Market & Deli**
451 N. Higgins Ave., Missoula. 549-1293.
www.wordens.com

One of Missoula's most fun stores is also one of it's oldest! Worden's Market was established around 1883, as Missoula's first grocery store and has been in continuous operation since it's inception. Worden's has developed a reputation for it's eclectic and worldly selection of award-winning wines, beers, specialty foods and candies and has established a full service, award-winning deli operation. The original character and commitment to customer service continues, in spite of it's growth. Why is it one of Missoula's favorite places to shop? No doubt it's because they carry the best selection of wines, beers, cheeses, cigars, and of course, the best deli and the most exciting gourmet groceries around. Not only will you find palate pleasing goods, but you'll have a great time. Open seven days a week. Check their web site!

**F Iron Horse Brew Pub**
501 N. Higgins, Missoula. 728-8866

A Missoula local's favorite. The towering ceilings, warm wood interior, and all glass walls provide a wide open atmosphere. Enjoy some of the finest handmade soups, sauces, and sandwiches found anywhere. They have over 18 of the local breweries' beers on tap, a wide selection of wine by the glass, and all of your favorite mixed drinks. Munch on Tami's world famous Iron Horse Snack Mix at their 36' bar. If the weather is right, sit outside on their deck, or stay inside and kick back while enjoying your favorite sport on one of nine TV screens. The Iron Horse is not just a great place to eat, it's a great place to linger.

**F Steelhead Grill**
140 W. Pine. Downtown Missoula. 541-3755.
www.moclub.com/steelheadgrill

Take two top chefs. Combine to form one restaurant. What do you get? Some of the most creative, eclectic cuisine found anywhere. Chefs Charles Davidson and Adam Young may tempt you with anything from Cajun to Pan Asian, Southwestern to Italian. For starters try their Fried Green Tomatoes with Chipotle Remoulade or Stoneground Corn Fries. Move on to a hearty New Orleans-style Gumbo. Then on to one of their unique entree's such as a Green Chile Pork Chop or Cornmeal Crusted Trout with Fried Green Tomatoes. Try their flatbreads and calzones as an entrée. Each dish unique, every night something new from the grill. The chefs say the one thing all of their creations have in common are the ingredients—always the freshest available. An excellent selection of wine and beer is available. Check their website for a sample menu. Dinner is served from 5 p.m. to 10 p.m. Tuesday through Saturday.

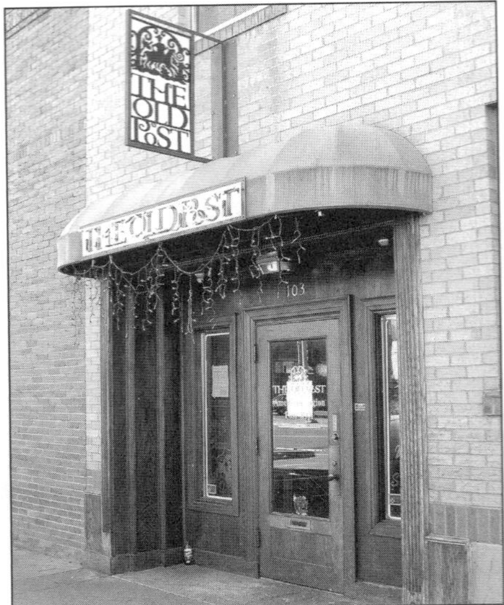


**F The Old Post**
103 W. Spruce in downtown Missouls. 721-7399

The brick and wood ambience of The Old Post reminds you of a neighborhood pub where everybody knows your name. It is actually the American Legion Post, but is open to the public. If you want to sample the microbreweries of Montana in a relaxed, friendly atmosphere, this is a place to do it. While they have a full selection of your favorite spirits, they also have some of the best sandwiches and pub fare to be found anywhere. If you come on the weekend, there's a good chance you'll also sample some of the better live music in the area.

**F Sushi Hana**
403 N. Higgins, Missoula. 549-7979

Featuring fine Japanese cuisine, Sushi Hana is one of the few authentic Japanese restaurants in Montana. Their fish is flown in fresh, and the finest ingredients are used to create a variety of sushi and other Japanese entrées including tempura, yakitori, udon, sobas, and combination plates. There is a great selection of appetizers, soups, salads, and daily specials to choose from as well. You can enjoy the a la carte sushi bar, and watch as the rolls are prepared, or enjoy a table in the dining room. Owner and chef, Chris Nagata has years of experience in fine Japanese cuisine. Stop in or call ahead for to go orders. Open for lunch and dinner daily.

**F Sean Kelly's, A Public House**
130 W. Pine St., Missoula. 542-1471

An American pub with an Irish feel..

**F Zimorino's Red Pies Over Montana**
424 N. Higgins, Missoula. 728-6686

**F Two Sisters**
127 W. Alder in downtown Missoula. 327-8438.
napigirl@in-tch.com

Voted "Best New Restaurant - 2001" by both the Independent and the Missoulian, Two Sisters is a unique, colorful restaurant featuring hand crafted cuisine by New Orleans trained chef (and Sister!) Beth Higgins. You can join them on one of the best patios in Missoula for a fabulous breakfast, lunch, or dinner of hand crafted, seasonal fare. Featuring daily specials for all meals, Two Sisters offers an exceptional dining experience finishing with absolutely sinful desserts. Beer and wine as well as a private party room and off site catering available. Check out their original location adjacent to Glacier National Park!

## Montana Trivia

It took John Mullan and his 250-man crew only three years (1859-1862) to build a road that stretched 624 miles from Fort Benton to Walla Walla, Washington. The road was the last link in the transportation route between the Atlantic and the Pacific. It took the average traveler forty-seven days to travel the full length of the road. The road was built at a cost of $100,000. A century later, it cost $1.2 billion to build the interstate highway system in Montana.

**L Orange St. Inn**
801 N. Orange St. at I-90 Orange St. Exit in Missoula. 721-3610. 800-328-0801 (Reservations only).

For travelers looking to take advantage of Missoula's attractions without paying top dollar for lodging, Orange Street Inn is an excellent choice. Located minutes from Missoula's downtown shops and restaurants, Orange Street Inn caters to budget-minded families and business travelers. The Inn's large, comfortable rooms have been recently remodeled, and rates include free continental breakfast, cable TV and 24-hour front desk assistance. The Inn even offers a fully furnished apartment with kitchen that's ideal for extended stays, such as visiting nearby St. Patrick Hospital. Great rooms, ideal location and affordable rates make Orange Street Inn one of Montana's best lodging values. Missoula's Orange Street Inn is close to downtown, but far from expensive.

**6.** *Gas, Food, Lodging, Shopping*

**L Inn on Broadway**
1609 W. Broadway, Missoula. 543-7231 or 800-286-2316

Located close to the airport, bus depot, and just a couple miles from downtown, the Inn on Broadway is a great family spot, for fun & relaxation in Missoula. There is an outdoor pool and patio area. The lounge and casino offer different entertainment and activities every night of the week. The rooms feature king and double beds, air-conditioning, and microwaves and refrigerators are available upon request. They offer non-smoking rooms, airport shuttle service, and have discounted rates for seniors, AAA, off-season, and business travelers. Long term rates are also available.

## Montana Trivia

The Gideons placed their first bibles in the Superior Hotel in Superior in 1908.

### L Red Lion Inn

700 W. Broadway, Missoula, 728-3300 or 800-733-5466(RED LION). www.redlion.com

The Red Lion is conveniently located off I-90 at Orange Street exit, near downtown, and just 10 minutes from the airport, the Red Lion Inn offers 76 air-conditioned guest rooms. Each is equipped with a data port telephone, coffee maker, iron and ironing board, cable TV with HBO & ESPN, and a complimentary continental breakfast buffet. They have a heated swimming pool and spa, a river front park with walking/biking paths, and a tennis court and fishing pond across the street. They offer complimentary airport transportation and a restaurant and 24-hour grocery right next door. Located near Glacier National Park, four public golf courses, and many recreational activities.

### L Travelodge

420 W. Broadway. I-90 Exit 104 at Orange St. 6 blks to Broadway, 1/2 blk right. West edge of downtown. 800-578-7878. 728-4500. www.travelodge.com.

## 7. *Attraction, Food*

### T Big Sky Brewing Company

120-A Hickory St., Missoula. 549-2777, www.bigskybrew.com

No visit to Missoula is complete without dropping in to the tasting room and gift shop at Big Sky Brewing Company. You can sample all of the beers made on premise while you look over the vast array of merchandise that supports the breweries beers: Moose Drool Brown Ale, Slow Elk Oatmeal Stout, Scape Goat Pale Ale, Summer Honey and Powder Hound. About a mile south of the Interstate, just off the Orange Street Bridge, across from McCormick Park. Monday through Friday 11:00 a.m. to 6:00 p.m. and Saturday Noon to 5:00. Check them out on the web at www.moose-drool.com.

## 8. *Attraction, Gas, Food, Shopping*

### F Tipu's Indian Cafe

115 1/2 S. 4th St. W. Half block west of Higgins behind Holiday Station. 592-0622. www.tipustiger.com. tiger@montana.com

What makes Tipu's unique is a combination of high quality, hearty, flavorful vegetarian food, a pleasant and unusual dining space, and a friendly atmosphere. So far they are the only Indian restaurant in Montana. They have blended traditional Indian cuisine with international influence and an emphasis on healthy organic ingredients. Some of their specials include authentic homemade chai, homemade paneer cheese, and delicious samosas. They have received "Best of Missoula" awards for four years running including "Best Vegetarian" and "Best Ethnic" categories. Visit their new location and try a new adventure in ethnic dining.

### S Unique Fair Trade Global Gifts: The Jeannette Rankin Peace Center

519 S. Higgins Ave. Missoula. 543-3955. www.jrpc.org

*The Clark's Fork River winds through the city of Missoula. The University of Montana campus sits in the foreground.*

## 9. *Attraction, Food, Miscellaneous,*

### T Museum of Fine Arts

University of Montana. 243-2019

The museum is located on the university campus and collects, exhibits, and preserves works of art for the education of university students, the scholarly study of research professionals and the enjoyment of the public. The large, 8,500 piece collection is rotated in the galleries located in the Performing Arts and Radio/Television Center on campus. Collections include antiques, sculpture, paintings, drawings, textiles, photographs, and ceramics. There is also a Museum Shop. The museum is open Monday through Friday.

### F Valentino's Italian and Greek Restaurant

1901 Stephens in Missoula. 1/2 blk north of Brooks. 542-8100

### F The Montana Club Restaurant & Casino

2620 Brooks St., Missoula. 543-3200

The Montana Club is conveniently located on the 93 strip near Southgate Mall. Enjoy one of Missoula's finest examples of how food was meant to be prepared. Savor scratch-made breakfast, lunch, and dinner. Enjoy different daily specials prepared with the freshest ingredients. They are consistently voted one of Missoula's favorite restaurants. Relax while you dine in upscale casual comfort while enjoying a true sense of Montana surroundings. From the 100 year-old exposed wood beams, to the tastefully reproduced photo's of old Montana, you'll know you had a "true" Montana experience. Open early till late. Large parties are welcome.

### M Lambros Real Estate

1001 S. Higgins Ave., Missoula. 532-9200. www.lambros.com

Lambros Real Estate, is often referred to as one of Montana's leading real estate companies, has been in business for over 40 years. They offer a full array of real estate services and are a leader in sales and technology. Lambros offices are located in Missoula, Polson, Seeley Lake, and Hamilton, providing service to all of western Montana. There are over 70 experienced sales associates specializing in residential, commercial, ranch and land, recreational, lake properties, property management and rentals. Access their web site for more information on all of their listings and Missoula County Multiple listings. Across western Montana, they are just what you are looking for.

### M University of Montana

Missoula. 243-0211 or 800-462-8636, www.umt.edu

The University of Montana was founded in 1893, the oldest university in the state, is also known as the home of the Montana "Grizzlies". Today it is the state's leading liberal arts institution comprised of the College of Arts and Sciences, the Graduate School, Davidson Honors College and seven professional schools. It offers fifty eight undergraduate degrees, fifty-two master's degrees, and twn doctoral degrees and maintains several arms in communities throughout the state. Current enrollment at the Missoula Campus is approximately 12,200 students.

### M Goodweb's Internet Cafe

800 Kensington in Missoula. Behind Baskin-Robbins on Brooks. 543-6080. www.goodwebs.net. goodweb@goodwebs.net

## 10. *Gas, Food, Shopping*

### F The Mustard Seed

2901 Brooks St., Southgate Mall, Missoula. 542-7333(SEED)

Contemporary cuisine since 1978, prepared with fresh vegetables, lean meats, and light sauces. Everything at the Mustard Seed is prepared from scratch—whole shrimp are hand peeled, fresh vegetables are cut every day, and the signature sauces and dressings are all handmade. They provide healthy meals with the best quality, for reasonable prices, in a fresh, casual and comfortable atmosphere. Stop in for a quick meal or a leisurely dinner out. Take out is available, and they offer delivery service to most areas in town.

#### It Happened in Montana

October 9, 1920. The University of Montana football team racked up the largest point total ever scored by a Montana college football team. They thrashed Mount Saint Charles College (now Carroll College) in Helena by the lopsided score of 133-0.

## 11. *Gas, Food, Miscellaneous*

### F Mongos Mongolian Grill

3521 Brooks, Missoula. 829-8888

Mongos offers a one-of-a-kind dining experience! You create you own entree by choosing from an amazing selection of fresh ingredients including favorite meats, seafood, noodles, vegetables, and specialty sauces ranging from mild Teriyaki to fiery Szechwan. If you are shy there are suggestions for favorite from their regulars. Just pick your own favorites and watch as the cooks prepare your creation on a large open grill. Enjoy a great selection of appetizers, wines, micro-brews, and sakes with your meal. Remember to leave room for an array of desserts as well. Stop in to Mongos for an experience you won't forget. They are open daily.

#### Montana Trivia

Lieutenant James Moss may be the first person to receive a sports endorsement contract. In 1897 he had his troops at Fort Missoula try out bicycles. Spaulding provided the bicycles and used his photos, reports, and notes in their advertisements.

### F Diamond Jim's

3700 Brooks, corner of Brooks and Reserve in Missoula. 251-3922.

When Diamond Jim Brady invited his friends to his place, he took exceptionally good care of them. They always had more than enough to eat and drink, and they were always well entertained. How could Diamond Jim's Casinos do any less? They are proud of the hospitality they offer, and the friendliness of the staff is an important part of their package. Here you'll find well-prepared meals, with breakfast and lunch menus, and evening dinner specials. Diamond Jim's Casino was voted "Missoula's Best Casino" in the 2002 Independent Record reader's survey. Package liquor is available. Visit their Eastgate location at 900 E. Broadway (casino, bar, and packaged liquor) and at Crossroads Truck Center on I90 and 93 (casino and bar).

### F Fiesta en Jalisco

3701 Brooks in Missoula. One block east of Brooks and Reserve. 728-1323

This recently opened authentic Mexican restaurant is quickly becoming a locals' favorite. Owner Raul Gomez is a purist who doesn't believe in the American version of his native Mexican cuisine. He serves up only authentic Mexican fare. His

#### It Happened in Montana

February 21, 1863. Montana's first civil suit was filed in Missoula by Tin-Cup Joe. Seems that Tin-Cup and his Indian wife asked "Baron" Cornelius O'Keefe if he and his wife could spend the night. The Baron and his brother David were just leaving to find Captain Mullen at his camp east of the Missoula Valley. They Told Tin-Cup he could stay, but to keep his horse out of the seed oats. Seems the O'Keefe brothers had raised a prize crop of oats the year before and had saved the seed in hopes of an even better crop the next year. When they returned from their journey, there was Tin-Cup's horse feasting on the oat seeds. The Baron went into a rage and frightened the horse so much that it stumbled into a root cellar and died. Tin-Cup and his wife barely escaped with their lives.

Tin-Cup told a fellow named Frank Woody about his experience. Woody said "file suit!" He did. Tin-Cup and the Baron faced off in front of one Judge Brooks. Frank Woody represented Tin-Cup and the Baron represented himself. When he came up to the bench, the Baron demanded the judge tell him by whose authority he was judging. The judge pulled a pack of cards from his pocket and told the Baron that these were his credentials. The judge then asked how the Baron suddenly became a lawyer. If credentials were so important, what credentials did the Baron have? The Baron punched the judge between the eyes and replied, "These are my credentials!" Pandemonium ensued and the judge ran for his life. Later, he fined the Baron $40. No one had the courage to approach the Baron for the money, Since there was no sheriff to do the court's bidding, the money was never paid..

Present ad at check-in to receive discount. Offer good only at the motels listed.
Not valid with other offers or discounts.

Chile Verde is the real thing. Other house specials include Chile Colorado, Carnitas de Res, Carne Adobada, and Steak Picado. His "Fiesta Favorites" include Sopitos, Flautas, and Taquitos Rancheros. The service here is just as great as the food. Raul's motto is ¡Comida fina y servicio fino! (fine food and fine service).This is Raul's first restaurant in Montana. If you're traveling west of Montana check out his others in Spokane, WA, Ellensburg, WA and Orofino, ID.

### F Paradise Falls

3621 Brooks St., Missoula. 728-3228

It's no wonder that Paradise Falls is a taste of paradise in Missoula. The spacious restaurant, lounge, and casino are all separated under one roof and open 7 a.m. to 2 a.m. daily. They serve breakfast, lunch, and dinner in the 100% smoke-free restaurant. The diverse menu includes steaks, seafood, baby back ribs, pizza, and special selections for kids. Reservations are recommended. The lounge features a unique oak bar and your favorite cocktails, wine, and a selection of 16 beers and micro brews on tap. You won't have to miss your favorite sporting event either. There are 9 TV's with satellite for everyone's pleasure. The casino is loaded with 20 machines and an ATM machine for your enjoyment.

### L Val-U Inn

3001 Brooks St., Missoula. 721-9600 or 800-443-7777

The Val-U Inn is the perfect location for the family. It is located next to Southgate Mall, near the University of Montana, fairgrounds, casinos, family and fine dining, and easy access to the Missoula Outdoor Theatre. Featuring a continental breakfast, cable TV with HBO, hot tub and sauna, guest laundry, courtesy van, and a friendly 24-hour desk staff. All rooms have queen size beds and waterbeds are available. They also offer non-smoking rooms and senior citizen rates.

### M College of Technology of The University of Montana

909 South Avenue West, Missoula. 243-7882 or 800-542-6882 in MT, www.cte.umt.edu

This arm of the University of Montana provides occupational education in thirty four areas ranging from health care, business, culinary arts, computers, electronics and other industries. Associate degrees, certificates and licensing exam preparation ore available.

## 12. *Adventure, Attraction, Gas, Food, Lodging, Shopping*

### T Blue Mountain Recreation

From Missoula. travel 2 miles south of Reserve Street on Highway 93 South. Turn right onto the Blue Mountain Road (County Road #30).

See sidebar.

### V The Canoe Rack

5020 US Hwy 93 S., Missoula. 251-0040. www.canoerack.com

For over 25 years, the Canoe Rack has been providing high quality paddling equipment for sale or rent, as well as expert advice on every aspect of paddle sports. Canoes and kayaks can be rented daily, weekly, or as long as your adventure lasts. You're more than welcome to begin or end your paddle at the store which sits along the Bitterroot River just south of Missoula. Shuttle service is also available. Taking advantage of Montana's wilderness is easy given its vast river systems and lakes. Wildlife viewing is optimal from the water when your vessel runs quiet. Lightweight and easy to transport through Montana's rough countryside, canoes were the chosen mode of transportation by the early explorers, Lewis and Clark. Many of those historic trails can be accessed within a few minutes of the Canoe Rack. Let their staff help you explore and enjoy a calm float or a whitewater adrenaline rush through the waters of Western Montana.

### L Super 8 Motel

3901 S. Brooks, Missoula. 251-2255 or 800-888-8000

Located close to Southgate Mall and a variety of restaurants, the 103 newly remodeled rooms are complete with data ports, cable TV with remotes, Showtime, free local calls, guest laundry facilities, fax & copy services, and microwaves and refrigerators are available. There is a shuttle available, and a complimentary toast and pastry bar every morning. Single rooms with recliners are available and children under 12 are free.

### L Best Inn South and Conference Center

3803 Brooks St. in Missoula. Corner of Brooks and Reserve. 251-2665. 800-272-9500. mtgs-4-u@bigsky.net. www.bestinn.com

Comfort is the key word at the Best Inns of Missoula. They are one of the rare places that cater to people with severe allergies. Their Evergreen™ rooms are allergen free with both air and water filtration. Their Business Plus Rooms have a data port, coffee maker, hair dryer, and ironing boards. Larger deluxe rooms are also available with sofa, microwave, and refrigerator. They offer a deluxe continental breakfast, free local calls, and a guest laundry. Relax after a busy day in their hot tub. They are an excellent choice for a business conference and are able to accommodate up to 250 people.

## 13. *Attraction, Gas, Food, Shopping*

### T Lolo Peak Winery

2506 Mount Ave. in Missoula. Corner of Mount and Reserve. 549-1111. wine@lolopeak.com

This is arguably Montana's most unique winery. Lolo Peak Winery makes wines exclusively from fruits of western Montana's agricultural bounty. The wines range from rhubarb and raspberry to plum and cherry. Apples from the Bitterroot Valley make both a dry apple wine and the "Winter Warmer" a sweetened spice wine ideal for that winter evening around the fireplace (Sold November thru March). The raspberry is a sweet dessert wine that is almost a port in style. It is wonderful with chocolate, or simply sipped alone. The plum wine is an excellent addition to any oriental dinner. Visit them at their brand new location and sample their wines. There's bound to be one you'll call your favorite. They are open from 10 a.m. to 6 p.m. Monday through Saturday.

### T Bayern Brewing

2600 S. 3rd St., W. Suite E, Missoula. 721-1482, www.bayernbrewery.com

Bayern Brewing began in Missoula, Montana, in 1987, and is the only German brewery in the Rocky Mountains. Owner and Brewmaster, Jürgen Knöller, is a German diploma Master Brewer. He began brewing in 1978 at age 16, receiving a rigorous and lengthy education in Germany. Jürgen focuses on quality and he is truly dedicated to his profession. Combine his education, experience and personal dedication and you have amazing beer. Every part of the process in the production of their beer is done in Missoula. They produce a superior product with Jürgen and his authentic dedication to the art of brewing, technologically superior equipment and old-fashioned hard work. See for yourself with a visit to the tap room and gift shop. Open daily.

### T Fort Missoula

South Ave. West, Missoula. 728-3476. www.montana.com/ftmslamuseum

On this 32-acre site rests a fort that was built in 1877 during the flight of the Nez Perce. It is now home to a museum possessing more than 22,000 artifacts including 13 historical structures documenting the history of the fort and the forestry in the area. There is a self-guided tour on an outdoor, interpretive trail describing a dozen historic buildings of the fort property. The Bitterroot River runs adjacent to the property which adds to your enjoyment and there is ample space to hike and view animals.

The Rocky Mountain Museum of Military History promotes the commemoration and study of the U.S. armed services, from the Frontier Period to the War on Terrorism. The Museum strives to impart a greater understainding of the roles played by America's service-men and service-women through this period of dramatic global change. The U.S. Fourth Infantry Regiment and the Civilian Conservation Corps constructed the Museum buildings in 1936 during the Great Depression. Headquartered in Buildings T-310 and T-316 by special arrangement with the Montana National Guard, the Museum exhibits from a wide collection of documents and artifacts, ranging from Civil War artillery to Vietnam-Era anti-tank missiles. The museum is open year round. Memorial Day through Labor Day hours are 10 a.m. to 5 p.m. Monday through Saturday, and noon to 5 p.m. on Sundays. Winter hours are noon to 5 p.m. Tuesday through Sunday, closed on Mondays. There is a nominal admission fee.

## 14. *Attraction, Gas, Food, Lodging*

### T Rocky Mountain Elk Foundation Visitor Center

2291 W. Broadway, Missoula. 800-325-5355(CALLELK)

Developed primarily by hunters and dedicated to the conservation of wildlife habitat, this center features a life-size bull elk bronze, a wildlife theater, beautiful wildlife artwork, and natural history displays. One display allows the children to feel furs and guess the animal. There are also many taxidermy mounts, and wildlife films are shown in the 50-seat theater.

### F Perugia Restaurant & Gallery

1106 W. Broadway, Missoula. 543-3757

The Risho family invites you to experience the Perugia adventure. Perugia, an authentic family-run restaurant, is owned and operated by chef Ray Risho, wife/artist Susie, eldest son Sam, youngest son Abe, and nephew Chris Robertson. The menu features authentic European and Mediterranean cuisine that evokes a taste and feel of the old world. There is an extensive wine list, cocktails and live music nightly. Theme nights, Italian Night Tuesdays and Greek Night Thursdays are perhaps the most popular nights of the week at Perugia, when heaping platters of popular dishes are served. The regular menu is extensive and offers a wide array of pastas, lamb, veal, steaks, chicken and seafood all served in three courses. Plan to join the Rishos for a memorable evening of old world hospitality and cooking. Open Tues.–Thurs. 5-9, Fri. & Sat. 5–10.

## 15. *Gas, Food, Lodging, Shopping*

### T Museum of Mountain Flying

Missoula International Airport

This museum traces the history of civil aviation in some of the country's toughest flying environments. It commemorates the legendary "Tall Timber" mountain pilots of the Northern Rockies, along with their great planes and extraordinary exploits iin the realm of mercy flights, forest-fire suppression and back-country cargo delivery. The museum's mission is to preserve the legends, lore and historical legacy of pilots and other individuals whose pioneering aviation exploits helped bring America's Rocky Mountain West into the Air Age. They display items related to this region's mountain-flying history, including, but not limited to, appropriate vintage aircraft, memorabilia, artifacts, historical documents, photographs, personal narrative and diaries, motion-picture footage, tape recordings, newspaper stories, magazine articles and books. Included in the current collection is a C-45 Twin Beech, a 1941 Stearman, three home-builts, a 1947 Federal flatbed airport truck, a World War II Jeep, a large model aircraft collection, and displays of smokejumper memorabilia, parachutes, and historic photos. The Douglas C-47 that dropped smokejumpers on Montana's notorious 1949 Mann Gulch fire. Twelve of the jumpers and a wilderness guard perished in the fire which inspired the Norman Maclean book *Young Men and Fire*.

### F Perkins Family Restaurant

2275 N. Reserve, Missoula. 543-3330

There's always something new cooking at Perkins! Located just two miles off the I-90 Reserve Street exit and close to many hotels, Perkins Family Restaurant and Bakery is the perfect place for travelers. They have fast, friendly service, great prices, and great food in a pleasant, non-smoking family atmosphere, with unique antiques hanging from the walls. The in-house bakery features fresh pies, muffins, cookies, and more. They offer daily soups and fantastic bread bowl salads. All your favorites are available all day and all night. Open 24-hours a day, you can dine-in or get food to go.

# Pattee Canyon Recreation Area

**The large picnic area and system of** roads and trails make Pattee Canyon one of the most popular recreation areas close to Missoula.

## Facilities

The picnic area includes tables, fire rings, toilets (some handicapped accessible), parking and group Picnic facilities, but no running water, electricity or shelters.

Three group picnic sites, with their extra large tables, extra grills and parking lots, can accommodate from 40 to 200 people. Arrangements for using the group sites are made through the Missoula Ranger District office at 329-3814.

Volunteer hosts are on duty in the picnic area during the summer. The Pattee Canyon Recreation Area is day use only.

## Trails & Roads

The extensive year-round system of trails and roads is open to non-motorized use. A person can get all the way from the picnic area to the Clark Fork river on these trails and roads.

During winter some of the trails, like the Southside Ski Trail, are groomed and maintained for crosscountry skiing. The groomed trails north of the road were developed in the 1980s by the Missoula Nordic Ski Club and the Forest Service.

Not all ski trails are groomed. The 3 1/2-mile-long Sam Braxton National Recreation trail is an ungroomed loop featuring big, old trees and pretty views. In the 1970s, Sam Braxton and the University of Montana Ski Team developed a network of cross-country ski trails near the Larch Camp Road. These trails are no longer used.

## Natural History

Besides being so close to town, the reason Pattee Canyon is so popular is because of its big, old trees. Most are ponderosa pine, or "yellow pine," the Montana state tree.

Photographs and surveys from the late 1800s show open, sunny meadows with a few big trees, large ponderosa pines spaced from 25 to 50 feet apart, with little but grass growing under them. A survey conducted between 1870 and 1900 recorded trees up to 5 feet in diameter!

Research has shown that since at least the mid-1500s, low-intensity ground fires have burned this area about once every seven years. These ground fires killed brush and young trees, but the thick bark of the yellow pines protected them from serious harm. The ground fires have produced a "fire-dependent old-growth" condition here.

When people started fighting fires at the turn of the century, the ecology of this area changed. It's been invaded by brush and Douglas-fir. The brush and young trees are a fire danger to the old trees, because they serve as fire ladders, leading ground fire into the tops of the mature trees, where it can kill them.

In 1977, the 1,200-acre Pattee Canyon fire killed many of the old trees in its path. This human caused fire burned intensely hot, largely because of all the brush and small tree fuels feeding it. You can see the result from Missoula, a large burned-over area at the southeast edge of town.

## Human History

- "Es Nin Paks." The Nez Perce and Salish Indians used Pattee Canyon on their way to the plains for buffalo hunting. The Native Americans called it "es nin paks," the crooked trail. They used it as a detour to avoid ambush by Blackfeet warriors in the narrow Hellgate Canyon of the Clark Fork river, where Interstate 90 now leads into Missoula.
- David Pattee. The Canyon takes its present name from David Pattee, who in 1871 filed a homestead claim on some land near the mouth of the canyon. In 1856, he came to the Bitterroot Valley from New Hampshire, to rebuild saw- and gristmills owned by Major John Owen. (The Fort Owen State Monument at Stevensville is named after him.) Pattee was active in several local businesses, but sold out and moved to Tacoma in 1878.
- Army timber reserve. In 1877, the US Army started building Fort Missoula. Since some of the largest trees in the area grew at the top of Pattee Canyon, it set aside a timber reserve of some 1,600 acres here. The old timber reserve is the basis of this recreation area.

The Army pushed logging roads up every drainage and draw. The main road, now used as a trail, turned north up Crazy Canyon (see map).

In the 1920s, the Army built a rifle range in the meadow at the pass. The long loop of the Meadow Loop Trail goes around the old rifle range, where earthen backstops and concrete foundations still can be seen. The range was closed in 1945.

## Opportunities

- Picnics
- Toilets (some handicapped accessible)
- Hiking
- Horseback Riding
- Jogging and running
- Bicycling
- Cross-country skiing
- Group picnics by permit only - call 329-3814
- Picnic area gate open from 9 am until sundown daily from Memorial Day until Labor Day
- Campfires allowed in facilities provided
- All trail open to a variety of uses yearlong, but no motorized vehicles allowed off roads
- Day use only, no overnight camping
- Shooting firearms and fireworks prohibited
- No running water or electricity available. Leave No Trace.

### F Sushi Hana
3075 N. Reserve, Ste. K, Missoula. 327-0731

Featuring fine Japanese cuisine, Sushi Hana is one of the few authentic Japanese restaurants in Montana. Their fish is flown in fresh, and the finest ingredients are used to create a variety of sushi and other Japanese entrees including tempura, yakitori, udon, sobas and combination plates. There is a great selection of appetizers, soups, salads and daily specials to choose from as well. You can enjoy the a la carte sushi bar, and watch as the rolls are prepared, or enjoy a table in the dining room. Owner and chef Chris Nagata has 15 years experience in fine Japanese cuisine. Stop in or call up for to go orders. Open for lunch and dinner daily.

### F Ambrosia Greek Food
2230 N. Reserve at Albertson's Shopping Center in Missoula. 542-7072

### F Old Country Buffet
3333 N. Reserve St., Missoula. 541-3463

## 16. *Gas, Food, Lodging*

### F MacKenzie River Pizza Co./ Rowdy's Cabin
4880 N. Reserve, Missoula. 721-0099.

Famous for gourmet pizzas, super sandwiches and extraordinary salads, everything is made fresh daily right down to the salad dressings and the pizza dough! They are easy to find directly off I-90 on the Reserve Street exit in the Rustic Rowdy's Cabin. Enjoy the fireplace and atrium while taking a break from the road.

### L C'mon Inn
2775 Expo Parkway, Missoula, (406) 543-4600 or (888) 989-5569.

At the C'mon Inn, you are welcome to enjoy a rustic, Montana decor complete with a river rock fireplace and waterfall. Their friendly staff believes

it is their responsibility to ensure that every guest is well taken care of and enjoys their visit. Located just off I-90 at the Reserve Street exit, the 119 brand new comfortable rooms will accommodate any weary travellers. The C'mon Inn features three different types of suite including: kitchenette suites, jacuzzi suites, and two-room suites. All guests are invited to use the exercise room, the large swimming pool, children's pool, or one of

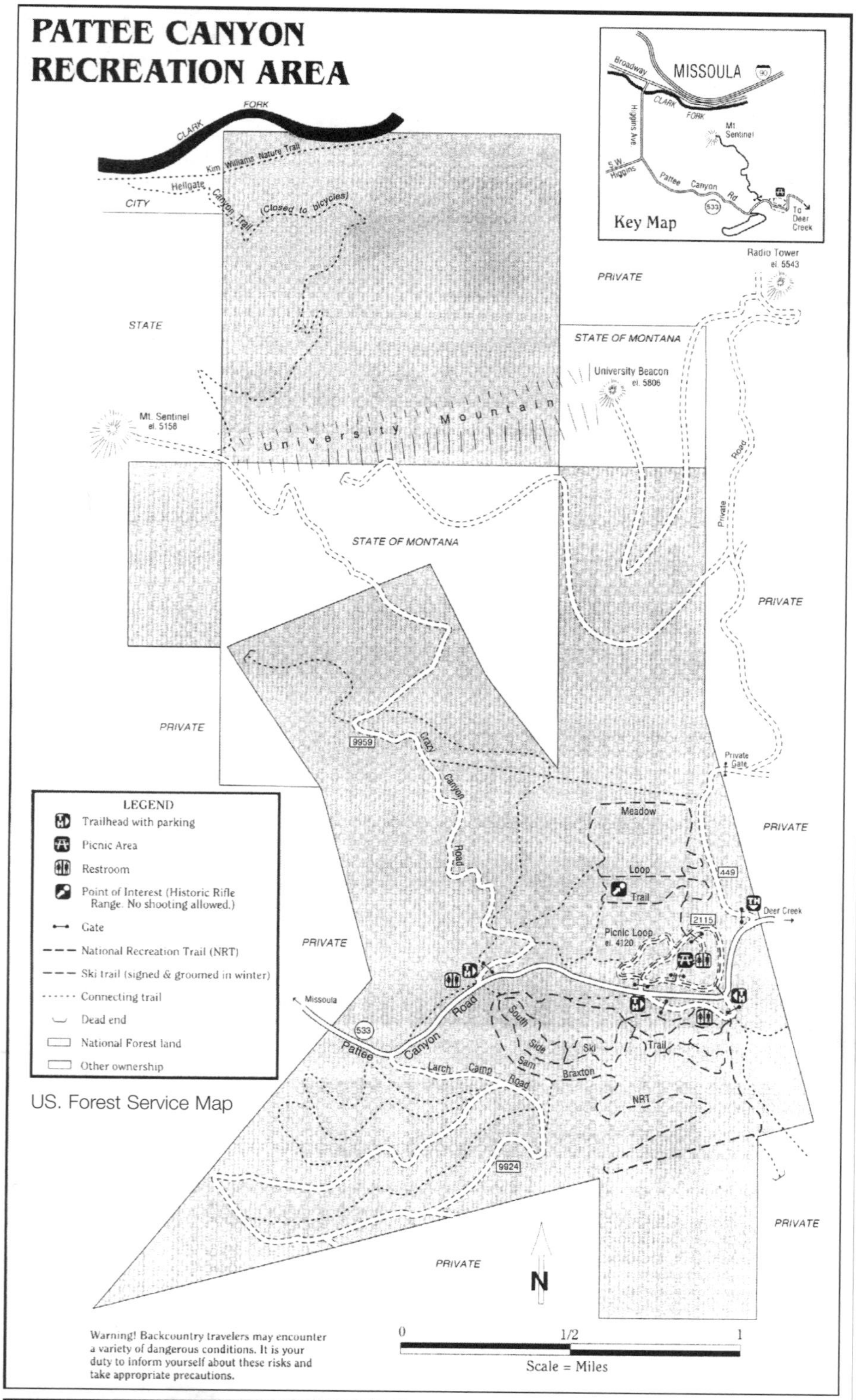

## PATTEE CANYON RECREATION AREA

LEGEND
- Trailhead with parking
- Picnic Area
- Restroom
- Point of Interest (Historic Rifle Range. No shooting allowed.)
- Gate
- National Recreation Trail (NRT)
- Ski trail (signed & groomed in winter)
- Connecting trail
- Dead end
- National Forest land
- Other ownership

Warning! Backcountry travelers may encounter a variety of dangerous conditions. It is your duty to inform yourself about these risks and take appropriate precautions.

0 1/2 1
Scale = Miles

US. Forest Service Map

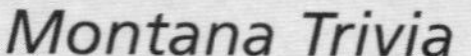

### Montana Trivia

Frank Burke wrote: "You can never judge anything in these Western places by their names, for the people seem to have a peculiar habit of giving high-sounding names to the most insignificant places." He was referring to the town of Superior.

the five hot tubs located in the spacious courtyard. Enjoy the arcade, ping pong table, and dining right next door. There is a complimentary continental breakfast and children under 12 are free.

### L Best Western Grant Creek Inn

5280 Grant Creek Rd., Missoula. 543-0700 or 800-528-1234

The beautiful Grant Creek Inn is conveniently located off I-90 Exit 101, Reserve Street in Missoula, overlooking the Missoula Valley. It is

only minutes from shopping, the University, dining, recreation, and the Missoula International Airport. Pamper yourself in their indoor pool, fitness center, whirlpool, sauna, or steam room. A complimentary European style breakfast buffet will satisfy you with sliced meats and cheeses, fresh pastries, bagels, hot and cold cereals, fresh fruits, juices, tea selections, and freshly ground coffee. Guest rooms feature king or two queen beds, coffee makers, ironing boards and irons, thermostat controlled heating and air conditioning, in-room voice mail, data ports, cable, Pay Per View movies, Nintendo, and ten suites with fireplaces. Additionally, they offer free airport shuttle, a guest laundry, lovely gift shop, ample parking including, park and fly. Conference facilities are available for 10 to 175 people. Learn more by visiting them at their web site.

### L Comfort Inn of Missoula

4545 N. Reserve, Missoula. 542-0888

You can always count on a Comfort Inn to provide quality accommodations and their famous Choice hospitality at down to earth prices. When you walk in their front door you will immediatly notice a clean, fresh look and warm family feeling that comes from a tradition of service. They offer an indoor heated pool and a relaxing spa. Their deluxe continental breakfast is complimentary with your stay. Their guest rooms are spacious and offer a business desk with computer data ports. The suites include a sofa, microwave and refrigerator. If you're in the mood, they offer suites with Jacuzzis. Coffee makers in the rooms assure you a hot cup of brew within minutes of waking up. 24 hour coffee and tea is always available in their breakfast room. For the business folks a copier and fax service is available. Packing kids? Under 18s are free when staying with a parent. And of course they offer non-smoking rooms and remote control cable TV with HBO, Fox News, and ESPN. They are only two minutes from I-90 and close to everything Missoula has to offer.

# Blue Mountain Recreation

There are three major access points off this road:

- The trailhead for the National Recreation Trail, about 1/2 mile north on Blue Mountain Road.
- Forest Road #365, turns left off Blue Mountain Road about 1.4 miles from Highway 93 South.
- Maclay Flat turnoff, on the right about 1.5 miles from Highway 93 South.

## The Recreation Area

Located just two miles west of Missoula, Blue Mountain Recreation Area is a great place to explore.

Once a U.S. Army Military Reservation, the 5,500 acres of valley bottom and mountain top became part of the Lolo National Forest in 1952. In 1975, a number of civic groups joined the Forest Service in a major clean-up project. Abandoned vehicles and garbage were removed, a system of trails was built, and regulations were established to protect people from indiscriminate shooting. In 1986, Blue Mountain was formally designated a Recreation Area.

## Maclay Flat Trails

At the base of Blue Mountain, two connecting loop trails at Maclay Flat offer an easy stroll through open grasslands and ponderosa pine. Parallel to the Bitterroot River, these trails (1-1/4 and 1-3/4 miles long) feature interpretive signs, benches, and wide wheelchair friendly paths. Maclay Flat also has picnic tables and wheel chair accessible toilets. Be considerate of other users and wildlife in the area. If you bring a dog, bring and use a leash.

## Mountain Trails

- Blue Mountain National Recreation Trail — 8 miles long. This trail is for hiking and horses. Vehicles and mountain bikes are prohibited!
- Blue Mountain Nature Trail — 1/4-mile-long loop trail. Wheelchair accessible up to the viewpoint. Information about the numbered posts along the trail is contained in a separate brochure, available at the trailhead or the Missoula Ranger District office.

## Scenic Drive/Fire Lookout

A rare sight awaits those who travel to the top of Blue Mountain: a working Forest Service lookout. Open from spring through fall—depending on snow conditions—and suitable for passenger cars and trucks, the mountain's gravelled road offers an easy climb and some great views of the Missoula valley and distant peaks.

During fire season, Blue Mountain visitors can climb the 50-foot lookout for a personal tour. Safety regulations, however, limit visitors to three at a time. Hours are 9 a.m. to 6 p.m. Remember, the lookout staff is on duty—the job of watching out for fires must come first! Please don't disturb this important work.

To reach the lookout, take Road #365 almost to the top, then continue on Road #2137 to the peak. Note: Road #2137 is open mainly in July and August.

## Camping and Campfires

Camping and campfires are allowed beginning 4.5 miles up the mountain, west of Road #365.

*Reprinted from U.S. Forest Service brochure.*

## L Best Inn North

4953 N. Reserve St. in Missoula. I-90 Exit 101. 542-7550. 800-272-9500. mtgs-4-u@bigsky.net. www.bestinn.com

There is more than one way to get comfortable at the Best Inn North. They are one of the rare places that cater to people with severe allergies. Their Evergreen™ rooms are allergen free with both air and water filtration. Their Business Plus Rooms have a data port, coffee maker, hair dryer, and ironing boards. Larger deluxe rooms are also available with sofa, microwave, and refrigerator. They offer a deluxe continental breakfast, free local calls, and a guest laundry. Relax after a busy day in their hot tub. They are just 5 miles from the Missoula airport and minutes from the UM campus.

## L Microtel Inn & Suites of Missoula

5059 N. Reserve St., I-90 exit 101, Missoula. 543-0959

The Microtel Inn & Suites is one of Missoula's newest hotels and offers a casino, lounge, cafe', convenience store and gas station. You will find 81 beautifully appointed rooms, all with very comfortable, chiropractor approved beds. Select rooms from the Queen Double, Spa Room, Spa Suite, or the Executive Suite with spa, all with the highest housekeeping standards. Children 16 and under

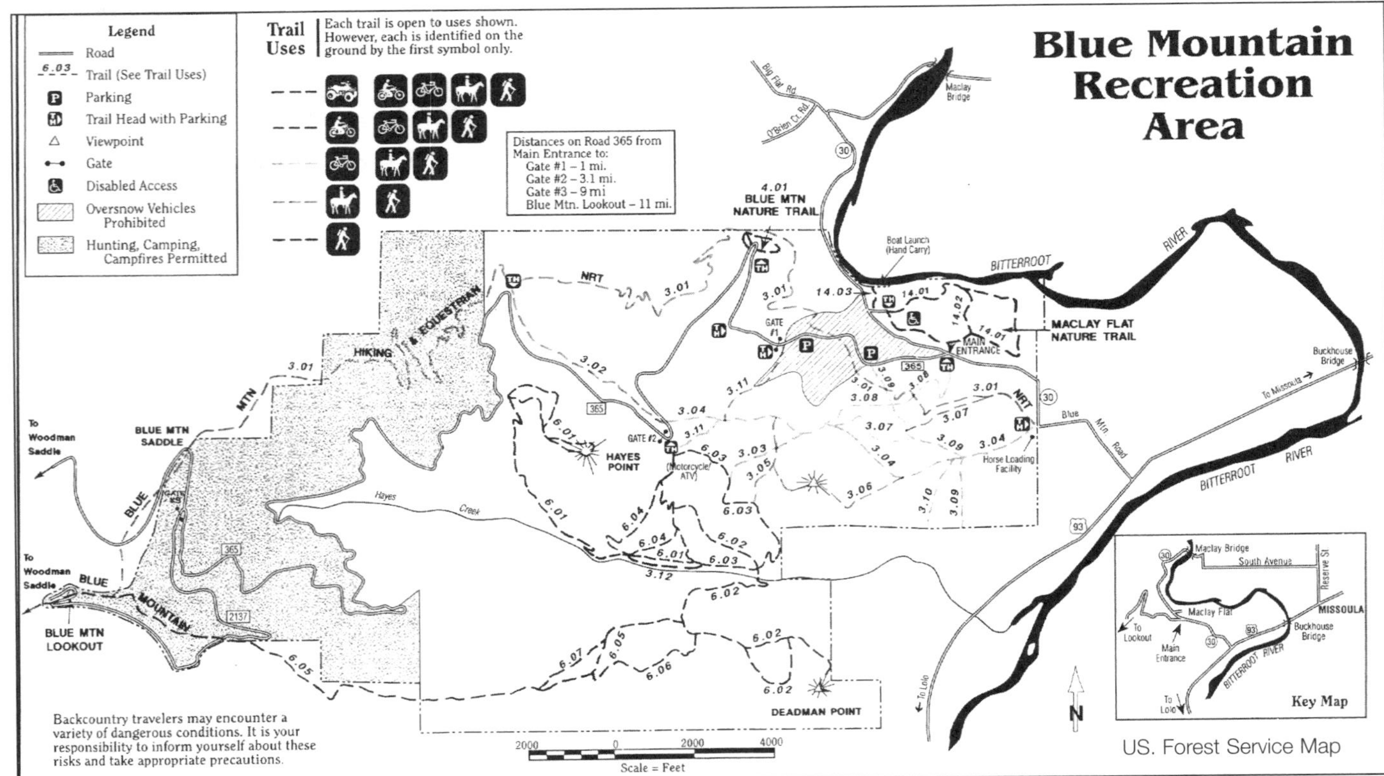


US. Forest Service Map

stay free with parents. Every night's stay comes with a free hot breakfast at the cafe', along with discount coupons for the casino, lounge, C-store, and gas pumps. They are conveniently located to all Missoula attractions, shopping, the University, Downtown, and the Clark River. Whether you are in town for business or pleasure their staff can point you in the right direction. Your complete comfort is their goal.

### L Super 8 Motel

4703 N. Reserve, Missoula. 549-0677 or 800-888-8000

Located close to the airport, Snowbowl Ski Area, and many local restaurants, the Super 8 features 58 rooms complete with data ports, cable TV with remotes, showtime, free local calls, guest laundry facilities, fax & copy services and microwaves and refrigerators are available. Relax in the indoor hot tub, or enjoy your own private jacuzzi suite. There is a shuttle available, and a complimentary toast and pastry bar every morning. Children under 12 are free.

### L Hampton Inn

4805 N. Reserve St. in Missoula at I-90 Reserve St. Exit. 549-1800. 800-426-7866. www.hampton-inn.com

## 17. *Attraction*

### T Pattee Canyon Recreation Area

In Missoula, from the corner where South Ave. and Southwest Higgins Ave. intersect Pattee Canyon Drive (paved road #553), go 3.5 miles east to the recreation area. Or from US highway 20 in East Missoula, drive 8 miles south up the Deer Creek Road.

The large picnic area and system of roads and trails make Pattee Canyon one of the most popular recreation areas close to Missoula.See sidebar

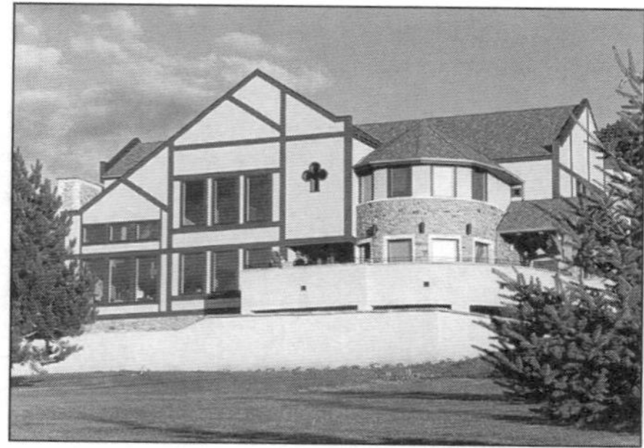

### F Shadow's Keep Restaurant

102 Ben Hogan Dr., Missoula. 728-5132

Look out over the Missoula Valley through The Keep's true post and beam interiors. Enjoy casual fine dining in a relaxed atmosphere. Reservations suggested.

## 18. *Attraction*

### T Council Grove State Park (Day Use Only)

In Missoula on 1-90 at Reserve St Exit, 2 miles south on Reserve St., then 10 miles west on Mullan Rd.

Council Grove is the site where the Hellgate treaty was signed, which established the Flathead Indian Reservation. The park preserves the location of the 1855 council between Isaac Stevens and the Flathead Kootenai, and the Pend d'Oreille Indians.

## 19. *Attraction, Gas, Food*

### Frenchtown

The early inhabitants of this area were French-Canadians from Quebec and Ontario. They settled this area in the 1860s.

### T Smoke Jumper Training and Aerial Fire Depot Visitor Center

West of Missoula airport on Hwy. 10. 329-4900

When a forest fire breaks out in the west, it is probable that smokejumpers trained here are busy fighting it. This is the oldest and largest of several centers operated nationally by the U.S. Forest Service. The visitor's center is a museum of the history of fire fighting since 1939, and includes photographs, murals and motion pictures. See an authentic fire lookout building, the water bomb and an exhibit on how parachutes are folded and lines are straightened. The Center is open from mid-May through mid-September with tours on the hour.

### T Frenchtown Pond State Park (Day Use Only)

15 miles west of Missoula on 1-90 at Frenchtown Exit #89, then 1 mile west on Frontage Rd. 542-5500

Frenchtown Pond State Park is a 41-acre recreational park which contains a spring-fed lake, making this an ideal area for fishing, swimming and boating.

## 20. *Gas, Food, Lodging*

### Alberton

This town was homesteaded by the Alberts family when the only roads here were Indian trails.

## 21.

### H The Natural Pier Bridge

I-90 Exit 75 just west of Alberton.

*This structure is an example of how engineers incorporated a natural feature into the design of a bridge. Designed by Montana Highway Commission bridge engineers, the bridge is a standard riveted Warren through truss. The bridge is unusual in that one of the piers is anchored to a rocky outcrop in the Clark Fork River. The bridge was once a component of the Yellowstone Trail—which traversed Montana from Lookout Pass to North Dakota.*

*Responding to pressure from the lumber companies and the Yellowstone Trail Association, Mineral County embarked on an ambitious bridge-building program in 1916. Although the county was responsible for the construction of the bridge, fiscal limitations and its location near the Lolo National Forest forced the county commissioners to seek financial aid from the federal government. In early 1917, the county contracted with the Wisconsin-based Wausau Iron Works Company to build the bridge. Work progressed steadily on the bridge for several months when the county ran out of money for its construction. After securing additional federal funds, the county commissioners called a referendum to raise money to complete construction of the bridge. Because of the law, however, the vote could not be held for several months. With the money eventually acquired, the bridge was completed in 1918 at a cost of $100,000.*

### H The Iron Mountain Mine

I-90 at milepost 58 between Superior and Alberton.

*The Iron Mountain Mine, one of the largest and most successful quartz mines in western Montana, was located about 12 miles north of here. L. T. Jones, a former Northern Pacific Railroad brakeman, discovered the ore body in 1888. Jones and his partners, D. R. Frazier and Frank Hall, located the Iron Mountain and Iron Tower lode claims on upper Hall Gulch. Later they bonded the property for $100,000 to J. K. Pardee, a prominent Montana mining entrepreneur, and Iron Mountain Company was born.*

*Intensive development began by 1889. Getting the ore to smelters was a major undertaking until 1891 when the Northern Pacific built a rail line from Missoula through Superior, four miles south of the mine.*

*By 1891 the company had built a concentrator that could reduce 100 tons daily. The concentrates were sent to the American Smelting and Refining Co. at Omaha, Nebraska, or East Helena, Montana, or, later, to Globe Smelter and Reduction Works of Denver, Colorado.*

*An 1897 state law forced the Iron Mountain Mine to close. It required all mines to have an escape shaft in addition to the main tunnel, and the Iron Mountain had only a main tunnel. From 1889 to 1898, the mine had produced over $1,000,000 and paid out $507,000 in dividends.*

*Later efforts to reopen the mine had only minor success and all that now remains are several wooden buildings, the railroad grade, many tramway routes, the concrete foundations of the mill, the stone and concrete powder houses, the tailings piles, and the collapsed adits and shafts.*

## 22. *Attraction, Gas, Food, Lodging*

### Superior

Superior, a county seat located at the mouth of Cedar Creek, was settled in 1869, named after the founders' hometown of Superior, Wisconsin. Just ten miles from the Idaho border, the Clark Fork River cuts through the town. Mining, logging, and Forest Service activities collectively contribute to the area's colorful history. About 900 hundred residents still live in Superior, close to several ghost towns in the area. Originally named Carter, the Keystone camp was a wild town where a rich silver lode was discovered in the 1880s.

Behind Superior and a few miles north lies Pardee. The remains can be reached by car with some hiking or 4WD. A rich vein of silver was discovered during the late 1800s by a worker for the Iron Mountain Mining Co. Because of it's remote location, safety laws, and dropping silver prices, operations closed in 1930. The museum in Superior is a great source of information for the various camps that have disappeared.

### Montana Trivia

Frank Burke wrote: "You can never judge anything in these Western places by their names, for the people seem to have a peculiar habit of giving high-sounding names to the most insignificant places." He was referring at the time to the town of Superior.

## Ninemile Remount Depot

Take a historical journey to the days of the early fire fighting in rugged wilderness of the mountain west. From 1930 until 1953, the Ninemile Remount Depot provided experienced packers and pack animals for fighting fires and for backcountry work projects throughout the vast roadless areas of the northern Rockies. Modeled after U.S. Army Cavalry remount depots which supplied fresh horses to troops, the Ninemile Remount depot is listed on the National Register of Historic Places for its unique role as a Forest Service Remount Depot and for its distinct Cape Cod style architecture.

### 1. This Bell Meant Business

During the summer fire season, 35 packers and wranglers were stationed at Ninemile. The ringing of the bell signaled that either dinner was ready in the cookhouse on your left, or there was a fire in the mountains, perhaps awakening the men in the bunkhouse.

Today, these buildings serve as administrative headquarters for the Ranger District and fire calls come over mobile radios.

The Cape Cod style of architecture was chosen to create an image of a well run horse farm along the lines of those found in New England or Kentucky. The buildings are maintained to preserve their original character and integrity.

### 2. A Working Ranch

Today, as in the past, Ninemile remains a working ranch. The smell of fresh cut alfalfa from the field to your left fills the air in July as provisions for the wintering animals are put up. The thundering hooves of up to 200 horses and mules can still be heard as wranglers move the animals between the 10 pastures on the 5000-acre "ranch."

The concrete slab here is all that remains of a garage and bunkhouse that burned down in 1982.

Today, as during the Remount era, lookouts are a vital link in detecting and reporting fires. You can see the lookout on the distant peak across the valley.

### 3. The Corrals, Load 'Em Up!

The fire call stirred up a cloud of dust and plenty of hee-hawing from anxious mules in the corrals. The driver backed to the loading ramp, men collected equipment from the barn, and the packer gathered, haltered and loaded the animals into the waiting truck.

Throughout the fire season, which generally ran from July through mid-September, 4 packtrains of 10 animals each waited in the corrals for the next fire call. Each packtrain carried enough gear to supply a 25-man backcountry fire camp

Stock still runs through these chutes to be wormed, inoculated, roached (the mule version of a shave and haircut) and sorted before returning to their summer homes—mountain Ranger Stations located in some of the finest backcountry and wilderness in North America! Twenty-five head remain at Ninemile year-round.

### 4. The Blacksmith Shop—Where Iron Meets The Trail

Horses and mules were shod here on the wooden floor by "farriers." Not all horses and mules appreciate the need for shoes but according to one packer, any animal that went in the building came out with shoes on! One reluctant mule jumped through the small window in front of the hitch rack!

With smoke pouring from the forge and continual ringing of the hammer on the anvils, the shop provided shoes for all the Forest Service stock across the Nation. The Blacksmiths hammered out 9 shoes an hour and 72 a day, totaling 15,000 per year.

Today, over 100 horses and mules are fitted with shoes here each year to prepare them for their backcountry missions. A working horse or mule wears out 4 sets of shoes in a busy summer season.

### 5. Outfitting the String—The Saddle Shop

The smell of horse sweat and leather still permeates this shop. Packers made and repaired all the gear necessary to outfit a string of mules in the mountains—saddles, halters and harnesses. Each packer marked the equipment to make sure it ended up on the right mule. This saddle shop supplied leather goods to the entire Northern Region of the Forest Service. Between fire calls, the packers "broke" young mules and horses in the adjacent corrals to ready them for "mountain" work.

Winter finds our packer still building, repairing and maintaining saddles and packing equipment for next summer in the mountains.

### 6. Retired With Honors

Mules, sired by a stallion donkey and born to a mare horse, are especially well suited for backcountry work. They have a strong survival instinct which keeps them from injuring themselves in sticky situations. Mules are surefooted on the trail and will carry a heavy load without one whinny of complaint!

Mules usually begin their careers as "green-broke" 5 year olds, knowing the feel of a saddle on their backs and how to lead on a halter. The experienced lead mules will quickly teach young mules the rules of the trail. A good mule may pack for 25 years.

### 7. Grand Menard's Castle—The Stud Barn

What better way to overcome a shortage of horses and mules than a breeding program? The stallions, such as Grand Menard, were bred to Forest Service mares in pursuit of the perfect mountain horse. After much experimenting, the consensus was that purebred horses, like Grand Menard, did not produce a good mountain horse. When mixed-blood mares were crossed with saddlebred stallions, most Rangers were happy with the resulting offspring.

Today the stud bam houses injured stock and the Forest Service buys their horses and mules!

### 8. The Barn

The centerpiece of the compound, the bam housed animals as well as grain and equipment. Big draft mules lifted hay into the loft using a system of nets and pulleys. Hay was dropped from the loft into a manger as you see in the stall to your left. Stallions were kept in these two stalls; however, they created such a ruckus during official visits that Regional Forester Kelley ordered the men to make a new home for the stallions—the stud barn just described.

Originally, the barn floor was wood. As you can imagine, keeping the floor clean was quite a chore. With a continual string of visitors to the Remount Depot, Regional Forester Kelley demanded a spit and polish image—so the floor was replaced with concrete.

When you visit the bam, note the distinctive weathervanes on the roof

Today the barn is used to store equipment for all aspects of Ranger District operations.

### 9. Fire Fighting Today

The fire engine, rather than a packtrain of mules, responds to today's fire calls. Engines, capable of carrying up to 750 gallons of water, can reach much of the 400,000-acre Ranger District via roads. Smoke Jumpers and mules are still used for backcountry fire-fighting efforts.

If the engines are gone, look for smoke on the horizon!

### 10. Can They Make It?

Within 15 minutes after the fire bell rang, trucks loaded with nine mules, a horse, and supplies for 25 men stopped here briefly to weigh the loads and ensure that the bridges along the planned route would handle the load.

*Reprinted from U.S. Forest Service Brochure*

### T Ninemile Remount Depot & Ranger Station

I-90 at Huson Exit 82. 626-5201

See sidebar.

### T Mineral County Museum

301 Second Ave. E, Superior. 822-4626

The Mineral County Museum in Superior opened by volunteers in 1977. It features local history, exhibits on mining, logging, and the USFS activities. It is also a repository of local newspapers and many historical documents concerning the area. John Mullan and the Mullan Road is another feature of the museum's exhibits. Admission is free. Call for hours.

## 23. *Attraction, Adventure, Gas, Food, Lodging*

### St. Regis

St. Regis, named for the St. Regis River, is a shipping point for the lumber industry. A bridge over the Clark Fork River lies in the center of town.

### T Quinn's Hot Springs

East of St. Regis on Hwy.135.

Find a pool and jacuzzi, on a privately owned resort overlooking the Clark Fork River. The pool water temperature is maintained at 75 to 105 degrees F. The springs were discovered by an Irishman, M.E. Quinn in the late 1880s. The springs have been maintained as a resort since 1905 with continuous improvements including campgrounds, restaurant, and lodging.

### V Taft Tunnel Bike Trail

From Lookout Pass (location of Bike Rentals) or Missoula, Montana go to the Taft Exit #5 of I-90 and turn right at the bottom of the off ramp. You will

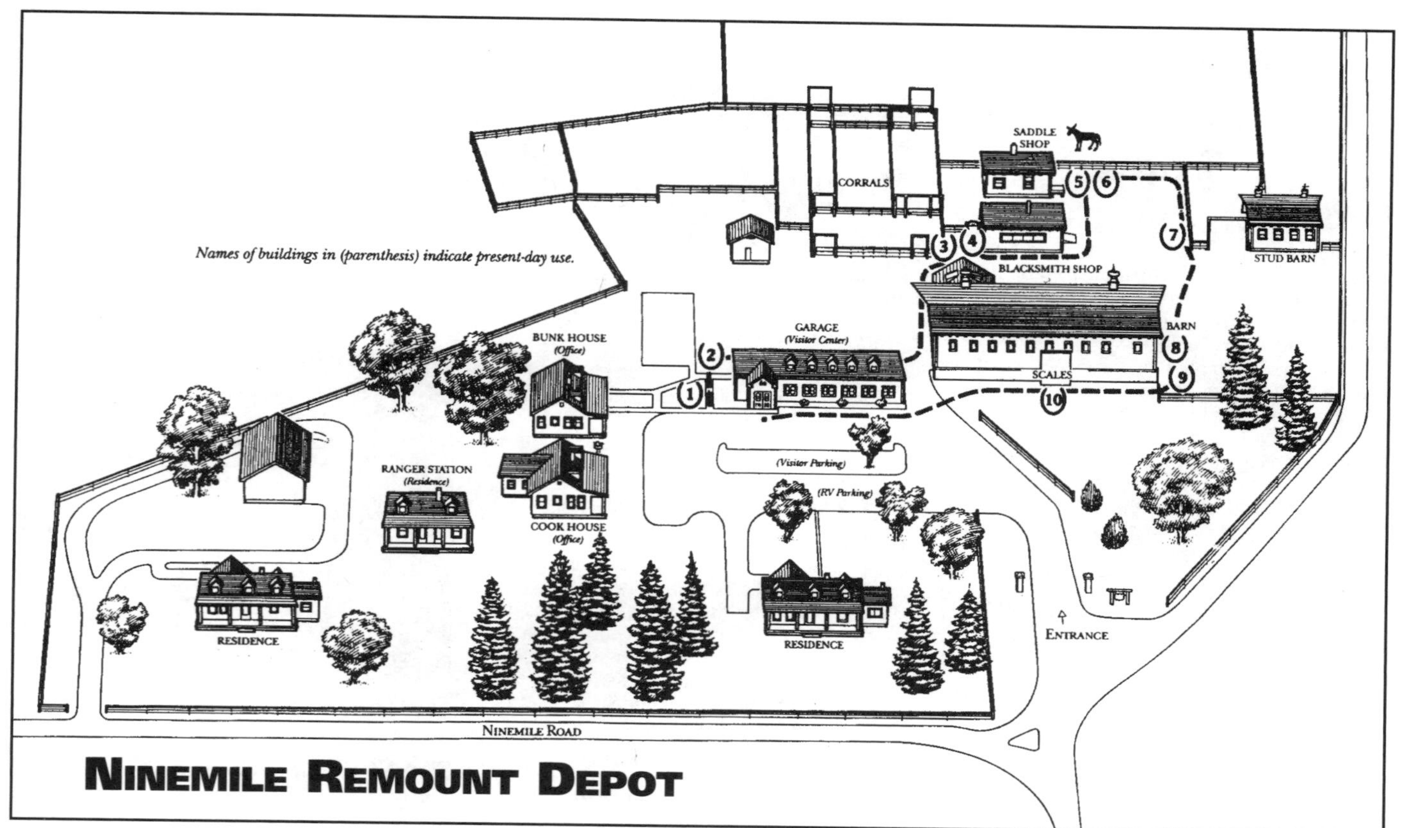


then turn left at the stop sign, go over a small bridge then just follow the signs south for 7 miles on Rainy Creek Road #506, follow this road up and over Roland Pass going forward at the top of Roland Pass and down to the historic townsite and trail head of Roland (7 miles from I-90).

An old rail line was transformed, abandoned tunnels were cleared and trestles were made safe, creating one of the most electrifying recreational trails in the United States. This is undoubtedly an extraordinary bike route and hiking trail. At the center of the trail is the 8,771-foot Taft Tunnel which was cut through solid rock from the Montana side of Lookout Pass to Idaho. The trestles proceed along abrupt cliffs and over craggy rock canyons. As the track descends into Idaho, the trail meanders through another nine tunnels and over seven wooden trestles before arriving at the valley floor. Flashlights are recommended for hikers and headlights are a necessity for bikers. To reach the trail and Taft Tunnel, go over Lookout Pass on I-90 and take Exit 5 for the Taft area. Turn south and follow Rainy Creek Rd. for two miles. Take the road toward East Portal at the Y-junction and then the parking area is immediately ahead. For more information, call the Lookout Pass Ski Area 208-744-1392.

## F Jasper's Restaurant

13 Old US Hwy 10, St. Regis. 649-2405

This sophisticated family style restaurant is a step above the rest! Jasper's offers homemade soups and specials for lunch and dinner daily, and a great variety of homemade meals. Offering steaks, seafood specials, and great lunches. The casino features poker and keno machines and a full service bar. Jasper's is a great place to find a delicious meal in a nice setting, or simply relax for a drink after a long day.

### *Montana Trivia*

One of the largest forest fires in the history of the United States swept over Idaho and Montana on August 20 and 21, 1910. The fire burned three million acres, destroyed eight billion board feet of timber and killed 86 people. Hurricane-force winds shot fireballs for miles across the mountains. The sky turned dark as far east as Colorado. An army of 10,000 firefighters made dramatic, but ultimately futil efforts to stop the blaze.

## 24. *Gas, Food, Lodging*

## DeBorgia

DeBorgia sits on the banks of the Regis River and originated as a station on the Northern Pacific twenty miles from Lookout Pass, which divides Montana and Idaho. The name is derived from the St. Regis de Borgia River.

## 25. *Historical Marker, Attraction, Gas, Food, Lodging*

## Haugan

Another town named for another railroad official, Haugan is the first town you arrive at when entering Montana on I-90 or the last town you see leaving. It is now more a traveler's oasis than a town. Center of the services is the 10,000 Silver $ Saloon. And, yes, there really are 10,000 silver dollars in the bar. In fact, there are more than 33,000 silver dollars in the bar. This should be your first stop in the state, or last stop leaving.

## Saltese

The town was named for Chief Saltese of the Nez Perce Indians. The site was known by the early prospectors, trappers and packers as Packer's Meadow as it was a good campground and resting place on the difficult trail to the Mullan Road. It was later called Silver City and was a supply point for the many small silver and gold mines in the surrounding mountains. In 1891 its name was changed for the final time.

## H Savenac Nursery Historic District

*Creation of the National Forest Service in 1905 brought Elers Koch, one of the nation's first professional foresters, to inspect and evaluate the Forest Reserves of Montana and Wyoming. Appointed Forest Supervisor of the Bitterroot and Lolo National Forests in 1907, Koch happened upon the abandoned homestead of a German settler named Savennach. He thought it a perfect spot to establish a tree nursery. Work began in 1908 and just as the first pine seedlings were ready for transplanting in 1910, fire swept through the region scorching 3 million acres of timberland. The nursery was destroyed, but the disaster influenced Forest Service policy, making fire prevention and conservation its primary mission. Reforestation of burned and logged areas figured prominently in that goal. Savenac Nursery was ideally situated along two railroad routes and the historic Mullan Road ran right through the property. The nursery was immediately rebuilt. Circa 1912 national road improvements incorporated the new Yellowstone Trail into this segment of the Mullan Road and by 1916, Savenac shipped several million seedlings to the vast Northern Region. The Civilian Conservation Corps rebuilt and modernized the facility a final time between 1932 and 1948. Savenac became the largest tree nursery in the northwest producing up to twelve million trees annually. The nursery operated until regional reorganization brought closure in 1969. Savenac Nursery, where much of the*

# Hiawatha Mountain Bike Trail

Imagine mountain biking a 15-mile historic railbed trail through cavernous train tunnels, across sky high train trestles, past sparkling mountain creeks with deer, elk, moose and endless views of the towering Bitterroots. The best part is—it's all downhill!

Located just off I-90 on the Idaho / Montana border, *The Route of the Hiawatha* is a scenic section of abandoned rail-bed from the "Milwaukee Road" that the Taft Tunnel Preservation Society, Silver Country, and the U.S. Forest Service have turned into a world class non-motorized trail in the area around the Montana and Idaho Border. In fact, this stretch has been called one of the most breathtaking scenic stretches of railroad in the country. This adventurous 13 mile trail takes mountain bikers (and hikers) through 10 cavernous tunnels and over 7 sky high trestles. The first tunnel you pass through is the 1.8 mile long Taft Tunnel reopened in 2001. This tunnel burrows 1.66 miles under the Idaho-Montana border

The trail is operated and maintained by the Taft Tunnel Preservation Society with fees collected from all users. A shuttle bus can transport you and your bike between trail heads.

| Trail Fees* | Adults | Children (3-13) |
|---|---|---|
| Day Use | $7.00 | $3.00 |
| Season Pass | $25.00 | $20.00 |
| Shuttle Bus (one way) | $9.00 | $6.00 |
| Helmets (required) | | $6.00 |
| Lights | | $4.00 |
| Helmet & Lights | | $9.00 |
| Bike Rentals (comfort suspension) | | $22 & $26 |
| $16 for child's bikes & trailers | | |

*plus sales tax

Rentals are located at Lookout Pass Ski Area.

**Shuttle Service**

Weekday shuttle service
11 to 4:15 pm.

Weekend shuttle service
11 to 5:45 pm.

Weekends only after Sept 4
12:00 to 5:15 pm.

Children under 14 years of age require adult supervision. Helmets & lights required. No dogs or pets allowed.

The Hiawatha shuttle will run between the top and bottom of the trail throughout the days scheduled.

Tickets, rentals and guided tours:
Call 208-744-1301.
www.skilookout.com/bike_home_page.html

Getting There
Take the Taft Exit (5) and turn south. Following the signs to the parking area. Representatives will meet you there to sell you permit and shuttle service.

*Interpretive signs tell the story of the railway and towns along the route.*

## The Route of the Hiawatha

In 1905, The Milwaukee and St. Paul Railway began looking for a route for their western extension over the Bitterroot Mountains. After five and a half months, exploring 930 miles, the railroad chose a route over St. Paul Pass. In laying out the route from the St. Paul Pass Tunnel the surveyors planned a line descending at a 1.7% gradient along the mountain slope. A big consideration in choosing this route was the potential for future traffic. This route down the St. Joe River offered exclusive access to huge quantities of old growth white pine and cedar timber. *Interpretive sign on trail.*

*Chance encounters with wildlife are a common occurance on the trail.*

## The Last Transcontinental Railroad

The Chicago, Milwaukee and St. Paul Railway's Pacific Extension survived for 71 colorful years. Racing silk trains sped along the route, and long, rumbling troop trains carried men and materiel through four wars. The Milwaukee's famed electric locomotives hosted presidents and celebrities and showcased the streamlined Olympian Hiawatha passenger train. The Route of the Hiawatha Rail-Trail, traces the most costly and difficult to build section of the railroad from Chicago to Tacoma. Today, thousands enjoy traveling over this scenic, historic trail helping keep alive the spirit of the Milwaukee Road.

The trail follows the trains and historians trace the history along the trail. When the Milwaukee Road abandoned its route over the Bitterroot Mountains, salvage companies striped the line of all the rails, ties, signals posts and everything else of value. The small fragments left behind are the remains of one of America's proudest railroads. From 1907 to 1911 thousands of people lived, worked and played in this secluded part of the Bitterroot Mountains. They constructed a railroad while leaving faint signs of their own passing. Today you may see archaeologists digging and sifting along the Route of the Hiawatha Trail lookinf for clues about people and places not found in written documents. Historical research and archaeological field work helps breate life into the history of the Milwaukee Road years. *Interpretive sign on trail.*

*Seven sky-high trestles line the route.*

## The St. Paul Pass Tunnel

The Milwaukee Road faced the daunting task of drilling a tunnel 23 feet high, 16 feet wide and 1.7 miles long into Idaho. It was a damp, dark, dirty dig. After the approaches were prepared in 1906, and a faltering start in 1907, work began in earnest in 1908. East and west crews toiled around the clock in wet, miserable conditions, and at their best could tunnel 20 feet a day. A company official remembered that:

*"Men were hard to keep as the work was disagreeable and hard. Several large veins of water were encountered and at times the working conditions were almost unbearable."*

It took 750 men—400 tunneling inside, 200 outside removing the dirt and rock, and 150 running the dig's power plant yards—two and a half years to complete. The steam-driven electric power plant set up four miles away in Taft, Montana powered both ends of the dig. Compressed air provided safe, smokeless power to the giant steam shovels that loaded the blasted, broken rock into electric rail cars for removal. *Interpretive sign on trail.*

*One of the shorter tunnels along the trail.*

## Montana Trivia

The forest fires of August, 1910, burned millions of acres in Idaho, Montana and Washington. On the night of August 20, engineer Johnnie Mackedon, returning from a trip to St. Paul Pass, found the Falcon siding on fire. Over one hundred terrified men, women, and children were gathered on the platform of the smoldering depot. He coupled to a flat-car on the adjoining siding and everyone scrambled on board for a harrowing ride to the safety of Tunnel 27.

*"Why, all that you could see of a bridge was a wall of flame, but we crossed it. I hooked her up, threw her wide open, and then we lay down on the deck to protect ourselves from the heat."* -Train Engineer Johnnie Mackedon.

*theory and practice of silviculture was pioneered, reflects the conservation ethic of the Forest Service.*

### H The Holacaust

West of Saltese.

*In 1910, this was a remote neck of the woods and hard to reach. Forest fire protection was relatively new. That dry summer many small fires started. Public apathy, together with manpower shortage, lack of organization and good equipment and inaccessibility permitted them to spread and join. Hell broke loose in August. Whipped by 50-mile gales, the combined blaze covered 3,000 square miles in three days. Animals were trapped, 87 human lives were lost, settlements and railroad trestles were destroyed, six billion board feet of timber burned like kindling. The pungent smoke pall stretched to eastern Montana.*

*Some good came from this costly burnt sacrifice to inadequate organization, funds and public understanding. Legislation was enacted, appropriations were increased, cooperative effort was developed, and the public became forest fire conscious. Now U.S. Forest Service lookouts and aerial patrols discover fires while small, then smokechasers by trail and smoke-jumpers by parachute reach and control most of the fires in record time. This devastated area has been restocked with trees that will again produce commercial timber, provide homes for wildlife and recreation for people. Fire protection methods, equipment and organization capable of handling future threats of dry summers will pay off in healthy watersheds and abundant forest products. An uncontrolled forest fire is a terrifying, destructive beast. Please be careful with your matches, cigarettes and campfires, won't you?*

### H Mullan Road

West of Saltese.

*During the years 1855-62 Captain John Mullan, 2nd Artillery, U.S.A., located and built what was known as the Mullan Road. Congress authorized the construction of the road under the supervision of the War Department to connect Ft. Benton, the head of navigation on the Missouri, with Ft. Walla Walla, the head of navigation on the Columbia.*

*In the winter of 1859-60, Capt. Mullan established a winter camp at this point which he called Cantonment Jordan. The Captain had selected this route in preference to the Clark's Fork route because he thought it would have a climatic advantage since it was farther south. However, he later expressed regret for making this choice because investigation showed that the more northerly route was highly favored with chinook winds and the snowfall in consequence was much lighter. The Captain also predicted that both of these routes might eventually be used by transcontinental railroads. His prophesy was correct.*

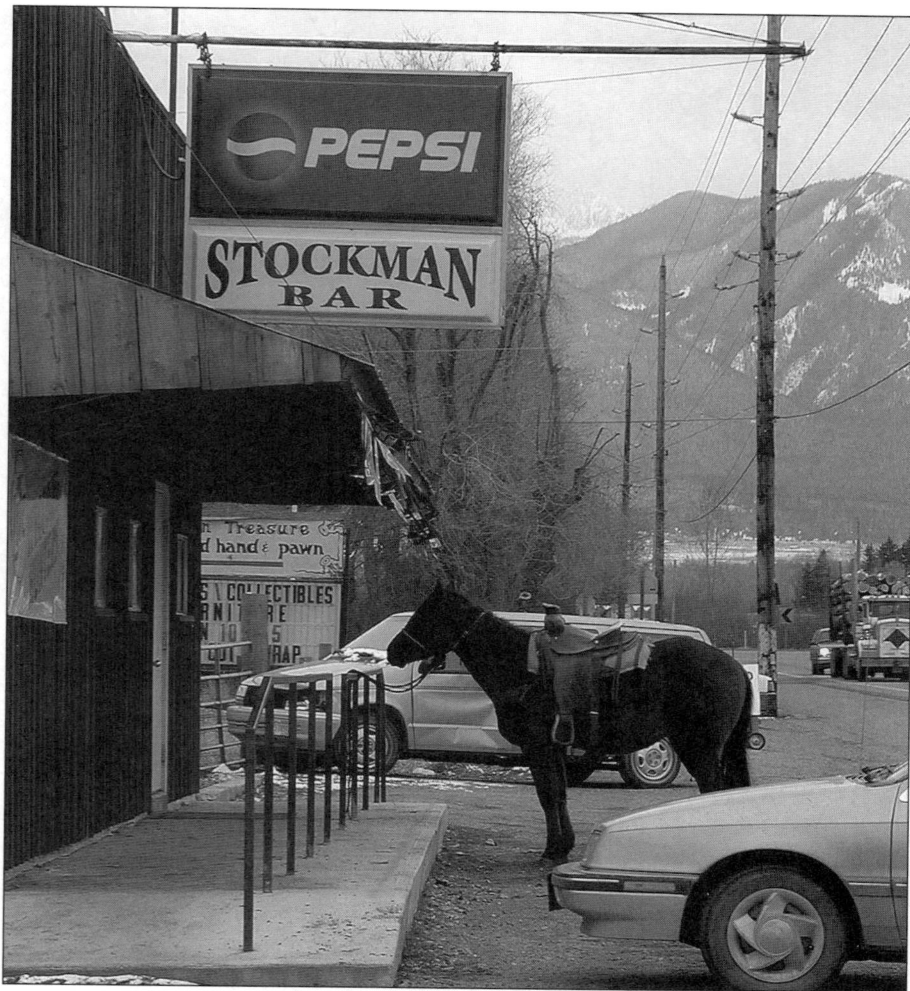


## 26. *Gas, Food, Lodging*

### Evaro

There are conflicting stories of how this town got its name. Some say it was named after a French count who journeyed through here in the early days. Certainly the most colorful story is that of a young bride named Eva Roe. In the days when trains pulled by steam engines moved most of the lumber, it took two engines to pull the loads up the steep hill near the town. It was a busy place and one where men significantly outnumbered women. Mail order brides were very popular, and one in particular stole the hearts of the locals. She was a beautiful young girl who, upon her arrival, insisted on a trial engagement. Her and her fiance fell madly in love immediately and the whole town watched with a heavy sigh as romance bloomed between the young couple. One day as she visited her beau at the lumber docks, a worker yelled "LOOK OUT!" As she rounded the bend, a pile of logs fell on her and crushed her to death. The townsfolk, as a show of love for the young woman, renamed the town Evaro.

## 27. *Historical Marker, Attraction, Gas, Food, Lodging, Camping*

### Arlee

Arlee was named for Chief Alee of the Salish tribe. The name, which means "red night" was corrupted in its English version when the "r" was added. Arlee was named Chief of the tribe when then Chief Charlo refused to move onto the new reservation.

### H The Jocko Valley

South of Arlee.

*Named for Jacco (Jacques) Raphael Finlay, a fur trader and trapper in the Kootenai and Flathead Indian country, 1806-09.*

*By treaty of Aug. 27, 1872, the Flathead Indians were supposed to have relinquished claim to their hereditary lands in the Bitterroot Valley, accepting the present reservation in lieu thereof Charlot, head chief of the Flatheads, always denied signing the treaty although when the papers were filed in Washington his name appeared on them, possibly a forgery.*

*Arlee (pronounced Ahlee by the Indians) was a war chief and did sign the treaty so the Government recognized him thereafter as head chief. Charlot never spoke to him afterwards.*

### T Arlee Historical Society

655 South Valley Creek Road, Arlee. 726-3167

### FA Buddy G'S Family Diner, Casino & Gas Station

Hwy 93, Arlee. 726-3100

Serving breakfast, lunch, and dinner seven days a week, Buddy G's is a great place to stop for hearty

Section 13

*Clark Fork River between Plains and Ravalli*

home cooking. They have hot lunch and soup & sandwich specials offered everyday, mouthwatering fresh-baked pies, and huckleberry shakes. The drive-thru window is open seven days a week for fast service to go. Check out the casino, where they hold daily drawings. Buddy G's convenient store offers gas & propane, a full line of groceries, fountain drinks, espresso, and fresh baked brownies and cookies.

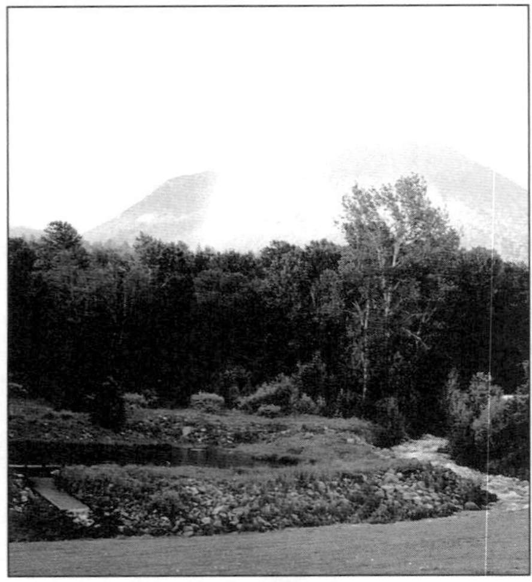

*The back yard of Sheep Ranch Inn.*

### FLC Creekside B&B - Sheep Ranch Inn

23580 Hwy 93 N., Arlee. 726-3332

Enjoy certified angus beef and open pit BBQs at the Sheep Ranch Inn, with dynamic views of the creek and trout ponds in back. They specialize in seafood, steaks, burgers and are located right off the highway, a perfect stopping point after a long drive. The bed & breakfast offers four rooms located creekside, with trails around the property, a 3D archery range, and a dining room & lounge on the premises at the Sheep Ranch Inn. They also have 12 RV sites with electrical hookups.

## 28. *Historical Marker, Gas, Food*

### Ravalli

Named for Father Ravalli of the St. Mary's Mission in Stevensville. He was a man of many talents. Not only a revered clergyman, but a physician as well. He built the first lumber and flour mills in Montana. While he was still living, the Northern Pacific Railroad paid tribute to him by giving this reservation town his name.

### H Flathead Reservation

West of Ravalli.

*The Native Americans on this reservation belong to the Salish, Kalispel, Spokane, Kootenai and Pend d'Oreille tribes. Lewis and Clark met the Salish in 1805 and described them and their allies, the Nez Perce, as being friendly and exceptional people. "Flathead" was a misnomer applied to the Salish by Lewis and Clark. No one knows for sure where it came from, but like many early names for tribes, it stuck. It seems that the whites almost always had a handle to hang on a tribe before they met anyone who could tell them their own name for themselves.*

*The Flatheads frequently crossed the mountains to the plains to hunt buffalo and there clash with the Blackfeet, their hereditary enemies. Many of the French and Scotch names amongst them came from marriage with the Hudson Bay Co. trappers and traders in the early fur days.*

### F Bison Inn Cafe & Gift Shop

Hwy. 93 N., Ravalli. 745-4470

Famous for their huckleberry shakes and buffalo burgers, this family restaurant and cafe offers great breakfasts and home cooking. Enjoy their huckleberry pies in the clean (all non-smoking), cozy atmosphere complete with fireplace. When you're through enjoying their great food, browse through their extensive gift shop loaded with jewelry, Native American crafts and art, clothing, and western gifts.

## 29. *Attraction*

### Moiese

This town was named for a subchief of the Flathead Indians.

### Perma

Both the Salish and Kootenai tribes came to this spot annually to dig the bulbs of the camas plant.

### T National Bison Range

132 Bison Range Road, Moiese. 644-2211

The National Bison Range is administered by the U.S. Fish and Wildlife Service as part of the National Wildlife Refuge System. It was established in 1908 when bison were nearly extinct, and is one of the oldest Wildlife Refuges in the nation.

A large portion of the 18,500-acre Range consists of native Palouse Prairie. Forests, wetlands and streams are also found here providing a wide range of habitats for wildlife. Elk, deer, pronghorn, black bear, coyote and ground squirrels are just some of the mammals that share the area with 350-500 bison. Over 200 species of birds also call this home including eagles, hawks, meadowlarks, bluebirds, ducks and geese. In May or June, you can enjoy a splendid display of wildflowers including Montana's state flower, the bitterroot. For birdwatchers there are ring-necked pheasants, gray partridges and grouse.

The best place to start your visit is at the Visitor Center. Here you will find informative displays and handouts, restrooms, videos, a bookstore and staff to answer your questions. This is where you pay the entrance fee. Fees are charged during the summer (mid-May to late October). The Range is part of the U.S. Fee System and accepts Golden Passes and Federal Waterfowl Stamps. Pay fees at the Visitor Center. The range is closed at night and there is no camping allowed on the Range.

#### Wildlife Viewing

Prairie Drive/West Loop: a 5-mile gravel road that travels through the flats. It is open to trailers and large RVs. It goes by the bison display pasture. Plan for 1/2 hour. Open year round.

Red Sleep Mountain Drive: a 19-mile, one-way gravel road which gains 2,000 feet. There are many switchbacks and 10% grades along the drive. No trailers or vehicles over 32 feet are allowed on this drive. Allow 1 1/2 to 2 hours. Open mid-May to late October.

Winter Drive: a 10-mile gravel road traveling through the flats and along Mission Creek. Allow 1 hour. Open late October to mid-May.

#### Walking Trails

Hiking is limited on the Range to a few short walking trails. A mile-long Nature Trail is located at the Picnic Area and the 1/4-mile Grassland Trail is at the visitor Center. The 1/2-mile Bitterroot Trail and 1-mile High Point trail are both located off the Red Sleep Mountain Drive. Walking away from your vehicle is prohibited except for these designated trails.

#### Picnic Area

The Range has a picnic area near Mission

## It Happened in Montana

May 3, 1933. A partially albino calf is born at the National Bison Range in Moiese. The baby bull came to be known as "Big Medicine," and lived on the reserve until he died in 1959. The stuffed remains of Big Medicine are one of the most popular exhibits at the Montana Historical Society in Helena.

Creek. There are tables, grills, water and accessible toilets. A covered pavilion is available on a first-come, first-served basis. There are no garbage cans, so please pack out all trash.

### Directions

The National Bison Range is located in the Mission Valley of Northwest Montana. Located 50 miles north of Missoula, Montana. Drive to the Refuge by taking Highway 93 north to Ravalli, turning west on Highway 200. Approximately 5 miles from Ravalli is the junction for State Highway 212. Travel north for about 5 miles to the entrance to the Bison Range. There is a sign on Highways 93 and 212 indicating the National Bison Range. If traveling from the north, the visitor must take either State Highway 35 around the east side of Flathead Lake, or Highway 93 around the west side. Proceed south from Polson 10 miles to the junction of Highway 93 with State Highway 212; it is about 13 miles to the entrance. There are signs on Highway 93 indicating the National Bison Range. When traveling from the west, turn north at St. Regis, Montana, off US Interstate 90 onto State Highway 135. Highway 135 junctions Highway 200, turn east until the junction of Highway 200 with State Highway 212 just east of Dixon, Montana. There is a sign at this junction indicating the National Bison Range. Travel north on Highway 212 for about 5 miles to the entrance. It is approximately 50 miles from St. Regis to the entrance to National Bison Range.
Reprinted from www.recreation.gov

**30.** *Gas, Food, Lodging, Camping*

### Paradise

This town didn't get its name the way you might think. Although not all agree, the most widely accepted story is that a roadhouse on the trail through here in the early days was named "Pair o' Dice." The name was modified from that. Paradise was a division point on the Northern Pacific Railroad, and the spot where the trainmen changed their watches from Mountain time to Pacific before heading over the mountains into Idaho.

## Montana Trivia

Montana inspires many artists. Plains, however, is home to the unique Haun's Cement Art. Bill and Kolene Haun have been pouring and painting cement vultures, cows, dogs, frogs, penguins, skunks, bears, bunnies, and hundreds of other critters for quite some time now. All the critters are made from cement and painted to last a heck of a long time. You'll know you have found them when you drive by.

### Plains

This was a popular wintering spot for Indians and their horses and was originally called Horse Plains. In later years, stockmen from as far away as Walla Walla, Washington found it a hospitable place to winter their herds in the protected open pasture.

### L Crossroads Motel & RV Park

Junction Hwy 28 & 200, Plains. 826-3623

Located on the Clark Fork River, Crossroads Motel offers 19 clean, nicely decorated guest rooms with great rates. They are all complete with in-room coffee and cable TV with HBO, Cinemax, and Showtime. The locally owned and operated establishment is beautifully landscaped and offers nice grassy spots for full hookup RV sites and tent sites. Crossroads is right on the edge of town, within walking distance to fishing and to downtown restaurants and shopping. Owners Rollie & Liz Larson will be there to welcome you to their part of the state.

**31.** *Historical Marker, Attraction, Gas, Food, Lodging, Shopping*

### St. Ignatius

St. Ignatius, named after St. Ignatius of Loyola, this town is the center of the Flathead Reservation at the foot of the magnificent Mission Range. Home to 2,500 residents, agriculture, timber and small businesses support its economy, although the Flathead Lake also attracts many visitors.

### H Fort Connah

North of St. Ignatius.

*Fort Connah, the last of the Hudson Bay Co. trading posts established within the present borders of the United States, was built about 1/4 mile east of here. Begun by Neil McArthur in fall 1846, his replacement, Angus McDonald, completed it in 1847. It remained an important trading center for the Flatheads until 1871. The old store house is still standing.*

*Mission Valley was thrown open for settlement in 1910. Prior to that time it was almost entirely virgin prairie, unplowed, unfenced and beautiful to see. You rode a saddle horse to get places. Some people wish it were still like that.*

### H The Mission Valley

St. Ignatius

*The Mission Valley, called by the Indians "Place of Encirclement," was occupied by bands of Salish and Kalispel speaking people when the white man came. By treaty with the Government in 1855 it became a part of the reservation of the Confederated Salish and Kootenai Tribes and included some Pend d'Oreille, Kalispel, and Nez Perce.*

*St. Ignatius Mission, the second built in Montana, was established in 1854 by the Jesuits. The first church was built of whipsawed timber and was held together with wooden pins. Through efforts of the priests the Mission prospered. Four Sisters of Providence from Montreal opened the first school in 1864. The Ursulines arrived in 1890 and opened a school for younger children.*

*In 1910 the unallotted land on the reservation was thrown open to settlement. The whites and barbed wire moved in.*

## Montana Trivia

Brother Joseph Carignano, a cook with no art training, painted fifty-eight murals on the walls and ceiling of the St. Ignatious Mission church.

### T St. Ignatius Mission

Just off Hwy. 93 in St. Ignatius. 745-2768

Much of the earliest history of the settlement of Montana started here. The St. Ignatius Mission gave its name to the surrounding Mission Valley, St. Ignatius, and the magnificent Mission Mountain Range.

The mission was founded in 1854, ten years after Montana became a territory and 35 years before it attained statehood, by Father Peter DeSmet, S.J. As a response to repeated appeals from Indians who had visited St. Louis, Father DeSmet moved here after founding the St. Mary Mission in Stevensville to the south in the 1840s. That mission is also still standing. The Flathead, Kootenai and Kalispel (Upper Pend d'Oreille) tribes brought Father DeSmet and the Jesuits to this valley they called the "surrounded." In time, the St. Ignatius Mission became one of the major missions of its day in the Northwest.

The massive church was built with local materials by the Indians and missionaries in 1891. One of the most striking characteristics of the building is the series of murals painted in only 14 months by the cook, Brother Joseph Carignano.

The complex of schools and hospitals that grew up around the church were lost to fires. Despite their absence, the Jesuit Fathers and the Dominican Sisters of Sparkhill, N.Y., continue the tradition of service to the current day reservation. You can view the mission with its 58 murals, the museum and nun's first residence, the original log-cabin residence and chapel daily from 8 a.m. to 7 p.m. Admission is free, but contributions are welcome to help maintain the historic structure.

### ST Allard's Flathead Indian Museum & Trading Post

US Hwy 93 in St. Ignatius. 746-2951

Featuring an interesting collection of Native American clothing and regalia of the Salish and Kootenai tribes, as well as others from the United States and Canada. This two story log trading post offers local handmade beadwork, penalty blankets, t-shirts, jewelry, regional books, clothing, and local artwork. Pick out gifts and souvenirs representing the area, and get a feel for the Native American culture in the Flathead Valley. The Huckleberry Jam Factory next door is open seasonally, featuring products made from wild huckleberrys including jam, jelly, ice cream, pie, shakes, and a large assortment of gifts. Also look out for the live buffalo exhibit with a private viewing platform.

### F Stoneheart Inn Bed & Breakfast

26 N. Main, St. Ignatius. 745-4999

### LAS Lodge Pole Museum, Motel & General Store

1 Museum Lane, St. Ignatius. 745-2951

## 32. *Historical Marker, Attraction, Gas, Food, Lodging, Shopping, Miscellaneous*

### H The Mission Mountain Wilderness

Ronan

*The mountains rising to the east lie in the Mission Mountain Wilderness Area and the Mission Mountain Tribal Wilderness. The range is more than a natural wonder; it is the first place in America where an Indian nation has designated tribal lands as a wilderness preserve. The crest of the range forms the eastern boundary of the Flathead Reservation. On the east side, 73,877 acres are managed by the Flathead National Forest; on this side, 89,500 acres are under the purview of the Confederated Salish and Kootenai (Flathead) Tribes. Both wildernesses are managed cooperatively and are open to everyone, though differences in management styles reflect tribal needs and traditions on the west side.*

*A few tribal elders can still trace the routes of old hunting trails through the Missions. Hunters used them to cross to the eastern Montana plains to hunt buffalo. The mountains hold sacred sites where tribal members go alone to fast and seek spiritual guidance for their lives. Other spots are traditional summer camps where families pick berries, gather medicinal herbs, plants, and roots, and cut tipi poles.*

*Clarence Woodcock of the Flathead Cultural Committee expressed the tribes's deeprooted spiritual and cultural ties to the mountains: "They are lands where our people walked and lived. Lands and landmarks carved into the minds of our ancestors through Coyote stories and actual experiences. Lands, landmarks, trees, mountain tops, crevices that we should look up to with respect."*

### T Flathead Indian Reservation

The Flathead Indian Reservation, created in 1855, mainly Salish, Pend d'Oreilles and Kootenai, is the longest occupied reservation in Montana. The seasons and available resources set the pattern of life for the Flathead tribe. In May and June, they lived where they could harvest camas root, bitterroot bulbs and wild onions. During the summers, they collected different varieties of berries: from huckleberries and chokecherries to raspberries and gooseberries. Near summer's end they gathered wild carrots and parsnips. They crossed the Rockies to hunt bison on the plains; eventually they became less dependent on buffalo and hunted smaller animals more and more. The economy today is based largely on the timber and hospitality industries.

### Pablo

Pablo is the home of the government offices of the Confederated Salish and Kootenai Tribes. The town was named for Michel Pablo, a Flathead chief and a rancher and stockman. Pablo was one of the first to raise buffalo and is credited for saving the bison from extinction.

Sam Walking Coyote, was a young Pend d'Orielle living among the Salish. While hunting with the Blackfeet in Milk River country, he married a Blackfeet woman. No problem, except that he already had a wife on the Flathead reservation. Tribal rules were pretty strict about polygamy. To atone for his sins, he trained six bison calves to follow his horse and brought them into the Mission Valley as a peace offering. As he resumed his life among the Salish, his herd grew to almost 300 animals. In 1884, he decided to sell them to Pablo and another rancher named Charles Allard for $3,000. He took the money to Missoula where he literally had the party of his life. He was found murdered under the Higgins Street Bridge after several days of revelry, his money gone. His herd was the nucleus for the herd that now roams the National Bison Range in Moiese.

### T The Peoples Center

Hwy. 93, 6 miles south of Polson, 675-0160 or (800) 883-5344. www.peoplescenter.org

In the heart of western Montana, encounter the ways of the region's original creators of fine arts and crafts—the Salish, Kootenai and Pend d'Oreille people of the Flathead Indian Reservation.

Traverse northwestern United States and southwestern Canada to admire the grandeur of the indigenous homelands of the Salish, Kootenai, and Pend d'Oreille people. Explore the headwaters of the Columbia River. Imagine crossing the Rocky Mountains through present day Glacier Park to hunt buffalo on horseback, or on foot. Envision a purely subsistence lifestyle, within an economic system based on bison, fish, roots, berries, and nature's other provisions.

Imagine, too, the changes in centuries-old lifeways when Europeans came—new foods, new tools, new weapons, new diseases, new economies, new blood, Mother Earth, the provider and sustainer of all needs, became a possession—a territory-land to be "owned" and occupied by white settlers. The aboriginal lands, 22 million acres, to which the people belonged, were ceded to the United States government in exchange for a reservation of 1,245,000 acres, which belonged to the people. Thus, the Flathead Indian Reservation, through the Treaty of Hellgate in 1855, brought together three tribes—two of which (Salish and Pend d'Oreille) were related by language and lifeways, and one whose language and lifeways were totally different (Kootenai).

Sweeping changes in culture were largely influenced by the Jesuit Fathers who founded St. Ignatius Mission, French fur traders, homesteaders, treaty negotiators, and federal Indian agents.

Against this backdrop, the Confederated Salish and Kootenai Tribes of the Flathead Indian Reservation have forged a government, an economy, health care, Salish Kootenai College, and many social services for the people. The people are lawyers, nurses, farmers, homemakers, loggers, teachers, and business owners. They manage forests, water, land, and mineral resources. They have adapted, yet they remain true to their culture.

Once again, imagine melding ancient lifeways with contemporary life. This is The People's Center. Born of proud traditions, enriching a living culture with a sense of place for the people to gather, share, learn, and tell their story to their own and to visitors. Enjoy exhibits which take you back to "The Beginning: The First Sun." Learn the languages which are still being spoken by families. Partake in a feast including buffalo, elk, venison, fry bread, huckleberries. See beadwork and quillwork on buckskin, still scraped, tanned, and smoked by hand. Immerse yourself in the culture of the people who invented "Made in Montana."

The museum is open from 9 a.m. to 5 p.m. weekdays. From Memorial Day through Labor Day it is open weekends also from 10 a.m. to 5 p.m. A small admission fee is charged. *Source: Peoples Center brochure.*

### Ronan

This town was founded in 1885 and named for an early Indian Reservation Superintendent, Major Peter Ronan. Ronan served for 16 years as an honest and compassionate administrator until his death in 1892. At the time of his death, he was the oldest commissioned Indian Agent in service. He was also known for his book on the history of the Flathead Indians. The area boomed when the area, which was once part of the Flathead Reservation, was opened to settlement in 1910, and thousands of small farms and ranches were established on the irrigated land.

In 1912, a fire broke out in an automobile garage. A windstorm caused the fire to spread rapidly to the other businesses in the downtown area. By the time the firemen rolled into action, half the town was in flames. By the time it was over, most of the business district and the flour mill lay in ruins.

### T Ninepipe Bird Sanctuary and Wildlife Preserve

Charlo, 664-2211

This 4,500 acre preserve of marsh, water and grass is the feeding, nesting, and resting area for a large number of birds and waterfowl. The area is covered with ponds created by receding glaciers. The number of waterfowl at the preserve can reach as high as 80,000 in the fall and 40,000 in the early spring. The most common nesting birds are snow geese, Canada geese, mallards, pintails, redheads, blue herons, cormorants, shovelers, mergansers and coots. Almost 190 species have been observed in the preserve at one time or another. To reach the preserve, take Hwy. 212 out of Charlo to the road crossing the dam, then drive or walk along the dike for the best view of the birds.

### T Garden of the Rockies Museum

5 blocks west of U.S. Hwy. 93 on Round Butte Road in Ronan. 676-4220

This is one of those quaint little off the road places we all love to "discover." On entering this former Catholic church you will find Indian exhibits on your right and cowboy exhibits on your left. Notice the embossed tin walls and ceiling as you enter. There are three old-time stores—Brandjord's, Sterling's, Scearce's. There is also a doctor's office, barber shop, music room, living room, American Legion exhibits, laundry and bedroom. See the first two-way radio in the Mission Valley and other vet memorabilia. In the school room are pictures of Ronan alumni.

There is a kitchen with a large collection of old utensils and appliances. Walk out the back door and find a machine shed with a buggy, belly dump, binder, fanning mill, drill press and a vintage speed boat, "Miss Ronan."

The Stage Stop is a hand-hewn log building

## Montana Trivia

Near Rogers Pass, about 20 miles northeast of Lincoln, H.M. Kleinschmidt was on duty as a volunteer weather observer. On the calm morning of January 20, 1954, the skies had cleared after a lengthy snowfall. Kleinschmidt reported he heard popping sounds in the cabin he occupied. He went outside to check the thermometer about 2 a.m. The thermometer he had only went as low as -65° F. The mercury had shrunk as far as it could go into the thermometer's bulb. Kleinschmidt sent the thermometer to the Weather Service in Washington D.C. and described the event. They determined that the temperature had reached at least -69.7° F—a record low for the continental forty-eight states.

featuring dove-tail joinery and is an excellent example of frontier workmanship. Inside the building is a reading room with many old books, a logging display and many other old farming, ranching and mining tools.

The museum is open Memorial Day through Labor Day, Monday through Saturday from 11 a.m. to 4 p.m. Admission is free, but good will offerings are gratefully accepted.

### T Ninepipes Museum of Early Montana

40962 US Hwy 93, Charlo. 644-3434

### F Ranch House Restaurant

1 Eisenhower St. S.W., Ronan. 676-0500

### M Salish Kootenai College

Pablo. 675-4800, www.skc.edu

Salish Kootenai College (SKC) is a Tribal College serving the Confederated Salish and Kootenai Tribes, located on the Flathead Indian Reservation.The College provides Adult Basic Education, Vocational Education, and associates degree and bachelor degree programs. It was founded in 1972 by the American Indian Higher Education Consortium and enrolls approximately 1,000 students.

### L Starlite Motel

18 Main St., S.W., Ronan. 676-7000

## 33. *Attraction, Gas, Food, Lodging, Shopping, Miscellaneous*

### Lincoln

Lincoln is entombed under heavy snow in the winter and becomes a vacation haven in the summer. This small community is surrounded by forests and lakes with the Blackfoot River serving as a gateway to some of Montana's most popular back-country. Some of Montana's largest pines surround this mountain village.

Like many of the mountain towns in western Montana, Lincoln has its roots in gold mining. In the mid 1800s, gold was discovered in what became known as Lincoln Gulch. By 1867, Abe Lincoln Gulch stretched for ten miles with a population of over 500 hardy souls. There were two saloons, a bakery, general store, and butcher shop. They were soon followed by a hotel and livery stable. Until the gold played out in 1926, miners took a reported $7 million out of the ground. Word is, that much again was removed and not reported.

Like so many mining towns, when the gold ran out, so did the townsfolk. The settlement almost disappeared until homesteaders began ranching in the upper Blackfoot River valley. The area became a popular place for vacation cabins for people from Great Falls and Helena. In 1919, a British immigrant and his wife, James and Mary Lambkin, bought the tiny hotel in Lincoln. They replaced the old hotel with a larger log structure and built several log cabins surrounding the hotel to provide lodging for tourists.

During the prohibition area, Lincoln stills kept Helena's government offices, stores, and politicians wet. In its prime, the Lincoln booze industry was producing over 300 gallons of illegal hooch per month. If they arrested the farmer-moonshiner, his wife took over until he left jail.

Lincoln got its fifteen minutes of fame in 1996 when FBI agents moved in on the cabin of Ted Kaczynski. Lincoln residents were somewhat shocked to find out their mild mannered neighbor was the so called Unabomber and the villain of an eighteen year manhunt.

### T The Blackfoot Valley

When glaciers carved the Blackfoot Valley, they left behind a corridor for people and wildlife. Before human settlement, hundreds of wildlife species passed through or made their homes in the river valley and its tributaries. Then, for centuries, Native Americans ascended the winding river bottom enroute to bison hunting grounds in the plains. Lewis and Clark took the same pathway in 1806, noting the remains of many Indian lodges and named the area "the Prairie of the Knobs." Almost a hundred years later, ranchers settled in the valley. Weathered homesteads still bear witness to the early days of ranching.

Today, the Blackfoot Valley continues to be home and haven for a breathtaking array of wildlife, from elegant sandhill cranes to herds of elk. The Bob Marshall Wilderness, the northern boundary of the valley, shelters creatures as wild as wolverines and grizzly bears. This link with the vast wilderness is a key reason for the spectacular wildlife viewing in the Blackfoot Valley. *Reprinted from brochure "Blackfoot Valley Wildlife Viewing Guide."*

### T The Blackfoot River

Along the Blackfoot River, you can see wild creatures that thrive on the river's edge.

## On The Trail of Lewis & Clark

After separating from Capt. Clark, Lewis and his men traveled up the Bitterroot River to its confluence with the Clark's Fork. From there they traveled up the Blackfoot River Valley making good time, sometimes 20 to 30 miles per day, following a Nez Perce path to the buffalo country.

Several public access sites along Highway 200 provide easy access to the river. Common mergansers —diving ducks—fly low along the river or swim in pairs or family groups undaunted by rapids. Just outside of Bonner, in winter and spring, bighorn sheep clamber up cliffs or graze on the flats. In the scenic Potomac Valley, red-tailed hawks cruise above the meadows in search of Columbian ground squirrels. At dusk, if you are extremely lucky, you might see a great-horned owl swoop from the forest edge.

Roundup Bridge and Clearwater Junction mark two river access points for wildlife viewing or catch-and-release fishing. The native trout fishery is improving after a decline in the 1970s and 1980s. Stricter fishing regulations and improved grazing and logging practices contribute to a healthier aquatic community.

Just west of Lincoln, the Blackfoot Canyon shelters elk, deer, and moose among dense forests. Keep a sharp lookout for river otters cavorting in the swift waters and ducks dabbling in marsh ponds. *Reprinted from brochure "Blackfoot Valley Wildlife Viewing Guide."*

### T Blackfoot Valley Museum

1 Lincoln Gulch Rd., Lincoln. 362-4203.

### A Doug's Tire & Auto

Highway 200, Lincoln. 362-4360

This NAPA Auto Care Center specializes in tires, tire repairs, brakes, engine, electrical work, and oil & lube. The NAPA warranty is good throughout

*The Blackfoot River between Lincoln and Ovando.*

the US. These professional and honest mechanics provide service for just about any of your auto needs. Stop in for quality service, any special travel needs, and a good selection of parts.

### S Garland's Town & Country
524 Main St., Lincoln. 362-4244

For 44 years Garland's has offered a broad selection of merchandise in the Lincoln area. If you need it they probably have it. They offer an excellent selection of regional books, a large gift department featuring Montana-made products and souvenirs, a sizable selection of greeting cards, a large selection of Montana souvenir T-shirts, a full range of sporting goods and clothing, fishing & hunting licenses and supplies, and a full range of outdoor clothing, shoes, and camping gear. Also check out the flower shop, offering a beautiful selection of plants and arrangements. Owner Teresa Garland will make you feel welcome.

### S Hi Country Trading Post/Free Blackfoot Valley Museum
1 Lincoln Gulch Road, Lincoln. 362-4203 or toll free 800-433-3916. www.hicountry.com
or email: mt@hicountry.com.

The Hi-Country Trading Post is home to the Upper Blackfoot Valley Historical Society Museum. The museum access is free. The museum contains a unique blend of artifacts collected in the Upper Blackfoot Valley region from Lincoln's logging and mining era. One unique item of interest is an actual signature from C.M. Russell when he signeed the Old Lincoln Hotel register in 1918. There are prints from the painting of Old Lincoln in the 1920s done by Bob Morgan along with a documented history of Lincoln in "Gold Pans and Singletrees." The museum also ahs a trophy colleciton of American big game mounts.

### L Blue Sky Motel
Hwy. 200, Lincoln. 800- 293-4521

### L Snowie Pines Inn
Hwy. 200, Lincoln. 362-4481

### M Lincoln Villa Styling Salon
223 Main Street, Lincoln. 362-4966

## 34. *Historical Marker*

### H The Bob Marshall Wilderness Country ("The Bob")
Junction MT 200 & 141

*North of here lies the second largest wilderness in the lower 48 states. Made up of the Bob Marshall, Scapegoat, and Great Bear wilderness areas, its north end abuts Glacier National Park, creating a continuous corridor of unspoiled mountains and valleys that harbor grizzly bears, mountain goats, wolverines, elk, moose, deer, and wolves.*

*Montana first protected part of this country in 1913 when the Sun River Game Preserve was created on the east side of the continental divide. Years of market hunting to supply miners and settlers with meat had decimated the elk herds.*

*Bob Marshall (1901-1939), pioneer forester and conservationist of the 1930s, was years ahead of his time in recognizing and campaigning for the inherent value of wilderness. His vision helped awaken the U.S. Forest Service to the need to conserve a portion of the vanishing wildlands from which our American heritage had been formed. Before his premature death, he had secured protection for nearly 5.5 million acres, including most of the area that was later to bear his name. Montanans convinced Congress to add the Scapegoat in 1972 and the Great Bear in 1978. Though wilderness must be balanced with other uses of Nations Forests, it protects resources for us all, like watersheds, fisheries, and wildlife. Someone once asked Bob Marshall how much wilderness America really needs. In reply he asked, "How many Brahms symphonies do we need?"*

*The tiny hamlet of Ovando.*

### T Browns Lake and Blackfoot WPA

The glaciers that receded 10,000 years ago left potholes in the prairie that are today watery refuges for Canada geese, swans, ducks and even white pelicans in spring.

Browns Lake is well known to anglers for rainbow trout. For wildlife watchers, the lake is a mecca too. In spring, hundreds of ducks and geese stop at the lake to rest and feed before continu-ing their migration north. In the hot summer months, American coots and red-necked grebes float in the lake, while yellow-headed blackbirds, and black terns call from the cattails.

The Blackfoot Waterfowl Production Area (WPA) is an example of a restored wetland. Look for ducks and geese on the four ponds, and watch for white-tailed and mule deer among the cottonwoods and aspen.

## 35. *Historical Marker, Lewis & Clark, Attraction, Gas, Food, Lodging*

### Ovando

Ovando, is located northeast of Missoula and serves as a supply point for logging camps, hay, and sheep ranches. The post office opened in 1883 and the town was named after the first postmaster, Ovando Hoyt.

### H Lewis minus Clark Expedition

*On their return trip from the Pacific Coast, the Corps of Discovery split into two parties at Travelers Rest (just south of Missoula, Montana) on July 1, 1806. Clark proceeded south down the route they had come in 1805 along the Bitterroot River. Lewis went north along the Blackfoot River. Their plan was to rendezvous at the Missouri River in late August.*

*Lewis traveled through this area accompanied by nine mounted soldiers, 17 horses, and his Newfoundland dog, Seaman. On July 5, 1806, they camped near here at the confluence of the Big Blackfoot River and a creek. Lewis named that creek Seaman's Creek after his dog. Today Seaman Creek is called Monture Creek, named after George Monture, an early day U.S. Army scout. Lewis described this part of the valley as* "prarie of the knobs" *because of the mounds along the trail, some of which can still be seen today. The trail was called* "COKALAHJSHKJT" *or "The River of the Road to the Buffalo" as it was known to the Nez perce.*

*The "knobs" that Lewis described were caused by glaciers dumping rocks along their edges and down icy holes and cracks within the glacier. The glaciers that left these knobs began to melt and slowly retreat to the north some 10,000 to 12,000 years ago.*

*From here they* "Proceeded On" *to the east, past Lincoln, up Alice Creek, and across the Continental Divide. The place they crossed the Continental Divide is known today as "Lewis and Clark Pass," even though Clark was never here!*

### D Meriwether Lewis
July 6, 1806

*"these plains I called the prairie of the knobs from the number of knobs being irregularly scattered through it. . .on the border of which we passed the remains of 32 old lodges"*

### T Ovando Museum
Ovando

### FL Blackfoot Inn
722 Pine, Ovando. 793-5555.
www.blackfoot-inn.com

Getting a little road weary? Looking for a taste of Montana history? Would you like a free cup of great coffee? Then take the Ovando turnoff and visit one of the oldest towns in Montana. Located on the Lewis and Clark trail, the town still has most of its original buildings intact. Gas up, stock up on snacks, and if you're ready to call it a day, stay at this historic bed and breakfast. Your hosts, Howard and Peggy Fly will make you feel right at home. Their rooms are comfortable and clean and they'll fix you a Montana size breakfast to start your day after a great night's sleep. While you're there, ask Howard to show you the local museum across the street (he has the keys). He'll also act as your tour guide.

## F Blackfoot Steamer
Ovando

## 36. *Lewis & Clark, Attraction*

## D Meriwether Lewis
July 4, 1806

*"these affectionate people our (Nez Perce) guides betrayed every emmotion unfeigned regreat at seperating from us."*

## T Garnet Ghost Town
Located about 35 miles east of Missoula in the Garnet Range. 329-3914

Garnet Recreation Area The 12-mile long Garnet Back Country Byway climbs 2,000 feet through the scenic Garnet Range to Garnet Ghost Town. To get there turn south at mile marker 22 just east of Potomac or on north access road just off Bearmouth exit on I-90.

Garnet is a glimpse of the real "Old West" and is one of the best preserved ghost towns in Montana.

Mining in Garnet began in the late 1800s and continued into the 1930s. During the boom days of 1895-1911 the population reached several thousand. As the gold thinned out, so did the population. Attempts were made to revive the town during the depression, but failed. By 1950 the only residents remaining were "ghosts".

A hotel, store, Chinese laundry, school, several saloons, drug store, assay office, barber shop, and private cabins for the miners and their families were constructed. The buildings were put up quickly and without foundations, which contributed to eventual collapse.

A self guided tour brochure is available at the Visitor's Center in Garnet. It contains interesting facts about each of the buildings. Some of the buildings and land are privately owned, so please do not trespass.

The road to Garnet is closed to wheeled vehicles from January 1 to March 31. Snowmobilers and skiers are welcome during this period. The best accessibility for wheeled passenger vehicles is from mid-May through November. *Reprinted from BLM brochure.*

## 37. *Gas, Food*

## 38. *Attraction*

## T Salmon Lake & Placid Lakes State Parks
5 miles south of Seeley Lake on Montana 83. 542-5500

Salmon Lake and Placid Lake are part of the beautiful links in a chain of lakes fed by the Clearwater River. Fishing, boating, and a variety of other water sports are popular activities in this woodland setting of western larch, ponderosa pine, and Douglas fir.

## T Seeley Chain of Lakes

Some of western Montana's best wildlife viewing can be found along the Clearwater River "chain of lakes," rich wetlands lined by larch, spruce, alder, willow and reed. Not far from the Seeley Lake Ranger Station, you can walk through an old-growth larch forest to a wildlife viewing blind. From the blind you may see birds such as northern harrier, American bittern, common yellowthroat, yellow-headed blackbird, and green-winged teal. Watch also for muskrat, spotted frog and an occasional moose.

The "chain of lakes" is loon country. Home to a part of the largest population of breeding common loons west of the Mississippi, these lakes provide the wilderness and quiet loons need. Listen for their haunting wails in May and June. Throughout the summer, you may see loons and their chicks on the larger lakes. Nesting loons and young chicks are very vulnerable to disturbance, so please view them and all wildlife from a distance.

Although migratory birds leave the area by October, you can see wildlife year-round. Abundant snow and frozen lakes offer great opportunities to spot animal tracks of all kinds, from mountain lions to bald eagles to deer mice.*Reprinted from brochure "Blackfoot Valley Wildlife Viewing Guide."*

## 39. *Attraction, Adventure, Gas, Food, Camping Lodging, Shopping,*

## Seeley Lake

Seeley Lake, a community of about 2,000, is located 45 miles northeast of Missoula and serves as a popular recreational area. The town has an information center called Seeley Lake Ranger Station and three forest service campgrounds on Seeley Lake. Seeley Lake, built near several lakes, has over 300 miles of well-developed and maintained snowmobile trails. These trails cover the beautiful Clearwater Valley and lead to scenic lookouts, back-country lakes and cozy lodges.

## T Timber Heritage Museum
Wapiti Resort in Seeley Lake. 677-2775

This museum is located on the original townsite of Seeley Lake. This replica of the "Olde Town" has been reconstructed to the era of the late 1800s through the early 1900s. There is a general store, schoolhouse, church, livery stable, leather shop and more. The museum is open from June 1 through September 1 from 1 p.m. to 4 p.m. Friday and Saturday.

## T Old Towne Historic Village
Seeley Lake. 677-2775

## T Clearwater Canoe Trail
Put in is 1 mile north of the Seeley Lake Ranger Station. 677-2233

This calm water float down the winding Clearwater River will take you anywhere from one to two hours to complete. The three mile float ends at the lake near the Seeley Lake Ranger Station. From here, you can hike the 1.5 miles back to your car along the Clearwater River. Expect to see lots of wildlife on this float: river otters, beavers, muskrats, turtles, ducks, loons, deer, moose, eagles, and osprey.

## T Blackfoot-Clearwater Wildlife Management Area
Turnoff is about 2.5 miles north of Clearwater Junction on Hwy. 83. 542-5500

Like the wildebeest of Africa's Serengeti, the annual elk migration to and from the Blackfoot-Clearwater Wildlife Management Area (WMA) each winter attracts a myriad of wild followers. Bald and golden eagles, mountain lions, lynx, weasels, magpies, ravens, coyotes, gray jays, even small rodents and ticks all form part of a process ion of predatory, scavenging or parasitic wildlile linked to elk herds.

The Blackloot-Clearwatcr WMA has become one of western Montana's premier elk winter ranges. In the 1940s, only a few elk mingled with 1,200 cattle and 6,000 sheep. Today 1,400 elk migrate from their summer wilderness home in the Bob Marshall Wilderness to spend the winter on land where cattle grazing is carefully prescribed. Elk in winter need native grasses for food, forests for shelter from wind and deep snow, and

*Seeley Lake.*

Section 13

a haven from human disturbance.

To protect the elk from disturbance in the winter, yon must watch from pullouts along Highways 83 or 200. Scan the grassy slopes with binoculars at dawn or dusk in December, January or late March.

This WMA is open to the public during May 15-November 15. *Reprinted from brochure "Blackfoot Valley Wildlife Viewing Guide."*

### V Seeley Lake Fun Center

Highway 83 N., Seeley Lake. 677-CATS(2287) seeleyfunrentals@montana.com or www.seeleylakefuncenter.com

Enjoy the Seeley Swan Valley from the best perspective. This is the place to rent top line equipment for winter and summer outdoor activities. Located between the Bob Marshall Wilderness and the Mission Mountains, Seeley Lake Fun Center is a year round recreational rental & Arctic cat dealership with rental snowmobiles, cross-country skis, snowshoes, and ice fishing rentals in winter; pontoon boats, watercraft, rafts, canoes, mountain bikes, and fishing equipment for summer. Their factory certified technicians will make sure all equipment is in tip top shape.

### F Lindey's Prime Steakhouse

Highway 83, Seeley Lake. 677-9229. www.seeleyswanpathfinder.com

Lindey's offers a unique dining experience—one that will stay with you for years to come. The combination of a beautiful setting on the shores of Seeley Lake, a one-of-a kind menu, mouth watering steaks and attentive and friendly service makes for a unforgettable evening. Originally from Minnesota, Lindey's opened it's doors in Seeley Lake in 1980, and has been rated one of the top ten steakhouses in the U.S. The menu is short, offering only choice cuts of beef which all come with a salad, side of potatoes and tasty garlic bread. Lakefront views are available from any seat in the house. Lindey's is wonderful for casual family dining or a romantic evening out. Either way, you are guaranteed to leave happy and full. In the summer, try Lindey's Landing West Bayburgers for a casual fare on the waterfront.

### FC The Filling Station

Hwy 83, Seeley Lake. 677-2080

The Filling Station is a family restaurant offering a wide selection of truly great and affordable meals. They have a variety of sandwiches, burgers, pizza and huckleberry BBQ ribs that should not be missed. Your hosts Kris and Leon Martin and their very friendly staff will make your dining experience as good as the food they serve. Save room for their homemade soups, bread, cakes and pies. Relax and enjoy your favorite wine, beer or cocktail and a variety of appetizers in front of their fireplace. While at The Filling Station you will enjoy seeing their unique collection of antique gas pumps and memorabilia. Daily lunch and dinner specials and breakfast served on the weekends. Also check out their RV park and laundromat located nearby in a pleasant and relaxed setting.

### FL Double Arrow Resort

Mile Marker 12, Highway 83, Seeley Lake. 677-2777 or 468-0777

The Double Arrow Lodge, in its serene mountain valley, is home to the traveler as it was when the main lodge was crafted over 60 years ago. The handsome, sturdy log structures capture a unique blend of European grace and Western hospitality. The Double Arrow Resort provides a variety of lodging styles to fit all of your accommodation needs, as well as conference and retreat facilities, food and beverage services, an indoor pool and year-round activities that include: golfing, scenic hikes and trail rides, old-fashioned sleigh and wagon rides, fishing, hunting, snowmobiling, skiing, swimming, tennis and more. Make your stay in the beautiful Seeley Lake area complete with a stay at the Double Arrow Resort.

### FS The Stage Station

Hwy 83. Seeley Lake. 677-2227

If you like the outside of this historic stage station, you'll absolutely love the inside. Not only kids, but adults too, love the old-fashioned ice cream parlor with an original Montana back bar. Select from a variety of espresso drinks, ice cream treats, muffins, and cookies. The store is filled with an eclectic mix of quality gifts, interesting antiques, Montana arts, crafts, pottery, jewelry, and wonderful clothing. The Stage Station is home to the wares of many local artists. The Stage Stop is one stop you won't want to miss.

### LC Seeley Lake Motor Lodge

Hwy 83, Mile Marker 15, Seeley Lake. 677-2335 or 800-237-9978. Email: slkmotorlodge@blackfoot.net www.seeleylakemotorlodge.com

The clean, quiet rooms at the Seeley Lake Motor Lodge feature color, cable TV with remotes, nonsmoking rooms, kitchenette, and rooms accommodating up to five people. Featuring a convenient coffee room with freshly brewed morning coffee, a microwave, and refrigerator. There are tent and RV sites with full and partial hookups. Located in the heart of Seeley Lake, you can wander through town enjoying gift shops, art galleries and more. Recreation in the surrounding area is endless, with Seeley Lake only 1/2 mile away. Enjoy hiking, wildlife viewing, and walking to nearby dining or shopping. In the winter, enjoy snowmobiling, dog sledding or cross country skiing with 300 miles of groomed trails out your front door. The area has great hunting and fishing as well.

### LC Tamaracks Resort

Highway 83 Mile 17, Seeley Lake. 677-2433 or 800-477-7216, www.tamaracksresort.com, email at heagy@aol.com

This resort is located on the north end of Seeley Lake and nestled among the towering trees of Lolo National Forest. Tamaracks Resort offers quiet, restful, secluded cabins and camping in a beautiful waterfront setting. They are open year all year long offering 13 individual cabins with fully equipped kitchens that sleep from 1-10 people. The quiet campground has tent sites and full RV hookups with a bathhouse, showers and laundry facilities. In the summer, guests can enjoy the lake with boat rentals, swimming or just relaxing in the

#### Montana Trivia

The Montana Children's Theater group tours around the world visiting schools and encouraging more than fifty thousand kids each year to get up on stage and perform.

sun. In the winter guests can take advantage of the many miles of cross country ski trails with ski and skate rentals in the shop. Reserve now for the vacation you deserve and will thoroughly enjoy.

## L Whitetail Guest Cabins

3806 Hwy 83 N., mile marker 19.4, Seeley Lake. 677-2024. www.whitetailcabins.com

The Whitetail Guest Cabins are tucked between the Mission Mountains and the Swan Range in one of Montana's most popular year-round recreation areas. From your cabin enjoy easy access to Seeley Lake and all that it has to offer. In the winter you can snowmobile from your door to over 230 miles of groomed snowmobile trails or cross country skiing or even go dogsledding. Eight cozy cabins are all non-smoking, with fully equipped kitchens, full baths, and satellite TV, private decks, and comfortable bedrooms. Each will accommodate 2 to 4 guests comfortably. Available on a daily or weekly basis. Pets are permitted on a preapproved and preregistered basis. Visit them on the web for more information.

## S Annie's Emporium

3166 Hwy. 83 N., Bison and Bear Trading Center. 677-0999 Seeley Lake. www.AnniesEmporium.com

A trip to Seeley Lake is not complete until you've been to Annie's Emporium, a browser's delight. Located in the Bison & Bear Trading Center you will find Annie's loaded to the rafters with a huge selection of unique, high quality Montana Made products, antiques, gifts, collectibles, and fresh fudge in a multitude of mouth watering flavors. Their constantly changing inventory includes distinct Montana gifts, Wrangler clothing, Huckleberry products, pottery, Victoria's Towels, Winterhawk Woodworks, Antler Iron Works, and remarkable treasures from the past. They top all of this off with free gift wrapping, packing and shipping services, and of course, they can create and deliver the perfect gift basket.

## S Deer Country Quilts

Hwy. 83, Bison & Bear Trading Center, Seeley Lake. 677-2730. www.deercountryquilts.com

Deer Country Quilts has earned a widespread reputation based on excellent customer service and

outstanding quality merchandise. Over 2,500 bolts of 100 percent cotton and a growing selection of polar fleece are in stock. They carefully select from the finest fabrics, notions, books and patterns available. In keeping with their quest for quality, they are also an authorized dealer for Bernina sewing machines and feature a full line of Bernina products. A full schedule of classes for all levels of quilters is offered, featuring many teachers with local and national reputations. They also work with local lodges, resorts and bed & breakfasts to offer retreats for guilds and quilting groups from around the country. Learn more at their web site.

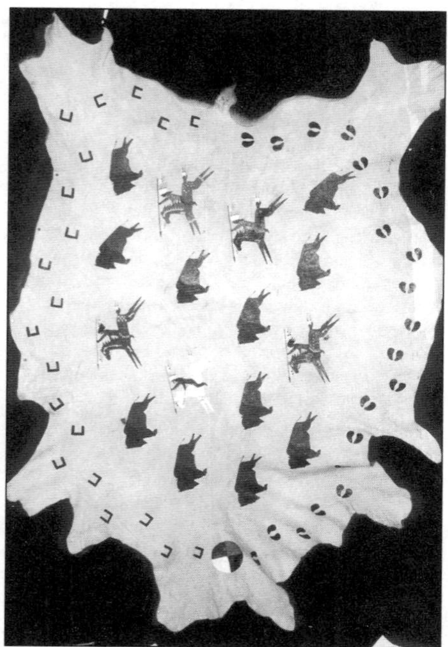

## S Grizzly Claw Trading Co.

Hwy. 83, Seeley Lake. 677-0008 or 888-551-0008. www.grizzlyclaw.com

Grizzly Claw Trading Company is where you'll find goods from the Old West rendezvous to the New Western Crafts of many diverse artists—woodcarvings, bronzes, stained glass, photography, paintings, and jewelry. The synergy is felt immediately upon entering the store. You'll be captivated by hundreds of items that are uniquely displayed, many exclusive to the Grizzly Claw. Discover pelts, painted robes, horns, skulls, knives, pipes, medicine bags, drums, and other Native American artifacts. For the home: lamps, pillows, rugs, pottery, and log furniture. Apparel includes: fleece, moccasins, jackets, vests, and shirts. Choose from a great selection of beading, crafting, leather and jewelry supplies. Enjoy Montana made foods and espresso while visiting this intriguing store. Visit there website at grizzlyclaw.com.

## S Good Times Clothing, Gifts & Videos

Hwy. 83 N., Seeley Lake. 677-2140

Located in the Filling Station Mall, Good Times features a wide selection of gifts, clothing, souvenirs, and momentos of Montana. They have all the items you can imagine to fit your vacation needs, including a variety of Montana made products, huckleberry products, 93 different styles of t-shirts and sweatshirt designs, candles, ornaments, bathing suits, hats, shoes, indian blankets, stuffed animals, handmade crafts, toys, candy, jewelry and much more. They also carry a full line of video rentals with all the new releases, and TV & VCR rentals for a relaxing evening after a full day of fun around the Seeley Lake area.

## S High Basin Sports

Hwy. 83, Seeley Lake. 677-3605

## S Spirit Mountain Health Products & Gifts

Hwy 83., Filling Station Mall, Seeley Lake. 677-2080

# Scenic Drives

## Lincoln Area

### Alice Creek Road

This road is eight miles east of Lincoln. The turnoff is to the north just before the turnoff to Hwy. 279. The road parallels Alice Creek to its headwaters. It is a single lane dirt road with the first seven miles crossing private land. The road will take you to several mountain meadows that are filled with wildflowers in the summer. You can also observe numerous beaver dams along the willow lined bottoms of the creek.

### Beaver Creek Road

Find this road two miles west of Lincoln on the north side of Hwy. 200. The road is accessible from mid-June through mid-November and travels a length of about 25 miles. The Reservoir Lake and Dry Creek trailheads can be found along this road. A number of logging areas provide good berry picking sites at the right time of the year. Watch for Grizzly bears frequenting these areas. This is a mountain drive through dense conifer cover that is interrupted only by logging areas. You will cross numerous small streams along the way. Huckleberry Pass is the highest elevation you will cross at 5,994 feet. There are some panoramic views of Coopers Lake and Kleinschmid Flat at the end of the road.

### Copper Creek Road

To find this road drive six miles east of Lincoln and look for Landers Fork Road just past the bridge. Take this north about four miles until it connects with Copper Creek Road. This road goes a little over 14 miles and reaches an elevation of 6,160 feet. This is a popular route which provides access to the Meadows Trail Head, Snowbank Lake Recreation Area and Copper Creek Campground. It parallels Copper Creek most of its length. From Snowbank Lake to the end of the road are some spectacular views of Red Mountain.

### Sucker Creek-Keep Cool Contour Road

This short scenic loop takes you to some great views of the Continental Divide and surrounding mountain ranges. Sucker Creek Road is at the eastern edge of Lincoln. The road winds up the mountain for about ten miles where it connects with Copper Creek Road. Turn right on Copper Creek to head back to Hwy. 200, or if you want to

# LOLO NATIONAL FOREST

Located in the "big sky country" of Montana, lies the Lolo National Forest. The Forest surrounds the western Montana community of Missoula. The crest of the Bitterroot Mountains divides Montana from Idaho and serve as the forest's western boundary. The Continental Divide through the Scapegoat wilderness defines the forest's eastern boundary. Four major rivers and their streams offer some of the best fishing in the Rocky Mountains. The topography varies from remote, high alpine lakes to whitewater streams and from heavily forested ridges to smooth rolling meadows. The Rattlesnake National Recreation Area offers many recreation opportunities right on the edge of Missoula.

Directions
Lolo National Forest
USDA Forest Service
Building 24
Fort Missoula
Missoula, MT 59804
Phone: 406-329-3750
Email:Mailroom_R1_Lolo@fs.fed.us

*Reprinted from www.recreation.gov*

keep exploring, turn left to head up to Snowbank Lake. Keep Cool Lakes is a popular spot for campers and picnickers and is a great place to take a break and relax.

**Ogden Road**
Head west of Lincoln on Hwy. 200 for about 11 miles. The road is marked with a sign on the south side of the Hwy. Ogden Road is a single lane road with some wide spots for passing that runs along the mountainside for about 14 miles. The highest elevation the road reaches is 4,411 feet. It travels through forest, meadows, and open hillsides. High points along the road offer excellent vistas of Helmville Valley and the surrounding mountain ranges.

## HIKES

### Lincoln Area

**Gould-Helmville Trail**
From Hwy. 200 just east of Lincoln turn onto Flesher Pass Road. Follow this approximately 12 miles to Stemple Pass Road. Follow this road to Stemple Pass and turn south onto Marsh Creek Road 485. Follow this to the trailhead. An alternate access can be reached by going just west of Lincoln to the Dalton Mountain Road. Turn south and go approximately 8 miles to the trailhead. The trail heads east from here. This trail is especially scenic as it follows the ridge tops its entire length. It extends for 13 miles and is not a loop trail. You can either hike partway and return, arrange for a pick up at the other end, or make it an overnighter. There are several ridge top meadows that make excellent camp sites.

**Stonewall Ridge Tail**
From Hwy. 200 on the east edge of Lincoln go north on Sucker Creek Road for 2.5 miles. Look for trailhead sign on the left. The hike begins on Trail #418 and heads up the mountain. The junction with the Ridge Trail is unmarked but is located on top of the ridge and heads west along the ridge. The total hike to the top is approximately 7 miles and the first 4.5 are a gradual uphill. This is a very scenic hike and provides some outstanding views of the Blackfoot Valley. Be aware that fog and high winds on Stonewall Mountain are a frequent occurrence. Most of the hike up is through a closed canopy environment with occasional glimpses of the Lincoln Valley. The real view is from atop Stonewall Mountain. On a clear summer day, the Garnet and Flint Mountain Ranges are a breathtaking sight. There are campsites available along the trail.

**Arrastra Creek Trail**
From Hwy. 200 just west of Lincoln, head north on Beaver Creek Road (FR 4106) for approximately 9 miles to the trailhead. There is ample parking here. This is a relatively easy trail which follows Arrastra Creek its entire length with very few inclines. The hike is very scenic and crosses talus slopes as well as stretches of close canopied Douglas Fir. There are several open meadows which make excellent camping and picnicking areas.

**Snowbank-Liverpool Trail**
Take Hwy. 200 six miles east of Lincoln and look for Landers Fork Road just past the bridge. Take this north about four miles until it connects with Copper Creek Road. Follow the road to Snowbank Lake. The trail head is on the northwest side of the parking area. This is an excellent trail, but you may share it with motorcyclists and horseback riders. The hike begins at Snowbank Lake and shortly reaches an old clearcut. Look across this clearcut for a Forest Service blaze mark. The trail starts through the forest at this point. For the first two miles you will follow Snowbank Creek. There are a number of smaller creeks crossing the trail. After crossing Snowbank Creek, the trail begins to get steeper on its way up to the ridge. You probably want to turn around here and head back to the parking area, as continuing on takes you further from your starting point with no loop back.

**Sauerkraut Trail**
This trail takes you to the old Lincoln View Mine. To access it, travel three miles west of Lincoln on Hwy. 200 and turn south on Dalton Mountain Road. Drive approximately four miles, the trail head is just past the bridge and is marked with a sign. The trail is in excellent condition and follows the creek up to the mine through a closed canopy of Douglas fir and lodgepole pine. If you are in huckleberry season, you will find ample pickings along this trail. As with any old mine, there are plenty of hazards. Be careful and watch your kids closely. This trail was originally constructed for purposes other than recreation. It is fairly short and is an excellent family hike.

### Missoula Area

**Hike to the M**
Certainly most popular hike in the area for locals, you can get spectacular views of the city by taking the trail up Mount Sentinel which towers over the University of Montana Campus. The trailhead is on the backside of the campus and very easy to find. The first M was built in 1909 out of white-washed rocks by the junior class of UM. The second M was built of wood by the freshman class of 1912. It had a lighting system with a 2 horse-power generator for special occasions. In 1915, the freshman class moved the M 200 feet higher up the mountain. The newest M was made of concrete and completed in 1968 at a cost of $4,328.01.

**Sawmill-Curry Trail System**
From East Broadway at 1-90 Exit 104, drive 4 miles north on Van Buren Street and Rattlesnake Drive to Sawmill Gulch Road (6300 Rattlesnake Drive). Turn left, cross Rattlesnake Creek and pass the Main Trailhead parking area. Continue 1.2 miles to the locked gate, via a single-lane county road with few turnouts. Bear right at both Intersections. Note: Parking space at the end of Sawmill Gulch Road is limited to four vehicles. There is not enough room to park or turn around a vehicle with a trailer.

The trails In this system have evolved over more than a century. Some were made by prospectors, settlers, and their livestock, beginning in the 1880s and 90s. Others—the steepest routes started as skid roads when woodcutters salvaged timber after the great fire of 1919. The gentler, wider roads were built when the maturing regrowth began to be harvested in the 1960s and 70s.

Big game animals have kept many of these trails well-worn, including some spurs that lead nowhere but into browse or cover. Some trails enter private land. Users are urged to respect the rights of private landowners.

All of the Sawmill-Curry Trail System lies within the South Zone, where camping, camp and picnic fires, and the discharging of firearms are prohibited. The South Zone includes Sawmill, Woods, Spring and Curry Gulches, and the area south of the Curry Trail to Kench Meadow, over to Poe Meadow, then southeast to the recreation area boundary.

**Riverfront Trails in Missoula**
This three mile loop begins and ends at Caras Park in downtown Missoula. This pleasant stroll ambles along the Clark Fork River. It crosses the river at the footbridge on the University of Montana campus and at the Orange Street Bridge. The north side trail links a number of parks on that side of town. The south side trail was once the bed of the Old Milwaukee Railroad. You can extend your walk another 2.5 miles by taking the Kim Williams Nature Trail east at the footbridge.

**Kim Williams Nature Trail**
This trail takes off of the Southside Clark Fork Trail on the south side of the Van Buren footbridge. It is a wide, flat, 2.5 mile trail built on an abandoned railroad bed and travels through a scenic 134-acre natural area in Hellgate Canyon. If you have the energy, you can take a spur after about a mile and connect with the Crazy Canyon Road. The hike from here is a rigorous 1.4 miles to the top of Mount Sentinel. You can complete the loop by connecting with the "M" trail and following it back to the trailhead.

**Greenough Park Trails**
These are a series of intermingling trails in a city park. Take I-90 exit 105 (Van Buren St.) and head northeast on Head north on Van Buren to Locust St. Turn left here and go four blocks to Monroe. Turn right and drive to Greenough Park entrance. The main trail is a 1-mile paved walking and bicycling path with numerous offshoots. There are interpretive signs along the trail. If you're a bird watcher, this is a great place to spot over 100 varieties of winged critters.

**Rattlesnake Valley National Recreation Area Trails**
This is a series of trails that wander through the hills north of Missoula and lead into the Rattlesnake Wilderness Area. To get there take I-

90 exit 105 (Van Buren St.) and head northeast on Van Buren. Stay on Van Buren until it turns into Rattlesnake Drive. Turn left on an unmarked road just past Wildcat Road. There is a parking area at the mouth of Sawmill Gulch just beyond the bridge.

### Seeley Lake Area

**Morrell Falls**
This is a fairly easy five-mile loop hike with only a 250-foot elevation gain. The falls cascade about 100 feet dumping incredible amounts of water. During spring runoff, you may see two waterfalls. Morrell Lake along the trail is a great place for a swim. To get there go north of Seeley Lake to Cottonwood Lakes Road FR 477. Turn east for about 1 mile to Morrell Creek Road. Go left (north) here and drive for about 7 miles till you cross the Morrell Creek bridge. Take a left at the next junction and drive 1 mile to the trailhead.

**Holland Lake and Falls Trail**
This 4-mile loop trail follows the shore of Holland Lake and takes you to a spectacular 40-foot waterfall. This is one of the gateways to the million acre Bob Marshall Wilderness area. To get there find the turnoff 8.3 miles south of Condon. It is well marked. You will find the trailhead just past the campground and lodge. There is ample parking available.

## Cross-Country Ski Trails

### Lolo National Forest

**Pattee Canyon Complex—5.5 mi. SE Missoula**
For more information contact: District Ranger, Bldg. 24-A, Fort Missoula, Missoula, MT 59804(406)329-3814
*1.6 km Easiest, 4 km More Difficult, 5.4 km Most Difficult; intermittent grooming*
Parking capacity, 40 cars; closed to motorized vehicles; 2 trails. Dogs prohibited on groomed trails.

**Seeley Lake Ski Trails, Seeley Creek Trailhead-1 mi. NE Seeley Lake**
For more information contact: District Ranger, Seeley Lake, MT 59868 (406) 677-2233
*3 km Easiest, 12 km More Difficult, 3 km Most Difficult; intermittent grooming*
Snowmobiles prohibited. Parking for 12 cars. Maps available at and District Office. Dogs prohibited on groomed trails.

**Lookout Pass Recreation Area Ski Trails—Lookout Pass, Montana/Idaho State Line**
For more information contact: District Ranger, Superior, MT 59872 (406) 822-4233
*3.6 km Easiest. 3.5 km More Difficult, 4.5 km Most Difficult; no grooming*
Parking available at Lookout Pass Ski Area. Maps available at Lookout Pass ski rental shop and District Office. Portions of some trails shared with snowmobiles.

## Information Please

All Montana area codes are 406

### Road Information

Montana Road Condition Report
800-226-7623, 800-335-7592 or local 444-7696
Montana Highway Patrol 444-7696
**Local Road Reports**
Missoula 728-8553
Statewide Weather Reports 453-2081

### Tourism Information

Travel Montana 800-847-4868 outside Montana
444-2654 in Montana
http://travel.mt.gov/.
Gold West Country 846-1943 or 800-879-1159
Glacier Country 837-6211 or 800-338-5072
Northern Rodeo Association 252-1122
**Chambers of Commerce**
Lincoln 362-4949
Missoula 543-6623
Plains 826-4700
Ronan 676-8300
Seeley Lake Area 677-2880
St. Ignatius 745-4935
Superior 822-4891

### Airports

Condon 754-2295
Lincoln 444-2506
Missoula 728-4381
Ronan 883-6211
Seeley Lake 677-9229
St Ignatius 745-3363
Superior 822-2980
Whitefish 257-5994

### Government Offices

State BLM Office 255-2885, 238-1540
Bureau of Land Management
Missoula Field Office 329-3914
Butte Field Office 494-5059
Bitterroot National Forest 363-7161
Lolo National Forest 329-3750
Flathead National Forest 758-5200
Lee Metcalf National Wildlife Refuge 777-5552
National Bison Range Wildlife Refuge 644-2211
Ninepipe and Pablo National Wildlife Refuge 644-2211
Montana Fish, Wildlife & Parks 542-5500
U.S. Bureau of Reclamation
Helena Field Office 475-3310

### Hospitals

Community Medical Center•Missoula 728-4100
St. Patrick Hospital • Missoula 542-0341
St Patrick Hospital • Missoula 543-7271
Clark Fork Valley Hospital • Plains 826-3601
St. Luke Community Hospital•Ronan 676-4441
Mineral County Hospital • Superior 822-4841

### Golf Courses

**Double Arrow Golf Course**
Seeley Lake 677-3247
King Ranch Golf Course • Frenchtown 626-4000
Highlands Golf Club • Missoula 728-7360
Linda Vista Golf Course • Missoula 251-3655
The Univ Of Montana Golf Course
Missoula 728-8629
Wild Horse Plains Golf Course
Plains 826-5626
Mission Mountain Country Club
Ronan 676-4653
Trestle Creek Golf Course • Saint Regis 649-2680

### Bed & Breakfasts

**Creekside B&B** • Arlee 726-3332
**Foxglove Cottage B&B** • Missoula 543-2927
**Stoneheart Inn** • St. Ignatius 745-4999
Blackfoot Commercial Co. • Ovando 793-5555
Cappuccino Cowboy Ranch
St. Ignatius 676-2255
Cougar Ranch B&B • Missoula 726-3745
Gibson Mansion B&B • Missoula 251-1345
Goldsmith's B&B Inn • Missoula 721-6732
Gracenote Garden B&B • Missoula 543-3480
Guest House, L.L.P. • Plains 826-3230
Hotel Albert B&B • De Borgia 678-4303

Eagle Watch B&B • Huson 626-4441
Emily A B&B • Seeley Lake 677-3474
Kozy Kountry B&B • Seeley Lake 677-3436
LumiVista B&B • Ronan 676-7877
Mandorla Ranch B&B
Montana Hotel • Alberton 722-4990
Lumberjack Inn • Lincoln 362-4001
Outlook Inn B&B • Somers 857-2060
Rocky Mountain Retreat • Seeley Lake 677-3023
Schoolhouse & Teacherage • Huson 626-5879
33-Bar Ranch B&B • Condon 754-2820
Timbers B&B • Ronan 676-4373
Twin Creek B&B • Ronan 676-8800
Zarephath Inn B&B • Ronan 676-3451

### Vacation Homes & Cabins

**Whitetail Guest Cabins** • Seeley Lake 677-2024
Big Cir Lodge • De Borgia 678-4364
Broken Heart • Haugan 678-4325
Rock Creek Cabins • Missoula 251-6611
Ruggs Outfitting • Superior 822-4240
Trout Bums • Missoula 825-6146

### Guest Ranches & Resorts

**Double Arrow Resort** • Seeley Lake 677-2777
Bar 1 Ranch • Huson 626-4780
Bob Marshall Wilderness Ranch
St.Ignatius 745-4466
Broken Heart Ranch • Haugan 678-4325
Cabinet Mountain Guest Ranch•Plains 826-3971

Center at Salmon Lake • Seeley Lake 677-3620
Cheff's Guest Ranch • Charlo 644-2557
Clearwater Guest Ranch • Greenough 244-5244
Deer Lick Resort • Swan Lake 886-2321
E Bar L Ranch • Bonner 244-5571
Gold Creek Lodge • Missoula 549-5987
Grizzly Hackle • Missoula 721-8996
Holland Lake Lodge • Condon 754-2282
Horseshoe Hills • Seeley Lake 677-2276
Lake Upsata Guest Ranch Llc
Ovando 793-5890
L Diamond E Ranch • Missoula 825-6295
The Lodges On Seeley Lake
Seeley Lake 677-2376
Montana Pines Hideaway Resort
Seeley Lake 677-2775
Quinn's Hot Springs Resort • Paradise 826-3150
Raptor Room • Condon 754-2880
Rich Ranch • Seeley Lake 677-2317
Rock Creek Cabin • Missoula 251-6611
Sheep Mountain Lodge • Superior 822-3382
Swan River Valley Lodge • Condon 754-2780
Tamaracks Resort • Seeley Lake 677-2433
White Tail Guest Ranch • Ovando 793-5627

### Forest Service Cabins

***Flathead National Forest***
**Condon House**
70 mi. S of Kalispell at Condon work Center, Condon, MT on State Hwy 83. 837-7500
Capacity: 6 Nightly fee: $50 Available: All year
Seven night limit. Electric heat, stove & refrigerator. Drinking water, flush toilets & shower. Paved road. No pets or livestock.

***Helena National Forest***
**Cummings Cabin**
8 1/2 mi. E of Lincoln, MT. (l-1/2 mi. SE off Hogum Crk. Rd) 362-4265

Capacity: 4 Nightly fee: $25 Available: All year, except big game hunting season. (max stay 5 nights)
Cross-country ski or snowmobile access in winter. Road usually plowed within 1-1/2 miles of cabin.

*Lolo National Forest*
**Hogback Homestead Cabin**
25 mi E of Missoula, MT, on I-90; then 29 mi. S on Rock Creek Rd. 329-3814
Capacity: 8 Nightly fee: $50 Available: All year
2-story, 3-bedroom; water pump, wood stove, furnished; winter access limited (1/2 mi. walk). 3 season drive in. First floor is wheelchair accessible.

**Savenac Cookhouse & Bunkhouse.**
90 mi. W of Missoula on I-90 Haugan Exit 16. 822-4233
Capacity: 30 Nightly fee: $100
Available: 8/1 - 3/1
Heated bunkhouse w/showers. Adjacent cookhouse w/dining room, kitchen on the grounds of the historic Savenac Nursery.

**Up Up 40' Lookout Tower.**
80 mi. W of Missoula, MT on I-90 Ward Creek Exit 26. Then approx. 18 mi. on FS Rds. 889 and 3816 822-4233
Capacity: 4 Nightly fee: $25 Available: 6/15 - 11/15
Drive directly to Tower. Discourage bringing children.

**West Cottage**
90 mi. W of Missoula on I-90 Haugan Exit 16 822-4233
Capacity: 4 Nightly fee: $25 Available: 9/8 - 3/1
Two bedroom, one bath cottage w/fuel oil heat, hot water, & kitchen on the grounds of historic Savenac Nursery.

**Thompson Peak Lookout Tower**
55 mi. W of Missoula on I-990 Superior Exit 47, 12 mi. SW of Superior 822-4233
Capacity: 4 Nightly fee: $30 Available: 5/26-10/15
Drive directly to tower. Microwave, refrigerator, heat

## Private Campgrounds

Best Holiday Trav-L-Park • Saint Regis 649-2470
Elkhorn Guest Ranch • Missoula 825-3220
Filling Station RV Park • Seeley Park 677-2080
Jocko Hollow Campground • Arlee 726-3336
Jellystone Park • Missoula 543-9400
Jim & Mary's Adult RV Park • Missoula 549-4416
KOA Kampgrounds • Missoula 549-0881
Out Post Campground • Missoula 549-2016
Crossroads Motel & RV Park • Plains 826-3623
Diamond S RV Park • Ronan 676-3641
Ronan Mission Meadows TRL & RV Park Ronan 676-5182
River Edge Campground • Alberton 722-3338
St. Ignatius Campground & Hostel St. Ignatius 745-3959
St Regis KOA • Saint Regis 649-2122
Coyle's RV Park • Seeley Lake 677-2214
Montana Pines Resort • Seeley Lake 677-2775
Turah RV Park • Missoula 258-9773
Willow Creek Campground • Charlo 644-2356

## Car Rental

Avis Rent-A-Car 549-4711
Budget of Missoula 543-7001
Dollar Rent-A-Car 542-2311
Enterprise Rent-A-Car 721-1888
Grizzly Auto Center 721-5000
Hertz Rent-A-Car 541-9511
National Car Rental 543-3131
Paradise RV Rentals 721-6729
Practical Rent-A-Car 721-4391
Rent A Wreck 721-3838
Thrifty Car Rental 549-2277
Xpress Rent-A-Car 542-8459

## Outfitters & Guides

*F=Fishing H=Hunting R=River Guides*
*E=Horseback Rides G=General Guide Services*

**10,000 Waves-raft & Kayak Adventures** R 549-6670
Big Salmon Outfitters HFE 676-3999
Broken Heart Guest Ranch HF 678-4325
Cabin Creek Outfitters G 726-3381
Cabinet Mountain Outfitters GFHER 826-3970
Clark Fork River Outfitters F 826-4220
Diamond N Outfitters HF 626-4022
Eustance Pack & Tack Outfitters G 362-4748
Four Rivers Fly Shop GF 721-4796
Five Valley Flyfishers F 728-9434
Grizzly Hackle Fishing Co. F 721-8996
High Plains Drifter F 721-2703
Joe Cantrell Outfitting HFER 649-2566
John Perry's Montana Fly Fishing F 258-2997
The King Fisher F 721-6141
Lewis & Clark Trail Adventures GR 728-7609
Missoulian Angler GF 728-7766
Montana Equestrian Tours E 754-2900
Montana Flyfishing FE 543-8824
Montana River Guides R 273-4718
Monture Face Outfitters HFE 244-5763
Mountain Trail Rides E 549-7759
North American Retreats G 793-5824
North Fork Crossing G 793-5046
Outdoor Adventures F 542-1230
Rugg's Outfitting GHFER 822-4240
Pangaea Expeditions R 721-7719
Pine Hills Outfitters H 754-2244
Pine Hills Outfitters E 362-4664
Rich Ranch HF 677-2317
Riding Inc E 721-5946
River Resource Outfitters GF 728-7477
Rocky Mountain Whitewater GR 728-2984
Rocky Point Outfitters HFGER 826-3766
Shamrock Sports & Outdoors R 721-5456
Snowcrest Sled Dog Adventures G
Sunchasers Inc R 825-6580
Thunder Bow Outfitters Inc G 754-2701
Trail Creek Stables E 677-2166
Venture West Vacations G 825-6200
Water Master Rafts R 251-3337
Western Waters GR 543-3203
Western Waters & Woods FR 822-9900
Western Timberline Outfitters HFE 826-3874
White Tail Ranch Outfitters G 793-5666
Wild Women G 543-3747
Wilderness Outfitters HF 728-0550
WTR Outfitters, LLC HF 793-5666
Blackfoot River Outfitters F 542-7411
Crain Outfitting & Guide Service G 826-5566
K Lazy Three Ranch G 362-
4258Malson Jerry Outfitting G 847-5582

## Cross-Country Ski Centers

Alice Creek Ranch
8 mi. E of Lincoln on Alice Creek Road 494-4235

Holland Lake Lodge
25 mi. N of Seeley Lake in Swan Valley 689-3611

## Downhill Ski Areas

Lookout Pass Ski & Recreation Area 744-1301
Marshall Mountain 258-6000
Snowbowl Ski & Summer Resort 549-9777

## Snowmobile Rentals

**Seeley Lake Fun Center** •Seeley Lake 677-2287
Summit Seekers Inc • Lincoln 362-4078

## Notes:

## Public Campgrounds

# Campsite Directions

| Campsite | Season | Camping | Trailers | Toilets | Water | Boat Launch | Fishing | Swimming | Trails | Stay Limit | Fee |
|---|---|---|---|---|---|---|---|---|---|---|---|
| **252•Gold Rush FS**<br>9 mi. S of Thompson Falls on Forest Rd. 352 | 6/1-10/15 | 7 | 18′ | • | • | | • | | | 14 | |
| **253•Cabin City FS**<br>3 mi. SE of De Borgia on I-90, exit 22•2.5 mi. NE on Camels Hump Rd. 353 •.2 mi. N of Forest Rd. 353 | 5/22-9/6 | 24 | 34′ | • | • | | • | | | 14 | • |
| **254•Sloway FS**<br>7 mi. SE of St. Regis on I-90•3 mi. W on Dry Creek Rd. on Clark Fork River | 5/17-9/30 | 16 | 40′ | • | • | | • | | | 14 | • |
| **255•Cascade FS**<br>9 mi. S of Paradise | 5/15-10/15 | 12 | 22′ | D | • | A | • | | • | 14 | • |
| **256•Trout Creek FS**<br>7 mi. SE of Superior on R. 269•3 mi. SW on Forest Rd. 250 | 5/22-9/6 | 12 | 30′ | .• | • | | • | | • | 14 | |
| **257•Quartz Flat FS**<br>11 mi. E of Superior near I-90 at rest area | 5/10-9/30 | 52 | 40′ | D | • | | • | | • | 14 | • |
| **258•Big Pine FWP**<br>18 mi. E of Superior on I-90 to Fish Creek EXit•5 mi. SW on Cty. Rd. | All Year | 10 | • | • | | | • | | | 7 | |
| **259•Holland Lake FS**<br>9 mi. SE of Condon on MT 83•3 mi. E on Forest Rd. 44 (Holland Lake Rd.) | 5/15-10/1 | 40 | 50′ | 0 | 0 | C | • | • | • | 14 | • |
| **260•Lake Alva FS**<br>12 mi. N of Seeley Lake on MT 83 | 5/15-9/30 | 43 | 22′ | D | • | C | • | • | | 14 | • |
| **261•Seeley Lake FS**<br>.3 mi. S of Seeley Lake on MT 83•3.3 mi. NW on Boy Scout Rd. | 5/22-9/5 | 29 | 32′ | D | • | C | • | • | • | 14 | • |
| **262•Big Larch FS**<br>1 mi. N of Seeley Lake MT 83•.5 mi. on Forest Rd. 2199 | 5/15-9/30 | 50 | 32′ | D | • | C | • | • | • | 14 | • |
| **263•River Point FS**<br>.3 mi. S of Seeley Lake on Mt 83•2.2 mi NW on Boy Scout Rd. | 6/25-9/5 | 26 | 22′ | D | • | | • | • | | 14 | • |
| **264•Placid Lake FWP**<br>3 mi. S of Seeley Lake on MT 83•3 mi. W on Cty. Rd. | 5/1-11/30 | 40 | • | D | • | C | • | • | | 14 | • |
| **265•Salmon Lake FWP**<br>5 mi. S of Seeley Lake on MT 83 | 5/1-11/30 | 20 | • | D | • | C | • | • | N | 14 | |
| **266•Russell Gates Memorial FWP**<br>35 mi. E of Bonner on MT 200 to Milepost 35 | All Year | 12 | • | D | • | A | • | | | 7 | • |
| **267•Big Nelson FS**<br>8 mi. E of Ovando on MT 200•11 mi. NE on Forest Rd. 500 | 6/15-9/15 | 4 | 16′ | • | | A | • | | • | 14 | |
| **268•Copper Creek FS**<br>6.5 mi. E of Lincoln on MT 200•8 mi. NW on Forest Rd. 330• | 5/24-9/1 | 20 | • | • | • | | • | | • | 14 | • |
| **269•Aspen Grove FS**<br>7 mi. E of Lincoln on MT 200•Group Reservations 362-4265 | 5/29-10/15 | 20 | • | • | • | | • | | • | 14 | • |
| **270•Hooper Park**<br>In Lincoln on MT 200 | 4/1-10/31 | 15 | 25′ | D | • | | | | • | | • |

**Agency**
FS—U.S.D.A Forest Service
FWP—Montana Fish, Wildlife & Parks
NPS—National Park Service
BLM—U.S. Bureau of Land Management
USBR—U.S. Bureau of Reclamation
CE—Corps of Engineers

**Camping**
Camping is allowed at this site. Number indicates camping spaces available
H—Hard sided units only; no tents

**Trailers**
Trailer units allowed. Number indicates maximum length.

**Toilets**
Toilets on site. D—Disabled access

**Water**
Drinkable water on site

**Fishing**
Visitors may fish on site

**Boat**
Type of boat ramp on site:
A—Hand launch
B—4-wheel drive with trailer
C—2-wheel drive with trailer

**Swimming**
Designated swimming areas on site

**Trails**
Trails on site
B—Backpacking N—Nature/Interpretive

**Stay Limit**
Maximum length of stay in days

**Fee**
Camping and/or day-use fee

**Section 13**

## Notes:

## Dining Quick Reference

Price Range refers to the average cost of a meal per person: ($) $1-$6, ($$) $7-$11, ($$$) $12-up. Cocktails: "Yes" indicates full bar; Beer (B)/Wine (W), Service: Breakfast (B), Brunch (BR), Lunch (L), Dinner (D). Businesses in bold print will have additional information under the appropriate map locator number in the body of this section.

| RESTAURANT | TYPE CUISINE | PRICE RANGE | CHILD MENU | COCKTAILS BEER WINE | SERVICE | CREDIT CARDS | MAP LOCATOR NUMBER |
|---|---|---|---|---|---|---|---|
| Burger King | Fast Food | $ | Yes | | B/L/D | | 2 |
| Finnegan's Family Restaurant | Family | $ | Yes | | B/L/D | Major | 2 |
| Little Caesar's | Pizza | $ | | | L/D | | 2 |
| McDonald's | Fast Food | $ | Yes | | B/L/D | | 2 |
| Pizza Hut | Pizza | $/$$ | Yes | B | L/D | V/M/D | 2 |
| Press Box Restaurant Casino | American | $ | | Yes | B/L/D | Major | 2 |
| Quizno's Classic Subs | Subs | $ | Yes | | L/D | | 2 |
| Taco Bell | Fast Food | $ | Yes | | L/D | | 2 |
| Waterfront Pasta House | Italian | $$ | Yes | W/B | D | V/M/D | 2 |
| Del's Place | American | $ | Yes | | B/L/D | | 3 |
| Raven Cafe | Coffee House | $ | | | B/L/D | | 3 |
| Robin's Sandwich Shop | American | $ | | | L | | 3 |
| **Butterfly Herbs** | Coffee House | $ | | | L | Major | 4 |
| **Sean Kelly's, A Public House** | Pub Fare | $/$$ | | Yes | L/D | A/V/M | 4 |
| **Shadow's Keep Restaurant** | Casual Fine Dining | $$$ | Yes | Yes | D | Major | 4 |
| **MacKenzie River Pizza Co.** | Pizza | $/$$ | | B/W | L/D | Major | 4 |
| Red Bird | Fine Dining | $$/$$$ | | B/W | L/D | Major | 4 |
| Dinasour Cafe | American | $ | | Yes | L/D | V/M | 4 |
| Doc's Gourmet Sandwich Express | Deli | $ | | | L/D | | 4 |
| El Cazador | Mexican | $/$$ | Yes | B/W | L/D | V/M | 4 |
| Locos Burrito Bus | Mexican | $ | | | L/D | | 4 |
| Taco del Sol | Fast Food | $ | Yes | | L/D | | 4 |
| Uptown Diner | 50s Diner | $ | Yes | | B/L/D | V/M/D | 4 |
| Zimorino's Red Pies Over Montana | Italian | $$/$$$ | Yes | B/W | D | V/M | 4 |
| Hunter Bay Coffee Roasters | Coffee House | | | | | | 4 |
| Kadenas | Eclectic | $$ | | | L/D | V/M/D | 4 |
| Northwest Noodles 'n Wrap | Asian | $ | Yes | | L/D | V/M | 4 |
| Thai Spicy | Thai/Chinese | $/$$ | | | L/D | V/M | 4 |
| Oxford Cafe | American | $$ | | Yes | L/D | Major | 4 |
| Double Front Cafe | American | $$ | | | | | 4 |
| Break Expresso | Coffee House | | | | | | 4 |
| Two Sisters | Eclectic | $/$$ | | | B/L/D | Major | 4 |
| **Iron Horse Brew Pub** | American | $/$$ | Yes | Yes | L/D | A/V/M | 5 |
| **Zimorino's** | Pizza/Italian | $$ | Yes | B/W | L/D | Major | 5 |
| **Steelhead Grill** | Eclectic | $$/$$$ | | B/W | D | Major | 5 |
| **Sushi Hana** | Fine Japanese | $$/$$$ | Yes | Yes | L/D | A/V | 5 |
| **Old Post** | Pubfare | $$ | | Yes | L/D | V/M | 5 |
| **Worden's Deli** | Deli/Gourmet | $/$$ | Yes | Yes | | Major | 5 |
| Hong Kong Chef | Chinese | $$ | Yes | B/W | L/D | V/M | 5 |
| Depot Restaurant & Bar | American | $$ | | Yes | | Major | 5 |
| Pagoda Chinese Food | Chinese | $/$$ | | | L/D | V/M | 5 |
| Subway | Fast Food | $ | Yes | | L/D | | 5 |
| Bagels On Broadway | Deli | $ | | | B/L | | 6 |
| Black Dog Cafe | Vegetarian | $/$$ | | B/W | L/D | | 6 |
| Casa Pablo's | Mexican | $/$$ | | Yes | L/D | V/M | 6 |
| Sawaddee Thai Restaurant | Thai | $$ | | | L/D | Major | 6 |
| Salad Bar & Sandwich Company | Deli | $ | | | B/L | | 6 |
| Taco John's | Fast Food | $ | Yes | | L/D | | 6 |
| **Chinook Restaurant** | French | $$$ | | B/W | D | Major | 7 |
| Pizza Pipeliine | Pizza | $/$$ | Yes | | L/D | | 8 |
| Second Thought News & Deli | Deli | $ | | | B/L/D | V/M | 8 |
| Tipu's Tiger | East-Indian | $/$$ | | | L/D | Major | 8 |
| **Valentino's** | Italian/Greek | $$ | | B/W | L/D | Major | 9 |
| Little Caesar's | Pizza | $ | | | L/D | | 9 |
| Montana Club | Steakhouse | $$ | Yes | Yes | B/L/D | Major | 9 |
| Papa John's Pizza | Pizza | $ | Yes | | L/D | | 9 |
| Paul's Pancake Parlor & Cafe | American | $$/$$$ | Yes | | B/L/D | Major | 9 |
| Ruby's Cafe | American | $ | Yes | | B/L/D | | 9 |
| Squire's Olde English Pub | Sandwiches | $$ | | Yes | L/D | Major | 9 |
| Subway | Fast Food | $ | Yes | | L/D | | 9 |
| Taco Time | Fast Food | $ | Yes | | L/D | | 9 |

## Dining Quick Reference-Continued

Price Range refers to the average cost of a meal per person: ($) $1-$6, ($$) $7-$11, ($$$) $12-up. Cocktails: "Yes" indicates full bar; Beer (B)/Wine (W), Service: Breakfast (B), Brunch (BR), Lunch (L), Dinner (D). Businesses in bold print will have additional information under the appropriate map locator number in the body of this section.

| RESTAURANT | TYPE CUISINE | PRICE RANGE | CHILD MENU | COCKTAILS BEER WINE | SERVICE | CREDIT CARDS | MAP LOCATOR NUMBER |
|---|---|---|---|---|---|---|---|
| The Bangkok | Thai | $$ | | | L/D | | 9 |
| Torrey's Home Cooking | Family | $ | | | L/D | | 9 |
| Trenary's Irish Pub | Family | $/$$ | Yes | B/W | B/L/D | Major | 9 |
| **The Mustard Seed** | Asian | $$ | Yes | Yes | L/D | Major | 10 |
| Bob's Pizza Plus | Fast Food | $ | Yes | | L/D | | 10 |
| Caffe Dolce | Coffee/Italian | $ | | | L/D | | 10 |
| Country Harvest Buffet | Buffet | $ | Yes | | B/L/D | V/M | 10 |
| Dairy Queen | Fast Food | $ | Yes | | L/D | | 10 |
| El Matador Mexican Restaurant | Mexican | $–$$$ | Yes | Yes | L/D | Major | 10 |
| Greek Gyros | Greek | $ | | | L/D | | 10 |
| Hoagieville | Fast Food | $ | | | L/D | | 10 |
| Noodle Express | Asian | $ | | | L/D | | 10 |
| Orange Julius | Fast Food | $ | Yes | | B/L/D | | 10 |
| Southgate Grill | American | $$/$$$ | | Yes | B/L/D | Major | 10 |
| 93 Drive Thru | Fast Food | $ | Yes | | L/D | | 10 |
| Burger King | Fast Food | $ | Yes | | B/L/D | | 10 |
| China Garden Restaurant | Chinese | $$ | | | L/D | V/M | 10 |
| Dairy Queen | Fast Food | $ | Yes | | L/D | | 10 |
| Hardee's | Fast Food | $ | Yes | | B/L/D | | 10 |
| **Mongos Mongolian Grill** | Asian Grill | $/$$ | Yes | W/B | L/D | Major | 11 |
| Arby's | Fast Food | $ | Yes | | B/L/D | | 11 |
| Deano's Restaurant | Pizza/Subs | $/$$ | | | L/D | V/M | 11 |
| Diamond Jim's | American | $ | | Yes | L/D | | 11 |
| Honey Teriyaki Express | Fast Food | $ | | | L/D | | 11 |
| Jaker's Steak Ribs & Fish House | Steak/Seafood | $$ | | Yes | L/D | Major | 11 |
| Joey's Seafood Restaurant | Family | $-$$$ | | | B/L | Major | 11 |
| McDonald's | Fast Food | $ | Yes | | B/L/D | | 11 |
| Mustang Sally's Grill | American | $$ | | Yes | L/D | Major | 11 |
| Paradise Falls | Family | $$ | Yes | Yes | B/L/D | Major | 11 |
| Sizzler | Steakhouse | $/$$ | Yes | | L/D | Major | 11 |
| Taco Bell | Fast Food | $ | Yes | | L/D | | 11 |
| Tower Pizza | Pizza | $ | | | L/D | | 11 |
| Village Inn Pizza | Pizza | $/$$ | Yes | B | L/D | V/M | 11 |
| Wendy's | Fast Food | $ | Yes | | L/D | | 11 |
| Lisa's Pasty Pantry | Regional | $$ | Yes | | L/D | Major | 11 |
| Rosa's Pizza | Pizza | $ | | | L/D | V/M | 11 |
| Viva Mexico | Mexican | $$ | | B/W | L/D | V/M | 11 |
| 4B's Restaurant | Family | $ | Yes | | B/L/D | V/M/D | 12 |
| Applebee's Neighborhood Grill | Eclectic | $$/$$$ | Yes | Yes | L/D | Major | 12 |
| Golden Corral | Steakhouse | $$ | Yes | | L/D | Major | 12 |
| Pizza Hut | Pizza | $/$$ | Yes | B | L/D | V/M/D | 12 |
| Zimorino's Red Pies Too | Italian | $$/$$$ | Yes | B/W | D | V/M | 12 |
| Reserve St. Drive-Inn | Fast Food | $ | Yes | | L/D | | 13 |
| Taco John's | Fast Food | $ | Yes | | L/D | | 13 |
| **Perugia Restaurant & Gallery** | Old World Cooking | $$/$$$ | | Yes | D | Major | 14 |
| Big Sky Drive In | Fast Food | $ | | | L/D | | 14 |
| Cruise In | Fast Food | $ | | | L/D | | 14 |
| Hoagieville | Fast Food | $ | | | L/D | | 14 |
| Limelight Restaurant | American | $$/$$$ | | Yes | | Major | 14 |
| McDonalds | Fast Food | $ | Yes | | B/L/D | | 14 |
| Prime Time Grill | Steakhouse | $/$$ | Yes | Yes | B/L/D | Major | 14 |
| Rocky Mountain Grill | American | $/$$ | | Yes | B/L/D | Major | 14 |
| Subway | Fast Food | $ | Yes | | L/D | | 14 |
| **Perkins Family Restaurant** | Family | $/$$ | Yes | | B/L/D | Major | 15 |
| **Sushi Hana** | Japanese Cuisine | $$/$$$ | Yes | W/B | L/D | A/V/M | 15 |
| **Ambrosia Greek Food** | Ambrosia | $$/$$$ | | | L/D | V/M | 15 |
| Arby's | Fast Food | $ | Yes | | B/L/D | | 15 |
| Burger King | Fast Food | $ | Yes | | B/L/D | | 15 |
| China Bowl | Chinese | $/$$ | | | L/D | V/M | 15 |
| Fuddruckers | American | $-$$ | Yes | Yes | L/D | Major | 15 |
| Granny's Buffet | Buffet | $ | Yes | | L/D/BR | V/M | 15 |

## Dining Quick Reference-Continued

Price Range refers to the average cost of a meal per person: ($) $1-$6, ($$) $7-$11, ($$$) $12-up. Cocktails: "Yes" indicates full bar; Beer (B)/Wine (W), Service: Breakfast (B), Brunch (BR), Lunch (L), Dinner (D). Businesses in bold print will have additional information under the appropriate map locator number in the body of this section.

| RESTAURANT | TYPE CUISINE | PRICE RANGE | CHILD MENU | COCKTAILS BEER WINE | SERVICE | CREDIT CARDS | MAP LOCATOR NUMBER |
|---|---|---|---|---|---|---|---|
| Pizza Hut | Pizza | $/$$ | Yes | B | L/D | V/M/D | 15 |
| Taco Bell | Fast Food | $ | Yes | | L/D | | 15 |
| Vietnam Noodle Express | Vietnamese | $$ | | | L/D | V/M | 15 |
| Wendy's | Fast Food | $ | Yes | | L/D | | 15 |
| **MacKenzie River Pizza Co./ Rowdy's Cabin** | Pizza | $/$$ | | B/W | L/D | Major | 16 |
| 4B's Restaurant | Family | $ | Yes | | B/L/D | V/M/D | 16 |
| Cracker Barrel | Family | $ | Yes | | B/L/D | V/M | 16 |
| Four B'S Restaurant | Family | $-$$ | Yes | | B/L/D | Major | 16 |
| Jokers Wild Bar & Restaurant | American | $$ | | Bar | L/D | | 16 |
| McDonald's | Fast Food | $ | Yes | | B/L/D | | 16 |
| Taco Time | Fast Food | $ | Yes | | L/D | | 16 |
| Muralt's Travel Plaza Conoco | Family | $$ | Yes | | B/L/D | Major | 16 |
| **Shadow's Keep** | Casual Fine Dining | $$/$$$ | Yes | W/B | L/D | V/M | 17 |
| Outback | Steakhouse | $$/$$$ | Yes | yes | L/D | Major | 17 |
| Friends | Deli | $/$$ | | | L/D | V/M | 19 |
| Grant Creek Deli | Deli | $/$$ | | | L/D | V/M | 17 |
| Hoagieville | fast food | $ | | | L/D | | 17 |
| Alcan Cafe | American | $$ | | yes | B/L/D | V/M | 17 |
| Silvertip Restaurant | American | $$ | | yes | L/D | V/M | 19 |
| King Ranch Restaurant | American | $$/$$$ | | Yes | L/D | Major | 19 |
| Sidetrack Cafe | Family | $ | Yes | | B/L/D | | 20 |
| Nine Mile House | Steaks & Seafood | $$ | Yes | Yes | L/D | V/M | 20 |
| Four Aces Cafe | Family | $ | Yes | Yes | B/L/D | Major | 22 |
| Lozeau Stagecoach | American | $ | | Yes | L/D | V/M | 22 |
| Sullivan's Rock'n Roll Rodeo | Family | $ | Yes | B/W | L/D | Major | 22 |
| Durango's Restaurant | Family | $ | Yes | Yes | B/L/D | Major | 22 |
| **Jasper's Restaurant** | Family | $ | Yes | Yes | B/L/D | Major | 23 |
| Frosty's Drive In | Fast Food | $ | Yes | | L/D | V/M/A | 23 |
| OK Cafe & Casino | American | $$ | | Yes | L/D | V/M | 23 |
| St Regis Travel Center | Family | $ | Yes | B/W | B/L/D | Major | 23 |
| St. Regis Exxon Express | Pizza | $ | | | L/D | Major | 23 |
| Pinecrest Lodge Restaurant | Family | $$ | | Yes | B/L/D | V/M | 24 |
| Lincoln's Silver Dollar Restaurant | Family | $/$$ | Yes | Yes | B/L/D | Major | 25 |
| Buck Snort Restaurant | American | $$ | | Yes | L/D | Major | 26 |
| **Buddy G'S Family Diner, Casino & Gas Station** | Family | $$ | Yes | Yes | B/L/D | Major | 27 |
| **Creekside B&B - Sheep Ranch Inn** | American | $$/$$$ | Yes | Yes | D | Major | 27 |
| Riverside Bar & Grille | American | $$ | | Yes | L/D | | 27 |
| **Bison Inn Cafe & Gift Shop** | Family | $ | | B/W | B/L/D | V/M | 28 |
| 4-Star Bar/Morigeau Restaurant | American | $$ | | Yes | L/D | Major | 28 |
| The Buffalo Grill | Burgers | $ | Yes | Yes | L/D | | 28 |
| Pair-a-Dice Bar | Steakhouse | $$ | | Yes | L/D | | 30 |
| Hilltop Cafe | Family | $ | | | B/L/D | | 30 |
| The Circle | Family | $ | Yes | | B/L/D | | 30 |
| Wild Horse Plains Club | American | $ | | Yes | L/D | | 30 |
| Benji's Restaurant | Fine Dining | $$ | Yes | | B/L/D | V/M | 30 |
| Cold Creek Cafe | Eclectic/Family | $ | Yes | | B/L | | 31 |
| Silver Dollar Bar & Grill | Steakhouse | $$$ | | Yes | D | Major | 31 |
| Malt Shop | American | $ | | | L/D | | 31 |
| 44 Bar & Cafe | American | $/$$ | | Yes | L/D | V/M/D | 31 |
| **Ranch House Restaurant** | Family | $/$$ | Yes | | B/L/D | V/M | 32 |
| Dairy Queen | Fast Food | $ | Yes | | L/D | | 32 |
| Lynn's Drive In | Fast Food | $ | | | L/D | | 32 |
| McDonald's | Fast Food | $ | Yes | | B/L/D | | 32 |
| Murph's Restaurant | Family | $/$$ | | | L/D | | 32 |
| Seven Acres Restaurant | American/Chinese | $ | | | L/D | | 32 |
| Stageline Pizza | Pizza | $/$$ | | | L/D | | 32 |
| Subway | Fast Food | $ | Yes | | L/D | | 32 |
| Trapper's Food Emporium | Family | $ | | | L/D | | 32 |
| Countryside Cafe | American | $$ | | Yes | L/D | Major | 32 |
| Connie's Countryside Cafe | Family | $ | Yes | | B/L/D | | 32 |
| Time Out Drive In | Fast Food | $ | | | L/D | | 32 |

## Dining Quick Reference-Continued

Price Range refers to the average cost of a meal per person: ($) $1-$6, ($$) $7-$11, ($$$) $12-up. Cocktails: "Yes" indicates full bar; Beer (B)/Wine (W), Service: Breakfast (B), Brunch (BR), Lunch (L), Dinner (D). Businesses in bold print will have additional information under the appropriate map locator number in the body of this section.

| RESTAURANT | TYPE CUISINE | PRICE RANGE | CHILD MENU | COCKTAILS BEER WINE | SERVICE | CREDIT CARDS | MAP LOCATOR NUMBER |
|---|---|---|---|---|---|---|---|
| Ninepipes Lodge, Restaurant, & Trading Post | Continental | $-$$$ | Yes | Yes | B/L/D | Major | 32 |
| Bootlegger Inn | American | $ | | Yes | B/L | | 33 |
| Lambkin's Restaurant | Family | $ | | Yes | B/L/D | V/M/D | 33 |
| Rainbow Cafe | Home Cooking | $ | | | B/L/D | | 33 |
| Scapegoat Eatery | American | $ | | Yes | L/D | | 33 |
| Stonewall Steakhouse & Bar | Steakhouse | $$/$$$ | Yes | Yes | D | Major | 33 |
| Subway | Fast Food | $ | Yes | | L/D | | 33 |
| The Lincoln Pit Stop & Pizza Parlor | Family | $ | Yes | | L/D | | 33 |
| The Lost Woodsman | Coffee House/Cafe | $ | | B/W | B/L/D | Major | 33 |
| The Wheel Inn | American | $ | Yes | Yes | L/D | | 33 |
| Hotel Lincoln | Fine Dining | $$ | | Yes | D | Major | 33 |
| Seven-Up Ranch Supper Club | Steakhouse | $$$ | Yes | Yes | D | Major | 33 |
| Trixi's Antler Saloon | American | $$ | | Yes | B/L/D | | 35 |
| Stoney's Kwik-Stop | Fast Food | $ | | Yes | B/L/D | V/M/D | 37 |
| **Lindey's Prime Steakhouse** | Steakhouse | $$$ | | Yes | D | | 39 |
| **The Filling Station** | Family | $$ | | Yes | B/L/D | | 39 |
| **Double Arrow Resort** | Fine Dining | $$$ | Yes | Yes | B/D/BR | V/M/D | 39 |
| **The Stage Station** | Coffee House | $ | | | B/L | Major | 39 |
| Chicken Coop & Lounge | American | $/$$ | | | | | 39 |
| Elkhorn Cafe | American | $/$$ | | | B/L/D | V/M | 39 |
| Hot Stuff Pizza/Smash Hit Subs | Fast Food | $ | Yes | | B/L/D | | 39 |
| Pop's Family Restaurant | family | $/$$ | Yes | | B/L/D | | 39 |
| Wild Horse Grill | American | $ | | Yes | L/D | | 39 |
| One Stop Convenience Center | American | $ | | Yes | L/D | | 39 |

**NOTES:**

## Motel Quick Reference

Price Range: ($) Under $40 ; ($$) $40-$60; ($$$) $60-$80, ($$$$) Over $80. Pets [check with the motel for specific policies] (P), Dining (D), Lounge (L), Disabled Access (DA), Full Breakfast (FB), Cont. Breakfast (CB), Indoor Pool (IP), Outdoor Pool (OP), Hot Tub (HT), Sauna (S), Refrigerator (R), Microwave (M) (Microwave and Refrigerator indicated only if in majority of rooms), Kitchenette (K). All Montana area codes are 406.

| HOTEL | PHONE | NUMBER ROOMS | PRICE RANGE | BREAKFAST | POOL/ HOT TUB SAUNA | NON SMOKE ROOMS | OTHER AMENITIES | CREDIT CARDS | MAP LOCATOR NUMBER |
|---|---|---|---|---|---|---|---|---|---|
| **Holiday Inn Express Hotel Riverside** | 549-7600 | 95 | $$$ | CB | | Yes | R/DA | Major | 2 |
| **Thunderbird Motel** | 543-7251 | 31 | $$$ | CB | IP/HT | Yes | R/CB/DA | Major | 2 |
| **Creekside Inn** | 549-2387 | 54 | $$ | | OP | Yes | P/K/R | Major | 2 |
| Campus Inn | 549-5134 | 82 | $ | CB | OP/HT | Yes | P/R/DA | Major | 2 |
| Hubbard's Ponderosa Lodge | 543-3102 | 40 | $$ | | | Yes | | Major | 2 |
| **Doubletree** | 728-3100 | 100 | $$$$ | | OP | Yes | P/D/L/DA | Major | 3 |
| **City Center Motel** | 543-3193 | 15 | $ | | | Yes | M/R | Major | 3 |
| Downtown Motel | 549-5191 | 22 | $ | | | Yes | M/R | V/M | 3 |
| **Uptown Motel** | 549-5141 | 13 | $ | | | Yes | P/M/R | Major | 4 |
| **Holiday Inn Parkside** | 721-8550 | 200 | $$$$ | | IP | Yes | R/L/D | Major | 4 |
| Best Western Executive Motor Inn | 543-7221 | 51 | $$/$$$ | | OP | Yes | P | Major | 4 |
| Orange Street Inn | 721-3610 | 81 | $$ | CB | | Yes | DA | Major | 5 |
| **Inn on Broadway** | 543-7231 | 79 | $-$$ | | OP | Yes | P/M/R/L/DA | Major | 6 |
| **Red Lion Inn** | 728-3300 | 76 | $$–$$$$ | CB | OP/HT | Yes | P/DA | Major | 6 |
| **Travelodge** | 728-4500 | 60 | $$ | | | Yes | R/M/R/DA | Major | 6 |
| **Val-U Inn** | 721-9600 | 84 | $$$ | | HT | Yes | | Major | 11 |
| Brooks St. Motor Inn | 549-5115 | 61 | $/$$ | CB | | Yes | P/R/DA | Major | 11 |
| Southgate Inn | 251-2250 | 81 | $$/$$$ | CB | OP/HT/S | Yes | P/M/R/DA | Major | 11 |
| Sleep Inn of Missoula | 543-5883 | 59 | $$ | CB | IP/HT | Yes | P/DA | Major | 11 |
| **Super 8 Motel** | 251-2255 | 104 | $ | CB | | Yes | P/DA | Major | 12 |
| **Best Inn South** | 542-7550 | 91 | $$ | | HT | Yes | P/D/DA | Major | 12 |
| Brownies Plus Motel | 543-6614 | 25 | $ | | | Yes | P | Major | 14 |
| Super 7 Motel | 549-2358 | 45 | $ | | | Yes | K/P/R | Major | 14 |
| Economy 1 Motel | 549-2381 | 21 | $$ | | | | K/M | Major | 14 |
| Sleepy Inn | 549-6484 | 35 | $ | | | Yes | K/R | Major | 14 |
| **Super 8 Motel** | 549-0677 | 58 | $$ | CB | HT | Yes | DA | Major | 16 |
| **Best Western Grant Creek Inn** | 543-0700 | 126 | $$$/$$$$ | CB | IP/HT/S | Yes | P/R/DA | Major | 16 |
| **Best Inn North** | 542-7550 | 67 | $$ | | HT | Yes | R/M/R/DA | Major | 16 |
| **Comfort Inn** | 542-0888 | 52 | $$/$$$ | CB | IP/HT | Yes | P/M/R/DA | Major | 16 |
| **Hampton Inn** | 549-1800 | 60 | $$$ | CB | IP/HT | Yes | DA/P | Major | 16 |
| **Microtel Inn & Suites** | 543-0959 | 81 | $$ | FB | | Yes | DA | Major | 16 |
| **C'mon Inn** | 543-4600 | 119 | $$$ | CB | HT | Yes | R/M/K/DA | Major | 16 |
| Motel 6 | 549-7773 | 65 | $$ | | | Yes | DA/P | Major | 16 |
| Ruby's Reserve Inn | 721-0990 | 127 | $$$ | CB | IP/HT | Yes | D/DA/P | Major | 16 |
| Travelers Inn Motel | 728-8330 | 29 | $$ | CB | | Yes | P | Major | 16 |
| Days Inn | 721-9776 | 69 | $$ | | | Yes | P/D/L/DA | Major | 16 |
| Redwood Lodge | 721-2110 | 41 | $$ | CB | HT | Yes | P/DA | Major | 16 |
| River Edge Motel | 722-4418 | 10 | $$ | CB | HT | Yes | P/D | Major | 20 |
| Bellevue Hotel-Motel | 822-4692 | 22 | $ | | | Yes | P | V/M | 22 |
| Budget Host Inn | 822-4831 | 24 | $$ | CB | | Yes | P | Major | 22 |
| Hilltop Motel | 822-4781 | 13 | $ | | | Yes | K/P/R | Major | 22 |
| St. Regis Camp Motel | 649-2428 | 14 | $ | | | Yes | K/P/R | V/M | 23 |
| Super 8 Motel | 649-2422 | 53 | $$ | | HT | Yes | K/P/DA | Major | 23 |
| Little River Motel | 649-2713 | 12 | $$ | | | Yes | K/P | Major | 23 |
| Black Diamond Guest Ranch | 678-4000 | 4 | $$ | | | | K/DA | | 24 |
| Hotel Albert B&B | 678-4303 | | | FB | | | | | 24 |
| Lincoln Silver Dollar | 678-4271 | 40 | $$$ | | Ht | Yes | P/D/L/DA | Major | 25 |
| Mangold's General Store & Motel | 678-4328 | 6 | $ | | | Yes | K/P/DA | | 25 |
| **Creekside B&B - Sheep Ranch Inn** | 726-3332 | | | CB | | | | | 27 |
| **Crossroads Motel & RV Park** | 826-3623 | 13 | $$ | | | Yes | P/M/R/AD | Major | 30 |
| Benji's | 826-5662 | 2 | $ | | | Yes | D | V/M | 30 |
| Tops Motel | 826-3412 | 9 | $ | | | | P/R/DA | Major | 30 |
| **Lodge Pole Motel** | 745-2951 | 7 | $ | | | | K/R/L | Major | 31 |
| **Stonehart Inn B&B** | 745-4999 | | | | | | | | 31 |
| Sunset Motel | 745-3900 | 10 | $ | | | Yes | P | Major | 31 |
| **Starlite Motel** | 676-7000 | 15 | $$ | | | Yes | P/M/R | Major | 32 |
| Ninepipes Lodge, Restaurant, & Trading Post | 644-2588 | 25 | $$$ | | | Yes | L/D | Major | 32 |
| **Blue Sky Motel** | 362-4450 | 9 | $ | | | Yes | K/P/M/R/DA | Major | 33 |
| **Snowie Pines Inn** | 362-4481 | 9 | $/$$ | | | Yes | P/M/R | Major | 33 |
| Hotel Lincoln | 362-4396 | 16 | $$ | CB | | Yes | P/D/L | Major | 33 |

## Motel Quick Reference-Continued

Price Range: ($) Under $40 ; ($$) $40-$60; ($$$) $60-$80, ($$$$) Over $80. Pets [check with the motel for specific policies] (P), Dining (D), Lounge (L), Disabled Access (DA), Full Breakfast (FB), Cont. Breakfast (CB), Indoor Pool (IP), Outdoor Pool (OP), Hot Tub (HT), Sauna (S), Refrigerator (R), Microwave (M) (Microwave and Refrigerator indicated only if in majority of rooms), Kitchenette (K). All Montana area codes are 406.

| HOTEL | PHONE | NUMBER ROOMS | PRICE RANGE | BREAKFAST | POOL/ HOT TUB SAUNA | NON SMOKE ROOMS | OTHER AMENITIES | CREDIT CARDS | MAP LOCATOR NUMBER |
|---|---|---|---|---|---|---|---|---|---|
| Seven-Up Ranch Supper Club | 362-4255 | 16 | $ | | | Yes | P/DA | Major | 33 |
| Leeper's Ponderosa Motel | 362-4333 | 15 | $ | CB | HT/S | Yes | K/P/M/R/DA | Major | 33 |
| The Roost | 362-4308 | 5 | $ | | | | K/P/R | | 33 |
| Three Bears Motel | 362-4355 | 15 | $ | | | Yes | K/P/R | Major | 33 |
| **Blackfoot Inn** | 793-5555 | | | FB | | | | | 35 |
| **Double Arrow Resort** | 677-2777 | 25 | $$$$ | CB | HT | Yes | K/D/L/DA | V/M/D | 39 |
| **The Stage Station** | 677-2227 | | | | | | | | 39 |
| **Seeley Lake Motor Lodge** | 677-2335 | 9 | $$ | | | Yes | K/M/R | Major | 39 |
| **Tamaracks Resort** | 677-2433 | 14 | $$$/$$$$ | | | Yes | K/M/R/DA | Major | 39 |
| **White Tail Guest Cabins** | 677-2024 | | | | | | | | 8 |
| Wilderness Gateway Inn | 677-2095 | 19 | $$ | | HT | Yes | | V/M/D | 39 |

## NOTES:

## Fishery

| Fishery | Brook Trout | Mt. Whitefish | Lake Whitefish | Golden Trout | Cutthroat Trout | Brown Trout | Rainbow Trout | Kokanee Salmon | Bull Trout | Lake Trout | Arctic Grayling | Burbot | Largemouth Bass | Smallmouth Bass | Walleye | Sauger | Northern Pike | Shovelnose Sturgeon | Channel Catfish | Yellow Perch | Crappie | Paddlefish | Vehicle Access | Campgrounds | Toilets | Docks | Boat Ramps | Motor Restrictions |
|---|---|---|---|---|---|---|---|---|---|---|---|---|---|---|---|---|---|---|---|---|---|---|---|---|---|---|---|---|
| | **Cold Water Species** | | | | | | | | | | | | **Warm Water Species** | | | | | | | | | | **Services** | | | | | |
| 305. Clark Fork alpine lakes | • | | | | • | | • | | | | | | | | | | | | | | | | | | | | | |
| 306. Fish Creek | • | • | | | • | • | • | | • | | | | | | | | | | | | | | • | • | • | | | |
| 307. Clark Fork River | | • | | | • | • | • | | • | | | | • | | | | • | | | | | | • | • | • | | • | |
| 308. Ninemile Creek | • | • | | | • | • | • | | | | | | | | | | | | | | | | • | | | | | |
| 309. Blackfoot River | • | • | | | • | • | • | | • | | | | | | | | | | | | | | • | • | • | | • | |
| 310. Harper's Lake | | | | | | | • | | | | | | | | | | | | | | | | • | • | • | | • | |
| 311. Salmon Lake | | • | | | • | • | • | • | • | | | | • | | | | | | | • | | | • | • | • | • | • | |
| 312. Placid Lake | | • | | | • | | • | • | • | | | | • | | | | | | | • | | | • | • | • | • | • | |
| 313. Rattlesnake Creek | | • | | | • | | | | • | | | | | | | | | | | | | | | | | | | |
| 314. Seeley Lake | | • | | | • | | • | • | • | | | | • | | | | | | | • | | | • | • | • | • | • | |
| 315. Lake Inez | | • | | | • | | | • | • | | | | • | | | | | | | • | | | • | • | • | | • | |
| 316. Lake Alva | | • | | | • | | | • | • | | | | • | | | | | | | • | | | • | • | • | | • | |
| 317. Rainy Lake | | • | | | • | | | | • | | | | | | | | | | | | | | | • | • | | | |
| 318. Mission Mtn. Wilderness lakes | • | | | • | • | | • | | | | | | | | | | | | | | | | | | | | | • |
| 319. Flathead River | | • | • | | • | | | | • | • | | | • | | | | • | | | | | | • | • | • | | • | |
| 320. South Fork Flathead River | | • | | | • | | | | • | | | | | | | | | | | | | | • | • | • | | • | • |
| 321. Cottonwood Creek | • | • | | | • | • | • | | | | | | | | | | | | | | | | | | | | | |
| 322. Upsata Lake | | | | | | | | | | | | | • | | | | | | | | | | | | | | | |
| 323. Coopers Lake | | | | | • | | | | | | | | | | | | | | | | | | • | • | • | | • | |
| 324. Blackfoot River | | • | | | • | • | • | | • | | | | | | | | | | | | | | • | • | • | | • | |
| 325. Browns Lake | | | | | | | • | | | | | | | | | | | | | | | | • | • | • | | • | |
| 326. Kicking Horse Reservoir | | | | | | | | | | | | • | | | | | | | • | | | • | | | | | | |
| 327. Ninepipe Reservoir | | | | | | | | | | | | • | | | | | | | • | | | • | | | | | | |

Section 13

**Notes:**

Section 13

# Section 14

## Flathead Lake and Glacier Park Area
## Including Kalispell, Whitefish, Bigfork and Polson

*Swan Lake*

## Weather Averages

**Kalispell**

| January | |
|---|---|
| Average High: | 28.2° F |
| Average Low: | 12.7° F |
| Record High : | 53.0° F |
| Record Low : | -38.0° F |
| Average Precip.: | 1.53 in |
| Rain/Snow Days: | |
| **April** | |
| Average High: | 55.2° F |
| Average Low: | 31.1° F |
| Record High : | 84.0° F |
| Record Low : | 10.0° F |
| Average Precip.: | 1.10 in |
| Rain/Snow Days: | 10 days |
| **July** | |
| Average High: | 80.1° F |
| Average Low: | 47.1° F |
| Record High : | 104.0° F |
| Record Low : | 31.0° F |
| Average Precip.: | 1.12 in |
| Rain/Snow Days: | 7 days |
| **October** | |
| Average High: | 54.4° F |
| Average Low: | 29.4° F |
| Record High : | 86.0° F |
| Record Low : | -3.0° F |
| Average Precip.: | 0.87 in |
| Rain/Snow Days: | 9 days |

**Big Mountain Ski Area**

| January | |
|---|---|
| Average High: | 28.3° F |
| Average Low: | 13.6° F |
| Average Precip.: | 1.41 in |
| **April** | |
| Average High: | 54.9° F |
| Average Low: | 32.1° F |
| Average Precip.: | 1.09 in |
| **July** | |
| Average High: | 81.1° F |
| Average Low: | 49.7° F |
| Average Precip.: | 1.12 in |
| **October** | |
| Average High: | 55.0° F |
| Average Low: | 31.7° F |
| Average Precip.: | 1.09 in |

**Hungry Horse Reservoir**

| January | |
|---|---|
| Average High: | 28.3° F |
| Average Low: | 13.6° F |
| Average Precip.: | 1.41 in |
| **April** | |
| Average High: | 54.9° F |
| Average Low: | 32.1° F |
| Average Precip.: | 1.09 in |
| **July** | |
| Average High: | 81.1° F |
| Average Low: | 49.7° F |
| Average Precip.: | 1.12 in |
| **October** | |
| Average High: | 55.0° F |
| Average Low: | 31.7° F |
| Average Precip.: | 1.09 in |

**Flathead Lake**

| January | |
|---|---|
| Average High: | 28.3° F |
| Average Low: | 13.6° F |
| Average Precip.: | 1.41 in |
| **April** | |
| Average High: | 54.9° F |
| Average Low: | 32.1° F |
| Average Precip.: | 1.09 in |
| **July** | |
| Average High: | 81.1° F |
| Average Low: | 49.7° F |
| Average Precip.: | 1.12 in |
| **October** | |
| Average High: | 55.0° F |
| Average Low: | 31.7° F |
| Average Precip.: | 1.09 in |

**Polson**

| January | |
|---|---|
| Average High: | 33.1° F |
| Average Low: | 17.1° F |
| Average Precip.: | 1.01 in |
| **April** | |
| Average High: | 58.7° F |
| Average Low: | 32.8° F |
| Average Precip.: | 1.45 in |
| **July** | |
| Average High: | 84.6° F |
| Average Low: | 49.5° F |
| Average Precip.: | 1.13 in |
| **October** | |
| Average High: | 58.5° F |
| Average Low: | 33.6° F |
| Average Precip.: | 1.17 in |

**1.** *Adventure, Gas, Food, Lodging, Camping*

### Babb

This town took its name from the district engineer in charge of the St. Mary's Irrigation Project. In 1912, the town became the headquarters for the Reclamation Service Project. This project diverted water from the St. Mary's River over the Hudson's Bay Divide to the Milk River. At one time, the Glacier Park Saddle Horse Company, five miles down the road, took as many as 10,000 people a year into Glacier Park on horseback. The business folded in 1942 when the park virtually shut down during World War II.

### St. Mary

There are many stories abouthow St. Mary was named. One of the more popular is the story of Father DeSmet, a jesuit priest, who was caught in a heavy fog coming off of Divide on the old Beaverslide trail. When the fog lifted, the first thing he saw was the face of St. Mary on the mountainside. He was able to use this as a landmark to help guide himself down to St. Mary Lake. The face of St. Mary appears in the rocks of Single Shot Mountain. The face can be best seen when looking at the mountain from about four miles north of St. Mary.

### Montana Trivia

Ten percent of grizzly bears in the northern Rockies die of natural causes. The other 90 percent are killed by humans. On average, only one human is killed each year by a grizzly.

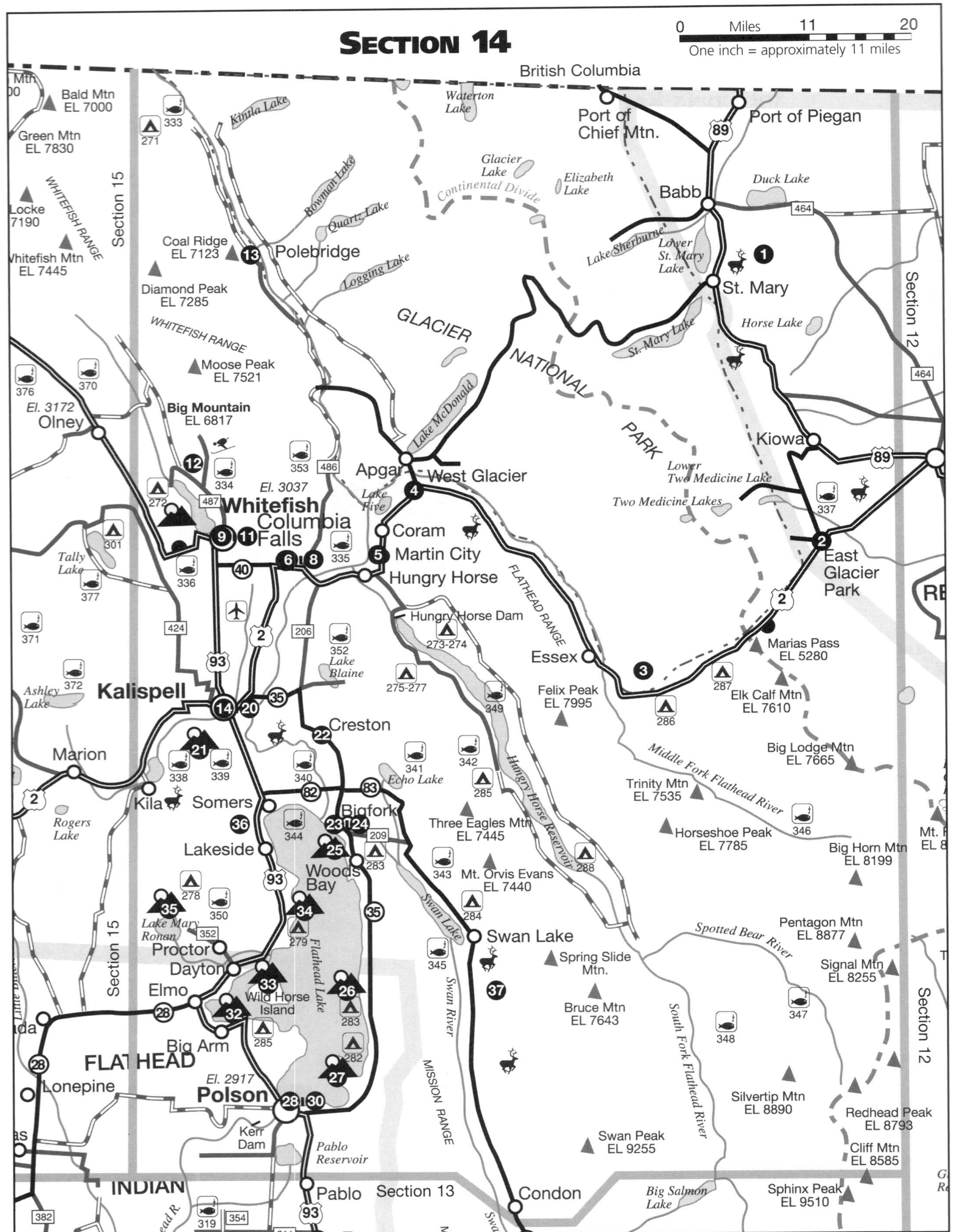
SECTION 14
0 Miles 11 20
One inch = approximately 11 miles
British Columbia
Port of Chief Mtn.
Port of Piegan
Waterton Lake
Kintla Lake
Bowman Lake
Quartz Lake
Polebridge
Logging Lake
Glacier Lake
Elizabeth Lake
Continental Divide
Duck Lake
Babb
Lake Sherburne
Lower St. Mary Lake
St. Mary
St. Mary Lake
Horse Lake
GLACIER NATIONAL PARK
Lake McDonald
Kiowa
Lower Two Medicine Lake
Two Medicine Lakes
East Glacier Park
Apgar
West Glacier
Lake Five
Coram
Martin City
Hungry Horse
Hungry Horse Dam
FLATHEAD RANGE
Essex
Marias Pass EL 5280
Elk Calf Mtn EL 7610
Felix Peak EL 7995
Big Lodge Mtn EL 7665
Middle Fork Flathead River
Trinity Mtn EL 7535
Horseshoe Peak EL 7785
Big Horn Mtn EL 8199
Bald Mtn EL 7000
Green Mtn EL 7830
Locke 7190
Whitefish Mtn EL 7445
WHITEFISH RANGE
Section 15
Coal Ridge EL 7123
Diamond Peak EL 7285
Moose Peak EL 7521
Big Mountain EL 6817
El. 3172
Olney
El. 3037
Whitefish
Columbia Falls
Tally Lake
Ashley Lake
Kalispell
Marion
Kila
Somers
Rogers Lake
Lakeside
Creston
Lake Blaine
Echo Lake
Bigfork
Three Eagles Mtn EL 7445
Hungry Horse Reservoir
Woods Bay
Mt. Orvis Evans EL 7440
Swan Lake
Lake Mary Ronan
Proctor
Dayton
Elmo
Wild Horse Island
Flathead Lake
Big Arm
FLATHEAD
Lonepine
El. 2917
Polson
Kerr Dam
Pablo Reservoir
Pablo
INDIAN
Section 13
Spring Slide Mtn.
Bruce Mtn EL 7643
Swan River
MISSION RANGE
South Fork Flathead River
Spotted Bear River
Pentagon Mtn EL 8877
Signal Mtn EL 8255
Silvertip Mtn EL 8890
Redhead Peak EL 8793
Swan Peak EL 9255
Cliff Mtn EL 8585
Big Salmon Lake
Sphinx Peak EL 9510
Condon
Section 12

All Montana Area Codes are 406

**Legend**

Locator number (matches numeric listing in section)

Wildlife viewing

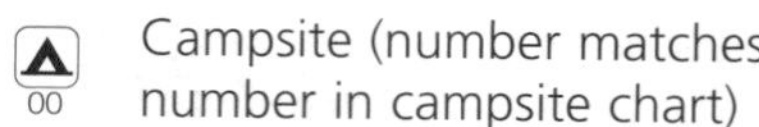
Campsite (number matches number in campsite chart)

State Park

Fishing Site (number matches number in fishing chart)

Rest stop

Interstate

us Highway

State Highway

County Road

Gravel/unpaved road

### VL Montana Ranch Adventures, Cabins and Trailrides

us Hwy. 464, Noffsinger Road, Duck Lake, St. Mary. 338-3333 or toll free 888-338-3054, www.montanaranchadventures.com

### F Babb Bar Cattle Baron Supper Club

Hwy. 89, Babb. 732-4033. www.babbbarcattlebaron.com

The Babb Bar Cattle Baron Supper Club is a part of Glacier Country history. Once famous as the second rowdiest bar in the country, now, known worldwide for the size and the flavor of its steaks. A secret sauce is the key ingredient and the reason people proclaim it as the best steak ever. The menu includes other delicious entrées such as lobster, chicken, and lamb. People actually fly into a small runway in Babb just to dine at the Cattle Baron. The Native American art collection displayed in this large building is another fascinating element. You will also learn the story of the Blackfeet Indians during your visit. A second Cattle Baron is now open in Shelby, Montana at the Sports Club Cattle Baron, where the same great menu is served. Reservations are recommended.

### F BNC Taco Shack

MT Hwy. 89 S., St. Mary. 732-9202

The BNC Taco Shack is home of the "Big Fat Burrito." You'll also enjoy their sandwiches, pasta, soup, and specials of the day. Vegetarians and vegans welcomed. They are located next to the east

*BNC Taco Shack*

entrance to Glacier National Park with beautiful patio dining surrounded by shady trees. Everyone will appreciate their quick service and reasonable prices. They'll even pack your lunch for all those day hikes. Recipes are made from scratch by native New Mexicans. Only green chile from Hatch, New Mexico is served. For a great experience, try the Salsa #17 caliente! A locals' favorite.

### FLC Johnson's of St. Mary Restaurant, Campground, and Bed & Breakfast

Hwy. 89,Star Route, St. Mary. 732-5565. www.johnsonsofstmary.com

Johnson's of St. Mary is more than just a world famous restaurant, campground and B&B— it's been a Montana tradition for over 50 years and it's in walking distance of Glacier Park. Johnson's is famous for their family style meals that include homemade soups, and lots of fresh bread and pies which are made daily. The large full service campground with fantastic views include a view of both upper and lower St. Mary lakes. Additionally, they offer shuttle buses, camping cabins, Internet access, showers, laundromat, and a gift shop. Your stay at Johnson's will leave you with wonderful Montana memories. If you're very lucky and call early you may get to spend the night in the Johnson Bed and Breakfast.

### FC Two Sisters

4 miles north of St. Mary on us 89 near Babb. 732-5535, napigirl@in-tch.com

Located north of the eastern entry to Glacier National Park, this colorful treasure really is owned by Two Sisters—Beth and Susan Higgins. With an eye-catching exterior of bright colors and abstract figures, it's hard to miss on us 89 from St Mary to Many Glacier. Famous for their Map of America in license plates, the Sisters are also celebrated for their homemade desserts and pies. The Cafe has full bar service available, with great fresh lime or berry Margaritas, a good wine list, and Montana Microbrews. Serving terrific hand crafted American fare for breakfast, lunch, and dinner, they can accommodate large parties of up to thirty people. Check out their second location in downtown Missoula!

### L Glacier Trailhead Cabins

Hwy. 89,2.5 miles N. of St. Mary, Babb. 732-4143 or 800-311-1041. www.glaciertrailheadcabins.com

Glacier Trailhead Cabins provide four-season log cabin accommodations, just north of St. Mary, near the eastern entrance to Glacier National Park. The cabins are in private wooded settings with spectacular views of the surrounding mountains. They are quiet, simple, and very comfortable, with modern bathrooms, microwaves, small refrigerators, and covered porches. There is a common fire pit, barbeque area, and picnic tables, and no television by popular demand. The perfect "home base" for hiking, fishing, wildlife photography, sightseeing, family reunions, or business retreats. The hosts are available, yet unobtrusive, and their goal is to make you feel comfortable and settled while providing lodging that is affordable and different from the ordinary.

### L Red Eagle Motel

Hwy. 89, Star Route, North End of St. Mary. 732-4453. www.redeaglemotel.com

### LC Chief Mountain Junction

Junction Hwy. 17 & 89, 5 miles north of Babb. 732-9253

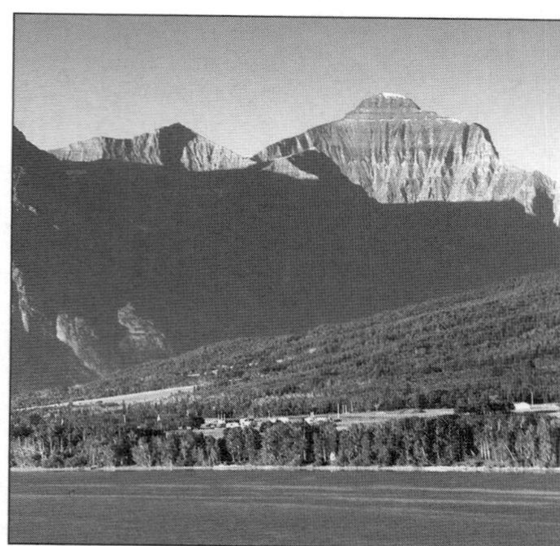

### C St Mary - Glacier Park KOA Campground

106 West Shore, St. Mary. 732-4122 or toll free 800-562-1504. www.goglacier.com

Experience camping as never before at St. Mary-Glacier Park KOA in the heart of Glacier country. Fresh mountain air, natural wonders, exhilarating views and first-class camping accommodations are available here. Centrally located near Waterton Park, West Glacier, East Glacier, Going-to-the-Sun Road, with direct access to St. Mary Lake. There are over 200 grassy, wooded tent sites and full-service RV sites, clean rest rooms and hot showers, laundry facilities, scenic outdoor hot tubs, game room, and children's playground. You can also choose to stay in their Kamping Kabin, or deluxe Kamping Kottage. Additional conveniences include an espresso, pizza, ice cream, grocery store, gift shop, and U-Save Auto Rentals. See information and photos on their web site.

### C Glacier Entrance Campground & Go Karts

Hwy. 89 S., St Mary. 732-4616

### S Mountain Chief Trading Post

Star Route, 1 mile north of St. Mary. 732-9242

## 2. *Gas, Food, Lodging, Camping*

### East Glacier

East Glacier is a recreational center serving as the eastern gateway to Glacier National Park. Scenic boat cruises operate on park lakes including one launch trip that takes you across Two Medicine

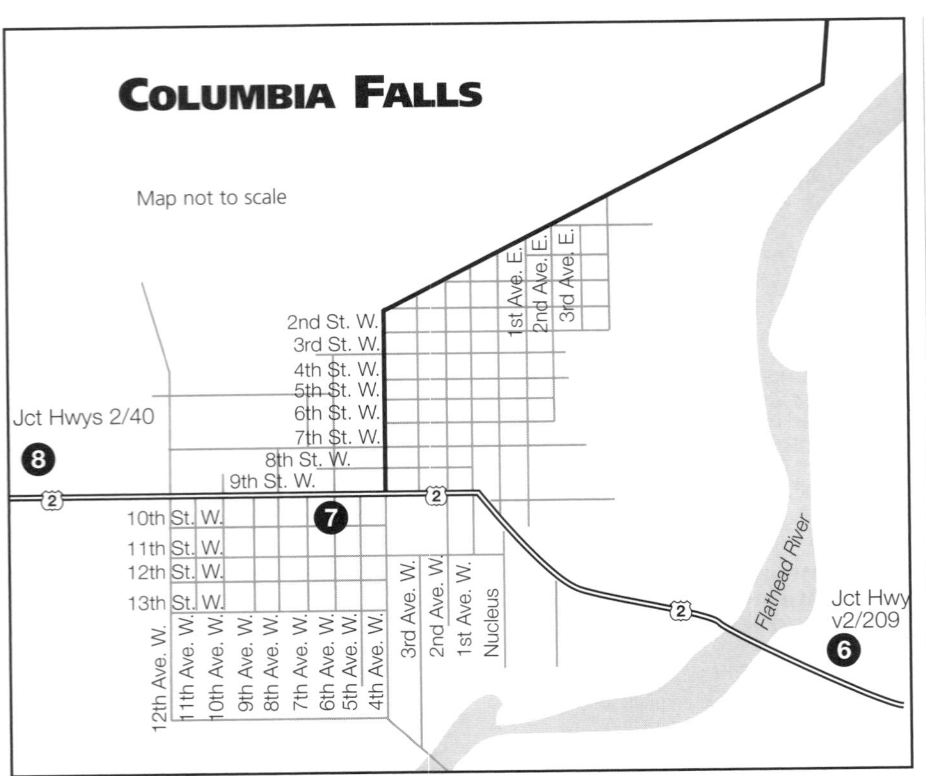

## F World Famous Whistle Stop Restaurant

1020 Hwy.. 49, Est Glacier. 226-9292

Enjoy the outdoor patio overlooking the majestic mountains of Glacier National Park at the World Famous Whistle Stop Restaurant while enjoying the food that made them famous. They feature delicious homemade desserts, world famous huckleberry pies, stuffed baked potatoes, a wide array of meat dishes, including excellent BBQ chicken and ribs, along with a nice selection of vegetarian dishes. All meals are served with fresh homemade bread and rolls. Breakfast find their awesome omelets and fabulous French toast. They are open 7 days a week from 7 a.m. to 9 p.m.. In the Great Falls area visit them at Mozart's Bistro across from the fairgrounds.

Lake, through a dense evergreen forest, to the foot of Twin Falls. Whether driving, hiking or on horseback, you'll enjoy the scenery and the unbeatable hospitality of the people.

## T John L. Clarke Western Art Gallery & Memorial Museum

900 Hwy.. 49, East Glacier Park. 226-9238

## F Glacier Village Restaurant and Buzz's Brew Station

Town Center, us Hwy. 2, East Glacier. 226-4464

Glacier Village Restaurant and Buzz's Brew Station has been family owned and operated since 1954. The unique and popular menu includes Blackfeet traditional dishes interspersed with great international cuisine, comfort foods, and Montana favorites. Renowned for its pastries, baked goods, and decadent desserts made on the premises. The restaurant also features over 30 huckleberry products, including huckleberry pork chops, fish, Buffalo short ribs, and homemade soups just to name a few. Authentic fry bread is served with huckleberry butter. They have a full beer and wine selection, along with a full espresso and tea bar. Enjoy their collection of historical photos from the area that compliments the warm and friendly atmosphere.

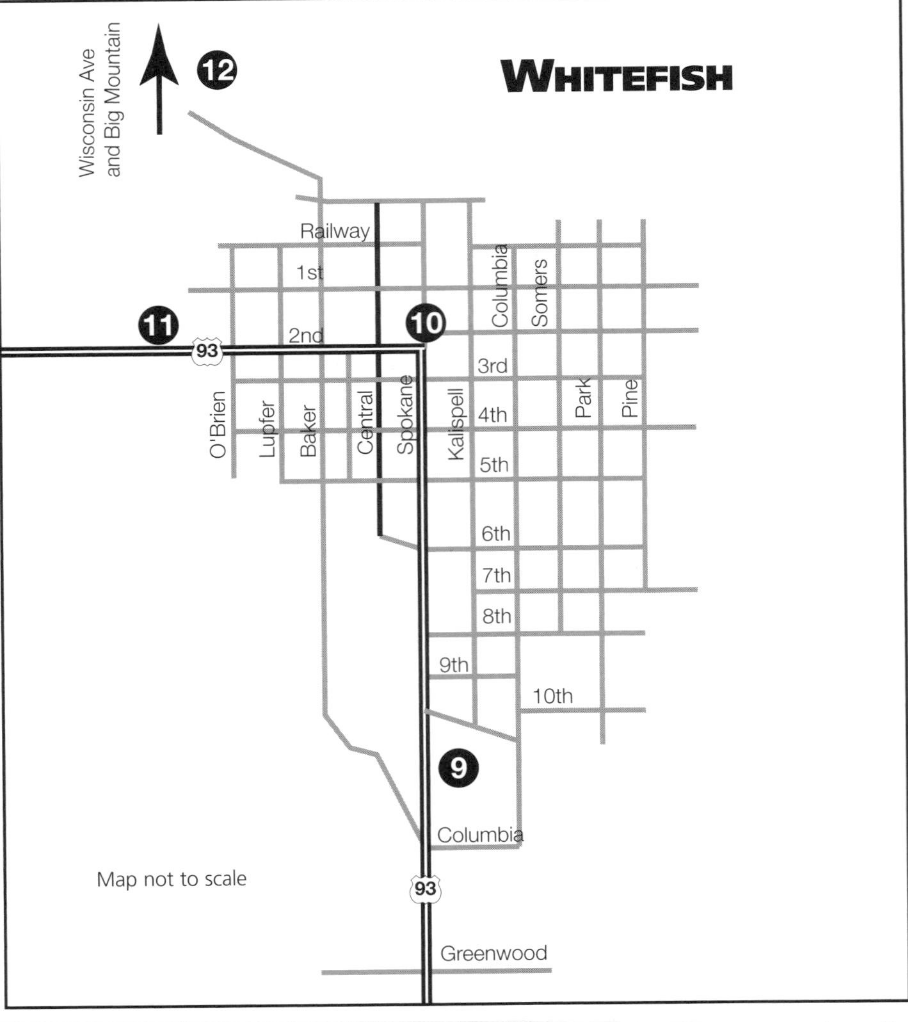

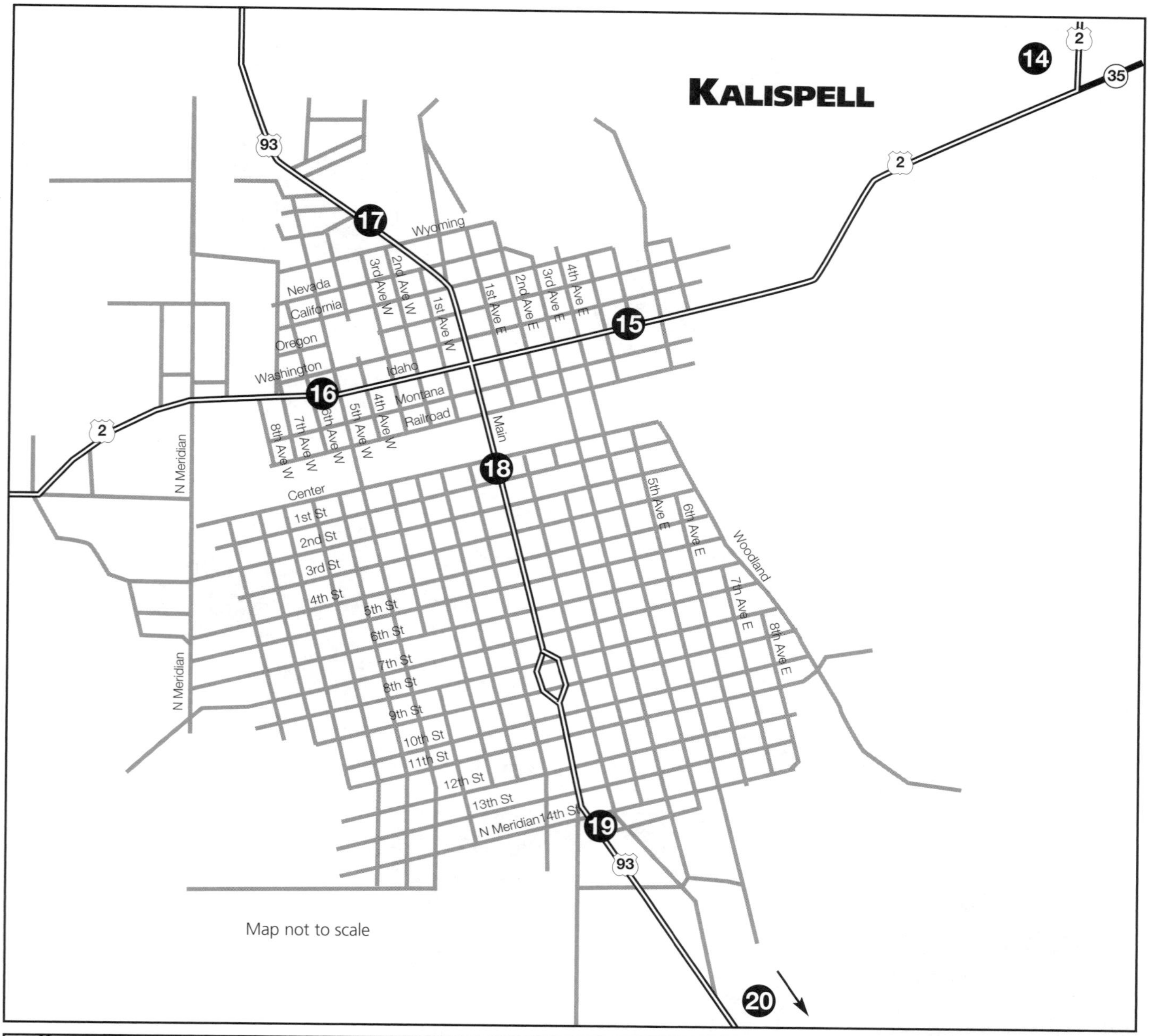

# KALISPELL

93
17
Wyoming
Nevada
California
Oregon
Washington
3rd Ave W
2nd Ave W
1st Ave W
1st Ave E
2nd Ave E
3rd Ave E
4th Ave E
15
2
14
2
35
16
Idaho
Montana
Railroad
8th Ave W
7th Ave W
6th Ave W
5th Ave W
4th Ave W
2
N Meridian
Main
18
Center
1st St
2nd St
3rd St
4th St
5th St
6th St
7th St
8th St
9th St
10th St
11th St
12th St
13th St
N Meridian
14th St
5th Ave E
6th Ave E
Woodland
7th Ave E
8th Ave E
N Meridian
19
93
20

Map not to scale

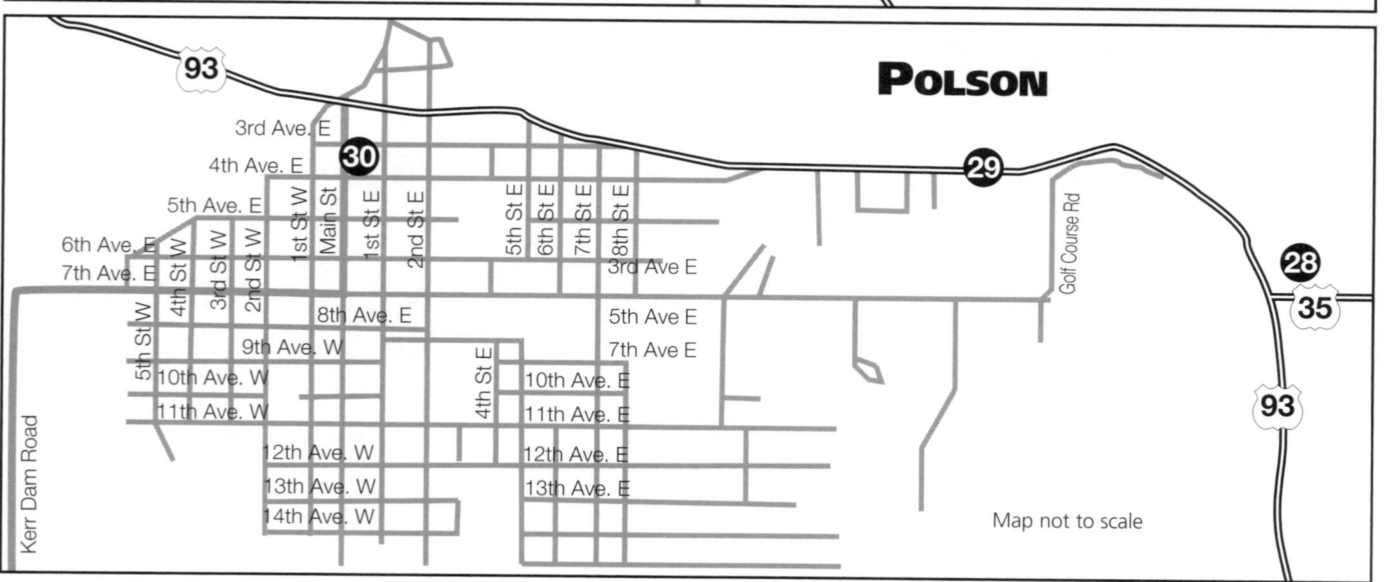

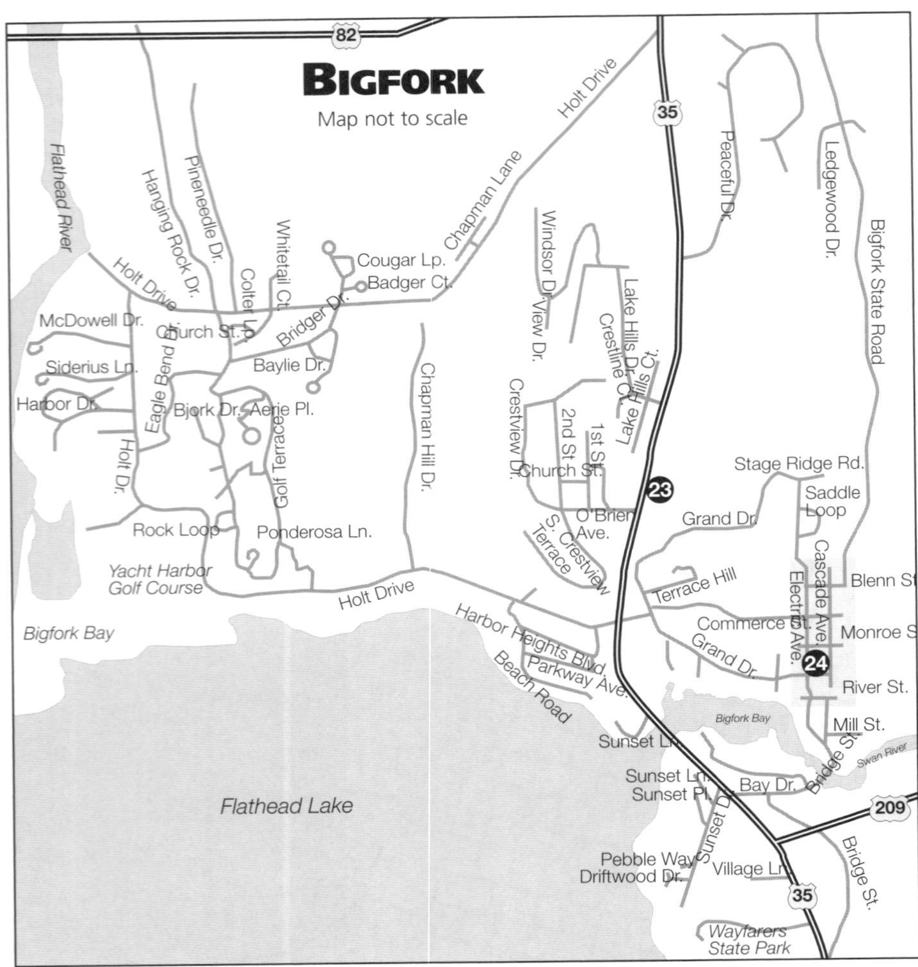


**F Two Medicine Grill**
314 Hwy. 2, East Glacier. 226-5572

**L Brownie's American Youth Hostel, Groceries and Bakery**
1020 Hwy. 49, East Glacier. 226-4426.
www.brownieshostel.com

Brownies Hostel and Grocery is nestled in the heart of the Blackfeet Indian Reservation. This rustic log building houses a grocery store and deli on the main floor, and a hostel on the second floor. The second story porch looks out at the majestic Rocky Mountains. The hostel offers an Internet café, separate men's and women's rooms, private rooms, common lounge, kitchen facilities, hot showers, laundry, bicycle storage, and is only 6 blocks from Amtrak. The grocery also sells deli sandwiches and salads, gourmet coffee and espresso, fresh baked pastries and bread, hand-dipped cones, sundaes, and shakes. Brownies offers you a unique opportunity to view a different culture and environmental experience you'll never forget.

**L East Glacier Motel & Cabins**
1107 Hwy. 49, East Glacier. 226-5593.
www.eastglacier.com

East Glacier Motel and Cabins is a favorite of families and hikers alike. With both cozy cabins and beautiful motel rooms it has something for everyone. The cabins are free standing, complete with TV, bedding, linens, and bathrooms. The motels are beautiful and spacious. Rooms with kitchenettes have microwaves, refrigerators, and hot plates. There is a central park area complete with picnic table and barbeque pit. If you don't feel like cooking there are two wonderful restaurants across the street. You are sure to enjoy your stay at East Glacier Motel and Cabins. Visit them on the web.

**L Glacier Park Circle R Motel**
416 Hwy. 2, East Glacier Park. 226-9331.
www.circlermotel.com

This motel is owned and operated by Ali and John Ray, both natives of the area. Ali is a native

*Glacier Park Circle R Motel*

American, and John grew up in St. Mary. Both have a wealth of information about the area and are happy to share it with guests. The cozy comfortable rooms all have in-room coffee machines and cable TV. The motel is centrally located on Hwy. 2 in East Glacier, close to shops, gift stores and restaurants. They offer reasonable rates in season and special off-season rates. Free area information is provided for all and free pickup and drop off for guests arriving on Amtrak.

**L Jacobson's Scenic View Cottages**
1204 Hwy. 49, East Glacier Park. 226-4422
or toll free 888-226-4422.

Jacobson's Cottages are 12 quiet and comfortable individual units tucked in among the pines and aspens next to Glacier National Park. These incredibly immaculate units are fully modern with electric heat, cable TV, and bathrooms with tub/shower combinations. Portable microwaves and refrigerators are available. The rates are among the most reasonable in the area. Take a pleasant stroll to nearby shops and restaurants, or jump in the car to visit Glacier National Park, just half a mile north on Highway 49. Open May through October.

**L Whistling Swan Motel**
512 us Hwy. 2, East Glacier. 226-4412.
www.whistlingswanmotel.com

The Whistling Swan Motel is the perfect base camp for your exploration of Glacier National Park. Whether you are walking local park trails, or angling for trophy trout on the world class lakes of the Blackfeet Reservation, you'll find the Whistling Swan Motel to be clean and accommodating and conveniently located within minutes of all town services. Choose between double, queen or kitchenette rooms. Amtrack shuttle is provided at no charge. Be sure and ask about AAA and Senior Citizens' discounts. Call early for the best availability. Visit them on the web or give them a call with your questions regarding area activities.

### LCS Sears Motel and Gift Shop

1023 Hwy. 49 N, East Glacier. 226-4432

Located on the quiet side of East Glacier, the Sears Motel and Gift Ship is your one stop for all your Glacier needs offering reasonable accommodations at a good value after a hard day of sightseeing, hiking, or lounging by a lake. Their 16 non-smoking rooms offer cable TV, showers, private facilities, and a choice of one or two double beds. They also offer wooded campsites for tents or full hookup RV's and is the area's Dollar Car Rental agency, with free shuttle service to and from the Amtrak depot. Sears is one of the largest gift shops in the Glacier area with "Almost a million shirts in stock!", film, guidebooks, railroad items, a wide assortment of huckleberry items, and everything you need to remember your visit, as well as gasoline to get you on your way. Family owned service with a personal touch. . .The reason guests return year after year. Stop in and you will too.

### S The Dead Mule

1012 Hwy. 49. East Glacier Park. 226-4558

The Dead Mule, an eclectic gift shop, boasts the only Made in Montana Foods Tasting Bar in the area. Stop in and have a free sample of chocolate, salsa, coffee, granola, mustard, fudge and other taste-tempting treats. They also carry beautifully handcrafted boxes, clocks, plus new and vintage items including jewelry, embroidered clothing, knickknacks and artwork, both local and regional. They are open from 9:30 a.m. to 7 p.m., six days a week. Don't miss The Dead Mule, you'll love their quaint setting and you're sure to find something to suit your taste and pocketbook.

### S The Spiral Spoon

1012 Hwy. 49, East Glacier Park. 226-4558

The Spiral Spoon is one of Montana's most unexpected experiences. This is where Jo Wagner spends the winter carving her one-of-a-kind wooden utensils and bowls. During the summer she sells her own work and delights in telling you all about her useable folk art. The Spiral Spoon also has carvings, turnings and chainsaw bears by other Montana artists as well as vintage kitchen collectibles and a variety of unusual gifts. Even if you are only browsing, stop by, be entertained and watch Jo carve. Shop hours are usually 9 a.m. -7 p.m., but if you're late, go to the house behind the shop and put Jo back to work.

*Montana Trivia*

The edible root of camus was a staple of the early Native American diet. It used to grow so abundantly, that fields full of its blue flowers could be mistaken for lakes.

## 3. *Attraction, Food, Lodging*

### Essex

Essex is a historic railroad village located twenty miles south of the West Glacier entrance to the park. Outdoor opportunities are limitless in the wilderness surrounding this little town. Summer provides numerous hiking and fishing experiences, autumn ushers in hunting season while winter invites you to cross country ski and snowmobile in terrain lavished by nature's finest paintings. In the spring, it is time to look for spring elk and deer in the open river bottoms and slopes.

### Summit

Summit, now only a ghost town, was the last settlement in the Gulch. In its day riches of up to $500,000 were packed out, and like many towns its population melted when gold was depleted.

### T Goat Lick Overlook

Hwy. 2, East of Essex.

The exposed river bank cliffs above the Middle Fork of the Flathead River provide an excellent

## HUCKLEBERRIES

You won't get through Montana without seeing huckleberry products. These little gems are made into preserves, candies, syrups, candles lotions and soaps. The huckleberry is very similar to the blueberry, and incredibly sweet and tart at the same time. They have a long history in the northwest. The Native Americans used them as an important source of food, drink, and rich dyes. Because of the huckleberry's unique flavor and challenge to harvest it has become one of Montana's hottest commodities and the main ingredient in one of the state's fastest growing industries.

The huckleberry that grows in the mountains and forests of Montana is special. The berries only grow in the wild on bushes. They won't bear fruit when transplanted or grown commercially, and availability varies year by year according to the whims of Mother Nature. In order to harvest huckleberries, pickers must go into the high mountain, Montana back country to find the bushes. "Bearing" in mind that huckleberries are a favorite food of grizzly bears, picking these tasty morsels isn't just hard, but can be darn hazardous.

No one knows just why huckleberry bushes reproduce or what makes one patch of berries good picking one year and not the next. To really enjoy huckleberries for yourself try some of the wonderful products that you'll see sold throughout the state. During the summer you can often find a special treat of fresh huckleberries for sale at the local farmers markets.

wildlife viewing area. Mountain goats, elk and deer stop to lick the minerals from the cliffs. You may even see billy goats and nannies with kids.

### FLS Half-Way Motel, Restaurant & Store

14840 Hwy. 2 East, Essex. 888-5650

The Half-Way Motel, Restaurant & Store is located on the Southern tip of Glacier National Park, halfway between the Park entrances of East Glacier and West Glacier on Highway #2. It is nestled in Montana's great wilderness and borders the Middle Fork of the Flathead River. Summer activities include hiking, biking, rafting, horseback riding and fishing. Winter activities include cross-country skiing and snowmobiling. Essex is only 55 miles from the Big Mountain. All of the large Motel rooms have two double beds, a full shower/bath combination, refrigerators, microwaves, and cable TV. The popular restaurant has a full-service menu, excelling in breakfast, lunch and dinner. The Store has many essential items for your convenience. Transportation is provided to and from the Amtrak stop less than a a mile away.

### FL Izaak Walton Inn

Izaak Walton Inn Rd., off Hwy 2, Essex. 888-5700. www.izaakwaltoninn.com, Email: stay@izaakwaltoninn.com

The Historic Izaak Walton Inn is snuggled between the southern tip of Glacier National Park and the Bob Marshall Wilderness. The resort offers comfy accommodations, a large fireplace to gather around, and a place where time stands still and lets you catch up. Where memories are made. Summer opportunities include hiking, rafting, fishing, horseback, riding and photographing trains. In the winter the Inn has 33 km of groomed cross country trails plus guided tours into Glacier Park, along with snowshoeing and ice skating. The Inn is an Amtrak stop with 33 rooms and four caboose cottages with kitchens. The Inn preserves it's railroad heritage with country style charm and a relaxing, peaceful atmosphere. Visit their web site for details.

### FL Snow Slip Inn - Bar, Motel, & Cafe

Hwy. 2 E., Mile Marker 191, Essex. 226-9381

**4.** *Attraction, Adventure, Gas, Food, Lodging, Camping, Shopping*

### West Glacier

West Glacier serves as the western rail and highway entrance to the magnificent Glacier National Park. West Glacier lies at the middle fork of the Flathead River. In a community carved into a region home to over 50 glaciers and 200 lakes, one might guess that recreation is West Glacier's backbone. There is no limiting the possibilities for recreation; the town offers easy access to both the park and the Bob Marshall Wilderness. One activity that has gained popularity is whitewater rafting on the Flathead River. The town provides chalets, motels and mountain views for your pleasure.

### T North American Wildlife Museum

U.S. Hwy. 2, West Glacier. 387-4018

For those who would like to learn more about area wildlife, this museum holds 85 animal and bird mounts in a simulated outdoor setting. Exhibits include elk, deer, moose, grizzly, black, and polar bears, coyotes, wolves, foxes and birds. All are portrayed in realistic dioramas. Experience the sound of the loon or the elk bugle as if you were hiking a trail. You will also see a tepee display in the complex. The museum is open daily May 1 through October from 9 a.m. to 9 p.m. A small admission fee is charged.

### V Kruger Helicopter Tours

1 1/2 Miles West of West Glacier, 387-4565 or 800-220-6565, www.vtown.com/kruger/

Featuring scenic helicopter flights over Glacier National Park and the beautiful Flathead Valley, Kruger Helicop-Tours offers a truly unique way to see this amazing area. With over 20 years experience in scenic tours, and 24 years flying experience with the park service in Glacier, Owners Jim & Jean Kruger offer quality experience and safety. Stop in for the "height" of your vacation and an unforgettable experience!

### VLS Glacier Raft Company and Glacier Outdoor Center

11957 Hwy. 2 E., West Glacier. 888-5454 or toll free 800-235-6781. www.glacierraftco.com

Glacier Raft Company provides daily trips from West Glacier, offering full or half day whitewater and scenic adventures for all levels. A steak lunch barbecue along the river highlights the full day of adventure. Also available are two or three day rafting, camping and fishing trips along the borders of Glacier National Park, a four-day Great Bear Wilderness whitewater trip, or guided fly-fishing trip with only two anglers per drift boat or raft. Take one-day self-guided trips or a variety of ride-and-raft trips, combining horseback riding, fishing, camping, and rafting. Consider staying in their log cabins with separate sleeping and living areas, complete kitchen, linens, full bath, television, covered deck, gas grill and gas fireplace. Handicap accommodations available. All cabins are nonsmoking and no pets allowed. Complete outdoor store open year 'round, with X-country skis and snowshoe rentals.

### VFS Rawhide Steakhouse, Trail Rides & Gift Shop

12000 Hwy.. 2 E., West Glacier. 387-5999 www.rawhidetradingpost.com

Offering a rustic western style dining room with a comfortable and enjoyable atmosphere, Rawhide Restaurant features Montana home cooking at its best. Serving breakfast, lunch and dinner daily with mouth watering mesquite broiled steaks. The gift shop offers a variety of Montana-made gifts & souvenirs, Indian artifacts, western art, jewelry and much more. For a truly western experience, try a family trail ride on mountain trails with scenic views of Glacier National Park. They also feature overnight horse trips, ride & raft combinations, four-day combination trips and wilderness fishing & scenic trips.

### VL Glacier Wilderness Guides Montana Raft Company/ Granite Park Chalet

West Glacier. 387-5555 or 800- 521-RAFT(7238), www.glacierguides.com, glguides@cyberport.net

Join Glacier Wilderness Guides for rafting, fishing and hiking adventures of a lifetime, or reserve a night at Granite Park Chalet, Glacier's historic alpine hut in the heart of the backcountry. Montana Raft Company offers rafting trips with smaller groups, superb food and warm, personal service resulting in unique summer experiences that are both exhilarating and satisfying. In 1983 the National Park Service chose Glacier Wilderness Guides to be the exclusive backpacking and day hiking guide service in Glacier National Park. Call their friendly staff today for Glacier's definitive rafting and hiking experiences.

### A West Glacier Exxon

West Glacier, 888-9974

### AFLS Glacier Highland Resort, Restaurant, & Gift Shop

us Hwy.. 2 E., West Glacier. 888-5427
or toll free, 800-766-0811

The Glacier Highland Resort is located in three rustic, yet modern buildings tucked away in the trees with great views Glacier National Park and abundant wildlife. It is conveniently located at the West Entrance to the park and across the road from the Amtrak Depot. Relax and enjoy great meals in their restaurant, especially fresh pies from their bakery. You will enjoy your restful sleep in their 33 immaculately clean knotty-pine finished rooms, on comfortable beds that bring visitors back time after time. The gift shop offers many treasures to remember your trip to Glacier Country, including an extensive clothing selection. They have it all! One stop for great food and lodging, car rentals, and groceries, beer, wine, and snacks.

### F West Glacier Restaurant

West Glacier, 888-5359

You can't miss it on the Going-to-the-Sun Road. The West Glacier Restaurant has served visitors and local residents for over 50 years! Open Memorial Day through late September, they offer casual, family-friendly dining., breakfast, lunch and dinner daily, featuring homemade soups and pies. Wine, beer, and cocktails are available and a lounge is adjacent to the restaurant.

### FS Cedar Tree Gift Shop & Deli

Apgar Village, Glacier Park, 888-5232

One of the largest gift shops in Glacier, offering a wonderful selection of fine gifts including pottery, jewelry, local art, T-shirts and huckleberry products. Marvel at the cedar trees preserved within the building's architecture. The deli serves a light breakfast, espresso, delicious sandwiches, ice cream and frozen huckleberry yogurt.

### FS West Glacier Mercantile

West Glacier, 888-5362

You will not want to miss this classic general store in West Glacier! You'll find everything you need, groceries, produce, meat, beer, wine, camping supplies, fishing licenses, tackle, and more than you can imagine.

### LC Lake Five Resort

540 Belton Stage Rd., West Glacier. 387-5601. www.lakefiveresort.com or email: lakefive@digisys.net

The Lake Five Resort offers tranquility hard to find in today's world. It's nestled in the foothills of Glacier Park just 1/3 mile off us Highway 2, three miles west of West Glacier. The resort sits on 235 acre Lake Five. Cabins, RV sites, campsites and tipi lodges are located from 60 feet to 250 feet from lake shore, an easy barefoot walk. Canoes and paddleboats are available for rent. A playground area satisfies the kids. Horseshoe pits and volleyball are options for older players. Swimming, boating and an occasional bite from a fish round out the fun. Families and friends have enjoyed the unspoiled beauty of this unique Montana resort for years.

### L Apgar Village Lodge

Apgar Village, Glacier National Park West Entrance, 888-5484

### L West Glacier Motel

West Glacier, 888-5662 or 888- 838-2363

This property located at the banks of the Flathead River in West Glacier, offers motel rooms and cabins at very reasonable rates. It's a great location just on the edge of Glacier National Park.

### L Moccasin Lodge Vacation Home

Hwy. 2 E., mile marker 162, West Glacier. 888-5545. www.royalvacation.net/glacier.htm

### C San-Suz-Ed RV Park & Campground

Hwy. 2 West, Milepost 150 & 151, West Glacier. 387-5280 or toll free 800-305-4616. www.san-suz-edrvpark.com

### S West Glacier Shirt Co.

West Glacier, 888-5350

Find them adjacent to the Exxon. The perfect place to find T-shirts, hats, sandals, shorts, sunglasses, and disposable cameras. Fax and photocopy service are also available. You can get an espresso too!

### S West Glacier Gift Shop

West Glacier, 888-5247

Next to the general store in West Glacier, this large shop carries an extensive variety of gifts, books, T-shirts, film, and Glacier Park mementos.

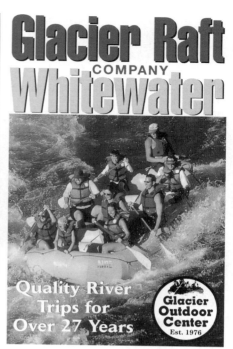



## 5. *Attraction, Gas, Food, Lodging*

### Coram

This town was originally the Coram-Nyack station on the Great Northern rail line.

### Hungry Horse

Hungry Horse is located at the mouth of a lake formed by a government dam, which towers 564 feet. In the midst of some of the most beautiful scenery in the Northwest, this town enjoys several lakes and nearby mountain ranges. Its unusual name was authored by two draft horses used for logging. The horses, named Tex and Jerry, wandered off during the severe winter of 1900 and were found about a month later, scraggly and hungry, but alive. The town survived as well and boasts great fishing in late summer on the Hungry Horse Reservoir.

### Martin City

This was a busy town when the Hungry Horse Dam project began. The town was accused of being brash and pompous prompting one writer to comment, "Martin City, for instance, is busily planning a 'Pioneer Days' fete in the spring to honor its 'oldtimers;' the town will be one year old then... Martin City occasionally sings hymns of praise to its pioneer 'business men'—barkeeps; it has seven bars and that's about all it has. ..."

### T Hungry Horse Dam and Reservoir

4 miles off Hwy.. 2 from Hungry Horse. 387-5241

The nation's 10th tallest dam towers over the South Fork of the Flathead River just a few miles from the town of Hungry Horse. The 564-foot-high Hungry Horse Dam is visited each year by more than 40,000 people. The reservoir behind the dam is one of the most scenic locations for water recreation, fishing, and camping in the state. The reservoir is 34 miles long and 23,800 acres. It is located just 15 miles from the west entrance to Glacier National Park and 20 miles northeast of Kalispell. There is a visitor center at the north end of the dam which is open from May 30th through Labor Day from 8:30 a.m. to 5 p.m. There are abundant campsites along the lakes shore, with eight campgrounds on the shore and campgrounds on Elk and Fire islands in the lake. There are also four boat launching facilities available.

### T House of Mystery
Between Hungry Horse & Columbia Falls, Hwy. 2, 892-1210. vortex1booth@netscape.net

Located 13 miles west of Glacier National Park near Hungry Horse, The House of Mystery is Montana's only natural vortex, producing unusual gravitational energies and mystifying phenomena. A popular family-oriented attraction, the gift shop offers old-time portraits and assorted curios, including crystals and prisms. Stop in for a tour and actually feel the strange forces at work. See where you can grow or shrink six inches just by moving three feet ahead, where birds don't fly, and trees grow in weird shapes and odd angles. Don't forget to bring your camera to prove it!

### T Great Bear Adventure
Hwy. 2, Coram.

This drive requires admission and is a drive-through an enclosed park where bears roam the area freely.

### FS The Huckleberry Patch
8858 Hwy. 2 E., Hungry Horse. 387-5000, www.huckleberrypatch.com

The Huckleberry Patch has been known as the, "Huckleberry Headquarters for over 45 years." Although they specialize in huckleberries and other wild berries that grow in their area, they also offer a family restaurant, cannery, fudgery, and gift shop. The restaurant serves breakfast all day, and a wide range of entrees for lunch and dinner, salad bar, and delicious Mexican specialties. The wildberry products available in the gift shop range from preserves, jams, jellies, syrups, toppings, fudge, and many other unique gifts that can also be ordered through the mail order catalogs. Located only 9 miles from the West Entrance of Glacier National Park, the Huckleberry Patch is a necessary stop on your way to or from the park. Visit them on the web!

### F Canyon Deli & Pizza Shoppe
10126 Hwy. 2., Coram. 387-4223

### L Abbott Valley Cabins
800 Spotted Bear Road, Martin City. 387-4436 or toll free at 888-307-4436, www.abbottvalley.com

Abbott Valley Homestead cabins are rustically romantic, yet comfortably convenient, located just 10 minutes from Glacier National Park. An excellent "base-camp", from which you can hike, bike, fish, golf, swim, or whatever your heart desires. The area is home to a multitude of animals, particularly deer, moose and elk in the meadows, while beaver, geese, loons, ducks and blue heron frequent the creeks and ponds. The cabins are each privately located on a working 260 acre family ranch. Each has a fully appointed kitchen, two bedrooms, full bath, laundry, wood stove, picnic table, gas barbeque, bedding, and linens. There are no telephones or televisions, but each cabin has a CD/tape player. Telephone, facsimile and e-mail service are available.

### L Glacier Cabins
9478 Hwy. 2 E., Martin City. 387-5339 or toll free 888-387-5339.

Your trip through Glacier Country will be even more special with a stay at Glacier Cabins, located just 8 miles from the west entrance to Glacier National Park and minutes from the Hungry Horse Dam and Recreation area. Five squeaky clean, comfortable, modern log cabins are rustic outside, and surrounded by pristine forests and clean mountain air. All cabins are equipped with private bathrooms, electric heat, cable TV, coffee makers with coffee, microwave ovens, refrigerators, gas barbeques, and picnic tables. Three cabins offer fully equipped kitchens complete with pots and pans and utensils. Each cabin has a porch swing with sitting chairs to relax and enjoy the flowered landscape and large shade trees.

### L Glacier Park Inn Bed & Breakfast
9128 Hwy. 2 East, Hungry Horse. 387-5099 or toll free 877-295-7417. www.glacierparkinn.com

Enjoy breathtaking views of the wild and scenic Flathead River and the Apgar Mountains of Glacier National Park from the deck of the octagonal shaped Glacier Park Inn Bed & Breakfast. Imagine fresh mountain air, while enjoying breakfast fit for a king or queen. The bed and breakfast has four bedrooms, each with private baths and two have private entrances as well. The commons areas are spacious and comfortable with soaring 25 foot ceilings. This unique bed and breakfast is only 9 miles from Glacier Park and is convenient to the plentiful year around activities that the area has to offer. Visit them on the web!

### L Evergreen Motel
Hwy. 2 East, Coram. 387-5365. www.anglefire.com/mt/evergreenmotel/picutres.html

### L Historic 1907 Tamarack Lodge, B&B, & Motel
9549 Hwy. 2 East, Hungry Horse. 387-4420

## 6. *Historical Marker, Adventure, Gas, Food, Lodging, Shopping*

### Columbia Falls
Columbia Falls, located at the north end of the Flathead Valley, is positioned as the western gateway to Glacier Park. It lies at the foot of Mount Columbia just two miles from the scenic Bad Rock Canyon. Don't be fooled by the name; Columbia Falls had no falls when it was named. Columbia was the first choice for a name but when that name was already taken "Falls" was added. In 1997, a waterfall complete with a small park was finally built behind Glacier Bank at the heart of the "old" Columbia Falls.

The town was established in the 1890s and has one of the world's largest aluminum extrusion plants, Columbia Falls Aluminum Company. The abundance of water and timber support this company as well as Plum Creek Timber Company. The two serve as the city's major industries.

In sharp contrast to industry, recreation also abounds here. There are many magnificent areas within a short distance including Glacier National Park, the North Fork of the Flathead River, Hungry Horse Reservoir, as well as the Great Bear and Bob Marshall Wilderness. Nine water parks with recreational areas are located within a few miles. Beckoning the avid golfer is the 18-hole Meadow Lake Golf Course nestled between towering pines, rivers and ponds. Horse rentals are available for special adventures into the wilderness.

### H Surrounded by Wilderness
Columbia Falls

*You are at the gateway to the upper Flathead River, which drains Glacier National Park, the Bob Marshall Wilderness Complex (the "Bob") and the southeastern corner of British Columbia. Two hundred nineteen miles of the three forks of the Flathead are designated as federal wild and scenic river, which means they are managed to maintain their natural primitive environments and unpolluted waters.*

*Directly to the south of here is the Swan Mountain Range, which stretches in an unbroken line for 100 miles. No road crosses the top of it. East of the Swan Range is the Bob.*

*Just around the next corner going toward the park, you can look east into the Great Bear Wilderness created in 1978 to link vital habitat in the Park and the Bob for the grizzly bear and other wildlife.*

### H Badrock Canyon
Columbia Falls

*The Great Northern Railway was constructed through Badrock Canyon in 1891. Prior to that, in 1890, the railroad contracted with Shepard Siems & Company to construct a road on the opposite side of the river to carry supplies to the railroad workers. The high canyon walls on the south side of the river were a major obstacle to the contractor, requiring extensive blasting to carve the road high above the canyon's floor. When completed in 1891, the road was so steep in places that wagons had to be lowered down it by ropes tied to trees-thus it was called the "Tote Road" by the local residents. It was not until sometime between 1906 and 1914 that the county built a new highway through the canyon, bypassing the old tote road with a more user-friendly thoroughfare.*

*Pioneer Billy Berne owned a small homesite at the west entrance to the canyon. Berne and his brother Mike came to Columbia Falls from Butte in 1889. For years the brothers manufactured bricks, which were used to construct many buildings in the area. In 1929, the construction of us Highway 2 destroyed much of the Berne homesite. In 1953, a niece of the Berne Brothers sold a tract of canyon land to the State of Montana for use as a roadside park dedicated to the memory of her uncles.*

### V Grizzly Go Karts
7480 Hwy. 2 E., Columbia Falls. 892-3132

Batting cages, bumper boats, mini golf—the track you can't bear to miss! Stop at the largest track in the Northwest, on the way to Glacier National Park, just 1/4 mile north of the waterslide! Open summer only.

### F Silver Bullet Bar, Pizza & Casino
1700 Hwy. 206, Columbia Falls. 755-3339

### L Glacier Park Super 8
7336 Hwy. 2 E., Columbia Falls. 892-0888 or 800-800-8000. www.super8.com

With a rustic style, log cabin atmosphere, the Glacier Park Super 8 features 32 spacious, beautifully designed rooms, located just 15 miles from Glacier National Park. Main level rooms offer convenient outside entrances, and upper level rooms have great views of the mountains where elk or deer can be seen in the early morning or late evenings. Jaccuzi suites, rooms with kitchenettes, and non-smoking rooms are also available. You will wake up in the mornings to a complimentary toast bar with tea, and coffee. The AAA approved rooms also offer cable TV, free local calls, and a friendly staff. Don't forget to ask about their honeymoon suites.

*Whitefish Lake*

### S Some Lady in Montana, Jewelry Design & Repair
418 Nucleus Ave., Columbia Falls. 892-9093

## 7. *Gas, Food, Lodging, Shopping*

### L Park View Inn B&B
904 4th Ave. W., Columbia Falls. 892-7275

## 8. *Gas, Food*

## 9. *Gas, Food, Lodging, Miscellaneous*

### Whitefish

Whitefish is a recreational town located fifteen miles north of Kalispell and 23 miles from Glacier National Park.. Located on the main east-west Amtrak line, it is situated on the south shore of the seven-mile-long Whitefish Lake and is only eight miles from The Big Mountain, a long established ski area. This town of about 5,000 people offers year-round recreational activities such as skiing, fishing, boating, hiking and backpacking, mountain biking, and golfing. Or for the really adventurous, get ready for an authentic cowboy evening: wagon rides, roping steer and spinning rope tricks. Then sit back to enjoy a hearty dinner Montana style while soaking up some cowboy lore.

The name "Whitefish" was given to this area by trappers in the mid 1850s when they discovered Indians catching native whitefish from the lake. The first permanent settler was John Morton who in 1883 built a cabin on the shore of Whitefish Lake just west of the river mouth. He was followed by loggers, Baker and the Hutchinson brothers, who logged around the lake in the early 1890s. But the actual town-site wasn't surveyed and dedicated until 1903 when timber clearing and building earnestly began. Timber and farming, in addition to the budding railroad, formed the bulk of Whitefish economy for the next fifty years.

As the timber industry waned and the force of the railroad diminished, a large golf course and club house were built, which at the time was the largest in the state. Golf gave Whitefish an economic facelift and a few adventurous folks had begun skiing the Hellroaring Mountain north of Whitefish. In time a ski lift was built and today The Big Mountain Ski and Summer Resort extends a wide variety of year-round recreational opportunities, making it a recreational and retirement haven. Glacier National Park practically lies in the backyard of Whitefish. Whitefish has also gained international recognition as a special place to retreat or even raise a family and has been coined the holiday village of the Flathead Valley with lots of friendly people, good entertainment and great restaurants.

### F Whitefish Brewing Co.
5650 Hwy.. 93, Whitefish. 862-2482

### F Hungry Hunter Restaurant & Casino
6550 Hwy. 93 S., Whitefish, 862-5303

### F China Wall Restaurant
6422 Hwy. 93 S., Whitefish, 862-2604

### L Best Western Rocky Mountain Lodge
6510 Hwy. 93 S., Whitefish. 862-2569 or 800-862-2569

The Rocky Mountain Lodge features 79 beautifully designed hotel rooms in a cozy mountain atmosphere. Unwind in front of the cozy fireplace in their spacious lobby. The rooms include a complimentary continental breakfast and guests can take advantage of the outdoor heated pool and jacuzzi, exercise room, complimentary shuttle service, and laundry facilities. Executives and families may want to try the mini-suites which include a fireplace, sofa bed, jacuzzi, microwave and refrigerator. Close to downtown, The Big Mountain Ski & Summer Resort, Glacier National Park, and numerous outdoor activities in the area.

### L Cheap Sleep Motel
6400 Hwy. 93 S., Whitefish. 862-5515 or toll free 800-862-3711. www.cheapsleepmotel.com

The folks at the Cheap Sleep Motel believe that there are a lot more interesting ways to spend hard-earned money than for a bed to sleep in. So they offer nice clean rooms real cheap. The Cheap Sleep Motel has 48 rooms, all with queen beds, outdoor pool, indoor hot tub, color cable TV, voice mail, and a guest laundry. More subtle amenities include plenty of hot water, Western hospitality, and the best motel coffee in Whitefish. They are just a short walk to several restaurants. The Cheap Sleep believes in a good night's rest with some money in your pocket. That should make good cents to everyone.

## Montana Trivia

In 2000, one of the hottest fire seasons in the history of the state, 884,666 acres burned. This is an area larger than the state of Rhode Island. It was, however, less than 1 percent of the state's total land area. 20 percent of those fires were caused by humans. In general, about 50 percent of fires are caused by humans. The rest are caused by lightning.

### L Gasthaus Wendlingen B&B

700 Monegan Rd., Whitefish. 862-4886 or toll free at 800-811-8002. www.whitefishmt.com/gasthaus. Email: gasthaus@aboutmontana.net

The Gasthaus Wendlingen Bed & Breakfast is a beautiful cedar and log home on 8 acres, surrounded by fantastic views of Big Mountain and Bad Rock Canyon, Glacier Park's gateway. They offer 4 comfortable rooms, with queen beds, twins, or king set-up. The rooms have fantastic views of mountains, water, and ski trails. Private baths and a steam room are available. Relax by the river rock fireplace, on the patio overlooking Haskill Creek, or on the front porch watching the alpenglow and visiting wildlife. Upon arrival you will be greeted with appetizers and refreshing beverages and wake up to a full breakfast served with homemade family recipes. They are close to attractions and great dining, while a quiet atmosphere beckons you at Gasthaus Wendlingen.

### L Allen's Motel

6540 Hwy.. 93 S., Whitefish, 862-3995

### L Norskman Hotel

6400 Hwy.. 93 S., Whitefish. 862-5515 or 800-862-3711

### L Whitefish Motel

620 8th St., Whitefish. 862-3507

### L Super 8 Motel

800 Spokana, Whitefish. 862-8255 or 800-800-8000

### M Montana Magic Casino

6426 Hwy. 93 S., Whitefish. 863-2920

## 10. *Attraction, Adventure, Gas, Food, Lodging, Shopping*

### T Whitefish Museum

North end of Central Ave., Whitefish. 862-0067

Once a depot for the Burlington Northern Railroad, this museum holds interesting local history with numerous railroad artifacts. The station's architecture is a reminder of times when first-class travel was by rail, and Glacier National Park was a favored destination for rich Easterners.

Today the depot still houses the Amtrak offices. A 1942 restored locomotive is displayed outdoors. This diesel is one of the first ever made and has been beautifully restored and repainted to the Great Northern Railway's Omaha orange and Pullman green. The museum is open Monday through Friday from 11 a.m. to 5 p.m. and on Saturday from 11 a.m. to 3 p.m. Admission is free, but contributions are welcome.

### VS Stumptown Anglers

222 Central Ave., Whitefish. 862-4554 or toll free 877-906-9949

Stumptown Anglers is a full ORVIS fly fishing dealer in downtown Whitefish. They offer everything from your fishing needs to angler themed gifts for the home to destination salt water fishing trips on tropical islands. This is your source for private casting lessons and fly tying classes. They make it easy to schedule full & half day guided float trips for beginners to expert fishermen with the Flathead Valley's most experienced guides. Mention their ad in this section and receive the "Hot Fly of the day", free! Stop in, email, or call and their friendly staff will inform you of the weekly hot spot and the area's best fishing tips.

*Wetting a line with Stumptown Anglers.*

### V Halcyon Sea Kayaking

103 Central Ave., Whitefish, 862-2658

An experience with Halcyon Sea Kayaking is a unique way to introduce yourself to the world of sea kayaking. This does not require great strength or expertise—sea kayaking is enjoyed by anyone who merely has the urge to experience the wonder of the water! All trips include a basic paddling safety lesson and a guided tour with individual instruction on some of Montana's beautiful waters. Your tour is guided with no more than five other people, so plenty of individual attention will be given. You can enjoy a morning trip which includes lunch, and afternoon trip, a sunset trip, overnight trips, and even a catered group trip. Sea kayaking is surprisingly simple and very fun, so grab a friend or two and enjoy the water today! Boat rentals are also available.

### F Truby's Wood Fired Pizza

115 Central Ave., Whitefish. 862-4979

Truby's Wood Fired Pizza is a local institution, serving the only authentic brick oven fired pizza in the Flathead Valley area. The diverse menu also includes superb steaks, their own smoked ribs, homemade soups, pasta, burgers, and daily specials. An extensive beer and wine selection and full bar includes hand crafted micro brews and all your other thirst quenching libations. Truby's is known for dishing up plenty of fun with a casual, yet elegant ambiance. Bring the family and enjoy the smoke-free restaurant inside or relax outside on the deck and enjoy the views for lunch or dinner.

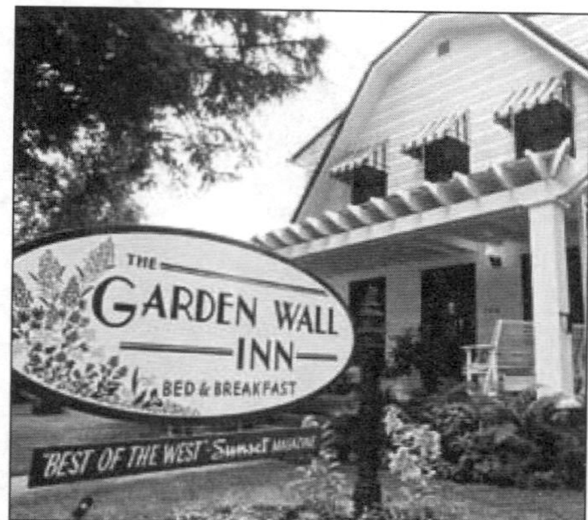


### L The Garden Wall Inn

504 Spokane Ave., Whitefish. 862-3440 or toll free 888-530-1700. www.gardenwallinn.com

The Garden Wall Inn, one of the finest old homes in Whitefish, has been catering to discerning travelers since 1987. Five luxurious guest rooms, each furnished with period antiques. Scrumptious 3-course breakfast prepared by their chef and the best location in Whitefish—right downtown. Nationally acclaimed for excellence and attention to detail. The innkeepers are keen explorers of the outdoors, and are happy to share their extensive knowledge of Glacier National Park, Whitefish, Big Mountain Ski Resort and the surrounding area. Tranquility, privacy, warm hospitality and attentive service are their trademarks. Chosen "Best of the West" by *Sunset Magazine*.

### L Whitefish Property Management

505 East 2nd, Whitefish. 863-4651 or fax 863-4655.
Email: wpminc@aboutmontana.net.
www.whitefishvacation.com

### S Hit the Hay

415 E. 2nd St., Whitefish. 862-3454 or fax 562-1721

Hit the Hay is one of the best sources in the Flathead Valley for beautiful bedding and exquisite accessories for the bath. Spoil yourself or someone special with something from their sumptuous collections of warm and colorful blankets, cozy pajamas, goose down comforters, bed sheets, merino throws, bath linen, and glorious gifts. Fine bedding from Hit the Hay will culminate the beauty of your home or cabin to accentuate subtle features and your personal style. Peruse textiles and designs from Yves Delorme, Frette, Peacock Alley, Brahms Mount and Morgan Collection. They specialize in little accessories that go a long way.

### S Artistic Touch, Northwest Crafts of Merit

209 Central Ave., Whitefish. 862-4813 or orders at 888-ART-TUCH (278-8824)

For over 15 years, Artistic Touch has been selling Northwest crafts of merit, offering Whitefish shoppers the best in local and regional art and crafts. This eclectic store is owned by Metal Worker, Mary K. Huff. Step inside and you ll find a wonderful selection of unique contemporary works in wood, metal, ceramics, glass and more. Check out their great jewelry selection, find that perfect gift, decorate your home or just enjoy one of their summer gallery shows which attracts artists from across the state. This is a shop you won't want to miss.

### S Sappari

215 Central Ave., Whitefish. 862-6848

Sappari has been a local favorite for the past 22 years. As their motto states, "It's the store where you never know what to expect." You can count on a fabulous selection of jewelry, clothing, eclectic home décor, and antiques at affordable prices. Their clothing is contemporary in feeling with an emphasis on natural fibers. Fun, unique, and always that vintage feminine influence that Rita is known for. They carry an outstanding selection of jewelry from local artisans, sterling silver with semiprecious stones, romantic vintage reproductions, to sparkle and glitter galore. When furnishing your new home or cabin in Montana, it's a must stop. They specialize in unique items that make your house a home, such as rugs, lamps, mirrors, tables, pictures, and textiles. Rita and Connie love what they're doing! Their fun friendly staff provide great service (and secrets to local life) that enhances your visit to Whitefish.

**S Sprouts - Fresh Cotton Clothing for Kids**
242 Central Ave., Whitefish. 862-7821 or toll free 888-821-6344

Located in the heart of downtown Whitefish, Sprouts offers fresh cotton clothing for children ages newborn through size 10. A unique specialty store, with a variety of name brands to choose from such as, Baby Lulu, Mulberri Bush, Sweet Potatoes, Zutano, April Cornell, Hartstrings, Woes & Willy, Le Top, Petit Bateau, Mustela, plus many more! You'll be sure to find something special for your little one at Sprouts. They are open Monday through Saturday and Sunday afternoons during the summer.

**S The Toggery**
122 Central Ave., Whitefish. 862-2271

**S General Store & Quilt Shop**
121 Central Ave., Whitefish. 862-5986

**S Whitefish Gallery**
213 W. 2nd St., Whitefish. 862-5120

**11.** *Gas, Food*

**F Whitefish Lake Golf Club Restaurant**
1200 us Hwy. 93 N., Whitefish. 862-5285

The Whitefish Lake Golf Club Restaurant features fine dining in an historic Montana setting. Built in 1936, the clubhouse features a restaurant that many consider the best in the Flathead. Prime rib, hand-cut steaks, fresh seafood and house specialties such as Braised Lamb Shank and BBQ pork ribs with sweet Cajun rub and apple butter BBQ sauce await you. The bar offers a vast wine list and a specialty martini menu. Lunch is served during the summer and a casual evening menu is offered on the patio overlooking the golf course. Dinner starts at 5:30 nightly and reservations are recommended for the dining room.

**12.**

**T Whitefish Lake State Park**
1 mile west of Whitefish on us. 93, then 1 mile north. Summer: 862-3991 Winter: 752-5501.

This popular, 10 acre park has a mature spruce/fir forest which contributes to the ambiance of the campground and beach. Boating, swimming, and fishing opportunities are abundant.

**T Whitefish Lake City Beach**
Northwest edge of Whitefish. 863-2470

Yes Virginia, there are beaches in Montana, and this is one of the better ones. This free-use city beach has lifeguards, swimming docks, picnic tables and shelters. Paddle boats, kayaks and sea cycles can be rented here too. Open in the summertime from 11 a.m. to 7 p.m.

**T The Big Mountain Ski & Summer Resort**
North of Whitefish

**FL Alpinglow Inn & Restaurant**
Big Mountain Ski & Summer Resort Village, Whitefish, 3900 Big Mountain Road, 862-6966 or 800-SKI-6760.

Located in the village of The Big Mountain Ski & Summer Resort, the Alpinglow is surrounded by spectacular views and outdoor sporting activities. Open winter and summer, the 54 newly remodeled rooms are complemented by a glass enclosed restaurant, two outdoor hot tubs, and a friendly outgoing staff. Full service dining is available during the winter season, including meal plans for guests. During the summer, the restaurant offers a continental breakfast buffet included in the room rate. The Alpinglow Inn is the closest hotel to all The Big Mountain ski lifts and summer activities. Children under 12 are free and non-smoking rooms are available.

*Alpinglow Inn & Restaurant*

**FL Kandahar Lodge & Cafe**
The Big Mountain Rd., Whitefish, 862-6098 or 800-862-6094, www.kandaharlodge.com

Located right near The Big Mountain Ski & Summer Resort Village, the Kandahar Lodge has the romantic charm you have always imagined. You can curl up in front of the huge rock fireplace, enjoy an intimate gourmet dinner in Cafe Kandahar, and take advantage of the endless winter and summer activities right out the front door. The 48 tastefully furnished guest units feature studio apartments, two bedroom suites with kitchens, and lofts with or without kitchens. Take advantage of the luxurious spa, jacuzzi, and steam rooms. They have a wood trimmed, elegant lounge, guest laundry, and a guest shuttle. Visit them at their web site for a look inside.

**L Good Medicine Lodge**
537 Wisconsin Ave., Whitefish. 862-5488 or toll free 800-860-5488 www.goodmedicinelodge.com or Email: info@goodmedicinelodge.com

Good Medicine Lodge, named one of America's Top Ten Romantic Inns (Travel America

Magazine). A classic Montana getaway hewn from solid cedar timbers and decorated in a western motif with fabrics influenced by native American textiles. Nine spacious rooms and suites all have private baths, vaulted wood ceilings, telephones and most have balconies with mountain views. The largest suite can sleep up to 5 guests. The lodge features crackling fireplaces, an outdoor spa and a smoke free environment for their guest's enjoyment. Additionally, a guest laundry and ski room complete with boot and glove dryers are available. Enjoy their full breakfast served daily. It is located minutes from skiing, hiking, golf, biking, Glacier Park, shopping and dining. Good Medicine Lodge has a three diamond rating with AAA..

### L Kristianna Mountain Homes

3842 Winter Ln., The Big Mountain Village, Whitefish, 862-2860 or 800-754-0040. www.kristianna.com

Nestled at the base on The Big Mountain Ski & Summer Resort, Kristianna Mountain Homes offers a collection of privately owned condominiums and upscale townhomes with ski-in/ski-out convenience. The units are complete with unsurpassed comfort, luxury, and service including daily housekeeping. The units range from two to four bedrooms that can accommodate groups of all sizes from a couple to a family reunion to a ski club. Each has a spacious living room with TV, VCR, and wood stove or gas fireplace. The kitchens are well equipped and easy to work in. If you like, they will do your grocery shopping for you so you are stocked upon arrival!

### L Crestwood Resort Condominiums

1301 Wisconson Ave., Whitefish. 862-7574 or toll free 800-862-7574. www.crestwoodresort.com

Crestwood Resort is a timeshare community of owners from around the United States and Canada. Ownership at Crestwood allows you to use your unit in Whitefish or trade it for any of the other 25,000 resorts in eighty countries. The resort is affiliated with Resort Condominiums International (RCI), the world's largest timeshare exchange and leisure Travel Company. Crestwood also has excellent weekly rentals available. They pride themselves on their knowledge and love of the Flathead and Whitefish. Give them a call or visit them on their web site. If you visit—we know you will buy!

### L Grouse Mountain Lodge

2 Fairway Drive, Whitefish. 862-3000 or reservations at 877-862-1505. wwwgrmtlodge.com

Picture a grand Northwest Montana lodge nestled in the heart of a mountain valley. Sunsets over crystal clear lakes. Wildlife among mature pine and larch forests. This picture comes to life at Grouse Mountain Lodge, just west of Glacier National Park and minutes from The Big Mountain ski area. Every day is a celebration of the great outdoors, with all the luxuries and service of a first-class resort. The magnificent lobby welcomes you to an atmosphere that is both elegant and casual. The friendly and professional staff will make you feel special. Excellent dining is available in the Wine Room, The Grill, and The Deck & Patio restaurants, with a backdrop of the Whitefish Mountain Range, overlooking 36 hole Whitefish Golf Course.

### L Hidden Moose Lodge

1735 E. Lakeshore Dr., Whitefish. 862-6516 or toll free 888-SEEMOOSE(733-6667). www.hiddenmooselodge.com

The Hidden Moose Lodge was designed to reflect the rustic, rugged history that is Montana. The lodge has vaulted ceilings with large picture windows, and spectacular views. It is built into the side of a hill and surrounded by large pine, birch and aspen trees. Nature trails wander through the property, some to Whitefish Lake, some through gardens, some to the nature conservancy only 300 fee away, and others lead deep into the forest. Each guest is greeted in the morning with a hearty Montana sized breakfast and complimentary beverages and snacks are served in the afternoon.

*Montana Trivia*

Tally Lake, near Whitefish, is the deepest natural lake in the state. it is over 500 feet deep.

Mountain bicycles are provided for guest use. The convenient location serves as a gateway to the wilderness and area attractions.

*Montana Trivia*

Flathead Lake is the largest natural freshwater lake west of the Great Lakes. It has 124 miles of shoreline and 188 square miles of surface.

### L Anapurna/Edelweiss Condominiums

3840 Big Mountain Rd., Whitefish, 862-3687 or 800-243-7547, wwwanapurnaproperties.com

Stay at the Big Mountain Ski & Summer Resort and enjoy affordable luxury in a priceless location. Spectacular scenery surrounds these homes and condominiums. All units have access to an indoor swimming pool and outdoor hot tub. Most units have decks with barbecues and fireplaces and all have completely equipped kitchens and cable TV with VCR. The rates offer a terrific value providing your base camp for exploring Glacier Park and enjoying the activities and attractions of Northwest Montana. Within walking distance are hiking and mountain biking trails, horseback riding, tennis, restaurants and shopping. AAA discount, children 12 and under free, some non-smoking, some allow pets. Call for reservations. Visit them at www.anapurnaproperties.com.

# Rivers and Streams

by Roland Cheek

Few places in the world—if any—can match the Flathead region for flowing water. Within this area are 21 listed rivers. Three—the main Flathead, the Kootenai, and the Clark Fork of the Columbia—are major rivers in any sense. Others, such as the Thompson, Swan, Whitefish, Stillwater, and the North, Middle, and South Forks of the Flathead are all large enough to be excellent for fishing, drift floating, or whitewater adventure.

Still other streams listed as mere creeks would rate as rivers elsewhere. McDonald Creek, up in Glacier, is a good example. Big Salmon Creek, deep within the Bob Marshall Wilderness is another. And then there are simply dozens of swift-flowing brooks that would be counted as rivers in Texas.

Shotgun pellets wouldn't carry across the lower Flathead, the Kootenai, or the Clark Fork. From there, streams range in size down to tiny neighborhood creeks fished by local kids. Cedar Creek near Columbia Falls and Ashley Creek near Kalispell are examples, as is Trumble Creek between Whitefish and Columbia Falls, and Abbott Creek near Martin City.

Many streams run through private land, but most are well within National Park or state and National Forests, or else a significant portion of them are. Floatable streams, such as those listed above, are all available to floaters by law throughout their navigable reaches, even though passing through private lands.

However, access through that same private land Is not afforded by law, and one must either obtain permission or utilize a public access site.

Fish inhabit most streams in the Flathead country, but they differ in size, specie and catchability, depending on the stream. Specie, of course, has a direct bearing on size. Big cutthroats, Dolly Varden and whitefish most often are migratory, traveling from lakes and lower rivers, sometimes for many miles upstream. Native fish are usually smaller, especially in the smaller streams. They tend to be cutthroat blocked by some natural migration barrier, or "brookies."

Brown trout are seldom found in the Flathead, but do exist in a few surprising places. So can one find an occasional northern pike, especially in larger Flathead Valley streams.

To give any of 'em a try, though, you must (depending on where you fish) purchase the appropriate Montana fishing license, a Flathead or Blackfeet Tribal Permit, or obtain a free Glacier Park fishing permit.

So ... take something along to cook your fish in and have a good lunch.

*Roland Cheek has lived the better part of fifty years living in Columbia Falls in the heart of the Flathead area. A good many of those years he spent as an outfitter. Most of the rest of that he's spent observing the area and its wildlife and writing about bears, elk, and the great outdoors surrounding him. His "Trails to Outdoor Adventure" has been syndicated in print and radio. He is the author of six books and countless outdoor articles. Find out more about him at www.rolandcheek.com.*

# A Land of Lakes

by Roland Cheek

**Minnesota claims to be the "Land** of Ten Thousand Lakes." And if they really have that many, we can't match 'em. But the Flathead area does contain well over 700, ranging in size from tiny reed-filled ponds, to gargantuan Flathead—at its extremities, 28 miles long and 15 miles wide.

It's a water wonderland, never far from a freshwater lake of some sort. One can easily test the placid waters of a remote warm-water lake with a canoe, or watch powerboat races at the Whitefish Regatta. One can manhandle a cartop dory into a little known forest gem, or pack a rubber raft into an isolated high mountain lake. Or simply relax, still fishing from shore along one of the many "oxbow sloughs."

They range in popularity, too. Many have first or second homes and condominiums scattered around their shores, while others have excellent state, federal or private campgrounds, picnic areas, boat docks, launching ramps, boat rental facilities, and repair shops. There are many lakes that are served by no roads, some by poor or no trails. Still others are so remote as to even require days to reach by horseback.

There are lakes near the top of 10,000-foot mountain peaks, glistening like jewels in beautiful glacial cirques. There are others, shallow and warm in the valley bottoms, thick with waterfowl and marsh life.

There are lakes with flashing, tail-dancing rainbows; others with tackle-busting lunker Dolly Varden, mackinaw, or northern Pike; still others with tasty kokanee salmon, cutthroat trout, or whitefish, several with slashing largemouth bass or fun-to-catch perch.

There are easy-access lakes where the water skiing is excellent and the people few, others with no-wake speed limits, and Wilderness and National Park lakes where only oar-powered boats can be used.

All in all, there's a lake to suit you, no matter your taste. All you must do is look.

In this corner of Montana, there are 17 lakes and four reservoirs each with over 1,000 surface acres. Flathead Lake is, of course, the largest at 126,080 acres. It is followed in size by two long, narrow reservoirs - Koocanusa and Hungry Horse.

Others within the list includes Lake McDonald, St. Mary, Kintla, Bowman, Logging and Sherburne within Glacier Park; Lower St. Mary and Duck on the Blackfeet Indian Reservation; Ninepipe and Pablo Reservoirs on the Flathead Indian Reservation; and Whitefish, Swan, Little Bitterroot, Ashley, McGregor, Lake Mary Ronan, Tally, Placid and Seeley, all within surrounding forests.

Opportunities for the highest quality recreation abound in these lakes; including pleasure boating, fishing, water skiing, swimming, diving, sailboating, and wind surfing on the half dozen largest (Flathead, Whitefish, McDonald, etc.).

Fishing can range from a simple relaxing way to while away an afternoon, to an outstanding tackle-busting, gut-wrenching adventure. All the big lakes contain a variety of fish, but the variety is different from lake to lake. Depending on the one you fish, your catch could include cutthroat, rainbow, Dolly Varden, and brown trout; bass, northern pike, kokanee salmon, and perch.

Most larger lakes (and some smaller ones) have boat rentals available at various locations, and boat ramps are always around somewhere.

There are a couple of tour boats plying the waters of Flathead Lake, for those wanting to relax and enjoy. One boat is based in Polson, the other in Somers. There are also tour boats based on Glacier Park's McDonald, St. Mary, Swiftcurrent and Two Medicine Lakes.

Any of these huge lakes contain enough surface area to be dangerous to boaters during storms. Especially so, is that true of Flathead Lake, where a sudden storm could catch unwary boaters several miles from shore. Take care.

*Roland Cheek has lived the better part of fifty years living in Columbia Falls in the heart of the Flathead area. A good many of those years he spent as an outfitter. Most of the rest of that he's spent observing the area and its wildlife and writing about bears, elk, and the great outdoors surrounding him. His "Trails to Outdoor Adventure" has been syndicated in print and radio. He is the author of six books and countless outdoor articles. Find out more about him at www.rolandcheek.com.*

## S Heather Candles

510 Wisconsin Ave., Whitefish, 862-5049.
www.heathercandles.com

Stop by and watch candle making and decorating in progress. Heather Candles are 100% hand crafted, using real flowers and leaves that have been grown, gathered and pressed on the grounds of the factory. The floras are artistically placed on the candles, creating unique floral and wildlife themes, and no two are alike! The entire process begins in the spring, when Heather plants flower beds complete with pansies and wildflowers, sowing the seeds from scratch each year. This unique process is what makes Heather Candles so special. Custom orders, wedding and special occasion candles are welcome. Heather invites you stop in!

**13.** *Shopping*

## Polebridge

In the early 1900s, resident Bill Adair opened a hotel along the North Fork of the Flathead. When Glacier National Park was established in 1910, Adair packed up his belongings and moved to the spot now known as Polebridge. Included in the move was the building now known as the Northern Lights Saloon. Today the town stands as a lone outpost at the remote northwest edge and entrance to Glacier Park.

**14.** *Gas, Food, Lodging*

## Kalispell

Kalispell was founded in 1891 and is the northern gateway to the Flathead Valley. The name means "prairie above the lake" in the Pend Orielle language. The town is located 32 miles from West Glacier and eight miles north of Flathead Lake, the largest natural freshwater lake west of the Mississippi River. The lake is twenty-eight miles long and fifteen miles wide at its widest point, boasting 185 miles of shoreline. This town of 13,000 people is located within a bustling tourist region, with supplemental lumber and fruit-growing industries. This region is especially known for its Flathead cherries.

The area's founding father, Charles Conrad, made a fortune as a Missouri River trader after his family lost its Virginia plantation during the Civil War. In 1895, he built a new estate now known as the Conrad Mansion which boasts three stories and 26 rooms set on three acres of gardens. Kalispell's art museum, the Hockaday Center for the Arts is time-worthy, displaying the works of regional and national artists in three galleries, along with a permanent collection of Western art.

## S Powder Horn Trading Co.

2052 Hwy.. 2 E., Kalispell. 752-6669
or fax 752-6748

A visit to Powder Horn Trading Co. is truly like stepping into the past. An old time trading post with every thing from buffalo robes to colorful Pendleton blankets as well as gifts and accents for every home on the range. They also stock the largest bead selection in northwest Montana, including many vintage trade beads. The sporting goods department offers modern as well as collectable firearms. At Powder Horn Trading Co., their motto is "The most interesting store in Montana". You just have to see it for yourself and you're sure to agree!

## S Willow Wind Studio

Call for directions 752-4686 or fax 752-5664.
www.willowwindstudio.com

Willow Wind Studio features the art of selected Flathead Valley artists, and the frame shop is recognized regionally for award winning framing design. Watercolors, pastels, and mixed media landscapes are featured, as well as black and white photography. For specialized framing needs, the gallery offers unique shadow box design, needlework stretching, prints on canvas stretching, drymounting, laminating, and shrink-wrapping. Round, oval, and specialty shaped frames are also available. The gallery is open Monday 12-5. Tuesday through Friday 10-5:30, Saturday by appointment. Be sure and visit them on the web.

## Winter Is Big In The Flathead

by Roland Cheek

**Winter sports are big in the Flathead.** And why not? Winter is big in the Flathead. Snow generally comes to the high country—the snow that lays all winter—in late October. And it still hangs on the north slopes and in some of the high passes into late May. Snow in the main valleys is different though.

Oh sure, snow flurries will come earlier than October. And it's not at all unusual to have late flurries into April. But winter seldom gets really serious—even in the high country—before the end of October. Nor does it hang on in the main valleys much past late March—that's when the ground begins to thaw.

Still, you can expect to experience five or six months of winter every year. Despite occasional "Chinook" winds from the Pacific, bringing warming, melting periods to the lower valleys, deep snow and freezing temperatures in the mountains ensure great winter recreation opportunities everywhere.

Most serious Montana skiers know the Big Mountain—located just north of Whitefish—is one of the most popular ski areas in the entire Treasure State. With more than 33 miles of ski terrain in 41 different runs; with 2,170 vertical feet above the 4,600-foot base area; with an uphill lift capacity of 8,430 skiers per hour - it's no wonder the Big Mountain is head and shoulders in popularity above many other Montana ski resorts.

But the real reason is SNOW. It's deep fine powder, usually blanketing the mountain beginning in October. Always open by Christmas, sometimes opening by Thanksgiving— depending on snow pack—Big Mountain's average snow is four to seven feet at base, seven to 10 feet at summit. And skiing usually lasts through April.

If sliding madly downhill on a couple of flat boards scares the socks off you, then take up cross country skiing as I did. Certainly one of the fastest growing outdoor recreational pursuits in Montana, there's unlimited opportunity in National Forests, state lands and Glacier Park. The sport's burgeoning popularity has led to several sporadically groomed-trail ski areas throughout the Flathead.

For those who seek solitude, that can be found virtually anywhere on the millions of acres of public lands in the Flathead. All you need is enough snow and enough willpower to seek out a suitable place. Snowshoes would help, too.

Yet another popular wintertime sport in the Flathead is snowmobiling. The expense of the sport has resulted in some decline over the last decade, but there are still substantial advocates around the valley.

Most snowmobiling is conducted in the Whitefish Range, north of Columbia Falls, the Swan Valley-Seeley Lake area, the Tally Lake country west of Whitefish, southeast of Eureka, the Flathead's South Fork above Hungry Horse Dam, and the Skyland Road area near Marias Pass.

Ice fishing is a wintertime activity pursued by many Flathead visitors and residents alike. Though to some folks, the sport would play better in August while they're bucking hay bales during the dog days of mid-summer, others like nothing better than to perch on an ice-covered lake, jigging for grandpa trout, through a six-inch hole— weather be damned!

Opportunities are plentiful for winter recreation; especially follow those folks who can't abide propping their feet up by the fire and sipping hot-buttered rums for an entire frigid season.

*Roland Cheek has lived the better part of fifty years living in Columbia Falls in the heart of the Flathead area. A good many of those years he spent as an outfitter. Most of the rest of that he's spent observing the area and its wildlife and writing about bears, elk, and the great outdoors surrounding him. His "Trails to Outdoor Adventure" has been syndicated in print and radio. He is the author of six books and countless outdoor articles. Find out more about him at www.rolandcheek.com.*

**S Glacier Quilts**
2960 Hwy. 2 East, Kalispell. 257-6966. www.glacierquilts.com or email: info@glacierquilts.com

## 15. *Gas, Food, Lodging*

**L Alpine Friendship Inn**
1009 Hwy. 2 E., Kalispell. 257-7155

Located in Kalispell, just 35 miles from Glacier National Park and close to The Big Mountain Ski Area, the Alpine Friendship Inn offers 30 newly appointed rooms. All units are complete with color cable TV, direct dial phones, air conditioning, free local calls and complimentary continental breakfast. Kitchenette, non-smoking, and handicapped access rooms are available upon request. Call now to find out about the great ski, snowmobile, and golf packages as well as a The Family Plan, The Weekender and many more specialty discounts. Save an automatic 10% with advance reservations. So call now to reserve your stay!

**L Vacationer Motel**
285 7th Ave. East N., Kalispell. 755-7144 or 888- 755-7155

The Vacationer Motel, will welcome you with family owned Montana hospitality in the heart of the beautiful Flathead Valley. "Your base camp to Glacier National Park" (32 miles). All 22 units offer color, cable TV, microwaves, refrigerators and direct dial phones with free local calls. Relax in the hot tub after a fun filled day. Guests may also enjoy a complimentary toast bar, coffee or tea. Call for summer reservations today. Your room is waiting for you.

### Montana Trivia

If Montana's 3,442,416 acres of federally designated wilderness areas were combined, they would form an area the size of Connecticut. 64 percent of Montana's forested land is owned by the federal government.

## 16.

**L Red Lion Inn**
1330 Hwy. 2 W., Kalispell. 755-6700 or 800-RED-LION(733-5466). www.relion.com/properties/kalispell

The 64 spacious rooms and suites, adjacent restaurant and lounge, heated pool and spa at the Red Lion Inn provide a comfortable base of operations as you explore destinations like Glacier National Park, ski Big Mountain Resort, or take advantage of the many opportunities for river rafting, fishing, horseback riding, and golf. They offer free continental breakfast buffet, free daily newspaper, computer data port phones, remote color TV's with cable, in-room coffee maker, hair dryer and in-room iron/ironing board. Fax and copy service is also available. Close to downtown. Visit and contact them at www.redlion/prperties/kalispell.

**L All Pro Rental Property Management**
376 W. Washington St., Kalispell. 755-1332 or toll free 866-755-1332. www.allprorental.net

All Pro Rental Property Management and Rental Agency specializes in deluxe vacation homes in the beautiful Flathead Valley. A wide variety of attractive properties are available—fully furnished homes or apartments, vacation cabins, and more. Their goal is to please and create long lasting relationships. Most homes include laundry facilities, linens, kitchen accessories, barbecues, and all the amenities, including bedding, pillows, linens, furniture and all necessary kitchen items. All Pro Rental vacation homes do not allow smoking or pets unless specific permission has been granted by the owner. They can help you find your home away from home in beautiful Montana. Visit them on the web.

### Montana Trivia

Supposedly you can predict the weather by watching mountain goats. If they're high on the mountain, expect good weather. If they're congregating in low lying areas, there is probably a storm on the way. The mountain goat, by the way is really not a goat. It is related to the antelope.

## 17.

**M Flathead Valley Community College**
777 Grandview Drive, Kalispell. 756-3846, www.fvcc.cc.mt.us

Flathead Valley Community College is the largest community college in Montana, located in Kalispell with an additional campus in Libby, Montana. Students are offered occupational two-year associate degrees and certificate programs, that prepare them for immediate job placement.

**T Lawrence Park**
Hwy.. 93 3 blocks north of Hwy.. 2 junction. Bear right on N. Main. Watch for signs to park. 758-7718

This park sits between the Stillwater River and the Buffalo Hills Golf Course. This is an urban park with several short trails that meander through the woods, a children's playground and a picnic area.

**L Four Seasons Motor Inn**
350 N. Main St., Kalispell. 755-6123 or 800-545-6399, www.fourseasonsmotor.inn.com

Stay at the Four Seasons Motor inn and experience the hospitality of a friendly, caring, community-minded small town facility located in beautiful Big Sky Country!. They offer clean, comfortable and affordable lodging with nonsmoking and smoking rooms, queen size beds, suites to accommodate up to six people, individually controlled heat and air conditioning, tub and shower combinations, in-room coffeemakers, cable TV for your personal comfort. Ample covered parking with winter plug-ins is provided. They are just three short blocks from uptown Kalispell featuring fantastic shopping, art galleries, theatres, and dining. A full service, Cimmerron Café, serving breakfast, lunch and dinner and boasting the best homemade pies in the Flathead Valley, is on-site.

**L Glacier Gateway Motel**
264 N. Main, Kalispell. 755-3330 or toll free 877-755-3337

The Glacier Gateway Motel is the perfect place to be your home away from home while in Glacier Country. Enjoy their down home hospitality with reasonable rates whether you stay for a day or a week. The motel is conveniently located to restaurants, the airport, mall and downtown shopping. They provide ample parking for all sizes of vehicles and include winter plug-ins. Additional amenities in all rooms include data ports in all rooms, air conditioning, small dogs allowed, smoking and nonsmoking rooms, exterior corridors, air conditioning, premium channel television, and free continental breakfast. There are 8 rooms available with fully equipped kitchenettes. Find The Glacier Gateway Motel at the intersection Hwy. 2. & Hwy. 93.

### Montana Trivia

The seeds of the cow parsnip are 70 percent more likely to sprout when eaten by a bear.

**L Days Inn**
1550 Hwy.. 93 N. Kai, Kalispell. 756-3222
or 800-329-7466 (DAYSINN)

**M Help-U-Sell Real Estate of Flathead Valley, Inc.**
17 E. Oregon, Kalispell. 755-4357 or fax 257-2237.
24 hour service 755-HELP (4357).
www.helpusellmontana.com

Help-U-Sell Real Estate of Flathead Valley, Inc., founded in 1994, bridges the gap between for-sale-by-owner and traditional style real estate. They are the only fee for service, real estate company in the valley, providing sellers savings on commissions, while providing the service they need and expect. As members of the local Multiple Listing Service, they can service buyers with virtually all listings available in the area. Help-U-sell services the entire area and looks forward to taking care of your real estate needs, whether you are selling or buying a home in the beautiful Flathead Valley. Their office is easy to find, 2 blocks north of the intersection of Hwy. 93 and Hwy. 2 in Kalispell. See virtual tours on their web site.

## 18. *Attraction, Gas, Food, Lodging, Shopping*

**T Conrad Mansion**
330 Woodland Ave. (6 blocks off Main St. on 4th St. East), Kalispell. 755-2166

The Conrad Mansion is one of the most outstanding examples of luxurious living and period architecture in the Pacific Northwest. The building itself remains unchanged since Spokane architect Kirtland Cutter designed and built the home in 1895. Ownership and occupation of this beautiful Norman-style mansion remained in the Conrad family until 1975, when it was given to the City of Kalispell.

The youngest of the Conrad children, Alicia Conrad Campbell, gave the Mansion to the city to be maintained in perpetuity as an historic site. It was her wish that the ancestral home be preserved in memory of and as a tribute to her pioneer parents, Charles E. and Alicia Conrad.

In 1868, at the age of 18, Charles Conrad left his boyhood home in Virginia and traveled to Fort Benton, Montana Territory. There he built a trading and freighting empire on the Missouri River that lasted more than twenty years. In his lifetime C.E. Conrad lived through the Civil War and the settling of the West, and he left an indelible mark on the history of Montana.

The Mansion kitchen showcases a custom-made range, a Southern beaten biscuit machine, and a servants' call board. The dining room has the original Chippendale table and complete set of chairs. The bedrooms, with their imported marble lavatories, sleigh beds and canopied four-posters, appear as they did when many notable guests were shown by the servants to their rooms.

The Great Hall, with its massive stone fireplace and golden oak woodwork, provided the setting for the legendary two-story Christmas tree, ablaze with the light of hundreds of beeswax candles. This beautiful scene is recreated during an exciting three-day social event, "Christmas At The Mansion," held every October.

During the life of the Mansion, there have been no architectural changes in the building. Both the exterior and interior (all three floors!) have been completely restored to their original beauty. From its exquisitely landscaped gardens to its collection of original furniture, toys and clothing, the Conrad Mansion offers the most complete example of privileged life in turn-of-the-century Montana.

Visit the most beautifully preserved pre-1900 mansion in Montana and experience the elegance of a bygone era. The museum is open from May 15 to October 15. Special events include Christmas at the Mansion, a Victorian holiday bazaar.

*Source: Conrad Mansion brochure.*

**T Central School Museum**
124 Second Ave. E., Kalispell. 756-8381

As the name implies, this museum is housed in a school built in 1894. The building has been used for everything from elementary classes to high school classes to classrooms for the fledgling Flathead Community College. The museum actually contains a classroom appearing as it did over 100 years ago.

Featured are the photos, sculptures, drawings, and writings of Frank Linderman, who came to Montana in 1865 at the age of sixteen. A young trapper who eventually became a statesman, artist, author and was a true friend and champion of Native Americans.

There is a large display of arrowheads, a collection of old cameras, a display of surveying equipment, and a large collection of household furniture from the 1880s. The museum is open from Tuesday through Saturday from 11 a.m. to 5 p.m. There is a small admission charge.

**T Hockaday Museum of Art**
302 Second Ave. East in Kalispell. 755-5268.
hockaday@bigsky.net. www.hockadaymuseum.org

The major visual art museum in northwest Montana is located in Kalispell's Carnegie Library building minutes from Glacier National Park, Flathead Lake, and other area attractions. Exhibits feature the historic and contemporary art of Montana. The permanent collection includes Ace Powell, Russell Chatham, Gary Schildt and Robert Scriver. The Hockaday is found two blocks east of Main on the corner of Second Ave. East at Third Street. The museum is open year round Tuesday through Saturday from 10 a.m. to 6 p.m. On Wednesdays from 10 a.m. to 8 p.m. A small admission is charged.

**T Woodland Park**
2nd St. E. (Conrad Drive), Kalispell.

Filled with all the ingredients for family fun, this park furnishes a pool with a waterslide, playground, rose garden, running/jogging/walking course, playing fields, horseshoe pits, picnic gazebos and barbeque pits. A popular attraction is a large pond with black swans. Kids on rollerblades can enjoy the swans resting around the paved path surrounding the lake.

### T Mark Ogle Studio

101 E. Center St., Kalispell. 752-421., www.markogle.com

Mark Ogle has traveled worldwide as an artist, while keeping his studio and gallery in Kalispell. He was the featured artist in the first western art exhibition ever in the the Republic of Ireland. His work was completely sold out and received great critical acclaim. Mark has also been a delegate to represent Montana and the Arts, by the Montana Chamber of Commerce, traveling to Komoto, Japan as an honored guest of the Japanese. From painting in the vast and beautiful locations of our national parks, to dock side marinas, to quaint street scenes, he is at home. He has produced and sold volumes of originals and limited edition prints of Glacier, Yellowstone, Grand Teton, Yosemite, Grand Canyon, Denali, Banff, Waterton, and Jaspar. Visit the studio or check the web site at www.markogle.com, for a further look at Mark Ogle's work.

### F Cafe Max

121 Main St., Kalispell. 755-7687

Voted "Best Chef in the Flathead Valley," Chef Douglas Day has created an enchanting eating experience at his busy downtown Kalispell restaurant. His menus range from duck to veal and include grilled seafood and premium angus beef. Café Max is famed for its spectacular desserts and friendly, professional service. The staff is willing to share information ranging from favorite hiking trails in Glacier Park to the attributes of the restaurant's daily wine features. Café Max offers an extensive list of fine wine and beer. Dinner is served Tuesday through Saturday from 5:30 p.m. Reservations are recommended.

### F Bulldog Pub & Steak House

208 1st Ave. E., Kalispell. 752-7522

### F Sweet P's Cafe & Grille

200 East Center St., Corner of 1st Ave. E. & Central. Kalispell. 257-0217

### FL WestCoast Kalispell Center Hotel

20 N. Main, Kalispell Center Mall, Kalispell. 751-5050 or 800-325-4000 www.westcoasthotels.com

WestCoast Kalispell Center Hotel in a unique Montana setting offers 132 deluxe guest rooms and the spacious Kalispell Center Mall all under the same roof. Your stay will be even more enjoyable with amenities such as a solarium pool, indoor/outdoor whirlpool, fitness center, in-room coffee, pay movies, hair dryers, irons, ironing boards, Nintendo, voicemail and dataports. Executive and family suites with wet bars, kitchenettes and fireplaces are also available. The

Northwest Bounty Co., Restaurant offers dining beneath an 80-foot skylit atrium with rustic Montana décor, serving breakfast, lunch and dinner in a relaxed atmosphere. The Black Diamond Casino features fine wines and spirits, hors d' oeuvres, and gaming. Ample parking and the airport shuttle service is free.

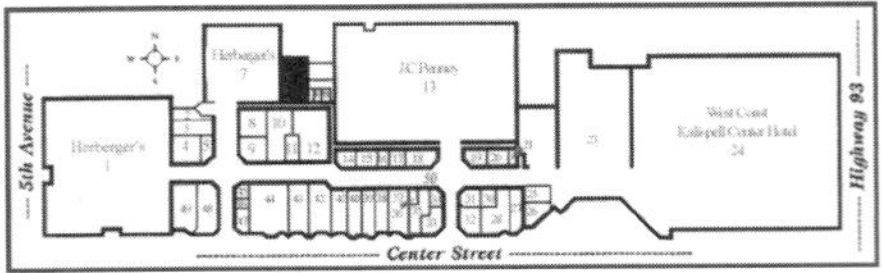

### S Kalispell Center Mall

20 North Main St., Kalispell. 751-5050. www.kalispellcentermall.com

Shop at the Kalispell Center Mall and take home some Montana memories from two major department stores; Herberger's and JC Penney. You'll also be delighted with an assortment of wonderful one-of-a-kind specialty shops. Adjoining is a full service hotel, West Coast Kalispell Center which will comfort you after a full day of shopping and touring. At the Kalispell Center Mall shopping is Tax Free! The Mall is open Monday through Friday, 10 am - 9 pm, Saturday, 10 am -7 pm, and Sunday 11 am - 5 pm. The Mall is conveniently located in downtown Kalispell at the corner of Hwy. 93 and Center, at 20 North Main. For additional information and mall events visit www.kalispellcentermall.com.

### S Kalispell Antiques Market
Corner of 1st & Main, Kalispell. 257-2800

The Kalispell Antiques Market, established in 1989, occupies 10,000 square feet and represents 35 of the Northwest's finest dealers. Collectors will be thrilled with a complete spectrum of antiques. The past comes alive with thousands of quality items such as first-edition books, out of print Montana books, posters, toys, wonderful jewelry, furniture, and other legacies from previous generations and Montana's past are for sale. Wonderful art pottery such as Roseville, Hull, and Weller can be found here as well. Enjoy exploring the cleverly appointed booths. They are located in the historic building that once served as the Opera House, now the centerpiece of Downtown.

## 19.

### F MacKenzie River Pizza Co.
1645 Hwy. 93 S., Kalispell. 756-0060

Famous for gourmet pizzas, super sandwiches and extraordinary salads, everything is made fresh daily right down to the salad dressings and the pizza dough! Be sure and stop as you head for Glacier Park from the South. Enjoy their great food, great decor, and great people all under a MacKenzie River Float Boat.

### F Sawbuck Saloon
1301 S. Main, Kalispell. 755-4778

The Sawbuck Saloon is loads of fun and is located next to six major motels and the bus depot, this restaurant, casino and sports bar is complete with homestyle cooking, three live poker tables, 20 keno & poker machines, a full service bar, and a great rustic atmosphere that gives off a taste of Montana. The separate sports bar features OTB with dog & horse racing, 27 TV's displaying all major sporting events, karaoke four nights a week, laser dancing, pool tables, and lots of space to move around. The restaurant & casino features daily specials, like the 8oz. sirloin steak dinner for only $5.95, and an ATM machine for your convenience. Stop into the Sawbuck Saloon for great food at great prices and lots of fun.

### L WestCoast Outlaw Hotel
1701 Hwy. 93 N., Kalispell. 755-6100 or 800-325-4000.
www.westcoasthotels.com/Outlaw

You'll be pampered at the WestCoast Outlaw Hotel, a full service hotel located in the middle of the Flathead Valley. 220 air-conditioned guest rooms and suites are equipped with in-room coffee, hair dryers, irons, ironing boards, Nintendo, voicemail dataports, and pay movies. A guest fitness center, racquetball and tennis courts, two indoor swimming pools, sauna, and four whirlpools are provided for your pleasure. The hotel is home to Hennessy's Restaurant and Outlaw Lounge & Casino. Open daily, Hennessy's has been the Flathead Valley's most famous restaurant since 1946. Steaks, ribs, seafood and Sunday brunch are their specialties. Complimentary parking and complimentary airport shuttle service is available for your convenience.

### L Diamond Lil Inn
1680 us Hwy.. 93 S., Kalispell. 752-3467 or 800-843-7301. diamondlilinn@in-tch.com

## 20. *Attraction, Lodging*

### T Creston Fish Hatchery
Hwy. 35, 10 miles south of Kalispell.

### L White Oak of Montana
4834 Hwy. 93 S., south of Kalispell at Somers. 857-2388 or 888-226-1003.
www.whiteoakofmontan.com

White Oak of Montana is centrally located in the Flathead Valley. It is a great headquarters to relax and enjoy the beautiful scenery and bountiful activities while in the Flathead Lake area. Over 100 rooms are available with exercise facilities including a pool and indoor track. A complimentary continental breakfast is served to guests. White Oak is in the heart of sweet cherry country and recreational access includes skiing, snowmobiling, hiking, and river and lake access for boating, sailing, and fishing. Five banquets rooms that can accommodate from 50 to 750 making White Oak a great place for weddings, family gatherings, and business meetings. Discount wedding packages are offered. Visit them on the web!

*White Oak of Montana*

## 21. *Historical Marker, Attraction, Miscellaneous*

### H Kalispell-Somers Railroad Spur Line
South of Kalispell.

*In 1901, Great Northern Railway tycoon James J. Hill and local businessman John O'Brien joined forces to build and operate a 11-mile railroad line to a sawmill on the north shore of Flathead Lake. Hill built this spur line in record time and provided financial assistance for the construction of the sawmill. In return, O'Brien supplied 600,000 railroad ties annually to the Great Northern Railway until 1906 when Hill acquired sole ownership of the sawmill. At Somers, O'Brien built 122 residences and a general store to provide housing and support services to the workers and their families. By 1910, the Somers Lumber Company sawmill was the largest in the Flathead Valley, producing over 30 million board feet of lumber every year. Freight and passenger trains passed over the spur line daily carrying travelers between the Great Northern depot in Kalispell and the steamboat terminal at Somers. The sawmill closed and was dismantled in 1949. The Burlington Northern Railroad used this spur line until 1985.*

### T Lone Pine State Park
4 miles southwest of Kalispell on Foy Lake Rd., then 1 mile east of Lone Pine Rd. 755-2706.

Located near Kalispell, Lone Pine offers outdoor wilderness close to the city. This park offers panoramic views of the valley and mountains, several easy trails in a wooded area, and a self-guided interpretive trail with three overlooks. For added fun there are horseshoe pits and a volleyball net.

**M Neville Log Homes**
2036 Hwy.. 93 N., Victor. 642-3091 or 800-635-7911. www.nevilog.com or email: neville@nevilog.com

## 22. *Attraction, Gas*

**T Gattis Gardens**
Hwy.. 35 in Creston. 755-2418

These are arguably some of the prettiest gardens to be found anywhere. A 1.25-mile walk takes you through the 4-acre through more than 2,000 varieties of flowers, most identified with signs. The trail rambles along Mill Creek. While enjoying the flowers you will often hear the strains of classical music drifting from the tool shed. Open daily in the summer from 9 a.m. to 9 p.m.

## 23. *Attraction, Gas, Food, Lodging, Camping, Shopping*

### Bigfork

Bigfork was founded in 1902 and is located on a bay where the Swan River empties into the Flathead Lake. Bigfork is one of the valley's most picturesque and cultured villages. The lovely resort community averages a population of 1,500, although it can swell exponentially during the summer. It houses many art galleries and shops, as well as some of the finest restaurants in the valley which are touted for their exceptional menus. The Bigfork Playhouse is acclaimed for its professional performances in the summer. Bigfork also has one of the best 18-hole golf courses in the west, keeping with its role as a resort village.

In 1901, Everit Sliter platted this site for a township. It was named for its location where the Swan River, a "big fork" of the Flathead River pours into the lake. Sliter was the town's first postmaster and ran the town's first hotel and general store and planted the first orchard there. The steamers that navigated the lake used Bigfork Bay as a harbor. The construction of a dam, power plant and road by Bigfork Power and Light along the Swan River in the early 1900s brought a boom to the town with the influx of construction workers. Heavy logging in the years prior to World War I brought loggers and carpenters.

Bigfork later grew as a tourist town when convict labor built the East Shore Highway from 1911 to 1914. The town became a convenient stopping point for travelers on the way to Glacier National Park. The town settled into a quiet existence and changed little for almost 50 years.

In the 1980s and 1990s when Montana became a destination for urban escapees, Bigfork began a metamorphosis. Eagle Bend Golf Course was constructed, and the area evolved to a resort town. In 1986, Bigfork was selected as one of the "50 Great Towns of the West" by journalist David Vokac in his book *"Great Towns of the West."*

**TS Kehoe's Agate Shop**
In Bigfork take Hwy.. 35 to flashing yellow light (Holt Drive) and turn toward lake (west). Drive 2.3 miles on Holt Drive and follow signs to shop. 1020 Holt Drive. 837-4467. email: ljkehoe@digisys.net

This rustic shop, built in 1932, sits where the community of Holt once stood. The town was a steamboat stop for the steamers that cruised the lake. The shop is like a lapidary museum containing rocks, jewelry, gems, fossils, petrified wood, minerals, and thunder eggs collected from around the world. Open from 10 a.m. to 6 p.m. in the Summer. Closed Mondays in the winter with shorter hours.

**L Candlewycke Inn Bed & Breakfast**
311 Aero Lane, Bigfork. 837-6406 or 888-617-8805. www.candlewyckeinn.com

Retreat to 10 acres of total seclusion. The Candlewycke Inn B&B is open all year with seasonal prices for singles as well as groups. Quilts and antiques adorn each spacious, theme decorated, king and queen size room. Pillowtop beds ensure the best nights sleep you'll ever experience away from home. Private baths, personal refrigerators and TV's are available in each room. A full breakfast is served each morning in the large country dining room. Slip into a relaxing hot tub and wrap yourself in plush terry robes. Enjoy water sports on Flathead Lake less than 3 miles or the majestic Glacier National Park only 45 minutes away from the Inn. All of this and more awaits you with an abundance of activities for all seasons.

**L O'Duachain Country Inn**
675 North Ferndale Drive, Bigfork. 837-6851 or reservations at 800-837-7460. www.MontanaInn.com

The O'Duachain (O-dew-cane) Country Inn was established in 1985. The gracious three-level log home and guest house are located on five scenic acres between Flathead and Swan Lakes. Enjoy the wrap-around deck, relax in the outdoor hot tub, view the local wildlife and Peacocks that roam the grounds, or explore surrounding countryside. The rooms offer rustic elegance with private baths, including a wheelchair accessible suite. Nearby activities include golf, tennis, boating, fishing, sailing, hiking, climbing, biking, tubing, rafting, and touring Glacier National Park. Dine at nearby world-class restaurants, but don't leave till after you've enjoyed the inn's famous breakfast. As an added treat to your stay, they provide libations and baked goods for snacking fare or a late night apres cordial. This is an ideal location for wedding receptions and reunions.

**S Architectural Innovations Interior Design and The French Conncection Antiques**
7975 Hwy. 35, Bigfork. 837-2334

**S Swan River Trading Co. & The Pine Box**
8560 Hwy. 35, Junction Hwy.s 35 & 209, Bigfork. 837-4121

Experience this unique decorative gift and furniture store where western elegance and rustic charm come together. The Pine Box builds rustically crafted pine furniture on site. There is no better keepsake of Montana than a piece of furniture that will last a lifetime and provide endless memories. Swan River Trading Co. can provide that finishing touch with one-of-a-kind western and Montana-made home furnishings.

## 24. *Attraction, Adventure, Food, Lodging, Shopping*

**T Everitt L. Sliter Memorial Park**
On south edge of downtown Bigfork. 837-4848

From late-June to late-August musicians from around the state perform every Sunday night at 8 p.m. in the open amphitheater called Riverbend Stage. There are restrooms, playground equipment and picnic tables here also. Bring your own lawnchairs or blankets for the performance.

**V Wildhorse Island Boat Trips**
452 Grand Dr., BigFork, 837-5617

Pointer Scenic Cruises-Flathead Lake Boat Trips.

**F Brookies Cookies**
191 Mill St., Bigfork, 837-2447. www.brookiescookies.com

Experience the taste of all-natural baked goods made fresh from scratch daily. From fresh breakfast goodies like muffins, scones and cinnamon rolls to an array of cookies, afternoon treats, and gourmet desserts, you'll see (and taste) why Brookies has earned so many blue ribbons. Locals stand in line waiting for the famous lowfat applesauce cinnamon rolls. Brookies prepares handmade pies and cakes that are elegant and delicious, along with many other gourmet desserts. While savoring their baked goods, enjoy a full service coffee/espresso/tea bar. In season, relax on the scenic deck overlooking the Swan River. Brookies Cookies does gift mail orders worldwide, call 800-697-6487 for a catalog or shop online.

### Montana Trivia

The Bob Marshall Wilderness was named for Bob Marshall who, along with some friends, formed The Wilderness Society. When asked "How much wilderness does America really need?", he replied, "How many Brahms symphonies do we need?"

**F Showthyme**
548 Electric Ave., Bigfork, 837-0707

Showthyme is a casually elegant restaurant that serves exceptional food. Known throughout the Northwest as one of the best food and wine experiences in the region. Their creative American style menu ranges from daily fresh fish specials, pasta dishes, wild game, fine cuts of beef, a mouth watering Chili Relleno and much more. Enjoy an excellent selection of wine, beer, and cocktails for the adults. A children's menu is available and there is outside dining in season. Dinner is served starting at 5 p.m. every evening. The entire restaurant is non-smoking. All major credit cards are accepted. Join hosts Blu and Rose Funk for a truly outstanding dining experience.

## The Flathead Monster

**If you think Scotland has a lock on** lake monsters you might be surprised to find Montana has its own version of "Nessie" in Flathead Lake. The monster was first spotted in 1889 by passengers of the lake steamer us Grant who first thought it to be an approaching boat. A passenger toting a rifle fired at it. He missed, but did scare it (whatever it was) away.

Since then scores of people have viewed the creature. Sightings were documented in the early 1900s, 1912, 1919, 1922-23, 1934, 1937, 1939 and regularly in every decade until today.

One of the more notable accounts came from a Polson couple and their four children on July 10, 1949. They reported a big fish near the Narrows. The fish appeared about 150 feet from them and had about a six foot length of its back visible. For over 30 seconds they watched it as it swam southeasterly leaving a wake 6" to 8" high as it slowly sank beneath the surface. They believed it to be a 10 to 12-foot long sturgeon. The man later became a chairman of the Montana State Fish and Game Commission.

1993 holds the record for the most sightings—nine in all. On July 13, near Woods Bay, a Seattle bank officer and a district sales manager actually managed to get some video footage of the creature. The video shows a dark shape on the surface. The sales manager swears he saw the eye's of the monster before they were able to get the tape rolling. He described it as the head of a sturgeon, but the body of a large eel at least 12 feet long. On July 29 in the early afternoon, a vacationing Illinois policeman, his wife and three children saw "Nessie" surface about 50 yards from their boat in calm waters near Wild Horse Island. The monster appeared to be following a school of bait-sized fish. The policeman described the creature as shiny with shiny humps, about 15 to 20 feet in length, and with a bowling ball-sized head. He claimed it looked like two seals swimming.

There seems to be no consistency to where or when "Nessie" will show. The creature has appeared at all times of the year, in all parts of the lake. Sightings of the creature have been reported by all manner of people—teachers, professionals, farmers, ranchers, military officers, law enforcement officers, business people, mill workers, and tourists of all ages.

There was a time when folks thought the mystery was solved. On May 28, 1955, the late C. Leslie Griffith claimed he snagged a big sturgeon near Dayton on the western side of the lake. He finally managed to gaff it several miles downlake near Big Arm State Park, after fighting it for nearly five hours. Not everyone believed his story. Some believe the 7-1/2 foot, 181 lb. white sturgeon was trucked in from somewhere else. The giant fish can be seen in the Polson Flathead Historical Museum today. Griffith did swear in court under oath that the fish was caught in Flathead Lake. A dispute later arose between Griffith and Big Fish Unlimited Inc. as to ownership of the fish and distribution of money from showing it. The case went all the way to the Montana Supreme Court. BFU retained ownership but had to give Griffith a cut of the proceeds.

### *Montana Trivia*

Over 90% of the mint grown in Montana is grown in the Flathead Valley with over 9,500 acres in cultivation. A typical acre of mint plants will yield 100 pounds of mint oil, enough to flavor 1.25 million sticks of gum

**F The Village Well**
260 River St., Bigfork, 837-5251

The Village Well is a locally owned establishment known for hand rolled, homemade pizza and outstanding live entertainment different nights during the week. They also have a variety of succulent sandwiches and burgers. They feature over a dozen beers on tap, with a large selection of micro-brews, and virtually every Montana Microbrew available. They have the only ping pong table in the area, with weekly tournaments year-round, billiards, and a casino. This is a regular stop off for kayakers, skiers, rock climbers, and other local adventure seekers from the Bigfork area.

**F Tuscany's Ristorante**
331 Bridge St., Bigfork, 837-2505

Experience fine dining in the Northern Italian Tradition at Tuscany's, a unique dining stop in downtown Bigfork. Tucked back into the surrounding birch trees right by the Swan River, the atmosphere offers a one-of-a-kind for outside dining experience in the summer. The cozy interior also offers inside dining that is perfect for both a romantic dinner or family outing. Experience live jazz music on the deck Thursday and Friday evenings throughout the summer. Call for summer/winter hours.

**F La Provence**
408 Bridge Street, Bigfork. 837-2923.
www.bigforklaprovencecom

Chef Marc Guizol brings years of European and U.S. culinary experience to guests at La Provence. The unique menu choices are typical of French Mediterranean Cuisine. The atmosphere is gracious and comfortable with high quality service and attention to their guests needs, with a warm welcome from Caroline, Marc's wife. The menu changes seasonally, and is complimented by a fine selection of the world's best wines earning the Wine Spectator Award. Reservations are recommended. Additionally, La Petite Provence offers a French Deli with fresh gourmet sandwiches, soups, salads, quiches, and pastries, and seating on the deck. A wonderful choice for memorable dining, party planning, or a box lunch for a day on the lake.

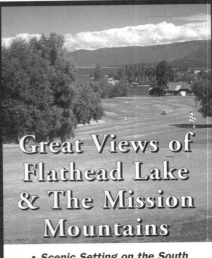

## F Swan River Café

360 Grand Ave., Bigfork. 837-2220

The Swan River Café is definitely not your ordinary café. Join them on the shaded deck overlooking the Big Fork Bay for one of Bigfork's premier dining experiences. Inside enjoy a romantic dinner by the fireplace, surrounded by a casual, yet elegant ambiance. They are well known for American and European gourmet dining, an extensive wine list, a mouthwatering selection of fresh seafood and house specialties, and their friendly staff. Order your favorite cocktail from their full bar. Make a point to try their lunch omelets and homemade coffee cake. They are open seven days a week for breakfast, lunch, and dinner from 8 a.m. to 10 p.m.

## FL Marina Cay Resort & Quincy's At Marina Cay

180 Vista Ln., Bigfork. 837-5861 or 800-433-6516, www.marinacay.com

Nestled into the water's edge of Bigfork Bay where the Swan River spills into the Flathead Lake, Marina Cay presents its guests with a remarkable year round blend of outdoor adventure and effortless luxury. Accommodations vary from single rooms and mini suites to spacious condos, some with whirlpool tubs, fireplaces, and waterfront views. At the marina you can rent a ski boat, wave runner, canoe, or other watercraft, take part in guided fishing charters, and experience the excitement and beauty of Flathead Lake. The gourmet diner will appreciate Quincy's Restaurant featuring fine cuisine and specialty wines. Overlooking Bigfork Bay, casual, but elegant dinners are served in this award-winning restaurant with live entertainment. Champ's Sports Pub and Grill and the waterfront Tiki Bar serve casual lunches and dinners as well. Learn more about this wonderful resort at their web site.

## FL Coyote Roadhouse Inn and Riverside Cabins

602 Three Eagle Lane. Bigfork. 837-1233 or 837-4250. www.coyoteroadhouse.com

*Coyote Café chef and owner Gary Hastings*

The Coyote Roadhouse Inn restaurant, established in 1986, instantly achieved a Mobile Guide 3-star rating and became known as "Montana's best restaurant," according to Travel and Leisure magazine. Executive Chef and owner Gary Hastings has created a "true roadhouse" in the elegant country style of dining and lodging. The nightly menu consists of Cajun, Southwestern, Mayan, and Tuscan cooking. Reservations are required. The main lodge has 2 master suites with private baths, 2 queen suites share a bath, and one queen studio suite with private bath. Additionally, five cabins have kitchenettes, private bath and Jacuzzi, and private decks overlooking the Swan River. All are exquisitely decorated with antiques and elegant country amenities and have spectacular views of the Mission and Swan mountain ranges.

## FL Mountain Lake Lodge

1950 Sylvan Drive, 5 miles south of Bigfork. 837-4210. Toll free at 877-823-4923. www.mountainlakelodge.com

Mountain Lake Lodge, features 30 luxurious suites each with views of Flathead Lake. Each of the suites includes a gas fireplace, cable TV, wet bar, microwave, and small refrigerator. Enjoy their distinctive waterfall swimming pool and outdoor hot tub. Other amenities include an exercise room, a Conference Room for Executive Retreats, and the Jest Gallery, presenting fine regional art and Coffee Bar. The Lodge boasts two outstanding restaurants. Louis' offers fine dining with a regional and international cuisine in an elegant setting. Riley's Sports Bar and Pub, provides a more casual atmosphere and features wood fired pizza and a selection of micro brews. The friendly and accommodating staff adds to the total experience of this lodge.

## L Swan River Inn

360 Grand Ave., Bigfork. 837-2220.

The Swan River Inn is conveniently located in Downtown Bigfork's stunning artists' community. The Inn offers spectacular views of the Bigfork Bay and the flower gardens that grace the property. The innkeepers offer a casual Montana atmos-

# Steamboat Days on Flathead Lake

**There was a time when there were no** roads around Flathead Lake. Until the Great Northern Railway made its way to the valley over Marias Pass in 1892, the primary mode of transportation was the steamboat. Passengers and freight were hauled overland from the Northern Pacific Depot at Ravalli to Polson. From there, steamboats completed the journey from across the lake to Demersville via the Flathead River.

Things changed considerably when the Great Northern put Kalispell on the main line. Now supplies could be shipped by steamboat to Polson eliminating the wagon trip from Ravalli.

Stops were made just about anywhere on the lake by boats with names like us Grant, Montana, Wasco, Crescent, Kalispell, Demersville, City of Polson, Flyer, Cassie D and Klondike. Some were large and some were small. The Klondike was 120 feet long and could carry 425 passengers and 118 tons of freight. Some of the smaller boats continued in service until the late 1920s.

Some of the more popular stops on the west side were Lakeside (at that time known as Chautauqua or Stoner), Rollins, Angel Point, Dayton (a lumber company dock), Big Arm, Elmo and Salish Point at Polson. On the east shore, Yellow and Woods Bays and Bigfork were popular stops.

While driving around the lake, you can see old dock pilings used by the steamboats. A rail line to Polson, passable roads around the lake and the depression finally sank the steamboat trade. The steamer Helena was tied up at the old ferry-crossing town of Holt, where it eventually sank and rotted. The pilot house of the Helena is displayed outside of Kehoe's Agate Shop, along with a descriptive sign.

*Swan River Inn*

phere with European charm. Six suites are offered and each is uniquely furnished with old world antiques, original artwork, and goose down comforters. They offer European friendliness and Swiss cleanliness. Your stay will be a culinary experience at the adjacent Swan River Café that blends American and European gastronomy. Rooms are nonsmoking and behaving pets are allowed.

## L Accommodations Flathead Lake
East Shore Route, Bigfork, 837-5617

Weekly Vacation Home Rentals.

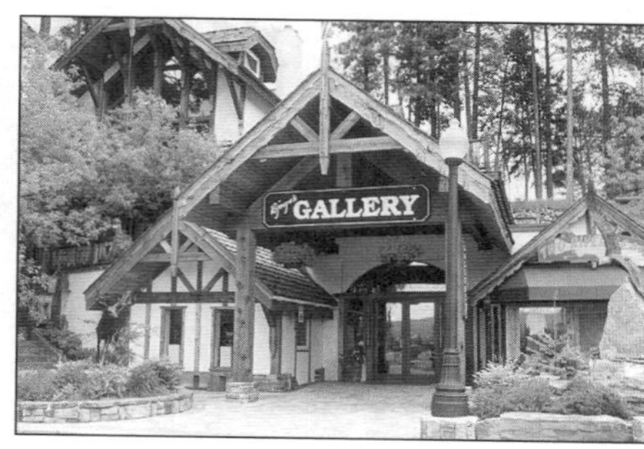


## S Bjorge's Gallery
603 Electric Ave., Bigfork. 837-3839.
www.bjorgesculpturegallery.com

Walk into Bjorge's Gallery and studio and you're likely to find sculptor Ken Bjorge at work on his latest limited-edition creation. This fine art gallery features Ken's representations of wildlife and the west, cast in bronze. Scenes of the old west and Montana's beautiful landscapes adorn the walls, all original oil paintings by such accomplished artists as Marnell Brown, Brent Cotton, Joe Ferrara, Jack Koonce and Margaret Graziano. You'll also find a selection of fine jewelry, hand-crafted knives and wool rugs, hand-loomed in Mexico. Stroll through to Two River Gear where you'll find a wonderful selection of fly fishing gear, flies, clothing, information and more.

## S ARTfusion
471 Electric Ave., Bigfork, 837-3526

A blending of contemporary art and crafts, Art Fusion is a visually stimulating gallery that represents over 60 Montana artists. Their emphasis is on ceramics and paintings. They also have jewelry, photography, and works in wood, glass, fiber and metal. "Colorful, playful art that invites you to feel good!". . .says it all!

### Montana Trivia

The worst way to tell the difference between a black bear and a grizzly bear is to climb a tree. If it follows you up the tree, it's a black bear. If it pushes the tree down, it's a griz.

## S Corbett Gallery
459 Electric Ave. Suite B, Bigfork, 837-2400

Corbett Gallery specializes in the fine western and wildlife art of several renowned Northwestern artists. Originals, sculptures, carvings, pottery, and prints grace this lovely gallery. View a wide range of unique western lighting by artist Roc Corbett. These fascinating pieces range from lamps to chandeliers in sculptured steel, bronze, brass and antlers.

## S Brett Thuma Gallery
459 Electric Ave., Bigfork, 837-4604

The gallery features artist Brett Thuma, with original wildlife and landscape paintings as well as limited edition prints. There is also a selection of bronzes created by Montana artists, inlaid wood mirrors and boxes, and a beautiful collection of jewelry. Artist and owner Brett Thuma invites you to browse leisurely through their unique collection. Located in the Twin Birches Mall.

## S Eva Gates Homemade Preserves
456 Electric Ave., Downtown Bigfork, 837-4356 or 800-682-4283. evagates@digisys.net

For over 50 years the Gates family has helped define the delicious taste of Northwest Montana. Passed down through the generations, this family business is the oldest of its kind in Montana and makes Montana's original huckleberry products. The company produces six varieties of gourmet fruit preserves and three syrups in Eva's time honored method—five pints at a time. When you stop by the gift shop and kitchen you can watch every-

Eva Gates

thing being made and sample the delicious results. This is a must-see while in Bigfork. Open seven days a week, all year long.

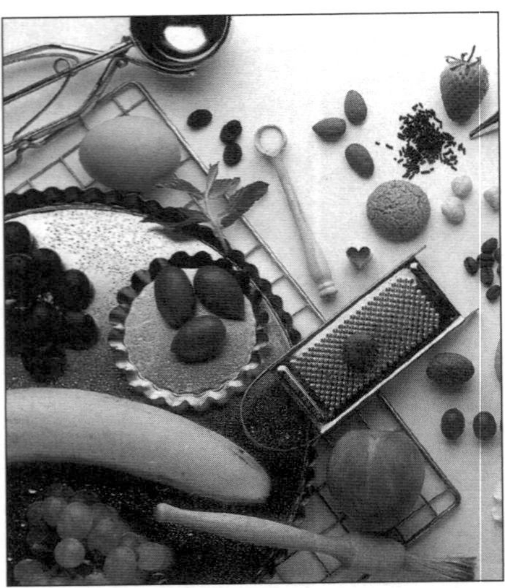

### S Roma's Eclectic on Electric

470 Electric Ave., Bigfork, 837-2332

Roma's Eclectic on Electric is a specialty shop for cooks. Owner Roma Taylor defines "eclectic" by bringing her customers the very best in cooking tools, tableware, and gourmet foods from a variety of sources around the world. By focusing on fine cooking utensils that combine high design and function, Roma's offers a selection that will make your cooking and entertaining an even more enjoyable experience. You are invited to stop by Roma's Electric Avenue, shop any time of the year and get your "kitchen shop fix" fulfilled!

## 25. *Historical Marker, Attraction, Gas, Food, Lodging*

### H A Permanent and Substantial Road

Rte 35, south of Bigfork.

*In the early 20th century many roads in Montana were constructed by convicts from the state prison in Deer Lodge. The warden believed that manual labor not only taught the men a skill, but also increased their self-esteem and reduced the chances they would later return to prison.*

*When created in 1913, the Montana Highway Commission had no money to build roads. Instead they funded "demonstration" projects which often used convict labor. The state paid 50¢ a day for each convict, while the counties provided the equipment. About a third of the penitentiary's 600 inmates worked outside the walls building roads and bridges throughout western Montana. This road was constructed by convict labor in 1913 and 1914.*

*About 111 prisoners worked on the road and lived in two tent camps. They enjoyed a measure of freedom not present in the prison. The food was generally good and the men were treated to evening band concerts performed by their musically inclined comrades. Despite this, thirteen men fled the camps; all were eventually recaptured and returned to prison. Built entirely by hand labor with horse-drawn scrapers and graders, the road cost $31,825 when completed. This was the longest section of road built by convicts before the program ended in 1927. Although upgraded over the years, the highway retains the same alignment established by Montana's convict laborers before World War 1.*

### T Flathead Lake State Park — Wayfarers Unit

5 miles south of Bigfork on Montana 35. Summer: 837-4196 Winter: 752-5501

Located near the resort town of Bigfork on the northeast shore of Flathead Lake. A mature mixed conifer forest makes this site very pleasant for camping and picnicking. Visitors can also enjoy a beach, wildflowers, walking trails, and the best sunsets in the valley. Trailer and boat sewage dump stations are available at this park.

### T Flathead Lake

Flathead Lake is located between Kalispell and Polson on Highways 93 and 35. This beautiful lake is renowned for boating, sailing, fishing, camping, and swimming. The parks six units offer public access to portions of Flathead Lake. One of the units—Wildhorse Island—is accessible only by boat.

Flathead Lake is the largest freshwater lake west of the Mississippi River, and was dredged out by receding glaciers during the Wisconsin period of glaciation. The Lake is 38 miles long and between 5 and 15 miles wide. Encompassing 188 square miles at an elevation of 2,892 feet, the lake's maximum depth is 339 feet, with 185 miles of shoreline.

### AS Bob's Woods Bay Market

26787 Hwy. 35, Bigfork, 837-4884

Bob's can supply you with gas, diesel, and propane among many other things. They have an outdoor fresh produce stand in season, a laundromat, deli sandwiches, ice cream, a nice selection of wine & beer, full groceries, film & batteries, T-shirts, Montana souvenirs, lottery tickets, us Post Office and UPS service, and 25¢ coffee. They can set you up with fishing licenses and they even have their own guide service. Stop in on your way through the Bigfork area.

### L Cherry Way Inn Family Bed & Breakfast

26400 East Shore Route, Bigfork. 837-2640

## 26. *Attraction*

### T Flathead Lake State Park — Yellow Bay Unit

15 miles north of Polson on Montana 35. 752-5501

Located in the heart of Montana's famous sweet cherry orchards, this park includes a walk-in tent area, Yellow Bay Creek and a wide, gravelly beach. Visitors enjoy swimming, boating, lake trout fishing, and bird watching.

## Flathead National Forest

**Horseback riding fun! Located in** northwestern Montana in the Rocky Mountain Province, lies the Flathead National Forest. All of the major landforms are structurally controlled with most of the mountain ranges being formed by block faults. Glaciation from the last ice age influenced the shape of the land as well as the composition of the soil.

From Kalispell, us highway 93 north and State highway 83 south provide primary access to the forest. 758-5200.

## 27. *Attraction*

### T Flathead Lake State Park — Finley Point Unit

11 miles north of Polson on Montana 35, then 4 miles west on county road. Summer: 849-5255 Winter: 752-5501

Finley Point is located in a secluded, mature conifer forest near the south end of Flathead Lake. Lake trout and yellow perch fishing are often excellent. Slips are available for boats up to 25 feet long, along with campsites with the capacity for 40 foot RVs. A boat pump-out station and overnight boat slips (including utilities) are also available.

## 28. *Attraction, Gas, Food, Lodging, Shopping, Miscellaneous*

### Polson

Polson has a thriving resort business heavily oriented toward boating and fishing on Flathead Lake. Fishermen come from all over North America to set their reel to the deep waters of the Flathead Lake, gouged by the last glaciers. Located in the middle of the Flathead Indian Reservation, Paul Bunyan is said to have gouged the sheer walls of the Flathead River Gorge which allows drainage of the lake. Kerr Dam regulates the flow of water at a rate of half-million gallons per second. At 204 feet, the concrete dam is more than 50 feet higher than Niagara Falls. Watch for the glorious sunrises and sunsets which accent the beautiful Mission Mountains.

### T Miracle of America Museum

Junction of Hwy.s. 93 and 35, south of Polson. 883-6804

When you first see this museum from the road, you know there is more inside (and outside) than you can see in a few minute walk through. In fact, there's so much here that visitors have named it the "Smithsonian of the West."

Gil Mangels founded this non-profit museum in 1984 and has grown it to 26 buildings, including a one-room schoolhouse, a furnished trapper's cabin, a sod-roofed log cabin, and a 1950 soda fountain. Most of these buildings are authentic, and a few are rebuilt to original specifications.

On the grounds of the museum you will see two Huey and two MASH helicopters, an A-7 Corsair attack bomber, a 1920 Model T Ford delivery truck, a 1910 Maytag car, a 1916 Model T Ford chain-driven dump truck, more than 30 military vehicles, over 30 vintage motorcycles, farm equipment, an authentic Flathead Lake logging tow boat, an antique snowmobile, Native American artifacts, hundreds of early household appliances and children's antique toys. Exhibits here range from the commonplace to the bizarre.

The museum is open daily from 8 a.m. to 8 p.m. A small admission fee is charged.

### L Mission Mountain Resort

257 Fulkerson Lane, 3 miles E. of Polson. 883-1883. www.polsonmtresort.com

### L Super 8 Motel

Jct. of Hwy.. 35 and 93, Polson. 883-6252 or 800-800-8000

### M Coldwell Banker / Kingsley & Associates

59046 Hwy. 93 S., Polson. 883-6711 or fax 883-2677. Toll free 888-830-6722. www.coldwellbankerkingsley.com

Whether you are a first time homebuyer or stepping up to your dream home, Coldwell Banker/Kingsley & Associates is a great place to begin. They are available 24/7 and only a click away at coldwellbankerkingsley.com. They are experts on the local market, offering expertise from waterfront properties to cattle ranches, cottages to shopping centers. For 95 years, the Coldwell Banker organization has been a premier provider of full-service real estate. The company is an industry leader in residential and commercial real estate. Their sales associates are dedicated to helping you with all of the details before, during and after the sale.

### M Linda Kingsley /Coldwell Banker

1615 Hillcrest Drive, Polson. 883-6711 or cell 250-6236 or toll free at 888-883-8706. email: lindakingsley@yahoo.com

Linda Kingsley of Coldwell Bank Kingsley & Associates can be found at the south end of Flathead Lake. She is known as a Realtor with warm, friendly, professional service, specializing in residential, waterfront, vacation, second homes, ranch land, and summer rentals. She goes the extra mile making clients her #1 priority and that's just one of many reasons why she is recognized as a top real estate professional in northwest Montana, the Flathead Lake, and Mission Valley areas. From the moment you meet Linda you will know she has your interests in mind and will assist you in every way possible. Her office is located at the gateway to all of northwest Montana, where she is known for negotiating skills and for putting the impossible together.

## 29. *Gas, Food, Lodging, Miscellaneous*

### F Regatta Pizza

59047 us Hwy.. 93, Polson. 883-6818.

### L Port Polson Inn

502 Hwy. 93, Polson. 883-5385 or 800-654-0682 (us & Canada). portpolsoninn@compuplus.net

From your room at the Port Polson Inn you will be treated to spectacular views of Flathead Lake and the Mission Mountain Range. The 43 rooms feature some kitchens, cable TV with HBO, and a complimentary continental breakfast. The hotel is complete with indoor and outdoor hot tubs, an exercise room, laundry facilities, and a fax service. They offer great golf packages and have exciting whitewater rafting in the area. They are only one hour from Glacier National Park and a 1/2 hour from the National Bison Range and the historic St. Ignatius Mission. Whether it is golf, dining, summer theatre or water recreation, Port Polson Inn is close to it all!

### L Bayview Inn

914 Hwy. 93, Polson. 883-3120 or 800-735-6862. www.angelfire.com/mt/polson

Built in 1984, the Bayview Inn of Polson is clean quiet, and modern—located within walking distance of restaurants and the downtown shopping area. Every one of the 25 rooms provides a magnificent view of beautiful Flathead Lake and the Mission Mountains. They are complete with cable TV with HBO and air-conditioning, and some even have microwaves, refrigerators, and coffee pots. Your stay includes a complimentary breakfast bar with coffee, juice, fresh fruit, and fresh doughnuts. Enjoy summer fun, with waterfront recreation and Glacier National Park not far away. The toll free number rings right to the front desk, and reservations are recommended, especially in the summer.

### M Lambros Real Estate

1201 1/2 Hwy. 93 E., Polson. 883-1372 or toll free at 800-432-6828. Email: millie@homesmt.com or tony@homesmt.com. www.lambros.com

Lambros Real Estate is the leading source for Flathead Lake, Montana real estate. Tillie and Tony Marshall (GRI) are both brokers and for approximately 10 years have been the leading real estate team in their market area, serving property buyers and sellers in the Flathead Lake area and the beautiful Mission Valley, serving all lake and valley communities including Polson, Ronan and St. Ignatius. For professional real estate services, see Tillie or Tony. They obviously enjoy what they do, and they enjoy their northwest Montana lifestyle. Visit their web site, email them, give them a call, or visit their office in Polson.

## 30. *Attraction, Gas, Food, Lodging*

### T Polson-Flathead Historical Museum

708 Main St. in Polson. 883-3049

Displays that depict the late 1800s and early 1900s are exhibited both inside the Museum building and in the spacious yard. In the yard, old buggies and wagons, a jail cell, farm equipment from old-time homesteads and a historic trading post (1881) that's been restored and contains other exhibits. In The Museum, the visitor can take a few minutes or a few hours and rub elbows with Flathead history, finding fascinating displays of the hardy valley homesteaders, the steamboaters, the cattle ranchers, the development of the City of Poison, as well as a pictorial history of the construction of Kerr Dam, area wildlife and Indian artifacts.

Visitors are invited to share in the heritage of the Mission Valley and Flathead Lake area that is preserved in the Poison Flathead Historical Museum. The development of the Flathead Indian Reservation by the white man and the Indian is reflected in many of the exhibits. Letters and periodicals describe the early experiences of the pioneers and document the growth of the area. Immersing yourself in the history aids in understanding how the valley grew and expanded. There is something for everyone in the Museum, young and old alike. Whether the visitor is recalling the good old days or wondering how it was back then, the time will be well spent.

The museum is open to the public Memorial

Day through Labor Day from 9 a.m. to 6 p.m. Monday through Saturday and Noon to 6 p.m. on Sundays.

F **Rancho Deluxe Steakhouse**
602 6th St. W., on the river, Polson. 883-2300

The Rancho Deluxe Supper Club is casual dining with a sensational views of Flathead Lake year round. The Rancho Deluxe is best known for it's Prime Rib, but the menu also has fantastic appetizers, seafood, pasta, prime rib, and great salads and sandwich selections. They have several micro brews on tap, a great wine selection, and your favorite cocktail. Top off your dining experience at Rancho Deluxe with one of their famous desserts. The historic Ranch has been a favorite steak house in Polson since the 1930's, with the first liquor license to be issued in Lake County. There is a separate casino and lounge for your added pleasure. They even have boat access with docks available. Reservations are suggested.

F **Historic Old Mill Place**
501 Main St., Polson. 883-3190

A great deli and ice cream shop in an historic feed mill.

F **Ponderae**
315 Main St., Polson. 883-1899

L **Ruth's Bed & Breakfast**
802 7th Ave. W, Polson. 883-2460

S **Wild-Side Chocolates and Gifts**
#6 2nd Ave East, Polson. 883-1722 or toll free 877-354-8237. www.wildsidechocolates.com

S **Art Forms Gallery**
215 Main St., Polson. 883-3135

A wonderful gallery filled with paintings, etchings, sculptures, pottery, jewelry & basketry.

M **Real Estate Buyers Solutions**
1st St. E., Polson. 883-8037 or fax 8831849 or toll free at 800-770-7995. www.cindywillis.com or email: realsol@cindywillis.com

## 31. *Attraction*

T **Kerr Dam**
8 miles southwest of Polson. 883-4550

Just a few miles southwest of Polson, the 204-foot-high Kerr Dam straddles the Buffalo Rapids Canyon. The dam was completed in 1938 for Montana Power Co., and will be taken over in 2015 by the Confederated Salish and Kootenai Tribes. It is capable of generating up to 190 megawatts of electricity. There is an English-style village at the powerhouse with a recreation area and raft launching facility. A trail and stairsteps on the canyon's rim lead to an excellent view of the dam. The views are at their finest in late May and early June when the spillway gates are open. The balance of the year, the river is diverted through 800 foot long tunnels and sent directly to the powerhouse. You can call the number above to arrange a tour of the dam, but be patient. The crew is often working outdoors and you may have to call back several times. Tours are available from 8 a.m. to 4:30 p.m. daily. To reach the dam, turn south at the first stoplight past the bridge in downtown Polson and follow the signs.

## 32.

### Big Arm

The town takes its name from the "big arm" of Flathead Lake on which it sits.

T **Flathead Lake State Park — Big Arm Unit**
12 miles north of Polson. on us 93. Summer: 849-5255 Winter: 752-5501 Reservations: 755-2706

Locked on Flathead Lake's Big Arm Bay, this park is a popular jump-off point for boat trips to Wildhorse Island. Big Arm's long pebble beach is popular with sunbathers, and Canada geese watchers. The Big Arm Unit offers camping on the shores of clear, cold Flathead Lake, the largest lake west of the Mississippi River.

## 33. *Attraction*

T **Flathead Lake State Park — Wild Horse Island (Day use Only)**
Access from Big Arm via boat. 752-5501

A glacier scoured mountain rises from the depths of the 200 square mile Flathead lake to form Wild Horse Island. The 2,163 acre island is one of the largest islands in the inland us and is large enough to support its own diverse ecosystem. An assortment of flora, including the endangered palouse prairie plant species, thrives on the mountainsides, wooded slopes, sheltered bays, open grasslands and rocky shores of the island. Abundant wildlife, including bighorn sheep, mule deer, bald eagles, ospreys, and the token herd of wild horses also reside here.

In times past, the Flathead and Pend d'Oreille Indians hid their horses on this island to protect them from the raiding parties of the Blackfeet. Today the island is on the Flathead Reservation portion of the lake. Fishing here requires a tribal fishing permit.

The channel that runs between the island and its neighbor, Melita Island, locally known as Mackinaw Island. Large lake trout are known to linger in the depths of the channel.

If you wish to visit the island, you will need at least an 18 ft. motorboat. Anything less is risky. The route to the island covers a considerable amount of open water, and sudden storms are not uncommon. You can rent boats at Big Arm Marina, 849-5622. Scenic cruises are also available from Pointer Scenic Cruises in Bigfork, 837-5617. There are no paid attendants here, and there is no fee. Camping, fires, and dogs are prohibited on the island.

T **Mission Mountain Winery**
Dayton

## 34. *Attraction, Gas, Food*

T **Flathead Lake State Park — West Shore Unit**
20 miles south of Kalispell on us 93. Summer: 844-3901 Winter: 752-5501

West Shore is located in a mature forest overlooking Flathead Lake. The park's glacially carved rock outcrops give spectacular views of Flathead Lake and the Mission and Swan Mountain Ranges. Fishing and boating are popular at this park. The campground is located above the rocky lakeshore in a fir, pine, and larch forest.

## 35. *Attraction*

T **Lake Mary Ronan**
us 93 at Dayton, then 7 miles northwest. 752-5501, Reservations: 755-2706.

Located on the east shore of Lake Mary Ronan, this 76-acre park is shaded by a forest of douglas fir and western larch. Attractions include fishing for trout, bass, and kokanee salmon, bird watching, huckleberry picking, swimming, and mushroom hunting.

## 36. *Gas, Food, Lodging*

### Lakeside

This town owes its existence to the tourists who come to visit Flathead Lake and Glacier Park.

### Somers

At the end of the 1800s, the lumber industry was booming on Flathead Lake. Somers was a sawmill town that reached its peak in 1901.

F **Tiebuckers Pub & Eatery**
75 Somers Rd., Somers. 857-3335

L **Bayshore Resort Motel**
Hwy. 93, Lakeside. 844-3131

Situated in the beautiful Rocky Mountains and located right on Flathead Lake, close to Glacier National Park, Canada, and Blacktail Downhill Ski Area, the Bayshore offers you a change of scenery. Most rooms have a view of Flathead Lake! They have a swimming beach and boat dock with slips, with fishing charters also available. All rooms have kitchenettes and you choose king or queen size beds, along with family style units, and large suites with private decks. There is a large meeting room at the water's edge that can be used for business meetings, family reunions, or wedding receptions. Join them for beautiful outdoor fun in the summers and fantastic downhill skiing in the winter.

## 37. *Attraction, Gas, Food, Lodging*

### Condon/Swan Valley

Most of the homes and businesses that have a Condon address are spread for several miles up and down Hwy.. 83 between Seeley Lake and Swan Lake for about 10 miles. Residents once petitioned the Post Office to have the name changed to Swan Valley and conceded to allow them to use either name as their address.

### Swan Lake

Swan Lake is located in the Seeley-Swan Valley near the south end of Swan Lake. It's named either for the swans that often visit or Emmett Swan, an early resident.

**T Swan Lake Recreation Area**
Swan Lake

**FL Laughing Horse Lodge**
71284 Hwy. 83, Swan Lake.
www.laughinghorselodge.com or
email: laughinghorsemontana@yahoo.com



## Scenic Drives

**The North Fork**

Take the windy gravel road northward along the North Fork of the Flathead River for some spectacular views of wildlife, and Glacier Park peaks. This drive is a local's favorite. To begin this trip take Nucleus Avenue north through Columbia Falls. The road takes a bend at the train depot then winds north. The road is paved for the first ten miles then turns to gravel. While the road gets oiled occasionally, expect some dust as you travel. The only town along this stretch is Polebridge. The mercantile store and saloon are both worth a visit. After 37 miles of driving, you'll need a break anyway. You can go into the park here jog north then east to Bowman Lake, or continue north to Kintla Lake, or go back to the road and continue north until the road leaves the river and head back.

**Goat Lick**

Mountain goats like to hang around this natural salt lick. And kids like to hang around and watch the goats. The lick is just east of Essex between West Glacier and East Glacier sitting atop cliffs that overlook the scenic Middle Fork of the Flathead River. Allow 60–90 minutes drive time from Kalispell or Whitefish. The best time to visit here is in the late spring and early summer. The nannies visit the lick with their kids about this time.

**Flathead Lake**

It's easy to spend an entire day exploring the nooks, crannies, and unique hamlets surrounding Flathead Lake. You can start just about anywhere on Hwy.. 93 or Hwy.. 35 and drive until you return to your starting point.

## Hikes

**Danny On Memorial Trail**

This trail was named after a northwest Montana nature photographer and Forest Service silviculturist. It offers stunning views of Glacier Park and the Flathead Valley. On a clear day you can see the snowclad peaks of the Mission Mountains to the south, Glacier Park to the east, the Canadian Peaks to the north, and the Cabinet Mountains in the distant west. The trail starts on Big Mountain. The hike can be a 5.6 mile one way, or a shorter 3.8 mile one way by taking the Flower Point Trail. If you want to cut some climbing and distance off, you can take the lift to the top of the mountain. Wildlife and wildflowers flourish here. If you can't hike without your dog, pass this one up. Dogs are not allowed on Big Mountain.

**East Rim Trail**

This hike is less than a mile, but inch for inch packs in as much scenery as any in the state. The hike takes you to the top of Big Mountain. Take the lift up to the summit of Big Mountain. Take the Danny On Trailhead about 100 yards from the Summit House. In a short distance the trail will separate from the Danny On trail, travel the edge of the eastern summit and return.

**Jewel Basin**

This is really more of a hiking area than a hike. As it is designated strictly hiking, you don't have to contend the horse pies and ATV's. There are over 35 miles of trail here with over 25 mountain lakes along them. The trails, usually clear by July are accessible from the Hungry Horse Reservoir or from Jewel Basin Road near Bigfork. The main parking area can be reached by turning on Echo Lake Road off MT Hwy.. 83 and then onto Jewel Basin Road No. 5392. The road goes for approximately seven roller coaster miles. There is usually snow in the parking lot until mid-June. There is a ranger station here with information on the various hiking opportunities. Abundant high altitude wildflowers and wildlife are the norm here.

**Swan River Nature Trail**

From the downtown area of Bigfork, head straight up Grand Avenue to access this relaxed stroll. The gated, non-motorized portion of this road extends for a mile of level walking along the churning whitewater of the Swan River.

**Crane Mountain Lookout**

This is more of a scenic drive with a short walk at the end. Take Hwy.. 209 southeast of Bigfork to Ferndale Drive (just past the fire station) and turn south. Go straight to the Y then bear right. Follow Crane Mountain Road for about six miles until you reach Road 498A. Park at the gated area then hike about 1/4 to the old fire lookout tower. Here you will get incredible views of both Flathead Lake to the west, and Swan Lake directly beneath you to the east.

**The Sally Tollefson Memorial Trail on the Swan River Oxbow Preserve**

2.5 miles south of Swan Lake on Hwy.. 83, turn right onto Porcupine Creek Road and drive for .25 mile to the sign which points the way to the parking area and kiosk. The trail covers about a mile through the 400 acre preserve with identification plaques describing the various flora and fauna. The Nature Conservancy established this preserve to protect several rare plant species and the diverse wetland community in the oxbow left by the Swan River as it changed course. Visitors are asked to stay on the trails to minimize the impact on the plant communities. This is an excellent hike for viewing a range of wildlife including moose, elk, deer, bald eagles, osprey, and a variety of other bird species. It is also a good place to see a grizzly, which makes it a high risk walk from mid-April to mid-June. Be prepared for mosquitoes and wet boggy ground.

**Sprunger-Whitney Nature Trail**

The Point Pleasant Campground, seven miles south of Swan Lake and 1/2 mile south of mile marker 64, is the trailhead of this two mile loop trail. As you walk from the old logging site

# How To Fool A Trout

by Roland Cheek

**Bob Hirsch, a fishing fool/outdoor writer** friend from sunnier climes, once whispered two simple fishing rules he swears are essential for the successful fisherman: "Light is right, and no drag—no brag."

Bob has a penchant for getting to the heart of a subject. He also wastes few words. However, realizing me and most of my readers aren't as sophisticated at it as this master angler, I asked him to illucidate. In his own words:

"Even hatchery trout soon learn to avoid the fisherman's offering. And wild, stream-hatched fish are so spooky and suspicious that catching one can be a real challenge, The most important single thing you can do to improve your trout take is to use light line. Load your reel with the best-quality line you can buy. It will cast further and come off the spool smoothly, and not in those stiff coils of 'memory.'

"There's not a trout in the state that can't be hooked and landed on 4-pound test monofilament. The light line will let you cast smaller lures and bait further. It also will help you fool fish, which you must do if you want to catch them.

"So re-spool with 4-pound mono, the best you can buy. Now really get crafty and tie on about four or five feet of 2-pound leader to guarantee more trout. Don't worry, it won't break. use a small (about No. 12 or 14), unsnelled hook and cover it completely with bait, even the eye.

"Snelled hooks, with their stiff, 20-pound mono leader, negate your 2-pound leader. use loose (unsnelled) hooks.

"Lastly, use as little weight as possible. None is best; it will let your bait look as natural as possible. If you must have weight to cast, try one split shot and add more only if needed. A big chunk of lead will only spook the trout when it picks up your bait and moves off.

"To land a big fish on light line, your reel's drag must be set properly. When you hear a fisherman say 'that lunker took off and popped my line like it was thread,' you can bet his drag wasn't set properly. Somewhere on every reel is an adjustable wheel or knob that tightens or loosens, permitting line to be stripped from the reel without turning the handle.

"Set this before you begin fishing each day. Best way is to have a friend hold the end of your line tightly while you raise the rod sharply, just as you would do when you strike a fish. The drag should slip slightly at the top of your rod's upward sweep.

"If in doubt, set the drag on the light side. It's easy to tighten it a bit while you're fighting a fish, but if it's too tight and the line breaks, loosening it won't help get the fish back.

"When the reel 'sings' as the drag is engaged and line is pulled out by the fish, stop reeling and let the trout run and tire itself. Always keep the rod tip up, so the fish is fighting the bend and not pulling directly on the line."

"These techniques work," Bob says, and I've tried 'em enough to know he's not just a-woofin.

## Fishing the Lakes

Freeze-up comes to most of the lowland lakes in December and sometimes even January, to where they're solid enough to fish through the ice.

Spring comes to the Flathead anywhere from late March on. usually, ice break-up occurs on lower valley lakes then, but the ice has been altogether too rotten to safely support anglers for quite a while prior to break-up. Ice retreats from some of the higher valley lakes in April and even into May. And it's not uncommon to find some high mountain lakes covered with ice well into June, or even early July.

My experiences tell me a darned good time to hit these lakes is just as the ice is beginning to break and "leads" open wide enough along shore to allow you spin-fishing room. After a winter of enforced repose, trout are apt to cast off all restraints at the sheer ecstasy of open surface water, and it's a lucky fisherman who chances by at just that moment, (Caution: stay off the ice!)

Small wobbling lures are best. Choose something in silver or white, and red—red is a must. Mepps are good too, with or without bucktail—No. 1 or 2. Super Duper, Panther Martin, ZRay—they're all good. For plugs, Flatfish or sinking Rapala in silver or gold, white with red spots, orange with black spots, or green with orange spots.

After the first feeding frenzy at break-up, most lake fishing settles gradually back to normal, where experience plays a more important role in success. Fishing still tends to be best for the first few weeks after the ice is gone. Trout are hungrier then, and are likelier to be feeding in the shallows. Big mackinaw (lake trout) can sometimes be taken at that time by wading fly fishermen, using big streamers fished wet. What a thrill!

Spin casting from shore is also good at that time. Later, trolling comes into its own as the waters warm and fish return to the depths. Still, cutthroat and rainbow return periodically to the shore on feeding forays. That's when the bait fisherman is likely to limit.

Unless you find trout cruising over a submerged weed bed, it's best to get down on or near the bottom with whatever you use.

Trolling is a tried and true method of taking trout and those long collections of spinners called "cowbells" or "Ford tenders" are often used for this purpose. They have no hook of their own, but serve as an attractor. Attach three feet of 2- to 4-pound monofilament and trail a lure, fly or a hook full of worms. Very effective.

Trolling with a lure or fly, usually with a split shot or two crimped on the line to get it down, is also good.

And, of course, boaters can anchor and fish with bait. If you do anchor, look long and hard at the weed beds—they're food factories for trout. Fish near 'em if you can.

Trout relish baits such as worms, crayfish, grasshoppers and crickets. Salmon eggs, whole kernel corn, Velveeta cheese and bite-sized marshmallows are widely used. Don't forget to use light leaders and small hooks.

Flies? I'm partial to gray flies—I just think Flathead country trout are partial to 'em, too. Gray hackle, Joe's Hopper, caddis—they're all good. So are others—coachman (bucktail and royal), wooly worm (size 8-10-12) in black, brown, or green. Royal Wulff is good, too. So are stone flies. And one heckuva lot of others,too.

In fact, one mighty fine fisherman who'd been on a week's float trip with us down the remote Wild and Scenic South Fork of the Flathead explained it best when I asked him what type of fly was best: "Anything," he said. "Anything at all."

## Fishing the Streams

Snow melt in the high mountains of our country usually begins in earnest sometime in May, The average date for high water to peak in the main Flathead River is May 27, but I've seen the peak vary from May 10 to June 19, depending on snow depths and spring temperatures.

The real point of the run-off is that the rivers can be very high and roily then, and fishing consequently can be good, but catching darned disappointing. However, one must remember that some fine catches can be made before run-off peaks, depending on stream opening dates. And during low snow pack and early run-off years, fishing can be good much earlier than normal. Nobody can second-guess the run-off, though. One must simply keep an open mind about the thing and fish when the water is right.

Flathead area streams vary tremendously in size. The really big ones are too broad to cast across and must be drift-floated to reach all the best places. Spinners, cast to overhanging banks, around submerged logs and upthrust boulders, retrieved in short jerks, are good. Or any of the above flies fished the same manner can be rewarding.

Many Flathead streams are small and the banks are lined with willows and brush, so they are difficult to fish. Because trout nearly always lie facing upstream, prudence dictates wading upstream and casting ahead.

But some streams are so small and brush-choked that it's impossible to cast far enough to be effective. In that case let your bait or fly drift downstream while you feed out line. Or you can use cover to sneak up to the stream and stick your rod through the brush to drop your fly directly into the pool or riffle.

On stretches where the stream opens up and has grass banks, it's perfectly okay to get down on your hands and knees and sneak up on a pool. Don't try to see if the pool has fish. When you see them—and they see you—fishing is over for a while at that spot.

Many of the intermediate-sized streams—small rivers, big creeks—can be fished effectively with some of the above mentioned lures. The secret is to make short upstream casts and to reel just enough to keep the spinner's blades flashing in stream and casting ahead.

But some streams are so small and brush-choked that it's impossible to cast far enough to be effective. In that case let your bait or fly drift downstream while you feed out line. Or you can use cover to sneak up to the stream and stick your rod through the brush to drop your fly directly into the pool or riffle.

On stretches where the stream opens up and has grass banks, it's perfectly okay to get down on your hands and knees and sneak up on a pool. Don't try to see if the pool has fish. When you see them—and they see you—fishing is over for a while at that spot.

Many of the intermediate sized streams—small rivers, big creeks—can be fished effectively with some of the above mentioned lures. The secret is to make short upstream casts and to reel just enough to keep the spinner's blades flashing in those deep holes across the stream. Be ready for a strike when the current starts sweeping your lure into mid-channel.

Incidentally, grasshoppers, caught streamside, have fooled a lot of big fish for centuries.

## When to Fish

The best time to go fishing is when you have a chance, but generally, early and late seasons of the year are best in Flathead area lakes and streams. As mentioned earlier in this section, lakes are good from ice break-up to water warm-up. Then they usually turn good again, come September and October. Best method for the "dog days" of summer is to troll slow and deep, or to fish dry flies near shore in early morning or late evening.

Streams are usually better for big migrating cutthroat around mid-May to mid-June, as they school for spawning runs. But beware the spring runoff bogey. Small streams are better during the aforementioned "dog days," wading or sneaking surreptitiously, drifting flies or bait.

Perhaps the best thing of all for you to remember is this quote from Herbert Hoover:

*"The good Lord does not subtract from a man's span of life the hours he spends fishing."*

*Roland Cheek's "Trails to Outdoor Adventure" has been syndicated in print and radio. He is the author of six books and countless outdoor articles. Find out more about him at www.roland-cheek.com.*

through the heavy old growth forest, you will see a wide variety of tree species and wildlife.

**Old Squeezer Loop Road**
This is an area of interconnecting trails that wander through meadow and forest and offer excellent wildlife viewing opportunities. On Hwy.. 83 about 13 miles south of Swan Lake at about mile marker 58 is the turnoff on Goat Creek FR 554. Go east for 1.5 miles. Take the fork right onto Old Squeezer Loop Road and go for about 2 miles to the parking area.

**Cold Lakes**
The easy 1.5 mile trail here leads to Lower Cold Lake. There is an Upper Cold Lake, but no real trail to it. You'll have to bushwack your way up if you want to see it. This is a pleasant hike here with lots of opportunities to see wildlife. You can even take a swim in the lake. Go south of Swan Lake on Hwy.. 83 about 23 miles to .7 miles north of mile marker 46. Turn west onto Cold Creek FR 903 and drive southwest for 3 miles. Turn right on FR 9568 and take another left on FR 9599. From the highway to the trailhead is about 7 miles.

## Cross-Country Ski Trails

### Flathead National Forest

**Essex Trail Complex-Izaak Walton Inn, Essex**
For more information contact: District Ranger, Hungry Horse, MT 59919 (406) 387-5243
*16.3 km Easiest 12.5 km More Difficult: 2 km Most Difficult; intermittent grooming*
System consists of 7 trails; park at Izaak Walton hm. Trails maintained and groomed by Izaak Walton Inn. $5 per person trail fee required.

**Glacier Wilderness Ranch-20 mii E Hungry Horse on Highway 2**
For more information contact: District Ranger, Hungry Horse, MT 59919 (406) 387-5243
*20.2 km varying from Easiest to Most Difficult; intermittent grooming*
Trails use old Highway 2.

**Round Meadows—15 mi NW Whitefish**
For more information contact: District Ranger, Whitefish, MT 59937 (406) 863-5400
*3.5 mi Easiest: 3.5 mi More Difficult: 2 mi More Difficult; intermittent grooming December 20 -March 15*
Trailhead parking 50 vehicles plus accessible restroom. Trail maps available at entrance sign. Please leave dogs at home.

**Blacktail Mountain-8 mi W Lakeside**
For more information contact: District Ranger, Bigfork, MT 59911(406)837-7500
*10 km Easiest, 29.5 km More Difficult; intermittent grooming*
No skiing on plowed Blacktail Mountain Road.

## Information Please

All Montana area codes are 406

### Road Information

Montana Road Condition Report
800-226-7623, 800-335-7592 or local 444-7696
Montana Highway Patrol444-7696

**Local Road Reports**
Missoula 728-8553
Kalispell 751-2037
Statewide Weather Reports 453-2081

### Tourism Information

Travel Montana 800-847-4868 outside Montana
444-2654 in Montana
http://travel.mt.gov/.
Glacier Country 837-6211 or 800-338-5072
Northern Rodeo Association 252-1122

**Chambers of Commerce**
Bigfork 837-5888
Columbia Falls 892-2072
East Glacier Park 226-4403
Kalispell 758-2800
Lakeside/Somers 844-3715
Polson 883-5969
Swan Lake 837-5086
Whitefish 862-3501

### Airports

Bigfork 257-5994
Kalispell 752-6600
Meadows Creek 752-7345
Polebridge 755-5401
Polson 883-6787

### Government Offices

State BLM Office 255-2885, 238-1540
Bureau of Land Management
Missoula Field Office 329-3914
Butte Field Office 494-5059
Flathead National Forest 758-5200
Montana Fish, Wildlife & Parks 752-5501
us Bureau of Reclamation
Helena Field Office 475-3310

### Hospitals

Flathead Outpatient Surgical • Kalispell 752-8484
Glacier View Hospital • Kalispell 752-5422
Kalispell Regional Hospital • Kalispell 752-1780
St Joseph Hospital • Polson 883-5377
North Valley Hospital • Whitefish 862-2501

### Golf Courses

Eagle Bend Golf Course • Bigfork 837-7300
Meadow Lake Golf Resort
Columbia Falls 892-2111
Glacier Park Lodge • East Glacier 226-5600
Buffalo Hill Golf Club • Kalispell 756-4548
Glacier Village Greens Golf Course
Kalispell 752-4666
Northern Pines Golf Club • Kalispell 751-1950
Mission Bay-residential Golf • Polson 883-1730
Polson City Golf Course • Polson 883-8230
Mountain Meadows Resort • Proctor 849-5459
Glacier View Golf Club • West Glacier 888-5471
Par 3 On Golf Course • Whitefish 862-7273
Whitefish Lake Golf Club • Whitefish 862-5960

# Definitely Wild, Certainly Scenic

by Roland Cheek

**The 1976 addition of all three forks** of the Flathead into America's Wild and Scenic Rivers System assures these free flowing streams in perpetuity for your children and grandchildren.

The Flathead System consists of three gradations: Wild, Scenic and Recreational.

A Wild River is preserved in its natural primitive condition, free of impoundments and generally inaccessible except by trail, with its watersheds or shorelines essentially primitive and its waters unpolluted. The sections of the Flathead River designated as wild are from the headwaters of the Middle Fork to Bear Creek and from the headwaters of the South Fork to Spotted Bear.

A Scenic River is free of impoundments and accessible in places by roads, with shorelines or watersheds still largely primitive and undeveloped. Emphasis is placed on preserving the high scenic quality of the area. The part of the Flathead River classified as a scenic river is from the United States-Canada border to Camas Bridge, on the North Fork.

A Recreational River is categorized. Though some development has occurred along their shorelines, some stretches are in a near natural setting, and high quality recreation experiences are available. Recreational segments are: on the North Fork, from Camas Bridge to the confluence with the Middle Fork at Blankenship; on the Middle Fork, from Bear Creek to the confluence of the South Fork below Hungry Horse; on the South Fork, from Spotted Bear to Hungry Horse Reservoir.

All three forks of the Flathead are popular whitewater rivers for floaters using inflatable rafts. The Middle Fork is far and away the most popular river because of its relatively easy access and proximity to the West Glacier entrance into Glacier National Park. For instance, the two-hour float segment immediately upstream from the Park entrance records some 11,500 floaters per year. That high volume, of course, reflects an unusually exciting stretch of river, where access is easily afforded and quickly accomplished.

The rest of the Middle Fork, some of it equally exciting, totaling some 125 miles, receives only an additional 1,000 user days. From these figures, one may better analyze the inordinate popularity of the Nyack to West Glacier stretch so heavily used—the one that carries such dramatic rapid christenings as *Jaws*, *Bonecrusher*, *Narrows* and *Pumphose*.

Professional raft companies are located in the West Glacier vicinity. Each provide a variety of whitewater float options to folks interested in an exciting two-day, day or afternoon float.

Access to the Middle Fork's Wilderness portion is via aircraft landing at Schafer airstrip. This Schafer to Bear Creek segment is a wild whitewater stream of first rank, and should only be attempted by those with good equipment and lots of experience.

The North Fork is considered a much more gentle stream for its entire American length, though two or three challenging rapids are just downstream from Great Northern Flats. The greatest upstream challenge for the floater, from the Canadian border to Camas Bridge could be low water and log jams. Consider the North Fork a better learning stream for novice or intermediate.

One or two of the West Glacier raft companies also provide float trips on the North Fork.

The Flathead's South Fork is very different. Except for a gentle five mile stretch from Spotted Bear to Hungry Horse Reservoir, this river is tough to access. There is one four-mile segment called Meadow Creek Gorge that is considered not navigable by even the most experienced whitewater rats.

There is one access trail leading to the river below the gorge. The trail is currently unmarked, about 1-1/2 miles north of the Meadow Creek Gorge trail bridge. Watch carefully for a small track leading east from the Meadow Creek Road. The trail is at the north foot of a steep hill. Parking is limited and it's a tough carry to get your rafts down to the river. But for those who do, the rewards of floating this isolated stretch (12 miles to Spotted Bear) of the South Fork make it all worthwhile.

Otherwise, the South Fork is a horseback show only. From the Meadow Creek pack bridge on, there are only trails accessing this most remote of all Flathead streams. The South Fork is navigable from some 40 upstream miles, down to the beginning of Meadow Creek Gorge. Surprisingly, there is little whitewater excitement along the South Fork, above the gorge. But it may well be the finest cutthroat trout fishery in the world.

One procedure for rating a river is the International Scale For Grading River Difficulty. It rates an entire river, or whole sections of a river according to the most difficult rapids to be encountered. Thus, if even one rapid rates a Class IV, the entire river or section being described must be rated as Class IV.

### The International Scale For Grading River Difficulty:

I. Practiced beginner: Easy sand banks, bends without difficulty, occasional small rapids with waves regular and low. Correct course easy to find; but care needed with minor obstacles like pebble banks, fallen trees, etc., especially on narrow rivers. River speed less than hard back-paddling speed.

II. Intermediate: Medium, fairly frequent but unobstructed rapids, usually with regular waves, easy eddies, and easy bends. Course generally easy to recognize. River speeds occasionally exceeding hard backpaddling speed.

III. Experienced: Difficult maneuvering in rapids necessary. Small falls, large regular waves covering boat, numerous rapids. Main current may swing under bushes, branches or overhangs. Course not always easily recognizable. Current speed usually less than fast forward paddling speed.

IV. Highly Skilled: Very difficult, long rocky rapids with difficult and completely irregular broken water which must be run head on. Very fast eddies, abrupt bends and vigorous cross currents. Difficult landings increase hazard. Frequent inspections necessary. Extensive experience necessary.

V. Team of Experts: Exceedingly difficult. Either very long or very mean waves, usually wild turbulence capable of picking up a boat and boater and throwing them several feet. Extreme congestion in cross current. Scouting difficult from shore and some danger to life in the event of a mishap.

VI. Team of Experts: Limit of Navigability - all previously mentioned difficulties increased to the limit. Only negotiable at favorable water levels. Cannot be attempted without risk of life.

Whitewater ratings for the three forks of the Flathead, as agreed upon by Flathead Wild and Scenic River administrators, in consultation with experienced floaters on their best known segments is as follows:

**North Fork**

| | |
|---|---|
| Border to Polebridge | II |
| Polebridge to Camas Bridge | I |
| Camas Bridge to Middle Fork | III |

**Middle Fork**

| | |
|---|---|
| Headwaters to Schafer Meadows | III |
| Schafer Meadows to Spruce Park | V |
| Spruce Park to Bear Creek | V |
| Bear Creek to West Glacier | IV |

**South Fork**

| | |
|---|---|
| Headwaters to Big Salmon | I |
| Big Salmon to Meadow Creek Gorge | II |
| Meadow Creek Gorge to Harrison Creek | V |
| Harrison Creek to Reservoir | II |

*Roland Cheek's "Trails to Outdoor Adventure" has been syndicated in print and radio. He is the author of six books and countless outdoor articles. Find out more about him at www.roland-cheek.com.*

## Bed & Breakfasts

| | |
|---|---|
| **Candlewycke Inn B&B** • Bigfork | 837-6406 |
| **Cherry Way Inn** • Bigfork | 837-6803 |
| **Coyote Roadhouse Inn** • Bigfork | 837-4250 |
| **Garden Wall B&B** • Whitefish | 862-3440 |
| **Gasthaus Wendlingen** • Whitefish | 862-4886 |
| **Glacier Park B&B** • Hungry Horse | 387-5099 |
| **Good Medicine Lodge** • Whitefish | 862-5488 |
| **Historic 1907 Tamarack LodgeB&B & Motel** Hungry Horse | 387-4420 |
| **Hidden Moose Lodge** • Whitefish | 862-6516 |
| **O'Duachain B&B** • Bigfork | 837-6851 |
| **Park View Inn B&B** • Columbia Falls | 892-7275 |
| **Ruth's B&B** • Polson | 883-2460 |
| **Swan River Inn B&B** • Bigfork | 387-2220 |
| A Wild Rose • Coram | 387-4900 |
| At The Rivers Edge B & B • Bigfork | 837-4600 |
| Bonnie's B&B • Kalispell | 755-3776 |
| Burggraf's Countrylane • Bigfork | 837-4608 |
| Bad Rock Country B & B Columbia Falls | 892-2829 |
| Cottonwood Hill Inn • Kalispell | 756-6404 |
| Duck Inn Lodge • Whitefish | 862-3825 |
| Flathead Lake B&B • Bigfork | 982-3493 |
| Hawthorne House • Polson | 883-2723 |
| Jubilee Orchards Lake Resort • Bigfork | 837-4256 |
| La Villa Montana • Columbia Falls | 892-0689 |
| Meadow Lake View B & B Columbia Falls | 892-0900 |
| Mountain Timbers Wilderness Columbia Falls | 387-5830 |
| Park View Inn B&B • Columbia Falls | 892-7275 |
| Plum Creek House • Columbia Falls | 892-1816 |
| Point Of View • Columbia Falls | 892-2525 |
| Glacier B&B • Hungry Horse | 387-4153 |
| Blaine Creek B&B • Kalispell | 752-2519 |
| Creston Country Inn • Kalispell | 755-7517 |
| Cutshaw Country Inn • Kalispell | 756-1409 |

Keith House B&B • Kalispell 752-7913
Logan House B&B • Kalispell 755-5588
Lonesome Dove Ranch • Kalispell 756-3056
River-rock B&B • Kalispell 756-6901
Soiree Ranch • Kalispell 257-5770
Stillwßater Inn B & B • Kalispell 755-7080
Switzer House Inn • Kalispell 257-5837
Shoreline Inn • Lakeside 844-3222
Mission Meadow B&B • Polson 883-5970
Mitchell House B&B • Polson 883-5484
Swan Hill B&B • Polson 883-5292
Llamas & Llodging • Somers 857-2447
Osprey Inn B&B • Somers 857-2042
Outlook Inn B&B • Somers 857-2060
Paola Creek B&B • West Glacier 888-5061
Silverwolf Chalets • West Glacier 387-4448
Smoky Bear Ranch • Columbia Falls
Crenshaw House • Whitefish 862-3496
Eagles Roost B&B • Whitefish 862-5198
Edgewood B&B • Whitefish 862-9663
Lake Lodge B&B • Whitefish 862-9765
Timber Wolf • Hungry Horse 387-9653
Wagner's Lodge • Babb 338-5770
The Way Less Traveled • Polebridge 261-5880
Whitefish Bend B&B • Whitefish 862-3825

## Guest Ranches & Resorts

**Jacobson's Cottages** • East Glacier 226-4422
**Crestwood Resort Condominiums**
Whitefish 862-7574
**Abbott Valley Homestead**
Hungry Horse 387-5774
**Lake Five Resort** • Hungry Horse 387-5601
**Marina Cay Resort** • Bigfork 837-5861
**Anapurna Condominium Rentals**
Whitefish 862-3687
Bayshore Resort • Lakeside 844-3131
**Big Mountain Ski & Summer Resort**
Whitefish 862-1900
**Brownie's American Youth Hostel**
East Glacier 226-4426
**Crestwood Resort** • Whitefish 862-7574
**Johnson's of St. Mary** • St. Mary 732-5565
**Mission Mountain Resort** • Polson 883-1883
**Montana Ranch Adventures** • St.Mary338-3333
**Mountain Lake Lodge** • Bigfork 837-4210
**White Oak of Montana** • Kalispell 857-2388
North Fork Hostel & Square Peg Ranch
Polebridge 888-5241
Bear Creek Guest Ranch & Outfitters
E. Glacier 226-4489
Bison Creek Ranch • E. Glacier 226-4482
Dillon's Resort Marina • Big Arm 849-5838
Happy Landing Resort • Big Arm 849-5663
Bayview Resort • Bigfork 837-4843
Woods Bay Resort • Bigfork 837-3333
Meadow Lake Resort • Columbia Falls 892-7601
North Forty Resort • Columbia Falls 862-7740
Arrowhead Resort • Elmo 849-5545
Day Star Guest Ranch • Hungry Horse 387-5685
Timber Wolf Resort • Hungry Horse 387-9653
Diamond R Guest Ranch • Kalispell 756-1573
Lake Blaine Resort • Kalispell 755-2891
Tee Pee Lodge • Kalispell 752-6533
Peaceful Bay Resort • Lakeside 844-2800
Hidden Rock Resort • Polson 887-2241
Mission Mountain Resort • Polson 883-1883
Camp Tuffit • Proctor 849-5220
Mountain Meadows Resort • Proctor 849-5459
Lake Mary Ronan Lodge • Proctor 849-5454
Alpine Homes • Whitefish 862-1982
Eagles Nest Rentals • Whitefish 862-1872
Gaynor's River Bend Ranch •Whitefish 862-3802
Log House On The Hill • Whitefish 862-1071
Wildwood Condominiums •Whitefish 863-4652

# He Mapped The West

**In 2007, the Flathead Valley will join** our Canadian neighbors to commemorate the life and work of David Thompson. Considered by many as the foremost land geographer of the American continent, Thompson mapped more than 1.5 million square miles in both Canada and the United States. In March 1812, he became the first white man to document Flathead Lake, then known as the Saleesh Lake. His name appears on our landscape and yet, American history books say little about this remarkable man and his achievements.

Born in Wales and educated at London's Greycoat School, Thompson prepared for a career in the military. At age 14 he found there was little demand for new recruits so he signed on with the Hudson Bay Company and sailed for Canada. In 1786, he was selected to travel inland to the prairies and by the next year he had traveled to the Rocky Mountains where he wintered with the Piegan.

In 1788, an accident resulted in a broken leg, probably a compound fracture. During his long recuperation Thompson met Hudson Bay Company surveyor Philip Tumor who taught him about celestial observation, navigation and cartography. Following his recovery, Thompson spent the next seven years traveling, trading furs and surveying his routes on the Canadian plains.

When Hudson Bay Company wanted him to stop his exploration, Thompson quit and joined the Northwest Company where he first surveyed the Mandan territory along the Missouri River. Lewis and Clark used his survey and maps on their famous journey west.

Thompson finally journeyed over the Continental Divide in 1807 and for the last five years of his western career, he explored and traded in the Northwest Company's Columbia Department. It was during this period that he traveled and mapped the entire 1,100 miles of the Columbia River, not to mention much of the Columbia Plateau. He mapped and established trading posts in Northwest Montana, Idaho, and Western Canada.

While in Montana, Thompson established Saleesh House, the first Montana trading post west of the Rockies. The Kootenai gave him the name Koo Koo Sint, or Star Looker, because of his nightly astronomical observations. Thompson mapped more than a million square miles of western North America, traveling 80,000 miles in the wilderness (contrasted to the 7,000 miles logged by Lewis and Clark). He was usually accompanied by his wife, Charlotte, a Cree who bore him 13 children.

Thompson was more than a geographer and cartographer. His daily journals detailed not only the natural world, but the people he encountered and their ways of life. He wrote 77 field journals followed by his Narrative that details his western explorations, providing details for several generations of historians.

The year 2007 will mark the 150th anniversary of Thompson's death in 1857 and the 200th anniversary of his first crossing of the Rocky Mountains in 1807. The David Thompson Bicentennial is a project of Parks Canada and the Mountain Parks Heritage tourism Councils in Canada.

For more information on events relating to David Thompson in the Flathead Valley go to the Flathead Valley Convention and Visitor Bureau website at www.montanasflatheadvalley.com.

*Article by Carol Edgar, courtesy of Flathead Valley Convention and Visitor Bureau.*

## Vacation Homes & Cabins

**Abbott Valley Cabins** • Martin City 387-4436
**All Pro Rental Property Management**
Kalispell 755-1332
**Anapurna/Edelweiss Condominiums**
Whitefish 862-3687
**Glacier Raft Company Cabins**
West Glacier 888-5454
**Glacier Trailhead Cabins** •St. Mary 732-4143
**Izaak Walton Inn** • Essex 888-5700
**East Glacier Cabins & Motel**
East Glacier 226-5593
**Coyote Roadhouse Cabins**
Bigfork 837-4250
**Moccasin Lodge Vacation Home**
West Glacier 888-5545
**Glacier Cabins** • Martin City 387-5339
**Accomodations Flatehead Lake**
Bigfork 837-5617
**Kristiana Mountain Homes**
Whitefish 862-2860
**Crestwood Resort Condominiums**
Whitefish 862-7574
A&A Montana Vacation Rentals
Lakeside 752-4783
Angel Point Guest Suites • Lakeside 844-2204
Authentic Montana Log Cabin
Bigfork 837-6898
Bay Point on the Lake • Whitefish 862-2331
Beardance Inn & Cabins • Bigfork 837-4551'
C Barr Heart Ranch • Coram 387-5617
Bigfork Rental Agency • Bigfork 837-6424
Bitterroot Lake Vacation Rental
Kalispell 756-6023
Cabins In Glacier National Park
Kalispell 756-2444
Cedar Shore Cabins • Columbia Falls 755-7520

Columbia Mountain Cabins
Columbia Falls 892-3005
Eagle Bend Flathead Vacation Rentals
Bigfork 837-4942
Echoing Jewel Vacation Home
Bigfork 257-4237
Essex Cabins • Essex 863-2355
Five Star Rentals • Whitefish 862-5994
Flathead Lake Beach Homes • Somers 857-2079
Full Circle Herb Farm • Kalispell 257-8133
Glacier Village Property Management
Whitefish 862-1960
Glacier River Ranch • Coram 387-4151
Gordon Ranch • Condon 252-8228
Gustin Orchards • Bigfork 982-3329
Harbor Mountain Properties
Bigfork 862-5511
Heartwood • Coram 387-5541
Inspiration Condos • Whitefish 862-0569
Jubilee Orchards Vacation Rentals
Bigfork 837-4256
Montana Ranch Adventures • St.Mary 338-3333
Montana Treasures & Retreats • Coram387-5498
Orchard House • Bigfork 837-3588
Polebridge Mercantile • Polebridge 888-5105

# Swan River NWR

**The Swan River National Wildlife** Refuge is located in northwest Montana, 32 miles southeast of the town of Creston, in the serene and picturesque Swan Valley Mountain Range. The refuge boundary lies within the floodplain of the Swan River above Swan Lake and between the Swan Mountain Range to the east and the Mission Mountain Range to the west. The valley was formed when glacial ice poured down the steep slopes of the Mission Range The valley floor is generally flat, but rises steeply to adjacent forested mountain sides. Most of the refuge lies within this valley floodplain, which is composed mainly of reed canary grass. Deciduous and coniferous forests comprise the rest. Swan River, which once meandered through the floodplain, has been forced to the west side of the refuge by deposits of silt, leaving a series of oxbow sloughs within the refuge floodplain. Objectives of the refuge are to provide for waterfowl habitat and production and to provide for other migratory bird habitat. The refuge also provides a nesting site for a pair of southern bald eagles and a variety of other avian species. In addition, deer, elk, moose, beaver, bobcat, black bear and grizzly bears are known to inhabit the area. There are no significant developments or facilities on the refuge and present management is directed at maintaining the area in its natural state.

Directions:
Swan River National Wildlife Refuge is 40 miles from Kalispell, Montana. Travel south from Kalispell on State Highway 35. At the town of Bigfork, travel south on State Highway 83. The Refuge entrance is one mile south of the town of Swan Lake.

Swan River NWR
Fish and Wildlife Service
National Wildlife Refuge System
132 Bison Range Road
Moiese, MT 59824
Phone: 406- 758-687
Email:R6FFA_CRE@fws.gov

Rach Outfitters • Bigfork 837-3632
River Ranch Retreat • Kalsipell 257-1622
Salish Mountains Lodge • Whitefish 881-3031
Shiloh Valley • Coram 387-5635
Silverwolf Log Chalet • West Glacier 387-4448
Stanton Creek Lodge • Essex 888-5040
Swan Lake Guest Cabins • Bigfork 837-1137
Swan Nest • Bigfork 387-5819
Swan River Valley Lodge • Condon 754-2780
Sweet Loretta's • Polebridge 888-5575
West Glacier Home ¶ Coram 387-4151
Whitefish Property Management
Whitefish 863-4651
Withrow House • Kalispell 752-2446
Woods Bay Point Retreat
Bigfork 837-5617
Yellow Bay Hideaway • Bigfork 982-3073

## Forest Service Cabins

*Flathead National Forest*

**Challenge Cabin**
51 mi. E of Hungry Horse, MT on us Hwy. 2 and 7 mi. E trail sys. on Skyland Rd 387-3800
Capacity: 6 Nightly fee: $25 Available: 12/1 - 3/31
Three night limit. Propane cooking/lights, wood heat, no water. Parking off us 2, next 7 mi. on snowmobile or cross-country skis. no pets.

**Ford Cabin**
45.2 mi. N of Columbia Falls, MT on N Fork Rd 210. 387-3800
Capacity: 8 Nightly fee: $25 Available: 5/20 - 3/10
Three night limit. Propane cooking/lights & heat. No refrig. Hand pump well. No pets. No snowmobiles in Ford Access area from 10/15 - 5/10.

**Hornet Lookout Cabin**
44 mi. N of Columbia Falls, MT 387-3800
Capacity: 4 Nightly fee: $15 Available: All year
Three night limit. Winter access can be difficult. No water. No pets.

**Mission Lookout**
3 mi. SW of Swan Lake, MT at end of Forest Road 9803 837-7500
Capacity: 4 Nightly fee: $25 Available: 6/1 - 8/15 & 9/15 - 10/20
Three night limit. Propane cooking. No water available. Pit toilet. Discourage bringing children. No pets. Grizzly bear restrictions apply.

**Ninko Cabin**
44 mi. N of Columbia Falls, MT 387-3800
Capacity: 6 Nightly fee: $25 Available: 12/1 - 3/31
Three night limit. Firewood is provided. Access is by snowmobile or cross-country skiing. No pets.

**Zip's Place Cabin**
48 mi. E of Hungry Horse, MT on us Hwy. 2, then 2 mi. S on a gravel county road. 387-3800
Capacity: 8 Nightly fee: $40 Available: 6/1 - 3/31
Three night limit. Propane heat/cooking, electricity. Hand pump well. No water at other times. Winter park off us 2, next 2 mi. on snowmobile/cross-country skis. Grizzly bear restrictions apply. No pets.

**Ben Rover Cabin**
35 mi. N of Columbia Falls, MT on N Fork Rd 210, then E l mi. to Polebridge 387-3800
Capacity: 8 Nightly fee: $40 Available: All year
Three night limit. Propane heat/cooking/refrig & lights. Hand pump well. No pets.

**Schnaus Cabin**
42 mi. N of Columbia Falls, MT on N Fork Road 210 387-3800
Capacity: 12 Nightly fee: $40
Available: All year
Three night stay limit. Propane heat/cooking/refrig & lights. Winter ski, snowshoe, or snowmbile a short distance from Rd. 210. No pets.

## Private Campgrounds

**Chief Mountain Junction** • Babb 732-9253
**Glacier Entrance Camground**
St. Mary 732-4616
**Johnson's of St. Mary** • St. Mary 732-5565
**Lake Five Resort** • West Glacier 387-5601
**San-SUZ-Ed Trailer Park**•West Glacier387-5280
**Sears Motel & Gift Shop**
East Glacier 226-4432
**St.Mary Glacier Park KOA**
St. Mary 732-4122
**Two Sisters** • St. Mary 732-5535
Barnacle Bob's RV Park • Big Arm 849-5882
Big Sky RV Resort & Campground
Rollins 844-3501
Coram RV Park • Coram 387-5552
Glacier Campground • West Glacier 387-5689
Glacier Mountain Shadows Resort
Columbia Falls 892-7686
Glacier Pines Campground • Kalispell 752-2760
Greenwood Village Campground
Kalispell 257-7719
Glacier Peaks RV • Columbia Falls 892-2133
KOA Kampgrounds • West Glacier 387-5341
Dillon's Resort Marina • Big Arm 849-5838
Blue Bay Campground • Bigfork 982-3077
Flathead East Shore Trailer • Bigfork 982-3324
KOA Kampgrounds • Polson 883-2151
Outback Montana, Inc • Bigfork 837-6973
Columbia Falls RV Resort
Columbia Falls 892-1122
La Salle Campgrounds
Columbia Falls 892-4668

North American RV Park • Coram 387-5800
Sundance RV Campground • Coram 387-5016
Firebrand Campgrounds
East Glacier Park 226-5573
Canyon RV & Campground
Hungry Horse 387-9393
Mountain Meadow RV Park
Hungry Horse 387-9125
Lake Blaine Resort • Kalispell 755-2891
Rocky Mountain Hi Campground
Kalispell 755-9573
Spruce Park Village Campground
Kalispell 752-6321
White Birch RV & Campground
Kalispell 752-4008
Edgewater Motel & RV Park•Lakeside 844-3644
Eagle Nest RV Resort • Polson 883-5904
Flathead Lake RV Resort • Polson 883-5940
LaSalle RV Park & Campground
C olumbia Falls 892-4668
Lodgepole Gallery & Tipi Village
Browning 338-2787
Moosehead Campground & Store
Sula 821-3327
RV Timbers Park • Bigfork 837-6999
Rondévue Park • Bigfork 837-6973
Rocking-C-Ranch • Polson 887-2537
Sleeping Wolf Campground & RV Park
Browning 338-7933
Stanton Creek Lodge • Essex 888-5040
Timber Wolf Resort • Hungry Horse 387-9653
White Birch Motel & RV Park
Kalispell 752-4008
Whitefish KOA Kampgrounds
Whitefish 862-8824
Whitefish RV Park • Whitefish 862-7275
Woods Bay Marina & RV Resort
Bigfork 837-6191

## Car Rental

Avis Rent-A-Car 226-4433
Dollar Rent-A-Car 226-4432
U Save Auto Rental 226-4412
Avis Rent-A-Car 257-2727
Budget Car & Truck Rental 755-7500
Dollar Rent-A-Car 892-0009
Enterprise Rent-A-Car 755-4848
National Car Rental 257-7144
Payless Car Rental 755-4022
Practical Rent-A-Car 755-3700
Rent A Wreck 755-4555
U Save Auto Rental 257-1900

# The Wild in Wilderness

by Roland Cheek

**The Flathead country is an especially** blessed section of the North American Continent and has been for ... oh, 50 or 100 million years—give or take a dozen or two. Rugged towering mountains, freshwater lakes, wild free flowing streams, varied wildlife, and the lush greenness of it all ... who could doubt our blessings.

Perhaps the most important manifestation of that blessing can be found in the folk living here. Unlike many similarly hallowed places, ours is not paradise lost. Though historical lessons are brief and experience scant among the populace, wisdom prevails and an undercurrent of preservation runs deep. The result has been that substantial portions of this wonderful country is preserved in its natural state for ours and future generations.

## Glacier National Park

Glacier is, of course, known far and wide as America's trail park. Deservedly so, for it contains hundreds of miles of well maintained trails for rider or hiker. However, Glacier's wild backcountry provides only one option among many.

## Bob Marshall Wilderness

Bigger than Glacier, the Bob Marshall is another option. Many folk's choice for America's finest wilderness, the huge, sprawling Bob Marshall encompasses entire river valleys and whole mountain ranges. Within its boundaries are a few well maintained trails and a bunch of remote wildlands with trails running the gamut from poor to none. It's wild, it's vast, and it's difficult to see without lots of time, good equipment, and a commitment to a demanding horseback or backpack vacation. But it's worth every second of it!

## Great Bear Wilderness

Between Glacier and the "Bob" is another fine wilderness area—the Great Bear Wilderness. It serves as a critical wildland connecting link, securing forever a tremendous wilderness ecosystem along America's northern Rockies. Though much of the Great Bear is trailless, access is not as difficult as one might think, with an enclave airstrip at Schafer Meadows in one section, and highway and forest road access around the perimeter of another section. I've been there often. Let me assure you it's worth visiting.

## Mission Mountains Wilderness

To the Bob Marshall's west, across the incredibly beautiful Swan Valley, is an equally incredibly beautiful wilderness—the 73,000 acre Mission Mountains Wilderness. Chocked full of many lakes and few trails, spectacular mountains and glacier scoured basins, the Mission Range is a seldom-tapped adventure for anyone.

But I've only told half the story!

## Mission Mountains Tribal Wilderness

The Mission Mountains Wilderness spreads along the mountain range's east slope. Immediately adjacent to the west, spreading along the Mission's western slope, is America's first voluntary Indian Wilderness—the 89,500 acre Mission Mountains Tribal Wilderness.

The Mission Mountains Tribal Wilderness is a magnificent piece of wild mountain country, seen by every daylight traveler driving us 93 between Missoula and Flathead Lake. This wilderness perfectly blends with its earlier-established National Forest sister wilderness to the east to round out protection for one of the most exquisite mountain ranges in America.

Their Tribal Wilderness Statement of Policy makes interesting reading:

*Wilderness has played a paramount role in shaping the character of the people and the culture of the Salish and Kootenai Tribes; It is the essence of traditional Indian religion and has served the Indian people of these Tribes as a place to hunt, as a place to gather medicinal herbs and roots as a vision seeking ground, as a sanctuary, and in countless other ways for thousands of years. Because maintaining an enduring resource of wilderness, is vitally Important to the people of the Confederated Salish and Kootenai Tribes and the perpetuation of their culture, there is hereby established a Mission Mountains Tribal Wilderness Area and this Area, described herein, shall be administered to protect and preserve wilderness values.*

This wilderness, along with most Tribal Lands on the Flathead Reservation, is open to non-Indian visitors—with purchase of Tribal Recreation use Permit, sold at various locations throughout the Flathead Valley area.

One word of caution, however, to Tribal wilderness visitors: There is a seasonal visitor closure currently in effect for the McDonald Peak area. The closure is for protection of wildlife (humans, too) during an apparent gathering time for grizzly bear. It seems as many as 11 different grizzlies have been sighted at one time, feeding on unusually high protein insects (ladybugs and army cutworm moths for you protein-deficient humans), in huge, open Grizzly Basin (Cliff Lake). Human/bear conflicts have occurred. The Tribe has ordered the area closed from mid-July to October 1.

## Jewel Basin

Some 25 miles north of the extreme northwest corner of the Bob Marshall Wilderness, along the rugged crest of the Swan Range Mountains, is the 15,000 acre Jewel Basin Hiking Area.

Administratively designated by the us Forest Service as a restricted area in 1970, this lake studded series of small basins has proven quite popular because of its proximity to the Flathead's major recreation centers, its magnificent view of Flathead Lake and the upper Flathead Valley, and its own intrinsic beauty.

Access is easy—follow the Jewel Basin Road east of Echo Lake, to Camp Misery, near 7,000 feet elevation. From there, trails lead in two directions. Both are relatively simple hikes into different sections of Jewel Basin.

More demanding trails can be readily found for those pressing on beyond day users.

Take your fishing pole with you, too. Some of Jewel Basin's better fishing lakes are Clayton, Wildcat, Black and Big Hawk.

## De facto Wildlands

There are other excellent wild places within the Flathead area. How long they'll remain so is anyone's guess.

Up the Flathead's North Fork, hugging the Forty-Ninth Parallel boundary with Canada, is an especially isolated and wildlife-rich region known roughly as the North End. Spraddling yet another series of mountains—the Whitefish Range—the North End is composed of several roadless areas carrying such quintessential names as Tuchuck, Nashukoin, Thompson-Seton. Yet, just a short while ago, the us Forest Service tried to peddle a timber sale in an isolated drainage where researchers had recorded critical wildlife habitat for 17 different grizzly bears. Fortunately for us and the bears, timber in the area was of such inferior quality, no local sawmills were interested. Since that time, efforts have accelerated to achieve wilderness status for the area.

Incidentally, the Forest Service also granted oil exploration leases there, too.

Presently, thank God, both key de facto wildernesses—the Swan Crest and the North End—are still intact. How long? Perhaps that depends on us..

*Roland Cheek's "Trails to Outdoor Adventure" has been syndicated in print and radio. He is the author of six books and countless outdoor articles. Find out more about him at www.roland-cheek.com.*

| | |
|---|---|
| Hertz Rent-A-Car | 758-2220 |
| Rent A Wreck | 883-4400 |
| Budget Rent-A-Car | 888-5427 |
| Budget Car & Truck Rental | 862-8170 |
| DePrato Car Rental | 862-3825 |
| Hertz Rent-A-Car | 863-1210 |

## Outfitters & Guides

*F=Fishing H=Hunting R=River Guides E=Horseback Rides G=General Guide Services*

| | | |
|---|---|---|
| **Glacier Raft Co** | GFR | 888-5454 |
| **Montana Ranch Adventures** | GE | 338-3333 |
| **Glacier Wilderness Guides** | GE | 387-5555 |
| **Kruger Helicopter Tours** | G | 387-4565 |
| **Rawhide Trailrides** | E | 387-5999 |
| **Stumptown Anglers** | F | 862-4554 |
| **Halcyon Sea Kayaking** | R | 862-2658 |
| **Wildhorse Island Boat Trips** | R | 837-5617 |
| A-1 Fishing | G | 857-2588 |
| Alpine Adventures | HFE | 755-7337 |
| Bagley Guide Service Fishing | F | 837-3618 |
| B&D Outfitters | HF | 752-7842 |
| Bob Marshall Wilderness Ranch | HFE | 745-4466 |
| Crane Mountain Guide Service | HF | 837-6933 |
| Flathead Lake Charters Svc | G | 857-3439 |
| Flathead Raft Co | FR | 883-5838 |
| Flying Eagle Ranch | HFE | 387-5999 |
| Glacier Country Outfitters | G | 756-1175 |
| Glacier Fishing Charters | HF | 892-2377 |
| Glacier Gateway Outfitters | F | 226-4408 |
| Glacier Park Tours | G | 756-2444 |
| Glacier Wilderness Guides | G | 387-5555 |
| Great Bear Oufitters | HF | 755-3210 |
| Great Northern Whitewater | R | 387-5340 |
| High Country Trails | FE | 755-1283 |
| Lion Creek Outfitters | HFE | 755-3723 |
| Montana Old West Oufitters | F | 336-3966 |
| Montana River Anglers | FE | 261-2033 |
| No Cut Throats Outfitting | G | 755-2368 |
| Northern Rockies Outfitter | G | 892-1188 |
| Northern Rocky Adventures | G | 862-6884 |

| | | |
|---|---|---|
| Old West Angler & Outfitters | GF | 322-5472 |
| Rach Outfitters | H | 837-3632 |
| Rising Wolf Guided Adventures | F | 338-3016 |
| Running Waters Ranch | H | 755-2041 |
| Salmon Forks Outfitters | HF | 892-5468 |
| Simon & Simon Co | G | 863-9696 |
| Sky Blue Basecamp | G | 756-7465 |
| Skyline Outfitter Inc | G | 387-4051 |
| Snowy Springs Outfitters | G | 755-2137 |
| Spotted Bear Ranch | G | 755-7337 |
| Stillwater Shooting Preserve | F | 755-1959 |
| Triple Divide Ranch Outfitters | F | 338-5048 |
| Two Medicine River Outfitters | GF | 226-4408 |
| Whitefish Lake Fishing | GF | 862-5313 |
| Whitefish Sea Kayaking | R | 862-3513 |
| Wild Trout Adventures | F | 837-3838 |
| Wild River Adventures | G | 387-9453 |
| Wilderness Lodge | HFER | 3887-4051 |
| World Class Adventures Inc | G | 755-8820 |
| Wright, Ed | G | 837-2623 |
| A Able Fishing Charters | F | 257-5214 |

## Cross-Country Ski Centers

| | |
|---|---|
| Big Mountain Nordic Center<br>8 mi. N of Whitefish | 862-1900 |
| Glacier Nordic Center | 862-9498 |
| Izaak Walton Inn • Essex | 888-5700 |
| Mountain Timbers Wilderness Lodge<br>West Glacier | 387-5830 |

Corinne Gaffner

## Downhill Ski Areas

| | |
|---|---|
| Blacktail Mountain Ski Area | 844-0999 |
| Big Mountain | 862-1900 |

## Snowmobile Rentals

| | |
|---|---|
| Winter Wonderland Sports<br>Kalispell | 257-2627 |

All Montana Area Codes are 406

| Fishery | Cold Water Species | | | | | | | | | | | | Warm Water Species | | | | | | | | | | Services | | | | | |
|---|---|---|---|---|---|---|---|---|---|---|---|---|---|---|---|---|---|---|---|---|---|---|---|---|---|---|---|---|
| | Brook Trout | Mt. Whitefish | Lake Whitefish | Golden Trout | Cutthroat Trout | Brown Trout | Rainbow Trout | Kokanee Salmon | Bull Trout | Lake Trout | Arctic Grayling | Burbot | Largemouth Bass | Smallmouth Bass | Walleye | Sauger | Northern Pike | Shovelnose Sturgeon | Channel Catfish | Yellow Perch | Crappie | Paddlefish | Vehicle Access | Campgrounds | Toilets | Docks | Boat Ramps | Motor Restrictions |
| 333. North Fork Flathead River | | • | | | • | | | | • | | | | | | | | | | | | | | • | • | • | | • | • |
| 334. Whitefish Lake | | | • | | • | | | | • | • | | | | | | | • | | | | | | • | • | • | • | • | |
| 335. Flathead River | | • | • | | • | | | | • | • | | | • | | | | • | | | | | | • | • | • | | • | |
| 336. Blanchard Lake | | | | | | | | | | | | | • | | | | | | • | | | | • | | | | | |
| 337. S. Fork Two Medicine River | | | | | • | | • | | | | | | | | | | | | | | | | | | | | | |
| 338. Smith Lake | | | | | | | | | | | | | | | | | | | | • | | | • | | • | • | • | |
| 339. Foy Lake | | | | | | | • | | | | | | | | | | | | | | | | • | | | • | • | |
| 340. Church Slough | | | | | | | | | | | | | • | | | | • | | | • | | | • | | | | • | |
| 341. Echo Lake | | | | | | | | | | | | | • | | | | • | | | • | | | • | • | • | • | • | |
| 342. Handkerchief Lake | | | | | • | | | | | | • | | | | | | | | | | | | • | • | • | | | |
| 343. Swan Lake | | | | | • | | • | • | • | | | | | | | | • | | | • | | | • | • | • | | • | |
| 344. Flathead Lake | | | • | | • | | | | • | • | | | | | | | | | | • | | | • | • | • | • | • | |
| 345. Swan River | • | • | | | • | | • | | • | | | | | | | | | | | | | | • | • | • | | | |
| 346. Middle Fork Flathead River | | • | | | • | | | | • | | | | | | | | | | | | | | • | • | • | | • | • |
| 347. Spotted Bear River | | • | | | • | | | | • | | | | | | | | | | | | | | • | • | • | | | |
| 348. Bob Marshall Wilderness lakes | | • | | | • | | | | • | | | | | | | | | | | | | | | | | | | • |
| 349. Hungry Horse Reservoir | | • | | | • | | | | • | | | | | | | | | | | | | | • | • | • | | • | |
| 350. Lake Mary Ronan | | | | | • | | • | • | | | | | • | | | | | | | | | | • | • | • | • | • | |
| 351. Duck Lake | | | | | | | • | | | | | | | | | | | | | | | | • | | | | | |
| 352. Lake Blaine | | | | | | | | | | | | | • | | | | • | | | • | | | • | | | | | |
| 353. Lake Five & Horseshoe Lake | | | | | | | | | | | | | • | | | | | | | • | | | • | | | | | |

## Public Campgrounds

# Campsite Directions

| Campground | Season | Camping | Trailers | Toilets | Water | Boat Launch | Fishing | Swimming | Trails | Stay Limit | Fee |
|---|---|---|---|---|---|---|---|---|---|---|---|
| **271•Tuchuck FS**<br>53 mi. N of Columbia Falls on Trail Creek Rd. 1665 | 6/15-9/30 | 7 | 22′ | • | | | • | | | 14 | |
| **272•Whitefish Lake State Park FWP**<br>1 mi. W of Whitefish on us 93 | 5/1-9/30 | 25 | 40′ | • | • | C | • | | | 7 | • |
| **273•Emery Bay FS**<br>6 mi. SE of Martin City on Forest Rd. 38 | 6/1-9/15 | 8 | 22′ | • | • | C | • | • | | 14 | |
| **274•Murray Bay FS**<br>22 mi. SE of Martin City on forest Rd. 38 | 6/1-9/15 | 18 | 22′ | • | • | C | • | • | | 14 | |
| **275•Doris Point FS**<br>8 mi. SE of Hungary Horse on Forest Rd. 895 | 6/15-9/30 | 18 | | • | | | • | • | | 14 | |
| **276•Lost Johnny Point FS**<br>9 mi. SE of Hungry Horse on Forest Rd. 895 | 6/1-9/15 | 21 | 22′ | • | • | c | • | • | • | 14 | • |
| **277•Lid Creek FS**<br>15 mi. SE of Hungry Horse on Forest Rd. 895• | 6/1-9/15 | 22 | 16′ | • | | C | • | • | | 14 | |
| **278•Lake Mary Ronan State Park FWP**<br>us 93 at Dayton•7 mi. NW | 5/19-9/30 | 27 | 35′ | • | • | C | • | | | 14 | • |
| **279•Flathead Lake State Park West Shore FWP**<br>6 mi. S of Lakeside on us 93 | 5/1-9/30 | 26 | 35′ | • | • | C | C | | N | 7 | • |
| **280•Flathead Lake State Park Wayfarers FWP**<br>W of Bigfork | 5/1-9/30 | 30 | 40′ | D | | C | • | | N | 7 | • |
| **281•Flathead Lake State Park Big Arm FWP**<br>15 mi. N of Polson on us 93 | 5/1-9/30 | 52 | 40′ | • | | C | • | | N | 7 | • |
| **282•Flathead Lake State Park Finley Point FWP**<br>9 mi. N of Polson on MT 35•4 mi. W | 5/1-9/30 | 16 | 40′ | • | | C | • | | | 7 | • |
| **283•Flathead Lake State Park Yellow Bay FWP**<br>15 mi. N of Polson on MT 35•Milepost 17 | 5/1-9/30 | 4 | | • | | C | • | | | 7 | |
| **284•Swan Lake FS**<br>.5 mi. NW of Swan Lake on MT 83•Group area by reservation only 837-3577 | 5/15-9/30 | 42 | 55′ | • | • | • | • | • | • | 14 | • |
| **285•Handkerchief Lake FS**<br>35 mi. SE of Hungry Horse on Forest Rd. 895•2 mi. NW on Forest Rd. 897 | 6/1-9/15 | 9 | 22′ | • | | | • | | | 14 | |
| **286•Devil Creek FS**<br>45 mi. SE of Hungry Horse on us 2 | 6/1-9/15 | 14 | 50′ | • | • | | • | | • | 14 | |
| **287•Summit FS**<br>13 mi. SW of East Glacier on us 2 | Summer | 17 | 36′ | D | • | | | | • | 14 | • |
| **288•Spotted Bear FS**<br>55 mi. SE of Martin City on forest Rd.38 | 6/20-9/10 | 13 | 22′ | • | • | | • | | • | 14 | |

**Agency**
FS—usD.A Forest Service
FWP—Montana Fish, Wildlife & Parks
NPS—National Park Service
BLM—us Bureau of Land Management
usBR—us Bureau of Reclamation
CE—Corps of Engineers

**Camping**
Camping is allowed at this site. Number indicates camping spaces available
H—Hard sided units only; no tents

**Trailers**
Trailer units allowed. Number indicates maximum length.

**Toilets**
Toilets on site. D—Disabled access

**Water**
Drinkable water on site

**Fishing**
Visitors may fish on site

**Boat**
Type of boat ramp on site:
A—Hand launch
B—4-wheel drive with trailer
C—2-wheel drive with trailer

**Swimming**
Designated swimming areas on site

**Trails**
Trails on site
B—Backpacking N—Nature/Interpretive

**Stay Limit**
Maximum length of stay in days

**Fee**
Camping and/or day-use fee

## Notes:

## Dining Quick Reference

Price Range refers to the average cost of a meal per person: ($) $1-$6, ($$) $7-$11, ($$$) $12-up. Cocktails: "Yes" indicates full bar; Beer (B)/Wine (W), Service: Breakfast (B), Brunch (BR), Lunch (L), Dinner (D). Businesses in bold print will have additional information under the appropriate map locator number in the body of this section.

| RESTAURANT | TYPE CUISINE | PRICE RANGE | CHILD MENU | COCKTAILS BEER WINE | SERVICE | CREDIT CARDS | MAP LOCATOR NUMBER |
|---|---|---|---|---|---|---|---|
| **Bab Bar Cattle Baron** | Steakhouse | $$$ | | Yes | D | Major | 1 |
| **Two Sisters Cafe & Campgrounds** | American | $ | | | | | 1 |
| **Johnson's of St. Mary** | Family | $/$$ | Yes | | B/L/D | | 1 |
| **BNC Taco Shack** | Fresh Mexican | $ | | | L/D | | 1 |
| **Silver Bullet** | Pizza/Bar | $/$$ | Yes | Yes | L/D | Major | 1 |
| **Glacier Village Restaurant** | Montana/American | $/$$ | Yes | B/W | B/L/D | Major | 2 |
| Firebrand Food & Ale | Seafood & Steak | $$ | Yes | Yes | D | | 2 |
| Serranos Mexican Restaurant | Mexican | $/$$ | | | L/D | | 2 |
| Summit Station Restaurant | American | $/$$ | | | L/D | | 2 |
| Thimbleberry Restaurant | American | $/$$$ | Yes | | B/L/D | | 2 |
| **Two Medicine Grill** | American | $/$$ | Yes | | B/L/D | V/M | 2 |
| **World Famous Whistle Stop Restaurant** | American | $ | Yes | B/W | B/L/D | V/M/D | 2 |
| Stanton Creek Lodge | American | $ | | Yes | B/L/D | Major | 3 |
| **West Glacier Restaurant** | Family | $/$$ | Yes | Yes | B/L/D | | 4 |
| **Cedar Tree Gift Shop & Deli** | Deli | $ | | | B/L/D | Major | 4 |
| **West Glacier Mercantile** | Grocery | | | | | | 4 |
| **Rawhide Steakhouse, Trail Rides & Gift Shop** | Steakhouse | $-$$$ | Yes | B/W | B/L/D | Major | 4 |
| **The Huckleberry Patch** | Family | $ | Yes | | B/L | Major | 5 |
| **Canyon Deli & Pizza Shoppe** | Family | $/$$ | | B | B/L/D | V/M | 5 |
| Burgers-N-Treats | Fast Food | $ | Yes | | B/L/D | | 5 |
| Log Cabin Cafe | Grill | $ | | Yes | B/L/D | | 5 |
| Peggy's Pizza | Pizza | $$ | | | L/D | | 5 |
| Going to the Sun | Coffee House | $ | | | | | 5 |
| Charlie Wong International Cuisine | International | $/$$ | | B/W | L/D | Major | 5 |
| Packer's Roost | Grill | $ | | Yes | L/D | | 5 |
| Spruce Park Cafe | Family | $ | | | B/L/D | Major | 5 |
| **Silver Bullet Bar, Pizza & Casino** | Pizza/Hamburgers | $/$$ | | Yes | L/D | V/M | 6 |
| A & W Family Restaurant | Fast Food | $ | Yes | | L/D | | 6 |
| Phyggs Deli | | | | | | | 6 |
| Ol' River Bridge Inn | American | $/$$ | Yes | Yes | B/L/D | Major | 6 |
| Blimpie's Subs | Fast Food | $ | Yes | | L/D | | 7 |
| Burger King | Fast Food | $ | Yes | | B/L/D | | 7 |
| Charlie Wong International Cuisine | International | $/$$ | | B/W | L/D | Major | 7 |
| Dairy Queen | Fast Food | $ | Yes | | L/D | | 7 |
| Fox's Drive In | Fast Food | $ | Yes | | L/D | | 7 |
| Pizza Hut | Pizza | $/$$ | Yes | B | L/D | V/M/D | 7 |
| Stageline Pizza | Pizza | $/$$ | | | L/D | | 7 |
| Sunrise Bakery | Bakery | | | | | | 7 |
| The Nite Owl Restaurant/Back Room | American | $/$$ | | Yes | B/L/D | | 7 |
| Blue Moon Grill | American | $/$$ | Yes | Yes | B/L/D | | 8 |
| **Whitefish Brewing Co.** | Brewery | | | | | | 9 |
| **Hungry Hunter Restaurant & Casino** | Chinese & American | $/$$ | | B/W | L/D | Major | 9 |
| **China Wall Restaurant** | Chinese | $/$$ | | | L/D | Major | 9 |
| Dairy Queen | Fast Food | $ | Yes | | L/D | | 9 |
| Denny's | Family | $ | Yes | | B/L/D | V/M | 9 |
| Cafe al Dente | Italian | $$/$$$ | Yes | Yes | L/D | V/M/D | 9 |
| Dos Amigos Mexican Restaurant | Mexican | $/$$ | Yes | Yes | L/D | Major | 9 |
| McDonald's | Fast Food | $ | Yes | | B/L/D | | 9 |
| Orient Express | Chinese | $$ | | | L/D | Major | 9 |
| Pizza Hut | Pizza | $/$$ | Yes | B | L/D | V/M/D | 9 |
| Subway | Fast Food | $ | Yes | | L/D | | 9 |
| Taco John's | Fast Food | $ | Yes | | L/D | | 9 |
| Wendy's | Fast Food | $ | Yes | | L/D | | 9 |
| Buffalo Cafe | Breakfast | $ | | | B/L | V/M | 10 |
| Great Northern Bar & Grill | American | $$/$$$ | | Yes | L/D | Major | 10 |
| Serrano's | Mexican | $$ | | Yes | D | Major | 10 |
| Swift Creek Cafe | Grille | $/$$ | | B/W | B/L/D | Major | 10 |
| **Truby's Wood Fired Pizza** | Gourmet Pizza | $$/$$$ | Yes | Yes | L/D | Major | 10 |
| Tupelo Grille | Eclectic | $$ | Yes | B/W | D | Major | 10 |
| Wasabi Sushi Bar | Sushi | $$ | | | L/D | Major | 10 |
| **Whitefish Lake Golf Restaurant** | Steak/Seafood | $$$ | Yes | Yes | L/D | Major | 11 |

All Montana Area Codes are 406

## Dining Quick Reference-Continued

Price Range refers to the average cost of a meal per person: ($) $1-$6, ($$) $7-$11, ($$$) $12-up. Cocktails: "Yes" indicates full bar; Beer (B)/Wine (W), Service: Breakfast (B), Brunch (BR), Lunch (L), Dinner (D). Businesses in bold print will have additional information under the appropriate map locator number in the body of this section.

| RESTAURANT | TYPE CUISINE | PRICE RANGE | CHILD MENU | COCKTAILS BEER WINE | SERVICE | CREDIT CARDS | MAP LOCATOR NUMBER |
|---|---|---|---|---|---|---|---|
| **Grouse Mountain Lodge** | Fine Dining | $$/$$$ | | Yes | B/L/D | Major | 12 |
| **Alpinglow Inn & Restaurant** | American | $/$$ | Yes | B/W | B/L/D | Major | 12 |
| **Kandahar Lodge & Cafe** | Fine Dining | $$/$$$ | | Yes | B/D | Major | 12 |
| Dire Wolf Pub | American | $ | | B/W | L/D | V/M | 12 |
| Pollo Grill | Grill | $$$ | Yes | B/W | D | Major | 12 |
| Wildwood Bakery Cafe | Bakery/Cafe | $ | Yes | | L | | 12 |
| Hellroaring Saloon & Eatery | American | $/$$ | | Yes | L/D | Major | 12 |
| Moguls Bar & Grille | American | $$ | | Yes | L/D | V/M | 12 |
| Rendezvous Room | Mexican/ American | $/$$ | | Yes | L/D | V/M | 12 |
| The Stube & Chuckwagon Grill | American Grill | $/$$ | Yes | Yes | L/D | Major | 12 |
| Big League Bagels & Deli | Deli | $/$$ | | | B/L/D | Major | 14 |
| Cislo's Family Restaurant | Family | $ | Yes | | B/L/D | | 14 |
| Hot Stuff Pizza/Smash Hit Subs | Fast Food | $ | Yes | | B/L/D | | 14 |
| McDonalds | Fast Food | $ | Yes | | B/L/D | | 14 |
| Rocco's | Italian | $$ | Yes | Yes | D | V/M | 14 |
| Wendy's | Fast Food | $ | Yes | | L/D | | 14 |
| Mountain Crossroads Restaurant | Family | $ | Yes | Yes | B/L/D | V/M/D | 14 |
| Evergreen Gas & Deli | Deli | $ | | | B/L/D | Major | 14 |
| Applebee's Neighborhood Grill | Eclectic | $$/$$$ | Yes | Yes | L/D | Major | 15 |
| Arctic Circle | Fast Food | $ | Yes | | L/D | | 15 |
| Barley's Brewhouse & Grill | Steak/Pizza | $$/$$$ | Yes | | B/W | Major | 15 |
| Burger King | Fast Food | $ | Yes | | B/L/D | | 15 |
| Dairy Queen | Fast Food | $ | Yes | | L/D | | 15 |
| Domino's Pizza | Pizza | $ | | | L/D | | 15 |
| Finnegan's Restaurant | Family | $ | Yes | | B/L/D | Major | 15 |
| McDonald's | Fast Food | $ | Yes | | B/L/D | | 15 |
| Nickel Charlie's | American | $ | Yes | B/W | B/L/D | V/M/D | 15 |
| Perkins Family Restaurant | Family | $/$$ | Yes | | B/L/D | Major | 15 |
| Taco Bell | Fast Food | $ | Yes | | L/D | | 15 |
| Wendy's | Fast Food | $ | Yes | | L/D | | 15 |
| Los Caporales | Mexican | $/$$ | Yes | Yes | L/D | Major | 15 |
| Subway | Fast Food | $ | Yes | | L/D | | 15 |
| Ole's Conoco | Fast Food | $ | | | B/L/D | Major | 15 |
| Arby's | Fast Food | $ | Yes | | B/L/D | | 16 |
| Black Angus Steak House | Steakhouse | $–$$$ | Yes | Yes | B/L/D | Major | 16 |
| Bojangles Family Restaurant | Family | $ | Yes | | B/L/D | V/M/D | 16 |
| CastleRock Steaks & Seafood | Steakhouse | $$/$$$ | Yes | Yes | D | Major | 16 |
| Hardee's | Fast Food | $ | Yes | | B/L/D | | 16 |
| McDonald's | Fast Food | $ | Yes | | B/L/D | | 16 |
| Quizno's Classic Subs | Subs | $ | Yes | | L/D | | 16 |
| Sizzler | Steakhouse | $$ | Yes | | L/D/BR | Major | 16 |
| Skipper's Seafood 'n Chowder | Fast Food | $ | Yes | | L/D | | 16 |
| Subway | Fast Food | $ | Yes | | L/D | | 16 |
| LBM Pizza | Pizza | $$ | | | L/D | Major | 16 |
| Fender's Restaurant | Fine Dining | $$/$$$ | Yes | Yes | L/D | Major | 17 |
| Four Seasons Restaurant | Chinese | $/$$ | | B/W | L/D | V/M/D | 17 |
| Spencer & Co. Steakhouse | Steakhouse | $$ | Yes | Yes | L/D | Major | 17 |
| **Café Max** | Fine Dining | $$$ | | B/W | D | Major | 18 |
| **Bulldog Pub & Steakhouse** | Steakhouse | $/$$$ | Yes | Yes | L/D | Major | 18 |
| **Sawbuck's** | American | $/$$ | Yes | Yes | B/L/D | M/V | 18 |
| **Northest Bounty** | Regional | $/$$/$$$ | Yes | Yes | B/L/D | Major | 18 |
| **Hennessey's** | Steak/Seafood | $$/$$$ | Yes | Yes | B/L/D/BR | Major | 18 |
| **Sweet P's** | American | $/$$ | Yes | | B/L | | 18 |
| **Sawbuck's** | American | $/$$ | Yes | Yes | B/L/D | M/V | 18 |
| Orange Julius | Fast Food | $ | Yes | | B/L/D | | 18 |
| Alley Connection | International | $$/$$$ | Yes | Yes | B/L | Major | 18 |
| Avalanche Creek Restaurant & Coffeehouse | coffeehouse/family | $ | | | B/D/D | Major | 18 |
| Kentucky Fried Chicken/A&W | Fast Food | $ | Yes | | L/D | | 18 |
| Knead Cafe & Bakery | American | $ | | B/W | B/L/D/BR | Major | 18 |
| Painted Horse Grill | Continental | $$/$$$ | Yes | B/W | L/D | Major | 18 |
| Pizza Hut | Pizza | $/$$ | Yes | B | L/D | V/M/D | 18 |

## Dining Quick Reference-Continued

Price Range refers to the average cost of a meal per person: ($) $1-$6, ($$) $7-$11, ($$$) $12-up. Cocktails: "Yes" indicates full bar; Beer (B)/Wine (W), Service: Breakfast (B), Brunch (BR), Lunch (L), Dinner (D). Businesses in bold print will have additional information under the appropriate map locator number in the body of this section.

| RESTAURANT | TYPE CUISINE | PRICE RANGE | CHILD MENU | COCKTAILS BEER WINE | SERVICE | CREDIT CARDS | MAP LOCATOR NUMBER |
|---|---|---|---|---|---|---|---|
| Serendepity Street Coffeehouse & Cafe | Coffeehouse/Cafe | $ | Yes | | L/D | | 18 |
| Taco John's | Fast Food | $ | Yes | | L/D | | 18 |
| Vivienne's 5th Street Cafe | cafe/tea | $ | | | B/L | | 18 |
| Anna's Greek Gyro | Greek | $ | | | L/D | | 18 |
| Dairy Queen | Fast Food | $ | Yes | | L/D | | 18 |
| Wolfgangs | Hot Dogs | $ | Yes | | L/D | | 18 |
| **MacKenzie River Pizza Co.** | Pizza | $/$$ | | B/W | L/D | Major | 19 |
| **Sawbuck Saloon** | American | $/$$ | | Yes | B/L/D | A/V/M | 19 |
| Best Bet Restaurant | American | $$ | Yes | Yes | B/L/D | Major | 19 |
| Big League Bagels & Deli | Deli | $ | | | B/L/D | | 19 |
| Blimpie's Subs | Fast Food | $ | Yes | | L/D | | 19 |
| Cattleman's Restaurant | Steakhouse | $/$$ | | B/W | L/D | Major | 19 |
| Taco Time Express | Fast Food | $ | Yes | | L/D | | 19 |
| White Oak Lodge | Fine Dining | $/$$$ | Yes | Yes | B/L/D | Major | 20 |
| Burgertown Dairy Freeze | Fast Food | $ | Yes | | B/L/D | | 23 |
| Dairy Queen | Fast Food | $ | Yes | | L/D | | 23 |
| El Topo | Mexican | $ | Yes | Yes | D | Major | 23 |
| North Shore Restaurant | Family | $ | Yes | Yes | B/L/D | Major | 23 |
| Pair-A-Dice Restaurant | Family | $-$$$ | Yes | Yes | L/D | Major | 23 |
| Korner Kitchen | Family | $ | Yes | Yes | B/L/D | V/M | 23 |
| Pizza Hut | Pizza | $/$$ | Yes | B | L/D | V/M/D | 23 |
| Subway | Fast Food | $ | Yes | | L/D | | 23 |
| Tall Pine Restaurant | American | $ | | Yes | L/D | Major | 23 |
| Echo Lake Cafe | American | $ | Yes | | B/L | Major | 23 |
| Bigfork Stage Stop Sinclair & Diner | Family | $ | | | B/L/D | Major | 23 |
| Bill's Conoco/Taco Maker | Mexican | $ | | | L/D | Major | 23 |
| **Marina Cay Resort & Quincy's At Marina Cay** | Fine Dining | $$/$$$ | | Yes | D | Major | 24 |
| **Brookies Cookies** | Bakery/Coffee House | $ | | | | V/M | 24 |
| **Showthyme** | Creative | $–$$$ | Yes | Yes | D | Major | 24 |
| **The Village Well** | Burgers & Sandwiches | $ | | Yes | L/D | V/M | 24 |
| **Tuscany's Ristorante** | Fine Dining | $$/$$$ | | B/W | D | V/M | 24 |
| **Swan River Cafe** | Creative | $$ | Yes | Yes | B/L/D/BR | Major | 24 |
| **La Provence** | French/Mediterranean | $$/$$$ | | B/W | D | V/M | 24 |
| Bigfork Inn | International | $$$ | Yes | B/W | L/D | Major | 24 |
| Champs Pub & Grill/The Waterfront Tiki Bar | American | $/$$ | | Yes | L/D | Major | 24 |
| Del Norte | Mexican | $ | Yes | B/W | L/D | | 24 |
| Garden Bar & Grill | American | $ | | Yes | L/D | V/M | 24 |
| RT Jingles Steak & Seafood House | Steakhouse | $$/$$$ | | Yes | L/D | Major | 24 |
| Raven Brew Pub & Grill | Grill | $/$$ | | W/B | D | | 25 |
| Sitting Duck | American | $$ | | Yes | L/D | Major | 25 |
| Woods Bay Grill | American | $ | Yes | | B/L | | 25 |
| Mountain Lake Lodge Restaurant & Lodging | International | $/$$$ | Yes | Yes | B/L/D | Major | 25 |
| Steamers Seafood House | Seafood | $$/$$$ | | Yes | L/D | Major | 28 |
| 4B's Restaurant | Family | $ | Yes | | B/L/D | V/M/D | 28 |
| Burger King | Fast Food | $ | Yes | | B/L/D | | 28 |
| Pajaritos | Mexican | $ | Yes | B | L/D | | 28 |
| Y Ribs | BBQ | $$ | | | L/D | | 28 |
| **Regatta Pizza** | Pizza | $ | Yes | Yes | L/D | Major | 29 |
| Driftwood Cafe | American | $ | Yes | | B/L/D/BR | V/M | 29 |
| McDonald's | Fast Food | $ | Yes | | B/L/D | | 29 |
| China Gate Restaurant | Chinese | | | | | | 29 |
| Pizza Hut | Pizza | $/$$ | Yes | B | L/D | V/M/D | 29 |
| Rae's Moka Express | Coffeehouse/Sandwich | $ | | B/L | | | 29 |
| Subway | Fast Food | $ | Yes | | L/D | | 29 |
| Taco Time | Fast Food | $ | Yes | | L/D | | 29 |
| Best Western Kwataqnuk Resort | American | $$ | Yes | Yes | B/BR/L/D | Major | 29 |
| **Historic Old Mill Place** | Deli/Ice Cream | $ | Yes | | L/D | | 30 |
| **Ponderae** | Family/Steak | $-$$$ | Yes | Yes | B/L/D/BR | V/M | 30 |
| Buddeez Pizza | Pizza | $$ | | | L/D | V/M | 30 |
| Charlie Wong International Cuisine | International | $/$$ | | B/W | L/D | Major | 30 |
| Rancho Deluxe Supper Club | Steakhouse | $/$$$ | Yes | Yes | L./D | Major | 30 |

## Dining Quick Reference-Continued

Price Range refers to the average cost of a meal per person: ($) $1-$6, ($$) $7-$11, ($$$) $12-up. Cocktails: "Yes" indicates full bar; Beer (B)/Wine (W), Service: Breakfast (B), Brunch (BR), Lunch (L), Dinner (D). Businesses in bold print will have additional information under the appropriate map locator number in the body of this section.

| RESTAURANT | TYPE CUISINE | PRICE RANGE | CHILD MENU | COCKTAILS BEER WINE | SERVICE | CREDIT CARDS | MAP LOCATOR NUMBER |
|---|---|---|---|---|---|---|---|
| Watusi Cafe | Cafe | $ | | | B/L | | 30 |
| Lake City Bakery & Eatery | Bakery | $ | | | B/L | | 30 |
| Idle Spur | American | $ | | Yes | L/D | Major | 33 |
| Big Sky RV Resort & Camp | American | $ | | | B/L/D | | 34 |
| **Tiebuckers Pub & Eatery** | Fine Dining | $$$ | Yes | Yes | D | Major | 36 |
| Bugzy's Pizza Pub | Gourmet Pizza | $$ | | B/W | L/D | Major | 36 |
| Montana Grill | Steaks & Seafood | $$/$$$ | Yes | Yes | L/D | Major | 36 |
| Somers Bay Cafe | American | $ | | B/W | B/L/D | | 36 |
| Dairy Queen | Fast Food | $ | Yes | | L/D | | 36 |
| Homestead Cafe | American | $ | Yes | Yes | B/L/D | | 36 |
| Rosario's Restaurant | Fine Dining | $$/$$$ | Yes | Yes | D | V/M/D | 36 |
| The Spinnaker | American | $ | | Yes | L/D | Major | 36 |
| Burrheads Gas & Cafe | American | $ | | | L/D | Major | 36 |
| City Market & Deli | Deli | $ | | | B/L/D | Major | 36 |
| **The Laughing Horse Lodge** | Western | $$/$$$ | | B/W | B/L/D | Major | 37 |
| Hungry Bear Steakhouse | Steakhouse | $/$$$ | | Yes | B/L/D | V/M/D | 37 |
| Swan Bar & Grill | American | $ | | Yes | L/D | V/M | 37 |
| Montana Charlie's | Italian | $$/$$$ | | Yes | L/D | Major | 37 |
| Mission Mountains Sinclair | Deli | $ | | | L/D | Major | 37 |
| Swan Valley Center | Deli | | | | L/D | Major | 37 |

**NOTES:**

## Motel Quick Reference

Price Range: ($) Under $40 ; ($$) $40-$60; ($$$) $60-$80, ($$$$) Over $80. Pets [check with the motel for specific policies] (P), Dining (D), Lounge (L), Disabled Access (DA), Full Breakfast (FB), Cont. Breakfast (CB), Indoor Pool (IP), Outdoor Pool (OP), Hot Tub (HT), Sauna (S), Refrigerator (R), Microwave (M) (Microwave and Refrigerator indicated only if in majority of rooms), Kitchenette (K). All Montana area codes are 406.

| HOTEL | PHONE | NUMBER ROOMS | PRICE RANGE | BREAKFAST | POOL/ HOT TUB SAUNA | NON SMOKE ROOMS | OTHER AMENITIES | CREDIT CARDS | MAP LOCATOR NUMBER |
|---|---|---|---|---|---|---|---|---|---|
| Johnson's of St. Mary | 732-5565 | 22 | $$/$$$ | | | | DA | V/M | 1 |
| Montana Ranch Adventures | 338-3333 | 3 | $$$ | | | Yes | R/M/K | M/V/D | 1 |
| Chief Mountain Junction | 732-9253 | 5 | $ | | | | P/K | Major | 1 |
| Red Eagle Motel | 732-4453 | 23 | $$$ | | | Yes | P/DA | V/M | 1 |
| St Mary Lodge & Resort | 732-4431 | 80 | $$$$ | | | Yes | P/L | | 1 |
| Thronson's General Store & Motel | 732-5530 | 14 | $$ | | | Yes | P | Major | 1 |
| Whistling Swan Motel | 226-4412 | 8 | $$ | | | Yes | K/M/R/P | Major | 2 |
| Sears Motel, Campground & Gift Shop | 226-4432 | 16 | $$ | | | Yes | | Major | 2 |
| East Glacier Motel | 226-5593 | 17 | $$ | | | Yes | K/P | Major | 2 |
| Glacier Park Circle R Motel | 226-9331 | 8 | $$ | | | Yes | | Major | 2 |
| Jacobson's Cottages | 226-4422 | 12 | $$/$$$ | | | | K/DA/P | Major | 2 |
| Brownie's American Youth Hostel | 226-4426 | 9/2 | $ | | | Yes | R/M/K | V/MD | 2 |
| Dancing Bear Inn | 226-4402 | 14 | $$ | | | Yes | K/P/M/R | Major | 2 |
| Mountain Pine Motel | 226-4403 | 25 | $$ | | | Yes | DA | Major | 2 |
| Izaak Walton Inn | 888-5700 | 37 | $$$$ | | | Yes | K | | 3 |
| The Halfway Motel | 888-5650 | 4 | $$ | | S | | D/L/DA | Major | 3 |
| Snow Slip Inn - Bar, Motel & Café | 226-9381 | 6 | $ | | | | D/L/P | | 3 |
| Moccasin Lodge Vacation Home | 888-5545 | | | | | | | | 3 |
| Stanton Creek Lodge | 888-5040 | 6 | $$ | | | Yes | | Major | 3 |
| Apgar Village Lodge | 888-5484 | 48 | | | | | K/M/R | V/M/D | 4 |
| West Glacier Motel | 888-5662 | 30 | $$-$$$$ | | | | K/M/R | Major | 4 |
| Glacier Highland Motel & Conoco | 888-5427 | 33 | $$/$$$ | | HT | Yes | | Major | 4 |
| Lake Five Resort | 387-5601 | 9 | $$/$$$ | | | Yes | P/R/K | | 4 |
| Belton Chalet & Lodge | 888-5000 | 27 | $$-$$$$ | CB | | Yes | D/L/DA | V/M/A | 4 |
| Great Northern Whitewater Rafting Resort | 387-5340 | 5 | $$$$ | | IP/HT | Yes | K/R | Major | 4 |
| Vista Motel | 888-5311 | 26 | $$$ | | OP | | K/M/R | Major | 4 |
| Abbott Valley Cabins | 387-4436 | 5 | $$$$ | | | Yes | R/K | Major | 5 |
| Glacier Cabins | 387-5339 | 5 | $$/$$$ | | | Yes | R/M/K | M/V | 5 |
| Glacier Park Inn B&B | 387-5099 | | | | | | | | 5 |
| Historic 1907 Tamarack Lodge, B&B, Motel | 387-4420 | 8 | $$$/$$$$ | CB | | Yes | DA | Major | 5 |
| Evergreen Motel | 387-5365 | 9 | $$$ | | | Yes | P/K/M/R | M/V | 5 |
| Mini Golden Inns Motel | 387-4317 | 38 | $$-$$$$ | CB | | Yes | K/P/M/R/DA | Major | 5 |
| Timber Wolf Resort | 387-9653 | 17 | $/$$ | CB | | Yes | P/DA | Major | 5 |
| Crooked Tree Motel & RV Park | 387-5531 | 8 | $ | | IP/S | Yes | K/P | V/M | 5 |
| Silverwolf Chalets | 387-4448 | | | | | | | | 5 |
| Glacier Park Super 8 | 892-0888 | 32 | $$/$$$ | CB | HT | Yes | M/F | Major | 6 |
| Ol' River Bridge Inn | 892-2181 | 31 | $$ | No | IP | Yes | R/L/D | Major | 6 |
| Western Inns-Glacier Mountain Shadows | 892-7686 | 23 | $$/$$$ | CB | HT/OP | Yes | P/M | V/M | 6 |
| Park View Inn B&B | 892-7275 | | | | | | | | 7 |
| Glacier Inn Motel | 892-4341 | 19 | $$ | | | Yes | R | Major | 7 |
| Lazy Bear Lodge | 862-4020 | 66 | $$ | | HT | Yes | P/D | Major | 9 |
| Best Western Rocky Mountain Lodge | 862-2569 | 79 | $$$ | CB | OP/HT | Yes | P/M/R/DA | Major | 9 |
| Allen's Motel | 862-3995 | 17 | $ | | | Yes | K/P/M/R | Major | 9 |
| Norskman Hotel | 862-5515 | 48 | $$ | CB | OP/HT | Yes | P | Major | 9 |
| Whitefish Motel | 862-3507 | 18 | $$ | | | Yes | K/P/M/R/DA | Major | 9 |
| Super 8 Motel | 862-8255 | 40 | $$/$$$ | CB | HT | Yes | P/DA | Major | 9 |
| Cheap Sleep Motel | 862-5515 | 48 | $/$$ | | HT/OP | Yes | P | Major | 9 |
| Gasthaus Wendlingen B&B | 862-4886 | | | | | | | | 9 |
| North Forty Resort | 862-7740 | | | | | | | | 9 |
| Pine Lodge | 862-7600 | 76 | $$$/$$$$ | CB | IP/OP/HT | Yes | K/P/M/R/DA | Major | 9 |
| Chalet Motel | 862-5581 | 33 | $$/$$$ | | IP/ HT | Yes | K/P/D/M/R/DA | Major | 9 |
| The Garden Wall B&B | 862-3440 | | | | | | | | 10 |
| Whitefish Property Management | 863-4651 | | | | | | | | 10 |
| Downtowner Motel | 862-2535 | 13 | $/$$$ | CB | HT/S | | | | 10 |
| Alpinglow Inn & Restaurant | 862-6966 | 54 | $$$$ | CB | HT/S | Yes | P/D/DA | Major | 12 |
| Kandahar Lodge & Cafe | 862-6098 | 48 | $$$ | | HT/S | Yes | DA/R/M/D/L/K | Major | 12 |
| Good Medicine Lodge | 862-5488 | | | FB | | | | | 12 |
| Kristianna Mountain Homes | 862-2860 | 20 | $$$$ | | HT/S | | K/M/R | Major | 12 |
| Edelweiss Condominiums | 862-5252 | 49 | $$$$ | FB | IP/HT | Yes | FB/K/M/R | Major | 12 |
| Anapurna Edelweiss | 862-3687 | 65 | $$$$ | | IP/HT | Yes | K/P/M/R | Major | 12 |
| Crestwood Resort Condominiums | 86-7574 | | | | | | | | 12 |

## Motel Quick Reference-Continued

Price Range: ($) Under $40 ; ($$) $40-$60; ($$$) $60-$80, ($$$$) Over $80. Pets [check with the motel for specific policies] (P), Dining (D), Lounge (L), Disabled Access (DA), Full Breakfast (FB), Cont. Breakfast (CB), Indoor Pool (IP), Outdoor Pool (OP), Hot Tub (HT), Sauna (S), Refrigerator (R), Microwave (M) (Microwave and Refrigerator indicated only if in majority of rooms), Kitchenette (K). All Montana area codes are 406.

| HOTEL | PHONE | NUMBER ROOMS | PRICE RANGE | BREAKFAST | POOL/ HOT TUB SAUNA | NON SMOKE ROOMS | OTHER AMENITIES | CREDIT CARDS | MAP LOCATOR NUMBER |
|---|---|---|---|---|---|---|---|---|---|
| **Grouse Mountain Lodge** | 862-3000 | 145 | $$$$ | | HT/IP/S | Yes | D/L/DA | Major | 12 |
| Eagles Roost Bed & Breakfast | 862-5198 | 3 | $$$/$$$$ | FB | HT | Yes | BB/PB | A/V/M | 12 |
| Whitefish Lake Lodge Resort | 862-2929 | 27 | $$$$ | CB | OP/HT | Yes | CB/K/M/R/DA | V/M | 12 |
| Black Diamond Lodge | 8622-3687 | 4 | $$$$ | FB | IP | Yes | | Major | 12 |
| **Alpine Friendship Inn** | 257-7155 | 30 | $$/$$$ | CB | HT | Yes | CB/K/P/M/R/DA | Major | 15 |
| Blue & White Motel | 755-4311 | 107 | $$/$$$ | CB | OP/ HT | Yes | P/DA | Major | 15 |
| Hilltop Inn | 755-4455 | 25 | $$ | | | Yes | K/R | Major | 15 |
| El Rancho Motel | 752-2941 | 18 | $$ | | | | R | Major | 15 |
| White Birch Motel | 752-408 | 10 | $$/$$$ | | | | K/P/R | Major | 15 |
| **All Pro Rental** | 755-1332 | | | | | | | | 16 |
| **Red Lion Inn** | 755-6700 | 64 | $$-$$$$ | CB | OP/HT | Yes | P/D/L/DA | Major | 16 |
| Hampton Inn | 755-7900 | 120 | $$$ | CB | IP/ HT | Yes | K/P/R/DA | Major | 16 |
| **Four Seasons Motor Inn** | 755-6123 | 101 | $$ | | HT | Yes | P/D/DA | Major | 17 |
| **Days Inn** | 756-3222 | 53 | $$/$$$ | CB | | Yes | DA | Major | 17 |
| **Glacier Gateway Motel** | 755-3330 | 15 | $$ | | | Yes | K/P/R/DA | Major | 17 |
| Kalispell Grand Hotel | 755-8100 | 40 | $$ | CB | | Yes | P/D/L | Major | 18 |
| **WestCoast Kalispell Center Hotel** | 752-6660 | 132 | $$$$ | | IP/HT/S | Yes | P/D/L/D | Major | 18 |
| Super 8 Motel Of Kalispell | 755-1888 | 74 | $$ | CB | | Yes | P/DA | Major | 18 |
| **Diamond Lil Inn** | 752-3467 | 62 | $$$ | | OP/HT | Yes | P/D/L | Major | 19 |
| Aero Inn | 755-3798 | 62 | $$ | CB | IP/HT/S | Yes | K/P/DA | Major | 19 |
| **WestCoast Outlaw Hotel** | 755-6100 | 220 | $$$$ | | IP/HT | Yes | D/L/DA | Major | 19 |
| Motel 6 | 752-6355 | 114 | $$ | | OP | Yes | P/DA | Major | 19 |
| **White oak of Montana** | 857-2388 | 100 | $$/$$$ | CB | IP | Yes | DA | | 20 |
| **Candlewycke B&B** | 837-6406 | | | | | | | | 23 |
| **O'Duachain Country Inn** | 837-6851 | | | | | | | Major | 23 |
| Timbers Motel & RV Park | 837-6200 | 40 | $$/$$$ | CB | OP/HT/S | Yes | P/DA | Major | 23 |
| **Coyote Inn & Riverside Cabins** | 837-1233 | 11 | $$$$ | CB | HT | Yes | DA/R/M/K | | 24 |
| **Marina Cay Resort** | 837-5861 | 120 | $$$ | | IP/HT | Yes | D/L/DA | Major | 24 |
| **Accommodations Flathead Lake** | 837-5617 | 4 | $$$$ | | | Yes | K/M/R | | 24 |
| **Swan River Inn** | 837-2220 | | | | | | | | 24 |
| **Cherry Way Inn Family B&B** | 837-260 | | | | | | | | 25 |
| Hotel Bigfork | 837-7377 | 6 | $$/$$$ | | HT | Yes | K/D/L | Major | 25 |
| Woods Bay Resort | 837-3333 | 10 | $$ | CB | | | K/P/R | Major | 25 |
| **Mission Mountain Resort** | 837-6200 | 7 | $$$/$$$$ | | | Yes | R/M/K | Major | 28 |
| **Super 8 Motel** | 883-6252 | 44 | $$ | CB | | Yes | K/P/R/DA | Major | 28 |
| **Port Polson Inn** | 883-5385 | 43 | $$ | CB | HT/S | Yes | K/M/R | Major | 29 |
| **Bayview Inn** | 883-3120 | 26 | $$/$$$ | CB | | Yes | P/M/R | Major | 29 |
| Best Western Kwataqnuk Resort | 883-3636 | 112 | $$$ | | IP/OP/HT | Yes | D/DA | Major | 29 |
| Cherry Hill Motel | 883-2737 | 15 | $$-$$$ | | HT | Yes | K/R/DA | V/M/D | 29 |
| **Ruth's B&B** | 883-2460 | | | | | | | | 30 |
| **Bayshore Resort Motel** | 844-3131 | 14 | $-$$$ | CB | HT | Yes | K/M/R | Major | 36 |
| Lakeshore Motel | 844-3304 | 7 | $$ | | | | DA | Major | 36 |
| Lakeside Resort Motel | 844-3570 | 15 | $$$ | | HT | Yes | K/M/R/DA | Major | 36 |
| Sunrise Vista Inn | 844-3864 | 9 | $$ | | | Yes | K/P/M/R/DA | V/M | 36 |
| Edgewater Motel & RV Park | 844-3644 | 20 | $$/$$$ | | | Yes | K/P/R/DA | Major | 36 |
| Somers Bay Log Cabin Lodging | 857-3881 | 6 | $$$$ | | | Yes | K/M/R | Major | 36 |
| **The Laughing Horse Lodge** | 886-2080 | 8 | $$/$$$ | | HT | Yes | P/D/L | Major | 37 |
| Swan Valley Super 8 | 754-2688 | 22 | $$/$$$ | CB | | Yes | K/M/R/DA | Major | 37 |

**NOTES:**

**NOTES:**

# Section 15

## Northwest Corner

## Including Libby, Thompson Falls and Eureka

*Kootenai River near Troy.*

### Weather Averages

**Libby**

| | |
|---|---|
| January | |
| Average High: | 31.3° F |
| Average Low: | 14.7° F |
| Average Precip.: | 2.06 in |
| April | |
| Average High: | 61.6° F |
| Average Low: | 30.2° F |
| Average Precip.: | 1.03 in |
| July | |
| Average High: | 88.0° F |
| Average Low: | 46.3° F |
| Average Precip.: | 0.91 in |
| October | |
| Average High: | 59.0° F |
| Average Low: | 32.6° F |
| Average Precip.: | 1.64 in |

**Thompson Falls**

| | |
|---|---|
| January | |
| Average High: | 31.9° F |
| Average Low: | 12.8° F |
| Average Precip.: | 4.13 in |
| April | |
| Average High: | 57.3° F |
| Average Low: | 27.5° F |
| Average Precip.: | 1.79 in |
| July | |
| Average High: | 84.4° F |
| Average Low: | 41.4° F |
| Average Precip.: | 0.86 in |
| October | |
| Average High: | 59.1° F |
| Average Low: | 29.7° F |
| Average Precip.: | 2.37 in |

**Lake Koocanusa**

| | |
|---|---|
| January | |
| Average High: | 31.3° F |
| Average Low: | 14.7° F |
| Average Precip.: | 2.06 in |
| April | |
| Average High: | 61.6° F |
| Average Low: | 30.2° F |
| Average Precip.: | 1.03 in |
| July | |
| Average High: | 88.0° F |
| Average Low: | 46.3° F |
| Average Precip.: | 0.91 in |
| October | |
| Average High: | 59.0° F |
| Average Low: | 32.6° F |
| Average Precip.: | 1.64 in |

**1.** *Attraction, Gas, Food, Lodging, Shopping*

### Hot Springs

The town is aptly named after its abundance of hot mineral springs and mud baths. The local Indians and settlers believed the natural waters and hot mud had healing powers. There are three locations where you can indulge yourself and soak away your mental and physical aches and pains.

One location is at the edge of town. It was originally called Camas Hot Springs and is owned by the Confederated Salish and Kootenai Tribes. The springs receive little upkeep, but they are free. This site includes two hot water plunges, each roughly three feet deep. There is also a gazebo with a shallow mud bath to soak in. The "corn hole" is a mud foot bath which is rumored to remove corns by soaking your feet for several hours in it. There are no lifeguards here and alcohol of any sort is prohibited. There is a public restroom equipped with water hoses to wash off the mud. A nearby grassy area is a good spot for picnicking or just relaxing with a good book after a soak.

If you want to move upscale a notch for your soaks, try the historic Symes Hotel in town. They have baths and a new outdoor mineral swimming pool and spa which are open to the public for a small admission charge.

Near Hot Springs off of Hwy. 28 is the Wild Horse Hot Springs. Here you can rent private rooms with plunges and steam saunas and restrooms by the hour.

Call the Hot Springs Chamber of Commerce at 741-2662 for more information.

### TL Symes Hot Springs Hotel & Mineral Baths

209 Wall St., Hot Springs. 741-2361.
www.ronan.net/~hscofc/symes.htm

Built in 1928, the historic Symes Hot Springs Hotel has 28 rooms, 9 apartments and 9 cozy cabins to suit any of your accommodation needs. The unique atmosphere is also complete with a large lobby and a sunroom area where guests are encouraged to relax, shops, a beauty salon, private baths, a jacuzzi suite and a new artesian mineral pool. The services in the spa include massage, watsu, body wraps, reiki and chiropractics. Enjoy an espresso drink in the lobby, mountain bike rentals and local horseback rides. Dining is also available on-site. Enjoy the healing waters in the beautiful historic atmosphere at Symes Hotel.

### TL Wild Horse Hot Springs

North of Hot Springs on Hwy 28.

The springs are located on a privately owned resort that is open year round. The bathhouse offers six private soaking rooms complete with bathroom and sauna with an hourly charge. The water is maintained at 104 degrees F in the soaking rooms and can be adjusted by the bathers preference. The springs were discovered around 1912 when Molly Bartlett decided to drill her own well and the hot water burst from the earth. She continued to share her good fortune of water with guests for bathing and later as "Camp Aqua" for children suffering from polio. A public resort was built is the 1980s, retaining the name of "Camp Aqua", and changed to Wild Horse Hot Springs in the 1990.

### FS Herb Store & More

300 Main St., Hot Springs. 741-5670

Stop in for a delicious lunch, where everything is made from scratch. Choose from homemade breads, pizza, sandwiches, salads, and great daily

All Montana Area Codes are 406

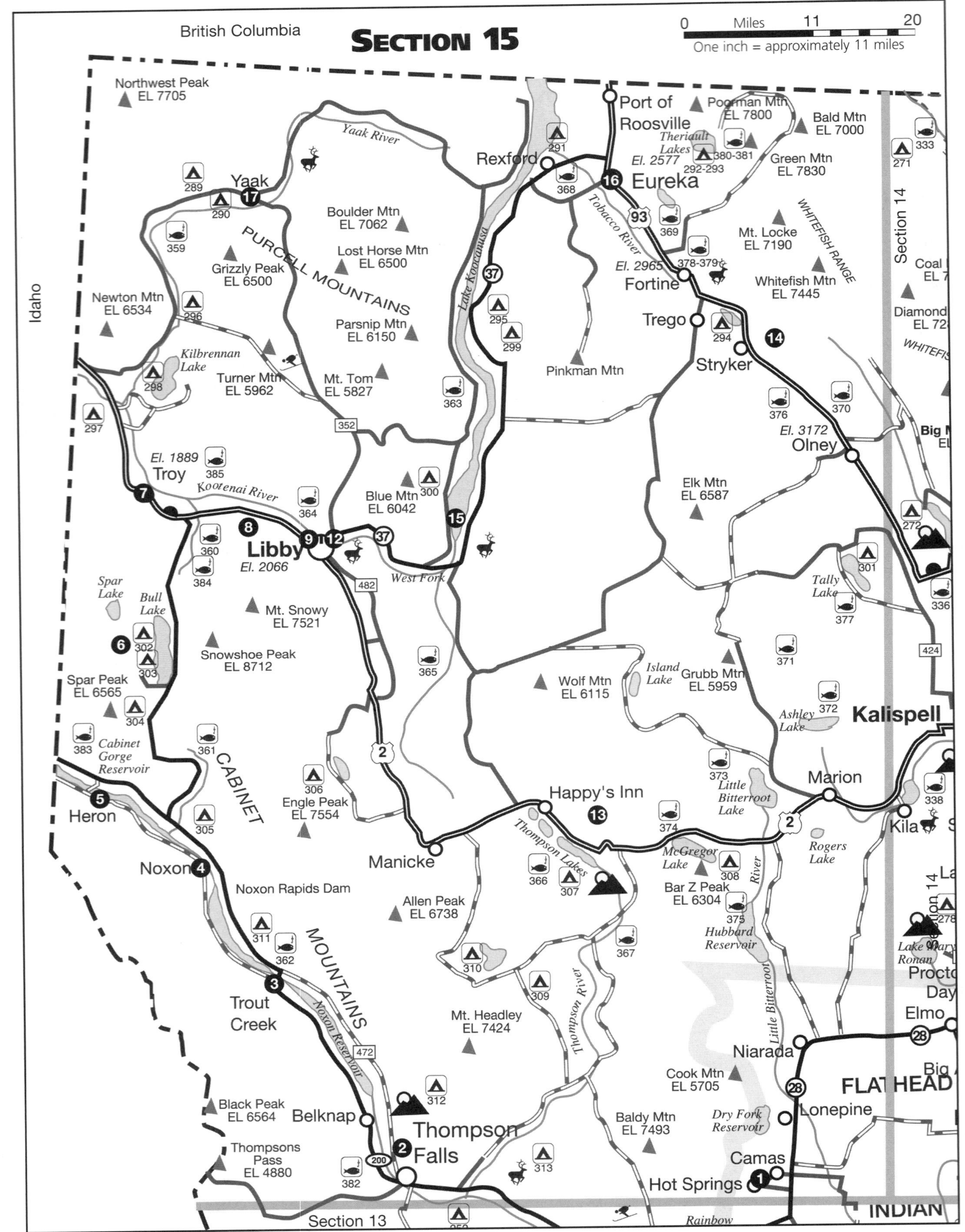

**Legend**

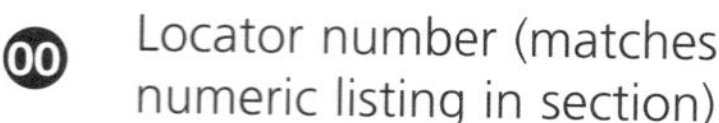

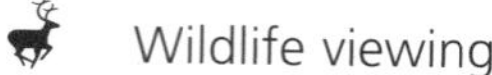

- Locator number (matches numeric listing in section)
- Wildlife viewing
- Campsite (number matches number in campsite chart)
- State Park
- Fishing Site (number matches number in fishing chart)
- Rest stop
- Interstate
- U.S. Highway
- State Highway
- County Road
- Gravel/unpaved road

lunch specials. This unique shop also offers a wide range of gift items, jewelry, and homeopathic products. They specialize in herbs and have a large variety of bulk and packaged herbs, spices, and teas. They offer interesting cards and gifts—with imported goods, books, tinctures, salves, incense, candles, snacks, and organic coffee. Donna's Jewelry is located in the store, with a nice variety and low prices. Owners Beverly and Karen can help you find the right herbs or gifts. Open 10–6, seven days a week.

### FA Y Quick Stop, Deli, Casino, & Lounge

1893 Hwy. 28, Hot Springs. 741-3210

### M Coldwell Banker/Kingsley & Associates

## 2. *Attraction, Gas, Food, Lodging Miscellaneous*

### Thompson Falls

Thompson Falls lies at the western edge of Montana within the Lolo National Forest. It is hedged by the Bitterroot Mountain Range on the west and the Cabinet Mountains on the north. Among other beautiful scenery, the Rose Garden Park is a popular stop. The Sanders County Museum and the Thompson Falls State Recreation area are other attractions.

### Belknap

For a brief time between 1883 and 1884, Belknap was a booming railroad town and outfitting point for miners. In 1884, it burned to the ground and never quite recovered. During its brief heyday, its population exceeded 3,000.

*Noxon bridge.*

### T Thompson Falls State Park

1 mile northwest of Thompson Falls on MT 200. 752-5501.

A mature, mixed pine forest makes this 36-acre park cool and private. Attractions include bird watching; fishing for bass, trout, and ling; nature walks; and boating on Noxon Rapids Reservoir.

### T The Heritage Museum

1367 Hwy 2 S., Libby. 293-7521

The Heritage Museum, a 12-sided log structure, 130 feet in diameter, is filled with Libby's old musical instruments, household implements and logging equipment. Special displays give an understanding of the region's wildlife, logging industry and mining. The exhibits portray the various peoples that came into the area— Kootenai Indians, trappers, miners, lumbermen, and women. Animal life exhibits in native habitats present the natural history of the surrounding terrain, and includes a silver-tipped grizzly and a mural of the local skyline.

A small house, furnished in turn of the century styles; an art gallery; exhibits by the Forest Service, mining interests, and the lumber industries are also featured in the main building. On the grounds there is a miner's cabin furnished by the Libby Woman's Club, an old forestry cookhouse, an equipment shed for old wagons, and other old buildings which are used to house special features. The museum is open June, July, and August.

> *Montana Trivia*
>
> Considering year-round temperatures, Thompson Falls is the hottest town in the state.

### T Old Jail Museum

Corner of Maiden Lane and S. Madison, Thompson Falls. 827-3496

This two-story Italianate style jail was built in 1907 at a cost of $5,000. Edward Donlan, a timber baron donated land for the new county courthouse and jail. It is Thompson Falls' oldest surviving county building. It was originally divided into incarceration cells on the second level with living quarters for the sheriff and his family on the first level.

There are four cells, each designed to hold four individuals. One cell, separate from the others, was for women and children detainees. Steel bars fastened by beams to a concrete floor and cement ceiling assured strict security within the cell room, while an 18" solid brick wall with steel door and locks isolated it from the stairway entrance. In the 1950s, it was considered the finest jail in the state. The museum is open from

> *Montana Trivia*
>
> Montana reaches its lowest altitude of 1,820 feet in the Northwest corner where the Kootenai flows into Idaho

Mother's Day to Labor Day, 7 days a week from noon to 4 p.m.

**L Falls Motel**
112 S. Gallatin, Thompson Falls. 827-3559 or 800-521-2184

The Falls Motel offers 22 rooms all on ground level with parking in front of your door. All rooms have a microwave, refrigerator, in-room coffee & tea, cable TV with HBO, and queen sized beds. Smoking & non-smoking rooms are available. They offer an on-site jacuzzi and free use of the local gym. Conveniently located near attractions and the Clark Fork River, guests enjoy the scenic trek across the pedestrian bridge to a beautifully wooded island with views of the Thompson Falls Dam and the rugged gorge below. The surrounding area provides a challenging 9-hole golf course and acres of National Forest, an outdoor enthusiast's paradise.

**L Thompson Falls Bed & Breakfast**
10 Mountain Meadows Lane, Thompson Falls. 827-0282 or toll free 866-fallsbb(325-5722). www.thompsonfallsbnb.net

The Thompson Falls Bed and Breakfast is located in a spectacular Rocky Mountain setting, cradled within the Cabinet Mountains, on a scenic route to Glacier Park. A central location to a wide variety of outdoor activities and awe-inspiring landscapes including the Clark Fork River, Thompson River, golf course, & The Old Jail Museum. Also nearby are ski resorts, lakes, Idaho, & Spokane, WA. Three charming bedrooms and a sitting room are available year round. You can also enjoy their covered deck with seating and comfortable hammocks while enjoying the peaceful, quiet setting and beautifully manicured yard. A delicious full breakfast is served daily. Give them a call or visit their web site.

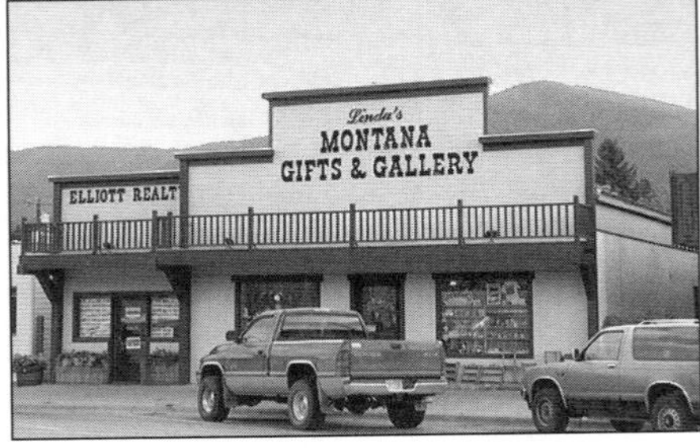


**S Linda's Montana Gifts & Gallery**
1219 Main St., Thompson Falls. 827-4383

**FLC Rimrock Lodge**
4946 Hwy. 200, Thompson Falls. 827-3536 or 888-418-2701. Email, tfl3536@montana.com. www.vacationalndandtravel.com

All 25 rooms at the Rimrock Lodge have river views. They are clean and comfortable with cable TV, direct dial phones, and easy access trails to the river where you can spot deer, elk, moose, and eagles. Their RV park has over 30 sites with hookups and showers. The restaurant serves breakfast, lunch and dinner seven days a week in a unique, cozy atmosphere with a mining decor, wood trimmed bar and fireplace. The full service menu offers seafood, steak, chicken dishes, burgers & sandwiches, a large salad bar, homemade soups daily, and a prime rib special on weekends. The baker prepares fresh dinner rolls, pastries and pies daily. They have a full lounge with poker and keno machines and a six lane bowling alley where you can try "cosmic bowling."

**S Antiques Plus**
915 Main Street, Thompson Falls. 827-0314

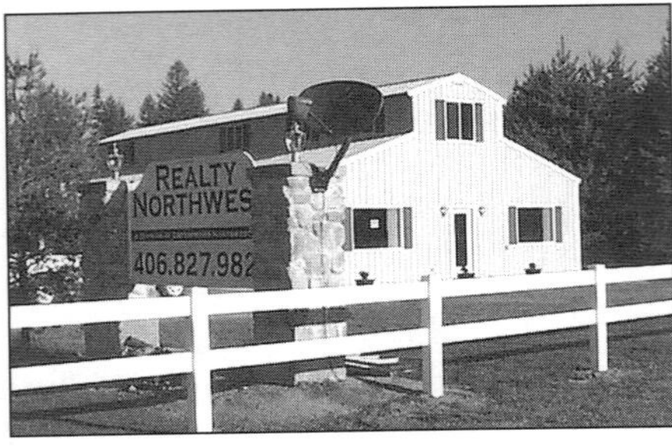


**M Realty Northwest**
4540 Hwy 200, Thompson Falls. 827-9829 or toll free 888-842-4266. www.realty-northwest.com or email: sales@realty-northwest.com

The dedicated Realtors at Realty Northwest will help you find just what you are looking for when it comes to real estate. Whether you are looking for bare land, waterfront property, ranches, commercial opportunities, or your Montana dream home, Realty Northwest will help you fulfill your real estate goals through professionalism, integrity and knowledge of today's real estate market. Serving Northwestern Montana, Realty Northwest strives for excellence in meeting the needs of customers and clients. They love the area and would love to introduce you to it. Stop by their office, visit them on the web or give them a call. They are open seven days a week and holidays by appointment.

**M Bennett Homes & Realty**
223 Main Street, Thompson Falls. 827-4663. www.thompsonfalls.com

**M Hurd-bush Realtors**
1013 Main St. in Thompson Falls. 827-3260

### *Montana Trivia*

In 1856, Congress appropriated $30,000 in an experiment to outfit western packers in Montana and several other states with camel caravans to transport goods. The experiment failed because horses and mules stampeded at the sight (or smell) of the strange critters.

## 3. *Gas, Food, Lodging*

### Trout Creek

Trout Creek, a flourishing town in the 1800s, derived much of its early commerce from mining, logging and the railroad. Today, it is an oasis of Montanan hospitality. The sparkling waters of the Clark Fork are full of trout and bass. The surrounding scenery is fantastic and attracts browsing wildlife, while the rushing of the mountain streams and sparkling blue alpine lakes are purely exhilarating.

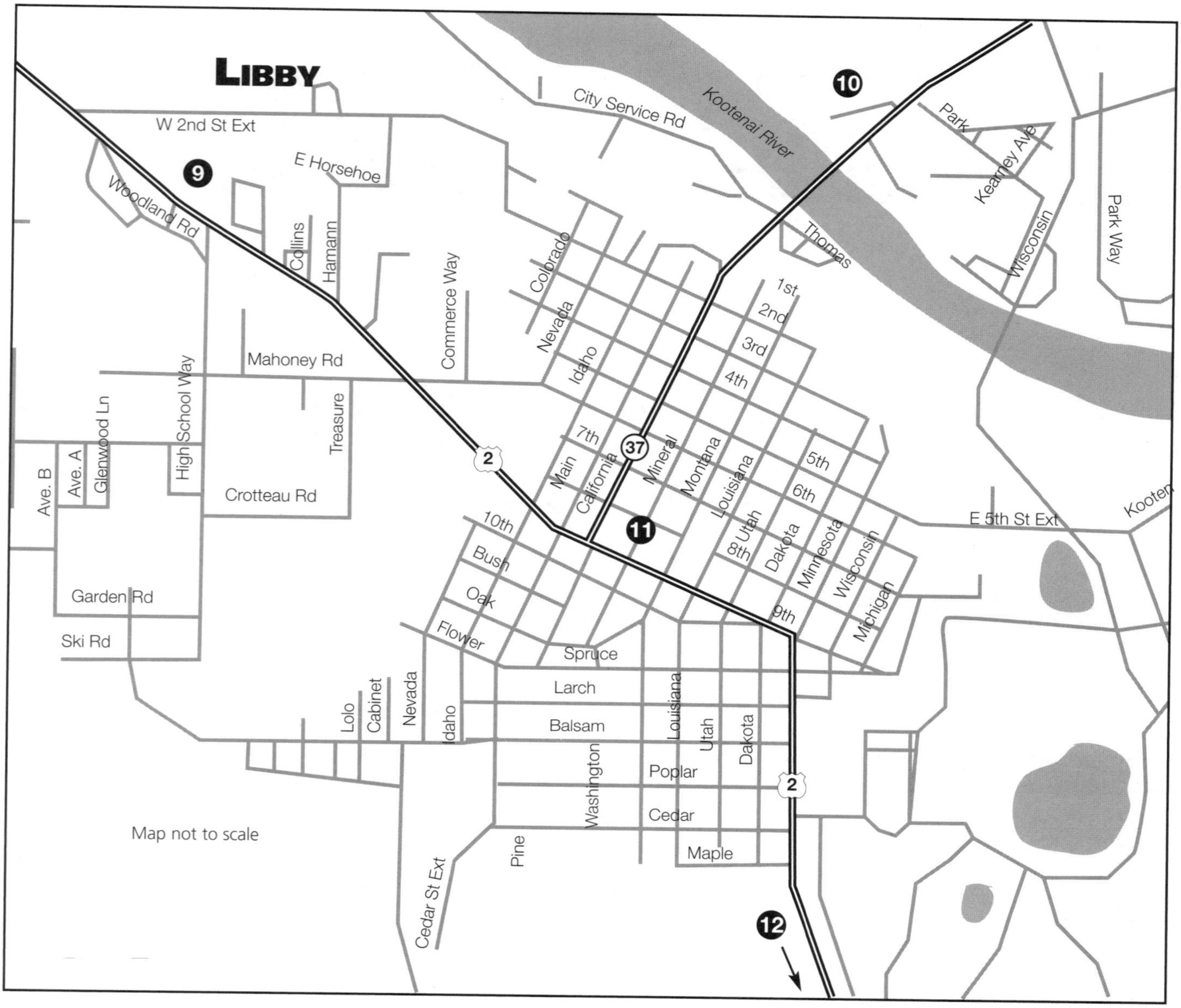

**LIBBY**

Map not to scale

## L Lakeside Motel

2957 Hwy. 200, Trout Creek. 827-4458

Located right on Noxon Reservoir in the heart of Trout Creek is the Lakeside Motel where you can take your pick of rooms. The regular motel rooms are spacious with vaulted ceilings, the rustic lakeside cabins are complete with kitchens and microwaves, and there is the luxurious two story jacuzzi suite with a balcony. All the rooms are very clean, and have cable TV with HBO, Disney, ESPN and more. You can enjoy waterfront activities with the public boat launch and dock. There are excellent outdoor recreational activities available in the area with hunting, fishing, and a great restaurant right next door.

## LC Trout Creek Motel & RV Park

2972 Hwy. 200, Trout Creek. 827-3268

The 8 room motel has clean, cozy rooms with double and queen size beds, kitchenettes, color TV, direct dial phones, free local calls, in-room coffee, room front parking, and plenty of room for truck and trailer parking (boats, snowmobiles, etc.). The RV park is off the road in a beautiful, serene setting surrounded by towering pine trees, and offers full RV hookups. Owners Glen & Kathy Ikola are very knowledgeable about the surrounding area and can help you plan recreational activities during your stay.

## F Katie Jack's Cafe

2981 Hwy. 200, Trout Creek. 827-3183

"Good food—one ugly waitress!" That's their motto at Katie Jack's Cafe located on the water in the heart of Trout Creek. Stop into this locally owned and operated restaurant for mouthwatering homestyle cooking with daily specials. Featuring a variety of huckleberry desserts including cheesecake, pie and milkshakes. The Katie Jack omelette special is a favorite among locals. Enjoy the beautiful surrounding wilderness and relax with a great home cooked meal.

### *Montana Trivia*

Over seventy percent of Montana's streamflow originates from melting snow.

### F Naughty Pine Saloon

2951 Hwy. 200, Trout Creek. 827-3282

Located right on the lake, this steakhouse, saloon, and casino is one of the the local's favorites for great steaks and seafood. The lively atmosphere is accentuated by wood trimmings and a rustic cabin atmosphere. In the summer months they offer outside dining on the waterfront. They feature volleyball, horseshoes, Monday night football specials, pool tables, darts, gaming machines, entertainment on special events, dances monthly, water recreation with river access and boat docks, and they sponsor several bass fishing tournaments throughout the year. The Naughty Pine can also be reserved for private parties.

## 4. *Food, Lodging*

### Noxon

Sitting in a heavily forested area, the town was known for its excellent trapping in the past, and its abundant crops of huckleberries today. The town saw a brief boom period when the railroad was under construction.

### L Bighorn Lodge Bed & Breakfast

2 Bighorn Lane, Mile Marker 7. Noxon. 847-4676 or toll 888-347-8477. www.bighornlodgemontana.com

The Bighorn Lodge Bed and Breakfast is designed for comfort and beauty with a unique blend of southern plantation and western contemporary architecture. 5 large guest rooms, each with private baths are uniquely appointed with furnishings of exceptional quality to insure your comfort and enjoyment. Outstanding hospitality and service at the Bighorn Lodge includes a full breakfast served daily. A 1,200 square foot cabin is available complete with 2 bedrooms/2 baths, kitchen, dining area, and living room with fireplace, television, and a large deck overlooking the Bull River. Relax and enjoy views from the veranda or lounging on the lodge deck after a day of recreation. A perfect destination for weekend getaways, corporate retreats, family reunions, weddings, and big game and guided fishing trips.

## 5.

### Heron

Virtually on the Idaho border on Hwy. 200, the town probably took its name from the birds that occasionally visit the nearby Clark's Fork River.

## 6. *Attraction*

### T Ross Creek Cedar Grove Scenic Area

Hwy 56 south from Hwy 2. Signs mark the turnoff for the 4-mile drive to the grove. Troy. 295-4693

This 10 acre preserve is home to huge western red cedars, some more than 500 years old. This is a favorite place for kids who love to crawl inside many of the trees which are hollowed out. Some of the trees are 175 feet tall and 12 feet in diameter. There is a paved nature trail and benches along the way. The self-guided nature trail winds in and out of the majestic trees for a mile. Keep alert for the elves and trolls that inhabit this fantasy land.

## 7. *Attraction, Gas, Food, Lodging, Shopping*

### Troy

Because of the deep ravines, dense forests and the steep mountains that characterize this area, the southern loop of the Kootenai was known as the Montana Wilds. Its ruggedness along with the fear of Indians kept it unsettled until gold was discovered in the mid 1860s. But not until the Great Northern railroad establish a freight division on the current townsite, did it really begin to flourish.

As construction crews filled the area, the town gained a reputation for rowdiness. One settler recalled, "fifteen saloons gaily lit were filled to the doors with wild men and wild women yelling, singing, dancing, cursing with glasses lifted high." In fact, the reputation for lawlessness in the settlement was so profound, trains locked their doors as they rolled through town to avoid holdups.

In 1910, the great forest fires that raged through the area almost claimed the town. Railroad hoses soaked the downtown buildings while a locomotive was kept steamed up ready to evacuate the remaining residents and crews should the fire overtake them. A little luck and a shift in the wind saved the town.

The town sits within walking distance of the Idaho border and the line which divides the Mountain Standard Time Zone from the Pacific Standard Time Zone. It has the distinction of being the town with the lowest elevation in Montana at only 1,889 feet above sea level.

There is some disagreement over how Troy got its name. Some say it took its name for a civil engineer working for the Great Northern. Others think the town was named for the Troy weight system, which was used to weigh silver and gold. Still others say that E.L. Preston named the town for Troy Morrow, the son of a family that was providing him with room and board while he surveyed the area for track and laid out the townsite. It is this latter theory that is most accepted.

### T Troy Museum & Visitor's Center
Troy

### L Holiday Motel
213 E. Missoula Ave., Troy. 295-4933

Enjoy your stay in this simple, quiet, very clean & comfortable establishment offering small town charm & decor. The rooms are nicely decorated and have HBO. Three of the rooms are two-bedroom suites. Enjoy a picnic at one of the tables outside or relax in the coziness of your room.

## 8.

### H Kootenai River
West of Libby.

The river is named for the Kootenai tribe that lived and hunted in this part of Montana and adjoining territory in Idaho and Canada. They were settled south of Flathead Lake in 1855 with the Salish on the Flathead Reservation.

They were friendly with neighboring mountain tribes but suffered frequently from the incursions of their bitter enemies, the Blackfeet, who came across the Continental Divide from the plains on horsestealing and scalp-raising expeditions.

First white men in here were trappers and traders for British fur companies as early as 1809. Placer discoveries were made and mining operations commenced about sixty years later.

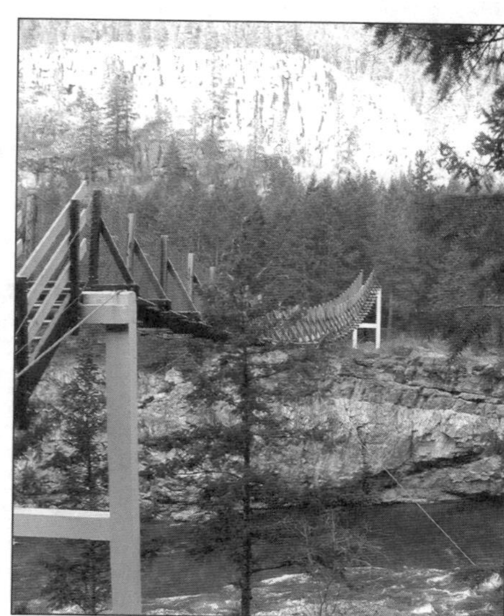

*A suspension foot bridge across the Kootenai River near Libby.*

### T Kootenai Falls
5 miles west of Libby.

Don't miss this spectacular cascading, 200-foot-drop falls; one of the few waterfalls on a major Northwest river whose power hasn't been harnessed to electrical generators. From Highway 2 there's a turnout approximately five miles west of Libby.

*Kootenai Falls.*

## 9. *Gas, Food, Lodging, Shopping*

### Libby

Libby is a timber town through and through. Initially trees were harvested for mine timbers, later for railroad bridges and ties; but ultimately the timber industry eclipsed both mining and the railroad and remains the mainstay for this town of approximately 2,600. The town is spread along the Kootenai River Valley, making it a very long town. The Cabinet Mountains border the south, the Purcell Mountains the northwest, and the Salish Mountains are the fortress to the northeast.

The Kootenai Indians roamed the region where Libby is located for about 300 years before the white man came. Explorers and trappers passed through this area, but the rugged physical terrain and deep forests discouraged settlers until late in the 1800s.

The town of Libby was built on the railroad right of way in 1892, as settlers joined the miners and trappers who had erected tent or simple log dwellings. Originally called Libby Creek, the name was shortened to Libby in 1904. The town was incorporated in 1909.

A typical small western town, early structures included log and wood frame buildings. The wood was supplied by the Libby Lumber and Development Company mill. Other building supplies came from two brick yards and a local marble quarry. A building boom took place between 1892 and 1894. Sixteen blocks had been laid out in the downtown area and lots were sold. But the boom was brief and the town slumbered through the depression of 1893. It wasn't until 1906, when Libby's lumbering industry gained momentum,

## Kootenai National Forest

**Libby is in the heart of the forest.** US Hwy. 2 is the primary travel route bisecting the forest. Access into the Forest is available from U.S. Highways 2 and 93, and ßState Highways 37, 56, 200, and 508. 293-6211

Located in the extreme northwest corner of Montana, bordered on the north by Canada and on the west by Idaho, lies the The Kootenai National Forest. Of the total 2.2 million acres, 50,384 are in the State of Idaho. Mountainous, rugged terrain runs north/south through the center of the Forest. High mountain peaks, notably Snowshoe, A Peak, and others ranging from 7,618 feet to 8,738 feet, provide a scenic backdrop for Libby and the surrounding area. More than 20 trails leading into the Wilderness give access to dozens of small lakes, ridgetop panoramas, and alpine meadows.

that consistent growth began. Prior to 1906, most of the timber harvested in the area was floated down the Kootenai in log drives to Bonner's Ferry and the mill there.

*Portions reprinted from Libby Chamber of Commerce data sheet.*

**L Venture Motor Inn**
443 Hwy 2 W., Libby. 293-7711 or 800-221-0166

The Venture Motor Inn boasts an indoor heated pool, hot tub, and an excellent family restaurant. The 72 spacious rooms include cable color TV, and king and queen size beds. Non-smoking rooms are available. Their restaurant is a locals' favorite and has a salad bar and a great view of the surrounding area from the second story perch. And here's something to talk about—free continental breakfast or $2 off breakfast! The restaurant also offers a kid's menu. For the business traveler, fax and copy services are available, along with 24-hour front desk service, and data ports in the rooms. Conference, banquet facilities, and meeting rooms are also available.

### Montana Trivia

From the source of a typical Montana river, to the point where it exits the state, it descends in altitude an average of three thousand feet.

**L Sandman Motel**
688 Hwy 2 W., Libby. 293-8831

Impeccably clean rooms! This incredibly quiet motel is situated away from the highway but nearby area restaurants & attractions. Microwaves & refrigerators are in all the rooms, and the facility is air-conditioned and handicap-accessible. Pets are welcome and kids under 10 stay free! They offer winter plug-ins and have a picnic and bar-b-que area. Their rates start at $33 (inquire about weekly and monthly rates) and all major credit cards are accepted. Their wealth of information on all local attractions will surely overwhelm you. Located on the west end of town on highway 2. For the friendliest service, and impeccably clean rooms drop in and say "G'day" to hosts Shane & Yvonne.

**10.** *Gas*

**11.** *Food*

### Montana Trivia

In 1900, moose were thought to be extinct in Montana outside of Yellowstone Park. Today, there are over 8,000 roaming the state.

**12.** *Attraction, Gas, Food, Lodging*

**T Montana City Old Town**
Main St., south of Hwy 2, Libby. 239-8426

Revisit Libby's history by visiting Montana City Old Town. There are false-fronted stores and a theater which does vaudeville acts and dramas in the Opera House.

**T The Heritage Museum**
1367 Hwy 2 S., Libby.

**F Pizza Hut**
903 California Ave., Libby. 293-7744

You know the name. You know the great pizza they serve. Besides great pizza, they have pasta, breadsticks, a salad bar, and dessert pizzas. You'll recognize the clean pleasant family atmosphere that is part of their trademark. They're right on the highway and easy to find.

**L Mountain Magic Motel**
919 Mineral Ave., Libby. 293-7795

Located in the heart of Libby, the Mountain Magic offers an outdoor heated pool and hot tub, color cable TV, air conditioning, and direct dial phones. Close to the town center and several good restaurants. Some rooms available with kitchenettes. Weekly rates available in the winter. Commercial rates available. Locally owned and operated.

**13.** *Attraction, Gas, Food, Lodging*

**Marion**

Believed to have been settled first in 1879 and the railroad came through over a decade later. During the years Marion was a base camp for the railroad workers. The train years were short lived when better and less treacherous routes were built. During the construction of the route to Marion about 20 Chinese men were killed during a terrible blast and buried along the now deserted grade. Marion eventually became a lumber town and when that industry faded so did Marion.

**T Logan State Park**
45 miles west of Kalispell on U.S. 2. Summer: 293-7190 Winter: 752-5501 Reservations: 755-2706

Surrounded by a 17-acre mature forest of western larch and ponderosa pine, this park is on the north shore of Middle Thompson Lake. Visitors enjoy swimming, boating, camping, waterskiing, and fishing for rainbow trout, largemouth bass, kokanee salmon, and yellow perch. A trailer sewage dump station is also available.

**14.** *Attraction, Gas, Food, Lodging*

**T Tally Lake State Park**
10 miles northwest of Kalispell. 862-2508

At 500 feet deep, Tally Lake is reputed to be the deepest natural lake in Montana. It is an excellent place to view birds, particularly raptors and waterfowl. There is a day-use fee charged here. To reach the park take Hwy. 93 north from the junction of Hwy. 2 to Reserve St. Go west for 4 miles to Farm-to-Market Road. Turn north and drive approximately 8 miles to Star Meadow Road FR 913. 10 miles to the campground.

**15.**

**T Libby Dam**
17 miles north of Libby. 293-5577

Libby Dam spans the Kootenai River 17 miles upstream from the town of Libby in the heart of beautiful northwestern Montana.

Libby Dam is 422 feet tall and 3,055 feet long. Lake Koocanusa is 90 miles long with a maximum depth of about 370 feet. Forty-two miles of Lake Koocanusa are in British Columbia, Canada.

The Kootenai River is the third largest tributary to the Columbia River, contributing almost 20 percent of the total water in the lower Columbia. Only the Snake and Pend Oreille/Clark Fork Rivers contribute more.

Libby Dam holds back 5.8 million acre-feet of water. An acre-foot of water is one acre of land covered with one foot of water, equaling 325,804 gallons. Spread out one foot deep, the lake would cover an area larger than the state of Massachusetts!

Surprisingly, Koocanusa is not an Indian name. Mrs. Alice Beers from Rexford, Montana, won a contest in 1971 to name the Libby Dam reservoir. She combined the first three letters from

KOOtenai River, the first three letters of CANada, and USA.

Libby Dam is a "straight-axis, concrete gravity" structure solidly anchored in bedrock. "Straight-axis" means the dam is built straight across the river instead of curved or arched. "Concrete gravity" means Libby Dam is made of concrete and holds back the water of the Kootenai River with its own massive weight. The 7.6 million tons of concrete in Libby Dam is enough to build a two-lane highway from Libby, Montana, to

Washington, D.C. (2,290 miles).

Libby Dam was built to provide flood protection for the Kootenai and lower Columbia Rivers, as well as to provide an additional source of hydroelectric power to meet increasing energy demands. Water stored behind Libby Dam also provides increased stream flows to downriver dams and powerhouses when water levels are low during winter months and in times of drought.

The Kootenai River flowed wildly before Libby Dam was built, causing floods in Montana, Idaho and British Columbia.

Historically, May and June were months of sandbags and anxiety! A total of $522 million in flood damages were caused by the Kootenai River from 1948 through 1961.

The Dam was built here because a large amount of water could effectively be stored. Any other site in the area would have required a longer, more costly structure and may have flooded more land.

At the peak of construction, the project employed over 2,000 workers. To offset this burden on the local communities, the Corps built three new schools, additions to several other schools, and the Libby airport. The Corps moved the town of Rexford to higher ground and built a new school, a water system, a sewage system, a fire station, a post office and roads. State highway 37 was also relocated. A forest development road was established along the west side of the reservoir. Koocanusa Bridge, Montana's longest (2,437 feet) and highest (270 feet), was built to provide access across the reservoir. Relocating the Great Northern Railroad line was one of the most complex of all the projects. Relocation cost more than $100.6 million - nearly 20 percent of the total dam construction budget-and included a seven-mile railroad tunnel through Elk Mountain.

Congress authorized construction of Libby Dam in 1951. The Columbia River Treaty between Canada and the United States was signed in 1961 and ratified in 1964. This treaty provided for construction of three storage dams in the Canadian portion of the Columbia River Basin (Duncan, Mica, and Hugh Keenleyside) and permitted the United States to construct Libby Dam. The four dams provide 25.5 million acre-feet of water storage to be used by both countries.

Construction began in 1966. It took the U.S. Army Corps of Engineers and its prime contractor, Morrison Knudsen Construction Company, until 1972 to complete Libby Dam. President Ford and Minister of Energy McDonald dedicated the facilities and ceremonially put the first power on line in August 1975. The powerhouse, was completed in 1976.

*Reprint of Corps of Engineers pamphlet.*

## 16. *Historical Marker, Attraction, Gas, Food, Lodging*

### Eureka

In recent years the term, "Last Best Place" has been used to describe the State of Montana. Few

who live in this vast and varied state would argue the point and what's more, those who live in the Tobacco Plains country consider it to be the "Last of the Last." It was not until the late 1880s that a handful of cattlemen found their way to this remote valley. Until then, it was strictly the domain of the Kootenai Indians who moved freely back and forth across the border with Canada, not knowing or caring about the imaginary line.

Not until 1904, when the Great Northern Railroad rerouted its tracks through here, was there any significant movement of settlers into the valley. Before that, the only commercial hubs in the area were the small settlements of Tobacco and Mills Spring. Oddly enough, they were about one half mile apart and considered themselves to be rivals. Their rivalry was ended, however, when the railroad missed both towns by less than two miles. The center of commerce was moved south to what was to become Eureka.

There was no shortage of entrepreneurs and homesteaders who came here looking for opportunity. Those people faced the future with unbridled optimism. Eureka began as a "flag station," but within two or three years, every passenger train stopped here. The editor of the Tobacco Plains Journal was one of the area's greatest promoters with weekly exhortations meant to draw more settlers this way. G. E. Shawler could not say enough about the potential riches that this country had to offer. Number one, of course, were the seemingly unlimited timber resources. Once the trains came through, the loggers and saw mills followed. But beyond that, Shawler foresaw the Tobacco Valley as an ideal place for families to come and grow fruits, grains and vegetables as well as livestock and poultry. Talk started almost immediately about the prospects of building a "big ditch" from the water rich mountains to provide irrigation for the semi-desert plains country to the north of Eureka. That project, begun in 1910, continues to improve even to this day, providing water to many small farmers and ranchers and gardeners all around Eureka.

Many thought that the surrounding mountains were rich with mineral resources. Prospectors poked and prodded every rock outcropping they could find, and while there were eventually some copper mines in the mountains to the east, gold and silver were never found in any worthwhile amounts.

By 1908, the town claimed over 60 businesses, including two each of banks, drug stores, meat markets, confectioners, barbers, doctors and lawyers. There was a school, a library, a newspaper, four churches and plenty of saloons. By 1910, a handful of people had driven automobiles into the valley over the wagon road that ran up from Kalispell.

Eureka boomed throughout the teens and into the roaring twenties. With its close proximity to Canada, the Prohibition era saw many dramas, great and small, played out between bootleggers and the "dry squad."

By the mid-twenties, the writing was on the wall as the area began to suffer some setbacks. Mainly, the Eureka Lumber Company planer burned and was not rebuilt. As for the farmers, the "Big Ditch," did not provide many of them with enough water and the Farmers and Merchants Bank foreclosed on them and then the bank failed. Eureka and the Tobacco Valley lay virtually dormant then for the next four decades. But since the early seventies, the trend has been reversed as more and more people come here seeking a less harried existence.

*Source: U.S. Forest Service pamphlet researched and written by Lost Trail Publishing.*

### Rexford

Most of what was originally Rexford is under Lake Koocanusa now. The small community on the lakeshore is the remnant of the original.

### H Tobacco Plains

Eureka

*During the fur trapping and trading days in the early part of the last century this corner of the state was remote and inaccessible from the customary trapping grounds and operating bases of the Americans. Representatives of the British and Canadian companies came in from the north and established posts along the Kootenai River.*

*The Tobacco Plains were so named by the Indians who planted tobacco for religious uses.*

*In prehistoric times the valley of the Kootenai was filled with an enormous ice sheet.*

### T Tobacco Valley Historical Village and Museum

South edge of Eureka. 882-4467

This museum chronicles the original settlement of the valley by the whites and the Kootenai Indians through present day. The valley is named for the tobacco that Indians were able to grow in the area. The museum is actually a collection of several historic buildings which were moved to the site. Among them are a museum and general store, school, library, church, Forest Service cabin, train depot, freight room, and a hand-hewn timber cabin—the first to be built in the Eureka area. A boardwalk connects the buildings. The museum is open daily Memorial Day to Labor Day from 1-5 p.m. Admission is free, but donations are appreciated.

### S Heavens Peak Health
407 Dewey Ave., Eureka. 296-3504.

Heavens Peak Health is the place for all the necessities of healthy living. They offer a wide selection of produce & snack foods, herbs, vitamins, organic foods & produce, as well as "alternatives for your four-footed friends." You can purchase bulk teas, coffees & grains, along with health & beauty supplies and body oils & soaps. They offer a wide array of beverage and fruit juices and have a jewelry and craft selection by local artists.

### S Northwest Sports Center
800 Hwy. 93 N., Eureka. 296-0888

Northwest Sports Center is your connection to the great outdoors. Eureka is an outdoorsman's wonderland with great hunting, fishing and camping throughout the whole general area. This is the place for all your supplies for hunting, flyfishing and trolling the big lake for salmon. They also carry outdoor clothing, camping supplies, hiking and athletic shoes, bait and lures, ammunition and archery supplies. Owners, Tom and Pat Moss, are more than happy to give great local advice on the area and local fishing tips. Stop in year round—plenty of RV parking!

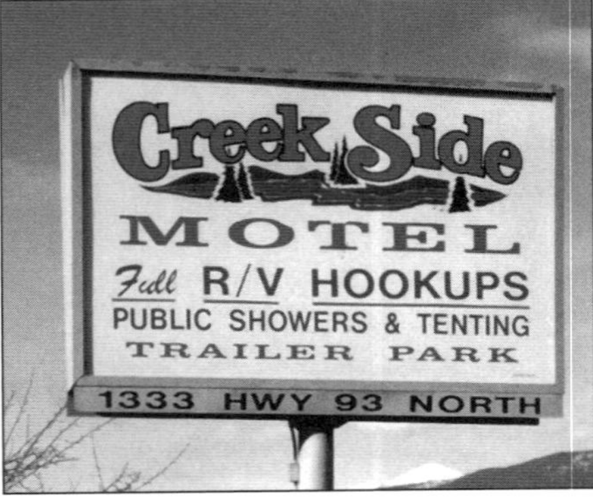


### LC Creekside Motel & RV Park
1333 Hwy. 93 N., Eureka. 296-2361

While dominantly an RV park and campground, the Creekside does offer three fully equipped kitchenettes. Pets are welcome! Enjoy views of the surrounding mountains while relaxing on the porches. Unlimited tent sites are also available. Toilets, water/electrical hookups, showers and a laundry all contribute to a comfortable stay. A creek runs through the property, and there are fresh flowers in the rooms all summer long.

## Eureka Lumber Company

**Eureka's past is inextricably tied to** the Eureka Lumber Company. Formed in 1905 shortly after the railroad pushed through, it was the focal point of the economy and without it, the town would have grown to little more than a whistle stop as was the fate of so many other settlements along the line. The June 19, 1908 issue of the Tobacco Plains Journal extolled the virtues of the company in a front page article:

"The passing traveler who takes occasion to note the circumstance from a railway car window will see an almost solid pack of logs in the river above Eureka for a distance of twenty miles. He will need no other evidence to understand that something is doing in the lumber manufacturing line in the vicinity. The vicinity is Eureka."

With over 100 men employed at the mill and another 150 employed in logging camps, the company's payroll amounted to $10,000 a month. In the spring when the logs that were decked along the Tobacco River throughout the winter were "driven" to the mill, the payroll grew by another $5,000. When one considers the trickle down effect of such a payroll, it becomes clear that the operation was the foundation of the local economy.

There were other far reaching effects. Three dams were built upriver in 1905. Environmental impact was not a consideration in those heydays of the lumber industry. Railroad spur lines were built to access more timber. A three mile flume brought more water into the Tobacco River from Glen Lake. Few signs of any of these "improvements" are in evidence today.

The Eureka Lumber Company went beyond simply providing jobs. It also was a stalwart supporter of all enterprises of a public nature whether the company was directly interested or not. Long about 1911, P. L. Howe, involved in the company from its inception, bought the controlling interest and changed the name to the P.L. Howe Lumber Company. By 1917, the International Workers of the World (I.W.W.) was making headway in organizing the mill workers and river drivers. They called strikes in 1917, 1918, and 1919 in an effort to halt the spring drive. This coincided with the United States entry into WW I and patriotism was at a fever pitch. Howe, who detested the I.W.W., used his influence to call in Federal troops, claiming the labor union intended to destroy infrastructure such as dams and railroad bridges.

The company flourished and died in less than 20 years, but in that time Eureka became a permanent spot on the map. Though the mill's closure staggered the town's economy, particularly when the Great Depression hit just four years later, the people found ways to diversify and have proved that Eureka is here to stay.

It is proper that the site of the Eureka Lumber Company is presently occupied by the Historical Village where its contribution to the foundation of Eureka can be preserved and remembered.

*Source: U.S. Forest Service pamphlet researched and written by Lost Trail Publishing.*

### 17. *Attraction*
### Yaak

This is the northwestern-most town in Montana and took its name from the nearby river. *Yaak* is an Indian word for "arrow. " The Indians thought the river cut like an arrow across the Kootenai.

### T Keystone Mines
north of Hwy. 2, Yaak.

A good deal of gold was produced here although it was never a major strike. Some structures are still standing but quite a challenge to get to. The site is in some of the state's most wild and rough country.

## Scenic Drives

**Lake Koocanusa**

Take Hwy. 37 just north of Libby to the dam. Stop at the visitors center then head north on the west side of the lake to the bridge just below Rexford. Cross the bridge back to Hwy. 37 and head south to complete the loop. If you have some extra time, head north on Hwy. 37 off the bridge to the quaint little town of Eureka, a town built on the timber industry. After knocking around the town, head back south on Hwy. 37 to complete the loop.

**Thompson River Road**

Whether you're looking for some great secluded fishing spots, or just a leisurely drive along a scenic mountain river, this is a delightful drive. You can either pick up the road just east of Thompson Falls and head north, or approximately 15 miles west of Kalispell and head south. If you're coming from Kalispell, follow the road along the river to the junction of Hwy. 200 and head east to Plains. Connect with Hwy. 28 and go north. You'll come to the small town of Hot Springs. If you have time, stop for a soak in one of three mineral pools or mud baths. Continue on Hwy. 28 to Elmo where you will catch 93 back to Kalispell.

## Hikes

**LeBeau Roadless Area and Finger Lake**

This is not so much a hiking trail as an area to hide. The area is roadless and pretty much trail-less. There is however, a short trail to Finger Lake. Follow Hwy. 93 northwest out of Whitefish for about 22 miles. You will see a turnoff to the west marked Legoni Lake. About 100 feet from the sign, turn at the third dirt road and follow it across a creek and the railroad tracks. Just past the tracks, the road makes a hairpin turn to the left. The campground is just under a half mile from here. Stay on the main road. Just before the campground you will see the trailhead sign. Park in the area just before the campground. Park and walk along the logging road until you see the sign for Finger Lake. The trail forks about half way to the lake. Take the fork to the ridgetop.

## Cross-Country Trails

### Kootenai National Forest

**Ross Creek Trail No. 4005-Highway 56, 17 mi. S Troy**

For more information contact: District Ranger, Troy Ranger Station, 1437 NHwy. 2, Troy, MT 59935 (406) 295-4693

*11 km Easiest. 2 km Most Difficult; intermittent grooming*
Parking capacity, 6 cars. Motor vehicles prohibited after December 1.

*For more information on following trails contact: District Ranger, Canoe Gulch Ranger Station, 12557 Hwy. 37. Libby, MT 59923 (406) 293-7773*

**Bear Creek-7 mi. S Libby**
*2.3 km Easiest. 1.8 km More Difficult. 1.4 km Most Difficult; intermittent grooming*
Parking capacity, 20 cars; motorized vehicles prohibited.

**Rainbow Ridge-22 mi. N Libby**
*2.8 km More Difficult; intermittent grooming*
Parking capacity, 10 cars; trail shared with snowmobiles.

**Flatiron Summit—24 mi. N Libby**
*2.5 km Most Difficult; intermittent grooming*
Parking capacity, 10 cars; motorized vehicles prohibited.

**Timberlane Campground-9 mi. N Libby**
*2.5 km Easiest, .8 km More Difficult; intermittent grooming*
Ski play hill and sledding; picnic shelter, fire ring; parking capacity, 10 cars.

**South Flower—4 mi. SW Libby**
*2.4 km Easiest, 5.5 km More Difficult, .5 km Most Difficult; intermittent grooming*
Parking capacity, 30 cars.

*For more information on following trails contact: District Ranger, Murphy Lake Ranger Station, Highway 93 N, Fortine. MT 59918(406) 882-4451*

**Grave Creek Road—16 mi. SE Eureka**
*35 km Easiest; 10 km More Difficult; intermittent grooming.*
Grooming by Ten Lakes Snowmobile Club. Parking available at Birch Creek Recreation Area. Grooming branches off Grave Creek Road to Stahl and Clarence Creek Roads (approx. 8 km each one way). Weasel Lake (3 km) and Weasel Cabin (2 km).

**Birch Creek-16 mi. SE Eureka**
*6 km Easiest, .6 km Most Difficult; intermittent grooming*
Parking available at Birch Creek Recreation Area.

**Therriault-10 mi. SE Eureka**
*16 km More Difficult 2 km Most Difficult; intermittent grooming*
Parking available at junction of Roads 756 and 7077.

**Williams Creek-16 mi. SE Eureka**
*19 km More Difficult; no grooming*
Limited parking; trails shared with snowmobiles.

**Deep Creek—15 mi. S Eureka**
*1.8 km Easiest, 6.2 km More Difficult; no grooming. If road not plowed, another 8 km Easiest included. See above*
Deep Creek road provides access to the North Fork of Deep Creek trail, Deep Creek trail, and Deep Divide road which accesses Williams Creek road.

**Laughing Water Creek-adjacent to Ranger Station**
*Up to 17 km More Difficult; intermittent grooming*
Limited parking; closed to snowmobiles.

*For more information on following contact: District Ranger, Eureka Ranger Station, 1299 Highway 93 N, Eureka, MT 59917 (406) 296-2536*

**Black Butte Road-5 mi. W Eureka**
*4.1 km More Difficult; no grooming*
Limited parking.

**Swisher Lake-10 mi. NW Eureka**
*4.8 km Easiest; no grooming*
Low elevation; limited parking.

**McGuire Mountain—25 mL S Eureka**
*5.6 to 15.1km More Difficult; no grooming*
Trail length depends on snow plowing of access road: limited parking.

**Virginia Hill—11 mi. S Eureka**
*8.2 km More Difficult; no grooming*
Mid-elevation, holds snow most of the season; limited parking on Road 7912 just off Pinkham Creek Road 854.

## Information Please

All Montana area codes are 406

### Road Information

Montana Road Condition Report
800-226-7623, 800-335-7592 or local 444-7696
Montana Highway Patrol 444-7696

**Local Road Reports**
Missoula 728-8553
Kalispell 751-2037
Statewide Weather Reports 453-2081

### Tourism Information

Travel Montana 800-847-4868 outside Montana
444-2654 in Montana
http://travel.mt.gov/.
Glacier Country 837-6211 or 800-338-5072
Northern Rodeo Association 252-1122

**Chambers of Commerce**
Libby 293-4167
Thompson Falls 827-4930
Tobacco Valley 297-2221
Troy 295-4175

### Airports

Eureka 296-2738
Hot Springs 741-3477
Libby 293-9776
Thompson Falls 285-3475
Troy 295-4480

### Government Offices

State BLM Office 255-2885, 238-1540
Bureau of Land Management
Missoula Field Office 329-3914
Flathead National Forest 758-5200
Kootenai National Forest 293-7713
Montana Fish, Wildlife & Parks 752-5501
U.S. Bureau of Reclamation
Helena Field Office 475-3310

### Hospitals

St. John's Lutheran Hospital • Libby 293-7761

### Golf Courses

Cabinet View Country Club • Libby 293-7332
Rivers Bend Golf Course
Thompson Falls 827-3438

### Bed & Breakfasts

**Bighorn Lodge** • Noxon 847-4676
**Thompson Falls B& B**
Thompson Falls 827-0282
Bull Lake Guest Ranch
Thompson Falls 295-4228
Kootinai River B&B • Thompson Falls 295-1501
Laughing Water Ranch • Fortine 882-4680
Lake Koocanusa Ranch • Rexford 889-3809
Blue Creek B&B • Heron 847-5555
River Bend B&B • Yaak 295-5493
Wilderness Lodge Hideaway • Heron 847-2063
Kootenai Country B&B • Libby 293-7878

### Guest Ranches & Resorts

**Bighorn Lodge** • Noxon 847-4676
RJR Guest Ranch • Eureka 889-3393
Mc Ginnis Meadows Cattle Ranch
Libby 293-5000
Hargrave Cattle & Guest Ranch
Marion 858-2284
Blue Spruce Lodge • Trout Creek 827-4762
Eda Ranch • Eureka 889-3141
Mc Gregor Lake Resort • Marion 858-2253
Loon's Echo Resort • Stryker 882-4791
Peacefull Lodge • Eureka 889-3981
Tucker's Inn • Trego 882-4200

### Vacations Homes & Cabins

Ksanka Mountain Ranch • Eureka 889-5684
Bower's Cabins • Fortine 889-5891
Jackson's McGregor Lake Summer Rental
Marion 858-2278

### Forest Service Cabins

***Kootenai National Forest***

**Big Creek Baldy Mtn. (Lookout Tower)**
20 mi. N of Libby, MT. 293-7773
Capacity: 6 Nightly fee: $25 Available: 6/1 - 10/1
Access depends on weather conditions. Primitive road access. Discourage bringing children.

**Gem Peak (Lookout Tower)**
15 mi. SW of Trout Creek, MT. 827-3533
Capacity: 4 Nightly fee: $25 Available: 6/15 - 10/15
Access depends on weather conditions. Drive directly to tower. Discourage bringing children.

**Mt. Baldy Buckhorn Ridge (Lookout Tower)**
25 mi. N of Troy, MT. 295-4693
Capacity: 4 Nightly fee: $25 Available: 7/1 - 10/31
Access depends on weather. Primitive road access; low clearance. Discourage bringing children.

**Sex Peak (Lookout Cabin)**
8 mi. S of Trout Creek, MT. 827-3533
Capacity: 4 Nightly fee: $25 Available: 6/15 - 10/15
Access depends on weather conditions. Drive directly to cabin.

**Webb Mtn. (Lookout Cabin)**
15 mi. SW of Rexford, MT. 296-2536
Capacity: 5 Nightly fee: $20 Available: All year
Primitive road access; low clearance. Normally plowed within 15 miles of cabin.

**McGuire (Lookout Cabin)**
14 mi. S of Eureka 296-2536
Capacity: 4 Nightly fee: $20 Available: All year
Trail access 3 miles from Road No. 494. Normally plowed within 14 miles of cabin.

**Mt. Wam Lookout Cabin**
17 mi. N of Fortine 882-4451
Capacity: 4 Nightly fee: $25 Available: All year
Access depends on weather conditions. 3 access trails: closest is from Rd 7022, 5 mi. hike to cabin.

***Lolo National Forest***

**Bend Guard Station**
32 mi. N of Thompson Falls, MT 827-3589
Capacity: 5 Nightly fee: $40; $5 persons, up to max. of 16 Available: All year
1 mile from plowed road in winter. Electric heat;

hot showers; fully furnished kitchen. Check for current road conditions.

**Cougar Peak (Lookout Cabin)**
10 mi. NW of Thompson Falls, MT. 827-3589
Capacity: 4 Nightly fee: $25 Available: 6/1-10/1
Lookout cabin sits near the end of Rd. 403. 150 ft walk to lookout. Snow may limit vehicle access.

**Priscilla Peak (Lookout Cabin)**
10 mi. NE of Thompson Falls, MT. 827-3589
Capacity: 4 Nightly fee: $15 Available: 6/1-10/1
Steep four-mile climb via trail to lookout. No heat source. Weather extremes probable.

## Private Campgrounds

**Rimrock Lodge** • Thompson Falls 827-3536
**Trout Creek Motel** • Trout Creek 827-3268
Blue Mountains RV Park • Eureka 889-3868
Creek Side Trailer Park • Eureka 296-2361
Big Bend • Libby 293-4536
Birdland Bay RV • Thompson Falls 827-4757
Cabinet Mountain Conoco • Libby 293-4942
Cooper's Woodland RV Park • Libby 293-8395
Happy's Inn & Resort • Libby 293-7810
Hook-U-Up RV Park • Libby 293-6869
Koocanusa Marina & Resort • Libby 293-7548
Meadowlark RV Park • Libby 293-8323
Woodland Park • Libby 293-8395
Rest A Day Campground • Marion 854-2292
Cabinet Gorge RV Park • Noxon 847-2291
Dog Creek Campground • Olney 881-2472
EZ-K • Rexford 296-2000
McGregor Lake Resort • Marion 858-2253
Mariner's Haven Campground • Rexford 296-3252
Birdland Bay RV • Thompson Falls 827-4757
Riverfront RV Park • Thompson Falls 827-3460
Sportsman's RV Park • Libby 293-7365
Two Bit Outfit RV Park • Libby 293-8323
Kootenai River Camp Ground • Troy 295-4090
LA-VI RV Park • Troy 295-4252

## Car Rental

Jenkins Motors 293-4104
Libby Auto Sales and Rental 293-7717
Timberline Auto Center, Inc. 293-4128

## Outfitters & Guides

*F=Fishing H=Hunting R=River Guides*
*E=Horseback Rides G=General Guide Services*

**Northwest Sports Center** G 296-0888
Blue River Valley Outfitting G 295-5881
Buckhorn Ranch Outfitters HF 889-3762
Bullseye Outfitting H 827-4932
Dave Blackburn's Kootenai Angler HF 293-7578
Elk Creek Outfitting F 847-5593
Hargrave Cattle & Guest Ranch HFE 858-2284
Hawkins Outfitters G 296-2642
Jerry Malson Outfitting G 847-5582
Koocanusa Marina & Resort G 293-7548
Kootenai Angler F 293-7578
Kootenai High Country Hunting G 882-4868
Lazy JR Outfitters HFER 293-9494
Lineham Outfitting Co F 293-8285
Linehan Outfitting Co G 295-4872
Montana Hight Country Outfitters H 847-2279
Montana Ranch Adventures FEG 338-3333
O'Brien Creek Fam GE 295-1809
Silverbow Outfitters HF 293-4868
Tamarack Lodge G 295-4880
Treasure State Outfitting F 293-8666
Wayne Hill Outfitting H 847-5563
Weare's Oufitting H 295-5861

## Downhill Ski Areas

Turner Mountain 293-4317

## Snowmobile Rentals

Snedigar Service • Fortine 882-4419
Big Red Ranch • Trego 882-4857

| Fishery | Cold Water Species | | | | | | | | | | | | Warm Water Species | | | | | | | | | | Services | | | | | |
|---|---|---|---|---|---|---|---|---|---|---|---|---|---|---|---|---|---|---|---|---|---|---|---|---|---|---|---|---|
| | Brook Trout | Mt. Whitefish | Lake Whitefish | Golden Trout | Cutthroat Trout | Brown Trout | Rainbow Trout | Kokanee Salmon | Bull Trout | Lake Trout | Arctic Grayling | Burbot | Largemouth Bass | Smallmouth Bass | Walleye | Sauger | Northern Pike | Shovelnose Sturgeon | Channel Catfish | Yellow Perch | Crappie | Paddlefish | Vehicle Access | Campgrounds | Toilets | Docks | Boat Ramps | Motor Restrictions |
| 359. Yaak River | • | • | | | • | | • | | | | | | | | | | | | | | | | • | • | • | | • | |
| 360. Lake Creek | • | • | | | • | | • | | | | | | | | | | | | | | | | | | | | | |
| 361. Bull River | • | • | | | • | • | | | | | | | | | | | | | | | | | • | • | | | | |
| 362. Noxon Rapids Reservoir | | • | • | | • | • | • | | • | | | | • | • | | | • | | | • | | | • | • | • | • | • | |
| 363. Lake Koocanusa | | • | | | • | | • | • | • | | | • | | | | | | | | | | | • | • | • | • | • | |
| 364. Kootenai River | | • | | | | | • | • | • | | | | | | | | | | | | | | • | • | • | | • | |
| 365. Fisher River | • | • | | | | | • | | | | | | | | | | | | | | | | • | | | | | |
| 366. Thompson Lakes | | | | | | • | • | • | | | | | • | • | | | • | | | • | | | • | • | • | • | • | |
| 367. Thompson River | • | • | | | • | • | • | | • | | | | | | | | | | | | | | • | • | • | | | |
| 368. Tobacco River | | | | | | | • | • | • | | | | | | | | | | | | | | • | | | | | |
| 369. Glen Lake | | • | | | | | • | • | | | | | | | | | | | | | | | • | • | • | | • | |
| 370. Upper Stillwater Lake | | | | | • | | | | | | | | | | | | • | | | • | | | • | | | | • | |
| 371. Logan Creek | • | • | | | • | | | | • | | | | | | | | | | | | | | • | • | | | | |
| 372. Ashley Lake | | | | | • | | | • | | | | | | | | | | | | • | | | • | • | • | | • | |
| 373. Little Bitterroot Lake | | | | | | | • | • | | | | | | | | | | | | | | | • | • | • | | • | |
| 374. McGregor Lake | | • | | | | | • | | | • | | | | | | | | | | • | | | • | • | • | • | • | |
| 375. Hubbart Reservoir | • | | | | | | • | • | | | | | | | | | | | | | | | • | | | | • | |
| 376. Lower Stillwater Lake | | | | | | | | | | | | | | | | | • | | | • | | | • | | | | • | |
| 377. Tally Lake | | | | | | | | | | | | | | | | | • | | | | | | • | • | • | | | • |
| 378. Dickey Lake | | | | | | | | | | | | | • | | | | • | | | | | | • | • | • | | | • |
| 379. Murphy Lake | | | | | | | | | | | | | • | | | | • | | | • | | | • | | | | | • |
| 380. Tetrault (Carpenter) Lake | | | | | | | | | | | | | • | | | | | | | | | | • | • | • | | | • |
| 381. Sophie Lake | | | | | | | | | | | | | • | | | | • | | | | | | • | | | | | • |
| 382. Thompson Falls Reservoir | | | | | | | | | | | | | | | | | • | | | | | | • | • | • | | | |
| 383. Cabinet Gorge Reservoir | | | | | | | | | | | | | • | • | | | • | | | • | • | | • | | | | | |
| 384. Savage Lake | | | | | | | | | | | | | • | | | | | | | | | | • | | | | | |
| 385. Alvord Lake | | | | | | | | | | | | | • | | | | | | | • | | | • | | | | | |

# Campsite Directions

| Campsite / Directions | Season | Camping | Trailers | Toilets | Water | Boat Launch | Fishing | Swimming | Trails | Stay Limit | Fee |
|---|---|---|---|---|---|---|---|---|---|---|---|
| **289•Whitetail FS**<br>7 mi. NW of Troy on US 2•12 mi. NE on Rt. 508•10 mi. NE on Forest Rd. 92 | 5/20-9/30 | 12 | 32′ | • | • | | • | | • | 14 | • |
| **290•Pete Creek FS**<br>7 mi. NW of Troy on US 2 • 12 mi. NE on rt. 508 • 12 mi. NE on Forest Road 92 | 5/20-9/30 | 12 | 32′ | • | • | | | • | • | 14 | • |
| **291•Rexford Bench FS**<br>7 mi. SW of Eureka on MT 37•Reservations 800-280-CAMP | 5/15-10/1 | 154 | 75′ | D | • | C | • | • | • | 14 | • |
| **292•Little Therriault FS**<br>7 mi. SE of Eureka on US 93•3 mi. NE on Cty. Rd. 114<br>•11 mi. NE on Forest Rd. 114•13 mi. W on Forest Rd. 319 | 5/20-10/15 | 6 | 32′ | • | • | | • | | • | 14 | • |
| **293•Big Therriault FS**<br>7 mi. SE of Eureka on US 93•3 mi NE on Cty. Rd. 114<br>•11 mi. NE on Forest Rd. 114•13 mi. W on Forest Rd. 319 | 5/20-10/15 | 10 | 32′ | • | • | C | • | | • | 14 | • |
| **294•North Dickey Lake FS**<br>13 mi. SE of Eureka on US 93 | 5/10-10/15 | 25 | 50′ | D | • | C • | • | • | • | 14 | • |
| **295•Peck Gulch FS**<br>23 mi. SW of Eureka on MT 37 | 5/15-10/1 | 75 | 32′ | D | • | C | • | • | • | 14 | • |
| **296•Yaak Falls FS**<br>10 mi. NW of Troy on US 2•6 mi. NE on Rt. 508 | 5/20-9/30 | 7 | 32 | • | | | • | | • | 14 | |
| **297•Yaak River FS**<br>7 mi. NW of Troy on US 2 | 5/20-9/30 | 44 | 32′ | D | • | | • | • | • | 14 | • |
| **298•Killbrennan Lake FS**<br>3 mi. NW of Troy on US 2•10 mi. NE on Forest Rd. 2394 | 5/20-9/30 | 7 | 32′ | • | | • | • | | | 14 | |
| **299•Rocky Gorge FS**<br>30 mi. SW of Eureka on MT 37 | 6/1-9/30 | 120 | 32′ | D | • | C | • | | • | 14 | • |
| **300•McGillivray FS**<br>15 mi. E of Libby on MT 37•10 mi. N on Forest Rd. 228•Reservations 800-280-CAMP | 5/23-9/15 | 50 | 32′ | D | • | C | • | • | • | 14 | • |
| **301•Tally Lake FS**<br>6 mi. W of Whitefish on US 93•15 mi. W on Forest Rd. 113 | 5/29-9/7 | 39 | 22′ | • | • | C | • | • | • | 14 | • |
| **302•Spar Lake FS**<br>3 mi. SE of Troy on US 2•16 mi. S on Forest Rd. 384 | 5/20-9/30 | 8 | 32′ | • | • | | • | | • | 14 | • |
| **303•Dorr Skeels FS**<br>3 mi. SE of Troy on US 2•14 mi. S on MT 56 | 5/20-9/30 | 6 | 32′ | • | | C | • | • | | 14 | |
| **304•Bad Medicine**<br>3 mi. SE of Troy on Us 2•18 mi. S on MT 56•1 mi. W on Forest R. 398<br>•1 mi. N on Forest Rd 7170 | 5/20-9/30 | 17 | 32′ | • | • | c | • | • | • | 14 | • |
| **305•Bull River FS**<br>6 mi. West of Noxon on MT 200 | 5/15-9/30 | 26 | 32′ | D | • | C | • | • | • | 14 | • |
| **306•Howard Lake FS**<br>12 mi. S of Libby on US 2•14 mi. SW on Forest Rd. 231 | 6/1-10/1 | 10 | 20′ | D | • | C | • | • | • | 14 | • |
| **307•Logan State Park FWP**<br>45 mi. W of Kalispell on US 2 | 5/1-9/30 | 39 | 40′ | • | • | C | • | • | | 14 | • |
| **308•McGregor Lake FS**<br>Temporarily closed | | | | | | | | | | | |
| **309•Fishtrap Lake FS**<br>5 mi. E of Thompson Falls on MT 200•13 mi. NE on Forest Rd. 56<br>•15 mi. NW on Forest Rd. 516•2 mi. W on Forest Rd. 7593 | 6/1-10/15 | 11 | 18′ | • | • | C | • | | 0 | 14 | |
| **310•Willow Creek FS**<br>19 mi. E of Trout Creek on forest Rd. 154 | 5/15-9/30 | 4 | 20′ | • | | | • | | • | 14 | |
| **311•North Shore FS**<br>2 mi. NW of Trout Creek on MT 200 | 5/15-9/30 | 13 | 40′ | • | • | C | • | • | | 14 | • |
| **312•Thompson Falls State Park FWP**<br>1 mi. NW of Thompson Falls on MT 200 | 5/1-9/30 | 17 | 55′ | • | • | C | • | • | | 14 | • |
| **313•Copper King FS**<br>5 mi. E of Thompson Falls on MT 200•4 mi. NE on Forest Rd.56 | 6/1-10/15 | 5 | | • | | | • | | | 14 | |

**Agency**
FS—U.S.D.A Forest Service
FWP—Montana Fish, Wildlife & Parks
NPS—National Park Service
BLM—U.S. Bureau of Land Management
USBR—U.S. Bureau of Reclamation
CE—Corps of Engineers

**Camping**
Camping is allowed at this site. Number indicates camping spaces available
H—Hard sided units only; no tents

**Trailers**
Trailer units allowed. Number indicates maximum length.

**Toilets**
Toilets on site. D—Disabled access

**Water**
Drinkable water on site

**Fishing**
Visitors may fish on site

**Boat**
Type of boat ramp on site:
A—Hand launch
B—4-wheel drive with trailer
C—2-wheel drive with trailer

**Swimming**
Designated swimming areas on site

**Trails**
Trails on site
B—Backpacking N—Nature/Interpretive

**Stay Limit**
Maximum length of stay in days

**Fee**
Camping and/or day-use fee

## Dining Quick Reference

Price Range refers to the average cost of a meal per person: ($) $1-$6, ($$) $7-$11, ($$$) $12-up. Cocktails: "Yes" indicates full bar; Beer (B)/Wine (W), Service: Breakfast (B), Brunch (BR), Lunch (L), Dinner (D). Businesses in bold print will have additional information under the appropriate map locator number in the body of this section.

| RESTAURANT | TYPE CUISINE | PRICE RANGE | CHILD MENU | COCKTAILS BEER WINE | SERVICE | CREDIT CARDS | MAP LOCATOR NUMBER |
|---|---|---|---|---|---|---|---|
| **Herb Store & More** | Home Cooking | $ | | | L | | 1 |
| **Y Quick Stop, Deli, Casino, & Lounge** | Deli | $ | Yes | | L/D | Major | 1 |
| Red Tail Cafe at the Symes | Fine Dining | $$ | | | B/D | Major | 1 |
| Running Iron Restaurant | Family | $ | Yes | | B/L/D | | 1 |
| Second Home Restaurant | Family | $/$$ | Yes | B/W | L/D | V/M | 1 |
| **Rimrock Lodge** | Family | | Yes | Yes | B/L/D | Major | 2 |
| **Naughty Pine Saloon** | American | $/$$ | Yes | Yes | L/D | | 3 |
| **Katie Jack's Cafe** | Family | $ | Yes | | B/L/D | V/M/D | 3 |
| Burger Express | Fast Food | $ | Yes | | B/L/D | | 2 |
| Granny's Cafe | Family | $ | Yes | | B/L | V/M | 2 |
| Laws Hometown PIzza | Pizza | $ | | | L/D | | 2 |
| New Asia Garden | Chinese | $$ | | | L/D | Major | 2 |
| Subway | Fast Food | $ | Yes | | L/D | | 2 |
| The Little Bear | Creative | $ | Yes | | L/D | | 2 |
| Wayside Bar | Burgers & Sandwiches | $ | | Yes | L/D | | 3 |
| Big Sky Pantry | Bakery | | | | | | 4 |
| Noxon Cafe | American | $ | | | B/L/D | | 4 |
| Hereford Bar & Restaurant | American | $/$$ | Yes | Yes | L/D | V/M | 4 |
| Beck's Cafe II & Casino | American | $/$$ | | B/W | B/L/D | Major | 7 |
| Boondocks Restaurant | American | $/$$ | Yes | B/W | L/D | | 7 |
| R Place | Fast Food | $ | Yes | | L/D | | 7 |
| Silver Spur Restaurant | American | $/$$ | Yes | Yes | B/L/D | V/M | 7 |
| Trojan Lanes Cafe | American | $ | Yes | Yes | L/D | | 7 |
| **Venture Motor Inn** | Family | $/$$ | Yes | | B/L/D | Major | 9 |
| 4B's Restaurant | Family | $ | Yes | | B/L/D | V/M/D | 9 |
| Beck's Montana Cafe | Family | $/$$ | Yes | | B/L/D | Major | 9 |
| Henry's Restaurant | Family | $/$$ | | | B/L/D | V/M | 9 |
| Ho Wun Chinese Restaurant | Chinese | $/$$ | | B/W | L/D | Major | 9 |
| J D'S Zip Inn | Fast Food | $ | | | B/L/D | Major | 9 |
| Little Joe's Restaurant & Bar | American | $ | | Yes | L/D | | 9 |
| Treasure Mountain Restaurant & Casino | American | $/$$ | Yes | Yes | B/L/D | Major | 9 |
| La Casa De Amigos Mexican | Mexican | $ | Yes | | L/D | V/M | 11 |
| Libby Cafe | American | $ | Yes | | B/L | | 11 |
| Marcia's Fine Dining | Family | $ | Yes | B/W | L/D | | 11 |
| **Pizza Hut** | Pizza | $/$$ | Yes | B | L/D | V/M/D | 12 |
| Copper Creek Coffee House | Deli | $ | | | L | | 12 |
| Dairy Queen | Fast Food | $ | Yes | | L/D | | 12 |
| Hidden Chapel Restaurant | Eclectic/Family | $-$$$ | | W/B | L/D/BR | V/M | 12 |
| M K Steak House | Steakhouse | $$$ | Yes | Yes | D | Major | 12 |
| McDonald's | Fast Food | $ | Yes | | B/L/D | | 12 |
| Subway | Fast Food | $ | Yes | | L/D | | 12 |
| The Express Burgers | Fast Food | $ | Yes | | L/D | | 12 |
| Happy's Inn & Resort | American | $$ | Yes | Yes | B/L/D | Major | 13 |
| Mc Gregor Lake Resort | American | $/$$ | Yes | Yes | B/L/D | V/M/D | 13 |
| Hilltop Hitching Post & Motel | American | $ | | Yes | L/D | Major | 13 |
| Sawmill Restaurant | American | $ | | B/W | B/L/D | Major | 14 |
| Point of Rocks Restaurant | Steakhouse | $$/$$$ | Yes | Yes | D/BR | V/M | 14 |
| Stillwater Bar & Restaurant | American | $ | | Yes | L/D | | 14 |
| 4 Corner's Casino & Restaurant | Family | $/$$ | Yes | B/W | B/L/D | V/M | 16 |
| Big E's Restaurant | Fast Food | $ | Yes | | B/L/D | | 16 |
| Bullwinkle's | Bistro | $/$$ | Yes | | L/D | V/M | 16 |
| Cafe Jax | Family | $/$$ | Yes | | B/L/D | V/M | 16 |
| Carmen's Little Kitchen | Family | $ | | | B/L | | 16 |
| Montana Chilly Willies | Deli/Ice Cream | $ | | | L/D | | 16 |
| TJ's China House | Chinese | $ | | Yes | L/D | Major | 16 |
| Valley Pizza | Pizza | $$ | | Yes | L/D | V/M | 16 |
| Ksanka Motor Inn & Deli | Deli | | | | B/L/D | Major | 16 |

## Motel Quick Reference

Price Range: ($) Under $40 ; ($$) $40-$60; ($$$) $60-$80, ($$$$) Over $80. Pets [check with the motel for specific policies] (P), Dining (D), Lounge (L), Disabled Access (DA), Full Breakfast (FB), Cont. Breakfast (CB), Indoor Pool (IP), Outdoor Pool (OP), Hot Tub (HT), Sauna (S), Refrigerator (R), Microwave (M) (Microwave and Refrigerator indicated only if in majority of rooms), Kitchenette (K). All Montana area codes are 406.

| HOTEL | PHONE | NUMBER ROOMS | PRICE RANGE | BREAKFAST | POOL/ HOT TUB SAUNA | NON SMOKE ROOMS | OTHER AMENITIES | CREDIT CARDS | MAP LOCATOR NUMBER |
|---|---|---|---|---|---|---|---|---|---|
| **Symes Hot Springs Hotel & Mineral Baths** | 741-2361 | 45 | $-$$$ | | OP/HT/S | Yes | K/P/R | Major | 1 |
| Hot Springs Lodge & Motel | 741-5642 | | | | | | | | 1 |
| Hot Springs Spa | 741-2283 | | | | | | | | 1 |
| Wild Horse Hot Springs | 741-3777 | 2 | $$ | | HT | | K/M/R | | 1 |
| **Rimrock Lodge** | 827-3536 | 25 | $/$$ | FB | | Yes | P/D/M/L/DA | Major | 2 |
| **Thompson Falls B&B** | 827-0282 | | | | | | | | 2 |
| **Falls Motel** | 827-3559 | 22 | $$ | | HT | Yes | P/R/M | Major | 2 |
| Lodge Motel | 827-3603 | 8 | $ | | | Yes | K/DA | | 2 |
| The Riverfront | 827-360 | 2 | $$/$$$ | | | Yes | DA/P/M/R/K | Major | 2 |
| **Trout Creek Motel & RV Park** | 827-3268 | 8 | $ | | | | K/P/M/R | V/M/D | 3 |
| **Lakeside Motel** | 827-4458 | 9 | $$ | | HT | Yes | K/M/R | Major | 3 |
| **Bighorn Lodge B&B** | 847-4676 | | | | | | | | 2 |
| Hereford Bar & Restaurant | 847-2635 | 4 | $ | | | | K/P/D/M/R/L | V/M | 4 |
| Noxon Motel | 847-2600 | 9 | $ | | HT | Yes | P | V/M | 4 |
| **Holiday Motel** | 295-4933 | 6 | $ | | | | DA | Major | 7 |
| Ranch Motel | 295-4332 | 14 | $ | | | | | Major | 7 |
| **Venture Motor Inn** | 293-7711 | 72 | $$/$$$ | | IP/HT | Yes | D/R/DA | Major | 9 |
| **Sandman Motel** | 293-8831 | 16 | $ | | | Yes | P/M/R/K/DA | Major | 9 |
| Caboose Motel | 293-6201 | 28 | $/$$ | | | Yes | P/R/D | Major | 9 |
| Libby Cabins & Motel | 293-3131 | 13 | $ | | | | K/P/R | V/M | 9 |
| Super 8 Motel | 293-2771 | 42 | $$ | | IP | Yes | P/DA | Major | 9 |
| **Mountain Magic Motel** | 293-7795 | 18 | $/$$ | | OP/HT | Yes | K/P/R | Major | 12 |
| Evergreen Motel | 293-4178 | 15 | $ | | | Yes | P/K/M/R | V/M | 12 |
| Happy's Inn & Resort | 293-7810 | 4 | $ | | | | K/D/L/R | Major | 13 |
| Mc Gregor Lake Resort | 858-2253 | 11 | $ | | | | | P/D/L | 13 |
| Hilltop Hitching Post & Motel | 854-2442 | 7 | $$ | | | | R/L/DA | Major | 13 |
| Potters Field Ranch | 881-2472 | 4 | $ | No | No | | | Major | 14 |
| **Creekside Motel & RV Park** | 296-2361 | 3 | $$ | | | | K/F | | 16 |
| Ksanka Motor Inn & Deli | 296-3127 | 30 | $$ | | | Yes | K/D/M/R | Major | 16 |
| Bear Berry Cabin | 889-3967 | 1 | $$$$ | | | Yes | K/M/R/DA | V/M | 16 |
| Silverado Motel | 296-3166 | 16 | $$ | CB | | Yes | P/L/DA | Major | 16 |

**NOTES:**

**NOTES:**

Section 15

# YELLOWSTONE

## THE FIRST NATIONAL PARK

NPS Photo

### BASIC DATA

**Area:** approximately 2.2 million acres or 3,472 square miles in Wyoming, Montana, and Idaho.

**Elevations:** 5,300 ft (1,608 m) at the North Entrance to almost 11,358 feet (3,640 m) at Eagle Peak on the east boundary; most roads lie at 7,500-8,000 feet (2,275-2,427 m).

**Speed limit:** 45 mph (73 kph) or lower where posted.

**Yellowstone Lake:** about 110 miles (170 km) of shoreline and approximately 136 square miles (354 sq km) of surface area.

**Thermal features:** About 10,000 thermal features are known, including more than 300 geysers.

**Grand Loop Road** provides access to major scenic attractions. Some, such as Old Faithful Geyser or the Grand Canyon, can only be seen by parking and walking to the feature. 142 miles (229 km) total around; Upper Loop, 70 miles (113 km); Lower Loop, 96 miles (155 km).

**Quick tour:** Explore one area instead of seeing the entire park from the road. Many people believe that to fully appreciate just the major attractions in Yellowstone, you must spend at least three days.

**General park information:** 307-344-7381 (long distance from some park locations).

**Lodging and services:** 307-344-7311 (long distance from some park locations).

**Yellowstone National Park Official Web Site:** www.nps.gov/yell.

### IN BRIEF

By Act of Congress on March 1, 1872, Yellowstone National Park was "dedicated and set apart as a public park or pleasuring ground for the benefit and enjoyment of the people" and "for the preservation, from injury or spoilation, of all timber, mineral deposits, natural curiosities, or wonders. . . and their retention in their natural condition." Yellowstone is the first and oldest national park in the world.

The commanding features that initially attracted interest, and led to the preservation of Yellowstone as a national park, were geological: the geothermal phenomena (there are more geysers and hot springs here than in the rest of the world combined), the colorful Grand Canyon of the Yellowstone River, fossil forests, and the size and elevation of Yellowstone Lake.

The human history of the park is evidenced by cultural sites dating back 12,000 years. More recent history can be seen in the historic structures and sites that represent the various periods of park administration and visitor facilities development.

### OPERATING HOURS, SEASONS

**Summer:** Park entrances open on different dates when snow crews are able to clear the roads. Visit the following Web address to learn the projected dates for this year. (http://www.nps.gov/yell/planvisit/orientation/travel/roadopen.htm) The season runs from mid-April to late-October. Once an entrance/road opens it is open 24 hours. The only exceptions are caused by road construction and weather-caused restrictions.

**Winter:** The season runs from mid-December to mid-March. The road for the North Entrance at Gardiner, MT to the Northeast Entrance at Cooke City, MT is open to wheeled-vehicle use year around. Only over-snow vehicles are allowed on other park roads.

### VISITOR INFORMATION STATIONS

**Albright Visitor Center, Mammoth:** Daily, year-round, 9 a.m.-6 p.m., through Sept. 24; 9 a.m.-5 p.m. thereafter. Information, bookstore, and exhibits on wildlife, early history, exploration, and establishment of the park. Films on the national park idea and artist Thomas Moran are shown throughout the day. Call 307-344-2263.

**Norris Geyser Basin Museum:** Daily, through Oct. 9, 9 a.m.-5 p.m.. Information, bookstore, and exhibits on the geothermal features of Yellowstone. Call 307-344-2812.

**Museum of the National Park Ranger, Norris:** Daily, through Sept. 30, 9 a.m.-5 p.m. Exhibits at historic soldier station trace development of the park ranger profession; video shown. Chat with former National Park Service employees who volunteer at the museum.

**Madison Information Station:** Daily, through Oct. 9, 9 a.m.-5 p.m.. Information and bookstore. Call 307-344-2821.

**Canyon Visitor Center:** Daily, through Oct. 9, 9 a.m.-6 p.m.. Information, bison exhibit, and bookstore. Call 307-242-2550.

**Grant Visitor Center:** Daily, through Oct. 1, 9 a.m.-6 p.m. Information, bookstore, exhibits, video on the role of fire in Yellowstone. Call 307-242-2650.

**Fishing Bridge Visitor Center:** Daily, through Oct. 1, 9 a.m.-6 p.m.. Information, bookstore, and exhibits on the park's birds and other wildlife. Call 307-242-2450.

**Old Faithful Visitor Center:** Daily, 8 a.m.-6 p.m., through Sept. 30; 9 a.m.-5 p.m. thereafter. Information, bookstore, and geyser eruption predictions. A short movie on thermal life is shown throughout the day. Call 307-545-2750.

**West Thumb Information Station:** Daily, through Oct. 1, 9 a.m.-5 p.m. Information and bookstore.

### WEATHER & CLIMATE

Summer: Daytime temperatures are often in the 70s (25C) and occasionally in the 80s (30C) in lower elevations. Nights are usually cool and temperatures may drop below freezing at higher elevations. Thunderstorms are common in the afternoons. Winter: Temperatures often range from zero to 20F(-20 to -5C) throughout the day. Sub-zero temperatures over-night are common. The record low temperature is -66F (-54C). Snowfall is highly variable. While the average is 150 inches per year, it is not uncommon for higher elevations to get twice that amount. Spring & Fall: Daytime temperatures range from the 30s to the 60s (0 to 20C) with overnight lows in the teens to single digits (-5 to -20C). Snow is common in the Spring and Fall with regular accumulations of 12" in a 24 hour period. At any time of year, be prepared for sudden changes. Unpredictability, more than anything else, characterizes Yellowstone's weather. Always be equipped with a wide range of clothing options. Be sure to bring a warm jacket and rain gear even in the summer.

Yellowstone

## Spring Weather

Cold and snow linger into April and May, although temperatures gradually climb. Average daytime readings fall in the 40s to 50s (5-15C), reaching the 60s and 70s (15-25C) by late May and June. Over-night temperatures fall below freezing and may plunge near zero (-20C). These are statistical averages; actual conditions can be vastly different from longterm "norms." At any time of year, be prepared for sudden changes; unpredictability, more than anything else, characterizes Yellowstone's weather. Storms in late May and early June may result in significant accumulations of snow—up to a foot of snow in 24 hours is not uncommon.

We recommend that you bring a warm jacket and rain gear. Spring visitors should be prepared for any type of weather. Call ahead for current weather and road information since sudden storms may result in cold temperatures, snow and/or temporary road closures. Yellowstone's weather is always unpredictable. Carry extra clothing when hiking. Good walking shoes and layers of clothing are recommended throughout the year.

## Summer Weather

Average maximum summer temperatures are usually in the 70s (25C) and occasionally in the 80s (30C) in the lower elevations. Nights are cool and temperatures may drop into the 30s and 40s (0-10C). Depending on the elevation, temperatures may even fall into the 20s (-5C) with a light freeze. June can be cool and rainy; July and August tend to be somewhat drier, although afternoon thundershowers and lightning storms are common. During lightning storms get off water or beaches and stay away from ridges, exposed places, and isolated trees. At any time of year, be prepared for sudden changes; unpredictability, more than anything else, characterizes Yellowstone's weather.

We recommend that you bring a warm jacket and rain gear even in the summer. If you plan to visit Yellowstone during spring or fall, call ahead for current weather and road information since sudden storms may result in cold temperatures, snow and/or temporary road closures. In summer, stop at visitor centers or ranger stations for weather forecasts. Always carry extra clothing when hiking. Good walking shoes and layers of clothing are recommended throughout the year.

## Autumn Weather

Autumn weather can be pleasant, although temperatures average 10 to 20 degrees lower than summer readings—highs in the 40s to 60s (5-20C). Over-night temperatures can fall into the teens and single digits (-10 to -20C). Snowstorms increase in frequency and intensity as the weeks go by. At any time of year be prepared for sudden changes; unpredictability, more than anything else, characterizes Yellowstone's weather.

Sudden storms can cause a drop in temperature or result in precipitation. Always carry extra clothing when hiking. Good walking shoes and layers of clothing are recommended throughout the year. If you plan to visit Yellowstone during spring or fall, call ahead for current weather and road information since sudden storms may result in cold temperatures, snow and/or temporary road closures.

## Winter Weather

Winter temperatures often hover near zero (-20C) throughout the day but may reach highs in the 20s (-5C). Subzero over-night temperatures are common. Occasionally, warm "chinook" winds will push daytime temperatures into the 40s (5-10C), causing significant melting of snowpack—especially at lower elevations. Yellowstone also typically experiences periods of bitterly cold weather. The lowest temperature recorded in Yellowstone was -66F (-54C) near West Yellowstone on February 9, 1933. Annual snowfall averages near 150 inches (380cm) in most of the park. At higher elevations, 200-400 inches (5-10m) of snowfall have been recorded. At any time of year, be prepared for sudden changes; unpredictability, more than anything else, characterizes Yellowstone's weather.

Snowmobilers and skiers should always check on temperatures and wind chill forecasts; subzero weather can make travel dangerous even with proper gear. Always carry extra clothing when hiking, skiing, or snowmobiling. Take advantage of the warming huts (heated shelters) provided in some park areas. Good walking shoes and layers of clothing are recommended throughout the year, but in the winter you'll also need warm boots. Cross-country skis or snowshoes are a 'must' in winter if you plan to go beyond the main roads and boardwalks.

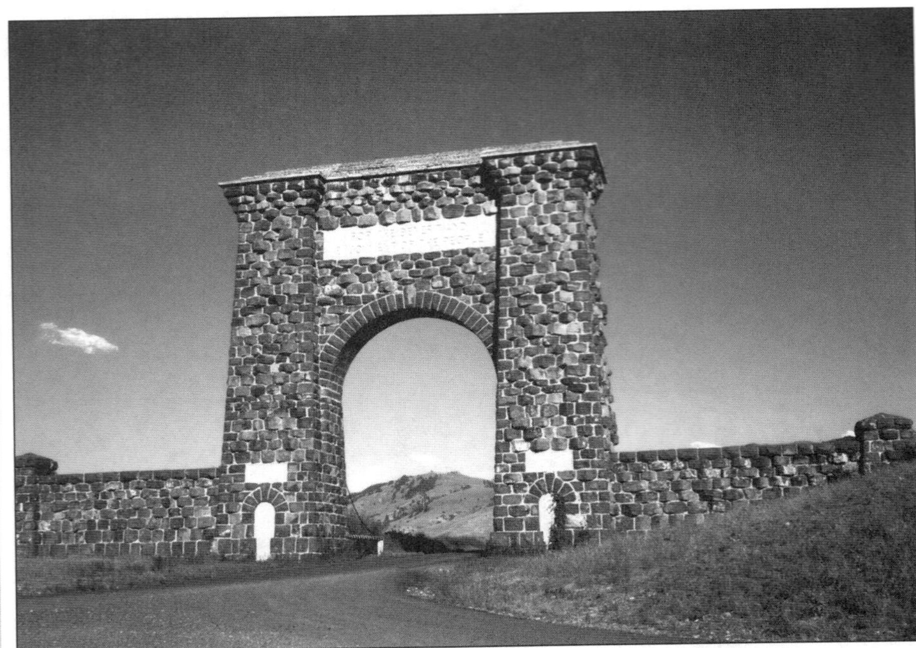

*The Roosevelt Arch at the North Entrance to the park at Gardiner. This is the only year round entrance to the park. NPS photo.*

## You Need to Know

**Anglers and Boaters:** Yellowstone National Park's fishing season opens the Saturday of Memorial Day weekend and closes the first Sunday in November. Boats and float tubes require permits.

**Back Country Permits:** *Permits are required for overnight backcountry use* and may be obtained in person up to 48 hours in advance from any ranger station. Rangers will provide information on weather, trails and other conditions.

**Bicycling:** Bicycling is permitted on established public roads, parking areas, and designated routes. There are no bicycle paths along roadways. Bicycles are prohibited on backcountry trails and boardwalks.

We strongly recommend that safety gear, including helmet and high visibility clothing, be worn by all bicyclists. Park roads are narrow and winding; most do not have a shoulder, or shoulders are covered with gravel. During April, May, and June, high snowbanks make travel more dangerous. Road elevations range from 5,300 to 8,860 feet (1,615-2,700 m); relatively long distances exist between services and facilities.

Motorists frequently do not see bicyclists or fail to give them sufficient space on the road. Drivers sometimes pass on hill crests, blind curves or in oncoming traffic. Vehicles, especially motor homes or those towing trailers, may have wide mirrors, posing an additional hazard. For more information about bicycling in Yellowstone, inquire at a visitor center.

**Falling Trees:** Following the fires of 1988, thousands of dead trees, known as snags, were left standing in Yellowstone. These snags may fall with very little warning.

Be cautious and alert for falling snags along trails and roadways, and in campsites and picnic areas. Avoid areas with large numbers of dead trees. Again, there is no guarantee of your safety.

**Weapons:**No firearms or weapons, including state-permitted concealed weapons, are allowed in Yellowstone. However, unloaded firearms may be transported in a vehicle when the weapon is cased, broken down or rendered inoperable, and kept out of sight. Ammunition must be placed in a separate compartment of the vehicle.

**Pets:** Pets must be leashed. They are prohibited on any trails, in the backcountry, and in thermal basins. Pets are not allowed more than 100 feet from a road or parking area. Leaving a pet unattended and/or tied to an object is prohibited.

**Traffic:** Yellowstone has more than 350 miles (564 km) of roads. Most are narrow rough, and busy! Some sections are steep with sharp drop-offs. Drive cautiously and courteously; **slow moving vehicles must use pullouts to observe wildlife or scenery and to allow safe passing by other**

**vehicles.** Watch for animals on the road, especially at night.

Bicycles and motorcycles present special hazards. Drive defensively and wear seat belts. *Yellowstone has a mandatory seat belt requirement for all passengers.* Be especially cautious of ice and road damage; cool temperatures may occur any time of the year. *The maximum speed limit is 45 mph (73 kru per hour) unless otherwise posted,* and they will stop you. Rangers are constantly patrolling the road with radar. The tickets are expensive and next to impossible to argue.

**High Altitude:** Visitors with a cardiac or respiratory medical history should be aware that most park roads range between 5,300 to 8,860 feet (1,615-2,700 m) in elevation. We recommend contacting a physician prior to your visit.

Be aware of your physical limitations, Don't over exert and drink plenty of fluids to forestall the dehydrating effects of the park's dry climate. Stop and rest frequently.

**Picnic Areas:** Overnight camping is not allowed in any of the park's picnic areas. Fires may be built only in fire grates available in picnic areas at Snake River, Grant Village, Bridge Bay, Cascade, Norris Meadows, Yellowstone River, Spring Creek, Nez Perce, and the east parking lot of Old Faithful. Liquid fuel stoves may be used for cooking at other locations. Most picnic areas have pit toilets, but none have drinking water.

## Avoid These Situations

Your visit may be marred by tragedy if you violate park rules. Law enforcement rangers strictly enforce park regulations to protect you and the park. Please help keep their contacts with you pleasant by paying special attention to park regulations and avoiding. these problems:

- speeding (radar enforced)
- driving while intoxicated (open container law is enforced)
- off-road travel by Vehicle or bicycle
- improper food storage
- camping violations
- pets off leash
- littering
- swimming in thermal pools
- removal or possession of natural (flowers, antlers, etc.) or cultural (artifacts) features
- feeding or approaching wildlife
- spotlighting (viewing animals with artificial light)
- boating and fishing violations
- failure to remove detachable side mirrors when not pulling trailers.

## Getting Around

Most visits use private vehicles to get around inside Yellowstone National Park. There is no public transportation service provided within the park.

AmFac Parks & Resorts provides bus tours within the park during the summer season. The Lower Loop Tour departs from locations in the southern part of the Park only. The Upper Loop Tour departs from Lake Hotel, Fishing Bridge RV Park, and Canyon Lodge to tour the northern section of the park only. The Grand Loop Tour departs from Gardiner, MT and Mammoth Hot Springs Hotel to tour the entire park in one day. During the winter season, they provide several snowcoach tours from various locations. Please call 307-344-7311 for information or reservations.

*Traffic jams like this usually indicate that there are watchable wildlife nearby. NPS photo.*

During the summer season, commercial businesses offer tours originating from many area towns and cities. During the winter season, some businesses provide snowcoach tours for most park roads or bus transportation on the Mammoth Hot Springs to Cooke City road.

## Seasonal Road Opening and Closing Schedule

**Winter:** The winter season of snowmobile and snowcoach travel runs from the third Monday of December to mid-March. All roads and entrances, with one exception, are closed to motor vehicle travel and are groomed for oversnow vehicles. The exception is the North Entrance and the road from Gardiner, MT, through the Northeast Entrance to Cooke City, MT, which is open only to wheeled vehicles. Plowing stops at Cooke City, so you must return to the North Entrance to leave the park.

**Spring:** Plowing begins in early March. Depending on weather, the first stretches of road to open to motor vehicles include Mammoth-Norris, Norris-Madison, and West Yellowstone-Old Faithful; these roads open in mid-April. Roads on the east and south sides of the park, including East and South Entrances, typically open in early May. The Sunlight Basin Road, between Cooke City, MT and Cody, WY and Craig Pass, between Old Faithful and West Thumb, open by early May as conditions allow. Dunraven Pass, between Tower and Canyon Junctions, and the Beartooth Highway, connecting Cooke City to Red Lodge, MT generally open by Memorial Day weekend. Weather can especially affect road openings over the higher passes. Spring storms may cause restrictions or temporary closures on some roads.

**Summer:** Park roads are generally open for travel, barring accidents, rock/mud slides or road construction.

**Fall:** Storms may cause temporary restrictions (snow tire or chain requirements) or closures of park roads. Large road reconstruction projects are underway in Yellowstone resulting in some closures of major sections of road. (See Road Construction Information.) The Beartooth Highway, connecting Cooke City to Red Lodge, MT closes for the season in mid-October. Depending on weather, park roads close for the season on the first Sunday of November. The only exception is the year round road from Gardiner to Cooke City, MT. The winter season of snowmobile and snowcoach travel begins in mid-December.

## Trip Checklist

- Barring road construction, most park roads are open to automobiles from about May 1 to the first Sunday in November; please plan with this in mind.
- Make lodging reservations as early as possible.
- Plan your arrival to secure your campsite early in the day.
- Review park regulation and permit information before your arrival.
- Pack clothes that can be layered and that are appropriate for the season of your visit.
- Get up-to-date road and weather information close to your time of visit by calling 307-344-7381.

## Bicycling in Yellowstone

Bicycles are not available for rent at the park. If you plan to bring one, remember it is subject to the same traffic rules as automobiles. Bicycling is permitted on established public roads, parking areas, and designated routes. Bikes are prohibited on backcountry trails and boardwalks.

Use extreme caution when riding on park roads; roads are winding and narrow while shoulders are either narrow or nonexistent. Vehicle traffic is heavy most of the time. There are no bicycle paths along roadways.

We strongly recommend that safety gear, including helmet and high visibility clothing, be worn by all bicyclists. During April, May, and June, high snowbanks make travel more dangerous. Road elevations range from 5,300 to 8,860 feet (1615 to 2700 meters), and services and facilities are relatively far apart—typically 20 to 30 miles (37 to 56 kilometers).

Motorists frequently do not see bicyclists or fail to give them sufficient space on the road. Drivers sometimes pass on hill crests, blind curves, or in oncoming traffic. Vehicles, especially motor homes or those towing trailers, may have wide mirrors, posing an additional hazard. For more information about bicycling, stop at a visitor center.

Before the roads open to general automobile traffic in the Spring, some of them are opened to bicycling.

## Boating in Yellowstone

**Private Boats** A permit is required for all vessels (motorized and non-motorized including float tubes) and must be obtained in person at any of the following locations: South Entrance, Lewis Lake Campground, Grant Village Visitor Center, Bridge Bay Ranger Station, and Lake Ranger Station. At Canyon and Mammoth Visitor Centers, only non-motorized boating permits are available. The fee is $20 (annual) or $10 (7 day) for motorized vessels and $10 (annual) or $5 (7 day) for non-motorized vessels. A Coast Guard approved wearable personal flotation device is required for each person boating.

Grand Teton National Park's boat permit will be honored as a one-time 7 day permit or can be applied toward a Yellowstone annual permit.

All vessels are prohibited on park rivers and streams except the channel between Lewis and Shoshone Lakes, where only hand-propelled vessels are permitted.

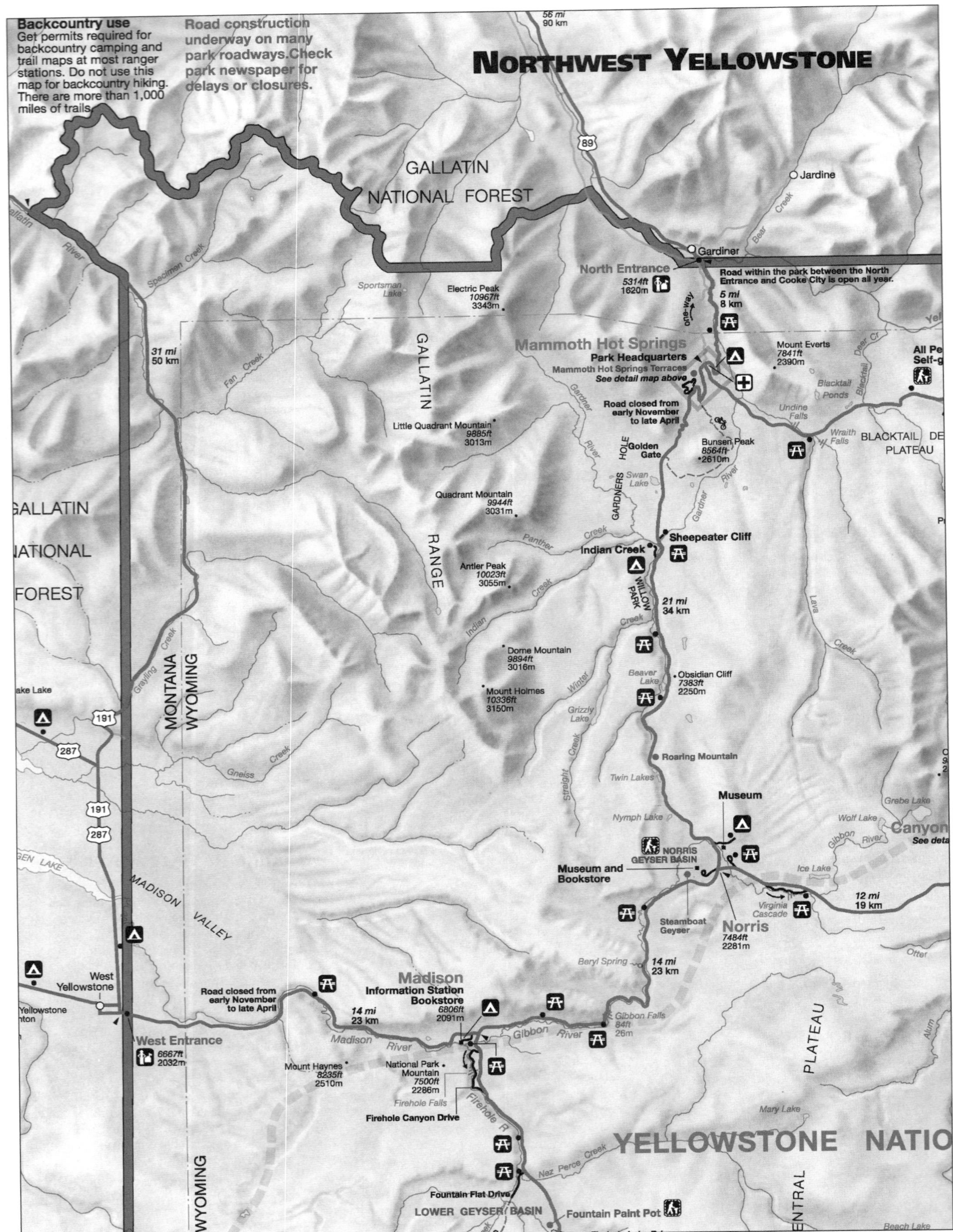
NORTHWEST YELLOWSTONE
Backcountry use
Get permits required for backcountry camping and trail maps at most ranger stations. Do not use this map for backcountry hiking. There are more than 1,000 miles of trails.
Road construction underway on many park roadways.Check park newspaper for delays or closures.
56 mi
90 km
GALLATIN
NATIONAL FOREST
Jardine
Gardiner
North Entrance
5314ft
1620m
Road within the park between the North Entrance and Cooke City is open all year.
5 mi
8 km
Electric Peak
10967ft
3343m
Sportsman Lake
Mammoth Hot Springs
Park Headquarters
Mammoth Hot Springs Terraces
See detail map above
Mount Everts
7841ft
2390m
Blacktail Ponds
Undine Falls
Wraith Falls
BLACKTAIL
PLATEAU
Road closed from early November to late April
Golden Gate
Bunsen Peak
8564ft
2610m
Little Quadrant Mountain
9885ft
3013m
GALLATIN
RANGE
31 mi
50 km
Quadrant Mountain
9944ft
3031m
Swan Lake
GARDNERS HOLE
Sheepeater Cliff
Indian Creek
WILLOW PARK
21 mi
34 km
Antler Peak
10023ft
3055m
Dome Mountain
9894ft
3016m
Mount Holmes
10336ft
3150m
Obsidian Cliff
7383ft
2250m
Beaver Lake
Grizzly Lake
Roaring Mountain
Twin Lakes
Nymph Lake
Museum
NORRIS GEYSER BASIN
Museum and Bookstore
Steamboat Geyser
Norris
7484ft
2281m
Virginia Cascade
12 mi
19 km
Grebe Lake
Wolf Lake
Ice Lake
Canyon
GALLATIN
NATIONAL
FOREST
MONTANA
WYOMING
MADISON VALLEY
West Yellowstone
West Entrance
6667ft
2032m
Road closed from early November to late April
14 mi
23 km
Madison
Information Station
Bookstore
6806ft
2091m
Beryl Spring
14 mi
23 km
Gibbon Falls
84ft
26m
Gibbon River
Madison River
Mount Haynes
8235ft
2510m
National Park Mountain
7500ft
2286m
Firehole Falls
Firehole Canyon Drive
Fountain Flat Drive
LOWER GEYSER BASIN
Fountain Paint Pot
Nez Perce Creek
YELLOWSTONE NATIO
PLATEAU
Mary Lake
WYOMING
Beach Lake
89
191
287

# Northeast Yellowstone

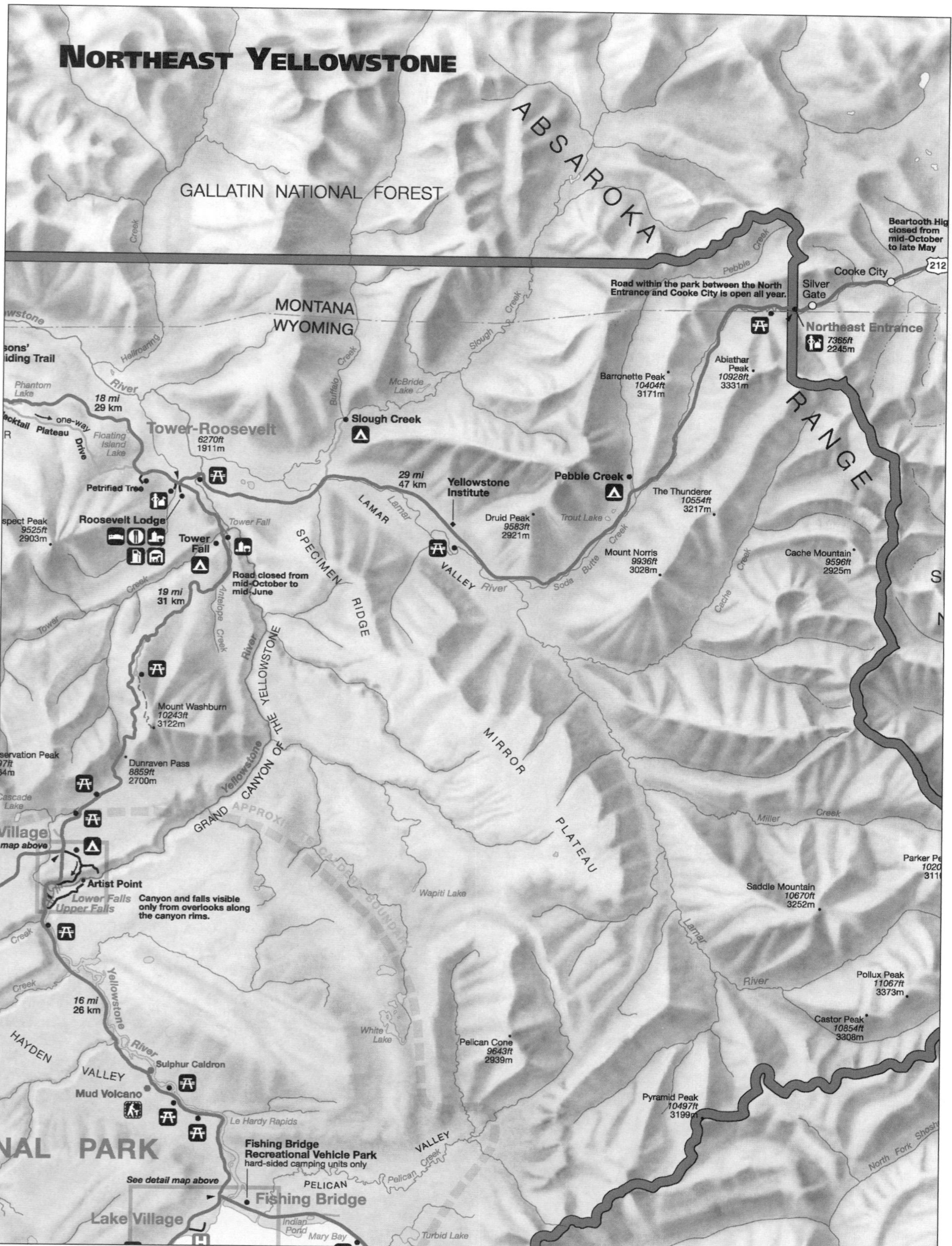

ABSAROKA RANGE
GALLATIN NATIONAL FOREST
MONTANA
WYOMING
Beartooth Hig closed from mid-October to late May
212
Cooke City
Silver Gate
Road within the park between the North Entrance and Cooke City is open all year.
Northeast Entrance
7365ft 2245m
Abiathar Peak 10928ft 3331m
Barronette Peak 10404ft 3171m
Slough Creek
McBride Lake
Tower-Roosevelt 6270ft 1911m
18 mi 29 km
Phantom Lake
one-way
Plateau
Drive
Floating Island Lake
Petrified Tree
Roosevelt Lodge
Tower Fall
Road closed from mid-October to mid-June
19 mi 31 km
29 mi 47 km
Yellowstone Institute
Pebble Creek
The Thunderer 10554ft 3217m
Druid Peak 9583ft 2921m
Trout Lake
Mount Norris 9936ft 3028m
Cache Mountain 9596ft 2925m
LAMAR VALLEY
SPECIMEN RIDGE
Lamar River
Soda Butte Creek
Mount Washburn 10243ft 3122m
Dunraven Pass 8859ft 2700m
GRAND CANYON OF THE YELLOWSTONE
MIRROR PLATEAU
Miller Creek
Artist Point
Lower Falls
Upper Falls
Canyon and falls visible only from overlooks along the canyon rims.
Wapiti Lake
Parker Pe
Saddle Mountain 10670ft 3252m
Pollux Peak 11067ft 3373m
Castor Peak 10854ft 3308m
16 mi 26 km
HAYDEN VALLEY
White Lake
Pelican Cone 9643ft 2939m
Sulphur Caldron
Mud Volcano
Le Hardy Rapids
Pyramid Peak 10497ft 3199m
NAL PARK
Fishing Bridge Recreational Vehicle Park
hard-sided camping units only
See detail map above
PELICAN VALLEY
Pelican Creek
Fishing Bridge
Lake Village
Indian Pond
Mary Bay
Turbid Lake
North Fork Shosh

# Southwest Yellowstone

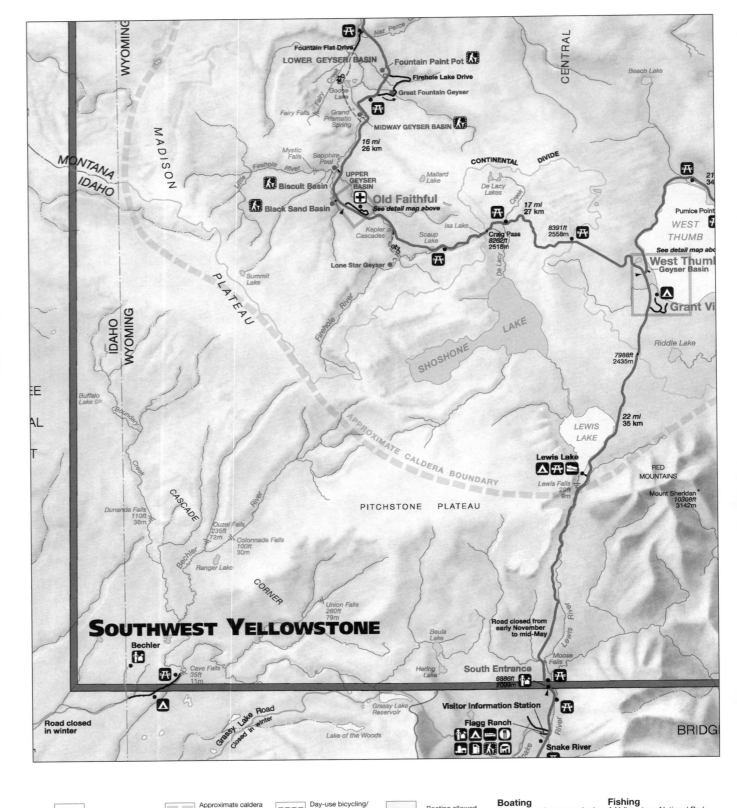

Fountain Flat Drive
LOWER GEYSER BASIN
Fountain Paint Pot
Firehole Lake Drive
Great Fountain Geyser
Nez Perce
Goose Lake
Fairy Falls
Fairy Creek
Grand Prismatic Spring
MIDWAY GEYSER BASIN
16 mi 26 km
Mystic Falls
Sapphire Pool
Little Firehole River
UPPER GEYSER BASIN
Biscuit Basin
Black Sand Basin
Old Faithful
See detail map above
Kepler Cascades
Lone Star Geyser
Scaup Lake
Mallard Lake
CONTINENTAL DIVIDE
De Lacy Lakes
De Lacy Creek
Isa Lake
Craig Pass 8262ft 2518m
17 mi 27 km
8391ft 2558m
CENTRAL
Beach Lake
Pumice Point
WEST THUMB
See detail map above
West Thumb Geyser Basin
Grant Village
Riddle Lake
7988ft 2435m
MONTANA
IDAHO
WYOMING
MADISON PLATEAU
Summit Lake
Firehole River
SHOSHONE LAKE
Buffalo Lake
Boundary Creek
LEWIS LAKE
22 mi 35 km
APPROXIMATE CALDERA BOUNDARY
Lewis Lake
Lewis Falls 29ft 9m
RED MOUNTAINS
Mount Sheridan 10308ft 3142m
PITCHSTONE PLATEAU
CASCADE CORNER
Dunanda Falls 110ft 36m
Ouzel Falls 235ft 72m
Colonnade Falls 100ft 30m
Bechler River
Ranger Lake
Union Falls 260ft 79m
Road closed from early November to mid-May
Lewis River
Beula Lake
Hering Lake
Moose Falls
South Entrance 6886ft 2099m
Bechler
Cave Falls 35ft 11m
Road closed in winter
Grassy Lake Road Closed in winter
Grassy Lake Reservoir
Lake of the Woods
Visitor Information Station
Flagg Ranch
Snake River
BRIDGER

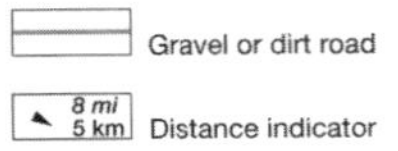

Gravel or dirt road
8 mi 5 km Distance indicator
One-way road
Approximate caldera boundary
Geothermal feature
Continental Divide
Day-use bicycling/ hiking trail (ask for more information)
Parking lot
Boating allowed
5 mph zone
Hand-propelled craft only

**Boating**
Boating permits are required for all watercraft. Inquire at ranger stations. Areas closed to watercraft include all rivers except Lewis River between Lewis and Shoshone lakes.

**Fishing**
A Yellowstone National Park fishing permit is required. State permits are not valid in the park and state regulations do not apply.

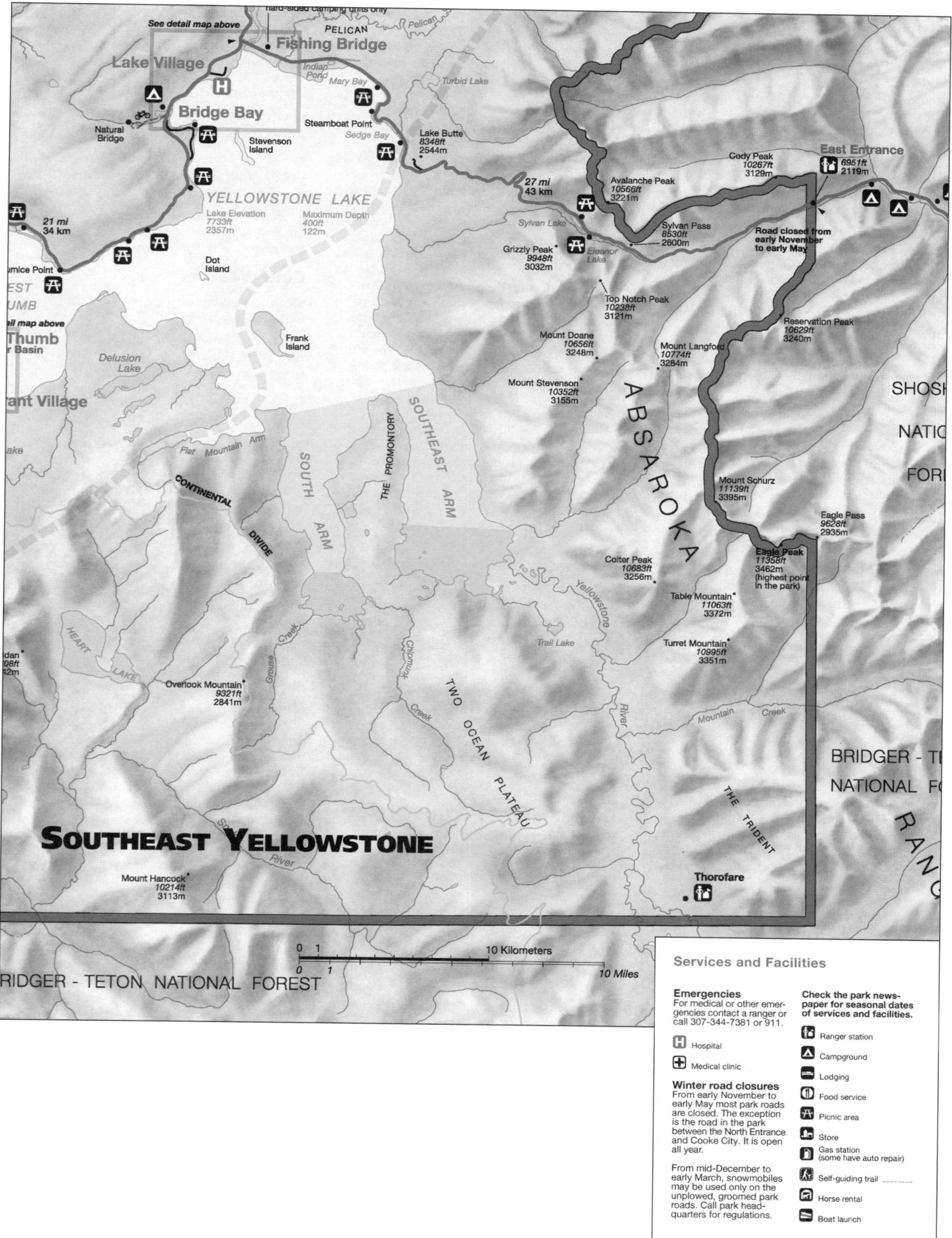

SOUTHEAST YELLOWSTONE
See detail map above
hard-sided camping units only
PELICAN
Pelican
Fishing Bridge
Lake Village
Indian Pond
Mary Bay
Turbid Lake
Bridge Bay
Natural Bridge
Steamboat Point
Sedge Bay
Stevenson Island
Lake Butte
8348ft
2544m
YELLOWSTONE LAKE
Lake Elevation
7733ft
2357m
Maximum Depth
400ft
122m
27 mi
43 km
21 mi
34 km
Dot Island
Frank Island
Delusion Lake
Thumb
Sylvan Lake
Eleanor Lake
Grizzly Peak
9948ft
3032m
Avalanche Peak
10566ft
3221m
Cody Peak
10267ft
3129m
East Entrance
6951ft
2119m
Sylvan Pass
8530ft
2600m
Road closed from early November to early May
Top Notch Peak
10238ft
3121m
Reservation Peak
10629ft
3240m
Mount Doane
10656ft
3248m
Mount Langford
10774ft
3284m
Mount Stevenson
10352ft
3155m
ABSAROKA
SHOSH
NATIC
FOR
Flat Mountain Arm
SOUTH ARM
THE PROMONTORY
SOUTHEAST ARM
CONTINENTAL DIVIDE
Mount Schurz
11139ft
3395m
Eagle Pass
9628ft
2935m
Eagle Peak
11358ft
3462m
(highest point in the park)
Colter Peak
10683ft
3256m
Table Mountain
11063ft
3372m
Turret Mountain
10995ft
3351m
Yellowstone River
Trail Lake
HEART LAKE
Grouse Creek
Overlook Mountain
9321ft
2841m
Chipmunk Creek
TWO OCEAN PLATEAU
Mountain Creek
BRIDGER - TE
NATIONAL F
RANG
THE TRIDENT
Thorofare
Snake River
Mount Hancock
10214ft
3113m
10 Kilometers
10 Miles
BRIDGER - TETON NATIONAL FOREST
Services and Facilities
Emergencies
For medical or other emergencies contact a ranger or call 307-344-7381 or 911.
Hospital
Medical clinic
Winter road closures
From early November to early May most park roads are closed. The exception is the road in the park between the North Entrance and Cooke City. It is open all year.
From mid-December to early March, snowmobiles may be used only on the unplowed, groomed park roads. Call park headquarters for regulations.
Check the park newspaper for seasonal dates of services and facilities.
Ranger station
Campground
Lodging
Food service
Picnic area
Store
Gas station (some have auto repair)
Self-guiding trail
Horse rental
Boat launch

Yellowstone

## Where Do I Go?

**Geysers & Hot Springs:** An unparalleled array of geothermal phenomena—geysers, hot springs, mudpots, and steam vents—are evidence of a volcanic past and the active earth beneath our feet. Many of the most famous features can be found between Mammoth Hot Springs and Old Faithful. Thermal areas include Mammoth Hot Springs, Norris Geyser Basin, Fountain Paint Pot, Midway Geyser Basin, and the Old Faithful area. West Thumb Geyser Basin is 17 miles east of Old Faithful; Mud Volcano is north of Yellowstone Lake.

**Grand Canyon:** The Grand Canyon of the Yellowstone extends from Canyon Village north to Tower Junction. The most famous and spectacular section, including the Upper and Lower Falls of the Yellowstone River, is seen from overlooks along the North and South Rim roads in the Canyon Village area. The northernmost extent of the canyon is visible from Tower Falls and Calcite Springs overlooks, 19 miles (31 km) north of Canyon Village.

The road between **Tower Junction and Canyon Village** goes over Dunraven Pass, the highest road in the park at 8,600 feet (2700 m). Along the way you will find spectacular views of the Absaroka Mountains, the Yellowstone caldera, and, on a clear day, the Teton Range to the south.

**Lake Area:** Yellowstone Lake is North America's largest high-altitude lake. The area is prime habitat for a variety of birds and mammals.

**Viewing Wildlife:** Yellowstone is home to a variety and abundance of wildlife unparalleled in the lower 48 states. The numbers and variety of animals you see are largely a matter of luck and coincidence, but the viewing tips on page 8 can help.

*Please be safe when you stop: Use pullouts, never stop in the middle of the road or block traffic.*

## Photographing Yellowstone

Photography has always played an important role in Yellowstone's history.

To help prove that the natural oddities described by mountain men and explorers did indeed exist, Ferdinand Hayden hired William Henry Jackson to produce photographs of the scenery, waterfalls, canyons, and thermal features viewed by the Hayden Expedition of 1871. Jackson used two cameras, and a bulky, time-consuming method of photography known as the wet plate process. One camera measured 6-1/2 inches by 8-1/2 inches, and the other was 8 inches by 10 inches. Due to slow shutter speeds of five to 15 seconds, the camera needed to be held steady by a heavy tripod. Just prior to taking a photograph, Jackson would prepare a light-sensitive emulsion layer to coat a piece of glass the same size as the camera. After exposing the glass plate negative, Jackson would immediately develop the negative in his darkroom tent before the emulsion layer dried. The average time to make a single photograph was 45 minutes.

Jackson carried hundreds of pounds of fragile glass plates, chemicals and solutions, cameras and tripod on pack mules. He would frequently take his equipment to some very difficult and sometimes precarious locations to get just the view he wanted.

The photographs taken by Jackson in 1871 were instrumental in persuading Congress to establish Yellowstone as the world's first national park in 1872.

Frank J. Haynes was another important photographer in the early days of the park, first journeying here in 1881. Haynes recognized the unique beauty of Yellowstone and realized that this first look would lead to some significant changes in his own career and life.

Haynes was the official photographer for Yellowstone National Park from 1884-1916. By 1897, Haynes had two photo studios in Yellowstone. The first was located in the Upper Geyser Basin, and the second at Mammoth Hot Springs. The Haynes studios sold black and white photographs, and hand-tinted postcards and stereocards to park visitors.

One of Haynes' most important accomplishments was documenting the early development of Yellowstone Park to accommodate increasing numbers of visitors. Haynes photographed park roads and bridges, stagecoaches, steamships on Yellowstone Lake, train stations in Gardiner and West Yellowstone, hotels, lodges, campgrounds, and visitors. Haynes also photographed the natural beauty of Yellowstone. Some of these photographs are of particular importance as they show thermal features displaying activity that differs from today.

Photography still plays an important role today in Yellowstone. Even though nearly every visitor today has a still or video camera, there remains the importance of recording today's cultural, natural and historical features, documenting gradual changes, and events of significant importance such as the restoration of the wolf.

Photo by Corinne Gaffner

## Taking Great Photos in Yellowstone

### The Basics

• Pay attention to light. At noon or with a bright background, use the flash to even out the light and bring out people's features.

• Take photos early or late in the day. The light is warmer, people I aren't squinting, crowds have thinned, animals are more active.

• Be careful with metering, whether automatic or manual. Sunlit reflective surfaces such as snow, or bright backgrounds such as a thermal basin, can cause inaccurate readings.

• Take photos in all kinds of weather. For example, colors are brighter on cloudy, damp days.

Learn about your subject. To take great photos of elk, read about their behavior, talk to park rangers about the best places to observe elk, etc.

### Home Video

• Reduce camera shake by using a tripod or image stabilizer, or filming at lower magnification. Use zoom sparingly. Show where the wildlife live in addition to the animals themselves. Remember to get in scenes yourself! Hand the camera to someone else in your group from time to time.

**Thermal Areas**

• For extra mood, take pictures early in the day.

• Include boardwalks for extra depth and people for size comparison.

• Use a polarizing filter to increase the brilliance of colorful algae.

• Protect your camera lens from geyser spray; it can leave a permanent deposit if not removed immediately with lens tissue.

### Cold Weather

• Cold is hard on batteries, so start with new batteries and carry spares.

• Keep your camera, film, and batteries in a warm place, such as inside your jacket. Avoid sudden temperature changes. Keep the lens and viewfinder free of fog and spray; expose as little glass as possible.

## Fishing in Yellowstone

Yellowstone National Park is managed as a natural area to protect plants, wildlife, geology, and scenery. Angling has been a major visitor activity for over a century. Present regulations reflect the park's primary purposes of resource protection and visitor use. The objectives of the fishing program are to:

1. Manage aquatic resources as an important part of the ecosystem.

2. Preserve and restore native fishes and their habitats.

3. Provide recreational fishing opportunities for the enjoyment of park visitors, consistent with the first two objectives.

In Yellowstone, bald eagles, ospreys, pelicans, otters, grizzly bears, and other wildlife take precedence over humans in utilizing fish as food. None of the fish in Yellowstone are stocked, and populations depend on sufficient number of spawning adults to maintain natural reproduction and genetic diversity. In Yellowstone National Park, we place less emphasis upon providing fishing for human consumption and put more emphasis upon the quality for recreational fishing. Anglers, in return, have the opportunity to fish for wild trout in a natural setting.

Because of the increasing number of anglers in the park, more restrictive regulations have been adopted in Yellowstone. These restrictions include: season opening/closing dates, restrictive use of bait, catch-and-release only areas, and number/size limits according to species. A few places are closed to the public to protect threatened and endangered species, sensitive nesting birds, and to provide scenic viewing areas for visitors seeking undisturbed wildlife.

### Permits and Fees

A permit is required to fish in Yellowstone. Anglers 16 years of age and older are required to purchase either a $10 ten-day or $20 season permit. Anglers 12 to 15 years of age are required to obtain a non-fee permit. Children 11 years of age or younger may fish without a permit when supervised by an adult. The adult is responsible for the child's actions. Fishing permits are available at all ranger stations, visitor centers, and Hamilton General Stores. No state fishing license is required in Yellowstone National Park.

## Fishing Season

Yellowstone's fishing season generally begins on the Saturday of Memorial Day weekend and continues through the first Sunday of November. Major exceptions: Yellowstone Lake opens June 1; Yellowstone Lake's tributary streams open July 15; Yellowstone River and its tributaries between Canyon and Yellowstone Lake open July 15.

## Boats & Float Tubes

You also must obtain a permit in person for boats and float tubes from the following locations: South Entrance, Lewis Lake Campground, Grant Village backcountry office, Bridge Bay Marina, and Lake Ranger Station. Non-motorized boating permits only are available at the Canyon, Mammoth, and Old Faithful backcountry offices, Bechler Ranger Station, and West and Northeast Entrances. You must have a Coast Guard approved "wearable" personal flotation device for each person boating.

## Non-toxic Fishing

Yellowstone National Park has implemented a non-toxic fishing program. Nationwide, over three million waterfowl die from lead poisoning through ingestion. Because lead from fishing tackle concentrates in aquatic environments, tackle such as leaded split shot sinkers, weighted jigs, and soft weighted ribbon for fly fishing are prohibited. Only non-toxic alternatives to lead are allowed.

## Releasing Fish

The following suggestions will insure that a released fish has the best chance for survival:

1. Play fish as rapidly as possible, do not play to total exhaustion.

2. Keep fish in water as much as possible when handling and removing hook.

3. Remove hook gently—do not squeeze fish or put fingers in gills. The use of barbless hooks is encouraged to make release easier.

4. If deeply hooked—cut line—do not pull hook out. Most fish survive with hooks left in them.

5. Release fish only after its equilibrium is maintained. If necessary, gently hold fish upright, facing upstream.

6. Release fish in quiet water, close to area where it was hooked.

7. Never release lake trout. They are an exotic threat to the fishery. All lake trout you catch must be kept and killed.

## Bears, Backcountry, and Anglers

Yellowstone is bear country, and there is no guarantee of your safety. Bears often utilize trails, streams, and lakeshores. Entry into some areas may be restricted; check with a ranger for specific bear management information. Traveling alone in bear country is not recommended. Make enough noise to make your presence known to bears. If you should encounter a bear, give it plenty of room, detour if possible, or wait for the bear to move on. If a bear should charge or attack and the situation allows, climb a tree. If you are caught by a bear, try playing dead. Do not run; this may excite the bear. Carefully read all bear country guidelines and regulations and be prepared for any situation.

*Yellowstone Park provides some of the finest angling in the world.*

## Garbage Disposal and Fish Cleaning

Please pick up all trash, including items such as monofilament fishing line and six pack holders, which may cause injury to wildlife, and properly dispose in trash receptacles.

When fish cleaning and disposal areas are not provided, dispose of fish entrails by puncturing the air bladder and dropping into deep water.

# Camping in Yellowstone

**First Come—First Served Campsites:** There are 12 campgrounds in Yellowstone National Park. Seven of these campgrounds are operated by the National Park Service: Indian Creek, Lewis Lake, Mammoth, Norris, Pebble Creek, Slough Creek, and Tower Fall. Sites at these campgrounds are available on a first-come, first-served basis.

**Reserved Campsites:** Yellowstone National Park Lodges operates campgrounds at Bridge Bay, Canyon, Grant Village, Madison, and Fishing Bridge RV Park. Same day reservations can be made by calling 307-344-7901 or by asking at lodging activities desks. Future reservations can be made by calling 307-344-7311 or by writing Yellowstone National Park Lodges, P.O. Box 165, YNP, WY 82100; www.travelyellowstone.com. Fishing Bridge RV Park is the only campground offering water, sewer, and electrical hookups, and it is for hardsided vehicles only (no tents or tent trailers are allowed).

*Make your reservations early and/or plan on securing your campsite as early in the day as possible; campgrounds may fill by early morning.*

**Camping Rules:** Camping or overnight vehicle parking in pullouts, parking areas, picnic grounds, or any place other than a designated campground are not permitted, and there are no overflow camping facilities. However, camping is often available in neighboring communities and forests outside the park.

Camping is limited to 14 days between June 15 and September 15 and to 30 days the rest of the year; there is no limit at Fishing Bridge RV Park. Check-out time for all campgrounds is 10 AM.

**Guest Hours:** Camping in Yellowstone is a special experience. Each visitor deserves the opportunity to hear the birds, wildlife, and streams in this beautiful environment. Respect the rights of other campers and comply with the law by adhering to quiet hours, 8 p.m. to 8 a.m. (10 p.m.-7 a.m. at Fishing Bridge RV Park). No generators, loud audio devices, or other noise disturbances will be allowed during this time. Generators are only permitted in six campgrounds and the Fishing Bridge RV Park.

**Holders of Golden Age and Golden Access passes** will be given approximately 50% discount on camping fees; this discount does not apply at the Fishing Bridge RV Park.

**Group Camping:** Group camping areas are available at Madison, Grant, and Bridge Bay campgrounds from late May through closing date for large organized groups with a designated leader such as youth groups or educational groups. The fees range from $40-$70 per night, depending on the size of the group. Advance reservations are required and can be made by writing Yellowstone National Park Lodges, P.O. Box 165, YNP, WY 82190 or by phoning 307-344-7311.

# Wildlife Viewing

Yellowstone's abundant and diverse wildlife are as famous as its geysers. Habitat preferences and seasonal cycles of movement determine, in a general sense, where a particular animal may be at a particular time. Early morning and evening hours are when animals tend to be feeding and thus are more easily seen. But remember that the numbers and variety of animals you see are largely a matter of luck and coincidence. Check at visitor centers for detailed information.

Wild animals, especially females with young, are unpredictable. Keep a safe distance from all wildlife. Each year a number of park visitors are injured by wildlife when approaching too closely. Approaching on foot within 100 yards (91 m) of bears or within 25 yards (23 m) of other wildlife is prohibited. Please use roadside pullouts when viewing wildlife. Use binoculars or telephoto lenses for safe viewing and to avoid disturbing them. By being sensitive to its needs, you will see more of an animal's natural behavior and activity. If you cause an animal to move, you are too close!

## WHERE TO WATCH WILDLIFE

Yellowstone National Park is home to one of the greatest concentrations of free-roaming, large mammals in the lower 48 states. With the restoration of the gray wolf, the variety of species found here now includes all those large mammals present when Euro-Americans first arrived here.

Habitat preferences and seasonal cycles of movement determine, in a general sense, where a particular animal may be at a particular time. Generally, you are more likely to see mammals in the early morning and late evening hours when they tend to feed.

**Grizzly bears:** Look around sunrise or sunset in the open meadows of the Lamar and Hayden valleys, Lake and Fishing Bridge areas, and along the road from Tower to Canyon. Also look along the road to the East Entrance. Backcountry travelers should be alert for bears at all times.

**Black bears:** Look in small openings within or near forested areas, especially along the roads from Mammoth to Tower and the Northeast Entrance, and in the Old Faithful, Madison, and Canyon areas. Black bears may also be seen on any backcountry trail.

**Wolves:** Most active at dawn and dusk; most often seen in the open areas along the Lamar River and Soda Butte Creek.

**Elk:** Look around Mammoth Hot Springs, Lamar Valley, Hayden Valley, and the north slope of Mount Washburn.

**Pronghorn:** Look in the grasslands between Mammoth and the Northeast Entrance.

**Moose:** Look for this elusive animal in willow thickets bordering streams, especially between Mammoth and Norris, near Lake, and along the road to the Northeast Entrance.

**Mule deer:** Look during cooler parts of the day near edges of forests.

**Mountain Lion:** Rare sightings occur at night, especially along the road to the Northeast Entrance.

**Bighorn Sheep:** Look on cliffs along the Gardner River and between Calcite Springs and Tower Fall, and on Mount Washburn.

**Beaver:** May be seen early mornings and evenings in streams and ponds such as at Willow Park and Harlequin Lake.

## BE A WISE WILDLIFE WATCHER

*Remember that you are a guest in the home of wildlife.*

• Stay at least 100 yards (91 m.) away from bears and at least 25 yards (23 m.) from all other animals.

• Stop in a pullout instead of the middle of the road.

• Turn off your engine.

• Always talk quietly.

• To find out what people are observing, get out of your car, approach them, and speak quietly. Never call or shout from your car.

## CALL OF THE WILD

As you travel through Yellowstone in autumn, stop often to listen for one of the most haunting sounds in nature—the bugle of a bull elk. His high pitched, melodic call echoes off of the canyons and hills of the park, and the final grunts finish off his vocal advertisement to all around that he is ready for the rut, or the mating season.

To a female elk, known as a cow, the bugle provides clues to the size and fitness of a bull. Each bull's bugle is different, but generally the older, larger bulls bugle more loudly than younger bulls.

Bugling often precedes a sparring match. During these matches, bulls lock antlers and shove each other until one retreats. Their sparring matches are shows of strength, not battles to the death.

All this action begins in September and goes on through the month, tapering off into October. Enjoy the sounds and sights of the elk mating season, but remember to keep yourself safe. Stay far away from them and use binoculars to view the action.

## KEEPING THE WILD IN WILDLIFE

Animals in Yellowstone are ***wild***; they are not like animals in zoos or on ranches and farms. Respect their need for undisturbed space, and you will be rewarded by seeing more of their natural activities and discovering how they live in the wild. You'll also expand your opportunities and have a safer, more rewarding visit.

When an animal is disturbed:

• It may move from a good feeding area to a less desirable area, thereby losing vital nourishment.

• Its heart rate increases due to stress, costing the animal vital energy.

• Through time and large numbers of human contacts, it becomes habituated to humans and is less likely to run from a potential poacher.

It may become annoyed and charge the photographer, sometimes causing serious injury.

### Minimize your impact:

• Consider your impact before you approach.

• Use an appropriate telephoto lens to take photos of an animal acting naturally in its own environment.

Do not approach animals closely. In Yellowstone, you are required to stay 100 yards (91 m) from a bear and 25 yards (23 m) from all other animals-including the "friendly" elk around Mammoth Hot Springs.

• Pull off the road and use your vehicle as a photo blind.

• Do not bait animals or tempt them with handouts, It's against the law and harms the animals.

## UNPREDICTABLE WILDLIFE—KEEP YOUR DISTANCE

You will see more of an animal's natural behavior and activity if you are sensitive to its need for space. Do not approach any wildlife, especially those with young. View them from the safety of your vehicle. If an animal reacts to your presence, you are too close.

Each year a number of park visitors are injured by wildlife when they approach animals too closely. You must stay at least 100 yards (91

| Campground | Sites | Dates | Fee | Elev (ft) | Toilet | Showers/ Laundry Nearby | Dump Station | Generators Permitted (8 AM-8 PM) |
|---|---|---|---|---|---|---|---|---|
| Bridge Bay* | 430 | 5/26-9/17 | $15.00** | 700 | Flush | | X | X |
| Canyon* | 272 | 6/2-9/10 | 15.00** | 8,000 | Flush | X | X | X |
| Grant Village* | 425 | 6/21-10/1 | 15.00** | 7,800 | Flush | X | X | X |
| Madison* | 280 | 5/5-10/22 | 15.00** | 6,800 | Flush | | X | X |
| Mammoth | 85 | All Year | 12.00 | 6,200 | Flush | | | X |
| Norris | 116 | 5/19-9/25 | 12.00 | 7,500 | Flush | | | X |
| Indian Creek | 75 | 6/9-9/18 | 10.00 | 7,300 | Vault | | | |
| Lewis Laki | 85 | 6/23-11/5 | 10.00 | 7,800 | Vault | | | |
| Pebble Creek | 32 | 6/2-9/25 | 10.00 | 6,900 | Vault | | | |
| Slough Creek | 29 | 5/26-10/31 | 10.00 | 6,250 | Vault | | | |
| Tower Fall | 32 | 5/19-79/25 | 10.00' | 6,600 | Vault | | | |
| Fishing Bridge RV* | 340 | 5/12-9/24 | 27.00"t | 7,800 | Flush | X | Sewer | X |

*Reserve through Yellowstone National Park Lodges; call 307-344-7311 or TDD 307-344-5305.
**Plus sales tax
† 1-4 people
Dates are approximate and may change because of weather or resource management concerns.
Bridge Bay, Canyon, Grant Village, and Madison campgrounds all contain accessible sites.

m) away from bears and at least 25 yards (23 m) away from all other large animals—bison, elk, bighorn sheep, deer, moose, wolves, and coyotes.

Bison may appear tame and slow but they are unpredictable and dangerous. They weigh up to 2,000 pounds (900 kg) and sprint at 30 miles per hour (48 kph)—three times faster than you can run! Every year visitors are gored, and some have been killed.

Coyotes quickly learn bad habits like roadside begging. This may lead to aggressive behavior toward humans.

Bears—be alert for tracks and sign. The best way to avoid being injured by a bear is to take all necessary precautions to avoid surprise encounters.

If precautionary measures fail and you are charged by a bear, you can usually defuse the situation. Pepper spray is a good last line of defense, it has been effective in more than 90% of the reported cases where it has been used. Become familiar with your pepper spray, read all instructions, and know its limitations. Pepper spray must be instantly available, not in your pack. Remember, carrying pepper spray is not a substitute for vigilance and good safety precautions.

If you are injured by a bear (regardless of how minor), or if you observe a bear or bear sign, report it to a park ranger as soon as possible. Someone's safety may depend on it.

## Bighorn Sheep

Bighorn sheep (*Ovis canadensis*) once numbered in the millions in western United States and were an important food source for humans. The "Sheepeaters", related to the Shoshoni tribe, lived year-round in Yellowstone until 1880. Their principal food was bighorn sheep and they made their bows from sheep horns. By 1900, during an "*epoch of relentless destruction by the skin hunters*" (Seton 1913), bighorn numbers were reduced to a few hundred in the United States. In 1897 Seton spent several months roaming the upper ranges of Yellowstone Park and did not see any, although about 100-150 were estimated to be present. He reported that by 1912, despite a disease (scab) contracted from domestic sheep, bighorns in the park had increased to more than 200 and travelers could find them with fair certainty by devoting a few days to searching around Mt. Everts, Mt. Washburn or other well-known ranges. In winter, small bands of sheep could then be seen every day between Mammoth and Gardiner ... "*4 great rams with about 40 other sheep...so tame that one could get pictures within ten feet...*"

Bighorn sheep are named for the large, curved horns borne by the males, or rams. Females, or ewes, also have horns, but they are short with only a slight curvature. Sheep range in color from light brown to grayish or dark, chocolate brown, with a white rump and lining on the back of all four legs. Rocky Mountain bighorn females weigh up to 200 pounds, and males occasionally exceed 300 pounds. During the mating season or "rut", occurring in November and December, the rams butt heads in apparent sparring for females. Rams' horns can weigh more than 40 pounds, and frequently show broken or "broomed" tips from repeated clashes. Lambs, usually only one per mother, are born in May and June. They graze on grasses and browse shrubby plants, particularly in fall and winter, and seek minerals at natural salt licks. Bighorns are well adapted to climbing steep terrain where they seek cover from predators such as coyotes, eagles, and mountain lions. They are susceptible to disease such as lungworm, and sometimes fall off cliffs.

By 1914 there were about 210 sheep in Yellowstone and by 1922 there were 300 (Seton 1929). Censuses since the 1920s have never indicated more than 500 sheep. In recent years, bighorns have been systematically counted by aerial surveys in early spring. An annual ground count is also conducted on the winter range in the northern part of the park.

In the winter of 1981-82, an outbreak of pinkeye occurred among bighorns in the Mt. Everts area. Many sheep were blinded and/or killed on the adjacent park road or by falling from cliffs. No evidence of the disease, a natural occurrence, has been seen since. Winter visitors to the park still enjoy watching and photographing bighorns along the cliffs between Gardiner and Mammoth, as they did 80 years ago. Annual surveys of bighorn indicate that the resident herd on Yellowstone's northern range consists of at least 150-225 animals.

In 1997, a new study done by researchers at Montana State University began to investigate bighorn population status and behavior in northern Yellowstone. Of particular interest to these investigators is the effect of road use on the bighorns' ability to use their summer and winter range. Sheep are commonly seen along the road through the Gardner River Canyon, where visitors should be alert for bighorns crossing between their preferred cliffs and the river where they drink.

Summering bands are found in the Gallatin and Washburn Ranges, the Absarokas, and occasionally in the Red Mountains. On Dunraven Pass, a section of the Grand Loop Road in the park, a band of ewes and lambs has become somewhat habituated to summer traffic. These bighorns cause numerous traffic jams and are sometimes illegally fed by visitors, posing traffic hazards and danger to sheep. Park staff and visitors are encouraged to educate others about the importance of the "no feeding" regulation to the long-term welfare of wild animals.

## Bison

Bison are the largest mammals in Yellowstone National Park. They are strictly vegetarian, a grazer of grasslands and sedges in the meadows, the foothills, and even the high-elevation, forested plateaus of Yellowstone. Bison males, called bulls, can weigh upwards of 1,800 pounds. Females (cows) average about 1,000 pounds. Both stand approximately six feet tall at the shoulder, and can move with surprising speed to defend their young or when approached too closely by people. Bison breed from mid-July to mid-August, and bear one calf in April and May. Some wolf predation of bison is documented in Canada and has recently been observed in Yellowstone.

Yellowstone is the only place in the lower 48 states where a population of wild bison has persisted since prehistoric times, although fewer than 50 native bison remained here in 1902. Fearing extinction, the park imported 21 bison from two privately-owned herds, as foundation stock for a bison ranching project that spanned 50 years at the Buffalo Ranch in Yellowstone's Lamar Valley. Activities there included irrigation, hay-feeding, roundups, culling, and predator control, to artificially ensure herd survival. By the 1920s, some intermingling of the introduced and wild bison had begun. With protection from poaching, the native and transplanted populations increased. In 1936, bison were transplanted to historic habitats in the Firehole River and Hayden Valley. In 1954, the entire population numbered 1,477. Bison were trapped and herds periodically reduced until 1967, when only 397 bison were counted parkwide. All bison herd reduction activities were phased out after 1966, again allowing natural ecological processes to determine bison numbers and distribution. Although winterkill takes a toll, by 1996 bison numbers had increased to about 3,500.

*A bison bull. NPS Photo*

Bison are nomadic grazers, wandering high on Yellowstone's grassy plateaus in summer. Despite their slow gait, bison are surprisingly fast for animals that weigh more than half a ton. In winter, they use their large heads like a plow to push aside snow and find winter food. In the park interior where snows are deep, they winter in thermally influenced areas and around the geyser basins. Bison also move to winter range in the northern part of Yellowstone.

Bison are enjoyed by visitors, celebrated by conservationists, and revered by Native Americans. Why are they a management challenge? One reason is that about half of Yellowstone's bison have been exposed to brucellosis, a bacterial disease that came to this continent with European cattle and may cause cattle to miscarry. The disease has little effect on park bison and has never been transmitted from wild bison to a visitor or to domestic livestock. Despite the very low risk to humans and livestock today, since the possibility of contagion exists, the State of Montana believes its "brucellosis-free" status may be jeopardized if bison are in proximity to cattle. Although the risk is very low, if cattle become infected, ranchers can be prevented from shipping livestock out of state until stringent testing and quarantine requirements are met. Although scien-

## The Grizzly Bear

NPS Photo

**The Yellowstone ecosystem provides** vital habitat for grizzlies in its two national parks (Yellowstone and Grand Teton), six national forests, state lands, and private lands. Some bears live either totally inside or outside of Yellowstone National Park; others may use portions of various different agency holdings.

Because grizzly bears range widely and are usually solitary, they are difficult to count. Biologists estimate their population within the Yellowstone ecosystem to be 280-610 bears.

The Yellowstone ecosystem is unique among areas inhabited by grizzly bears in North America because of the foods it provides. Here, grizzly bears depend more on animals, ranging from ants and moths to elk and bison. Bears here and elsewhere also eat large amounts of plants, but Yellowstone lacks the lush vegetation and berries found in northern Montana.

When Yellowstone grizzly bears emerge from hibernation in March and April, there is still a lot of snow and very little vegetation in most of the park. The bears move to the low country where elk and other ungulates (hoofed mammals) spent the winter. There, the bears feed on carcasses of ungulates that died during the winter. (Never approach a carcass-a bear may be nearby and it will often defend its food source.) Bears are not the only animal that depends on winter-killed ungulates for survival. Wolves, coyotes, wolverines, badgers, foxes, eagles, ravens, magpies, and carrion beetles also feed on the carcasses.

Grizzly bears prey on elk calves in the spring, usually from mid-May through early July. After early July, most elk calves can outrun bears. Some bears will feed on spawning cutthroat trout in the Yellowstone Lake area during the early summer. Bears also dig for small rodents (primarily pocket gophers), ants, roots, and tubers. Later in the summer, grizzly bears feed on army cutworm moths and whitebark pine nuts at high elevations. Despite their small size, these foods are important, high-protein foods for grizzly bears, especially as autumn approaches.

The restoration of wolves to the park appears to be providing bears more opportunities to obtain meat. During the years since the 1995 release of wolves into the park, bears have been observed successfully taking wolf-killed ungulates away from wolf packs. Will this new opportunity increase the grizzly bear population in Yellowstone? No one knows.

tists are studying new possibilities, there is yet no known safe, effective brucellosis vaccine for bison. Ironically, elk in the ecosystem also carry the disease, but this popular game species is not considered a threat to livestock.

Yellowstone wildlife freely move across boundaries set a century ago without knowledge of each animal's habitat needs. But bison are not always unwelcome outside the park. In the park managers have tried to limit bison use of lands outside the park through public hunting, hazing bison back inside park boundaries, capture, testing for exposure to brucellosis, and shipping them to slaughter. Since 1990, state and federal agency personnel have shot bison that leave the park. During the severe winter of 1996-1997, nearly 1,100 bison were sent to slaughter. The carcasses sold at public auction, or shot and given to Native Americans. These actions reduced the bison population to about 2,200 in 1997-1998. In the mild winter of 1997-1998, only 11 bison were killed in management actions, all in January, and all from the West Yellowstone area. Six bison were shot and five were sent to slaughter. Through the winter another 21 bison are known to have died, 12 of natural causes, and 9 from other causes such as collisions with vehicles.

The NPS, U.S.D.A. Forest Service, U.S.D.A. Animal and Plant Health Inspection Service, and the State of Montana completed a Draft Environmental Impact Statement for the Interagency Bison Management Plan for the State of Montana and Yellowstone National Park for public release on June 12, 1998. The purpose is to maintain a wild free-ranging bison population and to address the risk of brucellosis transmissions to protect the economic interest and viability of the livestock industry in Montana. Alternatives being considered range from: allowing bison to freely range over a large portion of public land inside and outside the park; managing bison like elk and other wildlife through controlled hunting outside park boundaries; and attempting to eradicate brucellosis by capturing, testing, and slaughtering infected bison at numerous facilities constructed inside the park. Additional options include purchase of additional winter range; attacking brucellosis with a (yet unknown) safe and effective vaccine for bison; and quarantine of animals at appropriate locations such as Indian Reservations or other suitable sites outside Yellowstone.

## Bobcats

Bobcats (*Felix rufus*) are small wild cats with reddish-brown or yellowish-brown coats, streaked with black or dark brown. They have prominent, pointed ears with a tuft of black hair at the tip. Females average 20 pounds and males weigh from 16 to 30 pounds. They breed in late winter or early spring and have a gestation period of about two months. A female may have one to six kittens each year. Although adapted to a variety of habitats across the country, they do not tolerate the deep snows found in much of Yellowstone, and thus they are usually reported in the northern portion of the park. Bobcats move about their home ranges most actively in the hours near dawn and dusk, hunting small mammals such as mice, rabbits, hares, and deer. They seek cover in conifer stands and on rocky ledges.

In the early years of this century, bobcats were reported as "somewhat common" in the park. In the last 64 years, there have been at least 43 reports of bobcats sighted in the park, 9 to 14 reports in each decade since 1960. These sightings have occurred throughout the park; about 80 percent have occurred in the northern half. Bobcats have been reported in about equal numbers during all seasons. In 1960, a bobcat was killed by a car near Squaw Lake (now Indian Pond) on the north shore of Yellowstone Lake; its skull was deposited in the Yellowstone Museum collection. Other roadkilled bobcats were reported in 1993 and 1996. In 1960, a young bobcat was reported on the porch of the administration building at Mammoth; other young bobcats have been reported at Pebble Creek bridge (Feb. 1977) and at Canyon campground (July 1986), where one accompanied an adult bobcat.

No research has been conducted in Yellowstone to determine the numbers or distribution of this elusive animal that usually is solitary, nocturnal, and widely scattered over its range.

Unlike lynx, which they resemble, bobcats elsewhere have been highly adaptable to human-caused changes in environmental conditions; some biologists believe that there are more bobcats in the United States today than in colonial times. Yellowstone has many rock outcrops, canyons bordered by rock ledges, conifer forests, and semi-open areas that seem to offer conditions favorable for bobcats—adequate shelter, a variety of rodents, rabbits, hares, birds, and other small animals as well as seasonal carrion, for food. Carrion is seldom used if live prey is available. Studies elsewhere have shown that bobcats also may kill both young and adult antelope and deer; they stalk bedded adults and may be carried long distances while biting their prey in the neck.

Bobcats are known to hole-up and wait out severe winter storms elsewhere, but whether they are able to tolerate the severe midwinter conditions of the park interior is unknown. These elusive cats are most active at night, so even those who study them seldom have an opportunity to see one. If you are so fortunate, look for the black bars on the inside of the forelegs. Black bars mean bobcat, and not the similar-looking lynx! If you see tracks, measure and photograph them carefully, then consult a track field guide. Bobcat tracks

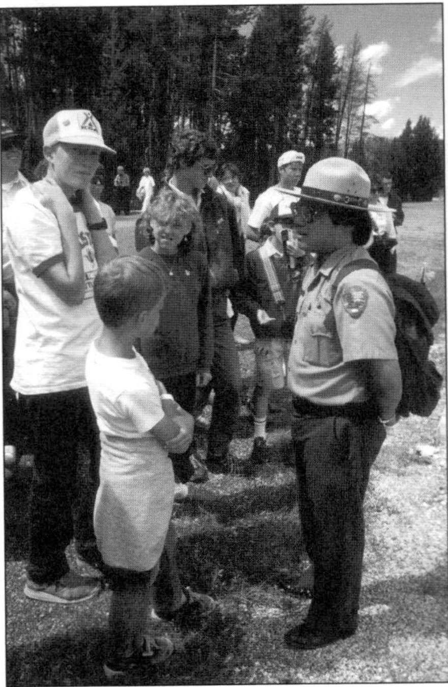

*Park rangers are one of your best sources of information while visiting the park.*

seldom exceed 2 1/4 inches in length; lynx tracks usually are longer than 3 1/2 inches.

If you see a bobcat or bobcat tracks, please report them promptly to a ranger or visitor center. For animals so seldom recorded, every observation is useful and important.

## Hiking and Camping in Bear Country

**Although the risk of an encounter with** a bear is low, there are no guarantees of your safety. Minimize your risks by following the guidelines below.

### A Fed Bear is a Dead Bear

Do not leave packs containing food unattended, even for a few minutes. Allowing a bear to obtain human food even once often results in the bear becoming aggressive about obtaining such food in the future. Aggressive bears present a threat to human safety and eventually may be destroyed or removed from the park.

### While Hiking

Make bears aware of your presence on trails by making loud noises, shouting, or singing. This lessens the chance of sudden encounters, which are the cause of most bear-caused human injuries in the park. Hike in groups and use caution where vision is obstructed. Do not hike after dark. Avoid carcasses; bears often defend this source of food.

### If You Encounter a Bear

Do not run. Bears can run 30 mph (48 kph), or 44 feet/second (13 m/second), which is faster than Olympic sprinters. Running may elicit an attack from an otherwise nonaggressive bear. If the bear is unaware of you, keep out of sight and detour behind and downwind of the bear. If the bear is aware of you and nearby, but has not acted aggressively, slowly back away.

Tree climbing to avoid bears is popular advice, but not very practical in many circumstances. All black bears, all grizzly cubs, and some adult grizzlies can climb trees. Plus, running to a tree may provoke an otherwise uncertain bear to chase you.

### If A Bear Charges or Approaches You

Do not run. Some bears will bluff their way out of a threatening situation by charging, then veering off or stopping abruptly at the last second. Bear experts generally recommend standing still until the bear stops and then slowly backing away. If you are attacked, lie on the ground completely flat. Spread your legs and clasp your hands over the back of your neck. Another alternative is to play dead: drop to the ground, lift your legs up to your chest, and clasp your hands over the back of your neck.

### When Camping

Never camp in an area that has obvious evidence of bear activity such as digging, tracks, scat, or where animal carcasses are present.

Odors attract bears. Avoid carrying or cooking odorous foods or other products. Keep a clean camp; do not cook or store food in your tent. All food, garbage, or other odorous items used for preparing or cooking food must be secured from bears. Hang all such items at least 10 feet (3 m) above the ground and at least 4 feet (1.2 m) out from tree trunks. Treat all odorous products such as soap, deodorant, or toiletries in the same manner as food.

Sleep a minimum of 100 yards (91m) from where you hang, cook, and eat your food. Keep your sleeping gear clean and free of food odor. Don't sleep in the same clothes worn while cooking and eating; hang those clothes in plastic bags.

*Coyotes are some of the more common critters seen in Yellowstone.*

## Coyotes

Yellowstone's coyotes (*Canis latrans*) are among the largest coyotes in the United States; adults average about 30 lbs. and some weigh around 40 lbs. This canid (member of the dog family) stands less than two feet tall and varies in color from gray to tan with sometimes a reddish tint to its coat. Coyotes live an average of about 6 years, although one Yellowstone coyote lived to be more than 13 before she was killed and eaten by a cougar. A coyote's ears and nose appear long and pointed, especially in relation to the size of its head. It can generally be distinguished from its much larger relative, the gray wolf, by its overall slight appearance compared to the massive 75 to 125-pound stockiness of the bigger dog. The coyote is a common predator in the park, often seen alone or in packs, traveling through the park's wide open valleys hunting small mammals. But they are widely distributed and their sign can also be found in the forests and thermal areas throughout Yellowstone. They are capable of killing large prey, especially when they cooperatively hunt.Yellowstone's coyotes (Canis latrans) are among the largest coyotes in the United States; adults average about 30 lbs. and some weigh around 40 lbs. This canid (member of the dog family) stands less than two feet tall and varies in color from gray to tan with sometimes a reddish tint to its coat. Coyotes live an average of about 6 years, although one Yellowstone coyote lived to be more than 13 before she was killed and eaten by a cougar. A coyote's ears and nose appear long and pointed, especially in relation to the size of its head. It can generally be distinguished from its much larger relative, the gray wolf, by its overall slight appearance compared to the massive 75 to 125-pound stockiness of the bigger dog. The coyote is a common predator in the park, often seen alone or in packs, traveling through the park's wide open valleys hunting small mammals. But they are widely distributed and their sign can also be found in the forests and thermal areas throughout Yellowstone. They are capable of killing large prey, especially when they cooperatively hunt.

*Mountain lions are seldom seen, but ever present. NPS photo*

## Mountain Lions

The mountain lion (*Felis concolor*), also called the cougar, is the largest member of the cat family living in Yellowstone. Mountain lions can weigh up to 200 pounds, although lions in Yellowstone are thought to range between 140 and 160 pounds for males and around 100 pounds for females. Two to three kittens may be born at any time of year, although most arrive in summer and fall. For reasons that are not clear, only about 50 percent of kittens survive their first year. The current population of lions in Yellowstone is estimated to be 18-24 animals and is thought to be increasing.

Mountain lions are rather secretive, consequently, most visitors are unaware of their existence in Yellowstone. Lions probably live throughout the park in summer. In winter, difficulty of movement and lack of available prey causes most lions to move to lower elevations. Lions are territorial and will kill other lions. The dominant animals reside in the northern range areas of the park where prey is available year-round. Mountain lions prey chiefly upon elk and deer, although their diet probably varies based upon opportunity, porcupines provide an important supplement to the lion's diet.

Mountain lions were significantly reduced by predator control measures during the early 1900s. It is reported that 121 lions were removed from the park between the years 1904 and 1925. At that time, the remaining population was estimated to be 12 individuals. Mountain lions apparently existed at very low numbers between 1925 and 1940. Reports of lions in Yellowstone have increased steadily from 1 each year between 1930

*A bison herd grazes in a meadow. NPS Photo*

and 1939 to about 16 each year between 1980 and 1988. However, increases in visitor travel in Yellowstone and improvements in record keeping during this period probably contributed to this trend.

In 1987, the first study of mountain lion ecology was initiated in Yellowstone National Park. The research documented population dynamics of mountain lions in the northern Yellowstone ecosystem inside and outside the park boundary, determined home ranges and habitat requirements, and assessed the role of lions as a predator in the ecosystem. In recent years in other areas of the West, mountain lions have occasionally attacked humans. No documented lion/human confrontations have occurred in Yellowstone.

*Elk are the most commonly observed animal in Yellowstone.*

## Elk

Elk (*Cervus elaphus*) are the most abundant large mammal found in Yellowstone; paleontological evidence confirms their continuous presence for at least 1,000 years. Yellowstone National Park was established in 1872, when market hunting of all large grazing animals was rampant. Not until after 1886, when the U.S. Army was called in to protect the park and wildlife slaughter was brought under control, did the large animals increase in number.

More than 30,000 elk from 7-8 different herds summer in Yellowstone and approximately 15,000 to 22,000 winter in the park. The subspecies of elk that lives here are found from Arizona to northern Canada along the Rocky Mountain chain; other species of elk were historically distributed from coast to coast, but disappeared from the eastern United States in the early 1800s. Some other subspecies of elk still occupy coastal regions of California, Washington, and Oregon. Elk are the second largest member of the deer family (moose are larger). Adult males, or bulls, range upwards of 700 pounds while females, or cows, average 500-525 pounds. Their coats are reddish brown with heavy, darker-colored manes and a distinct yellowish rump patch.

Bulls grow antlers annually from the time they are nearly one year old. When mature, a bull's "rack" may have 6 to 8 points or tines on each side and weigh more than 30 pounds. The antlers are usually shed in March or April, and begin regrowing in May, when the bony growth is nourished by blood vessels and covered by furry-looking "velvet." Antler growth ceases each year by August, when the velvet dries up and bulls begin to scrape it off by rubbing against trees, in preparation for the autumn mating season or rut. A bull may gather 20-30 cows into his harem during the mating season, often clashing or locking antlers with another mature male for the privilege of dominating the herd group. By November, mating season ends and elk generally move to their winter ranges. Calves weighing 25-40 pounds are born in late May or early June.

Climate is the most important factor affecting the size and distribution of elk herds here. Nearly the whole park—approximately 2.2 million acres—provides summer range for elk. However, winter snowfalls force elk and other ungulates to leave the greater part of the park. Only the northern, lower-elevation portion of Yellowstone, where temperatures are more moderate and snowfall less than in the park interior, can support large numbers of wintering elk. Annual precipitation, which occurs mostly as snow, averages as high as 75" in the southern, high-mountain plateaus of the park; minimum temperatures there are often well below 0° F, and have been as low as -66° F. In contrast, most of the northern range averages less than 30" of precipitation annually, and winter temperatures are considerably warmer.

## Moose

Moose (*Alces alces shirasi Nelson*), the largest member of the deer family, were reportedly very rare in northwest Wyoming when Yellowstone National Park was established in 1872. Subsequent protection from hunting and wolf control programs may have contributed to increased numbers but suppression of forest fires probably was the most important factor, since moose here depend on mature fir forests for winter survival.

Moose breed from early September to November and one to three calves are born in May or June. Calves weigh 25 to 35 pounds at birth but grow rapidly; adult females (cows) weigh up to 800 pounds and males (bulls) up to 1300 pounds. Bulls are readily identified by their large, palmate antlers, which are shed annually, and their bells, an apparently useless dewlap of skin and hair that dangles from the throat. Moose live mostly solitary lives, and die from disease, starvation, or predation by wolves and, occasionally, by grizzly bears.

Surveys in the late 1980s suggested a total park population of fewer than 1000 moose.

*Bull moose lock antlers. NPS photo*

Research on radio-collared moose in northern Yellowstone has shown that when snow depth forces moose from low-elevation willow stands in November, they move up to as high as 8500 feet, to winter in mature stands of subalpine fir and Douglas-fir. They browse fir almost exclusively during the deep-snow winter months. Tyers (unpubl. data) found that moose ate 39.6 percent subalpine fir, 25.5 percent willows, 10.6 percent lodgepole pine, 4.6 percent gooseberry, and 4 percent buffaloberry. Snow is not as deep under a canopy of conifer branches since some snow remains on them, and a crust that may restrict moose movements is less likely to form on shaded snow. However, Tyers found that moose could winter in areas where snow considerably deeper than that which elk could withstand.

The moose calf crop has been declining since the fires of 1988. During that summer there was also high predation of moose by grizzly bears in small patches of surviving timber. The winter following the fires many old moose died, probably as a combined result of the loss of good moose forage and a harsh winter. The fires forced some moose into poorer habitats, with the result that some almost doubled their home range, using deeper snow areas than previously, and sometimes browsing burned lodgepole pines. Unlike moose habitat elsewhere, northern Yellowstone does not have woody browse species that will come in quickly after a fire and extend above the snowpack to provide winter food. Therefore, the overall effects of the fires were probably detrimental to moose populations. Park managers, in cooperation with staff from the adjacent Gallatin National Forest and the Montana Department of Fish, Wildlife and Parks continue to seek good methods to monitor the status of moose in northern Yellowstone. Aerial surveys of willow habitats in spring have shown some promise of providing an index of moose population trends in Yellowstone, although their current population and distribution remain largely unknown.

Moose are commonly observed in the park's southwestern corner along the Bechler and Falls rivers, in the riparian zones around Yellowstone Lake, in the Soda Butte Creek, Pelican Creek, Lewis River, and Gallatin river drainages, and in the Willow Park area between Mammoth and Norris. Summer moose migrations from south and west of the park into Yellowstone have been confirmed by radiotelemetry.

## Self-Guiding Trails

Slow down and stretch your legs on these self-guiding trails. At each location, you can purchase a trail guide with a map, photos, and information.

**Mammoth Hot Springs.** Visitors marvel at the surreal appearance of these travertine terraces. As an early visitor described them: "the hot springs fall over a lofty hill of snowy whiteness, resembling cascades." The trail winds through the area, and you can also drive through the Upper Terraces.

**Fort Yellowstone Historic Trail.** Most of the buildings constructed in Mammoth during the time that the U.S. Army managed the park (1886-1918) are now used by the National Park Service as its headquarters.

**Norris Geyser Basin.** Explore the hottest, most dynamic geyser basin in the park. Porcelain Basin features hundreds of geothermal features in an open area; Back Basin trail winds through more forested terrain past a number of springs and geysers. Steamboat, the world's tallest geyser, erupted in May 2000—its first eruption since October 1991.

**Fountain Paint Pot.** Active, ever-changing mudpots; constant geysers; hissing fumaroles; and colorful, boiling hot springs await you on this trail and on Firehole Lake Drive. Park in the large parking area 8 miles (12.9 km) north of Old Faithful on the road to Madison Junction.

**Upper Geyser Basin.** The world's largest concentration of geysers is located here, including Old Faithful. View that famous feature, then walk the trails that wind past hundreds of geysers and hot springs. Names such as Beehive, Grotto, Castle, Riverside, and Morning Glory hint at the wonders you will see.

**Grand Canyon of the Yellowstone.** The Canyon and the Upper and Lower Falls can be seen from overlooks along the rims, which you can reach by car or foot. See for yourself why viewpoints are named Inspiration, Grandview, and Artist Point.

**West Thumb Geyser Basin.** The boiling springs in this basin, including the famous Fishing Cone, discharge their waters into chilly Yellowstone Lake. With mountains as a backdrop to the east, this is one of the prettiest self-guiding trails.

**Mud Volcano Area.** Discover turbulent and explosive mudpots, including Mud Volcano and Dragon's Mouth. View—and smell—Sulphur Caldron. Located on the road between Lake and Canyon, 6 miles (9.6 km) north of Fishing Bridge Junction.

## Natural Highlights of the Mammoth Area

### Mammoth Hot Springs

Mammoth Hot Springs are the main attraction of the Mammoth District. These features are quite different from thermal areas elsewhere in the park. Travertine formations grow much more rapidly than sinter formations due to the softer nature of limestone. As hot water rises through limestone, large quantities of rock are dissolved by the hot water, and a white chalky mineral is deposited on the surface.

Although visitors are sometimes confused by the rapidly shifting activity of the hot springs and disappointed when a favorite spring appears to have "died," it is important to realize that the location of springs and the rate of flow changes daily, that "on-again-off-again" is the rule, and that the overall volume of water discharged by all of the springs fluctuates little.

### The Gardner River and Gardner River Canyon

The North Entrance Road from Gardiner, Montana, to Mammoth Hot Springs, Wyoming, runs along the Gardner River. The road winds into the park, up the canyon, past crumbling walls of sandstone and ancient mudflows. The vegetation is much thicker in the canyon than on the open prairie down below, the common trees being Rocky Mountain juniper, cottonwood, and Douglas-fir. Low-growing willows also crowd the river's edge in the flatter, flood-prone sections of the canyon.

Watch for wildlife in season: eagles, osprey, dippers, and kingfishers along the river and bighorn sheep in the steeper parts of the canyon.

### 45th Parallel Bridge and Boiling River

A sign near where the road crosses the Gardner River marks the 45th parallel of latitude. The 45th parallel is an imaginary line that circles the globe halfway between the equator and the North Pole. This same line passes through Minneapolis-St. Paul, Ottawa, Bordeaux, Venice, Belgrade, and the northern tip of the Japanese islands. It is, here in Yellowstone, roughly aligned with the Montana-Wyoming border.

A parking area on the east side of the road is used by bathers in the "Boiling River." Bathers must walk upstream about a half mile from the parking area to the place where the footpath reaches the river. This spot is also marked by large clouds of steam, especially in cold weather. Here, a large hot spring, known as Boiling River, enters the Gardner River. The hot and the cold water mix in pools along the river's edge. Bathers are allowed in the river during daylight hours only. Bathing suits are required, and no alcoholic beverages are allowed. Boiling River is closed in the springtime due to hazardous high water and often does not reopen until mid-summer. The Yellowstone Park Foundation funded the Boiling River Trail Project. They are a non-profit organization whose mission is to fund projects and programs that protect, preserve and enhance Yellowstone National Park.

### Mt. Everts

Mt. Everts was named for explorer Truman Everts of the 1870 Washburn Expedition who became separated from his camping buddies, lost his glasses, lost his horse, and spent the next 37 days starving and freezing and hallucinating as he made his way through the untracked and inhospitable wilderness. Upon rescue, he was, according to his rescuers, within but a few hours of death. Everts never made it quite as far as Mt. Everts. He was found near the "Cut" on the Blacktail Plateau Drive and was mistaken for a black bear and nearly shot. His story, which he later published in Scribner's Monthly Magazine, remains one of Yellowstone's best known, lost-in-the-wilderness stories. It has also been published in book form, edited by Yellowstone's archivist Lee Whittlesey under the name *Lost in the Yellowstone*.

Mt. Everts is made up of distinctly layered sandstones and shales—sedimentary rocks deposited when this area was covered by a shallow inland sea, 70 to 140 million years ago.

### Bunsen Peak

Bunsen Peak and the "Bunsen burner" were both named for the German physicist, Robert Wilhelm Bunsen. Although most people are familiar with the "Bunsen burner," few people know why his students gave the burner that name. He was involved in pioneering research about geysers, and a "Bunsen burner" has a resemblance to a geyser. His theory on geysers was published in the 1800s, and it is still believed to be accurate.

Bunsen Peak is 8,564 feet high (2,612 meters) and may be climbed via a trail that starts at the Golden Gate. Another trail, the old Bunsen Peak road, skirts around the flank of the peak from the YCC camp to the Golden Gate. This old road may be used by hikers, mountain-bikers, and skiers in winter.

The peak is also interesting because it burned in the 1880s and then again in 1988. A series of old photos show the creep of trees up Bunsen following the 1880 fires, and the new patterns of open space created by the fires of 1988.

## Geological Overview of the Mammoth Area

### Mammoth Hot Springs

Mammoth Hot Springs are a surficial expression of the deep volcanic forces at work in Yellowstone. Although these springs lie outside the caldera boundary, their energy is attributed to the same magmatic system that fuels other Yellowstone thermal areas. Hot water flows from Norris to Mammoth along a fault line roughly associated with the Norris to Mammoth road. Shallow circulation along this corridor allows Norris' superheated water to cool somewhat before surfacing at Mammoth, generally at about 170° F.

Thermal activity here is extensive both over time and distance. Terrace Mountain, northwest of Golden Gate, has a thick cap of travertine. The Mammoth Terraces extend all the way from the hillside where we see them today, across the Parade Ground, and down to Boiling River. The Mammoth Hotel, as well as all of Fort Yellowstone, is built upon an old terrace formation known as Hotel Terrace. There was some concern when construction began in 1891 on the Fort site that the hollow ground would not support the weight of the buildings. Several large sink holes (fenced off) can be seen out on the Parade Ground. This area has been thermally active for several thousand years.

The Mammoth area exhibits much evidence of glacial activity from the Pinedale Glaciation. The summit of Terrace Mountain is covered with glacial till, thereby dating the travertine formation there to earlier than the end of the Pinedale Glaciation. Several thermal kames, including

NPS photo

### Opal Terrace

Opal Spring flows from the base of Capitol Hill, which is across the road from Liberty Cap. After years of dormancy, this spring became active in 1926 and began depositing up to one foot (0.3m) of travertine per year. In 1947, a tennis court was removed to allow natural expansion of the terrace. Further growth threatens the historic home next to Opal Terrace. Designed by Robert Reamer and built in 1908, the house is an example of Prairie Style architecture. Among Reamer's other designs are the Old Faithful Inn and the Roosevelt Arch at Yellowstone's North Entrance. Today sandbags and an earthen wall protect the house. The National Park Service strives to protect both historic and natural resources. At Opal Terrace both types of resources must be considered.

### Palette Spring

Water flows from a flat area and then down a steep ridge, creating a colorful hillside palette of brown, green, and orange (the colors are due to the presence of different heat-tolerant bacteria). This effect is much the same as an artist would achieve by allowing wet paint to run down a vertical surface.

NPS photo

### Liberty Cap

This 37-foot (11-m) hot spring cone marks the northern portion of Mammoth Hot Springs.

## Wolves

**As of August 2000, about 115-120** wolves inhabit the Yellowstone ecosystem. Approximately eighty-three known wolf mortalities have occurred in the ecosystem since wolf restoration began six years ago. There are about fourteen packs or groups in the ecosystem, most of which inhabit territories within the Yellowstone National Park or Grand Teton National Park. There are currently about eleven breeding pairs in the ecosystem.

Northern Rocky Mountain wolves, a subspecies of the gray wolf (Canis lupus), were native to Yellowstone when the park was established in 1872. Predator control was practiced here in the late 1800s and early 1900s. Between 1914 and 1926, at least 136 wolves were killed in the park; by the 1940s, wolf packs were rarely reported. By the 1970s, scientists found no evidence of a wolf population in Yellowstone; wolves persisted in the lower 48 states only in northern Minnesota and on Isle Royale in Michigan. An occasional wolf likely wandered into the Yellowstone area; however, no verifiable evidence of a breeding pair of wolves existed through the mid 1990s. In the early 1980s, wolves began to reestablish themselves near Glacier National Park in northern Montana; an estimated 75 wolves inhabited Montana in 1996. At the same time, wolf reports were increasing in central and north-central Idaho, and wolves were occasionally reported in the state of Washington. The wolf is listed as "endangered" throughout its historic range in the lower 48 states except in Minnesota, where it is "threatened."

National Park Service (NPS) policy calls for restoring native species when: a) sufficient habitat exists to support a self-perpetuating population, b) management can prevent serious threats to outside interests, c) the restored subspecies most nearly resembles the extirpated subspecies, and d) extirpation resulted from human activities.

The U.S. Fish & Wildlife Service 1987 Northern Rocky Mountain Wolf Recovery Plan proposed reintroduction of an "experimental population" of wolves into Yellowstone. In a report to Congress, scientists from the University of Wyoming predicted reductions of elk (15%-25%), bison (5%-15%), moose, and mule deer could result from wolf restoration in Yellowstone. A separate panel of 15 experts predicted decreases in moose (10%-15%) and mule deer (20%-30%). Minor effects were predicted for grizzly bears and mountain lions. Coyotes probably would decline and red foxes probably would increase.

In October 1991, Congress provided funds to the U.S Fish & Wildlife Service (USFWS) to prepare, in consultation with the NPS and the U.S. Forest Service, an Environmental Impact Statement (EIS) on restoring wolves to Yellowstone and central Idaho. After several years and a near-record number of public comments, the Secretary of Interior signed the Record of Decision on the Final Environmental Impact Statement (FEIS) for reintroduction of gray wolves to both areas. Staff from Yellowstone, the USFWS, and participating states prepared to implement wolf restoration. The USFWS prepared special regulations outlining how wolves would be managed as a nonessential experimental population under section 10(j) of the Endangered Species Act. These regulations took effect in November 1994. As outlined in the Record of Decision, the states and tribes would implement and lead wolf management outside the boundaries of national parks and wildlife refuges, within federal guidelines. The states of Idaho, Wyoming, and Montana have begun preparation of wolf management plans.

Park staff assisted with planning for a soft release of wolves in Yellowstone. This technique has been used to restore red wolves in the southeastern United States and swift fox in the Great Plains and involves holding animals temporarily in areas of suitable habitat. Penning of the animals is intended to discourage immediate long-distance dispersal. In contrast, a hard release allows animals to disperse immediately wherever they choose, and has been used in Idaho where there is limited access to the central Idaho wilderness.

In the autumn of 1995 at three sites in the Lamar Valley, park staff completed site planning, and archaeological and sensitive plant surveys. Approximately 1 acre was enclosed at each site with 9-gauge chain link fence in 10' x 10' panels. These enclosures could be dismantled and reconstructed at other sites if necessary. The fences had a 2' overhang and a 4' skirt at the bottom to discourage climbing over or digging under the enclosure. Each pen had a small holding area attached, to allow a wolf to be separated from the group for medical treatment. Inside each pen were several plywood security boxes to provide shelter. For the 1996 release, one pen was relocated to Blacktail Plateau and another was constructed in the Firehole Valley in central Yellowstone. Subsequently pens have been relocated from Lamar to other areas in the park interior to facilitate releases into other geographic areas or the park or special circumstances that require the temporary penning of wolves.

*While wolves are elusive, they have been sighted frequently by visitors in the park. NPS Photo*

USFWS and Canadian wildlife biologists captured wolves in Canada and released them in both recovery areas in 1995 and 1996. As planned, wolves of dispersal age (1-2 years old) were released in Idaho, while Yellowstone released pups of the year (7+ months old), together with one or more of the alpha pair (breeding adults). Young pups weigh about 75 lbs. and are less likely to have established a home range. The goal was to have 5-7 wolves from one social group together in each release pen.

Each wolf was radio-collared when captured in Canada. For about 8-10 weeks while

*The wolf is the subject of more stories, myths, and legends than any other creature that exists today. NPS Photo*

temporarily penned, the wolves experienced minimal human contact. Approximately once each week, they were fed roadkills. They were guarded by rangers and other volunteers who minimized the amount of visual contact between wolves and humans. The pen sites and surrounding areas were closed and marked to prevent unauthorized entry. Biologists used radio-telemetry to check on the welfare of wolves.

Although concern was expressed about the wolves becoming habituated to humans or to the captive conditions, the temporary holding period was not long in the life of a wolf. In Alaska and Canada, wolves are seldom known to develop the habituated behaviors seen more commonly in grizzly bears. Wolves, while social among their own kind, typically avoid human contact. They are highly efficient predators with well-developed predatory instincts. Their social structure and pack behavior minimizes their need to scavenge food or garbage available from human sources. Compared to bears, whose diet is predominantly vegetarian, wolves have less specific habitat requirements. The wolves' primary need is for prey, which is most likely to be elk, deer, and other ungulates in these recovery areas.

In 1995, fourteen wolves were released into Yellowstone National Park. In 1996, seventeen more wolves were brought from Canada and released. After release, several thousand visitors were lucky to view wolves chasing and killing elk or interacting with bears during spring. A park ranger and a group of visitors watched a most exciting encounter between two packs which likely resulted in one young wolf's death. This was not the first fatal encounter between wolves, although human-caused mortalities still outnumber inter-pack strife as a cause of wolf deaths.

Yellowstone's first fourteen wolves bore two litters totalling nine pups. In 1996, four packs produced fourteen pups. After the wolves' release in 1996, plans to transplant additional wolves were terminated due to reduced funding and due to the wolves' unexpected early reproductive success.

In early 1997, ten young wolves, orphaned when their parents were involved in livestock depredation on the Rocky Mountain Front in northwestern Montana, were released into the park. In the spring of the wolf restoration project's third year, nine packs of wolves produced 13 litters of 64 pups. Three of the packs produced multiple litters which, while documented in the literature, is still unusual. Alpha male wolves generally do not breed with their own offspring, possibly to prevent inbreeding. However, as wolves were matched up during temporary periods of penning and as pack members shifted or were killed and replaced by other dispersing wolves, the occasional result has been packs in which one or both of the alpha pair were not the parents of subordinate pack members. Consequently, the alpha males probably had less incentive to breed with only one female, especially since food was abundant and the packs were still in the early stages of establishing their territories. Lone wolves continued to roam widely, but most of the wolves remained primarily within the boundaries of Yellowstone National Park

An estimated 20,000 park visitors have observed wolves since their return in 1995. The program's visibility has resulted in opportunities to educate audiences about predator-prey relationships, endangered species restoration, and the importance of maintaining intact ecosystems. The program has also generated numerous partnerships with private groups and individuals who generously donated their time and money—critical in an era of reduced budgets and staff downsizing.

For both Idaho and Yellowstone, wolf population recovery is defined as having about 100 wolves, or approximately 10 breeding pairs, established in each area for 3 successive years. The goal to restore wolves and begin delisting them by approximately 2002 appears within reach. The return of the only species known to be missing from the world's first national park for the past half-century has been a milestone in ecological restoration. It has not only restored the wildlife complement of greater Yellowstone; it has been a symbolic victory for conservationists who patiently and persistently reversed the once-dominant attitude against predators to one of acceptance. We believe that Aldo Leopold would be proud that so many humans have come to respect even these "killer creatures" with whom we share the Earth.

Capitol Hill and Dude Hill, are major features of the Mammoth Village area. Ice-marginal stream beds are in evidence in the small, narrow valleys where Floating Island Lake and Phantom Lake are found. In Gardner Canyon, one can see the old, sorted gravel bed of the Gardner River covered by unsorted glacial till.

## Mammoth Tour

Several key ingredients combine to make the Mammoth Hot Springs Terraces: heat, water, limestone, and a rock fracture system through which hot water can reach the earth's surface.

Today's geothermal activity is a link to past volcanism. A partially molten magma chamber, remnant of a cataclysmic volcanic explosion 600,000 years ago in central Yellowstone, supplies one of the ingredients, heat.

Hot water is the creative force of the terraces. Without it, terrace growth ceases and color vanishes. The source of the water flowing out of Yellowstone's geothermal features is rain and snow. Falling high on the slopes in and around Yellowstone, water seeps deep into the earth. This cold ground water is warmed by heat radiating from the magma chamber before rising back to the surface.

Hot water must be able to reach the earth's surface in relatively large volumes to erupt as a geyser or flow as a hot spring. In Yellowstone, many conduits remain from the collapse of the giant caldera; frequent earthquakes keep this underground "plumbing" system open. Even though Mammoth lies north of the caldera ring-fracture system, a fault trending north from Norris Geyser Basin, 21 miles (34 km) away, may connect Mammoth to the hot water of that system. A system of small fissures carries water upward to create approximately 50 hot springs in the Mammoth Hot Springs area.

Another necessary ingredient for terrace growth is the mineral calcium carbonate. Thick layers of sedimentary limestone, deposited millions of years ago by vast seas, lie beneath the Mammoth area. As ground water seeps slowly downward and laterally, it comes in contact with hot gases charged with carbon dioxide rising from the magma chamber. Some carbon dioxide is readily dissolved in the hot water to form a weak carbonic acid solution. This hot, acidic solution dissolves great quantities of limestone as it works up through the rock layers to the surface hot springs. Once exposed to the open air, some of the carbon dioxide escapes from solution. As this happens, limestone can no longer remain in solution. A solid mineral reforms and is deposited as the travertine that forms the terraces.

Terrace features can change rapidly in appearance. Don't be surprised to find that some of these features look very different if you visit in person.

## Mammoth Hot Springs

*6239ft* 1902m

0 0.1 Km 0.5
0 0.1 Mi 0.5

Mammoth Hot Springs Hotel
To Gardiner
Post Office
Amphitheater
Ice
Park Headquarters
Upper Terrace Loop Drive: no buses, RVs, or trailers; closed in winter
Upper Terraces Area
one-way
Lower Terraces Area
HISTORIC FORT YELLOWSTONE
Chapel
To North Entrance and Gardiner
Albright Visitor Center
To Old Faithful via Norris and Madison
**Road closed from early November to late April**
To Tower-Roosevelt

Liberty Cap was named in 1871 by the Hayden Survey party because of its marked resemblance to the peaked caps worn during the French Revolution. Its unusual formation was created by a hot spring whose plumbing remained open and in one location for a long time. Its internal pressure was sufficient to raise the water to a great height, allowing mineral deposits to build continuously for perhaps hundreds of years.

### Minerva Terrace

Minerva Spring is a favorite not only because of its wide range of bright colors but also for its ornate travertine formations. Since the 1890s, when records were first kept on the activity of Mammoth Hot Springs, Minerva has gone through both active and inactive periods. For several years in the early 1900s, it was completely dry, but by 1951 reports state that Minerva was again active.

During some cycles of activity, water discharge and mineral deposition have been so great that boardwalks have been buried beneath mounds of newly deposited travertine. Consequently, an elevated and movable boardwalk now spans the hill in the vicinity of Minerva. In recent years, hot spring activity has shifted dramatically from Minerva to other features on the Lower Terraces, and back again.

### Cleopatra Terrace

Due to confusion related to the intermittent nature of many of the springs in the Mammoth Area, the name Cleopatra Spring has been given to at least three different springs over the years. As the confusion developed the original Cleopatra Spring came to be called Minerva Spring

### Jupiter Terrace

Jupiter Terrace displays cycles of activity and has been dry since 1992. When active, its color and intricate terraces make Jupiter an appealing spring.

### Overlook

From the Overlook visitors have a great view of the Main Terrace and the surrounding mountains.

### Main Terrace

Looking across the Main Terrace the red-roofed buildings of historic Fort Yellowstone are visible in the distance. The fort was built and occupied by the U.S. Cavalry during their tour of duty here from 1886 to 1918.

NPS photo

### Canary Spring

So named for its bright yellow color, Canary owes its brilliance to sulfur dependent filamentous bacteria. The colors blend here in delicate tints on the creamy rock face.

### Prospect Terrace

This terrace was referred to as the "Eleventh Terrace" by Dr. Peale in 1872. In the late 1880s a U.S Geological Service party led by Arnold Hague gave it the name Prospect Terrace. While the reason for its receiving this name is uncertain, it is likely that it was named simply because of the spectacular "prospective" views it affords.

### New Highland Terrace

Tree skeletons, engulfed by travertine, stand as monuments to a landscape created in the 1950s. In recent years, activity has shifted to other locations.

### Orange Spring Mound

Bacteria and algae create the streaks of color on Orange Spring Mound. It is noticeably different from many of the other terrace formations nearby. Its large mounded shape is the result of very slow water flow and mineral deposition.

### Bath Lake

At the bottom of a short but very steep hill lies Bath Lake, named by some of the local residents in the 1880s. Through the years, this "lake" has been empty as often as full. Though soldiers in the late 1880s once bathed in this pool, we now know that such activity destroys fragile formations and may cause dramatic changes in the behavior of thermal features. Bathing in any of Yellowstone's thermal features is unsafe and unlawful.

### White Elephant Back Terrace

Here, a long ridge replaces the terrace shape seen so frequently elsewhere in Mammoth. Water flowing from a rift in the earth's crust has built the mounded formation, which someone thought looked like the vertebral column of an elephant. Portions of the Upper Terraces beyond White Elephant Back are very old and have been inactive for hundreds of years.

### Angel Terrace

Known both for the pure white formations and colorful microorganisms of its active periods, Angel Terrace is one of the area's most unpredictable features. For decades it was dry and crumbling. More recently, hot springs have been intermittently active in parts of the formation.

## Historic Highlights of the Mammoth Area

Due to its year-round access and comparatively mild winters, Mammoth has always been the headquarters for the park. The hot springs were an early commercialized attraction for those seeking relief from ailments in the mineral waters. Two historic events taking place at Mammoth were the Nez Perce flight in 1877 and President Teddy Roosevelt's visit in 1903.

### Archaeological Resources

There are several wickiups in the vicinity as well as the Bannock Indian trail, roasting pits, and the Obsidian Cliff quarry site. In 1959, a Clovis point that was dated to more than 10,000 years ago was found at the site of the old Gardiner post office.

### Fort Yellowstone

All of the red-roofed, many-chimneyed buildings in the Mammoth area are part of historic Fort Yellowstone. Beginning in 1886, after 14 years of poor civilian management of the park, the Cavalry was called upon to manage the park's resources and visitors. Because the Cavalry only expected to be here a short while, they built a temporary post near the base of the Terraces called Camp Sheridan. After five cold, harsh winters, they realized that their stay in the park was going to be longer than expected, so they built Fort Yellowstone, a permanent post.

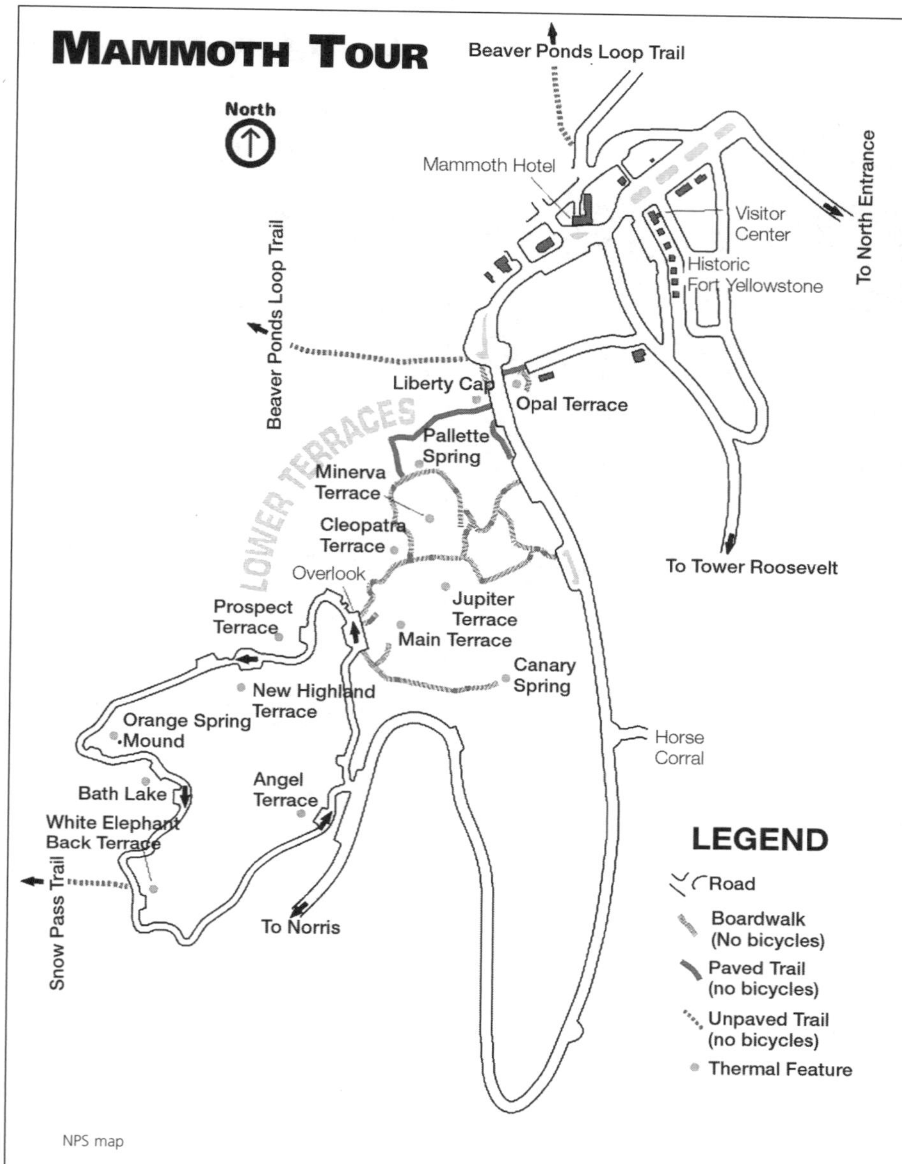

*Fort Yellowstone. NPS Photo.*

In 1891, the first building to be constructed was the guard house because it directly coincided with the Cavalry's mission—protection and management. There were three stages of construction at Fort Yellowstone. The first set of clapboard buildings were built in 1891, the second set in 1897 as the Fort expanded to a two-troop fort, and, finally, the stone buildings were built in 1909 making the fort's capacity 400 men or four troops. By 1916, the National Park Service was established, and the Cavalry gave control of Yellowstone back to the civilians. After a short time away, the Cavalry returned in 1917 and finished their duty completely in 1918. Since that time, historic Fort Yellowstone has been Yellowstone's headquarters.

### Roosevelt Arch

The first major entrance for Yellowstone was at the north boundary. Before 1903, trains would bring visitors to Cinnabar, Montana, which was a few miles northwest of Gardiner, Montana, and people would climb onto horse-drawn coaches there to enter the park. In 1903, the railway finally came to Gardiner, and people entered through an enormous stone archway. Robert Reamer, a famous architect in Yellowstone, designed the immense stone arch for coaches to travel through on their way into the park. At the time of the arch's construction, President Theodore Roosevelt was visiting the park. He consequently placed the cornerstone for the arch, which then took his name. The top of the Roosevelt Arch is inscribed with "For the benefit and enjoyment of the people," which is from the Organic Act of 1872, the enabling legislation for Yellowstone National Park.

### Obsidian Cliff

Obsidian Cliff is located 11 miles south of Mammoth Hot Springs and rises 150-200 feet above Obsidian Creek. The wayside exhibit here is one of the first of its kind in Yellowstone, built in the 1920s. Obsidian is created when lava cools so quickly that it does not have time to form crystals. A massive outcrop the size of Obsidian Cliff is quite rare because obsidian is usually found as small sections of other rock outcrops. Obsidian Cliff probably formed because the molten rock that erupted from the earth had very little water. The absence of water discourages the nucleation of atoms and causes faster cooling. Obsidian can be dated by measuring the hydration rate (absorption of water) of the rock. Because there are so few outcrops of obsidian, matching a projectile point to an outcrop is fairly easy.

For centuries, many Native Americans made their projectile points from obsidian. The rock itself is dark and glassy in appearance and, when broken, fractures into round pieces with sharp edges. Projectile points found as far away as Ohio have had their origin traced back to the Obsidian Cliff area. Tracking obsidian from Yellowstone to the Midwest indicates that the quality of obsidian found here was very good. In 1996, Obsidian Cliff was named a National Historic Landmark.

### Other Historic Sites

The list includes: the Engineer's office, designed in 1903 by Hiram Chittenden of the U.S. Army Corps of Engineers; Scottish Rite Chapel, 1913; Capitol Hill, former site of Superintendent Norris' headquarters blockhouse; Kite Hill cemetery, 1880s, containing graves of early settlers and employees; Reamer House, designed in 1908 by well-known architect Robert Reamer, an example of Prairie-style architecture; Haynes Picture Shop, photographic studio used by the Haynes family; old roads, railroad beds, bridges; and historic structures in Gardiner.

## Natural Highlights of the Norris Area

### Norris Geyser Basin

Norris Geyser Basin is the hottest, oldest, and most dynamic of Yellowstone's thermal areas. The highest temperature yet recorded in any geothermal area in Yellowstone was measured in a scientific drill hole at Norris: 459°F (237°C) just 1,087 feet (326 meters) below the surface! There are very few thermal features at Norris under the boiling point (199°F at this elevation). Norris shows evidence of having had thermal features for at least 115,000 years. The features in the basin change daily, with frequent disturbances from seismic activity and water fluctuations. The vast majority of the waters at Norris are acidic, including acid geysers which are very rare.

Steamboat Geyser, the tallest geyser in the world (300 to 400 feet) and Echinus Geyser (pH 3.5 or so) are the most popular features. The basin consists of three areas: Porcelain Basin, Back Basin, and One Hundred Springs Plain. Porcelain Basin is barren of trees and provides a sensory experience in sound, color, and smell; a 3/4 mile dirt and boardwalk trail accesses this area. Back Basin is more heavily wooded with features scattered throughout the area; a 1.5 mile trail of boardwalk and dirt encircles this part of the basin. One Hundred Springs Plain is an off-trail section of the Norris Geyser Basin that is very acidic, hol-

Yellowstone

*Bunsen Peak with Aspens Looking East from Fawn Pass Trail. NPS Photo*

low, and dangerous. Travel is discouraged without the guidance of knowledgeable staff members. The area was named after Philetus W. Norris, the second superintendent of Yellowstone, who provided the first detailed information about the thermal features.

### Roaring Mountain

Located just north of Norris on the Norris-Mammoth section of the Grand Loop Road, Roaring Mountain is a large, acidic thermal area (solfatara) that contains many steam vents (fumaroles). In the late 1800s and early 1900s, the number, size, and power of the fumaroles was much greater than today.

### Gibbon River

The Gibbon River flows from Wolf Lake through the Norris area and meets the Firehole River at Madison Junction to form the Madison River. Both cold and hot springs are responsible for the majority of the Gibbon's flow. Brook trout, brown trout, grayling, and rainbow trout find the Gibbon to their liking. The Gibbon River is fly-fishing only below Gibbon Falls.

### Virginia Cascades

A three-mile section of the old road takes visitors past 60-foot high Virginia Cascades. This cascading waterfall is formed by the very small (at that point) Gibbon River.

### Norris-Canyon Blowdown

This is a 22-mile swath of lodgepole pine blown down by wind-shear action in 1984. It was then burned during the North Fork fire in 1988. This is the site where a famous news anchor said, "Tonight, this is all that's left of Yellowstone." A wayside exhibit there tells the story.

## Geological Overview of the Norris Area

Norris sits on the intersection of three major faults. The Norris-Mammoth Corridor is a fault that runs from Norris north through Mammoth to the Gardiner, Montana, area. The Hebgen Lake fault runs from northwest of West Yellowstone, Montana, to Norris. This fault experienced an earthquake in 1959 that measured 7.4 on the Richter scale (sources vary on exact magnitude between 7.1 and 7.8). These two faults intersect with a ring fracture that resulted from the Yellowstone Caldera of 600,000 years ago. These faults are the primary reason that Norris Geyser Basin is so hot and dynamic. The Ragged Hills that lie between Back Basin and One Hundred Springs Plain are thermally altered glacial moraines. As glaciers receded, the underlying thermal features began to express themselves once again, melting remnants of the ice and causing masses of debris to be dumped. These debris piles were then altered by steam and hot water flowing through them.

Madison lies within the eroded stream channels cut through lava flows formed after the caldera eruption. The Gibbon Falls lies on the caldera boundary as does Virginia Cascades.

## Historic Highlights of the Norris Area

### The Norris Soldier Station

The Norris Soldier Station (Museum of the National Park Ranger) was an outlying station for soldiers to patrol and watch over Norris Geyser Basin. It was among the longest occupied stations in the park. A prior structure was built in 1886, replaced after fire in 1897, and modified in 1908. After the Army years, the building was used as a Ranger Station and residence until the 1959 earthquake caused structural damage. The building was restored in 1991.

### The Norris Geyser Basin Museum

The Norris Geyser Basin Museum is one of the park's original trailside museums built in 1929-30. It has always been a museum. It is an outstanding example of stone-and-log architecture.

### Archeological Resources

Digs by the Midwest Archaeological Center in Norris and Madison campgrounds reveal that people have camped in these areas for at least 10,000 years. Campfire remnants, obsidian flakes, and chips and bone fragments show that these campgrounds have always been favorites! Other such sites abound throughout the Norris area, particularly along the Solfatara Trail that connects Norris Campground with the Obsidian Cliff area.

## World's Tallest Geyser Erupts

**With a thunderous roar, the world's** tallest geyser erupted on the morning of May 2, 2000 for the first time in more than eight years. Steamboat—in Norris Geyser Basin—blasted water 300 feet (30 stories!) into the air for about a half hour, then settled into a steam phase that reached hundreds more feet into the sky. During a major eruption, Steamboat ejects several hundred thousand gallons of water. Much of the water falls to the slope above the geyser and collects in torrents of mud, sand, and rock that rush back into the vent and are blown back out again and again. Water rushes downhill, carving wide gullies and washing away trees.

Most of Steamboat's power comes from the steam that follows the eruption of water. Geysers release energy via steam and hot water. Some geysers release copious amounts of water but run out of energy before they run out of water. Steamboat, on the other hand, has so much energy that it cannot be dissipated by hot water alone and thus much steam is released.

After its massive eruption on May 2, Steamboat roared with steam for hours. The clouds billowed and condensed, falling as mist that shifted with the breeze. Water dripped off hoods and hats, benches and signs. People looked straight up and still could not see the top of the steam.

Steamboat's massive eruptions were first recorded by Park Superintendent P.W. Norris:

*"The new crater which burst forth in the Norris Geyser Plateau, with such upturning and hurling of rocks and trees, August 11, 1878, ... seems this year to have settled down to business as a very powerful flowing geyser, having in common with many others, a double period of eruption, one some 30 feet high about each half hour, and another 100 feet and long continued, each 6 or 7 days, and is doubtless still changing."*

Will Steamboat blow again? No one knows. Even so, it's still an impressive feature. The summer of 2000, Steamboat was splashing water higher than most of the park's geysers. So stop by Norris Geyser Basin and check out Steamboat. As Yellowstone's geyser observers like to say, "Go, Steamboat, Go!"

## Norris Tour

Norris Geyser Basin is the hottest and most changeable thermal area in Yellowstone. We will explore many of the features you would see if you

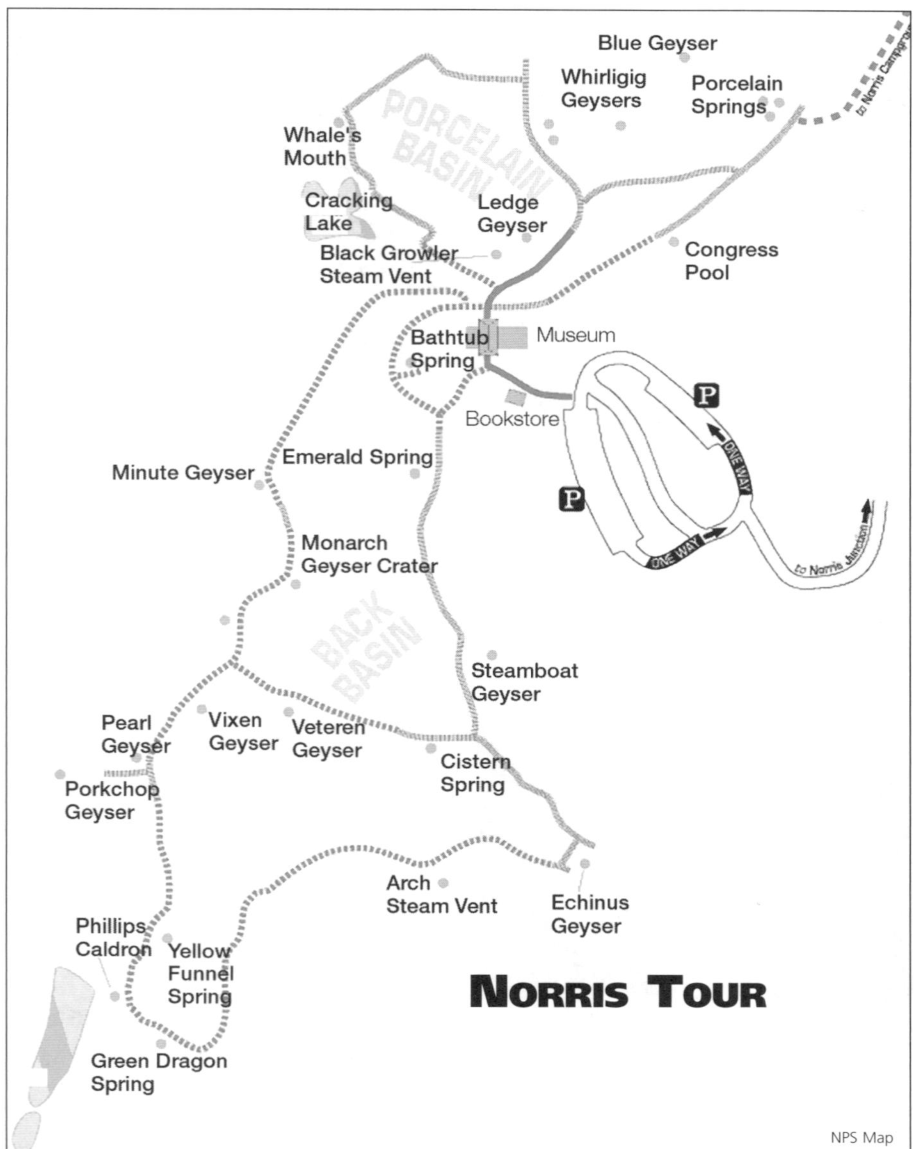

NPS Map

walked the 2 1/4 miles (3.6 km) of trails. Discover the location of the tallest active geyser, colorful hot springs, and microscopic life in one of the most extreme environments on earth.

Our tour starts at the Norris Museum. The museum houses exhibits relating to the origins of the geothermal features found at the basin. Two loop trails leave from here. They provide a safe route for viewing the Porcelain Basin and Back Basin.

Rainbow Colors, hissing steam, and pungent odors combine to create an experience unique in Yellowstone. Porcelain Basin is open terrain with hundreds of densely packed geothermal features; in contrast, Back Basin is forested and its features are more scattered and isolated.

## Porcelain Basin

Parts of the whitish rock-sheet before you pulsate from the pressure of steam and boiling water beneath them. A number of geysers and other features here have been born suddenly in small hydrothermal explosions. Some features are ephemeral, their activity lasting a few hours, days, or weeks. A few others have become relatively permanent fixtures in the scene.

NPS photo

## Congress Pool

A visit most times of the year will show a Congress Pool that appears pale blue in color. Due to the variable nature of Norris features it is possible to see the same pool looking muddy and boiling violently.

At Norris, "disturbances" of geothermal activity take place annually. No other thermal area in Yellowstone exhibits this phenomenon. Mysteriously features throughout the Norris area undergo dramatic behavioral changes literally overnight. Clear pools become muddy and boil violently, and some temporarily become geysers. These "disturbances" often occur in late summer and early fall but have been observed throughout the year.

Features that typically behave as geysers may display altered eruption cycles or temporarily cease erupting. New features may be created during a disturbance, although they seldom remain long-term attractions at the basin. Disturbances tend to last from a few days to more than a week. Gradually, most features revert to "normal" activity.

Why this happens is not fully understood. Further study will no doubt yield new clues that will help unravel the mystery of this phenomenon and lead to a greater understanding of the earth's hidden geologic forces.

## Black Growler Steam Vent

The hottest of Yellowstone's geothermal features are steam vents (fumaroles). Black Growler Steam Vent, on the hillside in front of you, has measured 199 to 280 degrees F (93 to 138 degrees C). A plentiful water supply would help cool these features; however, steam vents are usually found on hillsides or higher ground, above the basin's water supply. They rapidly boil away what little water they contain, releasing steam and other gases forcefully from underground.

NPS photo

## Ledge Geyser

Ledge is the second largest geyser in the Norris Geyser Basin, capable of shooting water 125 feet into the air. Because it erupts at an angle, however, the water will sometimes reach the ground 220 feet away. It has at times in the past erupted at regular intervals of 14 hours. The geyser became inactive between 1979 and late 1993. It erupted on a fairly regular cycle of every four to six days in 1994 and 1995.

## Hot Springs of Porcelain Basin

The milky color of the mineral deposited here inspired the naming of Porcelain Basin. The mineral, siliceous sinter, is brought to the surface by hot water and forms a sinter "sheet" over this flat area as the water flows across the ground and the mineral settles out. This is the fastest changing area in Norris Geyser Basin, and siliceous sinter is one of the agents of change. If the mineral seals off a hot spring or geyser by accumulating in its vent, the hot, pressurized water may flow underground to another weak area and blow through it.

Siliceous sinter is also called geyserite. Deposits usually accumulate very slowly, less than one inch (2.5cm) per century, and form the geyser cones and mounds seen in most geyser basins.

## Colorful Water

Many of Norris' features release acidic water.

Amazingly living organisms thrive even in the extreme environments of these acid hot springs! The overflow channels of geysers and hot springs are often brightly colored with minerals and microscopic life forms. Hardy, microscopic, lime-green Cyanidium algae thrives in these warm acid waters. Orange cyanobacteria may be found in the runoff streams in Porcelain Basin. From a distance these bacteria look like rusty, iron-rich mineral deposits.

These and other microscopic life forms are links to the emergence of life on earth billions of years ago. They are also a focus of research in the fields of medicine and criminal investigation. New tools for use in such complex areas as AIDS research and DNA "fingerprinting" have been developed from the microscopic thermal organisms found in Yellowstone's hot springs.

### Blue Geyser

Blue Geyser was called Iris Spring in 1886. Due to a misread map label, in 1904 the feature was inadvertently given its current name. It was observed to erupt to heights of over 60 feet from 1993 to 1996. It became almost dormant in 1997 and has remained very quiet ever since. Blue Geyser's last observed eruption was in February of 1997.

### Whirligig Geysers

Little Whirligig got its name because of its close proximity to Whirligig Geyser. Whirligig was so named because while erupting its water swirls in its crater. The orange-yellow iron oxide deposits around Little Whirligig make it one of the most colorful features in Porcelain Basin. It has been dormant for several years.

### Cistern Spring

Cistern Spring and Steamboat Geyser are linked underground. During a major eruption of Steamboat, the water in Cistern Spring's pool drains. Normally Cistern is a beautiful blue pool from which water continually overflows. It is quite creative, depositing as much as 1/2 inch (12mm) of grayish sinter each year. By comparison Old Faithful Geyser and many other thermal features may build at the rate of 1/2 to 1 inch (12–25mm) per century. Cistern Spring's influence expands throughout the lodgepole pine forest below. This forest has been slowly flooded with silica rich water since 1965. The pioneering lodgepole pine forest at Norris is in constant flux, retreating here and in other areas of increasing heat while advancing in places of diminished thermal activity.

### Emerald Spring

A hot spring's color often indicates the presence of minerals. In a clear blue pool, the water is absorbing all colors of sunlight except one, blue, which is reflected back to our eyes. Here in Emerald Spring's pool, another factor joins with light refraction to give this spring its color. The 27-foot (8 meter) deep pool is lined with yellow sulfur deposits. The yellow color from the sulfur combines with the reflected blue light, making the hot spring appear a magnificent emerald green.

Hot spring water can dissolve and transport sulfur from underground. The mineral can deposit and crystallize at the earth's surface, sometimes in hot spring pools.

### Echinus Geyser

Echinus (e-KI-nus) Geyser was a perennial crowd-pleaser which typically erupted every 35 to 75 minutes. Late in 1998 this geyser altered its interval and now erupts only a few times per day at best. Its pool fills gradually with water; then suddenly, bursts of steam and water explode 40 to 60 feet (12 to 18 m) skyward. Eruptions usually last about 4 minutes but in the past major eruptions have lasted as long as 118 minutes. The major eruptions were believed to be caused by a secondary water source which has mysteriously vanished. There has not been a major eruption in 3 years. In late 1998 Echinus' performance diminished and became erratic. As of mid-1999 its eruptions remain unpredictable.

Echinus is the largest acid-water geyser known. Its waters are almost as acidic as vinegar with a pH ranging from 3.3 to 3.6 . Acid geysers are extremely rare with the majority of the planet's total being found here at Norris Geyser Basin.

NPS photo

### Steamboat Geyser

The world's tallest active geyser, Steamboat can erupt to more than 300 feet (90m), showering viewers with its mineral-rich waters. For hours following its rare 3 to 40 minute major eruptions, Steamboat thunders with powerful jets of steam. As befitting such an awesome event, full eruptions are entirely unpredictable. Recently, Steamboat had one major eruption on May 2, 2000. More commonly, Steamboat has minor eruptions and ejects water in frequent bursts of 10 to 40 feet.

### Porkchop Geyser

Dramatic behavioral changes have characterized Porkchop Geyser during the last decade. Once a small hot spring that occasionally erupted, Porkchop Geyser became a continuous spouter in the spring of 1985. The force of the spray caused a roar that could be heard at the museum over 660 yards (603m) away. On September 5, 1989, Porkchop Geyser exploded. Rocks surrounding the old vent were upended and some were thrown more than 216 feet (66m) from the feature. Porkchop Geyser is now a gently rolling hot spring.

### Green Dragon Spring

Except on warm summer afternoons, steam frequently fills the cavern of this intriguing hot spring. Visitors must wait patiently for a glimpse of the sulfur-lined cave and boiling green water.

*Green Dragon Spring - NPS photo*

### Whale's Mouth

This hot spring was named by a park naturalist in 1967 because its shape "resembles the mouth and gullet of a giant fish".

### Crackling Lake

The name of this thermal feature was proposed by Ed Leigh in 1967 because of popping sounds from nearby springs on its southern shore. It was formerly simply called Spring #39 in Dr. Peale's publication entitled Gibbon Geyser Basin.

### Minute Geyser

Minute Geyser's eruptions have changed dramatically. Its larger west vent is clogged with rocks tossed in by early visitors when the park's main road was near this trail and passed within 70 feet of the geyser. Minute once erupted every 60 seconds, sometimes to heights of 40 to 50 feet (12 to 15 meters). Eruptions now are irregular and originate from its smaller east vent. Removal of the west vent's mineral-cemented rocks would require the use of heavy equipment resulting in severe damage.

Minute Geyser's destruction stands today as a sad reminder of thoughtless behavior on the part of some visitors.

## Natural Highlights of the Old Faithful Area

### The Upper Geyser Basin

Yellowstone, as a whole, possesses close to 60 percent of the world's geysers. The Upper Geyser Basin is home to the largest numbers of this fragile feature found in the park. Within one square mile there are at least 150 of these hydrothermal wonders. Of this remarkable number, only five major geysers are predicted regularly by the naturalist staff. They are Castle, Grand, Daisy, Riverside, and Old Faithful. There are many frequent, smaller geysers to be seen and marveled at in this basin as well as numerous hot springs and one recently developed mudpot (if it lasts).

### Lower Geyser Basin

This large area of hydrothermal activity can be viewed by foot along the boardwalk trail at Fountain Paint Pots and by car along the three mile Firehole Lake Drive. The latter is a one-way drive where you will find the sixth geyser predicted by the Old Faithful staff: Great Fountain. Its splashy eruptions send jets of diamond droplets bursting 100-200 feet in the air, while waves of water cascade down the raised terraces. Patience is a virtue with this twice-a-day geyser, as the predictions allow a 2 hour +/- window of opportunity.

Fountain Flats Drive departs the Grand Loop Road just south of the Nez Perce picnic area and follows along the Firehole River to a trailhead 1.5

# Fire: a Natural Force

**Fire, climate, erosion, and a vast assortment** of life forms ranging from microbes to insects to mammals, including humans, have all played roles in the creation of the vegetative landscape of Yellowstone. Vegetation here has adapted to fire and, in some cases, may be dependent on it.

Ecologists have known for many years that wildfire is essential to the evolution of a natural setting. Records kept in Yellowstone since 1931 show that lightning starts an average of 22 fires each year. Large-scale fires burn through the conifer forests of the Yellowstone plateau every 250 to 400 years and take place in the low-elevation grass-lands on average every 25 to 60 years. When fires are, suppressed the habitat gradually becomes less diverse. This, in turn, affects the variety of animals able to successfully inhabit a particular area.

In the first few decades after Yellowstone was established as the world's first national park in 1872, no effective fire fighting was done. Then, during the Army administration of Yellowstone (1886-1918), fire suppression occurred most frequently on the grass lands of the northern range. Throughout the rest of the park, which is largely covered by a lodgepole pine forest, reliable and consistent fire suppression began with the era of modern airborne firefighting techniques of the past 30 to 40 years.

In natural areas such as Yellowstone National Park, preserving a state of wildness is a primary goal of management. In 1972, Yellowstone was one of several national parks that initiated programs to allow some naturally caused fires to burn. By 1988, scientists had learned much about the occurrence and behavior of fire. Tens of thousands of lightning strikes simply fizzled out with no acreage burned. While 140 lightning strikes produced fires, most burned only a small area. Eighty percent of the lightning starts in this period went out by themselves.

## The Historic Fires of 1988

The summer of 1988 was the driest on record in Yellowstone. Though substantial precipitation fell during April and May, practically no rain fell in June, July, or August—an event previously unrecorded in the park's 112-year written record of weather conditions. In early summer, about 20 lightning-caused fires had been allowed to burn, and eleven of these fires burned themselves out.

But fires that continued to burn into the extremely dry weeks of late June and July met dramatically changed conditions. By late July, moisture content of grasses and small branches had dropped as low as 2 or 3 percent, and downed trees measured at 7 percent (kiln-dried lumber is 12 percent). After July 15, no new natural fires were allowed to burn and after July 21, all fires were fought.

The extreme weather conditions and heavy, dry accumulations of "fuel' (vegetation of various types) presented even the most skilled professional fire fighters with conditions rarely observed. Typical firefighting techniques were frequently ineffective because fires spread long distances by "spotting," a phenomenon in which wind carries embers from the tops of 200-foot flames far across unburned forest to start spot fires well ahead of the main fire. Fires routinely jumped barriers that normally stopped them such as rivers, roads, and major topographic features such as the Grand Canyon of the Yellowstone River. Fires advanced rapidly, making frontal attacks dangerous and impossible.

By the last week of September, about 50 lightning-caused fires had occurred in the park, 8 of which were still burning. More than $120,000,000 had been spent on fire control efforts in the greater Yellowstone area, and most major park developments—and a few surrounding communities—had been evacuated at least once as fire approached within a few miles of them. At the operation's peak, 9,000 firefighters (including Army and Marine units), more than 100 fire engines, and dozens of helicopters participated in the complex effort to control the fires and protect developments. It was the largest such cooperative effort ever undertaken in the United States.

## Changes Since 1988

Changes in both the natural landscape of Yellowstone and the management of naturally-caused fires have taken place since the historic fires of 1988. Scientists knew that the vegetative cover of Yellowstone was, in large part, the product of fires that had burned for millennia before the arrival of European humans. The growth of new plants and entire plant communities began immediately. In most places, plant growth is unusually lush because minerals and other nutrients are released by fire into the soil and because increased light stimulates growth in what was previously shaded forest floor.

These fires did not annihilate all life in their paths. Burning at a variety of temperatures, sometimes as ground fires, sometimes as crown fires (burning through treetops), fires killed many lodgepole pines and other trees but did not kill most other plants. Instead, they burned off the tops, leaving roots to regenerate. The fires created a mosaic of burns, partial burns, and unburned areas that provide new habitats for plants and animals.

Yellowstone National Park is one of the greatest living laboratories on the planet. Here, we can observe the effects of fire and other natural forces and processes, and learn from them. And what we learn is that change is constant in the natural world, flowing from the past into the present—continuing into the future to outcomes both predictable and mysterious,

## Facts About the Fires of 1988

### Why They Occurred

Conditions occurred that were never before seen in the history of Yellowstone: extended drought & high winds.

#### Statistics

- 9 fires caused by humans
- 42 fires caused by lightning
- 36% of the park burned (793,880 acres)
- Fires begun outside of the park burned more than half of the total acreage
- About 400 large mammals, primarily elk, perished
- $120 million spent fighting the fires
- 25,000 people employed in these efforts

#### Fighting the Fires

- Until July 21, naturally-caused fires allowed to burn.
- After that, all fires fought, regardless of their cause.
- Largest fire-fighting effort in the history of the U.S.
- Effort saved human life and property, but probably had little impact on the fires themselves.
- Rain and snow finally stopped the advance of the fires.

#### After the Fires

- Enormous public controversy occurred.
- Several high-level task forces formed to review NPS fire policies.
- Their recommendations reaffirmed the importance of natural fire in an ecosystem.
- They recommended additional guidelines be established to manage natural fire in Yellowstone.

miles distant. From there, the Fountain Freight Road hiking/biking trail continues along the old roadbed giving hikers access to the Sentinel Meadows Trail and the Fairy Falls Trail. Also along this path is the only handicapped-accessible backcountry site in the Old Faithful district at Goose Lake.

### Midway Geyser Basin

This geyser basin, though small in size compared to its companions along the Firehole River, holds large wonders for the visitor. Excelsior Geyser reveals a gaping crater 200 x 300 feet with a constant discharge of more than 4,000 gallons of water per minute into the Firehole River. Also in this surprising basin is Yellowstone's largest hot springs, Grand Prismatic Spring. This feature is 370 feet in diameter and more than 121 feet in depth.

### Lone Star Geyser Basin

This backcountry geyser basin is easily reached by a 5-mile roundtrip hike from the trailhead south of Old Faithful. Lone Star Geyser erupts about every three hours. There is a logbook, located in a cache near the geyser, for observations of geyser times and types of eruptions.

### Shoshone Geyser Basin

Shoshone Geyser Basin is reached by a 17-mile roundtrip hike that crosses the Continental Divide at Grant's Pass. This basin has no boardwalks, and extreme caution should be exercised when travelling through it. Trails in the basin must be used. Remote thermal areas, such as this, should be approached with respect, knowledge, and care. Be sure to emphasize personal safety and resource protection when entering a backcountry basin.

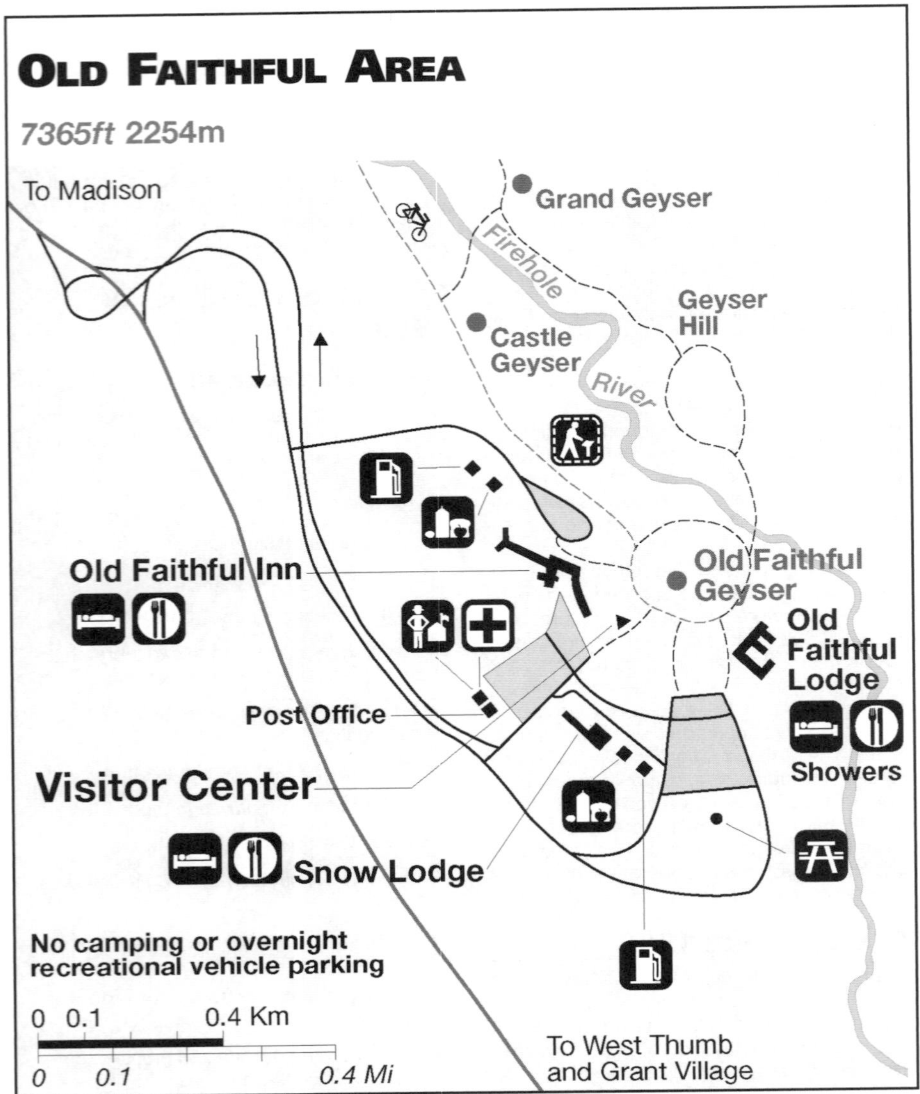


## Firehole River

The river derives its name from the steam (which they thought was smoke from fires) witnessed by early trappers to the area. Their term for a mountain valley was "hole," and the designation was born. The Firehole River boasts a world-famous reputation for challenging fly-fishing. Brown, rainbow, and brook trout give the angler a wary target in this stream.

## Craig Pass/Isa Lake

Both names are used to describe the same location seven miles south of Old Faithful on the Grand Loop Road. At 8,262 feet along the Continental Divide, Isa Lake is a uniquely confusing feature. During spring runoff, it drains into both the Atlantic and Pacific Oceans at the same time! (And backwards, too!) The west side of the lake flows into the Firehole drainage and, eventually, the Atlantic throughout the year. The east side, during spring, flows toward the Snake River drainage and the Pacific.

## Waterfall

Kepler Cascades is the most easily reached waterfall in the district. A marked pullout just south of Old Faithful and a short walk from the car offers the visitor easy access to view this 125-foot cascade.

# Geological Overview of the Old Faithful Area

Evidence of the geological forces that have shaped Yellowstone are found in abundance in this district. The hills surrounding Old Faithful and the Upper Geyser Basin are reminders of Quaternary rhyolitic lava flows. These flows, occurring long after the catastrophic eruption of 600,000 years ago, flowed across the landscape like stiff mounds of bread dough due to their high silica content.

Evidence of glacial activity is common, and it is one of the keys that allows geysers to exist. Glacier till deposits underlie the geyser basins providing storage areas for the water used in eruptions. Many landforms, such as Porcupine Hills north of Fountain Flats, are comprised of glacial gravel and are reminders that as recently as 13,000 years ago, this area was buried under ice.

Signs of the forces of erosion can be seen everywhere, from runoff channels carved across the sinter in the geyser basins to the drainage created by the Firehole River.

Mountain building is evident as you drive south of Old Faithful, toward Craig Pass. Here the Rocky Mountains reach a height of 8,262 feet, dividing the country into two distinct watersheds.

Yellowstone is a vast land containing a landscape that is continually being shaped by geological forces.

# Historic Highlights of the Old Faithful Area

## Old Faithful Historic District

This designation applies to the developed area adjacent to Old Faithful Geyser, which contains many historic structures.

NPS photo

## Old Faithful Inn

Built during the winter of 1903-04, the Old Faithful Inn was designed by Robert C. Reamer, who wanted the asymmetry of the building to reflect the chaos of nature. The lobby of the hotel features a 65-foot ceiling, a massive rhyolite fireplace, and railings made of contorted lodgepole pine. Wings were added to the hotel in 1915 and 1927, and today there are 327 rooms available to guests in this National Historic Landmark.

*The lobby of the Old Faithful Inn. NPS photo*

## Old Faithful Lodge

Unlike the Inn, the current Old Faithful Lodge is a result of numerous changes dating back to the early days of tent camps provided by companies like Shaw and Powell Camping Company and Wylie Permanent Camping Company. These camps were erected throughout the park and offered shelter before hotels and lodges were built. Both companies had facilities at Old Faithful. By 1917, auto traffic into the park was increasing, and it was decided that some camps could be eliminated. Yellowstone Park Camping Company emerged and operated on the old site of the Shaw and Powell camp, the present day site of the Lodge. In 1918, a laundry was built on the site and construction continued on the facility until 1928 when the Lodge reached its present configuration.

Cabin-style accommodations are available at Old Faithful Lodge. Often confused with the other two hotels in the area, Old Faithful Lodge houses a cafeteria, gift shop, coffee shop, and the front desk where guests check in.

### Lower Hamilton Store

Built in 1897, this is the oldest structure in the Old Faithful area still in use. The "knotty pine" porch is a popular resting place for visitors, providing a great view of Geyser Hill. (The oldest building at Old Faithful was built as a photo studio in 1897 for F. Jay Haynes. Originally located 700 feet southwest of Beehive Geyser and about 350 feet northwest of the front of the Old Faithful Inn, it now stands near the intersection of the Grand Loop Road and the fire lane, near the crosswalk.)

### Nez Perce Creek Wayside

This exhibit tells the story of the flight of the Nez Perce through Yellowstone in 1877. A band of 700 men, women, and children entered the park on the evening of August 23rd, fleeing 600 Army regulars commanded by General O.O. Howard. The Nez Perce had been told to leave their homeland and move to a reservation. They fled their ancestral home in the Wallowa Valley in northeastern Oregon on June 17, 1877, and by the time they entered the park, several battles, including a fight at Big Hole (another NPS site), had occurred.

During the two weeks they were in the park, the Nez Perce bumped into all 25 known people visiting the new park at that time, some more than once. Camps were plundered, hostages taken, and several people were killed or wounded.

After leaving the park, the Nez Perce tried reaching the Canadian border but were stopped by General Nelson Miles, who had reinforced General Howard's command. Some Nez Perce were able to slip into Canada, but the remaining 350 tribal members led by Chief Joseph surrendered to General Miles. This is where Chief Joseph gave his famous speech, "I will fight no more forever." The 1,700-mile flight that included Yellowstone National Park had come to an end. Today, Nez Perce Creek and the nearby wayside exhibit are reminders of their visit.

### Howard Eaton Trail

Named for an early park outfitter and guide, the Howard Eaton Trail paralleled the Grand Loop Road in many places. Remnants of this old horse trail are maintained and used by hikers today. Here in the Old Faithful District, the trail provides a less traveled route to Lone Star Geyser from the developed area.

## Old Faithful Tour

The largest concentration of geysers in the world is in the Upper Geyser Basin. Several of the more prominent geysers and hot springs are included on this tour with information concerning their eruption patterns, names, and relationships with other geothermal features.

### Old Faithful Geyser

Old Faithful erupts more frequently than any of the other big geysers, although it is not the largest or most regular geyser in the park. Its average interval between eruptions is about 76 minutes, varying from 45–110 minutes. An eruption lasts 1 1/2 to 5 minutes, expels 3,700–8,400 gallons (14,000–32,000 liters) of boiling water, and reaches heights of 106–184 feet (30–55m). It was named for its consistent performance by members of the Washburn Expedition in 1870. Although its average interval has lengthened through the years (due to earthquakes and vandalism), Old Faithful is still as spectacular and predictable as it was a century ago.

The largest active geyser in the world is Steamboat Geyser in the Norris Geyser Basin.

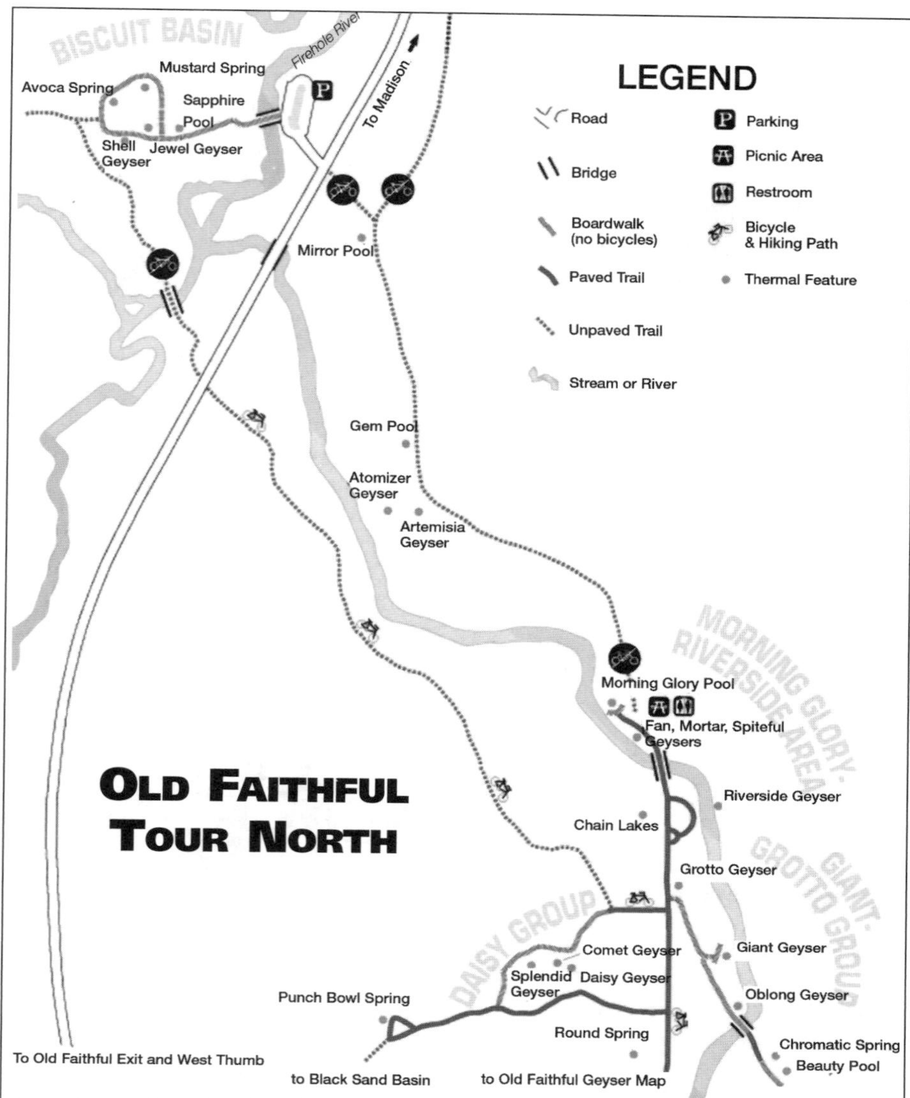

NPS photo

### Solitary Geyser

When Yellowstone National Park was established this feature was known as Solitary Spring and it did not erupt. Water was diverted from the spring to a swimming pool which lowered the water level sufficiently to start eruptions. Even though the diversion channel was filled and the water returned to its original level in the late 1940s, this thermal feature has not returned to its stable hot spring condition. A temporary change in the water level has led to a long-term change in the nature of this portion of the geyser basin illustrating the delicate nature of these geothermal systems. Most eruptions today occur every 4–8 minutes and last about 1 minute. They are typically less than 6 ft in height.*

**This information was found in the book The Geysers of Yellowstone, by: T. Scott Bryan.*

### Giantess Geyser

Infrequent but violent eruptions characterize Giantess Geyser. This fountain-type geyser erupts in several bursts 100–200 ft (30–60m) high. Eruptions generally occur 2–6 times a year. The surrounding area may shake from underground steam explosions just before the initial water and/or steam eruptions. Eruptions may occur

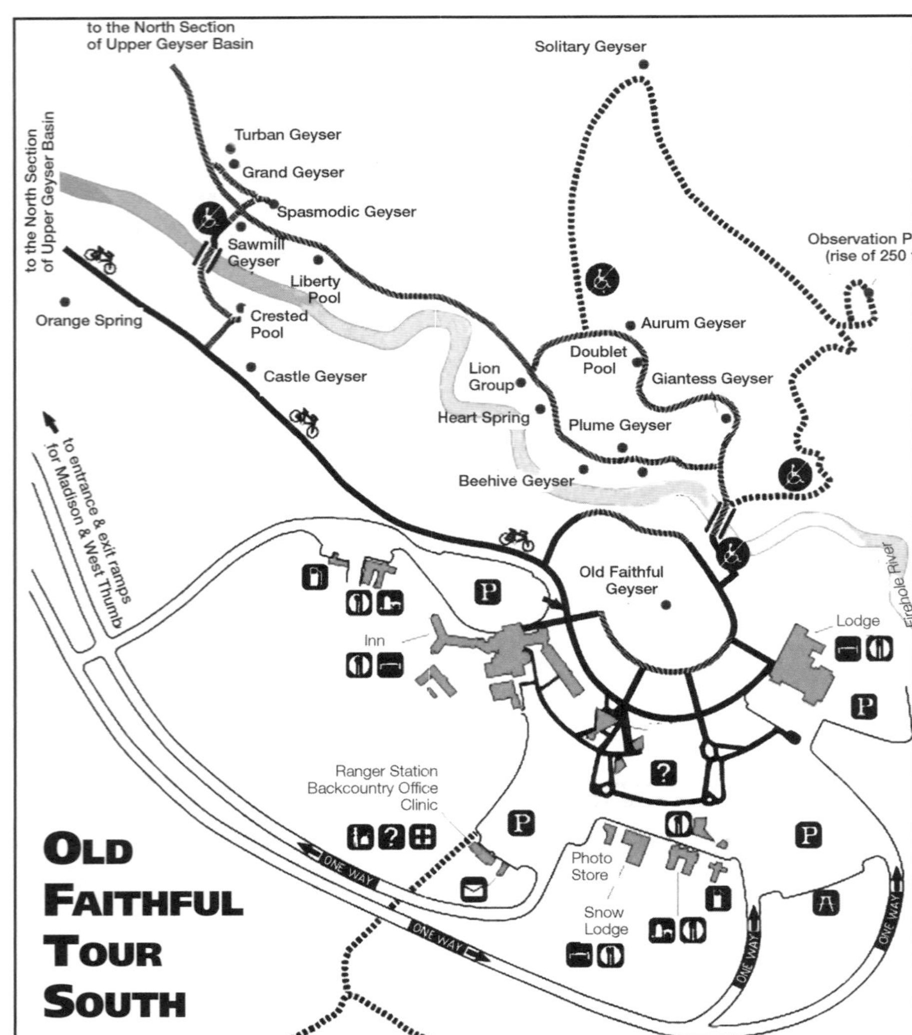


twice hourly and continue for 12–43 hours.

## Doublet Pool

Especially striking for its complex series of ledges, elaborate border ornamentation, and deep blue waters, Doublet Pool is an attractive subject for photographers. Occasionally, Doublet produces periodic vibrations underfoot, surface wave motion, and audible thumping. This is most likely the result of collapsing gas and steam bubbles deep underground.

## View from Observation Point

Climbing the hill to Observation Point allows you to take in one of the best views of the Upper Geyser Basin. From this vantage point 250 ft above Old Faithful the panorama is spectacular.

## Plume Geyser

Plume Geyser erupts about every 20 minutes. Its 3–5 quick bursts can reach heights of 25 ft (8m). This is a relatively young geyser that came into existence when a steam explosion created its vent in 1922.

## Beehive Geyser

Beehive Geyser is magnificent. Eruptions usually occur twice each day with displays lasting 4–5 minutes. During an eruption, the narrow cone acts like a nozzle, projecting the water column to heights of 130–190 ft (40–55m).

## The Lion Group

The Lion Group consists of four geysers: Lion, Lioness, Big Cub, and Little Cub, which are all connected underground. Of these Lion has the largest cone and eruptions. Active phases normally occur each day. Eruptions of Lion Geyser last 1–7 minutes and are often preceded by sudden gushes of steam and a deep roaring sound, hence the name Lion.

## Heart Spring

Heart Spring was named by park geologist George Marler in or about 1959 apparently because its shape resembles a human heart. It is 7-1/2 by 10 feet at the surface and 15 feet deep.

## Sawmill Geyser

Sawmill Geyser's eruptions are highly variable, some lasting only 9 minutes while others may last over 4 hours. The typical interval between eruptions is 1–3 hours. Overall it is erupting about 30% of the time. Sawmill received its name because water spins in its crater as it erupts looking somewhat like the rotating circular blade of a lumber mill.

## Grand Geyser

An eruption of Grand Geyser, the tallest predictable geyser in the world, occurs every 7–15 hours. A classic fountain geyser, Grand erupts from a large pool with powerful bursts rather than a steady column like Old Faithful. An average eruption lasts 9–12 minutes and consists of 1–4 bursts, sometimes reaching 200 feet (60m).

## Crested Pool

Crested pool is 42 feet deep and is constantly superheated. At times the temperature drops to a mere simmer but it occasionally comes to a full rolling boil as well. When boiling violently the water may dome to heights of 8–10 feet.

NPS photo

## Castle Geyser

Castle Geyser has the largest cone and may be the oldest of all geysers in the basin. Its eruption pattern has changed considerably throughout its recorded history. Castle is currently erupting about every 10–12 hours. A water eruption frequently reaches 90 feet (27m) and lasts about 20 minutes. The water phase is followed by a noisy steam phase lasting 30–40 minutes.

## Beauty Pool

Truly deserving its name, Beauty Pool is noted for its rich, blue water framed by rainbow-colored bacteria. It's plumbing system is closely related to the neighboring Chromatic Spring. Click "Next Stop" below for more details.

## Chromatic Spring

Chromatic Spring is closely related to Beauty Pool. During periodic energy shifts the level of one spring descends while the other rises and overflows. The time interval between shifts has ranged from a few weeks to several years.

## Giant Geyser

Giant Geyser was dormant for many years after the energy shift in 1955. Since then, it has slowly become active again. During 1997, its eruptions occurred every 3–10 days. This spectacular geyser's eruptions last about an hour and can reach heights of 180–250 feet (55–76m). During eruptions small geysers nearby may also erupt.

## Comet Geyser

Comet Geyser is a member of the Daisy Group

# Geothermal Features and How They Work

With half of the earth's geothermal features, Yellowstone holds the planet's most diverse and intact collection of geysers, hot springs, mudpots, and fumaroles. Its more than 300 geysers make up two thirds of all those found on earth. Combine this with more than 10,000 thermal features comprised of brilliantly colored hot springs, bubbling mudpots, and steaming fumaroles, and you have a place like no other. Geyserland, fairyland, wonderland—through the years, all have been used to describe the natural wonder and magic of this unique park that contains more geothermal features than any other place on earth.

Yellowstone's vast collection of thermal features provides a constant reminder of the park's recent volcanic past. Indeed, the caldera provides the setting that allows such features as Old Faithful to exist and to exist in such great concentrations.

## Hot Springs and How They Work

In the high mountains surrounding the Yellowstone Plateau, water falls as snow or rain and slowly percolates through layers of porous rock, finding its way through cracks and fissures in the earth's crust created by the ring fracturing and collapse of the caldera. Sinking to a depth of nearly 10,000 feet, this cold water comes into contact with the hot rocks associated with the shallow magma chamber beneath the surface. As the water is heated, its temperatures rise well above the boiling point to become superheated. This superheated water, however, remains in a liquid state due to the great pressure and weight pushing down on it from overlying rock and water. The result is something akin to a giant pressure cooker, with water temperatures in excess of 400°F.

The highly energized water is less dense than the colder, heavier water sinking around it. This creates convection currents that allow the lighter, more buoyant, superheated water to begin its slow, arduous journey back toward the surface through rhyolitic lava flows, following the cracks, fissures, and weak areas of the earth's crust. Rhyolite is essential to geysers because it contains an abundance of silica, the mineral from which glass is made. As the hot water travels through this "natural plumbing system," the high temperatures dissolve some of the silica in the rhyolite, yielding a solution of silica within the water.

At the surface, these silica-laden waters form a rock called geyserite, or sinter, creating the massive geyser cones; the scalloped edges of hot springs; and the expansive, light- colored, barren landscape characteristic of geyser basins. While in solution underground, some of this silica deposits as geyserite on the walls of the plumbing system forming a pressure-tight seal, locking in the hot water and creating a system that can withstand the great pressure needed to produce a geyser.

With the rise of superheated water through this complex plumbing system, the immense pressure exerted over the water drops as it nears the surface. The heat energy, if released in a slow steady manner, gives rise to a hot spring, the most abundant and colorful thermal feature in the park. Hot springs with names like Morning Glory, Grand Prismatic, Abyss, Emerald, and Sapphire, glisten like jewels in a host of colors across the park's harsh volcanic plain.

## Mudpots & How They Work

Where hot water is limited and hydrogen sulfide gas is present (emitting the "rotten egg" smell common to thermal areas), sulfuric acid is generated. The acid dissolves the surrounding rock into fine particles of silica and clay that mix with what little water there is to form the seething and bubbling mudpots. The sights, sounds, and smells of areas like Artist and Fountain paint pots and Mud Volcano make these curious features some of the most memorable in the park.

## Fumeroles (Steam Vents) and How They Work

Fumaroles, or steam vents, are hot springs with a lot of heat, but so little water that it all boils away before reaching the surface. At places like Roaring Mountain, the result is a loud hissing vent of steam and gases.

NPS photo

## Mammoth Hot Springs Terraces and How They Work

At Mammoth Hot Springs, a rarer kind of spring is born when the hot water ascends through the ancient limestone deposits of the area instead of the silica-rich lava flows of the hot springs common elsewhere in the park. The results are strikingly different and unique. They invoke a landscape that resembles a cave turned inside out, with its delicate features exposed for all to see. The flowing waters spill across the surface to sculpt magnificent travertine limestone terraces. As one early visitor described them, "No human architect ever designed such intricate fountains as these. The water trickles over the edges from one to another, blending them together with the effect of a frozen waterfall."

## How They Work

As ground water seeps slowly downward and laterally, it comes in contact with hot gases charged with carbon dioxide rising from the magma chamber. Some carbon dioxide is readily dissolved in the hot water to form a weak carbonic acid solution. This hot, acidic solution dissolves great quantities of limestone as it works up through the rock layers to the surface hot springs. Once exposed to the open air, some of the carbon dioxide escapes from solution. As this happens, limestone can no longer remain in solution. A solid mineral reforms and is deposited as the travertine that forms the terraces.

## Geysers and How They Work

Sprinkled amid the hot springs are the rarest fountains of all, the geysers. What makes them rare and distinguishes them from hot springs is that somewhere, usually near the surface in the plumbing system of a geyser, there are one or more constrictions. Expanding steam bubbles generated from the rising hot water build up behind these constrictions, ultimately squeezing through the narrow passageways and forcing the water above to overflow from the geyser. The release of water at the surface prompts a sudden decline in pressure of the hotter waters at great depth, triggering a violent chain reaction of tremendous steam explosions in which the volume of rising, now boiling, water expands 1,500 times or more. This expanding body of boiling superheated water bursts into the sky as one of Yellowstone's many famous geysers.

There are more geysers here than anywhere else on earth. Old Faithful, certainly the most famous geyser, is joined by numerous others big and small, named and unnamed. Though born of the same water and rock, what is enchanting is how differently they play in the sky. Riverside Geyser shoots at an angle across the Firehole River, often forming a rainbow in its mist. Castle erupts from a cone shaped like the ruins of some medieval fortress. Grand explodes in a series of powerful bursts, towering above the surrounding trees. Echinus spouts up and out to all sides like a fireworks display of water. And Steamboat, the largest in the world, pulsates like a massive steam engine in a rare, but remarkably memorable eruption, reaching heights of 300 to 400 feet.

which also contains Daisy and Splendid Geysers. Comet has the largest cone of the three but has, by far, the smallest eruptions. The nearly constant splashing of Comet over a long period of time has resulted in its large cone. Eruptions rarely exceed 6 feet in height.

## Splendid Geyser

Splendid Geyser's eruptions are at times over 200 feet in height, making it among the tallest geysers in Yellowstone. Its eruptions are infrequent and difficult to predict except for the fact that it is more likely to erupt when a storm front rapidly reduces the barometric pressure in the area. This slightly reduces the boiling temperature in the plumbing system and occasionally triggers a splendid eruption.

## Punch Bowl Spring

This boiling, intermittent spring has produced a sinter lip that raises it above the basin floor. That "punch bowl" appearance gave this feature its name.

## Daisy Geyser

Daisy Geyser erupts at an angle to a height of 75 feet (23m) for 3–5 minutes. Typically, Daisy is quite predictable, with eruption intervals of 90–115 minutes. An exception to this is when nearby Splendid Geyser erupts.

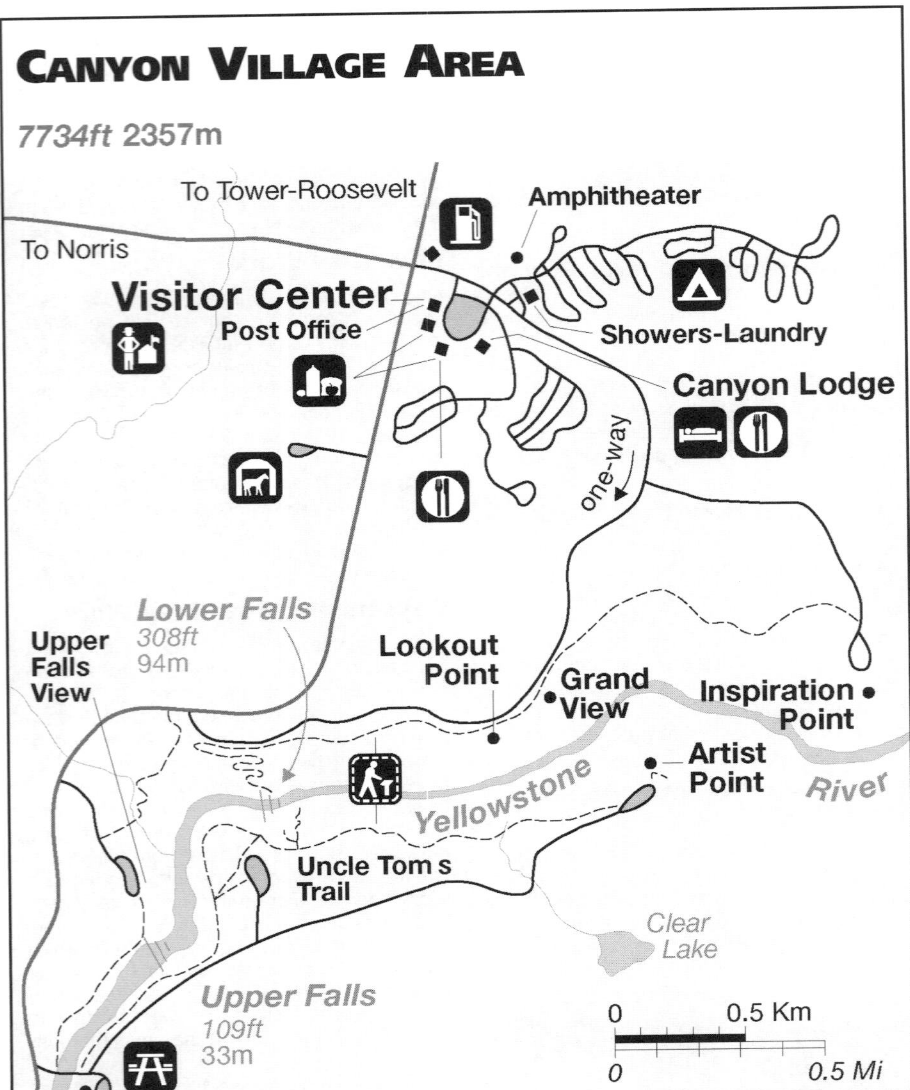


### Grotto Geyser

Grotto Geyser erupts about every eight hours. It splashes to a height of 10 feet (3m) for 1 1/2 to more than 10 hours. The weirdly shaped cone, that gives this geyser its name, may have resulted from geyserite covering the trunks of trees that once grew there.

### Morning Glory Pool

Long a favored destination for park visitors, Morning Glory Pool was named in the 1880s for its remarkable likeness to its namesake flower. However, this beautiful pool has fallen victim to vandalism. People have thrown literally tons of coins, trash, rocks, and logs into the pool. Much of the debris subsequently became embedded in the sides and vent of the spring, affecting water circulation and accelerating the loss of thermal energy. Through the years Morning Glory's appearance has changed as its temperature dropped. Orange and yellow bacteria that formerly colored only the periphery of the spring now spread toward its center.

### Riverside Geyser

Situated on the bank of the Firehole River, Riverside Geyser is one of the most picturesque geysers in the park. During its 20-minute eruptions, a 75 foot (23m) column of water arches gracefully over the river. Eruptions are about 5-1/2 to 6-1/2 hours apart. There is water runoff over the edge of Riverside's cone for an hour or two before each eruption. Many geysers have similar "indications" that they are about to erupt.

*Riverside Geyser. NPS photo.*

### Fan & Mortar Geysers

Fan and Mortar Geysers are in close proximity to one another and almost always erupt in concert. The interval between eruptions ranges from 1-1/2 days to months. Most eruptions last about 45 minutes. Mortar Geyser, pictured here, erupts to heights of 40–80 feet while Fan can reach heights of 100–125 feet.

### Sapphire Pool

Three miles north of Old Faithful is Biscuit Basin, named for the unusual biscuit-like deposits formerly surrounding Sapphire Pool. Following the 1959 Hebgen Lake earthquake, Sapphire erupted, and the "biscuits" were blown away. Other notable colorful features in the basin are Jewel Geyser, Shell Geyser, Avoca Spring, and Mustard Spring.

## NATURAL HIGHLIGHTS OF THE CANYON VILLAGE AREA

### The Grand Canyon of the Yellowstone

The Grand Canyon of the Yellowstone is the primary geologic feature in the Canyon District. It is roughly 20 miles long, measured from the Upper Falls to the Tower Fall area. Depth is 800 to 1,200 ft.; width is 1,500 to 4,000 ft. The canyon as we know it today is a very recent geologic feature. The present canyon is no more than 10,000 to 14,000 years old, although there has probably been a canyon in this location for a much longer period. The exact sequence of events in the formation of the canyon is not well understood, as there has been little field work done in the area. The few studies that are available are thought to be inaccurate. We do know that the canyon was formed by erosion rather than by glaciation. A more complete explanation can be found in the Geological Overview section. The geologic story of the canyon, its historical significance as a barrier to travel, its significance as destination/attraction, and its appearance in Native American lore and in the accounts of early explorers are all important interpretive points. The "ooh-ahh" factor is also important: its beauty and grandeur, its significance as a feature to be preserved, and the development of the national park idea.

### The Upper and Lower Falls of the Yellowstone

The falls are erosional features formed by the Yellowstone River as it flows over progressively softer, less resistant rock. The Upper Falls is upstream of the Lower Falls and is 109 ft. high. It can be seen from the Brink of the Upper Falls Trail and from Uncle Tom's Trail.

The Lower Falls is 308 ft. high and can be seen from Lookout Point, Red Rock Point, Artist Point, Brink of the Lower Falls Trail, and from various points on the South Rim Trail. The Lower Falls is often described as being more than twice the size of Niagara, although this only refers to its height and not the volume of water flowing over it. The volume of water flowing over the falls can vary from 63,500 gal/sec at peak runoff to 5,000 gal/sec in the fall.

A third falls can be found in the canyon

between the Upper and Lower falls. Crystal Falls is the outfall of Cascade Creek into the canyon. It can be seen from the South Rim Trail just east of the Uncle Tom's area.

### The Yellowstone River

The Yellowstone River is the force that created the canyon and the falls. It begins on the slopes of Yount Peak, south of the park, and travels more than 600 miles to its terminus in North Dakota where it empties into the Missouri River. It is the longest undammed river in the continental United States.

### Hayden Valley

Hayden Valley is one of the best places in the park to view a wide variety of wildlife. It is an excellent place to look for grizzly bears, particularly in the spring and early summer when they may be preying upon newborn bison and elk calves. Large herds of bison may be viewed in the spring, early summer, and during the fall rut, which usually begins late July to early August. Coyotes can almost always be seen in the valley.

Bird life is abundant in and along the river. A variety of shore birds may be seen in the mud flats at Alum Creek. A pair of sandhill cranes usually nests at the south end of the valley. Ducks, geese, and American white pelicans cruise the river. The valley is also an excellent place to look for bald eagles and northern harriers.

### Mt. Washburn

Mt. Washburn is the main peak in the Washburn Range, rising 10,243 ft. above the west side of the canyon. It is the remnant of volcanic activity that took place long before the formation of the present canyon. It is an excellent example of subalpine habitat and is very accessible to the average visitor. Bighorn sheep and an abundance of wildflowers can be found on its slopes in the summer. Mt. Washburn was named for Gen. Henry Dana Washburn, leader of the 1870 Washburn-Langford-Doane Expedition.

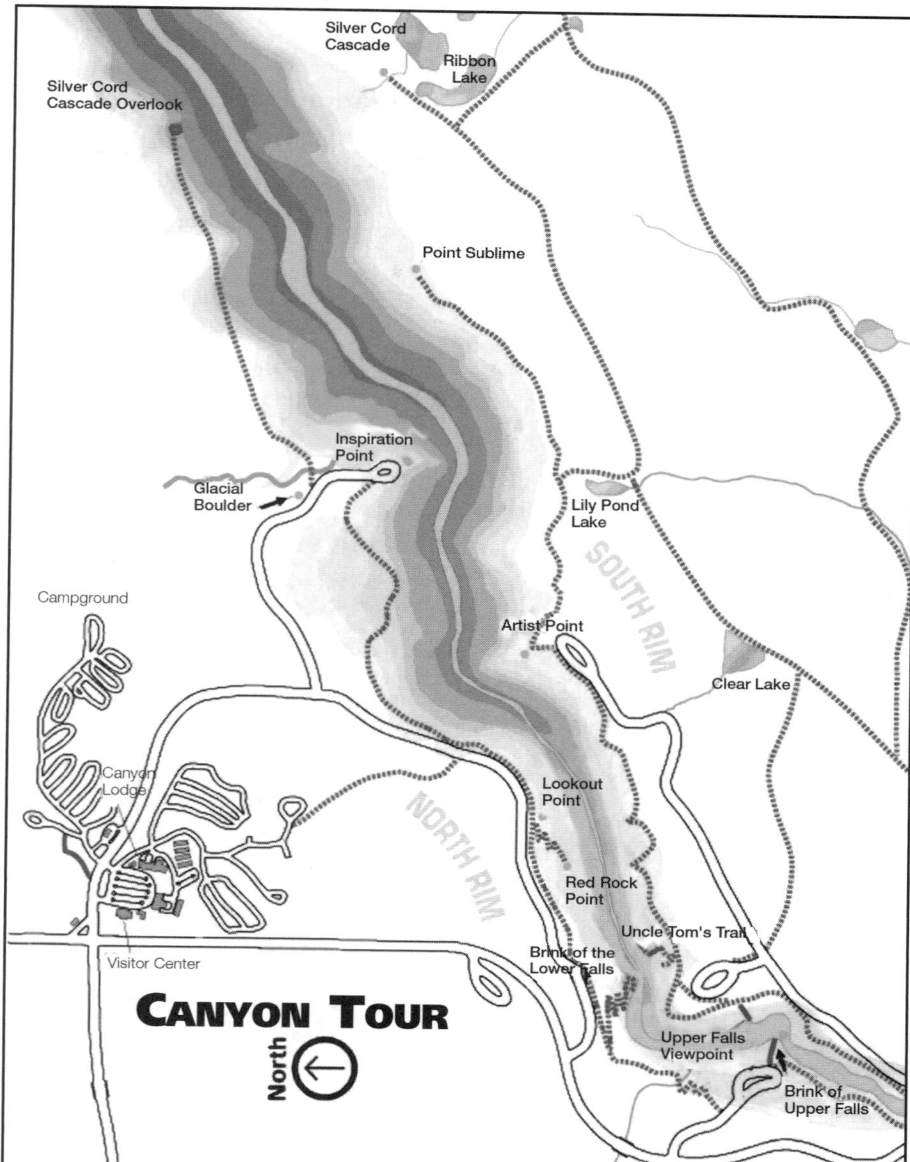


## Geological Overview of the Canyon Area

### The Grand Canyon of the Yellowstone

The specifics of the geology of the canyon are not well understood, except that it is an erosional feature rather than the result of glaciation. After the caldera eruption of about 600,000 years ago, the area was covered by a series of lava flows. The area was also faulted by the doming action of the caldera before the eruption. The site of the present canyon, as well as any previous canyons, was probably the result of this faulting, which allowed erosion to proceed at an accelerated rate. The area was also covered by the glaciers that followed the volcanic activity. Glacial deposits probably filled the canyon at one time, but have since been eroded away, leaving little or no evidence of their presence.

The canyon below the Lower Falls was at one time the site of a geyser basin that was the result of rhyolite lava flows, extensive faulting, and heat beneath the surface (related to the hot spot). No one is sure exactly when the geyser basin was formed in the area, although it was probably present at the time of the last glaciation. The chemical and heat action of the geyser basin caused the rhyolite rock to become hydrothermally altered, making it very soft and brittle and more easily erodible (sometimes likened to baking a potato). Evidence of this thermal activity still exists in the canyon in the form of geysers and hot springs that are still active and visible. The Clear Lake area (Clear Lake is fed by hot springs) south of the canyon is probably also a remnant of this activity.

According to Ken Pierce, U.S. Geological Survey geologist, at the end of the last glacial period, about 14,000 to 18,000 years ago, ice dams formed at the mouth of Yellowstone Lake. When the ice dams melted, a great volume of water was released downstream causing massive flash floods and immediate and catastrophic erosion of the present-day canyon. These flash floods probably happened more than once. The canyon is a classic V-shaped valley, indicative of river-type erosion rather than glaciation. The canyon is still being eroded by the Yellowstone River.

The colors in the canyon are also a result of hydrothermal alteration. The rhyolite in the canyon contains a variety of different iron compounds. When the old geyser basin was active, the "cooking" of the rock caused chemical alterations in these iron compounds. Exposure to the elements caused the rocks to change colors. The rocks are, in effect, oxidizing; the canyon is rusting. The colors indicate the presence or absence of water in the individual iron compounds. Most of the yellows in the canyon are the result of iron present in the rock rather than sulfur, as many people think.

## Historic Highlights of the Canyon Area

### Canyon Village

The Canyon Village complex is part of the Mission 66 project in the park. The Visitor Center was completed in 1957, and the new lodge was open for business in the same year. Though some people consider the development representative of the architecture of the time, none of the present buildings in the complex can be considered historic. There are, however, still remnants of the old hotel, lodge, and related facilities. These constitute the cultural resources of the district.

### The Canyon Hotel (no longer standing)

The old Canyon Hotel was located about 1 mile south of Canyon Junction at the present site of the horse corrals. It was a huge building, nearly a mile around its perimeter. It was dismantled and burned in 1962. See Aubrey Haines' account of this in *The Yellowstone Story, Vol. II.* Photographs of the hotel are available for viewing in an album at the Visitor Center and in the park's historic photo collection. Little if anything is left of the hotel building itself, but the hotel's cistern and the dump remain. The winterkeeper's house, in which Steve Fuller (a concession employee) lives, is also from this era. The cistern is being studied for removal, the dump is an archeological site that must be evaluated before further action is taken, and the house is being considered for the National Register of Historic Places.

### The Old Canyon Lodge (no longer standing)

The old Canyon Lodge was located at the present site of Uncle Tom's parking lot and in the meadows just east of the rest rooms. Remnants of this complex can still be found in the meadows.

### Other Cultural Resources

The remaining cultural resources associated with earlier developments are far from the public eye and not easily accessible. One has to know where to look for them. They include, but are not limited to, the Ram pump on Cascade Creek, the concrete apron (for water supply) on Cascade Creek, the hotel water tank, and the water tank at the Brink of the Upper Falls. All are slated for some kind of mitigation, depending upon funding, staffing, and priority by the resource management staff.

## Yellowstone-Canyon Tour

About 600,000 years ago, huge volcanic eruptions occurred in Yellowstone, emptying a large underground magma chamber. Volcanic debris spread for thousands of square miles in a matter of minutes. The roof of this chamber collapsed, forming a giant smoldering pit. This caldera was 30 miles (45 km) across, 45 miles (75 km) long, and several thousand feet deep. Eventually the caldera was filled with lava.

One of these lava flows was the Canyon Rhyolite flow, approximately 590,000 years ago which came from the east and ended just west of the present canyon. A thermal basin developed in this lava flow, altering and weakening the rhyolite lava by action of the hot steam and gases. Steam rises from vents in the canyon today and the multi-hued rocks of the canyon walls are also evidence of hydrothermally altered rhyolite.

Other lava flows blocked rivers and streams forming lakes that overflowed and cut through the various hard and soft rhyolites, creating the canyon. Later the canyon was blocked three different times by glaciers. Each time these glaciers formed lakes, which filled with sand and gravel. Floods from the melting glaciers at the end of each glacial period recarved the canyon, deepened it, and removed most of the sand and gravel.

The present appearance of the canyon dates from about 10,000 years ago when the last glaciers melted. Since that time, erosional forces (water, wind, earthquakes, and other natural forces) have continued to sculpt the canyon.

### Glacial Boulder

Along the road to Inspiration Point there is a house-sized granite boulder sitting in the pine forest alongside the road. It was plucked from the Beartooth Mountains by an early Pinedale Glacier and dropped on the north rim of the Grand Canyon of the Yellowstone nearly 80,000 years ago. Continued glacial advances and retreats led to the present-day appearance of the canyon and surrounding area.

### Inspiration Point Platform

Inspiration Point is a natural observation point. It is at a location where the canyon wall juts far out into the canyon allowing spectacular views both upstream and down.

A member of the Washburn party in 1870, Nathanial P. Langford, used these words to describe his visit to this point:

*"The place where I obtained the best and most terrible view of the canyon was a narrow projecting point situated two to three miles below the lower fall. Standing there or rather lying there for greater safety, I thought how utterly impossible it would be to describe to another the sensations inspired by such a presence. As I took in the scene, I realized my own littleness, my helplessness, my dread exposure to destruction, my inability to cope with or even comprehend the mighty architecture of nature."*

### Lookout Point

This was a popular lookout for many early visitors to the park. Noticing that it got regular visitation, in 1880 Superintendent P.W. Norris built a railing here and the location has been called Lookout Point ever since. It is likely that this was the superintendents preferred name for the spot. It had been called many things prior to 1880 including Point Lookout, Lookout Rock, Mount Lookout, and Prospect Point.

### Red Rock Point

Red Rock Point is near the tall reddish pinnacle of rock below the Lower Falls. Iron oxide is the cause of this rock's red pigmentation. The pinnacle has had several names relating to its color including Red Pinnacles and Cinnabar Tower. It was finally given its present-day name of Red Rock by the 1886 Park Photographer, F. Jay Haynes.

### Brink of the Lower Falls

The Lower Falls is the tallest waterfall in the park at 308 feet. The arrow at the top of the photo points at a group of visitors on the platform at the Brink of the Lower Falls.

Over the years the estimates of the height of this falls has varied dramatically. In 1851 Jim Bridger estimated its height at 250 feet. One outrageous newspaper story from 1867 placed its height at "thousands of feet". A map from 1869 gives the falls its current name of Lower Falls for the first time and estimates the height at 350 feet.

It mattered little how tall the observers thought the falls was. They consistently write journal entries that comment on its awe-inspiring nature. A member of the 1870 Washburn party N. P. Langford gave this brief but poetic description: *"A grander scene than the lower cataract of the Yellowstone was never witnessed by mortal eyes."*

### The Brink of the Upper Falls

This is the smaller of the two famous waterfalls on the Yellowstone River at 109 feet tall. To get a feel for its magnitude notice that the arrow at the top of the photo points at three people standing on the platform at the Brink of the Upper Falls.

This falls was called the "upper falls" for the first time by members of the 1869 Folsom party who estimated its height at 115 feet. Visitors to the Brink of the Upper Falls have throughout time found the power of the experience worthy of detailed description.

In 1870 N.P. Langford of the Washburn party wrote of his visit to the brink:

*The Lower Falls of the Yellowstone. NPS photo.*

*"Mr. Hedges and I made our way down to this table rock, where we sat for a long time. As from this spot we looked up at the descending waters, we insensibly felt that the slightest protrusion in them would hurl us backwards into the gulf below. A thousand arrows of foam, apparently aimed at us, leaped from the verge, and passed rapidly down the sheet. But as the view grew upon us, and we comprehended the power, majesty and beauty of the scene, we became insensible to the danger and gave ourselves up to the full enjoyment of it."*

### Upper Falls Viewpoint

Of the two famous Yellowstone River waterfalls this one stands at a higher elevation, but it is considerably shorter in height than its downstream neighbor, the Lower Falls. The height of the Upper Falls is 109 feet.

According to a companion, the famous mountain man Jim Bridger visited this waterfall in 1846. Word spread of its existence and in the 1860s some prospectors went out of their way to visit it.

### View of the Lower Falls from Uncle Tom's Trail

Uncle Tom's Trail was first constructed in 1898 by "Uncle" Tom Richardson. The five years following its construction, Uncle Tom led visitors on tours which included crossing the river upstream from the present day Chittenden Bridge, and then following his rough trail to the base of the Lower Falls. The tour was concluded with a picnic and a return trip across the river.

Today Uncle Tom's Trail is very different from the simple trail used by Mr. Richardson and his visitors. It is still, however, a very strenuous walk into the canyon. The trail drops 500 feet (150 m) in a series of more than 300 stairs and paved inclines.

### Artist Point

Many people thought that this was the point where Thomas Moran made the sketches he used to produce his famous painting of the canyon in 1872. In fact those sketches were made from the north rim in a location known today as Moran

Point.

The name Artist Point is believed to have been given to this location around 1883 by Park Photographer F. Jay Haynes. The name appeared in print for the first time in Mr. Haynes guidebook, published in 1890.

### Point Sublime

When the Cook-Folsom expedition stepped out of the woods on the south rim of the canyon in 1869 the staggering view prompted Folsom to use the following adjectives in his description of it: "pretty, beautiful, picturesque, magnificent, grand, sublime, awful, terrible". It is thought to be that description which prompted the naming of Point Sublime in the early 1920s.

### Silver Cord Cascade

Surface Creek flows passed this overlook and then falls abruptly in a long series of falls down to the river. While not a single waterfall, this cascade may well have given rise to the stories of a waterfall over 1000 feet tall that was hidden in the mountains.

Members of the Washburn party discovered the cascade in 1870 and named it Silverthread Fall. In 1885 the USGS Hague parties gave it the name that survives today, Silver Cord Cascade.

## Natural Highlights of the Tower-Roosevelt Area

### Specimen Ridge

Specimen Ridge, located along the Northeast Entrance Road east of Tower Junction, contains the largest concentration of petrified trees in the world. There are also excellent samples of petrified leaf impressions, conifer needles, and microscopic pollen from numerous species no longer growing in the park. Specimen Ridge provides a superb "window" into the distant past when plant communities and climactic conditions were much different than today.

### Petrified Tree

The Petrified Tree, located near the Lost Lake trailhead, is an excellent example of an ancient redwood, similar to many found on Specimen Ridge, that is easily accessible to park visitors. The interpretive message here also applies to those trees found on Specimen Ridge.

Petrified trees in the park are evidence of its volcanic history. Trees buried by volcanic ash slowly had their organic structure replaced by minerals. These tree trunks were literally turned to stone. The petrified tree pictured here was placed behind the fence to protect it from vandals and collectors. Two other petrified trees that were nearby were totally removed one piece at a time by thoughtless visitors in the past.

### Tower Fall

Tower Fall is the most recognizable natural feature in the district. The 132-foot drop of Tower Creek, framed by eroded volcanic pinnacles has been documented by park visitors from the earliest trips of Europeans into the Yellowstone region. Its idyllic setting has inspired numerous artists, including Thomas Moran. His painting of Tower Fall played a crucial role in the establishment of Yellowstone National Park in 1872. The nearby Bannock Ford on the Yellowstone River was an important travel route for early Native Americans as well as for early European visitors and miners up to the late 19th century.

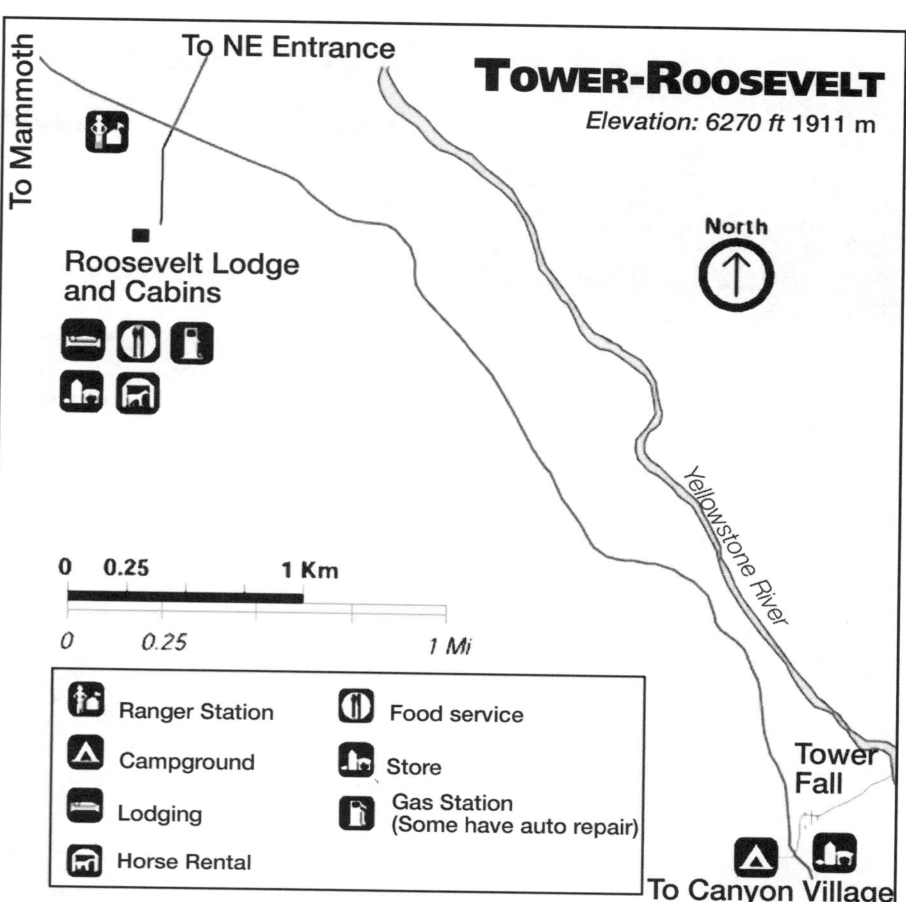


### Calcite Springs

This grouping of thermal springs along the Yellowstone River signals the downstream end of the Grand Canyon of the Yellowstone. The geothermally altered rhyolite inspired the artist Moran; his paintings of this scene were among those presented to Congress in 1872, leading to the establishment of the park. The steep, columnar basalt cliffs on the opposite side of the river from the overlook are remnants of an ancient lava flow, providing a window into the past volcanic forces that shaped much of the Yellowstone landscape. The gorge and cliffs provide habitat for numerous wildlife species including bighorn sheep, red-tailed hawks, and osprey.

### Yellowstone River and its Tributaries

The Yellowstone River and its tributaries provide habitat for numerous bird and fish species.

## Geological Overview of the Tower-Roosevelt Area

The geology of the Tower district is incredibly varied. Major landforms are expressions of geologic events that helped shape much of the Yellowstone area. Absaroka volcanics, glaciation, and erosion have left features as varied as Specimen Ridge's petrified trees to the gorges along the Yellowstone River's Black Canyon and the Grand Canyon of the Yellowstone.

Mt. Washburn and the Absaroka Range are both remnants of ancient volcanic events that formed the highest peaks in the Tower District. Ancient eruptions, perhaps 45 to 50 million years ago, buried the forests of Specimen Ridge in ash and debris flows. The columnar basalt formations near Tower Fall, the volcanic breccias of the "towers" themselves, and numerous igneous outcrops all reflect the district's volcanic history.

Later, glacial events scoured the landscape, exposing the stone forests and leaving evidence of their passage throughout the district. The glacial ponds and huge boulders (erratics) between the Lamar and Yellowstone rivers are remnants left by the retreating glaciers. Lateral and terminal moraines are common in these areas. Such evidence can also be found in the Hellroaring and Slough creek drainages, on Blacktail Plateau, and in the Lamar Valley.

The eroding power of running water has been at work in the district for many millions of years. The pinnacles of Tower Fall, the exposed rainbow colors of the Grand Canyon of the Yellowstone at Calcite Springs, and the fearsome gorge of the Black Canyon all are due, at least in part, to the forces of running water and gravity.

In the Lamar River Canyon lie exposed outcrops of gneiss and schist which are among the oldest rocks known in Yellowstone, perhaps more than two billion years old. Little is known about their origin due to their extreme age. Through time, heat and pressure have altered these rocks from their original state, further obscuring their early history. Only in the Gallatin Range are older outcrops found within the boundaries of the park.

## Historic Highlights of the Tower-Roosevelt Area

### The Buffalo Ranch

The Lamar Buffalo Ranch was built in the early

NPS photo

part of the century in an effort to increase the herd size of the few remaining bison in Yellowstone, preventing the feared extinction of the species. Buffalo ranching operations continued at Lamar until the 1950s. The valley was irrigated for hay pastures, and corrals and fencing were scattered throughout the area. Remnants of irrigation ditches, fencing, and water troughs can still be found. Four remaining buildings from the original ranch compound are contained within the Lamar Buffalo Ranch Historic District (two residences, the bunkhouse, and the barn) and are on the National Register of Historic Places. In the early 1980s, old tourist cabins from Fishing Bridge were brought to Lamar to be used for Yellowstone Institute classes. In 1993, a cabin replacement project, funded by the Yellowstone Association, was begun. At this time all of the old cabins have been replaced with new insulated and heated structures. The facility is also used in the spring and fall for the Park Service's residential environmental education program, Expedition: Yellowstone!

You are welcome to drive by to view the historic buffalo ranch, however, there are no facilities open to the general public at this location.

*Tower Falls. NPS photo*

### The Tower Ranger Station & Roosevelt National Historic District

The Tower Ranger Station, though not on the National Register of Historic Places, is a remodeled reconstruction of the second Tower Soldier Station, which was built in 1907. The Roosevelt Lodge was constructed in 1920 and has been determined eligible for the National Register of Historic Places. The Roosevelt National Historic District also includes the Roosevelt cabins. Interestingly, one of the reasons Roosevelt Lodge was nominated for the National Register was due to its important role in early park interpretation.

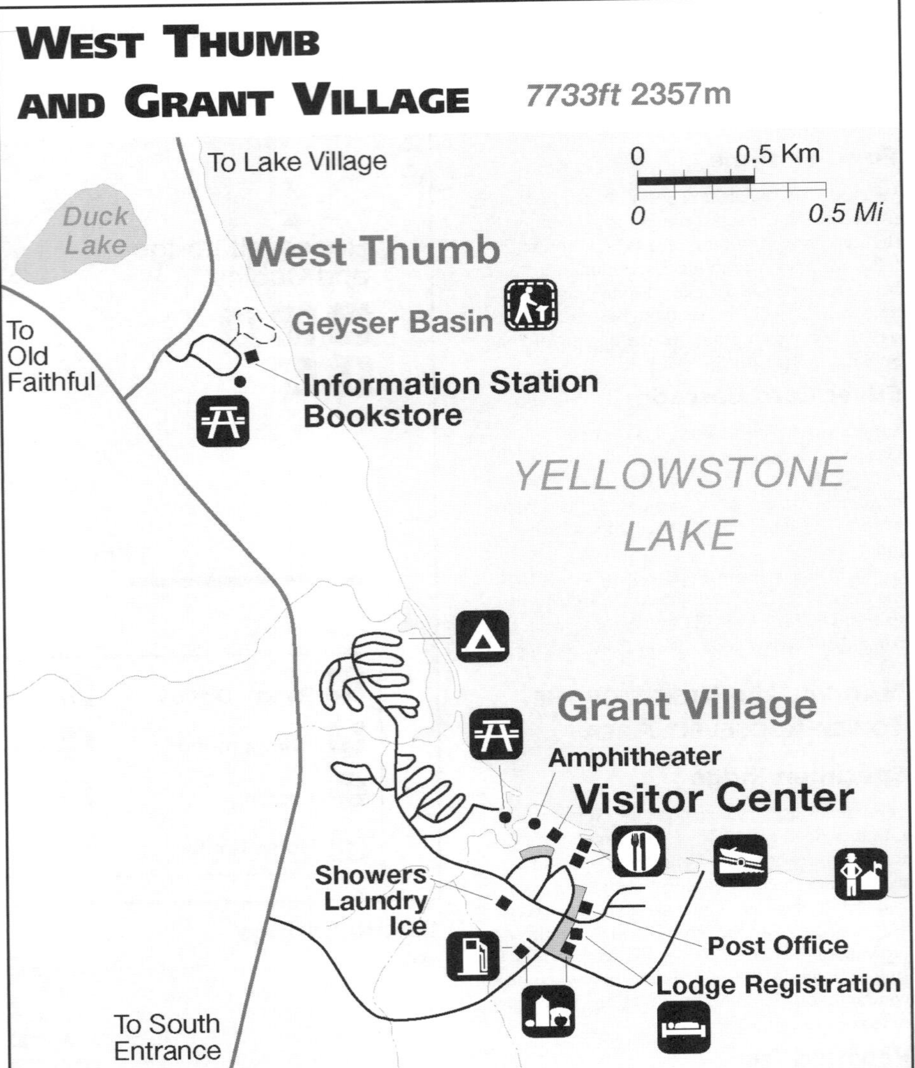


### Pleasant Valley

Pleasant Valley was the sight of "Uncle John" Yancey's Pleasant Valley Hotel, one of the earliest lodging facilities in Yellowstone. The hotel and outbuildings were built between 1884 and 1893 and served early park visitors as well as miners passing through en route to the mining district near Cooke City. Currently, the site is used by the park's main concessioner, Amfac, for their "Old West" cookouts. None of the original buildings remain.

### The Northeast Entrance Ranger Station

The Northeast Entrance Ranger Station was constructed in 1934-35 and is a National Historic Landmark. It's rustic log construction is characteristic of "parkitecture" common in the national parks of the west during that period.

### The Bannock Trail

The Bannock Trail, once used by Native Americans to access the buffalo plains east of the park from the Snake River plains in Idaho, was extensively used from approximately 1840 to 1876. A lengthy portion of the trail extends through the Tower District from the Blacktail Plateau (closely paralleling or actually covered by the existing road) to where it crosses the Yellowstone River at the Bannock Ford upstream from Tower Creek. From the river, the trail's main fork ascends the Lamar River splitting at Soda Butte Creek. From there, one fork ascends the creek before leaving the park. Traces of the trail can still be plainly seen in various locations, particularly on the Blacktail Plateau and at the Lamar-Soda Butte confluence.

### Archeological Resources

There are many archaeological sites in the Tower District. In fact, sites are found in a greater density here than in most other areas of the park. Unfortunately, most have yet to be extensively catalogued or studied.

## NATURAL HIGHLIGHTS OF THE

## WEST THUMB AND GRANT VILLAGE AREAS

### Yellowstone Lake

The park's largest lake is Yellowstone Lake. This "matchless mountain lake" was probably seen by John Colter on his famous winter trip of discovery in 1807-1808. Before that, Native Americans surely camped on its shores every summer. Although it is unlikely that Native Americans lived here, many arrowheads, spearheads, and other artifacts have been found near the lake.

William Clark's map of 1806-1811 showed what was probably Yellowstone Lake as "Eustis Lake," the name of the Secretary of War under President Jefferson. An 1814 map maker changed Clark's "Lake Biddle" (probably Jackson Lake) to "Lake Riddle," and it may at times also have referred to Yellowstone Lake. The name "Bridger Lake" (now applied to a small lake southeast of the park) may also have applied at times to Yellowstone Lake. In 1826, a party of fur trappers that included Daniel Potts, Bill Sublette, and Jedidiah Smith called Yellowstone Lake "Sublette Lake," and some historians credit Sublette with discovering the lake. Daniel Potts, one of the chroniclers of that 1826 trip, wrote to his family on July 8, 1827, and said that near the headwaters of the Yellowstone River is "a large fresh water lake…on the very top of the mountain which is about one hundred by forty miles in diameter and as clear as crystal" (letter, Yellowstone Park Research Library). Trapper Warren Ferris knew the name "Yellow Stone Lake" by 1831, and he showed it on his map of 1836. By the 1860s, Yellowstone Lake was well-known among former fur trappers, army personnel, and other frequent western explorers.

The 1871 Hayden Survey was the first to sail a boat, the Anna, on the waters of Yellowstone Lake, although some fur trappers or Indians may have floated rafts on the lake much earlier. Other early boats used to explore the lake were the Topping in 1874 (see Topping Point), a raft containing government surveyors in 1874, the Explorer in 1880 (see Explorer's Creek), a USGS boat destroyed by lightning in 1885, the Zillah in 1889, and the E.C. Waters (test runs only) in 1905. A boat piloted by Billy Hofer and William D. Pickett made at least one trip on the lake in 1880.

Yellowstone Lake covers 136 square miles and is 20 miles long by 14 miles wide. It has 110 miles of shoreline. The lake is at least 320 feet deep in the West Thumb area and has an average depth of 140 feet. Situated at an elevation of 7,733 feet, the lake remains cold the year-round, with an average temperature of 41°F.

Yellowstone Lake is the largest natural freshwater lake in the United States that is above 7,000 feet and is one of the largest such lakes in the world. Because of its size and depth and the area's prevailing winds, the lake can sometimes be whipped into a tempestuous inland ocean. During late summer, Yellowstone Lake becomes thermally stratified with each of several water layers having a different temperature. The topmost layer rarely exceeds 66°F, and the lower layers are much colder. Because of the extremely cold water, swimming is not recommended. Survival time is estimated to be only 20 to 30 minutes in water of this temperature.

The lake has the largest population of wild cutthroat trout in North America. Just how these Pacific Ocean cutthroat got trapped in a lake that drains to the Atlantic Ocean puzzled experts for years. There is now a theory that Yellowstone Lake once drained to the Pacific Ocean (via Outlet Canyon to Snake River) and that fish could pass across the Continental Divide at Two Ocean Pass. Lake trout, an illegally introduced, exotic species, is now found in Yellowstone Lake and threatens the existence of the native cutthroat trout.

Yellowstone Lake freezes over completely in winter, with ice thicknesses varying from a few inches to more than two feet. The lake's basin has an estimated capacity of 12,095,264 acre-feet of water. Because its annual outflow is about 1,100,000 acre-feet, the lake's water is completely replaced only about every eight to ten years. Since 1952, the annual water level fluctuation has been less than six feet.

### West Thumb of Yellowstone Lake

Members of the 1870 Washburn party noted that Yellowstone Lake was shaped like "a human hand with the fingers extended and spread apart as much as possible," with the large west bay representing the thumb. In 1878, however, the Hayden Survey used the name "West Arm" for the bay; "West Bay" was also used. Norris' maps of 1880 and 1881 used "West Bay or Thumb." During the 1930s, park personnel attempted to change the name back to "West Arm," but West Thumb remains the accepted name.

### West Thumb Geyser Basin

While many of the park's features had been described by mountain men and other explorers, the West Thumb area was the first Yellowstone feature to be written about in a publication. Daniel T. Potts, a trapper in the Yellowstone region in the 1820s, wrote a letter to his brother in Philadelphia, Pennsylvania, regarding his experiences in this area. The letter was later corrected for punctuation and spelling and printed in the Philadelphia Gazette on September 27, 1827. Part of the letter describing the northern part of the West Thumb Geyser Basin, which is currently known as "Potts Basin" follows:

*…on the south borders of this lake is a number of hot and boiling springs some of water and others of most beautiful fine clay and resembles that of a mush pot and throws its particles to the immense height of from twenty to thirty feet in height[.] The clay is white and of a pink and water appears fathomless as it appears to be entirely hollow under neath. There is also a number of places where the pure sulfur is sent forth in abundance[.] One of our men visited one of those whilst taking his recreation[.] There at an instant the earth began a tremendous trembling and he with difficulty made his escape when an explosion took place resembling that of thunder. During our stay in that quarter I heard it every day[.]*

In 1869, the first scientific expedition to explore the Yellowstone area, the Folsom-Cook-Peterson Expedition, visited the West Thumb Geyser Basin. David Folsom described the area as follows:

*"Among these were springs differing from any we had previously seen. They were situated along the shore for a distance of two miles, extending back from it about five hundred yards and into the lake perhaps as many feet. There were several hundred springs here, varying in size from miniature fountains to pools or wells seventy-five feet in diameter and of great depth. The water had a pale violet tinge, and was very clear, enabling us to discern small objects fifty or sixty feet below the surface. A small cluster of mud springs near by claimed our attention. These were filled with mud, resembling thick paint of the finest quality, differing in color from pure white to the various shades of yellow, pink, red and violet. During the afternoon they threw mud to the height of fifteen feet… ."*

Historically, visitors travelling to Yellowstone would arrive at West Thumb via stagecoach from the Old Faithful area. At West Thumb, they had the choice of continuing on the dusty, bumpy stagecoach or boarding the steamship "Zillah" to continue the journey to the Lake Hotel. The boat dock was located near the south end of the basin near Lakeside Spring.

The West Thumb area used to be the site of a large campground, cabins, a photo shop, a cafeteria, and a gas station. This development was located immediately next to the geyser basin with the park road passing between the two. In an effort to further protect the scenic quality and the very resource that visitors were coming to see, the National Park Service removed this development in the 1980s.

### Abyss Pool

In 1935, Chief Park Naturalist C.M. Bauer named Abyss Pool, a hot spring of the West Thumb Geyser Basin, for its impressive deepness. Bauer may have taken the name from Lieutenant G.C. Doane's 1870 description of a spring in this area: "*the distance to which objects are visible down in [its] deep abysses is truly wonderful*" (Bonney and Bonney, *Battle Drums*, p. 330). Abyss Pool may also be the spring that visitors referred to during the 1880s as "Tapering Spring" because of its sloping walls.

Nineteenth century observers were impressed with the pool's beauty. In 1871, F.V. Hayden reported that this spring's "ultramarine hue of the transparent depth in the bright sunlight was the most dazzlingly beautiful sight I have ever beheld" (*Preliminary Reports*, p. 101). And W.W. Wylie observed in 1882 that the spring's walls, "*coral-like in formation and singular in shape, tinted by the water's color, are surely good representations of fairy palaces*".

### Fishing Cone

Fishing Cone is a hot spring located in the West Thumb Geyser Basin. The Folsom party probably saw it in 1869, but the first recorded description of Fishing Cone comes from the 1870 Washburn Expedition. Party member Walter Trumball wrote about Cornelius Hedges's experience fishing:

*"A gentleman was fishing from one of the narrow isthmuses or shelves of rock, which divided one of these hot springs from the [Yellowstone] lake, when, in swinging a trout ashore, it accidentally got off the hook and fell into the spring. For a moment it darted about with wonderful rapidity, as if seeking an outlet. Then it came to the top, dead, and literally boiled (Overland Monthly, June 1871, p. 492)."*

From that time on, and perhaps even earlier, visitor after visitor performed this feat, catching fish from the cold lake and cooking them on the hook. Hayden Survey members did it in 1871, and the next year they named the spring "Fish Pot" or "Hot Spring Cone." Later names were "Fisherman's Kettle," "Fish Cone," "Fishpot Spring," "Crater Island," and "Chowder Pot." The name Fishing Cone came about gradually through the generic use of the term in guidebooks.

The cooking-on-the-hook feat at Fishing Cone soon became famous. For years, Park Superintendent P.W. Norris (1877-1882) demonstrated it to incredulous tourists, and in 1894 members of Congress hooted at their colleagues who described the process. A national magazine reported in 1903 that no visit to the park was complete without this experience, and tourists often dressed in a cook's hat and apron to have their pictures taken at Fishing Cone. The fishing and cooking practice, regarded today as unhealthy, is now prohibited.

Fishing at the cone can be dangerous. A known geyser, Fishing Cone erupted frequently to the height of 40 feet in 1919 and to lesser heights in 1939. One fisherman was badly burned in Fishing Cone in 1921.

## Lodgepole Pine Forests & Fire

This area is in a lodgepole pine forest, and the fires of 1988 greatly affected this part of the park. Several trails including the Lake Overlook Trail, Duck Lake Trail, and Riddle Lake Trail provide excellent opportunities to examine the various stages of lodgepole pine forest succession and development as well as fire ecology.

On July 12, 1988, a small fire started near the Falls River in the southeastern corner of the park. For several weeks, the fire grew slowly as crews attempted to contain it. On August 20, the winds picked up. This day would later become known as "Black Saturday" because more acres burned on this day alone than in the entire history of Yellowstone prior to this day. During that week, high winds drove the fire for miles until it approached the Lewis River. Defying all conventional understanding of fire behavior and driven by 60 mph winds that gusted to 80 mph, the fire blew all the way across the Lewis River Canyon on August 23.

Firefighters were astounded. Even the most experienced Incident Commanders had never seen fire burn like it did in 1988. While the fires shocked the nation and the world, scientists had long known that a fire of this magnitude would burn through a lodgepole pine forest like Yellowstone's on an average of once every 300 years. In fact, lodgepole pine forests are adapted to fire. Some of the pine cones need the intense heat of fire to open the cones and drop the seeds for the next generation of forests. While fire is often difficult for people to understand, for the lodgepole pine forests it is as important and necessary as other natural processes like rain and sunshine, death and rebirth.

## Cutthroat Trout Spawning Streams

Big Thumb Creek and Little Thumb Creek along with several other intermittent streams serve as cutthroat trout spawning streams, thus as major feeding areas for both grizzly and black bears during spawning season.

## Heart Lake

Lying in the Snake River watershed west of Lewis Lake and south of Yellowstone Lake, Heart Lake was named sometime before 1871 for Hart Hunney, an early hunter. The name does not refer to the heart-like shape of the lake. During the 1890s, historian Hiram Chittenden learned from Richard "Beaver Dick" Leigh, one of Hunney's cronies, about the naming of the lake. Evidently, Capt. John W. Barlow (see Barlow Peak), who explored Yellowstone in 1871, made the incorrect connection between the lake's name and its shape. Chittenden wrote to Barlow, who could recall nothing about the naming, but Leigh "was so positive and gave so much detail" that Chittenden concluded that he was right. Chittenden petitioned Arnold Hague of the USGS to change the spelling back to "Hart Lake," but Hague refused, convinced the shape of the lake determined the name.

As for Hart Hunney, Leigh said that Hunney operated in the vicinity of Heart Lake between 1840 and 1850 and died in a fight with Crow Indians in 1852. Chittenden thought it was possible that Hunney was one of Capt. Benjamin Bonneville's men.

NPS photo

## Isa Lake

Hiram Chittenden of the U.S. Army Corps of Engineers claimed to have discovered this lake on the Continental Divide at Craig Pass in 1891. Chittenden, who built many early roads in Yellowstone, was searching for a practicable route to locate his new road between Old Faithful and West Thumb. It was not until 1893 that Northern Pacific Railroad (NPRR) officials named the lake for Isabel Jelke of Cincinnati. Little is known about Jelke or about her relationship to Chittenden, the NPRR, and Yellowstone. Chittenden's 1916 poetic tribute to the lake and his discovery includes the puzzling line: "Thou hast no name; pray, wilt thou deign to bear/The name of her who first has sung of thee" (Verse, p. 53). Perhaps Isabel Jelke was already associated with the lake when Chittenden "discovered" it. Isa Lake is noteworthy as probably the only lake on earth that drains naturally to two oceans backwards, the east side draining to the Pacific and the west side to the Atlantic.

NPS photo

## Craig Pass

Craig Pass, at 8,262 feet on the Continental Divide, is about eight miles east of Old Faithful on the Grand Loop Road. In 1891, road engineer Captain Hiram Chittenden discovered Craig Pass while he was surveying for the first road between Old Faithful and West Thumb. It was probably Chittenden who named the pass for Ida M. Craig (Wilcox), "the first tourist to cross the pass" on Chittenden's new road, on about September 10, 1891. At the time that her name was given to the pass, Ida Wilcox (1847-1930) had been married 24 years. So why did Chittenden use her maiden name? Perhaps it was to honor her singularly for being the first tourist to cross the pass. It is also possible that through his connection with the military, Chittenden knew her father (Gen. James Craig) or her brother (Malin Craig, Sr.) and was really honoring the Craig family.

## DeLacy Creek

DeLacy Creek flows south from DeLacy Lakes to Shoshone Lake. Park Superintendent P.W. Norris named the creek in 1881 for Walter Washington DeLacy (1819-1892), the leader of a prospecting expedition that passed through the Yellowstone region in 1863. DeLacy, a surveyor and engineer, compiled the first accurate map of the Yellowstone area in 1865.

In 1863, DeLacy led a group of prospectors from Jackson Hole across the Pitchstone Plateau and discovered Shoshone Lake, which he named "DeLacy's Lake." He was the first to note the "strange" drainage of that lake south to the Snake River rather than west to the Madison River. But he did not publish his discoveries until 1876, which kept him from receiving credit for being the man who discovered Yellowstone and from leaving his name on present-day Shoshone Lake.

DeLacy also recognized the importance of Yellowstone's thermal features. In a published letter in 1869, he wrote: "At the head of the South Snake, and also on the south fork of the Madison [present-day Shoshone Lake and Firehole River], there are hundreds of hot springs, many of which are 'geysers'" (Raymond, "Mineral Resources," p. 142). In 1871, Hayden changed the name of "DeLacy's Lake" to "Madison Lake." In 1872, Frank Bradley criticized DeLacy for the "numerous errors" on his map and named the lake Shoshone.

Park Superintendent P.W. Norris felt sorry for DeLacy and named the present stream for him in 1881, stating:

*"The . . . narrative, the high character of its writer [DeLacy], his mainly correct descriptions of the region visited, and the traces which I have found of this party [campsite remains, etc.], proves alike its entire truthfulness, and the injustice of changing the name of De Lacy's Lake [to Shoshone Lake]; and fearing it is now too late to restore the proper name to it, I have, as a small token of deserved justice, named the stream and Park crossed by our trail above the Shoshone Lake after their discoverer (Fifth Annual Report, p. 44)."*

## Factory Hill

Factory Hill is a 9,607-foot-high peak in the Red Mountains. By 1876, the peak was called "Red Mountain," a name that had originally been given to present-day Mount Sheridan by members of the 1871 Hayden Survey. Eventually, the name "Red" was applied to the entire small mountain range.

Members of the Hague parties named Factory Hill in about 1885 because N.P. Langford's description of steam vents near the mountain. In the June 1871 issue of Scribner's, Langford had written: "Through the hazy atmosphere we beheld, on the shore of the inlet opposite our camp, the steam ascending in jets from more than fifty craters, giving it much the appearance of a New England factory village" (p. 120).

## Lewis River

This river drains Shoshone and Lewis lakes and is a tributary of the Snake River. In 1872, members of the second Hayden survey called the river "Lake Fork" because it was a fork of the Snake that began in those two lakes. An 1876 map showed the river marked "Lewis Fork" (of the Snake), named from Lewis Lake.

## Red Mountains

This small range of mountains, located just west of Heart Lake, is completely contained within the boundaries of Yellowstone National Park. In 1871, F.V. Hayden named present-day Mount Sheridan "Red Mountain." In 1872, members of the second Hayden Survey transferred that name to the entire range. The name was "derived from the prevailing color of the volcanic rocks which compose them" (Hayden, Twelfth Annual Report, p. 470). In 1878, Henry Gannett reported that there were 12 peaks in the range, with 10,308-foot-high Mount Sheridan being the highest.

## Riddle Lake

This small lake is located about three miles south of the West Thumb bay of Yellowstone Lake. Rudolph Hering (see Hering Lake) of the Hayden Survey named Riddle Lake in 1872. Frank Bradley of the Survey wrote:

*"Lake Riddle" is a fugitive name, which has been located at several places, but nowhere permanently. It is supposed to have been used originally to designate the mythical lake, among the mountains, whence, according to the hunters, water flowed to both oceans. I have agreed to Mr. Hering's proposal to attach the name to the lake, which is directly upon the [Continental] divide at a point where the waters of the two oceans start so nearly together, and thus to solve the insolvable "riddle" of the "two-ocean water" (in Hayden, Sixth Annual Report, p. 250).*

This "insolvable riddle" of the "mythical lake among the mountains" where water flowed to both oceans probably originated from (or at least was fueled by) "Lake Biddle," which appeared on the Lewis and Clark map of 1806 (named after their editor, Nicholas Biddle). The lake then appeared on the Samuel Lewis version of the map in 1814 as "Lake Riddle." Riddle Lake is not "directly on the divide"; it drains to the Atlantic Ocean by way of its outlet, Solution Creek, which flows to Yellowstone Lake. Thus, the name was the result of a mapping error combined with fur-trapper stories of two-ocean water.

## Shoshone Lake

Shoshone Lake, the park's second largest lake, is located at the head of the Lewis River southwest of West Thumb. It is possible that fur trapper Jim Bridger visited this lake in 1833, and fellow trapper Osborne Russell certainly reached the lake in 1839. According to James Gemmell, he and Bridger visited the lake in 1846 (in Wheeler, "*The Late James Gemmell*," pp. 131-136). Gemmell referred to it then as "Snake Lake," a name apparently used by the hunters.

Fr. Pierre-Jean DeSmet's 1851 map showed a "DeSmet's L." in the approximate position of present-day Shoshone Lake. In 1863, prospector Walter DeLacy visited the lake and named it "DeLacy's Lake." The lake was also called "Madison Lake" because it was erroneously thought to be the head of the Madison River. Cornelius Hedges of the 1870 Washburn Expedition named the lake after the party's leader, Gen. H.D. Washburn. By 1872, Shoshone Lake had already borne four or five names when Frank Bradley of the second Hayden Survey added a sixth. Bradley wrote: "Upon crossing the divide to the larger lake, we found it to belong to the Snake River drainage, and therefore called it Shoshone Lake, adopting the Indian name of the Snake [River]" (American Journal of Science and Arts, September 1873, p. 201). Bradley's name thus returned in spirit to Gemmell's and the fur trappers' name "Snake Lake."

Park Superintendent P.W. Norris thought that the name Shoshone Lake was "a fitting record of the name of the Indians who frequented it" (Fifth Annual Report, p. 44). The Shoshones lived mainly to the west and south of present-day Yellowstone National Park, but there is evidence that they occasionally entered the area and may have visited the lake each summer. Their arrowheads and other artifacts have been found in various places around the park.

The meaning of "Shoshone" has long been debated. Some authorities believe that the word represented an uncomplimentary Sioux expression given to the tribe by their Crow neighbors. David Shaul, a University of Arizona linguist, believes that the word literally translates as "those who camp together in wickiups" or "grass house people."

Shoshone Lake is 205 feet at its maximum depth, has an area of 8,050 acres, and contains lake trout, brown trout, and Utah chubs. Originally, Shoshone Lake was barren of fish owing to waterfalls on the Lewis River. The two types of trout were planted beginning in 1890, and the Utah chub was apparently introduced by bait fishermen. This large lake is the source of the Lewis River, which flows to the Pacific Ocean via the Snake River system. The U.S. Fish and Wildlife Service believes that Shoshone Lake may be the largest lake in the lower 48 states that cannot be reached by road. No motorboats are allowed on the lake.

## Shoshone Point

This point on the Grand Loop Road is located halfway between West Thumb and Old Faithful. It was named in 1891 because Shoshone Lake could be seen from here. In that year, Hiram M. Chittenden began constructing the first road between Old Faithful and West Thumb, and he probably named the point himself.

Shoshone Point was the scene of a stagecoach holdup in 1914. One bandit, armed and masked, stopped the first coaches of a long line of vehicles and robbed the 82 passengers in 15 coaches of $915.35 and about $130 in jewelry. Edward Trafton was convicted of the robbery and sentenced to five years in federal prison at Leavenworth, Kansas.

## Snake River

The Snake River is a major tributary of the Columbia River and has its headwaters just inside Yellowstone on the Two Ocean Plateau. Various stretches of this important river have had at least 15 different names. The name, which comes from the Snake (Shoshone) Indians, was applied to the river as early as 1812, making it one of the oldest place names in the park. Shoshone Indians referred to some parts of the stream as "Yampa-pah," meaning "stream where the Yampa grows" (yampa is a food plant) and later as "Po-og-way" meaning "road river" (a reference to the Oregon Trail, which followed sections of the river) or, less often, "sagebrush river."

In 1872, the second Hayden Survey to Yellowstone gave the name "Barlow's Fork" (of the Snake) to the part of the river above the mouth of Harebell Creek, honoring J.W. Barlow who had explored that area in 1871. The group thought that Harebell Creek was the Snake River's main channel, an interpretation of the stream that was changed by the Hague surveys during the 1880s. Frank Bradley of the 1872 survey gave the name "Lewis Fork" (of the Snake) to the present-day Lewis River. The Snake name comes from sign language—a serpentine movement of the hand with the index finger extended—that referred to the weaving of baskets or grass lodges of the Snake or Shoshone Indians.

The source of the Snake River was debated for a long time. The problem was to find the longest branch in the Two Ocean Plateau, which is thoroughly crisscrossed with streams. Current maps show the head of the Snake to be about 3 miles north of Phelps Pass, at a point on the Continental Divide inside Yellowstone National Park. In 1926, John G. White showed a photo in his hand-typed book Souvenir of Wyoming of the "true source of the Snake," writing that "it is near the Continental Divide upon two ocean plateau. A number of springs gush forth upon the hillside. Uniting, they form a small stream, which, at an altitude of two miles above sea level, begins its arduous journey…to the Pacific" (p. 309). The Snake River is the nation's fourth largest river; 42 miles of it are in Yellowstone National Park.

# Geological Overview of the Grant Village & West Thumb Areas

## West Thumb Geyser Basin

The West Thumb Geyser Basin, including Potts Basin to the north, is unique in that it is the largest geyser basin on the shores of Yellowstone Lake. The heat source of the thermal features in this location is thought to be relatively close to the surface, only 10,000 feet down! The West Thumb of Yellowstone Lake was formed by a large volcanic explosion that occurred approximately 150,000 years ago (125,000-200,000). The resulting collapsed volcano, called a caldera ("boiling pot" or caldron), later filled with water forming an extension of Yellowstone Lake. The West Thumb is about the same size as another famous volcanic caldera, Crater Lake in Oregon, but much smaller than the great Yellowstone caldera which formed 600,000 years ago. It is interesting to note that West Thumb is a caldera within a caldera.

Ring fractures formed as the magma chamber bulged up under the surface of the earth and subsequently cracked, releasing the enclosed magma. This created the source of heat for the West Thumb Geyser Basin today.

## West Thumb Thermal Features

The thermal features at West Thumb are found not only on the lake shore, but extend under the surface of the lake as well. Several underwater geysers were discovered in the early 1990s and can be seen as slick spots or slight bulges in the summer. During the winter, the underwater thermal features are visible as melt holes in the icy surface of the lake. The ice averages about three feet thick during the winter.

# Historic Highlights of the West Thumb & Grant Village Areas

## West Thumb Ranger Station

Built in 1925, with the open breezeway enclosed in 1966, the West Thumb Ranger Station is an excellent example of historic architecture associated with ranger stations in Yellowstone.

## Archeological Resources

The shoreline of West Thumb is the location of

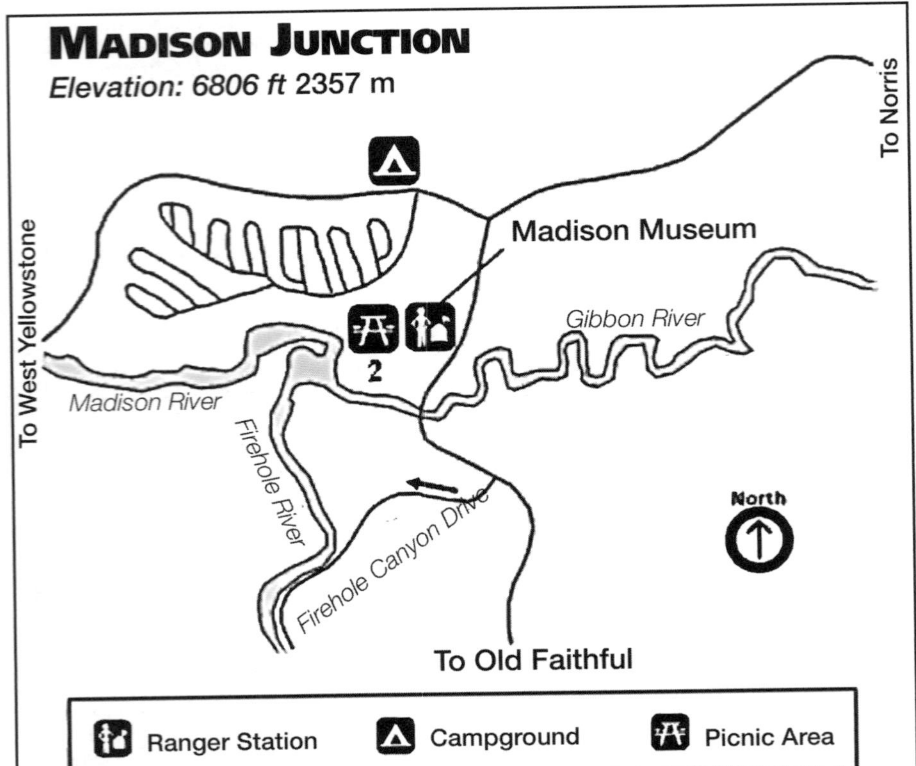


several Native American hearth sites providing evidence that native peoples once used this area as a travel route, camping ground, and food-gathering area.

## Natural Highlights of the Madison Area

### Gibbon Falls

This 84-foot (26-meter) waterfall tumbles over remnants of the Yellowstone Caldera rim. The rock wall on the opposite side of the road from the waterfall is the inner rim of the caldera.

NPS photo

### Artist Paint Pots

Artist Paint Pots is a small but lovely thermal area just south of Norris Junction. A one-mile round trip trail takes visitors to colorful hot springs, two large mudpots, and through a section of forest burned in 1988. Adjacent to this area are three other off-trail, backcountry thermal areas: Sylvan Springs, Gibbon Hill Geyser Basin, and Geyser Creek Thermal area. These areas are fragile, dangerous, and difficult to get to; travel without knowledgeable personnel is discouraged.

### Firehole River

The Firehole River starts south of Old Faithful, runs through the thermal areas northward to join the Gibbon and form the Madison River. The Firehole is world famous among anglers for its pristine beauty and healthy brown, brook, and rainbow trout.

### Firehole Canyon Drive and Firehole Falls

Firehole Canyon Drive, a side road, follows the Firehole River upstream from Madison Junction to just above Firehole Falls. The drive takes sightseers past 800-foot thick lava flows. Firehole Falls is a 40-foot waterfall. An unstaffed swimming area here is very popular in the warmest of the summer season. Cliff diving is illegal.

### Monument Geyser Basin

This small, nearly dormant basin lies at the top of a very steep one-mile trail. Thermos-bottle shaped geyser cones are remnants of a much more active time.

### Madison River

The Madison River is formed at the junction of the Gibbon and Firehole rivers, hence Madison Junction. The Madison joins the Jefferson and the Gallatin rivers at Three Forks, Montana, to form the Missouri River. The Madison is a blue-ribbon fly fishing stream with healthy stocks of brown and rainbow trout and mountain whitefish.

### Terrace Springs

The small thermal area just north of Madison Junction. This area provides the visitor with a short boardwalk tour of hot springs.

### National Park Mountain

The mountain is actually part of the lava flows that encircle the Madison Junction area. Near this site, in 1870, the Washburn-Langford-Doane Expedition is said to have camped and discussed the future of the region they were exploring. Legend has it that this was where the idea of the national park was discussed. It should be noted that there is no evidence of the campfire conversation ever taking place, and there is certainly no evidence to show that the idea of a national park was discussed.

## Natural Highlights of the Lake, Bridge Bay and Fishing Bridge Areas

### Yellowstone Lake

With a surface area of 136 square miles, Yellowstone Lake is the largest lake at high elevation (i.e., more than 7,000 ft.) in North America. It is a natural lake, situated at 7,733 ft. above sea level. It is roughly 20 miles long and 14 miles wide with 110 miles of shoreline. It is frozen nearly half the year. It freezes in late December or early January and thaws in late May or early June.

Recent research by Dr. Val Klump of the Center for Great Lakes Research and the University of Wisconsin has revolutionized the way we look at Yellowstone Lake. Figuratively, if one could pour all the water out of Yellowstone Lake, what would be found on the bottom is similar to what is found on land in Yellowstone; geysers, hot springs, and deep canyons. With a small submersible robot submarine, the researchers found a canyon just east of Stevenson Island which was 390 ft. deep. Prior to this finding, the deepest spot in the lake was thought to be 320 ft. at West Thumb. Underwater geysers, hot springs, and fumaroles were found at West Thumb and Mary and Sedge bays. The hottest spot in the lake was found at Mary Bay where the temperature was recorded at 252° F (122° C). Hollow pipes, or chimneys of silica, several feet in height, were found rising up from the lake bottom at Mary Bay. It is thought that these are the old plumbing systems of now dormant geysers. Rock spires up to 20-feet tall were found underwater near Bridge Bay. Samples of this rock are being analyzed, though it is believed that these features are probably related to underwater thermal activity.

This group of researchers also found that the conditions in Yellowstone Lake are similar to those that occur near the famous hydrothermal vents on the Pacific Ocean's mid- ocean ridge. Nutrient- and mineral-rich submarine fountains support incredible plant and animal communities, including bacterial mats, sponges, and earthworms.

### Yellowstone River

The Yellowstone River is the last major undammed river in the lower 48 states, flowing 671 miles from its source southeast of Yellowstone into the Missouri River and then, eventually, into the Atlantic Ocean. It begins in the Absaroka Mountain Range on Yount Peak. The river enters the park and meanders through the Thorofare region into Yellowstone Lake. It leaves the lake at Fishing Bridge and flows north over LeHardy Rapids and through Hayden Valley. After this peaceful stretch, it crashes over the Upper and Lower falls of the Grand Canyon. It then flows generally northwest, meeting it's largest tributary, the Lamar River, at Tower Junction. It continues through the Black Canyon and leaves the park near Gardiner, Montana. The Yellowstone River continues north and east through the state of Montana and joins the Missouri River near the eastern boundary line of the state. The Missouri

River eventually joins the Mississippi River, which flows into the Atlantic Ocean at the Gulf of Mexico.

In addition to the Yellowstone River, many of the spawning streams in the Lake/Fishing Bridge/Bridge Bay area provide critical food sources for grizzly bears in the spring time. Therefore, ecologically speaking, these river and streams are a primary resource in the district. The LeHardy Rapids are a cascade on the Yellowstone River, three miles north of Fishing Bridge. Geomorphologically, it is thought that this is the actual spot where the lake ends and the river continues it's northward flow. In the spring, many cutthroat trout may be seen here, resting in the shallow pools before expending bursts of energy to leap up the rapids on the their way to spawn under Fishing Bridge.

The rapids were named for Paul LeHardy, a civilian topographer with the Jones Expedition in 1873. Jones and a partner started off on a raft with the intent of surveying the river, planning to meet the rest of their party at the Lower Falls. Upon hitting the rapids, the raft capsized, and many of the supplies were lost, including guns, bedding, and food. LeHardy and his partner saved what they could and continued their journey to the falls on foot.

The rapids became a popular visitor attraction when a boardwalk was built in 1984 providing access to the area. Due to increased visitation, a group of harlequin ducks, which once frequented this area in spring, have not been seen for several years. The boardwalk has consequently been closed in early spring to protect this sensitive habitat, but the harlequins have not returned.

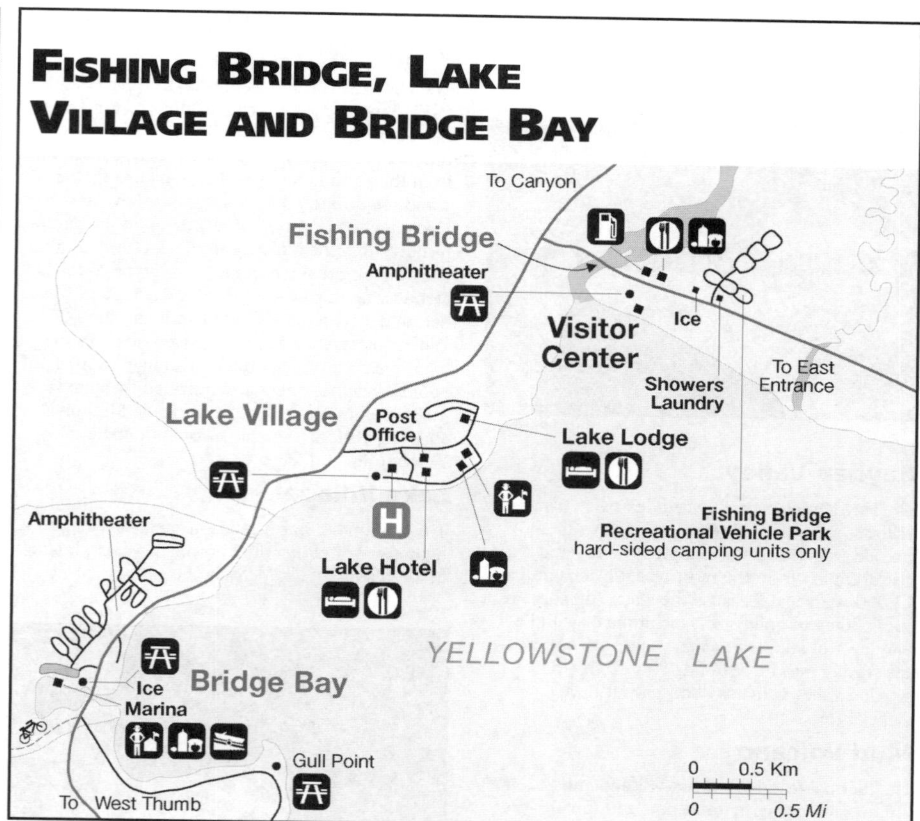


## Mud Volcano/Sulphur Caldron

When the Washburn Expedition explored the area in 1870, Nathaniel Langford described Mud Volcano as "greatest marvel we have yet met with." Although the Mud Volcano can no longer be heard from a mile away nor does it throw mud from it's massive crater, the area is still eerily intriguing.

The short loop from the parking lot past the Dragon's Mouth and the Mud Volcano is handicapped accessible. The half-mile upper loop trail via Sour Lake and the Black Dragon's Caldron is relatively steep. Two of the most popular features in the Mud Volcano front country are the Dragon's Mouth and the Black Dragon's Caldron. The rhythmic belching of steam and the flashing tongue of water give the Dragon's Mouth Spring it's name, though its activity has decreased notably since December 1994. The Black Dragon's Caldron exploded onto the landscape in 1948, blowing trees out by their roots and covering the surrounding forest with mud. The large roil in one end of the Caldron gives one the sense that the Black Dragon itself might rear it's head at any time.

In January 1995, a new feature on the south bank of Mud Geyser became extremely active. It covers an area of 20 by 8 feet and is comprised of fumaroles, small pools, and frying-pan type features. Much of the hillside to the south and southwest of Mud Geyser is steaming and hissing with a few mudpots intermixed. This increase in activity precipitated a great deal of visitor interest and subsequent illegal entry into the area.

The most dramatic features of the Mud Volcano area however, are not open to the public. The huge seething mud pot known as the "Gumper" is located off-boardwalk behind Sour Lake. The more recent features just south of the Gumper are some of the hottest and most active in the area. Ranger-guided walks are offered to provide visitors an opportunity to view this interesting place.

Farther in the backcountry behind Mud Volcano, several features are being tested for the existence of thermophilic microbes, which may offer insights into origin of life theories as well as having medical/environmental applications.

The Sulphur Caldron area can be viewed from a staging area just north of Mud Volcano. The Sulphur Caldron is among the most acidic springs in the park with a pH of 1.3. Its yellow, turbulent splashing waters bring to mind images of Shakespeare's soothsayers. Other features which can be viewed from this overlook are Turbulent Pool (which is no longer "turbulent") and the crater of a large, active mudpot.

For more specific information on the features of the Mud Volcano/Sulphur Caldron area, consult the annual reports that are available in the Ranger Naturalist Office adjacent to the Fishing Bridge Visitor Center.

## Hayden and Pelican Valleys

The Hayden Valley is located six miles north of Fishing Bridge Junction. The Pelican Valley is situated three miles east of Fishing Bridge. These two vast valleys comprise some of the best habitat in the lower 48 states for grizzly bears, bison, elk, and other wildlife species.

## Natural Bridge

Located just south of Bridge Bay Campground, it is an easy one-mile walk to the Natural Bridge. There is also a bicycle trail leading to the bridge. The Natural Bridge was formed by erosion of this rhyolite outcrop by Bridge Creek. The top of the bridge is approximately 51 ft. above the creek. A short switchback trail leads to the top, though travel across the bridge is now prohibited to protect this feature.

# Geological Overview of the Lake, Bridge Bay & Fishing Bridge Areas

## Yellowstone Lake

Geologists indicate that large volcanic eruptions have occurred in Yellowstone on an approximate interval of 600,000 years. The most recent of these (600,000 years ago) erupted from two large vents, one near Old Faithful, the Mallard Lake Dome, and one just north of Fishing Bridge, the Sour Creek Dome. Ash from this huge explosion, 1,000 times the size of Mt. St. Helens, has been found all across the continent. The magma chamber then collapsed, forming a large caldera filled partially by subsequent lava flows. Part of this caldera is the 136-square mile basin of Yellowstone Lake. The original lake was 200 ft. higher than the present-day lake, extending northward across Hayden Valley to the base of Mt. Washburn.

It is thought that Yellowstone Lake originally drained south into the Pacific Ocean via the Snake River. The lake currently drains north from its only outlet, the Yellowstone River, at Fishing Bridge. The elevation of the lake's north end does not drop substantially until LeHardy Rapids. Therefore, this spot is considered the actual northern boundary of Yellowstone Lake.

In the last decade, geological research has determined that the two volcanic vents, now known as "resurgent domes", are rising again. From year to year, they either rise or fall, with an average net uplift of about one inch per year. During the period between 1923 and 1985, the Sour Creek Dome was rising. In the years since 1986, it has either declined or remained the same. The resurgence of the Sour Creek dome, just north of Fishing Bridge is causing Yellowstone

Lake to "tilt" southward. Larger sandy beaches can now be found on the north shore of the lake, and flooded areas can be found in the southern arms.

NPS photo

### Hayden Valley

The Hayden Valley was once filled by an arm of Yellowstone Lake. Therefore, it contains fine-grained lake sediments that are now covered with glacial till left from the most recent glacial retreat 13,000 years ago. Because the glacial till contains many different grain sizes, including clay and a thin layer of lake sediments, water cannot percolate readily into the ground. This is why the Hayden Valley is marshy and has little encroachment of trees.

### Mud Volcano

The thermal features at Mud Volcano and Sulphur Caldron are primarily mud pots and fumaroles because the area is situated on a perched water system with little water available. Fumaroles or "steam vents" occur when the ground water boils away faster than it can be recharged. Also, the vapors are rich in sulfuric acid that leaches the rock, breaking it down into clay. Because no water washes away the acid or leached rock, it remains as sticky clay to form a mud pot. Hydrogen sulfide gas is present deep in the earth at Mud Volcano. As this gas combines with water and the sulfur is metabolized by cyanobacteria, a solution of sulfuric acid is formed that dissolves the surface soils to create pools and cones of clay and mud. Along with hydrogen sulfide, steam, carbon dioxide, and other gases explode through the layers of mud.

A series of shallow earthquakes associated with the volcanic activity in Yellowstone struck this area in 1978. Soil temperatures increased to nearly 200° F (93° C). The slope between Sizzling Basin and Mud Geyser, once covered with green grass and trees, became a barren landscape of fallen trees known as "the cooking hillside."

## Historic Highlights of the Lake, Bridge Bay, and Fishing Bridge Areas

### Fishing Bridge

The original bridge was built in 1902. It was a rough-hewn corduroy log bridge with a slightly different alignment than the current bridge. The existing bridge was built in 1937. The Fishing Bridge was historically a tremendously popular place to fish. Angling from the bridge was quite good, due to the fact that it was a major spawning area for cutthroat trout. However, because of the decline of the cutthroat population (in part, a result of this practice), the bridge was closed to fishing in 1973. Since that time, it has become a popular place to observe fish.

### Fishing Bridge Museum and Visitor Center

The Fishing Bridge Museum was completed in 1931. Built of native rock and stone, it appears to rise out of a rock outcrop. The structure was built to reflect the beauty of nature itself. Approaching from the parking lot, it was designed so that one could see through the building to Yellowstone Lake, hence the notion of focussing on the natural resource that the building was created to interpret. It would eventually become a prototype of rustic architecture in parks all over the nation and was declared a National Historic Landmark in 1987. When automobiles replaced stagecoaches as the main means of transportation through the park, people were no longer accompanied by a guide. The Museum was built as a "Trailside Museum," allowing visitors to obtain information about Yellowstone on their own.

### Lake Village

The buildings comprising historic Lake Village are figuratively, and literally in some cases, landmarks in the history of the Yellowstone story.

NPS photo

### The Lake Yellowstone Hotel

Built on a site long known as a meeting place for Indians, trappers, and mountain men, the Lake Yellowstone Hotel was ready to serve guests in 1891. At that time, it was not particularly distinctive, resembling any other railroad hotel financed by the Northern Pacific Railroad.

In 1903, the architect of the Old Faithful Inn, Robert Reamer, masterminded the renovation of the Hotel, designing the ionic columns, extending the roof in three places, and adding the 15 false balconies, which prompted it to be known for several years as the "Lake Colonial Hotel." A number of further changes by 1929, including the addition of the dining room, porte-cochere (portico), and sunroom as well as the refurbishing of the interior created the gracious landmark we see today.

By the 1970s, the Hotel had fallen into serious disrepair. In 1981, the National Park Service and the park concessioner, TW Recreational Services, embarked upon a ten-year project to restore the Lake Hotel in appearance to its days of glory in the 1920s. The work was finished for the celebration of the hotel's centennial in 1991. The Hotel was placed on the National Register of Historic Places that year.

The hotel is currently operated by AmFac Parks & Resorts. Information regarding room availability and reservation procedures is available through their website.

### The Lake Ranger Station

After a decade of military administration in Yellowstone, Congress created the National Park Service in 1916. Ranger stations began to replace

NPS photo

soldier stations throughout the park. The Lake Ranger Station was completed in 1923. The first Director of the National Park Service, Steven Mather, suggested that the station should blend in with its natural and cultural environment. A local woodsman used pioneer building techniques to give the station its "trapper cabin" style. With park architects, Superintendent Horace Albright designed a large octagonal "community room" with a central stone fireplace. This rustic hall served an informational function by day, and, in the evening, it became the scene of a folksy gathering around a log fire.

NPS photo

### The Lake Lodge

The advent of the auto in the park in 1915 created a great influx of visitors. The need arose for an intermediate style of lodging between the luxury of the Lake Hotel and the rustic accommodations of the tent camps. In 1926, the Lake Lodge (also a Robert Reamer design) was completed, one of four lodges in the park. The park was no longer primarily accessible to only affluent "dudes" or hearty "sagebrushers." Democracy had come to Yellowstone.

The lodge is currently operated by AmFac Parks & Resorts. Information regarding room availability and reservation procedures is available throughout their website.

### Archeological Research

For compliance purposes associated with the reconstruction of the East Entrance Road, recent archeological research has been conducted by the Mid-West Archeological Center of the National Park Service. Preliminary studies indicate that indigenous people inhabited the Lake area 9,600 years before present. Numerous projectile points have been found in addition to a hearth (cooking) structure, middens, and a bison harvest site.

## Winter Activities

### Skiing in Yellowstone

Most of Yellowstone is backcountry and managed as wilderness; many miles of trails are available for skiing. Track is set only on a few trails. All unplowed roads and trails are open to cross country skiing and showshoeing. When skiing on unplowed roadways used by snowmobiles, keep to the right to avoid accidents.

There are dangers inherent in wilderness: unpredictable wildlife, changing weather conditions, remote thermal areas, deep snow, open streams, and rugged mountains with extreme avalanche danger. When you choose to explore Yellowstone, you experience the land on its own terms; there is no guarantee of your safety. Be prepared for any situation. Carefully read all backcountry guidelines and regulations, and know the limit of your ability.

Most trails are marked with orange metal markers attached to trees. Few streams have bridges. Parties venturing into the backcountry should carry a USGS topographic map and a compass and know how to use them. Even on a well-marked trail, it is easy to get lost in a "whiteout" or blizzard. Only skiers thoroughly familiar with the area should attempt off-trail travel. When planning your trip, get specific information on conditions from rangers at a ranger station or visitor center.

Park elevations with adequate skiable snow range from 7,000 to 10,000 feet (2133 - 3048 meters.) Skiers and snowshoers who live at lower elevations should take a short day or overnight trip to test their capabilities before attempting longer outings.

A Backcountry Use Permit is required for all overnight ski trips. Contact a park ranger at a ranger station or visitor center before you begin a ski trip— whether for a few hours or several days. Trip planning should include allowances for limited daylight, snow conditions, temperature extremes, and the number of people in the group, their experience and physical condition. Overnight ski and snowshoe trips during December and January are difficult due to short days, extreme temperatures, and soft snow. Learn as much as you can about winter survival. Talk with park rangers before you leave on any trip.

Choose skis and boots made for touring or mountaineering. Narrow racing skis won't provide enough surface area to break trail.

Many of Yellowstone's roads are groomed and open to snowmobiles though this may change soon. Personal snowmobiles may be brought into the park or they may be rented in several different locations. Businesses with permits to rent snowmobiles or conduct guided snowmobile tours can be found on our Permitted Winter Businesses page. the park's lodging concessioner, Amfac Parks & Resorts, also provides snowmobile tours & rentals along with various other winter services and activities.

## Snowmobile Regulations & other Safety Tips

Snowmobile operators must have a valid state motor vehicle driver's license in their possession. Persons possessing a learners permit may operate a snowmobile when supervised one-to-one within line of sight (but no more than 100 yards) by a licensed person 21 years old or older.

Operate snowmobiles as you would an automobile. Use hand signals when turning or stopping. Allow enough distance in between snowmobiles when traveling. Passing is allowed only when safe. If you turn around, you must do so within the road width.

Maximum speed limit is 45 mph (72 kph) or less where posted or as conditions warrant. Speed is checked by radar. Obey all speed limit signs and stop signs.

Drive on the right side of the road and in single file. When stopping, pull to the far right and park in single file. Stay to the right even if the roads are rough.

*Cross Country skiing is one of the more "personal" ways to enjoy the park in the winter. NPS photo*

Snowmobiles may be driven on designated roads only. Sidehilling, berm-riding, or any off-road travel is prohibited and carries a fine of up to $5000. Report accidents to a ranger.

Operating a snowmobile while intoxicated is illegal. Possession of open alcoholic beverage containers, including botabags, is illegal.

Snowmobiles must be registered according to applicable state law. Muffler, lights, and brakes must be in good working condition.

Snowmobile exhaust and muffler systems must be in good working order. The maximum noise allowed is 78 decibels when measured during full acceleration at a distance of 50 feet. Most stock exhaust systems meet this standard; "after-market" ("piped") exhaust systems often do not. Snowmobiles exceeding the decibel standard will be denied entry into the park.

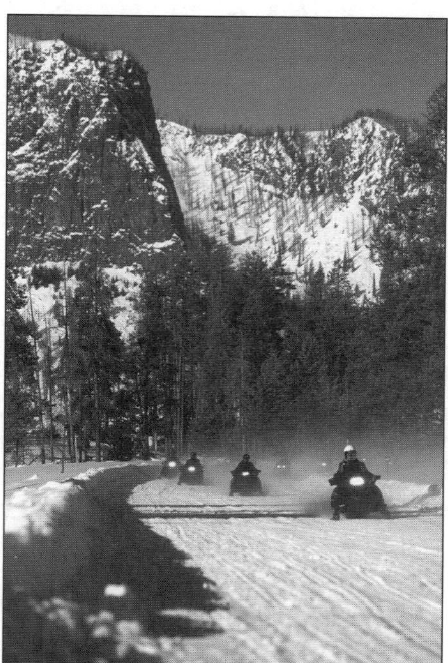

*The future of snowmobiles in the park is under discussion at this time. NPS photo*

Thermal basins, viewpoints, and walkways are snowpacked and icy during winter; fog reduces visibility. When walking, stay on boardwalks or maintained trails; walk carefully. Watch your children. Your hand or voice may be too far away if your child leaves your side.

Wild animals have the right of way. Wildlife are dangerous and unpredictable. Winter is a time of great stress. When you force an animal to move, it uses energy which is vital to its survival. Approaching, chasing, molesting, or feeding animals is prohibited.

If bison or other wildlife are on the road, stop at least 25 yards away and/or pull your machine as far as possible to the opposite side of the road; give them a chance to get off the road. If they run toward you, and you can confidently turn around, do so and move to a safe place to reassess the situation. If they walk or run toward you, and you cannot turn around, get off your machine and stand to the side of it, keeping the machine between you and the animal(s). If they are standing calmly, inch toward them and access their behavior. If they remain calm, pass on the opposite side of the road at a moderate speed. Do not make sudden or erratic movements; use groomed pullouts where possible. If the animal(s) appear agitated, do not attempt to pass as any advance may cause the animal(s) to charge. Do not chase animals or cause them to stampede. There is no guarantee of your safety.

## Winter Services

Snowmobile Fuel is available at Old Faithful, Canyon, Fishing Bridge, and Mammoth Hot Springs.

Lodging is available at the Old Faithful Snow Lodge and Mammoth Hot Springs Hotel. Reservations are strongly recommended; call 307-344-7311.

Restaurants are available at the Old Faithful Snow Lodge and Mammoth Hot Springs Hotel Dining Room. Dinner reservations are required; call 307-344-7901.

Fast Food is available at the Old Faithful Snow Lodge - Geyser Grill and at the Canyon and

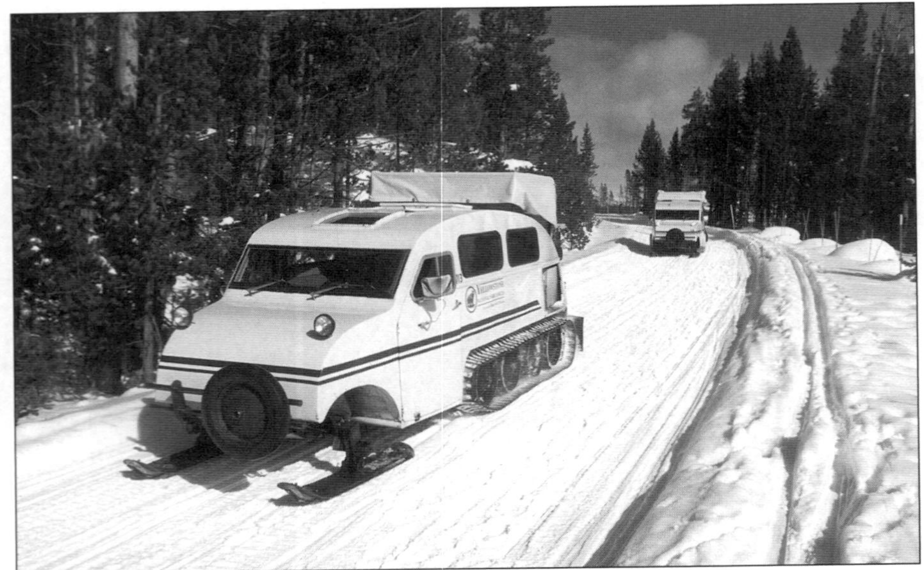

*Snowcoaches are a great way to enjoy Yellowstone in the winter. NPS photo*

Madison warming huts.

Lunch Counter & Groceries are available at Hamilton's Store at Mammoth Hot Springs.

**Restrooms:** Heated restroom facilities are located at Mammoth Hot Springs campground, Mammoth Visitor Center, Old Faithful Visitor Center, Madison warming hut, and Canyon warming hut. Vault toilets are found at other locations throughout the park.

**Camping:** The only campground open in winter is located at Mammoth Hot Springs. A backcountry permit is required for camping at any other location, including the winter camping area at Old Faithful. Permits may be obtained at ranger stations open in winter.

**Clinics:** Mammoth Clinic open weekdays 8:30 AM - 1 PM and 2-5 PM; closed Wednesday afternoons; call 307-344-7965. Old Faithful Clinic open every other Friday starting December 29th.

**Snowcoach Tours:** Tours depart from Mammoth Hot Springs, Old Faithful Snow Lodge, West Yellowstone, and Flagg Ranch outside the South Entrance.

**Snowmobile Rentals & Tours:** Depart from Mammoth Hot Springs Hotel, Old Faithful Snow Lodge, and nearby communities.

**Ski and Snowshoe Rentals and Tours:** Bear Den Ski Shops at Mammoth Hot Springs Hotel and Old Faithful Snow Lodge.

### Equipment and Clothing

Choose skis and boots made for touring or mountaineering. Narrow racing skis won't provide enough surface area to break trail. Low shoes won't give enough ankle support. Before you rent or borrow equipment, check for fit and suitability for wilderness use. Equipment that fits both you and park conditions can make or break your trip.

Winter temperatures are severe in Yellowstone, but you can be comfortable and confident if you are properly dressed. Prepare for changing conditions by wearing clothes in several adjustable layers. It is as important to prevent overheating as it is to prevent chilling.

Be sure your clothing includes a windproof hooded outer layer with wool or other insulated garments underneath. Wool or synthetic trousers and long underwear will help to keep your legs warm and dry in deep snow. Wind or rain-pants are lightweight and provide extra warmth on windy days. Avoid cotton jeans and sweatshirts. Thick wool socks and gaiters over boots help to keep your feet warm and dry. Wear gloves or wool mittens with shells that breathe to allow moisture to escape from sweaty hands.

Since you lose more heat through your head than any other part of your body, wear a face mask-style stocking cap or parka hood when you need maximum protection. Dark sunglasses are a must for sunny days. High altitude sunlight reflected from snow is much more intense than at lower elevations; snow-blindness may occur if sunglasses are not worn. Apply sunscreen lotion to exposed skin to avoid sunburn.

## Backcountry Rules

To preserve Yellowstone's backcountry and enhance your wilderness experience, the National Park Service has established the following regulations and guidelines. **Contact a park ranger before you begin a day hike or overnight trip.**

### Permits

Yellowstone National Park has a designated backcountry campsite system; permits are required for all overnight trips. Permits must be obtained at a ranger station no more than 48 hours before your camping date. Advance reservations for some backcountry campsites may be made in writing or in person for a $15 fee. To obtain the necessary forms, write the Backcountry Office, P.O. Box 168, YNP, WY 82190 or check at a ranger station.

You must also have a permit for fishing, boats, and float tubes.

### Limits

Each designated campsite has a maximum limit for the number of people and stock allowed per night. The maximum stay per campsite varies from 1 to 3 nights per trip. To protect resources and visitors, some hiking and camping restrictions may apply. Firearms, pets, motorized equipment, and any type of wheeled vehicle (except wheelchairs) are prohibited in the backcountry.

### Campfires

Campfires are permitted only in established fire pits. Burn only dead-and-down wood. Wood and ground fires are not allowed in some campsites. Your fire must be attended at all times and be completely extinguished before you leave.

### Pack It In-Pack It Out

All refuse must be carried out of the backcountry. This includes items partly burned in fire pits (foil, tin, glass, etc).

### Sanitation

Bury human waste 6 to 8 inches (15-20 cm) below the ground and a minimum of 100 feet (30 in) from water. Waste water should be disposed of at least 100 feet (30 in) from water or a campsite. Do not pollute lakes, ponds, rivers, or streams by washing yourself, clothing, or dishes in them.

### Should You Drink the Water?

Intestinal infections from drinking untreated water are increasingly common. Waters may be polluted by animal and/or human wastes. When possible, carry a supply of water from a domestic source. If you drink water from lakes or streams, boil it a minimum of two minutes to reduce the chance of infection or disease.

### Storms

Yellowstone's weather is unpredictable. A sunny warm day may become fiercely stormy with wind, rain, sleet, and, sometimes snow. Lightning storms are common; get off water or beaches and stay away from ridges, exposed places, and isolated trees.

Without adequate clothing and gear, an easy day hike or boat trip can turn into a battle for survival. Exposure to wind, rain, or cold can result in hypothermia. This rapid loss of body heat can cause death if not treated. Early warning signs include shivering, slurred speech, memory lapses, drowsiness, and exhaustion. Cold water is a special hazard to anglers and boaters. Get into dry clothes and drink warm fluids at the first signs of hypothermia.

### Stock Use

Overnight stock (horses, mules, burros, and llamas) use is not permitted prior to July 1, due to forage conditions and/or wet trail conditions. Horses are not allowed in frontcountry campgrounds.

### Stream Crossings

Fording a stream can be hazardous, especially during spring snow melt or high water. Check at local ranger stations for current trail and stream conditions.

### Trails

Yellowstone has more than 800 miles (1,280 km) of trails, allowing access to all major backcountry lakes, numerous waterfalls, mountain peaks, and thermal areas. Trails are minimally marked in keeping with the wilderness nature of the backcountry. Cross country travel is difficult because of the terrain and the amount of downed trees. Backcountry hikers should carry a map and compass, and know how to use both.

## Day Hiking in Yellowstone

Yellowstone National Park, encompassing 2.2 million acres, is one of America's premier wilderness areas. Most of the park is backcountry and managed as wilderness. Over 1,100 miles (1770 km) of trails are available for hiking. However, there are dangers inherent in wilderness: unpredictable wildlife, changing weather conditions, remote thermal areas, cold water lakes, turbulent streams, and rugged mountains with loose, "rotten" rock. Visiting wilderness means experiencing the land on its terms. If you choose to explore and enjoy the natural wonders of Yellowstone, there is no guarantee of your safety. Be prepared for any situation. Carefully read all backcountry guidelines and regulations.

There are numerous trails suitable for day hiking. Begin your hike by stopping at a ranger station or visitor center for information. Trail conditions may change suddenly and unexpectedly. Bear activity, rain or snow storms, high water, and fires may temporarily close trails. At a minimum, carry water, a raincoat or poncho, a warm hat, insect repellent, sunscreen, and a first aid kit. It is recommended that you hike with another person. No permit is required for day hiking.

## Day Hikes Near Mammoth

Begin your hike by stopping at a ranger station or visitor center for information. Trail conditions may change suddenly and unexpectedly. Bear activity, rain or snow storms, high water, and fires may temporarily close trails.

### Beaver Ponds Loop Trail

The trail follows the creek up Clematis Gulch, climbing 350 feet through Douglas-fir trees. The beaver ponds are reached after hiking 2.5 miles through open meadows of sagebrush and stands of aspen. Elk, mule deer, pronghorn, moose, beaver dams and lodges, and the occasional beaver and black bear may be sighted in the area. There are spectacular views as you wind your way back to Mammoth.
**Trailhead:** Clematis Gulch between Liberty Cap and the stone house (Judge's house)
**Distance:** 5 mile (8 km) loop
**Level of Difficulty:** Moderate

### Bunsen Peak Trail

This gradual 1,300 foot climb to the summit of Bunsen Peak provides a panoramic view of the Blacktail Plateau, Swan Lake Flats, Gallatin Mountain Range, and the Yellowstone River Valley. Return by the same route or take the trail down the back side to Osprey Falls trailhead (about 2 miles) and return via the Old Bunsen Peak Road Trail. Or visit Osprey Falls (an additional 2.8 miles, see below). Please plan for the additional mileage.
**Trailhead:** Entrance of the Old Bunsen Peak Road, five miles south of Mammoth toward Norris
**Distance:** 10 miles (16.1 km) roundtrip depending on side trips, 2 miles to the summit.
**Level of Difficulty:** Moderate

### Osprey Falls Trail

The trail follows the old roadbed for 2.5 miles through grassland and burnt forest. The Osprey Falls trail veers off the old road and follows the rim of Sheepeater Canyon before descending in a series of switchbacks to the bottom of Sheepeater Canyon. The Gardner River plunges over a 150-foot drop, forming Osprey Falls. Vertical cliffs rise 500 feet above you, making it one of the deepest canyons in Yellowstone.
**Trailhead:** 5 miles south of Mammoth on the Old Bunsen Peak Road Trail
**Distance:** 8 miles (12.9 km) roundtrip
**Level of Difficulty:** Difficult

### Lava Creek Trail

This trail follows Lava Creek downstream past Undine Falls (50 feet), descending gradually. Lava Creek meets the Gardner River farther downstream. The trail crosses a foot bridge on the Gardner River, and there is one final ascent to a pullout on the North Entrance Road just north of the Mammoth Campground.
**Trailhead:** The bridge at Lava Creek picnic area on the Mammoth-Tower Road
**Distance:** 3.5 miles (5.6 km) one way; 7 miles (11.3 km) roundtrip
**Level of Difficulty:** Moderate

### Rescue Creek Trail

This trail follows the Blacktail Deer Creek trail for the first 3/4 mile until meeting Rescue Creek trail. The trail climbs gradually through aspens and open meadows before beginning a 1,400 foot descent to the Gardner River. The trail crosses a foot bridge over the river and ends one mile south of the North Entrance Station.
**Trailhead:** Blacktail Trailhead on the Mammoth-Tower Road, seven miles east of Mammoth
**Distance:** 8 miles (12.9 km) on way; 16 miles (25.7 km) roundtrip
**Level of Difficulty:** Moderate

### Sepulcher Mountain Trail

This trail follows the Beaver Ponds Trail to the Sepulcher Mountain Trail junction. This trail rises 3,400 feet through pine trees and open meadows until the 9,652 foot summit of Sepulcher is reached. To complete the loop, continue along the opposite side of the mountain through a broad open slope to the junction of the Snow Pass Trail. Continue down until you reach the junction with the Howard Eaton Trail. This will lead you west of the Mammoth Terraces and back to your original trailhead.
**Trailhead:** Clematis Gulch between Liberty Cap and the stone house
**Distance:** 11 mile (17.7 km) loop trail
**Level of Difficulty:** Strenuous

### Wraith Falls

This short, easy hike through open sagebrush and Douglas-fir forest to the foot of Wraith Falls cascade on Lupine Creek.
**Trailhead:** Pullout 1/4 mile east of Lava Creek Picnic area on the Mammoth-Tower Road
**Distance:** 1 mile (1 km) round trip
**Level of Difficulty:** Easy

### Blacktail Deer Creek-Yellowstone River Trail

This trail follows Blacktail Deer Creek as it descends 1,100 feet through rolling, grassy hills and Douglas-fir where it reaches the Yellowstone River. The trail continues across the Yellowstone River on a steel suspension bridge and joins the Yellowstone River Trail. The trail continues downriver, passing Knowles Falls and into arid terrain until it ends in Gardiner, Montana.
**Trailhead:** Blacktail Trailhead on the Mammoth-Tower Road, seven miles east of Mammoth
**Distance:** 12.5 miles (21 km) one way
**Level of Difficulty:** Moderate due to length

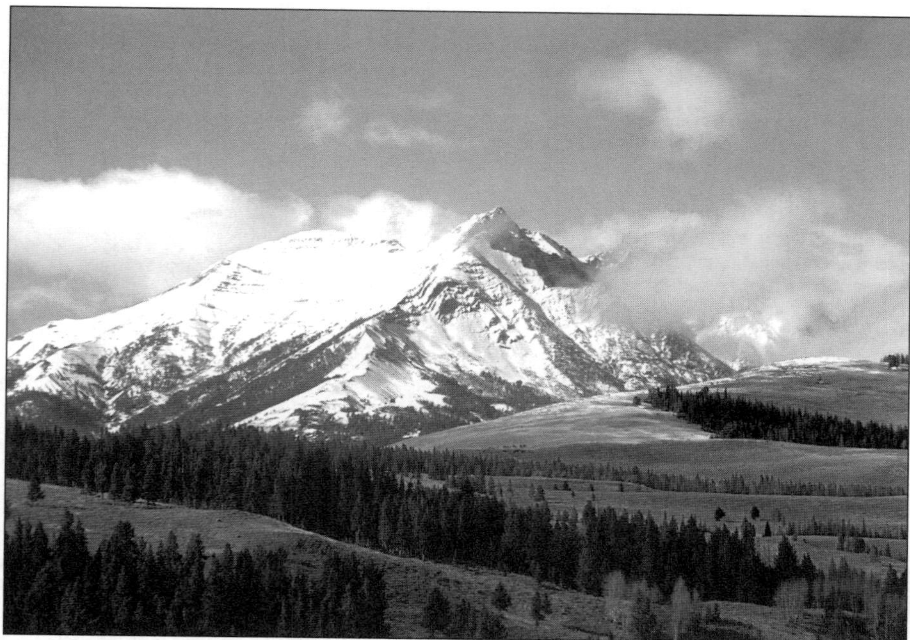

*Electric Peak, Snow-covered Gallatin Mountain Range. NPS Photo*

## Day Hikes near Norris

Begin your hike by stopping at a ranger station or visitor center for information. Trail conditions may change suddenly and unexpectedly. Bear activity, rain or snow storms, high water, and fires may temporarily close trails.

### Grizzly Lake

This trail passes through a twice-burned lodgepole pine stand (1976 and 1988) and through nice meadows. The lake is long, narrow, and heavily wooded. It can be difficult to access beyond the trail end of the lake. Marshiness and mosquitoes can make travel difficult early in the season. The lake is popular with anglers due to a strong population of small brook trout.
**Trailhead:** 1 mile (1 km) south of Beaver Lake on the Mammoth-Norris road
**Distance:** 4 miles (6 km) roundtrip
**Level of difficulty:** Moderate with some short, steep climbs and rolling terrain. A log jam crossing is required to continue past Grizzly Lake.

### Solfatara Creek

The trail follows Solfatara Creek for a short distance to the junction with Ice Lake Trail, it then parallels a power line for most of the way to Whiterock Springs. It climbs a short distance up to Lake of the Woods (difficult to find as it's off trail a bit) and passes Amphitheater Springs and

Lemonade Creek (don't drink it). These are small, but pretty thermal areas in the otherwise non-descript lodgepole pine forest. The trail then continues on to meet the road. There is no trail connection back to the campground except the way you came. Parking a car at both ends is desirable. This is a good place for folks who don't want to see many other hikers, but it can be under bear restrictions so check before starting out.
**Trailhead:** Beginning of Loop C in Norris Campground and 3/4 mile south of Beaver Lake Picnic Area on the Mammoth-Norris road
**Distance:** Campground to trailhead on the Mammoth-Norris road it is 13 miles (20 km) roundtrip
**Level of Difficulty:** Easy to moderate with one climb and descent of about 400 feet.

**Ice Lake Trail (direct route)**
Ice Lake is a lovely, small lake nestled in the thick lodgepole pine forest. Some of the area was heavily burned in 1988. Hikers can continue from Ice Lake to Wolf Lake, Grebe Lake, and Cascade Lake, and then on to Canyon.
**Trailhead:** 3.5 miles east of Norris on the Norris-Canyon road
**Distance:** 0.3 miles (0.5 km)
**Level of Difficulty:** Easy, handicapped accessible backcountry site on lake, may need assistance to reach lake due to some terrain level change

**Wolf Lake Cut-off Trail**
The trail follows the Gibbon River for at least 1 mile (1 km), passing Little Gibbon Falls. Dense, partially burned lodgepole pine forest is your main companion the rest of the way to Wolf Lake. Trailhead: Big pull-out about 1/4 miles east of Ice Lake Trailhead on Canyon-Norris Road. There is no trailhead sign due to lack of regular maintenance on the trail, but orange markers can be seen once hikers cross the road from the trailhead.
**Distance:** 6 miles (10 km) roundtrip; 1 mile (1.6 km) to junction with Wolf Lake Trail, then 2+ miles to Wolf Lake
**Level of Difficulty:** Moderate due to stream crossings and downfall; trail may be difficult to find at times

**Cygnet Lakes Trail**
This trail travels through intermittently burned lodgepole pine forest and past small marshy ephemeral ponds to the lush meadows surrounding Cygnet Lakes (small and boggy). Day use only! Trail not maintained beyond Cygnet Lakes.
**Trailhead:** Pullout on south side of Norris-Canyon road approximately 5.5 miles west of Canyon Junction
**Distance:** 8 miles (14.4 km) roundtrip
**Level of Difficulty:** Easy

**Artist Paint Pots**
This is one of the overlooked yet wonderful short hikes of Yellowstone. The trail winds across a wet meadow on boardwalk then enters a partially burned lodgepole pine forest. The thermal area within the short loop at the end of the trail contains some of the most colorful hot springs and small geysers found in the area. Two mudpots at the top of the hill allow closer access than Fountain Paint Pots. Caution for flying mud! Remind folks to stay on the trail throughout the area.
**Trailhead:** 4.5 miles south of Norris on the Norris-Madison road
**Distance:** 1 mile (1 km) roundtrip
**Level of Difficulty:** Easy with one steep uphill/downhill section, trail erodes easily so may be rutted after rains.

**Monument Geyser Basin**
This trail meanders along a gentle gradient following the Gibbon River then it turns sharply uphill and climbs 500 feet in 1/2 mile to the top of the mountain! Footing is on eroding geyserite and rhyolite, somewhat reminiscent of ball bearings. The geyser basin is a very interesting collection of dormant cones of varying sizes. One resembles a thermos bottle! Most of the activity here has dried up; hikers looking for exciting thermal activity will be disappointed, but those looking for adventure will find it. Remind folks to stay on trail!
**Trailhead:** 5 miles south of Norris Junction on the Norris-Madison road, just after Gibbon River Bridge
**Distance:** 2 miles (3 km)

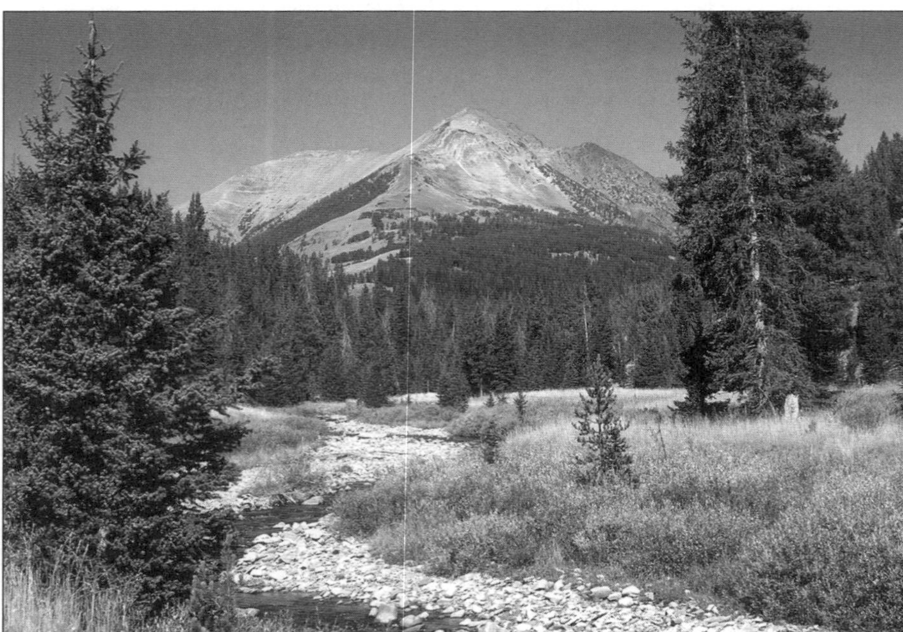

*Electric Peak with Stream in Foreground Gallatin Mountain Range. NPS Photo*

NPS photo

**Level of Difficulty:** Deceptively easy, then difficult!

## Day Hikes Near Madison

Begin your hike by stopping at a ranger station or visitor center for information. Trail conditions may change suddenly and unexpectedly. Bear activity, rain or snow storms, high water, and fires may temporarily close trails.

**Purple Mountain**
This trail ascends through intermittent burned lodgepole pine forest and ends with a nice view of the Firehole Valley and lower Gibbon Valley; some views of the Madison Junction area are also visible. Close to Madison Campground.
**Trailhead:** 1/4 mile north of Madison Junction on the Madison-Norris road, limited parking
**Distance:** 6 miles (10 km) roundtrip
**Level of Difficulty:** Moderate with steady climb of 1,500 feet

**Harlequin Lake**
This is a gentle ascent through burned lodgepole pines to a small, marshy lake popular with mosquitoes and waterfowl (but not harlequin ducks). Nice quick hike to escape the road for a little bit.
**Trailhead:** 1.5 miles west of Madison Campground on the West Entrance road
**Distance:** 1 mile (1 km) roundtrip
**Level of Difficulty:** Easy

**Two Ribbons Trail**
This is a completely boardwalked trail that winds through burned lodgepole pine and sagebrush communities next to the Madison River. Good examples of fire recovery and regrowth as well as buffalo wallows. There are no interpretive signs or brochures other than the wayside exhibits at the trailheads.
**Trailhead:** Approximately 5 miles east of the West Entrance, no marked trailhead, look for wayside exhibits next to boardwalk in large pull-outs
**Distance:** Approximately 1.5 miles (2 km) roundtrip
**Level of Difficulty:** Easy, mostly accessible

## Gallatin Area

There are many excellent hiking opportunities in the Gallatin area. Most of these, however, are longer and steeper than the average day hike. They include Daily Creek, the Sky Rim, Black Butte, Specimen Creek, Crescent Lake/High Lake, Sportsman Lake, Bighorn Pass and Fawn Pass. For more information, consult a Visitor Center or one of the hiking trail guides available from the Yellowstone Association.

## Day Hikes Near Old Faithful

Begin your hike by stopping at a ranger station or visitor center for information. Trail conditions may change suddenly and unexpectedly. Bear activity, rain or snow storms, high water, and fires may temporarily close trails.

**Geyser Hill Loop Trail**
This short loop trail gives visitors a good chance of seeing a variety of geysers, from the ever-entertaining Anemone with its short intervals of 5-10 minutes to the impressive Beehive with its unpredictable eruptions reaching 100-150 feet!
**Trailhead:** Boardwalk in front of Old Faithful Visitor Center
**Distance:** 1.3 mile (1.2 km) loop
**Level of Difficulty:** Easy

Numerous other combination loops or one-way walks can be chosen in the Upper Geyser Basin. Features such as Castle, Grand, Riverside, and Daisy geysers along with Morning Glory Pool are easily accessed using the Old Faithful self-guiding trail map. Details on geyser prediction times may be obtained by stopping by the visitor center.

**Observation Point Loop Trail**
This trail gains about 200 ft. in elevation to a prominent overlook providing a great view of the Upper Geyser Basin.
Trailhead: Firehole River footbridge behind Old Faithful Geyser
**Distance:** 1.1 mile (1 km) loop
**Level of Difficulty:** Moderate

**Mallard Lake Trail**
This trail climbs through lodgepole pine forest (some burned areas from the 1988 fires) and along meadows and rocky slopes before terminating at Mallard Lake.
**Trailhead:** Old Faithful Lodge cabin area
**Distance:** 6.8 miles (5.3 km) roundtrip
**Level of Difficulty:** Moderate

**Lone Star Geyser Trail**
This mostly level trail follows an old service road along the Firehole River through unburned forests of lodgepole pine. The geyser, which erupts approximately every 3 hours, puts on a delightful show. This trail can be accessed by bicycle with the final approach to the geyser on foot.
**Trailhead:** 3.5 miles southeast of the Old Faithful area, just beyond Kepler Cascades parking area.
**Distance:** 5 miles (8 km) roundtrip
**Level of Difficulty:** Easy

**Black Sand and Biscuit Basin Trails**
Easily accessed by boardwalks less than a mile in length, Emerald Pool, Sunset Lake, Jewel Geyser, and Sapphire Pool are among the features found in these less visited basins. Both areas are included in the Old Faithful area trail guide.
**Trailhead:** 0.5 and 2 miles north of Old Faithful area, respectively
**Distance:** Less than 0.5 (0.5 km) miles each
**Level of Difficulty:** Easy

**Midway Geyser Basin Trail**
The boardwalk leads visitors by impressive features including Excelsior Geyser and Grand Prismatic Spring.
**Trailhead:** Parking area 6 miles north of Old Faithful
**Distance:** 0.5 mile (0.5 km) loop
**Level of Difficulty:** Easy

**Fountain Paint Pot Trail**
Yellowstone's four types of thermal features can be seen in one short walk along this loop trail: geysers, hot springs, mudpots, and fumaroles. A trail guide is available for this area, which also includes the Firehole Lake Drive area.
**Trailhead:** Parking area 8 miles north of Old Faithful
**Distance:** 0.5 mile (0.5 km) loop
**Level of Difficulty:** Easy

**Mystic Falls Trail**
This trail follows a lovely creek through a lodgepole pine forest before reaching the 70- foot falls. By following a series of switchbacks, an overlook of the Upper Geyser Basin can be reached before looping back to join the main trail.
**Trailhead:** Back of the Biscuit Basin boardwalk
**Distance:** 2.4 miles (4 km) roundtrip
**Level of Difficulty:** Moderate

**Fairy Falls Trail**
At 200 feet high, Fairy Falls is an impressive backcountry sight. It can be reached from two different trailheads. The first trailhead, 1 mile south of the Midway Geyser Basin, begins at a steel bridge across the Firehole River and follows the Fountain Freight Road hiking/biking trail for approximately 1 mile before the hiking-only trail to Fairy Falls branches off on the left. The second trailhead, 1/2 mile south of the Nez Perce picnic area on the Fountain Freight Road, follows the hiking/biking path from the northern end, 1-3/4 miles to the junction with the Fairy Falls trail.
**Trailhead:** 1) Steel Bridge parking area 1 mile south of the Midway Geyser Basin
2) Fountain Freight Road parking area 1 mile south of Nez Perce picnic area on the Fountain Freight Road
**Distance:** 5 miles (8 km) from trailhead #1; 7 miles (5.5 km) from trailhead #2
**Level of Difficulty:** Easy

## Day Hikes near Grant Village & West Thumb

Begin your hike by stopping at a ranger station or visitor center for information. Trail conditions may change suddenly and unexpectedly. Bear activity, rain or snow storms, high water, and fires may temporarily close trails.

**West Thumb Geyser Basin Trail**
Stroll through a geyser basin of colorful hot springs and dormant lakeshore geysers situated on the scenic shores of Yellowstone Lake. Trails and boardwalks are handicapped accessible with assistance.
**Trailhead:** West Thumb Geyser Basin, 1/4 mile east of West Thumb Junction
**Distance:** 3/8 mile (1 km) roundtrip
**Level of Difficulty:** Easy; boardwalk trail with slight grade as trail descends to and climbs up from the lake shore

**Yellowstone Lake Overlook Trail**
Hike to a high mountain meadow for a commanding view of the West Thumb of Yellowstone Lake and the Absaroka Mountains.
**Trailhead:** Trailhead sign at entrance to West Thumb Geyser Basin parking area
**Distance:** 2 miles (3 km) roundtrip
**Level of Difficulty:** Moderate; mostly level terrain with a moderately strenuous 400-foot elevation gain near the overlook.

**Shoshone Lake Trail (via DeLacy Creek)**
Hike along a forest's edge and through open meadows to the shores of Yellowstone's largest backcountry lake. Look for wildlife in meadows.
**Trailhead:** Trailhead sign at DeLacy Creek, 8.8 miles west of West Thumb Junction
**Distance:** 6 miles (10 km) roundtrip
**Level of Difficulty:** Moderate; flat trail with no steep grades

**Riddle Lake Trail**
Crossing the Continental Divide, hike through small mountain meadows and forests to the shores

*Hiking a wildflower-covered hillside Rescue Creek Trail. NPS photo*

Yellowstone

*Park Ranger assisting visitors Canyon Visitor Center information desk. NPS photo*

of a picturesque little lake. Look for moose in the marshy meadows and for birds near the lake. Bear Management Area—trail opens July 15.
**Trailhead:** Approximately 3 miles south of the Grant Village intersection, immediately south of the Continental Divide sign
**Distance:** 5 miles (8 km) roundtrip
**Level of Difficulty:** Moderate; level walking

**Lewis River Channel/Shoshone Lake Loop Trail**
Get a feel for Yellowstone's backcountry…hike through a forested area to the colorful waters of the Lewis River Channel. Look for eagles and osprey fishing for trout in the shallow waters. For an all-day hike, follow the channel to Shoshone Lake and return via the forested Dogshead Trail.
**Trailhead:** Approximately 5 miles south of Grant Village intersection, just north of Lewis Lake on west side of the road
**Roundtrip Distance:** To channel outlet—7 miles (11 km) roundtrip; Loop—11 miles (17.5) roundtrip
**Level of Difficulty:** Moderate; mostly level, some rolling terrain

**Duck Lake Trail**
Climb a small hill for a view of Duck and Yellowstone lakes and explore the effects of the 1988 fires that swept through this area. Trail descends to lakeshore.
**Trailhead:** Trail begins in West Thumb Geyser Basin parking area, across the lot from Lake Overlook trailhead.
**Distance:** 1 mile (1.6 km) roundtrip
**Level of Difficulty:** Moderate

## Day Hikes Near Lake Village

Begin your hike by stopping at a ranger station or visitor center for information. Trail conditions may change suddenly and unexpectedly. Bear activity, rain or snow storms, high water, and fires may temporarily close trails.

**Pelican Creek Trail**
This short but diverse trail passes through the forest to the lakeshore before looping back across the marsh along Pelican Creek to the trailhead. It is a scenic introduction to a variety of Yellowstone's habitats and a good place for birding.
**Trailhead:** West end of Pelican Creek Bridge, 1 mile (1.5 km) east of Fishing Bridge Visitor Center
**Distance:** 1 mile (1.5 km) loop
**Level of Difficulty:** Easy

**Natural Bridge Trail**
The natural bridge is a 51 ft. (18 m) high cliff of rhyolite rock that has been cut through by the erosional forces of Bridge Creek. The trail from the campground meanders through the forest for 1.2 mile (0.8 km). It then joins the road and continues to the right (west) for 1 mile (1.5 km) before reaching the Natural Bridge. The short but steep switchback trail to the top of the bridge starts in front of the interpretive exhibit. To protect this fragile resource, the top of the bridge is closed to hiking. However, good views may be attained next to the bridge. The bicycle trail to the bridge begins just south of the marina off the main road.

The trail is closed from late spring to early summer due to bears feeding on spawning trout in Bridge Creek. Inquire at the Visitor Center about trail closures before hiking or bicycling these trails.
**Trailhead:** Bridge Bay Marina parking lot near the campground entrance road
**Distance:** 3 miles (5 km) roundtrip
**Level of Difficulty:** Easy

**Storm Point Trail**
This trail begins in the open meadows overlooking Indian Pond and Yellowstone Lake. The trail passes by the pond before turning right (west) into the forest. It continues through the trees and out to scenic, windswept Storm Point. The rocky area near the point is home to a large colony of yellow-bellied marmots. Following the shoreline to the west, the trail eventually loops through the lodgepole pine forest and returns to Indian Pond.
**Trailhead:** Pullout at Indian Pond, 3 miles (5 km) east of Fishing Bridge Visitor Center
**Distance:** 2 mile (3 km) loop
**Level of Difficulty:** Easy

**Elephant Back Mountain Trail**
This trail climbs 800 ft (244 km) in 1-1/2 miles (2.4 km) through a dense lodgepole pine forest. After a mile, the trail splits into a loop. The left fork is the shortest and least steep route to the top. The overlook provides a sweeping panoramic view of Yellowstone Lake and the surrounding area.
**Trailhead:** Pullout 1 mile (1.5 km) south of Fishing Bridge Junction
**Distance:** 3 mile (5 km) loop
**Level of Difficulty:** Moderately strenuous

**Howard Eaton Trail**
From the east side of Fishing Bridge, the trail follows the Yellowstone River for a short distance before joining a service road; the trail continues on the road for 1/4 mile (0.4 km). Leaving the road, the trail meanders for three miles (5 km) through meadow, forest, and sagebrush flats with frequent views of the river. Wildlife and waterfowl are commonly seen here. The last mile (1.5 km) passes through a dense lodgepole pine forest before reaching an overview of LeHardy Rapids.

To return, follow the same trail back to the trailhead. The trail does continue on for another 12 miles (19 km) to the South Rim Drive at Canyon, but is not well maintained. This trip would require planning for a full day's hike and a return ride to the trailhead.
This area is good grizzly bear habitat, and the trail is closed when bears are known to be in the area. Inquire at the Visitor Center before hiking.
**Trailhead:** Parking lot on east side of Fishing Bridge
**Distance:** 7 miles (11.3 km) roundtrip
**Level of Difficulty:** Easy

**Avalanche Peak Trail**
This trail climbs steeply (1,800 ft in 2.5 miles) without the benefit of switchbacks. It passes through the forest and into an old avalanche slide area. It continues through the whitebark pine forest to a small meadow at the base of the bowl of Avalanche Peak, affording some of the best panoramic views in the park. The trail continues up a scree slope along the narrow ridgeline of Avalanche Peak. An unmarked trail drops down the northeast side of the bowl and returns to the meadow. Since whitebark pine cones are a favored food of grizzly bears in the fall, avoid this trail at that time.
**Trailhead:** West end of Eleanor Lake across the road to the east of the small creek
**Distance:** 5 miles (8 km) roundtrip
**Level of Difficulty:** Strenuous

**Pelican Valley Trail**
This trail winds through the Pelican Valley providing views of the broad open valley and forest, some of the best grizzly habitat in the lower 48 states. It reaches the footbridge in 3 miles (5 km). The trail continues on through the valley. Due to grizzly bears in the area, the trail is not open until July 4th, and then it is recommended (not required) for use by groups of four people or more.
**Trailhead:** Dirt road 3 miles (5 km) east of Fishing Bridge Visitor Center, across the road from Indian Pond
**Distance:** 6 miles (10 km) roundtrip to footbridge
**Level of Difficulty:** Moderate

## Day Hikes Near Canyon Village

Begin your hike by stopping at a ranger station or visitor center for information. Trail conditions may change suddenly and unexpectedly. Bear activity, rain or snow storms, high water, and fires may temporarily close trails.

**Canyon Rims**

There are numerous trails and viewpoints of the canyon falls, both from the north and south rim.

**Mary Mountain Trail**
This trail climbs gradually up over Mary Mountain and the park's Central Plateau to the Nez Perce trailhead between Madison and Old Faithful. Elk and bison can sometimes be seen in the distant meadows. The trail through Hayden Valley is often difficult to follow as bison regularly knock down the trail markers.
**Trailhead:** North of Alum Creek pullout, 4 miles south of Canyon Junction
**Distance:** 21 miles one way
**Level of Difficulty:** Moderately strenuous due to length

**Howard Eaton Trail**
This hike, with little vertical rise, will take 2-8 hours. It passes through forest, meadow, and marshland to Cascade Lake (3 mi; 4.8 km), Grebe Lake (4.25 mi; 6.8 km), Wolf Lake (6.25 mi; 10 km), Ice Lake (8.25 mi; 13.7 km), and Norris Campground (12 mi; 19.3 km). Most years, this trail remains very wet and muddy through July. Insects can be very annoying.
**Trailhead:** 0.5 miles (0.8 km) west of Canyon Junction on the Norris-Canyon Road
**Distance:** From 3-12 miles one way, depending on destination
**Level of Difficulty:** Moderately easy

**Cascade Lake Trail**
This hike takes 3 hours and is an enjoyable walk through open meadows and over small creeks for those with limited time. Look for wildlife and wildflowers in season. Most years, this trail remains very wet and muddy through July.
**Trailhead:** Cascade Lake Picnic Area, 1.5 miles north of Canyon Jct. on the Tower-Canyon Road.
**Distance:** 4.5 miles (7.2 km) roundtrip
**Level of Difficulty:** Easy

**Observation Peak**
Hike to Cascade Lake from either of its two trailheads. From the lake, this strenuous, 1,400 foot climb in 3 miles will take roughly 3 hours. The hike takes you to a high mountain peak for an outstanding view of the Yellowstone wilderness. The trail passes through open meadows and some whitebark pine forests. Past Cascade Lake, no water is available along the trail. Not recommended for persons with heart and/or respiratory problems.
**Trailhead:** Cascade Lake Picnic Area, 1.5 miles north of Canyon Jct. on the Tower- Canyon Road. The other trailhead is accessed from a pullout 1/4 mile west of Canyon on the Norris-Canyon Road.
**Distance:** 11 miles roundtrip
**Level of Difficulty:** Strenuous

**Grebe Lake Trail**
There is little vertical rise on this 3-4 hour hike. This trail follows an old fire road through meadows and forest, some of which burned during the fires of 1988. Once at the lake you can connect with the Howard Eaton Trail.
**Trailhead:** 3.5 miles (5.6 km) west of Canyon Junction on the Norris-Canyon Road
**Distance:** 6 miles (9.7 km) roundtrip
**Level of Difficulty:** Moderately easy

**Seven Mile Hole Trail**
This hike takes 6-8 hours to complete. Following the Canyon Rim for the first 1.5 miles (2.4 km), you will be rewarded with views of Silver Cord Cascade. Continue north another 0.5 mile (0.8 km) to join the Washburn Spur Trail; at 3 miles (4.8 km), the trail drops off to Seven Mile Hole, a 1.5 mile (2.4 km), 1,400 foot (425 m) drop. Hike it carefully, watch your footing, and conserve your energy. Depending on your condition and the weather, it can be a long hike back out. Be especially careful where the trail passes both dormant and active hot springs. Off-trail travel is prohibited. Not recommended for persons with heart and/or respiratory problems.
**Trailhead:** Glacial Boulder Trailhead on Inspiration Point Road
**Distance:** 11 miles (17.7 km) roundtrip
**Level of Difficulty:** Strenuous

**Washburn Trail/Washburn Spur Trail**
This hike begins at the Dunraven Pass trailhead to Mount Washburn and ends at the Glacial Boulder on Inspiration Point Road. This strenuous hike takes 6-8 hours to complete. Starting at the Washburn Trailhead at Dunraven Pass, you ascend Mt. Washburn on a trail complete with (in season) wildflowers, bighorn sheep, and spectacular views. After this three mile ascent, the Washburn Spur Trail descends very steeply from the east side of the Fire Lookout to Washburn Hot Springs in another 3.7 miles (6 km). Here you will find some interesting thermal features, including mud pots. Continue past the turnoff to Seven Mile Hole and follow the trail to the Glacial Boulder and the Canyon area. Not recommended for persons with heart and/or respiratory problems.
**Trailhead:** Dunraven Pass, Washburn Trailhead, 4.5 miles north of Canyon Junction
**Distance:** 11.5 miles (18.5 km) one way
**Level of Difficulty:** Strenuous

## Day Hikes near Tower-Roosevelt

Begin your hike by stopping at a ranger station or visitor center for information. Trail conditions may change suddenly and unexpectedly. Bear activity, rain or snow storms, high water, and fires may temporarily close trails.

**Lost Lake Trail**
This loop trail departs from behind Roosevelt Lodge and climbs 300 feet (91 m) onto the bench. Here the trail joins the Roosevelt horse trail and continues west to Lost Lake. (If you take the trail east, you loop back to the Roosevelt corrals on the horse trail or continue on to Tower Fall Campground.) From Lost Lake, the trail follows the contour around the hillside to the Petrified Tree parking area. Cross the parking lot and climb the hill at its northeast end to loop back behind Tower Ranger Station. Cross the creek and return to the Roosevelt Lodge cabins.

Offering views of Lost Lake, waterfowl, wet meadows, sagebrush hilltops, wildflowers, and quite often black bears, this trail has a bit of everything. Parts of the trail are used by horse parties. For your safety when meeting horses, we recommend you move to the downhill side of the trail and remain still until they have passed.
**Trailhead:** Behind Roosevelt Lodge
**Distance:** 4 miles (6.4 km) roundtrip
**Level of difficulty:** Moderately strenuous

**Garnet Hill and Hellroaring Trails**
To access the Garnet Hill Loop Trail, park in the large parking area to the east of the service station at Tower Junction. Walk down the road toward the Northeast Entrance Road (approximately 100 yards/91 m) and head west on the dirt stagecoach road about 1.5 miles to the cookout shelter. Continue north along Elk Creek until nearly reaching the Yellowstone River. Here the trail divides, with the west fork joining the Hellroaring Trail and the east fork continuing around Garnet Hill and eventually returning to the Northeast Entrance Road where it is a short walk back to Tower Junction.

The Hellroaring Trail can be reached from the fork of Garnet Hill Trail (see above) or you can start from the Hellroaring parking area 3.5 miles (5.6 km) west of Tower Junction. Follow the trail over the Yellowstone River Suspension Bridge, cross a sagebrush plateau, and drop down to Hellroaring Creek. The Yellowstone River and Hellroaring Creek are both popular fishing areas. Note: This trail can be hot and dry during the summer months. Please remember to take water! Also, watch your footing if you go off-trail and onto the smooth river boulders along the Yellowstone River.
**Trailhead:** Tower Junction or 3.5 miles (5.6 km)

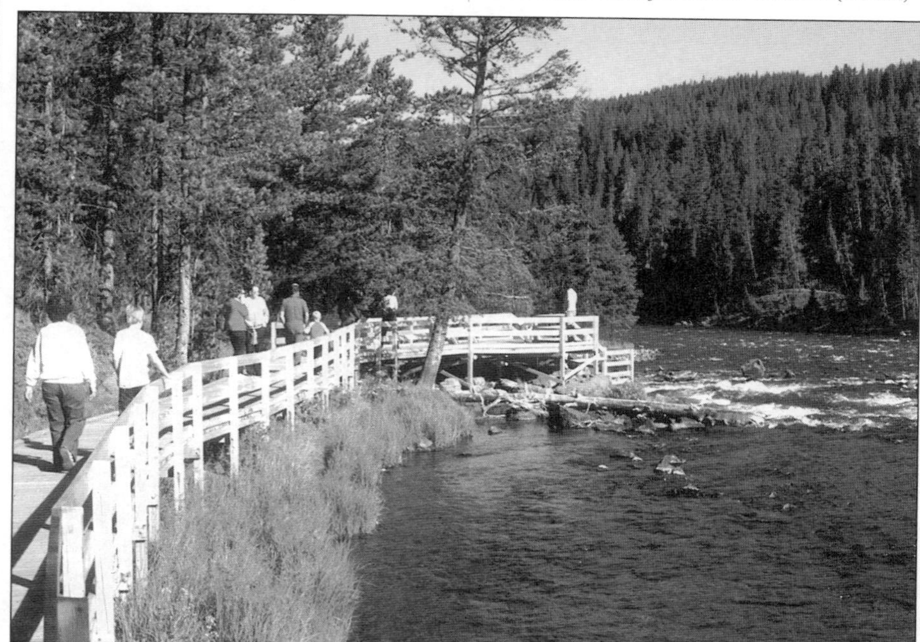

*Visitors on the boardwalk at LeHardy Rapids on the Yellowstone River. NPS photo*

Yellowstone

Yellowstone

west of Tower Junction
**Distance:**
1) Garnet Hill Loop: 7.5 miles (11.8 km) roundtrip
2) To Hellroaring Creek and back via Garnet Hill: 10 miles (16 km) roundtrip
3) To Hellroaring Creek and back via Hellroaring Trailhead: 4 miles (4.6 km) roundtrip
**Level of difficulty:** Moderately strenuous

**Yellowstone River Picnic Area Trail**
This often overlooked trail along the east rim of the Yellowstone River offers views of the Narrows of the Yellowstone, the Overhanging Cliff area, the towers of Tower Fall, basalt columns, and the historic Bannock Indian Ford. Tower Fall itself is not visible, but the store and highway across the river can be seen for reference purposes. The trail ties into the Specimen Ridge Trail above the Bannock Ford. (Continue up to Specimen Ridge only if you are prepared for a longer hike with few trail markers.) Otherwise continue north about one mile (1.6 km) to the Specimen Ridge Trailhead. Walk west along the road for another 0.7 mile (1.1 km) to the Yellowstone River Picnic Area. Watch for bighorn sheep along this trail but please don't approach them! Use caution along the river canyon with its steep dropoffs.
**Trailhead:** Yellowstone Picnic Area, 1.25 miles (2 km) northeast of Tower Junction on the road to the Northeast Entrance and Cooke City
**Distance:** 3.7 miles (5.9 km) roundtrip
**Level of difficulty:** Moderately strenuous

**Slough Creek Trail**
This is both a scenic walk and a fishing trail, a favorite of catch-and-release anglers from around the country. The trail follows a historic wagon trail up Slough Creek through several meadows and over Plateau and Elk Tongue creeks. From the trailhead, the trail switchbacks up a moderately steep trail and rejoins Slough Creek in about 2 miles (3.2 km) at the first meadow. While wildlife do not abound in this meadow during the summer, moose are commonly seen. Grizzly and black bears also use this valley. As on all Yellowstone trails, be alert for the possibility of bears in the backcountry. You may encounter the horse drawn wagons of Silver Tip Ranch, a private ranch north of the park boundary that has a historic right of access.
**Trailhead:** Near the vault toilet on the road to Slough Creek Campground
**Distance:** 2 miles (3.2 km) one way to First Meadow; 5 miles (8 km) one way to Second Meadow
**Level of difficulty:** Moderately strenuous for first 1.5 miles (2.4 km), then easy.

**Mt. Washburn Trail**
The hike to the top of Mt. Washburn is one of the most popular hikes in Yellowstone. Two trails, each 3 miles (4.8 km) in length, switchback to the summit where expansive views of much of Yellowstone unfold below on clear, summer days. An enclosed observation area allows you to get out of the wind. Bighorn sheep are seen quite frequently during the summer on the upper parts of the trails. Harsh alpine conditions contribute to short growing seasons for the fragile alpine vegetation on the mountain. Please stay on the trails and do not approach sheep or other wildlife to help preserve the wildness of this area.

The northern trail begins at the Chittenden Road parking area. The southern trail begins at Dunraven Pass parking area. More parking is available at the Chittenden Road Trailhead, although hikers using this trail may encounter bicycles and occasionally vehicles accessing Mt. Washburn for maintenance purposes.
**Trailheads:** Chittenden Road Parking Area, 8.7 miles (13.9 km) or Dunraven Pass Parking Area, 13.6 miles (21.8 km) south of Tower Junction on the Tower-Canyon Road
**Distance:** 6 miles (9.6 km) roundtrip
**Level of difficulty:** Moderately strenuous.

*The contents of this section are reprinted from National Park Service information publications.*

## NOTES:

# Glacier National Park

## The Crown Jewel of the Treasure State

*Lake McDonald greets visitors to the park at the West Glacier entrance. NPS Photo*

### The Basics

Created in 1910, Glacier National Park provides over one million acres of habitat and protection for a wonderful variety of wildlife and wildflowers.

The geologic history of Glacier is read in the numerous exposed layers of Precambrian sedimentary rocks. These extremely well preserved sediments date back to over 1 billion years. Subsequent sculpting by massive bodies of ice has transformed this area into a dramatic example of glacial landforms. Today several small alpine glaciers of relatively recent origin dot the mountains.

Glacier National Park contains a particularly rich biological diversity of plant and animal species. This combination of spectacular scenery, diverse flora and fauna, and relative isolation from major population centers have combined to make Glacier National Park the center of one of the largest and most intact ecosystems in North America.

Glacier National Park and Waterton Lakes National Park in Alberta were joined together by the governments of Canada and the United States in 1932 as Waterton-Glacier International Peace Park, the first park of its kind in the world.

Both parks have been designated Biosphere Reserves. In December of 1995 they were jointly designated the "Waterton-Glacier International Peace Park World Heritage Site."

Glacier National Park and the area claim some of the most astonishing geology in the country. The rocks that form the mountains were laid when the area was resting under a primordial sea dating back as far as 1.5 million years ago. The highest peaks of Glacier Park at 7,000 feet contrast with the deeply glaciered valleys. Colliding plates caused buckling and warping that in turn formed the mountains some 150 million years ago. During the last ice age, glaciers filled the park; the largest glaciers are located in the St. Mary and McDonald Valleys. Ten thousand years later the glaciers melted revealing Glacier Park as we see it today.

The Salish and Blackfeet tribes were the first to traverse this rugged land in the 1700s. In 1792 the first white frontiersman toured the Glacier Park area and twenty years later a trapper named Finan McDonald crossed the Marias Pass only to be ambushed by Blackfeet Indians. Under the pressure of the railroads, miners and white settlers, the Blackfeet sold the eastern slope of the park in 1895 for 1.5 million. Although copper mining and oil exploration were booming, conservationists joined forces with railroad interests to preserve the area as a national park. In 1910 President Taft signed a bill creating Glacier National Park. In 1933 the Going-to-the-Sun Road was completed which opened a new experience to those traveling by car.

Lake McDonald in West Glacier, the largest lake in Glacier National Park, is a springboard for many exciting activities. The lake is a fisherman's paradise teeming with all kinds of trout—cutthroat, bull, rainbow and brook. Walk atop Sperry Glacier or hike one of over 700 miles of hiking trails with differing levels of difficulty, from the most leisurely nature walks to brutally steep back country treks. For those who prefer the comfort of their car, the 50-mile Going-to-the-Sun Road is a beautiful drive and runs between West Glacier and St. Mary, offering easy access through the Glacier wilderness. During the summer the road is snow free, although snow occasionally falls well into the season in the 6,680-foot-high Logan Pass. You will not be disappointed by the extravagant parade of splendid views offered of glaciers, waterfalls and abundant wildlife.

### Glacier's Weather

Glacier's summer weather is as varied as its landscape.The western valleys generally receive the most rainfall, but daytime temperatures can exceed 90° F. It is frequently 10 to 15 degrees cooler at higher elevations. Sunny days often predominate on the east side of the park; however, strong winds frequently occur. Overnight lows in the park can drop to near 20° F, and snow can fall anytime.

Prepare for a variety of conditions and pack accordingly. You may start in a T-shirt and shorts, and need a parka by evening. Dress in layers. Always bring raingear.

The data shown on the next page was collected over the last ten years at Park Headquarters in West Glacier, at an elevation of 3,200 ft. Temperatures and rainfall amounts are often much different in other parts of the park.

### Visitor Centers

#### Apgar Visitor Center

May 20–June 24 . . . . . . . . .8 a.m. to 4:30 p.m.
June 25–Sept. 9 . . . . . . . . . . .8 a.m. to 8 p.m.
Sept. 10–Oct. 31 . . . . . . . . .8 a.m. to 4:30 p.m.

#### Logan Pass Visitor Center

early June–June 24 . . . . . . . .9 a.m. to 4:30 p.m.
June 25–Sept. 4 . . . . . . . . . . . .9 a.m. to 7 p.m.
Sept. 5–Sept. 30 . . . . . . . .10 a.m. to 4:30 p.m.
Oct. 1–Oct.14 . . . . . . . . . . . .10 a.m. to 4 p.m.

#### St. Mary Visitor Center

May 20–June 17 . . . . . . . . . . .8 a.m. to 5 p.m.
June 18–June 24 . . . . . . . . . . .8 a.m. to 6 p.m.
June 25–Sept. 4 . . . . . . . . . . . .8 a.m. to 9 p.m.
Sept. 5–Oct. 14 . . . . . . . . . . . . .8 a.m. to 5 p.m.

#### Many Glacier Ranger Station

May 26–June 24 . . . . . . . . . .8 a.m. to 4:30 p.m.
June 25–Sept. 4 . . . . . . . . . . . .8 a.m. to 6 p.m.
Sept. 5–Sept. 21 . . . . . . . . . 8 a.m. to 4:30 p.m.

#### Headquarters Building - West Glacier

Weekdays . . . . . . . . . . . . . .8 a.m. to 4:30 p.m.

### Entrance Fees

Single Vehicle Pass . . . . . . . . . . . . . . . . . .$10.00
Valid at Glacier National Park for 7 days.

Single Person Entry . . . . . . . . . . . . . . . . . . .$5.00

Entry into Glacier National Park by foot, bicycle, or motorcycle for 7 days.
Glacier National Park Pass . . . . . . . . . . . .$20.00

Valid for 1 year from month of purchase.
National Parks Pass . . . . . . . . . . . . . . . . .$50.00

Valid for 1 year from month of purchase.
Good at all National Park Service areas, that charge an entrance fee.

#### Other Accepted Passes

Golden Age and Golden Access passes are also accepted for entry into Glacier. Golden Eagle Passports are good for entry into any Federal Fee area, including Glacier. Golden Eagle Passports are no longer sold in National Parks. The National Parks Pass may be upgraded to a Golden Eagle for $15.00. Special fees are charged for commercial tour vehicles.

| Precipatation | Jan | Feb | Mar | Apr | May | Jun | Jul | Aug | Sep | Oct | Nov | Dec |
|---|---|---|---|---|---|---|---|---|---|---|---|---|
| Ave. precipitation | 3.25" | 1.86" | 2.06" | 2.07" | 2.97" | 3.35" | 1.95" | 1.45" | 1.83" | 2.93" | 3.76" | 3.09" |
| Average number of days with precipitation | 5 rain | 4 rain | 7 rain | 14 rain | 16 rain | 15 rain | 11 rain | 9 rain | 9 rain | 14 rain | 9 rain | 2 rain |
| | 16 snow | 11 snow | 8 snow | 2 snow | 1 snow | 0 snow | 0 snow | 0 snow | 0 snow | 1 snow | 11 snow | 17 snow |
| Average snowfall | 35.4" | 16.8" | 14.8" | 3.1" | .3" | 0" | 0" | 0" | 0" | 2.0" | 24.7" | 41.5" |

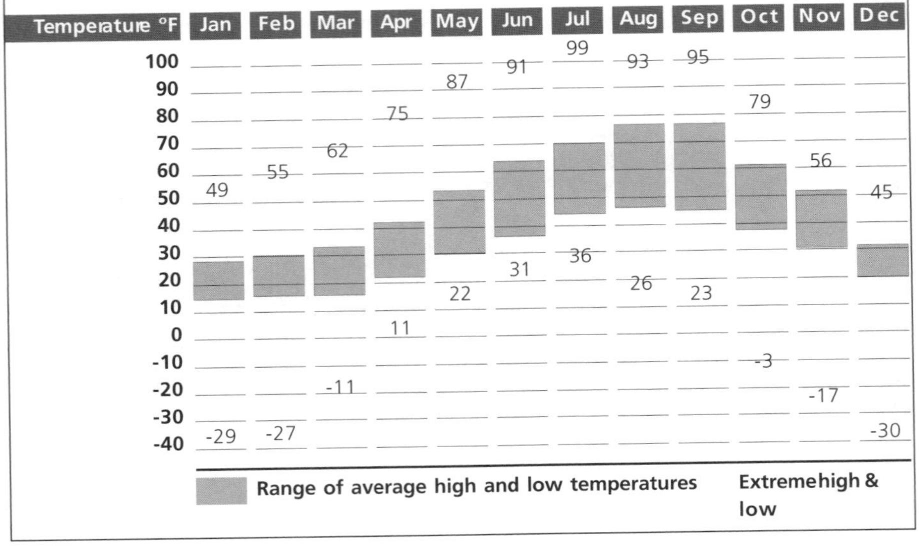

| Temperature °F | Jan | Feb | Mar | Apr | May | Jun | Jul | Aug | Sep | Oct | Nov | Dec |
|---|---|---|---|---|---|---|---|---|---|---|---|---|
| Extreme high | 49 | 55 | 62 | 75 | 87 | 91 | 99 | 93 | 95 | 79 | 56 | 45 |
| Extreme low | -29 | -27 | -11 | 11 | 22 | 31 | 36 | 26 | 23 | -3 | -17 | -30 |

Range of average high and low temperatures

Extreme high & low

## Historical Overview

### Before the Park

Recent archaeological surveys have found evidence of human use dating back over 10,000 years. These people may have been the ancestors of tribes that live in the area today. By the time the first European explorers came to this region, several different tribes inhabited the area. The Blackfeet Indians controlled the vast prairies east of the mountains. The Salish and Kootenai Indians lived and hunted in the western valleys. They also traveled east of the mountains to hunt buffalo.

In the early 1800's, French, English, and Spanish trappers came in search of beaver. In 1806, the Lewis and Clark Expedition came within 50 miles of the area that is now the park.

As the number of people moving west steadily increased, the Blackfeet, Salish, and Kootenai were forced onto reservations. The Blackfeet Reservation adjoins the east side of the park. The Salish and Kootenai reservation is southwest of Glacier. This entire area holds great spiritual importance to the Blackfeet, Salish, and Kootenai people.

The railroad over Marias Pass was completed in 1891. The completion of the Great Northern Railway allowed more people to enter the area. Homesteaders settled in the valleys west of Marias Pass and soon small towns developed.

Under pressure from miners, the mountains east of the Continental Divide were acquired in 1895 from the Blackfeet. Miners came searching for copper and gold. They hoped to strike it rich, but no large copper or gold deposits were ever located. Although the mining boom lasted only a few years, abandoned mine shafts are still found in several places in the park.

### Establishing the Park

Around the turn of the century, people started to look at the land differently. Rather than just seeing the minerals they could mine or land to settle on, they started to recognize the value of its spectacular scenic beauty. Facilities for tourists started to spring up. In the late 1890's, visitors arriving at Belton (now called West Glacier) could get off the train, take a stagecoach ride a few miles to Lake McDonald, and then board a boat for an eight mile trip to the Snyder Hotel. No roads existed in the mountains, but the lakes allowed boat travel into the wilderness.

Soon people, like George Bird Grinnell, pushed for the creation of a national park. Grinnell was an early explorer to this part of Montana and spent many years working to get the park established. The area was made a Forest Preserve in 1900, but was open to mining and homesteading. Grinnell and others sought the added protection a national park would provide. Grinnell saw his efforts rewarded in 1910 when President Taft signed the bill establishing Glacier as the country's 10th national park.

After the creation of the park, the growing staff of park rangers needed housing and offices to help protect the new park. The increasing number of park visitors made the need for roads, trails, and hotels urgent. The Great Northern Railway built a series of hotels and small backcountry lodges, called chalets, throughout the park. A typical visit to Glacier involved a train ride to the park, followed by a multi-day journey on horseback. Each day after a long ride in the mountains, guests would stay at a different hotel or chalet. The lack of roads meant that, to see the interior of the park, visitors had to hike or ride a horse. Eventually, the demand for a road across the mountains led to the building of the Going-to-the-Sun Road.

### A Heritage for the Future

The construction of the Going-to-the-Sun Road was a huge undertaking. Even today, visitors to the park marvel at how such a road could have been built. The final section of the Going-to-the-Sun Road, over Logan Pass, was completed in 1932 after 11 years of work. The road is considered an engineering feat and is a National Historic Landmark. It is one of the most scenic roads in North America. The construction of the road forever changed the way visitors would experience Glacier National Park. Future visitors would drive over sections of the park that previously had taken days of horseback riding to see.

Just across the border, in Canada, is Waterton Lakes National Park. In 1931, members of the Rotary Clubs of Alberta and Montana suggested joining the two parks as a symbol of the peace and friendship between our two countries. In 1932, the United States and Canadian governments voted to designate the parks as Waterton-Glacier International Peace Park, the world's first. More recently the parks have received two other international honors. The parks are both Biosphere Reserves, and were named as a World Heritage Site in 1995. This international recognition highlights the importance of this area, not just to the United States and Canada, but to the entire world.

While much has changed since the first visitors came to Glacier, it is possible to relive some of Glacier's early history. You can take a horseback ride like an early visitor. Miles of hiking trails follow routes first used by trappers in the early 1800's. Several hotels and chalets, built by the Great Northern Railway in the early 1900's, house summer guests to the park. A visit to Glacier National Park is still a great adventure!

## Geology

### Lewis Overthrust Fault

The Lewis Overthrust of Waterton/ Glacier provides scientists with insight about the massive dynamics of geologic processes that are going on today in other parts of the world, such as the Andes and the Himalaya Mountains. Because of the high degree of preservation of the original rock characteristics, the recent glacial sculpturing of the rocks, and the access by roads and trails, this major geologic structure in Waterton/Glacier Park is available for study by scientists from around the world.

The Lewis Overthrust began 170 million years ago, when a collision of the Earth s crustal plates elevated numerous mountain chains and formed the ancestral Rocky Mountains. Ever-increasing stresses near the end of this great event shoved a huge rock wedge, several miles thick and several hundred miles wide, eastward more than 50 miles. Large masses of relatively stronger rocks were shoved over softer and more easily deformed rocks. Erosion stripped away the upper part of the original rock wedge and exposed the rocks and structures visible in the park today. Rarely have rocks of such ancient age been thrust over rocks that are so much younger. The overlying Proterozoic rocks are over 1,500 million years older than the underlying Cretaceous age rocks.

Thus, the Lewis Overthrust is significant as a structural feature, for the extent of lateral displacement (up to 80 kilometers), and because it has functioned to expose ancient sediments possessing an unparalleled degree of preservation.

Of particular scenic and geologic note is Chief Mountain, a spectacular monolith towering above the prairie along the eastern margin of Waterton/ Glacier. Chief Mountain is an erosionally isolated remnant of the eastern edge of the upper plate of the Lewis Overthrust -- a feature known as a Klippen ranking with the Matterhorn as an example of this structural and erosional phenomenon.

## Proterozoic Sedimentary Rocks

Most of the rocks exposed in the park are sedimentary rocks of Proterozoic age, which were deposited from 1,600 to 800 million years ago. Rocks of that age in other parts of the world have been greatly altered by mountain building processes and no longer exhibit their original characteristics. These virtually unaltered Proterozoic rocks of Waterton/Glacier are unique in that they have preserved the subtle features of sedimentation such as ripple marks, mud cracks, salt-crystal casts, raindrop impressions, oolites, six species of fossil algae, mudchip breccias, and many other bedding characteristics.

These Proterozoic sedimentary rocks, while outcropping over an area extending from southern Montana to southern British Columbia, are most impressively exposed in Waterton/ Glacier. Due to the extreme relief and unexcelled exposures, over 2,100 meters of stratigraphic thickness is exposed to scientific examination. These features plus their chemical characteristics make the Proterozoic sediments of Glacier and Waterton National Parks unique for studying the physical and chemical conditions that existed on the Earth over a billion years ago. Such information is of great importance to scientists in understanding the stability or changes of the Earth s climates through geologic time. The recent glacial carving of these rocks has left them unusually fresh and beautifully exposed.

## Stromatolites

Several of the sedimentary rock layers described above, contain fossils called stromatolites. They were colonial organisms of blue-green algae that lived in warm shallow seas marginal to ancient lands. Six species representing three genera of stromatolites are preserved in the ancient sediments of the park. Because of the high degree of preservation of the rocks in which these fossils occur, the stromatolites of Waterton/Glacier contain such detail as to make them unique. Paleontologists from around the world come to Waterton/Glacier to study these fossils because of their preservation, diversity, and antiquity. These fossils are a major source of information concerning the physical and chemical conditions on the Earth for a time period of about 800 million years, at a time over a billion years ago. A professional geologist for the United States Geological Survey recently compared these ancient rocks and fossils of Waterton/Glacier to the rare book section of the world's geological library.

*Reachable only by boat from Canada, Goat Haunt is a tiny pocket of civilization in the wilderness. Goat Haunt Overlook, accessible by a steep one mile trail from the ranger station, offers an expansive view of Waterton Lake, looking north into Canada. During the summer, boats from Waterton cross the border several times a day, allowing visitors a truly international visit to Waterton-Glacier International Peace Park.NPS photo.*

## Glaciers

### What is a Glacier?

A glacier forms when more snow falls each winter than melts the next summer. The accumulation of snow above presses down on the layers below, and compacts them into ice. Ice near the surface of the glacier is often hard and brittle but, due to the pressure of ice above, the ice near the bottom of the glacier becomes flexible. This flexible layer allows the ice to move. Depending on the amount of ice, the angle of the mountainside, and the pull of gravity, the ice may start to move downhill. Once this mass of snow and ice begins to move, it is called a glacier.

### Glaciers Past and Present

The glaciers in Glacier National Park today are all geologically new having formed in the last few thousand years. Presently, all the glaciers in the park are shrinking. More snow melts each summer than accumulates each winter. As the climate changed over the last two million years, glaciers formed and melted away several times. What will happen to today's glaciers if the climate becomes colder, wetter, or warmer?

Geologists theorize that about 20,000 years ago the climate became cooler and/or wetter. This allowed for the formation of huge glaciers that filled the valleys with thousands of feet of ice. Imagine the valleys of Glacier National Park filled with ice, and just the tops of the highest peaks sticking out. These giant rivers of ice sculpted the mountains and valleys into their present appearance. Today's glaciers are carving at the mountains as well. Although smaller, they work in the same way as the larger glaciers of the past, and teach us about Glacier National Park's geologic history.

### Sculpting the Land

As the ice moves, it plucks rock and debris from the sides and bottom of the valleys. Rocks falling on the glacier from above mix with the glacial ice as well. A glacier is filled with rock and gravel. Over long periods of time the sandpaper-like quality of the moving ice scours and reshapes the land into, broad U-shaped valleys, sharp peaks, and lake filled basins. Massive ancient glaciers grinding over he bedrock below produced the spectacular landforms seen today.

### Glacial Landforms

The Park is filled with horns, cirques, arêtes, hanging valleys, and moraines; landforms given special names because they were produced by the action of glaciers.

## Horns

A horn is a steep mountain peak caused by several glaciers carving different sides of the same mountain. Mt. Reynolds at Logan Pass is a good example of a horn.

## Cirques

A cirque is a large bowl formed at the head of a glacier. Often as the ice melts away a small lake will form in the depression gouged by the glacier. Avalanche, Iceberg, and Gunsight are all excellent examples of cirque lakes.

## Arêtes

An arête (French for fish-bone) forms when two glaciers work on opposite sides of the same wall, leaving a long narrow ridge. One of Glacier National Parks more prominent features, the Garden Wall, is an arête separating the Lake McDonald Valley from the Many Glacier Valley.

## Hanging Valleys

Hanging Valleys are found throughout the park. As large glaciers scoured the main valleys, tributary glaciers worked the smaller side canyons. Unable to cut as deep as the valley glaciers, they left behind small valleys high up on the mountainsides. Frequently hanging valleys have waterfalls cascading out of their mouths into the valleys below. Birdwoman Falls, seen from the Going-to-the-Sun Road, plummets from a hanging valley on Mt. Oberlin.

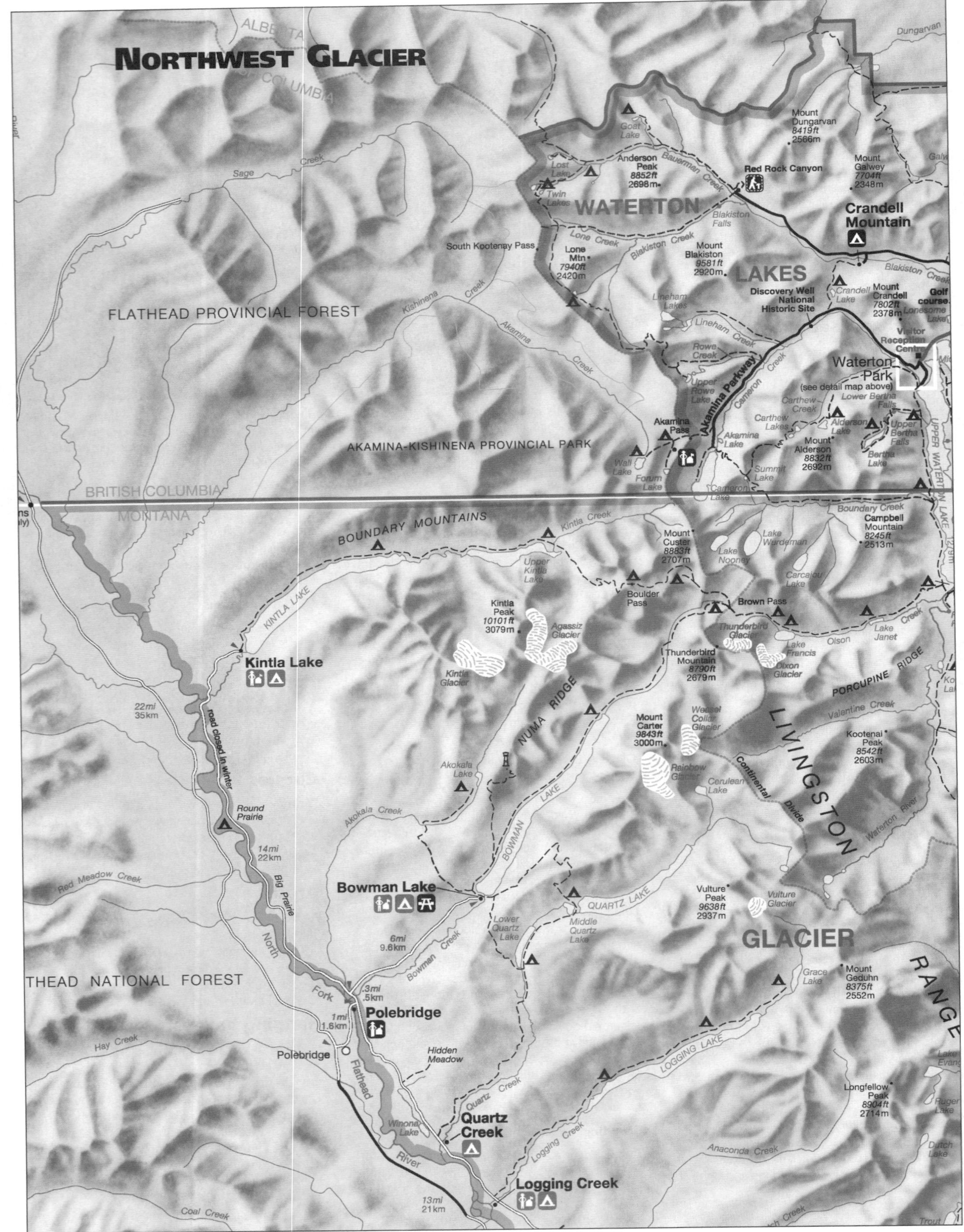
NORTHWEST GLACIER
FLATHEAD PROVINCIAL FOREST
AKAMINA-KISHINENA PROVINCIAL PARK
BRITISH COLUMBIA
MONTANA
WATERTON
LAKES
GLACIER
LIVINGSTON
RANGE
BOUNDARY MOUNTAINS
NUMA RIDGE
PORCUPINE RIDGE
THEAD NATIONAL FOREST
Mount Dungarvan 8419ft 2566m
Anderson Peak 8852ft 2698m
Red Rock Canyon
Mount Galwey 7704ft 2348m
Crandell Mountain
South Kootenay Pass
Lone Mtn 7940ft 2420m
Mount Blakiston 9581ft 2920m
Discovery Well National Historic Site
Mount Crandell 7802ft 2378m
Golf course
Visitor Reception Centre
Waterton Park (see detail map above)
Akamina Pass
Akamina Parkway
Mount Alderson 8832ft 2692m
Mount Custer 8883ft 2707m
Campbell Mountain 8245ft 2513m
Boulder Pass
Brown Pass
Kintla Peak 10101ft 3079m
Agassiz Glacier
Kintla Glacier
Thunderbird Mountain 8790ft 2679m
Thunderbird Glacier
Dixon Glacier
Kintla Lake
Mount Carter 9843ft 3000m
Weasel Collar Glacier
Rainbow Glacier
Continental Divide
Kootenai Peak 8542ft 2603m
road closed in winter
Round Prairie
Bowman Lake
Vulture Peak 9638ft 2937m
Vulture Glacier
Mount Geduhn 8375ft 2552m
Polebridge
Longfellow Peak 8904ft 2714m
Quartz Creek
Logging Creek
22mi 35km
14mi 22km
6mi 9.6km
.3mi .5km
1mi 1.6km
13mi 21km

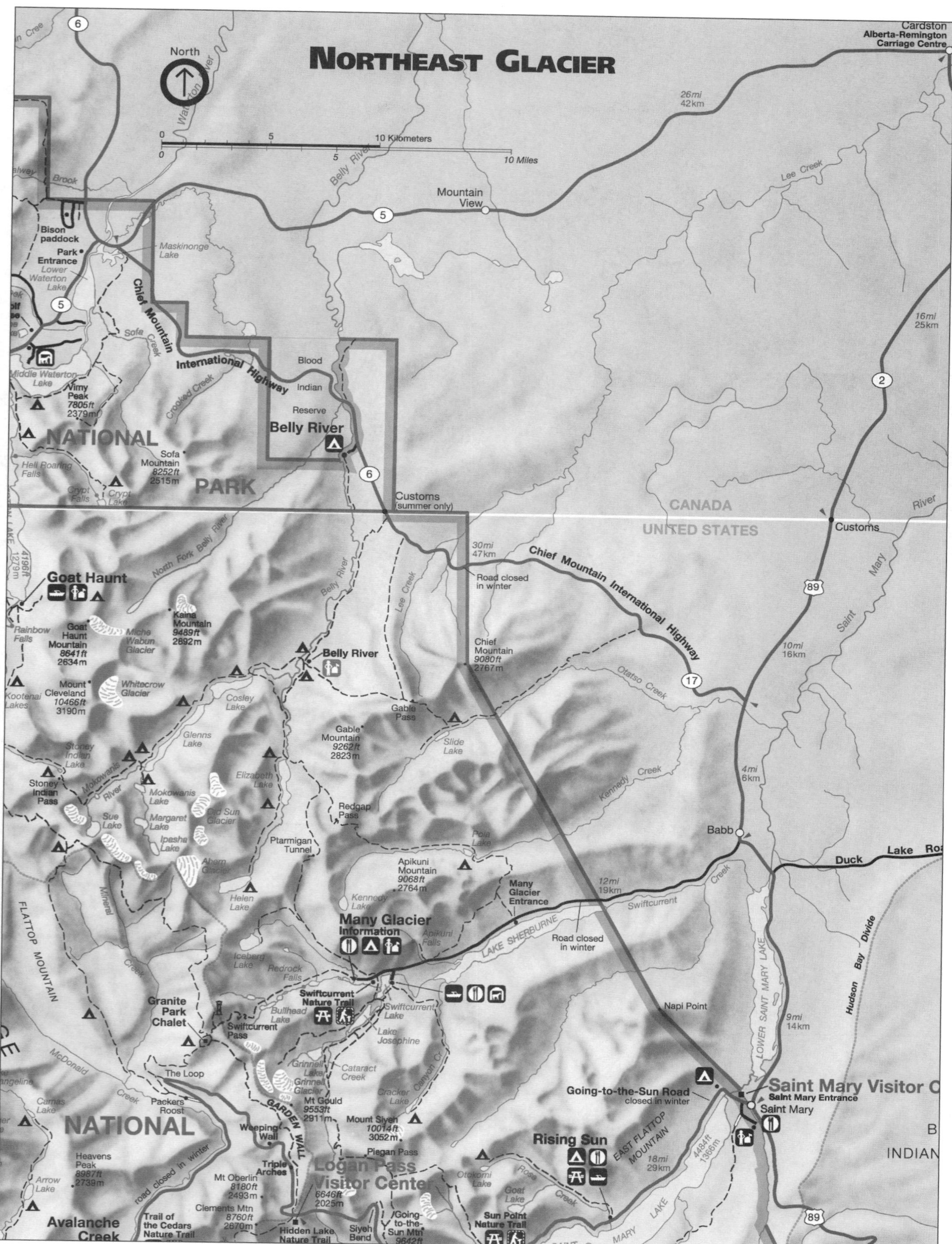

NORTHEAST GLACIER
North
Cardston
Alberta-Remington
Carriage Centre
26mi
42km
0
5
10 Kilometers
0
5
10 Miles
Waterton River
Belly River
Lee Creek
Mountain
View
Brook
Bison
paddock
Park
Entrance
Lower
Waterton
Lake
Maskinonge
Lake
Chief Mountain
International Highway
Sofa
Creek
Crooked Creek
Blood
Indian
Reserve
Belly River
Middle Waterton
Lake
Vimy
Peak
7805ft
2379m
NATIONAL
PARK
Sofa
Mountain
8252ft
2515m
Hell Roaring
Falls
Crypt
Falls
Crypt
Lake
Customs
(summer only)
16mi
25km
CANADA
UNITED STATES
Customs
River
30mi
47km
Chief Mountain International Highway
Road closed
in winter
Goat Haunt
North Fork Belly River
Kaina
Mountain
9489ft
2892m
Rainbow
Falls
Goat
Haunt
Mountain
8641ft
2634m
Miche
Wabun
Glacier
Belly River
Lee Creek
Chief
Mountain
9080ft
2767m
Saint Mary
10mi
16km
Mount
Cleveland
10466ft
3190m
Whitecrow
Glacier
Kootenai
Lakes
Cosley
Lake
Otatso Creek
Gable
Pass
Gable
Mountain
9262ft
2823m
Slide
Lake
Glenns
Lake
Stoney
Indian
Lake
Stoney
Indian
Pass
Mokowanis
River
Elizabeth
Lake
Kennedy Creek
4mi
6km
Mokowanis
Lake
Margaret
Lake
Old Sun
Glacier
Sue
Lake
Ipasha
Lake
Redgap
Pass
Poia
Lake
Babb
Duck
Lake
Ptarmigan
Tunnel
Ahern
Glacier
Apikuni
Mountain
9068ft
2764m
Helen
Lake
Kennedy
Lake
Many
Glacier
Entrance
12mi
19km
Swiftcurrent
Creek
FLATTOP MOUNTAIN
Mineral
Creek
Many Glacier
Information
Apikuni
Falls
LAKE SHERBURNE
Road closed
in winter
Iceberg
Lake
Redrock
Falls
Hudson Bay Divide
Granite
Park
Chalet
Swiftcurrent
Nature Trail
Bullhead
Lake
Swiftcurrent
Lake
Swiftcurrent
Pass
Lake
Josephine
Napi Point
LOWER SAINT MARY LAKE
9mi
14km
McDonald
The Loop
Grinnell
Lake
Grinnell
Glacier
Cataract
Creek
Canyon Cr
Cracker
Lake
Camas
Lake
Creek
Packers
Roost
GARDEN WALL
Mt Gould
9553ft
2911m
Mount Siyeh
10014ft
3052m
Going-to-the-Sun Road
closed in winter
Saint Mary Visitor C
Saint Mary Entrance
Saint Mary
NATIONAL
Weeping
Wall
Rising Sun
EAST FLATTOP MOUNTAIN
18mi
29km
4484ft
1366m
INDIAN
Heavens
Peak
8987ft
2739m
road closed in winter
Triple
Arches
Piegan Pass
Logan Pass
Visitor Center
6646ft
2025m
Otokomi
Lake
Goat
Lake
Rose
Creek
Arrow
Lake
Mt Oberlin
8180ft
2493m
Clements Mtn
8760ft
2670m
Avalanche
Creek
Trail of
the Cedars
Nature Trail
Hidden Lake
Nature Trail
Siyeh
Bend
Going-
to-the-
Sun Mtn
9642ft
Sun Point
Nature Trail
MARY LAKE

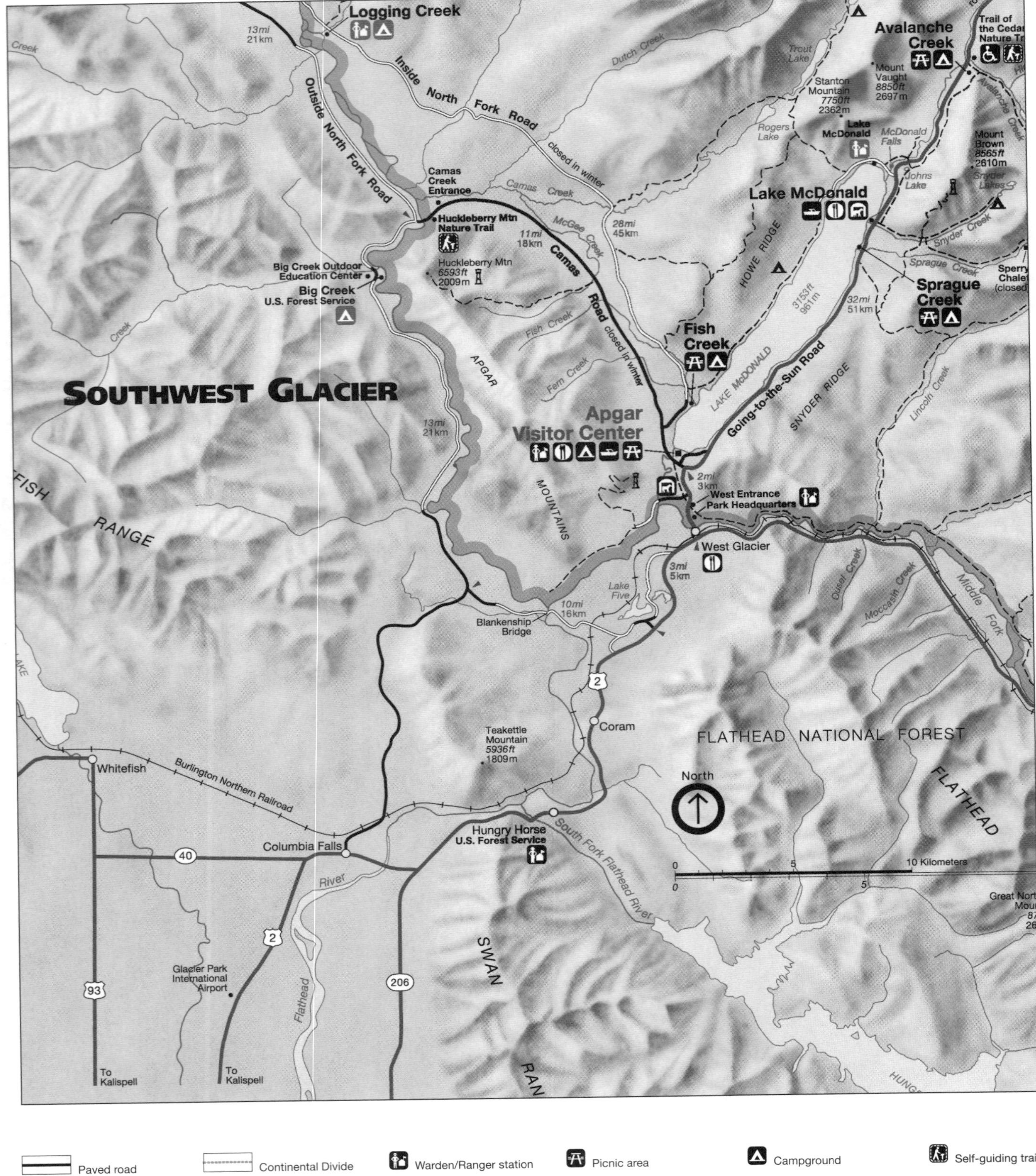


Paved road
Unpaved road
Trail
Continental Divide
Glacier
0.5mi 0.8km Distance indicator
Warden/Ranger station
Warden/Ranger station (infrequently staffed)
Food service and lodging
Picnic area
Riding stable
Boat tour/rentals
Campground
Primitive campground
Backcountry campsite
Self-guiding trail
Wheelchair accessible trail
Lookout tower

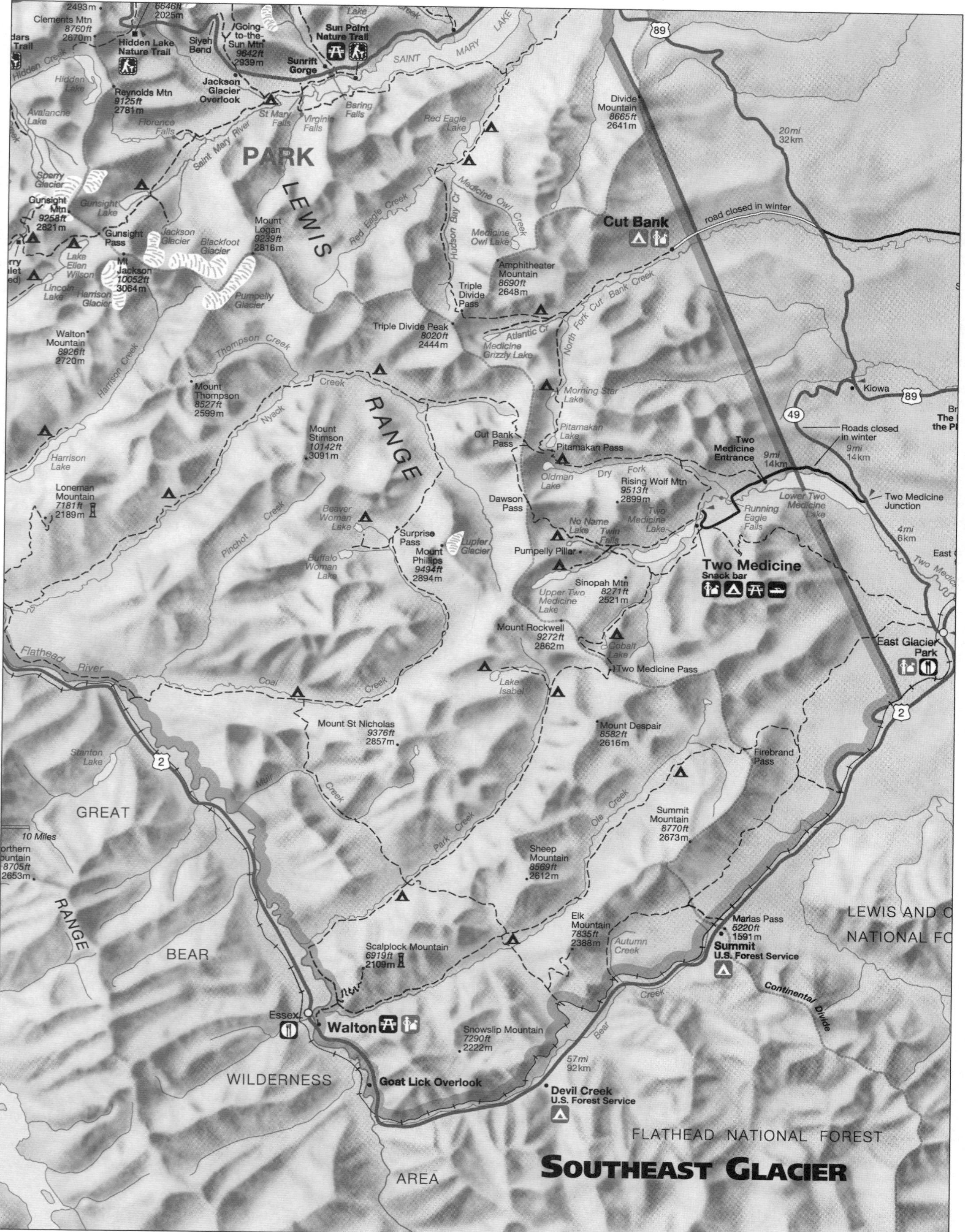
SOUTHEAST GLACIER
PARK
LEWIS
RANGE
Cut Bank
Two Medicine
Snack bar
East Glacier Park
Walton
Essex
Goat Lick Overlook
Summit
U.S. Forest Service
Devil Creek
U.S. Forest Service
Marias Pass
5220ft
1591m
Two Medicine Entrance
Two Medicine Junction
Kiowa
road closed in winter
Roads closed in winter
GREAT
BEAR
WILDERNESS
AREA
FLATHEAD NATIONAL FOREST
LEWIS AND C
NATIONAL FO
Continental Divide
Mount St Nicholas
9376ft
2857m
Mount Rockwell
9272ft
2862m
Rising Wolf Mtn
9513ft
2899m
Sinopah Mtn
8271ft
2521m
Mount Stimson
10142ft
3091m
Mount Phillips
9494ft
2894m
Summit Mountain
8770ft
2673m
Sheep Mountain
8569ft
2612m
Elk Mountain
7835ft
2388m
Scalplock Mountain
6919ft
2109m
Snowslip Mountain
7290ft
2222m
Mount Despair
8582ft
2616m
Triple Divide Peak
8020ft
2444m
Divide Mountain
8665ft
2641m
Amphitheater Mountain
8690ft
2648m
Mount Logan
9239ft
2816m
Mount Thompson
8527ft
2599m
Walton Mountain
8926ft
2720m
Loneman Mountain
7181ft
2189m
Mt Jackson
10052ft
3064m
Gunsight Mtn
9258ft
2821m
Reynolds Mtn
9125ft
2781m
Clements Mtn
8760ft
2670m
Going-to-the-Sun Mtn
9642ft
2939m
Jackson Glacier Overlook
Hidden Lake Nature Trail
Sun Point Nature Trail
Sunrift Gorge
Pitamakan Pass
Cut Bank Pass
Dawson Pass
Surprise Pass
Two Medicine Pass
Firebrand Pass
Triple Divide Pass
Gunsight Pass
Pumpelly Pillar
Flathead River
20mi
32km
9mi
14km
4mi
6km
57mi
92km

*Mt. Reynolds dominates the skyline at busy Logan Pass. From this view a few miles away in Preston Park, it is a pillar of serene majesty. Mt. Reynolds is the classic glacial horn, a peak carved by glaciers working on several sides of the mountain. As the glaciers carved at the mountainsides, they ground further and further back and up the peak, creating a towering pyramid shaped peak.*

### Moraines

Moraines form at the sides and front of a glacier. In a glacier there is always a flow of ice from the head to the toe. This conveyor belt like flow brings with it the rock and debris trapped in the ice. As it reaches the sides or front and the ice melts, this trapped material is released forming large piles. These piles of glacially transported material are called moraines. Moraines from the present glaciers are visible as mounds of rock and gravel along the sides and front of the ice. Plants soon colonize this new soil. Forests and meadows cover many ancient moraines making them harder to spot.

## Glacier at a Glimpse

### Apgar—elev. 3200 ft.

Apgar services are generally available mid-May through October and include: boat rentals, campground, campstore, gift shops, horseback rides, picnic area, restaurants, and a visitor center. Lodging is available at the Village Inn and the Apgar Village Lodge.

### Goat Haunt—elev. 4200 ft.

Reached only by boat or foot, Goat Haunt Ranger Station is open daily (limited hours) in summer. Exhibits, restrooms, camping (permit required) and picnicking are available.

### Lake McDonald—elev. 3150 ft.

At Lake McDonald, services are generally available June through late September and include: boat rentals, boat cruises, campstore, gift shops, horseback rides, and restaurants. Lodging is available at Lake McDonald Lodge. Camping is available at Sprague Creek Campground two miles south of the lodge.

### Rising Sun—elev. 4550 ft.

Services at Rising Sun are generally available June through early September and include: boat cruises, campground, campstore, gift shops, restaurant, and showers. Lodging is available at the Rising Sun Motor Inn. The Sun Point Nature Trail and picnic area are two miles west.

### St. Mary—elev. 4500 ft.

In-park services are generally available mid-May through mid-October at the St. Mary Visitor Center and Campground.

### Two Medicine—elev. 5150 ft.

Services are generally available June through mid-September and include: boat cruises, boat rentals, campground, campstore, gift shop, and picnic area. No overnight lodging is available.

### Walton—elev. 3900 ft.

There is a picnic area at Walton. Two miles south is the Goat Lick wildlife viewing area. The Goat Lick parking area is generally open May through October. Mountain goat sightings are best in early summer.

### Waterton—elev. 4200 ft.

Most services available June through September. Some services available year-round.

### Logan Pass—elev. 6640 ft.

The visitor center at Logan Pass is generally open mid-June through mid-October. Book sales are available in the visitor center and the Hidden Lake Nature Trail starts behind it. There is no phone, food, or beverage service available at Logan Pass.

### Many Glacier—elev. 4900 ft.

Services are generally available June through late-September and include: boat rentals, boat cruises, campstore, campground, gift shops, horseback rides, restaurants, and showers. Lodging is available at the Many Glacier Hotel and the Swiftcurrent Motor Inn. The Many Glacier Ranger Station is open daily in the summer for information and book sales. Swiftcurrent Nature Trail starts at the picnic area, just east of the ranger station.

### Polebridge—elev. 3600 ft.

Services are located outside the park in the community of Polebridge. The ranger station at the entrance to the park has book sales and information in the summer.

## Be Aware That

- Feeding or disturbing wildlife is prohibited.
- Open containers of alcohol in a motor vehicle are prohibited.
- Removal of any natural or cultural feature like flowers, rocks, artifacts, or antlers is prohibited.
- Picking of berries (including huckleberries) is limited to one quart per person.
- Picking of mushrooms is prohibited.
- Carrying or possessing loaded weapons is prohibited. Unloaded firearms may be trans-ported in a vehicle if cased, broken down or rendered inoperable, and kept out of sight.

## Pets

- Pets are permitted in campgrounds, along roads, and in parking areas, but they must be on a leash of 6 feet or less, caged, or in a vehicle at all times. They are not allowed in restaurants, stores, or visitor centers. *Pet owners are required to pick up after their pets and dispose of waste properly. Pets may not be left unattended and are not permitted on trails, along lake shores, or in the backcountry.*

## Bicycling

Bicycles are allowed on roadways, bike routes, and parking areas. They are not al-lowed on trails. Observe all traffic regulations. Keep to the right side of the road and ride in single file. Pull over if four or more vehicles stack up behind you. During periods of low visibility a white light or reflector, visible from a distance of at least 500 feet to the front, and a red light or reflector, visible from at least 200 feet to the rear, are required. Be visible! Attach a bright flag on a pole and wear light-colored clothing. Watch for falling rocks, drainage grates, and ice on road.

## Driving in the Park

The roads of Glacier National Park offer access to some of the most spectacular mountain scenery in the world.

Take time to enjoy the views. If more than four vehicles stack up behind you, please use a pullout to let them pass safely. Be aware of wildlife along the roads, especially at dusk or at night. Animals often dart out in front of vehicles. Please watch for and give the right of way to children and pedestrians. Obey the posted speed limit at all times.

### Road Construction

Due to the long snowy winters and late spring thaw, road construction/repair can only be accomplished in the summer months. All construction activities in the park are undertaken with care to insure that visitors are inconvenienced as little as possible.

## Going-to-the-Sun Road

Completed in 1932, this 52-mile road combines

both history and unparalleled scenery. It bisects the heart of Glacier. Its construction made accessible the remote backcountry of the park to everyone. While portions of this scenic route remain open year-round, the higher sections are generally not open until late May or June and close the third Monday in October, unless closed earlier by snowfall. To help reduce congestion along this narrow winding road, vehicle size restrictions are in effect. Over time, it became apparent that the road was not designed for the number or size of today's vehicles. Larger vehicles frequently had difficulty negotiating the sharp corners and often caused considerable traffic delays. To allow for a safe and enjoyable experience, vehicle size restrictions are in effect at all times.

## Going-to-the-Sun Road—Vehicle Size Restrictions

Vehicles, and vehicle combinations, longer than 21 feet (including bumpers) and wider than 8 feet (including mirrors), are prohibited between Avalanche Campground and the Sun Point parking area. Alternative transportation is available

## Logan Pass

A drive over Logan Pass is spectacular. The Going-to-the-Sun Road provides access to the alpine zone for vast numbers of people who otherwise would not be able to enjoy this beautiful, yet fragile, section of the park. However, with increased visitation it becomes more difficult every year to accommodate the growing number of park visitors. Frequently, in July and August, the parking lot at Logan Pass fills beyond capacity and visitors are forced to drive on without stopping. To avoid the crowds, plan on visiting Logan Pass early in the day or late in the afternoon. Most guided tours also stop at Logan Pass.

Frequently, in July and August, the parking lot at Logan Pass fills beyond capacity, forcing visitors to drive on without stopping. To avoid the crowds, plan on visiting Logan Pass early in the day or late in the afternoon. Guided tours, that stop at Logan Pass, are available, and help provide valuable service to those with oversized vehicles.

## Safety

### Water

**Rivers and Lakes:** Use extreme caution near water. Swift, cold glacial streams and rivers, moss-covered rocks, and slippery logs all present dangers. Children, photographers, boaters, rafters, swimmers, and fishermen have fallen victim to these rapid, frigid streams and deep glacial lakes.

Avoid wading in or fording swift streams. Never walk, play, or climb on slippery rocks and logs, especially around waterfalls. When boating, don't stand up or lean over the side, and always wear a lifejacket.

**Drowning:** Sudden immersion in cold water (below 80° F, 27° C) may trigger the "mammalian diving reflex." This reflex restricts blood from outlying areas of the body and routes it to vital organs like the heart, lungs, and brain. The colder the water, the younger the victim, and the quicker the rescue, the better the chance for survival. Some cold-water drowning victims have survived with no brain damage after being submerged for over 30 minutes.

**Revival Procedure:**
- Retrieve victim from water without endangering yourself.
- Prevent further body heat loss, but do not rewarm.
- Near-drowning victims may look dead. Don't let this stop you from trying to revive them! If there is no pulse, start CPR regardless of the duration of submersion.
- Delayed symptoms may occur within 24 hours.Victims must be evaluated by a physician.

**Giardia:** Giardiasis can be caused by a parasite (Giardia lamblia) found in park lakes and streams. Persistent, severe diarrhea, abdominal cramps, and nausea are the main symptoms of this disease. If you experience any symptoms, contact a physician. When hiking, carry water from one of the park's treated water systems. If you plan to camp in the backcountry, follow recommendations received with your permit. The easiest effective water treatments are either to bring water to a boil or to use an approved filter.

**Hypothermia:** Hypothermia, the "progressive physical collapse and reduced mental capacity resulting from the chilling of the inner core of the human body," can occur even at temperatures above freezing.Temperatures can drop rapidly. Sudden mountain storms can change a warm and pleasant hike into a drenching, bitterly cold and life-threatening experience. People in poor physical shape or who are exhausted are particularly at risk.

*Prevention:*
- Avoid hypothermia by using water-resistant clothing before you become wet.
- Wear clothing that wicks moisture away.
- Minimize wind exposure and if your clothes become wet, replace them.
- Avoid sweating by dressing in layers, rather than in a single bulky garment.
- Pack a sweater, warm hat, and raingear for any hike.

*Warning Signs:*
- Uncontrolled shivering, slow or slurred speech, memory lapses and incoherence, lack of coordination such as immobile or fumbling hands, stumbling, a lurching gait, drowsiness, and exhaustion.

*Immediate Treatment*
- Seek shelter from weather and get the victim into dry clothes.
- Give warm non-alcoholic drinks.
- Build a fire and keep victim awake.
- Strip victim and yourself, and get into sleeping bag making skin-to-skin contact.
- If victim is semi-conscious or worse, get professional help immediately.

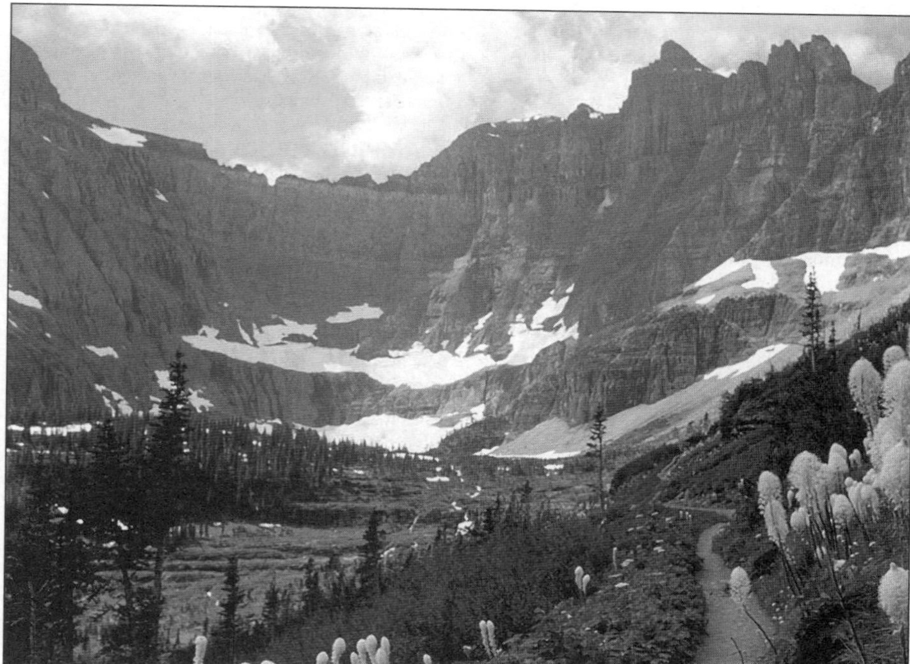

*Iceberg Cirque. NPS Photo*

### Wildlife Hazards

**Bears:** Recommended safety precautions and procedures for bears are found elsewhere in this chapter.

**Mountain Lions:** A glimpse of one of these magnificent cats would be a vacation highlight, but you need to take precautions to protect you and your children from an accidental encounter. *Don't hike alone. Make noise to avoid surprising a lion and keep children close to you at all times. If you do encounter a lion, do not run.Talk calmly, avert your gaze, stand tall, and back away. Unlike with bears, if attack seems imminent, act aggressively. Do not crouch and do not turn away. Lions may be scared away by being struck with rocks or sticks, or by being kicked or hit.* Lions are primarily nocturnal, but they have attacked in broad daylight.They rarely prey on humans, but such behavior occasionally does occur. Children and small adults are particularly vulnerable. Report all mountain lion encounters immediately!

***Whether bears, mountain lions, goats, sheep, deer, squirrels, marmots, or any other species, all park wildlife can present a very real and painful threat, especially females with young. Always***

*enjoy wildlife from the safety of your car or from a safe distance. Feeding, harassing, or molesting wildlife is strictly prohibited and subject to fine.*

## Medical Services

If you are injured or suddenly become ill while visiting the parks, please contact a warden or ranger for information and assistance. To ensure adequate staffing on your arrival at a hospital, call before setting out.

**Montana Hospitals**
Glacier County Medical Center
892-2nd St. E., Cut Bank, MT
873-2251

Kalispell Regional Hospital
310 SunnyView Lane, Kalispell, MT
752-5111

NorthValley Hospital
Highway 93 South, Whitefish, MT
862-2501

Teton Medical Center
915 4 NW, Choteau, MT
466-5763

## Watch Your Step

**Mountainous Terrain:** Many accidents occur when people fall after stepping off trails or roadsides, or by venturing onto very steep slopes. Stay on designated trails and don't go beyond protective fencing or guard rails. Supervise children closely in such areas. At upper elevations, trails should be followed carefully, noting directions given by trail signs and markers.

**Snow and Ice:** Snowfields and glaciers present serious hazards. Snowbridges may conceal deep crevasses on glaciers or large hidden cavities under snowfields, and collapse under the weight of an unsuspecting hiker. Don't slide on snowbanks. People often lose control and slide into rocks or trees. Exercise caution around any snowfield in the parks.

**Ticks:** Ticks are most active in spring and early summer. Most bites don't result in illness, but several serious diseases, like Rocky Mountain Spotted Fever, can be transmitted. Completely remove attached ticks and disinfect the site. If rashes or lesions form around the bite, or if unexplained symptoms occur, consult a physician.

**Rodents and Hantavirus:** Deer mice and other rodents are possible carriers of Hantavirus, an acute respiratory disease affecting the lungs. The most likely source of infection is from rodent urine and droppings inhaled as aerosols or dust.

Avoid areas where rodents may congregate such as burrows or nests, old uncleaned cabins, or other rodent-infested structures. Try to camp away from possible rodent burrows or shelters (garbage dumps and woodpiles), and keep food in rodent-proof containers. To prevent the spread of dust in the air, spray affected areas with a disinfectant before cleaning.

Initial symptoms are almost identical to the onset of flu. If you have potentially been exposed and exhibit flu-like symptoms, you should seek medical care immediately.

# Camping Regulations & Information

## Finding a Site

- Reservations are required at Fish Creek and St. Mary Campgrounds through the National Park Reservation Service (800-365-CAMP). Campers without advance reservations may inquire about site availability at kiosks located near the campground entrance.
- To register for your campsite at a "first-come, first-served" campground, stop at the registration and information bulletin board located at the entrance to campgrounds or campground loops. Select a site, fill out a fee envelope completely, and deposit it in the fee tube within 30 minutes. Pay for only 1 night at a time. Park rangers can not give refunds.
- Check out time is 12:00 noon.
- If staying an additional night, pay for the site and place a new receipt on your site post before leaving the campground.
- Camp only in designated sites in campgrounds. There are no overflow facilities.
- Camping or sleeping in vehicles along roadways is prohibited.
- Pitch tents on designated tent pads where available or on bare ground, not vegetated areas.
- Leave tables, grates, logs, and rocks as you find them.
- There is a camping limit of 7 days during July and August, with a maximum of 14 days in a calendar year.
- Park all vehicles only in the space provided for your campsite. Do not obstruct the road or other sites.

## Saving Your Site

- Place envelope fee receipt in the clip on your numbered site post.
- A paper plate strung across the entrance to your site with your name and date will show the site is taken. Do not place bags over the numbered site posts. Remove all markings when vacating the site.
- Sites are not to be left unattended for over 24 hours.

## Campsite Capacity

- There is a limit per site of 8 people and 2 tents, or a maximum of 2 vehicles per site where space is available.
- Campsites for groups of 9-24 campers are available at Apgar, Many Glacier, St. Mary, and Two Medicine.

## Food Storage Regulations

- Keep a clean camp!
- When it is not being consumed, all food, beverages, coolers, cooking utensils, food containers, and pet food must be kept in a closed, hard-sided vehicle, day or night.

# Points of Interest Along the Going-to-the-Sun Road

Driving the Going-to-the-Sun Road is a highlight of any park visit. Because of the steep, narrow nature of the road vehicle length limitations are in effect on the 24-mile section between Avalanche Campground (#5), west of Logan Pass, and Sun Point (#12) to the east.

A maximum vehicle length of 21 feet and a maximum width of 8 feet, including mirrors, is allowed on the Going-To-The-Sun Road.

All other vehicles must use an alternate route. Shuttle service and trailer parking are available.

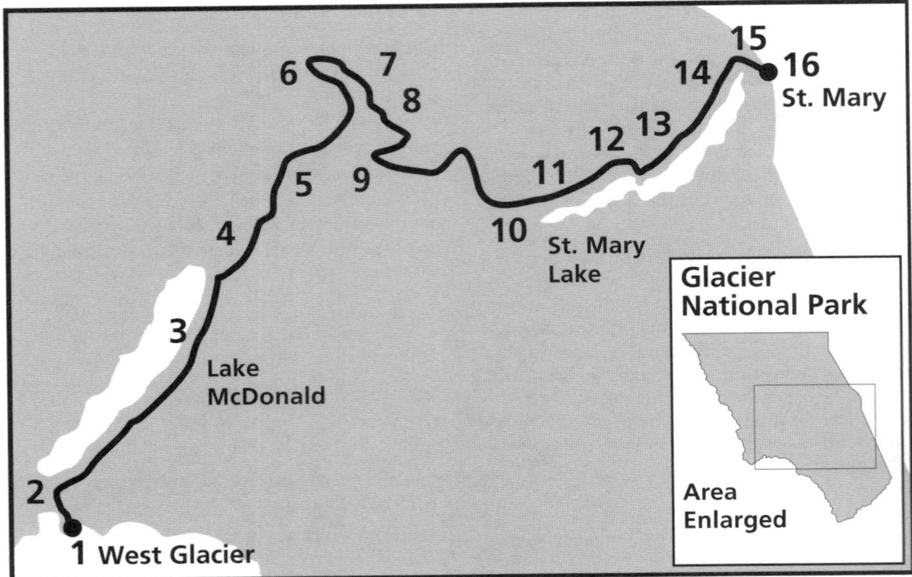

| Miles from: | West Glacier | St. Mary | |
|---|---|---|---|
| 1. **West Glacier** | 0.0 | 50.1 | All services available in this community just outside the park. |
| 2. **Apgar** | 2.6 | 47.5 | Visitor center, boat dock, all services except gas. |
| 3. **Lake McDonald Historic District** | 10.8 | 39.3 | Situated on the shores of Lake McDonald, the lodge is reminiscent of a Swiss chalet with a hunting lodge atmosphere. All services are available. |
| 4. **Johns Lake Pullout** | 12.8 | 37.3 | Enjoy a short 0.5 mile walk through a red cedar/hemlock forest to boggy Johns Lake. Look for moose and waterfowl. |
| 5. **Trail of the Cedars Avalanche Campground** | 16.2 | 33.9 | This 0.3 mile handicapped accessible trail winds through an old cedar/hemlock forest. Such old growth forests provide critical habitat for a variety of wildlife. |
| 6. **The Loop** | 24.6 | 25.5 | The Loop affords a scenic view of Heaven's Peak. A strenuous 4 mile hike to Granite Park Chalet begins here. |
| 7. **Bird Woman Falls Overlook** | 26.8 | 23.3 | Across the valley Bird Woman Falls cascades from a hanging valley on the slopes of Mt. Oberlin. Haystack Creek flows under the road directly ahead. |
| 8. **Weeping Wall** | 28.7 | 21.4 | Roll up your windows as you pass the Weeping Wall. A gushing waterfall in spring, the flow reduces to a mere trickle in fall. |
| 9. **Logan Pass** | 32.0 | 18.1 | At an elevation of 6680 ft., the Logan Pass Visitor Center sits atop the Continental Divide. Exhibits, publications, and informative programs available. |
| 10. **Jackson Glacier Overlook** | 36.1 | 14.0 | This is the best view of a glacier from the Going-to-the-Sun Road. Trailhead for Gunsight Lake and Gunsight Pass. |
| 11. **Sunrift Gorge** | 39.4 | 10.7 | A spectacular view of a water carved gorge is just a short 75' walk. Look for water ouzels in the creek. This chunky slate-grey bird is often sighted along rushing streams, foraging for aquatic insects. |
| 12. **Sun Point** **Park oversize vehicles here to continue over the Going-to-the-Sun Road.* | 40.0 | 10.1 | Stretch your legs, as you explore the effects of water, wind, ice, and sunlight on the 1.2 mile Sun Point Nature Trail. Views of Baring Falls and St. Mary Lake are highlights. |
| 13. **Rising Sun** | 43.8 | 6.3 | Campground, boat dock, all services available. |
| 14. **Two Dog Flats** | 48.0 | 2.1 | This native grassland community provides important habitat for a number of species. Hawks prey upon small mammals while songbirds forage on seeds and insects. Two Dog Flats supplies needed winter range for a large elk population. |
| 15. **St. Mary Visitor Center** | 49.3 | 0.8 | Exhibits, publications, and informative programs available. |
| 16. **St. Mary** | 50.1 | 0.0 | All services available in this community just outside the park. |

• Campers without vehicles, must use available food lockers or hanging devices for all food storage (check with a ranger or campground host for locations).

• Garbage must be properly stored at all times. Use bearproof trash cans provided. Violation of these regulations will likely result in a $50 fine and/or confiscation of these items.

## Sanitation and Showers

• All waste water from showers and sinks, especially dishwater, must be contained, and disposed of in utility sinks or RV dump stations. Do not leave waste water unattended. Human waste must be disposed of in toilets or RV dump stations. Recreational vehicles must use drain hoses at dump stations.

• No utility hook-ups are provided in any park campground. Individual hookups to water, sewage, or electrical outlets are prohibited.

• Washing dishes, clothing, people, or cleaning fish at water faucets is prohibited. Wash dishes at campsite; filter food scraps and dispose of them in bearproof trash cans.

• Fee showers are available at Rising Sun and Swiftcurrent Motor Inns and private campgrounds adjacent to the park.

## Quiet Hours

• Quiet hours are from 8:00 p.m. to 8:00 a.m. Please be considerate of your neighbor. All noise must be kept to a level that does not unreasonably disturb others.

• Generators may not be operated during quiet hours.

• The use of fireworks is prohibited within Glacier National Park.

## Vehicle and Bicycle Use

• Campground speed limits are 10 miles per hour.

• Bicycles are permitted only on roadways.

## Pets

• Pets are not permitted on trails or along lake shores. All unplowed roadways are "trails" in the winter.

• Pets must be on a leash of 6 feet or less, caged, or in vehicles at all times. Pets are not to be left unattended at any time.

# Hiking and Camping in Bear Country

**Although the risk of an encounter with a bear is low, there are no guarantees of your safety.** Minimize your risks by following the guidelines below.

While most visitors never see a bear, all of the park is bear country. Whether you plan to hike the trails, drive the roads, or stay overnight in a campground or lodge, take the time to learn the special precautions bear country demands. Report all sighting of bears as soon as possible!

## Hiking in Bear Country

### Don't Surprise Bears!

Bears will usually move out of the way if they hear people approaching, so make noise. Most bells are not loud enough. Calling out and clapping hands loudly at regular intervals is are better ways to make your presence known. Hiking quietly endangers you, the bear, and other hikers.

When bears charge hikers, the trail may be temporarily closed for public safety. While the trail remains closed, other visitors miss the opportunity to enjoy it. A bear constantly surprised by people may become habituated to close human contact and less likely to avoid people. This sets up a dangerous situation for both visitors and bears.

### Don't Make Assumptions!

You can't predict when and where bears might be encountered along a trail. People often assume they don't have to make noise while hiking on a well-used trail. Some of the most frequently used trails in the park are surrounded by excellent bear habitat. People have been charged and injured by bears fleeing from silent hikers who unwittingly surprised bears along the trail. Even if other hikers haven't seen bears along a trail section recently, don't assume there are no bears present.

Don't assume a bear's hearing is any better than your own. Some trail conditions make it hard for bears to see, hear, or smell approaching hikers. Be particularly careful by streams, against the wind, or in dense vegetation. A blind corner or a rise in the trail also requires special attention.

Keep children close by. Hike in groups and avoid hiking early in the morning, late in the day, or after dark.

### Inform Yourself About Bears

Park staff can help you identify signs of bear activity like tracks, torn-up logs, trampled vegetation, droppings, and overturned rocks. Bears spend a lot of time eating, so avoid hiking in obvious feeding areas like berry patches, cow parsnip thickets, or fields of glacier lilies.

### Don't Approach Bears!

Never intentionally get close to a bear. Individual bears have their own personal space requirements which vary depending on their mood. Each will react differently and its behavior can't be predicted. All bears are dangerous and should be respected equally.

**A fed bear is a dead bear! Bears are intelligent and learn very quickly how to obtain human food once they have tasted it. Bears that obtain human food may have to be destroyed. Leaving food, packs, or garbage unattended, even for a few minutes, sets up a potentially dangerous situation.**

### Pepper Spray

This aerosol pepper derivative triggers temporarily incapacitating discomfort in bears. It is a non-toxic and non-lethal means of deterring bears.

There have been cases where pepper spray apparently repelled aggressive or attacking bears and accounts where it has not worked as well as expected.

Factors influencing effectiveness include distance, wind, rainy weather, temperature extremes, and product shelf life.

If you decide to carry spray, use it only in situations where aggressive bear behavior justifies its use. Pepper spray is intended to be sprayed into the face of an oncoming bear. It is not intended to act as a repellent. Do not spray gear or around camp with pepper spray. **Under no circumstances should pepper spray create a false sense of security or serve as a substitute for standard safety precautions in bear country.** Be aware that you may not be able to cross the U.S./Canada border with pepper spray; check before attempting.

### Roadside Bears

It's exciting to see bears up close but we must act responsibly to keep them wild and alive. Do not approach bears for pictures or entice them to come closer. Never feed bears! Bears that receive human food may have to be destroyed.

If you see a bear from your car, stay inside. Leaving your vehicle endangers your safety and the bear's, and exposes you to traffic hazards. If traffic is heavy, keep your eyes on the road and don't stop. Accept the fact that, while your passengers may get a quick look, you may not. If traffic is light, slow down and pull over when it is safe to do so. Don't stop in the middle of the road, or close to a hill or curve where other drivers may not see you in time to avoid a collision. Exercising some common sense during the excitement of sighting a bear is important to you, the bear, and other visitors.

### If You Encounter a Bear

A commonly asked question is "What do I do if I run into a bear?" There is no easy answer. Like people, bears react differently to each situation. The best thing you can do is to make sure you have read all the suggestions for hiking and camping in bear country and follow them. Avoid encounters by being alert and making noise.

Bears may appear tolerant of people and then attack without warning. A bear's body language can help determine its mood. In general, bears show agitation by swaying their heads, huffing, and clacking their teeth. Lowered head and laid-back ears also indicate aggression. Bears may stand on their hind legs or approach to get a better view, but these actions are not necessarily signs of aggression. The bear may not have identified you as a person and is unable to smell or hear you from a distance.

### Bear Attacks

Almost 2 million people visit Waterton-Glacier yearly, and it seems that one or two bear attacks occur each year. The vast majority of these occur because people have surprised the bear. In this type of situation the bear may attack as a defensive maneuver.

If you surprise a bear, here are a few guidelines to follow that may help:

- Talk quietly or not at all; the time to make loud noise is before you encounter a bear. Try to detour around the bear if possible.

- Do not run! Back away slowly, but stop if it seems to agitate the bear.
- Assume a nonthreatening posture. Turn sideways, or bend at the knees to appear smaller.
- Use peripheral vision. Bears appear to interpret direct eye contact as threatening.
- Drop something (not food) to distract the bear. Keep your pack on for protection in case of an attack.
- If a bear attacks and you have pepper spray, use it!
- If the bear makes contact, protect your chest and abdomen by falling to the ground on your stomach, or assuming a fetal position to reduce the severity of an attack. Cover the back of your neck with your hands. Do not move until you are certain the bear has left.

In rare cases bears may attack at night or after stalking people.

This kind of attack is very rare. It can be very serious because it often means the bear is looking for food and preying on you.

- If you are attacked at night or if you feel you have been stalked and attacked as prey, try to escape. If you cannot escape, or if the bear follows, use pepper spray, or shout and try to intimidate the bear with a branch or rock. Do whatever it takes to let the bear know you are not easy prey.

### Camping & Bears

Odors attract bears. The campground and developed areas can remain "unattractive" to bears if each visitor manages food and trash properly. Regulations require that all edibles (including pet food), food containers (empty or not), and cookware (clean or not) be stored in a hard-sided vehicle or food locker when not in use, day or night.

• Keep a clean camp! Improperly stored or unattended food will likely result in confiscation of items and/or issuance of a Vio-lation Notice.

• Inspect campsites for bear sign and for careless campers nearby. Notify a ranger or warden of potential problems.

• Place all trash in bearproof containers

• Pets, especially dogs, must be kept under physical restraint.

• Report all bear sightings to the nearest ranger or warden immediately.

## Grizzly or Black Bear?

### What Kind of Bear Is That?

Waterton-Glacier International Peace Park is home to both black and grizzly bears. Even for experts, it is often difficult to distinguish between the species. The following clues will help to tell the species apart:

### Color

Color is not a reliable indicator of species. Contrary to their name black bears also come in brown, cinnamon, and blond. Grizzlies range from blond to nearly black. Grizzlies sometimes have silver-tipped guard hairs that give them a "grizzled" appearance.

## Physical Features

Grizzly bears often have a dished-in face and a large hump of heavy muscle above the shoulders. Their claws are around four inches (10 cm) long. A black bear's facial profile is much straighter from tip of nose to ears, without the dished-in look. Black bears lack the distinctive hump of a grizzly and have shorter claws, generally around one and a half inches (4 cm) long.

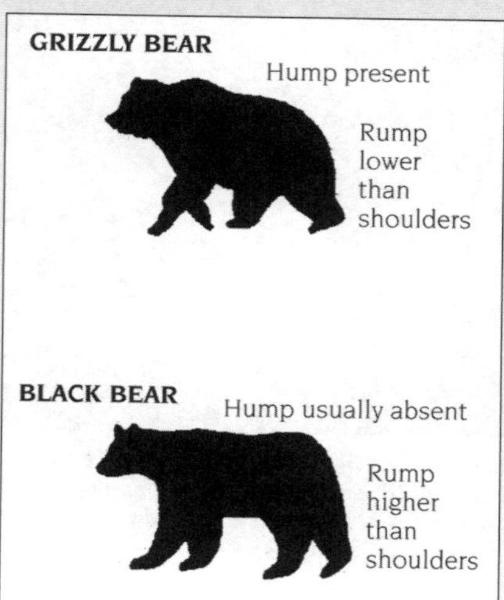


• Pets must be restrained while in open bed pick-up trucks.

• Pet waste must be collected and deposited in a trash receptacle.

### Fires and Firewood

• Gathering of firewood is prohibited EXCEPT in the following areas:

- Along the Inside North Fork Road from one mile north of Fish Creek Campground to Kintla Lake Campground.

- Along the Bowman Lake Road.

• In the areas listed above, only dead wood on the ground may be collected for use as fuel for campfires within Glacier National Park. Chainsaws are not permitted.

• Fires must be kept inside the fire grates and attended at all times. Be sure your fire is dead out when leaving your site for any reason.

• Firewood is available for sale at most campstores.

### Preserving the Natural Scene

• LEAVE NO TRACE is a national program which promotes outdoor skills and ethics for recreational users of our public lands—practice Leave No Trace techniques.

• Removal of any natural or cultural feature, like plants, rocks, artifacts, or antlers is prohibited.

• Do not dig, trench, or level the ground. Do not drive nails into, or strip bark from trees.

• Human food is harmful to all animals, including deer, birds, and chipmunks! Feeding wildlife is prohibited. Violations can result in a minimum $100.00 fine.

## Fishing

Fishing in Glacier National Park does not require a license, but there are regulations governing fishing that need to be followed. The general park fishing season is from the third Saturday in May to November 30. Several park streams are either closed to fishing or are catch-and- release only. Stop at a visitor center to obtain a copy of the regulations. Fishing from mid-channel to the west bank of the North Fork of the Flathead and all of the Middle Fork of the Flathead requires a Montana fishing license. The Blackfeet Reservation, just east of the park, requires their own fishing permit.

## Boating

Glacier National Park offers a variety of boating experiences. Boat launching ramps are available on Bowman and McDonald Lakes on the west side, and St. Mary and Two Medicine Lakes on the east side of the park.

Canoes or rafts can be carried to many smaller waters. White water canoeing, kayaking, or rafting can be enjoyed on the Flathead River which forms the south and west boundary of Glacier.

The rivers and lakes in this mountainous region are very cold. All water users (boaters, swimmers, and skiers) should be aware of the dangers of hypothermia at any time of the year.

### Accidents & Reports

Any accident resulting in death, personal injury, or property damage shall be reported (by each boat operator involved) to a park ranger as soon as possible, and no later than 24 hours after the incident. Boaters should render assistance to all persons needing help.

Give in writing the name and address of the boat operator and the identification of the boat to any injured person or to the owner of any property damaged.

### Registration

All motorboats and sailboats 12 feet in length and longer must be registered and numbered according to State of Montana regulations. Hand propelled boats are exempt, and boats from other states or countries may be used temporarily without Montana registration.

### Rules of the Waterways

• Keep to the right in channels when safe & practicable.

• Keep to the right when approaching another boat head-on or nearly so.

• Boats propelled by a motor shall keep clear of boats propelled by oars, paddles, or sails.

• Yield right-of-way to vessels on your right side in crossing situations.

• Yield right-of-way to vessels you overtake or pass.

### Where Permitted

Hand-propelled boats and sailboats are permitted on all park waters. From April 1 through September 30, the section of Upper McDonald Creek between Mineral Creek and Lake McDonald is closed to all types of boating and floating to protect nesting Harlequin ducks.

Privately owned motorboats and motor vessels are prohibited from all park waters with the exception of the following:

• Motorboats and motor vessels are allowed on McDonald, Sherburne, St. Mary, Two Medicine, and Waterton Lakes (no boat launch ramps exist on Sherburne Lake; only hand carried craft are permitted).

• Motorboats and motor vessels are allowed on Bowman and Two Medicine Lakes but are limited to ten (10) horsepower or less.

### Required Equipment

• A wearable type personal floatation device for each person on board, classified as Type I, II, III, or V. The throwable (Type IV) floatation device, such as a cushion or ring buoy, can no longer be substituted.

• Children under 12 must wear a personal floatation device.

• Flame arrestor (USCG approved) on each carburetor on inboard gasoline engines.

•Fire extinguisher(s) (B-1 type) or a fixed fire extinguisher system for all inboard engines and outboards with enclosed fuel compartments.

• Sound producing device for each motorboat 16 feet and longer.

• Navigation lights for motorboats and sailboats used between sunset & sunrise.

*Backcountry travelers to this spectacular lake may hear the added treat of wolves howling in the distance. Just over 15 years ago wolves from Canada moved into this area of Glacier. In 1984 the first documented den of wolf pups born in Glacier in over 60 years was discovered. Several packs of wolves now roam the wilds of the park adding a special magic to the character of Glacier. NPS Photo*

## Water Skiing

While water skiing, at least two competent persons must be in the towing boat, one of whom (other than the operator) must observe the person being towed. Each person being towed must wear a lifesaving device. If device being worn is not approved by the USCG, an approved device must be readily available in towing boat. Anyone water skiing must wear personal floatation device—ski belts are not USCG approved and are no longer acceptable.

Water skiing is permitted only on Lake McDonald and St. Mary Lake, and only from sunrise to sunset.

Towing is prohibited within 100 feet of any person swimming or diving.

## Not Allowed

- Reckless or negligent boat handling so as to endanger or be likely to endanger the lives of others.
- Boat handling by any person under the influence of alcohol or drugs.
- Riding the gunwales, transom, or foredeck while boat is moving faster than 5 mph.
- Swimming from boat while underway.
- Interference with other boats or with free & proper navigation of waterways.
- Leaving a boat unattended for more than 24 hours without specific authority from the superintendent or his/her duly authorized representative.
- Using trailers to launch or recover vessels at a site other than at a designated boat launching site.
- Overloading of boats.
- Installation of any obstruction whatever in the water.
- Operating "airboats."
- "Para-sailing"
- Use of personal watercraft on any park waters.
- Operating a vessel in excess of 5 mph within 100 feet of a diver's marker, downed water skier, or swimmer.
- Discharging toilet wastes into the water.
- Depositing trash, refuse, or debris of any kind in the water.

## Noise Level

A federal regulation prohibits the use of watercraft exceeding 82 decibels of noise within all national parks. This regulation is strictly enforced on all park waters. Those operating personal watercraft and other high-powered boats should check their engine noise levels to be sure they comply with the regulations.

Personal watercraft (jet skis) are prohibited.

## Shoreline Restrictions

Boating may be restricted in certain areas for safety or to protect sensitive wildlife habitat throughout the park. Marker buoys and/or signing will be placed to designate the closures.

Lake McDonald: To provide for the safety of the general public using beaches for swimming and other similar activities, a "No Wake Zone" has been established 300 feet north of the south shore (end) of Lake McDonald from the Going-to-the-Sun Road to the lake outlet located at Lower McDonald Creek. Mark buoys will replaced annually to delineate the zone.

## Camping

Undesignated camping is not allowed on lakes or lakeshores.

A Backcountry Use Permit is required for all designated backcountry campsites.

A fee of $4 per person per night will be

| Campground | Dates | Fee | Sites | Maximum Lengths & Number of Max Length Sites | Toilet | Dump Station | Special Information |
|---|---|---|---|---|---|---|---|
| Apgar | 5/5 - 10/16 | $14.00 | 196 | 25 sites up to 40' | Yes | Yes | 1, 3 |
| Avalanche | 6/16 - 9/5 | $14.00 | 87 | 50 sites up to 26' | Yes | Yes | 3 |
| Bowman Lake | 5/19 - 9/15 | $12.00 | 48 | RV's not recommended | No | No | 1, 2 |
| Cut Bank | 5/27 - 9/14 | $12.00 | 19 | RV's not recommended | No | No | 2 |
| Fish Creek | 6/1 - 9/5 | $17.00 | 180 | 3 sites up to 35' | Yes | Yes | 3, 4 |
| Kintla Lake | 5/19 - 9/15 | $12.00 | 13 | RV's not recommended | No | No | 1, 2 |
| Logging Creek | 7/1 - 9/5 | $12.00 | 8 | RV's not recommended | No | No | 1, 2 |
| Many Glacier | 5/27 - 9/22 | $14.00 | 110 | 13 sites up to 35' | Yes | Yes | 1, 3 |
| Quartz Creek | 7/1 - 9/5 | $12.00 | 7 | RV's not recommended | No | No | 1, 2 |
| Rising Sun | 5/27 - 9/14 | $14.00 | 83 | 3 sites up to 30' | Yes | Yes | 3 |
| Sprague Creek | 5/19 - 9/25 | $14.00 | 25 | No Towed Units | Yes | No | 3 |
| St. Mary | 5/31 - 9/14 | $17.00 | 148 | 25 sites up to 35' | Yes | Yes | 1, 3, 4 |
| Two Medicine | 5/27 - 9/14 | $14.00 | 99 | 13 sites up to 32' | Yes | Yes | 1, 3 |

Special Information
1 - Primitive camping available after the listed dates, road conditions permitting.
2 - Primitive campground accessible by dirt road only, large units not recommended
3 - Hiker/Biker sites available
4 - Campground may be reserved in advance by calling 800-365-CAMP.

Winter camping is available at the Apgar Picnic Area and the St. Mary Campground. No reservations are accepted for winter camping.

charged at the time of permit issuance (June 1 through September 30). There is no fee for campers aged 16 and under. An additional fee of $20 will be charged for confirmed advance reservations.

## Regulation

National Park Service boating regulations will be found in Title 36, Part 3, of the Code of Federal Regulations and are available at park headquarters and staffed ranger stations.

It is your responsibility to know and obey the U.S. Coast Guard and State of Montana regulations for boat operation & safety.

Park rangers may inspect or board any boat for the purpose of examining documents, licenses, and/or other permits relating to the operation of the boat and to inspect the boat to determine compliance with regulations.

## Pets

- Pets are allowed in vessels on lakes where motorized watercraft are permitted.
- Pets are prohibited on lake shores except at the boat launch.

# Scenic Drives

The Entrance Road provides 8 kilometres (5 miles) of magnificent views that beautifully illustrate the park's theme, "where the mountains meet the prairie." Colorful prairie flowers and grasses, and the glittering blue chain of the Waterton Lakes are set against a mountain backdrop. The sight of the historic Prince of Wales Hotel, on a knoll above the lakes, indicates you will soon arrive at our lakeside townsite. The Akamina Highway begins near the townsite and runs for 16km (10 miles) along the Cameron Valley. Points of interest include the site of western Canada's first producing oil well, the Oil City site, and scenic Cameron Lake.

The Red Rock Parkway meanders over rolling prairie and through the Blakiston Valley. It ends at the strikingly colored rocks and cascading creeks of Red Rock Canyon, a distance of 15km (9 miles). The drive features views of magnificent mountains, including Mt. Blakiston, the park's highest peak.

The Chief Mountain Highway is the primary route between Waterton Lakes and Glacier National Parks. The highway climbs from the grasslands near Maskinonge Lake to a viewpoint giving a magnificent vista of the Front Range of the Rockies and Waterton Valley. Enroute from the border crossing, the road traverses fields and forests, dotted with wetlands created by Crooked Creek.

The Bison Paddock, near the north entrance to the park off Highway 6, features a small herd of plains bison, maintained to commemorate the larger herds that once roamed freely in this area. The bison can be seen while driving a narrow road through the paddock. Please do not leave your vehicles. The road is not suitable for vehicles with trailers.

# Bicycling

Cyclists must observe all traffic regulations. Keep well to the right side of the road and ride in single file only. Pull off the road if four or more vehicles stack up behind you. In fog or after dark a white light in front and a red reflector on the rear of your bicycle are required. Be visible! Helmets are strongly advised. Attach a bright flag on a pole and wear light-colored clothing. Watch for falling rocks, drainage grates, and ice on road.

For safety and to ease congestion, restrictions are in effect on sections of the Going-to-the-Sun Road, from June 15 through Labor Day:

From Apgar Campground to Sprague Creek Campground bicycles are prohibited, both directions, between 11 a.m. and 4 p.m.

From Logan Creek to Logan Pass east-bound (uphill) bicycle traffic is prohibited between 11 a.m. and 4 p.m.

Start early! It takes about 45 minutes to ride from Sprague Creek to Logan Creek and about three hours from Logan Creek to Logan Pass.

Bicycle rentals are not available inside the park.

## Hiker/Biker Campsites

A limited number of sites at Apgar, Fish Creek, Sprague Creek, Avalanche, Many Glacier, Rising Sun, Two Medicine, and St. Mary campgrounds are held until 9:00 p.m. for bicyclists, pedestrians, and motorcyclists. Sites are shared and have a capacity of 8 people; larger groups must split up. The fee is $3.00 per person. If hiker/biker sites are full, campers must use regular unoccupied campsites.

*The high country of Glacier National Park is filled with incredible vistas like this scene. Flinsch Peak, and the ridge that stretches away to the right, lie on the Continental Divide. One of the more popular overnight hikes in the park follows along this ridge. Campers can stay at either Oldman Lake (just behind the hikers head) or No Name Lake. The view of Young Man Lake is reserved for hikers (like this one) willing to scale the summit of Rising Wolf Mountain. NPS Photo*

# Hiking

## Planning a Hike

Over half of the visitors to Glacier National Park report taking a hike. That's a lot of hikers, but over 700 miles of trail provide many outstanding opportunities for both short hikes and extended backpacking trips.

Hikers need to assume individual responsibility for planning their trips and hiking safely. Before setting out on your hike, stop by a park visitor center to obtain needed warnings and recommendations. You will increase your odds of a safe hike, decrease your disturbance to park wildlife, and lessen cumulative damage to resources.

Visitor center bookstores carry a complete line of trail guides, topographic maps and field guides to aid the hiker. Publications are also available by mail. Call the Glacier Natural History Association at 888-5756, to request a catalog.

Five self-guided walks interpret trailside features with brochures and signs. The Trail of the Cedars, Huckleberry Mountain, Hidden Lake, Sun Point, and Swiftcurrent Nature Trails encourage hikers to experience Glacier National Park at their own pace. The Trail of the Cedars is wheelchair accessible.

Good day hikes are plentiful. Visitor center staff will be happy to assist you with your choices and provide free maps of popular trails in park. Maps to four of the more popular hiking areas are available online as well at the links above.

## Overnight Trips

Hikers planning to camp overnight in Glacier's backcountry must stop at a visitor center or ranger station and obtain a backcountry permit.

## Backpacking

Permits are required to camp in the backcountry. *Permits are available only during the hours listed.* There is a $4.00 per person per night charge. Permits are is-sued no more than 24 hours in advance of the start of the trip.

Advanced reservations (more than 24 hours in advance) are available, but only at Apgar, St. Mary, or by mail. There is a $20.00 reservation fee.

Visitors entering the backcountry at Goat Haunt or Belly River, may obtain a backcountry permit at the Waterton Visitor Reception Centre (credit cards only).

**Apgar Backcountry Permit Center**

May 1–July 1 . . . . . . . . . . . . . . .8 a.m. to 4 p.m.
July 2–Sept. 11 . . . . . . . . . . . . .7 a.m. to 4 p.m.
Sept. 12–Oct. 31 . . . . . . . . . . . .8 a.m. to 4 p.m.

**St. Mary Visitor Center***

June 26–Sept. 30 . . . . . . . . .8 a.m. to 4:30 p.m.

Glacier National Park

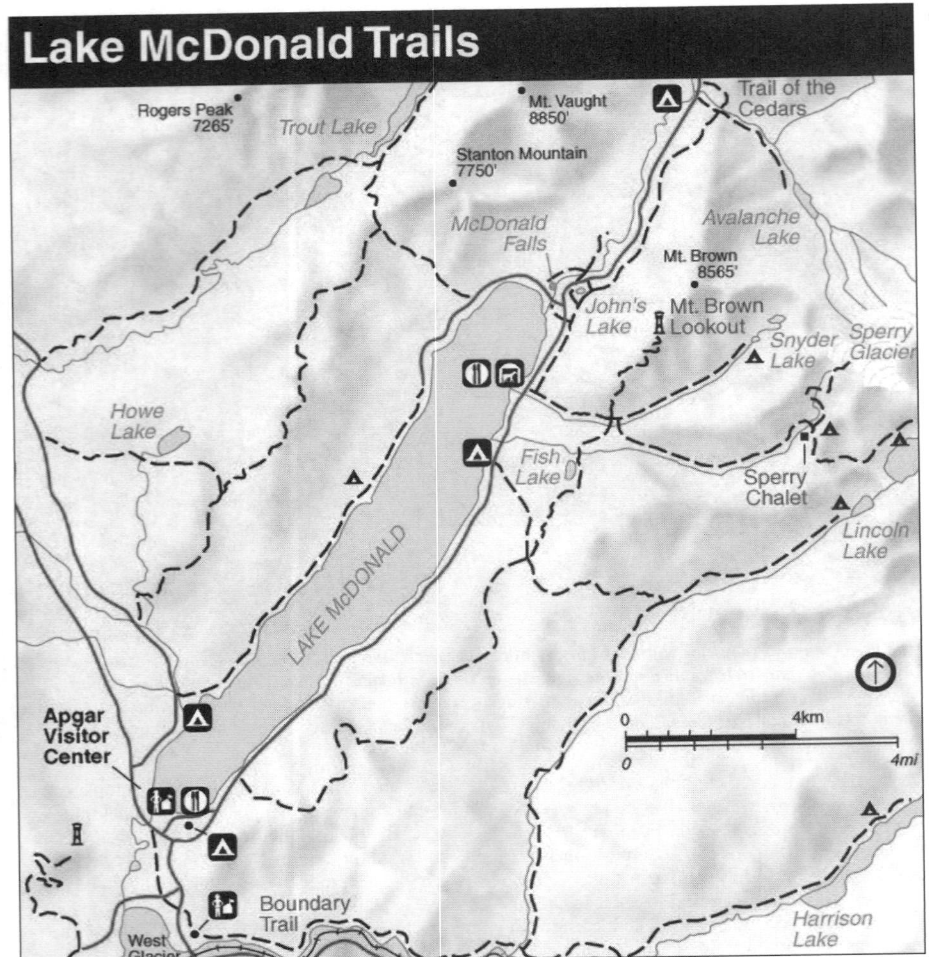


**Many Glacier Ranger Station***
May 26–Sept. 21 . . . . . . . . . .8 a.m. to 4:30 p.m.

**Two Medicine Ranger Station***
May 26–Sept. 16 . . . . . . . . . .8 a.m. to 4:30 p.m.

**Polebridge Ranger Station**
May 26–Sept. 11 . . . . . . . . . . . .9 a.m. to 5 p.m.

*Closed daily for a one hour lunch

## Glacier National Park Hikes

To view most of Glacier Park, you have to leave the roads and hit the trails. There are countless hikes throughout the park. Here are a few of the more popular ones.

### Avalanche Lake

This was one of John Muir's favorites. The hike starts a few miles east of Lake McDonald on Going-to-the-Sun Road at the mouth of Avalanche Creek. The early part of the trail is a boardwalk which travels through cool, mossy, old-growth cedars. This part is known as the Trail of the Cedars. Once you cross the footbridge over Avalanche Gorge and its foaming whitewater, you break into the magnificent Avalanche Lake cirque. Here you are surrounded by jagged alpine peaks. The hike is handicapped accessible at the beginning. The rest of the hike is vigorous, but not exhausting. The entire hike offers breathtaking scenery and abundant wildlife viewing opportunities.

### The Highline Trail

This trail begins at Logan Pass. Parking is limited at the trailhead, so you will want to get an early start. Begin by heading due north to the Granite Park Chalet. You will be hiking along the Garden Wall. Once you reach the Chalet your best option is to return by the same route. You can pick up the Loop Trail here, but the scenery isn't as good, and your more likely to have a grizzly invade your personal space—or the other way around. The best part of this hike is that it is a fairly level grade. The scenery along here is spectacular. Keep your eyes open for mountain goats, and an occasional grizzly. Plan a full day for this hike.

### Dawson-Pitamakan Loop

This 18.8 mile rugged hike in the Two Medicine Area has a difficulty rating of 4 on a scale of 5. The hike is at best an all day event. The highlight is a traverse around Rising Wolf Mountain (elev. 9,513) offering excellent views of the Park's interior. Start at Two Medicine Campground up Dry Fork Creek, past Oldman Lake to Pitamakan Pass. From there hike south to Dawson Pass, through Bighorn Basin and return to Two Medicine Lake. Plan B? Catch the Two Medicine boat for the last few miles back.

### Ptarmigan Tunnel

Certainly among the most popular hikes is the Ptarmigan Tunnel Trail. Find the trailhead at Swiftcurrent and climb about 4 miles to Ptarmigan Tunnel. This fine example of backcountry engineering is a path blasted right through the mountain by park trail crews. On the other side of the tunnel you will be treated to great views of the Belly River drainage. Keep your eyes open for grizzlies. This is one of the best areas in the park to see them.

### Triple Divide Pass Trail

This 14 plus mile trail is rated a 3 on a scale of 5 for difficulty. Most of this hike is in areas of the park that are well off the beaten path. The hike begins at the Cutbank Creek Campground where it follows the north fork of Cutbank Creek before it starts the assent to Triple Divide Peak. At the top, you are standing at the source of three major watersheds: the Pacific Ocean, Hudson's Bay, and

*Avalanche Lake*

the Gulf of Mexico.

### Red Eagle Trail

This is a fairly easy 15 mile hike along an old buffalo hunters' route to Red Eagle Lake behind the St. Mary Mountains. The trailhead begins at the St. Mary Ranger Station.

## Lake McDonald Hikes

**Avalanche**
Lake South of the Avalanche Gorge footbridge on the Trail of the Cedars 2.0 mile climbs 500'.

**Boundary Trail Park at Park Headquarters.**
The Trailhead is at the south end of Mather Drive in the employee housing area. 5.3 miles to the Lincoln Creek junction. Trail continues approx. 15 miles to Coal Creek gentle up and down along the Middle Fork of the Flathead.

**Fish Lake Sperry**
Trailhead across from Lake McDonald Lodge 3.0 miles climbs 1,000'.

**Howe Lake**
5 miles forth of Fish Creek Campground on the unpaved Inside North Fork Road 2.0 miles climbs 240'.

**John's Lake Loop Trail**
Watch for sign on Going-to-the-Sun Road north of Lake McDonald Lodge 3.0 mile loop climbs 160'.

**McDonald Falls**
North end of Lake McDonald on the North Lake McDonald Road View falls from bridge or take a very short walk up stream mostly level.

**Mt. Brown Lookout**
Trailhead across from Lake McDonald Lodge 5.4 miles climbs 4,325' (strenuous).

**Snyder Lake**
Trailhead across from Lake McDonald Lodge 4.4 miles climbs 2,147'.

**Sperry Chalet**
Trailhead across from Lake McDonald Lodge 6.4 mile climbs 3,432'.

**Sperry Glacier**
Trailhead across from Lake McDonald Lodge 10.4 mile climbs 3,432'.

**Trail of the Cedars**
Across from the Avalanche Campground Ranger Station 0.4 mile loop level boardwalk (wheelchair accessible).

**Trout Lake**
1.5 miles west on North Lake McDonald Road (1.1 miles of unpaved road) 4.2 miles climbs 2,100' then drops 2,100' to the lake.

## Logan Pass Hikes

**Avalanche Lake**
South of the Avalanche Gorge footbridge on the Trail of the Cedars 2.0 miles climbs 500'.

**Florence Falls**
Gunsight Lake Trailhead, 14 miles west of St. Mary 4.6 miles drops 500' then climbs 150'.

**Granite Park Chalet via the Highline Trail**
Logan Pass Parking Area 7.6 miles climbs 200'.

**Granite Park Chalet via the Loop Trail**

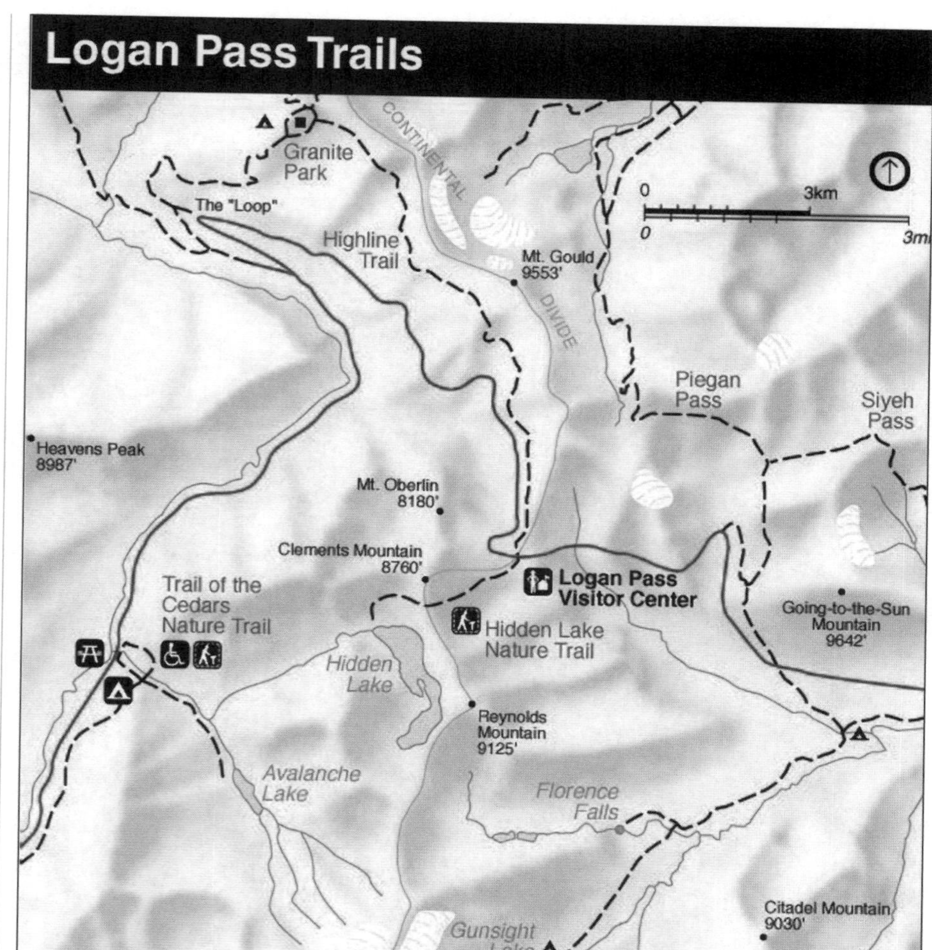


Loop Parking Area 3.5 miles climbs 2,200'.

**Gunsight Lake**
Gunsight Lake Trailhead, 14 miles west of St. Mary 6.2 miles drops then climbs 500'.

**Hidden Lake Nature Trail**
Upper level of the Logan Pass Visitor Center 1.5 miles to overlook of the lake climbs 460'.

**Piegan Pass**
Piegan Pass Trailhead, 3 miles east of Logan Pass 4.5 miles climbs 1,750'.

**Siyeh Pass**
Piegan Pass Trailhead, 3 miles east of Logan Pass 4.7 miles climbs 1,900'.

**Trail of the Cedars**
Across from the Avalanche Campground Ranger Station 0.4 mile loop level boardwalk (wheelchair accessible)

## Many Glacier Trails

**Appekunny Falls**
Grinnell Glacier Wayside Exhibit, 1.1 miles east of the Many Glacier Hotel 1.0 mile climbs 700'.

**Cracker Lake**
Cracker Lake Trailhead, south end of the Many Glacier Hotel parking area 6.1 miles climbs 1,400'.

**Granite Park Chalet**
Swiftcurrent Pass Trailhead at the west end of the Swiftcurrent Motor Inn parking area 7.3 miles climbs 2,300' then drops 500' to the chalet.

**Grinnell Glacier**
Grinnell Glacier Trailhead at the Many Glacier Picnic Area or the south end of the Many Glacier Hotel 5.5 miles or 3.8 miles via boat and hike climbs 1,600'.

**Grinnell Lake**
Grinnell Glacier Trailhead at the Many Glacier Picnic Area or the south end of the Many Glacier Hotel 3.4 miles or 0.9 mile via boat and hike climbs 60'

**Iceberg Lake**
Iceberg/Ptarmigan Trailhead, behind the Swiftcurrent Motor Inn cabin area 4.7 miles climbs 1,200'.

**Poia Lake**
Grinnell Glacier Wayside Exhibit, 1.1 miles east of the Many Glacier Hotel 6.4 mile climbs 1,300' then drops 415' to the lake.

**Ptarmigan Falls**
Iceberg/Ptarmigan Trailhead, behind the Swiftcurrent Motor Inn cabin area 2.5 miles climbs 700'.

**Ptarmigan Lake**
Iceberg/Ptarmigan Trailhead, behind the Swiftcurrent Motor Inn cabin area 4.3 miles climbs 1,700'.

**Ptarmigan Tunnel**
Iceberg/Ptarmigan Trailhead, behind the Swiftcurrent Motor Inn cabin area 5.2 miles climbs 2,300'.

## Many Glacier Trails

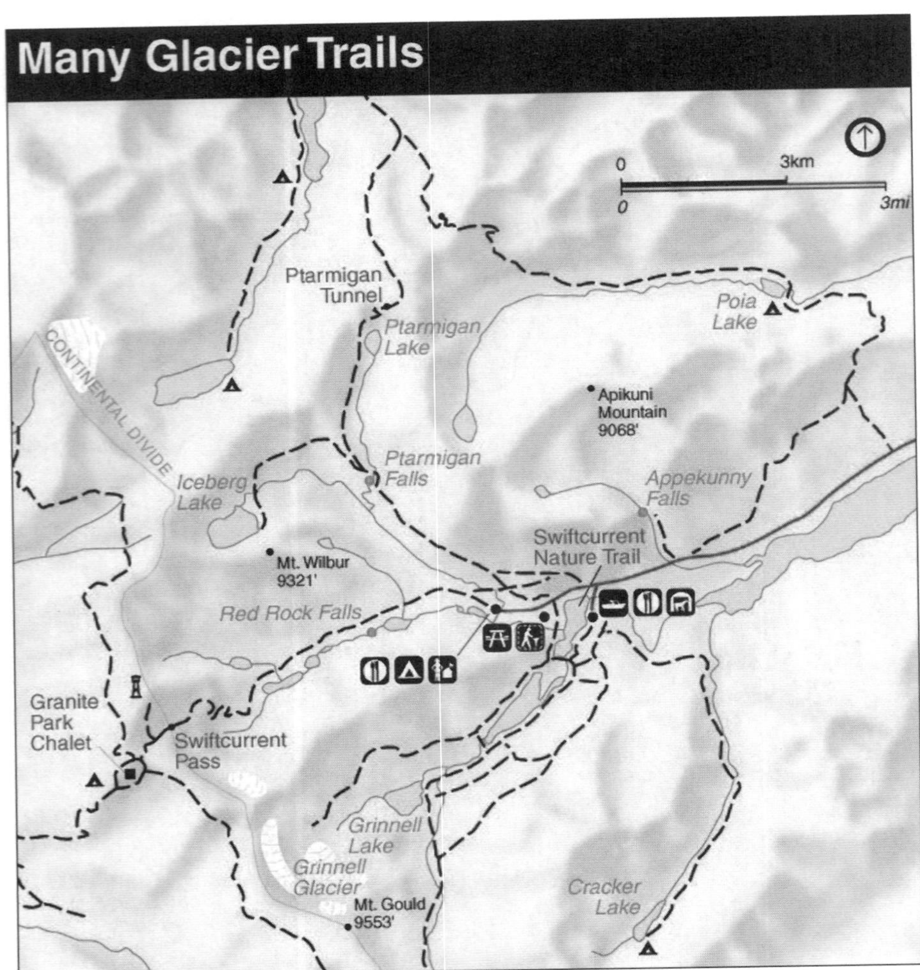


**Red Rock Falls**
Swiftcurrent Pass Trailhead at the west end of the Swiftcurrent Motor Inn parking area 1.8 miles climbs 100'.

**Swiftcurrent Nature Trail**
Grinnell Glacier Trailhead at the Many Glacier Picnic Area or the south end of the Many Glacier Hotel 2.4 mile loop trail mostly level.

**Swiftcurrent Pass**
Swiftcurrent Pass Trailhead at the west end of the Swiftcurrent Motor Inn parking area.

### St. Mary Trails

**Baring Falls**
Sunrift Gorge Parking Area, 10 miles west of St. Mary 0.3 miles drops 100'.

**Beaver Pond Trail**
1913 Ranger Station Parking Lot 1.8 miles gentle slopes.

**Otokomi Lake**
Beyond Rising Sun Motor Inn cabin 9a, 6 miles west of St. Mary 5.0 miles climbs 1,900'.

**Red Eagle Lake**
1913 Ranger Station Parking Lot 7.5 miles climbs 200'.

**St. Mary**
Falls St. Mary Falls Trailhead, just west of Sunrift Gorge .8 miles drops 150'.

**Siyeh Pass**
Piegan Pass Trailhead, 3 miles east of Logan Pass 4.7 miles climbs 1,900'.

**Sun Point Nature Trail**
Sun Point Parking Area, 9 miles west of St. Mary 0.7 miles gentle slopes.

**Virginia Falls**
St. Mary Falls Trailhead, just west of Sunrift Gorge 1.5 miles drops 150' then climbs 100'.

### Two Medicine Lake Trails

**Aster Park Viewpoint**
Two Medicine Lake South Shore Trailhead, just past the boat dock 1.9 miles climbs 670'.

**Cobalt Lake**
Two Medicine Lake South Shore Trailhead, just past the boat dock 5.7 miles climbs 1,400'.

**Dawson Pass****
Two Medicine Campground Trailhead 6.7 miles climbs 2,450'.

**No Name Lake**
Two Medicine Campground Trailhead 5.0 miles climbs 800' Oldman Lake Two Medicine Campground Trailhead 5.5 miles climbs 1,500'.

**Pitamakan Pass****
Two Medicine Campground Trailhead 6.9 miles climbs 2,400'.

**Rockwell Falls**
Two Medicine Lake South Shore Trailhead, just past the boat dock 3.4 miles climbs 375'.

**Running Eagle Falls**
Running Eagle Falls Trailhead, 1 mile west of the Entrance Station 0.3 miles climbs 60'.

**Scenic Point**
Mt. Henry Trailhead, 0.25 miles east of the Two Medicine Ranger Station 3.1 miles climbs 2,350'.

**Twin Falls**
Two Medicine Campground Trailhead 3.8 miles or 0.9 miles via boat & hike* climbs 75'.

**Two Medicine Pass**
Two Medicine Lake South Shore Trailhead, just past the boat dock 7.9 miles climbs 2,350'.

**Upper Two Medicine Lake**
Two Medicine Campground Trailhead 5.0 mles or 2.2 miles via boat & hike* climbs 350'.

* Boat trips depart from the Two Medicine Boat Dock

** Dawson Pass and Pitamakan Pass trips can be linked together to form a 16.9 mile loop.

### Cross Country Skiing

Enjoy Glacier's winter landscape on one of the following ski trips. Take into account your skiing ability, and check with rangers for local weather and snow conditions. Severe weather, lack of snow, winter rains, or melting conditions can quickly alter the difficulty of any winter trip. Ice is common on roads and on heavily skied trails. Plan to break trail on less popular routes. The Middle and North Forks of the Flathead River present major barriers to travel on the west side of the park. Skiing on frozen lakes is dangerous and not recommended. Skiers, snowshoers, and hikers are asked to maintain separate tracks.

As winter snows start to melt, emerging vegetation is revealed. Please stay off these fragile areas. Spring skiing opportunities remain at Granite Park, Many Glacier, and Logan Pass, but remember, warming conditions greatly increase avalanche activity.

Most ski routes are not marked. Pay attention to descriptions and local landmarks. A topograph-

## Apgar Area Ski Trails

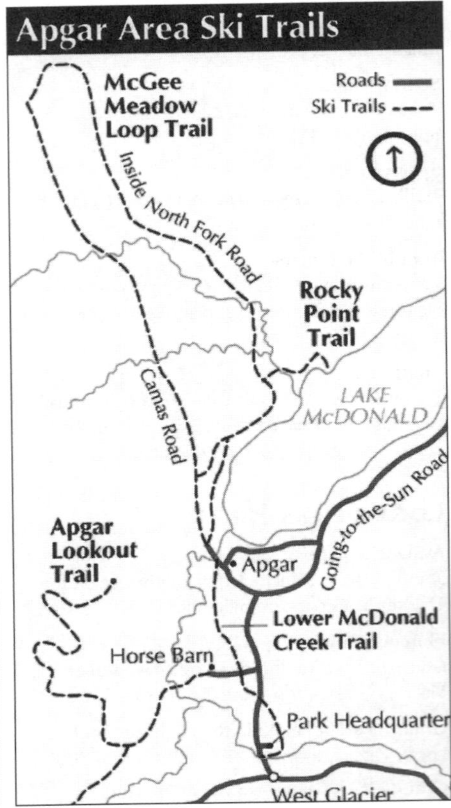

St. Mary Trails

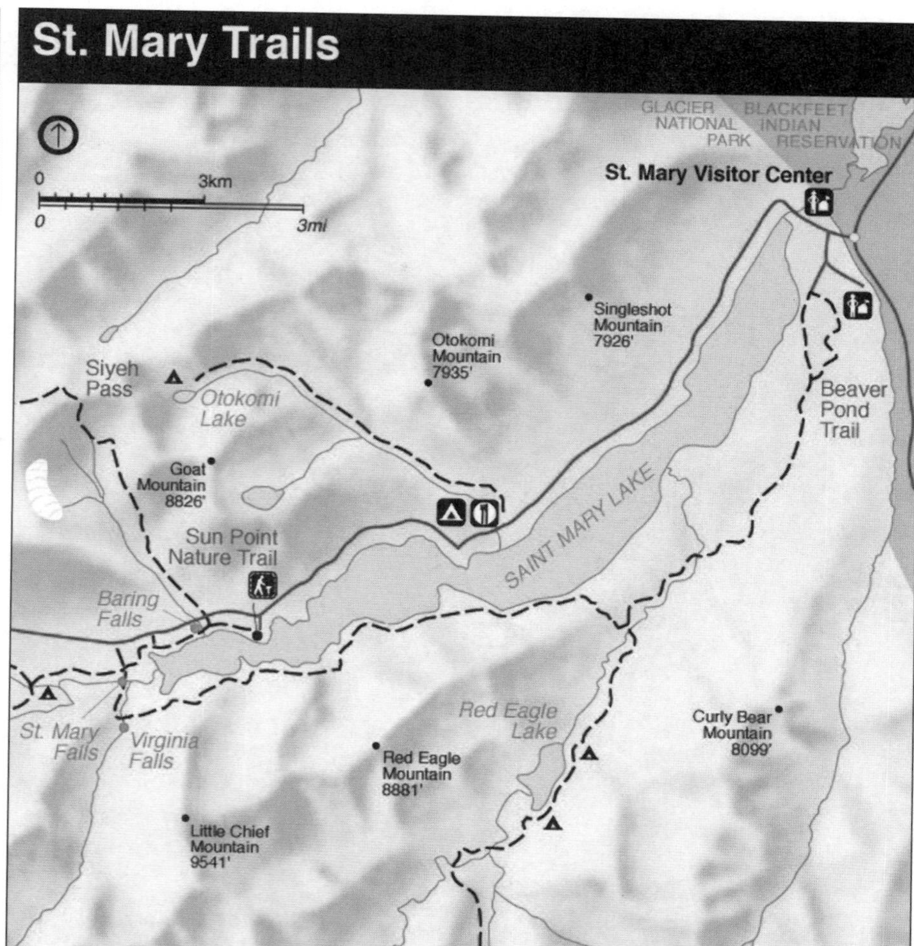


ic map will help.

Arduous cross park trips contain extreme avalanche and terrain hazards and should be attempted only by experienced and well equipped parties.

A permit is required for backcountry camping. Practice "Leave No Trace" camping techniques described in the information provided with your permit.

Skiers and snowshoers please register at the trailhead registration boxes. Climbers should complete the Voluntary Climbers Registration form, available at ranger stations and the Apgar Visitor Center.

Pets are not allowed on trails, unplowed roads, in the backcountry or off leash. Snowmobiles are not permitted anywhere in Glacier National Park.

## Avalanches

Avalanches are a major danger and potential killer to winter backcountry travelers. An understanding of avalanche conditions is the skier's best defense. Watch the signs of previous activity. These include old avalanche paths, downed trees, recent slides, and clumps of snow. Choose the safest route. Stay off cornices, steep to moderate open slopes, and stay out of gullies. If you must travel on a dangerous slope, go straight up or down; never traverse back and forth.

Glacier is part of the Northwest Montana Avalanche Warning System, which provides a weekly assessment of local avalanche conditions. Forecasts are updated each Friday morning during the avalanche season, and broadcast by local radio stations. Information can also be obtained by calling 257-8402 or 1-800-526-5329.

About 80% of avalanches occur during and immediately after storms. Avalanche activity increases with a foot or more of new snow, snowfall of one inch or more per hour, sustained winds over 15 miles per hour, changing temperatures, and during spring warming. Learn to recognize dangerous weather conditions. Carry rescue equipment including rescue shovels, ski probe poles, and transceivers. If you must cross a steep slope, cross one at a time, loosen all pack straps, remove ski pole straps, fasten all layers of clothing, and put on a hat and gloves.

McDonald Creek Ski Trails

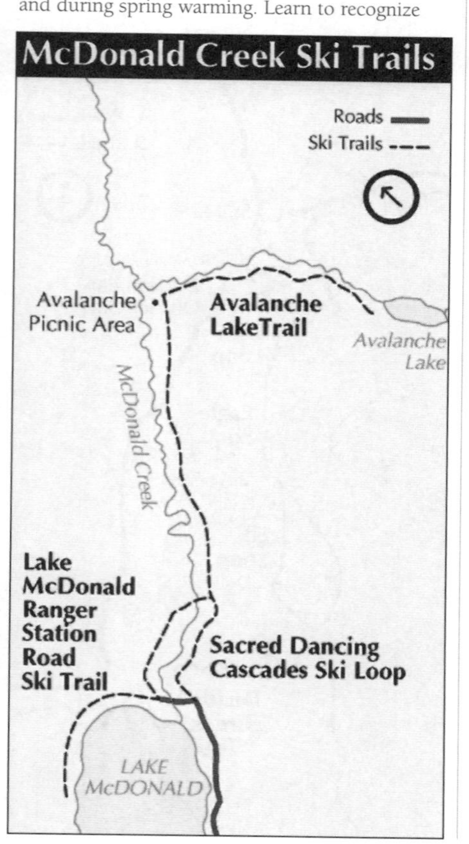


If caught in an avalanche, discard all equipment and make swimming motions toward the surface. As the sole survivor, do not go for help unless it is only a few minutes away. After 30 minutes, the buried victim has only a 50% chance of surviving. Mark the place where the victim was last seen, search directly downslope from this point for clues, and begin to probe immediately at the most likely location. Use probes, ski poles, skis, or anything available. With more than one survivor, send for help while the rest search.

Hypothermia Winter backcountry travel increases the risk of hypothermia and frostbite. Hypothermia, the "progressive physical collapse and reduced mental capacity resulting from the chilling of the inner core of the body", is the primary killer of outdoor enthusiasts. Drink liquids, stay dry, carry survival equipment, wear layers of warm clothing, and snack frequently. Be alert to symptoms of drowsiness and confusion. Once hypothermia sets in, external sources of warmth are necessary to revive the victim. Frostbite can occur on the ears, fingers, toes, face, or any exposed skin.

Wildlife viewing remains very rewarding in winter. Remember, survival during the long winter is difficult for Glacier's wildlife. Human contact adds unnecessary stress. Avoid approaching or startling any animals or birds. All park animals are wild and should never be fed. Bears, asleep for most of the winter, sometimes awaken for short periods of time. As always in bear country, exercise extreme caution, especially with food and garbage. If approached by a mountain lion, act aggressively. Do not run! Lions may be scared away by being struck with rocks or sticks, or by being kicked or hit.

Listed below are the three most popular areas in the park for cross country skiing and snowshoeing. Information on other areas is available at the Apgar Visitor Center, Park Headquarters, and the Hudson Bay District Office.

## Apgar Area Ski Trails

The routes described in this area begin at two parking locations:

- the concession horse barn, reached by taking the first left off the Going-to-the-Sun Road, past the West Entrance Station, and
- the road closure gate just beyond the McDonald Creek Bridge on the Camas Road.

**Lower McDonald Creek**

*2 to 3 miles to the meadow*

The trail begins just south of the McDonald Creek Bridge. The best access is the rather straight summer bike/foot path. This entire area is a good place to explore on your own. The gentle terrain along lower McDonald Creek provides an easy ski through the forest with side trips along the creek.

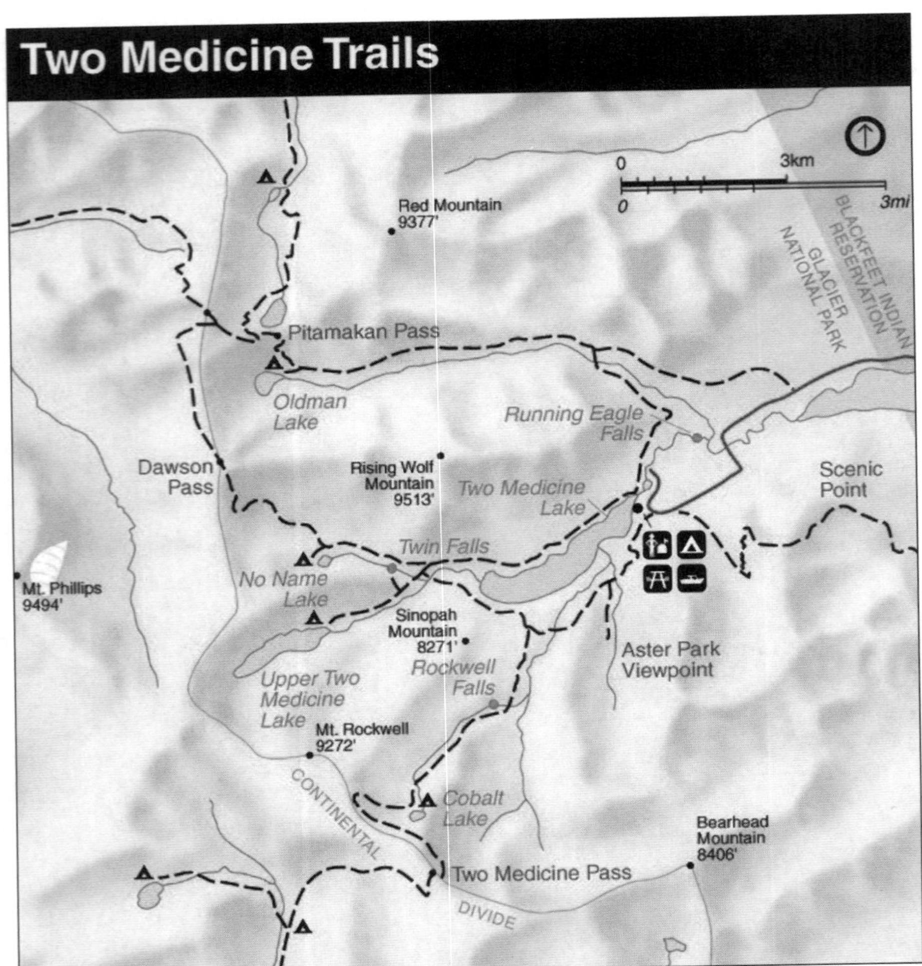


**Rocky Point**

*6 miles round trip*

Follow the same route as MeGee Meadow until .2 miles north of the Fish Creek Campground. Take the McDonald Lake Trail on the right, just before the gate on the road. The trail winds down a short hill but the route is fairly level for the most part. Ski left at the first trail junction then right at the next one shortly thereafter. The forest opens as you approach Rocky Point, where there are beautiful views up and down Lake McDonald.

**Apgar Lookout**

*101/2 miles round trip*

Park at the plowed area in front of the barn and follow the left fork of the unplowed road across the Quarter Circle Bridge Take the right fork and follow the road .5 mile until the actual Apgar Lookout trailhead is reached. After an easy start the trail steepens and climbing skins may be necessary for the trip if conditions are icy. The views are great from the lookout but this trail may be very difficult for beginning skiers.

**McGee Meadow Loop**

*111/2 miles round trip*

Take the right fork of the road at the closure and ski past the houses until the road turns to a trail. The trail soon joins the road to Fish Creek Campground and the Inside North Fork Road. Bear left past the campground. The improved road soon turns to a narrow climbing gravel road. From this point it is 3 miles to the first meadow. Continue over the crest of the hill to an orange marker identifying the trail to McGee Meadow. Ski along the northern edge of the meadow until you see the opening for the car pullout to the west on the Camas Road. After a couple of short uphill sections, the route descends to the road closure. This trip can be done in either direction, but going up the open Camas Road Hill is more tedious.

## McDonald Creek Ski Trails

Gentle terrain, generally ample snow, and easy access to wonderful winter scenery make this the most popular skiing area in the park. Follow the Going-to-the-Sun Road about 10 miles up the lake, past Lake McDonald Lodge to the road closure and the parking area.

**Sacred Dancing Cascade**

*2 miles round trip*

Ski up the unplowed road from the closure to the foot bridge across McDonald Creek. Turn left at the junction just across the creek and ski downstream along the west bank of the creek. The trail leaves the forest on the Lake McDonald Ranger Station Road where it is a short ski east to the closure.

**Lake McDonald Ranger Station Road**

*Mileage varies*

This trail starts with a gentle ski across the bridge over McDonald Creek and continues through the forest beyond with occasional views of the lake.

**Avalanche Picnic Area**

*8 miles round trip*

The route up the Going-to-the-Sun Road offers easy skiing and good views of the cedar/hemlock forest, McDonald Creek, and the mountains surrounding the McDonald Valley. Avalanche Picnic Area is a good destination. Longer trips up the road are possible. The forested valley trails, especially along Sacred Dancing Cascade, are also popular. Snow conditions may be variable under the tree canopy. Avalanche Lake is a popular destination with some steep narrow sections that can be difficult to ski up or down, especially when icy. The Trail of the Cedars is generally not good skiing.

## St. Mary Ski Trails

The main skiing trailhead for this area is a special parking area near the Hudson Bay District Office. Turn off U.S. Highway 89 at the winter park entrance (just south of the town of St. Mary) make a right after the bridge, then take the first left to the parking area by the trailhead information board.

**Red Eagle Loops**

*Mileage varies*

These specially designated and marked loops offer fine skiing through the aspens, meadows and mixed conifer stands in the rolling hills east of St. Mary Lake. The distances are one mile for the Lion Loop, 2.5 miles for the Eagle Loop, and 3.5 miles for the Elk Loop, Red Eagle Lake Trail 8 miles round trip Follow the first part of the Lion or Eagle Loops to the old fire road.

**Divide Creek Trail**

*7 miles*

This trail is much easier to ski downhill from the highway on Hudson Bay Divide to the Hudson

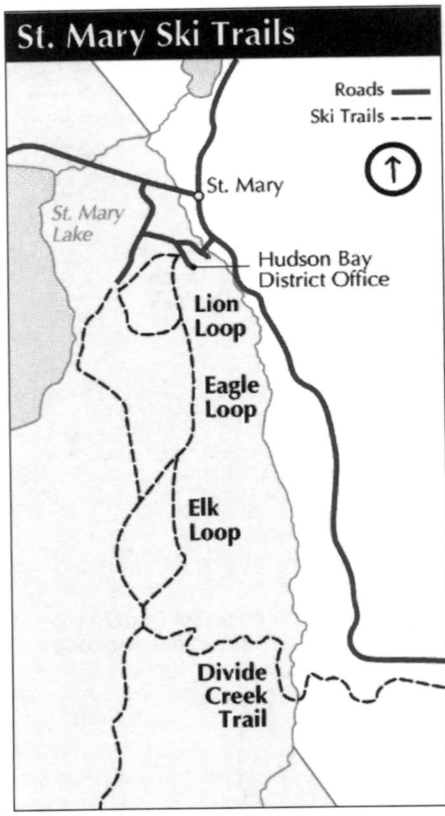

Bay District Office trailhead. Start at an orange stake on Highway 89, 4.5 miles south of St. Mary. Begin on the logging access road which skirts the bottom edge of several clear-cuts, then descends to Divide Creek. Use caution when crossing the creek and climbing out along a steep, narrow side-hill. The route then follows the old highway route to the Red Eagle Trail and back to the ranger station via one of the loop accesses. This route is for intermediate to advanced skiers.

The Blackfeet Tribe requires a permit, obtainable at the tribal Fish & Game office in Browning, to ski on the reservation.

## Services and Activities

Services are generally available from late May through mid-September.

### Guided bus tours

Narrated tours and shuttle services are offered by Glacier Park Incorporated. For reservations and information contact:

**Glacier Park, Inc.**
1850 North Central Avenue
Phoenix, AZ 85077-0928
Phone 602-207-6000
http://www.glacierparkinc.com

Sun Tours offers interpretive tours in Glacier National Park from mid-June to September 30. Tours highlight Blackfeet culture and history relating to Glacier National Park's natural features. Tours begin from St. Mary, East Glacier, and Browning. For reservation information, contact:

**Sun Tours**
P. O. Box 234
East Glacier, MT 59434
800-SUN-9220 or 226-9220

### Horseback rides

Horseback rides are provided by Mule Shoe Outfitters at the following locations: Lake McDonald Lodge, Apgar, and Many Glacier Hotel. For information contact:

Summer address & phone
**Mule Shoe Outfitters, LLC**
P.O. Box 322
West Glacier, MT 59936
732-4203
Winter address & phone
P.O. Box 1108
Wickenberg, AZ 88358
888-684-2338 or 520-684-2328
http://www.muleshoe.com

### Backcountry guides

Glacier Wilderness Guides offers guided day hikes and backpacking trips into the backcountry. For information contact:

**Glacier Wilderness Guides, Inc.**
Box 535
West Glacier, MT 59936
Phone 387-5555
Phone 800-521-7238
http://www.glacierguides.com

### Boat trips & rentals

Narrated boat cruises are offered at Lake McDonald, Many Glacier, Rising Sun, and Two Medicine. Optional free guided hikes are offered in conjunction with some trips. Boat and canoe rentals are also available. For information contact:

**Glacier Park Boat Company**
P.O. Box 5262, Kalispell, MT 59903
Phone 257-2426
http://www.montanaweb.com/gpboats

### Raft trips

Raft trips are not available within Glacier. Many local rafting companies offer trips on the Middle and North Forks of the Flathead River, immediately adjacent to the park. For information contact the following companies:

**Glacier Raft Company**
P.O. Box 210
West Glacier, MT 59936
888-5454 or 800-235-6781
http://www.glacierraftco.com

**Great Northern Whitewater**
P.O. Box 278
West Glacier, MT 59936
387-5340 or 800-735-7897
http://www.gnwhitewater.com

**Montana Raft Company**
P.O. Box 535-PS
West Glacier, MT 59936
387-5555 or 800-521-RAFT
http://www.glacierguides.com

**Wild River Adventures**
P.O. Box 272
West Glacier, MT 59936
387-9453 or 800-700-7056
http://www.riverwild.com

**Gasoline is not available within Glacier National Park boundaries. Be sure to fill up your gas tank before entering the park.**

*The contents of this section are reprinted from National Park Service publications.*

## Notes:

**Notes:**

# INDEX



Index

## C

## I



## J



## K



## L



Index

## M



## N

**O**



**P**



**Q**



**R**

Rosebud Battlefield 48-51

Rosebud County Pioneer Museum 43

Stuart, Granville 207, 230

## U



## V



## W



## Y



## Z